Peterson's Graduate Programs in the Physical Sciences, Mathematics, Agricultural Sciences, the Environment & Natural Resources

2014

About Peterson's

Peterson's provides the accurate, dependable, high-quality education content and guidance you need to succeed. No matter where you are on your academic or professional path, you can rely on Peterson's print and digital publications for the most up-to-date education exploration data, expert test-prep tools, and top-notch career success resources—everything you need to achieve your goals.

Visit us online at www.petersonsbooks.com and let Peterson's help you achieve your goals.

For more information, contact Peterson's Publishing, 3 Columbia Circle, Suite 205, Albany, NY 12203-5158; 800-338-3282 Ext. 54229; or find us on the World Wide Web at www.petersonsbooks.com.

Bernadette Webster, Managing Editor; Jill C. Schwartz, Editor; Ken Britschge, Research Project Manager; Jim Bonar, Research Operations Data Analyst; Nicole Gallo, Amy L. Weber, Research Associates; Phyllis Johnson, Software Engineer; Ray Golaszewski, Publishing Operations Manager; Linda M. Williams, Composition Manager; Carrie Hansen, Christine Lucht, Kiele Nowak, Mark Watts, Bailey Williams, Elayne Woods, Client Fulfillment Coordinators

ISSN 1093-8443
ISBN-13: 978-0-7689-3770-1

Printed in the United States of America

10 9 8 7 6 5 4 3 2 1   16 15 14

Forty-eighth Edition

Sustainability—Its Importance to Peterson's

What does sustainability mean to Peterson's? As a leading publisher, we are aware that our business has a direct impact on vital resources—most especially the trees that are used to make our books. Peterson's is proud that its products are certified to the Sustainable Forestry Initiative (SFI) chain-of-custody standard and that all of its books are printed on paper that is 40 percent post-consumer waste using vegetable-based ink.

Being a part of the Sustainable Forestry Initiative (SFI) means that all of out vendors—from paper suppliers to printers—have undergone rigorous audits to demonstrate that they are maintaining a sustainable environment.

Peterson's continuously strives to find new ways to incorporate sustainability throughout all aspects of its business.

CONTENTS

vi www.petersonsbooks.com

Peterson's Graduate Programs in the Physical Sciences, Mathematics, Agricultural Sciences, the Environment & Natural Resources 2014

A Note from the Peterson's Editors

The six volumes of Peterson's *Graduate and Professional Programs*, the only annually updated reference work of its kind, provide wideranging information on the graduate and professional programs offered by accredited colleges and universities in the United States, U.S. territories, and Canada and by those institutions outside the United States that are accredited by U.S. accrediting bodies. Nearly 36,000 individual academic and professional programs at more than 2,200 institutions are listed. Peterson's *Graduate and Professional Programs* have been used for more than forty years by prospective graduate and professional students, placement counselors, faculty advisers, and all others interested in postbaccalaureate education.

Graduate & Professional Programs: An Overview contains information on institutions as a whole, while the other books in the series are devoted to specific academic and professional fields:

Graduate Programs in the Humanities, Arts & Social Sciences
Graduate Programs in the Biological/Biomedical Sciences & Health-Related Medical Professions
Graduate Programs in the Physical Sciences, Mathematics, Agricultural Sciences, the Environment & Natural Resources
Graduate Programs in Engineering & Applied Sciences
Graduate Programs in Business, Education, Information Studies, Law & Social Work

The books may be used individually or as a set. For example, if you have chosen a field of study but do not know what institution you want to attend or if you have a college or university in mind but have not chosen an academic field of study, it is best to begin with the Overview guide.

Graduate & Professional Programs: An Overview presents several directories to help you identify programs of study that might interest you; you can then research those programs further in the other books in the series by using the Directory of Graduate and Professional Programs by Field, which lists 500 fields and gives the names of those institutions that offer graduate degree programs in each.

For geographical or financial reasons, you may be interested in attending a particular institution and will want to know what it has to offer. You should turn to the Directory of Institutions and Their Offerings, which lists the degree programs available at each institution. As in the Directory of Graduate and Professional Programs by Field, the level of degrees offered is also indicated.

All books in the series include advice on graduate education, including topics such as admissions tests, financial aid, and accreditation. **The Graduate Adviser** includes two essays and information about accreditation. The first essay, "The Admissions Process," discusses general admission requirements, admission tests, factors to consider when selecting a graduate school or program, when and how to apply, and how admission decisions are made. Special information for international students and tips for minority students are also included. The second essay, "Financial Support," is an overview of the broad range of support available at the graduate level. Fellowships, scholarships, and grants; assistantships and internships; federal and private loan programs, as well as Federal Work-Study; and the GI bill are detailed. This essay concludes with advice on applying for need-based financial aid. "Accreditation and Accrediting Agencies" gives information on accreditation and its purpose and lists institutional accrediting agencies first and then specialized accrediting agencies relevant to each volume's specific fields of study.

With information on more than 44,000 graduate programs in more than 500 disciplines, Peterson's *Graduate and Professional Programs* give you all the information you need about the programs that are of interest to you in three formats: **Profiles** (capsule summaries of basic information), **Displays** (information that an institution or program wants to emphasize), and **Close-Ups** (written by administrators, with more expansive information than the **Profiles**, emphasizing different aspects of the programs). By using these various formats of program information, coupled with **Appendixes** and **Indexes** covering directories and subject areas for all six books, you will find that these guides provide the most comprehensive, accurate, and up-to-date graduate study information available.

Peterson's publishes a full line of resources with information you need to guide you through the graduate admissions process. Peterson's publications can be found at college libraries and career centers and your local bookstore or library—or visit us on the Web at www.petersonsbooks.com. Peterson's books are now also available as ebooks.

Colleges and universities will be pleased to know that Peterson's helped you in your selection. Admissions staff members are more than happy to answer questions, address specific problems, and help in any way they can. The editors at Peterson's wish you great success in your graduate program search!

THE GRADUATE ADVISER

The Admissions Process

Generalizations about graduate admissions practices are not always helpful because each institution has its own set of guidelines and procedures. Nevertheless, some broad statements can be made about the admissions process that may help you plan your strategy.

Factors Involved in Selecting a Graduate School or Program

Selecting a graduate school and a specific program of study is a complex matter. Quality of the faculty; program and course offerings; the nature, size, and location of the institution; admission requirements; cost; and the availability of financial assistance are among the many factors that affect one's choice of institution. Other considerations are job placement and achievements of the program's graduates and the institution's resources, such as libraries, laboratories, and computer facilities. If you are to make the best possible choice, you need to learn as much as you can about the schools and programs you are considering before you apply.

The following steps may help you narrow your choices.

- Talk to alumni of the programs or institutions you are considering to get their impressions of how well they were prepared for work in their fields of study.
- Remember that graduate school requirements change, so be sure to get the most up-to-date information possible.
- Talk to department faculty members and the graduate adviser at your undergraduate institution. They often have information about programs of study at other institutions.
- Visit the Web sites of the graduate schools in which you are interested to request a graduate catalog. Contact the department chair in your chosen field of study for additional information about the department and the field.
- Visit as many campuses as possible. Call ahead for an appointment with the graduate adviser in your field of interest and be sure to check out the facilities and talk to students.

General Requirements

Graduate schools and departments have requirements that applicants for admission must meet. Typically, these requirements include undergraduate transcripts (which provide information about undergraduate grade point average and course work applied toward a major), admission test scores, and letters of recommendation. Most graduate programs also ask for an essay or personal statement that describes your personal reasons for seeking graduate study. In some fields, such as art and music, portfolios or auditions may be required in addition to other evidence of talent. Some institutions require that the applicant have an undergraduate degree in the same subject as the intended graduate major.

Most institutions evaluate each applicant on the basis of the applicant's total record, and the weight accorded any given factor varies widely from institution to institution and from program to program.

The Application Process

You should begin the application process at least one year before you expect to begin your graduate study. Find out the application deadline for each institution (many are provided in the **Profile** section of this guide). Go to the institution's Web site and find out if you can apply online. If not, request a paper application form. Fill out this form thoroughly and neatly. Assume that the school needs all the information it is requesting and that the admissions officer will be sensitive to the neatness and overall quality of what you submit. Do not supply more information than the school requires.

The institution may ask at least one question that will require a three or four-paragraph answer. Compose your response on the assumption that the admissions officer is interested in both what you think and how you express yourself. Keep your statement brief and to the point, but, at the same time, include all pertinent information about your past experiences and your educational goals. Individual statements vary greatly in style and content, which helps admissions officers differentiate among applicants. Many graduate departments give considerable weight to the statement in making their admissions decisions, so be sure to take the time to prepare a thoughtful and concise statement.

If recommendations are a part of the admissions requirements, carefully choose the individuals you ask to write them. It is generally best to ask current or former professors to write the recommendations, provided they are able to attest to your intellectual ability and motivation for doing the work required of a graduate student. It is advisable to provide stamped, preaddressed envelopes to people being asked to submit recommendations on your behalf.

Completed applications, including references, transcripts, and admission test scores, should be received at the institution by the specified date.

Be advised that institutions do not usually make admissions decisions until all materials have been received. Enclose a self-addressed postcard with your application, requesting confirmation of receipt. Allow at least ten days for the return of the postcard before making further inquiries.

If you plan to apply for financial support, it is imperative that you file your application early.

ADMISSION TESTS

The major testing program used in graduate admissions is the Graduate Record Examinations (GRE) testing program, sponsored by the GRE Board and administered by Educational Testing Service, Princeton, New Jersey.

The Graduate Record Examinations testing program consists of a General Test and eight Subject Tests. The General Test measures critical thinking, verbal reasoning, quantitative reasoning, and analytical writing skills. It is offered as an Internet-based test (iBT) in the United States, Canada, and many other countries.

The Graduate Record Examinations testing program consists of the revised General Test and eight Subject Tests. The GRE® revised General Test, introduced in August 2011, features a new test-taker friendly design and new question types. It reflects the kind of thinking students need to do in graduate or business school and demonstrates that students are indeed ready for graduate-level work.

- **Verbal Reasoning**—Measures ability to analyze and evaluate written material and synthesize information obtained from it, analyze relationships among component parts of sentences, and recognize relationships among words and concepts.
- **Quantitative Reasoning**—Measures problem-solving ability, focusing on basic concepts of arithmetic, algebra, geometry, and data analysis.
- **Analytical Writing**—Measures critical thinking and analytical writing skills, specifically the ability to articulate and support complex ideas clearly and effectively.

The GRE® revised General Test is available at about 700 test centers in more than 160 countries. It is offered as a computer-based test year-round at most locations around the world and as a paper-based test up to three times a year in areas where computer-based testing is not available.

Three scores are reported on the revised General Test:

1. A **Verbal Reasoning score** is reported on a 130–170 score scale, in 1-point increments.

2. A **Quantitative Reasoning score** is reported on a 130–170 score scale, in 1-point increments.

3. An **Analytical Writing score** is reported on a 0–6 score level, in half-point increments.

The GRE Subject Tests measure achievement and assume undergraduate majors or extensive background in the following eight disciplines:

- Biochemistry, Cell and Molecular Biology
- Biology
- Chemistry
- Computer Science
- Literature in English
- Mathematics
- Physics
- Psychology

The Subject Tests are available three times per year as paper-based administrations around the world. Testing time is approximately 2 hours and 50 minutes. You can obtain more information about the GRE by visiting the ETS Web site at www.ets.org or consulting the *GRE Information and Registration Bulletin.* The *Bulletin* can be obtained at many undergraduate colleges. You can also download it from the ETS Web site or obtain it by contacting Graduate Record Examinations, Educational Testing Service, P.O. Box 6000, Princeton, NJ 08541-6000; phone: 609-771-7670.

If you expect to apply for admission to a program that requires any of the GRE tests, you should select a test date well in advance of the application deadline. Scores on the computer-based General Test are reported within ten to fifteen days; scores on the paper-based Subject Tests are reported within six weeks.

Another testing program, the Miller Analogies Test (MAT), is administered at more than 500 Controlled Testing Centers, licensed by Harcourt Assessment, Inc., in the United States, Canada, and other countries. The MAT computer-based test is now available. Testing time is 60 minutes. The test consists of 120 partial analogies. You can obtain the *Candidate Information Booklet,* which contains a list of test centers and instructions for taking the test, from http://www.milleranalogies.com or by calling 800-622-3231 (toll-free).

Check the specific requirements of the programs to which you are applying.

How Admission Decisions Are Made

The program you apply to is directly involved in the admissions process. Although the final decision is usually made by the graduate dean (or an associate) or the faculty admissions committee, recommendations from faculty members in your intended field are important. At some institutions, an interview is incorporated into the decision process.

A Special Note for International Students

In addition to the steps already described, there are some special considerations for international students who intend to apply for graduate study in the United States. All graduate schools require an indication of competence in English. The purpose of the Test of English as a Foreign Language (TOEFL) is to evaluate the English proficiency of people who are nonnative speakers of English and want to study at colleges and universities where English is the language of instruction. The TOEFL is administered by Educational Testing Service (ETS) under the general direction of a policy board established by the College Board and the Graduate Record Examinations Board.

The TOEFL iBT assesses the four basic language skills: listening, reading, writing, and speaking. It was administered for the first time in September 2005, and ETS continues to introduce the TOEFL iBT in selected cities. The Internet-based test is administered at secure, official test centers. The testing time is approximately 4 hours. Because the TOEFL iBT includes a speaking section, the Test of Spoken English (TSE) is no longer needed.

The TOEFL is also offered in the paper-based format in areas of the world where Internet-based testing is not available. The paper-based TOEFL consists of three sections—listening comprehension, structure and written expression, and reading comprehension. The testing time is approximately 3 hours. The Test of Written English (TWE) is also given. The TWE is a 30-minute essay that measures the examinee's ability to compose in English. Examinees receive a TWE score separate from their TOEFL score. The *Information Bulletin* contains information on local fees and registration procedures.

The TOEFL® paper-based test (TOEFL PBT) began being phased out in mid-2012. For those who may have taken the TOEFL PBT, scores remain valid for two years after the test date. The Test of Written English (TWE) is also given. The TWE is a 30-minute essay that measures the examinee's ability to compose in English. Examinees receive a TWE score separate from their TOEFL score. The Information Bulletin contains information on local fees and registration procedures.

Additional information and registration materials are available from TOEFL Services, Educational Testing Service, P.O. Box 6151, Princeton, New Jersey 08541-6151. Phone: 609-771-7100. Web site: www.toefl.org.

International students should apply especially early because of the number of steps required to complete the admissions process. Furthermore, many United States graduate schools have a limited number of spaces for international students, and many more students apply than the schools can accommodate.

International students may find financial assistance from institutions very limited. The U.S. government requires international applicants to submit a certification of support, which is a statement attesting to the applicant's financial resources. In addition, international students *must* have health insurance coverage.

Tips for Minority Students

Indicators of a university's values in terms of diversity are found both in its recruitment programs and its resources directed to student success. Important questions: Does the institution vigorously recruit minorities for its graduate programs? Is there funding available to help with the costs associated with visiting the school? Are minorities represented in the institution's brochures or Web site or on their faculty rolls? What campus-based resources or services (including assistance in locating housing or career counseling and placement) are available? Is funding available to members of underrepresented groups?

At the program level, it is particularly important for minority students to investigate the "climate" of a program under consideration. How many minority students are enrolled and how many have graduated? What opportunities are there to work with diverse faculty and mentors whose research interests match yours? How are conflicts resolved or concerns addressed? How interested are faculty in building strong and supportive relations with students? "Climate" concerns should be addressed by posing questions to various individuals, including faculty members, current students, and alumni.

Information is also available through various organizations, such as the Hispanic Association of Colleges & Universities (HACU), and publications such as *Diverse Issues in Higher Education* and *Hispanic Outlook* magazine. There are also books devoted to this topic, such as *The Multicultural Student's Guide to Colleges* by Robert Mitchell.

4   www.petersonsbooks.com

Peterson's Graduate Programs in the Physical Sciences, Mathematics, Agricultural Sciences, the Environment & Natural Resources 2014

Financial Support

The range of financial support at the graduate level is very broad. The following descriptions will give you a general idea of what you might expect and what will be expected of you as a financial support recipient.

Fellowships, Scholarships, and Grants

These are usually outright awards of a few hundred to many thousands of dollars with no service to the institution required in return. Fellowships and scholarships are usually awarded on the basis of merit and are highly competitive. Grants are made on the basis of financial need or special talent in a field of study. Many fellowships, scholarships, and grants not only cover tuition, fees, and supplies but also include stipends for living expenses with allowances for dependents. However, the terms of each should be examined because some do not permit recipients to supplement their income with outside work. Fellowships, scholarships, and grants may vary in the number of years for which they are awarded.

In addition to the availability of these funds at the university or program level, many excellent fellowship programs are available at the national level and may be applied for before and during enrollment in a graduate program. A listing of many of these programs can be found at the Council of Graduate Schools' Web site: http://www. cgsnet.org. There is a wealth of information in the "Programs" and "Awards" sections.

Assistantships and Internships

Many graduate students receive financial support through assistantships, particularly involving teaching or research duties. It is important to recognize that such appointments should not be viewed simply as employment relationships but rather should constitute an integral and important part of a student's graduate education. As such, the appointments should be accompanied by strong faculty mentoring and increasingly responsible apprenticeship experiences. The specific nature of these appointments in a given program should be considered in selecting that graduate program.

TEACHING ASSISTANTSHIPS

These usually provide a salary and full or partial tuition remission and may also provide health benefits. Unlike fellowships, scholarships, and grants, which require no service to the institution, teaching assistantships require recipients to provide the institution with a specific amount of undergraduate teaching, ideally related to the student's field of study. Some teaching assistants are limited to grading papers, compiling bibliographies, taking notes, or monitoring laboratories. At some graduate schools, teaching assistants must carry lighter course loads than regular full-time students.

RESEARCH ASSISTANTSHIPS

These are very similar to teaching assistantships in the manner in which financial assistance is provided. The difference is that recipients are given basic research assignments in their disciplines rather than teaching responsibilities. The work required is normally related to the student's field of study; in most instances, the assistantship supports the student's thesis or dissertation research.

ADMINISTRATIVE INTERNSHIPS

These are similar to assistantships in application of financial assistance funds, but the student is given an assignment on a part-time basis, usually as a special assistant with one of the university's administrative offices. The assignment may not necessarily be directly related to the recipient's discipline.

RESIDENCE HALL AND COUNSELING ASSISTANTSHIPS

These assistantships are frequently assigned to graduate students in psychology, counseling, and social work, but they may be offered to students in other disciplines, especially if the student has worked in this capacity during his or her undergraduate years. Duties can vary from being available in a dean's office for a specific number of hours for consultation with undergraduates to living in campus residences and being responsible for both counseling and administrative tasks or advising student activity groups. Residence hall assistantships often include a room and board allowance and, in some cases, tuition assistance and stipends. Contact the Housing and Student Life Office for more information.

Health Insurance

The availability and affordability of health insurance is an important issue and one that should be considered in an applicant's choice of institution and program. While often included with assistantships and fellowships, this is not always the case and, even if provided, the benefits may be limited. It is important to note that the U.S. government requires international students to have health insurance.

The GI Bill

This provides financial assistance for students who are veterans of the United States armed forces. If you are a veteran, contact your local Veterans Administration office to determine your eligibility and to get full details about benefits. There are a number of programs that offer educational benefits to current military enlistees. Some states have tuition assistance programs for members of the National Guard. Contact the VA office at the college for more information.

Federal Work-Study Program (FWS)

Employment is another way some students finance their graduate studies. The federally funded Federal Work-Study Program provides eligible students with employment opportunities, usually in public and private nonprofit organizations. Federal funds pay up to 75 percent of the wages, with the remainder paid by the employing agency. FWS is available to graduate students who demonstrate financial need. Not all schools have these funds, and some only award them to undergraduates. Each school sets its application deadline and workstudy earnings limits. Wages vary and are related to the type of work done. You must file the Free Application for Federal Student Aid (FAFSA) to be eligible for this program.

Loans

Many graduate students borrow to finance their graduate programs when other sources of assistance (which do not have to be repaid) prove insufficient. You should always read and understand the terms of any loan program before submitting your application.

FEDERAL DIRECT LOANS

Federal Direct Stafford Loans. The Federal Direct Stafford Loan Program offers a fixed interest rate loan to graduate students with the Department of Education acting as the lender. Beginning with loans made on or after July 1, 2013, the interest rate for loans made each July 1st to June 30th period are determined based on the last 10-year Treasury note auction prior to June 1st of that year. The interest rate can be no higher than 9.5%.

Beginning July 1, 2012, the Federal Direct Stafford Loan for graduate students is an unsubsidized loan. Under the *unsubsidized* program, you pay the interest on the loan from the day proceeds are issued.

Graduate students may borrow up to $20,500 per year through the Direct Stafford Loan Program, up to a cumulative maximum of $138,500, including undergraduate borrowing. You may borrow up to the cost of attendance at the school in which you are enrolled or will attend, minus estimated financial assistance from other federal, state, and private sources, up to a maximum of $20,500.

Direct Stafford Graduate Loans made on or after July 1, 2006 and before July 1, 2013, carry a fixed interest rate of 6.8% both for in-school and in-repayment borrowers.

A fee is deducted from the loan proceeds upon disbursement. Loans with a first disbursement on or after July 1, 2010 but before July 1, 2012, have a borrower origination fee of 1 percent. For loans disbursed after July 1, 2012, these fee deductions no longer apply. The Budget Control Act of 2011, signed into law on August 2, 2011, eliminated Direct Subsidized Loan eligibility for graduate and professional students for periods of enrollment beginning on or after July 1, 2012 and terminated the authority of the Department of Education to offer most repayment incentives to Direct Loan borrowers for loans disbursed on or after July 1, 2012.

Under the *subsidized* Federal Direct Stafford Loan Program, repayment begins six months after your last date of enrollment on at least a half-time basis. Under the *unsubsidized* program, repayment of interest begins within thirty days from disbursement of the loan proceeds, and repayment of the principal begins six months after your last enrollment on at least a half-time basis. Some borrowers may choose to defer interest payments while they are in school. The accrued interest is added to the loan balance when the borrower begins repayment. There are several repayment options.

Federal Perkins Loans. The Federal Perkins Loan is available to students demonstrating financial need and is administered directly by the school. Not all schools have these funds, and some may award them to undergraduates only. Eligibility is determined from the information you provide on the FAFSA. The school will notify you of your eligibility.

Eligible graduate students may borrow up to $6,000 per year, up to a maximum of $40,000, including undergraduate borrowing (even if your previous Perkins Loans have been repaid). The interest rate for Federal Perkins Loans is 5 percent, and no interest accrues while you remain in school at least half-time. There are no guarantee, loan, or disbursement fees. Repayment begins nine months after your last date of enrollment on at least a half-time basis and may extend over a maximum of ten years with no prepayment penalty.

Federal Direct Graduate PLUS Loans. Effective July 1, 2006, graduate and professional students are eligible for Graduate PLUS loans. This program allows students to borrow up to the cost of attendance, less any other aid received. These loans have a fixed interest rate, and interest begins to accrue at the time of disbursement. Beginning with loans made on or after July 1, 2013, the interest rate for loans made each July 1st to June 30th period are determined based on the last 10-year Treasury note auction prior to June 1st of that year. The interest rate can be no higher than 10.5%. The PLUS loans do involve a credit check; a PLUS borrower may obtain a loan with a cosigner if his or her credit is not good enough. Grad PLUS loans may be deferred while a student is in school and for the six months following a drop below half-time enrollment. For more information, you should contact a representative in your college's financial aid office.

Deferring Your Federal Loan Repayments. If you borrowed under the Federal Direct Stafford Loan Program, Federal Direct PLUS Loan Program, or the Federal Perkins Loan Program for previous undergraduate or graduate study, your payments may be deferred when you return to graduate school, depending on when you borrowed and under which program.

There are other deferment options available if you are temporarily unable to repay your loan. Information about these deferments is provided at your entrance and exit interviews. If you believe you are eligible for a deferment of your loan payments, you must contact your lender or loan servicer to request a deferment. The deferment must be filed prior to the time your payment is due, and it must be re-filed when it expires if you remain eligible for deferment at that time.

SUPPLEMENTAL (PRIVATE) LOANS

Many lending institutions offer supplemental loan programs and other financing plans, such as the ones described here, to students seeking additional assistance in meeting their education expenses. Some loan programs target all types of graduate students; others are designed specifically for business, law, or medical students. In addition, you can use private loans not specifically designed for education to help finance your graduate degree.

If you are considering borrowing through a supplemental or private loan program, you should carefully consider the terms and be sure to read the fine print. Check with the program sponsor for the most current terms that will be applicable to the amounts you intend to borrow for graduate study. Most supplemental loan programs for graduate study offer unsubsidized, credit-based loans. In general, a credit-ready borrower is one who has a satisfactory credit history or no credit history at all. A creditworthy borrower generally must pass a credit test to be eligible to borrow or act as a cosigner for the loan funds.

Many supplemental loan programs have minimum and maximum annual loan limits. Some offer amounts equal to the cost of attendance minus any other aid you will receive for graduate study. If you are planning to borrow for several years of graduate study, consider whether there is a cumulative or aggregate limit on the amount you may borrow. Often this cumulative or aggregate limit will include any amounts you borrowed and have not repaid for undergraduate or previous graduate study.

The combination of the annual interest rate, loan fees, and the repayment terms you choose will determine how much you will repay over time. Compare these features in combination before you decide which loan program to use. Some loans offer interest rates that are adjusted monthly, quarterly, or annually. Some offer interest rates that are lower during the in-school, grace, and deferment periods and then increase when you begin repayment. Some programs include a loan origination fee, which is usually deducted from the principal amount you receive when the loan is disbursed and must be repaid along with the interest and other principal when you graduate, withdraw from school, or drop below half-time study. Sometimes the loan fees are reduced if you borrow with a qualified cosigner. Some programs allow you to defer interest and/or principal payments while you are enrolled in graduate school. Many programs allow you to capitalize your interest payments; the interest due on your loan is added to the outstanding balance of your loan, so you don't have to repay immediately, but this increases the amount you owe. Other programs allow you to pay the interest as you go, which reduces the amount you later have to repay. The private loan market is very competitive, and your financial aid office can help you evaluate these programs.

Applying for Need-Based Financial Aid

Schools that award federal and institutional financial assistance based on need will require you to complete the FAFSA and, in some cases, an institutional financial aid application.

If you are applying for federal student assistance, you **must** complete the FAFSA. A service of the U.S. Department of Education, the FAFSA is free to all applicants. Most applicants apply online at www.fafsa.ed.gov. Paper applications are available at the financial aid office of your local college.

After your FAFSA information has been processed, you will receive a Student Aid Report (SAR). If you provided an e-mail address on the FAFSA, this will be sent to you electronically; otherwise, it will be mailed to your home address.

Follow the instructions on the SAR if you need to correct information reported on your original application. If your situation changes after you file your FAFSA, contact your financial aid officer to discuss amending your information. You can also appeal your financial aid award if you have extenuating circumstances.

6 www.petersonsbooks.com

Peterson's Graduate Programs in the Physical Sciences, Mathematics, Agricultural Sciences, the Environment & Natural Resources 2014

If you would like more information on federal student financial aid, visit the FAFSA Web site or download the most recent version of *Funding Education Beyond High School: The Guide to Federal Student Aid* at http://studentaid.ed.gov/students/publications/student_guide/index.html. This guide is also available in Spanish.

The U.S. Department of Education also has a toll-free number for questions concerning federal student aid programs. The number is 1-800-4-FED AID (1-800-433-3243). If you are hearing impaired, call toll-free, 1-800-730-8913.

Summary

Remember that these are generalized statements about financial assistance at the graduate level. Because each institution allots its aid differently, you should communicate directly with the school and the specific department of interest to you. It is not unusual, for example, to find that an endowment vested within a specific department supports one or more fellowships. You may fit its requirements and specifications precisely.

Peterson's Graduate Programs in the Physical Sciences, Mathematics, Agricultural Sciences, the Environment & Natural Resources 2014

www.petersonsbooks.com **7**

Accreditation and Accrediting Agencies

Colleges and universities in the United States, and their individual academic and professional programs, are accredited by nongovernmental agencies concerned with monitoring the quality of education in this country. Agencies with both regional and national jurisdictions grant accreditation to institutions as a whole, while specialized bodies acting on a nationwide basis—often national professional associations—grant accreditation to departments and programs in specific fields.

Institutional and specialized accrediting agencies share the same basic concerns: the purpose an academic unit—whether university or program—has set for itself and how well it fulfills that purpose, the adequacy of its financial and other resources, the quality of its academic offerings, and the level of services it provides. Agencies that grant institutional accreditation take a broader view, of course, and examine university-wide or college-wide services with which a specialized agency may not concern itself.

Both types of agencies follow the same general procedures when considering an application for accreditation. The academic unit prepares a self-evaluation, focusing on the concerns mentioned above and usually including an assessment of both its strengths and weaknesses; a team of representatives of the accrediting body reviews this evaluation, visits the campus, and makes its own report; and finally, the accrediting body makes a decision on the application. Often, even when accreditation is granted, the agency makes a recommendation regarding how the institution or program can improve. All institutions and programs are also reviewed every few years to determine whether they continue to meet established standards; if they do not, they may lose their accreditation.

Accrediting agencies themselves are reviewed and evaluated periodically by the U.S. Department of Education and the Council for Higher Education Accreditation (CHEA). Recognized agencies adhere to certain standards and practices, and their authority in matters of accreditation is widely accepted in the educational community.

This does not mean, however, that accreditation is a simple matter, either for schools wishing to become accredited or for students deciding where to apply. Indeed, in certain fields the very meaning and methods of accreditation are the subject of a good deal of debate. For their part, those applying to graduate school should be aware of the safeguards provided by regional accreditation, especially in terms of degree acceptance and institutional longevity. Beyond this, applicants should understand the role that specialized accreditation plays in their field, as this varies considerably from one discipline to another. In certain professional fields, it is necessary to have graduated from a program that is accredited in order to be eligible for a license to practice, and in some fields the federal government also makes this a hiring requirement. In other disciplines, however, accreditation is not as essential, and there can be excellent programs that are not accredited. In fact, some programs choose not to seek accreditation, although most do.

Institutions and programs that present themselves for accreditation are sometimes granted the status of candidate for accreditation, or what is known as "preaccreditation." This may happen, for example, when an academic unit is too new to have met all the requirements for accreditation. Such status signifies initial recognition and indicates that the school or program in question is working to fulfill all requirements; it does not, however, guarantee that accreditation will be granted.

Institutional Accrediting Agencies—Regional

MIDDLE STATES ASSOCIATION OF COLLEGES AND SCHOOLS

Accredits institutions in Delaware, District of Columbia, Maryland, New Jersey, New York, Pennsylvania, Puerto Rico, and the Virgin Islands.

Dr. Elizabeth Sibolski, President
Middle States Commission on Higher Education
3624 Market Street, Second Floor West
Philadelphia, Pennsylvania 19104
Phone: 267-284-5000
Fax: 215-662-5501
E-mail: info@msche.org
Web: www.msche.org

NEW ENGLAND ASSOCIATION OF SCHOOLS AND COLLEGES

Accredits institutions in Connecticut, Maine, Massachusetts, New Hampshire, Rhode Island, and Vermont.

Dr. Barbara E. Brittingham, President/Director
Commission on Institutions of Higher Education
3 Burlington Road, Suite 100
Bedford, Massachusetts 01803-4531
Phone: 781-425-7714
Fax: 781-425-1001
E-mail: cihe@neasc.org
Web: http://cihe.neasc.org

NORTH CENTRAL ASSOCIATION OF COLLEGES AND SCHOOLS

Accredits institutions in Arizona, Arkansas, Colorado, Illinois, Indiana, Iowa, Kansas, Michigan, Minnesota, Missouri, Nebraska, New Mexico, North Dakota, Ohio, Oklahoma, South Dakota, West Virginia, Wisconsin, and Wyoming.

Dr. Sylvia Manning, President
The Higher Learning Commission
230 South LaSalle Street, Suite 7-500
Chicago, Illinois 60604-1413
Phone: 312-263-0456
Fax: 312-263-7462
E-mail: smanning@hlcommission.org
Web: www.ncahlc.org

NORTHWEST COMMISSION ON COLLEGES AND UNIVERSITIES

Accredits institutions in Alaska, Idaho, Montana, Nevada, Oregon, Utah, and Washington.

Dr. Sandra E. Elman, President
8060 165th Avenue, NE, Suite 100
Redmond, Washington 98052
Phone: 425-558-4224
Fax: 425-376-0596
E-mail: selman@nwccu.org
Web: www.nwccu.org

SOUTHERN ASSOCIATION OF COLLEGES AND SCHOOLS

Accredits institutions in Alabama, Florida, Georgia, Kentucky, Louisiana, Mississippi, North Carolina, South Carolina, Tennessee, Texas, and Virginia.

Dr. Belle S. Wheelan, President
Commission on Colleges
1866 Southern Lane
Decatur, Georgia 30033-4097
Phone: 404-679-4500
Fax: 404-679-4558
E-mail: questions@sacscoc.org
Web: www.sacscoc.org

WESTERN ASSOCIATION OF SCHOOLS AND COLLEGES

Accredits institutions in California, Guam, and Hawaii.

Dr. Mary Ellen Petrisko, President
Accrediting Commission for Senior Colleges and Universities
985 Atlantic Avenue, Suite 100
Alameda, California 94501
Phone: 510-748-9001
Fax: 510-748-9797
E-mail: wascsr@wascsenior.org
Web: http://www.wascsenior.org/

Institutional Accrediting Agencies—Other

ACCREDITING COUNCIL FOR INDEPENDENT COLLEGES AND SCHOOLS

Albert C. Gray, Ph.D., Executive Director and CEO
750 First Street, NE, Suite 980
Washington, DC 20002-4241
Phone: 202-336-6780
Fax: 202-842-2593
E-mail: info@acics.org
Web: www.acics.org

DISTANCE EDUCATION AND TRAINING COUNCIL (DETC)

Accrediting Commission
Michael P. Lambert, Executive Director
1601 18th Street, NW, Suite 2
Washington, DC 20009
Phone: 202-234-5100
Fax: 202-332-1386
E-mail: Brianna@detc.org
Web: www.detc.org

Specialized Accrediting Agencies

ACUPUNCTURE AND ORIENTAL MEDICINE

Mark S. McKenzie, LAc MsOM DiplOM, Executive Director
Accreditation Commission for Acupuncture and Oriental Medicine
8941 Aztec Drive
Eden Prairie, Minnesota 55347
Phone: 301-313-0855
Fax: 301-313-0912
E-mail: coordinator@acaom.org
Web: www.acaom.org

ART AND DESIGN

Samuel Hope, Executive Director
Karen P. Moynahan, Associate Director
National Association of Schools of Art and Design (NASAD)
Commission on Accreditation
11250 Roger Bacon Drive, Suite 21
Reston, Virginia 20190-5243
Phone: 703-437-0700
Fax: 703-437-6312
E-mail: info@arts-accredit.org
Web: http://nasad.arts-accredit.org/

BUSINESS

Jerry Trapnell, Executive Vice President/Chief Accreditation Officer
AACSB International—The Association to Advance Collegiate Schools of Business
777 South Harbour Island Boulevard, Suite 750
Tampa, Florida 33602
Phone: 813-769-6500
Fax: 813-769-6559
E-mail: jerryt@aacsb.edu
Web: www.aacsb.edu

CHIROPRACTIC

S. Ray Bennett, Director of Accreditation Services
Council on Chiropractic Education (CCE)
Commission on Accreditation
8049 North 85th Way
Scottsdale, Arizona 85258-4321
Phone: 480-443-8877
Fax: 480-483-7333
E-mail: cce@cce-usa.org
Web: www.cce-usa.org

CLINICAL LABORATORY SCIENCES

Dianne M. Cearlock, Ph.D., Chief Executive Officer
National Accrediting Agency for Clinical Laboratory Sciences
5600 North River Road, Suite 720
Rosemont, Illinois 60018-5119
Phone: 773-714-8880
Fax: 773-714-8886
E-mail: info@naacls.org
Web: www.naacls.org

CLINICAL PASTORAL EDUCATION

Deryck Durston, Interim Executive Director
Association for Clinical Pastoral Education, Inc.
1549 Claremont Road, Suite 103
Decatur, Georgia 30033-4611
Phone: 404-320-1472
Fax: 404-320-0849
E-mail: acpe@acpe.edu
Web: www.acpe.edu

DANCE

Samuel Hope, Executive Director
Karen P. Moynahan, Associate Director
National Association of Schools of Dance (NASD)
Commission on Accreditation
11250 Roger Bacon Drive, Suite 21
Reston, Virginia 20190-5248
Phone: 703-437-0700
Fax: 703-437-6312
E-mail: info@arts-accredit.org
Web: http://nasd.arts-accredit.org

DENTISTRY

Anthony Ziebert, Director
Commission on Dental Accreditation
American Dental Association
211 East Chicago Avenue, Suite 1900
Chicago, Illinois 60611
Phone: 312-440-4643
E-mail: accreditation@ada.org
Web: www.ada.org

DIETETICS

Ulric K. Chung, Ph.D., Executive Director
American Dietetic Association
Commission on Accreditation for Dietetics Education (CADE-ADA)
120 South Riverside Plaza, Suite 2000
Chicago, Illinois 60606-6995
Phone: 800-877-1600
Fax: 312-899-4817
E-mail: cade@eatright.org
Web: www.eatright.org/cade

ENGINEERING

Michael Milligan, Ph.D., PE, Executive Director
Accreditation Board for Engineering and Technology, Inc. (ABET)
111 Market Place, Suite 1050
Baltimore, Maryland 21202
Phone: 410-347-7700
Fax: 410-625-2238
E-mail: accreditation@abet.org
Web: www.abet.org

FORESTRY

Carol L. Redelsheimer, Director of Science and Education
Society of American Foresters
5400 Grosvenor Lane
Bethesda, Maryland 20814-2198
Phone: 301-897-8720 Ext. 123
Fax: 301-897-3690
E-mail: redelsheimerc@safnet.org
Web: www.safnet.org

10 www.petersonsbooks.com

Peterson's Graduate Programs in the Physical Sciences, Mathematics, Agricultural Sciences, the Environment & Natural Resources 2014

HEALTH SERVICES ADMINISTRATION

Margaret Schulte, President and CEO
Commission on Accreditation of Healthcare Management
    Education (CAHME)
1700 Rockville Pike
Suite 400
Rockville, Maryland 20852
Phone: 301-998-6101
E-mail: info@cahme.org
Web: www.cahme.org

INTERIOR DESIGN

Holly Mattson, Executive Director
Council for Interior Design Accreditation
206 Grandview Avenue, Suite 350
Grand Rapids, Michigan 49503-4014
Phone: 616-458-0400
Fax: 616-458-0460
E-mail: info@accredit-id.org
Web: www.accredit-id.org

JOURNALISM AND MASS COMMUNICATIONS

Susanne Shaw, Executive Director
Accrediting Council on Education in Journalism and Mass
    Communications (ACEJMC)
School of Journalism
Stauffer-Flint Hall
University of Kansas
1435 Jayhawk Boulevard
Lawrence, Kansas 66045-7575
Phone: 785-864-3973
Fax: 785-864-5225
E-mail: sshaw@ku.edu
Web: http://www2.ku.edu/~acejmc/

LANDSCAPE ARCHITECTURE

Ronald C. Leighton, Executive Director
Landscape Architectural Accreditation Board (LAAB)
American Society of Landscape Architects (ASLA)
636 Eye Street, NW
Washington, DC 20001-3736
Phone: 202-898-2444
Fax: 202-898-1185
E-mail: info@asla.org
Web: www.asla.org

LAW

Barry Currier, Managing Director
American Bar Association
321 North Clark Street, 21st Floor
Chicago, Illinois 60654
Phone: 312-988-6738
Fax: 312-988-5681
E-mail: legaled@americanbar.org
Web: www.abanet.org/legaled/

LIBRARY

Karen O'Brien, Director
Office for Accreditation
American Library Association
50 East Huron Street
Chicago, Illinois 60611
Phone: 800-545-2433 Ext. 2432
Fax: 312-280-2433
E-mail: accred@ala.org
Web: www.ala.org/accreditation/

MARRIAGE AND FAMILY THERAPY

Tanya A. Tamarkin, Director of Educational Affairs
Commission on Accreditation for Marriage and Family Therapy
    Education
American Association for Marriage and Family Therapy
112 South Alfred Street
Alexandria, Virginia 22314-3061
Phone: 703-838-9808
Fax: 703-838-9805
E-mail: coamfte@aamft.org
Web: www.aamft.org

MEDICAL ILLUSTRATION

Commission on Accreditation of Allied Health Education Programs
    (CAAHEP)
Kathleen Megivern, Executive Director
1361 Park Street
Clearwater, Florida 33756
Phone: 727-210-2350
Fax: 727-210-2354
E-mail: mail@caahep.org
Web: www.caahep.org

MEDICINE

Liaison Committee on Medical Education (LCME)
In odd-numbered years beginning each July 1, contact:
Barbara Barzansky, Ph.D., LCME Secretary
American Medical Association
Council on Medical Education
515 North State Street
Chicago, Illinois 60654
Phone: 312-464-4933
Fax: 312-464-5830
E-mail: cme@aamc.org
Web: www.ama-assn.org

In even-numbered years beginning each July 1, contact:
Dan Hunt, M.D., LCME Secretary
Association of American Medical Colleges
2450 N Street, NW Washington, DC 20037
Phone: 202-828-0596
Fax: 202-828-1125
E-mail: dhunt@aamc.org
Web: www.lcme.org

MUSIC

Samuel Hope, Executive Director
Karen P. Moynahan, Associate Director
National Association of Schools of Music (NASM)
Commission on Accreditation
11250 Roger Bacon Drive, Suite 21
Reston, Virginia 20190-5248
Phone: 703-437-0700
Fax: 703-437-6312
E-mail: info@arts-accredit.org
Web: http://nasm.arts-accredit.org/

NATUROPATHIC MEDICINE

Daniel Seitz, J.D., Ed.D., Executive Director
Council on Naturopathic Medical Education
P.O. Box 178
Great Barrington, Massachusetts 01230
Phone: 413-528-8877
Fax: 413-528-8880
E-mail: council@cnme.org
Web: www.cnme.org

Peterson's Graduate Programs in the Physical Sciences, Mathematics, Agricultural Sciences, the Environment & Natural Resources 2014

www.petersonsbooks.com 11

NURSE ANESTHESIA
Francis R. Gerbasi, Executive Director
Council on Accreditation of Nurse Anesthesia Educational Programs
American Association of Nurse Anesthetists
222 South Prospect Avenue, Suite 304
Park Ridge, Illinois 60068
Phone: 847-692-7050 Ext. 1154
Fax: 847-692-6968
E-mail: fgerbasi@aana.com
Web: http://home.coa.us.com

NURSE EDUCATION
Jennifer L. Butlin, Director
Commission on Collegiate Nursing Education (CCNE)
One Dupont Circle, NW, Suite 530
Washington, DC 20036-1120
Phone: 202-887-6791
Fax: 202-887-8476
E-mail: jbutlin@aacn.nche.edu
Web: www.aacn.nche.edu/accreditation

NURSE MIDWIFERY
Lorrie Kaplan, Executive Director
Accreditation Commission for Midwifery Education
American College of Nurse-Midwives
Nurse-Midwifery Program
8403 Colesville Road, Suite 1550
Silver Spring, Maryland 20910
Phone: 240-485-1800
Fax: 240-485-1818
E-mail: lkaplan@acnm.org
Web: www.midwife.org/acme.cfm

Sandra Bitonti Stewart, Executive Director
Midwifery Education Accreditation Council
1935 Pauline Boulevard, Suite 100B
Ann Arbor, Michigan 48103
Phone: 360-466-2080
Fax: 480-907-2936
E-mail: info@meacschools.org
Web: www.meacschools.org

NURSE PRACTITIONER
Gay Johnson, Acting CEO
National Association of Nurse Practitioners in Women's Health
Council on Accreditation
505 C Street, NE Washington, DC 20002
Phone: 202-543-9693 Ext. 1
Fax: 202-543-9858
E-mail: info@npwh.org
Web: www.npwh.org

NURSING
Sharon J. Tanner, Ed.D., RN, Executive Director
National League for Nursing Accrediting Commission (NLNAC)
3343 Peachtree Road, NE, Suite 500
Atlanta, Georgia 30326
Phone: 404-975-5000
Fax: 404-975-5020
E-mail: nlnac@nlnac.org
Web: www.nlnac.org

OCCUPATIONAL THERAPY
Neil Harvison, Ph.D., OTR/L
Director of Accreditation and Academic Affairs
The American Occupational Therapy Association
4720 Montgomery Lane
P.O. Box 31220
Bethesda, Maryland 20824-1220
Phone: 301-652-2682 Ext. 2912
Fax: 301-652-7711
E-mail: accred@aota.org
Web: www.aota.org

OPTOMETRY
Joyce L. Urbeck, Administrative Director
Accreditation Council on Optometric Education
American Optometric Association (AOA)
243 North Lindbergh Boulevard
St. Louis, Missouri 63141
Phone: 314-991-4000 Ext. 246
Fax: 314-991-4101
E-mail: acoe@aoa.org
Web: www.theacoe.org

OSTEOPATHIC MEDICINE
Konrad C. Miskowicz-Retz, Ph.D., CAE
Director, Department of Education
Commission on Osteopathic College Accreditation
American Osteopathic Association
142 East Ontario Street
Chicago, Illinois 60611
Phone: 312-202-8048
Fax: 312-202-8202
E-mail: kretz@osteopathic.org
Web: www.osteopathic.org

PHARMACY
Peter H. Vlasses, Executive Director
Accreditation Council for Pharmacy Education
135 South LaSalle Street, Suite 4100
Chicago, Illinois 60603-4810
Phone: 312-664-3575
Fax: 312-664-4652
E-mail: csinfo@acpe-accredit.org
Web: www.acpe-accredit.org

PHYSICAL THERAPY
Mary Jane Harris, Director
Commission on Accreditation in Physical Therapy Education (CAPTE)
American Physical Therapy Association (APTA)
1111 North Fairfax Street
Alexandria, Virginia 22314
Phone: 703-706-3245
Fax: 703-706-3387
E-mail: accreditation@apta.org
Web: www.capteonline.org

PHYSICIAN ASSISTANT STUDIES
John E. McCarty, Executive Director
Accreditation Review Commission on Education for the Physician
    Assistant, Inc. (ARC-PA)
12000 Findley Road, Suite 150
Johns Creek, Georgia 30097
Phone: 770-476-1224
Fax: 770-476-1738
E-mail: arc-pa@arc-pa.org
Web: www.arc-pa.org

PLANNING
Shonagh Merits, Executive Director
American Institute of Certified Planners/Association of Collegiate
    Schools of Planning/American Planning Association
Planning Accreditation Board (PAB)
53 W. Jackson Boulevard, Suite 1315
Chicago, Illinois 60604
Phone: 312-334-1271
Fax: 312-334-1273
E-mail: smerits@planningaccreditationboard.org
Web: www.planningaccreditationboard.org

12   www.petersonsbooks.com

*Peterson's Graduate Programs in the Physical Sciences, Mathematics,
Agricultural Sciences, the Environment & Natural Resources 2014*

PODIATRIC MEDICINE
Alan R. Tinkleman, Executive Director
Council on Podiatric Medical Education (CPME)
American Podiatric Medical Association
9312 Old Georgetown Road
Bethesda, Maryland 20814-1621
Phone: 301-571-9200
Fax: 301-571-4903
E-mail: artinkleman@apma.org
Web: www.cpme.org

PSYCHOLOGY AND COUNSELING
Susan Zlotlow, Executive Director
Office of Program Consultation and Accreditation
American Psychological Association
750 First Street, NE Washington, DC 20002-4242
Phone: 202-336-5979
Fax: 202-336-5978
E-mail: apaaccred@apa.org
Web: www.apa.org/ed/accreditation

Carol L. Bobby, Executive Director
Council for Accreditation of Counseling and Related Educational
    Programs (CACREP)
1001 North Fairfax Street, Suite 510
Alexandria, Virginia 22314
Phone: 703-535-5990
Fax: 703-739-6209
E-mail: cacrep@cacrep.org
Web: www.cacrcp.org

PUBLIC AFFAIRS AND ADMINISTRATION
Crystal Calarusso, Executive Director
Commission on Peer Review and Accreditation
National Association of Schools of Public Affairs and Administration
1029 Vermont Avenue, NW, Suite 1100
Washington, DC 20005
Phone: 202-628-8965
Fax: 202-626-4978
E-mail: copra@naspaa.org
Web: www.naspaa.org

PUBLIC HEALTH
Laura Rasar King, M.P.H., MCHES, Executive Director
Council on Education for Public Health
1010 Wayne Avenue, Suite 220
Silver Spring, Maryland 20910
Phone: 202-789-1050
Fax: 202-789-1895
E-mail: Lking@ceph.org
Web: www.ceph.org

REHABILITATION EDUCATION
Dr. Tom Evenson, President
Council on Rehabilitation Education (CORE)
Commission on Standards and Accreditation
1699 Woodfield Road, Suite 300
Schaumburg, Illinois 60173
Phone: 847-944-1345
Fax: 847-944-1324
E-mail: evenson@unt.edu
Web: www.core-rehab.org

SOCIAL WORK
Jo Ann Regan, Director of Accreditation
Commission on Accreditation
Council on Social Work Education
1701 Duke Street, Suite 200
Alexandria, Virginia 22314
Phone: 703-683-8080
Fax: 703-683-8099
E-mail: jregan@cswe.org
Web: www.cswe.org

SPEECH-LANGUAGE PATHOLOGY AND AUDIOLOGY
Patrima L. Tice, Director of Accreditation
American Speech-Language-Hearing Association
Council on Academic Accreditation in Audiology and Speech-Language
    Pathology
2200 Research Boulevard
Rockville, Maryland 20850-3289
Phone: 301-296-5796
Fax: 301-296-8750
E-mail: ptice@asha.org
Web: www.asha.org/academic/accreditation/default.htm

TECHNOLOGY
Michale S. McComis, Ed.D., Executive Director
Accrediting Commission of Career Schools and Colleges
2101 Wilson Boulevard, Suite 302
Arlington, Virginia 22201
Phone: 703-247-4212
Fax: 703-247-4533
E-mail: mccomis@accsc.org
Web: www.accsc.org

TEACHER EDUCATION
James G. Cibulka, President
National Council for Accreditation of Teacher Education
2010 Massachusetts Avenue, NW, Suite 500
Washington, DC 20036-1023
Phone: 202-466-7496
Fax: 202-296-6620
E-mail: ncate@ncate.org
Web: www.ncate.org

Mark LaCelle-Peterson, President
Teacher Education Accreditation Council (TEAC)
Accreditation Committee
One Dupont Circle, Suite 320
Washington, DC 20036-0110
Phone: 202-831-0400
Fax: 202-831-3013
E-mail: teac@teac.org
Web: www.teac.org

THEATER
Samuel Hope, Executive Director
Karen P. Moynahan, Associate Director
National Association of Schools of Theatre Commission on
    Accreditation
11250 Roger Bacon Drive, Suite 21
Reston, Virginia 20190
Phone: 703-437-0700
Fax: 703-437-6312
E-mail: info@arts-accredit.org
Web: http://nast.arts-accredit.org/

THEOLOGY
Bernard Fryshman, Executive Vice President
Association of Advanced Rabbinical and Talmudic Schools (AARTS)
Accreditation Commission
11 Broadway, Suite 405
New York, New York 10004
Phone: 212-363-1991
Fax: 212-533-5335
E-mail: BFryshman@nyit.edu

Daniel O. Aleshire, Executive Director
Association of Theological Schools in the United States and Canada
    (ATS)
Commission on Accrediting
10 Summit Park Drive
Pittsburgh, Pennsylvania 15275-1110
Phone: 412-788-6505
Fax: 412-788-6510
E-mail: ats@ats.edu
Web: www.ats.edu

*Peterson's Graduate Programs in the Physical Sciences, Mathematics,
Agricultural Sciences, the Environment & Natural Resources 2014*

www.petersonsbooks.com **13**

Paul Boatner, President
Transnational Association of Christian Colleges and Schools (TRACS)
Accreditation Commission
15935 Forest Road
Forest, Virginia 24551
Phone: 434-525-9539
Fax: 434-525-9538
E-mail: info@tracs.org
Web: www.tracs.org

VETERINARY MEDICINE
David Granstrom, Executive Director
Education and Research Division
American Veterinary Medical Association (AVMA)
Council on Education
1931 North Meacham Road, Suite 100
Schaumburg, Illinois 60173
Phone: 847-925-8070 Ext. 6674
Fax: 847-925-9329
E-mail: info@avma.org
Web: www.avma.org

14 www.petersonsbooks.com

*Peterson's Graduate Programs in the Physical Sciences, Mathematics,
Agricultural Sciences, the Environment & Natural Resources 2014*

How to Use These Guides

As you identify the particular programs and institutions that interest you, you can use both the *Graduate & Professional Programs: An Overview* volume and the specialized volumes in the series to obtain detailed information.

- *Graduate Programs in the Physical Sciences, Mathematics, Agricultural Sciences, the Environment & Natural Resources*
- *Graduate Programs in Engineering & Applied Sciences*
- *Graduate Programs the Humanities, Arts & Social Sciences*
- *Graduate Programs in the Biological/Biomedical Sciences & Health-Related Professions*
- *Graduate Programs in Business, Education, Information Studies, Law & Social Work*

Each of the specialized volumes in the series is divided into sections that contain one or more directories devoted to programs in a particular field. If you do not find a directory devoted to your field of interest in a specific volume, consult "Directories and Subject Areas" (located at the end of each volume). After you have identified the correct volume, consult the "Directories and Subject Areas in This Book" index, which shows (as does the more general directory) what directories cover subjects not specifically named in a directory or section title.

Each of the specialized volumes in the series has a number of general directories. These directories have entries for the largest unit at an institution granting graduate degrees in that field. For example, the general Engineering and Applied Sciences directory in the *Graduate Programs in Engineering & Applied Sciences* volume consists of **Profiles** for colleges, schools, and departments of engineering and applied sciences.

General directories are followed by other directories, or sections, that give more detailed information about programs in particular areas of the general field that has been covered. The general Engineering and Applied Sciences directory, in the previous example, is followed by nineteen sections with directories in specific areas of engineering, such as Chemical Engineering, Industrial/Management Engineering, and Mechanical Engineering.

Because of the broad nature of many fields, any system of organization is bound to involve a certain amount of overlap. Environmental studies, for example, is a field whose various aspects are studied in several types of departments and schools. Readers interested in such studies will find information on relevant programs in the *Graduate Programs in the Biological/Biomedical Sciences & Health-Related Professions* volume under Ecology and Environmental Biology and Environmental and Occupational Health; in the *Graduate Programs in the Physical Sciences, Mathematics, Agricultural Sciences, the Environment & Natural Resources* volume under Environmental Management and Policy and Natural Resources; and in the *Graduate Programs in Engineering & Applied Sciences* volume under Energy Management and Policy and Environmental Engineering. To help you find all of the programs of interest to you, the introduction to each section within the specialized volumes includes, if applicable, a paragraph suggesting other sections and directories with information on related areas of study.

Directory of Institutions with Programs in the Physical Sciences, Mathematics, Agricultural Sciences, the Environment & Natural Resources

This directory lists institutions in alphabetical order and includes beneath each name the academic fields in which each institution offers graduate programs. The degree level in each field is also indicated, provided

that the institution has supplied that information in response to Peterson's Annual Survey of Graduate and Professional Institutions.

An M indicates that a master's degree program is offered; a D indicates that a doctoral degree program is offered; a P indicates that the first professional degree is offered; an O signifies that other advanced degrees (e.g., certificates or specialist degrees) are offered; and an * (asterisk) indicates that a **Close-Up** and/or **Display** is located in this volume. See the index, "Close-Ups and Displays," for the specific page number.

Profiles of Academic and Professional Programs in the Specialized Volumes

Each section of **Profiles** has a table of contents that lists the Program Directories, **Displays**, and **Close-Ups**. Program Directories consist of the **Profiles** of programs in the relevant fields, with **Displays** following if programs have chosen to include them. **Close-Ups,** which are more individualized statements, again if programs have chosen to submit them, are also listed.

The **Profiles** found in the 500 directories in the specialized volumes provide basic data about the graduate units in capsule form for quick reference. To make these directories as useful as possible, **Profiles** are generally listed for an institution's smallest academic unit within a subject area. In other words, if an institution has a College of Liberal Arts that administers many related programs, the **Profile** for the individual program (e.g., Program in History), not the entire College, appears in the directory.

There are some programs that do not fit into any current directory and are not given individual **Profiles**. The directory structure is reviewed annually in order to keep this number to a minimum and to accommodate major trends in graduate education.

The following outline describes the **Profile** information found in the guides and explains how best to use that information. Any item that does not apply to or was not provided by a graduate unit is omitted from its listing. The format of the **Profiles** is constant, making it easy to compare one institution with another and one program with another.

Identifying Information. The institution's name, in boldface type, is followed by a complete listing of the administrative structure for that field of study. (For example, University of Akron, Buchtel College of Arts and Sciences, Department of Theoretical and Applied Mathematics, Program in Mathematics.) The last unit listed is the one to which all information in the **Profile** pertains. The institution's city, state, and zip code follow.

Offerings. Each field of study offered by the unit is listed with all postbaccalaureate degrees awarded. Degrees that are not preceded by a specific concentration are awarded in the general field listed in the unit name. Frequently, fields of study are broken down into subspecializations, and those appear following the degrees awarded; for example, "Offerings in secondary education (M.Ed.), including English education, mathematics education, science education." Students enrolled in the M.Ed. program would be able to specialize in any of the three fields mentioned.

Professional Accreditation. Some **Profiles** indicate whether a program is professionally accredited. Because it is possible for a program to receive or lose professional accreditation at any time, students entering fields in which accreditation is important to a career should verify the status of programs by contacting either the chairperson or the appropriate accrediting association.

Jointly Offered Degrees. Explanatory statements concerning programs that are offered in cooperation with other institutions are included in the list of degrees offered. This occurs most commonly on a regional basis (for example, two state universities offering a cooperative Ph.D. in special education) or where the specialized nature of the institutions encourages joint efforts (a J.D./M.B.A. offered by a law school at an institution with no formal business programs and an institution with a business school but lacking a law school). Only programs that are truly cooperative are listed; those involving only limited course work at another institution are not. Interested students should contact the heads of such units for further information.

Part-Time and Evening/Weekend Programs. When information regarding the availability of part-time or evening/weekend study appears in the **Profile**, it means that students are able to earn a degree exclusively through such study.

Postbaccalaureate Distance Learning Degrees. A postbaccalaureate distance learning degree program signifies that course requirements can be fulfilled with minimal or no on-campus study.

Faculty. Figures on the number of faculty members actively involved with graduate students through teaching or research are separated into full- and part-time as well as men and women whenever the information has been supplied.

Students. Figures for the number of students enrolled in graduate and professional programs pertain to the semester of highest enrollment from the 2012–13 academic year. These figures are broken down into full- and part-time and men and women whenever the data have been supplied. Information on the number of matriculated students enrolled in the unit who are members of a minority group or are international students appears here. The average age of the matriculated students is followed by the number of applicants, the percentage accepted, and the number enrolled for fall 2012.

Degrees Awarded. The number of degrees awarded in the calendar year is listed. Many doctoral programs offer a terminal master's degree if students leave the program after completing only part of the requirements for a doctoral degree; that is indicated here. All degrees are classified into one of four types: master's, doctoral, first professional, and other advanced degrees. A unit may award one or several degrees at a given level; however, the data are only collected by type and may therefore represent several different degree programs.

Degree Requirements. The information in this section is also broken down by type of degree, and all information for a degree level pertains to all degrees of that type unless otherwise specified. Degree requirements are collected in a simplified form to provide some very basic information on the nature of the program and on foreign language, thesis or dissertation, comprehensive exam, and registration requirements. Many units also provide a short list of additional requirements, such as fieldwork or an internship. For complete information on graduation requirements, contact the graduate school or program directly.

Entrance Requirements. Entrance requirements are broken down into the four degree levels of master's, doctoral, first professional, and other advanced degrees. Within each level, information may be provided in two basic categories: entrance exams and other requirements. The entrance exams are identified by the standard acronyms used by the testing agencies, unless they are not well known. Other entrance requirements are quite varied, but they often contain an undergraduate or graduate grade point average (GPA). Unless otherwise stated, the GPA is calculated on a 4.0 scale and is listed as a minimum required for admission. Additional exam requirements/recommendations for international students may be listed here. Application deadlines for domestic and international students, the application fee, and whether electronic applications are accepted may be listed here. Note that the deadline should be used for reference only; these dates are subject to change, and students interested in applying should always contact the graduate unit directly about application procedures and deadlines.

Expenses. The typical cost of study for the 2012–13 academic year is given in two basic categories: tuition and fees. Cost of study may be quite complex at a graduate institution. There are often sliding scales for part-time study, a different cost for first-year students, and other variables that make it impossible to completely cover the cost of study for each graduate program. To provide the most usable information, figures are given for full-time study for a full year where available and for part-time study in terms of a per-unit rate (per credit, per semester hour, etc.). Occasionally, variances may be noted in tuition and fees for reasons such as the type of program, whether courses are taken during the day or evening, whether courses are at the master's or doctoral level, or other institution-specific reasons. Expenses are usually subject to change; for exact costs at any given time, contact your

chosen schools and programs directly. Keep in mind that the tuition of Canadian institutions is usually given in Canadian dollars.

Financial Support. This section contains data on the number of awards administered by the institution and given to graduate students during the 2012–13 academic year. The first figure given represents the total number of students receiving financial support enrolled in that unit. If the unit has provided information on graduate appointments, these are broken down into three major categories: fellowships give money to graduate students to cover the cost of study and living expenses and are not based on a work obligation or research commitment, research assistantships provide stipends to graduate students for assistance in a formal research project with a faculty member, and teaching assistantships provide stipends to graduate students for teaching or for assisting faculty members in teaching undergraduate classes. Within each category, figures are given for the total number of awards, the average yearly amount per award, and whether full or partial tuition reimbursements are awarded. In addition to graduate appointments, the availability of several other financial aid sources is covered in this section. Tuition waivers are routinely part of a graduate appointment, but units sometimes waive part or all of a student's tuition even if a graduate appointment is not available. Federal WorkStudy is made available to students who demonstrate need and meet the federal guidelines; this form of aid normally includes 10 or more hours of work per week in an office of the institution. Institutionally sponsored loans are low-interest loans available to graduate students to cover both educational and living expenses. Career-related internships or fieldwork offer money to students who are participating in a formal off-campus research project or practicum. Grants, scholarships, traineeships, unspecified assistantships, and other awards may also be noted. The availability of financial support to part-time students is also indicated here.

Some programs list the financial aid application deadline and the forms that need to be completed for students to be eligible for financial awards. There are two forms: FAFSA, the Free Application for Federal Student Aid, which is required for federal aid, and the CSS PROFILE®.

Faculty Research. Each unit has the opportunity to list several keyword phrases describing the current research involving faculty members and graduate students. Space limitations prevent the unit from listing complete information on all research programs. The total expenditure for funded research from the previous academic year may also be included.

Unit Head and Application Contact. The head of the graduate program for each unit is listed with academic title and telephone and fax numbers and e-mail address if available. In addition to the unit head, many graduate programs list a separate contact for application and admission information, which follows the listing for the unit head. If no unit head or application contact is given, you should contact the overall institution for information on graduate admissions.

Displays and Close-Ups

The **Displays** and **Close-Ups** are supplementary insertions submitted by deans, chairs, and other administrators who wish to offer an additional, more individualized statement to readers. A number of graduate school and program administrators have attached a **Display** ad near the **Profile** listing. Here you will find information that an institution or program wants to emphasize. The **Close-Ups** are by their very nature more expansive and flexible than the **Profiles**, and the administrators who have written them may emphasize different aspects of their programs. All of the **Close-Ups** are organized in the same way (with the exception of a few that describe research and training opportunities instead of degree programs), and in each one you will find information on the same basic topics, such as programs of study, research facilities, tuition and fees, financial aid, and application procedures. If an institution or program has submitted a **Close-Up**, a boldface cross-reference appears below its **Profile**. As with the **Displays**, all of the **Close-Ups** in the guides have been submitted by choice; the absence of a **Display** or **Close-Up** does not reflect any type of editorial judgment on the part of Peterson's, and their presence in the guides should not be taken as an indication of status, quality, or approval. Statements regarding a university's objectives and accomplish-

16 www.petersonsbooks.com

Peterson's Graduate Programs in the Physical Sciences, Mathematics, Agricultural Sciences, the Environment & Natural Resources 2014

ments are a reflection of its own beliefs and are not the opinions of the Peterson's editors.

Appendixes

This section contains two appendixes. The first, "Institutional Changes Since the 2013 Edition," lists institutions that have closed, merged, or changed their name or status since the last edition of the guides. The second, "Abbreviations Used in the Guides," gives abbreviations of degree names, along with what those abbreviations stand for. These appendixes are identical in all six volumes of *Peterson's Graduate and Professional Programs*.

Indexes

There are three indexes presented here. The first index, "Close-Ups and Displays," gives page references for all programs that have chosen to place **Close-Ups** and **Displays** in this volume. It is arranged alphabetically by institution; within institutions, the arrangement is alphabetical by subject area. It is not an index to all programs in the book's directories of **Profiles**; readers must refer to the directories themselves for **Profile** information on programs that have not submitted the additional, more individualized statements. The second index, "Directories and Subject Areas in Other Books in This Series", gives book references for the directories in the specialized volumes and also includes cross-references for subject area names not used in the directory structure, for example, "Computing Technology (see Computer Science)." The third index, "Directories and Subject Areas in This Book," gives page references for the directories in this volume and cross-references for subject area names not used in this volume's directory structure.

Data Collection Procedures

The information published in the directories and **Profiles** of all the books is collected through Peterson's Annual Survey of Graduate and Professional Institutions. The survey is sent each spring to nearly 2,400 institutions offering postbaccalaureate degree programs, including accredited institutions in the United States, U.S. territories, and Canada and those institutions outside the United States that are accredited by U.S. accrediting bodies. Deans and other administrators complete these surveys, providing information on programs in the 500 academic and professional fields covered in the guides as well as overall institutional information. While every effort has been made to ensure the accuracy and completeness of the data, information is sometimes unavailable or changes occur after publication deadlines. All usable information received in time for publication has been included. The omission of any particular item from a directory or **Profile** signifies either that the item is not applicable to the institution or program or that information was not available. **Profiles** of programs scheduled to begin during the 2013–14 academic year cannot, obviously, include statistics on enrollment or, in many cases, the number of faculty members. If no usable data were submitted by an institution, its name, address, and program name appear in order to indicate the availability of graduate work.

Criteria for Inclusion in This Guide

To be included in this guide, an institution must have full accreditation or be a candidate for accreditation (preaccreditation) status by an institutional or specialized accrediting body recognized by the U.S. Department of Education or the Council for Higher Education Accreditation (CHEA). Institutional accrediting bodies, which review each institution as a whole, include the six regional associations of schools and colleges (Middle States, New England, North Central, Northwest, Southern, and Western), each of which is responsible for a specified portion of the United States and its territories. Other institutional accrediting bodies are national in scope and accredit specific kinds of institutions (e.g., Bible colleges, independent colleges, and rabbinical and Talmudic schools). Program registration by the New York State Board of Regents is considered to be the equivalent of institutional accreditation, since the board requires that all programs offered by an institution meet its standards before recognition is granted. A Canadian institution must be chartered and authorized to grant degrees by the provincial government, affiliated with a chartered institution, or accredited by a recognized U.S. accrediting body. This guide also includes institutions outside the United States that are accredited by these U.S. accrediting bodies. There are recognized specialized or professional accrediting bodies in more than fifty different fields, each of which is authorized to accredit institutions or specific programs in its particular field. For specialized institutions that offer programs in one field only, we designate this to be the equivalent of institutional accreditation. A full explanation of the accrediting process and complete information on recognized institutional (regional and national) and specialized accrediting bodies can be found online at www.chea.org or at www.ed.gov/admins/finaid/accred/index.html.

NOTICE: Certain portions of or information contained in this book have been submitted and paid for by the educational institution identified, and such institutions take full responsibility for the accuracy, timeliness, completeness and functionality of such contents. Such portions or information include (i) each display ad that comprises a half page of information covering a single educational institution or program and (ii) each two-page description or Close-Up of a graduate school or program that appear in the different sections of this guide. The "Close-Ups and Displays" are listed in various sections throughout the book.

Peterson's Graduate Programs in the Physical Sciences, Mathematics, Agricultural Sciences, the Environment & Natural Resources 2014

www.petersonsbooks.com **17**

DIRECTORY OF INSTITUTIONS AND THEIR OFFERINGS

ACADIA UNIVERSITY
Applied Mathematics	M
Chemistry	M
Geology	M
Statistics	M

ADELPHI UNIVERSITY
| Environmental Management and Policy | M |
| Environmental Sciences | M* |

AIR FORCE INSTITUTE OF TECHNOLOGY
Applied Mathematics	M,D
Applied Physics	M,D
Astrophysics	M,D
Environmental Management and Policy	M
Optical Sciences	M,D
Planetary and Space Sciences	M,D

ALABAMA AGRICULTURAL AND MECHANICAL UNIVERSITY
Agricultural Sciences— General	M,D
Agronomy and Soil Sciences	M,D
Applied Physics	M,D
Food Science and Technology	M,D
Optical Sciences	M,D
Physics	M,D
Plant Sciences	M,D

ALABAMA STATE UNIVERSITY
| Mathematics | M,O |

ALASKA PACIFIC UNIVERSITY
| Environmental Sciences | M |

ALBANY STATE UNIVERSITY
| Water Resources | M |

ALCORN STATE UNIVERSITY
Agricultural Sciences— General	M
Agronomy and Soil Sciences	M
Animal Sciences	M

AMERICAN PUBLIC UNIVERSITY SYSTEM
Environmental Management and Policy	M
Fish, Game, and Wildlife Management	M
Marine Affairs	M
Planetary and Space Sciences	M

AMERICAN UNIVERSITY
Applied Statistics	M,O
Environmental Management and Policy	M,D,O
Environmental Sciences	M,O
Mathematics	M,O
Natural Resources	M,D,O
Statistics	M,O

THE AMERICAN UNIVERSITY IN CAIRO
| Chemistry | M |

AMERICAN UNIVERSITY OF BEIRUT
Animal Sciences	M
Aquaculture	M
Biostatistics	M
Chemistry	M,D
Computational Sciences	M,D
Environmental Management and Policy	M,D

ANDREWS UNIVERSITY
| Mathematics | M |

ANGELO STATE UNIVERSITY
| Agricultural Sciences— General | M |
| Animal Sciences | M |

ANTIOCH UNIVERSITY NEW ENGLAND
| Environmental Management and Policy | M,D |
| Environmental Sciences | M,D |

ANTIOCH UNIVERSITY SEATTLE
| Environmental Management and Policy | M |

APPALACHIAN STATE UNIVERSITY
| Environmental Management and Policy | M |
| Mathematics | M |

AQUINAS COLLEGE
| Environmental Management and Policy | M |

ARIZONA STATE UNIVERSITY
Applied Mathematics	M,D,O
Astrophysics	M,D
Atmospheric Sciences	M,D,O
Chemistry	M,D
Environmental Management and Policy	M
Environmental Sciences	M,D,O
Geology	M,D
Geosciences	M,D
Mathematics	M,D
Physics	M,D
Planetary and Space Sciences	M,D
Statistics	M,D,O

ARKANSAS STATE UNIVERSITY
Agricultural Sciences— General	M,O
Chemistry	M,O
Environmental Sciences	M,D
Mathematics	M

ARKANSAS TECH UNIVERSITY
| Fish, Game, and Wildlife Management | M |

AUBURN UNIVERSITY
Agricultural Sciences— General	M,D
Agronomy and Soil Sciences	M,D
Analytical Chemistry	M,D
Animal Sciences	M,D
Applied Mathematics	M,D
Aquaculture	M,D
Chemistry	M,D
Fish, Game, and Wildlife Management	M,D
Food Science and Technology	M,D,O
Forestry	M,D
Geology	M

ANDREWS

Environmental Sciences	M,D
Food Science and Technology	M
Geology	M,D
Mathematics	M,D
Physics	M,D
Plant Sciences	M
Statistics	M,D
Theoretical Physics	M,D

Horticulture — (continued)
Horticulture	M,D
Hydrology	M,D
Inorganic Chemistry	M,D
Mathematics	M,D
Natural Resources	M,D
Organic Chemistry	M,D
Physical Chemistry	M,D
Physics	M,D
Statistics	M,D

AURORA UNIVERSITY
| Mathematics | M |

BALL STATE UNIVERSITY
Chemistry	M
Environmental Sciences	D
Geology	M
Mathematics	M
Natural Resources	M
Physics	M
Statistics	M

BARD COLLEGE
| Atmospheric Sciences | M,O |
| Environmental Management and Policy | M,O |

BARUCH COLLEGE OF THE CITY UNIVERSITY OF NEW YORK
| Mathematical and Computational Finance | M |
| Statistics | M |

BAYLOR UNIVERSITY
Chemistry	M,D
Environmental Management and Policy	M
Environmental Sciences	D
Geology	M,D
Geosciences	M,D
Limnology	M,D
Mathematics	M,D
Physics	M,D
Statistics	M,D

BEMIDJI STATE UNIVERSITY
| Environmental Management and Policy | M |
| Mathematics | M |

BERGIN UNIVERSITY OF CANINE STUDIES
| Animal Sciences | M |

BINGHAMTON UNIVERSITY, STATE UNIVERSITY OF NEW YORK
Analytical Chemistry	M,D
Applied Physics	M,D
Chemistry	M,D
Environmental Sciences	M,D
Geology	M,D
Inorganic Chemistry	M,D
Mathematics	M,D
Organic Chemistry	M,D
Physical Chemistry	M,D
Physics	M,D

BOISE STATE UNIVERSITY
Animal Sciences	M
Chemistry	M,D
Environmental Management and Policy	M,O
Geology	M,D
Geophysics	M,D
Hydrology	M,D
Mathematics	M

BOSTON COLLEGE
| Chemistry | M,D |

BOSTON COLLEGE (continued)
Geology	M
Geophysics	M
Inorganic Chemistry	M,D
Mathematics	D
Organic Chemistry	M,D
Physical Chemistry	M,D
Physics	M,D

BOSTON UNIVERSITY
Astronomy	M,D
Biostatistics	M,D
Chemistry	M,D
Environmental Management and Policy	M,D,O
Environmental Sciences	M,D
Food Science and Technology	M
Geosciences	M,D
Mathematical and Computational Finance	M,D
Mathematics	M,D
Photonics	M,D
Physics	M,D

BOWIE STATE UNIVERSITY
| Applied Mathematics | M |

BOWLING GREEN STATE UNIVERSITY
Applied Statistics	M,D
Chemistry	M,D
Geology	M
Geophysics	M
Mathematics	M,D
Physics	M
Statistics	M,D

BRADLEY UNIVERSITY
| Chemistry | M |

BRANDEIS UNIVERSITY
Chemistry	M,D
Inorganic Chemistry	M,D
Mathematics	M,D,O
Organic Chemistry	M,D
Physical Chemistry	M,D
Physics	M,D

BRIGHAM YOUNG UNIVERSITY
Agricultural Sciences— General	M,D
Analytical Chemistry	M,D
Animal Sciences	M,D
Applied Statistics	M
Astronomy	M,D
Chemistry	M,D
Environmental Sciences	M,D
Fish, Game, and Wildlife Management	M,D
Food Science and Technology	M
Geology	M
Mathematics	M,D
Physics	M,D
Plant Sciences	M,D
Statistics	M

BROCK UNIVERSITY
Chemistry	M,D
Geosciences	M
Mathematics	M
Physics	M
Statistics	M

BROOKLYN COLLEGE OF THE CITY UNIVERSITY OF NEW YORK
Chemistry	M,D
Geology	M,D
Geosciences	M,O
Mathematics	M,D
Physics	M,D

20 www.petersonsbooks.com

Petersons Graduate Programs in the Physical Sciences, Mathematics, Agricultural Sciences, the Environment & Natural Resources 2014

BROWN UNIVERSITY

Applied Mathematics	M,D
Biostatistics	M,D
Chemistry	M,D
Geosciences	M,D
Mathematics	M,D
Physics	M,D

BRYN MAWR COLLEGE

Chemistry	M,D
Mathematics	M,D
Physics	M,D

BUCKNELL UNIVERSITY

Chemistry	M
Mathematics	M

BUFFALO STATE COLLEGE, STATE UNIVERSITY OF NEW YORK

Chemistry	M

CALIFORNIA INSTITUTE OF TECHNOLOGY

Applied Mathematics	M,D
Applied Physics	M,D
Astronomy	D
Chemistry	M,D
Computational Sciences	M,D
Environmental Sciences	M,D
Geochemistry	M,D
Geology	M,D
Geophysics	M,D
Mathematics	D
Physics	D
Planetary and Space Sciences	M,D

CALIFORNIA POLYTECHNIC STATE UNIVERSITY, SAN LUIS OBISPO

Agricultural Sciences— General	M
Chemistry	M
Forestry	M
Mathematics	M
Natural Resources	M

CALIFORNIA STATE POLYTECHNIC UNIVERSITY, POMONA

Agricultural Sciences— General	M
Applied Mathematics	M
Chemistry	M
Environmental Sciences	M
Geology	M
Mathematics	M

CALIFORNIA STATE UNIVERSITY, BAKERSFIELD

Geology	M,O
Hydrogeology	M,O
Hydrology	M,O

CALIFORNIA STATE UNIVERSITY CHANNEL ISLANDS

Mathematics	M

CALIFORNIA STATE UNIVERSITY, CHICO

Environmental Management and Policy	M
Environmental Sciences	M
Geology	M
Geosciences	M
Hydrogeology	M
Hydrology	M

CALIFORNIA STATE UNIVERSITY, DOMINGUEZ HILLS

Environmental Sciences	M

CALIFORNIA STATE UNIVERSITY, EAST BAY

Applied Mathematics	M
Applied Statistics	M
Biostatistics	M
Chemistry	M
Environmental Sciences	M
Geology	M
Marine Sciences	M
Mathematics	M
Statistics	M

CALIFORNIA STATE UNIVERSITY, FRESNO

Animal Sciences	M
Chemistry	M
Food Science and Technology	M
Geology	M
Marine Sciences	M
Mathematics	M
Physics	M
Plant Sciences	M
Viticulture and Enology	M

CALIFORNIA STATE UNIVERSITY, FULLERTON

Applied Mathematics	M
Chemistry	M
Environmental Management and Policy	M
Geochemistry	M
Geology	M
Mathematics	M
Physics	M

CALIFORNIA STATE UNIVERSITY, LONG BEACH

Applied Mathematics	M,D
Applied Statistics	M
Chemistry	M
Food Science and Technology	M
Geology	M
Geophysics	M
Mathematics	M
Physics	M

CALIFORNIA STATE UNIVERSITY, LOS ANGELES

Analytical Chemistry	M
Applied Mathematics	M
Chemistry	M
Geology	M
Inorganic Chemistry	M
Mathematics	M
Organic Chemistry	M
Physical Chemistry	M
Physics	M

CALIFORNIA STATE UNIVERSITY, MONTEREY BAY

Marine Sciences	M
Water Resources	M

CALIFORNIA STATE UNIVERSITY, NORTHRIDGE

Applied Mathematics	M
Chemistry	M
Environmental Sciences	M
Geology	M
Mathematics	M
Physics	M

CALIFORNIA STATE UNIVERSITY, SACRAMENTO

Chemistry	M
Marine Sciences	M
Mathematics	M
Statistics	M

CALIFORNIA STATE UNIVERSITY, SAN BERNARDINO

Chemistry	M
Environmental Sciences	M
Mathematics	M

CALIFORNIA STATE UNIVERSITY, SAN MARCOS

Mathematics	M

CARLETON UNIVERSITY

Chemistry	M,D
Geosciences	M,D
Mathematics	M,D
Physics	M,D

CARNEGIE MELLON UNIVERSITY

Applied Mathematics	M,D
Applied Physics	M,D
Chemistry	M,D
Computational Sciences	D
Inorganic Chemistry	M,D
Mathematical and Computational Finance	M,D
Mathematics	M,D
Organic Chemistry	M,D
Physics	M,D
Statistics	M,D
Theoretical Chemistry	M,D

CASE WESTERN RESERVE UNIVERSITY

Applied Mathematics	M,D
Astronomy	M,D
Biostatistics	M,D
Chemistry	M,D
Geology	M,D
Geosciences	M,D
Mathematics	M,D
Physics	M,D
Statistics	M,D

THE CATHOLIC UNIVERSITY OF AMERICA

Physics	M,D

CENTRAL CONNECTICUT STATE UNIVERSITY

Chemistry	O
Geosciences	M,O
Mathematics	M,O
Physics	M,O
Statistics	M,O

CENTRAL EUROPEAN UNIVERSITY

Applied Mathematics	M,D
Environmental Management and Policy	M,D
Mathematics	M,D

CENTRAL MICHIGAN UNIVERSITY

Chemistry	M
Mathematics	M,D
Physics	M,D

CENTRAL WASHINGTON UNIVERSITY

Chemistry	M
Geology	M

CHAPMAN UNIVERSITY

Mathematics	M
Natural Resources	M
Computational Sciences	M
Food Science and Technology	M
Geosciences	M

CHICAGO STATE UNIVERSITY

Mathematics	M

CHRISTOPHER NEWPORT UNIVERSITY

Applied Physics	M
Chemistry	M
Environmental Sciences	M
Physics	M

CITY COLLEGE OF THE CITY UNIVERSITY OF NEW YORK

Atmospheric Sciences	M,D
Chemistry	M,D
Environmental Sciences	M,D
Geosciences	M,D
Mathematics	M
Physics	M,D

CLAREMONT GRADUATE UNIVERSITY

Applied Mathematics	M,D
Computational Sciences	M,D
Mathematics	M,D
Statistics	M,D

CLARK ATLANTA UNIVERSITY

Chemistry	M,D
Mathematics	M
Physics	M

CLARKSON UNIVERSITY

Chemistry	M,D
Environmental Management and Policy	M
Environmental Sciences	M,D
Mathematics	M,D
Physics	M,D

CLARK UNIVERSITY

Chemistry	M,D
Environmental Management and Policy	M
Physics	M,D

CLEMSON UNIVERSITY

Agricultural Sciences— General	M,D
Animal Sciences	M,D
Applied Mathematics	M,D
Aquaculture	M,D
Astronomy	M,D
Astrophysics	M,D
Atmospheric Sciences	M,D
Chemistry	M,D
Computational Sciences	M,D
Environmental Management and Policy	M,D
Environmental Sciences	M,D
Fish, Game, and Wildlife Management	M,D
Food Science and Technology	M,D
Forestry	M,D
Hydrogeology	M
Mathematics	M,D
Physics	M,D
Plant Sciences	M,D
Statistics	M,D

M—master's degree; P—first professional degree; D—doctorate; O—other advanced degree; *—Close-Up and/or Display

Petersons Graduate Programs in the Physical Sciences, Mathematics, Agricultural Sciences, the Environment & Natural Resources 2014

www.petersonsbooks.com **21**

CLEVELAND STATE UNIVERSITY

Analytical Chemistry	M,D
Applied Statistics	M
Chemistry	M,D
Condensed Matter Physics	M
Environmental Management and Policy	M,O
Environmental Sciences	M,D
Inorganic Chemistry	M,D
Mathematics	M
Optical Sciences	M
Organic Chemistry	M,D
Physical Chemistry	M,D
Physics	M

COASTAL CAROLINA UNIVERSITY

Marine Sciences	M

THE COLLEGE AT BROCKPORT, STATE UNIVERSITY OF NEW YORK

Environmental Sciences	M
Mathematics	M

COLLEGE OF CHARLESTON

Environmental Sciences	M
Marine Sciences	M
Mathematics	M,O

COLLEGE OF STATEN ISLAND OF THE CITY UNIVERSITY OF NEW YORK

Environmental Sciences	M

COLLEGE OF THE ATLANTIC

Environmental Management and Policy	M

THE COLLEGE OF WILLIAM AND MARY

Applied Mathematics	M,D
Applied Physics	M,D
Atmospheric Sciences	M,D
Chemistry	M
Computational Sciences	M
Geosciences	M,D
Marine Sciences	M,D
Optical Sciences	M,D
Physics	M,D

COLORADO SCHOOL OF MINES

Applied Mathematics	M,D
Applied Physics	M,D
Chemistry	M,D
Environmental Sciences	M,D
Geochemistry	M,D
Geology	M,D
Geophysics	M,D
Hydrology	M,D
Mathematics	M,D
Physics	M,D

COLORADO STATE UNIVERSITY

Agricultural Sciences—General	M,D
Agronomy and Soil Sciences	M,D
Animal Sciences	M,D
Atmospheric Sciences	M,D
Chemistry	M,D
Fish, Game, and Wildlife Management	M,D
Food Science and Technology	M,D
Forestry	M,D
Geosciences	M,D
Horticulture	M,D
Hydrology	M,D
Mathematics	M,D
Natural Resources	M,D
Physics	M,D
Plant Sciences	M,D
Range Science	M,D
Statistics	M,D
Water Resources	M,D

COLORADO STATE UNIVERSITY–PUEBLO

Chemistry	M

COLUMBIA UNIVERSITY

Applied Mathematics	M,D,O
Applied Physics	M,D,O
Astronomy	M,D
Atmospheric Sciences	M,D
Biostatistics	M,D
Chemical Physics	M,D
Chemistry	M,D
Environmental Management and Policy	M
Environmental Sciences	M
Geochemistry	M,D
Geodetic Sciences	M,D
Geophysics	M,D
Geosciences	M,D
Inorganic Chemistry	M,D
Mathematics	M,D
Meteorology	M
Oceanography	M,D
Organic Chemistry	M,D
Physics	M,D
Planetary and Space Sciences	M,D
Statistics	M,D

COLUMBUS STATE UNIVERSITY

Environmental Sciences	M

CONCORDIA UNIVERSITY (CANADA)

Chemistry	M,D
Environmental Management and Policy	M,O
Mathematics	M,D
Physics	M,D

CORNELL UNIVERSITY

Agronomy and Soil Sciences	M,D
Analytical Chemistry	D
Animal Sciences	M,D
Applied Mathematics	M,D
Applied Physics	M,D
Applied Statistics	M,D
Astronomy	D
Astrophysics	D
Atmospheric Sciences	M,D
Biometry	M,D
Chemical Physics	D
Chemistry	D
Computational Sciences	M,D
Environmental Management and Policy	M,D
Environmental Sciences	M,D
Fish, Game, and Wildlife Management	M,D
Food Science and Technology	M,D
Forestry	M,D
Geochemistry	M,D
Geology	M,D
Geophysics	M,D
Geosciences	M,D
Horticulture	M,D
Hydrology	M,D
Inorganic Chemistry	D
Limnology	D
Marine Geology	M,D
Marine Sciences	M,D
Mathematics	D
Mineralogy	M,D
Natural Resources	M,D
Oceanography	D
Organic Chemistry	D
Paleontology	M,D
Physical Chemistry	D

CREIGHTON UNIVERSITY

Atmospheric Sciences	M
Physics	M

DALHOUSIE UNIVERSITY

Agricultural Sciences—General	M
Agronomy and Soil Sciences	M
Animal Sciences	M
Applied Mathematics	M,D
Aquaculture	M
Chemistry	M,D
Environmental Management and Policy	M
Environmental Sciences	M
Food Science and Technology	M,D
Geosciences	M,D
Horticulture	M
Marine Affairs	M
Mathematics	M,D
Natural Resources	M
Oceanography	M,D
Physics	M,D
Statistics	M,D
Water Resources	M

DARTMOUTH COLLEGE

Astronomy	M,D
Chemistry	D
Geosciences	M,D
Mathematics	D
Physics	M,D

DELAWARE STATE UNIVERSITY

Applied Mathematics	M,D
Chemistry	M,D
Mathematics	M
Natural Resources	M
Optical Sciences	M,D
Physics	M,D
Plant Sciences	M
Theoretical Physics	D

DEPAUL UNIVERSITY

Analytical Chemistry	M
Applied Mathematics	M,O
Applied Statistics	M,O
Chemistry	M
Mathematical and Computational Finance	M,D
Mathematics	M,O
Physical Chemistry	M
Physics	M

DOWLING COLLEGE

Mathematics	M

DREW UNIVERSITY

Chemistry	M
Physics	M

DREXEL UNIVERSITY

Biostatistics	M,D,O
Chemistry	M,D
Environmental Management and Policy	M
Environmental Sciences	M,D
Food Science and Technology	M
Hydrology	M,D
Mathematics	M,D
Physics	M,D

DUKE UNIVERSITY

Biostatistics	M
Chemistry	D
Environmental Management and Policy	M,D
Environmental Sciences	M,D
Forestry	M,D
Geology	M,D
Marine Sciences	M
Mathematics	D
Natural Resources	M,D
Optical Sciences	M
Paleontology	D
Photonics	M
Physics	D
Statistics	D

DUQUESNE UNIVERSITY

Chemistry	M,D
Environmental Management and Policy	M,O
Environmental Sciences	M,O
Mathematics	M

EAST CAROLINA UNIVERSITY

Applied Physics	M,D
Chemistry	M
Geology	M,O
Hydrogeology	M,O
Mathematics	M,O
Physics	M,D
Statistics	M,O

EASTERN ILLINOIS UNIVERSITY

Chemistry	M
Mathematics	M

EASTERN KENTUCKY UNIVERSITY

Chemistry	M
Geology	M,D
Mathematics	M

EASTERN MICHIGAN UNIVERSITY

Applied Statistics	M
Chemistry	M
Geosciences	M
Mathematics	M
Physics	M
Water Resources	M,O

EASTERN NEW MEXICO UNIVERSITY

Analytical Chemistry	M
Chemistry	M
Inorganic Chemistry	M
Organic Chemistry	M
Physical Chemistry	M

EASTERN WASHINGTON UNIVERSITY

Mathematics	M

EAST TENNESSEE STATE UNIVERSITY

Biostatistics	M,O
Chemistry	M
Geosciences	M
Inorganic Chemistry	M
Mathematics	M
Organic Chemistry	M
Paleontology	M
Physical Chemistry	M

ÉCOLE POLYTECHNIQUE DE MONTRÉAL

Applied Mathematics	M,D,O
Optical Sciences	M,D,O

22 www.petersonsbooks.com

Petersons Graduate Programs in the Physical Sciences, Mathematics, Agricultural Sciences, the Environment & Natural Resources 2014

ELIZABETH CITY STATE UNIVERSITY
Applied Mathematics — M
Mathematics — M

EMORY UNIVERSITY
Biostatistics — M,D
Chemistry — D
Computational Sciences — D
Mathematics — M,D
Physics — D
Theoretical Physics — D

EMPORIA STATE UNIVERSITY
Geosciences — M,O
Mathematics — M

THE EVERGREEN STATE COLLEGE
Environmental Management and Policy — M

FAIRFIELD UNIVERSITY
Mathematics — M

FAIRLEIGH DICKINSON UNIVERSITY, COLLEGE AT FLORHAM
Chemistry — M

FAIRLEIGH DICKINSON UNIVERSITY, METROPOLITAN CAMPUS
Chemistry — M
Mathematics — M

FAYETTEVILLE STATE UNIVERSITY
Mathematics — M

FISK UNIVERSITY
Chemistry — M
Physics — M

FLORIDA AGRICULTURAL AND MECHANICAL UNIVERSITY
Chemistry — M
Environmental Sciences — M,D
Physics — M,D

FLORIDA ATLANTIC UNIVERSITY
Applied Mathematics — M,D
Chemistry — M,D
Environmental Management and Policy — M,O
Geology — M,D
Geosciences — M,D
Mathematics — M,D
Physics — M,D
Statistics — M,D

FLORIDA GULF COAST UNIVERSITY
Environmental Management and Policy — M
Environmental Sciences — M

FLORIDA INSTITUTE OF TECHNOLOGY
Applied Mathematics — M,D
Chemistry — M,D
Environmental Management and Policy — M,D
Environmental Sciences — M,D
Marine Sciences — M,D
Meteorology — M,D
Oceanography — M,D

Physics — M,D
Planetary and Space Sciences — M,D

FLORIDA INTERNATIONAL UNIVERSITY
Biostatistics — M,D
Chemistry — M,D
Environmental Management and Policy — M
Environmental Sciences — M
Geosciences — M,D
Mathematics — M
Physics — M,D
Statistics — M

FLORIDA STATE UNIVERSITY
Analytical Chemistry — M,D
Applied Mathematics — M,D
Applied Statistics — M,D
Atmospheric Sciences — M,D
Biostatistics — M,D
Chemistry — M,D
Computational Sciences — M,D
Environmental Sciences — M,D
Food Science and Technology — M,D
Geology — M,D
Geophysics — D
Geosciences — M,D
Inorganic Chemistry — M,D
Marine Sciences — M,D
Mathematical and Computational Finance — M,D
Mathematics — M,D
Meteorology — M,D
Oceanography — M,D
Organic Chemistry — M,D
Physical Chemistry — M,D
Physics — M,D
Statistics — M,D,O

FORT HAYS STATE UNIVERSITY
Geology — M
Geosciences — M

FORT VALLEY STATE UNIVERSITY
Animal Sciences — M

FRAMINGHAM STATE UNIVERSITY
Food Science and Technology — M

FRIENDS UNIVERSITY
Environmental Sciences — M

FROSTBURG STATE UNIVERSITY
Fish, Game, and Wildlife Management — M

FURMAN UNIVERSITY
Chemistry — M

GANNON UNIVERSITY
Environmental Sciences — M,O

GEORGE MASON UNIVERSITY
Applied Physics — M,D,O
Atmospheric Sciences — D
Biostatistics — M,O
Chemistry — M,D
Computational Sciences — M,D,O
Environmental Management and Policy — M,D,O
Environmental Sciences — M,D,O
Geosciences — M,D,O
Mathematics — M,D,O

Physics — M,D,O
Statistics — M,D,O

GEORGETOWN UNIVERSITY
Analytical Chemistry — D
Biostatistics — M
Chemistry — D
Inorganic Chemistry — D
Mathematics — M
Organic Chemistry — D
Physical Chemistry — D
Statistics — M
Theoretical Chemistry — D

THE GEORGE WASHINGTON UNIVERSITY
Analytical Chemistry — M,D
Applied Mathematics — M,D
Biostatistics — M,D
Chemistry — M,D
Environmental Management and Policy — M
Inorganic Chemistry — M,D
Mathematics — M,D
Organic Chemistry — M,D
Physical Chemistry — M,D
Physics — M,D
Statistics — M,D,O

GEORGIA INSTITUTE OF TECHNOLOGY
Applied Mathematics — M,D
Atmospheric Sciences — M,D
Chemistry — M,D
Environmental Management and Policy — M,D
Environmental Sciences — M,D
Geochemistry — M,D
Geophysics — M,D
Geosciences — M,D
Marine Sciences — M,D
Mathematical and Computational Finance — M,D
Mathematics — M,D
Meteorology — M,D
Natural Resources — M,D
Oceanography — M,D
Physics — M,D
Planetary and Space Sciences — M,D
Statistics — M,D

GEORGIA REGENTS UNIVERSITY
Biostatistics — M,D

GEORGIA SOUTHERN UNIVERSITY
Biostatistics — M,D
Mathematics — M

GEORGIA STATE UNIVERSITY
Analytical Chemistry — M,D
Astronomy — D
Biostatistics — M,D
Chemistry — M,D
Environmental Management and Policy — M,D,O
Geochemistry — M,D
Geology — M
Geosciences — M,D,O
Mathematics — M,D
Organic Chemistry — M,D
Physical Chemistry — M,D
Physics — M,D
Statistics — M,D

GODDARD COLLEGE
Environmental Management and Policy — M

GOVERNORS STATE UNIVERSITY
Analytical Chemistry — M

GRADUATE SCHOOL AND UNIVERSITY CENTER OF THE CITY UNIVERSITY OF NEW YORK
Chemistry — D
Environmental Sciences — D
Geosciences — D
Mathematics — D
Physics — D

GRAND VALLEY STATE UNIVERSITY
Biostatistics — M

GREEN MOUNTAIN COLLEGE
Environmental Management and Policy — M

HAMPTON UNIVERSITY
Applied Mathematics — M
Atmospheric Sciences — M,D
Chemistry — M
Computational Sciences — M
Physics — M,D
Planetary and Space Sciences — M,D
Statistics — M

HARDIN-SIMMONS UNIVERSITY
Environmental Management and Policy — M
Mathematics — M,D

HARVARD UNIVERSITY
Applied Mathematics — M,D
Applied Physics — M,D
Astronomy — D
Astrophysics — D
Biostatistics — M,D
Chemical Physics — D
Chemistry — D*
Environmental Management and Policy — M,O
Environmental Sciences — M,D
Forestry — M
Geosciences — M,D
Inorganic Chemistry — D
Mathematics — D
Organic Chemistry — D
Physical Chemistry — D
Physics — D
Planetary and Space Sciences — M,D
Statistics — M,D
Theoretical Physics — D

HAWAI'I PACIFIC UNIVERSITY
Marine Sciences — M

HOFSTRA UNIVERSITY
Chemistry — M,O
Geology — M,O
Geosciences — M,O
Physics — M,O

HOWARD UNIVERSITY
Analytical Chemistry — M,D
Applied Mathematics — M,D
Atmospheric Sciences — M,D
Chemistry — M,D
Environmental Sciences — M,D
Inorganic Chemistry — M,D
Mathematics — M,D
Organic Chemistry — M,D
Physical Chemistry — M,D
Physics — M,D

*M—master's degree; P—first professional degree; D—doctorate; O—other advanced degree; *—Close-Up and/or Display*

Petersons Graduate Programs in the Physical Sciences, Mathematics, Agricultural Sciences, the Environment & Natural Resources 2014

www.petersonsbooks.com   **23**

HUMBOLDT STATE UNIVERSITY

Environmental Management and Policy	M
Environmental Sciences	M
Fish, Game, and Wildlife Management	M
Forestry	M
Geology	M
Natural Resources	M
Water Resources	M

HUNTER COLLEGE OF THE CITY UNIVERSITY OF NEW YORK

Applied Mathematics	M
Biostatistics	M
Chemistry	M,D
Environmental Sciences	M,O
Geosciences	M,O
Mathematics	M
Physics	M,D

ICR GRADUATE SCHOOL

Astrophysics	M
Geology	M
Geophysics	M

IDAHO STATE UNIVERSITY

Applied Physics	M,D
Chemistry	M
Environmental Management and Policy	M
Environmental Sciences	M,O
Geology	M,O
Geophysics	M,O
Geosciences	M,O
Hydrology	M,O
Mathematics	M,D
Physics	M,D

ILLINOIS INSTITUTE OF TECHNOLOGY

Analytical Chemistry	M,D
Applied Mathematics	M,D
Applied Physics	M,D
Chemistry	M,D
Environmental Management and Policy	M
Food Science and Technology	M
Mathematical and Computational Finance	M
Physics	M,D

ILLINOIS STATE UNIVERSITY

Agricultural Sciences— General	M
Chemistry	M
Hydrogeology	M
Hydrology	M
Mathematics	M
Plant Sciences	M,D

INDIANA STATE UNIVERSITY

Mathematics	M

INDIANA UNIVERSITY BLOOMINGTON

Analytical Chemistry	M,D
Applied Mathematics	M,D
Applied Statistics	M,D
Astronomy	M,D
Astrophysics	M,D
Biostatistics	M,D
Chemistry	M,D
Environmental Management and Policy	M,D,O
Environmental Sciences	M,D
Geochemistry	M,D
Geology	M,D
Geophysics	M,D
Geosciences	M,D
Hydrogeology	M,D

Inorganic Chemistry	M,D
Mathematical Physics	M,D
Mathematics	M,D
Mineralogy	M,D
Organic Chemistry	M,D
Physical Chemistry	M,D
Physics	M,D
Statistics	M,D

INDIANA UNIVERSITY NORTHWEST

Environmental Management and Policy	M,O

INDIANA UNIVERSITY OF PENNSYLVANIA

Applied Mathematics	M
Chemistry	M
Environmental Management and Policy	M
Mathematics	M
Physics	M

INDIANA UNIVERSITY–PURDUE UNIVERSITY FORT WAYNE

Applied Mathematics	M,O
Applied Statistics	M,O
Mathematics	M,O

INDIANA UNIVERSITY–PURDUE UNIVERSITY INDIANAPOLIS

Applied Mathematics	M,D
Applied Statistics	M,D
Biostatistics	D
Chemistry	M,D
Geology	M,D
Geosciences	M,D
Mathematics	M,D
Physics	M,D
Statistics	M,D

INDIANA UNIVERSITY SOUTH BEND

Applied Mathematics	M

INSTITUTO TECNOLOGICO DE SANTO DOMINGO

Environmental Management and Policy	M,D,O
Environmental Sciences	M,D,O
Marine Sciences	M,D,O
Mathematics	M,D,O
Natural Resources	M,D,O

INSTITUTO TECNOLÓGICO Y DE ESTUDIOS SUPERIORES DE MONTERREY, CAMPUS CIUDAD DE MÉXICO

Environmental Sciences	M,D

INSTITUTO TECNOLÓGICO Y DE ESTUDIOS SUPERIORES DE MONTERREY, CAMPUS ESTADO DE MÉXICO

Environmental Management and Policy	M,D

INSTITUTO TECNOLÓGICO Y DE ESTUDIOS SUPERIORES DE MONTERREY, CAMPUS IRAPUATO

Environmental Management and Policy	M,D

INSTITUTO TECNOLÓGICO Y DE ESTUDIOS SUPERIORES DE MONTERREY, CAMPUS MONTERREY

Agricultural Sciences— General	M,D
Applied Statistics	M,D

Chemistry	M,D
Organic Chemistry	M,D

INTER AMERICAN UNIVERSITY OF PUERTO RICO, METROPOLITAN CAMPUS

Environmental Management and Policy	M

INTER AMERICAN UNIVERSITY OF PUERTO RICO, SAN GERMÁN CAMPUS

Applied Mathematics	M
Environmental Sciences	M

IOWA STATE UNIVERSITY OF SCIENCE AND TECHNOLOGY

Agricultural Sciences— General	M,D
Agronomy and Soil Sciences	M,D
Analytical Chemistry	D
Animal Sciences	M,D
Applied Mathematics	M,D
Applied Physics	M,D
Astrophysics	M,D
Biostatistics	M,D
Chemistry	M,D
Condensed Matter Physics	M,D
Environmental Sciences	M,D
Fish, Game, and Wildlife Management	M,D
Food Science and Technology	M,D
Forestry	M,D
Geology	M,D
Geosciences	M,D
Horticulture	M,D
Inorganic Chemistry	M,D
Mathematics	M,D
Meteorology	M,D
Natural Resources	M,D
Organic Chemistry	M,D
Physical Chemistry	M,D
Physics	M,D
Plant Sciences	M,D
Statistics	M,D

JACKSON STATE UNIVERSITY

Chemistry	M,D
Environmental Sciences	M,D
Mathematics	M

JACKSONVILLE STATE UNIVERSITY

Mathematics	M

JACKSONVILLE UNIVERSITY

Marine Sciences	M

JAMES MADISON UNIVERSITY

Mathematics	M
Statistics	M

JOHN CARROLL UNIVERSITY

Mathematics	M

THE JOHNS HOPKINS UNIVERSITY

Applied Mathematics	M,D,O
Applied Physics	M,O
Astronomy	D
Biostatistics	M,D
Chemistry	D
Environmental Management and Policy	M,O
Environmental Sciences	M
Geosciences	M,D
Mathematical and Computational Finance	M,D
Mathematics	D

Physics	D
Statistics	M,D

KANSAS STATE UNIVERSITY

Agricultural Sciences— General	M,D
Agronomy and Soil Sciences	M,D
Analytical Chemistry	M,D
Animal Sciences	M,D
Chemistry	M,D
Food Science and Technology	M,D
Geology	M
Horticulture	M,D
Inorganic Chemistry	M,D
Mathematics	M,D
Organic Chemistry	M,D
Physical Chemistry	M,D
Physics	M,D
Plant Sciences	M,D
Range Science	M,D
Statistics	M,D

KEAN UNIVERSITY

Environmental Management and Policy	M

KENNESAW STATE UNIVERSITY

Applied Statistics	M

KENT STATE UNIVERSITY

Analytical Chemistry	M,D
Applied Mathematics	M,D
Chemical Physics	M,D
Chemistry	M,D*
Geology	M,D
Inorganic Chemistry	M,D
Mathematics	M,D
Organic Chemistry	M,D
Physical Chemistry	M,D
Physics	M,D

KENTUCKY STATE UNIVERSITY

Aquaculture	M
Environmental Management and Policy	M

LAKEHEAD UNIVERSITY

Chemistry	M
Forestry	M,D
Geology	M
Mathematics	M
Physics	M

LAMAR UNIVERSITY

Chemistry	M
Environmental Management and Policy	M,D
Mathematics	M

LAURENTIAN UNIVERSITY

Analytical Chemistry	M
Applied Physics	M
Chemistry	M
Environmental Sciences	M
Geology	M,D
Natural Resources	M,D
Organic Chemistry	M
Physical Chemistry	M
Theoretical Chemistry	M

LEHIGH UNIVERSITY

Applied Mathematics	M,D
Chemistry	M,D
Computational Sciences	M,D
Environmental Management and Policy	M,O
Environmental Sciences	M,D
Geology	M,D
Geosciences	M,D
Mathematics	M,D

24 www.petersonsbooks.com

Petersons Graduate Programs in the Physical Sciences, Mathematics, Agricultural Sciences, the Environment & Natural Resources 2014

Photonics	M,D
Physics	M,D
Statistics	M,D

LEHMAN COLLEGE OF THE CITY UNIVERSITY OF NEW YORK
Mathematics	M
Plant Sciences	D

LOMA LINDA UNIVERSITY
Biostatistics	M,D,O
Geosciences	M,D

LONG ISLAND UNIVERSITY–BROOKLYN CAMPUS
Chemistry	M

LONG ISLAND UNIVERSITY–C. W. POST CAMPUS
Applied Mathematics	M
Environmental Management and Policy	M
Geosciences	M
Mathematics	M

LOUISIANA STATE UNIVERSITY AND AGRICULTURAL AND MECHANICAL COLLEGE
Agricultural Sciences—General	M,D
Agronomy and Soil Sciences	M,D
Animal Sciences	M,D
Applied Statistics	M
Astronomy	M,D
Astrophysics	M,D
Chemistry	M,D
Environmental Management and Policy	M
Environmental Sciences	M,D
Fish, Game, and Wildlife Management	M,D
Food Science and Technology	M,D
Forestry	M,D
Geology	M,D
Geophysics	M,D
Horticulture	M,D
Marine Affairs	M,D
Mathematics	M,D
Natural Resources	M,D
Oceanography	M,D
Physics	M,D
Statistics	M

LOUISIANA STATE UNIVERSITY HEALTH SCIENCES CENTER
Biostatistics	M,D

LOUISIANA TECH UNIVERSITY
Chemistry	M
Mathematics	M
Physics	M,D
Statistics	M

LOYOLA MARYMOUNT UNIVERSITY
Environmental Sciences	M

LOYOLA UNIVERSITY CHICAGO
Applied Statistics	M
Chemistry	M,D
Mathematics	M
Statistics	M

MARQUETTE UNIVERSITY
Analytical Chemistry	M,D
Chemical Physics	M,D
Chemistry	M,D

Computational Sciences	M,D
Inorganic Chemistry	M,D
Mathematics	M,D
Organic Chemistry	M,D
Physical Chemistry	M,D
Water Resources	M,D,O

MARSHALL UNIVERSITY
Chemistry	M
Environmental Sciences	M
Mathematics	M
Physics	M

MARYLHURST UNIVERSITY
Environmental Management and Policy	M
Natural Resources	M

MASSACHUSETTS COLLEGE OF PHARMACY AND HEALTH SCIENCES
Chemistry	M,D

MASSACHUSETTS INSTITUTE OF TECHNOLOGY
Atmospheric Sciences	M,D
Chemistry	D
Computational Sciences	M
Environmental Sciences	M,D,O
Geochemistry	M,D
Geology	M,D
Geophysics	M,D
Geosciences	M,D
Hydrology	M,D,O
Inorganic Chemistry	D
Marine Geology	M,D
Mathematics	D
Oceanography	M,D,O
Organic Chemistry	M,D,O
Physical Chemistry	D
Physics	M,D
Planetary and Space Sciences	M,D

MCGILL UNIVERSITY
Agricultural Sciences—General	M,D,O
Agronomy and Soil Sciences	M,D
Animal Sciences	M,D
Applied Mathematics	M,D
Atmospheric Sciences	M,D
Biostatistics	M,D,O
Chemistry	M,D
Computational Sciences	M,D
Environmental Management and Policy	M,D
Fish, Game, and Wildlife Management	M,D
Food Science and Technology	M,D
Forestry	M,D
Geosciences	M,D
Mathematics	M,D
Meteorology	M,D
Natural Resources	M,D
Oceanography	M,D
Physics	M,D
Planetary and Space Sciences	M,D
Plant Sciences	M,D,O
Statistics	M,D,O

MCMASTER UNIVERSITY
Analytical Chemistry	M,D
Applied Statistics	M
Astrophysics	D
Chemical Physics	M,D
Chemistry	M,D
Geochemistry	M,D
Geology	M,D

Geosciences	M,D
Inorganic Chemistry	M,D
Mathematics	M,D
Organic Chemistry	M,D
Physical Chemistry	M,D
Physics	D
Statistics	M

MCNEESE STATE UNIVERSITY
Agricultural Sciences—General	M
Chemistry	M
Environmental Sciences	M
Mathematics	M
Statistics	M

MEDICAL COLLEGE OF WISCONSIN
Biostatistics	D

MEDICAL UNIVERSITY OF SOUTH CAROLINA
Biostatistics	M,D
Marine Sciences	D

MEMORIAL UNIVERSITY OF NEWFOUNDLAND
Aquaculture	M
Chemistry	M,D
Computational Sciences	M
Condensed Matter Physics	M,D
Environmental Sciences	M
Fish, Game, and Wildlife Management	M,O
Food Science and Technology	M,D
Geology	M,D
Geophysics	M,D
Geosciences	M,D
Marine Affairs	M,D,O
Marine Sciences	M,O
Mathematics	M,D
Oceanography	M,D
Physics	M,D
Statistics	M,D

MERCER UNIVERSITY
Environmental Sciences	M

MIAMI UNIVERSITY
Chemistry	M,D
Computational Sciences	M
Environmental Sciences	M
Geology	M,D
Mathematics	M
Physics	M
Plant Sciences	M,D
Statistics	M

MICHIGAN STATE UNIVERSITY
Agricultural Sciences—General	M,D
Agronomy and Soil Sciences	M,D
Animal Sciences	M,D
Applied Mathematics	M,D
Applied Statistics	M,D
Astronomy	M,D
Astrophysics	M,D
Chemical Physics	M,D
Chemistry	M,D
Environmental Sciences	M,D
Fish, Game, and Wildlife Management	M,D
Food Science and Technology	M,D
Forestry	M,D
Geosciences	M,D
Horticulture	M,D
Mathematics	M,D

Natural Resources	M,D
Physics	M,D
Plant Sciences	M,D
Statistics	M,D

MICHIGAN TECHNOLOGICAL UNIVERSITY
Atmospheric Sciences	D
Chemistry	M,D
Computational Sciences	D
Environmental Management and Policy	M,D
Forestry	M,D
Geology	M,D
Geophysics	M,D
Mathematics	M,D
Physics	M,D

MIDDLE TENNESSEE STATE UNIVERSITY
Biostatistics	M
Chemistry	M,D
Geosciences	O
Mathematics	M,D

MILLERSVILLE UNIVERSITY OF PENNSYLVANIA
Atmospheric Sciences	M
Environmental Management and Policy	M
Meteorology	M

MINNESOTA STATE UNIVERSITY MANKATO
Astronomy	M
Environmental Sciences	M
Mathematics	M
Physics	M
Statistics	M

MISSISSIPPI COLLEGE
Chemistry	M
Mathematics	M

MISSISSIPPI STATE UNIVERSITY
Agricultural Sciences—General	M,D
Agronomy and Soil Sciences	M,D
Animal Sciences	M,D
Applied Physics	M,D
Atmospheric Sciences	M,D
Chemistry	M,D
Fish, Game, and Wildlife Management	M,D
Food Science and Technology	M,D
Forestry	M,D
Geology	M,D
Geosciences	M,D
Horticulture	M,D
Mathematics	M,D
Meteorology	M,D
Physics	M,D
Plant Sciences	M,D
Statistics	M,D

MISSOURI STATE UNIVERSITY
Agricultural Sciences—General	M
Chemistry	M
Environmental Management and Policy	M
Geology	M
Geosciences	M
Mathematics	M
Natural Resources	M
Plant Sciences	M

*M—master's degree; P—first professional degree; D—doctorate; O—other advanced degree; *—Close-Up and/or Display*

Petersons Graduate Programs in the Physical Sciences, Mathematics, Agricultural Sciences, the Environment & Natural Resources 2014

www.petersonsbooks.com **25**

MISSOURI UNIVERSITY OF SCIENCE AND TECHNOLOGY

Applied Mathematics	M,D
Chemistry	M,D
Geochemistry	M,D
Geology	M,D
Geophysics	M,D
Hydrology	M,D
Mathematics	M,D
Physics	M,D
Statistics	M,D
Water Resources	M,D

MISSOURI WESTERN STATE UNIVERSITY

Chemistry	M

MONMOUTH UNIVERSITY

Mathematical and Computational Finance	M

MONTANA STATE UNIVERSITY

Agricultural Sciences— General	M,D
Animal Sciences	M,D
Chemistry	M,D
Environmental Sciences	M,D
Fish, Game, and Wildlife Management	M,D
Geosciences	M,D
Mathematics	M,D
Natural Resources	M
Physics	M,D
Plant Sciences	M,D
Range Science	M,D
Statistics	M,D

MONTANA TECH OF THE UNIVERSITY OF MONTANA

Geochemistry	M
Geology	M
Geosciences	M
Hydrogeology	M

MONTCLAIR STATE UNIVERSITY

Applied Mathematics	M
Chemistry	M
Environmental Management and Policy	M,D
Environmental Sciences	M
Geosciences	M
Mathematics	M
Statistics	M

MONTEREY INSTITUTE OF INTERNATIONAL STUDIES

Environmental Management and Policy	M

MOREHEAD STATE UNIVERSITY

Agricultural Sciences— General	M
Environmental Management and Policy	M

MORGAN STATE UNIVERSITY

Chemistry	M
Mathematics	M

MOUNT ALLISON UNIVERSITY

Chemistry	M

MURRAY STATE UNIVERSITY

Agricultural Sciences— General	M
Chemistry	M
Environmental Sciences	M
Geosciences	M
Hydrology	M
Mathematics	M
Statistics	M

NAROPA UNIVERSITY

Environmental Management and Policy	M

NAVAL POSTGRADUATE SCHOOL

Acoustics	M,D
Applied Mathematics	M,D
Applied Physics	M,D,O
Meteorology	M,D
Oceanography	M,D
Physics	M,D

NEW JERSEY INSTITUTE OF TECHNOLOGY

Applied Mathematics	M
Applied Physics	M,D
Applied Statistics	M
Biostatistics	M
Chemistry	M,D
Environmental Management and Policy	M
Environmental Sciences	M,D
Mathematical and Computational Finance	M
Mathematics	D

NEW MEXICO HIGHLANDS UNIVERSITY

Chemistry	M
Environmental Management and Policy	M
Environmental Sciences	M
Geology	M
Natural Resources	M

NEW MEXICO INSTITUTE OF MINING AND TECHNOLOGY

Applied Mathematics	M,D
Astrophysics	M,D
Atmospheric Sciences	M,D
Chemistry	M,D
Geochemistry	M,D
Geology	M,D
Geophysics	M,D
Geosciences	M,D
Hydrology	M,D
Mathematical Physics	M,D
Mathematics	M,D
Physics	M,D
Statistics	M,D

NEW MEXICO STATE UNIVERSITY

Agricultural Sciences— General	M
Animal Sciences	M,D
Applied Statistics	M,D
Astronomy	M,D
Astrophysics	M,D
Chemistry	M,D
Environmental Sciences	M,D
Fish, Game, and Wildlife Management	M
Food Science and Technology	M
Geology	M
Horticulture	M,D
Hydrology	M,D
Mathematics	M,D
Physics	M,D
Plant Sciences	M,D
Range Science	M,D

THE NEW SCHOOL

Environmental Management and Policy	M

NEW YORK INSTITUTE OF TECHNOLOGY

Environmental Management and Policy	M,O

NEW YORK UNIVERSITY

Chemistry	M,D
Environmental Management and Policy	M
Food Science and Technology	M,D
Mathematical and Computational Finance	M,D
Mathematics	M,D
Physics	M,D
Statistics	M,D

NICHOLLS STATE UNIVERSITY

Mathematics	M

NORFOLK STATE UNIVERSITY

Optical Sciences	M

NORTH CAROLINA AGRICULTURAL AND TECHNICAL STATE UNIVERSITY

Agricultural Sciences— General	M
Agronomy and Soil Sciences	M
Animal Sciences	M
Applied Mathematics	M
Chemistry	M,D
Computational Sciences	M
Environmental Sciences	M
Mathematics	M
Optical Sciences	M,D
Physics	M
Plant Sciences	M

NORTH CAROLINA CENTRAL UNIVERSITY

Applied Mathematics	M
Chemistry	M
Geosciences	M
Mathematics	M
Physics	M

NORTH CAROLINA STATE UNIVERSITY

Agricultural Sciences— General	M,D,O
Agronomy and Soil Sciences	M,D
Animal Sciences	M,D
Applied Mathematics	M,D
Atmospheric Sciences	M,D
Biomathematics	M,D
Chemistry	M,D
Fish, Game, and Wildlife Management	M,D
Food Science and Technology	M,D
Forestry	M,D
Geosciences	M,D
Horticulture	M,D,O
Marine Sciences	M,D
Mathematical and Computational Finance	M
Mathematics	M,D
Meteorology	M,D
Natural Resources	M,D
Oceanography	M,D
Physics	M,D
Statistics	M,D

NORTH DAKOTA STATE UNIVERSITY

Agricultural Sciences— General	M,D
Agronomy and Soil Sciences	M,D
Animal Sciences	M,D
Applied Mathematics	M,D
Applied Statistics	M,D,O
Chemistry	M,D
Environmental Sciences	M,D
Food Science and Technology	M,D,O

NEW YORK UNIVERSITY (cont.)

Mathematics	M,D
Natural Resources	M,D
Physics	M,D
Plant Sciences	M,D
Range Science	M,D
Statistics	M,D,O

NORTHEASTERN ILLINOIS UNIVERSITY

Applied Mathematics	M
Chemistry	M
Environmental Management and Policy	M
Mathematics	M

NORTHEASTERN STATE UNIVERSITY

Environmental Management and Policy	M
Natural Resources	M

NORTHEASTERN UNIVERSITY

Applied Mathematics	M,D
Chemistry	M,D
Mathematics	M,D
Physics	M,D

NORTHERN ARIZONA UNIVERSITY

Applied Physics	M
Applied Statistics	M,O
Atmospheric Sciences	M,D
Chemistry	M
Environmental Management and Policy	M,D
Environmental Sciences	M,D
Forestry	M,D
Geology	M,D
Mathematics	M,O
Meteorology	M,D
Physics	M
Statistics	M,O

NORTHERN ILLINOIS UNIVERSITY

Chemistry	M,D
Geology	M,D
Mathematics	M,D
Physics	M,D
Statistics	M

NORTHWESTERN UNIVERSITY

Applied Mathematics	M,D
Astronomy	M,D
Astrophysics	M,D
Chemistry	D
Geology	M,D
Geosciences	M,D
Mathematics	D
Physics	M,D
Statistics	M,D

NORTHWEST MISSOURI STATE UNIVERSITY

Agricultural Sciences— General	M

NOVA SOUTHEASTERN UNIVERSITY

Environmental Sciences	M,D
Marine Affairs	M,D
Marine Sciences	M,D
Oceanography	M,D

OAKLAND UNIVERSITY

Applied Mathematics	M,D
Applied Statistics	M
Chemistry	M,D
Environmental Sciences	M
Mathematics	M
Physics	M,D
Statistics	O

26   www.petersonsbooks.com

Petersons Graduate Programs in the Physical Sciences, Mathematics, Agricultural Sciences, the Environment & Natural Resources 2014

THE OHIO STATE UNIVERSITY

Agricultural Sciences—General	M,D
Agronomy and Soil Sciences	M,D
Animal Sciences	M,D
Astronomy	M,D
Atmospheric Sciences	M,D
Biostatistics	M,D
Chemical Physics	M,D
Chemistry	M,D
Environmental Sciences	M,D
Food Science and Technology	M,D
Geodetic Sciences	M,D
Geology	M,D
Horticulture	M,D
Mathematics	M,D
Natural Resources	M,D
Optical Sciences	M,D
Physics	M,D
Statistics	M,D

OHIO UNIVERSITY

Astronomy	M,D
Environmental Management and Policy	M
Geochemistry	M
Geology	M
Geophysics	M
Hydrogeology	M
Mathematics	M,D
Physics	M,D*

OKLAHOMA STATE UNIVERSITY

Agricultural Sciences—General	M,D
Agronomy and Soil Sciences	M,D
Animal Sciences	M,D
Applied Mathematics	M,D
Chemistry	M,D
Environmental Sciences	M,D,O
Food Science and Technology	M,D
Forestry	M,D
Geology	M,D
Horticulture	M,D
Mathematics	M,D
Natural Resources	M,D
Photonics	M,D,O
Physics	M,D
Plant Sciences	M,D,O
Statistics	M,D

OLD DOMINION UNIVERSITY

Analytical Chemistry	M,D
Chemistry	M,D
Marine Affairs	M
Mathematics	M,D
Oceanography	M,D
Organic Chemistry	M,D
Physical Chemistry	M,D
Physics	M,D

OREGON HEALTH & SCIENCE UNIVERSITY

Biostatistics	M,O
Environmental Sciences	M,D

OREGON STATE UNIVERSITY

Agricultural Sciences—General	M,D
Agronomy and Soil Sciences	M,D
Analytical Chemistry	M,D
Animal Sciences	M,D
Applied Physics	M
Atmospheric Sciences	M,D
Biostatistics	M,D
Chemistry	M,D
Environmental Sciences	M,D
Fish, Game, and Wildlife Management	M,D
Food Science and Technology	M,D
Forestry	M,D
Geology	M,D
Geophysics	M,D
Horticulture	M,D
Inorganic Chemistry	M,D
Marine Affairs	M,O
Marine Sciences	M,O
Mathematics	M,D
Natural Resources	M
Oceanography	M,D
Organic Chemistry	M,D
Physical Chemistry	M,D
Physics	M,D
Range Science	M,D
Statistics	M,D
Water Resources	M,D

PACE UNIVERSITY

Environmental Management and Policy	M
Environmental Sciences	M

PENN STATE HARRISBURG

Environmental Sciences	M

PENN STATE UNIVERSITY PARK

Acoustics	M,D
Agricultural Sciences—General	M,D,O
Agronomy and Soil Sciences	M,D
Animal Sciences	M,D
Applied Mathematics	M,D
Applied Statistics	M,D
Astronomy	M,D
Astrophysics	M,D
Chemistry	M,D
Environmental Management and Policy	M
Environmental Sciences	M
Fish, Game, and Wildlife Management	M,D
Food Science and Technology	M,D
Forestry	M,D
Geosciences	M,D
Horticulture	M,D
Mathematics	M,D
Meteorology	M,D
Physics	M,D
Plant Sciences	M,D
Statistics	M,D

PITTSBURG STATE UNIVERSITY

Applied Physics	M
Chemistry	M
Mathematics	M
Physics	M

PLYMOUTH STATE UNIVERSITY

Environmental Management and Policy	M
Meteorology	M

POINT PARK UNIVERSITY

Environmental Management and Policy	M

POLYTECHNIC INSTITUTE OF NEW YORK UNIVERSITY

Applied Physics	M,D
Chemistry	M,D
Environmental Sciences	M
Mathematical and Computational Finance	M,O
Mathematics	M,D

POLYTECHNIC INSTITUTE OF NYU, LONG ISLAND GRADUATE CENTER

Chemistry	M

POLYTECHNIC INSTITUTE OF NYU, WESTCHESTER GRADUATE CENTER

Chemistry	M

POLYTECHNIC UNIVERSITY OF PUERTO RICO

Environmental Management and Policy	M

POLYTECHNIC UNIVERSITY OF PUERTO RICO, MIAMI CAMPUS

Environmental Management and Policy	M

POLYTECHNIC UNIVERSITY OF PUERTO RICO, ORLANDO CAMPUS

Environmental Management and Policy	M

PONTIFICAL CATHOLIC UNIVERSITY OF PUERTO RICO

Chemistry	M
Environmental Sciences	M

PORTLAND STATE UNIVERSITY

Chemistry	M,D
Environmental Management and Policy	M,D
Environmental Sciences	M,D
Geology	M,D
Mathematics	M,D,O
Physics	M,D
Statistics	M,D

PRAIRIE VIEW A&M UNIVERSITY

Agricultural Sciences—General	M
Agronomy and Soil Sciences	M
Animal Sciences	M
Chemistry	M
Mathematics	M

PRESCOTT COLLEGE

Environmental Management and Policy	M

PRINCETON UNIVERSITY

Applied Mathematics	D
Astronomy	D
Astrophysics	D
Atmospheric Sciences	D
Chemistry	M,D
Computational Sciences	D
Geosciences	D
Mathematics	D
Oceanography	D
Photonics	D
Physics	D
Plasma Physics	D

PURDUE UNIVERSITY

Agricultural Sciences—General	M,D
Agronomy and Soil Sciences	M,D
Analytical Chemistry	M,D
Animal Sciences	M,D
Aquaculture	M,D
Atmospheric Sciences	M,D
Chemistry	M,D
Computational Sciences	D
Environmental Management and Policy	M,D
Fish, Game, and Wildlife Management	M,D
Food Science and Technology	M,D
Forestry	M,D
Geosciences	M,D
Horticulture	M,D
Inorganic Chemistry	M,D
Mathematics	M,D
Natural Resources	M,D
Organic Chemistry	M,D
Physical Chemistry	M,D
Physics	M,D
Plant Sciences	D
Statistics	M,D

PURDUE UNIVERSITY CALUMET

Mathematics	M

QUEENS COLLEGE OF THE CITY UNIVERSITY OF NEW YORK

Chemistry	M
Environmental Sciences	M
Geology	M
Mathematics	M
Physics	M,D

QUEEN'S UNIVERSITY AT KINGSTON

Chemistry	M,D
Geology	M,D
Mathematics	M,D
Physics	M,D
Statistics	M,D

RENSSELAER POLYTECHNIC INSTITUTE

Acoustics	M,D
Applied Mathematics	M
Chemistry	M,D
Geology	M,D
Mathematics	M,D
Physics	M,D

RHODE ISLAND COLLEGE

Mathematics	M,O

RICE UNIVERSITY

Applied Mathematics	M,D
Applied Physics	M,D
Astronomy	M,D
Biostatistics	M,D
Chemistry	M,D
Computational Sciences	M,D
Environmental Management and Policy	M
Environmental Sciences	M,D
Geophysics	M
Geosciences	M,D
Inorganic Chemistry	M,D
Mathematical and Computational Finance	M,D
Mathematics	D
Organic Chemistry	M,D
Physical Chemistry	M,D
Physics	M,D
Statistics	M,D

THE RICHARD STOCKTON COLLEGE OF NEW JERSEY

Computational Sciences	M
Environmental Sciences	M

RIVIER UNIVERSITY

Mathematics	M

---

*M—master's degree; P—first professional degree; D—doctorate; O—other advanced degree; *—Close-Up and/or Display*

Petersons Graduate Programs in the Physical Sciences, Mathematics, Agricultural Sciences, the Environment & Natural Resources 2014

www.petersonsbooks.com **27**

ROCHESTER INSTITUTE OF TECHNOLOGY

Applied Mathematics	M
Applied Statistics	M,O
Astrophysics	M,D
Chemistry	M
Environmental Management and Policy	M
Environmental Sciences	M
Optical Sciences	M,D
Statistics	M,O

ROOSEVELT UNIVERSITY

Chemistry	M
Mathematics	M

ROSE-HULMAN INSTITUTE OF TECHNOLOGY

Optical Sciences	M

ROWAN UNIVERSITY

Mathematics	M

ROYAL MILITARY COLLEGE OF CANADA

Chemistry	M,D
Environmental Sciences	M,D
Mathematics	M
Physics	M

ROYAL ROADS UNIVERSITY

Environmental Management and Policy	M,O

RUTGERS, THE STATE UNIVERSITY OF NEW JERSEY, CAMDEN

Applied Mathematics	M
Chemistry	M
Mathematics	M

RUTGERS, THE STATE UNIVERSITY OF NEW JERSEY, NEWARK

Analytical Chemistry	M,D
Applied Physics	M,D
Chemistry	M,D
Environmental Sciences	M,D
Geology	M
Inorganic Chemistry	M,D
Mathematics	D
Organic Chemistry	M,D
Physical Chemistry	M,D

RUTGERS, THE STATE UNIVERSITY OF NEW JERSEY, NEW BRUNSWICK

Animal Sciences	M,D
Applied Mathematics	M,D
Applied Statistics	M,D
Astronomy	M,D
Atmospheric Sciences	M,D
Biostatistics	M,D
Chemistry	M,D
Condensed Matter Physics	M,D
Environmental Sciences	M,D
Food Science and Technology	M,D
Geology	M,D
Horticulture	M,D
Inorganic Chemistry	M,D
Mathematics	M,D
Oceanography	M,D
Organic Chemistry	M,D
Physical Chemistry	M,D
Physics	M,D
Statistics	M,D
Theoretical Physics	M,D
Water Resources	M,D

SACRED HEART UNIVERSITY

Chemistry	M
Environmental Management and Policy	M

ST. CLOUD STATE UNIVERSITY

Applied Statistics	M
Environmental Management and Policy	M
Mathematics	M

ST. EDWARD'S UNIVERSITY

Environmental Management and Policy	M

ST. FRANCIS XAVIER UNIVERSITY

Chemistry	M
Geology	M
Geosciences	M
Physics	M

ST. JOHN'S UNIVERSITY (NY)

Chemistry	M

SAINT JOSEPH'S UNIVERSITY

Mathematics	M,O

SAINT LOUIS UNIVERSITY

Chemistry	M,D
Geophysics	M,D
Geosciences	M,D
Mathematics	M,D
Meteorology	M,D

SAINT MARY'S UNIVERSITY (CANADA)

Astronomy	M,D

ST. THOMAS UNIVERSITY

Geosciences	M,D,O
Planetary and Space Sciences	M,D,O

SALEM STATE UNIVERSITY

Mathematics	M

SAMFORD UNIVERSITY

Environmental Management and Policy	M

SAM HOUSTON STATE UNIVERSITY

Agricultural Sciences— General	M
Chemistry	M
Computational Sciences	M
Mathematics	M
Statistics	M

SAN DIEGO STATE UNIVERSITY

Applied Mathematics	M
Astronomy	M
Biometry	M
Biostatistics	M,D
Chemistry	M,D
Computational Sciences	M,D
Geology	M
Mathematics	M,D
Physics	M
Statistics	M

SAN FRANCISCO STATE UNIVERSITY

Chemistry	M
Environmental Management and Policy	M
Geosciences	M
Marine Sciences	M
Mathematics	M

Natural Resources	M
Physics	M

SAN JOSE STATE UNIVERSITY

Applied Mathematics	M
Chemistry	M
Environmental Management and Policy	M
Geology	M
Marine Sciences	M
Mathematics	M
Meteorology	M
Physics	M
Statistics	M

SANTA CLARA UNIVERSITY

Applied Mathematics	M,D,O

SAVANNAH STATE UNIVERSITY

Marine Sciences	M

THE SCRIPPS RESEARCH INSTITUTE

Chemistry	D

SETON HALL UNIVERSITY

Analytical Chemistry	M,D
Chemistry	M,D
Inorganic Chemistry	M,D
Organic Chemistry	M,D
Physical Chemistry	M,D

SHIPPENSBURG UNIVERSITY OF PENNSYLVANIA

Environmental Management and Policy	M

SIMON FRASER UNIVERSITY

Applied Mathematics	M,D
Chemistry	M,D
Computational Sciences	M,D
Environmental Management and Policy	M,D,O
Fish, Game, and Wildlife Management	M,D,O
Geosciences	M,D
Mathematics	M,D
Physics	M,D
Statistics	M,D

SLIPPERY ROCK UNIVERSITY OF PENNSYLVANIA

Environmental Management and Policy	M

SMITH COLLEGE

Chemistry	M
Mathematics	O

SOUTH DAKOTA SCHOOL OF MINES AND TECHNOLOGY

Atmospheric Sciences	M,D
Environmental Sciences	D
Geology	M,D
Paleontology	M,D
Physics	M,D

SOUTH DAKOTA STATE UNIVERSITY

Agricultural Sciences— General	M,D
Agronomy and Soil Sciences	M,D
Animal Sciences	M,D
Chemistry	M,D
Computational Sciences	M,D
Fish, Game, and Wildlife Management	M,D
Food Science and Technology	M,D
Geosciences	D

Mathematics	M,D
Physics	M
Plant Sciences	M,D
Statistics	M,D

SOUTHEAST MISSOURI STATE UNIVERSITY

Chemistry	M
Environmental Management and Policy	M
Environmental Sciences	M
Mathematics	M

SOUTHERN ARKANSAS UNIVERSITY–MAGNOLIA

Agricultural Sciences— General	M

SOUTHERN CONNECTICUT STATE UNIVERSITY

Chemistry	M
Mathematics	M

SOUTHERN ILLINOIS UNIVERSITY CARBONDALE

Agricultural Sciences— General	M
Agronomy and Soil Sciences	M
Animal Sciences	M
Applied Physics	M,D
Chemistry	M,D
Environmental Management and Policy	M,D
Environmental Sciences	D
Forestry	M
Geology	M,D
Horticulture	M
Mathematics	M,D
Physics	M,D
Plant Sciences	M
Statistics	M,D

SOUTHERN ILLINOIS UNIVERSITY EDWARDSVILLE

Chemistry	M
Computational Sciences	M
Environmental Management and Policy	M
Environmental Sciences	M
Mathematics	M
Statistics	M

SOUTHERN METHODIST UNIVERSITY

Applied Mathematics	M,D
Atmospheric Sciences	M,D
Chemistry	M,D
Computational Sciences	M,D
Environmental Sciences	M,D
Geology	M,D
Geophysics	M,D
Mathematics	M,D
Physics	M,D
Statistics	M,D

SOUTHERN OREGON UNIVERSITY

Applied Mathematics	M

SOUTHERN UNIVERSITY AND AGRICULTURAL AND MECHANICAL COLLEGE

Agricultural Sciences— General	M
Analytical Chemistry	M
Chemistry	M
Environmental Sciences	M
Forestry	M
Inorganic Chemistry	M
Mathematics	M
Organic Chemistry	M

Petersons Graduate Programs in the Physical Sciences, Mathematics, Agricultural Sciences, the Environment & Natural Resources 2014

Physical Chemistry M
Physics M

STANFORD UNIVERSITY
Applied Physics M,D
Chemistry D
Computational Sciences M,D
Environmental Management
   and Policy M
Environmental Sciences M,D,O
Geophysics M,D
Geosciences M,D,O
Mathematical and
   Computational Finance M,D
Mathematics M,D
Physics D
Statistics M,D

**STATE UNIVERSITY OF NEW
YORK AT FREDONIA**
Chemistry M
Mathematics M

**STATE UNIVERSITY OF NEW
YORK AT NEW PALTZ**
Chemistry M,O
Geosciences M,O

**STATE UNIVERSITY OF NEW
YORK AT OSWEGO**
Chemistry M

**STATE UNIVERSITY OF NEW
YORK COLLEGE AT CORTLAND**
Mathematics M

**STATE UNIVERSITY OF NEW
YORK COLLEGE AT ONEONTA**
Geosciences M

**STATE UNIVERSITY OF NEW
YORK COLLEGE AT POTSDAM**
Mathematics M

**STATE UNIVERSITY OF NEW
YORK COLLEGE OF
ENVIRONMENTAL SCIENCE AND
FORESTRY**
Chemistry M,D
Environmental Management
   and Policy M,D
Environmental Sciences M,D
Fish, Game, and Wildlife
   Management M,D
Forestry M,D
Natural Resources M,D
Organic Chemistry M,D
Plant Sciences M,D
Water Resources M,D

**STEPHEN F. AUSTIN STATE
UNIVERSITY**
Chemistry M
Environmental Sciences M
Forestry M,D
Geology M
Mathematics M
Physics M
Statistics M

**STEVENS INSTITUTE OF
TECHNOLOGY**
Analytical Chemistry M,D,O
Applied Mathematics M
Applied Statistics O
Chemistry M,D,O
Hydrology M,D,O
Marine Affairs M

Mathematics M,D
Organic Chemistry M,D,O
Photonics M,D,O
Physical Chemistry M,D,O
Physics M,D,O
Statistics M,O

**STONY BROOK UNIVERSITY,
STATE UNIVERSITY OF NEW
YORK**
Applied Mathematics M,D
Astronomy D
Atmospheric Sciences M,D
Chemistry M,D
Environmental Management
   and Policy M,O
Geosciences M,D
Marine Affairs M
Marine Sciences M,D
Mathematics M,D
Physics M,D
Statistics M,D

SUL ROSS STATE UNIVERSITY
Animal Sciences M
Fish, Game, and Wildlife
   Management M
Geology M
Natural Resources M
Range Science M

SYRACUSE UNIVERSITY
Applied Statistics M
Chemistry M,D
Geology M,D
Mathematics M,D
Physics M,D

TARLETON STATE UNIVERSITY
Agricultural Sciences—
   General M
Environmental Sciences M
Mathematics M

TEMPLE UNIVERSITY
Applied Mathematics M,D
Chemistry M,D
Computational Sciences M,D
Geology M
Mathematics M,D
Physics M,D
Statistics M,D

TENNESSEE STATE UNIVERSITY
Agricultural Sciences—
   General M
Chemistry M
Mathematics M

**TENNESSEE TECHNOLOGICAL
UNIVERSITY**
Chemistry M,D
Environmental Sciences D
Fish, Game, and Wildlife
   Management M
Mathematics M

**TEXAS A&M INTERNATIONAL
UNIVERSITY**
Mathematics M

TEXAS A&M UNIVERSITY
Agricultural Sciences—
   General M,D
Agronomy and Soil Sciences M,D
Animal Sciences M,D
Applied Physics M,D
Chemistry M,D

Fish, Game, and Wildlife
   Management M,D
Food Science and
   Technology M,D
Forestry M,D
Geology M,D
Geophysics M,D
Horticulture M,D
Mathematics M,D
Meteorology M,D
Natural Resources M,D
Oceanography M,D
Physics M,D
Plant Sciences M,D
Range Science M,D
Statistics M,D

**TEXAS A&M UNIVERSITY AT
GALVESTON**
Marine Sciences M

**TEXAS A&M UNIVERSITY–
COMMERCE**
Agricultural Sciences—
   General M
Chemistry M
Environmental Sciences M,O
Mathematics M
Physics M

**TEXAS A&M UNIVERSITY–
CORPUS CHRISTI**
Applied Mathematics M
Aquaculture M
Environmental Sciences M
Marine Sciences D
Mathematics M

**TEXAS A&M UNIVERSITY–
KINGSVILLE**
Agricultural Sciences—
   General M,D
Agronomy and Soil Sciences M,D
Animal Sciences M
Chemistry M
Fish, Game, and Wildlife
   Management M,D
Geology M
Mathematics M
Plant Sciences M,D
Range Science M

TEXAS CHRISTIAN UNIVERSITY
Applied Mathematics M,D
Astrophysics M,D
Chemistry M,D
Environmental Management
   and Policy M
Environmental Sciences M
Geology M
Inorganic Chemistry M,D
Mathematics M,D
Organic Chemistry M,D
Physical Chemistry M,D
Physics M,D

TEXAS SOUTHERN UNIVERSITY
Chemistry M
Environmental Management
   and Policy M,D
Mathematics M

**TEXAS STATE UNIVERSITY–SAN
MARCOS**
Applied Mathematics M
Chemistry M
Environmental Management
   and Policy M

Fish, Game, and Wildlife
   Management M
Mathematics M,D
Physics M

TEXAS TECH UNIVERSITY
Agricultural Sciences—
   General M,D
Agronomy and Soil Sciences M,D
Animal Sciences M,D
Applied Physics M,D
Atmospheric Sciences M,D
Chemistry M,D
Environmental Management
   and Policy D
Environmental Sciences M,D
Fish, Game, and Wildlife
   Management M,D
Food Science and
   Technology M,D
Geosciences M,D
Horticulture M,D
Mathematics M,D
Natural Resources M,D
Physics M,D
Plant Sciences M,D
Range Science M,D
Statistics M,D

TEXAS WOMAN'S UNIVERSITY
Chemistry M
Food Science and
   Technology M,D
Mathematics M

THOMPSON RIVERS UNIVERSITY
Environmental Sciences M

TOWSON UNIVERSITY
Applied Mathematics M
Applied Physics M
Environmental Management
   and Policy M
Environmental Sciences M,O

TRENT UNIVERSITY
Chemistry M
Environmental Management
   and Policy M,D
Physics M

**TROPICAL AGRICULTURE
RESEARCH AND HIGHER
EDUCATION CENTER**
Agricultural Sciences—
   General M,D
Environmental Management
   and Policy M,D
Forestry M,D
Water Resources M,D

TROY UNIVERSITY
Environmental Management
   and Policy M
Environmental Sciences M

TUFTS UNIVERSITY
Analytical Chemistry M,D
Animal Sciences M
Biostatistics M,D
Chemistry M,D
Environmental Management
   and Policy M,D,O
Environmental Sciences M,D
Inorganic Chemistry M,D
Mathematics M,D
Organic Chemistry M,D
Physical Chemistry M,D
Physics M,D

*M—master's degree; P—first professional degree; D—doctorate; O—other advanced degree; *—Close-Up and/or Display*

*Petersons Graduate Programs in the Physical Sciences, Mathematics,
Agricultural Sciences, the Environment & Natural Resources 2014*

www.petersonsbooks.com   **29**

TULANE UNIVERSITY

Applied Mathematics	M,D
Biostatistics	M,D
Chemistry	M,D
Mathematics	M,D
Physics	D
Statistics	M,D

TUSKEGEE UNIVERSITY

Agronomy and Soil Sciences	M
Animal Sciences	M
Chemistry	M
Environmental Sciences	M
Food Science and Technology	M
Plant Sciences	M

UNIVERSIDAD AUTONOMA DE GUADALAJARA

Environmental Management and Policy	M,D

UNIVERSIDAD DE LAS AMÉRICAS PUEBLA

Food Science and Technology	M

UNIVERSIDAD DEL TURABO

Chemistry	M,D
Environmental Management and Policy	M,D
Environmental Sciences	M,D

UNIVERSIDAD METROPOLITANA

Environmental Management and Policy	M
Natural Resources	M

UNIVERSIDAD NACIONAL PEDRO HENRIQUEZ URENA

Agricultural Sciences— General	M
Animal Sciences	M
Environmental Sciences	M
Horticulture	M
Natural Resources	M

UNIVERSITÉ DE MONCTON

Astronomy	M
Chemistry	M
Food Science and Technology	M
Mathematics	M
Physics	M

UNIVERSITÉ DE MONTRÉAL

Chemistry	M,D
Environmental Management and Policy	O
Mathematical and Computational Finance	M,D,O
Mathematics	M,D,O
Physics	M,D
Statistics	M,D,O

UNIVERSITÉ DE SHERBROOKE

Chemistry	M,D,O
Environmental Sciences	M,O
Mathematics	M,D
Physics	M,D

UNIVERSITÉ DU QUÉBEC À CHICOUTIMI

Environmental Management and Policy	M
Geosciences	M
Mineralogy	D

UNIVERSITÉ DU QUÉBEC À MONTRÉAL

Atmospheric Sciences	M,D,O
Chemistry	M,D
Environmental Sciences	M,D,O
Geology	M,D,O
Geosciences	M,D,O
Mathematics	M,D
Meteorology	M,D,O
Mineralogy	M,D,O
Natural Resources	M,D,O

UNIVERSITÉ DU QUÉBEC À RIMOUSKI

Fish, Game, and Wildlife Management	M,D,O
Marine Affairs	M,O
Oceanography	M,D

UNIVERSITÉ DU QUÉBEC À TROIS-RIVIÈRES

Chemistry	M
Environmental Sciences	M,D
Mathematics	M
Physics	M,D

UNIVERSITÉ DU QUÉBEC EN ABITIBI-TÉMISCAMINGUE

Environmental Sciences	M,D
Forestry	M,D
Natural Resources	M,D

UNIVERSITÉ DU QUÉBEC, INSTITUT NATIONAL DE LA RECHERCHE SCIENTIFIQUE

Environmental Management and Policy	M,D
Geosciences	M,D
Hydrology	M,D

UNIVERSITÉ LAVAL

Agricultural Sciences— General	M,D,O
Agronomy and Soil Sciences	M,D
Animal Sciences	M,D
Chemistry	M,D
Environmental Management and Policy	M,D,O
Environmental Sciences	M,D
Food Science and Technology	M,D
Forestry	M,D
Geodetic Sciences	M,D
Geology	M,D
Geosciences	M,D
Mathematics	M,D
Oceanography	D
Physics	M,D
Statistics	M

UNIVERSITY AT ALBANY, STATE UNIVERSITY OF NEW YORK

Atmospheric Sciences	M,D
Biostatistics	M,D
Chemistry	M,D
Environmental Management and Policy	M
Environmental Sciences	M
Geology	M,D
Geosciences	M,D
Mathematics	M,D
Physics	M,D
Statistics	M,D,O

UNIVERSITY AT BUFFALO, THE STATE UNIVERSITY OF NEW YORK

Biostatistics	M,D
Chemistry	M,D
Computational Sciences	O
Environmental Sciences	M,D,O
Geology	M,D

Geosciences	M,D,O
Mathematics	M,D
Physics	M,D

THE UNIVERSITY OF AKRON

Applied Mathematics	M,D
Chemistry	M,D
Geology	M
Geophysics	M
Geosciences	M
Mathematics	M
Physics	M

THE UNIVERSITY OF ALABAMA

Applied Mathematics	M,D
Applied Statistics	M,D
Chemistry	M,D
Geology	M,D
Mathematics	M,D
Physics	M,D

THE UNIVERSITY OF ALABAMA AT BIRMINGHAM

Applied Mathematics	D
Biostatistics	M,D
Chemistry	M,D
Computational Sciences	D
Mathematics	M
Physics	M,D

THE UNIVERSITY OF ALABAMA IN HUNTSVILLE

Applied Mathematics	M,D
Atmospheric Sciences	M,D
Chemistry	M,D
Environmental Sciences	M,D
Geosciences	M,D
Mathematics	M,D
Optical Sciences	M,D
Photonics	M,D
Physics	M,D

UNIVERSITY OF ALASKA ANCHORAGE

Environmental Sciences	M

UNIVERSITY OF ALASKA FAIRBANKS

Astrophysics	M,D
Atmospheric Sciences	M,D
Chemistry	M,D
Computational Sciences	M,D
Environmental Management and Policy	M,D
Environmental Sciences	M,D
Fish, Game, and Wildlife Management	M,D
Geology	M,D
Geophysics	M,D
Limnology	M,D
Marine Sciences	M,D
Mathematics	M,D,O
Natural Resources	M,D
Oceanography	M,D
Physics	M,D
Statistics	M,D,O
Water Resources	M,D

UNIVERSITY OF ALBERTA

Agricultural Sciences— General	M,D
Agronomy and Soil Sciences	M,D
Applied Mathematics	M,D,O
Astrophysics	M,D
Biostatistics	M,D,O
Chemistry	M,D
Condensed Matter Physics	M,D
Environmental Management and Policy	M,D
Environmental Sciences	M,D
Forestry	M,D
Geophysics	M,D

Geosciences	M,D
Mathematical and Computational Finance	M,D,O
Mathematical Physics	M,D,O
Mathematics	M,D,O
Natural Resources	M,D
Physics	M,D
Statistics	M,D,O

THE UNIVERSITY OF ARIZONA

Agricultural Sciences— General	M,D
Agronomy and Soil Sciences	M,D
Animal Sciences	M,D
Applied Mathematics	M,D
Applied Physics	M
Astronomy	M,D
Atmospheric Sciences	M,D
Biostatistics	D
Chemistry	D
Environmental Management and Policy	M,D
Environmental Sciences	M,D
Fish, Game, and Wildlife Management	M,D
Forestry	M,D
Geosciences	M,D
Hydrology	M,D
Mathematics	M,D
Natural Resources	M,D
Optical Sciences	M,D
Physics	M,D
Planetary and Space Sciences	M,D
Plant Sciences	M,D
Range Science	M,D
Statistics	M,D
Water Resources	M,D

UNIVERSITY OF ARKANSAS

Agricultural Sciences— General	M,D
Agronomy and Soil Sciences	M,D
Animal Sciences	M,D
Applied Physics	M,D
Chemistry	M,D
Food Science and Technology	M,D
Geology	M
Horticulture	M
Mathematics	M,D
Photonics	M,D
Physics	M,D
Planetary and Space Sciences	M,D
Plant Sciences	D
Statistics	M

UNIVERSITY OF ARKANSAS AT LITTLE ROCK

Applied Mathematics	M,O
Applied Statistics	M,O
Chemistry	M
Geosciences	O
Mathematics	M,O

UNIVERSITY OF ARKANSAS AT MONTICELLO

Forestry	M
Natural Resources	M

UNIVERSITY OF ARKANSAS AT PINE BLUFF

Aquaculture	M
Fish, Game, and Wildlife Management	M

THE UNIVERSITY OF BRITISH COLUMBIA

Agricultural Sciences— General	M,D
Agronomy and Soil Sciences	M,D

30 www.petersonsbooks.com

Petersons Graduate Programs in the Physical Sciences, Mathematics, Agricultural Sciences, the Environment & Natural Resources 2014

Animal Sciences M,D
Applied Mathematics M,D
Astronomy M,D
Atmospheric Sciences M,D
Chemistry M,D
Food Science and
   Technology M,D
Forestry M,D
Geology M,D
Geophysics M,D
Marine Sciences M,D
Mathematics M,D
Natural Resources M,D
Oceanography M,D
Physics M,D
Plant Sciences M,D
Statistics M,D

UNIVERSITY OF CALGARY
Analytical Chemistry M,D
Astronomy M,D
Chemistry M,D
Environmental Management
   and Policy M,D,O
Geology M,D
Geophysics M,D
Inorganic Chemistry M,D
Mathematics M,D
Organic Chemistry M,D
Physical Chemistry M,D
Physics M,D
Statistics M,D
Theoretical Chemistry M,D

UNIVERSITY OF CALIFORNIA, BERKELEY
Applied Mathematics D
Astrophysics D
Biostatistics M,D
Chemistry D
Environmental Management
   and Policy M,D,O
Environmental Sciences M,D
Forestry M,D
Geology M,D
Geophysics M,D
Mathematics M,D
Natural Resources M,D
Physics D
Range Science M
Statistics M,D

UNIVERSITY OF CALIFORNIA, DAVIS
Agricultural Sciences—
   General M
Agronomy and Soil Sciences M,D
Animal Sciences M,D
Applied Mathematics M,D
Atmospheric Sciences M,D
Biostatistics M,D
Chemistry M,D
Environmental Sciences M,D
Food Science and
   Technology M,D
Geology M,D
Horticulture M
Hydrology M,D
Mathematics M,D
Physics M,D
Statistics M,D
Viticulture and Enology M,D

UNIVERSITY OF CALIFORNIA, IRVINE
Chemistry M,D
Geosciences M,D
Mathematics M,D
Physics M,D
Statistics M,D

UNIVERSITY OF CALIFORNIA, LOS ANGELES
Astronomy M,D
Astrophysics M,D
Atmospheric Sciences M,D
Biomathematics M,D
Biostatistics M,D
Chemistry M,D
Environmental Sciences M,D
Geochemistry M,D
Geology M,D
Geophysics M,D
Geosciences M,D
Mathematics M,D
Oceanography M,D
Physics M,D
Planetary and Space
   Sciences M,D
Statistics M,D

UNIVERSITY OF CALIFORNIA, MERCED
Applied Mathematics M,D
Chemistry M,D
Physics M,D

UNIVERSITY OF CALIFORNIA, RIVERSIDE
Agronomy and Soil Sciences M,D
Applied Statistics M,D
Chemistry M,D
Environmental Sciences M,D
Geology M,D
Mathematics M,D
Physics M,D
Plant Sciences M,D
Statistics M,D
Water Resources M,D

UNIVERSITY OF CALIFORNIA, SAN DIEGO
Applied Mathematics M,D
Applied Physics M,D
Chemistry M,D
Geosciences D
Marine Sciences M
Mathematics M,D
Oceanography D
Photonics M,D
Physics M,D
Statistics M,D

UNIVERSITY OF CALIFORNIA, SAN FRANCISCO
Chemistry D

UNIVERSITY OF CALIFORNIA, SANTA BARBARA
Applied Mathematics M,D
Applied Statistics M,D
Chemistry D
Computational Sciences M,D
Environmental Management
   and Policy M,D
Environmental Sciences M,D
Geology M,D
Geophysics M,D
Geosciences M,D
Marine Sciences M,D
Mathematical and
   Computational Finance M,D
Mathematics M,D
Photonics M,D
Physics D
Statistics M,D

UNIVERSITY OF CALIFORNIA, SANTA CRUZ
Applied Mathematics M,D
Astronomy D

Astrophysics D
Chemistry M,D
Environmental Management
   and Policy D
Geosciences M,D
Marine Sciences M,D
Mathematics M,D
Physics M,D
Planetary and Space
   Sciences M,D
Statistics M,D

UNIVERSITY OF CENTRAL ARKANSAS
Applied Mathematics M
Mathematics M

UNIVERSITY OF CENTRAL FLORIDA
Chemistry M,D,O
Mathematics M,D,O
Optical Sciences M,D
Photonics M,D
Physics M,D
Statistics M,O

UNIVERSITY OF CENTRAL MISSOURI
Applied Mathematics M,D,O
Environmental Management
   and Policy M,D,O
Mathematics M,D,O

UNIVERSITY OF CENTRAL OKLAHOMA
Applied Mathematics M
Chemistry M
Mathematics M
Statistics M

UNIVERSITY OF CHICAGO
Applied Mathematics M,D
Applied Statistics M
Astronomy M,D
Astrophysics M,D
Atmospheric Sciences M,D
Chemistry D
Environmental Management
   and Policy M,D
Environmental Sciences M,D
Geochemistry M,D
Geophysics M,D
Geosciences M,D
Mathematical and
   Computational Finance M
Mathematics M,D
Paleontology M,D
Physics M,D
Planetary and Space
   Sciences M,D
Statistics M,D,O

UNIVERSITY OF CINCINNATI
Analytical Chemistry M,D
Applied Mathematics M,D
Biostatistics M,D
Chemistry M,D
Environmental Sciences M,D
Geology M,D
Inorganic Chemistry M,D
Mathematics M,D
Organic Chemistry M,D
Physical Chemistry M,D
Physics M,D
Statistics M,D

UNIVERSITY OF COLORADO BOULDER
Applied Mathematics M,D

Astrophysics M,D
Atmospheric Sciences M,D
Chemical Physics M,D
Chemistry M,D
Environmental Management
   and Policy M,D
Geology M,D
Geophysics M,D
Hydrology M,D
Mathematical Physics M,D
Mathematics M,D
Oceanography M,D
Optical Sciences M,D
Physics M,D
Plasma Physics M,D

UNIVERSITY OF COLORADO COLORADO SPRINGS
Applied Mathematics M,D
Chemistry M
Environmental Sciences M
Mathematics M,D
Physics M

UNIVERSITY OF COLORADO DENVER
Applied Mathematics M,D
Applied Statistics M,D
Biostatistics M,D
Chemistry M
Computational Sciences M,D
Environmental Management
   and Policy M,D
Environmental Sciences M
Hydrology M,D
Mathematics M,D
Statistics M,D
Water Resources M

UNIVERSITY OF CONNECTICUT
Agricultural Sciences—
   General M,D
Agronomy and Soil Sciences M,D
Animal Sciences M,D
Applied Mathematics M
Chemistry M,D
Geology M,D
Marine Sciences M,D
Mathematical and
   Computational Finance M
Mathematics M,D
Natural Resources M,D
Oceanography M,D
Physics M,D
Plant Sciences M,D
Statistics M,D

UNIVERSITY OF DAYTON
Applied Mathematics M
Chemistry M
Environmental Management
   and Policy M,D
Mathematical and
   Computational Finance M
Optical Sciences M,D

UNIVERSITY OF DELAWARE
Agricultural Sciences—
   General M,D
Agronomy and Soil Sciences M,D
Animal Sciences M,D
Applied Mathematics M,D
Astronomy M,D
Chemistry M,D
Environmental Management
   and Policy M,D
Fish, Game, and Wildlife
   Management M,D
Food Science and
   Technology M,D

M—master's degree; P—first professional degree; D—doctorate; O—other advanced degree; *—Close-Up and/or Display

Petersons Graduate Programs in the Physical Sciences, Mathematics,
Agricultural Sciences, the Environment & Natural Resources 2014

www.petersonsbooks.com   **31**

Geology	M,D
Horticulture	M
Marine Affairs	M,D
Marine Geology	M,D
Marine Sciences	M,D
Mathematics	M,D
Natural Resources	M
Oceanography	M,D
Physics	M,D
Plant Sciences	M,D
Statistics	M

UNIVERSITY OF DENVER

Applied Physics	M,D
Astronomy	M,D
Chemistry	M,D
Environmental Management and Policy	M,O
Mathematics	M,D
Natural Resources	M,O
Physics	M,D
Statistics	M,D,O

UNIVERSITY OF DETROIT MERCY

Chemistry	M

THE UNIVERSITY OF FINDLAY

Environmental Management and Policy	M

UNIVERSITY OF FLORIDA

Agricultural Sciences— General	M,D
Agronomy and Soil Sciences	M,D
Animal Sciences	M,D
Aquaculture	M,D
Astronomy	M,D
Biostatistics	M,D
Chemistry	M,D
Fish, Game, and Wildlife Management	M,D
Food Science and Technology	M,D
Forestry	M,D
Geology	M,D
Geosciences	M,D
Horticulture	M,D
Hydrology	M,D
Limnology	M,D
Marine Sciences	M,D
Mathematics	M,D
Natural Resources	M,D
Physics	M,D
Plant Sciences	D
Statistics	M,D
Water Resources	M,D

UNIVERSITY OF GEORGIA

Agricultural Sciences— General	M,D
Agronomy and Soil Sciences	M,D
Analytical Chemistry	M,D
Animal Sciences	M,D
Applied Mathematics	M,D
Chemistry	M,D
Food Science and Technology	M,D
Forestry	M,D
Geology	M,D
Horticulture	M,D
Inorganic Chemistry	M,D
Marine Sciences	M,D
Mathematics	M,D
Natural Resources	M,D
Organic Chemistry	M,D
Physical Chemistry	M,D
Physics	M,D
Plant Sciences	M,D
Statistics	M,D

UNIVERSITY OF GUAM

Environmental Sciences	M

UNIVERSITY OF GUELPH

Agricultural Sciences— General	M,D,O
Agronomy and Soil Sciences	M,D
Animal Sciences	M,D
Applied Mathematics	M,D
Applied Statistics	M,D
Aquaculture	M
Atmospheric Sciences	M,D
Chemistry	M,D
Environmental Management and Policy	M,D
Environmental Sciences	M,D
Food Science and Technology	M,D
Horticulture	M,D
Mathematics	M,D
Natural Resources	M,D
Physics	M,D
Statistics	M,D

UNIVERSITY OF HAWAII AT HILO

Environmental Sciences	M

UNIVERSITY OF HAWAII AT MANOA

Agricultural Sciences— General	M,D
Animal Sciences	M
Astronomy	M,D
Chemistry	M,D
Environmental Management and Policy	M,D,O
Food Science and Technology	M
Geochemistry	M,D
Geology	M,D
Geophysics	M,D
Horticulture	M,D
Hydrogeology	M,D
Marine Geology	M,D
Marine Sciences	O
Mathematics	M,D
Meteorology	M,D
Natural Resources	M,D
Oceanography	M,D
Physics	M,D
Planetary and Space Sciences	M,D
Plant Sciences	M,D

UNIVERSITY OF HOUSTON

Applied Mathematics	M,D
Atmospheric Sciences	M,D
Chemistry	M,D
Geology	M,D
Geophysics	M,D
Mathematics	M,D
Physics	M,D
Planetary and Space Sciences	M,D

UNIVERSITY OF HOUSTON–CLEAR LAKE

Chemistry	M
Environmental Management and Policy	M
Environmental Sciences	M
Mathematics	M
Physics	M
Statistics	M

UNIVERSITY OF IDAHO

Agronomy and Soil Sciences	M,D
Animal Sciences	M,D
Chemistry	M,D
Environmental Management and Policy	M
Environmental Sciences	M,D
Food Science and Technology	M,D
Geology	M,D

Hydrology	M,D
Mathematics	M,D
Natural Resources	M,D
Physics	M,D
Plant Sciences	M,D
Statistics	M

UNIVERSITY OF ILLINOIS AT CHICAGO

Applied Mathematics	M,D
Biostatistics	M,D
Chemistry	M,D
Geology	M,D
Geosciences	M,D
Mathematical and Computational Finance	M,D
Mathematics	M,D
Physics	M,D
Statistics	M,D

UNIVERSITY OF ILLINOIS AT SPRINGFIELD

Environmental Management and Policy	M
Environmental Sciences	M

UNIVERSITY OF ILLINOIS AT URBANA–CHAMPAIGN

Agricultural Sciences— General	M
Agronomy and Soil Sciences	M,D
Animal Sciences	M,D
Applied Mathematics	M,D
Applied Statistics	M,D
Astronomy	M,D
Atmospheric Sciences	M,D
Chemical Physics	M,D
Chemistry	M,D
Environmental Sciences	M,D
Food Science and Technology	M,D
Geology	M,D
Geosciences	M,D
Mathematics	M,D
Natural Resources	M,D
Physics	M,D
Statistics	M,D

THE UNIVERSITY OF IOWA

Applied Mathematics	D
Astronomy	M
Biostatistics	M,D
Chemistry	M,D
Computational Sciences	D
Geosciences	M,D
Mathematics	M,D
Physics	M,D
Statistics	M,D,O

THE UNIVERSITY OF KANSAS

Astronomy	M,D
Atmospheric Sciences	M,D
Biostatistics	M,D
Chemistry	M,D
Computational Sciences	M,D
Environmental Sciences	M,D
Geology	M,D
Mathematics	M,D
Physics	M,D

UNIVERSITY OF KENTUCKY

Agricultural Sciences— General	M,D
Agronomy and Soil Sciences	M,D
Animal Sciences	M,D
Applied Mathematics	M,D
Astronomy	M,D
Chemistry	M,D
Forestry	M
Geology	M,D
Mathematics	M,D
Physics	M,D

Plant Sciences	M
Statistics	M,D

UNIVERSITY OF LETHBRIDGE

Agricultural Sciences— General	M,D
Chemistry	M,D
Computational Sciences	M,D
Environmental Sciences	M,D
Mathematics	M,D
Physics	M,D

UNIVERSITY OF LOUISIANA AT LAFAYETTE

Geology	M
Mathematics	M,D
Physics	M

UNIVERSITY OF LOUISVILLE

Analytical Chemistry	M,D
Applied Mathematics	M,D
Biostatistics	M,D
Chemical Physics	M,D
Chemistry	M,D
Inorganic Chemistry	M,D
Mathematics	M,D
Organic Chemistry	M,D
Physical Chemistry	M,D
Physics	M,D

UNIVERSITY OF MAINE

Agricultural Sciences— General	M,D,O
Agronomy and Soil Sciences	M
Animal Sciences	M
Chemistry	M,D
Environmental Management and Policy	M,D
Environmental Sciences	M,D
Fish, Game, and Wildlife Management	M,D
Food Science and Technology	M,D,O
Forestry	M,D
Geology	M
Geosciences	M
Horticulture	M
Marine Affairs	M,D
Marine Sciences	M,D
Mathematics	M
Natural Resources	M,D
Oceanography	M,D
Physics	M,D
Plant Sciences	M,D
Water Resources	M,D

THE UNIVERSITY OF MANCHESTER

Analytical Chemistry	M,D
Applied Mathematics	M,D
Astronomy	M,D
Astrophysics	M,D
Atmospheric Sciences	M,D
Chemistry	M,D
Condensed Matter Physics	M,D
Environmental Management and Policy	M,D
Environmental Sciences	M,D
Geochemistry	M,D
Geosciences	M,D
Inorganic Chemistry	M,D
Mathematical and Computational Finance	M,D
Mathematics	M,D
Natural Resources	M,D
Organic Chemistry	M,D
Paleontology	M,D
Physical Chemistry	M,D
Physics	M,D
Plant Sciences	M,D
Statistics	M,D
Theoretical Chemistry	M,D
Theoretical Physics	M,D

32 www.petersonsbooks.com

Petersons Graduate Programs in the Physical Sciences, Mathematics, Agricultural Sciences, the Environment & Natural Resources 2014

UNIVERSITY OF MANITOBA

Agricultural Sciences—General	M,D
Agronomy and Soil Sciences	M,D
Animal Sciences	M,D
Chemistry	M,D
Computational Sciences	M
Environmental Sciences	M,D
Food Science and Technology	M,D
Geology	M,D
Geophysics	M,D
Horticulture	M,D
Mathematics	M,D
Natural Resources	M,D
Physics	M,D
Plant Sciences	M,D
Statistics	M,D

UNIVERSITY OF MARYLAND, BALTIMORE

Biostatistics	M,D
Environmental Sciences	M,D
Marine Sciences	M,D

UNIVERSITY OF MARYLAND, BALTIMORE COUNTY

Applied Mathematics	M,D
Applied Physics	M,D
Atmospheric Sciences	M,D
Biostatistics	M,D
Chemistry	M,D,O
Environmental Management and Policy	M,D
Environmental Sciences	M,D,O
Marine Sciences	M,D,O
Physics	M,D
Planetary and Space Sciences	M
Statistics	M,D

UNIVERSITY OF MARYLAND, COLLEGE PARK

Agricultural Sciences—General	M,D
Analytical Chemistry	M,D
Animal Sciences	M,D
Applied Mathematics	M,D
Astronomy	M,D
Biostatistics	M,D
Chemical Physics	M,D
Chemistry	M,D
Environmental Sciences	M,D
Food Science and Technology	M,D
Geology	M,D
Horticulture	M,D
Inorganic Chemistry	M,D
Marine Sciences	M,D
Mathematics	M,D
Meteorology	M,D
Natural Resources	M,D
Oceanography	M,D
Organic Chemistry	M,D
Physical Chemistry	M,D
Physics	M,D
Statistics	M,D

UNIVERSITY OF MARYLAND EASTERN SHORE

Agricultural Sciences—General	M,D
Environmental Sciences	M,D
Food Science and Technology	M,D
Marine Sciences	M,D

UNIVERSITY OF MARYLAND UNIVERSITY COLLEGE

Environmental Management and Policy	M,O

UNIVERSITY OF MASSACHUSETTS AMHERST

Animal Sciences	M,D
Applied Mathematics	M,D
Astronomy	M,D
Biostatistics	M,D
Chemistry	M,D
Environmental Management and Policy	M,D
Fish, Game, and Wildlife Management	M,D
Food Science and Technology	M,D
Forestry	M,D
Geosciences	M,D
Marine Sciences	M,D
Mathematics	M,D
Physics	M,D
Plant Sciences	M,D
Statistics	M,D
Water Resources	M,D

UNIVERSITY OF MASSACHUSETTS BOSTON

Applied Physics	M
Chemistry	M
Environmental Sciences	D
Marine Sciences	D

UNIVERSITY OF MASSACHUSETTS DARTMOUTH

Acoustics	M,D,O
Chemistry	M,D
Environmental Management and Policy	M,O
Marine Affairs	M,D
Marine Sciences	M,D
Physics	M

UNIVERSITY OF MASSACHUSETTS LOWELL

Analytical Chemistry	M,D
Applied Mathematics	M,D
Applied Physics	M,D
Atmospheric Sciences	M,D
Chemistry	M,D
Computational Sciences	M,D
Environmental Management and Policy	M,D,O
Environmental Sciences	M,D,O
Inorganic Chemistry	M,D
Mathematics	M,D
Optical Sciences	M,D
Organic Chemistry	M,D
Physics	M,D

UNIVERSITY OF MEDICINE AND DENTISTRY OF NEW JERSEY

Biostatistics	M,D,O
Environmental Sciences	D

UNIVERSITY OF MEMPHIS

Analytical Chemistry	M,D
Applied Mathematics	M,D
Applied Statistics	M,D
Biostatistics	M
Chemistry	M,D
Geology	M,D,O
Geophysics	M,D,O
Inorganic Chemistry	M,D
Mathematics	M,D
Organic Chemistry	M,D
Physical Chemistry	M,D
Physics	M
Statistics	M,D

UNIVERSITY OF MIAMI

Chemistry	M,D
Environmental Management and Policy	M,D

Fish, Game, and Wildlife Management	M,D
Geophysics	M,D
Inorganic Chemistry	M,D
Marine Affairs	M
Marine Geology	M,D
Marine Sciences	M,D
Mathematics	M,D
Meteorology	M,D
Oceanography	M,D
Organic Chemistry	M,D
Physical Chemistry	M,D
Physics	M,D

UNIVERSITY OF MICHIGAN

Analytical Chemistry	D
Applied Physics	D
Applied Statistics	M,D
Astronomy	D
Astrophysics	D
Atmospheric Sciences	M,D
Biostatistics	M,D
Chemistry	D
Environmental Management and Policy	M,D
Environmental Sciences	M,D
Geosciences	M,D
Inorganic Chemistry	D
Marine Sciences	M,D
Mathematics	M,D
Natural Resources	M,D
Organic Chemistry	D
Physical Chemistry	D
Physics	D
Planetary and Space Sciences	M,D
Statistics	M,D

UNIVERSITY OF MICHIGAN–DEARBORN

Applied Mathematics	M
Computational Sciences	M
Environmental Sciences	M

UNIVERSITY OF MINNESOTA, DULUTH

Applied Mathematics	M
Chemistry	M
Computational Sciences	M
Geology	M,D
Physics	M

UNIVERSITY OF MINNESOTA, TWIN CITIES CAMPUS

Agricultural Sciences—General	M,D
Agronomy and Soil Sciences	M,D
Animal Sciences	M,D
Astrophysics	M,D
Biostatistics	M,D
Chemistry	M,D
Computational Sciences	M,D
Environmental Management and Policy	M
Food Science and Technology	M,D
Geology	M,D
Geophysics	M,D
Mathematics	M,D,O
Natural Resources	M,D
Physics	M,D
Plant Sciences	M,D
Statistics	M,D
Water Resources	M,D

UNIVERSITY OF MISSISSIPPI

Chemistry	M,D
Mathematics	M,D
Physics	M,D

UNIVERSITY OF MISSOURI

Agricultural Sciences—General	M,D,O
Agronomy and Soil Sciences	M,D
Analytical Chemistry	M,D
Animal Sciences	M,D
Applied Mathematics	M,D
Astronomy	M,D
Atmospheric Sciences	M,D
Chemistry	M,D
Fish, Game, and Wildlife Management	M,D,O
Food Science and Technology	M,D
Forestry	M,D
Geology	M,D
Horticulture	M,D
Inorganic Chemistry	M,D
Mathematics	M,D
Natural Resources	M
Organic Chemistry	M,D
Physical Chemistry	M,D
Physics	M,D
Plant Sciences	M,D
Statistics	M,D

UNIVERSITY OF MISSOURI–KANSAS CITY

Analytical Chemistry	M,D
Chemistry	M,D
Geology	M,D
Geosciences	M,D
Inorganic Chemistry	M,D
Mathematics	M,D
Organic Chemistry	M,D
Physical Chemistry	M,D
Physics	M,D
Statistics	M,D

UNIVERSITY OF MISSOURI–ST. LOUIS

Applied Mathematics	M,D
Applied Physics	M,D
Astrophysics	M,D
Chemistry	M,D
Inorganic Chemistry	M,D
Mathematics	M,D
Organic Chemistry	M,D
Physical Chemistry	M,D
Physics	M,D

THE UNIVERSITY OF MONTANA

Analytical Chemistry	M,D
Chemistry	M,D
Environmental Management and Policy	M
Environmental Sciences	M
Fish, Game, and Wildlife Management	M,D
Forestry	M,D
Geology	M,D
Geosciences	M,D
Inorganic Chemistry	M,D
Mathematics	M,D
Natural Resources	M,D
Organic Chemistry	M,D
Physical Chemistry	M,D

UNIVERSITY OF NEBRASKA AT OMAHA

Mathematics	M

UNIVERSITY OF NEBRASKA–LINCOLN

Agricultural Sciences—General	M,D
Agronomy and Soil Sciences	M,D
Analytical Chemistry	M,D
Animal Sciences	M,D
Astronomy	M,D

---

*M—master's degree; P—first professional degree; D—doctorate; O—other advanced degree; *—Close-Up and/or Display*

Petersons Graduate Programs in the Physical Sciences, Mathematics, Agricultural Sciences, the Environment & Natural Resources 2014

www.petersonsbooks.com   **33**

Chemistry	M,D
Food Science and Technology	M,D
Geosciences	M,D
Horticulture	M,D
Inorganic Chemistry	M,D
Mathematics	M,D
Natural Resources	M,D
Organic Chemistry	M,D
Physical Chemistry	M,D
Physics	M,D
Statistics	M,D

UNIVERSITY OF NEVADA, LAS VEGAS

Astronomy	M,D
Chemistry	M,D
Environmental Sciences	M,D,O
Geosciences	M,D
Mathematics	M,D
Physics	M,D
Water Resources	M

UNIVERSITY OF NEVADA, RENO

Agricultural Sciences—General	M,D
Animal Sciences	M
Atmospheric Sciences	M,D
Chemical Physics	D
Chemistry	M,D
Environmental Management and Policy	M
Environmental Sciences	M,D
Geochemistry	M,D
Geology	M,D
Geophysics	M,D
Hydrogeology	M,D
Hydrology	M,D
Mathematics	M
Physics	M,D

UNIVERSITY OF NEW BRUNSWICK FREDERICTON

Chemistry	M,D
Environmental Management and Policy	M,D
Forestry	M,D
Geodetic Sciences	M,D
Geology	M,D
Hydrology	M,D
Mathematics	M,D
Physics	M,D
Statistics	M,D
Water Resources	M,D

UNIVERSITY OF NEW BRUNSWICK SAINT JOHN

Natural Resources	M

UNIVERSITY OF NEW ENGLAND

Marine Sciences	M

UNIVERSITY OF NEW HAMPSHIRE

Animal Sciences	M,D
Applied Mathematics	M,D,O
Chemistry	M,D
Environmental Management and Policy	M
Fish, Game, and Wildlife Management	M
Forestry	M
Geology	M
Geosciences	M
Hydrology	M
Marine Sciences	M
Mathematics	M,D,O
Natural Resources	M,D
Oceanography	M,D,O
Physics	M,D
Statistics	M,D,O
Water Resources	M

UNIVERSITY OF NEW HAVEN

Environmental Management and Policy	M,O
Environmental Sciences	M,O
Geosciences	M,O

UNIVERSITY OF NEW MEXICO

Chemistry	M,D
Computational Sciences	O
Environmental Management and Policy	M
Geosciences	M,D
Mathematics	M,D
Natural Resources	M,D
Optical Sciences	M,D
Photonics	M,D
Physics	M,D
Planetary and Space Sciences	M,D
Statistics	M,D
Water Resources	M

UNIVERSITY OF NEW ORLEANS

Chemistry	M,D
Environmental Sciences	M
Geosciences	M
Mathematics	M
Physics	M,D

THE UNIVERSITY OF NORTH CAROLINA AT CHAPEL HILL

Astronomy	M,D
Astrophysics	M,D
Atmospheric Sciences	M,D
Biostatistics	M,D
Chemistry	M,D
Environmental Management and Policy	M,D
Environmental Sciences	M,D
Geology	M,D
Marine Sciences	M,D
Mathematics	M,D
Physics	M,D
Statistics	M,D

THE UNIVERSITY OF NORTH CAROLINA AT CHARLOTTE

Applied Mathematics	M,D
Applied Physics	M,D
Applied Statistics	M,D
Chemistry	M,D
Geosciences	M,D
Mathematical and Computational Finance	M,D
Mathematics	M,D
Optical Sciences	M,D

THE UNIVERSITY OF NORTH CAROLINA AT GREENSBORO

Chemistry	M
Mathematics	M,D

THE UNIVERSITY OF NORTH CAROLINA WILMINGTON

Chemistry	M
Environmental Management and Policy	M
Geology	M
Geosciences	M
Marine Sciences	M,D
Mathematics	M
Statistics	M

UNIVERSITY OF NORTH DAKOTA

Atmospheric Sciences	M,D
Chemistry	M,D
Fish, Game, and Wildlife Management	M,D
Geology	M,D
Geosciences	M,D
Mathematics	M

Physics	M,D
Planetary and Space Sciences	M

UNIVERSITY OF NORTHERN BRITISH COLUMBIA

Environmental Management and Policy	M,D,O
Mathematics	M,D,O
Natural Resources	M,D,O

UNIVERSITY OF NORTHERN COLORADO

Applied Statistics	M,D
Chemistry	M,D
Geosciences	M
Mathematics	M,D

UNIVERSITY OF NORTHERN IOWA

Applied Mathematics	M
Applied Physics	M
Chemistry	M
Environmental Sciences	M
Geosciences	M
Mathematics	M
Natural Resources	M
Physics	M

UNIVERSITY OF NORTH FLORIDA

Mathematics	M
Statistics	M

UNIVERSITY OF NORTH TEXAS

Chemistry	M,D,O
Environmental Sciences	M,D,O
Mathematics	M,D,O
Physics	M,D,O
Statistics	M,D,O

UNIVERSITY OF NORTH TEXAS HEALTH SCIENCE CENTER AT FORT WORTH

Biostatistics	M,D

UNIVERSITY OF NOTRE DAME

Applied Mathematics	M,D
Applied Statistics	M,D
Chemistry	M,D
Computational Sciences	M,D
Geosciences	M,D
Inorganic Chemistry	M,D
Mathematical and Computational Finance	M,D
Mathematics	M,D
Organic Chemistry	M,D
Physical Chemistry	M,D
Physics	M,D
Statistics	M,D

UNIVERSITY OF OKLAHOMA

Chemistry	M,D
Environmental Sciences	M,D
Geology	M,D
Geophysics	M,D
Mathematics	M,D*
Meteorology	M,D
Physics	M,D

UNIVERSITY OF OKLAHOMA HEALTH SCIENCES CENTER

Biostatistics	M,D

UNIVERSITY OF OREGON

Chemistry	M,D
Environmental Management and Policy	M,D
Geology	M,D
Mathematics	M,D
Physics	M,D

UNIVERSITY OF OTTAWA

Chemistry	M,D
Geosciences	M,D
Mathematics	M,D
Physics	M,D
Statistics	M,D

UNIVERSITY OF PENNSYLVANIA

Applied Mathematics	D
Biostatistics	M,D
Chemistry	M,D
Computational Sciences	D
Environmental Management and Policy	M
Environmental Sciences	M,D
Geosciences	M,D
Mathematics	M,D
Physics	M,D
Statistics	M,D

UNIVERSITY OF PITTSBURGH

Applied Mathematics	M,D
Applied Statistics	M,D
Biostatistics	M,D
Chemistry	M,D
Environmental Management and Policy	M
Geology	M,D
Mathematics	M,D
Physics	M,D*
Planetary and Space Sciences	M,D
Statistics	M,D

UNIVERSITY OF PRINCE EDWARD ISLAND

Chemistry	M

UNIVERSITY OF PUERTO RICO, MAYAGÜEZ CAMPUS

Agricultural Sciences—General	M
Agronomy and Soil Sciences	M
Animal Sciences	M
Applied Mathematics	M
Chemistry	M,D
Computational Sciences	M
Food Science and Technology	M
Geology	M
Horticulture	M
Marine Sciences	M,D
Mathematics	M
Physics	M
Statistics	M

UNIVERSITY OF PUERTO RICO, MEDICAL SCIENCES CAMPUS

Biostatistics	M

UNIVERSITY OF PUERTO RICO, RÍO PIEDRAS

Chemistry	M,D
Environmental Management and Policy	M
Environmental Sciences	M,D
Mathematics	M,D
Physics	M,D

UNIVERSITY OF REGINA

Analytical Chemistry	M,D
Chemistry	M,D
Geology	M,D
Inorganic Chemistry	M,D
Mathematics	M,D
Organic Chemistry	M,D
Physics	M,D
Statistics	M,D
Theoretical Chemistry	M,D

34 www.petersonsbooks.com

Petersons Graduate Programs in the Physical Sciences, Mathematics, Agricultural Sciences, the Environment & Natural Resources 2014

UNIVERSITY OF RHODE ISLAND

Animal Sciences	M,D
Applied Mathematics	M,D,O
Aquaculture	M,D
Chemistry	M,D
Environmental Management and Policy	M,D
Environmental Sciences	M,D
Fish, Game, and Wildlife Management	M,D
Food Science and Technology	M,D
Geosciences	M,D
Marine Affairs	M,D
Marine Sciences	M,D
Mathematics	M,D
Natural Resources	M,D
Oceanography	M,D
Physics	M,D
Statistics	M,D,O

UNIVERSITY OF ROCHESTER

Astronomy	M,D
Biostatistics	M
Chemistry	D
Environmental Management and Policy	M
Geology	M,D
Geosciences	M,D
Mathematics	D
Optical Sciences	M,D
Physics	M,D
Statistics	M,D

UNIVERSITY OF SAINT FRANCIS (IN)

Environmental Sciences	M

UNIVERSITY OF SAINT JOSEPH

Chemistry	M

UNIVERSITY OF SAN DIEGO

Marine Affairs	M
Marine Sciences	M

UNIVERSITY OF SAN FRANCISCO

Chemistry	M
Natural Resources	M

UNIVERSITY OF SASKATCHEWAN

Agricultural Sciences— General	M,D,O
Agronomy and Soil Sciences	M,D,O
Animal Sciences	M,D
Chemistry	M,D
Environmental Sciences	M
Food Science and Technology	M,D
Geology	M,D,O
Mathematics	M,D
Physics	M,D
Plant Sciences	M,D
Statistics	M,D

THE UNIVERSITY OF SCRANTON

Chemistry	M

UNIVERSITY OF SOUTH AFRICA

Agricultural Sciences— General	M,D
Environmental Management and Policy	M,D
Environmental Sciences	M,D
Horticulture	M,D
Natural Resources	M,D
Statistics	M,D

UNIVERSITY OF SOUTH ALABAMA

Marine Sciences	M,D
Mathematics	M

UNIVERSITY OF SOUTH CAROLINA

Applied Statistics	M,D,O
Astronomy	M,D
Biostatistics	M,D
Chemistry	M,D
Environmental Management and Policy	M
Geology	M,D
Geosciences	M,D
Marine Sciences	M,D
Mathematics	M,D
Physics	M,D
Statistics	M,D,O

THE UNIVERSITY OF SOUTH DAKOTA

Chemistry	M,D
Mathematics	M
Physics	M,D

UNIVERSITY OF SOUTHERN CALIFORNIA

Applied Mathematics	M,D
Biostatistics	M,D
Chemistry	D
Food Science and Technology	M,D,O
Geosciences	M,D
Marine Sciences	M,D
Mathematical and Computational Finance	M,D
Mathematics	M,D
Oceanography	M,D
Physical Chemistry	D
Physics	M,D
Statistics	M,D
Water Resources	M,D,O

UNIVERSITY OF SOUTHERN MAINE

Statistics	M

UNIVERSITY OF SOUTHERN MISSISSIPPI

Analytical Chemistry	M,D
Biostatistics	M
Chemistry	M,D
Computational Sciences	M,D
Geology	M,D
Hydrology	M,D
Inorganic Chemistry	M,D
Marine Sciences	M,D
Mathematics	M,D
Organic Chemistry	M,D
Physical Chemistry	M,D
Physics	M,D

UNIVERSITY OF SOUTH FLORIDA

Analytical Chemistry	M,D
Applied Physics	M,D
Biostatistics	M,D
Chemistry	M,D
Environmental Management and Policy	M,D
Environmental Sciences	M,D
Geology	M,D
Inorganic Chemistry	M,D
Marine Sciences	M,D
Mathematics	M,D
Oceanography	M,D
Organic Chemistry	M,D
Physical Chemistry	M,D
Physics	M,D
Statistics	M,D

UNIVERSITY OF SOUTH FLORIDA– ST. PETERSBURG CAMPUS

Environmental Management and Policy	M
Environmental Sciences	M

THE UNIVERSITY OF TENNESSEE

Agricultural Sciences— General	M,D
Analytical Chemistry	M,D
Animal Sciences	M,D
Applied Mathematics	M,D
Chemical Physics	M,D
Chemistry	M,D
Environmental Management and Policy	M,D
Fish, Game, and Wildlife Management	M
Food Science and Technology	M,D
Forestry	M
Geology	M,D
Inorganic Chemistry	M,D
Mathematics	M,D
Organic Chemistry	M,D
Physical Chemistry	M,D
Physics	M,D
Plant Sciences	M
Statistics	M,D
Theoretical Chemistry	M,D

THE UNIVERSITY OF TENNESSEE AT CHATTANOOGA

Applied Mathematics	M
Applied Statistics	M
Computational Sciences	M,D
Environmental Sciences	M
Mathematics	M

THE UNIVERSITY OF TENNESSEE AT MARTIN

Agricultural Sciences— General	M
Food Science and Technology	M

THE UNIVERSITY OF TENNESSEE SPACE INSTITUTE

Physics	M,D

THE UNIVERSITY OF TEXAS AT ARLINGTON

Applied Mathematics	M,D
Chemistry	M,D
Environmental Sciences	M,D
Geology	M,D
Mathematics	M,D
Physics	M,D

THE UNIVERSITY OF TEXAS AT AUSTIN

Analytical Chemistry	D
Applied Mathematics	M,D
Applied Physics	M,D
Astronomy	M,D
Chemistry	D
Computational Sciences	M,D
Environmental Management and Policy	M
Geology	M,D
Geosciences	M,D
Inorganic Chemistry	D
Marine Sciences	M,D
Mathematics	M,D
Natural Resources	M
Organic Chemistry	D
Physical Chemistry	D
Physics	M,D
Statistics	M,D

THE UNIVERSITY OF TEXAS AT BROWNSVILLE

Mathematics	M
Physics	M

THE UNIVERSITY OF TEXAS AT DALLAS

Applied Mathematics	M,D
Chemistry	M,D
Geochemistry	M,D
Geophysics	M,D
Geosciences	M,D
Hydrogeology	M,D
Mathematics	M,D
Paleontology	M,D
Physics	M,D
Statistics	M,D

THE UNIVERSITY OF TEXAS AT EL PASO

Chemistry	M,D
Computational Sciences	M,D
Environmental Sciences	M,D
Geology	M,D
Geophysics	M
Mathematics	M
Physics	M
Statistics	M

THE UNIVERSITY OF TEXAS AT SAN ANTONIO

Applied Mathematics	M
Applied Statistics	M,D
Chemistry	M,D
Environmental Sciences	M,D
Geology	M
Mathematics	M
Physics	M,D
Statistics	M,D

THE UNIVERSITY OF TEXAS AT TYLER

Mathematics	M

THE UNIVERSITY OF TEXAS HEALTH SCIENCE CENTER AT HOUSTON

Biomathematics	M,D
Biostatistics	M,D

THE UNIVERSITY OF TEXAS OF THE PERMIAN BASIN

Geology	M

THE UNIVERSITY OF TEXAS–PAN AMERICAN

Chemistry	M
Mathematics	M

UNIVERSITY OF THE DISTRICT OF COLUMBIA

Applied Statistics	M

UNIVERSITY OF THE INCARNATE WORD

Mathematics	M
Statistics	M

UNIVERSITY OF THE PACIFIC

Water Resources	M,D

UNIVERSITY OF THE SCIENCES

Chemistry	M,D

*M—master's degree; P—first professional degree; D—doctorate; O—other advanced degree; *—Close-Up and/or Display*

Petersons Graduate Programs in the Physical Sciences, Mathematics, Agricultural Sciences, the Environment & Natural Resources 2014

www.petersonsbooks.com **35**

UNIVERSITY OF THE VIRGIN ISLANDS
Environmental Sciences	M
Marine Sciences	M

THE UNIVERSITY OF TOLEDO
Analytical Chemistry	M,D
Applied Mathematics	M,D
Astrophysics	M,D
Biostatistics	M,O
Chemistry	M,D
Environmental Sciences	M,D
Geology	M,D
Inorganic Chemistry	M,D
Mathematics	M,D
Organic Chemistry	M,D
Physical Chemistry	M,D
Physics	M,D
Statistics	M,D

UNIVERSITY OF TORONTO
Astronomy	M,D
Astrophysics	M,D
Biostatistics	M,D
Chemistry	M,D
Environmental Sciences	M,D
Forestry	M,D
Geology	M,D
Mathematical and Computational Finance	M
Mathematics	M,D
Physics	M,D
Statistics	M,D

UNIVERSITY OF TULSA
Applied Mathematics	
Chemistry	M,D
Geosciences	M,D
Mathematics	M,D
Physics	M,D

UNIVERSITY OF UTAH
Atmospheric Sciences	M,D
Biostatistics	M,D
Chemical Physics	M,D
Chemistry	M,D
Computational Sciences	M
Environmental Sciences	M
Geology	M,D
Geophysics	M,D
Mathematics	M,D
Physics	M,D
Statistics	M,D

UNIVERSITY OF VERMONT
Agricultural Sciences—General	M,D
Agronomy and Soil Sciences	M,D
Animal Sciences	M,D
Biostatistics	M
Chemistry	M,D
Food Science and Technology	D
Forestry	M,D
Geology	M
Horticulture	M,D
Mathematics	M,D
Natural Resources	M,D
Physics	M
Plant Sciences	M,D
Statistics	M

UNIVERSITY OF VICTORIA
Astronomy	M,D
Astrophysics	M,D
Chemistry	M,D
Condensed Matter Physics	M,D
Geophysics	M,D
Geosciences	M,D
Mathematics	M,D
Oceanography	M,D

Physics	M,D
Statistics	M,D
Theoretical Physics	M,D

UNIVERSITY OF VIRGINIA
Astronomy	M,D
Chemistry	M,D
Environmental Sciences	M,D
Mathematics	M,D
Physics	M,D
Statistics	M,D

UNIVERSITY OF WASHINGTON
Applied Mathematics	M,D
Applied Physics	M,D
Astronomy	M,D
Atmospheric Sciences	M,D
Biostatistics	M,D
Chemistry	M,D
Computational Sciences	M,D
Environmental Management and Policy	M,D
Fish, Game, and Wildlife Management	M,D
Forestry	M,D
Geology	M,D
Geophysics	M,D
Horticulture	M,D
Hydrology	M,D
Marine Affairs	M,O
Marine Geology	M,D
Mathematics	M,D
Natural Resources	M,D
Oceanography	M,D
Physics	M,D
Statistics	M,D

UNIVERSITY OF WATERLOO
Applied Mathematics	M,D
Biostatistics	M,D
Chemistry	M,D
Environmental Management and Policy	M
Geosciences	M,D
Mathematics	M,D
Physics	M,D
Statistics	M,D

THE UNIVERSITY OF WESTERN ONTARIO
Applied Mathematics	M,D
Astronomy	M,D
Biostatistics	M,D
Chemistry	M,D
Environmental Sciences	M,D
Geology	M,D
Geophysics	M,D
Geosciences	M,D
Mathematics	M,D
Physics	M,D
Plant Sciences	M,D
Statistics	M,D

UNIVERSITY OF WEST FLORIDA
Applied Statistics	M
Environmental Sciences	M
Marine Affairs	M
Mathematics	M

UNIVERSITY OF WEST GEORGIA
Applied Mathematics	M
Mathematics	M

UNIVERSITY OF WINDSOR
Chemistry	M,D
Environmental Sciences	M,D
Geosciences	M,D
Mathematics	M,D
Physics	M,D
Statistics	M,D

UNIVERSITY OF WISCONSIN–GREEN BAY
Environmental Management and Policy	M
Environmental Sciences	M

UNIVERSITY OF WISCONSIN–LA CROSSE
Marine Sciences	M

UNIVERSITY OF WISCONSIN–MADISON
Agricultural Sciences—General	M,D
Agronomy and Soil Sciences	M,D
Animal Sciences	M,D
Astronomy	D
Atmospheric Sciences	M,D
Biometry	M
Chemistry	M,D
Environmental Sciences	M,D
Fish, Game, and Wildlife Management	M,D
Food Science and Technology	M,D
Forestry	M,D
Geology	M,D
Geophysics	M,D
Horticulture	M,D
Limnology	M,D
Marine Sciences	M,D
Mathematics	D
Natural Resources	M,D
Oceanography	M,D
Physics	M,D
Plant Sciences	M,D
Statistics	M,D
Water Resources	M

UNIVERSITY OF WISCONSIN–MILWAUKEE
Chemistry	M,D
Geochemistry	M,D
Geology	M,D
Mathematics	M,D
Physics	M,D
Water Resources	M,D

UNIVERSITY OF WISCONSIN–RIVER FALLS
Agricultural Sciences—General	M

UNIVERSITY OF WISCONSIN–STEVENS POINT
Natural Resources	M

UNIVERSITY OF WISCONSIN–STOUT
Food Science and Technology	M

UNIVERSITY OF WYOMING
Agricultural Sciences—General	M,D
Agronomy and Soil Sciences	M,D
Animal Sciences	M,D
Atmospheric Sciences	M,D
Chemistry	M,D
Food Science and Technology	M
Geology	M,D
Geophysics	M,D
Mathematics	M,D
Natural Resources	M,D
Range Science	M,D
Statistics	M,D
Water Resources	M,D

UTAH STATE UNIVERSITY
Agricultural Sciences—General	M,D
Agronomy and Soil Sciences	M,D

Animal Sciences	M,D
Applied Mathematics	M,D
Chemistry	M,D
Environmental Management and Policy	M,D
Fish, Game, and Wildlife Management	M,D
Food Science and Technology	M,D
Forestry	M,D
Geology	M
Mathematics	M,D
Meteorology	M,D
Natural Resources	M
Physics	M,D
Plant Sciences	M,D
Range Science	M,D
Statistics	M,D
Water Resources	M,D

VANDERBILT UNIVERSITY
Analytical Chemistry	M,D
Astronomy	M,D
Chemistry	M,D
Environmental Management and Policy	M,D
Environmental Sciences	M
Geology	M
Inorganic Chemistry	M,D
Mathematics	M,D
Organic Chemistry	M,D
Physical Chemistry	M,D
Physics	M,D
Theoretical Chemistry	M,D

VERMONT LAW SCHOOL
Environmental Management and Policy	M

VILLANOVA UNIVERSITY
Applied Statistics	M
Chemistry	M
Mathematics	M

VIRGINIA COMMONWEALTH UNIVERSITY
Analytical Chemistry	M,D
Applied Mathematics	M
Applied Physics	M
Biostatistics	M,D
Chemical Physics	M,D
Chemistry	M,D
Environmental Management and Policy	M
Inorganic Chemistry	M,D
Mathematics	M
Organic Chemistry	M,D
Physical Chemistry	M,D
Physics	M
Statistics	M,D

VIRGINIA POLYTECHNIC INSTITUTE AND STATE UNIVERSITY
Agricultural Sciences—General	M,D,O
Agronomy and Soil Sciences	M,D
Animal Sciences	M,D
Chemistry	M,D
Environmental Management and Policy	M,D,O
Environmental Sciences	M,D,O
Fish, Game, and Wildlife Management	M,D
Forestry	M,D
Geosciences	M,D
Horticulture	M,D
Mathematics	M,D
Natural Resources	M,D,O
Physics	M,D
Statistics	M,D

36 www.petersonsbooks.com

Petersons Graduate Programs in the Physical Sciences, Mathematics, Agricultural Sciences, the Environment & Natural Resources 2014

VIRGINIA STATE UNIVERSITY

Agricultural Sciences—	
General	M
Mathematics	M
Physics	M
Plant Sciences	M

WAKE FOREST UNIVERSITY

Analytical Chemistry	M,D
Chemistry	M,D
Inorganic Chemistry	M,D
Mathematics	M
Organic Chemistry	M,D
Physical Chemistry	M,D
Physics	M,D

WASHINGTON STATE UNIVERSITY

Agricultural Sciences—	
General	M
Agronomy and Soil Sciences	M,D
Animal Sciences	M,D
Applied Mathematics	M,D
Astrophysics	M,D
Chemistry	M,D
Environmental Sciences	M,D
Food Science and	
Technology	M,D
Geology	M,D
Horticulture	M,D
Mathematical and	
Computational Finance	M,D
Mathematics	M,D
Natural Resources	M,D
Optical Sciences	M,D
Physics	M,D

WASHINGTON STATE UNIVERSITY TRI-CITIES

Chemistry	M
Environmental Sciences	M,D
Natural Resources	M,D

WASHINGTON STATE UNIVERSITY VANCOUVER

Environmental Sciences	M

WASHINGTON UNIVERSITY IN ST. LOUIS

Biostatistics	M,O
Chemistry	D
Geosciences	M,D
Mathematics	M,D
Physics	D
Planetary and Space	
Sciences	M,D
Statistics	M,D

WAYNE STATE UNIVERSITY

Analytical Chemistry	M,D
Applied Mathematics	M,D
Chemistry	M,D
Food Science and	
Technology	M,D
Geology	M
Inorganic Chemistry	M,D
Mathematics	M,D
Organic Chemistry	M,D
Physical Chemistry	M,D
Physics	M,D
Statistics	M,D

WEBSTER UNIVERSITY

Environmental Management	
and Policy	M,D,O

WESLEYAN UNIVERSITY

Astronomy	M
Chemical Physics	D
Chemistry	D
Environmental Sciences	M
Geosciences	M
Inorganic Chemistry	D
Mathematics	M,D*
Organic Chemistry	D
Physics	D
Theoretical Chemistry	D

WESLEY COLLEGE

Environmental Management	
and Policy	M

WEST CHESTER UNIVERSITY OF PENNSYLVANIA

Applied Statistics	M,O
Astronomy	M,O
Chemistry	O
Geology	M,O
Geosciences	M,O
Mathematics	M,O
Planetary and Space	
Sciences	M,O

WESTERN CAROLINA UNIVERSITY

Chemistry	M
Mathematics	M

WESTERN CONNECTICUT STATE UNIVERSITY

Environmental Sciences	M
Geosciences	M
Mathematics	M
Planetary and Space	
Sciences	M

WESTERN ILLINOIS UNIVERSITY

Applied Mathematics	M,O
Chemistry	M
Mathematics	M,O
Physics	M

WESTERN KENTUCKY UNIVERSITY

Agricultural Sciences—	
General	M
Chemistry	M
Computational Sciences	M
Geology	M
Geosciences	M
Mathematics	M
Physics	M

WESTERN MICHIGAN UNIVERSITY

Applied Mathematics	M
Chemistry	M,D
Computational Sciences	M
Geosciences	M,D
Mathematics	M,D
Physics	M,D
Statistics	M,D

WESTERN WASHINGTON UNIVERSITY

Chemistry	M
Environmental Sciences	M
Geology	M
Marine Sciences	M
Mathematics	M

WEST TEXAS A&M UNIVERSITY

Agricultural Sciences—	
General	M,D
Animal Sciences	M
Chemistry	M
Environmental Sciences	M
Mathematics	M
Plant Sciences	M

WEST VIRGINIA UNIVERSITY

Agricultural Sciences—	
General	M,D
Agronomy and Soil Sciences	D
Analytical Chemistry	M,D
Animal Sciences	M,D
Applied Mathematics	M,D
Applied Physics	M,D
Chemical Physics	M,D
Chemistry	M,D
Condensed Matter Physics	M,D
Environmental Management	
and Policy	M,D
Fish, Game, and Wildlife	
Management	M
Food Science and	
Technology	M,D
Forestry	M,D
Geology	M,D
Geophysics	M,D
Horticulture	M,D
Hydrogeology	M,D
Inorganic Chemistry	M,D
Mathematics	M,D
Natural Resources	M,D
Organic Chemistry	M,D
Paleontology	M,D
Physical Chemistry	M,D
Physics	M,D
Plant Sciences	D
Plasma Physics	M,D
Statistics	M,D
Theoretical Chemistry	M,D
Theoretical Physics	M,D

WICHITA STATE UNIVERSITY

Applied Mathematics	M,D
Chemistry	M,D
Environmental Sciences	M
Geology	M
Mathematics	M,D

WILFRID LAURIER UNIVERSITY

Chemistry	M
Environmental Management	
and Policy	M,D
Environmental Sciences	M,D
Mathematics	M

WILKES UNIVERSITY

Mathematics	M

WILLAMETTE UNIVERSITY

Environmental Management	
and Policy	M

WILMINGTON UNIVERSITY

Environmental Management	
and Policy	M,D

WOODS HOLE OCEANOGRAPHIC INSTITUTION

Marine Geology	D
Oceanography	D

WORCESTER POLYTECHNIC INSTITUTE

Applied Mathematics	M,D,O
Applied Statistics	M,D,O
Chemistry	M,D
Mathematics	M,D,O
Physics	M,D

WRIGHT STATE UNIVERSITY

Applied Mathematics	M
Applied Statistics	M
Chemistry	M
Environmental Sciences	M,D
Geology	M
Geophysics	M
Mathematics	M
Physics	M

YALE UNIVERSITY

Applied Mathematics	M,D
Applied Physics	M,D
Astronomy	M,D
Astrophysics	M,D
Atmospheric Sciences	D
Biostatistics	M,D
Chemistry	D
Environmental Management	
and Policy	M,D
Environmental Sciences	M,D
Forestry	M,D
Geochemistry	D
Geology	D
Geophysics	D
Geosciences	D
Inorganic Chemistry	D
Mathematics	M,D
Meteorology	D
Oceanography	D
Organic Chemistry	D
Paleontology	D
Physical Chemistry	D
Physics	D
Planetary and Space	
Sciences	M,D
Statistics	M,D
Theoretical Chemistry	D

YORK UNIVERSITY

Applied Mathematics	M,D
Astronomy	M,D
Chemistry	M,D
Environmental Management	
and Policy	M,D
Geosciences	M,D
Mathematics	M,D
Physics	M,D
Planetary and Space	
Sciences	M,D
Statistics	M,D

YOUNGSTOWN STATE UNIVERSITY

Analytical Chemistry	M
Applied Mathematics	M
Chemistry	M
Environmental Management	
and Policy	M,O
Inorganic Chemistry	M
Mathematics	M
Organic Chemistry	M
Physical Chemistry	M
Statistics	M

---

*M—master's degree; P—first professional degree; D—doctorate; O—other advanced degree; *—Close-Up and/or Display*

Petersons Graduate Programs in the Physical Sciences, Mathematics, Agricultural Sciences, the Environment & Natural Resources 2014

www.petersonsbooks.com **37**

ACADEMIC AND PROFESSIONAL
PROGRAMS IN THE PHYSICAL SCIENCES

Section 1
Astronomy and Astrophysics

This section contains a directory of institutions offering graduate work in astronomy and astrophysics. Additional information about programs listed in the directory but not augmented by an in-depth entry may be obtained by writing directly to the dean of a graduate school or chair of a department at the address given in the directory.

For programs offering related work, see also in this book *Geosciences, Meteorology and Atmospheric Sciences,* and *Physics.* In the other guides in this series:

Graduate Programs in the Biological/Biomedical Sciences & Health-Related Medical Professions
    See *Biological and Biomedical Sciences* and *Biophysics*
Graduate Programs in Engineering & Applied Sciences
    See *Aerospace/Aeronautical Engineering, Energy and Power Engineering (Nuclear Engineering), Engineering and Applied Sciences,* and *Mechanical Engineering and Mechanics*

CONTENTS

Astronomy

Boston University, Graduate School of Arts and Sciences, Department of Astronomy, Boston, MA 02215. Offers MA, PhD. *Students:* 33 full-time (14 women); includes 5 minority (3 Asian, non-Hispanic/Latino; 2 Hispanic/Latino), 5 international. Average age 27. 99 applicants, 16% accepted, 5 enrolled. In 2012, 5 master's, 6 doctorates awarded. Terminal master's awarded for partial completion of doctoral program. *Degree requirements:* For master's, one foreign language, comprehensive exam, thesis or alternative; for doctorate, one foreign language, comprehensive exam, thesis/dissertation. *Entrance requirements:* For master's and doctorate, GRE General Test, GRE Subject Test (physics), 3 letters of recommendation. Additional exam requirements/recommendations for international students: Required—TOEFL (minimum score 550 paper-based; 85 iBT). *Application deadline:* For fall admission, 12/15 for domestic and international students. Application fee: $80. *Expenses: Tuition:* Full-time $42,400; part-time $1325 per credit. *Required fees:* $40 per semester. *Financial support:* In 2012–13, 1 fellowship with full tuition reimbursement (averaging $20,300 per year), 24 research assistantships with full tuition reimbursements (averaging $19,800 per year), 9 teaching assistantships with full tuition reimbursements (averaging $19,800 per year) were awarded; Federal Work-Study, health care benefits, and unspecified assistantships also available. Support available to part-time students. Financial award application deadline: 12/15. *Unit head:* Tereasa Brainerd, Chairman, 617-353-7412, Fax: 617-353-6463, E-mail: brainerd@bu.edu. *Application contact:* John-Albert Mosely, Department Administrator, 617-363-2625, Fax: 617-353-5704, E-mail: jmosely@bu.edu. Website: http://www.bu.edu/dbin/astronomy.

Brigham Young University, Graduate Studies, College of Physical and Mathematical Sciences, Department of Physics and Astronomy, Provo, UT 84602-1001. Offers physics (MS, PhD); physics and astronomy (PhD). Part-time programs available. *Faculty:* 30 full-time (2 women). *Students:* 37 full-time (7 women); includes 4 minority (2 Asian, non-Hispanic/Latino; 2 Hispanic/Latino), 1 international. Average age 29. 20 applicants, 50% accepted, 6 enrolled. In 2012, 6 master's, 4 doctorates awarded. Terminal master's awarded for partial completion of doctoral program. *Degree requirements:* For master's, thesis; for doctorate, thesis/dissertation, qualifying exam. *Entrance requirements:* For master's and doctorate, GRE Subject Test (physics), GRE General Test, minimum GPA of 3.0 in last 60 hours, ecclesiastical endorsement. Additional exam requirements/recommendations for international students: Required—TOEFL (minimum score 580 paper-based; 85 iBT), IELTS (minimum score 7). *Application deadline:* For fall admission, 1/15 priority date for domestic students, 1/15 for international students. Application fee: $50. Electronic applications accepted. *Expenses: Tuition:* Full-time $5950; part-time $331 per credit hour. Tuition and fees vary according to program and student's religious affiliation. *Financial support:* In 2012–13, 27 students received support, including 16 research assistantships with full tuition reimbursements available (averaging $20,640 per year), 15 teaching assistantships with full tuition reimbursements available (averaging $19,680 per year); fellowships with full tuition reimbursements available, institutionally sponsored loans, and tuition waivers (full) also available. Support available to part-time students. Financial award application deadline: 1/15. *Faculty research:* Acoustics; atomic, molecular, and optical physics; theoretical and mathematical physics; condensed matter; astrophysics and plasma. *Total annual research expenditures:* $1.8 million. *Unit head:* Dr. Ross L. Spencer, Chair, 801-422-2341, Fax: 801-422-0553, E-mail: ross_spencer@byu.edu. *Application contact:* Dr. Eric W. Hirschmann, Graduate Coordinator, 801-422-9271, Fax: 801-422-0553, E-mail: eric_hirschmann@byu.edu. Website: http://physics.byu.edu/.

California Institute of Technology, Division of Physics, Mathematics and Astronomy, Department of Astronomy, Pasadena, CA 91125-0001. Offers PhD. *Degree requirements:* For doctorate, one foreign language, thesis/dissertation, candidacy and final exams. *Entrance requirements:* For doctorate, GRE General Test, GRE Subject Test. Additional exam requirements/recommendations for international students: Required—TOEFL. *Faculty research:* Observational and theoretical astrophysics, cosmology, radio astronomy, solar physics.

Case Western Reserve University, School of Graduate Studies, Department of Astronomy, Cleveland, OH 44106. Offers MS, PhD. Part-time programs available. *Faculty:* 5 full-time (2 women), 3 part-time/adjunct (0 women). *Students:* 6 full-time (1 woman), 2 international. Average age 26. 12 applicants, 25% accepted, 3 enrolled. *Degree requirements:* For doctorate, comprehensive exam, thesis/dissertation. *Entrance requirements:* For doctorate, GRE General Test, GRE Subject Test (physics). Additional exam requirements/recommendations for international students: Required—TOEFL (minimum score 577 paper-based; 90 iBT), IELTS (minimum score 7). *Application deadline:* For fall admission, 1/15 priority date for domestic students. Applications are processed on a rolling basis. Application fee: $50. Electronic applications accepted. *Financial support:* Fellowships and research assistantships available. Financial award application deadline: 2/15; financial award applicants required to submit FAFSA. *Faculty research:* Optical observational astronomy, high- and low-dispersion spectroscopy, theoretical astrophysics, galactic structure. *Unit head:* Prof. James Christopher Mihos, Chair, 216-368-3729, Fax: 216-368-5406, E-mail: mihos@case.edu. *Application contact:* Agnes Torontalli, Department Assistant, 216-368-3728, Fax: 216-368-5406, E-mail: agnes@case.edu. Website: http://astroweb.case.edu/.

Clemson University, Graduate School, College of Engineering and Science, Department of Physics and Astronomy, Clemson, SC 29634. Offers physics (MS, PhD), including astronomy and astrophysics, atmospheric physics, biophysics. Part-time programs available. *Faculty:* 24 full-time (3 women). *Students:* 62 full-time (15 women), 1 part-time (0 women); includes 2 minority (1 Black or African American, non-Hispanic/Latino; 1 Hispanic/Latino), 28 international. Average age 26. 66 applicants, 41% accepted, 12 enrolled. In 2012, 8 master's, 5 doctorates awarded. Terminal master's awarded for partial completion of doctoral program. *Degree requirements:* For master's, thesis or alternative; for doctorate, thesis/dissertation. *Entrance requirements:* For master's and doctorate, GRE General Test. Additional exam requirements/recommendations for international students: Required—TOEFL. *Application deadline:* For fall admission, 1/15 priority date for domestic students; for spring admission, 9/15 priority date for domestic students. Applications are processed on a rolling basis. Application fee: $70 ($80 for international students). Electronic applications accepted. *Financial support:* In 2012–13, 60 students received support, including 1 fellowship with full and partial tuition reimbursement available (averaging $7,000 per year), 25 research assistantships with partial tuition reimbursements available (averaging $13,151 per year), 44 teaching assistantships with partial tuition reimbursements available (averaging $15,956 per year); career-related internships or fieldwork, institutionally sponsored loans, scholarships/grants, health care benefits, and unspecified assistantships also available. Support available to part-time students. Financial award application deadline: 6/1; financial award applicants required to submit FAFSA. *Faculty research:* Radiation physics, solid-state physics, nuclear physics, radar and lidar studies of atmosphere. *Total annual research expenditures:* $2.6 million. *Unit head:* Dr. Peter Barnes, Chair, 864-656-3419, Fax: 864-656-0805, E-mail: peterb@clemson.edu. *Application contact:* Graduate Coordinator, 864-656-6702, Fax: 864-656-0805, E-mail: physgradinfo-l@clemson.edu. Website: http://physicsnt.clemson.edu/.

Columbia University, Graduate School of Arts and Sciences, Division of Natural Sciences, Department of Astronomy, New York, NY 10027. Offers M Phil, MA, PhD. Part-time programs available. *Degree requirements:* For doctorate, thesis/dissertation. *Entrance requirements:* For master's and doctorate, GRE General Test, major in astronomy or physics. Additional exam requirements/recommendations for international students: Required—TOEFL. *Faculty research:* Theoretical astrophysics, x-ray astronomy, radio astronomy.

Cornell University, Graduate School, Graduate Fields of Arts and Sciences, Field of Astronomy and Space Sciences, Ithaca, NY 14853-0001. Offers astronomy (PhD); astrophysics (PhD); general space sciences (PhD); infrared astronomy (PhD); planetary studies (PhD); radio astronomy (PhD); radiophysics (PhD); theoretical astrophysics (PhD). *Faculty:* 31 full-time (2 women). *Students:* 27 full-time (9 women); includes 6 minority (3 Asian, non-Hispanic/Latino; 2 Hispanic/Latino; 1 Two or more races, non-Hispanic/Latino), 8 international. Average age 26. 84 applicants, 8% accepted, 1 enrolled. In 2012, 6 doctorates awarded. *Degree requirements:* For doctorate, comprehensive exam, thesis/dissertation. *Entrance requirements:* For doctorate, GRE General Test, GRE Subject Test (physics), 3 letters of recommendation. Additional exam requirements/recommendations for international students: Required—TOEFL (minimum score 600 paper-based; 77 iBT). *Application deadline:* For fall admission, 1/15 for domestic students. Application fee: $95. Electronic applications accepted. *Financial support:* In 2012–13, 27 students received support, including 11 fellowships with full tuition reimbursements available, 8 research assistantships with full tuition reimbursements available, 8 teaching assistantships with full tuition reimbursements available; institutionally sponsored loans, scholarships/grants, health care benefits, tuition waivers (full and partial), and unspecified assistantships also available. Financial award applicants required to submit FAFSA. *Faculty research:* Observational astrophysics, planetary sciences, cosmology, instrumentation, gravitational astrophysics. *Unit head:* Director of Graduate Studies, 607-255-4341. *Application contact:* Graduate Field Assistant, 607-255-4341, E-mail: oconnor@astro.cornell.edu. Website: http://www.gradschool.cornell.edu/fields.php?id-24&a-2.

Dartmouth College, Arts and Sciences Graduate Programs, Department of Physics and Astronomy, Hanover, NH 03755. Offers MS, PhD. Terminal master's awarded for partial completion of doctoral program. *Degree requirements:* For master's, thesis; for doctorate, thesis/dissertation. *Entrance requirements:* For master's and doctorate, GRE General Test, GRE Subject Test. Additional exam requirements/recommendations for international students: Required—TOEFL. *Faculty research:* Matter physics, plasma and beam physics, space physics, astronomy, cosmology.

Georgia State University, College of Arts and Sciences, Department of Physics and Astronomy, Program in Astronomy, Atlanta, GA 30302-3083. Offers PhD. *Faculty:* 5 full-time (1 woman), 2 part-time/adjunct (0 women). *Students:* 22 full-time (10 women); includes 3 minority (1 Asian, non-Hispanic/Latino; 2 Hispanic/Latino), 1 international. Average age 27. 32 applicants, 34% accepted, 4 enrolled. In 2012, 4 doctorates awarded. Terminal master's awarded for partial completion

42 www.petersonsbooks.com

Peterson's Graduate Programs in the Physical Sciences, Mathematics, Agricultural Sciences, the Environment & Natural Resources 2014

of doctoral program. *Degree requirements:* For doctorate, 2 foreign languages, comprehensive exam, thesis/dissertation. *Entrance requirements:* For doctorate, GRE General Test, GRE Subject Test (physics). Additional exam requirements/recommendations for international students: Required—TOEFL (minimum score 550 paper-based; 80 iBT). *Application deadline:* For fall admission, 1/15 for domestic and international students; for spring admission, 11/15 for domestic and international students. Application fee: $50. Electronic applications accepted. *Expenses:* Tuition, state resident: full-time $8064; part-time $336 per credit hour. Tuition, nonresident: full-time $28,800; part-time $1200 per credit hour. *Required fees:* $2128; $1064 per semester. Tuition and fees vary according to course load and program. *Financial support:* In 2012–13, 23 students received support, including 7 fellowships with full tuition reimbursements available (averaging $22,000 per year), 4 research assistantships with full tuition reimbursements available (averaging $22,000 per year), 12 teaching assistantships with full tuition reimbursements available (averaging $20,500 per year); institutionally sponsored loans, scholarships/grants, and unspecified assistantships also available. Financial award application deadline: 1/15. *Faculty research:* Astrophysics, active galactic nuclei, exoplanet searches, missing mass and dark matter stellare. *Total annual research expenditures:* $880,278. *Unit head:* Dr. Mike Crenshaw, Chair, 404-413-6020, E-mail: crenshaw@chara.gsu.edu. *Application contact:* Todd Henry, Graduate Director, 404-413-6054, E-mail: thenry@chara.gsu.edu. Website: http://www.phy-astr.gsu.edu/.

Harvard University, Graduate School of Arts and Sciences, Department of Astronomy, Cambridge, MA 02138. Offers astronomy (PhD); astrophysics (PhD). *Degree requirements:* For doctorate, thesis/dissertation, paper, research project, 2 semesters of teaching. *Entrance requirements:* For doctorate, GRE General Test, GRE Subject Test (physics). Additional exam requirements/recommendations for international students: Required—TOEFL. Electronic applications accepted. *Expenses: Tuition:* Full-time $37,576. *Required fees:* $930. Tuition and fees vary according to program and student level. *Faculty research:* Atomic and molecular physics, electromagnetism, solar physics, nuclear physics, fluid dynamics.

Indiana University Bloomington, University Graduate School, College of Arts and Sciences, Department of Astronomy, Bloomington, IN 47405-7000. Offers astronomy (MA, PhD); astrophysics (PhD). *Faculty:* 9 full-time (5 women), 2 part-time/adjunct (0 women). *Students:* 20 full-time (9 women); includes 5 minority (2 Asian, non-Hispanic/Latino; 1 Hispanic/Latino; 2 Two or more races, non-Hispanic/Latino), 1 international. 37 applicants, 16% accepted, 3 enrolled. In 2012, 4 master's, 4 doctorates awarded. Terminal master's awarded for partial completion of doctoral program. *Degree requirements:* For master's, thesis or alternative, oral exam; for doctorate, comprehensive exam, thesis/dissertation, oral defense. *Entrance requirements:* For master's and doctorate, GRE General Test, GRE Subject Test (physics), BA or BS in science. Additional exam requirements/recommendations for international students: Required—TOEFL. *Application deadline:* For fall admission, 1/15 for domestic students, 12/1 for international students; for spring admission, 9/1 for domestic students. Application fee: $55 ($65 for international students). Electronic applications accepted. *Financial support:* In 2012–13, 18 students received support, including 3 fellowships with full tuition reimbursements available (averaging $14,333 per year), 7 research assistantships with full tuition reimbursements available (averaging $19,850 per year), 8 teaching assistantships with full tuition reimbursements available (averaging $17,950 per year); scholarships/grants, health care benefits, and unspecified assistantships also available. Financial award application deadline: 1/15. *Faculty research:* Stellar and galaxy dynamics, stellar chemical abundances, galaxy evolution, observational cosmology. *Total annual research expenditures:* $772,980. *Unit head:* Dr. John Salzer, Chair, 812-855-6911, Fax: 812-855-8725, E-mail: josalzer@indiana.edu. *Application contact:* Julie Wilson, Graduate Secretary, 812-855-6911, Fax: 812-855-8725, E-mail: jaw@indiana.edu. Website: http://www.astro.indiana.edu/.

The Johns Hopkins University, Zanvyl Krieger School of Arts and Sciences, Henry A. Rowland Department of Physics and Astronomy, Baltimore, MD 21218-2699. Offers astronomy (PhD); physics (PhD). *Degree requirements:* For doctorate, comprehensive exam, thesis/dissertation, minimum B- average on required coursework. *Entrance requirements:* For doctorate, GRE General Test, GRE Subject Test. Additional exam requirements/recommendations for international students: Required—TOEFL (minimum score 600 paper-based; 100 iBT), IELTS. Electronic applications accepted. *Faculty research:* High-energy physics, condensed-matter, astrophysics, particle and experimental physics, plasma physics.

Louisiana State University and Agricultural and Mechanical College, Graduate School, College of Science, Department of Physics and Astronomy, Baton Rouge, LA 70803. Offers astronomy (PhD); astrophysics (PhD); medical physics (MS); physics (MS, PhD). *Faculty:* 45 full-time (5 women), 1 part-time/adjunct (0 women). *Students:* 106 full-time (21 women), 3 part-time (1 woman); includes 5 minority (1 Black or African American, non-Hispanic/Latino; 4 Hispanic/Latino), 52 international. Average age 27. 135 applicants, 16% accepted, 20 enrolled. In 2012, 8 master's, 8 doctorates awarded. Terminal master's awarded for partial completion of doctoral program. *Degree requirements:* For master's, thesis or alternative; for doctorate, thesis/dissertation. *Entrance requirements:* For master's and doctorate, GRE General Test, minimum GPA of 3.0. Additional exam requirements/recommendations for international students: Required—TOEFL (minimum score 550 paper-based; 79 iBT) or IELTS (minimum score 6.5). *Application deadline:* For fall admission, 1/25 priority date for domestic students, 5/15 for international students; for spring admission, 10/15 for international students. Applications are processed on a rolling basis. Application fee: $50 ($70 for international students). Electronic applications accepted. *Financial support:* In 2012–13, 108 students received support, including 12 fellowships with full tuition reimbursements available (averaging $26,748 per year), 60 research assistantships with full and partial tuition reimbursements available (averaging $22,794 per year), 35 teaching assistantships with full and partial tuition reimbursements available (averaging $19,046 per year); Federal Work-Study, institutionally sponsored loans, health care benefits, tuition waivers (full and partial), and unspecified assistantships also available. Financial award application deadline: 3/15; financial award applicants required to submit FAFSA. *Faculty research:* Experimentation and numerical relativity, condensed matter astrophysics, quantum computing, medical physics. *Total annual research expenditures:* $9.6 million. *Unit head:* Dr. Michael Cherry, Chair, 225-578-2262, Fax: 225-578-5855, E-mail: cherry@phys.lsu.edu. *Application contact:* Arnell Dangerfield, Administrative Coordinator, 225-578-1193, Fax: 225-578-5855, E-mail: adanger@lsu.edu. Website: http://www.phys.lsu.edu/.

Michigan State University, The Graduate School, College of Natural Science, Department of Physics and Astronomy, East Lansing, MI 48824. Offers astrophysics and astronomy (MS, PhD); physics (MS, PhD). *Entrance requirements:* Additional exam requirements/recommendations for international students: Required—TOEFL (minimum score 550 paper-based), Michigan State University ELT (minimum score 85), Michigan English Language Assessment Battery (minimum score 83). Electronic applications accepted. *Faculty research:* Nuclear and accelerator physics, high energy physics, condensed matter physics, biophysics, astrophysics and astronomy.

Minnesota State University Mankato, College of Graduate Studies, College of Science, Engineering and Technology, Department of Physics and Astronomy, Mankato, MN 56001. Offers MS. *Students:* 2 full-time (0 women), 8 part-time (0 women). *Degree requirements:* For master's, one foreign language, comprehensive exam, thesis or alternative. *Entrance requirements:* For master's, minimum GPA of 3.0 during previous 2 years, recommendation letters. Additional exam requirements/recommendations for international students: Required—TOEFL. *Application deadline:* For fall admission, 7/1 priority date for domestic students; for spring admission, 11/1 for domestic students. Applications are processed on a rolling basis. Application fee: $40. Electronic applications accepted. *Financial support:* Research assistantships, teaching assistantships with full tuition reimbursements, Federal Work-Study, and unspecified assistantships available. Support available to part-time students. Financial award application deadline: 3/15; financial award applicants required to submit FAFSA. *Unit head:* Dr. Mark Pickar, Chairperson, 507-389-2721. *Application contact:* 507-389-2321, E-mail: grad@mnsu.edu. Website: http://cset.mnsu.edu/pa/.

New Mexico State University, Graduate School, College of Arts and Sciences, Department of Astronomy, Las Cruces, NM 88003-8001. Offers MS, PhD. Part-time programs available. *Faculty:* 10 full-time (2 women). *Students:* 30 full-time (12 women), 3 part-time (1 woman); includes 3 minority (1 Asian, non-Hispanic/Latino; 2 Hispanic/Latino), 2 international. Average age 27. 46 applicants, 11% accepted, 5 enrolled. In 2012, 4 master's, 3 doctorates awarded. Terminal master's awarded for partial completion of doctoral program. *Degree requirements:* For master's, comprehensive exam (for some programs), thesis (for some programs); for doctorate, comprehensive exam, thesis/dissertation. *Entrance requirements:* For master's and doctorate, GRE General Test, GRE Subject Test (advanced physics). Additional exam requirements/recommendations for international students: Required—TOEFL (minimum score 550 paper-based; 79 iBT), IELTS (minimum score 6.5). *Application deadline:* For fall admission, 2/1 priority date for domestic students, 2/15 for international students. Applications are processed on a rolling basis. Application fee: $40 ($50 for international students). Electronic applications accepted. *Expenses:* Tuition, state resident: full-time $5239; part-time $218 per credit. Tuition, nonresident: full-time $18,266; part-time $761 per credit. *Required fees:* $1274; $53 per credit. *Financial support:* In 2012–13, 30 students received support, including 2 fellowships (averaging $4,456 per year), 17 research assistantships (averaging $18,823 per year), 13 teaching assistantships (averaging $13,762 per year); scholarships/grants, health care benefits, and unspecified assistantships also available. Financial award application deadline: 3/1. *Faculty research:* Planetary systems, solar and stellar physics, stellar populations, galaxies, interstellar medium. *Total annual research expenditures:* $6.2 million. *Unit head:* Dr. Jon Holtzman, Head, 575-646-8181, Fax: 575-646-1602, E-mail: holtz@nmsu.edu. *Application contact:* Dr. Nancy Chanover, Coordinator, 575-646-2567, Fax: 575-646-1602, E-mail: gradapps@astronomy.nmsu.edu. Website: http://astronomy.nmsu.edu/.

Northwestern University, The Graduate School, Judd A. and Marjorie Weinberg College of Arts and Sciences, Department of Physics and Astronomy, Evanston, IL 60208. Offers astrophysics (PhD); physics (MS, PhD). Admissions and degrees offered through The Graduate School. *Degree requirements:* For doctorate, thesis/dissertation, qualifying exam. *Entrance requirements:* For doctorate, GRE General Test, GRE Subject Test. Additional exam requirements/recommendations for international students: Required—TOEFL. *Faculty research:* Nuclear and particle physics, condensed-matter physics, nonlinear physics, astrophysics.

The Ohio State University, Graduate School, College of Arts and Sciences, Division of Natural and Mathematical Sciences, Department of Astronomy, Columbus, OH 43210. Offers MS, PhD. *Faculty:* 16. *Students:* 11 full-time (1 woman), 13 part-time (6 women); includes 3 minority (1 Hispanic/Latino; 2 Two or more races, non-Hispanic/Latino), 4 international. Average age 26. In 2012, 6 master's, 6 doctorates awarded. Terminal master's awarded for partial completion of doctoral program. *Degree requirements:* For master's, comprehensive exam, thesis; for doctorate, comprehensive exam, thesis/dissertation. *Entrance requirements:* For master's and doctorate, GRE General Test, GRE Subject Test (physics). Additional exam requirements/recommendations for international students: Required—TOEFL (minimum score 550 paper-based; 79 iBT), Michigan English Language Assessment Battery (minimum score 82); Recommended—IELTS (minimum score 7). *Application deadline:* For fall admission, 1/4 priority date for domestic students, 11/30 for international students; for winter admission, 12/1 for domestic students, 11/1 for international students; for spring admission, 3/1 for domestic students, 2/1 for international students. Applications are processed on a rolling basis. Application fee: $40 ($50 for international students). Electronic applications accepted. *Financial support:* Fellowships, research assistantships, teaching assistantships, Federal Work-Study, and institutionally sponsored loans available. Support available to part-time students. *Unit head:* Bradley M. Peterson, Chair, 614-292-2022, Fax: 614-292-2928, E-mail: peterson.12@osu.edu. *Application contact:* Todd Thompson, Graduate Admissions Chair, 614-292-1773, Fax: 614-292-2928, E-mail: gradchair@astronomy.ohio-state.edu. Website: http://www.astronomy.ohio-state.edu/.

Ohio University, Graduate College, College of Arts and Sciences, Department of Physics and Astronomy, Athens, OH 45701. Offers astronomy (MS, PhD); physics (MS, PhD). Terminal master's awarded for partial completion of doctoral program. *Degree requirements:* For master's, thesis or alternative; for doctorate, comprehensive exam, thesis/dissertation. *Entrance requirements:* For master's and doctorate, minimum GPA of 3.0. Additional exam requirements/recommendations for international students: Required—TOEFL (minimum score 600 paper-based; 100 iBT), IELTS (minimum score 7), TWE (minimum score 4). Electronic applications accepted. Application fee is waived when completed online. *Faculty research:* Nuclear physics, condensed-matter physics, nonlinear systems, astrophysics, biophysics.

See Display on page 240 and Close-Up on page 259.

Penn State University Park, Graduate School, Eberly College of Science, Department of Astronomy and Astrophysics, State College, University Park, PA 16802-1503. Offers MS, PhD. *Unit head:* Dr. Daniel J. Larson, Dean, 814-865-9591, Fax: 814-865-3634. *Application contact:* Cynthia E. Nicosia, Director, Graduate Enrollment Services, 814-865-1795, Fax: 814-865-4627, E-mail: cey1@psu.edu. Website: http://www.astro.psu.edu/.

Princeton University, Graduate School, Department of Astrophysical Sciences, Princeton, NJ 08544-1019. Offers astronomy (PhD); plasma physics (PhD). *Degree requirements:* For doctorate, thesis/dissertation. *Entrance requirements:* For doctorate, GRE General Test, GRE Subject Test (physics). Additional exam requirements/recommendations for international students: Required—TOEFL (minimum score 600 paper-based). Electronic applications accepted. *Faculty research:* Theoretical astrophysics, cosmology, galaxy formation, galactic dynamics, interstellar and intergalactic matter.

Rice University, Graduate Programs, Wiess School of Natural Sciences, Department of Physics and Astronomy, Houston, TX 77251-1892. Offers nanoscale physics (MS); physics and astronomy (PhD); science teaching (MST). Part-time programs available. *Degree requirements:* For master's, thesis (for some programs); for doctorate, thesis/dissertation, minimum B average. *Entrance requirements:* For master's, GRE General Test; for doctorate, GRE General Test, GRE Subject Test. Additional exam requirements/recommendations for international students: Required—TOEFL (minimum score 600 paper-based; 90 iBT). Electronic applications accepted. *Faculty research:* Optical physics; ultra cold atoms; membrane electr-statics, peptides, proteins and lipids; solar astrophysics; stellar activity; magnetic fields; young stars.

Rutgers, The State University of New Jersey, New Brunswick, Graduate School-New Brunswick, Department of Physics and Astronomy, Piscataway, NJ 08854-8097. Offers astronomy (MS, PhD); biophysics (PhD); condensed matter physics (MS, PhD); elementary particle physics (MS, PhD); intermediate energy nuclear physics (MS); nuclear physics (MS, PhD); physics (MST); surface science (PhD); theoretical physics (MS, PhD). Part-time programs available. Terminal master's awarded for partial completion of doctoral program. *Degree requirements:* For master's, comprehensive exam, thesis or alternative; for doctorate, comprehensive exam, thesis/dissertation. *Entrance requirements:* For master's and doctorate, GRE General Test, GRE Subject Test. Additional exam requirements/recommendations for international students: Required—TOEFL (minimum score 560 paper-based). Electronic applications accepted. *Faculty research:* Astronomy, high energy, condensed matter, surface, nuclear physics.

Saint Mary's University, Faculty of Science, Department of Astronomy and Physics, Halifax, NS B3H 3C3, Canada. Offers astronomy (M Sc, PhD). Part-time programs available. *Degree requirements:* For master's, thesis optional; for doctorate, comprehensive exam, thesis/dissertation. *Entrance requirements:* For master's, honors degree with minimum GPA of 3.0. Additional exam requirements/recommendations for international students: Required—TOEFL. *Faculty research:* Young stellar objects, interstellar medium, star clusters, galactic structure, early-type galaxies.

San Diego State University, Graduate and Research Affairs, College of Sciences, Department of Astronomy, San Diego, CA 92182. Offers MS. *Degree requirements:* For master's, thesis. *Entrance requirements:* For master's, GRE General Test, letters of reference. Additional exam requirements/recommendations for international students: Required—TOEFL. Electronic applications accepted. *Faculty research:* CCD, classical and dwarf novae, photometry, interactive binaries.

Stony Brook University, State University of New York, Graduate School, College of Arts and Sciences, Department of Physics and Astronomy, Program in Astronomy, Stony Brook, NY 11794. Offers PhD. *Degree requirements:* For doctorate, thesis/dissertation. *Entrance requirements:* For doctorate, GRE General Test, minimum GPA of 3.0. Additional exam requirements/recommendations for international students: Required—TOEFL. *Application deadline:* For fall admission, 1/15 for domestic students. Application fee: $100. *Expenses:* Tuition, state resident: full-time $9370. Tuition, nonresident: full-time $16,680. *Required fees:* $1214. *Financial support:* Fellowships, research assistantships, and teaching assistantships available. Financial award application deadline: 2/1. *Unit head:* Dr. Laszlo Mihaly, Chair, 631-632-8100, Fax: 631-632-8176, E-mail: laszlo.mihaly@stonybrook.edu. *Application contact:* Dr. Jacobus Verbaarschot, Director, 631-403-0754, Fax: 631-632-8176, E-mail: jacobus.verbaarschot@stonybrook.edu.

Université de Moncton, Faculty of Sciences, Department of Physics and Astronomy, Moncton, NB E1A 3E9, Canada. Offers M Sc. Part-time programs available. *Degree requirements:* For master's, thesis. *Entrance requirements:* For master's, proficiency in French. Electronic applications accepted. *Faculty research:* Thin films, optical properties, solar selective surfaces, microgravity and photonic materials.

The University of Arizona, College of Science, Department of Astronomy, Tucson, AZ 85721. Offers MS, PhD. *Faculty:* 26 full-time (4 women), 2 part-time/adjunct (0 women). *Students:* 38 full-time (15 women), 3 part-time (0 women); includes 3 minority (all Two or more races, non-Hispanic/Latino), 6 international. Average age 27. 125 applicants, 10% accepted, 7 enrolled. In 2012, 4 master's, 6 doctorates awarded. *Degree requirements:* For doctorate, thesis/dissertation. *Entrance requirements:* For doctorate, GRE General Test, GRE Subject Test (physics), minimum GPA of 3.5, 3 letters of recommendation. Additional exam requirements/recommendations for international students: Required—TOEFL (minimum score 550 paper-based; 79 iBT). *Application deadline:* For fall admission, 1/15 for domestic students, 12/1 for international students. Applications are processed on a rolling basis. Application fee: $75. Electronic applications accepted. *Financial support:* In 2012–13, 47 research assistantships with full tuition reimbursements (averaging $23,605 per year), 3 teaching assistantships with full tuition reimbursements (averaging $23,515 per year) were awarded; scholarships/grants, health care benefits, and unspecified assistantships also available. *Faculty research:* Astrophysics, submillimeter astronomy, infrared astronomy, Near Infrared Camera and Multi-Object Spectrometer (NICMOS), Spitzer Space Telescope. *Total annual research expenditures:* $79.7 million. *Unit head:* Dr. Peter A. Strittmatter, Head, 520-621-6524, Fax: 520-621-1532, E-mail: pstrittm@as.arizona.edu. *Application contact:* Erin L. Carlson, Administrative Associate, 520-621-6538, Fax: 520-621-1532, E-mail: ecarlson@as.arizona.edu. Website: http://www.as.arizona.edu.

The University of British Columbia, Faculty of Science, Program in Astronomy, Vancouver, BC V6T 1Z1, Canada. Offers M Sc, PhD.

University of Calgary, Faculty of Graduate Studies, Faculty of Science, Department of Physics and Astronomy, Calgary, AB T2N 1N4, Canada. Offers M Sc, PhD. Part-time programs available. *Degree requirements:* For master's, thesis; for doctorate, thesis/dissertation, oral candidacy exam, written qualifying exam. *Entrance requirements:* For master's and doctorate, GRE General Test, GRE Subject Test. Additional exam requirements/recommendations for international students: Required—TOEFL (minimum score 550 paper-based). Electronic applications accepted. *Faculty research:* Astronomy and astrophysics, mass spectrometry, atmospheric physics, space physics, medical physics.

University of California, Los Angeles, Graduate Division, College of Letters and Science, Department of Physics and Astronomy, Program in Astronomy, Los Angeles, CA 90095. Offers MAT, MS, PhD. *Faculty:* 58 full-time (7 women). *Students:* 23 full-time (13 women); includes 3 minority (all Asian, non-Hispanic/Latino), 2 international. Average age 24. 99 applicants, 21% accepted, 5 enrolled. In 2012, 5 master's, 3 doctorates awarded. Terminal master's awarded for partial completion of doctoral program. *Degree requirements:* For master's, comprehensive exam; for doctorate, thesis/dissertation, oral and written qualifying exams; 3 quarters of teaching experience. *Entrance requirements:* For master's and doctorate, GRE General Test, GRE Subject Test (physics), bachelor's degree; minimum undergraduate GPA of 3.0 (or its equivalent if letter grade system not used). Additional exam requirements/recommendations for international students: Required—TOEFL. *Application deadline:* For fall admission, 12/15 for domestic and international students. Application fee: $80 ($100 for international students). Electronic applications accepted. *Expenses:* Tuition, nonresident: full-time $15,102. *Required fees:* $14,809.19. Full-time tuition and fees vary according to program. *Financial support:* In 2012–13, 25 students received support, including 17 fellowships with full and partial tuition reimbursements available, 25 research assistantships with full and partial tuition reimbursements available, 13 teaching assistantships with full and partial tuition reimbursements available; Federal Work-Study, scholarships/grants, health care benefits, tuition waivers (full and partial), and unspecified assistantships also available. Financial award application deadline: 3/2; financial award applicants required to submit FAFSA. *Unit head:* Dr. James Rosenzweig, Chair, 310-206-4541, E-mail: rosenzweig@physics.ucla.edu. *Application contact:* Student Affairs Officer, 310-825-2307, E-mail: apply@physics.ucla.edu. Website: http://www.astro.ucla.edu.

University of California, Santa Cruz, Division of Graduate Studies, Division of Physical and Biological Sciences, Department of Astronomy and Astrophysics, Santa Cruz, CA 95064. Offers PhD. *Degree requirements:* For doctorate, one foreign language, thesis/dissertation, qualifying exam. *Entrance requirements:* For doctorate, GRE General Test, GRE Subject Test. Additional exam requirements/recommendations for international students: Required—TOEFL (minimum score 550 paper-based; 83 iBT); Recommended—IELTS (minimum score 8). Electronic applications accepted. *Faculty research:* Solar system and the Milky Way to the most distant galaxies in the Universe, fundamental questions of cosmology.

University of Chicago, Division of the Physical Sciences, Department of Astronomy and Astrophysics, Chicago, IL 60637-1513. Offers MS, PhD. Terminal master's awarded for partial completion of doctoral program. *Degree requirements:* For master's, comprehensive exam, thesis optional, candidacy exam; for doctorate, comprehensive exam, thesis/dissertation, dissertation for publication. *Entrance requirements:* For master's, department candidacy examination, minimum GPA of 3.0; for doctorate, GRE General Test, GRE Subject Test, minimum GPA of 3.0. Additional exam requirements/recommendations for international students: Required—TOEFL (minimum score 600 paper-based); Recommended—IELTS. Electronic applications accepted. *Faculty research:* Quasi-stellar object absorption lines, fluid dynamics, interstellar matter, particle physics, cosmology.

University of Delaware, College of Arts and Sciences, Department of Physics and Astronomy, Newark, DE 19716. Offers MS, PhD. Part-time programs available. Terminal master's awarded for partial completion of doctoral program. *Degree requirements:* For master's, thesis; for doctorate, thesis/dissertation. *Entrance requirements:* For master's and doctorate, GRE General Test, GRE Subject Test. Additional exam requirements/recommendations for international students: Required—TOEFL (minimum score 600 paper-based). Electronic applications accepted. *Faculty research:* Magnetoresistance and magnetic materials, ultrafast optical phenomena, superfluidity, elementary particle physics, stellar atmospheres and interiors.

University of Denver, Faculty of Natural Sciences and Mathematics, Department of Physics and Astronomy, Denver, CO 80208. Offers applied physics (MS); physics (MS, PhD). Part-time programs available. *Faculty:* 11 full-time (3 women), 5 part-time/adjunct (0 women). *Students:* 7 full-time (4 women), 7 part-time (3 women), 2 international. Average age 30. 41 applicants, 37% accepted, 4 enrolled. In 2012, 1 master's, 2 doctorates awarded. Terminal master's awarded for partial completion of doctoral program. *Degree requirements:* For master's, thesis optional; for doctorate, thesis/dissertation. *Entrance requirements:* For master's and doctorate, GRE General Test, GRE Subject Test in physics (strongly preferred), three letters of recommendation, personal statement. Additional exam requirements/recommendations for international students: Required—TOEFL (minimum score 550 paper-based; 80 iBT). *Application deadline:* For fall admission, 3/1 priority date for domestic students. Applications are processed on a rolling basis. Application fee: $60. Electronic applications accepted. *Expenses: Tuition:* Full-time $38,232; part-time $1062 per credit hour. *Required fees:* $744. Tuition and fees vary according to program. *Financial support:* In 2012–13, 15 students received support, including 7 research assistantships with full and partial tuition reimbursements available (averaging $15,683 per year), 10 teaching assistantships with full and partial tuition reimbursements available (averaging $23,085 per year); career-related internships or fieldwork, Federal Work-Study, institutionally sponsored loans, scholarships/grants, and unspecified assistantships also available. Support available to part-time students. Financial award application deadline: 2/15; financial award applicants required to submit FAFSA. *Faculty research:* Atomic and molecular beams and collisions, infrared astronomy, acoustic emission from stressed solids, nano materials. *Unit head:* Dr. Davor Balzar, Chair, 303-871-2238, E-mail: davor.balzar@du.edu. *Application contact:* Barbara Stephen, Assistant to the Chair, 303-871-2238, E-mail: barbara.stephen@du.edu. Website: http://www.physics.du.edu.

University of Florida, Graduate School, College of Liberal Arts and Sciences, Department of Astronomy, Gainesville, FL 32611. Offers MS, MST, PhD. *Degree requirements:* For doctorate, one foreign language, comprehensive exam, thesis/dissertation. *Entrance requirements:* For master's and doctorate, GRE General Test, GRE Subject Test (physics), minimum GPA of 3.0. Additional exam requirements/recommendations for international students: Required—TOEFL (minimum score 550 paper-based; 80 iBT), IELTS (minimum score 6). Electronic applications accepted. *Faculty research:* Solar systems, stars and stellar populations, star formation and interstellar medium, structure and evolution of galaxies, extragalactic astronomy and cosmology, extrasolar planets and instrumentation.

University of Hawaii at Manoa, Graduate Division, College of Natural Sciences, Department of Physics and Astronomy, Program in Astronomy, Honolulu, HI 96822. Offers MS, PhD. Part-time programs available. *Degree requirements:* For master's, thesis optional; for doctorate, comprehensive exam, thesis/dissertation. *Entrance requirements:* For master's and doctorate, GRE General Test. Additional exam requirements/recommendations for international students: Required—TOEFL (minimum score 560 paper-based; 83 iBT), IELTS (minimum score 5).

University of Illinois at Urbana–Champaign, Graduate College, College of Liberal Arts and Sciences, Department of Astronomy, Champaign, IL 61820. Offers astronomy (PhD). *Students:* 23 (8 women). Application fee: $75 ($90 for international students). *Unit head:* Charles Gammie, Chair, 217-333-8646, Fax: 217-244-7638, E-mail: gammie@illinois.edu. *Application contact:* Jeri Cochran, Administrative Assistant, 217-333-9784, Fax: 217-244-7638, E-mail: jcochran@illinois.edu. Website: http://www.astro.illinois.edu.

The University of Iowa, Graduate College, College of Liberal Arts and Sciences, Department of Physics and Astronomy, Program in Astronomy, Iowa City, IA 52242-1316. Offers MS. *Degree requirements:* For master's, thesis optional, exam. *Entrance requirements:* For master's, GRE General Test, minimum GPA of 3.0. Additional exam requirements/recommendations for international students: Required—TOEFL (minimum score 550 paper-based; 81 iBT). Electronic applications accepted.

The University of Kansas, Graduate Studies, College of Liberal Arts and Sciences, Department of Physics and Astronomy, Lawrence, KS 66045. Offers computational physics and astronomy (MS); physics (MS, PhD). *Faculty:* 27. *Students:* 47 full-time (5 women), 3 part-time (0 women); includes 3 minority (1 Black or African American, non-Hispanic/Latino; 2 Two or more races, non-Hispanic/Latino), 13 international. Average age 29. 69 applicants, 39% accepted, 14 enrolled. In 2012, 1 master's, 5 doctorates awarded. Terminal master's awarded for partial completion of doctoral program. *Degree requirements:* For master's, thesis (for some programs); for doctorate, comprehensive exam, thesis/dissertation, computer skills, communication skills. *Entrance requirements:* For master's and doctorate, GRE Subject Test (physics), undergraduate degree. Additional exam requirements/recommendations for international students: Required—TOEFL (minimum score 53 paper-based; 20 iBT). *Application deadline:* For fall admission, 12/1 priority date for domestic students, 12/1 for international students; for spring admission, 10/1 priority date for domestic students, 10/1 for international students. Applications are processed on a rolling basis. Application fee: $55 ($65 for international students). Electronic applications accepted. *Financial support:* Fellowships with full and partial tuition reimbursements, research assistantships with full and partial tuition reimbursements, teaching assistantships with full and partial tuition reimbursements, health care benefits, and unspecified assistantships available. Financial award application deadline: 4/1; financial award applicants required to submit FAFSA. *Faculty research:* Astrophysics, biophysics, high energy physics, nanophysics, nuclear physics. *Unit head:* Dr. Stephen J. Sanders, Chair, 785-864-4626, Fax: 785-864-5262, E-mail: ssanders@ku.edu. *Application contact:* Hume Feldman, Graduate Director, 785-864-4626, Fax: 785-864-5262, E-mail: humef@ku.edu. Website: http://www.physics.ku.edu.

University of Kentucky, Graduate School, College of Arts and Sciences, Program in Physics and Astronomy, Lexington, KY 40506-0032. Offers physics (MS, PhD). *Degree requirements:* For master's, comprehensive exam, thesis optional; for doctorate, comprehensive exam, thesis/dissertation. *Entrance requirements:* For master's, GRE General Test, minimum undergraduate GPA of 2.75; for doctorate, GRE General Test, minimum graduate GPA of 3.0. Additional exam requirements/recommendations for international students: Required—TOEFL (minimum score 550 paper-based). Electronic applications accepted. *Faculty research:* Astrophysics, active galactic nuclei, and radio astronomy; Rydbert atoms, and electron scattering; TOF spectroscopy, hyperon interactions and muons; particle theory, lattice gauge theory, quark, and skyrmion models.

The University of Manchester, School of Physics and Astronomy, Manchester, United Kingdom. Offers astronomy and astrophysics (M Sc, PhD); biological physics (M Sc, PhD); condensed matter physics (M Sc, PhD); nonlinear and liquid crystals physics (M Sc, PhD); nuclear physics (M Sc, PhD); particle physics (M Sc, PhD); photon physics (M Sc, PhD); physics (M Sc, PhD); theoretical physics (M Sc, PhD).

University of Maryland, College Park, Academic Affairs, College of Computer, Mathematical and Natural Sciences, Department of Astronomy, College Park, MD 20742. Offers MS, PhD. Part-time and evening/weekend programs available. *Faculty:* 77 full-time (17 women), 13 part-time/adjunct (3 women). *Students:* 42 full-time (17 women); includes 2 minority (both Asian, non-Hispanic/Latino), 15 international. 126 applicants, 16% accepted, 6 enrolled. In 2012, 7 master's, 5 doctorates awarded. Terminal master's awarded for partial completion of doctoral program. *Degree requirements:* For master's, thesis or alternative, written exam; for doctorate, thesis/dissertation, research project. *Entrance requirements:* For master's, GRE General Test, GRE Subject Test (physics), minimum GPA of 3.0, 3 letters of recommendation; for doctorate, GRE General Test, GRE Subject Test (physics), 3 letters of recommendation. *Application deadline:* For fall admission, 1/15 for domestic and international students. Applications are processed on a rolling basis. Application fee: $75. Electronic applications accepted. *Expenses:* Tuition, state resident: part-time $551 per credit. Tuition, nonresident: part-time $1188 per credit. Part-time tuition and fees vary according to program. *Financial support:* In 2012–13, 3 fellowships with full and partial tuition reimbursements (averaging $14,034 per year), 21 research assistantships with tuition reimbursements (averaging $21,700 per year), 16 teaching assistantships with tuition reimbursements (averaging $19,022 per year) were awarded; career-related internships or fieldwork, Federal Work-Study, and scholarships/grants also available. Support available to part-time students. Financial award applicants required to submit FAFSA. *Faculty research:* Solar radio astronomy, plasma and high-energy astrophysics, galactic and extragalactic astronomy. *Total annual research expenditures:* $22.8 million. *Unit head:* Stuart N. Vogel, Chair, 301-405-1508, Fax: 301-314-9067, E-mail: svogel@umd.edu. *Application contact:* Dr. Charles A. Caramello, Dean of Graduate School, 301-405-0358, Fax: 301-314-9305, E-mail: ccaramel@umd.edu.

University of Massachusetts Amherst, Graduate School, College of Natural Sciences, Department of Astronomy, Amherst, MA 01003. Offers MS, PhD. Part-time programs available. *Faculty:* 16 full-time (3 women). *Students:* 22 full-time (5 women), 1 part-time (0 women); includes 2 minority (1 American Indian or Alaska Native, non-Hispanic/Latino; 1 Hispanic/Latino), 9 international. Average age 27. 48 applicants, 21% accepted, 4 enrolled. In 2012, 2 master's, 4 doctorates awarded. Terminal master's awarded for partial completion of doctoral program. *Degree requirements:* For master's, thesis or alternative; for doctorate, comprehensive exam, thesis/dissertation. *Entrance requirements:* For master's and doctorate, GRE General Test, GRE Subject Test (physics). Additional exam requirements/recommendations for international students: Required—TOEFL (minimum score 550 paper-based; 80 iBT), IELTS (minimum score 6.5). *Application deadline:* For fall admission, 2/1 for domestic and international students; for spring admission, 10/1 for domestic and international students. Applications are processed on a rolling basis. Application fee: $75. Electronic applications accepted. *Expenses:* Tuition, state resident: full-time $1980; part-time $110 per credit. Tuition, nonresident: full-time $13,314; part-time $414 per credit. *Required fees:* $10,338; $3594 per semester. One-time fee: $357. *Financial support:* Fellowships with full and partial tuition reimbursements, research assistantships with full and partial tuition reimbursements, teaching assistantships with full and partial tuition reimbursements, career-related internships or fieldwork, Federal Work-Study, scholarships/grants, traineeships, health care benefits, tuition waivers (full and partial), and unspecified assistantships available. Support available to part-time students. Financial award application deadline: 2/1. *Unit head:* Dr. Daniela Calzetti, Graduate Program Director, 413-545-2194, Fax: 413-545-4223. *Application contact:* Lindsay DeSantis, Supervisor of Admissions, 413-545-0722, Fax: 413-577-0010, E-mail: gradadm@grad.umass.edu. Website: http://www-astro.phast.umass.edu/.

University of Michigan, Horace H. Rackham School of Graduate Studies, College of Literature, Science, and the Arts, Department of Astronomy, Ann Arbor, MI 48109-1042. Offers astronomy and astrophysics (PhD). *Faculty:* 21 full-time (6 women). *Students:* 30 full-time (13 women); includes 4 minority (all Asian, non-Hispanic/Latino). In 2012, 6 doctorates awarded. Terminal master's awarded for partial completion of doctoral program. *Degree requirements:* For doctorate, thesis/dissertation, oral defense of dissertation, preliminary exam. *Entrance requirements:* For doctorate, GRE General Test, GRE Subject Test (physics). Additional exam requirements/recommendations for international students: Required—TOEFL. *Application deadline:* For fall admission, 1/6 for domestic and international students. Application fee: $65 ($75 for international students). Electronic applications accepted. *Financial support:* In 2012–13, 5 fellowships with full tuition reimbursements (averaging $22,800 per year), 23 research assistantships with full tuition reimbursements (averaging $22,800 per year), 13 teaching assistantships with full tuition reimbursements (averaging $22,800 per year) were awarded; institutionally sponsored loans, scholarships/grants, health care benefits, and unspecified assistantships also available. Financial award applicants required to submit FAFSA. *Faculty research:* Extragalactic and galactic astronomy, cosmology, star and planet formation, high energy astrophysics. *Total annual research expenditures:* $2.1 million. *Unit head:* Dr. Joel Bregman, Chair and Professor, 734-764-3440, Fax: 734-763-6317, E-mail: jbregman@umich.edu. *Application contact:* Brian Cox, Student Services Coordinator, 734-764-3440, Fax: 734-763-6317, E-mail: bmcox@umich.edu. Website: http://www.lsa.umich.edu/astro.

University of Missouri, Graduate School, College of Arts and Sciences, Department of Physics and Astronomy, Columbia, MO 65211. Offers MS, PhD. *Faculty:* 27 full-time (8 women), 1 (woman) part-time/adjunct. *Students:* 35 full-time (7 women), 19 part-time (2 women); includes 5 minority (1 Black or African American, non-Hispanic/Latino; 1 Asian, non-Hispanic/Latino; 1 Hispanic/Latino; 2 Two or more races, non-Hispanic/Latino), 26 international. Average age 28. 63 applicants, 16% accepted, 9 enrolled. In 2012, 6 master's, 8 doctorates awarded. Terminal master's awarded for partial completion of doctoral program. *Degree requirements:* For doctorate, one foreign language, comprehensive exam, thesis/dissertation. *Entrance requirements:* For master's and doctorate, GRE General Test, minimum GPA of 3.0. Additional exam requirements/recommendations for international students: Required—TOEFL (minimum score 550 paper-based; 80 iBT). *Application deadline:* For fall admission, 3/15 priority date for domestic students, 3/15 for international students. Applications are processed on a rolling basis. Application fee: $55 ($75 for international students). Electronic applications accepted. *Expenses:* Tuition, state resident: full-time $6057. Tuition, nonresident: full-time $15,683. *Required fees:* $1000. *Financial support:* In 2012–13, 35 research assistantships with full tuition reimbursements, 10 teaching assistantships with full tuition reimbursements were awarded; institutionally sponsored loans, health care benefits, and unspecified assistantships also available. *Faculty research:* Experimental and theoretical condensed-matter physics, biological physics, astronomy/astrophysics. *Unit head:* Dr. Peter Pfeifer, Department Chair, 573-882-2335, E-mail: pfeiferp@missouri.edu. *Application contact:* Dr. Carsten Ullrich, Director of Graduate Studies, 573-882-3335, E-mail: ullrichc@missouri.edu. Website: http://physics.missouri.edu/graduate/.

University of Nebraska–Lincoln, Graduate College, College of Arts and Sciences, Department of Physics and Astronomy, Lincoln, NE 68588. Offers astronomy (MS, PhD); physics (MS, PhD). *Degree requirements:* For master's, thesis optional; for doctorate, comprehensive exam, thesis/dissertation. *Entrance requirements:* For master's and doctorate, GRE General Test. Additional exam requirements/recommendations for international students: Required—TOEFL (minimum score 550 paper-based). Electronic applications accepted. *Faculty research:* Electromagnetics of solids and thin films, photoionization, ion collisions with atoms, molecules and surfaces, nanostructures.

University of Nevada, Las Vegas, Graduate College, College of Science, Department of Physics, Las Vegas, NV 89154-4002. Offers astronomy (MS, PhD); physics (MS, PhD). Part-time programs available. *Faculty:* 23 full-time (3 women), 10 part-time/adjunct (5 women). *Students:* 12 full-time (1 woman), 4 part-time (0 women); includes 7 minority (all Two or more races, non-Hispanic/Latino), 6 international. Average age 31. 15 applicants, 47% accepted, 4 enrolled. In 2012, 4 master's, 2 doctorates awarded. *Degree requirements:* For master's, thesis, oral exam; for doctorate, comprehensive exam, thesis/dissertation. *Entrance requirements:* For master's and doctorate, GRE General Test. Additional exam requirements/recommendations for international students: Required—TOEFL (minimum score 550 paper-based; 80 iBT), IELTS (minimum score 7). *Application deadline:* For fall admission, 8/1 priority date for domestic students, 5/1 for international students; for spring admission, 10/1 priority date for domestic students, 10/1 for international students. Applications are processed on a rolling basis. Application fee: $60 ($95 for international students). Electronic applications accepted. *Expenses:* Tuition, state resident: full-time $4752; part-time $264 per credit. Tuition, nonresident: full-time $18,662; part-time $527.50 per credit. *Required fees:* $12 per credit. $266 per semester. One-time fee: $35. Tuition and fees vary according to course load, program and reciprocity agreements. *Financial support:* In 2012–13, 14 students received support, including 14 teaching assistantships with partial tuition reimbursements available (averaging $16,120 per year); institutionally sponsored loans, scholarships/grants, health care benefits, and unspecified assistantships also available. Financial award application deadline: 3/1. *Faculty research:* Gamma-ray bursters astrophysics, cosmology and dark matter astrophysics, experimental high pressure physics, theoretical condensed matter physics, laser-plasma atomic physics. *Total annual research expenditures:* $4.2 million. *Unit head:* Stephen Lepp, Chair/Professor, 702-895-4455, E-mail: lepp@physics.unlv.edu. *Application contact:* Graduate College Admissions Evaluator, 702-895-3320, Fax: 702-895-4180, E-mail: gradcollege@unlv.edu. Website: http://www.physics.unlv.edu/graduate.html.

The University of North Carolina at Chapel Hill, Graduate School, College of Arts and Sciences, Department of Physics and Astronomy, Chapel Hill, NC 27599. Offers physics (MS, PhD). Terminal master's awarded for partial completion of doctoral program. *Degree requirements:* For master's, comprehensive exam; for doctorate, comprehensive exam, thesis/dissertation. *Entrance requirements:* For master's and doctorate, GRE General Test, minimum GPA of 3.0. Electronic applications accepted. *Faculty research:* Observational astronomy, fullerenes, polarized beams, nanotubes, nucleosynthesis in stars and supernovae, superstring theory, ballistic transport in semiconductors, gravitation.

University of Rochester, School of Arts and Sciences, Department of Physics and Astronomy, Rochester, NY 14627. Offers physics (MA, MS, PhD); physics and astronomy (PhD). Part-time programs available. Terminal master's awarded for partial completion of doctoral program. *Degree requirements:* For master's, comprehensive exam, thesis (for some programs); for doctorate, comprehensive exam, thesis/dissertation, qualifying exam. *Entrance requirements:* For master's and doctorate, GRE General Test. Additional exam requirements/recommendations for international students: Required—TOEFL. *Faculty research:* Astronomy and astrophysics, biological physics, condensed matter physics, high energy/nuclear physics, quantum optics.

University of South Carolina, The Graduate School, College of Arts and Sciences, Department of Physics and Astronomy, Columbia, SC 29208. Offers IMA, MAT, MS, PSM, PhD. IMA and MAT offered in cooperation with the College of Education. Part-time programs available. Terminal master's awarded for partial completion of doctoral program. *Degree requirements:* For master's, comprehensive exam, thesis; for doctorate, one foreign language, comprehensive exam, thesis/dissertation. *Entrance requirements:* For master's and doctorate, GRE General Test, GRE Subject Test. Additional exam requirements/recommendations for international students: Required—TOEFL (minimum score 570 paper-based; 75 iBT). Electronic applications accepted. *Faculty research:* Condensed matter, intermediate-energy nuclear physics, foundations of quantum mechanics, astronomy/astrophysics.

The University of Texas at Austin, Graduate School, College of Natural Sciences, Department of Astronomy, Austin, TX 78712-1111. Offers MA, PhD. *Entrance requirements:* For master's and doctorate, GRE General Test, GRE Subject Test (physics). Additional exam requirements/recommendations for international students: Required—TOEFL. Electronic applications accepted. *Faculty research:* Stars, interstellar medium, galaxies, planetary astronomy, cosmology.

University of Toronto, School of Graduate Studies, Faculty of Arts and Science, Department of Astronomy and Astrophysics, Toronto, ON M5S 1A1, Canada. Offers M Sc, PhD. Part-time programs available. *Degree requirements:* For doctorate, thesis/dissertation, qualifying exam, thesis defense. *Entrance requirements:* For master's, minimum B average, bachelor's degree in astronomy

46 www.petersonsbooks.com

Peterson's Graduate Programs in the Physical Sciences, Mathematics, Agricultural Sciences, the Environment & Natural Resources 2014

or equivalent, 3 letters of reference; for doctorate, GRE General Test, minimum B+ average, master's degree in astronomy or equivalent, demonstrated research competence, 3 letters of reference. Additional exam requirements/recommendations for international students: Required—TOEFL (minimum score 580 paper-based; 93 iBT), TWE (minimum score 4). Electronic applications accepted.

University of Victoria, Faculty of Graduate Studies, Faculty of Science, Department of Physics and Astronomy, Victoria, BC V8W 2Y2, Canada. Offers astronomy and astrophysics (M Sc, PhD); condensed matter physics (M Sc, PhD); experimental particle physics (M Sc, PhD); medical physics (M Sc, PhD); ocean physics (M Sc, PhD); theoretical physics (M Sc, PhD). *Degree requirements:* For master's, thesis; for doctorate, comprehensive exam, thesis/dissertation, candidacy exam. *Entrance requirements:* For master's and doctorate, GRE. Additional exam requirements/recommendations for international students: Required—TOEFL (minimum score 575 paper-based), IELTS (minimum score 7). Electronic applications accepted. *Faculty research:* Old stellar populations; observational cosmology and large scale structure; cp violation; atlas.

University of Virginia, College and Graduate School of Arts and Sciences, Department of Astronomy, Charlottesville, VA 22903. Offers MS, PhD. *Faculty:* 15 full-time (2 women). *Students:* 31 full-time (9 women), 10 international. Average age 25. 84 applicants, 24% accepted, 7 enrolled. In 2012, 10 master's, 7 doctorates awarded. *Degree requirements:* For master's, comprehensive exam, thesis or alternative; for doctorate, comprehensive exam, thesis/dissertation. *Entrance requirements:* For master's and doctorate, GRE General Test, GRE Subject Test. Additional exam requirements/recommendations for international students: Required—TOEFL (minimum score 650 paper-based; 90 iBT), IELTS (minimum score 7). *Application deadline:* For fall admission, 12/31 for domestic and international students. Applications are processed on a rolling basis. Application fee: $60. Electronic applications accepted. *Expenses:* Tuition, state resident: full-time $13,278; part-time $717 per credit hour. Tuition, nonresident: full-time $22,602; part-time $1235 per credit hour. *Required fees:* $2384. *Financial support:* Fellowships, research assistantships, and teaching assistantships available. Financial award application deadline: 12/3; financial award applicants required to submit FAFSA. *Unit head:* Mike Skrutskie, Chair, 434-924-4328, Fax: 434-924-3104, E-mail: mfc4n@virginia.edu. *Application contact:* Kelsey Johnson, Co-Chair, Graduate Admissions, 434-924-7494, Fax: 434-924-3104, E-mail: gradadm@mail.astro.virginia.edu. Website: http://www.astro.virginia.edu/.

University of Washington, Graduate School, College of Arts and Sciences, Department of Astronomy, Seattle, WA 98195. Offers MS, PhD. Terminal master's awarded for partial completion of doctoral program. *Degree requirements:* For doctorate, thesis/dissertation. *Entrance requirements:* For master's and doctorate, GRE General Test, GRE Subject Test, minimum GPA of 3.0. Additional exam requirements/recommendations for international students: Required—TOEFL. *Faculty research:* Solar system dust, space astronomy, high-energy astrophysics, galactic and extragalactic astronomy, stellar astrophysics.

The University of Western Ontario, Faculty of Graduate Studies, Physical Sciences Division, Department of Physics and Astronomy, Program in Astronomy, London, ON N6A 5B8, Canada. Offers M Sc, PhD. Terminal master's awarded for partial completion of doctoral program. *Degree requirements:* For master's, thesis optional; for doctorate, comprehensive exam, thesis/dissertation. *Entrance requirements:* For master's, GRE Subject Test (physics), honors B Sc degree, minimum B average (Canadian), A - (international); for doctorate, M Sc degree, minimum B average (Canadian), A - (international). Additional exam requirements/recommendations for international students: Required—TOEFL (minimum score 580 paper-based). *Faculty research:* Observational and theoretical astrophysics spectroscopy, photometry, spectro-polarimetry, variable stars, cosmology.

University of Wisconsin–Madison, Graduate School, College of Letters and Science, Department of Astronomy, Madison, WI 53706-1380. Offers PhD. *Degree requirements:* For doctorate, comprehensive exam, thesis/dissertation. *Entrance requirements:* For doctorate, GRE General Test, GRE Subject Test (physics), bachelor's degree in related field. Additional exam requirements/recommendations for international students: Required—TOEFL. Electronic applications accepted. *Expenses:* Tuition, state resident: full-time $10,728; part-time $743 per credit. Tuition, nonresident: full-time $24,054; part-time $1575 per credit. *Required fees:* $1111; $72 per credit. *Faculty research:* Kinematics, evolution of galaxies, cosmic distance, scale and large-scale structures, interstellar intergalactic medium, star formation and evolution, solar system chemistry and dynamics.

Vanderbilt University, Graduate School, Department of Physics and Astronomy, Nashville, TN 87240-1001. Offers astronomy (MS); health physics (MA); physics (MAT, MS, PhD). *Faculty:* 33 full-time (4 women). *Students:* 78 full-time (21 women), 1 part-time (0 women); includes 12 minority (5 Black or African American, non-Hispanic/Latino; 1 Asian, non-Hispanic/Latino; 4 Hispanic/Latino; 2 Two or more races, non-Hispanic/Latino), 24 international. Average age 28. 199 applicants, 17% accepted, 12 enrolled. In 2012, 7 master's, 7 doctorates awarded. *Degree requirements:* For master's, thesis; for doctorate, comprehensive exam, thesis/dissertation, final and qualifying exams. *Entrance requirements:* For master's, GRE General Test; for doctorate, GRE General Test, GRE Subject Test. Additional exam requirements/recommendations for international students: Required—TOEFL (minimum score 570 paper-based; 88 iBT). *Application deadline:* For fall admission, 1/15 for domestic and international students. Electronic applications accepted. *Financial support:* Fellowships with full and partial tuition reimbursements, research assistantships with full tuition reimbursements, teaching assistantships with full tuition reimbursements, career-related internships or fieldwork, Federal Work-Study, and institutionally sponsored loans available. Financial award application deadline: 1/15; financial award applicants required to submit CSS PROFILE or FAFSA. *Faculty research:* Experimental and theoretical physics, free electron laser, living-state physics, heavy-ion physics, nuclear structure. *Unit head:* Dr. Julia Velkovska, Director of Graduate Studies, 615-322-0656, Fax: 615-343-7263, E-mail: julia.velkovska@vanderbilt.edu. *Application contact:* Donald Pickert, Administrative Assistant, 615-343-1026, Fax: 615-343-7263, E-mail: donald.pickert@vanderbilt.edu. Website: http://www.vanderbilt.edu/physics/.

Wesleyan University, Graduate Studies, Department of Astronomy, Middletown, CT 06459. Offers MA. *Degree requirements:* For master's, thesis. *Entrance requirements:* For master's, GRE General Test; GRE Subject Test in physics (recommended). Additional exam requirements/recommendations for international students: Required—TOEFL. *Application deadline:* For fall admission, 3/1 for domestic and international students. Application fee: $0. Electronic applications accepted. *Financial support:* Research assistantships, teaching assistantships with full tuition reimbursements, tuition waivers (full), and full-year stipends available. Financial award application deadline: 4/15; financial award applicants required to submit FAFSA. *Faculty research:* Observational-theoretical astronomy and astrophysics. *Unit head:* Dr. William Herbst, Chair, 860-685-3672, E-mail: wherbst@wesleyan.edu. *Application contact:* Linda Shettleworth, Administrative Assistant, 860-685-2130, E-mail: shettleworth@wesleyan.edu. Website: http://www.wesleyan.edu/astro/.

West Chester University of Pennsylvania, College of Arts and Sciences, Department of Geology and Astronomy, West Chester, PA 19383. Offers earth-space science (Teaching Certificate); general science (Teaching Certificate); geoscience (MA). Part-time and evening/weekend programs available. *Faculty:* 7 full-time (2 women). *Students:* 1 (woman) full-time, 16 part-time (3 women); includes 2 minority (1 Black or African American, non-Hispanic/Latino; 1 Hispanic/Latino). Average age 35. 5 applicants, 100% accepted, 4 enrolled. In 2012, 8 master's awarded. *Degree requirements:* For master's, comprehensive exam (for some programs), thesis or alternative. *Entrance requirements:* For master's, minimum GPA of 2.5. Additional exam requirements/recommendations for international students: Required—TOEFL (minimum score 550 paper-based; 80 iBT). *Application deadline:* For fall admission, 4/15 priority date for domestic students, 3/15 for international students; for spring admission, 10/15 priority date for domestic students, 9/1 for international students. Applications are processed on a rolling basis. Application fee: $45. Electronic applications accepted. *Expenses:* Tuition, state resident: full-time $7722; part-time $429 per credit. Tuition, nonresident: full-time $11,592; part-time $644 per credit. *Required fees:* $2108; $105.05 per credit. Tuition and fees vary according to campus/location and program. *Financial support:* Unspecified assistantships available. Support available to part-time students. Financial award application deadline: 2/15; financial award applicants required to submit FAFSA. *Faculty research:* Geoscience education, environmental geology, energy and sustainability, astronomy, meteorology. *Unit head:* Dr. Lee Anne Srogi, Chair, 610-436-2727, Fax: 610-436-3036, E-mail: lsrogi@wcupa.edu. *Application contact:* Dr. Martin Helmke, Graduate Coordinator, 610-436-3565, Fax: 610-436-3036, E-mail: mhelmke@wcupa.edu. Website: http://www.wcupa.edu/_academics/sch_cas.esc/.

Yale University, Graduate School of Arts and Sciences, Department of Astronomy, New Haven, CT 06520. Offers astronomy (PhD); solar and terrestrial physics (PhD). *Degree requirements:* For doctorate, thesis/dissertation. *Entrance requirements:* For doctorate, GRE General Test, GRE Subject Test (physics).

York University, Faculty of Graduate Studies, Faculty of Science and Engineering, Program in Physics and Astronomy, Toronto, ON M3J 1P3, Canada. Offers M Sc, PhD. Part-time and evening/weekend programs available. *Degree requirements:* For master's, thesis or alternative; for doctorate, comprehensive exam, thesis/dissertation. Electronic applications accepted.

Peterson's Graduate Programs in the Physical Sciences, Mathematics, Agricultural Sciences, the Environment & Natural Resources 2014

www.petersonsbooks.com **47**

Astrophysics

Air Force Institute of Technology, Graduate School of Engineering and Management, Department of Engineering Physics, Dayton, OH 45433-7765. Offers applied physics (MS, PhD); electro-optics (MS, PhD); materials science (PhD); nuclear engineering (MS, PhD); space physics (MS). Part-time programs available. *Degree requirements:* For master's, thesis; for doctorate, thesis/dissertation. *Entrance requirements:* For master's and doctorate, GRE General Test, minimum GPA of 3.0, U.S. citizenship. *Faculty research:* High-energy lasers, space physics, nuclear weapon effects, semiconductor physics.

Arizona State University, College of Liberal Arts and Sciences, School of Earth and Space Exploration, Tempe, AZ 85287-1404. Offers astrophysics (MS, PhD); exploration systems design (PhD); geological sciences (MS, PhD). PhD in exploration systems design is offered in collaboration with the Fulton Schools of Engineering. Terminal master's awarded for partial completion of doctoral program. *Degree requirements:* For master's, thesis, interactive Program of Study (iPOS) submitted before completing 50 percent of required credit hours; for doctorate, thesis/dissertation, interactive Program of Study (iPOS) submitted before completing 50 percent of required credit hours. *Entrance requirements:* For master's and doctorate, GRE, minimum GPA of 3.0 or equivalent in last 2 years of work leading to bachelor's degree. Additional exam requirements/recommendations for international students: Required—TOEFL (minimum score 80 iBT), TOEFL, IELTS, or Pearson Test of English. Electronic applications accepted.

Clemson University, Graduate School, College of Engineering and Science, Department of Physics and Astronomy, Clemson, SC 29634. Offers physics (MS, PhD), including astronomy and astrophysics, atmospheric physics, biophysics. Part-time programs available. *Faculty:* 24 full-time (3 women). *Students:* 62 full-time (15 women), 1 part-time (0 women); includes 2 minority (1 Black or African American, non-Hispanic/Latino; 1 Hispanic/Latino), 28 international. Average age 26. 66 applicants, 41% accepted, 12 enrolled. In 2012, 8 master's, 5 doctorates awarded. Terminal master's awarded for partial completion of doctoral program. *Degree requirements:* For master's, thesis or alternative; for doctorate, thesis/dissertation. *Entrance requirements:* For master's and doctorate, GRE General Test. Additional exam requirements/recommendations for international students: Required—TOEFL. *Application deadline:* For fall admission, 1/15 priority date for domestic students; for spring admission, 9/15 priority date for domestic students. Applications are processed on a rolling basis. Application fee: $70 ($80 for international students). Electronic applications accepted. *Financial support:* In 2012–13, 60 students received support, including 1 fellowship with full and partial tuition reimbursement available (averaging $7,000 per year), 25 research assistantships with partial tuition reimbursements available (averaging $13,151 per year), 44 teaching assistantships with partial tuition reimbursements available (averaging $15,956 per year); career-related internships or fieldwork, institutionally sponsored loans, scholarships/grants, health care benefits, and unspecified assistantships also available. Support available to part-time students. Financial award application deadline: 6/1; financial award applicants required to submit FAFSA. *Faculty research:* Radiation physics, solid-state physics, nuclear physics, radar and lidar studies of atmosphere. *Total annual research expenditures:* $2.6 million. *Unit head:* Dr. Peter Barnes, Chair, 864-656-3419, Fax: 864-656-0805, E-mail: peterb@clemson.edu. *Application contact:* Graduate Coordinator, 864-656-6702, Fax: 864-656-0805, E-mail: physgradinfo-l@clemson.edu. Website: http://physicsnt.clemson.edu/.

Cornell University, Graduate School, Graduate Fields of Arts and Sciences, Field of Astronomy and Space Sciences, Ithaca, NY 14853-0001. Offers astronomy (PhD); astrophysics (PhD); general space sciences (PhD); infrared astronomy (PhD); planetary studies (PhD); radio astronomy (PhD); radiophysics (PhD); theoretical astrophysics (PhD). *Faculty:* 31 full-time (2 women). *Students:* 27 full-time (9 women); includes 6 minority (3 Asian, non-Hispanic/Latino; 2 Hispanic/Latino; 1 Two or more races, non-Hispanic/Latino), 8 international. Average age 26. 84 applicants, 8% accepted, 1 enrolled. In 2012, 6 doctorates awarded. *Degree requirements:* For doctorate, comprehensive exam, thesis/dissertation. *Entrance requirements:* For doctorate, GRE General Test, GRE Subject Test (physics), 3 letters of recommendation. Additional exam requirements/recommendations for international students: Required—TOEFL (minimum score 600 paper-based; 77 iBT). *Application deadline:* For fall admission, 1/15 for domestic students. Application fee: $95. Electronic applications accepted. *Financial support:* In 2012–13, 27 students received support, including 11 fellowships with full tuition reimbursements available, 8 research assistantships with full tuition reimbursements available; 8 teaching assistantships with full tuition reimbursements available; institutionally sponsored loans, scholarships/grants, health care benefits, tuition waivers (full and partial), and unspecified assistantships also available. Financial award applicants required to submit FAFSA. *Faculty research:* Observational astrophysics, planetary sciences, cosmology, instrumentation, gravitational astrophysics. *Unit head:* Director of Graduate Studies, 607-255-4341. *Application contact:* Graduate Field Assistant, 607-255-4341, E-mail: oconnor@astro.cornell.edu. Website: http://www.gradschool.cornell.edu/fields.php?id-24&a-2.

Harvard University, Graduate School of Arts and Sciences, Department of Astronomy, Cambridge, MA 02138. Offers astronomy (PhD); astrophysics (PhD).

Degree requirements: For doctorate, thesis/dissertation, paper, research project, 2 semesters of teaching. *Entrance requirements:* For doctorate, GRE General Test, GRE Subject Test (physics). Additional exam requirements/recommendations for international students: Required—TOEFL. Electronic applications accepted. *Expenses: Tuition:* Full-time $37,576. *Required fees:* $930. Tuition and fees vary according to program and student level. *Faculty research:* Atomic and molecular physics, electromagnetism, solar physics, nuclear physics, fluid dynamics.

ICR Graduate School, Graduate Programs, Santee, CA 92071. Offers astro/geophysics (MS); biology (MS); geology (MS); science education (MS). Part-time programs available. *Degree requirements:* For master's, comprehensive exam (for some programs), thesis (for some programs). *Entrance requirements:* For master's, minimum undergraduate GPA of 3.0, bachelor's degree in science or science education. *Faculty research:* Age of the earth, limits of variation, catastrophe, optimum methods for teaching.

Indiana University Bloomington, University Graduate School, College of Arts and Sciences, Department of Astronomy, Bloomington, IN 47405-7000. Offers astronomy (MA, PhD); astrophysics (PhD). *Faculty:* 9 full-time (5 women), 2 part-time/adjunct (0 women). *Students:* 20 full-time (9 women); includes 5 minority (2 Asian, non-Hispanic/Latino; 1 Hispanic/Latino; 2 Two or more races, non-Hispanic/Latino), 1 international. 37 applicants, 16% accepted, 3 enrolled. In 2012, 4 master's, 4 doctorates awarded. Terminal master's awarded for partial completion of doctoral program. *Degree requirements:* For master's, thesis or alternative, oral exam; for doctorate, comprehensive exam, thesis/dissertation, oral defense. *Entrance requirements:* For master's and doctorate, GRE General Test, GRE Subject Test (physics), BA or BS in science. Additional exam requirements/recommendations for international students: Required—TOEFL. *Application deadline:* For fall admission, 1/15 for domestic students, 12/1 for international students; for spring admission, 9/1 for domestic students. Application fee: $55 ($65 for international students). Electronic applications accepted. *Financial support:* In 2012–13, 18 students received support, including 3 fellowships with full tuition reimbursements available (averaging $14,333 per year), 7 research assistantships with full tuition reimbursements available (averaging $19,850 per year), 8 teaching assistantships with full tuition reimbursements available (averaging $17,950 per year); scholarships/grants, health care benefits, and unspecified assistantships also available. Financial award application deadline: 1/15. *Faculty research:* Stellar and galaxy dynamics, stellar chemical abundances, galaxy evolution, observational cosmology. *Total annual research expenditures:* $772,980. *Unit head:* Dr. John Salzer, Chair, 812-855-6911, Fax: 812-855-8725, E-mail: josalzer@indiana.edu. *Application contact:* Julie Wilson, Graduate Secretary, 812-855-6911, Fax: 812-855-8725, E-mail: jaw@indiana.edu. Website: http://www.astro.indiana.edu/.

Iowa State University of Science and Technology, Department of Physics and Astronomy, Ames, IA 50011. Offers applied physics (MS, PhD); astrophysics (MS, PhD); condensed matter physics (MS, PhD); high energy physics (MS, PhD); nuclear physics (MS, PhD); physics (MS, PhD). *Degree requirements:* For master's, thesis (for some programs); for doctorate, thesis/dissertation. *Entrance requirements:* For master's and doctorate, GRE General Test, GRE Subject Test (physics). Additional exam requirements/recommendations for international students: Required—TOEFL (minimum score 550 paper-based; 79 iBT), IELTS (minimum score 6.5). *Application deadline:* For fall admission, 2/15 priority date for domestic students, 2/15 for international students; for spring admission, 10/15 for domestic and international students. Applications are processed on a rolling basis. Application fee: $60 ($90 for international students). Electronic applications accepted. *Financial support:* Application deadline: 2/15. *Faculty research:* Condensed-matter physics, including superconductivity and new materials; high-energy and nuclear physics; astronomy and astrophysics; atmospheric and environmental physics. *Total annual research expenditures:* $8.8 million. *Application contact:* Lori Hockett, Application Contact, 515-294-5870, Fax: 515-294-6027, E-mail: physastro@iastate.edu. Website: http://www.physastro.iastate.edu.

Iowa State University of Science and Technology, Program in Astrophysics, Ames, IA 50011. Offers MS, PhD. *Entrance requirements:* For master's and doctorate, GRE. Additional exam requirements/recommendations for international students: Required—TOEFL (minimum score 550 paper-based; 79 iBT), IELTS (minimum score 6.5). *Application deadline:* For fall admission, 2/15 for domestic students; for spring admission, 10/15 for domestic students. *Application contact:* Lori Hockett, Application Contact, 515-294-5870, Fax: 515-294-6027, E-mail: physastro@iastate.edu. Website: http://www.physastro@iastate.edu.

Louisiana State University and Agricultural and Mechanical College, Graduate School, College of Science, Department of Physics and Astronomy, Baton Rouge, LA 70803. Offers astronomy (PhD); astrophysics (PhD); medical physics (MS); physics (MS, PhD). *Faculty:* 45 full-time (5 women), 1 part-time/adjunct (0 women). *Students:* 106 full-time (21 women), 3 part-time (1 woman); includes 5 minority (1 Black or African American, non-Hispanic/Latino; 4 Hispanic/Latino), 52 international. Average age 27. 135 applicants, 16% accepted, 20 enrolled. In 2012, 8 master's, 8 doctorates awarded. Terminal master's awarded

48 www.petersonsbooks.com

Peterson's Graduate Programs in the Physical Sciences, Mathematics, Agricultural Sciences, the Environment & Natural Resources 2014

for partial completion of doctoral program. *Degree requirements:* For master's, thesis or alternative; for doctorate, thesis/dissertation. *Entrance requirements:* For master's and doctorate, GRE General Test, minimum GPA of 3.0. Additional exam requirements/recommendations for international students: Required—TOEFL (minimum score 550 paper-based; 79 iBT) or IELTS (minimum score 6.5). *Application deadline:* For fall admission, 1/25 priority date for domestic students, 5/15 for international students; for spring admission, 10/15 for international students. Applications are processed on a rolling basis. Application fee: $50 ($70 for international students). Electronic applications accepted. *Financial support:* In 2012–13, 108 students received support, including 12 fellowships with full tuition reimbursements available (averaging $26,748 per year), 60 research assistantships with full and partial tuition reimbursements available (averaging $22,794 per year), 35 teaching assistantships with full and partial tuition reimbursements available (averaging $19,046 per year); Federal Work-Study, institutionally sponsored loans, health care benefits, tuition waivers (full and partial), and unspecified assistantships also available. Financial award application deadline: 3/15; financial award applicants required to submit FAFSA. *Faculty research:* Experimentation and numerical relativity, condensed matter astrophysics, quantum computing, medical physics. *Total annual research expenditures:* $9.6 million. *Unit head:* Dr. Michael Cherry, Chair, 225-578-2262, Fax: 225-578-5855, E-mail: cherry@phys.lsu.edu. *Application contact:* Arnell Dangerfield, Administrative Coordinator, 225-578-1193, Fax: 225-578-5855, E-mail: adanger@lsu.edu. Website: http://www.phys.lsu.edu/.

McMaster University, School of Graduate Studies, Faculty of Science, Department of Physics and Astronomy, Hamilton, ON L8S 4M2, Canada. Offers astrophysics (PhD); physics (PhD). Part-time programs available. *Degree requirements:* For doctorate, comprehensive exam, thesis/dissertation. *Entrance requirements:* For doctorate, minimum B+ average. Additional exam requirements/recommendations for international students: Required—TOEFL (minimum score 550 paper-based). *Faculty research:* Condensed matter, astrophysics, nuclear, medical, nonlinear dynamics.

Michigan State University, The Graduate School, College of Natural Science, Department of Physics and Astronomy, East Lansing, MI 48824. Offers astrophysics and astronomy (MS, PhD); physics (MS, PhD). *Entrance requirements:* Additional exam requirements/recommendations for international students: Required—TOEFL (minimum score 550 paper-based), Michigan State University ELT (minimum score 85), Michigan English Language Assessment Battery (minimum score 83). Electronic applications accepted. *Faculty research:* Nuclear and accelerator physics, high energy physics, condensed matter physics, biophysics, astrophysics and astronomy.

New Mexico Institute of Mining and Technology, Graduate Studies, Department of Physics, Socorro, NM 87801. Offers astrophysics (PhD); atmospheric physics (PhD); instrumentation (MS); mathematical physics (PhD); physics (MS). *Faculty:* 12 full-time (3 women), 1 part-time/adjunct (0 women). *Students:* 30 full-time (12 women), 2 part-time (1 woman); includes 1 minority (Asian, non-Hispanic/Latino), 6 international. Average age 29. 15 applicants, 47% accepted, 4 enrolled. In 2012, 1 master's, 2 doctorates awarded. *Degree requirements:* For master's, thesis optional; for doctorate, thesis/dissertation. *Entrance requirements:* For master's, GRE General Test; for doctorate, GRE General Test, GRE Subject Test. Additional exam requirements/recommendations for international students: Required—TOEFL (minimum score 540 paper-based). *Application deadline:* For fall admission, 3/1 priority date for domestic students; for spring admission, 6/1 for domestic students. Applications are processed on a rolling basis. Application fee: $16 ($30 for international students). *Expenses:* Tuition, state resident: full-time $5043; part-time $280 per credit hour. Tuition, nonresident: full-time $16,682; part-time $927 per credit hour. *Required fees:* $648; $18 per credit hour. $108 per semester. Part-time tuition and fees vary according to course load. *Financial support:* In 2012–13, 19 research assistantships (averaging $18,770 per year), 13 teaching assistantships with full and partial tuition reimbursements (averaging $14,078 per year) were awarded; fellowships, Federal Work-Study, institutionally sponsored loans, and unspecified assistantships also available. Financial award application deadline: 3/1; financial award applicants required to submit CSS PROFILE or FAFSA. *Faculty research:* Cloud physics, stellar and extragalactic processes. *Total annual research expenditures:* $3 million. *Unit head:* Dr. Kenneth Eack, Chairman, 575-835-5328, Fax: 575-835-5707, E-mail: dwestpfa@nmt.edu. *Application contact:* Dr. Lorie Liebrock, Dean of Graduate Studies, 575-835-5513, Fax: 575-835-5476, E-mail: graduate@nmt.edu. Website: http://www.physics.nmt.edu/.

New Mexico State University, Graduate School, College of Arts and Sciences, Department of Physics, Las Cruces, NM 88003-8001. Offers physics (MS, PhD); space physics (MS). Part-time programs available. *Faculty:* 13 full-time (1 woman), 3 part-time/adjunct (0 women). *Students:* 39 full-time (13 women), 1 part-time (0 women); includes 5 minority (1 Black or African American, non-Hispanic/Latino; 4 Hispanic/Latino), 26 international. Average age 29. 73 applicants, 25% accepted, 9 enrolled. In 2012, 4 master's, 6 doctorates awarded. Terminal master's awarded for partial completion of doctoral program. *Degree requirements:* For master's, comprehensive exam, thesis optional, written qualifying exam; for doctorate, comprehensive exam, thesis/dissertation. *Entrance requirements:* For master's and doctorate, GRE General Test, GRE Subject Test. Additional exam requirements/recommendations for international students: Required—TOEFL (minimum score 550 paper-based; 79 iBT), IELTS (minimum score 6.5). *Application deadline:* For fall admission, 2/15 priority date for domestic students, 2/15 for international students; for spring admission, 9/1 priority date for domestic students, 9/1 for

international students. Applications are processed on a rolling basis. Application fee: $40 ($50 for international students). Electronic applications accepted. *Expenses:* Tuition, state resident: full-time $5239; part-time $218 per credit. Tuition, nonresident: full-time $18,266; part-time $761 per credit. *Required fees:* $1274; $53 per credit. *Financial support:* In 2012–13, 39 students received support, including 1 fellowship (averaging $3,930 per year), 20 research assistantships (averaging $18,980 per year), 16 teaching assistantships (averaging $17,206 per year); scholarships/grants, health care benefits, tuition waivers (partial), and unspecified assistantships also available. Financial award application deadline: 2/15; financial award applicants required to submit FAFSA. *Faculty research:* Nuclear and particle physics, optics, materials science, geophysics, physics education, atmospheric physics. *Total annual research expenditures:* $1.8 million. *Unit head:* Dr. Stefan Zollner, Head, 575-646-7627, Fax: 575-646-1934, E-mail: zollner@nmsu.edu. *Application contact:* Dr. Vassilios Papavassiliou, Associate Professor/Recruiting Contact, 575-646-3831, Fax: 575-646-1934, E-mail: graduate_advisor@physics.nmsu.edu. Website: http://physics.nmsu.edu.

Northwestern University, The Graduate School, Judd A. and Marjorie Weinberg College of Arts and Sciences, Department of Physics and Astronomy, Evanston, IL 60208. Offers astrophysics (PhD); physics (MS, PhD). Admissions and degrees offered through The Graduate School. *Degree requirements:* For doctorate, thesis/dissertation, qualifying exam. *Entrance requirements:* For doctorate, GRE General Test, GRE Subject Test. Additional exam requirements/recommendations for international students: Required—TOEFL. *Faculty research:* Nuclear and particle physics, condensed-matter physics, nonlinear physics, astrophysics.

Penn State University Park, Graduate School, Eberly College of Science, Department of Astronomy and Astrophysics, State College, University Park, PA 16802-1503. Offers MS, PhD. *Unit head:* Dr. Daniel J. Larson, Dean, 814-865-9591, Fax: 814-865-3634. *Application contact:* Cynthia E. Nicosia, Director, Graduate Enrollment Services, 814-865-1795, Fax: 814-865-4627, E-mail: cey1@psu.edu. Website: http://www.astro.psu.edu/.

Princeton University, Graduate School, Department of Astrophysical Sciences, Princeton, NJ 08544-1019. Offers astronomy (PhD); plasma physics (PhD). *Degree requirements:* For doctorate, thesis/dissertation. *Entrance requirements:* For doctorate, GRE General Test, GRE Subject Test (physics). Additional exam requirements/recommendations for international students: Required—TOEFL (minimum score 600 paper-based). Electronic applications accepted. *Faculty research:* Theoretical astrophysics, cosmology, galaxy formation, galactic dynamics, interstellar and intergalactic matter.

Rochester Institute of Technology, Graduate Enrollment Services, College of Science, Graduate Studies in Astrophysical Sciences and Technology, Rochester, NY 14623-5603. Offers MS, PhD. *Students:* 7 full-time (2 women), 10 part-time (3 women); includes 3 minority (1 Black or African American, non-Hispanic/Latino; 2 Hispanic/Latino), 4 international. Average age 28. 44 applicants, 20% accepted, 6 enrolled. In 2012, 1 doctorate awarded. Terminal master's awarded for partial completion of doctoral program. *Degree requirements:* For master's, comprehensive exam, thesis. *Entrance requirements:* For master's, GRE. Additional exam requirements/recommendations for international students: Required—TOEFL (minimum score 550 paper-based; 79 iBT) or IELTS (minimum score 6.5). *Application deadline:* For fall admission, 1/15 priority date for domestic students, 1/15 for international students. Application fee: $60. *Expenses: Tuition:* Full-time $35,976; part-time $999 per credit hour. *Required fees:* $240; $80 per quarter. *Financial support:* Fellowships with full and partial tuition reimbursements, research assistantships with full and partial tuition reimbursements, teaching assistantships with full and partial tuition reimbursements, Federal Work-Study, scholarships/grants, health care benefits, and unspecified assistantships available. *Faculty research:* Supermassive black holes, dark energy, gravitational waves, supernovae, massive stars, the galactic center, star formation, clusters of galaxies, active galactic nuclei, astroinformatics, computational astrophysics, instrument and detector development. *Unit head:* Dr. Andrew Robinson, Graduate Program Director, 585-475-2726, E-mail: axrsps@rit.edu. *Application contact:* Diane Ellison, Assistant Vice President, Graduate Enrollment Services, 585-475-2229, Fax: 585-475-7164, E-mail: gradinfo@rit.edu. Website: http://www.rit.edu/cos/astrophysics/.

Texas Christian University, College of Science and Engineering, Department of Physics and Astronomy, Fort Worth, TX 76129. Offers physics (MA, MS, PhD), including astrophysics (PhD), biophysics (PhD), business (PhD), physics (PhD); PhD/MBA. *Faculty:* 7 full-time (0 women). *Students:* 14 part-time (4 women); includes 2 minority (1 Asian, non-Hispanic/Latino; 1 Hispanic/Latino), 7 international. Average age 30. 31 applicants, 90% accepted, 2 enrolled. In 2012, 1 degree awarded. Terminal master's awarded for partial completion of doctoral program. *Median time to degree:* Of those who began their doctoral program in fall 2004, 100% received their degree in 8 years or less. *Degree requirements:* For master's, comprehensive exam, thesis; for doctorate, comprehensive exam, thesis/dissertation, paper submitted to scientific journal. *Entrance requirements:* For master's and doctorate, GRE General Test, minimum GPA of 3.0. Additional exam requirements/recommendations for international students: Required—TOEFL (minimum score 600 paper-based). *Application deadline:* For fall admission, 2/1 for domestic and international students; for spring admission, 10/1 for domestic and international students. Applications are processed on a rolling basis. Application fee: $60. Electronic applications accepted. *Expenses: Tuition:* Full-time $21,600; part-time $1200 per credit. *Required fees:* $48. Tuition and fees vary according to program. *Financial support:* In 2012–13, 14 students

Peterson's Graduate Programs in the Physical Sciences, Mathematics, Agricultural Sciences, the Environment & Natural Resources 2014

www.petersonsbooks.com **49**

received support, including 1 research assistantship with full tuition reimbursement available (averaging $20,500 per year), 11 teaching assistantships with full tuition reimbursements available (averaging $19,500 per year); tuition waivers also available. Financial award application deadline: 2/1. *Faculty research:* Biophysics, astrophysics, molecular physics, solid state physics, spectroscopy. *Total annual research expenditures:* $190,000. *Unit head:* Dr. William R. Graham, Professor and Chair, 817-257-7375 Ext. 6383, Fax: 817-257-7742, E-mail: w.graham@tcu.edu. *Application contact:* Dr. Yuri Strzhemechny, Associate Professor and Director, Graduate Program, 817-257-7375 Ext. 5793, Fax: 817-257-7742, E-mail: y.strzhemechny@tcu.edu. Website: http://www.phys.tcu.edu/grad_program.asp.

University of Alaska Fairbanks, College of Natural Sciences and Mathematics, Department of Physics, Fairbanks, AK 99775-5920. Offers computational physics (MS); physics (MAT, MS, PhD); space physics (MS, PhD). Part-time programs available. *Faculty:* 10 full-time (2 women). *Students:* 22 full-time (5 women), 3 part-time (0 women); includes 2 minority (1 American Indian or Alaska Native, non-Hispanic/Latino; 1 Asian, non-Hispanic/Latino), 7 international. Average age 30. 17 applicants, 24% accepted, 4 enrolled. In 2012, 3 master's, 2 doctorates awarded. Terminal master's awarded for partial completion of doctoral program. *Degree requirements:* For master's, comprehensive exam, thesis or alternative; for doctorate, comprehensive exam, thesis/dissertation, oral defense. *Entrance requirements:* Additional exam requirements/recommendations for international students: Required—TOEFL (minimum score 550 paper-based; 80 iBT). *Application deadline:* For fall admission, 6/1 for domestic students, 3/1 for international students; for spring admission, 10/15 for domestic students, 9/1 for international students. Applications are processed on a rolling basis. Application fee: $60. Electronic applications accepted. *Expenses:* Tuition, state resident: full-time $7038. Tuition, nonresident: full-time $14,382. Tuition and fees vary according to course level, course load and reciprocity agreements. *Financial support:* In 2012–13, 12 research assistantships with tuition reimbursements (averaging $16,543 per year), 10 teaching assistantships with tuition reimbursements (averaging $10,640 per year) were awarded; fellowships with tuition reimbursements, Federal Work-Study, scholarships/grants, health care benefits, and unspecified assistantships also available. Support available to part-time students. Financial award application deadline: 2/15; financial award applicants required to submit FAFSA. *Faculty research:* Atmospheric and ionospheric radar studies, space plasma theory, magnetospheric dynamics, space weather and auroral studies, turbulence and complex systems. *Unit head:* Ataur Chowdhury, Chair, 907-474-7339, Fax: 907-474-6130, E-mail: physics@uaf.edu. *Application contact:* Libby Eddy, Registrar and Director of Admissions, 907-474-7500, Fax: 907-474-7097, E-mail: admissions@uaf.edu. Website: http://www.uaf.edu/physics/.

University of Alberta, Faculty of Graduate Studies and Research, Department of Physics, Edmonton, AB T6G 2E1, Canada. Offers astrophysics (M Sc, PhD); condensed matter (M Sc, PhD); geophysics (M Sc, PhD); medical physics (M Sc, PhD); subatomic physics (M Sc, PhD). *Degree requirements:* For master's, thesis; for doctorate, thesis/dissertation. *Entrance requirements:* For master's and doctorate, minimum GPA of 7.0 on a 9.0 scale. Additional exam requirements/recommendations for international students: Required—TOEFL. *Faculty research:* Cosmology, astroparticle physics, high-intermediate energy, magnetism, superconductivity.

University of California, Berkeley, Graduate Division, College of Letters and Science, Department of Astrophysics, Berkeley, CA 94720-1500. Offers PhD. *Degree requirements:* For doctorate, thesis/dissertation, qualifying exam. *Entrance requirements:* For doctorate, GRE General Test, GRE Subject Test, minimum GPA of 3.0, 3 letters of recommendation. *Faculty research:* Theory, cosmology, radio astronomy, extra solar planets, infrared instrumentation.

University of California, Los Angeles, Graduate Division, College of Letters and Science, Department of Earth and Space Sciences, Program in Geophysics and Space Physics, Los Angeles, CA 90095. Offers MS, PhD. *Faculty:* 23 full-time (3 women). *Students:* 32 full-time (13 women); includes 7 minority (1 Black or African American, non-Hispanic/Latino; 3 Asian, non-Hispanic/Latino; 1 Hispanic/Latino; 2 Two or more races, non-Hispanic/Latino), 11 international. Average age 27. 56 applicants, 11% accepted, 2 enrolled. In 2012, 6 master's, 8 doctorates awarded. Terminal master's awarded for partial completion of doctoral program. *Degree requirements:* For master's, comprehensive exam or thesis; for doctorate, thesis/dissertation, oral and written qualifying exams. *Entrance requirements:* For master's and doctorate, GRE General Test, bachelor's degree; minimum undergraduate GPA of 3.0 (or its equivalent if letter grade system not used). Additional exam requirements/recommendations for international students: Required—TOEFL. *Application deadline:* For fall admission, 1/15 for domestic and international students. Application fee: $80 ($100 for international students). Electronic applications accepted. *Expenses:* Tuition, nonresident: full-time $15,102. *Required fees:* $14,809.19. Full-time tuition and fees vary according to program. *Financial support:* In 2012–13, 38 students received support, including 37 fellowships with full and partial tuition reimbursements available, 34 research assistantships with full and partial tuition reimbursements available, 8 teaching assistantships with full and partial tuition reimbursements available; Federal Work-Study, scholarships/grants, health care benefits, tuition waivers (full and partial), and unspecified assistantships also available. Financial award application deadline: 3/2; financial award applicants required to submit FAFSA. *Unit head:* Dr. Kevin McKeegan, Chair, 310-825-1475, E-mail: mckeegan@ess.ucla.edu. *Application contact:* Student Affairs Officer, 310-825-3917, Fax: 310-825-2779, E-mail: holbrook@ess.ucla.edu. Website: http://www.ess.ucla.edu/.

University of California, Santa Cruz, Division of Graduate Studies, Division of Physical and Biological Sciences, Department of Astronomy and Astrophysics, Santa Cruz, CA 95064. Offers PhD. *Degree requirements:* For doctorate, one foreign language, thesis/dissertation, qualifying exam. *Entrance requirements:* For doctorate, GRE General Test, GRE Subject Test. Additional exam requirements/recommendations for international students: Required—TOEFL (minimum score 550 paper-based; 83 iBT); Recommended—IELTS (minimum score 8). Electronic applications accepted. *Faculty research:* Solar system and the Milky Way to the most distant galaxies in the Universe, fundamental questions of cosmology.

University of Chicago, Division of the Physical Sciences, Department of Astronomy and Astrophysics, Chicago, IL 60637-1513. Offers MS, PhD. Terminal master's awarded for partial completion of doctoral program. *Degree requirements:* For master's, comprehensive exam, thesis optional, candidacy exam; for doctorate, comprehensive exam, thesis/dissertation, dissertation for publication. *Entrance requirements:* For master's, department candidacy examination, minimum GPA of 3.0; for doctorate, GRE General Test, GRE Subject Test, minimum GPA of 3.0. Additional exam requirements/recommendations for international students: Required—TOEFL (minimum score 600 paper-based); Recommended—IELTS. Electronic applications accepted. *Faculty research:* Quasi-stellar object absorption lines, fluid dynamics, interstellar matter, particle physics, cosmology.

University of Colorado Boulder, Graduate School, College of Arts and Sciences, Department of Astrophysical and Planetary Sciences, Boulder, CO 80309. Offers astrophysics (MS, PhD); planetary science (MS, PhD). *Faculty:* 22 full-time (3 women). *Students:* 53 full-time (13 women); includes 3 minority (1 Black or African American, non-Hispanic/Latino; 1 American Indian or Alaska Native, non-Hispanic/Latino; 1 Asian, non-Hispanic/Latino), 5 international. Average age 26. 175 applicants, 21% accepted, 11 enrolled. Terminal master's awarded for partial completion of doctoral program. *Degree requirements:* For master's, comprehensive exam, thesis or alternative; for doctorate, one foreign language, thesis/dissertation. *Entrance requirements:* For master's, GRE General Test, GRE Subject Test, minimum undergraduate GPA of 3.0; for doctorate, GRE General Test, GRE Subject Test. *Application deadline:* For fall admission, 1/15 priority date for domestic students, 12/1 for international students. Applications are processed on a rolling basis. Application fee: $50 ($60 for international students). Electronic applications accepted. *Financial support:* In 2012–13, 23 fellowships (averaging $13,475 per year), 31 research assistantships with full and partial tuition reimbursements (averaging $25,396 per year), 15 teaching assistantships with full and partial tuition reimbursements (averaging $23,435 per year) were awarded; institutionally sponsored loans, scholarships/grants, health care benefits, and unspecified assistantships also available. Financial award application deadline: 1/15; financial award applicants required to submit FAFSA. *Faculty research:* Astrophysics, astronomy, galaxies: stellar systems, infrared/optical astronomy, spectroscopy. *Total annual research expenditures:* $40 million. *Application contact:* E-mail: apsgradsec@colorado.edu. Website: http://aps.colorado.edu/.

The University of Manchester, School of Physics and Astronomy, Manchester, United Kingdom. Offers astronomy and astrophysics (M Sc, PhD); biological physics (M Sc, PhD); condensed matter physics (M Sc, PhD); nonlinear and liquid crystals physics (M Sc, PhD); nuclear physics (M Sc, PhD); particle physics (M Sc, PhD); photon physics (M Sc, PhD); physics (M Sc, PhD); theoretical physics (M Sc, PhD).

University of Michigan, Horace H. Rackham School of Graduate Studies, College of Literature, Science, and the Arts, Department of Astronomy, Ann Arbor, MI 48109-1042. Offers astronomy and astrophysics (PhD). *Faculty:* 21 full-time (6 women). *Students:* 30 full-time (13 women); includes 4 minority (all Asian, non-Hispanic/Latino). In 2012, 6 doctorates awarded. Terminal master's awarded for partial completion of doctoral program. *Degree requirements:* For doctorate, thesis/dissertation, oral defense of dissertation, preliminary exam. *Entrance requirements:* For doctorate, GRE General Test, GRE Subject Test (physics). Additional exam requirements/recommendations for international students: Required—TOEFL. *Application deadline:* For fall admission, 1/6 for domestic and international students. Application fee: $65 ($75 for international students). Electronic applications accepted. *Financial support:* In 2012–13, 5 fellowships with full tuition reimbursements (averaging $22,800 per year), 23 research assistantships with full tuition reimbursements (averaging $22,800 per year), 13 teaching assistantships with full tuition reimbursements (averaging $22,800 per year) were awarded; institutionally sponsored loans, scholarships/grants, health care benefits, and unspecified assistantships also available. Financial award applicants required to submit FAFSA. *Faculty research:* Extragalactic and galactic astronomy, cosmology, star and planet formation, high energy astrophysics. *Total annual research expenditures:* $2.1 million. *Unit head:* Dr. Joel Bregman, Chair and Professor, 734-764-3440, Fax: 734-763-6317, E-mail: jbregman@umich.edu. *Application contact:* Brian Cox, Student Services Coordinator, 734-764-3440, Fax: 734-763-6317, E-mail: bmcox@umich.edu. Website: http://www.lsa.umich.edu/astro.

University of Minnesota, Twin Cities Campus, College of Science and Engineering, School of Physics and Astronomy, Program in Astrophysics, Minneapolis, MN 55455-0213. Offers MS, PhD. Terminal master's awarded for partial completion of doctoral program. *Degree requirements:* For master's, thesis optional; for doctorate, thesis/dissertation. *Entrance requirements:* For master's and doctorate, GRE General Test, GRE Subject Test. Additional exam requirements/recommendations for international students: Required—TOEFL. *Faculty research:* Evolution of stars and galaxies; the interstellar medium; cosmology; observational, optical, infrared, and radio astronomy; computational astrophysics.

University of Missouri–St. Louis, College of Arts and Sciences, Department of Physics and Astronomy, St. Louis, MO 63121. Offers applied physics (MS); astrophysics (MS); physics (PhD). Part-time and evening/weekend programs available. *Faculty:* 9 full-time (2 women), 5 part-time/adjunct (0 women). *Students:* 14 full-time (3 women), 9 part-time (5 women); includes 2 minority (1 American Indian or Alaska Native, non-Hispanic/Latino; 1 Asian, non-Hispanic/Latino), 4 international. Average age 31. 21 applicants, 48% accepted, 6 enrolled. In 2012, 7 master's, 1 doctorate awarded. Terminal master's awarded for partial completion of doctoral program. *Degree requirements:* For master's, thesis optional; for doctorate, thesis/dissertation. *Entrance requirements:* For master's, GRE General Test; for doctorate, GRE General Test, 2 letters of recommendation. Additional exam requirements/recommendations for international students: Required—TOEFL (minimum score 550 paper-based; 79 iBT), IELTS (minimum score 6.5). *Application deadline:* For fall admission, 7/1 for domestic and international students; for spring admission, 12/1 for domestic students, 11/1 for international students. Application fee: $35 ($40 for international students). Electronic applications accepted. *Expenses:* Tuition, state resident: full-time $7364; part-time $409.10 per credit hour. Tuition, nonresident: full-time $18,153; part-time $1008.50 per credit hour. *Financial support:* In 2012–13, 5 research assistantships with full and partial tuition reimbursements (averaging $17,125 per year), 11 teaching assistantships with full and partial tuition reimbursements (averaging $14,500 per year) were awarded; fellowships with full tuition reimbursements and career-related internships or fieldwork also available. Financial award applicants required to submit FAFSA. *Faculty research:* Biophysics, atomic physics, nonlinear dynamics, materials science. *Unit head:* Dr. Bruce Wilking, Director of Graduate Studies, 314-516-5931, Fax: 314-516-6152, E-mail: bwilking@umsl.edu. *Application contact:* 314-516-5458, Fax: 314-516-6996, E-mail: gradadm@umsl.edu. Website: http://www.umsl.edu/~physics/.

The University of North Carolina at Chapel Hill, Graduate School, College of Arts and Sciences, Department of Physics and Astronomy, Chapel Hill, NC 27599. Offers physics (MS, PhD). Terminal master's awarded for partial completion of doctoral program. *Degree requirements:* For master's, comprehensive exam; for doctorate, comprehensive exam, thesis/dissertation. *Entrance requirements:* For master's and doctorate, GRE General Test, minimum GPA of 3.0. Electronic applications accepted. *Faculty research:* Observational astronomy, fullerenes, polarized beams, nanotubes, nucleosynthesis in stars and supernovae, superstring theory, ballistic transport in semiconductors, gravitation.

The University of Toledo, College of Graduate Studies, College of Natural Sciences and Mathematics, Department of Physics and Astronomy, Toledo, OH 43606-3390. Offers photovoltaics (PSM); physics (MS, PhD), including astrophysics (PhD), materials science, medical physics (PhD); MS/PhD. *Faculty:* 35. *Students:* 60 full-time (12 women), 8 part-time (1 woman); includes 2 minority (1 Black or African American, non-Hispanic/Latino; 1 Asian, non-Hispanic/Latino), 30 international. Average age 28. 75 applicants, 49% accepted, 19 enrolled. In 2012, 2 master's, 6 doctorates awarded. *Degree requirements:* For master's, thesis; for doctorate, thesis/dissertation, departmental qualifying exam. *Entrance requirements:* For master's and doctorate, GRE General Test, GRE Subject Test, minimum cumulative point-hour ratio of 2.7 for all previous academic work, three letters of recommendation, statement of purpose, transcripts from all prior institutions attended. Additional exam requirements/recommendations for international students: Required—TOEFL (minimum score 550 paper-based; 80 iBT), IELTS (minimum score 6.5). *Application deadline:* For fall admission, 1/15 priority date for domestic students, 1/15 for international students. Applications are processed on a rolling basis. Application fee: $45 ($75 for international students). Electronic applications accepted. *Financial support:* In 2012–13, 39 research assistantships with full and partial tuition reimbursements (averaging $17,207 per year), 25 teaching assistantships with full and partial tuition reimbursements (averaging $15,130 per year) were awarded; Federal Work-Study, institutionally sponsored loans, scholarships/grants, tuition waivers (full),

and unspecified assistantships also available. Support available to part-time students. *Faculty research:* Atomic physics, solid-state physics, materials science, astrophysics. *Unit head:* Dr. Lawrence Anderson-Huang, Chair, 419-530-7257, E-mail: lawrence.anderson@utoledo.edu. *Application contact:* Graduate School Office, 419-530-4723, Fax: 419-537-4724, E-mail: grdsch@utnet.utoledo.edu. Website: http://www.utoledo.edu/nsm/.

University of Toronto, School of Graduate Studies, Faculty of Arts and Science, Department of Astronomy and Astrophysics, Toronto, ON M5S 1A1, Canada. Offers M Sc, PhD. Part-time programs available. *Degree requirements:* For doctorate, thesis/dissertation, qualifying exam, thesis defense. *Entrance requirements:* For master's, minimum B average, bachelor's degree in astronomy or equivalent, 3 letters of reference; for doctorate, GRE General Test, minimum B+ average, master's degree in astronomy or equivalent, demonstrated research competence, 3 letters of reference. Additional exam requirements/recommendations for international students: Required—TOEFL (minimum score 580 paper-based; 93 iBT), TWE (minimum score 4). Electronic applications accepted.

University of Victoria, Faculty of Graduate Studies, Faculty of Science, Department of Physics and Astronomy, Victoria, BC V8W 2Y2, Canada. Offers astronomy and astrophysics (M Sc, PhD); condensed matter physics (M Sc, PhD); experimental particle physics (M Sc, PhD); medical physics (M Sc, PhD); ocean physics (M Sc, PhD); theoretical physics (M Sc, PhD). *Degree requirements:* For master's, thesis; for doctorate, comprehensive exam, thesis/dissertation, candidacy exam. *Entrance requirements:* For master's and doctorate, GRE. Additional exam requirements/recommendations for international students: Required—TOEFL (minimum score 575 paper-based), IELTS (minimum score 7). Electronic applications accepted. *Faculty research:* Old stellar populations; observational cosmology and large scale structure; cp violation; atlas.

Washington State University, Graduate School, College of Arts and Sciences, Department of Physics and Astronomy, Pullman, WA 99164-2814. Offers physics (MS, PhD), including astrophysics (PhD), extreme matter (PhD), materials and optics (PhD). *Faculty:* 18 full-time (2 women), 2 part-time/adjunct (1 woman). *Students:* 68 full-time (16 women), 5 part-time (2 women); includes 1 minority (Hispanic/Latino), 30 international. Average age 29. 89 applicants, 45% accepted, 17 enrolled. In 2012, 9 master's, 6 doctorates awarded. Terminal master's awarded for partial completion of doctoral program. *Degree requirements:* For master's, comprehensive exam (for some programs), thesis optional, oral exam; for doctorate, comprehensive exam, thesis/dissertation, oral exam, written exam. *Entrance requirements:* For master's and doctorate, GRE General Test, GRE Subject Test (recommended), minimum GPA of 3.0 in last half of undergraduate work completed. Additional exam requirements/recommendations for international students: Required—TOEFL (minimum score 550 paper-based; 80 iBT), IELTS. *Application deadline:* For fall admission, 3/1 priority date for domestic students, 3/1 for international students; for spring admission, 11/1 for domestic and international students. Applications are processed on a rolling basis. Application fee: $75. Electronic applications accepted. *Financial support:* In 2012–13, 67 students received support, including 1 fellowship with full and partial tuition reimbursement available (averaging $18,000 per year), 15 research assistantships with full and partial tuition reimbursements available (averaging $16,169 per year), 25 teaching assistantships with full and partial tuition reimbursements available (averaging $15,075 per year); Federal Work-Study, institutionally sponsored loans, scholarships/grants, health care benefits, and unspecified assistantships also available. Financial award application deadline: 2/1; financial award applicants required to submit FAFSA. *Faculty research:* Linear and nonlinear acoustics and optics, shock wave dynamics, solid-state physics, surface physics, high-pressure and semiconductor physics. *Total annual research expenditures:* $3.1 million. *Unit head:* Matthew D. McCluskey, Chair, 509-335-5356, Fax: 509-335-7816, E-mail: mattmcc@wsu.edu. *Application contact:* Graduate School Admissions, 800-GRADWSU, Fax: 509-335-1949, E-mail: gradsch@wsu.edu. Website: http://www.physics.wsu.edu/.

Yale University, Graduate School of Arts and Sciences, Department of Astronomy, New Haven, CT 06520. Offers astronomy (PhD); solar and terrestrial physics (PhD). *Degree requirements:* For doctorate, thesis/dissertation. *Entrance requirements:* For doctorate, GRE General Test, GRE Subject Test (physics).

Peterson's Graduate Programs in the Physical Sciences, Mathematics, Agricultural Sciences, the Environment & Natural Resources 2014

www.petersonsbooks.com **51**

Section 2
Chemistry

This section contains a directory of institutions offering graduate work in chemistry, followed by in-depth entries submitted by institutions that chose to prepare detailed program descriptions. Additional information about programs listed in the directory but not augmented by an in-depth entry may be obtained by writing directly to the dean of a graduate school or chair of a department at the address given in the directory.

For programs offering related work, see also in this book *Geosciences* and *Physics.* In the other guides in this series:

Graduate Programs in the Biological/Biomedical Sciences & Health-Related Medical Professions

See *Biological and Biomedical Sciences, Biochemistry, Biophysics, Nutrition, Pharmacology and Toxicology,* and *Pharmacy and Pharmaceutical Sciences*

Graduate Programs in Engineering & Applied Sciences

See *Engineering and Applied Sciences; Agricultural Engineering; Chemical Engineering; Geological, Mineral/Mining, and Petroleum Engineering; Materials Sciences and Engineering;* and *Pharmaceutical Engineering*

CONTENTS

Analytical Chemistry

Auburn University, Graduate School, College of Sciences and Mathematics, Department of Chemistry and Biochemistry, Auburn University, AL 36849. Offers analytical chemistry (MS, PhD); biochemistry (MS, PhD); inorganic chemistry (MS, PhD); organic chemistry (MS, PhD); physical chemistry (MS, PhD). Part-time programs available. *Faculty:* 28 full-time (5 women), 1 part-time/adjunct (0 women). *Students:* 37 full-time (14 women), 30 part-time (15 women); includes 6 minority (3 Black or African American, non-Hispanic/Latino; 1 American Indian or Alaska Native, non-Hispanic/Latino; 1 Asian, non-Hispanic/Latino; 1 Hispanic/Latino), 41 international. Average age 28. 38 applicants, 39% accepted, 12 enrolled. In 2012, 1 master's, 9 doctorates awarded. *Degree requirements:* For master's, thesis (for some programs); for doctorate, thesis/dissertation, oral and written exams. *Entrance requirements:* For master's and doctorate, GRE General Test. *Application deadline:* For fall admission, 7/7 for domestic students; for spring admission, 11/24 for domestic students. Applications are processed on a rolling basis. Application fee: $50 ($60 for international students). Electronic applications accepted. *Expenses:* Tuition, state resident: full-time $7866; part-time $437 per credit. Tuition, nonresident: full-time $23,598; part-time $1311 per credit. *Required fees:* $787 per semester. Tuition and fees vary according to degree level and program. *Financial support:* Fellowships, research assistantships, and teaching assistantships available. Financial award application deadline: 3/15; financial award applicants required to submit FAFSA. *Unit head:* Dr. J. V. Ortiz, Chair, 334-844-4043, Fax: 334-844-4043. *Application contact:* Dr. George Flowers, Dean of the Graduate School, 334-844-2125. Website: http://www.auburn.edu/cosam/departments/chemistry/.

Binghamton University, State University of New York, Graduate School, School of Arts and Sciences, Department of Chemistry, Binghamton, NY 13902-6000. Offers analytical chemistry (PhD); chemistry (MA, MS); environmental (PhD); inorganic chemistry (PhD); organic chemistry (PhD); physical chemistry (PhD). Part-time programs available. *Faculty:* 16 full-time (4 women), 4 part-time/adjunct (1 woman). *Students:* 25 full-time (10 women), 26 part-time (10 women); includes 4 minority (3 Black or African American, non-Hispanic/Latino; 1 Hispanic/Latino), 33 international. Average age 28. 53 applicants, 49% accepted, 11 enrolled. In 2012, 3 master's, 6 doctorates awarded. Terminal master's awarded for partial completion of doctoral program. *Degree requirements:* For master's, thesis or alternative, oral exam, seminar presentation; for doctorate, thesis/dissertation, cumulative exams. *Entrance requirements:* For master's and doctorate, GRE General Test, GRE Subject Test. Additional exam requirements/recommendations for international students: Required—TOEFL (minimum score 550 paper-based; 80 iBT). *Application deadline:* For fall admission, 1/15 priority date for domestic students, 1/15 for international students; for spring admission, 10/15 priority date for domestic students, 10/15 for international students. Applications are processed on a rolling basis. Application fee: $75. Electronic applications accepted. *Expenses:* Tuition, state resident: full-time $9370. Tuition, nonresident: full-time $16,680. *Financial support:* In 2012–13, 47 students received support, including 5 research assistantships with full tuition reimbursements available (averaging $18,000 per year), 34 teaching assistantships with full tuition reimbursements available (averaging $18,000 per year); career-related internships or fieldwork, Federal Work-Study, institutionally sponsored loans, scholarships/grants, health care benefits, tuition waivers (full), and unspecified assistantships also available. Financial award application deadline: 2/15; financial award applicants required to submit FAFSA. *Unit head:* Dr. Wayne E. Jones, Chairperson, 607-777-2421, E-mail: wjones@binghamton.edu. *Application contact:* Kishan Zuber, Recruiting and Admissions Coordinator, 607-777-2151, Fax: 607-777-2501, E-mail: kzuber@binghamton.edu.

Brigham Young University, Graduate Studies, College of Physical and Mathematical Sciences, Department of Chemistry and Biochemistry, Provo, UT 84602. Offers biochemistry (MS, PhD); chemistry (MS, PhD). *Faculty:* 33 full-time (2 women). *Students:* 101 full-time (41 women); includes 1 minority (Asian, non-Hispanic/Latino), 56 international. Average age 28. 75 applicants, 41% accepted, 16 enrolled. In 2012, 2 master's, 14 doctorates awarded. *Degree requirements:* For master's, thesis; for doctorate, comprehensive exam, thesis/dissertation, qualifying exam. *Entrance requirements:* For master's and doctorate, GRE General Test, minimum GPA of 3.0 in last 60 hours. Additional exam requirements/recommendations for international students: Required—TOEFL (minimum score 580 paper-based; 85 iBT), IELTS (minimum score 7); Recommended—TWE. *Application deadline:* For fall admission, 2/1 priority date for domestic students, 2/1 for international students. Applications are processed on a rolling basis. Application fee: $50. Electronic applications accepted. *Expenses: Tuition:* Full-time $5950; part-time $331 per credit hour. Tuition and fees vary according to program and student's religious affiliation. *Financial support:* In 2012–13, 101 students received support, including 12 fellowships with full tuition reimbursements available (averaging $21,250 per year), 51 research assistantships with full tuition reimbursements available (averaging $21,250 per year), 38 teaching assistantships with full tuition reimbursements available (averaging $21,250 per year); institutionally sponsored loans, scholarships/grants, health care benefits, tuition waivers (full), and unspecified assistantships also available. Financial award application deadline: 2/1. *Faculty research:* Separation science, molecular recognition, organic synthesis and biomedical application, biochemistry and molecular biology, molecular spectroscopy. *Total annual research expenditures:* $5.6 million. *Unit head:* Dr. Gregory F. Burton, Chair, 801-422-4917, Fax: 801-422-0153, E-mail: gburton@byu.edu. *Application contact:* Dr. Paul B. Farnsworth, Graduate Coordinator, 801-422-6502, Fax: 801-422-0153, E-mail: pbfarnsw@byu.edu. Website: http://www.chem.byu.edu/.

California State University, Los Angeles, Graduate Studies, College of Natural and Social Sciences, Department of Chemistry and Biochemistry, Los Angeles, CA 90032-8530. Offers analytical chemistry (MS); biochemistry (MS); chemistry (MS); inorganic chemistry (MS); organic chemistry (MS); physical chemistry (MS). Part-time and evening/weekend programs available. *Faculty:* 2 full-time (1 woman). *Students:* 3 full-time (1 woman), 16 part-time (9 women); includes 16 minority (all Hispanic/Latino). Average age 32. 21 applicants, 52% accepted, 8 enrolled. In 2012, 2 master's awarded. *Degree requirements:* For master's, one foreign language, comprehensive exam or thesis. *Entrance requirements:* Additional exam requirements/recommendations for international students: Required—TOEFL. *Application deadline:* For fall admission, 5/1 for domestic and international students. Applications are processed on a rolling basis. Application fee: $55. *Financial support:* Federal Work-Study available. Support available to part-time students. Financial award application deadline: 3/1. *Faculty research:* Intercalation of heavy metal, carborane chemistry, conductive polymers and fabrics, titanium reagents, computer modeling and synthesis. *Unit head:* Dr. Robert L. Vellanoweth, Chair, 323-343-2300, Fax: 323-343-6490, E-mail: rvellan@calstatela.edu. *Application contact:* Dr. Larry Fritz, Dean of Graduate Studies, 323-343-3820 Ext. 3827, Fax: 323-343-5653, E-mail: lfritz@calstatela.edu. Website: http://www.calstatela.edu/dept/chem/index.htm.

Cleveland State University, College of Graduate Studies, College of Sciences and Health Professions, Department of Chemistry, Cleveland, OH 44115. Offers analytical chemistry (MS); clinical chemistry (MS); clinical/bioanalytical chemistry (PhD), including cellular and molecular medicine, clinical chemistry, clinical/bioanalytical chemistry; environmental chemistry (MS); inorganic chemistry (MS); pharmaceutical/organic chemistry (MS); physical chemistry (MS). Part-time and evening/weekend programs available. *Faculty:* 12 full-time (0 women). *Students:* 10 full-time (6 women), 92 part-time (46 women); includes 7 minority (6 Black or African American, non-Hispanic/Latino; 1 Asian, non-Hispanic/Latino), 68 international. Average age 27. 119 applicants, 86% accepted, 18 enrolled. In 2012, 15 master's, 5 doctorates awarded. *Degree requirements:* For master's, thesis optional; for doctorate, comprehensive exam, thesis/dissertation. *Entrance requirements:* For master's and doctorate, GRE General Test. Additional exam requirements/recommendations for international students: Required—TOEFL (minimum score 525 paper-based; 65 iBT). *Application deadline:* For fall admission, 1/15 priority date for domestic students, 1/15 for international students. Applications are processed on a rolling basis. Application fee: $30. Electronic applications accepted. *Expenses:* Tuition, state resident: full-time $8172; part-time $510.75 per credit hour. Tuition, nonresident: full-time $15,372; part-time $960.75 per credit hour. *Required fees:* $25 per semester. Tuition and fees vary according to course load and program. *Financial support:* In 2012–13, 44 students received support, including 5 fellowships with full tuition reimbursements available (averaging $22,500 per year), 13 research assistantships with full tuition reimbursements available (averaging $22,500 per year), 24 teaching assistantships with full tuition reimbursements available (averaging $21,000 per year); scholarships/grants and unspecified assistantships also available. Financial award application deadline: 1/15. *Faculty research:* Bioanalytical techniques and molecular diagnostics, glycoproteomics and antithrombotic agents, drug discovery and innovation, analytical pharmacology, inflammatory disease research. *Total annual research expenditures:* $3 million. *Unit head:* Dr. David J. Anderson, Interim Chair, 216-687-2467, Fax: 216-687-9298, E-mail: d.anderson@csuohio.edu. *Application contact:* Richelle P. Emery, Administrative Coordinator, 216-687-2457, Fax: 216-687-9298, E-mail: r.emery@csuohio.edu. Website: http://www.csuohio.edu/chemistry/.

Cornell University, Graduate School, Graduate Fields of Arts and Sciences, Field of Chemistry and Chemical Biology, Ithaca, NY 14853-0001. Offers analytical chemistry (PhD); bio-organic chemistry (PhD); biophysical chemistry (PhD); chemical biology (PhD); chemical physics (PhD); inorganic chemistry (PhD); materials chemistry (PhD); organic chemistry (PhD); organometallic chemistry (PhD); physical chemistry (PhD); polymer chemistry (PhD); theoretical chemistry (PhD). *Faculty:* 48 full-time (5 women). *Students:* 161 full-time (70 women); includes 28 minority (1 Black or African American, non-Hispanic/Latino; 16 Asian, non-Hispanic/Latino; 4 Hispanic/Latino; 7 Two or more races, non-Hispanic/Latino), 48 international. Average age 25. 340 applicants, 33% accepted, 40 enrolled. In 2012, 15 doctorates awarded. *Degree requirements:* For doctorate, comprehensive exam, thesis/dissertation. *Entrance requirements:* For doctorate, GRE General Test, GRE Subject Test (chemistry), 3 letters of recommendation. Additional exam requirements/recommendations for international students: Required—TOEFL (minimum score 600 paper-based; 77 iBT). *Application deadline:* For fall admission, 1/10 for domestic students. Application fee: $95. Electronic applications accepted. *Financial support:* In 2012–13, 155 students received support, including 37 fellowships with full tuition reimbursements available, 50 research assistantships with full tuition reimbursements available, 68 teaching assistantships with full tuition reimbursements available; institutionally sponsored loans, scholarships/grants, health care benefits, tuition waivers (full and partial), and unspecified assistantships also available. Financial award applicants required to submit FAFSA. *Faculty research:* Analytical, organic, inorganic, physical, materials, chemical biology. *Unit head:* Director of Graduate Studies, 607-255-4139, Fax: 607-255-4137. *Application contact:* Graduate Field Assistant, 607-255-4139, Fax: 607-255-4137, E-mail: chemgrad@cornell.edu. Website: http://www.gradschool.cornell.edu/fields.php?id-26&a-2.

DePaul University, College of Science and Health, Department of Chemistry, Chicago, IL 60614. Offers analytical/physical chemistry (MS); biochemistry/medicinal chemistry (MS); polymer chemistry and coatings technology (MS); synthetic chemistry (MS). Part-time and evening/weekend programs available. *Faculty:* 7 full-time (4 women). *Students:* 5 full-time (2 women), 11 part-time (6 women); includes 5 minority (1 Asian, non-Hispanic/Latino; 3 Hispanic/Latino; 1 Two or more races, non-Hispanic/Latino), 1 international. Average age 26. In 2012, 4 master's awarded. *Degree requirements:* For master's, thesis (for some programs), oral exam (for select programs). *Entrance requirements:* For master's, BS in chemistry or equivalent. Additional exam requirements/recommendations for international students: Required—TOEFL (minimum score 590 paper-based; 96 iBT) or Pearson Test of English. *Application deadline:* For fall admission, 7/15 for domestic students, 5/1 for international students; for winter admission, 11/15 for domestic students, 9/1 for international students; for spring admission, 2/15 for domestic students, 12/1 for international students. Application fee: $40. Electronic applications accepted. *Financial support:* In 2012–13, 6 teaching assistantships with partial tuition reimbursements (averaging $9,000 per year) were awarded. Financial award application deadline: 6/1; financial award applicants required to submit FAFSA. *Faculty research:* Computational chemistry, organic synthesis, inorganic synthesis, polymer synthesis, biochemistry. *Total annual research expenditures:* $30,000. *Unit head:* Dr. Matthew Dintzner, Chairperson, 773-325-4726, Fax: 773-325-7421, E-mail: mdintzne@depaul.edu. *Application contact:* Ann Spittle, Director of Graduate Admission, 773-325-7315, Fax: 312-476-3244, E-mail: graddepaul@depaul.edu. Website: http://chemistry.depaul.edu.

Eastern New Mexico University, Graduate School, College of Liberal Arts and Sciences, Department of Physical Sciences, Portales, NM 88130. Offers chemistry (MS), including analytical, biochemistry, inorganic, organic, physical. Part-time programs available. *Faculty:* 2 full-time (0 women). *Students:* 2 full-time (0 women), 12 part-time (4 women), 12 international. Average age 25. 14 applicants, 93% accepted, 11 enrolled. In 2012, 5 master's awarded. *Degree requirements:* For master's, thesis optional, seminar, oral and written comprehensive exams. *Entrance requirements:* For master's, ACS placement examination, minimum GPA of 3.0; 2 letters of recommendation; personal statement of career goals; bachelor's degree with one year minimum each of general, organic, and analytical chemistry. Additional exam requirements/recommendations for international students: Required—TOEFL (minimum score 550 paper-based; 79 iBT), IELTS (minimum score 6). *Application deadline:* For fall admission, 7/20 priority date for domestic students, 6/20 for international students; for spring admission, 12/15 priority date for domestic students, 11/15 for international students. Applications are processed on a rolling basis. Application fee: $10. Electronic applications accepted. *Expenses:* Tuition, state resident: full-time $3356; part-time $139.85 per credit hour. Tuition, nonresident: full-time $9030; part-time $376.25 per credit hour. *Required fees:* $1425.60; $59.40 per credit hour. $712.80 per semester. *Financial support:* In 2012–13, 1 research assistantship with partial tuition reimbursement (averaging $8,500 per year), 10 teaching assistantships with partial tuition reimbursements (averaging $8,500 per year) were awarded; career-related internships or fieldwork and unspecified assistantships also available. Support available to part-time students. Financial award application deadline: 3/1; financial award applicants required to submit FAFSA. *Faculty research:* Synfuel, electrochemistry, protein chemistry. *Unit head:* Dr. Juacho Yan, Graduate Coordinator, 575-562-2494, Fax: 575-562-2192, E-mail: juacho.yan@enmu.edu. *Application contact:* Sharon Potter, Department Secretary, Biology and Physical Sciences, 575-562-2174, Fax: 575-562-2192, E-mail: sharon.potter@enmu.edu. Website: http://liberal-arts.enmu.edu/sciences/grad-chemistry.shtml.

Florida State University, The Graduate School, College of Arts and Sciences, Department of Chemistry and Biochemistry, Tallahassee, FL 32306-4390. Offers analytical chemistry (MS, PhD); biochemistry (MS, PhD); inorganic chemistry (MS, PhD); materials chemistry (PhD); organic chemistry (MS, PhD); physical chemistry (MS, PhD). *Faculty:* 37 full-time (4 women), 1 (woman) part-time/adjunct. *Students:* 138 full-time (52 women), 8 part-time (1 woman); includes 14 minority (6 Black or African American, non-Hispanic/Latino; 3 Asian, non-Hispanic/Latino; 2 Hispanic/Latino; 3 Two or more races, non-Hispanic/Latino), 63 international. Average age 25. 147 applicants, 40% accepted, 28 enrolled. In 2012, 7 master's, 27 doctorates awarded. Terminal master's awarded for partial completion of doctoral program. *Degree requirements:* For master's, comprehensive exam, thesis (for some programs); for doctorate, comprehensive exam, thesis/dissertation. *Entrance requirements:* For master's and doctorate, GRE General Test (minimum scores: 150 verbal, 151 quantitative; 1100 total on the old scale), minimum GPA of 3.1 in undergraduate course work. Additional exam requirements/recommendations for international students: Required—TOEFL (minimum score 90 iBT). *Application deadline:* For fall admission, 12/15 priority date for domestic students, 12/15 for international students; for spring admission, 9/15 for domestic and international students. Applications are processed on a rolling basis. Application fee: $30. Electronic applications accepted. *Expenses:* Contact institution. *Financial support:* In 2012–13, 140 students received support, including 7 fellowships with full and partial tuition reimbursements available (averaging $10,000 per year), 50 research assistantships with full tuition reimbursements available (averaging $20,000 per year), 100 teaching assistantships with full tuition reimbursements available (averaging $20,000 per year); health care benefits also available. Financial award application deadline: 12/15; financial award applicants required to submit FAFSA. *Faculty research:* Bioanalytical chemistry, including separations, microfluidics, petroleomics; materials chemistry, including magnets, polymers, catalysts, nanomaterials; spectroscopy, including NMR and EPR, ultrafast, Raman, and mass spectrometry; organic synthesis, natural products, photochemistry, and supramolecular chemistry; biochemistry, with focus on structural biology, metabolomics, and anticancer drugs. *Total annual research expenditures:* $9.8 million. *Unit head:* Dr. Timothy Logan, Chairman, 850-644-3810, Fax: 850-644-8281, E-mail: gradinfo@chem.fsu.edu. *Application contact:* Dr. Michael Shatruk, Associate Chair for Graduate Studies, 850-417-8417, Fax: 850-644-8281, E-mail: gradinfo@chem.fsu.edu. Website: http://www.chem.fsu.edu/.

Georgetown University, Graduate School of Arts and Sciences, Department of Chemistry, Washington, DC 20057. Offers analytical chemistry (PhD); biochemistry (PhD); computational chemistry (PhD); inorganic chemistry (PhD); materials chemistry (PhD); organic chemistry (PhD); physical chemistry (PhD); theoretical chemistry (PhD). Terminal master's awarded for partial completion of doctoral program. *Degree requirements:* For doctorate, comprehensive exam, thesis/dissertation. *Entrance requirements:* For doctorate, GRE General Test. Additional exam requirements/recommendations for international students: Required—TOEFL.

The George Washington University, Columbian College of Arts and Sciences, Department of Chemistry, Washington, DC 20052. Offers analytical chemistry (MS, PhD); inorganic chemistry (MS, PhD); materials science (MS, PhD); organic chemistry (MS, PhD); physical chemistry (MS, PhD). Part-time and evening/weekend programs available. *Faculty:* 17 full-time (6 women). *Students:* 30 full-time (16 women), 8 part-time (6 women); includes 3 minority (2 Asian, non-Hispanic/Latino; 1 Hispanic/Latino), 8 international. Average age 27. 66 applicants, 24% accepted, 10 enrolled. In 2012, 2 master's, 3 doctorates awarded. Terminal master's awarded for partial completion of doctoral program. *Degree requirements:* For master's, comprehensive exam, thesis or alternative; for doctorate, thesis/dissertation, general exam. *Entrance requirements:* For master's and doctorate, GRE General Test, interview, minimum GPA of 3.0. Additional exam requirements/recommendations for international students: Required—TOEFL (minimum score 550 paper-based; 80 iBT). *Application deadline:* For fall admission, 1/15 priority date for domestic students, 1/15 for international students; for spring admission, 9/1 priority date for domestic students, 9/1 for international students. Applications are processed on a rolling basis. Application fee: $75. Electronic applications accepted. *Financial support:* In 2012–13, 27 students received support. Fellowships with tuition reimbursements available, research assistantships, teaching assistantships with tuition reimbursements available, Federal Work-Study, and tuition waivers available. Financial award application deadline: 1/15. *Unit head:* Dr. Michael King, Chair, 202-994-6488. *Application contact:* Information Contact, 202-994-6121, E-mail: gwchem@gwu.edu. Website: http://www.gwu.edu/~gwchem/.

Georgia State University, College of Arts and Sciences, Department of Chemistry, Atlanta, GA 30302-3083. Offers analytical chemistry (MS, PhD); biochemistry (MS, PhD); bioinformatics (MS, PhD); biophysical chemistry (PhD); computational chemistry (MS, PhD); geochemistry (PhD); organic/medicinal chemistry (MS, PhD); physical chemistry (MS). PhD in geochemistry offered jointly with Department of Geology. Part-time programs available. *Faculty:* 38 full-time (11 women), 10 part-time/adjunct (3 women). *Students:* 107 full-time (57 women), 6 part-time (3 women); includes 25 minority (13 Black or African American, non-Hispanic/Latino; 1 American Indian or Alaska Native, non-Hispanic/Latino; 6 Asian, non-Hispanic/Latino; 4 Hispanic/Latino; 1 Two or more races, non-Hispanic/Latino), 57 international. Average age 28. 125 applicants, 39% accepted, 36 enrolled. In 2012, 28 master's, 12 doctorates awarded. Terminal master's awarded for partial completion of doctoral program. *Degree requirements:* For master's, one foreign language, comprehensive exam (for some programs), thesis (for some programs); for doctorate, one foreign language, comprehensive exam, thesis/dissertation. *Entrance requirements:* For master's and doctorate, GRE. Additional exam requirements/recommendations for international students: Required—TOEFL (minimum score 550 paper-based, 80 iBT) or IELTS (minimum score 6.5). *Application deadline:* For fall admission, 7/1 priority date for domestic students, 7/1 for international students; for winter admission, 11/15 priority date for domestic students, 11/15 for international students; for spring admission, 4/15 priority date for domestic students, 4/15 for international students. Applications are processed on a rolling basis. Application fee: $50. Electronic applications accepted. *Expenses:* Tuition, state resident: full-time $8064; part-time $336 per credit hour. Tuition, nonresident: full-time $28,800; part-time $1200 per credit hour. *Required fees:* $2128; $1064 per semester. Tuition and fees vary according to course load and program. *Financial support:* Fellowships with full tuition reimbursements, research assistantships with full tuition reimbursements, and teaching assistantships with full tuition reimbursements available. *Faculty research:* Analytical chemistry, biological/biochemistry, biophysical/computational chemistry, chemical education, organic/medicinal chemistry. *Total annual research expenditures:* $4 million. *Unit head:* Dr. Binghe Wang, Department Chair, 404-413-5500, Fax: 404-413-5506, E-mail: chemchair@gsu.edu. *Application contact:* Rita S. Bennett, Academic Specialist,

Peterson's Graduate Programs in the Physical Sciences, Mathematics, Agricultural Sciences, the Environment & Natural Resources 2014
www.petersonsbooks.com 55

404-413-5497, Fax: 404-413-5505, E-mail: rsb423@gsu.edu. Website: http://chemistry.gsu.edu/.

Governors State University, College of Arts and Sciences, Program in Analytical Chemistry, University Park, IL 60484. Offers MS. Part-time and evening/weekend programs available. *Degree requirements:* For master's, thesis or alternative. *Expenses: Tuition, area resident:* Part-time $272 per credit hour. Tuition, state resident: part-time $272 per credit hour. Tuition, nonresident: part-time $544 per credit hour. *Required fees:* $46 per credit hour. $133 per term. Tuition and fees vary according to degree level and program. *Faculty research:* Electrochemistry, photochemistry, spectrochemistry, biochemistry.

Howard University, Graduate School, Department of Chemistry, Washington, DC 20059-0002. Offers analytical chemistry (MS, PhD); atmospheric (MS, PhD); biochemistry (MS, PhD); environmental (MS, PhD); inorganic chemistry (MS, PhD); organic chemistry (MS, PhD); physical chemistry (MS, PhD). Terminal master's awarded for partial completion of doctoral program. *Degree requirements:* For master's, comprehensive exam, thesis, teaching experience; for doctorate, comprehensive exam, thesis/dissertation, teaching experience. *Entrance requirements:* For master's, GRE General Test, minimum GPA of 2.7; for doctorate, GRE General Test, minimum GPA of 3.0. Additional exam requirements/recommendations for international students: Required—TOEFL. Electronic applications accepted. *Faculty research:* Synthetic organics, materials, natural products, mass spectrometry.

Illinois Institute of Technology, Graduate College, College of Science and Letters, Department of Biological and Chemical Sciences, Chemistry Division, Chicago, IL 60616. Offers analytical chemistry (M Ch); chemistry (M Chem, MS, PhD); materials and chemical synthesis (M Ch). Part-time and evening/weekend programs available. Postbaccalaureate distance learning degree programs offered (no on-campus study). *Faculty:* 12 full-time (4 women). *Students:* 41 full-time (17 women), 51 part-time (25 women); includes 6 minority (2 Black or African American, non-Hispanic/Latino; 1 Asian, non-Hispanic/Latino; 2 Hispanic/Latino; 1 Two or more races, non-Hispanic/Latino), 36 international. Average age 29. 151 applicants, 84% accepted, 36 enrolled. In 2012, 13 master's awarded. Terminal master's awarded for partial completion of doctoral program. *Degree requirements:* For master's, comprehensive exam, thesis (for some programs); for doctorate, comprehensive exam, thesis/dissertation. *Entrance requirements:* For master's, GRE General Test (minimum score 1000 Quantitative and Verbal, 2.5 Analytical Writing), minimum undergraduate GPA of 3.0; for doctorate, GRE General Test (minimum score 1100 Quantitative and Verbal, 3.0 Analytical Writing), GRE Subject Test, minimum undergraduate GPA of 3.0. Additional exam requirements/recommendations for international students: Required—TOEFL (minimum score 523 paper-based; 70 iBT); Recommended—IELTS. *Application deadline:* For fall admission, 5/1 for domestic and international students; for spring admission, 10/15 for domestic and international students. Applications are processed on a rolling basis. Application fee: $40. Electronic applications accepted. *Expenses: Tuition:* Full-time $20,142; part-time $1119 per credit hour. *Required fees:* $605 per semester. One-time fee: $255. Tuition and fees vary according to program and student level. *Financial support:* Fellowships with full and partial tuition reimbursements, research assistantships with full and partial tuition reimbursements, teaching assistantships with full and partial tuition reimbursements, Federal Work-Study, institutionally sponsored loans, scholarships/grants, health care benefits, tuition waivers (partial), and unspecified assistantships available. Support available to part-time students. Financial award applicants required to submit FAFSA. *Faculty research:* Synthesis and analysis of inorganic nanoparticles; synthetic and mechanistic organic chemistry; synthesis of penicillin-related compounds; design, synthesis and property studies of nanomaterials for applications in chemical sensing, energy storage and biomedical usage; scanning probe microscopy. *Total annual research expenditures:* $201,793. *Unit head:* Dr. Rong Wang, Associate Chair, 312-567-3121, Fax: 312-567-3494, E-mail: wangr@iit.edu. *Application contact:* Deborah Gibson, Director, Graduate Admission, 866-472-3448, Fax: 312-567-3138, E-mail: inquiry.grad@iit.edu. Website: http://www.iit.edu/csl/che/.

Indiana University Bloomington, University Graduate School, College of Arts and Sciences, Department of Chemistry, Bloomington, IN 47405. Offers analytical chemistry (PhD); chemical biology chemistry (PhD); chemistry (MAT); inorganic chemistry (PhD); materials chemistry (PhD); organic chemistry (PhD); physical chemistry (PhD). *Faculty:* 42 full-time (4 women). *Students:* 215 full-time (85 women), 4 part-time (1 woman); includes 21 minority (8 Black or African American, non-Hispanic/Latino; 9 Asian, non-Hispanic/Latino; 1 Hispanic/Latino; 3 Two or more races, non-Hispanic/Latino), 69 international. Average age 27. 329 applicants, 40% accepted, 50 enrolled. In 2012, 12 master's, 20 doctorates awarded. Terminal master's awarded for partial completion of doctoral program. *Degree requirements:* For master's, thesis; for doctorate, thesis/dissertation. *Entrance requirements:* For master's and doctorate, GRE General Test, GRE Subject Test. Additional exam requirements/recommendations for international students: Required—TOEFL. *Application deadline:* For fall admission, 1/15 priority date for domestic students, 12/15 for international students. Applications are processed on a rolling basis. Application fee: $55 ($65 for international students). *Financial support:* In 2012–13, 200 students received support, including 10 fellowships with full tuition reimbursements available, 76 research assistantships with full tuition reimbursements available, 111 teaching assistantships with full tuition reimbursements available; Federal Work-Study and institutionally sponsored loans also available. *Faculty research:* Synthesis of complex natural products, organic reaction mechanisms, organic electrochemistry, transitive-metal chemistry, solid-state and surface chemistry. *Total annual research expenditures:* $7.7 million. *Unit head:* David Giedroc, Chairperson, 812-855-6239, E-mail: chemchair@indiana.edu. *Application contact:* Daniel Mindiola, Director of Graduate Admissions, 812-855-2069, Fax: 812-855-8385, E-mail: mindiola@indiana.edu. Website: http://www.chem.indiana.edu/.

Iowa State University of Science and Technology, Program in Analytical Chemistry, Ames, IA 50011. Offers PhD. *Entrance requirements:* For doctorate, official academic transcripts, resume, three letters of recommendation. Additional exam requirements/recommendations for international students: Required—TOEFL (minimum score 570 paper-based; 89 iBT), IELTS (minimum score 6.5). *Application deadline:* For fall admission, 2/1 for domestic and international students. Application fee: $60 ($90 for international students). Electronic applications accepted. *Application contact:* Lynette Edsall, Application Contact, 800-521-2436, Fax: 515-294-0105, E-mail: chemgrad@iastate.edu.

Kansas State University, Graduate School, College of Arts and Sciences, Department of Chemistry, Manhattan, KS 66506. Offers analytical chemistry (MS); biological chemistry (MS); chemistry (PhD); inorganic chemistry (MS); materials chemistry (MS); organic chemistry (MS); physical chemistry (MS). *Faculty:* 17 full-time (1 woman). *Students:* 71 full-time (36 women); includes 1 minority (Asian, non-Hispanic/Latino), 59 international. Average age 28. 108 applicants, 35% accepted, 15 enrolled. In 2012, 5 master's, 9 doctorates awarded. Terminal master's awarded for partial completion of doctoral program. *Degree requirements:* For master's, thesis; for doctorate, thesis/dissertation. *Entrance requirements:* For master's and doctorate, GRE, minimum GPA of 3.0. Additional exam requirements/recommendations for international students: Required—TOEFL (minimum score 550 paper-based). *Application deadline:* For fall admission, 2/1 priority date for domestic students, 2/1 for international students; for spring admission, 8/1 priority date for domestic students, 8/1 for international students. Applications are processed on a rolling basis. Application fee: $50 ($75 for international students). Electronic applications accepted. *Financial support:* In 2012–13, 39 research assistantships (averaging $18,182 per year), 24 teaching assistantships with full tuition reimbursements (averaging $18,106 per year) were awarded; institutionally sponsored loans and scholarships/grants also available. Support available to part-time students. Financial award application deadline: 3/1; financial award applicants required to submit FAFSA. *Faculty research:* Inorganic chemistry, organic and biological chemistry, analytical chemistry, physical chemistry, materials chemistry and nanotechnology. *Total annual research expenditures:* $2.8 million. *Unit head:* Eric Maatta, Head, 785-532-6665, Fax: 785-532-6666, E-mail: eam@ksu.edu. *Application contact:* Christer Aakeroy, Director, 785-532-6096, Fax: 785-532-6666, E-mail: aakeroy@ksu.edu. Website: http://www.k-state.edu/chem/.

Kent State University, College of Arts and Sciences, Department of Chemistry and Biochemistry, Kent, OH 44242-0001. Offers analytical chemistry (MS, PhD); biochemistry (MS, PhD); chemistry (MA); inorganic chemistry (MS, PhD); organic chemistry (MS, PhD); physical chemistry (MS, PhD). Terminal master's awarded for partial completion of doctoral program. *Degree requirements:* For master's, comprehensive exam, thesis; for doctorate, comprehensive exam, thesis/dissertation. *Entrance requirements:* For master's and doctorate, placement exam, GRE General Test, GRE Subject Test (recommended), minimum GPA of 2.75. Additional exam requirements/recommendations for international students: Required—TOEFL (minimum score 525 paper-based; 71 iBT). Electronic applications accepted. *Expenses:* Tuition, state resident: full-time $8424; part-time $468 per credit hour. Tuition, nonresident: full-time $14,580; part-time $810 per credit hour. Tuition and fees vary according to course load. *Faculty research:* Biological chemistry, materials chemistry, molecular spectroscopy.

See Display on page 73 and Close-Up on page 127.

Laurentian University, School of Graduate Studies and Research, Programme in Chemistry and Biochemistry, Sudbury, ON P3E 2C6, Canada. Offers analytical chemistry (M Sc); biochemistry (M Sc); environmental chemistry (M Sc); organic chemistry (M Sc); physical/theoretical chemistry (M Sc). Part-time programs available. *Degree requirements:* For master's, thesis or alternative. *Entrance requirements:* For master's, honors degree with minimum second class. *Faculty research:* Cell cycle checkpoints, kinetic modeling, toxicology to metal stress, quantum chemistry, biogeochemistry metal speciation.

Marquette University, Graduate School, College of Arts and Sciences, Department of Chemistry, Milwaukee, WI 53201-1881. Offers analytical chemistry (MS, PhD); bioanalytical chemistry (MS, PhD); biophysical chemistry (MS, PhD); chemical physics (MS, PhD); inorganic chemistry (MS, PhD); organic chemistry (MS, PhD); physical chemistry (MS, PhD). Part-time programs available. Terminal master's awarded for partial completion of doctoral program. *Degree requirements:* For master's, comprehensive exam; for doctorate, thesis/dissertation, cumulative exams. *Entrance requirements:* For master's and doctorate, official transcripts from all current and previous colleges/universities except Marquette, three letters of recommendation from individuals familiar with the applicant's academic work. Additional exam requirements/recommendations for international students: Required—TOEFL (minimum score 530 paper-based). Electronic applications accepted. *Faculty research:* Inorganic complexes, laser Raman spectroscopy, organic synthesis, synthetic bioinorganic chemistry, electro-active organic molecules.

McMaster University, School of Graduate Studies, Faculty of Science, Department of Chemistry, Hamilton, ON L8S 4M2, Canada. Offers analytical chemistry (M Sc, PhD); chemical physics (M Sc, PhD); chemistry (M Sc, PhD); inorganic chemistry (M Sc, PhD); organic chemistry (M Sc, PhD); physical chemistry (M Sc, PhD); polymer chemistry (M Sc, PhD). Part-time programs available. Terminal master's awarded for partial completion of doctoral program. *Degree requirements:* For master's, thesis; for doctorate, comprehensive exam, thesis/dissertation. *Entrance requirements:* For master's, minimum B+ average. Additional exam requirements/recommendations for international students: Required—TOEFL (minimum score 550 paper-based).

Old Dominion University, College of Sciences, Program in Chemistry, Norfolk, VA 23529. Offers analytical chemistry (MS); biochemistry (MS); chemistry (PhD); environmental chemistry (MS); organic chemistry (MS); physical chemistry (MS). Part-time and evening/weekend programs available. *Faculty:* 19 full-time (7 women), 3 part-time/adjunct (all women). *Students:* 36 full-time (20 women); includes 1 minority (Black or African American, non-Hispanic/Latino), 14 international. Average age 27. 35 applicants, 60% accepted, 8 enrolled. In 2012, 4 master's, 1 doctorate awarded. *Degree requirements:* For master's, comprehensive exam, thesis. *Entrance requirements:* For master's, GRE General Test, minimum GPA of 3.0 in major, 2.5 overall; for doctorate, GRE General Test. Additional exam requirements/recommendations for international students: Required—TOEFL. *Application deadline:* For fall admission, 7/1 for domestic students, 1/15 for international students; for spring admission, 11/1 for domestic students, 8/15 for international students. Applications are processed on a rolling basis. Application fee: $30. Electronic applications accepted. *Expenses:* Tuition, state resident: full-time $9432; part-time $393 per credit hour. Tuition, nonresident: full-time $23,928; part-time $997 per credit hour. *Required fees:* $59 per semester. One-time fee: $50. *Financial support:* In 2012–13, 6 students received support, including fellowships (averaging $18,000 per year), research assistantships with tuition reimbursements available (averaging $21,000 per year), teaching assistantships with tuition reimbursements available (averaging $18,000 per year); career-related internships or fieldwork, scholarships/grants, and unspecified assistantships also available. Financial award application deadline: 2/15; financial award applicants required to submit FAFSA. *Faculty research:* Biogeochemistry, materials chemistry, computational chemistry, organic chemistry, biofuels. *Total annual research expenditures:* $2.6 million. *Unit head:* Dr. Craig A. Bayse, Graduate Program Director, 757-683-4097, Fax: 757-683-4628, E-mail: chemgpd@odu.edu. *Application contact:* Valerie DeCosta, Grants and Graduate Program Assistant, 757-683-6979, Fax: 757-683-4628, E-mail: chemgpd@odu.edu.

Oregon State University, College of Science, Department of Chemistry, Corvallis, OR 97331. Offers analytical chemistry (MS, PhD); chemistry (MA, MAIS); inorganic chemistry (MS, PhD); nuclear and radiation chemistry (MS, PhD); organic chemistry (MS, PhD); physical chemistry (MS, PhD). Part-time programs available. *Faculty:* 28 full-time (7 women), 9 part-time/adjunct (1 woman). *Students:* 101 full-time (28 women), 1 part-time (0 women); includes 5 minority (2 Asian, non-Hispanic/Latino; 1 Hispanic/Latino; 2 Two or more races, non-Hispanic/Latino), 54 international. Average age 28. 98 applicants, 30% accepted, 27 enrolled. In 2012, 4 master's, 16 doctorates awarded. Terminal master's awarded for partial completion of doctoral program. *Degree requirements:* For master's, one foreign language, thesis; for doctorate, one foreign language, thesis/dissertation. *Entrance requirements:* For master's and doctorate, minimum GPA of 3.0 in last 90 hours of course work. Additional exam requirements/recommendations for international students: Required—TOEFL. *Application deadline:* For fall admission, 3/1 priority date for domestic students. Applications are processed on a rolling basis. Application fee: $50. *Expenses:* Tuition, state resident: full-time $11,367; part-time $421 per credit hour. Tuition, nonresident: full-time $18,279; part-time $677 per credit hour. *Required fees:* $1478. One-time fee: $300 full-time. Tuition and fees vary according to course load and program. *Financial support:* Fellowships, research assistantships, teaching assistantships, and institutionally sponsored loans available. Support available to part-time students. Financial award application deadline: 2/1. *Faculty research:* Solid state chemistry, enzyme reaction mechanisms, structure and dynamics of gas molecules, chemiluminescence, nonlinear optical spectroscopy. *Unit head:* Dr. Rich G. Carter, Professor/Chair, 541-737-9486, E-mail: rich.carter@oregonstate.edu.

Purdue University, Graduate School, College of Science, Department of Chemistry, West Lafayette, IN 47907. Offers analytical chemistry (MS, PhD); biochemistry (MS, PhD); chemical education (MS, PhD); inorganic chemistry (MS, PhD); organic chemistry (MS, PhD); physical chemistry (MS, PhD). *Faculty:* 42 full-time (14 women), 7 part-time/adjunct (0 women). *Students:* 275 full-time (102 women), 23 part-time (8 women); includes 34 minority (16 Black or African American, non-Hispanic/Latino; 5 Asian, non-Hispanic/Latino; 11 Hispanic/Latino; 2 Two or more races, non-Hispanic/Latino), 94 international. Average age 27. 716 applicants, 26% accepted, 66 enrolled. In 2012, 18 master's, 52 doctorates awarded. Terminal master's awarded for partial completion of doctoral program. *Degree requirements:* For master's, thesis; for doctorate, comprehensive exam, thesis/dissertation. *Entrance requirements:* For master's and doctorate, minimum undergraduate GPA of 3.0. Additional exam requirements/recommendations for international students: Required—TOEFL (minimum score 77 iBT); Recommended—TWE. *Application deadline:* For fall admission, 2/15 priority date for domestic students, 1/1 for international students. Applications are processed on a rolling basis. Application fee: $60 ($75 for international students). Electronic applications accepted. *Financial support:* In 2012–13, 2 fellowships with partial tuition reimbursements (averaging $18,000 per year), 55 teaching assistantships with partial tuition reimbursements (averaging $18,000 per year) were awarded; research assistantships with partial tuition reimbursements and tuition waivers (partial) also available. Support available to part-time students. Financial award applicants required to submit FAFSA. *Unit head:* Dr. Paul B. Shepson, Head, 765-494-5203, E-mail: pshepson@purdue.edu. *Application contact:* Betty L. Hatfield, Director of Graduate Admissions, 765-494-5208, E-mail: bettyh@purdue.edu.

Rutgers, The State University of New Jersey, Newark, Graduate School, Program in Chemistry, Newark, NJ 07102. Offers analytical chemistry (MS, PhD); biochemistry (MS, PhD); inorganic chemistry (MS, PhD); organic chemistry (MS, PhD); physical chemistry (MS, PhD). Part-time and evening/weekend programs available. Terminal master's awarded for partial completion of doctoral program. *Degree requirements:* For master's, thesis optional, cumulative exams; for doctorate, thesis/dissertation, exams, research proposal. *Entrance requirements:* For master's and doctorate, GRE General Test, minimum undergraduate B average. Additional exam requirements/recommendations for international students: Required—TOEFL. Electronic applications accepted. *Faculty research:* Medicinal chemistry, natural products, isotope effects, biophysics and biorganic approaches to enzyme mechanisms, organic and organometallic synthesis.

Seton Hall University, College of Arts and Sciences, Department of Chemistry and Biochemistry, South Orange, NJ 07079-2697. Offers analytical chemistry (MS, PhD); biochemistry (MS, PhD); chemistry (MS); inorganic chemistry (MS, PhD); organic chemistry (MS, PhD); physical chemistry (MS, PhD). Part-time and evening/weekend programs available. Terminal master's awarded for partial completion of doctoral program. *Degree requirements:* For master's, thesis optional; for doctorate, comprehensive exam, thesis/dissertation. *Entrance requirements:* Additional exam requirements/recommendations for international students: Required—TOEFL. Electronic applications accepted. *Faculty research:* DNA metal reactions; chromatography; bioinorganic, biophysical, organometallic, polymer chemistry; heterogeneous catalyst; synthetic organic and carbohydrate chemistry.

Southern University and Agricultural and Mechanical College, Graduate School, College of Sciences, Department of Chemistry, Baton Rouge, LA 70813. Offers analytical chemistry (MS); biochemistry (MS); environmental sciences (MS); inorganic chemistry (MS); organic chemistry (MS); physical chemistry (MS). *Degree requirements:* For master's, thesis. *Entrance requirements:* For master's, GMAT or GRE General Test. Additional exam requirements/recommendations for international students: Required—TOEFL (minimum score 525 paper-based). *Faculty research:* Synthesis of macrocyclic ligands, latex accelerators, anticancer drugs, biosensors, absorption isotheums, isolation of specific enzymes from plants.

Stevens Institute of Technology, Graduate School, Charles V. Schaefer Jr. School of Engineering, Department of Chemistry, Chemical Biology and Biomedical Engineering, Hoboken, NJ 07030. Offers analytical chemistry (PhD, Certificate); bioinformatics (PhD, Certificate); biomedical chemistry (Certificate); biomedical engineering (M Eng, Certificate); chemical biology (MS, PhD, Certificate); chemical physiology (Certificate); chemistry (MS, PhD); organic chemistry (PhD); physical chemistry (PhD); polymer chemistry (PhD, Certificate). Part-time and evening/weekend programs available. Postbaccalaureate distance learning degree programs offered (no on-campus study). Terminal master's awarded for partial completion of doctoral program. *Degree requirements:* For master's, thesis or alternative; for doctorate, one foreign language, thesis/dissertation; for Certificate, project or thesis. *Entrance requirements:* Additional exam requirements/recommendations for international students: Required—TOEFL. Electronic applications accepted. *Faculty research:* Biochemical reaction engineering, polymerization engineering, reactor design, biochemical process control and synthesis.

Tufts University, Graduate School of Arts and Sciences, Department of Chemistry, Medford, MA 02155. Offers analytical chemistry (MS, PhD); bioorganic chemistry (MS, PhD); environmental chemistry (MS, PhD); inorganic chemistry (MS, PhD); organic chemistry (MS, PhD); physical chemistry (MS, PhD). Terminal master's awarded for partial completion of doctoral program. *Degree requirements:* For master's, thesis optional; for doctorate, thesis/dissertation. *Entrance requirements:* For master's and doctorate, GRE General Test, GRE Subject Test. Additional exam requirements/recommendations for international students: Required—TOEFL (minimum score 600 paper-based; 80 iBT). Electronic applications accepted. *Expenses: Tuition:* Full-time $42,856; part-time $1072 per credit hour. *Required fees:* $730. Full-time tuition and fees vary according to degree level, program and student level. Part-time tuition and fees vary according to course load.

University of Calgary, Faculty of Graduate Studies, Faculty of Science, Department of Chemistry, Calgary, AB T2N 1N4, Canada. Offers analytical chemistry (M Sc, PhD); applied chemistry (M Sc, PhD); inorganic chemistry (M Sc, PhD); organic chemistry (M Sc, PhD); physical chemistry (M Sc, PhD); polymer chemistry (M Sc, PhD); theoretical chemistry (M Sc, PhD). *Degree requirements:* For master's, thesis; for doctorate, thesis/dissertation, candidacy exam. *Entrance requirements:* For master's, minimum GPA of 3.0; for doctorate, honors B Sc degree with minimum GPA of 3.7 or M Sc with minimum GPA of 3.3. Additional exam requirements/recommendations for international students: Required—TOEFL (minimum score 580 paper-based). Electronic applications accepted. *Faculty research:* Chemical analysis, chemical dynamics, synthesis theory.

University of Cincinnati, Graduate School, McMicken College of Arts and Sciences, Department of Chemistry, Cincinnati, OH 45221. Offers analytical chemistry (MS, PhD); biochemistry (MS, PhD); inorganic chemistry (MS, PhD); organic chemistry (MS, PhD); physical chemistry (MS, PhD); polymer chemistry (MS, PhD); sensors (PhD). Part-time and evening/weekend programs available. Terminal master's awarded for partial completion of doctoral program. *Degree requirements:* For master's, thesis optional; for doctorate, comprehensive exam, thesis/dissertation. *Entrance requirements:* For master's and doctorate, GRE General Test. Additional exam requirements/recommendations for international students: Required—TOEFL (minimum score 580 paper-based). Electronic applications accepted. *Faculty research:* Biomedical chemistry, laser chemistry, surface science, chemical sensors, synthesis.

University of Georgia, Franklin College of Arts and Sciences, Department of Chemistry, Athens, GA 30602. Offers analytical chemistry (MS, PhD); inorganic chemistry (MS, PhD); organic chemistry (MS, PhD); physical chemistry (MS, PhD). Terminal master's awarded for partial completion of doctoral program. *Degree requirements:* For master's, thesis; for doctorate, one foreign language, thesis/dissertation. *Entrance requirements:* For master's and doctorate, GRE General Test. Additional exam requirements/recommendations for international students: Required—TOEFL. Electronic applications accepted.

University of Louisville, Graduate School, College of Arts and Sciences, Department of Chemistry, Louisville, KY 40292-0001. Offers analytical chemistry (MS, PhD); biochemistry (MS, PhD); chemical physics (PhD); inorganic chemistry (MS, PhD); organic chemistry (MS, PhD); physical chemistry (MS, PhD). *Students:* 45 full-time (21 women), 5 part-time (1 woman); includes 1 minority (Hispanic/Latino), 35 international. Average age 28. 78 applicants, 17% accepted, 9 enrolled. In 2012, 19 master's, 7 doctorates awarded. Terminal master's awarded for partial completion of doctoral program. *Degree requirements:* For master's, variable foreign language requirement, comprehensive exam, thesis optional; for doctorate, variable foreign language requirement, comprehensive exam, thesis/dissertation. *Entrance requirements:* For master's and doctorate, BA or BS coursework. Additional exam requirements/recommendations for international students: Required—TOEFL. *Application deadline:* For fall admission, 3/15 for domestic and international students; for winter admission, 9/15 for domestic and international students. Applications are processed on a rolling basis. Application fee: $60. Electronic applications accepted. *Financial support:* In 2012–13, 33 teaching assistantships with full tuition reimbursements (averaging $22,000 per year) were awarded; fellowships with full tuition reimbursements, research assistantships with full tuition reimbursements, career-related internships or fieldwork, scholarships/grants, traineeships, health care benefits, and unspecified assistantships also available. Support available to part-time students. Financial award application deadline: 3/15. *Faculty research:* Computational chemistry, biophysics nuclear magnetic resonance, synthetic organic chemistry, synthetic inorganic chemistry, medicinal chemistry, protein chemistry, enzymology, nanochemistry, electrochemistry, analytical chemistry, synthetic biology, bioinformatics. *Total annual research expenditures:* $2.5 million. *Unit head:* Dr. Richard J. Wittebort, Professor/Chair, 502-852-6613. *Application contact:* Sherry Nalley, Administrator, 502-852-6798.

The University of Manchester, School of Chemical Engineering and Analytical Science, Manchester, United Kingdom. Offers biocatalysis (M Phil, PhD); chemical engineering (M Phil, PhD); chemical engineering and analytical science (M Phil, D Eng, PhD); colloids, crystals, interfaces and materials (M Phil, PhD); environment and sustainable technology (M Phil, PhD); instrumentation (M Phil, PhD); multi-scale modeling (M Phil, PhD); process integration (M Phil, PhD); systems biology (M Phil, PhD).

University of Maryland, College Park, Academic Affairs, College of Computer, Mathematical and Natural Sciences, Department of Chemistry and Biochemistry, Chemistry Program, College Park, MD 20742. Offers analytical chemistry (MS, PhD); inorganic chemistry (MS, PhD); organic chemistry (MS, PhD); physical chemistry (MS, PhD). Part-time and evening/weekend programs available. *Students:* 113 full-time (64 women), 2 part-time (0 women); includes 19 minority (11 Black or African American, non-Hispanic/Latino; 4 Asian, non-Hispanic/Latino; 2 Hispanic/Latino; 2 Two or more races, non-Hispanic/Latino), 44 international. 339 applicants, 27% accepted, 20 enrolled. In 2012, 7 master's, 14 doctorates awarded. Terminal master's awarded for partial completion of doctoral program. *Degree requirements:* For master's, thesis optional; for doctorate, thesis/dissertation, 2 seminar presentations, oral exam. *Entrance requirements:* For master's and doctorate, GRE General Test, GRE Subject Test (recommended), minimum GPA of 3.0, 3 letters of recommendation. Additional exam requirements/recommendations for international students: Required—TOEFL. *Application deadline:* For fall admission, 2/1 for domestic and international students; for spring admission, 6/1 for domestic and international students. Applications are processed on a rolling basis. Application fee: $75. Electronic applications accepted. *Expenses:* Tuition, state resident: part-time $551 per credit. Tuition, nonresident: part-time $1188 per credit. Part-time tuition and fees vary according to program. *Financial support:* In 2012–13, 14 fellowships with full and partial tuition reimbursements (averaging $20,017 per year), 52 research assistantships (averaging $19,868 per year), 44 teaching assistantships (averaging $19,209 per year) were awarded. Financial award applicants required to submit FAFSA. *Faculty research:* Environmental chemistry, nuclear chemistry, lunar and environmental analysis, x-ray crystallography. *Unit head:* Dr. Michael Doyle, Chairperson, 301-405-1795, Fax: 301-314-2779, E-mail: mdoyle3@umd.edu. *Application contact:* Dr. Charles A. Caramello, Dean of Graduate School, 301-405-0358, Fax: 301-314-9305.

University of Massachusetts Lowell, College of Sciences, Department of Chemistry, Lowell, MA 01854-2881. Offers analytical chemistry (PhD); biochemistry (PhD); chemistry (MS, PhD); environmental studies (PhD); green chemistry (PhD); inorganic chemistry (PhD); organic chemistry (PhD); polymer science (MS). Terminal master's awarded for partial completion of doctoral program. *Degree requirements:* For master's, thesis; for doctorate, 2 foreign languages, thesis/dissertation. *Entrance requirements:* For master's and doctorate, GRE General Test. Electronic applications accepted.

University of Memphis, Graduate School, College of Arts and Sciences, Department of Chemistry, Memphis, TN 38152. Offers analytical chemistry (MS, PhD); computational chemistry (MS, PhD); inorganic chemistry (MS, PhD); organic chemistry (MS, PhD); physical chemistry (MS, PhD). Part-time programs available. Terminal master's awarded for partial completion of doctoral program. *Degree requirements:* For master's, comprehensive exam, thesis or alternative; for doctorate, comprehensive exam, thesis/dissertation. *Entrance requirements:* For master's and doctorate, GRE General Test, admission to Graduate School plus 32 undergraduate hours in chemistry. Additional exam requirements/recommendations for international students: Required—TOEFL. Electronic applications accepted. *Faculty research:* Computational chemistry, materials chemistry, organic/polymer synthesis, drug design/delivery, water chemistry.

University of Michigan, Horace H. Rackham School of Graduate Studies, College of Literature, Science, and the Arts, Department of Chemistry, Ann Arbor, MI 48109-1055. Offers analytical chemistry (PhD); chemical biology (PhD); inorganic chemistry (PhD); material chemistry (PhD); organic chemistry (PhD); physical chemistry (PhD). *Degree requirements:* For doctorate, thesis/dissertation, oral defense of dissertation, organic cumulative proficiency exams. *Entrance requirements:* For doctorate, GRE General Test, GRE Subject Test (recommended), 3 letters of recommendation. Additional exam requirements/recommendations for international students: Required—TOEFL (minimum score 560 paper-based; 84 iBT). Electronic applications accepted. *Faculty research:* Biological catalysis, protein engineering, chemical sensors, de novo metalloprotein design, supramolecular architecture.

University of Missouri, Graduate School, College of Arts and Sciences, Department of Chemistry, Columbia, MO 65211. Offers analytical chemistry (MS, PhD); inorganic chemistry (MS, PhD); organic chemistry (MS, PhD); physical chemistry (MS, PhD). *Faculty:* 22 full-time (4 women), 1 part-time/adjunct (0 women). *Students:* 110 full-time (42 women), 9 part-time (5 women); includes 10 minority (3 Black or African American, non-Hispanic/Latino; 3 Asian, non-Hispanic/Latino; 2 Hispanic/Latino; 2 Two or more races, non-Hispanic/Latino), 47 international. Average age 27. 94 applicants, 21% accepted, 15 enrolled. In 2012, 2 master's, 5 doctorates awarded. *Degree requirements:* For master's, thesis; for doctorate, one foreign language, comprehensive exam, thesis/dissertation. *Entrance requirements:* For master's, GRE General Test, minimum GPA of 3.0; for doctorate, GRE General Test (minimum score: Verbal 450, Quantitative 600, Analytical 3), minimum GPA of 3.0. Additional exam requirements/recommendations for international students: Required—TOEFL (minimum score 600 paper-based; 100 iBT). *Application deadline:* For fall admission, 2/1 priority date for domestic students, 2/1 for international students; for winter admission, 10/15 for domestic and international students. Applications are processed on a rolling basis. Application fee: $55 ($75 for international students). Electronic applications accepted. *Expenses:* Tuition, state resident: full-time $6057. Tuition, nonresident: full-time $15,683. *Required fees:* $1000. *Financial support:* In 2012–13, 9 fellowships with full tuition reimbursements, 15 research assistantships with full tuition reimbursements, 78 teaching assistantships with full tuition reimbursements were awarded; institutionally sponsored loans, traineeships, health care benefits, and unspecified assistantships also available. *Faculty research:* Analytical, organic, biological, physical, inorganic and radiochemistry. *Unit head:* Dr. Jerry Atwood, Department Chair, 573-882-8374, E-mail: atwoodj@missouri.edu. *Application contact:* Jerry Brightwell, Administrative Assistant, 573-884-6832, E-mail: brightwellj@missouri.edu. Website: http://chemistry.missouri.edu/.

University of Missouri–Kansas City, College of Arts and Sciences, Department of Chemistry, Kansas City, MO 64110-2499. Offers analytical chemistry (MS, PhD); inorganic chemistry (MS, PhD); organic chemistry (MS, PhD); physical chemistry (MS, PhD); polymer chemistry (MS, PhD). PhD (interdisciplinary) offered through the School of Graduate Studies. Part-time and evening/weekend programs available. *Faculty:* 15 full-time (3 women), 2 part-time/adjunct (0 women). *Students:* 7 part-time (3 women); includes 3 minority (2 Black or African American, non-Hispanic/Latino; 1 Hispanic/Latino). Average age 38. 19 applicants, 37% accepted, 3 enrolled. In 2012, 2 master's awarded. *Degree requirements:* For master's, thesis (for some programs); for doctorate, thesis/dissertation. *Entrance requirements:* For master's, equivalent of American Chemical Society approved bachelor's degree in chemistry; for doctorate, GRE General Test, equivalent of American Chemical Society approved bachelor's degree in chemistry. Additional exam requirements/recommendations for international students: Required—TOEFL (minimum score 550 paper-based; 80 iBT), TWE. *Application deadline:* For fall admission, 4/15 for domestic and international students; for spring admission, 10/15 for domestic and international students. Applications are processed on a rolling basis. Application fee: $45 ($50 for international students). Electronic applications accepted. *Expenses:* Tuition, state resident: full-time $5972.40; part-time $331.80 per credit hour. Tuition, nonresident: full-time $15,417; part-time $856.50 per credit hour. *Required fees:* $95.89 per credit hour. Full-time tuition and fees vary according to program.

Financial support: In 2012–13, 6 research assistantships with partial tuition reimbursements (averaging $18,817 per year), 16 teaching assistantships with partial tuition reimbursements (averaging $18,132 per year) were awarded; Federal Work-Study, institutionally sponsored loans, and scholarships/grants also available. Support available to part-time students. Financial award application deadline: 3/1; financial award applicants required to submit FAFSA. *Faculty research:* Molecular spectroscopy, characterization and synthesis of materials and compounds, computational chemistry, natural products, drug delivery systems and anti-tumor agents. *Unit head:* Dr. Kathleen V. Kilway, Chair, 816-235-2289, Fax: 816-235-5502. *Application contact:* Graduate Recruiting Committee, 816-235-2272, Fax: 816-235-5502, E-mail: umkc-chemdept@umkc.edu. Website: http://cas.umkc.edu/chem/.

The University of Montana, Graduate School, College of Arts and Sciences, Department of Chemistry and Biochemistry, Missoula, MT 59812-0002. Offers chemistry (MS, PhD), including environmental/analytical chemistry, inorganic chemistry, organic chemistry, physical chemistry. Terminal master's awarded for partial completion of doctoral program. *Degree requirements:* For master's, thesis (for some programs); for doctorate, thesis/dissertation. *Entrance requirements:* For master's and doctorate, GRE General Test. Additional exam requirements/recommendations for international students: Required—TOEFL (minimum score 575 paper-based). *Faculty research:* Reaction mechanisms and kinetics, inorganic and organic synthesis, analytical chemistry, natural products.

University of Nebraska–Lincoln, Graduate College, College of Arts and Sciences, Department of Chemistry, Lincoln, NE 68588. Offers analytical chemistry (PhD); biochemistry (PhD); chemistry (MS); inorganic chemistry (PhD); materials chemistry (PhD); organic chemistry (PhD); physical chemistry (PhD). *Degree requirements:* For master's, one foreign language, thesis optional, departmental qualifying exam; for doctorate, one foreign language, comprehensive exam, thesis/dissertation, departmental qualifying exams. *Entrance requirements:* For master's and doctorate, GRE. Additional exam requirements/recommendations for international students: Required—TOEFL (minimum score 550 paper-based). Electronic applications accepted. *Faculty research:* Bioorganic and bioinorganic chemistry, biophysical and bioanalytical chemistry, structure-function of DNA and proteins, organometallics, mass spectrometry.

University of Regina, Faculty of Graduate Studies and Research, Faculty of Science, Department of Chemistry and Biochemistry, Regina, SK S4S 0A2, Canada. Offers analytical/environmental chemistry (M Sc, PhD); biophysics of biological interfaces (M Sc, PhD); enzymology/chemical biology (M Sc, PhD); inorganic/organometallic chemistry (M Sc, PhD); signal transduction and mechanisms of cancer cell regulation (M Sc, PhD); supramolecular organic photochemistry and photophysics (M Sc, PhD); synthetic organic chemistry (M Sc, PhD); theoretical/computational chemistry (M Sc, PhD). *Faculty:* 12 full-time (2 women), 3 part-time/adjunct (0 women). *Students:* 11 full-time (6 women), 2 part-time (0 women). 32 applicants, 19% accepted. In 2012, 7 master's awarded. *Degree requirements:* For master's, thesis; for doctorate, thesis/dissertation. *Entrance requirements:* Additional exam requirements/recommendations for international students: Required—TOEFL (minimum score 580 paper-based; 80 iBT), IELTS (minimum score 6.5). *Application deadline:* Applications are processed on a rolling basis. Application fee: $100. Electronic applications accepted. Tuition and fees charges are reported in Canadian dollars. *Expenses: Tuition, area resident:* Full-time $3942 Canadian dollars; part-time $219 Canadian dollars per credit hour. *International tuition:* $4742 Canadian dollars full-time. *Required fees:* $421.55 Canadian dollars; $93.60 Canadian dollars per credit hour. Tuition and fees vary according to course load, degree level and program. *Financial support:* In 2012–13, 5 fellowships (averaging $7,000 per year), 10 teaching assistantships (averaging $2,470 per year) were awarded; research assistantships and scholarships/grants also available. Financial award application deadline: 6/15. *Faculty research:* Asymmetric synthesis and methodology, theoretical and computational chemistry, biophysical biochemistry, analytical and environmental chemistry, chemical biology. *Unit head:* Dr. Lynn Mihichuk, Head, 306-585-4793, Fax: 306-337-2409, E-mail: lynn.mihichuk@uregina.ca. *Application contact:* Dr. Brian Sterenberg, Graduate Program Coordinator, 306-585-4106, Fax: 306-337-2409, E-mail: brian.sterenberg@uregina.ca. Website: http://www.chem.uregina.ca/.

University of Southern Mississippi, Graduate School, College of Science and Technology, Department of Chemistry and Biochemistry, Hattiesburg, MS 39406-0001. Offers analytical chemistry (MS, PhD); biochemistry (MS, PhD); inorganic chemistry (MS, PhD); organic chemistry (MS, PhD); physical chemistry (MS, PhD). *Faculty:* 16 full-time (4 women). *Students:* 26 full-time (9 women); includes 2 minority (1 Black or African American, non-Hispanic/Latino; 1 Asian, non-Hispanic/Latino), 8 international. Average age 27. 63 applicants, 13% accepted, 4 enrolled. In 2012, 2 master's, 4 doctorates awarded. *Degree requirements:* For master's, comprehensive exam, thesis; for doctorate, comprehensive exam, thesis/dissertation. *Entrance requirements:* For master's, GRE General Test, minimum GPA of 2.75 in last 60 hours; for doctorate, GRE General Test, minimum GPA of 3.5. Additional exam requirements/recommendations for international students: Required—TOEFL, IELTS. *Application deadline:* For fall admission, 3/1 priority date for domestic students, 3/1 for international students. Applications are processed on a rolling basis. Application fee: $50. *Financial support:* In 2012–13, 3 research assistantships with full tuition reimbursements (averaging $17,000 per year), 19 teaching assistantships with full tuition reimbursements (averaging $20,700 per year) were awarded; fellowships, Federal Work-Study, institutionally sponsored loans, scholarships/grants, health care benefits, and unspecified assistantships also available. Support available to part-time students. Financial award application deadline: 3/15; financial award applicants required to submit FAFSA. *Faculty research:* Plant biochemistry, photo chemistry, polymer chemistry, x-ray analysis, enzyme chemistry. *Unit head:* Dr. Sabine Heinhorst, Chair, 601-266-4701, Fax: 601-266-6075. Website: http://www.usm.edu/graduateschool/table.php.

University of South Florida, Graduate School, College of Arts and Sciences, Department of Chemistry, Tampa, FL 33620-9951. Offers analytical chemistry (MS, PhD); biochemistry (MS, PhD); computational chemistry (MS, PhD); environmental chemistry (MS, PhD); inorganic chemistry (MS, PhD); organic chemistry (MS); physical chemistry (MS, PhD); polymer chemistry (PhD). Part-time programs available. Terminal master's awarded for partial completion of doctoral program. *Degree requirements:* For master's, comprehensive exam, thesis (for some programs); for doctorate, comprehensive exam, thesis/dissertation. *Entrance requirements:* For master's and doctorate, GRE General Test, minimum GPA of 3.0. Additional exam requirements/recommendations for international students: Required—TOEFL (minimum score 550 paper-based; 79 iBT) or IELTS (minimum score 6.5). Electronic applications accepted. *Faculty research:* Synthesis, bio-organic chemistry, bioinorganic chemistry, environmental chemistry, nuclear magnetic resonance (NMR).

The University of Tennessee, Graduate School, College of Arts and Sciences, Department of Chemistry, Knoxville, TN 37996. Offers analytical chemistry (MS, PhD); chemical physics (PhD); environmental chemistry (MS, PhD); inorganic chemistry (MS, PhD); organic chemistry (MS, PhD); physical chemistry (MS, PhD); polymer chemistry (MS, PhD); theoretical chemistry (PhD). Part-time programs available. Terminal master's awarded for partial completion of doctoral program. *Degree requirements:* For master's, thesis; for doctorate, thesis/dissertation. *Entrance requirements:* For master's and doctorate, GRE General Test, minimum GPA of 2.7. Additional exam requirements/recommendations for international students: Required—TOEFL. Electronic applications accepted. *Expenses:* Tuition, state resident: full-time $9000; part-time $501 per credit hour. Tuition, nonresident: full-time $27,188; part-time $1512 per credit hour. *Required fees:* $1280; $62 per credit hour. Tuition and fees vary according to program.

The University of Texas at Austin, Graduate School, College of Natural Sciences, Department of Chemistry and Biochemistry, Austin, TX 78712-1111. Offers analytical chemistry (PhD); biochemistry (PhD); inorganic chemistry (PhD); organic chemistry (PhD); physical chemistry (PhD). *Entrance requirements:* For doctorate, GRE General Test.

The University of Toledo, College of Graduate Studies, College of Natural Sciences and Mathematics, Department of Chemistry, Toledo, OH 43606-3390. Offers analytical chemistry (MS, PhD); biological chemistry (MS, PhD); inorganic chemistry (MS, PhD); organic chemistry (MS, PhD); physical chemistry (MS, PhD). Part-time programs available. *Faculty:* 23. *Students:* 66 full-time (20 women), 9 part-time (2 women); includes 3 minority (1 Asian, non-Hispanic/Latino; 2 Hispanic/Latino), 50 international. Average age 27. 84 applicants, 26% accepted, 19 enrolled. In 2012, 6 master's, 7 doctorates awarded. *Degree requirements:* For master's, thesis or alternative; for doctorate, thesis/dissertation. *Entrance requirements:* For master's and doctorate, GRE General Test, GRE Subject Test, minimum cumulative point-hour ratio of 2.7 for all previous academic work, three letters of recommendation, statement of purpose, transcripts from all prior institutions attended. Additional exam requirements/recommendations for international students: Required—TOEFL (minimum score 550 paper-based; 80 iBT), IELTS (minimum score 6.5). *Application deadline:* For fall admission, 1/15 priority date for domestic students, 1/15 for international students. Applications are processed on a rolling basis. Application fee: $45 ($75 for international students). Electronic applications accepted. *Financial support:* In 2012–13, 29 research assistantships with full and partial tuition reimbursements (averaging $16,200 per year), 49 teaching assistantships with full and partial tuition reimbursements (averaging $15,682 per year) were awarded; Federal Work-Study, institutionally sponsored loans, scholarships/grants, tuition waivers (full), and unspecified assistantships also available. Support available to part-time students. *Faculty research:* Enzymology, materials chemistry, crystallography, theoretical chemistry. *Unit head:* Dr. Ronald Viola, Chair, 419-530-1582, Fax: 419-530-4033, E-mail: ronald.viola@utoledo.edu. *Application contact:* Graduate School Office, 419-530-4723, Fax: 419-530-4724, E-mail: grdsch@utnet.utoledo.edu. Website: http://www.utoledo.edu/nsm/.

Vanderbilt University, Graduate School, Department of Chemistry, Nashville, TN 37240-1001. Offers analytical chemistry (MAT, MS, PhD); inorganic chemistry (MAT, MS, PhD); organic chemistry (MAT, MS, PhD); physical chemistry (MAT, MS, PhD); theoretical chemistry (MAT, MS). *Faculty:* 21 full-time (3 women). *Students:* 123 full-time (46 women); includes 22 minority (5 Black or African American, non-Hispanic/Latino; 1 American Indian or Alaska Native, non-Hispanic/Latino; 3 Asian, non-Hispanic/Latino; 5 Hispanic/Latino; 8 Two or more races, non-Hispanic/Latino), 14 international. Average age 25. 430 applicants, 15% accepted, 29 enrolled. In 2012, 6 master's, 14 doctorates awarded. Terminal master's awarded for partial completion of doctoral program. *Degree requirements:* For master's, thesis; for doctorate, thesis/dissertation, area, qualifying, and final exams. *Entrance requirements:* For master's and doctorate, GRE General Test, GRE Subject Test (recommended). Additional exam requirements/recommendations for international students: Required—TOEFL (minimum score 570 paper-based; 88 iBT). *Application deadline:* For fall admission, 1/15 for domestic and international students. Application fee: $0.

Analytical Chemistry

Electronic applications accepted. *Financial support:* Fellowships with full and partial tuition reimbursements, research assistantships with full tuition reimbursements, teaching assistantships with full tuition reimbursements, Federal Work-Study, institutionally sponsored loans, scholarships/grants, traineeships, and health care benefits available. Financial award application deadline: 1/15; financial award applicants required to submit CSS PROFILE or FAFSA. *Faculty research:* Chemical synthesis; mechanistic, theoretical, bioorganic, analytical, and spectroscopic chemistry. *Unit head:* Dr. David Cliffel, Director of Graduate Studies, 615-343-3937, Fax: 615-322-4936, E-mail: d.cliffel@vanderbilt.edu. *Application contact:* Sandra Ford, Administrative Assistant, 615-322-8695, Fax: 615-322-4936, E-mail: sandra.e.ford@Vanderbilt.Edu. Website: http://www.vanderbilt.edu/chemistry/.

Virginia Commonwealth University, Graduate School, College of Humanities and Sciences, Department of Chemistry, Richmond, VA 23284-9005. Offers analytical chemistry (MS, PhD); chemical physics (PhD); inorganic chemistry (MS, PhD); organic chemistry (MS, PhD); physical chemistry (MS, PhD). Part-time programs available. Terminal master's awarded for partial completion of doctoral program. *Degree requirements:* For master's, thesis; for doctorate, thesis/dissertation, comprehensive cumulative exams, research proposal. *Entrance requirements:* For master's, GRE General Test, 30 undergraduate credits in chemistry; for doctorate, GRE General Test. Additional exam requirements/recommendations for international students: Required—TOEFL (minimum score 600 paper-based; 100 iBT) or IELTS (minimum score 6.5). Electronic applications accepted. *Faculty research:* Physical, organic, inorganic, analytical, and polymer chemistry; chemical physics.

Wake Forest University, Graduate School of Arts and Sciences, Department of Chemistry, Winston-Salem, NC 27109. Offers analytical chemistry (MS, PhD); inorganic chemistry (MS, PhD); organic chemistry (MS, PhD); physical chemistry (MS, PhD). Part-time programs available. *Degree requirements:* For master's, one foreign language, comprehensive exam, thesis; for doctorate, 2 foreign languages, comprehensive exam, thesis/dissertation. *Entrance requirements:* For master's and doctorate, GRE General Test. Additional exam requirements/recommendations for international students: Required—TOEFL. Electronic applications accepted.

Wayne State University, College of Liberal Arts and Sciences, Department of Chemistry, Detroit, MI 48202. Offers analytical chemistry (PhD); biochemistry (PhD); chemistry (MA, MS); inorganic chemistry (PhD); organic chemistry (PhD); physical chemistry (PhD). *Students:* 167 full-time (79 women), 1 part-time (0 women); includes 12 minority (3 Black or African American, non-Hispanic/Latino; 2 American Indian or Alaska Native, non-Hispanic/Latino; 5 Asian, non-Hispanic/Latino; 2 Hispanic/Latino), 113 international. Average age 28. 440 applicants, 23% accepted, 50 enrolled. In 2012, 5 master's, 15 doctorates awarded. *Degree requirements:* For master's, thesis (for some programs), oral exam; for doctorate, thesis/dissertation, oral exam. *Entrance requirements:* For master's, one year of physics, math through calculus, general chemistry (8 credits), organic chemistry (8 credits), physical chemistry (six credits), quantitative analysis (four credits), and advanced chemistry (three credits); advanced biology (for biochemistry applicants); minimum undergraduate GPA of 2.75 in chemistry and cognate sciences; for doctorate, minimum undergraduate GPA of 3.0 in chemistry and cognate science. Additional exam requirements/recommendations for international students: Required—TOEFL (minimum score 550 paper-based; 79 iBT); Recommended—TWE (minimum score 5.5). *Application deadline:* For fall admission, 2/10 priority date for domestic students, 2/10 for international students; for winter admission, 10/1 priority date for domestic students, 9/1 for international students; for spring admission, 2/1 priority date for domestic students, 1/1 for international students. Applications are processed on a rolling basis. Application fee: $50. Electronic applications accepted. *Expenses:* Tuition, state resident: full-time $12,788; part-time $532.85 per credit hour. Tuition, nonresident: full-time $28,243; part-time $1176.80 per credit hour. *Required fees:* $1367.30; $39.75 per credit hour. $206.65 per semester. Tuition and fees vary according to course load and program. *Financial support:* In 2012–13, 154 students received support, including 10 fellowships with tuition reimbursements available (averaging $23,000 per year), 60 research assistantships with tuition reimbursements available (averaging $19,682 per year), 81 teaching assistantships with tuition reimbursements available (averaging $20,788 per year); scholarships/grants, health care benefits, and unspecified assistantships also available. Financial award application deadline: 7/1. *Faculty research:* Natural products synthesis, molecular biology, molecular mechanics calculations, organometallic chemistry, experimental physical chemistry. *Total annual research expenditures:* $7.2 million. *Unit head:* Dr. James Rigby, Chair, 313-577-3472, Fax: 313-577-8822, E-mail: aa392@wayne.edu. *Application contact:* Dr. Charles Winter, Graduate Director, 313-577-5224, E-mail: chw@chem.wayne.edu. Website: http://chem.wayne.edu/.

West Virginia University, Eberly College of Arts and Sciences, Department of Chemistry, Morgantown, WV 26506. Offers analytical chemistry (MS, PhD); inorganic chemistry (MS, PhD); organic chemistry (MS, PhD); physical chemistry (MS, PhD); theoretical chemistry (MS, PhD). Part-time programs available. Postbaccalaureate distance learning degree programs offered (no on-campus study). Terminal master's awarded for partial completion of doctoral program. *Degree requirements:* For master's, thesis; for doctorate, thesis/dissertation. *Entrance requirements:* For master's, GRE General Test, GRE Subject Test (recommended), minimum GPA of 2.5; for doctorate, GRE General Test, GRE Subject Test (recommended), minimum GPA of 2.75. Additional exam requirements/recommendations for international students: Required—TOEFL. Electronic applications accepted. *Faculty research:* Analysis of proteins, drug interactions, solids and effluents by advanced separation methods; new synthetic strategies for complex organic molecules; synthesis and structural characterization of metal complexes for polymerization catalysis, nonlinear science, spectroscopy.

Youngstown State University, Graduate School, College of Science, Technology, Engineering and Mathematics, Department of Chemistry, Youngstown, OH 44555-0001. Offers analytical chemistry (MS); biochemistry (MS); chemistry education (MS); inorganic chemistry (MS); organic chemistry (MS); physical chemistry (MS). Part-time programs available. *Degree requirements:* For master's, thesis. *Entrance requirements:* For master's, bachelor's degree in chemistry, minimum GPA of 2.7. Additional exam requirements/recommendations for international students: Required—TOEFL. *Faculty research:* Analysis of antioxidants, chromatography, defects and disorder in crystalline oxides, hydrogen bonding, novel organic and organometallic materials.

Chemistry

Acadia University, Faculty of Pure and Applied Science, Department of Chemistry, Wolfville, NS B4P 2R6, Canada. Offers M Sc. *Faculty:* 2 full-time (0 women). *Students:* 3 full-time (1 woman), 1 (woman) part-time. Average age 26. 17 applicants, 29% accepted, 2 enrolled. In 2012, 2 master's awarded. *Degree requirements:* For master's, thesis. *Entrance requirements:* Additional exam requirements/recommendations for international students: Required—TOEFL (minimum score 580 paper-based; 93 iBT), IELTS (minimum score 6.5). *Application deadline:* For fall admission, 2/1 for domestic and international students. Applications are processed on a rolling basis. Application fee: $50. *Financial support:* Research assistantships, teaching assistantships, scholarships/grants, and unspecified assistantships available. Financial award application deadline: 2/1. *Faculty research:* Atmospheric chemistry, chemical kinetics, bioelectrochemistry of proteins, self-assembling monolayers. *Unit head:* Dr. John Murimboh, Department Head, 902-585-1172, Fax: 902-585-1114, E-mail: john.murimboh@acadiau.ca. *Application contact:* Avril Bird, Secretary, 902-585-1242, Fax: 902-585-1114, E-mail: avril.bird@acadiau.ca. Website: http://chemistry.acadiau.ca/.

The American University in Cairo, School of Sciences and Engineering, Department of Chemistry, Cairo, Egypt. Offers food chemistry (M Chem). *Degree requirements:* For master's, thesis. *Entrance requirements:* For master's, bachelor's degree in chemistry or related discipline with minimum GPA of 3.0. *Expenses: Tuition:* Full-time $10,000. Tuition and fees vary according to course load, degree level and program.

American University of Beirut, Graduate Programs, Faculty of Arts and Sciences, Beirut, Lebanon. Offers anthropology (MA); Arab and Middle Eastern history (PhD); Arabic language and literature (MA, PhD); archaeology (MA); biology (MS); cell and molecular biology (PhD); chemistry (MS); clinical psychology (MA); computational science (MS); computer science (MS); economics (MA); education (MA); English language (MA); English literature (MA); environmental policy planning (MSES); financial economics (MAFE); general psychology (MA); geology (MS); history (MA); mathematics (MA, MS); media studies (MA); Middle Eastern studies (MA); philosophy (MA); physics (MS); political studies (MA); public administration (MA); sociology (MA); statistics (MA, MS); theoretical physics (PhD); transnational American studies (MA). Part-time programs available. *Faculty:* 238 full-time (80 women), 7 part-time/adjunct (3 women). *Students:* 253 full-time (169 women), 139 part-time (105 women). Average age 26. 306 applicants, 47% accepted, 90 enrolled. In 2012, 126 degrees awarded. *Degree requirements:* For master's, one foreign language, comprehensive exam, thesis (for some programs); for doctorate, one foreign language, comprehensive exam, thesis/dissertation. *Entrance requirements:* For master's, GRE, letter of recommendation; for doctorate, GRE, letters of recommendation. Additional exam requirements/recommendations for international students: Required—TOEFL (minimum score 600 paper-based; 97 iBT), IELTS (minimum score 7). *Application deadline:* For fall admission, 4/30 for domestic students, 4/18 for international students; for spring admission, 11/1 for domestic and international students. Application fee: $50. *Expenses: Tuition:* Full-time $13,896; part-time $772 per credit. *Financial support:* In 2012–13, 20 students received support. Career-related internships or fieldwork, institutionally sponsored loans, scholarships/grants, health care benefits, and unspecified assistantships available. Financial award application deadline: 2/4; financial award applicants required to submit FAFSA. *Faculty research:* Modern Middle East history; Near Eastern archaeology; Islamic history; European history; software engineering; scientific computing; data mining; the applications of cooperative learning in language teaching and teacher education; world/comparative literature; rhetoric and composition; creative writing; public management; public policy and international affairs; hydrogeology; mineralogy, petrology, and geochemistry; tectonics and structural geology; cell and molecular biology; ecology. *Unit head:* Dr. Patrick McGreevy, Dean, 961-1374374 Ext. 3800, Fax: 961-1744461, E-mail: pm07@aub.edu.lb. *Application contact:* Dr. Salim Kanaan, Director, Admissions Office, 961-1-350000 Ext. 2594, Fax: 961-1750775, E-mail: sk00@aub.edu.lb. Website: http://staff.aub.edu.lb/~webfas.

Arizona State University, College of Liberal Arts and Sciences, Department of Chemistry and Biochemistry, Tempe, AZ 85287-1604. Offers biochemistry (MS, PhD); chemistry (MS, PhD); nanoscience (PSM). Terminal master's awarded for partial completion of doctoral program. *Degree requirements:* For master's, thesis, interactive Program of Study (iPOS) submitted before completing 50 percent of required credit hours; for doctorate, comprehensive exam, thesis/dissertation, interactive Program of Study (iPOS) submitted before completing 50 percent of required credit hours. *Entrance requirements:* For master's and doctorate, GRE, minimum GPA of 3.0 or equivalent in last 2 years of work leading to bachelor's degree. Additional exam requirements/recommendations for international students: Required—TOEFL (minimum score 80 iBT), TOEFL, IELTS, or Pearson Test of English. Electronic applications accepted.

Arkansas State University, Graduate School, College of Sciences and Mathematics, Department of Chemistry and Physics, Jonesboro, State University, AR 72467. Offers chemistry (MS); chemistry education (MSE, SCCT). Part-time programs available. *Faculty:* 12 full-time (1 woman). *Students:* 6 full-time (3 women), 5 part-time (3 women); includes 3 minority (2 Black or African American, non-Hispanic/Latino; 1 Asian, non-Hispanic/Latino), 4 international. Average age 27. 18 applicants, 39% accepted, 3 enrolled. In 2012, 6 master's awarded. *Degree requirements:* For master's, comprehensive exam, thesis or alternative; for SCCT, comprehensive exam. *Entrance requirements:* For master's, GRE General Test or MAT, appropriate bachelor's degree, official transcript, immunization records, valid teaching certificate (for MSE); for SCCT, GRE General Test or MAT, interview, master's degree, official transcript, immunization records. Additional exam requirements/recommendations for international students: Required—TOEFL (minimum score 550 paper-based; 79 iBT), IELTS (minimum score 6), Pearson Test of English (minimum score 56). *Application deadline:* For fall admission, 7/1 for domestic and international students; for spring admission, 11/15 for domestic students, 11/14 for international students. Applications are processed on a rolling basis. Application fee: $30 ($40 for international students). Electronic applications accepted. *Expenses:* Tuition, state resident: full-time $4140; part-time $230 per credit hour. Tuition, nonresident: full-time $8280; part-time $460 per credit hour. *Required fees:* $56 per credit hour. $25 per term. Tuition and fees vary according to course load and program. *Financial support:* In 2012–13, 1 student received support. Teaching assistantships, career-related internships or fieldwork, scholarships/grants, and unspecified assistantships available. Financial award application deadline: 7/1; financial award applicants required to submit FAFSA. *Unit head:* Dr. William Burns, Interim Chair, 870-972-3086, Fax: 870-972-3089, E-mail: wburns@astate.edu. *Application contact:* Vickey Ring, Graduate Admissions Coordinator, 870-972-3029, Fax: 870-972-3857, E-mail: vickeyring@astate.edu. Website: http://www.astate.edu/college/sciences-and-mathematics/departments/chemistry-physics/index.dot.

Auburn University, Graduate School, College of Sciences and Mathematics, Department of Chemistry and Biochemistry, Auburn University, AL 36849. Offers analytical chemistry (MS, PhD); biochemistry (MS, PhD); inorganic chemistry (MS, PhD); organic chemistry (MS, PhD); physical chemistry (MS, PhD). Part-time programs available. *Faculty:* 28 full-time (5 women), 1 part-time/adjunct (0 women). *Students:* 37 full-time (14 women), 30 part-time (15 women); includes 6 minority (3 Black or African American, non-Hispanic/Latino; 1 American Indian or Alaska Native, non-Hispanic/Latino; 1 Asian, non-Hispanic/Latino; 1 Hispanic/Latino), 41 international. Average age 28. 38 applicants, 39% accepted, 12 enrolled. In 2012, 1 master's, 9 doctorates awarded. *Degree requirements:* For master's, thesis (for some programs); for doctorate, thesis/dissertation, oral and written exams. *Entrance requirements:* For master's and doctorate, GRE General Test. *Application deadline:* For fall admission, 7/7 for domestic students; for spring admission, 11/24 for domestic students. Applications are processed on a rolling basis. Application fee: $50 ($60 for international students). Electronic applications accepted. *Expenses:* Tuition, state resident: full-time $7866; part-time $437 per credit. Tuition, nonresident: full-time $23,598; part-time $1311 per credit. *Required fees:* $787 per semester. Tuition and fees vary according to degree level and program. *Financial support:* Fellowships, research assistantships, and teaching assistantships available. Financial award application deadline: 3/15; financial award applicants required to submit FAFSA. *Unit head:* Dr. J. V. Ortiz, Chair, 334-844-4043, Fax: 334-844-4043. *Application contact:* Dr. George Flowers, Dean of the Graduate School, 334-844-2125. Website: http://www.auburn.edu/cosam/departments/chemistry/.

Ball State University, Graduate School, College of Sciences and Humanities, Department of Chemistry, Muncie, IN 47306-1099. Offers MA, MS. *Faculty:* 13 full-time (2 women). *Students:* 6 full-time (3 women), 11 part-time (5 women), 4 international. Average age 22. 20 applicants, 60% accepted, 5 enrolled. In 2012, 5 master's awarded. *Entrance requirements:* For master's, GRE General Test. Application fee: $50. *Expenses:* Tuition, state resident: full-time $7666. Tuition, nonresident: full-time $19,114. *Required fees:* $782. *Financial support:* In 2012–13, 14 students received support, including 13 teaching assistantships with full and partial tuition reimbursements available (averaging $4,520 per year); research assistantships with full tuition reimbursements available also available. Financial award application deadline: 3/1. *Faculty research:* Synthetic and analytical chemistry, biochemistry, theoretical chemistry. *Unit head:* Dr. Patti Lang, Interim Chair, 765-285-8060, Fax: 765-285-2351, E-mail: plang@bsu.edu. *Application contact:* Dr. James Poole, Associate Provost for Research and Dean of the Graduate School, 765-285-8071, E-mail: jpoole@bsu.edu. Website: http://www.bsu.edu/csh/chemistry/.

Baylor University, Graduate School, College of Arts and Sciences, Department of Chemistry and Biochemistry, Waco, TX 76798. Offers chemistry (MS, PhD). Part-time programs available. *Faculty:* 14 full-time (2 women). *Students:* 57 full-time (24 women), 1 part-time (0 women); includes 8 minority (4 Asian, non-Hispanic/Latino; 2 Hispanic/Latino; 2 Two or more races, non-Hispanic/Latino), 22 international. In 2012, 1 master's, 6 doctorates awarded. Terminal master's awarded for partial completion of doctoral program. *Degree requirements:* For master's, thesis; for doctorate, comprehensive exam, thesis/dissertation. *Entrance requirements:* For master's and doctorate, GRE General Test, GRE Subject Test. Additional exam requirements/recommendations for international students: Required—TOEFL. *Application deadline:* For fall admission, 8/1 for domestic students. Applications are processed on a rolling basis. Application fee: $25. *Expenses: Tuition:* Full-time $24,426; part-time $1357 per semester hour. *Required fees:* $2556; $142 per semester hour. *Financial support:* In 2012–13, 20 students received support. Fellowships, research assistantships, teaching assistantships, Federal Work-Study, institutionally sponsored loans, and tuition waivers (full) available. Support available to part-time students. *Unit head:* Dr. Charles Garner, Graduate Program Director, 254-710-6862, Fax: 254-710-2403, E-mail: charles_garner@baylor.edu. *Application contact:* Nancy Kallas, Administrative Assistant, 254-710-6844, Fax: 254-710-2403, E-mail: nancy_kallas@baylor.edu. Website: http://www.baylor.edu/chemistry/.

Binghamton University, State University of New York, Graduate School, School of Arts and Sciences, Department of Chemistry, Binghamton, NY 13902-6000. Offers analytical chemistry (PhD); chemistry (MA, MS); environmental (PhD); inorganic chemistry (PhD); organic chemistry (PhD); physical chemistry (PhD). Part-time programs available. *Faculty:* 16 full-time (4 women), 4 part-time/adjunct (1 woman). *Students:* 25 full-time (10 women), 26 part-time (10 women); includes 4 minority (3 Black or African American, non-Hispanic/Latino; 1 Hispanic/Latino), 33 international. Average age 28. 53 applicants, 49% accepted, 11 enrolled. In 2012, 3 master's, 6 doctorates awarded. Terminal master's awarded for partial completion of doctoral program. *Degree requirements:* For master's, thesis or alternative, oral exam, seminar presentation; for doctorate, thesis/dissertation, cumulative exams. *Entrance requirements:* For master's and doctorate, GRE General Test, GRE Subject Test. Additional exam requirements/recommendations for international students: Required—TOEFL (minimum score 550 paper-based; 80 iBT). *Application deadline:* For fall admission, 1/15 priority date for domestic students, 1/15 for international students; for spring admission, 10/15 priority date for domestic students, 10/15 for international students. Applications are processed on a rolling basis. Application fee: $75. Electronic applications accepted. *Expenses:* Tuition, state resident: full-time $9370. Tuition, nonresident: full-time $16,680. *Financial support:* In 2012–13, 47 students received support, including 5 research assistantships with full tuition reimbursements available (averaging $18,000 per year), 34 teaching assistantships with full tuition reimbursements available (averaging $18,000 per year); career-related internships or fieldwork, Federal Work-Study, institutionally sponsored loans, scholarships/grants, health care benefits, tuition waivers (full), and unspecified assistantships also available. Financial award application deadline: 2/15; financial award applicants required to submit FAFSA. *Unit head:* Dr. Wayne E. Jones, Chairperson, 607-777-2421, E-mail: wjones@binghamton.edu. *Application contact:* Kishan Zuber, Recruiting and Admissions Coordinator, 607-777-2151, Fax: 607-777-2501, E-mail: kzuber@binghamton.edu.

Boise State University, College of Arts and Sciences, Department of Chemistry and Biochemistry, Boise, ID 83725-0399. Offers biomolecular sciences (PhD); chemistry (MS). *Faculty:* 15 full-time, 1 part-time/adjunct. *Students:* 9 full-time (4 women), 2 part-time (1 woman); includes 1 minority (Asian, non-Hispanic/Latino), 1 international. 27 applicants, 70% accepted, 10 enrolled. In 2012, 1 master's awarded. Application fee: $55. *Expenses:* Tuition, state resident: full-time $3486; part-time $312 per credit. Tuition, nonresident: full-time $5720; part-time $413 per credit. *Financial support:* In 2012–13, 3 students received support, including 1 research assistantship, 2 teaching assistantships. *Application contact:* Linda Platt, Office Services Supervisor, Graduate Admission and Degree Services, 208-426-1074, Fax: 208-426-2789, E-mail: lplatt@boisestate.edu. Website: http://chemistry.boisestate.edu/.

Boston College, Graduate School of Arts and Sciences, Department of Chemistry, Chestnut Hill, MA 02467-3800. Offers biochemistry (PhD); inorganic chemistry (PhD); organic chemistry (PhD); physical chemistry (PhD); science education (MST). *Degree requirements:* For doctorate, thesis/dissertation, qualifying exam. *Entrance requirements:* For doctorate, GRE General Test, GRE Subject Test. Additional exam requirements/recommendations for international students: Required—TOEFL (minimum score 600 paper-based; 100 iBT). Electronic applications accepted.

Boston University, Graduate School of Arts and Sciences, Department of Chemistry, Boston, MA 02215. Offers MA, PhD. *Students:* 116 full-time (53 women), 1 (woman) part-time; includes 18 minority (2 American Indian or Alaska Native, non-Hispanic/Latino; 11 Asian, non-Hispanic/Latino; 4 Hispanic/Latino; 1 Two or more races, non-Hispanic/Latino), 41 international. Average age 24. 288 applicants, 21% accepted, 22 enrolled. In 2012, 22 master's, 13 doctorates awarded. Terminal master's awarded for partial completion of doctoral program. *Degree requirements:* For master's, one foreign language; for doctorate, one foreign language, comprehensive exam, thesis/dissertation. *Entrance requirements:* For master's and doctorate, GRE General Test, GRE Subject Test (recommended), 3 letters of recommendation. Additional exam requirements/recommendations for international students: Required—TOEFL (minimum score 550 paper-based; 84 iBT). *Application deadline:* For fall admission, 1/1 for domestic and international students. Application fee: $80. Electronic applications accepted. *Expenses: Tuition:* Full-time $42,400; part-time $1325 per credit. *Required fees:* $40 per semester. *Financial support:* In 2012–13, 5 fellowships with full tuition reimbursements (averaging $20,300 per year), 53 research assistantships with full tuition reimbursements (averaging $19,800 per year), 59 teaching assistantships with full tuition reimbursements (averaging $19,800 per year) were awarded; Federal Work-Study, scholarships/grants, health care benefits, and tuition waivers (full) also available. Support available to part-time students. Financial award application deadline: 1/1. *Unit head:* Lawrence Ziegler, Chairman, 617-353-8663, Fax: 617-353-6466, E-mail: lziegler@bu.edu. *Application contact:* Ruth Moritz, Academic Administrator, 617-353-2503, Fax: 617-353-6466, E-mail: rmoritz@bu.edu. Website: http://www.bu.edu/chemistry/.

Bowling Green State University, Graduate College, College of Arts and Sciences, Center for Photochemical Sciences, Bowling Green, OH 43403. Offers PhD. *Degree requirements:* For doctorate, comprehensive exam, thesis/dissertation. *Entrance requirements:* For doctorate, GRE General Test. Additional exam requirements/recommendations for international students: Required—TOEFL. Electronic applications accepted. *Faculty research:* Laser-initiated photopolymerization, spectroscopic and kinetic studies, optoelectronics of semiconductor multiple quantum wells, electron transfer processes, carotenoid pigments.

Bowling Green State University, Graduate College, College of Arts and Sciences, Department of Chemistry, Bowling Green, OH 43403. Offers MAT, MS. Part-time programs available. *Degree requirements:* For master's, thesis or alternative. *Entrance requirements:* For master's, GRE General Test. Additional exam requirements/recommendations for international students: Required—TOEFL. Electronic applications accepted. *Faculty research:* Organic, inorganic, physical, and analytical chemistry; biochemistry; surface science.

Bradley University, Graduate School, College of Liberal Arts and Sciences, Department of Chemistry and Biochemistry, Peoria, IL 61625-0002. Offers chemistry (MS). Part-time and evening/weekend programs available. *Degree requirements:* For master's, comprehensive exam, thesis. *Entrance requirements:* For master's, 2 letters of recommendation. Additional exam requirements/recommendations for international students: Required—TOEFL (minimum score 550 paper-based; 79 iBT).

Brandeis University, Graduate School of Arts and Sciences, Department of Chemistry, Waltham, MA 02454. Offers inorganic chemistry (MA, MS, PhD); organic chemistry (MA, MS, PhD); physical chemistry (MS, PhD). *Students:* 44 full-time (20 women); includes 3 minority (1 Black or African American, non-Hispanic/Latino; 2 Asian, non-Hispanic/Latino). 121 applicants, 26% accepted, 11 enrolled. In 2012, 6 master's, 7 doctorates awarded. Terminal master's awarded for partial completion of doctoral program. *Degree requirements:* For master's, thesis, 1 year of residency (for MA); 2 years of residency (for MS); for doctorate, comprehensive exam, thesis/dissertation, 3 years of residency; 2 seminars, qualifying exams. *Entrance requirements:* For master's and doctorate, GRE General Test, resume, statement of purpose, letters of recommendation. Additional exam requirements/recommendations for international students: Required—TOEFL (minimum score 600 paper-based; 100 iBT); Recommended—IELTS (minimum score 7). *Application deadline:* For fall admission, 1/15 priority date for domestic students. Application fee: $75. Electronic applications accepted. *Financial support:* In 2012–13, 16 research assistantships with full tuition reimbursements (averaging $25,000 per year) were awarded; fellowships with full tuition reimbursements, Federal Work-Study, scholarships/grants, health care benefits, tuition waivers (partial), and unspecified assistantships also available. Support available to part-time students. Financial award application deadline: 4/15; financial award applicants required to submit FAFSA. *Faculty research:* Oscillating chemical reactions, molecular recognition systems, protein crystallography, synthesis of natural product spectroscopy and magnetic resonance. *Unit head:* Dr. Judith Herzfeld, Chair, Graduate Program, 781-736-2540, Fax: 781-736-2516, E-mail: herzfeld@brandeis.edu. *Application contact:* Charlotte Haygazian, Coordinator, 781-736-2500, Fax: 781-736-2516, E-mail: chemadm@brandeis.edu. Website: http://www.brandeis.edu/gsas.

Brigham Young University, Graduate Studies, College of Physical and Mathematical Sciences, Department of Chemistry and Biochemistry, Provo, UT 84602. Offers biochemistry (MS, PhD); chemistry (MS, PhD). *Faculty:* 33 full-time (2 women). *Students:* 101 full-time (41 women); includes 1 minority (Asian, non-Hispanic/Latino), 56 international. Average age 28. 75 applicants, 41% accepted, 16 enrolled. In 2012, 2 master's, 14 doctorates awarded. *Degree requirements:* For master's, thesis; for doctorate, comprehensive exam, thesis/dissertation, qualifying exam. *Entrance requirements:* For master's and doctorate, GRE General Test, minimum GPA of 3.0 in last 60 hours. Additional exam requirements/recommendations for international students: Required—TOEFL (minimum score 580 paper-based; 85 iBT), IELTS (minimum score 7); Recommended—TWE. *Application deadline:* For fall admission, 2/1 priority date for domestic students, 2/1 for international students. Applications are processed on a rolling basis. Application fee: $50. Electronic applications accepted. *Expenses: Tuition:* Full-time $5950; part-time $331 per credit hour. Tuition and fees vary according to program and student's religious affiliation. *Financial support:* In 2012–13, 101 students received support, including 12 fellowships with full tuition reimbursements available (averaging $21,250 per year), 51 research assistantships with full tuition reimbursements available (averaging $21,250 per year), 38 teaching assistantships with full tuition reimbursements available (averaging $21,250 per year); institutionally sponsored loans, scholarships/grants, health care benefits, tuition waivers (full), and unspecified assistantships also available. Financial award application deadline: 2/1. *Faculty research:* Separation science, molecular recognition, organic synthesis and biomedical application, biochemistry and molecular biology, molecular spectroscopy. *Total annual research expenditures:* $5.6 million. *Unit head:* Dr. Gregory F. Burton, Chair, 801-422-4917, Fax: 801-422-0153, E-mail: gburton@byu.edu. *Application contact:* Dr. Paul B. Farnsworth, Graduate Coordinator, 801-422-6502, Fax: 801-422-0153, E-mail: pbfarnsw@byu.edu. Website: http://www.chem.byu.edu/.

Brock University, Faculty of Graduate Studies, Faculty of Mathematics and Science, Program in Chemistry, St. Catharines, ON L2S 3A1, Canada. Offers M Sc, PhD. Part-time programs available. *Degree requirements:* For master's, thesis; for doctorate, thesis/dissertation. *Entrance requirements:* For master's, honors B Sc in chemistry; for doctorate, M Sc. Additional exam requirements/recommendations for international students: Required—TOEFL (minimum score 550 paper-based; 80 iBT), IELTS (minimum score 6.5), TWE (minimum score 4). Electronic applications accepted. *Faculty research:* Bioorganic chemistry, trace element analysis, organic synthesis, electrochemistry, structural inorganic chemistry.

Brooklyn College of the City University of New York, Division of Graduate Studies, Department of Chemistry, Brooklyn, NY 11210-2889. Offers MA, PhD. Part-time programs available. *Degree requirements:* For master's, one foreign language, thesis or alternative, 30 credits. *Entrance requirements:* For master's, 2 letters of recommendation. Additional exam requirements/recommendations for international students: Required—TOEFL (minimum score 500 paper-based; 61 iBT). Electronic applications accepted.

Brooklyn College of the City University of New York, Division of Graduate Studies, School of Education, Program in Middle Childhood Education (Science), Brooklyn, NY 11210-2889. Offers biology (MA); chemistry (MA); earth science (MA); general science (MA); physics (MA). Part-time and evening/weekend programs available. *Entrance requirements:* For master's, LAST, interview, previous course work in education and mathematics, resume, 2 letters of recommendation, essay. Additional exam requirements/recommendations for international students: Required—TOEFL (minimum score 500 paper-based; 61 iBT). Electronic applications accepted. *Faculty research:* Geometric thinking, mastery of basic facts, problem-solving strategies, history of mathematics.

Brown University, Graduate School, Department of Chemistry, Providence, RI 02912. Offers biochemistry (PhD); chemistry (AM, Sc M, PhD). *Degree requirements:* For master's, thesis; for doctorate, one foreign language, thesis/dissertation, cumulative exam.

Bryn Mawr College, Graduate School of Arts and Sciences, Department of Chemistry, Bryn Mawr, PA 19010-2899. Offers MA, PhD. *Faculty:* 6. *Students:* 5 full-time (3 women), 6 part-time (3 women). Average age 31. 8 applicants, 38% accepted, 0 enrolled. In 2012, 2 master's awarded. *Degree requirements:* For master's, one foreign language, thesis; for doctorate, 2 foreign languages, comprehensive exam, thesis/dissertation. *Entrance requirements:* For master's and doctorate, GRE General Test, GRE Subject Test. Additional exam requirements/recommendations for international students: Required—TOEFL (minimum score 600 paper-based). *Application deadline:* For fall admission, 1/3 for domestic and international students. Application fee: $50. *Expenses: Tuition:* Full-time $35,280. *Financial support:* In 2012–13, 1 research assistantship with full tuition reimbursement (averaging $15,500 per year), 4 teaching assistantships with partial tuition reimbursements (averaging $15,500 per year) were awarded; Federal Work-Study, scholarships/grants, and tuition waivers (partial) also available. Support available to part-time students. Financial award application deadline: 1/3. *Unit head:* Dr. William Malachowski, Chair, 610-526-5104. *Application contact:* Lea R. Miller, Secretary, 610-526-5072, Fax: 610-526-5076, E-mail: lrmiller@brynmawr.edu.

Bucknell University, Graduate Studies, College of Arts and Sciences, Department of Chemistry, Lewisburg, PA 17837. Offers MA, MS. *Degree requirements:* For master's, thesis. *Entrance requirements:* For master's, GRE General Test, GRE Subject Test, minimum GPA of 3.0. Additional exam requirements/recommendations for international students: Required—TOEFL (minimum score 600 paper-based).

Buffalo State College, State University of New York, The Graduate School, Faculty of Natural and Social Sciences, Department of Chemistry, Buffalo, NY 14222-1095. Offers chemistry (MA); secondary education (MS Ed), including chemistry. Part-time and evening/weekend programs available. *Degree requirements:* For master's, thesis (for some programs), project. *Entrance requirements:* For master's, minimum GPA of 2.6, New York teaching certificate (MS Ed). Additional exam requirements/recommendations for international students: Required—TOEFL (minimum score 550 paper-based).

California Institute of Technology, Division of Chemistry and Chemical Engineering, Program in Chemistry, Pasadena, CA 91125-0001. Offers MS, PhD. Part-time and evening/weekend programs available. Postbaccalaureate distance learning degree programs offered (minimal on-campus study). *Faculty:* 43 full-time (8 women). *Students:* 215 full-time (77 women). Average age 26. 443 applicants, 26% accepted, 37 enrolled. In 2012, 8 master's, 25 doctorates awarded. Terminal master's awarded for partial completion of doctoral program. *Degree requirements:* For master's, thesis; for doctorate, thesis/dissertation. *Entrance requirements:* Additional exam requirements/recommendations for international students: Required—TOEFL; Recommended—IELTS, TWE. *Application deadline:* For fall admission, 12/15 for domestic students, 1/1 for international students. Application fee: $80. Electronic applications accepted. *Financial support:* Fellowships, research assistantships, teaching assistantships, Federal Work-Study, institutionally sponsored loans, scholarships/grants, traineeships, health care benefits, and unspecified assistantships available. Financial award application deadline: 1/1. *Unit head:* Prof. Jacqueline K. Barton, Chair, Chemistry and Chemical Engineering, 626-395-3646, Fax: 626-568-8824, E-mail: jkbarton@caltech.edu. *Application contact:* Agnes Tong, Option Secretary, 626-395-6111, E-mail: agnest@caltech.edu. Website: http://chemistry.caltech.edu/.

California Polytechnic State University, San Luis Obispo, College of Science and Mathematics, Department of Chemistry and Biochemistry, San Luis Obispo, CA 93407. Offers polymers and coating science (MS). Part-time programs available. *Faculty:* 2 full-time (1 woman). *Students:* 9 full-time (1 woman), 3 part-time (0 women); includes 5 minority (2 Asian, non-Hispanic/Latino; 1 Hispanic/Latino; 2 Two or more races, non-Hispanic/Latino), 1 international. Average age 23. 11 applicants, 64% accepted, 7 enrolled. In 2012, 4 master's awarded. *Degree requirements:* For master's, comprehensive exam (for some programs), thesis (for some programs), comprehensive oral exam. *Entrance requirements:* For master's, minimum GPA of 2.5 in last 90 quarter units of course work. Additional exam requirements/recommendations for international students: Required—TOEFL (minimum score 550 paper-based) or IELTS (minimum score 6). *Application deadline:* For fall admission, 7/1 for domestic students, 11/30 for international students; for winter admission, 11/1 for domestic students, 6/30 for international students; for spring admission, 2/1 for domestic students. Applications are processed on a rolling basis. Application fee: $55. Electronic applications accepted. *Expenses:* Tuition, state resident: full-time $6738; part-time $3906 per year. Tuition, nonresident: full-time $17,898; part-time $8370 per year. *Required fees:* $3051; $874 per term. One-time fee: $3051 full-time; $2622 part-time. *Financial support:* Fellowships, research assistantships, career-related internships or fieldwork, Federal Work-Study, and scholarships/grants available. Support available to part-time students. Financial award application deadline: 3/2; financial award applicants required to submit FAFSA. *Faculty research:* Polymer physical chemistry and analysis, polymer synthesis, coatings formulation. *Unit head:* Dr. Ray Fernando, Graduate Coordinator, 805-756-2395, Fax: 805-756-5500, E-mail: rhfernan@calpoly.edu. *Application contact:* Dr. James Maraviglia, Associate Vice Provost for Marketing and Enrollment Development, 805-756-2311, Fax: 805-756-5400, E-mail: admissions@calpoly.edu. Website: http://polymerscoatings.calpoly.edu/graduate.htm.

California State Polytechnic University, Pomona, Academic Affairs, College of Science, Program in Chemistry, Pomona, CA 91768-2557. Offers MS. Part-time programs available. *Students:* 3 full-time (2 women), 11 part-time (5 women); includes 6 minority (3 Asian, non-Hispanic/Latino; 2 Hispanic/Latino; 1 Two or more races, non-Hispanic/Latino), 2 international. Average age 27. 31 applicants, 42% accepted, 3 enrolled. In 2012, 3 master's awarded. *Degree requirements:* For master's, thesis. *Entrance requirements:* For master's, GRE General Test. *Application deadline:* For fall admission, 5/1 priority date for domestic students; for winter admission, 10/15 priority date for domestic students; for spring admission, 1/20 priority date for domestic students. Applications are processed on a rolling basis. Application fee: $55. Electronic applications accepted. *Financial support:* In 2012–13, 2 students received support. Career-related internships or fieldwork, Federal Work-Study, and institutionally sponsored loans available. Support available to part-time students. Financial award application deadline: 3/2; financial award applicants required to submit FAFSA. *Unit head:* Dr. Floyd Klavetter, Graduate Coordinator, 909-869-3677, E-mail: flklavetter@csupomona.edu. *Application contact:* Deborah L. Brandon, Executive Director, Admissions and Outreach, 909-869-3427, Fax: 909-869-5315, E-mail: dlbrandon@csupomona.edu. Website: http://www.csupomona.edu/~chemistry/grad/index.htm.

California State University, East Bay, Office of Academic Programs and Graduate Studies, College of Science, Department of Chemistry, Hayward, CA 94542-3000. Offers biochemistry (MS); chemistry (MS). *Degree requirements:* For master's, comprehensive exam or thesis. *Entrance requirements:* For master's, minimum GPA of 2.6 in field during previous 2 years of course work. Additional exam requirements/recommendations for international students: Required—TOEFL (minimum score 550 paper-based). Electronic applications accepted.

California State University, Fresno, Division of Graduate Studies, College of Science and Mathematics, Department of Chemistry, Fresno, CA 93740-8027. Offers MS. Part-time programs available. *Degree requirements:* For master's, thesis or alternative. *Entrance requirements:* For master's, GRE General Test, minimum GPA of 2.5. Additional exam requirements/recommendations for international students: Required—TOEFL. Electronic applications accepted. *Faculty research:* Genetics, viticulture, DNA, soils, molecular modeling, analysis of quinone.

California State University, Fullerton, Graduate Studies, College of Natural Science and Mathematics, Department of Chemistry and Biochemistry, Fullerton, CA 92834-9480. Offers chemistry (MA, MS); geochemistry (MS). Part-time programs available. *Students:* 5 full-time (1 woman), 23 part-time (6 women); includes 11 minority (6 Asian, non-Hispanic/Latino; 4 Hispanic/Latino; 1 Two or more races, non-Hispanic/Latino), 1 international. Average age 27. 50 applicants, 40% accepted, 11 enrolled. In 2012, 10 master's awarded. *Degree requirements:* For master's, thesis, departmental qualifying exam. *Entrance requirements:* For master's, minimum GPA of 2.5 in last 60 units of course work, major in chemistry or related field. Application fee: $55. *Financial support:* Research assistantships, teaching assistantships, career-related internships or fieldwork, Federal Work-Study, institutionally sponsored loans, and scholarships/grants available. Support available to part-time students. Financial award application deadline: 3/1; financial award applicants required to submit FAFSA. *Unit head:* Dr. Christopher Meyer, Chair, 657-278-3621. *Application contact:* Admissions/Applications, 657-278-2371.

California State University, Long Beach, Graduate Studies, College of Natural Sciences and Mathematics, Department of Chemistry and Biochemistry, Long Beach, CA 90840. Offers biochemistry (MS); chemistry (MS). Part-time programs available. *Degree requirements:* For master's, thesis, departmental qualifying exam. Electronic applications accepted. *Faculty research:* Enzymology, organic synthesis, molecular modeling, environmental chemistry, reaction kinetics.

California State University, Los Angeles, Graduate Studies, College of Natural and Social Sciences, Department of Chemistry and Biochemistry, Los Angeles, CA 90032-8530. Offers analytical chemistry (MS); biochemistry (MS); chemistry (MS); inorganic chemistry (MS); organic chemistry (MS); physical chemistry (MS). Part-time and evening/weekend programs available. *Faculty:* 2 full-time (1 woman). *Students:* 3 full-time (1 woman), 16 part-time (9 women); includes 16 minority (all Hispanic/Latino). Average age 32. 21 applicants, 52% accepted, 8 enrolled. In 2012, 2 master's awarded. *Degree requirements:* For master's, one foreign language, comprehensive exam or thesis. *Entrance requirements:* Additional exam requirements/recommendations for international students: Required—TOEFL. *Application deadline:* For fall admission, 5/1 for domestic and international students. Applications are processed on a rolling basis. Application fee: $55. *Financial support:* Federal Work-Study available. Support available to part-time students. Financial award application deadline: 3/1. *Faculty research:* Intercalation of heavy metal, carborane chemistry, conductive polymers and fabrics, titanium reagents, computer modeling and synthesis. *Unit head:* Dr. Robert L. Vellanoweth, Chair, 323-343-2300, Fax: 323-343-6490, E-mail: rvellan@calstatela.edu. *Application contact:* Dr. Larry Fritz, Dean of Graduate Studies, 323-343-3820 Ext. 3827, Fax: 323-343-5653, E-mail: lfritz@calstatela.edu. Website: http://www.calstatela.edu/dept/chem/index.htm.

California State University, Northridge, Graduate Studies, College of Science and Mathematics, Department of Chemistry and Biochemistry, Northridge, CA 91330. Offers biochemistry (MS); chemistry (MS), including chemistry, environmental chemistry. *Degree requirements:* For master's, thesis. *Entrance requirements:* For master's, GRE General Test or minimum GPA of 3.0. Additional exam requirements/recommendations for international students: Required—TOEFL. Electronic applications accepted.

California State University, Sacramento, Office of Graduate Studies, College of Natural Sciences and Mathematics, Department of Chemistry, Sacramento, CA 95819-6057. Offers MS. Part-time programs available. *Degree requirements:* For master's, thesis or project; qualifying exam; writing proficiency exam. *Entrance requirements:* For master's, minimum GPA of 2.5 during previous 2 years of course work, BA in chemistry or equivalent. Additional exam requirements/recommendations for international students: Required—TOEFL. Electronic applications accepted.

California State University, San Bernardino, Graduate Studies, College of Social and Behavioral Sciences, Program in Environmental Sciences, San Bernardino, CA 92407-2397. Offers MS. *Students:* 4 full-time (2 women), 12 part-time (6 women); includes 9 minority (3 Asian, non-Hispanic/Latino; 5 Hispanic/Latino; 1 Two or more races, non-Hispanic/Latino), 1 international. Average age 33. 2 applicants, 50% accepted, 0 enrolled. In 2012, 2 master's awarded. *Unit head:* Dr. Joan E. Frysxell, Graduate Coordinator, 909-537-5311, E-mail: jfryxell@csusb.edu. *Application contact:* Dr. Jeffrey Thompson, Dean of Graduate Studies, 909-537-5058, E-mail: jthompso@csusb.edu.

Carleton University, Faculty of Graduate Studies, Faculty of Science, Department of Chemistry, Ottawa, ON K1S 5B6, Canada. Offers M Sc, PhD. Programs offered jointly with University of Ottawa. *Degree requirements:* For master's, thesis; for doctorate, comprehensive exam, thesis/dissertation. *Entrance requirements:* For master's, honors degree; for doctorate, M Sc. Additional exam requirements/recommendations for international students: Required—TOEFL. *Faculty research:* Bioorganic chemistry, analytical toxicology, theoretical and physical chemistry, inorganic chemistry.

Chemistry

Carnegie Mellon University, Mellon College of Science, Department of Chemistry, Pittsburgh, PA 15213-3891. Offers biotechnology and management (MS); chemistry (PhD), including bioinorganic, bioorganic, organic and materials, biophysics and spectroscopy, computational and theoretical, polymer; colloids, polymers and surfaces (MS). Part-time programs available. Terminal master's awarded for partial completion of doctoral program. *Degree requirements:* For doctorate, thesis/dissertation, departmental qualifying and oral exams, teaching experience. *Entrance requirements:* For master's, GRE General Test; for doctorate, GRE General Test, GRE Subject Test. Additional exam requirements/ recommendations for international students: Required—TOEFL. Electronic applications accepted. *Faculty research:* Physical and theoretical chemistry, chemical synthesis, biophysical/bioinorganic chemistry.

Case Western Reserve University, School of Graduate Studies, Department of Chemistry, Cleveland, OH 44106. Offers MS, PhD. Part-time programs available. *Faculty:* 21 full-time (5 women), 1 part-time/adjunct (0 women). *Students:* 98 full-time (43 women); includes 2 minority (both Asian, non-Hispanic/Latino), 61 international. Average age 26. 224 applicants, 21% accepted, 28 enrolled. In 2012, 6 master's, 12 doctorates awarded. Terminal master's awarded for partial completion of doctoral program. *Degree requirements:* For master's, thesis optional; for doctorate, thesis/dissertation. *Entrance requirements:* For master's and doctorate, GRE General Test, GRE Subject Test. Additional exam requirements/recommendations for international students: Required—TOEFL (minimum score 577 paper-based; 90 iBT); Recommended—IELTS (minimum score 7). *Application deadline:* For fall admission, 4/15 priority date for domestic students. Applications are processed on a rolling basis. Application fee: $0. Electronic applications accepted. *Financial support:* Fellowships, research assistantships, teaching assistantships, and unspecified assistantships available. Financial award application deadline: 2/15. *Faculty research:* Electrochemistry, synthetic chemistry, chemistry of life process, spectroscopy, kinetics. *Unit head:* Prof. Mary Barkley, Chair, 216-368-3622, Fax: 216-368-3006, E-mail: mary.barkley@case.edu. *Application contact:* Julie Ilhan, Graduate Affairs Coordinator, 216-368-5030, Fax: 216-368-3006, E-mail: julie.ilhan@case.edu. Website: http://www.case.edu/artsci/chem/.

Central Connecticut State University, School of Graduate Studies, School of Arts and Sciences, Department of Chemistry and Biochemistry, New Britain, CT 06050-4010. Offers Certificate. Part-time and evening/weekend programs available. *Degree requirements:* For Certificate, qualifying exam. *Entrance requirements:* Additional exam requirements/recommendations for international students: Required—TOEFL (minimum score 550 paper-based; 79 iBT). *Application deadline:* For fall admission, 6/1 for domestic students, 5/1 for international students; for spring admission, 11/1 for domestic and international students. Applications are processed on a rolling basis. Application fee: $50. Electronic applications accepted. *Expenses: Tuition, area resident:* Full-time $5337; part-time $498 per credit. Tuition, state resident: full-time $8008; part-time $510 per credit. Tuition, nonresident: full-time $14,869; part-time $510 per credit. *Required fees:* $3970. One-time fee: $62 part-time. *Unit head:* Dr. Barry Westcott, Chair, 860-832-2675, E-mail: westcottb@ccsu.edu. *Application contact:* Patricia Gardner, Associate Director of Graduate Studies, 860-832-2350, Fax: 860-832-2362, E-mail: graduateadmissions@ccsu.edu. Website: http://you.ccsu.edu/chemistry/.

Central Michigan University, College of Graduate Studies, College of Science and Technology, Department of Chemistry, Mount Pleasant, MI 48859. Offers chemistry (MS); teaching chemistry (MA), including teaching college chemistry, teaching high school chemistry. Part-time programs available. *Faculty:* 11 full-time (6 women). *Students:* 26 (7 women); includes 1 minority (Asian, non-Hispanic/ Latino), 9 international. Average age 26. 17 applicants, 18% accepted, 3 enrolled. In 2012, 8 master's awarded. *Degree requirements:* For master's, comprehensive exam, thesis or alternative. *Entrance requirements:* For master's, GRE. *Application deadline:* For fall admission, 7/1 for international students; for spring admission, 10/1 for international students. Applications are processed on a rolling basis. Application fee: $35 ($45 for international students). Electronic applications accepted. *Expenses:* Tuition, state resident: full-time $8730; part-time $485 per credit hour. Tuition, nonresident: full-time $13,788; part-time $766 per credit hour. One-time fee: $75. Tuition and fees vary according to degree level, campus/ location and reciprocity agreements. *Financial support:* Research assistantships, career-related internships or fieldwork, Federal Work-Study, unspecified assistantships, and out-of-state merit awards available. Financial award application deadline: 2/1. *Faculty research:* Analytical and organic-inorganic chemistry, biochemistry, catalysis, dendrimer and polymer studies, nanotechnology. *Unit head:* Dr. David Ash, Chairperson, 989-774-3981, Fax: 989-774-3883, E-mail: ash1de@cmich.edu. *Application contact:* Dr. Mary Tecklenburg, Graduate Program Coordinator, 989-774-3078, Fax: 989-774-3883, E-mail: teckl1mm@cmich.edu. Website: http://www.cst.cmich.edu.

Central Washington University, Graduate Studies and Research, College of the Sciences, Department of Chemistry, Ellensburg, WA 98926. Offers MS. Part-time programs available. *Faculty:* 12 full-time (4 women). *Students:* 7 full-time (0 women), 1 (woman) part-time; includes 3 minority (1 Asian, non-Hispanic/Latino; 2 Two or more races, non-Hispanic/Latino), 1 international. 11 applicants, 73% accepted, 8 enrolled. In 2012, 1 master's awarded. *Degree requirements:* For master's, thesis. *Entrance requirements:* For master's, GRE General Test, minimum GPA of 3.0. Additional exam requirements/recommendations for international students: Required—TOEFL (minimum score 550 paper-based; 79 iBT), IELTS (minimum score 6.5). *Application deadline:* For fall admission, 2/1 for

domestic students; for winter admission, 10/1 for domestic students; for spring admission, 1/1 for domestic students. Applications are processed on a rolling basis. Application fee: $50. Electronic applications accepted. *Expenses:* Tuition, state resident: full-time $8517. Tuition, nonresident: full-time $18,972. *Required fees:* $978. *Financial support:* In 2012–13, 3 research assistantships with full and partial tuition reimbursements (averaging $9,677 per year), 5 teaching assistantships with full and partial tuition reimbursements (averaging $9,677 per year) were awarded; career-related internships or fieldwork, Federal Work-Study, and health care benefits also available. Financial award application deadline: 3/1; financial award applicants required to submit FAFSA. *Unit head:* Dr. Dion Rivera, Program Director, 509-963-2883, Fax: 509-963-1050, E-mail: riverad@cwu.edu. *Application contact:* Justine Eason, Admissions Program Coordinator, 509-963-3103, Fax: 509-963-1799, E-mail: masters@cwu.edu.

Christopher Newport University, Graduate Studies, Department of Teacher Preparation, Newport News, VA 23606-2998. Offers art (PK-12) (MAT); biology (6-12) (MAT); chemistry (6-12) (MAT); computer science (6-12) (MAT); elementary (PK-6) (MAT); English (6-12) (MAT); English as second language (PK-12) (MAT); French (PK-12) (MAT); history and social science (6-12) (MAT); mathematics (6-12) (MAT); music (PK-12) (MAT), including choral, instrumental; physics (6-12) (MAT); Spanish (PK-12) (MAT). Part-time and evening/weekend programs available. *Degree requirements:* For master's, comprehensive exam, thesis or alternative. *Entrance requirements:* For master's, PRAXIS I, minimum GPA of 3.0. Additional exam requirements/recommendations for international students: Required—TOEFL (minimum score 580 paper-based; 92 iBT). Electronic applications accepted. *Faculty research:* Early literacy development, instructional innovations, professional teaching standards, multicultural issues, aesthetic education.

City College of the City University of New York, Graduate School, College of Liberal Arts and Science, Division of Science, Department of Chemistry, Program in Chemistry, New York, NY 10031-9198. Offers MA, PhD. PhD program offered jointly with Graduate School and University Center of the City University of New York. Terminal master's awarded for partial completion of doctoral program. *Degree requirements:* For doctorate, one foreign language, thesis/dissertation. *Entrance requirements:* For master's and doctorate, GRE. Additional exam requirements/recommendations for international students: Required—TOEFL (minimum score 500 paper-based). *Faculty research:* Laser spectroscopy, bioorganic chemistry, polymer chemistry and crystallography, electroanalytical chemistry, ESR of metal clusters.

Clark Atlanta University, School of Arts and Sciences, Department of Chemistry, Atlanta, GA 30314. Offers MS, PhD. Part-time programs available. *Faculty:* 7 full-time (0 women). *Students:* 14 full-time (8 women), 17 part-time (10 women); includes 24 minority (all Black or African American, non-Hispanic/Latino), 6 international. Average age 30. 9 applicants, 100% accepted, 9 enrolled. In 2012, 2 master's, 1 doctorate awarded. *Degree requirements:* For master's, one foreign language, thesis; for doctorate, 2 foreign languages, thesis/dissertation. *Entrance requirements:* For master's, GRE General Test, minimum GPA of 2.5; for doctorate, GRE General Test, GRE Subject Test, minimum graduate GPA of 3.0. Additional exam requirements/recommendations for international students: Required—TOEFL (minimum score 500 paper-based; 61 iBT). *Application deadline:* For fall admission, 4/1 for domestic and international students; for spring admission, 11/1 for domestic and international students. Applications are processed on a rolling basis. Application fee: $40 ($55 for international students). *Expenses:* Tuition: Full-time $14,256; part-time $792 per credit hour. *Required fees:* $818; $409 per semester. *Financial support:* In 2012–13, 6 teaching assistantships were awarded; fellowships, research assistantships, career-related internships or fieldwork, Federal Work-Study, scholarships/grants, traineeships, and unspecified assistantships also available. Support available to part-time students. Financial award application deadline: 4/30; financial award applicants required to submit FAFSA. *Unit head:* Dr. Cass Parker, Chairperson, 404-880-6858, E-mail: cparker@cau.edu. *Application contact:* Michelle Clark-Davis, Graduate Program Admissions, 404-880-6605, E-mail: cauadmissions@cau.edu.

Clarkson University, Graduate School, School of Arts and Sciences, Department of Chemistry and Biomolecular Science, Potsdam, NY 13699. Offers chemistry (MS, PhD). Part-time programs available. *Faculty:* 23 full-time (4 women), 2 part-time/adjunct (1 woman). *Students:* 40 full-time (15 women); includes 1 minority (Two or more races, non-Hispanic/Latino), 22 international. Average age 25. 30 applicants, 53% accepted, 8 enrolled. In 2012, 8 master's, 5 doctorates awarded. *Degree requirements:* For doctorate, comprehensive exam, thesis/dissertation, departmental qualifying exam. *Entrance requirements:* For master's and doctorate, GRE, transcripts of all college coursework, three letters of recommendation; resume and personal statement (recommended). Additional exam requirements/recommendations for international students: Required—TOEFL. *Application deadline:* For fall admission, 1/30 priority date for domestic students, 1/30 for international students; for spring admission, 9/1 priority date for domestic students, 9/1 for international students. Applications are processed on a rolling basis. Application fee: $25 ($35 for international students). Electronic applications accepted. *Expenses:* Tuition: Full-time $15,108; part-time $1259 per credit hour. *Required fees:* $295 per semester. *Financial support:* In 2012–13, 34 students received support, including fellowships with full tuition reimbursements available (averaging $22,650 per year), 13 research assistantships with full tuition reimbursements available (averaging $22,650 per year), 20 teaching assistantships with full tuition reimbursements available (averaging $22,650 per year); scholarships/grants, tuition waivers (partial), and unspecified assistantships also available. *Faculty research:* Real-time monitoring of neurotransmitters, tumor differentiation, chemical catalysis, multi-enzyme biomolecular computing networks. *Total annual research expenditures:* $1.6 million. *Unit head:* Dr. Phillip Christiansen, Chair, 315-268-2389, Fax: 315-268-6610, E-mail: pac@clarkson.edu. *Application contact:* Jennifer Reed, Graduate Coordinator, School of Arts and Sciences, 315-268-3802, Fax: 315-268-3989, E-mail: sciencegrad@clarkson.edu. Website: http://www.clarkson.edu/biosci_chemistry/.

Clark University, Graduate School, Department of Chemistry, Worcester, MA 01610-1477. Offers MA, PhD. *Faculty:* 10 full-time (1 woman), 2 part-time/adjunct (0 women). *Students:* 17 full-time (3 women); includes 1 minority (Asian, non-Hispanic/Latino), 7 international. Average age 27. 37 applicants, 24% accepted, 7 enrolled. In 2012, 6 master's, 1 doctorate awarded. Terminal master's awarded for partial completion of doctoral program. *Degree requirements:* For master's, thesis or alternative; for doctorate, one foreign language, thesis/dissertation. *Entrance requirements:* For master's and doctorate, GRE General Test. Additional exam requirements/recommendations for international students: Required—TOEFL. *Application deadline:* For fall admission, 2/15 priority date for domestic students. Applications are processed on a rolling basis. Application fee: $50. *Expenses: Tuition:* Full-time $38,100; part-time $4762.50 per course. *Required fees:* $30. Tuition and fees vary according to course load and program. *Financial support:* In 2012–13, fellowships with tuition reimbursements (averaging $19,025 per year), 6 research assistantships with full tuition reimbursements (averaging $19,825 per year), 8 teaching assistantships with full tuition reimbursements (averaging $19,825 per year) were awarded; tuition waivers (full) also available. *Faculty research:* Nuclear chemistry, molecular biology simulation, NMR studies, biochemistry, protein folding mechanisms. *Total annual research expenditures:* $550,000. *Unit head:* Dr. Luis Smith, Chair, 508-793-7116. *Application contact:* Rene Baril, Department Secretary, 528-793-7173, Fax: 528-793-8861, E-mail: chemistry@clarku.edu. Website: http://www.clarku.edu/departments/chemistry/graduate/index.cfm.

Clemson University, Graduate School, College of Engineering and Science, Department of Chemistry, Clemson, SC 29634. Offers MS, PhD. *Faculty:* 34 full-time (5 women), 3 part-time/adjunct (1 woman). *Students:* 90 full-time (36 women), 4 part-time (1 woman); includes 9 minority (3 Black or African American, non-Hispanic/Latino; 4 Asian, non-Hispanic/Latino; 1 Hispanic/Latino; 1 Two or more races, non-Hispanic/Latino), 48 international. Average age 27. 186 applicants, 19% accepted, 13 enrolled. In 2012, 6 master's, 10 doctorates awarded. *Degree requirements:* For master's, one foreign language, thesis; for doctorate, one foreign language, thesis/dissertation. *Entrance requirements:* For master's and doctorate, GRE General Test. Additional exam requirements/recommendations for international students: Required—TOEFL. *Application deadline:* For fall admission, 3/1 for domestic students, 4/15 for international students; for spring admission, 9/15 for international students. Applications are processed on a rolling basis. Application fee: $70 ($80 for international students). Electronic applications accepted. *Financial support:* In 2012–13, 88 students received support, including 3 fellowships with full and partial tuition reimbursements available (averaging $11,383 per year), 19 research assistantships with partial tuition reimbursements available (averaging $14,089 per year), 78 teaching assistantships with partial tuition reimbursements available (averaging $19,738 per year); career-related internships or fieldwork, institutionally sponsored loans, scholarships/grants, health care benefits, and unspecified assistantships also available. Support available to part-time students. Financial award applicants required to submit FAFSA. *Faculty research:* Fluorine chemistry, organic synthetic methods and natural products, metal and non-metal clusters, analytical spectroscopies, polymers. *Total annual research expenditures:* $2.7 million. *Unit head:* Dr. Stephen E. Creager, Chair, 864-656-3065, Fax: 864-656-6613, E-mail: screage@clemson.edu. *Application contact:* Dr. Steve Stuart, Coordinator, 864-656-5013, Fax: 864-656-6613, E-mail: ss@clemson.edu. Website: http://chemistry.clemson.edu/.

Cleveland State University, College of Graduate Studies, College of Sciences and Health Professions, Department of Chemistry, Cleveland, OH 44115. Offers analytical chemistry (MS); clinical chemistry (MS); clinical/bioanalytical chemistry (PhD), including cellular and molecular medicine, clinical chemistry, clinical/bioanalytical chemistry; environmental chemistry (MS); inorganic chemistry (MS); pharmaceutical/organic chemistry (MS); physical chemistry (MS). Part-time and evening/weekend programs available. *Faculty:* 12 full-time (0 women). *Students:* 10 full-time (6 women), 92 part-time (46 women); includes 7 minority (6 Black or African American, non-Hispanic/Latino; 1 Asian, non-Hispanic/Latino), 68 international. Average age 27. 119 applicants, 86% accepted, 18 enrolled. In 2012, 15 master's, 5 doctorates awarded. *Degree requirements:* For master's, thesis optional; for doctorate, comprehensive exam, thesis/dissertation. *Entrance requirements:* For master's and doctorate, GRE General Test. Additional exam requirements/recommendations for international students: Required—TOEFL (minimum score 525 paper-based; 65 iBT). *Application deadline:* For fall admission, 1/15 priority date for domestic students, 1/15 for international students. Applications are processed on a rolling basis. Application fee: $30. Electronic applications accepted. *Expenses: Tuition,* state resident: full-time $8172; part-time $510.75 per credit hour. Tuition, nonresident: full-time $15,372; part-time $960.75 per credit hour. *Required fees:* $25 per semester. Tuition and fees vary according to course load and program. *Financial support:* In 2012–13, 44 students received support, including 5 fellowships with full tuition reimbursements available (averaging $22,500 per year), 13 research assistantships with full tuition reimbursements available (averaging $22,500 per year), 24 teaching assistantships with full tuition reimbursements available (averaging $21,000 per year); scholarships/grants and unspecified

assistantships also available. Financial award application deadline: 1/15. *Faculty research:* Bioanalytical techniques and molecular diagnostics, glycoproteomics and antithrombotic agents, drug discovery and innovation, analytical pharmacology, inflammatory disease research. *Total annual research expenditures:* $3 million. *Unit head:* Dr. David J. Anderson, Interim Chair, 216-687-2467, Fax: 216-687-9298, E-mail: d.anderson@csuohio.edu. *Application contact:* Richelle P. Emery, Administrative Coordinator, 216-687-2457, Fax: 216-687-9298, E-mail: r.emery@csuohio.edu. Website: http://www.csuohio.edu/chemistry/.

The College of William and Mary, Faculty of Arts and Sciences, Department of Chemistry, Williamsburg, VA 23187-8795. Offers MA, MS. *Faculty:* 17 full-time (4 women), 3 part-time/adjunct (0 women). *Students:* 10 full-time (6 women), 1 part-time (0 women), 2 international. Average age 24. 33 applicants, 48% accepted, 4 enrolled. In 2012, 7 master's awarded. *Degree requirements:* For master's, comprehensive exam, thesis (for some programs). *Entrance requirements:* For master's, GRE, minimum GPA of 2.5. Additional exam requirements/recommendations for international students: Required—TOEFL. *Application deadline:* For fall admission, 3/1 priority date for domestic students, 3/1 for international students. Applications are processed on a rolling basis. Application fee: $45. Electronic applications accepted. *Expenses:* Tuition, state resident: full-time $6779; part-time $385 per credit hour. Tuition, nonresident: full-time $20,608; part-time $1000 per credit hour. *Required fees:* $4625. *Financial support:* In 2012–13, 10 students received support, including 11 fellowships (averaging $2,218 per year), 1 research assistantship with full tuition reimbursement available (averaging $15,850 per year), 9 teaching assistantships with full tuition reimbursements available (averaging $15,850 per year); health care benefits and unspecified assistantships also available. Financial award application deadline: 3/1; financial award applicants required to submit FAFSA. *Faculty research:* Organic, physical, polymer and analytic chemistry; biochemistry. *Total annual research expenditures:* $771,561. *Unit head:* Dr. Chris Abelt, Chair, 757-221-2540, Fax: 757-221-2715, E-mail: cjabel@wm.edu. *Application contact:* Dr. Deborah C. Bebout, Graduate Director, 757-221-2558, Fax: 757-221-2715, E-mail: dcbebo@wm.edu. Website: http://www.wm.edu/as/chemistry.

Colorado School of Mines, Graduate School, Department of Chemistry and Geochemistry, Program in Chemistry, Golden, CO 80401-1887. Offers applied chemistry (PhD); chemistry (MS). Part-time programs available. *Students:* 43 full-time (15 women), 2 part-time (1 woman); includes 5 minority (3 Asian, non-Hispanic/Latino; 2 Hispanic/Latino), 13 international. Average age 28. 57 applicants, 26% accepted, 5 enrolled. In 2012, 3 master's, 2 doctorates awarded. *Degree requirements:* For master's, thesis (for some programs); for doctorate, comprehensive exam, thesis/dissertation. *Entrance requirements:* For master's and doctorate, GRE General Test. Additional exam requirements/recommendations for international students: Required—TOEFL (minimum score 550 paper-based; 80 iBT). *Application deadline:* For fall admission, 1/15 priority date for domestic students, 1/15 for international students; for spring admission, 10/15 priority date for domestic students, 10/15 for international students. Application fee: $50 ($70 for international students). Electronic applications accepted. *Financial support:* In 2012–13, fellowships with full tuition reimbursements (averaging $20,000 per year), research assistantships with full tuition reimbursements (averaging $20,000 per year), teaching assistantships with full tuition reimbursements (averaging $20,000 per year) were awarded; scholarships/grants, health care benefits, and unspecified assistantships also available. Financial award application deadline: 1/15; financial award applicants required to submit FAFSA. *Unit head:* Dr. Dan Knauss, Department Head, 303-273-3625 Ext. 303, Fax: 303-273-3629. *Application contact:* Prof. Tina Voelker, Associate Professor, 303-273-3152, Fax: 303-273-3629, E-mail: tvoelker@mines.edu. Website: http://chemistry.mines.edu.

Colorado State University, Graduate School, College of Natural Sciences, Department of Chemistry, Fort Collins, CO 80523-1872. Offers MS, PhD. *Faculty:* 28 full-time (9 women). *Students:* 63 full-time (25 women), 78 part-time (26 women); includes 18 minority (2 American Indian or Alaska Native, non-Hispanic/Latino; 4 Asian, non-Hispanic/Latino; 6 Hispanic/Latino; 6 Two or more races, non-Hispanic/Latino), 10 international. Average age 26. 47 applicants, 57% accepted, 27 enrolled. In 2012, 10 master's, 23 doctorates awarded. Terminal master's awarded for partial completion of doctoral program. *Degree requirements:* For master's, comprehensive exam, thesis (for some programs), seminar; for doctorate, comprehensive exam, thesis/dissertation, seminar. *Entrance requirements:* For master's and doctorate, GRE General Test, minimum GPA of 3.0. Additional exam requirements/recommendations for international students: Required—TOEFL (minimum score 550 paper-based; 80 iBT). *Application deadline:* For fall admission, 2/15 for domestic and international students; for spring admission, 9/15 for domestic and international students. Applications are processed on a rolling basis. Application fee: $50. Electronic applications accepted. *Expenses:* Tuition, state resident: full-time $8811; part-time $490 per credit. Tuition, nonresident: full-time $21,600; part-time $1200 per credit. *Required fees:* $1819; $61 per credit. *Financial support:* In 2012–13, 203 students received support, including 31 fellowships (averaging $24,237 per year), 97 research assistantships with full tuition reimbursements available (averaging $12,725 per year), 75 teaching assistantships with full tuition reimbursements available (averaging $13,030 per year); career-related internships or fieldwork, scholarships/grants, health care benefits, tuition waivers, and unspecified assistantships also available. Financial award application deadline: 1/15; financial award applicants required to submit FAFSA. *Faculty research:* Molecular spectroscopy and dynamics, environmental and analytical chemistry, synthesis, biological chemistry, sustainable and renewable chemistry. *Total annual research*

Peterson's Graduate Programs in the Physical Sciences, Mathematics, Agricultural Sciences, the Environment & Natural Resources 2014

www.petersonsbooks.com **65**

expenditures: $5.4 million. *Unit head:* Dr. Ellen R. Fisher, Department Head, 970-491-5931, Fax: 970-491-1801, E-mail: ellen.fisher@colostate.edu. *Application contact:* Kathy Gibson, Graduate Contact, 970-491-0502, Fax: 970-491-1801, E-mail: kathy.gibson@colostate.edu. Website: http://www.chem.colostate.edu/.

Colorado State University–Pueblo, College of Science and Mathematics, Pueblo, CO 81001-4901. Offers applied natural science (MS), including biochemistry, biology, chemistry. Part-time and evening/weekend programs available. *Degree requirements:* For master's, comprehensive exam (for some programs), thesis (for some programs), internship report (if non-thesis). *Entrance requirements:* For master's, GRE General Test (minimum score 1000), 2 letters of reference, minimum GPA of 3.0. Additional exam requirements/recommendations for international students: Required—TOEFL (minimum score 500 paper-based), IELTS (minimum score 5). *Faculty research:* Fungal cell walls, molecular biology, bioactive materials synthesis, atomic force microscopy-surface chemistry, nanoscience.

Columbia University, Graduate School of Arts and Sciences, Division of Natural Sciences, Department of Chemistry, New York, NY 10027. Offers chemical physics (M Phil, PhD); inorganic chemistry (M Phil, MA, PhD); organic chemistry (M Phil, MA, PhD); MD/PhD. *Degree requirements:* For master's, one foreign language, teaching experience, oral/written exams (M Phil); for doctorate, one foreign language, thesis/dissertation. *Entrance requirements:* For master's and doctorate, GRE General Test, GRE Subject Test. Additional exam requirements/recommendations for international students: Required—TOEFL. *Faculty research:* Biophysics.

Concordia University, School of Graduate Studies, Faculty of Arts and Science, Department of Chemistry and Biochemistry, Montréal, QC H3G 1M8, Canada. Offers chemistry (M Sc, PhD). *Degree requirements:* For master's, thesis; for doctorate, thesis/dissertation. *Entrance requirements:* For master's, honors degree in chemistry; for doctorate, M Sc in biochemistry, biology, or chemistry. *Faculty research:* Bioanalytical, bio-organic, and inorganic chemistry; materials and solid-state chemistry.

Cornell University, Graduate School, Graduate Fields of Arts and Sciences, Field of Chemistry and Chemical Biology, Ithaca, NY 14853-0001. Offers analytical chemistry (PhD); bio-organic chemistry (PhD); biophysical chemistry (PhD); chemical biology (PhD); chemical physics (PhD); inorganic chemistry (PhD); materials chemistry (PhD); organic chemistry (PhD); organometallic chemistry (PhD); physical chemistry (PhD); polymer chemistry (PhD); theoretical chemistry (PhD). *Faculty:* 48 full-time (5 women). *Students:* 161 full-time (70 women); includes 28 minority (1 Black or African American, non-Hispanic/Latino; 16 Asian, non-Hispanic/Latino; 4 Hispanic/Latino; 7 Two or more races, non-Hispanic/Latino), 48 international. Average age 25. 340 applicants, 33% accepted, 40 enrolled. In 2012, 15 doctorates awarded. *Degree requirements:* For doctorate, comprehensive exam, thesis/dissertation. *Entrance requirements:* For doctorate, GRE General Test, GRE Subject Test (chemistry), 3 letters of recommendation. Additional exam requirements/recommendations for international students: Required—TOEFL (minimum score 600 paper-based; 77 iBT). *Application deadline:* For fall admission, 1/10 for domestic students. Application fee: $95. Electronic applications accepted. *Financial support:* In 2012–13, 155 students received support, including 37 fellowships with full tuition reimbursements available, 50 research assistantships with full tuition reimbursements available, 68 teaching assistantships with full tuition reimbursements available; institutionally sponsored loans, scholarships/grants, health care benefits, tuition waivers (full and partial), and unspecified assistantships also available. Financial award applicants required to submit FAFSA. *Faculty research:* Analytical, organic, inorganic, physical, materials, chemical biology. *Unit head:* Director of Graduate Studies, 607-255-4139, Fax: 607-255-4137. *Application contact:* Graduate Field Assistant, 607-255-4139, Fax: 607-255-4137, E-mail: chemgrad@cornell.edu. Website: http://www.gradschool.cornell.edu/fields.php?id-26&a-2.

Dalhousie University, Faculty of Science, Department of Chemistry, Halifax, NS B3H 4R2, Canada. Offers M Sc, PhD. Part-time programs available. Terminal master's awarded for partial completion of doctoral program. *Degree requirements:* For master's, thesis; for doctorate, thesis/dissertation. *Entrance requirements:* Additional exam requirements/recommendations for international students: Required—TOEFL (minimum score 600 paper-based; 92 iBT), IELTS (minimum score 7). Electronic applications accepted. *Faculty research:* Analytical, inorganic, organic, physical, and theoretical chemistry.

Dartmouth College, Arts and Sciences Graduate Programs, Department of Chemistry, Hanover, NH 03755. Offers PhD. *Degree requirements:* For doctorate, thesis/dissertation, departmental qualifying exams. *Entrance requirements:* For doctorate, GRE General Test, GRE Subject Test. Additional exam requirements/recommendations for international students: Required—TOEFL. Electronic applications accepted. *Faculty research:* Organic and polymer synthesis, bioinorganic chemistry, magnetic resonance parameters.

Delaware State University, Graduate Programs, Department of Chemistry, Dover, DE 19901-2277. Offers applied chemistry (MS, PhD); chemistry (MS). Part-time and evening/weekend programs available. *Entrance requirements:* For master's, GRE, minimum GPA of 3.0 in major, 2.75 overall; for doctorate, GRE. Additional exam requirements/recommendations for international students: Required—TOEFL (minimum score 550 paper-based). Electronic applications accepted. *Faculty research:* Chemiluminescence, environmental chemistry, forensic chemistry, heteropoly anions anti-cancer and antiviral agents, low temperature infrared studies of lithium salts.

DePaul University, College of Science and Health, Department of Chemistry, Chicago, IL 60614. Offers analytical/physical chemistry (MS); biochemistry/medicinal chemistry (MS); polymer chemistry and coatings technology (MS); synthetic chemistry (MS). Part-time and evening/weekend programs available. *Faculty:* 7 full-time (4 women). *Students:* 5 full-time (2 women), 11 part-time (6 women); includes 5 minority (1 Asian, non-Hispanic/Latino; 3 Hispanic/Latino; 1 Two or more races, non-Hispanic/Latino), 1 international. Average age 26. In 2012, 4 master's awarded. *Degree requirements:* For master's, thesis (for some programs), oral exam (for select programs). *Entrance requirements:* For master's, BS in chemistry or equivalent. Additional exam requirements/recommendations for international students: Required—TOEFL (minimum score 590 paper-based; 96 iBT) or Pearson Test of English. *Application deadline:* For fall admission, 7/15 for domestic students, 5/1 for international students; for winter admission, 11/15 for domestic students, 9/1 for international students; for spring admission, 2/15 for domestic students, 12/1 for international students. Application fee: $40. Electronic applications accepted. *Financial support:* In 2012–13, 6 teaching assistantships with partial tuition reimbursements (averaging $9,000 per year) were awarded. Financial award application deadline: 6/1; financial award applicants required to submit FAFSA. *Faculty research:* Computational chemistry, organic synthesis, inorganic synthesis, polymer synthesis, biochemistry. *Total annual research expenditures:* $30,000. *Unit head:* Dr. Matthew Dintzner, Chairperson, 773-325-4726, Fax: 773-325-7421, E-mail: mdintzne@depaul.edu. *Application contact:* Ann Spittle, Director of Graduate Admission, 773-325-7315, Fax: 312-476-3244, E-mail: graddepaul@depaul.edu. Website: http://chemistry.depaul.edu.

Drew University, Caspersen School of Graduate Studies, Program in Education, Madison, NJ 07940-1493. Offers biology (MAT); chemistry (MAT); English (MAT); French (MAT); Italian (MAT); math (MAT); physics (MAT); social studies (MAT); Spanish (MAT); theatre arts (MAT). Part-time programs available. *Entrance requirements:* For master's, transcripts, personal statement, recommendations. Additional exam requirements/recommendations for international students: Required—TOEFL, TWE. *Expenses:* Contact institution.

Drexel University, College of Arts and Sciences, Department of Chemistry, Philadelphia, PA 19104-2875. Offers MS, PhD. Part-time programs available. Terminal master's awarded for partial completion of doctoral program. *Degree requirements:* For master's, thesis optional; for doctorate, one foreign language, thesis/dissertation. *Entrance requirements:* For master's and doctorate, GRE. Additional exam requirements/recommendations for international students: Required—TOEFL. Electronic applications accepted. *Faculty research:* Inorganic, analytical, organic, physical, and atmospheric polymer chemistry.

Duke University, Graduate School, Department of Chemistry, Durham, NC 27708. Offers PhD. *Faculty:* 23 full-time. *Students:* 92 full-time (42 women); includes 8 minority (4 Black or African American, non-Hispanic/Latino; 4 Hispanic/Latino), 41 international. 291 applicants, 22% accepted, 20 enrolled. In 2012, 19 doctorates awarded. *Degree requirements:* For doctorate, one foreign language, thesis/dissertation. *Entrance requirements:* For doctorate, GRE General Test, GRE Subject Test (recommended). Additional exam requirements/recommendations for international students: Required—TOEFL (minimum score 550 paper-based; 83 iBT), IELTS (minimum score 7). *Application deadline:* For fall admission, 12/8 priority date for domestic students, 12/8 for international students. Application fee: $80. Electronic applications accepted. *Financial support:* Fellowships, research assistantships, and teaching assistantships available. Financial award application deadline: 12/8. *Unit head:* Baldwin Steve, Director of Graduate Studies, 919-660-1503, Fax: 919-660-1605, E-mail: caroline.morris@duke.edu. *Application contact:* Elizabeth Hutton, Director of Admissions, 919-684-3913, Fax: 919-684-2277, E-mail: grad-admissions@duke.edu. Website: http://www.chem.duke.edu/graduates/.

Duquesne University, Bayer School of Natural and Environmental Sciences, Department of Chemistry and Biochemistry, Pittsburgh, PA 15282-0001. Offers chemistry (MS, PhD). Part-time programs available. *Faculty:* 14 full-time (3 women), 1 (woman) part-time/adjunct. *Students:* 39 full-time (18 women), 2 part-time (0 women); includes 4 minority (1 Black or African American, non-Hispanic/Latino; 2 Asian, non-Hispanic/Latino; 1 Hispanic/Latino), 8 international. Average age 27. 54 applicants, 30% accepted, 8 enrolled. In 2012, 1 master's, 8 doctorates awarded. Terminal master's awarded for partial completion of doctoral program. *Degree requirements:* For master's, thesis (for some programs); for doctorate, thesis/dissertation. *Entrance requirements:* For master's, GRE General Test, BS in chemistry or related field, 3 letters of recommendation, official transcripts, statement of purpose; for doctorate, GRE General Test, BS in chemistry or related field, statement of purpose, official transcripts, 3 letters of recommendation with recommendation forms. Additional exam requirements/recommendations for international students: Required—TOEFL (minimum score 100 iBT). *Application deadline:* For fall admission, 2/15 priority date for domestic students, 2/15 for international students; for spring admission, 10/1 priority date for domestic students, 10/1 for international students. Applications are processed on a rolling basis. Application fee: $0 ($40 for international students). Electronic applications accepted. *Expenses:* Contact institution. *Financial support:* In 2012–13, 39 students received support, including 1 fellowship with tuition reimbursement available (averaging $22,320 per year), 9 research assistantships with full tuition reimbursements available (averaging $22,070 per year), 27 teaching assistantships with full tuition reimbursements available (averaging $22,070 per year); scholarships/grants and unspecified assistantships also available. Financial award application deadline: 5/31. *Faculty research:* Computational physical chemistry, bioinorganic chemistry, analytical chemistry, biophysics, synthetic organic chemistry. *Total annual research expenditures:* $2.4 million. *Unit head:* Dr. Ralph Wheeler, Chair, 412-396-6341, Fax: 412-396-5683, E-mail: wheeler7@duq.edu. *Application contact:* Heather Costello, Graduate Academic Advisor, 412-396-6339, Fax: 412-396-4881, E-mail: costelloh@duq.edu. Website: http://www.duq.edu/academics/schools/natural-and-environmental-sciences/academic-programs/chemistry-and-biochemistry.

East Carolina University, Graduate School, Thomas Harriot College of Arts and Sciences, Department of Chemistry, Greenville, NC 27858-4353. Offers MS. Part-time programs available. *Degree requirements:* For master's, one foreign language, comprehensive exam, thesis. *Entrance requirements:* For master's, GRE General Test. Additional exam requirements/recommendations for international students: Required—TOEFL. *Expenses:* Tuition, state resident: full-time $4009. Tuition, nonresident: full-time $15,840. *Required fees:* $2111. *Faculty research:* Organometallic, natural-product syntheses; chemometrics; electroanalytical method development; microcomputer adaptations for handicapped students.

Eastern Illinois University, Graduate School, College of Sciences, Department of Chemistry, Charleston, IL 61920-3099. Offers MS. *Degree requirements:* For master's, thesis. *Entrance requirements:* For master's, GRE General Test.

Eastern Kentucky University, The Graduate School, College of Arts and Sciences, Department of Chemistry, Richmond, KY 40475-3102. Offers MS. Part-time and evening/weekend programs available. *Entrance requirements:* For master's, GRE General Test, minimum GPA of 2.5. *Faculty research:* Organic synthesis, surface chemistry, inorganic chemistry, analytical chemistry.

Eastern Michigan University, Graduate School, College of Arts and Sciences, Department of Chemistry, Ypsilanti, MI 48197. Offers MS. Part-time and evening/weekend programs available. *Faculty:* 20 full-time (9 women). *Students:* 1 (woman) full-time, 32 part-time (18 women); includes 3 minority (1 Black or African American, non-Hispanic/Latino; 2 Asian, non-Hispanic/Latino), 16 international. Average age 29. 41 applicants, 44% accepted, 6 enrolled. In 2012, 10 master's awarded. *Degree requirements:* For master's, thesis. *Entrance requirements:* For master's, GRE General Test. Additional exam requirements/recommendations for international students: Required—TOEFL. *Application deadline:* For fall admission, 8/1 for domestic students, 5/1 for international students; for winter admission, 12/1 for domestic students, 8/1 for international students; for spring admission, 4/1 for domestic students, 3/1 for international students. Applications are processed on a rolling basis. Application fee: $35. *Expenses:* Tuition, state resident: full-time $10,776; part-time $449 per credit hour. Tuition, nonresident: full-time $21,242; part-time $885 per credit hour. *Required fees:* $41 per credit hour. $48 per term. One-time fee: $100. Tuition and fees vary according to course level, degree level and reciprocity agreements. *Financial support:* Fellowships, research assistantships with full tuition reimbursements, teaching assistantships with full tuition reimbursements, career-related internships or fieldwork, Federal Work-Study, institutionally sponsored loans, scholarships/grants, tuition waivers (partial), and unspecified assistantships available. Support available to part-time students. Financial award applicants required to submit FAFSA. *Unit head:* Dr. Steven Pernecky, Department Head, 734-487-0106, Fax: 734-487-1496, E-mail: spernecky@emich.edu. *Application contact:* Dr. Timothy Brewer, Graduate Coordinator, 734-487-9613, Fax: 734-487-1496, E-mail: tbrewer@emich.edu. Website: http://www.emich.edu/public/chemistry/chmhome.htm.

Eastern New Mexico University, Graduate School, College of Liberal Arts and Sciences, Department of Physical Sciences, Portales, NM 88130. Offers chemistry (MS), including analytical, biochemistry, inorganic, organic, physical. Part-time programs available. *Faculty:* 2 full-time (0 women). *Students:* 2 full-time (0 women), 12 part-time (4 women), 12 international. Average age 25. 14 applicants, 93% accepted, 11 enrolled. In 2012, 5 master's awarded. *Degree requirements:* For master's, thesis optional, seminar, oral and written comprehensive exams. *Entrance requirements:* For master's, ACS placement examination, minimum GPA of 3.0; 2 letters of recommendation; personal statement of career goals; bachelor's degree with one year minimum each of general, organic, and analytical chemistry. Additional exam requirements/recommendations for international students: Required—TOEFL (minimum score 550 paper-based; 79 iBT), IELTS (minimum score 6). *Application deadline:* For fall admission, 7/20 priority date for domestic students, 6/20 for international students; for spring admission, 12/15 priority date for domestic students, 11/15 for international students. Applications are processed on a rolling basis. Application fee: $10. Electronic applications accepted. *Expenses:* Tuition, state resident: full-time $3356; part-time $139.85 per credit hour. Tuition, nonresident: full-time $9030; part-time $376.25 per credit hour. *Required fees:* $1425.60; $59.40 per credit hour. $712.80 per semester. *Financial support:* In 2012–13, 1 research assistantship with partial tuition reimbursement (averaging $8,500 per year), 10 teaching assistantships with partial tuition reimbursements (averaging $8,500 per year) were awarded; career-related internships or fieldwork and unspecified assistantships also available. Support available to part-time students. Financial award application deadline: 3/1; financial award applicants required to submit FAFSA. *Faculty research:* Synfuel, electrochemistry, protein chemistry. *Unit head:* Dr. Juacho Yan, Graduate Coordinator, 575-562-2494, Fax: 575-562-2192, E-mail: juacho.yan@enmu.edu. *Application contact:* Sharon Potter, Department Secretary, Biology and Physical Sciences, 575-562-2174, Fax: 575-562-2192, E-mail: sharon.potter@enmu.edu. Website: http://liberal-arts.enmu.edu/sciences/grad-chemistry.shtml.

East Tennessee State University, School of Graduate Studies, College of Arts and Sciences, Department of Chemistry, Johnson City, TN 37614. Offers chemistry (MS), including inorganic chemistry, organic chemistry, physical chemistry. Part-time and evening/weekend programs available. *Faculty:* 10 full-time (4 women), 1 part-time/adjunct (0 women). *Students:* 17 full-time (3 women), 6 part-time (3 women); includes 4 minority (1 Black or African American, non-Hispanic/Latino; 1 American Indian or Alaska Native, non-Hispanic/Latino; 1 Asian, non-Hispanic/Latino; 1 Two or more races, non-Hispanic/Latino), 14 international. 40 applicants, 53% accepted, 15 enrolled. In 2012, 13 master's awarded. *Degree requirements:* For master's, comprehensive exam, thesis. *Entrance requirements:* For master's, prerequisites in physical chemistry with lab requiring calculus; two letters of recommendation. Additional exam requirements/recommendations for international students: Required—TOEFL (minimum score 550 paper-based; 79 iBT). *Application deadline:* For fall admission, 6/1 for domestic students, 4/30 for international students; for spring admission, 11/1 for domestic students, 9/30 for international students. Application fee: $35 ($45 for international students). Electronic applications accepted. *Financial support:* In 2012–13, 18 students received support, including 18 teaching assistantships with full and partial tuition reimbursements available (averaging $8,300 per year); career-related internships or fieldwork, institutionally sponsored loans, scholarships/grants, and unspecified assistantships also available. Financial award application deadline: 7/1; financial award applicants required to submit FAFSA. *Faculty research:* Analytical chemistry, inorganic chemistry, organic chemistry, physical chemistry. *Unit head:* Dr. Cassandra Eagle, Chair, 423-439-4367, Fax: 423-439-5835, E-mail: eaglec@etsu.edu. *Application contact:* Gail Powers, Graduate Specialist, 423-439-4703, Fax: 423-439-5624, E-mail: powersg@etsu.edu. Website: http://www.etsu.edu/cas/chemistry/.

Emory University, Laney Graduate School, Department of Chemistry, Atlanta, GA 30322-1100. Offers PhD. *Faculty:* 22 full-time (2 women), 5 part-time/adjunct (1 woman). *Students:* 127 full-time (60 women); includes 10 minority (1 Black or African American, non-Hispanic/Latino; 4 Asian, non-Hispanic/Latino; 4 Hispanic/Latino; 1 Two or more races, non-Hispanic/Latino), 52 international. Average age 25. 377 applicants, 18% accepted, 25 enrolled. In 2012, 10 doctorates awarded. *Degree requirements:* For doctorate, comprehensive exam, thesis/dissertation. *Entrance requirements:* For doctorate, GRE General Test, 3 letters of recommendation, curriculum vitae. Additional exam requirements/recommendations for international students: Required—TOEFL. *Application deadline:* For fall admission, 1/3 priority date for domestic students, 1/3 for international students. Application fee: $75. Electronic applications accepted. *Financial support:* Fellowships, research assistantships, teaching assistantships, career-related internships or fieldwork, Federal Work-Study, institutionally sponsored loans, scholarships/grants, health care benefits, and tuition waivers (full and partial) available. Support available to part-time students. Financial award application deadline: 1/3; financial award applicants required to submit FAFSA. *Faculty research:* Organometallic synthesis and catalysis, synthesis of natural products, x-ray crystallography, mass spectrometry, analytical neurochemistry. *Unit head:* Prof. David Lynn, Chair, 404-727-9348. *Application contact:* Prof. Vincent Conticello, Director of Graduate Studies, 404-727-2779, Fax: 404-727-6586, E-mail: vcontic@emory.edu. Website: http://www.chemistry.emory.edu/.

Fairleigh Dickinson University, College at Florham, Maxwell Becton College of Arts and Sciences, Department of Chemistry and Geological Sciences, Program in Chemistry, Madison, NJ 07940-1099. Offers MS.

Fairleigh Dickinson University, Metropolitan Campus, University College: Arts, Sciences, and Professional Studies, School of Natural Sciences, Program in Chemistry, Teaneck, NJ 07666-1914. Offers MS.

Fairleigh Dickinson University, Metropolitan Campus, University College: Arts, Sciences, and Professional Studies, School of Natural Sciences, Program in Cosmetic Science, Teaneck, NJ 07666-1914. Offers MS.

Fisk University, Division of Graduate Studies, Department of Chemistry, Nashville, TN 37208-3051. Offers MA. Part-time programs available. *Degree requirements:* For master's, comprehensive exam, thesis. *Entrance requirements:* For master's, GRE General Test, minimum GPA of 3.0. Electronic applications accepted. *Faculty research:* Environmental studies, lithium compound synthesis, HIU compound synthesis.

Florida Agricultural and Mechanical University, Division of Graduate Studies, Research, and Continuing Education, College of Arts and Sciences, Department of Chemistry, Tallahassee, FL 32307-3200. Offers MS. *Degree requirements:* For master's, comprehensive exam, thesis optional. *Entrance requirements:* For master's, GRE General Test, minimum GPA of 3.0.

Florida Atlantic University, Charles E. Schmidt College of Science, Department of Chemistry and Biochemistry, Boca Raton, FL 33431-0991. Offers chemistry (MS, MST, PhD). Part-time programs available. *Faculty:* 13 full-time (1 woman), 1 (woman) part-time/adjunct. *Students:* 24 full-time (11 women), 6 part-time (4 women); includes 2 minority (1 Asian, non-Hispanic/Latino; 1 Hispanic/Latino), 12 international. Average age 27. 42 applicants, 5% accepted, 2 enrolled. In 2012, 6 doctorates awarded. Terminal master's awarded for partial completion of doctoral program. *Degree requirements:* For master's, thesis; for doctorate, comprehensive exam, thesis/dissertation. *Entrance requirements:* For master's,

GRE General Test, minimum GPA of 3.0; for doctorate, GRE, minimum GPA of 3.0. Additional exam requirements/recommendations for international students: Required—TOEFL. *Application deadline:* For fall admission, 7/1 priority date for domestic students, 2/15 for international students; for spring admission, 11/1 priority date for domestic students, 7/15 for international students. Applications are processed on a rolling basis. Application fee: $30. *Expenses:* Tuition, state resident: full-time $8876; part-time $369.82 per credit hour. Tuition, nonresident: full-time $24,595; part-time $1024.81 per credit hour. *Financial support:* Fellowships, research assistantships with full tuition reimbursements, teaching assistantships with full tuition reimbursements, and Federal Work-Study available. *Faculty research:* Polymer synthesis and characterization, spectroscopy, geochemistry, environmental chemistry, biomedical chemistry. *Unit head:* Dr. Cyril Parkanyi, Chair, 561-297-2093, Fax: 561-297-2759, E-mail: parkanyi@fau.edu. *Application contact:* Dr. Salvatore D. Lepore, Professor, 561-297-0330, Fax: 561-297-2759, E-mail: slepore@fau.edu. Website: http://www.science.fau.edu/chemistry/.

Florida Institute of Technology, Graduate Programs, College of Science, Department of Chemistry, Melbourne, FL 32901-6975. Offers biochemistry (MS); chemistry (MS, PhD). Part-time programs available. *Faculty:* 7 full-time (0 women). *Students:* 51 full-time (27 women), 1 part-time (0 women); includes 2 minority (both Black or African American, non-Hispanic/Latino), 39 international. Average age 28. 73 applicants, 63% accepted, 15 enrolled. In 2012, 9 master's, 5 doctorates awarded. Terminal master's awarded for partial completion of doctoral program. *Degree requirements:* For master's, comprehensive exam, thesis, research proposal, oral examination in defense of the thesis, proficiency examination; for doctorate, comprehensive exam, thesis/dissertation, oral defense of dissertation, dissertation research publishable to standards, complete original research study. *Entrance requirements:* For master's, proficiency exams, minimum GPA of 3.0, 3 letters of recommendation, resume, statement of objectives; for doctorate, minimum GPA of 3.3, resume, 3 letters of recommendation, statement of objectives. Additional exam requirements/recommendations for international students: Required—TOEFL (minimum score 550 paper-based; 79 iBT). *Application deadline:* For fall admission, 4/1 for international students; for spring admission, 9/30 for international students. Applications are processed on a rolling basis. Electronic applications accepted. *Expenses: Tuition:* Full-time $20,214; part-time $1123 per credit hour. Tuition and fees vary according to campus/location. *Financial support:* In 2012–13, 5 research assistantships with full and partial tuition reimbursements (averaging $8,863 per year), 11 teaching assistantships with full and partial tuition reimbursements (averaging $10,481 per year) were awarded; career-related internships or fieldwork, institutionally sponsored loans, tuition waivers (partial), unspecified assistantships, and tuition remissions also available. Support available to part-time students. Financial award application deadline: 3/1; financial award applicants required to submit FAFSA. *Faculty research:* Energy storage applications, marine and organic chemistry, stereochemistry, medicinal chemistry, environmental chemistry. *Total annual research expenditures:* $502,321. *Unit head:* Dr. Michael W. Babich, Department Head, 321-674-8046, Fax: 321-674-8951, E-mail: babich@fit.edu. *Application contact:* Cheryl A. Brown, Associate Director of Graduate Admissions, 321-674-7581, Fax: 321-723-9468, E-mail: cbrown@fit.edu. Website: http://cos.fit.edu/chemistry/.

Florida International University, College of Arts and Sciences, Department of Chemistry, Chemistry Program, Miami, FL 33199. Offers MS, PhD. *Degree requirements:* For master's, thesis; for doctorate, comprehensive exam, thesis/dissertation. *Entrance requirements:* For master's and doctorate, GRE, minimum GPA of 3.0, 3 letters of recommendation. Additional exam requirements/recommendations for international students: Required—TOEFL (minimum score 550 paper-based). Electronic applications accepted.

Florida State University, The Graduate School, College of Arts and Sciences, Department of Chemistry and Biochemistry, Tallahassee, FL 32306-4390. Offers analytical chemistry (MS, PhD); biochemistry (MS, PhD); inorganic chemistry (MS, PhD); materials chemistry (PhD); organic chemistry (MS, PhD); physical chemistry (MS, PhD). *Faculty:* 37 full-time (4 women), 1 (woman) part-time/adjunct. *Students:* 138 full-time (52 women), 8 part-time (1 woman); includes 14 minority (6 Black or African American, non-Hispanic/Latino; 3 Asian, non-Hispanic/Latino; 2 Hispanic/Latino; 3 Two or more races, non-Hispanic/Latino), 63 international. Average age 25. 147 applicants, 40% accepted, 28 enrolled. In 2012, 7 master's, 27 doctorates awarded. Terminal master's awarded for partial completion of doctoral program. *Degree requirements:* For master's, comprehensive exam, thesis (for some programs); for doctorate, comprehensive exam, thesis/dissertation. *Entrance requirements:* For master's and doctorate, GRE General Test (minimum scores: 150 verbal, 151 quantitative; 1100 total on the old scale), minimum GPA of 3.1 in undergraduate course work. Additional exam requirements/recommendations for international students: Required—TOEFL (minimum score 90 iBT). *Application deadline:* For fall admission, 12/15 priority date for domestic students, 12/15 for international students; for spring admission, 9/15 for domestic and international students. Applications are processed on a rolling basis. Application fee: $30. Electronic applications accepted. *Expenses:* Contact institution. *Financial support:* In 2012–13, 140 students received support, including 7 fellowships with full and partial tuition reimbursements available (averaging $10,000 per year), 50 research assistantships with full tuition reimbursements available (averaging $20,000 per year), 100 teaching assistantships with full tuition reimbursements available (averaging $20,000 per year); health care benefits also available. Financial award application deadline: 12/15; financial award applicants required to submit FAFSA. *Faculty research:* Bioanalytical chemistry, including separations, microfluidics, petroleomics; materials chemistry, including magnets, polymers, catalysts, nanomaterials; spectroscopy, including NMR and EPR, ultrafast, Raman, and mass spectrometry; organic synthesis, natural products, photochemistry, and supramolecular chemistry; biochemistry, with focus on structural biology, metabolomics, and anticancer drugs. *Total annual research expenditures:* $9.8 million. *Unit head:* Dr. Timothy Logan, Chairman, 850-644-3810, Fax: 850-644-8281, E-mail: gradinfo@chem.fsu.edu. *Application contact:* Dr. Michael Shatruk, Associate Chair for Graduate Studies, 850-417-8417, Fax: 850-644-8281, E-mail: gradinfo@chem.fsu.edu. Website: http://www.chem.fsu.edu/.

Furman University, Graduate Division, Department of Chemistry, Greenville, SC 29613. Offers MS. *Faculty:* 9 full-time (3 women). *Students:* 6 full-time (1 woman); includes 3 minority (1 Black or African American, non-Hispanic/Latino; 2 Asian, non-Hispanic/Latino). Average age 23. 4 applicants, 100% accepted, 4 enrolled. In 2012, 1 master's awarded. *Degree requirements:* For master's, comprehensive exam, thesis. *Entrance requirements:* For master's, GRE General Test, GRE Subject Test. *Application deadline:* For fall admission, 8/1 for domestic and international students; for spring admission, 12/10 for domestic and international students. Applications are processed on a rolling basis. Application fee: $50. *Financial support:* In 2012–13, 6 students received support, including 6 fellowships (averaging $5,122 per year); research assistantships, scholarships/grants, and unspecified assistantships also available. Financial award application deadline: 7/1; financial award applicants required to submit FAFSA. *Faculty research:* Computer-assisted chemical analysis, DNA-metal interactions, laser-initiated reactions, nucleic acid chemistry and biochemistry. *Unit head:* Dr. Lon B. Knight, Jr., Professor, 864-294-3372, Fax: 864-294-3559, E-mail: lon.knight@furman.edu. *Application contact:* Dian Hall, Information Contact, 864-294-2056, Fax: 864-294-3559, E-mail: dian.hall@furman.edu.

George Mason University, College of Science, Department of Chemistry and Biochemistry, Fairfax, VA 22030. Offers chemistry (MS); chemistry and biochemistry (PhD). *Faculty:* 17 full-time (3 women), 5 part-time/adjunct (3 women). *Students:* 32 full-time (13 women), 24 part-time (13 women); includes 20 minority (4 Black or African American, non-Hispanic/Latino; 1 American Indian or Alaska Native, non-Hispanic/Latino; 12 Asian, non-Hispanic/Latino; 3 Hispanic/Latino), 4 international. Average age 29. 57 applicants, 58% accepted, 17 enrolled. In 2012, 7 master's, 1 doctorate awarded. *Degree requirements:* For master's, thesis or alternative; for doctorate, comprehensive exam, thesis/dissertation, exit seminar. *Entrance requirements:* For master's, GRE, bachelor's degree in related field; 2 official copies of transcripts; expanded goals statement; 3 letters of recommendation; resume for those whose bachelor's degree is 5 years or older; for doctorate, GRE, undergraduate degree in related field; BS with minimum GPA of 3.0; 3 letters of recommendation; 2 copies of official transcripts; expanded goals statement; resume. Additional exam requirements/recommendations for international students: Required—TOEFL (minimum score 570 paper-based; 88 iBT), IELTS (minimum score 6.5), Pearson Test of English. *Application deadline:* For fall admission, 4/15 priority date for domestic students; for spring admission, 11/1 priority date for domestic students. Application fee: $65 ($80 for international students). Electronic applications accepted. *Expenses:* Tuition, state resident: full-time $9080; part-time $378.33 per credit hour. Tuition, nonresident: full-time $25,010; part-time $1042.08 per credit hour. *Required fees:* $2610; $108.75 per credit hour. Tuition and fees vary according to program. *Financial support:* In 2012–13, 21 students received support, including 5 research assistantships with full and partial tuition reimbursements available (averaging $15,628 per year), 16 teaching assistantships with full and partial tuition reimbursements available (averaging $14,000 per year); career-related internships or fieldwork, Federal Work-Study, scholarships/grants, unspecified assistantships, and health care benefits (for full-time research or teaching assistantship recipients) also available. Support available to part-time students. Financial award application deadline: 3/1; financial award applicants required to submit FAFSA. *Faculty research:* Electroanalytical techniques for the study of toxic species in the environment, problems associated with the solid-gas interface, applying peptide/protein engineering principles to investigate biomolecules, enzymes, isoprene biosynthesis, contaminants in the aquatic environment, radioactivity, middle distillate fuels. *Total annual research expenditures:* $52,469. *Unit head:* John A. Schreifels, Chair, 703-993-1082, Fax: 703-993-1055, E-mail: jschreif@gmu.edu. *Application contact:* Mery Tucker, Administrative Specialist, 703-993-1070, Fax: 703-993-1055, E-mail: mtucker2@gmu.edu. Website: http://chemistry.gmu.edu/.

Georgetown University, Graduate School of Arts and Sciences, Department of Chemistry, Washington, DC 20057. Offers analytical chemistry (PhD); biochemistry (PhD); computational chemistry (PhD); inorganic chemistry (PhD); materials chemistry (PhD); organic chemistry (PhD); physical chemistry (PhD); theoretical chemistry (PhD). Terminal master's awarded for partial completion of doctoral program. *Degree requirements:* For doctorate, comprehensive exam, thesis/dissertation. *Entrance requirements:* For doctorate, GRE General Test. Additional exam requirements/recommendations for international students: Required—TOEFL.

The George Washington University, Columbian College of Arts and Sciences, Department of Chemistry, Washington, DC 20052. Offers analytical chemistry (MS, PhD); inorganic chemistry (MS, PhD); materials science (MS, PhD); organic chemistry (MS, PhD); physical chemistry (MS, PhD). Part-time and evening/weekend programs available. *Faculty:* 17 full-time (6 women). *Students:* 30 full-time (16 women), 8 part-time (6 women); includes 3 minority (2 Asian, non-

Hispanic/Latino; 1 Hispanic/Latino), 8 international. Average age 27. 66 applicants, 24% accepted, 10 enrolled. In 2012, 2 master's, 3 doctorates awarded. Terminal master's awarded for partial completion of doctoral program. *Degree requirements:* For master's, comprehensive exam, thesis or alternative; for doctorate, thesis/dissertation, general exam. *Entrance requirements:* For master's and doctorate, GRE General Test, interview, minimum GPA of 3.0. Additional exam requirements/recommendations for international students: Required—TOEFL (minimum score 550 paper-based; 80 iBT). *Application deadline:* For fall admission, 1/15 priority date for domestic students, 1/15 for international students; for spring admission, 9/1 priority date for domestic students, 9/1 for international students. Applications are processed on a rolling basis. Application fee: $75. Electronic applications accepted. *Financial support:* In 2012–13, 27 students received support. Fellowships with tuition reimbursements available, research assistantships, teaching assistantships with tuition reimbursements available, Federal Work-Study, and tuition waivers available. Financial award application deadline: 1/15. *Unit head:* Dr. Michael King, Chair, 202-994-6488. *Application contact:* Information Contact, 202-994-6121, E-mail: gwchem@gwu.edu. Website: http://www.gwu.edu/~gwchem/.

Georgia Institute of Technology, Graduate Studies and Research, College of Sciences, School of Chemistry and Biochemistry, Atlanta, GA 30332-0001. Offers MS, MS Chem, PhD. Terminal master's awarded for partial completion of doctoral program. *Degree requirements:* For master's, thesis (for some programs); for doctorate, thesis/dissertation. *Entrance requirements:* For master's and doctorate, GRE General Test, GRE Subject Test, minimum GPA of 2.7. Additional exam requirements/recommendations for international students: Required—TOEFL. Electronic applications accepted. *Faculty research:* Inorganic, organic, physical, and analytical chemistry.

Georgia State University, College of Arts and Sciences, Department of Chemistry, Atlanta, GA 30302-3083. Offers analytical chemistry (MS, PhD); biochemistry (MS, PhD); bioinformatics (MS, PhD); biophysical chemistry (PhD); computational chemistry (MS, PhD); geochemistry (PhD); organic/medicinal chemistry (MS, PhD); physical chemistry (MS). PhD in geochemistry offered jointly with Department of Geology. Part-time programs available. *Faculty:* 38 full-time (11 women), 10 part-time/adjunct (3 women). *Students:* 107 full-time (57 women), 6 part-time (3 women); includes 25 minority (13 Black or African American, non-Hispanic/Latino; 1 American Indian or Alaska Native, non-Hispanic/Latino; 6 Asian, non-Hispanic/Latino; 4 Hispanic/Latino; 1 Two or more races, non-Hispanic/Latino), 57 international. Average age 28. 125 applicants, 39% accepted, 36 enrolled. In 2012, 28 master's, 12 doctorates awarded. Terminal master's awarded for partial completion of doctoral program. *Degree requirements:* For master's, one foreign language, comprehensive exam (for some programs), thesis (for some programs); for doctorate, one foreign language, comprehensive exam, thesis/dissertation. *Entrance requirements:* For master's and doctorate, GRE. Additional exam requirements/recommendations for international students: Required—TOEFL (minimum score 550 paper-based, 80 iBT) or IELTS (minimum score 6.5). *Application deadline:* For fall admission, 7/1 priority date for domestic students, 7/1 for international students; for winter admission, 11/15 priority date for domestic students, 11/15 for international students; for spring admission, 4/15 priority date for domestic students, 4/15 for international students. Applications are processed on a rolling basis. Application fee: $50. Electronic applications accepted. *Expenses:* Tuition, state resident: full-time $8064; part-time $336 per credit hour. Tuition, nonresident: full-time $28,800; part-time $1200 per credit hour. *Required fees:* $2128; $1064 per semester. Tuition and fees vary according to course load and program. *Financial support:* Fellowships with full tuition reimbursements, research assistantships with full tuition reimbursements, and teaching assistantships with full tuition reimbursements available. *Faculty research:* Analytical chemistry, biological/biochemistry, biophysical/computational chemistry, chemical education, organic/medicinal chemistry. *Total annual research expenditures:* $4 million. *Unit head:* Dr. Binghe Wang, Department Chair, 404-413-5500, Fax: 404-413-5506, E-mail: chemchair@gsu.edu. *Application contact:* Rita S. Bennett, Academic Specialist, 404-413-5497, Fax: 404-413-5505, E-mail: rsb423@gsu.edu. Website: http://chemistry.gsu.edu/.

Georgia State University, College of Education, Department of Middle-Secondary Education and Instructional Technology, Atlanta, GA 30302-3083. Offers English education (M Ed, MAT); English speakers of other languages (MAT); instructional design and technology (online) (MS); instructional technology (PhD), including alternative instructional delivery systems, consulting, instructional design, management, research; mathematics education (M Ed, MAT); middle level education (MAT); reading, language and literacy education (M Ed), including reading instruction; science education (MAT), including biology, broad field science, chemistry, earth science, physics; social studies education (M Ed, MAT), including economics (MAT), geography (MAT), history (MAT), political science (MAT); teaching and learning (PhD), including language and literacy, mathematics education, music education, science education, social studies, teaching and teacher education. *Accreditation:* NCATE. Part-time and evening/weekend programs available. Postbaccalaureate distance learning degree programs offered (minimal on-campus study). *Faculty:* 38 full-time (30 women), 7 part-time/adjunct (all women). *Students:* 268 full-time (191 women), 243 part-time (172 women); includes 212 minority (148 Black or African American, non-Hispanic/Latino; 1 American Indian or Alaska Native, non-Hispanic/Latino; 26 Asian, non-Hispanic/Latino; 20 Hispanic/Latino; 1 Native Hawaiian or other Pacific Islander, non-Hispanic/Latino; 16 Two or more races, non-Hispanic/Latino), 15 international. Average age 34. 149 applicants, 67% accepted, 67 enrolled. In 2012, 253 master's, 18 doctorates awarded. *Degree requirements:* For master's, comprehensive exam (for some programs), thesis or alternative, exit portfolio; for doctorate, comprehensive exam, thesis/dissertation. *Entrance requirements:* For master's, GRE; GACE I (for initial teacher preparation degree programs), baccalaureate degree or equivalent, resume, goals statement, two letters of recommendation, minimum undergraduate GPA of 2.5; proof of initial teacher certification in the content area (for M Ed); for doctorate, GRE, resume, goals statement, writing sample, two letters of recommendation, minimum graduate GPA of 3.3, interview. Additional exam requirements/recommendations for international students: Required—TOEFL (minimum score 550 paper-based, 79 iBT) or IELTS (minimum score 6.5). *Application deadline:* For fall admission, 1/15 priority date for domestic students, 1/15 for international students; for spring admission, 10/1 for domestic and international students. Application fee: $50. Electronic applications accepted. *Expenses:* Tuition, state resident: full-time $8064; part-time $336 per credit hour. Tuition, nonresident: full-time $28,800; part-time $1200 per credit hour. *Required fees:* $2128; $1064 per semester. Tuition and fees vary according to course load and program. *Financial support:* In 2012–13, 110 students received support, including 3 fellowships with full tuition reimbursements available (averaging $19,667 per year), 68 research assistantships with full tuition reimbursements available (averaging $5,436 per year), 29 teaching assistantships with full tuition reimbursements available (averaging $2,779 per year); career-related internships or fieldwork, Federal Work-Study, scholarships/grants, health care benefits, tuition waivers (full and partial), and unspecified assistantships also available. Financial award application deadline: 3/15. *Faculty research:* Teacher education in language and literacy, mathematics, science, and social studies in urban middle and secondary school settings; learning technologies in school, community, and corporate settings; multicultural education and education for social justice; urban education; international education. *Total annual research expenditures:* $761,493. *Unit head:* Dr. Dana L. Fox, Chair, 404-413-8060, Fax: 404-413-8063, E-mail: dfox@gsu.edu. *Application contact:* Bobbie Turner, Administrative Coordinator I, 404-413-8405, Fax: 404-413-8063, E-mail: bnturner@gsu.edu. Website: http://msit.gsu.edu/msit_programs.htm

Graduate School and University Center of the City University of New York, Graduate Studies, Program in Chemistry, New York, NY 10016-4039. Offers PhD. *Degree requirements:* For doctorate, one foreign language, thesis/dissertation. *Entrance requirements:* For doctorate, GRE General Test. Additional exam requirements/recommendations for international students: Required—TOEFL. Electronic applications accepted.

Hampton University, Graduate College, Department of Chemistry, Hampton, VA 23668. Offers MS. Part-time and evening/weekend programs available. *Degree requirements:* For master's, thesis. *Entrance requirements:* For master's, GRE General Test.

Harvard University, Graduate School of Arts and Sciences, Department of Chemistry and Chemical Biology, Cambridge, MA 02138. Offers biochemical chemistry (PhD); inorganic chemistry (PhD); organic chemistry (PhD); physical chemistry (PhD). *Degree requirements:* For doctorate, thesis/dissertation, cumulative exams. *Entrance requirements:* For doctorate, GRE General Test, GRE Subject Test. Additional exam requirements/recommendations for international students: Required—TOEFL. *Expenses: Tuition:* Full-time $37,576. *Required fees:* $930. Tuition and fees vary according to program and student level.

See Display on next page and Close-Up on page 125.

Hofstra University, School of Education, Programs in Teaching - Secondary Education, Hempstead, NY 11549. Offers business education (MS Ed); education technology (Advanced Certificate); English education (MA, MS Ed); foreign language and TESOL (MS Ed); foreign language education (MA, MS Ed), including French, German, Russian, Spanish; mathematics education (MA, MS Ed); science education (MA, MS Ed), including biology, chemistry, earth science, geology, physics; secondary education (Advanced Certificate); social studies education (MA, MS Ed); technology for learning (MA). Part-time and evening/weekend programs available. Postbaccalaureate distance learning degree programs offered (minimal on-campus study). *Students:* 64 full-time (36 women), 41 part-time (22 women); includes 17 minority (9 Black or African American, non-Hispanic/Latino; 3 Asian, non-Hispanic/Latino; 4 Hispanic/Latino; 1 Native Hawaiian or other Pacific Islander, non-Hispanic/Latino). Average age 28. 87 applicants, 87% accepted, 46 enrolled. In 2012, 57 master's, 7 other advanced degrees awarded. *Degree requirements:* For master's, one foreign language, comprehensive exam (for some programs), thesis (for some programs), exit project, electronic portfolio, student teaching, fieldwork, curriculum project, minimum GPA of 3.0; for Advanced Certificate, 3 foreign languages, comprehensive exam (for some programs), thesis project. *Entrance requirements:* For master's, 2 letters of recommendation, teacher certification (MA), essay; for Advanced Certificate, 2 letters of recommendation, essay, interview and/or portfolio. Additional exam requirements/recommendations for international students: Required—TOEFL (minimum score 550 paper-based; 80 iBT); Recommended—IELTS (minimum score 6.5). *Application deadline:* Applications are processed on a rolling basis. Application fee: $70 ($75 for international students). Electronic applications accepted. *Expenses: Tuition:* Full-time $19,800; part-time $1100 per credit hour. *Required fees:* $970; $165 per term. Tuition and fees vary according to program. *Financial support:* In 2012–13, 82 students received support, including 17 fellowships with full and partial tuition reimbursements available (averaging $3,142 per year), 1 research assistantship

Chemistry

with full and partial tuition reimbursement available (averaging $16,527 per year); career-related internships or fieldwork, Federal Work-Study, institutionally sponsored loans, scholarships/grants, tuition waivers (full and partial), and unspecified assistantships also available. Support available to part-time students. Financial award applicants required to submit FAFSA. *Faculty research:* Appropriate content in secondary school disciplines, appropriate pedagogy in secondary school disciplines, adolescent development, secondary school organization, preparation for EDTPA addition to the curriculum. *Unit head:* Dr. Esther Fusco, Chairperson, 516-463-7704, Fax: 516-463-6196, E-mail: catezf@hofstra.edu. *Application contact:* Carol Drummer, Dean of Graduate Admissions, 516-463-4876, Fax: 516-463-4664, E-mail: gradstudent@hofstra.edu. Website: http://www.hofstra.edu/education/.

Howard University, Graduate School, Department of Chemistry, Washington, DC 20059-0002. Offers analytical chemistry (MS, PhD); atmospheric (MS, PhD); biochemistry (MS, PhD); environmental (MS, PhD); inorganic chemistry (MS, PhD); organic chemistry (MS, PhD); physical chemistry (MS, PhD). Terminal master's awarded for partial completion of doctoral program. *Degree requirements:* For master's, comprehensive exam, thesis, teaching experience; for doctorate, comprehensive exam, thesis/dissertation, teaching experience. *Entrance requirements:* For master's, GRE General Test, minimum GPA of 2.7; for doctorate, GRE General Test, minimum GPA of 3.0. Additional exam requirements/recommendations for international students: Required—TOEFL. Electronic applications accepted. *Faculty research:* Synthetic organics, materials, natural products, mass spectrometry.

Hunter College of the City University of New York, Graduate School, School of Arts and Sciences, Department of Chemistry, New York, NY 10021-5085. Offers biochemistry (MA, PhD); chemistry (PhD). Part-time programs available. *Faculty:* 10 full-time (2 women). *Students:* 1 full-time (0 women), 7 part-time (6 women); includes 4 minority (all Asian, non-Hispanic/Latino), 1 international. Average age 26. 13 applicants, 54% accepted, 5 enrolled. In 2012, 8 master's awarded. *Degree requirements:* For master's, comprehensive exam or thesis. *Entrance requirements:* For master's, GRE General Test, 1 year of course work in chemistry, quantitative analysis, organic chemistry, physical chemistry, biology, biochemistry lecture and laboratory. Additional exam requirements/recommendations for international students: Required—TOEFL. *Application deadline:* For fall admission, 4/1 for domestic students; for spring admission, 11/1 for domestic students. Application fee: $125. *Expenses:* Tuition, state resident: full-time $8690; part-time $365 per credit. Tuition, nonresident: full-time $16,200; part-time $675 per credit. *Required fees:* $320 per semester. One-time fee: $125. Tuition and fees vary according to class time, campus/location and program. *Financial support:* Teaching assistantships and tuition waivers (partial) available. Support available to part-time students. *Faculty research:* Theoretical chemistry, vibrational optical activity, Raman spectroscopy. *Unit head:* Dr. Gary J. Quigley,

Chairperson, 212-772-5330, E-mail: gary.quilgley@hunter.cuny.edu. *Application contact:* William Zlata, Director for Graduate Admissions, 212-772-4482, Fax: 212-650-3336, E-mail: admissions@hunter.cuny.edu.

Idaho State University, Office of Graduate Studies, College of Science and Engineering, Department of Chemistry, Pocatello, ID 83209-8023. Offers MNS, MS. MS students must enter as undergraduates. Part-time programs available. *Degree requirements:* For master's, comprehensive exam, thesis (for some programs). *Entrance requirements:* For master's, GRE General Test, minimum GPA of 3.0 in all upper-division classes; 1 semester of calculus, inorganic chemistry, and analytical chemistry; 1 year of physics, organic chemistry and physical chemistry. Additional exam requirements/recommendations for international students: Required—TOEFL (minimum score 550 paper-based; 80 iBT). Electronic applications accepted. *Faculty research:* Low temperature plasma, organic chemistry, physical chemistry, inorganic chemistry, analytical chemistry.

Illinois Institute of Technology, Graduate College, College of Science and Letters, Department of Biological and Chemical Sciences, Chemistry Division, Chicago, IL 60616. Offers analytical chemistry (M Ch); chemistry (M Chem, MS, PhD); materials and chemical synthesis (M Ch). Part-time and evening/weekend programs available. Postbaccalaureate distance learning degree programs offered (no on-campus study). *Faculty:* 12 full-time (4 women). *Students:* 41 full-time (17 women), 51 part-time (25 women); includes 6 minority (2 Black or African American, non-Hispanic/Latino; 1 Asian, non-Hispanic/Latino; 2 Hispanic/Latino; 1 Two or more races, non-Hispanic/Latino), 36 international. Average age 29. 151 applicants, 84% accepted, 36 enrolled. In 2012, 13 master's awarded. Terminal master's awarded for partial completion of doctoral program. *Degree requirements:* For master's, comprehensive exam, thesis (for some programs); for doctorate, comprehensive exam, thesis/dissertation. *Entrance requirements:* For master's, GRE General Test (minimum score 1000 Quantitative and Verbal, 2.5 Analytical Writing), minimum undergraduate GPA of 3.0; for doctorate, GRE General Test (minimum score 1100 Quantitative and Verbal, 3.0 Analytical Writing), GRE Subject Test, minimum undergraduate GPA of 3.0. Additional exam requirements/recommendations for international students: Required—TOEFL (minimum score 523 paper-based; 70 iBT); Recommended—IELTS. *Application deadline:* For fall admission, 5/1 for domestic and international students; for spring admission, 10/15 for domestic and international students. Applications are processed on a rolling basis. Application fee: $40. Electronic applications accepted. *Expenses: Tuition:* Full-time $20,142; part-time $1119 per credit hour. *Required fees:* $605 per semester. One-time fee: $255. Tuition and fees vary according to program and student level. *Financial support:* Fellowships with full and partial tuition reimbursements, research assistantships with full and partial tuition reimbursements, teaching assistantships with full and partial tuition reimbursements, Federal Work-Study, institutionally sponsored loans,

70 www.petersonsbooks.com

Peterson's Graduate Programs in the Physical Sciences, Mathematics, Agricultural Sciences, the Environment & Natural Resources 2014

scholarships/grants, health care benefits, tuition waivers (partial), and unspecified assistantships available. Support available to part-time students. Financial award applicants required to submit FAFSA. *Faculty research:* Synthesis and analysis of inorganic nanoparticles; synthetic and mechanistic organic chemistry; synthesis of penicillin-related compounds; design, synthesis and property studies of nanomaterials for applications in chemical sensing, energy storage and biomedical usage; scanning probe microscopy. *Total annual research expenditures:* $201,793. *Unit head:* Dr. Rong Wang, Associate Chair, 312-567-3121, Fax: 312-567-3494, E-mail: wangr@iit.edu. *Application contact:* Deborah Gibson, Director, Graduate Admission, 866-472-3448, Fax: 312-567-3138, E-mail: inquiry.grad@iit.edu. Website: http://www.iit.edu/csl/che/.

Illinois State University, Graduate School, College of Arts and Sciences, Department of Chemistry, Normal, IL 61790-2200. Offers MS. *Degree requirements:* For master's, thesis. *Entrance requirements:* For master's, GRE General Test, minimum GPA of 2.6 in last 60 hours of course work. *Faculty research:* Solid-state and solution behavior of lanthanide scorpionates and porphyrinoids; CAREER: Versatile Vanadium: biology, materials science and education through its diverse coordinator carbaporphyrins and other highly modified porphyrinoid systems; oxadiazines: structurally novel templates for catalytic asymmetric synthesis.

Indiana University Bloomington, University Graduate School, College of Arts and Sciences, Department of Chemistry, Bloomington, IN 47405. Offers analytical chemistry (PhD); chemical biology chemistry (PhD); chemistry (MAT); inorganic chemistry (PhD); materials chemistry (PhD); organic chemistry (PhD); physical chemistry (PhD). *Faculty:* 42 full-time (4 women). *Students:* 215 full-time (85 women), 4 part-time (1 woman); includes 21 minority (8 Black or African American, non-Hispanic/Latino; 9 Asian, non-Hispanic/Latino; 1 Hispanic/Latino; 3 Two or more races, non-Hispanic/Latino), 69 international. Average age 27. 329 applicants, 40% accepted, 50 enrolled. In 2012, 12 master's, 20 doctorates awarded. Terminal master's awarded for partial completion of doctoral program. *Degree requirements:* For master's, thesis; for doctorate, thesis/dissertation. *Entrance requirements:* For master's and doctorate, GRE General Test, GRE Subject Test. Additional exam requirements/recommendations for international students: Required—TOEFL. *Application deadline:* For fall admission, 1/15 priority date for domestic students, 12/15 for international students. Applications are processed on a rolling basis. Application fee: $55 ($65 for international students). *Financial support:* In 2012–13, 200 students received support, including 10 fellowships with full tuition reimbursements available, 76 research assistantships with full tuition reimbursements available, 111 teaching assistantships with full tuition reimbursements available; Federal Work-Study and institutionally sponsored loans also available. *Faculty research:* Synthesis of complex natural products, organic reaction mechanisms, organic electrochemistry, transitive-metal chemistry, solid-state and surface chemistry. *Total annual research expenditures:* $7.7 million. *Unit head:* David Giedroc, Chairperson, 812-855-6239, E-mail: chemchair@indiana.edu. *Application contact:* Daniel Mindiola, Director of Graduate Admissions, 812-855-2069, Fax: 812-855-8385, E-mail: mindiola@indiana.edu. Website: http://www.chem.indiana.edu/.

Indiana University of Pennsylvania, School of Graduate Studies and Research, College of Natural Sciences and Mathematics, Department of Chemistry, MA Program in Chemistry, Indiana, PA 15705-1087. Offers MA. Part-time programs available. *Faculty:* 7 full-time (2 women). *Students:* 2 full-time (0 women), 1 part-time (0 women), 1 international. Average age 34. *Degree requirements:* For master's, thesis optional. *Entrance requirements:* For master's, 2 letters of recommendation. Additional exam requirements/recommendations for international students: Required—TOEFL (minimum score 540 paper-based). *Application deadline:* Applications are processed on a rolling basis. Application fee: $50. Electronic applications accepted. *Expenses:* Tuition, state resident: part-time $429 per credit hour. Tuition, nonresident: part-time $644 per credit hour. *Required fees:* $110.60 per credit hour. One-time fee: $180 part-time. *Financial support:* Research assistantships with full and partial tuition reimbursements available. Financial award application deadline: 4/15; financial award applicants required to submit FAFSA. *Unit head:* Dr. Keith Kyler, Graduate Coordinator, 724-357-5702, E-mail: keith.kyler@iup.edu. *Application contact:* Dr. Lawrence Kupchella, Graduate Coordinator, 724-357-5702, E-mail: lkup@iup.edu. Website: http://www.iup.edu/upper.aspx?id=90471.

Indiana University of Pennsylvania, School of Graduate Studies and Research, College of Natural Sciences and Mathematics, Department of Chemistry, MS Program in Chemistry, Indiana, PA 15705-1087. Offers MS. *Faculty:* 7 full-time (2 women). *Students:* 13 full-time (5 women), 2 part-time (1 woman); includes 3 minority (1 Black or African American, non-Hispanic/Latino; 2 Asian, non-Hispanic/Latino), 5 international. Average age 25. 26 applicants, 46% accepted, 5 enrolled. In 2012, 3 master's awarded. *Degree requirements:* For master's, thesis. *Entrance requirements:* For master's, 2 letters of recommendation. Additional exam requirements/recommendations for international students: Required—TOEFL (minimum score 540 paper-based). *Application deadline:* Applications are processed on a rolling basis. Application fee: $50. Electronic applications accepted. *Expenses:* Tuition, state resident: part-time $429 per credit hour. Tuition, nonresident: part-time $644 per credit hour. *Required fees:* $110.60 per credit hour. One-time fee: $180 part-time. *Financial support:* Research assistantships available. *Unit head:* Dr. John C. Woolcock, Chairperson, 724-357-2361. *Application contact:* Dr. Lawrence Kupchella, Graduate Coordinator, 724-357-5702, E-mail: lkup@iup.edu. Website: http://www.iup.edu/upper.aspx?id=90471.

Indiana University–Purdue University Indianapolis, School of Science, Department of Chemistry and Chemical Biology, Indianapolis, IN 46202-2896. Offers MS, PhD, MD/PhD. MD/PhD offered jointly with Indiana University School of Medicine and Purdue University. Part-time and evening/weekend programs available. *Faculty:* 10 full-time (2 women). *Students:* 20 full-time (12 women), 24 part-time (12 women); includes 4 minority (1 Asian, non-Hispanic/Latino; 1 Hispanic/Latino; 2 Two or more races, non-Hispanic/Latino), 10 international. Average age 31. 16 applicants, 44% accepted, 6 enrolled. In 2012, 7 master's awarded. Terminal master's awarded for partial completion of doctoral program. *Degree requirements:* For master's, thesis (for some programs); for doctorate, thesis/dissertation. *Entrance requirements:* For master's and doctorate, minimum GPA of 3.0. Additional exam requirements/recommendations for international students: Required—TOEFL. *Application deadline:* Applications are processed on a rolling basis. Application fee: $55 ($65 for international students). *Financial support:* In 2012–13, fellowships with partial tuition reimbursements (averaging $13,500 per year), teaching assistantships with partial tuition reimbursements (averaging $17,440 per year) were awarded; research assistantships with partial tuition reimbursements, career-related internships or fieldwork, institutionally sponsored loans, tuition waivers (partial), and cooperative positions also available. Financial award application deadline: 3/1. *Faculty research:* Analytical, biological, inorganic, organic, and physical chemistry. *Total annual research expenditures:* $1.6 million. *Unit head:* Jay A. Siegel, Chair, 317-274-6872. *Application contact:* Eric Long, Associate Chair, 317-274-6888, Fax: 317-274-4701, E-mail: long@chem.iupui.edu. Website: http://www.chem.iupui.edu/.

Instituto Tecnológico y de Estudios Superiores de Monterrey, Campus Monterrey, Graduate and Research Division, Program in Natural and Social Sciences, Monterrey, Mexico. Offers biotechnology (MS); chemistry (MS, PhD); communications (MS); education (MA). Part-time programs available. *Degree requirements:* For master's, one foreign language, thesis; for doctorate, one foreign language, thesis/dissertation. *Entrance requirements:* For master's, EXADEP; for doctorate, EXADEP, master's degree in related field. Additional exam requirements/recommendations for international students: Required—TOEFL. *Faculty research:* Cultural industries, mineral substances, bioremediation, food processing, CQ in industrial chemical processing.

Iowa State University of Science and Technology, Department of Chemistry, Ames, IA 50011. Offers MS, PhD. *Degree requirements:* For master's, thesis; for doctorate, thesis/dissertation. *Entrance requirements:* Additional exam requirements/recommendations for international students: Required—TOEFL (minimum score 570 paper-based; 89 iBT), IELTS (minimum score 6.5). *Application deadline:* For fall admission, 2/1 priority date for domestic students, 2/1 for international students. Application fee: $60 ($90 for international students). Electronic applications accepted. *Application contact:* Lynette Edsall, Application Contact, 800-521-2436, Fax: 515-294-0105, E-mail: chemgrad@iastate.edu. Website: http://www.chem.iastate.edu/.

Jackson State University, Graduate School, College of Science, Engineering and Technology, Department of Chemistry and Biochemistry, Jackson, MS 39217. Offers MS, PhD. Part-time and evening/weekend programs available. *Degree requirements:* For master's, comprehensive exam, thesis; for doctorate, comprehensive exam, thesis/dissertation. *Entrance requirements:* For master's, GRE General Test; for doctorate, MAT. Additional exam requirements/recommendations for international students: Required—TOEFL (minimum score 520 paper-based; 67 iBT). *Faculty research:* Electrochemical and spectroscopic studies on charge transfer and energy transfer processes, spectroscopy of trapped molecular ions, respirable mine dust.

The Johns Hopkins University, Zanvyl Krieger School of Arts and Sciences, Chemistry-Biology Interface Program, Baltimore, MD 21218-2699. Offers PhD. Terminal master's awarded for partial completion of doctoral program. *Degree requirements:* For doctorate, comprehensive exam, thesis/dissertation, 8 one-semester courses, literature seminar, research proposal. *Entrance requirements:* For doctorate, GRE General Test, GRE Subject Test in biochemistry, cell and molecular biology, biology or chemistry (strongly recommended), 3 letters of recommendation, interview. Electronic applications accepted. *Faculty research:* Enzyme mechanisms, inhibitors, and metabolic pathways; DNA replication, damaged, and repair; using small molecules to probe signal transduction, gene regulation, angiogenesis, and other biological processes; synthetic methods and medicinal chemistry; synthetic modeling of metalloenzymes.

The Johns Hopkins University, Zanvyl Krieger School of Arts and Sciences, Department of Chemistry, Baltimore, MD 21218-2699. Offers PhD. Terminal master's awarded for partial completion of doctoral program. *Degree requirements:* For doctorate, comprehensive exam, thesis/dissertation, 8 one-semester courses, literature seminar. *Entrance requirements:* For doctorate, GRE General Test, GRE Subject Test. Additional exam requirements/recommendations for international students: Required—TOEFL (minimum score 600 paper-based), IELTS. Electronic applications accepted. *Faculty research:* Experimental physical, biophysical, inorganic/materials, organic/bioorganic theoretical.

Kansas State University, Graduate School, College of Arts and Sciences, Department of Chemistry, Manhattan, KS 66506. Offers analytical chemistry (MS); biological chemistry (MS); chemistry (PhD); inorganic chemistry (MS); materials chemistry (MS); organic chemistry (MS); physical chemistry (MS).

Faculty: 17 full-time (1 woman). *Students:* 71 full-time (36 women); includes 1 minority (Asian, non-Hispanic/Latino), 59 international. Average age 28. 108 applicants, 35% accepted, 15 enrolled. In 2012, 5 master's, 9 doctorates awarded. Terminal master's awarded for partial completion of doctoral program. *Degree requirements:* For master's, thesis; for doctorate, thesis/dissertation. *Entrance requirements:* For master's and doctorate, GRE, minimum GPA of 3.0. Additional exam requirements/recommendations for international students: Required—TOEFL (minimum score 550 paper-based). *Application deadline:* For fall admission, 2/1 priority date for domestic students, 2/1 for international students; for spring admission, 8/1 priority date for domestic students, 8/1 for international students. Applications are processed on a rolling basis. Application fee: $50 ($75 for international students). Electronic applications accepted. *Financial support:* In 2012–13, 39 research assistantships (averaging $18,182 per year), 24 teaching assistantships with full tuition reimbursements (averaging $18,106 per year) were awarded; institutionally sponsored loans and scholarships/grants also available. Support available to part-time students. Financial award application deadline: 3/1; financial award applicants required to submit FAFSA. *Faculty research:* Inorganic chemistry, organic and biological chemistry, analytical chemistry, physical chemistry, materials chemistry and nanotechnology. *Total annual research expenditures:* $2.8 million. *Unit head:* Eric Maatta, Head, 785-532-6665, Fax: 785-532-6666, E-mail: eam@ksu.edu. *Application contact:* Christer Aakeroy, Director, 785-532-6096, Fax: 785-532-6666, E-mail: aakeroy@ksu.edu. Website: http://www.k-state.edu/chem/.

Kent State University, College of Arts and Sciences, Department of Chemistry and Biochemistry, Kent, OH 44242-0001. Offers analytical chemistry (MS, PhD); biochemistry (MS, PhD); chemistry (MA); inorganic chemistry (MS, PhD); organic chemistry (MS, PhD); physical chemistry (MS, PhD). Terminal master's awarded for partial completion of doctoral program. *Degree requirements:* For master's, comprehensive exam, thesis; for doctorate, comprehensive exam, thesis/dissertation. *Entrance requirements:* For master's and doctorate, placement exam, GRE General Test, GRE Subject Test (recommended), minimum GPA of 2.75. Additional exam requirements/recommendations for international students: Required—TOEFL (minimum score 525 paper-based; 71 iBT). Electronic applications accepted. *Expenses:* Tuition, state resident: full-time $8424; part-time $468 per credit hour. Tuition, nonresident: full-time $14,580; part-time $810 per credit hour. Tuition and fees vary according to course load. *Faculty research:* Biological chemistry, materials chemistry, molecular spectroscopy.

See Display on next page and Close-Up on page 127.

Lakehead University, Graduate Studies, Faculty of Social Sciences and Humanities, Department of Chemistry, Thunder Bay, ON P7B 5E1, Canada. Offers M Sc. Part-time and evening/weekend programs available. *Degree requirements:* For master's, thesis, oral examination. *Entrance requirements:* For master's, minimum B+ average. Additional exam requirements/recommendations for international students: Required—TOEFL. *Faculty research:* Physical inorganic chemistry, photochemistry, physical chemistry.

Lamar University, College of Graduate Studies, College of Arts and Sciences, Department of Chemistry and Biochemistry, Beaumont, TX 77710. Offers chemistry (MS). Part-time programs available. *Faculty:* 10 full-time (3 women). *Students:* 97 full-time (39 women), 10 part-time (5 women); includes 3 minority (1 Black or African American, non-Hispanic/Latino; 1 Hispanic/Latino; 1 Two or more races, non-Hispanic/Latino), 99 international. Average age 24. 130 applicants, 92% accepted, 37 enrolled. In 2012, 19 master's awarded. *Degree requirements:* For master's, thesis, practicum. *Entrance requirements:* For master's, GRE General Test, minimum GPA of 2.5 in last 60 hours of course work. Additional exam requirements/recommendations for international students: Required—TOEFL, TWE. *Application deadline:* For fall admission, 8/1 for domestic students, 7/1 for international students; for spring admission, 12/1 for domestic students, 11/1 for international students. Applications are processed on a rolling basis. Application fee: $25 ($50 for international students). *Expenses:* Tuition, state resident: full-time $5364; part-time $298 per credit hour. Tuition, nonresident: full-time $12,582; part-time $699 per credit hour. *Required fees:* $1844. *Financial support:* In 2012–13, 6 students received support, including 5 teaching assistantships with partial tuition reimbursements available (averaging $9,000 per year); tuition waivers (partial) and unspecified assistantships also available. Financial award application deadline: 4/1. *Faculty research:* Environmental chemistry, surface chemistry, polymer chemistry, organic synthesis, computational chemistry. *Unit head:* Dr. Richard S. Lumpkin, Chair, 409-880-8267, Fax: 409-880-8270, E-mail: lumpkines@hal.lamar.edu. *Application contact:* Dr. Paul Bernazzani, Graduate Advisor, 409-880-8272, Fax: 409-880-8270, E-mail: bernazzapx@hal.lamar.edu.

Laurentian University, School of Graduate Studies and Research, Programme in Chemistry and Biochemistry, Sudbury, ON P3E 2C6, Canada. Offers analytical chemistry (M Sc); biochemistry (M Sc); environmental chemistry (M Sc); organic chemistry (M Sc); physical/theoretical chemistry (M Sc). Part-time programs available. *Degree requirements:* For master's, thesis or alternative. *Entrance requirements:* For master's, honors degree with minimum second class. *Faculty research:* Cell cycle checkpoints, kinetic modeling, toxicology to metal stress, quantum chemistry, biogeochemistry metal speciation.

Lehigh University, College of Arts and Sciences, Department of Chemistry, Bethlehem, PA 18015. Offers MS, PhD. Part-time programs available. Postbaccalaureate distance learning degree programs offered (no on-campus study). *Faculty:* 15 full-time (1 woman), 5 part-time/adjunct (1 woman). *Students:* 44 full-time (22 women), 60 part-time (30 women); includes 10 minority (2 Black or African American, non-Hispanic/Latino; 6 Asian, non-Hispanic/Latino; 1 Hispanic/Latino; 1 Two or more races, non-Hispanic/Latino), 17 international. Average age 30. 113 applicants, 40% accepted, 30 enrolled. In 2012, 34 master's, 2 doctorates awarded. Terminal master's awarded for partial completion of doctoral program. *Degree requirements:* For master's, comprehensive exam, thesis; for doctorate, comprehensive exam, thesis/dissertation. *Entrance requirements:* Additional exam requirements/recommendations for international students: Required—TOEFL (minimum score 85 iBT). *Application deadline:* For fall admission, 1/15 priority date for domestic students, 1/15 for international students. Applications are processed on a rolling basis. Application fee: $75. Electronic applications accepted. *Financial support:* In 2012–13, 3 fellowships with full tuition reimbursements (averaging $25,000 per year), 8 research assistantships with full tuition reimbursements (averaging $25,000 per year), 19 teaching assistantships with full tuition reimbursements (averaging $25,000 per year) were awarded; career-related internships or fieldwork, Federal Work-Study, institutionally sponsored loans, scholarships/grants, tuition waivers (full and partial), and unspecified assistantships also available. Support available to part-time students. Financial award application deadline: 1/15. *Faculty research:* Materials chemistry, biological chemistry, surface chemistry, nano science. *Total annual research expenditures:* $2.6 million. *Unit head:* Prof. Robert A. Flowers, II, Professor/Chair, 610-758-3470, Fax: 610-758-6536, E-mail: rof2@lehigh.edu. *Application contact:* Dr. Rebecca Miller, Graduate Coordinator, 610-758-3471, Fax: 610-758-6536, E-mail: inluchem@lehigh.edu. Website: http://www.lehigh.edu/chemistry.

Long Island University–Brooklyn Campus, Richard L. Conolly College of Liberal Arts and Sciences, Department of Chemistry, Brooklyn, NY 11201-8423. Offers MS. Part-time and evening/weekend programs available. *Degree requirements:* For master's, thesis or alternative. *Entrance requirements:* For master's, 2 letters of recommendation. Additional exam requirements/recommendations for international students: Required—TOEFL (minimum score 500 paper-based). Electronic applications accepted. *Faculty research:* Clinical chemistry, free radicals, heats of hydrogenation.

Louisiana State University and Agricultural and Mechanical College, Graduate School, College of Science, Department of Chemistry, Baton Rouge, LA 70803. Offers MS, PhD. Part-time programs available. *Faculty:* 27 full-time (6 women), 1 part-time/adjunct (0 women). *Students:* 158 full-time (68 women), 6 part-time (2 women); includes 38 minority (26 Black or African American, non-Hispanic/Latino; 5 Asian, non-Hispanic/Latino; 5 Hispanic/Latino; 2 Two or more races, non-Hispanic/Latino), 67 international. Average age 28. 147 applicants, 34% accepted, 29 enrolled. In 2012, 4 master's, 25 doctorates awarded. Terminal master's awarded for partial completion of doctoral program. *Degree requirements:* For master's, thesis (for some programs); for doctorate, thesis/dissertation, general exam. *Entrance requirements:* For master's and doctorate, GRE General Test, minimum GPA of 3.0. Additional exam requirements/recommendations for international students: Required—TOEFL (minimum score 550 paper-based; 79 iBT) or IELTS (minimum score 6.5). *Application deadline:* For fall admission, 3/1 priority date for domestic students, 5/15 for international students; for spring admission, 8/1 for domestic students, 10/15 for international students. Applications are processed on a rolling basis. Application fee: $25. Electronic applications accepted. *Financial support:* In 2012–13, 161 students received support, including 26 fellowships with full tuition reimbursements available (averaging $31,082 per year), 54 research assistantships with full and partial tuition reimbursements available (averaging $22,171 per year), 84 teaching assistantships with full and partial tuition reimbursements available (averaging $22,000 per year); career-related internships or fieldwork, Federal Work-Study, scholarships/grants, traineeships, and unspecified assistantships also available. Support available to part-time students. Financial award application deadline: 7/1; financial award applicants required to submit FAFSA. *Faculty research:* Materials, biological, environmental. *Total annual research expenditures:* $6.7 million. *Unit head:* Dr. Luigi Marzilli, Chair, 225-578-3465, Fax: 225-578-3458, E-mail: lmarzil@lsu.edu. *Application contact:* Dr. John Pojman, Director of Graduate Studies, 225-578-7202, Fax: 225-578-3458, E-mail: japojman@lsu.edu. Website: http://chemistry.lsu.edu/.

Louisiana Tech University, Graduate School, College of Engineering and Science, Department of Chemistry, Ruston, LA 71272. Offers MS. Part-time programs available. *Degree requirements:* For master's, thesis. *Entrance requirements:* For master's, GRE General Test, minimum GPA of 3.0 in last 60 hours. Additional exam requirements/recommendations for international students: Required—TOEFL. *Faculty research:* Vibrational spectroscopy, quantum studies of chemical reactions, enzyme kinetics, synthesis of transition metal compounds, NMR spectrometry.

Loyola University Chicago, Graduate School, Department of Chemistry, Chicago, IL 60660. Offers MS, PhD. Part-time and evening/weekend programs available. *Faculty:* 14 full-time (2 women). *Students:* 38 full-time (19 women), 4 part-time (3 women); includes 15 minority (4 Black or African American, non-Hispanic/Latino; 5 Asian, non-Hispanic/Latino; 4 Hispanic/Latino; 1 Native Hawaiian or other Pacific Islander, non-Hispanic/Latino; 1 Two or more races, non-Hispanic/Latino), 8 international. Average age 28. 56 applicants, 34% accepted, 12 enrolled. In 2012, 10 master's, 1 doctorate awarded. Terminal master's awarded for partial completion of doctoral program. *Degree requirements:* For master's, thesis (for some programs); for doctorate, comprehensive exam, thesis/dissertation. *Entrance requirements:* For master's and doctorate, GRE General Test, GRE Subject Test. Additional exam

requirements/recommendations for international students: Required—TOEFL (minimum score 550 paper-based). *Application deadline:* For fall admission, 8/1 priority date for domestic students; for spring admission, 12/1 for domestic students. Applications are processed on a rolling basis. Application fee: $50. Electronic applications accepted. Application fee is waived when completed online. *Expenses: Tuition:* Full-time $16,290. *Required fees:* $128 per semester. Tuition and fees vary according to course load and program. *Financial support:* In 2012–13, 19 students received support, including 3 fellowships with full tuition reimbursements available (averaging $22,000 per year), 6 research assistantships with full and partial tuition reimbursements available (averaging $22,000 per year), 16 teaching assistantships with full tuition reimbursements available (averaging $22,000 per year); Federal Work-Study, scholarships/grants, traineeships, and unspecified assistantships also available. Financial award application deadline: 2/1; financial award applicants required to submit FAFSA. *Faculty research:* Magnetic resonance of membrane/protein systems, organometallic catalysis, novel synthesis of natural products. *Total annual research expenditures:* $682,510. *Unit head:* Dr. Duarte Freitas, Chair, 773-508-7045, Fax: 773-508-3086, E-mail: dfreita@luc.edu. *Application contact:* Stacey N. Lind, Graduate Program Coordinator, 773-508-3104, Fax: 773-508-3086, E-mail: slind@luc.edu. Website: http://www.luc.edu/chemistry/.

Marquette University, Graduate School, College of Arts and Sciences, Department of Chemistry, Milwaukee, WI 53201-1881. Offers analytical chemistry (MS, PhD); bioanalytical chemistry (MS, PhD); biophysical chemistry (MS, PhD); chemical physics (MS, PhD); inorganic chemistry (MS, PhD); organic chemistry (MS, PhD); physical chemistry (MS, PhD). Part-time programs available. Terminal master's awarded for partial completion of doctoral program. *Degree requirements:* For master's, comprehensive exam; for doctorate, thesis/dissertation, cumulative exams. *Entrance requirements:* For master's and doctorate, official transcripts from all current and previous colleges/universities except Marquette, three letters of recommendation from individuals familiar with the applicant's academic work. Additional exam requirements/recommendations for international students: Required—TOEFL (minimum score 530 paper-based). Electronic applications accepted. *Faculty research:* Inorganic complexes, laser Raman spectroscopy, organic synthesis, synthetic bioinorganic chemistry, electro-active organic molecules.

Marshall University, Academic Affairs Division, College of Science, Department of Chemistry, Huntington, WV 25755. Offers MS. *Faculty:* 10 full-time (3 women). *Students:* 5 full-time (3 women). Average age 24. In 2012, 2 master's awarded. *Degree requirements:* For master's, thesis. Application fee: $40. *Financial support:* Career-related internships or fieldwork available. *Unit head:* Dr. Michael Casteliani, Chairperson, 304-696-6486, E-mail: castella@marshall.edu. *Application contact:* Dr. John Hubbard, Information Contact, 304-696-2430, Fax: 304-746-1902, E-mail: hubbard@marshall.edu.

Massachusetts College of Pharmacy and Health Sciences, Graduate Studies, Program in Medicinal Chemistry, Boston, MA 02115-5896. Offers MS, PhD. *Students:* 9 full-time (4 women), all international. Average age 27. 20 applicants, 70% accepted, 10 enrolled. Terminal master's awarded for partial completion of doctoral program. *Degree requirements:* For master's, thesis, oral defense of thesis; for doctorate, one foreign language, comprehensive exam, thesis/dissertation, oral defense of dissertation, qualifying exam. *Entrance requirements:* For master's and doctorate, GRE General Test, minimum GPA of 3.0. Additional exam requirements/recommendations for international students: Required—TOEFL (minimum score 550 paper-based; 79 iBT). *Application deadline:* For fall admission, 2/1 priority date for domestic students, 2/1 for international students. Application fee: $0. Electronic applications accepted. *Financial support:* Fellowships with partial tuition reimbursements, research assistantships with partial tuition reimbursements, teaching assistantships with full tuition reimbursements, tuition waivers (partial), and unspecified assistantships available. Financial award application deadline: 3/15. *Faculty research:* Analytical chemistry, medicinal chemistry, organic chemistry, neurochemistry. *Unit head:* Dr. Ahmed Mehanna, Professor, 617-732-2955, E-mail: ahmed.mehanna@mcphs.edu. *Application contact:* Brian Barilone, Coordinator of Graduate Admission, 617-879-5032, E-mail: admissions@mcphs.edu.

Massachusetts Institute of Technology, School of Science, Department of Chemistry, Cambridge, MA 02139. Offers biological chemistry (PhD, Sc D); inorganic chemistry (PhD, Sc D); organic chemistry (PhD, Sc D); physical chemistry (PhD, Sc D). *Faculty:* 27 full-time (5 women). *Students:* 228 full-time (80 women), 4 part-time (2 women); includes 54 minority (6 Black or African American, non-Hispanic/Latino; 1 American Indian or Alaska Native, non-Hispanic/Latino; 31 Asian, non-Hispanic/Latino; 13 Hispanic/Latino; 3 Two or more races, non-Hispanic/Latino), 69 international. Average age 26. 651 applicants, 17% accepted, 44 enrolled. In 2012, 30 doctorates awarded. *Degree requirements:* For doctorate, comprehensive exam, thesis/dissertation. *Entrance requirements:* For doctorate, GRE General Test. Additional exam requirements/recommendations for international students: Required—IELTS (minimum score 7); Recommended—TOEFL (minimum score 600 paper-based). *Application deadline:* For fall admission, 12/15 for domestic and international students. Application fee: $75. Electronic applications accepted. *Expenses: Tuition:* Full-time $41,770; part-time $650 per credit hour. *Required fees:* $280. *Financial support:* In 2012–13, 194 students received support, including 71 fellowships (averaging $36,300 per year), 111 research assistantships (averaging $31,400 per year), 41 teaching assistantships (averaging $34,600 per year); Federal Work-Study, institutionally sponsored loans, scholarships/grants, traineeships,

Peterson's Graduate Programs in the Physical Sciences, Mathematics, Agricultural Sciences, the Environment & Natural Resources 2014

www.petersonsbooks.com **73**

health care benefits, and unspecified assistantships also available. *Faculty research:* Synthetic organic and organometallic chemistry including catalysis; biological chemistry including bioorganic chemistry; physical chemistry including chemical dynamics and biophysical chemistry; inorganic chemistry including synthesis, catalysis, bioinorganic and physical inorganic chemistry; materials chemistry including surface science, nanoscience and polymers. *Total annual research expenditures:* $28.4 million. *Unit head:* Prof. Sylvia T. Ceyer, Head, 617-253-1803, Fax: 617-258-7500. *Application contact:* Graduate Administrator, 617-253-1845, Fax: 617-258-0241, E-mail: chemgradeducation@mit.edu. Website: http://web.mit.edu/chemistry/www/.

McGill University, Faculty of Graduate and Postdoctoral Studies, Faculty of Science, Department of Chemistry, Montréal, QC H3A 2T5, Canada. Offers chemical biology (M Sc, PhD); chemistry (M Sc, PhD).

McMaster University, School of Graduate Studies, Faculty of Science, Department of Chemistry, Hamilton, ON L8S 4M2, Canada. Offers analytical chemistry (M Sc, PhD); chemical physics (M Sc, PhD); chemistry (M Sc, PhD); inorganic chemistry (M Sc, PhD); organic chemistry (M Sc, PhD); physical chemistry (M Sc, PhD); polymer chemistry (M Sc, PhD). Part-time programs available. Terminal master's awarded for partial completion of doctoral program. *Degree requirements:* For master's, thesis; for doctorate, comprehensive exam, thesis/dissertation. *Entrance requirements:* For master's, minimum B+ average. Additional exam requirements/recommendations for international students: Required—TOEFL (minimum score 550 paper-based).

McNeese State University, Doré School of Graduate Studies, College of Science, Department of Chemistry, Program in Environmental and Chemical Sciences, Lake Charles, LA 70609. Offers chemistry (MS); chemistry/environmental science education (MS). Evening/weekend programs available. *Students:* 14 full-time (3 women), 1 (woman) part-time; includes 1 minority (Black or African American, non-Hispanic/Latino), 10 international. In 2012, 12 master's awarded. *Degree requirements:* For master's, comprehensive exam, thesis or alternative. *Entrance requirements:* For master's, GRE. *Application deadline:* For fall admission, 5/15 priority date for domestic students, 5/15 for international students; for spring admission, 10/15 priority date for domestic students, 10/15 for international students. Applications are processed on a rolling basis. Application fee: $20 ($30 for international students). *Expenses:* Tuition, state resident: full-time $4287; part-time $587 per credit hour. *Required fees:* $1177. Tuition and fees vary according to course load. *Financial support:* Application deadline: 5/1. *Unit head:* Dr. Ron W. Darbeau, Department Head, 337-475-5777, Fax: 337-475-5950, E-mail: rdarbeau@mcneese.edu.

Memorial University of Newfoundland, School of Graduate Studies, Department of Chemistry, St. John's, NL A1C 5S7, Canada. Offers chemistry (M Sc, PhD); instrumental analysis (M Sc). Part-time programs available. *Degree requirements:* For master's, thesis, research seminar, American Chemical Society Exam; for doctorate, comprehensive exam, thesis/dissertation, seminars, oral thesis defense, American Chemical Society Exam. *Entrance requirements:* For master's, B Sc or honors degree in chemistry (preferred); for doctorate, master's degree in chemistry or honors bachelor's degree. Electronic applications accepted. *Faculty research:* Analytical/environmental chemistry; medicinal electrochemistry; inorganic, marine, organic, physical, and theoretical/computational chemistry, environmental science and instrumental analysis.

Miami University, College of Arts and Science, Department of Chemistry and Biochemistry, Oxford, OH 45056. Offers MS, PhD. *Students:* 63 full-time (28 women), 2 part-time (0 women); includes 6 minority (2 Black or African American, non-Hispanic/Latino; 3 Asian, non-Hispanic/Latino; 1 Hispanic/Latino), 29 international. Average age 27. In 2012, 9 master's, 11 doctorates awarded. *Entrance requirements:* For master's and doctorate, GRE General Test; GRE Subject Test (recommended), minimum undergraduate GPA of 2.75. Additional exam requirements/recommendations for international students: Required—TOEFL (minimum score 550 paper-based). *Application deadline:* Applications are processed on a rolling basis. Application fee: $50. Electronic applications accepted. *Expenses:* Tuition, state resident: full-time $12,444; part-time $519 per credit hour. Tuition, nonresident: full-time $27,484; part-time $1145 per credit hour. *Required fees:* $468. Part-time tuition and fees vary according to course load, campus/location and program. *Financial support:* Fellowships with full tuition reimbursements, research assistantships with full tuition reimbursements, teaching assistantships with full tuition reimbursements, Federal Work-Study, institutionally sponsored loans, tuition waivers (full), and unspecified assistantships available. Financial award application deadline: 2/15; financial award applicants required to submit FAFSA. *Unit head:* Dr. Richard Taylor, Professor and Interim Chair, 513-529-2826, E-mail: taylorrt@miamioh.edu. *Application contact:* Dr. Stacey Lowery Bretz, Professor, 513-529-3731, E-mail: bretzsl@miamioh.edu. Website: http://www.chemistry.MiamiOH.edu.

Michigan State University, The Graduate School, College of Natural Science, Department of Chemistry, East Lansing, MI 48824. Offers chemical physics (PhD); chemistry (MS, PhD); chemistry-environmental toxicology (PhD); computational chemistry (MS). *Entrance requirements:* Additional exam requirements/recommendations for international students: Required—TOEFL. Electronic applications accepted. *Faculty research:* Analytical chemistry, inorganic and organic chemistry, nuclear chemistry, physical chemistry, theoretical and computational chemistry.

Michigan State University, National Superconducting Cyclotron Laboratory, East Lansing, MI 48824. Offers chemistry (PhD); physics (PhD).

Michigan Technological University, Graduate School, College of Sciences and Arts, Department of Chemistry, Houghton, MI 49931. Offers MS, PhD. Part-time programs available. Terminal master's awarded for partial completion of doctoral program. *Degree requirements:* For master's, comprehensive exam (for some programs), thesis (for some programs); for doctorate, comprehensive exam, thesis/dissertation. *Entrance requirements:* For master's and doctorate, GRE, statement of purpose, official transcripts, 3 letters of recommendation. Additional exam requirements/recommendations for international students: Required—TOEFL (minimum score 79 iBT) or IELTS. Electronic applications accepted. *Faculty research:* Inorganic chemistry, physical/theoretical chemistry, bio/organic chemistry, polymer/materials chemistry, analytical/environmental chemistry.

Middle Tennessee State University, College of Graduate Studies, College of Basic and Applied Sciences, Department of Chemistry, Murfreesboro, TN 37132. Offers MS, DA. Part-time and evening/weekend programs available. Postbaccalaureate distance learning degree programs offered. *Degree requirements:* For master's, comprehensive exam, thesis. *Entrance requirements:* For master's and doctorate, GRE. Additional exam requirements/recommendations for international students: Required—TOEFL (minimum score 525 paper-based; 71 iBT) or IELTS (minimum score 6). Electronic applications accepted. *Faculty research:* Chemical education.

Mississippi College, Graduate School, College of Arts and Sciences, School of Science and Mathematics, Department of Chemistry and Biochemistry, Clinton, MS 39058. Offers MCS, MS. Part-time programs available. *Degree requirements:* For master's, comprehensive exam, thesis (for some programs). *Entrance requirements:* For master's, GRE. Additional exam requirements/recommendations for international students: Recommended—TOEFL, IELTS. Electronic applications accepted.

Mississippi State University, College of Arts and Sciences, Department of Chemistry, Mississippi State, MS 39762. Offers MA, MS, PhD. MA program available online only. *Faculty:* 12 full-time (0 women), 1 part-time/adjunct (0 women). *Students:* 54 full-time (20 women), 3 part-time (0 women); includes 4 minority (2 Black or African American, non-Hispanic/Latino; 1 Hispanic/Latino; 1 Two or more races, non-Hispanic/Latino), 41 international. Average age 29. 127 applicants, 13% accepted, 11 enrolled. In 2012, 3 master's, 6 doctorates awarded. Terminal master's awarded for partial completion of doctoral program. *Degree requirements:* For master's, thesis, comprehensive oral or written exam; for doctorate, thesis/dissertation, comprehensive oral or written exam. *Entrance requirements:* For master's, minimum GPA of 2.75 on last two years of undergraduate courses; for doctorate, minimum GPA of 2.75. Additional exam requirements/recommendations for international students: Required—TOEFL (minimum score 477 paper-based; 53 iBT); Recommended—IELTS (minimum score 4.5). *Application deadline:* For fall admission, 7/1 for domestic students, 5/1 for international students; for spring admission, 11/1 for domestic students, 9/1 for international students. Applications are processed on a rolling basis. Application fee: $60. Electronic applications accepted. *Financial support:* In 2012–13, 5 research assistantships with full tuition reimbursements (averaging $17,505 per year), 47 teaching assistantships with full tuition reimbursements (averaging $17,265 per year) were awarded; Federal Work-Study, institutionally sponsored loans, scholarships/grants, and unspecified assistantships also available. Financial award application deadline: 4/1; financial award applicants required to submit FAFSA. *Faculty research:* Spectroscopy, fluorometry, organic and inorganic synthesis, electrochemistry. *Total annual research expenditures:* $4.3 million. *Unit head:* Dr. Edwin A. Lewis, Department Head, 662-325-3584, Fax: 662-325-1618, E-mail: elewis@chemistry.msstate.edu. *Application contact:* Dr. Stephen Foster, Graduate Coordinator, 662-325-8854, E-mail: grad@chemistry.msstate.edu. Website: http://www.chemistry.msstate.edu/graduate/.

Missouri State University, Graduate College, College of Natural and Applied Sciences, Department of Chemistry, Springfield, MO 65897. Offers chemistry (MS); natural and applied science (MNAS), including chemistry (MNAS, MS Ed); secondary education (MS Ed), including chemistry (MNAS, MS Ed). Part-time programs available. *Degree requirements:* For master's, comprehensive exam, thesis. *Entrance requirements:* For master's, GRE General Test (MS, MNAS), minimum undergraduate GPA of 3.0 (MS and MNAS), 9-12 teacher certification (MS Ed). Additional exam requirements/recommendations for international students: Required—TOEFL (minimum score 550 paper-based; 79 iBT). Electronic applications accepted. *Faculty research:* Polyethylene glycol derivatives, electrochemiluminescence of environmental systems, enzymology, environmental organic pollutants, DNA repair via NMR.

Missouri University of Science and Technology, Graduate School, Department of Chemistry, Rolla, MO 65409. Offers MS, MST, PhD. Terminal master's awarded for partial completion of doctoral program. *Degree requirements:* For doctorate, one foreign language, thesis/dissertation. *Entrance requirements:* For master's, GRE (minimum score 600 quantitative, 3 writing), minimum GPA of 3.0; for doctorate, GRE (minimum score: quantitative 600, writing 3.5), minimum GPA of 3.0. Additional exam requirements/recommendations for international students: Required—TOEFL (minimum score 550 paper-based). Electronic applications accepted. *Faculty research:* Structure and properties of materials; bioanalytical, environmental, and polymer chemistry.

Missouri Western State University, Program in Applied Science, St. Joseph, MO 64507-2294. Offers chemistry (MAS); engineering technology management (MAS); human factors and usability testing (MAS); information technology management (MAS); sport and fitness management (MAS). Part-time programs available. *Students:* 17 full-time (6 women), 16 part-time (4 women); includes 2 minority (both Black or African American, non-Hispanic/Latino), 11 international. Average age 30. 29 applicants, 69% accepted, 13 enrolled. In 2012, 10 master's awarded. *Entrance requirements:* Additional exam requirements/recommendations for international students: Recommended—TOEFL (minimum score 500 paper-based; 61 iBT), IELTS (minimum score 5.5). *Application deadline:* For fall admission, 7/15 for domestic students, 6/15 for international students; for spring admission, 10/1 for domestic students, 10/15 for international students. Applications are processed on a rolling basis. Application fee: $45 ($50 for international students). Electronic applications accepted. *Expenses:* Tuition, state resident: full-time $5619; part-time $280.96 per credit hour. Tuition, nonresident: full-time $10,794; part-time $539.71 per credit hour. *Required fees:* $99 per credit hour. $176 per semester. Tuition and fees vary according to course load and program. *Financial support:* Scholarships/grants and unspecified assistantships available. Support available to part-time students. *Unit head:* Dr. Benjamin D. Caldwell, Dean of the Graduate School, 816-271-4394, Fax: 816-271-4525, E-mail: graduate@missouriwestern.edu.

Montana State University, College of Graduate Studies, College of Letters and Science, Department of Chemistry and Biochemistry, Bozeman, MT 59717. Offers biochemistry (MS, PhD); chemistry (MS, PhD). Part-time programs available. *Degree requirements:* For master's, comprehensive exam, thesis (for some programs); for doctorate, comprehensive exam, thesis/dissertation. *Entrance requirements:* For master's and doctorate, GRE General Test, transcripts, letter of recommendation. Additional exam requirements/recommendations for international students: Required—TOEFL (minimum score 550 paper-based). Electronic applications accepted. *Faculty research:* Proteomics, nano-materials chemistry, computational chemistry, optical spectroscopy, photochemistry.

Montclair State University, The Graduate School, College of Science and Mathematics, Department of Chemistry and Biochemistry, Program in Chemistry, Montclair, NJ 07043-1624. Offers MS. *Degree requirements:* For master's, thesis. *Entrance requirements:* For master's, GRE General Test, 24 undergraduate credits in chemistry, 2 letters of recommendation, essay. Additional exam requirements/recommendations for international students: Required—TOEFL (minimum score 83 iBT), IELTS (minimum score 6.5). Electronic applications accepted. *Faculty research:* Computational chemistry, nanochemistry, pharmaceutical biochemistry, medicinal chemistry, biophysical chemistry.

Morgan State University, School of Graduate Studies, School of Computer, Mathematical, and Natural Sciences, Department of Chemistry, Baltimore, MD 21251. Offers MS. *Degree requirements:* For master's, comprehensive exam, thesis, oral defense of thesis. *Entrance requirements:* For master's, GRE General Test, minimum GPA of 2.5.

Mount Allison University, Department of Chemistry, Sackville, NB E4L 1E4, Canada. Offers M Sc. *Degree requirements:* For master's, thesis. *Entrance requirements:* For master's, honors degree in chemistry. *Faculty research:* Biophysical chemistry of model biomembranes, organic synthesis, fast-reaction kinetics, physical chemistry of micelles.

Murray State University, College of Science, Engineering and Technology, Program in Chemistry, Murray, KY 42071. Offers MS. Part-time programs available. *Degree requirements:* For master's, comprehensive exam (for some programs), thesis (for some programs). *Entrance requirements:* For master's, GRE General Test. Additional exam requirements/recommendations for international students: Required—TOEFL. *Faculty research:* Environmental, organic, biochemistry, analytical.

New Jersey Institute of Technology, Office of Graduate Studies, College of Science and Liberal Arts, Department of Chemistry and Environmental Science, Program in Chemistry, Newark, NJ 07102. Offers MS, PhD. Part-time and evening/weekend programs available. Terminal master's awarded for partial completion of doctoral program. *Degree requirements:* For master's, thesis optional; for doctorate, thesis/dissertation. *Entrance requirements:* For master's, GRE General Test; for doctorate, GRE General Test, minimum graduate GPA of 3.5. Additional exam requirements/recommendations for international students: Required—TOEFL (minimum score 550 paper-based; 79 iBT). Electronic applications accepted. *Expenses:* Tuition, state resident: full-time $16,836; part-time $915 per credit. Tuition, nonresident: full-time $24,370; part-time $1286 per credit. *Required fees:* $2318; $242 per credit. *Faculty research:* Medical instrumentation, prosthesis design, biodegradation of hazardous waste, orthopedic biomechanics, image processing.

New Mexico Highlands University, Graduate Studies, College of Arts and Sciences, Department of Chemistry, Las Vegas, NM 87701. Offers MS. Part-time programs available. *Degree requirements:* For master's, comprehensive exam, thesis. *Entrance requirements:* For master's, minimum undergraduate GPA of 3.0. Additional exam requirements/recommendations for international students: Required—TOEFL (minimum score 540 paper-based). *Application deadline:* For fall admission, 8/1 priority date for domestic students. Applications are processed on a rolling basis. Application fee: $15. *Expenses:* Tuition, state resident: full-time $4277; part-time $178.22 per hour. Tuition, nonresident: full-time $6715; part-time $279.81 per hour. *International tuition:* $8510 full-time. Part-time tuition and fees vary according to campus/location. *Financial support:* Career-related internships or fieldwork, Federal Work-Study, institutionally sponsored loans, scholarships/grants, tuition waivers (full and partial), and unspecified assistantships available. Support available to part-time students. Financial award application deadline: 3/1. *Faculty research:* Invasive organisms in managed and wildland ecosystems, juniper and pinyon ecology and management, vegetation and community structure, big game management, quantitative forestry. *Unit head:* Prof. David Sammeth, Department Head, 505-454-3407, E-mail: d7sammeth@nmhu.edu. *Application contact:* Diane Trujillo, Administrative Assistant, Graduate Studies, 505-454-3266, Fax: 505-426-2117, E-mail: dtrujillo@nmhu.edu.

New Mexico Institute of Mining and Technology, Graduate Studies, Department of Chemistry, Socorro, NM 87801. Offers MS, PhD. Part-time programs available. *Faculty:* 8 full-time (1 woman), 2 part-time/adjunct (both women). *Students:* 16 full-time (5 women); includes 3 minority (2 Hispanic/Latino; 1 Two or more races, non-Hispanic/Latino), 5 international. Average age 29. 15 applicants, 60% accepted, 4 enrolled. In 2012, 1 master's, 1 doctorate awarded. *Degree requirements:* For master's, thesis; for doctorate, thesis/dissertation. *Entrance requirements:* For master's, GRE General Test; for doctorate, GRE General Test, GRE Subject Test. Additional exam requirements/recommendations for international students: Required—TOEFL (minimum score 540 paper-based). *Application deadline:* For fall admission, 3/1 priority date for domestic students; for spring admission, 6/1 priority date for domestic students. Applications are processed on a rolling basis. Application fee: $16 ($30 for international students). Electronic applications accepted. *Expenses:* Tuition, state resident: full-time $5043; part-time $280 per credit hour. Tuition, nonresident: full-time $16,682; part-time $927 per credit hour. *Required fees:* $640; $10 per credit hour. $108 per semester. Part-time tuition and fees vary according to course load. *Financial support:* In 2012–13, 5 research assistantships (averaging $18,665 per year), 10 teaching assistantships with full and partial tuition reimbursements (averaging $18,092 per year) were awarded; fellowships, Federal Work-Study, institutionally sponsored loans, and unspecified assistantships also available. Financial award application deadline: 3/1; financial award applicants required to submit CSS PROFILE or FAFSA. *Faculty research:* Organic, analytical, environmental, and explosives chemistry. *Total annual research expenditures:* $927,139. *Unit head:* Dr. Michael Pullin, Chair, 575-835-6185, Fax: 575-835-5364, E-mail: mpullin@nmt.edu. *Application contact:* Dr. Lorie Liebrock, Dean of Graduate Studies, 575-835-5513, Fax: 575-835-5476, E-mail: graduate@nmt.edu. Website: http://infohost.nmt.edu/~chem/.

New Mexico State University, Graduate School, College of Arts and Sciences, Department of Chemistry and Biochemistry, Las Cruces, NM 88003-8001. Offers chemistry (MS, PhD). Part-time programs available. *Faculty:* 18 full-time (3 women). *Students:* 41 full-time (13 women), 6 part-time (2 women); includes 5 minority (1 American Indian or Alaska Native, non-Hispanic/Latino; 1 Asian, non-Hispanic/Latino; 2 Hispanic/Latino; 1 Native Hawaiian or other Pacific Islander, non-Hispanic/Latino), 34 international. Average age 31. 16 applicants, 63% accepted, 6 enrolled. In 2012, 5 master's, 6 doctorates awarded. *Degree requirements:* For master's, comprehensive exam, thesis; for doctorate, comprehensive exam, thesis/dissertation. *Entrance requirements:* For master's and doctorate, GRE, BS in chemistry or biochemistry, minimum GPA of 3.0. Additional exam requirements/recommendations for international students: Required—TOEFL (minimum score 550 paper-based; 79 iBT), IELTS (minimum score 6.5). *Application deadline:* For fall admission, 7/1 priority date for domestic students, 3/1 for international students; for spring admission, 11/1 for domestic students. Applications are processed on a rolling basis. Application fee: $40 ($50 for international students). Electronic applications accepted. *Expenses:* Tuition, state resident: full-time $5239; part-time $218 per credit. Tuition, nonresident: full-time $18,266; part-time $761 per credit. *Required fees:* $1274; $53 per credit. *Financial support:* In 2012–13, 41 students received support, including 16 research assistantships (averaging $16,931 per year), 29 teaching assistantships (averaging $17,200 per year); career-related internships or fieldwork, Federal Work-Study, health care benefits, and unspecified assistantships also available. Support available to part-time students. Financial award application deadline: 4/1. *Faculty research:* Clays, surfaces, and water structure; electroanalytical and environmental chemistry; organometallic synthesis and organobiomimetics; molecular genetics, DNA recombination mechanisms, and NMR spectroscopy of protein interactions; spectroscopy and reaction kinetics. *Total annual research expenditures:* $6.2 million. *Unit head:* Dr. William Quintana, Head/Recruiting Contact, 575-646-5877, Fax: 575-646-2649, E-mail: wquintan@nmsu.edu. *Application contact:* Dr. Jeremy M. Smith, Associate Professor, Chemistry, 575-646-3346, Fax: 575-646-2649, E-mail: jesmith@nmsu.edu. Website: http://www.chemistry.nmsu.edu/.

New York University, Graduate School of Arts and Science, Department of Chemistry, New York, NY 10012-1019. Offers MS, PhD. *Faculty:* 23 full-time (1 woman). *Students:* 115 full-time (48 women), 6 part-time (2 women); includes 12 minority (2 Black or African American, non-Hispanic/Latino; 5 Asian, non-Hispanic/Latino; 4 Hispanic/Latino; 1 Two or more races, non-Hispanic/Latino), 68 international. Average age 27. 220 applicants, 23% accepted, 24 enrolled. In 2012, 2 master's, 10 doctorates awarded. *Degree requirements:* For master's, thesis or alternative; for doctorate, one foreign language, thesis/dissertation. *Entrance requirements:* For master's and doctorate, GRE General Test, GRE Subject Test. Additional exam requirements/recommendations for international students: Required—TOEFL. *Application deadline:* For fall admission, 12/12 for domestic and international students. Application fee: $90. *Expenses: Tuition:* Full-time $34,488; part-time $1437 per credit. *Required fees:* $2332; $1437 per credit. Tuition and fees vary according to program. *Financial support:* Fellowships with tuition reimbursements, research assistantships with tuition reimbursements, teaching assistantships with tuition reimbursements, career-related internships or fieldwork, Federal Work-Study, institutionally sponsored loans, scholarships/grants, health care benefits, and unspecified assistantships available. Financial award application deadline: 12/12; financial award applicants required to submit FAFSA. *Faculty research:* Biomolecular chemistry, theoretical and computational chemistry, physical chemistry, nanotechnology, bio-organic chemistry. *Unit head:* Michael Ward, Chair, 212-998-8400, Fax: 212-260-7905, E-mail: grad.chem@nyu.edu. *Application contact:* Marcus Weck, Director of Graduate Studies, 212-998-8400, Fax: 212-260-7905, E-mail: grad.chem@nyu.edu. Website: http://www.nyu.edu/pages/chemistry/.

North Carolina Agricultural and Technical State University, School of Graduate Studies, College of Arts and Sciences, Department of Chemistry, Greensboro, NC 27411. Offers MS, PhD. Part-time and evening/weekend programs available. *Degree requirements:* For master's, comprehensive exam, thesis or alternative, qualifying exam. *Entrance requirements:* For master's, GRE General Test, minimum GPA of 3.0. *Faculty research:* Tobacco pesticides.

North Carolina Central University, Division of Academic Affairs, College of Science and Technology, Department of Chemistry, Durham, NC 27707-3129. Offers MS. *Degree requirements:* For master's, one foreign language, comprehensive exam, thesis. *Entrance requirements:* For master's, GRE, minimum GPA of 3.0 in major, 2.5 overall. Additional exam requirements/recommendations for international students: Required—TOEFL.

North Carolina State University, Graduate School, College of Physical and Mathematical Sciences, Department of Chemistry, Raleigh, NC 27695. Offers MS, PhD. Part-time programs available. Terminal master's awarded for partial completion of doctoral program. *Degree requirements:* For master's, thesis (for some programs); for doctorate, thesis/dissertation. *Entrance requirements:* For master's and doctorate, GRE General Test (recommended). Electronic applications accepted. *Faculty research:* Biological chemistry, electrochemistry, organic/inorganic materials, natural products, organometallics.

North Dakota State University, College of Graduate and Interdisciplinary Studies, College of Science and Mathematics, Department of Biochemistry and Molecular Biology, Program in Chemistry, Fargo, ND 58108. Offers MS, PhD. *Students:* 39 full-time (12 women), 3 part-time (0 women); includes 4 minority (3 Black or African American, non-Hispanic/Latino; 1 Two or more races, non-Hispanic/Latino), 18 international. Average age 28. 48 applicants, 35% accepted, 11 enrolled. In 2012, 2 doctorates awarded. Application fee: $35. *Unit head:* Dr. Gregory Cook, Chair, 701-231-8694, Fax: 701-231-8831, E-mail: gregory.cook@ndsu.edu.

Northeastern Illinois University, Graduate College, College of Arts and Sciences, Department of Chemistry, Program in Chemistry, Chicago, IL 60625-4699. Offers MS. Part-time and evening/weekend programs available. *Degree requirements:* For master's, comprehensive exam, final exam or thesis. *Entrance requirements:* For master's, 2 semesters of chemistry, calculus, organic chemistry, physical chemistry, and physics; 1 semester analytic chemistry; minimum GPA of 2.75. Additional exam requirements/recommendations for international students: Required—TOEFL (minimum score 550 paper-based; 79 iBT). Electronic applications accepted. *Faculty research:* Liquid chromatographic separation of pharmaceuticals, Diels-Alder reaction products, organogermanium chemistry, mass spectroscopy.

Northeastern University, College of Science, Department of Chemistry and Chemical Biology, Boston, MA 02115-5096. Offers chemistry (MS, PhD). Part-time programs available. *Students:* 118 full-time (63 women), 37 part-time (18 women). 241 applicants, 24% accepted, 30 enrolled. In 2012, 23 master's, 16 doctorates awarded. Terminal master's awarded for partial completion of doctoral program. *Degree requirements:* For master's, thesis (for some programs); for doctorate, thesis/dissertation, qualifying exam in specialty area. *Entrance requirements:* Additional exam requirements/recommendations for international students: Required—TOEFL (minimum score 100 iBT). *Application deadline:* For fall admission, 1/1 priority date for domestic students, 1/1 for international students. Applications are processed on a rolling basis. Application fee: $75. Electronic applications accepted. *Financial support:* Fellowships with tuition reimbursements, research assistantships with tuition reimbursements, teaching assistantships with tuition reimbursements, career-related internships or fieldwork, Federal Work-Study, scholarships/grants, health care benefits, and unspecified assistantships available. Financial award application deadline: 3/1; financial award applicants required to submit FAFSA. *Faculty research:* Bioanalysis, bioorganic and medicinal chemistry, biophysical chemistry, nanomaterials, proteomics. *Unit head:* Dr. Carla N. Mattos, Graduate Coordinator, 617-373-6616, Fax: 617-373-8795, E-mail: chemistry-grad-info@neu.edu. *Application contact:* Cara Shockley, Department Admissions Contact, 617-373-2824, Fax: 617-373-7281, E-mail: chemistry-grad-info@neu.edu. Website: http://www.northeastern.edu/chem/.

Northern Arizona University, Graduate College, College of Engineering, Forestry and Natural Sciences, Department of Chemistry and Biochemistry, Flagstaff, AZ 86011. Offers chemistry (MS). Part-time programs available. *Degree requirements:* For master's, thesis. *Entrance requirements:* For master's, minimum GPA of 3.0. Additional exam requirements/recommendations for international students: Required—TOEFL (minimum score 550 paper-based; 80 iBT), IELTS (minimum score 7). Electronic applications accepted. *Faculty research:* Biochemistry of exercise, organic and inorganic mechanism studies, inhibition of ice mutation, polymer separation.

Northern Illinois University, Graduate School, College of Liberal Arts and Sciences, Department of Chemistry and Biochemistry, De Kalb, IL 60115-2854. Offers chemistry (MS, PhD). *Faculty:* 16 full-time (1 woman), 3 part-time/adjunct (1 woman). *Students:* 41 full-time (19 women), 3 part-time (all women); includes 4 minority (2 Black or African American, non-Hispanic/Latino; 1 Asian, non-Hispanic/Latino; 1 Two or more races, non-Hispanic/Latino), 13 international. Average age 28. 63 applicants, 27% accepted, 4 enrolled. In 2012, 4 master's, 3 doctorates awarded. Terminal master's awarded for partial completion of doctoral program. *Degree requirements:* For master's, comprehensive exam, thesis optional, research seminar; for doctorate, one foreign language, thesis/dissertation, candidacy exam, dissertation defense, research seminar. *Entrance requirements:* For master's, GRE General Test, bachelor's degree in mathematics or science, minimum GPA of 2.75; for doctorate, GRE General Test, bachelor's degree in mathematics or science; minimum undergraduate GPA of 2.75, 3.2 graduate. Additional exam requirements/recommendations for international students: Required—TOEFL (minimum score 550 paper-based). *Application deadline:* For fall admission, 6/1 for domestic students, 5/1 for international students; for spring admission, 11/1 for domestic students, 10/1 for international students. Applications are processed on a rolling basis. Application fee: $40. Electronic applications accepted. *Financial support:* In 2012–13, 10 research assistantships with full tuition reimbursements, 30 teaching assistantships with full tuition reimbursements were awarded; fellowships with full tuition reimbursements, career-related internships or fieldwork, Federal Work-Study, scholarships/grants, tuition waivers (full), and unspecified assistantships also available. Support available to part-time students. Financial award applicants required to submit FAFSA. *Faculty research:* Viscoelastic properties of polymers, lig and buding tocytochrome coxidases, computational inorganic chemistry, chemistry of organosilanes. *Unit head:* Dr. Jon Carnahan, Chair, 815-753-1181, Fax: 815-753-4802, E-mail: carnahan@niu.edu. *Application contact:* Graduate School Office, 815-753-0395, E-mail: gradsch@niu.edu. Website: http://www.chembio.niu.edu/.

Northwestern University, The Graduate School, Judd A. and Marjorie Weinberg College of Arts and Sciences, Department of Chemistry, Evanston, IL 60208. Offers PhD. Admissions and degrees offered through The Graduate School. *Degree requirements:* For doctorate, thesis/dissertation. *Entrance requirements:* For doctorate, GRE General Test, GRE Subject Test (chemistry). Additional exam requirements/recommendations for international students: Required—TOEFL. Electronic applications accepted. *Faculty research:* Inorganic, organic, physical, environmental, materials, and chemistry of life processes.

Oakland University, Graduate Study and Lifelong Learning, College of Arts and Sciences, Department of Chemistry, Rochester, MI 48309-4401. Offers biological sciences: health and environmental chemistry (PhD); chemistry (MS). *Degree requirements:* For master's, thesis; for doctorate, thesis/dissertation. *Entrance requirements:* For master's, minimum GPA of 3.0 for unconditional admission; for doctorate, GRE Subject Test, minimum GPA of 3.0 for unconditional admission. Additional exam requirements/recommendations for international students: Required—TOEFL (minimum score 550 paper-based). Electronic applications accepted. *Faculty research:* Chemistry of free radical species generated from biological intermediates; fate of toxic organic compounds in the environment; electroanalytical and surface chemistry at solid/liquid interface; computational modeling of intermolecular interactions and surface phenomena; metabolism and biological activity of modified fatty acids and xenobiotic carboxylic acids; physiologic and pathologic mechanisms that modulate immune responses.

The Ohio State University, Graduate School, College of Arts and Sciences, Division of Natural and Mathematical Sciences, Departments of Chemistry and Biochemistry, Columbus, OH 43210. Offers biochemistry (MS); chemistry (MS, PhD). *Faculty:* 45. *Students:* 198 full-time (65 women), 70 part-time (24 women); includes 26 minority (9 Black or African American, non-Hispanic/Latino; 1 American Indian or Alaska Native, non-Hispanic/Latino; 8 Asian, non-Hispanic/Latino; 6 Hispanic/Latino; 2 Two or more races, non-Hispanic/Latino), 131 international. Average age 26. In 2012, 18 master's, 30 doctorates awarded. *Degree requirements:* For master's, thesis optional; for doctorate, thesis/dissertation. *Entrance requirements:* For master's and doctorate, GRE General Test. Additional exam requirements/recommendations for international students: Required—TOEFL (minimum score 550 paper-based; 79 iBT), Michigan English Language Assessment Battery (minimum score 82); Recommended—IELTS (minimum score 7). *Application deadline:* For fall admission, 12/16 for domestic and international students; for winter admission, 12/1 for domestic students, 11/1 for international students; for spring admission, 3/1 for domestic students, 2/1 for international students. Applications are processed on a rolling basis. Application fee: $40 ($50 for international students). Electronic applications accepted. *Financial support:* Fellowships, research assistantships, teaching assistantships, Federal Work-Study, and institutionally sponsored loans available. Support available to part-time students. *Unit head:* Dr. Susan V. Olesik, Chair, 614-292-0733, E-mail: olesik.1@osu.edu. *Application contact:* Dr. Claudia Turro, Vice Chair, 614-292-6708, Fax: 614-292-1685, E-mail: turro.1@osu.edu. Website: https://chemistry.osu.edu/.

Oklahoma State University, College of Arts and Sciences, Department of Chemistry, Stillwater, OK 74078. Offers MS, PhD. *Faculty:* 24 full-time (3 women), 1 (woman) part-time/adjunct. *Students:* 18 full-time (7 women), 52 part-time (22 women); includes 3 minority (1 Black or African American, non-Hispanic/Latino; 1 Hispanic/Latino; 1 Two or more races, non-Hispanic/Latino), 50 international. Average age 29. 134 applicants, 22% accepted, 16 enrolled. In 2012, 3 master's, 10 doctorates awarded. *Degree requirements:* For master's, thesis; for doctorate, comprehensive exam, thesis/dissertation. *Entrance requirements:* For master's and doctorate, GRE or GMAT. Additional exam requirements/recommendations for international students: Required—TOEFL (minimum score 550 paper-based; 79 iBT). *Application deadline:* For fall admission, 3/1 for international students; for spring admission, 8/1 for international students. Applications are processed on a rolling basis. Application fee: $40 ($75 for international students). Electronic applications accepted. *Expenses:* Tuition, state resident: full-time $4272; part-time $178 per credit hour. Tuition, nonresident: full-time $17,016; part-time $709 per credit hour. *Required fees:* $2188; $91.17 per credit hour. One-time fee: $50 full-time. Part-time tuition and fees vary according to course load and campus/location. *Financial support:* In 2012–13, 22 research assistantships (averaging $19,094 per year), 45 teaching assistantships (averaging $17,840 per year) were awarded; career-related internships or fieldwork, Federal Work-Study, scholarships/grants, health care benefits, tuition waivers (partial), and unspecified assistantships also available. Support available to part-time students. Financial award application deadline: 3/1; financial award applicants required to submit FAFSA. *Faculty research:* Materials science, surface chemistry, and nanoparticles; theoretical physical chemistry; synthetic and medicinal chemistry; bioanalytical chemistry; electromagnetic (UV, VIS, IR, Raman), mass, and x-ray spectroscopes. *Unit head:* Dr. Frank Blum, Interim Head, 405-744-5920, Fax: 405-744-6007. *Application contact:* Dr. Sheryl Tucker, Dean, 405-744-7099, Fax: 405-744-0355, E-mail: grad-i@okstate.edu. Website: http://chemistry.okstate.edu.

Old Dominion University, College of Sciences, Program in Chemistry, Norfolk, VA 23529. Offers analytical chemistry (MS); biochemistry (MS); chemistry (PhD); environmental chemistry (MS); organic chemistry (MS); physical chemistry (MS). Part-time and evening/weekend programs available. *Faculty:* 19 full-time (7 women), 3 part-time/adjunct (all women). *Students:* 36 full-time (20 women); includes 1 minority (Black or African American, non-Hispanic/Latino), 14 international. Average age 27. 35 applicants, 60% accepted, 8 enrolled. In 2012, 4 master's, 1 doctorate awarded. *Degree requirements:* For master's, comprehensive exam, thesis. *Entrance requirements:* For master's, GRE General Test, minimum GPA of 3.0 in major, 2.5 overall; for doctorate, GRE General Test. Additional exam requirements/recommendations for international students: Required—TOEFL. *Application deadline:* For fall admission, 7/1 for domestic students, 1/15 for international students; for spring admission, 11/1 for domestic students, 8/15 for international students. Applications are processed on a rolling basis. Application fee: $30. Electronic applications accepted. *Expenses:* Tuition, state resident: full-time $9432; part-time $393 per credit hour. Tuition, nonresident: full-time $23,928; part-time $997 per credit hour. *Required fees:* $59 per semester. One-time fee: $50. *Financial support:* In 2012–13, 6 students received support, including fellowships (averaging $18,000 per year), research assistantships with tuition reimbursements available (averaging $21,000 per year), teaching assistantships with tuition reimbursements available (averaging $18,000 per year); career-related internships or fieldwork, scholarships/grants, and unspecified assistantships also available. Financial award application deadline: 2/15; financial award applicants required to submit FAFSA. *Faculty research:* Biogeochemistry, materials chemistry, computational chemistry, organic chemistry, biofuels. *Total annual research expenditures:* $2.6 million. *Unit head:* Dr. Craig A. Bayse, Graduate Program Director, 757-683-4097, Fax: 757-683-4628, E-mail: chemgpd@odu.edu. *Application contact:* Valerie DeCosta, Grants and Graduate Program Assistant, 757-683-6979, Fax: 757-683-4628, E-mail: chemgpd@odu.edu.

Old Dominion University, Darden College of Education, Programs in Secondary Education, Norfolk, VA 23529. Offers biology (MS Ed); chemistry (MS Ed); English (MS Ed); instructional technology (MS Ed); library science (MS Ed); secondary education (MS Ed). *Accreditation:* NCATE. Part-time and evening/weekend programs available. Postbaccalaureate distance learning degree programs offered (minimal on-campus study). *Faculty:* 10 full-time (6 women), 22 part-time/adjunct (10 women). *Students:* 74 full-time (46 women), 87 part-time (60 women); includes 32 minority (17 Black or African American, non-Hispanic/Latino; 8 Hispanic/Latino; 7 Two or more races, non-Hispanic/Latino). Average age 33. 75 applicants, 71% accepted, 53 enrolled. In 2012, 66 master's awarded. *Degree requirements:* For master's, comprehensive exam, thesis. *Entrance requirements:* For master's, GRE General Test or MAT, PRAXIS I (for licensure), minimum GPA of 2.8, teaching certificate. Additional exam requirements/recommendations for international students: Required—TOEFL. *Application deadline:* For fall admission, 6/1 for domestic and international students; for winter admission, 11/1 for domestic and international students; for spring admission, 3/1 for domestic and international students. Applications are processed on a rolling basis. Application fee: $50. Electronic applications accepted. *Expenses:* Tuition, state resident: full-time $9432; part-time $393 per credit hour. Tuition, nonresident: full-time $23,928; part-time $997 per credit hour. *Required fees:* $59 per semester. One-time fee: $50. *Financial support:* In 2012–13, 56 students received support, including fellowships (averaging $15,000 per year), research assistantships with tuition reimbursements available (averaging $9,000 per year), teaching assistantships with tuition reimbursements available (averaging $15,000 per year); career-related internships or fieldwork, Federal Work-Study, institutionally sponsored loans, scholarships/grants, and tuition waivers (partial) also available. Support available to part-time students. Financial award application deadline: 2/15; financial award applicants required to submit FAFSA. *Faculty research:* Use of technology, writing project for teachers, geography teaching, reading. *Unit head:* Dr. Robert Lucking, Graduate Program Director, 757-683-5545, Fax: 757-683-5862, E-mail: rlucking@odu.edu. *Application contact:* William Heffelfinger, Director of Graduate Admissions, 757-683-5554, Fax: 757-683-3255, E-mail: gradadmit@odu.edu. Website: http://education.odu.edu/eci/secondary/.

Oregon State University, College of Science, Department of Chemistry, Corvallis, OR 97331. Offers analytical chemistry (MS, PhD); chemistry (MA, MAIS); inorganic chemistry (MS, PhD); nuclear and radiation chemistry (MS, PhD); organic chemistry (MS, PhD); physical chemistry (MS, PhD). Part-time programs available. *Faculty:* 28 full-time (7 women), 9 part-time/adjunct (1 woman). *Students:* 101 full-time (28 women), 1 part-time (0 women); includes 5 minority (2 Asian, non-Hispanic/Latino; 1 Hispanic/Latino; 2 Two or more races, non-Hispanic/Latino), 54 international. Average age 28. 98 applicants, 30% accepted, 27 enrolled. In 2012, 4 master's, 16 doctorates awarded. Terminal master's awarded for partial completion of doctoral program. *Degree requirements:* For master's, one foreign language, thesis; for doctorate, one foreign language, thesis/dissertation. *Entrance requirements:* For master's and doctorate, minimum GPA of 3.0 in last 90 hours of course work. Additional exam requirements/recommendations for international students: Required—TOEFL. *Application deadline:* For fall admission, 3/1 priority date for domestic students. Applications are processed on a rolling basis. Application fee: $50. *Expenses:* Tuition, state resident: full-time $11,367; part-time $421 per credit hour. Tuition, nonresident: full-time $18,279; part-time $677 per credit hour. *Required fees:* $1478. One-time fee: $300 full-time. Tuition and fees vary according to course load and program. *Financial support:* Fellowships, research assistantships, teaching assistantships, and institutionally sponsored loans available. Support available to part-time students. Financial award application deadline: 2/1. *Faculty research:* Solid state chemistry, enzyme reaction mechanisms, structure and dynamics of gas molecules, chemiluminescence, nonlinear optical spectroscopy. *Unit head:* Dr. Rich G. Carter, Professor/Chair, 541-737-9486, E-mail: rich.carter@oregonstate.edu.

Penn State University Park, Graduate School, Eberly College of Science, Department of Chemistry, State College, University Park, PA 16802-1503. Offers MS, PhD. *Unit head:* Dr. Barbara J. Garrison, Head, 814-863-2103, E-mail: bjg@psu.edu. *Application contact:* Dana Coval-Dinant, Graduate Student Recruiting Manager, 814-865-1383, Fax: 814-865-3228, E-mail: dmc6@psu.edu. Website: http://www.chem.psu.edu/.

Pittsburg State University, Graduate School, College of Arts and Sciences, Department of Chemistry, Pittsburg, KS 66762. Offers MS. *Degree requirements:* For master's, thesis or alternative.

Polytechnic Institute of New York University, Department of Chemical and Biomolecular Engineering, Major in Chemistry, Brooklyn, NY 11201-2990. Offers MS. Part-time and evening/weekend programs available. *Students:* 15 full-time (5 women), 2 part-time (0 women); includes 1 minority (Asian, non-Hispanic/Latino), 15 international. Average age 29. 57 applicants, 40% accepted, 7 enrolled. In 2012, 11 master's awarded. *Degree requirements:* For master's, comprehensive exam (for some programs), thesis (for some programs). *Entrance requirements:* For master's, GRE General Test, GRE Subject Test. Additional exam requirements/recommendations for international students: Required—TOEFL (minimum score 550 paper-based; 80 iBT); Recommended—IELTS (minimum score 6.5). *Application deadline:* For fall admission, 7/31 priority date for domestic students, 4/30 for international students; for spring admission, 12/31 priority date for domestic students, 10/30 for international students. Applications are processed on a rolling basis. Application fee: $75. Electronic applications accepted. *Financial support:* Fellowships, research assistantships, teaching assistantships, institutionally sponsored loans, scholarships/grants, and unspecified assistantships available. Support available to part-time students. Financial award applicants required to submit FAFSA. *Faculty research:* Optical rotation of light by plastic films, supramolecular chemistry, unusual stereochemical opportunities, polyaniline copolymers. *Unit head:* Dr. Walter Zurawksy, Department Head, 718-260-3725, E-mail: zurawsky@poly.edu. *Application contact:* Raymond Lutzky, Director, Graduate Enrollment Management, 718-637-5984, Fax: 718-260-3624, E-mail: gradinfo@poly.edu.

Polytechnic Institute of New York University, Department of Chemical and Biomolecular Engineering, Major in Materials Chemistry, Brooklyn, NY 11201-2990. Offers PhD. Part-time and evening/weekend programs available. *Students:* 9 full-time (3 women), 16 part-time (5 women); includes 2 minority (both Asian, non-Hispanic/Latino), 17 international. 21 applicants, 29% accepted, 6 enrolled. In 2012, 1 doctorate awarded. *Degree requirements:* For doctorate, comprehensive exam, thesis/dissertation. *Entrance requirements:* Additional exam requirements/recommendations for international students: Required—TOEFL (minimum score 550 paper-based; 80 iBT); Recommended—IELTS (minimum score 6.5). *Application deadline:* For fall admission, 7/31 priority date for domestic students, 4/30 for international students; for spring admission, 12/31 priority date for domestic students, 10/30 for international students. Applications are processed on a rolling basis. Application fee: $75. Electronic applications accepted. *Financial support:* Fellowships, research assistantships, teaching assistantships, institutionally sponsored loans, scholarships/grants, and unspecified assistantships available. Support available to part-time students. Financial award applicants required to submit FAFSA. *Unit head:* Dr. Walter Zurawsky, Department Head, 718-260-3725, E-mail: zurawsky@poly.edu. *Application contact:* Raymond Lutzky, Director, Graduate Enrollment Management, 718-637-5984, Fax: 718-260-3624, E-mail: rlutzky@poly.edu.

Polytechnic Institute of NYU, Long Island Graduate Center, Graduate Programs, Department of Chemical and Biomolecular Engineering, Major in Chemistry, Melville, NY 11747. Offers MS. *Students:* 17 applicants, 82% accepted, 13 enrolled. *Degree requirements:* For master's, comprehensive exam (for some programs), thesis (for some programs). *Entrance requirements:*

Peterson's Graduate Programs in the Physical Sciences, Mathematics, Agricultural Sciences, the Environment & Natural Resources 2014

www.petersonsbooks.com **77**

Additional exam requirements/recommendations for international students: Required—TOEFL (minimum score 550 paper-based; 80 iBT); Recommended—IELTS (minimum score 6.5). *Application deadline:* For fall admission, 7/31 priority date for domestic students, 4/30 for international students; for spring admission, 12/31 priority date for domestic students, 11/30 for international students. Applications are processed on a rolling basis. Application fee: $75. Electronic applications accepted. *Financial support:* Institutionally sponsored loans, scholarships/grants, and unspecified assistantships available. Support available to part-time students. *Unit head:* Prof. Bruce A. Garetz, Department Head, 718-260-3287, E-mail: bgaretz@poly.edu. *Application contact:* JeanCarlo Bonilla, Director of Graduate Enrollment Management, 718-260-3182, Fax: 718-260-3624, E-mail: gradinfo@poly.edu.

Polytechnic Institute of NYU, Westchester Graduate Center, Graduate Programs, Department of Chemical and Biological Engineering, Major in Chemistry, Hawthorne, NY 10532-1507. Offers MS. *Degree requirements:* For master's, comprehensive exam (for some programs), thesis (for some programs). *Entrance requirements:* Additional exam requirements/recommendations for international students: Required—TOEFL (minimum score 550 paper-based; 80 iBT); Recommended—IELTS (minimum score 6.5). *Application deadline:* For fall admission, 7/31 priority date for domestic students, 4/30 for international students; for spring admission, 12/31 priority date for domestic students, 11/30 for international students. Applications are processed on a rolling basis. Application fee: $75. Electronic applications accepted. *Financial support:* Institutionally sponsored loans, scholarships/grants, and unspecified assistantships available. Support available to part-time students. *Unit head:* Dr. Bruce Garetz, Department Head, 718-260-3287, E-mail: bgaretz@poly.edu. *Application contact:* Raymond Lutzky, Director of Graduate Enrollment Management, 718-637-5984, Fax: 718-260-3624, E-mail: rlutzky@poly.edu.

Pontifical Catholic University of Puerto Rico, College of Sciences, Department of Chemistry, Ponce, PR 00717-0777. Offers MS. Part-time and evening/weekend programs available. *Degree requirements:* For master's, thesis. *Entrance requirements:* For master's, GRE General Test, 2 letters of recommendation, minimum GPA of 3.0, minimum 37 credits in chemistry. Electronic applications accepted.

Portland State University, Graduate Studies, College of Liberal Arts and Sciences, Department of Chemistry, Portland, OR 97207-0751. Offers MA, MS, PhD. Part-time programs available. *Degree requirements:* For master's, one foreign language, thesis; for doctorate, one foreign language, thesis/dissertation, cumulative exams, seminar presentations. *Entrance requirements:* For master's, GRE General Test, GRE Subject Test, minimum GPA of 3.0 in upper-division course work or 2.75 overall, 2 letters of recommendation. Additional exam requirements/recommendations for international students: Required—TOEFL (minimum score 550 paper-based). *Faculty research:* Synthetic inorganic chemistry, atmospheric chemistry, organic photochemistry, enzymology, analytical chemistry.

Prairie View A&M University, College of Arts and Sciences, Department of Chemistry, Prairie View, TX 77446-0519. Offers MS. Part-time and evening/weekend programs available. *Degree requirements:* For master's, thesis. *Entrance requirements:* For master's, GRE General Test. Additional exam requirements/recommendations for international students: Recommended—TOEFL. Electronic applications accepted. *Faculty research:* Material science, environmental characterization (surface phenomena), activation of plasminogens, polymer modifications, organic synthesis.

Princeton University, Graduate School, Department of Chemistry, Princeton, NJ 08544-1019. Offers chemistry (PhD); industrial chemistry (MS). *Degree requirements:* For doctorate, thesis/dissertation, general exams. *Entrance requirements:* For master's, GRE General Test; for doctorate, GRE General Test, GRE Subject Test (recommended). Additional exam requirements/recommendations for international students: Required—TOEFL. Electronic applications accepted. *Faculty research:* Chemistry of interfaces, organic synthesis, organometallic chemistry, inorganic reactions, biostructural chemistry.

Purdue University, Graduate School, College of Science, Department of Chemistry, West Lafayette, IN 47907. Offers analytical chemistry (MS, PhD); biochemistry (MS, PhD); chemical education (MS, PhD); inorganic chemistry (MS, PhD); organic chemistry (MS, PhD); physical chemistry (MS, PhD). *Faculty:* 42 full-time (14 women), 7 part-time/adjunct (0 women). *Students:* 275 full-time (102 women), 23 part-time (8 women); includes 34 minority (16 Black or African American, non-Hispanic/Latino; 5 Asian, non-Hispanic/Latino; 11 Hispanic/Latino; 2 Two or more races, non-Hispanic/Latino), 94 international. Average age 27. 716 applicants, 26% accepted, 66 enrolled. In 2012, 18 master's, 52 doctorates awarded. Terminal master's awarded for partial completion of doctoral program. *Degree requirements:* For master's, thesis; for doctorate, comprehensive exam, thesis/dissertation. *Entrance requirements:* For master's and doctorate, minimum undergraduate GPA of 3.0. Additional exam requirements/recommendations for international students: Required—TOEFL (minimum score 77 iBT); Recommended—TWE. *Application deadline:* For fall admission, 2/15 priority date for domestic students, 1/1 for international students. Applications are processed on a rolling basis. Application fee: $60 ($75 for international students). Electronic applications accepted. *Financial support:* In 2012–13, 2 fellowships with partial tuition reimbursements (averaging $18,000 per year), 55 teaching assistantships with partial tuition reimbursements (averaging $18,000 per year) were awarded; research assistantships with partial tuition reimbursements and tuition waivers (partial) also available. Support available to part-time students. Financial award applicants required to submit FAFSA. *Unit head:* Dr. Paul B. Shepson, Head, 765-494-5203, E-mail: pshepson@purdue.edu. *Application contact:* Betty L. Hatfield, Director of Graduate Admissions, 765-494-5208, E-mail: bettyh@purdue.edu.

Queens College of the City University of New York, Division of Graduate Studies, Mathematics and Natural Sciences Division, Department of Chemistry and Biochemistry, Flushing, NY 11367-1597. Offers biochemistry (MA); chemistry (MA). Part-time and evening/weekend programs available. *Faculty:* 17 full-time (3 women), 19 part-time/adjunct (8 women). *Students:* 7 full-time (5 women), 16 part-time (7 women); includes 16 minority (4 Black or African American, non-Hispanic/Latino; 8 Asian, non-Hispanic/Latino; 4 Hispanic/Latino), 3 international. 18 applicants, 89% accepted, 6 enrolled. In 2012, 4 master's awarded. *Degree requirements:* For master's, comprehensive exam. *Entrance requirements:* For master's, GRE, previous course work in calculus and physics, minimum GPA of 3.0. Additional exam requirements/recommendations for international students: Required—TOEFL. *Application deadline:* For fall admission, 4/1 for domestic students; for spring admission, 11/1 for domestic students. Applications are processed on a rolling basis. Application fee: $125. *Expenses:* Tuition, state resident: full-time $8690; part-time $365 per credit. Tuition, nonresident: full-time $16,200; part-time $675 per credit. Full-time tuition and fees vary according to course load. *Financial support:* Career-related internships or fieldwork and unspecified assistantships available. Financial award application deadline: 4/1; financial award applicants required to submit FAFSA. *Unit head:* Dr. Wilma Saffran, Chairperson, 718-997-4144. *Application contact:* Graduate Adviser, 718-997-4100.

Queen's University at Kingston, School of Graduate Studies and Research, Faculty of Arts and Sciences, Department of Chemistry, Kingston, ON K7L 3N6, Canada. Offers M Sc, PhD. Part-time programs available. *Degree requirements:* For master's, thesis (for some programs); for doctorate, comprehensive exam, thesis/dissertation. *Entrance requirements:* Additional exam requirements/recommendations for international students: Required—TOEFL (minimum score 580 paper-based). *Faculty research:* Medicinal/biological chemistry, materials chemistry, environmental/analytical chemistry, theoretical/computational chemistry.

Rensselaer Polytechnic Institute, Graduate School, School of Science, Program in Chemistry, Troy, NY 12180-3590. Offers MS, PhD. *Faculty:* 14 full-time (2 women), 3 part-time/adjunct (2 women). *Students:* 36 full-time (19 women), 2 part-time (1 woman); includes 3 minority (2 Asian, non-Hispanic/Latino; 1 Two or more races, non-Hispanic/Latino), 15 international. Average age 26. 123 applicants, 28% accepted, 11 enrolled. In 2012, 5 master's, 8 doctorates awarded. Terminal master's awarded for partial completion of doctoral program. *Degree requirements:* For master's, thesis (for some programs); for doctorate, comprehensive exam, thesis/dissertation. *Entrance requirements:* For master's and doctorate, GRE. Additional exam requirements/recommendations for international students: Required—TOEFL (minimum score 600 paper-based, 100 iBT), IELTS (minimum score 7), or Pearson Test of English (minimum score 68). *Application deadline:* For fall admission, 1/1 priority date for domestic students; for spring admission, 8/15 priority date for domestic students. Applications are processed on a rolling basis. Application fee: $75. Electronic applications accepted. *Financial support:* In 2012–13, research assistantships (averaging $18,500 per year), teaching assistantships (averaging $18,500 per year) were awarded; fellowships also available. Financial award application deadline: 1/1. *Faculty research:* Analytical and bioanalytical chemistry, biotechnology, chemical biology and biochemistry, chemistry, inorganic and organometallic chemistry, nanotechnology, organic and medicinal chemistry, physical and computational chemistry, polymer and materials chemistry. *Application contact:* Office of Graduate Admissions, 518-276-6216, E-mail: gradadmissions@rpi.edu. Website: http://www.rpi.edu/dept/chem/academic/graduate.html.

Rice University, Graduate Programs, Wiess School of Natural Sciences, Department of Chemistry, Houston, TX 77251-1892. Offers chemistry (MA); inorganic chemistry (PhD); organic chemistry (PhD); physical chemistry (PhD). Terminal master's awarded for partial completion of doctoral program. *Degree requirements:* For master's, thesis; for doctorate, thesis/dissertation. *Entrance requirements:* For master's and doctorate, GRE General Test, minimum GPA of 3.0. Additional exam requirements/recommendations for international students: Required—TOEFL (minimum score 600 paper-based; 90 iBT). Electronic applications accepted. *Faculty research:* Nanoscience, biomaterials, nanobioinformatics, fullerene pharmaceuticals.

Rochester Institute of Technology, Graduate Enrollment Services, College of Science, Department of Chemistry, Rochester, NY 14623-5603. Offers MS. Part-time and evening/weekend programs available. Postbaccalaureate distance learning degree programs offered (minimal on-campus study). *Students:* 1 full-time (0 women), 14 part-time (3 women); includes 1 minority (Hispanic/Latino), 2 international. Average age 24. 28 applicants, 46% accepted, 7 enrolled. In 2012, 2 master's awarded. *Degree requirements:* For master's, thesis. *Entrance requirements:* For master's, GRE, minimum GPA of 3.0. Additional exam requirements/recommendations for international students: Required—TOEFL (minimum score 550 paper-based; 79 iBT) or IELTS (minimum score 6.5). *Application deadline:* For fall admission, 2/15 priority date for domestic students, 2/15 for international students; for winter admission, 11/1 for domestic students; for spring admission, 2/1 for domestic students. Applications are processed on a rolling basis. Application fee: $60. Electronic applications accepted. *Expenses: Tuition:* Full-time $35,976; part-time $999 per credit hour. *Required fees:* $240;

$80 per quarter. *Financial support:* Fellowships with full and partial tuition reimbursements, research assistantships with full and partial tuition reimbursements, teaching assistantships with full and partial tuition reimbursements, career-related internships or fieldwork, scholarships/grants, and unspecified assistantships available. Support available to part-time students. Financial award applicants required to submit FAFSA. *Faculty research:* Organic polymer chemistry, magnetic resonance and imaging, inorganic coordination polymers, biophysical chemistry, physical polymer chemistry. *Unit head:* Dr. Paul Rosenberg, Department Head, 585-475-2497, Fax: 585-475-7800, E-mail: lprsch@rit.edu. *Application contact:* Diane Ellison, Assistant Vice President, Graduate Enrollment Services, 585-475-2229, Fax: 585-475-7164, E-mail: gradinfo@rit.edu. Website: http://www.rit.edu/cos/chemistry/department_info.html.

Roosevelt University, Graduate Division, College of Arts and Sciences, Department of Biological, Chemical, and Physical Sciences, Chicago, IL 60605. Offers biotechnology and chemical science (MS). Part-time and evening/weekend programs available. *Degree requirements:* For master's, thesis optional. *Entrance requirements:* For master's, minimum GPA of 2.7, undergraduate course work in science and mathematics. *Faculty research:* Phase-transfer catalysts, bioinorganic chemistry, long chain dicarboxylic acids, organosilicon compounds, spectroscopic studies.

Royal Military College of Canada, Division of Graduate Studies and Research, Science Division, Department of Chemistry and Chemical and Materials Engineering, Kingston, ON K7K 7B4, Canada. Offers chemical engineering (M Eng, MA Sc, PhD); chemistry (M Sc, PhD). *Degree requirements:* For master's, thesis; for doctorate, comprehensive exam, thesis/dissertation. *Entrance requirements:* For master's, honour's degree with second-class standing; for doctorate, master's degree. Electronic applications accepted.

Rutgers, The State University of New Jersey, Camden, Graduate School of Arts and Sciences, Program in Chemistry, Camden, NJ 08102. Offers MS. Part-time and evening/weekend programs available. *Degree requirements:* For master's, comprehensive exam, thesis (for some programs), 30 credits. *Entrance requirements:* For master's, GRE (for assistantships), 3 letters of recommendation; statement of personal, professional and academic goals; chemistry or related undergraduate degree (preferred). Additional exam requirements/recommendations for international students: Required—TOEFL, IELTS; Recommended—TWE. Electronic applications accepted. *Faculty research:* Organic and inorganic synthesis, enzyme biochemistry, trace metal analysis, theoretical and molecular modeling.

Rutgers, The State University of New Jersey, Newark, Graduate School, Program in Chemistry, Newark, NJ 07102. Offers analytical chemistry (MS, PhD); biochemistry (MS, PhD); inorganic chemistry (MS, PhD); organic chemistry (MS, PhD); physical chemistry (MS, PhD). Part-time and evening/weekend programs available. Terminal master's awarded for partial completion of doctoral program. *Degree requirements:* For master's, thesis optional, cumulative exams; for doctorate, thesis/dissertation, exams, research proposal. *Entrance requirements:* For master's and doctorate, GRE General Test, minimum undergraduate B average. Additional exam requirements/recommendations for international students: Required—TOEFL. Electronic applications accepted. *Faculty research:* Medicinal chemistry, natural products, isotope effects, biophysics and biorganic approaches to enzyme mechanisms, organic and organometallic synthesis.

Rutgers, The State University of New Jersey, New Brunswick, Graduate School-New Brunswick, Department of Chemistry and Chemical Biology, Piscataway, NJ 08854-8097. Offers biological chemistry (MS, PhD); inorganic chemistry (MS, PhD); organic chemistry (MS, PhD); physical chemistry (MS, PhD). Part-time and evening/weekend programs available. Terminal master's awarded for partial completion of doctoral program. *Degree requirements:* For master's, thesis or alternative, exam; for doctorate, thesis/dissertation, 1 year residency. *Entrance requirements:* For master's and doctorate, GRE General Test, GRE Subject Test. Additional exam requirements/recommendations for international students: Required—TOEFL. Electronic applications accepted. *Faculty research:* Biophysical organic/bioorganic, inorganic/bioinorganic, theoretical, and solid-state/surface chemistry.

Rutgers, The State University of New Jersey, New Brunswick, Graduate School-New Brunswick, Department of Environmental Sciences, Piscataway, NJ 08854-8097. Offers air pollution and resources (MS, PhD); aquatic biology (MS, PhD); aquatic chemistry (MS, PhD); atmospheric science (MS, PhD); chemistry and physics of aerosol and hydrosol systems (MS, PhD); environmental chemistry (MS, PhD); environmental microbiology (MS, PhD); environmental toxicology (PhD); exposure assessment (PhD); fate and effects of pollutants (MS, PhD); pollution prevention and control (MS, PhD); water and wastewater treatment (MS, PhD); water resources (MS, PhD). Terminal master's awarded for partial completion of doctoral program. *Degree requirements:* For master's, comprehensive exam, thesis or alternative, oral final exam; for doctorate, comprehensive exam, thesis/dissertation, thesis defense, qualifying exam. *Entrance requirements:* For master's and doctorate, GRE General Test. Additional exam requirements/recommendations for international students: Required—TOEFL. Electronic applications accepted. *Faculty research:* Biological waste treatment; contaminant fate and transport; air, soil and water quality.

Sacred Heart University, Graduate Programs, College of Arts and Sciences, Department of Chemistry, Fairfield, CT 06825-1000. Offers MS. Part-time and evening/weekend programs available. *Faculty:* 7 full-time (1 woman), 1 part-time/adjunct (0 women). *Students:* 26 full-time, 26 part-time; includes 3 minority (2 Asian, non-Hispanic/Latino; 1 Hispanic/Latino), 33 international. 76 applicants, 72% accepted, 10 enrolled. In 2012, 18 master's awarded. *Degree requirements:* For master's, thesis optional. *Entrance requirements:* For master's, bachelor's degree in related area (natural science with a heavy concentration in chemistry), minimum GPA of 2.75. Additional exam requirements/recommendations for international students: Recommended—TOEFL (minimum score 80 iBT), IELTS (minimum score 5.5). *Application deadline:* Applications are processed on a rolling basis. Application fee: $60. Electronic applications accepted. Tuition and fees vary according to program. *Financial support:* Career-related internships or fieldwork, institutionally sponsored loans, and unspecified assistantships available. Support available to part-time students. Financial award applicants required to submit FAFSA. *Unit head:* Dr. Eid Alkhatib, Chair, 203-365-7546, E-mail: gradstudies@sacredheart.edu. *Application contact:* Kathy Dilks, Executive Director of Graduate Admissions, 203-365-7619, Fax: 203-365-4732, E-mail: dilksk@sacredheart.edu. Website: http://www.sacredheart.edu/academics/collegeofartssciences/academicdepartments/chemistry/graduatedegreesandcertificates/.

St. Francis Xavier University, Graduate Studies, Department of Chemistry, Antigonish, NS B2G 2W5, Canada. Offers M Sc. *Degree requirements:* For master's, thesis. *Entrance requirements:* Additional exam requirements/recommendations for international students: Required—TOEFL (minimum score 580 paper-based). *Faculty research:* Photoelectron spectroscopy, synthesis and properties of surfactants, nucleic acid synthesis, transition metal chemistry, colloids.

St. John's University, St. John's College of Liberal Arts and Sciences, Department of Chemistry, Queens, NY 11439. Offers MS. Part-time and evening/weekend programs available. *Students:* 11 full-time (7 women), 16 part-time (13 women); includes 10 minority (1 Black or African American, non-Hispanic/Latino; 3 Asian, non-Hispanic/Latino; 6 Hispanic/Latino), 9 international. Average age 27. 28 applicants, 50% accepted, 12 enrolled. In 2012, 11 master's awarded. *Degree requirements:* For master's, comprehensive exam, thesis optional. *Entrance requirements:* For master's, GRE, minimum GPA of 3.0 (overall); 3.5 (in chemistry). Additional exam requirements/recommendations for international students: Required—TOEFL (minimum score 600 paper-based; 100 iBT), IELTS (minimum score 5.5). *Application deadline:* For fall admission, 5/1 priority date for domestic students, 5/1 for international students; for spring admission, 11/1 priority date for domestic students, 11/1 for international students. Applications are processed on a rolling basis. Application fee: $70. Electronic applications accepted. *Expenses: Tuition:* Full-time $18,900; part-time $1050 per credit. *Required fees:* $170 per semester. Tuition and fees vary according to program. *Financial support:* Research assistantships, teaching assistantships, and scholarships/grants available. Support available to part-time students. Financial award application deadline: 3/1; financial award applicants required to submit FAFSA. *Faculty research:* Synthesis and reactions of a-lactams, NMR spectroscopy or nucleosides, analytical chemistry, environment chemistry and photochemistry of transition metal complexes. *Unit head:* Dr. Alison G. Hyslop, Chair, 718-990-6297, E-mail: hyslopa@stjohns.edu. *Application contact:* Robert Medrano, Director of Graduate Admission, 718-990-1601, Fax: 718-990-5686, E-mail: gradhelp@stjohns.edu.

Saint Louis University, Graduate Education, College of Arts and Sciences and Graduate Education, Department of Chemistry, St. Louis, MO 63103-2097. Offers MS, MS-R, PhD. Part-time and evening/weekend programs available. *Degree requirements:* For master's, thesis; for doctorate, comprehensive exam, thesis/dissertation. *Entrance requirements:* For master's, letters of recommendation, resume, interview; for doctorate, letters of recommendation, resumé, interview, transcripts, goal statement. Additional exam requirements/recommendations for international students: Required—TOEFL (minimum score 550 paper-based; 80 iBT). Electronic applications accepted. *Faculty research:* Photochemistry, energy, materials, biomaterials, nanomaterials.

Sam Houston State University, College of Sciences, Department of Chemistry, Huntsville, TX 77341. Offers MS. Part-time programs available. *Faculty:* 10 full-time (1 woman). *Students:* 11 full-time (6 women), 1 part-time (0 women); includes 1 minority (Hispanic/Latino), 8 international. Average age 27. 13 applicants, 46% accepted, 5 enrolled. In 2012, 5 master's awarded. *Degree requirements:* For master's, comprehensive exam, thesis optional. *Entrance requirements:* For master's, GRE General Test. Additional exam requirements/recommendations for international students: Required—TOEFL (minimum score 550 paper-based; 79 iBT). *Application deadline:* For fall admission, 8/1 for domestic students, 6/25 for international students; for spring admission, 12/1 for domestic students, 11/12 for international students. Applications are processed on a rolling basis. Application fee: $45 ($75 for international students). Electronic applications accepted. *Expenses:* Tuition, state resident: full-time $2205; part-time $245 per credit hour. Tuition, nonresident: full-time $5391; part-time $599 per credit hour. *Required fees:* $67 per credit hour. $367 per semester. Tuition and fees vary according to course load and campus/location. *Financial support:* In 2012–13, 1 research assistantship (averaging $2,890 per year), 5 teaching assistantships (averaging $13,005 per year) were awarded; Federal Work-Study, institutionally sponsored loans, scholarships/grants, tuition waivers (partial), and unspecified assistantships also available. Support available to part-time students. Financial award application deadline: 5/31; financial award applicants required to submit FAFSA. *Total annual research expenditures:* $298,912. *Unit head:* Dr. Rick Norman, Chair, 936-294-1527, Fax: 936-294-4996, E-mail: chm_ren@

shsu.edu. *Application contact:* Dr. Thomas Chasteen, Advisor, 936-294-1971, E-mail: chm_tgc@shsu.edu. Website: http://www.shsu.edu/~chemistry/.

San Diego State University, Graduate and Research Affairs, College of Sciences, Department of Chemistry and Biochemistry, San Diego, CA 92182. Offers MA, MS, PhD. PhD offered jointly with University of California, San Diego. Terminal master's awarded for partial completion of doctoral program. *Degree requirements:* For doctorate, thesis/dissertation. *Entrance requirements:* For master's, GRE General Test, bachelor's degree in related field, 3 letters of reference; for doctorate, GRE General Test, GRE Subject Test. Additional exam requirements/recommendations for international students: Required—TOEFL. Electronic applications accepted. *Faculty research:* Nonlinear, laser, and electrochemistry; surface reaction dynamics; catalysis, synthesis, and organometallics; proteins, enzymology, and gene expression regulation.

San Francisco State University, Division of Graduate Studies, College of Science and Engineering, Department of Chemistry and Biochemistry, San Francisco, CA 94132-1722. Offers chemistry (MS), including biochemistry. Part-time programs available. *Application deadline:* Applications are processed on a rolling basis. Electronic applications accepted. *Unit head:* Dr. Jane DeWitt, Chair, 415-338-1288, Fax: 415-338-2384, E-mail: gradchem@sfsu.edu. *Application contact:* Dr. Andrew Ichimura, Graduate Coordinator, 415-405-0721, Fax: 415-338-2384, E-mail: ichimura@sfsu.edu. Website: http://lewis.sfsu.edu.

San Jose State University, Graduate Studies and Research, College of Science, Department of Chemistry, San Jose, CA 95192-0001. Offers MA, MS. Part-time and evening/weekend programs available. *Degree requirements:* For master's, thesis or alternative. *Entrance requirements:* For master's, GRE. Electronic applications accepted. *Faculty research:* Intercalated compounds, organic/biochemical reaction mechanisms, complexing agents in biochemistry, DNA repair, metabolic inhibitors.

The Scripps Research Institute, Kellogg School of Science and Technology, La Jolla, CA 92037. Offers chemical and biological sciences (PhD). *Faculty:* 168 full-time (32 women). *Students:* 203 full-time (60 women). *Degree requirements:* For doctorate, thesis/dissertation. *Entrance requirements:* For doctorate, GRE General Test, GRE Subject Test, 3 letters of recommendation, official transcripts. Additional exam requirements/recommendations for international students: Required—TOEFL. *Application deadline:* For fall admission, 12/1 for domestic and international students. Application fee: $0. Electronic applications accepted. *Financial support:* Fellowships, institutionally sponsored loans, tuition waivers (full), and annual stipends available. *Faculty research:* Molecular structure and function, plant biology, immunology, bioorganic chemistry and molecular design, synthetic organic chemistry and natural product synthesis. *Unit head:* Dr. James R. Williamson, Dean of Graduate and Postdoctoral Studies, 858-784-8469, Fax: 858-784-2802, E-mail: gradprgm@scripps.edu. *Application contact:* Marylyn Rinaldi, Administrative Director, 858-784-8469, Fax: 858-784-2802, E-mail: mrinaldi@scripps.edu. Website: http://education.scripps.edu/.

Seton Hall University, College of Arts and Sciences, Department of Chemistry and Biochemistry, South Orange, NJ 07079-2697. Offers analytical chemistry (MS, PhD); biochemistry (MS, PhD); chemistry (MS); inorganic chemistry (MS, PhD); organic chemistry (MS, PhD); physical chemistry (MS, PhD). Part-time and evening/weekend programs available. Terminal master's awarded for partial completion of doctoral program. *Degree requirements:* For master's, thesis optional; for doctorate, comprehensive exam, thesis/dissertation. *Entrance requirements:* Additional exam requirements/recommendations for international students: Required—TOEFL. Electronic applications accepted. *Faculty research:* DNA metal reactions; chromatography; bioinorganic, biophysical, organometallic, polymer chemistry; heterogeneous catalyst; synthetic organic and carbohydrate chemistry.

Simon Fraser University, Office of Graduate Studies, Faculty of Science, Department of Chemistry, Burnaby, BC V5A 1S6, Canada. Offers M Sc, PhD. *Faculty:* 27 full-time (4 women). *Students:* 107 full-time (44 women). 43 applicants, 60% accepted, 16 enrolled. In 2012, 8 master's, 11 doctorates awarded. *Degree requirements:* For master's, thesis; for doctorate, thesis/dissertation. *Entrance requirements:* For master's, minimum GPA of 3.0 (on scale of 4.33), or 3.33 based on last 60 credits of undergraduate courses; for doctorate, minimum GPA of 3.5 (on scale of 4.33). Additional exam requirements/recommendations for international students: Recommended—TOEFL (minimum score 580 paper-based; 93 iBT), IELTS (minimum score 7), TWE (minimum score 5). *Application deadline:* Applications are processed on a rolling basis. Application fee: $90 Canadian dollars ($125 Canadian dollars for international students). Electronic applications accepted. Tuition and fees charges are reported in Canadian dollars. *Expenses: Tuition, area resident:* Full-time $5000 Canadian dollars; part-time $275 Canadian dollars per credit hour. *Required fees:* $780 Canadian dollars. *Financial support:* In 2012–13, 59 students received support, including 62 fellowships (averaging $6,250 per year), teaching assistantships (averaging $5,608 per year); research assistantships and scholarships/grants also available. *Faculty research:* Analytical chemistry, inorganic and bioinorganic chemistry, organic and biological chemistry, physical and nuclear chemistry, chemical biology. *Unit head:* Dr. Rob Britton, Graduate Chair, 778-782-4889, Fax: 778-782-3530. *Application contact:* Lynn Wood, Graduate Secretary, 778-782-3345, Fax: 778-782-3530, E-mail: chemgdin@sfu.ca. Website: http://www.chemistry.sfu.ca/.

Smith College, Graduate and Special Programs, Department of Chemistry, Northampton, MA 01063. Offers MAT. Part-time programs available. *Faculty:* 9 full-time (6 women). In 2012, 1 master's awarded. *Entrance requirements:* For master's, GRE General Test. Additional exam requirements/recommendations for international students: Required—TOEFL (minimum score 590 paper-based; 97 iBT). *Application deadline:* For fall admission, 4/1 for domestic students, 1/15 for international students; for spring admission, 12/1 for domestic students. Application fee: $60. *Expenses: Tuition:* Full-time $15,480; part-time $1290 per credit. *Financial support:* Career-related internships or fieldwork and institutionally sponsored loans available. Support available to part-time students. Financial award application deadline: 1/15; financial award applicants required to submit CSS PROFILE or FAFSA. *Unit head:* Kate Queeney, Chair, 413-585-3835, E-mail: kqueeney@smith.edu. *Application contact:* Ruth Morgan, Administrative Assistant, 413-585-3050, Fax: 413-585-3054, E-mail: gradstdy@smith.edu. Website: http://www.science.smith.edu/departments/chem/.

South Dakota State University, Graduate School, College of Arts and Science, Department of Chemistry, Brookings, SD 57007. Offers MS, PhD. *Degree requirements:* For master's, thesis, oral exam; for doctorate, thesis/dissertation, preliminary oral and written exams, research tool. *Entrance requirements:* For master's and doctorate, bachelor's degree in chemistry or closely related discipline. Additional exam requirements/recommendations for international students: Required—TOEFL (minimum score 580 paper-based; 92 iBT). *Faculty research:* Environmental chemistry, computational chemistry, organic synthesis and photochemistry, novel material development and characterization.

Southeast Missouri State University, School of Graduate Studies, Department of Chemistry, Cape Girardeau, MO 63701-4799. Offers MNS. Part-time programs available. *Faculty:* 9 full-time (1 woman). *Students:* 8 full-time (6 women), 2 part-time (both women), 6 international. Average age 25. 32 applicants, 41% accepted, 4 enrolled. In 2012, 13 master's awarded. *Degree requirements:* For master's, comprehensive exam (for some programs), thesis (for some programs). *Entrance requirements:* For master's, GRE General Test, minimum undergraduate GPA of 2.5, 2.75 in last 30 semester hours of undergraduate science or math courses; 2 letters of recommendation; minimum C grade in selected chemistry courses. Additional exam requirements/recommendations for international students: Required—TOEFL (minimum score 550 paper-based; 79 iBT), IELTS (minimum score 6). *Application deadline:* For fall admission, 8/1 for domestic students, 6/1 for international students; for spring admission, 11/21 for domestic students, 10/1 for international students. Applications are processed on a rolling basis. Application fee: $30 ($40 for international students). Electronic applications accepted. *Financial support:* In 2012–13, 7 students received support, including 6 teaching assistantships with full tuition reimbursements available (averaging $7,900 per year); career-related internships or fieldwork, Federal Work-Study, scholarships/grants, traineeships, tuition waivers (full), and unspecified assistantships also available. Financial award application deadline: 6/30; financial award applicants required to submit FAFSA. *Faculty research:* Crystallography, trace metal detection, electrochemistry of metalloporphyrins, organic reactions with supported reagents, synthesis of molecules of biological interest. *Unit head:* Dr. Philip W. Crawford, Chairperson and Professor, 573-651-2166, E-mail: pcrawford@semo.edu. *Application contact:* Alisa Aleen McFerron, Assistant Director of Admissions for Operations, 573-651-5937, E-mail: amcferron@semo.edu. Website: http://www.semo.edu/chemistry/.

Southern Connecticut State University, School of Graduate Studies, School of Arts and Sciences, Department of Chemistry, New Haven, CT 06515-1355. Offers MS. Part-time and evening/weekend programs available. *Degree requirements:* For master's, thesis or alternative. *Entrance requirements:* For master's, interview, undergraduate work in chemistry. Electronic applications accepted. *Expenses:* Tuition, state resident: full-time $5617; part-time $314 per credit. Tuition, nonresident: full-time $15,650. *Required fees:* $4355; $253 per credit. $55 per semester.

Southern Illinois University Carbondale, Graduate School, College of Science, Department of Chemistry and Biochemistry, Carbondale, IL 62901-4701. Offers MS, PhD. Part-time programs available. *Faculty:* 18 full-time (1 woman), 2 part-time/adjunct (0 women). *Students:* 43 full-time (19 women), 15 part-time (8 women); includes 3 minority (1 Black or African American, non-Hispanic/Latino; 2 Asian, non-Hispanic/Latino), 38 international. Average age 25. 54 applicants, 13% accepted, 4 enrolled. In 2012, 1 master's, 3 doctorates awarded. Terminal master's awarded for partial completion of doctoral program. *Degree requirements:* For master's, one foreign language, thesis; for doctorate, variable foreign language requirement, thesis/dissertation. *Entrance requirements:* For master's, minimum GPA of 2.7; for doctorate, GRE General Test, minimum GPA of 3.25. Additional exam requirements/recommendations for international students: Required—TOEFL. *Application deadline:* Applications are processed on a rolling basis. Application fee: $50. *Financial support:* In 2012–13, 17 research assistantships with full tuition reimbursements, 23 teaching assistantships with full tuition reimbursements were awarded; fellowships with full tuition reimbursements, Federal Work-Study, institutionally sponsored loans, and tuition waivers (full) also available. Support available to part-time students. *Faculty research:* Materials, separations, computational chemistry, synthetics. *Total annual research expenditures:* $1 million. *Unit head:* Gary Kinsel, Chair, 618-453-6482, Fax: 618-453-6408. *Application contact:* Doug Coons, Office Specialist, 618-453-6496, Fax: 618-453-6408, E-mail: dcoons@chem.siu.edu.

Southern Illinois University Edwardsville, Graduate School, College of Arts and Sciences, Department of Chemistry, Edwardsville, IL 62026. Offers MS. Part-time and evening/weekend programs available. *Faculty:* 17 full-time (4 women). *Students:* 9 full-time (7 women), 22 part-time (14 women); includes 1 minority

(Two or more races, non-Hispanic/Latino), 15 international. 29 applicants, 52% accepted. In 2012, 15 master's awarded. *Degree requirements:* For master's, thesis (for some programs), research paper. *Entrance requirements:* Additional exam requirements/recommendations for international students: Required—TOEFL (minimum score 550 paper-based; 79 iBT), IELTS (minimum score 6.5). *Application deadline:* For fall admission, 7/26 for domestic students, 6/1 for international students; for spring admission, 12/6 for domestic students, 10/1 for international students. Applications are processed on a rolling basis. Application fee: $30. Electronic applications accepted. *Expenses:* Tuition, state resident: full-time $6504; part-time $3252 per semester. Tuition, nonresident: full-time $8130; part-time $4065 per semester. *Required fees:* $705.50 per semester. Tuition and fees vary according to course level, course load, degree level, program and student level. *Financial support:* In 2012–13, 4 research assistantships with full tuition reimbursements (averaging $9,585 per year), 31 teaching assistantships with full tuition reimbursements (averaging $9,585 per year) were awarded; fellowships with full tuition reimbursements, institutionally sponsored loans, scholarships/grants, and unspecified assistantships also available. Financial award application deadline: 3/1; financial award applicants required to submit FAFSA. *Unit head:* Dr. Yun Lu, Program Director, 618-650-2042, E-mail: yulu@siue.edu. *Application contact:* Michelle Robinson, Coordinator of Graduate Recruitment, 618-650-2811, Fax: 618-650-3523, E-mail: michero@siue.edu. Website: http://www.siue.edu/artsandsciences/chemistry/.

Southern Methodist University, Dedman College, Department of Chemistry, Dallas, TX 75275-0314. Offers chemistry (MS, PhD); materials science and engineering (MS, PhD). Terminal master's awarded for partial completion of doctoral program. *Degree requirements:* For master's, thesis; for doctorate, comprehensive exam, thesis/dissertation. *Entrance requirements:* For master's, GRE General Test, bachelor's degree in chemistry, minimum GPA of 3.0; for doctorate, GRE General Test, bachelor's degree in chemistry or closely related field, minimum GPA of 3.0. Additional exam requirements/recommendations for international students: Required—TOEFL (minimum score 550 paper-based; 80 iBT). Electronic applications accepted. *Faculty research:* Materials/polymer, medicinal/bioorganic, theoretical and computational, organic/inorganic/organometallic synthesis, inorganic polymer chemistry.

Southern University and Agricultural and Mechanical College, Graduate School, College of Sciences, Department of Chemistry, Baton Rouge, LA 70813. Offers analytical chemistry (MS); biochemistry (MS); environmental sciences (MS); inorganic chemistry (MS); organic chemistry (MS); physical chemistry (MS). *Degree requirements:* For master's, thesis. *Entrance requirements:* For master's, GMAT or GRE General Test. Additional exam requirements/recommendations for international students: Required—TOEFL (minimum score 525 paper-based). *Faculty research:* Synthesis of macrocyclic ligands, latex accelerators, anticancer drugs, biosensors, absorption isotheums, isolation of specific enzymes from plants.

Stanford University, School of Humanities and Sciences, Department of Chemistry, Stanford, CA 94305-5080. Offers PhD. *Degree requirements:* For doctorate, thesis/dissertation. *Entrance requirements:* For doctorate, GRE General Test, GRE Subject Test. Additional exam requirements/recommendations for international students: Required—TOEFL. Electronic applications accepted. *Expenses: Tuition:* Full-time $41,250; part-time $917 per credit hour.

State University of New York at Fredonia, Graduate Studies, Department of Chemistry and Biochemistry, Fredonia, NY 14063-1136. Offers chemistry (MS); curriculum and instruction science education (MS Ed). Part-time and evening/weekend programs available. *Degree requirements:* For master's, thesis optional. *Expenses:* Tuition, state resident: full-time $7020; part-time $390 per credit hour. Tuition, nonresident: full-time $12,510; part-time $695 per credit hour. *Required fees:* $1113.30; $61.85 per credit hour. Tuition and fees vary according to course load.

State University of New York at New Paltz, Graduate School, School of Education, Department of Secondary Education, New Paltz, NY 12561. Offers adolescence education: biology (MAT, MS Ed); adolescence education: chemistry (MAT, MS Ed); adolescence education: earth science (MAT, MS Ed); adolescence education: English (MAT, MS Ed); adolescence education: French (MAT, MS Ed); adolescence education: social studies (MAT, MS Ed); adolescence education: Spanish (MAT, MS Ed); second language education (MS Ed, AC), including second language education (MS Ed), teaching English language learners (AC). *Accreditation:* NCATE. Part-time and evening/weekend programs available. *Faculty:* 25 full-time (10 women), 7 part-time/adjunct (4 women). *Students:* 75 full-time (44 women), 61 part-time (41 women); includes 26 minority (3 Black or African American, non-Hispanic/Latino; 4 Asian, non-Hispanic/Latino; 16 Hispanic/Latino; 3 Two or more races, non-Hispanic/Latino), 1 international. Average age 30. 93 applicants, 70% accepted, 48 enrolled. In 2012, 71 master's awarded. *Degree requirements:* For master's, comprehensive exam (for some programs), portfolio. *Entrance requirements:* For master's, minimum GPA of 3.0, New York state teaching certificate (MS Ed). Additional exam requirements/recommendations for international students: Required—TOEFL (minimum score 550 paper-based; 80 iBT), IELTS (minimum score 6.5). *Application deadline:* For fall admission, 3/1 priority date for domestic students, 3/1 for international students; for spring admission, 10/1 priority date for domestic students, 10/1 for international students. Application fee: $50. Electronic applications accepted. *Expenses:* Tuition, state resident: full-time $9370; part-time $390 per credit hour. Tuition, nonresident: full-time $16,680; part-time $695 per credit hour. *Required fees:* $1188; $68.40 per credit hour. $184 per semester. *Financial support:* In 2012–13, 7 students received support, including 1 fellowship with partial tuition reimbursement available (averaging $3,000 per year); Federal Work-Study, institutionally sponsored loans, and tuition waivers (full and partial) also available. Financial award application deadline: 8/1; financial award applicants required to submit FAFSA. *Unit head:* Dr. Devon Duhaney, Chair, 845-257-2850, E-mail: duhaneyd@newpaltz.edu. *Application contact:* Caroline Murphy, Graduate Admissions Advisor, 845-257-3285, Fax: 845-257-3284, E-mail: gradschool@newpaltz.edu. Website: http://www.newpaltz.edu/secondaryed/.

State University of New York at Oswego, Graduate Studies, College of Liberal Arts and Sciences, Department of Chemistry, Oswego, NY 13126. Offers MS. Part-time programs available. *Degree requirements:* For master's, comprehensive exam, thesis. *Entrance requirements:* For master's, GRE General Test, GRE Subject Test, BA or BS in chemistry. Additional exam requirements/recommendations for international students: Required—TOEFL (minimum score 560 paper-based).

State University of New York College of Environmental Science and Forestry, Department of Chemistry, Syracuse, NY 13210-2779. Offers biochemistry (MPS, MS, PhD); environmental chemistry (MPS, MS, PhD); organic chemistry of natural products (MPS, MS, PhD); polymer chemistry (MPS, MS, PhD). *Degree requirements:* For master's, thesis; for doctorate, comprehensive exam, thesis/dissertation. *Entrance requirements:* For master's and doctorate, GRE General Test, GRE Subject Test, minimum GPA of 3.0. Additional exam requirements/recommendations for international students: Required—TOEFL (minimum score 550 paper-based; 80 iBT), IELTS (minimum score 6). Electronic applications accepted. *Expenses:* Tuition, state resident: full-time $9370; part-time $390 per credit hour. Tuition, nonresident: full-time $16,680; part-time $695 per credit hour. *Required fees:* $981. Tuition and fees vary according to course load and program. *Faculty research:* Polymer chemistry, biochemistry.

Stephen F. Austin State University, Graduate School, College of Sciences and Mathematics, Department of Chemistry, Nacogdoches, TX 75962. Offers MS. Part-time programs available. *Degree requirements:* For master's, comprehensive exam. *Entrance requirements:* For master's, GRE General Test, minimum GPA of 2.8 in last 60 hours, 2.5 overall. Additional exam requirements/recommendations for international students: Required—TOEFL. *Faculty research:* Synthesis and chemistry of ferrate ion, properties of fluoroberyllates, polymer chemistry.

Stevens Institute of Technology, Graduate School, Charles V. Schaefer Jr. School of Engineering, Department of Chemistry, Chemical Biology and Biomedical Engineering, Hoboken, NJ 07030. Offers analytical chemistry (PhD, Certificate); bioinformatics (PhD, Certificate); biomedical chemistry (Certificate); biomedical engineering (M Eng, Certificate); chemical biology (MS, PhD, Certificate); chemical physiology (Certificate); chemistry (MS, PhD); organic chemistry (PhD); physical chemistry (PhD); polymer chemistry (PhD, Certificate). Part-time and evening/weekend programs available. Postbaccalaureate distance learning degree programs offered (no on-campus study). Terminal master's awarded for partial completion of doctoral program. *Degree requirements:* For master's, thesis or alternative; for doctorate, one foreign language, thesis/dissertation; for Certificate, project or thesis. *Entrance requirements:* Additional exam requirements/recommendations for international students: Required—TOEFL. Electronic applications accepted. *Faculty research:* Biochemical reaction engineering, polymerization engineering, reactor design, biochemical process control and synthesis.

Stony Brook University, State University of New York, Graduate School, College of Arts and Sciences, Department of Chemistry, Stony Brook, NY 11794. Offers MS, PhD. *Faculty:* 32 full-time (7 women), 4 part-time/adjunct (1 woman). *Students:* 200 full-time (94 women), 2 part-time (both women); includes 30 minority (7 Black or African American, non-Hispanic/Latino; 15 Asian, non-Hispanic/Latino; 8 Hispanic/Latino), 121 international. Average age 28. 430 applicants, 34% accepted, 46 enrolled. In 2012, 15 master's, 22 doctorates awarded. Terminal master's awarded for partial completion of doctoral program. *Degree requirements:* For master's, thesis; for doctorate, one foreign language, thesis/dissertation. *Entrance requirements:* For master's and doctorate, GRE General Test. Additional exam requirements/recommendations for international students: Required—TOEFL. *Application deadline:* For fall admission, 1/15 for domestic students. Application fee: $100. *Expenses:* Tuition, state resident: full-time $9370. Tuition, nonresident: full-time $16,680. *Required fees:* $1214. *Financial support:* In 2012–13, 6 fellowships, 109 research assistantships, 40 teaching assistantships were awarded. *Faculty research:* Chemistry, bioimaging, chemical sciences, organic chemistry, spectroscopy, nanostructured materials. *Total annual research expenditures:* $10.9 million. *Unit head:* Prof. Nicole Sampson, Chairman, 631-632-7880, Fax: 631-632-7960, E-mail: nicole.sampson@stonybrook.edu. *Application contact:* Melissa Jordan, Assistant Dean for Records and Admission, 631-632-9712, Fax: 631-632-7243. Website: http://ws.cc.stonybrook.edu/chemistry/.

Syracuse University, College of Arts and Sciences, Program in Chemistry, Syracuse, NY 13244. Offers MS, PhD. *Degree requirements:* For master's, comprehensive exam, thesis (for some programs); for doctorate, comprehensive exam, thesis/dissertation. *Entrance requirements:* For master's and doctorate, GRE General Test. Additional exam requirements/recommendations for international students: Required—TOEFL (minimum score 100 iBT). Electronic applications accepted. *Faculty research:* Synthetic organic chemistry, biophysical spectroscopy, solid state in organic chemistry, biochemistry, organometallic chemistry.

Temple University, College of Science and Technology, Department of Chemistry, Philadelphia, PA 19122-6096. Offers MA, PhD. Evening/weekend programs available. *Faculty:* 40 full-time (8 women). *Students:* 98 full-time (35 women), 5 part-time (2 women); includes 10 minority (3 Black or African American, non-Hispanic/Latino; 7 Asian, non-Hispanic/Latino), 47 international. 142 applicants, 18% accepted, 22 enrolled. In 2012, 5 master's, 18 doctorates awarded. Terminal master's awarded for partial completion of doctoral program. *Degree requirements:* For master's, thesis (for some programs); for doctorate, thesis/dissertation, teaching experience. *Entrance requirements:* For master's and doctorate, GRE General Test, minimum GPA of 3.0. Additional exam requirements/recommendations for international students: Required—TOEFL (minimum score 550 paper-based; 79 iBT). *Application deadline:* For fall admission, 2/15 for domestic students, 12/15 for international students; for spring admission, 9/15 for domestic students, 8/1 for international students. Applications are processed on a rolling basis. Application fee: $60. Electronic applications accepted. *Financial support:* Fellowships, research assistantships, and teaching assistantships available. Financial award application deadline: 1/15; financial award applicants required to submit FAFSA. *Faculty research:* Polymers, nonlinear optics, natural products, materials science, enantioselective synthesis. *Unit head:* Dr. Robert Levis, Chair, 215-204-5241, Fax: 215-204-1532, E-mail: rjlevis@temple.edu. *Application contact:* Tiffany Gilles, Program Coordinator, 215-204-3379, Fax: 215-204-1532, E-mail: tgilles@temple.edu. Website: http://www.temple.edu/chemistry.

Tennessee State University, The School of Graduate Studies and Research, College of Arts and Sciences, Department of Chemistry, Nashville, TN 37209-1561. Offers MS. Part-time programs available. *Degree requirements:* For master's, thesis optional. *Entrance requirements:* For master's, GRE General Test. Electronic applications accepted.

Tennessee Technological University, Graduate School, College of Arts and Sciences, Department of Chemistry, Cookeville, TN 38505. Offers MS. Part-time programs available. *Faculty:* 16 full-time (1 woman). *Students:* 11 full-time (4 women), 8 part-time (5 women); includes 4 minority (2 Asian, non-Hispanic/Latino; 2 Hispanic/Latino), 9 international. Average age 28. 26 applicants, 38% accepted, 6 enrolled. In 2012, 5 master's awarded. *Degree requirements:* For master's, thesis. *Entrance requirements:* For master's, GRE. Additional exam requirements/recommendations for international students: Required—TOEFL (minimum score 527 paper-based; 71 iBT), IELTS (minimum score 5.5), Pearson Test of English. *Application deadline:* For fall admission, 8/1 for domestic students, 5/1 for international students; for spring admission, 12/1 for domestic students, 10/1 for international students. Application fee: $35 ($40 for international students). Electronic applications accepted. *Expenses:* Tuition, state resident: full-time $8444; part-time $441 per credit hour. Tuition, nonresident: full-time $21,404; part-time $1089 per credit hour. *Financial support:* In 2012–13, 1 research assistantship (averaging $10,000 per year), 6 teaching assistantships (averaging $7,500 per year) were awarded; career-related internships or fieldwork also available. Financial award application deadline: 4/1. *Unit head:* Dr. Jeffrey Boles, Interim Chairperson, 931-372-3421, Fax: 931-372-3434, E-mail: jboles@tntech.edu. *Application contact:* Shelia K. Kendrick, Coordinator of Graduate Admissions, 931-372-3808, Fax: 931-372-3497, E-mail: skendrick@tntech.edu.

Tennessee Technological University, Graduate School, College of Arts and Sciences, Department of Environmental Sciences, Cookeville, TN 38505. Offers biology (PhD); chemistry (PhD). Part-time programs available. *Students:* 2 full-time (1 woman), 15 part-time (5 women); includes 3 minority (1 Black or African American, non-Hispanic/Latino; 1 American Indian or Alaska Native, non-Hispanic/Latino; 1 Hispanic/Latino), 5 international. 14 applicants, 43% accepted, 3 enrolled. In 2012, 1 doctorate awarded. *Degree requirements:* For doctorate, comprehensive exam, thesis/dissertation. *Entrance requirements:* For doctorate, GRE. Additional exam requirements/recommendations for international students: Required—TOEFL (minimum score 527 paper-based; 71 iBT), IELTS (minimum score 5.5), Pearson Test of English. *Application deadline:* For fall admission, 8/1 for domestic students, 5/1 for international students; for spring admission, 12/1 for domestic students, 10/2 for international students. Application fee: $35 ($40 for international students). Electronic applications accepted. *Expenses:* Tuition, state resident: full-time $8444; part-time $441 per credit hour. Tuition, nonresident: full-time $21,404; part-time $1089 per credit hour. *Financial support:* In 2012–13, 5 research assistantships (averaging $10,000 per year), 3 teaching assistantships (averaging $10,000 per year) were awarded; fellowships also available. Financial award application deadline: 4/1. *Application contact:* Shelia K. Kendrick, Coordinator of Graduate Admissions, 931-372-3808, Fax: 931-372-3497, E-mail: skendrick@tntech.edu.

Texas A&M University, College of Science, Department of Chemistry, College Station, TX 77843. Offers MS, PhD. *Faculty:* 38. *Students:* 277 full-time (106 women), 5 part-time (2 women); includes 37 minority (5 Black or African American, non-Hispanic/Latino; 1 American Indian or Alaska Native, non-Hispanic/Latino; 12 Asian, non-Hispanic/Latino; 18 Hispanic/Latino; 1 Two or more races, non-Hispanic/Latino), 144 international. Average age 26. In 2012, 4 master's, 45 doctorates awarded. Terminal master's awarded for partial completion of doctoral program. *Degree requirements:* For master's, thesis; for doctorate, thesis/dissertation. *Entrance requirements:* For master's and doctorate, GRE General Test. Additional exam requirements/recommendations for international students: Required—TOEFL. *Application deadline:* For fall admission, 3/1 priority date for domestic students. Applications are processed on a rolling basis. Electronic applications accepted. *Financial support:* In 2012–13, fellowships with full tuition reimbursements (averaging $21,600 per year), research assistantships with full tuition reimbursements (averaging $18,600 per year), teaching assistantships with full tuition reimbursements (averaging $18,600 per year) were awarded. Financial award application deadline: 3/1; financial award applicants required to submit FAFSA. *Faculty research:* Biological chemistry, spectroscopy, structure and bonding, reactions and mechanisms, theoretical chemistry. *Unit head:* Dr. David Russell, Head, 979-845-3345, E-mail: russell@chem.tamu.edu. *Application contact:* Dr. Michael P. Rosynek, Graduate Advisor, 979-845-2233, Fax: 979-845-4719, E-mail: rosynek@chem.tamu.edu. Website: http://www.chem.tamu.edu/.

Texas A&M University–Commerce, Graduate School, College of Science, Engineering and Agriculture, Department of Chemistry, Commerce, TX 75429-3011. Offers M Ed, MS. Part-time programs available. *Degree requirements:* For master's, comprehensive exam, thesis (for some programs). *Entrance requirements:* For master's, GRE General Test. Electronic applications accepted. *Expenses:* Tuition, state resident: full-time $3630; part-time $2420 per year. Tuition, nonresident: full-time $9948; part-time $6632.16 per year. *Required fees:* $1006 per year. *Faculty research:* Analytical organic.

Texas A&M University–Kingsville, College of Graduate Studies, College of Arts and Sciences, Department of Chemistry, Kingsville, TX 78363. Offers MS. Part-time programs available. *Degree requirements:* For master's, comprehensive exam, thesis or alternative. *Entrance requirements:* For master's, GRE General Test, minimum GPA of 3.0. Additional exam requirements/recommendations for international students: Required—TOEFL. *Faculty research:* Organic heterocycles, amino alcohol complexes, rare earth arsine complexes.

Texas Christian University, College of Science and Engineering, Department of Chemistry, Fort Worth, TX 76129. Offers biochemistry (MS, PhD); chemistry (MA); inorganic (MS, PhD); organic (MS, PhD); physical (MS, PhD). Part-time programs available. *Faculty:* 11 full-time (2 women). *Students:* 7 full-time (3 women), 17 part-time (10 women); includes 4 minority (1 Asian, non-Hispanic/Latino; 3 Hispanic/Latino), 13 international. Average age 27. 34 applicants, 24% accepted, 5 enrolled. In 2012, 1 master's, 1 doctorate awarded. *Degree requirements:* For master's, thesis; for doctorate, thesis/dissertation, literature seminar, cumulative exams, research progress report, original proposal. *Entrance requirements:* For master's and doctorate, GRE General Test. Additional exam requirements/recommendations for international students: Required—TOEFL (minimum score 80 iBT). *Application deadline:* For fall admission, 2/1 priority date for domestic students, 2/1 for international students; for spring admission, 9/1 priority date for domestic students, 9/1 for international students. Application fee: $50. Electronic applications accepted. *Expenses: Tuition:* Full-time $21,600; part-time $1200 per credit. *Required fees:* $48. Tuition and fees vary according to program. *Financial support:* In 2012–13, 16 students received support, including 16 teaching assistantships with full tuition reimbursements available; tuition waivers (full and partial) and unspecified assistantships also available. Financial award application deadline: 2/1. *Faculty research:* Phase transitions and transport properties of bio/macromolecular solutions, nanoscale biomaterials, electronic structure theory, synthetic methodology and total synthesis of natural products, chemistry and biology of (bio)polymers. *Unit head:* Dr. Robert Neilson, Chairperson/Professor, 817-257-7345, Fax: 817-257-5851, E-mail: r.neilson@tcu.edu. *Application contact:* Dr. Sergei V. Dzyuba, Director of Graduate Studies/Assistant Professor, 817-257-6218, Fax: 817-257-5851, E-mail: s.dzyuba@tcu.edu. Website: http://www.chm.tcu.edu/.

Texas Southern University, School of Science and Technology, Department of Chemistry, Houston, TX 77004-4584. Offers MS. *Faculty:* 8 full-time (1 woman), 1 part-time/adjunct (0 women). *Students:* 7 full-time (3 women), 9 part-time (2 women); includes 15 minority (9 Black or African American, non-Hispanic/Latino; 5 Asian, non-Hispanic/Latino; 1 Hispanic/Latino), 1 international. Average age 33. 15 applicants, 40% accepted, 4 enrolled. In 2012, 2 master's awarded. *Degree requirements:* For master's, one foreign language, comprehensive exam, thesis. *Entrance requirements:* For master's, GRE General Test, minimum GPA of 2.5. Additional exam requirements/recommendations for international students: Required—TOEFL. *Application deadline:* For fall admission, 7/1 for domestic and international students; for spring admission, 11/1 for domestic and international students. Applications are processed on a rolling basis. Application fee: $50 ($75 for international students). Electronic applications accepted. *Expenses:* Tuition, state resident: full-time $1836; part-time $100 per credit hour. Tuition, nonresident: full-time $7128; part-time $360 per credit hour. *Required fees:* $6268. *Financial support:* In 2012–13, 2 research assistantships (averaging $5,880 per year), 6 teaching assistantships (averaging $3,650 per year) were awarded; fellowships, scholarships/grants, and unspecified assistantships also available. Financial award application deadline: 5/1. *Faculty research:* Analytical and physical chemistry, geochemistry, inorganic chemistry, biochemistry, organic chemistry. *Unit head:* Dr. John Sapp, Chair, 713-313-7831, E-mail: sapp_jb@tsu.edu. *Application contact:* Delois Smith-Johnson, Administrative Secretary, 713-313-7831, E-mail: johnson_ds@tsu.edu. Website: http://www.cost.tsu.edu/WebPages/Chemistry.html.

Texas State University–San Marcos, Graduate School, College of Science and Engineering, Department of Chemistry and Biochemistry, Program in Chemistry, San Marcos, TX 78666. Offers MA, MS. *Faculty:* 7 full-time (2 women). *Students:* 9 full-time (3 women), 2 part-time (both women); includes 2 minority (1 Hispanic/Latino; 1 Two or more races, non-Hispanic/Latino), 2 international. Average age

28. 9 applicants, 67% accepted, 5 enrolled. In 2012, 3 master's awarded. *Degree requirements:* For master's, comprehensive exam, thesis (for some programs). *Entrance requirements:* For master's, minimum GPA of 2.75 in last 60 hours of course work. Additional exam requirements/recommendations for international students: Required—TOEFL (minimum score 550 paper-based; 78 iBT). *Application deadline:* For fall admission, 6/15 for domestic students, 6/1 for international students; for spring admission, 10/15 for domestic students, 10/1 for international students. Applications are processed on a rolling basis. Application fee: $40 ($90 for international students). *Expenses:* Tuition, state resident: full-time $6408; part-time $3204 per semester. Tuition, nonresident: full-time $14,832; part-time $7416 per semester. *Required fees:* $1824; $618. Tuition and fees vary according to course load. *Financial support:* In 2012–13, 10 students received support, including 3 research assistantships (averaging $12,230 per year), 7 teaching assistantships (averaging $12,710 per year); career-related internships or fieldwork, Federal Work-Study, institutionally sponsored loans, scholarships/grants, health care benefits, and unspecified assistantships also available. Support available to part-time students. Financial award application deadline: 4/1; financial award applicants required to submit FAFSA. *Unit head:* Dr. Chad Booth, Graduate Advisor, 512-245-8789, Fax: 512-245-2374, E-mail: chadbooth@txstate.edu. *Application contact:* Dr. J. Michael Willoughby, Dean of Graduate School, 512-245-2581, Fax: 512-245-8365, E-mail: gradcollege@txstate.edu. Website: http://www.txstate.edu/chemistry/

Texas Tech University, Graduate School, College of Arts and Sciences, Department of Chemistry and Biochemistry, Lubbock, TX 79409. Offers chemistry (MS, PhD). Part-time programs available. *Degree requirements:* For master's, thesis; for doctorate, thesis/dissertation. *Entrance requirements:* For master's and doctorate, GRE General Test, diagnostic examination in area of specialization. Additional exam requirements/recommendations for international students: Required—TOEFL (minimum score 550 paper-based; 79 iBT). Electronic applications accepted. *Faculty research:* Theoretical and computational chemistry, plant biochemistry and chemical biology, materials and supramolecular chemistry, nanotechnology, spectroscopic analysis.

Texas Woman's University, Graduate School, College of Arts and Sciences, Department of Chemistry and Biochemistry, Denton, TX 76201. Offers chemistry (MS). Part-time programs available. *Degree requirements:* For master's, comprehensive exam, thesis. *Entrance requirements:* For master's, GRE General Test (preferred minimum score 146 [400 old version] verbal, 146 [550 old version] quantitative), 2 reference contacts. Additional exam requirements/recommendations for international students: Required—TOEFL (minimum score 550 paper-based; 79 iBT). Electronic applications accepted. *Faculty research:* Glutathione synthetase, conformational properties of DNA quadruplexes, constriction and analysis of aqueous enzyme phase diagrams, development of metallopolymers, basic chemical research.

Trent University, Graduate Studies, Program in Applications of Modeling in the Natural and Social Sciences, Department of Chemistry, Peterborough, ON K9J 7B8, Canada. Offers M Sc. Part-time programs available. *Degree requirements:* For master's, thesis. *Entrance requirements:* For master's, honours degree. *Faculty research:* Synthetic-organic chemistry, mass spectrometry and ion storage.

Tufts University, Graduate School of Arts and Sciences, Department of Chemistry, Medford, MA 02155. Offers analytical chemistry (MS, PhD); bioorganic chemistry (MS, PhD); environmental chemistry (MS, PhD); inorganic chemistry (MS, PhD); organic chemistry (MS, PhD); physical chemistry (MS, PhD). Terminal master's awarded for partial completion of doctoral program. *Degree requirements:* For master's, thesis optional; for doctorate, thesis/dissertation. *Entrance requirements:* For master's and doctorate, GRE General Test, GRE Subject Test. Additional exam requirements/recommendations for international students: Required—TOEFL (minimum score 600 paper-based; 80 iBT). Electronic applications accepted. *Expenses: Tuition:* Full-time $42,856; part-time $1072 per credit hour. *Required fees:* $730. Full-time tuition and fees vary according to degree level, program and student level. Part-time tuition and fees vary according to course load.

Tulane University, School of Science and Engineering, Department of Chemistry, New Orleans, LA 70118-5669. Offers MS, PhD. Terminal master's awarded for partial completion of doctoral program. *Degree requirements:* For master's, thesis; for doctorate, thesis/dissertation. *Entrance requirements:* For master's, GRE General Test, minimum B average in undergraduate course work; for doctorate, GRE General Test. Additional exam requirements/recommendations for international students: Required—TOEFL. Electronic applications accepted. *Faculty research:* Enzyme mechanisms, organic synthesis, photochemistry, theory of polymer dynamics.

Tuskegee University, Graduate Programs, College of Agricultural, Environmental and Natural Sciences, Department of Chemistry, Tuskegee, AL 36088. Offers MS. *Degree requirements:* For master's, thesis. *Entrance requirements:* For master's, GRE General Test. Additional exam requirements/recommendations for international students: Required—TOEFL (minimum score 500 paper-based). *Expenses: Tuition:* Full-time $18,100; part-time $575 per credit hour. *Required fees:* $800.

Universidad del Turabo, Graduate Programs, Programs in Science and Technology, Gurabo, PR 00778-3030. Offers environmental analysis (MSE), including environmental chemistry; environmental management (MSE), including pollution management; environmental science (D Sc), including environmental biology. *Students:* 12 full-time (10 women), 97 part-time (63 women); all minorities (all Hispanic/Latino). Average age 38. 60 applicants, 90% accepted, 40 enrolled. In 2012, 17 master's, 1 doctorate awarded. *Entrance requirements:* For master's, GRE, EXADEP, interview. *Application deadline:* For fall admission, 8/5 for domestic students. Application fee: $25. *Unit head:* Teresa Lipsett, Dean, 787-743-7979. *Application contact:* Virginia Gonzalez, Admissions Officer, 787-746-3009.

Université de Moncton, Faculty of Sciences, Department of Chemistry and Biochemistry, Moncton, NB E1A 3E9, Canada. Offers biochemistry (M Sc); chemistry (M Sc). Part-time programs available. *Degree requirements:* For master's, one foreign language, thesis. *Entrance requirements:* For master's, minimum GPA of 3.0. Electronic applications accepted. *Faculty research:* Environmental contaminants, natural products synthesis, nutraceutical, organic catalysis, molecular biology of cancer.

Université de Montréal, Faculty of Arts and Sciences, Department of Chemistry, Montréal, QC H3C 3J7, Canada. Offers M Sc, PhD. *Degree requirements:* For master's, thesis; for doctorate, thesis/dissertation, general exam. *Entrance requirements:* For master's, B Sc in chemistry or the equivalent; for doctorate, M Sc in chemistry or equivalent. Electronic applications accepted. *Faculty research:* Analytical, inorganic, physical, and organic chemistry.

Université de Sherbrooke, Faculty of Sciences, Department of Chemistry, Sherbrooke, QC J1K 2R1, Canada. Offers M Sc, PhD, Diploma. *Degree requirements:* For master's, thesis; for doctorate, thesis/dissertation. *Entrance requirements:* For doctorate, master's degree. Electronic applications accepted. *Faculty research:* Organic, electro-, theoretical, and physical chemistry.

Université du Québec à Montréal, Graduate Programs, Program in Chemistry, Montréal, QC H3C 3P8, Canada. Offers M Sc, PhD. M Sc offered jointly with Université du Québec à Trois-Rivières. Part-time programs available. *Degree requirements:* For master's, thesis. *Entrance requirements:* For master's, appropriate bachelor's degree or equivalent and proficiency in French.

Université du Québec à Trois-Rivières, Graduate Programs, Program in Chemistry, Trois-Rivières, QC G9A 5H7, Canada. Offers M Sc. Part-time programs available. *Degree requirements:* For master's, thesis. *Entrance requirements:* For master's, appropriate bachelor's degree, proficiency in French.

Université Laval, Faculty of Sciences and Engineering, Department of Chemistry, Programs in Chemistry, Québec, QC G1K 7P4, Canada. Offers M Sc, PhD. Part-time programs available. Terminal master's awarded for partial completion of doctoral program. *Degree requirements:* For master's, thesis; for doctorate, comprehensive exam, thesis/dissertation. *Entrance requirements:* For master's and doctorate, knowledge of French, comprehension of written English. Electronic applications accepted.

University at Albany, State University of New York, College of Arts and Sciences, Department of Chemistry, Albany, NY 12222-0001. Offers MS, PhD. *Degree requirements:* For master's, one foreign language, thesis, major field exam; for doctorate, 2 foreign languages, thesis/dissertation, cumulative exams, oral proposition. *Entrance requirements:* For doctorate, GRE. Additional exam requirements/recommendations for international students: Required—TOEFL (minimum score 550 paper-based). Electronic applications accepted. *Faculty research:* Synthetic, organic, and inorganic chemistry; polymer chemistry; ESR and NMR spectroscopy; theoretical chemistry; physical biochemistry.

University at Albany, State University of New York, School of Public Health, Department of Environmental Health Sciences, Albany, NY 12222-0001. Offers environmental and analytical chemistry (MS, PhD); environmental and occupational health (MS, PhD); toxicology (MS, PhD). *Degree requirements:* For master's, thesis; for doctorate, comprehensive exam, thesis/dissertation. *Entrance requirements:* For master's and doctorate, GRE General Test, GRE Subject Test, 3 letters of reference. Additional exam requirements/recommendations for international students: Required—TOEFL (minimum score 600 paper-based). Electronic applications accepted. *Faculty research:* Xenobiotic metabolism, neurotoxicity of halogenated hydrocarbons, pharmac/toxicogenomics, environmental analytical chemistry.

University at Buffalo, the State University of New York, Graduate School, College of Arts and Sciences, Department of Chemistry, Buffalo, NY 14260. Offers chemistry (MA, PhD); medicinal chemistry (MS, PhD). Part-time programs available. *Faculty:* 28 full-time (4 women), 1 (woman) part-time/adjunct. *Students:* 144 full-time (56 women), 1 part-time (0 women); includes 17 minority (8 Black or African American, non-Hispanic/Latino; 2 Asian, non-Hispanic/Latino; 7 Hispanic/Latino), 40 international. Average age 26. 227 applicants, 32% accepted, 34 enrolled. In 2012, 10 master's, 24 doctorates awarded. Terminal master's awarded for partial completion of doctoral program. *Degree requirements:* For master's, thesis or alternative, project; for doctorate, thesis/dissertation, synopsis proposal. *Entrance requirements:* For master's and doctorate, GRE General Test. Additional exam requirements/recommendations for international students: Required—TOEFL (minimum score 550 paper-based; 79 iBT). *Application deadline:* For fall admission, 3/1 priority date for domestic students, 3/1 for international students; for spring admission, 11/1 priority date for domestic students. Applications are processed on a rolling basis. Application fee: $75. Electronic applications accepted. *Financial support:* In 2012–13, 3 students received support, including 3 fellowships with full tuition reimbursements available (averaging $22,080 per year), 33 research assistantships with full tuition reimbursements available (averaging $22,080 per year), 91 teaching assistantships with full tuition reimbursements available (averaging $22,080 per year); Federal Work-Study, institutionally sponsored loans, and unspecified assistantships also available. Financial award application deadline: 6/15; financial award applicants required to submit FAFSA. *Faculty research:* Synthesis, measurements, structure theory, translation. *Total annual research expenditures:* $8 million. *Unit head:* Dr. Michael R. Detty, Chairman, 716-645-6824, Fax: 716-645-6963, E-mail: chechair@buffalo.edu. *Application contact:* Dr. Diana S. Aga, Director of Graduate Studies, 716-645-4220, Fax: 716-645-6963, E-mail: dianaaga@buffalo.edu. Website: http://www.chemistry.buffalo.edu/.

The University of Akron, Graduate School, Buchtel College of Arts and Sciences, Department of Chemistry, Akron, OH 44325. Offers MS, PhD. Part-time and evening/weekend programs available. *Faculty:* 16 full-time (2 women), 5 part-time/adjunct (2 women). *Students:* 57 full-time (28 women), 3 part-time (2 women); includes 2 minority (both Black or African American, non-Hispanic/Latino), 31 international. Average age 28. 93 applicants, 23% accepted, 11 enrolled. In 2012, 1 master's, 13 doctorates awarded. Terminal master's awarded for partial completion of doctoral program. *Degree requirements:* For master's, thesis, seminar presentation; for doctorate, comprehensive exam, thesis/dissertation, cumulative exams, oral exam, defense of dissertation. *Entrance requirements:* For master's, baccalaureate degree in chemistry, biochemistry, or a related field, minimum GPA of 2.75, 3 letters of recommendation, statement of purpose; for doctorate, baccalaureate degree in chemistry, biochemistry, or a related field, minimum GPA of 2.75, three letters of recommendation, statement of purpose. Additional exam requirements/recommendations for international students: Required—TOEFL (minimum score 550 paper-based; 79 iBT). *Application deadline:* For fall admission, 6/1 for domestic and international students; for spring admission, 11/15 for domestic and international students. Application fee: $40 ($60 for international students). Electronic applications accepted. *Expenses:* Tuition, state resident: full-time $7285; part-time $404.70 per credit hour. Tuition, nonresident: full-time $12,473; part-time $692.95 per credit hour. *Required fees:* $34.05 per credit hour. Tuition and fees vary according to course load. *Financial support:* In 2012–13, 10 research assistantships with full tuition reimbursements, 42 teaching assistantships with full tuition reimbursements were awarded; tuition waivers (partial) also available. *Faculty research:* NMR and mass spectrometric characterization of biological and synthetic polymers, synthesis and characterization of new organic and inorganic material, metals in medicine, enzymology of gene regulation, high-resolution spectroscopy and ultrafast characterization of organic materials. *Total annual research expenditures:* $1.5 million. *Unit head:* Dr. Michael Taschner, Chair, 330-972-6068, E-mail: mtaschner@uakron.edu. *Application contact:* Dr. Mark Tausig, Associate Dean, 330-972-6266, Fax: 330-972-6475, E-mail: mtausig@uakron.edu. Website: http://www.uakron.edu/chemistry/.

The University of Alabama, Graduate School, College of Arts and Sciences, Department of Chemistry, Tuscaloosa, AL 35487-0336. Offers MS, PhD. *Faculty:* 22 full-time (1 woman), 1 (woman) part-time/adjunct. *Students:* 85 full-time (35 women), 8 part-time (3 women); includes 14 minority (9 Black or African American, non-Hispanic/Latino; 2 Asian, non-Hispanic/Latino; 2 Hispanic/Latino; 1 Two or more races, non-Hispanic/Latino), 30 international. Average age 28. 145 applicants, 34% accepted, 21 enrolled. In 2012, 7 master's, 7 doctorates awarded. Terminal master's awarded for partial completion of doctoral program. *Degree requirements:* For master's, comprehensive exam, thesis (for some programs), literature seminar; for doctorate, comprehensive exam, thesis/dissertation, exams, research proposal, oral defense. *Entrance requirements:* For master's, GRE, minimum GPA of 3.0; for doctorate, GRE General Test, MAT, minimum GPA of 3.0. Additional exam requirements/recommendations for international students: Required—Pearson Test of English (minimum score 59); Recommended—TOEFL (minimum score 550 paper-based; 79 iBT), IELTS (minimum score 6.5). *Application deadline:* For fall admission, 1/15 priority date for domestic students, 1/15 for international students. Applications are processed on a rolling basis. Application fee: $50 ($60 for international students). Electronic applications accepted. *Expenses:* Tuition, state resident: full-time $9200. Tuition, nonresident: full-time $22,950. *Financial support:* In 2012–13, 13 fellowships with full tuition reimbursements (averaging $22,560 per year), 26 research assistantships with full tuition reimbursements (averaging $22,560 per year), 45 teaching assistantships with full tuition reimbursements (averaging $22,560 per year) were awarded; career-related internships or fieldwork, scholarships/grants, health care benefits, and unspecified assistantships also available. *Faculty research:* Molecular synthesis and assembly, materials and measurements for alternative energy, electronic and magnetic nanomaterials, biochemical processes and biomaterials, environmental and green chemistry. *Total annual research expenditures:* $3.7 million. *Unit head:* Dr. Kevin H. Shaughnessy, Associate Professor and Chair of Chemistry, 205-348-8436, Fax: 205-348-9104, E-mail: kshaughn@bama.ua.edu. *Application contact:* Dr. Shane C. Street, Associate Professor and Director of Graduate Recruiting, 205-348-5957, Fax: 205-348-9104, E-mail: sstreet@bama.ua.edu. Website: http://www.bama.ua.edu/~chem/.

The University of Alabama at Birmingham, College of Arts and Sciences, Program in Chemistry, Birmingham, AL 35294-1240. Offers MS, PhD. *Students:* 33 full-time (21 women), 4 part-time (3 women); includes 7 minority (2 Black or African American, non-Hispanic/Latino; 3 Asian, non-Hispanic/Latino; 2 Hispanic/Latino), 16 international. Average age 28. In 2012, 13 master's, 3 doctorates awarded. *Degree requirements:* For master's, thesis (for some programs); for doctorate, thesis/dissertation. *Entrance requirements:* For master's and doctorate, GRE General Test, letters of recommendation. Additional exam requirements/recommendations for international students: Required—TOEFL. *Application deadline:* For fall admission, 7/1 for domestic students; for spring admission, 11/1 for domestic students. Applications are processed on a rolling basis. Application fee: $45 ($60 for international students). *Expenses:* Tuition, state resident: full-time $6420; part-time $335 per credit hour. Tuition, nonresident: full-time $14,574; part-time $788 per credit hour. Tuition and fees vary according to course load and program. *Financial support:* Fellowships with full tuition reimbursements, research assistantships with full tuition reimbursements, teaching assistantships with full tuition reimbursements, career-related internships or fieldwork, Federal Work-Study, institutionally sponsored loans, health care benefits, and unspecified assistantships available. Support available to part-time students. Financial award application deadline: 5/1; financial award applicants required to submit FAFSA. *Faculty research:* Drug discovery and synthesis, structural biochemistry and physical biochemistry, synthesis and characterization of advanced materials and polymers. *Total annual research expenditures:* $707,000. *Unit head:* Dr. David E. Graves, Chair, 205-975-5381, Fax: 205-934-2543, E-mail: dgraves@uab.edu. Website: http://www.uab.edu/chemistry/graduate.

The University of Alabama in Huntsville, School of Graduate Studies, College of Science, Department of Chemistry, Huntsville, AL 35899. Offers biotechnology science and engineering (PhD); chemistry (MS); education (MS); materials science (PhD). Part-time and evening/weekend programs available. *Faculty:* 12 full-time (2 women). *Students:* 11 full-time (5 women), 7 part-time (5 women); includes 5 minority (2 Black or African American, non-Hispanic/Latino; 1 American Indian or Alaska Native, non-Hispanic/Latino; 1 Asian, non-Hispanic/Latino; 1 Two or more races, non-Hispanic/Latino), 3 international. Average age 29. 14 applicants, 86% accepted, 6 enrolled. In 2012, 3 master's awarded. *Degree requirements:* For master's, comprehensive exam, thesis or alternative, oral and written exams. *Entrance requirements:* For master's, GRE General Test, minimum GPA of 3.0. Additional exam requirements/recommendations for international students: Required—TOEFL (minimum score 550 paper-based; 80 iBT), IELTS (minimum score 6.5). *Application deadline:* For fall admission, 7/15 priority date for domestic students, 4/1 for international students; for spring admission, 11/30 priority date for domestic students, 9/1 for international students. Applications are processed on a rolling basis. Application fee: $40 ($50 for international students). Electronic applications accepted. *Expenses:* Tuition, state resident: full-time $8516; part-time $515 per credit hour. Tuition, nonresident: full-time $20,384; part-time $1229 per credit hour. *Required fees:* $148 per semester. One-time fee: $150. *Financial support:* In 2012–13, 9 students received support, including 9 teaching assistantships with full tuition reimbursements available (averaging $11,566 per year); career-related internships or fieldwork, Federal Work-Study, institutionally sponsored loans, scholarships/grants, health care benefits, tuition waivers, and unspecified assistantships also available. Support available to part-time students. Financial award application deadline: 4/1; financial award applicants required to submit FAFSA. *Faculty research:* Natural products drug discovery, protein biochemistry, macromolecular biophysics, polymer synthesis, surface modification and analysis of materials. *Total annual research expenditures:* $1.1 million. *Unit head:* Dr. William Setzer, Chair, 256-824-6153, Fax: 256-824-6349, E-mail: setzerw@uah.edu. *Application contact:* Kim Gray, Graduate Studies Admissions Coordinator, 256-824-6002, Fax: 256-824-6405, E-mail: deangrad@uah.edu. Website: http://chemistry.uah.edu.

University of Alaska Fairbanks, College of Natural Sciences and Mathematics, Department of Chemistry and Biochemistry, Fairbanks, AK 99775-6160. Offers biochemistry and molecular biology (MS, PhD); chemistry (MA, MS); environmental chemistry (MS, PhD). Part-time programs available. *Faculty:* 11 full-time (2 women). *Students:* 29 full-time (14 women), 5 part-time (3 women); includes 6 minority (1 American Indian or Alaska Native, non-Hispanic/Latino; 1 Asian, non-Hispanic/Latino; 4 Hispanic/Latino), 9 international. Average age 29. 34 applicants, 24% accepted, 8 enrolled. In 2012, 8 master's, 2 doctorates awarded. *Degree requirements:* For master's, comprehensive exam, thesis or alternative; for doctorate, comprehensive exam, thesis/dissertation, oral defense. *Entrance requirements:* Additional exam requirements/recommendations for international students: Required—TOEFL (minimum score 550 paper-based). *Application deadline:* For fall admission, 6/1 for domestic students, 3/1 for international students; for spring admission, 10/15 for domestic students, 9/1 for international students. Applications are processed on a rolling basis. Application fee: $60. Electronic applications accepted. *Expenses:* Tuition, state resident: full-time $7038. Tuition, nonresident: full-time $14,382. Tuition and fees vary according to course level, course load and reciprocity agreements. *Financial support:* In 2012–13, 10 research assistantships with tuition reimbursements (averaging $14,528 per year), 17 teaching assistantships with tuition reimbursements (averaging $17,756 per year) were awarded; fellowships with tuition reimbursements, Federal Work-Study, scholarships/grants, health care benefits, and unspecified assistantships also available. Support available to part-time students. Financial award application deadline: 7/1; financial award applicants required to submit FAFSA. *Faculty research:* Atmospheric aerosols, cold adaptation, hibernation and neuroprotection, liganogated ion channels, arctic contaminants. *Unit head:* Bill Simpson, Department Chair, 907-474-5510, Fax: 907-474-5640, E-mail: chemistry.uaf@alaska.edu. *Application contact:* Libby Eddy, Registrar and Director of Admissions, 907-474-7500, Fax: 907-474-7097, E-mail: admissions@uaf.edu. Website: http://www.uaf.edu/chem.

University of Alberta, Faculty of Graduate Studies and Research, Department of Chemistry, Edmonton, AB T6G 2E1, Canada. Offers M Sc, PhD. Part-time programs available. Terminal master's awarded for partial completion of doctoral program. *Degree requirements:* For master's, thesis; for doctorate, thesis/

dissertation. *Entrance requirements:* For master's and doctorate, minimum GPA of 6.5 on 9.0 scale. *Expenses:* Contact institution. *Faculty research:* Synthetic inorganic and organic chemistry, chemical biology and biochemical analysis, materials and surface chemistry, spectroscopy and instrumentation, computational chemistry.

The University of Arizona, College of Science, Department of Chemistry and Biochemistry, Tucson, AZ 85721. Offers biochemistry (PhD); chemistry (PhD). Part-time programs available. *Faculty:* 32 full-time (6 women), 4 part-time/adjunct (2 women). *Students:* 181 full-time (74 women), 5 part-time (2 women); includes 24 minority (1 Black or African American, non-Hispanic/Latino; 1 American Indian or Alaska Native, non-Hispanic/Latino; 1 Asian, non-Hispanic/Latino; 10 Hispanic/Latino; 1 Native Hawaiian or other Pacific Islander, non-Hispanic/Latino; 10 Two or more races, non-Hispanic/Latino), 66 international. Average age 28. 380 applicants, 18% accepted, 47 enrolled. In 2012, 24 doctorates awarded. *Degree requirements:* For doctorate, comprehensive exam, thesis/dissertation. *Entrance requirements:* For doctorate, GRE General Test, 3 letters of recommendation, statement of purpose. Additional exam requirements/recommendations for international students: Required—TOEFL (minimum score 550 paper-based; 79 iBT). *Application deadline:* For fall admission, 2/1 for domestic students, 1/1 for international students; for spring admission, 10/15 for domestic and international students. Applications are processed on a rolling basis. Application fee: $75. Electronic applications accepted. *Financial support:* In 2012–13, 45 research assistantships with full tuition reimbursements (averaging $24,349 per year), 98 teaching assistantships with full tuition reimbursements (averaging $24,878 per year) were awarded; institutionally sponsored loans, scholarships/grants, health care benefits, tuition waivers (partial), and unspecified assistantships also available. Financial award applicants required to submit FAFSA. *Faculty research:* Analytical, inorganic, organic, physical chemistry, biological chemistry. *Total annual research expenditures:* $9.4 million. *Unit head:* Dr. Vicki Wysocki, Head, 520-621-2628, Fax: 520-621-8407, E-mail: vwysocki@u.arizona.edu. *Application contact:* Lori Boyd, Senior Program Coordinator, 800-545-5814, Fax: 520-621-8407, E-mail: chemistry@arizona.edu. Website: http://www.chem.arizona.edu/.

University of Arkansas, Graduate School, J. William Fulbright College of Arts and Sciences, Department of Chemistry and Biochemistry, Fayetteville, AR 72701-1201. Offers chemistry (MS, PhD). *Students:* 19 full-time (9 women), 39 part-time (16 women); includes 2 minority (1 Asian, non-Hispanic/Latino; 1 Two or more races, non-Hispanic/Latino), 21 international. In 2012, 2 master's, 7 doctorates awarded. *Degree requirements:* For master's, one foreign language, thesis; for doctorate, one foreign language, thesis/dissertation. *Application deadline:* For fall admission, 4/1 for international students; for spring admission, 10/1 for international students. Applications are processed on a rolling basis. Application fee: $40 ($50 for international students). Electronic applications accepted. *Financial support:* In 2012–13, 17 research assistantships, 32 teaching assistantships were awarded; fellowships with tuition reimbursements, career-related internships or fieldwork, and Federal Work-Study also available. Support available to part-time students. Financial award application deadline: 4/1; financial award applicants required to submit FAFSA. *Unit head:* Dr. Dan Davis, Departmental Chairperson, 479-575-4601, Fax: 479-575-4049, E-mail: cheminfo@uark.edu. *Application contact:* Graduate Admissions, 479-575 6246, Fax: 479-575-5908, E-mail: gradinfo@uark.edu. Website: http://chemistry.uark.edu/.

University of Arkansas at Little Rock, Graduate School, College of Science and Mathematics, Department of Chemistry, Little Rock, AR 72204-1099. Offers MA, MS. Part-time and evening/weekend programs available. *Degree requirements:* For master's, thesis (MS). *Entrance requirements:* For master's, minimum GPA of 2.7.

The University of British Columbia, Faculty of Science, Program in Chemistry, Vancouver, BC V6T 1Z1, Canada. Offers M Sc, PhD. Terminal master's awarded for partial completion of doctoral program. *Degree requirements:* For master's, thesis; for doctorate, comprehensive exam, thesis/dissertation. *Entrance requirements:* For master's and doctorate, GRE General Test, GRE Subject Test. Additional exam requirements/recommendations for international students: Required—TOEFL (minimum score 580 paper-based). Electronic applications accepted. *Faculty research:* Organic, physical, analytical, inorganic, and bio-chemical projects.

University of Calgary, Faculty of Graduate Studies, Faculty of Science, Department of Chemistry, Calgary, AB T2N 1N4, Canada. Offers analytical chemistry (M Sc, PhD); applied chemistry (M Sc, PhD); inorganic chemistry (M Sc, PhD); organic chemistry (M Sc, PhD); physical chemistry (M Sc, PhD); polymer chemistry (M Sc, PhD); theoretical chemistry (M Sc, PhD). *Degree requirements:* For master's, thesis; for doctorate, thesis/dissertation, candidacy exam. *Entrance requirements:* For master's, minimum GPA of 3.0; for doctorate, honors B Sc degree with minimum GPA of 3.7 or M Sc with minimum GPA of 3.3. Additional exam requirements/recommendations for international students: Required—TOEFL (minimum score 580 paper-based). Electronic applications accepted. *Faculty research:* Chemical analysis, chemical dynamics, synthesis theory.

University of California, Berkeley, Graduate Division, College of Chemistry, Department of Chemistry, Berkeley, CA 94720-1500. Offers PhD. *Degree requirements:* For doctorate, thesis/dissertation, qualifying exam. *Entrance requirements:* For doctorate, GRE General Test, GRE Subject Test, minimum GPA of 3.0, 3 letters of recommendation. Additional exam requirements/recommendations for international students: Required—TOEFL. Electronic applications accepted. *Faculty research:* Analytical bioinorganic, bio-organic, biophysical environmental, inorganic and organometallic.

University of California, Davis, Graduate Studies, Graduate Group in Agricultural and Environmental Chemistry, Davis, CA 95616. Offers MS, PhD. *Degree requirements:* For master's, thesis; for doctorate, thesis/dissertation. *Entrance requirements:* For master's and doctorate, GRE General Test, minimum GPA of 3.0. Additional exam requirements/recommendations for international students: Required—TOEFL (minimum score 550 paper-based). Electronic applications accepted.

University of California, Davis, Graduate Studies, Program in Chemistry, Davis, CA 95616. Offers MS, PhD. Terminal master's awarded for partial completion of doctoral program. *Degree requirements:* For master's, thesis; for doctorate, thesis/dissertation. *Entrance requirements:* For master's, minimum GPA of 3.0; for doctorate, GRE, minimum GPA of 3.0. Additional exam requirements/recommendations for international students: Required—TOEFL (minimum score 550 paper-based). Electronic applications accepted. *Faculty research:* Analytical, biological, organic, inorganic, and theoretical chemistry.

University of California, Irvine, School of Physical Sciences, Department of Chemistry, Irvine, CA 92697. Offers chemical and material physics (PhD); chemical and materials physics (MS); chemistry (MS, PhD). *Students:* 210 full-time (91 women), 5 part-time (1 woman); includes 48 minority (1 Black or African American, non-Hispanic/Latino; 32 Asian, non-Hispanic/Latino; 10 Hispanic/Latino; 1 Native Hawaiian or other Pacific Islander, non-Hispanic/Latino; 4 Two or more races, non-Hispanic/Latino), 28 international. Average age 26. 379 applicants, 49% accepted, 65 enrolled. In 2012, 7 master's, 40 doctorates awarded. *Degree requirements:* For doctorate, thesis/dissertation. *Entrance requirements:* For master's and doctorate, GRE General Test, GRE Subject Test, minimum GPA of 3.0. Additional exam requirements/recommendations for international students: Required—TOEFL (minimum score 550 paper-based). *Application deadline:* For fall admission, 1/15 priority date for domestic students, 1/15 for international students. Applications are processed on a rolling basis. Application fee: $80 ($100 for international students). Electronic applications accepted. *Financial support:* Fellowships, research assistantships with full tuition reimbursements, teaching assistantships, institutionally sponsored loans, traineeships, health care benefits, and unspecified assistantships available. Financial award application deadline: 3/1; financial award applicants required to submit FAFSA. *Faculty research:* Analytical, organic, inorganic, physical, and atmospheric chemistry; biogeochemistry and climate; synthetic chemistry. *Unit head:* Dr. Scott Rychnovsky, Chair, 949-824-8292, Fax: 949-824-6379, E-mail: srychnov@uci.edu. *Application contact:* Jaime M. Albano, Graduate Affairs Officer, 949-824-4261, Fax: 949-824-8571, E-mail: jmalbano@uci.edu. Website: http://www.chem.uci.edu/.

University of California, Los Angeles, Graduate Division, College of Letters and Science, Department of Chemistry and Biochemistry, Program in Chemistry, Los Angeles, CA 90095. Offers MS, PhD. *Faculty:* 47 full-time (10 women). *Students:* 215 full-time (69 women); includes 65 minority (2 Black or African American, non-Hispanic/Latino; 35 Asian, non-Hispanic/Latino; 22 Hispanic/Latino; 6 Two or more races, non-Hispanic/Latino), 44 international. Average age 26. 363 applicants, 39% accepted, 46 enrolled. In 2012, 24 master's, 28 doctorates awarded. *Degree requirements:* For master's, comprehensive exam or thesis; for doctorate, thesis/dissertation, oral and written exams, 1 year of teaching experience. *Entrance requirements:* For doctorate, GRE General Test, GRE Subject Test (recommended), bachelor's degree; minimum undergraduate GPA of 3.0 (or its equivalent if letter grade system not used). Additional exam requirements/recommendations for international students: Required—TOEFL, GRE Subject Test. *Application deadline:* For fall admission, 12/15 for domestic and international students. Application fee: $80 ($100 for international students). Electronic applications accepted. *Expenses:* Tuition, nonresident: full-time $15,102. *Required fees:* $14,809.19. Full-time tuition and fees vary according to program. *Financial support:* In 2012–13, 215 students received support, including 213 fellowships with full and partial tuition reimbursements available, 140 research assistantships with full and partial tuition reimbursements available, 161 teaching assistantships with full and partial tuition reimbursements available; Federal Work-Study, scholarships/grants, health care benefits, tuition waivers (full and partial), and unspecified assistantships also available. Financial award application deadline: 3/2; financial award applicants required to submit FAFSA. *Unit head:* Dr. Miguel Garcia-Garibay, Chair, 310-825-3159, E-mail: mgg@chem.ucla.edu. *Application contact:* Student Affairs Officer, 310-825-3150, Fax: 310-267-0204, E-mail: chemgrad@chem.ucla.edu. Website: http://www.chem.ucla.edu.

University of California, Merced, Graduate Division, School of Natural Sciences, Merced, CA 95343. Offers applied mathematics (MS, PhD); physics and chemistry (MS, PhD); quantitative and systems biology (MS, PhD). *Students:* 121 full-time (50 women); includes 38 minority (3 Black or African American, non-Hispanic/Latino; 12 Asian, non-Hispanic/Latino; 18 Hispanic/Latino; 5 Two or more races, non-Hispanic/Latino), 34 international. Average age 28. 161 applicants, 47% accepted, 42 enrolled. In 2012, 9 master's, 5 doctorates awarded. *Financial support:* In 2012–13, 120 students received support, including 108 fellowships with full and partial tuition reimbursements available (averaging $11,590 per year), 34 research assistantships with full and partial tuition reimbursements available (averaging $8,960 per year), 103 teaching assistantships with partial tuition reimbursements available (averaging $12,560 per year); health care benefits also available. Financial award applicants required to submit FAFSA. *Unit head:* Dr. Juan Meza, Dean, 209-228-4487, Fax: 209-228-4060, E-mail: jcmeza@ucmerced.edu. *Application contact:* Tsu Ya, Graduate Admissions and Academic Services Manager, 209-228-4723, Fax: 209-228-6906, E-mail: tya@ucmerced.edu.

University of California, Riverside, Graduate Division, Department of Chemistry, Riverside, CA 92521-0403. Offers MS, PhD. Terminal master's awarded for partial completion of doctoral program. *Degree requirements:* For master's, qualifying exams or thesis; for doctorate, thesis/dissertation, qualifying exams, 3 quarters of teaching experience, research proposition. *Entrance requirements:* For master's and doctorate, GRE General Test, minimum GPA of 3.0. Additional exam requirements/recommendations for international students: Required—TOEFL (minimum score 550 paper-based; 80 iBT). Electronic applications accepted. *Expenses:* Tuition, state resident: full-time $14,646. Tuition, nonresident: full-time $29,748. *Faculty research:* Analytical, inorganic, organic, and physical chemistry; chemical physics.

University of California, San Diego, Office of Graduate Studies, Department of Chemistry and Biochemistry, La Jolla, CA 92093. Offers chemistry (MS, PhD). *Degree requirements:* For doctorate, thesis/dissertation. *Entrance requirements:* For doctorate, GRE General Test, GRE Subject Test. Electronic applications accepted.

University of California, San Francisco, School of Pharmacy and Graduate Division, Chemistry and Chemical Biology Graduate Program, San Francisco, CA 94143. Offers PhD. *Degree requirements:* For doctorate, thesis/dissertation. *Entrance requirements:* For doctorate, GRE General Test, GRE Subject Test, minimum GPA of 3.0. Additional exam requirements/recommendations for international students: Required—TOEFL (minimum score 550 paper-based; 80 iBT). Electronic applications accepted. *Faculty research:* Biochemistry, macromolecular structure, cellular and molecular pharmacology, physical chemistry and computational biology, synthetic chemistry.

University of California, Santa Barbara, Graduate Division, College of Letters and Sciences, Division of Mathematics, Life, and Physical Sciences, Department of Chemistry and Biochemistry, Santa Barbara, CA 93106-9510. Offers chemistry (PhD). *Faculty:* 36 full-time (9 women), 3 part-time/adjunct (0 women). *Students:* 163 full-time (45 women); includes 30 minority (3 Black or African American, non-Hispanic/Latino; 2 American Indian or Alaska Native, non-Hispanic/Latino; 18 Asian, non-Hispanic/Latino; 7 Hispanic/Latino), 29 international. Average age 27. 242 applicants, 48% accepted, 46 enrolled. In 2012, 30 doctorates awarded. *Median time to degree:* Of those who began their doctoral program in fall 2004, 58% received their degree in 8 years or less. *Degree requirements:* For doctorate, comprehensive exam, thesis/dissertation, annual faculty committee meetings; minimum 1 year of teaching experience. *Entrance requirements:* For doctorate, GRE, 3 letters of recommendation, statement of purpose, personal achievements essay, resume/curriculum vitae, transcripts. Additional exam requirements/recommendations for international students: Required—TOEFL (minimum score 550 paper-based; 80 iBT), IELTS (minimum score 7). *Application deadline:* For fall admission, 12/15 priority date for domestic students, 2/15 for international students. Application fee: $80 ($100 for international students). Electronic applications accepted. *Financial support:* In 2012–13, 115 students received support, including 78 fellowships with full and partial tuition reimbursements available (averaging $9,949 per year), 63 research assistantships with full and partial tuition reimbursements available (averaging $15,046 per year), 83 teaching assistantships with full and partial tuition reimbursements available (averaging $17,655 per year); career-related internships or fieldwork, Federal Work-Study, institutionally sponsored loans, scholarships/grants, traineeships, health care benefits, tuition waivers (full and partial), and unspecified assistantships also available. Support available to part-time students. Financial award application deadline: 12/15; financial award applicants required to submit FAFSA. *Faculty research:* Organic, inorganic, physical, and materials chemistry, biochemistry. *Unit head:* Dr. Fredrick W. Dahlquist, Department Chair, 805-893-5326, Fax: 805-893-4120, E-mail: dahlquist@chem.ucsb.edu. *Application contact:* Mallarie A. Stevens, Graduate Program Advisor/Student Affairs Manager, 805-893-5675, Fax: 805-893-4120, E-mail: gradprog@chem.ucsb.edu. Website: http://www.chem.ucsb.edu/.

University of California, Santa Cruz, Division of Graduate Studies, Division of Physical and Biological Sciences, Department of Chemistry and Biochemistry, Santa Cruz, CA 95064. Offers MS, PhD. *Degree requirements:* For master's, thesis optional; for doctorate, one foreign language, thesis/dissertation, qualifying exam. *Entrance requirements:* For master's and doctorate, GRE General Test, GRE Subject Test. Additional exam requirements/recommendations for international students: Required—TOEFL (minimum score 570 paper-based; 89 iBT); Recommended—IELTS (minimum score 8). Electronic applications accepted. *Faculty research:* Marine chemistry; biochemistry; inorganic, organic, and physical chemistry.

University of Central Florida, College of Sciences, Department of Chemistry, Orlando, FL 32816. Offers chemistry (MS, PhD); computer forensics (Certificate); forensic science (MS). Part-time and evening/weekend programs available. *Faculty:* 29 full-time (2 women), 6 part-time/adjunct (3 women). *Students:* 76 full-time (37 women), 17 part-time (5 women); includes 29 minority (4 Black or African American, non-Hispanic/Latino; 10 Asian, non-Hispanic/Latino; 14 Hispanic/Latino; 1 Two or more races, non-Hispanic/Latino), 26 international. Average age 29. 102 applicants, 50% accepted, 21 enrolled. In 2012, 6 master's, 7 doctorates, 6 other advanced degrees awarded. *Degree requirements:* For master's, thesis, final exam. *Entrance requirements:* For master's, GRE General Test, minimum GPA of 3.0 in last 60 hours. Additional exam requirements/recommendations for international students: Required—TOEFL. *Application deadline:* For fall admission, 7/15 for domestic students; for spring admission, 12/1 for domestic students. Application fee: $30. Electronic applications accepted. *Financial support:* In 2012–13, 64 students received support, including 10 fellowships with partial tuition reimbursements available (averaging $3,900 per year), 17 research assistantships with partial tuition reimbursements available (averaging $13,300 per year), 45 teaching assistantships with partial tuition reimbursements available (averaging $11,800 per year); career-related internships or fieldwork, Federal Work-Study, institutionally sponsored loans, tuition waivers (partial), and unspecified assistantships also available. Financial award application deadline: 3/1; financial award applicants required to submit FAFSA. *Faculty research:* Physical and synthetic organic chemistry, lasers, polymers, biochemical action of pesticides, environmental analysis. *Unit head:* Dr. Kevin D. Belfield, Chair, 407-823-2246, Fax: 407-823-2252, E-mail: belfield@ucf.edu. *Application contact:* Barbara Rodriguez, Director, Admissions and Registration, 407-823-2766, Fax: 407-823-6442, E-mail: gradadmissions@ucf.edu. Website: http://chemistry.cos.ucf.edu/.

University of Central Oklahoma, The Jackson College of Graduate Studies, College of Mathematics and Science, Department of Chemistry, Edmond, OK 73034-5209. Offers MS. Part-time programs available. *Faculty:* 3 full-time (1 woman), 3 part-time/adjunct (0 women). *Students:* 16 full-time (11 women), 24 part-time (21 women); includes 9 minority (3 Black or African American, non-Hispanic/Latino; 2 Asian, non-Hispanic/Latino; 4 Hispanic/Latino), 1 international. Average age 28. In 2012, 18 master's awarded. *Entrance requirements:* For master's, GRE General Test. *Application deadline:* For fall admission, 7/1 for international students; for spring admission, 11/1 for international students. Applications are processed on a rolling basis. Application fee: $25. Electronic applications accepted. *Expenses:* Tuition, state resident: full-time $3718; part-time $195.65 per credit hour. Tuition, nonresident: full-time $9309; part-time $489.95 per credit hour. *Required fees:* $399.95; $21.50 per credit hour. One-time fee: $50. Tuition and fees vary according to program. *Financial support:* Application deadline: 3/31; applicants required to submit FAFSA. *Unit head:* Dr. Cheryl Frech, Chairperson, 405-974-5476. *Application contact:* Dr. John Garic, Interim Dean, Graduate College, 405-974-3341, Fax: 405-974-3852, E-mail: gradcoll@ucok.edu.

University of Chicago, Division of the Physical Sciences, Department of Chemistry, Chicago, IL 60637-1513. Offers PhD. *Degree requirements:* For doctorate, comprehensive exam, thesis/dissertation. *Entrance requirements:* For doctorate, GRE General Test, GRE Subject Test. Additional exam requirements/recommendations for international students: Required—TOEFL (minimum score 600 paper-based; 104 iBT), IELTS (minimum score 7). Electronic applications accepted. *Expenses:* Contact institution. *Faculty research:* Organic, inorganic, physical, biological chemistry.

University of Cincinnati, Graduate School, McMicken College of Arts and Sciences, Department of Chemistry, Cincinnati, OH 45221. Offers analytical chemistry (MS, PhD); biochemistry (MS, PhD); inorganic chemistry (MS, PhD); organic chemistry (MS, PhD); physical chemistry (MS, PhD); polymer chemistry (MS, PhD); sensors (PhD). Part-time and evening/weekend programs available. Terminal master's awarded for partial completion of doctoral program. *Degree requirements:* For master's, thesis optional; for doctorate, comprehensive exam, thesis/dissertation. *Entrance requirements:* For master's and doctorate, GRE General Test. Additional exam requirements/recommendations for international students: Required—TOEFL (minimum score 580 paper-based). Electronic applications accepted. *Faculty research:* Biomedical chemistry, laser chemistry, surface science, chemical sensors, synthesis.

University of Colorado Boulder, Graduate School, College of Arts and Sciences, Department of Chemistry and Biochemistry, Boulder, CO 80309. Offers biochemistry (PhD); chemistry (MS). *Faculty:* 40 full-time (7 women). *Students:* 229 full-time (92 women), 1 part-time (0 women); includes 31 minority (3 Black or African American, non-Hispanic/Latino; 7 Asian, non-Hispanic/Latino; 17 Hispanic/Latino; 4 Two or more races, non-Hispanic/Latino), 44 international. Average age 27. 559 applicants, 27% accepted, 53 enrolled. Terminal master's awarded for partial completion of doctoral program. *Degree requirements:* For master's, comprehensive exam or thesis; for doctorate, comprehensive exam, thesis/dissertation, cumulative exam. *Entrance requirements:* For master's, GRE General Test, GRE Subject Test, minimum undergraduate GPA of 2.75; for doctorate, GRE General Test, GRE Subject Test, minimum GPA of 3.0. *Application deadline:* For fall admission, 12/15 priority date for domestic students, 12/15 for international students. Applications are processed on a rolling basis. Application fee: $50 ($60 for international students). Electronic applications accepted. *Financial support:* In 2012–13, 80 fellowships (averaging $12,459 per year), 128 research assistantships with full and partial tuition reimbursements (averaging $22,685 per year), 83 teaching assistantships with full and partial tuition reimbursements (averaging $20,982 per year) were awarded; institutionally sponsored loans, scholarships/grants, health care benefits, and unspecified assistantships also available. Financial award applicants required to submit FAFSA. *Faculty research:* Analytical, atmospheric, biochemistry, biophysical, chemical physics, environmental, inorganic, organic and physical chemistry. *Total annual research expenditures:* $31.8 million. *Application contact:* E-mail: gradassist.chembiochem@colorado.edu. Website: http://chem.colorado.edu.

University of Colorado Colorado Springs, College of Letters, Arts and Sciences, Master of Sciences Program, Colorado Springs, CO 80933-7150. Offers biology (M Sc); chemistry (M Sc); education (M Sc); forensic science (M Sc); health promotion (M Sc); mathematics (M Sc); physics (M Sc); sports medicine (M Sc); sports nutrition (M Sc). Part-time programs available. *Students:* 67 full-time (48 women), 27 part-time (17 women); includes 12 minority (2 American Indian or Alaska Native, non-Hispanic/Latino; 2 Asian, non-Hispanic/Latino; 6 Hispanic/Latino; 2 Two or more races, non-Hispanic/Latino), 5 international. Average age 28. In 2012, 41 master's awarded. *Degree requirements:* For master's, thesis or alternative. *Entrance requirements:* For master's, minimum GPA of 2.75. Additional exam requirements/recommendations for international students: Required—TOEFL (minimum score 525 paper-based). *Application deadline:* For fall admission, 6/1 priority date for domestic students; for spring admission, 12/1 for domestic students. Applications are processed on a rolling basis. Application fee: $60 ($75 for international students). Electronic applications accepted. *Expenses:* Contact institution. *Financial support:* In 2012–13, 17 students received support, including 2 fellowships; research assistantships, teaching assistantships, career-related internships or fieldwork, Federal Work-Study, and scholarships/grants also available. Support available to part-time students. Financial award application deadline: 3/1; financial award applicants required to submit FAFSA. *Faculty research:* Biomechanics and physiology of elite athletic training, genetic engineering in yeast and bacteria including phage display and DNA repair, immunology and cell biology, synthetic organic chemistry. *Unit head:* Dr. Peter A. Braza, Dean, 719-255-4550, Fax: 719-255-4200, E-mail: pbraza@uccs.edu. *Application contact:* Taryn Bailey, Graduate Recruitment Specialist, 719-255-3702, Fax: 719-255-3037, E-mail: gradinfo@uccs.edu.

University of Colorado Denver, College of Liberal Arts and Sciences, Department of Chemistry, Denver, CO 80217. Offers MS. Part-time programs available. *Faculty:* 14 full-time (4 women). *Students:* 5 full-time (2 women), 9 part-time (2 women); includes 5 minority (1 Black or African American, non-Hispanic/Latino; 3 Asian, non-Hispanic/Latino; 1 Hispanic/Latino), 1 international. Average age 31. 19 applicants, 32% accepted, 3 enrolled. In 2012, 8 master's awarded. *Degree requirements:* For master's, comprehensive exam, thesis or alternative, 30-33 credit hours. *Entrance requirements:* For master's, GRE General Test and GRE Subject Test in chemistry (recommended), undergraduate degree in chemistry; minimum undergraduate GPA of 3.0. Additional exam requirements/recommendations for international students: Required—TOEFL (minimum score 537 paper-based; 75 iBT); Recommended—IELTS (minimum score 6.5). *Application deadline:* For fall admission, 5/1 priority date for domestic students, 4/1 for international students; for spring admission, 10/1 priority date for domestic students, 9/1 for international students. Applications are processed on a rolling basis. Application fee: $50 ($75 for international students). Electronic applications accepted. *Expenses:* Tuition, state resident: full-time $7712; part-time $355 per credit hour. Tuition, nonresident: full-time $22,038; part-time $1087 per credit hour. *Required fees:* $1110; $1. Tuition and fees vary according to course load, campus/location and program. *Financial support:* In 2012–13, 2 students received support. Fellowships, research assistantships, teaching assistantships, Federal Work-Study, institutionally sponsored loans, scholarships/grants, traineeships, and unspecified assistantships available. Financial award application deadline: 4/1; financial award applicants required to submit FAFSA. *Faculty research:* Enzymology of proteinases, computational chemistry, metal-organic coordination and materials chemistry, environmental chemistry, materials chemistry. *Unit head:* Dr. Douglas Dyckes, Professor and Chair, 303-556-3204, Fax: 303-556-4776, E-mail: douglas.dyckes@ucdenver.edu. *Application contact:* Laura Cuellar, Program Assistant, 303-556-4885, Fax: 303-556-4776, E-mail: laura.cuellar@ucdenver.edu. Website: http://www.ucdenver.edu/academics/colleges/CLAS/Departments/chemistry/Programs/Masters/Pages/Masters.aspx.

University of Connecticut, Graduate School, College of Liberal Arts and Sciences, Department of Chemistry, Storrs, CT 06269. Offers MS, PhD. Terminal master's awarded for partial completion of doctoral program. *Degree requirements:* For master's, comprehensive exam; for doctorate, thesis/dissertation. *Entrance requirements:* For master's and doctorate, GRE General Test, GRE Subject Test. Additional exam requirements/recommendations for international students: Required—TOEFL (minimum score 550 paper-based). Electronic applications accepted.

University of Dayton, Department of Chemistry, Dayton, OH 45469-1300. Offers MS. Part-time programs available. *Faculty:* 10 full-time (1 woman). *Students:* 4 full-time (1 woman), 2 part-time (1 woman), 2 international. Average age 25. 43 applicants, 7% accepted, 2 enrolled. In 2012, 4 master's awarded. *Degree requirements:* For master's, thesis and 30 credit hours (21 course and 9 research) or 30 hours course credit. *Entrance requirements:* For master's, GRE, American Chemical Society standardized exams, BS in chemistry or closely-related discipline. Additional exam requirements/recommendations for international students: Required—TOEFL (minimum score 550 paper-based; 80 iBT), TWE. *Application deadline:* For fall admission, 5/1 priority date for domestic students, 5/1 for international students; for winter admission, 7/1 for international students; for spring admission, 11/1 for international students. Applications are processed on a rolling basis. Application fee: $0. Electronic applications accepted. *Expenses: Tuition:* Part-time $708 per credit hour. *Required fees:* $25 per semester. Tuition and fees vary according to course level, course load, degree level and program. *Financial support:* In 2012–13, 4 teaching assistantships with full tuition reimbursements (averaging $12,286 per year) were awarded; institutionally sponsored loans, health care benefits, and unspecified assistantships also available. Financial award applicants required to submit FAFSA. *Faculty research:* Organic synthesis, medicinal chemistry, enzyme purification, physical organic, materials chemistry and nanotechnology. *Total annual research expenditures:* $20,000. *Unit head:* Dr. Mark Masthay, Chair, 937-229-2631, E-mail: mmasthay1@udayton.edu. *Application contact:* Dr. Kevin Church, Graduate Program Director, 937-229-2659, E-mail: kchurch1@udayton.edu.

University of Delaware, College of Arts and Sciences, Department of Chemistry and Biochemistry, Newark, DE 19716. Offers biochemistry (MA, MS, PhD); chemistry (MA, MS, PhD). Part-time programs available. Terminal master's awarded for partial completion of doctoral program. *Degree requirements:* For master's, one foreign language, thesis (for some programs); for doctorate, one foreign language, thesis/dissertation, cumulative exam. *Entrance requirements:* For master's and doctorate, GRE General Test. Additional exam requirements/recommendations for international students: Required—TOEFL (minimum score 600 paper-based). Electronic applications accepted. *Faculty research:* Micro-organisms, bone, cancer metastosis, developmental biology, cell biology, molecular biology.

University of Denver, Faculty of Natural Sciences and Mathematics, Department of Chemistry and Biochemistry, Denver, CO 80208. Offers MA, MS, PhD. Part-time programs available. *Faculty:* 15 full-time (3 women), 4 part-time/adjunct (1 woman). *Students:* 13 full-time (7 women), 18 part-time (9 women); includes 3 minority (1 Black or African American, non-Hispanic/Latino; 1 American Indian or Alaska Native, non-Hispanic/Latino; 1 Two or more races, non-Hispanic/Latino), 14 international. Average age 28. 43 applicants, 58% accepted, 12 enrolled. In 2012, 1 master's, 4 doctorates awarded. Terminal master's awarded for partial completion of doctoral program. *Degree requirements:* For master's, comprehensive exam (for some programs), thesis; for doctorate, comprehensive exam, thesis/dissertation. *Entrance requirements:* For master's, GRE General Test (for MS). Additional exam requirements/recommendations for international students: Required—TOEFL (minimum score 550 paper-based; 80 iBT). *Application deadline:* For fall admission, 3/1 priority date for domestic students. Applications are processed on a rolling basis. Application fee: $60. Electronic applications accepted. *Expenses: Tuition:* Full-time $38,232; part-time $1062 per credit hour. *Required fees:* $744. Tuition and fees vary according to program. *Financial support:* In 2012–13, 19 students received support, including 9 research assistantships with full and partial tuition reimbursements available (averaging $18,149 per year), 19 teaching assistantships with full and partial tuition reimbursements available (averaging $21,924 per year); career-related internships or fieldwork, Federal Work-Study, institutionally sponsored loans, and scholarships/grants also available. Support available to part-time students. Financial award application deadline: 2/15; financial award applicants required to submit FAFSA. *Faculty research:* Atmospheric chemistry, magnetic resonance, molecular spectroscopy, laser photolysis, biophysical chemistry. *Unit head:* Dr. Sandra S. Eaton, Chair, 303-871-3100, Fax: 303-871-2254, E-mail: seaton@du.edu. *Application contact:* Christine Stutzman, Office Assistant, 303-871-2435, Fax: 303-871-2254, E-mail: cheminfo@du.edu. Website: http://www.du.edu/nsm/departments/chemistryandbiochemistry/.

University of Detroit Mercy, College of Engineering and Science, Department of Chemistry and Biochemistry, Detroit, MI 48221. Offers chemistry (MS). Evening/weekend programs available. *Degree requirements:* For master's, thesis. *Entrance requirements:* For master's, GRE General Test, minimum GPA of 3.0. *Faculty research:* Polymer and physical chemistry, industrial aspects of chemistry.

University of Florida, Graduate School, College of Liberal Arts and Sciences, Department of Chemistry, Gainesville, FL 32611. Offers chemistry (MS, MST); clinical and translational science (PhD); imaging science and technology (PhD). Terminal master's awarded for partial completion of doctoral program. *Degree requirements:* For master's, thesis; for doctorate, comprehensive exam, thesis/dissertation. *Entrance requirements:* For master's and doctorate, GRE General Test, minimum GPA of 3.0. Additional exam requirements/recommendations for international students: Required—TOEFL (minimum score 550 paper-based; 80 iBT), IELTS (minimum score 6). Electronic applications accepted. *Faculty research:* Organic, analytical, physical, inorganic, and biological chemistry.

University of Georgia, Franklin College of Arts and Sciences, Department of Chemistry, Athens, GA 30602. Offers analytical chemistry (MS, PhD); inorganic chemistry (MS, PhD); organic chemistry (MS, PhD); physical chemistry (MS, PhD). Terminal master's awarded for partial completion of doctoral program. *Degree requirements:* For master's, thesis; for doctorate, one foreign language, thesis/dissertation. *Entrance requirements:* For master's and doctorate, GRE General Test. Additional exam requirements/recommendations for international students: Required—TOEFL. Electronic applications accepted.

University of Guelph, Graduate Studies, College of Physical and Engineering Science, Guelph-Waterloo Centre for Graduate Work in Chemistry and Biochemistry, Guelph, ON N1G 2W1, Canada. Offers M Sc, PhD. M Sc, PhD offered jointly with University of Waterloo. Part-time programs available. *Degree requirements:* For master's, thesis; for doctorate, thesis/dissertation. *Faculty research:* Inorganic, analytical, biological, physical/theoretical, polymer, and organic chemistry.

University of Hawaii at Manoa, Graduate Division, College of Natural Sciences, Department of Chemistry, Honolulu, HI 96822. Offers MS, PhD. Part-time programs available. *Degree requirements:* For master's, comprehensive exam, thesis; for doctorate, comprehensive exam, thesis/dissertation. *Entrance requirements:* For master's and doctorate, GRE General Test, GRE Subject Test.

Additional exam requirements/recommendations for international students: Required—TOEFL (minimum score 500 paper-based; 61 iBT), IELTS (minimum score 5). *Faculty research:* Marine natural products, biophysical spectroscopy, zeolites, organometallic hydrides, new visual pigments, theory of surfaces.

University of Houston, College of Natural Sciences and Mathematics, Department of Chemistry, Houston, TX 77204. Offers MA, PhD. Part-time programs available. Terminal master's awarded for partial completion of doctoral program. *Degree requirements:* For master's, thesis; for doctorate, thesis/dissertation, oral presentation. *Entrance requirements:* For master's and doctorate, GRE General Test. Additional exam requirements/recommendations for international students: Required—TOEFL (minimum score 79 iBT), IELTS (minimum score 6.5). Electronic applications accepted. *Faculty research:* Materials, molecular design, surface science, structural chemistry, synthesis.

University of Houston–Clear Lake, School of Science and Computer Engineering, Program in Chemistry, Houston, TX 77058-1098. Offers MS. Part-time and evening/weekend programs available. *Entrance requirements:* For master's, GRE General Test. Additional exam requirements/recommendations for international students: Required—TOEFL (minimum score 550 paper-based).

University of Idaho, College of Graduate Studies, College of Science, Department of Chemistry, Moscow, ID 83844-2343. Offers MS, PhD. *Faculty:* 11 full-time. *Students:* 25 full-time, 3 part-time. Average age 30. In 2012, 5 master's, 2 doctorates awarded. *Degree requirements:* For master's, thesis or alternative; for doctorate, one foreign language, thesis/dissertation. *Entrance requirements:* For master's, minimum GPA of 2.8; for doctorate, minimum undergraduate GPA of 2.8, 3.0 graduate. *Application deadline:* For fall admission, 8/1 for domestic students; for spring admission, 12/15 for domestic students. Applications are processed on a rolling basis. Application fee: $60. Electronic applications accepted. *Expenses:* Tuition, state resident: full-time $4230; part-time $252 per credit hour. Tuition, nonresident: full-time $17,018; part-time $891 per credit hour. *Required fees:* $2932; $107 per credit hour. *Financial support:* Fellowships, research assistantships, and teaching assistantships available. Financial award applicants required to submit FAFSA. *Faculty research:* Analytical chemistry, inorganic chemistry, organic chemistry, physical chemistry. *Unit head:* Dr. Ray von Wandruska, Chair, 208-885-6552, E-mail: chemoff@uidaho.edu. *Application contact:* Erick Larson, Director of Graduate Admissions, 208-885-4723, E-mail: gadms@uidaho.edu. Website: http://www.uidaho.edu/sci/chem.

University of Illinois at Chicago, College of Pharmacy and Graduate College, Graduate Programs in Pharmacy, Chicago, IL 60607-7128. Offers biopharmaceutical sciences (PhD); forensic science (MS); medicinal chemistry (MS, PhD); pharmacognosy (MS, PhD); pharmacy administration (MS, PhD). *Students:* 85 full-time (54 women), 55 part-time (26 women); includes 17 minority (4 Black or African American, non-Hispanic/Latino; 10 Asian, non-Hispanic/Latino; 3 Hispanic/Latino), 77 international. Average age 23. 285 applicants, 29% accepted, 26 enrolled. In 2012, 5 master's, 17 doctorates awarded. Terminal master's awarded for partial completion of doctoral program. *Degree requirements:* For master's, variable foreign language requirement, thesis; for doctorate, variable foreign language requirement, thesis/dissertation. *Entrance requirements:* For master's and doctorate, GRE General Test. Additional exam requirements/recommendations for international students: Required—TOEFL. *Application deadline:* For fall admission, 2/1 for domestic students. Applications are processed on a rolling basis. Application fee: $40 ($50 for international students). Electronic applications accepted. *Expenses:* Contact institution. *Financial support:* In 2012–13, 122 students received support, including 2 fellowships with full tuition reimbursements available; research assistantships with full tuition reimbursements available, teaching assistantships with full tuition reimbursements available, career-related internships or fieldwork, Federal Work-Study, institutionally sponsored loans, traineeships, tuition waivers (full), and unspecified assistantships also available. Financial award application deadline: 3/1; financial award applicants required to submit FAFSA. *Unit head:* Janet P. Engle, Executive Associate Dean for Academic Affairs, 312-996-6212. *Application contact:* Jackie Perry, Graduate College Receptionist, 312-413-2550, Fax: 312-413-0185, E-mail: gradcoll@uic.edu.

University of Illinois at Chicago, Graduate College, College of Liberal Arts and Sciences, Department of Chemistry, Chicago, IL 60607-7128. Offers MS, PhD. Part-time programs available. *Students:* 141 full-time (65 women), 1 part-time (0 women); includes 14 minority (2 Black or African American, non-Hispanic/Latino; 9 Asian, non-Hispanic/Latino; 3 Hispanic/Latino), 91 international. Average age 27. 130 applicants, 48% accepted, 30 enrolled. In 2012, 12 master's, 10 doctorates awarded. Terminal master's awarded for partial completion of doctoral program. *Degree requirements:* For master's, thesis or cumulative exam; for doctorate, one foreign language, thesis/dissertation, cumulative exams. *Entrance requirements:* For master's and doctorate, GRE Subject Test, minimum GPA of 3.0. Additional exam requirements/recommendations for international students: Required—TOEFL. *Application deadline:* For fall admission, 1/1 priority date for domestic students, 2/15 for international students; for spring admission, 10/1 priority date for domestic students, 7/15 for international students. Applications are processed on a rolling basis. Application fee: $40 ($50 for international students). Electronic applications accepted. *Expenses:* Tuition, state resident: full-time $10,882; part-time $3627 per term. Tuition, nonresident: full-time $22,880; part-time $7627 per term. *Required fees:* $1170 per semester. Tuition and fees vary according to course load, degree level and program. *Financial support:* In 2012–13, 1 fellowship with full tuition reimbursement was awarded; research assistantships with full tuition reimbursements, teaching assistantships with full tuition reimbursements, Federal Work-Study, institutionally sponsored loans, scholarships/grants, traineeships, tuition waivers (full), and unspecified assistantships also available. Financial award application deadline: 3/1; financial award applicants required to submit FAFSA. *Unit head:* Prof. Luke Hanley, Professor and Head, 312-996-3161, E-mail: lhanley@uic.edu. Website: http://www.chem.uic.edu/.

University of Illinois at Urbana–Champaign, Graduate College, College of Liberal Arts and Sciences, School of Chemical Sciences, Department of Chemistry, Champaign, IL 61820. Offers astrochemistry (PhD); chemical physics (PhD); chemistry (MA, MS, PhD); teaching of chemistry (MS); MS/JD; MS/MBA. *Students:* 282 (100 women). Application fee: $75 ($90 for international students). *Unit head:* Jeffrey Moore, Head, 217-333-0711, Fax: 217-244-5943, E-mail: jsmoore@illinois.edu. *Application contact:* Krista Smith, Program Coordinator, 217-244-4844, Fax: 217-244-5943, E-mail: kristasm@illinois.edu. Website: http://chemistry.illinois.edu/.

The University of Iowa, Graduate College, College of Liberal Arts and Sciences, Department of Chemistry, Iowa City, IA 52242-1316. Offers MS, PhD. *Degree requirements:* For master's, thesis optional, exam; for doctorate, comprehensive exam, thesis/dissertation. *Entrance requirements:* For master's and doctorate, GRE General Test, minimum GPA of 3.0. Additional exam requirements/recommendations for international students: Required—TOEFL (minimum score 550 paper-based; 81 iBT). Electronic applications accepted.

The University of Kansas, Graduate Studies, College of Liberal Arts and Sciences, Department of Chemistry, Lawrence, KS 66045. Offers MS, PhD. *Faculty:* 28. *Students:* 105 full-time (41 women), 3 part-time (0 women); includes 8 minority (4 Asian, non-Hispanic/Latino; 1 Hispanic/Latino; 3 Two or more races, non-Hispanic/Latino), 28 international. Average age 28. 199 applicants, 27% accepted, 19 enrolled. In 2012, 10 doctorates awarded. *Degree requirements:* For master's, thesis; for doctorate, comprehensive exam, thesis/dissertation. *Entrance requirements:* For master's and doctorate, GRE General Test. Additional exam requirements/recommendations for international students: Required—TOEFL. *Application deadline:* For fall admission, 1/15 priority date for domestic students, 1/15 for international students; for spring admission, 9/1 priority date for domestic students, 9/1 for international students. Applications are processed on a rolling basis. Application fee: $55 ($65 for international students). Electronic applications accepted. *Financial support:* Fellowships with full tuition reimbursements, research assistantships with full and partial tuition reimbursements, teaching assistantships with full and partial tuition reimbursements, scholarships/grants, traineeships, tuition waivers (full), and unspecified assistantships available. Financial award application deadline: 4/15. *Faculty research:* Organometallic and inorganic synthetic methodology, bioanalytical chemistry, computational materials science, proteomics, physical chemistry. *Unit head:* Prof. Craig E. Lunte, Chair, 785-864-4670, Fax: 785-864-5396, E-mail: clunte@ku.edu. *Application contact:* Prof. Brian B. Laird, Graduate Director, 785-864-4670, Fax: 785-864-5396, E-mail: blaird@ku.edu. Website: http://www.chem.ku.edu/.

University of Kentucky, Graduate School, College of Arts and Sciences, Program in Chemistry, Lexington, KY 40506-0032. Offers MS, PhD. Part-time programs available. Terminal master's awarded for partial completion of doctoral program. *Degree requirements:* For master's, comprehensive exam, thesis optional; for doctorate, comprehensive exam, thesis/dissertation. *Entrance requirements:* For master's, GRE General Test, minimum undergraduate GPA of 2.75; for doctorate, GRE General Test, minimum graduate GPA of 3.0. Additional exam requirements/recommendations for international students: Required—TOEFL (minimum score 550 paper-based). Electronic applications accepted. *Faculty research:* Analytical, inorganic, organic, and physical chemistry; biological chemistry; nuclear chemistry; radiochemistry; materials chemistry.

University of Lethbridge, School of Graduate Studies, Lethbridge, AB T1K 3M4, Canada. Offers accounting (MScM); addictions counseling (M Sc); agricultural biotechnology (M Sc); agricultural studies (M Sc, MA); anthropology (MA); archaeology (MA); art (MA, MFA); biochemistry (M Sc); biological sciences (M Sc); biomolecular science (PhD); biosystems and biodiversity (PhD); Canadian studies (MA); chemistry (M Sc); computer science (M Sc); computer science and geographical information science (M Sc); counseling psychology (M Ed); dramatic arts (MA); earth, space, and physical science (PhD); economics (MA); educational leadership (M Ed); English (MA); environmental science (M Sc); evolution and behavior (PhD); exercise science (M Sc); finance (MScM); French (MA); French/German (MA); French/Spanish (MA); general education (M Ed); general management (MScM); geography (M Sc, MA); German (MA); health science (M Sc); history (MA); human resource management and labour relations (MScM); individualized multidisciplinary (M Sc, MA); information systems (MScM); international management (MScM); kinesiology (M Sc, MA); management (M Sc, MA); marketing (MScM); mathematics (M Sc); music (M Mus, MA); Native American studies (MA); neuroscience (M Sc, PhD); new media (MA); nursing (M Sc); philosophy (MA); physics (M Sc); policy and strategy (MScM); political science (MA); psychology (M Sc, MA); religious studies (MA); social sciences (MA); sociology (MA); theatre and dramatic arts (MFA); theoretical and computational science (PhD); urban and regional studies (MA); women's studies (MA). Part-time and evening/weekend programs available. *Degree requirements:* For doctorate, comprehensive exam, thesis/dissertation. *Entrance requirements:* For master's, GMAT (M Sc in management), bachelor's degree in related field, minimum GPA of 3.0 during previous 20 graded semester courses, 2 years teaching or related experience (M Ed); for doctorate, master's degree, minimum graduate GPA of 3.5. Additional exam requirements/recommendations for international students: Required—TOEFL. *Faculty research:* Movement and brain plasticity, gibberellin physiology, photosynthesis, carbon cycling, molecular properties of main-group ring components.

University of Louisville, Graduate School, College of Arts and Sciences, Department of Chemistry, Louisville, KY 40292-0001. Offers analytical chemistry (MS, PhD); biochemistry (MS, PhD); chemical physics (PhD); inorganic chemistry (MS, PhD); organic chemistry (MS, PhD); physical chemistry (MS, PhD). *Students:* 45 full-time (21 women), 5 part-time (1 woman); includes 1 minority (Hispanic/Latino), 35 international. Average age 28. 78 applicants, 17% accepted, 9 enrolled. In 2012, 19 master's, 7 doctorates awarded. Terminal master's awarded for partial completion of doctoral program. *Degree requirements:* For master's, variable foreign language requirement, comprehensive exam, thesis optional; for doctorate, variable foreign language requirement, comprehensive exam, thesis/dissertation. *Entrance requirements:* For master's and doctorate, BA or BS coursework. Additional exam requirements/recommendations for international students: Required—TOEFL. *Application deadline:* For fall admission, 3/15 for domestic and international students; for winter admission, 9/15 for domestic and international students. Applications are processed on a rolling basis. Application fee: $60. Electronic applications accepted. *Financial support:* In 2012–13, 33 teaching assistantships with full tuition reimbursements (averaging $22,000 per year) were awarded; fellowships with full tuition reimbursements, research assistantships with full tuition reimbursements, career-related internships or fieldwork, scholarships/grants, traineeships, health care benefits, and unspecified assistantships also available. Support available to part-time students. Financial award application deadline: 3/15. *Faculty research:* Computational chemistry, biophysics nuclear magnetic resonance, synthetic organic chemistry, synthetic inorganic chemistry, medicinal chemistry, protein chemistry, enzymology, nanochemistry, electrochemistry, analytical chemistry, synthetic biology, bioinformatics. *Total annual research expenditures:* $2.5 million. *Unit head:* Dr. Richard J. Wittebort, Professor/Chair, 502-852-6613. *Application contact:* Sherry Nalley, Administrator, 502-852-6798.

University of Maine, Graduate School, College of Liberal Arts and Sciences, Department of Chemistry, Orono, ME 04469. Offers MS, PhD. *Faculty:* 12 full-time (3 women), 1 part-time/adjunct (0 women). *Students:* 24 full-time (9 women), 5 part-time (0 women); includes 1 minority (Asian, non-Hispanic/Latino), 15 international. Average age 30. 27 applicants, 26% accepted, 5 enrolled. In 2012, 4 master's, 3 doctorates awarded. Terminal master's awarded for partial completion of doctoral program. *Degree requirements:* For master's, thesis; for doctorate, comprehensive exam, thesis/dissertation. *Entrance requirements:* For master's and doctorate, GRE General Test. Additional exam requirements/recommendations for international students: Required—TOEFL. *Application deadline:* For fall admission, 2/1 priority date for domestic students. Applications are processed on a rolling basis. Application fee: $65. Electronic applications accepted. *Financial support:* In 2012–13, 2 research assistantships with full tuition reimbursements (averaging $12,900 per year), 15 teaching assistantships with full tuition reimbursements (averaging $17,184 per year) were awarded; tuition waivers (full and partial) also available. Financial award application deadline: 3/1. *Faculty research:* Quantum mechanics, insect chemistry, organic synthesis. *Unit head:* Dr. Francois Amar, Chair, 207-581-1196. *Application contact:* Scott G. Delcourt, Associate Dean of the Graduate School, 207-581-3291, Fax: 207-581-3232, E-mail: graduate@maine.edu. Website: http://www2.umaine.edu/graduate/.

The University of Manchester, School of Chemical Engineering and Analytical Science, Manchester, United Kingdom. Offers biocatalysis (M Phil, PhD); chemical engineering (M Phil, PhD); chemical engineering and analytical science (M Phil, D Eng, PhD); colloids, crystals, interfaces and materials (M Phil, PhD); environment and sustainable technology (M Phil, PhD); instrumentation (M Phil, PhD); multi-scale modeling (M Phil, PhD); process integration (M Phil, PhD); systems biology (M Phil, PhD).

The University of Manchester, School of Chemistry, Manchester, United Kingdom. Offers biological chemistry (PhD); chemistry (M Ent, M Phil, M Sc, D Ent, PhD); inorganic chemistry (PhD); materials chemistry (PhD); nanoscience (PhD); nuclear fission (PhD); organic chemistry (PhD); physical chemistry (PhD); theoretical chemistry (PhD).

The University of Manchester, School of Earth, Atmospheric and Environmental Sciences, Manchester, United Kingdom. Offers atmospheric sciences (M Phil, M Sc, PhD); basin studies and petroleum geosciences (M Phil, M Sc, PhD); earth, atmospheric and environmental sciences (M Phil, M Sc, PhD); environmental geochemistry and cosmochemistry (M Phil, M Sc, PhD); isotope geochemistry and cosmochemistry (M Phil, M Sc, PhD); paleontology (M Phil, M Sc, PhD); physics and chemistry of minerals and fluids (M Phil, M Sc, PhD); structural and petrological geosciences (M Phil, M Sc, PhD).

University of Manitoba, Faculty of Graduate Studies, Faculty of Science, Department of Chemistry, Winnipeg, MB R3T 2N2, Canada. Offers M Sc, PhD. *Degree requirements:* For master's, thesis; for doctorate, one foreign language, thesis/dissertation.

University of Maryland, Baltimore County, Graduate School, College of Arts, Humanities and Social Sciences, Department of Education, Program in Teaching, Baltimore, MD 21250. Offers early childhood education (MAT); elementary education (MAT); secondary education (MAT), including art, biology, chemistry, dance, earth/space science, English, foreign language, mathematics, music, physics, social studies, theatre. Part-time and evening/weekend programs available. *Faculty:* 24 full-time (18 women), 25 part-time/adjunct (19 women). *Students:* 53 full-time (40 women), 43 part-time (28 women); includes 22 minority (14 Black or African American, non-Hispanic/Latino; 3 Asian, non-Hispanic/Latino; 4 Hispanic/Latino; 1 Two or more races, non-Hispanic/Latino), 1 international. Average age 30. 40 applicants, 95% accepted, 35 enrolled. In 2012, 106 master's awarded. *Degree requirements:* For master's, comprehensive exam (for some programs), thesis (for some programs). *Entrance requirements:* For master's, PRAXIS I or SAT (minimum score of 1000), minimum GPA of 3.0. Additional exam requirements/recommendations for international students: Required—TOEFL. *Application deadline:* For fall admission, 6/1 for domestic students; for spring admission, 11/1 for domestic students. Applications are processed on a rolling basis. Application fee: $50. Electronic applications accepted. *Financial support:* In 2012–13, 6 students received support, including teaching assistantships with full and partial tuition reimbursements available (averaging $12,000 per year); career-related internships or fieldwork, Federal Work-Study, scholarships/grants, tuition waivers, and unspecified assistantships also available. Financial award application deadline: 3/1. *Faculty research:* STEM teacher education, culturally sensitive pedagogy, ESOL/bilingual education, early childhood education, language, literacy and culture. *Unit head:* Dr. Susan M. Blunck, Graduate Program Director, 410-455-2869, Fax: 410-455-3986, E-mail: blunck@umbc.edu. Website: http://www.umbc.edu/education/.

University of Maryland, Baltimore County, Graduate School, College of Natural and Mathematical Sciences, Department of Chemistry and Biochemistry, Baltimore, MD 21250. Offers biochemistry (PhD); chemistry (MS, PhD); chemistry and biochemistry (Postbaccalaureate Certificate). Part-time programs available. *Faculty:* 19 full-time (4 women), 3 part-time/adjunct (0 women). *Students:* 50 full-time (25 women), 1 part-time (0 women); includes 6 minority (3 Black or African American, non-Hispanic/Latino; 1 Asian, non-Hispanic/Latino; 2 Hispanic/Latino), 18 international. Average age 26. 95 applicants, 26% accepted, 14 enrolled. In 2012, 4 master's, 8 doctorates awarded. Terminal master's awarded for partial completion of doctoral program. *Degree requirements:* For master's, comprehensive exam (for some programs), thesis (for some programs); for doctorate, comprehensive exam, thesis/dissertation. *Entrance requirements:* For master's, GRE General Test, minimum GPA of 3.0; for doctorate, GRE General Test, GRE Subject Test (recommended), minimum GPA of 3.0. Additional exam requirements/recommendations for international students: Required—TOEFL (minimum score 550 paper-based; 80 iBT). *Application deadline:* For fall admission, 6/1 priority date for domestic students, 1/1 for international students; for spring admission, 11/1 priority date for domestic students, 5/1 for international students. Applications are processed on a rolling basis. Application fee: $50. Electronic applications accepted. *Financial support:* In 2012–13, 4 fellowships with full tuition reimbursements (averaging $24,000 per year), 11 research assistantships with full tuition reimbursements (averaging $21,000 per year), 31 teaching assistantships with full tuition reimbursements (averaging $21,000 per year) were awarded; health care benefits also available. *Faculty research:* Protein structures, bio-organic chemistry, enzyme catalysis, molecular biology, metabolism. *Total annual research expenditures:* $3.3 million. *Unit head:* Dr. Dale R. Whalen, Director, Graduate Program, 410-455-2491, Fax: 410-455-2608, E-mail: chemgrad@umbc.edu. *Application contact:* Patricia Gagne, Graduate Coordinator, 866-PhD-UMBC, Fax: 410-455-2608, E-mail: pgagne1@umbc.edu. Website: http://www.umbc.edu/chem.

University of Maryland, College Park, Academic Affairs, College of Computer, Mathematical and Natural Sciences, Department of Chemistry and Biochemistry, Chemistry Program, College Park, MD 20742. Offers analytical chemistry (MS, PhD); inorganic chemistry (MS, PhD); organic chemistry (MS, PhD); physical chemistry (MS, PhD). Part-time and evening/weekend programs available. *Students:* 113 full-time (64 women), 2 part-time (0 women); includes 19 minority (11 Black or African American, non-Hispanic/Latino; 4 Asian, non-Hispanic/Latino; 2 Hispanic/Latino; 2 Two or more races, non-Hispanic/Latino), 44 international. 339 applicants, 27% accepted, 20 enrolled. In 2012, 7 master's, 14 doctorates awarded. Terminal master's awarded for partial completion of doctoral program. *Degree requirements:* For master's, thesis optional; for doctorate, thesis/dissertation, 2 seminar presentations, oral exam. *Entrance requirements:* For master's and doctorate, GRE General Test, GRE Subject Test (recommended), minimum GPA of 3.0, 3 letters of recommendation. Additional exam requirements/recommendations for international students: Required—TOEFL. *Application deadline:* For fall admission, 2/1 for domestic and international students; for spring admission, 6/1 for domestic and international students. Applications are processed on a rolling basis. Application fee: $75. Electronic applications accepted. *Expenses:* Tuition, state resident: part-time $551 per credit. Tuition, nonresident: part-time $1188 per credit. Part-time tuition and fees vary according to program. *Financial support:* In 2012–13, 14 fellowships with full and partial tuition reimbursements (averaging $20,017 per year), 52 research assistantships (averaging $19,868 per year), 44 teaching assistantships (averaging $19,209 per year) were awarded. Financial award applicants required to submit FAFSA. *Faculty research:* Environmental chemistry, nuclear chemistry, lunar and environmental analysis, x-ray crystallography. *Unit head:* Dr. Michael Doyle, Chairperson, 301-405-1795, Fax: 301-314-2779, E-mail: mdoyle3@umd.edu. *Application contact:* Dr. Charles A. Caramello, Dean of Graduate School, 301-405-0358, Fax: 301-314-9305.

University of Massachusetts Amherst, Graduate School, College of Natural Sciences, Department of Chemistry, Amherst, MA 01003. Offers MS, PhD. Part-time programs available. *Faculty:* 30 full-time (5 women). *Students:* 135 full-time (62 women), 9 part-time (3 women); includes 14 minority (5 Black or African

American, non-Hispanic/Latino; 5 Asian, non-Hispanic/Latino; 4 Hispanic/Latino), 83 international. Average age 27. 269 applicants, 27% accepted, 25 enrolled. In 2012, 6 master's, 14 doctorates awarded. Terminal master's awarded for partial completion of doctoral program. *Degree requirements:* For master's, thesis (for some programs); for doctorate, comprehensive exam, thesis/dissertation. *Entrance requirements:* For master's and doctorate, GRE General Test. Additional exam requirements/recommendations for international students: Required—TOEFL (minimum score 550 paper-based; 80 iBT), IELTS (minimum score 6.5). *Application deadline:* For fall admission, 12/15 for domestic and international students. Applications are processed on a rolling basis. Application fee: $75. Electronic applications accepted. *Expenses:* Tuition, state resident: full-time $1980; part-time $110 per credit. Tuition, nonresident: full-time $13,314; part-time $414 per credit. *Required fees:* $10,338; $3594 per semester. One-time fee: $357. *Financial support:* Fellowships with full and partial tuition reimbursements, research assistantships with full and partial tuition reimbursements, teaching assistantships with full and partial tuition reimbursements, career-related internships or fieldwork, Federal Work-Study, scholarships/grants, traineeships, health care benefits, tuition waivers (full and partial), and unspecified assistantships available. Support available to part-time students. Financial award application deadline: 12/15. *Unit head:* Dr. Edward Voigtman, Graduate Program Director, 413-545-2664, Fax: 413-545-4490. *Application contact:* Lindsay DeSantis, Supervisor of Admissions, 413-545-0722, Fax: 413-577-0010, E-mail: gradadm@grad.umass.edu. Website: http://www.chem.umass.edu/.

University of Massachusetts Boston, Office of Graduate Studies, College of Science and Mathematics, Program in Chemistry, Boston, MA 02125-3393. Offers MS. Part-time and evening/weekend programs available. *Degree requirements:* For master's, comprehensive exam, thesis, oral exams. *Entrance requirements:* For master's, GRE General Test, GRE Subject Test, minimum GPA of 2.75. *Faculty research:* Synthesis and mechanisms of organic nitrogen compounds, application of spin resonance in the study of structure and dynamics, chemical education and teacher training, new synthetic reagents, structural study of inorganic solids by infrared and Raman spectroscopy.

University of Massachusetts Dartmouth, Graduate School, College of Arts and Sciences, Department of Chemistry, North Dartmouth, MA 02747-2300. Offers MS, PhD. Part-time programs available. *Faculty:* 16 full-time (4 women). *Students:* 16 full-time (8 women), 12 part-time (4 women); includes 2 minority (1 Black or African American, non-Hispanic/Latino; 1 Hispanic/Latino), 19 international. Average age 27. 18 applicants, 89% accepted, 7 enrolled. In 2012, 11 master's awarded. *Degree requirements:* For master's, comprehensive exam (for some programs), thesis or alternative; for doctorate, thesis/dissertation (for some programs). *Entrance requirements:* For master's and doctorate, GRE (recommended), statement of purpose (minimum of 300 words), resume, 2 letters of recommendation, official transcripts. Additional exam requirements/recommendations for international students: Required—TOEFL (minimum score 550 paper-based). *Application deadline:* For fall admission, 3/15 priority date for domestic students, 2/15 for international students; for spring admission, 11/1 priority date for domestic students, 10/1 for international students. Applications are processed on a rolling basis. Application fee: $60. Electronic applications accepted. *Expenses:* Tuition, state resident: part-time $86.29 per credit. Tuition, nonresident: part-time $337.46 per credit. *Required fees:* $631.03 per credit. Tuition and fees vary according to course load and reciprocity agreements. *Financial support:* In 2012–13, 1 fellowship with full tuition reimbursement (averaging $10,000 per year), 4 research assistantships with full and partial tuition reimbursements (averaging $3,778 per year), 15 teaching assistantships with full and partial tuition reimbursements (averaging $8,000 per year) were awarded; Federal Work-Study also available. Support available to part-time students. Financial award application deadline: 3/1; financial award applicants required to submit FAFSA. *Faculty research:* Inorganic chemistry, biochemical kinetics, photochemistry, ion-molecule reactions, atmosphere chemistry. *Total annual research expenditures:* $1.6 million. *Unit head:* Dr. Yuegang Zuo, Graduate Program Director, 508-999-8959, Fax: 508-999-9167, E-mail: yzuo@umassd.edu. *Application contact:* Steven Briggs, Director of Marketing and Recruitment, 508-999-8604, Fax: 508-999-8183, E-mail: graduate@umassd.edu. Website: http://www.umassd.edu/cas/chemistry/.

University of Massachusetts Lowell, College of Sciences, Department of Chemistry, Lowell, MA 01854-2881. Offers analytical chemistry (PhD); biochemistry (PhD); chemistry (MS, PhD); environmental studies (PhD); green chemistry (PhD); inorganic chemistry (PhD); organic chemistry (PhD); polymer science (MS). Terminal master's awarded for partial completion of doctoral program. *Degree requirements:* For master's, thesis; for doctorate, 2 foreign languages, thesis/dissertation. *Entrance requirements:* For master's and doctorate, GRE General Test. Electronic applications accepted.

University of Memphis, Graduate School, College of Arts and Sciences, Department of Chemistry, Memphis, TN 38152. Offers analytical chemistry (MS, PhD); computational chemistry (MS, PhD); inorganic chemistry (MS, PhD); organic chemistry (MS, PhD); physical chemistry (MS, PhD). Part-time programs available. Terminal master's awarded for partial completion of doctoral program. *Degree requirements:* For master's, comprehensive exam, thesis or alternative; for doctorate, comprehensive exam, thesis/dissertation. *Entrance requirements:* For master's and doctorate, GRE General Test, admission to Graduate School plus 32 undergraduate hours in chemistry. Additional exam requirements/recommendations for international students: Required—TOEFL. Electronic applications accepted. *Faculty research:* Computational chemistry, materials chemistry, organic/polymer synthesis, drug design/delivery, water chemistry.

University of Miami, Graduate School, College of Arts and Sciences, Department of Chemistry, Coral Gables, FL 33124. Offers chemistry (MS); inorganic chemistry (PhD); organic chemistry (PhD); physical chemistry (PhD). Terminal master's awarded for partial completion of doctoral program. *Degree requirements:* For master's, comprehensive exam; for doctorate, comprehensive exam, thesis/dissertation. *Entrance requirements:* For master's and doctorate, GRE General Test. Additional exam requirements/recommendations for international students: Required—TOEFL (minimum score 550 paper-based). Electronic applications accepted. *Faculty research:* Supramolecular chemistry, electrochemistry, surface chemistry, catalysis, organometalic.

University of Michigan, Horace H. Rackham School of Graduate Studies, College of Literature, Science, and the Arts, Department of Chemistry, Ann Arbor, MI 48109-1055. Offers analytical chemistry (PhD); chemical biology (PhD); inorganic chemistry (PhD); material chemistry (PhD); organic chemistry (PhD); physical chemistry (PhD). *Degree requirements:* For doctorate, thesis/dissertation, oral defense of dissertation, organic cumulative proficiency exams. *Entrance requirements:* For doctorate, GRE General Test, GRE Subject Test (recommended), 3 letters of recommendation. Additional exam requirements/recommendations for international students: Required—TOEFL (minimum score 560 paper-based; 84 iBT). Electronic applications accepted. *Faculty research:* Biological catalysis, protein engineering, chemical sensors, de novo metalloprotein design, supramolecular architecture.

University of Minnesota, Duluth, Graduate School, Swenson College of Science and Engineering, Department of Chemistry and Biochemistry, Duluth, MN 55812-2496. Offers MS. Part-time programs available. *Degree requirements:* For master's, thesis. *Entrance requirements:* For master's, bachelor's degree in chemistry, minimum GPA of 3.0. Additional exam requirements/recommendations for international students: Required—TOEFL (minimum score 550 paper-based; 79 iBT), IELTS (minimum score 6.5). *Faculty research:* Physical, inorganic, organic, and analytical chemistry; biochemistry and molecular biology.

University of Minnesota, Twin Cities Campus, College of Science and Engineering, Department of Chemistry, Minneapolis, MN 55455-0213. Offers MS, PhD. Part-time programs available. Terminal master's awarded for partial completion of doctoral program. *Degree requirements:* For master's, thesis or alternative; for doctorate, thesis/dissertation, preliminary candidacy exams. *Entrance requirements:* For master's and doctorate, GRE General Test. Additional exam requirements/recommendations for international students: Required—TOEFL. *Faculty research:* Analytical, biological, inorganic, organic, and physical chemistry.

University of Minnesota, Twin Cities Campus, School of Public Health, Division of Environmental Health Sciences, Area in Environmental Chemistry, Minneapolis, MN 55455-0213. Offers MS, PhD. *Degree requirements:* For doctorate, thesis/dissertation. *Entrance requirements:* For master's and doctorate, GRE General Test. Electronic applications accepted.

University of Mississippi, Graduate School, College of Liberal Arts, Department of Chemistry and Biochemistry, Oxford, University, MS 38677. Offers MS, DA, PhD. *Faculty:* 20 full-time (2 women). *Students:* 42 full-time (13 women), 2 part-time (0 women); includes 13 minority (4 Black or African American, non-Hispanic/Latino; 3 Asian, non-Hispanic/Latino; 4 Hispanic/Latino; 2 Two or more races, non-Hispanic/Latino), 14 international. In 2012, 1 master's, 4 doctorates awarded. *Degree requirements:* For master's, thesis; for doctorate, one foreign language, thesis/dissertation. *Entrance requirements:* For master's, GRE General Test, minimum GPA of 3.0; for doctorate, GRE General Test. Additional exam requirements/recommendations for international students: Required—TOEFL. *Application deadline:* For fall admission, 4/1 for domestic students; for spring admission, 10/1 for domestic students. Applications are processed on a rolling basis. Application fee: $25. Electronic applications accepted. *Expenses:* Tuition, state resident: full-time $6282; part-time $349 per credit hour. Tuition, nonresident: full-time $16,266; part-time $903.50 per credit hour. *Financial support:* Scholarships/grants available. Financial award application deadline: 3/1; financial award applicants required to submit FAFSA. *Unit head:* Dr. Charles Hussey, Chairman, 662-915-7301, Fax: 662-915-7300, E-mail: chemistry@olemiss.edu. *Application contact:* Dr. Christy M. Wyandt, Associate Dean, 662-915-7474, Fax: 662-915-7577, E-mail: cwyandt@olemiss.edu.

University of Missouri, Graduate School, College of Arts and Sciences, Department of Chemistry, Columbia, MO 65211. Offers analytical chemistry (MS, PhD); inorganic chemistry (MS, PhD); organic chemistry (MS, PhD); physical chemistry (MS, PhD). *Faculty:* 22 full-time (4 women), 1 part-time/adjunct (0 women). *Students:* 110 full-time (42 women), 9 part-time (5 women); includes 10 minority (3 Black or African American, non-Hispanic/Latino; 3 Asian, non-Hispanic/Latino; 2 Hispanic/Latino; 2 Two or more races, non-Hispanic/Latino), 47 international. Average age 27. 94 applicants, 21% accepted, 15 enrolled. In 2012, 2 master's, 5 doctorates awarded. *Degree requirements:* For master's, thesis; for doctorate, one foreign language, comprehensive exam, thesis/dissertation. *Entrance requirements:* For master's, GRE General Test, minimum GPA of 3.0; for doctorate, GRE General Test (minimum score: Verbal 450, Quantitative 600, Analytical 3), minimum GPA of 3.0. Additional exam requirements/recommendations for international students: Required—TOEFL (minimum score 600 paper-based; 100 iBT). *Application deadline:* For fall admission, 2/1 priority date for domestic students, 2/1 for international students; for winter admission, 10/

15 for domestic and international students. Applications are processed on a rolling basis. Application fee: $55 ($75 for international students). Electronic applications accepted. *Expenses:* Tuition, state resident: full-time $6057. Tuition, nonresident: full-time $15,683. *Required fees:* $1000. *Financial support:* In 2012–13, 9 fellowships with full tuition reimbursements, 15 research assistantships with full tuition reimbursements, 78 teaching assistantships with full tuition reimbursements were awarded; institutionally sponsored loans, traineeships, health care benefits, and unspecified assistantships also available. *Faculty research:* Analytical, organic, biological, physical, inorganic and radiochemistry. *Unit head:* Dr. Jerry Atwood, Department Chair, 573-882-8374, E-mail: atwoodj@missouri.edu. *Application contact:* Jerry Brightwell, Administrative Assistant, 573-884-6832, E-mail: brightwellj@missouri.edu. Website: http://chemistry.missouri.edu/.

University of Missouri–Kansas City, College of Arts and Sciences, Department of Chemistry, Kansas City, MO 64110-2499. Offers analytical chemistry (MS, PhD); inorganic chemistry (MS, PhD); organic chemistry (MS, PhD); physical chemistry (MS, PhD); polymer chemistry (MS, PhD). PhD (interdisciplinary) offered through the School of Graduate Studies. Part-time and evening/weekend programs available. *Faculty:* 15 full-time (3 women), 2 part-time/adjunct (0 women). *Students:* 7 part-time (3 women); includes 3 minority (2 Black or African American, non-Hispanic/Latino; 1 Hispanic/Latino). Average age 38. 19 applicants, 37% accepted, 3 enrolled. In 2012, 2 master's awarded. *Degree requirements:* For master's, thesis (for some programs); for doctorate, thesis/dissertation. *Entrance requirements:* For master's, equivalent of American Chemical Society approved bachelor's degree in chemistry; for doctorate, GRE General Test, equivalent of American Chemical Society approved bachelor's degree in chemistry. Additional exam requirements/recommendations for international students: Required—TOEFL (minimum score 550 paper-based; 80 iBT), TWE. *Application deadline:* For fall admission, 4/15 for domestic and international students; for spring admission, 10/15 for domestic and international students. Applications are processed on a rolling basis. Application fee: $45 ($50 for international students). Electronic applications accepted. *Expenses:* Tuition, state resident: full-time $5972.40; part-time $331.80 per credit hour. Tuition, nonresident: full-time $15,417; part-time $856.50 per credit hour. *Required fees:* $95.89 per credit hour. Full-time tuition and fees vary according to program. *Financial support:* In 2012–13, 6 research assistantships with partial tuition reimbursements (averaging $18,817 per year), 16 teaching assistantships with partial tuition reimbursements (averaging $18,132 per year) were awarded; Federal Work-Study, institutionally sponsored loans, and scholarships/grants also available. Support available to part-time students. Financial award application deadline: 3/1; financial award applicants required to submit FAFSA. *Faculty research:* Molecular spectroscopy, characterization and synthesis of materials and compounds, computational chemistry, natural products, drug delivery systems and anti-tumor agents. *Unit head:* Dr. Kathleen V. Kilway, Chair, 816-235-2289, Fax: 816-235-5502. *Application contact:* Graduate Recruiting Committee, 816-235-2272, Fax: 816-235-5502, E-mail: umkc-chemdept@umkc.edu. Website: http://cas.umkc.edu/chem/.

University of Missouri–St. Louis, College of Arts and Sciences, Department of Chemistry and Biochemistry, St. Louis, MO 63121. Offers chemistry (MS, PhD), including biochemistry, inorganic chemistry, organic chemistry, physical chemistry. Part-time and evening/weekend programs available. *Faculty:* 19 full-time (3 women), 6 part-time/adjunct (1 woman). *Students:* 37 full-time (15 women), 25 part-time (16 women); includes 6 minority (2 Black or African American, non-Hispanic/Latino; 1 Asian, non-Hispanic/Latino; 3 Hispanic/Latino), 18 international. Average age 30. 85 applicants, 22% accepted, 7 enrolled. In 2012, 18 master's, 5 doctorates awarded. Terminal master's awarded for partial completion of doctoral program. *Degree requirements:* For master's, thesis optional; for doctorate, thesis/dissertation. *Entrance requirements:* For master's, 2 letters of recommendation; for doctorate, GRE General Test, 3 letters of recommendation. Additional exam requirements/recommendations for international students: Required—TOEFL (minimum score 550 paper-based; 79 iBT), IELTS (minimum score 6.5). *Application deadline:* For fall admission, 7/1 priority date for domestic students, 7/1 for international students; for spring admission, 12/1 priority date for domestic students, 12/1 for international students. Applications are processed on a rolling basis. Application fee: $35 ($40 for international students). Electronic applications accepted. *Expenses:* Tuition, state resident: full-time $7364; part-time $409.10 per credit hour. Tuition, nonresident: full-time $18,153; part-time $1008.50 per credit hour. *Financial support:* In 2012–13, 16 research assistantships with full and partial tuition reimbursements (averaging $13,500 per year), 20 teaching assistantships with full and partial tuition reimbursements (averaging $13,500 per year) were awarded; fellowships with full and partial tuition reimbursements also available. *Faculty research:* Metallaborane chemistry, serum transferrin chemistry, natural products chemistry, organic synthesis. *Unit head:* Dr. Janet Wilking, Director of Graduate Studies, 314-516-5311, Fax: 314-516-5342, E-mail: gradchem@umsl.edu. *Application contact:* Graduate Admissions, 314-516-5458, Fax: 314-516-6996, E-mail: gradadm@umsl.edu. Website: http://www.umsl.edu/chemistry/.

The University of Montana, Graduate School, College of Arts and Sciences, Department of Chemistry and Biochemistry, Missoula, MT 59812-0002. Offers chemistry (MS, PhD), including environmental/analytical chemistry, inorganic chemistry, organic chemistry, physical chemistry. Terminal master's awarded for partial completion of doctoral program. *Degree requirements:* For master's, thesis (for some programs); for doctorate, thesis/dissertation. *Entrance requirements:* For master's and doctorate, GRE General Test. Additional exam requirements/

recommendations for international students: Required—TOEFL (minimum score 575 paper-based). *Faculty research:* Reaction mechanisms and kinetics, inorganic and organic synthesis, analytical chemistry, natural products.

University of Nebraska–Lincoln, Graduate College, College of Arts and Sciences, Department of Chemistry, Lincoln, NE 68588. Offers analytical chemistry (PhD); biochemistry (PhD); chemistry (MS); inorganic chemistry (PhD); materials chemistry (PhD); organic chemistry (PhD); physical chemistry (PhD). *Degree requirements:* For master's, one foreign language, thesis optional, departmental qualifying exam; for doctorate, one foreign language, comprehensive exam, thesis/dissertation, departmental qualifying exams. *Entrance requirements:* For master's and doctorate, GRE. Additional exam requirements/recommendations for international students: Required—TOEFL (minimum score 550 paper-based). Electronic applications accepted. *Faculty research:* Bioorganic and bioinorganic chemistry, biophysical and bioanalytical chemistry, structure-function of DNA and proteins, organometallics, mass spectrometry.

University of Nevada, Las Vegas, Graduate College, College of Science, Department of Chemistry, Las Vegas, NV 89154-4003. Offers biochemistry (MS); chemistry (MS, PhD); radiochemistry (PhD). Part-time programs available. *Faculty:* 23 full-time (4 women), 10 part-time/adjunct (5 women). *Students:* 37 full-time (20 women), 13 part-time (3 women); includes 29 minority (1 Black or African American, non-Hispanic/Latino; 1 Asian, non-Hispanic/Latino; 1 Hispanic/Latino; 26 Two or more races, non-Hispanic/Latino), 10 international. Average age 29. 25 applicants, 60% accepted, 13 enrolled. In 2012, 3 master's, 4 doctorates awarded. *Degree requirements:* For master's, thesis. *Entrance requirements:* For master's and doctorate, GRE General Test. Additional exam requirements/recommendations for international students: Required—TOEFL (minimum score 550 paper-based; 80 iBT), IELTS (minimum score 7). *Application deadline:* For fall admission, 2/1 priority date for domestic students, 5/1 for international students; for spring admission, 10/1 priority date for domestic students, 10/1 for international students. Applications are processed on a rolling basis. Application fee: $60 ($95 for international students). Electronic applications accepted. *Expenses:* Tuition, state resident: full-time $4752; part-time $264 per credit. Tuition, nonresident: full-time $18,662; part-time $527.50 per credit. *Required fees:* $12 per credit. $266 per semester. One-time fee: $35. Tuition and fees vary according to course load, program and reciprocity agreements. *Financial support:* In 2012–13, 43 students received support, including 29 research assistantships with partial tuition reimbursements available (averaging $15,349 per year), 14 teaching assistantships with partial tuition reimbursements available (averaging $14,719 per year); institutionally sponsored loans, scholarships/grants, health care benefits, and unspecified assistantships also available. Financial award application deadline: 3/1. *Faculty research:* Material science, biochemistry, chemical education, physical chemistry and theoretical computation, analytical and organic chemistry. *Total annual research expenditures:* $2 million. *Unit head:* Dr. Dennis Lindle, Chair/Professor, 702-895-4426, Fax: 702-895-4072, E-mail: lindle@unlv.nevada.edu. *Application contact:* Graduate Coordinator, 702-895-3320, Fax: 702-895-4180, E-mail: gradcollege@unlv.edu. Website: http://www.unlv.edu/chemistry.

University of Nevada, Reno, Graduate School, College of Science, Department of Chemistry, Reno, NV 89557. Offers MS, PhD. Terminal master's awarded for partial completion of doctoral program. *Degree requirements:* For master's, thesis; for doctorate, one foreign language, thesis/dissertation. *Entrance requirements:* For master's, GRE, minimum GPA of 2.75; for doctorate, GRE, minimum GPA of 3.0. Additional exam requirements/recommendations for international students: Required—TOEFL (minimum score 500 paper-based; 61 iBT), IELTS (minimum score 6). Electronic applications accepted. *Faculty research:* Organic/inorganic chemistry, physical chemistry, chemical chemistry, physics, organometallic chemistry.

University of New Brunswick Fredericton, School of Graduate Studies, Faculty of Science, Department of Chemistry, Fredericton, NB E3B 5A3, Canada. Offers M Sc, PhD. *Faculty:* 15 full-time (2 women), 1 (woman) part-time/adjunct. *Students:* 21 full-time (10 women); includes 10 minority (1 Black or African American, non-Hispanic/Latino; 9 Asian, non-Hispanic/Latino). In 2012, 3 master's, 1 doctorate awarded. Terminal master's awarded for partial completion of doctoral program. *Degree requirements:* For master's, thesis; for doctorate, comprehensive exam, thesis/dissertation. *Entrance requirements:* For master's, bachelor's degree in chemistry or biochemistry; minimum GPA of 3.0; for doctorate, minimum GPA of 3.0. Additional exam requirements/recommendations for international students: Required—TOEFL (minimum score 580 paper-based), IELTS (minimum score 7.5), TWE (minimum score 4). *Application deadline:* For fall admission, 3/1 for domestic students. Applications are processed on a rolling basis. Application fee: $50 Canadian dollars. Electronic applications accepted. Tuition and fees charges are reported in Canadian dollars. *Expenses: Tuition, area resident:* Full-time $3956 Canadian dollars. *Required fees:* $579.50 Canadian dollars; $55 Canadian dollars per semester. *Financial support:* In 2012–13, fellowships (averaging $18,000 per year), 32 research assistantships (averaging $1,595 per year), 38 teaching assistantships (averaging $3,800 per year) were awarded; scholarships/grants also available. *Faculty research:* Inorganic, organic, bio-organic, physical chemistry, pulp and paper, theoretical and computation chemistry. *Total annual research expenditures:* $1.1 million. *Unit head:* Dr. Saba Mattar, Director of Graduate Studies, 506-447-3091, Fax: 506-453-4981, E-mail: mattar@unb.ca. *Application contact:* Krista Coy, Graduate

Peterson's Graduate Programs in the Physical Sciences, Mathematics, Agricultural Sciences, the Environment & Natural Resources 2014

www.petersonsbooks.com **91**

Secretary, 506-453-4781, Fax: 506-453-4981, E-mail: krista.coy@unb.ca. Website: http://go.unb.ca/gradprograms.

University of New Hampshire, Graduate School, College of Engineering and Physical Sciences, Department of Chemistry, Durham, NH 03824. Offers chemistry (MS, MST, PhD); chemistry education (PhD). *Faculty:* 28 full-time (17 women). *Students:* 51 full-time (23 women), 10 part-time (5 women); includes 6 minority (1 Black or African American, non-Hispanic/Latino; 3 Hispanic/Latino; 2 Two or more races, non-Hispanic/Latino), 26 international. Average age 27. 66 applicants, 50% accepted, 16 enrolled. In 2012, 4 master's, 3 doctorates awarded. Terminal master's awarded for partial completion of doctoral program. *Degree requirements:* For master's, thesis; for doctorate, one foreign language, thesis/dissertation. *Entrance requirements:* Additional exam requirements/recommendations for international students: Required—TOEFL (minimum score 550 paper-based; 80 iBT). *Application deadline:* For fall admission, 4/1 priority date for domestic students, 4/1 for international students; for spring admission, 12/1 for domestic students. Applications are processed on a rolling basis. Application fee: $65. *Expenses:* Tuition, state resident: full-time $13,500; part-time $750 per credit. Tuition, nonresident: full-time $25,940; part-time $1089 per credit. *Required fees:* $1699; $424.75 per semester. *Financial support:* In 2012–13, 48 students received support, including 2 fellowships, 12 research assistantships, 39 teaching assistantships; Federal Work-Study, scholarships/grants, and tuition waivers (full and partial) also available. Support available to part-time students. Financial award application deadline: 2/15. *Faculty research:* Analytical, physical, organic, and inorganic chemistry. *Unit head:* Dr. Chuck Zercher, Chairperson, 603-862-1550. *Application contact:* Cindi Rohwer, Coordinator, 603-862-1550, E-mail: chem.dept@unh.edu. Website: http://www.unh.edu/chemistry/.

University of New Mexico, Graduate School, College of Arts and Sciences, Department of Chemistry and Chemical Biology, Albuquerque, NM 87131-2039. Offers MS, PhD. *Faculty:* 17 full-time (3 women), 3 part-time/adjunct (1 woman). *Students:* 42 full-time (16 women), 9 part-time (1 woman); includes 4 minority (all Hispanic/Latino), 32 international. Average age 28. 27 applicants, 67% accepted, 13 enrolled. In 2012, 2 master's, 6 doctorates awarded. Terminal master's awarded for partial completion of doctoral program. *Degree requirements:* For master's, comprehensive exam, thesis (for some programs); for doctorate, comprehensive exam, thesis/dissertation. *Entrance requirements:* For master's and doctorate, department exams. Additional exam requirements/recommendations for international students: Required—TOEFL (minimum score 550 paper-based; 79 iBT). *Application deadline:* For fall admission, 2/1 for domestic and international students. Applications are processed on a rolling basis. Application fee: $50 ($100 for international students). *Expenses:* Tuition, state resident: full-time $3296; part-time $276.73 per credit hour. Tuition, nonresident: full-time $10,604; part-time $885.74 per credit hour. *Required fees:* $628. *Financial support:* In 2012–13, 50 students received support, including 11 fellowships (averaging $986 per year), 33 research assistantships with tuition reimbursements available (averaging $11,215 per year), 30 teaching assistantships (averaging $15,341 per year); scholarships/grants, health care benefits, and unspecified assistantships also available. Financial award application deadline: 2/1; financial award applicants required to submit FAFSA. *Faculty research:* Materials, inorganic, organic, physical, and biological chemistry. *Total annual research expenditures:* $1.8 million. *Unit head:* Dr. Stephen Cabaniss, Chair, 505-277-6655, Fax: 505-277-2609, E-mail: cabaniss@unm.edu. *Application contact:* Coordinator, Program Advisement, 505-277-6655, Fax: 505-277-2609, E-mail: kamc@unm.edu. Website: http://chemistry.unm.edu/.

University of New Orleans, Graduate School, College of Sciences, Department of Chemistry, New Orleans, LA 70148. Offers MS, PhD. *Students:* 51 (25 women). Average age 29. In 2012, 8 master's, 17 doctorates awarded. *Degree requirements:* For master's, variable foreign language requirement, thesis, departmental qualifying exam; for doctorate, variable foreign language requirement, thesis/dissertation, departmental qualifying exam. *Entrance requirements:* For master's and doctorate, GRE General Test. Additional exam requirements/recommendations for international students: Required—TOEFL (minimum score 550 paper-based; 79 iBT), IELTS (minimum score 6.5). *Application deadline:* For fall admission, 7/1 priority date for domestic students, 6/1 for international students; for spring admission, 11/1 priority date for domestic students, 10/1 for international students. Applications are processed on a rolling basis. Application fee: $20. Electronic applications accepted. *Expenses: Required fees:* $2165 per semester. *Financial support:* Application deadline: 5/15; applicants required to submit FAFSA. *Faculty research:* Synthesis and reactions of novel compounds, high-temperature kinetics, calculations of molecular electrostatic potentials, structures and reactions of metal complexes. *Unit head:* Dr. Edwin Stevens, Chairperson, 504-280-5849, Fax: 504-280-6860, E-mail: estevens@uno.edu. *Application contact:* Dr. Mark Trudell, Graduate Coordinator, 504-280-7337, Fax: 504-280-6860, E-mail: mtrudell@uno.edu. Website: http://chem.uno.edu.

The University of North Carolina at Chapel Hill, Graduate School, College of Arts and Sciences, Department of Chemistry, Chapel Hill, NC 27599. Offers MA, MS, PhD. *Degree requirements:* For master's, comprehensive exam, thesis (for some programs); for doctorate, comprehensive exam, thesis/dissertation. *Entrance requirements:* For master's and doctorate, GRE General Test, GRE Subject Test, minimum GPA of 3.0.

The University of North Carolina at Charlotte, The Graduate School, College of Liberal Arts and Sciences, Department of Chemistry, Charlotte, NC 28223-0001. Offers chemistry (MS); nanoscale science (PhD). Part-time programs available. *Faculty:* 21 full-time (4 women), 1 (woman) part-time/adjunct. *Students:* 17 full-time (4 women), 21 part-time (11 women); includes 8 minority (5 Black or African American, non-Hispanic/Latino; 2 Asian, non-Hispanic/Latino; 1 Hispanic/Latino), 4 international. Average age 26. 35 applicants, 49% accepted, 14 enrolled. In 2012, 6 master's awarded. Terminal master's awarded for partial completion of doctoral program. *Degree requirements:* For master's, thesis; for doctorate, thesis/dissertation. *Entrance requirements:* For master's, GRE General Test, minimum GPA of 3.0 in undergraduate major, 2.75 overall. Additional exam requirements/recommendations for international students: Required—TOEFL (minimum score 557 paper-based; 83 iBT). *Application deadline:* For fall admission, 7/1 for domestic students, 5/1 for international students; for spring admission, 11/1 for domestic students, 10/1 for international students. Applications are processed on a rolling basis. Application fee: $65 ($75 for international students). Electronic applications accepted. *Expenses:* Tuition, state resident: full-time $3453. Tuition, nonresident: full-time $15,982. *Required fees:* $2420. Tuition and fees vary according to course load and program. *Financial support:* In 2012–13, 34 students received support, including 7 research assistantships (averaging $11,558 per year), 27 teaching assistantships (averaging $16,993 per year); career-related internships or fieldwork, Federal Work-Study, institutionally sponsored loans, scholarships/grants, and unspecified assistantships also available. Support available to part-time students. Financial award application deadline: 4/1; financial award applicants required to submit FAFSA. *Faculty research:* Organometallic reagents as chiral auxiliaries for organic synthesis, fluorinated molecular tweezers of different molecular architecture in a convergent approach from various tether scaffolds and fluoroarene building blocks, using capillary electrophoresis (CE) to analyze and characterize proteins, the synthesis and integration of organic conjugated polymers and dye molecules for solar energy conversion applications. *Total annual research expenditures:* $372,638. *Unit head:* Dr. Bernadette T. Donovan-Merkert, Chair, 704-687-4765, Fax: 704-687-0960, E-mail: bdonovan@uncc.edu. *Application contact:* Kathy B. Giddings, Director of Graduate Admissions, 704-687-5503, Fax: 704-687-1668, E-mail: gradadm@uncc.edu. Website: http://chemistry.uncc.edu/graduate-programs.

The University of North Carolina at Greensboro, Graduate School, College of Arts and Sciences, Department of Chemistry and Biochemistry, Greensboro, NC 27412-5001. Offers biochemistry (MS); chemistry (MS). *Degree requirements:* For master's, one foreign language, thesis. *Entrance requirements:* For master's, GRE General Test. Additional exam requirements/recommendations for international students: Required—TOEFL. Electronic applications accepted. *Faculty research:* Synthesis of novel cyclopentadienes, molybdenum hydroxylase-cata ladder polymers, vinyl silicones.

The University of North Carolina Wilmington, College of Arts and Sciences, Department of Chemistry and Biochemistry, Wilmington, NC 28403-3297. Offers MS. Part-time programs available. *Degree requirements:* For master's, comprehensive exam, thesis. *Entrance requirements:* For master's, GRE General Test, minimum B average in undergraduate major. Additional exam requirements/recommendations for international students: Required—TOEFL (minimum score 550 paper-based; 79 iBT), IELTS (minimum score 6.5).

University of North Dakota, Graduate School, College of Arts and Sciences, Department of Chemistry, Grand Forks, ND 58202. Offers MS, PhD. Terminal master's awarded for partial completion of doctoral program. *Degree requirements:* For master's, thesis, final exam; for doctorate, comprehensive exam, thesis/dissertation, final exam. *Entrance requirements:* For master's and doctorate, GRE General Test, GRE Subject Test, minimum GPA of 3.0. Additional exam requirements/recommendations for international students: Required—TOEFL (minimum score 550 paper-based; 79 iBT), IELTS (minimum score 6.5). Electronic applications accepted. *Faculty research:* Synthetic and structural organometallic chemistry, photochemistry, theoretical chemistry, chromatographic chemistry, x-ray crystallography.

University of Northern Colorado, Graduate School, College of Natural and Health Sciences, Department of Chemistry and Biochemistry, Greeley, CO 80639. Offers chemical education (MS, PhD); chemistry (MS). Part-time programs available. *Degree requirements:* For master's, comprehensive exam, thesis or alternative; for doctorate, comprehensive exam, thesis/dissertation. *Entrance requirements:* For master's, 3 letters of reference; for doctorate, GRE General Test, 3 letters of reference. Electronic applications accepted.

University of Northern Iowa, Graduate College, College of Humanities, Arts and Sciences, Department of Chemistry, Cedar Falls, IA 50614. Offers applied chemistry and biochemistry (PSM); chemistry (MA, MS). Part-time programs available. *Students:* 2 full-time (1 woman), 1 part-time (0 women). 4 applicants, 50% accepted, 1 enrolled. In 2012, 2 master's awarded. *Degree requirements:* For master's, comprehensive exam (for some programs), thesis (for some programs). *Entrance requirements:* For master's, minimum GPA of 3.0, 3 letters of recommendation. Additional exam requirements/recommendations for international students: Required—TOEFL (minimum score 500 paper-based; 61 iBT). *Application deadline:* For fall admission, 8/1 priority date for domestic students. Applications are processed on a rolling basis. Application fee: $50 ($70 for international students). Electronic applications accepted. *Financial support:* Career-related internships or fieldwork, Federal Work-Study, scholarships/grants, and tuition waivers (full and partial) available. Support available to part-time students. Financial award application deadline: 2/1. *Unit head:* Dr. William S. Harwood, Head, 319-273-2052, Fax: 319-273-7127, E-mail: bill.harwood@

92 www.petersonsbooks.com

Peterson's Graduate Programs in the Physical Sciences, Mathematics, Agricultural Sciences, the Environment & Natural Resources 2014

uni.edu. *Application contact:* Laurie S. Russell, Record Analyst, 319-273-2623, Fax: 319-273-2885, E-mail: laurie.russell@uni.edu. Website: http://www.chem.uni.edu/.

University of North Texas, Robert B. Toulouse School of Graduate Studies, Denton, TN 750603. Offers accounting (MS, PhD); applied anthropology (MA, MS); applied behavior analysis (Certificate); applied technology and performance improvement (M Ed, MS, PhD); art education (MA, PhD); art history (MA); art museum education (Certificate); arts leadership (Certificate); audiology (Au D); behavior analysis (MS); biochemistry and molecular biology (MS, PhD); biology (MA, MS, PhD); business (PhD); business computer information systems (PhD); chemistry (MS, PhD); clinical psychology (PhD); communication studies (MA, MS); computer engineering (MS); computer science (MS); computer science and engineering (PhD); counseling (M Ed, MS, PhD), including clinical mental health counseling (MS), college and university counseling (M Ed, MS), elementary school counseling (M Ed, MS), secondary school counseling (M Ed, MS); counseling psychology (PhD); creative writing (MA); criminal justice (MS); curriculum and instruction (M Ed, PhD), including curriculum studies (PhD), early childhood studies (PhD), language and literacy studies (PhD); decision sciences (MBA); design (MA, MFA), including fashion design (MFA), innovation studies, interior design (MFA); early childhood studies (MS); economics (MS); educational leadership (M Ed, Ed D, PhD); educational psychology (MS), including family studies, gifted and talented (MS, PhD), human development, learning and cognition, research, measurement and evaluation; educational research (PhD), including gifted and talented (MS, PhD), human development and family studies, psychological aspects of sports and exercise, research, measurement and statistics; electrical engineering (MS); emergency management (MPA); engineering systems (MS); English (MA, PhD); environmental science (MS, PhD); experimental psychology (PhD); finance (MBA, MS, PhD); financial management (MPA); French (MA); health psychology and behavioral medicine (PhD); health services management (MBA); higher education (M Ed, Ed D, PhD); history (MA, MS, PhD), including European history (PhD), military history (PhD), United States history (PhD); hospitality management (MS); human resources management (MPA); information science (MS, PhD); information technologies (MBA); information technology and decision sciences (MS); interdisciplinary studies (MA, MS); international sustainable tourism (MS); jazz studies (MM); journalism (MA, MJ, Graduate Certificate), including interactive and virtual digital communication (Graduate Certificate), narrative journalism (Graduate Certificate), public relations (Graduate Certificate); kinesiology (MS); learning technologies (MS, PhD); library science (MS); local government management (MPA); logistics and supply chain management (MBA, PhD); long-term care, senior housing, and aging services (MA, MS); management science (PhD); marketing (MBA, PhD); materials science and engineering (MS, PhD); mathematics (MA, PhD); merchandising (MS); music (MA, MM Ed, PhD), including ethnomusicology (MA), music education (MM Ed, PhD), music theory (MA, PhD), musicology (MA, PhD), performance (MA); nonprofit management (MPA); operations and supply chain management (MBA); performance (MM, DMA); philosophy (MA, PhD); physics (MS, PhD); political science (MA, MS, PhD); public administration and management (PhD), including emergency management, nonprofit management, public financial management, urban management; radio, television and film (MA, MFA); recreation, event and sport management (MS); rehabilitation counseling (MS, Certificate); sociology (MA, MS, PhD); Spanish (MA); special education (M Ed, PhD), including autism intervention (PhD), emotional/behavioral disorders (PhD), mild/moderate disabilities (PhD); speech-language pathology (MA, MS); strategic management (MBA); studio art (MFA); taxation (MS); teaching (M Ed); MBA/MS; MS/MPH; MSES/MBA. Part-time and evening/weekend programs available. Postbaccalaureate distance learning degree programs offered. *Faculty:* 665 full-time (219 women), 237 part-time/adjunct (135 women). *Students:* 3,206 full-time (1,712 women), 3,623 part-time (2,305 women); includes 1,742 minority (575 Black or African American, non-Hispanic/Latino; 16 American Indian or Alaska Native, non-Hispanic/Latino; 294 Asian, non-Hispanic/Latino; 690 Hispanic/Latino; 2 Native Hawaiian or other Pacific Islander, non-Hispanic/Latino; 165 Two or more races, non-Hispanic/Latino), 1,125 international. Average age 32. 6,094 applicants, 43% accepted, 1692 enrolled. In 2012, 1,910 master's, 237 doctorates awarded. Terminal master's awarded for partial completion of doctoral program. *Degree requirements:* For master's, variable foreign language requirement, comprehensive exam (for some programs), thesis (for some programs); for doctorate, variable foreign language requirement, comprehensive exam (for some programs), thesis/dissertation; for other advanced degree, variable foreign language requirement, comprehensive exam (for some programs). *Entrance requirements:* For master's and doctorate, GRE, GMAT. Additional exam requirements/recommendations for international students: Required—TOEFL (minimum score 550 paper-based; 79 iBT). *Application deadline:* For fall admission, 7/15 for domestic students, 3/15 for international students; for spring admission, 11/15 for domestic students, 9/15 for international students. Applications are processed on a rolling basis. Application fee: $60. Electronic applications accepted. *Expenses:* Tuition, state resident: full-time $5242; part-time $216 per credit hour. Tuition, nonresident: full-time $11,560; part-time $567 per credit hour. *Required fees:* $730 per semester. *Financial support:* Fellowships with partial tuition reimbursements, research assistantships with partial tuition reimbursements, teaching assistantships, career-related internships or fieldwork, Federal Work-Study, institutionally sponsored loans, scholarships/grants, and library assistantships available. Support available to part-time students. Financial award applicants required to submit FAFSA. *Unit head:* Mark Wardell, Dean, 940-565-2383, E-mail: mark.wardell@unt.edu. *Application contact:* Toulouse School of Graduate Studies, 940-565-2383, Fax: 940-565-2141, E-mail: gradsch@unt.edu. Website: http://www.tsgs.unt.edu/.

University of Notre Dame, Graduate School, College of Science, Department of Chemistry and Biochemistry, Notre Dame, IN 46556. Offers biochemistry (MS, PhD); inorganic chemistry (MS, PhD); organic chemistry (MS, PhD); physical chemistry (MS, PhD). Terminal master's awarded for partial completion of doctoral program. *Degree requirements:* For master's, comprehensive exam, thesis; for doctorate, thesis/dissertation, qualifying exam. *Entrance requirements:* For master's and doctorate, GRE General Test, GRE Subject Test (strongly recommended). Additional exam requirements/recommendations for international students: Required—TOEFL (minimum score 600 paper-based; 80 iBT). Electronic applications accepted. *Faculty research:* Reaction design and mechanistic studies; reactive intermediates; synthesis, structure and reactivity of organometallic cluster complexes and biologically active natural products; bioorganic chemistry; enzymology.

University of Oklahoma, College of Arts and Sciences, Department of Chemistry and Biochemistry, Norman, OK 73019. Offers bioinformatics (MS); chemistry (PhD). Part-time programs available. *Faculty:* 24 full-time (5 women). *Students:* 74 full-time (25 women), 23 part-time (10 women); includes 15 minority (3 Black or African American, non-Hispanic/Latino; 2 American Indian or Alaska Native, non-Hispanic/Latino; 2 Asian, non-Hispanic/Latino; 5 Hispanic/Latino; 3 Two or more races, non-Hispanic/Latino), 32 international. Average age 27. 127 applicants, 17% accepted, 22 enrolled. In 2012, 18 master's, 11 doctorates awarded. Terminal master's awarded for partial completion of doctoral program. *Degree requirements:* For master's, comprehensive exam (for some programs), thesis (for some programs); for doctorate, comprehensive exam, thesis/dissertation. *Entrance requirements:* For master's and doctorate, GRE. Additional exam requirements/recommendations for international students: Required—TOEFL (minimum score 550 paper-based; 79 iBT). *Application deadline:* For fall admission, 2/1 for domestic and international students; for spring admission, 9/1 for domestic and international students. Applications are processed on a rolling basis. Application fee: $40 ($90 for international students). Electronic applications accepted. *Expenses:* Tuition, state resident: full-time $4205; part-time $175.20 per credit hour. Tuition, nonresident: full-time $15,667; part-time $653 per credit hour. *Required fees:* $2745; $103.85 per credit hour. Tuition and fees vary according to course load and degree level. *Financial support:* In 2012–13, 3 fellowships with full tuition reimbursements (averaging $5,000 per year), 22 research assistantships with partial tuition reimbursements (averaging $16,019 per year), 57 teaching assistantships with partial tuition reimbursements (averaging $16,864 per year) were awarded; institutionally sponsored loans, scholarships/grants, health care benefits, tuition waivers (full), and unspecified assistantships also available. Support available to part-time students. Financial award application deadline: 6/1; financial award applicants required to submit FAFSA. *Faculty research:* Structural biology, synthesis and catalysis, natural products, membrane biochemistry, genomics. *Total annual research expenditures:* $6.5 million. *Unit head:* Dr. George Richter-Addo, Professor and Chair, 405-325-4812, Fax: 405-325-6111, E-mail: grichteraddo@ou.edu. *Application contact:* Angelika Tietz, Graduate Program Assistant, 405-325-4811 Ext. 62946, Fax: 405-325-6111, E-mail: atietz@ou.edu. Website: http://chem.ou.edu.

University of Oregon, Graduate School, College of Arts and Sciences, Department of Chemistry, Eugene, OR 97403. Offers biochemistry (MA, MS, PhD); chemistry (MA, MS, PhD). Terminal master's awarded for partial completion of doctoral program. *Degree requirements:* For doctorate, thesis/dissertation. *Entrance requirements:* For master's and doctorate, GRE General Test, minimum GPA of 3.0. Additional exam requirements/recommendations for international students: Required—TOEFL. *Faculty research:* Organic chemistry, organometallic chemistry, inorganic chemistry, physical chemistry, materials science, biochemistry, chemical physics, molecular or cell biology.

University of Ottawa, Faculty of Graduate and Postdoctoral Studies, Faculty of Science, Ottawa-Carleton Chemistry Institute, Ottawa, ON K1N 6N5, Canada. Offers M Sc, PhD. M Sc, PhD offered jointly with Carleton University. *Degree requirements:* For master's, thesis, seminar; for doctorate, comprehensive exam, thesis/dissertation, 2 seminars. *Entrance requirements:* For master's, honors B Sc degree or equivalent, minimum B average; for doctorate, honors B Sc with minimum B average or M Sc in chemistry with minimum B+ average. Electronic applications accepted. Tuition and fees charges are reported in Canadian dollars. *Expenses: Tuition, area resident:* Full-time $7074 Canadian dollars; part-time $256 Canadian dollars per credit. *International tuition:* $16,334 Canadian dollars full-time. *Required fees:* $738 Canadian dollars; $110 Canadian dollars per term. Part-time tuition and fees vary according to course load, program and student level. *Faculty research:* Organic chemistry, physical chemistry, inorganic chemistry.

University of Pennsylvania, School of Arts and Sciences, Graduate Group in Chemistry, Philadelphia, PA 19104. Offers MS, PhD. *Faculty:* 30 full-time (5 women), 11 part-time/adjunct (1 woman). *Students:* 190 full-time (81 women), 3 part-time (0 women); includes 24 minority (4 Black or African American, non-Hispanic/Latino; 12 Asian, non-Hispanic/Latino; 5 Hispanic/Latino; 3 Two or more races, non-Hispanic/Latino), 85 international. 501 applicants, 28% accepted, 45 enrolled. In 2012, 16 master's, 27 doctorates awarded. *Degree requirements:* For doctorate, thesis/dissertation. *Entrance requirements:* For doctorate, GRE General Test, GRE Subject Test, previous graduate course work in organic, inorganic, and physical chemistry, and general physics, each with a lab, as well as differential and integral calculus. Additional exam requirements/recommendations for international students: Required—TOEFL. *Application deadline:* For fall admission, 12/1 priority date for domestic students. Application fee: $70. Electronic applications accepted. *Financial support:* Fellowships, research assistantships, teaching assistantships, institutionally sponsored loans, scholarships/grants, traineeships, health care benefits, and unspecified assistantships available. Financial award application deadline: 12/15. *Application contact:* Arts and Sciences Graduate Admissions, 215-573-5816, Fax: 215-573-8068, E-mail: gdasadmis@sas.upenn.edu. Website: http://www.sas.upenn.edu/graduate-division.

University of Pittsburgh, Dietrich School of Arts and Sciences, Department of Chemistry, Pittsburgh, PA 15260. Offers MS, PhD. Part-time and evening/weekend programs available. *Faculty:* 33 full-time (5 women), 16 part-time/adjunct (4 women). *Students:* 199 full-time (49 women), 2 part-time (1 woman); includes 6 minority (2 Black or African American, non-Hispanic/Latino; 2 Asian, non-Hispanic/Latino; 2 Hispanic/Latino), 86 international. Average age 24. 279 applicants, 44% accepted, 45 enrolled. In 2012, 5 master's, 22 doctorates awarded. Terminal master's awarded for partial completion of doctoral program. *Degree requirements:* For master's, comprehensive exam, thesis; for doctorate, comprehensive exam, thesis/dissertation. *Entrance requirements:* For master's and doctorate, GRE General Test, GRE Subject Test. Additional exam requirements/recommendations for international students: Required—TOEFL (minimum score 600 paper-based; 100 iBT). *Application deadline:* For fall admission, 2/15 priority date for domestic students, 2/15 for international students. Applications are processed on a rolling basis. Application fee: $50. Electronic applications accepted. *Expenses:* Tuition, state resident: full-time $19,336; part-time $782 per credit. Tuition, nonresident: full-time $31,658; part-time $1295 per credit. *Required fees:* $740; $200 per term. Tuition and fees vary according to program. *Financial support:* In 2012–13, 201 students received support, including 8 fellowships with tuition reimbursements available (averaging $26,955 per year), 111 research assistantships with tuition reimbursements available (averaging $23,265 per year), 72 teaching assistantships with tuition reimbursements available (averaging $23,745 per year); Federal Work-Study, scholarships/grants, health care benefits, and unspecified assistantships also available. Financial award application deadline: 2/15. *Faculty research:* Analytical, biological, inorganic and materials including nanostructured materials, organic, physical and theoretical. *Total annual research expenditures:* $10.1 million. *Unit head:* Dr. David H. Waldeck, Chairman, 412-624-0415, Fax: 412-624-1649, E-mail: chemchr@pitt.edu. *Application contact:* Christie D. Hay, Graduate Program Administrator, 412-624-8501, Fax: 412-624-8611, E-mail: gradadm@pitt.edu. Website: http://www.chem.pitt.edu.

University of Prince Edward Island, Faculty of Science, Charlottetown, PE C1A 4P3, Canada. Offers biology (M Sc); chemistry (M Sc). *Degree requirements:* For master's, thesis. *Entrance requirements:* Additional exam requirements/recommendations for international students: Required—TOEFL (minimum score 550 paper-based; 80 iBT), Canadian Academic English Language Assessment, Michigan English Language Assessment Battery, Canadian Test of English for Scholars and Trainees. *Faculty research:* Ecology and wildlife biology, molecular, genetics and biotechnology, organametallic, bio-organic, supramolecular and synthetic organic chemistry, neurobiology and stoke materials science.

University of Puerto Rico, Mayagüez Campus, Graduate Studies, College of Arts and Sciences, Department of Chemistry, Mayagüez, PR 00681-9000. Offers chemistry (MS, PhD). Part-time programs available. *Faculty:* 37 full-time (19 women), 1 part-time/adjunct (0 women). *Students:* 80 full-time (45 women); includes 75 minority (all Hispanic/Latino), 24 international. 15 applicants, 100% accepted, 10 enrolled. In 2012, 3 master's, 2 doctorates awarded. *Degree requirements:* For master's, one foreign language, comprehensive exam, thesis; for doctorate, comprehensive exam, thesis/dissertation. *Entrance requirements:* For master's, GRE, BS in chemistry or the equivalent. *Application deadline:* For fall admission, 2/15 for domestic and international students; for spring admission, 9/15 for domestic and international students. Applications are processed on a rolling basis. Application fee: $25. Tuition and fees vary according to course level and course load. *Financial support:* In 2012–13, 29 research assistantships (averaging $15,000 per year), 34 teaching assistantships (averaging $8,500 per year) were awarded; Federal Work-Study and institutionally sponsored loans also available. *Faculty research:* Biochemistry, spectroscopy, food chemistry, physical chemistry, electrochemistry. *Unit head:* Dr. Rene Vieta, Director, 787-265-5458, Fax: 787-265-3849, E-mail: rene.vieta@upr.edu. Website: http://www.uprm.edu/wquim/.

University of Puerto Rico, Río Piedras, College of Natural Sciences, Department of Chemistry, San Juan, PR 00931-3300. Offers MS, PhD. Part-time programs available. *Degree requirements:* For master's, one foreign language, comprehensive exam, thesis; for doctorate, one foreign language, comprehensive exam, thesis/dissertation. *Entrance requirements:* For master's, GRE General Test, GRE Subject Test, interview, minimum GPA of 3.0, letter of recommendation; for doctorate, GRE General Test, GRE Subject Test, minimum GPA of 3.0, letter of recommendation. Additional exam requirements/recommendations for international students: Required—TOEFL.

University of Regina, Faculty of Graduate Studies and Research, Faculty of Science, Department of Chemistry and Biochemistry, Regina, SK S4S 0A2, Canada. Offers analytical/environmental chemistry (M Sc, PhD); biophysics of biological interfaces (M Sc, PhD); enzymology/chemical biology (M Sc, PhD); inorganic/organometallic chemistry (M Sc, PhD); signal transduction and mechanisms of cancer cell regulation (M Sc, PhD); supramolecular organic photochemistry and photophysics (M Sc, PhD); synthetic organic chemistry (M Sc, PhD); theoretical/computational chemistry (M Sc, PhD). *Faculty:* 12 full-time (2 women), 3 part-time/adjunct (0 women). *Students:* 11 full-time (6 women), 2 part-time (0 women). 32 applicants, 19% accepted. In 2012, 7 master's awarded. *Degree requirements:* For master's, thesis; for doctorate, thesis/dissertation. *Entrance requirements:* Additional exam requirements/recommendations for international students: Required—TOEFL (minimum score 580 paper-based; 80 iBT), IELTS (minimum score 6.5). *Application deadline:* Applications are processed on a rolling basis. Application fee: $100. Electronic applications accepted. Tuition and fees charges are reported in Canadian dollars. *Expenses: Tuition, area resident:* Full-time $3942 Canadian dollars; part-time $219 Canadian dollars per credit hour. *International tuition:* $4742 Canadian dollars full-time. *Required fees:* $421.55 Canadian dollars; $93.60 Canadian dollars per credit hour. Tuition and fees vary according to course load, degree level and program. *Financial support:* In 2012–13, 5 fellowships (averaging $7,000 per year), 10 teaching assistantships (averaging $2,470 per year) were awarded; research assistantships and scholarships/grants also available. Financial award application deadline: 6/15. *Faculty research:* Asymmetric synthesis and methodology, theoretical and computational chemistry, biophysical biochemistry, analytical and environmental chemistry, chemical biology. *Unit head:* Dr. Lynn Mihichuk, Head, 306-585-4793, Fax: 306-337-2409, E-mail: lynn.mihichuk@uregina.ca. *Application contact:* Dr. Brian Sterenberg, Graduate Program Coordinator, 306-585-4106, Fax: 306-337-2409, E-mail: brian.sterenberg@uregina.ca. Website: http://www.chem.uregina.ca/.

University of Rhode Island, Graduate School, College of Arts and Sciences, Department of Chemistry, Kingston, RI 02881. Offers MS, PhD. Part-time and evening/weekend programs available. *Faculty:* 18 full-time (6 women). *Students:* 54 full-time (24 women), 5 part-time (2 women); includes 6 minority (2 Black or African American, non-Hispanic/Latino; 3 Asian, non-Hispanic/Latino; 1 Hispanic/Latino), 15 international. In 2012, 9 master's, 6 doctorates awarded. *Degree requirements:* For master's, comprehensive exam (for some programs), thesis optional; for doctorate, comprehensive exam, thesis/dissertation. *Entrance requirements:* For master's and doctorate, GRE (for graduates of non-U.S. universities), 2 letters of recommendation. Additional exam requirements/recommendations for international students: Required—TOEFL (minimum score 550 paper-based). *Application deadline:* For fall admission, 7/15 for domestic students, 1/15 for international students; for spring admission, 11/15 for domestic students, 9/15 for international students. Application fee: $65. Electronic applications accepted. *Expenses:* Tuition, state resident: full-time $11,532; part-time $641 per credit. Tuition, nonresident: full-time $23,606; part-time $1311 per credit. *Required fees:* $1388; $36 per credit. $35 per semester. One-time fee: $130. *Financial support:* In 2012–13, 6 research assistantships with full tuition reimbursements (averaging $7,900 per year), 36 teaching assistantships with full tuition reimbursements (averaging $13,918 per year) were awarded. Financial award applicants required to submit FAFSA. *Faculty research:* Analytical chemistry, biochemistry, analytical/nanoscience, materials/analytical, theoretical chemistry. *Unit head:* Dr. William Euler, Chairperson, 401-874-5090, Fax: 401-874-5072, E-mail: weuler@chm.uri.edu. Website: http://www.chm.uri.edu/index.php.

University of Rochester, School of Arts and Sciences, Department of Chemistry, Rochester, NY 14627. Offers PhD. Terminal master's awarded for partial completion of doctoral program. *Degree requirements:* For doctorate, thesis/dissertation, qualifying exam. *Entrance requirements:* For doctorate, GRE General Test, undergraduate transcript, three letters of recommendation. Additional exam requirements/recommendations for international students: Required—TOEFL. Electronic applications accepted. *Faculty research:* Organic, inorganic, physical, biological, theoretical.

University of Saint Joseph, Department of Chemistry, West Hartford, CT 06117-2700. Offers biochemistry (MS); chemistry (MS). Part-time and evening/weekend programs available. Postbaccalaureate distance learning degree programs offered. *Degree requirements:* For master's, comprehensive exam, thesis optional. *Entrance requirements:* For master's, 2 letters of recommendation. Electronic applications accepted. Application fee is waived when completed online. *Expenses: Tuition:* Full-time $30,408; part-time $670 per credit. *Required fees:* $1418; $40 per credit. Tuition and fees vary according to course load, degree level and program.

University of San Francisco, College of Arts and Sciences, Chemistry Program, San Francisco, CA 94117-1080. Offers MS. Part-time and evening/weekend programs available. *Faculty:* 3 full-time (1 woman). *Students:* 13 full-time (6 women); includes 3 minority (2 Asian, non-Hispanic/Latino; 1 Hispanic/Latino), 2 international. Average age 25. 51 applicants, 6% accepted, 3 enrolled. In 2012, 1 master's awarded. *Degree requirements:* For master's, thesis. *Entrance requirements:* For master's, GRE General Test, GRE Subject Test, BS in chemistry or related field. *Application deadline:* For fall admission, 2/1 for domestic students; for spring admission, 10/15 for domestic students. Applications are processed on a rolling basis. Application fee: $55 ($65 for international students). *Expenses: Tuition:* Full-time $20,340; part-time $1130 per credit hour. Part-time tuition and fees vary according to course load, degree level, campus/location and program. *Financial support:* In 2012–13, 13 students received support. Fellowships, research assistantships, teaching assistantships, career-related internships or fieldwork, Federal Work-Study, institutionally sponsored loans, and tuition waivers (partial) available. Support available to part-time students. Financial award application deadline: 3/2; financial award applicants required to submit FAFSA. *Faculty research:* Organic photochemistry, genetics of chromatic adaptation, electron transfer processes in solution, metabolism of protein hormones. *Total annual research expenditures:* $75,000. *Unit head:* Dr. Jeff Curtis, Chair, 415-422-6157, Fax: 415-422-5157. *Application contact:* Information Contact, 415-422-5135, Fax: 415-422-2217, E-mail: asgraduate@usfca.edu. Website: http://www.usfca.edu/artsci/chemg/.

University of Saskatchewan, College of Graduate Studies and Research, College of Arts and Science, Department of Chemistry, Saskatoon, SK S7N 5A2, Canada. Offers M Sc, PhD. *Degree requirements:* For master's, thesis; for doctorate, comprehensive exam (for some programs), thesis/dissertation. *Entrance requirements:* Additional exam requirements/recommendations for international students: Required—TOEFL (minimum score 80 iBT); Recommended—IELTS (minimum score 6.5). Electronic applications accepted.

The University of Scranton, College of Graduate and Continuing Education, Department of Chemistry, Program in Chemistry, Scranton, PA 18510. Offers MA, MS. Part-time and evening/weekend programs available. *Faculty:* 10 full-time (3 women), 1 part-time/adjunct (0 women). *Students:* 8 full-time (5 women), 3 part-time (1 woman), 4 international. Average age 29. 28 applicants, 11% accepted. In 2012, 1 master's awarded. *Degree requirements:* For master's, comprehensive exam (for some programs), thesis (for some programs), capstone experience. *Entrance requirements:* For master's, minimum GPA of 3.0. Additional exam requirements/recommendations for international students: Required—TOEFL (minimum score 500 paper-based), IELTS (minimum score 6). *Application deadline:* Applications are processed on a rolling basis. Application fee: $0. *Financial support:* Fellowships, teaching assistantships, career-related internships or fieldwork, Federal Work-Study, and unspecified assistantships available. Support available to part-time students. Financial award application deadline: 3/1. *Unit head:* Dr. Christopher A. Baumann, Director, 570-941-6389, Fax: 570-941-7510, E-mail: cab@scranton.edu.

The University of Scranton, College of Graduate and Continuing Education, Department of Chemistry, Program in Clinical Chemistry, Scranton, PA 18510. Offers MA, MS. Part-time and evening/weekend programs available. *Faculty:* 10 full-time (3 women), 1 part-time/adjunct (0 women). *Students:* 18 full-time (15 women), 2 part-time (both women), 11 international. Average age 26. 17 applicants, 29% accepted. In 2012, 5 master's awarded. *Degree requirements:* For master's, comprehensive exam (for some programs), thesis (for some programs), capstone experience. *Entrance requirements:* For master's, minimum GPA of 3.0. Additional exam requirements/recommendations for international students: Required—TOEFL (minimum score 500 paper-based), IELTS (minimum score 6). *Application deadline:* Applications are processed on a rolling basis. Application fee: $0. *Financial support:* Fellowships, teaching assistantships, career-related internships or fieldwork, Federal Work-Study, and unspecified assistantships available. Support available to part-time students. Financial award application deadline: 3/1. *Unit head:* Dr. Christopher A. Baumann, Director, 570-941-6389, Fax: 570-941-7510, E-mail: cab@scranton.edu.

University of South Carolina, The Graduate School, College of Arts and Sciences, Department of Chemistry and Biochemistry, Columbia, SC 29208. Offers IMA, MAT, MS, PhD. IMA and MAT offered in cooperation with the College of Education. Part-time programs available. Terminal master's awarded for partial completion of doctoral program. *Degree requirements:* For master's, comprehensive exam, thesis; for doctorate, comprehensive exam, thesis/dissertation. *Entrance requirements:* For master's and doctorate, GRE General Test. Additional exam requirements/recommendations for international students: Required—TOEFL. Electronic applications accepted. *Faculty research:* Spectroscopy, crystallography, organic and organometallic synthesis, analytical chemistry, materials.

The University of South Dakota, Graduate School, College of Arts and Sciences, Department of Chemistry, Vermillion, SD 57069-2390. Offers MS, PhD. *Degree requirements:* For master's, comprehensive exam, thesis. *Entrance requirements:* For master's, minimum GPA of 2.7; for doctorate, GRE, minimum GPA of 2.7. Additional exam requirements/recommendations for international students: Required—TOEFL (minimum score 550 paper-based; 79 iBT), GRE. Electronic applications accepted. *Faculty research:* Electrochemistry, photochemistry, inorganic synthesis, environmental and solid-state chemistry.

University of Southern California, Graduate School, Dana and David Dornsife College of Letters, Arts and Sciences, Department of Chemistry, Los Angeles, CA 90089. Offers chemistry (PhD); physical chemistry (PhD). Terminal master's awarded for partial completion of doctoral program. *Degree requirements:* For doctorate, thesis/dissertation. *Entrance requirements:* For doctorate, GRE General Test. Additional exam requirements/recommendations for international students: Required—TOEFL. Electronic applications accepted. *Faculty research:* Biological chemistry, inorganic chemistry, organic chemistry, physical chemistry, theoretical chemistry.

University of Southern Mississippi, Graduate School, College of Science and Technology, Department of Chemistry and Biochemistry, Hattiesburg, MS 39406-0001. Offers analytical chemistry (MS, PhD); biochemistry (MS, PhD); inorganic chemistry (MS, PhD); organic chemistry (MS, PhD); physical chemistry (MS, PhD). *Faculty:* 16 full-time (4 women). *Students:* 26 full-time (9 women); includes 2 minority (1 Black or African American, non-Hispanic/Latino; 1 Asian, non-Hispanic/Latino), 8 international. Average age 27. 63 applicants, 13% accepted, 4 enrolled. In 2012, 2 master's, 4 doctorates awarded. *Degree requirements:* For master's, comprehensive exam, thesis; for doctorate, comprehensive exam, thesis/dissertation. *Entrance requirements:* For master's, GRE General Test, minimum GPA of 2.75 in last 60 hours; for doctorate, GRE General Test, minimum GPA of 3.5. Additional exam requirements/recommendations for international students: Required—TOEFL, IELTS. *Application deadline:* For fall admission, 3/1 priority date for domestic students, 3/1 for international students. Applications are processed on a rolling basis. Application fee: $50. *Financial support:* In 2012–13, 3 research assistantships with full tuition reimbursements (averaging $17,000 per year), 19 teaching assistantships with full tuition reimbursements (averaging $20,700 per year) were awarded; fellowships, Federal Work-Study, institutionally sponsored loans, scholarships/grants, health care benefits, and unspecified assistantships also available. Support available to part-time students. Financial award application deadline: 3/15; financial award applicants required to submit FAFSA. *Faculty research:* Plant biochemistry, photo chemistry, polymer chemistry, x-ray analysis, enzyme chemistry. *Unit head:* Dr. Sabine Heinhorst, Chair, 601-266-4701, Fax: 601-266-6075. Website: http://www.usm.edu/graduateschool/table.php.

University of South Florida, Graduate School, College of Arts and Sciences, Department of Chemistry, Tampa, FL 33620-9951. Offers analytical chemistry (MS, PhD); biochemistry (MS, PhD); computational chemistry (MS, PhD); environmental chemistry (MS, PhD); inorganic chemistry (MS, PhD); organic chemistry (MS); physical chemistry (MS, PhD); polymer chemistry (PhD). Part-time programs available. Terminal master's awarded for partial completion of doctoral program. *Degree requirements:* For master's, comprehensive exam, thesis (for some programs); for doctorate, comprehensive exam, thesis/dissertation. *Entrance requirements:* For master's and doctorate, GRE General Test, minimum GPA of 3.0. Additional exam requirements/recommendations for international students: Required—TOEFL (minimum score 550 paper-based; 79 iBT) or IELTS (minimum score 6.5). Electronic applications accepted. *Faculty research:* Synthesis, bio-organic chemistry, bioinorganic chemistry, environmental chemistry, nuclear magnetic resonance (NMR).

The University of Tennessee, Graduate School, College of Arts and Sciences, Department of Chemistry, Knoxville, TN 37996. Offers analytical chemistry (MS, PhD); chemical physics (PhD); environmental chemistry (MS, PhD); inorganic chemistry (MS, PhD); organic chemistry (MS, PhD); physical chemistry (MS, PhD); polymer chemistry (MS, PhD); theoretical chemistry (PhD). Part-time programs available. Terminal master's awarded for partial completion of doctoral program. *Degree requirements:* For master's, thesis; for doctorate, thesis/dissertation. *Entrance requirements:* For master's and doctorate, GRE General Test, minimum GPA of 2.7. Additional exam requirements/recommendations for international students: Required—TOEFL. Electronic applications accepted. *Expenses:* Tuition, state resident: full-time $9000; part-time $501 per credit hour. Tuition, nonresident: full-time $27,188; part-time $1512 per credit hour. *Required fees:* $1280; $62 per credit hour. Tuition and fees vary according to program.

The University of Texas at Arlington, Graduate School, College of Science, Department of Chemistry and Biochemistry, Arlington, TX 76019. Offers chemistry (MS, PhD). Part-time programs available. Terminal master's awarded for partial completion of doctoral program. *Degree requirements:* For master's, comprehensive exam (for some programs), thesis optional; for doctorate, comprehensive exam, thesis/dissertation, internship, oral defense of dissertation. *Entrance requirements:* For master's and doctorate, GRE General Test, minimum GPA of 3.0 in last 60 hours of course work; BS in STEM field (preferably chemistry or biochemistry) or equivalent 4-year minimum program. Additional exam requirements/recommendations for international students: Required—TOEFL (minimum score 550 paper-based; 80 iBT). Electronic applications accepted.

The University of Texas at Austin, Graduate School, College of Natural Sciences, Department of Chemistry and Biochemistry, Austin, TX 78712-1111. Offers analytical chemistry (PhD); biochemistry (PhD); inorganic chemistry (PhD); organic chemistry (PhD); physical chemistry (PhD). *Entrance requirements:* For doctorate, GRE General Test.

The University of Texas at Dallas, School of Natural Sciences and Mathematics, Department of Chemistry, Richardson, TX 75080. Offers MS, PhD. Part-time and evening/weekend programs available. *Faculty:* 20 full-time (2 women), 5 part-time/adjunct (4 women). *Students:* 65 full-time (33 women), 6 part-time (5 women); includes 8 minority (5 Asian, non-Hispanic/Latino; 3 Hispanic/Latino), 46 international. Average age 28. 116 applicants, 22% accepted, 22 enrolled. In 2012, 5 master's, 4 doctorates awarded. *Degree requirements:* For master's, thesis or internship; for doctorate, comprehensive exam, thesis/dissertation, research practica. *Entrance requirements:* For master's and doctorate, GRE General Test, minimum GPA of 3.0 in upper-level course work in field. Additional exam requirements/recommendations for international students: Required—TOEFL (minimum score 600 paper-based). *Application deadline:* For fall admission, 7/15 for domestic students, 5/1 for international students; for spring admission, 11/15 for domestic students, 9/1 for international students. Applications are processed on a rolling basis. Application fee: $50 ($100 for international students). Electronic applications accepted. *Expenses:* Tuition, state resident: full-time $11,940; part-time $663.33 per credit hour. Tuition, nonresident: full-time $21,606; part-time $1200.33 per credit hour. Tuition and fees vary according to course load. *Financial support:* In 2012–13, 58 students received support, including 32 research assistantships with partial tuition reimbursements available (averaging $21,750 per year), 31 teaching assistantships with partial tuition reimbursements available (averaging $15,474 per year); career-related internships or fieldwork, Federal Work-Study, institutionally sponsored loans,

Peterson's Graduate Programs in the Physical Sciences, Mathematics, Agricultural Sciences, the Environment & Natural Resources 2014

www.petersonsbooks.com 95

scholarships/grants, and unspecified assistantships also available. Support available to part-time students. Financial award application deadline: 4/30; financial award applicants required to submit FAFSA. *Faculty research:* Advanced nano-materials; novel MRI agents; peptidomimetics to treat diabetes; semiconducting polymers for organic electronics; macrocyclic receptors for catalysis, medicine, materials science; electroactive polymers. *Unit head:* Dr. John P. Ferraris, Department Head, 972-883-2901, Fax: 972-883-2925, E-mail: chemistry@utdallas.edu. *Application contact:* Dr. Inga Holl Musselman, Associate Department Head, 972-883-2706, Fax: 972-883-2925, E-mail: imusselm@utdallas.edu. Website: http://www.utdallas.edu/chemistry/.

The University of Texas at El Paso, Graduate School, College of Science, Department of Chemistry, El Paso, TX 79968-0001. Offers MS, PhD. Part-time and evening/weekend programs available. *Degree requirements:* For master's, thesis; for doctorate, thesis/dissertation. *Entrance requirements:* For master's, GRE, minimum GPA of 3.0; for doctorate, GRE, letters of recommendation. Additional exam requirements/recommendations for international students: Required—TOEFL; Recommended—IELTS. Electronic applications accepted.

The University of Texas at San Antonio, College of Sciences, Department of Chemistry, San Antonio, TX 78249-0617. Offers MS, PhD. *Faculty:* 15 full-time (1 woman), 2 part-time/adjunct (0 women). *Students:* 39 full-time (24 women), 22 part-time (9 women); includes 20 minority (1 Black or African American, non-Hispanic/Latino; 5 Asian, non-Hispanic/Latino; 9 Hispanic/Latino; 5 Two or more races, non-Hispanic/Latino), 21 international. Average age 28. 73 applicants, 44% accepted, 22 enrolled. In 2012, 7 master's, 3 doctorates awarded. *Degree requirements:* For master's, comprehensive exam, thesis optional; for doctorate, comprehensive exam, thesis/dissertation. *Entrance requirements:* For master's, GRE General Test, minimum GPA of 3.0 in all undergraduate chemistry courses, 2 letters of recommendation; for doctorate, GRE, official transcripts from all colleges and universities attended, resume or curriculum vitae, at least 2 letters of recommendation, statement of purpose. Additional exam requirements/recommendations for international students: Required—TOEFL (minimum score 500 paper-based; 61 iBT), IELTS (minimum score 5). *Application deadline:* For fall admission, 7/1 for domestic students, 4/1 for international students; for spring admission, 11/1 for domestic students, 9/1 for international students. Application fee: $45 ($85 for international students). *Financial support:* In 2012–13, 48 students received support, including 12 fellowships with full tuition reimbursements available (averaging $21,000 per year), 12 research assistantships with full tuition reimbursements available (averaging $25,000 per year), 24 teaching assistantships with full tuition reimbursements available (averaging $13,000 per year). *Faculty research:* Medicinal chemistry, biosensors, mass spectrometry, organic synthesis, enzymatic mechanisms. *Total annual research expenditures:* $1.7 million. *Unit head:* Dr. Waldemar Gorski, Department Chair, 210-458-5469, Fax: 210-458-7428, E-mail: waldemar.gorski@utsa.edu. *Application contact:* Dr. Stephan Bach, Graduate Advisor of Record, 210-458-6896, Fax: 210-458-7428, E-mail: stephan.bach@utsa.edu.

The University of Texas–Pan American, College of Science and Mathematics, Department of Chemistry, Edinburg, TX 78539. Offers MS, MSIS. *Expenses:* Tuition, state resident: full-time $1800; part-time $100 per credit hour. Tuition, nonresident: full-time $8118; part-time $451 per credit hour. *Required fees:* $403.45 per credit hour. Tuition and fees vary according to course load.

University of the Sciences, College of Graduate Studies, Program in Chemistry, Biochemistry and Pharmacognosy, Philadelphia, PA 19104-4495. Offers biochemistry (MS, PhD); chemistry (MS, PhD); pharmacognosy (MS, PhD). Part-time programs available. *Degree requirements:* For master's, thesis, qualifying exams; for doctorate, comprehensive exam, thesis/dissertation, qualifying exams. *Entrance requirements:* For master's and doctorate, GRE General Test, GRE Subject Test. Additional exam requirements/recommendations for international students: Required—TOEFL, TWE. *Expenses:* Contact institution. *Faculty research:* Organic and medicinal synthesis, mass spectroscopy use in protein analysis, study of analogues of taxol, cholesteryl esters.

The University of Toledo, College of Graduate Studies, College of Natural Sciences and Mathematics, Department of Chemistry, Toledo, OH 43606-3390. Offers analytical chemistry (MS, PhD); biological chemistry (MS, PhD); inorganic chemistry (MS, PhD); organic chemistry (MS, PhD); physical chemistry (MS, PhD). Part-time programs available. *Faculty:* 23. *Students:* 66 full-time (20 women), 9 part-time (2 women); includes 3 minority (1 Asian, non-Hispanic/Latino; 2 Hispanic/Latino), 50 international. Average age 27. 84 applicants, 26% accepted, 19 enrolled. In 2012, 6 master's, 7 doctorates awarded. *Degree requirements:* For master's, thesis or alternative; for doctorate, thesis/dissertation. *Entrance requirements:* For master's and doctorate, GRE General Test; GRE Subject Test, minimum cumulative point-hour ratio of 2.7 for all previous academic work, three letters of recommendation, statement of purpose, transcripts from all prior institutions attended. Additional exam requirements/recommendations for international students: Required—TOEFL (minimum score 550 paper-based; 80 iBT), IELTS (minimum score 6.5). *Application deadline:* For fall admission, 1/15 priority date for domestic students, 1/15 for international students. Applications are processed on a rolling basis. Application fee: $45 ($75 for international students). Electronic applications accepted. *Financial support:* In 2012–13, 29 research assistantships with full and partial tuition reimbursements (averaging $16,200 per year), 49 teaching assistantships with full and partial tuition reimbursements (averaging $15,682 per year) were awarded; Federal Work-Study, institutionally sponsored loans, scholarships/grants, tuition waivers (full), and unspecified assistantships also available. Support available to part-time students. *Faculty research:* Enzymology, materials chemistry, crystallography, theoretical chemistry. *Unit head:* Dr. Ronald Viola, Chair, 419-530-1582, Fax: 419-530-4033, E-mail: ronald.viola@utoledo.edu. *Application contact:* Graduate School Office, 419-530-4723, Fax: 419-530-4724, E-mail: grdsch@utnet.utoledo.edu. Website: http://www.utoledo.edu/nsm/.

University of Toronto, School of Graduate Studies, Faculty of Arts and Science, Department of Chemistry, Toronto, ON M5S 1A1, Canada. Offers M Sc, PhD. *Degree requirements:* For master's, thesis; for doctorate, thesis/dissertation, oral exam, thesis defense. *Entrance requirements:* For master's, bachelor's degree in chemistry or a related field; for doctorate, master's degree in chemistry or a related field. Additional exam requirements/recommendations for international students: Required—TOEFL (minimum score 580 paper-based; 93 iBT), TWE (minimum score 4). Electronic applications accepted.

University of Tulsa, Graduate School, College of Engineering and Natural Sciences, Department of Chemistry and Biochemistry, Program in Chemistry, Tulsa, OK 74104-3189. Offers MS, PhD. Part-time programs available. *Faculty:* 10 full-time (1 woman). *Students:* 15 full-time (6 women), 2 part-time (1 woman), 5 international. Average age 30. 20 applicants, 60% accepted, 5 enrolled. In 2012, 1 doctorate awarded. Terminal master's awarded for partial completion of doctoral program. *Degree requirements:* For master's, thesis (for some programs); for doctorate, comprehensive exam, thesis/dissertation. *Entrance requirements:* For master's, GRE General Test. Additional exam requirements/recommendations for international students: Required—TOEFL (minimum score 550 paper-based; 80 iBT), IELTS (minimum score 6). *Application deadline:* Applications are processed on a rolling basis. Application fee: $40. Electronic applications accepted. *Expenses: Tuition:* Full-time $18,630. *Required fees:* $1340; $5 per credit hour. $75 per semester. Tuition and fees vary according to course load. *Financial support:* In 2012–13, 17 students received support, including 4 fellowships (averaging $1,510 per year), 7 research assistantships with full tuition reimbursements available (averaging $11,721 per year), 8 teaching assistantships with full tuition reimbursements available (averaging $12,583 per year); career-related internships or fieldwork, Federal Work-Study, scholarships/grants, health care benefits, tuition waivers (full and partial), and unspecified assistantships also available. Support available to part-time students. Financial award application deadline: 2/1; financial award applicants required to submit FAFSA. *Total annual research expenditures:* $333,602. *Unit head:* Dr. Dale C. Teeters, Chairperson, 918-631-2515, Fax: 918-631-3404, E-mail: dale-teeters@utulsa.edu. *Application contact:* Dr. Kenneth Roberts, Advisor, 918-631-3090, Fax: 918-631-3404, E-mail: kproberts@utulsa.edu. Website: http://www.chemistry.utulsa.edu/.

University of Utah, Graduate School, College of Science, Department of Chemistry, Salt Lake City, UT 84112-0850. Offers chemical physics (PhD); chemistry (M Phil, MA, MS, PhD); science teacher education (MS). Part-time programs available. Postbaccalaureate distance learning degree programs offered. *Faculty:* 32 full-time (7 women), 1 part-time/adjunct (0 women). *Students:* 146 full-time (43 women), 29 part-time (14 women); includes 4 minority (1 Black or African American, non-Hispanic/Latino; 1 Asian, non-Hispanic/Latino; 1 Hispanic/Latino; 1 Two or more races, non-Hispanic/Latino), 51 international. Average age 28. 290 applicants, 32% accepted, 38 enrolled. In 2012, 14 master's, 22 doctorates awarded. Terminal master's awarded for partial completion of doctoral program. *Degree requirements:* For master's, thesis optional, 20 hours of course work, 10 hours of research; for doctorate, thesis/dissertation, 18 hours of course work, 14 hours of research. *Entrance requirements:* For master's and doctorate, GRE General Test, minimum GPA of 3.0. Additional exam requirements/recommendations for international students: Required—TOEFL (minimum score 620 paper-based; 105 iBT). *Application deadline:* For fall admission, 4/1 for domestic students, 2/1 for international students; for spring admission, 11/1 for domestic and international students. Application fee: $55 ($65 for international students). Electronic applications accepted. Application fee is waived when completed online. *Financial support:* In 2012–13, 1 fellowship with tuition reimbursement (averaging $22,000 per year), 119 research assistantships with tuition reimbursements (averaging $22,500 per year), 55 teaching assistantships with tuition reimbursements (averaging $22,000 per year) were awarded; scholarships/grants and tuition waivers (full) also available. Financial award application deadline: 4/1; financial award applicants required to submit FAFSA. *Faculty research:* Biological, theoretical, inorganic, organic, and physical-analytical chemistry. *Total annual research expenditures:* $13.3 million. *Unit head:* Dr. Henry S. White, Chair, 801-585-6256, Fax: 801-581-8433, E-mail: chair@chemistry.utah.edu. *Application contact:* Jo Hoovey, Graduate Coordinator, 801-581-4393, Fax: 801-581-5408, E-mail: jhoovey@chem.utah.edu. Website: http://www.chem.utah.edu/.

University of Vermont, Graduate College, College of Arts and Sciences, Department of Chemistry, Burlington, VT 05405. Offers chemistry (MS, PhD). *Students:* 41 (17 women); includes 1 minority (American Indian or Alaska Native, non-Hispanic/Latino), 12 international. 70 applicants, 47% accepted, 9 enrolled. In 2012, 3 master's, 5 doctorates awarded. *Degree requirements:* For master's, one foreign language, thesis; for doctorate, 2 foreign languages, thesis/dissertation. *Entrance requirements:* For master's and doctorate, GRE General Test. Additional exam requirements/recommendations for international students: Required—TOEFL (minimum score 550 paper-based; 80 iBT). *Application deadline:* For fall admission, 4/1 priority date for domestic students, 4/1 for international students. Applications are processed on a rolling basis. Application fee: $40. Electronic applications accepted. *Expenses: Tuition, area resident:* Part-time $572 per credit. Tuition, nonresident: part-time $1444 per credit. *Financial support:* Fellowships, research assistantships, and teaching assistantships available. Financial award application deadline: 3/1. *Unit head:* Dr. Dwight Matthews, Chairperson, 802-656-2594. *Application contact:* Dr. Rory Waterman, Coordinator, 802-656-2594.

University of Victoria, Faculty of Graduate Studies, Faculty of Science, Department of Chemistry, Victoria, BC V8W 2Y2, Canada. Offers M Sc, PhD. *Degree requirements:* For master's, thesis; for doctorate, thesis/dissertation, candidacy exam. *Entrance requirements:* For master's and doctorate, GRE Subject Test. Additional exam requirements/recommendations for international students: Required—TOEFL (minimum score 575 paper-based), IELTS (minimum score 7). Electronic applications accepted. *Faculty research:* Laser spectroscopy and dynamics; inorganic, organic, and organometallic synthesis; electro and surface chemistry.

University of Virginia, College and Graduate School of Arts and Sciences, Department of Chemistry, Charlottesville, VA 22903. Offers MA, MS, PhD. *Faculty:* 24 full-time (4 women), 1 (woman) part-time/adjunct. *Students:* 100 full-time (42 women); includes 6 minority (2 Black or African American, non-Hispanic/Latino; 3 Asian, non-Hispanic/Latino; 1 Hispanic/Latino), 24 international. Average age 25. 218 applicants, 35% accepted, 27 enrolled. In 2012, 8 master's, 15 doctorates awarded. *Degree requirements:* For master's, comprehensive exam, thesis; for doctorate, comprehensive exam, thesis/dissertation. *Entrance requirements:* For master's and doctorate, GRE General Test; GRE Subject Test (recommended). Additional exam requirements/recommendations for international students: Required—TOEFL (minimum score 600 paper-based; 90 iBT), IELTS (minimum score 7). *Application deadline:* For fall admission, 2/1 for domestic and international students. Application fee: $60. Electronic applications accepted. *Expenses:* Tuition, state resident: full-time $13,278; part-time $717 per credit hour. Tuition, nonresident: full-time $22,602; part-time $1235 per credit hour. *Required fees:* $2384. *Financial support:* Fellowships and teaching assistantships available. Financial award applicants required to submit FAFSA. *Unit head:* Dean Harman, Chairman, 434-924-3344, Fax: 434-924-3710, E-mail: chem@virginia.edu. *Application contact:* Susan Marshall, Graduate Studies Administrative Assistant, 434-924-7014, Fax: 434-924-6737, E-mail: sem8h@virginia.edu. Website: http://www.virginia.edu/chem/.

University of Washington, Graduate School, College of Arts and Sciences, Department of Chemistry, Seattle, WA 98195. Offers MS, PhD. Terminal master's awarded for partial completion of doctoral program. *Degree requirements:* For master's, thesis (for some programs); for doctorate, thesis/dissertation. *Entrance requirements:* For master's and doctorate, GRE Subject Test, minimum GPA of 3.0. Additional exam requirements/recommendations for international students: Required—TOEFL. *Faculty research:* Biopolymers, material science and nanotechnology, organometallic chemistry, analytical chemistry, bioorganic chemistry.

University of Waterloo, Graduate Studies, Faculty of Science, Guelph-Waterloo Centre for Graduate Work in Chemistry and Biochemistry, Waterloo, ON N2L 3G1, Canada. Offers M Sc, PhD. M Sc, PhD offered jointly with University of Guelph. Part-time programs available. *Degree requirements:* For master's and doctorate, project or thesis. *Entrance requirements:* For master's, GRE, honors degree, minimum B average; for doctorate, GRE, master's degree, minimum B average. Additional exam requirements/recommendations for international students: Required—TOEFL, TWE. Electronic applications accepted. *Faculty research:* Polymer, physical, inorganic, organic, and theoretical chemistry.

The University of Western Ontario, Faculty of Graduate Studies, Physical Sciences Division, Department of Chemistry, London, ON N6A 5B8, Canada. Offers M Sc, PhD. *Degree requirements:* For master's, thesis; for doctorate, thesis/dissertation. *Entrance requirements:* For master's, minimum B+ average, honors B Sc in chemistry; for doctorate, M Sc or equivalent in chemistry. Additional exam requirements/recommendations for international students: Required—TOEFL (paper-based 570) or IELTS (6). *Faculty research:* Materials, inorganic, organic, physical and theoretical chemistry.

University of Windsor, Faculty of Graduate Studies, Faculty of Science, Department of Chemistry and Biochemistry, Windsor, ON N9B 3P4, Canada. Offers M Sc, PhD. Part-time programs available. *Degree requirements:* For master's, thesis; for doctorate, comprehensive exam, thesis/dissertation. *Entrance requirements:* For master's and doctorate, minimum B average. Additional exam requirements/recommendations for international students: Required—TOEFL (minimum score 560 paper-based). Electronic applications accepted. *Faculty research:* Molecular biology/recombinant DNA techniques (PCR, cloning mutagenesis), No/02 detectors, western immunoblotting and detection, CD/NMR protein/peptide structure determination, confocal/electron microscopes.

University of Wisconsin–Madison, Graduate School, College of Engineering, Program in Environmental Chemistry and Technology, Madison, WI 53706. Offers MS, PhD. Part-time programs available. *Faculty:* 17 full-time (3 women). *Students:* 18 full-time (12 women); includes 3 minority (1 Black or African American, non-Hispanic/Latino; 2 Hispanic/Latino), 3 international. 58 applicants. In 2012, 2 doctorates awarded. Terminal master's awarded for partial completion of doctoral program. *Degree requirements:* For master's, thesis or alternative; for doctorate, thesis/dissertation. *Entrance requirements:* For master's and doctorate, GRE General Test. Additional exam requirements/recommendations for international students: Required—TOEFL. *Application deadline:* For fall admission, 1/1 priority date for domestic students, 1/1 for international students. Application fee: $45. Electronic applications accepted. *Expenses:* Tuition, state resident: full-time $10,728; part-time $743 per credit. Tuition, nonresident: full-time $24,054; part-time $1575 per credit. *Required fees:* $1111; $72 per credit. *Financial support:* In 2012–13, 3 fellowships with full tuition reimbursements (averaging $20,200 per year), 15 research assistantships with full tuition reimbursements (averaging $20,200 per year) were awarded; Federal Work-Study and institutionally sponsored loans also available. Financial award application deadline: 1/1. *Faculty research:* Chemical limnology, chemical remediation, geochemistry, photocatalysis, water quality. *Unit head:* Dr. Marc A. Anderson, Chair, 608-263-3264, E-mail: nanopor@wisc.edu. *Application contact:* Mary Possin, Student Services Coordinator, 608-263-3264, Fax: 608-265-2340, E-mail: mcpossin@wisc.edu. Website: http://www.engr.edu/interd/wcp/.

University of Wisconsin–Madison, Graduate School, College of Letters and Science, Department of Chemistry, Madison, WI 53706-1380. Offers MS, PhD. Part-time programs available. Terminal master's awarded for partial completion of doctoral program. *Degree requirements:* For master's, thesis (for some programs); for doctorate, thesis/dissertation, cumulative exams, research proposal, seminar. *Entrance requirements:* For master's and doctorate, GRE, minimum GPA of 3.0. Additional exam requirements/recommendations for international students: Required—TOEFL. Electronic applications accepted. *Expenses:* Tuition, state resident: full-time $10,728; part-time $743 per credit. Tuition, nonresident: full-time $24,054; part-time $1575 per credit. *Required fees:* $1111; $72 per credit. *Faculty research:* Analytical, inorganic, organic, physical, and macromolecular chemistry.

University of Wisconsin–Milwaukee, Graduate School, College of Letters and Sciences, Department of Chemistry, Milwaukee, WI 53201-0413. Offers biogeochemistry (PhD); chemistry (MS, PhD). *Faculty:* 20 full-time (4 women). *Students:* 60 full-time (27 women), 16 part-time (9 women); includes 11 minority (2 Black or African American, non-Hispanic/Latino; 6 Asian, non-Hispanic/Latino; 3 Two or more races, non-Hispanic/Latino), 30 international. Average age 30. 70 applicants, 61% accepted, 10 enrolled. In 2012, 5 master's, 4 doctorates awarded. *Degree requirements:* For master's, thesis or alternative; for doctorate, thesis/dissertation. *Entrance requirements:* For doctorate, GRE General Test. Additional exam requirements/recommendations for international students: Required—TOEFL (minimum score 600 paper-based; 79 iBT), IELTS (minimum score 6.5). *Application deadline:* For fall admission, 1/1 priority date for domestic students; for spring admission, 9/1 for domestic students. Applications are processed on a rolling basis. Application fee: $56 ($96 for international students). *Financial support:* In 2012–13, 3 fellowships, 30 research assistantships, 46 teaching assistantships were awarded; career-related internships or fieldwork, unspecified assistantships, and project assistantships also available. Support available to part-time students. Financial award application deadline: 4/15; financial award applicants required to submit FAFSA. *Faculty research:* Analytical chemistry, biochemistry, inorganic chemistry, organic chemistry, physical chemistry. *Unit head:* Peter Geissinger, Department Chair, 414-229-5230, Fax: 414-229-5530, E-mail: geissing@uwm.edu. *Application contact:* General Information Contact, 414-229-4982, Fax: 414-229-6967, E-mail: gradschool@uwm.edu. Website: http://www.uwm.edu/dept/chemistry/.

University of Wyoming, College of Arts and Sciences, Department of Chemistry, Laramie, WY 82070. Offers MS, PhD. *Degree requirements:* For master's, thesis; for doctorate, thesis/dissertation. *Entrance requirements:* For master's and doctorate, GRE General Test, minimum GPA of 3.0. Additional exam requirements/recommendations for international students: Required—TOEFL (minimum score 600 paper-based). Electronic applications accepted. *Faculty research:* Organic chemistry, inorganic chemistry, analytical chemistry, physical chemistry.

Utah State University, School of Graduate Studies, College of Science, Department of Chemistry and Biochemistry, Logan, UT 84322. Offers biochemistry (MS, PhD); chemistry (MS, PhD). Part-time programs available. Terminal master's awarded for partial completion of doctoral program. *Degree requirements:* For master's, thesis, oral and written exams; for doctorate, thesis/dissertation, oral and written exams. *Entrance requirements:* For master's and doctorate, GRE General Test, minimum GPA of 3.0. Additional exam requirements/recommendations for international students: Required—TOEFL. *Faculty research:* Analytical, inorganic, organic, and physical chemistry; iron in asbestos chemistry and carcinogenicity; dicopper complexes; photothermal spectrometry; metal molecule clusters.

Vanderbilt University, Graduate School, Department of Chemistry, Nashville, TN 37240-1001. Offers analytical chemistry (MAT, MS, PhD); inorganic chemistry (MAT, MS, PhD); organic chemistry (MAT, MS, PhD); physical chemistry (MAT, MS, PhD); theoretical chemistry (MAT, MS). *Faculty:* 21 full-time (3 women). *Students:* 123 full-time (46 women); includes 22 minority (5 Black or African American, non-Hispanic/Latino; 1 American Indian or Alaska Native, non-Hispanic/Latino; 3 Asian, non-Hispanic/Latino; 5 Hispanic/Latino; 8 Two or more races, non-Hispanic/Latino), 14 international. Average age 25. 430 applicants, 15% accepted, 29 enrolled. In 2012, 6 master's, 14 doctorates awarded. Terminal master's awarded for partial completion of doctoral program. *Degree requirements:* For master's, thesis; for doctorate, thesis/dissertation, area, qualifying, and final exams. *Entrance requirements:* For master's and doctorate, GRE General Test, GRE Subject Test (recommended). Additional exam requirements/recommendations for international students: Required—TOEFL (minimum score 570 paper-based; 88 iBT). *Application deadline:* For fall

Peterson's Graduate Programs in the Physical Sciences, Mathematics, Agricultural Sciences, the Environment & Natural Resources 2014

www.petersonsbooks.com **97**

admission, 1/15 for domestic and international students. Application fee: $0. Electronic applications accepted. *Financial support:* Fellowships with full and partial tuition reimbursements, research assistantships with full tuition reimbursements, teaching assistantships with full tuition reimbursements, Federal Work-Study, institutionally sponsored loans, scholarships/grants, traineeships, and health care benefits available. Financial award application deadline: 1/15; financial award applicants required to submit CSS PROFILE or FAFSA. *Faculty research:* Chemical synthesis; mechanistic, theoretical, bioorganic, analytical, and spectroscopic chemistry. *Unit head:* Dr. David Cliffel, Director of Graduate Studies, 615-343-3937, Fax: 615-322-4936, E-mail: d.cliffel@vanderbilt.edu. *Application contact:* Sandra Ford, Administrative Assistant, 615-322-8695, Fax: 615-322-4936, E-mail: sandra.e.ford@Vanderbilt.Edu. Website: http://www.vanderbilt.edu/chemistry/.

Villanova University, Graduate School of Liberal Arts and Sciences, Department of Chemistry, Villanova, PA 19085-1699. Offers MS. Part-time and evening/weekend programs available. *Faculty:* 7 full-time (1 woman). *Students:* 22 full-time (12 women), 9 part-time (4 women); includes 2 minority (1 Asian, non-Hispanic/Latino; 1 Hispanic/Latino), 1 international. Average age 26. 23 applicants, 78% accepted, 11 enrolled. In 2012, 11 master's awarded. *Degree requirements:* For master's, comprehensive exam (for some programs), thesis (for some programs). *Entrance requirements:* For master's, GRE General Test, minimum GPA of 3.0, 3 recommendation letters. Additional exam requirements/recommendations for international students: Required—TOEFL. *Application deadline:* For fall admission, 5/1 for international students; for spring admission, 10/15 for international students. Applications are processed on a rolling basis. Application fee: $50. Electronic applications accepted. *Expenses:* Contact institution. *Financial support:* Research assistantships, teaching assistantships, scholarships/grants, and unspecified assistantships available. Financial award applicants required to submit FAFSA. *Unit head:* Dr. Temer Ahmadi, Chair, 610-519-7796. *Application contact:* Dean, Graduate School of Liberal Arts and Sciences. Website: http://www.villanova.edu/artsci/chemistry/graduate/.

Virginia Commonwealth University, Graduate School, College of Humanities and Sciences, Department of Chemistry, Richmond, VA 23284-9005. Offers analytical chemistry (MS, PhD); chemical physics (PhD); inorganic chemistry (MS, PhD); organic chemistry (MS, PhD); physical chemistry (MS, PhD). Part-time programs available. Terminal master's awarded for partial completion of doctoral program. *Degree requirements:* For master's, thesis; for doctorate, thesis/dissertation, comprehensive cumulative exams, research proposal. *Entrance requirements:* For master's, GRE General Test, 30 undergraduate credits in chemistry; for doctorate, GRE General Test. Additional exam requirements/recommendations for international students: Required—TOEFL (minimum score 600 paper-based; 100 iBT) or IELTS (minimum score 6.5). Electronic applications accepted. *Faculty research:* Physical, organic, inorganic, analytical, and polymer chemistry; chemical physics.

Virginia Polytechnic Institute and State University, Graduate School, College of Science, Blacksburg, VA 24061. Offers biological sciences (MS, PhD); biomedical technology development and management (MS); chemistry (MS, PhD); economics (MA, PhD); geosciences (MS, PhD); mathematics (MS, PhD); physics (MS, PhD); psychology (MS, PhD); statistics (MS, PhD). *Faculty:* 259 full-time (68 women), 3 part-time/adjunct (all women). *Students:* 555 full-time (230 women), 31 part-time (12 women); includes 44 minority (10 Black or African American, non-Hispanic/Latino; 1 American Indian or Alaska Native, non-Hispanic/Latino; 11 Asian, non-Hispanic/Latino; 14 Hispanic/Latino; 8 Two or more races, non-Hispanic/Latino), 250 international. Average age 28. 1,091 applicants, 24% accepted, 137 enrolled. In 2012, 65 master's, 89 doctorates awarded. *Median time to degree:* Of those who began their doctoral program in fall 2004, 68% received their degree in 8 years or less. *Degree requirements:* For master's, comprehensive exam (for some programs), thesis (for some programs); for doctorate, comprehensive exam (for some programs), thesis/dissertation (for some programs). *Entrance requirements:* For master's and doctorate, GRE/GMAT (may vary by department). Additional exam requirements/recommendations for international students: Required—TOEFL (minimum score 550 paper-based). *Application deadline:* For fall admission, 8/1 for domestic students, 4/1 for international students; for spring admission, 1/1 for domestic students, 9/1 for international students. Applications are processed on a rolling basis. Application fee: $65. Electronic applications accepted. *Expenses:* Tuition, state resident: full-time $10,677; part-time $593.25 per credit hour. Tuition, nonresident: full-time $20,926; part-time $1162.50 per credit hour. *Required fees:* $427.75 per semester. Tuition and fees vary according to course load, campus/location and program. *Financial support:* In 2012–13, 1 fellowship with full tuition reimbursement (averaging $21,606 per year), 159 research assistantships with full tuition reimbursements (averaging $19,950 per year), 331 teaching assistantships with full tuition reimbursements (averaging $17,426 per year) were awarded. Financial award application deadline: 3/1; financial award applicants required to submit FAFSA. *Total annual research expenditures:* $23.4 million. *Unit head:* Dr. Lay Nam Chang, Dean, 540-231-5422, Fax: 540-231-3380, E-mail: laynam@vt.edu. *Application contact:* Diane Stearns, Assistant to the Dean, 540-231-7515, Fax: 540-231-3380, E-mail: dstearns@vt.edu. Website: http://www.science.vt.edu/.

Wake Forest University, Graduate School of Arts and Sciences, Department of Chemistry, Winston-Salem, NC 27109. Offers analytical chemistry (MS, PhD); inorganic chemistry (MS, PhD); organic chemistry (MS, PhD); physical chemistry (MS, PhD). Part-time programs available. *Degree requirements:* For master's, one foreign language, comprehensive exam, thesis; for doctorate, 2 foreign languages, comprehensive exam, thesis/dissertation. *Entrance requirements:* For master's and doctorate, GRE General Test. Additional exam requirements/recommendations for international students: Required—TOEFL. Electronic applications accepted.

Washington State University, Graduate School, College of Arts and Sciences, Department of Chemistry, Pullman, WA 99164. Offers MS, PhD. *Faculty:* 23 full-time (5 women). *Students:* 86 full-time (28 women); includes 6 minority (5 Asian, non-Hispanic/Latino; 1 Hispanic/Latino), 24 international. Average age 24. 72 applicants, 40% accepted, 19 enrolled. In 2012, 10 master's, 10 doctorates awarded. Terminal master's awarded for partial completion of doctoral program. *Degree requirements:* For master's, comprehensive exam (for some programs), thesis (for some programs), oral exam, teaching experience; for doctorate, comprehensive exam, thesis/dissertation, oral exam, written exam, teaching experience. *Entrance requirements:* For master's and doctorate, GRE General Test, GRE Subject Test (recommended), transcripts from each post-secondary school attended (photocopies acceptable); three letters of recommendation. Additional exam requirements/recommendations for international students: Required—TOEFL. *Application deadline:* For fall admission, 1/15 priority date for domestic students, 3/1 for international students; for spring admission, 10/1 priority date for domestic students, 7/1 for international students. Applications are processed on a rolling basis. Application fee: $75. Electronic applications accepted. *Financial support:* In 2012–13, 100 students received support, including 44 research assistantships with full and partial tuition reimbursements available (averaging $36,000 per year), 44 teaching assistantships with full and partial tuition reimbursements available (averaging $36,000 per year); fellowships, career-related internships or fieldwork, Federal Work-Study, institutionally sponsored loans, scholarships/grants, health care benefits, and unspecified assistantships also available. Financial award application deadline: 2/15; financial award applicants required to submit FAFSA. *Faculty research:* Environmental chemistry, materials chemistry, radio chemistry, bio-organic, computational chemistry. *Unit head:* Kerry W. Hipps, Chair, 509-335-8866, Fax: 509-335-8867, E-mail: chemistry@wsu.edu. *Application contact:* Graduate School Admissions, 800-GRADWSU, Fax: 509-335-1949, E-mail: gradsch@wsu.edu. Website: http://www.chem.wsu.edu/.

Washington State University Tri-Cities, Graduate Programs, Program in Chemistry, Richland, WA 99354-1671. Offers MS. Part-time and evening/weekend programs available. *Faculty:* 1 full-time, 8 part-time/adjunct (2 women). *Students:* 10 part-time (6 women); includes 2 minority (1 Black or African American, non-Hispanic/Latino; 1 Hispanic/Latino). Average age 31. 2 applicants, 50% accepted, 1 enrolled. In 2012, 2 master's awarded. Terminal master's awarded for partial completion of doctoral program. *Degree requirements:* For master's, comprehensive exam (for some programs), thesis optional. *Entrance requirements:* For master's, GRE, minimum GPA of 3.0, 3 letters of recommendation. Additional exam requirements/recommendations for international students: Required—TOEFL. *Application deadline:* For fall admission, 3/1 priority date for domestic students, 3/1 for international students; for spring admission, 10/1 priority date for domestic students, 7/1 for international students. Applications are processed on a rolling basis. Application fee: $75. Electronic applications accepted. *Financial support:* In 2012–13, 1 student received support, including 3 teaching assistantships (averaging $3,300 per year); career-related internships or fieldwork, Federal Work-Study, institutionally sponsored loans, scholarships/grants, health care benefits, and unspecified assistantships also available. Financial award application deadline: 2/15; financial award applicants required to submit FAFSA. *Faculty research:* Proteomics, environmental chemistry, organic green chemistry, electron microscopy, organic mass spectrometry, inorganic infrared spectroscopy, organometallics, nuclear magnetic resonance, natural product chemistry, chemical physics. *Unit head:* Dr. Kerry Hipps, Chair, 509-335-3442, E-mail: hipps@wsu.edu. *Application contact:* Karen Grant, Chemistry Program Director, 509-372-7276, E-mail: kgrant@tricity.wsu.edu. Website: http://www.tricity.wsu.edu/science/chemistry.html.

Washington University in St. Louis, Graduate School of Arts and Sciences, Department of Chemistry, St. Louis, MO 63130-4899. Offers PhD. Terminal master's awarded for partial completion of doctoral program. *Degree requirements:* For doctorate, thesis/dissertation. *Entrance requirements:* For doctorate, GRE General Test, GRE Subject Test. Electronic applications accepted.

Wayne State University, College of Liberal Arts and Sciences, Department of Chemistry, Detroit, MI 48202. Offers analytical chemistry (PhD); biochemistry (PhD); chemistry (MA, MS); inorganic chemistry (PhD); organic chemistry (PhD); physical chemistry (PhD). *Students:* 167 full-time (79 women), 1 part-time (0 women); includes 12 minority (3 Black or African American, non-Hispanic/Latino; 2 American Indian or Alaska Native, non-Hispanic/Latino; 5 Asian, non-Hispanic/Latino; 2 Hispanic/Latino), 113 international. Average age 28. 440 applicants, 23% accepted, 50 enrolled. In 2012, 5 master's, 15 doctorates awarded. *Degree requirements:* For master's, thesis (for some programs), oral exam; for doctorate, thesis/dissertation, oral exam. *Entrance requirements:* For master's, one year of physics, math through calculus, general chemistry (8 credits), organic chemistry (8 credits), physical chemistry (six credits), quantitative analysis (four credits), and advanced chemistry (three credits); advanced biology (for biochemistry applicants); minimum undergraduate GPA of 2.75 in chemistry and cognate sciences; for doctorate, minimum undergraduate GPA of 3.0 in chemistry and cognate science. Additional exam requirements/recommendations for international students: Required—TOEFL (minimum score 550 paper-based; 79 iBT); Recommended—TWE (minimum score 5.5). *Application deadline:* For fall admission, 2/10 priority date for domestic students, 2/10 for international students; for winter admission, 10/1 priority date for domestic students, 9/1 for international students; for spring admission, 2/1 priority date for domestic students, 1/1 for international students. Applications are processed on a rolling basis. Application fee: $50. Electronic applications accepted. *Expenses:* Tuition, state resident: full-time $12,788; part-time $532.85 per credit hour. Tuition, nonresident: full-time $28,243; part-time $1176.80 per credit hour. *Required fees:* $1367.30; $39.75 per credit hour. $206.65 per semester. Tuition and fees vary according to course load and program. *Financial support:* In 2012–13, 154 students received support, including 10 fellowships with tuition reimbursements available (averaging $23,000 per year), 60 research assistantships with tuition reimbursements available (averaging $19,682 per year), 81 teaching assistantships with tuition reimbursements available (averaging $20,788 per year); scholarships/grants, health care benefits, and unspecified assistantships also available. Financial award application deadline: 7/1. *Faculty research:* Natural products synthesis, molecular biology, molecular mechanics calculations, organometallic chemistry, experimental physical chemistry. *Total annual research expenditures:* $7.2 million. *Unit head:* Dr. James Rigby, Chair, 313-577-3472, Fax: 313-577-8822, E-mail: aa392@wayne.edu. *Application contact:* Dr. Charles Winter, Graduate Director, 313-577-5224, E-mail: chw@chem.wayne.edu. Website: http://chem.wayne.edu/.

Wesleyan University, Graduate Studies, Department of Chemistry, Middletown, CT 06459-0180. Offers biochemistry (PhD); chemical physics (PhD); inorganic chemistry (PhD); organic chemistry (PhD); physical chemistry (PhD); theoretical chemistry (PhD). Terminal master's awarded for partial completion of doctoral program. *Degree requirements:* For doctorate, thesis/dissertation, proposal. *Entrance requirements:* For doctorate, GRE General Test, 3 recommendations. Additional exam requirements/recommendations for international students: Required—TOEFL. *Application deadline:* Applications are processed on a rolling basis. Application fee: $0. Electronic applications accepted. *Financial support:* Research assistantships with full tuition reimbursements, teaching assistantships with full tuition reimbursements, and institutionally sponsored loans available. Financial award application deadline: 4/15; financial award applicants required to submit FAFSA. *Unit head:* Prof. Rex F. Pratt, Chair, 860-685-2727. *Application contact:* Sarah Atwell, Administrative Assistant IV/Graduate Program Coordinator, 860-685-2573, Fax: 860-685-2211, E-mail: satwell@wesleyan.edu. Website: http://www.wesleyan.edu/chem/.

West Chester University of Pennsylvania, College of Arts and Sciences, Department of Chemistry, West Chester, PA 19383. Offers Teaching Certificate. *Students:* 1 (woman) part-time. Average age 42. *Degree requirements:* For Teaching Certificate, minimum overall GPA of 3.0, pass PAPA and Chemistry PRAXIS. *Entrance requirements:* For degree, minimum GPA of 2.8 in most recent 48 credits. Additional exam requirements/recommendations for international students: Required—TOEFL (minimum score 550 paper-based; 80 iBT). *Application deadline:* For fall admission, 4/15 priority date for domestic students, 3/15 for international students; for spring admission, 10/15 priority date for domestic students, 9/1 for international students. Applications are processed on a rolling basis. Electronic applications accepted. *Expenses:* Tuition, state resident: full-time $7722; part-time $429 per credit. Tuition, nonresident: full-time $11,592; part-time $644 per credit. *Required fees:* $2108; $105.05 per credit. Tuition and fees vary according to campus/location and program. *Financial support:* Unspecified assistantships available. Support available to part-time students. Financial award application deadline: 2/15; financial award applicants required to submit FAFSA. *Faculty research:* Solids, polymers, chromatography, nucleic acids, chemical education. *Unit head:* Dr. Blaise Frost, Chair, 610-436-2526, E-mail: bfrost@wcupa.edu. *Application contact:* Dr. John Townsend, Secondary Education Advisor, 610-436-1063, E-mail: jtownsend@wcupa.edu. Website: http://www.wcupa.edu/_academics/sch_cas.che/.

Western Carolina University, Graduate School, College of Arts and Sciences, Department of Chemistry and Physics, Cullowhee, NC 28723. Offers chemistry (MS). *Degree requirements:* For master's, thesis. *Entrance requirements:* For master's, GRE General Test, undergraduate science degree with minimum GPA of 3.0, 3 letters of recommendation. Additional exam requirements/recommendations for international students: Required—TOEFL (minimum score 550 paper-based; 79 iBT). *Faculty research:* Trace metal analysis, metal waste reduction, supramolecular chemistry, free radical biophysical chemistry.

Western Illinois University, School of Graduate Studies, College of Arts and Sciences, Department of Chemistry, Macomb, IL 61455-1390. Offers MS. Part-time programs available. *Students:* 33 full-time (14 women), 2 part-time (1 woman); includes 3 minority (2 Black or African American, non-Hispanic/Latino; 1 Asian, non-Hispanic/Latino), 24 international. Average age 24. In 2012, 24 master's awarded. *Degree requirements:* For master's, thesis or alternative. *Entrance requirements:* Additional exam requirements/recommendations for international students: Required—TOEFL (minimum score 530 paper-based; 71 iBT). *Application deadline:* Applications are processed on a rolling basis. Application fee: $30. Electronic applications accepted. *Financial support:* In 2012–13, 21 students received support, including 1 research assistantship with full tuition reimbursement available (averaging $7,544 per year), 20 teaching assistantships with full tuition reimbursements available (averaging $8,688 per year). Financial award applicants required to submit FAFSA. *Unit head:* Dr. Rose McConnell, Chairperson, 309-298-1538. *Application contact:* Dr. Nancy Parsons, Interim Associate Provost and Director of Graduate Studies, 309-298-1806, Fax: 309-298-2345, E-mail: grad-office@wiu.edu. Website: http://wiu.edu/chemistry.

Western Kentucky University, Graduate Studies, Ogden College of Science and Engineering, Department of Chemistry, Bowling Green, KY 42101. Offers MA Ed, MS. *Degree requirements:* For master's, comprehensive exam, thesis. *Entrance requirements:* For master's, GRE General Test, minimum GPA of 2.75. Additional exam requirements/recommendations for international students: Required—TOEFL (minimum score 555 paper-based). *Faculty research:* Catatonic surfactants, directed orthometalation reactions, thermal stability and degradation mechanisms, co-firing refused derived fuels, laser fluorescence.

Western Michigan University, Graduate College, College of Arts and Sciences, Department of Chemistry, Kalamazoo, MI 49008. Offers MS, PhD. *Degree requirements:* For master's, thesis, departmental qualifying and oral exams; for doctorate, thesis/dissertation.

Western Michigan University, Graduate College, College of Arts and Sciences, Mallinson Institute for Science Education, Kalamazoo, MI 49008. Offers science education (MA, PhD); science education: biological sciences (PhD); science education: chemistry (PhD); science education: geosciences (PhD); science education: physical geography (PhD); science education: physics (PhD). *Degree requirements:* For doctorate, thesis/dissertation, oral and written exams. *Entrance requirements:* For master's, undergraduate degree in a science or science education, teacher certification (or appropriate education courses); for doctorate, GRE General Test, master's degree in a science or science education. Additional exam requirements/recommendations for international students: Recommended—TOEFL. Electronic applications accepted. *Faculty research:* History and philosophy of science, curriculum and instruction, science content learning, college science teaching and learning, social and cultural factors in science education.

Western Washington University, Graduate School, College of Sciences and Technology, Department of Chemistry, Bellingham, WA 98225-5996. Offers MS. Part-time programs available. *Degree requirements:* For master's, thesis (for some programs). *Entrance requirements:* For master's, GRE General Test, minimum GPA of 3.0 in last 60 semester hours or last 90 quarter hours. Additional exam requirements/recommendations for international students: Required—TOEFL (minimum score 567 paper-based). Electronic applications accepted. *Faculty research:* Bio-, organic, inorganic, physical, analytical chemistry.

West Texas A&M University, College of Agriculture, Science and Engineering, Department of Mathematics, Physical Sciences and Engineering Technology, Program in Chemistry, Canyon, TX 79016-0001. Offers MS. Part-time programs available. *Degree requirements:* For master's, comprehensive exam, thesis optional. *Entrance requirements:* For master's, GRE General Test. Additional exam requirements/recommendations for international students: Required—TOEFL (minimum score 550 paper-based). Electronic applications accepted. *Faculty research:* Biochemistry; inorganic, organic, and physical chemistry; vibrational spectroscopy; magnetic susceptibilities; carbene chemistry.

West Virginia University, Eberly College of Arts and Sciences, Department of Chemistry, Morgantown, WV 26506. Offers analytical chemistry (MS, PhD); inorganic chemistry (MS, PhD); organic chemistry (MS, PhD); physical chemistry (MS, PhD); theoretical chemistry (MS, PhD). Part-time programs available. Postbaccalaureate distance learning degree programs offered (no on-campus study). Terminal master's awarded for partial completion of doctoral program. *Degree requirements:* For master's, thesis; for doctorate, thesis/dissertation. *Entrance requirements:* For master's, GRE General Test, GRE Subject Test (recommended), minimum GPA of 2.5; for doctorate, GRE General Test, GRE Subject Test (recommended), minimum GPA of 2.75. Additional exam requirements/recommendations for international students: Required—TOEFL. Electronic applications accepted. *Faculty research:* Analysis of proteins, drug interactions, solids and effluents by advanced separation methods; new synthetic strategies for complex organic molecules; synthesis and structural characterization of metal complexes for polymerization catalysis, nonlinear science, spectroscopy.

Wichita State University, Graduate School, Fairmount College of Liberal Arts and Sciences, Department of Chemistry, Wichita, KS 67260. Offers MS, PhD. *Unit head:* Dr. David Eichhorn, Chair, 316-978-3120, Fax: 316-978-3431, E-mail: david.eichhorn@wichita.edu. *Application contact:* Jordan Oleson, Admission Coordinator, 316-978-3095, E-mail: jordan.oleson@wichita.edu. Website: http://www.wichita.edu/.

Wilfrid Laurier University, Faculty of Graduate and Postdoctoral Studies, Faculty of Science, Department of Chemistry, Waterloo, ON N2L 3C5, Canada. Offers M Sc. *Degree requirements:* For master's, thesis. *Entrance requirements:* For master's, honors degree or equivalent in chemistry, biochemistry or a related discipline; minimum B average in last two full-time undergraduate years. Additional exam requirements/recommendations for international students: Required—TOEFL (minimum score 89 iBT). Electronic applications accepted. *Faculty research:* Cold regions water science, biophysical methods, biochemistry, nanochemistry.

Worcester Polytechnic Institute, Graduate Studies and Research, Department of Chemistry and Biochemistry, Worcester, MA 01609-2280. Offers biochemistry (MS, PhD); chemistry (MS, PhD). Evening/weekend programs available. *Faculty:* 7 full-time (1 woman), 1 part-time/adjunct (0 women). *Students:* 19 full-time (9 women); includes 2 minority (1 Asian, non-Hispanic/Latino; 1 Two or more races,

Chemistry

non-Hispanic/Latino), 8 international. 63 applicants, 13% accepted, 6 enrolled. In 2012, 11 master's awarded. *Degree requirements:* For master's, thesis; for doctorate, comprehensive exam, thesis/dissertation. *Entrance requirements:* For master's and doctorate, GRE General Test, 3 letters of recommendation, statement of purpose. Additional exam requirements/recommendations for international students: Required—TOEFL (minimum score 563 paper-based; 84 iBT), IELTS (minimum score 7). *Application deadline:* For fall admission, 1/1 priority date for domestic students, 1/1 for international students; for spring admission, 10/1 priority date for domestic students, 10/1 for international students. Applications are processed on a rolling basis. Application fee: $70. Electronic applications accepted. *Financial support:* Research assistantships, teaching assistantships, career-related internships or fieldwork, institutionally sponsored loans, scholarships/grants, and unspecified assistantships available. Financial award application deadline: 1/1; financial award applicants required to submit FAFSA. *Faculty research:* Catalysis experimental and computational protein biophysics, biological metals, synthetic methods, surface chemistry, computational chemistry. *Unit head:* Dr. Arne Gericke, Department Head, 508-831-5371, Fax: 508-831-5933, E-mail: agericke@wpi.edu. *Application contact:* Dr. George Kaminski, Graduate Coordinator, 508-831-5371, Fax: 508-831-5933, E-mail: gkaminski@wpi.edu. Website: http://www.wpi.edu/Academics/Depts/Chemistry/.

Wright State University, School of Graduate Studies, College of Science and Mathematics, Department of Chemistry, Dayton, OH 45435. Offers chemistry (MS); environmental sciences (MS). Part-time and evening/weekend programs available. *Degree requirements:* For master's, oral defense of thesis, seminar. *Entrance requirements:* Additional exam requirements/recommendations for international students: Required—TOEFL. *Faculty research:* Polymer synthesis and characterization, laser kinetics, organic and inorganic synthesis, analytical and environmental chemistry.

Yale University, Graduate School of Arts and Sciences, Department of Chemistry, New Haven, CT 06520. Offers biophysical chemistry (PhD); inorganic chemistry (PhD); organic chemistry (PhD); physical and theoretical chemistry (PhD). *Degree requirements:* For doctorate, thesis/dissertation. *Entrance requirements:* For doctorate, GRE General Test, GRE Subject Test. Additional exam requirements/recommendations for international students: Required—TOEFL.

York University, Faculty of Graduate Studies, Faculty of Science and Engineering, Program in Chemistry, Toronto, ON M3J 1P3, Canada. Offers M Sc, PhD. Part-time and evening/weekend programs available. *Degree requirements:* For master's, thesis or alternative; for doctorate, thesis/dissertation. Electronic applications accepted.

Youngstown State University, Graduate School, College of Science, Technology, Engineering and Mathematics, Department of Chemistry, Youngstown, OH 44555-0001. Offers analytical chemistry (MS); biochemistry (MS); chemistry education (MS); inorganic chemistry (MS); organic chemistry (MS); physical chemistry (MS). Part-time programs available. *Degree requirements:* For master's, thesis. *Entrance requirements:* For master's, bachelor's degree in chemistry, minimum GPA of 2.7. Additional exam requirements/recommendations for international students: Required—TOEFL. *Faculty research:* Analysis of antioxidants, chromatography, defects and disorder in crystalline oxides, hydrogen bonding, novel organic and organometallic materials.

Inorganic Chemistry

Auburn University, Graduate School, College of Sciences and Mathematics, Department of Chemistry and Biochemistry, Auburn University, AL 36849. Offers analytical chemistry (MS, PhD); biochemistry (MS, PhD); inorganic chemistry (MS, PhD); organic chemistry (MS, PhD); physical chemistry (MS, PhD). Part-time programs available. *Faculty:* 28 full-time (5 women), 1 part-time/adjunct (0 women). *Students:* 37 full-time (14 women), 30 part-time (15 women); includes 6 minority (3 Black or African American, non-Hispanic/Latino; 1 American Indian or Alaska Native, non-Hispanic/Latino; 1 Asian, non-Hispanic/Latino; 1 Hispanic/Latino), 41 international. Average age 28. 38 applicants, 39% accepted, 12 enrolled. In 2012, 1 master's, 9 doctorates awarded. *Degree requirements:* For master's, thesis (for some programs); for doctorate, thesis/dissertation, oral and written exams. *Entrance requirements:* For master's and doctorate, GRE General Test. *Application deadline:* For fall admission, 7/7 for domestic students; for spring admission, 11/24 for domestic students. Applications are processed on a rolling basis. Application fee: $50 ($60 for international students). Electronic applications accepted. *Expenses:* Tuition, state resident: full-time $7866; part-time $437 per credit. Tuition, nonresident: full-time $23,598; part-time $1311 per credit. *Required fees:* $787 per semester. Tuition and fees vary according to degree level and program. *Financial support:* Fellowships, research assistantships, and teaching assistantships available. Financial award application deadline: 3/15; financial award applicants required to submit FAFSA. *Unit head:* Dr. J. V. Ortiz, Chair, 334-844-4043, Fax: 334-844-4043. *Application contact:* Dr. George Flowers, Dean of the Graduate School, 334-844-2125. Website: http://www.auburn.edu/cosam/departments/chemistry/.

Binghamton University, State University of New York, Graduate School, School of Arts and Sciences, Department of Chemistry, Binghamton, NY 13902-6000. Offers analytical chemistry (PhD); chemistry (MA, MS); environmental (PhD); inorganic chemistry (PhD); organic chemistry (PhD); physical chemistry (PhD). Part-time programs available. *Faculty:* 16 full-time (4 women), 4 part-time/adjunct (1 woman). *Students:* 25 full-time (10 women), 26 part-time (10 women); includes 4 minority (3 Black or African American, non-Hispanic/Latino; 1 Hispanic/Latino), 33 international. Average age 28. 53 applicants, 49% accepted, 11 enrolled. In 2012, 3 master's, 6 doctorates awarded. Terminal master's awarded for partial completion of doctoral program. *Degree requirements:* For master's, thesis or alternative, oral exam, seminar presentation; for doctorate, thesis/dissertation, cumulative exams. *Entrance requirements:* For master's and doctorate, GRE General Test, GRE Subject Test. Additional exam requirements/recommendations for international students: Required—TOEFL (minimum score 550 paper-based; 80 iBT). *Application deadline:* For fall admission, 1/15 priority date for domestic students, 1/15 for international students; for spring admission, 10/15 priority date for domestic students, 10/15 for international students. Applications are processed on a rolling basis. Application fee: $75. Electronic applications accepted. *Expenses:* Tuition, state resident: full-time $9370. Tuition, nonresident: full-time $16,680. *Financial support:* In 2012–13, 47 students received support, including 5 research assistantships with full tuition reimbursements available (averaging $18,000 per year), 34 teaching assistantships with full tuition reimbursements available (averaging $18,000 per year); career-related internships or fieldwork, Federal Work-Study, institutionally sponsored loans, scholarships/grants, health care benefits, tuition waivers (full), and unspecified assistantships also available. Financial award application deadline: 2/15; financial award applicants required to submit FAFSA. *Unit head:* Dr. Wayne E. Jones, Chairperson, 607-777-2421, E-mail: wjones@binghamton.edu. *Application contact:* Kishan Zuber, Recruiting and Admissions Coordinator, 607-777-2151, Fax: 607-777-2501, E-mail: kzuber@binghamton.edu.

Boston College, Graduate School of Arts and Sciences, Department of Chemistry, Chestnut Hill, MA 02467-3800. Offers biochemistry (PhD); inorganic chemistry (PhD); organic chemistry (PhD); physical chemistry (PhD); science education (MST). *Degree requirements:* For doctorate, thesis/dissertation, qualifying exam. *Entrance requirements:* For doctorate, GRE General Test, GRE Subject Test. Additional exam requirements/recommendations for international students: Required—TOEFL (minimum score 600 paper-based; 100 iBT). Electronic applications accepted.

Brandeis University, Graduate School of Arts and Sciences, Department of Chemistry, Waltham, MA 02454. Offers inorganic chemistry (MA, MS, PhD); organic chemistry (MA, MS, PhD); physical chemistry (MS, PhD). *Students:* 44 full-time (20 women); includes 3 minority (1 Black or African American, non-Hispanic/Latino; 2 Asian, non-Hispanic/Latino). 121 applicants, 26% accepted, 11 enrolled. In 2012, 6 master's, 7 doctorates awarded. Terminal master's awarded for partial completion of doctoral program. *Degree requirements:* For master's, thesis, 1 year of residency (for MA); 2 years of residency (for MS); for doctorate, comprehensive exam, thesis/dissertation, 3 years of residency; 2 seminars, qualifying exams. *Entrance requirements:* For master's and doctorate, GRE General Test, resume, statement of purpose, letters of recommendation. Additional exam requirements/recommendations for international students: Required—TOEFL (minimum score 600 paper-based; 100 iBT); Recommended—IELTS (minimum score 7). *Application deadline:* For fall admission, 1/15 priority date for domestic students. Application fee: $75. Electronic applications accepted. *Financial support:* In 2012–13, 16 research assistantships with full tuition reimbursements (averaging $25,000 per year) were awarded; fellowships with full tuition reimbursements, Federal Work-Study, scholarships/grants, health care benefits, tuition waivers (partial), and unspecified assistantships also available. Support available to part-time students. Financial award application deadline: 4/15; financial award applicants required to submit FAFSA. *Faculty research:* Oscillating chemical reactions, molecular recognition systems, protein crystallography, synthesis of natural product spectroscopy and magnetic resonance. *Unit head:* Dr. Judith Herzfeld, Chair, Graduate Program, 781-736-2540, Fax: 781-736-2516, E-mail: herzfeld@brandeis.edu. *Application contact:* Charlotte Haygazian, Coordinator, 781-736-2500, Fax: 781-736-2516, E-mail: chemadm@brandeis.edu. Website: http://www.brandeis.edu/gsas.

California State University, Los Angeles, Graduate Studies, College of Natural and Social Sciences, Department of Chemistry and Biochemistry, Los Angeles, CA 90032-8530. Offers analytical chemistry (MS); biochemistry (MS); chemistry (MS); inorganic chemistry (MS); organic chemistry (MS); physical chemistry (MS). Part-time and evening/weekend programs available. *Faculty:* 2 full-time (1 woman). *Students:* 3 full-time (1 woman), 16 part-time (9 women); includes 16 minority (all Hispanic/Latino). Average age 32. 21 applicants, 52% accepted, 8

100 www.petersonsbooks.com

Peterson's Graduate Programs in the Physical Sciences, Mathematics, Agricultural Sciences, the Environment & Natural Resources 2014

enrolled. In 2012, 2 master's awarded. *Degree requirements:* For master's, one foreign language, comprehensive exam or thesis. *Entrance requirements:* Additional exam requirements/recommendations for international students: Required—TOEFL. *Application deadline:* For fall admission, 5/1 for domestic and international students. Applications are processed on a rolling basis. Application fee: $55. *Financial support:* Federal Work-Study available. Support available to part-time students. Financial award application deadline: 3/1. *Faculty research:* Intercalation of heavy metal, carborane chemistry, conductive polymers and fabrics, titanium reagents, computer modeling and synthesis. *Unit head:* Dr. Robert L. Vellanoweth, Chair, 323-343-2300, Fax: 323-343-6490, E-mail: rvellan@calstatela.edu. *Application contact:* Dr. Larry Fritz, Dean of Graduate Studies, 323-343-3820 Ext. 3827, Fax: 323-343-5653, E-mail: lfritz@calstatela.edu. Website: http://www.calstatela.edu/dept/chem/index.htm.

Carnegie Mellon University, Mellon College of Science, Department of Chemistry, Pittsburgh, PA 15213-3891. Offers biotechnology and management (MS); chemistry (PhD), including bioinorganic, bioorganic, organic and materials, biophysics and spectroscopy, computational and theoretical, polymer; colloids, polymers and surfaces (MS). Part-time programs available. Terminal master's awarded for partial completion of doctoral program. *Degree requirements:* For doctorate, thesis/dissertation, departmental qualifying and oral exams, teaching experience. *Entrance requirements:* For master's, GRE General Test; for doctorate, GRE General Test, GRE Subject Test. Additional exam requirements/recommendations for international students: Required—TOEFL. Electronic applications accepted. *Faculty research:* Physical and theoretical chemistry, chemical synthesis, biophysical/bioinorganic chemistry.

Cleveland State University, College of Graduate Studies, College of Sciences and Health Professions, Department of Chemistry, Cleveland, OH 44115. Offers analytical chemistry (MS); clinical chemistry (MS); clinical/bioanalytical chemistry (PhD), including cellular and molecular medicine, clinical chemistry, clinical/bioanalytical chemistry; environmental chemistry (MS); inorganic chemistry (MS); pharmaceutical/organic chemistry (MS); physical chemistry (MS). Part-time and evening/weekend programs available. *Faculty:* 12 full-time (0 women). *Students:* 10 full-time (6 women), 92 part-time (46 women); includes 7 minority (6 Black or African American, non-Hispanic/Latino; 1 Asian, non-Hispanic/Latino), 68 international. Average age 27. 119 applicants, 86% accepted, 18 enrolled. In 2012, 15 master's, 5 doctorates awarded. *Degree requirements:* For master's, thesis optional; for doctorate, comprehensive exam, thesis/dissertation. *Entrance requirements:* For master's and doctorate, GRE General Test. Additional exam requirements/recommendations for international students: Required—TOEFL (minimum score 525 paper-based; 65 iBT). *Application deadline:* For fall admission, 1/15 priority date for domestic students, 1/15 for international students. Applications are processed on a rolling basis. Application fee: $30. Electronic applications accepted. *Expenses:* Tuition, state resident: full-time $8172; part-time $510.75 per credit hour. Tuition, nonresident: full-time $15,372; part-time $960.75 per credit hour. *Required fees:* $25 per semester. Tuition and fees vary according to course load and program. *Financial support:* In 2012–13, 44 students received support, including 5 fellowships with full tuition reimbursements available (averaging $22,500 per year), 13 research assistantships with full tuition reimbursements available (averaging $22,500 per year), 24 teaching assistantships with full tuition reimbursements available (averaging $21,000 per year); scholarships/grants and unspecified assistantships also available. Financial award application deadline: 1/15. *Faculty research:* Bioanalytical techniques and molecular diagnostics, glycoproteomics and antithrombotic agents, drug discovery and innovation, analytical pharmacology, inflammatory disease research. *Total annual research expenditures:* $3 million. *Unit head:* Dr. David J. Anderson, Interim Chair, 216-687-2467, Fax: 216-687-9298, E-mail: d.anderson@csuohio.edu. *Application contact:* Richelle P. Emery, Administrative Coordinator, 216-687-2457, Fax: 216-687-9298, E-mail: r.emery@csuohio.edu. Website: http://www.csuohio.edu/chemistry/.

Columbia University, Graduate School of Arts and Sciences, Division of Natural Sciences, Department of Chemistry, New York, NY 10027. Offers chemical physics (M Phil, PhD); inorganic chemistry (M Phil, MA, PhD); organic chemistry (M Phil, MA, PhD); MD/PhD. *Degree requirements:* For master's, one foreign language, teaching experience, oral/written exams (M Phil); for doctorate, one foreign language, thesis/dissertation. *Entrance requirements:* For master's and doctorate, GRE General Test, GRE Subject Test. Additional exam requirements/recommendations for international students: Required—TOEFL. *Faculty research:* Biophysics.

Cornell University, Graduate School, Graduate Fields of Arts and Sciences, Field of Chemistry and Chemical Biology, Ithaca, NY 14853-0001. Offers analytical chemistry (PhD); bio-organic chemistry (PhD); biophysical chemistry (PhD); chemical biology (PhD); chemical physics (PhD); inorganic chemistry (PhD); materials chemistry (PhD); organic chemistry (PhD); organometallic chemistry (PhD); physical chemistry (PhD); polymer chemistry (PhD); theoretical chemistry (PhD). *Faculty:* 48 full-time (5 women). *Students:* 161 full-time (70 women); includes 28 minority (1 Black or African American, non-Hispanic/Latino; 16 Asian, non-Hispanic/Latino; 4 Hispanic/Latino; 7 Two or more races, non-Hispanic/Latino), 48 international. Average age 25. 340 applicants, 33% accepted, 40 enrolled. In 2012, 15 doctorates awarded. *Degree requirements:* For doctorate, comprehensive exam, thesis/dissertation. *Entrance requirements:* For doctorate, GRE General Test, GRE Subject Test (chemistry), 3 letters of recommendation. Additional exam requirements/recommendations for international students: Required—TOEFL (minimum score 600 paper-based; 77 iBT). *Application deadline:* For fall admission, 1/10 for domestic students. Application fee: $95. Electronic applications accepted. *Financial support:* In 2012–13, 155 students received support, including 37 fellowships with full tuition reimbursements available, 50 research assistantships with full tuition reimbursements available, 68 teaching assistantships with full tuition reimbursements available; institutionally sponsored loans, scholarships/grants, health care benefits, tuition waivers (full and partial), and unspecified assistantships also available. Financial award applicants required to submit FAFSA. *Faculty research:* Analytical, organic, inorganic, physical, materials, chemical biology. *Unit head:* Director of Graduate Studies, 607-255-4139, Fax: 607-255-4137. *Application contact:* Graduate Field Assistant, 607-255-4139, Fax: 607-255-4137, E-mail: chemgrad@cornell.edu. Website: http://www.gradschool.cornell.edu/fields.php?id-26&a-2.

Eastern New Mexico University, Graduate School, College of Liberal Arts and Sciences, Department of Physical Sciences, Portales, NM 88130. Offers chemistry (MS), including analytical, biochemistry, inorganic, organic, physical. Part-time programs available. *Faculty:* 2 full-time (0 women). *Students:* 2 full-time (0 women), 12 part-time (4 women), 12 international. Average age 25. 14 applicants, 93% accepted, 11 enrolled. In 2012, 5 master's awarded. *Degree requirements:* For master's, thesis optional, seminar, oral and written comprehensive exams. *Entrance requirements:* For master's, ACS placement examination, minimum GPA of 3.0; 2 letters of recommendation; personal statement of career goals; bachelor's degree with one year minimum each of general, organic, and analytical chemistry. Additional exam requirements/recommendations for international students: Required—TOEFL (minimum score 550 paper-based; 79 iBT), IELTS (minimum score 6). *Application deadline:* For fall admission, 7/20 priority date for domestic students, 6/20 for international students; for spring admission, 12/15 priority date for domestic students, 11/15 for international students. Applications are processed on a rolling basis. Application fee: $10. Electronic applications accepted. *Expenses:* Tuition, state resident: full-time $3356; part-time $139.85 per credit hour. Tuition, nonresident: full-time $9030; part-time $376.25 per credit hour. *Required fees:* $1425.60; $59.40 per credit hour. $712.80 per semester. *Financial support:* In 2012–13, 1 research assistantship with partial tuition reimbursement (averaging $8,500 per year), 10 teaching assistantships with partial tuition reimbursements (averaging $8,500 per year) were awarded; career-related internships or fieldwork and unspecified assistantships also available. Support available to part-time students. Financial award application deadline: 3/1; financial award applicants required to submit FAFSA. *Faculty research:* Synfuel, electrochemistry, protein chemistry. *Unit head:* Dr. Juacho Yan, Graduate Coordinator, 575-562-2494, Fax: 575-562-2192, E-mail: juacho.yan@enmu.edu. *Application contact:* Sharon Potter, Department Secretary, Biology and Physical Sciences, 575-562-2174, Fax: 575-562-2192, E-mail: sharon.potter@enmu.edu. Website: http://liberal-arts.enmu.edu/sciences/grad-chemistry.shtml.

East Tennessee State University, School of Graduate Studies, College of Arts and Sciences, Department of Chemistry, Johnson City, TN 37614. Offers chemistry (MS), including inorganic chemistry, organic chemistry, physical chemistry. Part-time and evening/weekend programs available. *Faculty:* 10 full-time (4 women), 1 part-time/adjunct (0 women). *Students:* 17 full-time (3 women), 6 part-time (3 women); includes 4 minority (1 Black or African American, non-Hispanic/Latino; 1 American Indian or Alaska Native, non-Hispanic/Latino; 1 Asian, non-Hispanic/Latino; 1 Two or more races, non-Hispanic/Latino), 14 international. 40 applicants, 53% accepted, 15 enrolled. In 2012, 13 master's awarded. *Degree requirements:* For master's, comprehensive exam, thesis. *Entrance requirements:* For master's, prerequisites in physical chemistry with lab requiring calculus; two letters of recommendation. Additional exam requirements/recommendations for international students: Required—TOEFL (minimum score 550 paper-based; 79 iBT). *Application deadline:* For fall admission, 6/1 for domestic students, 4/30 for international students; for spring admission, 11/1 for domestic students, 9/30 for international students. Application fee: $35 ($45 for international students). Electronic applications accepted. *Financial support:* In 2012–13, 18 students received support, including 18 teaching assistantships with full and partial tuition reimbursements available (averaging $8,300 per year); career-related internships or fieldwork, institutionally sponsored loans, scholarships/grants, and unspecified assistantships also available. Financial award application deadline: 7/1; financial award applicants required to submit FAFSA. *Faculty research:* Analytical chemistry, inorganic chemistry, organic chemistry, physical chemistry. *Unit head:* Dr. Cassandra Eagle, Chair, 423-439-4367, Fax: 423-439-5835, E-mail: eaglec@etsu.edu. *Application contact:* Gail Powers, Graduate Specialist, 423-439-4703, Fax: 423-439-5624, E-mail: powersg@etsu.edu. Website: http://www.etsu.edu/cas/chemistry/.

Florida State University, The Graduate School, College of Arts and Sciences, Department of Chemistry and Biochemistry, Tallahassee, FL 32306-4390. Offers analytical chemistry (MS, PhD); biochemistry (MS, PhD); inorganic chemistry (MS, PhD); materials chemistry (PhD); organic chemistry (MS, PhD); physical chemistry (MS, PhD). *Faculty:* 37 full-time (4 women), 1 (woman) part-time/adjunct. *Students:* 138 full-time (52 women), 8 part-time (1 woman); includes 14 minority (6 Black or African American, non-Hispanic/Latino; 3 Asian, non-Hispanic/Latino; 2 Hispanic/Latino; 3 Two or more races, non-Hispanic/Latino), 63 international. Average age 25. 147 applicants, 40% accepted, 28 enrolled. In 2012, 7 master's, 27 doctorates awarded. Terminal master's awarded for partial completion of doctoral program. *Degree requirements:* For master's, comprehensive exam, thesis (for some programs); for doctorate, comprehensive exam, thesis/dissertation. *Entrance requirements:* For master's and doctorate, GRE General Test (minimum scores: 150 verbal, 151 quantitative; 1100 total on

Peterson's Graduate Programs in the Physical Sciences, Mathematics, Agricultural Sciences, the Environment & Natural Resources 2014

www.petersonsbooks.com 101

the old scale), minimum GPA of 3.1 in undergraduate course work. Additional exam requirements/recommendations for international students: Required—TOEFL (minimum score 90 iBT). *Application deadline:* For fall admission, 12/15 priority date for domestic students, 12/15 for international students; for spring admission, 9/15 for domestic and international students. Applications are processed on a rolling basis. Application fee: $30. Electronic applications accepted. *Expenses:* Contact institution. *Financial support:* In 2012–13, 140 students received support, including 7 fellowships with full and partial tuition reimbursements available (averaging $10,000 per year), 50 research assistantships with full tuition reimbursements available (averaging $20,000 per year), 100 teaching assistantships with full tuition reimbursements available (averaging $20,000 per year); health care benefits also available. Financial award application deadline: 12/15; financial award applicants required to submit FAFSA. *Faculty research:* Bioanalytical chemistry, including separations, microfluidics, pertroleomics; materials chemistry, including magnets, polymers, catalysts, nanomaterials; spectroscopy, including NMR and EPR, ultrafast, Raman, and mass spectrometry; organic synthesis, natural products, photochemistry, and supramolecular chemistry; biochemistry, with focus on structural biology, metabolomics, and anticancer drugs. *Total annual research expenditures:* $9.8 million. *Unit head:* Dr. Timothy Logan, Chairman, 850-644-3810, Fax: 850-644-8281, E-mail: gradinfo@chem.fsu.edu. *Application contact:* Dr. Michael Shatruk, Associate Chair for Graduate Studies, 850-417-8417, Fax: 850-644-8281, E-mail: gradinfo@chem.fsu.edu. Website: http://www.chem.fsu.edu/.

Georgetown University, Graduate School of Arts and Sciences, Department of Chemistry, Washington, DC 20057. Offers analytical chemistry (PhD); biochemistry (PhD); computational chemistry (PhD); inorganic chemistry (PhD); materials chemistry (PhD); organic chemistry (PhD); physical chemistry (PhD); theoretical chemistry (PhD). Terminal master's awarded for partial completion of doctoral program. *Degree requirements:* For doctorate, comprehensive exam, thesis/dissertation. *Entrance requirements:* For doctorate, GRE General Test. Additional exam requirements/recommendations for international students: Required—TOEFL.

The George Washington University, Columbian College of Arts and Sciences, Department of Chemistry, Washington, DC 20052. Offers analytical chemistry (MS, PhD); inorganic chemistry (MS, PhD); materials science (MS, PhD); organic chemistry (MS, PhD); physical chemistry (MS, PhD). Part-time and evening/weekend programs available. *Faculty:* 17 full-time (6 women). *Students:* 30 full-time (16 women), 8 part-time (6 women); includes 3 minority (2 Asian, non-Hispanic/Latino; 1 Hispanic/Latino), 8 international. Average age 27. 66 applicants, 24% accepted, 10 enrolled. In 2012, 2 master's, 3 doctorates awarded. Terminal master's awarded for partial completion of doctoral program. *Degree requirements:* For master's, comprehensive exam, thesis or alternative; for doctorate, thesis/dissertation, general exam. *Entrance requirements:* For master's and doctorate, GRE General Test, interview, minimum GPA of 3.0. Additional exam requirements/recommendations for international students: Required—TOEFL (minimum score 550 paper-based; 80 iBT). *Application deadline:* For fall admission, 1/15 priority date for domestic students, 1/15 for international students; for spring admission, 9/1 priority date for domestic students, 9/1 for international students. Applications are processed on a rolling basis. Application fee: $75. Electronic applications accepted. *Financial support:* In 2012–13, 27 students received support. Fellowships with tuition reimbursements available, research assistantships, teaching assistantships with tuition reimbursements available, Federal Work-Study, and tuition waivers available. Financial award application deadline: 1/15. *Unit head:* Dr. Michael King, Chair, 202-994-6488. *Application contact:* Information Contact, 202-994-6121, E-mail: gwchem@gwu.edu. Website: http://www.gwu.edu/~gwchem/.

Harvard University, Graduate School of Arts and Sciences, Department of Chemistry and Chemical Biology, Cambridge, MA 02138. Offers biochemical chemistry (PhD); inorganic chemistry (PhD); organic chemistry (PhD); physical chemistry (PhD). *Degree requirements:* For doctorate, thesis/dissertation, cumulative exams. *Entrance requirements:* For doctorate, GRE General Test, GRE Subject Test. Additional exam requirements/recommendations for international students: Required—TOEFL. *Expenses: Tuition:* Full-time $37,576. *Required fees:* $930. Tuition and fees vary according to program and student level.

See Display on page 70 and Close-Up on page 125.

Howard University, Graduate School, Department of Chemistry, Washington, DC 20059-0002. Offers analytical chemistry (MS, PhD); atmospheric (MS, PhD); biochemistry (MS, PhD); environmental (MS, PhD); inorganic chemistry (MS, PhD); organic chemistry (MS, PhD); physical chemistry (MS, PhD). Terminal master's awarded for partial completion of doctoral program. *Degree requirements:* For master's, comprehensive exam, thesis, teaching experience; for doctorate, comprehensive exam, thesis/dissertation, teaching experience. *Entrance requirements:* For master's, GRE General Test, minimum GPA of 2.7; for doctorate, GRE General Test, minimum GPA of 3.0. Additional exam requirements/recommendations for international students: Required—TOEFL. Electronic applications accepted. *Faculty research:* Synthetic organics, materials, natural products, mass spectrometry.

Indiana University Bloomington, University Graduate School, College of Arts and Sciences, Department of Chemistry, Bloomington, IN 47405. Offers analytical chemistry (PhD); chemical biology chemistry (PhD); chemistry (MAT); inorganic chemistry (PhD); materials chemistry (PhD); organic chemistry (PhD); physical chemistry (PhD). *Faculty:* 42 full-time (4 women). *Students:* 215 full-time (85 women), 4 part-time (1 woman); includes 21 minority (8 Black or African American, non-Hispanic/Latino; 9 Asian, non-Hispanic/Latino; 1 Hispanic/Latino; 3 Two or more races, non-Hispanic/Latino), 69 international. Average age 27. 329 applicants, 40% accepted, 50 enrolled. In 2012, 12 master's, 20 doctorates awarded. Terminal master's awarded for partial completion of doctoral program. *Degree requirements:* For master's, thesis; for doctorate, thesis/dissertation. *Entrance requirements:* For master's and doctorate, GRE General Test, GRE Subject Test. Additional exam requirements/recommendations for international students: Required—TOEFL. *Application deadline:* For fall admission, 1/15 priority date for domestic students, 12/15 for international students. Applications are processed on a rolling basis. Application fee: $55 ($65 for international students). *Financial support:* In 2012–13, 200 students received support, including 10 fellowships with full tuition reimbursements available, 76 research assistantships with full tuition reimbursements available, 111 teaching assistantships with full tuition reimbursements available; Federal Work-Study and institutionally sponsored loans also available. *Faculty research:* Synthesis of complex natural products, organic reaction mechanisms, organic electrochemistry, transitive-metal chemistry, solid-state and surface chemistry. *Total annual research expenditures:* $7.7 million. *Unit head:* David Giedroc, Chairperson, 812-855-6239, E-mail: chemchair@indiana.edu. *Application contact:* Daniel Mindiola, Director of Graduate Admissions, 812-855-2069, Fax: 812-855-8385, E-mail: mindiola@indiana.edu. Website: http://www.chem.indiana.edu/.

Iowa State University of Science and Technology, Program in Inorganic Chemistry, Ames, IA 50011. Offers MS, PhD. *Entrance requirements:* Additional exam requirements/recommendations for international students: Required—TOEFL (minimum score 570 paper-based; 89 iBT), IELTS (minimum score 6.5). *Application deadline:* For fall admission, 2/1 for domestic students. Application fee: $60 ($90 for international students). Electronic applications accepted. *Application contact:* Lynette Edsall, Application Contact, 515-294-7810, Fax: 515-294-0105, E-mail: chemgrad@iastate.edu. Website: http://www.chem.iastate.edu.

Kansas State University, Graduate School, College of Arts and Sciences, Department of Chemistry, Manhattan, KS 66506. Offers analytical chemistry (MS); biological chemistry (MS); chemistry (PhD); inorganic chemistry (MS); materials chemistry (MS); organic chemistry (MS); physical chemistry (MS). *Faculty:* 17 full-time (1 woman). *Students:* 71 full-time (36 women); includes 1 minority (Asian, non-Hispanic/Latino), 59 international. Average age 28. 108 applicants, 35% accepted, 15 enrolled. In 2012, 5 master's, 9 doctorates awarded. Terminal master's awarded for partial completion of doctoral program. *Degree requirements:* For master's, thesis; for doctorate, thesis/dissertation. *Entrance requirements:* For master's and doctorate, GRE, minimum GPA of 3.0. Additional exam requirements/recommendations for international students: Required—TOEFL (minimum score 550 paper-based). *Application deadline:* For fall admission, 2/1 priority date for domestic students, 2/1 for international students; for spring admission, 8/1 priority date for domestic students, 8/1 for international students. Applications are processed on a rolling basis. Application fee: $50 ($75 for international students). Electronic applications accepted. *Financial support:* In 2012–13, 39 research assistantships (averaging $18,182 per year), 24 teaching assistantships with full tuition reimbursements (averaging $18,106 per year) were awarded; institutionally sponsored loans and scholarships/grants also available. Support available to part-time students. Financial award application deadline: 3/1; financial award applicants required to submit FAFSA. *Faculty research:* Inorganic chemistry, organic and biological chemistry, analytical chemistry, physical chemistry, materials chemistry and nanotechnology. *Total annual research expenditures:* $2.8 million. *Unit head:* Eric Maatta, Head, 785-532-6665, Fax: 785-532-6666, E-mail: eam@ksu.edu. *Application contact:* Christer Aakeroy, Director, 785-532-6096, Fax: 785-532-6666, E-mail: aakeroy@ksu.edu. Website: http://www.k-state.edu/chem/.

Kent State University, College of Arts and Sciences, Department of Chemistry and Biochemistry, Kent, OH 44242-0001. Offers analytical chemistry (MS, PhD); biochemistry (MS, PhD); chemistry (MA); inorganic chemistry (MS, PhD); organic chemistry (MS, PhD); physical chemistry (MS, PhD). Terminal master's awarded for partial completion of doctoral program. *Degree requirements:* For master's, comprehensive exam, thesis; for doctorate, comprehensive exam, thesis/dissertation. *Entrance requirements:* For master's and doctorate, placement exam, GRE General Test, GRE Subject Test (recommended), minimum GPA of 2.75. Additional exam requirements/recommendations for international students: Required—TOEFL (minimum score 525 paper-based; 71 iBT). Electronic applications accepted. *Expenses:* Tuition, state resident: full-time $8424; part-time $468 per credit hour. Tuition, nonresident: full-time $14,580; part-time $810 per credit hour. Tuition and fees vary according to course load. *Faculty research:* Biological chemistry, materials chemistry, molecular spectroscopy.

See Display on page 73 and Close-Up on page 127.

Marquette University, Graduate School, College of Arts and Sciences, Department of Chemistry, Milwaukee, WI 53201-1881. Offers analytical chemistry (MS, PhD); bioanalytical chemistry (MS, PhD); biophysical chemistry (MS, PhD); chemical physics (MS, PhD); inorganic chemistry (MS, PhD); organic chemistry (MS, PhD); physical chemistry (MS, PhD). Part-time programs available. Terminal master's awarded for partial completion of doctoral program. *Degree requirements:* For master's, comprehensive exam; for doctorate, thesis/dissertation, cumulative exams. *Entrance requirements:* For master's and doctorate, official transcripts from all current and previous colleges/universities except Marquette, three letters of recommendation from individuals familiar with the applicant's academic work. Additional exam requirements/recommendations for international students: Required—TOEFL (minimum score 530 paper-based). Electronic applications accepted. *Faculty research:* Inorganic complexes, laser Raman spectroscopy, organic synthesis, synthetic bioinorganic chemistry, electro-active organic molecules.

Massachusetts Institute of Technology, School of Science, Department of Chemistry, Cambridge, MA 02139. Offers biological chemistry (PhD, Sc D); inorganic chemistry (PhD, Sc D); organic chemistry (PhD, Sc D); physical chemistry (PhD, Sc D). *Faculty:* 27 full-time (5 women). *Students:* 228 full-time (80 women), 4 part-time (2 women); includes 54 minority (6 Black or African American, non-Hispanic/Latino; 1 American Indian or Alaska Native, non-Hispanic/Latino; 31 Asian, non-Hispanic/Latino; 13 Hispanic/Latino; 3 Two or more races, non-Hispanic/Latino), 69 international. Average age 26. 651 applicants, 17% accepted, 44 enrolled. In 2012, 30 doctorates awarded. *Degree requirements:* For doctorate, comprehensive exam, thesis/dissertation. *Entrance requirements:* For doctorate, GRE General Test. Additional exam requirements/recommendations for international students: Required—IELTS (minimum score 7); Recommended—TOEFL (minimum score 600 paper-based). *Application deadline:* For fall admission, 12/15 for domestic and international students. Application fee: $75. Electronic applications accepted. *Expenses: Tuition:* Full-time $41,770; part-time $650 per credit hour. *Required fees:* $280. *Financial support:* In 2012–13, 194 students received support, including 71 fellowships (averaging $36,300 per year), 111 research assistantships (averaging $31,400 per year), 41 teaching assistantships (averaging $34,600 per year); Federal Work-Study, institutionally sponsored loans, scholarships/grants, traineeships, health care benefits, and unspecified assistantships also available. *Faculty research:* Synthetic organic and organometallic chemistry including catalysis; biological chemistry including bioorganic chemistry; physical chemistry including chemical dynamics and biophysical chemistry; inorganic chemistry including synthesis, catalysis, bioinorganic and physical inorganic chemistry; materials chemistry including surface science, nanoscience and polymers. *Total annual research expenditures:* $28.1 million. *Unit head:* Prof. Sylvia T. Ceyer, Head, 617-253-1803, Fax: 617-258-7500. *Application contact:* Graduate Administrator, 617-253-1845, Fax: 617-258-0241, E-mail: chemgradeducation@mit.edu. Website: http://web.mit.edu/chemistry/www/.

McMaster University, School of Graduate Studies, Faculty of Science, Department of Chemistry, Hamilton, ON L8S 4M2, Canada. Offers analytical chemistry (M Sc, PhD); chemical physics (M Sc, PhD); chemistry (M Sc, PhD); inorganic chemistry (M Sc, PhD); organic chemistry (M Sc, PhD); physical chemistry (M Sc, PhD); polymer chemistry (M Sc, PhD). Part-time programs available. Terminal master's awarded for partial completion of doctoral program. *Degree requirements:* For master's, thesis; for doctorate, comprehensive exam, thesis/dissertation. *Entrance requirements:* For master's, minimum B+ average. Additional exam requirements/recommendations for international students: Required—TOEFL (minimum score 550 paper-based).

Oregon State University, College of Science, Department of Chemistry, Corvallis, OR 97331. Offers analytical chemistry (MS, PhD); chemistry (MA, MAIS); inorganic chemistry (MS, PhD); nuclear and radiation chemistry (MS, PhD); organic chemistry (MS, PhD); physical chemistry (MS, PhD). Part-time programs available. *Faculty:* 28 full-time (7 women), 9 part-time/adjunct (1 woman). *Students:* 101 full-time (28 women), 1 part-time (0 women); includes 5 minority (2 Asian, non-Hispanic/Latino; 1 Hispanic/Latino; 2 Two or more races, non-Hispanic/Latino), 54 international. Average age 28. 98 applicants, 30% accepted, 27 enrolled. In 2012, 4 master's, 16 doctorates awarded. Terminal master's awarded for partial completion of doctoral program. *Degree requirements:* For master's, one foreign language, thesis; for doctorate, one foreign language, thesis/dissertation. *Entrance requirements:* For master's and doctorate, minimum GPA of 3.0 in last 90 hours of course work. Additional exam requirements/recommendations for international students: Required—TOEFL. *Application deadline:* For fall admission, 3/1 priority date for domestic students. Applications are processed on a rolling basis. Application fee: $50. *Expenses:* Tuition, state resident: full-time $11,367; part-time $421 per credit hour. Tuition, nonresident: full-time $18,279; part-time $677 per credit hour. *Required fees:* $1478. One-time fee: $300 full-time. Tuition and fees vary according to course load and program. *Financial support:* Fellowships, research assistantships, teaching assistantships, and institutionally sponsored loans available. Support available to part-time students. Financial award application deadline: 2/1. *Faculty research:* Solid state chemistry, enzyme reaction mechanisms, structure and dynamics of gas molecules, chemiluminescence, nonlinear optical spectroscopy. *Unit head:* Dr. Rich G. Carter, Professor/Chair, 541-737-0486, E-mail: rich.carter@oregonstate.edu.

Purdue University, Graduate School, College of Science, Department of Chemistry, West Lafayette, IN 47907. Offers analytical chemistry (MS, PhD); biochemistry (MS, PhD); chemical education (MS, PhD); inorganic chemistry (MS, PhD); organic chemistry (MS, PhD); physical chemistry (MS, PhD). *Faculty:* 42 full-time (14 women), 7 part-time/adjunct (0 women). *Students:* 275 full-time (102 women), 23 part-time (8 women); includes 34 minority (16 Black or African American, non-Hispanic/Latino; 5 Asian, non-Hispanic/Latino; 11 Hispanic/Latino; 2 Two or more races, non-Hispanic/Latino), 94 international. Average age 27. 716 applicants, 26% accepted, 66 enrolled. In 2012, 18 master's, 52 doctorates awarded. Terminal master's awarded for partial completion of doctoral program. *Degree requirements:* For master's, thesis; for doctorate, comprehensive exam, thesis/dissertation. *Entrance requirements:* For master's and doctorate, minimum undergraduate GPA of 3.0. Additional exam requirements/recommendations for international students: Required—TOEFL (minimum score 77 iBT); Recommended—TWE. *Application deadline:* For fall admission, 2/15 priority date for domestic students, 1/1 for international students. Applications are processed on a rolling basis. Application fee: $60 ($75 for international students). Electronic applications accepted. *Financial support:* In 2012–13, 2 fellowships with partial tuition reimbursements (averaging $18,000 per year), 55 teaching assistantships with partial tuition reimbursements (averaging $18,000 per year) were awarded; research assistantships with partial tuition reimbursements and tuition waivers (partial) also available. Support available to part-time students. Financial award applicants required to submit FAFSA. *Unit head:* Dr. Paul B. Shepson, Head, 765-494-5203, E-mail: pshepson@purdue.edu. *Application contact:* Betty L. Hatfield, Director of Graduate Admissions, 765-494-5208, E-mail: bettyh@purdue.edu.

Rice University, Graduate Programs, Wiess School of Natural Sciences, Department of Chemistry, Houston, TX 77251-1892. Offers chemistry (MA); inorganic chemistry (PhD); organic chemistry (PhD); physical chemistry (PhD). Terminal master's awarded for partial completion of doctoral program. *Degree requirements:* For master's, thesis; for doctorate, thesis/dissertation. *Entrance requirements:* For master's and doctorate, GRE General Test, minimum GPA of 3.0. Additional exam requirements/recommendations for international students: Required—TOEFL (minimum score 600 paper-based; 90 iBT). Electronic applications accepted. *Faculty research:* Nanoscience, biomaterials, nanobioinformatics, fullerene pharmaceuticals.

Rutgers, The State University of New Jersey, Newark, Graduate School, Program in Chemistry, Newark, NJ 07102. Offers analytical chemistry (MS, PhD); biochemistry (MS, PhD); inorganic chemistry (MS, PhD); organic chemistry (MS, PhD); physical chemistry (MS, PhD). Part-time and evening/weekend programs available. Terminal master's awarded for partial completion of doctoral program. *Degree requirements:* For master's, thesis optional, cumulative exams; for doctorate, thesis/dissertation, exams, research proposal. *Entrance requirements:* For master's and doctorate, GRE General Test, minimum undergraduate B average. Additional exam requirements/recommendations for international students: Required—TOEFL. Electronic applications accepted. *Faculty research:* Medicinal chemistry, natural products, isotope effects, biophysics and biorganic approaches to enzyme mechanisms, organic and organometallic synthesis.

Rutgers, The State University of New Jersey, New Brunswick, Graduate School-New Brunswick, Department of Chemistry and Chemical Biology, Piscataway, NJ 08854-8097. Offers biological chemistry (MS, PhD); inorganic chemistry (MS, PhD); organic chemistry (MS, PhD); physical chemistry (MS, PhD). Part-time and evening/weekend programs available. Terminal master's awarded for partial completion of doctoral program. *Degree requirements:* For master's, thesis or alternative, exam; for doctorate, thesis/dissertation, 1 year residency. *Entrance requirements:* For master's and doctorate, GRE General Test, GRE Subject Test. Additional exam requirements/recommendations for international students: Required—TOEFL. Electronic applications accepted. *Faculty research:* Biophysical organic/bioorganic, inorganic/bioinorganic, theoretical, and solid-state/surface chemistry.

Seton Hall University, College of Arts and Sciences, Department of Chemistry and Biochemistry, South Orange, NJ 07079-2697. Offers analytical chemistry (MS, PhD); biochemistry (MS, PhD); chemistry (MS); inorganic chemistry (MS, PhD); organic chemistry (MS, PhD); physical chemistry (MS, PhD). Part-time and evening/weekend programs available. Terminal master's awarded for partial completion of doctoral program. *Degree requirements:* For master's, thesis optional; for doctorate, comprehensive exam, thesis/dissertation. *Entrance requirements:* Additional exam requirements/recommendations for international students: Required—TOEFL. Electronic applications accepted. *Faculty research:* DNA metal reactions; chromatography; bioinorganic, biophysical, organometallic, polymer chemistry; heterogeneous catalyst; synthetic organic and carbohydrate chemistry.

Southern University and Agricultural and Mechanical College, Graduate School, College of Sciences, Department of Chemistry, Baton Rouge, LA 70813. Offers analytical chemistry (MS); biochemistry (MS); environmental sciences (MS); inorganic chemistry (MS); organic chemistry (MS); physical chemistry (MS). *Degree requirements:* For master's, thesis. *Entrance requirements:* For master's, GMAT or GRE General Test. Additional exam requirements/recommendations for international students: Required—TOEFL (minimum score 525 paper-based). *Faculty research:* Synthesis of macrocyclic ligands, latex accelerators, anticancer drugs, biosensors, absorption isotheums, isolation of specific enzymes from plants.

Texas Christian University, College of Science and Engineering, Department of Chemistry, Fort Worth, TX 76129. Offers biochemistry (MS, PhD); chemistry (MA); inorganic (MS, PhD); organic (MS, PhD); physical (MS, PhD). Part-time programs available. *Faculty:* 11 full-time (2 women). *Students:* 7 full-time (3 women), 17 part-time (10 women); includes 4 minority (1 Asian, non-Hispanic/Latino; 3 Hispanic/Latino), 13 international. Average age 27. 34 applicants, 24% accepted, 5 enrolled. In 2012, 1 master's, 1 doctorate awarded. *Degree requirements:* For master's, thesis; for doctorate, thesis/dissertation, literature seminar, cumulative exams, research progress report, original proposal. *Entrance requirements:* For master's and doctorate, GRE General Test. Additional exam requirements/recommendations for international students: Required—TOEFL (minimum score 80 iBT). *Application deadline:* For fall admission, 2/1 priority date for domestic students, 2/1 for international students; for spring admission, 9/1 priority date for domestic students, 9/1 for international students. Application fee: $50. Electronic applications accepted. *Expenses: Tuition:* Full-time $21,600; part-time $1200 per credit. *Required fees:* $48. Tuition and fees vary according to program. *Financial support:* In 2012–13, 16 students received support, including 16 teaching assistantships with full tuition reimbursements available; tuition waivers (full and partial) and unspecified assistantships also available. Financial award application deadline: 2/1. *Faculty research:* Phase transitions and transport properties of bio/macromolecular solutions, nanoscale biomaterials, electronic structure theory, synthetic methodology and total synthesis of natural products, chemistry and biology of (bio)polymers. *Unit head:* Dr. Robert Neilson, Chairperson/Professor, 817-257-7345, Fax: 817-257-5851, E-mail: r.neilson@tcu.edu. *Application contact:* Dr. Sergei V. Dzyuba, Director of Graduate Studies/ Assistant Professor, 817-257-6218, Fax: 817-257-5851, E-mail: s.dzyuba@tcu.edu. Website: http://www.chm.tcu.edu/.

Tufts University, Graduate School of Arts and Sciences, Department of Chemistry, Medford, MA 02155. Offers analytical chemistry (MS, PhD); bioorganic chemistry (MS, PhD); environmental chemistry (MS, PhD); inorganic chemistry (MS, PhD); organic chemistry (MS, PhD); physical chemistry (MS, PhD). Terminal master's awarded for partial completion of doctoral program. *Degree requirements:* For master's, thesis optional; for doctorate, thesis/dissertation. *Entrance requirements:* For master's and doctorate, GRE General Test, GRE Subject Test. Additional exam requirements/recommendations for international students: Required—TOEFL (minimum score 600 paper-based; 80 iBT). Electronic applications accepted. *Expenses: Tuition:* Full-time $42,856; part-time $1072 per credit hour. *Required fees:* $730. Full-time tuition and fees vary according to degree level, program and student level. Part-time tuition and fees vary according to course load.

University of Calgary, Faculty of Graduate Studies, Faculty of Science, Department of Chemistry, Calgary, AB T2N 1N4, Canada. Offers analytical chemistry (M Sc, PhD); applied chemistry (M Sc, PhD); inorganic chemistry (M Sc, PhD); organic chemistry (M Sc, PhD); physical chemistry (M Sc, PhD); polymer chemistry (M Sc, PhD); theoretical chemistry (M Sc, PhD). *Degree requirements:* For master's, thesis; for doctorate, thesis/dissertation, candidacy exam. *Entrance requirements:* For master's, minimum GPA of 3.0; for doctorate, honors B Sc degree with minimum GPA of 3.7 or M Sc with minimum GPA of 3.3. Additional exam requirements/recommendations for international students: Required—TOEFL (minimum score 580 paper-based). Electronic applications accepted. *Faculty research:* Chemical analysis, chemical dynamics, synthesis theory.

University of Cincinnati, Graduate School, McMicken College of Arts and Sciences, Department of Chemistry, Cincinnati, OH 45221. Offers analytical chemistry (MS, PhD); biochemistry (MS, PhD); inorganic chemistry (MS, PhD); organic chemistry (MS, PhD); physical chemistry (MS, PhD); polymer chemistry (MS, PhD); sensors (PhD). Part-time and evening/weekend programs available. Terminal master's awarded for partial completion of doctoral program. *Degree requirements:* For master's, thesis optional; for doctorate, comprehensive exam, thesis/dissertation. *Entrance requirements:* For master's and doctorate, GRE General Test. Additional exam requirements/recommendations for international students: Required—TOEFL (minimum score 580 paper-based). Electronic applications accepted. *Faculty research:* Biomedical chemistry, laser chemistry, surface science, chemical sensors, synthesis.

University of Georgia, Franklin College of Arts and Sciences, Department of Chemistry, Athens, GA 30602. Offers analytical chemistry (MS, PhD); inorganic chemistry (MS, PhD); organic chemistry (MS, PhD); physical chemistry (MS, PhD). Terminal master's awarded for partial completion of doctoral program. *Degree requirements:* For master's, thesis; for doctorate, one foreign language, thesis/dissertation. *Entrance requirements:* For master's and doctorate, GRE General Test. Additional exam requirements/recommendations for international students: Required—TOEFL. Electronic applications accepted.

University of Louisville, Graduate School, College of Arts and Sciences, Department of Chemistry, Louisville, KY 40292-0001. Offers analytical chemistry (MS, PhD); biochemistry (MS, PhD); chemical physics (PhD); inorganic chemistry (MS, PhD); organic chemistry (MS, PhD); physical chemistry (MS, PhD). *Students:* 45 full-time (21 women), 5 part-time (1 woman); includes 1 minority (Hispanic/Latino), 35 international. Average age 28. 78 applicants, 17% accepted, 9 enrolled. In 2012, 19 master's, 7 doctorates awarded. Terminal master's awarded for partial completion of doctoral program. *Degree requirements:* For master's, variable foreign language requirement, comprehensive exam, thesis optional; for doctorate, variable foreign language requirement, comprehensive exam, thesis/dissertation. *Entrance requirements:* For master's and doctorate, BA or BS coursework. Additional exam requirements/recommendations for international students: Required—TOEFL. *Application deadline:* For fall admission, 3/15 for domestic and international students; for winter admission, 9/15 for domestic and international students. Applications are processed on a rolling basis. Application fee: $60. Electronic applications accepted. *Financial support:* In 2012–13, 33 teaching assistantships with full tuition reimbursements (averaging $22,000 per year) were awarded; fellowships with full tuition reimbursements, research assistantships with full tuition reimbursements, career-related internships or fieldwork, scholarships/grants, traineeships, health care benefits, and unspecified assistantships also available. Support available to part-time students. Financial award application deadline: 3/15. *Faculty research:* Computational chemistry, biophysics nuclear magnetic resonance, synthetic organic chemistry, synthetic inorganic chemistry, medicinal chemistry, protein chemistry, enzymology, nanochemistry, electrochemistry, analytical chemistry, synthetic biology, bioinformatics. *Total annual research expenditures:* $2.5 million. *Unit head:* Dr. Richard J. Wittebort, Professor/Chair, 502-852-6613. *Application contact:* Sherry Nalley, Administrator, 502-852-6798.

The University of Manchester, School of Chemistry, Manchester, United Kingdom. Offers biological chemistry (PhD); chemistry (M Ent, M Phil, M Sc, D Ent, PhD); inorganic chemistry (PhD); materials chemistry (PhD); nanoscience (PhD); nuclear fission (PhD); organic chemistry (PhD); physical chemistry (PhD); theoretical chemistry (PhD).

University of Maryland, College Park, Academic Affairs, College of Computer, Mathematical and Natural Sciences, Department of Chemistry and Biochemistry, Chemistry Program, College Park, MD 20742. Offers analytical chemistry (MS, PhD); inorganic chemistry (MS, PhD); organic chemistry (MS, PhD); physical chemistry (MS, PhD). Part-time and evening/weekend programs available. *Students:* 113 full-time (64 women), 2 part-time (0 women); includes 19 minority (11 Black or African American, non-Hispanic/Latino; 4 Asian, non-Hispanic/Latino; 2 Hispanic/Latino; 2 Two or more races, non-Hispanic/Latino), 44 international. 339 applicants, 27% accepted, 20 enrolled. In 2012, 7 master's, 14 doctorates awarded. Terminal master's awarded for partial completion of doctoral program. *Degree requirements:* For master's, thesis optional; for doctorate, thesis/dissertation, 2 seminar presentations, oral exam. *Entrance requirements:* For master's and doctorate, GRE General Test, GRE Subject Test (recommended), minimum GPA of 3.0, 3 letters of recommendation. Additional exam requirements/recommendations for international students: Required—TOEFL. *Application deadline:* For fall admission, 2/1 for domestic and international students; for spring admission, 6/1 for domestic and international students. Applications are processed on a rolling basis. Application fee: $75. Electronic applications accepted. *Expenses:* Tuition, state resident: part-time $551 per credit. Tuition, nonresident: part-time $1188 per credit. Part-time tuition and fees vary according to program. *Financial support:* In 2012–13, 14 fellowships with full and partial tuition reimbursements (averaging $20,017 per year), 52 research assistantships (averaging $19,868 per year), 44 teaching assistantships (averaging $19,209 per year) were awarded. Financial award applicants required to submit FAFSA. *Faculty research:* Environmental chemistry, nuclear chemistry, lunar and environmental analysis, x-ray crystallography. *Unit head:* Dr. Michael Doyle, Chairperson, 301-405-1795, Fax: 301-314-2779, E-mail: mdoyle3@umd.edu. *Application contact:* Dr. Charles A. Caramello, Dean of Graduate School, 301-405-0358, Fax: 301-314-9305.

University of Massachusetts Lowell, College of Sciences, Department of Chemistry, Lowell, MA 01854-2881. Offers analytical chemistry (PhD); biochemistry (PhD); chemistry (MS, PhD); environmental studies (PhD); green chemistry (PhD); inorganic chemistry (PhD); organic chemistry (PhD); polymer science (MS). Terminal master's awarded for partial completion of doctoral program. *Degree requirements:* For master's, thesis; for doctorate, 2 foreign languages, thesis/dissertation. *Entrance requirements:* For master's and doctorate, GRE General Test. Electronic applications accepted.

University of Memphis, Graduate School, College of Arts and Sciences, Department of Chemistry, Memphis, TN 38152. Offers analytical chemistry (MS, PhD); computational chemistry (MS, PhD); inorganic chemistry (MS, PhD); organic chemistry (MS, PhD); physical chemistry (MS, PhD). Part-time programs available. Terminal master's awarded for partial completion of doctoral program. *Degree requirements:* For master's, comprehensive exam, thesis or alternative; for doctorate, comprehensive exam, thesis/dissertation. *Entrance requirements:* For master's and doctorate, GRE General Test, admission to Graduate School plus 32 undergraduate hours in chemistry. Additional exam requirements/recommendations for international students: Required—TOEFL. Electronic applications accepted. *Faculty research:* Computational chemistry, materials chemistry, organic/polymer synthesis, drug design/delivery, water chemistry.

University of Miami, Graduate School, College of Arts and Sciences, Department of Chemistry, Coral Gables, FL 33124. Offers chemistry (MS); inorganic chemistry (PhD); organic chemistry (PhD); physical chemistry (PhD). Terminal master's awarded for partial completion of doctoral program. *Degree requirements:* For master's, comprehensive exam; for doctorate, comprehensive exam, thesis/dissertation. *Entrance requirements:* For master's and doctorate, GRE General Test. Additional exam requirements/recommendations for international students: Required—TOEFL (minimum score 550 paper-based). Electronic applications accepted. *Faculty research:* Supramolecular chemistry, electrochemistry, surface chemistry, catalysis, organometalic.

University of Michigan, Horace H. Rackham School of Graduate Studies, College of Literature, Science, and the Arts, Department of Chemistry, Ann Arbor, MI 48109-1055. Offers analytical chemistry (PhD); chemical biology (PhD); inorganic chemistry (PhD); material chemistry (PhD); organic chemistry (PhD); physical chemistry (PhD). *Degree requirements:* For doctorate, thesis/dissertation, oral defense of dissertation, organic cumulative proficiency exams. *Entrance requirements:* For doctorate, GRE General Test, GRE Subject Test (recommended), 3 letters of recommendation. Additional exam requirements/recommendations for international students: Required—TOEFL (minimum score 560 paper-based; 84 iBT). Electronic applications accepted. *Faculty research:* Biological catalysis, protein engineering, chemical sensors, de novo metalloprotein design, supramolecular architecture.

University of Missouri, Graduate School, College of Arts and Sciences, Department of Chemistry, Columbia, MO 65211. Offers analytical chemistry (MS, PhD); inorganic chemistry (MS, PhD); organic chemistry (MS, PhD); physical chemistry (MS, PhD). *Faculty:* 22 full-time (4 women), 1 part-time/adjunct (0 women). *Students:* 110 full-time (42 women), 9 part-time (5 women); includes 10 minority (3 Black or African American, non-Hispanic/Latino; 3 Asian, non-Hispanic/Latino; 2 Hispanic/Latino; 2 Two or more races, non-Hispanic/Latino), 47 international. Average age 27. 94 applicants, 21% accepted, 15 enrolled. In 2012, 2 master's, 5 doctorates awarded. *Degree requirements:* For master's, thesis; for doctorate, one foreign language, comprehensive exam, thesis/dissertation. *Entrance requirements:* For master's, GRE General Test, minimum GPA of 3.0; for doctorate, GRE General Test (minimum score: Verbal 450, Quantitative 600, Analytical 3), minimum GPA of 3.0. Additional exam requirements/recommendations for international students: Required—TOEFL (minimum score 600 paper-based; 100 iBT). *Application deadline:* For fall admission, 2/1 priority date for domestic students, 2/1 for international students; for winter admission, 10/15 for domestic and international students. Applications are processed on a rolling basis. Application fee: $55 ($75 for international students). Electronic applications accepted. *Expenses:* Tuition, state resident: full-time $6057. Tuition, nonresident: full-time $15,683. *Required fees:* $1000. *Financial support:* In 2012–13, 9 fellowships with full tuition reimbursements, 15 research assistantships with full tuition reimbursements, 78 teaching assistantships with full tuition reimbursements were awarded; institutionally sponsored loans, traineeships, health care benefits, and unspecified assistantships also available. *Faculty research:* Analytical, organic, biological, physical, inorganic and radiochemistry. *Unit head:* Dr. Jerry Atwood, Department Chair, 573-882-8374, E-mail: atwoodj@missouri.edu. *Application contact:* Jerry Brightwell, Administrative Assistant, 573-884-6832, E-mail: brightwellj@missouri.edu. Website: http://chemistry.missouri.edu/.

University of Missouri–Kansas City, College of Arts and Sciences, Department of Chemistry, Kansas City, MO 64110-2499. Offers analytical chemistry (MS, PhD); inorganic chemistry (MS, PhD); organic chemistry (MS, PhD); physical chemistry (MS, PhD); polymer chemistry (MS, PhD). PhD (interdisciplinary) offered through the School of Graduate Studies. Part-time and evening/weekend programs available. *Faculty:* 15 full-time (3 women), 2 part-time/adjunct (0 women). *Students:* 7 part-time (3 women); includes 3 minority (2 Black or African American, non-Hispanic/Latino, 1 Hispanic/Latino). Average age 38. 19 applicants, 37% accepted, 3 enrolled. In 2012, 2 master's awarded. *Degree requirements:* For master's, thesis (for some programs); for doctorate, thesis/dissertation. *Entrance requirements:* For master's, equivalent of American Chemical Society approved bachelor's degree in chemistry; for doctorate, GRE General Test, equivalent of American Chemical Society approved bachelor's degree in chemistry. Additional exam requirements/recommendations for international students: Required—TOEFL (minimum score 550 paper-based; 80 iBT), TWE. *Application deadline:* For fall admission, 4/15 for domestic and international students; for spring admission, 10/15 for domestic and international students. Applications are processed on a rolling basis. Application fee: $45 ($50 for international students). Electronic applications accepted. *Expenses:* Tuition, state resident: full-time $5972.40; part-time $331.80 per credit hour. Tuition, nonresident: full-time $15,417; part-time $856.50 per credit hour. *Required fees:* $95.89 per credit hour. Full-time tuition and fees vary according to program. *Financial support:* In 2012–13, 6 research assistantships with partial tuition reimbursements (averaging $18,817 per year), 16 teaching assistantships with partial tuition reimbursements (averaging $18,132 per year) were awarded; Federal Work-Study, institutionally sponsored loans, and scholarships/grants also available. Support available to part-time students. Financial award application deadline: 3/1; financial award applicants required to submit FAFSA. *Faculty research:* Molecular spectroscopy, characterization and synthesis of materials and compounds, computational chemistry, natural products, drug delivery systems and anti-tumor agents. *Unit head:* Dr. Kathleen V. Kilway, Chair, 816-235-2289, Fax: 816-235-5502. *Application contact:* Graduate Recruiting Committee, 816-235-2272, Fax: 816-235-5502, E-mail: umkc-chemdept@umkc.edu. Website: http://cas.umkc.edu/chem/.

University of Missouri–St. Louis, College of Arts and Sciences, Department of Chemistry and Biochemistry, St. Louis, MO 63121. Offers chemistry (MS, PhD), including biochemistry, inorganic chemistry, organic chemistry, physical chemistry. Part-time and evening/weekend programs available. *Faculty:* 19 full-time (3 women), 6 part-time/adjunct (1 woman). *Students:* 37 full-time (15 women), 25 part-time (16 women); includes 6 minority (2 Black or African American, non-Hispanic/Latino; 1 Asian, non-Hispanic/Latino; 3 Hispanic/Latino), 18 international. Average age 30. 85 applicants, 22% accepted, 7 enrolled. In 2012, 10 master's, 5 doctorates awarded. Terminal master's awarded for partial completion of doctoral program. *Degree requirements:* For master's, thesis optional; for doctorate, thesis/dissertation. *Entrance requirements:* For master's, 2 letters of recommendation; for doctorate, GRE General Test, 3 letters of recommendation. Additional exam requirements/recommendations for international students: Required—TOEFL (minimum score 550 paper-based; 79 iBT), IELTS (minimum score 6.5). *Application deadline:* For fall admission, 7/1 priority date for domestic students, 7/1 for international students; for spring admission, 12/1 priority date for domestic students, 12/1 for international students. Applications are processed on a rolling basis. Application fee: $35 ($40 for international students). Electronic applications accepted. *Expenses:* Tuition, state resident: full-time $7364; part-time $409.10 per credit hour. Tuition, nonresident: full-time $18,153; part-time $1008.50 per credit hour. *Financial support:* In 2012–13, 16 research assistantships with full and partial tuition reimbursements (averaging $13,500 per year), 20 teaching assistantships with full and partial tuition reimbursements (averaging $13,500 per year) were awarded; fellowships with full and partial tuition reimbursements also available. *Faculty research:* Metallaborane chemistry, serum transferrin chemistry, natural products chemistry, organic synthesis. *Unit head:* Dr. Janet Wilking, Director of Graduate Studies, 314-516-5311, Fax: 314-516-5342, E-mail: gradchem@umsl.edu. *Application contact:* Graduate Admissions, 314-516-5458, Fax: 314-516-6996, E-mail: gradadm@umsl.edu. Website: http://www.umsl.edu/chemistry/.

The University of Montana, Graduate School, College of Arts and Sciences, Department of Chemistry and Biochemistry, Missoula, MT 59812-0002. Offers chemistry (MS, PhD), including environmental/analytical chemistry, inorganic chemistry, organic chemistry, physical chemistry. Terminal master's awarded for partial completion of doctoral program. *Degree requirements:* For master's, thesis (for some programs); for doctorate, thesis/dissertation. *Entrance requirements:* For master's and doctorate, GRE General Test. Additional exam requirements/recommendations for international students: Required—TOEFL (minimum score 575 paper-based). *Faculty research:* Reaction mechanisms and kinetics, inorganic and organic synthesis, analytical chemistry, natural products.

University of Nebraska–Lincoln, Graduate College, College of Arts and Sciences, Department of Chemistry, Lincoln, NE 68588. Offers analytical chemistry (PhD); biochemistry (PhD); chemistry (MS); inorganic chemistry (PhD); materials chemistry (PhD); organic chemistry (PhD); physical chemistry (PhD). *Degree requirements:* For master's, one foreign language, thesis optional, departmental qualifying exam; for doctorate, one foreign language, comprehensive exam, thesis/dissertation, departmental qualifying exams. *Entrance requirements:* For master's and doctorate, GRE. Additional exam requirements/recommendations for international students: Required—TOEFL (minimum score 550 paper-based). Electronic applications accepted. *Faculty research:* Bioorganic and bioinorganic chemistry, biophysical and bioanalytical chemistry, structure-function of DNA and proteins, organometallics, mass spectrometry.

University of Notre Dame, Graduate School, College of Science, Department of Chemistry and Biochemistry, Notre Dame, IN 46556. Offers biochemistry (MS, PhD); inorganic chemistry (MS, PhD); organic chemistry (MS, PhD); physical chemistry (MS, PhD). Terminal master's awarded for partial completion of doctoral program. *Degree requirements:* For master's, comprehensive exam, thesis; for doctorate, thesis/dissertation, qualifying exam. *Entrance requirements:* For master's and doctorate, GRE General Test, GRE Subject Test (strongly recommended). Additional exam requirements/recommendations for international students: Required—TOEFL (minimum score 600 paper-based; 80 iBT). Electronic applications accepted. *Faculty research:* Reaction design and mechanistic studies; reactive intermediates; synthesis, structure and reactivity of organometallic cluster complexes and biologically active natural products; bioorganic chemistry, enzymology.

University of Regina, Faculty of Graduate Studies and Research, Faculty of Science, Department of Chemistry and Biochemistry, Regina, SK S4S 0A2, Canada. Offers analytical/environmental chemistry (M Sc, PhD); biophysics of biological interfaces (M Sc, PhD); enzymology/chemical biology (M Sc, PhD); inorganic/organometallic chemistry (M Sc, PhD); signal transduction and mechanisms of cancer cell regulation (M Sc, PhD); supramolecular organic photochemistry and photophysics (M Sc, PhD); synthetic organic chemistry (M Sc, PhD); theoretical/computational chemistry (M Sc, PhD). *Faculty:* 12 full-time (2 women), 3 part-time/adjunct (0 women). *Students:* 11 full-time (6 women), 2 part-time (0 women). 32 applicants, 19% accepted. In 2012, 7 master's awarded. *Degree requirements:* For master's, thesis; for doctorate, thesis/dissertation. *Entrance requirements:* Additional exam requirements/recommendations for international students: Required—TOEFL (minimum score 580 paper-based; 80 iBT), IELTS (minimum score 6.5). *Application deadline:* Applications are processed on a rolling basis. Application fee: $100. Electronic applications accepted. Tuition and fees charges are reported in Canadian dollars. *Expenses: Tuition, area resident:* Full-time $3942 Canadian dollars; part-time $219 Canadian dollars per credit hour. *International tuition:* $4742 Canadian dollars full-time. *Required fees:* $421.55 Canadian dollars; $93.60 Canadian dollars per credit hour. Tuition and fees vary according to course load, degree level and program. *Financial support:* In 2012–13, 5 fellowships (averaging $7,000 per year), 10 teaching assistantships (averaging $2,470 per year) were awarded; research assistantships and scholarships/grants also available. Financial award application deadline: 6/15. *Faculty research:* Asymmetric synthesis and methodology, theoretical and computational chemistry, biophysical biochemistry, analytical and environmental chemistry, chemical biology. *Unit head:* Dr. Lynn Mihichuk, Head, 306-585-4793, Fax: 306-337-2409, E-mail: lynn.mihichuk@uregina.ca. *Application contact:* Dr. Brian Sterenberg, Graduate Program Coordinator, 306-585-4106, Fax: 306-337-2409, E-mail: brian.sterenberg@uregina.ca. Website: http://www.chem.uregina.ca/.

University of Southern Mississippi, Graduate School, College of Science and Technology, Department of Chemistry and Biochemistry, Hattiesburg, MS 39406-0001. Offers analytical chemistry (MS, PhD); biochemistry (MS, PhD); inorganic chemistry (MS, PhD); organic chemistry (MS, PhD); physical chemistry (MS, PhD). *Faculty:* 16 full-time (4 women). *Students:* 26 full-time (9 women); includes 2 minority (1 Black or African American, non-Hispanic/Latino; 1 Asian, non-Hispanic/Latino), 8 international. Average age 27. 63 applicants, 13% accepted, 4 enrolled. In 2012, 2 master's, 4 doctorates awarded. *Degree requirements:* For

Peterson's Graduate Programs in the Physical Sciences, Mathematics, Agricultural Sciences, the Environment & Natural Resources 2014

www.petersonsbooks.com **105**

master's, comprehensive exam, thesis; for doctorate, comprehensive exam, thesis/dissertation. *Entrance requirements:* For master's, GRE General Test, minimum GPA of 2.75 in last 60 hours; for doctorate, GRE General Test, minimum GPA of 3.5. Additional exam requirements/recommendations for international students: Required—TOEFL, IELTS. *Application deadline:* For fall admission, 3/1 priority date for domestic students, 3/1 for international students. Applications are processed on a rolling basis. Application fee: $50. *Financial support:* In 2012–13, 3 research assistantships with full tuition reimbursements (averaging $17,000 per year), 19 teaching assistantships with full tuition reimbursements (averaging $20,700 per year) were awarded; fellowships, Federal Work-Study, institutionally sponsored loans, scholarships/grants, health care benefits, and unspecified assistantships also available. Support available to part-time students. Financial award application deadline: 3/15; financial award applicants required to submit FAFSA. *Faculty research:* Plant biochemistry, photo chemistry, polymer chemistry, x-ray analysis, enzyme chemistry. *Unit head:* Dr. Sabine Heinhorst, Chair, 601-266-4701, Fax: 601-266-6075. Website: http://www.usm.edu/graduateschool/table.php.

University of South Florida, Graduate School, College of Arts and Sciences, Department of Chemistry, Tampa, FL 33620-9951. Offers analytical chemistry (MS, PhD); biochemistry (MS, PhD); computational chemistry (MS, PhD); environmental chemistry (MS, PhD); inorganic chemistry (MS, PhD); organic chemistry (MS); physical chemistry (MS, PhD); polymer chemistry (PhD). Part-time programs available. Terminal master's awarded for partial completion of doctoral program. *Degree requirements:* For master's, comprehensive exam, thesis (for some programs); for doctorate, comprehensive exam, thesis/dissertation. *Entrance requirements:* For master's and doctorate, GRE General Test, minimum GPA of 3.0. Additional exam requirements/recommendations for international students: Required—TOEFL (minimum score 550 paper-based; 79 iBT) or IELTS (minimum score 6.5). Electronic applications accepted. *Faculty research:* Synthesis, bio-organic chemistry, bioinorganic chemistry, environmental chemistry, nuclear magnetic resonance (NMR).

The University of Tennessee, Graduate School, College of Arts and Sciences, Department of Chemistry, Knoxville, TN 37996. Offers analytical chemistry (MS, PhD); chemical physics (PhD); environmental chemistry (MS, PhD); inorganic chemistry (MS, PhD); organic chemistry (MS, PhD); physical chemistry (MS, PhD); polymer chemistry (MS, PhD); theoretical chemistry (PhD). Part-time programs available. Terminal master's awarded for partial completion of doctoral program. *Degree requirements:* For master's, thesis; for doctorate, thesis/dissertation. *Entrance requirements:* For master's and doctorate, GRE General Test, minimum GPA of 2.7. Additional exam requirements/recommendations for international students: Required—TOEFL. Electronic applications accepted. *Expenses:* Tuition, state resident: full-time $9000; part-time $501 per credit hour. Tuition, nonresident: full-time $27,188; part-time $1512 per credit hour. *Required fees:* $1280; $62 per credit hour. Tuition and fees vary according to program.

The University of Texas at Austin, Graduate School, College of Natural Sciences, Department of Chemistry and Biochemistry, Austin, TX 78712-1111. Offers analytical chemistry (PhD); biochemistry (PhD); inorganic chemistry (PhD); organic chemistry (PhD); physical chemistry (PhD). *Entrance requirements:* For doctorate, GRE General Test.

The University of Toledo, College of Graduate Studies, College of Natural Sciences and Mathematics, Department of Chemistry, Toledo, OH 43606-3390. Offers analytical chemistry (MS, PhD); biological chemistry (MS, PhD); inorganic chemistry (MS, PhD); organic chemistry (MS, PhD); physical chemistry (MS, PhD). Part-time programs available. *Faculty:* 23. *Students:* 66 full-time (20 women), 9 part-time (2 women); includes 3 minority (1 Asian, non-Hispanic/Latino; 2 Hispanic/Latino), 50 international. Average age 27. 84 applicants, 26% accepted, 19 enrolled. In 2012, 6 master's, 7 doctorates awarded. *Degree requirements:* For master's, thesis or alternative; for doctorate, thesis/dissertation. *Entrance requirements:* For master's and doctorate, GRE General Test, GRE Subject Test, minimum cumulative point-hour ratio of 2.7 for all previous academic work, three letters of recommendation, statement of purpose, transcripts from all prior institutions attended. Additional exam requirements/recommendations for international students: Required—TOEFL (minimum score 550 paper-based; 80 iBT), IELTS (minimum score 6.5). *Application deadline:* For fall admission, 1/15 priority date for domestic students, 1/15 for international students. Applications are processed on a rolling basis. Application fee: $45 ($75 for international students). Electronic applications accepted. *Financial support:* In 2012–13, 29 research assistantships with full and partial tuition reimbursements (averaging $16,200 per year), 49 teaching assistantships with full and partial tuition reimbursements (averaging $15,682 per year) were awarded; Federal Work-Study, institutionally sponsored loans, scholarships/grants, tuition waivers (full), and unspecified assistantships also available. Support available to part-time students. *Faculty research:* Enzymology, materials chemistry, crystallography, theoretical chemistry. *Unit head:* Dr. Ronald Viola, Chair, 419-530-1582, Fax: 419-530-4033, E-mail: ronald.viola@utoledo.edu. *Application contact:* Graduate School Office, 419-530-4723, Fax: 419-530-4724, E-mail: grdsch@utnet.utoledo.edu. Website: http://www.utoledo.edu/nsm/.

Vanderbilt University, Graduate School, Department of Chemistry, Nashville, TN 37240-1001. Offers analytical chemistry (MAT, MS, PhD); inorganic chemistry (MAT, MS, PhD); organic chemistry (MAT, MS, PhD); physical chemistry (MAT, MS, PhD); theoretical chemistry (MAT, MS). *Faculty:* 21 full-time (3 women). *Students:* 123 full-time (46 women); includes 22 minority (5 Black or African American, non-Hispanic/Latino; 1 American Indian or Alaska Native, non-Hispanic/Latino; 3 Asian, non-Hispanic/Latino; 5 Hispanic/Latino; 8 Two or more races, non-Hispanic/Latino), 14 international. Average age 25. 430 applicants, 15% accepted, 29 enrolled. In 2012, 6 master's, 14 doctorates awarded. Terminal master's awarded for partial completion of doctoral program. *Degree requirements:* For master's, thesis; for doctorate, thesis/dissertation, area, qualifying, and final exams. *Entrance requirements:* For master's and doctorate, GRE General Test, GRE Subject Test (recommended). Additional exam requirements/recommendations for international students: Required—TOEFL (minimum score 570 paper-based; 88 iBT). *Application deadline:* For fall admission, 1/15 for domestic and international students. Application fee: $0. Electronic applications accepted. *Financial support:* Fellowships with full and partial tuition reimbursements, research assistantships with full tuition reimbursements, teaching assistantships with full tuition reimbursements, Federal Work-Study, institutionally sponsored loans, scholarships/grants, traineeships, and health care benefits available. Financial award application deadline: 1/15; financial award applicants required to submit CSS PROFILE or FAFSA. *Faculty research:* Chemical synthesis; mechanistic, theoretical, bioorganic, analytical, and spectroscopic chemistry. *Unit head:* Dr. David Cliffel, Director of Graduate Studies, 615-343-3937, Fax: 615-322-4936, E-mail: d.cliffel@vanderbilt.edu. *Application contact:* Sandra Ford, Administrative Assistant, 615-322-8695, Fax: 615-322-4936, E-mail: sandra.e.ford@Vanderbilt.Edu. Website: http://www.vanderbilt.edu/chemistry/.

Virginia Commonwealth University, Graduate School, College of Humanities and Sciences, Department of Chemistry, Richmond, VA 23284-9005. Offers analytical chemistry (MS, PhD); chemical physics (PhD); inorganic chemistry (MS, PhD); organic chemistry (MS, PhD); physical chemistry (MS, PhD). Part-time programs available. Terminal master's awarded for partial completion of doctoral program. *Degree requirements:* For master's, thesis; for doctorate, thesis/dissertation, comprehensive cumulative exams, research proposal. *Entrance requirements:* For master's, GRE General Test, 30 undergraduate credits in chemistry; for doctorate, GRE General Test. Additional exam requirements/recommendations for international students: Required—TOEFL (minimum score 600 paper-based; 100 iBT) or IELTS (minimum score 6.5). Electronic applications accepted. *Faculty research:* Physical, organic, inorganic, analytical, and polymer chemistry; chemical physics.

Wake Forest University, Graduate School of Arts and Sciences, Department of Chemistry, Winston-Salem, NC 27109. Offers analytical chemistry (MS, PhD); inorganic chemistry (MS, PhD); organic chemistry (MS, PhD); physical chemistry (MS, PhD). Part-time programs available. *Degree requirements:* For master's, one foreign language, comprehensive exam, thesis; for doctorate, 2 foreign languages, comprehensive exam, thesis/dissertation. *Entrance requirements:* For master's and doctorate, GRE General Test. Additional exam requirements/recommendations for international students: Required—TOEFL. Electronic applications accepted.

Wayne State University, College of Liberal Arts and Sciences, Department of Chemistry, Detroit, MI 48202. Offers analytical chemistry (PhD); biochemistry (PhD); chemistry (MA, MS); inorganic chemistry (PhD); organic chemistry (PhD); physical chemistry (PhD). *Students:* 167 full-time (79 women), 1 part-time (0 women); includes 12 minority (3 Black or African American, non-Hispanic/Latino; 2 American Indian or Alaska Native, non-Hispanic/Latino; 5 Asian, non-Hispanic/Latino; 2 Hispanic/Latino), 113 international. Average age 28. 440 applicants, 23% accepted, 50 enrolled. In 2012, 5 master's, 15 doctorates awarded. *Degree requirements:* For master's, thesis (for some programs), oral exam; for doctorate, thesis/dissertation, oral exam. *Entrance requirements:* For master's, one year of physics, math through calculus, general chemistry (8 credits), organic chemistry (8 credits), physical chemistry (six credits), quantitative analysis (four credits), and advanced chemistry (three credits); advanced biology (for biochemistry applicants); minimum undergraduate GPA of 2.75 in chemistry and cognate sciences; for doctorate, minimum undergraduate GPA of 3.0 in chemistry and cognate science. Additional exam requirements/recommendations for international students: Required—TOEFL (minimum score 550 paper-based; 79 iBT); Recommended—TWE (minimum score 5.5). *Application deadline:* For fall admission, 2/10 priority date for domestic students, 2/10 for international students; for winter admission, 10/1 priority date for domestic students, 9/1 for international students; for spring admission, 2/1 priority date for domestic students, 1/1 for international students. Applications are processed on a rolling basis. Application fee: $50. Electronic applications accepted. *Expenses:* Tuition, state resident: full-time $12,788; part-time $532.85 per credit hour. Tuition, nonresident: full-time $28,243; part-time $1176.80 per credit hour. *Required fees:* $1367.30; $39.75 per credit hour. $206.65 per semester. Tuition and fees vary according to course load and program. *Financial support:* In 2012–13, 154 students received support, including 10 fellowships with tuition reimbursements available (averaging $23,000 per year), 60 research assistantships with tuition reimbursements available (averaging $19,682 per year), 81 teaching assistantships with tuition reimbursements available (averaging $20,788 per year); scholarships/grants, health care benefits, and unspecified assistantships also available. Financial award application deadline: 7/1. *Faculty research:* Natural products synthesis, molecular biology, molecular mechanics calculations, organometallic chemistry, experimental physical chemistry. *Total annual research expenditures:* $7.2 million. *Unit head:* Dr. James Rigby, Chair, 313-577-3472, Fax: 313-577-8822, E-mail: aa392@wayne.edu. *Application contact:* Dr. Charles Winter, Graduate Director, 313-577-5224, E-mail: chw@chem.wayne.edu. Website: http://chem.wayne.edu/.

Wesleyan University, Graduate Studies, Department of Chemistry, Middletown, CT 06459-0180. Offers biochemistry (PhD); chemical physics (PhD); inorganic chemistry (PhD); organic chemistry (PhD); physical chemistry (PhD); theoretical chemistry (PhD). Terminal master's awarded for partial completion of doctoral program. *Degree requirements:* For doctorate, thesis/dissertation, proposal. *Entrance requirements:* For doctorate, GRE General Test, 3 recommendations. Additional exam requirements/recommendations for international students: Required—TOEFL. *Application deadline:* Applications are processed on a rolling basis. Application fee: $0. Electronic applications accepted. *Financial support:* Research assistantships with full tuition reimbursements, teaching assistantships with full tuition reimbursements, and institutionally sponsored loans available. Financial award application deadline: 4/15; financial award applicants required to submit FAFSA. *Unit head:* Prof. Rex F. Pratt, Chair, 860-685-2727. *Application contact:* Sarah Atwell, Administrative Assistant IV/Graduate Program Coordinator, 860-685-2573, Fax: 860-685-2211, E-mail: satwell@wesleyan.edu. Website: http://www.wesleyan.edu/chem/.

West Virginia University, Eberly College of Arts and Sciences, Department of Chemistry, Morgantown, WV 26506. Offers analytical chemistry (MS, PhD); inorganic chemistry (MS, PhD); organic chemistry (MS, PhD); physical chemistry (MS, PhD); theoretical chemistry (MS, PhD). Part-time programs available. Postbaccalaureate distance learning degree programs offered (no on-campus study). Terminal master's awarded for partial completion of doctoral program. *Degree requirements:* For master's, thesis; for doctorate, thesis/dissertation. *Entrance requirements:* For master's, GRE General Test, GRE Subject Test (recommended), minimum GPA of 2.5; for doctorate, GRE General Test, GRE Subject Test (recommended), minimum GPA of 2.75. Additional exam

requirements/recommendations for international students: Required—TOEFL. Electronic applications accepted. *Faculty research:* Analysis of proteins, drug interactions, solids and effluents by advanced separation methods; new synthetic strategies for complex organic molecules; synthesis and structural characterization of metal complexes for polymerization catalysis, nonlinear science, spectroscopy.

Yale University, Graduate School of Arts and Sciences, Department of Chemistry, New Haven, CT 06520. Offers biophysical chemistry (PhD); inorganic chemistry (PhD); organic chemistry (PhD); physical and theoretical chemistry (PhD). *Degree requirements:* For doctorate, thesis/dissertation. *Entrance requirements:* For doctorate, GRE General Test, GRE Subject Test. Additional exam requirements/recommendations for international students: Required—TOEFL.

Youngstown State University, Graduate School, College of Science, Technology, Engineering and Mathematics, Department of Chemistry, Youngstown, OH 44555-0001. Offers analytical chemistry (MS); biochemistry (MS); chemistry education (MS); inorganic chemistry (MS); organic chemistry (MS); physical chemistry (MS). Part-time programs available. *Degree requirements:* For master's, thesis. *Entrance requirements:* For master's, bachelor's degree in chemistry, minimum GPA of 2.7. Additional exam requirements/recommendations for international students: Required—TOEFL. *Faculty research:* Analysis of antioxidants, chromatography, defects and disorder in crystalline oxides, hydrogen bonding, novel organic and organometallic materials.

Organic Chemistry

Auburn University, Graduate School, College of Sciences and Mathematics, Department of Chemistry and Biochemistry, Auburn University, AL 36849. Offers analytical chemistry (MS, PhD); biochemistry (MS, PhD); inorganic chemistry (MS, PhD); organic chemistry (MS, PhD); physical chemistry (MS, PhD). Part-time programs available. *Faculty:* 28 full-time (5 women), 1 part-time/adjunct (0 women). *Students:* 37 full-time (14 women), 30 part-time (15 women); includes 6 minority (3 Black or African American, non-Hispanic/Latino; 1 American Indian or Alaska Native, non-Hispanic/Latino; 1 Asian, non-Hispanic/Latino; 1 Hispanic/Latino), 41 international. Average age 28. 38 applicants, 39% accepted, 12 enrolled. In 2012, 1 master's, 9 doctorates awarded. *Degree requirements:* For master's, thesis (for some programs); for doctorate, thesis/dissertation, oral and written exams. *Entrance requirements:* For master's and doctorate, GRE General Test. *Application deadline:* For fall admission, 7/7 for domestic students; for spring admission, 11/24 for domestic students. Applications are processed on a rolling basis. Application fee: $50 ($60 for international students). Electronic applications accepted. *Expenses:* Tuition, state resident: full-time $7866; part-time $437 per credit. Tuition, nonresident: full-time $23,598; part-time $1311 per credit. *Required fees:* $787 per semester. Tuition and fees vary according to degree level and program. *Financial support:* Fellowships, research assistantships, and teaching assistantships available. Financial award application deadline: 3/15; financial award applicants required to submit FAFSA. *Unit head:* Dr. J. V. Ortiz, Chair, 334-844-4043, Fax: 334-844-4043. *Application contact:* Dr. George Flowers, Dean of the Graduate School, 334-844-2125. Website: http://www.auburn.edu/cosam/departments/chemistry/.

Binghamton University, State University of New York, Graduate School, School of Arts and Sciences, Department of Chemistry, Binghamton, NY 13902-6000. Offers analytical chemistry (PhD); chemistry (MA, MS); environmental (PhD); inorganic chemistry (PhD); organic chemistry (PhD); physical chemistry (PhD). Part-time programs available. *Faculty:* 16 full-time (4 women), 4 part-time/adjunct (1 woman). *Students:* 25 full-time (10 women), 26 part-time (10 women); includes 4 minority (3 Black or African American, non-Hispanic/Latino; 1 Hispanic/Latino), 33 international. Average age 28. 53 applicants, 49% accepted, 11 enrolled. In 2012, 3 master's, 6 doctorates awarded. Terminal master's awarded for partial completion of doctoral program. *Degree requirements:* For master's, thesis or alternative, oral exam, seminar presentation; for doctorate, thesis/dissertation, cumulative exams. *Entrance requirements:* For master's and doctorate, GRE General Test, GRE Subject Test. Additional exam requirements/recommendations for international students: Required—TOEFL (minimum score 550 paper-based; 80 iBT). *Application deadline:* For fall admission, 1/15 priority date for domestic students, 1/15 for international students; for spring admission, 10/15 priority date for domestic students, 10/15 for international students. Applications are processed on a rolling basis. Application fee: $75. Electronic applications accepted. *Expenses:* Tuition, state resident: full-time $9370. Tuition, nonresident: full-time $16,680. *Financial support:* In 2012–13, 47 students received support, including 5 research assistantships with full tuition reimbursements available (averaging $18,000 per year), 34 teaching assistantships with full tuition reimbursements available (averaging $18,000 per year); career-related internships or fieldwork, Federal Work-Study, institutionally sponsored loans, scholarships/grants, health care benefits, tuition waivers (full), and unspecified assistantships also available. Financial award application

deadline: 2/15; financial award applicants required to submit FAFSA. *Unit head:* Dr. Wayne E. Jones, Chairperson, 607-777-2421, E-mail: wjones@binghamton.edu. *Application contact:* Kishan Zuber, Recruiting and Admissions Coordinator, 607-777-2151, Fax: 607-777-2501, E-mail: kzuber@binghamton.edu.

Boston College, Graduate School of Arts and Sciences, Department of Chemistry, Chestnut Hill, MA 02467-3800. Offers biochemistry (PhD); inorganic chemistry (PhD); organic chemistry (PhD); physical chemistry (PhD); science education (MST). *Degree requirements:* For doctorate, thesis/dissertation, qualifying exam. *Entrance requirements:* For doctorate, GRE General Test, GRE Subject Test. Additional exam requirements/recommendations for international students: Required—TOEFL (minimum score 600 paper-based; 100 iBT). Electronic applications accepted.

Brandeis University, Graduate School of Arts and Sciences, Department of Chemistry, Waltham, MA 02454. Offers inorganic chemistry (MA, MS, PhD); organic chemistry (MA, MS, PhD); physical chemistry (MS, PhD). *Students:* 44 full-time (20 women); includes 3 minority (1 Black or African American, non-Hispanic/Latino; 2 Asian, non-Hispanic/Latino). 121 applicants, 26% accepted, 11 enrolled. In 2012, 6 master's, 7 doctorates awarded. Terminal master's awarded for partial completion of doctoral program. *Degree requirements:* For master's, thesis, 1 year of residency (for MA); 2 years of residency (for MS); for doctorate, comprehensive exam, thesis/dissertation, 3 years of residency; 2 seminars, qualifying exams. *Entrance requirements:* For master's and doctorate, GRE General Test, resume, statement of purpose, letters of recommendation. Additional exam requirements/recommendations for international students: Required—TOEFL (minimum score 600 paper-based; 100 iBT); Recommended—IELTS (minimum score 7). *Application deadline:* For fall admission, 1/15 priority date for domestic students. Application fee: $75. Electronic applications accepted. *Financial support:* In 2012–13, 16 research assistantships with full tuition reimbursements (averaging $25,000 per year) were awarded; fellowships with full tuition reimbursements, Federal Work-Study, scholarships/grants, health care benefits, tuition waivers (partial), and unspecified assistantships also available. Support available to part-time students. Financial award application deadline: 4/15; financial award applicants required to submit FAFSA. *Faculty research:* Oscillating chemical reactions, molecular recognition systems, protein crystallography, synthesis of natural product spectroscopy and magnetic resonance. *Unit head:* Dr. Judith Herzfeld, Chair, Graduate Program, 781-736-2540, Fax: 781-736-2516, E-mail: herzfeld@brandeis.edu. *Application contact:* Charlotte Haygazian, Coordinator, 781-736-2500, Fax: 781-736-2516, E-mail: chemadm@brandeis.edu. Website: http://www.brandeis.edu/gsas.

California State University, Los Angeles, Graduate Studies, College of Natural and Social Sciences, Department of Chemistry and Biochemistry, Los Angeles, CA 90032-8530. Offers analytical chemistry (MS); biochemistry (MS); chemistry (MS); inorganic chemistry (MS); organic chemistry (MS); physical chemistry (MS). Part-time and evening/weekend programs available. *Faculty:* 2 full-time (1 woman). *Students:* 3 full-time (1 woman), 16 part-time (9 women); includes 16 minority (all Hispanic/Latino). Average age 32. 21 applicants, 52% accepted, 8 enrolled. In 2012, 2 master's awarded. *Degree requirements:* For master's, one foreign language, comprehensive exam or thesis. *Entrance requirements:*

Peterson's Graduate Programs in the Physical Sciences, Mathematics, Agricultural Sciences, the Environment & Natural Resources 2014

www.petersonsbooks.com **107**

Additional exam requirements/recommendations for international students: Required—TOEFL. *Application deadline:* For fall admission, 5/1 for domestic and international students. Applications are processed on a rolling basis. Application fee: $55. *Financial support:* Federal Work-Study available. Support available to part-time students. Financial award application deadline: 3/1. *Faculty research:* Intercalation of heavy metal, carborane chemistry, conductive polymers and fabrics, titanium reagents, computer modeling and synthesis. *Unit head:* Dr. Robert L. Vellanoweth, Chair, 323-343-2300, Fax: 323-343-6490, E-mail: rvellan@calstatela.edu. *Application contact:* Dr. Larry Fritz, Dean of Graduate Studies, 323-343-3820 Ext. 3827, Fax: 323-343-5653, E-mail: lfritz@calstatela.edu. Website: http://www.calstatela.edu/dept/chem/index.htm.

Carnegie Mellon University, Mellon College of Science, Department of Chemistry, Pittsburgh, PA 15213-3891. Offers biotechnology and management (MS); chemistry (PhD), including bioinorganic, bioorganic, organic and materials, biophysics and spectroscopy, computational and theoretical, polymer; colloids, polymers and surfaces (MS). Part-time programs available. Terminal master's awarded for partial completion of doctoral program. *Degree requirements:* For doctorate, thesis/dissertation, departmental qualifying and oral exams, teaching experience. *Entrance requirements:* For master's, GRE General Test; for doctorate, GRE General Test, GRE Subject Test. Additional exam requirements/recommendations for international students: Required—TOEFL. Electronic applications accepted. *Faculty research:* Physical and theoretical chemistry, chemical synthesis, biophysical/bioinorganic chemistry.

Cleveland State University, College of Graduate Studies, College of Sciences and Health Professions, Department of Chemistry, Cleveland, OH 44115. Offers analytical chemistry (MS); clinical chemistry (MS); clinical/bioanalytical chemistry (PhD), including cellular and molecular medicine, clinical chemistry, clinical/bioanalytical chemistry; environmental chemistry (MS); inorganic chemistry (MS); pharmaceutical/organic chemistry (MS); physical chemistry (MS). Part-time and evening/weekend programs available. *Faculty:* 12 full-time (0 women). *Students:* 10 full-time (6 women), 92 part-time (46 women); includes 7 minority (6 Black or African American, non-Hispanic/Latino; 1 Asian, non-Hispanic/Latino), 68 international. Average age 27. 119 applicants, 86% accepted, 18 enrolled. In 2012, 15 master's, 5 doctorates awarded. *Degree requirements:* For master's, thesis optional; for doctorate, comprehensive exam, thesis/dissertation. *Entrance requirements:* For master's and doctorate, GRE General Test. Additional exam requirements/recommendations for international students: Required—TOEFL (minimum score 525 paper-based; 65 iBT). *Application deadline:* For fall admission, 1/15 priority date for domestic students, 1/15 for international students. Applications are processed on a rolling basis. Application fee: $30. Electronic applications accepted. *Expenses:* Tuition, state resident: full-time $8172; part-time $510.75 per credit hour. Tuition, nonresident: full-time $15,372; part-time $960.75 per credit hour. *Required fees:* $25 per semester. Tuition and fees vary according to course load and program. *Financial support:* In 2012–13, 44 students received support, including 5 fellowships with full tuition reimbursements available (averaging $22,500 per year), 13 research assistantships with full tuition reimbursements available (averaging $22,500 per year), 24 teaching assistantships with full tuition reimbursements available (averaging $21,000 per year); scholarships/grants and unspecified assistantships also available. Financial award application deadline: 1/15. *Faculty research:* Bioanalytical techniques and molecular diagnostics, glycoproteomics and antithrombotic agents, drug discovery and innovation, analytical pharmacology, inflammatory disease research. *Total annual research expenditures:* $3 million. *Unit head:* Dr. David J. Anderson, Interim Chair, 216-687-2467, Fax: 216-687-9298, E-mail: d.anderson@csuohio.edu. *Application contact:* Richelle P. Emery, Administrative Coordinator, 216-687-2457, Fax: 216-687-9298, E-mail: r.emery@csuohio.edu. Website: http://www.csuohio.edu/chemistry/.

Columbia University, Graduate School of Arts and Sciences, Division of Natural Sciences, Department of Chemistry, New York, NY 10027. Offers chemical physics (M Phil, PhD); inorganic chemistry (M Phil, MA, PhD); organic chemistry (M Phil, MA, PhD); MD/PhD. *Degree requirements:* For master's, one foreign language, teaching experience, oral/written exams (M Phil); for doctorate, one foreign language, thesis/dissertation. *Entrance requirements:* For master's and doctorate, GRE General Test, GRE Subject Test. Additional exam requirements/recommendations for international students: Required—TOEFL. *Faculty research:* Biophysics.

Cornell University, Graduate School, Graduate Fields of Arts and Sciences, Field of Chemistry and Chemical Biology, Ithaca, NY 14853-0001. Offers analytical chemistry (PhD); bio-organic chemistry (PhD); biophysical chemistry (PhD); chemical biology (PhD); chemical physics (PhD); inorganic chemistry (PhD); materials chemistry (PhD); organic chemistry (PhD); organometallic chemistry (PhD); physical chemistry (PhD); polymer chemistry (PhD); theoretical chemistry (PhD). *Faculty:* 48 full-time (5 women). *Students:* 161 full-time (70 women); includes 28 minority (1 Black or African American, non-Hispanic/Latino; 16 Asian, non-Hispanic/Latino; 4 Hispanic/Latino; 7 Two or more races, non-Hispanic/Latino), 48 international. Average age 25. 340 applicants, 33% accepted, 40 enrolled. In 2012, 15 doctorates awarded. *Degree requirements:* For doctorate, comprehensive exam, thesis/dissertation. *Entrance requirements:* For doctorate, GRE General Test, GRE Subject Test (chemistry), 3 letters of recommendation. Additional exam requirements/recommendations for international students: Required—TOEFL (minimum score 600 paper-based; 77 iBT). *Application deadline:* For fall admission, 1/10 for domestic students. Application fee: $95. Electronic applications accepted. *Financial support:* In 2012–13, 155 students received support, including 37 fellowships with full tuition reimbursements available, 50 research assistantships with full tuition reimbursements available, 68 teaching assistantships with full tuition reimbursements available; institutionally sponsored loans, scholarships/grants, health care benefits, tuition waivers (full and partial), and unspecified assistantships also available. Financial award applicants required to submit FAFSA. *Faculty research:* Analytical, organic, inorganic, physical, materials, chemical biology. *Unit head:* Director of Graduate Studies, 607-255-4139, Fax: 607-255-4137. *Application contact:* Graduate Field Assistant, 607-255-4139, Fax: 607-255-4137, E-mail: chemgrad@cornell.edu. Website: http://www.gradschool.cornell.edu/fields.php?id-26&a-2.

Eastern New Mexico University, Graduate School, College of Liberal Arts and Sciences, Department of Physical Sciences, Portales, NM 88130. Offers chemistry (MS), including analytical, biochemistry, inorganic, organic, physical. Part-time programs available. *Faculty:* 2 full-time (0 women). *Students:* 2 full-time (0 women), 12 part-time (4 women), 12 international. Average age 25. 14 applicants, 93% accepted, 11 enrolled. In 2012, 5 master's awarded. *Degree requirements:* For master's, thesis optional, seminar, oral and written comprehensive exams. *Entrance requirements:* For master's, ACS placement examination, minimum GPA of 3.0; 2 letters of recommendation; personal statement of career goals; bachelor's degree with one year minimum each of general, organic, and analytical chemistry. Additional exam requirements/recommendations for international students: Required—TOEFL (minimum score 550 paper-based; 79 iBT), IELTS (minimum score 6). *Application deadline:* For fall admission, 7/20 priority date for domestic students, 6/20 for international students; for spring admission, 12/15 priority date for domestic students, 11/15 for international students. Applications are processed on a rolling basis. Application fee: $10. Electronic applications accepted. *Expenses:* Tuition, state resident: full-time $3356; part-time $139.85 per credit hour. Tuition, nonresident: full-time $9030; part-time $376.25 per credit hour. *Required fees:* $1425.60; $59.40 per credit hour. $712.80 per semester. *Financial support:* In 2012–13, 1 research assistantship with partial tuition reimbursement (averaging $8,500 per year), 10 teaching assistantships with partial tuition reimbursements (averaging $8,500 per year) were awarded; career-related internships or fieldwork and unspecified assistantships also available. Support available to part-time students. Financial award application deadline: 3/1; financial award applicants required to submit FAFSA. *Faculty research:* Synfuel, electrochemistry, protein chemistry. *Unit head:* Dr. Juacho Yan, Graduate Coordinator, 575-562-2494, Fax: 575-562-2192, E-mail: juacho.yan@enmu.edu. *Application contact:* Sharon Potter, Department Secretary, Biology and Physical Sciences, 575-562-2174, Fax: 575-562-2192, E-mail: sharon.potter@enmu.edu. Website: http://liberal-arts.enmu.edu/sciences/grad-chemistry.shtml.

East Tennessee State University, School of Graduate Studies, College of Arts and Sciences, Department of Chemistry, Johnson City, TN 37614. Offers chemistry (MS), including inorganic chemistry, organic chemistry, physical chemistry. Part-time and evening/weekend programs available. *Faculty:* 10 full-time (4 women), 1 part-time/adjunct (0 women). *Students:* 17 full-time (3 women), 6 part-time (3 women); includes 4 minority (1 Black or African American, non-Hispanic/Latino; 1 American Indian or Alaska Native, non-Hispanic/Latino; 1 Asian, non-Hispanic/Latino; 1 Two or more races, non-Hispanic/Latino), 14 international. 40 applicants, 53% accepted, 15 enrolled. In 2012, 13 master's awarded. *Degree requirements:* For master's, comprehensive exam, thesis. *Entrance requirements:* For master's, prerequisites in physical chemistry with lab requiring calculus; two letters of recommendation. Additional exam requirements/recommendations for international students: Required—TOEFL (minimum score 550 paper-based; 79 iBT). *Application deadline:* For fall admission, 6/1 for domestic students, 4/30 for international students; for spring admission, 11/1 for domestic students, 9/30 for international students. Application fee: $35 ($45 for international students). Electronic applications accepted. *Financial support:* In 2012–13, 18 students received support, including 18 teaching assistantships with full and partial tuition reimbursements available (averaging $8,300 per year); career-related internships or fieldwork, institutionally sponsored loans, scholarships/grants, and unspecified assistantships also available. Financial award application deadline: 7/1; financial award applicants required to submit FAFSA. *Faculty research:* Analytical chemistry, inorganic chemistry, organic chemistry, physical chemistry. *Unit head:* Dr. Cassandra Eagle, Chair, 423-439-4367, Fax: 423-439-5835, E-mail: eaglec@etsu.edu. *Application contact:* Gail Powers, Graduate Specialist, 423-439-4703, Fax: 423-439-5624, E-mail: powersg@etsu.edu. Website: http://www.etsu.edu/cas/chemistry/.

Florida State University, The Graduate School, College of Arts and Sciences, Department of Chemistry and Biochemistry, Tallahassee, FL 32306-4390. Offers analytical chemistry (MS, PhD); biochemistry (MS, PhD); inorganic chemistry (MS, PhD); materials chemistry (PhD); organic chemistry (MS, PhD); physical chemistry (MS, PhD). *Faculty:* 37 full-time (4 women), 1 (woman) part-time/adjunct. *Students:* 138 full-time (52 women), 8 part-time (1 woman); includes 14 minority (6 Black or African American, non-Hispanic/Latino; 3 Asian, non-Hispanic/Latino; 2 Hispanic/Latino; 3 Two or more races, non-Hispanic/Latino), 63 international. Average age 25. 147 applicants, 40% accepted, 28 enrolled. In 2012, 7 master's, 27 doctorates awarded. Terminal master's awarded for partial completion of doctoral program. *Degree requirements:* For master's, comprehensive exam, thesis (for some programs); for doctorate, comprehensive exam, thesis/dissertation. *Entrance requirements:* For master's and doctorate, GRE General Test (minimum scores: 150 verbal, 151 quantitative; 1100 total on the old scale), minimum GPA of 3.1 in undergraduate course work. Additional exam requirements/recommendations for international students: Required—

TOEFL (minimum score 90 iBT). *Application deadline:* For fall admission, 12/15 priority date for domestic students, 12/15 for international students; for spring admission, 9/15 for domestic and international students. Applications are processed on a rolling basis. Application fee: $30. Electronic applications accepted. *Expenses:* Contact institution. *Financial support:* In 2012–13, 140 students received support, including 7 fellowships with full and partial tuition reimbursements available (averaging $10,000 per year), 50 research assistantships with full tuition reimbursements available (averaging $20,000 per year), 100 teaching assistantships with full tuition reimbursements available (averaging $20,000 per year); health care benefits also available. Financial award application deadline: 12/15; financial award applicants required to submit FAFSA. *Faculty research:* Bioanalytical chemistry, including separations, microfluidics, pertroleomics; materials chemistry, including magnets, polymers, catalysts, nanomaterials; spectroscopy, including NMR and EPR, ultrafast, Raman, and mass spectrometry; organic synthesis, natural products, photochemistry, and supramolecular chemistry; biochemistry, with focus on structural biology, metabolomics, and anticancer drugs. *Total annual research expenditures:* $9.8 million. *Unit head:* Dr. Timothy Logan, Chairman, 850-644-3810, Fax: 850-644-8281, E-mail: gradinfo@chem.fsu.edu. *Application contact:* Dr. Michael Shatruk, Associate Chair for Graduate Studies, 850-417-8417, Fax: 850-644-8281, E-mail: gradinfo@chem.fsu.edu. Website: http://www.chem.fsu.edu/.

Georgetown University, Graduate School of Arts and Sciences, Department of Chemistry, Washington, DC 20057. Offers analytical chemistry (PhD); biochemistry (PhD); computational chemistry (PhD); inorganic chemistry (PhD); materials chemistry (PhD); organic chemistry (PhD); physical chemistry (PhD); theoretical chemistry (PhD). Terminal master's awarded for partial completion of doctoral program. *Degree requirements:* For doctorate, comprehensive exam, thesis/dissertation. *Entrance requirements:* For doctorate, GRE General Test. Additional exam requirements/recommendations for international students: Required—TOEFL.

The George Washington University, Columbian College of Arts and Sciences, Department of Chemistry, Washington, DC 20052. Offers analytical chemistry (MS, PhD); inorganic chemistry (MS, PhD); materials science (MS, PhD); organic chemistry (MS, PhD); physical chemistry (MS, PhD). Part-time and evening/weekend programs available. *Faculty:* 17 full-time (6 women). *Students:* 30 full-time (16 women), 8 part-time (6 women); includes 3 minority (2 Asian, non-Hispanic/Latino; 1 Hispanic/Latino), 8 international. Average age 27. 66 applicants, 24% accepted, 10 enrolled. In 2012, 2 master's, 3 doctorates awarded. Terminal master's awarded for partial completion of doctoral program. *Degree requirements:* For master's, comprehensive exam, thesis or alternative; for doctorate, thesis/dissertation, general exam. *Entrance requirements:* For master's and doctorate, GRE General Test, interview, minimum GPA of 3.0. Additional exam requirements/recommendations for international students: Required—TOEFL (minimum score 550 paper-based; 80 iBT). *Application deadline:* For fall admission, 1/15 priority date for domestic students, 1/15 for international students; for spring admission, 9/1 priority date for domestic students, 9/1 for international students. Applications are processed on a rolling basis. Application fee: $75. Electronic applications accepted. *Financial support:* In 2012–13, 27 students received support. Fellowships with tuition reimbursements available, research assistantships, teaching assistantships with tuition reimbursements available, Federal Work-Study, and tuition waivers available. Financial award application deadline: 1/15. *Unit head:* Dr. Michael King, Chair, 202-994-6488. *Application contact:* Information Contact, 202-994-6121, E-mail: gwchem@gwu.edu. Website: http://www.gwu.edu/~gwchem/.

Georgia State University, College of Arts and Sciences, Department of Chemistry, Atlanta, GA 30302-3083. Offers analytical chemistry (MS, PhD); biochemistry (MS, PhD); bioinformatics (MS, PhD); biophysical chemistry (PhD); computational chemistry (MS, PhD); geochemistry (PhD); organic/medicinal chemistry (MS, PhD); physical chemistry (MS). PhD in geochemistry offered jointly with Department of Geology. Part-time programs available. *Faculty:* 38 full-time (11 women), 10 part-time/adjunct (3 women). *Students:* 107 full-time (57 women), 6 part-time (3 women); includes 25 minority (13 Black or African American, non-Hispanic/Latino; 1 American Indian or Alaska Native, non-Hispanic/Latino; 6 Asian, non-Hispanic/Latino; 4 Hispanic/Latino; 1 Two or more races, non-Hispanic/Latino), 57 international. Average age 28. 125 applicants, 39% accepted, 36 enrolled. In 2012, 28 master's, 12 doctorates awarded. Terminal master's awarded for partial completion of doctoral program. *Degree requirements:* For master's, one foreign language, comprehensive exam (for some programs), thesis (for some programs); for doctorate, one foreign language, comprehensive exam, thesis/dissertation. *Entrance requirements:* For master's and doctorate, GRE. Additional exam requirements/recommendations for international students: Required—TOEFL (minimum score 550 paper-based, 80 iBT) or IELTS (minimum score 6.5). *Application deadline:* For fall admission, 7/1 priority date for domestic students, 7/1 for international students; for winter admission, 11/15 priority date for domestic students, 11/15 for international students; for spring admission, 4/15 priority date for domestic students, 4/15 for international students. Applications are processed on a rolling basis. Application fee: $50. Electronic applications accepted. *Expenses:* Tuition, state resident: full-time $8064; part-time $336 per credit hour. Tuition, nonresident: full-time $28,800; part-time $1200 per credit hour. *Required fees:* $2128; $1064 per semester. Tuition and fees vary according to course load and program. *Financial support:* Fellowships with full tuition reimbursements, research assistantships with full tuition reimbursements, and teaching assistantships with full tuition reimbursements available. *Faculty research:* Analytical chemistry, biological/biochemistry, biophysical/computational chemistry, chemical education, organic/medicinal chemistry. *Total annual research expenditures:* $4 million. *Unit head:* Dr. Binghe Wang, Department Chair, 404-413-5500, Fax: 404-413-5506, E-mail: chemchair@gsu.edu. *Application contact:* Rita S. Bennett, Academic Specialist, 404-413-5497, Fax: 404-413-5505, E-mail: rsb423@gsu.edu. Website: http://chemistry.gsu.edu/.

Harvard University, Graduate School of Arts and Sciences, Department of Chemistry and Chemical Biology, Cambridge, MA 02138. Offers biochemical chemistry (PhD); inorganic chemistry (PhD); organic chemistry (PhD); physical chemistry (PhD). *Degree requirements:* For doctorate, thesis/dissertation, cumulative exams. *Entrance requirements:* For doctorate, GRE General Test, GRE Subject Test. Additional exam requirements/recommendations for international students: Required—TOEFL. *Expenses: Tuition:* Full-time $37,576. *Required fees:* $930. Tuition and fees vary according to program and student level.

See Display on page 70 and Close-Up on page 125.

Howard University, Graduate School, Department of Chemistry, Washington, DC 20059-0002. Offers analytical chemistry (MS, PhD); atmospheric (MS, PhD); biochemistry (MS, PhD); environmental (MS, PhD); inorganic chemistry (MS, PhD); organic chemistry (MS, PhD); physical chemistry (MS, PhD). Terminal master's awarded for partial completion of doctoral program. *Degree requirements:* For master's, comprehensive exam, thesis, teaching experience; for doctorate, comprehensive exam, thesis/dissertation, teaching experience. *Entrance requirements:* For master's, GRE General Test, minimum GPA of 2.7; for doctorate, GRE General Test, minimum GPA of 3.0. Additional exam requirements/recommendations for international students: Required—TOEFL. Electronic applications accepted. *Faculty research:* Synthetic organics, materials, natural products, mass spectrometry.

Indiana University Bloomington, University Graduate School, College of Arts and Sciences, Department of Chemistry, Bloomington, IN 47405. Offers analytical chemistry (PhD); chemical biology chemistry (PhD); chemistry (MAT); inorganic chemistry (PhD); materials chemistry (PhD); organic chemistry (PhD); physical chemistry (PhD). *Faculty:* 42 full-time (4 women). *Students:* 215 full-time (85 women), 4 part-time (1 woman); includes 21 minority (8 Black or African American, non-Hispanic/Latino; 9 Asian, non-Hispanic/Latino; 1 Hispanic/Latino; 3 Two or more races, non-Hispanic/Latino), 69 international. Average age 27. 329 applicants, 40% accepted, 50 enrolled. In 2012, 12 master's, 20 doctorates awarded. Terminal master's awarded for partial completion of doctoral program. *Degree requirements:* For master's, thesis; for doctorate, thesis/dissertation. *Entrance requirements:* For master's and doctorate, GRE General Test, GRE Subject Test. Additional exam requirements/recommendations for international students: Required—TOEFL. *Application deadline:* For fall admission, 1/15 priority date for domestic students, 12/15 for international students. Applications are processed on a rolling basis. Application fee: $55 ($65 for international students). *Financial support:* In 2012–13, 200 students received support, including 10 fellowships with full tuition reimbursements available, 76 research assistantships with full tuition reimbursements available, 111 teaching assistantships with full tuition reimbursements available; Federal Work-Study and institutionally sponsored loans also available. *Faculty research:* Synthesis of complex natural products, organic reaction mechanisms, organic electrochemistry, transitive-metal chemistry, solid-state and surface chemistry. *Total annual research expenditures:* $7.7 million. *Unit head:* David Giedroc, Chairperson, 812-855-6239, E-mail: chemchair@indiana.edu. *Application contact:* Daniel Mindiola, Director of Graduate Admissions, 812-855-2069, Fax: 812-855-8385, E-mail: mindiola@indiana.edu. Website: http://www.chem.indiana.edu/.

Instituto Tecnológico y de Estudios Superiores de Monterrey, Campus Monterrey, Graduate and Research Division, Program in Natural and Social Sciences, Monterrey, Mexico. Offers biotechnology (MS); chemistry (MS, PhD); communications (MS); education (MA). Part-time programs available. *Degree requirements:* For master's, one foreign language, thesis; for doctorate, one foreign language, thesis/dissertation. *Entrance requirements:* For master's, EXADEP; for doctorate, EXADEP, master's degree in related field. Additional exam requirements/recommendations for international students: Required—TOEFL. *Faculty research:* Cultural industries, mineral substances, bioremediation, food processing, CQ in industrial chemical processing.

Iowa State University of Science and Technology, Program in Organic Chemistry, Ames, IA 50011. Offers MS, PhD. *Entrance requirements:* Additional exam requirements/recommendations for international students: Required—TOEFL (minimum score 570 paper-based; 89 iBT), IELTS (minimum score 6.5). *Application deadline:* For fall admission, 2/1 for domestic students. Application fee: $60 ($90 for international students). Electronic applications accepted. *Application contact:* Lynette Edsall, Application Contact, 800-521-2436, Fax: 515-294-0105, E-mail: chemgrad@iastate.edu. Website: http://www.chem.iastate.edu.

Kansas State University, Graduate School, College of Arts and Sciences, Department of Chemistry, Manhattan, KS 66506. Offers analytical chemistry (MS); biological chemistry (MS); chemistry (PhD); inorganic chemistry (MS); materials chemistry (MS); organic chemistry (MS); physical chemistry (MS). *Faculty:* 17 full-time (1 woman). *Students:* 71 full-time (36 women); includes 1 minority (Asian, non-Hispanic/Latino), 59 international. Average age 28. 108 applicants, 35% accepted, 15 enrolled. In 2012, 5 master's, 9 doctorates awarded. Terminal master's awarded for partial completion of doctoral program.

Degree requirements: For master's, thesis; for doctorate, thesis/dissertation. *Entrance requirements:* For master's and doctorate, GRE, minimum GPA of 3.0. Additional exam requirements/recommendations for international students: Required—TOEFL (minimum score 550 paper-based). *Application deadline:* For fall admission, 2/1 priority date for domestic students, 2/1 for international students; for spring admission, 8/1 priority date for domestic students, 8/1 for international students. Applications are processed on a rolling basis. Application fee: $50 ($75 for international students). Electronic applications accepted. *Financial support:* In 2012–13, 39 research assistantships (averaging $18,182 per year), 24 teaching assistantships with full tuition reimbursements (averaging $18,106 per year) were awarded; institutionally sponsored loans and scholarships/grants also available. Support available to part-time students. Financial award application deadline: 3/1; financial award applicants required to submit FAFSA. *Faculty research:* Inorganic chemistry, organic and biological chemistry, analytical chemistry, physical chemistry, materials chemistry and nanotechnology. *Total annual research expenditures:* $2.8 million. *Unit head:* Eric Maatta, Head, 785-532-6665, Fax: 785-532-6666, E-mail: eam@ksu.edu. *Application contact:* Christer Aakeroy, Director, 785-532-6096, Fax: 785-532-6666, E-mail: aakeroy@ksu.edu. Website: http://www.k-state.edu/chem/.

Kent State University, College of Arts and Sciences, Department of Chemistry and Biochemistry, Kent, OH 44242-0001. Offers analytical chemistry (MS, PhD); biochemistry (MS, PhD); chemistry (MA); inorganic chemistry (MS, PhD); organic chemistry (MS, PhD); physical chemistry (MS, PhD). Terminal master's awarded for partial completion of doctoral program. *Degree requirements:* For master's, comprehensive exam, thesis; for doctorate, comprehensive exam, thesis/dissertation. *Entrance requirements:* For master's and doctorate, placement exam, GRE General Test, GRE Subject Test (recommended), minimum GPA of 2.75. Additional exam requirements/recommendations for international students: Required—TOEFL (minimum score 525 paper-based; 71 iBT). Electronic applications accepted. *Expenses:* Tuition, state resident: full-time $8424; part-time $468 per credit hour. Tuition, nonresident: full-time $14,580; part-time $810 per credit hour. Tuition and fees vary according to course load. *Faculty research:* Biological chemistry, materials chemistry, molecular spectroscopy.

See Display on page 73 and Close-Up on page 127.

Laurentian University, School of Graduate Studies and Research, Programme in Chemistry and Biochemistry, Sudbury, ON P3E 2C6, Canada. Offers analytical chemistry (M Sc); biochemistry (M Sc); environmental chemistry (M Sc); organic chemistry (M Sc); physical/theoretical chemistry (M Sc). Part-time programs available. *Degree requirements:* For master's, thesis or alternative. *Entrance requirements:* For master's, honors degree with minimum second class. *Faculty research:* Cell cycle checkpoints, kinetic modeling, toxicology to metal stress, quantum chemistry, biogeochemistry metal speciation.

Marquette University, Graduate School, College of Arts and Sciences, Department of Chemistry, Milwaukee, WI 53201-1881. Offers analytical chemistry (MS, PhD); bioanalytical chemistry (MS, PhD); biophysical chemistry (MS, PhD); chemical physics (MS, PhD); inorganic chemistry (MS, PhD); organic chemistry (MS, PhD); physical chemistry (MS, PhD). Part-time programs available. Terminal master's awarded for partial completion of doctoral program. *Degree requirements:* For master's, comprehensive exam; for doctorate, thesis/dissertation, cumulative exams. *Entrance requirements:* For master's and doctorate, official transcripts from all current and previous colleges/universities except Marquette, three letters of recommendation from individuals familiar with the applicant's academic work. Additional exam requirements/recommendations for international students: Required—TOEFL (minimum score 530 paper-based). Electronic applications accepted. *Faculty research:* Inorganic complexes, laser Raman spectroscopy, organic synthesis, synthetic bioinorganic chemistry, electro-active organic molecules.

Massachusetts Institute of Technology, School of Engineering, Department of Civil and Environmental Engineering, Cambridge, MA 02139. Offers biological oceanography (PhD, Sc D); chemical oceanography (PhD, Sc D); civil and environmental engineering (M Eng, SM, PhD, Sc D); civil and environmental systems (PhD, Sc D); civil engineering (PhD, Sc D, CE); coastal engineering (PhD, Sc D); construction engineering and management (PhD, Sc D); environmental biology (PhD, Sc D); environmental chemistry (PhD, Sc D); environmental engineering (PhD, Sc D); environmental fluid mechanics (PhD, Sc D); geotechnical and geoenvironmental engineering (PhD, Sc D); hydrology (PhD, Sc D); information technology (PhD, Sc D); oceanographic engineering (PhD, Sc D); structures and materials (PhD, Sc D); transportation (PhD, Sc D); SM/MBA. *Faculty:* 34 full-time (7 women), 1 part-time/adjunct (0 women). *Students:* 224 full-time (85 women); includes 29 minority (4 Black or African American, non-Hispanic/Latino; 13 Asian, non-Hispanic/Latino; 6 Hispanic/Latino; 6 Two or more races, non-Hispanic/Latino), 129 international. Average age 26. 636 applicants, 25% accepted, 95 enrolled. In 2012, 67 master's, 18 doctorates, 1 other advanced degree awarded. *Degree requirements:* For master's and CE, thesis; for doctorate, comprehensive exam, thesis/dissertation. *Entrance requirements:* For master's and doctorate, GRE General Test. Additional exam requirements/recommendations for international students: Required—TOEFL (minimum score 577 paper-based; 90 iBT), IELTS (minimum score 7). *Application deadline:* For fall admission, 12/15 for domestic and international students. Application fee: $75. Electronic applications accepted. *Expenses: Tuition:* Full-time $41,770; part-time $650 per credit hour. *Required fees:* $280. *Financial support:* In 2012–13, 180 students received support, including 46 fellowships (averaging $32,400 per year), 117 research assistantships (averaging $30,800 per year), 22 teaching assistantships (averaging $31,800 per year); career-related internships or fieldwork, Federal Work-Study, institutionally sponsored loans, scholarships/grants, health care benefits, and unspecified assistantships also available. *Faculty research:* Environmental chemistry; environmental fluid mechanics and coastal engineering; environmental microbiology; geotechnical engineering and geomechanics; hydrology and hydroclimatology; infrastructure systems; mechanics of materials and structures; transportation systems. *Total annual research expenditures:* $20.7 million. *Unit head:* Prof. Markus Buehler, Head, 617-253-7101. *Application contact:* Graduate Admissions Coordinator, 617-253-7119, E-mail: cee-admissions@mit.edu. Website: http://cee.mit.edu/.

Massachusetts Institute of Technology, School of Science, Department of Chemistry, Cambridge, MA 02139. Offers biological chemistry (PhD, Sc D); inorganic chemistry (PhD, Sc D); organic chemistry (PhD, Sc D); physical chemistry (PhD, Sc D). *Faculty:* 27 full-time (5 women). *Students:* 228 full-time (80 women), 4 part-time (2 women); includes 54 minority (6 Black or African American, non-Hispanic/Latino; 1 American Indian or Alaska Native, non-Hispanic/Latino; 31 Asian, non-Hispanic/Latino; 13 Hispanic/Latino; 3 Two or more races, non-Hispanic/Latino), 69 international. Average age 26. 651 applicants, 17% accepted, 44 enrolled. In 2012, 30 doctorates awarded. *Degree requirements:* For doctorate, comprehensive exam, thesis/dissertation. *Entrance requirements:* For doctorate, GRE General Test. Additional exam requirements/recommendations for international students: Required—IELTS (minimum score 7); Recommended—TOEFL (minimum score 600 paper-based). *Application deadline:* For fall admission, 12/15 for domestic and international students. Application fee: $75. Electronic applications accepted. *Expenses: Tuition:* Full-time $41,770; part-time $650 per credit hour. *Required fees:* $280. *Financial support:* In 2012–13, 194 students received support, including 71 fellowships (averaging $36,300 per year), 111 research assistantships (averaging $31,400 per year), 41 teaching assistantships (averaging $34,600 per year); Federal Work-Study, institutionally sponsored loans, scholarships/grants, traineeships, health care benefits, and unspecified assistantships also available. *Faculty research:* Synthetic organic and organometallic chemistry including catalysis; biological chemistry including bioorganic chemistry; physical chemistry including chemical dynamics and biophysical chemistry; inorganic chemistry including synthesis, catalysis, bioinorganic and physical inorganic chemistry; materials chemistry including surface science, nanoscience and polymers. *Total annual research expenditures:* $28.4 million. *Unit head:* Prof. Sylvia T. Ceyer, Head, 617-253-1803, Fax: 617-258-7500. *Application contact:* Graduate Administrator, 617-253-1845, Fax: 617-258-0241, E-mail: chemgradeducation@mit.edu. Website: http://web.mit.edu/chemistry/www/.

McMaster University, School of Graduate Studies, Faculty of Science, Department of Chemistry, Hamilton, ON L8S 4M2, Canada. Offers analytical chemistry (M Sc, PhD); chemical physics (M Sc, PhD); chemistry (M Sc, PhD); inorganic chemistry (M Sc, PhD); organic chemistry (M Sc, PhD); physical chemistry (M Sc, PhD); polymer chemistry (M Sc, PhD). Part-time programs available. Terminal master's awarded for partial completion of doctoral program. *Degree requirements:* For master's, thesis; for doctorate, comprehensive exam, thesis/dissertation. *Entrance requirements:* For master's, minimum B+ average. Additional exam requirements/recommendations for international students: Required—TOEFL (minimum score 550 paper-based).

Old Dominion University, College of Sciences, Program in Chemistry, Norfolk, VA 23529. Offers analytical chemistry (MS); biochemistry (MS); chemistry (PhD); environmental chemistry (MS); organic chemistry (MS); physical chemistry (MS). Part-time and evening/weekend programs available. *Faculty:* 19 full-time (7 women), 3 part-time/adjunct (all women). *Students:* 36 full-time (20 women); includes 1 minority (Black or African American, non-Hispanic/Latino), 14 international. Average age 27. 35 applicants, 60% accepted, 8 enrolled. In 2012, 4 master's, 1 doctorate awarded. *Degree requirements:* For master's, comprehensive exam, thesis. *Entrance requirements:* For master's, GRE General Test, minimum GPA of 3.0 in major, 2.5 overall; for doctorate, GRE General Test. Additional exam requirements/recommendations for international students: Required—TOEFL. *Application deadline:* For fall admission, 7/1 for domestic students, 1/15 for international students; for spring admission, 11/1 for domestic students, 8/15 for international students. Applications are processed on a rolling basis. Application fee: $30. Electronic applications accepted. *Expenses:* Tuition, state resident: full-time $9432; part-time $393 per credit hour. Tuition, nonresident: full-time $23,928; part-time $997 per credit hour. *Required fees:* $59 per semester. One-time fee: $50. *Financial support:* In 2012–13, 6 students received support, including fellowships (averaging $18,000 per year), research assistantships with tuition reimbursements available (averaging $21,000 per year), teaching assistantships with tuition reimbursements available (averaging $18,000 per year); career-related internships or fieldwork, scholarships/grants, and unspecified assistantships also available. Financial award application deadline: 2/15; financial award applicants required to submit FAFSA. *Faculty research:* Biogeochemistry, materials chemistry, computational chemistry, organic chemistry, biofuels. *Total annual research expenditures:* $2.6 million. *Unit head:* Dr. Craig A. Bayse, Graduate Program Director, 757-683-4097, Fax: 757-683-4628, E-mail: chemgpd@odu.edu. *Application contact:* Valerie DeCosta, Grants and Graduate Program Assistant, 757-683-6979, Fax: 757-683-4628, E-mail: chemgpd@odu.edu.

Oregon State University, College of Science, Department of Chemistry, Corvallis, OR 97331. Offers analytical chemistry (MS, PhD); chemistry (MA, MAIS); inorganic chemistry (MS, PhD); nuclear and radiation chemistry (MS,

PhD); organic chemistry (MS, PhD); physical chemistry (MS, PhD). Part-time programs available. *Faculty:* 28 full-time (7 women), 9 part-time/adjunct (1 woman). *Students:* 101 full-time (28 women), 1 part-time (0 women); includes 5 minority (2 Asian, non-Hispanic/Latino; 1 Hispanic/Latino; 2 Two or more races, non-Hispanic/Latino), 54 international. Average age 28. 98 applicants, 30% accepted, 27 enrolled. In 2012, 4 master's, 16 doctorates awarded. Terminal master's awarded for partial completion of doctoral program. *Degree requirements:* For master's, one foreign language, thesis; for doctorate, one foreign language, thesis/dissertation. *Entrance requirements:* For master's and doctorate, minimum GPA of 3.0 in last 90 hours of course work. Additional exam requirements/recommendations for international students: Required—TOEFL. *Application deadline:* For fall admission, 3/1 priority date for domestic students. Applications are processed on a rolling basis. Application fee: $50. *Expenses:* Tuition, state resident: full-time $11,367; part-time $421 per credit hour. Tuition, nonresident: full-time $18,279; part-time $677 per credit hour. *Required fees:* $1478. One-time fee: $300 full-time. Tuition and fees vary according to course load and program. *Financial support:* Fellowships, research assistantships, teaching assistantships, and institutionally sponsored loans available. Support available to part-time students. Financial award application deadline: 2/1. *Faculty research:* Solid state chemistry, enzyme reaction mechanisms, structure and dynamics of gas molecules, chemiluminescence, nonlinear optical spectroscopy. *Unit head:* Dr. Rich G. Carter, Professor/Chair, 541-737-9486, E-mail: rich.carter@oregonstate.edu.

Purdue University, Graduate School, College of Science, Department of Chemistry, West Lafayette, IN 47907. Offers analytical chemistry (MS, PhD); biochemistry (MS, PhD); chemical education (MS, PhD); inorganic chemistry (MS, PhD); organic chemistry (MS, PhD); physical chemistry (MS, PhD). *Faculty:* 42 full-time (14 women), 7 part-time/adjunct (0 women). *Students:* 275 full-time (102 women), 23 part-time (8 women); includes 34 minority (16 Black or African American, non-Hispanic/Latino; 5 Asian, non-Hispanic/Latino; 11 Hispanic/Latino; 2 Two or more races, non-Hispanic/Latino), 94 international. Average age 27. 716 applicants, 26% accepted, 66 enrolled. In 2012, 18 master's, 52 doctorates awarded. Terminal master's awarded for partial completion of doctoral program. *Degree requirements:* For master's, thesis; for doctorate, comprehensive exam, thesis/dissertation. *Entrance requirements:* For master's and doctorate, minimum undergraduate GPA of 3.0. Additional exam requirements/recommendations for international students: Required—TOEFL (minimum score 77 iBT); Recommended—TWE. *Application deadline:* For fall admission, 2/15 priority date for domestic students, 1/1 for international students. Applications are processed on a rolling basis. Application fee: $60 ($75 for international students). Electronic applications accepted. *Financial support:* In 2012–13, 2 fellowships with partial tuition reimbursements (averaging $18,000 per year), 55 teaching assistantships with partial tuition reimbursements (averaging $18,000 per year) were awarded; research assistantships with partial tuition reimbursements and tuition waivers (partial) also available. Support available to part-time students. Financial award applicants required to submit FAFSA. *Unit head:* Dr. Paul B. Shepson, Head, 765-494-5203, E-mail: pshepson@purdue.edu. *Application contact:* Betty L. Hatfield, Director of Graduate Admissions, 765-494-5208, E-mail: bettyh@purdue.edu.

Rice University, Graduate Programs, Wiess School of Natural Sciences, Department of Chemistry, Houston, TX 77251-1892. Offers chemistry (MA); inorganic chemistry (PhD); organic chemistry (PhD); physical chemistry (PhD). Terminal master's awarded for partial completion of doctoral program. *Degree requirements:* For master's, thesis; for doctorate, thesis/dissertation. *Entrance requirements:* For master's and doctorate, GRE General Test, minimum GPA of 3.0. Additional exam requirements/recommendations for international students: Required—TOEFL (minimum score 600 paper-based; 90 iBT). Electronic applications accepted. *Faculty research:* Nanoscience, biomaterials, nanobioinformatics, fullerene pharmaceuticals.

Rutgers, The State University of New Jersey, Newark, Graduate School, Program in Chemistry, Newark, NJ 07102. Offers analytical chemistry (MS, PhD); biochemistry (MS, PhD); inorganic chemistry (MS, PhD); organic chemistry (MS, PhD); physical chemistry (MS, PhD). Part-time and evening/weekend programs available. Terminal master's awarded for partial completion of doctoral program. *Degree requirements:* For master's, thesis optional, cumulative exams; for doctorate, thesis/dissertation, exams, research proposal. *Entrance requirements:* For master's and doctorate, GRE General Test, minimum undergraduate B average. Additional exam requirements/recommendations for international students: Required—TOEFL. Electronic applications accepted. *Faculty research:* Medicinal chemistry, natural products, isotope effects, biophysics and biorganic approaches to enzyme mechanisms, organic and organometallic synthesis.

Rutgers, The State University of New Jersey, New Brunswick, Graduate School-New Brunswick, Department of Chemistry and Chemical Biology, Piscataway, NJ 08854-8097. Offers biological chemistry (MS, PhD); inorganic chemistry (MS, PhD); organic chemistry (MS, PhD); physical chemistry (MS, PhD). Part-time and evening/weekend programs available. Terminal master's awarded for partial completion of doctoral program. *Degree requirements:* For master's, thesis or alternative, exam; for doctorate, thesis/dissertation, 1 year residency. *Entrance requirements:* For master's and doctorate, GRE General Test, GRE Subject Test. Additional exam requirements/recommendations for international students: Required—TOEFL. Electronic applications accepted. *Faculty research:* Biophysical organic/bioorganic, inorganic/bioinorganic, theoretical, and solid-state/surface chemistry.

Seton Hall University, College of Arts and Sciences, Department of Chemistry and Biochemistry, South Orange, NJ 07079-2697. Offers analytical chemistry (MS, PhD); biochemistry (MS, PhD); chemistry (MS); inorganic chemistry (MS, PhD); organic chemistry (MS, PhD); physical chemistry (MS, PhD). Part-time and evening/weekend programs available. Terminal master's awarded for partial completion of doctoral program. *Degree requirements:* For master's, thesis optional; for doctorate, comprehensive exam, thesis/dissertation. *Entrance requirements:* Additional exam requirements/recommendations for international students: Required—TOEFL. Electronic applications accepted. *Faculty research:* DNA metal reactions; chromatography; bioinorganic, biophysical, organometallic, polymer chemistry; heterogeneous catalyst; synthetic organic and carbohydrate chemistry.

Southern University and Agricultural and Mechanical College, Graduate School, College of Sciences, Department of Chemistry, Baton Rouge, LA 70813. Offers analytical chemistry (MS); biochemistry (MS); environmental sciences (MS); inorganic chemistry (MS); organic chemistry (MS); physical chemistry (MS). *Degree requirements:* For master's, thesis. *Entrance requirements:* For master's, GMAT or GRE General Test. Additional exam requirements/recommendations for international students: Required—TOEFL (minimum score 525 paper-based). *Faculty research:* Synthesis of macrocyclic ligands, latex accelerators, anticancer drugs, biosensors, absorption isotherms, isolation of specific enzymes from plants.

State University of New York College of Environmental Science and Forestry, Department of Chemistry, Syracuse, NY 13210-2779. Offers biochemistry (MPS, MS, PhD); environmental chemistry (MPS, MS, PhD); organic chemistry of natural products (MPS, MS, PhD); polymer chemistry (MPS, MS, PhD). *Degree requirements:* For master's, thesis; for doctorate, comprehensive exam, thesis/dissertation. *Entrance requirements:* For master's and doctorate, GRE General Test, GRE Subject Test, minimum GPA of 3.0. Additional exam requirements/recommendations for international students: Required—TOEFL (minimum score 550 paper-based; 80 iBT), IELTS (minimum score 6). Electronic applications accepted. *Expenses:* Tuition, state resident: full-time $9370; part-time $390 per credit hour. Tuition, nonresident: full-time $16,680; part-time $695 per credit hour. *Required fees:* $981. Tuition and fees vary according to course load and program. *Faculty research:* Polymer chemistry, biochemistry.

Stevens Institute of Technology, Graduate School, Charles V. Schaefer Jr. School of Engineering, Department of Chemistry, Chemical Biology and Biomedical Engineering, Hoboken, NJ 07030. Offers analytical chemistry (PhD, Certificate); bioinformatics (PhD, Certificate); biomedical chemistry (Certificate); biomedical engineering (M Eng, Certificate); chemical biology (MS, PhD, Certificate); chemical physiology (Certificate); chemistry (MS, PhD); organic chemistry (PhD); physical chemistry (PhD); polymer chemistry (PhD, Certificate). Part-time and evening/weekend programs available. Postbaccalaureate distance learning degree programs offered (no on-campus study). Terminal master's awarded for partial completion of doctoral program. *Degree requirements:* For master's, thesis or alternative; for doctorate, one foreign language, thesis/dissertation; for Certificate, project or thesis. *Entrance requirements:* Additional exam requirements/recommendations for international students: Required—TOEFL. Electronic applications accepted. *Faculty research:* Biochemical reaction engineering, polymerization engineering, reactor design, biochemical process control and synthesis.

Texas Christian University, College of Science and Engineering, Department of Chemistry, Fort Worth, TX 76129. Offers biochemistry (MS, PhD); chemistry (MA); inorganic (MS, PhD); organic (MS, PhD); physical (MS, PhD). Part-time programs available. *Faculty:* 11 full-time (2 women). *Students:* 7 full-time (3 women), 17 part-time (10 women); includes 4 minority (1 Asian, non-Hispanic/Latino; 3 Hispanic/Latino), 13 international. Average age 27. 34 applicants, 24% accepted, 5 enrolled. In 2012, 1 master's, 1 doctorate awarded. *Degree requirements:* For master's, thesis; for doctorate, thesis/dissertation, literature seminar, cumulative exams, research progress report, original proposal. *Entrance requirements:* For master's and doctorate, GRE General Test. Additional exam requirements/recommendations for international students: Required—TOEFL (minimum score 80 iBT). *Application deadline:* For fall admission, 2/1 priority date for domestic students, 2/1 for international students; for spring admission, 9/1 priority date for domestic students, 9/1 for international students. Application fee: $50. Electronic applications accepted. *Expenses: Tuition:* Full-time $21,600; part-time $1200 per credit. *Required fees:* $48. Tuition and fees vary according to program. *Financial support:* In 2012–13, 16 students received support, including 16 teaching assistantships with full tuition reimbursements available; tuition waivers (full and partial) and unspecified assistantships also available. Financial award application deadline: 2/1. *Faculty research:* Phase transitions and transport properties of bio/macromolecular solutions, nanoscale biomaterials, electronic structure theory, synthetic methodology and total synthesis of natural products, chemistry and biology of (bio)polymers. *Unit head:* Dr. Robert Neilson, Chairperson/Professor, 817-257-7345, Fax: 817-257-5851, E-mail: r.neilson@tcu.edu. *Application contact:* Dr. Sergei V. Dzyuba, Director of Graduate Studies/Assistant Professor, 817-257-6218, Fax: 817-257-5851, E-mail: s.dzyuba@tcu.edu. Website: http://www.chm.tcu.edu/.

Tufts University, Graduate School of Arts and Sciences, Department of Chemistry, Medford, MA 02155. Offers analytical chemistry (MS, PhD); bioorganic chemistry (MS, PhD); environmental chemistry (MS, PhD); inorganic chemistry (MS, PhD); organic chemistry (MS, PhD); physical chemistry (MS, PhD). Terminal master's awarded for partial completion of doctoral program. *Degree* *requirements:* For master's, thesis optional; for doctorate, thesis/dissertation. *Entrance requirements:* For master's and doctorate, GRE General Test, GRE Subject Test. Additional exam requirements/recommendations for international students: Required—TOEFL (minimum score 600 paper-based; 80 iBT). Electronic applications accepted. *Expenses: Tuition:* Full-time $42,856; part-time $1072 per credit hour. *Required fees:* $730. Full-time tuition and fees vary according to degree level, program and student level. Part-time tuition and fees vary according to course load.

University of Calgary, Faculty of Graduate Studies, Faculty of Science, Department of Chemistry, Calgary, AB T2N 1N4, Canada. Offers analytical chemistry (M Sc, PhD); applied chemistry (M Sc, PhD); inorganic chemistry (M Sc, PhD); organic chemistry (M Sc, PhD); physical chemistry (M Sc, PhD); polymer chemistry (M Sc, PhD); theoretical chemistry (M Sc, PhD). *Degree requirements:* For master's, thesis; for doctorate, thesis/dissertation, candidacy exam. *Entrance requirements:* For master's, minimum GPA of 3.0; for doctorate, honors B Sc degree with minimum GPA of 3.7 or M Sc with minimum GPA of 3.3. Additional exam requirements/recommendations for international students: Required—TOEFL (minimum score 580 paper-based). Electronic applications accepted. *Faculty research:* Chemical analysis, chemical dynamics, synthesis theory.

University of Cincinnati, Graduate School, McMicken College of Arts and Sciences, Department of Chemistry, Cincinnati, OH 45221. Offers analytical chemistry (MS, PhD); biochemistry (MS, PhD); inorganic chemistry (MS, PhD); organic chemistry (MS, PhD); physical chemistry (MS, PhD); polymer chemistry (MS, PhD); sensors (PhD). Part-time and evening/weekend programs available. Terminal master's awarded for partial completion of doctoral program. *Degree requirements:* For master's, thesis optional; for doctorate, comprehensive exam, thesis/dissertation. *Entrance requirements:* For master's and doctorate, GRE General Test. Additional exam requirements/recommendations for international students: Required—TOEFL (minimum score 580 paper-based). Electronic applications accepted. *Faculty research:* Biomedical chemistry, laser chemistry, surface science, chemical sensors, synthesis.

University of Georgia, Franklin College of Arts and Sciences, Department of Chemistry, Athens, GA 30602. Offers analytical chemistry (MS, PhD); inorganic chemistry (MS, PhD); organic chemistry (MS, PhD); physical chemistry (MS, PhD). Terminal master's awarded for partial completion of doctoral program. *Degree requirements:* For master's, thesis; for doctorate, one foreign language, thesis/dissertation. *Entrance requirements:* For master's and doctorate, GRE General Test. Additional exam requirements/recommendations for international students: Required—TOEFL. Electronic applications accepted.

University of Louisville, Graduate School, College of Arts and Sciences, Department of Chemistry, Louisville, KY 40292-0001. Offers analytical chemistry (MS, PhD); biochemistry (MS, PhD); chemical physics (PhD); inorganic chemistry (MS, PhD); organic chemistry (MS, PhD); physical chemistry (MS, PhD). *Students:* 45 full-time (21 women), 5 part-time (1 woman); includes 1 minority (Hispanic/Latino), 35 international. Average age 28. 78 applicants, 17% accepted, 9 enrolled. In 2012, 19 master's, 7 doctorates awarded. Terminal master's awarded for partial completion of doctoral program. *Degree requirements:* For master's, variable foreign language requirement, comprehensive exam, thesis optional; for doctorate, variable foreign language requirement, comprehensive exam, thesis/dissertation. *Entrance requirements:* For master's and doctorate, BA or BS coursework. Additional exam requirements/recommendations for international students: Required—TOEFL. *Application deadline:* For fall admission, 3/15 for domestic and international students; for winter admission, 9/15 for domestic and international students. Applications are processed on a rolling basis. Application fee: $60. Electronic applications accepted. *Financial support:* In 2012–13, 33 teaching assistantships with full tuition reimbursements (averaging $22,000 per year) were awarded; fellowships with full tuition reimbursements, research assistantships with full tuition reimbursements, career-related internships or fieldwork, scholarships/grants, traineeships, health care benefits, and unspecified assistantships also available. Support available to part-time students. Financial award application deadline: 3/15. *Faculty research:* Computational chemistry, biophysics nuclear magnetic resonance, synthetic organic chemistry, synthetic inorganic chemistry, medicinal chemistry, protein chemistry, enzymology, nanochemistry, electrochemistry, analytical chemistry, synthetic biology, bioinformatics. *Total annual research expenditures:* $2.5 million. *Unit head:* Dr. Richard J. Wittebort, Professor/Chair, 502-852-6613. *Application contact:* Sherry Nalley, Administrator, 502-852-6798.

The University of Manchester, School of Chemistry, Manchester, United Kingdom. Offers biological chemistry (PhD); chemistry (M Ent, M Phil, M Sc, D Ent, PhD); inorganic chemistry (PhD); materials chemistry (PhD); nanoscience (PhD); nuclear fission (PhD); organic chemistry (PhD); physical chemistry (PhD); theoretical chemistry (PhD).

University of Maryland, College Park, Academic Affairs, College of Computer, Mathematical and Natural Sciences, Department of Chemistry and Biochemistry, Chemistry Program, College Park, MD 20742. Offers analytical chemistry (MS, PhD); inorganic chemistry (MS, PhD); organic chemistry (MS, PhD); physical chemistry (MS, PhD). Part-time and evening/weekend programs available. *Students:* 113 full-time (64 women), 2 part-time (0 women); includes 19 minority (11 Black or African American, non-Hispanic/Latino; 4 Asian, non-Hispanic/Latino; 2 Hispanic/Latino; 2 Two or more races, non-Hispanic/Latino), 44 international. 339 applicants, 27% accepted, 20 enrolled. In 2012, 7 master's, 14 doctorates awarded. Terminal master's awarded for partial completion of doctoral program. *Degree requirements:* For master's, thesis optional; for doctorate, thesis/dissertation, 2 seminar presentations, oral exam. *Entrance requirements:* For master's and doctorate, GRE General Test, GRE Subject Test (recommended), minimum GPA of 3.0, 3 letters of recommendation. Additional exam requirements/recommendations for international students: Required—TOEFL. *Application deadline:* For fall admission, 2/1 for domestic and international students; for spring admission, 6/1 for domestic and international students. Applications are processed on a rolling basis. Application fee: $75. Electronic applications accepted. *Expenses:* Tuition, state resident: part-time $551 per credit. Tuition, nonresident: part-time $1188 per credit. Part-time tuition and fees vary according to program. *Financial support:* In 2012–13, 14 fellowships with full and partial tuition reimbursements (averaging $20,017 per year), 52 research assistantships (averaging $19,868 per year), 44 teaching assistantships (averaging $19,209 per year) were awarded. Financial award applicants required to submit FAFSA. *Faculty research:* Environmental chemistry, nuclear chemistry, lunar and environmental analysis, x-ray crystallography. *Unit head:* Dr. Michael Doyle, Chairperson, 301-405-1795, Fax: 301-314-2779, E-mail: mdoyle3@umd.edu. *Application contact:* Dr. Charles A. Caramello, Dean of Graduate School, 301-405-0358, Fax: 301-314-9305.

University of Massachusetts Lowell, College of Sciences, Department of Chemistry, Lowell, MA 01854-2881. Offers analytical chemistry (PhD); biochemistry (PhD); chemistry (MS, PhD); environmental studies (PhD); green chemistry (PhD); inorganic chemistry (PhD); organic chemistry (PhD); polymer science (MS). Terminal master's awarded for partial completion of doctoral program. *Degree requirements:* For master's, thesis; for doctorate, 2 foreign languages, thesis/dissertation. *Entrance requirements:* For master's and doctorate, GRE General Test. Electronic applications accepted.

University of Memphis, Graduate School, College of Arts and Sciences, Department of Chemistry, Memphis, TN 38152. Offers analytical chemistry (MS, PhD); computational chemistry (MS, PhD); inorganic chemistry (MS, PhD); organic chemistry (MS, PhD); physical chemistry (MS, PhD). Part-time programs available. Terminal master's awarded for partial completion of doctoral program. *Degree requirements:* For master's, comprehensive exam, thesis or alternative; for doctorate, comprehensive exam, thesis/dissertation. *Entrance requirements:* For master's and doctorate, GRE General Test, admission to Graduate School plus 32 undergraduate hours in chemistry. Additional exam requirements/recommendations for international students: Required—TOEFL. Electronic applications accepted. *Faculty research:* Computational chemistry, materials chemistry, organic/polymer synthesis, drug design/delivery, water chemistry.

University of Miami, Graduate School, College of Arts and Sciences, Department of Chemistry, Coral Gables, FL 33124. Offers chemistry (MS); inorganic chemistry (PhD); organic chemistry (PhD); physical chemistry (PhD). Terminal master's awarded for partial completion of doctoral program. *Degree requirements:* For master's, comprehensive exam; for doctorate, comprehensive exam, thesis/dissertation. *Entrance requirements:* For master's and doctorate, GRE General Test. Additional exam requirements/recommendations for international students: Required—TOEFL (minimum score 550 paper-based). Electronic applications accepted. *Faculty research:* Supramolecular chemistry, electrochemistry, surface chemistry, catalysis, organometalic.

University of Michigan, Horace H. Rackham School of Graduate Studies, College of Literature, Science, and the Arts, Department of Chemistry, Ann Arbor, MI 48109-1055. Offers analytical chemistry (PhD); chemical biology (PhD); inorganic chemistry (PhD); material chemistry (PhD); organic chemistry (PhD); physical chemistry (PhD). *Degree requirements:* For doctorate, thesis/dissertation, oral defense of dissertation, organic cumulative proficiency exams. *Entrance requirements:* For doctorate, GRE General Test, GRE Subject Test (recommended), 3 letters of recommendation. Additional exam requirements/recommendations for international students: Required—TOEFL (minimum score 560 paper-based; 84 iBT). Electronic applications accepted. *Faculty research:* Biological catalysis, protein engineering, chemical sensors, de novo metalloprotein design, supramolecular architecture.

University of Missouri, Graduate School, College of Arts and Sciences, Department of Chemistry, Columbia, MO 65211. Offers analytical chemistry (MS, PhD); inorganic chemistry (MS, PhD); organic chemistry (MS, PhD); physical chemistry (MS, PhD). *Faculty:* 22 full-time (4 women), 1 part-time/adjunct (0 women). *Students:* 110 full-time (42 women), 9 part-time (5 women); includes 10 minority (3 Black or African American, non-Hispanic/Latino; 3 Asian, non-Hispanic/Latino; 2 Hispanic/Latino; 2 Two or more races, non-Hispanic/Latino), 47 international. Average age 27. 94 applicants, 21% accepted, 15 enrolled. In 2012, 2 master's, 5 doctorates awarded. *Degree requirements:* For master's, thesis; for doctorate, one foreign language, comprehensive exam, thesis/dissertation. *Entrance requirements:* For master's, GRE General Test, minimum GPA of 3.0; for doctorate, GRE General Test (minimum score: Verbal 450, Quantitative 600, Analytical 3), minimum GPA of 3.0. Additional exam requirements/recommendations for international students: Required—TOEFL (minimum score 600 paper-based; 100 iBT). *Application deadline:* For fall admission, 2/1 priority date for domestic students, 2/1 for international students; for winter admission, 10/15 for domestic and international students. Applications are processed on a rolling basis. Application fee: $55 ($75 for international students). Electronic applications accepted. *Expenses:* Tuition, state resident: full-time $6057. Tuition, nonresident: full-time $15,683. *Required fees:* $1000. *Financial support:* In 2012–13, 9 fellowships with full tuition reimbursements, 15 research assistantships with full tuition reimbursements, 78 teaching assistantships with full tuition reimbursements were awarded; institutionally sponsored loans, traineeships, health care benefits, and unspecified assistantships also available. *Faculty research:* Analytical, organic, biological, physical, inorganic and radiochemistry. *Unit head:* Dr. Jerry Atwood, Department Chair, 573-882-8374, E-mail: atwoodj@missouri.edu. *Application contact:* Jerry Brightwell, Administrative Assistant, 573-884-6832, E-mail: brightwellj@missouri.edu. Website: http://chemistry.missouri.edu/.

University of Missouri–Kansas City, College of Arts and Sciences, Department of Chemistry, Kansas City, MO 64110-2499. Offers analytical chemistry (MS, PhD); inorganic chemistry (MS, PhD); organic chemistry (MS, PhD); physical chemistry (MS, PhD); polymer chemistry (MS, PhD). PhD (interdisciplinary) offered through the School of Graduate Studies. Part-time and evening/weekend programs available. *Faculty:* 15 full-time (3 women), 2 part-time/adjunct (0 women). *Students:* 7 part-time (3 women); includes 3 minority (2 Black or African American, non-Hispanic/Latino; 1 Hispanic/Latino). Average age 38. 19 applicants, 37% accepted, 3 enrolled. In 2012, 2 master's awarded. *Degree requirements:* For master's, thesis (for some programs); for doctorate, thesis/dissertation. *Entrance requirements:* For master's, equivalent of American Chemical Society approved bachelor's degree in chemistry; for doctorate, GRE General Test, equivalent of American Chemical Society approved bachelor's degree in chemistry. Additional exam requirements/recommendations for international students: Required—TOEFL (minimum score 550 paper-based; 80 iBT), TWE. *Application deadline:* For fall admission, 4/15 for domestic and international students; for spring admission, 10/15 for domestic and international students. Applications are processed on a rolling basis. Application fee: $45 ($50 for international students). Electronic applications accepted. *Expenses:* Tuition, state resident: full-time $5972.40; part-time $331.80 per credit hour. Tuition, nonresident: full-time $15,417; part-time $856.50 per credit hour. *Required fees:* $95.89 per credit hour. Full-time tuition and fees vary according to program. *Financial support:* In 2012–13, 6 research assistantships with partial tuition reimbursements (averaging $18,817 per year), 16 teaching assistantships with partial tuition reimbursements (averaging $18,132 per year) were awarded; Federal Work-Study, institutionally sponsored loans, and scholarships/grants also available. Support available to part-time students. Financial award application deadline: 3/1; financial award applicants required to submit FAFSA. *Faculty research:* Molecular spectroscopy, characterization and synthesis of materials and compounds, computational chemistry, natural products, drug delivery systems and anti-tumor agents. *Unit head:* Dr. Kathleen V. Kilway, Chair, 816-235-2289, Fax: 816-235-5502. *Application contact:* Graduate Recruiting Committee, 816-235-2272, Fax: 816-235-5502, E-mail: umkc-chemdept@umkc.edu. Website: http://cas.umkc.edu/chem/.

University of Missouri–St. Louis, College of Arts and Sciences, Department of Chemistry and Biochemistry, St. Louis, MO 63121. Offers chemistry (MS, PhD), including biochemistry, inorganic chemistry, organic chemistry, physical chemistry. Part-time and evening/weekend programs available. *Faculty:* 19 full-time (3 women), 6 part-time/adjunct (1 woman). *Students:* 37 full-time (15 women), 25 part-time (16 women); includes 6 minority (2 Black or African American, non-Hispanic/Latino; 1 Asian, non-Hispanic/Latino; 3 Hispanic/Latino), 18 international. Average age 30. 85 applicants, 22% accepted, 7 enrolled. In 2012, 18 master's, 5 doctorates awarded. Terminal master's awarded for partial completion of doctoral program. *Degree requirements:* For master's, thesis optional; for doctorate, thesis/dissertation. *Entrance requirements:* For master's, 2 letters of recommendation; for doctorate, GRE General Test, 3 letters of recommendation. Additional exam requirements/recommendations for international students: Required—TOEFL (minimum score 550 paper-based; 79 iBT), IELTS (minimum score 6.5). *Application deadline:* For fall admission, 7/1 priority date for domestic students, 7/1 for international students; for spring admission, 12/1 priority date for domestic students, 12/1 for international students. Applications are processed on a rolling basis. Application fee: $35 ($40 for international students). Electronic applications accepted. *Expenses:* Tuition, state resident: full-time $7364; part-time $409.10 per credit hour. Tuition, nonresident: full-time $18,153; part-time $1008.50 per credit hour. *Financial support:* In 2012–13, 16 research assistantships with full and partial tuition reimbursements (averaging $13,500 per year), 20 teaching assistantships with full and partial tuition reimbursements (averaging $13,500 per year) were awarded; fellowships with full and partial tuition reimbursements also available. *Faculty research:* Metallaborane chemistry, serum transferrin chemistry, natural products chemistry, organic synthesis. *Unit head:* Dr. Janet Wilking, Director of Graduate Studies, 314-516-5311, Fax: 314-516-5342, E-mail: gradchem@umsl.edu. *Application contact:* Graduate Admissions, 314-516-5458, Fax: 314-516-6996, E-mail: gradadm@umsl.edu. Website: http://www.umsl.edu/chemistry/.

The University of Montana, Graduate School, College of Arts and Sciences, Department of Chemistry and Biochemistry, Missoula, MT 59812-0002. Offers chemistry (MS, PhD), including environmental/analytical chemistry, inorganic chemistry, organic chemistry, physical chemistry. Terminal master's awarded for partial completion of doctoral program. *Degree requirements:* For master's, thesis (for some programs); for doctorate, thesis/dissertation. *Entrance requirements:* For master's and doctorate, GRE General Test. Additional exam requirements/recommendations for international students: Required—TOEFL (minimum score 575 paper-based). *Faculty research:* Reaction mechanisms and kinetics, inorganic and organic synthesis, analytical chemistry, natural products.

University of Nebraska–Lincoln, Graduate College, College of Arts and Sciences, Department of Chemistry, Lincoln, NE 68588. Offers analytical chemistry (PhD); biochemistry (PhD); chemistry (MS); inorganic chemistry (PhD); materials chemistry (PhD); organic chemistry (PhD); physical chemistry (PhD). *Degree requirements:* For master's, one foreign language, thesis optional, departmental qualifying exam; for doctorate, one foreign language, comprehensive exam, thesis/dissertation, departmental qualifying exams. *Entrance requirements:* For master's and doctorate, GRE. Additional exam requirements/recommendations for international students: Required—TOEFL (minimum score 550 paper-based). Electronic applications accepted. *Faculty research:* Bioorganic and bioinorganic chemistry, biophysical and bioanalytical chemistry, structure-function of DNA and proteins, organometallics, mass spectrometry.

University of Notre Dame, Graduate School, College of Science, Department of Chemistry and Biochemistry, Notre Dame, IN 46556. Offers biochemistry (MS, PhD); inorganic chemistry (MS, PhD); organic chemistry (MS, PhD); physical chemistry (MS, PhD). Terminal master's awarded for partial completion of doctoral program. *Degree requirements:* For master's, comprehensive exam, thesis; for doctorate, thesis/dissertation, qualifying exam. *Entrance requirements:* For master's and doctorate, GRE General Test, GRE Subject Test (strongly recommended). Additional exam requirements/recommendations for international students: Required—TOEFL (minimum score 600 paper-based; 80 iBT). Electronic applications accepted. *Faculty research:* Reaction design and mechanistic studies; reactive intermediates; synthesis, structure and reactivity of organometallic cluster complexes and biologically active natural products; bioorganic chemistry; enzymology.

University of Regina, Faculty of Graduate Studies and Research, Faculty of Science, Department of Chemistry and Biochemistry, Regina, SK S4S 0A2, Canada. Offers analytical/environmental chemistry (M Sc, PhD); biophysics of biological interfaces (M Sc, PhD); enzymology/chemical biology (M Sc, PhD); inorganic/organometallic chemistry (M Sc, PhD); signal transduction and mechanisms of cancer cell regulation (M Sc, PhD); supramolecular organic photochemistry and photophysics (M Sc, PhD); synthetic organic chemistry (M Sc, PhD); theoretical/computational chemistry (M Sc, PhD). *Faculty:* 12 full-time (2 women), 3 part-time/adjunct (0 women). *Students:* 11 full-time (6 women), 2 part-time (0 women). 32 applicants, 19% accepted. In 2012, 7 master's awarded. *Degree requirements:* For master's, thesis; for doctorate, thesis/dissertation. *Entrance requirements:* Additional exam requirements/recommendations for international students: Required—TOEFL (minimum score 580 paper-based; 80 iBT), IELTS (minimum score 6.5). *Application deadline:* Applications are processed on a rolling basis. Application fee: $100. Electronic applications accepted. Tuition and fees charges are reported in Canadian dollars. *Expenses: Tuition, area resident:* Full-time $3942 Canadian dollars; part-time $219 Canadian dollars per credit hour. *International tuition:* $4742 Canadian dollars full-time. *Required fees:* $421.55 Canadian dollars; $93.60 Canadian dollars per credit hour. Tuition and fees vary according to course load, degree level and program. *Financial support:* In 2012–13, 5 fellowships (averaging $7,000 per year), 10 teaching assistantships (averaging $2,470 per year) were awarded; research assistantships and scholarships/grants also available. Financial award application deadline: 6/15. *Faculty research:* Asymmetric synthesis and methodology, theoretical and computational chemistry, biophysical biochemistry, analytical and environmental chemistry, chemical biology. *Unit head:* Dr. Lynn Mihichuk, Head, 306-585-4793, Fax: 306-337-2409, E-mail: lynn.mihichuk@uregina.ca. *Application contact:* Dr. Brian Sterenberg, Graduate Program Coordinator, 306-585-4106, Fax: 306-337-2409, E-mail: brian.sterenberg@uregina.ca. Website: http://www.chem.uregina.ca/.

University of Southern Mississippi, Graduate School, College of Science and Technology, Department of Chemistry and Biochemistry, Hattiesburg, MS 39406-0001. Offers analytical chemistry (MS, PhD); biochemistry (MS, PhD); inorganic chemistry (MS, PhD); organic chemistry (MS, PhD); physical chemistry (MS, PhD). *Faculty:* 16 full-time (4 women). *Students:* 26 full-time (9 women); includes 2 minority (1 Black or African American, non-Hispanic/Latino; 1 Asian, non-Hispanic/Latino), 8 international. Average age 27. 63 applicants, 13% accepted, 4 enrolled. In 2012, 2 master's, 4 doctorates awarded. *Degree requirements:* For master's, comprehensive exam, thesis; for doctorate, comprehensive exam, thesis/dissertation. *Entrance requirements:* For master's, GRE General Test, minimum GPA of 2.75 in last 60 hours; for doctorate, GRE General Test, minimum GPA of 3.5. Additional exam requirements/recommendations for international students: Required—TOEFL, IELTS. *Application deadline:* For fall admission, 3/1 priority date for domestic students, 3/1 for international students. Applications are processed on a rolling basis. Application fee: $50. *Financial support:* In 2012–13, 3 research assistantships with full tuition reimbursements (averaging $17,000 per year), 19 teaching assistantships with full tuition reimbursements (averaging $20,700 per year) were awarded; fellowships, Federal Work-Study, institutionally sponsored loans, scholarships/grants, health care benefits, and unspecified assistantships also available. Support available to part-time students. Financial award application deadline: 3/15; financial award applicants required to submit FAFSA. *Faculty research:* Plant biochemistry, photo chemistry, polymer chemistry, x-ray analysis, enzyme chemistry. *Unit head:* Dr. Sabine Heinhorst, Chair, 601-266-4701, Fax: 601-266-6075. Website: http://www.usm.edu/graduateschool/table.php.

University of South Florida, Graduate School, College of Arts and Sciences, Department of Chemistry, Tampa, FL 33620-9951. Offers analytical chemistry

Peterson's Graduate Programs in the Physical Sciences, Mathematics, Agricultural Sciences, the Environment & Natural Resources 2014

www.petersonsbooks.com **113**

(MS, PhD); biochemistry (MS, PhD); computational chemistry (MS, PhD); environmental chemistry (MS, PhD); inorganic chemistry (MS, PhD); organic chemistry (MS); physical chemistry (MS, PhD); polymer chemistry (PhD). Part-time programs available. Terminal master's awarded for partial completion of doctoral program. *Degree requirements:* For master's, comprehensive exam, thesis (for some programs); for doctorate, comprehensive exam, thesis/dissertation. *Entrance requirements:* For master's and doctorate, GRE General Test, minimum GPA of 3.0. Additional exam requirements/recommendations for international students: Required—TOEFL (minimum score 550 paper-based; 79 iBT) or IELTS (minimum score 6.5). Electronic applications accepted. *Faculty research:* Synthesis, bio-organic chemistry, bioinorganic chemistry, environmental chemistry, nuclear magnetic resonance (NMR).

The University of Tennessee, Graduate School, College of Arts and Sciences, Department of Chemistry, Knoxville, TN 37996. Offers analytical chemistry (MS, PhD); chemical physics (PhD); environmental chemistry (MS, PhD); inorganic chemistry (MS, PhD); organic chemistry (MS, PhD); physical chemistry (MS, PhD); polymer chemistry (MS, PhD); theoretical chemistry (PhD). Part-time programs available. Terminal master's awarded for partial completion of doctoral program. *Degree requirements:* For master's, thesis; for doctorate, thesis/dissertation. *Entrance requirements:* For master's and doctorate, GRE General Test, minimum GPA of 2.7. Additional exam requirements/recommendations for international students: Required—TOEFL. Electronic applications accepted. *Expenses:* Tuition, state resident: full-time $9000; part-time $501 per credit hour. Tuition, nonresident: full-time $27,188; part-time $1512 per credit hour. *Required fees:* $1280; $62 per credit hour. Tuition and fees vary according to program.

The University of Texas at Austin, Graduate School, College of Natural Sciences, Department of Chemistry and Biochemistry, Austin, TX 78712-1111. Offers analytical chemistry (PhD); biochemistry (PhD); inorganic chemistry (PhD); organic chemistry (PhD); physical chemistry (PhD). *Entrance requirements:* For doctorate, GRE General Test.

The University of Toledo, College of Graduate Studies, College of Natural Sciences and Mathematics, Department of Chemistry, Toledo, OH 43606-3390. Offers analytical chemistry (MS, PhD); biological chemistry (MS, PhD); inorganic chemistry (MS, PhD); organic chemistry (MS, PhD); physical chemistry (MS, PhD). Part-time programs available. *Faculty:* 23. *Students:* 66 full-time (20 women), 9 part-time (2 women); includes 3 minority (1 Asian, non-Hispanic/Latino; 2 Hispanic/Latino), 50 international. Average age 27. 84 applicants, 26% accepted, 19 enrolled. In 2012, 6 master's, 7 doctorates awarded. *Degree requirements:* For master's, thesis or alternative; for doctorate, thesis/dissertation. *Entrance requirements:* For master's and doctorate, GRE General Test, GRE Subject Test, minimum cumulative point-hour ratio of 2.7 for all previous academic work, three letters of recommendation, statement of purpose, transcripts from all prior institutions attended. Additional exam requirements/recommendations for international students: Required—TOEFL (minimum score 550 paper-based; 80 iBT), IELTS (minimum score 6.5). *Application deadline:* For fall admission, 1/15 priority date for domestic students, 1/15 for international students. Applications are processed on a rolling basis. Application fee: $45 ($75 for international students). Electronic applications accepted. *Financial support:* In 2012–13, 29 research assistantships with full and partial tuition reimbursements (averaging $16,200 per year), 49 teaching assistantships with full and partial tuition reimbursements (averaging $15,682 per year) were awarded; Federal Work-Study, institutionally sponsored loans, scholarships/grants, tuition waivers (full), and unspecified assistantships also available. Support available to part-time students. *Faculty research:* Enzymology, materials chemistry, crystallography, theoretical chemistry. *Unit head:* Dr. Ronald Viola, Chair, 419-530-1582, Fax: 419-530-4033, E-mail: ronald.viola@utoledo.edu. *Application contact:* Graduate School Office, 419-530-4723, Fax: 419-530-4724, E-mail: grdsch@utnet.utoledo.edu. Website: http://www.utoledo.edu/nsm/.

Vanderbilt University, Graduate School, Department of Chemistry, Nashville, TN 37240-1001. Offers analytical chemistry (MAT, MS, PhD); inorganic chemistry (MAT, MS, PhD); organic chemistry (MAT, MS, PhD); physical chemistry (MAT, MS, PhD); theoretical chemistry (MAT, MS). *Faculty:* 21 full-time (3 women). *Students:* 123 full-time (46 women); includes 22 minority (5 Black or African American, non-Hispanic/Latino; 1 American Indian or Alaska Native, non-Hispanic/Latino; 3 Asian, non-Hispanic/Latino; 5 Hispanic/Latino; 8 Two or more races, non-Hispanic/Latino), 14 international. Average age 25. 430 applicants, 15% accepted, 29 enrolled. In 2012, 6 master's, 14 doctorates awarded. Terminal master's awarded for partial completion of doctoral program. *Degree requirements:* For master's, thesis; for doctorate, thesis/dissertation, area, qualifying, and final exams. *Entrance requirements:* For master's and doctorate, GRE General Test, GRE Subject Test (recommended). Additional exam requirements/recommendations for international students: Required—TOEFL (minimum score 570 paper-based; 88 iBT). *Application deadline:* For fall admission, 1/15 for domestic and international students. Application fee: $0. Electronic applications accepted. *Financial support:* Fellowships with full and partial tuition reimbursements, research assistantships with full tuition reimbursements, teaching assistantships with full tuition reimbursements, Federal Work-Study, institutionally sponsored loans, scholarships/grants, traineeships, and health care benefits available. Financial award application deadline: 1/15; financial award applicants required to submit CSS PROFILE or FAFSA. *Faculty research:* Chemical synthesis; mechanistic, theoretical, bioorganic, analytical, and spectroscopic chemistry. *Unit head:* Dr. David Cliffel, Director of Graduate Studies, 615-343-3937, Fax: 615-322-4936, E-mail: d.cliffel@vanderbilt.edu. *Application contact:* Sandra Ford, Administrative Assistant, 615-322-8695, Fax: 615-322-4936, E-mail: sandra.e.ford@Vanderbilt.Edu. Website: http://www.vanderbilt.edu/chemistry/.

Virginia Commonwealth University, Graduate School, College of Humanities and Sciences, Department of Chemistry, Richmond, VA 23284-9005. Offers analytical chemistry (MS, PhD); chemical physics (PhD); inorganic chemistry (MS, PhD); organic chemistry (MS, PhD); physical chemistry (MS, PhD). Part-time programs available. Terminal master's awarded for partial completion of doctoral program. *Degree requirements:* For master's, thesis; for doctorate, thesis/dissertation, comprehensive cumulative exams, research proposal. *Entrance requirements:* For master's, GRE General Test, 30 undergraduate credits in chemistry; for doctorate, GRE General Test. Additional exam requirements/recommendations for international students: Required—TOEFL (minimum score 600 paper-based; 100 iBT) or IELTS (minimum score 6.5). Electronic applications accepted. *Faculty research:* Physical, organic, inorganic, analytical, and polymer chemistry; chemical physics.

Wake Forest University, Graduate School of Arts and Sciences, Department of Chemistry, Winston-Salem, NC 27109. Offers analytical chemistry (MS, PhD); inorganic chemistry (MS, PhD); organic chemistry (MS, PhD); physical chemistry (MS, PhD). Part-time programs available. *Degree requirements:* For master's, one foreign language, comprehensive exam, thesis; for doctorate, 2 foreign languages, comprehensive exam, thesis/dissertation. *Entrance requirements:* For master's and doctorate, GRE General Test. Additional exam requirements/recommendations for international students: Required—TOEFL. Electronic applications accepted.

Wayne State University, College of Liberal Arts and Sciences, Department of Chemistry, Detroit, MI 48202. Offers analytical chemistry (PhD); biochemistry (PhD); chemistry (MA, MS); inorganic chemistry (PhD); organic chemistry (PhD); physical chemistry (PhD). *Students:* 167 full-time (79 women), 1 part-time (0 women); includes 12 minority (3 Black or African American, non-Hispanic/Latino; 2 American Indian or Alaska Native, non-Hispanic/Latino; 5 Asian, non-Hispanic/Latino; 2 Hispanic/Latino), 113 international. Average age 28. 440 applicants, 23% accepted, 50 enrolled. In 2012, 5 master's, 15 doctorates awarded. *Degree requirements:* For master's, thesis (for some programs), oral exam; for doctorate, thesis/dissertation, oral exam. *Entrance requirements:* For master's, one year of physics, math through calculus, general chemistry (8 credits), organic chemistry (8 credits), physical chemistry (six credits), quantitative analysis (four credits), and advanced chemistry (three credits); advanced biology (for biochemistry applicants); minimum undergraduate GPA of 2.75 in chemistry and cognate sciences; for doctorate, minimum undergraduate GPA of 3.0 in chemistry and cognate science. Additional exam requirements/recommendations for international students: Required—TOEFL (minimum score 550 paper-based; 79 iBT); Recommended—TWE (minimum score 5.5). *Application deadline:* For fall admission, 2/10 priority date for domestic students, 2/10 for international students; for winter admission, 10/1 priority date for domestic students, 9/1 for international students; for spring admission, 2/1 priority date for domestic students, 1/1 for international students. Applications are processed on a rolling basis. Application fee: $50. Electronic applications accepted. *Expenses:* Tuition, state resident: full-time $12,788; part-time $532.85 per credit hour. Tuition, nonresident: full-time $28,243; part-time $1176.80 per credit hour. *Required fees:* $1367.30; $39.75 per credit hour. $206.65 per semester. Tuition and fees vary according to course load and program. *Financial support:* In 2012–13, 154 students received support, including 10 fellowships with tuition reimbursements available (averaging $23,000 per year), 60 research assistantships with tuition reimbursements available (averaging $19,682 per year), 81 teaching assistantships with tuition reimbursements available (averaging $20,788 per year); scholarships/grants, health care benefits, and unspecified assistantships also available. Financial award application deadline: 7/1. *Faculty research:* Natural products synthesis, molecular biology, molecular mechanics calculations, organometallic chemistry, experimental physical chemistry. *Total annual research expenditures:* $7.2 million. *Unit head:* Dr. James Rigby, Chair, 313-577-3472, Fax: 313-577-8822, E-mail: aa392@wayne.edu. *Application contact:* Dr. Charles Winter, Graduate Director, 313-577-5224, E-mail: chw@chem.wayne.edu. Website: http://chem.wayne.edu/.

Wesleyan University, Graduate Studies, Department of Chemistry, Middletown, CT 06459-0180. Offers biochemistry (PhD); chemical physics (PhD); inorganic chemistry (PhD); organic chemistry (PhD); physical chemistry (PhD); theoretical chemistry (PhD). Terminal master's awarded for partial completion of doctoral program. *Degree requirements:* For doctorate, thesis/dissertation, proposal. *Entrance requirements:* For doctorate, GRE General Test, 3 recommendations. Additional exam requirements/recommendations for international students: Required—TOEFL. *Application deadline:* Applications are processed on a rolling basis. Application fee: $0. Electronic applications accepted. *Financial support:* Research assistantships with full tuition reimbursements, teaching assistantships with full tuition reimbursements, and institutionally sponsored loans available. Financial award application deadline: 4/15; financial award applicants required to submit FAFSA. *Unit head:* Prof. Rex F. Pratt, Chair, 860-685-2727. *Application contact:* Sarah Atwell, Administrative Assistant IV/Graduate Program Coordinator, 860-685-2573, Fax: 860-685-2211, E-mail: satwell@wesleyan.edu. Website: http://www.wesleyan.edu/chem/.

West Virginia University, Eberly College of Arts and Sciences, Department of Chemistry, Morgantown, WV 26506. Offers analytical chemistry (MS, PhD); inorganic chemistry (MS, PhD); organic chemistry (MS, PhD); physical chemistry

(MS, PhD); theoretical chemistry (MS, PhD). Part-time programs available. Postbaccalaureate distance learning degree programs offered (no on-campus study). Terminal master's awarded for partial completion of doctoral program. *Degree requirements:* For master's, thesis; for doctorate, thesis/dissertation. *Entrance requirements:* For master's, GRE General Test, GRE Subject Test (recommended), minimum GPA of 2.5; for doctorate, GRE General Test, GRE Subject Test (recommended), minimum GPA of 2.75. Additional exam requirements/recommendations for international students: Required—TOEFL. Electronic applications accepted. *Faculty research:* Analysis of proteins, drug interactions, solids and effluents by advanced separation methods; new synthetic strategies for complex organic molecules; synthesis and structural characterization of metal complexes for polymerization catalysis, nonlinear science, spectroscopy.

Yale University, Graduate School of Arts and Sciences, Department of Chemistry, New Haven, CT 06520. Offers biophysical chemistry (PhD); inorganic chemistry (PhD); organic chemistry (PhD); physical and theoretical chemistry

(PhD). *Degree requirements:* For doctorate, thesis/dissertation. *Entrance requirements:* For doctorate, GRE General Test, GRE Subject Test. Additional exam requirements/recommendations for international students: Required—TOEFL.

Youngstown State University, Graduate School, College of Science, Technology, Engineering and Mathematics, Department of Chemistry, Youngstown, OH 44555-0001. Offers analytical chemistry (MS); biochemistry (MS); chemistry education (MS); inorganic chemistry (MS); organic chemistry (MS); physical chemistry (MS). Part-time programs available. *Degree requirements:* For master's, thesis. *Entrance requirements:* For master's, bachelor's degree in chemistry, minimum GPA of 2.7. Additional exam requirements/recommendations for international students: Required—TOEFL. *Faculty research:* Analysis of antioxidants, chromatography, defects and disorder in crystalline oxides, hydrogen bonding, novel organic and organometallic materials.

Physical Chemistry

Auburn University, Graduate School, College of Sciences and Mathematics, Department of Chemistry and Biochemistry, Auburn University, AL 36849. Offers analytical chemistry (MS, PhD); biochemistry (MS, PhD); inorganic chemistry (MS, PhD); organic chemistry (MS, PhD); physical chemistry (MS, PhD). Part-time programs available. *Faculty:* 28 full-time (5 women), 1 part-time/adjunct (0 women). *Students:* 37 full-time (14 women), 30 part-time (15 women); includes 6 minority (3 Black or African American, non-Hispanic/Latino; 1 American Indian or Alaska Native, non-Hispanic/Latino; 1 Asian, non-Hispanic/Latino; 1 Hispanic/Latino), 41 international. Average age 20. 38 applicants, 39% accepted, 12 enrolled. In 2012, 1 master's, 9 doctorates awarded. *Degree requirements:* For master's, thesis (for some programs); for doctorate, thesis/dissertation, oral and written exams. *Entrance requirements:* For master's and doctorate, GRE General Test. *Application deadline:* For fall admission, 7/7 for domestic students; for spring admission, 11/24 for domestic students. Applications are processed on a rolling basis. Application fee: $50 ($60 for international students). Electronic applications accepted. *Expenses:* Tuition, state resident: full-time $7866; part-time $437 per credit. Tuition, nonresident: full-time $23,598; part-time $1311 per credit. *Required fees:* $787 per semester. Tuition and fees vary according to degree level and program. *Financial support:* Fellowships, research assistantships, and teaching assistantships available. Financial award application deadline: 3/15; financial award applicants required to submit FAFSA. *Unit head:* Dr. J. V. Ortiz, Chair, 334-844-4043, Fax: 334-844-4043. *Application contact:* Dr. George Flowers, Dean of the Graduate School, 334-844-2125. Website: http://www.auburn.edu/cosam/departments/chemistry/.

Binghamton University, State University of New York, Graduate School, School of Arts and Sciences, Department of Chemistry, Binghamton, NY 13902-6000. Offers analytical chemistry (PhD); chemistry (MA, MS); environmental (PhD); inorganic chemistry (PhD); organic chemistry (PhD); physical chemistry (PhD). Part-time programs available. *Faculty:* 16 full-time (4 women), 4 part-time/adjunct (1 woman). *Students:* 25 full-time (10 women), 26 part-time (10 women); includes 4 minority (3 Black or African American, non-Hispanic/Latino; 1 Hispanic/Latino), 33 international. Average age 28. 53 applicants, 49% accepted, 11 enrolled. In 2012, 3 master's, 6 doctorates awarded. Terminal master's awarded for partial completion of doctoral program. *Degree requirements:* For master's, thesis or alternative, oral exam, seminar presentation; for doctorate, thesis/dissertation, cumulative exams. *Entrance requirements:* For master's and doctorate, GRE General Test, GRE Subject Test. Additional exam requirements/recommendations for international students: Required—TOEFL (minimum score 550 paper-based; 80 iBT). *Application deadline:* For fall admission, 1/15 priority date for domestic students, 1/15 for international students; for spring admission, 10/15 priority date for domestic students, 10/15 for international students. Applications are processed on a rolling basis. Application fee: $75. Electronic applications accepted. *Expenses:* Tuition, state resident: full-time $9370. Tuition, nonresident: full-time $16,680. *Financial support:* In 2012–13, 47 students received support, including 5 research assistantships with full tuition reimbursements available (averaging $18,000 per year), 34 teaching assistantships with full tuition reimbursements available (averaging $18,000 per year); career-related internships or fieldwork, Federal Work-Study, institutionally sponsored loans, scholarships/grants, health care benefits, tuition waivers (full), and unspecified assistantships also available. Financial award application deadline: 2/15; financial award applicants required to submit FAFSA. *Unit head:* Dr. Wayne E. Jones, Chairperson, 607-777-2421, E-mail: wjones@binghamton.edu. *Application contact:* Kishan Zuber, Recruiting and Admissions Coordinator, 607-777-2151, Fax: 607-777-2501, E-mail: kzuber@binghamton.edu.

Boston College, Graduate School of Arts and Sciences, Department of Chemistry, Chestnut Hill, MA 02467-3800. Offers biochemistry (PhD); inorganic chemistry (PhD); organic chemistry (PhD); physical chemistry (PhD); science education (MST). *Degree requirements:* For doctorate, thesis/dissertation,

qualifying exam. *Entrance requirements:* For doctorate, GRE General Test, GRE Subject Test. Additional exam requirements/recommendations for international students: Required—TOEFL (minimum score 600 paper-based; 100 iBT). Electronic applications accepted.

Brandeis University, Graduate School of Arts and Sciences, Department of Chemistry, Waltham, MA 02454. Offers inorganic chemistry (MA, MS, PhD); organic chemistry (MA, MS, PhD); physical chemistry (MS, PhD). *Students:* 44 full-time (20 women); includes 3 minority (1 Black or African American, non-Hispanic/Latino; 2 Asian, non-Hispanic/Latino). 121 applicants, 26% accepted, 11 enrolled. In 2012, 6 master's, 7 doctorates awarded. Terminal master's awarded for partial completion of doctoral program. *Degree requirements:* For master's, thesis, 1 year of residency (for MA); 2 years of residency (for MS); for doctorate, comprehensive exam, thesis/dissertation, 3 years of residency; 2 seminars, qualifying exams. *Entrance requirements:* For master's and doctorate, GRE General Test, resume, statement of purpose, letters of recommendation. Additional exam requirements/recommendations for international students: Required—TOEFL (minimum score 600 paper-based; 100 iBT); Recommended—IELTS (minimum score 7). *Application deadline:* For fall admission, 1/15 priority date for domestic students. Application fee: $75. Electronic applications accepted. *Financial support:* In 2012–13, 16 research assistantships with full tuition reimbursements (averaging $25,000 per year) were awarded; fellowships with full tuition reimbursements, Federal Work-Study, scholarships/grants, health care benefits, tuition waivers (partial), and unspecified assistantships also available. Support available to part-time students. Financial award application deadline: 4/15; financial award applicants required to submit FAFSA. *Faculty research:* Oscillating chemical reactions, molecular recognition systems, protein crystallography, synthesis of natural product spectroscopy and magnetic resonance. *Unit head:* Dr. Judith Herzfeld, Chair, Graduate Program, 781-736-2540, Fax: 781-736-2516, E-mail: herzfeld@brandeis.edu. *Application contact:* Charlotte Haygazian, Coordinator, 781-736-2500, Fax: 781-736-2516, E-mail: chemadm@brandeis.edu. Website: http://www.brandeis.edu/gsas.

California State University, Los Angeles, Graduate Studies, College of Natural and Social Sciences, Department of Chemistry and Biochemistry, Los Angeles, CA 90032-8530. Offers analytical chemistry (MS); biochemistry (MS); chemistry (MS); inorganic chemistry (MS); organic chemistry (MS); physical chemistry (MS). Part-time and evening/weekend programs available. *Faculty:* 2 full-time (1 woman). *Students:* 3 full-time (1 woman), 16 part-time (9 women); includes 16 minority (all Hispanic/Latino). Average age 32. 21 applicants, 52% accepted, 8 enrolled. In 2012, 2 master's awarded. *Degree requirements:* For master's, one foreign language, comprehensive exam or thesis. *Entrance requirements:* Additional exam requirements/recommendations for international students: Required—TOEFL. *Application deadline:* For fall admission, 5/1 for domestic and international students. Applications are processed on a rolling basis. Application fee: $55. *Financial support:* Federal Work-Study available. Support available to part-time students. Financial award application deadline: 3/1. *Faculty research:* Intercalation of heavy metal, carborane chemistry, conductive polymers and fabrics, titanium reagents, computer modeling and synthesis. *Unit head:* Dr. Robert L. Vellanoweth, Chair, 323-343-2300, Fax: 323-343-6490, E-mail: rvellan@calstatela.edu. *Application contact:* Dr. Larry Fritz, Dean of Graduate Studies, 323-343-3820 Ext. 3827, Fax: 323-343-5653, E-mail: lfritz@calstatela.edu. Website: http://www.calstatela.edu/dept/chem/index.htm.

Cleveland State University, College of Graduate Studies, College of Sciences and Health Professions, Department of Chemistry, Cleveland, OH 44115. Offers analytical chemistry (MS); clinical chemistry (MS); clinical/bioanalytical chemistry (PhD), including cellular and molecular medicine, clinical chemistry, clinical/bioanalytical chemistry; environmental chemistry (MS); inorganic chemistry (MS); pharmaceutical/organic chemistry (MS); physical chemistry (MS). Part-time and evening/weekend programs available. *Faculty:* 12 full-time (0 women). *Students:* 10 full-time (6 women), 92 part-time (46 women); includes 7 minority (6 Black or African

Peterson's Graduate Programs in the Physical Sciences, Mathematics, Agricultural Sciences, the Environment & Natural Resources 2014

www.petersonsbooks.com **115**

American, non-Hispanic/Latino; 1 Asian, non-Hispanic/Latino), 68 international. Average age 27. 119 applicants, 86% accepted, 18 enrolled. In 2012, 15 master's, 5 doctorates awarded. *Degree requirements:* For master's, thesis optional; for doctorate, comprehensive exam, thesis/dissertation. *Entrance requirements:* For master's and doctorate, GRE General Test. Additional exam requirements/recommendations for international students: Required—TOEFL (minimum score 525 paper-based; 65 iBT). *Application deadline:* For fall admission, 1/15 priority date for domestic students, 1/15 for international students. Applications are processed on a rolling basis. Application fee: $30. Electronic applications accepted. *Expenses:* Tuition, state resident: full-time $8172; part-time $510.75 per credit hour. Tuition, nonresident: full-time $15,372; part-time $960.75 per credit hour. *Required fees:* $25 per semester. Tuition and fees vary according to course load and program. *Financial support:* In 2012–13, 44 students received support, including 5 fellowships with full tuition reimbursements available (averaging $22,500 per year), 13 research assistantships with full tuition reimbursements available (averaging $22,500 per year), 24 teaching assistantships with full tuition reimbursements available (averaging $21,000 per year); scholarships/grants and unspecified assistantships also available. Financial award application deadline: 1/15. *Faculty research:* Bioanalytical techniques and molecular diagnostics, glycoproteomics and antithrombotic agents, drug discovery and innovation, analytical pharmacology, inflammatory disease research. *Total annual research expenditures:* $3 million. *Unit head:* Dr. David J. Anderson, Interim Chair, 216-687-2467, Fax: 216-687-9298, E-mail: d.anderson@csuohio.edu. *Application contact:* Richelle P. Emery, Administrative Coordinator, 216-687-2457, Fax: 216-687-9298, E-mail: r.emery@csuohio.edu. Website: http://www.csuohio.edu/chemistry/.

Cornell University, Graduate School, Graduate Fields of Arts and Sciences, Field of Chemistry and Chemical Biology, Ithaca, NY 14853-0001. Offers analytical chemistry (PhD); bio-organic chemistry (PhD); biophysical chemistry (PhD); chemical biology (PhD); chemical physics (PhD); inorganic chemistry (PhD); materials chemistry (PhD); organic chemistry (PhD); organometallic chemistry (PhD); physical chemistry (PhD); polymer chemistry (PhD); theoretical chemistry (PhD). *Faculty:* 48 full-time (5 women). *Students:* 161 full-time (70 women); includes 28 minority (1 Black or African American, non-Hispanic/Latino; 16 Asian, non-Hispanic/Latino; 4 Hispanic/Latino; 7 Two or more races, non-Hispanic/Latino), 48 international. Average age 25. 340 applicants, 33% accepted, 40 enrolled. In 2012, 15 doctorates awarded. *Degree requirements:* For doctorate, comprehensive exam, thesis/dissertation. *Entrance requirements:* For doctorate, GRE General Test, GRE Subject Test (chemistry), 3 letters of recommendation. Additional exam requirements/recommendations for international students: Required—TOEFL (minimum score 600 paper-based; 77 iBT). *Application deadline:* For fall admission, 1/10 for domestic students. Application fee: $95. Electronic applications accepted. *Financial support:* In 2012–13, 155 students received support, including 37 fellowships with full tuition reimbursements available, 50 research assistantships with full tuition reimbursements available, 68 teaching assistantships with full tuition reimbursements available; institutionally sponsored loans, scholarships/grants, health care benefits, tuition waivers (full and partial), and unspecified assistantships also available. Financial award applicants required to submit FAFSA. *Faculty research:* Analytical, organic, inorganic, physical, materials, chemical biology. *Unit head:* Director of Graduate Studies, 607-255-4139, Fax: 607-255-4137. *Application contact:* Graduate Field Assistant, 607-255-4139, Fax: 607-255-4137, E-mail: chemgrad@cornell.edu. Website: http://www.gradschool.cornell.edu/fields.php?id-26&a-2.

DePaul University, College of Science and Health, Department of Chemistry, Chicago, IL 60614. Offers analytical/physical chemistry (MS); biochemistry/medicinal chemistry (MS); polymer chemistry and coatings technology (MS); synthetic chemistry (MS). Part-time and evening/weekend programs available. *Faculty:* 7 full-time (4 women). *Students:* 5 full-time (2 women), 11 part-time (6 women); includes 5 minority (1 Asian, non-Hispanic/Latino; 3 Hispanic/Latino; 1 Two or more races, non-Hispanic/Latino), 1 international. Average age 26. In 2012, 4 master's awarded. *Degree requirements:* For master's, thesis (for some programs), oral exam (for select programs). *Entrance requirements:* For master's, BS in chemistry or equivalent. Additional exam requirements/recommendations for international students: Required—TOEFL (minimum score 590 paper-based; 96 iBT) or Pearson Test of English. *Application deadline:* For fall admission, 7/15 for domestic students, 5/1 for international students; for winter admission, 11/15 for domestic students, 9/1 for international students; for spring admission, 2/15 for domestic students, 12/1 for international students. Application fee: $40. Electronic applications accepted. *Financial support:* In 2012–13, 6 teaching assistantships with partial tuition reimbursements (averaging $9,000 per year) were awarded. Financial award application deadline: 6/1; financial award applicants required to submit FAFSA. *Faculty research:* Computational chemistry, organic synthesis, inorganic synthesis, polymer synthesis, biochemistry. *Total annual research expenditures:* $30,000. *Unit head:* Dr. Matthew Dintzner, Chairperson, 773-325-4726, Fax: 773-325-7421, E-mail: mdintzne@depaul.edu. *Application contact:* Ann Spittle, Director of Graduate Admission, 773-325-7315, Fax: 312-476-3244, E-mail: graddepaul@depaul.edu. Website: http://chemistry.depaul.edu.

Eastern New Mexico University, Graduate School, College of Liberal Arts and Sciences, Department of Physical Sciences, Portales, NM 88130. Offers chemistry (MS), including analytical, biochemistry, inorganic, organic, physical. Part-time programs available. *Faculty:* 2 full-time (0 women). *Students:* 2 full-time (0 women), 12 part-time (4 women), 12 international. Average age 25. 14 applicants, 93% accepted, 11 enrolled. In 2012, 5 master's awarded. *Degree requirements:* For master's, thesis optional, seminar, oral and written comprehensive exams. *Entrance requirements:* For master's, ACS placement examination, minimum GPA of 3.0; 2 letters of recommendation; personal statement of career goals; bachelor's degree with one year minimum each of general, organic, and analytical chemistry. Additional exam requirements/recommendations for international students: Required—TOEFL (minimum score 550 paper-based; 79 iBT), IELTS (minimum score 6). *Application deadline:* For fall admission, 7/20 priority date for domestic students, 6/20 for international students; for spring admission, 12/15 priority date for domestic students, 11/15 for international students. Applications are processed on a rolling basis. Application fee: $10. Electronic applications accepted. *Expenses:* Tuition, state resident: full-time $3356; part-time $139.85 per credit hour. Tuition, nonresident: full-time $9030; part-time $376.25 per credit hour. *Required fees:* $1425.60; $59.40 per credit hour. $712.80 per semester. *Financial support:* In 2012–13, 1 research assistantship with partial tuition reimbursement (averaging $8,500 per year), 10 teaching assistantships with partial tuition reimbursements (averaging $8,500 per year) were awarded; career-related internships or fieldwork and unspecified assistantships also available. Support available to part-time students. Financial award application deadline: 3/1; financial award applicants required to submit FAFSA. *Faculty research:* Synfuel, electrochemistry, protein chemistry. *Unit head:* Dr. Juacho Yan, Graduate Coordinator, 575-562-2494, Fax: 575-562-2192, E-mail: juacho.yan@enmu.edu. *Application contact:* Sharon Potter, Department Secretary, Biology and Physical Sciences, 575-562-2174, Fax: 575-562-2192, E-mail: sharon.potter@enmu.edu. Website: http://liberal-arts.enmu.edu/sciences/grad-chemistry.shtml.

East Tennessee State University, School of Graduate Studies, College of Arts and Sciences, Department of Chemistry, Johnson City, TN 37614. Offers chemistry (MS), including inorganic chemistry, organic chemistry, physical chemistry. Part-time and evening/weekend programs available. *Faculty:* 10 full-time (4 women), 1 part-time/adjunct (0 women). *Students:* 17 full-time (3 women), 6 part-time (3 women); includes 4 minority (1 Black or African American, non-Hispanic/Latino; 1 American Indian or Alaska Native, non-Hispanic/Latino; 1 Asian, non-Hispanic/Latino; 1 Two or more races, non-Hispanic/Latino), 14 international. 40 applicants, 53% accepted, 15 enrolled. In 2012, 13 master's awarded. *Degree requirements:* For master's, comprehensive exam, thesis. *Entrance requirements:* For master's, prerequisites in physical chemistry with lab requiring calculus; two letters of recommendation. Additional exam requirements/recommendations for international students: Required—TOEFL (minimum score 550 paper-based; 79 iBT). *Application deadline:* For fall admission, 6/1 for domestic students, 4/30 for international students; for spring admission, 11/1 for domestic students, 9/30 for international students. Application fee: $35 ($45 for international students). Electronic applications accepted. *Financial support:* In 2012–13, 18 students received support, including 18 teaching assistantships with full and partial tuition reimbursements available (averaging $8,300 per year); career-related internships or fieldwork, institutionally sponsored loans, scholarships/grants, and unspecified assistantships also available. Financial award application deadline: 7/1; financial award applicants required to submit FAFSA. *Faculty research:* Analytical chemistry, inorganic chemistry, organic chemistry, physical chemistry. *Unit head:* Dr. Cassandra Eagle, Chair, 423-439-4367, Fax: 423-439-5835, E-mail: eaglec@etsu.edu. *Application contact:* Gail Powers, Graduate Specialist, 423-439-4703, Fax: 423-439-5624, E-mail: powersg@etsu.edu. Website: http://www.etsu.edu/cas/chemistry/.

Florida State University, The Graduate School, College of Arts and Sciences, Department of Chemistry and Biochemistry, Tallahassee, FL 32306-4390. Offers analytical chemistry (MS, PhD); biochemistry (MS, PhD); inorganic chemistry (MS, PhD); materials chemistry (PhD); organic chemistry (MS, PhD); physical chemistry (MS, PhD). *Faculty:* 37 full-time (4 women), 1 (woman) part-time/adjunct. *Students:* 138 full-time (52 women), 8 part-time (1 woman); includes 14 minority (6 Black or African American, non-Hispanic/Latino; 3 Asian, non-Hispanic/Latino; 2 Hispanic/Latino; 3 Two or more races, non-Hispanic/Latino), 63 international. Average age 25. 147 applicants, 40% accepted, 28 enrolled. In 2012, 7 master's, 27 doctorates awarded. Terminal master's awarded for partial completion of doctoral program. *Degree requirements:* For master's, comprehensive exam, thesis (for some programs); for doctorate, comprehensive exam, thesis/dissertation. *Entrance requirements:* For master's and doctorate, GRE General Test (minimum scores: 150 verbal, 151 quantitative; 1100 total on the old scale), minimum GPA of 3.1 in undergraduate course work. Additional exam requirements/recommendations for international students: Required—TOEFL (minimum score 90 iBT). *Application deadline:* For fall admission, 12/15 priority date for domestic students, 12/15 for international students; for spring admission, 9/15 for domestic and international students. Applications are processed on a rolling basis. Application fee: $30. Electronic applications accepted. *Expenses:* Contact institution. *Financial support:* In 2012–13, 140 students received support, including 7 fellowships with full and partial tuition reimbursements available (averaging $10,000 per year), 50 research assistantships with full tuition reimbursements available (averaging $20,000 per year), 100 teaching assistantships with full tuition reimbursements available (averaging $20,000 per year); health care benefits also available. Financial award application deadline: 12/15; financial award applicants required to submit FAFSA. *Faculty research:* Bioanalytical chemistry, including separations, microfluidics, pertroleomics; materials chemistry, including magnets, polymers, catalysts, nanomaterials; spectroscopy, including NMR and EPR, ultrafast, Raman, and mass spectrometry; organic synthesis, natural products, photochemistry, and supramolecular chemistry; biochemistry, with focus on structural biology, metabolomics, and anticancer drugs. *Total annual research expenditures:* $9.8

116 www.petersonsbooks.com

Peterson's Graduate Programs in the Physical Sciences, Mathematics, Agricultural Sciences, the Environment & Natural Resources 2014

million. *Unit head:* Dr. Timothy Logan, Chairman, 850-644-3810, Fax: 850-644-8281, E-mail: gradinfo@chem.fsu.edu. *Application contact:* Dr. Michael Shatruk, Associate Chair for Graduate Studies, 850-417-8417, Fax: 850-644-8281, E-mail: gradinfo@chem.fsu.edu. Website: http://www.chem.fsu.edu/.

Georgetown University, Graduate School of Arts and Sciences, Department of Chemistry, Washington, DC 20057. Offers analytical chemistry (PhD); biochemistry (PhD); computational chemistry (PhD); inorganic chemistry (PhD); materials chemistry (PhD); organic chemistry (PhD); physical chemistry (PhD); theoretical chemistry (PhD). Terminal master's awarded for partial completion of doctoral program. *Degree requirements:* For doctorate, comprehensive exam, thesis/dissertation. *Entrance requirements:* For doctorate, GRE General Test. Additional exam requirements/recommendations for international students: Required—TOEFL.

The George Washington University, Columbian College of Arts and Sciences, Department of Chemistry, Washington, DC 20052. Offers analytical chemistry (MS, PhD); inorganic chemistry (MS, PhD); materials science (MS, PhD); organic chemistry (MS, PhD); physical chemistry (MS, PhD). Part-time and evening/weekend programs available. *Faculty:* 17 full-time (6 women). *Students:* 30 full-time (16 women), 8 part-time (6 women); includes 3 minority (2 Asian, non-Hispanic/Latino; 1 Hispanic/Latino), 8 international. Average age 27. 66 applicants, 24% accepted, 10 enrolled. In 2012, 2 master's, 3 doctorates awarded. Terminal master's awarded for partial completion of doctoral program. *Degree requirements:* For master's, comprehensive exam, thesis or alternative; for doctorate, thesis/dissertation, general exam. *Entrance requirements:* For master's and doctorate, GRE General Test, interview, minimum GPA of 3.0. Additional exam requirements/recommendations for international students: Required—TOEFL (minimum score 550 paper-based; 80 iBT). *Application deadline:* For fall admission, 1/15 priority date for domestic students, 1/15 for international students; for spring admission, 9/1 priority date for domestic students, 9/1 for international students. Applications are processed on a rolling basis. Application fee: $75. Electronic applications accepted. *Financial support:* In 2012–13, 27 students received support. Fellowships with tuition reimbursements available, research assistantships, teaching assistantships with tuition reimbursements available, Federal Work-Study, and tuition waivers available. Financial award application deadline: 1/15. *Unit head:* Dr. Michael King, Chair, 202-994-6488. *Application contact:* Information Contact, 202-994-6121, E-mail: gwchem@gwu.edu. Website: http://www.gwu.edu/~gwchem/.

Georgia State University, College of Arts and Sciences, Department of Chemistry, Atlanta, GA 30302-3083. Offers analytical chemistry (MS, PhD); biochemistry (MS, PhD); bioinformatics (MS, PhD); biophysical chemistry (PhD); computational chemistry (MS, PhD); geochemistry (PhD); organic/medicinal chemistry (MS, PhD); physical chemistry (MS). PhD in geochemistry offered jointly with Department of Geology. Part-time programs available. *Faculty:* 38 full-time (11 women), 10 part-time/adjunct (3 women). *Students:* 107 full-time (57 women), 6 part-time (3 women); includes 25 minority (13 Black or African American, non-Hispanic/Latino; 1 American Indian or Alaska Native, non-Hispanic/Latino; 6 Asian, non-Hispanic/Latino; 4 Hispanic/Latino; 1 Two or more races, non-Hispanic/Latino), 57 international. Average age 28. 125 applicants, 39% accepted, 36 enrolled. In 2012, 28 master's, 12 doctorates awarded. Terminal master's awarded for partial completion of doctoral program. *Degree requirements:* For master's, one foreign language, comprehensive exam (for some programs), thesis (for some programs); for doctorate, one foreign language, comprehensive exam, thesis/dissertation. *Entrance requirements:* For master's and doctorate, GRE. Additional exam requirements/recommendations for international students: Required—TOEFL (minimum score 550 paper-based, 80 iBT) or IELTS (minimum score 6.5). *Application deadline:* For fall admission, 7/1 priority date for domestic students, 7/1 for international students; for winter admission, 11/15 priority date for domestic students, 11/15 for international students; for spring admission, 4/15 priority date for domestic students, 4/15 for international students. Applications are processed on a rolling basis. Application fee: $50. Electronic applications accepted. *Expenses:* Tuition, state resident: full-time $8064; part-time $336 per credit hour. Tuition, nonresident: full-time $28,800; part-time $1200 per credit hour. *Required fees:* $2128; $1064 per semester. Tuition and fees vary according to course load and program. *Financial support:* Fellowships with full tuition reimbursements, research assistantships with full tuition reimbursements, and teaching assistantships with full tuition reimbursements available. *Faculty research:* Analytical chemistry, biological/biochemistry, biophysical/computational chemistry, chemical education, organic/medicinal chemistry. *Total annual research expenditures:* $4 million. *Unit head:* Dr. Binghe Wang, Department Chair, 404-413-5500, Fax: 404-413-5506, E-mail: chemchair@gsu.edu. *Application contact:* Rita S. Bennett, Academic Specialist, 404-413-5497, Fax: 404-413-5505, E-mail: rsb423@gsu.edu. Website: http://chemistry.gsu.edu/.

Harvard University, Graduate School of Arts and Sciences, Department of Chemistry and Chemical Biology, Cambridge, MA 02138. Offers biochemical chemistry (PhD); inorganic chemistry (PhD); organic chemistry (PhD); physical chemistry (PhD). *Degree requirements:* For doctorate, thesis/dissertation, cumulative exams. *Entrance requirements:* For doctorate, GRE General Test, GRE Subject Test. Additional exam requirements/recommendations for international students: Required—TOEFL. *Expenses: Tuition:* Full-time $37,576. *Required fees:* $930. Tuition and fees vary according to program and student level.

See Display on page 70 and Close-Up on page 125.

Howard University, Graduate School, Department of Chemistry, Washington, DC 20059-0002. Offers analytical chemistry (MS, PhD); atmospheric (MS, PhD); biochemistry (MS, PhD); environmental (MS, PhD); inorganic chemistry (MS, PhD); organic chemistry (MS, PhD); physical chemistry (MS, PhD). Terminal master's awarded for partial completion of doctoral program. *Degree requirements:* For master's, comprehensive exam, thesis, teaching experience; for doctorate, comprehensive exam, thesis/dissertation, teaching experience. *Entrance requirements:* For master's, GRE General Test, minimum GPA of 2.7; for doctorate, GRE General Test, minimum GPA of 3.0. Additional exam requirements/recommendations for international students: Required—TOEFL. Electronic applications accepted. *Faculty research:* Synthetic organics, materials, natural products, mass spectrometry.

Indiana University Bloomington, University Graduate School, College of Arts and Sciences, Department of Chemistry, Bloomington, IN 47405. Offers analytical chemistry (PhD); chemical biology chemistry (PhD); chemistry (MAT); inorganic chemistry (PhD); materials chemistry (PhD); organic chemistry (PhD); physical chemistry (PhD). *Faculty:* 42 full-time (4 women). *Students:* 215 full-time (85 women), 4 part-time (1 woman); includes 21 minority (8 Black or African American, non-Hispanic/Latino; 9 Asian, non-Hispanic/Latino; 1 Hispanic/Latino; 3 Two or more races, non-Hispanic/Latino), 69 international. Average age 27. 329 applicants, 40% accepted, 50 enrolled. In 2012, 12 master's, 20 doctorates awarded. Terminal master's awarded for partial completion of doctoral program. *Degree requirements:* For master's, thesis; for doctorate, thesis/dissertation. *Entrance requirements:* For master's and doctorate, GRE General Test, GRE Subject Test. Additional exam requirements/recommendations for international students: Required—TOEFL. *Application deadline:* For fall admission, 1/15 priority date for domestic students, 12/15 for international students. Applications are processed on a rolling basis. Application fee: $55 ($65 for international students). *Financial support:* In 2012–13, 200 students received support, including 10 fellowships with full tuition reimbursements available, 76 research assistantships with full tuition reimbursements available, 111 teaching assistantships with full tuition reimbursements available; Federal Work-Study and institutionally sponsored loans also available. *Faculty research:* Synthesis of complex natural products, organic reaction mechanisms, organic electrochemistry, transitive-metal chemistry, solid-state and surface chemistry. *Total annual research expenditures:* $7.7 million. *Unit head:* David Giedroc, Chairperson, 812-855-6239, E-mail: chemchair@indiana.edu. *Application contact:* Daniel Mindiola, Director of Graduate Admissions, 812-855-2069, Fax: 812-855-8385, E-mail: mindiola@indiana.edu. Website: http://www.chem.indiana.edu/.

Iowa State University of Science and Technology, Program in Physical Chemistry, Ames, IA 50011. Offers MS, PhD. *Entrance requirements:* Additional exam requirements/recommendations for international students: Required—TOEFL (minimum score 570 paper-based; 89 iBT), IELTS (minimum score 6.5). *Application deadline:* For fall admission, 2/1 for domestic students. Application fee: $60 ($90 for international students). Electronic applications accepted. *Application contact:* Lynette Edsall, Application Contact, 800-521-2436, Fax: 515-294-0105, E-mail: chemgrad@iastate.edu. Website: http://www.chem.iastate.edu.

Kansas State University, Graduate School, College of Arts and Sciences, Department of Chemistry, Manhattan, KS 66506. Offers analytical chemistry (MS); biological chemistry (MS); chemistry (PhD); inorganic chemistry (MS); materials chemistry (MS); organic chemistry (MS); physical chemistry (MS). *Faculty:* 17 full-time (1 woman). *Students:* 71 full-time (36 women); includes 1 minority (Asian, non-Hispanic/Latino), 59 international. Average age 28. 108 applicants, 35% accepted, 15 enrolled. In 2012, 5 master's, 9 doctorates awarded. Terminal master's awarded for partial completion of doctoral program. *Degree requirements:* For master's, thesis; for doctorate, thesis/dissertation. *Entrance requirements:* For master's and doctorate, GRE, minimum GPA of 3.0. Additional exam requirements/recommendations for international students: Required—TOEFL (minimum score 550 paper-based). *Application deadline:* For fall admission, 2/1 priority date for domestic students, 2/1 for international students; for spring admission, 8/1 priority date for domestic students, 8/1 for international students. Applications are processed on a rolling basis. Application fee: $50 ($75 for international students). Electronic applications accepted. *Financial support:* In 2012–13, 39 research assistantships (averaging $18,182 per year), 24 teaching assistantships with full tuition reimbursements (averaging $18,106 per year) were awarded; institutionally sponsored loans and scholarships/grants also available. Support available to part-time students. Financial award application deadline: 3/1; financial award applicants required to submit FAFSA. *Faculty research:* Inorganic chemistry, organic and biological chemistry, analytical chemistry, physical chemistry, materials chemistry and nanotechnology. *Total annual research expenditures:* $2.8 million. *Unit head:* Eric Maatta, Head, 785-532-6665, Fax: 785-532-6666, E-mail: eam@ksu.edu. *Application contact:* Christer Aakeroy, Director, 785-532-6096, Fax: 785-532-6666, E-mail: aakeroy@ksu.edu. Website: http://www.k-state.edu/chem/.

Kent State University, College of Arts and Sciences, Department of Chemistry and Biochemistry, Kent, OH 44242-0001. Offers analytical chemistry (MS, PhD); biochemistry (MS, PhD); chemistry (MA); inorganic chemistry (MS, PhD); organic chemistry (MS, PhD); physical chemistry (MS, PhD). Terminal master's awarded for partial completion of doctoral program. *Degree requirements:* For master's, comprehensive exam, thesis; for doctorate, comprehensive exam, thesis/dissertation. *Entrance requirements:* For master's and doctorate, placement exam, GRE General Test, GRE Subject Test (recommended), minimum GPA of

2.75. Additional exam requirements/recommendations for international students: Required—TOEFL (minimum score 525 paper-based; 71 iBT). Electronic applications accepted. *Expenses:* Tuition, state resident: full-time $8424; part-time $468 per credit hour. Tuition, nonresident: full-time $14,580; part-time $810 per credit hour. Tuition and fees vary according to course load. *Faculty research:* Biological chemistry, materials chemistry, molecular spectroscopy.

See Display on page 73 and Close-Up on page 127.

Laurentian University, School of Graduate Studies and Research, Programme in Chemistry and Biochemistry, Sudbury, ON P3E 2C6, Canada. Offers analytical chemistry (M Sc); biochemistry (M Sc); environmental chemistry (M Sc); organic chemistry (M Sc); physical/theoretical chemistry (M Sc). Part-time programs available. *Degree requirements:* For master's, thesis or alternative. *Entrance requirements:* For master's, honors degree with minimum second class. *Faculty research:* Cell cycle checkpoints, kinetic modeling, toxicology to metal stress, quantum chemistry, biogeochemistry metal speciation.

Marquette University, Graduate School, College of Arts and Sciences, Department of Chemistry, Milwaukee, WI 53201-1881. Offers analytical chemistry (MS, PhD); bioanalytical chemistry (MS, PhD); biophysical chemistry (MS, PhD); chemical physics (MS, PhD); inorganic chemistry (MS, PhD); organic chemistry (MS, PhD); physical chemistry (MS, PhD). Part-time programs available. Terminal master's awarded for partial completion of doctoral program. *Degree requirements:* For master's, comprehensive exam; for doctorate, thesis/dissertation, cumulative exams. *Entrance requirements:* For master's and doctorate, official transcripts from all current and previous colleges/universities except Marquette, three letters of recommendation from individuals familiar with the applicant's academic work. Additional exam requirements/recommendations for international students: Required—TOEFL (minimum score 530 paper-based). Electronic applications accepted. *Faculty research:* Inorganic complexes, laser Raman spectroscopy, organic synthesis, synthetic bioinorganic chemistry, electro-active organic molecules.

Massachusetts Institute of Technology, School of Science, Department of Chemistry, Cambridge, MA 02139. Offers biological chemistry (PhD, Sc D); inorganic chemistry (PhD, Sc D); organic chemistry (PhD, Sc D); physical chemistry (PhD, Sc D). *Faculty:* 27 full-time (5 women). *Students:* 228 full-time (80 women), 4 part-time (2 women); includes 54 minority (6 Black or African American, non-Hispanic/Latino; 1 American Indian or Alaska Native, non-Hispanic/Latino; 31 Asian, non-Hispanic/Latino; 13 Hispanic/Latino; 3 Two or more races, non-Hispanic/Latino), 69 international. Average age 26. 651 applicants, 17% accepted, 44 enrolled. In 2012, 30 doctorates awarded. *Degree requirements:* For doctorate, comprehensive exam, thesis/dissertation. *Entrance requirements:* For doctorate, GRE General Test. Additional exam requirements/recommendations for international students: Required—IELTS (minimum score 7); Recommended—TOEFL (minimum score 600 paper-based). *Application deadline:* For fall admission, 12/15 for domestic and international students. Application fee: $75. Electronic applications accepted. *Expenses: Tuition:* Full-time $41,770; part-time $650 per credit hour. *Required fees:* $280. *Financial support:* In 2012–13, 194 students received support, including 71 fellowships (averaging $36,300 per year), 111 research assistantships (averaging $31,400 per year), 41 teaching assistantships (averaging $34,600 per year); Federal Work-Study, institutionally sponsored loans, scholarships/grants, traineeships, health care benefits, and unspecified assistantships also available. *Faculty research:* Synthetic organic and organometallic chemistry including catalysis; biological chemistry including bioorganic chemistry; physical chemistry including chemical dynamics and biophysical chemistry; inorganic chemistry including synthesis, catalysis, bioinorganic and physical inorganic chemistry; materials chemistry including surface science, nanoscience and polymers. *Total annual research expenditures:* $28.4 million. *Unit head:* Prof. Sylvia T. Ceyer, Head, 617-253-1803, Fax: 617-258-7500. *Application contact:* Graduate Administrator, 617-253-1845, Fax: 617-258-0241, E-mail: chemgradeducation@mit.edu. Website: http://web.mit.edu/chemistry/www/.

McMaster University, School of Graduate Studies, Faculty of Science, Department of Chemistry, Hamilton, ON L8S 4M2, Canada. Offers analytical chemistry (M Sc, PhD); chemical physics (M Sc, PhD); chemistry (M Sc, PhD); inorganic chemistry (M Sc, PhD); organic chemistry (M Sc, PhD); physical chemistry (M Sc, PhD); polymer chemistry (M Sc, PhD). Part-time programs available. Terminal master's awarded for partial completion of doctoral program. *Degree requirements:* For master's, thesis; for doctorate, comprehensive exam, thesis/dissertation. *Entrance requirements:* For master's, minimum B+ average. Additional exam requirements/recommendations for international students: Required—TOEFL (minimum score 550 paper-based).

Old Dominion University, College of Sciences, Program in Chemistry, Norfolk, VA 23529. Offers analytical chemistry (MS); biochemistry (MS); chemistry (PhD); environmental chemistry (MS); organic chemistry (MS); physical chemistry (MS). Part-time and evening/weekend programs available. *Faculty:* 19 full-time (7 women), 3 part-time/adjunct (all women). *Students:* 36 full-time (20 women); includes 1 minority (Black or African American, non-Hispanic/Latino), 14 international. Average age 27. 35 applicants, 60% accepted, 8 enrolled. In 2012, 4 master's, 1 doctorate awarded. *Degree requirements:* For master's, comprehensive exam, thesis. *Entrance requirements:* For master's, GRE General Test, minimum GPA of 3.0 in major, 2.5 overall; for doctorate, GRE General Test. Additional exam requirements/recommendations for international students: Required—TOEFL. *Application deadline:* For fall admission, 7/1 for domestic students, 1/15 for international students; for spring admission, 11/1 for domestic students, 8/15 for international students. Applications are processed on a rolling basis. Application fee: $30. Electronic applications accepted. *Expenses:* Tuition, state resident: full-time $9432; part-time $393 per credit hour. Tuition, nonresident: full-time $23,928; part-time $997 per credit hour. *Required fees:* $59 per semester. One-time fee: $50. *Financial support:* In 2012–13, 6 students received support, including fellowships (averaging $18,000 per year), research assistantships with tuition reimbursements available (averaging $21,000 per year), teaching assistantships with tuition reimbursements available (averaging $18,000 per year); career-related internships or fieldwork, scholarships/grants, and unspecified assistantships also available. Financial award application deadline: 2/15; financial award applicants required to submit FAFSA. *Faculty research:* Biogeochemistry, materials chemistry, computational chemistry, organic chemistry, biofuels. *Total annual research expenditures:* $2.6 million. *Unit head:* Dr. Craig A. Bayse, Graduate Program Director, 757-683-4097, Fax: 757-683-4628, E-mail: chemgpd@odu.edu. *Application contact:* Valerie DeCosta, Grants and Graduate Program Assistant, 757-683-6979, Fax: 757-683-4628, E-mail: chemgpd@odu.edu.

Oregon State University, College of Science, Department of Chemistry, Corvallis, OR 97331. Offers analytical chemistry (MS, PhD); chemistry (MA, MAIS); inorganic chemistry (MS, PhD); nuclear and radiation chemistry (MS, PhD); organic chemistry (MS, PhD); physical chemistry (MS, PhD). Part-time programs available. *Faculty:* 28 full-time (7 women), 9 part-time/adjunct (1 woman). *Students:* 101 full-time (28 women), 1 part-time (0 women); includes 5 minority (2 Asian, non-Hispanic/Latino; 1 Hispanic/Latino; 2 Two or more races, non-Hispanic/Latino), 54 international. Average age 28. 98 applicants, 30% accepted, 27 enrolled. In 2012, 4 master's, 16 doctorates awarded. Terminal master's awarded for partial completion of doctoral program. *Degree requirements:* For master's, one foreign language, thesis; for doctorate, one foreign language, thesis/dissertation. *Entrance requirements:* For master's and doctorate, minimum GPA of 3.0 in last 90 hours of course work. Additional exam requirements/recommendations for international students: Required—TOEFL. *Application deadline:* For fall admission, 3/1 priority date for domestic students. Applications are processed on a rolling basis. Application fee: $50. *Expenses:* Tuition, state resident: full-time $11,367; part-time $421 per credit hour. Tuition, nonresident: full-time $18,279; part-time $677 per credit hour. *Required fees:* $1478. One-time fee: $300 full-time. Tuition and fees vary according to course load and program. *Financial support:* Fellowships, research assistantships, teaching assistantships, and institutionally sponsored loans available. Support available to part-time students. Financial award application deadline: 2/1. *Faculty research:* Solid state chemistry, enzyme reaction mechanisms, structure and dynamics of gas molecules, chemiluminescence, nonlinear optical spectroscopy. *Unit head:* Dr. Rich G. Carter, Professor/Chair, 541-737-9486, E-mail: rich.carter@oregonstate.edu.

Purdue University, Graduate School, College of Science, Department of Chemistry, West Lafayette, IN 47907. Offers analytical chemistry (MS, PhD); biochemistry (MS, PhD); chemical education (MS, PhD); inorganic chemistry (MS, PhD); organic chemistry (MS, PhD); physical chemistry (MS, PhD). *Faculty:* 42 full-time (14 women), 7 part-time/adjunct (0 women). *Students:* 275 full-time (102 women), 23 part-time (8 women); includes 34 minority (16 Black or African American, non-Hispanic/Latino; 5 Asian, non-Hispanic/Latino; 11 Hispanic/Latino; 2 Two or more races, non-Hispanic/Latino), 94 international. Average age 27. 716 applicants, 26% accepted, 66 enrolled. In 2012, 18 master's, 52 doctorates awarded. Terminal master's awarded for partial completion of doctoral program. *Degree requirements:* For master's, thesis; for doctorate, comprehensive exam, thesis/dissertation. *Entrance requirements:* For master's and doctorate, minimum undergraduate GPA of 3.0. Additional exam requirements/recommendations for international students: Required—TOEFL (minimum score 77 iBT); Recommended—TWE. *Application deadline:* For fall admission, 2/15 priority date for domestic students, 1/1 for international students. Applications are processed on a rolling basis. Application fee: $60 ($75 for international students). Electronic applications accepted. *Financial support:* In 2012–13, 2 fellowships with partial tuition reimbursements (averaging $18,000 per year), 55 teaching assistantships with partial tuition reimbursements (averaging $18,000 per year) were awarded; research assistantships with partial tuition reimbursements and tuition waivers (partial) also available. Support available to part-time students. Financial award applicants required to submit FAFSA. *Unit head:* Dr. Paul B. Shepson, Head, 765-494-5203, E-mail: pshepson@purdue.edu. *Application contact:* Betty L. Hatfield, Director of Graduate Admissions, 765-494-5208, E-mail: bettyh@purdue.edu.

Rice University, Graduate Programs, Wiess School of Natural Sciences, Department of Chemistry, Houston, TX 77251-1892. Offers chemistry (MA); inorganic chemistry (PhD); organic chemistry (PhD); physical chemistry (PhD). Terminal master's awarded for partial completion of doctoral program. *Degree requirements:* For master's, thesis; for doctorate, thesis/dissertation. *Entrance requirements:* For master's and doctorate, GRE General Test, minimum GPA of 3.0. Additional exam requirements/recommendations for international students: Required—TOEFL (minimum score 600 paper-based; 90 iBT). Electronic applications accepted. *Faculty research:* Nanoscience, biomaterials, nanobioinformatics, fullerene pharmaceuticals.

Rutgers, The State University of New Jersey, Newark, Graduate School, Program in Chemistry, Newark, NJ 07102. Offers analytical chemistry (MS, PhD); biochemistry (MS, PhD); inorganic chemistry (MS, PhD); organic chemistry (MS, PhD); physical chemistry (MS, PhD). Part-time and evening/weekend programs available. Terminal master's awarded for partial completion of doctoral program. *Degree requirements:* For master's, thesis optional, cumulative exams; for doctorate, thesis/dissertation, exams, research proposal. *Entrance requirements:* For master's and doctorate, GRE General Test, minimum undergraduate B average. Additional exam requirements/recommendations for international students: Required—TOEFL. Electronic applications accepted. *Faculty research:* Medicinal chemistry, natural products, isotope effects, biophysics and biorganic approaches to enzyme mechanisms, organic and organometallic synthesis.

Rutgers, The State University of New Jersey, New Brunswick, Graduate School-New Brunswick, Department of Chemistry and Chemical Biology, Piscataway, NJ 08854-8097. Offers biological chemistry (MS, PhD); inorganic chemistry (MS, PhD); organic chemistry (MS, PhD); physical chemistry (MS, PhD). Part-time and evening/weekend programs available. Terminal master's awarded for partial completion of doctoral program. *Degree requirements:* For master's, thesis or alternative, exam; for doctorate, thesis/dissertation, 1 year residency. *Entrance requirements:* For master's and doctorate, GRE General Test, GRE Subject Test. Additional exam requirements/recommendations for international students: Required—TOEFL. Electronic applications accepted. *Faculty research:* Biophysical organic/bioorganic, inorganic/bioinorganic, theoretical, and solid-state/surface chemistry.

Seton Hall University, College of Arts and Sciences, Department of Chemistry and Biochemistry, South Orange, NJ 07079-2697. Offers analytical chemistry (MS, PhD); biochemistry (MS, PhD); chemistry (MS); inorganic chemistry (MS, PhD); organic chemistry (MS, PhD); physical chemistry (MS, PhD). Part-time and evening/weekend programs available. Terminal master's awarded for partial completion of doctoral program. *Degree requirements:* For master's, thesis optional; for doctorate, comprehensive exam, thesis/dissertation. *Entrance requirements:* Additional exam requirements/recommendations for international students: Required—TOEFL. Electronic applications accepted. *Faculty research:* DNA metal reactions; chromatography; bioinorganic, biophysical, organometallic, polymer chemistry; heterogeneous catalyst; synthetic organic and carbohydrate chemistry.

Southern University and Agricultural and Mechanical College, Graduate School, College of Sciences, Department of Chemistry, Baton Rouge, LA 70813. Offers analytical chemistry (MS); biochemistry (MS); environmental sciences (MS); inorganic chemistry (MS); organic chemistry (MS); physical chemistry (MS). *Degree requirements:* For master's, thesis. *Entrance requirements:* For master's, GMAT or GRE General Test. Additional exam requirements/recommendations for international students: Required—TOEFL (minimum score 525 paper-based). *Faculty research:* Synthesis of macrocyclic ligands, latex accelerators, anticancer drugs, biosensors, absorption isotheums, isolation of specific enzymes from plants.

Stevens Institute of Technology, Graduate School, Charles V. Schaefer Jr. School of Engineering, Department of Chemistry, Chemical Biology and Biomedical Engineering, Hoboken, NJ 07030. Offers analytical chemistry (PhD, Certificate); bioinformatics (PhD, Certificate); biomedical chemistry (Certificate); biomedical engineering (M Eng, Certificate); chemical biology (MS, PhD, Certificate); chemical physiology (Certificate); chemistry (MS, PhD); organic chemistry (PhD); physical chemistry (PhD); polymer chemistry (PhD, Certificate). Part-time and evening/weekend programs available. Postbaccalaureate distance learning degree programs offered (no on-campus study). Terminal master's awarded for partial completion of doctoral program. *Degree requirements:* For master's, thesis or alternative; for doctorate, one foreign language, thesis/dissertation; for Certificate, project or thesis. *Entrance requirements:* Additional exam requirements/recommendations for international students: Required—TOEFL. Electronic applications accepted. *Faculty research:* Biochemical reaction engineering, polymerization engineering, reactor design, biochemical process control and synthesis.

Texas Christian University, College of Science and Engineering, Department of Chemistry, Fort Worth, TX 76129. Offers biochemistry (MS, PhD); chemistry (MA); inorganic (MS, PhD); organic (MS, PhD); physical (MS, PhD). Part-time programs available. *Faculty:* 11 full-time (2 women). *Students:* 7 full-time (3 women), 17 part-time (10 women); includes 4 minority (1 Asian, non-Hispanic/Latino; 3 Hispanic/Latino), 13 international. Average age 27. 34 applicants, 24% accepted, 5 enrolled. In 2012, 1 master's, 1 doctorate awarded. *Degree requirements:* For master's, thesis; for doctorate, thesis/dissertation, literature seminar, cumulative exams, research progress report, original proposal. *Entrance requirements:* For master's and doctorate, GRE General Test. Additional exam requirements/recommendations for international students: Required—TOEFL (minimum score 80 iBT). *Application deadline:* For fall admission, 2/1 priority date for domestic students, 2/1 for international students; for spring admission, 9/1 priority date for domestic students, 9/1 for international students. Application fee: $50. Electronic applications accepted. *Expenses: Tuition:* Full-time $21,600; part-time $1200 per credit. *Required fees:* $48. Tuition and fees vary according to program. *Financial support:* In 2012–13, 16 students received support, including 16 teaching assistantships with full tuition reimbursements available; tuition waivers (full and partial) and unspecified assistantships also available. Financial award application deadline: 2/1. *Faculty research:* Phase transitions and transport properties of bio/macromolecular solutions, nanoscale biomaterials, electronic structure theory, synthetic methodology and total synthesis of natural products, chemistry and biology of (bio)polymers. *Unit head:* Dr. Robert Neilson, Chairperson/Professor, 817-257-7345, Fax: 817-257-5851, E-mail: r.neilson@tcu.edu. *Application contact:* Dr. Sergei V. Dzyuba, Director of Graduate Studies/Assistant Professor, 817-257-6218, Fax: 817-257-5851, E-mail: s.dzyuba@tcu.edu. Website: http://www.chm.tcu.edu/.

Tufts University, Graduate School of Arts and Sciences, Department of Chemistry, Medford, MA 02155. Offers analytical chemistry (MS, PhD); bioorganic chemistry (MS, PhD); environmental chemistry (MS, PhD); inorganic chemistry (MS, PhD); organic chemistry (MS, PhD); physical chemistry (MS, PhD). Terminal master's awarded for partial completion of doctoral program. *Degree requirements:* For master's, thesis optional; for doctorate, thesis/dissertation. *Entrance requirements:* For master's and doctorate, GRE General Test, GRE Subject Test. Additional exam requirements/recommendations for international students: Required—TOEFL (minimum score 600 paper-based; 80 iBT). Electronic applications accepted. *Expenses: Tuition:* Full-time $42,856; part-time $1072 per credit hour. *Required fees:* $730. Full-time tuition and fees vary according to degree level, program and student level. Part-time tuition and fees vary according to course load.

University of Calgary, Faculty of Graduate Studies, Faculty of Science, Department of Chemistry, Calgary, AB T2N 1N4, Canada. Offers analytical chemistry (M Sc, PhD); applied chemistry (M Sc, PhD); inorganic chemistry (M Sc, PhD); organic chemistry (M Sc, PhD); physical chemistry (M Sc, PhD); polymer chemistry (M Sc, PhD); theoretical chemistry (M Sc, PhD). *Degree requirements:* For master's, thesis; for doctorate, thesis/dissertation, candidacy exam. *Entrance requirements:* For master's, minimum GPA of 3.0; for doctorate, honors B Sc degree with minimum GPA of 3.7 or M Sc with minimum GPA of 3.3. Additional exam requirements/recommendations for international students: Required—TOEFL (minimum score 580 paper-based). Electronic applications accepted. *Faculty research:* Chemical analysis, chemical dynamics, synthesis theory.

University of Cincinnati, Graduate School, McMicken College of Arts and Sciences, Department of Chemistry, Cincinnati, OH 45221. Offers analytical chemistry (MS, PhD); biochemistry (MS, PhD); inorganic chemistry (MS, PhD); organic chemistry (MS, PhD); physical chemistry (MS, PhD); polymer chemistry (MS, PhD); sensors (PhD). Part-time and evening/weekend programs available. Terminal master's awarded for partial completion of doctoral program. *Degree requirements:* For master's, thesis optional; for doctorate, comprehensive exam, thesis/dissertation. *Entrance requirements:* For master's and doctorate, GRE General Test. Additional exam requirements/recommendations for international students: Required—TOEFL (minimum score 580 paper-based). Electronic applications accepted. *Faculty research:* Biomedical chemistry, laser chemistry, surface science, chemical sensors, synthesis.

University of Georgia, Franklin College of Arts and Sciences, Department of Chemistry, Athens, GA 30602. Offers analytical chemistry (MS, PhD); inorganic chemistry (MS, PhD); organic chemistry (MS, PhD); physical chemistry (MS, PhD). Terminal master's awarded for partial completion of doctoral program. *Degree requirements:* For master's, thesis; for doctorate, one foreign language, thesis/dissertation. *Entrance requirements:* For master's and doctorate, GRE General Test. Additional exam requirements/recommendations for international students: Required—TOEFL. Electronic applications accepted.

University of Louisville, Graduate School, College of Arts and Sciences, Department of Chemistry, Louisville, KY 40292-0001. Offers analytical chemistry (MS, PhD); biochemistry (MS, PhD); chemical physics (PhD); inorganic chemistry (MS, PhD); organic chemistry (MS, PhD); physical chemistry (MS, PhD). *Students:* 45 full-time (21 women), 5 part-time (1 woman); includes 1 minority (Hispanic/Latino), 35 international. Average age 28. 78 applicants, 17% accepted, 9 enrolled. In 2012, 19 master's, 7 doctorates awarded. Terminal master's awarded for partial completion of doctoral program. *Degree requirements:* For master's, variable foreign language requirement, comprehensive exam, thesis optional; for doctorate, variable foreign language requirement, comprehensive exam, thesis/dissertation. *Entrance requirements:* For master's and doctorate, BA or BS coursework. Additional exam requirements/recommendations for international students: Required—TOEFL. *Application deadline:* For fall admission, 3/15 for domestic and international students; for winter admission, 9/15 for domestic and international students. Applications are processed on a rolling basis. Application fee: $60. Electronic applications accepted. *Financial support:* In 2012–13, 33 teaching assistantships with full tuition reimbursements (averaging $22,000 per year) were awarded; fellowships with full tuition reimbursements, research assistantships with full tuition reimbursements, career-related internships or fieldwork, scholarships/grants, traineeships, health care benefits, and unspecified assistantships also available. Support available to part-time students. Financial award application deadline: 3/15. *Faculty research:* Computational chemistry, biophysics nuclear magnetic resonance, synthetic organic chemistry, synthetic inorganic chemistry, medicinal chemistry, protein chemistry, enzymology, nanochemistry, electrochemistry, analytical chemistry, synthetic biology, bioinformatics. *Total annual research expenditures:* $2.5 million. *Unit head:* Dr. Richard J. Wittebort, Professor/Chair, 502-852-6613. *Application contact:* Sherry Nalley, Administrator, 502-852-6798.

The University of Manchester, School of Chemistry, Manchester, United Kingdom. Offers biological chemistry (PhD); chemistry (M Ent, M Phil, M Sc, D Ent, PhD); inorganic chemistry (PhD); materials chemistry (PhD); nanoscience (PhD); nuclear fission (PhD); organic chemistry (PhD); physical chemistry (PhD); theoretical chemistry (PhD).

University of Maryland, College Park, Academic Affairs, College of Computer, Mathematical and Natural Sciences, Department of Chemistry and Biochemistry,

Chemistry Program, College Park, MD 20742. Offers analytical chemistry (MS, PhD); inorganic chemistry (MS, PhD); organic chemistry (MS, PhD); physical chemistry (MS, PhD). Part-time and evening/weekend programs available. *Students:* 113 full-time (64 women), 2 part-time (0 women); includes 19 minority (11 Black or African American, non-Hispanic/Latino; 4 Asian, non-Hispanic/Latino; 2 Hispanic/Latino; 2 Two or more races, non-Hispanic/Latino), 44 international. 339 applicants, 27% accepted, 20 enrolled. In 2012, 7 master's, 14 doctorates awarded. Terminal master's awarded for partial completion of doctoral program. *Degree requirements:* For master's, thesis optional; for doctorate, thesis/dissertation, 2 seminar presentations, oral exam. *Entrance requirements:* For master's and doctorate, GRE General Test, GRE Subject Test (recommended), minimum GPA of 3.0, 3 letters of recommendation. Additional exam requirements/recommendations for international students: Required—TOEFL. *Application deadline:* For fall admission, 2/1 for domestic and international students; for spring admission, 6/1 for domestic and international students. Applications are processed on a rolling basis. Application fee: $75. Electronic applications accepted. *Expenses:* Tuition, state resident: part-time $551 per credit. Tuition, nonresident: part-time $1188 per credit. Part-time tuition and fees vary according to program. *Financial support:* In 2012–13, 14 fellowships with full and partial tuition reimbursements (averaging $20,017 per year), 52 research assistantships (averaging $19,868 per year), 44 teaching assistantships (averaging $19,209 per year) were awarded. Financial award applicants required to submit FAFSA. *Faculty research:* Environmental chemistry, nuclear chemistry, lunar and environmental analysis, x-ray crystallography. *Unit head:* Dr. Michael Doyle, Chairperson, 301-405-1795, Fax: 301-314-2779, E-mail: mdoyle3@umd.edu. *Application contact:* Dr. Charles A. Caramello, Dean of Graduate School, 301-405-0358, Fax: 301-314-9305.

University of Memphis, Graduate School, College of Arts and Sciences, Department of Chemistry, Memphis, TN 38152. Offers analytical chemistry (MS, PhD); computational chemistry (MS, PhD); inorganic chemistry (MS, PhD); organic chemistry (MS, PhD); physical chemistry (MS, PhD). Part-time programs available. Terminal master's awarded for partial completion of doctoral program. *Degree requirements:* For master's, comprehensive exam, thesis or alternative; for doctorate, comprehensive exam, thesis/dissertation. *Entrance requirements:* For master's and doctorate, GRE General Test, admission to Graduate School plus 32 undergraduate hours in chemistry. Additional exam requirements/recommendations for international students: Required—TOEFL. Electronic applications accepted. *Faculty research:* Computational chemistry, materials chemistry, organic/polymer synthesis, drug design/delivery, water chemistry.

University of Miami, Graduate School, College of Arts and Sciences, Department of Chemistry, Coral Gables, FL 33124. Offers chemistry (MS); inorganic chemistry (PhD); organic chemistry (PhD); physical chemistry (PhD). Terminal master's awarded for partial completion of doctoral program. *Degree requirements:* For master's, comprehensive exam; for doctorate, comprehensive exam, thesis/dissertation. *Entrance requirements:* For master's and doctorate, GRE General Test. Additional exam requirements/recommendations for international students: Required—TOEFL (minimum score 550 paper-based). Electronic applications accepted. *Faculty research:* Supramolecular chemistry, electrochemistry, surface chemistry, catalysis, organometalic.

University of Michigan, Horace H. Rackham School of Graduate Studies, College of Literature, Science, and the Arts, Department of Chemistry, Ann Arbor, MI 48109-1055. Offers analytical chemistry (PhD); chemical biology (PhD); inorganic chemistry (PhD); material chemistry (PhD); organic chemistry (PhD); physical chemistry (PhD). *Degree requirements:* For doctorate, thesis/dissertation, oral defense of dissertation, organic cumulative proficiency exams. *Entrance requirements:* For doctorate, GRE General Test, GRE Subject Test (recommended), 3 letters of recommendation. Additional exam requirements/recommendations for international students: Required—TOEFL (minimum score 560 paper-based; 84 iBT). Electronic applications accepted. *Faculty research:* Biological catalysis, protein engineering, chemical sensors, de novo metalloprotein design, supramolecular architecture.

University of Missouri, Graduate School, College of Arts and Sciences, Department of Chemistry, Columbia, MO 65211. Offers analytical chemistry (MS, PhD); inorganic chemistry (MS, PhD); organic chemistry (MS, PhD); physical chemistry (MS, PhD). *Faculty:* 22 full-time (4 women), 1 part-time/adjunct (0 women). *Students:* 110 full-time (42 women), 9 part-time (5 women); includes 10 minority (3 Black or African American, non-Hispanic/Latino; 3 Asian, non-Hispanic/Latino; 2 Hispanic/Latino; 2 Two or more races, non-Hispanic/Latino), 47 international. Average age 27. 94 applicants, 21% accepted, 15 enrolled. In 2012, 2 master's, 5 doctorates awarded. *Degree requirements:* For master's, thesis; for doctorate, one foreign language, comprehensive exam, thesis/dissertation. *Entrance requirements:* For master's, GRE General Test, minimum GPA of 3.0; for doctorate, GRE General Test (minimum score: Verbal 450, Quantitative 600, Analytical 3), minimum GPA of 3.0. Additional exam requirements/recommendations for international students: Required—TOEFL (minimum score 600 paper-based; 100 iBT). *Application deadline:* For fall admission, 2/1 priority date for domestic students, 2/1 for international students; for winter admission, 10/15 for domestic and international students. Applications are processed on a rolling basis. Application fee: $55 ($75 for international students). Electronic applications accepted. *Expenses:* Tuition, state resident: full-time $6057. Tuition, nonresident: full-time $15,683. *Required fees:* $1000. *Financial support:* In 2012–13, 9 fellowships with full tuition reimbursements, 15 research assistantships with full tuition reimbursements, 78 teaching assistantships with full tuition reimbursements were awarded; institutionally sponsored loans, traineeships, health care benefits, and unspecified assistantships also available. *Faculty research:* Analytical, organic, biological, physical, inorganic and radiochemistry. *Unit head:* Dr. Jerry Atwood, Department Chair, 573-882-8374, E-mail: atwoodj@missouri.edu. *Application contact:* Jerry Brightwell, Administrative Assistant, 573-884-6832, E-mail: brightwellj@missouri.edu. Website: http://chemistry.missouri.edu/.

University of Missouri–Kansas City, College of Arts and Sciences, Department of Chemistry, Kansas City, MO 64110-2499. Offers analytical chemistry (MS, PhD); inorganic chemistry (MS, PhD); organic chemistry (MS, PhD); physical chemistry (MS, PhD); polymer chemistry (MS, PhD). PhD (interdisciplinary) offered through the School of Graduate Studies. Part-time and evening/weekend programs available. *Faculty:* 15 full-time (3 women), 2 part-time/adjunct (0 women). *Students:* 7 part-time (3 women); includes 3 minority (2 Black or African American, non-Hispanic/Latino; 1 Hispanic/Latino). Average age 38. 19 applicants, 37% accepted, 3 enrolled. In 2012, 2 master's awarded. *Degree requirements:* For master's, thesis (for some programs); for doctorate, thesis/dissertation. *Entrance requirements:* For master's, equivalent of American Chemical Society approved bachelor's degree in chemistry; for doctorate, GRE General Test, equivalent of American Chemical Society approved bachelor's degree in chemistry. Additional exam requirements/recommendations for international students: Required—TOEFL (minimum score 550 paper-based; 80 iBT), TWE. *Application deadline:* For fall admission, 4/15 for domestic and international students; for spring admission, 10/15 for domestic and international students. Applications are processed on a rolling basis. Application fee: $45 ($50 for international students). Electronic applications accepted. *Expenses:* Tuition, state resident: full-time $5972.40; part-time $331.80 per credit hour. Tuition, nonresident: full-time $15,417; part-time $856.50 per credit hour. *Required fees:* $95.89 per credit hour. Full-time tuition and fees vary according to program. *Financial support:* In 2012–13, 6 research assistantships with partial tuition reimbursements (averaging $18,817 per year), 16 teaching assistantships with partial tuition reimbursements (averaging $18,132 per year) were awarded; Federal Work-Study, institutionally sponsored loans, and scholarships/grants also available. Support available to part-time students. Financial award application deadline: 3/1; financial award applicants required to submit FAFSA. *Faculty research:* Molecular spectroscopy, characterization and synthesis of materials and compounds, computational chemistry, natural products, drug delivery systems and anti-tumor agents. *Unit head:* Dr. Kathleen V. Kilway, Chair, 816-235-2289, Fax: 816-235-5502. *Application contact:* Graduate Recruiting Committee, 816-235-2272, Fax: 816-235-5502, E-mail: umkc-chemdept@umkc.edu. Website: http://cas.umkc.edu/chem/.

University of Missouri–St. Louis, College of Arts and Sciences, Department of Chemistry and Biochemistry, St. Louis, MO 63121. Offers chemistry (MS, PhD), including biochemistry, inorganic chemistry, organic chemistry, physical chemistry. Part-time and evening/weekend programs available. *Faculty:* 19 full-time (3 women), 6 part-time/adjunct (1 woman). *Students:* 37 full-time (15 women), 25 part-time (16 women); includes 6 minority (2 Black or African American, non-Hispanic/Latino; 1 Asian, non-Hispanic/Latino; 3 Hispanic/Latino), 18 international. Average age 30. 85 applicants, 22% accepted, 7 enrolled. In 2012, 18 master's, 5 doctorates awarded. Terminal master's awarded for partial completion of doctoral program. *Degree requirements:* For master's, thesis optional; for doctorate, thesis/dissertation. *Entrance requirements:* For master's, 2 letters of recommendation; for doctorate, GRE General Test, 3 letters of recommendation. Additional exam requirements/recommendations for international students: Required—TOEFL (minimum score 550 paper-based; 79 iBT), IELTS (minimum score 6.5). *Application deadline:* For fall admission, 7/1 priority date for domestic students, 7/1 for international students; for spring admission, 12/1 priority date for domestic students, 12/1 for international students. Applications are processed on a rolling basis. Application fee: $35 ($40 for international students). Electronic applications accepted. *Expenses:* Tuition, state resident: full-time $7364; part-time $409.10 per credit hour. Tuition, nonresident: full-time $18,153; part-time $1008.50 per credit hour. *Financial support:* In 2012–13, 16 research assistantships with full and partial tuition reimbursements (averaging $13,500 per year), 20 teaching assistantships with full and partial tuition reimbursements (averaging $13,500 per year) were awarded; fellowships with full and partial tuition reimbursements also available. *Faculty research:* Metallaborane chemistry, serum transferrin chemistry, natural products chemistry, organic synthesis. *Unit head:* Dr. Janet Wilking, Director of Graduate Studies, 314-516-5311, Fax: 314-516-5342, E-mail: gradchem@umsl.edu. *Application contact:* Graduate Admissions, 314-516-5458, Fax: 314-516-6996, E-mail: gradadm@umsl.edu. Website: http://www.umsl.edu/chemistry/.

The University of Montana, Graduate School, College of Arts and Sciences, Department of Chemistry and Biochemistry, Missoula, MT 59812-0002. Offers chemistry (MS, PhD), including environmental/analytical chemistry, inorganic chemistry, organic chemistry, physical chemistry. Terminal master's awarded for partial completion of doctoral program. *Degree requirements:* For master's, thesis (for some programs); for doctorate, thesis/dissertation. *Entrance requirements:* For master's and doctorate, GRE General Test. Additional exam requirements/recommendations for international students: Required—TOEFL (minimum score 575 paper-based). *Faculty research:* Reaction mechanisms and kinetics, inorganic and organic synthesis, analytical chemistry, natural products.

University of Nebraska–Lincoln, Graduate College, College of Arts and Sciences, Department of Chemistry, Lincoln, NE 68588. Offers analytical chemistry (PhD); biochemistry (PhD); chemistry (MS); inorganic chemistry (PhD); materials chemistry (PhD); organic chemistry (PhD); physical chemistry (PhD). *Degree requirements:* For master's, one foreign language, thesis optional, departmental qualifying exam; for doctorate, one foreign language, comprehensive exam, thesis/dissertation, departmental qualifying exams. *Entrance requirements:* For master's and doctorate, GRE. Additional exam requirements/recommendations for international students: Required—TOEFL (minimum score 550 paper-based). Electronic applications accepted. *Faculty research:* Bioorganic and bioinorganic chemistry, biophysical and bioanalytical chemistry, structure-function of DNA and proteins, organometallics, mass spectrometry.

University of Notre Dame, Graduate School, College of Science, Department of Chemistry and Biochemistry, Notre Dame, IN 46556. Offers biochemistry (MS, PhD); inorganic chemistry (MS, PhD); organic chemistry (MS, PhD); physical chemistry (MS, PhD). Terminal master's awarded for partial completion of doctoral program. *Degree requirements:* For master's, comprehensive exam, thesis; for doctorate, thesis/dissertation, qualifying exam. *Entrance requirements:* For master's and doctorate, GRE General Test, GRE Subject Test (strongly recommended). Additional exam requirements/recommendations for international students: Required—TOEFL (minimum score 600 paper-based; 80 iBT). Electronic applications accepted. *Faculty research:* Reaction design and mechanistic studies, reactive intermediates; synthesis, structure and reactivity of organometallic cluster complexes and biologically active natural products; bioorganic chemistry; enzymology.

University of Southern California, Graduate School, Dana and David Dornsife College of Letters, Arts and Sciences, Department of Chemistry, Los Angeles, CA 90089. Offers chemistry (PhD); physical chemistry (PhD). Terminal master's awarded for partial completion of doctoral program. *Degree requirements:* For doctorate, thesis/dissertation. *Entrance requirements:* For doctorate, GRE General Test. Additional exam requirements/recommendations for international students: Required—TOEFL. Electronic applications accepted. *Faculty research:* Biological chemistry, inorganic chemistry, organic chemistry, physical chemistry, theoretical chemistry.

University of Southern Mississippi, Graduate School, College of Science and Technology, Department of Chemistry and Biochemistry, Hattiesburg, MS 39406-0001. Offers analytical chemistry (MS, PhD); biochemistry (MS, PhD); inorganic chemistry (MS, PhD); organic chemistry (MS, PhD); physical chemistry (MS, PhD). *Faculty:* 16 full-time (4 women). *Students:* 26 full-time (9 women); includes 2 minority (1 Black or African American, non-Hispanic/Latino; 1 Asian, non-Hispanic/Latino), 8 international. Average age 27. 63 applicants, 13% accepted, 4 enrolled. In 2012, 2 master's, 4 doctorates awarded. *Degree requirements:* For master's, comprehensive exam, thesis; for doctorate, comprehensive exam, thesis/dissertation. *Entrance requirements:* For master's, GRE General Test, minimum GPA of 2.75 in last 60 hours; for doctorate, GRE General Test, minimum GPA of 3.5. Additional exam requirements/recommendations for international students: Required—TOEFL, IELTS. *Application deadline:* For fall admission, 3/1 priority date for domestic students, 3/1 for international students. Applications are processed on a rolling basis. Application fee: $50. *Financial support:* In 2012–13, 3 research assistantships with full tuition reimbursements (averaging $17,000 per year), 19 teaching assistantships with full tuition reimbursements (averaging $20,700 per year) were awarded; fellowships, Federal Work-Study, institutionally sponsored loans, scholarships/grants, health care benefits, and unspecified assistantships also available. Support available to part-time students. Financial award application deadline: 3/15; financial award applicants required to submit FAFSA. *Faculty research:* Plant biochemistry, photo chemistry, polymer chemistry, x-ray analysis, enzyme chemistry. *Unit head:* Dr. Sabine Heinhorst, Chair, 601-266-4701, Fax: 601-266-6075. Website: http://www.usm.edu/graduateschool/table.php.

University of South Florida, Graduate School, College of Arts and Sciences, Department of Chemistry, Tampa, FL 33620-9951. Offers analytical chemistry (MS, PhD); biochemistry (MS, PhD); computational chemistry (MS, PhD); environmental chemistry (MS, PhD); inorganic chemistry (MS, PhD); organic chemistry (MS); physical chemistry (MS, PhD); polymer chemistry (PhD). Part-time programs available. Terminal master's awarded for partial completion of doctoral program. *Degree requirements:* For master's, comprehensive exam, thesis (for some programs); for doctorate, comprehensive exam, thesis/dissertation. *Entrance requirements:* For master's and doctorate, GRE General Test, minimum GPA of 3.0. Additional exam requirements/recommendations for international students: Required—TOEFL (minimum score 550 paper-based; 79 iBT) or IELTS (minimum score 6.5). Electronic applications accepted. *Faculty research:* Synthesis, bio-organic chemistry, bioinorganic chemistry, environmental chemistry, nuclear magnetic resonance (NMR).

The University of Tennessee, Graduate School, College of Arts and Sciences, Department of Chemistry, Knoxville, TN 37996. Offers analytical chemistry (MS, PhD); chemical physics (PhD); environmental chemistry (MS, PhD); inorganic chemistry (MS, PhD); organic chemistry (MS, PhD); physical chemistry (MS, PhD); polymer chemistry (MS, PhD); theoretical chemistry (PhD). Part-time programs available. Terminal master's awarded for partial completion of doctoral program. *Degree requirements:* For master's, thesis; for doctorate, thesis/dissertation. *Entrance requirements:* For master's and doctorate, GRE General Test, minimum GPA of 2.7. Additional exam requirements/recommendations for international students: Required—TOEFL. Electronic applications accepted. *Expenses:* Tuition, state resident: full-time $9000; part-time $501 per credit hour. Tuition, nonresident: full-time $27,188; part-time $1512 per credit hour. *Required fees:* $1280; $62 per credit hour. Tuition and fees vary according to program.

The University of Texas at Austin, Graduate School, College of Natural Sciences, Department of Chemistry and Biochemistry, Austin, TX 78712-1111. Offers analytical chemistry (PhD); biochemistry (PhD); inorganic chemistry (PhD); organic chemistry (PhD); physical chemistry (PhD). *Entrance requirements:* For doctorate, GRE General Test.

The University of Toledo, College of Graduate Studies, College of Natural Sciences and Mathematics, Department of Chemistry, Toledo, OH 43606-3390. Offers analytical chemistry (MS, PhD); biological chemistry (MS, PhD); inorganic chemistry (MS, PhD); organic chemistry (MS, PhD); physical chemistry (MS, PhD). Part-time programs available. *Faculty:* 23. *Students:* 66 full-time (20 women), 9 part-time (2 women); includes 3 minority (1 Asian, non-Hispanic/Latino; 2 Hispanic/Latino), 50 international. Average age 27. 84 applicants, 26% accepted, 19 enrolled. In 2012, 6 master's, 7 doctorates awarded. *Degree requirements:* For master's, thesis or alternative; for doctorate, thesis/dissertation. *Entrance requirements:* For master's and doctorate, GRE General Test, GRE Subject Test, minimum cumulative point-hour ratio of 2.7 for all previous academic work, three letters of recommendation, statement of purpose, transcripts from all prior institutions attended. Additional exam requirements/recommendations for international students: Required—TOEFL (minimum score 550 paper-based; 80 iBT), IELTS (minimum score 6.5). *Application deadline:* For fall admission, 1/15 priority date for domestic students, 1/15 for international students. Applications are processed on a rolling basis. Application fee: $45 ($75 for international students). Electronic applications accepted. *Financial support:* In 2012–13, 29 research assistantships with full and partial tuition reimbursements (averaging $16,200 per year), 49 teaching assistantships with full and partial tuition reimbursements (averaging $15,682 per year) were awarded; Federal Work-Study, institutionally sponsored loans, scholarships/grants, tuition waivers (full), and unspecified assistantships also available. Support available to part-time students. *Faculty research:* Enzymology, materials chemistry, crystallography, theoretical chemistry. *Unit head:* Dr. Ronald Viola, Chair, 419-530-1582, Fax: 419-530-4033, E-mail: ronald.viola@utoledo.edu. *Application contact:* Graduate School Office, 419-530-4723, Fax: 419-530-4724, E-mail: grdsch@utnet.utoledo.edu. Website: http://www.utoledo.edu/nsm/.

Vanderbilt University, Graduate School, Department of Chemistry, Nashville, TN 37240-1001. Offers analytical chemistry (MAT, MS, PhD); inorganic chemistry (MAT, MS, PhD); organic chemistry (MAT, MS, PhD); physical chemistry (MAT, MS, PhD); theoretical chemistry (MAT, MS). *Faculty:* 21 full-time (3 women). *Students:* 123 full-time (46 women); includes 22 minority (5 Black or African American, non-Hispanic/Latino; 1 American Indian or Alaska Native, non-Hispanic/Latino; 3 Asian, non-Hispanic/Latino; 5 Hispanic/Latino; 8 Two or more races, non-Hispanic/Latino), 14 international. Average age 25. 430 applicants, 15% accepted, 29 enrolled. In 2012, 6 master's, 14 doctorates awarded. Terminal master's awarded for partial completion of doctoral program. *Degree requirements:* For master's, thesis; for doctorate, thesis/dissertation, area, qualifying, and final exams. *Entrance requirements:* For master's and doctorate, GRE General Test, GRE Subject Test (recommended). Additional exam requirements/recommendations for international students: Required—TOEFL (minimum score 570 paper-based; 88 iBT). *Application deadline:* For fall admission, 1/15 for domestic and international students. Application fee: $0. Electronic applications accepted. *Financial support:* Fellowships with full and partial tuition reimbursements, research assistantships with full tuition reimbursements, teaching assistantships with full tuition reimbursements, Federal Work-Study, institutionally sponsored loans, scholarships/grants, traineeships, and health care benefits available. Financial award application deadline: 1/15; financial award applicants required to submit CSS PROFILE or FAFSA. *Faculty research:* Chemical synthesis; mechanistic, theoretical, bioorganic, analytical, and spectroscopic chemistry. *Unit head:* Dr. David Cliffel, Director of Graduate Studies, 615-343-3937, Fax: 615-322-4936, E-mail: d.cliffel@vanderbilt.edu. *Application contact:* Sandra Ford, Administrative Assistant, 615-322-8695, Fax: 615-322-4936, E-mail: sandra.e.ford@Vanderbilt.Edu. Website: http://www.vanderbilt.edu/chemistry/.

Virginia Commonwealth University, Graduate School, College of Humanities and Sciences, Department of Chemistry, Richmond, VA 23284-9005. Offers analytical chemistry (MS, PhD); chemical physics (PhD); inorganic chemistry (MS, PhD); organic chemistry (MS, PhD); physical chemistry (MS, PhD). Part-time programs available. Terminal master's awarded for partial completion of doctoral program. *Degree requirements:* For master's, thesis; for doctorate, thesis/dissertation, comprehensive cumulative exams, research proposal. *Entrance requirements:* For master's, GRE General Test, 30 undergraduate credits in chemistry; for doctorate, GRE General Test. Additional exam requirements/recommendations for international students: Required—TOEFL (minimum score 600 paper-based; 100 iBT) or IELTS (minimum score 6.5). Electronic applications accepted. *Faculty research:* Physical, organic, inorganic, analytical, and polymer chemistry; chemical physics.

Wake Forest University, Graduate School of Arts and Sciences, Department of Chemistry, Winston-Salem, NC 27109. Offers analytical chemistry (MS, PhD); inorganic chemistry (MS, PhD); organic chemistry (MS, PhD); physical chemistry (MS, PhD). Part-time programs available. *Degree requirements:* For master's, one foreign language, comprehensive exam, thesis; for doctorate, 2 foreign languages, comprehensive exam, thesis/dissertation. *Entrance requirements:* For master's and doctorate, GRE General Test. Additional exam requirements/

recommendations for international students: Required—TOEFL. Electronic applications accepted.

Wayne State University, College of Liberal Arts and Sciences, Department of Chemistry, Detroit, MI 48202. Offers analytical chemistry (PhD); biochemistry (PhD); chemistry (MA, MS); inorganic chemistry (PhD); organic chemistry (PhD); physical chemistry (PhD). *Students:* 167 full-time (79 women), 1 part-time (0 women); includes 12 minority (3 Black or African American, non-Hispanic/Latino; 2 American Indian or Alaska Native, non-Hispanic/Latino; 5 Asian, non-Hispanic/Latino; 2 Hispanic/Latino), 113 international. Average age 28. 440 applicants, 23% accepted, 50 enrolled. In 2012, 5 master's, 15 doctorates awarded. *Degree requirements:* For master's, thesis (for some programs), oral exam; for doctorate, thesis/dissertation, oral exam. *Entrance requirements:* For master's, one year of physics, math through calculus, general chemistry (8 credits), organic chemistry (8 credits), physical chemistry (six credits), quantitative analysis (four credits), and advanced chemistry (three credits); advanced biology (for biochemistry applicants); minimum undergraduate GPA of 2.75 in chemistry and cognate sciences; for doctorate, minimum undergraduate GPA of 3.0 in chemistry and cognate science. Additional exam requirements/recommendations for international students: Required—TOEFL (minimum score 550 paper-based; 79 iBT); Recommended—TWE (minimum score 5.5). *Application deadline:* For fall admission, 2/10 priority date for domestic students, 2/10 for international students; for winter admission, 10/1 priority date for domestic students, 9/1 for international students; for spring admission, 2/1 priority date for domestic students, 1/1 for international students. Applications are processed on a rolling basis. Application fee: $50. Electronic applications accepted. *Expenses:* Tuition, state resident: full-time $12,788; part-time $532.85 per credit hour. Tuition, nonresident: full-time $28,243; part-time $1176.80 per credit hour. *Required fees:* $1367.30; $39.75 per credit hour. $206.65 per semester. Tuition and fees vary according to course load and program. *Financial support:* In 2012–13, 154 students received support, including 10 fellowships with tuition reimbursements available (averaging $23,000 per year), 60 research assistantships with tuition reimbursements available (averaging $19,682 per year), 81 teaching assistantships with tuition reimbursements available (averaging $20,788 per year); scholarships/grants, health care benefits, and unspecified assistantships also available. Financial award application deadline: 7/1. *Faculty research:* Natural products synthesis, molecular biology, molecular mechanics calculations, organometallic chemistry, experimental physical chemistry. *Total annual research expenditures:* $7.2 million. *Unit head:* Dr. James Rigby, Chair, 313-577-3472, Fax: 313-577-8822, E-mail: aa392@wayne.edu. *Application contact:* Dr. Charles Winter, Graduate Director, 313-577-5224, E-mail: chw@chem.wayne.edu. Website: http://chem.wayne.edu/.

West Virginia University, Eberly College of Arts and Sciences, Department of Chemistry, Morgantown, WV 26506. Offers analytical chemistry (MS, PhD); inorganic chemistry (MS, PhD); organic chemistry (MS, PhD); physical chemistry (MS, PhD); theoretical chemistry (MS, PhD). Part-time programs available. Postbaccalaureate distance learning degree programs offered (no on-campus study). Terminal master's awarded for partial completion of doctoral program. *Degree requirements:* For master's, thesis; for doctorate, thesis/dissertation. *Entrance requirements:* For master's, GRE General Test, GRE Subject Test (recommended), minimum GPA of 2.5; for doctorate, GRE General Test, GRE Subject Test (recommended), minimum GPA of 2.75. Additional exam requirements/recommendations for international students: Required—TOEFL. Electronic applications accepted. *Faculty research:* Analysis of proteins, drug interactions, solids and effluents by advanced separation methods; new synthetic strategies for complex organic molecules; synthesis and structural characterization of metal complexes for polymerization catalysis, nonlinear science, spectroscopy.

Yale University, Graduate School of Arts and Sciences, Department of Chemistry, New Haven, CT 06520. Offers biophysical chemistry (PhD); inorganic chemistry (PhD); organic chemistry (PhD); physical and theoretical chemistry (PhD). *Degree requirements:* For doctorate, thesis/dissertation. *Entrance requirements:* For doctorate, GRE General Test, GRE Subject Test. Additional exam requirements/recommendations for international students: Required—TOEFL.

Youngstown State University, Graduate School, College of Science, Technology, Engineering and Mathematics, Department of Chemistry, Youngstown, OH 44555-0001. Offers analytical chemistry (MS); biochemistry (MS); chemistry education (MS); inorganic chemistry (MS); organic chemistry (MS); physical chemistry (MS). Part-time programs available. *Degree requirements:* For master's, thesis. *Entrance requirements:* For master's, bachelor's degree in chemistry, minimum GPA of 2.7. Additional exam requirements/recommendations for international students: Required—TOEFL. *Faculty research:* Analysis of antioxidants, chromatography, defects and disorder in crystalline oxides, hydrogen bonding, novel organic and organometallic materials.

Theoretical Chemistry

Carnegie Mellon University, Mellon College of Science, Department of Chemistry, Pittsburgh, PA 15213-3891. Offers biotechnology and management (MS); chemistry (PhD), including bioinorganic, bioorganic, organic and materials, biophysics and spectroscopy, computational and theoretical, polymer; colloids, polymers and surfaces (MS). Part-time programs available. Terminal master's awarded for partial completion of doctoral program. *Degree requirements:* For doctorate, thesis/dissertation, departmental qualifying and oral exams, teaching experience. *Entrance requirements:* For master's, GRE General Test; for doctorate, GRE General Test, GRE Subject Test. Additional exam requirements/recommendations for international students: Required—TOEFL. Electronic applications accepted. *Faculty research:* Physical and theoretical chemistry, chemical synthesis, biophysical/bioinorganic chemistry.

Cornell University, Graduate School, Graduate Fields of Arts and Sciences, Field of Chemistry and Chemical Biology, Ithaca, NY 14853-0001. Offers analytical chemistry (PhD); bio-organic chemistry (PhD); biophysical chemistry (PhD); chemical biology (PhD); chemical physics (PhD); inorganic chemistry (PhD); materials chemistry (PhD); organic chemistry (PhD); organometallic chemistry (PhD); physical chemistry (PhD); polymer chemistry (PhD); theoretical chemistry (PhD). *Faculty:* 48 full-time (5 women). *Students:* 161 full-time (70 women); includes 28 minority (1 Black or African American, non-Hispanic/Latino; 16 Asian, non-Hispanic/Latino; 4 Hispanic/Latino; 7 Two or more races, non-Hispanic/Latino), 48 international. Average age 25. 340 applicants, 33% accepted, 40 enrolled. In 2012, 15 doctorates awarded. *Degree requirements:* For doctorate, comprehensive exam, thesis/dissertation. *Entrance requirements:* For doctorate, GRE General Test, GRE Subject Test (chemistry), 3 letters of recommendation. Additional exam requirements/recommendations for international students: Required—TOEFL (minimum score 600 paper-based; 77 iBT). *Application deadline:* For fall admission, 1/10 for domestic students. Application fee: $95. Electronic applications accepted. *Financial support:* In 2012–13, 155 students received support, including 37 fellowships with full tuition reimbursements available, 50 research assistantships with full tuition reimbursements available, 68 teaching assistantships with full tuition reimbursements available; institutionally sponsored loans, scholarships/grants, health care benefits, tuition waivers (full and partial), and unspecified assistantships also available. Financial award applicants required to submit FAFSA. *Faculty research:* Analytical, organic, inorganic, physical, materials, chemical biology. *Unit head:* Director of Graduate Studies, 607-255-4139, Fax: 607-255-4137. *Application contact:* Graduate Field Assistant, 607-255-4139, Fax: 607-255-4137, E-mail: chemgrad@cornell.edu. Website: http://www.gradschool.cornell.edu/fields.php?id-26&a-2.

Georgetown University, Graduate School of Arts and Sciences, Department of Chemistry, Washington, DC 20057. Offers analytical chemistry (PhD); biochemistry (PhD); computational chemistry (PhD); inorganic chemistry (PhD); materials chemistry (PhD); organic chemistry (PhD); physical chemistry (PhD); theoretical chemistry (PhD). Terminal master's awarded for partial completion of doctoral program. *Degree requirements:* For doctorate, comprehensive exam, thesis/dissertation. *Entrance requirements:* For doctorate, GRE General Test. Additional exam requirements/recommendations for international students: Required—TOEFL.

Laurentian University, School of Graduate Studies and Research, Programme in Chemistry and Biochemistry, Sudbury, ON P3E 2C6, Canada. Offers analytical chemistry (M Sc); biochemistry (M Sc); environmental chemistry (M Sc); organic chemistry (M Sc); physical/theoretical chemistry (M Sc). Part-time programs available. *Degree requirements:* For master's, thesis or alternative. *Entrance requirements:* For master's, honors degree with minimum second class. *Faculty research:* Cell cycle checkpoints, kinetic modeling, toxicology to metal stress, quantum chemistry, biogeochemistry metal speciation.

University of Calgary, Faculty of Graduate Studies, Faculty of Science, Department of Chemistry, Calgary, AB T2N 1N4, Canada. Offers analytical chemistry (M Sc, PhD); applied chemistry (M Sc, PhD); inorganic chemistry (M Sc, PhD); organic chemistry (M Sc, PhD); physical chemistry (M Sc, PhD); polymer chemistry (M Sc, PhD); theoretical chemistry (M Sc, PhD). *Degree requirements:* For master's, thesis; for doctorate, thesis/dissertation, candidacy exam. *Entrance requirements:* For master's, minimum GPA of 3.0; for doctorate, honors B Sc degree with minimum GPA of 3.7 or M Sc with minimum GPA of 3.3. Additional exam requirements/recommendations for international students: Required—TOEFL (minimum score 580 paper-based). Electronic applications accepted. *Faculty research:* Chemical analysis, chemical dynamics, synthesis theory.

The University of Manchester, School of Chemistry, Manchester, United Kingdom. Offers biological chemistry (PhD); chemistry (M Ent, M Phil, M Sc, D Ent, PhD); inorganic chemistry (PhD); materials chemistry (PhD); nanoscience (PhD); nuclear fission (PhD); organic chemistry (PhD); physical chemistry (PhD); theoretical chemistry (PhD).

Peterson's Graduate Programs in the Physical Sciences, Mathematics, Agricultural Sciences, the Environment & Natural Resources 2014

University of Regina, Faculty of Graduate Studies and Research, Faculty of Science, Department of Chemistry and Biochemistry, Regina, SK S4S 0A2, Canada. Offers analytical/environmental chemistry (M Sc, PhD); biophysics of biological interfaces (M Sc, PhD); enzymology/chemical biology (M Sc, PhD); inorganic/organometallic chemistry (M Sc, PhD); signal transduction and mechanisms of cancer cell regulation (M Sc, PhD); supramolecular organic photochemistry and photophysics (M Sc, PhD); synthetic organic chemistry (M Sc, PhD); theoretical/computational chemistry (M Sc, PhD). *Faculty:* 12 full-time (2 women), 3 part-time/adjunct (0 women). *Students:* 11 full-time (6 women), 2 part-time (0 women). 32 applicants, 19% accepted. In 2012, 7 master's awarded. *Degree requirements:* For master's, thesis; for doctorate, thesis/dissertation. *Entrance requirements:* Additional exam requirements/recommendations for international students: Required—TOEFL (minimum score 580 paper-based; 80 iBT), IELTS (minimum score 6.5). *Application deadline:* Applications are processed on a rolling basis. Application fee: $100. Electronic applications accepted. Tuition and fees charges are reported in Canadian dollars. *Expenses: Tuition, area resident:* Full-time $3942 Canadian dollars; part-time $219 Canadian dollars per credit hour. *International tuition:* $4742 Canadian dollars full-time. *Required fees:* $421.55 Canadian dollars; $93.60 Canadian dollars per credit hour. Tuition and fees vary according to course load, degree level and program. *Financial support:* In 2012–13, 5 fellowships (averaging $7,000 per year), 10 teaching assistantships (averaging $2,470 per year) were awarded; research assistantships and scholarships/grants also available. Financial award application deadline: 6/15. *Faculty research:* Asymmetric synthesis and methodology, theoretical and computational chemistry, biophysical biochemistry, analytical and environmental chemistry, chemical biology. *Unit head:* Dr. Lynn Mihichuk, Head, 306-585-4793, Fax: 306-337-2409, E-mail: lynn.mihichuk@uregina.ca. *Application contact:* Dr. Brian Sterenberg, Graduate Program Coordinator, 306-585-4106, Fax: 306-337-2409, E-mail: brian.sterenberg@uregina.ca. Website: http://www.chem.uregina.ca/.

The University of Tennessee, Graduate School, College of Arts and Sciences, Department of Chemistry, Knoxville, TN 37996. Offers analytical chemistry (MS, PhD); chemical physics (PhD); environmental chemistry (MS, PhD); inorganic chemistry (MS, PhD); organic chemistry (MS, PhD); physical chemistry (MS, PhD); polymer chemistry (MS, PhD); theoretical chemistry (PhD). Part-time programs available. Terminal master's awarded for partial completion of doctoral program. *Degree requirements:* For master's, thesis; for doctorate, thesis/dissertation. *Entrance requirements:* For master's and doctorate, GRE General Test, minimum GPA of 2.7. Additional exam requirements/recommendations for international students: Required—TOEFL. Electronic applications accepted. *Expenses: Tuition, state resident:* full-time $9000; part-time $501 per credit hour. Tuition, nonresident: full-time $27,188; part-time $1512 per credit hour. *Required fees:* $1280; $62 per credit hour. Tuition and fees vary according to program.

Vanderbilt University, Graduate School, Department of Chemistry, Nashville, TN 37240-1001. Offers analytical chemistry (MAT, MS, PhD); inorganic chemistry (MAT, MS, PhD); organic chemistry (MAT, MS, PhD); physical chemistry (MAT, MS, PhD); theoretical chemistry (MAT, MS). *Faculty:* 21 full-time (3 women). *Students:* 123 full-time (46 women); includes 22 minority (5 Black or African American, non-Hispanic/Latino; 1 American Indian or Alaska Native, non-Hispanic/Latino; 3 Asian, non-Hispanic/Latino; 5 Hispanic/Latino; 8 Two or more races, non-Hispanic/Latino), 14 international. Average age 25. 430 applicants, 15% accepted, 29 enrolled. In 2012, 6 master's, 14 doctorates awarded. Terminal master's awarded for partial completion of doctoral program. *Degree requirements:* For master's, thesis; for doctorate, thesis/dissertation, area, qualifying, and final exams. *Entrance requirements:* For master's and doctorate, GRE General Test, GRE Subject Test (recommended). Additional exam requirements/recommendations for international students: Required—TOEFL (minimum score 570 paper-based; 88 iBT). *Application deadline:* For fall admission, 1/15 for domestic and international students. Application fee: $0. Electronic applications accepted. *Financial support:* Fellowships with full and partial tuition reimbursements, research assistantships with full tuition reimbursements, teaching assistantships with full tuition reimbursements, Federal Work-Study, institutionally sponsored loans, scholarships/grants, traineeships, and health care benefits available. Financial award application deadline: 1/15; financial award applicants required to submit CSS PROFILE or FAFSA. *Faculty research:* Chemical synthesis; mechanistic, theoretical, bioorganic, analytical, and spectroscopic chemistry. *Unit head:* Dr. David Cliffel, Director of Graduate Studies, 615-343-3937, Fax: 615-322-4936, E-mail: d.cliffel@vanderbilt.edu. *Application contact:* Sandra Ford, Administrative Assistant, 615-322-8695, Fax: 615-322-4936, E-mail: sandra.e.ford@Vanderbilt.Edu. Website: http://www.vanderbilt.edu/chemistry/.

Wesleyan University, Graduate Studies, Department of Chemistry, Middletown, CT 06459-0180. Offers biochemistry (PhD); chemical physics (PhD); inorganic chemistry (PhD); organic chemistry (PhD); physical chemistry (PhD); theoretical chemistry (PhD). Terminal master's awarded for partial completion of doctoral program. *Degree requirements:* For doctorate, thesis/dissertation, proposal. *Entrance requirements:* For doctorate, GRE General Test, 3 recommendations. Additional exam requirements/recommendations for international students: Required—TOEFL. *Application deadline:* Applications are processed on a rolling basis. Application fee: $0. Electronic applications accepted. *Financial support:* Research assistantships with full tuition reimbursements, teaching assistantships with full tuition reimbursements, and institutionally sponsored loans available. Financial award application deadline: 4/15; financial award applicants required to submit FAFSA. *Unit head:* Prof. Rex F. Pratt, Chair, 860-685-2727. *Application contact:* Sarah Atwell, Administrative Assistant IV/Graduate Program Coordinator, 860-685-2573, Fax: 860-685-2211, E-mail: satwell@wesleyan.edu. Website: http://www.wesleyan.edu/chem/.

West Virginia University, Eberly College of Arts and Sciences, Department of Chemistry, Morgantown, WV 26506. Offers analytical chemistry (MS, PhD); inorganic chemistry (MS, PhD); organic chemistry (MS, PhD); physical chemistry (MS, PhD); theoretical chemistry (MS, PhD). Part-time programs available. Postbaccalaureate distance learning degree programs offered (no on-campus study). Terminal master's awarded for partial completion of doctoral program. *Degree requirements:* For master's, thesis; for doctorate, thesis/dissertation. *Entrance requirements:* For master's, GRE General Test, GRE Subject Test (recommended), minimum GPA of 2.5; for doctorate, GRE General Test, GRE Subject Test (recommended), minimum GPA of 2.75. Additional exam requirements/recommendations for international students: Required—TOEFL. Electronic applications accepted. *Faculty research:* Analysis of proteins, drug interactions, solids and effluents by advanced separation methods; new synthetic strategies for complex organic molecules; synthesis and structural characterization of metal complexes for polymerization catalysis, nonlinear science, spectroscopy.

Yale University, Graduate School of Arts and Sciences, Department of Chemistry, New Haven, CT 06520. Offers biophysical chemistry (PhD); inorganic chemistry (PhD); organic chemistry (PhD); physical and theoretical chemistry (PhD). *Degree requirements:* For doctorate, thesis/dissertation. *Entrance requirements:* For doctorate, GRE General Test, GRE Subject Test. Additional exam requirements/recommendations for international students: Required—TOEFL.

Peterson's Graduate Programs in the Physical Sciences, Mathematics, Agricultural Sciences, the Environment & Natural Resources 2014

www.petersonsbooks.com **123**

HARVARD UNIVERSITY
Department of Chemistry and Chemical Biology

Programs of Study

The Department of Chemistry and Chemical Biology offers a program of study that leads to the degree of Doctor of Philosophy (Ph.D.) in chemistry in the special fields of biological, inorganic, organic, and physical chemistry. An interdepartmental Ph.D. program in chemical physics is also available. Upon entering the program, students formulate a plan of study in consultation with a Curriculum Advising Committee. Students must obtain honor grades in four advanced half courses (five for chemical physics). The course work is usually completed by the end of the second year of study. Students are expected to present and defend an independent research proposal anytime from the first semester of their second year through the end of their fourth year (June 30). Although the curriculum for the Ph.D. degree includes the course, research proposal, and oral defense requirements, the majority of the graduate student's time and energy is devoted to original investigations in a chosen field of research. Students are expected to join a research group in their second semester of residence, but no later than the third. The Ph.D. dissertation is based on independent scholarly research, which, upon conclusion, is defended in an oral examination before a Ph.D. committee. The preparation of a satisfactory thesis normally requires at least four years of full-time research.

Research Facilities

Departmental research facilities are located in six buildings on the historic main Harvard campus: Mallinckrodt, Conant, Converse, Naito, Bauer, and the Mallinckrodt/Hoffman "Link." These laboratories are adjacent to the Departments of Stem Cell and Regenerative Biology, Molecular and Cellular Biology, Organismic and Evolutionary Biology, Physics, Earth and Planetary Sciences, the Centers for Systems Biology and Brain Science, and the School of Engineering and Applied Sciences. Also nearby is the Science Center, which houses Mathematics, Statistics, and History of Science but is devoted primarily to undergraduate teaching facilities. In addition to the faculty research labs, the Chemistry and Chemical Biology complex contains facilities for analytical instrumentation (NMR, MS, X-ray Crystallography, and X-ray Diffractometry), a library, and computer workstations for molecular modeling and chemical information retrieval. A machine shop, electronics shop, and facilities for biological mass spectrometry, protein structure determination, materials synthesis, nanofabrication, and imaging are available in adjacent departments. Nearly all CCB faculty members are affiliated with multiple cross-departmental programs and research centers at Harvard.

Financial Aid

The Department of Chemistry and Chemical Biology meets the financial needs of its graduate students through Departmental scholarships, Departmental fellowships, teaching fellowships, research assistantships, and independent outside fellowships. Financial support is awarded on a twelve-month basis, enabling students to pursue their research throughout the year. Tuition is afforded to all graduate students in good standing for the tenure of the Ph.D. program.

Cost of Study

As stated in the Financial Aid section, tuition is waived for all Ph.D. students in good standing.

Living and Housing Costs

Dormitory rooms for single students are available, with costs (excluding meals) that ranged from $6,290 for a single room to $9,878 for a two-room suite in 2013–14. Married and single students may apply for apartments managed by Harvard Planning and Real Estate. The monthly costs are studio apartment, $1,080–$1,796; one-bedroom apartment, $1,576–$2,466; two-bedroom apartment, $1,882–$3,092; and three-bedroom apartment, $2,211–$4,560. There are also many privately owned apartments nearby and within commuting distance.

Student Group

The Graduate School of Arts and Sciences (GSAS) has an enrollment of approximately 4,000 graduate students. There are approximately 185 students in the Department of Chemistry and Chemical Biology, 43 percent of whom are international students.

Student Outcomes

In 2012, 14 percent of the Ph.D. recipients entered positions in academia, 17 percent accepted permanent positions in industry, 49 percent conducted postdoctoral research before accepting permanent positions in academia or industry, and 20 percent pursued other directions.

Location

Cambridge, a city of over 100,000, is just minutes from Boston. It is a scientific and intellectual center, teeming with activities in all areas of creativity and study. The Cambridge/Boston area is a major cultural center, with its many public and university museums, theaters, symphony, and numerous private, special interest, and historical collections and performances. New England abounds in possibilities for recreational pursuits, from camping, hiking, and skiing in the mountains of New Hampshire and Vermont to swimming, sailing, fishing, and surfing on the seashores of Cape Cod and Maine.

The University

Harvard College was established in 1636, and its charter, which still guides the University, was granted in 1650. An early brochure, published in 1643, justified the College's existence: "To advance Learning and perpetuate it to Posterity...." Today, Harvard University, with its network of graduate and professional schools, occupies a noteworthy position in the academic world, and the Department of Chemistry and Chemical Biology offers an educational program in keeping with the University's long-standing record of achievement.

Applying

Applications for admission to study for the Ph.D. degree in chemistry may be accessed at the GSAS website at http://www.gsas.harvard.edu/apply/apply.php. Applications are accepted online from students who have received a bachelor's degree or equivalent.

The application process should begin during the summer or fall of the year preceding desired entrance. Completed online applications and any paper supporting materials should be submitted to the GSAS Admissions Office by December 3, though this date may vary slightly from year to year.

Correspondence and Information

Graduate Admissions Office
Department of Chemistry and Chemical Biology
Harvard University
12 Oxford Street
Cambridge, Massachusetts 02138
United States
Phone: 617-496-3208
E-mail: admissions@chemistry.harvard.edu
Website: http://www.chem.harvard.edu

THE FACULTY AND THEIR RESEARCH

Joanna Aizenberg, Gordon McKay Professor of Materials Science, Susan S. and Kenneth L. Wallach Professor at the Radcliffe Institute for Advanced Study, and Professor of Chemistry and Chemical Biology; Ph.D., Weizmann (Israel), 1996. Biomimetic inorganic materials synthesis, self-assembly, crystal engineering, surface chemistry, nanofabrication, biomaterials, biomechanics, biooptics.

James G. Anderson, Philip S. Weld Professor of Atmospheric Chemistry; Ph.D., Colorado, 1970. Chemical reactivity of radical and radical-molecule systems; chemical catalysis sustained by free radical chain reactions in the earth's stratosphere and troposphere; mechanistic links between chemistry, radiation, and dynamics in the atmosphere that control climate; high-accuracy satellite observations for testing and systematic improvement of climate forecasts.

Alan Aspuru-Guzik, Professor of Chemistry and Chemical Biology; Ph.D., Berkeley, 2004. Theoretical physical chemistry; quantum computation

Peterson's Graduate Programs in the Physical Sciences, Mathematics, Agricultural Sciences, the Environment & Natural Resources 2014

www.petersonsbooks.com **125**

Harvard University

and its application to chemistry problems; development of electronic structure methods for atoms and molecules: density functional theory and quantum Monte Carlo; theoretical understanding and design of renewable energy materials.

Emily Balskus, Assistant Professor of Chemistry and Chemical Biology; Ph.D., Harvard, 2008. The elucidation and study of biosynthetic pathways and enzymes as well as the development of synthetic methods that are compatible with microbial chemistry.

Theodore A. Betley, Associate Professor of Chemistry and Chemical Biology; Ph.D., Caltech, 2005. Synthetic inorganic chemistry targeting chemical energy conversion, structure and reactivity of polymetallic and organometallic compounds.

Adam E. Cohen, Professor of Chemistry and Chemical Biology and of Physics; Ph.D., Cambridge, 2003; Ph.D., Stanford, 2007. Single-molecule spectroscopy and biophysics; Brownian motion and feedback control; electrokinetics, polymer physics, fluctuation-induced forces; nonequilibrium van der Waals/Casimir forces; instrumentation.

Cynthia M. Friend, Theodore William Richards Professor of Chemistry and Professor of Materials Science; Ph.D., Berkeley, 1981. Surface chemistry: heterogeneous catalysis, nanostructure growth, environmental chemistry, laser-assisted materials processing, heterogeneous chemistry relevant to origins of life, chemical sensor technology.

Roy Gerald Gordon, Thomas Dudley Cabot Professor of Chemistry; Ph.D., Harvard, 1964. Intermolecular forces, transport processes, and molecular motion; theory of crystal structures and phase transitions, kinetics of crystal growth; solar energy, chemical vapor deposition; synthesis of inorganic precursors to new materials, thin films and their applications to microelectronics and solar cells.

Eric J. Heller, Professor of Chemistry and Physics; Ph.D., Harvard, 1973. Few-body quantum mechanics, scattering theory, and quantum chaos; physics of semiconductor devices, ultracold molecular collisions, and nonadiabatic interactions in molecules and gases.

Eric N. Jacobsen, Sheldon Emery Professor of Chemistry; Ph.D., Berkeley, 1986. Mechanistic and synthetic organic chemistry; development of new synthetic methods with emphasis on asymmetric catalysis; physical-organic studies of reactivity and recognition phenomena in homogeneous catalysis; stereoselective synthesis of natural products.

Daniel Kahne, Professor of Chemistry and Chemical Biology and Professor of Biological Chemistry and Molecular Pharmacology; Ph.D., Columbia, 1986. Synthetic organic chemistry and its applications to problems in chemistry and biology.

Charles M. Lieber, Mark Hyman Jr. Professor of Chemistry; Ph.D., Stanford, 1985. Chemistry and physics of materials with an emphasis on nanoscale systems; rational synthesis of new nanoscale building blocks and nanostructured solids; development of methodologies for hierarchical assembly of nanoscale building blocks into complex and functional systems; investigation of fundamental electronic, optical, and optoelectronic properties of nanoscale materials; design and development of nanoelectronics and nanophotonic systems, with emphasis on electrically based biological detection, digital and quantum computing, and photonic systems.

David R. Liu, Professor of Chemistry and Chemical Biology and Howard Hughes Medical Institute Investigator; Ph.D., Berkeley, 1999. Organic chemistry and chemical biology of molecular evolution, nucleic acid–templated organic synthesis, reaction discovery, protein and nucleic acid evolution and engineering, synthetic polymer evolution; generally, effective molarity-based approaches to controlling reactivity and evolution-based approaches to the discovery of functional synthetic and biological molecules.

Andrew G. Myers, Professor of Chemistry and Chemical Biology and Amory Houghton Professor of Chemistry; Ph.D., Harvard, 1985. Synthesis and study of complex natural products; development of synthetic methodology.

Kang-Kuen Ni, Assistant Professor of Chemistry and Chemical Biology; Ph.D., Colorado, 2009. Quantum control and manipulation of molecular, atomic, and mesoscopic systems; developing techniques of cooling and trapping gases of polar molecules.

Daniel G. Nocera, Patterson Rockwood Professor of Energy; Ph.D., Caltech, 1984. Chemistry of renewable energy, solar energy conversion and storage, biological energy conversion with emphasis on mechanisms derived from proton-coupled electron transfer, applications of photochemistry including the development of nanocrystal-bioconjugate constructs for metabolic profiling of living systems, the physics of highly correlated systems derived from spin frustration.

Erin O'Shea, Professor of Molecular and Cellular Biology and of Chemistry and Chemical Biology, Howard Hughes Medical Institute Investigator, and Director of the Center for Systems Biology; Ph.D., MIT, 1992. Systems-level and molecular analysis of signaling pathways; transcriptional regulatory network architecture, function, and evolution; regulation and mechanism of oscillation of a circadian clock.

Hongkun Park, Professor of Chemistry and Chemical Biology and Professor of Physics; Ph.D., Stanford, 1996. Physics and chemistry of nanostructured materials; development of neuro-electronic interface; electron transport through individual molecules, nanowires, and nanotubes; single-molecule optoelectronics; synthesis and characterization of transition-metal-oxide and chalcogenide nanostructures; interrogation of complex neural networks using optical and electronic techniques.

Tobias Ritter, Professor of Chemistry and Chemical Biology; Ph.D., Swiss Federal Institute of Technology, 2004. Synthetic organic and organometallic chemistry, development of new synthetic methods based on transition-metal catalysis, stereoselective synthesis of biologically active natural and unnatural products.

Alan Saghatelian, Associate Professor of Chemistry and Chemical Biology; Ph.D., California, San Diego (Scripps), 2002. Development and application of global metabolite profiling (metabolomics) as a general discovery tool for chemical biology, elucidation of molecules and metabolic pathways that control phenotype at the cellular and physiological level.

Stuart L. Schreiber, Morris Loeb Professor of Chemistry and Chemical Biology and Howard Hughes Medical Institute Investigator; Ph.D., Harvard, 1981. Development of diversity-oriented synthesis, chemical genetics, and ChemBank; application to an understanding of cell circuitry and disease biology.

Matthew D. Shair, Professor of Chemistry and Chemical Biology; Ph.D., Columbia, 1995. Synthesis of small molecules that have interesting biological functions and elucidation of their cellular mechanisms; development of organic synthesis.

Eugene I. Shakhnovich, Professor of Chemistry and Chemical Biology; Ph.D., Moscow, 1984. Theoretical biomolecular science, including protein folding, theory of molecular evolution, structural bioinformatics, rational drug design, populational genomics, other complex systems including complex polymers and spin glasses.

Jack Szostak, Alexander A. Rich Distinguished Investigator, Massachusetts General Hospital; Professor of Genetics; Professor of Chemistry and Chemical Biology and Howard Hughes Medical Institute Investigator; Ph.D., Cornell, 1977. Design and synthesis of self-replicating artificial cell, chemical genetics, and ChemBank; origins and early evolution of life.

Gregory L. Verdine, Professor of Stem Cell and Regenerative Biology and Erving Professor of Chemistry; Ph.D., Columbia, 1986. Protein-nucleic acid interactions, transcriptional regulation, X-ray crystallography, structure and function of DNA-processing enzymes, discovery of novel ligands to peptide receptors.

George M. Whitesides, Woodford L. and Ann A. Flowers University Professor; Ph.D., Caltech, 1964. Physical organic chemistry, materials science, biophysics, complexity, surface science, microfluidics, self-assembly, microtechnology and nanotechnology, cell-surface biochemistry.

Xiaoliang Sunney Xie, Professor of Chemistry and Chemical Biology; Ph.D., California, San Diego, 1990. Single-molecule spectroscopy and dynamics, molecular interaction and chemical dynamics in biological systems, live cell imaging.

Xiaowei Zhuang, Professor of Chemistry and Chemical Biology and of Physics and Howard Hughes Medical Institute Investigator; Ph.D., Berkeley, 1996. Investigating complex biological processes at the single-molecule level, live cell imaging, development of new techniques for single-molecule sensing and imaging.

Affiliate Members of the Department of Chemistry and Chemical Biology

Jon Clardy, Professor of Biological Chemistry and Molecular Pharmacology (Medical School); Ph.D., Harvard, 1969. Discovery of biologically active small molecules using DNA-based approaches or high-throughput screening and chemical analysis, protein structure and enzymology, functioning of small molecules as carriers of biological information, new biosynthetic pathways, new microbial biology.

Efthimios Kaxiras, Gordon McKay Professor of Applied Physics and Professor of Physics (School of Engineering and Applied Sciences); Ph.D., MIT, 1987. Development of computational methodologies for coupling spatial and temporal scales; optical and electronic properties for nucleic acids, melanin, and flavonoids; structure and properties of carbon and other nanotubes, surface nanowires and nanodots, and graphene nanoflakes; effect of chemical impurities on the large-scale mechanical behavior of solids.

Suzanne Walker, Professor of Microbiology and Molecular Genetics (Medical School); Ph.D., Princeton, 1992. Chemical biology: synthetic organic chemistry applied to the study of biochemical molecules, enzymology, mechanism of action of antibiotics.

126   www.petersonsbooks.com

Peterson's Graduate Programs in the Physical Sciences, Mathematics, Agricultural Sciences, the Environment & Natural Resources 2014

KENT STATE UNIVERSITY
Department of Chemistry and Biochemistry

Programs of Study

The Department of Chemistry and Biochemistry offers programs leading to the Master of Science (M.S.) and Doctor of Philosophy (Ph.D.) degrees in the traditional divisions of analytical, inorganic, organic, and physical chemistry and biochemistry. A variety of interdisciplinary areas are covered in bioanalytical chemistry, bioinorganic chemistry, biophysics, and molecular/cell biology. Faculty members also have research interests in the specialty areas of liquid crystals, photonic materials, spectroscopy, nanomaterials, separations, and surface science.

Graduate students are required to complete a program of core courses in their area of specialization and at least one (for M.S. candidates) or two (for Ph.D. candidates) elective courses in other areas of chemistry. The extraordinary breadth of the program gives students considerable flexibility in curriculum design, ensuring a modern and dynamic graduate education. At the end of the second year, doctoral students must pass a written examination in their field of specialization and defend an original research proposal for their dissertation. Students typically complete their doctoral program with their thesis defense after 4.5 years.

Research Facilities

Kent State University is home to excellent research facilities. The chemistry department has advanced NMR, X-ray, mass spectrometry, and proteomics core facilities. Research laboratories are located primarily in Williams Hall and the attached Science Research Laboratory. In addition, excellent materials' characterization facilities and one of the largest academic clean room facilities in the nation are housed in the nearby Liquid Crystal Institute. A confocal microscopy core facility located in the biology department is also available to chemistry students. Williams Hall houses two large lecture halls, classrooms, undergraduate and research laboratories, chemical stockrooms, and glass and electronics shops. A machine shop, which is jointly operated with the physics department, is located in adjoining Smith Hall. Spectrometers include 500-MHz, 400-MHz (solids), and 300-MHz high-resolution NMR instruments; electrospray, MALDI-TOF, LC/ESI, protein chip SELDI mass spectrometers; various high-end FT-IR spectrometers, including a focal plane array FT-IR microscope for spectroscopic imaging; photon-counting fluorometer; circular dichroism; ESR, FPLC, UV/visible spectrometers; AA/AE equipment; and an EDX-700 energy dispersive X-ray spectrometer. An X-ray facility includes a Siemens D5000 Powder diffractometer and a Bruker AXS CCD instrument for single-crystal structural elucidation. Equipment available in specialty areas includes a microwave spectrometer, an LCQ electrospray mass spectrometer with MS/MS capability, a phosphorimager, Microcal VP DSC and ITC calorimeters, Bruker Vector 33 FTIR-NIR, Jobin Yvon Raman spectrometer with inverted microscope, laser tweezer instrumentation, particle sizer, Cary Eclipse fluorescence spectrophotometer, MF^2 Jobin Yvon fluorescence lifetime spectrometer, fluorescence correlation spectrometer, ThermoFinnigan Polaris Q115W GC-MS, a BAS electrochemical analyzer, various preparative centrifuges, a molecular dynamic Typhoon 8600 imaging system, and PCR and DNA sequencing and cell culture facilities. Individual research groups in the Department of Chemistry and Biochemistry maintain a variety of computer systems, including PCs and workstations. High-performance computing is made possible with access to the Ohio Supercomputer Center, which maintains Cray T94, Cray T3E, IBM SP2, and SGI Origin 2000 supercomputers. The Department has advanced molecular modeling facilities, including Cerius, Felix, Hyperchem, InsightII/Discover, Macromodel, and Spartan packages for modeling surfaces and interfaces, polymers, proteins, and nucleic acids, as well as facilities for performing ab initio calculations of molecular properties and molecular dynamics. A 3-D immersive classroom equipped with a rear projection system that generates 6' x 7' three-dimensional images when viewed with shutter glasses is available in Williams Hall and is frequently used for a variety of graduate classes. The University Library provides online access to virtually all chemical/biochemical journals as well as a broad variety of chemical databases, including the Chemical Abstracts SciFinder Service.

Financial Aid

Graduate students are generously supported through teaching and research assistantships as well as University fellowships. Students in good academic standing are guaranteed appointments for periods of at least 4½ years (Ph.D. candidates) or 2½ years (M.S. candidates). Stipends for 2013–14 range from $19,500 (M.S.) to $21,500 (Ph.D.) for a twelve-month appointment. A $1,010 credit is made toward the University's health insurance plan. First-year bonuses and renewable merit fellowships providing an additional $2,500 per year are available to outstanding doctoral applicants. In addition, first-year bonuses of $1,250 are available for highly talented students pursuing their Ph.D. in physical chemistry. Advanced Ph.D. students are typically funded through research assistantships ($21,500 or higher) provided by their respective advisors.

Cost of Study

Graduate tuition and fees for the 2013–14 academic year are $7,488, for which a tuition scholarship is provided.

Living and Housing Costs

Rooms in the graduate hall of residence are $3,234 to $4,318 per semester; married students' apartments may be rented for $830 per month (all utilities included). Information concerning off-campus housing may be obtained from the University housing office. Costs vary widely, but apartments typically rent for $600 to $700 per month.

Student Group

The ethnically diverse and highly talented chemistry graduate student population currently numbers about 50. There are approximately 28,000 students enrolled at the main campus of Kent State University; 13,000 additional students attend the seven regional campuses.

Location

Kent, a college town of about 28,000, is located 35 miles southeast of Cleveland and 12 miles east of Akron in a peaceful suburban setting. Kent offers the cultural advantages of a major metropolitan complex as well as the relaxed pace of semi-rural living. There are a number of music (e.g., Kent State's folk festival and free chamber music concerts in the summer), theater, and visual art groups at the University and in the community. Blossom Music Center, the summer home of the Cleveland Orchestra and the site of Kent State's cooperative programs in art, music, and theater, is only 15 miles from the main campus. This beautiful outdoor concert venue is also the site for many critically acclaimed rock concerts throughout the summer months. The newly expanded Akron and Cleveland art museums are within easy reach of the campus. Cleveland is also the home of the world-renowned Rock and Roll Hall of Fame and several professional sport teams. There are a wide variety of recreational facilities available on the campus and within the local area, including West Branch State Park and the Cuyahoga Valley National Park. Nearby Lake Erie and its beaches offer a broad range of water recreational activities. Winter activities include

Peterson's Graduate Programs in the Physical Sciences, Mathematics, Agricultural Sciences, the Environment & Natural Resources 2014

www.petersonsbooks.com **127**

ice skating as well as downhill and cross-country skiing. Kent State's state-of-the-art recreation and wellness center is available for graduate students free of charge.

The University

Established in 1910, Kent State University is one of Ohio's largest and oldest state universities. The campus contains 820 acres of wooded hillsides plus an airport and an eighteen-hole golf course. There are approximately 100 buildings on the main campus. Bachelor's, master's, and doctoral degrees are offered in more than thirty subject areas. The full-time faculty numbers approximately 1,200.

Applying

The online application system for the graduate program is located at: http://www.kent.edu/admissions/apply/. To ensure full consideration, candidates for admission for the upcoming fall semester should make certain that all their application material is received by the University no later than January 10. However, applications will be accepted until all positions are filled. In the case that late applications cannot be considered for fall admission, they will be automatically considered for admission the following spring semester. A limited number of positions are available for spring admission. Candidates should ensure that their application package is complete no later than September 1.

Application material must include all pertinent transcripts, general GRE exam, personal statement, three letters of recommendation, and a CV/resume. Domestic applicants can send all application materials to: Research and Graduate Studies, Office of Graduate Services, 16 Cartwright Hall, Kent State University, P. O. Box 5190, Kent, Ohio 44242-0001.

Foreign students must also provide TOEFL or IELTS exam scores. The minimum cutoff for the TOEFL is 525 on the paper-based exam, and 71 on the Internet-based test. The minimum cutoff for the IELTS is a score of six. Although the subject GRE is not required, candidates are encouraged to provide a subject GRE to strengthen their file. International applicants can send all application materials to: Office of International Affairs, Kent State University, 106 Van Campen Hall, 21 Loop Road, Kent, Ohio 44242, U.S.A.

Correspondence and Information

General Correspondence:
Graduate Coordinator
Department of Chemistry and Biochemistry
Kent State University
Kent, Ohio 44242
Phone: 330-672-2032
Fax: 330-672-3816
E-mail: chemgc@kent.edu
Website: http://www.kent.edu/chemistry

THE FACULTY AND THEIR RESEARCH

Research groups are supported through grants awarded by the National Science Foundation, the National Institutes of Health, the Department of Energy, the Department of Defense, and other federal and state funding agencies.

Soumitra Basu, Assistant Professor; Ph.D., Thomas Jefferson, 1996. Biochemistry: molecular modulation of RNA function, anticancer therapeutics using RNAi, alternative translation modes with implications for tumor angiogenesis, chemical modification of RNA, toxicoribonomics.

Nicola E. Brasch, Associate Professor; Ph.D., Otago (New Zealand), 1994. Bioinorganic and medicinal chemistry: vitamin B_{12} and the B_{12}-dependent enzyme reactions; vanadium chemistry; inorganic drug delivery systems; synthesis, kinetics, and mechanism.

Scott D. Bunge, Assistant Professor; Ph.D., Georgia Tech, 2001. Inorganic chemistry: molecular design, organometallics, coordination chemistry, air-sensitive synthesis, catalysis, X-ray crystallography, thin films, nanomaterials.

Bansidhar Datta, Associate Professor; Ph.D., Nebraska–Lincoln, 1989. Biochemistry and molecular biology: mechanism of protein synthesis initiation in mammals; studies of posttranslational modifications, such as O-glycosylation and phosphorylation of translational regulator, p67; molecular cloning of translational regulatory proteins; studies of the evolutionary origins of the regulatory/structural domains in p67.

Barry Dunietz, Assistant Professor; Ph.D., Columbia, 2000. Physical and quantum chemistry: electron transport processes through molecular and nanoscale bridges; proton transfer reactions and catalytic centers in enzymes; charge transfer in photovoltaic (PV) materials.

Roger B. Gregory, Professor; Ph.D., Sheffield (England), 1980. Biochemistry: protein conformational dynamics; the characterization of dynamic substructures in proteins; protein hydration and glass transition behavior; proteomics: development and application of high-sensitivity methods for protein characterization, including protein-protein interactions and protein chemical modifications.

Songping D. Huang, Associate Professor; Ph.D., Michigan State, 1993. Inorganic chemistry: molecule-based magnetic and nonlinear optical materials, organic conductors and superconductors, novel microporous and mesoporous materials, synthesis and crystal growth of metal oxides and chalcogenides.

Mietek Jaroniec, Professor; Ph.D., Lublin (Poland), 1976. Physical/analytical/materials chemistry: adsorption and chromatography at the gas/solid and liquid/solid interface; synthesis and modification of adsorbents, catalysts, and chromatographic packings with tailored surface and structural properties; self-assembled organic-inorganic nanomaterials; ordered mesoporous carbons synthesized via templating and imprinting methods; characterization of nanoporous materials.

Anatoly K. Khitrin, Associate Professor; Ph.D., Institute of Chemical Physics, Russian Academy of Sciences, 1985. Physical chemistry: NMR techniques, theory of magnetic resonance, material science, quantum computing and microimaging.

Hanbin Mao, Assistant Professor; Ph.D., Texas A&M, 2003. Bioanalytical and biophysical chemistry: micro total analysis systems ("lab-on-a-chip"), laser and magnetic tweezers, single-molecule DNA and DNA-protein interactions, drug-screening.

Paul Sampson, Professor; Ph.D., Birmingham (England), 1983. Synthetic organic chemistry: development of new synthetic methods; synthetic (stereoselective) organofluorine chemistry, with applications to the synthesis of fluorinated liquid crystals and carbohydrate analogs; development of new organometallic synthons as building blocks for organic synthesis.

Alexander J. Seed, Associate Professor; Ph.D., Hull (England), 1995. Organic chemistry, design, synthesis, and physical characterization of liquid crystals; ferroelectric, antiferroelectric, and high-twisting power materials for optical applications; new heterocyclic synthetic methodology.

Diane Stroup, Associate Professor; Ph.D., Ohio State, 1992. Biochemistry: control of mammalian gene expression by regulation of transcriptional and posttranscriptional processes, study of nuclear hormone receptors and signal transduction events.

Michael J. Tubergen, Associate Professor; Ph.D., Chicago, 1991. Physical chemistry: high-resolution microwave spectroscopy for molecular structure determination of hydrogen-bonded complexes and biological molecules.

Robert J. Twieg, Distinguished Professor; Ph.D., Berkeley, 1976. Organic chemistry and materials science: development of organic and polymeric materials with novel electronic and optoelectronic properties, including nonlinear optical chromophores, photorefractive chromophores, organic semiconductors, fluorescent tags, and liquid crystals, with emphasis on applications and durability issues.

John L. West, Professor; Ph.D., Carnegie Mellon, 1980. Physical chemistry: materials science; liquid crystal polymer formulations for display applications, basic studies of liquid crystal alignment.

SELECTED PUBLICATIONS

Basu, S., and S. A. Strobel. Identification of specific monovalent metal ion binding sites within RNA. *Methods* 122:264–75, 2001.

Basu, S., A. Szewczak, M. Cocco, and S. A. Strobel. Direct detection of specific monovalent metal ion binding to a DNA G-quartet by ^{205}T1 NMR. *J. Am. Chem. Soc.* 122:3240–1, 2000.

128 www.petersonsbooks.com

Peterson's Graduate Programs in the Physical Sciences, Mathematics, Agricultural Sciences, the Environment & Natural Resources 2014

Basu, S., and S. A. Strobel. Thiophilic metal ion rescue of phosphorothioate interference within the Tetrahymena ribozyme P4-P6 domain. *RNA* 5:1399–407, 1999.

Hannibal, L., C. A. Smith, D. W. Jacobsen, and **N. E. Brasch.** Nitroxylcob(III) alamin: Synthesis and X-ray structural characterization. *Angew. Chem.* 46:5140, 2007.

Hannibal, L., et al. **(N. E. Brasch).** X-ray structural characterization of imidazolylcobalamin and histidinylcobalamin: Cobalamin models for aquacobalamin bound to the B$_{12}$ transporter protein transcobalamin. *Inorg. Chem.* 46:3613, 2007.

Mukherjee, R., et al. **(N. E. Brasch).** Structural and spectroscopic evidence for the formation of trinuclear and tetranuclear V(III)/carboxylate complexes of acetate and related derivatives in aqueous solution. *Inorg. Chem.* 46:1575, 2007.

Bunge, S. D., J. A. Bertke, and T. L. Cleland. Synthesis, structure, and reactivity of low-coordinate 1,1,3,3-tetraethylguanidinate complexes. *Inorg. Chem.* 48(16):8037–43, 2009.

Bunge, S. D., J. A. Ocana, T. L. Cleland, and J. L. Steele. Synthetic, structural, and theoretical investigation of guanidinate complexes containing planar Cu$_6$ cores. *Inorg. Chem.* 48(11):4619–21, 2009.

Monegan, J. D., and **S. D. Bunge.** Structurally characterized 1,1,3,3-tetramethylguanidine solvated magnesium aryloxide complexes: [Mg(μ-OEt)(DBP)(H-TMG)]$_2$, [Mg(μ -OBc)(DBP)(H-TMG)]$_2$, [Mg(μ -TMBA) (DBP)(H-TMG)]$_2$, [Mg(μ -DPP)(DBP)(H-TMG)]$_2$, [Mg(BMP)$_2$(H-TMG)$_2$], [Mg(O-2,6-Ph$_2$C$_6$H$_3$)$_2$ (H-TMG)$_2$]. *Inorg. Chem.* 48(7):3248–56, 2009.

Datta, B., et al. Autoproteolysis of rat p67 generates several peptide fragments: The N-terminal fragment, p26, is required for the protection of eIF2 alpha from phosphorylation. *Biochemistry* 46(11):3465, 2007.

Ghosh, A., et al. **(B. Datta).** The N-terminal lysine residue-rich domain II and the 340-430 amino acid segment of eukaryotic initiation factor 2-associated glycoprotein p67 are the binding sites for the gamma subunit of eIF2. *Exp. Cell Res.* 312(16):3184, 2006.

Datta, B., et al. The binding between p67 and eukaryotic initiation factor 2 plays important roles in the protection of eIF2 alpha from phosphorylation by kinases. *Arch. Biochem. Biophys.* 452(2):138, 2006.

Zheng, S., et al. **(B. Dunietz).** *Ab initio* study of the emissive charge-transfer states of solvated chromophore-functionalized silsesquioxanes. *J. Am. Chem. Soc.* 134(16):6944–7, 2012.

Phillips, H., et al. **(B. Dunietz).** Calculating off-site excitations in symmetric donor-acceptor systems via time-dependent density functional theory with range-separated density functionals. *J. Chem. Theor. Comput.* 8(8):2661–8, 2012.

Balachandran, J., et al. **(B. Dunietz).** End-group-induced charge transfer in molecular junctions: Effect on electronic-structure and thermopower. *J. Phys. Chem. Lett.* 3(15):1962–7, 2012.

Roh, J. H., et al. **(R. B. Gregory).** Influence of hydration on the dynamics of lysozyme. *Biophys. J.* 91(7):2573, 2006.

Roh, J. H., et al. **(R. B. Gregory).** Onsets of anharmonicity in protein dynamics. *Phys. Rev. Lett.* 95(3): 038101, 2005.

Gregory, R. B. Protein hydration and glass transitions. In *The Properties of Water in Foods*, pp. 55–99, ed. D. Reid. New York: Chapman-Hall, 1997.

Fu, D. W., et al. **(S. D. Huang).** Dielectric anisotropy of a homochiral trinuclear nickel(II) complex. *J. Am. Chem. Soc.* 129(17):5346, 2007.

Ye, Q., et al. **(S. D. Huang).** Ferroelectric metal-organic framework with a high dielectric constant. *J. Am. Chem. Soc.* 128(20):6554, 2006.

Vanchura, B. A., et al. **(S. D. Huang).** Direct synthesis of mesostructured lamellar molybdenum disulfides using a molten neutral n-alkylamine as the solvent and template. *J. Am. Chem. Soc.* 124(41):12090, 2002.

Celer, E. B., and **M. Jaroniec.** Temperature-programmed microwave-assisted synthesis of SBA-15 ordered mesoporous silica. *J. Am. Chem. Soc.* 128(44):14408, 2006.

Gierszal, K. P., and **M. Jaroniec.** Carbons with extremely large volume of uniform mesopores synthesized by carbonization of phenolic resin film formed on colloidal silica template. *J. Am. Chem. Soc.* 128(31):10026, 2006.

Jaroniec, M. Materials science: Organosilica the conciliator. *Nature* 442(7103):638, 2006.

Lee, J. S., T. Adams, and **A. K. Khitrin.** Experimental demonstration of a stimulated polarization wave in a chain of nuclear spins. *New J. Phys.* 9(4): 83, 2007.

Lee, J. S., and **A. K. Khitrin.** Constant-time method for measuring inter-nuclear distances in static powders. *J. Magn. Reson.* 186:327, 2007.

Lee, J. S., and **A. K. Khitrin.** NMR quantum toys. *Concepts Magn. Reson.* 30A:194, 2007.

Luchette, P., N. Abiy, and **H. Mao.** Microanalysis of clouding process at the single droplet level. *Sensor. Actuator. B Chem.* 128:154–60, 2007.

Mao, H., et al. Temperature control methods in a laser-tweezers system. *Biophys. J.* 89:1308, 2005.

Mao, H., P. Cremer, and M. Manson. A versatile, sensitive microfluidic assay for bacterial chemotaxis. *Proc. Natl. Acad. Sci. U.S.A.* 100:5449, 2003.

Chumachenko, N., and **P. Sampson.** Synthesis of beta-hydroxy sulfones via opening of hydrophilic epoxides with zinc sulfinates in aqueous media. *Tetrahedron* 62(18):4540, 2006.

Novikov, Y. Y., and **P. Sampson.** 1-bromo-1-lithioethene: A practical reagent in organic synthesis. *J. Org. Chem.* 70(25):10247, 2005.

Chumachenko, N., **P. Sampson,** A. D. Hunter, and M. Zeller. β-acyloxysulfonyl tethers for intramolecular Diels-Alder cycloaddition reactions. *Org. Lett.* 7:3203, 2005.

Sybo, B., et al. **(P. Sampson** and **A. J. Seed).** 1,3,4-Thiadiazole-2-carboxylate esters: New synthetic methodology for the preparation of an elusive family of self-organizing materials. *J. Mater. Chem.* 17(32):3406–11, 2007.

Seed, A. J. Synthesis of self-organizing mesogenic materials containing a sulfur-based five-membered heterocyclic core. *Chem. Soc. Rev.* 36(12):2046–69, 2007.

McCoy, B. K., et al. **(A. J. Seed).** Smectic-$C^*\alpha$ phase with two coexistent helical pitch values and a first-order smectic-$C^*\alpha$ to smectic-C^* transition. *Phys. Rev. E* 75(5-1): 051706, 2007.

Tubergen, M. J., et al. Rotational spectra and conformational structures of 1-phenyl-2-propanol, methamphetamine, and 1-phenyl-2-propanone. *J. Phys. Chem. A* 110(49):13188, 2006.

Tubergen, M. J., et al. Rotational spectra, nuclear quadrupole hyperfine tensors, and conformational structures of the mustard gas simulent 2-chloroethyl ethyl sulfide. *J. Mol. Spectros.* 233(2):180, 2005.

Tubergen, M. J., C. R. Torok, and R. J. Lavrich. Effect of solvent on molecular conformation: Microwave spectra and structures of 2-aminoethanol van der Waals complexes. *J. Chem. Phys.* 119:8397–403, 2003.

Wang, H., et al. **(R. J. Twieg).** The influence of tetrahydroquinoline rings in dicyanomethylenedihydrofuran (DCDHF) single-molecule fluorophores. *Tetrahedron* 63(1):103, 2007.

Lu, Z. K., et al. **(R. J. Twieg).** Long-wavelength analogue of PRODAN: Synthesis and properties of Anthradan, a fluorophore with a 2,6-donor-acceptor anthracene structure. *J. Org. Chem.* 71(26):9651, 2006.

Ellman, B., et al. **(R. J. Twieg).** High mobility, low dispersion hole transport in 1,4-diiodobenzene. *Adv. Mater.* 18(17):2284, 2006.

Li, F. H., et al. **(J. West).** Orientational coupling amplification in ferroelectric nematic colloids. *Phys. Rev. Lett.* 97(14): 147801, 2006.

Buyuktanir, E. A., et al. **(J. L. West).** Field-induced polymer wall formation in a bistable smectic-A liquid crystal display. *Appl. Phys. Lett.* 89(3): 031101, 2006.

West, J. L., et al. Colloidal particles at a nematic-isotropic interface: Effects of confinement. *Eur. Phys. J. E* 20(2):237, 2006.

Peterson's Graduate Programs in the Physical Sciences, Mathematics, Agricultural Sciences, the Environment & Natural Resources 2014

www.petersonsbooks.com **129**

Section 3
Geosciences

This section contains a directory of institutions offering graduate work in geosciences. Additional information about programs listed in the directory may be obtained by writing directly to the dean of a graduate school or chair of a department at the address given in the directory.

For programs offering related work, see all other areas in this book. In the other guides in this series:

Graduate Programs in the Humanities, Arts & Social Sciences

See *Geography*

Graduate Programs in the Biological/Biomedical Sciences & Health-Related Medical Professions

See *Biological and Biomedical Sciences, Biophysics,* and *Botany and Plant Biology*

Graduate Programs in Engineering & Applied Sciences

See *Aerospace/Aeronautical Engineering; Agricultural Engineering and Bioengineering; Civil and Environmental Engineering; Energy and Power Engineering (Nuclear Engineering); Engineering and Applied Sciences; Geological, Mineral/Mining,* and *Petroleum Engineering;* and *Mechanical Engineering and Mechanics*

CONTENTS

Program Directories

Geochemistry

California Institute of Technology, Division of Geological and Planetary Sciences, Pasadena, CA 91125-0001. Offers environmental science and engineering (MS, PhD); geobiology (MS, PhD); geochemistry (MS, PhD); geology (MS, PhD); geophysics (MS, PhD); planetary science (MS, PhD). *Faculty:* 43 full-time (8 women). *Students:* 110 full-time (52 women); includes 9 minority (1 Black or African American, non-Hispanic/Latino; 7 Asian, non-Hispanic/Latino; 1 Hispanic/Latino), 30 international. Average age 26. 225 applicants, 19% accepted, 24 enrolled. In 2012, 7 master's, 13 doctorates awarded. *Degree requirements:* For doctorate, thesis/dissertation. *Entrance requirements:* For doctorate, GRE General Test. Additional exam requirements/recommendations for international students: Required—TOEFL; Recommended—IELTS, TWE. *Application deadline:* For fall admission, 1/1 for domestic and international students. Application fee: $80. Electronic applications accepted. *Financial support:* In 2012–13, 19 fellowships with full tuition reimbursements (averaging $29,000 per year), 72 research assistantships with full tuition reimbursements (averaging $29,000 per year) were awarded; teaching assistantships with full tuition reimbursements, institutionally sponsored loans, scholarships/grants, health care benefits, and unspecified assistantships also available. Financial award applicants required to submit FAFSA. *Faculty research:* Planetary surfaces, evolution of anaerobic respiratory processes, structural geology and tectonics, theoretical and numerical seismology, global biogeochemical cycles. *Unit head:* Dr. Kenneth A. Farley, Chairman, 626-395-6111, Fax: 626-795-6028, E-mail: dianb@gps.caltech.edu. *Application contact:* Dr. Robert W. Clayton, Academic Officer, 626-395-6909, Fax: 626-795-6028, E-mail: dianb@gps.caltech.edu. Website: http://www.gps.caltech.edu/.

California State University, Fullerton, Graduate Studies, College of Natural Science and Mathematics, Department of Chemistry and Biochemistry, Fullerton, CA 92834-9480. Offers chemistry (MA, MS); geochemistry (MS). Part-time programs available. *Students:* 5 full-time (1 woman), 23 part-time (6 women); includes 11 minority (6 Asian, non-Hispanic/Latino; 4 Hispanic/Latino; 1 Two or more races, non-Hispanic/Latino), 1 international. Average age 27. 50 applicants, 40% accepted, 11 enrolled. In 2012, 10 master's awarded. *Degree requirements:* For master's, thesis, departmental qualifying exam. *Entrance requirements:* For master's, minimum GPA of 2.5 in last 60 units of course work, major in chemistry or related field. Application fee: $55. *Financial support:* Research assistantships, teaching assistantships, career-related internships or fieldwork, Federal Work-Study, institutionally sponsored loans, and scholarships/grants available. Support available to part-time students. Financial award application deadline: 3/1; financial award applicants required to submit FAFSA. *Unit head:* Dr. Christopher Meyer, Chair, 657-278-3621. *Application contact:* Admissions/Applications, 657-278-2371.

Colorado School of Mines, Graduate School, Department of Chemistry and Geochemistry and Department of Geology and Geological Engineering, Program in Geochemistry, Golden, CO 80401-1887. Offers MS, PhD. Part-time programs available. *Students:* 6 full-time (4 women). Average age 29. 24 applicants, 13% accepted, 1 enrolled. *Degree requirements:* For master's, thesis (for some programs); for doctorate, comprehensive exam, thesis/dissertation. *Entrance requirements:* For master's and doctorate, GRE General Test. Additional exam requirements/recommendations for international students: Required—TOEFL (minimum score 550 paper-based; 80 iBT). *Application deadline:* For fall admission, 1/15 for domestic and international students; for spring admission, 10/15 priority date for domestic students, 10/15 for international students. Application fee: $50 ($70 for international students). Electronic applications accepted. *Financial support:* In 2012–13, fellowships with full tuition reimbursements (averaging $20,000 per year), research assistantships with full tuition reimbursements (averaging $20,000 per year), teaching assistantships with full tuition reimbursements (averaging $20,000 per year) were awarded; scholarships/grants, health care benefits, and unspecified assistantships also available. Financial award application deadline: 1/15; financial award applicants required to submit FAFSA. *Faculty research:* Geochemical analysis, organic geochemistry, hydrochemical systems, environmental microbiology, process control programming. *Unit head:* Dr. Dan Knauss, Department Head, 303-273-3625, Fax: 303-273-3629, E-mail: dknauss@mines.edu. *Application contact:* Tina Voelker, Associate Professor, 303-273-3152, Fax: 303-273-3629, E-mail: tvoelker@mines.edu. Website: http://geochem.mines.edu.

Colorado School of Mines, Graduate School, Department of Geology and Geological Engineering, Golden, CO 80401-1887. Offers geochemistry (MS, PMS, PhD); geological engineering (ME, MS, PhD); geology (MS, PhD). Part-time programs available. *Faculty:* 26 full-time (12 women), 7 part-time/adjunct (3 women). *Students:* 152 full-time (48 women), 34 part-time (10 women); includes 16 minority (1 Black or African American, non-Hispanic/Latino; 2 American Indian or Alaska Native, non-Hispanic/Latino; 2 Asian, non-Hispanic/Latino; 11 Hispanic/Latino), 27 international. Average age 31. 287 applicants, 48% accepted, 54 enrolled. In 2012, 35 master's, 3 doctorates awarded. *Degree requirements:* For master's, thesis (for some programs); for doctorate, comprehensive exam, thesis/dissertation. *Entrance requirements:* For master's and doctorate, GRE General Test. Additional exam requirements/recommendations for international students: Required—TOEFL (minimum score 550 paper-based; 80 iBT). *Application*

deadline: For fall admission, 1/15 for domestic and international students; for spring admission, 10/15 for domestic and international students. Application fee: $50 ($70 for international students). Electronic applications accepted. *Financial support:* In 2012–13, 98 students received support, including 14 fellowships with full tuition reimbursements available (averaging $21,120 per year), 65 research assistantships with full tuition reimbursements available (averaging $21,120 per year), 19 teaching assistantships with full tuition reimbursements available (averaging $21,120 per year); scholarships/grants, health care benefits, and unspecified assistantships also available. Financial award application deadline: 1/15; financial award applicants required to submit FAFSA. *Faculty research:* Predictive sediment modeling, petrophysics, aquifer-contaminant flow modeling, water-rock interactions, geotechnical engineering. *Total annual research expenditures:* $2.6 million. *Unit head:* Dr. John Humphrey, Head, 303-273-3819, Fax: 303-273-3859, E-mail: jhumphre@mines.edu. *Application contact:* Dr. Christian Shorey, Lecturer, 303-273-3556, Fax: 303-273-3859, E-mail: cshorey@mines.edu. Website: http://geology.mines.edu.

Columbia University, Graduate School of Arts and Sciences, Division of Natural Sciences, Department of Earth and Environmental Sciences, New York, NY 10027. Offers geochemistry (M Phil, MA, PhD); geodetic sciences (M Phil, MA, PhD); geophysics (M Phil, MA, PhD); oceanography (M Phil, MA, PhD). *Degree requirements:* For master's, thesis or alternative, fieldwork, written exam; for doctorate, one foreign language, thesis/dissertation. *Entrance requirements:* For master's and doctorate, GRE General Test, GRE Subject Test, major in natural or physical science. Additional exam requirements/recommendations for international students: Required—TOEFL. *Faculty research:* Structural geology and stratigraphy, petrology, paleontology, rare gas, isotope and aqueous geochemistry.

Cornell University, Graduate School, Graduate Fields of Engineering, Field of Geological Sciences, Ithaca, NY 14853. Offers economic geology (M Eng, MS, PhD); engineering geology (M Eng, MS, PhD); environmental geophysics (M Eng, MS, PhD); general geology (M Eng, MS, PhD); geobiology (M Eng, MS, PhD); geochemistry and isotope geology (M Eng, MS, PhD); geohydrology (M Eng, MS, PhD); geomorphology (M Eng, MS, PhD); geophysics (M Eng, MS, PhD); geotectonics (M Eng, MS, PhD); marine geology (MS, PhD); mineralogy (M Eng, MS, PhD); paleontology (M Eng, MS, PhD); petroleum geology (M Eng, MS, PhD); petrology (M Eng, MS, PhD); planetary geology (M Eng, MS, PhD); Precambrian geology (M Eng, MS, PhD); Quaternary geology (M Eng, MS, PhD); rock mechanics (M Eng, MS, PhD); sedimentology (M Eng, MS, PhD); seismology (M Eng, MS, PhD); stratigraphy (M Eng, MS, PhD); structural geology (M Eng, MS, PhD). *Faculty:* 37 full-time (5 women). *Students:* 32 full-time (13 women); includes 5 minority (2 Asian, non-Hispanic/Latino; 1 Hispanic/Latino; 2 Two or more races, non-Hispanic/Latino), 8 international. Average age 27. 58 applicants, 17% accepted, 6 enrolled. In 2012, 6 master's, 3 doctorates awarded. *Degree requirements:* For master's, thesis (MS); for doctorate, comprehensive exam, thesis/dissertation. *Entrance requirements:* For master's and doctorate, GRE General Test, 3 letters of recommendation. Additional exam requirements/recommendations for international students: Required—TOEFL (minimum score 550 paper-based; 77 iBT). *Application deadline:* For fall admission, 1/15 priority date for domestic students. Applications are processed on a rolling basis. Application fee: $95. Electronic applications accepted. *Financial support:* In 2012–13, 26 students received support, including 9 fellowships with full tuition reimbursements available, 16 research assistantships with full tuition reimbursements available, 1 teaching assistantship with full tuition reimbursement available; institutionally sponsored loans, scholarships/grants, health care benefits, tuition waivers (full and partial), and unspecified assistantships also available. Financial award applicants required to submit FAFSA. *Faculty research:* Geophysics, structural geology, petrology, geochemistry, geodynamics. *Unit head:* Director of Graduate Studies, 607-255-5466, Fax: 607-254-4780. *Application contact:* Graduate Field Assistant, 607-255-5466, Fax: 607-254-4780, E-mail: gradprog@geology.cornell.edu. Website: http://www.gradschool.cornell.edu/fields.php?id-30&a-2.

Georgia Institute of Technology, Graduate Studies and Research, College of Sciences, School of Earth and Atmospheric Sciences, Atlanta, GA 30332-0340. Offers atmospheric chemistry, aerosols and clouds (MS, PhD); dynamics of weather and climate (MS, PhD); geochemistry (MS, PhD); geophysics (MS, PhD); oceanography (MS, PhD); paleoclimate (MS, PhD); planetary science (MS, PhD); remote sensing (MS, PhD). Part-time programs available. Terminal master's awarded for partial completion of doctoral program. *Degree requirements:* For master's, thesis or alternative; for doctorate, comprehensive exam, thesis/dissertation. *Entrance requirements:* For master's, GRE, letters of recommendation; for doctorate, GRE, academic transcripts, letters of recommendation, personal statement. Additional exam requirements/recommendations for international students: Required—TOEFL (minimum score 550 paper-based; 79 iBT). *Faculty research:* Geophysics; atmospheric chemistry, aerosols and clouds; dynamics of weather and climate; geochemistry; oceanography; paleoclimate; planetary science; remote sensing.

Georgia State University, College of Arts and Sciences, Department of Chemistry, Atlanta, GA 30302-3083. Offers analytical chemistry (MS, PhD);

132 www.petersonsbooks.com

Peterson's Graduate Programs in the Physical Sciences, Mathematics, Agricultural Sciences, the Environment & Natural Resources 2014

biochemistry (MS, PhD); bioinformatics (MS, PhD); biophysical chemistry (PhD); computational chemistry (MS, PhD); geochemistry (PhD); organic/medicinal chemistry (MS, PhD); physical chemistry (MS). PhD in geochemistry offered jointly with Department of Geology. Part-time programs available. *Faculty:* 38 full-time (11 women), 10 part-time/adjunct (3 women). *Students:* 107 full-time (57 women), 6 part-time (3 women); includes 25 minority (13 Black or African American, non-Hispanic/Latino; 1 American Indian or Alaska Native, non-Hispanic/Latino; 6 Asian, non-Hispanic/Latino; 4 Hispanic/Latino; 1 Two or more races, non-Hispanic/Latino), 57 international. Average age 28. 125 applicants, 39% accepted, 36 enrolled. In 2012, 28 master's, 12 doctorates awarded. Terminal master's awarded for partial completion of doctoral program. *Degree requirements:* For master's, one foreign language, comprehensive exam (for some programs), thesis (for some programs); for doctorate, one foreign language, comprehensive exam, thesis/dissertation. *Entrance requirements:* For master's and doctorate, GRE. Additional exam requirements/recommendations for international students: Required—TOEFL (minimum score 550 paper-based, 80 iBT) or IELTS (minimum score 6.5). *Application deadline:* For fall admission, 7/1 priority date for domestic students, 7/1 for international students; for winter admission, 11/15 priority date for domestic students, 11/15 for international students; for spring admission, 4/15 priority date for domestic students, 4/15 for international students. Applications are processed on a rolling basis. Application fee: $50. Electronic applications accepted. *Expenses:* Tuition, state resident: full-time $8064; part-time $336 per credit hour. Tuition, nonresident: full-time $28,800; part-time $1200 per credit hour. *Required fees:* $2128; $1064 per semester. Tuition and fees vary according to course load and program. *Financial support:* Fellowships with full tuition reimbursements, research assistantships with full tuition reimbursements, and teaching assistantships with full tuition reimbursements available. *Faculty research:* Analytical chemistry, biological/biochemistry, biophysical/computational chemistry, chemical education, organic/medicinal chemistry. *Total annual research expenditures:* $4 million. *Unit head:* Dr. Binghe Wang, Department Chair, 404-413-5500, Fax: 404-413-5506, E-mail: chemchair@gsu.edu. *Application contact:* Rita S. Bennett, Academic Specialist, 404-413-5497, Fax: 404-413-5505, E-mail: rsb423@gsu.edu. Website: http://chemistry.gsu.edu/.

Indiana University Bloomington, University Graduate School, College of Arts and Sciences, Department of Geological Sciences, Bloomington, IN 47405-7000. Offers biogeochemistry (MS, PhD); economic geology (MS, PhD); geobiology (MS, PhD); geophysics, structural geology and tectonics (MS, PhD); hydrogeology (MS, PhD); mineralogy (MS, PhD); stratigraphy and sedimentology (MS, PhD). *Faculty:* 17 full-time (1 woman). *Students:* 63 full-time (23 women), 3 part-time (1 woman); includes 3 minority (1 Black or African American, non-Hispanic/Latino; 1 Hispanic/Latino; 1 Two or more races, non-Hispanic/Latino), 15 international. Average age 29. 82 applicants, 26% accepted, 15 enrolled. In 2012, 10 master's, 4 doctorates awarded. Terminal master's awarded for partial completion of doctoral program. *Degree requirements:* For master's, thesis or alternative; for doctorate, comprehensive exam, thesis/dissertation. *Entrance requirements:* For master's and doctorate, GRE General Test. Additional exam requirements/recommendations for international students: Required—TOEFL. *Application deadline:* For fall admission, 1/15 priority date for domestic students, 12/15 for international students; for spring admission, 9/1 priority date for domestic students, 9/1 for international students. Applications are processed on a rolling basis. Application fee: $55 ($65 for international students). *Financial support:* In 2012–13, fellowships with full tuition reimbursements (averaging $17,300 per year), research assistantships with full tuition reimbursements (averaging $16,370 per year), teaching assistantships with full tuition reimbursements (averaging $15,150 per year) were awarded; career-related internships or fieldwork, Federal Work-Study, and institutionally sponsored loans also available. *Faculty research:* Geophysics, geochemistry, hydrogeology, geobiology, planetary science. *Total annual research expenditures:* $644,299. *Unit head:* Simon Brassell, Chair, 812-855-5581, Fax: 812-855-7899, E-mail: geochair@indiana.edu. *Application contact:* Mary Iverson, Graduate Secretary, 812-855-7214, Fax: 812-855-7899, E-mail: miverson@indiana.edu. Website: http://www.indiana.edu/~geosci/.

Massachusetts Institute of Technology, School of Science, Department of Earth, Atmospheric, and Planetary Sciences, Cambridge, MA 02139. Offers atmospheric chemistry (PhD, Sc D); atmospheric science (SM, PhD, Sc D); chemical oceanography (SM, PhD, Sc D); climate physics and chemistry (SM, PhD, Sc D); earth and planetary sciences (SM); geochemistry (PhD, Sc D); geology (PhD, Sc D); geophysics (PhD, Sc D); marine geology and geophysics (SM, PhD, Sc D); physical oceanography (SM, PhD, Sc D); planetary sciences (PhD, Sc D). *Faculty:* 33 full-time (6 women), 1 (woman) part-time/adjunct. *Students:* 166 full-time (77 women); includes 24 minority (3 Black or African American, non-Hispanic/Latino; 1 American Indian or Alaska Native, non-Hispanic/Latino; 9 Asian, non-Hispanic/Latino; 6 Hispanic/Latino; 5 Two or more races, non-Hispanic/Latino), 58 international. Average age 27. 232 applicants, 23% accepted, 27 enrolled. In 2012, 12 master's, 22 doctorates awarded. Terminal master's awarded for partial completion of doctoral program. *Degree requirements:* For master's, thesis; for doctorate, comprehensive exam, thesis/dissertation. *Entrance requirements:* For master's, GRE General Test; for doctorate, GRE General Test, GRE Subject Test (chemistry or physics for planetary science area). Additional exam requirements/recommendations for international students: Required—TOEFL (minimum score 577 paper-based; 91 iBT), IELTS (minimum score 7). *Application deadline:* For fall admission, 1/5 for domestic and international students; for spring admission, 11/1 for domestic and international students. Application fee: $75. Electronic applications accepted. *Expenses:* *Tuition:* Full-time $41,770; part-time $650 per credit hour. *Required fees:* $280. *Financial support:* In 2012–13, 108 students received support, including 62 fellowships (averaging $30,700 per year), 87 research assistantships (averaging $32,600 per year), 15 teaching assistantships (averaging $30,800 per year); Federal Work-Study, institutionally sponsored loans, scholarships/grants, health care benefits, and unspecified assistantships also available. *Faculty research:* Formation, dynamics and evolution of planetary systems; origin, composition, structure and dynamics of the atmospheres, oceans, surfaces and interiors of the Earth and other planets; evolution and interaction of the physical, chemical, geological and biological components of the Earth system; characterization of past, present and potential future climates and the causes and consequences of climate change; interplay of energy and the environment. *Total annual research expenditures:* $28.1 million. *Unit head:* Prof. Robert van der Hilst, Head, 617-253-2127, Fax: 617-253-8298, E-mail: eapsinfo@mit.edu. *Application contact:* EAPS Education Office, 617-253-3381, Fax: 617-253-8298, E-mail: eapsinfo@mit.edu. Website: http://eapsweb.mit.edu/.

McMaster University, School of Graduate Studies, Faculty of Science, School of Geography and Earth Sciences, Hamilton, ON L8S 4M2, Canada. Offers geochemistry (PhD); geology (M Sc, PhD); human geography (MA, PhD); physical geography (M Sc, PhD). Part-time programs available. Terminal master's awarded for partial completion of doctoral program. *Degree requirements:* For master's, thesis; for doctorate, comprehensive exam, thesis/dissertation. *Entrance requirements:* For master's, minimum B+ average. Additional exam requirements/recommendations for international students: Required—TOEFL (minimum score 550 paper-based).

Missouri University of Science and Technology, Graduate School, Department of Geological Sciences and Engineering, Rolla, MO 65409. Offers geological engineering (MS, DE, PhD); geology and geophysics (MS, PhD), including geochemistry, geology, geophysics, groundwater and environmental geology; petroleum engineering (MS, DE, PhD). Part-time programs available. *Degree requirements:* For master's, thesis optional; for doctorate, comprehensive exam, thesis/dissertation. *Entrance requirements:* For master's, GRE General Test (minimum score 600 quantitative, writing 3.5), minimum GPA of 3.0 in last 4 semesters; for doctorate, GRE General Test (minimum: Q 600, GRE WR 3.5). Additional exam requirements/recommendations for international students: Required—TOEFL. Electronic applications accepted. *Faculty research:* Digital image processing and geographic information systems, mineralogy, igneous and sedimentary petrology-geochemistry, sedimentology groundwater hydrology and contaminant transport.

Montana Tech of The University of Montana, Graduate School, Geosciences Programs, Butte, MT 59701-8997. Offers geochemistry (MS); geological engineering (MS); geology (MS); geophysical engineering (MS); hydrogeological engineering (MS); hydrogeology (MS). Part-time programs available. *Degree requirements:* For master's, comprehensive exam (for some programs), thesis (for some programs). *Entrance requirements:* For master's, GRE General Test, minimum GPA of 3.0. Additional exam requirements/recommendations for international students: Required—TOEFL (minimum score 525 paper-based; 71 iBT). Electronic applications accepted. *Faculty research:* Water resource development, seismic processing, petroleum reservoir characterization, environmental geochemistry, geologic mapping.

New Mexico Institute of Mining and Technology, Graduate Studies, Department of Earth and Environmental Science, Program in Geochemistry, Socorro, NM 87801. Offers MS, PhD. *Students:* 5 full-time (2 women), 1 (woman) part-time; includes 2 minority (1 Hispanic/Latino; 1 Two or more races, non-Hispanic/Latino). Average age 27. *Expenses:* Tuition, state resident: full-time $5043; part-time $280 per credit hour. Tuition, nonresident: full-time $16,682; part-time $927 per credit hour. *Required fees:* $648; $18 per credit hour. $108 per semester. Part-time tuition and fees vary according to course load. *Financial support:* In 2012–13, 4 research assistantships (averaging $19,605 per year) were awarded. *Unit head:* Dr. Gary Axen, Chair, 575-835-5178, Fax: 575-835-6436, E-mail: gaxen@ees.nmt.edu. *Application contact:* Dr. Lorie Liebrock, Dean of Graduate Studies, 575-835-5513, Fax: 575-835-5476, E-mail: graduate@nmt.edu.

Ohio University, Graduate College, College of Arts and Sciences, Department of Geological Sciences, Athens, OH 45701-2979. Offers environmental geochemistry (MS); environmental geology (MS); environmental/hydrology (MS); geology (MS); geology education (MS); geomorphology/surficial processes (MS); geophysics (MS); hydrogeology (MS); sedimentology (MS); structure/tectonics (MS). Part-time programs available. *Degree requirements:* For master's, thesis. *Entrance requirements:* Additional exam requirements/recommendations for international students: Required—TOEFL (minimum score 550 paper-based; 80 iBT) or IELTS (minimum score 6.5). Electronic applications accepted. *Faculty research:* Geoscience education, tectonics, fluvial geomorphology, invertebrate paleontology, mine/hydrology.

University of California, Los Angeles, Graduate Division, College of Letters and Science, Department of Earth and Space Sciences, Program in Geochemistry, Los Angeles, CA 90095. Offers MS, PhD. *Faculty:* 23 full-time (3 women). *Students:* 14 full-time (9 women); includes 4 minority (1 Black or African American, non-Hispanic/Latino; 1 American Indian or Alaska Native, non-Hispanic/Latino; 1 Asian, non-Hispanic/Latino; 1 Hispanic/Latino), 1 international. Average age 30. 14 applicants, 43% accepted, 3 enrolled. In 2012, 4 master's, 1

Geochemistry

doctorate awarded. *Degree requirements:* For master's, comprehensive exam, thesis; for doctorate, thesis/dissertation, oral and written qualifying exams. *Entrance requirements:* For master's, GRE General and Subject Tests, bachelor's degree; minimum undergraduate GPA of 3.0 (or its equivalent if letter grade system not used); for doctorate, bachelor's degree; minimum undergraduate GPA of 3.0 (or its equivalent if letter grade system not used). Additional exam requirements/recommendations for international students: Required—TOEFL. *Application deadline:* For fall admission, 1/15 for domestic and international students. Application fee: $80 ($100 for international students). Electronic applications accepted. *Expenses:* Tuition, nonresident: full-time $15,102. Required fees: $14,809.19. Full-time tuition and fees vary according to program. *Financial support:* In 2012–13, 13 students received support, including 12 fellowships with full and partial tuition reimbursements available, 11 research assistantships with full and partial tuition reimbursements available, 8 teaching assistantships with full and partial tuition reimbursements available; Federal Work-Study, scholarships/grants, health care benefits, tuition waivers (full and partial), and unspecified assistantships also available. Financial award application deadline: 3/2; financial award applicants required to submit FAFSA. *Unit head:* Dr. Kevin McKeegan, Chair, 310-825-1475, E-mail: mckeegan@ess.ucla.edu. *Application contact:* Student Affairs Officer, 310-825-3880, Fax: 310-825-2779, E-mail: info@ess.ucla.edu. Website: http://www.ess.ucla.edu/.

University of Chicago, Division of the Physical Sciences, Department of the Geophysical Sciences, Chicago, IL 60637-1513. Offers atmospheric sciences (SM, PhD); cosmochemistry (PhD); earth sciences (SM, PhD); paleobiology (PhD); planetary and space sciences (SM, PhD). Terminal master's awarded for partial completion of doctoral program. *Degree requirements:* For master's, thesis, seminar; for doctorate, variable foreign language requirement, comprehensive exam, thesis/dissertation. *Entrance requirements:* For doctorate, GRE General Test. Additional exam requirements/recommendations for international students: Required—TOEFL (minimum score 600 paper-based; 96 iBT), IELTS (minimum score 7). Electronic applications accepted. *Faculty research:* Climatology, evolutionary paleontology, cosmochemistry, geochemistry, oceanic sciences.

University of Hawaii at Manoa, Graduate Division, School of Ocean and Earth Science and Technology, Department of Geology and Geophysics, Honolulu, HI 96822. Offers high-pressure geophysics and geochemistry (MS, PhD); hydrogeology and engineering geology (MS, PhD); marine geology and geophysics (MS, PhD); planetary geosciences and remote sensing (MS, PhD); seismology and solid-earth geophysics (MS, PhD); volcanology, petrology, and geochemistry (MS, PhD). Part-time programs available. Terminal master's awarded for partial completion of doctoral program. *Degree requirements:* For master's, thesis optional; for doctorate, comprehensive exam, thesis/dissertation. *Entrance requirements:* For master's and doctorate, GRE General Test, minimum GPA of 3.0. Additional exam requirements/recommendations for international students: Required—TOEFL (minimum score 580 paper-based; 92 iBT), IELTS (minimum score 5).

The University of Manchester, School of Earth, Atmospheric and Environmental Sciences, Manchester, United Kingdom. Offers atmospheric sciences (M Phil, M Sc, PhD); basin studies and petroleum geosciences (M Phil, M Sc, PhD); earth, atmospheric and environmental sciences (M Phil, M Sc, PhD); environmental geochemistry and cosmochemistry (M Phil, M Sc, PhD); isotope geochemistry and cosmochemistry (M Phil, M Sc, PhD); paleontology (M Phil, M Sc, PhD); physics and chemistry of minerals and fluids (M Phil, M Sc, PhD); structural and petrological geosciences (M Phil, M Sc, PhD).

University of Nevada, Reno, Graduate School, College of Science, Mackay School of Earth Sciences and Engineering, Department of Geological Sciences and Engineering, Program in Geochemistry, Reno, NV 89557. Offers MS, PhD. Terminal master's awarded for partial completion of doctoral program. *Degree requirements:* For master's, thesis optional; for doctorate, thesis/dissertation. *Entrance requirements:* For master's, GRE General Test, minimum GPA of 2.75; for doctorate, GRE General Test, minimum GPA of 3.0. Additional exam requirements/recommendations for international students: Required—TOEFL (minimum score 500 paper-based; 61 iBT), IELTS (minimum score 6). Electronic applications accepted.

The University of Texas at Dallas, School of Natural Sciences and Mathematics, Department of Geosciences, Richardson, TX 75080. Offers

geochemistry (MS, PhD); geophysics (MS, PhD); geospatial information sciences (MS, PhD); hydrogeology (MS, PhD); sedimentary, stratigraphy, paleontology (PhD); stratigraphy, paleontology (MS); structural geology and tectonics (MS, PhD). Part-time and evening/weekend programs available. *Faculty:* 10 full-time (1 woman). *Students:* 45 full-time (18 women), 26 part-time (11 women); includes 9 minority (2 Black or African American, non-Hispanic/Latino; 4 Asian, non-Hispanic/Latino; 3 Hispanic/Latino), 23 international. Average age 30. 90 applicants, 31% accepted, 18 enrolled. In 2012, 7 master's, 4 doctorates awarded. *Degree requirements:* For master's, thesis optional; for doctorate, thesis/dissertation. *Entrance requirements:* For master's and doctorate, GRE General Test, minimum GPA of 3.0 in upper-level course work in field. Additional exam requirements/recommendations for international students: Required—TOEFL (minimum score 550 paper-based). *Application deadline:* For fall admission, 7/15 for domestic students, 5/1 for international students; for spring admission, 11/15 for domestic students, 9/1 for international students. Applications are processed on a rolling basis. Application fee: $50 ($100 for international students). Electronic applications accepted. *Expenses:* Tuition, state resident: full-time $11,940; part-time $663.33 per credit hour. Tuition, nonresident: full-time $21,606; part-time $1200.33 per credit hour. Tuition and fees vary according to course load. *Financial support:* In 2012–13, 33 students received support, including 12 research assistantships with partial tuition reimbursements available (averaging $22,270 per year), 9 teaching assistantships with partial tuition reimbursements available (averaging $15,300 per year); career-related internships or fieldwork, Federal Work-Study, institutionally sponsored loans, scholarships/grants, and unspecified assistantships also available. Support available to part-time students. Financial award application deadline: 4/30; financial award applicants required to submit FAFSA. *Faculty research:* Cybermapping, GPS applications for geophysics and geology, seismology and ground-penetrating radar, numerical modeling, signal processing and inverse modeling techniques in seismology. *Unit head:* Dr. John Oldow, Department Head, 972-883-2401, Fax: 972-883-2537, E-mail: geosciences@utdallas.edu. *Application contact:* Gloria Eby, Graduate Support Assistant, 972-883-2404, Fax: 972-883-2537, E-mail: geosciences@utdallas.edu. Website: http://www.utdallas.edu/geosciences.

University of Wisconsin–Milwaukee, Graduate School, College of Letters and Sciences, Department of Chemistry, Milwaukee, WI 53201-0413. Offers biogeochemistry (PhD); chemistry (MS, PhD). *Faculty:* 20 full-time (4 women). *Students:* 60 full-time (27 women), 16 part-time (9 women); includes 11 minority (2 Black or African American, non-Hispanic/Latino; 6 Asian, non-Hispanic/Latino; 3 Two or more races, non-Hispanic/Latino), 30 international. Average age 30. 70 applicants, 61% accepted, 10 enrolled. In 2012, 5 master's, 4 doctorates awarded. *Degree requirements:* For master's, thesis or alternative; for doctorate, thesis/dissertation. *Entrance requirements:* For doctorate, GRE General Test. Additional exam requirements/recommendations for international students: Required—TOEFL (minimum score 600 paper-based; 79 iBT), IELTS (minimum score 6.5). *Application deadline:* For fall admission, 1/1 priority date for domestic students; for spring admission, 9/1 for domestic students. Applications are processed on a rolling basis. Application fee: $56 ($96 for international students). *Financial support:* In 2012–13, 3 fellowships, 30 research assistantships, 46 teaching assistantships were awarded; career-related internships or fieldwork, unspecified assistantships, and project assistantships also available. Support available to part-time students. Financial award application deadline: 4/15; financial award applicants required to submit FAFSA. *Faculty research:* Analytical chemistry, biochemistry, inorganic chemistry, organic chemistry, physical chemistry. *Unit head:* Peter Geissinger, Department Chair, 414-229-5230, Fax: 414-229-5530, E-mail: geissing@uwm.edu. *Application contact:* General Information Contact, 414-229-4982, Fax: 414-229-6967, E-mail: gradschool@uwm.edu. Website: http://www.uwm.edu/dept/chemistry/.

Yale University, Graduate School of Arts and Sciences, Department of Geology and Geophysics, New Haven, CT 06520. Offers biogeochemistry (PhD); climate dynamics (PhD); geochemistry (PhD); geophysics (PhD); meteorology (PhD); oceanography (PhD); paleontology (PhD); paleooceanography (PhD); petrology (PhD); tectonics (PhD). *Degree requirements:* For doctorate, thesis/dissertation. *Entrance requirements:* For doctorate, GRE General Test. Additional exam requirements/recommendations for international students: Required—TOEFL.

Geodetic Sciences

Columbia University, Graduate School of Arts and Sciences, Division of Natural Sciences, Department of Earth and Environmental Sciences, New York, NY 10027. Offers geochemistry (M Phil, MA, PhD); geodetic sciences (M Phil, MA, PhD); geophysics (M Phil, MA, PhD); oceanography (M Phil, MA, PhD). *Degree requirements:* For master's, thesis or alternative, fieldwork, written exam; for doctorate, one foreign language, thesis/dissertation. *Entrance requirements:* For master's and doctorate, GRE General Test, GRE Subject Test, major in natural or physical science. Additional exam requirements/recommendations for international students: Required—TOEFL. *Faculty research:* Structural geology

and stratigraphy, petrology, paleontology, rare gas, isotope and aqueous geochemistry.

The Ohio State University, Graduate School, College of Arts and Sciences, Division of Natural and Mathematical Sciences, School of Earth Sciences, Columbus, OH 43210. Offers geodetic science (MS, PhD); geological sciences (MS, PhD). *Faculty:* 28. *Students:* 48 full-time (18 women), 23 part-time (8 women); includes 5 minority (1 Black or African American, non-Hispanic/Latino; 1 American Indian or Alaska Native, non-Hispanic/Latino; 2 Hispanic/Latino; 1 Two or more races, non-Hispanic/Latino), 25 international. Average age 29. In 2012,

134 www.petersonsbooks.com

Peterson's Graduate Programs in the Physical Sciences, Mathematics, Agricultural Sciences, the Environment & Natural Resources 2014

21 master's, 7 doctorates awarded. *Degree requirements:* For master's, thesis; for doctorate, thesis/dissertation. *Entrance requirements:* For master's, GRE, undergraduate degree in biological science, geological sciences, physical science or engineering (recommended); minimum GPA of 3.2; for doctorate, GRE, undergraduate degree in biological science, geological sciences, physical science or engineering (recommended); minimum GPA of 3.4. Additional exam requirements/recommendations for international students: Required—TOEFL (minimum score 550 paper-based; 79 iBT), Michigan English Language Assessment Battery (minimum score 82), TSE (minimum score 230); Recommended—IELTS (minimum score 8). *Application deadline:* For fall admission, 1/7 priority date for domestic students, 11/30 for international students; for winter admission, 12/1 for domestic students, 11/1 for international students; for spring admission, 12/1 for domestic students, 11/1 for international students. Applications are processed on a rolling basis. Application fee: $40 ($50 for international students). Electronic applications accepted. *Unit head:* W. Berry Lyons, Director, 614-688-3241, Fax: 614-292-7688, E-mail: lyons.142@osu.edu. *Application contact:* Graduate Admissions, 614-292-9444, Fax: 614-292-3895, E-mail: domestic.grad@osu.edu. Website: http://www.earthsciences.osu.edu/.

Université Laval, Faculty of Forestry, Geography and Geomatics, Department of Geomatics Sciences, Programs in Geomatics Sciences, Québec, QC G1K 7P4, Canada. Offers M Sc, PhD. Terminal master's awarded for partial completion of doctoral program. *Degree requirements:* For master's, thesis (for some programs); for doctorate, comprehensive exam, thesis/dissertation. *Entrance requirements:* For master's and doctorate, knowledge of French and English. Electronic applications accepted.

University of New Brunswick Fredericton, School of Graduate Studies, Faculty of Engineering, Department of Geodesy and Geomatics, Fredericton, NB E3B 5A3, Canada. Offers environmental engineering (M Eng), including geomatics; surveying engineering (M Eng, M Sc E, PhD). *Faculty:* 9 full-time (1 woman), 7 part-time/adjunct (3 women). *Students:* 45 full-time (10 women), 7 part-time (1 woman). In 2012, 10 master's, 2 doctorates awarded. *Degree requirements:* For master's, thesis; for doctorate, comprehensive exam, thesis/dissertation, qualifying exam. *Entrance requirements:* For master's and doctorate, minimum GPA of 3.0. Additional exam requirements/recommendations for international students: Required—TOEFL (minimum score 550 paper-based; 80 iBT), IELTS (minimum score 7), TWE (minimum score 4), Michigan English Language Assessment Battery (minimum score 85), CanTest (minimum score 4.5). *Application deadline:* For fall admission, 3/1 for domestic students. Applications are processed on a rolling basis. Application fee: $50 Canadian dollars. Electronic applications accepted. Tuition and fees charges are reported in Canadian dollars. *Expenses: Tuition, area resident:* Full-time $3956 Canadian dollars. *Required fees:* $579.50 Canadian dollars; $55 Canadian dollars per semester. *Financial support:* In 2012–13, 28 fellowships, 28 research assistantships, 27 teaching assistantships were awarded. *Faculty research:* GIS, GPS, remote sensing, ocean mapping, land administration, hydrography, engineering surveys. *Unit head:* Dr. Sue Nichols, Director of Graduate Studies, 506-453-5141, Fax: 506-453-4943, E-mail: nichols@unb.ca. *Application contact:* Sylvia Whitaker, Graduate Secretary, 506-458-7085, Fax: 506-453-4943, E-mail: swhitake@unb.ca. Website: http://go.unb.ca/gradprograms.

Geology

Acadia University, Faculty of Pure and Applied Science, Department of Earth and Environmental Science, Wolfville, NS B4P 2R6, Canada. Offers M Sc. *Faculty:* 8 full-time (2 women), 5 part-time/adjunct (0 women). *Students:* 2 full-time (0 women). Average age 24. 6 applicants, 67% accepted, 2 enrolled. In 2012, 5 master's awarded. *Degree requirements:* For master's, thesis. *Entrance requirements:* For master's, BSC (honours) in geology or equivalent. Additional exam requirements/recommendations for international students: Required—TOEFL (minimum score 580 paper-based; 93 iBT), IELTS (minimum score 6.5). *Application deadline:* For fall admission, 2/1 priority date for domestic students, 2/1 for international students. Applications are processed on a rolling basis. Application fee: $50. *Financial support:* Research assistantships, teaching assistantships, scholarships/grants, and unspecified assistantships available. Financial award application deadline: 2/1. *Faculty research:* Igneous, metamorphic, and Quaternary geology; stratigraphy; remote sensing; tectonics, carbonate sedimentology. *Unit head:* Dr. Robert Raeside, Head, 902-585-1323, Fax: 902-585-1816, E-mail: rob.raeside@acadiau.ca. *Application contact:* Theresa Starratt, Graduate Studies Officer, 902-585-1914, Fax: 902-585-1096, E-mail: gradadmissions@acadiau.ca. Website: http://ees.acadiau.ca/.

American University of Beirut, Graduate Programs, Faculty of Arts and Sciences, Beirut, Lebanon. Offers anthropology (MA); Arab and Middle Eastern history (PhD); Arabic language and literature (MA, PhD); archaeology (MA); biology (MS); cell and molecular biology (PhD); chemistry (MS); clinical psychology (MA); computational science (MS); computer science (MS); economics (MA); education (MA); English language (MA); English literature (MA); environmental policy planning (MSES); financial economics (MAFE); general psychology (MA); geology (MS); history (MA); mathematics (MA, MS); media studies (MA); Middle Eastern studies (MA); philosophy (MA); physics (MS); political studies (MA); public administration (MA); sociology (MA); statistics (MA, MS); theoretical physics (PhD); transnational American studies (MA). Part-time programs available. *Faculty:* 238 full-time (80 women), 7 part-time/adjunct (3 women). *Students:* 253 full-time (169 women), 139 part-time (105 women). Average age 26. 306 applicants, 47% accepted, 90 enrolled. In 2012, 126 degrees awarded. *Degree requirements:* For master's, one foreign language, comprehensive exam, thesis (for some programs); for doctorate, one foreign language, comprehensive exam, thesis/dissertation. *Entrance requirements:* For master's, GRE, letter of recommendation; for doctorate, GRE, letters of recommendation. Additional exam requirements/recommendations for international students: Required—TOEFL (minimum score 600 paper-based; 97 iBT), IELTS (minimum score 7). *Application deadline:* For fall admission, 4/30 for domestic students, 4/18 for international students; for spring admission, 11/1 for domestic and international students. Application fee: $50. *Expenses: Tuition:* Full-time $13,896; part-time $772 per credit. *Financial support:* In 2012–13, 20 students received support. Career-related internships or fieldwork, institutionally sponsored loans, scholarships/grants, health care benefits, and unspecified assistantships available. Financial award application deadline: 2/4; financial award applicants required to submit FAFSA. *Faculty research:* Modern Middle East history; Near Eastern archaeology; Islamic history; European history; software engineering; scientific computing; data mining; the applications of cooperative learning in language teaching and teacher education; world/comparative literature; rhetoric and composition; creative writing; public management; public policy and international affairs; hydrogeology; mineralogy, petrology, and geochemistry; tectonics and structural geology; cell and molecular biology; ecology. *Unit head:* Dr. Patrick McGreevy, Dean, 961-1374374 Ext. 3800, Fax: 961-1744461, E-mail: pm07@aub.edu.lb. *Application contact:* Dr. Salim Kanaan, Director, Admissions Office, 961-1-350000 Ext. 2594, Fax: 961-1750775, E-mail: sk00@aub.edu.lb. Website: http://staff.aub.edu.lb/~webfas.

Arizona State University, College of Liberal Arts and Sciences, School of Earth and Space Exploration, Tempe, AZ 85287-1404. Offers astrophysics (MS, PhD); exploration systems design (PhD); geological sciences (MS, PhD). PhD in exploration systems design is offered in collaboration with the Fulton Schools of Engineering. Terminal master's awarded for partial completion of doctoral program. *Degree requirements:* For master's, thesis, interactive Program of Study (iPOS) submitted before completing 50 percent of required credit hours; for doctorate, thesis/dissertation, interactive Program of Study (iPOS) submitted before completing 50 percent of required credit hours. *Entrance requirements:* For master's and doctorate, GRE, minimum GPA of 3.0 or equivalent in last 2 years of work leading to bachelor's degree. Additional exam requirements/recommendations for international students: Required—TOEFL (minimum score 80 iBT), TOEFL, IELTS, or Pearson Test of English. Electronic applications accepted.

Auburn University, Graduate School, College of Sciences and Mathematics, Department of Geology and Geography, Auburn University, AL 36849. Offers geography (MS); geology (MS). Part-time programs available. *Faculty:* 11 full-time (2 women). *Students:* 16 full-time (7 women), 17 part-time (4 women); includes 1 minority (American Indian or Alaska Native, non-Hispanic/Latino), 7 international. Average age 28. 23 applicants, 48% accepted, 9 enrolled. In 2012, 5 master's awarded. *Degree requirements:* For master's, computer language or geographic information systems, field camp. *Entrance requirements:* For master's, GRE General Test. *Application deadline:* For fall admission, 7/7 for domestic students; for spring admission, 11/24 for domestic students. Applications are processed on a rolling basis. Application fee: $50 ($60 for international students). Electronic applications accepted. *Expenses: Tuition, state resident:* full-time $7866; part-time $437 per credit. Tuition, nonresident: full-time $23,598; part-time $1311 per credit. *Required fees:* $787 per semester. Tuition and fees vary according to degree level and program. *Financial support:* Research assistantships, teaching assistantships, and Federal Work-Study available. Support available to part-time students. Financial award application deadline: 3/15; financial award applicants required to submit FAFSA. *Faculty research:* Empirical magma dynamics and melt migration, ore mineralogy, role of terrestrial plant biomass in deposition, metamorphic petrology and isotope geochemistry, reef development, crinoid topology. *Unit head:* Dr. Mark Steltenpohl, Interim Chair, 334-844-4893. *Application contact:* Dr. George Flowers, Dean of the Graduate School, 334-844-2125.

Ball State University, Graduate School, College of Sciences and Humanities, Department of Geology, Muncie, IN 47306-1099. Offers MA, MS. *Faculty:* 4 full-time (1 woman). *Students:* 8 full-time (2 women), 6 part-time (5 women), 4 international. Average age 39. 9 applicants, 78% accepted, 4 enrolled. In 2012, 1 master's awarded. *Degree requirements:* For master's, thesis (for some programs). *Entrance requirements:* For master's, GRE General Test. Application fee: $50. *Expenses: Tuition, state resident:* full-time $7666. Tuition, nonresident: full-time $19,114. *Required fees:* $782. *Financial support:* In 2012–13, 6 students

Peterson's Graduate Programs in the Physical Sciences, Mathematics, Agricultural Sciences, the Environment & Natural Resources 2014

www.petersonsbooks.com **135**

received support, including 8 teaching assistantships with full tuition reimbursements available (averaging $14,044 per year); research assistantships and career-related internships or fieldwork also available. Financial award application deadline: 3/1. *Faculty research:* Environmental geology, geophysics, stratigraphy. *Unit head:* Scott Rice-Snow, Interim Chairman, 765-285-8269, E-mail: ricesnow@bsu.edu. *Application contact:* Dr. Kirsten Nicholson, Professor, 765-285-8268, E-mail: knichols@bsu.edu. Website: http://www.bsu.edu/geology/.

Baylor University, Graduate School, College of Arts and Sciences, Department of Geology, Waco, TX 76798. Offers earth science (MA); geology (MS, PhD). *Faculty:* 12 full-time (1 woman). *Students:* 30 full-time (11 women); includes 4 minority (2 Asian, non-Hispanic/Latino; 2 Hispanic/Latino), 6 international. In 2012, 10 master's awarded. *Degree requirements:* For master's, thesis; for doctorate, thesis/dissertation. *Entrance requirements:* For master's and doctorate, GRE General Test. *Application deadline:* For fall admission, 3/15 priority date for domestic students. Applications are processed on a rolling basis. Application fee: $25. *Expenses: Tuition:* Full-time $24,426; part-time $1357 per semester hour. *Required fees:* $2556; $142 per semester hour. *Financial support:* In 2012–13, 18 teaching assistantships were awarded; Federal Work-Study and institutionally sponsored loans also available. *Faculty research:* Petroleum geology, geophysics, engineering geology, hydrogeology. *Unit head:* Dr. Steve Dworkin, Graduate Program Director, 254-710-2186, Fax: 254-710-2673, E-mail: steve_dworkin@baylor.edu. *Application contact:* Paulette Penney, Administrative Assistant, 254-710-2361, Fax: 254-710-3870, E-mail: paulette_penney@baylor.edu. Website: http://www.baylor.edu/geology/.

Binghamton University, State University of New York, Graduate School, School of Arts and Sciences, Department of Geological Sciences, Binghamton, NY 13902-6000. Offers MA, PhD. Part-time programs available. *Faculty:* 11 full-time (1 woman). *Students:* 10 full-time (6 women), 21 part-time (6 women); includes 3 minority (2 Hispanic/Latino; 1 Native Hawaiian or other Pacific Islander, non-Hispanic/Latino), 2 international. Average age 30. 26 applicants, 35% accepted, 3 enrolled. In 2012, 2 master's awarded. Terminal master's awarded for partial completion of doctoral program. *Degree requirements:* For master's, thesis or alternative; for doctorate, variable foreign language requirement, thesis/dissertation, departmental qualifying exam. *Entrance requirements:* For master's and doctorate, GRE General Test, GRE Subject Test. Additional exam requirements/recommendations for international students: Required—TOEFL (minimum score 550 paper-based; 80 iBT). *Application deadline:* For fall admission, 2/15 priority date for domestic students, 2/15 for international students; for spring admission, 9/15 priority date for domestic students, 9/15 for international students. Applications are processed on a rolling basis. Application fee: $75. Electronic applications accepted. *Expenses:* Tuition, state resident: full-time $9370. Tuition, nonresident: full-time $16,680. *Financial support:* In 2012–13, 17 students received support, including 6 research assistantships with full tuition reimbursements available (averaging $10,000 per year), 10 teaching assistantships with full tuition reimbursements available (averaging $15,500 per year); career-related internships or fieldwork, Federal Work-Study, institutionally sponsored loans, scholarships/grants, health care benefits, tuition waivers (full and partial), and unspecified assistantships also available. Financial award application deadline: 2/15; financial award applicants required to submit FAFSA. *Unit head:* Dr. Joseph R. Graney, Chairperson, 607-777-6347, E-mail: jgraney@binghamton.edu. *Application contact:* Kishan Zuber, Recruiting and Admissions Coordinator, 607-777-2151, Fax: 607-777-2501, E-mail: kzuber@binghamton.edu.

Boise State University, College of Arts and Sciences, Department of Geosciences, Boise, ID 83725-0399. Offers earth science (M E Sci); geology (MS, PhD); geophysics (MS, PhD); hydrology (MS). Part-time programs available. *Faculty:* 16 full-time, 30 part-time/adjunct. *Students:* 43 full-time (11 women), 15 part-time (6 women); includes 1 minority (Black or African American, non-Hispanic/Latino), 3 international. 74 applicants, 78% accepted, 16 enrolled. In 2012, 15 master's, 3 doctorates awarded. *Degree requirements:* For master's, thesis. *Entrance requirements:* For master's, GRE General Test, BS in related field, minimum GPA of 3.0; for doctorate, GRE General Test. *Application deadline:* For fall admission, 3/1 priority date for domestic students; for spring admission, 10/1 priority date for domestic students. Applications are processed on a rolling basis. Application fee: $55. Electronic applications accepted. *Expenses:* Tuition, state resident: full-time $3486; part-time $312 per credit. Tuition, nonresident: full-time $5720; part-time $413 per credit. *Financial support:* In 2012–13, 4 fellowships with full and partial tuition reimbursements (averaging $11,333 per year), 19 research assistantships with full tuition reimbursements (averaging $11,153 per year), 11 teaching assistantships (averaging $10,834 per year) were awarded; career-related internships or fieldwork, Federal Work-Study, institutionally sponsored loans, scholarships/grants, tuition waivers (partial), and unspecified assistantships also available. Support available to part-time students. Financial award application deadline: 3/1. *Faculty research:* Seismology, geothermal aquifers, sedimentation, tectonics, seismo-acoustic propagation. *Unit head:* Dr. Clyde J. Northrup, Chairman, 208-426-1631, Fax: 208-426-4061. *Application contact:* Linda Platt, Office Services Supervisor, Graduate Admission and Degree Services, 208-426-1074, Fax: 208-426-2789, E-mail: lplatt@boisestate.edu.

Boston College, Graduate School of Arts and Sciences, Department of Earth and Environmental Sciences, Chestnut Hill, MA 02467-3800. Offers MS, MBA/MS. *Degree requirements:* For master's, thesis. *Entrance requirements:* For master's, GRE General Test, GRE Subject Test. Additional exam requirements/recommendations for international students: Required—TOEFL (minimum score 600 paper-based; 100 iBT). Electronic applications accepted. *Faculty research:* Coastal and marine geology, experimental sedimentology, geomagnetism, igneous petrology, paleontology.

Bowling Green State University, Graduate College, College of Arts and Sciences, Department of Geology, Bowling Green, OH 43403. Offers MS. Part-time programs available. *Degree requirements:* For master's, thesis. *Entrance requirements:* For master's, GRE General Test. Additional exam requirements/recommendations for international students: Required—TOEFL. Electronic applications accepted. *Faculty research:* Remote sensing, environmental geology, geological information systems, structural geology, geochemistry.

Brigham Young University, Graduate Studies, College of Physical and Mathematical Sciences, Department of Geological Sciences, Provo, UT 84602. Offers MS. *Faculty:* 14 full-time (2 women). *Students:* 17 full-time (3 women), 15 part-time (4 women); includes 3 minority (1 American Indian or Alaska Native, non-Hispanic/Latino; 2 Asian, non-Hispanic/Latino). Average age 27. 17 applicants, 65% accepted, 11 enrolled. In 2012, 6 master's awarded. *Degree requirements:* For master's, thesis. *Entrance requirements:* For master's, GRE General Test, minimum GPA of 3.0 in last 60 hours of course work. Additional exam requirements/recommendations for international students: Required—TOEFL. *Application deadline:* For fall admission, 2/1 priority date for domestic students, 2/1 for international students; for winter admission, 9/15 priority date for domestic students, 9/15 for international students. Applications are processed on a rolling basis. Application fee: $50. *Expenses: Tuition:* Full-time $5950; part-time $331 per credit hour. Tuition and fees vary according to program and student's religious affiliation. *Financial support:* In 2012–13, 24 students received support, including 4 research assistantships with partial tuition reimbursements available (averaging $17,920 per year), 23 teaching assistantships with partial tuition reimbursements available (averaging $17,920 per year); career-related internships or fieldwork, institutionally sponsored loans, scholarships/grants, and tuition waivers (partial) also available. Financial award application deadline: 2/1. *Faculty research:* Regional tectonics, hydrogeochemistry, crystal chemistry and crystallography, stratigraphy, environmental geophysics, petrology. *Total annual research expenditures:* $110,000. *Unit head:* Dr. Scott Ritter, Chairman, 801-422-4239, Fax: 801-422-0267, E-mail: scott_ritter@byu.edu. *Application contact:* Dr. Michael J. Dorais, Graduate Coordinator, 801-422-1347, Fax: 801-422-0267, E-mail: dorais@byu.edu. Website: http://www.geology.byu.edu/.

Brooklyn College of the City University of New York, Division of Graduate Studies, Department of Earth and Environmental Sciences, Brooklyn, NY 11210-2889. Offers MA, PhD. Evening/weekend programs available. Terminal master's awarded for partial completion of doctoral program. *Degree requirements:* For master's, comprehensive exam, thesis or alternative, qualifying exams, 30 credits. *Entrance requirements:* For master's, bachelor's degree in geology or equivalent, 2 letters of recommendation; for doctorate, GRE. Additional exam requirements/recommendations for international students: Required—TOEFL (minimum score 550 paper-based; 79 iBT). Electronic applications accepted. *Faculty research:* Geochemistry, petrology, tectonophysics, hydrogeology, sedimentary geology, environmental geology.

California Institute of Technology, Division of Geological and Planetary Sciences, Pasadena, CA 91125-0001. Offers environmental science and engineering (MS, PhD); geobiology (MS, PhD); geochemistry (MS, PhD); geology (MS, PhD); geophysics (MS, PhD); planetary science (MS, PhD). *Faculty:* 43 full-time (8 women). *Students:* 110 full-time (52 women); includes 9 minority (1 Black or African American, non-Hispanic/Latino; 7 Asian, non-Hispanic/Latino; 1 Hispanic/Latino), 30 international. Average age 26. 225 applicants, 19% accepted, 24 enrolled. In 2012, 7 master's, 13 doctorates awarded. *Degree requirements:* For doctorate, thesis/dissertation. *Entrance requirements:* For doctorate, GRE General Test. Additional exam requirements/recommendations for international students: Required—TOEFL; Recommended—IELTS, TWE. *Application deadline:* For fall admission, 1/1 for domestic and international students. Application fee: $80. Electronic applications accepted. *Financial support:* In 2012–13, 19 fellowships with full tuition reimbursements (averaging $29,000 per year), 72 research assistantships with full tuition reimbursements (averaging $29,000 per year) were awarded; teaching assistantships with full tuition reimbursements, institutionally sponsored loans, scholarships/grants, health care benefits, and unspecified assistantships also available. Financial award applicants required to submit FAFSA. *Faculty research:* Planetary surfaces, evolution of anaerobic respiratory processes, structural geology and tectonics, theoretical and numerical seismology, global biogeochemical cycles. *Unit head:* Dr. Kenneth A. Farley, Chairman, 626-395-6111, Fax: 626-795-6028, E-mail: dianb@gps.caltech.edu. *Application contact:* Dr. Robert W. Clayton, Academic Officer, 626-395-6909, Fax: 626-795-6028, E-mail: dianb@gps.caltech.edu. Website: http://www.gps.caltech.edu/.

California State Polytechnic University, Pomona, Academic Affairs, College of the Extended University, Program in Geology, Pomona, CA 91768-2557. Offers MS. Program held jointly with the College of Science. *Students:* 8 full-time (2 women), 1 (woman) part-time; includes 2 minority (1 Asian, non-Hispanic/Latino; 1 Hispanic/Latino). 14 applicants, 93% accepted, 9 enrolled. *Unit head:* Laura L. Smith, Program Development Manager, 909-869-3996, E-mail: lauralsmith@csupomona.edu. *Application contact:* Deborah L. Brandon, Executive Director, Admissions and Outreach, 909-869-3427, Fax: 909-869-5315, E-mail: dlbrandon@csupomona.edu. Website: http://www.ceu.csupomona.edu/specialsessions/degree_programs/gs.html.

California State University, Bakersfield, Division of Graduate Studies, School of Natural Sciences, Mathematics, and Engineering, Program in Geology, Bakersfield, CA 93311. Offers geology (MS); hydrogeology (MS, Postbaccalaureate Certificate); petroleum geology (MS). Part-time and evening/weekend programs available. *Degree requirements:* For master's, thesis. *Entrance requirements:* For master's, GRE General Test, BS in geology.

California State University, Chico, Office of Graduate Studies, College of Natural Sciences, Department of Geological and Environmental Sciences, Chico, CA 95929-0722. Offers environmental science (MS); geosciences (MS), including hydrology/hydrogeology. Part-time programs available. *Faculty:* 5 full-time (2 women), 3 part-time/adjunct (1 woman). *Students:* 15 full-time (7 women), 4 part-time (1 woman); includes 3 minority (all Asian; non-Hispanic/Latino), 2 international. Average age 32. 20 applicants, 55% accepted, 7 enrolled. In 2012, 7 master's awarded. *Degree requirements:* For master's, thesis or project. *Entrance requirements:* For master's, GRE General Test, two letters of recommendation, faculty mentor, statement of purpose. Additional exam requirements/recommendations for international students: Required—TOEFL (minimum score 550 paper-based; 80 iBT), IELTS (minimum score 6.5), Pearson Test of English (minimum score 59). *Application deadline:* For fall admission, 3/1 priority date for domestic students, 3/1 for international students; for spring admission, 9/15 priority date for domestic students, 9/15 for international students. Application fee: $55. Electronic applications accepted. *Expenses:* Tuition, state resident: part-time $372 per unit. Tuition, nonresident: part-time $372 per unit. *Required fees:* $2687 per semester. Tuition and fees vary according to course level and program. *Financial support:* Fellowships, teaching assistantships, career-related internships or fieldwork, and scholarships/grants available. Financial award application deadline: 3/1; financial award applicants required to submit FAFSA. *Unit head:* Dr. David L. Brown, Chair, 530-898-5262, Fax: 530-898-5234, E-mail: geos@csuchico.edu. *Application contact:* Judy L. Rice, Graduate Admissions Coordinator, 530-898-5416, Fax: 530-898-3342, E-mail: jlrice@csuchico.edu. Website: http://www.csuchico.edu/geos/.

California State University, East Bay, Office of Academic Programs and Graduate Studies, College of Science, Department of Earth and Environmental Sciences, Hayward, CA 94542-3000. Offers geology (MS), including environmental geology, geology. Part-time and evening/weekend programs available. *Degree requirements:* For master's, thesis or project. *Entrance requirements:* For master's, GRE, minimum GPA of 2.75 in field, 2.5 overall; 2 letters of recommendation. Additional exam requirements/recommendations for international students: Required—TOEFL (minimum score 550 paper-based). Electronic applications accepted. *Faculty research:* Hydrology, seismic activity; origins of life.

California State University, Fresno, Division of Graduate Studies, College of Science and Mathematics, Department of Earth and Environmental Sciences, Fresno, CA 93740-8027. Offers geology (MS). Part-time programs available. *Degree requirements:* For master's, thesis. *Entrance requirements:* For master's, GRE General Test, undergraduate geology degree, minimum GPA of 2.7. Additional exam requirements/recommendations for international students: Required—TOEFL. Electronic applications accepted. *Faculty research:* Water drainage, pollution, cartography, creek restoration, nitrate contamination.

California State University, Fullerton, Graduate Studies, College of Natural Science and Mathematics, Department of Geological Sciences, Fullerton, CA 92834-9480. Offers MS. Part-time programs available. *Students:* 3 full-time (2 women), 10 part-time (5 women); includes 1 minority (Hispanic/Latino), 1 international. Average age 29. 27 applicants, 33% accepted, 6 enrolled. In 2012, 8 master's awarded. *Degree requirements:* For master's, thesis. *Entrance requirements:* For master's, bachelor's degree in geology, minimum GPA of 3.0 in geology courses. Application fee: $55. *Financial support:* Research assistantships, teaching assistantships, career-related internships or fieldwork, Federal Work-Study, institutionally sponsored loans, and scholarships/grants available. Support available to part-time students. Financial award application deadline: 3/1; financial award applicants required to submit FAFSA. *Unit head:* Dr. David Bowman, Chair, 657-278-3882. *Application contact:* Admissions/Applications, 657-278-2371.

California State University, Long Beach, Graduate Studies, College of Natural Sciences and Mathematics, Department of Geological Sciences, Long Beach, CA 90840. Offers geology (MS); geophysics (MS). Part-time programs available. *Degree requirements:* For master's, thesis. *Entrance requirements:* For master's, GRE General Test. Electronic applications accepted. *Faculty research:* Paleontology, geophysics, structural geology, organic geochemistry, sedimentary geology.

California State University, Los Angeles, Graduate Studies, College of Natural and Social Sciences, Department of Geological Sciences, Los Angeles, CA 90032-8530. Offers MS. Program offered jointly with California State University, Northridge. Part-time and evening/weekend programs available. *Faculty:* 3 full-time (0 women), 1 part-time/adjunct (0 women). *Students:* 15 full-time (11 women), 22 part-time (14 women); includes 20 minority (1 Black or African American, non-Hispanic/Latino; 7 Asian, non-Hispanic/Latino; 9 Hispanic/Latino; 1 Native Hawaiian or other Pacific Islander, non-Hispanic/Latino; 2 Two or more races, non-Hispanic/Latino), 1 international. Average age 30. 33 applicants, 52% accepted, 13 enrolled. In 2012, 5 master's awarded. *Degree requirements:* For master's, comprehensive exam or thesis. *Entrance requirements:* Additional exam requirements/recommendations for international students: Required—TOEFL (minimum score 500 paper-based). *Application deadline:* For fall admission, 5/1 for domestic and international students. Applications are processed on a rolling basis. Application fee: $55. Electronic applications accepted. *Financial support:* Federal Work-Study available. Support available to part-time students. Financial award application deadline: 3/1. *Unit head:* Dr. Ali Modarres, Chair, 323-343-2435, Fax: 323-343-5609, E-mail: amodarr@calstatela.edu. *Application contact:* Dr. Larry Fritz, Dean of Graduate Studies, 323-343-3820, Fax: 323-343-5653, E-mail: lfritz@calstatela.edu. Website: http://www.calstatela.edu/dept/geology/index.htm.

California State University, Northridge, Graduate Studies, College of Science and Mathematics, Department of Geological Sciences, Northridge, CA 91330. Offers geology (MS). Part-time and evening/weekend programs available. *Degree requirements:* For master's, thesis. *Entrance requirements:* For master's, GRE General Test, minimum GPA of 2.75. Additional exam requirements/recommendations for international students: Required—TOEFL. *Faculty research:* Petrology of California Miocene volcanics, sedimentology of California Miocene formations, Eocene gastropods, structure of White/Inyo Mountains, seismology of Californian and Mexican earthquakes.

Case Western Reserve University, School of Graduate Studies, Earth, Environmental, and Planetary Sciences, Cleveland, OH 44106. Offers MS, PhD. Part-time programs available. *Faculty:* 7 full-time (1 woman), 7 part-time/adjunct (1 woman). *Students:* 8 full-time (3 women), 3 international. Average age 28. 14 applicants, 21% accepted, 2 enrolled. In 2012, 1 doctorate awarded. Terminal master's awarded for partial completion of doctoral program. *Degree requirements:* For master's, thesis or alternative; for doctorate, thesis/dissertation. *Entrance requirements:* For master's and doctorate, GRE General Test, GRE Subject Test. Additional exam requirements/recommendations for international students: Required—TOEFL (minimum score 577 paper-based; 90 iBT); Recommended—IELTS (minimum score 7). *Application deadline:* For fall admission, 1/15 priority date for domestic students; for spring admission, 11/15 for domestic students. Applications are processed on a rolling basis. Application fee: $50. Electronic applications accepted. *Financial support:* Research assistantships, teaching assistantships, Federal Work-Study, and tuition waivers (partial) available. Support available to part-time students. Financial award application deadline: 1/15; financial award applicants required to submit FAFSA. *Faculty research:* Geochemistry, hydrology, ecology, geomorphology, planetary science, stratigraphy and basin analysis, igneous petrology. *Unit head:* Gerald Matisoff, Chairman, 216-368-3677, Fax: 216-368-3691, E-mail: gerald.matisoff@case.edu. *Application contact:* James Van Orman, Chair, Graduate Admission Committee, 216-368-3690, Fax: 216-368-3691, E-mail: james.vanorman@case.edu. Website: http://geology.case.edu/.

Central Washington University, Graduate Studies and Research, College of the Sciences, Department of Geological Sciences, Ellensburg, WA 98926. Offers MS. Part-time programs available. *Faculty:* 12 full-time (8 women). *Students:* 19 full-time (11 women), 3 part-time (2 women); includes 2 minority (1 Black or African American, non-Hispanic/Latino; 1 Asian, non-Hispanic/Latino). 33 applicants, 58% accepted, 19 enrolled. In 2012, 5 master's awarded. *Degree requirements:* For master's, thesis. *Entrance requirements:* For master's, GRE General Test, minimum GPA of 3.0. Additional exam requirements/recommendations for international students: Required—TOEFL (minimum score 550 paper-based; 79 iBT) or IELTS. *Application deadline:* For fall admission, 2/1 priority date for domestic students; for winter admission, 10/1 for domestic students; for spring admission, 1/1 for domestic students. Applications are processed on a rolling basis. Application fee: $50. Electronic applications accepted. *Expenses:* Tuition, state resident: full-time $8517. Tuition, nonresident: full-time $18,972. *Required fees:* $978. *Financial support:* In 2012–13, 9 research assistantships with full and partial tuition reimbursements (averaging $9,677 per year), 8 teaching assistantships with full and partial tuition reimbursements (averaging $9,677 per year) were awarded; career-related internships or fieldwork, Federal Work-Study, health care benefits, and unspecified assistantships also available. Financial award application deadline: 3/1; financial award applicants required to submit FAFSA. *Unit head:* Dr. Christopher Mattinson, Graduate Coordinator, 509-963-2702. *Application contact:* Justine Eason, Admissions Program Coordinator, 509-963-3103, Fax: 509-963-1799, E-mail: masters@cwu.edu. Website: http://www.geology.cwu.edu/.

Colorado School of Mines, Graduate School, Department of Geology and Geological Engineering, Golden, CO 80401-1887. Offers geochemistry (MS, PMS, PhD); geological engineering (ME, MS, PhD); geology (MS, PhD). Part-time programs available. *Faculty:* 26 full-time (12 women), 7 part-time/adjunct (3 women). *Students:* 152 full-time (48 women), 34 part-time (10 women); includes 16 minority (1 Black or African American, non-Hispanic/Latino; 2 American Indian or Alaska Native, non-Hispanic/Latino; 2 Asian, non-Hispanic/Latino; 11 Hispanic/Latino), 27 international. Average age 31. 287 applicants, 48% accepted, 54 enrolled. In 2012, 35 master's, 3 doctorates awarded. *Degree requirements:* For master's, thesis (for some programs); for doctorate, comprehensive exam, thesis/dissertation. *Entrance requirements:* For master's and doctorate, GRE General Test. Additional exam requirements/recommendations for international students: Required—TOEFL (minimum score 550 paper-based; 80 iBT). *Application deadline:* For fall admission, 1/15 for domestic and international students; for spring admission, 10/15 for domestic and international students. Application fee: $50 ($70 for international students). Electronic applications accepted. *Financial support:* In 2012–13, 98 students received support, including 14 fellowships with full tuition reimbursements available (averaging $21,120 per year), 65 research assistantships with full tuition reimbursements available (averaging $21,120 per year), 19 teaching assistantships with full tuition reimbursements available (averaging $21,120 per year); scholarships/grants, health care benefits, and unspecified assistantships also available. Financial award application deadline: 1/15; financial award applicants required to submit FAFSA. *Faculty research:* Predictive sediment modeling, petrophysics, aquifer-contaminant flow modeling, water-rock interactions, geotechnical engineering. *Total annual research expenditures:* $2.6 million. *Unit head:* Dr. John Humphrey, Head, 303-273-3819, Fax: 303-273-3859, E-mail: jhumphre@mines.edu. *Application contact:* Dr. Christian Shorey, Lecturer, 303-273-3556, Fax: 303-273-3859, E-mail: cshorey@mines.edu. Website: http://geology.mines.edu.

Cornell University, Graduate School, Graduate Fields of Engineering, Field of Geological Sciences, Ithaca, NY 14853. Offers economic geology (M Eng, MS, PhD); engineering geology (M Eng, MS, PhD); environmental geophysics (M Eng, MS, PhD); general geology (M Eng, MS, PhD); geobiology (M Eng, MS, PhD); geochemistry and isotope geology (M Eng, MS, PhD); geohydrology (M Eng, MS, PhD); geomorphology (M Eng, MS, PhD); geophysics (M Eng, MS, PhD); geotectonics (M Eng, MS, PhD); marine geology (MS, PhD); mineralogy (M Eng, MS, PhD); paleontology (M Eng, MS, PhD); petroleum geology (M Eng, MS, PhD); petrology (M Eng, MS, PhD); planetary geology (M Eng, MS, PhD); Precambrian geology (M Eng, MS, PhD); Quaternary geology (M Eng, MS, PhD); rock mechanics (M Eng, MS, PhD); sedimentology (M Eng, MS, PhD); seismology (M Eng, MS, PhD); stratigraphy (M Eng, MS, PhD); structural geology (M Eng, MS, PhD). *Faculty:* 37 full-time (5 women). *Students:* 32 full-time (13 women); includes 5 minority (2 Asian, non-Hispanic/Latino; 1 Hispanic/Latino; 2 Two or more races, non-Hispanic/Latino), 8 international. Average age 27. 58 applicants, 17% accepted, 6 enrolled. In 2012, 6 master's, 3 doctorates awarded. *Degree requirements:* For master's, thesis (MS); for doctorate, comprehensive exam, thesis/dissertation. *Entrance requirements:* For master's and doctorate, GRE General Test, 3 letters of recommendation. Additional exam requirements/recommendations for international students: Required—TOEFL (minimum score 550 paper-based; 77 iBT). *Application deadline:* For fall admission, 1/15 priority date for domestic students. Applications are processed on a rolling basis. Application fee: $95. Electronic applications accepted. *Financial support:* In 2012–13, 26 students received support, including 9 fellowships with full tuition reimbursements available, 16 research assistantships with full tuition reimbursements available, 1 teaching assistantship with full tuition reimbursement available; institutionally sponsored loans, scholarships/grants, health care benefits, tuition waivers (full and partial), and unspecified assistantships also available. Financial award applicants required to submit FAFSA. *Faculty research:* Geophysics, structural geology, petrology, geochemistry, geodynamics. *Unit head:* Director of Graduate Studies, 607-255-5466, Fax: 607-254-4780. *Application contact:* Graduate Field Assistant, 607-255-5466, Fax: 607-254-4780, E-mail: gradprog@geology.cornell.edu. Website: http://www.gradschool.cornell.edu/fields.php?id-30&a-2.

Duke University, Graduate School, Division of Earth and Ocean Sciences, Durham, NC 27708. Offers MS, PhD. Part-time programs available. *Faculty:* 11 full-time. *Students:* 19 full-time (11 women); includes 1 minority (Hispanic/Latino), 3 international. 30 applicants, 30% accepted, 7 enrolled. In 2012, 7 doctorates awarded. Terminal master's awarded for partial completion of doctoral program. *Degree requirements:* For master's, thesis; for doctorate, thesis/dissertation. *Entrance requirements:* For master's and doctorate, GRE General Test. Additional exam requirements/recommendations for international students: Required—TOEFL (minimum score 550 paper-based; 83 iBT), IELTS (minimum score 7). *Application deadline:* For fall admission, 12/8 priority date for domestic students, 12/8 for international students; for spring admission, 10/15 for domestic and international students. Application fee: $80. Electronic applications accepted. *Financial support:* Fellowships, research assistantships, teaching assistantships, and Federal Work-Study available. Financial award application deadline: 12/8. *Unit head:* Peter Haff, Director of Graduate Studies, 919-681-4426, Fax: 919-684-5833, E-mail: cabrera@duke.edu. *Application contact:* Elizabeth Hutton, Director of Admissions, 919-684-3913, Fax: 919-684-2277, E-mail: grad-admissions@duke.edu. Website: http://www.nicholas.duke.edu/eos/.

East Carolina University, Graduate School, Thomas Harriot College of Arts and Sciences, Department of Geology, Greenville, NC 27858-4353. Offers geology (MS); hydrogeology and environmental geology (Certificate). Part-time programs available. *Degree requirements:* For master's, one foreign language, comprehensive exam, thesis. *Entrance requirements:* For master's, GRE General Test. Additional exam requirements/recommendations for international students: Required—TOEFL. *Expenses:* Tuition, state resident: full-time $4009. Tuition, nonresident: full-time $15,840. *Required fees:* $2111.

Eastern Kentucky University, The Graduate School, College of Arts and Sciences, Department of Earth Sciences, Richmond, KY 40475-3102. Offers geology (MS, PhD). PhD program offered jointly with University of Kentucky. Part-time programs available. *Degree requirements:* For master's, thesis. *Entrance requirements:* For master's, GRE General Test, minimum GPA of 2.5. *Faculty research:* Hydrogeology, sedimentary geology, geochemistry, environmental geology, tectonics.

Florida Atlantic University, Charles E. Schmidt College of Science, Department of Geosciences, Boca Raton, FL 33431-0991. Offers geography (MA); geology (MS); geosciences (PhD). Part-time programs available. *Faculty:* 11 full-time (3 women), 2 part-time/adjunct (0 women). *Students:* 29 full-time (16 women), 16 part-time (8 women); includes 12 minority (1 Black or African American, non-Hispanic/Latino; 4 Asian, non-Hispanic/Latino; 7 Hispanic/Latino), 1 international. Average age 34. 28 applicants, 68% accepted, 14 enrolled. In 2012, 9 master's, 2 doctorates awarded. *Degree requirements:* For master's, thesis (for some programs). *Entrance requirements:* For master's, GRE General Test, minimum GPA of 3.0. *Application deadline:* For fall admission, 3/15 for domestic and international students; for spring admission, 10/15 for domestic and international students. Applications are processed on a rolling basis. Application fee: $30. Electronic applications accepted. *Expenses:* Tuition, state resident: full-time $8876; part-time $369.82 per credit hour. Tuition, nonresident: full-time $24,595; part-time $1024.81 per credit hour. *Financial support:* Research assistantships with partial tuition reimbursements, teaching assistantships with partial tuition reimbursements, career-related internships or fieldwork, Federal Work-Study, institutionally sponsored loans, and unspecified assistantships available. *Faculty research:* GIS applications, paleontology, hydrogeology, economic development. *Unit head:* Dr. Russell Ivy, Chair, 561-297-3295, Fax: 561-297-2745, E-mail: ivy@fau.edu. *Application contact:* Dr. David Warburton, Graduate Coordinator, 561-297-3312, Fax: 561-297-2745, E-mail: warburto@fau.edu. Website: http://www.geosciences.fau.edu/.

Florida State University, The Graduate School, College of Arts and Sciences, Department of Earth, Ocean and Atmospheric Science, Program in Geological Sciences, Tallahassee, FL 32306. Offers MS, PhD. *Faculty:* 11 full-time (1 woman). *Students:* 31 full-time (16 women), 4 part-time (3 women); includes 2 minority (1 Black or African American, non-Hispanic/Latino; 1 Asian, non-Hispanic/Latino), 14 international. Average age 27. *Degree requirements:* For master's, comprehensive exam, thesis; for doctorate, comprehensive exam, thesis/dissertation. *Entrance requirements:* For master's and doctorate, GRE General Test, minimum GPA of 3.0. Additional exam requirements/recommendations for international students: Required—TOEFL (minimum score 550 paper-based; 80 iBT). *Application deadline:* For fall admission, 3/1 priority date for domestic students, 3/1 for international students; for spring admission, 8/1 priority date for domestic students, 8/1 for international students. Applications are processed on a rolling basis. Application fee: $35. Electronic applications accepted. *Expenses:* Tuition, state resident: full-time $7263; part-time $403.51 per credit hour. Tuition, nonresident: full-time $18,087; part-time $1004.85 per credit hour. *Required fees:* $1335.42; $74.19 per credit hour. $445.14 per semester. One-time fee: $40 full-time; $20 part-time. Tuition and fees vary according to program. *Financial support:* In 2012–13, 25 students received support. Fellowships, research assistantships, teaching assistantships, career-related internships or fieldwork, and Federal Work-Study available. Financial award application deadline: 2/7; financial award applicants required to submit FAFSA. *Faculty research:* Appalachian and collisional tectonics, surface and groundwater hydrogeology, micropaleontology, isotope and trace element geochemistry, coastal and estuarine studies. *Total annual research expenditures:* $2.3 million. *Unit head:* Dr. Lynn Dudley, Chairman, 850-644-6205, Fax: 850-644-4214, E-mail: ldudley@fsu.edu. *Application contact:* Michaela Lupiani, Academic Coordinator, 850-644-6205, Fax: 850-644-4214, E-mail: mlupiani@fsu.edu. Website: http://www.eoas.fsu.edu.

Fort Hays State University, Graduate School, College of Arts and Sciences, Department of Geosciences, Program in Geosciences, Hays, KS 67601-4099. Offers geography (MS); geology (MS). *Degree requirements:* For master's, comprehensive exam, thesis. *Entrance requirements:* For master's, GRE General Test. Additional exam requirements/recommendations for international students: Required—TOEFL (minimum score 550 paper-based). Electronic applications accepted. *Faculty research:* Cretaceous and late Cenozoic stratigraphy, sedimentation, paleontology.

Georgia State University, College of Arts and Sciences, Department of Geosciences, Program in Geology, Atlanta, GA 30302-3083. Offers MS. *Degree requirements:* For master's, one foreign language, comprehensive exam (for some programs), thesis or alternative. *Entrance requirements:* For master's, GRE General Test, minimum GPA of 2.75. Additional exam requirements/recommendations for international students: Required—TOEFL. *Application deadline:* For fall admission, 4/15 for domestic and international students; for spring admission, 9/15 for domestic and international students. Application fee: $50. *Expenses:* Tuition, state resident: full-time $8064; part-time $336 per credit hour. Tuition, nonresident: full-time $28,800; part-time $1200 per credit hour. *Required fees:* $2128; $1064 per semester. Tuition and fees vary according to course load and program. *Financial support:* Research assistantships with tuition reimbursements, teaching assistantships with tuition reimbursements, and tuition waivers (partial) available. *Unit head:* Dr. W. Crawford Elliott, Chair, 404-413-5756, E-mail: wcelliott@gsu.edu. *Application contact:* Dr. Jeremy Diem, Director of Graduate Studies, 404-413-5770, E-mail: jdiem@gsu.edu. Website: http://geosciences.gsu.edu/11199.html.

Hofstra University, School of Education, Programs in Teaching - Secondary Education, Hempstead, NY 11549. Offers business education (MS Ed); education technology (Advanced Certificate); English education (MA, MS Ed); foreign language and TESOL (MS Ed); foreign language education (MA, MS Ed), including French, German, Russian, Spanish; mathematics education (MA, MS Ed); science education (MA, MS Ed), including biology, chemistry, earth science, geology, physics; secondary education (Advanced Certificate); social studies education (MA, MS Ed); technology for learning (MA). Part-time and evening/weekend programs available. Postbaccalaureate distance learning degree programs offered (minimal on-campus study). *Students:* 64 full-time (36 women), 41 part-time (22 women); includes 17 minority (9 Black or African

American, non-Hispanic/Latino; 3 Asian, non-Hispanic/Latino; 4 Hispanic/Latino; 1 Native Hawaiian or other Pacific Islander, non-Hispanic/Latino). Average age 28. 87 applicants, 87% accepted, 46 enrolled. In 2012, 57 master's, 7 other advanced degrees awarded. *Degree requirements:* For master's, one foreign language, comprehensive exam (for some programs), thesis (for some programs), exit project, electronic portfolio, student teaching, fieldwork, curriculum project, minimum GPA of 3.0; for Advanced Certificate, 3 foreign languages, comprehensive exam (for some programs), thesis project. *Entrance requirements:* For master's, 2 letters of recommendation, teacher certification (MA), essay; for Advanced Certificate, 2 letters of recommendation, essay, interview and/or portfolio. Additional exam requirements/recommendations for international students: Required—TOEFL (minimum score 550 paper-based; 80 iBT); Recommended—IELTS (minimum score 6.5). *Application deadline:* Applications are processed on a rolling basis. Application fee: $70 ($75 for international students). Electronic applications accepted. *Expenses: Tuition:* Full-time $19,800; part-time $1100 per credit hour. *Required fees:* $970; $165 per term. Tuition and fees vary according to program. *Financial support:* In 2012–13, 82 students received support, including 17 fellowships with full and partial tuition reimbursements available (averaging $3,142 per year), 1 research assistantship with full and partial tuition reimbursement available (averaging $16,527 per year); career-related internships or fieldwork, Federal Work-Study, institutionally sponsored loans, scholarships/grants, tuition waivers (full and partial), and unspecified assistantships also available. Support available to part-time students. Financial award applicants required to submit FAFSA. *Faculty research:* Appropriate content in secondary school disciplines, appropriate pedagogy in secondary school disciplines, adolescent development, secondary school organization, preparation for EDTPA addition to the curriculum. *Unit head:* Dr. Esther Fusco, Chairperson, 516-463-7704, Fax: 516-463-6196, E-mail: catezf@hofstra.edu. *Application contact:* Carol Drummer, Dean of Graduate Admissions, 516-463-4876, Fax: 516-463-4664, E-mail: gradstudent@hofstra.edu. Website: http://www.hofstra.edu/education/.

Humboldt State University, Academic Programs, College of Natural Resources and Sciences, Programs in Environmental Systems, Arcata, CA 95521-8299. Offers environmental systems (MS), including energy, environment and society, environmental resources engineering, geology, math modeling. *Students:* 35 full-time (11 women), 5 part-time (2 women); includes 4 minority (1 Asian, non-Hispanic/Latino; 3 Two or more races, non-Hispanic/Latino), 1 international. Average age 27. 71 applicants, 42% accepted, 20 enrolled. In 2012, 18 master's awarded. *Degree requirements:* For master's, thesis. *Entrance requirements:* For master's, GRE, appropriate bachelor's degree, minimum GPA of 2.5, 3 letters of recommendation. Additional exam requirements/recommendations for international students: Required—TOEFL. *Application deadline:* For fall admission, 2/15 for domestic students; for spring admission, 10/15 for domestic students. Applications are processed on a rolling basis. Application fee: $55. *Expenses:* Tuition, state resident: full-time $8396. Tuition, nonresident: full-time $17,324. Tuition and fees vary according to program. *Financial support:* Application deadline: 3/1; applicants required to submit FAFSA. *Faculty research:* Mathematical modeling, international development technology, geology, environmental resources engineering. *Unit head:* Dr. Chris Dugaw, Chair, 707-826-4251, Fax: 707-826-4145, E-mail: dugaw@humboldt.edu. *Application contact:* Dr. Dale Oliver, Coordinator, 707-826-4921, Fax: 707-826-3140, E-mail: dale.oliver@humboldt.edu.

ICR Graduate School, Graduate Programs, Santee, CA 92071. Offers astro/geophysics (MS); biology (MS); geology (MS); science education (MS). Part-time programs available. *Degree requirements:* For master's, comprehensive exam (for some programs), thesis (for some programs). *Entrance requirements:* For master's, minimum undergraduate GPA of 3.0, bachelor's degree in science or science education. *Faculty research:* Age of the earth, limits of variation, catastrophe, optimum methods for teaching.

Idaho State University, Office of Graduate Studies, College of Science and Engineering, Department of Geosciences, Pocatello, ID 83209-8072. Offers geographic information science (MS); geology (MNS, MS); geology with emphasis in environmental geoscience (MS); geophysics/hydrology/geology (MS); geotechnology (Postbaccalaureate Certificate). Part-time programs available. *Degree requirements:* For master's, comprehensive exam, thesis, oral colloquium; for Postbaccalaureate Certificate, thesis optional, minimum 19 credits. *Entrance requirements:* For master's, GRE General Test (minimum 50th percentile in 2 sections), 3 letters of recommendation; for Postbaccalaureate Certificate, GRE General Test, 3 letters of recommendation, bachelor's degree, statement of goals. Additional exam requirements/recommendations for international students: Required—TOEFL (minimum score 550 paper-based, 80 iBT). Electronic applications accepted. *Faculty research:* Quantitative field mapping and sampling: microscopic, geochemical, and isotopic analysis of rocks, minerals and water; remote sensing, geographic information systems, and global positioning systems: environmental and watershed management; surficial and fluvial processes: landscape change; regional tectonics, structural geology; planetary geology.

Indiana University Bloomington, University Graduate School, College of Arts and Sciences, Department of Geological Sciences, Bloomington, IN 47405-7000. Offers biogeochemistry (MS, PhD); economic geology (MS, PhD); geobiology (MS, PhD); geophysics, structural geology and tectonics (MS, PhD); hydrogeology (MS, PhD); mineralogy (MS, PhD); stratigraphy and sedimentology (MS, PhD). *Faculty:* 17 full-time (1 woman). *Students:* 63 full-time (23 women), 3 part-time (1 woman); includes 3 minority (1 Black or African American, non-Hispanic/Latino; 1 Hispanic/Latino; 1 Two or more races, non-Hispanic/Latino), 15 international. Average age 29. 82 applicants, 26% accepted, 15 enrolled. In 2012, 10 master's, 4 doctorates awarded. Terminal master's awarded for partial completion of doctoral program. *Degree requirements:* For master's, thesis or alternative; for doctorate, comprehensive exam, thesis/dissertation. *Entrance requirements:* For master's and doctorate, GRE General Test. Additional exam requirements/recommendations for international students: Required—TOEFL. *Application deadline:* For fall admission, 1/15 priority date for domestic students, 12/15 for international students; for spring admission, 9/1 priority date for domestic students, 9/1 for international students. Applications are processed on a rolling basis. Application fee: $55 ($65 for international students). *Financial support:* In 2012–13, fellowships with full tuition reimbursements (averaging $17,300 per year), research assistantships with full tuition reimbursements (averaging $16,370 per year), teaching assistantships with full tuition reimbursements (averaging $15,150 per year) were awarded; career-related internships or fieldwork, Federal Work-Study, and institutionally sponsored loans also available. *Faculty research:* Geophysics, geochemistry, hydrogeology, geobiology, planetary science. *Total annual research expenditures:* $644,299. *Unit head:* Simon Brassell, Chair, 812-855-5581, Fax: 812-855-7899, E-mail: geochair@indiana.edu. *Application contact:* Mary Iverson, Graduate Secretary, 812-855-7214, Fax: 812-855-7899, E-mail: miverson@indiana.edu. Website: http://www.indiana.edu/~geosci/.

Indiana University–Purdue University Indianapolis, School of Science, Department of Earth Sciences, Indianapolis, IN 46202-3272. Offers applied earth sciences (PhD); geology (MS). Part-time and evening/weekend programs available. *Faculty:* 8 full-time (2 women). *Students:* 6 full-time (4 women), 14 part-time (7 women), 6 international. Average age 29. 12 applicants, 42% accepted, 4 enrolled. In 2012, 8 master's awarded. *Degree requirements:* For master's, thesis (for some programs). *Entrance requirements:* For master's, GRE General Test, minimum GPA of 3.0. Application fee: $55 ($65 for international students). *Financial support:* In 2012–13, fellowships with full tuition reimbursements (averaging $12,000 per year), teaching assistantships with full tuition reimbursements (averaging $12,103 per year) were awarded; research assistantships with full tuition reimbursements and scholarships/grants also available. Financial award application deadline: 3/1. *Faculty research:* Wetland hydrology, groundwater contamination, soils, sedimentology, sediment chemistry. *Unit head:* Gabriel Filippelli, Chair, 317-274-7484, Fax: 317-274-7966. *Application contact:* Lenore P. Tedesco, Associate Professor, 317-274-7484, Fax: 317-274-7966, E-mail: ltedesco@iupui.edu. Website: http://www.geology.iupui.edu/.

Iowa State University of Science and Technology, Department of Geological and Atmospheric Sciences, Ames, IA 50011. Offers earth science (MS, PhD); environmental science (MS, PhD); geology (MS, PhD); meteorology (MS, PhD). *Degree requirements:* For master's, thesis (for some programs); for doctorate, thesis/dissertation. *Entrance requirements:* For master's and doctorate, GRE General Test. Additional exam requirements/recommendations for international students: Required—TOEFL (minimum score 550 paper-based; 79 iBT), IELTS (minimum score 6.5). *Application deadline:* For fall admission, 1/1 priority date for domestic students. Application fee: $60 ($90 for international students). Electronic applications accepted. *Application contact:* Deann Frisk, Application Contact, 515-294-4477, Fax: 515-294-6049, E-mail: geology@iastate.edu. Website: http://www.ge-at.iastate.edu/.

Kansas State University, Graduate School, College of Arts and Sciences, Department of Geology, Manhattan, KS 66506. Offers MS. *Faculty:* 8 full-time (0 women), 6 part-time/adjunct (0 women). *Students:* 15 full-time (3 women), 7 part-time (2 women); includes 2 minority (1 Black or African American, non-Hispanic/Latino; 1 Hispanic/Latino), 5 international. Average age 26. 21 applicants, 71% accepted, 6 enrolled. In 2012, 6 master's awarded. *Degree requirements:* For master's, thesis. *Entrance requirements:* For master's, GRE General Test. Additional exam requirements/recommendations for international students: Required—TOEFL. *Application deadline:* For fall admission, 2/1 priority date for domestic students, 2/1 for international students; for spring admission, 8/1 priority date for domestic students, 8/1 for international students. Applications are processed on a rolling basis. Application fee: $50 ($75 for international students). Electronic applications accepted. *Financial support:* In 2012–13, 10 students received support, including 4 research assistantships (averaging $16,875 per year), 10 teaching assistantships with full tuition reimbursements available (averaging $10,469 per year); career-related internships or fieldwork, institutionally sponsored loans, scholarships/grants, unspecified assistantships, and stipends also available. Support available to part-time students. Financial award application deadline: 3/1; financial award applicants required to submit FAFSA. *Faculty research:* Chemical hydrogeology, petroleum geology, exploration seismic and near surface geophysics, late Pleistocene geochronology, igneous petrology, volcanology, climate change, tidal sedimentation processes, luminescence dating, biomineralization. *Total annual research expenditures:* $208,620. *Unit head:* Dr. George Clark, Head, 785-532-2242, Fax: 785-532-5159, E-mail: grc@ksu.edu. *Application contact:* Dr. Matthew Brueseke, Interim Director of Domestic Graduate Studies, 785-532-1908, Fax: 785-532-5159, E-mail: brueseke@ksu.edu. Website: http://www.k-state.edu/geology/.

Kent State University, College of Arts and Sciences, Department of Geology, Kent, OH 44242-0001. Offers applied geology (PhD); geology (MS). *Degree requirements:* For master's, thesis; for doctorate, one foreign language, thesis/

dissertation. *Entrance requirements:* For master's, minimum GPA of 2.75; for doctorate, GRE General Test, GRE Subject Test, minimum GPA of 3.0. Additional exam requirements/recommendations for international students: Required—TOEFL (minimum score 575 paper-based). Electronic applications accepted. *Expenses:* Tuition, state resident: full-time $8424; part-time $468 per credit hour. Tuition, nonresident: full-time $14,580; part-time $810 per credit hour. Tuition and fees vary according to course load. *Faculty research:* Groundwater, surface water, engineering geology, paleontology, structural geology.

Lakehead University, Graduate Studies, Department of Geology, Thunder Bay, ON P7B 5E1, Canada. Offers M Sc. Part-time and evening/weekend programs available. *Degree requirements:* For master's, thesis, department seminar, oral exam. *Entrance requirements:* For master's, minimum B average, honours bachelors degree in geology. Additional exam requirements/recommendations for international students: Required—TOEFL. *Faculty research:* Rock physics, sedimentology, mineralogy and economic geology, geochemistry, petrology of alkaline rocks.

Laurentian University, School of Graduate Studies and Research, Programme in Geology (Earth Sciences), Sudbury, ON P3E 2C6, Canada. Offers geology (M Sc); mineral deposits and precambrian geology (PhD); mineral exploration (M Sc). Part-time programs available. *Degree requirements:* For master's, thesis. *Entrance requirements:* For master's, honors degree with second class or better. *Faculty research:* Localization and metallogenesis of Ni-Cu-(PGE) sulfide mineralization in the Thompson Nickel Belt, mapping lithology and ore-grade and monitoring dissolved organic carbon in lakes using remote sensing, global reefs, volcanic effects on VMS deposits.

Lehigh University, College of Arts and Sciences, Department of Earth and Environmental Sciences, Bethlehem, PA 18015. Offers MS, PhD. *Faculty:* 15 full-time (2 women). *Students:* 21 full-time (7 women), 4 part-time (2 women), 4 international. Average age 27. 56 applicants, 23% accepted, 5 enrolled. In 2012, 8 master's, 3 doctorates awarded. Terminal master's awarded for partial completion of doctoral program. *Degree requirements:* For master's, thesis; for doctorate, thesis/dissertation. *Entrance requirements:* For master's and doctorate, GRE General Test, transcripts, recommendation letters, research statement, faculty advocates. Additional exam requirements/recommendations for international students: Required—TOEFL (minimum score 85 iBT). *Application deadline:* For fall admission, 1/1 for domestic and international students. Applications are processed on a rolling basis. Application fee: $75. Electronic applications accepted. *Financial support:* In 2012–13, 14 students received support, including 2 fellowships with full tuition reimbursements available (averaging $25,000 per year), 5 research assistantships with full tuition reimbursements available (averaging $25,000 per year), 10 teaching assistantships with full tuition reimbursements available (averaging $25,000 per year); career-related internships or fieldwork, Federal Work-Study, institutionally sponsored loans, scholarships/grants, tuition waivers (full and partial), and unspecified assistantships also available. Support available to part-time students. Financial award application deadline: 1/1. *Faculty research:* Tectonics, surficial processes, ecology, environmental change. *Total annual research expenditures:* $1.6 million. *Unit head:* Dr. Frank J. Pazzaglia, Chairman, 610-758-3667, Fax: 610-758-3677, E-mail: fjp3@lehigh.edu. *Application contact:* Dr. Stephen Peters, Graduate Coordinator, 610-758-3957, Fax: 610-758-3677, E-mail: scp2@lehigh.edu. Website: http://www.ees.lehigh.edu/.

Louisiana State University and Agricultural and Mechanical College, Graduate School, College of Science, Department of Geology and Geophysics, Baton Rouge, LA 70803. Offers MS, PhD. *Faculty:* 26 full-time (4 women). *Students:* 42 full-time (20 women), 6 part-time (1 woman); includes 3 minority (1 Hispanic/Latino, 2 Two or more races, non-Hispanic/Latino), 8 international. Average age 27. 86 applicants, 14% accepted, 5 enrolled. In 2012, 19 master's awarded. Terminal master's awarded for partial completion of doctoral program. *Degree requirements:* For master's, thesis; for doctorate, thesis/dissertation. *Entrance requirements:* For master's and doctorate, GRE General Test, minimum GPA of 3.0. Additional exam requirements/recommendations for international students: Required—TOEFL (minimum score 550 paper-based; 79 iBT) or IELTS (minimum score 6.5). *Application deadline:* For fall admission, 1/25 priority date for domestic students, 5/15 for international students; for spring admission, 10/15 for international students. Applications are processed on a rolling basis. Application fee: $50 ($70 for international students). Electronic applications accepted. *Financial support:* In 2012–13, 38 students received support, including 3 fellowships with full tuition reimbursements available (averaging $33,665 per year), 18 research assistantships with full and partial tuition reimbursements available (averaging $19,403 per year), 17 teaching assistantships with full and partial tuition reimbursements available (averaging $13,765 per year); career-related internships or fieldwork, Federal Work-Study, institutionally sponsored loans, health care benefits, tuition waivers (full and partial), and unspecified assistantships also available. Financial award application deadline: 3/15; financial award applicants required to submit FAFSA. *Faculty research:* Geophysics, sedimentology, geochemistry, geomicrobiology, tectonics. *Total annual research expenditures:* $1 million. *Unit head:* Dr. Carol Wicks, Chair, 225-578-3353, Fax: 225-578-2302, E-mail: cwicks@lsu.edu. *Application contact:* Dr. Sam Bentley, Graduate Adviser, 225-578-5735, E-mail: sjb@lsu.edu. Website: http://www.geol.lsu.edu/.

Massachusetts Institute of Technology, School of Science, Department of Earth, Atmospheric, and Planetary Sciences, Cambridge, MA 02139. Offers atmospheric chemistry (PhD, Sc D); atmospheric science (SM, PhD, Sc D); chemical oceanography (SM, PhD, Sc D); climate physics and chemistry (SM, PhD, Sc D); earth and planetary sciences (SM); geochemistry (PhD, Sc D); geology (PhD, Sc D); geophysics (PhD, Sc D); marine geology and geophysics (SM, PhD, Sc D); physical oceanography (SM, PhD, Sc D); planetary sciences (PhD, Sc D). *Faculty:* 33 full-time (6 women), 1 (woman) part-time/adjunct. *Students:* 166 full-time (77 women); includes 24 minority (3 Black or African American, non-Hispanic/Latino; 1 American Indian or Alaska Native, non-Hispanic/Latino; 9 Asian, non-Hispanic/Latino; 6 Hispanic/Latino; 5 Two or more races, non-Hispanic/Latino), 58 international. Average age 27. 232 applicants, 23% accepted, 27 enrolled. In 2012, 12 master's, 22 doctorates awarded. Terminal master's awarded for partial completion of doctoral program. *Degree requirements:* For master's, thesis; for doctorate, comprehensive exam, thesis/dissertation. *Entrance requirements:* For master's, GRE General Test; for doctorate, GRE General Test, GRE Subject Test (chemistry or physics for planetary science area). Additional exam requirements/recommendations for international students: Required—TOEFL (minimum score 577 paper-based; 91 iBT), IELTS (minimum score 7). *Application deadline:* For fall admission, 1/5 for domestic and international students; for spring admission, 11/1 for domestic and international students. Application fee: $75. Electronic applications accepted. *Expenses: Tuition:* Full-time $41,770; part-time $650 per credit hour. *Required fees:* $280. *Financial support:* In 2012–13, 108 students received support, including 62 fellowships (averaging $30,700 per year), 87 research assistantships (averaging $32,600 per year), 15 teaching assistantships (averaging $30,800 per year); Federal Work-Study, institutionally sponsored loans, scholarships/grants, health care benefits, and unspecified assistantships also available. *Faculty research:* Formation, dynamics and evolution of planetary systems; origin, composition, structure and dynamics of the atmospheres, oceans, surfaces and interiors of the Earth and other planets; evolution and interaction of the physical, chemical, geological and biological components of the Earth system; characterization of past, present and potential future climates and the causes and consequences of climate change; interplay of energy and the environment. *Total annual research expenditures:* $28.1 million. *Unit head:* Prof. Robert van der Hilst, Head, 617-253-2127, Fax: 617-253-8298, E-mail: eapsinfo@mit.edu. *Application contact:* EAPS Education Office, 617-253-3381, Fax: 617-253-8298, E-mail: eapsinfo@mit.edu. Website: http://eapsweb.mit.edu/.

McMaster University, School of Graduate Studies, Faculty of Science, School of Geography and Earth Sciences, Hamilton, ON L8S 4M2, Canada. Offers geochemistry (PhD); geology (M Sc, PhD); human geography (MA, PhD); physical geography (M Sc, PhD). Part-time programs available. Terminal master's awarded for partial completion of doctoral program. *Degree requirements:* For master's, thesis; for doctorate, comprehensive exam, thesis/dissertation. *Entrance requirements:* For master's, minimum B+ average. Additional exam requirements/recommendations for international students: Required—TOEFL (minimum score 550 paper-based).

Memorial University of Newfoundland, School of Graduate Studies, Department of Earth Sciences, St. John's, NL A1C 5S7, Canada. Offers geology (M Sc, PhD); geophysics (M Sc, PhD). Part-time programs available. *Degree requirements:* For master's, thesis; for doctorate, comprehensive exam, thesis/dissertation, oral thesis defense, entry evaluation. *Entrance requirements:* For master's, honors B Sc; for doctorate, M Sc. Electronic applications accepted. *Faculty research:* Geochemistry, sedimentology, paleoceanography and global change, mineral deposits, petroleum geology, hydrology.

Miami University, College of Arts and Science, Department of Geology, Oxford, OH 45056. Offers MA, MS, PhD. Part-time programs available. *Students:* 35 full-time (19 women); includes 4 minority (1 Black or African American, non-Hispanic/Latino; 1 American Indian or Alaska Native, non-Hispanic/Latino; 1 Asian, non-Hispanic/Latino; 1 Two or more races, non-Hispanic/Latino), 18 international. Average age 28. In 2012, 2 master's, 3 doctorates awarded. *Entrance requirements:* For master's, GRE, minimum undergraduate GPA of 2.75 overall; for doctorate, GRE, minimum GPA of 2.75 (undergraduate) or 3.0 (graduate). Additional exam requirements/recommendations for international students: Required—TOEFL (minimum score 550 paper-based). *Application deadline:* For fall admission, 2/1 for domestic and international students. Application fee: $50. Electronic applications accepted. *Expenses:* Tuition, state resident: full-time $12,444; part-time $519 per credit hour. Tuition, nonresident: full-time $27,484; part-time $1145 per credit hour. *Required fees:* $468. Part-time tuition and fees vary according to course load, campus/location and program. *Financial support:* Fellowships with full tuition reimbursements, research assistantships with full tuition reimbursements, teaching assistantships with full tuition reimbursements, Federal Work-Study, institutionally sponsored loans, health care benefits, tuition waivers (full), and unspecified assistantships available. Financial award application deadline: 2/15; financial award applicants required to submit FAFSA. *Unit head:* Dr. William Hart, Department Chair and Professor, 513-529-3216, Fax: 513-529-1542, E-mail: hartwk@miamioh.edu. *Application contact:* Dr. Elisabeth Widom, Professor, 513-529-5048, E-mail: widome@miamioh.edu. Website: http://www.MiamiOH.edu/geology/.

Michigan Technological University, Graduate School, College of Engineering, Department of Geological and Mining Engineering and Sciences, Houghton, MI 49931. Offers geological engineering (MS, PhD); geology (MS, PhD); geophysics (MS, PhD); mining engineering (MS, PhD). Part-time programs available. Terminal master's awarded for partial completion of doctoral program. *Degree requirements:* For master's, comprehensive exam (for some programs), thesis (for some programs); for doctorate, comprehensive exam, thesis/dissertation.

Entrance requirements: For master's and doctorate, GRE, statement of purpose, official transcripts, 3 letters of recommendation. Additional exam requirements/recommendations for international students: Required—TOEFL (minimum score 79 iBT) or IELTS. Electronic applications accepted. *Faculty research:* Volcanic hazards and volcanic clouds, oil and gas exploration and development, groundwater measurement and modeling, geophysics, environmental paleomagnetism.

Mississippi State University, College of Arts and Sciences, Department of Geosciences, Mississippi State, MS 39762. Offers applied meteorology (MS); broadcast meteorology (MS); earth and atmospheric science (PhD); environmental geoscience (MS); geography (MS); geology (MS); geospatial sciences (MS); professional meteorology/climatology (MS); teachers in geoscience (MS). Postbaccalaureate distance learning degree programs offered (no on-campus study). *Faculty:* 14 full-time (3 women), 2 part-time/adjunct (0 women). *Students:* 62 full-time (27 women), 273 part-time (117 women); includes 29 minority (7 Black or African American, non-Hispanic/Latino; 4 Asian, non-Hispanic/Latino; 13 Hispanic/Latino; 5 Two or more races, non-Hispanic/Latino), 8 international. Average age 34. 235 applicants, 70% accepted, 135 enrolled. In 2012, 101 master's, 2 doctorates awarded. *Degree requirements:* For master's, thesis (for some programs), comprehensive oral or written exam; for doctorate, thesis/dissertation, comprehensive oral or written exam. *Entrance requirements:* For master's, GRE (for on-campus applicants), minimum undergraduate GPA of 2.75; for doctorate, completed thesis-based MS with background in one department emphasis area. Additional exam requirements/recommendations for international students: Required—TOEFL (minimum score 477 paper-based; 53 iBT); Recommended—IELTS (minimum score 4.5). *Application deadline:* For fall admission, 7/1 for domestic students, 5/1 for international students; for spring admission, 11/1 for domestic students, 9/1 for international students. Applications are processed on a rolling basis. Application fee: $60. Electronic applications accepted. *Financial support:* In 2012–13, 12 research assistantships with full tuition reimbursements (averaging $20,723 per year), 30 teaching assistantships with full tuition reimbursements (averaging $14,091 per year) were awarded; Federal Work-Study, institutionally sponsored loans, scholarships/grants, tuition waivers (partial), and unspecified assistantships also available. Financial award application deadline: 4/1; financial award applicants required to submit FAFSA. *Faculty research:* Climatology, hydrogeology, sedimentology, meteorology. *Total annual research expenditures:* $6.8 million. *Unit head:* Dr. Darrel Schmitz, Professor and Head, 662-325-3915, Fax: 662-325-9423, E-mail: schmitz@geosci.msstate.edu. *Application contact:* Dr. Mike Brown, Associate Professor/Graduate Coordinator, 662-325-3915, Fax: 662-325-9423, E-mail: tina@gesci.msstate.edu. Website: http://www.geosciences.msstate.edu.

Missouri State University, Graduate College, College of Natural and Applied Sciences, Department of Geography, Geology, and Planning, Springfield, MO 65897. Offers geospatial sciences (MS, MS Ed), including earth science (MS Ed), geology (MS), human geography and planning (MS), physical geography (MS Ed); natural and applied science (MNAS), including geography, geology and planning; secondary education (MS Ed), including geography. *Accreditation:* ACSP. Part-time and evening/weekend programs available. *Degree requirements:* For master's, comprehensive exam, thesis (for some programs). *Entrance requirements:* For master's, GRE General Test (MS, MNAS), minimum undergraduate GPA of 3.0 (MS, MNAS), 9-12 teacher certification (MS Ed). Additional exam requirements/recommendations for international students: Required—TOEFL (minimum score 550 paper-based; 79 iBT). Electronic applications accepted. *Faculty research:* Stratigraphy and ancient meteorite impacts, environmental geochemistry of karst, hyperspectral image processing, water quality, small town planning.

Missouri University of Science and Technology, Graduate School, Department of Geological Sciences and Engineering, Rolla, MO 65409. Offers geological engineering (MS, DE, PhD); geology and geophysics (MS, PhD), including geochemistry, geology, geophysics, groundwater and environmental geology; petroleum engineering (MS, DE, PhD). Part-time programs available. *Degree requirements:* For master's, thesis optional; for doctorate, comprehensive exam, thesis/dissertation. *Entrance requirements:* For master's, GRE General Test (minimum score 600 quantitative, writing 3.5), minimum GPA of 3.0 in last 4 semesters; for doctorate, GRE General Test (minimum: Q 600, GRE WR 3.5). Additional exam requirements/recommendations for international students: Required—TOEFL. Electronic applications accepted. *Faculty research:* Digital image processing and geographic information systems, mineralogy, igneous and sedimentary petrology-geochemistry, sedimentology groundwater hydrology and contaminant transport.

Montana Tech of The University of Montana, Graduate School, Geosciences Programs, Butte, MT 59701-8997. Offers geochemistry (MS); geological engineering (MS); geology (MS); geophysical engineering (MS); hydrogeological engineering (MS); hydrogeology (MS). Part-time programs available. *Degree requirements:* For master's, comprehensive exam (for some programs), thesis (for some programs). *Entrance requirements:* For master's, GRE General Test, minimum GPA of 3.0. Additional exam requirements/recommendations for international students: Required—TOEFL (minimum score 525 paper-based; 71 iBT). Electronic applications accepted. *Faculty research:* Water resource development, seismic processing, petroleum reservoir characterization, environmental geochemistry, geologic mapping.

New Mexico Highlands University, Graduate Studies, College of Arts and Sciences, Program in Natural Science, Las Vegas, NM 87701. Offers biology (MS); environmental science and management (MS); geology (MS). *Expenses:* Tuition, state resident: full-time $4277; part-time $178.22 per hour. Tuition, nonresident: full-time $6715; part-time $279.81 per hour. *International tuition:* $8510 full-time. Part-time tuition and fees vary according to campus/location. *Application contact:* Diane Trujillo, Administrative Assistant, Graduate Studies, 505-454-3266, Fax: 505-454-3558, E-mail: dtrujillo@nmhu.edu. Website: http://www.nmhu.edu/academics/graduate/arts_science_grad/natural_science/index.aspx.

New Mexico Institute of Mining and Technology, Graduate Studies, Department of Earth and Environmental Science, Program in Geology, Socorro, NM 87801. Offers MS, PhD. *Students:* 23 full-time (12 women), 2 part-time (1 woman); includes 6 minority (3 American Indian or Alaska Native, non-Hispanic/Latino; 1 Hispanic/Latino; 2 Two or more races, non-Hispanic/Latino), 3 international. Average age 29. In 2012, 3 master's, 2 doctorates awarded. *Degree requirements:* For master's, thesis optional; for doctorate, thesis/dissertation. *Entrance requirements:* For master's, GRE General Test; for doctorate, GRE General Test, GRE Subject Test. Additional exam requirements/recommendations for international students: Required—TOEFL (minimum score 540 paper-based). *Application deadline:* For fall admission, 3/1 priority date for domestic students; for spring admission, 6/1 for domestic students. Applications are processed on a rolling basis. Application fee: $16 ($30 for international students). Electronic applications accepted. *Expenses:* Tuition, state resident: full-time $5043; part-time $280 per credit hour. Tuition, nonresident: full-time $16,682; part-time $927 per credit hour. *Required fees:* $648; $18 per credit hour. $108 per semester. Part-time tuition and fees vary according to course load. *Financial support:* In 2012–13, 8 research assistantships (averaging $10,322 per year), 7 teaching assistantships (averaging $12,777 per year) were awarded; Federal Work-Study, institutionally sponsored loans, and unspecified assistantships also available. Financial award application deadline: 3/1; financial award applicants required to submit CSS PROFILE or FAFSA. *Faculty research:* Care and karst topography, soil/water chemistry and properties, geochemistry of ore deposits. *Unit head:* Dr. Andrew Campbell, Coordinator, 575-835-5327, Fax: 575-835-6436, E-mail: campbell@nmt.edu. *Application contact:* Dr. Lorie Liebrock, Dean of Graduate Studies, 575-835-5513, Fax: 575-835-5476, E-mail: graduate@nmt.edu.

New Mexico State University, Graduate School, College of Arts and Sciences, Department of Geological Sciences, Las Cruces, NM 88003-8001. Offers MS. Part-time programs available. *Faculty:* 3 full-time (1 woman), 3 part-time/adjunct (0 women). *Students:* 12 full-time (3 women), 3 part-time (all women); includes 1 minority (Hispanic/Latino). Average age 29. 25 applicants, 44% accepted, 7 enrolled. In 2012, 10 master's awarded. *Degree requirements:* For master's, thesis. *Entrance requirements:* For master's, GRE General Test, BS in geology or the equivalent. Additional exam requirements/recommendations for international students: Required—TOEFL (minimum score 550 paper-based; 79 iBT), IELTS (minimum score 6.5). *Application deadline:* For fall admission, 7/1 priority date for domestic students, 7/1 for international students; for spring admission, 11/1 priority date for domestic students, 11/1 for international students. Applications are processed on a rolling basis. Application fee: $40 ($50 for international students). Electronic applications accepted. *Expenses:* Tuition, state resident: full-time $5239; part-time $218 per credit. Tuition, nonresident: full-time $18,266; part-time $761 per credit. *Required fees:* $1274; $53 per credit. *Financial support:* In 2012–13, 11 students received support, including 11 teaching assistantships (averaging $17,577 per year); career-related internships or fieldwork, Federal Work-Study, institutionally sponsored loans, scholarships/grants, health care benefits, and unspecified assistantships also available. Support available to part-time students. Financial award application deadline: 2/15; financial award applicants required to submit FAFSA. *Faculty research:* Geochemistry, tectonics, sedimentology, stratigraphy, igneous petrology. *Total annual research expenditures:* $289,451. *Unit head:* Dr. Nancy J. McMillan, Head/Recruiting Contact, 575-646-5000, Fax: 575-646-1056, E-mail: nmcmilla@nmsu.edu. Website: http://www.nmsu.edu/~geology/.

Northern Arizona University, Graduate College, College of Engineering, Forestry and Natural Sciences, School of Earth Sciences and Environmental Sustainability, Flagstaff, AZ 86011. Offers climate science and solutions (MS); earth science (MS); earth sciences and environmental sustainability (PhD); environmental sciences and policy (MS); geology (MS). *Degree requirements:* For master's, comprehensive exam (for some programs), thesis (for some programs). *Entrance requirements:* Additional exam requirements/recommendations for international students: Required—TOEFL (minimum score 550 paper-based; 80 iBT), IELTS (minimum score 7). Electronic applications accepted.

Northern Illinois University, Graduate School, College of Liberal Arts and Sciences, Department of Geology and Environmental Geosciences, De Kalb, IL 60115-2854. Offers geology (MS, PhD). Part-time programs available. *Faculty:* 11 full-time (1 woman), 1 (woman) part-time/adjunct. *Students:* 20 full-time (7 women), 18 part-time (9 women); includes 2 minority (1 Asian, non-Hispanic/Latino; 1 Hispanic/Latino), 3 international. Average age 29. 26 applicants, 65% accepted, 9 enrolled. In 2012, 6 master's awarded. Terminal master's awarded for partial completion of doctoral program. *Degree requirements:* For master's, comprehensive exam, thesis optional, research seminar; for doctorate, thesis/dissertation, candidacy exam, dissertation defense, internship, research seminar. *Entrance requirements:* For master's, GRE General Test, bachelor's degree in engineering or science, minimum GPA of 2.75; for doctorate, GRE General Test, bachelor's or master's degree in engineering or science, minimum graduate GPA of 3.2. Additional exam requirements/recommendations for international students: Required—TOEFL (minimum score 550 paper-based). *Application deadline:* For fall admission, 6/1 for domestic students, 5/1 for international students; for spring admission, 11/1 for domestic students, 10/1 for international students. Applications are processed on a rolling basis. Application fee: $40. Electronic applications accepted. *Financial support:* In 2012–13, 4 research assistantships with full tuition reimbursements, 20 teaching assistantships with full tuition reimbursements were awarded; fellowships with full tuition reimbursements, career-related internships or fieldwork, Federal Work-Study, scholarships/grants, tuition waivers (full), and unspecified assistantships also available. Support available to part-time students. Financial award applicants required to submit FAFSA. *Faculty research:* Micropaleontology, environmental geochemistry, glacial geology, igneous petrology, statistical analyses of fracture networks. *Unit head:* Dr. Colin Booth, Chair, 815-753-0523, Fax: 815-753-1945, E-mail: cbooth@niu.edu. *Application contact:* Dr. Mark Fischer, Graduate Program Director, 815-753-7939, E-mail: mfischer@niu.edu. Website: http://jove.geol.niu.edu/.

Northwestern University, The Graduate School, Judd A. and Marjorie Weinberg College of Arts and Sciences, Department of Geological Sciences, Evanston, IL 60208. Offers MS, PhD. Admissions and degrees offered through The Graduate School. Part-time programs available. *Degree requirements:* For doctorate, thesis/dissertation. *Entrance requirements:* For master's and doctorate, GRE General Test. Additional exam requirements/recommendations for international students: Required—TOEFL. Electronic applications accepted.

The Ohio State University, Graduate School, College of Arts and Sciences, Division of Natural and Mathematical Sciences, School of Earth Sciences, Columbus, OH 43210. Offers geodetic science (MS, PhD); geological sciences (MS, PhD). *Faculty:* 28. *Students:* 48 full-time (18 women), 23 part-time (8 women); includes 5 minority (1 Black or African American, non-Hispanic/Latino; 1 American Indian or Alaska Native, non-Hispanic/Latino; 2 Hispanic/Latino; 1 Two or more races, non-Hispanic/Latino), 25 international. Average age 29. In 2012, 21 master's, 7 doctorates awarded. *Degree requirements:* For master's, thesis; for doctorate, thesis/dissertation. *Entrance requirements:* For master's, GRE, undergraduate degree in biological science, geological sciences, physical science or engineering (recommended); minimum GPA of 3.2; for doctorate, GRE, undergraduate degree in biological science, geological sciences, physical science or engineering (recommended); minimum GPA of 3.4. Additional exam requirements/recommendations for international students: Required—TOEFL (minimum score 550 paper-based; 79 iBT), Michigan English Language Assessment Battery (minimum score 82), TSE (minimum score 230); Recommended—IELTS (minimum score 8). *Application deadline:* For fall admission, 1/7 priority date for domestic students, 11/30 for international students; for winter admission, 12/1 for domestic students, 11/1 for international students; for spring admission, 12/1 for domestic students, 11/1 for international students. Applications are processed on a rolling basis. Application fee: $40 ($50 for international students). Electronic applications accepted. *Unit head:* W. Berry Lyons, Director, 614-688-3241, Fax: 614-292-7688, E-mail: lyons.142@osu.edu. *Application contact:* Graduate Admissions, 614-292-9444, Fax: 614-292-3895, E-mail: domestic.grad@osu.edu. Website: http://www.earthsciences.osu.edu/.

Ohio University, Graduate College, College of Arts and Sciences, Department of Geological Sciences, Athens, OH 45701-2979. Offers environmental geochemistry (MS); environmental geology (MS); environmental/hydrology (MS); geology (MS); geology education (MS); geomorphology/surficial processes (MS); geophysics (MS); hydrogeology (MS); sedimentology (MS); structure/tectonics (MS). Part-time programs available. *Degree requirements:* For master's, thesis. *Entrance requirements:* Additional exam requirements/recommendations for international students: Required—TOEFL (minimum score 550 paper-based; 80 iBT) or IELTS (minimum score 6.5). Electronic applications accepted. *Faculty research:* Geoscience education, tectonics, fluvial geomorphology, invertebrate paleontology, mine/hydrology.

Oklahoma State University, College of Arts and Sciences, School of Geology, Stillwater, OK 74078. Offers MS, PhD. *Faculty:* 15 full-time (2 women), 2 part-time/adjunct (1 woman). *Students:* 41 full-time (14 women), 22 part-time (1 woman); includes 6 minority (1 Black or African American, non-Hispanic/Latino; 2 Hispanic/Latino; 3 Two or more races, non-Hispanic/Latino), 15 international. Average age 29. 96 applicants, 41% accepted, 23 enrolled. In 2012, 30 master's awarded. *Degree requirements:* For master's, thesis; for doctorate, comprehensive exam, thesis/dissertation. *Entrance requirements:* For master's, GRE; for doctorate, GRE. Additional exam requirements/recommendations for international students: Required—TOEFL (minimum score 550 paper-based; 79 iBT). *Application deadline:* For fall admission, 3/1 for international students; for spring admission, 8/1 for international students. Applications are processed on a rolling basis. Application fee: $40 ($75 for international students). Electronic applications accepted. *Expenses:* Tuition, state resident: full-time $4272; part-time $178 per credit hour. Tuition, nonresident: full-time $17,016; part-time $709 per credit hour. *Required fees:* $2188; $91.17 per credit hour. One-time fee: $50 full-time. Part-time tuition and fees vary according to course load and campus/location. *Financial support:* In 2012–13, 16 research assistantships (averaging $10,078 per year), 25 teaching assistantships (averaging $8,005 per year) were awarded; career-related internships or fieldwork, Federal Work-Study, scholarships/grants, health care benefits, tuition waivers (partial), and unspecified assistantships also available. Support available to part-time students. Financial award application deadline: 3/1; financial award applicants required to submit FAFSA. *Faculty research:* Groundwater hydrology, petroleum geology. *Unit head:*

Dr. Eliot Atekwana, Head, 405-744-6358, Fax: 405-744-7841. *Application contact:* Dr. Sheryl Tucker, Dean, 405-744-7099, Fax: 405-744-0355, E-mail: grad-i@okstate.edu. Website: http://geology.okstate.edu.

Oregon State University, College of Earth, Ocean, and Atmospheric Sciences, Program in Geology, Corvallis, OR 97331. Offers MA, MAIS, MS, PhD. Part-time programs available. *Students:* 33 full-time (14 women), 3 part-time (1 woman); includes 5 minority (1 Asian, non-Hispanic/Latino; 3 Hispanic/Latino; 1 Two or more races, non-Hispanic/Latino), 2 international. Average age 29. 77 applicants, 19% accepted, 10 enrolled. In 2012, 8 master's, 4 doctorates awarded. Terminal master's awarded for partial completion of doctoral program. *Degree requirements:* For master's, variable foreign language requirement, thesis; for doctorate, one foreign language, thesis/dissertation. *Entrance requirements:* For master's and doctorate, GRE General Test, GRE Subject Test, minimum GPA of 3.0 in last 90 hours. Additional exam requirements/recommendations for international students: Required—TOEFL. *Application deadline:* For fall admission, 2/1 for domestic students. Applications are processed on a rolling basis. Application fee: $50. *Expenses:* Tuition, state resident: full-time $11,367; part-time $421 per credit hour. Tuition, nonresident: full-time $18,279; part-time $677 per credit hour. *Required fees:* $1478. One-time fee: $300 full-time. Tuition and fees vary according to course load and program. *Financial support:* Fellowships, research assistantships, teaching assistantships, Federal Work-Study, and institutionally sponsored loans available. Support available to part-time students. Financial award application deadline: 2/1. *Faculty research:* Hydrogeology, geomorphology, ocean geology, geochemistry, earthquake geology. *Unit head:* Dr. Peter U. Clark, Professor, 541-737-1247, Fax: 541-737-1200, E-mail: clarkp@geo.oregonstate.edu.

Oregon State University, College of Earth, Ocean, and Atmospheric Sciences, Program in Ocean, Earth, and Atmospheric Sciences, Corvallis, OR 97331. Offers atmospheric sciences (MA, MS); geography (PhD); geology (PhD); geophysics (MA, MS); oceanography (MA, MS). *Students:* 33 full-time (17 women), 1 part-time (0 women); includes 5 minority (1 Asian, non-Hispanic/Latino; 2 Hispanic/Latino; 2 Two or more races, non-Hispanic/Latino), 7 international. Average age 28. 148 applicants, 15% accepted, 8 enrolled. In 2012, 10 master's, 3 doctorates awarded. *Expenses:* Tuition, state resident: full-time $11,367; part-time $421 per credit hour. Tuition, nonresident: full-time $18,279; part-time $677 per credit hour. *Required fees:* $1478. One-time fee: $300 full-time. Tuition and fees vary according to course load and program. *Unit head:* Dr. Mark R. Abbott, Dean, 541-737-5195, Fax: 541-737-2064, E-mail: mark@coas.oregonstate.edu. *Application contact:* Dr. Robert S. Allan, Assistant Director, Student Programs, 541-737-1340, Fax: 541-737-2064, E-mail: rallan@coas.oregonstate.edu. Website: http://ceoas.oregonstate.edu/academics/ocean/.

Portland State University, Graduate Studies, College of Liberal Arts and Sciences, Department of Geology, Portland, OR 97207-0751. Offers environmental sciences and resources (PhD); geology (MA, MS); science/geology (MAT, MST). Part-time programs available. *Degree requirements:* For master's, comprehensive exam, thesis, field comprehensive; for doctorate, thesis/dissertation, 2 years of residency. *Entrance requirements:* For master's, GRE General Test, GRE Subject Test, BA/BS in geology, minimum GPA of 3.0 in upper-division course work or 2.75 overall. Additional exam requirements/recommendations for international students: Required—TOEFL (minimum score 550 paper-based). *Faculty research:* Sediment transport, volcanic environmental geology, coastal and fluvial processes.

Queens College of the City University of New York, Division of Graduate Studies, Mathematics and Natural Sciences Division, School of Earth and Environmental Sciences, Flushing, NY 11367-1597. Offers MA. Part-time and evening/weekend programs available. *Faculty:* 16 full-time (4 women), 9 part-time/adjunct (3 women). *Students:* 9 part-time (5 women); includes 4 minority (1 Black or African American, non-Hispanic/Latino; 1 Asian, non-Hispanic/Latino; 2 Hispanic/Latino). 18 applicants, 56% accepted, 4 enrolled. In 2012, 10 master's awarded. *Degree requirements:* For master's, comprehensive exam, thesis. *Entrance requirements:* For master's, GRE, previous course work in calculus, physics, and chemistry; minimum GPA of 3.0. Additional exam requirements/recommendations for international students: Required—TOEFL. *Application deadline:* For fall admission, 4/1 for domestic students; for spring admission, 11/1 for domestic students. Applications are processed on a rolling basis. Application fee: $125. *Expenses:* Tuition, state resident: full-time $8690; part-time $365 per credit. Tuition, nonresident: full-time $16,200; part-time $675 per credit. Full-time tuition and fees vary according to course load. *Financial support:* Career-related internships or fieldwork and unspecified assistantships available. Financial award application deadline: 4/1; financial award applicants required to submit FAFSA. *Unit head:* Dr. Allan Ludman, Chairperson, 718-997-3300. *Application contact:* Dr. Hannes Brueckner, Graduate Adviser, 718-997-3300, E-mail: hannes_brueckner@qc.edu.

Queen's University at Kingston, School of Graduate Studies and Research, Faculty of Arts and Sciences, Department of Geological Sciences and Geological Engineering, Kingston, ON K7L 3N6, Canada. Offers M Sc, M Sc Eng, PhD. Part-time programs available. *Degree requirements:* For master's, thesis (for some programs); for doctorate, comprehensive exam, thesis/dissertation. *Entrance requirements:* Additional exam requirements/recommendations for international students: Required—TOEFL. *Faculty research:* Geochemistry, sedimentology, geophysics, economic geology, structural geology.

Rensselaer Polytechnic Institute, Graduate School, School of Science, Program in Geology, Troy, NY 12180-3590. Offers MS, PhD. *Faculty:* 6 full-time (1 woman), 1 part-time/adjunct (0 women). *Students:* 10 full-time (7 women). Average age 26. 30 applicants, 13% accepted, 3 enrolled. In 2012, 2 master's, 1 doctorate awarded. Terminal master's awarded for partial completion of doctoral program. *Degree requirements:* For master's, comprehensive exam, thesis (for some programs); for doctorate, comprehensive exam, thesis/dissertation. *Entrance requirements:* For master's and doctorate, GRE. Additional exam requirements/recommendations for international students: Required—TOEFL (minimum score 570 paper-based, 88 iBT), IELTS (minimum score 6.5), or Pearson Test of English (minimum score 60). *Application deadline:* For fall admission, 1/1 priority date for domestic students, 1/1 for international students; for spring admission, 8/15 priority date for domestic students, 8/15 for international students. Applications are processed on a rolling basis. Application fee: $75. Electronic applications accepted. *Financial support:* In 2012–13, research assistantships (averaging $18,500 per year), teaching assistantships (averaging $18,500 per year) were awarded; fellowships also available. Financial award application deadline: 1/1; financial award applicants required to submit FAFSA. *Faculty research:* Astrobiology, carbon in deep earth, climate assessment, ecosystem studies, environmental and freshwater geochemistry, geoinformatics, geomicrobiology, geophysical simulation, inorganic and igneous experimental geochemistry, isotopic and organic geochemistry, lithosphere dynamics and tectonophysics, metamorphic petrology and geochemistry, microbial geochemistry, paleoceanography and micropaleontology, seismology and solid earth geophysics. *Application contact:* Steven Roecker, Office of Graduate Admissions, 518-276-6216, E-mail: gradadmissions@rpi.edu. Website: http://www.rpi.edu/dept/geo/.

Rutgers, The State University of New Jersey, Newark, Graduate School, Program in Environmental Geology, Newark, NJ 07102. Offers MS. Part-time and evening/weekend programs available. *Degree requirements:* For master's, comprehensive exam, thesis optional. *Entrance requirements:* For master's, GRE General Test, minimum B average. Electronic applications accepted. *Faculty research:* Environmental geology, plate tectonics, geoarchaeology, geophysics, mineralogy-petrology.

Rutgers, The State University of New Jersey, New Brunswick, Graduate School-New Brunswick, Department of Earth and Planetary Sciences, Piscataway, NJ 08854-8097. Offers geological sciences (MS, PhD). Part-time programs available. *Degree requirements:* For master's, thesis; for doctorate, comprehensive exam, thesis/dissertation. *Entrance requirements:* For master's and doctorate, GRE General Test, GRE Subject Test (recommended). Electronic applications accepted. *Faculty research:* Basin analysis, volcanology, quaternary studies, engineering geophysics, marine geology, biogeochemistry and paleoceanography.

St. Francis Xavier University, Graduate Studies, Department of Earth Sciences, Antigonish, NS B2G 2W5, Canada. Offers M Sc. *Degree requirements:* For master's, thesis. *Entrance requirements:* Additional exam requirements/recommendations for international students: Required—TOEFL (minimum score 580 paper-based). *Faculty research:* Environmental earth sciences, global change tectonics, paleoclimatology, crustal fluids.

San Diego State University, Graduate and Research Affairs, College of Sciences, Department of Geological Sciences, San Diego, CA 92182. Offers MS. Part-time programs available. *Degree requirements:* For master's, thesis. *Entrance requirements:* For master's, GRE General Test, bachelor's degree in related field, 2 letters of reference. Additional exam requirements/recommendations for international students: Required—TOEFL. Electronic applications accepted. *Faculty research:* Earthquakes, hydrology, meteorological analysis and tomography studies.

San Jose State University, Graduate Studies and Research, College of Science, Department of Geology, San Jose, CA 95192-0001. Offers MS. *Degree requirements:* For master's, thesis. *Entrance requirements:* For master's, GRE. Electronic applications accepted.

South Dakota School of Mines and Technology, Graduate Division, Department of Geology and Geological Engineering, Rapid City, SD 57701-3995. Offers geology and geological engineering (MS, PhD); paleontology (MS). Part-time programs available. *Faculty:* 13 full-time (3 women). *Students:* 23 full-time (10 women), 12 part-time (4 women); includes 4 minority (1 American Indian or Alaska Native, non-Hispanic/Latino; 2 Hispanic/Latino; 1 Two or more races, non-Hispanic/Latino), 6 international. Average age 30. 19 applicants, 63% accepted, 8 enrolled. In 2012, 10 master's awarded. *Degree requirements:* For master's, thesis; for doctorate, thesis/dissertation. *Entrance requirements:* For master's and doctorate, GRE General Test, GRE Subject Test. Additional exam requirements/recommendations for international students: Required—TOEFL (minimum score 520 paper-based; 68 iBT), TWE. *Application deadline:* For fall admission, 7/1 priority date for domestic students, 4/1 for international students; for spring admission, 11/1 for domestic students, 9/1 for international students. Applications are processed on a rolling basis. Application fee: $35. Electronic applications accepted. *Expenses:* Tuition, state resident: full-time $4720; part-time $196.80 per credit hour. Tuition, nonresident: full-time $10,000; part-time $416.55 per credit hour. *Required fees:* $4360. *Financial support:* In 2012–13, 7 research assistantships with partial tuition reimbursements (averaging $3,724 per year), 9 teaching assistantships with partial tuition reimbursements (averaging $2,913 per year) were awarded; fellowships, Federal Work-Study, and institutionally sponsored loans also available. Support available to part-time students. Financial award application deadline: 5/15. *Faculty research:* Contaminants in soil, nitrate leaching, environmental changes, fracture formations, greenhouse effect. *Total annual research expenditures:* $787,393. *Unit head:* Dr. Maribeth Price, Chair, 605-394-1290, E-mail: laurie.anderson@sdsmt.edu. *Application contact:* Linda Carlson, Office of Graduate Education, 605-355-3468, Fax: 605-394-1767, E-mail: linda.carlson@sdsmt.edu.

Southern Illinois University Carbondale, Graduate School, College of Science, Department of Geology, Carbondale, IL 62901-4701. Offers environmental resources and policy (PhD); geology (MS, PhD). *Faculty:* 12 full-time (0 women). *Students:* 29 full-time (12 women), 46 part-time (9 women); includes 7 minority (4 Black or African American, non-Hispanic/Latino; 1 American Indian or Alaska Native, non-Hispanic/Latino; 1 Asian, non-Hispanic/Latino; 1 Hispanic/Latino), 13 international. Average age 25. 59 applicants, 42% accepted, 11 enrolled. In 2012, 12 master's, 1 doctorate awarded. *Degree requirements:* For master's, thesis; for doctorate, one foreign language, thesis/dissertation. *Entrance requirements:* For master's, GRE, minimum GPA of 2.7; for doctorate, GRE General Test, minimum GPA of 3.25. Additional exam requirements/recommendations for international students: Required—TOEFL. *Application deadline:* For fall admission, 2/15 priority date for domestic students. Applications are processed on a rolling basis. Application fee: $50. *Financial support:* In 2012–13, 17 students received support. Fellowships with full tuition reimbursements available, research assistantships with full tuition reimbursements available, teaching assistantships with full tuition reimbursements available, Federal Work-Study, institutionally sponsored loans, and tuition waivers (full) available. Support available to part-time students. *Total annual research expenditures:* $720,000. *Unit head:* Dr. Steven Esling, Chair, 618-453-3351, Fax: 618-453-7393, E-mail: esling@geo.siu.edu. *Application contact:* Sharon Simons, Office Specialist, 618-453-3351, E-mail: simons@geo.siu.edu.

Southern Methodist University, Dedman College, Department of Earth Sciences, Dallas, TX 75275. Offers applied geophysics (MS); earth sciences (MS, PhD). Part-time programs available. *Degree requirements:* For master's, thesis (for some programs), qualifying exam; for doctorate, thesis/dissertation, qualifying exam. *Entrance requirements:* For master's and doctorate, GRE General Test, minimum GPA of 3.0, letters of recommendation. Additional exam requirements/recommendations for international students: Required—TOEFL. Electronic applications accepted. *Faculty research:* Sedimentology, geochemistry, igneous and metamorphic petrology, vertebrate paleontology, seismology.

Stephen F. Austin State University, Graduate School, College of Sciences and Mathematics, Department of Geology, Nacogdoches, TX 75962. Offers MS, MSNS. *Degree requirements:* For master's, comprehensive exam. *Entrance requirements:* For master's, GRE General Test, minimum GPA of 2.8 in last 60 hours, 2.5 overall. Additional exam requirements/recommendations for international students: Required—TOEFL. *Faculty research:* Stratigraphy of Kaibab limestone, Utah; structure of Ouachita Mountains, Arkansas; groundwater chemistry of Carrizo Sand, Texas.

Sul Ross State University, School of Arts and Sciences, Department of Earth and Physical Sciences, Alpine, TX 79832. Offers geology (MS). Part-time programs available. *Degree requirements:* For master's, thesis optional. *Entrance requirements:* For master's, GRE General Test, minimum GPA of 2.5 in last 60 hours of undergraduate work.

Syracuse University, College of Arts and Sciences, Program in Earth Sciences, Syracuse, NY 13244. Offers MA, MS, PhD. Part-time programs available. *Degree requirements:* For master's, thesis (for some programs), research tool; for doctorate, thesis/dissertation, 2 research tools. *Entrance requirements:* For master's and doctorate, GRE General Test, GRE Subject Test. Additional exam requirements/recommendations for international students: Required—TOEFL (minimum score 100 iBT). Electronic applications accepted.

Temple University, College of Science and Technology, Department of Earth and Environmental Science, Philadelphia, PA 19122-6096. Offers MS. *Faculty:* 11 full-time (4 women). *Students:* 12 full-time (2 women). 13 applicants, 46% accepted, 4 enrolled. In 2012, 5 master's awarded. *Degree requirements:* For master's, thesis, qualifying exam. *Entrance requirements:* For master's, GRE General Test, minimum GPA of 3.0. Additional exam requirements/recommendations for international students: Required—TOEFL (minimum score 550 paper-based; 79 iBT). *Application deadline:* For fall admission, 2/1 for domestic students, 12/15 for international students; for spring admission, 10/1 for domestic students, 8/1 for international students. Application fee: $60. Electronic applications accepted. *Financial support:* Fellowships, research assistantships with full tuition reimbursements, teaching assistantships with full tuition reimbursements, and scholarships/grants available. Financial award application deadline: 1/15; financial award applicants required to submit FAFSA. *Faculty research:* Hydraulic modeling, environmental geochemistry and geophysics, paleosas, cyclic stratigraphy, materials research. *Unit head:* Dr. Jonathan Nyquist, Chair, 215-204-7484, Fax: 215-204-3496, E-mail: ees@temple.edu. *Application contact:* Shelah Cox, Administrative Assistant, 215-204-8227, E-mail: scox@temple.edu. Website: https://ees.cst.temple.edu/.

Texas A&M University, College of Geosciences, Department of Geology and Geophysics, College Station, TX 77843. Offers geology (MS, PhD); geophysics (MS, PhD). *Faculty:* 27. *Students:* 110 full-time (40 women), 28 part-time (17 women); includes 15 minority (3 Black or African American, non-Hispanic/Latino; 6 Asian, non-Hispanic/Latino; 4 Hispanic/Latino; 2 Two or more races, non-

Hispanic/Latino), 47 international. Average age 28. In 2012, 20 master's, 5 doctorates awarded. *Degree requirements:* For master's, thesis; for doctorate, thesis/dissertation. *Entrance requirements:* For master's and doctorate, GRE General Test. Additional exam requirements/recommendations for international students: Required—TOEFL. *Application deadline:* For fall admission, 3/1 priority date for domestic students, 1/15 for international students; for spring admission, 10/1 priority date for domestic students, 8/15 for international students. Applications are processed on a rolling basis. Application fee: $50 ($75 for international students). Electronic applications accepted. *Financial support:* In 2012–13, fellowships with partial tuition reimbursements (averaging $1,000 per year), research assistantships with partial tuition reimbursements (averaging $11,925 per year), teaching assistantships with partial tuition reimbursements (averaging $11,925 per year) were awarded; Federal Work-Study, institutionally sponsored loans, scholarships/grants, tuition waivers (partial), and unspecified assistantships also available. Financial award application deadline: 3/1; financial award applicants required to submit FAFSA. *Faculty research:* Environmental and engineering geology and geophysics, petroleum geology, tectonophysics, geochemistry. *Unit head:* Dr. Rick Giardino, Head, 979-845-3224, E-mail: giardino@geo.tamu.edu. *Application contact:* Graduate Admissions, 979-845-1044, E-mail: admissions@tamu.edu. Website: http://geoweb.tamu.edu.

Texas A&M University–Kingsville, College of Graduate Studies, College of Arts and Sciences, Department of Geosciences, Kingsville, TX 78363. Offers applied geology (MS). Part-time and evening/weekend programs available. *Degree requirements:* For master's, comprehensive exam, thesis. *Entrance requirements:* For master's, GRE General Test, minimum GPA of 3.0. Additional exam requirements/recommendations for international students: Required—TOEFL. *Faculty research:* Stratigraphy and sedimentology of modern coastal sediments, sandstone diagnosis, vertebrate paleontology, structural geology.

Texas Christian University, College of Science and Engineering, School of Geology, Energy and the Environment, Fort Worth, TX 76129. Offers environmental management (MEM); environmental science (MA, MS); geology (MS). Part-time programs available. *Faculty:* 7 full-time (1 woman). *Students:* 17 full-time (9 women), 24 part-time (11 women); includes 4 minority (1 Black or African American, non-Hispanic/Latino; 1 Asian, non-Hispanic/Latino; 2 Hispanic/Latino), 2 international. Average age 26. 30 applicants, 80% accepted, 16 enrolled. In 2012, 10 master's awarded. *Degree requirements:* For master's, comprehensive exam (for some programs), thesis (for some programs). *Entrance requirements:* For master's, GRE. Additional exam requirements/recommendations for international students: Required—TOEFL (minimum score 550 paper-based; 80 iBT). *Application deadline:* For fall admission, 2/28 priority date for domestic students, 2/28 for international students. Application fee: $60. *Expenses: Tuition:* Full-time $21,600; part-time $1200 per credit. *Required fees:* $48. Tuition and fees vary according to program. *Financial support:* In 2012–13, 15 teaching assistantships with full tuition reimbursements (averaging $15,000 per year) were awarded. Financial award application deadline: 2/28. *Unit head:* Dr. Phil Hartman, Dean, 817-257-7727, E-mail: p.hartman@tcu.edu. *Application contact:* Dr. Magnus Rittby, Associate Dean for Administration and Graduate Programs, 817-257-7729, Fax: 817-257-7736, E-mail: m.rittby@tcu.edu. Website: http://geo1.tcu.edu/graduate/graduate.html.

Université du Québec à Montréal, Graduate Programs, Program in Earth Sciences, Montreal, QC H3C 3P8, Canada. Offers earth sciences (M Sc); mineral resources (PhD); non-renewable resources (DESS). Part-time programs available. Terminal master's awarded for partial completion of doctoral program. *Degree requirements:* For master's, thesis (for some programs); for doctorate, thesis/dissertation. *Entrance requirements:* For master's, appropriate bachelor's degree or equivalent, proficiency in French. *Faculty research:* Economic geology, structural geology, geochemistry, Quaternary geology, isotopic geochemistry.

Université Laval, Faculty of Sciences and Engineering, Department of Geology and Geological Engineering, Québec, QC G1K 7P4, Canada. Offers earth sciences (M Sc, PhD), including earth sciences, environmental technologies (M Sc); geology (M Sc, PhD). Terminal master's awarded for partial completion of doctoral program. *Degree requirements:* For master's, thesis (for some programs); for doctorate, comprehensive exam, thesis/dissertation. *Entrance requirements:* For master's and doctorate, knowledge of French. Electronic applications accepted. *Faculty research:* Engineering, economics, regional geology.

University at Albany, State University of New York, College of Arts and Sciences, Department of Earth and Atmospheric Sciences, Albany, NY 12222-0001. Offers atmospheric science (MS, PhD); geology (MS, PhD). *Degree requirements:* For master's, one foreign language, comprehensive exam, thesis; for doctorate, 2 foreign languages, comprehensive exam, thesis/dissertation, oral exams. *Entrance requirements:* For master's and doctorate, GRE General Test. Additional exam requirements/recommendations for international students: Required—TOEFL (minimum score 550 paper-based). Electronic applications accepted. *Faculty research:* Environmental geochemistry, tectonics, mesoscale meteorology, atmospheric chemistry.

University at Buffalo, the State University of New York, Graduate School, College of Arts and Sciences, Department of Geology, Buffalo, NY 14260. Offers MA, MS, PhD. Part-time programs available. *Faculty:* 14 full-time (6 women), 1 part-time/adjunct (0 women). *Students:* 60 full-time (23 women); includes 3 minority (1 American Indian or Alaska Native, non-Hispanic/Latino; 2 Hispanic/Latino), 12 international. Average age 26. 63 applicants, 57% accepted, 24 enrolled. In 2012, 8 master's awarded. *Degree requirements:* For master's, project or thesis; for doctorate, thesis/dissertation, dissertation defense. *Entrance requirements:* For master's and doctorate, GRE General Test. Additional exam requirements/recommendations for international students: Required—TOEFL (minimum score 550 paper-based; 79 iBT). *Application deadline:* For fall admission, 2/1 priority date for domestic students, 2/1 for international students; for spring admission, 10/1 priority date for domestic students, 10/1 for international students. Applications are processed on a rolling basis. Application fee: $75. Electronic applications accepted. *Financial support:* In 2012–13, 31 students received support, including 7 fellowships with full tuition reimbursements available (averaging $6,000 per year), 16 research assistantships with full tuition reimbursements available (averaging $15,500 per year), 15 teaching assistantships with full tuition reimbursements available (averaging $15,500 per year); Federal Work-Study, scholarships/grants, health care benefits, and unspecified assistantships also available. Financial award application deadline: 2/1; financial award applicants required to submit FAFSA. *Faculty research:* Environmental geology, hydrogeology, geochemistry, fractured rocks, volcanology. *Total annual research expenditures:* $1.9 million. *Unit head:* Dr. Richelle M. Allen-King, Professor and Chair, 716-645-3489, Fax: 716-645-3999, E-mail: geology@buffalo.edu. *Application contact:* Dr. Eliza Calder, Director of Graduate Studies, 716-645-4329, Fax: 716-645-3999, E-mail: ecalder@buffalo.edu. Website: http://www.geology.buffalo.edu/.

The University of Akron, Graduate School, Buchtel College of Arts and Sciences, Department of Geology and Environmental Science, Akron, OH 44325. Offers earth science (MS); engineering geology (MS); environmental geology (MS); geology (MS); geophysics (MS). Part-time programs available. *Faculty:* 10 full-time (2 women), 8 part-time/adjunct (2 women). *Students:* 15 full-time (5 women). Average age 25. 24 applicants, 75% accepted, 5 enrolled. In 2012, 8 master's awarded. *Degree requirements:* For master's, comprehensive exam, thesis, seminar, proficiency exam. *Entrance requirements:* For master's, minimum GPA of 2.75, three letters of recommendation, statement of purpose. Additional exam requirements/recommendations for international students: Required—TOEFL (minimum score 550 paper-based; 79 iBT). *Application deadline:* Applications are processed on a rolling basis. Application fee: $40 ($60 for international students). Electronic applications accepted. *Expenses:* Tuition, state resident: full-time $7285; part-time $404.70 per credit hour. Tuition, nonresident: full-time $12,473; part-time $692.95 per credit hour. *Required fees:* $34.05 per credit hour. Tuition and fees vary according to course load. *Financial support:* In 2012–13, 14 teaching assistantships with full tuition reimbursements were awarded. *Faculty research:* Terrestrial environmental change, karst hydrogeology, lacustrine paleoenvironments, environmental magnetism and geophysics. *Total annual research expenditures:* $306,408. *Unit head:* Dr. John Szabo, Chair, 330-972-8039, E-mail: jszabo@uakron.edu. *Application contact:* Dr. LaVerne Friberg, Director of Graduate Studies, 330-972-8046, E-mail: lfribe1@uakron.edu. Website: http://www.uakron.edu/geology/.

The University of Alabama, Graduate School, College of Arts and Sciences, Department of Geological Sciences, Tuscaloosa, AL 35487. Offers MS, PhD. *Faculty:* 15 full-time (6 women). *Students:* 41 full-time (16 women), 13 part-time (3 women); includes 4 minority (2 Black or African American, non-Hispanic/Latino; 1 American Indian or Alaska Native, non-Hispanic/Latino; 1 Two or more races, non-Hispanic/Latino), 13 international. Average age 29. 53 applicants, 60% accepted, 15 enrolled. In 2012, 8 master's, 2 doctorates awarded. Terminal master's awarded for partial completion of doctoral program. *Degree requirements:* For master's, comprehensive exam, thesis; for doctorate, comprehensive exam, thesis/dissertation. *Entrance requirements:* For master's and doctorate, GRE. Additional exam requirements/recommendations for international students: Required—TOEFL (minimum score 550 paper-based; 79 iBT). *Application deadline:* For fall admission, 3/1 priority date for domestic students, 3/1 for international students; for spring admission, 10/1 priority date for domestic students, 10/1 for international students. Applications are processed on a rolling basis. Application fee: $50 ($60 for international students). Electronic applications accepted. *Expenses:* Tuition, state resident: full-time $9200. Tuition, nonresident: full-time $22,950. *Financial support:* In 2012–13, 11 research assistantships with full tuition reimbursements (averaging $13,595 per year), 29 teaching assistantships with full tuition reimbursements (averaging $13,365 per year) were awarded; career-related internships or fieldwork, Federal Work-Study, and institutionally sponsored loans also available. *Faculty research:* Structure, petrology, stratigraphy, geochemistry, hydrogeology, geophysics. *Total annual research expenditures:* $894,551. *Unit head:* Dr. Harold H. Stowell, Chairperson and Professor, 205-348-5095, E-mail: hstowell@wgs.geo.ua.edu. *Application contact:* Dr. Andrew Mark Goodliffe, Graduate Program Director, 205-348-7167, E-mail: amg@ua.edu. Website: http://www.geo.ua.edu/.

University of Alaska Fairbanks, College of Natural Sciences and Mathematics, Department of Geology and Geophysics, Fairbanks, AK 99775-5780. Offers geology (MS, PhD), including economic geology (PhD), petroleum geology (MS), quaternary geology (PhD), remote sensing, volcanology (PhD); geophysics (MS, PhD), including remote sensing, snow, ice, and permafrost geophysics (MS), solid-earth geophysics (MS). Part-time programs available. *Faculty:* 11 full-time (5 women). *Students:* 62 full-time (30 women), 12 part-time (5 women); includes 3 minority (1 Hispanic/Latino; 2 Two or more races, non-Hispanic/Latino), 25 international. Average age 29. 92 applicants, 21% accepted, 19 enrolled. In 2012, 4 master's, 7 doctorates awarded. Terminal master's awarded for partial completion of doctoral program. *Degree requirements:* For master's, comprehensive exam, thesis, oral exam, oral defense; for doctorate, comprehensive exam, thesis/dissertation, oral exam, oral defense. *Entrance requirements:* For master's and doctorate, GRE General Test. Additional exam requirements/recommendations for international students: Required—TOEFL (minimum score 550 paper-based). *Application deadline:* For fall admission, 6/1 for domestic students, 3/1 for international students; for spring admission, 10/15 for domestic students, 9/1 for international students. Applications are processed on a rolling basis. Application fee: $60. Electronic applications accepted. *Expenses:* Tuition, state resident: full-time $7038. Tuition, nonresident: full-time $14,382. Tuition and fees vary according to course level, course load and reciprocity agreements. *Financial support:* In 2012–13, 47 research assistantships with tuition reimbursements (averaging $15,895 per year), 7 teaching assistantships with tuition reimbursements (averaging $13,083 per year) were awarded; fellowships with tuition reimbursements, Federal Work-Study, scholarships/grants, health care benefits, and unspecified assistantships also available. Support available to part-time students. Financial award application deadline: 2/15; financial award applicants required to submit FAFSA. *Faculty research:* Glacial surging, volcanology, geochronology, impact cratering, permafrost geophysics. *Total annual research expenditures:* $45,000. *Unit head:* Dr. Sarah Fowell, Department Co-Chair, 907-474-7565, Fax: 907-474-5163, E-mail: geology@uaf.edu. *Application contact:* Libby Eddy, Registrar and Director of Admissions, 907-474-7500, Fax: 907-474-7097, E-mail: admissions@uaf.edu. Website: http://www.uaf.edu/geology/

University of Arkansas, Graduate School, J. William Fulbright College of Arts and Sciences, Department of Geosciences, Program in Geology, Fayetteville, AR 72701-1201. Offers MS. Part-time programs available. *Students:* 22 full-time (7 women), 10 part-time (2 women); includes 3 minority (2 Black or African American, non-Hispanic/Latino; 1 Hispanic/Latino), 1 international. In 2012, 5 master's awarded. *Degree requirements:* For master's, thesis. *Application deadline:* For fall admission, 4/1 for international students; for spring admission, 10/1 for international students. Applications are processed on a rolling basis. Application fee: $40 ($50 for international students). Electronic applications accepted. *Financial support:* In 2012–13, 1 research assistantship, 10 teaching assistantships were awarded; fellowships, career-related internships or fieldwork, and Federal Work-Study also available. Support available to part-time students. Financial award application deadline: 4/1; financial award applicants required to submit FAFSA. *Unit head:* Dr. Ralph Davis, Graduate Coordinator, 479-575-3355, Fax: 479-575-3469, E-mail: ralphd@uark.edu. *Application contact:* Dr. Doy Zachry, Graduate Admissions, 479-575-2785, E-mail: dzachry@uark.edu. Website: http://geosciences.uark.edu/.

The University of British Columbia, Faculty of Science, Department of Earth and Ocean Sciences, Vancouver, BC V6T 1Z4, Canada. Offers atmospheric science (M Sc, PhD); geological engineering (M Eng, MA Sc, PhD); geological sciences (M Sc, PhD); geophysics (M Sc, MA Sc, PhD); oceanography (M Sc, PhD). *Degree requirements:* For master's, thesis (for some programs); for doctorate, comprehensive exam, thesis/dissertation. *Entrance requirements:* Additional exam requirements/recommendations for international students: Required—TOEFL (minimum score 600 paper-based; 100 iBT). Electronic applications accepted. *Faculty research:* Oceans and atmosphere, environmental earth science, hydro geology, mineral deposits, geophysics.

University of Calgary, Faculty of Graduate Studies, Faculty of Science, Department of Geology and Geophysics, Calgary, AB T2N 1N4, Canada. Offers geology (M Sc, PhD); geophysics (M Sc, PhD). Part-time programs available. Terminal master's awarded for partial completion of doctoral program. *Degree requirements:* For master's, thesis; for doctorate, thesis/dissertation, candidacy exam. *Entrance requirements:* For master's, B Sc; for doctorate, honors B Sc or M Sc. Additional exam requirements/recommendations for international students: Required—TOEFL. Electronic applications accepted. *Faculty research:* Geochemistry, petrology, paleontology, stratigraphy, exploration and solid-earth geophysics.

University of California, Berkeley, Graduate Division, College of Letters and Science, Department of Earth and Planetary Science, Berkeley, CA 94720-1500. Offers geology (MA, MS, PhD); geophysics (MA, MS, PhD). Terminal master's awarded for partial completion of doctoral program. *Degree requirements:* For master's, oral exam (MA), thesis (MS); for doctorate, comprehensive exam, thesis/dissertation, candidacy exams. *Entrance requirements:* For master's and doctorate, GRE General Test, minimum GPA of 3.0, 3 letters of recommendation. Additional exam requirements/recommendations for international students: Required—TOEFL. *Faculty research:* Tectonics, environmental geology, high-pressure geophysics and seismology, economic geology, geochemistry.

University of California, Davis, Graduate Studies, Program in Geology, Davis, CA 95616. Offers MS, PhD. Terminal master's awarded for partial completion of doctoral program. *Degree requirements:* For master's, thesis; for doctorate, thesis/dissertation. *Entrance requirements:* For master's and doctorate, GRE General Test, GRE Subject Test, minimum GPA of 3.0. Additional exam requirements/recommendations for international students: Required—TOEFL (minimum score 550 paper-based). Electronic applications accepted. *Faculty research:* Petrology, paleontology, geophysics, sedimentology, structure/ tectonics.

University of California, Los Angeles, Graduate Division, College of Letters and Science, Department of Earth and Space Sciences, Program in Geology, Los Angeles, CA 90095. Offers MS, PhD. *Faculty:* 23 full-time (3 women). *Students:* 22 full-time (8 women); includes 6 minority (1 Black or African American, non-Hispanic/Latino; 4 Asian, non-Hispanic/Latino; 1 Hispanic/Latino), 3 international. Average age 27. 31 applicants, 19% accepted, 5 enrolled. In 2012, 5 master's, 2 doctorates awarded. Terminal master's awarded for partial completion of doctoral program. *Degree requirements:* For master's, comprehensive exam or thesis; for doctorate, thesis/dissertation, oral and written qualifying exams. *Entrance requirements:* For master's and doctorate, GRE General Test, bachelor's degree; minimum undergraduate GPA of 3.0 (or its equivalent if letter grade system not used). Additional exam requirements/recommendations for international students: Required—TOEFL. *Application deadline:* For fall admission, 1/15 for domestic and international students. Application fee: $80 ($100 for international students). Electronic applications accepted. *Expenses:* Tuition, nonresident: full-time $15,102. *Required fees:* $14,809.19. Full-time tuition and fees vary according to program. *Financial support:* In 2012–13, 21 students received support, including 20 fellowships with full and partial tuition reimbursements available, 12 research assistantships with full and partial tuition reimbursements available, 18 teaching assistantships with full and partial tuition reimbursements available; Federal Work-Study, scholarships/grants, health care benefits, tuition waivers (full and partial), and unspecified assistantships also available. Financial award application deadline: 3/2; financial award applicants required to submit FAFSA. *Unit head:* Dr. Kevin McKeegan, Chair, 310-825-1475, E-mail: mckeegan@ess.ucla.edu. *Application contact:* Student Affairs Officer, 310-825-3880, Fax: 310-825-2779, E-mail: info@ess.ucla.edu. Website: http://www.ess.ucla.edu.

University of California, Riverside, Graduate Division, Department of Earth Sciences, Riverside, CA 92521-0102. Offers geological sciences (MS, PhD). *Faculty:* 34 full-time (15 women). *Students:* 31 full-time (19 women), 1 part-time (0 women); includes 2 minority (both Hispanic/Latino), 2 international. Average age 30. In 2012, 2 doctorates awarded. Terminal master's awarded for partial completion of doctoral program. *Degree requirements:* For master's, thesis, final oral exam; for doctorate, thesis/dissertation, qualifying exams, final oral exam. *Entrance requirements:* For master's and doctorate, GRE General Test, minimum GPA of 3.2. Additional exam requirements/recommendations for international students: Required—TOEFL (minimum score 550 paper-based; 80 iBT). *Application deadline:* For fall admission, 12/1 priority date for domestic students, 2/1 for international students; for winter admission, 9/1 for domestic students, 7/1 for international students; for spring admission, 12/1 for domestic students, 10/1 for international students. Applications are processed on a rolling basis. Application fee: $80 ($100 for international students). Electronic applications accepted. *Expenses:* Tuition, state resident: full-time $14,646. Tuition, nonresident: full-time $29,748. *Financial support:* In 2012–13, fellowships with full and partial tuition reimbursements (averaging $12,000 per year), research assistantships with full and partial tuition reimbursements (averaging $16,000 per year), teaching assistantships with full and partial tuition reimbursements (averaging $16,500 per year) were awarded; career-related internships or fieldwork, Federal Work-Study, institutionally sponsored loans, health care benefits, tuition waivers (full and partial), and unspecified assistantships also available. Financial award application deadline: 1/5; financial award applicants required to submit FAFSA. *Faculty research:* Applied and solid earth geophysics, tectonic geomorphology, fluid-rock interaction, paleobiology-ecology, sedimentary-geochemistry. *Unit head:* Dr. Richard Minnich, Chair, 951-827-5515, Fax: 951-827-4324, E-mail: richard.minnich@ucr.edu. *Application contact:* John Herring, Graduate Program Assistant, 951-827-2441, Fax: 951-827-4324, E-mail: geology@ucr.edu. Website: http://vortex.ucr.edu/esdocs/gradstud.html.

University of California, Santa Barbara, Graduate Division, College of Letters and Sciences, Division of Mathematics, Life, and Physical Sciences, Department of Earth Science, Santa Barbara, CA 93106-9620. Offers geological sciences (MS, PhD); geophysics (MS). *Faculty:* 20 full-time (3 women), 6 part-time/adjunct (1 woman). *Students:* 43 full-time (18 women); includes 7 minority (1 American Indian or Alaska Native, non-Hispanic/Latino; 1 Asian, non-Hispanic/Latino; 5 Hispanic/Latino), 6 international. Average age 27. 116 applicants, 19% accepted, 13 enrolled. In 2012, 3 master's, 1 doctorate awarded. Terminal master's awarded for partial completion of doctoral program. *Degree requirements:* For master's, comprehensive exam, thesis, 30 units; for doctorate, comprehensive exam, thesis/dissertation, 30 units, oral qualifying exam. *Entrance requirements:* For master's and doctorate, GRE General Test. Additional exam requirements/ recommendations for international students: Required—TOEFL (minimum score 550 paper-based; 80 iBT), IELTS (minimum score 7). *Application deadline:* For fall admission, 2/1 for domestic and international students. Application fee: $80 ($100 for international students). Electronic applications accepted. *Financial support:* In 2012–13, 28 students received support, including 3 fellowships with full and partial tuition reimbursements available (averaging $22,000 per year), 11 research assistantships with full and partial tuition reimbursements available (averaging $5,500 per year), 41 teaching assistantships with full and partial tuition reimbursements available (averaging $5,885 per year). Financial award application deadline: 1/3; financial award applicants required to submit CSS PROFILE or FAFSA. *Faculty research:* Geology, geomaterials and earth's structure; geomorphology, tectonics; geophysics, seismology; paleoclimatology, paleooceanography and geochemistry; paleobiology, evolution and paleontology. *Unit head:* Dr. Douglas Burbank, Chair, 805-893-7858, Fax: 805-893-2314, E-mail: burbank@eri.ucsb.edu. *Application contact:* Hannah Smit, Graduate Program Assistant, 805-893-3329, Fax: 805-893-2314, E-mail: hsmit@ geol.ucsb.edu. Website: http://www.geol.ucsb.edu/.

University of Cincinnati, Graduate School, McMicken College of Arts and Sciences, Department of Geology, Cincinnati, OH 45221. Offers MS, PhD. Part-time programs available. *Degree requirements:* For master's, thesis; for doctorate, comprehensive exam, thesis/dissertation. *Entrance requirements:* For master's and doctorate, GRE General Test, 1 year of course work in physics, chemistry, and calculus. Additional exam requirements/recommendations for international students: Required—TOEFL. Electronic applications accepted. *Faculty research:* Paleobiology, sequence stratigraphy, earth systems history, quaternary, groundwater.

University of Colorado Boulder, Graduate School, College of Arts and Sciences, Department of Geological Sciences, Boulder, CO 80309. Offers geology (MS, PhD); geophysics (PhD). *Faculty:* 28 full-time (7 women). *Students:* 75 full-time (39 women), 12 part-time (2 women); includes 5 minority (1 American Indian or Alaska Native, non-Hispanic/Latino; 2 Hispanic/Latino; 2 Two or more races, non-Hispanic/Latino), 11 international. Average age 28. 221 applicants, 8% accepted, 17 enrolled. Terminal master's awarded for partial completion of doctoral program. *Degree requirements:* For master's, comprehensive exam, thesis; for doctorate, comprehensive exam, thesis/dissertation. *Entrance requirements:* For master's, GRE General Test, minimum undergraduate GPA of 3.0; for doctorate, GRE General Test, minimum GPA of 2.75. *Application deadline:* For fall admission, 1/10 priority date for domestic students, 12/1 for international students. Application fee: $50 ($60 for international students). Electronic applications accepted. *Financial support:* In 2012–13, 34 fellowships (averaging $12,016 per year), 34 research assistantships with full and partial tuition reimbursements (averaging $22,169 per year), 24 teaching assistantships with full and partial tuition reimbursements (averaging $19,553 per year) were awarded; institutionally sponsored loans, scholarships/grants, health care benefits, and unspecified assistantships also available. Financial award application deadline: 1/15; financial award applicants required to submit FAFSA. *Faculty research:* Sedimentology, stratigraphy, economic geology of mineral deposits, fossil fuels, hydrogeology and water resources, geophysics, isotope geology, paleobiology, mineralogy, remote sensing. *Total annual research expenditures:* $7.6 million. *Application contact:* E-mail: geolinfo@colorado.edu. Website: http://www.colorado.edu/GeolSci.

University of Connecticut, Graduate School, College of Liberal Arts and Sciences, Center for Integrative Geosciences, Storrs, CT 06269. Offers geological sciences (MS, PhD). *Degree requirements:* For doctorate, thesis/dissertation. *Entrance requirements:* For master's and doctorate, GRE General Test. Additional exam requirements/recommendations for international students: Required—TOEFL (minimum score 550 paper-based). Electronic applications accepted.

University of Delaware, College of Earth, Ocean, and Environment, Department of Geological Sciences, Newark, DE 19716. Offers MA, PhD.

University of Florida, Graduate School, College of Liberal Arts and Sciences, Department of Geological Sciences, Gainesville, FL 32611. Offers hydrologic sciences (MS, MST, PhD); tropical conservation and development (MS, MST, PhD); wetland sciences (MS, MST, PhD). Terminal master's awarded for partial completion of doctoral program. *Degree requirements:* For master's, thesis (for some programs); for doctorate, one foreign language, thesis/dissertation. *Entrance requirements:* For master's, GRE General Test (minimum score of 1000), minimum GPA of 3.0; for doctorate, GRE General Test (minimum score of 1100), minimum GPA of 3.0. Additional exam requirements/recommendations for international students: Required—TOEFL (minimum score 550 paper-based; 80 iBT), IELTS (minimum score 6). Electronic applications accepted. *Faculty research:* Paleoclimatology, tectonophysics, petrochemistry, marine geology, geochemistry, hydrology.

University of Georgia, Franklin College of Arts and Sciences, Department of Geology, Athens, GA 30602. Offers MS, PhD. *Degree requirements:* For master's, thesis; for doctorate, one foreign language, thesis/dissertation. *Entrance requirements:* For master's and doctorate, GRE General Test. Electronic applications accepted.

University of Hawaii at Manoa, Graduate Division, School of Ocean and Earth Science and Technology, Department of Geology and Geophysics, Honolulu, HI 96822. Offers high-pressure geophysics and geochemistry (MS, PhD); hydrogeology and engineering geology (MS, PhD); marine geology and geophysics (MS, PhD); planetary geosciences and remote sensing (MS, PhD); seismology and solid-earth geophysics (MS, PhD); volcanology, petrology, and geochemistry (MS, PhD). Part-time programs available. Terminal master's awarded for partial completion of doctoral program. *Degree requirements:* For master's, thesis optional; for doctorate, comprehensive exam, thesis/dissertation. *Entrance requirements:* For master's and doctorate, GRE General Test, minimum GPA of 3.0. Additional exam requirements/recommendations for international students: Required—TOEFL (minimum score 580 paper-based; 92 iBT), IELTS (minimum score 5).

University of Houston, College of Natural Sciences and Mathematics, Department of Earth and Atmospheric Sciences, Houston, TX 77204. Offers atmospheric science (PhD); geology (MA, PhD); geophysics (PhD). Part-time programs available. *Degree requirements:* For master's, thesis; for doctorate, comprehensive exam, thesis/dissertation. *Entrance requirements:* For master's and doctorate, GRE General Test. Additional exam requirements/recommendations for international students: Required—TOEFL (minimum score 550 paper-based; 79 iBT), IELTS (minimum score 6.5). Electronic applications accepted. *Faculty research:* Atmospherics sciences, seismic and solid earth geophysics, tectonics, environmental hydrochemistry, carbonates, micropaleontology, structure and tectonics, petroleum geology.

University of Idaho, College of Graduate Studies, College of Science, Department of Geological Sciences, Moscow, ID 83844-3022. Offers geology (MS, PhD); hydrology (MS). *Faculty:* 10 full-time, 1 part-time/adjunct. *Students:* 20 full-time, 13 part-time. Average age 33. In 2012, 8 master's, 3 doctorates awarded. *Degree requirements:* For doctorate, one foreign language, thesis/dissertation. *Entrance requirements:* For master's, minimum GPA of 2.8; for doctorate, minimum undergraduate GPA of 2.8, 3.0 graduate. *Application deadline:* For fall admission, 8/1 for domestic students; for spring admission, 12/15 for domestic students. Applications are processed on a rolling basis. Application fee: $60. Electronic applications accepted. *Expenses:* Tuition, state resident: full-time $4230; part-time $252 per credit hour. Tuition, nonresident: full-time $17,018; part-time $891 per credit hour. *Required fees:* $2932; $107 per credit hour. *Financial support:* Fellowships, research assistantships, and teaching assistantships available. Financial award applicants required to submit FAFSA. *Faculty research:* Health effects of mineral dust, geomicrobiology, glacial and arctic sciences, optical mineralogy, planetary and terrestrial geomechanics. *Unit head:* Dr. Mickey Gunter, Head, 208-885-6192, E-mail: geology@uidaho.edu. *Application contact:* Erick Larson, Director of Graduate Admissions, 208-885-4723, E-mail: gadms@uidaho.edu. Website: http://www.uidaho.edu/sci/geology.

University of Illinois at Chicago, Graduate College, College of Liberal Arts and Sciences, Department of Earth and Environmental Sciences, Chicago, IL 60607-7128. Offers MS, PhD. *Students:* 22 full-time (13 women); includes 1 minority (Asian, non-Hispanic/Latino), 6 international. Average age 28. 31 applicants, 26% accepted, 4 enrolled. In 2012, 2 master's, 1 doctorate awarded. *Degree requirements:* For master's, thesis; for doctorate, thesis/dissertation. *Entrance requirements:* For master's and doctorate, GRE General Test, minimum GPA of 2.75. Additional exam requirements/recommendations for international students: Required—TOEFL. *Application deadline:* For fall admission, 2/1 for domestic and international students; for spring admission, 11/15 for domestic students, 7/15 for international students. Applications are processed on a rolling basis. Application fee: $40 ($50 for international students). Electronic applications accepted. *Expenses:* Tuition, state resident: full-time $10,882; part-time $3627 per term. Tuition, nonresident: full-time $22,880; part-time $7627 per term. *Required fees:* $1170 per semester. Tuition and fees vary according to course load, degree level and program. *Financial support:* In 2012–13, 1 fellowship with full tuition reimbursement was awarded; research assistantships with full tuition reimbursements, teaching assistantships with full tuition reimbursements, Federal Work-Study, scholarships/grants, traineeships, tuition waivers (full), and unspecified assistantships also available. Financial award application deadline: 3/1; financial award applicants required to submit FAFSA. *Total annual research expenditures:* $1.3 million. *Unit head:* Dr. Kathryn Nagy, Head, 312-355-3276, E-mail: klnagy@uic.edu. *Application contact:* Andrew Dombard, Director of Graduate Studies, 312-996-9206, E-mail: adombard@uic.edu. Website: http://www.uic.edu/depts/geos/.

University of Illinois at Urbana–Champaign, Graduate College, College of Liberal Arts and Sciences, School of Earth, Society and Environment, Department of Geology, Champaign, IL 61820. Offers geology (MS, PhD); teaching of earth sciences (MS). *Students:* 29 (15 women). Terminal master's awarded for partial completion of doctoral program. Application fee: $75 ($90 for international students). *Unit head:* Thomas M. Johnson, Head, 217-244-2002, Fax: 217-244-4996, E-mail: tmjohnsn@illinois.edu. *Application contact:* Marilyn K. Whalen, Office Administrator, 217-333-3542, Fax: 217-244-4996, E-mail: mkt@illinois.edu. Website: http://www.geology.illinois.edu/.

The University of Kansas, Graduate Studies, College of Liberal Arts and Sciences, Department of Geology, Lawrence, KS 66045. Offers MS, PhD. PhD offered jointly with Kansas State University. *Students:* 77 full-time (30 women), 20 part-time (7 women); includes 10 minority (1 American Indian or Alaska Native, non-Hispanic/Latino; 6 Hispanic/Latino; 3 Two or more races, non-Hispanic/Latino), 13 international. Average age 28. 125 applicants, 48% accepted, 27 enrolled. In 2012, 20 master's, 3 doctorates awarded. *Degree requirements:* For master's, thesis or alternative; for doctorate, comprehensive exam, thesis/dissertation. *Entrance requirements:* For master's and doctorate, GRE General Test, 3 letters of recommendation. Additional exam requirements/recommendations for international students: Required—TOEFL. *Application deadline:* For fall admission, 2/1 priority date for domestic students, 2/1 for international students; for spring admission, 10/31 priority date for domestic students, 10/31 for international students. Applications are processed on a rolling basis. Application fee: $45 ($55 for international students). Electronic applications accepted. *Financial support:* Fellowships with full and partial tuition reimbursements, research assistantships with full and partial tuition reimbursements, teaching assistantships with full and partial tuition reimbursements, and unspecified assistantships available. Financial award application deadline: 2/1. *Faculty research:* Sedimentology, paleontology, tectonics, geophysics, hydrogeology. *Unit head:* Luis A. Gonzalez, Chair, 785-864-4974, Fax: 785-864-5276, E-mail: lgonzlez@ku.edu. *Application contact:* Gwen Macpherson, Graduate Director, 785-864-4974, Fax: 785-864-5276, E-mail: glmac@ku.edu. Website: http://www.geo.ku.edu.

University of Kentucky, Graduate School, College of Arts and Sciences, Program in Geology, Lexington, KY 40506-0032. Offers MS, PhD. *Degree requirements:* For master's, comprehensive exam, thesis; for doctorate, comprehensive exam, thesis/dissertation. *Entrance requirements:* For master's, GRE General Test, minimum undergraduate GPA of 2.75; for doctorate, GRE General Test, minimum graduate GPA of 3.0. Additional exam requirements/

recommendations for international students: Required—TOEFL (minimum score 550 paper-based). Electronic applications accepted. *Faculty research:* Structure tectonics, geophysics, stratigraphy, hydrogeology, coal geology.

University of Louisiana at Lafayette, College of Sciences, Department of Geology, Lafayette, LA 70504. Offers MS. Part-time programs available. *Degree requirements:* For master's, comprehensive exam, thesis. *Entrance requirements:* For master's, GRE General Test, minimum GPA of 2.75. Additional exam requirements/recommendations for international students: Required—TOEFL (minimum score 550 paper-based). Electronic applications accepted. *Faculty research:* Aquifer contamination, coastal erosion, geochemistry of peat, petroleum geology and geophysics, remote sensing and geographic information systems applications.

University of Maine, Graduate School, Climate Change Institute, Orono, ME 04469. Offers quaternary and climate studies (MS). Part-time programs available. *Faculty:* 37 full-time (0 women), 11 part-time/adjunct (0 women). *Students:* 8 full-time (4 women), 1 international. Average age 26. 24 applicants, 33% accepted, 5 enrolled. In 2012, 4 master's awarded. *Degree requirements:* For master's, thesis. *Entrance requirements:* For master's, GRE General Test. Additional exam requirements/recommendations for international students: Required—TOEFL. *Application deadline:* For fall admission, 2/1 priority date for domestic students. Applications are processed on a rolling basis. Application fee: $65. Electronic applications accepted. *Financial support:* In 2012–13, 3 research assistantships with full tuition reimbursements (averaging $14,780 per year), 3 teaching assistantships with full tuition reimbursements (averaging $14,100 per year) were awarded. Financial award application deadline: 3/1. *Faculty research:* Climate change, ecosystems, geology, glacial geology, anthropology. *Total annual research expenditures:* $14.2 million. *Unit head:* Dr. Paul Mayewski, Director, 207-581-3019, Fax: 207-581-1203. *Application contact:* Scott G. Delcourt, Associate Dean of the Graduate School, 207-581-3291, Fax: 207-581-3232, E-mail: graduate@maine.edu. Website: http://climatechange.umaine.edu/.

University of Manitoba, Faculty of Graduate Studies, Clayton H. Riddell Faculty of Environment, Earth, and Resources, Department of Geological Sciences, Winnipeg, MB R3T 2N2, Canada. Offers geology (M Sc, PhD); geophysics (M Sc, PhD). *Degree requirements:* For master's, thesis; for doctorate, thesis/dissertation. *Entrance requirements:* For master's and doctorate, GRE General Test, GRE Subject Test (geology), minimum GPA of 3.0. Additional exam requirements/recommendations for international students: Required—TOEFL.

University of Maryland, College Park, Academic Affairs, College of Computer, Mathematical and Natural Sciences, Department of Geology, College Park, MD 20742. Offers MS, PhD. *Faculty:* 37 full-time (9 women), 4 part-time/adjunct (2 women). *Students:* 31 full-time (16 women); includes 2 minority (both Hispanic/Latino), 10 international. 77 applicants, 14% accepted, 5 enrolled. In 2012, 6 master's, 6 doctorates awarded. *Degree requirements:* For master's, thesis, oral defense; for doctorate, thesis/dissertation. *Entrance requirements:* For master's, GRE General Test, minimum GPA of 3.0, 3 letters of recommendation; for doctorate, GRE General Test, 3 letters of recommendation. Additional exam requirements/recommendations for international students: Required—TOEFL. *Application deadline:* For fall admission, 3/15 for domestic students, 2/1 for international students; for spring admission, 10/15 for domestic students, 6/1 for international students. Applications are processed on a rolling basis. Application fee: $75. Electronic applications accepted. *Expenses:* Tuition, state resident: part-time $551 per credit. Tuition, nonresident: part-time $1188 per credit. Part-time tuition and fees vary according to program. *Financial support:* In 2012–13, 3 fellowships with full and partial tuition reimbursements (averaging $13,850 per year), 6 research assistantships (averaging $20,419 per year), 23 teaching assistantships (averaging $20,048 per year) were awarded; Federal Work-Study and scholarships/grants also available. Support available to part-time students. Financial award application deadline: 2/15; financial award applicants required to submit FAFSA. *Total annual research expenditures:* $2.7 million. *Unit head:* Roberta Rudnick, Chair, 301-405-4065, Fax: 301-314-9661, E-mail: rudnick@umd.edu. *Application contact:* Dr. Charles A. Caramello, Dean of Graduate School, 301-405-0358, Fax: 301-314-9305.

University of Memphis, Graduate School, College of Arts and Sciences, Department of Earth Sciences, Memphis, TN 38152. Offers archaeology (MS); earth sciences (PhD); geographic information systems (Graduate Certificate); geography (MA, MS); geology (MS); geophysics (MS); interdisciplinary (MS). Part-time and evening/weekend programs available. Terminal master's awarded for partial completion of doctoral program. *Degree requirements:* For master's, comprehensive exam, thesis, seminar presentation; for doctorate, thesis/dissertation. *Entrance requirements:* For master's, GRE General Test, 3 letters of recommendation, statement of research interests; for doctorate, GRE General Test, 2 letters of recommendation, resume, personal statement. Additional exam requirements/recommendations for international students: Required—TOEFL (minimum score 550 paper-based). Electronic applications accepted. *Faculty research:* Hazards, active tectonics, geophysics, hydrology and water resources, spatial analysis.

University of Minnesota, Duluth, Graduate School, Swenson College of Science and Engineering, Department of Geological Sciences, Duluth, MN 55812-2496. Offers MS, PhD. PhD offered jointly with University of Minnesota, Twin Cities Campus. Part-time programs available. *Degree requirements:* For master's, thesis, final oral exam, written and oral research proposal. *Entrance requirements:* For master's, GRE General Test, minimum GPA of 3.0. Additional exam requirements/recommendations for international students: Required—TOEFL (minimum score 550 paper-based). Electronic applications accepted. *Faculty research:* Surface processes, tectonics, planetary geology, paleoclimate, petrology.

University of Minnesota, Twin Cities Campus, College of Science and Engineering, Department of Earth Sciences, Minneapolis, MN 55455-0213. Offers MS, PhD. Terminal master's awarded for partial completion of doctoral program. *Degree requirements:* For master's, thesis; for doctorate, thesis/dissertation. *Entrance requirements:* For master's and doctorate, GRE General Test, 3 letters of recommendation. Additional exam requirements/recommendations for international students: Required—TOEFL (minimum score 550 paper-based). Electronic applications accepted. *Faculty research:* Geology, geophysics, geochemistry, geobiology, climate and environmental geosciences.

University of Missouri, Graduate School, College of Arts and Sciences, Department of Geological Sciences, Columbia, MO 65211. Offers MS, PhD. *Faculty:* 10 full-time (3 women), 1 part-time/adjunct (0 women). *Students:* 28 full-time (14 women), 7 part-time (0 women), 15 international. Average age 28. 38 applicants, 16% accepted, 3 enrolled. In 2012, 8 master's, 1 doctorate awarded. *Degree requirements:* For master's, thesis; for doctorate, variable foreign language requirement, thesis/dissertation. *Entrance requirements:* For master's and doctorate, GRE General Test, minimum GPA of 3.0. Additional exam requirements/recommendations for international students: Required—TOEFL (minimum score 530 paper-based; 71 iBT). *Application deadline:* For fall admission, 2/15 priority date for domestic students, 2/15 for international students. Applications are processed on a rolling basis. Application fee: $55 ($75 for international students). Electronic applications accepted. *Expenses:* Tuition, state resident: full-time $6057. Tuition, nonresident: full-time $15,683. *Required fees:* $1000. *Financial support:* In 2012–13, 2 fellowships with full tuition reimbursements, 17 research assistantships with full tuition reimbursements, 13 teaching assistantships with full tuition reimbursements were awarded; institutionally sponsored loans, health care benefits, and unspecified assistantships also available. *Faculty research:* Geochemistry, tectonics, economic geology, biogeochemistry, geophysics. *Unit head:* Dr. Kevin L. Shelton, Department Chair, 573-882-6568, E-mail: sheltonkl@missouri.edu. *Application contact:* Alice Thompson, Administrative Assistant, 573-882-6785, E-mail: thompsonao@missouri.edu. Website: http://geology.missouri.edu/degree/grad.html.

University of Missouri–Kansas City, College of Arts and Sciences, Department of Geosciences, Kansas City, MO 64110-2499. Offers environmental and urban geosciences (MS); geosciences (PhD). PhD (interdisciplinary) offered through the School of Graduate Studies. Part-time programs available. *Faculty:* 11 full-time (3 women), 5 part-time/adjunct (0 women). *Students:* 6 full-time (3 women), 21 part-time (11 women); includes 4 minority (2 Black or African American, non-Hispanic/Latino; 1 American Indian or Alaska Native, non-Hispanic/Latino; 1 Two or more races, non-Hispanic/Latino), 5 international. Average age 33. 24 applicants, 50% accepted, 9 enrolled. In 2012, 12 master's awarded. *Degree requirements:* For master's, thesis; for doctorate, thesis/dissertation, qualifying exam. *Entrance requirements:* For master's, GRE General Test, minimum GPA of 3.0. Additional exam requirements/recommendations for international students: Required—TOEFL (minimum score 550 paper-based; 80 iBT). *Application deadline:* For fall admission, 3/15 priority date for domestic students, 3/15 for international students. Applications are processed on a rolling basis. Application fee: $45 ($50 for international students). Electronic applications accepted. *Expenses:* Tuition, state resident: full-time $5972.40; part-time $331.80 per credit hour. Tuition, nonresident: full-time $15,417; part-time $856.50 per credit hour. *Required fees:* $95.89 per credit hour. Full-time tuition and fees vary according to program. *Financial support:* In 2012–13, 1 research assistantship with partial tuition reimbursement (averaging $15,750 per year), 14 teaching assistantships with partial tuition reimbursements (averaging $13,308 per year) were awarded; Federal Work-Study, institutionally sponsored loans, and tuition waivers (full and partial) also available. Support available to part-time students. Financial award application deadline: 3/1; financial award applicants required to submit FAFSA. *Faculty research:* Neotectonics and applied geophysics, environmental geosciences, urban geoscience, geoinformatics-remote sensing, atmospheric research. *Unit head:* Dr. James B. Murowchick, Chair, 816-235-2979, Fax: 816-235-5535, E-mail: murowchick@umkc.edu. *Application contact:* Dr. Jejung Lee, Associate Professor, 816-235-6495, Fax: 816-235-5535, E-mail: leej@umkc.edu. Website: http://cas.umkc.edu/geo/.

The University of Montana, Graduate School, College of Arts and Sciences, Department of Geology, Missoula, MT 59812-0002. Offers applied geoscience (PhD); geology (MS, PhD). *Degree requirements:* For doctorate, thesis/dissertation. *Entrance requirements:* For master's and doctorate, GRE General Test. Additional exam requirements/recommendations for international students: Required—TOEFL (minimum score 525 paper-based). *Faculty research:* Environmental geoscience, regional structure and tectonics, groundwater geology, petrology, mineral deposits.

University of Nevada, Reno, Graduate School, College of Science, Mackay School of Earth Sciences and Engineering, Department of Geological Sciences and Engineering, Program in Geology, Reno, NV 89557. Offers MS, PhD. Terminal master's awarded for partial completion of doctoral program. *Degree requirements:* For master's, thesis optional; for doctorate, thesis/dissertation. *Entrance requirements:* For master's, GRE General Test, minimum GPA of 2.75; for doctorate, GRE General Test, minimum GPA of 3.0. Additional exam requirements/recommendations for international students: Required—TOEFL (minimum score 500 paper-based; 61 iBT), IELTS (minimum score 6). Electronic applications accepted. *Faculty research:* Mineral exploration, geochemistry, hydrology.

University of New Brunswick Fredericton, School of Graduate Studies, Faculty of Science, Department of Earth Sciences, Fredericton, NB E3B 5A3, Canada. Offers M Sc, PhD. Part-time programs available. *Faculty:* 11 full-time (0 women). *Students:* 23 full-time (11 women), 6 part-time (4 women). In 2012, 5 master's, 4 doctorates awarded. *Degree requirements:* For master's, thesis; for doctorate, thesis/dissertation. *Entrance requirements:* For master's, minimum GPA of 3.0, B Sc in earth sciences or related subject; for doctorate, minimum GPA of 3.0; M Sc in earth science or related subject. Additional exam requirements/recommendations for international students: Required—TOEFL, IELTS, TWE. *Application deadline:* For fall admission, 3/1 for domestic students. Applications are processed on a rolling basis. Application fee: $50 Canadian dollars. Electronic applications accepted. Tuition and fees charges are reported in Canadian dollars. *Expenses: Tuition, area resident:* Full-time $3956 Canadian dollars. *Required fees:* $579.50 Canadian dollars; $55 Canadian dollars per semester. *Financial support:* In 2012–13, 1 fellowship was awarded; research assistantships and teaching assistantships also available. *Faculty research:* Applied geophysics and rock physics; applied glacial and quaternary geology; aqueous and environmental geochemistry and hydrogeology; lithogeochemistry and mineral deposits; igneous, metamorphic and experimental petrology; isotope geochemistry and U-Pb geochronology; paleontology and ichnology; sedimentology, stratigraphy and petroleum geology; shock metamorphism, impact and planetary geology; structural geology and rock mechanics. *Total annual research expenditures:* $133,936. *Unit head:* Dr. David Keighley, Director of Graduate Studies, 506-453-5196, Fax: 506-453-5055, E-mail: keig@unb.ca. *Application contact:* Christine Lodge, Office Support Staff, Administrative and Graduate Services, 506-453-4803, Fax: 506-453-5055, E-mail: lodge@unb.ca. Website: http://go.unb.ca/gradprograms.

University of New Hampshire, Graduate School, College of Engineering and Physical Sciences, Department of Earth Sciences, Durham, NH 03824. Offers general (MS); geology (MS); hydrology (MS); ocean mapping (MS). *Faculty:* 17 full-time (5 women). *Students:* 15 full-time (8 women), 15 part-time (5 women); includes 1 minority (Black or African American, non-Hispanic/Latino), 4 international. Average age 27. 43 applicants, 53% accepted, 8 enrolled. In 2012, 15 master's awarded. *Degree requirements:* For master's, thesis. *Entrance requirements:* For master's, GRE General Test. Additional exam requirements/recommendations for international students: Required—TOEFL (minimum score 550 paper-based; 80 iBT). *Application deadline:* For fall admission, 4/1 priority date for domestic students, 4/1 for international students; for spring admission, 12/1 for domestic students. Applications are processed on a rolling basis. Application fee: $65. Electronic applications accepted. *Expenses:* Tuition, state resident: full-time $13,500; part-time $750 per credit. Tuition, nonresident: full-time $25,940; part-time $1089 per credit. *Required fees:* $1699; $424.75 per semester. *Financial support:* In 2012–13, 24 students received support, including 11 research assistantships, 7 teaching assistantships; fellowships, career-related internships or fieldwork, Federal Work-Study, scholarships/grants, and tuition waivers (full and partial) also available. Support available to part-time students. Financial award application deadline: 2/15. *Unit head:* Dr. Julie Bryce, Chairperson, 603-862-3139, E-mail: earth.sciences@unh.edu. *Application contact:* Sue Clark, Administrative Assistant, 603-862-1718, E-mail: earth.sciences@unh.edu. Website: http://www.unh.edu/esci/.

The University of North Carolina at Chapel Hill, Graduate School, College of Arts and Sciences, Department of Geological Sciences, Chapel Hill, NC 27599. Offers MS, PhD. *Degree requirements:* For master's, comprehensive exam, thesis; for doctorate, one foreign language, comprehensive exam, thesis/dissertation. *Entrance requirements:* For master's and doctorate, GRE General Test, minimum GPA of 3.0. Electronic applications accepted. *Faculty research:* Paleoceanography, igneous petrology, paleontology, geophysics, structural geology.

The University of North Carolina Wilmington, College of Arts and Sciences, Department of Geography and Geology, Wilmington, NC 28403-3297. Offers geology (MS); marine science (MS). *Degree requirements:* For master's, comprehensive exam, thesis. *Entrance requirements:* For master's, GRE General Test, GRE Subject Test, minimum B average in undergraduate major and basic prerequisite geology courses.

University of North Dakota, Graduate School, School of Engineering and Mines, Department of Geology, Grand Forks, ND 58202. Offers MA, MS, PhD. *Degree requirements:* For master's, thesis, final exam; for doctorate, one foreign language, comprehensive exam, thesis/dissertation, final exam. *Entrance requirements:* For master's and doctorate, GRE General Test, minimum GPA of 3.0. Additional exam requirements/recommendations for international students: Required—TOEFL (minimum score 550 paper-based; 79 iBT), IELTS (minimum score 6.5). Electronic applications accepted. *Faculty research:* Hydrogeology, environmental geology, geological engineering, sedimentology, geomorphology.

University of Oklahoma, Mewbourne College of Earth and Energy, ConocoPhillips School of Geology and Geophysics, Program in Geology, Norman, OK 73019. Offers MS, PhD. Part-time programs available. *Students:* 49 full-time (17 women), 21 part-time (3 women); includes 4 minority (1 Black or African American, non-Hispanic/Latino; 1 American Indian or Alaska Native, non-

Hispanic/Latino; 1 Asian, non-Hispanic/Latino; 1 Hispanic/Latino), 24 international. Average age 27. 122 applicants, 20% accepted, 20 enrolled. In 2012, 22 master's, 5 doctorates awarded. *Degree requirements:* For master's, comprehensive exam, thesis; for doctorate, one foreign language, comprehensive exam, thesis/dissertation, proposal, colloquium and dissertation defense. *Entrance requirements:* Additional exam requirements/recommendations for international students: Required—TOEFL (minimum score 550 paper-based; 79 iBT). *Application deadline:* For fall admission, 2/1 for domestic and international students; for spring admission, 9/1 for domestic and international students. Applications are processed on a rolling basis. Application fee: $40 ($90 for international students). Electronic applications accepted. *Expenses:* Tuition, state resident: full-time $4205; part-time $175.20 per credit hour. Tuition, nonresident: full-time $15,667; part-time $653 per credit hour. *Required fees:* $2745; $103.85 per credit hour. Tuition and fees vary according to course load and degree level. *Financial support:* Career-related internships or fieldwork, scholarships/grants, and unspecified assistantships available. Financial award application deadline: 6/1; financial award applicants required to submit FAFSA. *Faculty research:* Earth systems, lithospheric dynamics, energy, geochemistry, and geophysics. *Unit head:* Dr. R. Douglas Elmore, Director and Associate Provost, 405-325-3253, Fax: 405-325-3140, E-mail: delmore@ou.edu. *Application contact:* Donna S. Mullins, Coordinator for Administrative Student Services, 405-325-3255, Fax: 405-325-3140, E-mail: dsmullins@ou.edu. Website: http://geology.ou.edu.

University of Oregon, Graduate School, College of Arts and Sciences, Department of Geological Sciences, Eugene, OR 97403. Offers MA, MS, PhD. *Degree requirements:* For master's, foreign language (MA). *Entrance requirements:* For master's and doctorate, GRE General Test, GRE Subject Test.

University of Pittsburgh, Dietrich School of Arts and Sciences, Department of Geology and Planetary Science, Pittsburgh, PA 15260-3332. Offers geographical information systems and remote sensing (Pro-MS); geology and planetary science (MS, PhD). Part-time programs available. *Faculty:* 7 full-time (2 women), 2 part-time/adjunct (1 woman). *Students:* 24 full-time (12 women), 7 part-time (3 women), 1 international. Average age 30. 48 applicants, 44% accepted, 12 enrolled. In 2012, 3 master's, 4 doctorates awarded. *Degree requirements:* For master's, thesis, oral thesis defense; for doctorate, comprehensive exam, thesis/dissertation, oral dissertation defense. *Entrance requirements:* For master's and doctorate, GRE General Test. Additional exam requirements/recommendations for international students: Required—TOEFL (minimum score 90 iBT), IELTS (minimum score 7.5). *Application deadline:* For fall admission, 1/15 priority date for domestic students, 1/15 for international students. Applications are processed on a rolling basis. Application fee: $50. Electronic applications accepted. *Expenses:* Tuition, state resident: full-time $19,336; part-time $782 per credit. Tuition, nonresident: full-time $31,658; part-time $1295 per credit. *Required fees:* $740; $200 per term. Tuition and fees vary according to program. *Financial support:* In 2012–13, 25 students received support, including 2 fellowships with full tuition reimbursements available (averaging $19,165 per year), 14 research assistantships with full and partial tuition reimbursements available (averaging $14,400 per year), 9 teaching assistantships with full and partial tuition reimbursements available (averaging $16,460 per year); career-related internships or fieldwork, Federal Work-Study, institutionally sponsored loans, scholarships/grants, health care benefits, and tuition waivers (full and partial) also available. Support available to part-time students. Financial award application deadline: 1/15; financial award applicants required to submit FAFSA. *Faculty research:* Geographical information systems, hydrology, low temperature geochemistry, volcanology, paleoclimatology. *Total annual research expenditures:* $1.6 million. *Unit head:* Dr. William Harbert, Chair, 412-624-8783, Fax: 412-624-3914, E-mail: harbert@pitt.edu. *Application contact:* Dr. Rosemary Capo, Director of Graduate Studies, 412-624-8873, Fax: 412-624-3914, E-mail: rcapo@pitt.edu. Website: http://www.geology.pitt.edu/.

University of Puerto Rico, Mayagüez Campus, Graduate Studies, College of Arts and Sciences, Department of Geology, Mayagüez, PR 00681-9000. Offers MS. Part-time programs available. *Faculty:* 10 full-time (2 women). *Students:* 19 full-time (12 women); includes 15 minority (all Hispanic/Latino), 1 international. 8 applicants, 88% accepted, 5 enrolled. In 2012, 2 master's awarded. *Degree requirements:* For master's, comprehensive exam, thesis. *Entrance requirements:* For master's, GRE General Test, BS in geology or the equivalent; minimum GPA of 2.8. *Application deadline:* For fall admission, 2/15 for domestic and international students; for spring admission, 9/15 for domestic and international students. Applications are processed on a rolling basis. Application fee: $25. Tuition and fees vary according to course level and course load. *Financial support:* In 2012–13, 14 students received support, including 6 research assistantships (averaging $15,000 per year), 9 teaching assistantships (averaging $8,500 per year). *Faculty research:* Seismology, applied geophysics, geographic information systems, environmental remote sensing, petrology. *Total annual research expenditures:* $363,164. *Unit head:* Dr. Lizzette Rodriguez, Interim Director, 787-832-4040 Ext. 3000, E-mail: lizzette.rodriguez1@upr.edu. *Application contact:* Marsha Irizarry, Administrative Secretary III, 787-832-4040 Ext. 2414, Fax: 787-265-3845, E-mail: irizarrym@uprm.edu. Website: http://geology.uprm.edu.

University of Regina, Faculty of Graduate Studies and Research, Faculty of Science, Department of Geology, Regina, SK S4S 0A2, Canada. Offers M Sc, PhD. PhD program offered on a special case basis only. *Faculty:* 8 full-time (3 women), 7 part-time/adjunct (0 women). *Students:* 13 full-time (5 women), 6 part-time (2 women). 20 applicants, 35% accepted. In 2012, 3 master's awarded. *Degree requirements:* For master's, thesis; for doctorate, thesis/dissertation.

148 www.petersonsbooks.com

Peterson's Graduate Programs in the Physical Sciences, Mathematics, Agricultural Sciences, the Environment & Natural Resources 2014

Entrance requirements: Additional exam requirements/recommendations for international students: Required—TOEFL (minimum score 580 paper-based; 80 iBT), IELTS (minimum score 6.5). *Application deadline:* Applications are processed on a rolling basis. Application fee: $100. Electronic applications accepted. Tuition and fees charges are reported in Canadian dollars. *Expenses: Tuition, area resident:* Full-time $3942 Canadian dollars; part-time $219 Canadian dollars per credit hour. *International tuition:* $4742 Canadian dollars full-time. *Required fees:* $421.55 Canadian dollars; $93.60 Canadian dollars per credit hour. Tuition and fees vary according to course load, degree level and program. *Financial support:* In 2012–13, 2 fellowships (averaging $6,000 per year), 2 research assistantships (averaging $5,500 per year), 5 teaching assistantships (averaging $2,400 per year) were awarded; scholarships/grants also available. Financial award application deadline: 6/15. *Faculty research:* Quaternary and economic geology; volcanology; organic, igneous, and metamorphic petrology; carbonate sedimentology and basin analysis; mineralogy. *Unit head:* Dr. Hairuo Qing, Head, 306-585-4677, Fax: 306-585-5433, E-mail: hairuo.qing@uregina.ca. *Application contact:* Dr. Osman Salad Hersi, Graduate Program Coordinator, 306-585-4663, Fax: 306-585-5433, E-mail: osman.salad.hersi@uregina.ca. Website: http://www.uregina.ca/geology/.

University of Rochester, School of Arts and Sciences, Department of Earth and Environmental Sciences, Rochester, NY 14627. Offers MS, PhD. *Degree requirements:* For doctorate, thesis/dissertation, qualifying exam. *Entrance requirements:* For master's and doctorate, GRE General Test. Additional exam requirements/recommendations for international students: Required—TOEFL. Electronic applications accepted. *Faculty research:* Geochemistry and environmental sciences; paleomagnetism, structure and tectonics.

University of Saskatchewan, College of Graduate Studies and Research, College of Arts and Science and College of Engineering, Department of Geological Sciences, Saskatoon, SK S7N 5A2, Canada. Offers M Sc, PhD, Diploma. *Degree requirements:* For master's, thesis; for doctorate, comprehensive exam (for some programs), thesis/dissertation. *Entrance requirements:* Additional exam requirements/recommendations for international students: Required—TOEFL (minimum score 80 iBT); Recommended—IELTS (minimum score 6.5). Electronic applications accepted.

University of South Carolina, The Graduate School, College of Arts and Sciences, Department of Geological Sciences, Columbia, SC 29208. Offers MS, PhD. Terminal master's awarded for partial completion of doctoral program. *Degree requirements:* For master's, thesis; for doctorate, comprehensive exam, thesis/dissertation, published paper. *Entrance requirements:* For master's and doctorate, GRE General Test. Additional exam requirements/recommendations for international students: Required—TOEFL (minimum score 570 paper-based; 75 iBT). Electronic applications accepted. *Faculty research:* Environmental geology, tectonics, petrology, coastal processes, paleoclimatology.

University of Southern Mississippi, Graduate School, College of Science and Technology, Department of Geography and Geology, Hattiesburg, MS 39406-0001. Offers geography (MS, PhD); geology (MS). Part-time programs available. *Faculty:* 11 full-time (2 women), 1 part-time/adjunct (0 women). *Students:* 16 full-time (4 women), 19 part-time (4 women); includes 3 minority (all Two or more races, non-Hispanic/Latino). Average age 32. 20 applicants, 40% accepted, 6 enrolled. In 2012, 5 master's, 1 doctorate awarded. *Degree requirements:* For master's, comprehensive exam, thesis (for some programs), internships; for doctorate, comprehensive exam, thesis/dissertation. *Entrance requirements:* For master's, GMAT, GRE General Test, minimum GPA of 3.0 for last 60 hours; for doctorate, GRE, minimum GPA of 3.5. Additional exam requirements/recommendations for international students: Required—TOEFL, IELTS. *Application deadline:* For fall admission, 3/15 for domestic and international students; for spring admission, 1/3 for domestic students. Applications are processed on a rolling basis. Application fee: $50. Electronic applications accepted. *Financial support:* In 2012–13, 1 research assistantship with tuition reimbursement (averaging $18,000 per year), 8 teaching assistantships with full tuition reimbursements (averaging $8,700 per year) were awarded; fellowships with full tuition reimbursements, career-related internships or fieldwork, Federal Work-Study, scholarships/grants, health care benefits, and unspecified assistantships also available. Financial award application deadline: 3/15; financial award applicants required to submit FAFSA. *Faculty research:* City and regional planning, geographic techniques, physical geography, human geography. *Unit head:* Dr. Clifton Dixon, Chair, 601-266-4729, Fax: 601-266-6219, E-mail: c.dixon@usm.edu. Website: http://www.usm.edu/graduateschool/table.php.

University of South Florida, Graduate School, College of Arts and Sciences, Department of Geology, Tampa, FL 33620-9951. Offers MS, PhD. Part-time programs available. *Degree requirements:* For master's, comprehensive exam, thesis (for some programs); for doctorate, comprehensive exam, thesis/dissertation. *Entrance requirements:* For master's and doctorate, GRE General Test, minimum GPA of 3.0, three letters of recommendation, personal statement. Additional exam requirements/recommendations for international students: Required—TOEFL (minimum score 550 paper-based; 79 iBT) or IELTS (minimum score 6.5). Electronic applications accepted.

The University of Tennessee, Graduate School, College of Arts and Sciences, Department of Geological Sciences, Knoxville, TN 37996. Offers geology (MS, PhD). Part-time programs available. *Degree requirements:* For master's, thesis; for doctorate, one foreign language, thesis/dissertation. *Entrance requirements:* For master's and doctorate, GRE General Test, minimum GPA of 2.7. Additional exam requirements/recommendations for international students: Required—TOEFL. Electronic applications accepted. *Expenses:* Tuition, state resident: full-time $9000; part-time $501 per credit hour. Tuition, nonresident: full-time $27,188; part-time $1512 per credit hour. *Required fees:* $1280; $62 per credit hour. Tuition and fees vary according to program.

The University of Texas at Arlington, Graduate School, College of Science, Department of Earth and Environmental Sciences, Program in Environmental and Earth Sciences, Arlington, TX 76019. Offers environmental science (MS, PhD); geology (MS, PhD). Part-time and evening/weekend programs available. Terminal master's awarded for partial completion of doctoral program. *Degree requirements:* For master's, thesis optional; for doctorate, comprehensive exam, thesis/dissertation. *Entrance requirements:* For master's, GRE General Test. Additional exam requirements/recommendations for international students: Required—TOEFL (minimum score 550 paper-based). Electronic applications accepted.

The University of Texas at Austin, Graduate School, Jackson School of Geosciences, Austin, TX 78712-1111. Offers MA, MS, PhD. Part-time programs available. *Degree requirements:* For master's, report (MA), thesis (MS); for doctorate, thesis/dissertation. *Entrance requirements:* For master's and doctorate, GRE General Test. Electronic applications accepted. *Faculty research:* Sedimentary geology, geophysics, hydrogeology, structure/tectonics, vertebrate paleontology.

The University of Texas at El Paso, Graduate School, College of Science, Department of Geological Sciences, El Paso, TX 79968-0001. Offers geological sciences (MS, PhD); geophysics (MS). Part-time and evening/weekend programs available. *Degree requirements:* For master's, thesis; for doctorate, one foreign language, thesis/dissertation. *Entrance requirements:* For master's, GRE, minimum GPA of 3.0, BS in geology or equivalent; for doctorate, GRE, minimum GPA of 3.0, MS in geology or equivalent. Additional exam requirements/recommendations for international students: Required—TOEFL. Electronic applications accepted.

The University of Texas at San Antonio, College of Sciences, Department of Geological Sciences, San Antonio, TX 78249-0617. Offers MS. Part-time programs available. *Faculty:* 12 full-time (3 women), 2 part-time/adjunct (0 women). *Students:* 21 full-time (10 women), 11 part-time (2 women); includes 5 minority (1 Black or African American, non-Hispanic/Latino; 1 Asian, non-Hispanic/Latino; 2 Hispanic/Latino; 1 Two or more races, non-Hispanic/Latino), 8 international. Average age 29. 33 applicants, 79% accepted, 17 enrolled. In 2012, 6 master's awarded. *Degree requirements:* For master's, comprehensive exam, thesis (for some programs). *Entrance requirements:* For master's, GRE General Test, three letters of recommendation, statement of research interest. Additional exam requirements/recommendations for international students: Required—TOEFL (minimum score 500 paper-based; 61 iBT), IELTS (minimum score 5). *Application deadline:* For fall admission, 7/1 for domestic students, 4/1 for international students; for spring admission, 11/1 for domestic students, 9/1 for international students. Application fee: $45 ($85 for international students). *Financial support:* Tuition waivers available. *Faculty research:* Low temperature geochemistry, aqueous geochemistry, hydrogeology, groundwater modeling, stratigraphy, carbonate petrology, paleontology, micropaleontology, remote sensing, geographic information systems, geoinformatics, tectonics, structural geology, metamorphic petrology, geochronology, sediment transports, methodology. *Unit head:* Dr. Alan R. Dutton, Department Chair, 210-458-4455, Fax: 210-458-4469, E-mail: alan.dutton@utsa.edu. *Application contact:* Graduate Advisor of Record, 210-458-4455, Fax: 210-458-4469, E-mail: geosciences@utsa.edu. Website: http://www.utsa.edu/geosci/.

The University of Texas of the Permian Basin, Office of Graduate Studies, College of Arts and Sciences, Department of Physical Sciences, Program in Geology, Odessa, TX 79762-0001. Offers MS. *Degree requirements:* For master's, comprehensive exam, thesis or alternative. *Entrance requirements:* For master's, GRE General Test. Additional exam requirements/recommendations for international students: Required—TOEFL (minimum score 550 paper-based).

The University of Toledo, College of Graduate Studies, College of Natural Sciences and Mathematics, Department of Environmental Sciences, Toledo, OH 43606-3390. Offers biology - ecology (PhD), including ecology (MS, PhD); geology (MS), including ecology (MS, PhD). Part-time programs available. *Faculty:* 35. *Students:* 6 full-time (0 women), 5 part-time (4 women), 1 international. Average age 30. 4 applicants, 50% accepted, 2 enrolled. In 2012, 3 master's awarded. *Degree requirements:* For master's, thesis or alternative. *Entrance requirements:* For master's, GRE General Test, minimum cumulative point-hour ratio of 2.7 for all previous academic work, three letters of recommendation, statement of purpose, transcripts from all prior institutions attended. Additional exam requirements/recommendations for international students: Required—TOEFL (minimum score 550 paper-based; 80 iBT), IELTS (minimum score 6.5). *Application deadline:* For fall admission, 1/15 priority date for domestic students, 1/15 for international students. Applications are processed on a rolling basis. Application fee: $45 ($75 for international students). Electronic applications accepted. *Financial support:* In 2012–13, 2 research assistantships with full and partial tuition reimbursements (averaging $18,700 per year), 4 teaching assistantships with full and partial tuition reimbursements (averaging $3,038 per year) were awarded; Federal Work-Study, institutionally sponsored loans, scholarships/grants, tuition waivers (full), and unspecified assistantships also available. Support available to part-time students. *Faculty research:*

Environmental geochemistry, geophysics, petrology and mineralogy, paleontology, geohydrology. *Unit head:* Dr. Timothy G. Fisher, Chair, 419-530-2883, E-mail: timothy.fisher@utoledo.edu. *Application contact:* Graduate School Office, 419-530-4723, Fax: 419-530-4724, E-mail: grdsch@utnet.utoledo.edu. Website: http://www.utoledo.edu/nsm/.

University of Toronto, School of Graduate Studies, Faculty of Arts and Science, Department of Geology, Toronto, ON M5S 1A1, Canada. Offers M Sc, MA Sc, PhD. Part-time programs available. *Degree requirements:* For master's, thesis (for some programs); for doctorate, thesis/dissertation. *Entrance requirements:* For master's, B Sc, BA Sc, or equivalent; letters of reference; for doctorate, M Sc or equivalent, minimum B+ average, letters of reference. Additional exam requirements/recommendations for international students: Required—TOEFL (minimum score 580 paper-based; 93 iBT), TWE (minimum score 4). Electronic applications accepted.

University of Utah, Graduate School, College of Mines and Earth Sciences, Department of Geology and Geophysics, Salt Lake City, UT 84112. Offers environmental engineering (ME, MS, PhD); geological engineering (ME, MS, PhD); geology (MS, PhD); geophysics (MS, PhD). *Faculty:* 21 full-time (5 women), 1 part-time/adjunct (0 women). *Students:* 58 full-time (21 women), 34 part-time (7 women); includes 5 minority (1 American Indian or Alaska Native, non-Hispanic/Latino; 2 Asian, non-Hispanic/Latino; 2 Hispanic/Latino), 22 international. Average age 30. 211 applicants, 20% accepted, 26 enrolled. In 2012, 6 master's, 4 doctorates awarded. Terminal master's awarded for partial completion of doctoral program. *Degree requirements:* For master's, comprehensive exam, thesis; for doctorate, thesis/dissertation, qualifying exam (written and oral). *Entrance requirements:* For master's and doctorate, GRE General Test, minimum GPA of 3.25. Additional exam requirements/recommendations for international students: Required—TOEFL (minimum score 500 paper-based; 61 iBT), IELTS. *Application deadline:* For fall admission, 1/15 priority date for domestic students, 1/15 for international students. Applications are processed on a rolling basis. Application fee: $55 ($65 for international students). Electronic applications accepted. *Financial support:* In 2012–13, 26 students received support, including 11 fellowships with full tuition reimbursements available (averaging $16,000 per year), 39 research assistantships with full tuition reimbursements available (averaging $22,000 per year), 15 teaching assistantships with full tuition reimbursements available (averaging $16,000 per year); career-related internships or fieldwork, institutionally sponsored loans, scholarships/grants, unspecified assistantships, and stipends also available. Financial award application deadline: 1/15; financial award applicants required to submit FAFSA. *Faculty research:* Igneous, metamorphic, and sedimentary petrology; ore deposits; aqueous geochemistry; isotope geochemistry; heat flow. *Total annual research expenditures:* $3.3 million. *Unit head:* Dr. Kip Solomon, Chair, 801-581-7231, Fax: 801-581-7065, E-mail: kip.solomon@utah.edu. *Application contact:* Dr. Cari L. Johnson, Director of Graduate Studies, 801-585-3782, Fax: 801-581-7065, E-mail: cari.johnson@utah.edu. Website: http://www.earth.utah.edu/.

University of Vermont, Graduate College, College of Arts and Sciences, Department of Geology, Burlington, VT 05405. Offers MS. *Students:* 12 (5 women); includes 1 minority (Hispanic/Latino). 32 applicants, 22% accepted, 6 enrolled. In 2012, 7 master's awarded. *Degree requirements:* For master's, thesis. *Entrance requirements:* For master's, GRE General Test. Additional exam requirements/recommendations for international students: Required—TOEFL (minimum score 550 paper-based; 80 iBT). *Application deadline:* For fall admission, 2/15 priority date for domestic students, 2/15 for international students. Applications are processed on a rolling basis. Application fee: $40. Electronic applications accepted. *Expenses: Tuition, area resident:* Part-time $572 per credit. Tuition, nonresident: part-time $1444 per credit. *Financial support:* Research assistantships and teaching assistantships available. Financial award application deadline: 3/1. *Faculty research:* Mineralogy, lake sediments, structural geology. *Unit head:* Dr. Andrea Lini, Chairperson, 802-656-3396. *Application contact:* Prof. Laura Webb, Coordinator, 802-656-3396.

University of Washington, Graduate School, College of the Environment, Department of Earth and Space Sciences, Seattle, WA 98195. Offers geology (MS, PhD); geophysics (MS, PhD). *Degree requirements:* For master's, thesis or alternative, departmental qualifying exam, final exam; for doctorate, thesis/dissertation, departmental qualifying exam, general and final exams. *Entrance requirements:* For master's and doctorate, GRE General Test, minimum GPA of 3.0. Additional exam requirements/recommendations for international students: Required—TOEFL (minimum score 580 paper-based). Electronic applications accepted.

The University of Western Ontario, Faculty of Graduate Studies, Physical Sciences Division, Department of Earth Sciences, London, ON N6A 5B8, Canada. Offers environment and sustainability (MES); geology (M Sc, PhD); geology and environmental science (M Sc, PhD); geophysics (M Sc, PhD); geophysics and environmental science (M Sc, PhD). *Degree requirements:* For master's, thesis; for doctorate, thesis/dissertation, qualifying exam. *Entrance requirements:* For master's, honors in B Sc; for doctorate, M Sc. Additional exam requirements/recommendations for international students: Required—TOEFL. *Faculty research:* Geophysics, geochemistry, paleontology, sedimentology/stratigraphy, glaciology/quaternary.

University of Wisconsin–Madison, Graduate School, College of Letters and Science, Department of Geology and Geophysics, Program in Geology, Madison, WI 53706-1380. Offers MS, PhD. *Degree requirements:* For master's, thesis; for doctorate, one foreign language, thesis/dissertation. *Entrance requirements:* For master's and doctorate, GRE General Test. *Expenses:* Tuition, state resident: full-time $10,728; part-time $743 per credit. Tuition, nonresident: full-time $24,054; part-time $1575 per credit. *Required fees:* $1111; $72 per credit.

University of Wisconsin–Milwaukee, Graduate School, College of Letters and Sciences, Department of Geosciences, Milwaukee, WI 53201-0413. Offers geological sciences (MS, PhD). *Faculty:* 8 full-time (2 women). *Students:* 11 full-time (8 women), 14 part-time (7 women); includes 1 minority (Two or more races, non-Hispanic/Latino), 2 international. Average age 30. 16 applicants, 69% accepted, 5 enrolled. In 2012, 8 master's awarded. *Degree requirements:* For master's, thesis; for doctorate, one foreign language, thesis/dissertation. *Entrance requirements:* For master's, GRE General Test, minimum GPA of 3.0; for doctorate, GRE General Test, master's degree. Additional exam requirements/recommendations for international students: Required—TOEFL (minimum score 550 paper-based; 79 iBT), IELTS (minimum score 6.5). *Application deadline:* For fall admission, 1/1 priority date for domestic students; for spring admission, 9/1 for domestic students. Applications are processed on a rolling basis. Application fee: $56 ($96 for international students). Electronic applications accepted. *Financial support:* In 2012–13, 4 research assistantships, 11 teaching assistantships were awarded; career-related internships or fieldwork and unspecified assistantships also available. Support available to part-time students. Financial award application deadline: 4/15; financial award applicants required to submit FAFSA. *Faculty research:* Geology, geosciences, geophysics, hydrogeology, paleontology. *Unit head:* Dr. Barry Cameron, Department Chair, 414-229-3136, E-mail: bcameron@uwm.edu. *Application contact:* General Information Contact, 414-229-4982, Fax: 414-229-6967, E-mail: gradschool@uwm.edu. Website: http://www.uwm.edu/dept/geosciences/.

University of Wyoming, College of Arts and Sciences, Department of Geology and Geophysics, Laramie, WY 82070. Offers geology (MS, PhD); geophysics (MS, PhD). Part-time programs available. *Degree requirements:* For master's, comprehensive exam, thesis; for doctorate, comprehensive exam, thesis/dissertation. *Entrance requirements:* For master's and doctorate, GRE General Test, minimum GPA of 3.0. *Faculty research:* Low-temp geochemistry, geohydrology, paleontology, structure/tectonics, sedimentation and petroleum geology, petrology, geophysics/seismology.

Utah State University, School of Graduate Studies, College of Science, Department of Geology, Logan, UT 84322. Offers MS. *Degree requirements:* For master's, thesis. *Entrance requirements:* For master's, GRE General Test, minimum GPA of 3.0. Additional exam requirements/recommendations for international students: Required—TOEFL. *Faculty research:* Sedimentary geology, structural geology, regional tectonics, hydrogeology petrology.

Vanderbilt University, Graduate School, Department of Earth and Environmental Sciences, Nashville, TN 37240-1001. Offers MAT, MS. *Faculty:* 8 full-time (2 women). *Students:* 15 full-time (6 women), 1 (woman) part-time, 1 international. Average age 25. 31 applicants, 32% accepted, 6 enrolled. In 2012, 3 master's awarded. *Degree requirements:* For master's, thesis. *Entrance requirements:* For master's, GRE General Test, GRE Subject Test (recommended). Additional exam requirements/recommendations for international students: Required—TOEFL (minimum score 570 paper-based; 88 iBT). *Application deadline:* For fall admission, 1/15 for domestic and international students. Application fee: $0. Electronic applications accepted. *Financial support:* Fellowships with full and partial tuition reimbursements, research assistantships with full and partial tuition reimbursements, teaching assistantships with full tuition reimbursements, career-related internships or fieldwork, Federal Work-Study, institutionally sponsored loans, and health care benefits available. Financial award application deadline: 1/15; financial award applicants required to submit CSS PROFILE or FAFSA. *Faculty research:* Geochemical processes, magmatic processes and crustal evolution, paleoecology and paleoenvironments, sedimentary systems, transport phenomena, environmental policy. *Unit head:* Dr. Calvin Miller, Director of Graduate Studies, 615-322-2232, E-mail: calvin.miller@vanderbilt.edu. *Application contact:* Teri Sparkman, Office Assistant, 615-322-2976, E-mail: teri.pugh@vanderbilt.edu. Website: http://www.vanderbilt.edu/ees/.

Washington State University, Graduate School, College of Agricultural, Human, and Natural Resource Sciences, School of the Environment, Pullman, WA 99164. Offers environmental and natural resource sciences (PhD); environmental sciences (MS); geology (MS, PhD); natural resources (MS). *Faculty:* 27 full-time (5 women), 7 part-time/adjunct (3 women). *Students:* 72 full-time (37 women), 7 part-time (4 women); includes 1 minority (Hispanic/Latino), 6 international. Average age 27. In 2012, 5 master's, 2 doctorates awarded. *Degree requirements:* For master's, comprehensive exam (for some programs), thesis (for some programs), oral exam; for doctorate, comprehensive exam, thesis/dissertation, oral exam. *Entrance requirements:* For master's, GRE General Test, official copies of all college transcripts, three letters of recommendation. Additional exam requirements/recommendations for international students: Required—TOEFL, IELTS. *Application deadline:* For fall admission, 1/10 priority date for domestic students, 1/10 for international students; for spring admission, 7/1 for domestic and international students. Applications are processed on a rolling basis. Application fee: $75. *Financial support:* In 2012–13, fellowships (averaging $2,333 per year), research assistantships with full and partial tuition reimbursements (averaging $13,917 per year), teaching assistantships with full and partial tuition reimbursements (averaging $13,056 per year) were awarded; career-related internships or fieldwork, Federal Work-Study, institutionally sponsored loans, tuition waivers (partial), and unspecified assistantships also available. Financial award application deadline: 2/15; financial award applicants required to submit FAFSA. *Faculty research:* Environmental and natural resources conservation and sustainability; earth sciences: earth systems and geology; wildlife ecology and conservation sciences. *Total annual research expenditures:* $967,000. *Unit head:* Dr. Steve Bollens, Director, 360-546-9116, E-mail: sbollens@vancouver.wsu.edu. *Application contact:* Graduate School Admissions, 800-GRADWSU, Fax: 509-335-1949, E-mail: gradsch@wsu.edu. Website: http://environment.wsu.edu/.

Washington State University, Graduate School, College of Arts and Sciences, School of the Environment, Department of Geology, Pullman, WA 99164. Offers MS, PhD. *Degree requirements:* For master's, comprehensive exam (for some programs), thesis, oral exam; for doctorate, one foreign language, comprehensive exam, thesis/dissertation, oral exam, written exam. *Entrance requirements:* For master's and doctorate, GRE General Test, official copies of college transcripts, minimum GPA of 3.0, 3 letters of recommendation. Additional exam requirements/recommendations for international students: Required—TOEFL (minimum score 560 paper-based). Electronic applications accepted. *Faculty research:* Genesis of ore deposits, geohydrology of the Pacific Northwest, geochemistry and petrology of plateau basalts.

Wayne State University, College of Liberal Arts and Sciences, Department of Geology, Detroit, MI 48202. Offers MS. *Students:* 5 full-time (2 women), 1 part time (0 women). Average age 27. 13 applicants, 38% accepted, 2 enrolled. In 2012, 4 master's awarded. *Degree requirements:* For master's, thesis. *Entrance requirements:* For master's, GRE General Test, undergraduate major in geology or strong background in geology, supported by courses in related sciences, minimum GPA of 3.0 in major, six or more credits in the field of geology, one year of calculus, chemistry, and physics, three letters of recommendation. Additional exam requirements/recommendations for international students: Required—TOEFL (minimum score 550 paper-based; 79 iBT); Recommended—TWE (minimum score 5.5). *Application deadline:* For fall admission, 6/1 priority date for domestic students, 5/1 for international students; for winter admission, 10/1 priority date for domestic students, 9/1 for international students; for spring admission, 2/1 priority date for domestic students, 10/1 for international students. Applications are processed on a rolling basis. Application fee: $50. Electronic applications accepted. *Expenses:* Tuition, state resident: full-time $12,788; part-time $532.85 per credit hour. Tuition, nonresident: full-time $28,243; part-time $1176.80 per credit hour. *Required fees:* $1367.30; $39.75 per credit hour. $206.65 per semester. Tuition and fees vary according to course load and program. *Financial support:* In 2012–13, 5 students received support, including 3 research assistantships with full and partial tuition reimbursements available (averaging $18,143 per year), 1 teaching assistantship with full and partial tuition reimbursement available (averaging $17,391 per year); fellowships with full and partial tuition reimbursements available, scholarships/grants, health care benefits, and unspecified assistantships also available. Support available to part-time students. Financial award applicants required to submit FAFSA. *Faculty research:* Glacial geology of Southeastern Michigan; applications of U-Th series, cosmogenic and anthrogenic radionuclides as tracers and chronometers in the environment; geochemical exploration of ore deposits using trace-elemental and stable isotopic (light-elemental) analytical tools; fate and transport of groundwater contaminants in glacial sediments; environmental radioactivity and geochronology. *Total annual research expenditures:* $195,567. *Unit head:* Dr. David Njus, Professor and Acting Chair, 313-577-3105, E-mail: ad5348@wayne.edu. Website: http://clasweb.clas.wayne.edu/geology.

West Chester University of Pennsylvania, College of Arts and Sciences, Department of Geology and Astronomy, West Chester, PA 19383. Offers earth-space science (Teaching Certificate); general science (Teaching Certificate); geoscience (MA). Part-time and evening/weekend programs available. *Faculty:* 7 full-time (2 women). *Students:* 1 (woman) full-time, 16 part-time (3 women); includes 2 minority (1 Black or African American, non-Hispanic/Latino; 1 Hispanic/Latino). Average age 35. 5 applicants, 100% accepted, 4 enrolled. In 2012, 8 master's awarded. *Degree requirements:* For master's, comprehensive exam (for some programs), thesis or alternative. *Entrance requirements:* For master's, minimum GPA of 2.5. Additional exam requirements/recommendations for international students: Required—TOEFL (minimum score 550 paper-based; 80

iBT). *Application deadline:* For fall admission, 4/15 priority date for domestic students, 3/15 for international students; for spring admission, 10/15 priority date for domestic students, 9/1 for international students. Applications are processed on a rolling basis. Application fee: $45. Electronic applications accepted. *Expenses:* Tuition, state resident: full-time $7722; part-time $429 per credit. Tuition, nonresident: full-time $11,592; part-time $644 per credit. *Required fees:* $2108; $105.05 per credit. Tuition and fees vary according to campus/location and program. *Financial support:* Unspecified assistantships available. Support available to part-time students. Financial award application deadline: 2/15; financial award applicants required to submit FAFSA. *Faculty research:* Geoscience education, environmental geology, energy and sustainability, astronomy, meteorology. *Unit head:* Dr. Lee Anne Srogi, Chair, 610-436-2727, Fax: 610-436-3036, E-mail: lsrogi@wcupa.edu. *Application contact:* Dr. Martin Helmke, Graduate Coordinator, 610-436-3565, Fax: 610-436-3036, E-mail: mhelmke@wcupa.edu. Website: http://www.wcupa.edu/_academics/sch_cas.esc/.

Western Kentucky University, Graduate Studies, Ogden College of Science and Engineering, Department of Geography and Geology, Bowling Green, KY 42101. Offers geoscience (MS). *Degree requirements:* For master's, comprehensive exam, thesis or alternative. *Entrance requirements:* For master's, GRE General Test, minimum GPA of 2.75. Additional exam requirements/recommendations for international students: Required—TOEFL (minimum score 555 paper-based; 79 iBT). *Faculty research:* Hydroclimatology, electronic data sets, groundwater, sinkhole liquification potential, meteorological analysis.

Western Washington University, Graduate School, College of Sciences and Technology, Department of Geology, Bellingham, WA 98225-5996. Offers MS. Part-time programs available. *Degree requirements:* For master's, thesis. *Entrance requirements:* For master's, GRE General Test, minimum GPA of 3.0 in last 60 semester hours or last 90 quarter hours. Additional exam requirements/recommendations for international students: Required—TOEFL (minimum score 567 paper-based). Electronic applications accepted. *Faculty research:* Structure/tectonics; sedimentary, glacial and quaternary geomorphology; igneous and metamorphic petrology; hydrology, geophysics.

West Virginia University, Eberly College of Arts and Sciences, Department of Geology and Geography, Program in Geology, Morgantown, WV 26506. Offers geomorphology (MS, PhD); geophysics (MS, PhD); hydrogeology (MS, PhD); paleontology (MS, PhD); petroleum geology (PhD); petrology (MS, PhD); stratigraphy (MS, PhD); structure (MS, PhD). Part-time programs available. Terminal master's awarded for partial completion of doctoral program. *Degree requirements:* For master's, thesis (for some programs); for doctorate, comprehensive exam, thesis/dissertation. *Entrance requirements:* For master's, GRE General Test, minimum GPA of 2.5; for doctorate, GRE General Test, minimum GPA of 3.3. Additional exam requirements/recommendations for international students: Required—TOEFL.

Wichita State University, Graduate School, Fairmount College of Liberal Arts and Sciences, Department of Geology, Wichita, KS 67260. Offers earth, environmental, and physical sciences (MS). Part-time programs available. *Unit head:* Dr. William Parcell, Chair, 316-978-3140, E-mail: william.parcell@wichita.edu. *Application contact:* Jordan Oleson, Admissions Coordinator, 316-978-3095, Fax: 316-978-3253, E-mail: jordan.oleson@wichita.edu. Website: http://www.wichita.edu/.

Wright State University, School of Graduate Studies, College of Science and Mathematics, Department of Earth and Environmental Sciences, Program in Geological Sciences, Dayton, OH 45435. Offers MS. Part-time programs available. *Degree requirements:* For master's, thesis. *Entrance requirements:* Additional exam requirements/recommendations for international students: Required—TOEFL.

Yale University, Graduate School of Arts and Sciences, Department of Geology and Geophysics, New Haven, CT 06520. Offers biogeochemistry (PhD); climate dynamics (PhD); geochemistry (PhD); geophysics (PhD); meteorology (PhD); oceanography (PhD); paleontology (PhD); paleooceanography (PhD); petrology (PhD); tectonics (PhD). *Degree requirements:* For doctorate, thesis/dissertation. *Entrance requirements:* For doctorate, GRE General Test. Additional exam requirements/recommendations for international students: Required—TOEFL.

Geophysics

Boise State University, College of Arts and Sciences, Department of Geosciences, Boise, ID 83725-0399. Offers earth science (M E Sci); geology (MS, PhD); geophysics (MS, PhD); hydrology (MS). Part-time programs available. *Faculty:* 16 full-time, 30 part-time/adjunct. *Students:* 43 full-time (11 women), 15 part-time (6 women); includes 1 minority (Black or African American, non-Hispanic/Latino), 3 international. 74 applicants, 78% accepted, 16 enrolled. In 2012, 15 master's, 3 doctorates awarded. *Degree requirements:* For master's, thesis. *Entrance requirements:* For master's, GRE General Test, BS in related field, minimum GPA of 3.0; for doctorate, GRE General Test. *Application deadline:* For fall admission, 3/1 priority date for domestic students; for spring admission, 10/1 priority date for domestic students. Applications are processed on

a rolling basis. Application fee: $55. Electronic applications accepted. *Expenses:* Tuition, state resident: full-time $3486; part-time $312 per credit. Tuition, nonresident: full-time $5720; part-time $413 per credit. *Financial support:* In 2012–13, 4 fellowships with full and partial tuition reimbursements (averaging $11,333 per year), 19 research assistantships with full tuition reimbursements (averaging $11,153 per year), 11 teaching assistantships (averaging $10,834 per year) were awarded; career-related internships or fieldwork, Federal Work-Study, institutionally sponsored loans, scholarships/grants, tuition waivers (partial), and unspecified assistantships also available. Support available to part-time students. Financial award application deadline: 3/1. *Faculty research:* Seismology, geothermal aquifers, sedimentation, tectonics, seismo-acoustic propagation. *Unit*

Peterson's Graduate Programs in the Physical Sciences, Mathematics, Agricultural Sciences, the Environment & Natural Resources 2014

www.petersonsbooks.com **151**

head: Dr. Clyde J. Northrup, Chairman, 208-426-1631, Fax: 208-426-4061. *Application contact:* Linda Platt, Office Services Supervisor, Graduate Admission and Degree Services, 208-426-1074, Fax: 208-426-2789, E-mail: lplatt@boisestate.edu.

Boston College, Graduate School of Arts and Sciences, Department of Earth and Environmental Sciences, Chestnut Hill, MA 02467-3800. Offers MS, MBA/MS. *Degree requirements:* For master's, thesis. *Entrance requirements:* For master's, GRE General Test, GRE Subject Test. Additional exam requirements/recommendations for international students: Required—TOEFL (minimum score 600 paper-based; 100 iBT). Electronic applications accepted. *Faculty research:* Coastal and marine geology, experimental sedimentology, geomagnetism, igneous petrology, paleontology.

Bowling Green State University, Graduate College, College of Arts and Sciences, Department of Physics and Astronomy, Bowling Green, OH 43403. Offers geophysics (MS); physics (MAT, MS). *Degree requirements:* For master's, thesis or alternative. *Entrance requirements:* For master's, GRE General Test. Additional exam requirements/recommendations for international students: Required—TOEFL. Electronic applications accepted. *Faculty research:* Computational physics, solid-state physics, materials science, theoretical physics.

California Institute of Technology, Division of Geological and Planetary Sciences, Pasadena, CA 91125-0001. Offers environmental science and engineering (MS, PhD); geobiology (MS, PhD); geochemistry (MS, PhD); geology (MS, PhD); geophysics (MS, PhD); planetary science (MS, PhD). *Faculty:* 43 full-time (8 women). *Students:* 110 full-time (52 women); includes 9 minority (1 Black or African American, non-Hispanic/Latino; 7 Asian, non-Hispanic/Latino; 1 Hispanic/Latino), 30 international. Average age 26. 225 applicants, 19% accepted, 24 enrolled. In 2012, 7 master's, 13 doctorates awarded. *Degree requirements:* For doctorate, thesis/dissertation. *Entrance requirements:* For doctorate, GRE General Test. Additional exam requirements/recommendations for international students: Required—TOEFL; Recommended—IELTS, TWE. *Application deadline:* For fall admission, 1/1 for domestic and international students. Application fee: $80. Electronic applications accepted. *Financial support:* In 2012–13, 19 fellowships with full tuition reimbursements (averaging $29,000 per year), 72 research assistantships with full tuition reimbursements (averaging $29,000 per year) were awarded; teaching assistantships with full tuition reimbursements, institutionally sponsored loans, scholarships/grants, health care benefits, and unspecified assistantships also available. Financial award applicants required to submit FAFSA. *Faculty research:* Planetary surfaces, evolution of anaerobic respiratory processes, structural geology and tectonics, theoretical and numerical seismology, global biogeochemical cycles. *Unit head:* Dr. Kenneth A. Farley, Chairman, 626-395-6111, Fax: 626-795-6028, E-mail: dianb@gps.caltech.edu. *Application contact:* Dr. Robert W. Clayton, Academic Officer, 626-395-6909, Fax: 626-795-6028, E-mail: dianb@gps.caltech.edu. Website: http://www.gps.caltech.edu/.

California State University, Long Beach, Graduate Studies, College of Natural Sciences and Mathematics, Department of Geological Sciences, Long Beach, CA 90840. Offers geology (MS); geophysics (MS). Part-time programs available. *Degree requirements:* For master's, thesis. *Entrance requirements:* For master's, GRE General Test. Electronic applications accepted. *Faculty research:* Paleontology, geophysics, structural geology, organic geochemistry, sedimentary geology.

Colorado School of Mines, Graduate School, Department of Geophysics, Golden, CO 80401-1887. Offers geophysical engineering (ME, MS, PhD); geophysics (MS, PhD); hydrology (MS, PhD); mineral exploration and mining geosciences (PMS). Part-time programs available. *Faculty:* 16 full-time (1 woman), 3 part-time/adjunct (0 women). *Students:* 90 full-time (28 women), 7 part-time (3 women); includes 12 minority (4 Black or African American, non-Hispanic/Latino; 1 American Indian or Alaska Native, non-Hispanic/Latino; 2 Asian, non-Hispanic/Latino; 5 Hispanic/Latino), 53 international. Average age 29. 183 applicants, 22% accepted, 29 enrolled. In 2012, 16 master's, 3 doctorates awarded. *Degree requirements:* For master's, thesis (for some programs); for doctorate, one foreign language, comprehensive exam, thesis/dissertation, oral exams. *Entrance requirements:* For master's and doctorate, GRE General Test. Additional exam requirements/recommendations for international students: Required—TOEFL (minimum score 550 paper-based; 80 iBT). *Application deadline:* For fall admission, 1/15 for domestic and international students; for spring admission, 10/15 for domestic and international students. Application fee: $50 ($70 for international students). Electronic applications accepted. *Financial support:* In 2012–13, 76 students received support, including 7 fellowships with full tuition reimbursements available (averaging $21,120 per year), 65 research assistantships with full tuition reimbursements available (averaging $21,120 per year), 4 teaching assistantships with full tuition reimbursements available (averaging $21,120 per year); scholarships/grants, health care benefits, and unspecified assistantships also available. Financial award application deadline: 1/15; financial award applicants required to submit FAFSA. *Faculty research:* Seismic exploration, gravity and geomagnetic fields, electrical mapping and sounding, bore hole measurements, environmental physics. *Total annual research expenditures:* $6.8 million. *Unit head:* Dr. Terence K. Young, Head, 303-273-3454, Fax: 303-273-3478, E-mail: tkyoung@mines.edu. *Application contact:* Michelle Szobody, Office Manager, 303-273-3935, Fax: 303-273-3478, E-mail: mszobody@mines.edu. Website: http://geophysics.mines.edu.

Columbia University, Graduate School of Arts and Sciences, Division of Natural Sciences, Department of Earth and Environmental Sciences, New York, NY 10027. Offers geochemistry (M Phil, MA, PhD); geodetic sciences (M Phil, MA, PhD); geophysics (M Phil, MA, PhD); oceanography (M Phil, MA, PhD). *Degree requirements:* For master's, thesis or alternative, fieldwork, written exam; for doctorate, one foreign language, thesis/dissertation. *Entrance requirements:* For master's and doctorate, GRE General Test, GRE Subject Test, major in natural or physical science. Additional exam requirements/recommendations for international students: Required—TOEFL. *Faculty research:* Structural geology and stratigraphy, petrology, paleontology, rare gas, isotope and aqueous geochemistry.

Cornell University, Graduate School, Graduate Fields of Engineering, Field of Geological Sciences, Ithaca, NY 14853. Offers economic geology (M Eng, MS, PhD); engineering geology (M Eng, MS, PhD); environmental geophysics (M Eng, MS, PhD); general geology (M Eng, MS, PhD); geobiology (M Eng, MS, PhD); geochemistry and isotope geology (M Eng, MS, PhD); geohydrology (M Eng, MS, PhD); geomorphology (M Eng, MS, PhD); geophysics (M Eng, MS, PhD); geotectonics (M Eng, MS, PhD); marine geology (MS, PhD); mineralogy (M Eng, MS, PhD); paleontology (M Eng, MS, PhD); petroleum geology (M Eng, MS, PhD); petrology (M Eng, MS, PhD); planetary geology (M Eng, MS, PhD); Precambrian geology (M Eng, MS, PhD); Quaternary geology (M Eng, MS, PhD); rock mechanics (M Eng, MS, PhD); sedimentology (M Eng, MS, PhD); seismology (M Eng, MS, PhD); stratigraphy (M Eng, MS, PhD); structural geology (M Eng, MS, PhD). *Faculty:* 37 full-time (5 women). *Students:* 32 full-time (13 women); includes 5 minority (2 Asian, non-Hispanic/Latino; 1 Hispanic/Latino; 2 Two or more races, non-Hispanic/Latino), 8 international. Average age 27. 58 applicants, 17% accepted, 6 enrolled. In 2012, 6 master's, 3 doctorates awarded. *Degree requirements:* For master's, thesis (MS); for doctorate, comprehensive exam, thesis/dissertation. *Entrance requirements:* For master's and doctorate, GRE General Test, 3 letters of recommendation. Additional exam requirements/recommendations for international students: Required—TOEFL (minimum score 550 paper-based; 77 iBT). *Application deadline:* For fall admission, 1/15 priority date for domestic students. Applications are processed on a rolling basis. Application fee: $95. Electronic applications accepted. *Financial support:* In 2012–13, 26 students received support, including 9 fellowships with full tuition reimbursements available, 16 research assistantships with full tuition reimbursements available, 1 teaching assistantship with full tuition reimbursement available; institutionally sponsored loans, scholarships/grants, health care benefits, tuition waivers (full and partial), and unspecified assistantships also available. Financial award applicants required to submit FAFSA. *Faculty research:* Geophysics, structural geology, petrology, geochemistry, geodynamics. *Unit head:* Director of Graduate Studies, 607-255-5466, Fax: 607-254-4780. *Application contact:* Graduate Field Assistant, 607-255-5466, Fax: 607-254-4780, E-mail: gradprog@geology.cornell.edu. Website: http://www.gradschool.cornell.edu/fields.php?id-30&a-2.

Florida State University, The Graduate School, College of Arts and Sciences, Interdisciplinary Program in Geophysical Fluid Dynamics, Tallahassee, FL 32306. Offers PhD. *Faculty:* 19 full-time (2 women). *Students:* 12 full-time (3 women), 2 part-time (0 women), 4 international. Average age 30. 5 applicants, 60% accepted, 1 enrolled. In 2012, 1 doctorate awarded. *Degree requirements:* For doctorate, thesis/dissertation, departmental qualifying exam. *Entrance requirements:* For doctorate, GRE General Test, GRE Subject Test, minimum GPA of 3.0. Additional exam requirements/recommendations for international students: Required—TOEFL (minimum score 550 paper-based; 80 iBT). *Application deadline:* For fall admission, 3/30 for domestic and international students. Application fee: $30. Electronic applications accepted. *Expenses:* Tuition, state resident: full-time $7263; part-time $403.51 per credit hour. Tuition, nonresident: full-time $18,087; part-time $1004.85 per credit hour. *Required fees:* $1335.42; $74.19 per credit hour. $445.14 per semester. One-time fee: $40 full-time; $20 part-time. Tuition and fees vary according to program. *Financial support:* In 2012–13, 1 research assistantship (averaging $21,500 per year) was awarded; fellowships and unspecified assistantships also available. Financial award applicants required to submit FAFSA. *Faculty research:* Hurricane dynamics, convection, air-sea interaction, wave-mean flow interaction, numerical models. *Total annual research expenditures:* $408,421. *Unit head:* Dr. Kevin Speer, Director, 850-645-5625, Fax: 850-644-8972, E-mail: kspeer@ocean.fsu.edu. *Application contact:* Vijaya Challa, Academic Coordinator, 850-644-5594, Fax: 850-644-8972, E-mail: vijaya@gfdi.fsu.edu. Website: http://www.gfdphd.fsu.edu/.

Georgia Institute of Technology, Graduate Studies and Research, College of Sciences, School of Earth and Atmospheric Sciences, Atlanta, GA 30332-0340. Offers atmospheric chemistry, aerosols and clouds (MS, PhD); dynamics of weather and climate (MS, PhD); geochemistry (MS, PhD); geophysics (MS, PhD); oceanography (MS, PhD); paleoclimate (MS, PhD); planetary science (MS, PhD); remote sensing (MS, PhD). Part-time programs available. Terminal master's awarded for partial completion of doctoral program. *Degree requirements:* For master's, thesis or alternative; for doctorate, comprehensive exam, thesis/dissertation. *Entrance requirements:* For master's, GRE, letters of recommendation; for doctorate, GRE, academic transcripts, letters of recommendation, personal statement. Additional exam requirements/recommendations for international students: Required—TOEFL (minimum score 550 paper-based; 79 iBT). *Faculty research:* Geophysics; atmospheric chemistry, aerosols and clouds; dynamics of weather and climate; geochemistry; oceanography; paleoclimate; planetary science; remote sensing.

ICR Graduate School, Graduate Programs, Santee, CA 92071. Offers astro/geophysics (MS); biology (MS); geology (MS); science education (MS). Part-time programs available. *Degree requirements:* For master's, comprehensive exam (for some programs), thesis (for some programs). *Entrance requirements:* For master's, minimum undergraduate GPA of 3.0, bachelor's degree in science or science education. *Faculty research:* Age of the earth, limits of variation, catastrophe, optimum methods for teaching.

Idaho State University, Office of Graduate Studies, College of Science and Engineering, Department of Geosciences, Pocatello, ID 83209-8072. Offers geographic information science (MS); geology (MNS, MS); geology with emphasis in environmental geoscience (MS); geophysics/hydrology/geology (MS); geotechnology (Postbaccalaureate Certificate). Part-time programs available. *Degree requirements:* For master's, comprehensive exam, thesis, oral colloquium; for Postbaccalaureate Certificate, thesis optional, minimum 19 credits. *Entrance requirements:* For master's, GRE General Test (minimum 50th percentile in 2 sections), 3 letters of recommendation; for Postbaccalaureate Certificate, GRE General Test, 3 letters of recommendation, bachelor's degree, statement of goals. Additional exam requirements/recommendations for international students: Required—TOEFL (minimum score 550 paper-based; 80 iBT). Electronic applications accepted. *Faculty research:* Quantitative field mapping and sampling: microscopic, geochemical, and isotopic analysis of rocks, minerals and water; remote sensing, geographic information systems, and global positioning systems: environmental and watershed management; surficial and fluvial processes: landscape change; regional tectonics, structural geology; planetary geology.

Indiana University Bloomington, University Graduate School, College of Arts and Sciences, Department of Geological Sciences, Bloomington, IN 47405-7000. Offers biogeochemistry (MS, PhD); economic geology (MS, PhD); geobiology (MS, PhD); geophysics, structural geology and tectonics (MS, PhD); hydrogeology (MS, PhD); mineralogy (MS, PhD); stratigraphy and sedimentology (MS, PhD). *Faculty:* 17 full-time (1 woman). *Students:* 63 full-time (23 women), 3 part-time (1 woman); includes 3 minority (1 Black or African American, non-Hispanic/Latino; 1 Hispanic/Latino; 1 Two or more races, non-Hispanic/Latino), 15 international. Average age 29. 82 applicants, 26% accepted, 15 enrolled. In 2012, 10 master's, 4 doctorates awarded. Terminal master's awarded for partial completion of doctoral program. *Degree requirements:* For master's, thesis or alternative; for doctorate, comprehensive exam, thesis/dissertation. *Entrance requirements:* For master's and doctorate, GRE General Test. Additional exam requirements/recommendations for international students: Required—TOEFL. *Application deadline:* For fall admission, 1/15 priority date for domestic students, 12/15 for international students; for spring admission, 9/1 priority date for domestic students, 9/1 for international students. Applications are processed on a rolling basis. Application fee: $55 ($65 for international students). *Financial support:* In 2012–13, fellowships with full tuition reimbursements (averaging $17,300 per year), research assistantships with full tuition reimbursements (averaging $16,370 per year), teaching assistantships with full tuition reimbursements (averaging $15,150 per year) were awarded; career-related internships or fieldwork, Federal Work-Study, and institutionally sponsored loans also available. *Faculty research:* Geophysics, geochemistry, hydrogeology, geobiology, planetary science. *Total annual research expenditures:* $644,299. *Unit head:* Simon Brassell, Chair, 812-855-5581, Fax: 812-855-7899, E-mail: geochair@indiana.edu. *Application contact:* Mary Iverson, Graduate Secretary, 812-855-7214, Fax: 812-855-7899, E-mail: miverson@indiana.edu. Website: http://www.indiana.edu/~geosci/.

Louisiana State University and Agricultural and Mechanical College, Graduate School, College of Science, Department of Geology and Geophysics, Baton Rouge, LA 70803. Offers MS, PhD. *Faculty:* 26 full-time (4 women). *Students:* 42 full-time (20 women), 6 part-time (1 woman); includes 3 minority (1 Hispanic/Latino; 2 Two or more races, non-Hispanic/Latino), 8 international. Average age 27. 86 applicants, 14% accepted, 5 enrolled. In 2012, 19 master's awarded. Terminal master's awarded for partial completion of doctoral program. *Degree requirements:* For master's, thesis; for doctorate, thesis/dissertation. *Entrance requirements:* For master's and doctorate, GRE General Test, minimum GPA of 3.0. Additional exam requirements/recommendations for international students: Required—TOEFL (minimum score 550 paper-based; 79 iBT) or IELTS (minimum score 6.5). *Application deadline:* For fall admission, 1/25 priority date for domestic students, 5/15 for international students; for spring admission, 10/15 for international students. Applications are processed on a rolling basis. Application fee: $50 ($70 for international students). Electronic applications accepted. *Financial support:* In 2012–13, 38 students received support, including 3 fellowships with full tuition reimbursements available (averaging $33,665 per year), 18 research assistantships with full and partial tuition reimbursements available (averaging $19,403 per year), 17 teaching assistantships with full and partial tuition reimbursements available (averaging $13,765 per year); career-related internships or fieldwork, Federal Work-Study, institutionally sponsored loans, health care benefits, tuition waivers (full and partial), and unspecified assistantships also available. Financial award application deadline: 3/15; financial award applicants required to submit FAFSA. *Faculty research:* Geophysics, sedimentology, geochemistry, geomicrobiology, tectonics. *Total annual research expenditures:* $1 million. *Unit head:* Dr. Carol Wicks, Chair, 225-578-3353, Fax: 225-578-2302, E-mail: cwicks@lsu.edu. *Application contact:* Dr. Sam Bentley, Graduate Adviser, 225-578-5735, E-mail: sjb@lsu.edu. Website: http://www.geol.lsu.edu/.

Massachusetts Institute of Technology, School of Science, Department of Earth, Atmospheric, and Planetary Sciences, Cambridge, MA 02139. Offers atmospheric chemistry (PhD, Sc D); atmospheric science (SM, PhD, Sc D); chemical oceanography (SM, PhD, Sc D); climate physics and chemistry (SM, PhD, Sc D); earth and planetary sciences (SM); geochemistry (PhD, Sc D); geology (PhD, Sc D); geophysics (PhD, Sc D); marine geology and geophysics (SM, PhD, Sc D); physical oceanography (SM, PhD, Sc D); planetary sciences (PhD, Sc D). *Faculty:* 33 full-time (6 women), 1 (woman) part-time/adjunct. *Students:* 166 full-time (77 women); includes 24 minority (3 Black or African American, non-Hispanic/Latino; 1 American Indian or Alaska Native, non-Hispanic/Latino; 9 Asian, non-Hispanic/Latino; 6 Hispanic/Latino; 5 Two or more races, non-Hispanic/Latino), 58 international. Average age 27. 232 applicants, 23% accepted, 27 enrolled. In 2012, 12 master's, 22 doctorates awarded. Terminal master's awarded for partial completion of doctoral program. *Degree requirements:* For master's, thesis; for doctorate, comprehensive exam, thesis/dissertation. *Entrance requirements:* For master's, GRE General Test; for doctorate, GRE General Test, GRE Subject Test (chemistry or physics for planetary science area). Additional exam requirements/recommendations for international students: Required—TOEFL (minimum score 577 paper-based; 91 iBT), IELTS (minimum score 7). *Application deadline:* For fall admission, 1/5 for domestic and international students; for spring admission, 11/1 for domestic and international students. Application fee: $75. Electronic applications accepted. *Expenses: Tuition:* Full-time $41,770; part-time $650 per credit hour. *Required fees:* $280. *Financial support:* In 2012–13, 108 students received support, including 62 fellowships (averaging $30,700 per year), 87 research assistantships (averaging $32,600 per year), 15 teaching assistantships (averaging $30,800 per year); Federal Work-Study, institutionally sponsored loans, scholarships/grants, health care benefits, and unspecified assistantships also available. *Faculty research:* Formation, dynamics and evolution of planetary systems; origin, composition, structure and dynamics of the atmospheres, oceans, surfaces and interiors of the Earth and other planets; evolution and interaction of the physical, chemical, geological and biological components of the Earth system; characterization of past, present and potential future climates and the causes and consequences of climate change; interplay of energy and the environment. *Total annual research expenditures:* $28.1 million. *Unit head:* Prof. Robert van der Hilst, Head, 617-253-2127, Fax: 617-253-8298, E-mail: eapsinfo@mit.edu. *Application contact:* EAPS Education Office, 617-253-3381, Fax: 617-253-8298, E-mail: eapsinfo@mit.edu. Website: http://eapsweb.mit.edu/.

Memorial University of Newfoundland, School of Graduate Studies, Department of Earth Sciences, St. John's, NL A1C 5S7, Canada. Offers geology (M Sc, PhD); geophysics (M Sc, PhD). Part-time programs available. *Degree requirements:* For master's, thesis; for doctorate, comprehensive exam, thesis/dissertation, oral thesis defense, entry evaluation. *Entrance requirements:* For master's, honors B Sc; for doctorate, M Sc. Electronic applications accepted. *Faculty research:* Geochemistry, sedimentology, paleoceanography and global change, mineral deposits, petroleum geology, hydrology.

Michigan Technological University, Graduate School, College of Engineering, Department of Geological and Mining Engineering and Sciences, Houghton, MI 49931. Offers geological engineering (MS, PhD); geology (MS, PhD); geophysics (MS, PhD); mining engineering (MS, PhD). Part-time programs available. Terminal master's awarded for partial completion of doctoral program. *Degree requirements:* For master's, comprehensive exam (for some programs), thesis (for some programs); for doctorate, comprehensive exam, thesis/dissertation. *Entrance requirements:* For master's and doctorate, GRE, statement of purpose, official transcripts, 3 letters of recommendation. Additional exam requirements/recommendations for international students: Required—TOEFL (minimum score 79 iBT) or IELTS. Electronic applications accepted. *Faculty research:* Volcanic hazards and volcanic clouds, oil and gas exploration and development, groundwater measurement and modeling, geophysics, environmental paleomagnetism.

Missouri University of Science and Technology, Graduate School, Department of Geological Sciences and Engineering, Rolla, MO 65409. Offers geological engineering (MS, DE, PhD); geology and geophysics (MS, PhD), including geochemistry, geology, geophysics, groundwater and environmental geology; petroleum engineering (MS, DE, PhD). Part-time programs available. *Degree requirements:* For master's, thesis optional; for doctorate, comprehensive exam, thesis/dissertation. *Entrance requirements:* For master's, GRE General Test (minimum score 600 quantitative, writing 3.5), minimum GPA of 3.0 in last 4 semesters; for doctorate, GRE General Test (minimum: Q 600, GRE WR 3.5). Additional exam requirements/recommendations for international students: Required—TOEFL. Electronic applications accepted. *Faculty research:* Digital image processing and geographic information systems, mineralogy, igneous and sedimentary petrology-geochemistry, sedimentology groundwater hydrology and contaminant transport.

New Mexico Institute of Mining and Technology, Graduate Studies, Department of Earth and Environmental Science, Program in Geophysics, Socorro, NM 87801. Offers MS, PhD. *Students:* 7 full-time (4 women), 3 part-time (all women), 2 international. Average age 27. In 2012, 1 master's, 3 doctorates awarded. *Degree requirements:* For master's, thesis optional; for doctorate, thesis/dissertation. *Entrance requirements:* For master's, GRE General Test; for doctorate, GRE General Test, GRE Subject Test. Additional exam requirements/recommendations for international students: Required—TOEFL (minimum score 540 paper-based). *Application deadline:* For fall admission, 3/1 priority date for domestic students; for spring admission, 6/1 for domestic students. Applications are processed on a rolling basis. Application fee: $16 ($30 for international students). *Expenses:* Tuition, state resident: full-time $5043; part-time $280 per credit hour. Tuition, nonresident: full-time $16,682; part-time $927 per credit hour. *Required fees:* $648; $18 per credit hour. $108 per semester. Part-time tuition and fees vary according to course load. *Financial support:* In 2012–13, 6 research assistantships (averaging $11,349 per year), 1 teaching assistantship (averaging $10,098 per year) were awarded; Federal Work-Study, institutionally sponsored loans, and unspecified assistantships also available. Financial award application deadline: 3/1; financial award applicants required to submit CSS PROFILE or FAFSA. *Faculty research:* Earthquake and volcanic seismology, subduction zone tectonics, network seismology, physical properties of sediments in fault zones. *Unit head:* Dr. Richard Aster, Coordinator, 575-835-5924, Fax: 575-835-6436, E-mail: aster@nmt.edu. *Application contact:* Dr. Lorie Liebrock, Dean of Graduate Studies, 575-835-5513, Fax: 575-835-5476, E-mail: graduate@nmt.edu.

Ohio University, Graduate College, College of Arts and Sciences, Department of Geological Sciences, Athens, OH 45701-2979. Offers environmental geochemistry (MS); environmental geology (MS); environmental/hydrology (MS); geology (MS); geology education (MS); geomorphology/surficial processes (MS); geophysics (MS); hydrogeology (MS); sedimentology (MS); structure/tectonics (MS). Part-time programs available. *Degree requirements:* For master's, thesis. *Entrance requirements:* Additional exam requirements/recommendations for international students: Required—TOEFL (minimum score 550 paper-based; 80 iBT) or IELTS (minimum score 6.5). Electronic applications accepted. *Faculty research:* Geoscience education, tectonics, fluvial geomorphology, invertebrate paleontology, mine/hydrology.

Oregon State University, College of Earth, Ocean, and Atmospheric Sciences, Program in Ocean, Earth, and Atmospheric Sciences, Corvallis, OR 97331. Offers atmospheric sciences (MA, MS); geography (PhD); geology (PhD); geophysics (MA, MS); oceanography (MA, MS). *Students:* 33 full-time (17 women), 1 part-time (0 women); includes 5 minority (1 Asian, non-Hispanic/Latino; 2 Hispanic/Latino; 2 Two or more races, non-Hispanic/Latino), 7 international. Average age 28. 148 applicants, 15% accepted, 8 enrolled. In 2012, 10 master's, 3 doctorates awarded. *Expenses:* Tuition, state resident: full-time $11,367; part-time $421 per credit hour. Tuition, nonresident: full-time $18,279; part-time $677 per credit hour. *Required fees:* $1478. One-time fee: $300 full-time. Tuition and fees vary according to course load and program. *Unit head:* Dr. Mark R. Abbott, Dean, 541-737-5195, Fax: 541-737-2064, E-mail: mark@coas.oregonstate.edu. *Application contact:* Dr. Robert S. Allan, Assistant Director, Student Programs, 541-737-1340, Fax: 541-737-2064, E-mail: rallan@coas.oregonstate.edu. Website: http://ceoas.oregonstate.edu/academics/ocean/.

Rice University, Graduate Programs, Wiess School–Professional Science Master's Programs, Professional Master's Program in Subsurface Geosciences, Houston, TX 77251-1892. Offers geophysics (MS). Part-time programs available. *Degree requirements:* For master's, internship. *Entrance requirements:* For master's, GRE, letters of recommendation (4). Additional exam requirements/recommendations for international students: Required—TOEFL (minimum score 600 paper-based; 90 iBT). Electronic applications accepted. *Faculty research:* Seismology, geodynamics, wave propagation, bio-geochemistry, remote sensing.

Saint Louis University, Graduate Education, College of Arts and Sciences, Department of Earth and Atmospheric Sciences, St. Louis, MO 63103-2097. Offers geophysics (PhD); geoscience (MS); meteorology (M Pr Met, MS-R, PhD). Part-time programs available. *Degree requirements:* For master's, thesis (for some programs), comprehensive oral exam; for doctorate, thesis/dissertation, preliminary exams. *Entrance requirements:* For master's, GRE General Test, letters of recommendation, resume; for doctorate, GRE General Test, letters of recommendation, resumé, goal statement, transcripts. Additional exam requirements/recommendations for international students: Required—TOEFL (minimum score 525 paper-based). Electronic applications accepted. *Faculty research:* Structural geology, mesoscale meteorology and severe storms, weather and climate change prediction.

Southern Methodist University, Dedman College, Department of Earth Sciences, Dallas, TX 75275. Offers applied geophysics (MS); earth sciences (MS, PhD). Part-time programs available. *Degree requirements:* For master's, thesis (for some programs), qualifying exam; for doctorate, thesis/dissertation, qualifying exam. *Entrance requirements:* For master's and doctorate, GRE General Test, minimum GPA of 3.0, letters of recommendation. Additional exam requirements/recommendations for international students: Required—TOEFL. Electronic applications accepted. *Faculty research:* Sedimentology, geochemistry, igneous and metamorphic petrology, vertebrate paleontology, seismology.

Stanford University, School of Earth Sciences, Department of Geophysics, Stanford, CA 94305-9991. Offers MS, PhD. Terminal master's awarded for partial completion of doctoral program. *Degree requirements:* For master's, thesis; for doctorate, thesis/dissertation. *Entrance requirements:* For master's and doctorate, GRE General Test. Additional exam requirements/recommendations for international students: Required—TOEFL. Electronic applications accepted. *Expenses: Tuition:* Full-time $41,250; part-time $917 per credit hour.

Texas A&M University, College of Geosciences, Department of Geology and Geophysics, College Station, TX 77843. Offers geology (MS, PhD); geophysics (MS, PhD). *Faculty:* 27. *Students:* 110 full-time (40 women), 28 part-time (17 women); includes 15 minority (3 Black or African American, non-Hispanic/Latino; 6 Asian, non-Hispanic/Latino; 4 Hispanic/Latino; 2 Two or more races, non-Hispanic/Latino), 47 international. Average age 28. In 2012, 20 master's, 5 doctorates awarded. *Degree requirements:* For master's, thesis; for doctorate, thesis/dissertation. *Entrance requirements:* For master's and doctorate, GRE General Test. Additional exam requirements/recommendations for international students: Required—TOEFL. *Application deadline:* For fall admission, 3/1 priority date for domestic students, 1/15 for international students; for spring admission, 10/1 priority date for domestic students, 8/15 for international students. Applications are processed on a rolling basis. Application fee: $50 ($75 for international students). Electronic applications accepted. *Financial support:* In 2012–13, fellowships with partial tuition reimbursements (averaging $1,000 per year), research assistantships with partial tuition reimbursements (averaging $11,925 per year), teaching assistantships with partial tuition reimbursements (averaging $11,925 per year) were awarded; Federal Work-Study, institutionally sponsored loans, scholarships/grants, tuition waivers (partial), and unspecified assistantships also available. Financial award application deadline: 3/1; financial award applicants required to submit FAFSA. *Faculty research:* Environmental and engineering geology and geophysics, petroleum geology, tectonophysics, geochemistry. *Unit head:* Dr. Rick Giardino, Head, 979-845-3224, E-mail: giardino@geo.tamu.edu. *Application contact:* Graduate Admissions, 979-845-1044, E-mail: admissions@tamu.edu. Website: http://geoweb.tamu.edu.

The University of Akron, Graduate School, Buchtel College of Arts and Sciences, Department of Geology and Environmental Science, Program in Geophysics, Akron, OH 44325. Offers MS. *Students:* 1 (woman) full-time. Average age 49. 3 applicants, 67% accepted, 0 enrolled. *Degree requirements:* For master's, comprehensive exam, thesis, seminar, proficiency exam. *Entrance requirements:* For master's, minimum GPA of 2.75, letters of recommendation, statement of purpose. Additional exam requirements/recommendations for international students: Required—TOEFL (minimum score 550 paper-based; 79 iBT). *Application deadline:* Applications are processed on a rolling basis. Application fee: $40 ($60 for international students). Electronic applications accepted. *Expenses:* Tuition, state resident: full-time $7285; part-time $404.70 per credit hour. Tuition, nonresident: full-time $12,473; part-time $692.95 per credit hour. *Required fees:* $34.05 per credit hour. Tuition and fees vary according to course load. *Application contact:* Dr. LaVerne Friberg, Director of Graduate Studies, 330-972-8046, E-mail: lfribe1@uakron.edu.

University of Alaska Fairbanks, College of Natural Sciences and Mathematics, Department of Geology and Geophysics, Fairbanks, AK 99775-5780. Offers geology (MS, PhD), including economic geology (PhD), petroleum geology (MS), quaternary geology (PhD), remote sensing, volcanology (PhD); geophysics (MS, PhD), including remote sensing, snow, ice, and permafrost geophysics (MS), solid-earth geophysics (MS). Part-time programs available. *Faculty:* 11 full-time (5 women). *Students:* 62 full-time (30 women), 12 part-time (5 women); includes 3 minority (1 Hispanic/Latino; 2 Two or more races, non-Hispanic/Latino), 25 international. Average age 29. 92 applicants, 21% accepted, 19 enrolled. In 2012, 4 master's, 7 doctorates awarded. Terminal master's awarded for partial completion of doctoral program. *Degree requirements:* For master's, comprehensive exam, thesis, oral exam, oral defense; for doctorate, comprehensive exam, thesis/dissertation, oral exam, oral defense. *Entrance requirements:* For master's and doctorate, GRE General Test. Additional exam requirements/recommendations for international students: Required—TOEFL (minimum score 550 paper-based). *Application deadline:* For fall admission, 6/1 for domestic students, 3/1 for international students; for spring admission, 10/15 for domestic students, 9/1 for international students. Applications are processed on a rolling basis. Application fee: $60. Electronic applications accepted. *Expenses:* Tuition, state resident: full-time $7038. Tuition, nonresident: full-time $14,382. Tuition and fees vary according to course level, course load and reciprocity agreements. *Financial support:* In 2012–13, 47 research assistantships with tuition reimbursements (averaging $15,895 per year), 7 teaching assistantships with tuition reimbursements (averaging $13,083 per year) were awarded; fellowships with tuition reimbursements, Federal Work-Study, scholarships/grants, health care benefits, and unspecified assistantships also available. Support available to part-time students. Financial award application deadline: 2/15; financial award applicants required to submit FAFSA. *Faculty research:* Glacial surging, volcanology, geochronology, impact cratering, permafrost geophysics. *Total annual research expenditures:* $45,000. *Unit head:* Dr. Sarah Fowell, Department Co-Chair, 907-474-7565, Fax: 907-474-5163, E-mail: geology@uaf.edu. *Application contact:* Libby Eddy, Registrar and Director of Admissions, 907-474-7500, Fax: 907-474-7097, E-mail: admissions@uaf.edu. Website: http://www.uaf.edu/geology/.

University of Alberta, Faculty of Graduate Studies and Research, Department of Physics, Edmonton, AB T6G 2E1, Canada. Offers astrophysics (M Sc, PhD); condensed matter (M Sc, PhD); geophysics (M Sc, PhD); medical physics (M Sc, PhD); subatomic physics (M Sc, PhD). *Degree requirements:* For master's, thesis; for doctorate, thesis/dissertation. *Entrance requirements:* For master's and doctorate, minimum GPA of 7.0 on a 9.0 scale. Additional exam requirements/recommendations for international students: Required—TOEFL. *Faculty research:* Cosmology, astroparticle physics, high-intermediate energy, magnetism, superconductivity.

The University of British Columbia, Faculty of Science, Department of Earth and Ocean Sciences, Vancouver, BC V6T 1Z4, Canada. Offers atmospheric science (M Sc, PhD); geological engineering (M Eng, MA Sc, PhD); geological sciences (M Sc, PhD); geophysics (M Sc, MA Sc, PhD); oceanography (M Sc, PhD). *Degree requirements:* For master's, thesis (for some programs); for doctorate, comprehensive exam, thesis/dissertation. *Entrance requirements:* Additional exam requirements/recommendations for international students: Required—TOEFL (minimum score 600 paper-based; 100 iBT). Electronic applications accepted. *Faculty research:* Oceans and atmosphere, environmental earth science, hydro geology, mineral deposits, geophysics.

University of Calgary, Faculty of Graduate Studies, Faculty of Science, Department of Geology and Geophysics, Calgary, AB T2N 1N4, Canada. Offers geology (M Sc, PhD); geophysics (M Sc, PhD). Part-time programs available. Terminal master's awarded for partial completion of doctoral program. *Degree requirements:* For master's, thesis; for doctorate, thesis/dissertation, candidacy exam. *Entrance requirements:* For master's, B Sc; for doctorate, honors B Sc or M Sc. Additional exam requirements/recommendations for international students: Required—TOEFL. Electronic applications accepted. *Faculty research:* Geochemistry, petrology, paleontology, stratigraphy, exploration and solid-earth geophysics.

University of California, Berkeley, Graduate Division, College of Letters and Science, Department of Earth and Planetary Science, Berkeley, CA 94720-1500. Offers geology (MA, MS, PhD); geophysics (MA, MS, PhD). Terminal master's awarded for partial completion of doctoral program. *Degree requirements:* For master's, oral exam (MA), thesis (MS); for doctorate, comprehensive exam, thesis/dissertation, candidacy exams. *Entrance requirements:* For master's and doctorate, GRE General Test, minimum GPA of 3.0, 3 letters of recommendation. Additional exam requirements/recommendations for international students: Required—TOEFL. *Faculty research:* Tectonics, environmental geology, high-pressure geophysics and seismology, economic geology, geochemistry.

University of California, Los Angeles, Graduate Division, College of Letters and Science, Department of Earth and Space Sciences, Program in Geophysics and Space Physics, Los Angeles, CA 90095. Offers MS, PhD. *Faculty:* 23 full-time (3 women). *Students:* 32 full-time (13 women); includes 7 minority (1 Black or African American, non-Hispanic/Latino; 3 Asian, non-Hispanic/Latino; 1 Hispanic/Latino; 2 Two or more races, non-Hispanic/Latino), 11 international. Average age 27. 56 applicants, 11% accepted, 2 enrolled. In 2012, 6 master's, 8 doctorates awarded. Terminal master's awarded for partial completion of doctoral program. *Degree requirements:* For master's, comprehensive exam or thesis; for doctorate, thesis/dissertation, oral and written qualifying exams. *Entrance requirements:* For master's and doctorate, GRE General Test, bachelor's degree, minimum undergraduate GPA of 3.0 (or its equivalent if letter grade system not used). Additional exam requirements/recommendations for international students: Required—TOEFL. *Application deadline:* For fall admission, 1/15 for domestic and international students. Application fee: $80 ($100 for international students). Electronic applications accepted. *Expenses:* Tuition, nonresident: full-time $15,102. *Required fees:* $14,809.19. Full-time tuition and fees vary according to program. *Financial support:* In 2012–13, 38 students received support, including 37 fellowships with full and partial tuition reimbursements available, 34 research assistantships with full and partial tuition reimbursements available, 8 teaching assistantships with full and partial tuition reimbursements available; Federal Work-Study, scholarships/grants, health care benefits, tuition waivers (full and partial), and unspecified assistantships also available. Financial award application deadline: 3/2; financial award applicants required to submit FAFSA. *Unit head:* Dr. Kevin McKeegan, Chair, 310-825-1475, E-mail: mckeegan@ess.ucla.edu. *Application contact:* Student Affairs Officer, 310-825-3917, Fax: 310-825-2779, E-mail: holbrook@ess.ucla.edu. Website: http://www.ess.ucla.edu/.

University of California, Santa Barbara, Graduate Division, College of Letters and Sciences, Division of Mathematics, Life, and Physical Sciences, Department of Earth Science, Santa Barbara, CA 93106-9620. Offers geological sciences (MS, PhD); geophysics (MS). *Faculty:* 20 full-time (3 women), 6 part-time/adjunct (1 woman). *Students:* 43 full-time (18 women); includes 7 minority (1 American Indian or Alaska Native, non-Hispanic/Latino; 1 Asian, non-Hispanic/Latino; 5 Hispanic/Latino), 6 international. Average age 27. 116 applicants, 19% accepted, 13 enrolled. In 2012, 3 master's, 1 doctorate awarded. Terminal master's awarded for partial completion of doctoral program. *Degree requirements:* For master's, comprehensive exam, thesis, 30 units; for doctorate, comprehensive exam, thesis/dissertation, 30 units, oral qualifying exam. *Entrance requirements:* For master's and doctorate, GRE General Test. Additional exam requirements/recommendations for international students: Required—TOEFL (minimum score 550 paper-based; 80 iBT), IELTS (minimum score 7). *Application deadline:* For fall admission, 2/1 for domestic and international students. Application fee: $80 ($100 for international students). Electronic applications accepted. *Financial support:* In 2012–13, 28 students received support, including 3 fellowships with full and partial tuition reimbursements available (averaging $22,000 per year), 11 research assistantships with full and partial tuition reimbursements available (averaging $5,500 per year), 41 teaching assistantships with full and partial tuition reimbursements available (averaging $5,885 per year). Financial award application deadline: 1/3; financial award applicants required to submit CSS PROFILE or FAFSA. *Faculty research:* Geology, geomaterials and earth's structure; geomorphology, tectonics; geophysics, seismology; paleoclimatology, paleooceanography and geochemistry; paleobiology, evolution and paleontology. *Unit head:* Dr. Douglas Burbank, Chair, 805-893-7858, Fax: 805-893-2314, E-mail: burbank@eri.ucsb.edu. *Application contact:* Hannah Smit, Graduate Program Assistant, 805-893-3329, Fax: 805-893-2314, E-mail: hsmit@geol.ucsb.edu. Website: http://www.geol.ucsb.edu/.

University of Chicago, Division of the Physical Sciences, Department of the Geophysical Sciences, Chicago, IL 60637-1513. Offers atmospheric sciences (SM, PhD); cosmochemistry (PhD); earth sciences (SM, PhD); paleobiology (PhD); planetary and space sciences (SM, PhD). Terminal master's awarded for partial completion of doctoral program. *Degree requirements:* For master's, thesis, seminar; for doctorate, variable foreign language requirement, comprehensive exam, thesis/dissertation. *Entrance requirements:* For doctorate, GRE General Test. Additional exam requirements/recommendations for international students: Required—TOEFL (minimum score 600 paper-based; 96 iBT), IELTS (minimum score 7). Electronic applications accepted. *Faculty research:* Climatology, evolutionary paleontology, cosmochemistry, geochemistry, oceanic sciences.

University of Colorado Boulder, Graduate School, College of Arts and Sciences, Department of Geological Sciences, Boulder, CO 80309. Offers geology (MS, PhD); geophysics (PhD). *Faculty:* 28 full-time (7 women). *Students:* 75 full-time (39 women), 12 part-time (2 women); includes 5 minority (1 American Indian or Alaska Native, non-Hispanic/Latino; 2 Hispanic/Latino; 2 Two or more races, non-Hispanic/Latino), 11 international. Average age 28. 221 applicants, 8% accepted, 17 enrolled. Terminal master's awarded for partial completion of doctoral program. *Degree requirements:* For master's, comprehensive exam, thesis; for doctorate, comprehensive exam, thesis/dissertation. *Entrance requirements:* For master's, GRE General Test, minimum undergraduate GPA of 3.0; for doctorate, GRE General Test, minimum GPA of 2.75. *Application deadline:* For fall admission, 1/10 priority date for domestic students, 12/1 for international students. Application fee: $50 ($60 for international students). Electronic applications accepted. *Financial support:* In 2012–13, 34 fellowships (averaging $12,016 per year), 34 research assistantships with full and partial tuition reimbursements (averaging $22,169 per year), 24 teaching assistantships with full and partial tuition reimbursements (averaging $19,553 per year) were awarded; institutionally sponsored loans, scholarships/grants, health care benefits, and unspecified assistantships also available. Financial award application deadline: 1/15; financial award applicants required to submit FAFSA. *Faculty research:* Sedimentology, stratigraphy, economic geology of mineral deposits, fossil fuels, hydrogeology and water resources, geophysics, isotope geology, paleobiology, mineralogy, remote sensing. *Total annual research expenditures:* $7.6 million. *Application contact:* E-mail: geolinfo@colorado.edu. Website: http://www.colorado.edu/GeolSci.

University of Colorado Boulder, Graduate School, College of Arts and Sciences, Department of Physics, Boulder, CO 80309. Offers chemical physics (PhD); geophysics (PhD); liquid crystal science and technology (PhD); mathematical physics (PhD); medical physics (PhD); optical sciences and engineering (PhD); physics (MS, PhD). *Faculty:* 50 full-time (7 women). *Students:* 158 full-time (32 women), 64 part-time (9 women); includes 11 minority (6 Asian, non-Hispanic/Latino; 5 Hispanic/Latino), 74 international. Average age 27. 600 applicants, 21% accepted, 32 enrolled. Terminal master's awarded for partial completion of doctoral program. *Degree requirements:* For master's, comprehensive exam, thesis or alternative; for doctorate, comprehensive exam, thesis/dissertation. *Entrance requirements:* For master's and doctorate, GRE General Test, GRE Subject Test, minimum undergraduate GPA of 3.0. Additional exam requirements/recommendations for international students: Required—TOEFL. *Application deadline:* For fall admission, 12/15 priority date for domestic students, 12/15 for international students. Applications are processed on a rolling basis. Application fee: $50 ($60 for international students). Electronic applications accepted. *Financial support:* In 2012–13, 38 fellowships (averaging $14,995 per year), 156 research assistantships with full and partial tuition reimbursements (averaging $25,043 per year), 48 teaching assistantships with full and partial tuition reimbursements (averaging $18,902 per year) were awarded; institutionally sponsored loans, scholarships/grants, health care benefits, and unspecified assistantships also available. Financial award application deadline: 1/15; financial award applicants required to submit FAFSA. *Faculty research:* Atomic and molecular physics, nuclear physics, condensed matter, elementary particle physics, laser or optical physics, plasma physics, geophysics, astrophysics and chemical physics. *Total annual research expenditures:* $23.7 million. *Application contact:* E-mail: physics@colorado.edu. Website: http://physics.colorado.edu/.

University of Hawaii at Manoa, Graduate Division, School of Ocean and Earth Science and Technology, Department of Geology and Geophysics, Honolulu, HI 96822. Offers high-pressure geophysics and geochemistry (MS, PhD); hydrogeology and engineering geology (MS, PhD); marine geology and geophysics (MS, PhD); planetary geosciences and remote sensing (MS, PhD); seismology and solid-earth geophysics (MS, PhD); volcanology, petrology, and geochemistry (MS, PhD). Part-time programs available. Terminal master's awarded for partial completion of doctoral program. *Degree requirements:* For master's, thesis optional; for doctorate, comprehensive exam, thesis/dissertation. *Entrance requirements:* For master's and doctorate, GRE General Test, minimum GPA of 3.0. Additional exam requirements/recommendations for international students: Required—TOEFL (minimum score 580 paper-based; 92 iBT), IELTS (minimum score 5).

University of Houston, College of Natural Sciences and Mathematics, Department of Earth and Atmospheric Sciences, Houston, TX 77204. Offers atmospheric science (PhD); geology (MA, PhD); geophysics (PhD). Part-time programs available. *Degree requirements:* For master's, thesis; for doctorate, comprehensive exam, thesis/dissertation. *Entrance requirements:* For master's and doctorate, GRE General Test. Additional exam requirements/recommendations for international students: Required—TOEFL (minimum score 550 paper-based; 79 iBT), IELTS (minimum score 6.5). Electronic applications accepted. *Faculty research:* Atmospherics sciences, seismic and solid earth geophysics, tectonics, environmental hydrochemistry, carbonates, micropaleontology, structure and tectonics, petroleum geology.

University of Manitoba, Faculty of Graduate Studies, Clayton H. Riddell Faculty of Environment, Earth, and Resources, Department of Geological Sciences, Winnipeg, MB R3T 2N2, Canada. Offers geology (M Sc, PhD); geophysics (M Sc, PhD). *Degree requirements:* For master's, thesis; for doctorate, thesis/dissertation. *Entrance requirements:* For master's and doctorate, GRE General Test, GRE Subject Test (geology), minimum GPA of 3.0. Additional exam requirements/recommendations for international students: Required—TOEFL.

University of Memphis, Graduate School, College of Arts and Sciences, Department of Earth Sciences, Memphis, TN 38152. Offers archaeology (MS); earth sciences (PhD); geographic information systems (Graduate Certificate); geography (MA, MS); geology (MS); geophysics (MS); interdisciplinary (MS). Part-time and evening/weekend programs available. Terminal master's awarded for partial completion of doctoral program. *Degree requirements:* For master's, comprehensive exam, thesis, seminar presentation; for doctorate, thesis/dissertation. *Entrance requirements:* For master's, GRE General Test, 3 letters of recommendation, statement of research interests; for doctorate, GRE General Test, 2 letters of recommendation, resume, personal statement. Additional exam requirements/recommendations for international students: Required—TOEFL (minimum score 550 paper-based). Electronic applications accepted. *Faculty research:* Hazards, active tectonics, geophysics, hydrology and water resources, spatial analysis.

University of Miami, Graduate School, Rosenstiel School of Marine and Atmospheric Science, Division of Marine Geology and Geophysics, Coral Gables, FL 33124. Offers MS, PhD. Terminal master's awarded for partial completion of doctoral program. *Degree requirements:* For master's, comprehensive exam, thesis; for doctorate, comprehensive exam, thesis/dissertation. *Entrance requirements:* For master's and doctorate, GRE General Test. Additional exam requirements/recommendations for international students: Required—TOEFL (minimum score 550 paper-based). Electronic applications accepted. *Faculty research:* Carbonate sedimentology, low-temperature geochemistry, paleoceanography, geodesy and tectonics.

University of Minnesota, Twin Cities Campus, College of Science and Engineering, Department of Earth Sciences, Minneapolis, MN 55455-0213. Offers MS, PhD. Terminal master's awarded for partial completion of doctoral program. *Degree requirements:* For master's, thesis; for doctorate, thesis/dissertation. *Entrance requirements:* For master's and doctorate, GRE General Test, 3 letters of recommendation. Additional exam requirements/recommendations for international students: Required—TOEFL (minimum score 550 paper-based). Electronic applications accepted. *Faculty research:* Geology, geophysics, geochemistry, geobiology, climate and environmental geosciences.

University of Nevada, Reno, Graduate School, College of Science, Mackay School of Earth Sciences and Engineering, Department of Geological Sciences and Engineering, Program in Geophysics, Reno, NV 89557. Offers MS, PhD. Terminal master's awarded for partial completion of doctoral program. *Degree requirements:* For master's, thesis optional; for doctorate, thesis/dissertation. *Entrance requirements:* For master's, GRE General Test, minimum GPA of 2.75; for doctorate, GRE General Test, minimum GPA of 3.0. Additional exam requirements/recommendations for international students: Required—TOEFL (minimum score 500 paper-based; 61 iBT), IELTS (minimum score 6). Electronic applications accepted. *Faculty research:* Geophysics exploration, seismology, remote sensing.

University of Oklahoma, Mewbourne College of Earth and Energy, ConocoPhillips School of Geology and Geophysics, Program in Geophysics, Norman, OK 73019. Offers MS, PhD. Part-time programs available. *Students:* 26 full-time (5 women), 12 part-time (2 women); includes 3 minority (1 Asian, non-Hispanic/Latino; 2 Hispanic/Latino), 22 international. Average age 27. 80 applicants, 14% accepted, 8 enrolled. In 2012, 5 master's, 1 doctorate awarded. *Degree requirements:* For master's, comprehensive exam, thesis; for doctorate, comprehensive exam, thesis/dissertation, proposal, colloquium and dissertation defense. *Entrance requirements:* Additional exam requirements/recommendations for international students: Required—TOEFL (minimum score 550 paper-based; 79 iBT). *Application deadline:* For fall admission, 2/1 for domestic and international students; for spring admission, 9/1 for domestic and international students. Applications are processed on a rolling basis. Application fee: $40 ($90 for international students). Electronic applications accepted. *Expenses:* Tuition, state resident: full-time $4205; part-time $175.20 per credit hour. Tuition, nonresident: full-time $15,667; part-time $653 per credit hour. *Required fees:* $2745; $103.85 per credit hour. Tuition and fees vary according to course load and degree level. *Financial support:* Career-related internships or fieldwork, scholarships/grants, and unspecified assistantships available. Financial award application deadline: 6/1; financial award applicants required to submit FAFSA. *Faculty research:* Lithospheric structure and evolution, basin analysis, outcrop-scale investigations of sand-bodies in turbidite channels. *Unit head:* Dr. R. Douglas Elmore, Director and Associate Provost, 405-325-3253, Fax: 405-325-3140, E-mail: delmore@ou.edu. *Application contact:* Donna S. Mullins, Coordinator of Administrative Student Services, 405-325-3255, Fax: 405-325-3140, E-mail: dsmullins@ou.edu. Website: http://geology.ou.edu.

The University of Texas at Dallas, School of Natural Sciences and Mathematics, Department of Geosciences, Richardson, TX 75080. Offers geochemistry (MS, PhD); geophysics (MS, PhD); geospatial information sciences (MS, PhD); hydrogeology (MS, PhD); sedimentary, stratigraphy, paleontology (PhD); stratigraphy, paleontology (MS); structural geology and tectonics (MS, PhD). Part-time and evening/weekend programs available. *Faculty:* 10 full-time (1 woman). *Students:* 45 full-time (18 women), 26 part-time (11 women); includes 9 minority (2 Black or African American, non-Hispanic/Latino; 4 Asian, non-Hispanic/Latino; 3 Hispanic/Latino), 23 international. Average age 30. 90 applicants, 31% accepted, 18 enrolled. In 2012, 7 master's, 4 doctorates awarded. *Degree requirements:* For master's, thesis optional; for doctorate, thesis/dissertation. *Entrance requirements:* For master's and doctorate, GRE General Test, minimum GPA of 3.0 in upper-level course work in field. Additional exam requirements/recommendations for international students: Required—TOEFL (minimum score 550 paper-based). *Application deadline:* For fall admission, 7/15 for domestic students, 5/1 for international students; for spring admission, 11/15 for domestic students, 9/1 for international students. Applications are processed on a rolling basis. Application fee: $50 ($100 for international students). Electronic applications accepted. *Expenses:* Tuition, state resident: full-time $11,940; part-time $663.33 per credit hour. Tuition, nonresident: full-time $21,606; part-time $1200.33 per credit hour. Tuition and fees vary according to course load. *Financial support:* In 2012–13, 33 students received support, including 12 research assistantships with partial tuition reimbursements available (averaging $22,270 per year), 9 teaching assistantships with partial tuition reimbursements available (averaging $15,300 per year); career-related internships or fieldwork, Federal Work-Study, institutionally sponsored loans, scholarships/grants, and unspecified assistantships also available. Support available to part-time students. Financial award application deadline: 4/30; financial award applicants required to submit FAFSA. *Faculty research:* Cybermapping, GPS applications for geophysics and geology, seismology and ground-penetrating radar, numerical modeling, signal processing and inverse modeling techniques in seismology. *Unit head:* Dr. John Oldow, Department Head, 972-883-2401, Fax: 972-883-2537, E-mail: geosciences@utdallas.edu. *Application contact:* Gloria Eby, Graduate Support Assistant, 972-883-2404, Fax: 972-883-2537, E-mail: geosciences@utdallas.edu. Website: http://www.utdallas.edu/geosciences.

The University of Texas at El Paso, Graduate School, College of Science, Department of Geological Sciences, Program in Geophysics, El Paso, TX 79968-0001. Offers MS. Part-time and evening/weekend programs available. *Degree requirements:* For master's, thesis. *Entrance requirements:* For master's, minimum GPA of 3.0, letters of recommendation. Additional exam requirements/recommendations for international students: Required—TOEFL; Recommended—IELTS. Electronic applications accepted.

University of Utah, Graduate School, College of Mines and Earth Sciences, Department of Geology and Geophysics, Salt Lake City, UT 84112. Offers environmental engineering (ME, MS, PhD); geological engineering (ME, MS, PhD); geology (MS, PhD); geophysics (MS, PhD). *Faculty:* 21 full-time (5 women), 1 part-time/adjunct (0 women). *Students:* 58 full-time (21 women), 34 part-time (7 women); includes 5 minority (1 American Indian or Alaska Native, non-Hispanic/Latino; 2 Asian, non-Hispanic/Latino; 2 Hispanic/Latino), 22 international. Average age 30. 211 applicants, 20% accepted, 26 enrolled. In 2012, 6 master's, 4 doctorates awarded. Terminal master's awarded for partial completion of doctoral program. *Degree requirements:* For master's, comprehensive exam, thesis; for doctorate, thesis/dissertation, qualifying exam (written and oral). *Entrance requirements:* For master's and doctorate, GRE General Test, minimum GPA of 3.25. Additional exam requirements/recommendations for international students: Required—TOEFL (minimum score 500 paper-based; 61 iBT), IELTS. *Application deadline:* For fall admission, 1/15 priority date for domestic students, 1/15 for international students. Applications are processed on a rolling basis. Application fee: $55 ($65 for international students). Electronic applications accepted. *Financial support:* In 2012–13, 26 students received support, including 11 fellowships with full tuition reimbursements available (averaging $16,000 per year), 39 research assistantships with full tuition reimbursements available (averaging $22,000 per year), 15 teaching assistantships with full tuition reimbursements available (averaging $16,000 per year); career-related internships or fieldwork, institutionally sponsored loans, scholarships/grants, unspecified assistantships, and stipends also available. Financial award application deadline: 1/15; financial award applicants required to submit FAFSA. *Faculty research:* Igneous, metamorphic, and sedimentary petrology; ore deposits; aqueous geochemistry; isotope geochemistry; heat flow. *Total annual research expenditures:* $3.3 million. *Unit head:* Dr. Kip Solomon, Chair, 801-581-7231, Fax: 801-581-7065, E-mail: kip.solomon@utah.edu. *Application contact:* Dr. Cari L. Johnson, Director of Graduate Studies, 801-585-3782, Fax: 801-581-7065, E-mail: cari.johnson@utah.edu. Website: http://www.earth.utah.edu/.

University of Victoria, Faculty of Graduate Studies, Faculty of Science, Department of Physics and Astronomy, Victoria, BC V8W 2Y2, Canada. Offers astronomy and astrophysics (M Sc, PhD); condensed matter physics (M Sc, PhD); experimental particle physics (M Sc, PhD); medical physics (M Sc, PhD); ocean physics (M Sc, PhD); theoretical physics (M Sc, PhD). *Degree requirements:* For master's, thesis; for doctorate, comprehensive exam, thesis/dissertation, candidacy exam. *Entrance requirements:* For master's and doctorate, GRE. Additional exam requirements/recommendations for international students: Required—TOEFL (minimum score 575 paper-based), IELTS (minimum score 7). Electronic applications accepted. *Faculty research:* Old stellar populations; observational cosmology and large scale structure; cp violation; atlas.

University of Washington, Graduate School, College of the Environment, Department of Earth and Space Sciences, Seattle, WA 98195. Offers geology (MS, PhD); geophysics (MS, PhD). *Degree requirements:* For master's, thesis or alternative, departmental qualifying exam, final exam; for doctorate, thesis/dissertation, departmental qualifying exam, general and final exams. *Entrance requirements:* For master's and doctorate, GRE General Test, minimum GPA of 3.0. Additional exam requirements/recommendations for international students: Required—TOEFL (minimum score 580 paper-based). Electronic applications accepted.

The University of Western Ontario, Faculty of Graduate Studies, Physical Sciences Division, Department of Earth Sciences, London, ON N6A 5B8, Canada. Offers environment and sustainability (MES); geology (M Sc, PhD); geology and environmental science (M Sc, PhD); geophysics (M Sc, PhD); geophysics and environmental science (M Sc, PhD). *Degree requirements:* For master's, thesis; for doctorate, thesis/dissertation, qualifying exam. *Entrance requirements:* For master's, honors in B Sc; for doctorate, M Sc. Additional exam requirements/recommendations for international students: Required—TOEFL. *Faculty research:* Geophysics, geochemistry, paleontology, sedimentology/stratigraphy, glaciology/quaternary.

University of Wisconsin–Madison, Graduate School, College of Letters and Science, Department of Geology and Geophysics, Program in Geophysics, Madison, WI 53706-1380. Offers MS, PhD. *Degree requirements:* For master's, thesis; for doctorate, one foreign language, thesis/dissertation. *Entrance requirements:* For master's and doctorate, GRE General Test. *Expenses:* Tuition, state resident: full-time $10,728; part-time $743 per credit. Tuition, nonresident: full-time $24,054; part-time $1575 per credit. *Required fees:* $1111; $72 per credit.

University of Wyoming, College of Arts and Sciences, Department of Geology and Geophysics, Laramie, WY 82070. Offers geology (MS, PhD); geophysics (MS, PhD). Part-time programs available. *Degree requirements:* For master's,

comprehensive exam, thesis; for doctorate, comprehensive exam, thesis/dissertation. *Entrance requirements:* For master's and doctorate, GRE General Test, minimum GPA of 3.0. *Faculty research:* Low-temp geochemistry, geohydrology, paleontology, structure/tectonics, sedimentation and petroleum geology, petrology, geophysics/seismology.

West Virginia University, Eberly College of Arts and Sciences, Department of Geology and Geography, Program in Geology, Morgantown, WV 26506. Offers geomorphology (MS, PhD); geophysics (MS, PhD); hydrogeology (MS, PhD); paleontology (MS, PhD); petroleum geology (PhD); petrology (MS, PhD); stratigraphy (MS, PhD); structure (MS, PhD). Part-time programs available. Terminal master's awarded for partial completion of doctoral program. *Degree requirements:* For master's, thesis (for some programs); for doctorate, comprehensive exam, thesis/dissertation. *Entrance requirements:* For master's, GRE General Test, minimum GPA of 2.5; for doctorate, GRE General Test, minimum GPA of 3.3. Additional exam requirements/recommendations for international students: Required—TOEFL.

Wright State University, School of Graduate Studies, College of Science and Mathematics, Department of Physics, Program in Physics, Dayton, OH 45435. Offers geophysics (MS); medical physics (MS). Part-time and evening/weekend programs available. *Degree requirements:* For master's, thesis. *Entrance requirements:* Additional exam requirements/recommendations for international students: Required—TOEFL. *Faculty research:* Solid-state physics, optics, geophysics.

Yale University, Graduate School of Arts and Sciences, Department of Geology and Geophysics, New Haven, CT 06520. Offers biogeochemistry (PhD); climate dynamics (PhD); geochemistry (PhD); geophysics (PhD); meteorology (PhD); oceanography (PhD); paleontology (PhD); paleooceanography (PhD); petrology (PhD); tectonics (PhD). *Degree requirements:* For doctorate, thesis/dissertation. *Entrance requirements:* For doctorate, GRE General Test. Additional exam requirements/recommendations for international students: Required—TOEFL.

Geosciences

Arizona State University, College of Liberal Arts and Sciences, School of Earth and Space Exploration, Tempe, AZ 85287-1404. Offers astrophysics (MS, PhD); exploration systems design (PhD); geological sciences (MS, PhD). PhD in exploration systems design is offered in collaboration with the Fulton Schools of Engineering. Terminal master's awarded for partial completion of doctoral program. *Degree requirements:* For master's, thesis, interactive Program of Study (iPOS) submitted before completing 50 percent of required credit hours; for doctorate, thesis/dissertation, interactive Program of Study (iPOS) submitted before completing 50 percent of required credit hours. *Entrance requirements:* For master's and doctorate, GRE, minimum GPA of 3.0 or equivalent in last 2 years of work leading to bachelor's degree. Additional exam requirements/recommendations for international students: Required—TOEFL (minimum score 80 iBT), TOEFL, IELTS, or Pearson Test of English. Electronic applications accepted.

Baylor University, Graduate School, College of Arts and Sciences, Department of Geology, Waco, TX 76798. Offers earth science (MA); geology (MS, PhD). *Faculty:* 12 full-time (1 woman). *Students:* 30 full-time (11 women); includes 4 minority (2 Asian, non-Hispanic/Latino; 2 Hispanic/Latino), 6 international. In 2012, 10 master's awarded. *Degree requirements:* For master's, thesis; for doctorate, thesis/dissertation. *Entrance requirements:* For master's and doctorate, GRE General Test. *Application deadline:* For fall admission, 3/15 priority date for domestic students. Applications are processed on a rolling basis. Application fee: $25. *Expenses: Tuition:* Full-time $24,426; part-time $1357 per semester hour. *Required fees:* $2556; $142 per semester hour. *Financial support:* In 2012–13, 18 teaching assistantships were awarded; Federal Work-Study and institutionally sponsored loans also available. *Faculty research:* Petroleum geology, geophysics, engineering geology, hydrogeology. *Unit head:* Dr. Steve Dworkin, Graduate Program Director, 254-710-2186, Fax: 254-710-2673, E-mail: steve_dworkin@baylor.edu. *Application contact:* Paulette Penney, Administrative Assistant, 254-710-2361, Fax: 254-710-3870, E-mail: paulette_penney@baylor.edu. Website: http://www.baylor.edu/geology/.

Baylor University, Graduate School, College of Arts and Sciences, The Institute of Ecological, Earth and Environmental Sciences, Waco, TX 76798. Offers PhD. *Students:* 10 full-time (3 women); includes 2 minority (1 Hispanic/Latino; 1 Two or more races, non-Hispanic/Latino), 5 international. In 2012, 1 doctorate awarded. *Degree requirements:* For doctorate, variable foreign language requirement, comprehensive exam, thesis/dissertation or alternative. *Entrance requirements:* For doctorate, GRE. Additional exam requirements/recommendations for international students: Required—TOEFL (minimum score 550 paper-based; 80 iBT); Recommended—IELTS (minimum score 6.5). *Application deadline:* For fall admission, 2/15 priority date for domestic students, 2/15 for international students; for spring admission, 11/15 for domestic and international students. Application fee: $40. Electronic applications accepted. *Expenses: Tuition:* Full-time $24,426; part-time $1357 per semester hour. *Required fees:* $2556; $142 per semester

hour. *Financial support:* In 2012–13, 5 students received support, including 5 research assistantships with full and partial tuition reimbursements available (averaging $20,000 per year), 5 teaching assistantships with full and partial tuition reimbursements available (averaging $20,000 per year); career-related internships or fieldwork, scholarships/grants, traineeships, health care benefits, tuition waivers (partial), unspecified assistantships, and Presidential Scholarship (Baylor University) also available. Financial award application deadline: 2/15. *Faculty research:* Ecosystem processes, environmental toxicology and risk assessment, biogeochemical cycling, chemical fate and transport, conservation management. *Unit head:* Dr. Joseph D. White, Director, 254-710-2911, E-mail: joseph_d_white@baylor.edu. *Application contact:* Shannon Koehler, Administrative Associate, 254-710-2224, Fax: 254-710-2580, E-mail: shannon_koehler@baylor.edu. Website: http://www.baylor.edu/TIEEES/.

Boston University, Graduate School of Arts and Sciences, Department of Earth and Environment, Boston, MA 02215. Offers earth sciences (MA, PhD); energy and environmental analysis (MA); environmental remote sensing and GIS (MA); geography and environment (MA, PhD); global development policy (MA); international relations and environmental policy (MA). *Students:* 77 full-time (39 women), 11 part-time (5 women); includes 2 minority (1 American Indian or Alaska Native, non-Hispanic/Latino; 1 Asian, non-Hispanic/Latino), 25 international. Average age 27. 288 applicants, 33% accepted, 23 enrolled. In 2012, 4 master's, 6 doctorates awarded. *Degree requirements:* For master's, comprehensive exam (for some programs), thesis (for some programs); for doctorate, comprehensive exam, thesis/dissertation. *Entrance requirements:* For master's and doctorate, GRE, 3 letters of recommendation, official transcripts, personal statement. Additional exam requirements/recommendations for international students: Required—TOEFL (minimum score 550 paper-based; 84 iBT). *Application deadline:* For fall admission, 1/15 for domestic students, 11/15 for international students. Application fee: $80. Electronic applications accepted. *Expenses: Tuition:* Full-time $42,400; part-time $1325 per credit. *Required fees:* $40 per semester. *Financial support:* In 2012–13, 2 fellowships with full tuition reimbursements (averaging $20,300 per year), 32 research assistantships with full tuition reimbursements (averaging $19,800 per year), 19 teaching assistantships with full tuition reimbursements (averaging $19,800 per year) were awarded; Federal Work-Study, scholarships/grants, traineeships, and health care benefits also available. Financial award application deadline: 1/15. *Faculty research:* Biogeosciences, climate and surface processes; energy, environment and society; geographical sciences; geology, geochemistry and geophysics. *Unit head:* Curtis Woodcock, Chair, 617-353-5746, E-mail: curtis@bu.edu. *Application contact:* Christian Cole, Graduate Program Coordinator, 617-353-2529, Fax: 617-353-8399, E-mail: ccole@bu.edu. Website: http://www.bu.edu/earth/.

Brock University, Faculty of Graduate Studies, Faculty of Mathematics and Science, Program in Earth Sciences, St. Catharines, ON L2S 3A1, Canada. Offers M Sc. Part-time programs available. *Degree requirements:* For master's,

Peterson's Graduate Programs in the Physical Sciences, Mathematics, Agricultural Sciences, the Environment & Natural Resources 2014

www.petersonsbooks.com   **157**

thesis. *Entrance requirements:* For master's, honors B Sc in earth sciences. Additional exam requirements/recommendations for international students: Required—TOEFL (minimum score 550 paper-based; 80 iBT), IELTS (minimum score 6.5), TWE (minimum score 4). Electronic applications accepted. *Faculty research:* Clastic sedimentology, environmental geology, geochemistry, micropaleontology, structural geology.

Brooklyn College of the City University of New York, Division of Graduate Studies, School of Education, Program in Adolescence Education and Special Subjects, Brooklyn, NY 11210-2889. Offers adolescence science education (MAT); art teacher (MA); biology teacher (MA); chemistry teacher (MA); earth science teacher (MAT); English teacher (MA); French teacher (MA); health and nutrition sciences: health teacher (MS Ed); mathematics teacher (MA); music education (CAS); music teacher (MA); physical education teacher (MS Ed); physics teacher (MA); social studies teacher (MA); Spanish teacher (MA). Part-time and evening/weekend programs available. *Degree requirements:* For master's, comprehensive exam (for some programs), thesis (for some programs). *Entrance requirements:* For master's, LAST, previous course work in education, resume, 2 letters of recommendation, essay. Additional exam requirements/recommendations for international students: Required—TOEFL (minimum score 500 paper-based; 61 iBT). Electronic applications accepted. *Faculty research:* Interdisciplinary education, semiotics, discourse analysis, autobiography, teacher identity.

Brooklyn College of the City University of New York, Division of Graduate Studies, School of Education, Program in Middle Childhood Education (Science), Brooklyn, NY 11210-2889. Offers biology (MA); chemistry (MA); earth science (MA); general science (MA); physics (MA). Part-time and evening/weekend programs available. *Entrance requirements:* For master's, LAST, interview, previous course work in education and mathematics, resume, 2 letters of recommendation, essay. Additional exam requirements/recommendations for international students: Required—TOEFL (minimum score 500 paper-based; 61 iBT). Electronic applications accepted. *Faculty research:* Geometric thinking, mastery of basic facts, problem-solving strategies, history of mathematics.

Brown University, Graduate School, Department of Geological Sciences, Providence, RI 02912. Offers MA, Sc M, PhD. *Degree requirements:* For doctorate, thesis/dissertation, 1 semester of teaching experience, preliminary exam. *Faculty research:* Geochemistry, mineral kinetics, igneous and metamorphic petrology, tectonophysics including geophysics and structural geology, paleoclimatology, paleoceanography, sedimentation, planetary geology.

California State University, Chico, Office of Graduate Studies, College of Natural Sciences, Department of Geological and Environmental Sciences, Program in Geosciences, Chico, CA 95929-0722. Offers hydrology/hydrogeology (MS). Part-time programs available. *Faculty:* 5 full-time (2 women), 3 part-time/adjunct (1 woman). *Students:* 6 full-time (4 women). Average age 33. 11 applicants, 45% accepted, 3 enrolled. In 2012, 1 master's awarded. *Degree requirements:* For master's, comprehensive exam, thesis. *Entrance requirements:* For master's, GRE, faculty mentor, statement of purpose. Additional exam requirements/recommendations for international students: Required—TOEFL (minimum score 550 paper-based; 80 iBT), IELTS (minimum score 6.5), Pearson Test of English (minimum score 59). *Application deadline:* For fall admission, 3/1 priority date for domestic students, 3/1 for international students; for spring admission, 9/15 priority date for domestic students, 9/15 for international students. Application fee: $55. Electronic applications accepted. *Expenses:* Tuition, state resident: part-time $372 per unit. Tuition, nonresident: part-time $372 per unit. *Required fees:* $2687 per semester. Tuition and fees vary according to course level and program. *Financial support:* Fellowships, research assistantships, teaching assistantships, and career-related internships or fieldwork available. *Unit head:* Dr. David L. Brown, Chair, 530-898-5262, Fax: 530-898-5234, E-mail: geos@csuchico.edu. *Application contact:* Judy L. Rice, Graduate Admissions Coordinator, 530-898-5416, Fax: 530-898-3342, E-mail: jlrice@csuchico.edu. Website: http://catalog.csuchico.edu/viewer/12/GEOS.html.

Carleton University, Faculty of Graduate Studies, Faculty of Science, Department of Earth Sciences, Ottawa, ON K1S 5B6, Canada. Offers M Sc, PhD. Programs offered jointly with University of Ottawa. *Degree requirements:* For master's, thesis, seminar; for doctorate, comprehensive exam, thesis/dissertation, seminar. *Entrance requirements:* For master's, honors degree in science; for doctorate, M Sc. Additional exam requirements/recommendations for international students: Required—TOEFL. *Faculty research:* Resource geology, geophysics, basin analysis, lithosphere dynamics.

Case Western Reserve University, School of Graduate Studies, Earth, Environmental, and Planetary Sciences, Cleveland, OH 44106. Offers MS, PhD. Part-time programs available. *Faculty:* 7 full-time (1 woman), 7 part-time/adjunct (1 woman). *Students:* 8 full-time (3 women), 3 international. Average age 28. 14 applicants, 21% accepted, 2 enrolled. In 2012, 1 doctorate awarded. Terminal master's awarded for partial completion of doctoral program. *Degree requirements:* For master's, thesis or alternative; for doctorate, thesis/dissertation. *Entrance requirements:* For master's and doctorate, GRE General Test, GRE Subject Test. Additional exam requirements/recommendations for international students: Required—TOEFL (minimum score 577 paper-based; 90 iBT); Recommended—IELTS (minimum score 7). *Application deadline:* For fall admission, 1/15 priority date for domestic students; for spring admission, 11/15 for domestic students. Applications are processed on a rolling basis. Application fee: $50. Electronic applications accepted. *Financial support:* Research assistantships, teaching assistantships, Federal Work-Study, and tuition waivers (partial) available. Support available to part-time students. Financial award application deadline: 1/15; financial award applicants required to submit FAFSA. *Faculty research:* Geochemistry, hydrology, ecology, geomorphology, planetary science, stratigraphy and basin analysis, igneous petrology. *Unit head:* Gerald Matisoff, Chairman, 216-368-3677, Fax: 216-368-3691, E-mail: gerald.matisoff@case.edu. *Application contact:* James Van Orman, Chair, Graduate Admission Committee, 216-368-3690, Fax: 216-368-3691, E-mail: james.vanorman@case.edu. Website: http://geology.case.edu/.

Central Connecticut State University, School of Graduate Studies, School of Arts and Sciences, Department of Physics and Earth Science, New Britain, CT 06050-4010. Offers natural sciences (MS); science education (Certificate). Part-time and evening/weekend programs available. *Faculty:* 3 full-time (1 woman). *Students:* 7 part-time (6 women). Average age 32. 3 applicants, 33% accepted, 1 enrolled. In 2012, 3 master's, 1 other advanced degree awarded. *Degree requirements:* For master's, comprehensive exam, thesis or alternative; for Certificate, qualifying exam. *Entrance requirements:* For master's, minimum undergraduate GPA of 2.7. Additional exam requirements/recommendations for international students: Required—TOEFL (minimum score 550 paper-based; 79 iBT). *Application deadline:* For fall admission, 6/1 for domestic students, 5/1 for international students; for spring admission, 11/1 for domestic and international students. Applications are processed on a rolling basis. Application fee: $50. Electronic applications accepted. *Expenses: Tuition, area resident:* Full-time $5337; part-time $498 per credit. Tuition, state resident: full-time $8008; part-time $510 per credit. Tuition, nonresident: full-time $14,869; part-time $510 per credit. *Required fees:* $3970. One-time fee: $62 part-time. *Financial support:* Career-related internships or fieldwork, Federal Work-Study, scholarships/grants, and unspecified assistantships available. Support available to part-time students. Financial award application deadline: 3/1; financial award applicants required to submit FAFSA. *Faculty research:* Elementary/secondary science education, particle and solid states, weather patterns, planetary studies. *Unit head:* Dr. Mark Evans, Chair, 860-832-2930, E-mail: evansmaa@ccsu.edu. *Application contact:* Patricia Gardner, Associate Director of Graduate Studies, 860-832-2350, Fax: 860-832-2362, E-mail: graduateadmissions@ccsu.edu. Website: http://www.physics.ccsu.edu/.

Chapman University, Schmid College of Science and Technology, Program in Hazards, Global and Environmental Change, Orange, CA 92866. Offers MS. Part-time programs available. *Faculty:* 14 full-time (1 woman), 3 part-time/adjunct (1 woman). *Students:* 5 full-time (2 women), 8 part-time (5 women); includes 4 minority (2 Asian, non-Hispanic/Latino; 1 Hispanic/Latino; 1 Native Hawaiian or other Pacific Islander, non-Hispanic/Latino), 4 international. Average age 27. 28 applicants, 71% accepted, 15 enrolled. In 2012, 1 master's awarded. *Entrance requirements:* Additional exam requirements/recommendations for international students: Required—TOEFL (minimum score 550 paper-based; 80 iBT). *Financial support:* Fellowships, Federal Work-Study, and scholarships/grants available. Financial award applicants required to submit FAFSA. *Unit head:* Dr. Menas Kafatos, Dean, 714-628-7223, E-mail: jhill@chapman.edu. *Application contact:* Saundra Hoover, Director of Graduate Admissions, 714-997-6786, Fax: 714-997-6713, E-mail: shoover@chapman.edu. Website: http://www.chapman.edu/SCS/EES/MSHGEC.asp.

City College of the City University of New York, Graduate School, College of Liberal Arts and Science, Division of Science, Department of Earth and Atmospheric Sciences, New York, NY 10031-9198. Offers earth and environmental science (PhD); earth systems science (MA). PhD program offered jointly with Graduate School and University Center of the City University of New York. *Degree requirements:* For master's, comprehensive exam, thesis. *Entrance requirements:* Additional exam requirements/recommendations for international students: Required—TOEFL (minimum score 500 paper-based; 61 iBT). Electronic applications accepted. *Faculty research:* Water resources, high-temperature geochemistry, sedimentary basin analysis, tectonics.

The College of William and Mary, Faculty of Arts and Sciences, Department of Applied Science, Williamsburg, VA 23187-8795. Offers accelerator science (PhD); applied mathematics (PhD); applied mechanics (PhD); applied robotics (PhD); applied science (MS); atmospheric and environmental science (PhD); computational neuroscience (PhD); interface, thin film and surface science (PhD); lasers and optics (PhD); magnetic resonance (PhD); materials science and engineering (PhD); mathematical and computational biology (PhD); medical imaging (PhD); nanotechnology (PhD); neuroscience (PhD); non-destructive evaluation (PhD); polymer chemistry (PhD); remote sensing (PhD). *Faculty:* 13 full-time (2 women), 1 part-time/adjunct (0 women). *Students:* 36 full-time (11 women); includes 2 minority (1 Black or African American, non-Hispanic/Latino; 1 Asian, non-Hispanic/Latino), 22 international. Average age 26. 40 applicants, 45% accepted, 8 enrolled. In 2012, 3 master's, 2 doctorates awarded. *Median time to degree:* Of those who began their doctoral program in fall 2004, 95% received their degree in 8 years or less. *Degree requirements:* For master's, comprehensive exam, thesis; for doctorate, comprehensive exam, thesis/dissertation, 4 core courses. *Entrance requirements:* For master's and doctorate, GRE General Test, GRE Subject Test. Additional exam requirements/recommendations for international students: Required—TOEFL, TWE. *Application deadline:* For fall admission, 2/3 priority date for domestic students, 2/3 for international students; for spring admission, 10/15 priority date for domestic students, 10/14 for international students. Applications are processed on a rolling basis. Application fee: $45. Electronic applications accepted. *Expenses:* Tuition, state resident: full-time $6779; part-time $385 per credit hour. Tuition, nonresident: full-time $20,608; part-time $1000 per credit hour. *Required fees:* $4625. *Financial support:* Fellowships, research assistantships, teaching assistantships, Federal Work-Study, health care benefits, tuition waivers (full), and unspecified assistantships available. Financial award application deadline: 4/15; financial award applicants required to submit FAFSA. *Faculty research:* Computational biology, non-destructive evaluation, neurophysiology, lasers and optics. *Unit head:* Dr. Christopher Del Negro, Chair, 757-221-7808, Fax: 757-221-2050, E-mail: cadeln@wm.edu. *Application contact:* Rosario Fox, Graduate Program Coordinator, 757-221-2563, Fax: 757-221-2050, E-mail: rxfoxx@wm.edu. Website: http://www.wm.edu/as/appliedscience.

Colorado State University, Graduate School, Warner College of Natural Resources, Department of Geosciences, Fort Collins, CO 80523-1482. Offers earth sciences (PhD); geosciences (MS). Part-time programs available. *Faculty:* 11 full-time (4 women). *Students:* 20 full-time (8 women), 43 part-time (22 women); includes 5 minority (1 American Indian or Alaska Native, non-Hispanic/Latino; 1 Asian, non-Hispanic/Latino; 2 Hispanic/Latino; 1 Two or more races, non-Hispanic/Latino), 8 international. Average age 31. 88 applicants, 36% accepted, 16 enrolled. In 2012, 8 master's, 1 doctorate awarded. *Degree requirements:* For master's, thesis; for doctorate, comprehensive exam, thesis/dissertation. *Entrance requirements:* For master's and doctorate, GRE General Test, minimum GPA of 3.0, letters of recommendation. Additional exam requirements/recommendations for international students: Required—TOEFL (minimum score 550 paper-based; 80 iBT); Recommended—IELTS (minimum score 6). *Application deadline:* For fall admission, 2/15 priority date for domestic students, 2/15 for international students; for spring admission, 7/15 priority date for domestic students, 7/15 for international students. Applications are processed on a rolling basis. Application fee: $50. Electronic applications accepted. *Expenses:* Tuition, state resident: full-time $8811; part-time $490 per credit. Tuition, nonresident: full-time $21,600; part-time $1200 per credit. *Required fees:* $1819; $61 per credit. *Financial support:* In 2012–13, 27 students received support, including 3 fellowships (averaging $39,500 per year), 16 research assistantships with full tuition reimbursements available (averaging $13,417 per year), 8 teaching assistantships with full tuition reimbursements available (averaging $11,200 per year); scholarships/grants also available. Financial award application deadline: 2/15; financial award applicants required to submit FAFSA. *Faculty research:* Snow, surface, and groundwater hydrology; fluvial geomorphology; geographic information systems; geochemistry; chemical weathering. *Total annual research expenditures:* $1.2 million. *Unit head:* Dr. John Ridley, Associate Professor/Interim Department Head, 970-491-5943, Fax: 970-491-6307, E-mail: jridley@cnr.colostate.edu. *Application contact:* Sharon Gale, Graduate Contact, 970-491-5661, Fax: 970-491-6307, E-mail: sharon.gale@colostate.edu. Website: http://warnercnr.colostate.edu/geosciences-home/.

Columbia University, Graduate School of Arts and Sciences, Division of Natural Sciences, Department of Earth and Environmental Sciences, New York, NY 10027. Offers geochemistry (M Phil, MA, PhD); geodetic sciences (M Phil, MA, PhD); geophysics (M Phil, MA, PhD); oceanography (M Phil, MA, PhD). *Degree requirements:* For master's, thesis or alternative, fieldwork, written exam; for doctorate, one foreign language, thesis/dissertation. *Entrance requirements:* For master's and doctorate, GRE General Test, GRE Subject Test, major in natural or physical science. Additional exam requirements/recommendations for international students: Required—TOEFL. *Faculty research:* Structural geology and stratigraphy, petrology, paleontology, rare gas, isotope and aqueous geochemistry.

Cornell University, Graduate School, Graduate Fields of Engineering, Field of Geological Sciences, Ithaca, NY 14853. Offers economic geology (M Eng, MS, PhD); engineering geology (M Eng, MS, PhD); environmental geophysics (M Eng, MS, PhD); general geology (M Eng, MS, PhD); geobiology (M Eng, MS, PhD); geochemistry and isotope geology (M Eng, MS, PhD); geohydrology (M Eng, MS, PhD); geomorphology (M Eng, MS, PhD); geophysics (M Eng, MS, PhD); geotectonics (M Eng, MS, PhD); marine geology (MS, PhD); mineralogy (M Eng, MS, PhD); paleontology (M Eng, MS, PhD); petroleum geology (M Eng, MS, PhD); petrology (M Eng, MS, PhD); planetary geology (M Eng, MS, PhD); Precambrian geology (M Eng, MS, PhD); Quaternary geology (M Eng, MS, PhD); rock mechanics (M Eng, MS, PhD); sedimentology (M Eng, MS, PhD); seismology (M Eng, MS, PhD); stratigraphy (M Eng, MS, PhD); structural geology (M Eng, MS, PhD). *Faculty:* 37 full-time (5 women). *Students:* 32 full-time (13 women); includes 5 minority (2 Asian, non-Hispanic/Latino; 1 Hispanic/Latino; 2 Two or more races, non-Hispanic/Latino), 8 international. Average age 27. 58 applicants, 17% accepted, 6 enrolled. In 2012, 6 master's, 3 doctorates awarded. *Degree requirements:* For master's, thesis (MS); for doctorate, comprehensive exam, thesis/dissertation. *Entrance requirements:* For master's and doctorate, GRE General Test, 3 letters of recommendation. Additional exam requirements/recommendations for international students: Required—TOEFL (minimum score 550 paper-based; 77 iBT). *Application deadline:* For fall admission, 1/15 priority date for domestic students. Applications are processed on a rolling basis. Application fee: $95. Electronic applications accepted. *Financial support:* In 2012–13, 26 students received support, including 9 fellowships with full tuition reimbursements available, 16 research assistantships with full tuition reimbursements available, 1 teaching assistantship with full tuition reimbursement available; institutionally sponsored loans, scholarships/grants, health care benefits, tuition waivers (full and partial), and unspecified assistantships also available. Financial award applicants required to submit FAFSA. *Faculty research:* Geophysics, structural geology, petrology, geochemistry, geodynamics. *Unit head:* Director of Graduate Studies, 607-255-5466, Fax: 607-254-4780. *Application contact:* Graduate Field Assistant, 607-255-5466, Fax: 607-254-4780, E-mail: gradprog@geology.cornell.edu. Website: http://www.gradschool.cornell.edu/fields.php?id-30&a-2.

Dalhousie University, Faculty of Science, Department of Earth Sciences, Halifax, NS B3H 4R2, Canada. Offers M Sc, PhD. *Degree requirements:* For master's, one foreign language, thesis; for doctorate, one foreign language, thesis/dissertation. *Entrance requirements:* Additional exam requirements/recommendations for international students: Required—TOEFL, IELTS, CANTEST, CAEL, or Michigan English Language Assessment Battery. *Faculty research:* Marine geology and geophysics, Appalachian and Grenville geology, micropaleontology, geodynamics and structural geology, geochronology.

Dartmouth College, Arts and Sciences Graduate Programs, Department of Earth Sciences, Hanover, NH 03755. Offers MS, PhD. Terminal master's awarded for partial completion of doctoral program. *Degree requirements:* For master's, thesis; for doctorate, thesis/dissertation. *Entrance requirements:* For master's and doctorate, GRE General Test, GRE Subject Test. Additional exam requirements/recommendations for international students: Required—TOEFL. *Faculty research:* Geochemistry, remote sensing, geophysics, hydrology, economic geology.

Eastern Michigan University, Graduate School, College of Arts and Sciences, Department of Geography and Geology, Program in Earth Science Education, Ypsilanti, MI 48197. Offers MS. *Students:* 1 (woman) full-time, 4 part-time (2 women). Average age 33. 1 applicant. In 2012, 4 master's awarded. Application fee: $35. *Expenses:* Tuition, state resident: full-time $10,776; part-time $449 per credit hour. Tuition, nonresident: full-time $21,242; part-time $885 per credit hour. *Required fees:* $41 per credit hour. $48 per term. One-time fee: $100. Tuition and fees vary according to course level, degree level and reciprocity agreements. *Application contact:* Dr. Thomas Kovacs, Program Advisor, 734-487-0218, Fax: 734-487-6979, E-mail: tkovacs@emich.edu.

East Tennessee State University, School of Graduate Studies, College of Arts and Sciences, Department of Geosciences, Johnson City, TN 37614. Offers geospatial analysis (MS); paleontology (MS). Part-time programs available. *Faculty:* 8 full-time (2 women), 2 part-time/adjunct (1 woman). *Students:* 11 full-time (3 women), 3 part-time (1 woman); includes 2 minority (both Two or more races, non-Hispanic/Latino). 13 applicants, 46% accepted, 5 enrolled. *Degree requirements:* For master's, thesis. *Entrance requirements:* For master's, bachelor's degree in geosciences or related discipline, minimum GPA of 3.0, three letters of recommendation, resume. Additional exam requirements/recommendations for international students: Required—TOEFL (minimum score 550 paper-based; 79 iBT). *Application deadline:* For fall admission, 2/1 for domestic and international students. Application fee: $35 ($45 for international students). Electronic applications accepted. *Financial support:* In 2012–13, 12 students received support, including 6 research assistantships with full tuition reimbursements available (averaging $8,000 per year), 6 teaching assistantships with full tuition reimbursements available (averaging $9,500 per year); career-related internships or fieldwork, institutionally sponsored loans, scholarships/grants, and unspecified assistantships also available. Financial award application deadline: 7/1; financial award applicants required to submit FAFSA. *Faculty research:* Vertebrate paleontology; volcanology; soils and geological engineering; geological hazards stemming from volcanoes and tsunamis and the sociological responses; applications of geospatial analysis to meteorology, weather and climate, and geomorphology/watershed management; shallow surface geophysics, sedimentology, and stratigraphy. *Unit head:* Dr. Jim Mead, Chair, 423-439-7515, Fax: 423-439-7520, E-mail: mead@etsu.edu. *Application contact:* Gail Powers, Graduate Specialist, 423-439-4703, Fax: 423-439-5624, E-mail: powersg@etsu.edu. Website: http://www.etsu.edu/cas/geosciences/.

Emporia State University, Department of Physical Sciences, Emporia, KS 66801-5087. Offers earth science (MS); geospatial analysis (Postbaccalaureate Certificate); physical science (MS). Part-time programs available. Postbaccalaureate distance learning degree programs offered (minimal on-campus study). *Faculty:* 14 full-time (4 women). *Students:* 8 full-time (5 women), 33 part-time (16 women); includes 4 minority (1 Black or African American, non-Hispanic/Latino; 1 American Indian or Alaska Native, non-Hispanic/Latino; 1 Hispanic/Latino; 1 Native Hawaiian or other Pacific Islander, non-Hispanic/Latino), 5 international. 18 applicants, 83% accepted, 6 enrolled. In 2012, 9 master's awarded. *Degree requirements:* For master's, comprehensive exam or thesis. *Entrance requirements:* For master's, physical science qualifying exam, appropriate undergraduate degree. Additional exam requirements/recommendations for international students: Required—TOEFL (minimum score 520 paper-based; 68 iBT). *Application deadline:* For fall admission, 8/15 priority date for domestic students. Applications are processed on a rolling basis. Application fee: $30 ($75 for international students). Electronic applications accepted. *Expenses:* Tuition, state resident: full-time $4968; part-time $207 per credit hour. Tuition, nonresident: full-time $15,432; part-time $643 per credit hour. *Required fees:* $70 per credit hour. Tuition and fees vary according to course load. *Financial support:* In 2012–13, 1 research assistantship with full tuition reimbursement (averaging $7,200 per year), 7 teaching assistantships with full tuition reimbursements (averaging $7,200 per year) were awarded; Federal Work-Study, institutionally sponsored loans, health care benefits, and unspecified assistantships also available. Financial award application deadline: 3/15; financial award applicants required to submit FAFSA. *Faculty research:* Bredigite, larnite, and dicalcium silicates from Marble Canyon. *Unit head:* Dr. Richard Sleezer,

Interim Chair, 620-341-5330, Fax: 620-341-6055, E-mail: rsleezer@emporia.edu. *Application contact:* Mary Sewell, Admissions Coordinator, 800-950-GRAD, Fax: 620-341-5909, E-mail: msewell@emporia.edu. Website: http://www.emporia.edu/physci/.

Florida Atlantic University, Charles E. Schmidt College of Science, Department of Geosciences, Boca Raton, FL 33431-0991. Offers geography (MA); geology (MS); geosciences (PhD). Part-time programs available. *Faculty:* 11 full-time (3 women), 2 part-time/adjunct (0 women). *Students:* 29 full-time (16 women), 16 part-time (8 women); includes 12 minority (1 Black or African American, non-Hispanic/Latino; 4 Asian, non-Hispanic/Latino; 7 Hispanic/Latino), 1 international. Average age 34. 28 applicants, 68% accepted, 14 enrolled. In 2012, 9 master's, 2 doctorates awarded. *Degree requirements:* For master's, thesis (for some programs). *Entrance requirements:* For master's, GRE General Test, minimum GPA of 3.0. *Application deadline:* For fall admission, 3/15 for domestic and international students; for spring admission, 10/15 for domestic and international students. Applications are processed on a rolling basis. Application fee: $30. Electronic applications accepted. *Expenses:* Tuition, state resident: full-time $8876; part-time $369.82 per credit hour. Tuition, nonresident: full-time $24,595; part-time $1024.81 per credit hour. *Financial support:* Research assistantships with partial tuition reimbursements, teaching assistantships with partial tuition reimbursements, career-related internships or fieldwork, Federal Work-Study, institutionally sponsored loans, and unspecified assistantships available. *Faculty research:* GIS applications, paleontology, hydrogeology, economic development. *Unit head:* Dr. Russell Ivy, Chair, 561-297-3295, Fax: 561-297-2745, E-mail: ivy@fau.edu. *Application contact:* Dr. David Warburton, Graduate Coordinator, 561-297-3312, Fax: 561-297-2745, E-mail: warburto@fau.edu. Website: http://www.geosciences.fau.edu/.

Florida International University, College of Arts and Sciences, Department of Earth and Environment, Program in Geosciences, Miami, FL 33199. Offers MS, PhD. Part-time and evening/weekend programs available. *Degree requirements:* For master's, thesis optional; for doctorate, comprehensive exam, thesis/dissertation. *Entrance requirements:* For master's, GRE (minimum score of 1000), minimum GPA of 3.0 during last two years of undergraduate study, letter of intent, 3 letters of recommendation, resume; for doctorate, GRE (minimum score of 1120), minimum GPA of 3.0 during last two years of undergraduate study, letter of intent, 3 letters of recommendation, resume. Additional exam requirements/recommendations for international students: Required—TOEFL (minimum score 550 paper-based; 80 iBT). Electronic applications accepted.

Florida State University, The Graduate School, College of Arts and Sciences, Department of Scientific Computing, Tallahassee, FL 32306-4120. Offers computational science (MS, PSM, PhD), including atmospheric science (PhD), biochemistry (PhD), biological science (PhD), computational molecular biology/bioinformatics (PSM), computational science (PhD), geological science (PhD), materials science (PhD), physics (PhD). Part-time programs available. *Faculty:* 14 full-time (2 women). *Students:* 28 full-time (5 women), 4 part-time (0 women); includes 12 minority (10 Asian, non-Hispanic/Latino; 2 Hispanic/Latino). Average age 28. 28 applicants, 43% accepted, 7 enrolled. In 2012, 11 master's, 5 doctorates awarded. Terminal master's awarded for partial completion of doctoral program. *Degree requirements:* For master's, thesis (for some programs); for doctorate, comprehensive exam, thesis/dissertation. *Entrance requirements:* For master's and doctorate, GRE General Test, knowledge of at least one object-oriented computing language, 3 letters of recommendations. Additional exam requirements/recommendations for international students: Required—TOEFL (minimum score 550 paper-based; 80 iBT). *Application deadline:* For fall admission, 1/15 for domestic and international students. Application fee: $30. Electronic applications accepted. *Expenses:* Tuition, state resident: full-time $7263; part-time $403.51 per credit hour. Tuition, nonresident: full-time $18,087; part-time $1004.85 per credit hour. *Required fees:* $1335.42; $74.19 per credit hour. $445.14 per semester. One-time fee: $40 full-time; $20 part-time. Tuition and fees vary according to program. *Financial support:* In 2012–13, 32 students received support, including 12 research assistantships with full tuition reimbursements available (averaging $20,000 per year), 17 teaching assistantships with full tuition reimbursements available (averaging $20,000 per year); scholarships/grants and unspecified assistantships also available. Financial award application deadline: 4/15. *Faculty research:* Morphometrics, mathematical and systems biology, mining proteomic and metabolic data, computational materials research, advanced 4-D Var data-assimilation methods in dynamic meteorology and oceanography, computational fluid dynamics, astrophysics. *Unit head:* Dr. Max Gunzburger, Chair, 850-644-1010, E-mail: mgunzburger@fsu.edu. *Application contact:* Maribel Amwake, Academic Coordinator, 850-644-0143, Fax: 850-644-0098, E-mail: mamwake@fsu.edu. Website: http://www.sc.fsu.edu.

Fort Hays State University, Graduate School, College of Arts and Sciences, Department of Geosciences, Program in Geosciences, Hays, KS 67601-4099. Offers geography (MS); geology (MS). *Degree requirements:* For master's, comprehensive exam, thesis. *Entrance requirements:* For master's, GRE General Test. Additional exam requirements/recommendations for international students: Required—TOEFL (minimum score 550 paper-based). Electronic applications accepted. *Faculty research:* Cretaceous and late Cenozoic stratigraphy, sedimentation, paleontology.

George Mason University, College of Science, Department of Geography and Geoinformation Science, Fairfax, VA 22030. Offers earth system science (MS); earth systems and geoinformation sciences (PhD); geographic and cartographic sciences (MS); geographic information sciences (Certificate); geoinformatics and geospatial intelligence (MS); geospatial intelligence (Certificate); remote sensing and image processing (Certificate). *Faculty:* 34 full-time (7 women), 8 part-time/adjunct (0 women). *Students:* 54 full-time (19 women), 149 part-time (44 women); includes 34 minority (8 Black or African American, non-Hispanic/Latino; 1 American Indian or Alaska Native, non-Hispanic/Latino; 9 Asian, non-Hispanic/Latino; 9 Hispanic/Latino; 7 Two or more races, non-Hispanic/Latino), 24 international. Average age 35. 114 applicants, 66% accepted, 46 enrolled. In 2012, 22 master's, 7 doctorates, 38 other advanced degrees awarded. *Degree requirements:* For master's, thesis optional. *Entrance requirements:* For master's, GRE (waived for those who have earned a master's degree from U.S. institution), bachelor's degree with minimum GPA of 3.0; 2 copies of official transcripts; current resume; expanded goals statement; 3 letters of recommendation; for doctorate, GRE (waived for those who have earned a master's degree from U.S. institution), bachelor's degree with minimum GPA of 3.0; 2 copies of official transcripts; 3 letters of recommendation; resume; expanded goals statement; for Certificate, GRE (waived for those who have earned a master's degree from U.S. institution), baccalaureate degree with minimum GPA of 3.0; 2 official copies of transcripts; expanded goals statement; 3 letters of recommendation; resume. Additional exam requirements/recommendations for international students: Required—TOEFL (minimum score 570 paper-based; 88 iBT), IELTS (minimum score 6.5), Pearson Test of English. *Application deadline:* For fall admission, 4/15 priority date for domestic students; for spring admission, 11/15 priority date for domestic students. Application fee: $65 ($80 for international students). Electronic applications accepted. *Expenses:* Tuition, state resident: full-time $9080; part-time $378.33 per credit hour. Tuition, nonresident: full-time $25,010; part-time $1042.08 per credit hour. *Required fees:* $2610; $108.75 per credit hour. Tuition and fees vary according to program. *Financial support:* In 2012–13, 25 students received support, including 1 fellowship (averaging $8,000 per year), 19 research assistantships with full and partial tuition reimbursements available (averaging $16,367 per year), 6 teaching assistantships with full and partial tuition reimbursements available (averaging $16,262 per year); career-related internships or fieldwork, Federal Work-Study, scholarships/grants, unspecified assistantships, and health care benefits (for full-time research or teaching assistantship recipients) also available. Support available to part-time students. Financial award application deadline: 3/1; financial award applicants required to submit FAFSA. *Faculty research:* Global environment climate monitoring, gender and earth science, earth science education, remote sensing, planetary geology, hydrology, theoretical issues of geographic information data acquisition and processing. *Total annual research expenditures:* $4.1 million. *Unit head:* Peggy Agouris, Chair, 703-993-9265, Fax: 703-993-9230, E-mail: pagouris@gmu.edu. *Application contact:* Sheryl Luzzadder Beach, Associate Chair/Academic Programs Director, 703-993-1213, Fax: 703-993-9299, E-mail: slbeach@gmu.edu. Website: http://ggs.gmu.edu/.

Georgia Institute of Technology, Graduate Studies and Research, College of Sciences, School of Earth and Atmospheric Sciences, Atlanta, GA 30332-0340. Offers atmospheric chemistry, aerosols and clouds (MS, PhD); dynamics of weather and climate (MS, PhD); geochemistry (MS, PhD); geophysics (MS, PhD); oceanography (MS, PhD); paleoclimate (MS, PhD); planetary science (MS, PhD); remote sensing (MS, PhD). Part-time programs available. Terminal master's awarded for partial completion of doctoral program. *Degree requirements:* For master's, thesis or alternative; for doctorate, comprehensive exam, thesis/dissertation. *Entrance requirements:* For master's, GRE, letters of recommendation; for doctorate, GRE, academic transcripts, letters of recommendation, personal statement. Additional exam requirements/recommendations for international students: Required—TOEFL (minimum score 550 paper-based; 79 iBT). *Faculty research:* Geophysics; atmospheric chemistry, aerosols and clouds; dynamics of weather and climate; geochemistry; oceanography; paleoclimate; planetary science; remote sensing.

Georgia State University, College of Arts and Sciences, Department of Geosciences, Atlanta, GA 30302-3083. Offers geographic information systems (Certificate); geography (MS); geology (MS). Part-time programs available. *Faculty:* 12 full-time (3 women), 3 part-time/adjunct (0 women). *Students:* 32 full-time (18 women), 15 part-time (6 women); includes 10 minority (4 Black or African American, non-Hispanic/Latino; 2 Asian, non-Hispanic/Latino; 2 Hispanic/Latino; 2 Two or more races, non-Hispanic/Latino), 2 international. Average age 32. 20 applicants, 65% accepted, 9 enrolled. In 2012, 13 master's, 1 other advanced degree awarded. *Degree requirements:* For master's, one foreign language, comprehensive exam (for some programs), thesis. *Entrance requirements:* For master's, GRE; for Certificate, GRE. Additional exam requirements/recommendations for international students: Required—TOEFL (minimum score 550 paper-based; 80 iBT). *Application deadline:* For fall admission, 4/15 for domestic and international students; for spring admission, 11/15 for domestic and international students. Applications are processed on a rolling basis. Application fee: $50. Electronic applications accepted. *Expenses:* Tuition, state resident: full-time $8064; part-time $336 per credit hour. Tuition, nonresident: full-time $28,800; part-time $1200 per credit hour. *Required fees:* $2128; $1064 per semester. Tuition and fees vary according to course load and program. *Financial support:* In 2012–13, 1 research assistantship with full tuition reimbursement (averaging $12,000 per year), 26 teaching assistantships with full tuition reimbursements (averaging $6,000 per year) were awarded; fellowships, career-related internships or fieldwork, Federal Work-Study, and unspecified assistantships also available. Support available to part-time students. Financial award application deadline: 4/15. *Faculty research:* Sedimentology, mineralogy, climatology, geographic information science, hydrology. *Unit head:* Dr. W. Crawford Elliott, Chair, 404-413-

5756, Fax: 404-413-5768, E-mail: wcelliott@gsu.edu. *Application contact:* Dr. Jeremy Diem, Director of Graduate Studies, 404-413-5770, Fax: 404-413-5768, E-mail: jdiem@gsu.edu. Website: http://monarch.gsu.edu/geosciences/.

Georgia State University, College of Education, Department of Middle-Secondary Education and Instructional Technology, Atlanta, GA 30302-3083. Offers English education (M Ed, MAT); English speakers of other languages (MAT); instructional design and technology (online) (MS); instructional technology (PhD), including alternative instructional delivery systems, consulting, instructional design, management, research; mathematics education (M Ed, MAT); middle level education (MAT); reading, language and literacy education (M Ed), including reading instruction; science education (MAT), including biology, broad field science, chemistry, earth science, physics; social studies education (M Ed, MAT), including economics (MAT), geography (MAT), history (MAT), political science (MAT); teaching and learning (PhD), including language and literacy, mathematics education, music education, science education, social studies, teaching and teacher education. *Accreditation:* NCATE. Part-time and evening/weekend programs available. Postbaccalaureate distance learning degree programs offered (minimal on-campus study). *Faculty:* 38 full-time (30 women), 7 part-time/adjunct (all women). *Students:* 268 full-time (191 women), 243 part-time (172 women); includes 212 minority (148 Black or African American, non-Hispanic/Latino; 1 American Indian or Alaska Native, non-Hispanic/Latino; 26 Asian, non-Hispanic/Latino; 20 Hispanic/Latino; 1 Native Hawaiian or other Pacific Islander, non-Hispanic/Latino; 16 Two or more races, non-Hispanic/Latino), 15 international. Average age 34. 149 applicants, 67% accepted, 67 enrolled. In 2012, 253 master's, 18 doctorates awarded. *Degree requirements:* For master's, comprehensive exam (for some programs), thesis or alternative, exit portfolio; for doctorate, comprehensive exam, thesis/dissertation. *Entrance requirements:* For master's, GRE; GACE I (for initial teacher preparation degree programs), baccalaureate degree or equivalent, resume, goals statement, two letters of recommendation, minimum undergraduate GPA of 2.5; proof of initial teacher certification in the content area (for M Ed); for doctorate, GRE, resume, goals statement, writing sample, two letters of recommendation, minimum graduate GPA of 3.3, interview. Additional exam requirements/recommendations for international students: Required—TOEFL (minimum score 550 paper-based, 79 iBT) or IELTS (minimum score 6.5). *Application deadline:* For fall admission, 1/15 priority date for domestic students, 1/15 for international students; for spring admission, 10/1 for domestic and international students. Application fee: $50. Electronic applications accepted. *Expenses:* Tuition, state resident: full-time $8064; part-time $336 per credit hour. Tuition, nonresident: full-time $28,800; part-time $1200 per credit hour. *Required fees:* $2128; $1064 per semester. Tuition and fees vary according to course load and program. *Financial support:* In 2012–13, 110 students received support, including 3 fellowships with full tuition reimbursements available (averaging $19,667 per year), 68 research assistantships with full tuition reimbursements available (averaging $5,436 per year), 29 teaching assistantships with full tuition reimbursements available (averaging $2,779 per year); career-related internships or fieldwork, Federal Work-Study, scholarships/grants, health care benefits, tuition waivers (full and partial), and unspecified assistantships also available. Financial award application deadline: 3/15. *Faculty research:* Teacher education in language and literacy, mathematics, science, and social studies in urban middle and secondary school settings; learning technologies in school, community, and corporate settings; multicultural education and education for social justice; urban education; international education. *Total annual research expenditures:* $761,493. *Unit head:* Dr. Dana L. Fox, Chair, 404-413-8060, Fax: 404-413-8063, E-mail: dfox@gsu.edu. *Application contact:* Bobbie Turner, Administrative Coordinator I, 404-413-8405, Fax: 404-413-8063, E-mail: bnturner@gsu.edu. Website: http://msit.gsu.edu/msit_programs.htm.

Graduate School and University Center of the City University of New York, Graduate Studies, Program in Earth and Environmental Sciences, New York, NY 10016-4039. Offers PhD. *Degree requirements:* For doctorate, one foreign language, comprehensive exam, thesis/dissertation. *Entrance requirements:* For doctorate, GRE General Test. Additional exam requirements/recommendations for international students: Required—TOEFL. Electronic applications accepted.

Harvard University, Graduate School of Arts and Sciences, Department of Earth and Planetary Sciences, Cambridge, MA 02138. Offers AM, PhD. Terminal master's awarded for partial completion of doctoral program. *Degree requirements:* For doctorate, comprehensive exam, thesis/dissertation. *Entrance requirements:* For doctorate, GRE General Test. Additional exam requirements/recommendations for international students: Required—TOEFL. Electronic applications accepted. *Expenses: Tuition:* Full-time $37,576. *Required fees:* $930. Tuition and fees vary according to program and student level. *Faculty research:* Economic geography, geochemistry, geophysics, mineralogy, crystallography.

Hofstra University, School of Education, Programs in Teaching - Secondary Education, Hempstead, NY 11549. Offers business education (MS Ed); education technology (Advanced Certificate); English education (MA, MS Ed); foreign language and TESOL (MS Ed); foreign language education (MA, MS Ed), including French, German, Russian, Spanish; mathematics education (MA, MS Ed); science education (MA, MS Ed), including biology, chemistry, earth science, geology, physics; secondary education (Advanced Certificate); social studies education (MA, MS Ed); technology for learning (MA). Part-time and evening/weekend programs available. Postbaccalaureate distance learning degree programs offered (minimal on-campus study). *Students:* 64 full-time (36 women), 41 part-time (22 women); includes 17 minority (9 Black or African American, non-Hispanic/Latino; 3 Asian, non-Hispanic/Latino; 4 Hispanic/Latino; 1 Native Hawaiian or other Pacific Islander, non-Hispanic/Latino). Average age 28. 87 applicants, 87% accepted, 46 enrolled. In 2012, 57 master's, 7 other advanced degrees awarded. *Degree requirements:* For master's, one foreign language, comprehensive exam (for some programs), thesis (for some programs), exit project, electronic portfolio, student teaching, fieldwork, curriculum project, minimum GPA of 3.0; for Advanced Certificate, 3 foreign languages, comprehensive exam (for some programs), thesis project. *Entrance requirements:* For master's, 2 letters of recommendation, teacher certification (MA), essay; for Advanced Certificate, 2 letters of recommendation, essay, interview and/or portfolio. Additional exam requirements/recommendations for international students: Required—TOEFL (minimum score 550 paper-based; 80 iBT); Recommended—IELTS (minimum score 6.5). *Application deadline:* Applications are processed on a rolling basis. Application fee: $70 ($75 for international students). Electronic applications accepted. *Expenses: Tuition:* Full-time $19,800; part-time $1100 per credit hour. *Required fees:* $970; $165 per term. Tuition and fees vary according to program. *Financial support:* In 2012–13, 82 students received support, including 17 fellowships with full and partial tuition reimbursements available (averaging $3,142 per year), 1 research assistantship with full and partial tuition reimbursement available (averaging $16,527 per year); career-related internships or fieldwork, Federal Work-Study, institutionally sponsored loans, scholarships/grants, tuition waivers (full and partial), and unspecified assistantships also available. Support available to part-time students. Financial award applicants required to submit FAFSA. *Faculty research:* Appropriate content in secondary school disciplines, appropriate pedagogy in secondary school disciplines, adolescent development, secondary school organization, preparation for EDTPA addition to the curriculum. *Unit head:* Dr. Esther Fusco, Chairperson, 516-463-7704, Fax: 516-463-6196, E-mail: catezf@hofstra.edu. *Application contact:* Carol Drummer, Dean of Graduate Admissions, 516-463-4876, Fax: 516-463-4664, E-mail: gradstudent@hofstra.edu. Website: http://www.hofstra.edu/education/.

Hunter College of the City University of New York, Graduate School, School of Arts and Sciences, Department of Geography, New York, NY 10021-5085. Offers analytical geography (MA); earth system science (MA); environmental and social issues (MA); geographic information science (Certificate); geographic information systems (MA); teaching earth science (MA). Part-time and evening/weekend programs available. *Faculty:* 8 full-time (4 women), 5 part-time/adjunct (0 women). *Students:* 2 full-time (1 woman), 58 part-time (30 women); includes 11 minority (1 Black or African American, non-Hispanic/Latino; 5 Asian, non-Hispanic/Latino; 5 Hispanic/Latino), 3 international. Average age 33. 22 applicants, 68% accepted, 7 enrolled. In 2012, 13 master's, 8 other advanced degrees awarded. *Degree requirements:* For master's, comprehensive exam or thesis. *Entrance requirements:* For master's, GRE General Test, minimum B average in major, B- overall; 18 credits of course work in geography; 2 letters of recommendation; for Certificate, minimum B average in major, B- overall. Additional exam requirements/recommendations for international students: Required—TOEFL. *Application deadline:* For fall admission, 4/1 for domestic students; for spring admission, 11/1 for domestic students. Applications are processed on a rolling basis. Application fee: $125. *Expenses:* Tuition, state resident: full-time $8690; part-time $365 per credit. Tuition, nonresident: full-time $16,200; part-time $675 per credit. *Required fees:* $320 per semester. One-time fee: $125. Tuition and fees vary according to class time, campus/location and program. *Financial support:* In 2012–13, 1 fellowship (averaging $3,000 per year), 2 research assistantships (averaging $10,000 per year), 10 teaching assistantships (averaging $6,000 per year) were awarded; career-related internships or fieldwork, Federal Work-Study, institutionally sponsored loans, and unspecified assistantships also available. Financial award application deadline: 3/1. *Faculty research:* Urban geography, economic geography, geographic information science, demographic methods, climate change. *Unit head:* Prof. William Solecki, Chair, 212-772-4536, Fax: 212-772-5268, E-mail: wsolecki@hunter.cuny.edu. *Application contact:* Prof. Marianna Pavlovskaya, Graduate Adviser, 212-772-5320, Fax: 212-772-5268, E-mail: mpavlov@geo.hunter.cuny.edu. Website: http://www.geo.hunter.cuny.edu/.

Hunter College of the City University of New York, Graduate School, School of Education, Programs in Secondary Education, New York, NY 10021-5085. Offers biology education (MA); chemistry education (MA); earth science (MA); English education (MA); French education (MA); Italian education (MA); mathematics education (MA); physics education (MA); social studies education (MA); Spanish education (MA). *Accreditation:* NCATE. *Faculty:* 40 full-time (24 women), 71 part-time/adjunct (55 women). *Students:* 35 full-time (24 women), 166 part-time (102 women); includes 68 minority (18 Black or African American, non-Hispanic/Latino; 31 Asian, non-Hispanic/Latino; 19 Hispanic/Latino), 5 international. Average age 30. 592 applicants, 59% accepted, 214 enrolled. In 2012, 110 master's awarded. *Degree requirements:* For master's, thesis. *Entrance requirements:* Additional exam requirements/recommendations for international students: Required—TOEFL. *Application deadline:* For fall admission, 4/1 for domestic students, 2/1 for international students; for spring admission, 11/1 for domestic students, 9/1 for international students. Applications are processed on a rolling basis. Application fee: $125. *Expenses:* Tuition, state resident: full-time $8690; part-time $365 per credit. Tuition, nonresident: full-time $16,200; part-time $675 per credit. *Required fees:* $320 per semester. One-time fee: $125. Tuition and fees vary according to class time, campus/location and program. *Financial support:* Fellowships and tuition waivers (full and partial) available. Support available to part-time students. *Unit head:* Dr. Kate Garret, Coordinator, 212-772-4700, E-mail: kgarret@hunter.cuny.edu. *Application contact:* Milena Solo, Director for Graduate

Admissions, 212-772-4482, Fax: 212-650-3336, E-mail: milena.solo@hunter.cuny.edu. Website: http://www.hunter.cuny.edu/school-of-education/programs/graduate.

Idaho State University, Office of Graduate Studies, College of Science and Engineering, Department of Geosciences, Pocatello, ID 83209-8072. Offers geographic information science (MS); geology (MNS, MS); geology with emphasis in environmental geoscience (MS); geophysics/hydrology/geology (MS); geotechnology (Postbaccalaureate Certificate). Part-time programs available. *Degree requirements:* For master's, comprehensive exam, thesis, oral colloquium; for Postbaccalaureate Certificate, thesis optional, minimum 19 credits. *Entrance requirements:* For master's, GRE General Test (minimum 50th percentile in 2 sections), 3 letters of recommendation; for Postbaccalaureate Certificate, GRE General Test, 3 letters of recommendation, bachelor's degree, statement of goals. Additional exam requirements/recommendations for international students: Required—TOEFL (minimum score 550 paper-based; 80 iBT). Electronic applications accepted. *Faculty research:* Quantitative field mapping and sampling: microscopic, geochemical, and isotopic analysis of rocks, minerals and water; remote sensing, geographic information systems, and global positioning systems: environmental and watershed management; surficial and fluvial processes: landscape change; regional tectonics, structural geology; planetary geology.

Indiana University Bloomington, University Graduate School, College of Arts and Sciences, Department of Geological Sciences, Bloomington, IN 47405-7000. Offers biogeochemistry (MS, PhD); economic geology (MS, PhD); geobiology (MS, PhD); geophysics, structural geology and tectonics (MS, PhD); hydrogeology (MS, PhD); mineralogy (MS, PhD); stratigraphy and sedimentology (MS, PhD). *Faculty:* 17 full-time (1 woman). *Students:* 63 full-time (23 women), 3 part-time (1 woman); includes 3 minority (1 Black or African American, non-Hispanic/Latino; 1 Hispanic/Latino; 1 Two or more races, non-Hispanic/Latino), 15 international. Average age 29. 82 applicants, 26% accepted, 15 enrolled. In 2012, 10 master's, 4 doctorates awarded. Terminal master's awarded for partial completion of doctoral program. *Degree requirements:* For master's, thesis or alternative; for doctorate, comprehensive exam, thesis/dissertation. *Entrance requirements:* For master's and doctorate, GRE General Test. Additional exam requirements/recommendations for international students: Required—TOEFL. *Application deadline:* For fall admission, 1/15 priority date for domestic students, 12/15 for international students; for spring admission, 9/1 priority date for domestic students, 9/1 for international students. Applications are processed on a rolling basis. Application fee: $55 ($65 for international students). *Financial support:* In 2012–13, fellowships with full tuition reimbursements (averaging $17,300 per year), research assistantships with full tuition reimbursements (averaging $16,370 per year), teaching assistantships with full tuition reimbursements (averaging $15,150 per year) were awarded; career-related internships or fieldwork, Federal Work-Study, and institutionally sponsored loans also available. *Faculty research:* Geophysics, geochemistry, hydrogeology, geobiology, planetary science. *Total annual research expenditures:* $644,299. *Unit head:* Simon Brassell, Chair, 812-855-5581, Fax: 812-855-7899, E-mail: geochair@indiana.edu. *Application contact:* Mary Iverson, Graduate Secretary, 812-855-7214, Fax: 812-855-7899, E-mail: miverson@indiana.edu. Website: http://www.indiana.edu/~geosci/.

Indiana University–Purdue University Indianapolis, School of Science, Department of Earth Sciences, Indianapolis, IN 46202-3272. Offers applied earth sciences (PhD); geology (MS). Part-time and evening/weekend programs available. *Faculty:* 8 full-time (2 women). *Students:* 6 full-time (4 women), 14 part-time (7 women), 6 international. Average age 29. 12 applicants, 42% accepted, 4 enrolled. In 2012, 8 master's awarded. *Degree requirements:* For master's, thesis (for some programs). *Entrance requirements:* For master's, GRE General Test, minimum GPA of 3.0. Application fee: $55 ($65 for international students). *Financial support:* In 2012–13, fellowships with full tuition reimbursements (averaging $12,000 per year), teaching assistantships with full tuition reimbursements (averaging $12,103 per year) were awarded; research assistantships with full tuition reimbursements and scholarships/grants also available. Financial award application deadline: 3/1. *Faculty research:* Wetland hydrology, groundwater contamination, soils, sedimentology, sediment chemistry. *Unit head:* Gabriel Filippelli, Chair, 317-274-7484, Fax: 317-274-7966. *Application contact:* Lenore P. Tedesco, Associate Professor, 317-274-7484, Fax: 317-274-7966, E-mail: ltedesco@iupui.edu. Website: http://www.geology.iupui.edu/.

Iowa State University of Science and Technology, Department of Geological and Atmospheric Sciences, Ames, IA 50011. Offers earth science (MS, PhD); environmental science (MS, PhD); geology (MS, PhD); meteorology (MS, PhD). *Degree requirements:* For master's, thesis (for some programs); for doctorate, thesis/dissertation. *Entrance requirements:* For master's and doctorate, GRE General Test. Additional exam requirements/recommendations for international students: Required—TOEFL (minimum score 550 paper-based; 79 iBT), IELTS (minimum score 6.5). *Application deadline:* For fall admission, 1/1 priority date for domestic students. Application fee: $60 ($90 for international students). Electronic applications accepted. *Application contact:* Deann Frisk, Application Contact, 515-294-4477, Fax: 515-294-6049, E-mail: geology@iastate.edu. Website: http://www.ge-at.iastate.edu/.

Iowa State University of Science and Technology, Program in Earth Science, Ames, IA 50011. Offers MS, PhD. *Entrance requirements:* For master's and doctorate, GRE. Additional exam requirements/recommendations for international students: Required—TOEFL (minimum score 550 paper-based; 79 iBT), IELTS (minimum score 6.5). *Application deadline:* For fall admission, 1/1 priority date for domestic students. Application fee: $60 ($90 for international students). Electronic applications accepted. *Application contact:* Deann Frisk, Application Contact, 515-294-4477, Fax: 515-294-6049, E-mail: geology@iastate.edu. Website: http://www.ge-at.iastate.edu.

The Johns Hopkins University, Zanvyl Krieger School of Arts and Sciences, The Morton K. Blaustein Department of Earth and Planetary Sciences, Baltimore, MD 21218-2699. Offers MA, PhD. *Degree requirements:* For doctorate, comprehensive exam, thesis/dissertation. *Entrance requirements:* For master's and doctorate, GRE General Test. Additional exam requirements/recommendations for international students: Required—TOEFL (minimum score 600 paper-based; 100 iBT), IELTS. Electronic applications accepted. *Faculty research:* Oceanography, atmospheric sciences, geophysics, geology, geochemistry.

Lehigh University, College of Arts and Sciences, Department of Earth and Environmental Sciences, Bethlehem, PA 18015. Offers MS, PhD. *Faculty:* 15 full-time (2 women). *Students:* 21 full-time (7 women), 4 part-time (2 women), 4 international. Average age 27. 56 applicants, 23% accepted, 5 enrolled. In 2012, 8 master's, 3 doctorates awarded. Terminal master's awarded for partial completion of doctoral program. *Degree requirements:* For master's, thesis; for doctorate, thesis/dissertation. *Entrance requirements:* For master's and doctorate, GRE General Test, transcripts, recommendation letters, research statement, faculty advocates. Additional exam requirements/recommendations for international students: Required—TOEFL (minimum score 85 iBT). *Application deadline:* For fall admission, 1/1 for domestic and international students. Applications are processed on a rolling basis. Application fee: $75. Electronic applications accepted. *Financial support:* In 2012–13, 14 students received support, including 2 fellowships with full tuition reimbursements available (averaging $25,000 per year), 5 research assistantships with full tuition reimbursements available (averaging $25,000 per year), 10 teaching assistantships with full tuition reimbursements available (averaging $25,000 per year); career-related internships or fieldwork, Federal Work-Study, institutionally sponsored loans, scholarships/grants, tuition waivers (full and partial), and unspecified assistantships also available. Support available to part-time students. Financial award application deadline: 1/1. *Faculty research:* Tectonics, surficial processes, ecology, environmental change. *Total annual research expenditures:* $1.6 million. *Unit head:* Dr. Frank J. Pazzaglia, Chairman, 610-758-3667, Fax: 610-758-3677, E-mail: fjp3@lehigh.edu. *Application contact:* Dr. Stephen Peters, Graduate Coordinator, 610-758-3957, Fax: 610-758-3677, E-mail: scp2@lehigh.edu. Website: http://www.ees.lehigh.edu/.

Loma Linda University, School of Science and Technology, Department of Biological and Earth Sciences, Loma Linda, CA 92350. Offers MS, PhD. *Degree requirements:* For master's, comprehensive exam, thesis; for doctorate, comprehensive exam, thesis/dissertation. *Entrance requirements:* For master's, minimum GPA of 3.0. Additional exam requirements/recommendations for international students: Required—TOEFL (minimum score 550 paper-based).

Long Island University–C. W. Post Campus, College of Liberal Arts and Sciences, Department of Earth and Environmental Science, Brookville, NY 11548-1300. Offers earth science (MS); earth science education (MS); environmental studies (MS).

Massachusetts Institute of Technology, School of Science, Department of Earth, Atmospheric, and Planetary Sciences, Cambridge, MA 02139. Offers atmospheric chemistry (PhD, Sc D); atmospheric science (SM, PhD, Sc D); chemical oceanography (SM, PhD, Sc D); climate physics and chemistry (SM, PhD, Sc D); earth and planetary sciences (SM); geochemistry (PhD, Sc D); geology (PhD, Sc D); geophysics (PhD, Sc D); marine geology and geophysics (SM, PhD, Sc D); physical oceanography (SM, PhD, Sc D); planetary sciences (PhD, Sc D). *Faculty:* 33 full-time (6 women), 1 (woman) part-time/adjunct. *Students:* 166 full-time (77 women); includes 24 minority (3 Black or African American, non-Hispanic/Latino; 1 American Indian or Alaska Native, non-Hispanic/Latino; 9 Asian, non-Hispanic/Latino; 6 Hispanic/Latino; 5 Two or more races, non-Hispanic/Latino), 58 international. Average age 27. 232 applicants, 23% accepted, 27 enrolled. In 2012, 12 master's, 22 doctorates awarded. Terminal master's awarded for partial completion of doctoral program. *Degree requirements:* For master's, thesis; for doctorate, comprehensive exam, thesis/dissertation. *Entrance requirements:* For master's, GRE General Test; for doctorate, GRE General Test, GRE Subject Test (chemistry or physics for planetary science area). Additional exam requirements/recommendations for international students: Required—TOEFL (minimum score 577 paper-based; 91 iBT), IELTS (minimum score 7). *Application deadline:* For fall admission, 1/5 for domestic and international students; for spring admission, 11/1 for domestic and international students. Application fee: $75. Electronic applications accepted. *Expenses: Tuition:* Full-time $41,770; part-time $650 per credit hour. *Required fees:* $280. *Financial support:* In 2012–13, 108 students received support, including 62 fellowships (averaging $30,700 per year), 87 research assistantships (averaging $32,600 per year), 15 teaching assistantships (averaging $30,800 per year); Federal Work-Study, institutionally sponsored loans, scholarships/grants, health care benefits, and unspecified assistantships also available. *Faculty research:* Formation, dynamics and evolution of planetary systems; origin, composition, structure and dynamics of the atmospheres, oceans, surfaces and interiors of the Earth and other planets; evolution and interaction of the physical, chemical, geological and biological components of the Earth system; characterization of past, present and potential future climates and the causes and consequences of climate change; interplay of energy and the environment. *Total annual research expenditures:* $28.1 million. *Unit head:* Prof. Robert van der Hilst, Head, 617-253-2127, Fax: 617-253-8298, E-mail: eapsinfo@mit.edu. *Application contact:* EAPS Education Office, 617-253-3381, Fax: 617-253-8298, E-mail: eapsinfo@mit.edu. Website: http://eapsweb.mit.edu/.

McGill University, Faculty of Graduate and Postdoctoral Studies, Faculty of Science, Department of Earth and Planetary Sciences, Montréal, QC H3A 2T5, Canada. Offers M Sc, PhD.

McMaster University, School of Graduate Studies, Faculty of Science, School of Geography and Earth Sciences, Hamilton, ON L8S 4M2, Canada. Offers geochemistry (PhD); geology (M Sc, PhD); human geography (MA, PhD); physical geography (M Sc, PhD). Part-time programs available. Terminal master's awarded for partial completion of doctoral program. *Degree requirements:* For master's, thesis; for doctorate, comprehensive exam, thesis/dissertation. *Entrance requirements:* For master's, minimum B+ average. Additional exam requirements/recommendations for international students: Required—TOEFL (minimum score 550 paper-based).

Memorial University of Newfoundland, School of Graduate Studies, Department of Earth Sciences, St. John's, NL A1C 5S7, Canada. Offers geology (M Sc, PhD); geophysics (M Sc, PhD). Part-time programs available. *Degree requirements:* For master's, thesis; for doctorate, comprehensive exam, thesis/dissertation, oral thesis defense, entry evaluation. *Entrance requirements:* For master's, honors B Sc; for doctorate, M Sc. Electronic applications accepted. *Faculty research:* Geochemistry, sedimentology, paleoceanography and global change, mineral deposits, petroleum geology, hydrology.

Michigan State University, The Graduate School, College of Natural Science, Department of Geological Sciences, East Lansing, MI 48824. Offers environmental geosciences (MS, PhD); environmental geosciences-environmental toxicology (PhD); geological sciences (MS, PhD). *Degree requirements:* For master's, thesis (for those without prior thesis work); for doctorate, thesis/dissertation. *Entrance requirements:* For master's, GRE General Test, minimum GPA of 3.0, course work in geoscience, 3 letters of recommendation; for doctorate, GRE General Test, 3 letters of recommendation. Additional exam requirements/recommendations for international students: Required—TOEFL (minimum score 550 paper-based), Michigan State University ELT (minimum score 85), Michigan English Language Assessment Battery (minimum score 83). Electronic applications accepted. *Faculty research:* Water in the environment, global and biological change, crystal dynamics.

Middle Tennessee State University, College of Graduate Studies, College of Liberal Arts, Department of Geosciences, Murfreesboro, TN 37132. Offers Graduate Certificate. Part-time and evening/weekend programs available. Postbaccalaureate distance learning degree programs offered. *Entrance requirements:* Additional exam requirements/recommendations for international students: Required—TOEFL (minimum score 525 paper-based; 71 iBT) or IELTS (minimum score 6).

Mississippi State University, College of Arts and Sciences, Department of Geosciences, Mississippi State, MS 39762. Offers applied meteorology (MS); broadcast meteorology (MS); earth and atmospheric science (PhD); environmental geoscience (MS); geography (MS); geology (MS); geospatial sciences (MS); professional meteorology/climatology (MS); teachers in geoscience (MS). Postbaccalaureate distance learning degree programs offered (no on-campus study). *Faculty:* 14 full-time (3 women), 2 part-time/adjunct (0 women). *Students:* 62 full-time (27 women), 273 part-time (117 women); includes 29 minority (7 Black or African American, non-Hispanic/Latino; 4 Asian, non-Hispanic/Latino; 13 Hispanic/Latino; 5 Two or more races, non-Hispanic/Latino), 8 international. Average age 34. 235 applicants, 70% accepted, 135 enrolled. In 2012, 101 master's, 2 doctorates awarded. *Degree requirements:* For master's, thesis (for some programs), comprehensive oral or written exam; for doctorate, thesis/dissertation, comprehensive oral or written exam. *Entrance requirements:* For master's, GRE (for on-campus applicants), minimum undergraduate GPA of 2.75; for doctorate, completed thesis-based MS with background in one department emphasis area. Additional exam requirements/recommendations for international students: Required—TOEFL (minimum score 477 paper-based; 53 iBT); Recommended—IELTS (minimum score 4.5). *Application deadline:* For fall admission, 7/1 for domestic students, 5/1 for international students; for spring admission, 11/1 for domestic students, 9/1 for international students. Applications are processed on a rolling basis. Application fee: $60. Electronic applications accepted. *Financial support:* In 2012–13, 12 research assistantships with full tuition reimbursements (averaging $20,723 per year), 30 teaching assistantships with full tuition reimbursements (averaging $14,091 per year) were awarded; Federal Work-Study, institutionally sponsored loans, scholarships/grants, tuition waivers (partial), and unspecified assistantships also available. Financial award application deadline: 4/1; financial award applicants required to submit FAFSA. *Faculty research:* Climatology, hydrogeology, sedimentology, meteorology. *Total annual research expenditures:* $6.8 million. *Unit head:* Dr. Darrel Schmitz, Professor and Head, 662-325-3915, Fax: 662-325-9423, E-mail: schmitz@geosci.msstate.edu. *Application contact:* Dr. Mike Brown, Associate Professor/Graduate Coordinator, 662-325-3915, Fax: 662-325-9423, E-mail: tina@gesci.msstate.edu. Website: http://www.geosciences.msstate.edu.

Missouri State University, Graduate College, College of Natural and Applied Sciences, Department of Geography, Geology, and Planning, Springfield, MO 65897. Offers geospatial sciences (MS, MS Ed), including earth science (MS Ed), geology (MS), human geography and planning (MS), physical geography (MS Ed); natural and applied science (MNAS), including geography, geology and planning; secondary education (MS Ed), including geography. *Accreditation:* ACSP. Part-time and evening/weekend programs available. *Degree requirements:* For master's, comprehensive exam, thesis (for some programs). *Entrance requirements:* For master's, GRE General Test (MS, MNAS), minimum undergraduate GPA of 3.0 (MS, MNAS), 9-12 teacher certification (MS Ed). Additional exam requirements/recommendations for international students: Required—TOEFL (minimum score 550 paper-based; 79 iBT). Electronic applications accepted. *Faculty research:* Stratigraphy and ancient meteorite impacts, environmental geochemistry of karst, hyperspectral image processing, water quality, small town planning.

Montana State University, College of Graduate Studies, College of Letters and Science, Department of Earth Sciences, Bozeman, MT 59717. Offers MS, PhD. Part-time programs available. *Degree requirements:* For master's, comprehensive exam, thesis (for some programs); for doctorate, comprehensive exam, thesis/dissertation. *Entrance requirements:* For master's and doctorate, GRE General Test, minimum GPA of 3.0. Additional exam requirements/recommendations for international students: Required—TOEFL (minimum score 550 paper-based). Electronic applications accepted. *Faculty research:* Dinosaur paleontology, climate history/geomicrobiology, stratigraphy/sedimentology/structure/carbon sequestration, igneous petrology South America, historical/urban economic geography western U. S. and China.

Montana Tech of The University of Montana, Graduate School, Geosciences Programs, Butte, MT 59701-8997. Offers geochemistry (MS); geological engineering (MS); geology (MS); geophysical engineering (MS); hydrogeological engineering (MS); hydrogeology (MS). Part-time programs available. *Degree requirements:* For master's, comprehensive exam (for some programs), thesis (for some programs). *Entrance requirements:* For master's, GRE General Test, minimum GPA of 3.0. Additional exam requirements/recommendations for international students: Required—TOEFL (minimum score 525 paper-based; 71 iBT). Electronic applications accepted. *Faculty research:* Water resource development, seismic processing, petroleum reservoir characterization, environmental geochemistry, geologic mapping.

Montclair State University, The Graduate School, College of Science and Mathematics, Department of Earth and Environmental Studies, Program in Geoscience, Montclair, NJ 07043-1624. Offers MS. Part-time and evening/weekend programs available. *Degree requirements:* For master's, thesis. *Entrance requirements:* Additional exam requirements/recommendations for international students: Required—TOEFL (minimum score 83 iBT), IELTS (minimum score 6.5). Electronic applications accepted. *Faculty research:* Environmental geochemisty, flood hydrology, geomorphology and weathering processes, regional climate modeling, remote sensing, Cenozoic marine sediment records from polar regions, igneous and metamorphic petrology.

Murray State University, College of Science, Engineering and Technology, Program in Geosciences, Murray, KY 42071. Offers MS. Part-time programs available. *Degree requirements:* For master's, comprehensive exam, thesis optional. *Entrance requirements:* Additional exam requirements/recommendations for international students: Required—TOEFL, IELTS.

New Mexico Institute of Mining and Technology, Graduate Studies, Department of Earth and Environmental Science, Socorro, NM 87801. Offers geochemistry (MS, PhD); geology (MS, PhD); geophysics (MS, PhD); hydrology (MS, PhD). *Faculty:* 17 full-time (2 women), 1 part-time/adjunct (0 women). *Students:* 52 full-time (24 women), 14 part-time (9 women); includes 12 minority (3 American Indian or Alaska Native, non-Hispanic/Latino; 5 Hispanic/Latino; 4 Two or more races, non-Hispanic/Latino), 9 international. Average age 28. 82 applicants, 35% accepted, 16 enrolled. In 2012, 10 master's, 6 doctorates awarded. *Degree requirements:* For master's, thesis optional; for doctorate, thesis/dissertation. *Entrance requirements:* For master's, GRE General Test; for doctorate, GRE General Test, GRE Subject Test. Additional exam requirements/recommendations for international students: Required—TOEFL. *Application deadline:* For fall admission, 3/1 priority date for domestic students; for spring admission, 6/1 for domestic students. Applications are processed on a rolling basis. Application fee: $16. *Expenses:* Tuition, state resident: full-time $5043; part-time $280 per credit hour. Tuition, nonresident: full-time $16,682; part-time $927 per credit hour. *Required fees:* $648; $18 per credit hour. $108 per semester. Part-time tuition and fees vary according to course load. *Financial support:* In 2012–13, 1 fellowship (averaging $3,210 per year), 30 research assistantships (averaging $13,700 per year), 11 teaching assistantships with full and partial tuition reimbursements (averaging $10,765 per year) were awarded; Federal Work-Study, institutionally sponsored loans, and unspecified assistantships also available. Financial award application deadline: 3/1; financial award applicants required to submit CSS PROFILE or FAFSA. *Faculty research:* Seismology, geochemistry, caves and karst topography, hydrology, volcanology. *Total annual research expenditures:* $2.2 million. *Unit head:* Dr. Gary Axen, Chair, 505-835-5178, Fax: 505-835-6436, E-mail: gaxen@ees.nmt.edu. *Application contact:* Dr. Lorie Liebrock, Dean of Graduate Studies, 505-835-5513, Fax: 505-835-5476, E-mail: graduate@nmt.edu. Website: http://www.ees.nmt.edu/.

North Carolina Central University, Division of Academic Affairs, College of Science and Technology, Department of Environmental, Earth and Geospatial Sciences, Durham, NC 27707-3129. Offers earth sciences (MS). *Degree requirements:* For master's, one foreign language, comprehensive exam.

Entrance requirements: For master's, GRE, minimum GPA of 3.0 in major, 2.5 overall. Additional exam requirements/recommendations for international students: Required—TOEFL.

North Carolina State University, Graduate School, College of Physical and Mathematical Sciences, Department of Marine, Earth, and Atmospheric Sciences, Raleigh, NC 27695. Offers marine, earth, and atmospheric sciences (MS, PhD); meteorology (MS, PhD); oceanography (MS, PhD). PhD offered jointly with The University of North Carolina Wilmington. Terminal master's awarded for partial completion of doctoral program. *Degree requirements:* For master's, thesis (for some programs), final oral exam; for doctorate, comprehensive exam, thesis/dissertation, final oral exam, preliminary oral and written exams. *Entrance requirements:* For master's, GRE General Test, minimum GPA of 3.0; for doctorate, GRE General Test, GRE Subject Test (for disciplines in biological oceanography and geology), minimum GPA of 3.0. Additional exam requirements/recommendations for international students: Required—TOEFL (minimum score 550 paper-based). Electronic applications accepted. *Faculty research:* Boundary layer and air quality meteorology; climate and mesoscale dynamics; biological, chemical, geological, and physical oceanography; hard rock, soft rock, environmental, and paleo-geology.

Northwestern University, The Graduate School, Judd A. and Marjorie Weinberg College of Arts and Sciences, Department of Geological Sciences, Evanston, IL 60208. Offers MS, PhD. Admissions and degrees offered through The Graduate School. Part-time programs available. *Degree requirements:* For doctorate, thesis/dissertation. *Entrance requirements:* For master's and doctorate, GRE General Test. Additional exam requirements/recommendations for international students: Required—TOEFL. Electronic applications accepted.

Penn State University Park, Graduate School, College of Earth and Mineral Sciences, Department of Geosciences, State College, University Park, PA 16802-1503. Offers earth science (M Ed); geosciences (MS, PhD). *Unit head:* Dr. William E. Easterling, III, Dean, 814-865-6546, Fax: 814-863-7708, E-mail: wee2@psu.edu. *Application contact:* Cynthia E. Nicosia, Director of Graduate Enrollment Services, 814-865-1834, E-mail: cey1@psu.edu. Website: http://www.geosc.psu.edu/.

Princeton University, Graduate School, Department of Geosciences, Princeton, NJ 08544-1019. Offers atmospheric and oceanic sciences (PhD); geosciences (PhD); ocean sciences and marine biology (PhD). *Degree requirements:* For doctorate, one foreign language, thesis/dissertation. *Entrance requirements:* For doctorate, GRE General Test. Additional exam requirements/recommendations for international students: Required—TOEFL (minimum score 600 paper-based). Electronic applications accepted. *Faculty research:* Biogeochemistry, climate science, earth history, regional geology and tectonics, solid–earth geophysics.

Purdue University, Graduate School, College of Science, Department of Earth and Atmospheric Sciences, West Lafayette, IN 47907. Offers MS, PhD. *Faculty:* 31 full-time (2 women), 3 part-time/adjunct (0 women). *Students:* 66 full-time (27 women), 6 part-time (3 women); includes 9 minority (3 Black or African American, non-Hispanic/Latino; 3 American Indian or Alaska Native, non-Hispanic/Latino; 1 Asian, non-Hispanic/Latino; 2 Hispanic/Latino), 26 international. Average age 27. 180 applicants, 17% accepted, 19 enrolled. In 2012, 9 master's, 9 doctorates awarded. *Degree requirements:* For master's, comprehensive exam, thesis; for doctorate, one foreign language, comprehensive exam, thesis/dissertation. *Entrance requirements:* For master's, GRE General Test, minimum undergraduate GPA of 3.0 or equivalent; for doctorate, GRE General Test, minimum undergraduate or master's GPA of 3.0 or equivalent. Additional exam requirements/recommendations for international students: Required—TOEFL (minimum score 550 paper-based; 77 iBT); Recommended—TWE. *Application deadline:* For fall admission, 1/2 priority date for domestic students, 1/2 for international students; for spring admission, 9/1 for domestic and international students. Applications are processed on a rolling basis. Application fee: $60 ($75 for international students). Electronic applications accepted. *Financial support:* Fellowships with partial tuition reimbursements, research assistantships with partial tuition reimbursements, and teaching assistantships with partial tuition reimbursements available. Support available to part-time students. Financial award application deadline: 3/1; financial award applicants required to submit FAFSA. *Faculty research:* Geology, geophysics, hydrogeology, paleoclimatology, environmental science. *Unit head:* Dr. Jonathan M. Harbor, Head, 765-494-4753. *Application contact:* Kathy S. Kincade, Graduate Secretary, 765-494-5984, Fax: 765-496-1210, E-mail: kkincade@purdue.edu. Website: http://www.eas.purdue.edu.

Rice University, Graduate Programs, Wiess School of Natural Sciences, Department of Earth Science, Houston, TX 77251-1892. Offers MS, PhD. Terminal master's awarded for partial completion of doctoral program. *Degree requirements:* For master's, comprehensive exam, thesis, annual department report and presentation, qualifying exam, orals, 2 publications; for doctorate, comprehensive exam, thesis/dissertation, annual department report and presentation, qualifying exam, orals, 3 publications. *Entrance requirements:* For master's and doctorate, GRE. Additional exam requirements/recommendations for international students: Required—TOEFL (minimum score 600 paper-based; 90 iBT), IELTS. Electronic applications accepted. *Faculty research:* Seismology, structural geology, tectonics and paleomagnetism, geodynamics, high temperature geochemistry, volcanic processes.

Rice University, Graduate Programs, Wiess School–Professional Science Master's Programs, Professional Master's Program in Subsurface Geosciences, Houston, TX 77251-1892. Offers geophysics (MS). Part-time programs available. *Degree requirements:* For master's, internship. *Entrance requirements:* For master's, GRE, letters of recommendation (4). Additional exam requirements/recommendations for international students: Required—TOEFL (minimum score 600 paper-based; 90 iBT). Electronic applications accepted. *Faculty research:* Seismology, geodynamics, wave propagation, bio-geochemistry, remote sensing.

St. Francis Xavier University, Graduate Studies, Department of Earth Sciences, Antigonish, NS B2G 2W5, Canada. Offers M Sc. *Degree requirements:* For master's, thesis. *Entrance requirements:* Additional exam requirements/recommendations for international students: Required—TOEFL (minimum score 580 paper-based). *Faculty research:* Environmental earth sciences, global change tectonics, paleoclimatology, crustal fluids.

Saint Louis University, Graduate Education, College of Arts and Sciences, Department of Earth and Atmospheric Sciences, St. Louis, MO 63103-2097. Offers geophysics (PhD); geoscience (MS); meteorology (M Pr Met, MS-R, PhD). Part-time programs available. *Degree requirements:* For master's, thesis (for some programs), comprehensive oral exam; for doctorate, thesis/dissertation, preliminary exams. *Entrance requirements:* For master's, GRE General Test, letters of recommendation, resume; for doctorate, GRE General Test, letters of recommendation, resumé, goal statement, transcripts. Additional exam requirements/recommendations for international students: Required—TOEFL (minimum score 525 paper-based). Electronic applications accepted. *Faculty research:* Structural geology, mesoscale meteorology and severe storms, weather and climate change prediction.

St. Thomas University, School of Leadership Studies, Institute for Education, Miami Gardens, FL 33054-6459. Offers earth/space science (Certificate); educational administration (MS, Certificate); educational leadership (Ed D); elementary education (MS); ESOL (Certificate); gifted education (Certificate); instructional technology (MS, Certificate); professional/studies (Certificate); reading (MS, Certificate); special education (MS). Part-time and evening/weekend programs available. *Degree requirements:* For master's, comprehensive exam; for doctorate, comprehensive exam, thesis/dissertation. *Entrance requirements:* For master's, interview, minimum GPA of 3.0 or GRE; for doctorate, GRE or MAT. Additional exam requirements/recommendations for international students: Required—TOEFL (minimum score 550 paper-based; 79 iBT). Electronic applications accepted.

San Francisco State University, Division of Graduate Studies, College of Science and Engineering, Department of Geosciences, San Francisco, CA 94132-1722. Offers MS. *Application deadline:* Applications are processed on a rolling basis. *Unit head:* Dr. Oswaldo Garcia, Chair, 415-338-2061, E-mail: ogarcia@sfsu.edu. *Application contact:* Dr. John Caskey, Graduate Coordinator, 415-405-0353, E-mail: caskey@sfsu.edu. Website: http://tornado.sfsu.edu.

Simon Fraser University, Office of Graduate Studies, Faculty of Science, Department of Earth Sciences, Burnaby, BC V5A 1S6, Canada. Offers M Sc, PhD. *Faculty:* 16 full-time (4 women). *Students:* 54 full-time (25 women). 15 applicants, 67% accepted, 7 enrolled. In 2012, 7 master's, 3 doctorates awarded. *Degree requirements:* For master's, thesis; for doctorate, comprehensive exam, thesis/dissertation. *Entrance requirements:* For master's, minimum GPA of 3.0 (on scale of 4.33), or 3.33 based on last 60 credits of undergraduate courses; for doctorate, minimum GPA of 3.5 (on scale of 4.33). Additional exam requirements/recommendations for international students: Recommended—TOEFL (minimum score 580 paper-based; 93 iBT), IELTS (minimum score 7), TWE (minimum score 5). *Application deadline:* For fall admission, 3/20 for domestic students; for spring admission, 9/30 for domestic students. Applications are processed on a rolling basis. Application fee: $90 ($125 for international students). Electronic applications accepted. Tuition and fees charges are reported in Canadian dollars. *Expenses: Tuition, area resident:* Full-time $5000 Canadian dollars; part-time $275 Canadian dollars per credit hour. *Required fees:* $780 Canadian dollars. *Financial support:* In 2012–13, 24 students received support, including 17 fellowships (averaging $6,250 per year), teaching assistantships (averaging $5,608 per year); research assistantships and scholarships/grants also available. *Faculty research:* Glaciology, structural geology, quaternary and environmental earth sciences, geochronology, and tectonics; exploration or earthquake seismology. *Unit head:* Dr. Dan Gibson, Graduate Chair, 778-782-7057, Fax: 778-782-4198, E-mail: easc-grad-chair@sfu.ca. *Application contact:* Glenda Pauls, Graduate Secretary, 778-782-5387, Fax: 778-782-4198, E-mail: eascgsec@sfu.ca. Website: http://www.sfu.ca/earth-sciences/.

South Dakota State University, Graduate School, College of Engineering, Geospatial Science and Engineering Program, Brookings, SD 57007. Offers PhD. Part-time programs available. *Degree requirements:* For doctorate, comprehensive exam, thesis/dissertation. *Entrance requirements:* For doctorate, GRE. Additional exam requirements/recommendations for international students: Required—TOEFL (minimum score 525 paper-based; 71 iBT). *Faculty research:* Deforestation, land use/cover change, GIS spatial modeling.

Stanford University, School of Earth Sciences, Department of Geological and Environmental Sciences, Stanford, CA 94305-9991. Offers MS, PhD, Eng. Terminal master's awarded for partial completion of doctoral program. *Degree requirements:* For master's and Eng, thesis; for doctorate, thesis/dissertation. *Entrance requirements:* For master's, doctorate, and Eng, GRE General Test. Additional exam requirements/recommendations for international students: Required—TOEFL. Electronic applications accepted. *Expenses: Tuition:* Full-time $41,250; part-time $917 per credit hour.

Stanford University, School of Earth Sciences, Earth Systems Program, Stanford, CA 94305-9991. Offers MS. Students admitted at the undergraduate level. Electronic applications accepted. *Expenses: Tuition:* Full-time $41,250; part-time $917 per credit hour.

State University of New York at New Paltz, Graduate School, School of Education, Department of Secondary Education, New Paltz, NY 12561. Offers adolescence education: biology (MAT, MS Ed); adolescence education: chemistry (MAT, MS Ed); adolescence education: earth science (MAT, MS Ed); adolescence education: English (MAT, MS Ed); adolescence education: French (MAT, MS Ed); adolescence education: social studies (MAT, MS Ed); adolescence education: Spanish (MAT, MS Ed); second language education (MS Ed, AC), including second language education (MS Ed), teaching English language learners (AC). *Accreditation:* NCATE. Part-time and evening/weekend programs available. *Faculty:* 25 full-time (10 women), 7 part-time/adjunct (4 women). *Students:* 75 full-time (44 women), 61 part-time (41 women); includes 26 minority (3 Black or African American, non-Hispanic/Latino; 4 Asian, non-Hispanic/Latino; 16 Hispanic/Latino; 3 Two or more races, non-Hispanic/Latino), 1 international. Average age 30. 93 applicants, 70% accepted, 48 enrolled. In 2012, 71 master's awarded. *Degree requirements:* For master's, comprehensive exam (for some programs), portfolio. *Entrance requirements:* For master's, minimum GPA of 3.0, New York state teaching certificate (MS Ed). Additional exam requirements/recommendations for international students: Required—TOEFL (minimum score 550 paper-based; 80 iBT), IELTS (minimum score 6.5). *Application deadline:* For fall admission, 3/1 priority date for domestic students, 3/1 for international students; for spring admission, 10/1 priority date for domestic students, 10/1 for international students. Application fee: $50. Electronic applications accepted. *Expenses:* Tuition, state resident: full-time $9370; part-time $390 per credit hour. Tuition, nonresident: full-time $16,680; part-time $695 per credit hour. *Required fees:* $1188; $68.40 per credit hour. $184 per semester. *Financial support:* In 2012–13, 7 students received support, including 1 fellowship with partial tuition reimbursement available (averaging $3,000 per year); Federal Work-Study, institutionally sponsored loans, and tuition waivers (full and partial) also available. Financial award application deadline: 8/1; financial award applicants required to submit FAFSA. *Unit head:* Dr. Devon Duhaney, Chair, 845-257-2850, E-mail: duhaneyd@newpaltz.edu. *Application contact:* Caroline Murphy, Graduate Admissions Advisor, 845-257-3285, Fax: 845-257-3284, E-mail: gradschool@newpaltz.edu. Website: http://www.newpaltz.edu/secondaryed/.

State University of New York College at Oneonta, Graduate Education, Department of Earth Sciences, Oneonta, NY 13820-4015. Offers MA. Part-time and evening/weekend programs available. *Degree requirements:* For master's, thesis. *Entrance requirements:* For master's, GRE General Test.

Stony Brook University, State University of New York, Graduate School, College of Arts and Sciences, Department of Geosciences, Stony Brook, NY 11794. Offers earth science (MAT); geosciences (MS, PhD). MAT offered through the School of Professional Development. *Faculty:* 16 full-time (4 women), 1 part-time/adjunct (0 women). *Students:* 46 full-time (32 women), 12 part-time (5 women); includes 7 minority (4 Black or African American, non-Hispanic/Latino; 2 Hispanic/Latino; 1 Two or more races, non-Hispanic/Latino), 20 international. Average age 29. 70 applicants, 50% accepted, 22 enrolled. In 2012, 5 master's, 1 doctorate awarded. Terminal master's awarded for partial completion of doctoral program. *Degree requirements:* For master's, thesis or alternative; for doctorate, thesis/dissertation. *Entrance requirements:* For master's and doctorate, GRE General Test, minimum GPA of 3.0. Additional exam requirements/recommendations for international students: Required—TOEFL. *Application deadline:* For fall admission, 1/15 for domestic students. Application fee: $100. *Expenses:* Tuition, state resident: full-time $9370. Tuition, nonresident: full-time $16,680. *Required fees:* $1214. *Financial support:* In 2012–13, 5 fellowships, 17 research assistantships, 15 teaching assistantships were awarded. *Faculty research:* Astronomy, theoretical and observational astrophysics, paleontology, petrology, crystallography. *Total annual research expenditures:* $2.8 million. *Unit head:* Dr. Richard Reeder, Chair, 631-632-8139, Fax: 631-632-8240, E-mail: rjreeder@stonybrook.edu. *Application contact:* Dr. Brian Phillips, Director, 631-632-8200, Fax: 631-632-8240, E-mail: brian.phillips@stonybrook.edu. Website: http://www.geosciences.stonybrook.edu/.

Texas Tech University, Graduate School, College of Arts and Sciences, Department of Geosciences, Lubbock, TX 79409. Offers atmospheric science (MS); geography (MS); geosciences (MS, PhD). Part-time programs available. *Degree requirements:* For master's, thesis or alternative; for doctorate, comprehensive exam, thesis/dissertation. *Entrance requirements:* For master's and doctorate, GRE General Test. Additional exam requirements/recommendations for international students: Required—TOEFL (minimum score 550 paper-based; 79 iBT). Electronic applications accepted. *Faculty research:* Sedimentology and paleontology, geophysics, geochemistry, geospatial technology, hurricanes and severe storms.

Université du Québec à Chicoutimi, Graduate Programs, Program in Earth Sciences, Chicoutimi, QC G7H 2B1, Canada. Offers M Sc A. Part-time programs available. *Degree requirements:* For master's, thesis. *Entrance requirements:* For master's, appropriate bachelor's degree, proficiency in French.

Université du Québec à Montréal, Graduate Programs, Program in Earth and Atmospheric Sciences, Montréal, QC H3C 3P8, Canada. Offers atmospheric sciences (M Sc); Earth and atmospheric sciences (PhD); Earth science (M Sc); meteorology (PhD, Diploma). PhD programs offered jointly with McGill University. Part-time programs available. *Degree requirements:* For master's, thesis. *Entrance requirements:* For master's and Diploma, appropriate bachelor's degree or equivalent, proficiency in French; for doctorate, appropriate master's degree or equivalent, proficiency in French.

Université du Québec à Montréal, Graduate Programs, Program in Earth Sciences, Montreal, QC H3C 3P8, Canada. Offers earth sciences (M Sc); mineral resources (PhD); non-renewable resources (DESS). Part-time programs available. Terminal master's awarded for partial completion of doctoral program. *Degree requirements:* For master's, thesis (for some programs); for doctorate, thesis/dissertation. *Entrance requirements:* For master's, appropriate bachelor's degree or equivalent, proficiency in French. *Faculty research:* Economic geology, structural geology, geochemistry, Quaternary geology, isotopic geochemistry.

Université du Québec, Institut National de la Recherche Scientifique, Graduate Programs, Research Center–Water, Earth and Environment, Québec, QC G1K 9A9, Canada. Offers earth sciences (M Sc, PhD); earth sciences-environmental technologies (M Sc); water sciences (M Sc, PhD). Part-time programs available. *Faculty:* 39. *Students:* 204 full-time (96 women), 20 part-time (9 women), 106 international. Average age 30. In 2012, 24 master's, 6 doctorates awarded. *Degree requirements:* For master's, thesis optional; for doctorate, thesis/dissertation. *Entrance requirements:* For master's, appropriate bachelor's degree, proficiency in French; for doctorate, appropriate master's degree, proficiency in French. *Application deadline:* For fall admission, 3/30 for domestic and international students; for winter admission, 11/1 for domestic and international students; for spring admission, 3/1 for domestic and international students. Application fee: $45. Electronic applications accepted. *Financial support:* In 2012–13, fellowships (averaging $16,500 per year) were awarded; research assistantships also available. *Faculty research:* Land use, impacts of climate change, adaptation to climate change, integrated management of resources (mineral and water). *Unit head:* Yves Begin, Director, 418-654-2524, Fax: 418-654-2600, E-mail: yves.begin@ete.inrs.ca. *Application contact:* Sylvie Richard, Registrar, 418 654-2518, Fax: 418-654-3858, E-mail: sylvie.richard@adm.inrs.ca. Website: http://www.ete.inrs.ca/.

Université Laval, Faculty of Sciences and Engineering, Department of Geology and Geological Engineering, Programs in Earth Sciences, Québec, QC G1K 7P4, Canada. Offers earth sciences (M Sc, PhD); environmental technologies (M Sc). Offered jointly with INRS-Géressources. Terminal master's awarded for partial completion of doctoral program. *Degree requirements:* For master's, thesis (for some programs); for doctorate, comprehensive exam, thesis/dissertation. *Entrance requirements:* For master's and doctorate, knowledge of French. Electronic applications accepted.

University at Albany, State University of New York, College of Arts and Sciences, Department of Earth and Atmospheric Sciences, Albany, NY 12222-0001. Offers atmospheric science (MS, PhD); geology (MS, PhD). *Degree requirements:* For master's, one foreign language, comprehensive exam, thesis; for doctorate, 2 foreign languages, comprehensive exam, thesis/dissertation, oral exams. *Entrance requirements:* For master's and doctorate, GRE General Test. Additional exam requirements/recommendations for international students: Required—TOEFL (minimum score 550 paper-based). Electronic applications accepted. *Faculty research:* Environmental geochemistry, tectonics, mesoscale meteorology, atmospheric chemistry.

University at Buffalo, the State University of New York, Graduate School, College of Arts and Sciences, Department of Geography, Buffalo, NY 14260. Offers Canadian studies (Certificate); earth systems science (MA, MS); economic geography and business geographics (MS); environmental modeling and analysis (MA); geographic information science (MA, MS); geography (MA, PhD); GIS and environmental analysis (Certificate); health geography (MS); international trade (MA); transportation and business geographics (MA); urban and regional analysis (MA). Part-time programs available. *Faculty:* 16 full-time (7 women), 1 part-time/adjunct (0 women). *Students:* 98 full-time (46 women), 17 part-time (6 women); includes 69 minority (66 Asian, non-Hispanic/Latino; 3 Hispanic/Latino). Average age 29. 157 applicants, 58% accepted, 43 enrolled. In 2012, 30 master's, 10 doctorates awarded. Terminal master's awarded for partial completion of doctoral program. *Degree requirements:* For master's, thesis (for some programs), project or portfolio; for doctorate, thesis/dissertation. *Entrance requirements:* For master's, GRE General Test, minimum GPA of 2.9; for doctorate, GRE General Test, minimum GPA of 3.0. Additional exam requirements/recommendations for international students: Required—TOEFL (minimum score 550 paper-based; 79 iBT). *Application deadline:* For fall admission, 5/1 priority date for domestic students, 3/10 for international students; for spring admission, 11/1 priority date for domestic students, 9/1 for international students. Applications are processed on a rolling basis. Application fee: $75. Electronic applications accepted. *Financial support:* In 2012–13, 13 students received support, including 8 fellowships with full tuition reimbursements available (averaging $5,500 per year), 13 teaching assistantships with full tuition reimbursements available (averaging $13,520 per year); research assistantships with full tuition reimbursements available, career-related internships or fieldwork, Federal Work-Study, institutionally sponsored loans, traineeships, health care benefits, and unspecified assistantships also available. Financial award application deadline: 1/10. *Faculty research:* International business and world trade, geographic information systems and cartography, transportation, urban and regional analysis, physical and environmental geography. *Total annual research expenditures:* $505,189. *Unit head:* Dr. Sharmistha Bagchi-Sen, Chairman, 716-645-0473, Fax: 716-645-2329,

Geosciences

E-mail: geosbs@buffalo.edu. *Application contact:* Betsy Crooks, Graduate Secretary, 716-645-0471, Fax: 716-645-2329, E-mail: babraham@buffalo.edu. Website: http://www.geog.buffalo.edu/.

The University of Akron, Graduate School, Buchtel College of Arts and Sciences, Department of Geology and Environmental Science, Program in Earth Science, Akron, OH 44325. Offers MS. *Students:* 1 applicant, 100% accepted, 0 enrolled. *Degree requirements:* For master's, comprehensive exam, thesis, seminar, proficiency exam. *Entrance requirements:* For master's, minimum GPA of 2.75, letters of recommendation, statement of purpose. Additional exam requirements/recommendations for international students: Required—TOEFL (minimum score 550 paper-based; 79 iBT). *Application deadline:* Applications are processed on a rolling basis. Application fee: $40 ($60 for international students). Electronic applications accepted. *Expenses:* Tuition, state resident: full-time $7285; part-time $404.70 per credit hour. Tuition, nonresident: full-time $12,473; part-time $692.95 per credit hour. *Required fees:* $34.05 per credit hour. Tuition and fees vary according to course load. *Application contact:* Dr. LaVerne Friberg, Director of Graduate Studies, 330-972-8046, E-mail: lfribe1@uakron.edu.

The University of Alabama in Huntsville, School of Graduate Studies, College of Science, Department of Atmospheric Science, Huntsville, AL 35899. Offers atmospheric science (MS, PhD); earth system science (MS). Part-time and evening/weekend programs available. *Faculty:* 10 full-time (0 women), 1 part-time/adjunct (0 women). *Students:* 42 full-time (14 women), 5 part-time (all women); includes 3 minority (1 Black or African American, non-Hispanic/Latino; 1 Asian, non-Hispanic/Latino; 1 Hispanic/Latino), 7 international. Average age 26. 49 applicants, 90% accepted, 17 enrolled. In 2012, 5 master's, 2 doctorates awarded. *Degree requirements:* For master's, comprehensive exam, thesis or alternative, oral and written exams; for doctorate, comprehensive exam, thesis/dissertation, oral and written exams. *Entrance requirements:* For master's, GRE General Test, minimum GPA of 3.0; sequence of courses in calculus (including the calculus of vector-valued functions); courses in linear algebra and ordinary differential equations; two semesters each of chemistry and calculus-based physics; proficiency in at least one high-level computer programming language; for doctorate, GRE General Test, minimum GPA of 3.0. Additional exam requirements/recommendations for international students: Required—TOEFL (minimum score 550 paper-based; 80 iBT), IELTS (minimum score 6.5). *Application deadline:* For fall admission, 7/15 priority date for domestic students, 4/1 for international students; for spring admission, 11/30 priority date for domestic students, 9/1 for international students. Applications are processed on a rolling basis. Application fee: $40 ($50 for international students). Electronic applications accepted. *Expenses:* Tuition, state resident: full-time $8516; part-time $515 per credit hour. Tuition, nonresident: full-time $20,384; part-time $1229 per credit hour. *Required fees:* $148 per semester. One-time fee: $150. *Financial support:* In 2012–13, 36 students received support, including 34 research assistantships with full and partial tuition reimbursements available (averaging $14,797 per year), 2 teaching assistantships with full and partial tuition reimbursements available (averaging $14,400 per year); career-related internships or fieldwork, Federal Work-Study, institutionally sponsored loans, scholarships/grants, health care benefits, and unspecified assistantships also available. Support available to part-time students. Financial award application deadline: 4/1; financial award applicants required to submit FAFSA. *Faculty research:* Severe weather, climate, satellite remote sensing, numerical modeling, air pollution. *Total annual research expenditures:* $9.6 million. *Unit head:* Dr. Sundar Christopher, Chair, 256-922-7872, Fax: 256-922-7755, E-mail: sundar@nsstc.uah.edu. *Application contact:* Kim Gray, Graduate Studies Admissions Coordinator, 256-824-6002, Fax: 256-824-6405, E-mail: deangrad@uah.edu. Website: http://www.nsstc.uah.edu/atmos/index.html.

University of Alberta, Faculty of Graduate Studies and Research, Department of Earth and Atmospheric Sciences, Edmonton, AB T6G 2E1, Canada. Offers M Sc, MA, PhD. *Degree requirements:* For master's, thesis, residency; for doctorate, thesis/dissertation, residency. *Entrance requirements:* For master's, B Sc, minimum GPA of 6.5 on a 9.0 scale; for doctorate, M Sc. Additional exam requirements/recommendations for international students: Required—TOEFL or Michigan English Language Assessment Battery. Electronic applications accepted. *Faculty research:* Geology, human geography, physical geography, meteorology.

The University of Arizona, College of Science, Department of Geosciences, Tucson, AZ 85721. Offers MS, PhD. Part-time programs available. *Faculty:* 16 full-time (2 women), 6 part-time/adjunct (2 women). *Students:* 66 full-time (24 women), 10 part-time (8 women); includes 6 minority (3 Hispanic/Latino; 3 Two or more races, non-Hispanic/Latino), 5 international. Average age 29. 187 applicants, 14% accepted, 18 enrolled. In 2012, 14 master's, 9 doctorates awarded. Terminal master's awarded for partial completion of doctoral program. *Degree requirements:* For master's, thesis or prepublication; for doctorate, comprehensive exam, thesis/dissertation. *Entrance requirements:* For master's, GRE General Test, 3 letters of recommendation, curriculum vitae; for doctorate, GRE General Test, statement of purpose, 3 letters of recommendation, curriculum vitae. Additional exam requirements/recommendations for international students: Required—TOEFL (minimum score 550 paper-based; 79 iBT). *Application deadline:* For fall admission, 1/15 for domestic and international students. Applications are processed on a rolling basis. Application fee: $75. Electronic applications accepted. *Financial support:* In 2012–13, 31 research assistantships with full tuition reimbursements (averaging $23,134 per year), 29 teaching assistantships with full tuition reimbursements (averaging $22,822 per year) were awarded; career-related internships or fieldwork, institutionally sponsored loans, scholarships/grants, health care benefits, tuition waivers (partial), and unspecified assistantships also available. Financial award application deadline: 1/15. *Faculty research:* Tectonics, geophysics, geochemistry/petrology, economic geology, Quaternary studies, stratigraphy/paleontology. *Total annual research expenditures:* $5 million. *Unit head:* Dr. Karl Flessa, Head, 520-621-7336, Fax: 520-621-2672, E-mail: kflessa@geo.arizona.edu. *Application contact:* Anne Chase, Graduate Program Office, 520-621-6004, Fax: 520-621-2672, E-mail: gradapps@geo.arizona.edu. Website: http://www.geo.arizona.edu/.

University of Arkansas at Little Rock, Graduate School, College of Science and Mathematics, Program in Geospatial Technology, Little Rock, AR 72204-1099. Offers Graduate Certificate.

University of California, Irvine, School of Physical Sciences, Department of Earth System Science, Irvine, CA 92697. Offers MS, PhD. *Students:* 47 full-time (27 women); includes 5 minority (1 Black or African American, non-Hispanic/Latino; 1 Asian, non-Hispanic/Latino; 1 Hispanic/Latino; 2 Two or more races, non-Hispanic/Latino), 21 international. Average age 28. 57 applicants, 30% accepted, 10 enrolled. In 2012, 6 master's, 4 doctorates awarded. *Degree requirements:* For doctorate, thesis/dissertation. *Entrance requirements:* For master's and doctorate, GRE General Test, GRE Subject Test, minimum GPA of 3.0. Additional exam requirements/recommendations for international students: Required—TOEFL (minimum score 550 paper-based). *Application deadline:* For fall admission, 1/15 priority date for domestic students, 1/15 for international students. Applications are processed on a rolling basis. Application fee: $80 ($100 for international students). Electronic applications accepted. *Financial support:* Fellowships, research assistantships with full tuition reimbursements, teaching assistantships, career-related internships or fieldwork, institutionally sponsored loans, traineeships, health care benefits, and unspecified assistantships available. Financial award application deadline: 3/1; financial award applicants required to submit FAFSA. *Faculty research:* Atmospheric chemistry, climate change, isotope biogeochemistry, global environmental chemistry. *Unit head:* Michael L. Goulden, Chair, 949-824-1983, Fax: 949-824-3874, E-mail: mgoulden@uci.edu. *Application contact:* Cynthia A. Dennis, Department Manager, 949-824-3876, Fax: 949-824-3874, E-mail: cadennis@uci.edu. Website: http://www.ess.uci.edu/.

University of California, Los Angeles, Graduate Division, College of Letters and Science, Department of Earth and Space Sciences, Los Angeles, CA 90095. Offers geochemistry (MS, PhD); geology (MS, PhD); geophysics and space physics (MS, PhD). *Faculty:* 23 full-time (3 women). *Students:* 68 full-time (30 women); includes 17 minority (3 Black or African American, non-Hispanic/Latino; 1 American Indian or Alaska Native, non-Hispanic/Latino; 8 Asian, non-Hispanic/Latino; 3 Hispanic/Latino; 2 Two or more races, non-Hispanic/Latino), 15 international. Average age 28. 101 applicants, 18% accepted, 10 enrolled. In 2012, 15 master's, 11 doctorates awarded. Terminal master's awarded for partial completion of doctoral program. *Degree requirements:* For master's, comprehensive exams or thesis; for doctorate, thesis/dissertation, oral and written qualifying exams. *Entrance requirements:* For master's, GRE General Test; GRE Subject Test, bachelor's degree; minimum undergraduate GPA of 3.0 (or its equivalent if letter grade system not used); for doctorate, GRE General Test, bachelor's degree; minimum undergraduate GPA of 3.0 (or its equivalent if letter grade system not used). Additional exam requirements/recommendations for international students: Required—TOEFL. *Application deadline:* For fall admission, 1/15 for domestic and international students. Application fee: $80 ($100 for international students). Electronic applications accepted. *Expenses:* Tuition, nonresident: full-time $15,102. *Required fees:* $14,809.19. Full-time tuition and fees vary according to program. *Financial support:* In 2012–13, 72 students received support, including 69 fellowships with full and partial tuition reimbursements available, 57 research assistantships with full and partial tuition reimbursements available, 34 teaching assistantships with full and partial tuition reimbursements available; Federal Work-Study, scholarships/grants, health care benefits, tuition waivers (full and partial), and unspecified assistantships also available. Financial award application deadline: 3/2; financial award applicants required to submit FAFSA. *Unit head:* Dr. Kevin McKeegan, Chair, 310-825-1475, E-mail: mckeegan@ess.ucla.edu. *Application contact:* Student Affairs Officer, 310-825-3917, E-mail: holbrook@ess.ucla.edu. Website: http://www.ess.ucla.edu/.

University of California, San Diego, Office of Graduate Studies, Scripps Institution of Oceanography, La Jolla, CA 92093. Offers earth sciences (PhD); marine biology (PhD); oceanography (PhD). *Degree requirements:* For doctorate, comprehensive exam, thesis/dissertation. *Entrance requirements:* For doctorate, GRE General Test. Additional exam requirements/recommendations for international students: Required—TOEFL (minimum score 550 paper-based; 80 iBT). Electronic applications accepted.

University of California, Santa Barbara, Graduate Division, College of Letters and Sciences, Division of Mathematics, Life, and Physical Sciences, Department of Earth Science, Santa Barbara, CA 93106-9620. Offers geological sciences (MS, PhD); geophysics (MS). *Faculty:* 20 full-time (3 women), 6 part-time/adjunct (1 woman). *Students:* 43 full-time (18 women); includes 7 minority (1 American Indian or Alaska Native, non-Hispanic/Latino; 1 Asian, non-Hispanic/Latino; 5 Hispanic/Latino), 6 international. Average age 27. 116 applicants, 19% accepted, 13 enrolled. In 2012, 3 master's, 1 doctorate awarded. Terminal master's awarded for partial completion of doctoral program. *Degree requirements:* For master's, comprehensive exam, thesis, 30 units; for doctorate, comprehensive exam, thesis/dissertation, 30 units, oral qualifying exam. *Entrance requirements:* For master's and doctorate, GRE General Test. Additional exam requirements/recommendations for international students: Required—TOEFL (minimum score 550 paper-based; 80 iBT), IELTS (minimum score 7). *Application deadline:* For fall admission, 2/1 for domestic and international students. Application fee: $80 ($100 for international students). Electronic applications accepted. *Financial support:* In 2012–13, 28 students received support, including 3 fellowships with full and partial tuition reimbursements available (averaging $22,000 per year), 11 research assistantships with full and partial tuition reimbursements available (averaging $5,500 per year), 41 teaching assistantships with full and partial tuition reimbursements available (averaging $5,885 per year). Financial award application deadline: 1/3; financial award applicants required to submit CSS PROFILE or FAFSA. *Faculty research:* Geology, geomaterials and earth's structure; geomorphology, tectonics; geophysics, seismology; paleoclimatology, paleooceanography and geochemistry; paleobiology, evolution and paleontology. *Unit head:* Dr. Douglas Burbank, Chair, 805-893-7858, Fax: 805-893-2314, E-mail: burbank@eri.ucsb.edu. *Application contact:* Hannah Smit, Graduate Program Assistant, 805-893-3329, Fax: 805-893-2314, E-mail: hsmit@geol.ucsb.edu. Website: http://www.geol.ucsb.edu/.

University of California, Santa Cruz, Division of Graduate Studies, Division of Physical and Biological Sciences, Department of Earth and Planetary Sciences, Santa Cruz, CA 95064. Offers MS, PhD. Terminal master's awarded for partial completion of doctoral program. *Degree requirements:* For master's, thesis; for doctorate, one foreign language, thesis/dissertation, qualifying exam. *Entrance requirements:* For master's and doctorate, GRE General Test. Additional exam requirements/recommendations for international students: Required—TOEFL (minimum score 550 paper-based; 83 iBT); Recommended—IELTS (minimum score 8). Electronic applications accepted. *Faculty research:* Evolution of continental margins and orogenic belts, geologic processes occurring at plate boundaries, deep-sea sediment diagenesis, paleoecology, hydrogeology.

University of Chicago, Division of the Physical Sciences, Department of the Geophysical Sciences, Chicago, IL 60637-1513. Offers atmospheric sciences (SM, PhD); cosmochemistry (PhD); earth sciences (SM, PhD); paleobiology (PhD); planetary and space sciences (SM, PhD). Terminal master's awarded for partial completion of doctoral program. *Degree requirements:* For master's, thesis, seminar; for doctorate, variable foreign language requirement, comprehensive exam, thesis/dissertation. *Entrance requirements:* For doctorate, GRE General Test. Additional exam requirements/recommendations for international students: Required—TOEFL (minimum score 600 paper-based; 96 iBT), IELTS (minimum score 7). Electronic applications accepted. *Faculty research:* Climatology, evolutionary paleontology, cosmochemistry, geochemistry, oceanic sciences.

University of Florida, Graduate School, College of Liberal Arts and Sciences, Department of Geological Sciences, Gainesville, FL 32611. Offers hydrologic sciences (MS, MST, PhD); tropical conservation and development (MS, MST, PhD); wetland sciences (MS, MST, PhD). Terminal master's awarded for partial completion of doctoral program. *Degree requirements:* For master's, thesis (for some programs); for doctorate, one foreign language, thesis/dissertation. *Entrance requirements:* For master's, GRE General Test (minimum score of 1000), minimum GPA of 3.0; for doctorate, GRE General Test (minimum score of 1100), minimum GPA of 3.0. Additional exam requirements/recommendations for international students: Required—TOEFL (minimum score 550 paper-based; 80 iBT), IELTS (minimum score 6). Electronic applications accepted. *Faculty research:* Paleoclimatology, tectonophysics, petrochemistry, marine geology, geochemistry, hydrology.

University of Illinois at Chicago, Graduate College, College of Liberal Arts and Sciences, Department of Earth and Environmental Sciences, Chicago, IL 60607-7128. Offers MS, PhD. *Students:* 22 full-time (13 women); includes 1 minority (Asian, non-Hispanic/Latino), 6 international. Average age 28. 31 applicants, 26% accepted, 4 enrolled. In 2012, 2 master's, 1 doctorate awarded. *Degree requirements:* For master's, thesis; for doctorate, thesis/dissertation. *Entrance requirements:* For master's and doctorate, GRE General Test, minimum GPA of 2.75. Additional exam requirements/recommendations for international students: Required—TOEFL. *Application deadline:* For fall admission, 2/1 for domestic and international students; for spring admission, 11/15 for domestic students, 7/15 for international students. Applications are processed on a rolling basis. Application fee: $40 ($50 for international students). Electronic applications accepted. *Expenses:* Tuition, state resident: full-time $10,882; part-time $3627 per term. Tuition, nonresident: full-time $22,880; part-time $7627 per term. *Required fees:* $1170 per semester. Tuition and fees vary according to course load, degree level and program. *Financial support:* In 2012–13, 1 fellowship with full tuition reimbursement was awarded; research assistantships with full tuition reimbursements, teaching assistantships with full tuition reimbursements, Federal Work-Study, scholarships/grants, traineeships, tuition waivers (full), and unspecified assistantships also available. Financial award application deadline: 3/1; financial award applicants required to submit FAFSA. *Total annual research expenditures:* $1.3 million. *Unit head:* Dr. Kathryn Nagy, Head, 312-355-3276, E-mail: klnagy@uic.edu. *Application contact:* Andrew Dombard, Director of Graduate Studies, 312-996-9206, E-mail: adombard@uic.edu. Website: http://www.uic.edu/depts/geos/.

University of Illinois at Urbana–Champaign, Graduate College, College of Liberal Arts and Sciences, School of Earth, Society and Environment, Department of Geology, Champaign, IL 61820. Offers geology (MS, PhD); teaching of earth sciences (MS). *Students:* 29 (15 women). Terminal master's awarded for partial completion of doctoral program. Application fee: $75 ($90 for international students). *Unit head:* Thomas M. Johnson, Head, 217-244-2002, Fax: 217-244-4996, E-mail: tmjohnsn@illinois.edu. *Application contact:* Marilyn K. Whalen, Office Administrator, 217-333-3542, Fax: 217-244-4996, E-mail: mkt@illinois.edu. Website: http://www.geology.illinois.edu/.

The University of Iowa, Graduate College, College of Liberal Arts and Sciences, Department of Geoscience, Iowa City, IA 52242-1316. Offers MS, PhD. *Degree requirements:* For master's, thesis optional, exam; for doctorate, comprehensive exam, thesis/dissertation. *Entrance requirements:* For master's and doctorate, GRE General Test, minimum GPA of 3.0. Additional exam requirements/recommendations for international students: Required—TOEFL (minimum score 550 paper-based; 81 iBT). Electronic applications accepted.

University of Maine, Graduate School, College of Education and Human Development, Master of Science in Teaching Program, Orono, ME 04469. Offers earth sciences (MST); general (MST); mathematics (MST); physics (MST). Part-time programs available. *Students:* 20 full-time (8 women), 5 part-time (2 women); includes 1 minority (Asian, non-Hispanic/Latino). Average age 40. 17 applicants, 71% accepted, 9 enrolled. In 2012, 3 master's awarded. *Degree requirements:* For master's, thesis. *Entrance requirements:* For master's, GRE General Test, MAT. Additional exam requirements/recommendations for international students: Required—TOEFL. Application fee: $65. *Financial support:* Application deadline: 3/1. *Unit head:* Dr. Susan McKay, Director, 207-581-1016. *Application contact:* Scott G. Delcourt, Associate Dean of the Graduate School, 207-581-3291, Fax: 207-581-3232, E-mail: graduate@maine.edu. Website: http://umaine.edu/center/mst-program/.

The University of Manchester, School of Earth, Atmospheric and Environmental Sciences, Manchester, United Kingdom. Offers atmospheric sciences (M Phil, M Sc, PhD); basin studies and petroleum geosciences (M Phil, M Sc, PhD); earth, atmospheric and environmental sciences (M Phil, M Sc, PhD); environmental geochemistry and cosmochemistry (M Phil, M Sc, PhD); isotope geochemistry and cosmochemistry (M Phil, M Sc, PhD); paleontology (M Phil, M Sc, PhD); physics and chemistry of minerals and fluids (M Phil, M Sc, PhD); structural and petrological geosciences (M Phil, M Sc, PhD).

University of Massachusetts Amherst, Graduate School, College of Natural Sciences, Department of Geosciences, Program in Geosciences, Amherst, MA 01003. Offers MS, PhD. Part-time programs available. *Students:* 40 full-time (16 women), 26 part-time (11 women); includes 9 minority (1 Black or African American, non-Hispanic/Latino; 1 American Indian or Alaska Native, non-Hispanic/Latino; 3 Asian, non-Hispanic/Latino; 1 Hispanic/Latino; 3 Two or more races, non-Hispanic/Latino), 10 international. Average age 32. 79 applicants, 52% accepted, 22 enrolled. In 2012, 8 master's, 8 doctorates awarded. Terminal master's awarded for partial completion of doctoral program. *Degree requirements:* For master's, thesis or alternative; for doctorate, comprehensive exam, thesis/dissertation. *Entrance requirements:* For master's and doctorate, GRE General Test. Additional exam requirements/recommendations for international students: Required—TOEFL (minimum score 550 paper-based; 80 iBT), IELTS (minimum score 6.5). *Application deadline:* For fall admission, 1/15 for domestic and international students; for spring admission, 10/1 for domestic and international students. Applications are processed on a rolling basis. Application fee: $75. Electronic applications accepted. *Expenses:* Tuition, state resident: full-time $1980; part-time $110 per credit. Tuition, nonresident: full-time $13,314; part-time $414 per credit. *Required fees:* $10,338; $3594 per semester. One-time fee: $357. *Financial support:* Fellowships with full and partial tuition reimbursements, research assistantships with full and partial tuition reimbursements, teaching assistantships with full and partial tuition reimbursements, career-related internships or fieldwork, Federal Work-Study, scholarships/grants, traineeships, health care benefits, tuition waivers (full and partial), and unspecified assistantships available. Support available to part-time students. Financial award application deadline: 1/15. *Unit head:* Dr. Laurie Brown, Graduate Program Director, 413-545-2286, Fax: 413-545-1200. *Application contact:* Lindsay DeSantis, Supervisor of Admissions, 413-545-0722, Fax: 413-577-0010, E-mail: gradadm@grad.umass.edu. Website: http://www.geo.umass.edu/.

University of Michigan, Horace H. Rackham School of Graduate Studies, College of Literature, Science, and the Arts, Department of Earth and Environmental Sciences, Ann Arbor, MI 48109-1005. Offers MS, PhD. *Faculty:* 28 full-time (6 women), 10 part-time/adjunct (5 women). *Students:* 67 full-time (31 women); includes 7 minority (1 Black or African American, non-Hispanic/Latino; 1 American Indian or Alaska Native, non-Hispanic/Latino; 1 Asian, non-Hispanic/Latino; 2 Hispanic/Latino; 2 Two or more races, non-Hispanic/Latino), 21 international. 139 applicants, 25% accepted, 24 enrolled. In 2012, 9 master's, 12 doctorates awarded. Terminal master's awarded for partial completion of doctoral program. *Degree requirements:* For master's, thesis; for doctorate, comprehensive exam, thesis/dissertation, oral defense of dissertation. *Entrance requirements:* For master's and doctorate, GRE General Test. Additional exam requirements/recommendations for international students: Required—TOEFL (minimum score 84 iBT). *Application deadline:* For fall admission, 1/5 for domestic and international students; for winter admission, 11/1 for domestic and international students. Application fee: $65 ($75 for international students). Electronic applications accepted. *Financial support:* Fellowships with full tuition reimbursements, research assistantships with full tuition reimbursements, teaching assistantships with full tuition reimbursements, career-related internships or fieldwork, scholarships/grants, health care benefits, and unspecified assistantships available. Financial award application deadline: 1/5; financial

Peterson's Graduate Programs in the Physical Sciences, Mathematics, Agricultural Sciences, the Environment & Natural Resources 2014

www.petersonsbooks.com **167**

award applicants required to submit FAFSA. *Faculty research:* Isotope geochemistry, paleoclimatology, mineral physics, tectonics, paleontology. *Unit head:* Dr. Rebecca Lange, Chair, 734-764-1435, Fax: 734-763-4690, E-mail: michiganearth@umich.edu. *Application contact:* Anne Hudon, Graduate Program Coordinator, 734-615-3034, Fax: 734-763-4690, E-mail: michiganearth@umich.edu. Website: http://www.lsa.umich.edu/earth.

University of Missouri–Kansas City, College of Arts and Sciences, Department of Geosciences, Kansas City, MO 64110-2499. Offers environmental and urban geosciences (MS); geosciences (PhD). PhD (interdisciplinary) offered through the School of Graduate Studies. Part-time programs available. *Faculty:* 11 full-time (3 women), 5 part-time/adjunct (0 women). *Students:* 6 full-time (3 women), 21 part-time (11 women); includes 4 minority (2 Black or African American, non-Hispanic/Latino; 1 American Indian or Alaska Native, non-Hispanic/Latino; 1 Two or more races, non-Hispanic/Latino), 5 international. Average age 33. 24 applicants, 50% accepted, 9 enrolled. In 2012, 12 master's awarded. *Degree requirements:* For master's, thesis; for doctorate, thesis/dissertation, qualifying exam. *Entrance requirements:* For master's, GRE General Test, minimum GPA of 3.0. Additional exam requirements/recommendations for international students: Required—TOEFL (minimum score 550 paper-based; 80 iBT). *Application deadline:* For fall admission, 3/15 priority date for domestic students, 3/15 for international students. Applications are processed on a rolling basis. Application fee: $45 ($50 for international students). Electronic applications accepted. *Expenses:* Tuition, state resident: full-time $5972.40; part-time $331.80 per credit hour. Tuition, nonresident: full-time $15,417; part-time $856.50 per credit hour. *Required fees:* $95.89 per credit hour. Full-time tuition and fees vary according to program. *Financial support:* In 2012–13, 1 research assistantship with partial tuition reimbursement (averaging $15,750 per year), 14 teaching assistantships with partial tuition reimbursements (averaging $13,308 per year) were awarded; Federal Work-Study, institutionally sponsored loans, and tuition waivers (full and partial) also available. Support available to part-time students. Financial award application deadline: 3/1; financial award applicants required to submit FAFSA. *Faculty research:* Neotectonics and applied geophysics, environmental geosciences, urban geoscience, geoinformatics-remote sensing, atmospheric research. *Unit head:* Dr. James B. Murowchick, Chair, 816-235-2979, Fax: 816-235-5535, E-mail: murowchick@umkc.edu. *Application contact:* Dr. Jejung Lee, Associate Professor, 816-235-6495, Fax: 816-235-5535, E-mail: leej@umkc.edu. Website: http://cas.umkc.edu/geo/.

The University of Montana, Graduate School, College of Arts and Sciences, Department of Geology, Missoula, MT 59812-0002. Offers applied geoscience (PhD); geology (MS, PhD). *Degree requirements:* For doctorate, thesis/dissertation. *Entrance requirements:* For master's and doctorate, GRE General Test. Additional exam requirements/recommendations for international students: Required—TOEFL (minimum score 525 paper-based). *Faculty research:* Environmental geoscience, regional structure and tectonics, groundwater geology, petrology, mineral deposits.

University of Nebraska–Lincoln, Graduate College, College of Arts and Sciences, Department of Geosciences, Lincoln, NE 68588. Offers MS, PhD. *Degree requirements:* For master's, thesis optional, departmental qualifying exam; for doctorate, comprehensive exam, thesis/dissertation, departmental qualifying exams. *Entrance requirements:* For master's and doctorate, GRE General Test. Additional exam requirements/recommendations for international students: Required—TOEFL (minimum score 550 paper-based). Electronic applications accepted. *Faculty research:* Hydrogeology, sedimentology, environmental geology, vertebrate paleontology.

University of Nevada, Las Vegas, Graduate College, College of Science, Department of Geoscience, Las Vegas, NV 89154-4010. Offers MS, PhD. Part-time programs available. *Faculty:* 22 full-time (6 women), 10 part-time/adjunct (0 women). *Students:* 36 full-time (18 women), 15 part-time (7 women); includes 37 minority (3 Hispanic/Latino; 34 Two or more races, non-Hispanic/Latino), 6 international. Average age 30. 52 applicants, 27% accepted, 12 enrolled. In 2012, 8 master's, 5 doctorates awarded. *Degree requirements:* For master's, comprehensive exam, thesis; for doctorate, comprehensive exam, thesis/dissertation. *Entrance requirements:* For master's and doctorate, GRE General Test. Additional exam requirements/recommendations for international students: Required—TOEFL (minimum score 550 paper-based; 80 iBT), IELTS (minimum score 7). *Application deadline:* For fall admission, 2/1 priority date for domestic students, 5/1 for international students; for spring admission, 10/1 priority date for domestic students, 10/1 for international students. Applications are processed on a rolling basis. Application fee: $60 ($95 for international students). Electronic applications accepted. *Expenses:* Tuition, state resident: full-time $4752; part-time $264 per credit. Tuition, nonresident: full-time $18,662; part-time $527.50 per credit. *Required fees:* $12 per credit. $266 per semester. One-time fee: $35. Tuition and fees vary according to course load, program and reciprocity agreements. *Financial support:* In 2012–13, 45 students received support, including 17 research assistantships with partial tuition reimbursements available (averaging $11,153 per year), 28 teaching assistantships with partial tuition reimbursements available (averaging $11,464 per year); institutionally sponsored loans, scholarships/grants, health care benefits, and unspecified assistantships also available. Financial award application deadline: 3/1. *Faculty research:* Petrology, geochemistry and economic geology; climate and earth surface processes; structural geology and tectonics; sedimentary geology and paleontology; hydrogeologic and environmental science. *Total annual research expenditures:* $990,889. *Unit head:* Dr. Michael Wells, Chair/Professor, 702-895-0828, Fax: 702-895-4064, E-mail: michael.wells@unlv.edu. *Application contact:* Graduate College Admissions Evaluator, 702-895-3320, Fax: 702-895-4180, E-mail: gradcollege@unlv.edu. Website: http://geoscience.unlv.edu/.

University of New Hampshire, Graduate School, College of Engineering and Physical Sciences, Department of Earth Sciences, Durham, NH 03824. Offers general (MS); geology (MS); hydrology (MS); ocean mapping (MS). *Faculty:* 17 full-time (5 women). *Students:* 15 full-time (8 women), 15 part-time (5 women); includes 1 minority (Black or African American, non-Hispanic/Latino), 4 international. Average age 27. 43 applicants, 53% accepted, 8 enrolled. In 2012, 15 master's awarded. *Degree requirements:* For master's, thesis. *Entrance requirements:* For master's, GRE General Test. Additional exam requirements/recommendations for international students: Required—TOEFL (minimum score 550 paper-based; 80 iBT). *Application deadline:* For fall admission, 4/1 priority date for domestic students, 4/1 for international students; for spring admission, 12/1 for domestic students. Applications are processed on a rolling basis. Application fee: $65. Electronic applications accepted. *Expenses:* Tuition, state resident: full-time $13,500; part-time $750 per credit. Tuition, nonresident: full-time $25,940; part-time $1089 per credit. *Required fees:* $1699; $424.75 per semester. *Financial support:* In 2012–13, 24 students received support, including 11 research assistantships, 7 teaching assistantships; fellowships, career-related internships or fieldwork, Federal Work-Study, scholarships/grants, and tuition waivers (full and partial) also available. Support available to part-time students. Financial award application deadline: 2/15. *Unit head:* Dr. Julie Bryce, Chairperson, 603-862-3139, E-mail: earth.sciences@unh.edu. *Application contact:* Sue Clark, Administrative Assistant, 603-862-1718, E-mail: earth.sciences@unh.edu. Website: http://www.unh.edu/esci/.

University of New Haven, Graduate School, College of Arts and Sciences, Program in Environmental Sciences, West Haven, CT 06516-1916. Offers environmental ecology (MS); environmental geoscience (MS); environmental health and management (MS); environmental science (MS); environmental science education (MS); geographical information systems (MS, Certificate). Part-time and evening/weekend programs available. *Students:* 23 full-time (14 women), 13 part-time (6 women); includes 5 minority (3 Black or African American, non-Hispanic/Latino; 2 Asian, non-Hispanic/Latino), 9 international. 43 applicants, 81% accepted, 21 enrolled. In 2012, 9 master's, 4 other advanced degrees awarded. *Degree requirements:* For master's, thesis optional, research project. *Entrance requirements:* Additional exam requirements/recommendations for international students: Required—TOEFL (minimum score 80 iBT), IELTS, Pearson Test of English (minimum score 53). *Application deadline:* For fall admission, 5/31 for international students; for winter admission, 10/15 for international students; for spring admission, 1/15 for international students. Applications are processed on a rolling basis. Application fee: $75. Electronic applications accepted. Application fee is waived when completed online. *Expenses: Tuition:* Part-time $775 per credit. *Required fees:* $45 per trimester. *Financial support:* Research assistantships with partial tuition reimbursements, teaching assistantships with partial tuition reimbursements, career-related internships or fieldwork, Federal Work-Study, scholarships/grants, and unspecified assistantships available. Support available to part-time students. Financial award applicants required to submit FAFSA. *Faculty research:* Mapping and assessing geological and living resources in Long Island Sound, geology, San Salvador Island, Bahamas. *Unit head:* Dr. Roman Zajac, Coordinator, 203-932-7114, E-mail: rzajac@newhaven.edu. *Application contact:* Eloise Gormley, Director of Graduate Admissions, 203-932-7440, E-mail: gradinfo@newhaven.edu. Website: http://www.newhaven.edu/4728/.

University of New Mexico, Graduate School, College of Arts and Sciences, Department of Earth and Planetary Sciences, Albuquerque, NM 87131. Offers MS, PhD. Part-time programs available. *Faculty:* 33 full-time (5 women), 22 part-time/adjunct (3 women). *Students:* 21 full-time (13 women), 30 part-time (17 women); includes 6 minority (1 American Indian or Alaska Native, non-Hispanic/Latino; 1 Asian, non-Hispanic/Latino; 4 Hispanic/Latino), 7 international. Average age 31. 74 applicants, 15% accepted, 7 enrolled. In 2012, 11 master's, 6 doctorates awarded. Terminal master's awarded for partial completion of doctoral program. *Degree requirements:* For master's, comprehensive exam, thesis; for doctorate, comprehensive exam, thesis/dissertation. *Entrance requirements:* For master's and doctorate, GRE General Test. Additional exam requirements/recommendations for international students: Required—TOEFL. *Application deadline:* For fall admission, 1/15 priority date for domestic students, 1/15 for international students; for spring admission, 11/1 priority date for domestic students, 11/1 for international students. Application fee: $50. Electronic applications accepted. *Expenses:* Tuition, state resident: full-time $3296; part-time $276.73 per credit hour. Tuition, nonresident: full-time $10,604; part-time $885.74 per credit hour. *Required fees:* $628. *Financial support:* In 2012–13, 51 students received support, including 3 fellowships with full tuition reimbursements available (averaging $2,714 per year), 14 research assistantships with full tuition reimbursements available (averaging $14,363 per year), 21 teaching assistantships with full tuition reimbursements available (averaging $1,982 per year); scholarships/grants and health care benefits also available. Financial award application deadline: 1/15. *Faculty research:* Climatology, experimental petrology, geochemistry, geographic information technologies, geomorphology, geophysics, hydrogeology, ingeneous petrology, metamorphic petrology, meteoritics, meteorology, micrometeorites, mineralogy, paleoclimatology, paleonology, pedology, petrology, physical volcanology, planetary sciences, precambrian geology, quantenary geology, sedimentary geochemistry, sedimentology, stable isotope geochemistry, stratigraphy, structural geology, tectonics, volcanology. *Total annual research expenditures:* $2.5 million. *Unit head:* Dr. Adrian J. Brearley, Chair, 505-277-4204, Fax: 505-277-8843, E-mail: brearley@unm.edu. *Application contact:* Cindy Jaramillo, Administrative Assistant III, 505-277-1635, Fax: 505-277-8843, E-mail: epsdept@unm.edu. Website: http://epswww.unm.edu/.

University of New Orleans, Graduate School, College of Sciences, Department of Earth and Environmental Sciences, New Orleans, LA 70148. Offers MS. Evening/weekend programs available. *Students:* 16 (7 women). Average age 27. 17 applicants, 41% accepted, 3 enrolled. In 2012, 7 master's awarded. *Degree requirements:* For master's, thesis. *Entrance requirements:* For master's, GRE General Test. Additional exam requirements/recommendations for international students: Required—TOEFL (minimum score 550 paper-based; 79 iBT), IELTS. *Application deadline:* For fall admission, 1/1 priority date for domestic students, 1/1 for international students; for spring admission, 10/15 priority date for domestic students, 10/1 for international students. Applications are processed on a rolling basis. Application fee: $20. Electronic applications accepted. *Expenses: Required fees:* $2165 per semester. *Financial support:* Fellowships, research assistantships, teaching assistantships, career-related internships or fieldwork, Federal Work-Study, and institutionally sponsored loans available. Financial award application deadline: 3/15; financial award applicants required to submit FAFSA. *Faculty research:* Continental margin structure and seismology, burial diagenesis of siliciastic sediments, tectonics at convergent plate margins, continental shelf sediment stability, early diagenesis of carbonates. *Unit head:* Dr. William Simmons, Chairperson, 504-280-6791, Fax: 504-280-7396, E-mail: wsimmons@uno.edu. *Application contact:* Dr. Ioannis Georgiou, Graduate Coordinator, 504-280-1373, Fax: 504-280-7396, E-mail: igeorgio@uno.edu. Website: http://ees.uno.edu.

The University of North Carolina at Charlotte, The Graduate School, College of Liberal Arts and Sciences, Department of Geography and Earth Sciences, Charlotte, NC 28223-0001. Offers earth sciences (MS); geography (MA), including community planning, geographic location science and technologies, location analysis, transportation studies, urban regional analysis; geography and urban regional analysis (PhD). Part-time and evening/weekend programs available. *Faculty:* 28 full-time (10 women), 2 part-time/adjunct (0 women). *Students:* 52 full-time (21 women), 47 part-time (20 women); includes 9 minority (4 Black or African American, non-Hispanic/Latino; 2 Hispanic/Latino; 1 Native Hawaiian or other Pacific Islander, non-Hispanic/Latino; 2 Two or more races, non-Hispanic/Latino), 17 international. Average age 31. 56 applicants, 68% accepted, 19 enrolled. In 2012, 16 master's awarded. Terminal master's awarded for partial completion of doctoral program. *Degree requirements:* For master's, comprehensive exam, thesis or alternative, project. *Entrance requirements:* For master's, GRE General Test or MAT, Doppelt Mathematical Reasoning Test, minimum GPA of 3.0 in undergraduate major, 2.75 overall. Additional exam requirements/recommendations for international students: Required—TOEFL (minimum score 557 paper-based; 83 iBT). *Application deadline:* For fall admission, 7/1 for domestic students, 5/1 for international students; for spring admission, 11/1 for domestic students, 10/1 for international students. Applications are processed on a rolling basis. Application fee: $65 ($75 for international students). Electronic applications accepted. *Expenses:* Tuition, state resident: full-time $3453. Tuition, nonresident: full-time $15,982. *Required fees:* $2420. Tuition and fees vary according to course load and program. *Financial support:* In 2012–13, 43 students received support, including 23 research assistantships (averaging $9,488 per year), 20 teaching assistantships (averaging $9,500 per year); fellowships, career-related internships or fieldwork, institutionally sponsored loans, scholarships/grants, and unspecified assistantships also available. Support available to part-time students. Financial award application deadline: 4/1; financial award applicants required to submit FAFSA. *Faculty research:* Improving geographic knowledge discovery and spatial reasoning with mobile and Web-based geographical information systems; an in-house supercomputing cluster for multi-scale science and collaborative research; feedback between a generalist pathogen, hosts and heterogeneous environments at multiple spatial and temporal scales. *Total annual research expenditures:* $601,790. *Unit head:* Dr. Craig Allan, Chair, 704-687-5999, Fax: 704-687-3182, E-mail: cjallan@uncc.edu. *Application contact:* Kathy B. Giddings, Director of Graduate Admissions, 704-687-5503, Fax: 704-687-1668, E-mail: gradadm@uncc.edu. Website: http://www.geoearch.uncc.edu/.

The University of North Carolina Wilmington, College of Arts and Sciences, Department of Geography and Geology, Wilmington, NC 28403-3297. Offers geology (MS); marine science (MS). *Degree requirements:* For master's, comprehensive exam, thesis. *Entrance requirements:* For master's, GRE General Test, GRE Subject Test, minimum B average in undergraduate major and basic prerequisite geology courses.

University of North Dakota, Graduate School, John D. Odegard School of Aerospace Sciences, Program in Earth System Science and Policy, Grand Forks, ND 58202. Offers MEM, MS, PhD. Part-time programs available. *Degree requirements:* For master's, thesis (for some programs); for doctorate, thesis/dissertation (for some programs). *Entrance requirements:* For master's and doctorate, GRE General Test, minimum GPA of 3.0. Additional exam requirements/recommendations for international students: Required—TOEFL (minimum score 550 paper-based; 79 iBT), IELTS (minimum score 6.5). Electronic applications accepted.

University of Northern Colorado, Graduate School, College of Natural and Health Sciences, School of Chemistry, Earth Sciences and Physics, Program in Earth Sciences, Greeley, CO 80639. Offers MA. Part-time programs available. *Degree requirements:* For master's, comprehensive exam. *Entrance requirements:* For master's, GRE General Test, 3 letters of recommendation. Electronic applications accepted.

University of Northern Iowa, Graduate College, College of Humanities, Arts and Sciences, Program in Science Education, Cedar Falls, IA 50614. Offers earth science education (MA); physics education (MA); science education (MA). *Students:* 4 full-time (2 women), 8 part-time (2 women); includes 1 minority (Two or more races, non-Hispanic/Latino). 1 applicant, 100% accepted, 1 enrolled. In 2012, 8 master's awarded. *Degree requirements:* For master's, comprehensive exam (for some programs), thesis or alternative. *Entrance requirements:* For master's, minimum GPA of 3.0. Additional exam requirements/recommendations for international students: Required—TOEFL (minimum score 500 paper-based; 61 iBT). *Application deadline:* For fall admission, 8/1 priority date for domestic students. Applications are processed on a rolling basis. Application fee: $50 ($70 for international students). Electronic applications accepted. *Financial support:* Application deadline: 2/1. *Unit head:* Dr. Cherin A. Lee, Director, 319-273-7357, Fax: 319-273-3051, E-mail: cherin.lee@uni.edu. *Application contact:* Laurie S. Russell, Record Analyst, 319-273-2623, Fax: 319-273-2885, E-mail: laurie.russell@uni.edu. Website: http://www.uni.edu/science-ed/.

University of Notre Dame, Graduate School, College of Engineering, Department of Civil Engineering and Geological Sciences, Notre Dame, IN 46556. Offers bioengineering (MS Bio E); civil engineering (MSCE); civil engineering and geological sciences (PhD); environmental engineering (MS Env E); geological sciences (MS). Terminal master's awarded for partial completion of doctoral program. *Degree requirements:* For master's, comprehensive exam; for doctorate, thesis/dissertation, candidacy exam. *Entrance requirements:* For master's and doctorate, GRE General Test. Additional exam requirements/recommendations for international students: Required—TOEFL (minimum score 600 paper-based; 80 iBT). Electronic applications accepted. *Faculty research:* Environmental modeling, biological-waste treatment, petrology, environmental geology, geochemistry.

University of Ottawa, Faculty of Graduate and Postdoctoral Studies, Faculty of Science, Ottawa-Carleton Geoscience Centre, Ottawa, ON K1N 6N5, Canada. Offers earth sciences (M Sc, PhD). M Sc, PhD offered jointly with Carleton University. *Degree requirements:* For master's, thesis, seminar; for doctorate, comprehensive exam, thesis/dissertation, seminar. *Entrance requirements:* For master's, honors B Sc degree or equivalent, minimum B average; for doctorate, honors B Sc with minimum B average or M Sc with minimum B+ average. Electronic applications accepted. Tuition and fees charges are reported in Canadian dollars. *Expenses: Tuition, area resident:* Full-time $7074 Canadian dollars; part-time $256 Canadian dollars per credit. *International tuition:* $16,334 Canadian dollars full-time. *Required fees:* $738 Canadian dollars; $110 Canadian dollars per term. Part-time tuition and fees vary according to course load, program and student level. *Faculty research:* Environmental geoscience, geochemistry/petrology, geomatics/geomathematics, mineral resource studies.

University of Pennsylvania, School of Arts and Sciences, Graduate Group in Earth and Environmental Science, Philadelphia, PA 19104. Offers MS, PhD. Part-time programs available. *Faculty:* 9 full-time (2 women), 4 part-time/adjunct (0 women). *Students:* 15 full-time (11 women), 1 (woman) part-time, 4 international. 31 applicants, 10% accepted, 1 enrolled. In 2012, 3 doctorates awarded. *Degree requirements:* For master's, one foreign language, thesis; for doctorate, one foreign language, thesis/dissertation. *Entrance requirements:* For master's and doctorate, GRE General Test. Additional exam requirements/recommendations for international students: Required—TOEFL. *Application deadline:* For fall admission, 12/1 priority date for domestic students. Application fee: $70. Electronic applications accepted. *Financial support:* Fellowships, research assistantships, teaching assistantships, institutionally sponsored loans, scholarships/grants, traineeships, health care benefits, and unspecified assistantships available. Financial award application deadline: 12/15. *Faculty research:* Isotope geochemistry, regional tectonics, environmental geology, metamorphic and igneous petrology, paleontology. *Application contact:* Arts and Sciences Graduate Admissions, 215-573-5816, Fax: 215-573-8068, E-mail: gdasadmis@sas.upenn.edu. Website: http://www.sas.upenn.edu/graduate-division.

University of Rhode Island, Graduate School, College of the Environment and Life Sciences, Department of Geosciences, Kingston, RI 02881. Offers environmental science and management (MESM); environmental sciences (MS, PhD). Part-time programs available. *Faculty:* 5 full-time (2 women). *Students:* 6 full-time (0 women), 2 part-time (1 woman). In 2012, 4 master's awarded. *Degree requirements:* For master's, comprehensive exam (for some programs), thesis optional; for doctorate, comprehensive exam, thesis/dissertation. *Entrance requirements:* For master's and doctorate, GRE, 2 letters of recommendation. Additional exam requirements/recommendations for international students: Required—TOEFL (minimum score 550 paper-based). *Application deadline:* For fall admission, 7/15 for domestic students, 2/1 for international students; for spring admission, 11/15 for domestic students, 7/15 for international students. Application fee: $65. Electronic applications accepted. *Expenses:* Tuition, state resident: full-time $11,532; part-time $641 per credit. Tuition, nonresident: full-time $23,606; part-time $1311 per credit. *Required fees:* $1388; $36 per credit. $35 per semester. One-time fee: $130. *Financial support:* In 2012–13, 4 research assistantships with full and partial tuition reimbursements (averaging $11,014 per year), 1 teaching assistantship with full and partial tuition reimbursement (averaging $15,800 per year) were awarded. Financial award application deadline: 7/15; financial award applicants required to submit FAFSA. *Faculty research:* Hydrology and water resources, interior of the earth, quaternary and modern depositional environments, geobiology of Mesozoic terrestrial ecosystems. *Unit head:* Dr. Daivd Fastovsky, Chair, 401-874-2185, Fax: 401-874-2190, E-mail: defastov@uri.edu. Website: http://www.uri.edu/cels/geo/.

University of Rochester, School of Arts and Sciences, Department of Earth and Environmental Sciences, Rochester, NY 14627. Offers MS, PhD. *Degree requirements:* For doctorate, thesis/dissertation, qualifying exam. *Entrance requirements:* For master's and doctorate, GRE General Test. Additional exam requirements/recommendations for international students: Required—TOEFL. Electronic applications accepted. *Faculty research:* Geochemistry and environmental sciences; paleomagnetism, structure and tectonics.

University of South Carolina, The Graduate School, College of Arts and Sciences, Department of Geological Sciences, Columbia, SC 29208. Offers MS, PhD. Terminal master's awarded for partial completion of doctoral program. *Degree requirements:* For master's, thesis; for doctorate, comprehensive exam, thesis/dissertation, published paper. *Entrance requirements:* For master's and doctorate, GRE General Test. Additional exam requirements/recommendations for international students: Required—TOEFL (minimum score 570 paper-based; 75 iBT). Electronic applications accepted. *Faculty research:* Environmental geology, tectonics, petrology, coastal processes, paleoclimatology.

University of Southern California, Graduate School, Dana and David Dornsife College of Letters, Arts and Sciences, Department of Earth Sciences, Los Angeles, CA 90089. Offers geological sciences (MS, PhD). Only Ph.D. and M.S./Ph.D. students are funded. Part-time programs available. Terminal master's awarded for partial completion of doctoral program. *Degree requirements:* For master's, thesis; for doctorate, comprehensive exam, thesis/dissertation. *Entrance requirements:* For master's and doctorate, GRE. Additional exam requirements/recommendations for international students: Required—TOEFL. Electronic applications accepted. *Faculty research:* Geophysics, paleoceanography, geochemistry, geobiology, structure, tectonics.

The University of Texas at Austin, Graduate School, Jackson School of Geosciences, Austin, TX 78712-1111. Offers MA, MS, PhD. Part-time programs available. *Degree requirements:* For master's, report (MA), thesis (MS); for doctorate, thesis/dissertation. *Entrance requirements:* For master's and doctorate, GRE General Test. Electronic applications accepted. *Faculty research:* Sedimentary geology, geophysics, hydrogeology, structure/tectonics, vertebrate paleontology.

The University of Texas at Dallas, School of Natural Sciences and Mathematics, Department of Geosciences, Richardson, TX 75080. Offers geochemistry (MS, PhD); geophysics (MS, PhD); geospatial information sciences (MS, PhD); hydrogeology (MS, PhD); sedimentary, stratigraphy, paleontology (PhD); stratigraphy, paleontology (MS); structural geology and tectonics (MS, PhD). Part-time and evening/weekend programs available. *Faculty:* 10 full-time (1 woman). *Students:* 45 full-time (18 women), 26 part-time (11 women); includes 9 minority (2 Black or African American, non-Hispanic/Latino; 4 Asian, non-Hispanic/Latino; 3 Hispanic/Latino), 23 international. Average age 30. 90 applicants, 31% accepted, 18 enrolled. In 2012, 7 master's, 4 doctorates awarded. *Degree requirements:* For master's, thesis optional; for doctorate, thesis/dissertation. *Entrance requirements:* For master's and doctorate, GRE General Test, minimum GPA of 3.0 in upper-level course work in field. Additional exam requirements/recommendations for international students: Required—TOEFL (minimum score 550 paper-based). *Application deadline:* For fall admission, 7/15 for domestic students, 5/1 for international students; for spring admission, 11/15 for domestic students, 9/1 for international students. Applications are processed on a rolling basis. Application fee: $50 ($100 for international students). Electronic applications accepted. *Expenses:* Tuition, state resident: full-time $11,940; part-time $663.33 per credit hour. Tuition, nonresident: full-time $21,606; part-time $1200.33 per credit hour. Tuition and fees vary according to course load. *Financial support:* In 2012–13, 33 students received support, including 12 research assistantships with partial tuition reimbursements available (averaging $22,270 per year), 9 teaching assistantships with partial tuition reimbursements available (averaging $15,300 per year); career-related internships or fieldwork, Federal Work-Study, institutionally sponsored loans, scholarships/grants, and unspecified assistantships also available. Support available to part-time students. Financial award application deadline: 4/30; financial award applicants required to submit FAFSA. *Faculty research:* Cybermapping, GPS applications for geophysics and geology, seismology and ground-penetrating radar, numerical modeling, signal processing and inverse modeling techniques in seismology. *Unit head:* Dr. John Oldow, Department Head, 972-883-2401, Fax: 972-883-2537, E-mail: geosciences@utdallas.edu. *Application contact:* Gloria Eby, Graduate Support Assistant, 972-883-2404, Fax: 972-883-2537, E-mail: geosciences@utdallas.edu. Website: http://www.utdallas.edu/geosciences.

University of Tulsa, Graduate School, College of Engineering and Natural Sciences, Department of Geosciences, Tulsa, OK 74104-3189. Offers MS, PhD, JD/MS. Part-time programs available. *Faculty:* 9 full-time (1 woman), 6 part-time/adjunct (1 woman). *Students:* 36 full-time (11 women), 10 part-time (5 women); includes 1 minority (American Indian or Alaska Native, non-Hispanic/Latino), 34 international. Average age 26. 82 applicants, 40% accepted, 19 enrolled. In 2012, 7 master's awarded. Terminal master's awarded for partial completion of doctoral program. *Degree requirements:* For master's, thesis (for some programs); for doctorate, comprehensive exam, thesis/dissertation. *Entrance requirements:* For master's and doctorate, GRE General Test. Additional exam requirements/recommendations for international students: Required—TOEFL (minimum score 550 paper-based; 80 iBT), IELTS (minimum score 6). *Application deadline:* Applications are processed on a rolling basis. Application fee: $40. Electronic applications accepted. *Expenses: Tuition:* Full-time $18,630. *Required fees:* $1340; $5 per credit hour. $75 per semester. Tuition and fees vary according to course load. *Financial support:* In 2012–13, 15 students received support, including 2 fellowships with full and partial tuition reimbursements available (averaging $3,750 per year), 2 research assistantships with full and partial tuition reimbursements available (averaging $8,105 per year), 6 teaching assistantships with full and partial tuition reimbursements available (averaging $10,250 per year); career-related internships or fieldwork, scholarships/grants, health care benefits, and unspecified assistantships also available. Support available to part-time students. Financial award application deadline: 2/1; financial award applicants required to submit FAFSA. *Faculty research:* Petroleum exploration/production and environmental science, including clastic sedimentology, petroleum seismology, seismic stratigraphy, structural geology, geochemistry, and biogeoscience. *Total annual research expenditures:* $115,247. *Unit head:* Dr. Bryan Tapp, Chairperson, 918-631-3018, Fax: 918-631-2091, E-mail: jbt@utulsa.edu. *Application contact:* Dr. Peter J. Michael, Adviser, 918-631-3017, Fax: 918-631-2156, E-mail: pjm@utulsa.edu. Website: http://www.geo.utulsa.edu/.

University of Victoria, Faculty of Graduate Studies, Faculty of Science, School of Earth and Ocean Sciences, Victoria, BC V8W 2Y2, Canada. Offers M Sc, PhD. Part-time programs available. *Degree requirements:* For master's, thesis; for doctorate, thesis/dissertation, candidacy exam. *Entrance requirements:* For master's and doctorate, GRE. Additional exam requirements/recommendations for international students: Required—TOEFL (minimum score 575 paper-based), IELTS (minimum score 7). Electronic applications accepted. *Faculty research:* Climate modeling, geology.

University of Waterloo, Graduate Studies, Faculty of Science, Department of Earth Sciences, Waterloo, ON N2L 3G1, Canada. Offers M Sc, PhD. Part-time programs available. *Degree requirements:* For master's, research paper or thesis; for doctorate, comprehensive exam, thesis/dissertation. *Entrance requirements:* For master's, GRE, honors degree, minimum B average; for doctorate, GRE, master's degree, minimum B average. Additional exam requirements/recommendations for international students: Required—TOEFL, TWE. Electronic applications accepted. *Faculty research:* Environmental geology, soil physics.

The University of Western Ontario, Faculty of Graduate Studies, Physical Sciences Division, Department of Earth Sciences, London, ON N6A 5B8, Canada. Offers environment and sustainability (MES); geology (M Sc, PhD); geology and environmental science (M Sc, PhD); geophysics (M Sc, PhD); geophysics and environmental science (M Sc, PhD). *Degree requirements:* For master's, thesis; for doctorate, thesis/dissertation, qualifying exam. *Entrance requirements:* For master's, honors in B Sc; for doctorate, M Sc. Additional exam requirements/recommendations for international students: Required—TOEFL. *Faculty research:* Geophysics, geochemistry, paleontology, sedimentology/stratigraphy, glaciology/quaternary.

University of Windsor, Faculty of Graduate Studies, Faculty of Science, Department of Earth and Environmental Sciences, Windsor, ON N9B 3P4, Canada. Offers earth sciences (M Sc, PhD). Part-time programs available. *Degree requirements:* For master's, thesis; for doctorate, comprehensive exam, thesis/dissertation. *Entrance requirements:* For master's, minimum B average; for doctorate, minimum B average, copies of publication abstract. Additional exam requirements/recommendations for international students: Required—TOEFL (minimum score 560 paper-based). *Faculty research:* Aqueous geochemistry and hydrothermal processes, igneous petrochemistry, radiogenic isotopes, radiometric age-dating, diagenetic and sedimentary geochemistry.

Virginia Polytechnic Institute and State University, Graduate School, College of Science, Blacksburg, VA 24061. Offers biological sciences (MS, PhD); biomedical technology development and management (MS); chemistry (MS, PhD); economics (MA, PhD); geosciences (MS, PhD); mathematics (MS, PhD); physics (MS, PhD); psychology (MS, PhD); statistics (MS, PhD). *Faculty:* 259 full-time (68 women), 3 part-time/adjunct (all women). *Students:* 555 full-time (230 women), 31 part-time (12 women); includes 44 minority (10 Black or African American, non-Hispanic/Latino; 1 American Indian or Alaska Native, non-Hispanic/Latino; 11 Asian, non-Hispanic/Latino; 14 Hispanic/Latino; 8 Two or more races, non-Hispanic/Latino), 250 international. Average age 28. 1,091 applicants, 24% accepted, 137 enrolled. In 2012, 65 master's, 89 doctorates awarded. *Median time to degree:* Of those who began their doctoral program in fall 2004, 68% received their degree in 8 years or less. *Degree requirements:* For master's, comprehensive exam (for some programs), thesis (for some programs); for doctorate, comprehensive exam (for some programs), thesis/dissertation (for some programs). *Entrance requirements:* For master's and doctorate, GRE/GMAT (may vary by department). Additional exam requirements/recommendations for international students: Required—TOEFL (minimum score 550 paper-based). *Application deadline:* For fall admission, 8/1 for domestic students, 4/1 for international students; for spring admission, 1/1 for domestic students, 9/1 for international students. Applications are processed on a rolling basis. Application fee: $65. Electronic applications accepted. *Expenses:* Tuition, state resident: full-time $10,677; part-time $593.25 per credit hour. Tuition, nonresident: full-time $20,926; part-time $1162.50 per credit hour. *Required fees:*

$427.75 per semester. Tuition and fees vary according to course load, campus/location and program. *Financial support:* In 2012–13, 1 fellowship with full tuition reimbursement (averaging $21,606 per year), 159 research assistantships with full tuition reimbursements (averaging $19,950 per year), 331 teaching assistantships with full tuition reimbursements (averaging $17,426 per year) were awarded. Financial award application deadline: 3/1; financial award applicants required to submit FAFSA. *Total annual research expenditures:* $23.4 million. *Unit head:* Dr. Lay Nam Chang, Dean, 540-231-5422, Fax: 540-231-3380, E-mail: laynam@vt.edu. *Application contact:* Diane Stearns, Assistant to the Dean, 540-231-7515, Fax: 540-231-3380, E-mail: dstearns@vt.edu. Website: http://www.science.vt.edu/.

Washington University in St. Louis, Graduate School of Arts and Sciences, Department of Earth and Planetary Sciences, St. Louis, MO 63130-4899. Offers MA, PhD. Terminal master's awarded for partial completion of doctoral program. *Degree requirements:* For master's, thesis; for doctorate, thesis/dissertation. *Entrance requirements:* For master's and doctorate, GRE General Test. Electronic applications accepted.

Wesleyan University, Graduate Studies, Department of Earth and Environmental Sciences, Middletown, CT 06459. Offers MA. *Degree requirements:* For master's, thesis. *Entrance requirements:* For master's, GRE General Test, official transcripts, three recommendation letters, essay. Additional exam requirements/recommendations for international students: Required—TOEFL. *Application deadline:* For fall admission, 2/15 priority date for domestic students, 2/15 for international students. Applications are processed on a rolling basis. Application fee: $0. Electronic applications accepted. *Financial support:* Teaching assistantships with full tuition reimbursements and tuition waivers (full and partial) available. Financial award application deadline: 4/15; financial award applicants required to submit FAFSA. *Faculty research:* Tectonics, volcanology, stratigraphy, coastal processes, geochemistry. *Unit head:* Dr. Martha Gilmore, Chair, 860-685-3129, E-mail: mgilmore@wesleyan.edu. *Application contact:* Ginny Harris, Administrative Assistant, 860-685-2244, E-mail: vharris@wesleyan.edu. Website: http://www.weslean.edu/ees/.

West Chester University of Pennsylvania, College of Arts and Sciences, Department of Geology and Astronomy, West Chester, PA 19383. Offers earth-space science (Teaching Certificate); general science (Teaching Certificate); geoscience (MA). Part time and evening/weekend programs available. *Faculty:* 7 full-time (2 women). *Students:* 1 (woman) full-time, 16 part-time (3 women); includes 2 minority (1 Black or African American, non-Hispanic/Latino; 1 Hispanic/Latino). Average age 35. 5 applicants, 100% accepted, 4 enrolled. In 2012, 8 master's awarded. *Degree requirements:* For master's, comprehensive exam (for some programs), thesis or alternative. *Entrance requirements:* For master's, minimum GPA of 2.5. Additional exam requirements/recommendations for international students: Required—TOEFL (minimum score 550 paper-based; 80 iBT). *Application deadline:* For fall admission, 4/15 priority date for domestic students, 3/15 for international students; for spring admission, 10/15 priority date for domestic students, 9/1 for international students. Applications are processed on a rolling basis. Application fee: $45. Electronic applications accepted. *Expenses:* Tuition, state resident: full-time $7722; part-time $429 per credit. Tuition, nonresident: full-time $11,592; part-time $644 per credit. *Required fees:* $2108; $105.05 per credit. Tuition and fees vary according to campus/location and program. *Financial support:* Unspecified assistantships available. Support available to part-time students. Financial award application deadline: 2/15; financial award applicants required to submit FAFSA. *Faculty research:* Geoscience education, environmental geology, energy and sustainability, astronomy, meteorology. *Unit head:* Dr. Lee Anne Srogi, Chair, 610-436-2727, Fax: 610-436-3036, E-mail: lsrogi@wcupa.edu. *Application contact:* Dr. Martin Helmke, Graduate Coordinator, 610-436-3565, Fax: 610-436-3036, E-mail: mhelmke@wcupa.edu. Website: http://www.wcupa.edu/_academics/sch_cas.esc/.

Western Connecticut State University, Division of Graduate Studies, School of Arts and Sciences, Department of Physics, Astronomy and Meteorology, Danbury, CT 06810-6885. Offers earth and planetary sciences (MA). Part-time programs available. *Faculty:* 2 full-time (0 women). *Students:* 1 (woman) full-time, 3 part-time (all women). Average age 26. 6 applicants, 50% accepted, 2 enrolled.

In 2012, 5 master's awarded. *Degree requirements:* For master's, thesis, completion of program in 6 years. *Entrance requirements:* For master's, minimum GPA of 2.5 or GRE; one year each of calculus-based physics and calculus; semester course in differential equations. Additional exam requirements/recommendations for international students: Recommended—TOEFL (minimum score 550 paper-based; 79 iBT), IELTS (minimum score 6). *Application deadline:* For fall admission, 8/5 priority date for domestic students; for spring admission, 1/5 priority date for domestic students. Applications are processed on a rolling basis. Application fee: $50. *Expenses:* Contact institution. *Financial support:* In 2012–13, 1 student received support. Application deadline: 5/1; applicants required to submit FAFSA. *Faculty research:* Data collection and analysis of Gulf Stream surface temperature and circulation; science for visually impaired students including investigations of a satellite orbit, the Moon's surface, spectra of chemical elements and stars, the rotation of the Sun, and the spiral structure of our galaxy. *Unit head:* Dr. Dennis Dawson, Department Chair, 203-837-8671, E-mail: dawson@wcsu.edu. *Application contact:* Chris Shankle, Associate Director of Graduate Admissions, 203-837-9005, Fax: 203-837-8326, E-mail: shanklec@wcsu.edu. Website: http://www.wcsu.edu/physics/.

Western Kentucky University, Graduate Studies, Ogden College of Science and Engineering, Department of Geography and Geology, Bowling Green, KY 42101. Offers geoscience (MS). *Degree requirements:* For master's, comprehensive exam, thesis or alternative. *Entrance requirements:* For master's, GRE General Test, minimum GPA of 2.75. Additional exam requirements/recommendations for international students: Required—TOEFL (minimum score 555 paper-based; 79 iBT). *Faculty research:* Hydroclimatology, electronic data sets, groundwater, sinkhole liquification potential, meteorological analysis.

Western Michigan University, Graduate College, College of Arts and Sciences, Department of Geosciences, Program in Earth Science, Kalamazoo, MI 49008. Offers MA. *Degree requirements:* For master's, thesis or alternative, oral exam. *Entrance requirements:* For master's, GRE General Test.

Western Michigan University, Graduate College, College of Arts and Sciences, Department of Geosciences, Program in Geosciences, Kalamazoo, MI 49008. Offers MS, PhD. *Degree requirements:* For master's, oral exam; for doctorate, thesis/dissertation, oral exam. *Entrance requirements:* For master's and doctorate, GRE General Test.

Western Michigan University, Graduate College, College of Arts and Sciences, Mallinson Institute for Science Education, Kalamazoo, MI 49008. Offers science education (MA, PhD); science education: biological sciences (PhD); science education: chemistry (PhD); science education: geosciences (PhD); science education: physical geography (PhD); science education: physics (PhD). *Degree requirements:* For doctorate, thesis/dissertation, oral and written exams. *Entrance requirements:* For master's, undergraduate degree in a science or science education, teacher certification (or appropriate education courses); for doctorate, GRE General Test, master's degree in a science or science education. Additional exam requirements/recommendations for international students: Recommended—TOEFL. Electronic applications accepted. *Faculty research:* History and philosophy of science, curriculum and instruction, science content learning, college science teaching and learning, social and cultural factors in science education.

Yale University, Graduate School of Arts and Sciences, Department of Geology and Geophysics, New Haven, CT 06520. Offers biogeochemistry (PhD); climate dynamics (PhD); geochemistry (PhD); geophysics (PhD); meteorology (PhD); oceanography (PhD); paleontology (PhD); paleooceanography (PhD); petrology (PhD); tectonics (PhD). *Degree requirements:* For doctorate, thesis/dissertation. *Entrance requirements:* For doctorate, GRE General Test. Additional exam requirements/recommendations for international students: Required—TOEFL.

York University, Faculty of Graduate Studies, Faculty of Science and Engineering, Program in Earth and Space Science, Toronto, ON M3J 1P3, Canada. Offers M Sc, PhD. Part-time and evening/weekend programs available. *Degree requirements:* For master's, thesis or alternative; for doctorate, thesis/dissertation. Electronic applications accepted.

Hydrogeology

California State University, Bakersfield, Division of Graduate Studies, School of Natural Sciences, Mathematics, and Engineering, Program in Geology, Bakersfield, CA 93311. Offers geology (MS); hydrogeology (MS, Postbaccalaureate Certificate); petroleum geology (MS). Part-time and evening/weekend programs available. *Degree requirements:* For master's, thesis. *Entrance requirements:* For master's, GRE General Test, BS in geology.

California State University, Chico, Office of Graduate Studies, College of Natural Sciences, Department of Geological and Environmental Sciences, Program in Geosciences, Chico, CA 95929-0722. Offers hydrology/hydrogeology (MS). Part-time programs available. *Faculty:* 5 full-time (2 women), 3 part-time/adjunct (1 woman). *Students:* 6 full-time (4 women). Average age 33. 11

applicants, 45% accepted, 3 enrolled. In 2012, 1 master's awarded. *Degree requirements:* For master's, comprehensive exam, thesis. *Entrance requirements:* For master's, GRE, faculty mentor, statement of purpose. Additional exam requirements/recommendations for international students: Required—TOEFL (minimum score 550 paper-based; 80 iBT), IELTS (minimum score 6.5), Pearson Test of English (minimum score 59). *Application deadline:* For fall admission, 3/1 priority date for domestic students, 3/1 for international students; for spring admission, 9/15 priority date for domestic students, 9/15 for international students. Application fee: $55. Electronic applications accepted. *Expenses:* Tuition, state resident: part-time $372 per unit. Tuition, nonresident: part-time $372 per unit. *Required fees:* $2687 per semester. Tuition and fees vary according to course level and program. *Financial support:* Fellowships, research assistantships,

Peterson's Graduate Programs in the Physical Sciences, Mathematics, Agricultural Sciences, the Environment & Natural Resources 2014

www.petersonsbooks.com **171**

Hydrogeology

teaching assistantships, and career-related internships or fieldwork available. *Unit head:* Dr. David L. Brown, Chair, 530-898-5262, Fax: 530-898-5234, E-mail: geos@csuchico.edu. *Application contact:* Judy L. Rice, Graduate Admissions Coordinator, 530-898-5416, Fax: 530-898-3342, E-mail: jlrice@csuchico.edu. Website: http://catalog.csuchico.edu/viewer/12/GEOS.html.

Clemson University, Graduate School, College of Engineering and Science, Department of Environmental Engineering and Earth Sciences, Program in Hydrogeology, Clemson, SC 29634. Offers MS. Part-time programs available. *Students:* 11 full-time (6 women), 3 part-time (1 woman), 2 international. Average age 26. 18 applicants, 83% accepted, 6 enrolled. In 2012, 9 master's awarded. *Degree requirements:* For master's, thesis optional. *Entrance requirements:* For master's, GRE General Test, minimum GPA of 3.0 during previous 2 years. Additional exam requirements/recommendations for international students: Required—TOEFL. *Application deadline:* Applications are processed on a rolling basis. Application fee: $70 ($80 for international students). Electronic applications accepted. *Financial support:* In 2012–13, 8 students received support, including 3 research assistantships with partial tuition reimbursements available (averaging $17,784 per year), 5 teaching assistantships with partial tuition reimbursements available (averaging $17,784 per year); fellowships with full and partial tuition reimbursements available, career-related internships or fieldwork, institutionally sponsored loans, scholarships/grants, health care benefits, and unspecified assistantships also available. Support available to part-time students. Financial award application deadline: 6/1; financial award applicants required to submit FAFSA. *Faculty research:* Groundwater, geology, environmental geology, geophysics, geochemistry, remediation, modeling, sedimentology. *Total annual research expenditures:* $670,000. *Unit head:* Dr. Tanju Karanfil, Chair, 864-653-1005, Fax: 864-656-5973, E-mail: tkaranf@clemson.edu. *Application contact:* Dr. Jim W. Castle, Hydrogeology Graduate Program Coordinator, 864-656-5015, Fax: 864-656-1041, E-mail: jcastle@clemson.edu. Website: http://www.clemson.edu/ces/eees/gradprog/hydro/index.html.

East Carolina University, Graduate School, Thomas Harriot College of Arts and Sciences, Department of Geology, Greenville, NC 27858-4353. Offers geology (MS); hydrogeology and environmental geology (Certificate). Part-time programs available. *Degree requirements:* For master's, one foreign language, comprehensive exam, thesis. *Entrance requirements:* For master's, GRE General Test. Additional exam requirements/recommendations for international students: Required—TOEFL. *Expenses:* Tuition, state resident: full-time $4009. Tuition, nonresident: full-time $15,840. *Required fees:* $2111.

Illinois State University, Graduate School, College of Arts and Sciences, Department of Geography-Geology, Normal, IL 61790-2200. Offers hydrogeology (MS). *Degree requirements:* For master's, thesis optional. *Entrance requirements:* For master's, GRE General Test. *Faculty research:* Thermal transport within the hyporheic zone, nutrient cycling in watersheds, water quality in karst systems, ground water dating using dissolved helium.

Indiana University Bloomington, University Graduate School, College of Arts and Sciences, Department of Geological Sciences, Bloomington, IN 47405-7000. Offers biogeochemistry (MS, PhD); economic geology (MS, PhD); geobiology (MS, PhD); geophysics, structural geology and tectonics (MS, PhD); hydrogeology (MS, PhD); mineralogy (MS, PhD); stratigraphy and sedimentology (MS, PhD). *Faculty:* 17 full-time (1 woman). *Students:* 63 full-time (23 women), 3 part-time (1 woman); includes 3 minority (1 Black or African American, non-Hispanic/Latino; 1 Hispanic/Latino; 1 Two or more races, non-Hispanic/Latino), 15 international. Average age 29. 82 applicants, 26% accepted, 15 enrolled. In 2012, 10 master's, 4 doctorates awarded. Terminal master's awarded for partial completion of doctoral program. *Degree requirements:* For master's, thesis or alternative; for doctorate, comprehensive exam, thesis/dissertation. *Entrance requirements:* For master's and doctorate, GRE General Test. Additional exam requirements/recommendations for international students: Required—TOEFL. *Application deadline:* For fall admission, 1/15 priority date for domestic students, 12/15 for international students; for spring admission, 9/1 priority date for domestic students, 9/1 for international students. Applications are processed on a rolling basis. Application fee: $55 ($65 for international students). *Financial support:* In 2012–13, fellowships with full tuition reimbursements (averaging $17,300 per year), research assistantships with full tuition reimbursements (averaging $16,370 per year), teaching assistantships with full tuition reimbursements (averaging $15,150 per year) were awarded; career-related internships or fieldwork, Federal Work-Study, and institutionally sponsored loans also available. *Faculty research:* Geophysics, geochemistry, hydrogeology, geobiology, planetary science. *Total annual research expenditures:* $644,299. *Unit head:* Simon Brassell, Chair, 812-855-5581, Fax: 812-855-7899, E-mail: geochair@indiana.edu. *Application contact:* Mary Iverson, Graduate Secretary, 812-855-7214, Fax: 812-855-7899, E-mail: miverson@indiana.edu. Website: http://www.indiana.edu/~geosci/.

Montana Tech of The University of Montana, Graduate School, Geosciences Programs, Butte, MT 59701-8997. Offers geochemistry (MS); geological engineering (MS); geology (MS); geophysical engineering (MS); hydrogeological engineering (MS); hydrogeology (MS). Part-time programs available. *Degree requirements:* For master's, comprehensive exam (for some programs), thesis (for some programs). *Entrance requirements:* For master's, GRE General Test, minimum GPA of 3.0. Additional exam requirements/recommendations for international students: Required—TOEFL (minimum score 525 paper-based; 71 iBT). Electronic applications accepted. *Faculty research:* Water resource development, seismic processing, petroleum reservoir characterization, environmental geochemistry, geologic mapping.

Ohio University, Graduate College, College of Arts and Sciences, Department of Geological Sciences, Athens, OH 45701-2979. Offers environmental geochemistry (MS); environmental geology (MS); environmental/hydrology (MS); geology (MS); geology education (MS); geomorphology/surficial processes (MS); geophysics (MS); hydrogeology (MS); sedimentology (MS); structure/tectonics (MS). Part-time programs available. *Degree requirements:* For master's, thesis. *Entrance requirements:* Additional exam requirements/recommendations for international students: Required—TOEFL (minimum score 550 paper-based; 80 iBT) or IELTS (minimum score 6.5). Electronic applications accepted. *Faculty research:* Geoscience education, tectonics, fluvial geomorphology, invertebrate paleontology, mine/hydrology.

University of Hawaii at Manoa, Graduate Division, School of Ocean and Earth Science and Technology, Department of Geology and Geophysics, Honolulu, HI 96822. Offers high-pressure geophysics and geochemistry (MS, PhD); hydrogeology and engineering geology (MS, PhD); marine geology and geophysics (MS, PhD); planetary geosciences and remote sensing (MS, PhD); seismology and solid-earth geophysics (MS, PhD); volcanology, petrology, and geochemistry (MS, PhD). Part-time programs available. Terminal master's awarded for partial completion of doctoral program. *Degree requirements:* For master's, thesis optional; for doctorate, comprehensive exam, thesis/dissertation. *Entrance requirements:* For master's and doctorate, GRE General Test, minimum GPA of 3.0. Additional exam requirements/recommendations for international students: Required—TOEFL (minimum score 580 paper-based; 92 iBT), IELTS (minimum score 5).

University of Nevada, Reno, Graduate School, Interdisciplinary Program in Hydrologic Sciences, Reno, NV 89557. Offers hydrogeology (MS, PhD); hydrology (MS, PhD). Offered through the M. C. Fleischmann College of Agriculture, the College of Engineering, the Mackay School of Mines, and the Desert Research Institute. Terminal master's awarded for partial completion of doctoral program. *Degree requirements:* For master's, thesis optional; for doctorate, thesis/dissertation. *Entrance requirements:* For master's and doctorate, GRE General Test, minimum GPA of 3.0. Additional exam requirements/recommendations for international students: Required—TOEFL (minimum score 500 paper-based; 61 iBT), IELTS (minimum score 6). Electronic applications accepted. *Faculty research:* Groundwater, water resources, surface water, soil science.

The University of Texas at Dallas, School of Natural Sciences and Mathematics, Department of Geosciences, Richardson, TX 75080. Offers geochemistry (MS, PhD); geophysics (MS, PhD); geospatial information sciences (MS, PhD); hydrogeology (MS, PhD); sedimentary, stratigraphy, paleontology (PhD); stratigraphy, paleontology (MS); structural geology and tectonics (MS, PhD). Part-time and evening/weekend programs available. *Faculty:* 10 full-time (1 woman). *Students:* 45 full-time (18 women), 26 part-time (11 women); includes 9 minority (2 Black or African American, non-Hispanic/Latino; 4 Asian, non-Hispanic/Latino; 3 Hispanic/Latino), 23 international. Average age 30. 90 applicants, 31% accepted, 18 enrolled. In 2012, 7 master's, 4 doctorates awarded. *Degree requirements:* For master's, thesis optional; for doctorate, thesis/dissertation. *Entrance requirements:* For master's and doctorate, GRE General Test, minimum GPA of 3.0 in upper-level course work in field. Additional exam requirements/recommendations for international students: Required—TOEFL (minimum score 550 paper-based). *Application deadline:* For fall admission, 7/15 for domestic students, 5/1 for international students; for spring admission, 11/15 for domestic students, 9/1 for international students. Applications are processed on a rolling basis. Application fee: $50 ($100 for international students). Electronic applications accepted. *Expenses:* Tuition, state resident: full-time $11,940; part-time $663.33 per credit hour. Tuition, nonresident: full-time $21,606; part-time $1200.33 per credit hour. Tuition and fees vary according to course load. *Financial support:* In 2012–13, 33 students received support, including 12 research assistantships with partial tuition reimbursements available (averaging $22,270 per year), 9 teaching assistantships with partial tuition reimbursements available (averaging $15,300 per year); career-related internships or fieldwork, Federal Work-Study, institutionally sponsored loans, scholarships/grants, and unspecified assistantships also available. Support available to part-time students. Financial award application deadline: 4/30; financial award applicants required to submit FAFSA. *Faculty research:* Cybermapping, GPS applications for geophysics and geology, seismology and ground-penetrating radar, numerical modeling, signal processing and inverse modeling techniques in seismology. *Unit head:* Dr. John Oldow, Department Head, 972-883-2401, Fax: 972-883-2537, E-mail: geosciences@utdallas.edu. *Application contact:* Gloria Eby, Graduate Support Assistant, 972-883-2404, Fax: 972-883-2537, E-mail: geosciences@utdallas.edu. Website: http://www.utdallas.edu/geosciences.

West Virginia University, Eberly College of Arts and Sciences, Department of Geology and Geography, Program in Geology, Morgantown, WV 26506. Offers geomorphology (MS, PhD); geophysics (MS, PhD); hydrogeology (MS, PhD); paleontology (MS, PhD); petroleum geology (PhD); petrology (MS, PhD); stratigraphy (MS, PhD); structure (MS, PhD). Part-time programs available. Terminal master's awarded for partial completion of doctoral program. *Degree requirements:* For master's, thesis (for some programs); for doctorate, comprehensive exam, thesis/dissertation. *Entrance requirements:* For master's, GRE General Test, minimum GPA of 2.5; for doctorate, GRE General Test,

Hydrology

minimum GPA of 3.3. Additional exam requirements/recommendations for international students: Required—TOEFL.

Auburn University, Graduate School, Ginn College of Engineering, Department of Civil Engineering, Auburn University, AL 36849. Offers construction engineering and management (MCE, MS, PhD); environmental engineering (MCE, MS, PhD); geotechnical/materials engineering (MCE, MS, PhD); hydraulics/hydrology (MCE, MS, PhD); structural engineering (MCE, MS, PhD); transportation engineering (MCE, MS, PhD). Part-time programs available. *Faculty:* 21 full-time (2 women), 1 part-time/adjunct (0 women). *Students:* 48 full-time (16 women), 62 part-time (14 women); includes 6 minority (4 Black or African American, non-Hispanic/Latino; 1 Asian, non-Hispanic/Latino; 1 Hispanic/Latino), 37 international. Average age 26. 111 applicants, 59% accepted, 25 enrolled. In 2012, 26 master's, 2 doctorates awarded. *Degree requirements:* For master's, project (MCE), thesis (MS); for doctorate, comprehensive exam, thesis/dissertation. *Entrance requirements:* For master's and doctorate, GRE General Test. *Application deadline:* For fall admission, 7/7 for domestic students; for spring admission, 11/24 for domestic students. Applications are processed on a rolling basis. Application fee: $50 ($60 for international students). Electronic applications accepted. *Expenses:* Tuition, state resident: full-time $7866; part-time $437 per credit. Tuition, nonresident: full-time $23,598; part-time $1311 per credit. *Required fees:* $787 per semester. Tuition and fees vary according to degree level and program. *Financial support:* Fellowships, research assistantships, teaching assistantships, and Federal Work-Study available. Support available to part-time students. Financial award application deadline: 3/15; financial award applicants required to submit FAFSA. *Unit head:* Dr. J. Michael Stallings, Head, 334-844-4320. *Application contact:* Dr. George Flowers, Dean of the Graduate School, 334-844-2125.

Boise State University, College of Arts and Sciences, Department of Geosciences, Boise, ID 83725-0399. Offers earth science (M E Sci); geology (MS, PhD); geophysics (MS, PhD); hydrology (MS). Part-time programs available. *Faculty:* 16 full-time, 30 part-time/adjunct. *Students:* 43 full-time (11 women), 15 part-time (6 women); includes 1 minority (Black or African American, non-Hispanic/Latino), 3 international. 74 applicants, 78% accepted, 16 enrolled. In 2012, 15 master's, 3 doctorates awarded. *Degree requirements:* For master's, thesis. *Entrance requirements:* For master's, GRE General Test, BS in related field, minimum GPA of 3.0; for doctorate, GRE General Test. *Application deadline:* For fall admission, 3/1 priority date for domestic students; for spring admission, 10/1 priority date for domestic students. Applications are processed on a rolling basis. Application fee: $55. Electronic applications accepted. *Expenses:* Tuition, state resident: full-time $3486; part-time $312 per credit. Tuition, nonresident: full-time $5720; part-time $413 per credit. *Financial support:* In 2012–13, 4 fellowships with full and partial tuition reimbursements (averaging $11,333 per year), 19 research assistantships with full tuition reimbursements (averaging $11,153 per year), 11 teaching assistantships (averaging $10,834 per year) were awarded; career-related internships or fieldwork, Federal Work-Study, institutionally sponsored loans, scholarships/grants, tuition waivers (partial), and unspecified assistantships also available. Support available to part-time students. Financial award application deadline: 3/1. *Faculty research:* Seismology, geothermal aquifers, sedimentation, tectonics, seismo-acoustic propagation. *Unit head:* Dr. Clyde J. Northrup, Chairman, 208-426-1631, Fax: 208-426-4061. *Application contact:* Linda Platt, Office Services Supervisor, Graduate Admission and Degree Services, 208-426-1074, Fax: 208-426-2789, E-mail: lplatt@boisestate.edu.

California State University, Bakersfield, Division of Graduate Studies, School of Natural Sciences, Mathematics, and Engineering, Program in Geology, Bakersfield, CA 93311. Offers geology (MS); hydrogeology (MS, Postbaccalaureate Certificate); petroleum geology (MS). Part-time and evening/weekend programs available. *Degree requirements:* For master's, thesis. *Entrance requirements:* For master's, GRE General Test, BS in geology.

California State University, Chico, Office of Graduate Studies, College of Natural Sciences, Department of Geological and Environmental Sciences, Program in Geosciences, Chico, CA 95929-0722. Offers hydrology/hydrogeology (MS). Part-time programs available. *Faculty:* 5 full-time (2 women), 3 part-time/adjunct (1 woman). *Students:* 6 full-time (4 women). Average age 33. 11 applicants, 45% accepted, 3 enrolled. In 2012, 1 master's awarded. *Degree requirements:* For master's, comprehensive exam, thesis. *Entrance requirements:* For master's, GRE, faculty mentor, statement of purpose. Additional exam requirements/recommendations for international students: Required—TOEFL (minimum score 550 paper-based; 80 iBT), IELTS (minimum score 6.5), Pearson Test of English (minimum score 59). *Application deadline:* For fall admission, 3/1 priority date for domestic students, 3/1 for international students; for spring admission, 9/15 priority date for domestic students, 9/15 for international students. Application fee: $55. Electronic applications accepted. *Expenses:* Tuition, state resident: part-time $372 per unit. Tuition, nonresident: part-time $372 per unit. *Required fees:* $2687 per semester. Tuition and fees vary according to course level and program. *Financial support:* Fellowships, research assistantships, teaching assistantships, and career-related internships or fieldwork available. *Unit head:* Dr. David L. Brown, Chair, 530-898-5262, Fax: 530-898-5234, E-mail: geos@csuchico.edu. *Application contact:* Judy L. Rice, Graduate Admissions Coordinator, 530-898-5416, Fax: 530-898-3342, E-mail: jlrice@csuchico.edu. Website: http://catalog.csuchico.edu/viewer/12/GEOS.html.

Colorado School of Mines, Graduate School, Department of Geophysics, Golden, CO 80401-1887. Offers geophysical engineering (ME, MS, PhD); geophysics (MS, PhD); hydrology (MS, PhD); mineral exploration and mining geosciences (PMS). Part-time programs available. *Faculty:* 16 full-time (1 woman), 3 part-time/adjunct (0 women). *Students:* 90 full-time (28 women), 7 part-time (3 women); includes 12 minority (4 Black or African American, non-Hispanic/Latino; 1 American Indian or Alaska Native, non-Hispanic/Latino; 2 Asian, non-Hispanic/Latino; 5 Hispanic/Latino), 53 international. Average age 29. 183 applicants, 22% accepted, 29 enrolled. In 2012, 16 master's, 3 doctorates awarded. *Degree requirements:* For master's, thesis (for some programs); for doctorate, one foreign language, comprehensive exam, thesis/dissertation, oral exams. *Entrance requirements:* For master's and doctorate, GRE General Test. Additional exam requirements/recommendations for international students: Required—TOEFL (minimum score 550 paper-based; 80 iBT). *Application deadline:* For fall admission, 1/15 for domestic and international students; for spring admission, 10/15 for domestic and international students. Application fee: $50 ($70 for international students). Electronic applications accepted. *Financial support:* In 2012–13, 76 students received support, including 7 fellowships with full tuition reimbursements available (averaging $21,120 per year), 65 research assistantships with full tuition reimbursements available (averaging $21,120 per year), 4 teaching assistantships with full tuition reimbursements available (averaging $21,120 per year); scholarships/grants, health care benefits, and unspecified assistantships also available. Financial award application deadline: 1/15; financial award applicants required to submit FAFSA. *Faculty research:* Seismic exploration, gravity and geomagnetic fields, electrical mapping and sounding, bore hole measurements, environmental physics. *Total annual research expenditures:* $6.8 million. *Unit head:* Dr. Terence K. Young, Head, 303-273-3454, Fax: 303-273-3478, E-mail: tkyoung@mines.edu. *Application contact:* Michelle Szobody, Office Manager, 303-273-3935, Fax: 303-273-3478, E-mail: mszobody@mines.edu. Website: http://geophysics.mines.edu.

Colorado State University, Graduate School, Warner College of Natural Resources, Department of Forest and Rangeland Stewardship, Fort Collins, CO 80523-1472. Offers forest sciences (MS, PhD); natural resources stewardship (MNRS); rangeland ecosystem science (MS, PhD); watershed science (MS). Part-time programs available. Postbaccalaureate distance learning degree programs offered (no on-campus study). *Faculty:* 12 full-time (2 women). *Students:* 26 full-time (7 women), 80 part-time (34 women); includes 6 minority (1 American Indian or Alaska Native, non-Hispanic/Latino; 5 Hispanic/Latino), 11 international. Average age 35. 20 applicants, 100% accepted, 17 enrolled. In 2012, 17 master's, 3 doctorates awarded. *Degree requirements:* For master's, thesis (for some programs); for doctorate, comprehensive exam, thesis/dissertation. *Entrance requirements:* For master's, GRE General Test (minimum score 1000 verbal and quantitative), minimum GPA of 3.0, 3 letters of recommendation; for doctorate, GRE General Test (combined minimum score of 1100 on the Verbal and Quantitative sections), minimum GPA of 3.0, 3 letters of recommendation, statement of research interest. Additional exam requirements/recommendations for international students: Required—TOEFL (minimum score 550 paper-based; 80 iBT), IELTS (minimum score 6.5). *Application deadline:* For fall admission, 2/15 priority date for domestic students, 2/15 for international students; for spring admission, 7/15 priority date for domestic students, 7/15 for international students. Applications are processed on a rolling basis. Application fee: $50. Electronic applications accepted. *Expenses:* Tuition, state resident: full-time $8811; part-time $490 per credit. Tuition, nonresident: full-time $21,600; part-time $1200 per credit. *Required fees:* $1819; $61 per credit. *Financial support:* In 2012–13, 53 students received support, including 3 fellowships (averaging $14,767 per year), 36 research assistantships with full and partial tuition reimbursements available (averaging $16,479 per year), 14 teaching assistantships with full and partial tuition reimbursements available (averaging $6,991 per year); Federal Work-Study, scholarships/grants, and unspecified assistantships also available. Financial award application deadline: 2/15; financial award applicants required to submit FAFSA. *Faculty research:* Ecology, natural resource management, hydrology, restoration, human dimensions. *Total annual research expenditures:* $2.4 million. *Unit head:* Dr. Frederick Smith, Department Head and Professor, 970-491-7505, Fax: 970-491-6754, E-mail: fwsmith@colostate.edu. *Application contact:* Sonya LeFebre, Coordinator, 970-491-1907, Fax: 970-491-6754, E-mail: sonya.lefebre@colostate.edu. Website: http://warnercnr.colostate.edu/frws-home/

Peterson's Graduate Programs in the Physical Sciences, Mathematics, Agricultural Sciences, the Environment & Natural Resources 2014

www.petersonsbooks.com **173**

Hydrology

Cornell University, Graduate School, Graduate Fields of Engineering, Field of Civil and Environmental Engineering, Ithaca, NY 14853-0001. Offers engineering management (M Eng, MS, PhD); environmental engineering (M Eng, MS, PhD); environmental fluid mechanics and hydrology (M Eng, MS, PhD); environmental systems engineering (M Eng, MS, PhD); geotechnical engineering (M Eng, MS, PhD); remote sensing (M Eng, MS, PhD); structural engineering (M Eng, MS, PhD); structural mechanics (M Eng, MS); transportation engineering (MS, PhD); transportation systems engineering (M Eng); water resource systems (M Eng, MS, PhD). *Faculty:* 38 full-time (4 women). *Students:* 144 full-time (62 women); includes 20 minority (2 Black or African American, non-Hispanic/Latino; 8 Asian, non-Hispanic/Latino; 7 Hispanic/Latino; 3 Two or more races, non-Hispanic/Latino), 80 international. Average age 25. 738 applicants, 45% accepted, 87 enrolled. In 2012, 87 master's, 12 doctorates awarded. Terminal master's awarded for partial completion of doctoral program. *Degree requirements:* For master's, thesis (MS); for doctorate, comprehensive exam, thesis/dissertation. *Entrance requirements:* For master's and doctorate, GRE General Test (recommended), 2 letters of recommendation. Additional exam requirements/recommendations for international students: Required—TOEFL (minimum score 600 paper-based; 77 iBT). *Application deadline:* For fall admission, 1/15 priority date for domestic students; for spring admission, 10/15 for domestic students. Application fee: $95. Electronic applications accepted. *Financial support:* In 2012–13, 60 students received support, including 35 fellowships with full tuition reimbursements available, 16 research assistantships with full tuition reimbursements available, 9 teaching assistantships with full tuition reimbursements available; institutionally sponsored loans, scholarships/grants, health care benefits, tuition waivers (full and partial), and unspecified assistantships also available. Financial award applicants required to submit FAFSA. *Faculty research:* Environmental engineering, geotechnical engineering, remote sensing, environmental fluid mechanics and hydrology, structural engineering. *Unit head:* Director of Graduate Studies, 607-255-7560, Fax: 607-255-9004. *Application contact:* Graduate Field Assistant, 607-255-7560, Fax: 607-255-9004, E-mail: cee_grad@cornell.edu. Website: http://www.gradschool.cornell.edu/fields.php?id-27&a-2.

Cornell University, Graduate School, Graduate Fields of Engineering, Field of Geological Sciences, Ithaca, NY 14853. Offers economic geology (M Eng, MS, PhD); engineering geology (M Eng, MS, PhD); environmental geophysics (M Eng, MS, PhD); general geology (M Eng, MS, PhD); geobiology (M Eng, MS, PhD); geochemistry and isotope geology (M Eng, MS, PhD); geohydrology (M Eng, MS, PhD); geomorphology (M Eng, MS, PhD); geophysics (M Eng, MS, PhD); geotectonics (M Eng, MS, PhD); marine geology (MS, PhD); mineralogy (M Eng, MS, PhD); paleontology (M Eng, MS, PhD); petroleum geology (M Eng, MS, PhD); petrology (M Eng, MS, PhD); planetary geology (M Eng, MS, PhD); Precambrian geology (M Eng, MS, PhD); Quaternary geology (M Eng, MS, PhD); rock mechanics (M Eng, MS, PhD); sedimentology (M Eng, MS, PhD); seismology (M Eng, MS, PhD); stratigraphy (M Eng, MS, PhD); structural geology (M Eng, MS, PhD). *Faculty:* 37 full-time (5 women). *Students:* 32 full-time (13 women); includes 5 minority (2 Asian, non-Hispanic/Latino; 1 Hispanic/Latino; 2 Two or more races, non-Hispanic/Latino), 8 international. Average age 27. 58 applicants, 17% accepted, 6 enrolled. In 2012, 6 master's, 3 doctorates awarded. *Degree requirements:* For master's, thesis (MS); for doctorate, comprehensive exam, thesis/dissertation. *Entrance requirements:* For master's and doctorate, GRE General Test, 3 letters of recommendation. Additional exam requirements/recommendations for international students: Required—TOEFL (minimum score 550 paper-based; 77 iBT). *Application deadline:* For fall admission, 1/15 priority date for domestic students. Applications are processed on a rolling basis. Application fee: $95. Electronic applications accepted. *Financial support:* In 2012–13, 26 students received support, including 9 fellowships with full tuition reimbursements available, 16 research assistantships with full tuition reimbursements available, 1 teaching assistantship with full tuition reimbursement available; institutionally sponsored loans, scholarships/grants, health care benefits, tuition waivers (full and partial), and unspecified assistantships also available. Financial award applicants required to submit FAFSA. *Faculty research:* Geophysics, structural geology, petrology, geochemistry, geodynamics. *Unit head:* Director of Graduate Studies, 607-255-5466, Fax: 607-254-4780. *Application contact:* Graduate Field Assistant, 607-255-5466, Fax: 607-254-4780, E-mail: gradprog@geology.cornell.edu. Website: http://www.gradschool.cornell.edu/fields.php?id-30&a-2.

Drexel University, College of Engineering, Department of Civil, Architectural, and Environmental Engineering, Philadelphia, PA 19104-2875. Offers architectural / building systems engineering (PhD); architectural/building systems engineering (MS); civil engineering (MS, PhD); environmental engineering (MS, PhD); geotechnical, geoenvironmental and geosynthetics engineering (MS, PhD); hydraulics, hydrology and water resources engineering (MS, PhD); structures (MS). Part-time and evening/weekend programs available. *Degree requirements:* For master's, thesis optional; for doctorate, thesis/dissertation. *Entrance requirements:* For master's, minimum GPA of 3.0; for doctorate, minimum GPA of 3.5, MS in civil engineering. Additional exam requirements/recommendations for international students: Required—TOEFL. Electronic applications accepted. *Faculty research:* Structural dynamics, hazardous wastes, water resources, pavement materials, groundwater.

Idaho State University, Office of Graduate Studies, College of Science and Engineering, Department of Geosciences, Pocatello, ID 83209-8072. Offers geographic information science (MS); geology (MNS, MS); geology with emphasis in environmental geoscience (MS); geophysics/hydrology/geology (MS); geotechnology (Postbaccalaureate Certificate). Part-time programs available. *Degree requirements:* For master's, comprehensive exam, thesis, oral colloquium; for Postbaccalaureate Certificate, thesis optional, minimum 19 credits. *Entrance requirements:* For master's, GRE General Test (minimum 50th percentile in 2 sections), 3 letters of recommendation; for Postbaccalaureate Certificate, GRE General Test, 3 letters of recommendation, bachelor's degree, statement of goals. Additional exam requirements/recommendations for international students: Required—TOEFL (minimum score 550 paper-based; 80 iBT). Electronic applications accepted. *Faculty research:* Quantitative field mapping and sampling: microscopic, geochemical, and isotopic analysis of rocks, minerals and water; remote sensing, geographic information systems, and global positioning systems: environmental and watershed management; surficial and fluvial processes: landscape change; regional tectonics, structural geology; planetary geology.

Illinois State University, Graduate School, College of Arts and Sciences, Department of Geography-Geology, Normal, IL 61790-2200. Offers hydrogeology (MS). *Degree requirements:* For master's, thesis optional. *Entrance requirements:* For master's, GRE General Test. *Faculty research:* Thermal transport within the hyporheic zone, nutrient cycling in watersheds, water quality in karst systems, ground water dating using dissolved helium.

Massachusetts Institute of Technology, School of Engineering, Department of Civil and Environmental Engineering, Cambridge, MA 02139. Offers biological oceanography (PhD, Sc D); chemical oceanography (PhD, Sc D); civil and environmental engineering (M Eng, SM, PhD, Sc D); civil and environmental systems (PhD, Sc D); civil engineering (PhD, Sc D, CE); coastal engineering (PhD, Sc D); construction engineering and management (PhD, Sc D); environmental biology (PhD, Sc D); environmental chemistry (PhD, Sc D); environmental engineering (PhD, Sc D); environmental fluid mechanics (PhD, Sc D); geotechnical and geoenvironmental engineering (PhD, Sc D); hydrology (PhD, Sc D); information technology (PhD, Sc D); oceanographic engineering (PhD, Sc D); structures and materials (PhD, Sc D); transportation (PhD, Sc D); SM/MBA. *Faculty:* 34 full-time (7 women), 1 part-time/adjunct (0 women). *Students:* 224 full-time (85 women); includes 29 minority (4 Black or African American, non-Hispanic/Latino; 13 Asian, non-Hispanic/Latino; 6 Hispanic/Latino; 6 Two or more races, non-Hispanic/Latino), 129 international. Average age 26. 636 applicants, 25% accepted, 95 enrolled. In 2012, 67 master's, 18 doctorates, 1 other advanced degree awarded. *Degree requirements:* For master's and CE, thesis; for doctorate, comprehensive exam, thesis/dissertation. *Entrance requirements:* For master's and doctorate, GRE General Test. Additional exam requirements/recommendations for international students: Required—TOEFL (minimum score 577 paper-based; 90 iBT), IELTS (minimum score 7). *Application deadline:* For fall admission, 12/15 for domestic and international students. Application fee: $75. Electronic applications accepted. *Expenses: Tuition:* Full-time $41,770; part-time $650 per credit hour. *Required fees:* $280. *Financial support:* In 2012–13, 180 students received support, including 46 fellowships (averaging $32,400 per year), 117 research assistantships (averaging $30,800 per year), 22 teaching assistantships (averaging $31,800 per year); career-related internships or fieldwork, Federal Work-Study, institutionally sponsored loans, scholarships/grants, health care benefits, and unspecified assistantships also available. *Faculty research:* Environmental chemistry; environmental fluid mechanics and coastal engineering; environmental microbiology; geotechnical engineering and geomechanics; hydrology and hydroclimatology; infrastructure systems; mechanics of materials and structures; transportation systems. *Total annual research expenditures:* $20.7 million. *Unit head:* Prof. Markus Buehler, Head, 617-253-7101. *Application contact:* Graduate Admissions Coordinator, 617-253-7119, E-mail: cee-admissions@mit.edu. Website: http://cee.mit.edu/.

Missouri University of Science and Technology, Graduate School, Department of Civil, Architectural, and Environmental Engineering, Rolla, MO 65409. Offers civil engineering (MS, DE, PhD); construction engineering (MS, DE, PhD); environmental engineering (MS); fluid mechanics (MS, DE, PhD); geotechnical engineering (MS, DE, PhD); hydrology and hydraulic engineering (MS, DE, PhD). Part-time and evening/weekend programs available. Terminal master's awarded for partial completion of doctoral program. *Degree requirements:* For master's, thesis optional; for doctorate, comprehensive exam, thesis/dissertation. *Entrance requirements:* For master's, GRE General Test (minimum combined score 1100), minimum GPA of 3.0; for doctorate, GRE General Test (minimum score: verbal and quantitative 400, writing 3.5), minimum GPA of 3.0. Additional exam requirements/recommendations for international students: Required—TOEFL. Electronic applications accepted. *Faculty research:* Earthquake engineering, structural optimization and control systems, structural health monitoring/damage detection, soil-structure interaction, soil mechanics and foundation engineering.

Murray State University, College of Science, Engineering and Technology, Program in Water Science, Murray, KY 42071. Offers MS. Part-time programs available. *Degree requirements:* For master's, comprehensive exam, thesis. *Entrance requirements:* For master's, GRE General Test. Electronic applications accepted. *Faculty research:* Water chemistry, GIS, amphibian biology, nutrient chemistry, limnology.

New Mexico Institute of Mining and Technology, Graduate Studies, Department of Earth and Environmental Science, Program in Hydrology, Socorro, NM 87801. Offers MS, PhD. *Students:* 17 full-time (6 women), 8 part-time (4 women); includes 4 minority (3 Hispanic/Latino; 1 Two or more races, non-Hispanic/Latino), 4 international. Average age 29. In 2012, 4 master's, 1 doctorate awarded. *Degree requirements:* For master's, thesis; for doctorate, thesis/dissertation. *Entrance requirements:* For master's, GRE General Test; for doctorate, GRE General Test, GRE Subject Test. Additional exam requirements/recommendations for international students: Required—TOEFL (minimum score 540 paper-based). *Application deadline:* For fall admission, 3/1 priority date for domestic students; for spring admission, 6/1 for domestic students. Applications are processed on a rolling basis. Application fee: $16 ($30 for international students). *Expenses:* Tuition, state resident: full-time $5043; part-time $280 per credit hour. Tuition, nonresident: full-time $16,682; part-time $927 per credit hour. *Required fees:* $648; $18 per credit hour. $108 per semester. Part-time tuition and fees vary according to course load. *Financial support:* In 2012–13, 1 fellowship (averaging $3,210 per year), 12 research assistantships (averaging $15,160 per year), 3 teaching assistantships (averaging $6,294 per year) were awarded; Federal Work-Study, institutionally sponsored loans, and unspecified assistantships also available. Financial award application deadline: 3/1; financial award applicants required to submit CSS PROFILE or FAFSA. *Faculty research:* Surface and subsurface hydrology, numerical simulation, stochastic hydrology, water quality, modeling. *Unit head:* Dr. Fred Phillips, Coordinator, 575-835-5540, Fax: 575-835-6436, E-mail: phillips@nmt.edu. *Application contact:* Dr. Lorie Liebrock, Dean of Graduate Studies, 575-835-5513, Fax: 575-835-5476, E-mail: graduate@nmt.edu.

New Mexico State University, Graduate School, College of Agricultural, Consumer and Environmental Sciences, Department of Agricultural Economics and Agricultural Business, Las Cruces, NM 88003-8001. Offers agribusiness (M Ag, MBA); agricultural economics (MS); economic development (DED); economics (MA); water science management (MS). Part-time programs available. *Faculty:* 10 full-time (2 women). *Students:* 6 full-time (3 women), 6 part-time (4 women); includes 5 minority (all Hispanic/Latino), 2 international. Average age 30. 13 applicants, 46% accepted, 2 enrolled. In 2012, 6 master's awarded. *Degree requirements:* For master's, thesis (for some programs); for doctorate, comprehensive exam, thesis/dissertation. *Entrance requirements:* For master's, previous course work in intermediate microeconomics, intermediate macroeconomics, college-level calculus, statistics; for doctorate, previous course work in intermediate microeconomics, intermediate macroeconomics, college-level calculus, statistics, related MS or equivalent, minimum GPA of 3.0. Additional exam requirements/recommendations for international students: Required—TOEFL (minimum score 550 paper-based, 79 iBT), IELTS (minimum score 6.5). *Application deadline:* For fall admission, 7/1 priority date for domestic students, 7/1 for international students; for spring admission, 11/1 priority date for domestic students, 11/1 for international students. Applications are processed on a rolling basis. Application fee: $40 ($50 for international students). Electronic applications accepted. *Expenses:* Tuition, state resident: full-time $5239; part-time $218 per credit. Tuition, nonresident: full-time $18,266; part-time $761 per credit. *Required fees:* $1274; $53 per credit. *Financial support:* In 2012–13, 7 students received support, including 3 research assistantships (averaging $16,233 per year), 5 teaching assistantships (averaging $11,270 per year); career-related internships or fieldwork, Federal Work-Study, scholarships/grants, traineeships, health care benefits, and unspecified assistantships also available. Support available to part-time students. Financial award application deadline: 3/1. *Faculty research:* Natural resource policy, production economics and farm/ranch management, agribusiness and marketing, international marketing and trade, agricultural risk management. *Total annual research expenditures:* $1.4 million. *Unit head:* Dr. Terry Crawford, Interim Head, 575-646-3215, Fax: 575-646-3808, E-mail: crawford@nmsu.edu. *Application contact:* Dr. L. Allen Torell, Professor/Recruiting Contact, 575-646-4732, Fax: 575-646-3808, E-mail: atorell@nmsu.edu. Website: http://aces.nmsu.edu/academics/aeab/.

Stevens Institute of Technology, Graduate School, Charles V. Schaefer Jr. School of Engineering, Department of Civil, Environmental, and Ocean Engineering, Program in Civil Engineering, Hoboken, NJ 07030. Offers civil engineering (PhD); geotechnical engineering (Certificate); geotechnical/geoenvironmental engineering (M Eng, Engr); hydrologic modeling (M Eng); stormwater management (M Eng); structural engineering (M Eng, Engr); water resources engineering (M Eng). *Degree requirements:* For master's, thesis optional; for doctorate, variable foreign language requirement, thesis/dissertation; for other advanced degree, project or thesis. *Entrance requirements:* For doctorate, GRE. Additional exam requirements/recommendations for international students: Required—TOEFL. Electronic applications accepted.

Université du Québec, Institut National de la Recherche Scientifique, Graduate Programs, Research Center–Water, Earth and Environment, Québec, QC G1K 9A9, Canada. Offers earth sciences (M Sc, PhD); earth sciences-environmental technologies (M Sc); water sciences (M Sc, PhD). Part-time programs available. *Faculty:* 39. *Students:* 204 full-time (96 women), 20 part-time (9 women), 106 international. Average age 30. In 2012, 24 master's, 6 doctorates awarded. *Degree requirements:* For master's, thesis optional; for doctorate, thesis/dissertation. *Entrance requirements:* For master's, appropriate bachelor's degree, proficiency in French; for doctorate, appropriate master's degree, proficiency in French. *Application deadline:* For fall admission, 3/30 for domestic and international students; for winter admission, 11/1 for domestic and international students; for spring admission, 3/1 for domestic and international students. Application fee: $45. Electronic applications accepted. *Financial support:* In 2012–13, fellowships (averaging $16,500 per year) were awarded; research assistantships also available. *Faculty research:* Land use, impacts of climate change, adaptation to climate change, integrated management of resources (mineral and water). *Unit head:* Yves Begin, Director, 418-654-2524, Fax: 418-654-2600, E-mail: yves.begin@ete.inrs.ca. *Application contact:* Sylvie Richard, Registrar, 418-654-2518, Fax: 418-654-3858, E-mail: sylvie.richard@adm.inrs.ca. Website: http://www.ete.inrs.ca/.

The University of Arizona, College of Science, Department of Hydrology and Water Resources, Tucson, AZ 85721. Offers MS, PhD. Part-time programs available. *Faculty:* 11 full-time (1 woman), 3 part-time/adjunct (0 women). *Students:* 52 full-time (16 women), 6 part-time (3 women); includes 11 minority (1 American Indian or Alaska Native, non-Hispanic/Latino; 1 Asian, non-Hispanic/Latino; 4 Hispanic/Latino; 5 Two or more races, non-Hispanic/Latino), 13 international. Average age 31. 59 applicants, 29% accepted, 7 enrolled. In 2012, 9 master's, 5 doctorates awarded. *Degree requirements:* For master's, thesis; for doctorate, thesis/dissertation. *Entrance requirements:* For master's, GRE General Test, 3 letters of recommendation, bachelor's degree in related field; for doctorate, GRE General Test, minimum undergraduate GPA of 3.2, graduate 3.4; 3 letters of recommendation; master's degree in related field; master's thesis abstract. Additional exam requirements/recommendations for international students: Required—TOEFL (minimum score 550 paper-based; 79 iBT). *Application deadline:* For fall admission, 5/1 for domestic students, 12/1 for international students; for spring admission, 10/1 for domestic students, 6/1 for international students. Applications are processed on a rolling basis. Application fee: $75. Electronic applications accepted. *Financial support:* In 2012–13, 16 research assistantships with full tuition reimbursements (averaging $23,223 per year), 4 teaching assistantships with full tuition reimbursements (averaging $23,586 per year) were awarded; institutionally sponsored loans, scholarships/grants, health care benefits, and unspecified assistantships also available. Financial award application deadline: 1/31. *Faculty research:* Subsurface and surface hydrology, hydrometeorology/climatology, applied remote sensing, water resource systems, environmental hydrology and water quality. *Total annual research expenditures:* $1.7 million. *Unit head:* Kevin E. Lansey, Department Head, 520-621-7120, E-mail: lansey@email.arizona.edu. *Application contact:* Terrie Thompson, Academic Advising Coordinator, 520-621-3131, Fax: 520-621-1422, E-mail: programs@hwr.arizona.edu. Website: http://www.hwr.arizona.edu/.

University of California, Davis, Graduate Studies, Graduate Group in Hydrologic Sciences, Davis, CA 95616. Offers MS, PhD. Terminal master's awarded for partial completion of doctoral program. *Degree requirements:* For master's, comprehensive exam (for some programs), thesis (for some programs); for doctorate, thesis/dissertation. *Entrance requirements:* For master's, GRE General Test, minimum GPA of 3.0; for doctorate, GRE. Additional exam requirements/recommendations for international students: Required—TOEFL (minimum score 550 paper-based). Electronic applications accepted. *Faculty research:* Pollutant transport in surface and subsurface waters, subsurface heterogeneity, micrometeorology evaporation, biodegradation.

University of Colorado Boulder, Graduate School, College of Engineering and Applied Science, Department of Civil, Environmental, and Architectural Engineering, Boulder, CO 80309. Offers building systems (MS, PhD); construction engineering management (MS, PhD); environmental engineering (MS, PhD); geotechnical engineering and geomechanics (MS, PhD); hydrology, water resources and environmental fluid mechanics (MS, PhD); structural engineering and structural mechanics (MS, PhD). *Faculty:* 34 full-time (7 women). *Students:* 234 full-time (86 women), 52 part-time (15 women); includes 34 minority (1 Black or African American, non-Hispanic/Latino; 2 American Indian or Alaska Native, non-Hispanic/Latino; 12 Asian, non-Hispanic/Latino; 16 Hispanic/Latino; 3 Two or more races, non-Hispanic/Latino), 69 international. Average age 28. 513 applicants, 53% accepted, 58 enrolled. Terminal master's awarded for partial completion of doctoral program. *Degree requirements:* For master's, comprehensive exam, thesis or alternative; for doctorate, thesis/dissertation. *Entrance requirements:* For master's, GRE General Test, minimum undergraduate GPA of 3.0. *Application deadline:* For fall admission, 1/15 for domestic students, 12/1 for international students; for spring admission, 10/1 for domestic and international students. Application fee: $50 ($60 for international students). Electronic applications accepted. *Financial support:* In 2012–13, 208 students received support, including 87 fellowships (averaging $8,489 per year), 83 research assistantships with full and partial tuition reimbursements available (averaging $22,120 per year), 12 teaching assistantships with full and partial tuition reimbursements available (averaging $18,545 per year); institutionally sponsored loans, scholarships/grants, health care benefits, and unspecified assistantships also available. Financial award application deadline: 1/15; financial award applicants required to submit FAFSA. *Faculty research:* Civil, architectural, mechanical and environmental engineering; continuum mechanics. *Total annual research expenditures:* $11.9 million. *Application contact:* E-mail: cvengrad@colorado.edu. Website: http://ceae.colorado.edu/.

University of Colorado Denver, College of Engineering and Applied Science, Department of Civil Engineering, Denver, CO 80217. Offers civil engineering (EASPh D); civil engineering systems (PhD); environmental and sustainability engineering (MS, PhD); geographic information systems (MS); geotechnical engineering (MS, PhD); hydrology and hydraulics (MS, PhD); structural engineering (MS, PhD); transportation engineering (MS, PhD). Part-time and evening/weekend programs available. *Faculty:* 13 full-time (2 women), 10 part-time/adjunct (1 woman). *Students:* 66 full-time (14 women), 52 part-time (9 women); includes 26 minority (10 Black or African American, non-Hispanic/Latino; 6 Asian, non-Hispanic/Latino; 8 Hispanic/Latino; 2 Two or more races, non-Hispanic/Latino), 15 international. Average age 33. 72 applicants, 64% accepted, 19 enrolled. In 2012, 27 master's, 7 doctorates awarded. *Degree requirements:*

For master's, comprehensive exam, 30 credit hours, project or thesis; for doctorate, comprehensive exam, thesis/dissertation, 60 credit hours (30 of which are dissertation research). *Entrance requirements:* For master's, GRE, statement of purpose, transcripts, three references; for doctorate, GRE, statement of purpose, transcripts, references, letter of support from faculty stating willingness to serve as dissertation advisor and outlining plan for financial support. Additional exam requirements/recommendations for international students: Required—TOEFL (minimum score 537 paper-based; 75 iBT); Recommended—IELTS (minimum score 6.5). *Application deadline:* For fall admission, 5/15 for domestic students, 4/15 for international students; for spring admission, 10/1 for domestic students, 9/1 for international students. Applications are processed on a rolling basis. Application fee: $50 ($75 for international students). Electronic applications accepted. *Expenses:* Contact institution. *Financial support:* In 2012–13, 38 students received support. Fellowships, research assistantships, teaching assistantships, career-related internships or fieldwork, Federal Work-Study, institutionally sponsored loans, scholarships/grants, traineeships, and unspecified assistantships available. Financial award application deadline: 4/1; financial award applicants required to submit FAFSA. *Faculty research:* Earthquake source physics, environmental biotechnology, hydrologic and hydraulic engineering, sustainability assessments, transportation energy use and greenhouse gas emissions. *Unit head:* Dr. Kevin Rens, Chair, 303-556-8017, Fax: 303-556-2368, E-mail: kevin.rens@ucdenver.edu. *Application contact:* Maria Rase, Program Assistant, 303-556-6712, Fax: 303-556-2368, E-mail: maria.rase@ucdenver.edu. Website: http://www.ucdenver.edu/academics/colleges/Engineering/Programs/Civil-Engineering/Pages/CivilEngineering.aspx.

University of Florida, Graduate School, College of Liberal Arts and Sciences, Department of Geological Sciences, Gainesville, FL 32611. Offers hydrologic sciences (MS, MST, PhD); tropical conservation and development (MS, MST, PhD); wetland sciences (MS, MST, PhD). Terminal master's awarded for partial completion of doctoral program. *Degree requirements:* For master's, thesis (for some programs); for doctorate, one foreign language, thesis/dissertation. *Entrance requirements:* For master's, GRE General Test (minimum score of 1000), minimum GPA of 3.0; for doctorate, GRE General Test (minimum score of 1100), minimum GPA of 3.0. Additional exam requirements/recommendations for international students: Required—TOEFL (minimum score 550 paper-based; 80 iBT), IELTS (minimum score 6). Electronic applications accepted. *Faculty research:* Paleoclimatology, tectonophysics, petrochemistry, marine geology, geochemistry, hydrology.

University of Idaho, College of Graduate Studies, College of Science, Department of Geological Sciences, Moscow, ID 83844-3022. Offers geology (MS, PhD); hydrology (MS). *Faculty:* 10 full-time, 1 part-time/adjunct. *Students:* 20 full-time, 13 part-time. Average age 33. In 2012, 8 master's, 3 doctorates awarded. *Degree requirements:* For doctorate, one foreign language, thesis/dissertation. *Entrance requirements:* For master's, minimum GPA of 2.8; for doctorate, minimum undergraduate GPA of 2.8, 3.0 graduate. *Application deadline:* For fall admission, 8/1 for domestic students; for spring admission, 12/15 for domestic students. Applications are processed on a rolling basis. Application fee: $60. Electronic applications accepted. *Expenses:* Tuition, state resident: full-time $4230; part-time $252 per credit hour. Tuition, nonresident: full-time $17,018; part-time $891 per credit hour. *Required fees:* $2932; $107 per credit hour. *Financial support:* Fellowships, research assistantships, and teaching assistantships available. Financial award applicants required to submit FAFSA. *Faculty research:* Health effects of mineral dust, geomicrobiology, glacial and arctic sciences, optical mineralogy, planetary and terrestrial geomechanics. *Unit head:* Dr. Mickey Gunter, Head, 208-885-6192, E-mail: geology@uidaho.edu. *Application contact:* Erick Larson, Director of Graduate Admissions, 208-885-4723, E-mail: gadms@uidaho.edu. Website: http://www.uidaho.edu/sci/geology.

University of Nevada, Reno, Graduate School, Interdisciplinary Program in Hydrologic Sciences, Reno, NV 89557. Offers hydrogeology (MS, PhD); hydrology (MS, PhD). Offered through the M. C. Fleischmann College of Agriculture, the College of Engineering, the Mackay School of Mines, and the Desert Research Institute. Terminal master's awarded for partial completion of doctoral program. *Degree requirements:* For master's, thesis optional; for doctorate, thesis/dissertation. *Entrance requirements:* For master's and doctorate, GRE General Test, minimum GPA of 3.0. Additional exam requirements/recommendations for international students: Required—TOEFL (minimum score 500 paper-based; 61 iBT), IELTS (minimum score 6). Electronic applications accepted. *Faculty research:* Groundwater, water resources, surface water, soil science.

University of New Brunswick Fredericton, School of Graduate Studies, Faculty of Engineering, Department of Civil Engineering, Fredericton, NB E3B 5A3, Canada. Offers construction engineering and management (M Eng, M Sc E, PhD); environmental engineering (M Eng, M Sc E, PhD); environmental studies (M Eng); geotechnical engineering (M Eng, M Sc E, PhD); groundwater/hydrology (M Eng, M Sc E, PhD); materials (M Eng, M Sc E, PhD); pavements (M Eng, M Sc E, PhD); structures (M Eng, M Sc E, PhD); transportation (M Eng, M Sc E, PhD). Part-time programs available. *Faculty:* 18 full-time (1 woman). *Students:* 22 full-time (6 women), 17 part-time (4 women). In 2012, 13 master's, 2 doctorates awarded. *Degree requirements:* For master's, thesis, proposal; for doctorate, comprehensive exam, thesis/dissertation, qualifying exam; proposal; 27 credit hours of courses. *Entrance requirements:* For master's, minimum GPA of 3.0; B Sc E in civil engineering or related engineering degree; for doctorate, minimum GPA of 3.0; graduate degree in engineering or applied science. Additional exam requirements/recommendations for international students: Required—IELTS (minimum score 7.5), TWE (minimum score 4), Michigan English Language Assessment Battery (minimum score 85), Can Test (minimum score 4.75). *Application deadline:* For fall admission, 5/1 for domestic students; for winter admission, 11/1 for domestic students. Applications are processed on a rolling basis. Application fee: $50 Canadian dollars. Electronic applications accepted. Tuition and fees charges are reported in Canadian dollars. *Expenses: Tuition, area resident:* Full-time $3956 Canadian dollars. *Required fees:* $579.50 Canadian dollars; $55 Canadian dollars per semester. *Financial support:* In 2012–13, 35 fellowships, 48 research assistantships, 35 teaching assistantships were awarded; career-related internships or fieldwork and scholarships/grants also available. *Faculty research:* Construction engineering and management; engineering materials and infrastructure renewal; highway and pavement research; structures and solid mechanics; geotechnical and geoenvironmental engineering; structure interaction; transportation and planning; environment, solid waste management; structural engineering; water and environmental engineering. *Unit head:* Dr. Peter Bischoff, Director of Graduate Studies, 506-453-5103, Fax: 506-453-3568, E-mail: bischoff@unb.ca. *Application contact:* Joyce Moore, Graduate Secretary, 506-452-6127, Fax: 506-453-3568, E-mail: joycem@unb.ca. Website: http://go.unb.ca/gradprograms.

University of New Hampshire, Graduate School, College of Engineering and Physical Sciences, Department of Earth Sciences, Durham, NH 03824. Offers general (MS); geology (MS); hydrology (MS); ocean mapping (MS). *Faculty:* 17 full-time (5 women). *Students:* 15 full-time (8 women), 15 part-time (5 women); includes 1 minority (Black or African American, non-Hispanic/Latino), 4 international. Average age 27. 43 applicants, 53% accepted, 8 enrolled. In 2012, 15 master's awarded. *Degree requirements:* For master's, thesis. *Entrance requirements:* For master's, GRE General Test. Additional exam requirements/recommendations for international students: Required—TOEFL (minimum score 550 paper-based; 80 iBT). *Application deadline:* For fall admission, 4/1 priority date for domestic students, 4/1 for international students; for spring admission, 12/1 for domestic students. Applications are processed on a rolling basis. Application fee: $65. Electronic applications accepted. *Expenses:* Tuition, state resident: full-time $13,500; part-time $750 per credit. Tuition, nonresident: full-time $25,940; part-time $1089 per credit. *Required fees:* $1699; $424.75 per semester. *Financial support:* In 2012–13, 24 students received support, including 11 research assistantships, 7 teaching assistantships; fellowships, career-related internships or fieldwork, Federal Work-Study, scholarships/grants, and tuition waivers (full and partial) also available. Support available to part-time students. Financial award application deadline: 2/15. *Unit head:* Dr. Julie Bryce, Chairperson, 603-862-3139, E-mail: earth.sciences@unh.edu. *Application contact:* Sue Clark, Administrative Assistant, 603-862-1718, E-mail: earth.sciences@unh.edu. Website: http://www.unh.edu/esci/.

University of Southern Mississippi, Graduate School, College of Science and Technology, Department of Marine Science, Stennis Space Center, MS 39529. Offers hydrographic science (MS); marine science (MS, PhD). Part-time programs available. *Faculty:* 16 full-time (2 women). *Students:* 37 full-time (15 women), 7 part-time (4 women); includes 15 minority (4 Black or African American, non-Hispanic/Latino; 9 Asian, non-Hispanic/Latino; 2 Hispanic/Latino). Average age 31. 46 applicants, 48% accepted, 17 enrolled. In 2012, 18 master's, 1 doctorate awarded. *Median time to degree:* Of those who began their doctoral program in fall 2004, 100% received their degree in 8 years or less. *Degree requirements:* For master's, comprehensive exam, thesis, oral qualifying exam (marine science); for doctorate, 2 foreign languages, comprehensive exam, thesis/dissertation, oral qualifying exam. *Entrance requirements:* For master's, GRE General Test, minimum GPA of 3.0; for doctorate, GRE General Test, minimum GPA of 3.0 (undergraduate), 3.5 (graduate). Additional exam requirements/recommendations for international students: Required—TOEFL. *Application deadline:* For fall admission, 3/1 priority date for domestic students, 3/1 for international students. Application fee: $50. Electronic applications accepted. *Financial support:* In 2012–13, 4 students received support, including 35 research assistantships with full tuition reimbursements available (averaging $20,400 per year), 2 teaching assistantships with full tuition reimbursements available (averaging $20,400 per year); Federal Work-Study and institutionally sponsored loans also available. Financial award application deadline: 3/15. *Faculty research:* Chemical, biological, physical, and geological marine science; remote sensing; bio-optics; numerical modeling; hydrography. *Total annual research expenditures:* $6.4 million. *Unit head:* Dr. William M. Graham, Chair/Professor, 228-688-3177, Fax: 228-688-1121, E-mail: marine.science@usm.edu. *Application contact:* Linda Downs, Senior Office Support Specialist, 228-688-3177, Fax: 228-688-1121, E-mail: marine.science@usm.edu. Website: http://www.usm.edu/marine/.

University of Washington, Graduate School, College of Engineering, Department of Civil and Environmental Engineering, Seattle, WA 98195-2700. Offers civil engineering (MS, MSE, PhD); construction engineering (MSCE); environmental engineering (MS, MSCE, MSE, PhD); global trade, transportation and logistics (MS); hydrology, water resources, and environmental fluid mechanics (MS, MSCE, MSE, PhD); structural and geotechnical engineering and mechanics (MS, MSCE, MSE, PhD); transportation and construction engineering (MS, MSE, PhD); transportation engineering (MSCE). Part-time programs available. Postbaccalaureate distance learning degree programs offered (no on-campus study). *Faculty:* 48 full-time (11 women), 14 part-time/adjunct (2 women). *Students:* 214 full-time (81 women), 94 part-time (25 women); includes 50 minority (5 Black or African American, non-Hispanic/Latino; 2 American Indian or Alaska Native, non-Hispanic/Latino; 30 Asian, non-Hispanic/Latino; 11 Hispanic/Latino; 2

Native Hawaiian or other Pacific Islander, non-Hispanic/Latino, 75 international. 784 applicants, 53% accepted, 148 enrolled. In 2012, 106 master's, 7 doctorates awarded. Terminal master's awarded for partial completion of doctoral program. *Degree requirements:* For master's, thesis (for some programs); for doctorate, comprehensive exam, thesis/dissertation, general, qualifying, and final exams; completion of degree within 10 years. *Entrance requirements:* For master's, GRE General Test, minimum GPA of 3.0, statement of purpose, letters of recommendation, transcripts; for doctorate, GRE General Test, minimum GPA of 3.5, statement of purpose, letters of recommendation, transcripts. Additional exam requirements/recommendations for international students: Required—TOEFL (minimum score 580 paper-based; 92 iBT); Recommended—IELTS (minimum score 7). *Application deadline:* For fall admission, 1/10 for domestic and international students. Applications are processed on a rolling basis. Application fee: $75. Electronic applications accepted. *Expenses:* Contact institution.

Financial support: In 2012–13, 105 students received support, including 22 fellowships with full and partial tuition reimbursements available (averaging $18,558 per year), 65 research assistantships with full tuition reimbursements available (averaging $16,524 per year), 15 teaching assistantships with full tuition reimbursements available (averaging $16,524 per year); scholarships/grants also available. Financial award application deadline: 1/10; financial award applicants required to submit FAFSA. *Faculty research:* Structural and geotechnical engineering, transportation and construction engineering, water and environmental engineering. *Total annual research expenditures:* $12 million. *Unit head:* Dr. Gregory R. Miller, Professor/Chair, 206-543-0350, Fax: 206-543-1543, E-mail: gmiller@uw.edu. *Application contact:* Lorna Latal, Graduate Adviser, 206-543-2574, Fax: 206-543-1543, E-mail: llatal@u.washington.edu. Website: http://www.ce.washington.edu/programs/prospective/grad/applying/gen_admission.html.

Limnology

Baylor University, Graduate School, College of Arts and Sciences, Department of Biology, Waco, TX 76798. Offers biology (MA, MS, PhD); environmental biology (MS); limnology (MS). Part-time programs available. *Faculty:* 13 full-time (3 women). *Students:* 37 full-time (21 women), 4 part-time (3 women); includes 7 minority (3 Asian, non-Hispanic/Latino; 4 Two or more races, non-Hispanic/Latino), 15 international. In 2012, 7 master's, 2 doctorates awarded. *Degree requirements:* For master's, thesis (for some programs); for doctorate, thesis/dissertation. *Entrance requirements:* For master's and doctorate, GRE General Test. *Application deadline:* For fall admission, 1/31 priority date for domestic students. Applications are processed on a rolling basis. Application fee: $25. *Expenses: Tuition:* Full-time $24,426; part-time $1357 per semester hour. *Required fees:* $2556; $142 per semester hour. *Financial support:* Teaching assistantships, career-related internships or fieldwork, Federal Work-Study, institutionally sponsored loans, and tuition waivers (full and partial) available. Support available to part-time students. Financial award application deadline: 2/28. *Faculty research:* Terrestrial ecology, aquatic ecology, genetics. *Unit head:* Dr. Myeongwoo Lee, Graduate Program Director, 254-710-2141, Fax: 254-710-2969, E-mail: myeongwoo_lee@baylor.edu. *Application contact:* Tamara Lehmann, Administrative Assistant, 254-710-2911, Fax: 254-710-2969, E-mail: tamara_lehmann@baylor.edu. Website: http://www.baylor.edu/biology/.

Cornell University, Graduate School, Graduate Fields of Agriculture and Life Sciences, Field of Ecology and Evolutionary Biology, Ithaca, NY 14853-0001. Offers ecology (PhD), including animal ecology, applied ecology, biogeochemistry, community and ecosystem ecology, limnology, oceanography, physiological ecology, plant ecology, population ecology, theoretical ecology, vertebrate zoology; evolutionary biology (PhD), including ecological genetics, paleobiology, population biology, systematics. *Faculty:* 53 full-time (14 women). *Students:* 53 full-time (35 women); includes 7 minority (2 Asian, non-Hispanic/Latino; 3 Hispanic/Latino; 2 Two or more races, non-Hispanic/Latino), 11 international. Average age 28. 72 applicants, 15% accepted, 5 enrolled. In 2012, 8 doctorates awarded. *Degree requirements:* For doctorate, comprehensive exam, thesis/dissertation, 2 semesters of teaching experience. *Entrance requirements:* For doctorate, GRE General Test, GRE Subject Test (biology), 2 letters of recommendation. Additional exam requirements/recommendations for international students: Required—TOEFL (minimum score 550 paper-based; 77 iBT). *Application deadline:* For fall admission, 12/15 for domestic students. Application fee: $95. Electronic applications accepted. *Financial support:* In 2012–13, 52 students received support, including 59 fellowships with full tuition reimbursements available, 2 research assistantships with full tuition reimbursements available, 25 teaching assistantships with full tuition reimbursements available; institutionally sponsored loans, scholarships/grants, health care benefits, tuition waivers (full and partial), and unspecified assistantships also available. Financial award applicants required to submit FAFSA. *Faculty research:* Population and organismal biology, population and evolutionary genetics, systematics and macroevolution, biochemistry, conservation biology. *Unit head:* Director of Graduate Studies, 607-254-4230. *Application contact:* Graduate Field Assistant, 607-254-4230, E-mail: eeb_grad_req@cornell.edu. Website: http://www.gradschool.cornell.edu/fields.php?id-46&a-2.

University of Alaska Fairbanks, School of Fisheries and Ocean Sciences, Program in Marine Sciences and Limnology, Fairbanks, AK 99775-7220. Offers marine biology (MS, PhD); oceanography (PhD), including biological oceanography, chemical oceanography, fisheries, geological oceanography, physical oceanography. Part-time programs available. *Faculty:* 5 full-time (2 women), 1 part-time/adjunct (0 women). *Students:* 45 full-time (33 women), 17 part-time (13 women); includes 8 minority (3 Asian, non-Hispanic/Latino; 5 Hispanic/Latino), 8 international. Average age 29. 52 applicants, 25% accepted, 12 enrolled. In 2012, 4 master's, 5 doctorates awarded. *Degree requirements:* For

master's, comprehensive exam, thesis, oral defense; for doctorate, comprehensive exam, thesis/dissertation, oral defense. *Entrance requirements:* For master's and doctorate, GRE General Test. Additional exam requirements/recommendations for international students: Required—TOEFL (minimum score 550 paper-based; 80 iBT). *Application deadline:* For fall admission, 6/1 for domestic students, 3/1 for international students; for spring admission, 10/15 for domestic students, 8/1 for international students. Applications are processed on a rolling basis. Application fee: $60. Electronic applications accepted. *Expenses:* Tuition, state resident: full-time $7038. Tuition, nonresident: full-time $14,382. Tuition and fees vary according to course level, course load and reciprocity agreements. *Financial support:* In 2012–13, 31 research assistantships with tuition reimbursements (averaging $11,137 per year), 7 teaching assistantships with tuition reimbursements (averaging $11,750 per year) were awarded; fellowships with tuition reimbursements, career-related internships or fieldwork, Federal Work-Study, scholarships/grants, health care benefits, and unspecified assistantships also available. Support available to part-time students. Financial award application deadline: 7/1; financial award applicants required to submit FAFSA. *Unit head:* Katrin Iken, Co-Chair, 907-474-7289, Fax: 907-474-5863, E-mail: academics@sfos.uaf.edu. *Application contact:* Libby Eddy, Registrar and Director of Admissions, 907-474-7500, Fax: 907-474-7097, E-mail: admissions@alaska.edu. Website: http://www.sfos.uaf.edu/prospective/graduate/marinebio.php.

University of Florida, Graduate School, College of Agricultural and Life Sciences, Department of Fisheries and Aquatic Sciences, Gainesville, FL 32611. Offers MFAS, MS, PhD. Part-time programs available. *Degree requirements:* For master's, thesis (for MS); technical paper (for MFAS); for doctorate, comprehensive exam, thesis/dissertation. *Entrance requirements:* For master's and doctorate, GRE General Test, minimum GPA of 3.0. Additional exam requirements/recommendations for international students: Required—TOEFL (minimum score 550 paper-based; 80 iBT), IELTS (minimum score 6). Electronic applications accepted. *Faculty research:* Conservation and management of aquatic ecosystems; aquatic animal health; water quality, nutrients, and eutrophication; sustainable and quantitative fisheries; aquaculture or ornamental fish, marine baitfish, and shellfish.

University of Wisconsin–Madison, Graduate School, College of Engineering, Program in Limnology and Marine Science, Madison, WI 53706. Offers MS, PhD. *Faculty:* 28 full-time (7 women). *Students:* 16 full-time (4 women), 2 international. 41 applicants, 10% accepted, 4 enrolled. In 2012, 1 master's, 1 doctorate awarded. Terminal master's awarded for partial completion of doctoral program. *Degree requirements:* For master's, thesis; for doctorate, thesis/dissertation. *Entrance requirements:* For master's and doctorate, GRE General Test. Additional exam requirements/recommendations for international students: Required—TOEFL. *Application deadline:* For fall admission, 1/1 priority date for domestic students, 1/1 for international students. Application fee: $45. Electronic applications accepted. *Expenses:* Tuition, state resident: full-time $10,728; part-time $743 per credit. Tuition, nonresident: full-time $24,054; part-time $1575 per credit. *Required fees:* $1111; $72 per credit. *Financial support:* In 2012–13, fellowships with full tuition reimbursements (averaging $20,200 per year), 14 research assistantships with full tuition reimbursements (averaging $20,200 per year), 4 teaching assistantships with full tuition reimbursements (averaging $20,200 per year) were awarded; Federal Work-Study and institutionally sponsored loans also available. Financial award application deadline: 1/1. *Faculty research:* Lake ecosystems, ecosystem modeling, geochemistry, physiological ecology, chemical limnology. *Unit head:* Steven Loheide, Chair, 608-263-3264, E-mail: loheide@wisc.edu. *Application contact:* Mary Possin, Student Services Coordinator, 608-263-3264, Fax: 608-265-2340, E-mail: mcpossin@wisc.edu. Website: http://www.engr.wisc.edu/interd/limnology/.

Peterson's Graduate Programs in the Physical Sciences, Mathematics, Agricultural Sciences, the Environment & Natural Resources 2014

www.petersonsbooks.com **177**

Marine Geology

Cornell University, Graduate School, Graduate Fields of Engineering, Field of Geological Sciences, Ithaca, NY 14853. Offers economic geology (M Eng, MS, PhD); engineering geology (M Eng, MS, PhD); environmental geophysics (M Eng, MS, PhD); general geology (M Eng, MS, PhD); geobiology (M Eng, MS, PhD); geochemistry and isotope geology (M Eng, MS, PhD); geohydrology (M Eng, MS, PhD); geomorphology (M Eng, MS, PhD); geophysics (M Eng, MS, PhD); geotectonics (M Eng, MS, PhD); marine geology (MS, PhD); mineralogy (M Eng, MS, PhD); paleontology (M Eng, MS, PhD); petroleum geology (M Eng, MS, PhD); petrology (M Eng, MS, PhD); planetary geology (M Eng, MS, PhD); Precambrian geology (M Eng, MS, PhD); Quaternary geology (M Eng, MS, PhD); rock mechanics (M Eng, MS, PhD); sedimentology (M Eng, MS, PhD); seismology (M Eng, MS, PhD); stratigraphy (M Eng, MS, PhD); structural geology (M Eng, MS, PhD). *Faculty:* 37 full-time (5 women). *Students:* 32 full-time (13 women); includes 5 minority (2 Asian, non-Hispanic/Latino; 1 Hispanic/Latino; 2 Two or more races, non-Hispanic/Latino), 8 international. Average age 27. 58 applicants, 17% accepted, 6 enrolled. In 2012, 6 master's, 3 doctorates awarded. *Degree requirements:* For master's, thesis (MS); for doctorate, comprehensive exam, thesis/dissertation. *Entrance requirements:* For master's and doctorate, GRE General Test, 3 letters of recommendation. Additional exam requirements/recommendations for international students: Required—TOEFL (minimum score 550 paper-based; 77 iBT). *Application deadline:* For fall admission, 1/15 priority date for domestic students. Applications are processed on a rolling basis. Application fee: $95. Electronic applications accepted. *Financial support:* In 2012–13, 26 students received support, including 9 fellowships with full tuition reimbursements available, 16 research assistantships with full tuition reimbursements available, 1 teaching assistantship with full tuition reimbursement available; institutionally sponsored loans, scholarships/grants, health care benefits, tuition waivers (full and partial), and unspecified assistantships also available. Financial award applicants required to submit FAFSA. *Faculty research:* Geophysics, structural geology, petrology, geochemistry, geodynamics. *Unit head:* Director of Graduate Studies, 607-255-5466, Fax: 607-254-4780. *Application contact:* Graduate Field Assistant, 607-255-5466, Fax: 607-254-4780, E-mail: gradprog@geology.cornell.edu. Website: http://www.gradschool.cornell.edu/fields.php?id-30&a-2.

Massachusetts Institute of Technology, School of Science, Department of Earth, Atmospheric, and Planetary Sciences, Cambridge, MA 02139. Offers atmospheric chemistry (PhD, Sc D); atmospheric science (SM, PhD, Sc D); chemical oceanography (SM, PhD, Sc D); climate physics and chemistry (SM, PhD, Sc D); earth and planetary sciences (SM); geochemistry (PhD, Sc D); geology (PhD, Sc D); geophysics (PhD, Sc D); marine geology and geophysics (SM, PhD, Sc D); physical oceanography (SM, PhD, Sc D); planetary sciences (PhD, Sc D). *Faculty:* 33 full-time (6 women), 1 (woman) part-time/adjunct. *Students:* 166 full-time (77 women); includes 24 minority (3 Black or African American, non-Hispanic/Latino; 1 American Indian or Alaska Native, non-Hispanic/Latino; 9 Asian, non-Hispanic/Latino; 6 Hispanic/Latino; 5 Two or more races, non-Hispanic/Latino), 58 international. Average age 27. 232 applicants, 23% accepted, 27 enrolled. In 2012, 12 master's, 22 doctorates awarded. Terminal master's awarded for partial completion of doctoral program. *Degree requirements:* For master's, thesis; for doctorate, comprehensive exam, thesis/dissertation. *Entrance requirements:* For master's, GRE General Test; for doctorate, GRE General Test, GRE Subject Test (chemistry or physics for planetary science area). Additional exam requirements/recommendations for international students: Required—TOEFL (minimum score 577 paper-based; 91 iBT), IELTS (minimum score 7). *Application deadline:* For fall admission, 1/5 for domestic and international students; for spring admission, 11/1 for domestic and international students. Application fee: $75. Electronic applications accepted. *Expenses: Tuition:* Full-time $41,770; part-time $650 per credit hour. *Required fees:* $280. *Financial support:* In 2012–13, 108 students received support, including 62 fellowships (averaging $30,700 per year), 87 research assistantships (averaging $32,600 per year), 15 teaching assistantships (averaging $30,800 per year); Federal Work-Study, institutionally sponsored loans, scholarships/grants, health care benefits, and unspecified assistantships also available. *Faculty research:* Formation, dynamics and evolution of planetary systems; origin, composition, structure and dynamics of the atmospheres, oceans, surfaces and interiors of the Earth and other planets; evolution and interaction of the physical, chemical, geological and biological components of the Earth system; characterization of past, present and potential future climates and the causes and consequences of climate change; interplay of energy and the environment. *Total annual research expenditures:* $28.1 million. *Unit head:* Prof. Robert van der Hilst, Head, 617-253-2127, Fax: 617-253-8298, E-mail: eapsinfo@mit.edu. *Application contact:* EAPS Education Office, 617-253-3381, Fax: 617-253-8298, E-mail: eapsinfo@mit.edu. Website: http://eapsweb.mit.edu/.

University of Delaware, College of Earth, Ocean, and Environment, Newark, DE 19716. Offers geography (MA, MS, PhD); geology (MS, PhD); marine science and policy (MMP, MS, PhD), including marine policy (MMP), marine studies (MS, PhD), oceanography (PhD); ocean engineering (MS, PhD). *Degree requirements:* For master's, thesis; for doctorate, thesis/dissertation. *Entrance requirements:* For master's and doctorate, GRE General Test. Additional exam requirements/recommendations for international students: Required—TOEFL. Electronic applications accepted. *Faculty research:* Marine biology and biochemistry, oceanography, marine policy, physical ocean science and engineering, ocean engineering.

University of Hawaii at Manoa, Graduate Division, School of Ocean and Earth Science and Technology, Department of Geology and Geophysics, Honolulu, HI 96822. Offers high-pressure geophysics and geochemistry (MS, PhD); hydrogeology and engineering geology (MS, PhD); marine geology and geophysics (MS, PhD); planetary geosciences and remote sensing (MS, PhD); seismology and solid-earth geophysics (MS, PhD); volcanology, petrology, and geochemistry (MS, PhD). Part-time programs available. Terminal master's awarded for partial completion of doctoral program. *Degree requirements:* For master's, thesis optional; for doctorate, comprehensive exam, thesis/dissertation. *Entrance requirements:* For master's and doctorate, GRE General Test, minimum GPA of 3.0. Additional exam requirements/recommendations for international students: Required—TOEFL (minimum score 580 paper-based; 92 iBT), IELTS (minimum score 5).

University of Miami, Graduate School, Rosenstiel School of Marine and Atmospheric Science, Division of Marine Geology and Geophysics, Coral Gables, FL 33124. Offers MS, PhD. Terminal master's awarded for partial completion of doctoral program. *Degree requirements:* For master's, comprehensive exam, thesis; for doctorate, comprehensive exam, thesis/dissertation. *Entrance requirements:* For master's and doctorate, GRE General Test. Additional exam requirements/recommendations for international students: Required—TOEFL (minimum score 550 paper-based). Electronic applications accepted. *Faculty research:* Carbonate sedimentology, low-temperature geochemistry, paleoceanography, geodesy and tectonics.

University of Washington, Graduate School, College of the Environment, School of Oceanography, Seattle, WA 98195. Offers biological oceanography (MS, PhD); chemical oceanography (MS, PhD); marine geology and geophysics (MS, PhD); physical oceanography (MS, PhD). Terminal master's awarded for partial completion of doctoral program. *Degree requirements:* For master's, research project; for doctorate, thesis/dissertation. *Entrance requirements:* For master's and doctorate, GRE General Test, minimum GPA of 3.0. Additional exam requirements/recommendations for international students: Required—TOEFL. Electronic applications accepted. *Faculty research:* Global climate change, hydrothermal vent systems, marine microbiology, marine and freshwater biogeochemistry, biological-physical interactions.

Woods Hole Oceanographic Institution, MIT/WHOI Joint Program in Oceanography/Applied Ocean Science and Engineering, Woods Hole, MA 02543-1541. Offers applied ocean science and engineering (PhD); biological oceanography (PhD); chemical oceanography (PhD); marine geology and geophysics (PhD); physical oceanography (PhD). Program offered jointly with Massachusetts Institute of Technology. *Degree requirements:* For doctorate, thesis/dissertation. *Entrance requirements:* For doctorate, GRE General Test, GRE Subject Test. Additional exam requirements/recommendations for international students: Required—TOEFL. Electronic applications accepted.

Mineralogy

Cornell University, Graduate School, Graduate Fields of Engineering, Field of Geological Sciences, Ithaca, NY 14853. Offers economic geology (M Eng, MS, PhD); engineering geology (M Eng, MS, PhD); environmental geophysics (M Eng, MS, PhD); general geology (M Eng, MS, PhD); geobiology (M Eng, MS, PhD); geochemistry and isotope geology (M Eng, MS, PhD); geohydrology (M Eng, MS, PhD); geomorphology (M Eng, MS, PhD); geophysics (M Eng, MS, PhD); geotectonics (M Eng, MS, PhD); marine geology (MS, PhD); mineralogy (M Eng, MS, PhD); paleontology (M Eng, MS, PhD); petroleum geology (M Eng, MS, PhD); petrology (M Eng, MS, PhD); planetary geology (M Eng, MS, PhD); Precambrian geology (M Eng, MS, PhD); Quaternary geology (M Eng, MS, PhD); rock mechanics (M Eng, MS, PhD); sedimentology (M Eng, MS, PhD); seismology (M Eng, MS, PhD); stratigraphy (M Eng, MS, PhD); structural geology (M Eng, MS, PhD). *Faculty:* 37 full-time (5 women). *Students:* 32 full-time (13 women); includes 5 minority (2 Asian, non-Hispanic/Latino; 1 Hispanic/Latino; 2 Two or

178 www.petersonsbooks.com

Peterson's Graduate Programs in the Physical Sciences, Mathematics, Agricultural Sciences, the Environment & Natural Resources 2014

more races, non-Hispanic/Latino), 8 international. Average age 27. 58 applicants, 17% accepted, 6 enrolled. In 2012, 6 master's, 3 doctorates awarded. *Degree requirements:* For master's, thesis (MS); for doctorate, comprehensive exam, thesis/dissertation. *Entrance requirements:* For master's and doctorate, GRE General Test, 3 letters of recommendation. Additional exam requirements/recommendations for international students: Required—TOEFL (minimum score 550 paper-based; 77 iBT). *Application deadline:* For fall admission, 1/15 priority date for domestic students. Applications are processed on a rolling basis. Application fee: $95. Electronic applications accepted. *Financial support:* In 2012–13, 26 students received support, including 9 fellowships with full tuition reimbursements available, 16 research assistantships with full tuition reimbursements available, 1 teaching assistantship with full tuition reimbursement available; institutionally sponsored loans, scholarships/grants, health care benefits, tuition waivers (full and partial), and unspecified assistantships also available. Financial award applicants required to submit FAFSA. *Faculty research:* Geophysics, structural geology, petrology, geochemistry, geodynamics. *Unit head:* Director of Graduate Studies, 607-255-5466, Fax: 607-254-4780. *Application contact:* Graduate Field Assistant, 607-255-5466, Fax: 607-254-4780, E-mail: gradprog@geology.cornell.edu. Website: http://www.gradschool.cornell.edu/fields.php?id-30&a-2.

Indiana University Bloomington, University Graduate School, College of Arts and Sciences, Department of Geological Sciences, Bloomington, IN 47405-7000. Offers biogeochemistry (MS, PhD); economic geology (MS, PhD); geobiology (MS, PhD); geophysics, structural geology and tectonics (MS, PhD); hydrogeology (MS, PhD); mineralogy (MS, PhD); stratigraphy and sedimentology (MS, PhD). *Faculty:* 17 full-time (1 woman). *Students:* 63 full-time (23 women), 3 part-time (1 woman); includes 3 minority (1 Black or African American, non-Hispanic/Latino; 1 Hispanic/Latino; 1 Two or more races, non-Hispanic/Latino), 15 international. Average age 29. 82 applicants, 26% accepted, 15 enrolled. In 2012, 10 master's, 4 doctorates awarded. Terminal master's awarded for partial completion of doctoral program. *Degree requirements:* For master's, thesis or alternative; for doctorate, comprehensive exam, thesis/dissertation. *Entrance requirements:* For master's and doctorate, GRE General Test. Additional exam requirements/recommendations for international students: Required—TOEFL.

Application deadline: For fall admission, 1/15 priority date for domestic students, 12/15 for international students; for spring admission, 9/1 priority date for domestic students, 9/1 for international students. Applications are processed on a rolling basis. Application fee: $55 ($65 for international students). *Financial support:* In 2012–13, fellowships with full tuition reimbursements (averaging $17,300 per year), research assistantships with full tuition reimbursements (averaging $16,370 per year), teaching assistantships with full tuition reimbursements (averaging $15,150 per year) were awarded; career-related internships or fieldwork, Federal Work-Study, and institutionally sponsored loans also available. *Faculty research:* Geophysics, geochemistry, hydrogeology, geobiology, planetary science. *Total annual research expenditures:* $644,299. *Unit head:* Simon Brassell, Chair, 812-855-5581, Fax: 812-855-7899, E-mail: geochair@indiana.edu. *Application contact:* Mary Iverson, Graduate Secretary, 812-855-7214, Fax: 812-855-7899, E-mail: miverson@indiana.edu. Website: http://www.indiana.edu/~geosci/.

Université du Québec à Chicoutimi, Graduate Programs, Program in Mineral Resources, Chicoutimi, QC G7H 2B1, Canada. Offers PhD. Program offered jointly with Université du Québec à Montréal. Part-time programs available. *Degree requirements:* For doctorate, thesis/dissertation. *Entrance requirements:* For doctorate, appropriate master's degree, proficiency in French.

Université du Québec à Montréal, Graduate Programs, Program in Earth Sciences, Montreal, QC H3C 3P8, Canada. Offers earth sciences (M Sc); mineral resources (PhD); non-renewable resources (DESS). Part-time programs available. Terminal master's awarded for partial completion of doctoral program. *Degree requirements:* For master's, thesis (for some programs); for doctorate, thesis/dissertation. *Entrance requirements:* For master's, appropriate bachelor's degree or equivalent, proficiency in French. *Faculty research:* Economic geology, structural geology, geochemistry, Quaternary geology, isotopic geochemistry.

Université du Québec à Montréal, Graduate Programs, Program in Mineral Resources, Montréal, QC H3C 3P8, Canada. Offers PhD. Program offered jointly with Université du Québec à Chicoutimi. Part-time programs available. *Degree requirements:* For doctorate, thesis/dissertation. *Entrance requirements:* For doctorate, appropriate master's degree or equivalent, proficiency in French.

Paleontology

Cornell University, Graduate School, Graduate Fields of Engineering, Field of Geological Sciences, Ithaca, NY 14853. Offers economic geology (M Eng, MS, PhD); engineering geology (M Eng, MS, PhD); environmental geophysics (M Eng, MS, PhD); general geology (M Eng, MS, PhD); geobiology (M Eng, MS, PhD); geochemistry and isotope geology (M Eng, MS, PhD); geohydrology (M Eng, MS, PhD); geomorphology (M Eng, MS, PhD); geophysics (M Eng, MS, PhD); geotectonics (M Eng, MS, PhD); marine geology (MS, PhD); mineralogy (M Eng, MS, PhD); paleontology (M Eng, MS, PhD); petroleum geology (M Eng, MS, PhD); petrology (M Eng, MS, PhD); planetary geology (M Eng, MS, PhD); Precambrian geology (M Eng, MS, PhD); Quaternary geology (M Eng, MS, PhD); rock mechanics (M Eng, MS, PhD); sedimentology (M Eng, MS, PhD); seismology (M Eng, MS, PhD); stratigraphy (M Eng, MS, PhD); structural geology (M Eng, MS, PhD). *Faculty:* 37 full-time (5 women). *Students:* 32 full-time (13 women); includes 5 minority (2 Asian, non-Hispanic/Latino; 1 Hispanic/Latino; 2 Two or more races, non-Hispanic/Latino), 8 international. Average age 27. 58 applicants, 17% accepted, 6 enrolled. In 2012, 6 master's, 3 doctorates awarded. *Degree requirements:* For master's, thesis (MS); for doctorate, comprehensive exam, thesis/dissertation. *Entrance requirements:* For master's and doctorate, GRE General Test, 3 letters of recommendation. Additional exam requirements/recommendations for international students: Required—TOEFL (minimum score 550 paper-based; 77 iBT). *Application deadline:* For fall admission, 1/15 priority date for domestic students. Applications are processed on a rolling basis. Application fee: $95. Electronic applications accepted. *Financial support:* In 2012–13, 26 students received support, including 9 fellowships with full tuition reimbursements available, 16 research assistantships with full tuition reimbursements available, 1 teaching assistantship with full tuition reimbursement available; institutionally sponsored loans, scholarships/grants, health care benefits, tuition waivers (full and partial), and unspecified assistantships also available. Financial award applicants required to submit FAFSA. *Faculty research:* Geophysics, structural geology, petrology, geochemistry, geodynamics. *Unit head:* Director of Graduate Studies, 607-255-5466, Fax: 607-254-4780. *Application contact:* Graduate Field Assistant, 607-255-5466, Fax: 607-254-4780, E-mail: gradprog@geology.cornell.edu. Website: http://www.gradschool.cornell.edu/fields.php?id-30&a-2.

Duke University, Graduate School, Department of Biological Anthropology and Anatomy, Durham, NC 27710. Offers cellular and molecular biology (PhD); gross anatomy and physical anthropology (PhD), including comparative morphology of human and non-human primates, primate social behavior, vertebrate paleoanatomy; neuroanatomy (PhD). *Faculty:* 9 full-time. *Students:* 13 full-time (7 women); includes 3 minority (1 Black or African American, non-Hispanic/Latino; 2 Hispanic/Latino), 7 international. 71 applicants, 3% accepted, 2 enrolled. In 2012, 1 doctorate awarded. *Degree requirements:* For doctorate, one foreign language, thesis/dissertation. *Entrance requirements:* For doctorate, GRE General Test. Additional exam requirements/recommendations for international students: Required—TOEFL (minimum score 550 paper-based; 83 iBT), IELTS (minimum score 7). *Application deadline:* For fall admission, 12/8 priority date for domestic students, 12/8 for international students. Application fee: $80. Electronic applications accepted. *Financial support:* Fellowships, teaching assistantships, and Federal Work Study available. Financial award application deadline: 12/31. *Unit head:* Daniel Schmitt, Director of Graduate Studies, 919-684-4124, Fax: 919-684-8542, E-mail: mlsquire@duke.edu. *Application contact:* Elizabeth Hutton, Director of Admissions, 919-684-3913, Fax: 919-684-2277, E-mail: grad-admissions@duke.edu. Website: http://www.baa.duke.edu/.

East Tennessee State University, School of Graduate Studies, College of Arts and Sciences, Department of Biological Sciences, Johnson City, TN 37614. Offers biology (MS); biomedical sciences (MS); microbiology (MS); paleontology (MS). *Faculty:* 21 full-time (5 women), 6 part-time/adjunct (1 woman). *Students:* 38 full-time (15 women), 3 part-time (1 woman); includes 3 minority (1 Black or African American, non-Hispanic/Latino; 2 Asian, non-Hispanic/Latino), 17 international. 64 applicants, 42% accepted, 24 enrolled. In 2012, 11 master's awarded. *Degree requirements:* For master's, comprehensive exam, thesis. *Entrance requirements:* For master's, GRE General Test or GRE Subject Test, minimum GPA of 3.0, undergraduate degree in life or physical sciences, two letters of recommendation. Additional exam requirements/recommendations for international students: Required—TOEFL (minimum score 550 paper-based; 79 iBT). *Application deadline:* For fall admission, 4/1 for domestic students, 2/1 for international students; for spring admission, 9/1 for domestic students, 7/1 for international students. Application fee: $35 ($45 for international students). Electronic applications accepted. *Financial support:* In 2012–13, 36 students received support, including 2 research assistantships with full tuition reimbursements available (averaging $9,000 per year), 30 teaching assistantships with full tuition reimbursements available (averaging $8,500 per year); institutionally sponsored loans, scholarships/grants, and unspecified assistantships also available. Financial award application deadline: 7/1; financial award applicants required to submit FAFSA. *Faculty research:* Neuroethology, chronobiology, molecular biology, behavioral ecology, systematics, paleobotany. *Unit head:* Dr. Darrell Moore, Interim Chair, 423-439-4329, Fax: 423-439-5958, E-mail: zavadam@etsu.edu. *Application contact:* Gail Powers, Graduate Specialist, 423-439-4703, Fax: 423-439-5624, E-mail: powersg@etsu.edu.

East Tennessee State University, School of Graduate Studies, College of Arts and Sciences, Department of Geosciences, Johnson City, TN 37614. Offers geospatial analysis (MS); paleontology (MS). Part-time programs available. *Faculty:* 8 full-time (2 women), 2 part-time/adjunct (1 woman). *Students:* 11 full-

Peterson's Graduate Programs in the Physical Sciences, Mathematics, Agricultural Sciences, the Environment & Natural Resources 2014

www.petersonsbooks.com **179**

time (3 women), 3 part-time (1 woman); includes 2 minority (both Two or more races, non-Hispanic/Latino). 13 applicants, 46% accepted, 5 enrolled. *Degree requirements:* For master's, thesis. *Entrance requirements:* For master's, bachelor's degree in geosciences or related discipline, minimum GPA of 3.0, three letters of recommendation, resume. Additional exam requirements/recommendations for international students: Required—TOEFL (minimum score 550 paper-based; 79 iBT). *Application deadline:* For fall admission, 2/1 for domestic and international students. Application fee: $35 ($45 for international students). Electronic applications accepted. *Financial support:* In 2012–13, 12 students received support, including 6 research assistantships with full tuition reimbursements available (averaging $8,000 per year), 6 teaching assistantships with full tuition reimbursements available (averaging $9,500 per year); career-related internships or fieldwork, institutionally sponsored loans, scholarships/grants, and unspecified assistantships also available. Financial award application deadline: 7/1; financial award applicants required to submit FAFSA. *Faculty research:* Vertebrate paleontology; volcanology; soils and geological engineering; geological hazards stemming from volcanoes and tsunamis and the sociological responses; applications of geospatial analysis to meteorology, weather and climate, and geomorphology/watershed management; shallow surface geophysics, sedimentology, and stratigraphy. *Unit head:* Dr. Jim Mead, Chair, 423-439-7515, Fax: 423-439-7520, E-mail: mead@etsu.edu. *Application contact:* Gail Powers, Graduate Specialist, 423-439-4703, Fax: 423-439-5624, E-mail: powersg@etsu.edu. Website: http://www.etsu.edu/cas/geosciences/.

South Dakota School of Mines and Technology, Graduate Division, Department of Geology and Geological Engineering, Rapid City, SD 57701-3995. Offers geology and geological engineering (MS, PhD); paleontology (MS). Part-time programs available. *Faculty:* 13 full-time (3 women). *Students:* 23 full-time (10 women), 12 part-time (4 women); includes 4 minority (1 American Indian or Alaska Native, non-Hispanic/Latino; 2 Hispanic/Latino; 1 Two or more races, non-Hispanic/Latino), 6 international. Average age 30. 19 applicants, 63% accepted, 8 enrolled. In 2012, 10 master's awarded. *Degree requirements:* For master's, thesis; for doctorate, thesis/dissertation. *Entrance requirements:* For master's and doctorate, GRE General Test, GRE Subject Test. Additional exam requirements/recommendations for international students: Required—TOEFL (minimum score 520 paper-based; 68 iBT), TWE. *Application deadline:* For fall admission, 7/1 priority date for domestic students, 4/1 for international students; for spring admission, 11/1 for domestic students, 9/1 for international students. Applications are processed on a rolling basis. Application fee: $35. Electronic applications accepted. *Expenses:* Tuition, state resident: full-time $4720; part-time $196.80 per credit hour. Tuition, nonresident: full-time $10,000; part-time $416.55 per credit hour. *Required fees:* $4360. *Financial support:* In 2012–13, 7 research assistantships with partial tuition reimbursements (averaging $3,724 per year), 9 teaching assistantships with partial tuition reimbursements (averaging $2,913 per year) were awarded; fellowships, Federal Work-Study, and institutionally sponsored loans also available. Support available to part-time students. Financial award application deadline: 5/15. *Faculty research:* Contaminants in soil, nitrate leaching, environmental changes, fracture formations, greenhouse effect. *Total annual research expenditures:* $787,393. *Unit head:* Dr. Maribeth Price, Chair, 605-394-1290, E-mail: laurie.anderson@sdsmt.edu. *Application contact:* Linda Carlson, Office of Graduate Education, 605-355-3468, Fax: 605-394-1767, E-mail: linda.carlson@sdsmt.edu.

South Dakota School of Mines and Technology, Graduate Division, Program in Paleontology, Rapid City, SD 57701-3995. Offers MS. Part-time programs available. *Faculty:* 13 full-time (3 women). *Students:* 9 full-time (5 women), 6 part-time (4 women). Average age 26. 6 applicants, 50% accepted, 2 enrolled. In 2012, 1 master's awarded. *Degree requirements:* For master's, thesis. *Entrance requirements:* For master's, GRE General Test, GRE Subject Test. Additional exam requirements/recommendations for international students: Required—TOEFL (minimum score 520 paper-based; 68 iBT), TWE. *Application deadline:* For fall admission, 7/1 priority date for domestic students, 4/1 for international students; for spring admission, 11/1 for domestic students, 9/1 for international students. Applications are processed on a rolling basis. Application fee: $35. Electronic applications accepted. *Expenses:* Tuition, state resident: full-time $4720; part-time $196.80 per credit hour. Tuition, nonresident: full-time $10,000; part-time $416.55 per credit hour. *Required fees:* $4360. *Financial support:* Fellowships, research assistantships with partial tuition reimbursements, teaching assistantships with partial tuition reimbursements, Federal Work-Study, and institutionally sponsored loans available. Support available to part-time students. Financial award application deadline: 5/15. *Faculty research:* Cretaceous, Miocene, and Oligocene vertebrates. *Unit head:* Dr. Laurie Anderson, Department Head, 605-394-1290, E-mail: laurie.anderson@sdsmt.edu. *Application contact:* Linda Carlson, Office of Graduate Education, 605-355-3468, Fax: 605-394-1767, E-mail: linda.carlson@sdsmt.edu. Website: http://www.sdsmt.edu/Academics/Departments/Geology-and-Geological-Engineering/Graduate-Education/Paleontology-MS/.

University of Chicago, Division of the Physical Sciences, Department of the Geophysical Sciences, Chicago, IL 60637-1513. Offers atmospheric sciences (SM, PhD); cosmochemistry (PhD); earth sciences (SM, PhD); paleobiology (PhD); planetary and space sciences (SM, PhD). Terminal master's awarded for partial completion of doctoral program. *Degree requirements:* For master's, thesis, seminar; for doctorate, variable foreign language requirement, comprehensive exam, thesis/dissertation. *Entrance requirements:* For doctorate, GRE General Test. Additional exam requirements/recommendations for international students: Required—TOEFL (minimum score 600 paper-based; 96 iBT), IELTS (minimum score 7). Electronic applications accepted. *Faculty research:* Climatology, evolutionary paleontology, cosmochemistry, geochemistry, oceanic sciences.

The University of Manchester, School of Earth, Atmospheric and Environmental Sciences, Manchester, United Kingdom. Offers atmospheric sciences (M Phil, M Sc, PhD); basin studies and petroleum geosciences (M Phil, M Sc, PhD); earth, atmospheric and environmental sciences (M Phil, M Sc, PhD); environmental geochemistry and cosmochemistry (M Phil, M Sc, PhD); isotope geochemistry and cosmochemistry (M Phil, M Sc, PhD); paleontology (M Phil, M Sc, PhD); physics and chemistry of minerals and fluids (M Phil, M Sc, PhD); structural and petrological geosciences (M Phil, M Sc, PhD).

The University of Texas at Dallas, School of Natural Sciences and Mathematics, Department of Geosciences, Richardson, TX 75080. Offers geochemistry (MS, PhD); geophysics (MS, PhD); geospatial information sciences (MS, PhD); hydrogeology (MS, PhD); sedimentary, stratigraphy, paleontology (PhD); stratigraphy, paleontology (MS); structural geology and tectonics (MS, PhD). Part-time and evening/weekend programs available. *Faculty:* 10 full-time (1 woman). *Students:* 45 full-time (18 women), 26 part-time (11 women); includes 9 minority (2 Black or African American, non-Hispanic/Latino; 4 Asian, non-Hispanic/Latino; 3 Hispanic/Latino), 23 international. Average age 30. 90 applicants, 31% accepted, 18 enrolled. In 2012, 7 master's, 4 doctorates awarded. *Degree requirements:* For master's, thesis optional; for doctorate, thesis/dissertation. *Entrance requirements:* For master's and doctorate, GRE General Test, minimum GPA of 3.0 in upper-level course work in field. Additional exam requirements/recommendations for international students: Required—TOEFL (minimum score 550 paper-based). *Application deadline:* For fall admission, 7/15 for domestic students, 5/1 for international students; for spring admission, 11/15 for domestic students, 9/1 for international students. Applications are processed on a rolling basis. Application fee: $50 ($100 for international students). Electronic applications accepted. *Expenses:* Tuition, state resident: full-time $11,940; part-time $663.33 per credit hour. Tuition, nonresident: full-time $21,606; part-time $1200.33 per credit hour. Tuition and fees vary according to course load. *Financial support:* In 2012–13, 33 students received support, including 12 research assistantships with partial tuition reimbursements available (averaging $22,270 per year), 9 teaching assistantships with partial tuition reimbursements available (averaging $15,300 per year); career-related internships or fieldwork, Federal Work-Study, institutionally sponsored loans, scholarships/grants, and unspecified assistantships also available. Support available to part-time students. Financial award application deadline: 4/30; financial award applicants required to submit FAFSA. *Faculty research:* Cybermapping, GPS applications for geophysics and geology, seismology and ground-penetrating radar, numerical modeling, signal processing and inverse modeling techniques in seismology. *Unit head:* Dr. John Oldow, Department Head, 972-883-2401, Fax: 972-883-2537, E-mail: geosciences@utdallas.edu. *Application contact:* Gloria Eby, Graduate Support Assistant, 972-883-2404, Fax: 972-883-2537, E-mail: geosciences@utdallas.edu. Website: http://www.utdallas.edu/geosciences.

West Virginia University, Eberly College of Arts and Sciences, Department of Geology and Geography, Program in Geology, Morgantown, WV 26506. Offers geomorphology (MS, PhD); geophysics (MS, PhD); hydrogeology (MS, PhD); paleontology (MS, PhD); petroleum geology (PhD); petrology (MS, PhD); stratigraphy (MS, PhD); structure (MS, PhD). Part-time programs available. Terminal master's awarded for partial completion of doctoral program. *Degree requirements:* For master's, thesis (for some programs); for doctorate, comprehensive exam, thesis/dissertation. *Entrance requirements:* For master's, GRE General Test, minimum GPA of 2.5; for doctorate, GRE General Test, minimum GPA of 3.3. Additional exam requirements/recommendations for international students: Required—TOEFL.

Yale University, Graduate School of Arts and Sciences, Department of Geology and Geophysics, New Haven, CT 06520. Offers biogeochemistry (PhD); climate dynamics (PhD); geochemistry (PhD); geophysics (PhD); meteorology (PhD); oceanography (PhD); paleontology (PhD); paleooceanography (PhD); petrology (PhD); tectonics (PhD). *Degree requirements:* For doctorate, thesis/dissertation. *Entrance requirements:* For doctorate, GRE General Test. Additional exam requirements/recommendations for international students: Required—TOEFL.

180 www.petersonsbooks.com

Peterson's Graduate Programs in the Physical Sciences, Mathematics, Agricultural Sciences, the Environment & Natural Resources 2014

Planetary and Space Sciences

Air Force Institute of Technology, Graduate School of Engineering and Management, Department of Operational Sciences, Dayton, OH 45433-7765. Offers logistics management (MS); operations research (MS, PhD); space operations (MS). Part-time programs available. *Degree requirements:* For master's, thesis; for doctorate, thesis/dissertation. *Entrance requirements:* For doctorate, GRE General Test, minimum GPA of 3.0, U.S. citizenship. *Faculty research:* Optimization, simulation, combat modeling and analysis, reliability and maintainability, resource scheduling.

American Public University System, AMU/APU Graduate Programs, Charles Town, WV 25414. Offers accounting (MBA, MS); criminal justice (MA), including business administration, emergency and disaster management, general (MA, MS); educational leadership (M Ed); emergency and disaster management (MA); entrepreneurship (MBA); environmental policy and management (MS), including environmental planning, environmental sustainability, fish and wildlife management, general (MA, MS), global environmental management; finance (MBA); general (MBA); global business management (MBA); history (MA), including American history, ancient and classical history, European history, global history, public history; homeland security (MA), including business administration, counter-terrorism studies, criminal justice, cyber, emergency management and public health, intelligence studies, transportation security; homeland security resource allocation (MBA); humanities (MA); information technology (MS), including digital forensics, enterprise software development, information assurance and security, IT project management; information technology management (MBA); intelligence studies (MA), including criminal intelligence, cyber, general (MA, MS), homeland security, intelligence analysis, intelligence collection, intelligence management, intelligence operations, terrorism studies; international relations and conflict resolution (MA), including comparative and security issues, conflict resolution, international and transnational security issues, peacekeeping; legal studies (MA); management (MA), including defense management, general (MA, MS), human resource management, organizational leadership, public administration; marketing (MBA); military history (MA), including American military history, American Revolution, civil war, war since 1945, World War II; military studies (MA), including joint warfare, strategic leadership; national security studies (MA), including general (MA, MS), homeland security, regional security studies, security and intelligence analysis, terrorism studies; nonprofit management (MBA); political science (MA), including American politics and government, comparative government and development, general (MA, MS), international relations, public policy; psychology (MA), including general (MA, MS), maritime engineering management, reverse logistics management; public administration (MPA), including disaster management, environmental policy, health policy, human resources, national security, organizational management, security management; public health (MPH); reverse logistics management (MA); school counseling (M Ed); security management (MA); space studies (MS), including aerospace science, general (MA, MS), planetary science; sports and health sciences (MS); sports management (MS), including coaching theory and strategy, general (MA, MS), sports administration; teaching (M Ed), including curriculum and instruction for elementary teachers, elementary reading, English language learners, instructional leadership, online learning, special education; transportation and logistics management (MA), including general (MA, MS), maritime engineering management, reverse logistics management. Programs offered via distance learning only. Part-time and evening/weekend programs available. Postbaccalaureate distance learning degree programs offered (no on-campus study). *Faculty:* 439 full-time (246 women), 1,493 part-time/adjunct (708 women). *Students:* 611 full-time (284 women), 11,732 part-time (4,476 women); includes 3,985 minority (2,112 Black or African American, non-Hispanic/Latino; 103 American Indian or Alaska Native, non-Hispanic/Latino; 336 Asian, non-Hispanic/Latino; 915 Hispanic/Latino; 113 Native Hawaiian or other Pacific Islander, non-Hispanic/Latino; 406 Two or more races, non-Hispanic/Latino), 167 international. Average age 36. In 2012, 2,761 master's awarded. *Degree requirements:* For master's, comprehensive exam or practicum. *Entrance requirements:* For master's, official transcript showing earned bachelor's degree from institution accredited by recognized accrediting body. Additional exam requirements/recommendations for international students: Required—TOEFL (minimum score 550 paper-based), IELTS (minimum score 6.5). *Application deadline:* Applications are processed on a rolling basis. Application fee: $0. Electronic applications accepted. *Financial support:* Applicants required to submit FAFSA. *Faculty research:* Military history, criminal justice, management performance, national security. *Unit head:* Dr. Karan Powell, Executive Vice President and Provost, 877-468-6268, Fax: 304-724-3780. *Application contact:* Terry Grant, Vice President of Enrollment Management, 877-468-6268, Fax: 304-724-3780, E-mail: info@apus.edu. Website: http://www.apus.edu.

Arizona State University, College of Liberal Arts and Sciences, School of Earth and Space Exploration, Tempe, AZ 85287-1404. Offers astrophysics (MS, PhD); exploration systems design (PhD); geological sciences (MS, PhD). PhD in exploration systems design is offered in collaboration with the Fulton Schools of Engineering. Terminal master's awarded for partial completion of doctoral program. *Degree requirements:* For master's, thesis, interactive Program of Study (iPOS) submitted before completing 50 percent of required credit hours; for doctorate, thesis/dissertation, interactive Program of Study (iPOS) submitted before completing 50 percent of required credit hours. *Entrance requirements:* For master's and doctorate, GRE, minimum GPA of 3.0 or equivalent in last 2 years of work leading to bachelor's degree. Additional exam requirements/recommendations for international students: Required—TOEFL (minimum score 80 iBT), TOEFL, IELTS, or Pearson Test of English. Electronic applications accepted.

California Institute of Technology, Division of Geological and Planetary Sciences, Pasadena, CA 91125-0001. Offers environmental science and engineering (MS, PhD); geobiology (MS, PhD); geochemistry (MS, PhD); geology (MS, PhD); geophysics (MS, PhD); planetary science (MS, PhD). *Faculty:* 43 full-time (8 women). *Students:* 110 full-time (52 women); includes 9 minority (1 Black or African American, non-Hispanic/Latino; 7 Asian, non-Hispanic/Latino; 1 Hispanic/Latino), 30 international. Average age 26. 225 applicants, 19% accepted, 24 enrolled. In 2012, 7 master's, 13 doctorates awarded. *Degree requirements:* For doctorate, thesis/dissertation. *Entrance requirements:* For doctorate, GRE General Test. Additional exam requirements/recommendations for international students: Required—TOEFL; Recommended—IELTS, TWE. *Application deadline:* For fall admission, 1/1 for domestic and international students. Application fee: $80. Electronic applications accepted. *Financial support:* In 2012–13, 19 fellowships with full tuition reimbursements (averaging $29,000 per year), 72 research assistantships with full tuition reimbursements (averaging $29,000 per year) were awarded; teaching assistantships with full tuition reimbursements, institutionally sponsored loans, scholarships/grants, health care benefits, and unspecified assistantships also available. Financial award applicants required to submit FAFSA. *Faculty research:* Planetary surfaces, evolution of anaerobic respiratory processes, structural geology and tectonics, theoretical and numerical seismology, global biogeochemical cycles. *Unit head:* Dr. Kenneth A. Farley, Chairman, 626-395-6111, Fax: 626-795-6028, E-mail: dianb@gps.caltech.edu. *Application contact:* Dr. Robert W. Clayton, Academic Officer, 626-395-6909, Fax: 626-795-6028, E-mail: dianb@gps.caltech.edu. Website: http://www.gps.caltech.edu/.

Columbia University, Graduate School of Arts and Sciences, Division of Natural Sciences, Program in Atmospheric and Planetary Science, New York, NY 10027. Offers M Phil, PhD. Offered jointly through the Departments of Geological Sciences, Astronomy, and Physics and in cooperation with NASA Goddard Space Flight Center's Institute for Space Studies. *Degree requirements:* For doctorate, variable foreign language requirement, thesis/dissertation. *Entrance requirements:* For doctorate, GRE General Test, GRE Subject Test, previous course work in mathematics and physics. Additional exam requirements/recommendations for international students: Required—TOEFL. *Faculty research:* Climate, weather prediction.

Cornell University, Graduate School, Graduate Fields of Arts and Sciences, Field of Astronomy and Space Sciences, Ithaca, NY 14853-0001. Offers astronomy (PhD); astrophysics (PhD); general space sciences (PhD); infrared astronomy (PhD); planetary studies (PhD); radio astronomy (PhD); radiophysics (PhD); theoretical astrophysics (PhD). *Faculty:* 31 full-time (2 women). *Students:* 27 full-time (9 women); includes 6 minority (3 Asian, non-Hispanic/Latino; 2 Hispanic/Latino; 1 Two or more races, non-Hispanic/Latino), 8 international. Average age 26. 84 applicants, 8% accepted, 1 enrolled. In 2012, 6 doctorates awarded. *Degree requirements:* For doctorate, comprehensive exam, thesis/dissertation. *Entrance requirements:* For doctorate, GRE General Test, GRE Subject Test (physics), 3 letters of recommendation. Additional exam requirements/recommendations for international students: Required—TOEFL (minimum score 600 paper-based; 77 iBT). *Application deadline:* For fall admission, 1/15 for domestic students. Application fee: $95. Electronic applications accepted. *Financial support:* In 2012–13, 27 students received support, including 11 fellowships with full tuition reimbursements available, 8 research assistantships with full tuition reimbursements available, 8 teaching assistantships with full tuition reimbursements available; institutionally sponsored loans, scholarships/grants, health care benefits, tuition waivers (full and partial), and unspecified assistantships also available. Financial award applicants required to submit FAFSA. *Faculty research:* Observational astrophysics, planetary sciences, cosmology, instrumentation, gravitational astrophysics. *Unit head:* Director of Graduate Studies, 607-255-4341. *Application contact:* Graduate Field Assistant, 607-255-4341, E-mail: oconnor@astro.cornell.edu. Website: http://www.gradschool.cornell.edu/fields.php?id-24&a-2.

Florida Institute of Technology, Graduate Programs, College of Science, Department of Physics and Space Sciences, Melbourne, FL 32901-6975. Offers physics (MS, PhD); space sciences (MS, PhD). Part-time programs available. *Faculty:* 12 full-time (1 woman). *Students:* 33 full-time (11 women), 7 part-time (4 women); includes 5 minority (3 Asian, non-Hispanic/Latino; 2 Hispanic/Latino), 9 international. Average age 31. 90 applicants, 24% accepted, 10 enrolled. In 2012, 7 master's, 1 doctorate awarded. Terminal master's awarded for partial completion of doctoral program. *Degree requirements:* For master's, comprehensive exam, thesis optional, oral exam, 6 credits of math methodology; for doctorate, one foreign language, comprehensive exam, thesis/dissertation, publication in referred journal, seminar on dissertation research, dissertation published in a major journal. *Entrance requirements:* For master's, minimum GPA of 3.0, resume, 3 letters of recommendation, vector analysis, statement of objectives; for doctorate, GRE General and Subject Tests (recommended), minimum GPA of 3.2, resume, 3 letters of recommendation, statement of objectives. Additional exam requirements/recommendations for international students: Required—TOEFL (minimum score 550 paper-based; 79 iBT). *Application deadline:* For fall admission, 4/1 for international students; for spring admission, 9/30 for international students. Applications are processed on a rolling basis. Electronic applications accepted. *Expenses: Tuition:* Full-time $20,214; part-time $1123 per credit hour. Tuition and fees vary according to campus/location. *Financial support:* In 2012–13, 14 research assistantships with full and partial tuition reimbursements (averaging $12,502 per year), 12 teaching assistantships with full and partial tuition reimbursements (averaging $12,510 per year) were awarded; career-related internships or fieldwork, institutionally sponsored loans, tuition waivers (partial), unspecified assistantships, and tuition remissions also available. Support available to part-time students. Financial award application deadline: 3/1; financial award applicants required to submit FAFSA. *Faculty research:* Lasers, semiconductors, magnetism, quantum devices, high energy physics. *Total annual research expenditures:* $1.9 million. *Unit head:* Dr. Terry D. Oswalt, Department Head, 321-674-7325, Fax: 321-674-7482, E-mail: toswalt@fit.edu. *Application contact:* Cheryl A. Brown, Associate Director of Graduate Admissions, 321-674-7581, Fax: 321-723-9468, E-mail: cbrown@fit.edu. Website: http://cos.fit.edu/pss/.

Georgia Institute of Technology, Graduate Studies and Research, College of Sciences, School of Earth and Atmospheric Sciences, Atlanta, GA 30332-0340. Offers atmospheric chemistry, aerosols and clouds (MS, PhD); dynamics of weather and climate (MS, PhD); geochemistry (MS, PhD); geophysics (MS, PhD); oceanography (MS, PhD); paleoclimate (MS, PhD); planetary science (MS, PhD); remote sensing (MS, PhD). Part-time programs available. Terminal master's awarded for partial completion of doctoral program. *Degree requirements:* For master's, thesis or alternative; for doctorate, comprehensive exam, thesis/dissertation. *Entrance requirements:* For master's, GRE, letters of recommendation; for doctorate, GRE, academic transcripts, letters of recommendation, personal statement. Additional exam requirements/recommendations for international students: Required—TOEFL (minimum score 550 paper-based; 79 iBT). *Faculty research:* Geophysics; atmospheric chemistry, aerosols and clouds; dynamics of weather and climate; geochemistry; oceanography; paleoclimate; planetary science; remote sensing.

Hampton University, Graduate College, Department of Atmospheric and Planetary Sciences, Hampton, VA 23668. Offers atmospheric sciences (MS, PhD); planetary sciences (MS, PhD).

Harvard University, Graduate School of Arts and Sciences, Department of Earth and Planetary Sciences, Cambridge, MA 02138. Offers AM, PhD. Terminal master's awarded for partial completion of doctoral program. *Degree requirements:* For doctorate, comprehensive exam, thesis/dissertation. *Entrance requirements:* For doctorate, GRE General Test. Additional exam requirements/recommendations for international students: Required—TOEFL. Electronic applications accepted. *Expenses: Tuition:* Full-time $37,576. *Required fees:* $930. Tuition and fees vary according to program and student level. *Faculty research:* Economic geography, geochemistry, geophysics, mineralogy, crystallography.

Massachusetts Institute of Technology, School of Science, Department of Earth, Atmospheric, and Planetary Sciences, Cambridge, MA 02139. Offers atmospheric chemistry (PhD, Sc D); atmospheric science (SM, PhD, Sc D); chemical oceanography (SM, PhD, Sc D); climate physics and chemistry (SM, PhD, Sc D); earth and planetary sciences (SM); geochemistry (PhD, Sc D); geology (PhD, Sc D); geophysics (PhD, Sc D); marine geology and geophysics (SM, PhD, Sc D); physical oceanography (SM, PhD, Sc D); planetary sciences (PhD, Sc D). *Faculty:* 33 full-time (6 women), 1 (woman) part-time/adjunct. *Students:* 166 full-time (77 women); includes 24 minority (3 Black or African American, non-Hispanic/Latino; 1 American Indian or Alaska Native, non-Hispanic/Latino; 9 Asian, non-Hispanic/Latino; 6 Hispanic/Latino; 5 Two or more races, non-Hispanic/Latino), 58 international. Average age 27. 232 applicants, 23% accepted, 27 enrolled. In 2012, 12 master's, 22 doctorates awarded. Terminal master's awarded for partial completion of doctoral program. *Degree requirements:* For master's, thesis; for doctorate, comprehensive exam, thesis/dissertation. *Entrance requirements:* For master's, GRE General Test; for doctorate, GRE General Test, GRE Subject Test (chemistry or physics for planetary science area). Additional exam requirements/recommendations for international students: Required—TOEFL (minimum score 577 paper-based; 91 iBT), IELTS (minimum score 7). *Application deadline:* For fall admission, 1/5 for domestic and international students; for spring admission, 11/1 for domestic and international students. Application fee: $75. Electronic applications accepted. *Expenses: Tuition:* Full-time $41,770; part-time $650 per credit hour. *Required fees:* $280. *Financial support:* In 2012–13, 108 students received support, including 62 fellowships (averaging $30,700 per year), 87 research assistantships (averaging $32,600 per year), 15 teaching assistantships (averaging $30,800 per year); Federal Work-Study, institutionally sponsored loans, scholarships/grants, health care benefits, and unspecified assistantships also available. *Faculty research:* Formation, dynamics and evolution of planetary systems; origin, composition, structure and dynamics of the atmospheres, oceans, surfaces and interiors of the Earth and other planets; evolution and interaction of the physical, chemical, geological and biological components of the Earth system; characterization of past, present and potential future climates and the causes and consequences of climate change; interplay of energy and the environment. *Total annual research expenditures:* $28.1 million. *Unit head:* Prof. Robert van der Hilst, Head, 617-253-2127, Fax: 617-253-8298, E-mail: eapsinfo@mit.edu. *Application contact:* EAPS Education Office, 617-253-3381, Fax: 617-253-8298, E-mail: eapsinfo@mit.edu. Website: http://eapsweb.mit.edu/.

McGill University, Faculty of Graduate and Postdoctoral Studies, Faculty of Science, Department of Earth and Planetary Sciences, Montréal, QC H3A 2T5, Canada. Offers M Sc, PhD.

St. Thomas University, School of Leadership Studies, Institute for Education, Miami Gardens, FL 33054-6459. Offers earth/space science (Certificate); educational administration (MS, Certificate); educational leadership (Ed D); elementary education (MS); ESOL (Certificate); gifted education (Certificate); instructional technology (MS, Certificate); professional/studies (Certificate); reading (MS, Certificate); special education (MS). Part-time and evening/weekend programs available. *Degree requirements:* For master's, comprehensive exam; for doctorate, comprehensive exam, thesis/dissertation. *Entrance requirements:* For master's, interview, minimum GPA of 3.0 or GRE; for doctorate, GRE or MAT. Additional exam requirements/recommendations for international students: Required—TOEFL (minimum score 550 paper-based; 79 iBT). Electronic applications accepted.

The University of Arizona, College of Science, Department of Planetary Sciences, Tucson, AZ 85721. Offers MS, PhD. *Faculty:* 24 full-time (10 women), 2 part-time/adjunct (1 woman). *Students:* 28 full-time (13 women), 1 (woman) part-time; includes 4 minority (1 Hispanic/Latino; 3 Two or more races, non-Hispanic/Latino), 8 international. Average age 28. 83 applicants, 5% accepted, 3 enrolled. In 2012, 5 doctorates awarded. *Degree requirements:* For master's, thesis (for some programs); for doctorate, one foreign language, thesis/dissertation. *Entrance requirements:* For master's and doctorate, 3 letters of recommendation. Additional exam requirements/recommendations for international students: Required—TOEFL (minimum score 550 paper-based; 79 iBT). *Application deadline:* For fall admission, 1/15 for domestic and international students. Applications are processed on a rolling basis. Application fee: $75. Electronic applications accepted. *Financial support:* In 2012–13, 8 research assistantships with full tuition reimbursements (averaging $21,652 per year), 8 teaching assistantships with full tuition reimbursements (averaging $20,954 per year) were awarded; scholarships/grants, health care benefits, tuition waivers (partial), and unspecified assistantships also available. Financial award application deadline: 2/15. *Faculty research:* Cosmochemistry, planetary geology, astronomy, space physics, planetary physics. *Total annual research expenditures:* $39 million. *Unit head:* Dr. Michael Drake, Professor/Head/Director, 520-621-6962, Fax: 520-621-4933, E-mail: drake@lpl.arizona.edu. *Application contact:* Pam Street, Information Contact, 520-621-2828, Fax: 520-621-4933, E-mail: admissions@lpl.arizona.edu. Website: http://www.lpl.arizona.edu/.

University of Arkansas, Graduate School, Interdisciplinary Program in Space and Planetary Sciences, Fayetteville, AR 72701-1201. Offers MS, PhD. *Students:* 1 (woman) full-time, 22 part-time (12 women); includes 1 minority (Two or more races, non-Hispanic/Latino), 6 international. In 2012, 1 master's, 2 doctorates awarded. *Application deadline:* For fall admission, 4/1 for international students; for spring admission, 10/1 for international students. Applications are processed on a rolling basis. Application fee: $40 ($50 for international students). Electronic applications accepted. *Financial support:* In 2012–13, 7 research assistantships, 12 teaching assistantships were awarded; fellowships also available. *Unit head:* Dr. Lin Oliver, Director, 479-575-6571, E-mail: woliver@uark.edu. *Application contact:* Graduate Admissions, 479-575-6246, Fax: 479-575-5908, E-mail: gradinfo@uark.edu. Website: http://spacecenter.uark.edu.

University of California, Los Angeles, Graduate Division, College of Letters and Science, Department of Earth and Space Sciences, Los Angeles, CA 90095. Offers geochemistry (MS, PhD); geology (MS, PhD); geophysics and space physics (MS, PhD). *Faculty:* 23 full-time (3 women). *Students:* 68 full-time (30 women); includes 17 minority (3 Black or African American, non-Hispanic/Latino; 1 American Indian or Alaska Native, non-Hispanic/Latino; 8 Asian, non-Hispanic/Latino; 3 Hispanic/Latino; 2 Two or more races, non-Hispanic/Latino), 15 international. Average age 28. 101 applicants, 18% accepted, 10 enrolled. In 2012, 15 master's, 11 doctorates awarded. Terminal master's awarded for partial completion of doctoral program. *Degree requirements:* For master's, comprehensive exams or thesis; for doctorate, thesis/dissertation, oral and written qualifying exams. *Entrance requirements:* For master's, GRE General Test; GRE Subject Test, bachelor's degree; minimum undergraduate GPA of 3.0 (or its equivalent if letter grade system not used); for doctorate, GRE General Test, bachelor's degree; minimum undergraduate GPA of 3.0 (or its equivalent if letter grade system not used). Additional exam requirements/recommendations for international students: Required—TOEFL. *Application deadline:* For fall admission, 1/15 for domestic and international students. Application fee: $80 ($100 for international students). Electronic applications accepted. *Expenses:* Tuition, nonresident: full-time $15,102. *Required fees:* $14,809.19. Full-time tuition and fees vary according to program. *Financial support:* In 2012–13, 72 students received support, including 69 fellowships with full and partial tuition reimbursements available, 57 research assistantships with full and partial tuition reimbursements available, 34 teaching assistantships with full and partial tuition reimbursements available; Federal Work-Study, scholarships/grants, health care benefits, tuition waivers (full and partial), and unspecified assistantships also available. Financial award application deadline: 3/2; financial award applicants required to submit FAFSA. *Unit head:* Dr. Kevin McKeegan, Chair, 310-825-1475, E-mail: mckeegan@ess.ucla.edu. *Application contact:* Student Affairs Officer,

310-825-3917, E-mail: holbrook@ess.ucla.edu. Website: http://www.ess.ucla.edu/.

University of California, Santa Cruz, Division of Graduate Studies, Division of Physical and Biological Sciences, Department of Earth and Planetary Sciences, Santa Cruz, CA 95064. Offers MS, PhD. Terminal master's awarded for partial completion of doctoral program. *Degree requirements:* For master's, thesis; for doctorate, one foreign language, thesis/dissertation, qualifying exam. *Entrance requirements:* For master's and doctorate, GRE General Test. Additional exam requirements/recommendations for international students: Required—TOEFL (minimum score 550 paper-based; 83 iBT); Recommended—IELTS (minimum score 8). Electronic applications accepted. *Faculty research:* Evolution of continental margins and orogenic belts, geologic processes occurring at plate boundaries, deep-sea sediment diagenesis, paleoecology, hydrogeology.

University of Chicago, Division of the Physical Sciences, Department of the Geophysical Sciences, Chicago, IL 60637-1513. Offers atmospheric sciences (SM, PhD); cosmochemistry (PhD); earth sciences (SM, PhD); paleobiology (PhD); planetary and space sciences (SM, PhD). Terminal master's awarded for partial completion of doctoral program. *Degree requirements:* For master's, thesis, seminar; for doctorate, variable foreign language requirement, comprehensive exam, thesis/dissertation. *Entrance requirements:* For doctorate, GRE General Test. Additional exam requirements/recommendations for international students: Required—TOEFL (minimum score 600 paper-based; 96 iBT), IELTS (minimum score 7). Electronic applications accepted. *Faculty research:* Climatology, evolutionary paleontology, cosmochemistry, geochemistry, oceanic sciences.

University of Hawaii at Manoa, Graduate Division, School of Ocean and Earth Science and Technology, Department of Geology and Geophysics, Honolulu, HI 96822. Offers high-pressure geophysics and geochemistry (MS, PhD); hydrogeology and engineering geology (MS, PhD); marine geology and geophysics (MS, PhD); planetary geosciences and remote sensing (MS, PhD); seismology and solid-earth geophysics (MS, PhD); volcanology, petrology, and geochemistry (MS, PhD). Part-time programs available. Terminal master's awarded for partial completion of doctoral program. *Degree requirements:* For master's, thesis optional; for doctorate, comprehensive exam, thesis/dissertation. *Entrance requirements:* For master's and doctorate, GRE General Test, minimum GPA of 3.0. Additional exam requirements/recommendations for international students: Required—TOEFL (minimum score 580 paper-based; 92 iBT), IELTS (minimum score 5).

University of Houston, College of Liberal Arts and Social Sciences, Department of Health and Human Performance, Houston, TX 77204. Offers exercise science (MS); human nutrition (MS); human space exploration sciences (MS); kinesiology (PhD); physical education (M Ed). *Accreditation:* NCATE (one or more programs are accredited). Part-time and evening/weekend programs available. *Degree requirements:* For master's, comprehensive exam (for some programs), thesis (for some programs); for doctorate, comprehensive exam, thesis/dissertation, qualifying exam, candidacy paper. *Entrance requirements:* For master's, GRE (minimum 35th percentile on each section), minimum cumulative GPA of 3.0; for doctorate, GRE (minimum 35th percentile on each section), minimum cumulative GPA of 3.3. Additional exam requirements/recommendations for international students: Required—TOEFL (minimum score 550 paper-based; 79 iBT). Electronic applications accepted. *Faculty research:* Biomechanics, exercise physiology, obesity, nutrition, space exploration science.

University of Maryland, Baltimore County, Graduate School, College of Arts, Humanities and Social Sciences, Department of Education, Program in Teaching, Baltimore, MD 21250. Offers early childhood education (MAT); elementary education (MAT); secondary education (MAT), including art, biology, chemistry, dance, earth/space science, English, foreign language, mathematics, music, physics, social studies, theatre. Part-time and evening/weekend programs available. *Faculty:* 24 full-time (18 women), 25 part-time/adjunct (19 women). *Students:* 53 full-time (40 women), 43 part-time (28 women); includes 22 minority (14 Black or African American, non-Hispanic/Latino; 3 Asian, non-Hispanic/Latino; 4 Hispanic/Latino; 1 Two or more races, non-Hispanic/Latino), 1 international. Average age 30. 40 applicants, 95% accepted, 35 enrolled. In 2012, 106 master's awarded. *Degree requirements:* For master's, comprehensive exam (for some programs), thesis (for some programs). *Entrance requirements:* For master's, PRAXIS I or SAT (minimum score of 1000), minimum GPA of 3.0. Additional exam requirements/recommendations for international students: Required—TOEFL. *Application deadline:* For fall admission, 6/1 for domestic students; for spring admission, 11/1 for domestic students. Applications are processed on a rolling basis. Application fee: $50. Electronic applications accepted. *Financial support:* In 2012–13, 6 students received support, including teaching assistantships with full and partial tuition reimbursements available (averaging $12,000 per year); career-related internships or fieldwork, Federal Work-Study, scholarships/grants, tuition waivers, and unspecified assistantships also available. Financial award application deadline: 3/1. *Faculty research:* STEM teacher education, culturally sensitive pedagogy, ESOL/bilingual education, early childhood education, language, literacy and culture. *Unit head:* Dr. Susan M. Blunck, Graduate Program Director, 410-455-2869, Fax: 410-455-3986, E-mail: blunck@umbc.edu. Website: http://www.umbc.edu/education/.

University of Michigan, College of Engineering, Department of Atmospheric, Oceanic, and Space Sciences, Ann Arbor, MI 48109. Offers atmospheric and space sciences (MS, PhD); geoscience and remote sensing (PhD); space and planetary sciences (PhD); space engineering (M Eng). Part-time programs available. *Students:* 106 full-time (37 women), 1 part-time (0 women). 141 applicants, 50% accepted, 42 enrolled. In 2012, 41 master's, 5 doctorates awarded. Terminal master's awarded for partial completion of doctoral program. *Degree requirements:* For master's, thesis (for some programs); for doctorate, thesis/dissertation, oral defense of dissertation, preliminary exams. *Entrance requirements:* For master's and doctorate, GRE General Test. Additional exam requirements/recommendations for international students: Required—TOEFL. *Application deadline:* Applications are processed on a rolling basis. Application fee: $65 ($75 for international students). Electronic applications accepted. *Financial support:* Fellowships, research assistantships, teaching assistantships, career-related internships or fieldwork, Federal Work-Study, institutionally sponsored loans, and health care benefits available. Support available to part-time students. Financial award applicants required to submit FAFSA. *Faculty research:* Planetary environments, space instrumentation, air pollution meteorology, global climate change, sun-earth connection, space weather. *Unit head:* Dr. James Slavin, Chair, 734-764-7221, Fax: 734-615-4645, E-mail: jaslavin@umich.edu. *Application contact:* Sandra Pytlinski, Student Services Associate, 734-936-0482, Fax: 734-763-0437, E-mail: aoss.um@umich.edu. Website: http://aoss.engin.umich.edu/.

University of New Mexico, Graduate School, College of Arts and Sciences, Department of Earth and Planetary Sciences, Albuquerque, NM 87131. Offers MS, PhD. Part-time programs available. *Faculty:* 33 full-time (5 women), 22 part-time/adjunct (3 women). *Students:* 21 full-time (13 women), 30 part-time (17 women); includes 6 minority (1 American Indian or Alaska Native, non-Hispanic/Latino; 1 Asian, non-Hispanic/Latino; 4 Hispanic/Latino), 7 international. Average age 31. 74 applicants, 15% accepted, 7 enrolled. In 2012, 11 master's, 6 doctorates awarded. Terminal master's awarded for partial completion of doctoral program. *Degree requirements:* For master's, comprehensive exam, thesis; for doctorate, comprehensive exam, thesis/dissertation. *Entrance requirements:* For master's and doctorate, GRE General Test. Additional exam requirements/recommendations for international students: Required—TOEFL. *Application deadline:* For fall admission, 1/15 priority date for domestic students, 1/15 for international students; for spring admission, 11/1 priority date for domestic students, 11/1 for international students. Application fee: $50. Electronic applications accepted. *Expenses:* Tuition, state resident: full-time $3296; part-time $276.73 per credit hour. Tuition, nonresident: full-time $10,604; part-time $885.74 per credit hour. *Required fees:* $628. *Financial support:* In 2012–13, 51 students received support, including 3 fellowships with full tuition reimbursements available (averaging $2,714 per year), 14 research assistantships with full tuition reimbursements available (averaging $14,363 per year), 21 teaching assistantships with full tuition reimbursements available (averaging $1,982 per year); scholarships/grants and health care benefits also available. Financial award application deadline: 1/15. *Faculty research:* Climatology, experimental petrology, geochemistry, geographic information technologies, geomorphology, geophysics, hydrogeology, ingeneous petrology, metamorphic petrology, meteoritics, meteorology, micrometeorites, mineralogy, paleoclimatology, paleonology, pedology, petrology, physical volcanology, planetary sciences, precambrian geology, quantenary geology, sedimentary geochemistry, sedimentology, stable isotope geochemistry, stratigraphy, structural geology, tectonics, volcanology. *Total annual research expenditures:* $2.5 million. *Unit head:* Dr. Adrian J. Brearley, Chair, 505-277-4204, Fax: 505-277-8843, E-mail: brearley@unm.edu. *Application contact:* Cindy Jaramillo, Administrative Assistant III, 505-277-1635, Fax: 505-277-8843, E-mail: epsdept@unm.edu. Website: http://epswww.unm.edu/.

University of North Dakota, Graduate School, John D. Odegard School of Aerospace Sciences, Space Studies Program, Grand Forks, ND 58202. Offers MS. Part-time programs available. Postbaccalaureate distance learning degree programs offered (minimal on-campus study). *Degree requirements:* For master's, comprehensive exam, thesis or alternative. *Entrance requirements:* For master's, minimum GPA of 3.0. Additional exam requirements/recommendations for international students: Required—TOEFL (minimum score 550 paper-based; 79 iBT), IELTS (minimum score 6.5). Electronic applications accepted. *Faculty research:* Earth-approaching asteroids, international remote sensing statutes, Mercury fly-by design, origin of meteorites, craters on Venus.

University of Pittsburgh, Dietrich School of Arts and Sciences, Department of Geology and Planetary Science, Pittsburgh, PA 15260-3332. Offers geographical information systems and remote sensing (Pro-MS); geology and planetary science (MS, PhD). Part-time programs available. *Faculty:* 7 full-time (2 women), 2 part-time/adjunct (1 woman). *Students:* 24 full-time (12 women), 7 part-time (3 women), 1 international. Average age 30. 48 applicants, 44% accepted, 12 enrolled. In 2012, 3 master's, 4 doctorates awarded. *Degree requirements:* For master's, thesis, oral thesis defense; for doctorate, comprehensive exam, thesis/dissertation, oral dissertation defense. *Entrance requirements:* For master's and doctorate, GRE General Test. Additional exam requirements/recommendations for international students: Required—TOEFL (minimum score 90 iBT), IELTS (minimum score 7.5). *Application deadline:* For fall admission, 1/15 priority date for domestic students, 1/15 for international students. Applications are processed on a rolling basis. Application fee: $50. Electronic applications accepted. *Expenses:* Tuition, state resident: full-time $19,336; part-time $782 per credit. Tuition, nonresident: full-time $31,658; part-time $1295 per credit. *Required fees:* $740; $200 per term. Tuition and fees vary according to program. *Financial support:* In 2012–13, 25 students received support, including 2 fellowships with full tuition reimbursements available (averaging $19,165 per year), 14 research assistantships with full and partial tuition reimbursements available (averaging $14,400 per year), 9 teaching assistantships with full and partial tuition reimbursements available (averaging $16,460 per year); career-related internships or fieldwork, Federal Work-Study, institutionally sponsored loans, scholarships/grants, health care benefits, and tuition waivers (full and partial) also available. Support available to part-time students. Financial award application deadline: 1/15; financial award applicants required to submit FAFSA. *Faculty research:* Geographical information systems, hydrology, low temperature geochemistry, volcanology, paleoclimatology. *Total annual research expenditures:* $1.6 million. *Unit head:* Dr. William Harbert, Chair, 412-624-8783, Fax: 412-624-3914, E-mail: harbert@pitt.edu. *Application contact:* Dr. Rosemary Capo, Director of Graduate Studies, 412-624-8873, Fax: 412-624-3914, E-mail: rcapo@pitt.edu. Website: http://www.geology.pitt.edu/.

Washington University in St. Louis, Graduate School of Arts and Sciences, Department of Earth and Planetary Sciences, St. Louis, MO 63130-4899. Offers MA, PhD. Terminal master's awarded for partial completion of doctoral program. *Degree requirements:* For master's, thesis; for doctorate, thesis/dissertation. *Entrance requirements:* For master's and doctorate, GRE General Test. Electronic applications accepted.

West Chester University of Pennsylvania, College of Arts and Sciences, Department of Geology and Astronomy, West Chester, PA 19383. Offers earth-space science (Teaching Certificate); general science (Teaching Certificate); geoscience (MA). Part-time and evening/weekend programs available. *Faculty:* 7 full-time (2 women). *Students:* 1 (woman) full-time, 16 part-time (3 women); includes 2 minority (1 Black or African American, non-Hispanic/Latino; 1 Hispanic/Latino). Average age 35. 5 applicants, 100% accepted, 4 enrolled. In 2012, 8 master's awarded. *Degree requirements:* For master's, comprehensive exam (for some programs), thesis or alternative. *Entrance requirements:* For master's, minimum GPA of 2.5. Additional exam requirements/recommendations for international students: Required—TOEFL (minimum score 550 paper-based; 80 iBT). *Application deadline:* For fall admission, 4/15 priority date for domestic students, 3/15 for international students; for spring admission, 10/15 priority date for domestic students, 9/1 for international students. Applications are processed on a rolling basis. Application fee: $45. Electronic applications accepted. *Expenses:* Tuition, state resident: full-time $7722; part-time $429 per credit. Tuition, nonresident: full-time $11,592; part-time $644 per credit. *Required fees:* $2108; $105.05 per credit. Tuition and fees vary according to campus/location and program. *Financial support:* Unspecified assistantships available. Support available to part-time students. Financial award application deadline: 2/15; financial award applicants required to submit FAFSA. *Faculty research:*

Geoscience education, environmental geology, energy and sustainability, astronomy, meteorology. *Unit head:* Dr. Lee Anne Srogi, Chair, 610-436-2727, Fax: 610-436-3036, E-mail: lsrogi@wcupa.edu. *Application contact:* Dr. Martin Helmke, Graduate Coordinator, 610-436-3565, Fax: 610-436-3036, E-mail: mhelmke@wcupa.edu. Website: http://www.wcupa.edu/_academics/sch_cas.esc/.

Western Connecticut State University, Division of Graduate Studies, School of Arts and Sciences, Department of Physics, Astronomy and Meteorology, Danbury, CT 06810-6885. Offers earth and planetary sciences (MA). Part-time programs available. *Faculty:* 2 full-time (0 women). *Students:* 1 (woman) full-time, 3 part-time (all women). Average age 26. 6 applicants, 50% accepted, 2 enrolled. In 2012, 5 master's awarded. *Degree requirements:* For master's, thesis, completion of program in 6 years. *Entrance requirements:* For master's, minimum GPA of 2.5 or GRE; one year each of calculus-based physics and calculus; semester course in differential equations. Additional exam requirements/recommendations for international students: Recommended—TOEFL (minimum score 550 paper-based; 79 iBT), IELTS (minimum score 6). *Application deadline:* For fall admission, 8/5 priority date for domestic students; for spring admission, 1/5 priority date for domestic students. Applications are processed on a rolling basis. Application fee: $50. *Expenses:* Contact institution. *Financial support:* In 2012–13, 1 student received support. Application deadline: 5/1; applicants required to submit FAFSA. *Faculty research:* Data collection and analysis of Gulf Stream surface temperature and circulation; science for visually impaired students including investigations of a satellite orbit, the Moon's surface, spectra of chemical elements and stars, the rotation of the Sun, and the spiral structure of our galaxy. *Unit head:* Dr. Dennis Dawson, Department Chair, 203-837-8671, E-mail: dawsond@wcsu.edu. *Application contact:* Chris Shankle, Associate Director of Graduate Admissions, 203-837-9005, Fax: 203-837-8326, E-mail: shanklec@wcsu.edu. Website: http://www.wcsu.edu/physics/.

Yale University, Graduate School of Arts and Sciences, Department of Astronomy, New Haven, CT 06520. Offers astronomy (PhD); solar and terrestrial physics (PhD). *Degree requirements:* For doctorate, thesis/dissertation. *Entrance requirements:* For doctorate, GRE General Test, GRE Subject Test (physics).

York University, Faculty of Graduate Studies, Faculty of Science and Engineering, Program in Earth and Space Science, Toronto, ON M3J 1P3, Canada. Offers M Sc, PhD. Part-time and evening/weekend programs available. *Degree requirements:* For master's, thesis or alternative; for doctorate, thesis/dissertation. Electronic applications accepted.

184 www.petersonsbooks.com

Peterson's Graduate Programs in the Physical Sciences, Mathematics, Agricultural Sciences, the Environment & Natural Resources 2014

Section 4
Marine Sciences and Oceanography

This section contains a directory of institutions offering graduate work in marine sciences and oceanography. Additional information about programs listed in the directory may be obtained by writing directly to the dean of a graduate school or chair of a department at the address given in the directory.

For programs offering related work, see also in this book *Chemistry, Geosciences, Meteorology and Atmospheric Sciences,* and *Physics.* In the other guides in this series:

Graduate Programs in the Biological/Biomedical Sciences & Health-Related Medical Professions

See *Biological and Biomedical Sciences; Environmental Biology, and Evolutionary Biology;* and *Marine Biology*

Graduate Programs in Engineering & Applied Sciences

See *Civil and Environmental Engineering, Engineering and Applied Sciences,* and *Ocean Engineering*

CONTENTS

Program Directories

Marine Sciences

California State University, East Bay, Office of Academic Programs and Graduate Studies, College of Science, Department of Biological Sciences, Marine Science Program, Moss Landing, CA 95039. Offers MS. *Degree requirements:* For master's, thesis. *Entrance requirements:* For master's, GRE Subject Test, minimum GPA of 3.0 in field, 2.75 overall; 3 letters of reference; statement of purpose. Additional exam requirements/recommendations for international students: Required—TOEFL.

California State University, Fresno, Division of Graduate Studies, College of Science and Mathematics, Program in Marine Sciences, Fresno, CA 93740-8027. Offers MS. Part-time programs available. Postbaccalaureate distance learning degree programs offered. *Degree requirements:* For master's, thesis. *Entrance requirements:* For master's, GRE General Test, minimum GPA of 3.0. Additional exam requirements/recommendations for international students: Required—TOEFL. Electronic applications accepted. *Faculty research:* Wetlands ecology, land/water conservation, water irrigation.

California State University, Monterey Bay, College of Science, Media Arts and Technology, Moss Landing Marine Laboratories, Seaside, CA 93955-8001. Offers MS. Part-time programs available. *Degree requirements:* For master's, thesis, thesis defense. *Entrance requirements:* For master's, selected MLML faculty member to serve as potential thesis advisor and selected consortium institution to serve as home campus. Additional exam requirements/recommendations for international students: Required—TOEFL (minimum score 525 paper-based; 71 iBT). Electronic applications accepted. *Faculty research:* Remote sensing microbiology trace elements, chemistry ecology of birds, mammals, turtles and fish, invasive species, marine phycology.

California State University, Sacramento, Office of Graduate Studies, College of Natural Sciences and Mathematics, Department of Biological Sciences, Sacramento, CA 95819-6077. Offers biological sciences (MA, MS); immunohematology (MS); marine science (MS). Part-time programs available. *Degree requirements:* For master's, thesis, writing proficiency exam. *Entrance requirements:* For master's, GRE, bachelor's degree in biology or equivalent; minimum GPA of 3.0 in biology, 2.75 overall during last 2 years of course work. Additional exam requirements/recommendations for international students: Required—TOEFL. Electronic applications accepted.

Coastal Carolina University, College of Science, Conway, SC 29528-6054. Offers coastal marine and wetland studies (MS). Part-time and evening/weekend programs available. *Faculty:* 19 full-time (3 women). *Students:* 16 full-time (6 women), 19 part-time (11 women); includes 2 minority (1 American Indian or Alaska Native, non-Hispanic/Latino; 1 Hispanic/Latino). Average age 27. 35 applicants, 80% accepted, 13 enrolled. In 2012, 7 master's awarded. *Degree requirements:* For master's, thesis optional. *Entrance requirements:* For master's, GRE, 2 letters of recommendation, resume, official transcripts, essay, written statement of educational and career goals, baccalaureate degree. Additional exam requirements/recommendations for international students: Required—TOEFL (minimum score 575 paper-based; 89 iBT). *Application deadline:* For fall admission, 3/1 priority date for domestic students, 3/1 for international students; for spring admission, 11/1 priority date for domestic students, 11/1 for international students. Applications are processed on a rolling basis. Application fee: $45. Electronic applications accepted. *Expenses:* Tuition, state resident: full-time $11,760; part-time $490 per credit hour. Tuition, nonresident: full-time $17,496; part-time $729 per credit hour. *Required fees:* $80; $40 per term. Tuition and fees vary according to program. *Financial support:* Fellowships, research assistantships, and unspecified assistantships available. Support available to part-time students. Financial award application deadline: 3/1; financial award applicants required to submit FAFSA. *Unit head:* Dr. Michael H. Roberts, Dean, 843-349-2282, Fax: 843-349-2545, E-mail: mroberts@coastal.edu. *Application contact:* Dr. James O. Luken, Associate Provost/Director of Graduate Studies, 843-349-2235, Fax: 843-349-6444, E-mail: joluken@coastal.edu. Website: http://www.coastal.edu/science/.

College of Charleston, Graduate School, School of Sciences and Mathematics, Program in Marine Biology, Charleston, SC 29412. Offers MS. *Degree requirements:* For master's, comprehensive exam, thesis. *Entrance requirements:* For master's, GRE General Test, 3 letters of recommendation. Additional exam requirements/recommendations for international students: Required—TOEFL (minimum score 81 iBT). Electronic applications accepted. *Faculty research:* Ecology, environmental physiology, marine genomics, bioinformatics, toxicology, cell biology, population biology, fisheries science, animal physiology, biodiversity, estuarine ecology, evolution and systematics, microbial processes, plant physiology, immunology.

The College of William and Mary, Virginia Institute of Marine Science, Gloucester Point, VA 23062. Offers MS, PhD. *Faculty:* 62 full-time (15 women), 2 part-time/adjunct (1 woman). *Students:* 87 full-time (49 women), 2 part-time (1 woman); includes 8 minority (2 Asian, non-Hispanic/Latino; 3 Hispanic/Latino; 1 Native Hawaiian or other Pacific Islander, non-Hispanic/Latino; 2 Two or more races, non-Hispanic/Latino), 12 international. Average age 28. 120 applicants, 21% accepted, 18 enrolled. In 2012, 12 master's, 6 doctorates awarded. *Degree requirements:* For master's, thesis, qualifying exam; for doctorate, comprehensive exam, thesis/dissertation, qualifying exam. *Entrance requirements:* For master's, GRE, appropriate bachelor's degree; for doctorate, GRE, appropriate bachelor's and master's degrees. Additional exam requirements/recommendations for international students: Required—TOEFL. *Application deadline:* For fall admission, 1/15 for domestic and international students. Application fee: $50. Electronic applications accepted. *Expenses:* Tuition, state resident: full-time $6779; part-time $385 per credit hour. Tuition, nonresident: full-time $20,608; part-time $1000 per credit hour. *Required fees:* $4625. *Financial support:* In 2012–13, 93 students received support, including 16 fellowships with full tuition reimbursements available (averaging $19,005 per year), 69 research assistantships with full tuition reimbursements available (averaging $19,005 per year), 8 teaching assistantships with partial tuition reimbursements available (averaging $6,500 per year); career-related internships or fieldwork, Federal Work-Study, scholarships/grants, health care benefits, and unspecified assistantships also available. Support available to part-time students. Financial award application deadline: 6/15; financial award applicants required to submit FAFSA. *Faculty research:* Marine science, oceanography, marine ecology, fisheries, environmental science and ecotoxicology. *Total annual research expenditures:* $18 million. *Unit head:* Dr. John T. Wells, Dean/Director, 804-684-7102, Fax: 804-684-7009, E-mail: wells@vims.edu. *Application contact:* Fonda J. Powell, Admissions Coordinator, 804-684-7105, Fax: 804-684-7881, E-mail: fonda@vims.edu. Website: http://www.vims.edu/.

Cornell University, Graduate School, Graduate Fields of Agriculture and Life Sciences, Field of Natural Resources, Ithaca, NY 14853-0001. Offers community-based natural resources management (MS, PhD); ecosystem biology and biogeochemistry (MPS, MS, PhD); environmental management (MPS); fishery and aquatic science (MPS, MS, PhD); forest science (MPS, MS, PhD); human dimensions of natural resources management (MPS, MS, PhD); program development and evaluation (MPS, MS, PhD); wildlife science (MPS, MS, PhD). *Faculty:* 40 full-time (8 women). *Students:* 56 full-time (23 women); includes 2 minority (1 Asian, non-Hispanic/Latino; 1 Two or more races, non-Hispanic/Latino), 12 international. Average age 32. 61 applicants, 33% accepted, 15 enrolled. In 2012, 7 master's, 6 doctorates awarded. *Degree requirements:* For master's, thesis (MS), project paper (MPS); for doctorate, comprehensive exam, thesis/dissertation. *Entrance requirements:* For master's and doctorate, GRE General Test, 2 letters of recommendation. Additional exam requirements/ recommendations for international students: Required—TOEFL (minimum score 550 paper-based; 77 iBT). *Application deadline:* For spring admission, 10/30 for domestic students. Applications are processed on a rolling basis. Application fee: $95. Electronic applications accepted. *Financial support:* In 2012–13, 46 students received support, including 14 fellowships with full tuition reimbursements available, 15 research assistantships with full tuition reimbursements available, 17 teaching assistantships with full tuition reimbursements available; institutionally sponsored loans, scholarships/grants, health care benefits, tuition waivers (full and partial), and unspecified assistantships also available. Financial award applicants required to submit FAFSA. *Faculty research:* Ecosystem-level dynamics, systems modeling, conservation biology/management, resource management's human dimensions, biogeochemistry. *Unit head:* Director of Graduate Studies, 607-255-2807, Fax: 607-255-0349. *Application contact:* Graduate Field Assistant, 607-255-2807, Fax: 607-255-0349, E-mail: nrgrad@cornell.edu. Website: http://www.gradschool.cornell.edu/fields.php?id-54&a-2.

Duke University, Graduate School, Program in Marine Science and Conservation, Beaufort, NC 28516. Offers MS. *Faculty:* 18 full-time. *Students:* 35 full-time (25 women); includes 3 minority (1 American Indian or Alaska Native, non-Hispanic/Latino; 1 Asian, non-Hispanic/Latino; 1 Hispanic/Latino), 7 international. 54 applicants, 11% accepted, 4 enrolled. *Entrance requirements:* Additional exam requirements/recommendations for international students: Required—TOEFL (minimum score 550 paper-based; 83 iBT), IELTS. *Application deadline:* For fall admission, 12/8 priority date for domestic students. Application fee: $80. *Financial support:* Fellowships, research assistantships, and teaching assistantships available. *Unit head:* Lisa Campbell, Director of Graduate Studies, 252-504-7585, Fax: 252-504-7648, E-mail: rachel.lopiccolo@duke.edu. *Application contact:* Elizabeth Hutton, Director of Admissions, 919-684-3913, Fax: 919-684-2277, E-mail: grad-admissions@duke.edu. Website: http://www.env.duke.edu/marinelab.

Florida Institute of Technology, Graduate Programs, College of Engineering, Department of Marine and Environmental Systems, Program in Oceanography, Melbourne, FL 32901-6975. Offers biological oceanography (MS); chemical oceanography (MS); coastal management (MS); geological oceanography (MS); oceanography (PhD); physical oceanography (MS). Part-time programs available. *Faculty:* 15 full-time (0 women), 2 part-time/adjunct (0 women). *Students:* 15 full-time (10 women), 4 part-time (0 women); includes 1 minority (Two or more races, non-Hispanic/Latino), 5 international. Average age 28. 25 applicants, 68% accepted, 8 enrolled. In 2012, 2 master's, 3 doctorates awarded. *Degree requirements:* For master's, comprehensive exam (for some programs), thesis (for some programs), seminar, field project, written final exam, internship, technical paper, oral presentation; for doctorate, comprehensive exam, thesis/dissertation,

186 facebook.com/petersonspublishing

Peterson's Graduate Programs in the Physical Sciences, Mathematics, Agricultural Sciences, the Environment & Natural Resources 2014

seminar, internships, publications. *Entrance requirements:* For master's, GRE General Test, minimum GPA of 3.0, 3 letters of recommendation, resume, transcripts, statement of objectives; for doctorate, GRE General Test, minimum GPA of 3.3, resume, 3 letters of recommendation, statement of objectives, on-campus interview (highly recommended). Additional exam requirements/recommendations for international students: Required—TOEFL (minimum score 550 paper-based; 79 iBT). *Application deadline:* Applications are processed on a rolling basis. Electronic applications accepted. *Expenses: Tuition:* Full-time $20,214; part-time $1123 per credit hour. Tuition and fees vary according to campus/location. *Financial support:* Career-related internships or fieldwork, institutionally sponsored loans, tuition waivers (partial), unspecified assistantships, and tuition remissions available. Support available to part-time students. Financial award application deadline: 3/1; financial award applicants required to submit FAFSA. *Faculty research:* Marine geochemistry, ecosystem dynamics, coastal processes, marine pollution, environmental modeling. *Total annual research expenditures:* $2.2 million. *Unit head:* Dr. George Maul, Department Head, 321-674-7453, Fax: 321-674-7212, E-mail: gmaul@fit.edu. *Application contact:* Cheryl A. Brown, Associate Director of Graduate Admission, 321-674-7581, Fax: 321-723-9468, E-mail: cbrown@fit.edu. Website: http://www.coe.fit.edu/dmes.

Florida State University, The Graduate School, College of Arts and Sciences, Department of Earth, Ocean and Atmospheric Science, Program in Oceanography, Tallahassee, FL 32306-4320. Offers aquatic environmental science (MS, PSM); oceanography (MS, PhD). *Faculty:* 10 full-time (1 woman), 1 (woman) part-time/adjunct. *Students:* 53 full-time (25 women); includes 5 minority (1 Black or African American, non-Hispanic/Latino; 4 Asian, non-Hispanic/Latino), 15 international. Average age 27. 60 applicants, 23% accepted, 12 enrolled. In 2012, 7 master's, 5 doctorates awarded. *Degree requirements:* For master's, thesis; for doctorate, comprehensive exam, thesis/dissertation. *Entrance requirements:* For master's and doctorate, GRE General Test, minimum upper-division GPA of 3.0. Additional exam requirements/recommendations for international students: Required—TOEFL (minimum score 550 paper-based; 80 iBT). *Application deadline:* For fall admission, 2/15 priority date for domestic students, 2/15 for international students; for spring admission, 7/15 priority date for domestic students, 7/15 for international students. Applications are processed on a rolling basis. Application fee: $35. Electronic applications accepted. *Expenses:* Tuition, state resident: full-time $7263; part-time $403.51 per credit hour. Tuition, nonresident: full-time $18,087; part-time $1004.85 per credit hour. *Required fees:* $1335.42; $74.19 per credit hour. $445.14 per semester. One-time fee: $40 full-time; $20 part-time. Tuition and fees vary according to program. *Financial support:* In 2012–13, 36 students received support, including 1 fellowship with full tuition reimbursement available, 27 research assistantships with full tuition reimbursements available, 10 teaching assistantships with full tuition reimbursements available. Financial award application deadline: 2/15; financial award applicants required to submit FAFSA. *Faculty research:* Trace metals in seawater, currents and waves, modeling, benthic ecology, marine biogeochemistry. *Unit head:* Dr. Jeffrey Chanton, Area Coordinator, 850-644-6700, Fax: 850-644-2581, E-mail: chanton@ocean.fsu.edu. *Application contact:* Michaela Lupiani, Academic Coordinator, 850-644-6700, Fax: 850-644-2581, E-mail: admissions@ocean.fsu.edu. Website: http://www.eoas.fsu.edu.

Georgia Institute of Technology, Graduate Studies and Research, College of Sciences, School of Earth and Atmospheric Sciences, Atlanta, GA 30332-0340. Offers atmospheric chemistry, aerosols and clouds (MS, PhD); dynamics of weather and climate (MS, PhD); geochemistry (MS, PhD); geophysics (MS, PhD); oceanography (MS, PhD); paleoclimate (MS, PhD); planetary science (MS, PhD); remote sensing (MS, PhD). Part-time programs available. Terminal master's awarded for partial completion of doctoral program. *Degree requirements:* For master's, thesis or alternative; for doctorate, comprehensive exam, thesis/dissertation. *Entrance requirements:* For master's, GRE, letters of recommendation; for doctorate, GRE, academic transcripts, letters of recommendation, personal statement. Additional exam requirements/recommendations for international students: Required—TOEFL (minimum score 550 paper-based; 79 iBT). *Faculty research:* Geophysics; atmospheric chemistry, aerosols and clouds; dynamics of weather and climate; geochemistry; oceanography; paleoclimate; planetary science; remote sensing.

Hawai`i Pacific University, College of Natural and Computational Sciences, Honolulu, HI 96813. Offers global leadership and sustainable development (MA); marine science (MS). Part-time and evening/weekend programs available. *Degree requirements:* For master's, thesis. *Entrance requirements:* For master's, GRE, bachelor's degree in science or marine science, minimum GPA of 3.0. Additional exam requirements/recommendations for international students: Recommended—TOEFL (minimum score 550 paper-based; 80 iBT), TWE (minimum score 5). Electronic applications accepted.

Instituto Tecnologico de Santo Domingo, Graduate School, Area of Basic And Environmental Sciences, Santo Domingo, Dominican Republic. Offers environmental science (M En S), including environmental education, environmental management, marine resources, natural resources management; mathematics (MS, PhD); renewable energy technology (MS, Certificate).

Jacksonville University, Marine Science Research Institute, Jacksonville, FL 32211. Offers MA, MS. *Degree requirements:* For master's, thesis (for MS).

Medical University of South Carolina, College of Graduate Studies, Program in Molecular and Cellular Biology and Pathobiology, Charleston, SC 29425. Offers cancer biology (PhD); cardiovascular biology (PhD); cardiovascular imaging (PhD); cell regulation (PhD); craniofacial biology (PhD); genetics and development (PhD); marine biomedicine (PhD); DMD/PhD; MD/PhD. *Degree requirements:* For doctorate, thesis/dissertation, oral and written exams. *Entrance requirements:* For doctorate, GRE General Test, interview, minimum GPA of 3.0. Additional exam requirements/recommendations for international students: Required—TOEFL (minimum score 600 paper-based; 100 iBT). Electronic applications accepted.

Memorial University of Newfoundland, School of Graduate Studies, Interdisciplinary Program in Marine Studies, St. John's, NL A1C 5S7, Canada. Offers fisheries resource management (MMS, Advanced Diploma). Part-time programs available. *Degree requirements:* For master's, report. *Entrance requirements:* For master's and Advanced Diploma, high 2nd class degree from a recognized university. *Faculty research:* Biological, ecological and oceanographic aspects of world fisheries; economics; political science; sociology.

North Carolina State University, Graduate School, College of Physical and Mathematical Sciences, Department of Marine, Earth, and Atmospheric Sciences, Raleigh, NC 27695. Offers marine, earth, and atmospheric sciences (MS, PhD); meteorology (MS, PhD); oceanography (MS, PhD). PhD offered jointly with The University of North Carolina Wilmington. Terminal master's awarded for partial completion of doctoral program. *Degree requirements:* For master's, thesis (for some programs), final oral exam; for doctorate, comprehensive exam, thesis/dissertation, final oral exam, preliminary oral and written exams. *Entrance requirements:* For master's, GRE General Test, minimum GPA of 3.0; for doctorate, GRE General Test, GRE Subject Test (for disciplines in biological oceanography and geology), minimum GPA of 3.0. Additional exam requirements/recommendations for international students: Required—TOEFL (minimum score 550 paper-based). Electronic applications accepted. *Faculty research:* Boundary layer and air quality meteorology; climate and mesoscale dynamics; biological, chemical, geological, and physical oceanography; hard rock, soft rock, environmental, and paleo-geology.

Nova Southeastern University, Oceanographic Center, Fort Lauderdale, FL 33314-7796. Offers biological sciences (MS); coastal zone management (MS); marine and coastal studies (MA); marine biology (MS); marine biology and oceanography (PhD), including marine biology, oceanography; marine environmental sciences (MS). Part-time and evening/weekend programs available. *Faculty:* 13 full-time (1 woman), 20 part-time/adjunct (5 women). *Students:* 123 full-time (84 women), 153 part-time (96 women); includes 36 minority (7 Black or African American, non-Hispanic/Latino; 1 American Indian or Alaska Native, non-Hispanic/Latino; 5 Asian, non-Hispanic/Latino; 18 Hispanic/Latino; 5 Two or more races, non-Hispanic/Latino), 6 international. Average age 29. 98 applicants, 81% accepted, 48 enrolled. In 2012, 26 master's, 1 doctorate awarded. *Degree requirements:* For master's, thesis; for doctorate, comprehensive exam, thesis/dissertation, departmental qualifying exam. *Entrance requirements:* For master's, GRE General Test, 3 letters of recommendation, BS/BA in natural science (for marine biology program), BS/BA in biology (for biological sciences program), minor in the natural sciences or equivalent (for coastal zone management and marine environmental sciences); for doctorate, GRE General Test, master's degree. Additional exam requirements/recommendations for international students: Required—TOEFL (minimum score 550 paper-based). *Application deadline:* Applications are processed on a rolling basis. Application fee: $50. *Expenses:* Contact institution. *Financial support:* In 2012–13, 2 fellowships with full and partial tuition reimbursements (averaging $16,300 per year), 50 research assistantships with full and partial tuition reimbursements (averaging $19,000 per year) were awarded; teaching assistantships, career-related internships or fieldwork, Federal Work-Study, scholarships/grants, health care benefits, tuition waivers (full and partial), and unspecified assistantships also available. Support available to part-time students. Financial award applicants required to submit FAFSA. *Faculty research:* Physical, geological, chemical, and biological oceanography. *Unit head:* Dr. Richard Dodge, Dean, 954-262-3600, Fax: 954-262-4020, E-mail: dodge@nsu.nova.edu. *Application contact:* Dr. Richard Spieler, Associate Dean of Academic Programs, 954-262-3600, Fax: 954-262-4020, E-mail: spieler@nova.edu. Website: http://www.nova.edu/ocean/.

Oregon State University, College of Earth, Ocean, and Atmospheric Sciences, Program in Marine Resource Management, Corvallis, OR 97331. Offers MA, MS, Certificate. *Students:* 23 full-time (15 women), 3 part-time (1 woman); includes 3 minority (2 Asian, non-Hispanic/Latino; 1 Hispanic/Latino), 2 international. Average age 28. 47 applicants, 30% accepted, 10 enrolled. In 2012, 10 master's awarded. *Degree requirements:* For master's, thesis optional. *Entrance requirements:* For master's, GRE General Test, minimum GPA of 3.0 in last 90 hours of course work. Additional exam requirements/recommendations for international students: Required—TOEFL. *Application deadline:* For fall admission, 2/1 priority date for domestic students. Applications are processed on a rolling basis. Application fee: $50. *Expenses:* Tuition, state resident: full-time $11,367; part-time $421 per credit hour. Tuition, nonresident: full-time $18,279; part-time $677 per credit hour. *Required fees:* $1478. One-time fee: $300 full-time. Tuition and fees vary according to course load and program. *Financial support:* Fellowships, research assistantships, teaching assistantships, career-related internships or fieldwork, Federal Work-Study, and institutionally sponsored loans available. Support available to part-time students. Financial award application deadline: 2/1. *Faculty research:* Ocean and coastal resources, fisheries resources, marine pollution, marine recreation and tourism. *Unit head:*

Marine Sciences

Dr. Flaxen Conway, Director/Professor, 541-737-1339, Fax: 541-737-2540, E-mail: fconway@coas.oregonstate.edu. *Application contact:* Anna Pakenham, Assistant Director, 541-737-8637, Fax: 541-737-2064, E-mail: apakenham@coas.oregonstate.edu.

San Francisco State University, Division of Graduate Studies, College of Science and Engineering, Department of Biology, Program in Marine Science, San Francisco, CA 94132-1722. Offers MS. Program offered through the Moss Landing Marine Laboratories. *Application deadline:* Applications are processed on a rolling basis. *Unit head:* Dr. Kenneth Coale, Director, 831-771-4400, E-mail: frontdesk@mlml.calstate.edu. *Application contact:* Drew Seals, Graduate Coordinator, 831-771-4400, E-mail: dseals@mlml.calstate.edu. Website: http://www.sfsu.edu/~bulletin/current/programs/marines.htm#282.

San Jose State University, Graduate Studies and Research, College of Science, Moss Landing Marine Laboratories, San Jose, CA 95192-0001. Offers MS. *Degree requirements:* For master's, thesis, qualifying exam. *Entrance requirements:* For master's, GRE. Electronic applications accepted. *Faculty research:* Physical oceanography, marine geology, ecology, ichthyology, invertebrate zoology.

Savannah State University, Master of Science in Marine Sciences Program, Savannah, GA 31404. Offers applied marine science (MS); marine science research (MS); professional advancement (MS). Part-time and evening/weekend programs available. *Faculty:* 5 full-time (3 women). *Students:* 5 full-time (all women), 11 part-time (6 women); includes 9 minority (7 Black or African American, non-Hispanic/Latino; 1 American Indian or Alaska Native, non-Hispanic/Latino; 1 Asian, non-Hispanic/Latino). Average age 28. 4 applicants, 100% accepted, 2 enrolled. In 2012, 7 master's awarded. *Degree requirements:* For master's, comprehensive exam, field paper or thesis. *Entrance requirements:* For master's, GRE General Test, minimum GPA of 3.0, 3 letters of recommendation, essay, official transcripts, resume, immunization certificate, interview (recommended). Additional exam requirements/recommendations for international students: Required—TOEFL. *Application deadline:* For fall admission, 5/23 for domestic students, 5/15 for international students; for spring admission, 10/31 for domestic students, 10/1 for international students. Applications are processed on a rolling basis. Application fee: $25. Electronic applications accepted. *Expenses:* Tuition, state resident: full-time $4372. Tuition, nonresident: full-time $16,254. *Required fees:* $1680. *Financial support:* Career-related internships or fieldwork, Federal Work-Study, institutionally sponsored loans, scholarships/grants, health care benefits, and unspecified assistantships available. Financial award applicants required to submit FAFSA. *Unit head:* Dr. Carol Pride, MSMS Coordinator, 912-358-4433, E-mail: msms@savannahstate.edu. Website: http://www.savannahstate.edu/prospective-student/degrees-grad-ms.shtml.

Stony Brook University, State University of New York, Graduate School, School of Marine and Atmospheric Sciences, Institute for Terrestrial and Planetary Atmospheres, Program in Marine Sciences, Stony Brook, NY 11794. Offers MS, PhD. Evening/weekend programs available. *Degree requirements:* For doctorate, one foreign language, comprehensive exam, thesis/dissertation. *Entrance requirements:* For master's, GRE General Test, official transcripts, minimum GPA of 3.0, 3 letters of recommendation; for doctorate, GRE General Test, minimum GPA of 3.0, 3 letters of recommendation. Additional exam requirements/recommendations for international students: Required—TOEFL (minimum score 600 paper-based). *Application deadline:* For fall admission, 1/15 priority date for domestic students; for spring admission, 10/1 priority date for domestic students. Application fee: $100. Electronic applications accepted. *Expenses:* Tuition, state resident: full-time $9370. Tuition, nonresident: full-time $16,680. *Required fees:* $1214. *Financial support:* Fellowships, research assistantships, teaching assistantships, and career-related internships or fieldwork available. *Unit head:* Dr. Minghua Zhang, Director, 631-632-8318. *Application contact:* Dr. Anne R. McElroy, Assistant Director, 631-632-8488, Fax: 631-632-8200, E-mail: nne.mcelroy@stonybrook.edu.

Texas A&M University at Galveston, Department of Marine Sciences, Galveston, TX 77553-1675. Offers marine resources management (MMRM). Part-time programs available. *Faculty:* 33 full-time (7 women). *Students:* 20 full-time (9 women), 13 part-time (7 women); includes 3 minority (2 Hispanic/Latino; 1 Two or more races, non-Hispanic/Latino). Average age 24. 16 applicants, 94% accepted, 13 enrolled. In 2012, 11 master's awarded. *Degree requirements:* For master's, thesis (for some programs). *Entrance requirements:* For master's, GRE, course work in economics. Additional exam requirements/recommendations for international students: Required—TOEFL (minimum score 550 paper-based; 80 iBT), IELTS (minimum score 6). *Application deadline:* For fall admission, 6/15 for domestic and international students; for spring admission, 10/15 for domestic and international students. Application fee: $50 ($90 for international students). Electronic applications accepted. *Financial support:* In 2012–13, 11 students received support, including 2 research assistantships, 9 teaching assistantships; scholarships/grants, health care benefits, and unspecified assistantships also available. Financial award applicants required to submit FAFSA. *Faculty research:* Biogeochemistry, physical oceanography, theoretical chemistry, marine policy. *Unit head:* Dr. Patrick Louchouarn, Professor/Head, 409-740-4710. *Application contact:* Dr. Frederick C. Schlemmer, II, Associate Professor/Graduate Advisor, 409-740-4518, Fax: 409-740-4429, E-mail: schlemme@tamug.edu.

Texas A&M University–Corpus Christi, Graduate Studies and Research, College of Science and Technology, Program in Coastal and Marine System Science, Corpus Christi, TX 78412-5503. Offers PhD.

University of Alaska Fairbanks, School of Fisheries and Ocean Sciences, Program in Marine Sciences and Limnology, Fairbanks, AK 99775-7220. Offers marine biology (MS, PhD); oceanography (PhD), including biological oceanography, chemical oceanography, fisheries, geological oceanography, physical oceanography. Part-time programs available. *Faculty:* 5 full-time (2 women), 1 part-time/adjunct (0 women). *Students:* 45 full-time (33 women), 17 part-time (13 women); includes 8 minority (3 Asian, non-Hispanic/Latino; 5 Hispanic/Latino), 8 international. Average age 29. 52 applicants, 25% accepted, 12 enrolled. In 2012, 4 master's, 5 doctorates awarded. *Degree requirements:* For master's, comprehensive exam, thesis, oral defense; for doctorate, comprehensive exam, thesis/dissertation, oral defense. *Entrance requirements:* For master's and doctorate, GRE General Test. Additional exam requirements/recommendations for international students: Required—TOEFL (minimum score 550 paper-based; 80 iBT). *Application deadline:* For fall admission, 6/1 for domestic students, 3/1 for international students; for spring admission, 10/15 for domestic students, 8/1 for international students. Applications are processed on a rolling basis. Application fee: $60. Electronic applications accepted. *Expenses:* Tuition, state resident: full-time $7038. Tuition, nonresident: full-time $14,382. Tuition and fees vary according to course level, course load and reciprocity agreements. *Financial support:* In 2012–13, 31 research assistantships with tuition reimbursements (averaging $11,137 per year), 7 teaching assistantships with tuition reimbursements (averaging $11,750 per year) were awarded; fellowships with tuition reimbursements, career-related internships or fieldwork, Federal Work-Study, scholarships/grants, health care benefits, and unspecified assistantships also available. Support available to part-time students. Financial award application deadline: 7/1; financial award applicants required to submit FAFSA. *Unit head:* Katrin Iken, Co-Chair, 907-474-7289, Fax: 907-474-5863, E-mail: academics@sfos.uaf.edu. *Application contact:* Libby Eddy, Registrar and Director of Admissions, 907-474-7500, Fax: 907-474-7097, E-mail: admissions@alaska.edu. Website: http://www.sfos.uaf.edu/prospective/graduate/marinebio.php.

The University of British Columbia, Faculty of Science, Department of Earth and Ocean Sciences, Vancouver, BC V6T 1Z4, Canada. Offers atmospheric science (M Sc, PhD); geological engineering (M Eng, MA Sc, PhD); geological sciences (M Sc, PhD); geophysics (M Sc, MA Sc, PhD); oceanography (M Sc, PhD). *Degree requirements:* For master's, thesis (for some programs); for doctorate, comprehensive exam, thesis/dissertation. *Entrance requirements:* Additional exam requirements/recommendations for international students: Required—TOEFL (minimum score 600 paper-based; 100 iBT). Electronic applications accepted. *Faculty research:* Oceans and atmosphere, environmental earth science, hydro geology, mineral deposits, geophysics.

University of California, San Diego, Office of Graduate Studies, Scripps Institution of Oceanography, Program in Marine Biodiversity and Conservation, La Jolla, CA 92093. Offers MAS. *Entrance requirements:* For master's, minimum 3 years post-baccalaureate work experience. Additional exam requirements/recommendations for international students: Required—TOEFL. Electronic applications accepted.

University of California, Santa Barbara, Graduate Division, College of Letters and Sciences, Division of Mathematics, Life, and Physical Sciences, Interdepartmental Graduate Program in Marine Science, Santa Barbara, CA 93106-9620. Offers MS, PhD. *Faculty:* 39 full-time (11 women). *Students:* 18 full-time (12 women); includes 1 minority (American Indian or Alaska Native, non-Hispanic/Latino), 3 international. Average age 28. 50 applicants, 18% accepted, 5 enrolled. In 2012, 3 master's, 7 doctorates awarded. *Degree requirements:* For master's, thesis, 39 units; for doctorate, comprehensive exam, thesis/dissertation, 31 units. *Entrance requirements:* For master's and doctorate, GRE. Additional exam requirements/recommendations for international students: Required—TOEFL (minimum score 550 paper-based; 80 iBT), IELTS (minimum score 7). *Application deadline:* For fall admission, 12/15 for domestic and international students. Application fee: $80 ($100 for international students). Electronic applications accepted. *Financial support:* In 2012–13, 10 students received support, including 15 fellowships with full tuition reimbursements available (averaging $11,468 per year), 13 research assistantships with full tuition reimbursements available (averaging $10,895 per year), 7 teaching assistantships with full tuition reimbursements available (averaging $7,908 per year); career-related internships or fieldwork, Federal Work-Study, institutionally sponsored loans, scholarships/grants, health care benefits, tuition waivers (full and partial), and unspecified assistantships also available. Support available to part-time students. Financial award application deadline: 12/15; financial award applicants required to submit FAFSA. *Faculty research:* Ocean carbon cycling, paleooceanography, physiology of marine organisms, bio-optical oceanography, biological oceanography. *Unit head:* Prof. Libe Washburn, Chair/Professor of Geography, 805-893-7367, Fax: 805-893-2578, E-mail: washburn@eri.ucsb.edu. *Application contact:* Melanie Fujii, Student Affairs Officer, 805-893-2979, Fax: 805-893-5885, E-mail: fujii@lifesci.ucsb.edu. Website: http://www.igpms.ucsb.edu/.

University of California, Santa Cruz, Division of Graduate Studies, Division of Physical and Biological Sciences, Department of Ocean Sciences, Santa Cruz, CA 95064. Offers MS, PhD. Terminal master's awarded for partial completion of doctoral program. *Degree requirements:* For master's, thesis; for doctorate,

188 facebook.com/petersonspublishing

Peterson's Graduate Programs in the Physical Sciences, Mathematics, Agricultural Sciences, the Environment & Natural Resources 2014

comprehensive exam, thesis/dissertation, seminar, qualifying exam. *Entrance requirements:* For master's and doctorate, GRE General Test, GRE Subject Test, 3 letters of recommendation. Additional exam requirements/recommendations for international students: Required—TOEFL (minimum score 550 paper-based; 83 iBT); Recommended—IELTS (minimum score 8). Electronic applications accepted. *Faculty research:* Sediment, marine organic and trace metal biogeochemistry; paleoceanography; remote sensing (satellite oceanography); coastal circulation processes; the development of software applications for real-time data acquisition and data visualization; climatology.

University of Connecticut, Graduate School, College of Liberal Arts and Sciences, Department of Marine Sciences, Storrs, CT 06269. Offers MS, PhD. Terminal master's awarded for partial completion of doctoral program. *Degree requirements:* For master's, comprehensive exam; for doctorate, thesis/dissertation. *Entrance requirements:* Additional exam requirements/recommendations for international students: Required—TOEFL (minimum score 550 paper-based). Electronic applications accepted.

University of Delaware, College of Earth, Ocean, and Environment, School of Marine Science and Policy, Newark, DE 19716. Offers marine policy (MMP); marine studies (MS, PhD), including marine biosciences, oceanography, physical ocean science and engineering; oceanography (PhD).

University of Florida, Graduate School, College of Agricultural and Life Sciences, Department of Fisheries and Aquatic Sciences, Gainesville, FL 32611. Offers MFAS, MS, PhD. Part-time programs available. *Degree requirements:* For master's, thesis (for MS); technical paper (for MFAS); for doctorate, comprehensive exam, thesis/dissertation. *Entrance requirements:* For master's and doctorate, GRE General Test, minimum GPA of 3.0. Additional exam requirements/recommendations for international students: Required—TOEFL (minimum score 550 paper-based; 80 iBT), IELTS (minimum score 6). Electronic applications accepted. *Faculty research:* Conservation and management of aquatic ecosystems; aquatic animal health; water quality, nutrients, and eutrophication; sustainable and quantitative fisheries; aquaculture or ornamental fish, marine baitfish, and shellfish.

University of Georgia, Franklin College of Arts and Sciences, Department of Marine Sciences, Athens, GA 30602. Offers MS, PhD. *Degree requirements:* For master's, thesis; for doctorate, comprehensive exam, thesis/dissertation, teaching experience, field research experience. *Entrance requirements:* For master's and doctorate, GRE General Test. Additional exam requirements/recommendations for international students: Required—TOEFL. Electronic applications accepted. *Faculty research:* Microbial ecology, biogeochemistry, polar biology, coastal ecology, coastal circulation.

University of Hawaii at Manoa, Graduate Division, College of Social Sciences, Department of Geography, Graduate Ocean Policy Certificate Program, Honolulu, HI 96822. Offers Graduate Certificate. Part-time programs available. *Entrance requirements:* Additional exam requirements/recommendations for international students: Required—TOEFL (minimum score 500 paper-based; 61 iBT), IELTS (minimum score 5).

University of Maine, Graduate School, College of Natural Sciences, Forestry, and Agriculture, School of Marine Sciences, Orono, ME 04469. Offers marine biology (MS, PhD); marine policy (MS); oceanography (MS, PhD). Part-time programs available. *Faculty:* 40 full-time (8 women), 60 part-time/adjunct (16 women). *Students:* 46 full-time (24 women), 16 part-time (5 women); includes 1 minority (Hispanic/Latino), 7 international. Average age 29. 71 applicants, 15% accepted, 10 enrolled. In 2012, 12 master's, 3 doctorates awarded. *Degree requirements:* For master's, thesis; for doctorate, comprehensive exam, thesis/dissertation. *Entrance requirements:* For master's and doctorate, GRE General Test. Additional exam requirements/recommendations for international students: Required—TOEFL. *Application deadline:* For fall admission, 2/1 priority date for domestic students. Applications are processed on a rolling basis. Application fee: $65. Electronic applications accepted. *Financial support:* In 2012–13, 41 research assistantships with tuition reimbursements (averaging $16,713 per year), 6 teaching assistantships with tuition reimbursements (averaging $13,600 per year) were awarded; career-related internships or fieldwork, Federal Work-Study, and tuition waivers (full and partial) also available. Support available to part-time students. Financial award application deadline: 3/1. *Faculty research:* Coastal processes, microbial ecology, crustacean systematics. *Total annual research expenditures:* $2 million. *Unit head:* Dr. Peter Jumars, Director, 207-581-3321, Fax: 207-581-4388. *Application contact:* Scott G. Delcourt, Associate Dean of the Graduate School, 207-581-3291, Fax: 207-581-3232, E-mail: graduate@maine.edu. Website: http://www.umaine.edu/marine/.

University of Maryland, Baltimore, Graduate School, Program in Marine-Estuarine-Environmental Sciences, College Park, MD 20742. Offers MS, PhD. Part-time programs available. *Faculty:* 7. *Students:* 1 applicant. Terminal master's awarded for partial completion of doctoral program. *Degree requirements:* For master's, thesis, oral defense; for doctorate, comprehensive exam, thesis/dissertation, proposal defense, oral defense. *Entrance requirements:* For master's and doctorate, GRE General Test, minimum GPA of 3.0. Additional exam requirements/recommendations for international students: Required—TOEFL. *Application deadline:* For fall admission, 2/1 for domestic students, 1/1 for international students; for spring admission, 9/1 for domestic students. Applications are processed on a rolling basis. Application fee: $50. Electronic applications accepted. *Financial support:* In 2012–13, 1 research assistantship with tuition reimbursement was awarded; fellowships with tuition reimbursements, teaching assistantships with tuition reimbursements, scholarships/grants, and unspecified assistantships also available. *Unit head:* Dr. Kennedy T. Paynter, Jr., Director, 301-405-6938, Fax: 301-314-4139, E-mail: mees@umd.edu. *Application contact:* Keith T. Brooks, Assistant Dean, 410-706-7131, Fax: 410-706-3473, E-mail: kbrooks@umaryland.edu. Website: http://www.mees.umd.edu/.

University of Maryland, Baltimore County, Graduate School, College of Natural and Mathematical Sciences, Department of Biological Sciences, Baltimore, MD 21250. Offers applied molecular biology (MS); biological sciences (MS, PhD); biotechnology (MPS), including biotechnology; biotechnology (Graduate Certificate), including biochemical regulatory engineering, biotechnology management; marine-estuarine-environmental sciences (MS); molecular and cell biology (PhD); neuroscience and cognitive sciences (PhD). Part-time programs available. *Faculty:* 34 full-time (17 women). *Students:* 84 full-time (48 women); includes 33 minority (11 Black or African American, non-Hispanic/Latino; 19 Asian, non-Hispanic/Latino; 3 Hispanic/Latino). Average age 27. 154 applicants, 21% accepted, 19 enrolled. In 2012, 9 master's, 10 doctorates awarded. *Entrance requirements:* For master's and doctorate, GRE General Test, minimum GPA of 3.0. Additional exam requirements/recommendations for international students: Required—TOEFL. *Application deadline:* For fall admission, 1/15 for domestic students, 12/15 for international students. Applications are processed on a rolling basis. Application fee: $50. Electronic applications accepted. *Financial support:* In 2012–13, 77 students received support, including fellowships (averaging $12,000 per year), 33 research assistantships (averaging $22,746 per year), 44 teaching assistantships (averaging $21,726 per year); career-related internships or fieldwork and tuition waivers (partial) also available. *Unit head:* Dr. Philip Farabaugh, Chairman, 410-455-3081, Fax: 410-455-3875, E-mail: farabaug@umbc.edu. *Application contact:* Dr. Stephen Miller, Director, 410-455-3381, Fax: 410-455-3875, E-mail: biograd@umbc.edu.

University of Maryland, Baltimore County, Graduate School, Marine-Estuarine-Environmental Sciences Graduate Program, College Park, MD 20742. Offers MS, PhD. Part-time programs available. *Faculty:* 11. *Students:* 2 full-time (1 woman). 6 applicants, 33% accepted, 2 enrolled. In 2012, 1 doctorate awarded. *Degree requirements:* For master's, thesis, oral defense; for doctorate, comprehensive exam, thesis/dissertation, proposal defense, oral defense. *Entrance requirements:* For master's and doctorate, GRE General Test, minimum GPA of 3.0. Additional exam requirements/recommendations for international students: Required—TOEFL. *Application deadline:* For fall admission, 2/1 for domestic students, 1/1 for international students; for spring admission, 9/1 for domestic students. Applications are processed on a rolling basis. Application fee: $50. Electronic applications accepted. *Financial support:* In 2012–13, 2 fellowships with tuition reimbursements (averaging $22,500 per year), 1 research assistantship with tuition reimbursement (averaging $21,000 per year), 1 teaching assistantship with tuition reimbursement (averaging $20,000 per year) were awarded; career-related internships or fieldwork, scholarships/grants, and unspecified assistantships also available. Financial award application deadline: 12/1. *Unit head:* Dr. Kennedy T. Paynter, Jr., Director, 301-405-6938, Fax: 301-314-4139, E-mail: mees@umd.edu. Website: http://www.mees.umd.edu.

University of Maryland, College Park, Academic Affairs, College of Computer, Mathematical and Natural Sciences, Program in Marine-Estuarine-Environmental Sciences, College Park, MD 20742. Offers MS, PhD. Part-time programs available. *Faculty:* 127. *Students:* 113 (73 women); includes 9 minority (3 Black or African American, non-Hispanic/Latino; 4 Asian, non-Hispanic/Latino; 2 Hispanic/Latino), 22 international. 141 applicants, 26% accepted, 23 enrolled. In 2012, 13 master's, 12 doctorates awarded. Terminal master's awarded for partial completion of doctoral program. *Degree requirements:* For master's, thesis, oral defense; for doctorate, comprehensive exam, thesis/dissertation, proposal defense, oral defense. *Entrance requirements:* For master's and doctorate, GRE General Test, minimum GPA of 3.0. Additional exam requirements/recommendations for international students: Required—TOEFL. *Application deadline:* For fall admission, 2/1 for domestic and international students; for spring admission, 9/1 for domestic students, 6/1 for international students. Applications are processed on a rolling basis. Application fee: $75. Electronic applications accepted. *Expenses:* Tuition, state resident: part-time $551 per credit. Tuition, nonresident: part-time $1188 per credit. Part-time tuition and fees vary according to program. *Financial support:* In 2012–13, 9 teaching assistantships with full tuition reimbursements were awarded; fellowships with full tuition reimbursements, research assistantships with full tuition reimbursements, Federal Work-Study, scholarships/grants, traineeships, health care benefits, and unspecified assistantships also available. Financial award application deadline: 1/1; financial award applicants required to submit FAFSA. *Faculty research:* Ecology, environmental chemistry, environmental molecular biology/biotechnology, environmental sciences, fisheries science, oceanography. *Unit head:* Dr. Kennedy T. Paynter, Jr., Director, 301-405-6938, Fax: 301-314-4139, E-mail: mees@umd.edu. Website: http://www.mees.umd.edu/.

University of Maryland Eastern Shore, Graduate Programs, Department of Natural Sciences, Princess Anne, MD 21853-1299. Offers marine-estuarine-environmental sciences (MS, PhD); toxicology (MS, PhD). *Degree requirements:* For master's, thesis; for doctorate, comprehensive exam, thesis/dissertation. *Entrance requirements:* For master's and doctorate, GRE General Test, minimum GPA of 3.0. Additional exam requirements/recommendations for international students: Required—TOEFL (minimum score 80 iBT). Electronic applications accepted. *Faculty research:* Environmental chemistry (air/water pollution), fin fish ecology.

Marine Sciences

University of Maryland Eastern Shore, Graduate Programs, Program in Marine-Estuarine-Environmental Sciences, College Park, MD 20742. Offers MS, PhD. Part-time programs available. *Faculty:* 26. *Students:* 30 full-time (20 women), 2 part-time (both women); includes 10 minority (8 Black or African American, non-Hispanic/Latino; 1 American Indian or Alaska Native, non-Hispanic/Latino; 1 Hispanic/Latino), 13 international. 12 applicants, 67% accepted, 5 enrolled. In 2012, 3 master's, 3 doctorates awarded. *Degree requirements:* For master's, thesis; for doctorate, comprehensive exam, thesis/dissertation, proposal defense. *Entrance requirements:* For master's and doctorate, GRE General Test, minimum GPA of 3.0. Additional exam requirements/recommendations for international students: Required—TOEFL. *Application deadline:* For fall admission, 2/1 for domestic and international students; for spring admission, 9/1 for domestic students, 8/1 for international students. Applications are processed on a rolling basis. Application fee: $45. Electronic applications accepted. *Financial support:* In 2012–13, 28 students received support. Fellowships with tuition reimbursements available, research assistantships with tuition reimbursements available, teaching assistantships with tuition reimbursements available, career-related internships or fieldwork, scholarships/grants, and unspecified assistantships available. Support available to part-time students. Financial award application deadline: 1/1. *Unit head:* Dr. Kennedy T. Paynter, Jr., Director, 301-405-6938, Fax: 301-314-4139, E-mail: mees@umd.edu. Website: http://www.mees.umd.edu/.

University of Massachusetts Amherst, Graduate School, Interdisciplinary Programs, Program in Marine Science and Technology, Amherst, MA 01003. Offers MS, PhD. Part-time programs available. *Students:* 4 full-time (3 women), 3 part-time (2 women). Average age 29. In 2012, 1 doctorate awarded. Terminal master's awarded for partial completion of doctoral program. *Degree requirements:* For master's, thesis or alternative; for doctorate, comprehensive exam, thesis/dissertation. *Entrance requirements:* For master's and doctorate, GRE General Test, 3 letters of recommendation. Additional exam requirements/recommendations for international students: Required—TOEFL (minimum score 550 paper-based; 80 iBT), IELTS (minimum score 6.5). *Application deadline:* For fall admission, 12/15 for domestic and international students; for spring admission, 10/1 for domestic and international students. Applications are processed on a rolling basis. Application fee: $75. Electronic applications accepted. *Expenses:* Tuition, state resident: full-time $1980; part-time $110 per credit. Tuition, nonresident: full-time $13,314; part-time $414 per credit. *Required fees:* $10,338; $3594 per semester. One-time fee: $357. *Financial support:* Fellowships, research assistantships, teaching assistantships, career-related internships or fieldwork, Federal Work-Study, scholarships/grants, traineeships, health care benefits, tuition waivers (full and partial), and unspecified assistantships available. Support available to part-time students. Financial award application deadline: 12/15; financial award applicants required to submit FAFSA. *Unit head:* Dr. Andy Danylchuk, Graduate Program Director, 413-545-2940. *Application contact:* Lindsay DeSantis, Supervisor of Admissions, 413-545-0722, Fax: 413-577-0010, E-mail: gradadm@grad.umass.edu. Website: http://www.umassmarine.net/.

University of Massachusetts Boston, Office of Graduate Studies, College of Science and Mathematics, Department of Environmental, Earth and Ocean Sciences, Track in Environmental, Earth and Ocean Sciences, Boston, MA 02125-3393. Offers PhD. Part-time and evening/weekend programs available. *Degree requirements:* For doctorate, comprehensive exam, thesis/dissertation, oral exams. *Entrance requirements:* For doctorate, GRE General Test, minimum GPA of 2.75. *Faculty research:* Conservation genetics, anthropogenic and natural influences on community structures of coral reef factors, geographical variation in mitochondrial DNA, protein chemistry and enzymology pertaining to insect cuticle.

University of Massachusetts Dartmouth, Graduate School, School of Marine Science and Technology, North Dartmouth, MA 02747-2300. Offers coastal and ocean administration science and technology (MS); marine science (MS, PhD). Part-time programs available. *Faculty:* 14 full-time (1 woman), 1 part-time/adjunct (0 women). *Students:* 32 full-time (14 women), 26 part-time (7 women); includes 1 minority (Hispanic/Latino), 15 international. Average age 32. 44 applicants, 73% accepted, 8 enrolled. In 2012, 7 master's, 1 doctorate awarded. Terminal master's awarded for partial completion of doctoral program. *Degree requirements:* For master's, thesis or alternative; for doctorate, comprehensive exam, thesis/dissertation. *Entrance requirements:* For master's and doctorate, GRE, resume, 3 letters of recommendation, official transcripts. Additional exam requirements/recommendations for international students: Required—TOEFL (minimum score 577 paper-based; 91 iBT). *Application deadline:* For fall admission, 2/15 priority date for domestic students, 1/15 for international students; for spring admission, 11/15 priority date for domestic students, 10/15 for international students. Applications are processed on a rolling basis. Application fee: $60. Electronic applications accepted. *Expenses:* Tuition, state resident: part-time $86.29 per credit. Tuition, nonresident: part-time $337.46 per credit. *Required fees:* $631.03 per credit. Tuition and fees vary according to course load and reciprocity agreements. *Financial support:* In 2012–13, 1 fellowship with full tuition reimbursement (averaging $30,000 per year), 30 research assistantships with full and partial tuition reimbursements (averaging $6,600 per year) were awarded. Financial award application deadline: 3/1; financial award applicants required to submit FAFSA. *Faculty research:* Storm-forced and internal wave dynamics, estuarine circulation, marine biogeochemical cycles, spatial distributions of marine fishes and invertebrates, plankton communities. *Total annual research expenditures:* $10.5 million. *Unit head:* Louis Goodman, Associate Dean, School of Marine Science and Technology, 508-910-6375, Fax: 508-910-6371, E-mail: lgoodman@umassd.edu. *Application contact:* Steven Briggs, Director of Marketing and Recruitment, 508-999-8604, Fax: 508-999-8183, E-mail: graduate@umassd.edu. Website: http://www.umassd.edu/smast.

University of Miami, Graduate School, Rosenstiel School of Marine and Atmospheric Science, Division of Applied Marine Physics, Coral Gables, FL 33124. Offers applied marine physics (MS, PhD), including coastal ocean dynamics, underwater acoustics and geoacoustics (PhD); wave surface dynamics and air-sea interaction (PhD). Part-time programs available. Terminal master's awarded for partial completion of doctoral program. *Degree requirements:* For master's, comprehensive exam, thesis; for doctorate, comprehensive exam, thesis/dissertation. *Entrance requirements:* For master's and doctorate, GRE General Test. Additional exam requirements/recommendations for international students: Required—TOEFL (minimum score 550 paper-based). Electronic applications accepted.

University of Miami, Graduate School, Rosenstiel School of Marine and Atmospheric Science, Division of Marine and Atmospheric Chemistry, Coral Gables, FL 33124. Offers MS, PhD. Terminal master's awarded for partial completion of doctoral program. *Degree requirements:* For master's, comprehensive exam, thesis; for doctorate, comprehensive exam, thesis/dissertation. *Entrance requirements:* For master's and doctorate, GRE General Test. Additional exam requirements/recommendations for international students: Required—TOEFL (minimum score 550 paper-based). Electronic applications accepted. *Faculty research:* Global change issues, chemistry of marine waters and marine atmosphere.

University of Michigan, School of Natural Resources and Environment, Program in Natural Resources and Environment, Ann Arbor, MI 48109-1041. Offers aquatic sciences: research and management (MS); behavior, education and communication (MS); conservation biology (MS); conservation ecology (MS); environmental informatics (MS); environmental justice (MS); environmental policy and planning (MS); natural resources and environment (PhD); sustainable systems (MS); terrestrial ecosystems (MS); MS/JD; MS/MBA; MUP/MS. *Faculty:* 45 full-time, 23 part-time/adjunct. *Students:* 399 full-time (221 women); includes 65 minority (4 Black or African American, non-Hispanic/Latino; 29 Asian, non-Hispanic/Latino; 23 Hispanic/Latino; 9 Two or more races, non-Hispanic/Latino), 68 international. Average age 27. 635 applicants. In 2012, 138 master's, 9 doctorates awarded. Terminal master's awarded for partial completion of doctoral program. *Degree requirements:* For master's, practicum or group project; for doctorate, comprehensive exam, thesis/dissertation, oral defense of dissertation, preliminary exam. *Entrance requirements:* For master's, GRE General Test; for doctorate, GRE General Test, master's degree. Additional exam requirements/recommendations for international students: Required—TOEFL (minimum score 560 paper-based; 84 iBT). *Application deadline:* For fall admission, 1/5 priority date for domestic students, 1/5 for international students. Applications are processed on a rolling basis. Application fee: $65 ($75 for international students). Electronic applications accepted. *Financial support:* Fellowships with tuition reimbursements, research assistantships with tuition reimbursements, teaching assistantships with tuition reimbursements, career-related internships or fieldwork, Federal Work-Study, institutionally sponsored loans, scholarships/grants, health care benefits, and unspecified assistantships available. Support available to part-time students. Financial award application deadline: 1/5; financial award applicants required to submit FAFSA. *Faculty research:* Stream ecology and fish biology, plant-insect interactions, environmental education, resource control and reproductive success, remote sensing, conservation ecology, sustainable systems. *Unit head:* Dr. Marie Lynn Miranda, Dean, 734-764-2550, Fax: 734-763-8965, E-mail: mlmirand@umich.edu. *Application contact:* Sondra R. Auerbach, Director of Academic Services, 734-764-6453, Fax: 734-936-2195, E-mail: snre.admissions@umich.edu. Website: http://www.snre.umich.edu/.

University of New England, College of Arts and Sciences, Program in Marine Sciences, Biddeford, ME 04005-9526. Offers MS. *Faculty:* 8 full-time (4 women). *Students:* 11 full-time (6 women), 8 part-time (all women); includes 1 minority (Asian, non-Hispanic/Latino). Average age 25. 37 applicants, 27% accepted, 8 enrolled. In 2012, 2 master's awarded. *Degree requirements:* For master's, thesis. *Entrance requirements:* For master's, GRE. *Application deadline:* For fall admission, 2/1 for domestic students. Application fee: $40. *Financial support:* Application deadline: 5/1; applicants required to submit FAFSA. *Unit head:* Barry Costa-Pierce, Chair and Professor, Department of Marine Sciences, 207-602-2440, E-mail: bcostapierce@une.edu. *Application contact:* Stacy Gato, Executive Director of University Admissions, 207-221-4225, Fax: 207-523-1925, E-mail: gradadmissions@une.edu. Website: http://www.une.edu/cas/marine/graduate/.

University of New Hampshire, Graduate School, College of Life Sciences and Agriculture, Department of Natural Resources, Durham, NH 03824. Offers environmental conservation (MS); forestry (MS); integrated coastal ecosystem science, policy, management (MS); natural resources (MS); water resources (MS); wildlife (MS). Part-time programs available. *Faculty:* 40 full-time. *Students:* 32 full-time (18 women), 29 part-time (16 women); includes 3 minority (all Hispanic/Latino), 3 international. Average age 28. 63 applicants, 43% accepted, 22 enrolled. In 2012, 14 master's awarded. *Degree requirements:* For master's, thesis or alternative. *Entrance requirements:* For master's, GRE General Test. Additional exam requirements/recommendations for international students: Required—TOEFL (minimum score 550 paper-based; 80 iBT). *Application deadline:* For fall admission, 6/1 for domestic students, 4/1 for international students; for spring admission, 12/1 for domestic students. Applications are processed on a rolling basis. Application fee: $65. Electronic applications accepted. *Expenses:* Tuition, state resident: full-time $13,500; part-time $750 per credit. Tuition, nonresident: full-time $25,940; part-time $1089 per credit. *Required fees:* $1699; $424.75 per semester. *Financial support:* In 2012–13, 35 students received support, including 1 fellowship, 15 research assistantships, 23 teaching assistantships; career-related internships or fieldwork, Federal Work-Study, scholarships/grants, and tuition waivers (full and partial) also available. Support available to part-time students. Financial award application deadline: 2/15. *Unit head:* Dr. Ted Howard, Chairperson, 603-862-2700, E-mail: natural.resources@unh.edu. *Application contact:* Nancy Brown, Administrative Assistant, 603-862-1022, E-mail: natural.resources@unh.edu. Website: http://www.nre.unh.edu/academics/.

The University of North Carolina at Chapel Hill, Graduate School, College of Arts and Sciences, Department of Marine Sciences, Chapel Hill, NC 27599. Offers MS, PhD. *Faculty:* 23 full-time (4 women), 12 part-time/adjunct (1 woman). *Students:* 40 full-time (23 women); includes 4 minority (2 Hispanic/Latino; 2 Two or more races, non-Hispanic/Latino), 5 international. Average age 28. 65 applicants, 22% accepted, 14 enrolled. In 2012, 3 master's, 3 doctorates awarded. *Degree requirements:* For master's, comprehensive exam, thesis; for doctorate, comprehensive exam, thesis/dissertation. *Entrance requirements:* For master's and doctorate, GRE General Test, minimum GPA of 3.0. Additional exam requirements/recommendations for international students: Required—TOEFL. *Application deadline:* For fall admission, 1/2 priority date for domestic students, 1/2 for international students. Application fee: $80. Electronic applications accepted. *Financial support:* In 2012–13, 37 students received support, including 4 fellowships with full tuition reimbursements available, 23 research assistantships with full tuition reimbursements available (averaging $20,500 per year), 10 teaching assistantships with full tuition reimbursements available (averaging $20,500 per year); scholarships/grants, traineeships, health care benefits, and unspecified assistantships also available. Financial award application deadline: 3/1. *Faculty research:* Physical oceanography, marine biology and ecology, marine geochemistry, marine geology and coastal meteorology. *Unit head:* Dr. Harvey Seim, Chairman, 919-962-2083, Fax: 919-962-1254, E-mail: harvey_seim@unc.edu. *Application contact:* Rachel Copeland, Student Services Manager, 919-843-0308, Fax: 919-962-1254, E-mail: rachelc@unc.edu. Website: http://marine.unc.edu/.

The University of North Carolina at Chapel Hill, Graduate School, Gillings School of Global Public Health, Department of Environmental Sciences and Engineering, Chapel Hill, NC 27599. Offers air, radiation and industrial hygiene (MPH, MS, MSEE, MSPH, PhD); aquatic and atmospheric sciences (MPH, MS, MSPH, PhD); environmental engineering (MPH, MS, MSEE, MSPH, PhD); environmental health sciences (MPH, MS, MSPH, PhD); environmental management and policy (MPH, MS, MSPH, PhD). *Faculty:* 31 full-time. *Students:* 131 full-time (74 women); includes 31 minority (3 Black or African American, non-Hispanic/Latino; 13 Asian, non-Hispanic/Latino; 9 Hispanic/Latino; 1 Native Hawaiian or other Pacific Islander, non-Hispanic/Latino; 5 Two or more races, non-Hispanic/Latino), 24 international. Average age 27. 262 applicants, 26% accepted, 30 enrolled. In 2012, 22 master's, 8 doctorates awarded. Terminal master's awarded for partial completion of doctoral program. *Degree requirements:* For master's, comprehensive exam, thesis (for some programs), research paper; for doctorate, comprehensive exam, thesis/dissertation. *Entrance requirements:* For master's and doctorate, GRE General Test, minimum GPA of 3.0 (recommended). Additional exam requirements/recommendations for international students: Required—TOEFL. *Application deadline:* For fall admission, 12/10 priority date for domestic students, 12/10 for international students; for spring admission, 9/10 for domestic students. Applications are processed on a rolling basis. Application fee: $85. Electronic applications accepted. *Financial support:* Fellowships with tuition reimbursements, research assistantships with tuition reimbursements, teaching assistantships with tuition reimbursements, career-related internships or fieldwork, Federal Work-Study, traineeships, health care benefits, and unspecified assistantships available. Support available to part-time students. Financial award application deadline: 12/10; financial award applicants required to submit FAFSA. *Faculty research:* Air, radiation and industrial hygiene, aquatic and atmospheric sciences, environmental health sciences, environmental management and policy, water resources engineering. *Unit head:* Dr. Michael Aitken, Chair, 919-966-1024, Fax: 919-966-7911, E-mail: mike_aitken@unc.edu. *Application contact:* Jack Whaley, Registrar, 919-966-3844, Fax: 919-966-7911, E-mail: jack_whaley@unc.edu. Website: http://www2.sph.unc.edu/envr/.

The University of North Carolina Wilmington, College of Arts and Sciences, Department of Biology and Marine Biology, Wilmington, NC 28403-3297. Offers biology (MS); marine biology (MS, PhD). Part-time programs available. *Degree requirements:* For master's, comprehensive exam, thesis; for doctorate, comprehensive exam, thesis/dissertation. *Entrance requirements:* For master's, GRE General Test, GRE Subject Test, minimum B average in undergraduate major; for doctorate, GRE General Test, minimum B average in undergraduate major and graduate courses. Additional exam requirements/recommendations for international students: Required—TOEFL (minimum score 550 paper-based; 79 iBT), IELTS (minimum score 6.5). Electronic applications accepted. *Faculty research:* Ecology, physiology, cell and molecular biology, systematics, biomechanics.

University of Puerto Rico, Mayagüez Campus, Graduate Studies, College of Arts and Sciences, Department of Marine Sciences, Mayagüez, PR 00681-9000. Offers MS, PhD. Part-time programs available. *Faculty:* 13 full-time (0 women). *Students:* 48 full-time (24 women), 1 (woman) part-time; includes 36 minority (all Hispanic/Latino), 7 international. 12 applicants, 100% accepted, 11 enrolled. In 2012, 2 master's, 1 doctorate awarded. *Degree requirements:* For master's, one foreign language, thesis, departmental and comprehensive final exams; for doctorate, one foreign language, thesis/dissertation, qualifying, comprehensive, and final exams. *Entrance requirements:* For master's, GRE, minimum GPA of 3.0; for doctorate, GRE, minimum GPA of 3.5. *Application deadline:* For fall admission, 2/15 for domestic and international students; for spring admission, 9/15 for domestic and international students. Applications are processed on a rolling basis. Application fee: $25. Tuition and fees vary according to course level and course load. *Financial support:* In 2012–13, 13 students received support, including 22 research assistantships (averaging $15,000 per year), 5 teaching assistantships (averaging $8,500 per year); Federal Work-Study and institutionally sponsored loans also available. *Faculty research:* Marine botany, ecology, chemistry, and parasitology; fisheries; ichthyology; aquaculture. *Unit head:* Dr. John Kubaryk, Director, 787-265-3838, Fax: 787-265-3838, E-mail: john.kubaryk@upr.edu. *Application contact:* Monserrate Casiano, Secretary, 787-832-4040 Ext. 3447, Fax: 787-265-3838, E-mail: monserrate.casiano@upr.edu. Website: http://cima.uprm.edu.

University of Rhode Island, Graduate School, College of the Environment and Life Sciences, Department of Fisheries, Animal and Veterinary Science, Kingston, RI 02881. Offers animal health and disease (MS); animal science (MS); aquaculture (MS); aquatic pathology (MS); environmental sciences (PhD), including animal science, aquacultural science, aquatic pathology, fisheries science; fisheries (MS). *Faculty:* 9 full-time (4 women). *Students:* 6 full-time (2 women), 1 part-time (0 women), 2 international. In 2012, 6 master's, 1 doctorate awarded. *Degree requirements:* For master's, comprehensive exam (for some programs), thesis optional; for doctorate, comprehensive exam, thesis/dissertation. *Entrance requirements:* For master's and doctorate, GRE, 2 letters of recommendation. Additional exam requirements/recommendations for international students: Required—TOEFL (minimum score 550 paper-based). *Application deadline:* For fall admission, 7/15 for domestic students, 2/1 for international students; for spring admission, 11/15 for domestic students, 7/15 for international students. Application fee: $65. Electronic applications accepted. *Expenses:* Tuition, state resident: full-time $11,532; part-time $641 per credit. Tuition, nonresident: full-time $23,606; part-time $1311 per credit. *Required fees:* $1388; $36 per credit. $35 per semester. One-time fee: $130. *Financial support:* In 2012–13, 3 research assistantships with full and partial tuition reimbursements (averaging $11,679 per year), 1 teaching assistantship with full and partial tuition reimbursement (averaging $9,818 per year) were awarded. Financial award application deadline: 7/15; financial award applicants required to submit FAFSA. *Unit head:* Dr. David Bengtson, Chair, 401-874-2668, Fax: 401-874-7575, E-mail: bengtson@uri.edu. Website: http://www.uri.edu/cels/favs/.

University of San Diego, College of Arts and Sciences, Program in Marine Science, San Diego, CA 92110-2492. Offers MS. Part-time programs available. *Faculty:* 4 full-time (1 woman). *Students:* 8 full-time (4 women), 12 part-time (10 women); includes 6 minority (1 Black or African American, non-Hispanic/Latino; 2 Hispanic/Latino; 3 Two or more races, non-Hispanic/Latino). Average age 27. 28 applicants, 21% accepted, 2 enrolled. In 2012, 2 master's awarded. *Degree requirements:* For master's, thesis. *Entrance requirements:* For master's, GRE General Test, minimum GPA of 3.0, 1 semester of biology with lab, 1 year of chemistry with lab, 1 year of physics with lab, 1 semester of calculus. Additional exam requirements/recommendations for international students: Required—TOEFL (minimum score 580 paper-based; 83 iBT), TWE. *Application deadline:* For fall admission, 4/1 for domestic and international students. Applications are processed on a rolling basis. Application fee: $45. Electronic applications accepted. *Expenses: Tuition:* Full-time $23,040; part-time $1280 per unit. *Required fees:* $270. Full-time tuition and fees vary according to course load and degree level. *Financial support:* In 2012–13, 13 students received support. Career-related internships or fieldwork, Federal Work-Study, institutionally sponsored loans, and unspecified assistantships available. Support available to part-time students. Financial award application deadline: 4/1; financial award applicants required to submit FAFSA. *Faculty research:* Marine ecology, environmental geology and geochemistry, climatology, physiological ecology, fisheries and aquaculture. *Unit head:* Dr. Ronald S. Kaufmann, Director, 619-260-4795, Fax: 619-260-6874, E-mail: andrewsk@sandiego.edu. *Application contact:* Monica Mahon, Associate Director of Graduate Admissions, 619-260-4524, Fax: 619-260-4158, E-mail: grads@sandiego.edu. Website: http://www.sandiego.edu/cas/marine_science_ms/.

University of South Alabama, Graduate School, College of Arts and Sciences, Department of Marine Sciences, Mobile, AL 36688-0002. Offers MS, PhD. *Faculty:* 6 full-time (1 woman). *Students:* 23 full-time (12 women), 16 part-time (9 women); includes 1 minority (Native Hawaiian or other Pacific Islander, non-Hispanic/Latino), 5 international. 47 applicants, 30% accepted, 6 enrolled. In 2012, 7 master's, 7 doctorates awarded. *Degree requirements:* For master's, comprehensive exam, thesis optional; for doctorate, one foreign language, comprehensive exam, thesis/dissertation, research project. *Entrance requirements:* For master's, GRE, minimum GPA of 3.0, BS in marine sciences or related discipline; for doctorate, GRE, BS or MS in marine sciences or related discipline; minimum undergraduate GPA of 3.0, graduate 3.25. Additional exam requirements/recommendations for international students: Required—TOEFL. *Application deadline:* For fall admission, 4/1 priority date for domestic students, 3/1 for international students. Applications are processed on a rolling basis. Application fee: $35. *Expenses:* Tuition, state resident: full-time $8592; part-time $358 per credit hour. Tuition, nonresident: full-time $17,184; part-time $716 per

Oceanography

credit hour. *Financial support:* In 2012–13, fellowships with tuition reimbursements (averaging $13,600 per year), research assistantships (averaging $16,000 per year) were awarded. Financial award application deadline: 4/1. *Unit head:* Dr. Robert Shipp, Chair, 251-460-7136, Fax: 251-460-7136. *Application contact:* Dr. Ronald Kiene, Graduate Coordinator, 251-460-7136, Fax: 251-460-7928. Website: http://www.southalabama.edu/marinesciences.

University of South Carolina, The Graduate School, College of Arts and Sciences, Marine Science Program, Columbia, SC 29208. Offers MS, PhD. *Degree requirements:* For master's, thesis; for doctorate, comprehensive exam, thesis/dissertation. *Entrance requirements:* For master's and doctorate, GRE General Test. Additional exam requirements/recommendations for international students: Required—TOEFL (minimum score 570 paper-based). Electronic applications accepted. *Faculty research:* Biological, chemical, geological, and physical oceanography; policy.

University of Southern California, Graduate School, Dana and David Dornsife College of Letters, Arts and Sciences, Graduate Program in Ocean Sciences, Los Angeles, CA 90089. Offers MS, PhD. Only Ph.D. and M.S./Ph.D. students are funded. Part-time programs available. Terminal master's awarded for partial completion of doctoral program. *Degree requirements:* For master's, thesis; for doctorate, comprehensive exam, thesis/dissertation. *Entrance requirements:* For master's and doctorate, GRE. Additional exam requirements/recommendations for international students: Required—TOEFL. Electronic applications accepted. *Faculty research:* Microbial ecology, biogeochemical cycles, marine chemistry, marine biology, global change.

University of Southern Mississippi, Graduate School, College of Science and Technology, Department of Coastal Sciences, Ocean Springs, MS 39566-7000. Offers MS, PhD. Part-time programs available. *Faculty:* 17 full-time (4 women), 2 part-time/adjunct (0 women). *Students:* 68 full-time (31 women), 22 part-time (11 women); includes 6 minority (1 Black or African American, non-Hispanic/Latino; 3 Hispanic/Latino; 2 Two or more races, non-Hispanic/Latino), 23 international. Average age 30. 65 applicants, 37% accepted, 19 enrolled. In 2012, 20 master's, 4 doctorates awarded. Terminal master's awarded for partial completion of doctoral program. *Degree requirements:* For master's, comprehensive exam, thesis; for doctorate, comprehensive exam, thesis/dissertation. *Entrance requirements:* For master's, GRE General Test, minimum GPA of 3.0 for last 60 hours; for doctorate, GRE General Test, minimum undergraduate GPA of 3.0, graduate 3.5. Additional exam requirements/recommendations for international students: Required—TOEFL, IELTS. *Application deadline:* For fall admission, 3/1 priority date for domestic students, 3/1 for international students. Applications are processed on a rolling basis. Application fee: $50. Electronic applications accepted. *Financial support:* In 2012–13, 1 fellowship with full tuition reimbursement (averaging $10,000 per year), 34 research assistantships with full tuition reimbursements (averaging $16,232 per year) were awarded; Federal Work-Study, scholarships/grants, health care benefits, and unspecified assistantships also available. Financial award application deadline: 3/15; financial award applicants required to submit FAFSA. *Unit head:* Dr. Jeffrey Lotz, Chair, 228-872-4215, Fax: 228-872-4295. *Application contact:* Kalin Buttrich, Administrative Assistant, 228-872-4201, Fax: 228-872-4295. Website: http://www.usm.edu/graduateschool/table.php.

University of Southern Mississippi, Graduate School, College of Science and Technology, Department of Marine Science, Stennis Space Center, MS 39529. Offers hydrographic science (MS); marine science (MS, PhD). Part-time programs available. *Faculty:* 16 full-time (2 women). *Students:* 37 full-time (15 women), 7 part-time (4 women); includes 15 minority (4 Black or African American, non-Hispanic/Latino; 9 Asian, non-Hispanic/Latino; 2 Hispanic/Latino). Average age 31. 46 applicants, 48% accepted, 17 enrolled. In 2012, 18 master's, 1 doctorate awarded. *Median time to degree:* Of those who began their doctoral program in fall 2004, 100% received their degree in 8 years or less. *Degree requirements:* For master's, comprehensive exam, thesis, oral qualifying exam (marine science); for doctorate, 2 foreign languages, comprehensive exam, thesis/dissertation, oral qualifying exam. *Entrance requirements:* For master's, GRE General Test, minimum GPA of 3.0; for doctorate, GRE General Test, minimum GPA of 3.0 (undergraduate), 3.5 (graduate). Additional exam requirements/recommendations for international students: Required—TOEFL. *Application deadline:* For fall admission, 3/1 priority date for domestic students, 3/1 for international students. Application fee: $50. Electronic applications accepted. *Financial support:* In 2012–

13, 4 students received support, including 35 research assistantships with full tuition reimbursements available (averaging $20,400 per year), 2 teaching assistantships with full tuition reimbursements available (averaging $20,400 per year); Federal Work-Study and institutionally sponsored loans also available. Financial award application deadline: 3/15. *Faculty research:* Chemical, biological, physical, and geological marine science; remote sensing; bio-optics; numerical modeling; hydrography. *Total annual research expenditures:* $6.4 million. *Unit head:* Dr. William M. Graham, Chair/Professor, 228-688-3177, Fax: 228-688-1121, E-mail: marine.science@usm.edu. *Application contact:* Linda Downs, Senior Office Support Specialist, 228-688-3177, Fax: 228-688-1121, E-mail: marine.science@usm.edu. Website: http://www.usm.edu/marine/.

University of South Florida, Graduate School, College of Marine Science, Saint Petersburg, FL 33701. Offers biological oceanography (MS, PhD); chemical oceanography (MS, PhD); geological oceanography (MS, PhD); interdisciplinary (PhD); marine resource assessment (MS, PhD); physical oceanography (MS, PhD). Part-time programs available. Terminal master's awarded for partial completion of doctoral program. *Degree requirements:* For master's, comprehensive exam, thesis; for doctorate, comprehensive exam, thesis/dissertation. *Entrance requirements:* For master's and doctorate, GRE, minimum GPA of 3.0 in last 60 hours, three letters of recommendation, research-interest statement, resume. Additional exam requirements/recommendations for international students: Required—TOEFL (minimum score 550 paper-based; 79 iBT) or IELTS (minimum score 6.5). *Faculty research:* Trace metal chemistry, water quality, organic and isotopic geochemistry, physical chemistry, nutrient chemistry.

The University of Texas at Austin, Graduate School, College of Natural Sciences, Department of Marine Science, Austin, TX 78712-1111. Offers MS, PhD. *Degree requirements:* For master's, thesis; for doctorate, thesis/dissertation. *Entrance requirements:* For master's and doctorate, GRE General Test. Additional exam requirements/recommendations for international students: Required—TOEFL.

University of the Virgin Islands, Graduate Programs, Division of Science and Mathematics, Program in Environmental and Marine Science, Saint Thomas, VI 00802-9990. Offers MS. *Entrance requirements:* For master's, GRE. Additional exam requirements/recommendations for international students: Required—TOEFL (minimum score 550 paper-based).

University of Wisconsin–La Crosse, Office of University Graduate Studies, College of Science and Health, Department of Biology, La Crosse, WI 54601-3742. Offers aquatic sciences (MS); biology (MS); cellular and molecular biology (MS); clinical microbiology (MS); microbiology (MS); nurse anesthesia (MS); physiology (MS). Part-time programs available. *Degree requirements:* For master's, comprehensive exam, thesis. *Entrance requirements:* For master's, GRE General Test, minimum GPA of 2.85. Additional exam requirements/recommendations for international students: Required—TOEFL (minimum score 550 paper-based; 79 iBT). Electronic applications accepted.

University of Wisconsin–Madison, Graduate School, College of Letters and Science, Department of Atmospheric and Oceanic Sciences, Madison, WI 53706-1380. Offers MS, PhD. Part-time programs available. *Degree requirements:* For master's, thesis (for some programs); for doctorate, thesis/dissertation. *Entrance requirements:* For master's and doctorate, GRE General Test, minimum GPA of 3.0; previous course work in chemistry, mathematics, and physics. Electronic applications accepted. *Expenses:* Tuition, state resident: full-time $10,728; part-time $743 per credit. Tuition, nonresident: full-time $24,054; part-time $1575 per credit. *Required fees:* $1111; $72 per credit. *Faculty research:* Satellite meteorology, weather systems, global climate change, numerical modeling, atmosphere-ocean interaction.

Western Washington University, Graduate School, Huxley College of the Environment, Department of Environmental Sciences, Bellingham, WA 98225-5996. Offers environmental science (MS); marine and estuarine science (MS). Part-time programs available. *Degree requirements:* For master's, thesis. *Entrance requirements:* For master's, GRE General Test, minimum GPA of 3.0 in last 60 semester hours or last 90 quarter hours. Additional exam requirements/recommendations for international students: Required—TOEFL (minimum score 567 paper-based). Electronic applications accepted. *Faculty research:* Landscape ecology, climate change, watershed studies, environmental toxicology and risk assessment, aquatic toxicology, toxic algae, invasive species.

Oceanography

Columbia University, Graduate School of Arts and Sciences, Division of Natural Sciences, Department of Earth and Environmental Sciences, New York, NY 10027. Offers geochemistry (M Phil, MA, PhD); geodetic sciences (M Phil, MA, PhD); geophysics (M Phil, MA, PhD); oceanography (M Phil, MA, PhD). *Degree requirements:* For master's, thesis or alternative, fieldwork, written exam; for doctorate, one foreign language, thesis/dissertation. *Entrance requirements:* For master's and doctorate, GRE General Test, GRE Subject Test, major in natural or physical science. Additional exam requirements/recommendations for

international students: Required—TOEFL. *Faculty research:* Structural geology and stratigraphy, petrology, paleontology, rare gas, isotope and aqueous geochemistry.

Cornell University, Graduate School, Graduate Fields of Agriculture and Life Sciences, Field of Ecology and Evolutionary Biology, Ithaca, NY 14853-0001. Offers ecology (PhD), including animal ecology, applied ecology, biogeochemistry, community and ecosystem ecology, limnology, oceanography,

192 facebook.com/petersonspublishing

Peterson's Graduate Programs in the Physical Sciences, Mathematics, Agricultural Sciences, the Environment & Natural Resources 2014

physiological ecology, plant ecology, population ecology, theoretical ecology, vertebrate zoology; evolutionary biology (PhD), including ecological genetics, paleobiology, population biology, systematics. *Faculty:* 53 full-time (14 women). *Students:* 53 full-time (35 women); includes 7 minority (2 Asian, non-Hispanic/Latino; 3 Hispanic/Latino; 2 Two or more races, non-Hispanic/Latino), 11 international. Average age 28. 72 applicants, 15% accepted, 5 enrolled. In 2012, 8 doctorates awarded. *Degree requirements:* For doctorate, comprehensive exam, thesis/dissertation, 2 semesters of teaching experience. *Entrance requirements:* For doctorate, GRE General Test, GRE Subject Test (biology), 2 letters of recommendation. Additional exam requirements/recommendations for international students: Required—TOEFL (minimum score 550 paper-based; 77 iBT). *Application deadline:* For fall admission, 12/15 for domestic students. Application fee: $95. Electronic applications accepted. *Financial support:* In 2012–13, 52 students received support, including 25 fellowships with full tuition reimbursements available, 2 research assistantships with full tuition reimbursements available, 25 teaching assistantships with full tuition reimbursements available; institutionally sponsored loans, scholarships/grants, health care benefits, tuition waivers (full and partial), and unspecified assistantships also available. Financial award applicants required to submit FAFSA. *Faculty research:* Population and organismal biology, population and evolutionary genetics, systematics and macroevolution, biochemistry, conservation biology. *Unit head:* Director of Graduate Studies, 607-254-4200. *Application contact:* Graduate Field Assistant, 607-254-4230, E-mail: eeb_grad_req@cornell.edu. Website: http://www.gradschool.cornell.edu/fields.php?id-46&a-2.

Dalhousie University, Faculty of Science, Department of Oceanography, Halifax, NS B3H 4R2, Canada. Offers M Sc, PhD. *Degree requirements:* For master's, thesis; for doctorate, thesis/dissertation. *Entrance requirements:* Additional exam requirements/recommendations for international students: Required—TOEFL, IELTS, CANTEST, CAEL, or Michigan English Language Assessment Battery. Electronic applications accepted. *Faculty research:* Biological and physical oceanography, chemical and geological oceanography, atmospheric sciences.

Florida Institute of Technology, Graduate Programs, College of Engineering, Department of Marine and Environmental Systems, Program in Oceanography, Melbourne, FL 32901-6975. Offers biological oceanography (MS); chemical oceanography (MS); coastal management (MS); geological oceanography (MS); oceanography (PhD); physical oceanography (MS). Part-time programs available. *Faculty:* 15 full-time (0 women), 2 part-time/adjunct (0 women). *Students:* 15 full-time (10 women), 4 part-time (0 women); includes 1 minority (Two or more races, non-Hispanic/Latino), 5 international. Average age 28. 25 applicants, 68% accepted, 8 enrolled. In 2012, 2 master's, 3 doctorates awarded. *Degree requirements:* For master's, comprehensive exam (for some programs), thesis (for some programs), seminar, field project, written final exam, internship, technical paper, oral presentation; for doctorate, comprehensive exam, thesis/dissertation, seminar, internships, publications. *Entrance requirements:* For master's, GRE General Test, minimum GPA of 3.0, 3 letters of recommendation, resume, transcripts, statement of objectives; for doctorate, GRE General Test, minimum GPA of 3.3, resume, 3 letters of recommendation, statement of objectives, on-campus interview (highly recommended). Additional exam requirements/recommendations for international students: Required—TOEFL (minimum score 550 paper-based; 79 iBT). *Application deadline:* Applications are processed on a rolling basis. Electronic applications accepted. *Expenses: Tuition:* Full-time $20,214; part-time $1123 per credit hour. Tuition and fees vary according to campus/location. *Financial support:* Career-related internships or fieldwork, institutionally sponsored loans, tuition waivers (partial), unspecified assistantships, and tuition remissions available. Support available to part-time students. Financial award application deadline: 3/1; financial award applicants required to submit FAFSA. *Faculty research:* Marine geochemistry, ecosystem dynamics, coastal processes, marine pollution, environmental modeling. *Total annual research expenditures:* $2.2 million. *Unit head:* Dr. George Maul, Department Head, 321-674-7453, Fax: 321-674-7212, E-mail: gmaul@fit.edu. *Application contact:* Cheryl A. Brown, Associate Director of Graduate Admission, 321-674-7581, Fax: 321-723-9468, E-mail: cbrown@fit.edu. Website: http://www.coe.fit.edu/dmes.

Florida State University, The Graduate School, College of Arts and Sciences, Department of Earth, Ocean and Atmospheric Science, Program in Oceanography, Tallahassee, FL 32306-4320. Offers aquatic environmental science (MS, PSM); oceanography (MS, PhD). *Faculty:* 10 full-time (1 woman), 1 (woman) part-time/adjunct. *Students:* 53 full-time (25 women); includes 5 minority (1 Black or African American, non-Hispanic/Latino; 4 Asian, non-Hispanic/Latino), 15 international. Average age 27. 60 applicants, 23% accepted, 12 enrolled. In 2012, 7 master's, 5 doctorates awarded. *Degree requirements:* For master's, thesis; for doctorate, comprehensive exam, thesis/dissertation. *Entrance requirements:* For master's and doctorate, GRE General Test, minimum upper-division GPA of 3.0. Additional exam requirements/recommendations for international students: Required—TOEFL (minimum score 550 paper-based; 80 iBT). *Application deadline:* For fall admission, 2/15 priority date for domestic students, 2/15 for international students; for spring admission, 7/15 priority date for domestic students, 7/15 for international students. Applications are processed on a rolling basis. Application fee: $35. Electronic applications accepted. *Expenses:* Tuition, state resident: full-time $7263; part-time $403.51 per credit hour. Tuition, nonresident: full-time $18,087; part-time $1004.85 per credit hour. *Required fees:* $1335.42; $74.19 per credit hour. $445.14 per semester. One-time fee: $40 full-time; $20 part-time. Tuition and fees vary according to program. *Financial support:* In 2012–13, 36 students received support, including 1 fellowship with full tuition reimbursement available, 27 research assistantships with full tuition reimbursements available, 10 teaching assistantships with full tuition reimbursements available. Financial award application deadline: 2/15; financial award applicants required to submit FAFSA. *Faculty research:* Trace metals in seawater, currents and waves, modeling, benthic ecology, marine biogeochemistry. *Unit head:* Dr. Jeffrey Chanton, Area Coordinator, 850-644-6700, Fax: 850-644-2581, E-mail: chanton@ocean.fsu.edu. *Application contact:* Michaela Lupiani, Academic Coordinator, 850-644-6700, Fax: 850-644-2581, E-mail: admissions@ocean.fsu.edu. Website: http://www.eoas.fsu.edu.

Georgia Institute of Technology, Graduate Studies and Research, College of Sciences, School of Earth and Atmospheric Sciences, Atlanta, GA 30332-0340. Offers atmospheric chemistry, aerosols and clouds (MS, PhD); dynamics of weather and climate (MS, PhD); geochemistry (MS, PhD); geophysics (MS, PhD); oceanography (MS, PhD); paleoclimate (MS, PhD); planetary science (MS, PhD); remote sensing (MS, PhD). Part-time programs available. Terminal master's awarded for partial completion of doctoral program. *Degree requirements:* For master's, thesis or alternative; for doctorate, comprehensive exam, thesis/dissertation. *Entrance requirements:* For master's, GRE, letters of recommendation; for doctorate, GRE, academic transcripts, letters of recommendation, personal statement. Additional exam requirements/recommendations for international students: Required—TOEFL (minimum score 550 paper-based; 79 iBT). *Faculty research:* Geophysics; atmospheric chemistry, aerosols and clouds; dynamics of weather and climate; geochemistry; oceanography; paleoclimate; planetary science; remote sensing.

Louisiana State University and Agricultural and Mechanical College, Graduate School, School of the Coast and Environment, Department of Oceanography and Coastal Sciences, Baton Rouge, LA 70803. Offers MS, PhD. *Faculty:* 25 full-time (3 women), 2 part-time/adjunct (0 women). *Students:* 51 full-time (24 women), 11 part-time (6 women); includes 1 minority (Hispanic/Latino), 11 international. Average age 29. 39 applicants, 33% accepted, 12 enrolled. In 2012, 7 master's, 9 doctorates awarded. *Degree requirements:* For master's, thesis (for some programs); for doctorate, one foreign language, thesis/dissertation. *Entrance requirements:* For master's, GRE General Test, minimum GPA of 3.0; for doctorate, GRE General Test, MA or MS, minimum GPA of 3.0. Additional exam requirements/recommendations for international students: Required—TOEFL (minimum score 550 paper-based; 79 iBT) or IELTS (minimum score 6.5). *Application deadline:* For fall admission, 1/25 priority date for domestic students, 5/15 for international students; for spring admission, 10/15 for international students. Applications are processed on a rolling basis. Application fee: $50 ($70 for international students). *Financial support:* In 2012–13, 59 students received support, including 6 fellowships (averaging $37,644 per year), 46 research assistantships with full and partial tuition reimbursements available (averaging $19,426 per year); teaching assistantships with full and partial tuition reimbursements available, Federal Work-Study, institutionally sponsored loans, scholarships/grants, health care benefits, tuition waivers (full and partial), and unspecified assistantships also available. Support available to part-time students. Financial award applicants required to submit FAFSA. *Faculty research:* Physical and geological oceanography, wetland sustainability and restoration fisheries, coastal ecology and biogeochemistry. *Total annual research expenditures:* $9.2 million. *Unit head:* Dr. Donald Baltz, Chair, 225-578-6512, Fax: 225-578-6513, E-mail: dbaltz@lsu.edu. *Application contact:* Dr. Charles Lindau, Graduate Adviser, 225-578-8766, Fax: 225-578-5328, E-mail: clinda1@lsu.edu. Website: http://www.oceanography.lsu.edu/.

Massachusetts Institute of Technology, School of Engineering, Department of Civil and Environmental Engineering, Cambridge, MA 02139. Offers biological oceanography (PhD, Sc D); chemical oceanography (PhD, Sc D); civil and environmental engineering (M Eng, SM, PhD, Sc D); civil and environmental systems (PhD, Sc D); civil engineering (PhD, Sc D, CE); coastal engineering (PhD, Sc D); construction engineering and management (PhD, Sc D); environmental biology (PhD, Sc D); environmental chemistry (PhD, Sc D); environmental engineering (PhD, Sc D); environmental fluid mechanics (PhD, Sc D); geotechnical and geoenvironmental engineering (PhD, Sc D); hydrology (PhD, Sc D); information technology (PhD, Sc D); oceanographic engineering (PhD, Sc D); structures and materials (PhD, Sc D); transportation (PhD, Sc D); SM/MBA. *Faculty:* 34 full-time (7 women), 1 part-time/adjunct (0 women). *Students:* 224 full-time (85 women); includes 29 minority (4 Black or African American, non-Hispanic/Latino; 13 Asian, non-Hispanic/Latino; 6 Hispanic/Latino; 6 Two or more races, non-Hispanic/Latino), 129 international. Average age 26. 636 applicants, 25% accepted, 95 enrolled. In 2012, 67 master's, 18 doctorates, 1 other advanced degree awarded. *Degree requirements:* For master's and CE, thesis; for doctorate, comprehensive exam, thesis/dissertation. *Entrance requirements:* For master's and doctorate, GRE General Test. Additional exam requirements/recommendations for international students: Required—TOEFL (minimum score 577 paper-based; 90 iBT), IELTS (minimum score 7). *Application deadline:* For fall admission, 12/15 for domestic and international students. Application fee: $75. Electronic applications accepted. *Expenses: Tuition:* Full-time $41,770; part-time $650 per credit hour. *Required fees:* $280. *Financial support:* In 2012–13, 180 students received support, including 46 fellowships (averaging $32,400 per year), 117 research assistantships (averaging $30,800 per year), 22 teaching assistantships (averaging $31,800 per year); career-related internships or fieldwork, Federal Work-Study, institutionally sponsored loans, scholarships/grants, health care benefits, and unspecified assistantships also available. *Faculty research:* Environmental chemistry; environmental fluid mechanics and coastal engineering; environmental microbiology; geotechnical engineering and geomechanics; hydrology and hydroclimatology; infrastructure systems; mechanics of materials and structures; transportation systems. *Total annual research expenditures:* $20.7 million. *Unit head:* Prof. Markus Buehler, Head, 617-253-7101. *Application contact:* Graduate Admissions Coordinator, 617-253-7119, E-mail: cee-admissions@mit.edu. Website: http://cee.mit.edu/.

Massachusetts Institute of Technology, School of Science, Department of Biology, Cambridge, MA 02139. Offers biochemistry (PhD); biological oceanography (PhD); biology (PhD); biophysical chemistry and molecular structure (PhD); cell biology (PhD); computational and systems biology (PhD); developmental biology (PhD); genetics (PhD); immunology (PhD); microbiology (PhD); molecular biology (PhD); neurobiology (PhD). *Faculty:* 58 full-time (15 women). *Students:* 260 full-time (137 women); includes 71 minority (4 Black or African American, non-Hispanic/Latino; 1 American Indian or Alaska Native, non-Hispanic/Latino; 28 Asian, non-Hispanic/Latino; 32 Hispanic/Latino; 6 Two or more races, non-Hispanic/Latino), 43 international. Average age 26. 708 applicants, 14% accepted, 47 enrolled. In 2012, 34 doctorates awarded. *Degree requirements:* For doctorate, comprehensive exam, thesis/dissertation. *Entrance requirements:* For doctorate, GRE General Test. Additional exam requirements/recommendations for international students: Required—TOEFL (minimum score 577 paper-based), IELTS (minimum score 6.5). *Application deadline:* For fall admission, 12/1 for domestic and international students. Application fee: $75. Electronic applications accepted. *Expenses: Tuition:* Full-time $41,770; part-time $650 per credit hour. *Required fees:* $280. *Financial support:* In 2012–13, 233 students received support, including 149 fellowships (averaging $34,500 per year), 107 research assistantships (averaging $34,100 per year), 1 teaching assistantship; Federal Work-Study, institutionally sponsored loans, scholarships/grants, traineeships, health care benefits, and unspecified assistantships also available. *Faculty research:* Cellular, developmental and molecular (plant and animal) biology; biochemistry, bioengineering, biophysics and structural biology; classical and molecular genetics, stem cell and epigenetics; immunology and microbiology; cancer biology, molecular medicine, neurobiology and human disease; computational and systems biology. *Total annual research expenditures:* $49.9 million. *Unit head:* Prof. Tania A. Baker, Head, 617-253-4701. *Application contact:* Biology Education Office, 617-253-3717, Fax: 617-258-9329, E-mail: gradbio@mit.edu. Website: https://biology.mit.edu/.

Massachusetts Institute of Technology, School of Science, Department of Earth, Atmospheric, and Planetary Sciences, Cambridge, MA 02139. Offers atmospheric chemistry (PhD, Sc D); atmospheric science (SM, PhD, Sc D); chemical oceanography (SM, PhD, Sc D); climate physics and chemistry (SM, PhD, Sc D); earth and planetary sciences (SM); geochemistry (PhD, Sc D); geology (PhD, Sc D); geophysics (PhD, Sc D); marine geology and geophysics (SM, PhD, Sc D); physical oceanography (SM, PhD, Sc D); planetary sciences (PhD, Sc D). *Faculty:* 33 full-time (6 women), 1 (woman) part-time/adjunct. *Students:* 166 full-time (77 women); includes 24 minority (3 Black or African American, non-Hispanic/Latino; 1 American Indian or Alaska Native, non-Hispanic/Latino; 9 Asian, non-Hispanic/Latino; 6 Hispanic/Latino; 5 Two or more races, non-Hispanic/Latino), 58 international. Average age 27. 232 applicants, 23% accepted, 27 enrolled. In 2012, 12 master's, 22 doctorates awarded. Terminal master's awarded for partial completion of doctoral program. *Degree requirements:* For master's, thesis; for doctorate, comprehensive exam, thesis/dissertation. *Entrance requirements:* For master's, GRE General Test; for doctorate, GRE General Test, GRE Subject Test (chemistry or physics for planetary science area). Additional exam requirements/recommendations for international students: Required—TOEFL (minimum score 577 paper-based; 91 iBT), IELTS (minimum score 7). *Application deadline:* For fall admission, 1/5 for domestic and international students; for spring admission, 11/1 for domestic and international students. Application fee: $75. Electronic applications accepted. *Expenses: Tuition:* Full-time $41,770; part-time $650 per credit hour. *Required fees:* $280. *Financial support:* In 2012–13, 108 students received support, including 62 fellowships (averaging $30,700 per year), 87 research assistantships (averaging $32,600 per year), 15 teaching assistantships (averaging $30,800 per year); Federal Work-Study, institutionally sponsored loans, scholarships/grants, health care benefits, and unspecified assistantships also available. *Faculty research:* Formation, dynamics and evolution of planetary systems; origin, composition, structure and dynamics of the atmospheres, oceans, surfaces and interiors of the Earth and other planets; evolution and interaction of the physical, chemical, geological and biological components of the Earth system; characterization of past, present and potential future climates and the causes and consequences of climate change; interplay of energy and the environment. *Total annual research expenditures:* $28.1 million. *Unit head:* Prof. Robert van der Hilst, Head, 617-253-2127, Fax: 617-253-8298, E-mail: eapsinfo@mit.edu. *Application contact:* EAPS Education Office, 617-253-3381, Fax: 617-253-8298, E-mail: eapsinfo@mit.edu. Website: http://eapsweb.mit.edu/.

McGill University, Faculty of Graduate and Postdoctoral Studies, Faculty of Science, Department of Atmospheric and Oceanic Sciences, Montréal, QC H3A 2T5, Canada. Offers atmospheric science (M Sc, PhD); physical oceanography (M Sc, PhD). PhD program in physical oceanography offered jointly with Université Laval.

Memorial University of Newfoundland, School of Graduate Studies, Department of Physics and Physical Oceanography, St. John's, NL A1C 5S7, Canada. Offers atomic and molecular physics (M Sc, PhD); condensed matter physics (M Sc, PhD); physical oceanography (M Sc, PhD); physics (M Sc). Part-time programs available. *Degree requirements:* For master's, thesis, seminar presentation on thesis topic; for doctorate, comprehensive exam, thesis/dissertation, oral defense of thesis. *Entrance requirements:* For master's, honors B Sc or equivalent; for doctorate, M Sc or equivalent. Electronic applications accepted. *Faculty research:* Experiment and theory in atomic and molecular physics, condensed matter physics, physical oceanography, theoretical geophysics and applied nuclear physics.

Naval Postgraduate School, Departments and Academic Groups, Department of Meteorology, Monterey, CA 93943. Offers meteorology (MS, PhD); meteorology and physical oceanography (MS). Program only open to commissioned officers of the United States and friendly nations and selected United States federal civilian employees. Part-time programs available. *Degree requirements:* For master's, thesis; for doctorate, one foreign language, thesis/dissertation. *Faculty research:* Air-sea interactions, boundary layer meteorology, climate dynamics, numerical weather prediction, tropical cyclones.

Naval Postgraduate School, Departments and Academic Groups, Department of Oceanography, Monterey, CA 93943. Offers physical oceanography (MS, PhD). Program only open to commissioned officers of the United States and friendly nations and selected United States federal civilian employees. Part-time programs available. *Degree requirements:* For master's, thesis; for doctorate, thesis/dissertation. *Faculty research:* Lagrangian acoustic subsurface technology, naval ocean analysis prediction, nearshore processes, unmanned vehicles, ocean acoustics, turbulence, waves.

Naval Postgraduate School, Departments and Academic Groups, Undersea Warfare Academic Group, Monterey, CA 93943. Offers applied mathematics (MS); applied physics (MS); applied science (MS), including acoustics, operations research, physical oceanography, signal processing; electrical engineering (MS); engineering acoustics (MS, PhD); engineering science (MS), including electrical engineering, mechanical engineering; mechanical engineer (ME); mechanical engineering (MS, MSME); meteorology (MS); operations research (MS); physical oceanography (MS). Program only open to commissioned officers of the United States and friendly nations and selected United States federal civilian employees. Part-time programs available. *Degree requirements:* For master's, thesis. *Faculty research:* Unmanned/autonomous vehicles, sea mines and countermeasures, submarine warfare in the twentieth and twenty-first centuries.

North Carolina State University, Graduate School, College of Physical and Mathematical Sciences, Department of Marine, Earth, and Atmospheric Sciences, Raleigh, NC 27695. Offers marine, earth, and atmospheric sciences (MS, PhD); meteorology (MS, PhD); oceanography (MS, PhD). PhD offered jointly with The University of North Carolina Wilmington. Terminal master's awarded for partial completion of doctoral program. *Degree requirements:* For master's, thesis (for some programs), final oral exam; for doctorate, comprehensive exam, thesis/dissertation, final oral exam, preliminary oral and written exams. *Entrance requirements:* For master's, GRE General Test, minimum GPA of 3.0; for doctorate, GRE General Test, GRE Subject Test (for disciplines in biological oceanography and geology), minimum GPA of 3.0. Additional exam requirements/recommendations for international students: Required—TOEFL (minimum score 550 paper-based). Electronic applications accepted. *Faculty research:* Boundary layer and air quality meteorology; climate and mesoscale dynamics; biological, chemical, geological, and physical oceanography; hard rock, soft rock, environmental, and paleo-geology.

Nova Southeastern University, Oceanographic Center, Fort Lauderdale, FL 33314-7796. Offers biological sciences (MS); coastal zone management (MS); marine and coastal studies (MA); marine biology (MS); marine biology and oceanography (PhD), including marine biology, oceanography; marine environmental sciences (MS). Part-time and evening/weekend programs available. *Faculty:* 13 full-time (1 woman), 20 part-time/adjunct (5 women). *Students:* 123 full-time (84 women), 153 part-time (96 women); includes 36 minority (7 Black or African American, non-Hispanic/Latino; 1 American Indian or Alaska Native, non-Hispanic/Latino; 5 Asian, non-Hispanic/Latino; 18 Hispanic/Latino; 5 Two or more races, non-Hispanic/Latino), 6 international. Average age 29. 98 applicants, 81% accepted, 48 enrolled. In 2012, 26 master's, 1 doctorate awarded. *Degree requirements:* For master's, thesis; for doctorate, comprehensive exam, thesis/dissertation, departmental qualifying exam. *Entrance requirements:* For master's, GRE General Test, 3 letters of recommendation, BS/BA in natural science (for marine biology program), BS/BA in biology (for biological sciences program), minor in the natural sciences or equivalent (for coastal zone management and marine environmental sciences); for doctorate, GRE General Test, master's degree. Additional exam requirements/recommendations for international students: Required—TOEFL (minimum score 550 paper-based). *Application deadline:* Applications are processed on a rolling basis. Application fee: $50. *Expenses:* Contact institution. *Financial support:* In 2012–13, 2 fellowships with full and partial tuition reimbursements (averaging $16,300 per year), 50 research assistantships with full and partial tuition reimbursements (averaging $19,000 per year) were awarded; teaching assistantships, career-related internships or fieldwork, Federal Work-Study, scholarships/grants, health care benefits, tuition waivers (full and partial), and unspecified assistantships also available. Support available to part-time students. Financial award applicants required to submit FAFSA. *Faculty research:* Physical, geological, chemical, and biological oceanography. *Unit head:* Dr. Richard Dodge, Dean, 954-262-3600, Fax: 954-262-4020, E-mail: dodge@nsu.nova.edu.

Application contact: Dr. Richard Spieler, Associate Dean of Academic Programs, 954-262-3600, Fax: 954-262-4020, E-mail: spieler@nova.edu. Website: http://www.nova.edu/ocean/.

Old Dominion University, College of Sciences, Department of Ocean, Earth and Atmospheric Sciences, Norfolk, VA 23529. Offers ocean and earth sciences (MS); oceanography (PhD). Part-time programs available. *Faculty:* 25 full-time (6 women), 1 part-time/adjunct (0 women). *Students:* 29 full-time (13 women), 13 part-time (5 women); includes 6 minority (1 Black or African American, non-Hispanic/Latino; 1 American Indian or Alaska Native, non-Hispanic/Latino; 1 Asian, non-Hispanic/Latino; 1 Hispanic/Latino; 2 Two or more races, non-Hispanic/Latino), 6 international. Average age 30. 33 applicants, 48% accepted, 11 enrolled. In 2012, 7 master's, 4 doctorates awarded. Terminal master's awarded for partial completion of doctoral program. *Degree requirements:* For master's, comprehensive exam (for some programs), thesis (for some programs), 10 days of ship time or fieldwork; for doctorate, comprehensive exam, thesis/dissertation, 10 days of ship time or fieldwork. *Entrance requirements:* For master's and doctorate, GRE General Test, minimum GPA of 3.0 in major, 2.8 overall. Additional exam requirements/recommendations for international students: Required—TOEFL (minimum score 550 paper-based). *Application deadline:* For fall admission, 2/1 priority date for domestic students, 2/1 for international students. Applications are processed on a rolling basis. Application fee: $50. Electronic applications accepted. *Expenses:* Tuition, state resident: full-time $9432; part-time $393 per credit hour. Tuition, nonresident: full-time $23,928; part-time $997 per credit hour. *Required fees:* $59 per semester. One-time fee: $50. *Financial support:* In 2012–13, 16 students received support, including 3 fellowships with full tuition reimbursements available (averaging $22,000 per year), 25 research assistantships with full tuition reimbursements available (averaging $22,000 per year), 14 teaching assistantships with full tuition reimbursements available (averaging $15,500 per year); career-related internships or fieldwork, scholarships/grants, and unspecified assistantships also available. Support available to part-time students. Financial award application deadline: 2/1; financial award applicants required to submit FAFSA. *Faculty research:* Biological, chemical, geological, and physical oceanography. *Unit head:* Dr. Rodger Harvey, Department Chair, 757-683-4285, Fax: 757-683-5303, E-mail: rharvey@odu.edu. *Application contact:* William Heffelfinger, Director of Graduate Admissions, 757-683-5554, Fax: 757-683-3255, E-mail: gradadmit@odu.edu. Website: http://www.odu.edu/sci/oceanography/.

Oregon State University, College of Earth, Ocean, and Atmospheric Sciences, Program in Ocean, Earth, and Atmospheric Sciences, Corvallis, OR 97331. Offers atmospheric sciences (MA, MS); geography (PhD); geology (PhD); geophysics (MA, MS); oceanography (MA, MS). *Students:* 33 full-time (17 women), 1 part-time (0 women); includes 5 minority (1 Asian, non-Hispanic/Latino; 2 Hispanic/Latino; 2 Two or more races, non-Hispanic/Latino), 7 international. Average age 28. 148 applicants, 15% accepted, 8 enrolled. In 2012, 10 master's, 3 doctorates awarded. *Expenses:* Tuition, state resident: full-time $11,367; part-time $421 per credit hour. Tuition, nonresident: full-time $18,279; part-time $677 per credit hour. *Required fees:* $1478. One-time fee: $300 full-time. Tuition and fees vary according to course load and program. *Unit head:* Dr. Mark R. Abbott, Dean, 541-737-5195, Fax: 541-737-2064, E-mail: mark@coas.oregonstate.edu. *Application contact:* Dr. Robert S. Allan, Assistant Director, Student Programs, 541-737-1340, Fax: 541-737-2064, E-mail: rallan@coas.oregonstate.edu. Website: http://ceoas.oregonstate.edu/academics/ocean/.

Princeton University, Graduate School, Department of Geosciences, Program in Atmospheric and Oceanic Sciences, Princeton, NJ 08544-1019. Offers PhD. *Degree requirements:* For doctorate, one foreign language, thesis/dissertation. *Entrance requirements:* For doctorate, GRE General Test, GRE Subject Test. Additional exam requirements/recommendations for international students: Required—TOEFL (minimum score 600 paper-based). Electronic applications accepted. *Faculty research:* Climate dynamics, middle atmosphere dynamics and chemistry, oceanic circulation, marine geochemistry, numerical modeling.

Rutgers, The State University of New Jersey, New Brunswick, Graduate School-New Brunswick, Program in Oceanography, Piscataway, NJ 08854-8097. Offers MS, PhD. Terminal master's awarded for partial completion of doctoral program. *Degree requirements:* For master's, thesis; for doctorate, comprehensive exam, thesis/dissertation. *Entrance requirements:* For master's and doctorate, GRE General Test, 1 year course work in calculus, physics, chemistry. Additional exam requirements/recommendations for international students: Required—TOEFL. Electronic applications accepted. *Faculty research:* Coastal observations and modeling, estuarine ecology/fish/benthos, geochemistry, deep sea ecology/hydrothermal vents, molecular biology applications.

Texas A&M University, College of Geosciences, Department of Oceanography, College Station, TX 77843. Offers MS, PhD. *Faculty:* 24. *Students:* 63 full-time (37 women), 17 part-time (6 women); includes 7 minority (1 Black or African American, non-Hispanic/Latino; 1 American Indian or Alaska Native, non-Hispanic/Latino; 1 Asian, non-Hispanic/Latino; 4 Hispanic/Latino), 27 international. Average age 29. In 2012, 10 master's, 7 doctorates awarded. *Degree requirements:* For master's, thesis; for doctorate, thesis/dissertation. *Entrance requirements:* For master's and doctorate, GRE General Test. Additional exam requirements/recommendations for international students: Required—TOEFL. *Application deadline:* For fall admission, 1/15 priority date for domestic students; for spring admission, 10/1 for domestic students. Applications are processed on a rolling basis. Application fee: $50 ($75 for international

students). Electronic applications accepted. *Financial support:* In 2012–13, fellowships with partial tuition reimbursements (averaging $18,000 per year), research assistantships with partial tuition reimbursements (averaging $18,000 per year), teaching assistantships with partial tuition reimbursements (averaging $18,000 per year) were awarded; Federal Work-Study, scholarships/grants, and tuition waivers (partial) also available. Financial award application deadline: 1/15. *Faculty research:* Ocean circulation, climate studies, coastal and shelf dynamics, marine phytoplankton, stable isotope geochemistry. *Unit head:* Piers Chapman, Head, 979-845-7211, Fax: 979-845-6331. *Application contact:* Christine Arnold, Academic Advisor II, 979-845-7688, Fax: 979-845-6331, E-mail: chrisarnold@tamu.edu. Website: http://ocean.tamu.edu.

Université du Québec à Rimouski, Graduate Programs, Program in Oceanography, Rimouski, QC G5L 3A1, Canada. Offers M Sc, PhD. Part-time programs available. *Students:* 49 full-time, 6 part-time, 28 international. 50 applicants, 74% accepted. In 2012, 11 master's, 6 doctorates awarded. *Degree requirements:* For master's, thesis; for doctorate, thesis/dissertation. *Entrance requirements:* For master's, appropriate bachelor's degree, proficiency in French; for doctorate, appropriate master's degree, proficiency in French. *Application deadline:* For fall admission, 5/1 priority date for domestic students. Application fee: $30. *Financial support:* Fellowships, research assistantships, and teaching assistantships available. *Unit head:* Jean-Francois Dumais, Director, 418-724-1770, Fax: 418-724-1525, E-mail: jean-francois_dumais@uqar.ca. *Application contact:* Jacques d'Astous, Conseiller en Recrutement et en Communication, 800-463-4712, Fax: 418-724-1869, E-mail: jacques_dastous@uqar.ca.

Université Laval, Faculty of Sciences and Engineering, Program in Oceanography, Québec, QC G1K 7P4, Canada. Offers PhD. Program offered jointly with McGill University and Université du Québec à Rimouski. *Degree requirements:* For doctorate, comprehensive exam, thesis/dissertation. *Entrance requirements:* For doctorate, knowledge of French, knowledge of English. Additional exam requirements/recommendations for international students: Required—TOEFL. Electronic applications accepted.

University of Alaska Fairbanks, School of Fisheries and Ocean Sciences, Program in Marine Sciences and Limnology, Fairbanks, AK 99775-7220. Offers marine biology (MS, PhD); oceanography (PhD), including biological oceanography, chemical oceanography, fisheries, geological oceanography, physical oceanography. Part-time programs available. *Faculty:* 5 full-time (2 women), 1 part-time/adjunct (0 women). *Students:* 45 full-time (33 women), 17 part-time (13 women); includes 8 minority (3 Asian, non-Hispanic/Latino; 5 Hispanic/Latino), 8 international. Average age 29. 52 applicants, 25% accepted, 12 enrolled. In 2012, 4 master's, 5 doctorates awarded. *Degree requirements:* For master's, comprehensive exam, thesis, oral defense; for doctorate, comprehensive exam, thesis/dissertation, oral defense. *Entrance requirements:* For master's and doctorate, GRE General Test. Additional exam requirements/recommendations for international students: Required—TOEFL (minimum score 550 paper-based; 80 iBT). *Application deadline:* For fall admission, 6/1 for domestic students, 3/1 for international students; for spring admission, 10/15 for domestic students, 8/1 for international students. Applications are processed on a rolling basis. Application fee: $60. Electronic applications accepted. *Expenses:* Tuition, state resident: full-time $7038. Tuition, nonresident: full-time $14,382. Tuition and fees vary according to course level, course load and reciprocity agreements. *Financial support:* In 2012–13, 31 research assistantships with tuition reimbursements (averaging $11,137 per year), 7 teaching assistantships with tuition reimbursements (averaging $11,750 per year) were awarded; fellowships with tuition reimbursements, career-related internships or fieldwork, Federal Work-Study, scholarships/grants, health care benefits, and unspecified assistantships also available. Support available to part-time students. Financial award application deadline: 7/1; financial award applicants required to submit FAFSA. *Unit head:* Katrin Iken, Co-Chair, 907-474-7289, Fax: 907-474-5863, E-mail: academics@sfos.uaf.edu. *Application contact:* Libby Eddy, Registrar and Director of Admissions, 907-474-7500, Fax: 907-474-7097, E-mail: admissions@alaska.edu. Website: http://www.sfos.uaf.edu/prospective/graduate/marinebio.php.

The University of British Columbia, Faculty of Science, Department of Earth and Ocean Sciences, Vancouver, BC V6T 1Z4, Canada. Offers atmospheric science (M Sc, PhD); geological engineering (M Eng, MA Sc, PhD); geological sciences (M Sc, PhD); geophysics (M Sc, MA Sc, PhD); oceanography (M Sc, PhD). *Degree requirements:* For master's, thesis (for some programs); for doctorate, comprehensive exam, thesis/dissertation. *Entrance requirements:* Additional exam requirements/recommendations for international students: Required—TOEFL (minimum score 600 paper-based; 100 iBT). Electronic applications accepted. *Faculty research:* Oceans and atmosphere, environmental earth science, hydro geology, mineral deposits, geophysics.

University of California, Los Angeles, Graduate Division, College of Letters and Science, Department of Atmospheric and Oceanic Sciences, Los Angeles, CA 90095. Offers MS, PhD. *Faculty:* 15 full-time (2 women). *Students:* 39 full-time (20 women); includes 9 minority (5 Asian, non-Hispanic/Latino; 4 Hispanic/Latino), 18 international. Average age 26. 89 applicants, 36% accepted, 9 enrolled. In 2012, 14 master's, 6 doctorates awarded. Terminal master's awarded for partial completion of doctoral program. *Degree requirements:* For master's, comprehensive exam or thesis; for doctorate, thesis/dissertation, oral and written qualifying exams; 2 quarters of teaching experience. *Entrance requirements:* For master's and doctorate, GRE General Test, bachelor's degree; minimum undergraduate GPA of 3.0 (or its equivalent if letter grade system not used).

Peterson's Graduate Programs in the Physical Sciences, Mathematics, Agricultural Sciences, the Environment & Natural Resources 2014

facebook.com/petersonspublishing **195**

Additional exam requirements/recommendations for international students: Required—TOEFL. *Application deadline:* For fall admission, 12/15 for domestic and international students. Application fee: $80 ($100 for international students). Electronic applications accepted. *Expenses:* Tuition, nonresident: full-time $15,102. *Required fees:* $14,809.19. Full-time tuition and fees vary according to program. *Financial support:* In 2012–13, 39 students received support, including 38 fellowships with full and partial tuition reimbursements available, 35 research assistantships with full and partial tuition reimbursements available, 14 teaching assistantships with full and partial tuition reimbursements available; Federal Work-Study, scholarships/grants, health care benefits, tuition waivers (full and partial), and unspecified assistantships also available. Financial award application deadline: 3/2; financial award applicants required to submit FAFSA. *Unit head:* Dr. David C. Neelin, Chair, 310-206-3734, E-mail: neelin@atmos.ucla.edu. *Application contact:* Departmental Office, 310-825-1217, Fax: 310-206-5219, E-mail: studentinfo@atmos.ucla.edu. Website: http://www.atmos.ucla.edu.

University of California, San Diego, Office of Graduate Studies, Scripps Institution of Oceanography, La Jolla, CA 92093. Offers earth sciences (PhD); marine biology (PhD); oceanography (PhD). *Degree requirements:* For doctorate, comprehensive exam, thesis/dissertation. *Entrance requirements:* For doctorate, GRE General Test. Additional exam requirements/recommendations for international students: Required—TOEFL (minimum score 550 paper-based; 80 iBT). Electronic applications accepted.

University of Colorado Boulder, Graduate School, College of Arts and Sciences, Department of Atmospheric and Oceanic Sciences, Boulder, CO 80309. Offers MS, PhD. *Faculty:* 12 full-time (5 women). *Students:* 57 full-time (26 women), 7 part-time (3 women); includes 6 minority (1 Black or African American, non-Hispanic/Latino; 2 Asian, non-Hispanic/Latino; 2 Hispanic/Latino; 1 Two or more races, non-Hispanic/Latino), 12 international. Average age 29. 128 applicants, 25% accepted, 13 enrolled. *Entrance requirements:* For master's, minimum undergraduate GPA of 3.0. *Application deadline:* For fall admission, 1/1 for domestic students, 12/1 for international students; for spring admission, 10/1 for domestic and international students. Electronic applications accepted. *Financial support:* In 2012–13, 55 students received support, including 9 fellowships (averaging $18,687 per year), 36 research assistantships with full and partial tuition reimbursements available (averaging $25,891 per year), 13 teaching assistantships with full and partial tuition reimbursements available (averaging $22,873 per year); institutionally sponsored loans, scholarships/grants, health care benefits, and unspecified assistantships also available. Financial award applicants required to submit FAFSA. *Faculty research:* Atmospheric sciences, atmospheric structure and dynamics, atmospheric models, atmospheric physics, global change. *Total annual research expenditures:* $15.9 million. *Application contact:* E-mail: atocasst@colorado.edu. Website: http://atoc.colorado.edu/.

University of Connecticut, Graduate School, College of Liberal Arts and Sciences, Department of Marine Sciences, Storrs, CT 06269. Offers MS, PhD. Terminal master's awarded for partial completion of doctoral program. *Degree requirements:* For master's, comprehensive exam; for doctorate, thesis/dissertation. *Entrance requirements:* Additional exam requirements/recommendations for international students: Required—TOEFL (minimum score 550 paper-based). Electronic applications accepted.

University of Delaware, College of Earth, Ocean, and Environment, School of Marine Science and Policy, Newark, DE 19716. Offers marine policy (MMP); marine studies (MS, PhD), including marine biosciences, oceanography, physical ocean science and engineering; oceanography (PhD).

University of Hawaii at Manoa, Graduate Division, School of Ocean and Earth Science and Technology, Department of Oceanography, Honolulu, HI 96822. Offers MS, PhD. Part-time programs available. Terminal master's awarded for partial completion of doctoral program. *Degree requirements:* For master's, one foreign language, comprehensive exam, thesis, field experience; for doctorate, one foreign language, comprehensive exam, thesis/dissertation, field experience. *Entrance requirements:* For master's and doctorate, GRE General Test. Additional exam requirements/recommendations for international students: Required—TOEFL (minimum score 560 paper-based; 83 iBT), IELTS (minimum score 5). *Faculty research:* Physical oceanography, marine chemistry, biological oceanography, atmospheric chemistry, marine geology.

University of Maine, Graduate School, College of Natural Sciences, Forestry, and Agriculture, School of Marine Sciences, Orono, ME 04469. Offers marine biology (MS, PhD); marine policy (MS); oceanography (MS, PhD). Part-time programs available. *Faculty:* 40 full-time (8 women), 60 part-time/adjunct (16 women). *Students:* 46 full-time (24 women), 16 part-time (5 women); includes 1 minority (Hispanic/Latino), 7 international. Average age 29. 71 applicants, 15% accepted, 10 enrolled. In 2012, 12 master's, 3 doctorates awarded. *Degree requirements:* For master's, thesis; for doctorate, comprehensive exam, thesis/dissertation. *Entrance requirements:* For master's and doctorate, GRE General Test. Additional exam requirements/recommendations for international students: Required—TOEFL. *Application deadline:* For fall admission, 2/1 priority date for domestic students. Applications are processed on a rolling basis. Application fee: $65. Electronic applications accepted. *Financial support:* In 2012–13, 41 research assistantships with tuition reimbursements (averaging $16,713 per year), 6 teaching assistantships with tuition reimbursements (averaging $13,600 per year) were awarded; career-related internships or fieldwork, Federal Work-Study, and tuition waivers (full and partial) also available. Support available to part-time students. Financial award application deadline: 3/1. *Faculty research:* Coastal processes, microbial ecology, crustacean systematics. *Total annual research expenditures:* $2 million. *Unit head:* Dr. Peter Jumars, Director, 207-581-3321, Fax: 207-581-4388. *Application contact:* Scott G. Delcourt, Associate Dean of the Graduate School, 207-581-3291, Fax: 207-581-3232, E-mail: graduate@maine.edu. Website: http://www.umaine.edu/marine/.

University of Maryland, College Park, Academic Affairs, College of Computer, Mathematical and Natural Sciences, Department of Atmospheric and Oceanic Science, College Park, MD 20742. Offers MS, PMS, PhD. Part-time and evening/weekend programs available. Postbaccalaureate distance learning degree programs offered. *Faculty:* 36 full-time (8 women), 7 part-time/adjunct (2 women). *Students:* 49 full-time (22 women), 13 part-time (7 women); includes 3 minority (2 Asian, non-Hispanic/Latino; 1 Hispanic/Latino), 21 international. 127 applicants, 13% accepted, 15 enrolled. In 2012, 7 master's, 7 doctorates awarded. Terminal master's awarded for partial completion of doctoral program. *Degree requirements:* For master's, comprehensive exam, scholarly paper, written and oral exams; for doctorate, thesis/dissertation, exam. *Entrance requirements:* For master's, GRE General Test, background in mathematics, experience in scientific computer languages, 3 letters of recommendation; for doctorate, GRE General Test. *Application deadline:* For fall admission, 1/15 priority date for domestic students, 1/15 for international students. Applications are processed on a rolling basis. Application fee: $75. Electronic applications accepted. *Expenses:* Tuition, state resident: part-time $551 per credit. Tuition, nonresident: part-time $1188 per credit. Part-time tuition and fees vary according to program. *Financial support:* In 2012–13, 2 fellowships with partial tuition reimbursements (averaging $9,750 per year), 16 research assistantships (averaging $20,344 per year), 26 teaching assistantships (averaging $20,210 per year) were awarded; Federal Work-Study and scholarships/grants also available. Support available to part-time students. Financial award applicants required to submit FAFSA. *Faculty research:* Weather, atmospheric chemistry, air pollution, global change, radiation. *Total annual research expenditures:* $2.8 million. *Unit head:* James A. Carton, Chair, 301-405-5365, Fax: 301-314-9482, E-mail: carton@umd.edu. *Application contact:* Dr. Charles A. Caramello, Dean of Graduate School, 301-405-0358, Fax: 301-314-9305.

University of Miami, Graduate School, Rosenstiel School of Marine and Atmospheric Science, Division of Meteorology and Physical Oceanography, Coral Gables, FL 33124. Offers meteorology (MS, PhD); physical oceanography (MS, PhD). Terminal master's awarded for partial completion of doctoral program. *Degree requirements:* For master's, comprehensive exam, thesis; for doctorate, comprehensive exam, thesis/dissertation. *Entrance requirements:* For master's and doctorate, GRE General Test. Additional exam requirements/recommendations for international students: Required—TOEFL (minimum score 550 paper-based). Electronic applications accepted.

University of New Hampshire, Graduate School, College of Engineering and Physical Sciences, Department of Earth Sciences, Durham, NH 03824. Offers general (MS); geology (MS); hydrology (MS); ocean mapping (MS). *Faculty:* 17 full-time (5 women). *Students:* 15 full-time (8 women), 15 part-time (5 women); includes 1 minority (Black or African American, non-Hispanic/Latino), 4 international. Average age 27. 43 applicants, 53% accepted, 8 enrolled. In 2012, 15 master's awarded. *Degree requirements:* For master's, thesis. *Entrance requirements:* For master's, GRE General Test. Additional exam requirements/recommendations for international students: Required—TOEFL (minimum score 550 paper-based; 80 iBT). *Application deadline:* For fall admission, 4/1 priority date for domestic students, 4/1 for international students; for spring admission, 12/1 for domestic students. Applications are processed on a rolling basis. Application fee: $65. Electronic applications accepted. *Expenses:* Tuition, state resident: full-time $13,500; part-time $750 per credit. Tuition, nonresident: full-time $25,940; part-time $1089 per credit. *Required fees:* $1699; $424.75 per semester. *Financial support:* In 2012–13, 24 students received support, including 11 research assistantships, 7 teaching assistantships; fellowships, career-related internships or fieldwork, Federal Work-Study, scholarships/grants, and tuition waivers (full and partial) also available. Support available to part-time students. Financial award application deadline: 2/15. *Unit head:* Dr. Julie Bryce, Chairperson, 603-862-3139, E-mail: earth.sciences@unh.edu. *Application contact:* Sue Clark, Administrative Assistant, 603-862-1718, E-mail: earth.sciences@unh.edu. Website: http://www.unh.edu/esci/.

University of New Hampshire, Graduate School, College of Engineering and Physical Sciences, Program in Ocean Engineering, Durham, NH 03824. Offers ocean engineering (MS, PhD); ocean mapping (MS, Postbaccalaureate Certificate). *Faculty:* 13 full-time (1 woman). *Students:* 18 full-time (8 women), 7 part-time (0 women); includes 1 minority (Hispanic/Latino), 15 international. Average age 30. 27 applicants, 63% accepted, 9 enrolled. In 2012, 3 master's, 7 other advanced degrees awarded. *Degree requirements:* For master's, thesis. *Entrance requirements:* Additional exam requirements/recommendations for international students: Required—TOEFL (minimum score 550 paper-based; 80 iBT). *Application deadline:* For fall admission, 4/1 priority date for domestic students; for spring admission, 12/1 for domestic students. Applications are processed on a rolling basis. Application fee: $65. Electronic applications accepted. *Expenses:* Tuition, state resident: full-time $13,500; part-time $750 per credit. Tuition, nonresident: full-time $25,940; part-time $1089 per credit. *Required fees:* $1699; $424.75 per semester. *Financial support:* In 2012–13, 18 students received support, including 16 research assistantships, 2 teaching assistantships; fellowships, Federal Work-Study, scholarships/grants, and tuition waivers (full and partial) also available. Support available to part-time students.

Financial award application deadline: 2/15. *Unit head:* Dr. Kenneth Baldwin, Chairperson, 603-862-1898. *Application contact:* Jennifer Bedsole, Information Contact, 603-862-0672, E-mail: ocean.engineering@unh.edu. Website: http://www.unh.edu/oe/.

University of Rhode Island, Graduate School, Graduate School of Oceanography, Narragansett, RI 02882. Offers MO, MS, PhD, MBA/MO, PhD/MA, PhD/MMA. Part-time programs available. *Faculty:* 28 full-time (8 women), 2 part-time/adjunct (0 women). *Students:* 73 full-time (47 women), 14 part-time (7 women); includes 2 minority (both Asian, non-Hispanic/Latino), 7 international. In 2012, 13 master's, 6 doctorates awarded. *Degree requirements:* For master's, comprehensive exam (for some programs), thesis optional; for doctorate, comprehensive exam, thesis/dissertation. *Entrance requirements:* For master's, GRE, 2 letters of recommendation; for doctorate, GRE, 3 letters of recommendation. Additional exam requirements/recommendations for international students: Required—TOEFL (minimum score 600 paper-based; 100 iBT). *Application deadline:* For fall admission, 1/15 for domestic and international students; for spring admission, 11/15 for domestic students, 7/15 for international students. Application fee: $65. Electronic applications accepted. *Expenses:* Tuition, state resident: full-time $11,532; part-time $641 per credit. Tuition, nonresident: full-time $23,606; part-time $1311 per credit. *Required fees:* $1388; $36 per credit. $35 per semester. One-time fee: $130. *Financial support:* In 2012–13, 30 research assistantships with full and partial tuition reimbursements (averaging $10,733 per year), 10 teaching assistantships with full and partial tuition reimbursements (averaging $10,275 per year) were awarded. Financial award application deadline: 1/15; financial award applicants required to submit FAFSA. *Faculty research:* Subduction, life in extreme environments, the marine nitrogen cycle, hurricane prediction, Antarctic ocean circulation. *Unit head:* Dr. Bruce Corliss, Dean, 401-874-6222, Fax: 401-874-6931, E-mail: bruce.corliss@gso.uri.edu. Website: http://www.gso.uri.edu/.

University of Southern California, Graduate School, Dana and David Dornsife College of Letters, Arts and Sciences, Department of Biological Sciences, Program in Marine Biology and Biological Oceanography, Los Angeles, CA 90089. Offers marine and environmental biology (MS); marine biology and biological oceanography (PhD). Terminal master's awarded for partial completion of doctoral program. *Degree requirements:* For master's, research paper; for doctorate, comprehensive exam, thesis/dissertation, qualifying examination, dissertation defense. *Entrance requirements:* For master's and doctorate, GRE, 3 letters of recommendation, personal statement, resume, minimum GPA of 3.0. Additional exam requirements/recommendations for international students: Required—TOEFL (minimum score 600 paper-based; 100 iBT). Electronic applications accepted. *Faculty research:* Microbial ecology, biogeochemistry, and geobiology; biodiversity and molecular ecology; integrative organismal biology; conservation biology; marine genomics.

University of South Florida, Graduate School, College of Marine Science, Saint Petersburg, FL 33701. Offers biological oceanography (MS, PhD); chemical oceanography (MS, PhD); geological oceanography (MS, PhD); interdisciplinary (PhD); marine resource assessment (MS, PhD); physical oceanography (MS, PhD). Part-time programs available. Terminal master's awarded for partial completion of doctoral program. *Degree requirements:* For master's, comprehensive exam, thesis; for doctorate, comprehensive exam, thesis/dissertation. *Entrance requirements:* For master's and doctorate, GRE, minimum GPA of 3.0 in last 60 hours, three letters of recommendation, research-interest statement, resume. Additional exam requirements/recommendations for international students: Required—TOEFL (minimum score 550 paper-based; 79 iBT) or IELTS (minimum score 6.5). *Faculty research:* Trace metal chemistry, water quality, organic and isotopic geochemistry, physical chemistry, nutrient chemistry.

University of Victoria, Faculty of Graduate Studies, Faculty of Science, School of Earth and Ocean Sciences, Victoria, BC V8W 2Y2, Canada. Offers M Sc, PhD. Part-time programs available. *Degree requirements:* For master's, thesis; for doctorate, thesis/dissertation, candidacy exam. *Entrance requirements:* For master's and doctorate, GRE. Additional exam requirements/recommendations for international students: Required—TOEFL (minimum score 575 paper-based),

IELTS (minimum score 7). Electronic applications accepted. *Faculty research:* Climate modeling, geology.

University of Washington, Graduate School, College of the Environment, School of Oceanography, Seattle, WA 98195. Offers biological oceanography (MS, PhD); chemical oceanography (MS, PhD); marine geology and geophysics (MS, PhD); physical oceanography (MS, PhD). Terminal master's awarded for partial completion of doctoral program. *Degree requirements:* For master's, research project; for doctorate, thesis/dissertation. *Entrance requirements:* For master's and doctorate, GRE General Test, minimum GPA of 3.0. Additional exam requirements/recommendations for international students: Required—TOEFL. Electronic applications accepted. *Faculty research:* Global climate change, hydrothermal vent systems, marine microbiology, marine and freshwater biogeochemistry, biological-physical interactions.

University of Wisconsin–Madison, Graduate School, College of Engineering, Program in Limnology and Marine Science, Madison, WI 53706. Offers MS, PhD. *Faculty:* 28 full-time (7 women). *Students:* 16 full-time (4 women), 2 international. 41 applicants, 10% accepted, 4 enrolled. In 2012, 1 master's, 1 doctorate awarded. Terminal master's awarded for partial completion of doctoral program. *Degree requirements:* For master's, thesis; for doctorate, thesis/dissertation. *Entrance requirements:* For master's and doctorate, GRE General Test. Additional exam requirements/recommendations for international students: Required—TOEFL. *Application deadline:* For fall admission, 1/1 priority date for domestic students, 1/1 for international students. Application fee: $45. Electronic applications accepted. *Expenses:* Tuition, state resident: full-time $10,728; part-time $743 per credit. Tuition, nonresident: full-time $24,054; part-time $1575 per credit. *Required fees:* $1111; $72 per credit. *Financial support:* In 2012–13, fellowships with full tuition reimbursements (averaging $20,200 per year), 14 research assistantships with full tuition reimbursements (averaging $20,200 per year), 4 teaching assistantships with full tuition reimbursements (averaging $20,200 per year) were awarded; Federal Work-Study and institutionally sponsored loans also available. Financial award application deadline: 1/1. *Faculty research:* Lake ecosystems, ecosystem modeling, geochemistry, physiological ecology, chemical limnology. *Unit head:* Steven Loheide, Chair, 608-263-3264, E-mail: loheide@wisc.edu. *Application contact:* Mary Possin, Student Services Coordinator, 608-263-3264, Fax: 608-265-2340, E-mail: mcpossin@wisc.edu. Website: http://www.engr.wisc.edu/interd/limnology/.

University of Wisconsin–Madison, Graduate School, College of Letters and Science, Department of Atmospheric and Oceanic Sciences, Madison, WI 53706-1380. Offers MS, PhD. Part-time programs available. *Degree requirements:* For master's, thesis (for some programs); for doctorate, thesis/dissertation. *Entrance requirements:* For master's and doctorate, GRE General Test, minimum GPA of 3.0; previous course work in chemistry, mathematics, and physics. Electronic applications accepted. *Expenses:* Tuition, state resident: full-time $10,728; part-time $743 per credit. Tuition, nonresident: full-time $24,054; part-time $1575 per credit. *Required fees:* $1111; $72 per credit. *Faculty research:* Satellite meteorology, weather systems, global climate change, numerical modeling, atmosphere-ocean interaction.

Woods Hole Oceanographic Institution, MIT/WHOI Joint Program in Oceanography/Applied Ocean Science and Engineering, Woods Hole, MA 02543-1541. Offers applied ocean science and engineering (PhD); biological oceanography (PhD); chemical oceanography (PhD); marine geology and geophysics (PhD); physical oceanography (PhD). Program offered jointly with Massachusetts Institute of Technology. *Degree requirements:* For doctorate, thesis/dissertation. *Entrance requirements:* For doctorate, GRE General Test, GRE Subject Test. Additional exam requirements/recommendations for international students: Required—TOEFL. Electronic applications accepted.

Yale University, Graduate School of Arts and Sciences, Department of Geology and Geophysics, New Haven, CT 06520. Offers biogeochemistry (PhD); climate dynamics (PhD); geochemistry (PhD); geophysics (PhD); meteorology (PhD); oceanography (PhD); paleontology (PhD); paleooceanography (PhD); petrology (PhD); tectonics (PhD). *Degree requirements:* For doctorate, thesis/dissertation. *Entrance requirements:* For doctorate, GRE General Test. Additional exam requirements/recommendations for international students: Required—TOEFL.

Peterson's Graduate Programs in the Physical Sciences, Mathematics, Agricultural Sciences, the Environment & Natural Resources 2014

facebook.com/petersonspublishing **197**

Section 5
Meteorology and Atmospheric Sciences

This section contains a directory of institutions offering graduate work in meteorology and atmospheric sciences. Additional information about programs listed in the directory may be obtained by writing directly to the dean of a graduate school or chair of a department at the address given in the directory.

For programs offering related work, see also in this book *Astronomy and Astrophysics, Geosciences, Marine Sciences and Oceanography,* and *Physics.* In the other guides in this series:

Graduate Programs in the Biological/Biomedical Sciences & Health-Related Medical Professions

See *Biological and Biomedical Sciences* and *Biophysics*

Graduate Programs in Engineering & Applied Sciences

See *Aerospace/Aeronautical Engineering, Civil and Environmental Engineering, Engineering and Applied Sciences,* and *Mechanical Engineering and Mechanics*

CONTENTS

Program Directories

Atmospheric Sciences

Arizona State University, College of Liberal Arts and Sciences, School of Geographical Sciences, Tempe, AZ 85287-5302. Offers atmospheric science (Graduate Certificate); geographic education (MAS); geographic information systems (MAS); geographical information science (Graduate Certificate); geography (MA, PhD); transportation systems (Graduate Certificate); urban and environmental planning (MUEP). Terminal master's awarded for partial completion of doctoral program. *Degree requirements:* For master's, thesis, interactive Program of Study (iPOS) submitted before completing 50 percent of required credit hours; for doctorate, comprehensive exam, thesis/dissertation, interactive Program of Study (iPOS) submitted before completing 50 percent of required credit hours. *Entrance requirements:* For master's and doctorate, GRE, minimum GPA of 3.0 or equivalent in last 2 years of work leading to bachelor's degree. Additional exam requirements/recommendations for international students: Required—TOEFL (minimum score 80 iBT), TOEFL, IELTS, or Pearson Test of English. Electronic applications accepted. *Expenses:* Contact institution.

Bard College, Bard Center for Environmental Policy, Annandale-on-Hudson, NY 12504. Offers climate science and policy (MS, Professional Certificate), including agriculture (MS), ecosystems (MS); environmental policy (MS, Professional Certificate); sustainability (MBA); MS/JD; MS/MAT. Part-time programs available. *Degree requirements:* For master's, thesis, 4-month, full-time internship. *Entrance requirements:* For master's, GRE, coursework in statistics, chemistry and one other semester of college science; personal statement; curriculum vitae; 3 letters of recommendation; sample of written work. Additional exam requirements/recommendations for international students: Required—TOEFL (minimum score 600 paper-based; 100 iBT). Electronic applications accepted. *Expenses:* Contact institution. *Faculty research:* Climate and agriculture, alternative energy, environmental economics, environmental toxicology, EPA law, sustainable development, international relations, literature and composition, human rights, agronomy, advocacy, leadership.

City College of the City University of New York, Graduate School, College of Liberal Arts and Science, Division of Science, Department of Earth and Atmospheric Sciences, New York, NY 10031-9198. Offers earth and environmental science (PhD); earth systems science (MA). PhD program offered jointly with Graduate School and University Center of the City University of New York. *Degree requirements:* For master's, comprehensive exam, thesis. *Entrance requirements:* Additional exam requirements/recommendations for international students: Required—TOEFL (minimum score 500 paper-based; 61 iBT). Electronic applications accepted. *Faculty research:* Water resources, high-temperature geochemistry, sedimentary basin analysis, tectonics.

Clemson University, Graduate School, College of Engineering and Science, Department of Physics and Astronomy, Clemson, SC 29634. Offers physics (MS, PhD), including astronomy and astrophysics, atmospheric physics, biophysics. Part-time programs available. *Faculty:* 24 full-time (3 women). *Students:* 62 full-time (15 women), 1 part-time (0 women); includes 2 minority (1 Black or African American, non-Hispanic/Latino; 1 Hispanic/Latino), 28 international. Average age 26. 66 applicants, 41% accepted, 12 enrolled. In 2012, 8 master's, 5 doctorates awarded. Terminal master's awarded for partial completion of doctoral program. *Degree requirements:* For master's, thesis or alternative; for doctorate, thesis/dissertation. *Entrance requirements:* For master's and doctorate, GRE General Test. Additional exam requirements/recommendations for international students: Required—TOEFL. *Application deadline:* For fall admission, 1/15 priority date for domestic students; for spring admission, 9/15 priority date for domestic students. Applications are processed on a rolling basis. Application fee: $70 ($80 for international students). Electronic applications accepted. *Financial support:* In 2012–13, 60 students received support, including 1 fellowship with full and partial tuition reimbursement available (averaging $7,000 per year), 25 research assistantships with partial tuition reimbursements available (averaging $13,151 per year), 44 teaching assistantships with partial tuition reimbursements available (averaging $15,956 per year); career-related internships or fieldwork, institutionally sponsored loans, scholarships/grants, health care benefits, and unspecified assistantships also available. Support available to part-time students. Financial award application deadline: 6/1; financial award applicants required to submit FAFSA. *Faculty research:* Radiation physics, solid-state physics, nuclear physics, radar and lidar studies of atmosphere. *Total annual research expenditures:* $2.6 million. *Unit head:* Dr. Peter Barnes, Chair, 864-656-3419, Fax: 864-656-0805, E-mail: peterb@clemson.edu. *Application contact:* Graduate Coordinator, 864-656-6702, Fax: 864-656-0805, E-mail: physgradinfo-l@clemson.edu. Website: http://physicsnt.clemson.edu/.

The College of William and Mary, Faculty of Arts and Sciences, Department of Applied Science, Williamsburg, VA 23187-8795. Offers accelerator science (PhD); applied mathematics (PhD); applied mechanics (PhD); applied robotics (PhD); applied science (MS); atmospheric and environmental science (PhD); computational neuroscience (PhD); interface, thin film and surface science (PhD); lasers and optics (PhD); magnetic resonance (PhD); materials science and engineering (PhD); mathematical and computational biology (PhD); medical imaging (PhD); nanotechnology (PhD); neuroscience (PhD); non-destructive evaluation (PhD); polymer chemistry (PhD); remote sensing (PhD). *Faculty:* 13 full-time (2 women), 1 part-time/adjunct (0 women). *Students:* 36 full-time (11 women); includes 2 minority (1 Black or African American, non-Hispanic/Latino; 1 Asian, non-Hispanic/Latino), 22 international. Average age 26. 40 applicants, 45% accepted, 8 enrolled. In 2012, 3 master's, 2 doctorates awarded. *Median time to degree:* Of those who began their doctoral program in fall 2004, 95% received their degree in 8 years or less. *Degree requirements:* For master's, comprehensive exam, thesis; for doctorate, comprehensive exam, thesis/dissertation, 4 core courses. *Entrance requirements:* For master's and doctorate, GRE General Test, GRE Subject Test. Additional exam requirements/recommendations for international students: Required—TOEFL, TWE. *Application deadline:* For fall admission, 2/3 priority date for domestic students, 2/3 for international students; for spring admission, 10/15 priority date for domestic students, 10/14 for international students. Applications are processed on a rolling basis. Application fee: $45. Electronic applications accepted. *Expenses:* Tuition, state resident: full-time $6779; part-time $385 per credit hour. Tuition, nonresident: full-time $20,608; part-time $1000 per credit hour. *Required fees:* $4625. *Financial support:* Fellowships, research assistantships, teaching assistantships, Federal Work-Study, health care benefits, tuition waivers (full), and unspecified assistantships available. Financial award application deadline: 4/15; financial award applicants required to submit FAFSA. *Faculty research:* Computational biology, non-destructive evaluation, neurophysiology, lasers and optics. *Unit head:* Dr. Christopher Del Negro, Chair, 757-221-7808, Fax: 757-221-2050, E-mail: cadeln@wm.edu. *Application contact:* Rosario Fox, Graduate Program Coordinator, 757-221-2563, Fax: 757-221-2050, E-mail: rxfoxx@wm.edu. Website: http://www.wm.edu/as/appliedscience.

Colorado State University, Graduate School, College of Engineering, Department of Atmospheric Science, Fort Collins, CO 80523-1371. Offers MS, PhD. Part-time programs available. *Faculty:* 12 full-time (2 women), 3 part-time/adjunct (0 women). *Students:* 67 full-time (25 women), 24 part-time (12 women); includes 14 minority (2 Black or African American, non-Hispanic/Latino; 9 Hispanic/Latino; 3 Two or more races, non-Hispanic/Latino), 7 international. Average age 27. 175 applicants, 10% accepted, 14 enrolled. In 2012, 14 master's, 15 doctorates awarded. *Degree requirements:* For master's, thesis optional; for doctorate, comprehensive exam, thesis/dissertation. *Entrance requirements:* For master's, GRE General Test, minimum GPA of 3.0; BS in physics, math, atmospheric science, engineering, chemistry or related major; calculus-based math and differential equations; calculus-based physics; letters of recommendation; for doctorate, GRE General Test, minimum GPA of 3.0; MS with thesis in atmospheric science or related field; statement with interests; curriculum vitae; letters of recommendation. Additional exam requirements/recommendations for international students: Required—TOEFL (minimum score 550 paper-based; 80 iBT), IELTS (minimum score 6). *Application deadline:* For fall admission, 1/15 priority date for domestic students, 1/15 for international students; for spring admission, 9/1 priority date for domestic students, 9/1 for international students. Applications are processed on a rolling basis. Application fee: $50. Electronic applications accepted. *Expenses:* Contact institution. *Financial support:* In 2012–13, 69 students received support, including 10 fellowships with full tuition reimbursements available (averaging $30,310 per year), 2 research assistantships with full tuition reimbursements available (averaging $26,685 per year), 2 teaching assistantships with partial tuition reimbursements available (averaging $1,505 per year); scholarships/grants and unspecified assistantships also available. Financial award application deadline: 1/1; financial award applicants required to submit FAFSA. *Faculty research:* Radiation and remote sensing; atmospheric chemistry; climate and atmosphere; ocean dynamics; cloud microphysics, severe storms, and mesoscale meteorology; global biogeochemical cycles and ecosystems. *Total annual research expenditures:* $12.5 million. *Unit head:* Dr. Jeffrey Collett, Jr., Head, 970-491-8360, Fax: 970-491-8449, E-mail: jeffrey.collett@colostate.edu. *Application contact:* Prof. Sonia Kreidenweis, Graduate Student Counselor and Professor, 970-491-8360, Fax: 970-491-8449, E-mail: info@atmos.colostate.edu. Website: http://www.ATMOS.colostate.edu/.

Columbia University, Graduate School of Arts and Sciences, Division of Natural Sciences, Program in Atmospheric and Planetary Science, New York, NY 10027. Offers M Phil, PhD. Offered jointly through the Departments of Geological Sciences, Astronomy, and Physics and in cooperation with NASA Goddard Space Flight Center's Institute for Space Studies. *Degree requirements:* For doctorate, variable foreign language requirement, thesis/dissertation. *Entrance requirements:* For doctorate, GRE General Test, GRE Subject Test, previous course work in mathematics and physics. Additional exam requirements/recommendations for international students: Required—TOEFL. *Faculty research:* Climate, weather prediction.

Columbia University, Graduate School of Arts and Sciences, Program in Climate and Society, New York, NY 10027. Offers MA.

Cornell University, Graduate School, Graduate Fields of Agriculture and Life Sciences, Field of Atmospheric Science, Ithaca, NY 14853-0001. Offers MS, PhD. *Faculty:* 15 full-time (1 woman). *Students:* 9 full-time (3 women), 3 international. Average age 26. 40 applicants, 5% accepted, 1 enrolled. In 2012, 1 master's, 3 doctorates awarded. *Degree requirements:* For master's, thesis; for doctorate, comprehensive exam, thesis/dissertation. *Entrance requirements:* For master's and doctorate, GRE General Test, 2 letters of recommendation. Additional exam requirements/recommendations for international students: Required—TOEFL (minimum score 550 paper-based; 77 iBT). *Application deadline:* For fall admission, 2/1 for domestic students; for spring admission, 8/1 priority date for domestic students. Application fee: $95. Electronic applications accepted. *Financial support:* In 2012–13, 8 students received support, including 7 research assistantships with full tuition reimbursements available, 1 teaching assistantship with full tuition reimbursement available; fellowships with full tuition reimbursements available, institutionally sponsored loans, traineeships, health care benefits, tuition waivers (full and partial), and unspecified assistantships also available. Financial award applicants required to submit FAFSA. *Faculty research:* Applied climatology, climate dynamics, statistical meteorology/climatology, synoptic meteorology, upper atmospheric science. *Unit head:* Director of Graduate Studies, 607-255-3034, Fax: 607-255-2106, E-mail: atmscigradfield@cornell.edu. *Application contact:* Graduate Field Assistant, 607-255-3034, Fax: 607-255-2106, E-mail: pmv2@cornell.edu. Website: http://www.gradschool.cornell.edu/fields.php?id-39&a-2.

Creighton University, Graduate School, College of Arts and Sciences, Program in Atmospheric Sciences, Omaha, NE 68178-0001. Offers MS. Part-time programs available. *Faculty:* 4 full-time (0 women). *Students:* 3 full-time (all women). Average age 24. 5 applicants, 60% accepted, 2 enrolled. In 2012, 1 master's awarded. *Degree requirements:* For master's, thesis optional. *Entrance requirements:* For master's, GRE General Test, 3 letters of recommendation. Additional exam requirements/recommendations for international students: Required—TOEFL (minimum score 550 paper-based; 80 iBT). *Application deadline:* For fall admission, 3/1 for domestic and international students. Application fee: $50. Electronic applications accepted. *Expenses: Tuition:* Full-time $13,250; part-time $730 per credit hour. *Required fees:* $144 per semester. Tuition and fees vary according to course load, campus/location, program, reciprocity agreements and student's religious affiliation. *Financial support:* In 2012–13, 1 research assistantship with full tuition reimbursement (averaging $14,000 per year), 3 teaching assistantships with full tuition reimbursements (averaging $10,913 per year) were awarded. Support available to part-time students. Financial award applicants required to submit FAFSA. *Unit head:* Dr. Joseph Zehnder, Chair, 402-280-2448, E-mail: zehnder@creighton.edu. *Application contact:* Taunya Plater, Senior Program Coordinator, 402-280-2870, Fax: 402-280-2423, E-mail: taunyaplater@creighton.edu.

Florida State University, The Graduate School, College of Arts and Sciences, Department of Scientific Computing, Tallahassee, FL 32306-4120. Offers computational science (MS, PSM, PhD), including atmospheric science (PhD), biochemistry (PhD), biological science (PhD), computational molecular biology/bioinformatics (PSM), computational science (PhD), geological science (PhD), materials science (PhD), physics (PhD). Part-time programs available. *Faculty:* 14 full-time (2 women). *Students:* 28 full-time (5 women), 4 part-time (0 women); includes 12 minority (10 Asian, non-Hispanic/Latino; 2 Hispanic/Latino). Average age 28. 28 applicants, 43% accepted, 7 enrolled. In 2012, 11 master's, 5 doctorates awarded. Terminal master's awarded for partial completion of doctoral program. *Degree requirements:* For master's, thesis (for some programs); for doctorate, comprehensive exam, thesis/dissertation. *Entrance requirements:* For master's and doctorate, GRE General Test, knowledge of at least one object oriented computing language, 3 letters of recommendations. Additional exam requirements/recommendations for international students: Required—TOEFL (minimum score 550 paper-based; 80 iBT). *Application deadline:* For fall admission, 1/15 for domestic and international students. Application fee: $30. Electronic applications accepted. *Expenses:* Tuition, state resident: full-time $7263; part-time $403.51 per credit hour. Tuition, nonresident: full-time $18,087; part-time $1004.85 per credit hour. *Required fees:* $1335.42; $74.19 per credit hour. $445.14 per semester. One-time fee: $40 full-time; $20 part-time. Tuition and fees vary according to program. *Financial support:* In 2012–13, 32 students received support, including 12 research assistantships with full tuition reimbursements available (averaging $20,000 per year), 17 teaching assistantships with full tuition reimbursements available (averaging $20,000 per year); scholarships/grants and unspecified assistantships also available. Financial award application deadline: 4/15. *Faculty research:* Morphometrics, mathematical and systems biology, mining proteomic and metabolic data, computational materials research, advanced 4-D Var data-assimilation methods in dynamic meteorology and oceanography, computational fluid dynamics, astrophysics. *Unit head:* Dr. Max Gunzburger, Chair, 850-644-1010, E-mail: mgunzburger@fsu.edu. *Application contact:* Maribel Amwake, Academic Coordinator, 850-644-0143, Fax: 850-644-0098, E-mail: mamwake@fsu.edu. Website: http://www.sc.fsu.edu.

George Mason University, College of Science, Program in Climate Dynamics, Fairfax, VA 22030. Offers PhD. *Faculty:* 17 full-time (5 women), 13 part-time/adjunct (4 women). *Students:* 17 full-time (8 women), 3 part-time (2 women), 14 international. Average age 31. 13 applicants, 69% accepted, 4 enrolled. In 2012, 3 doctorates awarded. *Degree requirements:* For doctorate, comprehensive exam, thesis/dissertation. *Entrance requirements:* For doctorate, GRE (waived for those who have earned a master's degree from U.S. institution), undergraduate degree with minimum GPA of 3.0; 2 copies of official transcripts; current resume; expanded goals statement; 3 letters of recommendation. Additional exam requirements/recommendations for international students: Required—TOEFL (minimum score 570 paper-based; 88 iBT), IELTS (minimum score 6.5), Pearson Test of English. *Application deadline:* For fall admission, 4/15 priority date for domestic students, 2/1 for international students; for spring admission, 11/15 priority date for domestic students. Application fee: $65 ($80 for international students). Electronic applications accepted. *Expenses:* Tuition, state resident: full-time $9080; part-time $378.33 per credit hour. Tuition, nonresident: full-time $25,010; part-time $1042.08 per credit hour. *Required fees:* $2610; $108.75 per credit hour. Tuition and fees vary according to program. *Financial support:* In 2012–13, 18 students received support, including 17 research assistantships with full and partial tuition reimbursements available (averaging $16,853 per year), 1 teaching assistantship with full and partial tuition reimbursement available (averaging $14,000 per year); career-related internships or fieldwork, Federal Work-Study, scholarships/grants, unspecified assistantships, and health care benefits (for full-time research or teaching assistantship recipients) also available. Support available to part-time students. Financial award application deadline: 3/1; financial award applicants required to submit FAFSA. *Faculty research:* Modeling and diagnosis of large-scale behavior of the climate system, anthropogenic climate changes, El Nino, prediction of climate events, ocean change in Antarctic. *Unit head:* Dr. David Straus, Chair, 703-993-9587, Fax: 703-993-9300, E-mail: dstraus@gmu.edu. *Application contact:* Dr. Barry Klinger, Graduate Coordinator, 703-993-9227, Fax: 703-993-9300, E-mail: bklinger@gmu.edu. Website: http://aoes.gmu.edu/academics/graduate/climate.

Georgia Institute of Technology, Graduate Studies and Research, College of Sciences, School of Earth and Atmospheric Sciences, Atlanta, GA 30332-0340. Offers atmospheric chemistry, aerosols and clouds (MS, PhD); dynamics of weather and climate (MS, PhD); geochemistry (MS, PhD); geophysics (MS, PhD); oceanography (MS, PhD); paleoclimate (MS, PhD); planetary science (MS, PhD); remote sensing (MS, PhD). Part-time programs available. Terminal master's awarded for partial completion of doctoral program. *Degree requirements:* For master's, thesis or alternative; for doctorate, comprehensive exam, thesis/dissertation. *Entrance requirements:* For master's, GRE, letters of recommendation; for doctorate, GRE, academic transcripts, letters of recommendation, personal statement. Additional exam requirements/recommendations for international students: Required—TOEFL (minimum score 550 paper-based; 79 iBT). *Faculty research:* Geophysics; atmospheric chemistry, aerosols and clouds; dynamics of weather and climate; geochemistry; oceanography; paleoclimate; planetary science; remote sensing.

Hampton University, Graduate College, Department of Atmospheric and Planetary Sciences, Hampton, VA 23668. Offers atmospheric sciences (MS, PhD); planetary sciences (MS, PhD).

Hampton University, Graduate College, Department of Physics, Hampton, VA 23668. Offers atmospheric physics (MS, PhD); medical physics (MS, PhD); nuclear physics (MS, PhD); optical physics (MS, PhD). Part-time and evening/weekend programs available. Terminal master's awarded for partial completion of doctoral program. *Degree requirements:* For master's, thesis optional; for doctorate, thesis/dissertation, oral defense, qualifying exam. *Entrance requirements:* For master's, GRE General Test; for doctorate, GRE General Test, minimum GPA of 3.0 or master's degree in physics or related field. *Faculty research:* Laser optics, remote sensing.

Howard University, Graduate School and School of Engineering and Computer Science, Department of Atmospheric Sciences, Washington, DC 20059-0002. Offers MS, PhD. Part-time programs available. Terminal master's awarded for partial completion of doctoral program. *Degree requirements:* For master's, thesis; for doctorate, one foreign language, comprehensive exam, thesis/dissertation. *Entrance requirements:* For master's, GRE General Test, minimum GPA of 3.0; for doctorate, GRE General Test, minimum GPA of 3.2. Additional exam requirements/recommendations for international students: Required—TOEFL (minimum score 550 paper-based). *Faculty research:* Atmospheric chemistry, climate, atmospheric radiation, gravity waves, aerosols, extraterrestrial atmospheres, turbulence.

Howard University, Graduate School, Department of Chemistry, Washington, DC 20059-0002. Offers analytical chemistry (MS, PhD); atmospheric (MS, PhD); biochemistry (MS, PhD); environmental (MS, PhD); inorganic chemistry (MS, PhD); organic chemistry (MS, PhD); physical chemistry (MS, PhD). Terminal master's awarded for partial completion of doctoral program. *Degree requirements:* For master's, comprehensive exam, thesis, teaching experience; for doctorate, comprehensive exam, thesis/dissertation, teaching experience. *Entrance requirements:* For master's, GRE General Test, minimum GPA of 2.7; for doctorate, GRE General Test, minimum GPA of 3.0. Additional exam requirements/recommendations for international students: Required—TOEFL. Electronic applications accepted. *Faculty research:* Synthetic organics, materials, natural products, mass spectrometry.

Massachusetts Institute of Technology, School of Science, Department of Earth, Atmospheric, and Planetary Sciences, Cambridge, MA 02139. Offers atmospheric chemistry (PhD, Sc D); atmospheric science (SM, PhD, Sc D); chemical oceanography (SM, PhD, Sc D); climate physics and chemistry (SM, PhD, Sc D); earth and planetary sciences (SM); geochemistry (PhD, Sc D); geology (PhD, Sc D); geophysics (PhD, Sc D); marine geology and geophysics (SM, PhD, Sc D); physical oceanography (SM, PhD, Sc D); planetary sciences (PhD, Sc D). *Faculty:* 33 full-time (6 women), 1 (woman) part-time/adjunct. *Students:* 166 full-time (77 women); includes 24 minority (3 Black or African American, non-Hispanic/Latino; 1 American Indian or Alaska Native, non-Hispanic/Latino; 9 Asian, non-Hispanic/Latino; 6 Hispanic/Latino; 5 Two or more races, non-Hispanic/Latino), 58 international. Average age 27. 232 applicants, 23% accepted, 27 enrolled. In 2012, 12 master's, 22 doctorates awarded. Terminal master's awarded for partial completion of doctoral program. *Degree requirements:* For master's, thesis; for doctorate, comprehensive exam, thesis/

dissertation. *Entrance requirements:* For master's, GRE General Test; for doctorate, GRE General Test, GRE Subject Test (chemistry or physics for planetary science area). Additional exam requirements/recommendations for international students: Required—TOEFL (minimum score 577 paper-based; 91 iBT), IELTS (minimum score 7). *Application deadline:* For fall admission, 1/5 for domestic and international students; for spring admission, 11/1 for domestic and international students. Application fee: $75. Electronic applications accepted. *Expenses: Tuition:* Full-time $41,770; part-time $650 per credit hour. *Required fees:* $280. *Financial support:* In 2012–13, 108 students received support, including 62 fellowships (averaging $30,700 per year), 87 research assistantships (averaging $32,600 per year), 15 teaching assistantships (averaging $30,800 per year); Federal Work-Study, institutionally sponsored loans, scholarships/grants, health care benefits, and unspecified assistantships also available. *Faculty research:* Formation, dynamics and evolution of planetary systems; origin, composition, structure and dynamics of the atmospheres, oceans, surfaces and interiors of the Earth and other planets; evolution and interaction of the physical, chemical, geological and biological components of the Earth system; characterization of past, present and potential future climates and the causes and consequences of climate change; interplay of energy and the environment. *Total annual research expenditures:* $28.1 million. *Unit head:* Prof. Robert van der Hilst, Head, 617-253-2127, Fax: 617-253-8298, E-mail: eapsinfo@mit.edu. *Application contact:* EAPS Education Office, 617-253-3381, Fax: 617-253-8298, E-mail: eapsinfo@mit.edu. Website: http://eapsweb.mit.edu/.

McGill University, Faculty of Graduate and Postdoctoral Studies, Faculty of Science, Department of Atmospheric and Oceanic Sciences, Montréal, QC H3A 2T5, Canada. Offers atmospheric science (M Sc, PhD); physical oceanography (M Sc, PhD). PhD program in physical oceanography offered jointly with Université Laval.

Michigan Technological University, Graduate School, Interdisciplinary Programs, Houghton, MI 49931. Offers atmospheric sciences (PhD); biochemistry and molecular biology (PhD); computational science and engineering (PhD); environmental engineering (PhD). *Degree requirements:* For doctorate, comprehensive exam, thesis/dissertation. *Entrance requirements:* For doctorate, GRE, statement of purpose, official transcripts, 3 letters of recommendation. Additional exam requirements/recommendations for international students: Required—TOEFL or IELTS.

Millersville University of Pennsylvania, College of Graduate and Professional Studies, School of Science and Mathematics, Department of Earth Sciences, Millersville, PA 17551-0302. Offers integrated scientific applications (MS), including climate science applications, environmental systems management, geoinformatics, weather intelligence and risk management. Part-time and evening/weekend programs available. *Faculty:* 10 full-time (2 women), 2 part-time/adjunct (1 woman). *Students:* 4 part-time (1 woman); includes 1 minority (Asian, non-Hispanic/Latino). Average age 23. 5 applicants, 100% accepted, 3 enrolled. *Degree requirements:* For master's, thesis optional, internship or applied research. *Entrance requirements:* For master's, GRE, MAT, or GMAT (if GPA is lower than 3.0), 3 letters of recommendation, resume, official transcripts, goal statement, telephone interview. Additional exam requirements/recommendations for international students: Required—TOEFL (minimum score 500 paper-based) or IELTS (minimum score 6). *Application deadline:* For fall admission, 1/15 priority date for domestic students, 1/15 for international students; for winter admission, 10/1 priority date for domestic students, 10/1 for international students; for spring admission, 10/1 priority date for domestic students, 10/1 for international students. Applications are processed on a rolling basis. Application fee: $40 ($50 for international students). Electronic applications accepted. *Expenses:* Tuition, state resident: full-time $7722; part-time $429 per credit. Tuition, nonresident: full-time $11,592; part-time $644 per credit. Tuition and fees vary according to course load. *Financial support:* In 2012–13, 2 students received support, including 2 research assistantships (averaging $5,000 per year). Financial award application deadline: 3/15; financial award applicants required to submit FAFSA. *Faculty research:* Climatology and meteorology. *Total annual research expenditures:* $229,000. *Unit head:* Dr. Richard D. Clark, Graduate Program Coordinator, 717-872-3930, E-mail: richard.clark@millersville.edu. *Application contact:* Dr. Victor S. DeSantis, Dean of Graduate and Professional Studies, 717-872-3099, Fax: 717-872-3453, E-mail: victor.desantis@millersville.edu. Website: http://www.millersville.edu/graduate/admissions/MSISA.php.

Mississippi State University, College of Arts and Sciences, Department of Geosciences, Mississippi State, MS 39762. Offers applied meteorology (MS); broadcast meteorology (MS); earth and atmospheric science (PhD); environmental geoscience (MS); geography (MS); geology (MS); geospatial sciences (MS); professional meteorology/climatology (MS); teachers in geoscience (MS). Postbaccalaureate distance learning degree programs offered (no on-campus study). *Faculty:* 14 full-time (3 women), 2 part-time/adjunct (0 women). *Students:* 62 full-time (27 women), 273 part-time (117 women); includes 29 minority (7 Black or African American, non-Hispanic/Latino; 4 Asian, non-Hispanic/Latino; 13 Hispanic/Latino; 5 Two or more races, non-Hispanic/Latino), 8 international. Average age 34. 235 applicants, 70% accepted, 135 enrolled. In 2012, 101 master's, 2 doctorates awarded. *Degree requirements:* For master's, thesis (for some programs), comprehensive oral or written exam; for doctorate, thesis/dissertation, comprehensive oral or written exam. *Entrance requirements:* For master's, GRE (for on-campus applicants), minimum undergraduate GPA of 2.75; for doctorate, completed thesis-based MS with background in one department emphasis area. Additional exam requirements/recommendations for international students: Required—TOEFL (minimum score 477 paper-based; 53 iBT); Recommended—IELTS (minimum score 4.5). *Application deadline:* For fall admission, 7/1 for domestic students, 5/1 for international students; for spring admission, 11/1 for domestic students, 9/1 for international students. Applications are processed on a rolling basis. Application fee: $60. Electronic applications accepted. *Financial support:* In 2012–13, 12 research assistantships with full tuition reimbursements (averaging $20,723 per year), 30 teaching assistantships with full tuition reimbursements (averaging $14,091 per year) were awarded; Federal Work-Study, institutionally sponsored loans, scholarships/grants, tuition waivers (partial), and unspecified assistantships also available. Financial award application deadline: 4/1; financial award applicants required to submit FAFSA. *Faculty research:* Climatology, hydrogeology, sedimentology, meteorology. *Total annual research expenditures:* $6.8 million. *Unit head:* Dr. Darrel Schmitz, Professor and Head, 662-325-3915, Fax: 662-325-9423, E-mail: schmitz@geosci.msstate.edu. *Application contact:* Dr. Mike Brown, Associate Professor/Graduate Coordinator, 662-325-3915, Fax: 662-325-9423, E-mail: tina@gesci.msstate.edu. Website: http://www.geosciences.msstate.edu.

New Mexico Institute of Mining and Technology, Graduate Studies, Department of Physics, Socorro, NM 87801. Offers astrophysics (PhD); atmospheric physics (PhD); instrumentation (MS); mathematical physics (PhD); physics (MS). *Faculty:* 12 full-time (3 women), 1 part-time/adjunct (0 women). *Students:* 30 full-time (12 women), 2 part-time (1 woman); includes 1 minority (Asian, non-Hispanic/Latino), 6 international. Average age 29. 15 applicants, 47% accepted, 4 enrolled. In 2012, 1 master's, 2 doctorates awarded. *Degree requirements:* For master's, thesis optional; for doctorate, thesis/dissertation. *Entrance requirements:* For master's, GRE General Test; for doctorate, GRE General Test, GRE Subject Test. Additional exam requirements/recommendations for international students: Required—TOEFL (minimum score 540 paper-based). *Application deadline:* For fall admission, 3/1 priority date for domestic students; for spring admission, 6/1 for domestic students. Applications are processed on a rolling basis. Application fee: $16 ($30 for international students). *Expenses:* Tuition, state resident: full-time $5043; part-time $280 per credit hour. Tuition, nonresident: full-time $16,682; part-time $927 per credit hour. *Required fees:* $648; $18 per credit hour. $108 per semester. Part-time tuition and fees vary according to course load. *Financial support:* In 2012–13, 19 research assistantships (averaging $18,770 per year), 13 teaching assistantships with full and partial tuition reimbursements (averaging $14,078 per year) were awarded; fellowships, Federal Work-Study, institutionally sponsored loans, and unspecified assistantships also available. Financial award application deadline: 3/1; financial award applicants required to submit CSS PROFILE or FAFSA. *Faculty research:* Cloud physics, stellar and extragalactic processes. *Total annual research expenditures:* $3 million. *Unit head:* Dr. Kenneth Eack, Chairman, 575-835-5328, Fax: 575-835-5707, E-mail: dwestpfa@nmt.edu. *Application contact:* Dr. Lorie Liebrock, Dean of Graduate Studies, 575-835-5513, Fax: 575-835-5476, E-mail: graduate@nmt.edu. Website: http://www.physics.nmt.edu/.

North Carolina State University, Graduate School, College of Physical and Mathematical Sciences, Department of Marine, Earth, and Atmospheric Sciences, Raleigh, NC 27695. Offers marine, earth, and atmospheric sciences (MS, PhD); meteorology (MS, PhD); oceanography (MS, PhD). PhD offered jointly with The University of North Carolina Wilmington. Terminal master's awarded for partial completion of doctoral program. *Degree requirements:* For master's, thesis (for some programs), final oral exam; for doctorate, comprehensive exam, thesis/dissertation, final oral exam, preliminary oral and written exams. *Entrance requirements:* For master's, GRE General Test, minimum GPA of 3.0; for doctorate, GRE General Test, GRE Subject Test (for disciplines in biological oceanography and geology), minimum GPA of 3.0. Additional exam requirements/recommendations for international students: Required—TOEFL (minimum score 550 paper-based). Electronic applications accepted. *Faculty research:* Boundary layer and air quality meteorology; climate and mesoscale dynamics; biological, chemical, geological, and physical oceanography; hard rock, soft rock, environmental, and paleo-geology.

Northern Arizona University, Graduate College, College of Engineering, Forestry and Natural Sciences, School of Earth Sciences and Environmental Sustainability, Flagstaff, AZ 86011. Offers climate science and solutions (MS); earth science (MS); earth sciences and environmental sustainability (PhD); environmental sciences and policy (MS); geology (MS). *Degree requirements:* For master's, comprehensive exam (for some programs), thesis (for some programs). *Entrance requirements:* Additional exam requirements/recommendations for international students: Required—TOEFL (minimum score 550 paper-based; 80 iBT), IELTS (minimum score 7). Electronic applications accepted.

The Ohio State University, Graduate School, College of Arts and Sciences, Division of Social and Behavioral Sciences, Department of Geography, Columbus, OH 43210. Offers atmospheric sciences (MS, PhD); geography (MA, PhD). *Faculty:* 24. *Students:* 42 full-time (18 women), 26 part-time (8 women); includes 6 minority (4 Asian, non-Hispanic/Latino; 1 Hispanic/Latino; 1 Two or more races, non-Hispanic/Latino), 24 international. Average age 28. In 2012, 11 master's, 4 doctorates awarded. *Degree requirements:* For doctorate, variable foreign language requirement, thesis/dissertation. *Entrance requirements:* For master's and doctorate, GRE. Additional exam requirements/recommendations for international students: Required—Michigan English Language Assessment Battery (minimum score 86); Recommended—TOEFL (minimum score 600 paper-based; 100 iBT), IELTS (minimum score 8). *Application deadline:* For fall admission, 12/15 priority date for domestic students, 11/30 for international students; for winter admission, 12/1 for domestic students, 11/1 for international students; for spring admission, 3/1 for domestic students, 2/1 for international students. Applications are processed on a rolling basis. Application fee: $40 ($50 for international students). Electronic applications accepted. *Financial support:* Fellowships, research assistantships, teaching assistantships, Federal Work-Study, and institutionally sponsored loans available. Support available to part-time students. *Unit head:* Daniel Sui, Chair, 614-688-5441, Fax: 614-292-6213, E-mail: sui.10@osu.edu. *Application contact:* Graduate Admissions, 614-292-9444, Fax: 614-292-3895, E-mail: gradadmissions@osu.edu. Website: http://www.geography.osu.edu/.

Oregon State University, College of Earth, Ocean, and Atmospheric Sciences, Program in Ocean, Earth, and Atmospheric Sciences, Corvallis, OR 97331. Offers atmospheric sciences (MA, MS); geography (PhD); geology (PhD); geophysics (MA, MS); oceanography (MA, MS). *Students:* 33 full-time (17 women), 1 part-time (0 women); includes 5 minority (1 Asian, non-Hispanic/Latino; 2 Hispanic/Latino; 2 Two or more races, non-Hispanic/Latino), 7 international. Average age 28. 148 applicants, 15% accepted, 8 enrolled. In 2012, 10 master's, 3 doctorates awarded. *Expenses:* Tuition, state resident: full-time $11,367; part-time $421 per credit hour. Tuition, nonresident: full-time $18,279; part-time $677 per credit hour. *Required fees:* $1478. One-time fee: $300 full-time. Tuition and fees vary according to course load and program. *Unit head:* Dr. Mark R. Abbott, Dean, 541-737-5195, Fax: 541-737-2064, E-mail: mark@coas.oregonstate.edu. *Application contact:* Dr. Robert S. Allan, Assistant Director, Student Programs, 541-737-1340, Fax: 541-737-2064, E-mail: rallan@coas.oregonstate.edu. Website: http://ceoas.oregonstate.edu/academics/ocean/.

Princeton University, Graduate School, Department of Geosciences, Program in Atmospheric and Oceanic Sciences, Princeton, NJ 08544-1019. Offers PhD. *Degree requirements:* For doctorate, one foreign language, thesis/dissertation. *Entrance requirements:* For doctorate, GRE General Test, GRE Subject Test. Additional exam requirements/recommendations for international students: Required—TOEFL (minimum score 600 paper-based). Electronic applications accepted. *Faculty research:* Climate dynamics, middle atmosphere dynamics and chemistry, oceanic circulation, marine geochemistry, numerical modeling.

Purdue University, Graduate School, College of Science, Department of Earth and Atmospheric Sciences, West Lafayette, IN 47907. Offers MS, PhD. *Faculty:* 31 full-time (2 women), 3 part-time/adjunct (0 women). *Students:* 66 full-time (27 women), 6 part-time (3 women); includes 9 minority (3 Black or African American, non-Hispanic/Latino; 3 American Indian or Alaska Native, non-Hispanic/Latino; 1 Asian, non-Hispanic/Latino; 2 Hispanic/Latino), 26 international. Average age 27. 180 applicants, 17% accepted, 19 enrolled. In 2012, 9 master's, 9 doctorates awarded. *Degree requirements:* For master's, comprehensive exam, thesis; for doctorate, one foreign language, comprehensive exam, thesis/dissertation. *Entrance requirements:* For master's, GRE General Test, minimum undergraduate GPA of 3.0 or equivalent; for doctorate, GRE General Test, minimum undergraduate or master's GPA of 3.0 or equivalent. Additional exam requirements/recommendations for international students: Required—TOEFL (minimum score 550 paper-based; 77 iBT); Recommended—TWE. *Application deadline:* For fall admission, 1/2 priority date for domestic students, 1/2 for international students; for spring admission, 9/1 for domestic and international students. Applications are processed on a rolling basis. Application fee: $60 ($75 for international students). Electronic applications accepted. *Financial support:* Fellowships with partial tuition reimbursements, research assistantships with partial tuition reimbursements, and teaching assistantships with partial tuition reimbursements available. Support available to part-time students. Financial award application deadline: 3/1; financial award applicants required to submit FAFSA. *Faculty research:* Geology, geophysics, hydrogeology, paleoclimatology, environmental science. *Unit head:* Dr. Jonathan M. Harbor, Head, 765-494-4753. *Application contact:* Kathy S. Kincade, Graduate Secretary, 765-494-5984, Fax: 765-496-1210, E-mail: kkincade@purdue.edu. Website: http://www.eas.purdue.edu.

Rutgers, The State University of New Jersey, New Brunswick, Graduate School-New Brunswick, Department of Environmental Sciences, Piscataway, NJ 08854-8097. Offers air pollution and resources (MS, PhD); aquatic biology (MS, PhD); aquatic chemistry (MS, PhD); atmospheric science (MS, PhD); chemistry and physics of aerosol and hydrosol systems (MS, PhD); environmental chemistry (MS, PhD); environmental microbiology (MS, PhD); environmental toxicology (PhD); exposure assessment (PhD); fate and effects of pollutants (MS, PhD); pollution prevention and control (MS, PhD); water and wastewater treatment (MS, PhD); water resources (MS, PhD). Terminal master's awarded for partial completion of doctoral program. *Degree requirements:* For master's, comprehensive exam, thesis or alternative, oral final exam; for doctorate, comprehensive exam, thesis/dissertation, thesis defense, qualifying exam. *Entrance requirements:* For master's and doctorate, GRE General Test. Additional exam requirements/recommendations for international students: Required—TOEFL. Electronic applications accepted. *Faculty research:* Biological waste treatment; contaminant fate and transport; air, soil and water quality.

South Dakota School of Mines and Technology, Graduate Division, PhD Program in Atmospheric and Environmental Sciences, Rapid City, SD 57701-3995. Offers PhD. Program offered jointly with South Dakota State University. Part-time programs available. *Faculty:* 6 full-time (1 woman), 2 part-time/adjunct (1 woman). *Students:* 3 full-time (0 women), 9 part-time (2 women); includes 1 minority (Two or more races, non-Hispanic/Latino), 3 international. Average age 38. 1 applicant. *Degree requirements:* For doctorate, comprehensive exam, thesis/dissertation. *Entrance requirements:* For doctorate, GRE General Test, GRE Subject Test. Additional exam requirements/recommendations for international students: Required—TOEFL (minimum score 520 paper-based; 68 iBT), TWE. *Application deadline:* For fall admission, 7/1 priority date for domestic students, 4/1 for international students; for spring admission, 11/1 for domestic students, 9/1 for international students. Applications are processed on a rolling basis. Application fee: $35. Electronic applications accepted. *Expenses:* Tuition, state resident: full-time $4720; part-time $196.80 per credit hour. Tuition, nonresident: full-time $10,000; part-time $416.55 per credit hour. *Required fees:* $4360. *Financial support:* Fellowships, research assistantships with partial tuition reimbursements, teaching assistantships with partial tuition reimbursements, and unspecified assistantships available. Financial award application deadline: 5/15. *Unit head:* Dr. William Capehart, Program Coordinator, 605-394-1994, E-mail: william.capehart@sdsmt.edu. *Application contact:* Linda Carlson, Office of Graduate Education, 605-355-3468, Fax: 605-394-1767, E-mail: linda.carlson@sdsmt.edu. Website: http://www.sdsmt.edu/Academics/Departments/Atmospheric-Sciences/Graduate-Education/Atmospheric-and-Environmental-Sciences—PhD-/.

South Dakota School of Mines and Technology, Graduate Division, Program in Atmospheric Sciences, Rapid City, SD 57701-3995. Offers MS. Part-time programs available. *Faculty:* 6 full-time (1 woman), 1 part-time/adjunct (0 women). *Students:* 12 full-time (4 women), 1 part-time (0 women). Average age 28. 14 applicants, 93% accepted, 13 enrolled. In 2012, 6 master's awarded. *Degree requirements:* For master's, thesis. *Entrance requirements:* For master's, GRE General Test. Additional exam requirements/recommendations for international students: Required—TOEFL (minimum score 520 paper-based; 68 iBT), TWE. *Application deadline:* For fall admission, 7/1 priority date for domestic students, 4/1 for international students; for spring admission, 11/1 for domestic students, 9/1 for international students. Applications are processed on a rolling basis. Application fee: $35. Electronic applications accepted. *Expenses:* Tuition, state resident: full-time $4720; part-time $196.80 per credit hour. Tuition, nonresident: full-time $10,000; part-time $416.55 per credit hour. *Required fees:* $4360. *Financial support:* Fellowships, research assistantships with partial tuition reimbursements, teaching assistantships with partial tuition reimbursements, Federal Work-Study, and institutionally sponsored loans available. Support available to part-time students. Financial award application deadline: 5/15. *Faculty research:* Hailstorm observations and numerical modeling, microbursts and lightning, radioactive transfer, remote sensing. *Unit head:* Dr. William Capehart, Program Coordinator, 605-394-1994, E-mail: william.capehart@sdsmt.edu. *Application contact:* Linda Carlson, Office of Graduate Education, 605-355-3468, Fax: 605-394-1767, E-mail: linda.carlson@sdsmt.edu. Website: http://www.sdsmt.edu/Academics/Departments/Atmospheric-Sciences/Graduate-Education/Atmospheric-and-Environmental-Sciences—MS-/.

Southern Methodist University, Bobby B. Lyle School of Engineering, Department of Environmental and Civil Engineering, Dallas, TX 75275-0340. Offers air pollution control and atmospheric sciences (PhD); civil engineering (MS); environmental engineering (MS); structural engineering (PhD); sustainability and development (MA); water and wastewater engineering (PhD). Part-time and evening/weekend programs available. Postbaccalaureate distance learning degree programs offered (no on-campus study). Terminal master's awarded for partial completion of doctoral program. *Degree requirements:* For master's, thesis optional; for doctorate, thesis/dissertation, oral and written qualifying exams. *Entrance requirements:* For master's, GRE General Test, minimum GPA of 3.0 in last 2 years; bachelor's degree in engineering, mathematics, or sciences; for doctorate, GRE, BS and MS in related field, minimum GPA of 3.3. Additional exam requirements/recommendations for international students: Required—TOEFL. Electronic applications accepted. *Faculty research:* Human and environmental health effects of endocrine disrupters, development of air pollution control systems for diesel engines, structural analysis and design, modeling and design of waste treatment systems.

Stony Brook University, State University of New York, Graduate School, School of Marine and Atmospheric Sciences, Institute for Terrestrial and Planetary Atmospheres, Program in Atmospheric Sciences, Stony Brook, NY 11794. Offers MS, PhD. Evening/weekend programs available. *Degree requirements:* For doctorate, one foreign language, comprehensive exam, thesis/dissertation. *Entrance requirements:* For master's, GRE, minimum GPA of 3.0, 3 letters of recommendation; for doctorate, GRE, official transcripts, minimum GPA of 3.0, 3 letters of recommendation. Additional exam requirements/recommendations for international students: Required—TOEFL (minimum score 600 paper-based). *Application deadline:* For fall admission, 1/15 priority date for domestic students; for spring admission, 10/1 priority date for domestic students. Application fee: $100. Electronic applications accepted. *Expenses:* Tuition, state resident: full-time $9370. Tuition, nonresident: full-time $16,680. *Required fees:* $1214. *Financial support:* Fellowships, research assistantships, teaching assistantships, and career-related internships or fieldwork available. *Unit head:* Dr. Minghua Zhang, Director, 631-632-8318. *Application contact:* Dr. Anne R. McElroy, Director of Graduate Programs, 631-632-8488, Fax: 631-632-8200, E-mail: anne.mcelroy@stonybrook.edu.

Texas Tech University, Graduate School, College of Arts and Sciences, Department of Geosciences, Lubbock, TX 79409. Offers atmospheric science (MS); geography (MS); geosciences (MS, PhD). Part-time programs available. *Degree requirements:* For master's, thesis or alternative; for doctorate, comprehensive exam, thesis/dissertation. *Entrance requirements:* For master's and doctorate, GRE General Test. Additional exam requirements/ recommendations for international students: Required—TOEFL (minimum score 550 paper-based; 79 iBT). Electronic applications accepted. *Faculty research:* Sedimentology and paleontology, geophysics, geochemistry, geospatial technology, hurricanes and severe storms.

Université du Québec à Montréal, Graduate Programs, Program in Earth and Atmospheric Sciences, Montréal, QC H3C 3P8, Canada. Offers atmospheric sciences (M Sc); Earth and atmospheric sciences (PhD); Earth science (M Sc); meteorology (PhD, Diploma). PhD programs offered jointly with McGill University. Part-time programs available. *Degree requirements:* For master's, thesis. *Entrance requirements:* For master's and Diploma, appropriate bachelor's degree or equivalent, proficiency in French; for doctorate, appropriate master's degree or equivalent, proficiency in French.

University at Albany, State University of New York, College of Arts and Sciences, Department of Earth and Atmospheric Sciences, Albany, NY 12222-0001. Offers atmospheric science (MS, PhD); geology (MS, PhD). *Degree requirements:* For master's, one foreign language, comprehensive exam, thesis; for doctorate, 2 foreign languages, comprehensive exam, thesis/dissertation, oral exams. *Entrance requirements:* For master's and doctorate, GRE General Test. Additional exam requirements/recommendations for international students: Required—TOEFL (minimum score 550 paper-based). Electronic applications accepted. *Faculty research:* Environmental geochemistry, tectonics, mesoscale meteorology, atmospheric chemistry.

The University of Alabama in Huntsville, School of Graduate Studies, College of Science, Department of Atmospheric Science, Huntsville, AL 35899. Offers atmospheric science (MS, PhD); earth system science (MS). Part-time and evening/weekend programs available. *Faculty:* 10 full-time (0 women), 1 part-time/adjunct (0 women). *Students:* 42 full-time (14 women), 5 part-time (all women); includes 3 minority (1 Black or African American, non-Hispanic/Latino; 1 Asian, non-Hispanic/Latino; 1 Hispanic/Latino), 7 international. Average age 26. 49 applicants, 90% accepted, 17 enrolled. In 2012, 5 master's, 2 doctorates awarded. *Degree requirements:* For master's, comprehensive exam, thesis or alternative, oral and written exams; for doctorate, comprehensive exam, thesis/dissertation, oral and written exams. *Entrance requirements:* For master's, GRE General Test, minimum GPA of 3.0; sequence of courses in calculus (including the calculus of vector-valued functions); courses in linear algebra and ordinary differential equations; two semesters each of chemistry and calculus-based physics; proficiency in at least one high-level computer programming language; for doctorate, GRE General Test, minimum GPA of 3.0. Additional exam requirements/recommendations for international students: Required—TOEFL (minimum score 550 paper-based; 80 iBT), IELTS (minimum score 6.5). *Application deadline:* For fall admission, 7/15 priority date for domestic students, 4/1 for international students; for spring admission, 11/30 priority date for domestic students, 9/1 for international students. Applications are processed on a rolling basis. Application fee: $40 ($50 for international students). Electronic applications accepted. *Expenses:* Tuition, state resident: full-time $8516; part-time $515 per credit hour. Tuition, nonresident: full-time $20,384; part-time $1229 per credit hour. *Required fees:* $148 per semester. One-time fee: $150. *Financial support:* In 2012–13, 36 students received support, including 34 research assistantships with full and partial tuition reimbursements available (averaging $14,797 per year), 2 teaching assistantships with full and partial tuition reimbursements available (averaging $14,400 per year); career-related internships or fieldwork, Federal Work-Study, institutionally sponsored loans, scholarships/grants, health care benefits, and unspecified assistantships also available. Support available to part-time students. Financial award application deadline: 4/1; financial award applicants required to submit FAFSA. *Faculty research:* Severe weather, climate, satellite remote sensing, numerical modeling, air pollution. *Total annual research expenditures:* $9.6 million. *Unit head:* Dr. Sundar Christopher, Chair, 256-922-7872, Fax: 256-922-7755, E-mail: sundar@nsstc.uah.edu. *Application contact:* Kim Gray, Graduate Studies Admissions Coordinator, 256-824-6002, Fax: 256-824-6405, E-mail: deangrad@uah.edu. Website: http://www.nsstc.uah.edu/atmos/index.html.

University of Alaska Fairbanks, College of Natural Sciences and Mathematics, Program in Atmospheric Science, Fairbanks, AK 99775-7320. Offers MS, PhD. Part-time programs available. *Students:* 18 full-time (4 women), 7 international. Average age 26. 20 applicants, 25% accepted, 5 enrolled. In 2012, 4 master's, 2 doctorates awarded. *Degree requirements:* For master's, comprehensive exam, thesis, oral defense; for doctorate, comprehensive exam, thesis/dissertation, oral defense. *Entrance requirements:* Additional exam requirements/ recommendations for international students: Required—TOEFL (minimum score 550 paper-based; 80 iBT). *Application deadline:* For fall admission, 6/1 for domestic students, 3/1 for international students; for spring admission, 10/15 for domestic students, 9/1 for international students. Applications are processed on a rolling basis. Application fee: $60. Electronic applications accepted. *Expenses:* Tuition, state resident: full-time $7038. Tuition, nonresident: full-time $14,382. Tuition and fees vary according to course level, course load and reciprocity agreements. *Financial support:* In 2012–13, 15 research assistantships with tuition reimbursements (averaging $16,644 per year), 2 teaching assistantships with tuition reimbursements (averaging $13,945 per year) were awarded; fellowships with tuition reimbursements, Federal Work-Study, scholarships/ grants, health care benefits, and unspecified assistantships also available. Support available to part-time students. Financial award application deadline: 2/15; financial award applicants required to submit FAFSA. *Faculty research:* Sea ice, climate modeling, atmospheric chemistry, global change, cloud and aerosol physics. *Unit head:* Dr. Nicole Moelders, Program Chair, 907-474-7368, Fax: 907-474-7379, E-mail: atmos@gi.alaska.edu. *Application contact:* Libby Eddy, Registrar and Director of Admissions, 907-474-7500, Fax: 907-474-7097, E-mail: admissions@uaf.edu. Website: http://www.gi.alaska.edu/research/atmo.

The University of Arizona, College of Science, Department of Atmospheric Sciences, Tucson, AZ 85721. Offers MS, PhD. *Faculty:* 6 full-time (2 women). *Students:* 23 full-time (11 women), 2 part-time (0 women); includes 2 minority (1 Hispanic/Latino; 1 Two or more races, non-Hispanic/Latino), 8 international. Average age 29. 18 applicants, 22% accepted, 4 enrolled. In 2012, 7 master's, 3 doctorates awarded. *Degree requirements:* For master's, thesis or alternative; for doctorate, comprehensive exam, thesis/dissertation. *Entrance requirements:* For master's, GRE General Test, 3 letters of recommendation; for doctorate, GRE General Test, 3 letters of recommendation, statement of purpose. Additional exam requirements/recommendations for international students: Required—TOEFL (minimum score 550 paper-based; 79 iBT). *Application deadline:* For fall admission, 2/1 for domestic students, 12/1 for international students. Applications are processed on a rolling basis. Application fee: $75. Electronic applications accepted. *Financial support:* In 2012–13, 1 research assistantship with full tuition reimbursement (averaging $20,979 per year), 5 teaching assistantships with full tuition reimbursements (averaging $22,137 per year) were awarded; scholarships/ grants, health care benefits, tuition waivers (full), and unspecified assistantships also available. *Faculty research:* Climate dynamics, radiative transfer and remote sensing, atmospheric chemistry, atmosphere dynamics, atmospheric electricity. *Total annual research expenditures:* $3 million. *Unit head:* Eric A. Betterton, Head, 520-621-6831, E-mail: betterton@atmo.arizona.edu. *Application contact:* Sonya Flores-Basurto, Information Contact, 520-621-6831, Fax: 520-621-6833, E-mail: sfloresb@email.arizona.edu. Website: http://www.atmo.arizona.edu.

The University of British Columbia, Faculty of Science, Department of Earth and Ocean Sciences, Vancouver, BC V6T 1Z4, Canada. Offers atmospheric science (M Sc, PhD); geological engineering (M Eng, MA Sc, PhD); geological sciences (M Sc, PhD); geophysics (M Sc, MA Sc, PhD); oceanography (M Sc, PhD). *Degree requirements:* For master's, thesis (for some programs); for doctorate, comprehensive exam, thesis/dissertation. *Entrance requirements:* Additional exam requirements/recommendations for international students: Required—TOEFL (minimum score 600 paper-based; 100 iBT). Electronic applications accepted. *Faculty research:* Oceans and atmosphere, environmental earth science, hydro geology, mineral deposits, geophysics.

University of California, Davis, Graduate Studies, Graduate Group in Atmospheric Sciences, Davis, CA 95616. Offers MS, PhD. *Degree requirements:* For master's, comprehensive exam or thesis; for doctorate, thesis/dissertation, 3 part qualifying exam. *Entrance requirements:* For master's and doctorate, GRE General Test, minimum GPA of 3.0. Additional exam requirements/ recommendations for international students: Required—TOEFL (minimum score 550 paper-based). Electronic applications accepted. *Faculty research:* Air quality, biometeorology, climate dynamics, boundary layer large-scale dynamics.

University of California, Los Angeles, Graduate Division, College of Letters and Science, Department of Atmospheric and Oceanic Sciences, Los Angeles, CA 90095. Offers MS, PhD. *Faculty:* 15 full-time (2 women). *Students:* 39 full-time (20 women); includes 9 minority (5 Asian, non-Hispanic/Latino; 4 Hispanic/Latino), 18 international. Average age 26. 89 applicants, 36% accepted, 9 enrolled. In 2012, 14 master's, 6 doctorates awarded. Terminal master's awarded for partial completion of doctoral program. *Degree requirements:* For master's, comprehensive exam or thesis; for doctorate, thesis/dissertation, oral and written qualifying exams; 2 quarters of teaching experience. *Entrance requirements:* For master's and doctorate, GRE General Test, bachelor's degree; minimum undergraduate GPA of 3.0 (or its equivalent if letter grade system not used). Additional exam requirements/recommendations for international students: Required—TOEFL. *Application deadline:* For fall admission, 12/15 for domestic and international students. Application fee: $80 ($100 for international students). Electronic applications accepted. *Expenses:* Tuition, nonresident: full-time $15,102. *Required fees:* $14,809.19. Full-time tuition and fees vary according to program. *Financial support:* In 2012–13, 39 students received support, including 38 fellowships with full and partial tuition reimbursements available, 35 research assistantships with full and partial tuition reimbursements available, 14 teaching assistantships with full and partial tuition reimbursements available; Federal Work-Study, scholarships/grants, health care benefits, tuition waivers (full and partial), and unspecified assistantships also available. Financial award application deadline: 3/2; financial award applicants required to submit FAFSA. *Unit head:* Dr. David C. Neelin, Chair, 310-206-3734, E-mail: neelin@atmos.ucla.edu. *Application contact:* Departmental Office, 310-825-1217, Fax: 310-206-5219, E-mail: studentinfo@atmos.ucla.edu. Website: http://www.atmos.ucla.edu.

University of Chicago, Division of the Physical Sciences, Department of the Geophysical Sciences, Chicago, IL 60637-1513. Offers atmospheric sciences (SM, PhD); cosmochemistry (PhD); earth sciences (SM, PhD); paleobiology (PhD); planetary and space sciences (SM, PhD). Terminal master's awarded for partial completion of doctoral program. *Degree requirements:* For master's, thesis, seminar; for doctorate, variable foreign language requirement, comprehensive exam, thesis/dissertation. *Entrance requirements:* For doctorate, GRE General Test. Additional exam requirements/recommendations for international students: Required—TOEFL (minimum score 600 paper-based; 96 iBT), IELTS (minimum score 7). Electronic applications accepted. *Faculty research:* Climatology, evolutionary paleontology, cosmochemistry, geochemistry, oceanic sciences.

University of Colorado Boulder, Graduate School, College of Arts and Sciences, Department of Atmospheric and Oceanic Sciences, Boulder, CO 80309. Offers MS, PhD. *Faculty:* 12 full-time (5 women). *Students:* 57 full-time (26 women), 7 part-time (3 women); includes 6 minority (1 Black or African American, non-Hispanic/Latino; 2 Asian, non-Hispanic/Latino; 2 Hispanic/Latino; 1 Two or more races, non-Hispanic/Latino), 12 international. Average age 29. 128 applicants, 25% accepted, 13 enrolled. *Entrance requirements:* For master's, minimum undergraduate GPA of 3.0. *Application deadline:* For fall admission, 1/1 for domestic students, 12/1 for international students; for spring admission, 10/1 for domestic and international students. Electronic applications accepted. *Financial support:* In 2012–13, 55 students received support, including 9 fellowships (averaging $18,687 per year), 36 research assistantships with full and partial tuition reimbursements available (averaging $25,891 per year), 13 teaching assistantships with full and partial tuition reimbursements available (averaging $22,873 per year); institutionally sponsored loans, scholarships/grants, health care benefits, and unspecified assistantships also available. Financial award applicants required to submit FAFSA. *Faculty research:* Atmospheric sciences, atmospheric structure and dynamics, atmospheric models, atmospheric physics, global change. *Total annual research expenditures:* $15.9 million. *Application contact:* E-mail: atocasst@colorado.edu. Website: http://atoc.colorado.edu/.

University of Guelph, Graduate Studies, Ontario Agricultural College, Department of Land Resource Science, Guelph, ON N1G 2W1, Canada. Offers atmospheric science (M Sc, PhD); environmental and agricultural earth sciences (M Sc, PhD); land resources management (M Sc, PhD); soil science (M Sc, PhD). Part-time programs available. *Degree requirements:* For master's, thesis (for some programs), research project (non-thesis track); for doctorate, comprehensive exam, thesis/dissertation. *Entrance requirements:* For master's, minimum B- average during previous 2 years of course work; for doctorate, minimum B average during previous 2 years of course work. Additional exam requirements/recommendations for international students: Required—TOEFL (minimum score 550 paper-based). Electronic applications accepted. *Faculty research:* Soil science, environmental earth science, land resource management.

University of Houston, College of Natural Sciences and Mathematics, Department of Earth and Atmospheric Sciences, Houston, TX 77204. Offers atmospheric science (PhD); geology (MA, PhD); geophysics (PhD). Part-time programs available. *Degree requirements:* For master's, thesis; for doctorate, comprehensive exam, thesis/dissertation. *Entrance requirements:* For master's and doctorate, GRE General Test. Additional exam requirements/ recommendations for international students: Required—TOEFL (minimum score 550 paper-based; 79 iBT), IELTS (minimum score 6.5). Electronic applications accepted. *Faculty research:* Atmospherics sciences, seismic and solid earth geophysics, tectonics, environmental hydrochemistry, carbonates, micropaleontology, structure and tectonics, petroleum geology.

University of Illinois at Urbana–Champaign, Graduate College, College of Liberal Arts and Sciences, School of Earth, Society and Environment, Department of Atmospheric Sciences, Champaign, IL 61820. Offers MS, PhD. *Students:* 43 (21 women). Application fee: $75 ($90 for international students). *Unit head:* Robert Rauber, Head, 217-333-2835, Fax: 217-244-4393, E-mail: r-rauber@illinois.edu. *Application contact:* Shirley Palmisano, Office Administrator, 217-333-2046, Fax: 217-244-4393, E-mail: sjpalm@illinois.edu. Website: http://www.atmos.illinois.edu/.

The University of Kansas, Graduate Studies, College of Liberal Arts and Sciences, Department of Geography, Lawrence, KS 66045-7613. Offers atmospheric science (MS); geography (MA, PhD); MUP/MA. Part-time programs available. *Faculty:* 24. *Students:* 87 full-time (35 women), 19 part-time (8 women); includes 10 minority (1 Black or African American, non-Hispanic/Latino; 8 American Indian or Alaska Native, non-Hispanic/Latino; 1 Hispanic/Latino), 15 international. Average age 32. 68 applicants, 50% accepted, 24 enrolled. In 2012, 5 master's, 10 doctorates awarded. *Degree requirements:* For master's, comprehensive exam, thesis, thesis defense; for doctorate, one foreign language, comprehensive exam, thesis/dissertation, dissertation defense. *Entrance requirements:* For master's and doctorate, GRE General Test, 3 letters of reference, transcripts, statement of interests. Additional exam requirements/ recommendations for international students: Required—TOEFL. *Application deadline:* For fall admission, 1/15 priority date for domestic students, 1/15 for international students; for spring admission, 11/1 for domestic students, 10/1 for international students. Applications are processed on a rolling basis. Application fee: $55 ($65 for international students). Electronic applications accepted. *Financial support:* Fellowships with full tuition reimbursements, research assistantships with full tuition reimbursements, teaching assistantships with full and partial tuition reimbursements, and unspecified assistantships available. Financial award application deadline: 1/15. *Faculty research:* Physical geography, human/cultural/regional geography, geographic information science, atmospheric science. *Unit head:* Johannes Feddema, Chair, 785-864-5143, Fax: 785-864-5378, E-mail: feddema@ku.edu. *Application contact:* Nathaniell Brunsell, Graduate Director, 785-864-5143, Fax: 785-864-5378, E-mail: brunsell@ku.edu. Website: http://www.geog.ku.edu/.

The University of Manchester, School of Earth, Atmospheric and Environmental Sciences, Manchester, United Kingdom. Offers atmospheric sciences (M Phil, M Sc, PhD); basin studies and petroleum geosciences (M Phil, M Sc, PhD); earth, atmospheric and environmental sciences (M Phil, M Sc, PhD); environmental geochemistry and cosmochemistry (M Phil, M Sc, PhD); isotope geochemistry and cosmochemistry (M Phil, M Sc, PhD); paleontology (M Phil, M Sc, PhD); physics and chemistry of minerals and fluids (M Phil, M Sc, PhD); structural and petrological geosciences (M Phil, M Sc, PhD).

University of Maryland, Baltimore County, Graduate School, College of Natural and Mathematical Sciences, Department of Physics, Program in Atmospheric Physics, Baltimore, MD 21250. Offers MS, PhD. Part-time programs available. *Faculty:* 23 full-time (4 women), 16 part-time/adjunct (4 women). *Students:* 14 full-time (3 women); includes 1 minority (Asian, non-Hispanic/Latino), 6 international. Average age 32. 5 applicants, 20% accepted, 1 enrolled. In 2012, 3 master's, 3 doctorates awarded. Terminal master's awarded for partial completion of doctoral program. *Degree requirements:* For master's, comprehensive exam (for some programs), thesis optional; for doctorate, comprehensive exam, thesis/ dissertation. *Entrance requirements:* For master's and doctorate, GRE General Test, minimum GPA of 3.0. Additional exam requirements/recommendations for international students: Required—TOEFL (minimum score 587 paper-based; 95 iBT). *Application deadline:* For fall admission, 1/1 for domestic and international students; for spring admission, 11/1 for domestic students, 5/1 for international students. Applications are processed on a rolling basis. Application fee: $50. Electronic applications accepted. *Financial support:* In 2012–13, 14 students received support, including 1 fellowship with full tuition reimbursement available (averaging $30,000 per year), 10 research assistantships with full tuition reimbursements available (averaging $26,400 per year), 3 teaching assistantships with full tuition reimbursements available (averaging $23,000 per year); career-related internships or fieldwork, scholarships/grants, health care benefits, and unspecified assistantships also available. Financial award application deadline: 5/31. *Faculty research:* Atmospheric dynamics, aerosols and clouds, satellite and aircraft remote sensing, optics and instrumentation development, lidar and in situ aerosol measurements. *Total annual research expenditures:* $4 million. *Unit head:* Dr. Vanderlei Martins, Graduate Program Director, 410-455-2764, Fax: 410-455-1072, E-mail: martins@umbc.edu. *Application contact:* Dr. Lazlo Takacs, Graduate Admissions Committee Chair, 410-455-2513, Fax: 410-455-1072, E-mail: takacs@umbc.edu. Website: http://www.physics.umbc.edu.

University of Massachusetts Lowell, College of Sciences, Department of Environmental, Earth and Atmospheric Sciences, Lowell, MA 01854-2881. Offers atmospheric science (MS, PhD).

University of Michigan, College of Engineering, Department of Atmospheric, Oceanic, and Space Sciences, Ann Arbor, MI 48109. Offers atmospheric and space sciences (MS, PhD); geoscience and remote sensing (PhD); space and planetary sciences (PhD); space engineering (M Eng). Part-time programs available. *Students:* 106 full-time (37 women), 1 part-time (0 women). 141 applicants, 50% accepted, 42 enrolled. In 2012, 41 master's, 5 doctorates awarded. Terminal master's awarded for partial completion of doctoral program. *Degree requirements:* For master's, thesis (for some programs); for doctorate, thesis/dissertation, oral defense of dissertation, preliminary exams. *Entrance requirements:* For master's and doctorate, GRE General Test. Additional exam requirements/recommendations for international students: Required—TOEFL. *Application deadline:* Applications are processed on a rolling basis. Application fee: $65 ($75 for international students). Electronic applications accepted. *Financial support:* Fellowships, research assistantships, teaching assistantships, career-related internships or fieldwork, Federal Work-Study, institutionally sponsored loans, and health care benefits available. Support available to part-time students. Financial award applicants required to submit FAFSA. *Faculty research:* Planetary environments, space instrumentation, air pollution meteorology, global climate change, sun-earth connection, space weather. *Unit head:* Dr. James Slavin, Chair, 734-764-7221, Fax: 734-615-4645, E-mail: jaslavin@umich.edu. *Application contact:* Sandra Pytlinski, Student Services Associate, 734-936-0482, Fax: 734-763-0437, E-mail: aoss.um@umich.edu. Website: http://aoss.engin.umich.edu/.

University of Missouri, Graduate School, School of Natural Resources, Department of Soil, Environmental, and Atmospheric Sciences, Columbia, MO 65211. Offers atmospheric science (MS, PhD); soil science (MS, PhD). *Faculty:* 9 full-time (0 women). *Students:* 24 full-time (10 women), 8 part-time (5 women); includes 4 minority (1 Black or African American, non-Hispanic/Latino; 1 Asian, non-Hispanic/Latino; 1 Hispanic/Latino; 1 Two or more races, non-Hispanic/ Latino), 6 international. Average age 30. 22 applicants, 45% accepted, 9 enrolled. In 2012, 6 master's, 2 doctorates awarded. *Degree requirements:* For doctorate, thesis/dissertation. *Entrance requirements:* For master's and doctorate, GRE General Test, minimum GPA of 3.0. Additional exam requirements/ recommendations for international students: Required—TOEFL (minimum score 530 paper-based; 71 iBT). *Application deadline:* Applications are processed on a rolling basis. Application fee: $55 ($75 for international students). *Expenses:* Tuition, state resident: full-time $6057. Tuition, nonresident: full-time $15,683. *Required fees:* $1000. *Financial support:* Fellowships, research assistantships, teaching assistantships, institutionally sponsored loans, and scholarships/grants available. *Faculty research:* Soil physics; x-ray tomography of soil systems; use of radar in forecasting; soil and water conservation and management and applied soil physics; soil chemical and biogeochemical investigations; fresh water supply regimes (quantity, timing); water quality disturbance mechanisms; best management practices (BMP's); environmental biophysics and ecohydrology; hydrologic scaling, modeling, and change; synoptic and mesoscale dynamics. *Unit head:* Dr. Stephen Anderson, Department Chair, 573-882-6303, E-mail: andersons@missouri.edu. Website: http://www.snr.missouri.edu/seas/academics/graduate-program.php.

Atmospheric Sciences

University of Nevada, Reno, Graduate School, Interdisciplinary Program in Atmospheric Sciences, Reno, NV 89557. Offers MS, PhD. Terminal master's awarded for partial completion of doctoral program. *Degree requirements:* For master's, thesis optional; for doctorate, thesis/dissertation. *Entrance requirements:* For master's, GRE (recommended), minimum GPA of 2.75; for doctorate, GRE (recommended), minimum GPA of 3.0. Additional exam requirements/recommendations for international students: Required—TOEFL (minimum score 500 paper-based; 61 iBT), IELTS (minimum score 6). Electronic applications accepted. *Faculty research:* Atmospheric chemistry, cloud and aerosol physics, atmospheric optics, mesoscale meterology.

The University of North Carolina at Chapel Hill, Graduate School, Gillings School of Global Public Health, Department of Environmental Sciences and Engineering, Chapel Hill, NC 27599. Offers air, radiation and industrial hygiene (MPH, MS, MSEE, MSPH, PhD); aquatic and atmospheric sciences (MPH, MS, MSPH, PhD); environmental engineering (MPH, MS, MSEE, MSPH, PhD); environmental health sciences (MPH, MS, MSPH, PhD); environmental management and policy (MPH, MS, MSPH, PhD). *Faculty:* 31 full-time. *Students:* 131 full-time (74 women); includes 31 minority (3 Black or African American, non-Hispanic/Latino; 13 Asian, non-Hispanic/Latino; 9 Hispanic/Latino; 1 Native Hawaiian or other Pacific Islander, non-Hispanic/Latino; 5 Two or more races, non-Hispanic/Latino), 24 international. Average age 27. 262 applicants, 26% accepted, 30 enrolled. In 2012, 22 master's, 8 doctorates awarded. Terminal master's awarded for partial completion of doctoral program. *Degree requirements:* For master's, comprehensive exam, thesis (for some programs), research paper; for doctorate, comprehensive exam, thesis/dissertation. *Entrance requirements:* For master's and doctorate, GRE General Test, minimum GPA of 3.0 (recommended). Additional exam requirements/recommendations for international students: Required—TOEFL. *Application deadline:* For fall admission, 12/10 priority date for domestic students, 12/10 for international students; for spring admission, 9/10 for domestic students. Applications are processed on a rolling basis. Application fee: $85. Electronic applications accepted. *Financial support:* Fellowships with tuition reimbursements, research assistantships with tuition reimbursements, teaching assistantships with tuition reimbursements, career-related internships or fieldwork, Federal Work-Study, traineeships, health care benefits, and unspecified assistantships available. Support available to part-time students. Financial award application deadline: 12/10; financial award applicants required to submit FAFSA. *Faculty research:* Air, radiation and industrial hygiene, aquatic and atmospheric sciences, environmental health sciences, environmental management and policy, water resources engineering. *Unit head:* Dr. Michael Aitken, Chair, 919-966-1024, Fax: 919-966-7911, E-mail: mike_aitken@unc.edu. *Application contact:* Jack Whaley, Registrar, 919-966-3844, Fax: 919-966-7911, E-mail: jack_whaley@unc.edu. Website: http://www2.sph.unc.edu/envr/.

University of North Dakota, Graduate School, John D. Odegard School of Aerospace Sciences, Department of Atmospheric Sciences, Grand Forks, ND 58202. Offers MS, PhD. Part-time programs available. *Degree requirements:* For master's, comprehensive exam, thesis or alternative. *Entrance requirements:* For master's and doctorate, GRE General Test, minimum GPA of 3.0. Additional exam requirements/recommendations for international students: Required—TOEFL (minimum score 550 paper-based; 79 iBT), IELTS (minimum score 6.5). Electronic applications accepted.

University of Utah, Graduate School, College of Mines and Earth Sciences, Department of Atmospheric Sciences, Salt Lake City, UT 84112. Offers MS, PhD. Part-time programs available. *Faculty:* 10 full-time (1 woman), 1 part-time/adjunct (0 women). *Students:* 31 full-time (10 women), 14 part-time (4 women); includes 3 minority (all Hispanic/Latino), 7 international. Average age 28. 69 applicants, 22% accepted, 10 enrolled. In 2012, 6 master's, 2 doctorates awarded. Terminal master's awarded for partial completion of doctoral program. *Degree requirements:* For master's, comprehensive exam, thesis optional; for doctorate, comprehensive exam, thesis/dissertation. *Entrance requirements:* For master's and doctorate, GRE General Test, minimum GPA of 3.0, 3 letters of reference, personal statement, resume/curriculum vitae, official transcript. Additional exam requirements/recommendations for international students: Required—TOEFL (minimum score 500 paper-based; 61 iBT); Recommended—IELTS (minimum score 6). *Application deadline:* For fall admission, 1/7 priority date for domestic students, 1/7 for international students. Applications are processed on a rolling basis. Application fee: $55 ($65 for international students). Electronic applications accepted. *Financial support:* In 2012–13, 30 students received support, including 7 fellowships (averaging $24,000 per year), 35 research assistantships (averaging $24,500 per year), 6 teaching assistantships (averaging $5,000 per year). Financial award application deadline: 2/15; financial award applicants required to submit FAFSA. *Faculty research:* Clouds, aerosols, and climate; numerical weather prediction; mountain weather and climate; tropical convection and storms; climate variability and change. *Total annual research expenditures:* $3.9 million. *Unit head:* Dr. Kevin D. Perry, Chair, 801-585-9482, Fax: 801-585-3681, E-mail: kevin.perry@utah.edu. *Application contact:* Michelle R. Brooks, Academic Coordinator, 801-581-6136, Fax: 801-585-3681, E-mail: atmos-advising@lists.utah.edu. Website: http://www.atmos.utah.edu/.

University of Washington, Graduate School, College of the Environment, Department of Atmospheric Sciences, Seattle, WA 98195. Offers MS, PhD. *Degree requirements:* For master's, thesis; for doctorate, thesis/dissertation, qualifying exam. *Entrance requirements:* For master's and doctorate, GRE General Test, minimum GPA of 3.0. Additional exam requirements/recommendations for international students: Required—TOEFL. *Faculty research:* Climate change, synoptic and mesoscale meteorology, atmospheric chemistry, cloud physics, dynamics of the atmosphere.

University of Wisconsin–Madison, Graduate School, College of Letters and Science, Department of Atmospheric and Oceanic Sciences, Madison, WI 53706-1380. Offers MS, PhD. Part-time programs available. *Degree requirements:* For master's, thesis (for some programs); for doctorate, thesis/dissertation. *Entrance requirements:* For master's and doctorate, GRE General Test, minimum GPA of 3.0; previous course work in chemistry, mathematics, and physics. Electronic applications accepted. *Expenses:* Tuition, state resident: full-time $10,728; part-time $743 per credit. Tuition, nonresident: full-time $24,054; part-time $1575 per credit. *Required fees:* $1111; $72 per credit. *Faculty research:* Satellite meteorology, weather systems, global climate change, numerical modeling, atmosphere-ocean interaction.

University of Wyoming, College of Engineering and Applied Sciences, Department of Atmospheric Science, Laramie, WY 82070. Offers MS, PhD. Postbaccalaureate distance learning degree programs offered (minimal on-campus study). Terminal master's awarded for partial completion of doctoral program. *Degree requirements:* For master's, thesis; for doctorate, comprehensive exam, thesis/dissertation. *Entrance requirements:* For master's and doctorate, GRE General Test, minimum GPA of 3.0. Additional exam requirements/recommendations for international students: Required—TOEFL (minimum score 525 paper-based). Electronic applications accepted. *Expenses:* Contact institution. *Faculty research:* Cloud physics; aerosols, boundary layer processes; airborne observations; stratospheric aerosols and gases.

Yale University, Graduate School of Arts and Sciences, Department of Geology and Geophysics, New Haven, CT 06520. Offers biogeochemistry (PhD); climate dynamics (PhD); geochemistry (PhD); geophysics (PhD); meteorology (PhD); oceanography (PhD); paleontology (PhD); paleooceanography (PhD); petrology (PhD); tectonics (PhD). *Degree requirements:* For doctorate, thesis/dissertation. *Entrance requirements:* For doctorate, GRE General Test. Additional exam requirements/recommendations for international students: Required—TOEFL.

Meteorology

Columbia University, Graduate School of Arts and Sciences, Program in Climate and Society, New York, NY 10027. Offers MA.

Florida Institute of Technology, Graduate Programs, College of Engineering, Department of Marine and Environmental Systems, Melbourne, FL 32901-6975. Offers earth remote sensing (MS); environmental resource management (MS); environmental science (MS, PhD); meteorology (MS); ocean engineering (MS, PhD); oceanography (MS, PhD), including biological oceanography (MS), chemical oceanography (MS), coastal management (MS), geological oceanography (MS), oceanography (PhD), physical oceanography (MS). Part-time programs available. *Faculty:* 15 full-time (0 women), 2 part-time/adjunct (0 women). *Students:* 53 full-time (19 women), 15 part-time (4 women); includes 3 minority (1 Asian, non-Hispanic/Latino; 1 Hispanic/Latino; 1 Two or more races, non-Hispanic/Latino), 23 international. Average age 27. 141 applicants, 45% accepted, 21 enrolled. In 2012, 16 master's, 4 doctorates awarded. *Degree requirements:* For master's, comprehensive exam (for some programs), thesis (for some programs), seminar, field project, written final exam, technical paper, oral presentation, or internship; for doctorate, comprehensive exam, thesis/ dissertation, seminar, internships (oceanography and environmental science), publications. *Entrance requirements:* For master's, GRE General Test (environmental science, oceanography, environmental resource management, meteorology, earth remote sensing), 3 letters of recommendation, minimum GPA of 3.0, resume, transcripts, statement of objectives; for doctorate, GRE General Test (oceanography, environmental science), resume, 3 letters of recommendation, minimum GPA of 3.3, statement of objectives, on-campus interview (highly recommended). Additional exam requirements/recommendations for international students: Required—TOEFL (minimum score 550 paper-based; 79 iBT). *Application deadline:* For fall admission, 4/1 for international students; for spring admission, 9/30 for international students. Applications are processed on a rolling basis. Electronic applications accepted. *Expenses: Tuition:* Full-time $20,214; part-time $1123 per credit hour. Tuition and fees vary according to campus/location. *Financial support:* In 2012–13, 5 fellowships with full and partial tuition reimbursements (averaging $5,400 per year), 8 research assistantships with full and partial tuition reimbursements (averaging $7,851 per year), 13 teaching assistantships with full and partial tuition reimbursements (averaging

206 www.petersonsbooks.com

Peterson's Graduate Programs in the Physical Sciences, Mathematics, Agricultural Sciences, the Environment & Natural Resources 2014

$5,565 per year) were awarded; career-related internships or fieldwork, institutionally sponsored loans, tuition waivers (partial), unspecified assistantships, and tuition remissions also available. Support available to part-time students. Financial award application deadline: 3/1; financial award applicants required to submit FAFSA. *Total annual research expenditures:* $2.2 million. *Unit head:* Dr. George Maul, Department Head, 321-674-7453, Fax: 321-674-7212, E-mail: gmaul@fit.edu. *Application contact:* Cheryl A. Brown, Associate Director of Graduate Admissions, 321-674-7581, Fax: 321-723-9468, E-mail: cbrown@fit.edu. Website: http://coe.fit.edu/dmes/.

Florida State University, The Graduate School, College of Arts and Sciences, Department of Earth, Ocean and Atmospheric Science, Program in Meteorology, Tallahassee, FL 32306-4520. Offers MS, PhD. *Faculty:* 14 full-time (2 women). *Students:* 70 full-time (19 women), 8 part-time (3 women); includes 7 minority (2 Black or African American, non-Hispanic/Latino; 5 Hispanic/Latino), 17 international. Average age 24. 113 applicants, 40% accepted, 22 enrolled. In 2012, 14 master's, 7 doctorates awarded. Terminal master's awarded for partial completion of doctoral program. *Degree requirements:* For master's, thesis optional; for doctorate, comprehensive exam, thesis/dissertation. *Entrance requirements:* For master's, GRE General Test (minimum score 1100 verbal and quantitative), minimum GPA of 3.0 in upper-division work; for doctorate, GRE General Test (minimum combined Verbal and Quantitative score: 1100), minimum GPA of 3.0, faculty sponsor. Additional exam requirements/recommendations for international students: Required—TOEFL (minimum score 550 paper-based; 80 iBT). *Application deadline:* For fall admission, 1/30 priority date for domestic students, 1/30 for international students; for spring admission, 11/1 for domestic students, 6/30 for international students. Applications are processed on a rolling basis. Application fee: $30. *Expenses:* Tuition, state resident: full-time $7263; part-time $403.51 per credit hour. Tuition, nonresident: full-time $18,087; part-time $1004.85 per credit hour. *Required fees:* $1335.42; $74.19 per credit hour. $445.14 per semester. One-time fee: $40 full-time; $20 part-time. Tuition and fees vary according to program. *Financial support:* In 2012–13, 56 students received support, including 2 fellowships with partial tuition reimbursements available (averaging $19,000 per year), 39 research assistantships with partial tuition reimbursements available (averaging $21,500 per year), 14 teaching assistantships with partial tuition reimbursements available (averaging $21,500 per year); career-related internships or fieldwork, scholarships/grants, and unspecified assistantships also available. Financial award applicants required to submit FAFSA. *Faculty research:* Physical, dynamic, and synoptic meteorology; climatology. *Total annual research expenditures:* $600,000. *Unit head:* Dr. Lynn Dudley, Chairman, 850-644-6205, Fax: 850-644-9642, E-mail: ldudley@fsu.edu. *Application contact:* Tim McGann, Academic Program Specialist, 850-644-8580, Fax: 850-644-9642, E-mail: tmcgann@fsu.edu. Website: http://www.met.fsu.edu/.

Georgia Institute of Technology, Graduate Studies and Research, College of Sciences, School of Earth and Atmospheric Sciences, Atlanta, GA 30332-0340. Offers atmospheric chemistry, aerosols and clouds (MS, PhD); dynamics of weather and climate (MS, PhD); geochemistry (MS, PhD); geophysics (MS, PhD); oceanography (MS, PhD); paleoclimate (MS, PhD); planetary science (MS, PhD); remote sensing (MS, PhD). Part-time programs available. Terminal master's awarded for partial completion of doctoral program. *Degree requirements:* For master's, thesis or alternative; for doctorate, comprehensive exam, thesis/dissertation. *Entrance requirements:* For master's, GRE, letters of recommendation; for doctorate, GRE, academic transcripts, letters of recommendation, personal statement. Additional exam requirements/recommendations for international students: Required—TOEFL (minimum score 550 paper-based; 79 iBT). *Faculty research:* Geophysics; atmospheric chemistry, aerosols and clouds; dynamics of weather and climate; geochemistry; oceanography; paleoclimate; planetary science; remote sensing.

Iowa State University of Science and Technology, Department of Geological and Atmospheric Sciences, Ames, IA 50011. Offers earth science (MS, PhD); environmental science (MS, PhD); geology (MS, PhD); meteorology (MS, PhD). *Degree requirements:* For master's, thesis (for some programs); for doctorate, thesis/dissertation. *Entrance requirements:* For master's and doctorate, GRE General Test. Additional exam requirements/recommendations for international students: Required—TOEFL (minimum score 550 paper-based; 79 iBT), IELTS (minimum score 6.5). *Application deadline:* For fall admission, 1/1 priority date for domestic students. Application fee: $60 ($90 for international students). Electronic applications accepted. *Application contact:* Deann Frisk, Application Contact, 515-294-4477, Fax: 515-294-6049, E-mail: geology@iastate.edu. Website: http://www.ge-at.iastate.edu/.

Iowa State University of Science and Technology, Program in Agricultural Meteorology, Ames, IA 50011. Offers MS, PhD. *Entrance requirements:* Additional exam requirements/recommendations for international students: Required—TOEFL (minimum score 550 paper-based; 79 iBT), IELTS (minimum score 6.5). *Application deadline:* Applications are processed on a rolling basis. Electronic applications accepted. *Application contact:* Jaci Severson, Application Contact, 515-294-1361, Fax: 515-294-8146, E-mail: gradprograms@agron.iastate.edu. Website: http://www.agron.iastate.edu.

Iowa State University of Science and Technology, Program in Meteorology, Ames, IA 50011. Offers MS, PhD. *Entrance requirements:* For master's and doctorate, GRE. Additional exam requirements/recommendations for international students: Required—TOEFL (minimum score 550 paper-based; 79 iBT), IELTS (minimum score 6.5). *Application deadline:* For fall admission, 12/1 priority date for domestic students. Application fee: $60 ($90 for international students). Electronic applications accepted. *Application contact:* Jaci Severson, Application Contact, 515-294-1361, Fax: 515-294-8146, E-mail: meteorologygraduateprograms@iastate.edu. Website: http://www.ge-at.iastate.edu.

McGill University, Faculty of Graduate and Postdoctoral Studies, Faculty of Agricultural and Environmental Sciences, Department of Natural Resource Sciences, Montréal, QC H3A 2T5, Canada. Offers entomology (M Sc, PhD); environmental assessment (M Sc); forest science (M Sc, PhD); microbiology (M Sc, PhD); micrometeorology (M Sc, PhD); neotropical environment (M Sc, PhD); soil science (M Sc, PhD); wildlife biology (M Sc, PhD).

Millersville University of Pennsylvania, College of Graduate and Professional Studies, School of Science and Mathematics, Department of Earth Sciences, Millersville, PA 17551-0302. Offers integrated scientific applications (MS), including climate science applications, environmental systems management, geoinformatics, weather intelligence and risk management. Part-time and evening/weekend programs available. *Faculty:* 10 full-time (2 women), 2 part-time/adjunct (1 woman). *Students:* 4 part-time (1 woman); includes 1 minority (Asian, non-Hispanic/Latino). Average age 23. 5 applicants, 100% accepted, 3 enrolled. *Degree requirements:* For master's, thesis optional, internship or applied research. *Entrance requirements:* For master's, GRE, MAT, or GMAT (if GPA is lower than 3.0), 3 letters of recommendation, resume, official transcripts, goal statement, telephone interview. Additional exam requirements/recommendations for international students: Required—TOEFL (minimum score 500 paper-based) or IELTS (minimum score 6). *Application deadline:* For fall admission, 1/15 priority date for domestic students, 1/15 for international students; for winter admission, 10/1 priority date for domestic students, 10/1 for international students; for spring admission, 10/1 priority date for domestic students, 10/1 for international students. Applications are processed on a rolling basis. Application fee: $40 ($50 for international students). Electronic applications accepted. *Expenses:* Tuition, state resident: full-time $7722; part-time $429 per credit. Tuition, nonresident: full-time $11,592; part-time $644 per credit. Tuition and fees vary according to course load. *Financial support:* In 2012–13, 2 students received support, including 2 research assistantships (averaging $5,000 per year). Financial award application deadline: 3/15; financial award applicants required to submit FAFSA. *Faculty research:* Climatology and meteorology. *Total annual research expenditures:* $229,000. *Unit head:* Dr. Richard D. Clark, Graduate Program Coordinator, 717 872 3030, E-mail: richard.clark@millersville.edu. *Application contact:* Dr. Victor S. DeSantis, Dean of Graduate and Professional Studies, 717-872-3099, Fax: 717-872-3453, E-mail: victor.desantis@millersville.edu. Website: http://www.millersville.edu/graduate/admissions/MSISA.php.

Millersville University of Pennsylvania, College of Graduate and Professional Studies, School of Science and Mathematics, Program in Integrated Scientific Applications, Millersville, PA 17551-0302. Offers climate science applications (MS); environmental systems management (MS); geoinformatics (MS); weather intelligence and risk management (MS). *Expenses:* Tuition, state resident: full-time $7722; part-time $429 per credit. Tuition, nonresident: full-time $11,592; part-time $644 per credit. Tuition and fees vary according to course load.

Mississippi State University, College of Arts and Sciences, Department of Geosciences, Mississippi State, MS 39762. Offers applied meteorology (MS); broadcast meteorology (MS); earth and atmospheric science (PhD); environmental geoscience (MS); geography (MS); geology (MS); geospatial sciences (MS); professional meteorology/climatology (MS); teachers in geoscience (MS). Postbaccalaureate distance learning degree programs offered (no on-campus study). *Faculty:* 14 full-time (3 women), 2 part-time/adjunct (0 women). *Students:* 62 full-time (27 women), 273 part-time (117 women); includes 29 minority (7 Black or African American, non-Hispanic/Latino; 4 Asian, non-Hispanic/Latino; 13 Hispanic/Latino; 5 Two or more races, non-Hispanic/Latino), 8 international. Average age 34. 235 applicants, 70% accepted, 135 enrolled. In 2012, 101 master's, 2 doctorates awarded. *Degree requirements:* For master's, thesis (for some programs), comprehensive oral or written exam; for doctorate, thesis/dissertation, comprehensive oral or written exam. *Entrance requirements:* For master's, GRE (for on-campus applicants), minimum undergraduate GPA of 2.75; for doctorate, completed thesis-based MS with background in one department emphasis area. Additional exam requirements/recommendations for international students: Required—TOEFL (minimum score 477 paper-based; 53 iBT); Recommended—IELTS (minimum score 4.5). *Application deadline:* For fall admission, 7/1 for domestic students, 5/1 for international students; for spring admission, 11/1 for domestic students, 9/1 for international students. Applications are processed on a rolling basis. Application fee: $60. Electronic applications accepted. *Financial support:* In 2012–13, 12 research assistantships with full tuition reimbursements (averaging $20,723 per year), 30 teaching assistantships with full tuition reimbursements (averaging $14,091 per year) were awarded; Federal Work-Study, institutionally sponsored loans, scholarships/grants, tuition waivers (partial), and unspecified assistantships also available. Financial award application deadline: 4/1; financial award applicants required to submit FAFSA. *Faculty research:* Climatology, hydrogeology, sedimentology, meteorology. *Total annual research expenditures:* $6.8 million. *Unit head:* Dr. Darrel Schmitz, Professor and Head, 662-325-3915, Fax: 662-325-9423, E-mail: schmitz@geosci.msstate.edu. *Application contact:* Dr. Mike Brown, Associate Professor/Graduate Coordinator, 662-325-3915, Fax: 662-325-9423, E-mail: tina@gesci.msstate.edu. Website: http://www.geosciences.msstate.edu.

Naval Postgraduate School, Departments and Academic Groups, Department of Meteorology, Monterey, CA 93943. Offers meteorology (MS, PhD);

meteorology and physical oceanography (MS). Program only open to commissioned officers of the United States and friendly nations and selected United States federal civilian employees. Part-time programs available. *Degree requirements:* For master's, thesis; for doctorate, one foreign language, thesis/dissertation. *Faculty research:* Air-sea interactions, boundary layer meteorology, climate dynamics, numerical weather prediction, tropical cyclones.

Naval Postgraduate School, Departments and Academic Groups, Undersea Warfare Academic Group, Monterey, CA 93943. Offers applied mathematics (MS); applied physics (MS); applied science (MS), including acoustics, operations research, physical oceanography, signal processing; electrical engineering (MS); engineering acoustics (MS, PhD); engineering science (MS), including electrical engineering, mechanical engineering; mechanical engineer (ME); mechanical engineering (MS, MSME); meteorology (MS); operations research (MS); physical oceanography (MS). Program only open to commissioned officers of the United States and friendly nations and selected United States federal civilian employees. Part-time programs available. *Degree requirements:* For master's, thesis. *Faculty research:* Unmanned/autonomous vehicles, sea mines and countermeasures, submarine warfare in the twentieth and twenty-first centuries.

North Carolina State University, Graduate School, College of Physical and Mathematical Sciences, Department of Marine, Earth, and Atmospheric Sciences, Raleigh, NC 27695. Offers marine, earth, and atmospheric sciences (MS, PhD); meteorology (MS, PhD); oceanography (MS, PhD). PhD offered jointly with The University of North Carolina Wilmington. Terminal master's awarded for partial completion of doctoral program. *Degree requirements:* For master's, thesis (for some programs), final oral exam; for doctorate, comprehensive exam, thesis/dissertation, final oral exam, preliminary oral and written exams. *Entrance requirements:* For master's, GRE General Test, minimum GPA of 3.0; for doctorate, GRE General Test, GRE Subject Test (for disciplines in biological oceanography and geology), minimum GPA of 3.0. Additional exam requirements/recommendations for international students: Required—TOEFL (minimum score 550 paper-based). Electronic applications accepted. *Faculty research:* Boundary layer and air quality meteorology; climate and mesoscale dynamics; biological, chemical, geological, and physical oceanography; hard rock, soft rock, environmental, and paleo-geology.

Northern Arizona University, Graduate College, College of Engineering, Forestry and Natural Sciences, School of Earth Sciences and Environmental Sustainability, Flagstaff, AZ 86011. Offers climate science and solutions (MS); earth science (MS); earth sciences and environmental sustainability (PhD); environmental sciences and policy (MS); geology (MS). *Degree requirements:* For master's, comprehensive exam (for some programs), thesis (for some programs). *Entrance requirements:* Additional exam requirements/recommendations for international students: Required—TOEFL (minimum score 550 paper-based; 80 iBT), IELTS (minimum score 7). Electronic applications accepted.

Penn State University Park, Graduate School, College of Earth and Mineral Sciences, Department of Meteorology, State College, University Park, PA 16802-1503. Offers MS, PhD. *Unit head:* Dr. William E. Easterling, III, Dean, 814-865-6546, Fax: 814-863-7708, E-mail: wee2@psu.edu. *Application contact:* Cynthia E. Nicosia, Director of Graduate Enrollment Services, 814-865-1834, E-mail: cey1@psu.edu. Website: http://ploneprod.met.psu.edu/.

Plymouth State University, College of Graduate Studies, Graduate Studies in Education, Program in Science, Plymouth, NH 03264-1595. Offers applied meteorology (MS); environmental science and policy (MS); science education (MS).

Saint Louis University, Graduate Education, College of Arts and Sciences, Department of Earth and Atmospheric Sciences, St. Louis, MO 63103-2097. Offers geophysics (PhD); geoscience (MS); meteorology (M Pr Met, MS-R, PhD). Part-time programs available. *Degree requirements:* For master's, thesis (for some programs), comprehensive oral exam; for doctorate, thesis/dissertation, preliminary exams. *Entrance requirements:* For master's, GRE General Test, letters of recommendation, resume; for doctorate, GRE General Test, letters of recommendation, resumé, goal statement, transcripts. Additional exam requirements/recommendations for international students: Required—TOEFL (minimum score 525 paper-based). Electronic applications accepted. *Faculty research:* Structural geology, mesoscale meteorology and severe storms, weather and climate change prediction.

San Jose State University, Graduate Studies and Research, College of Science, Department of Meteorology and Climate Science, San Jose, CA 95192-0001. Offers meteorology (MS). *Degree requirements:* For master's, thesis or alternative. *Entrance requirements:* For master's, GRE. Electronic applications accepted.

Texas A&M University, College of Geosciences, Department of Atmospheric Sciences, College Station, TX 77843. Offers MS, PhD. *Faculty:* 17. *Students:* 55 full-time (16 women), 4 part-time (0 women); includes 3 minority (1 Black or African American, non-Hispanic/Latino; 2 Hispanic/Latino), 21 international. Average age 27. In 2012, 7 master's, 5 doctorates awarded. *Degree requirements:* For master's, thesis; for doctorate, thesis/dissertation. *Entrance requirements:* For master's and doctorate, GRE General Test. Additional exam requirements/recommendations for international students: Required—TOEFL. *Application deadline:* For fall admission, 3/1 for domestic students; for spring admission, 10/1 for domestic students. Applications are processed on a rolling basis. Application fee: $50 ($75 for international students). Electronic applications accepted. *Financial support:* In 2012–13, fellowships (averaging $16,500 per year), research assistantships with tuition reimbursements (averaging $15,000 per year), teaching assistantships (averaging $15,000 per year) were awarded; career-related internships or fieldwork, institutionally sponsored loans, scholarships/grants, and tuition waivers (partial) also available. Financial award application deadline: 3/1; financial award applicants required to submit FAFSA. *Faculty research:* Radar and satellite rainfall relationships, mesoscale dynamics and numerical modeling, climatology. *Unit head:* Kenneth Bowman, Head, 979-862-7671, E-mail: k-bowman@tamu.edu. *Application contact:* Christine Arnold, Academic Advisor II, 979-845-7688, Fax: 979-862-4466, E-mail: chrisarnold@tamu.edu. Website: http://atmo.tamu.edu/.

Université du Québec à Montréal, Graduate Programs, Program in Earth and Atmospheric Sciences, Montréal, QC H3C 3P8, Canada. Offers atmospheric sciences (M Sc); Earth and atmospheric sciences (PhD); Earth science (M Sc); meteorology (PhD, Diploma). PhD programs offered jointly with McGill University. Part-time programs available. *Degree requirements:* For master's, thesis. *Entrance requirements:* For master's and Diploma, appropriate bachelor's degree or equivalent, proficiency in French; for doctorate, appropriate master's degree or equivalent, proficiency in French.

University of Hawaii at Manoa, Graduate Division, School of Ocean and Earth Science and Technology, Department of Meteorology, Honolulu, HI 96822. Offers MS, PhD. Part-time programs available. *Degree requirements:* For master's, comprehensive exam, thesis; for doctorate, comprehensive exam, thesis/dissertation. *Entrance requirements:* For master's and doctorate, GRE General Test. Additional exam requirements/recommendations for international students: Required—TOEFL (minimum score 560 paper-based; 83 iBT), IELTS (minimum score 5). *Faculty research:* Tropical cyclones, air-sea interactions, mesoscale meteorology, intraseasonal oscillations, tropical climate.

University of Maryland, College Park, Academic Affairs, College of Computer, Mathematical and Natural Sciences, Department of Atmospheric and Oceanic Science, College Park, MD 20742. Offers MS, PMS, PhD. Part-time and evening/weekend programs available. Postbaccalaureate distance learning degree programs offered. *Faculty:* 36 full-time (8 women), 7 part-time/adjunct (2 women). *Students:* 49 full-time (22 women), 13 part-time (7 women); includes 3 minority (2 Asian, non-Hispanic/Latino; 1 Hispanic/Latino), 21 international. 127 applicants, 13% accepted, 15 enrolled. In 2012, 7 master's, 7 doctorates awarded. Terminal master's awarded for partial completion of doctoral program. *Degree requirements:* For master's, comprehensive exam, scholarly paper, written and oral exams; for doctorate, thesis/dissertation, exam. *Entrance requirements:* For master's, GRE General Test, background in mathematics, experience in scientific computer languages, 3 letters of recommendation; for doctorate, GRE General Test. *Application deadline:* For fall admission, 1/15 priority date for domestic students, 1/15 for international students. Applications are processed on a rolling basis. Application fee: $75. Electronic applications accepted. *Expenses:* Tuition, state resident: part-time $551 per credit. Tuition, nonresident: part-time $1188 per credit. Part-time tuition and fees vary according to program. *Financial support:* In 2012–13, 2 fellowships with partial tuition reimbursements (averaging $9,750 per year), 16 research assistantships (averaging $20,344 per year), 26 teaching assistantships (averaging $20,210 per year) were awarded; Federal Work-Study and scholarships/grants also available. Support available to part-time students. Financial award applicants required to submit FAFSA. *Faculty research:* Weather, atmospheric chemistry, air pollution, global change, radiation. *Total annual research expenditures:* $2.8 million. *Unit head:* James A. Carton, Chair, 301-405-5365, Fax: 301-314-9482, E-mail: carton@umd.edu. *Application contact:* Dr. Charles A. Caramello, Dean of Graduate School, 301-405-0358, Fax: 301-314-9305.

University of Miami, Graduate School, Rosenstiel School of Marine and Atmospheric Science, Division of Meteorology and Physical Oceanography, Coral Gables, FL 33124. Offers meteorology (MS, PhD); physical oceanography (MS, PhD). Terminal master's awarded for partial completion of doctoral program. *Degree requirements:* For master's, comprehensive exam, thesis; for doctorate, comprehensive exam, thesis/dissertation. *Entrance requirements:* For master's and doctorate, GRE General Test. Additional exam requirements/recommendations for international students: Required—TOEFL (minimum score 550 paper-based). Electronic applications accepted.

University of Oklahoma, College of Atmospheric and Geographic Sciences, School of Meteorology, Norman, OK 73072. Offers meteorology (MS, PhD); professional meteorology (MS). *Faculty:* 35 full-time (4 women), 3 part-time/adjunct (0 women). *Students:* 70 full-time (21 women), 41 part-time (12 women); includes 7 minority (1 Black or African American, non-Hispanic/Latino; 4 Asian, non-Hispanic/Latino; 1 Hispanic/Latino; 1 Two or more races, non-Hispanic/Latino), 16 international. Average age 27. 100 applicants, 22% accepted, 18 enrolled. In 2012, 20 master's, 4 doctorates awarded. *Degree requirements:* For master's, comprehensive exam (for some programs), thesis (for some programs); for doctorate, one foreign language, comprehensive exam, thesis/dissertation, general exam. *Entrance requirements:* Additional exam requirements/recommendations for international students: Required—TOEFL (minimum score 550 paper-based; 79 iBT). *Application deadline:* For fall admission, 2/15 for domestic and international students; for spring admission, 10/15 for domestic students, 10/1 for international students. Applications are processed on a rolling basis. Application fee: $40 ($90 for international students). Electronic applications accepted. *Expenses:* Tuition, state resident: full-time $4205; part-time $175.20 per credit hour. Tuition, nonresident: full-time $15,667; part-time $653 per credit hour. *Required fees:* $2745; $103.85 per credit hour. Tuition and fees vary according to course load and degree level. *Financial support:* In 2012–13, 5 fellowships with full tuition reimbursements (averaging $5,000 per year), 63 research assistantships with partial tuition reimbursements (averaging $18,007 per year), 19 teaching assistantships with partial tuition reimbursements (averaging $17,442 per year) were awarded; health care benefits and unspecified assistantships also available. Financial award application deadline: 6/1; financial award applicants required to submit FAFSA. *Faculty research:* Convective and mesoscale dynamics, modeling and data assimilation, radar, climate, tropical and polar meteorology. *Total annual research expenditures:* $8.7 million. *Unit head:* David Parsons, Director, 405-325-8565, Fax: 405-325-7689, E-mail: dparsons@ou.edu. Website: http://som.ou.edu.

Utah State University, School of Graduate Studies, College of Agriculture, Department of Plants, Soils, and Biometeorology, Logan, UT 84322. Offers biometeorology (MS, PhD); ecology (MS, PhD); plant science (MS, PhD); soil science (MS, PhD). Part-time programs available. Terminal master's awarded for partial completion of doctoral program. *Degree requirements:* For master's, thesis; for doctorate, thesis/dissertation. *Entrance requirements:* For master's, GRE General Test, BS in plant, soil, atmospheric science, or related field; minimum GPA of 3.0; for doctorate, GRE General Test, minimum GPA of 3.0. Additional exam requirements/recommendations for international students: Required—TOEFL. Electronic applications accepted. *Faculty research:* Biotechnology and genomics, plant physiology and biology, nutrient and water efficient landscapes, physical-chemical-biological processes in soil, environmental biophysics and climate.

Yale University, Graduate School of Arts and Sciences, Department of Geology and Geophysics, New Haven, CT 06520. Offers biogeochemistry (PhD); climate dynamics (PhD); geochemistry (PhD); geophysics (PhD); meteorology (PhD); oceanography (PhD); paleontology (PhD); paleooceanography (PhD); petrology (PhD); tectonics (PhD). *Degree requirements:* For doctorate, thesis/dissertation. *Entrance requirements:* For doctorate, GRE General Test. Additional exam requirements/recommendations for international students: Required—TOEFL.

Peterson's Graduate Programs in the Physical Sciences, Mathematics, Agricultural Sciences, the Environment & Natural Resources 2014

www.petersonsbooks.com **209**

Section 6
Physics

This section contains a directory of institutions offering graduate work in physics, followed by in-depth entries submitted by institutions that chose to prepare detailed program descriptions. Additional information about programs listed in the directory but not augmented by an in-depth entry may be obtained by writing directly to the dean of a graduate school or chair of a department at the address given in the directory.

For programs offering related work, see all other areas in this book. In the other guides in this series:

Graduate Programs in the Biological/Biomedical Sciences & Health-Related Medical Professions

See *Allied Health, Biological and Biomedical Sciences, Biophysics,* and *Vision Sciences*

Graduate Programs in Engineering & Applied Sciences

See *Aerospace/Aeronautical Engineering, Electrical and Computer Engineering, Energy and Power Engineering (Nuclear Engineering), Engineering and Applied Sciences, Engineering Physics, Materials Sciences and Engineering,* and *Mechanical Engineering and Mechanics*

CONTENTS

Acoustics

Naval Postgraduate School, Departments and Academic Groups, Undersea Warfare Academic Group, Monterey, CA 93943. Offers applied mathematics (MS); applied physics (MS); applied science (MS), including acoustics, operations research, physical oceanography, signal processing; electrical engineering (MS); engineering acoustics (MS, PhD); engineering science (MS), including electrical engineering, mechanical engineering; mechanical engineer (ME); mechanical engineering (MS, MSME); meteorology (MS); operations research (MS); physical oceanography (MS). Program only open to commissioned officers of the United States and friendly nations and selected United States federal civilian employees. Part-time programs available. *Degree requirements:* For master's, thesis. *Faculty research:* Unmanned/autonomous vehicles, sea mines and countermeasures, submarine warfare in the twentieth and twenty-first centuries.

Penn State University Park, Graduate School, Intercollege Graduate Programs and College of Engineering, Intercollege Graduate Program in Acoustics, State College, University Park, PA 16802-1503. Offers M Eng, MS, PhD. *Unit head:* Dr. Anthony Atchley, Project Chair, 814-865-6364, Fax: 814-865-7595, E-mail: atchley@psu.edu. *Application contact:* Cynthia E. Nicosia, Director, Graduate Enrollment Services, 814-865-1795, Fax: 814-865-4627, E-mail: cey1@psu.edu.

Rensselaer Polytechnic Institute, Graduate School, School of Architecture, PhD Program in Architectural Sciences, Troy, NY 12180-3590. Offers acoustics (PhD); lighting (PhD). *Faculty:* 28 full-time (3 women), 16 part-time/adjunct (3 women). *Students:* 23 full-time (6 women), 3 part-time (2 women); includes 1 minority (Two or more races, non-Hispanic/Latino), 11 international. Average age 34. 38 applicants, 29% accepted, 4 enrolled. In 2012, 4 doctorates awarded. *Degree requirements:* For doctorate, comprehensive exam (for some programs), thesis/dissertation. *Entrance requirements:* For doctorate, GRE. Additional exam requirements/recommendations for international students: Required—TOEFL (minimum score 570 paper-based, 88 iBT),IELTS (minimum score 6.5), or Pearson Test of English (minimum score 60). *Application deadline:* For fall admission, 1/1 priority date for domestic students, 1/1 for international students. Applications are processed on a rolling basis. Application fee: $75. Electronic applications accepted. *Financial support:* In 2012–13, research assistantships (averaging $18,500 per year), teaching assistantships with full tuition reimbursements (averaging $18,500 per year) were awarded; fellowships also available. Financial award application deadline: 1/1. *Faculty research:* Lighting, acoustics, computation, building systems. *Application contact:* Office of Graduate Admissions, 518-276-6216, E-mail: gradadmissions@rpi.edu. Website: http://www.arch.rpi.edu/academic/graduate/phd-program/.

Rensselaer Polytechnic Institute, Graduate School, School of Architecture, Program in Architectural Acoustics, Troy, NY 12180-3590. Offers MS, PhD. *Faculty:* 28 full-time (3 women), 16 part-time/adjunct (3 women). *Students:* 14 full-time (5 women), 6 part-time (0 women); includes 3 minority (1 Black or African American, non-Hispanic/Latino; 1 Asian, non-Hispanic/Latino; 1 Hispanic/Latino), 3 international. Average age 26. 40 applicants, 60% accepted, 14 enrolled. In 2012, 6 master's awarded. *Degree requirements:* For master's, thesis; for doctorate, comprehensive exam, thesis/dissertation. *Entrance requirements:* For master's and doctorate, GRE. Additional exam requirements/recommendations for international students: Required—TOEFL (minimum score 570 paper-based, 88 iBT), IELTS (minimum score 6.5), or Pearson Test of English (minimum score 60). *Application deadline:* For fall admission, 1/1 priority date for domestic students, 1/1 for international students. Applications are processed on a rolling basis. Application fee: $75. Electronic applications accepted. *Financial support:* In 2012–13, research assistantships (averaging $18,500 per year), teaching assistantships (averaging $18,500 per year) were awarded; fellowships also available. Financial award application deadline: 1/1. *Application contact:* Office of Graduate Admissions, 518-276-6216, E-mail: gradadmissions@rpi.edu. Website: http://www.arch.rpi.edu/academic/graduate/architectural-acoustics-2/.

University of Massachusetts Dartmouth, Graduate School, College of Engineering, Department of Electrical and Computer Engineering, North Dartmouth, MA 02747-2300. Offers acoustics (Postbaccalaureate Certificate); communications (Postbaccalaureate Certificate); computer engineering (MS, PhD); computer systems engineering (Postbaccalaureate Certificate); digital signal processing (Postbaccalaureate Certificate); electrical engineering (MS, PhD); electrical engineering systems (Postbaccalaureate Certificate). Part-time programs available. *Faculty:* 15 full-time (4 women), 1 part-time/adjunct (0 women). *Students:* 27 full-time (3 women), 43 part-time (3 women); includes 7 minority (2 Black or African American, non-Hispanic/Latino; 1 Asian, non-Hispanic/Latino; 1 Hispanic/Latino; 3 Two or more races, non-Hispanic/Latino), 32 international. Average age 28. 83 applicants, 73% accepted, 15 enrolled. In 2012, 20 master's, 3 doctorates awarded. *Degree requirements:* For master's, culminating project or thesis; for doctorate, comprehensive exam, thesis/dissertation. *Entrance requirements:* For master's and doctorate, GRE, statement of purpose (minimum of 300 words), resume, 3 letters of recommendation, official transcripts; for Postbaccalaureate Certificate, statement of purpose (minimum of 300 words), resume, official transcripts. Additional exam requirements/recommendations for international students: Required—TOEFL (minimum score 533 paper-based; 72 iBT). *Application deadline:* For fall admission, 2/15 priority date for domestic students, 1/15 for international students; for spring admission, 11/1 priority date for domestic students, 10/1 for international students. Applications are processed on a rolling basis. Application fee: $60. Electronic applications accepted. *Expenses:* Tuition, state resident: part-time $86.29 per credit. Tuition, nonresident: part-time $337.46 per credit. *Required fees:* $631.03 per credit. Tuition and fees vary according to course load and reciprocity agreements. *Financial support:* In 2012–13, 1 fellowship with full tuition reimbursement (averaging $8,000 per year), 12 research assistantships with full and partial tuition reimbursements (averaging $7,315 per year), 12 teaching assistantships with full and partial tuition reimbursements (averaging $7,500 per year) were awarded; Federal Work-Study and unspecified assistantships also available. Support available to part-time students. Financial award application deadline: 3/1; financial award applicants required to submit FAFSA. *Faculty research:* Speech acoustics, marine applications, signals and systems, applied electromagnetics, intelligent agency. *Total annual research expenditures:* $1.5 million. *Unit head:* Dr. Karen Payton, Graduate Program Director, 508-999-8434, Fax: 508-999-8489, E-mail: kpayton@umassd.edu. *Application contact:* Steven Briggs, Director of Marketing and Recruitment, 508-999-8604, Fax: 508-999-8183, E-mail: graduate@umassd.edu. Website: http://www.umassd.edu/engineering/ece/.

Applied Physics

Air Force Institute of Technology, Graduate School of Engineering and Management, Department of Engineering Physics, Dayton, OH 45433-7765. Offers applied physics (MS, PhD); electro-optics (MS, PhD); materials science (PhD); nuclear engineering (MS, PhD); space physics (MS). Part-time programs available. *Degree requirements:* For master's, thesis; for doctorate, thesis/dissertation. *Entrance requirements:* For master's and doctorate, GRE General Test, minimum GPA of 3.0, U.S. citizenship. *Faculty research:* High-energy lasers, space physics, nuclear weapon effects, semiconductor physics.

Alabama Agricultural and Mechanical University, School of Graduate Studies, School of Arts and Sciences, Department of Physics, Huntsville, AL 35811. Offers physics (MS, PhD), including applied physics (PhD), materials science (PhD), optics/lasers (PhD). Part-time and evening/weekend programs available. *Degree requirements:* For doctorate, thesis/dissertation. *Entrance requirements:* For master's and doctorate, GRE General Test. Additional exam requirements/recommendations for international students: Required—TOEFL (minimum score 500 paper-based; 61 iBT). Electronic applications accepted.

Binghamton University, State University of New York, Graduate School, School of Arts and Sciences, Department of Physics, Applied Physics, and Astronomy, Binghamton, NY 13902-6000. Offers MS, PhD. *Faculty:* 13 full-time (1 woman), 7 part-time/adjunct (2 women). *Students:* 19 full-time (1 woman), 9 part-time (1 woman); includes 2 minority (1 Black or African American, non-Hispanic/Latino; 1 Native Hawaiian or other Pacific Islander, non-Hispanic/Latino), 9 international. Average age 27. 19 applicants, 68% accepted, 9 enrolled. *Degree requirements:* For master's, thesis or alternative. *Entrance requirements:* For master's, GRE General Test, GRE Subject Test. Additional exam requirements/recommendations for international students: Required—TOEFL (minimum score 550 paper-based; 80 iBT). *Application deadline:* For fall admission, 2/15 priority date for domestic students, 2/15 for international students; for spring admission, 10/15 priority date for domestic students, 10/15 for international students. Applications are processed on a rolling basis. Application fee: $75. Electronic applications accepted. *Expenses:* Tuition, state resident: full-time $9370. Tuition, nonresident: full-time $16,680. *Financial support:* In 2012–13, 27 students received support, including 2 research assistantships with full tuition reimbursements available (averaging $18,000 per year), 25 teaching assistantships with full tuition reimbursements available (averaging $18,000 per year); career-related internships or fieldwork, Federal Work-Study, institutionally sponsored loans, scholarships/grants, health care benefits, and unspecified assistantships also available. Financial award application deadline: 2/15; financial award applicants required to submit FAFSA. *Unit head:* Dr. Eric Cotts, Chairperson, 607-777-4371, E-mail: ecotts@binghamton.edu. *Application contact:* Kishan Zuber, Recruiting and Admissions Coordinator, 607-777-2151, Fax: 607-777-2501, E-mail: kzuber@binghamton.edu.

212 www.petersonsbooks.com

Peterson's Graduate Programs in the Physical Sciences, Mathematics, Agricultural Sciences, the Environment & Natural Resources 2014

California Institute of Technology, Division of Engineering and Applied Science, Option in Applied Physics, Pasadena, CA 91125-0001. Offers MS, PhD. *Degree requirements:* For doctorate, thesis/dissertation. Electronic applications accepted. *Faculty research:* Solid-state electronics, quantum electronics, plasmas, linear and nonlinear laser optics, electromagnetic theory.

Carnegie Mellon University, Mellon College of Science, Department of Physics, Pittsburgh, PA 15213-3891. Offers applied physics (PhD); physics (MS, PhD). *Degree requirements:* For doctorate, thesis/dissertation, qualifying exam. *Entrance requirements:* For doctorate, GRE General Test, GRE Subject Test. Additional exam requirements/recommendations for international students: Required—TOEFL. Electronic applications accepted. *Faculty research:* Astrophysics, condensed matter physics, biological physics, medium energy and nuclear physics, high-energy physics.

Christopher Newport University, Graduate Studies, Department of Physics, Computer Science, and Engineering, Newport News, VA 23606-2998. Offers applied physics and computer science (MS). Part-time and evening/weekend programs available. *Degree requirements:* For master's, comprehensive exam (for some programs), thesis optional. *Entrance requirements:* For master's, GRE General Test, minimum GPA of 3.0. Additional exam requirements/recommendations for international students: Required—TOEFL (minimum score 580 paper-based; 92 iBT). Electronic applications accepted. *Faculty research:* Advanced programming methodologies, experimental nuclear physics, computer architecture, semiconductor nanophysics, laser and optical fiber sensors.

The College of William and Mary, Faculty of Arts and Sciences, Department of Applied Science, Williamsburg, VA 23187-8795. Offers accelerator science (PhD); applied mathematics (PhD); applied mechanics (PhD); applied robotics (PhD); applied science (MS); atmospheric and environmental science (PhD); computational neuroscience (PhD); interface, thin film and surface science (PhD); lasers and optics (PhD); magnetic resonance (PhD); materials science and engineering (PhD); mathematical and computational biology (PhD); medical imaging (PhD); nanotechnology (PhD); neuroscience (PhD); non-destructive evaluation (PhD); polymer chemistry (PhD); remote sensing (PhD). *Faculty:* 13 full-time (2 women), 1 part-time/adjunct (0 women). *Students:* 36 full-time (11 women); includes 2 minority (1 Black or African American, non-Hispanic/Latino; 1 Asian, non-Hispanic/Latino), 22 international. Average age 26. 40 applicants, 45% accepted, 8 enrolled. In 2012, 3 master's, 2 doctorates awarded. *Median time to degree:* Of those who began their doctoral program in fall 2004, 95% received their degree in 8 years or less. *Degree requirements:* For master's, comprehensive exam, thesis; for doctorate, comprehensive exam, thesis/dissertation, 4 core courses. *Entrance requirements:* For master's and doctorate, GRE General Test, GRE Subject Test. Additional exam requirements/recommendations for international students: Required—TOEFL, TWE. *Application deadline:* For fall admission, 2/3 priority date for domestic students, 2/3 for international students; for spring admission, 10/15 priority date for domestic students, 10/14 for international students. Applications are processed on a rolling basis. Application fee: $45. Electronic applications accepted. *Expenses:* Tuition, state resident: full-time $6779; part-time $385 per credit hour. Tuition, nonresident: full-time $20,608; part-time $1000 per credit hour. *Required fees:* $4625. *Financial support:* Fellowships, research assistantships, teaching assistantships, Federal Work-Study, health care benefits, tuition waivers (full), and unspecified assistantships available. Financial award application deadline: 4/15; financial award applicants required to submit FAFSA. *Faculty research:* Computational biology, non-destructive evaluation, neurophysiology, lasers and optics. *Unit head:* Dr. Christopher Del Negro, Chair, 757-221-7808, Fax: 757-221-2050, E-mail: cadeln@wm.edu. *Application contact:* Rosario Fox, Graduate Program Coordinator, 757-221-2563, Fax: 757-221-2050, E-mail: rxfoxx@wm.edu. Website: http://www.wm.edu/as/appliedscience.

Colorado School of Mines, Graduate School, Department of Physics, Golden, CO 80401-1887. Offers applied physics (MS, PhD); materials science (MS, PhD); nuclear engineering (MS, PhD). Part-time programs available. *Faculty:* 37 full-time (4 women), 9 part-time/adjunct (5 women). *Students:* 65 full-time (21 women), 10 part-time (1 woman); includes 5 minority (1 Asian, non-Hispanic/Latino; 4 Hispanic/Latino), 16 international. Average age 27. 102 applicants, 34% accepted, 16 enrolled. In 2012, 10 master's, 3 doctorates awarded. *Degree requirements:* For master's, thesis (for some programs); for doctorate, comprehensive exam, thesis/dissertation. *Entrance requirements:* For master's and doctorate, GRE General Test, GRE Subject Test. Additional exam requirements/recommendations for international students: Required—TOEFL (minimum score 550 paper-based; 80 iBT). *Application deadline:* For fall admission, 1/15 priority date for domestic students, 1/15 for international students; for spring admission, 10/15 priority date for domestic students, 10/15 for international students. Application fee: $50 ($70 for international students). Electronic applications accepted. *Financial support:* In 2012–13, 52 students received support, including fellowships with full tuition reimbursements available (averaging $21,120 per year), 40 research assistantships with full tuition reimbursements available (averaging $21,120 per year), 12 teaching assistantships with full tuition reimbursements available (averaging $21,120 per year); scholarships/grants, health care benefits, and unspecified assistantships also available. Financial award application deadline: 1/15; financial award applicants required to submit FAFSA. *Faculty research:* Light scattering, low-energy nuclear physics, high fusion plasma diagnostics, laser operations, mathematical physics. *Total annual research expenditures:* $7.1 million. *Unit head:* Dr. Thomas Furtak, Head, 303-273-3843, Fax: 303-273-3919, E-mail: tfurtak@mines.edu. *Application contact:* Dr. David Wood, Professor, 303-273-3853, Fax: 303-273-3919, E-mail: dwood@mines.edu. Website: http://physics.mines.edu.

Columbia University, Fu Foundation School of Engineering and Applied Science, Department of Applied Physics and Applied Mathematics, New York, NY 10027. Offers applied physics (Eng Sc D); applied physics and applied mathematics (MS, PhD, Engr); materials science and engineering (MS, Eng Sc D, PhD); medical physics (MS). Part-time programs available. Postbaccalaureate distance learning degree programs offered (no on-campus study). *Faculty:* 32 full-time (2 women), 23 part-time/adjunct (2 women). *Students:* 111 full-time (22 women), 17 part-time (5 women); includes 19 minority (17 Asian, non-Hispanic/Latino; 1 Hispanic/Latino; 1 Two or more races, non-Hispanic/Latino), 53 international. Average age 28. 460 applicants, 26% accepted, 54 enrolled. In 2012, 41 master's, 17 doctorates awarded. Terminal master's awarded for partial completion of doctoral program. *Degree requirements:* For master's, comprehensive exam; for doctorate, thesis/dissertation, qualifying exam. *Entrance requirements:* For master's, GRE General Test, GRE Subject Test (strongly recommended); for doctorate, GRE General Test, GRE Subject Test (applied physics); for Engr, GRE General Test. Additional exam requirements/recommendations for international students: Required—TOEFL, IELTS. *Application deadline:* For fall admission, 12/15 priority date for domestic students, 12/15 for international students; for spring admission, 10/1 priority date for domestic students, 10/1 for international students. Application fee: $95. Electronic applications accepted. *Financial support:* In 2012–13, 73 students received support, including 2 fellowships with full tuition reimbursements available (averaging $31,140 per year), 55 research assistantships with full tuition reimbursements available (averaging $31,133 per year), 16 teaching assistantships with full tuition reimbursements available (averaging $31,133 per year); health care benefits also available. Financial award application deadline: 12/15; financial award applicants required to submit FAFSA. *Faculty research:* Plasma physics and fusion energy; optical and laser physics; atmospheric, oceanic and earth physics; applied mathematics; solid state science and processing of materials, their properties, and their structure; medical physics. *Unit head:* Dr. I. Cevdet Noyan, Professor/Chair, 212-854-8919, E-mail: icn2@columbia.edu. *Application contact:* Montserrat Fernandez-Pinkley, Student Services Coordinator, 212-854-4457, Fax: 212-854-8257, E-mail: mf2157@columbia.edu. Website: http://www.apam.columbia.edu/.

Cornell University, Graduate School, Graduate Fields of Engineering, Field of Applied Physics, Ithaca, NY 14853-0001. Offers applied physics (PhD); engineering physics (M Eng). *Faculty:* 43 full-time (5 women). *Students:* 101 full-time (20 women); includes 16 minority (6 Asian, non-Hispanic/Latino; 7 Hispanic/Latino; 3 Two or more races, non-Hispanic/Latino), 45 international. Average age 25. 215 applicants, 35% accepted, 34 enrolled. In 2012, 22 master's, 4 doctorates awarded. *Degree requirements:* For doctorate, comprehensive exam, thesis/dissertation, written exams. *Entrance requirements:* For master's, GRE General Test, 3 letters of recommendation; for doctorate, GRE General Test, GRE Subject Test (physics), GRE Writing Assessment, 3 letters of recommendation. Additional exam requirements/recommendations for international students: Required—TOEFL (minimum score 600 paper-based; 77 iBT). *Application deadline:* For fall admission, 1/15 for domestic students. Application fee: $95. Electronic applications accepted. *Financial support:* In 2012–13, 69 students received support, including 35 fellowships with full tuition reimbursements available, 26 research assistantships with full tuition reimbursements available, 8 teaching assistantships with full tuition reimbursements available; institutionally sponsored loans, scholarships/grants, health care benefits, tuition waivers (full and partial), and unspecified assistantships also available. *Faculty research:* Quantum and nonlinear optics, plasma physics, solid state physics, condensed matter physics and nanotechnology, electron and x-ray spectroscopy. *Unit head:* Graduate Faculty Representative, 607-255-0638. *Application contact:* Graduate Field Assistant, 607-255-0638, E-mail: aep_info@cornell.edu. Website: http://www.gradschool.cornell.edu/fields.php?id-23&a-2.

East Carolina University, Graduate School, Thomas Harriot College of Arts and Sciences, Department of Physics, Greenville, NC 27858-4353. Offers applied physics (MS); biomedical physics (PhD); health physics (MS); medical physics (MS). Part-time programs available. *Degree requirements:* For master's, one foreign language, comprehensive exam. *Entrance requirements:* For master's, GRE General Test. Additional exam requirements/recommendations for international students: Required—TOEFL. *Expenses:* Tuition, state resident: full-time $4009. Tuition, nonresident: full-time $15,840. *Required fees:* $2111.

George Mason University, College of Science, School of Physics, Astronomy and Computational Sciences, Fairfax, VA 22030. Offers applied and engineering physics (MS); computational science (MS); computational science and informatics (PhD); computational techniques and applications (Certificate); physics (PhD). *Faculty:* 48 full-time (11 women), 10 part-time/adjunct (1 woman). *Students:* 58 full-time (16 women), 97 part-time (19 women); includes 25 minority (6 Black or African American, non-Hispanic/Latino; 11 Asian, non-Hispanic/Latino; 6 Hispanic/Latino; 2 Two or more races, non-Hispanic/Latino), 26 international. Average age 35. 105 applicants, 49% accepted, 22 enrolled. In 2012, 20 master's, 15 doctorates, 1 other advanced degree awarded. *Degree requirements:* For master's, thesis optional; for doctorate, comprehensive exam, thesis/dissertation. *Entrance requirements:* For master's and doctorate, GRE, baccalaureate degree in related field with minimum GPA of 3.0 in last 60 credit hours; 3 letters of recommendation; expanded goals statement; resume; 2 copies of official transcripts. Additional exam requirements/recommendations for international students: Required—TOEFL (minimum score 570 paper-based; 88 iBT), IELTS (minimum score 6.5), Pearson Test of English. *Application deadline:* For fall admission, 4/15 priority date for domestic students; for spring admission, 11/15 priority date for domestic students. Application fee: $65 ($80 for international students). Electronic applications accepted. *Expenses:* Tuition, state resident: full-time $9080; part-time $378.33 per credit hour. Tuition, nonresident: full-time $25,010; part-time $1042.08 per credit hour. *Required fees:* $2610; $108.75 per credit hour. Tuition and fees vary according to program. *Financial support:* In 2012–13, 51 students received support, including 1 fellowship (averaging $8,000 per year), 37 research assistantships with full and partial tuition reimbursements available (averaging $18,917 per year), 16 teaching assistantships with full and partial tuition reimbursements available (averaging $13,676 per year); career-related internships or fieldwork, Federal Work-Study, scholarships/grants, unspecified assistantships, and health care benefits (for full-time research or teaching assistantship recipients) also available. Support available to part-time students. Financial award application deadline: 3/1; financial award applicants required to submit FAFSA. *Faculty research:* Particle and nuclear physics; computational statistics; astronomy, astrophysics, and space and planetary science; astronomy and physics education; atomic physics; biophysics and neuroscience; optical physics; fundamental theoretical studies; multidimensional data analysis. *Total annual research expenditures:* $5.8 million. *Unit head:* Dr. Michael Summers, Director, 703-993-3971, Fax: 703-993-1269, E-mail: msummers@gmu.edu. *Application contact:* Dr. Paul So, Graduate Advisor, 703-993-4377, Fax: 703-993-1269, E-mail: paso@gmu.edu. Website: http://spacs.gmu.edu/.

Harvard University, Graduate School of Arts and Sciences, Department of Physics, Cambridge, MA 02138. Offers experimental physics (PhD); medical engineering/medical physics (PhD), including applied physics, engineering sciences, physics; theoretical physics (PhD). *Degree requirements:* For doctorate, thesis/dissertation, final exams, laboratory experience, *Entrance requirements:* For doctorate, GRE General Test, GRE Subject Test. Additional exam requirements/recommendations for international students: Required—TOEFL. *Expenses: Tuition:* Full-time $37,576. *Required fees:* $930. Tuition and fees vary according to program and student level. *Faculty research:* Particle physics, condensed matter physics, atomic physics.

Harvard University, Graduate School of Arts and Sciences, School of Engineering and Applied Sciences, Cambridge, MA 02138. Offers applied mathematics (ME, SM, PhD); applied physics (ME, SM, PhD); computer science (ME, SM, PhD); engineering science (ME); engineering sciences (SM, PhD). Part-time programs available. Terminal master's awarded for partial completion of doctoral program. *Degree requirements:* For master's, thesis optional; for doctorate, comprehensive exam, thesis/dissertation. *Entrance requirements:* For master's and doctorate, GRE General Test, GRE Subject Test (recommended), 3 letters of recommendation. Additional exam requirements/recommendations for international students: Required—TOEFL (minimum score 80 iBT). Electronic applications accepted. *Expenses: Tuition:* Full-time $37,576. *Required fees:* $930. Tuition and fees vary according to program and student level. *Faculty research:* Applied mathematics, applied physics, computer science and electrical engineering, environmental engineering, mechanical and biomedical engineering.

Idaho State University, Office of Graduate Studies, College of Science and Engineering, Department of Physics, Pocatello, ID 83209-8106. Offers applied physics (PhD); health physics (MS); physics (MNS). Part-time programs available. *Degree requirements:* For master's, comprehensive exam, thesis (for some programs), oral exam (for some programs); for doctorate, comprehensive exam, thesis/dissertation (for some programs), oral exam, written qualifying exam in physics or health physics after 1st year. *Entrance requirements:* For master's, GRE General Test, 3 letters of recommendation, BS or BA in physics, teaching certificate (MNS); for doctorate, GRE General Test (minimum 50th percentile), 3 letters of recommendation, statement of career goals. Additional exam requirements/recommendations for international students: Required—TOEFL (minimum score 550 paper-based; 80 iBT). Electronic applications accepted. *Faculty research:* Ion beam applications, low-energy nuclear physics, relativity and cosmology, observational astronomy.

Illinois Institute of Technology, Graduate College, College of Science and Letters, Department of Physics, Chicago, IL 60616. Offers applied physics (MS); health physics (MHP); physics (MS, PhD). Part-time and evening/weekend programs available. Postbaccalaureate distance learning degree programs offered (minimal on-campus study). *Faculty:* 17 full-time (1 woman), 4 part-time/adjunct (1 woman). *Students:* 47 full-time (12 women), 36 part-time (5 women); includes 10 minority (2 Black or African American, non-Hispanic/Latino; 4 Asian, non-Hispanic/Latino; 1 Hispanic/Latino; 3 Two or more races, non-Hispanic/Latino), 27 international. Average age 31. 104 applicants, 83% accepted, 27 enrolled. In 2012, 13 master's, 2 doctorates awarded. Terminal master's awarded for partial completion of doctoral program. *Degree requirements:* For master's, comprehensive exam (for some programs), thesis (for some programs); for doctorate, comprehensive exam, thesis/dissertation. *Entrance requirements:* For master's, GRE General Test (minimum score 1000 Quantitative and Verbal, 2.5 Analytical Writing), minimum undergraduate GPA of 3.0; for doctorate, GRE General Test (minimum score 1100 Quantitative and Verbal, 3.0 Analytical Writing), minimum undergraduate GPA of 3.0. Additional exam requirements/recommendations for international students: Required—TOEFL (minimum score 523 paper-based; 70 iBT); Recommended—IELTS (minimum score 5.5). *Application deadline:* For fall admission, 5/1 for domestic and international students; for spring admission, 10/15 for domestic and international students. Applications are processed on a rolling basis. Application fee: $40. Electronic applications accepted. *Expenses: Tuition:* Full-time $20,142; part-time $1119 per credit hour. *Required fees:* $605 per semester. One-time fee: $255. Tuition and fees vary according to program and student level. *Financial support:* In 2012–13, 6 fellowships with full and partial tuition reimbursements (averaging $9,547 per year), 3 research assistantships with full and partial tuition reimbursements (averaging $9,848 per year), 3 teaching assistantships with full and partial tuition reimbursements (averaging $7,586 per year) were awarded; Federal Work-Study, institutionally sponsored loans, scholarships/grants, health care benefits, and unspecified assistantships also available. Support available to part-time students. Financial award applicants required to submit FAFSA. *Faculty research:* Elementary particle physics, accelerator and plasma physics, condensed-matter physics, biological physics, x-ray optics, x-ray imaging, quantum theory. *Total annual research expenditures:* $4.6 million. *Unit head:* Dr. Christopher White, Professor, 312-567-3734, Fax: 312-567-3289, E-mail: whitec@iit.edu. *Application contact:* Deborah Gibson, Director, Graduate Admission, 866-472-3448, Fax: 312-567-3138, E-mail: inquiry.grad@iit.edu. Website: http://www.iit.edu/csl/physics.

Iowa State University of Science and Technology, Department of Physics and Astronomy, Ames, IA 50011. Offers applied physics (MS, PhD); astrophysics (MS, PhD); condensed matter physics (MS, PhD); high energy physics (MS, PhD); nuclear physics (MS, PhD); physics (MS, PhD). *Degree requirements:* For master's, thesis (for some programs); for doctorate, thesis/dissertation. *Entrance requirements:* For master's and doctorate, GRE General Test, GRE Subject Test (physics). Additional exam requirements/recommendations for international students: Required—TOEFL (minimum score 550 paper-based; 79 iBT), IELTS (minimum score 6.5). *Application deadline:* For fall admission, 2/15 priority date for domestic students, 2/15 for international students; for spring admission, 10/15 for domestic and international students. Applications are processed on a rolling basis. Application fee: $60 ($90 for international students). Electronic applications accepted. *Financial support:* Application deadline: 2/15. *Faculty research:* Condensed-matter physics, including superconductivity and new materials; high-energy and nuclear physics; astronomy and astrophysics; atmospheric and environmental physics. *Total annual research expenditures:* $8.8 million. *Application contact:* Lori Hockett, Application Contact, 515-294-5870, Fax: 515-294-6027, E-mail: physastro@iastate.edu. Website: http://www.physastro.iastate.edu.

Iowa State University of Science and Technology, Program in Applied Physics, Ames, IA 50011. Offers MS, PhD. *Entrance requirements:* For master's and doctorate, GRE. Additional exam requirements/recommendations for international students: Required—TOEFL (minimum score 550 paper-based; 79 iBT), IELTS (minimum score 6.5). *Application deadline:* For fall admission, 2/15 for domestic and international students; for spring admission, 10/15 for domestic and international students. Electronic applications accepted. *Application contact:* Lori Hockett, Application Contact, 515-294-5870, Fax: 515-294-6027, E-mail: physastro@iastate.edu. Website: http://www.physastro.iastate.edu.

The Johns Hopkins University, Engineering Program for Professionals, Part-time Program in Applied Physics, Baltimore, MD 21218-2699. Offers MS, Post-Master's Certificate. Part-time and evening/weekend programs available. Electronic applications accepted.

Laurentian University, School of Graduate Studies and Research, Programme in Physics, Sudbury, ON P3E 2C6, Canada. Offers M Sc. Part-time programs available. *Degree requirements:* For master's, thesis or alternative. *Entrance requirements:* For master's, honors degree with second class or better. *Faculty research:* Solar neutrino physics and astrophysics, applied acoustics and ultrasonics, powder science and technology, solid state physics, theoretical physics.

Mississippi State University, College of Arts and Sciences, Department of Physics and Astronomy, Mississippi State, MS 39762. Offers engineering (PhD), including applied physics; physics (MS, PhD). Part-time programs available. *Faculty:* 12 full-time (0 women), 2 part-time/adjunct (0 women). *Students:* 42 full-time (6 women), 3 part-time (1 woman); includes 2 minority (both Hispanic/Latino), 35 international. Average age 30. 75 applicants, 17% accepted, 11 enrolled. In 2012, 7 master's, 3 doctorates awarded. *Degree requirements:* For master's, thesis optional, comprehensive oral or written exam; for doctorate, thesis/dissertation, comprehensive oral or written exam. *Entrance requirements:* For master's, GRE, minimum GPA of 2.75 on last two years of undergraduate courses; for doctorate, GRE. Additional exam requirements/recommendations for international students: Required—TOEFL (minimum score 477 paper-based; 53 iBT); Recommended—IELTS (minimum score 4.5). *Application deadline:* For fall admission, 7/1 priority date for domestic students, 5/1 for international students; for spring admission, 11/1 priority date for domestic students, 9/1 for international students. Applications are processed on a rolling basis. Application fee: $60. Electronic applications accepted. *Financial support:* In 2012–13, 14 research assistantships with full tuition reimbursements (averaging $14,594 per year), 20 teaching assistantships with full tuition reimbursements (averaging $13,950 per year) were awarded; Federal Work-Study, institutionally sponsored loans, and unspecified assistantships also available. Financial award application deadline: 3/15; financial award applicants required to submit FAFSA. *Faculty research:* Atomic/molecular spectroscopy, theoretical optics, gamma-ray astronomy, experimental nuclear physics, computational physics. *Total annual research* *expenditures:* $2.6 million. *Unit head:* Dr. Mark A. Novotny, Department Head and Professor, 662-325-2806, Fax: 662-325-8898, E-mail: man40@ra.msstate.edu. *Application contact:* Dr. David Monts, Professor and Graduate Coordinator, 662-325-2931, Fax: 662-325-8898, E-mail: physics@msstate.edu. Website: http://www.msstate.edu/dept/physics/.

Naval Postgraduate School, Departments and Academic Groups, Department of Physics, Monterey, CA 93943. Offers applied physics (MS, PhD); combat systems technology (MS); engineering acoustics (MS, PhD); physics (MS, PhD). Program only open to commissioned officers of the United States and friendly nations and selected United States federal civilian employees. Part-time programs available. *Degree requirements:* For master's, thesis; for doctorate, thesis/dissertation. *Faculty research:* Acoustics, free electron laser, sensors, weapons and effects.

Naval Postgraduate School, Departments and Academic Groups, Space Systems Academic Group, Monterey, CA 93943. Offers applied physics (MS); astronautical engineering (MS); computer science (MS); electrical engineering (MS); mechanical engineering (MS); space systems (Engr); space systems operations (MS). Program only open to commissioned officers of the United States and friendly nations and selected United States federal civilian employees. Part-time programs available. *Degree requirements:* For master's and Engr, thesis; for doctorate, thesis/dissertation. *Faculty research:* Military applications for space; space reconnaissance and remote sensing; radiation-hardened electronics for space; design, construction and operations of small satellites; satellite communications systems.

Naval Postgraduate School, Departments and Academic Groups, Undersea Warfare Academic Group, Monterey, CA 93943. Offers applied mathematics (MS); applied physics (MS); applied science (MS), including acoustics, operations research, physical oceanography, signal processing; electrical engineering (MS); engineering acoustics (MS, PhD); engineering science (MS), including electrical engineering, mechanical engineering; mechanical engineer (ME); mechanical engineering (MS, MSME); meteorology (MS); operations research (MS); physical oceanography (MS). Program only open to commissioned officers of the United States and friendly nations and selected United States federal civilian employees. Part-time programs available. *Degree requirements:* For master's, thesis. *Faculty research:* Unmanned/autonomous vehicles, sea mines and countermeasures, submarine warfare in the twentieth and twenty-first centuries.

New Jersey Institute of Technology, Office of Graduate Studies, College of Science and Liberal Arts, Department of Physics, Program in Applied Physics, Newark, NJ 07102. Offers MS, PhD. Part-time and evening/weekend programs available. Terminal master's awarded for partial completion of doctoral program. *Degree requirements:* For master's, thesis optional; for doctorate, thesis/dissertation, residency. *Entrance requirements:* For master's, GRE General Test; for doctorate, GRE General Test, minimum graduate GPA of 3.5. Additional exam requirements/recommendations for international students: Required—TOEFL (minimum score 550 paper-based; 79 iBT). Electronic applications accepted. *Expenses:* Tuition, state resident: full-time $16,836; part-time $915 per credit. Tuition, nonresident: full-time $24,370; part-time $1286 per credit. *Required fees:* $2318; $242 per credit.

Northern Arizona University, Graduate College, College of Engineering, Forestry and Natural Sciences, Department of Physics and Astronomy, Flagstaff, AZ 86011. Offers applied physics (MS). Part-time programs available. *Degree requirements:* For master's, thesis optional. *Entrance requirements:* Additional exam requirements/recommendations for international students: Required—TOEFL (minimum score 550 paper-based; 80 iBT), IELTS (minimum score 7). Electronic applications accepted.

Oregon State University, College of Science, Department of Physics, Program in Applied Physics, Corvallis, OR 97331. Offers MS. *Students:* 1. 2 applicants. *Expenses:* Tuition, state resident: full-time $11,367; part-time $421 per credit hour. Tuition, nonresident: full-time $18,279; part-time $677 per credit hour. *Required fees:* $1478. One-time fee: $300 full-time. Tuition and fees vary according to course load and program. *Unit head:* Dr. Henri J. F. Jansen, Chair, 541-737-1668, Fax: 541-737-1683, E-mail: physics.chair@science.oregonstate.edu. *Application contact:* Dr. Yun-Shik Lee, Head Graduate Advisor/Professor, 541-737-5057, E-mail: leeys@physics.oregonstate.edu.

Pittsburg State University, Graduate School, College of Arts and Sciences, Department of Physics, Pittsburg, KS 66762. Offers applied physics (MS); physics (MS); professional physics (MS). *Degree requirements:* For master's, thesis or alternative.

Polytechnic Institute of New York University, Department of Applied Physics, Brooklyn, NY 11201-2990. Offers MS, PhD. Part-time and evening/weekend programs available. *Faculty:* 5 full-time (0 women). *Students:* 1 (woman) full-time, 2 part-time (1 woman); includes 1 minority (Asian, non-Hispanic/Latino), 2 international. Average age 29. 10 applicants, 10% accepted, 1 enrolled. *Degree requirements:* For master's, comprehensive exam (for some programs), thesis (for some programs); for doctorate, comprehensive exam, thesis/dissertation. *Entrance requirements:* For master's, BA in physics; for doctorate, departmental qualifying exam, BS in physics. Additional exam requirements/recommendations for international students: Required—TOEFL (minimum score 550 paper-based; 80 iBT); Recommended—IELTS (minimum score 6.5). *Application deadline:* For fall admission, 7/31 priority date for domestic students, 4/30 for international students; for spring admission, 12/31 priority date for domestic students, 11/30 for international students. Applications are processed on a rolling basis. Application fee: $75. Electronic applications accepted. *Financial support:* Fellowships, research assistantships, teaching assistantships, and institutionally sponsored loans available. Support available to part-time students. Financial award applicants required to submit FAFSA. *Faculty research:* Combining microdroplets, UHV cryogenic scanning, tunneling, surface spectroscopy of a single aerosol particle. *Total annual research expenditures:* $40,634. *Unit head:* Dr. Lorcan M. Folan, Head, 718-260-3072, E-mail: lfolan@poly.edu. *Application contact:* Raymond Lutzky, Director of Graduate Enrollment Management, 718-637-5984, Fax: 718-260-3624, E-mail: rlutzky@poly.edu.

Rice University, Rice Quantum Institute, Houston, TX 77251-1892. Offers MS, PhD. *Degree requirements:* For master's, thesis; for doctorate, thesis/dissertation. *Entrance requirements:* For master's and doctorate, GRE General Test, GRE Subject Test (physics), minimum GPA of 3.0. Additional exam requirements/recommendations for international students: Required—TOEFL (minimum score 600 paper-based; 90 iBT). Electronic applications accepted. *Faculty research:* Nanotechnology, solid state materials, atomic physics, thin films.

Rutgers, The State University of New Jersey, Newark, Graduate School, Program in Applied Physics, Newark, NJ 07102. Offers MS, PhD. MS, PhD offered jointly with New Jersey Institute of Technology. *Entrance requirements:* For master's and doctorate, GRE. Additional exam requirements/recommendations for international students: Required—TOEFL.

Southern Illinois University Carbondale, Graduate School, College of Science, Department of Physics, Carbondale, IL 62901-4701. Offers MS, PhD. *Faculty:* 9 full-time (0 women). *Students:* 6 full-time (1 woman), 24 part-time (5 women); includes 2 minority (1 Asian, non-Hispanic/Latino; 1 Hispanic/Latino), 14 international. 37 applicants, 19% accepted, 5 enrolled. In 2012, 7 master's, 5 doctorates awarded. *Degree requirements:* For master's, one foreign language, thesis. *Entrance requirements:* For master's, minimum GPA of 2.7. Additional exam requirements/recommendations for international students: Required—TOEFL. *Application deadline:* Applications are processed on a rolling basis. Application fee: $50. *Financial support:* In 2012–13, 1 fellowship with full tuition reimbursement, 9 teaching assistantships with full tuition reimbursements were awarded; research assistantships with full tuition reimbursements, career-related internships or fieldwork, Federal Work-Study, institutionally sponsored loans, and tuition waivers (full) also available. Support available to part-time students. Financial award application deadline: 2/15. *Faculty research:* Atomic, molecular, nuclear, and mathematical physics; statistical mechanics; solid-state and low-temperature physics; rheology; material science. *Total annual research expenditures:* $773,352. *Unit head:* Dr. Naushad Ali, Chairperson, 618-453-1053, E-mail: nali@physics.siu.edu. Website: http://siuphysics.physics.siu.edu/.

Stanford University, School of Humanities and Sciences, Department of Applied Physics, Stanford, CA 94305-9991. Offers MS, PhD. Terminal master's awarded for partial completion of doctoral program. *Degree requirements:* For doctorate, thesis/dissertation. *Entrance requirements:* For master's and doctorate, GRE General Test, GRE Subject Test. Additional exam requirements/recommendations for international students: Required—TOEFL. Electronic applications accepted. *Expenses: Tuition:* Full-time $41,250; part-time $917 per credit hour.

Texas A&M University, College of Science, Department of Physics and Astronomy, College Station, TX 77843. Offers applied physics (PhD); physics (MS, PhD). *Faculty:* 54. *Students:* 177 full-time (21 women), 7 part-time (0 women); includes 28 minority (3 Black or African American, non-Hispanic/Latino; 1 American Indian or Alaska Native, non-Hispanic/Latino; 5 Asian, non-Hispanic/Latino; 13 Hispanic/Latino; 6 Two or more races, non-Hispanic/Latino), 90 international. Average age 27. In 2012, 13 master's, 10 doctorates awarded. Terminal master's awarded for partial completion of doctoral program. *Degree requirements:* For master's, thesis (for some programs); for doctorate, thesis/dissertation. *Entrance requirements:* For master's and doctorate, GRE General Test, GRE Subject Test. Additional exam requirements/recommendations for international students: Required—TOEFL. *Application deadline:* For fall admission, 3/1 priority date for domestic students; for spring admission, 8/1 for domestic students. Application fee: $50 ($75 for international students). Electronic applications accepted. *Financial support:* In 2012–13, research assistantships (averaging $16,200 per year), teaching assistantships (averaging $16,200 per year) were awarded; fellowships also available. Financial award application deadline: 3/1; financial award applicants required to submit FAFSA. *Faculty research:* Condensed-matter, atomic/molecular, high-energy, and nuclear physics; quantum optics. *Unit head:* Dr. Edward S. Fry, Head, 979-845-7717, E-mail: fry@physics.tamu.edu. *Application contact:* Dr. George W. Kattawar, Professor, 979-845-1180, Fax: 979-845-2590, E-mail: kattawar@tamu.edu. Website: http://physics.tamu.edu/.

Texas Tech University, Graduate School, College of Arts and Sciences, Department of Physics, Lubbock, TX 79409. Offers applied physics (MS); physics (MS, PhD). Part-time programs available. *Degree requirements:* For master's, variable foreign language requirement, thesis or alternative; for doctorate, variable foreign language requirement, thesis/dissertation. *Entrance requirements:* For master's and doctorate, GRE General Test. Additional exam requirements/recommendations for international students: Required—TOEFL (minimum score 550 paper-based; 79 iBT). Electronic applications accepted. *Faculty research:* Biophysics, high energy and nuclear physics, condensed matter physics, atomic and molecular physics, physics education.

Applied Physics

Towson University, Program in Applied Physics, Towson, MD 21252-0001. Offers MS.

The University of Arizona, College of Science, Department of Physics, Program in Applied and Industrial Physics, Tucson, AZ 85721. Offers PSM. Part-time programs available. *Students:* 1 full-time (0 women), 1 part-time (0 women); includes 1 minority (Hispanic/Latino), 1 international. Average age 29. 13 applicants, 38% accepted, 5 enrolled. In 2012, 4 master's awarded. *Degree requirements:* For master's, thesis or alternative, internship, colloquium, business courses. *Entrance requirements:* Additional exam requirements/recommendations for international students: Required—TOEFL (minimum score 550 paper-based; 79 iBT). Application fee: $75. Electronic applications accepted. *Financial support:* Career-related internships or fieldwork, Federal Work-Study, and scholarships/grants available. *Faculty research:* Nanotechnology, optics, medical imaging, high energy physics, biophysics. *Unit head:* Dr. Michael Shupe, Department Head, 520-621-2679, E-mail: shupe@physics.arizona.edu. *Application contact:* Lisa Shapouri, Graduate Coordinator, 520-621-2290, Fax: 520-621-4721, E-mail: lisas@physics.arizona.edu. Website: http://www.physics.arizona.edu/.

University of Arkansas, Graduate School, J. William Fulbright College of Arts and Sciences, Department of Physics, Fayetteville, AR 72701-1201. Offers applied physics (MS); physics (MS, PhD); physics education (MA). *Students:* 7 full-time (3 women), 45 part-time (7 women); includes 4 minority (1 American Indian or Alaska Native, non-Hispanic/Latino; 1 Asian, non-Hispanic/Latino; 1 Hispanic/Latino; 1 Two or more races, non-Hispanic/Latino), 31 international. In 2012, 3 master's, 1 doctorate awarded. *Degree requirements:* For master's, thesis; for doctorate, thesis/dissertation. *Application deadline:* For fall admission, 4/1 for international students; for spring admission, 10/1 for international students. Applications are processed on a rolling basis. Application fee: $40 ($50 for international students). Electronic applications accepted. *Financial support:* In 2012–13, 21 research assistantships, 22 teaching assistantships were awarded; fellowships with tuition reimbursements, career-related internships or fieldwork, and Federal Work-Study also available. Support available to part-time students. Financial award application deadline: 4/1; financial award applicants required to submit FAFSA. *Unit head:* Dr. Julio Gea-Banacloche, Departmental Chairperson, 479-575-2506, Fax: 479-575-4580, E-mail: jgeabana@uark.edu. *Application contact:* Dr. Reeta Vyas, Graduate Coordinator, 479-575-6058, E-mail: rvyas@uark.edu. Website: http://www.uark.edu/depts/physics/.

University of California, San Diego, Office of Graduate Studies, Department of Electrical and Computer Engineering, La Jolla, CA 92093. Offers applied ocean science (MS, PhD); applied physics (MS, PhD); communication theory and systems (MS, PhD); computer engineering (MS, PhD); electrical engineering (M Eng); electronic circuits and systems (MS, PhD); intelligent systems, robotics and control (MS, PhD); photonics (MS, PhD); signal and image processing (MS, PhD). MS only offered to students who have been admitted to the PhD program. *Entrance requirements:* For master's and doctorate, GRE General Test. Electronic applications accepted.

University of Denver, Faculty of Natural Sciences and Mathematics, Department of Physics and Astronomy, Denver, CO 80208. Offers applied physics (MS); physics (MS, PhD). Part-time programs available. *Faculty:* 11 full-time (3 women), 5 part-time/adjunct (0 women). *Students:* 7 full-time (4 women), 7 part-time (3 women), 2 international. Average age 30. 41 applicants, 37% accepted, 4 enrolled. In 2012, 1 master's, 2 doctorates awarded. Terminal master's awarded for partial completion of doctoral program. *Degree requirements:* For master's, thesis optional; for doctorate, thesis/dissertation. *Entrance requirements:* For master's and doctorate, GRE General Test, GRE Subject Test in physics (strongly preferred), three letters of recommendation, personal statement. Additional exam requirements/recommendations for international students: Required—TOEFL (minimum score 550 paper-based; 80 iBT). *Application deadline:* For fall admission, 3/1 priority date for domestic students. Applications are processed on a rolling basis. Application fee: $60. Electronic applications accepted. *Expenses:* Tuition: Full-time $38,232; part-time $1062 per credit hour. *Required fees:* $744. Tuition and fees vary according to program. *Financial support:* In 2012–13, 15 students received support, including 7 research assistantships with full and partial tuition reimbursements available (averaging $15,683 per year), 10 teaching assistantships with full and partial tuition reimbursements available (averaging $23,085 per year); career-related internships or fieldwork, Federal Work-Study, institutionally sponsored loans, scholarships/grants, and unspecified assistantships also available. Support available to part-time students. Financial award application deadline: 2/15; financial award applicants required to submit FAFSA. *Faculty research:* Atomic and molecular beams and collisions, infrared astronomy, acoustic emission from stressed solids, nano materials. *Unit head:* Dr. Davor Balzar, Chair, 303-871-2238, E-mail: davor.balzar@du.edu. *Application contact:* Barbara Stephen, Assistant to the Chair, 303-871-2238, E-mail: barbara.stephen@du.edu. Website: http://www.physics.du.edu.

University of Maryland, Baltimore County, Graduate School, College of Natural and Mathematical Sciences, Department of Physics, Program in Applied Physics, Baltimore, MD 21250. Offers MS, PhD. Part-time programs available. *Faculty:* 21 full-time (3 women), 16 part-time/adjunct (2 women). *Students:* 29 full-time (10 women), 3 part-time (0 women); includes 2 minority (both Black or African American, non-Hispanic/Latino), 10 international. Average age 24. 43 applicants, 30% accepted, 5 enrolled. In 2012, 1 master's, 5 doctorates awarded. Terminal master's awarded for partial completion of doctoral program. *Degree requirements:* For master's, thesis optional; for doctorate, comprehensive exam, thesis/dissertation. *Entrance requirements:* For master's and doctorate, GRE General Test, GRE Subject Test (recommended), minimum GPA of 3.0. Additional exam requirements/recommendations for international students: Required—TOEFL. *Application deadline:* For fall admission, 1/1 for domestic and international students; for spring admission, 11/30 for domestic students. Applications are processed on a rolling basis. Application fee: $50. Electronic applications accepted. *Financial support:* In 2012–13, 26 students received support, including 4 fellowships with full tuition reimbursements available (averaging $30,000 per year), 14 research assistantships with full tuition reimbursements available (averaging $26,000 per year), 12 teaching assistantships with full tuition reimbursements available (averaging $22,000 per year); career-related internships or fieldwork, scholarships/grants, health care benefits, and unspecified assistantships also available. Support available to part-time students. Financial award application deadline: 1/1. *Faculty research:* Astrophysics, atmospheric physics, nanoscale physics, quantum optics and quantum information science. *Total annual research expenditures:* $4.8 million. *Unit head:* Dr. Todd Pittman, Graduate Program Director, 410-455-2513, Fax: 410-455-1072, E-mail: todd.pittman@umbc.edu. *Application contact:* Dr. Lazlo Takacs, Graduate Admissions Committee Chair, 410-455-2524, Fax: 410-455-1072, E-mail: takacs@umbc.edu. Website: http://www.physics.umbc.edu.

University of Massachusetts Boston, Office of Graduate Studies, College of Science and Mathematics, Program in Applied Physics, Boston, MA 02125-3393. Offers MS. Part-time and evening/weekend programs available. *Degree requirements:* For master's, thesis optional. *Entrance requirements:* For master's, minimum GPA of 2.75. *Faculty research:* Experimental laser research, nonlinear optics, experimental and theoretical solid state physics, semiconductor devices, opto-electronics.

University of Massachusetts Lowell, College of Sciences, Department of Physics and Applied Physics, Program in Applied Physics, Lowell, MA 01854-2881. Offers applied mechanics (PhD); applied physics (MS, PhD), including optical sciences (MS). Terminal master's awarded for partial completion of doctoral program. *Degree requirements:* For master's, thesis; for doctorate, 2 foreign languages, thesis/dissertation. *Entrance requirements:* For master's, GRE General Test, 3 letters of reference; for doctorate, GRE General Test, transcripts, 3 letters of reference. Additional exam requirements/recommendations for international students: Required—TOEFL.

University of Michigan, Horace H. Rackham School of Graduate Studies, College of Literature, Science, and the Arts, Applied Physics Program, Ann Arbor, MI 48109. Offers PhD. *Degree requirements:* For doctorate, oral defense of dissertation, preliminary and qualifying exams. *Entrance requirements:* For doctorate, GRE General Test. Additional exam requirements/recommendations for international students: Required—TOEFL. Electronic applications accepted. *Faculty research:* Optical sciences, materials research, quantum structures, medical imaging, environment and science policy.

University of Missouri–St. Louis, College of Arts and Sciences, Department of Physics and Astronomy, St. Louis, MO 63121. Offers applied physics (MS); astrophysics (MS); physics (PhD). Part-time and evening/weekend programs available. *Faculty:* 9 full-time (2 women), 5 part-time/adjunct (0 women). *Students:* 14 full-time (3 women), 9 part-time (5 women); includes 2 minority (1 American Indian or Alaska Native, non-Hispanic/Latino; 1 Asian, non-Hispanic/Latino), 4 international. Average age 31. 21 applicants, 48% accepted, 6 enrolled. In 2012, 7 master's, 1 doctorate awarded. Terminal master's awarded for partial completion of doctoral program. *Degree requirements:* For master's, thesis optional; for doctorate, thesis/dissertation. *Entrance requirements:* For master's, GRE General Test; for doctorate, GRE General Test, 2 letters of recommendation. Additional exam requirements/recommendations for international students: Required—TOEFL (minimum score 550 paper-based; 79 iBT), IELTS (minimum score 6.5). *Application deadline:* For fall admission, 7/1 for domestic and international students; for spring admission, 12/1 for domestic students, 11/1 for international students. Application fee: $35 ($40 for international students). Electronic applications accepted. *Expenses:* Tuition, state resident: full-time $7364; part-time $409.10 per credit hour. Tuition, nonresident: full-time $18,153; part-time $1008.50 per credit hour. *Financial support:* In 2012–13, 5 research assistantships with full and partial tuition reimbursements (averaging $17,125 per year), 11 teaching assistantships with full and partial tuition reimbursements (averaging $14,500 per year) were awarded; fellowships with full tuition reimbursements and career-related internships or fieldwork also available. Financial award applicants required to submit FAFSA. *Faculty research:* Biophysics, atomic physics, nonlinear dynamics, materials science. *Unit head:* Dr. Bruce Wilking, Director of Graduate Studies, 314-516-5931, Fax: 314-516-6152, E-mail: bwilking@umsl.edu. *Application contact:* 314-516-5458, Fax: 314-516-6996, E-mail: gradadm@umsl.edu. Website: http://www.umsl.edu/~physics/.

The University of North Carolina at Charlotte, The Graduate School, College of Liberal Arts and Sciences, Department of Physics and Optical Science, Charlotte, NC 28223-0001. Offers applied physics (MS); optical science and engineering (MS, PhD). *Faculty:* 20 full-time (4 women). *Students:* 46 full-time (11 women), 11 part-time (3 women); includes 3 minority (2 Black or African American, non-Hispanic/Latino; 1 Hispanic/Latino), 27 international. Average age 29. 53 applicants, 42% accepted, 14 enrolled. In 2012, 8 master's, 8 doctorates awarded. Terminal master's awarded for partial completion of doctoral program. *Degree requirements:* For master's, comprehensive exam (for some programs), thesis optional, thesis or comprehensive exam; for doctorate, thesis/dissertation. *Entrance requirements:* For master's, GRE General Test, minimum GPA of 3.0 during previous 2 years, 2.75 overall; for doctorate, GRE, minimum GPA of 3.0, letters of recommendation. Additional exam requirements/recommendations for international students: Required—TOEFL (minimum score 557 paper-based; 83 iBT). *Application deadline:* For fall admission, 7/15 for domestic students, 5/1 for international students; for spring admission, 11/15 for domestic students, 10/1 for international students. Applications are processed on a rolling basis. Application fee: $65 ($75 for international students). Electronic applications accepted. *Expenses:* Tuition, state resident: full-time $3453. Tuition, nonresident: full-time $15,982. *Required fees:* $2420. Tuition and fees vary according to course load and program. *Financial support:* In 2012–13, 38 students received support, including 7 fellowships (averaging $42,271 per year), 9 research assistantships (averaging $9,781 per year), 22 teaching assistantships (averaging $7,705 per year); career-related internships or fieldwork, institutionally sponsored loans, scholarships/grants, and unspecified assistantships also available. Support available to part-time students. Financial award application deadline: 4/1; financial award applicants required to submit FAFSA. *Faculty research:* Experimental and computational material sciences, optoelectronics, quantum structures, electronic and electromagnetic waves in anisotropic media, nanoscale smart devices, infrared (IR) transmitting optical materials, low loss IR transmitting glass optical fibers and rugged transparent ceramic spinel windows. *Total annual research expenditures:* $1.3 million. *Unit head:* Dr. Glen Boreman, Chair, 704-687-8173, Fax: 704-687-3160, E-mail: gboreman@uncc.edu. *Application contact:* Kathy B. Giddings, Director of Graduate Admissions, 704-687-5503, Fax: 704-687-1668, E-mail: gradadm@uncc.edu. Website: http://physics.uncc.edu/graduate-programs.

University of Northern Iowa, Graduate College, College of Humanities, Arts and Sciences, Department of Physics, Cedar Falls, IA 50614. Offers applied physics (PSM). *Students:* 2 full-time (1 woman), 1 part-time (0 women), 1 international. 5 applicants, 40% accepted, 1 enrolled. In 2012, 5 degrees awarded. *Degree requirements:* For master's, comprehensive exam (for some programs), thesis or alternative. *Entrance requirements:* For master's, minimum GPA of 3.0. Additional exam requirements/recommendations for international students: Required—TOEFL (minimum score 500 paper-based; 61 iBT). *Application deadline:* For fall admission, 8/1 priority date for domestic students. Applications are processed on a rolling basis. Application fee: $50 ($70 for international students). Electronic applications accepted. *Financial support:* Career-related internships or fieldwork, Federal Work-Study, scholarships/grants, and tuition waivers (full and partial) available. Support available to part-time students. Financial award application deadline: 2/1. *Unit head:* Dr. C. Clifton Chancey, Head, 319-273-2420, E-mail: c.chancey@uni.edu. *Application contact:* Laurie S. Russell, Record Analyst, 319-273-2623, Fax: 319-273-2885, E-mail: laurie.russell@uni.edu. Website: http://www.physics.uni.edu/.

University of South Florida, Graduate School, College of Arts and Sciences, Department of Physics, Tampa, FL 33620-9951. Offers applied physics (PhD); physics (MS). Part-time programs available. *Degree requirements:* For master's, comprehensive exam, thesis optional; for doctorate, comprehensive exam, thesis/dissertation. *Entrance requirements:* For master's and doctorate, GRE, minimum GPA of 3.0, three letters of recommendation, statement of purpose. Additional exam requirements/recommendations for international students: Required—

TOEFL (minimum score 550 paper-based; 79 iBT) or IELTS (minimum score 6.5). Electronic applications accepted. *Faculty research:* Biophysics and biomedical physics, atomic molecular and optical physics, solid state and materials physics, physics education.

The University of Texas at Austin, Graduate School, College of Natural Sciences, Department of Physics, Austin, TX 78712-1111. Offers MA, MS, PhD. *Degree requirements:* For master's, thesis; for doctorate, thesis/dissertation. *Entrance requirements:* For master's and doctorate, GRE General Test, GRE Subject Test (physics). Electronic applications accepted.

University of Washington, Graduate School, College of Arts and Sciences, Department of Physics, Seattle, WA 98195. Offers MS, PhD. Part-time and evening/weekend programs available. Terminal master's awarded for partial completion of doctoral program. *Degree requirements:* For doctorate, thesis/dissertation. *Entrance requirements:* For master's, GRE; for doctorate, GRE General Test, GRE Subject Test. Additional exam requirements/recommendations for international students: Required—TOEFL. Electronic applications accepted. *Faculty research:* Astro-, atomic, condensed-matter, nuclear, and particle physics; physics education.

Virginia Commonwealth University, Graduate School, College of Humanities and Sciences, Department of Physics, Program in Physics and Applied Physics, Richmond, VA 23284-9005. Offers MS. *Entrance requirements:* For master's, GRE. Additional exam requirements/recommendations for international students: Required—TOEFL (minimum score 600 paper-based; 100 iBT); Recommended—IELTS (minimum score 6.5). Electronic applications accepted. *Faculty research:* Theoretical and experimental condensed matter physics, general relativity and cosmology, physics education.

West Virginia University, Eberly College of Arts and Sciences, Department of Physics, Morgantown, WV 26506. Offers applied physics (MS, PhD); astrophysics (MS, PhD); chemical physics (MS, PhD); condensed matter physics (MS, PhD); elementary particle physics (MS, PhD); materials physics (MS, PhD); plasma physics (MS, PhD); solid state physics (MS, PhD); statistical physics (MS, PhD); theoretical physics (MS, PhD). Terminal master's awarded for partial completion of doctoral program. *Degree requirements:* For master's, thesis or alternative, qualifying exam; for doctorate, thesis/dissertation, qualifying exam. *Entrance requirements:* For master's and doctorate, GRE General Test, minimum GPA of 3.0. Additional exam requirements/recommendations for international students: Required—TOEFL. *Faculty research:* Experimental and theoretical condensed-matter, plasma, high-energy theory, nonlinear dynamics, space physics.

Yale University, Graduate School of Arts and Sciences, School of Engineering and Applied Science, Department of Applied Physics, New Haven, CT 06520. Offers MS, PhD. Terminal master's awarded for partial completion of doctoral program. *Degree requirements:* For doctorate, thesis/dissertation, area exam. *Entrance requirements:* For master's and doctorate, GRE General Test. Additional exam requirements/recommendations for international students: Required—TOEFL. *Faculty research:* Condensed-matter physics, optical physics, materials science.

Chemical Physics

Columbia University, Graduate School of Arts and Sciences, Division of Natural Sciences, Department of Chemistry, Program in Chemical Physics, New York, NY 10027. Offers M Phil, PhD. *Entrance requirements:* For master's, GRE General Test, GRE Subject Test. Additional exam requirements/recommendations for international students: Required—TOEFL.

Cornell University, Graduate School, Graduate Fields of Arts and Sciences, Field of Chemistry and Chemical Biology, Ithaca, NY 14853-0001. Offers analytical chemistry (PhD); bio-organic chemistry (PhD); biophysical chemistry (PhD); chemical biology (PhD); chemical physics (PhD); inorganic chemistry (PhD); materials chemistry (PhD); organic chemistry (PhD); organometallic chemistry (PhD); physical chemistry (PhD); polymer chemistry (PhD); theoretical chemistry (PhD). *Faculty:* 48 full-time (5 women). *Students:* 161 full-time (70 women); includes 28 minority (1 Black or African American, non-Hispanic/Latino; 16 Asian, non-Hispanic/Latino; 4 Hispanic/Latino; 7 Two or more races, non-Hispanic/Latino), 48 international. Average age 25. 340 applicants, 33% accepted, 40 enrolled. In 2012, 15 doctorates awarded. *Degree requirements:* For doctorate, comprehensive exam, thesis/dissertation. *Entrance requirements:* For doctorate, GRE General Test, GRE Subject Test (chemistry), 3 letters of recommendation. Additional exam requirements/recommendations for international students: Required—TOEFL (minimum score 600 paper-based; 77 iBT). *Application deadline:* For fall admission, 1/10 for domestic students. Application fee: $95. Electronic applications accepted. *Financial support:* In 2012–13, 155 students received support, including 37 fellowships with full tuition reimbursements available, 50 research assistantships with full tuition reimbursements available, 68 teaching assistantships with full tuition reimbursements available; institutionally sponsored loans, scholarships/grants, health care benefits, tuition waivers (full and partial), and unspecified

assistantships also available. Financial award applicants required to submit FAFSA. *Faculty research:* Analytical, organic, inorganic, physical, materials, chemical biology. *Unit head:* Director of Graduate Studies, 607-255-4139, Fax: 607-255-4137. *Application contact:* Graduate Field Assistant, 607-255-4139, Fax: 607-255-4137, E-mail: chemgrad@cornell.edu. Website: http://www.gradschool.cornell.edu/fields.php?id-26&a-2.

Harvard University, Graduate School of Arts and Sciences, Committee on Chemical Physics, Cambridge, MA 02138. Offers PhD. *Degree requirements:* For doctorate, one foreign language, thesis/dissertation, cumulative exams. *Entrance requirements:* For doctorate, GRE General Test, GRE Subject Test. Additional exam requirements/recommendations for international students: Required—TOEFL. *Expenses: Tuition:* Full-time $37,576. *Required fees:* $930. Tuition and fees vary according to program and student level.

Kent State University, College of Arts and Sciences, Chemical Physics Interdisciplinary Program, Kent, OH 44242-0001. Offers MS, PhD. Program offered in cooperation with the Departments of Chemistry, Mathematics and Computer Science, and Physics and the Liquid Crystal Institute. Terminal master's awarded for partial completion of doctoral program. *Degree requirements:* For master's, thesis; for doctorate, thesis/dissertation, candidacy exam. *Entrance requirements:* For master's and doctorate, GRE. Additional exam requirements/recommendations for international students: Required—TOEFL (minimum score 525 paper-based). Electronic applications accepted. *Expenses:* Tuition, state resident: full-time $8424; part-time $468 per credit hour. Tuition, nonresident: full-time $14,580; part-time $810 per credit hour. Tuition and fees vary according to course load.

Peterson's Graduate Programs in the Physical Sciences, Mathematics, Agricultural Sciences, the Environment & Natural Resources 2014

www.petersonsbooks.com   **217**

Chemical Physics

Marquette University, Graduate School, College of Arts and Sciences, Department of Chemistry, Milwaukee, WI 53201-1881. Offers analytical chemistry (MS, PhD); bioanalytical chemistry (MS, PhD); biophysical chemistry (MS, PhD); chemical physics (MS, PhD); inorganic chemistry (MS, PhD); organic chemistry (MS, PhD); physical chemistry (MS, PhD). Part-time programs available. Terminal master's awarded for partial completion of doctoral program. *Degree requirements:* For master's, comprehensive exam; for doctorate, thesis/dissertation, cumulative exams. *Entrance requirements:* For master's and doctorate, official transcripts from all current and previous colleges/universities except Marquette, three letters of recommendation from individuals familiar with the applicant's academic work. Additional exam requirements/recommendations for international students: Required—TOEFL (minimum score 530 paper-based). Electronic applications accepted. *Faculty research:* Inorganic complexes, laser Raman spectroscopy, organic synthesis, synthetic bioinorganic chemistry, electro-active organic molecules.

McMaster University, School of Graduate Studies, Faculty of Science, Department of Chemistry, Hamilton, ON L8S 4M2, Canada. Offers analytical chemistry (M Sc, PhD); chemical physics (M Sc, PhD); chemistry (M Sc, PhD); inorganic chemistry (M Sc, PhD); organic chemistry (M Sc, PhD); physical chemistry (M Sc, PhD); polymer chemistry (M Sc, PhD). Part-time programs available. Terminal master's awarded for partial completion of doctoral program. *Degree requirements:* For master's, thesis; for doctorate, comprehensive exam, thesis/dissertation. *Entrance requirements:* For master's, minimum B+ average. Additional exam requirements/recommendations for international students: Required—TOEFL (minimum score 550 paper-based).

Michigan State University, The Graduate School, College of Natural Science, Department of Chemistry, East Lansing, MI 48824. Offers chemical physics (PhD); chemistry (MS, PhD); chemistry-environmental toxicology (PhD); computational chemistry (MS). *Entrance requirements:* Additional exam requirements/recommendations for international students: Required—TOEFL. Electronic applications accepted. *Faculty research:* Analytical chemistry, inorganic and organic chemistry, nuclear chemistry, physical chemistry, theoretical and computational chemistry.

The Ohio State University, Graduate School, College of Arts and Sciences, Division of Natural and Mathematical Sciences, Program in Chemical Physics, Columbus, OH 43210. Offers MS, PhD. *Faculty:* 32. *Students:* 3 full-time (1 woman), 4 part-time (1 woman), 4 international. Average age 25. In 2012, 1 master's, 2 doctorates awarded. *Degree requirements:* For master's, thesis optional; for doctorate, thesis/dissertation. *Entrance requirements:* For doctorate, GRE General Test, GRE Subject Test (chemistry or physics). Additional exam requirements/recommendations for international students: Required—Michigan English Language Assessment Battery (minimum score 86); Recommended—TOEFL (minimum score 600 paper-based; 100 iBT). *Application deadline:* For fall admission, 1/7 priority date for domestic students, 11/30 for international students; for winter admission, 12/1 for domestic students, 11/1 for international students; for spring admission, 3/1 for domestic students, 2/1 for international students. Applications are processed on a rolling basis. Application fee: $40 ($50 for international students). Electronic applications accepted. *Financial support:* Fellowships, research assistantships, teaching assistantships, Federal Work-Study, and institutionally sponsored loans available. Support available to part-time students. *Unit head:* Dr. Terry A. Miller, Chair, 614-292-2569, Fax: 614-292-1948, E-mail: miller.104@osu.edu. *Application contact:* Becky Gregory, Program Assistant, 614-292-2569, Fax: 614-292-1948, E-mail: gregory.10@osu.edu. Website: https://molspect.chemistry.ohio-state.edu/chemphys/.

University of Colorado Boulder, Graduate School, College of Arts and Sciences, Department of Physics, Boulder, CO 80309. Offers chemical physics (PhD); geophysics (PhD); liquid crystal science and technology (PhD); mathematical physics (PhD); medical physics (PhD); optical sciences and engineering (PhD); physics (MS, PhD). *Faculty:* 50 full-time (7 women). *Students:* 158 full-time (32 women), 64 part-time (9 women); includes 11 minority (6 Asian, non-Hispanic/Latino; 5 Hispanic/Latino), 74 international. Average age 27. 600 applicants, 21% accepted, 32 enrolled. Terminal master's awarded for partial completion of doctoral program. *Degree requirements:* For master's, comprehensive exam, thesis or alternative; for doctorate, comprehensive exam, thesis/dissertation. *Entrance requirements:* For master's and doctorate, GRE General Test, GRE Subject Test, minimum undergraduate GPA of 3.0. Additional exam requirements/recommendations for international students: Required—TOEFL. *Application deadline:* For fall admission, 12/15 priority date for domestic students, 12/15 for international students. Applications are processed on a rolling basis. Application fee: $50 ($60 for international students). Electronic applications accepted. *Financial support:* In 2012–13, 38 fellowships (averaging $14,995 per year), 156 research assistantships with full and partial tuition reimbursements (averaging $25,043 per year), 48 teaching assistantships with full and partial tuition reimbursements (averaging $18,902 per year) were awarded; institutionally sponsored loans, scholarships/grants, health care benefits, and unspecified assistantships also available. Financial award application deadline: 1/15; financial award applicants required to submit FAFSA. *Faculty research:* Atomic and molecular physics, nuclear physics, condensed matter, elementary particle physics, laser or optical physics, plasma physics, geophysics, astrophysics and chemical physics. *Total annual research expenditures:* $23.7 million. *Application contact:* E-mail: physics@colorado.edu. Website: http://physics.colorado.edu/.

University of Illinois at Urbana–Champaign, Graduate College, College of Liberal Arts and Sciences, School of Chemical Sciences, Department of Chemistry, Champaign, IL 61820. Offers astrochemistry (PhD); chemical physics (PhD); chemistry (MA, MS, PhD); teaching of chemistry (MS); MS/JD; MS/MBA. *Students:* 282 (100 women). Application fee: $75 ($90 for international students). *Unit head:* Jeffrey Moore, Head, 217-333-0711, Fax: 217-244-5943, E-mail: jsmoore@illinois.edu. *Application contact:* Krista Smith, Program Coordinator, 217-244-4844, Fax: 217-244-5943, E-mail: kristasm@illinois.edu. Website: http://chemistry.illinois.edu/.

University of Louisville, Graduate School, College of Arts and Sciences, Department of Chemistry, Louisville, KY 40292-0001. Offers analytical chemistry (MS, PhD); biochemistry (MS, PhD); chemical physics (PhD); inorganic chemistry (MS, PhD); organic chemistry (MS, PhD); physical chemistry (MS, PhD). *Students:* 45 full-time (21 women), 5 part-time (1 woman); includes 1 minority (Hispanic/Latino), 35 international. Average age 28. 78 applicants, 17% accepted, 9 enrolled. In 2012, 19 master's, 7 doctorates awarded. Terminal master's awarded for partial completion of doctoral program. *Degree requirements:* For master's, variable foreign language requirement, comprehensive exam, thesis optional; for doctorate, variable foreign language requirement, comprehensive exam, thesis/dissertation. *Entrance requirements:* For master's and doctorate, BA or BS coursework. Additional exam requirements/recommendations for international students: Required—TOEFL. *Application deadline:* For fall admission, 3/15 for domestic and international students; for winter admission, 9/15 for domestic and international students. Applications are processed on a rolling basis. Application fee: $60. Electronic applications accepted. *Financial support:* In 2012–13, 33 teaching assistantships with full tuition reimbursements (averaging $22,000 per year) were awarded; fellowships with full tuition reimbursements, research assistantships with full tuition reimbursements, career-related internships or fieldwork, scholarships/grants, traineeships, health care benefits, and unspecified assistantships also available. Support available to part-time students. Financial award application deadline: 3/15. *Faculty research:* Computational chemistry, biophysics nuclear magnetic resonance, synthetic organic chemistry, synthetic inorganic chemistry, medicinal chemistry, protein chemistry, enzymology, nanochemistry, electrochemistry, analytical chemistry, synthetic biology, bioinformatics. *Total annual research expenditures:* $2.5 million. *Unit head:* Dr. Richard J. Wittebort, Professor/Chair, 502-852-6613. *Application contact:* Sherry Nalley, Administrator, 502-852-6798.

University of Maryland, College Park, Academic Affairs, College of Computer, Mathematical and Natural Sciences, Institute for Physical Science and Technology, Program in Chemical Physics, College Park, MD 20742. Offers MS, PhD. Part-time and evening/weekend programs available. *Students:* 31 full-time (6 women), 2 part-time (0 women); includes 1 minority (Hispanic/Latino), 16 international. 27 applicants, 37% accepted, 6 enrolled. In 2012, 3 master's, 5 doctorates awarded. Terminal master's awarded for partial completion of doctoral program. *Degree requirements:* For master's, thesis optional, paper, qualifying exam; for doctorate, thesis/dissertation, seminars. *Entrance requirements:* For master's, GRE General Test, GRE Subject Test (chemistry, math or physics), minimum GPA of 3.3, 3 letters of recommendation; for doctorate, GRE Subject Test (chemistry, math, or physics), GRE General Test, minimum GPA of 3.3, 3 letters of recommendation. *Application deadline:* For fall admission, 2/1 for domestic and international students; for spring admission, 6/1 for domestic and international students. Applications are processed on a rolling basis. Application fee: $75. Electronic applications accepted. *Expenses:* Tuition, state resident: part-time $551 per credit. Tuition, nonresident: part-time $1188 per credit. Part-time tuition and fees vary according to program. *Financial support:* In 2012–13, 2 fellowships with partial tuition reimbursements (averaging $10,278 per year), 20 research assistantships (averaging $20,514 per year), 11 teaching assistantships (averaging $18,868 per year) were awarded; Federal Work-Study and scholarships/grants also available. Financial award applicants required to submit FAFSA. *Faculty research:* Discrete molecules and gases; dynamic phenomena; thermodynamics, statistical mechanical theory and quantum mechanical theory; atmospheric physics; biophysics. *Unit head:* Rajarshi Roy, Director, 301-405-4878, Fax: 301-314-9396, E-mail: rroy@umd.edu. *Application contact:* Dr. Charles A. Caramello, Dean of Graduate School, 301-405-0358, Fax: 301-314-9305.

University of Nevada, Reno, Graduate School, Interdisciplinary Program in Chemical Physics, Reno, NV 89557. Offers PhD. *Degree requirements:* For doctorate, thesis/dissertation. *Entrance requirements:* For doctorate, GRE, minimum GPA of 3.0. Additional exam requirements/recommendations for international students: Required—TOEFL (minimum score 500 paper-based; 61 iBT). Electronic applications accepted. *Faculty research:* Atomic and molecular physics, physical chemistry.

The University of Tennessee, Graduate School, College of Arts and Sciences, Department of Chemistry, Knoxville, TN 37996. Offers analytical chemistry (MS, PhD); chemical physics (PhD); environmental chemistry (MS, PhD); inorganic chemistry (MS, PhD); organic chemistry (MS, PhD); physical chemistry (MS, PhD); polymer chemistry (MS, PhD); theoretical chemistry (PhD). Part-time programs available. Terminal master's awarded for partial completion of doctoral program. *Degree requirements:* For master's, thesis; for doctorate, thesis/dissertation. *Entrance requirements:* For master's and doctorate, GRE General Test, minimum GPA of 2.7. Additional exam requirements/recommendations for international students: Required—TOEFL. Electronic applications accepted. *Expenses:* Tuition, state resident: full-time $9000; part-time $501 per credit hour. Tuition, nonresident: full-time $27,188; part-time $1512 per credit hour. *Required fees:* $1280; $62 per credit hour. Tuition and fees vary according to program.

University of Utah, Graduate School, College of Science, Department of Chemistry, Salt Lake City, UT 84112-0850. Offers chemical physics (PhD); chemistry (M Phil, MA, MS, PhD); science teacher education (MS). Part-time programs available. Postbaccalaureate distance learning degree programs offered. *Faculty:* 32 full-time (7 women), 1 part-time/adjunct (0 women). *Students:* 146 full-time (43 women), 29 part-time (14 women); includes 4 minority (1 Black or African American, non-Hispanic/Latino; 1 Asian, non-Hispanic/Latino; 1 Hispanic/Latino; 1 Two or more races, non-Hispanic/Latino), 51 international. Average age 28. 290 applicants, 32% accepted, 38 enrolled. In 2012, 14 master's, 22 doctorates awarded. Terminal master's awarded for partial completion of doctoral program. *Degree requirements:* For master's, thesis optional, 20 hours of course work, 10 hours of research; for doctorate, thesis/dissertation, 18 hours of course work, 14 hours of research. *Entrance requirements:* For master's and doctorate, GRE General Test, minimum GPA of 3.0. Additional exam requirements/recommendations for international students: Required—TOEFL (minimum score 620 paper-based; 105 iBT). *Application deadline:* For fall admission, 4/1 for domestic students, 2/1 for international students; for spring admission, 11/1 for domestic and international students. Application fee: $55 ($65 for international students). Electronic applications accepted. Application fee is waived when completed online. *Financial support:* In 2012–13, 1 fellowship with tuition reimbursement (averaging $22,000 per year), 119 research assistantships with tuition reimbursements (averaging $22,500 per year), 55 teaching assistantships with tuition reimbursements (averaging $22,000 per year) were awarded; scholarships/grants and tuition waivers (full) also available. Financial award application deadline: 4/1; financial award applicants required to submit FAFSA. *Faculty research:* Biological, theoretical, inorganic, organic, and physical-analytical chemistry. *Total annual research expenditures:* $13.3 million. *Unit head:* Dr. Henry S. White, Chair, 801-585-6256, Fax: 801-581-8433, E-mail: chair@chemistry.utah.edu. *Application contact:* Jo Hoovey, Graduate Coordinator, 801-581-4393, Fax: 801-581-5408, E-mail: jhoovey@chem.utah.edu. Website: http://www.chem.utah.edu/.

University of Utah, Graduate School, College of Science, Department of Physics and Astronomy, Salt Lake City, UT 84112. Offers chemical physics (PhD); medical physics (MS, PhD); physics (MA, MS, PhD); physics teaching (PhD). Part-time programs available. *Faculty:* 33 full-time (3 women), 3 part-time/adjunct (0 women). *Students:* 74 full-time (20 women), 17 part-time (4 women); includes 5 minority (4 Asian, non-Hispanic/Latino; 1 Hispanic/Latino), 45 international. Average age 29. 188 applicants, 14% accepted, 14 enrolled. In 2012, 9 master's, 11 doctorates awarded. Terminal master's awarded for partial completion of doctoral program. *Degree requirements:* For master's, comprehensive exam (for some programs), thesis or alternative, teaching experience, departmental exam; for doctorate, comprehensive exam, thesis/dissertation, departmental qualifying exam. *Entrance requirements:* For master's and doctorate, GRE General Test, GRE Subject Test, minimum GPA of 3.0. Additional exam requirements/recommendations for international students: Required—TOEFL (minimum score 500 paper-based; 69 iBT). *Application deadline:* For fall admission, 4/1 priority date for domestic students, 4/1 for international students. Applications are processed on a rolling basis. Application fee: $55 ($65 for international students). Electronic applications accepted. *Financial support:* In 2012–13, 41 research assistantships with full tuition reimbursements (averaging $23,500 per year), 31 teaching assistantships with full tuition reimbursements (averaging $20,641 per

year) were awarded; Federal Work-Study, institutionally sponsored loans, and scholarships/grants also available. Financial award application deadline: 2/15; financial award applicants required to submit FAFSA. *Faculty research:* High-energy, cosmic-ray, astrophysics, medical physics, condensed matter, relativity applied physics, biophysics, astronomy. *Total annual research expenditures:* $6.8 million. *Unit head:* Dr. David Kieda, Chair, 801-581-6901, Fax: 801-581-4801, E-mail: kieda@physics.utah.edu. *Application contact:* Jackie Hadley, Graduate Secretary, 801-581-6861, Fax: 801-581-4801, E-mail: jackie@physics.utah.edu. Website: http://www.physics.utah.edu/.

Virginia Commonwealth University, Graduate School, College of Humanities and Sciences, Department of Chemistry, Richmond, VA 23284-9005. Offers analytical chemistry (MS, PhD); chemical physics (PhD); inorganic chemistry (MS, PhD); organic chemistry (MS, PhD); physical chemistry (MS, PhD). Part-time programs available. Terminal master's awarded for partial completion of doctoral program. *Degree requirements:* For master's, thesis; for doctorate, thesis/dissertation, comprehensive cumulative exams, research proposal. *Entrance requirements:* For master's, GRE General Test, 30 undergraduate credits in chemistry; for doctorate, GRE General Test. Additional exam requirements/recommendations for international students: Required—TOEFL (minimum score 600 paper-based; 100 iBT) or IELTS (minimum score 6.5). Electronic applications accepted. *Faculty research:* Physical, organic, inorganic, analytical, and polymer chemistry; chemical physics.

Wesleyan University, Graduate Studies, Department of Chemistry, Middletown, CT 06459-0180. Offers biochemistry (PhD); chemical physics (PhD); inorganic chemistry (PhD); organic chemistry (PhD); physical chemistry (PhD); theoretical chemistry (PhD). Terminal master's awarded for partial completion of doctoral program. *Degree requirements:* For doctorate, thesis/dissertation, proposal. *Entrance requirements:* For doctorate, GRE General Test, 3 recommendations. Additional exam requirements/recommendations for international students: Required—TOEFL. *Application deadline:* Applications are processed on a rolling basis. Application fee: $0. Electronic applications accepted. *Financial support:* Research assistantships with full tuition reimbursements, teaching assistantships with full tuition reimbursements, and institutionally sponsored loans available. Financial award application deadline: 4/15; financial award applicants required to submit FAFSA. *Unit head:* Prof. Rex F. Pratt, Chair, 860-685-2727. *Application contact:* Sarah Atwell, Administrative Assistant IV/Graduate Program Coordinator, 860-685-2573, Fax: 860-685-2211, E-mail: satwell@wesleyan.edu. Website: http://www.wesleyan.edu/chem/.

West Virginia University, Eberly College of Arts and Sciences, Department of Physics, Morgantown, WV 26506. Offers applied physics (MS, PhD); astrophysics (MS, PhD); chemical physics (MS, PhD); condensed matter physics (MS, PhD); elementary particle physics (MS, PhD); materials physics (MS, PhD); plasma physics (MS, PhD); solid state physics (MS, PhD); statistical physics (MS, PhD); theoretical physics (MS, PhD). Terminal master's awarded for partial completion of doctoral program. *Degree requirements:* For master's, thesis or alternative, qualifying exam; for doctorate, thesis/dissertation, qualifying exam. *Entrance requirements:* For master's and doctorate, GRE General Test, minimum GPA of 3.0. Additional exam requirements/recommendations for international students: Required—TOEFL. *Faculty research:* Experimental and theoretical condensed-matter, plasma, high-energy theory, nonlinear dynamics, space physics.

Condensed Matter Physics

Cleveland State University, College of Graduate Studies, College of Sciences and Health Professions, Department of Physics, Cleveland, OH 44115. Offers applied optics (MS); condensed matter physics (MS); medical physics (MS); optics and materials (MS); optics and medical imaging (MS). Part-time and evening/weekend programs available. *Faculty:* 4 full-time (0 women), 1 part-time/adjunct (0 women). *Students:* 2 full-time (1 woman), 18 part-time (3 women); includes 1 minority (Asian, non-Hispanic/Latino), 3 international. Average age 31. 30 applicants, 87% accepted, 7 enrolled. In 2012, 3 master's awarded. *Entrance requirements:* For master's, undergraduate degree in engineering, physics, chemistry or mathematics. Additional exam requirements/recommendations for international students: Required—TOEFL (minimum score 525 paper-based). *Application deadline:* For fall admission, 7/15 priority date for domestic students, 7/15 for international students. Applications are processed on a rolling basis. Application fee: $30. Electronic applications accepted. *Expenses:* Tuition, state resident: full-time $8172; part-time $510.75 per credit hour. Tuition, nonresident: full-time $15,372; part-time $960.75 per credit hour. *Required fees:* $25 per semester. Tuition and fees vary according to course load and program. *Financial support:* In 2012–13, 1 research assistantship with full and partial tuition reimbursement (averaging $5,666 per year) was awarded; fellowships with tuition reimbursements, teaching assistantships, and tuition waivers (full) also available. *Faculty research:* Statistical physics, experimental solid-state physics, theoretical optics, experimental biological physics (macromolecular crystallography), experimental optics. *Total annual research expenditures:* $350,000. *Unit head:* Dr. Miron Kaufman, Chairperson, 216-687-2436, Fax: 216-523-7268, E-mail: m.kaufman@csuohio.edu. *Application contact:* Dr. James A. Lock, Director, 216-

687-2420, Fax: 216-523-7268, E-mail: j.lock@csuohio.edu. Website: http://www.csuohio.edu/sciences/dept/physics/index.html.

Iowa State University of Science and Technology, Department of Physics and Astronomy, Ames, IA 50011. Offers applied physics (MS, PhD); astrophysics (MS, PhD); condensed matter physics (MS, PhD); high energy physics (MS, PhD); nuclear physics (MS, PhD); physics (MS, PhD). *Degree requirements:* For master's, thesis (for some programs); for doctorate, thesis/dissertation. *Entrance requirements:* For master's and doctorate, GRE General Test, GRE Subject Test (physics). Additional exam requirements/recommendations for international students: Required—TOEFL (minimum score 550 paper-based; 79 iBT), IELTS (minimum score 6.5). *Application deadline:* For fall admission, 2/15 priority date for domestic students, 2/15 for international students; for spring admission, 10/15 for domestic and international students. Applications are processed on a rolling basis. Application fee: $60 ($90 for international students). Electronic applications accepted. *Financial support:* Application deadline: 2/15. *Faculty research:* Condensed-matter physics, including superconductivity and new materials; high-energy and nuclear physics; astronomy and astrophysics; atmospheric and environmental physics. *Total annual research expenditures:* $8.8 million. *Application contact:* Lori Hockett, Application Contact, 515-294-5870, Fax: 515-294-6027, E-mail: physastro@iastate.edu. Website: http://www.physastro.iastate.edu.

Iowa State University of Science and Technology, Program in Condensed Matter Physics, Ames, IA 50011. Offers MS, PhD. *Entrance requirements:* For master's and doctorate, GRE. Additional exam requirements/recommendations

Peterson's Graduate Programs in the Physical Sciences, Mathematics, Agricultural Sciences, the Environment & Natural Resources 2014

www.petersonsbooks.com **219**

for international students: Required—TOEFL (minimum score 550 paper-based; 79 iBT), IELTS (minimum score 6.5). *Application deadline:* For fall admission, 2/15 for domestic and international students; for spring admission, 10/15 for domestic and international students. Application fee: $60 ($90 for international students). Electronic applications accepted. *Application contact:* Lori Hockett, Information Contact, 515-294-5870, Fax: 515-294-6027, E-mail: physastro@iastate.edu. Website: http://www.physastro.iastate.edu.

Memorial University of Newfoundland, School of Graduate Studies, Department of Physics and Physical Oceanography, St. John's, NL A1C 5S7, Canada. Offers atomic and molecular physics (M Sc, PhD); condensed matter physics (M Sc, PhD); physical oceanography (M Sc, PhD); physics (M Sc). Part-time programs available. *Degree requirements:* For master's, thesis, seminar presentation on thesis topic; for doctorate, comprehensive exam, thesis/dissertation, oral defense of thesis. *Entrance requirements:* For master's, honors B Sc or equivalent; for doctorate, M Sc or equivalent. Electronic applications accepted. *Faculty research:* Experiment and theory in atomic and molecular physics, condensed matter physics, physical oceanography, theoretical geophysics and applied nuclear physics.

Rutgers, The State University of New Jersey, New Brunswick, Graduate School-New Brunswick, Department of Physics and Astronomy, Piscataway, NJ 08854-8097. Offers astronomy (MS, PhD); biophysics (PhD); condensed matter physics (MS, PhD); elementary particle physics (MS, PhD); intermediate energy nuclear physics (MS); nuclear physics (MS, PhD); physics (MST); surface science (PhD); theoretical physics (MS, PhD). Part-time programs available. Terminal master's awarded for partial completion of doctoral program. *Degree requirements:* For master's, comprehensive exam, thesis or alternative; for doctorate, comprehensive exam, thesis/dissertation. *Entrance requirements:* For master's and doctorate, GRE General Test, GRE Subject Test. Additional exam requirements/recommendations for international students: Required—TOEFL (minimum score 560 paper-based). Electronic applications accepted. *Faculty research:* Astronomy, high energy, condensed matter, surface, nuclear physics.

University of Alberta, Faculty of Graduate Studies and Research, Department of Physics, Edmonton, AB T6G 2E1, Canada. Offers astrophysics (M Sc, PhD); condensed matter (M Sc, PhD); geophysics (M Sc, PhD); medical physics (M Sc, PhD); subatomic physics (M Sc, PhD). *Degree requirements:* For master's, thesis; for doctorate, thesis/dissertation. *Entrance requirements:* For master's and doctorate, minimum GPA of 7.0 on a 9.0 scale. Additional exam requirements/recommendations for international students: Required—TOEFL. *Faculty research:* Cosmology, astroparticle physics, high-intermediate energy, magnetism, superconductivity.

The University of Manchester, School of Physics and Astronomy, Manchester, United Kingdom. Offers astronomy and astrophysics (M Sc, PhD); biological physics (M Sc, PhD); condensed matter physics (M Sc, PhD); nonlinear and liquid crystals physics (M Sc, PhD); nuclear physics (M Sc, PhD); particle physics (M Sc, PhD); photon physics (M Sc, PhD); physics (M Sc, PhD); theoretical physics (M Sc, PhD).

University of Victoria, Faculty of Graduate Studies, Faculty of Science, Department of Physics and Astronomy, Victoria, BC V8W 2Y2, Canada. Offers astronomy and astrophysics (M Sc, PhD); condensed matter physics (M Sc, PhD); experimental particle physics (M Sc, PhD); medical physics (M Sc, PhD); ocean physics (M Sc, PhD); theoretical physics (M Sc, PhD). *Degree requirements:* For master's, thesis; for doctorate, comprehensive exam, thesis/dissertation, candidacy exam. *Entrance requirements:* For master's and doctorate, GRE. Additional exam requirements/recommendations for international students: Required—TOEFL (minimum score 575 paper-based), IELTS (minimum score 7). Electronic applications accepted. *Faculty research:* Old stellar populations; observational cosmology and large scale structure; cp violation; atlas.

West Virginia University, Eberly College of Arts and Sciences, Department of Physics, Morgantown, WV 26506. Offers applied physics (MS, PhD); astrophysics (MS, PhD); chemical physics (MS, PhD); condensed matter physics (MS, PhD); elementary particle physics (MS, PhD); materials physics (MS, PhD); plasma physics (MS, PhD); solid state physics (MS, PhD); statistical physics (MS, PhD); theoretical physics (MS, PhD). Terminal master's awarded for partial completion of doctoral program. *Degree requirements:* For master's, thesis or alternative, qualifying exam; for doctorate, thesis/dissertation, qualifying exam. *Entrance requirements:* For master's and doctorate, GRE General Test, minimum GPA of 3.0. Additional exam requirements/recommendations for international students: Required—TOEFL. *Faculty research:* Experimental and theoretical condensed-matter, plasma, high-energy theory, nonlinear dynamics, space physics.

Mathematical Physics

Indiana University Bloomington, University Graduate School, College of Arts and Sciences, Department of Mathematics, Bloomington, IN 47405-7000. Offers applied mathematics (MA); mathematical physics (PhD); mathematics education (MAT); pure mathematics (MA, PhD). *Faculty:* 49 full-time (3 women). *Students:* 118 full-time (21 women), 1 part-time (0 women); includes 12 minority (2 Black or African American, non-Hispanic/Latino; 9 Asian, non-Hispanic/Latino; 1 Hispanic/Latino), 72 international. Average age 27. 218 applicants, 25% accepted, 28 enrolled. In 2012, 15 master's, 12 doctorates awarded. Terminal master's awarded for partial completion of doctoral program. *Degree requirements:* For doctorate, one foreign language, thesis/dissertation. *Entrance requirements:* For master's and doctorate, GRE General Test, GRE Subject Test. Additional exam requirements/recommendations for international students: Required—TOEFL. *Application deadline:* For fall admission, 1/15 priority date for domestic students, 1/15 for international students. Applications are processed on a rolling basis. Application fee: $55 ($65 for international students). Electronic applications accepted. *Financial support:* In 2012–13, 2 students received support, including 9 fellowships with full tuition reimbursements available (averaging $21,450 per year), 11 research assistantships with full tuition reimbursements available (averaging $16,045 per year), 96 teaching assistantships with full tuition reimbursements available (averaging $15,870 per year); scholarships/grants, health care benefits, and unspecified assistantships also available. Financial award application deadline: 1/15. *Faculty research:* Topology, geometry, algebra, applied, analysis. *Unit head:* Kevin Zumbrun, Chair, 812-855-2200. *Application contact:* Kate Forrest, Graduate Secretary, 812-855-2645, Fax: 812-855-0046, E-mail: gradmath@indiana.edu. Website: http://www.math.indiana.edu/.

New Mexico Institute of Mining and Technology, Graduate Studies, Department of Physics, Socorro, NM 87801. Offers astrophysics (PhD); atmospheric physics (PhD); instrumentation (MS); mathematical physics (PhD); physics (MS). *Faculty:* 12 full-time (3 women), 1 part-time/adjunct (0 women). *Students:* 30 full-time (12 women), 2 part-time (1 woman); includes 1 minority (Asian, non-Hispanic/Latino), 6 international. Average age 29. 15 applicants, 47% accepted, 4 enrolled. In 2012, 1 master's, 2 doctorates awarded. *Degree requirements:* For master's, thesis optional; for doctorate, thesis/dissertation. *Entrance requirements:* For master's, GRE General Test; for doctorate, GRE General Test, GRE Subject Test. Additional exam requirements/recommendations for international students: Required—TOEFL (minimum score 540 paper-based). *Application deadline:* For fall admission, 3/1 priority date for domestic students; for spring admission, 6/1 for domestic students. Applications are processed on a rolling basis. Application fee: $16 ($30 for international students). *Expenses:* Tuition, state resident: full-time $5043; part-time $280 per credit hour. Tuition, nonresident: full-time $16,682; part-time $927 per credit hour. *Required fees:* $648; $18 per credit hour. $108 per semester. Part-time tuition and fees vary according to course load. *Financial support:* In 2012–13, 19 research assistantships (averaging $18,770 per year), 13 teaching assistantships with full and partial tuition reimbursements (averaging $14,078 per year) were awarded; fellowships, Federal Work-Study, institutionally sponsored loans, and unspecified assistantships also available. Financial award application deadline: 3/1; financial award applicants required to submit CSS PROFILE or FAFSA. *Faculty research:* Cloud physics, stellar and extragalactic processes. *Total annual research expenditures:* $3 million. *Unit head:* Dr. Kenneth Eack, Chairman, 575-835-5328, Fax: 575-835-5707, E-mail: dwestpfa@nmt.edu. *Application contact:* Dr. Lorie Liebrock, Dean of Graduate Studies, 575-835-5513, Fax: 575-835-5476, E-mail: graduate@nmt.edu. Website: http://www.physics.nmt.edu/.

University of Alberta, Faculty of Graduate Studies and Research, Department of Mathematical and Statistical Sciences, Edmonton, AB T6G 2E1, Canada. Offers applied mathematics (M Sc, PhD); biostatistics (M Sc); mathematical finance (M Sc, PhD); mathematical physics (M Sc, PhD); mathematics (M Sc, PhD); statistics (M Sc, PhD, Postgraduate Diploma). Part-time programs available. Terminal master's awarded for partial completion of doctoral program. *Degree requirements:* For master's, thesis (for some programs); for doctorate, comprehensive exam, thesis/dissertation. *Entrance requirements:* Additional exam requirements/recommendations for international students: Required—TOEFL (minimum score 580 paper-based). Electronic applications accepted. *Faculty research:* Classical and functional analysis, algebra, differential equations, geometry.

University of Colorado Boulder, Graduate School, College of Arts and Sciences, Department of Physics, Boulder, CO 80309. Offers chemical physics (PhD); geophysics (PhD); liquid crystal science and technology (PhD); mathematical physics (PhD); medical physics (PhD); optical sciences and engineering (PhD); physics (MS, PhD). *Faculty:* 50 full-time (7 women). *Students:* 158 full-time (32 women), 64 part-time (9 women); includes 11 minority (6 Asian, non-Hispanic/Latino; 5 Hispanic/Latino), 74 international. Average age 27. 600 applicants, 21% accepted, 32 enrolled. Terminal master's awarded for partial completion of doctoral program. *Degree requirements:* For master's, comprehensive exam, thesis or alternative; for doctorate, comprehensive exam, thesis/dissertation. *Entrance requirements:* For master's and doctorate, GRE General Test, GRE Subject Test, minimum undergraduate GPA of 3.0. Additional exam requirements/recommendations for international students: Required—TOEFL. *Application deadline:* For fall admission, 12/15 priority date for domestic

220 www.petersonsbooks.com

Peterson's Graduate Programs in the Physical Sciences, Mathematics, Agricultural Sciences, the Environment & Natural Resources 2014

students, 12/15 for international students. Applications are processed on a rolling basis. Application fee: $50 ($60 for international students). Electronic applications accepted. *Financial support:* In 2012–13, 38 fellowships (averaging $14,995 per year), 156 research assistantships with full and partial tuition reimbursements (averaging $25,043 per year), 48 teaching assistantships with full and partial tuition reimbursements (averaging $18,902 per year) were awarded; institutionally sponsored loans, scholarships/grants, health care benefits, and unspecified assistantships also available. Financial award application deadline: 1/15; financial award applicants required to submit FAFSA. *Faculty research:* Atomic and molecular physics, nuclear physics, condensed matter, elementary particle physics, laser or optical physics, plasma physics, geophysics, astrophysics and chemical physics. *Total annual research expenditures:* $23.7 million. *Application contact:* E-mail: physics@colorado.edu. Website: http://physics.colorado.edu/.

Optical Sciences

Air Force Institute of Technology, Graduate School of Engineering and Management, Department of Electrical and Computer Engineering, Dayton, OH 45433-7765. Offers computer engineering (MS, PhD); computer systems/science (MS); electrical engineering (MS, PhD); electro-optics (MS, PhD). *Accreditation:* ABET (one or more programs are accredited). Part-time programs available. *Degree requirements:* For master's, thesis; for doctorate, thesis/dissertation. *Entrance requirements:* For master's and doctorate, GRE General Test, minimum GPA of 3.0, U.S. citizenship. *Faculty research:* Remote sensing, information survivability, microelectronics, computer networks, artificial intelligence.

Air Force Institute of Technology, Graduate School of Engineering and Management, Department of Engineering Physics, Dayton, OH 45433-7765. Offers applied physics (MS, PhD); electro-optics (MS, PhD); materials science (PhD); nuclear engineering (MS, PhD); space physics (MS). Part-time programs available. *Degree requirements:* For master's, thesis; for doctorate, thesis/dissertation. *Entrance requirements:* For master's and doctorate, GRE General Test, minimum GPA of 3.0, U.S. citizenship. *Faculty research:* High-energy lasers, space physics, nuclear weapon effects, semiconductor physics.

Alabama Agricultural and Mechanical University, School of Graduate Studies, School of Arts and Sciences, Department of Physics, Huntsville, AL 35811. Offers physics (MS, PhD), including applied physics (PhD); materials science (PhD); optics/lasers (PhD). Part-time and evening/weekend programs available. *Degree requirements:* For doctorate, thesis/dissertation. *Entrance requirements:* For master's and doctorate, GRE General Test. Additional exam requirements/recommendations for international students: Required—TOEFL (minimum score 500 paper-based; 61 iBT). Electronic applications accepted.

Cleveland State University, College of Graduate Studies, College of Sciences and Health Professions, Department of Physics, Cleveland, OH 44115. Offers applied optics (MS); condensed matter physics (MS); medical physics (MS); optics and materials (MS); optics and medical imaging (MS). Part-time and evening/weekend programs available. *Faculty:* 4 full-time (0 women), 1 part-time/adjunct (0 women). *Students:* 2 full-time (1 woman), 18 part-time (3 women); includes 1 minority (Asian, non-Hispanic/Latino), 3 international. Average age 31. 30 applicants, 87% accepted, 7 enrolled. In 2012, 3 master's awarded. *Entrance requirements:* For master's, undergraduate degree in engineering, physics, chemistry or mathematics. Additional exam requirements/recommendations for international students: Required—TOEFL (minimum score 525 paper-based). *Application deadline:* For fall admission, 7/15 priority date for domestic students, 7/15 for international students. Applications are processed on a rolling basis. Application fee: $30. Electronic applications accepted. *Expenses:* Tuition, state resident: full-time $8172; part-time $510.75 per credit hour. Tuition, nonresident: full-time $15,372; part-time $960.75 per credit hour. *Required fees:* $25 per semester. Tuition and fees vary according to course load and program. *Financial support:* In 2012–13, 1 research assistantship with full and partial tuition reimbursement (averaging $5,666 per year) was awarded; fellowships with tuition reimbursements, teaching assistantships, and tuition waivers (full) also available. *Faculty research:* Statistical physics, experimental solid-state physics, theoretical optics, experimental biological physics (macromolecular crystallography), experimental optics. *Total annual research expenditures:* $350,000. *Unit head:* Dr. Miron Kaufman, Chairperson, 216-687-2436, Fax: 216-523-7268, E-mail: m.kaufman@csuohio.edu. *Application contact:* Dr. James A. Lock, Director, 216-687-2420, Fax: 216-523-7268, E-mail: j.lock@csuohio.edu. Website: http://www.csuohio.edu/sciences/dept/physics/index.html.

The College of William and Mary, Faculty of Arts and Sciences, Department of Applied Science, Williamsburg, VA 23187-8795. Offers accelerator science (PhD); applied mathematics (PhD); applied mechanics (PhD); applied robotics (PhD); applied science (MS); atmospheric and environmental science (PhD); computational neuroscience (PhD); interface, thin film and surface science (PhD); lasers and optics (PhD); magnetic resonance (PhD); materials science and engineering (PhD); mathematical and computational biology (PhD); medical imaging (PhD); nanotechnology (PhD); neuroscience (PhD); non-destructive evaluation (PhD); polymer chemistry (PhD); remote sensing (PhD). *Faculty:* 13 full-time (2 women), 1 part-time/adjunct (0 women). *Students:* 36 full-time (11 women); includes 2 minority (1 Black or African American, non-Hispanic/Latino; 1 Asian, non-Hispanic/Latino), 22 international. Average age 26. 40 applicants, 45% accepted, 8 enrolled. In 2012, 3 master's, 2 doctorates awarded. *Median time to degree:* Of those who began their doctoral program in fall 2004, 95% received their degree in 8 years or less. *Degree requirements:* For master's, comprehensive exam, thesis; for doctorate, comprehensive exam, thesis/dissertation, 4 core courses. *Entrance requirements:* For master's and doctorate, GRE General Test, GRE Subject Test. Additional exam requirements/recommendations for international students: Required—TOEFL, TWE. *Application deadline:* For fall admission, 2/3 priority date for domestic students, 2/3 for international students; for spring admission, 10/15 priority date for domestic students, 10/14 for international students. Applications are processed on a rolling basis. Application fee: $45. Electronic applications accepted. *Expenses:* Tuition, state resident: full-time $6779; part-time $385 per credit hour. Tuition, nonresident: full-time $20,608; part-time $1000 per credit hour. *Required fees:* $4625. *Financial support:* Fellowships, research assistantships, teaching assistantships, Federal Work-Study, health care benefits, tuition waivers (full), and unspecified assistantships available. Financial award application deadline: 4/15; financial award applicants required to submit FAFSA. *Faculty research:* Computational biology, non-destructive evaluation, neurophysiology, lasers and optics. *Unit head:* Dr. Christopher Del Negro, Chair, 757-221-7808, Fax: 757-221-2050, E-mail: cadeln@wm.edu. *Application contact:* Rosario Fox, Graduate Program Coordinator, 757-221-2563, Fax: 757-221-2050, E-mail: rxfoxx@wm.edu. Website: http://www.wm.edu/as/appliedscience.

Delaware State University, Graduate Programs, Department of Physics, Dover, DE 19901-2277. Offers applied optics (MS); optics (PhD); physics (MS); physics teaching (MS). Part-time and evening/weekend programs available. *Entrance requirements:* For master's, minimum GPA of 3.0 in major, 2.75 overall. Additional exam requirements/recommendations for international students: Required—TOEFL. Electronic applications accepted. *Faculty research:* Thermal properties of solids, nuclear physics, radiation damage in solids.

Duke University, Graduate School, Pratt School of Engineering, Master of Engineering Program, Durham, NC 27708-0271. Offers biomedical engineering (M Eng); civil engineering (M Eng); electrical and computer engineering (M Eng); environmental engineering (M Eng); materials science and engineering (M Eng); mechanical engineering (M Eng); photonics and optical sciences (M Eng). Part-time programs available. *Entrance requirements:* For master's, GRE General Test, resume, 3 letters of recommendation, statement of purpose. Additional exam requirements/recommendations for international students: Required—TOEFL.

École Polytechnique de Montréal, Graduate Programs, Department of Engineering Physics, Montréal, QC H3C 3A7, Canada. Offers optical engineering (M Eng, M Sc A, PhD); solid-state physics and engineering (M Eng, M Sc A, PhD). Part-time programs available. *Degree requirements:* For master's, one foreign language, thesis; for doctorate, one foreign language, thesis/dissertation. *Entrance requirements:* For master's, minimum GPA of 2.75; for doctorate, minimum GPA of 3.0. *Faculty research:* Optics, thin-film physics, laser spectroscopy, plasmas, photonic devices.

Norfolk State University, School of Graduate Studies, School of Science and Technology, Program in Optical Engineering, Norfolk, VA 23504. Offers MS.

North Carolina Agricultural and Technical State University, School of Graduate Studies, College of Engineering, Department of Electrical and Computer Engineering, Greensboro, NC 27411. Offers electrical engineering (MSEE, PhD), including communications and signal processing, computer engineering, electronic and optical materials and devices, power systems and control. Part-time programs available. *Degree requirements:* For master's, project, thesis defense; for doctorate, thesis/dissertation. *Entrance requirements:* For master's, GRE General Test, GRE Subject Test, minimum GPA of 2.8; for doctorate, GRE General Test, minimum GPA of 3.0. *Faculty research:* Semiconductor compounds, VLSI design, image processing, optical systems and devices, fault-tolerant computing.

The Ohio State University, College of Optometry, Columbus, OH 43210. Offers optometry (OD); vision science (MS, PhD); OD/MS. Application fee is $40 (domestic), $50 (international) for all programs, except OD ($60/$70). *Accreditation:* AOA (one or more programs are accredited). *Faculty:* 21. *Students:* 258 full-time (144 women), 3 part-time (1 woman); includes 34 minority (2 Black or African American, non-Hispanic/Latino; 1 American Indian or Alaska Native, non-Hispanic/Latino; 24 Asian, non-Hispanic/Latino; 6 Hispanic/Latino; 1 Two or more races, non-Hispanic/Latino), 1 international. Average age 26. In 2012, 8 master's, 63 doctorates awarded. *Degree requirements:* For master's, thesis; for doctorate, thesis/dissertation. *Entrance requirements:* For master's, GRE; for doctorate, GRE (for PhD); OAT (for OD). Additional exam requirements/recommendations for international students: Required—TOEFL, TOEFL (minimum score 550 paper-

Peterson's Graduate Programs in the Physical Sciences, Mathematics, Agricultural Sciences, the Environment & Natural Resources 2014

www.petersonsbooks.com   **221**

based, 79 iBT), Michigan English Language Assessment Battery (minimum score 82), IELTS (minimum score 7) for MS and PhD; TOEFL (minimum score 577 paper-based, 90 iBT), Michigan English Language Assessment Battery (minimum score 84), IELTS (minimum score 7.5) for OD; Recommended—IELTS. *Application deadline:* For spring admission, 12/1 for domestic students, 11/1 for international students. Applications are processed on a rolling basis. Electronic applications accepted. *Expenses:* Contact institution. *Financial support:* Research assistantships with full tuition reimbursements, teaching assistantships with full tuition reimbursements, Federal Work-Study, institutionally sponsored loans, and scholarships/grants available. Financial award application deadline: 2/1; financial award applicants required to submit FAFSA. *Unit head:* Dr. Melvin Shipp, Dean, 614-292-3246, E-mail: shipp.25@osu.edu. *Application contact:* Graduate Admissions, 614-292-9444, Fax: 614-292-3895, E-mail: domestic.grad@osu.edu. Website: http://www.optometry.osu.edu/.

Rochester Institute of Technology, Graduate Enrollment Services, College of Science, Chester F. Carlson Center for Imaging Science, Rochester, NY 14623-5603. Offers MS, PhD. Part-time programs available. Postbaccalaureate distance learning degree programs offered (no on-campus study). *Students:* 37 full-time (9 women), 79 part-time (27 women); includes 7 minority (1 Black or African American, non-Hispanic/Latino; 1 American Indian or Alaska Native, non-Hispanic/Latino; 1 Hispanic/Latino; 1 Native Hawaiian or other Pacific Islander, non-Hispanic/Latino; 3 Two or more races, non-Hispanic/Latino), 54 international. Average age 29. 92 applicants, 48% accepted, 27 enrolled. In 2012, 8 master's, 8 doctorates awarded. Terminal master's awarded for partial completion of doctoral program. *Degree requirements:* For master's, thesis; for doctorate, thesis/dissertation. *Entrance requirements:* For master's, GRE, minimum GPA of 3.0. Additional exam requirements/recommendations for international students: Required—TOEFL (minimum score 600 paper-based; 100 iBT) or IELTS (minimum score 6.5). *Application deadline:* For fall admission, 1/15 priority date for domestic students, 1/15 for international students. Applications are processed on a rolling basis. Application fee: $60. Electronic applications accepted. *Expenses: Tuition:* Full-time $35,976; part-time $999 per credit hour. *Required fees:* $240; $80 per quarter. *Financial support:* Research assistantships, teaching assistantships, career-related internships or fieldwork, scholarships/grants, unspecified assistantships, and merit-based fellowships covering full tuition, stipends available. Support available to part-time students. Financial award applicants required to submit FAFSA. *Faculty research:* Biomedical imaging, nano-imaging, remote sensing, sensor development, vision and visual perception, astronomy and space weather alert technologies, computational photography, graphical display, emergency response, environmental forecasting, cultural heritage and the application of imaging science to green energy initiatives. *Unit head:* Dr. Stefi Baum, Director, 585-475-6220, Fax: 585-475-5988, E-mail: baum@cis.rit.edu. *Application contact:* Diane Ellison, Assistant Vice President, Graduate Enrollment Services, 585-475-2229, Fax: 585-475-7164, E-mail: gradinfo@rit.edu. Website: http://www.cis.rit.edu/.

Rose-Hulman Institute of Technology, Faculty of Engineering and Applied Sciences, Department of Physics and Optical Engineering, Terre Haute, IN 47803-3999. Offers optical engineering (MS). Part-time programs available. *Faculty:* 17 full-time (3 women). *Students:* 12 full-time (2 women), 2 part-time (1 woman), 8 international. Average age 24. 14 applicants, 100% accepted, 9 enrolled. In 2012, 1 master's awarded. *Degree requirements:* For master's, thesis. *Entrance requirements:* For master's, GRE, minimum GPA of 3.0. Additional exam requirements/recommendations for international students: Required—TOEFL (minimum score 580 paper-based; 92 iBT). *Application deadline:* For fall admission, 2/1 priority date for domestic students. Applications are processed on a rolling basis. Application fee: $0. *Financial support:* In 2012–13, 12 students received support. Fellowships with full and partial tuition reimbursements available, research assistantships with full and partial tuition reimbursements available, teaching assistantships, institutionally sponsored loans, scholarships/grants, and tuition waivers (full and partial) available. Financial award application deadline: 2/1. *Faculty research:* Optical design, laser systems, non-linear optics, metrology, optical microelectromechanical systems, bio-photonics. *Total annual research expenditures:* $166,944. *Unit head:* Dr. Charles Joenathan, Chairman, 812-877-8494, Fax: 812-877-8023, E-mail: charles.joenathan@rose-hulman.edu. *Application contact:* Dr. Azad Siahmakoun, Associate Dean of the Faculty, 812-877-8400, Fax: 812-877-8061, E-mail: siahmako@rose-hulman.edu. Website: http://www.rose-hulman.edu/phoe/.

The University of Alabama in Huntsville, School of Graduate Studies, College of Engineering, Department of Electrical and Computer Engineering, Huntsville, AL 35899. Offers computer engineering (MSE, PhD); electrical engineering (MSE, PhD), including optics and photonics technology (MSE), opto-electronics (MSE); information assurance (MS); optical science and engineering (PhD); optics and photonics (MSE); software engineering (MSSE). Part-time and evening/weekend programs available. *Faculty:* 25 full-time (3 women). *Students:* 56 full-time (13 women), 135 part-time (19 women); includes 20 minority (9 Black or African American, non-Hispanic/Latino; 1 American Indian or Alaska Native, non-Hispanic/Latino; 8 Asian, non-Hispanic/Latino; 2 Hispanic/Latino), 45 international. Average age 30. 131 applicants, 72% accepted, 44 enrolled. In 2012, 44 master's, 7 doctorates awarded. *Degree requirements:* For master's, comprehensive exam, thesis or alternative, oral and written exams; for doctorate, comprehensive exam, thesis/dissertation, oral and written exams. *Entrance requirements:* For master's, GRE General Test, appropriate bachelor's degree, minimum GPA of 3.0; for doctorate, GRE General Test, minimum GPA of 3.0. Additional exam requirements/recommendations for international students: Required—TOEFL (minimum score 500 paper-based; 80 iBT), IELTS (minimum score 6.5). *Application deadline:* For fall admission, 7/15 priority date for domestic students, 4/1 for international students; for spring admission, 11/30 priority date for domestic students, 9/1 for international students. Applications are processed on a rolling basis. Application fee: $40 ($50 for international students). Electronic applications accepted. *Expenses:* Tuition, state resident: full-time $8516; part-time $515 per credit hour. Tuition, nonresident: full-time $20,384; part-time $1229 per credit hour. *Required fees:* $148 per semester. One-time fee: $150. *Financial support:* In 2012–13, 30 students received support, including 9 research assistantships with full tuition reimbursements available (averaging $13,113 per year), 21 teaching assistantships with full tuition reimbursements available (averaging $11,376 per year); career-related internships or fieldwork, Federal Work-Study, institutionally sponsored loans, scholarships/grants, health care benefits, tuition waivers (full), and unspecified assistantships also available. Support available to part-time students. Financial award application deadline: 4/1; financial award applicants required to submit FAFSA. *Faculty research:* Advanced computer architecture and systems, fault tolerant computing and verification, computational electro-magnetics, nano-photonics and plasmonics, micro electro-mechanical (MEMS) systems. *Total annual research expenditures:* $18.6 million. *Unit head:* Dr. Robert Lindquist, Chair, 256-824-6316, Fax: 256-824-6803, E-mail: lindquis@ece.uah.edu. *Application contact:* Kim Gray, Graduate Studies Admissions Coordinator, 256-824-6002, Fax: 256-824-6405, E-mail: deangrad@uah.edu. Website: http://www.ece.uah.edu/.

The University of Alabama in Huntsville, School of Graduate Studies, Interdisciplinary Studies, Interdisciplinary Program in Optical Science and Engineering, Huntsville, AL 35899. Offers PhD. Part-time and evening/weekend programs available. *Faculty:* 8 full-time (0 women), 8 part-time/adjunct (0 women). *Students:* 1 (woman) full-time, 5 part-time (1 woman), 2 international. Average age 34. 12 applicants, 83% accepted, 0 enrolled. In 2012, 2 doctorates awarded. *Degree requirements:* For doctorate, comprehensive exam, thesis/dissertation, written and oral exams. *Entrance requirements:* For doctorate, GRE General Test, minimum GPA of 3.0, BS in physical science or engineering. Additional exam requirements/recommendations for international students: Required—TOEFL (minimum score 550 paper-based; 80 iBT), IELTS (minimum score 6.5). *Application deadline:* For fall admission, 7/15 priority date for domestic students, 4/1 for international students; for spring admission, 11/30 priority date for domestic students, 9/1 for international students. Applications are processed on a rolling basis. Application fee: $40 ($50 for international students). Electronic applications accepted. *Expenses:* Tuition, state resident: full-time $8516; part-time $515 per credit hour. Tuition, nonresident: full-time $20,384; part-time $1229 per credit hour. *Required fees:* $148 per semester. One-time fee: $150. *Financial support:* In 2012–13, 2 students received support, including 2 research assistantships with full tuition reimbursements available (averaging $7,124 per year); career-related internships or fieldwork, Federal Work-Study, institutionally sponsored loans, scholarships/grants, health care benefits, and unspecified assistantships also available. Support available to part-time students. Financial award application deadline: 4/1; financial award applicants required to submit FAFSA. *Faculty research:* Optoelectronics, optical communications, digital signal/image processing, computer-generated holography, semiconductor device modeling. *Total annual research expenditures:* $953,683. *Unit head:* Dr. Robert G. Lindquist, Program Director, 256-824-2882, Fax: 256-824-6618, E-mail: lindquist@ece.uah.edu. *Application contact:* Kim Gray, Graduate Studies Admissions Coordinator, 256-824-6002, Fax: 256-824-6405, E-mail: deangrad@uah.edu. Website: http://www.uah.edu/science/departments/optical-science-engineering.

The University of Arizona, College of Optical Sciences, Tucson, AZ 85721. Offers MS, PhD. Part-time programs available. *Faculty:* 26 full-time (3 women), 4 part-time/adjunct (0 women). *Students:* 188 full-time (51 women), 97 part-time (16 women); includes 53 minority (6 Black or African American, non-Hispanic/Latino; 1 American Indian or Alaska Native, non-Hispanic/Latino; 12 Asian, non-Hispanic/Latino; 15 Hispanic/Latino; 1 Native Hawaiian or other Pacific Islander, non-Hispanic/Latino; 18 Two or more races, non-Hispanic/Latino), 75 international. Average age 31. 233 applicants, 26% accepted, 46 enrolled. In 2012, 32 master's, 21 doctorates awarded. *Degree requirements:* For master's, thesis (for some programs), exam; for doctorate, thesis/dissertation, oral and written exams. *Entrance requirements:* For master's, GRE General Test, GRE Subject Test (recommended), minimum GPA of 3.0, 2 letters of recommendation, resume; for doctorate, GRE General Test, GRE Subject Test (recommended), minimum GPA of 3.0, 2 letters of recommendation, statement of purpose, resume. Additional exam requirements/recommendations for international students: Required—TOEFL. *Application deadline:* For fall admission, 1/1 for domestic students, 12/1 for international students. Applications are processed on a rolling basis. Application fee: $75. Electronic applications accepted. *Financial support:* In 2012–13, 100 research assistantships with full tuition reimbursements (averaging $23,145 per year), 29 teaching assistantships with full tuition reimbursements (averaging $17,656 per year) were awarded; fellowships and scholarships/grants also available. Financial award application deadline: 1/1. *Faculty research:* Medical optics, medical imaging, optical data storage, optical bistability, nonlinear optical effects. *Total annual research expenditures:* $31 million. *Unit head:* Dr. Thomas L. Koch, Dean, 520-621-6997, Fax: 520-621-9613, E-mail: tlkoch@email.arizona.edu. *Application contact:* Gail Varin, Coordinator, Graduate Academic Progress, 520-626-0888, E-mail: gail@optics.arizona.edu. Website: http://www.optics.arizona.edu.

University of Central Florida, College of Optics and Photonics, Orlando, FL 32816. Offers optics (MS, PhD). Part-time and evening/weekend programs available. *Faculty:* 42 full-time (6 women), 10 part-time/adjunct (3 women). *Students:* 111 full-time (17 women), 13 part-time (4 women); includes 11 minority (1 Black or African American, non-Hispanic/Latino; 5 Asian, non-Hispanic/Latino; 4 Hispanic/Latino; 1 Two or more races, non-Hispanic/Latino), 66 international. Average age 28. 229 applicants, 21% accepted, 26 enrolled. In 2012, 23 master's, 11 doctorates awarded. *Median time to degree:* Of those who began their doctoral program in fall 2004, 75% received their degree in 8 years or less. *Degree requirements:* For master's, thesis or alternative; for doctorate, thesis/dissertation, departmental qualifying exam, candidacy exam. *Entrance requirements:* For master's, GRE General Test, minimum GPA of 3.0 in last 60 hours; for doctorate, GRE General Test, minimum GPA of 3.5 in last 60 hours. Additional exam requirements/recommendations for international students: Required—TOEFL. *Application deadline:* For fall admission, 2/1 priority date for domestic students; for spring admission, 12/1 for domestic students. Application fee: $30. Electronic applications accepted. *Financial support:* In 2012–13, 70 students received support, including 19 fellowships with partial tuition reimbursements available (averaging $5,600 per year), 80 research assistantships with partial tuition reimbursements available (averaging $11,800 per year); career-related internships or fieldwork, Federal Work-Study, institutionally sponsored loans, tuition waivers (partial), and unspecified assistantships also available. Financial award application deadline: 3/1; financial award applicants required to submit FAFSA. *Unit head:* Dr. Bahaa E. Saleh, Dean and Director, 407-823-6817, E-mail: besaleh@creol.ucf.edu. *Application contact:* Barbara Rodriguez, Director, Admissions and Registration, 407-823-2766, Fax: 407-823-6442, E-mail: gradadmissions@ucf.edu. Website: http://www.creol.ucf.edu/.

University of Colorado Boulder, Graduate School, College of Arts and Sciences, Department of Physics, Boulder, CO 80309. Offers chemical physics (PhD); geophysics (PhD); liquid crystal science and technology (PhD); mathematical physics (PhD); medical physics (PhD); optical sciences and engineering (PhD); physics (MS, PhD). *Faculty:* 50 full-time (7 women). *Students:* 158 full-time (32 women), 64 part-time (9 women); includes 11 minority (6 Asian, non-Hispanic/Latino; 5 Hispanic/Latino), 74 international. Average age 27. 600 applicants, 21% accepted, 32 enrolled. Terminal master's awarded for partial completion of doctoral program. *Degree requirements:* For master's, comprehensive exam, thesis or alternative; for doctorate, comprehensive exam, thesis/dissertation. *Entrance requirements:* For master's and doctorate, GRE General Test, GRE Subject Test, minimum undergraduate GPA of 3.0. Additional exam requirements/recommendations for international students: Required—TOEFL. *Application deadline:* For fall admission, 12/15 priority date for domestic students, 12/15 for international students. Applications are processed on a rolling basis. Application fee: $50 ($60 for international students). Electronic applications accepted. *Financial support:* In 2012–13, 38 fellowships (averaging $14,995 per year), 156 research assistantships with full and partial tuition reimbursements (averaging $25,043 per year), 48 teaching assistantships with full and partial tuition reimbursements (averaging $18,902 per year) were awarded; institutionally sponsored loans, scholarships/grants, health care benefits, and unspecified assistantships also available. Financial award application deadline: 1/15; financial award applicants required to submit FAFSA. *Faculty research:* Atomic and molecular physics, nuclear physics, condensed matter, elementary particle physics, laser or optical physics, plasma physics, geophysics, astrophysics and chemical physics. *Total annual research expenditures:* $23.7 million. *Application contact:* E-mail: physics@colorado.edu. Website: http://physics.colorado.edu/.

University of Dayton, Program in Electro-Optics, Dayton, OH 45469-1300. Offers MSEO, PhD. Part-time and evening/weekend programs available. *Faculty:* 6 full-time (0 women), 8 part-time/adjunct (0 women). *Students:* 36 full-time (6 women), 11 part-time (2 women); includes 2 minority (1 Asian, non-Hispanic/Latino; 1 Hispanic/Latino), 24 international. Average age 27. 94 applicants, 43% accepted, 13 enrolled. In 2012, 11 master's, 3 doctorates awarded. *Degree requirements:* For master's, comprehensive exam (for some programs), thesis (for some programs); for doctorate, comprehensive exam, thesis/dissertation, departmental qualifying exam. *Entrance requirements:* Additional exam requirements/recommendations for international students: Required—TOEFL (minimum score 550 paper-based; 80 iBT). *Application deadline:* For fall admission, 8/1 for domestic students, 5/1 for international students; for winter admission, 11/1 for domestic students, 9/1 for international students; for spring admission, 11/1 for domestic and international students. Applications are processed on a rolling basis. Application fee: $0 ($50 for international students). Electronic applications accepted. *Expenses: Tuition:* Part-time $708 per credit hour. *Required fees:* $25 per semester. Tuition and fees vary according to course level, course load, degree level and program. *Financial support:* In 2012–13, 19 research assistantships with full tuition reimbursements (averaging $21,000 per year), 4 teaching assistantships with full tuition reimbursements (averaging $14,000 per year) were awarded; institutionally sponsored loans, health care benefits, and unspecified assistantships also available. Financial award applicants required to submit FAFSA. *Faculty research:* Spatial and spatiotemporal solitary waves and their stabilization in nonlinear negative index materials, stimulated photorefractive backscatter leading to six-wave mixing and phase conjugation in iron doped lithium niobate, modeling and characterization of PLZT adaptive microlenses, experimental investigation of self-starting operation in a F8L based on a symmetrical NOLM, negative refraction and sub-wavelength focusing in the visible range using transparent metallo-dielectric stacks. *Total annual research expenditures:* $1.8 million. *Unit head:* Dr. Partha P. Banerjee, Director, 937-229-2797, Fax: 937-229-2097, E-mail: pbanerjee1@udayton.edu. Website: http://www.udayton.edu/learn/graduate/engineering/major_electro_optics.php.

University of Massachusetts Lowell, College of Sciences, Department of Physics and Applied Physics, Program in Applied Physics, Lowell, MA 01854-2881. Offers applied mechanics (PhD); applied physics (MS, PhD), including optical sciences (MS). Terminal master's awarded for partial completion of doctoral program. *Degree requirements:* For master's, thesis; for doctorate, 2 foreign languages, thesis/dissertation. *Entrance requirements:* For master's, GRE General Test, 3 letters of reference; for doctorate, GRE General Test, transcripts, 3 letters of reference. Additional exam requirements/recommendations for international students: Required—TOEFL.

University of New Mexico, Graduate School, College of Arts and Sciences, Optical Science and Engineering Program, Albuquerque, NM 87106. Offers imaging science (MS, PhD); optical science and engineering (MS, PhD); photonics (MS, PhD). Program jointly administered by the Department of Physics and Astronomy and the Department of Electrical and Computer Engineering. Part-time programs available. *Faculty:* 34 full-time (2 women). *Students:* 24 full-time (4 women), 34 part-time (9 women); includes 3 minority (1 Asian, non-Hispanic/Latino; 2 Hispanic/Latino), 44 international. Average age 29. 51 applicants, 24% accepted, 11 enrolled. In 2012, 10 master's, 2 doctorates awarded. Terminal master's awarded for partial completion of doctoral program. *Degree requirements:* For master's, comprehensive exam (for some programs), thesis (for some programs); for doctorate, comprehensive exam, thesis/dissertation. *Entrance requirements:* For master's, GRE General Test, GRE Subject Test in physics (preferred), relevant undergraduate coursework, curriculum vitae, letters of recommendation, letter of intent/personal statement; for doctorate, GRE General Test, GRE Subject Test in physics (preferred), relevant undergraduate coursework, curriculum vitae, letters of recommendation. Additional exam requirements/recommendations for international students: Required—TOEFL (minimum score 575 paper-based; 79 iBT), IELTS (minimum score 7). *Application deadline:* For fall admission, 1/15 priority date for domestic students, 1/15 for international students; for spring admission, 8/1 priority date for domestic students, 8/1 for international students. Application fee: $50. Electronic applications accepted. *Expenses:* Tuition, state resident: full-time $3296; part-time $276.73 per credit hour. Tuition, nonresident: full-time $10,604; part-time $885.74 per credit hour. *Required fees:* $628. *Financial support:* In 2012–13, 34 students received support, including 29 research assistantships with full tuition reimbursements available (averaging $16,097 per year), 10 teaching assistantships with full tuition reimbursements available (averaging $14,400 per year); fellowships with full tuition reimbursements available, career-related internships or fieldwork, scholarships/grants, health care benefits, and unspecified assistantships also available. Support available to part-time students. Financial award application deadline: 2/1; financial award applicants required to submit FAFSA. *Faculty research:* Advanced materials, atom optics, biomedical optics, fiber optics, laser cooling, high intensity interactions, lithography, nano photonics, nonlinear optics, optical imaging, optical sensors, optoelectronics, quantum optics, spectroscopy, ultrafast phenomena. *Unit head:* Dr. Majeed Hayat, General Chair, 505-272-7095, Fax: 505-277-7801, E-mail: hayat@ece.unm.edu. *Application contact:* Doris Williams, Advisor, 505-277-7764, Fax: 505-277-7801, E-mail: dorisw@chtm.unm.edu. Website: http://www.optics.unm.edu/.

The University of North Carolina at Charlotte, The Graduate School, College of Liberal Arts and Sciences, Department of Physics and Optical Science, Charlotte, NC 28223-0001. Offers applied physics (MS); optical science and engineering (MS, PhD). *Faculty:* 20 full-time (4 women). *Students:* 46 full-time (11 women), 11 part-time (3 women); includes 3 minority (2 Black or African American, non-Hispanic/Latino; 1 Hispanic/Latino), 27 international. Average age 29. 53 applicants, 42% accepted, 14 enrolled. In 2012, 8 master's, 8 doctorates awarded. Terminal master's awarded for partial completion of doctoral program. *Degree requirements:* For master's, comprehensive exam (for some programs), thesis optional, thesis or comprehensive exam; for doctorate, thesis/dissertation. *Entrance requirements:* For master's, GRE General Test, minimum GPA of 3.0 during previous 2 years, 2.75 overall; for doctorate, GRE, minimum GPA of 3.0, letters of recommendation. Additional exam requirements/recommendations for international students: Required—TOEFL (minimum score 557 paper-based; 83 iBT). *Application deadline:* For fall admission, 7/15 for domestic students, 5/1 for international students; for spring admission, 11/15 for domestic students, 10/1 for international students. Applications are processed on a rolling basis. Application fee: $65 ($75 for international students). Electronic applications accepted. *Expenses:* Tuition, state resident: full-time $3453. Tuition, nonresident: full-time $15,982. *Required fees:* $2420. Tuition and fees vary according to course load and program. *Financial support:* In 2012–13, 38 students received support, including 7 fellowships (averaging $42,271 per year), 9 research assistantships (averaging $9,781 per year), 22 teaching assistantships (averaging $7,705 per year); career-related internships or fieldwork, institutionally sponsored loans, scholarships/grants, and unspecified assistantships also available. Support available to part-time students. Financial award application deadline: 4/1; financial award applicants required to submit FAFSA. *Faculty research:* Experimental and computational material sciences, optoelectronics, quantum structures, electronic and electromagnetic waves in anisotropic media, nanoscale smart devices, infrared (IR) transmitting optical materials, low loss IR transmitting glass optical fibers and rugged transparent ceramic spinel windows. *Total annual research expenditures:* $1.3 million. *Unit head:* Dr. Glen Boreman, Chair, 704-687-8173, Fax: 704-687-3160, E-mail: gboreman@uncc.edu. *Application contact:* Kathy B.

Optical Sciences

Giddings, Director of Graduate Admissions, 704-687-5503, Fax: 704-687-1668, E-mail: gradadm@uncc.edu. Website: http://physics.uncc.edu/graduate-programs.

University of Rochester, Hajim School of Engineering and Applied Sciences, Institute of Optics, Rochester, NY 14627. Offers MS, PhD. Terminal master's awarded for partial completion of doctoral program. *Degree requirements:* For master's, comprehensive exam; for doctorate, thesis/dissertation, preliminary and qualifying exams. *Entrance requirements:* For master's and doctorate, GRE. Additional exam requirements/recommendations for international students: Required—TOEFL. *Faculty research:* Biomedical, fiber and optical communication; image science and systems; ultrafast optics and highfield sciences.

University of Rochester, Hajim School of Engineering and Applied Sciences, Master of Science in Technical Entrepreneurship and Management Program, Rochester, NY 14627-0360. Offers biomedical engineering (MS); chemical engineering (MS); computer science (MS); electrical and computer engineering (MS); energy and the environment (MS); materials science (MS); mechanical engineering (MS); optics (MS). Program offered in collaboration with Simons School of Business. Part-time programs available. *Faculty:* 621 full-time, 21 part-time/adjunct. *Students:* 24 full-time (7 women); includes 2 minority (both Asian, non-Hispanic/Latino), 17 international. Average age 24. 170 applicants, 63% accepted, 24 enrolled. In 2012, 1 degree awarded. *Degree requirements:* For master's, comprehensive exam. *Entrance requirements:* For master's, GRE or GMAT, technical concentration of interest, 3 letters of recommendation, personal statement, official transcript, bachelor's degree (or equivalent for international students) in engineering, science, or mathematics. Additional exam requirements/recommendations for international students: Required—TOEFL or IELTS. *Application deadline:* For fall admission, 2/1 for domestic and international students. Applications are processed on a rolling basis. Application fee: $60. Electronic applications accepted. *Financial support:* In 2012–13, 23 students received support. Career-related internships or fieldwork and scholarships/grants available. Financial award application deadline: 2/1. *Faculty research:* High efficiency solar cells, macromolecular self-assembly, digital signal processing, memory hierarchy management, molecular and physical mechanisms in cell migration, optical imaging systems. *Unit head:* Duncan T. Moore, Vice Provost for Entrepreneurship, 585-275-5248, Fax: 585-473-6745, E-mail: moore@optics.rochester.edu. *Application contact:* Andrea M. Galati, Executive Director, 585-276-3407, Fax: 585-276-2357, E-mail: andrea.galati@rochester.edu. Website: http://www.rochester.edu/team.

University of Rochester, School of Nursing, Rochester, NY 14642. Offers acute care nurse practitioner (MS); adult nurse practitioner (MS); adult/geriatric nurse practitioner (MS); care of children and families/pediatric nurse practitioner (MS); care of children and families/pediatric nurse practitioner/neonatal nurse practitioner (MS); clinical nurse leader (MS); clinical research coordinator (MS); family nurse practitioner (MS); family psychiatric mental health nurse practitioner (MS); health care organization management and leadership (MS); health practice research (PhD); nursing (DNP). *Accreditation:* AACN. Part-time programs available. Postbaccalaureate distance learning degree programs offered (minimal on-campus study). Terminal master's awarded for partial completion of doctoral program. *Degree requirements:* For doctorate, thesis/dissertation. *Entrance requirements:* For master's, BS in nursing, minimum GPA of 3.0, course work in statistics; for doctorate, GRE General Test, MS in nursing, minimum GPA of 3.5. Additional exam requirements/recommendations for international students: Required—or IELTS (minimum score 6.5); Recommended—TOEFL (minimum score 560 paper-based; 88 iBT). Electronic applications accepted. *Faculty research:* Clinical research in aging, managing asthma in children, interventions to improve outcomes in critically ill children and their mothers, nurse home visitation studies, medical device evaluation, critical care clinical studies, high risk behavior and prevention, palliative care, pregnancy-related weight gain.

Washington State University, Graduate School, College of Arts and Sciences, Department of Physics and Astronomy, Pullman, WA 99164-2814. Offers physics (MS, PhD), including astrophysics (PhD), extreme matter (PhD), materials and optics (PhD). *Faculty:* 18 full-time (2 women), 2 part-time/adjunct (1 woman). *Students:* 68 full-time (16 women), 5 part-time (2 women); includes 1 minority (Hispanic/Latino), 30 international. Average age 29. 89 applicants, 45% accepted, 17 enrolled. In 2012, 9 master's, 6 doctorates awarded. Terminal master's awarded for partial completion of doctoral program. *Degree requirements:* For master's, comprehensive exam (for some programs), thesis optional, oral exam; for doctorate, comprehensive exam, thesis/dissertation, oral exam, written exam. *Entrance requirements:* For master's and doctorate, GRE General Test, GRE Subject Test (recommended), minimum GPA of 3.0 in last half of undergraduate work completed. Additional exam requirements/recommendations for international students: Required—TOEFL (minimum score 550 paper-based; 80 iBT), IELTS. *Application deadline:* For fall admission, 3/1 priority date for domestic students, 3/1 for international students; for spring admission, 11/1 for domestic and international students. Applications are processed on a rolling basis. Application fee: $75. Electronic applications accepted. *Financial support:* In 2012–13, 67 students received support, including 1 fellowship with full and partial tuition reimbursement available (averaging $18,000 per year), 15 research assistantships with full and partial tuition reimbursements available (averaging $16,169 per year), 25 teaching assistantships with full and partial tuition reimbursements available (averaging $15,075 per year); Federal Work-Study, institutionally sponsored loans, scholarships/grants, health care benefits, and unspecified assistantships also available. Financial award application deadline: 2/1; financial award applicants required to submit FAFSA. *Faculty research:* Linear and nonlinear acoustics and optics, shock wave dynamics, solid-state physics, surface physics, high-pressure and semiconductor physics. *Total annual research expenditures:* $3.1 million. *Unit head:* Matthew D. McCluskey, Chair, 509-335-5356, Fax: 509-335-7816, E-mail: mattmcc@wsu.edu. *Application contact:* Graduate School Admissions, 800-GRADWSU, Fax: 509-335-1949, E-mail: gradsch@wsu.edu. Website: http://www.physics.wsu.edu/.

Photonics

Boston University, College of Engineering, Department of Electrical and Computer Engineering, Boston, MA 02215. Offers computer engineering (M Eng, MS, PhD); electrical engineering (M Eng, MS, PhD); photonics (M Eng, MS). Part-time programs available. *Faculty:* 40 full-time (3 women), 5 part-time/adjunct (0 women). *Students:* 239 full-time (57 women), 26 part-time (all women); includes 27 minority (1 Black or African American, non-Hispanic/Latino; 1 American Indian or Alaska Native, non-Hispanic/Latino; 20 Asian, non-Hispanic/Latino; 4 Hispanic/Latino; 1 Two or more races, non-Hispanic/Latino), 191 international. Average age 24. 810 applicants, 25% accepted, 112 enrolled. In 2012, 55 master's, 13 doctorates awarded. Terminal master's awarded for partial completion of doctoral program. *Degree requirements:* For master's, thesis (for some programs); for doctorate, comprehensive exam, thesis/dissertation. *Entrance requirements:* For master's and doctorate, GRE General Test. Additional exam requirements/recommendations for international students: Required—TOEFL (minimum score 550 paper-based; 84 iBT), IELTS (minimum score 6.5). *Application deadline:* For fall admission, 3/15 for domestic and international students; for spring admission, 10/1 for domestic and international students. Applications are processed on a rolling basis. Application fee: $70. Electronic applications accepted. *Expenses:* Tuition: Full-time $42,400; part-time $1325 per credit. *Required fees:* $40 per semester. *Financial support:* In 2012–13, 126 students received support, including 8 fellowships with full tuition reimbursements available (averaging $28,950 per year), 82 research assistantships with full tuition reimbursements available (averaging $19,300 per year), 18 teaching assistantships with full tuition reimbursements available (averaging $19,300 per year); career-related internships or fieldwork, Federal Work-Study, institutionally sponsored loans, scholarships/grants, traineeships, and health care benefits also available. Financial award application deadline: 1/15; financial award applicants required to submit FAFSA. *Faculty research:* Communications and computer networks; signal, image, video, and multimedia processing; solid-state materials, devices, and photonics; systems, control, and reliable computing; VLSI, computer engineering and high-performance computing. *Unit head:* Dr. David Castanon, Interim Chairman, 617-353-9880, Fax: 617-353-6440, E-mail: dac@bu.edu. *Application contact:* Stephen Doherty, Director of Graduate Programs, 617-353-9760, Fax: 617-353-0259, E-mail: enggrad@bu.edu. Website: http://www.bu.edu/ece/.

Duke University, Graduate School, Pratt School of Engineering, Master of Engineering Program, Durham, NC 27708-0271. Offers biomedical engineering (M Eng); civil engineering (M Eng); electrical and computer engineering (M Eng); environmental engineering (M Eng); materials science and engineering (M Eng); mechanical engineering (M Eng); photonics and optical sciences (M Eng). Part-time programs available. *Entrance requirements:* For master's, GRE General Test, resume, 3 letters of recommendation, statement of purpose. Additional exam requirements/recommendations for international students: Required—TOEFL.

Lehigh University, College of Arts and Sciences, Department of Physics, Bethlehem, PA 18015. Offers photonics (MS); physics (MS, PhD); polymer science (MS, PhD). Part-time programs available. *Faculty:* 14 full-time (1 woman). *Students:* 41 full-time (14 women), 1 part-time (0 women); includes 1 minority (Black or African American, non-Hispanic/Latino), 15 international. Average age 26. 101 applicants, 20% accepted, 9 enrolled. In 2012, 6 master's, 5 doctorates awarded. *Degree requirements:* For doctorate, comprehensive exam, thesis/dissertation. *Entrance requirements:* For master's and doctorate, GRE General Test. Additional exam requirements/recommendations for international students: Required—TOEFL (minimum score 79 iBT). *Application deadline:* For fall admission, 2/15 priority date for domestic students, 2/15 for international students. Applications are processed on a rolling basis. Application fee: $75. Electronic applications accepted. *Financial support:* In 2012–13, 40 students received support, including 4 fellowships with full tuition reimbursements available (averaging $26,000 per year), 15 research assistantships with full tuition

224 www.petersonsbooks.com

Peterson's Graduate Programs in the Physical Sciences, Mathematics, Agricultural Sciences, the Environment & Natural Resources 2014

reimbursements available (averaging $25,640 per year), 21 teaching assistantships with full tuition reimbursements available (averaging $25,640 per year); career-related internships or fieldwork, Federal Work-Study, institutionally sponsored loans, scholarships/grants, tuition waivers (full and partial), and unspecified assistantships also available. Support available to part-time students. Financial award application deadline: 1/15. *Faculty research:* Condensed matter physics; atomic, molecular and optical physics; plasma physics; nonlinear optics and photonics; astronomy and astrophysics. *Total annual research expenditures:* $1.8 million. *Unit head:* Dr. Volkmar Dierolf, Chair, 610-758-3915, Fax: 610-758-5730, E-mail: vod2@lehigh.edu. *Application contact:* Dr. Dimitrios Vavylonis, Graduate Admissions Officer, 610-758-3724, Fax: 610-758-5730, E-mail: div206@lehigh.edu. Website: http://www.physics.lehigh.edu/.

Lehigh University, P.C. Rossin College of Engineering and Applied Science, Department of Electrical and Computer Engineering, Bethlehem, PA 18015. Offers electrical engineering (M Eng, MS, PhD); photonics (MS); wireless network engineering (MS). Part-time programs available. *Faculty:* 18 full-time (4 women). *Students:* 52 full-time (14 women), 7 part-time (1 woman); includes 2 minority (1 Asian, non-Hispanic/Latino; 1 Hispanic/Latino), 54 international. Average age 26. 418 applicants, 5% accepted, 14 enrolled. In 2012, 8 master's, 8 doctorates awarded. Terminal master's awarded for partial completion of doctoral program. *Degree requirements:* For master's, thesis optional; for doctorate, thesis/dissertation, qualifying or comprehensive exam for all 1st year PhD's; general exam 7 months or more prior to completion/dissertation defense. *Entrance requirements:* For master's and doctorate, GRE General Test, BS in field or related field. Additional exam requirements/recommendations for international students: Required—TOEFL (minimum score 79 iBT). *Application deadline:* For fall admission, 1/15 priority date for domestic students, 1/15 for international students; for spring admission, 11/1 for domestic and international students. Application fee: $75. Electronic applications accepted. *Financial support:* In 2012–13, 4 fellowships with full tuition reimbursements (averaging $18,360 per year), 42 research assistantships with full tuition reimbursements (averaging $21,600 per year), 5 teaching assistantships with full tuition reimbursements (averaging $18,819 per year) were awarded; career-related internships or fieldwork, Federal Work-Study, institutionally sponsored loans, scholarships/grants, tuition waivers (full and partial), and unspecified assistantships also available. Support available to part-time students. Financial award application deadline: 1/15. *Faculty research:* Nanostructures/nanodevices, terahertz generation, analog devices, mixed mode design and signal circuits, optoelectronic sensors, micro-fabrication technology and design, packaging/reliability of microsensors, coding and networking information theory, radio frequency, wireless and optical wireless communication, wireless networks. *Total annual research expenditures:* $2.8 million. *Unit head:* Dr. Filbert J. Bartoli, Chair, 610-758-4069, Fax: 610-758-6279, E-mail: fjb205@lehigh.edu. *Application contact:* Coley B. Burke, Graduate Coordinator, 610-758-4072, Fax: 610-758-6279, E-mail: cbb310@lehigh.edu. Website: http://www.ece.lehigh.edu/.

Lehigh University, P.C. Rossin College of Engineering and Applied Science, Department of Materials Science and Engineering, Bethlehem, PA 18015. Offers materials science and engineering (M Eng, MS, PhD); photonics (MS); polymer science/engineering (M Eng, MS, PhD); MBA/E. Part-time programs available. *Faculty:* 13 full-time (3 women), 1 part-time/adjunct (0 women). *Students:* 29 full-time (6 women), 3 part-time (1 woman); includes 2 minority (both Asian, non-Hispanic/Latino), 13 international. Average age 26. 331 applicants, 2% accepted, 6 enrolled. In 2012, 8 master's, 4 doctorates awarded. *Degree requirements:* For master's, thesis; for doctorate, comprehensive exam, thesis/dissertation. *Entrance requirements:* For master's and doctorate, GRE General Test, minimum GPA of 3.0. Additional exam requirements/recommendations for international students: Required—TOEFL (minimum score 487 paper-based; 85 iBT). *Application deadline:* For fall admission, 1/15 priority date for domestic students, 1/15 for international students; for spring admission, 12/1 priority date for domestic students, 12/1 for international students. Applications are processed on a rolling basis. Application fee: $75. Electronic applications accepted. *Financial support:* In 2012–13, 29 students received support, including 4 fellowships with full and partial tuition reimbursements available (averaging $25,092 per year), 25 research assistantships with full tuition reimbursements available (averaging $24,082 per year), 13 teaching assistantships with partial tuition reimbursements available (averaging $25,786 per year); career-related internships or fieldwork, Federal Work-Study, institutionally sponsored loans, scholarships/grants, and unspecified assistantships also available. Support available to part-time students. Financial award application deadline: 1/15. *Faculty research:* Metals, ceramics, crystals, polymers, fatigue crack propagation, biomaterials. *Total annual research expenditures:* $5.6 million. *Unit head:* Dr. Helen Chan, Chairperson, 610-758-5554, Fax: 610-758-4244, E-mail: hmc0@lehigh.edu. *Application contact:* Anne Marie Lobley, Graduate Administrative Coordinator, 610-758-4222, Fax: 610-758-4244, E-mail: amme@lehigh.edu. Website: http://www.lehigh.edu/~inmatsci/.

Oklahoma State University, College of Arts and Sciences, Department of Physics, Stillwater, OK 74078. Offers photonics (MS, PhD); physics (MS, PhD). *Faculty:* 27 full-time (4 women), 2 part-time/adjunct (0 women). *Students:* 3 full-time (0 women), 38 part-time (3 women); includes 2 minority (both Two or more races, non-Hispanic/Latino), 26 international. Average age 29. 65 applicants, 23% accepted, 9 enrolled. In 2012, 2 master's, 8 doctorates awarded. *Degree requirements:* For master's, thesis; for doctorate, comprehensive exam, thesis/dissertation, oral defense of dissertation, preliminary exam, qualifying exam. *Entrance requirements:* For master's and doctorate, GRE. Additional exam requirements/recommendations for international students: Required—TOEFL (minimum score 550 paper-based; 79 iBT). *Application deadline:* For fall admission, 3/1 for international students; for spring admission, 8/1 for international students. Applications are processed on a rolling basis. Application fee: $40 ($75 for international students). Electronic applications accepted. *Expenses:* Tuition, state resident: full-time $4272; part-time $178 per credit hour. Tuition, nonresident: full-time $17,016; part-time $709 per credit hour. *Required fees:* $2188; $91.17 per credit hour. One-time fee: $50 full-time. Part-time tuition and fees vary according to course load and campus/location. *Financial support:* In 2012–13, 16 research assistantships (averaging $19,560 per year), 35 teaching assistantships (averaging $16,530 per year) were awarded; career-related internships or fieldwork, Federal Work-Study, scholarships/grants, health care benefits, tuition waivers (partial), and unspecified assistantships also available. Support available to part-time students. Financial award application deadline: 3/1; financial award applicants required to submit FAFSA. *Faculty research:* Lasers and photonics, non-linear optical materials, turbulence, structure and function of biological membranes, particle theory. *Unit head:* Dr. John Mintmire, Head, 405-744-5796, Fax: 405-744-6811. *Application contact:* Dr. Sheryl Tucker, Dean, 405-744-7099, Fax: 405-744-0355, E-mail: grad-i@okstate.edu. Website: http://physics.okstate.edu/.

Oklahoma State University, Graduate College, Stillwater, OK 74078. Offers aerospace security (Graduate Certificate); biobased products and bioenergy (Graduate Certificate); bioinformatics (Graduate Certificate); business data mining (Graduate Certificate); engineering and technology management (Graduate Certificate); environmental science (MS); global issues (Graduate Certificate); information assurance (Graduate Certificate); international studies (MS); natural and applied science (MS); photonics (PhD); plant science (PhD); teaching English to speakers of other languages (Graduate Certificate). Programs are interdisciplinary. *Faculty:* 3 full-time (2 women), 2 part-time/adjunct (0 women). *Students:* 83 full-time (50 women), 169 part-time (90 women); includes 64 minority (16 Black or African American, non-Hispanic/Latino; 13 American Indian or Alaska Native, non-Hispanic/Latino; 13 Asian, non-Hispanic/Latino; 6 Hispanic/Latino; 1 Native Hawaiian or other Pacific Islander, non-Hispanic/Latino; 15 Two or more races, non-Hispanic/Latino), 51 international. Average age 32. 605 applicants, 71% accepted, 82 enrolled. In 2012, 76 master's, 7 doctorates awarded. *Degree requirements:* For master's, thesis (for some programs); for doctorate, comprehensive exam, thesis/dissertation. *Entrance requirements:* For master's and doctorate, GRE or GMAT. Additional exam requirements/recommendations for international students: Required—TOEFL (minimum score 550 paper-based; 79 iBT). *Application deadline:* For fall admission, 3/1 for international students; for spring admission, 8/1 for international students. Applications are processed on a rolling basis. Application fee: $40 ($75 for international students). Electronic applications accepted. *Expenses:* Tuition, state resident: full-time $4272; part-time $178 per credit hour. Tuition, nonresident: full-time $17,016; part-time $709 per credit hour. *Required fees:* $2188; $91.17 per credit hour. One-time fee: $50 full-time. Part-time tuition and fees vary according to course load and campus/location. *Financial support:* In 2012–13, 6 research assistantships (averaging $6,600 per year) were awarded; career-related internships or fieldwork, Federal Work-Study, scholarships/grants, health care benefits, tuition waivers (partial), and unspecified assistantships also available. Support available to part-time students. Financial award application deadline: 3/1; financial award applicants required to submit FAFSA. *Unit head:* Dr. Sheryl Tucker, Dean, 405-744-7099, Fax: 405-744-0355, E-mail: grad-i@okstate.edu. *Application contact:* Dr. Susan Mathew, Coordinator of Admissions, 405-744-6368, Fax: 405-744-0355, E-mail: grad-i@okstate.edu. Website: http://gradcollege.okstate.edu/.

Princeton University, Princeton Institute for the Science and Technology of Materials (PRISM), Princeton, NJ 08544-1019. Offers materials (PhD).

Stevens Institute of Technology, Graduate School, Charles V. Schaefer Jr. School of Engineering, Department of Electrical and Computer Engineering, Program in Electrical Engineering, Hoboken, NJ 07030. Offers computer architecture and digital systems (M Eng); electrical engineering (PhD); microelectronics and photonics science and technology (M Eng); signal processing for communications (M Eng); telecommunications systems engineering (M Eng); wireless communications (M Eng, Certificate). *Degree requirements:* For master's, thesis optional; for doctorate, variable foreign language requirement, thesis/dissertation. *Entrance requirements:* For master's, doctorate, and Certificate, GRE. Additional exam requirements/recommendations for international students: Required—TOEFL. Electronic applications accepted.

Stevens Institute of Technology, Graduate School, Charles V. Schaefer Jr. School of Engineering, Interdisciplinary Program in Microelectronics and Photonics, Hoboken, NJ 07030. Offers Certificate.

The University of Alabama in Huntsville, School of Graduate Studies, College of Engineering, Department of Electrical and Computer Engineering, Huntsville, AL 35899. Offers computer engineering (MSE, PhD); electrical engineering (MSE, PhD), including optics and photonics technology (MSE), opto-electronics (MSE); information assurance (MS); optical science and engineering (PhD); optics and photonics (MSE); software engineering (MSSE). Part-time and evening/weekend programs available. *Faculty:* 25 full-time (3 women). *Students:* 56 full-time (13 women), 135 part-time (19 women); includes 20 minority (9 Black or African American, non-Hispanic/Latino; 1 American Indian or Alaska Native, non-Hispanic/Latino; 8 Asian, non-Hispanic/Latino; 2 Hispanic/Latino), 45 international. Average age 30. 131 applicants, 72% accepted, 44 enrolled. In 2012, 44 master's, 7 doctorates awarded. *Degree requirements:* For master's, comprehensive exam, thesis or alternative, oral and written exams; for doctorate, comprehensive exam, thesis/dissertation, oral and written exams. *Entrance requirements:* For master's, GRE General Test, appropriate bachelor's degree, minimum GPA of 3.0; for doctorate, GRE General Test, minimum GPA of 3.0. Additional exam requirements/recommendations for international students: Required—TOEFL (minimum score 500 paper-based; 80 iBT), IELTS (minimum score 6.5). *Application deadline:* For fall admission, 7/15 priority date for domestic students, 4/1 for international students; for spring admission, 11/30 priority date for domestic students, 9/1 for international students. Applications are processed on a rolling basis. Application fee: $40 ($50 for international students). Electronic applications accepted. *Expenses:* Tuition, state resident: full-time $8516; part-time $515 per credit hour. Tuition, nonresident: full-time $20,384; part-time $1229 per credit hour. *Required fees:* $148 per semester. One-time fee: $150. *Financial support:* In 2012–13, 30 students received support, including 9 research assistantships with full tuition reimbursements available (averaging $13,113 per year), 21 teaching assistantships with full tuition reimbursements available (averaging $11,376 per year); career-related internships or fieldwork, Federal Work-Study, institutionally sponsored loans, scholarships/grants, health care benefits, tuition waivers (full), and unspecified assistantships also available. Support available to part-time students. Financial award application deadline: 4/1; financial award applicants required to submit FAFSA. *Faculty research:* Advanced computer architecture and systems, fault tolerant computing and verification, computational electro-magnetics, nano-photonics and plasmonics, micro electro-mechanical (MEMS) systems. *Total annual research expenditures:* $18.6 million. *Unit head:* Dr. Robert Lindquist, Chair, 256-824-6316, Fax: 256-824-6803, E-mail: lindquis@ece.uah.edu. *Application contact:* Kim Gray, Graduate Studies Admissions Coordinator, 256-824-6002, Fax: 256-824-6405, E-mail: deangrad@uah.edu. Website: http://www.ece.uah.edu/.

The University of Alabama in Huntsville, School of Graduate Studies, College of Science, Department of Physics, Huntsville, AL 35899. Offers education (MS); optics and photonics technology (MS); physics (MS, PhD). Part-time and evening/weekend programs available. *Faculty:* 18 full-time (0 women), 1 part-time/adjunct (0 women). *Students:* 41 full-time (11 women), 17 part-time (4 women); includes 3 minority (2 Asian, non-Hispanic/Latino; 1 Hispanic/Latino), 16 international. Average age 28. 41 applicants, 76% accepted, 17 enrolled. In 2012, 10 master's, 2 doctorates awarded. *Degree requirements:* For master's, comprehensive exam, thesis or alternative, oral and written exams; for doctorate, comprehensive exam, thesis/dissertation, oral and written exams. *Entrance requirements:* For master's and doctorate, GRE General Test, minimum GPA of 3.0. Additional exam requirements/recommendations for international students: Required—TOEFL (minimum score 550 paper-based; 80 iBT), IELTS (minimum score 6.5). *Application deadline:* For fall admission, 7/15 priority date for domestic students, 4/1 for international students; for spring admission, 11/30 priority date for domestic students, 9/1 for international students. Applications are processed on a rolling basis. Application fee: $40 ($50 for international students). Electronic applications accepted. *Expenses:* Tuition, state resident: full-time $8516; part-time $515 per credit hour. Tuition, nonresident: full-time $20,384; part-time $1229 per credit hour. *Required fees:* $148 per semester. One-time fee: $150. *Financial support:* In 2012–13, 34 students received support, including 1 fellowship with full tuition reimbursement available (averaging $17,455 per year), 22 research assistantships with full and partial tuition reimbursements available (averaging $16,424 per year), 12 teaching assistantships with full and partial tuition reimbursements available (averaging $17,547 per year); career-related internships or fieldwork, Federal Work-Study, institutionally sponsored loans, scholarships/grants, health care benefits, and unspecified assistantships also available. Support available to part-time students. Financial award application deadline: 4/1; financial award applicants required to submit FAFSA. *Faculty research:* Space and solar physics, computational physics, optics, high energy astrophysics. *Total annual research expenditures:* $6.5 million. *Unit head:* Dr. Gary Zank, Chair, 256-824-2481, Fax: 256-824-6873, E-mail: gary.zank@uah.edu. *Application contact:* Kim Gray, Graduate Studies Admissions Coordinator, 256-824-6002, Fax: 256-824-6405, E-mail: deangrad@uah.edu. Website: http://physics.uah.edu/.

University of Arkansas, Graduate School, Interdisciplinary Program in Microelectronics and Photonics, Fayetteville, AR 72701-1201. Offers MS, PhD. *Students:* 17 full-time (4 women), 47 part-time (6 women); includes 7 minority (6 Black or African American, non-Hispanic/Latino; 1 Asian, non-Hispanic/Latino), 28 international. In 2012, 9 master's, 3 doctorates awarded. *Degree requirements:* For doctorate, thesis/dissertation. *Application deadline:* For fall admission, 4/1 for international students; for spring admission, 10/1 for international students. Applications are processed on a rolling basis. Application fee: $40 ($50 for international students). Electronic applications accepted. *Financial support:* In 2012–13, 25 research assistantships, 4 teaching assistantships were awarded; fellowships with tuition reimbursements also available. Financial award application deadline: 4/1; financial award applicants required to submit FAFSA. *Unit head:* Dr. Ken Vickers, Head, 479-575-2875, Fax: 479-575-4580, E-mail: vickers@uark.edu. *Application contact:* Graduate Admissions, 479-575-6246, Fax: 479-575-5908, E-mail: gradinfo@uark.edu. Website: http://microep.uark.edu.

University of California, San Diego, Office of Graduate Studies, Department of Electrical and Computer Engineering, La Jolla, CA 92093. Offers applied ocean science (MS, PhD); applied physics (MS, PhD); communication theory and systems (MS, PhD); computer engineering (MS, PhD); electrical engineering (M Eng); electronic circuits and systems (MS, PhD); intelligent systems, robotics and control (MS, PhD); photonics (MS, PhD); signal and image processing (MS, PhD). MS only offered to students who have been admitted to the PhD program. *Entrance requirements:* For master's and doctorate, GRE General Test. Electronic applications accepted.

University of California, Santa Barbara, Graduate Division, College of Engineering, Department of Electrical and Computer Engineering, Santa Barbara, CA 93106-2014. Offers communications, control and signal processing (MS, PhD); computer engineering (MS, PhD); electronics and photonics (MS, PhD); MS/PhD. *Faculty:* 38 full-time (4 women), 1 part-time/adjunct (0 women). *Students:* 268 full-time (53 women); includes 32 minority (2 Black or African American, non-Hispanic/Latino; 2 American Indian or Alaska Native, non-Hispanic/Latino; 21 Asian, non-Hispanic/Latino; 5 Hispanic/Latino; 1 Native Hawaiian or other Pacific Islander, non-Hispanic/Latino; 1 Two or more races, non-Hispanic/Latino), 164 international. Average age 26. 1,515 applicants, 20% accepted, 83 enrolled. In 2012, 68 master's, 38 doctorates awarded. Terminal master's awarded for partial completion of doctoral program. *Degree requirements:* For master's, comprehensive exam, thesis; for doctorate, thesis/dissertation. *Entrance requirements:* For master's and doctorate, GRE General Test. Additional exam requirements/recommendations for international students: Required—TOEFL (minimum score 550 paper-based; 80 iBT), IELTS (minimum score 7). *Application deadline:* For fall admission, 12/15 for domestic and international students; for winter admission, 11/1 for domestic and international students; for spring admission, 1/1 for domestic and international students. Application fee: $80 ($100 for international students). Electronic applications accepted. *Financial support:* In 2012–13, 196 students received support, including 75 fellowships with full and partial tuition reimbursements available (averaging $7,595 per year), 125 research assistantships with full and partial tuition reimbursements available (averaging $26,949 per year), 65 teaching assistantships with full and partial tuition reimbursements available (averaging $10,659 per year); tuition waivers (full and partial) also available. Financial award application deadline: 12/15; financial award applicants required to submit FAFSA. *Faculty research:* Communications, signal processing, computer engineering, control, electronics and photonics. *Total annual research expenditures:* $25.5 million. *Unit head:* Prof. Jerry Gibson, Chair, 805-893-3821, Fax: 805-893-6262, E-mail: gibson@ece.ucsb.edu. *Application contact:* Erika Raquel Klukovich, Graduate Admissions Coordinator, 805-893-3114, Fax: 805-893-5402, E-mail: erika@ece.ucsb.edu. Website: http://www.ece.ucsb.edu/.

University of Central Florida, College of Optics and Photonics, Orlando, FL 32816. Offers optics (MS, PhD). Part-time and evening/weekend programs available. *Faculty:* 42 full-time (6 women), 10 part-time/adjunct (3 women). *Students:* 111 full-time (17 women), 13 part-time (4 women); includes 11 minority (1 Black or African American, non-Hispanic/Latino; 5 Asian, non-Hispanic/Latino; 4 Hispanic/Latino; 1 Two or more races, non-Hispanic/Latino), 66 international. Average age 28. 229 applicants, 21% accepted, 26 enrolled. In 2012, 23 master's, 11 doctorates awarded. *Median time to degree:* Of those who began their doctoral program in fall 2004, 75% received their degree in 8 years or less. *Degree requirements:* For master's, thesis or alternative; for doctorate, thesis/dissertation, departmental qualifying exam, candidacy exam. *Entrance requirements:* For master's, GRE General Test, minimum GPA of 3.0 in last 60 hours; for doctorate, GRE General Test, minimum GPA of 3.5 in last 60 hours. Additional exam requirements/recommendations for international students: Required—TOEFL. *Application deadline:* For fall admission, 2/1 priority date for domestic students; for spring admission, 12/1 for domestic students. Application fee: $30. Electronic applications accepted. *Financial support:* In 2012–13, 70 students received support, including 19 fellowships with partial tuition reimbursements available (averaging $5,600 per year), 80 research assistantships with partial tuition reimbursements available (averaging $11,800 per year); career-related internships or fieldwork, Federal Work-Study, institutionally sponsored loans, tuition waivers (partial), and unspecified assistantships also available. Financial award application deadline: 3/1; financial award applicants required to submit FAFSA. *Unit head:* Dr. Bahaa E. Saleh, Dean and Director, 407-823-6817, E-mail: besaleh@creol.ucf.edu. *Application contact:* Barbara Rodriguez, Director, Admissions and Registration, 407-823-2766, Fax: 407-823-6442, E-mail: gradadmissions@ucf.edu. Website: http://www.creol.ucf.edu/.

University of New Mexico, Graduate School, College of Arts and Sciences, Optical Science and Engineering Program, Albuquerque, NM 87106. Offers imaging science (MS, PhD); optical science and engineering (MS, PhD); photonics (MS, PhD). Program jointly administered by the Department of Physics and Astronomy and the Department of Electrical and Computer Engineering. Part-time programs available. *Faculty:* 34 full-time (2 women). *Students:* 24 full-time (4 women), 34 part-time (9 women); includes 3 minority (1 Asian, non-Hispanic/Latino; 2 Hispanic/Latino), 44 international. Average age 29. 51 applicants, 24% accepted, 11 enrolled. In 2012, 10 master's, 2 doctorates awarded. Terminal master's awarded for partial completion of doctoral program. *Degree requirements:* For master's, comprehensive exam (for some programs), thesis (for some programs); for doctorate, comprehensive exam, thesis/dissertation. *Entrance requirements:* For master's, GRE General Test, GRE Subject Test in physics (preferred), relevant undergraduate coursework, curriculum vitae, letters of recommendation, letter of intent/personal statement; for doctorate, GRE General Test, GRE Subject Test in physics (preferred), relevant undergraduate coursework, curriculum vitae, letters of recommendation. Additional exam requirements/recommendations for international students: Required—TOEFL (minimum score 575 paper-based; 79 iBT), IELTS (minimum score 7). *Application deadline:* For fall admission, 1/15 priority date for domestic students, 1/15 for international students; for spring admission, 8/1 priority date for domestic students, 8/1 for international students. Application fee: $50. Electronic

226 www.petersonsbooks.com

Peterson's Graduate Programs in the Physical Sciences, Mathematics, Agricultural Sciences, the Environment & Natural Resources 2014

applications accepted. *Expenses:* Tuition, state resident: full-time $3296; part-time $276.73 per credit hour. Tuition, nonresident: full-time $10,604; part-time $885.74 per credit hour. *Required fees:* $628. *Financial support:* In 2012–13, 34 students received support, including 29 research assistantships with full tuition reimbursements available (averaging $16,097 per year), 10 teaching assistantships with full tuition reimbursements available (averaging $14,400 per year); fellowships with full tuition reimbursements available, career-related internships or fieldwork, scholarships/grants, health care benefits, and unspecified assistantships also available. Support available to part-time students. Financial award application deadline: 2/1; financial award applicants required to submit FAFSA. *Faculty research:* Advanced materials, atom optics, biomedical optics, fiber optics, laser cooling, high intensity interactions, lithography, nano photonics, nonlinear optics, optical imaging, optical sensors, optoelectronics, quantum optics, spectroscopy, ultrafast phenomena. *Unit head:* Dr. Majeed Hayat, General Chair, 505-272-7095, Fax: 505-277-7801, E-mail: hayat@ece.unm.edu. *Application contact:* Doris Williams, Advisor, 505-277-7764, Fax: 505-277-7801, E-mail: dorisw@chtm.unm.edu. Website: http://www.optics.unm.edu/.

Physics

Alabama Agricultural and Mechanical University, School of Graduate Studies, School of Arts and Sciences, Department of Physics, Huntsville, AL 35811. Offers physics (MS, PhD), including applied physics (PhD), materials science (PhD), optics/lasers (PhD). Part-time and evening/weekend programs available. *Degree requirements:* For doctorate, thesis/dissertation. *Entrance requirements:* For master's and doctorate, GRE General Test. Additional exam requirements/recommendations for international students: Required—TOEFL (minimum score 500 paper-based; 61 iBT). Electronic applications accepted.

American University of Beirut, Graduate Programs, Faculty of Arts and Sciences, Beirut, Lebanon. Offers anthropology (MA); Arab and Middle Eastern history (PhD); Arabic language and literature (MA, PhD); archaeology (MA); biology (MS); cell and molecular biology (PhD); chemistry (MS); clinical psychology (MA); computational science (MS); computer science (MS); economics (MA); education (MA); English language (MA); English literature (MA); environmental policy planning (MSES); financial economics (MAFE); general psychology (MA); geology (MS); history (MA); mathematics (MA, MS); media studies (MA); Middle Eastern studies (MA); philosophy (MA); physics (MS); political studies (MA); public administration (MA); sociology (MA); statistics (MA, MS); theoretical physics (PhD); transnational American studies (MA). Part-time programs available. *Faculty:* 238 full-time (80 women), 7 part-time/adjunct (3 women). *Students:* 253 full-time (169 women), 139 part-time (105 women). Average age 26. 306 applicants, 47% accepted, 90 enrolled. In 2012, 126 degrees awarded. *Degree requirements:* For master's, one foreign language, comprehensive exam, thesis (for some programs); for doctorate, one foreign language, comprehensive exam, thesis/dissertation. *Entrance requirements:* For master's, GRE, letter of recommendation; for doctorate, GRE, letters of recommendation. Additional exam requirements/recommendations for international students: Required—TOEFL (minimum score 600 paper-based; 97 iBT), IELTS (minimum score 7). *Application deadline:* For fall admission, 4/30 for domestic students, 4/18 for international students; for spring admission, 11/1 for domestic and international students. Application fee: $50. *Expenses: Tuition:* Full-time $13,890; part-time $772 per credit. *Financial support:* In 2012–13, 20 students received support. Career-related internships or fieldwork, institutionally sponsored loans, scholarships/grants, health care benefits, and unspecified assistantships available. Financial award application deadline: 2/4; financial award applicants required to submit FAFSA. *Faculty research:* Modern Middle East history; Near Eastern archaeology; Islamic history; European history; software engineering; scientific computing; data mining; the applications of cooperative learning in language teaching and teacher education; world/comparative literature; rhetoric and composition; creative writing; public management; public policy and international affairs; hydrogeology; mineralogy, petrology, and geochemistry; tectonics and structural geology; cell and molecular biology; ecology. *Unit head:* Dr. Patrick McGreevy, Dean, 961-1374374 Ext. 3800, Fax: 961-1744461, E-mail: pm07@aub.edu.lb. *Application contact:* Dr. Salim Kanaan, Director, Admissions Office, 961-1-350000 Ext. 2594, Fax: 961-1750775, E-mail: sk00@aub.edu.lb. Website: http://staff.aub.edu.lb/~webfas.

Arizona State University, College of Liberal Arts and Sciences, Department of Physics, Tempe, AZ 85287-1504. Offers nanoscience (PSM); physics (MNS, PhD). Part-time programs available. Terminal master's awarded for partial completion of doctoral program. *Degree requirements:* For master's, comprehensive exam, thesis or alternative, interactive Program of Study (iPOS) submitted before completing 50 percent of required credit hours; for doctorate, comprehensive exam, thesis/dissertation, interactive Program of Study (iPOS) submitted before completing 50 percent of required credit hours. *Entrance requirements:* For master's and doctorate, GRE, minimum GPA of 3.0 or equivalent in last 2 years of work leading to bachelor's degree. Additional exam requirements/recommendations for international students: Required—TOEFL (minimum score 80 iBT), TOEFL, IELTS, or Pearson Test of English. Electronic applications accepted. *Expenses:* Contact institution.

Auburn University, Graduate School, College of Sciences and Mathematics, Department of Physics, Auburn University, AL 36849. Offers MS, PhD. Part-time programs available. *Faculty:* 22 full-time (1 woman), 3 part-time/adjunct (0 women). *Students:* 17 full-time (3 women), 38 part-time (9 women); includes 3 minority (1 Black or African American, non-Hispanic/Latino; 1 Asian, non-Hispanic/Latino; 1 Hispanic/Latino), 19 international. Average age 28. 20 applicants, 70% accepted, 13 enrolled. In 2012, 5 master's, 7 doctorates awarded. *Degree requirements:* For doctorate, thesis/dissertation, oral and written exams. *Entrance requirements:* For master's and doctorate, GRE General Test. *Application deadline:* For fall admission, 7/7 for domestic students; for spring admission, 11/24 for domestic students. Applications are processed on a rolling basis. Application fee: $50 ($60 for international students). Electronic applications accepted. *Expenses:* Tuition, state resident: full-time $7866; part-time $437 per credit. Tuition, nonresident: full-time $23,598; part-time $1311 per credit. *Required fees:* $787 per semester. Tuition and fees vary according to degree level and program. *Financial support:* Research assistantships, teaching assistantships, career-related internships or fieldwork, and Federal Work-Study available. Support available to part-time students. Financial award application deadline: 3/15; financial award applicants required to submit FAFSA. *Faculty research:* Atomic/radioactive physics, plasma physics, condensed matter physics, space physics, nonlinear dynamics. *Unit head:* Dr. Joe D. Perez, III, Head, 334-844-4264. *Application contact:* Dr. George Flowers, Dean of the Graduate School, 334-844-2125. Website: http://www.physics.auburn.edu/.

Ball State University, Graduate School, College of Sciences and Humanities, Department of Physics and Astronomy, Program in Physics, Muncie, IN 47306-1099. Offers MA, MAE, MS. *Students:* 15 full-time (4 women), 5 part-time (3 women), 5 international. Average age 26. 20 applicants, 75% accepted, 8 enrolled. In 2012, 8 master's awarded. *Entrance requirements:* For master's, GRE General Test. Application fee: $50. *Expenses:* Tuition, state resident: full-time $7666. Tuition, nonresident: full-time $19,114. *Required fees:* $782. *Financial support:* In 2012–13, 14 students received support, including 15 teaching assistantships with full tuition reimbursements available (averaging $8,811 per year); research assistantships with full tuition reimbursements available also available. Financial award application deadline: 3/1. *Faculty research:* Solar energy, particle physics, atomic spectroscopy. *Unit head:* Dr. Thomas Robertson, Chairperson, 765-285-8869, E-mail: troberton@bsu.edu. *Application contact:* Dr. Robert Morris, Associate Provost for Research and Dean of the Graduate School, 765-285-1300, E-mail: rmorris@bsu.edu. Website: http://www.bsu.edu/physics/.

Baylor University, Graduate School, College of Arts and Sciences, Department of Physics, Waco, TX 76798-7316. Offers MA, MS, PhD. *Faculty:* 15 full-time (3 women). *Students:* 29 full-time (5 women); includes 1 minority (Hispanic/Latino), 20 international. 93 applicants, 26% accepted, 8 enrolled. In 2012, 1 master's, 4 doctorates awarded. Terminal master's awarded for partial completion of doctoral program. *Degree requirements:* For master's, comprehensive exam (for some programs), thesis or alternative; for doctorate, one foreign language, comprehensive exam, thesis/dissertation. *Entrance requirements:* For master's and doctorate, GRE General Test. Additional exam requirements/recommendations for international students: Required—TOEFL (minimum score 550 paper-based; 80 iBT), IELTS (minimum score 6.5), or Pearson Test of English. *Application deadline:* For fall admission, 2/15 for domestic and international students; for spring admission, 12/15 for domestic and international students. Application fee: $50. Electronic applications accepted. *Expenses: Tuition:* Full-time $24,426; part-time $1357 per semester hour. *Required fees:* $2556; $142 per semester hour. *Financial support:* In 2012–13, 27 students received support, including 5 research assistantships with full tuition reimbursements available (averaging $23,402 per year), 24 teaching assistantships with full tuition reimbursements available (averaging $23,402 per year). *Faculty research:* Elementary particle physics and cosmology, condensed matter physics, space science physics, nonlinear dynamics, atomic and molecular physics. *Total annual research expenditures:* $545,988. *Unit head:* Dr. Gerald Cleaver, Graduate Program Director, 254-710-2283, Fax: 254-710-3878, E-mail: gerald_cleaver@baylor.edu. *Application contact:* Marian Nunn-Graves, Administrative Assistant, 254-710-2511, Fax: 254-710-3878, E-mail: marian_nunn-graves@baylor.edu. Website: http://www.baylor.edu/physics/.

Binghamton University, State University of New York, Graduate School, School of Arts and Sciences, Department of Physics, Applied Physics, and Astronomy, Binghamton, NY 13902-6000. Offers MS, PhD. *Faculty:* 13 full-time (1 woman), 7 part-time/adjunct (2 women). *Students:* 19 full-time (1 woman), 9 part-time (1 woman); includes 2 minority (1 Black or African American, non-Hispanic/Latino; 1 Native Hawaiian or other Pacific Islander, non-Hispanic/Latino), 9 international. Average age 27. 19 applicants, 68% accepted, 9 enrolled. *Degree requirements:* For master's, thesis or alternative. *Entrance requirements:* For master's, GRE General Test, GRE Subject Test. Additional exam requirements/

Peterson's Graduate Programs in the Physical Sciences, Mathematics, Agricultural Sciences, the Environment & Natural Resources 2014

www.petersonsbooks.com **227**

recommendations for international students: Required—TOEFL (minimum score 550 paper-based; 80 iBT). *Application deadline:* For fall admission, 2/15 priority date for domestic students, 2/15 for international students; for spring admission, 10/15 priority date for domestic students, 10/15 for international students. Applications are processed on a rolling basis. Application fee: $75. Electronic applications accepted. *Expenses:* Tuition, state resident: full-time $9370. Tuition, nonresident: full-time $16,680. *Financial support:* In 2012–13, 27 students received support, including 2 research assistantships with full tuition reimbursements available (averaging $18,000 per year), 25 teaching assistantships with full tuition reimbursements available (averaging $18,000 per year); career-related internships or fieldwork, Federal Work-Study, institutionally sponsored loans, scholarships/grants, health care benefits, and unspecified assistantships also available. Financial award application deadline: 2/15; financial award applicants required to submit FAFSA. *Unit head:* Dr. Eric Cotts, Chairperson, 607-777-4371, E-mail: ecotts@binghamton.edu. *Application contact:* Kishan Zuber, Recruiting and Admissions Coordinator, 607-777-2151, Fax: 607-777-2501, E-mail: kzuber@binghamton.edu.

Boston College, Graduate School of Arts and Sciences, Department of Physics, Chestnut Hill, MA 02467-3800. Offers MS, PhD. Terminal master's awarded for partial completion of doctoral program. *Degree requirements:* For master's, thesis (for some programs); for doctorate, thesis/dissertation. *Entrance requirements:* For master's and doctorate, GRE General Test, GRE Subject Test. Additional exam requirements/recommendations for international students: Required—TOEFL (minimum score 600 paper-based; 100 iBT). Electronic applications accepted. *Faculty research:* Atmospheric/space physics, astrophysics, atomic and molecular physics, fusion and plasmas, solid-state physics.

Boston University, Graduate School of Arts and Sciences, Department of Physics, Boston, MA 02215. Offers MA, PhD. *Students:* 106 full-time (16 women); includes 8 minority (5 Asian, non-Hispanic/Latino; 3 Hispanic/Latino), 56 international. Average age 25. 312 applicants, 22% accepted, 19 enrolled. In 2012, 22 master's, 17 doctorates awarded. Terminal master's awarded for partial completion of doctoral program. *Degree requirements:* For master's, one foreign language, comprehensive exam, thesis or alternative; for doctorate, one foreign language, comprehensive exam, thesis/dissertation. *Entrance requirements:* For master's and doctorate, GRE General Test, GRE Subject Test. Additional exam requirements/recommendations for international students: Required—TOEFL (minimum score 600 paper-based). *Application deadline:* For fall admission, 12/15 for domestic and international students. Application fee: $80. Electronic applications accepted. *Expenses: Tuition:* Full-time $42,400; part-time $1325 per credit. *Required fees:* $40 per semester. *Financial support:* In 2012–13, 2 fellowships with full tuition reimbursements (averaging $20,300 per year), 74 research assistantships with full tuition reimbursements (averaging $19,800 per year), 32 teaching assistantships with full tuition reimbursements (averaging $19,800 per year) were awarded; Federal Work-Study, scholarships/grants, and health care benefits also available. Support available to part-time students. Financial award application deadline: 12/15. *Unit head:* Dr. Sid Redner, Chairman, 617-353-2618, Fax: 617-353-9393, E-mail: redner@bu.edu. *Application contact:* Mirtha M. Cabello, Administrative Coordinator, 617-353-2623, Fax: 617-353-9393, E-mail: cabello@bu.edu. Website: http://buphy.bu.edu/.

Bowling Green State University, Graduate College, College of Arts and Sciences, Department of Physics and Astronomy, Bowling Green, OH 43403. Offers geophysics (MS); physics (MAT, MS). *Degree requirements:* For master's, thesis or alternative. *Entrance requirements:* For master's, GRE General Test. Additional exam requirements/recommendations for international students: Required—TOEFL. Electronic applications accepted. *Faculty research:* Computational physics, solid-state physics, materials science, theoretical physics.

Brandeis University, Graduate School of Arts and Sciences, Department of Physics, Waltham, MA 02454-9110. Offers physics (MS, PhD); quantitative biology (PhD). Part-time programs available. *Faculty:* 16 full-time (4 women), 2 part-time/adjunct (0 women). *Students:* 46 full-time (9 women); includes 1 minority (Asian, non-Hispanic/Latino), 22 international. 104 applicants, 16% accepted, 10 enrolled. In 2012, 3 master's, 4 doctorates awarded. Terminal master's awarded for partial completion of doctoral program. *Degree requirements:* For master's, thesis optional, qualifying exam, 1-year residency; for doctorate, comprehensive exam, thesis/dissertation, qualifying and advanced exams. *Entrance requirements:* For master's and doctorate, GRE General Test; GRE Subject Test (recommended), resume, 2 letters of recommendation, statement of purpose, transcript(s). Additional exam requirements/recommendations for international students: Required—TOEFL (minimum score 600 paper-based; 100 iBT), Pearson Test of English (minimum score 68); Recommended—IELTS (minimum score 7). *Application deadline:* For fall admission, 1/15 priority date for domestic students. Application fee: $75. Electronic applications accepted. *Financial support:* In 2012–13, fellowships with full tuition reimbursements (averaging $24,480 per year), 31 research assistantships with full tuition reimbursements (averaging $24,480 per year), 5 teaching assistantships with partial tuition reimbursements (averaging $1,250 per year) were awarded; Federal Work-Study, scholarships/grants, health care benefits, and tuition waivers (partial) also available. Support available to part-time students. Financial award application deadline: 1/15; financial award applicants required to submit FAFSA. *Faculty research:* Astrophysics, condensed-matter and biophysics, high energy and gravitational theory, particle physics, microfluidics, radio astronomy, string theory. *Unit head:* Dr. John Wardle, Director of Graduate Studies, 781-736-2800, E-mail: wardle@brandeis.edu. *Application contact:* Catherine Broderick, Department Administrator, 781-736-2800, E-mail: cbroderi@brandeis.edu. Website: http://www.brandeis.edu/gsas.

Brigham Young University, Graduate Studies, College of Physical and Mathematical Sciences, Department of Physics and Astronomy, Provo, UT 84602-1001. Offers physics (MS, PhD); physics and astronomy (PhD). Part-time programs available. *Faculty:* 30 full-time (2 women). *Students:* 37 full-time (7 women); includes 4 minority (2 Asian, non-Hispanic/Latino; 2 Hispanic/Latino), 1 international. Average age 29. 20 applicants, 50% accepted, 6 enrolled. In 2012, 6 master's, 4 doctorates awarded. Terminal master's awarded for partial completion of doctoral program. *Degree requirements:* For master's, thesis; for doctorate, thesis/dissertation, qualifying exam. *Entrance requirements:* For master's and doctorate, GRE Subject Test (physics), GRE General Test, minimum GPA of 3.0 in last 60 hours, ecclesiastical endorsement. Additional exam requirements/recommendations for international students: Required—TOEFL (minimum score 580 paper-based; 85 iBT), IELTS (minimum score 7). *Application deadline:* For fall admission, 1/15 priority date for domestic students, 1/15 for international students. Application fee: $50. Electronic applications accepted. *Expenses: Tuition:* Full-time $5950; part-time $331 per credit hour. Tuition and fees vary according to program and student's religious affiliation. *Financial support:* In 2012–13, 27 students received support, including 16 research assistantships with full tuition reimbursements available (averaging $20,640 per year), 15 teaching assistantships with full tuition reimbursements available (averaging $19,680 per year); fellowships with full tuition reimbursements available, institutionally sponsored loans, and tuition waivers (full) also available. Support available to part-time students. Financial award application deadline: 1/15. *Faculty research:* Acoustics; atomic, molecular, and optical physics; theoretical and mathematical physics; condensed matter; astrophysics and plasma. *Total annual research expenditures:* $1.8 million. *Unit head:* Dr. Ross L. Spencer, Chair, 801-422-2341, Fax: 801-422-0553, E-mail: ross_spencer@byu.edu. *Application contact:* Dr. Eric W. Hirschmann, Graduate Coordinator, 801-422-9271, Fax: 801-422-0553, E-mail: eric_hirschmann@byu.edu. Website: http://physics.byu.edu/.

Brock University, Faculty of Graduate Studies, Faculty of Mathematics and Science, Program in Physics, St. Catharines, ON L2S 3A1, Canada. Offers M Sc. Part-time programs available. *Degree requirements:* For master's, thesis. *Entrance requirements:* For master's, honors B Sc in physics. Additional exam requirements/recommendations for international students: Required—TOEFL (minimum score 550 paper-based; 80 iBT), IELTS (minimum score 6.5), TWE (minimum score 4). Electronic applications accepted. *Faculty research:* Quantum physics, optical properties, non-crystalline materials, condensed matter physics, biophysics.

Brooklyn College of the City University of New York, Division of Graduate Studies, Department of Physics, Brooklyn, NY 11210-2889. Offers MA, PhD. Part-time programs available. Terminal master's awarded for partial completion of doctoral program. *Degree requirements:* For master's, comprehensive exam, thesis or alternative, 30 credits. *Entrance requirements:* For master's, 2 letters of recommendation, 12 credits in advanced physics; for doctorate, GRE. Additional exam requirements/recommendations for international students: Required—TOEFL (minimum score 500 paper-based; 61 iBT). Electronic applications accepted.

Brooklyn College of the City University of New York, Division of Graduate Studies, School of Education, Program in Middle Childhood Education (Science), Brooklyn, NY 11210-2889. Offers biology (MA); chemistry (MA); earth science (MA); general science (MA); physics (MA). Part-time and evening/weekend programs available. *Entrance requirements:* For master's, LAST, interview, previous course work in education and mathematics, resume, 2 letters of recommendation, essay. Additional exam requirements/recommendations for international students: Required—TOEFL (minimum score 500 paper-based; 61 iBT). Electronic applications accepted. *Faculty research:* Geometric thinking, mastery of basic facts, problem-solving strategies, history of mathematics.

Brown University, Graduate School, Department of Physics, Providence, RI 02912. Offers Sc M, PhD. *Degree requirements:* For doctorate, thesis/dissertation, qualifying and oral exams.

Bryn Mawr College, Graduate School of Arts and Sciences, Department of Physics, Bryn Mawr, PA 19010-2899. Offers MA, PhD. *Faculty:* 2 full-time (0 women), 2 part-time/adjunct (0 women). *Students:* 5 full-time (1 woman), 1 (woman) part-time. Average age 24. 5 applicants, 40% accepted, 1 enrolled. In 2012, 1 doctorate awarded. *Degree requirements:* For master's, one foreign language, thesis; for doctorate, one foreign language, thesis/dissertation. *Entrance requirements:* For master's and doctorate, GRE General Test, GRE Subject Test. Additional exam requirements/recommendations for international students: Required—TOEFL (minimum score 600 paper-based). *Application deadline:* For fall admission, 1/3 for domestic and international students. Application fee: $50. *Expenses: Tuition:* Full-time $35,280. *Financial support:* In 2012–13, 5 research assistantships with full tuition reimbursements (averaging $3,900 per year), 4 teaching assistantships with partial tuition reimbursements (averaging $13,563 per year) were awarded; Federal Work-Study, scholarships/grants, tuition waivers (partial), and tuition awards also available. Support available to part-time students. Financial award application deadline: 1/3. *Unit head:* Dr. Elizabeth McCormack, Chair/Professor of Physics, 610-526-5656, E-mail: emccorma@brynmawr.edu. *Application contact:* Maria Dantis, Administrative Assistant to the Graduate School of Arts and Sciences Dean, 610-526-5074, E-mail: mdantis@brynmawr.edu.

228 www.petersonsbooks.com

Peterson's Graduate Programs in the Physical Sciences, Mathematics, Agricultural Sciences, the Environment & Natural Resources 2014

California Institute of Technology, Division of Physics, Mathematics and Astronomy, Department of Physics, Pasadena, CA 91125-0001. Offers PhD. *Degree requirements:* For doctorate, thesis/dissertation, candidacy and final exams. *Entrance requirements:* For doctorate, GRE General Test, GRE Subject Test. Additional exam requirements/recommendations for international students: Required—TOEFL. *Faculty research:* High-energy physics, nuclear physics, condensed-matter physics, theoretical physics and astrophysics, gravity physics.

California State University, Fresno, Division of Graduate Studies, College of Science and Mathematics, Department of Physics, Fresno, CA 93740-8027. Offers MS. Part-time programs available. *Degree requirements:* For master's, thesis or alternative. *Entrance requirements:* For master's, GRE General Test, minimum GPA of 2.5. Additional exam requirements/recommendations for international students: Required—TOEFL. Electronic applications accepted. *Faculty research:* Energy, astronomy, silicon vertex detector, neuroimaging, particle physics.

California State University, Fullerton, Graduate Studies, College of Natural Science and Mathematics, Department of Physics, Fullerton, CA 92834-9480. Offers MS. Part-time programs available. *Students:* 3 full-time (0 women), 14 part-time (3 women); includes 7 minority (2 Asian, non-Hispanic/Latino; 5 Hispanic/Latino), 1 international. Average age 26. 22 applicants, 73% accepted, 13 enrolled. In 2012, 3 master's awarded. Application fee: $55. *Financial support:* Research assistantships, teaching assistantships, career-related internships or fieldwork, Federal Work-Study, institutionally sponsored loans, and scholarships/grants available. Support available to part-time students. Financial award application deadline: 3/1; financial award applicants required to submit FAFSA. *Unit head:* Dr. Jim Feagin, Chair, 657-278-4827. *Application contact:* Admissions/Applications, 657-278-2371.

California State University, Long Beach, Graduate Studies, College of Natural Sciences and Mathematics, Department of Physics and Astronomy, Long Beach, CA 90840. Offers physics (MS). Part-time programs available. *Degree requirements:* For master's, comprehensive exam or thesis. Electronic applications accepted. *Faculty research:* Musical acoustics, modern optics, neutrino physics, quantum gravity, atomic physics.

California State University, Los Angeles, Graduate Studies, College of Natural and Social Sciences, Department of Physics and Astronomy, Los Angeles, CA 90032-8530. Offers physics (MS). Part-time and evening/weekend programs available. *Faculty:* 1 full-time (0 women), 4 part-time/adjunct (1 woman). *Students:* 12 full-time (5 women), 7 part-time (1 woman); includes 12 minority (2 Asian, non-Hispanic/Latino; 8 Hispanic/Latino; 2 Two or more races, non-Hispanic/Latino), 1 international. Average age 35. 25 applicants, 60% accepted, 6 enrolled. In 2012, 5 master's awarded. *Degree requirements:* For master's, comprehensive exam or thesis. *Entrance requirements:* Additional exam requirements/recommendations for international students: Required—TOEFL (minimum score 500 paper-based). *Application deadline:* For fall admission, 5/1 for domestic and international students. Applications are processed on a rolling basis. Application fee: $55. Electronic applications accepted. *Financial support:* Federal Work-Study available. Support available to part-time students. Financial award application deadline: 3/1. *Faculty research:* Intermediate energy, nuclear physics, condensed-matter physics, biophysics. *Unit head:* Dr. Oscar Bernal, Chair, 323-343-2100, Fax: 323-343-2497, E-mail: obernal@calstatela.edu. *Application contact:* Dr. Larry Fritz, Dean of Graduate Studies, 323-343-3820, Fax: 323-343-5653, E-mail: lfritz@calstatela.edu. Website: http://www.calstatela.edu/dept/physics/.

California State University, Northridge, Graduate Studies, College of Science and Mathematics, Department of Physics and Astronomy, Northridge, CA 91330. Offers physics (MS). Part-time and evening/weekend programs available. *Degree requirements:* For master's, thesis or comprehensive exam. *Entrance requirements:* For master's, GRE General Test or minimum GPA of 3.0. Additional exam requirements/recommendations for international students: Required—TOEFL.

Carleton University, Faculty of Graduate Studies, Faculty of Science, Department of Physics, Ottawa, ON K1S 5B6, Canada. Offers M Sc, PhD. Programs offered jointly with University of Ottawa. *Degree requirements:* For master's, thesis optional, seminar; for doctorate, comprehensive exam, thesis/dissertation, seminar. *Entrance requirements:* For master's, honors degree in science; for doctorate, M Sc. Additional exam requirements/recommendations for international students: Required—TOEFL. *Faculty research:* Experimental and theoretical elementary particle physics, medical physics.

Carnegie Mellon University, Mellon College of Science, Department of Physics, Pittsburgh, PA 15213-3891. Offers applied physics (PhD); physics (MS, PhD). *Degree requirements:* For doctorate, thesis/dissertation, qualifying exam. *Entrance requirements:* For doctorate, GRE General Test, GRE Subject Test. Additional exam requirements/recommendations for international students: Required—TOEFL. Electronic applications accepted. *Faculty research:* Astrophysics, condensed matter physics, biological physics, medium energy and nuclear physics, high-energy physics.

Case Western Reserve University, School of Graduate Studies, Department of Physics, Cleveland, OH 44106. Offers MS, PhD. Part-time programs available. *Faculty:* 23 full-time (4 women), 6 part-time/adjunct (1 woman). *Students:* 61 full-time (10 women), 1 part-time (0 women); includes 4 minority (1 Black or African American, non-Hispanic/Latino; 1 Hispanic/Latino; 2 Two or more races, non-Hispanic/Latino), 21 international. Average age 26. 171 applicants, 32% accepted, 13 enrolled. In 2012, 2 master's, 4 doctorates awarded. Terminal master's awarded for partial completion of doctoral program. *Degree requirements:* For master's, comprehensive exam, exam; for doctorate, thesis/dissertation, qualifying exam, topical exam. *Entrance requirements:* For master's and doctorate, GRE General Test, GRE Subject Test (physics), letters of recommendation. Additional exam requirements/recommendations for international students: Required—TOEFL (minimum score 577 paper-based; 90 iBT); Recommended—IELTS (minimum score 7). *Application deadline:* For fall admission, 1/15 priority date for domestic students. Application fee: $8. Electronic applications accepted. *Financial support:* Fellowships, research assistantships, teaching assistantships, tuition waivers, and unspecified assistantships available. Financial award application deadline: 1/15. *Faculty research:* Condensed-matter physics, imaging physics, nonlinear optics, high-energy physics, cosmology and astrophysics. *Unit head:* Prof. Kathleen Kash, Chair, 216-368-4000, E-mail: kathleen.kash@case.edu. *Application contact:* Prof. Corbin Covault, Admissions, 216-368-4000, Fax: 216-368-4671, E-mail: grad_dir@phys.case.edu. Website: http://www.phys.cwru.edu/.

The Catholic University of America, School of Arts and Sciences, Department of Physics, Washington, DC 20064. Offers MS, PhD. Part-time programs available. *Faculty:* 12 full-time (2 women), 2 part-time/adjunct (0 women). *Students:* 14 full-time (8 women), 23 part-time (9 women); includes 4 minority (1 Asian, non-Hispanic/Latino; 3 Hispanic/Latino), 15 international. Average age 28. 28 applicants, 64% accepted, 8 enrolled. In 2012, 4 master's, 1 doctorate awarded. *Degree requirements:* For master's, comprehensive exam, thesis or alternative; for doctorate, comprehensive exam, thesis/dissertation, oral exam. *Entrance requirements:* For master's and doctorate, GRE General Test, statement of purpose, official copies of academic transcripts, three letters of recommendation. Additional exam requirements/recommendations for international students: Required—TOEFL (minimum score 580 paper-based). *Application deadline:* For fall admission, 8/1 priority date for domestic students, 7/15 for international students; for spring admission, 12/1 priority date for domestic students, 10/15 for international students. Applications are processed on a rolling basis. Application fee: $55. Electronic applications accepted. *Expenses: Tuition:* Full-time $36,320; part-time $1420 per credit hour. *Required fees:* $400; $145 per semester hour. One-time fee: $425. Tuition and fees vary according to program. *Financial support:* Fellowships, research assistantships, teaching assistantships, Federal Work-Study, scholarships/grants, tuition waivers (full and partial), and unspecified assistantships available. Financial award application deadline: 2/1; financial award applicants required to submit FAFSA. *Faculty research:* Glass and ceramics technologies, astrophysics and computational sciences, the role of evolution in galaxy properties, nuclear physics, biophysics. *Total annual research expenditures:* $6.7 million. *Unit head:* Dr. Steve Kraemer, Chair, 202-319-5856, Fax: 202-319-4448, E-mail: kraemer@cua.edu. *Application contact:* Andrew Woodall, Director of Graduate Admissions, 202-319-5057, Fax: 202-319-6533, E-mail: cua-admissions@cua.edu. Website: http://physics.cua.edu/.

Central Connecticut State University, School of Graduate Studies, School of Arts and Sciences, Department of Physics and Earth Science, New Britain, CT 06050-4010. Offers natural sciences (MS); science education (Certificate). Part-time and evening/weekend programs available. *Faculty:* 3 full-time (1 woman). *Students:* 7 part-time (6 women). Average age 32. 3 applicants, 33% accepted, 1 enrolled. In 2012, 3 master's, 1 other advanced degree awarded. *Degree requirements:* For master's, comprehensive exam, thesis or alternative; for Certificate, qualifying exam. *Entrance requirements:* For master's, minimum undergraduate GPA of 2.7. Additional exam requirements/recommendations for international students: Required—TOEFL (minimum score 550 paper-based; 79 iBT). *Application deadline:* For fall admission, 6/1 for domestic students, 5/1 for international students; for spring admission, 11/1 for domestic and international students. Applications are processed on a rolling basis. Application fee: $50. Electronic applications accepted. *Expenses: Tuition, area resident:* Full-time $5337; part-time $498 per credit. Tuition, state resident: full-time $8008; part-time $510 per credit. Tuition, nonresident: full-time $14,869; part-time $510 per credit. *Required fees:* $3970. One-time fee: $62 part-time. *Financial support:* Career-related internships or fieldwork, Federal Work-Study, scholarships/grants, and unspecified assistantships available. Support available to part-time students. Financial award application deadline: 3/1; financial award applicants required to submit FAFSA. *Faculty research:* Elementary/secondary science education, particle and solid states, weather patterns, planetary studies. *Unit head:* Dr. Mark Evans, Chair, 860-832-2930, E-mail: evansmaa@ccsu.edu. *Application contact:* Patricia Gardner, Associate Director of Graduate Studies, 860-832-2350, Fax: 860-832-2362, E-mail: graduateadmissions@ccsu.edu. Website: http://www.physics.ccsu.edu/.

Central Michigan University, College of Graduate Studies, College of Science and Technology, Department of Physics, Mount Pleasant, MI 48859. Offers physics (MS); science of advanced materials (PhD). PhD is an interdisciplinary program. Part-time programs available. *Faculty:* 5 full-time (1 woman). *Students:* 30 (9 women); includes 2 minority (1 Black or African American, non-Hispanic/Latino; 1 Asian, non-Hispanic/Latino), 16 international. Average age 29. 39 applicants, 23% accepted, 6 enrolled. In 2012, 8 master's awarded. *Degree requirements:* For master's, thesis or alternative; for doctorate, comprehensive exam, thesis/dissertation. *Entrance requirements:* For doctorate, GRE, bachelor's degree in physics, chemistry, biochemistry, biology, geology, engineering, mathematics, or other relevant area. *Application deadline:* For fall admission, 6/1 for international students; for spring admission, 10/1 for international students.

Application fee: $35 ($45 for international students). Electronic applications accepted. *Expenses:* Tuition, state resident: full-time $8730; part-time $485 per credit hour. Tuition, nonresident: full-time $13,788; part-time $766 per credit hour. One-time fee: $75. Tuition and fees vary according to degree level, campus/location and reciprocity agreements. *Financial support:* Research assistantships, teaching assistantships, career-related internships or fieldwork, Federal Work-Study, unspecified assistantships, and out-of-state merit awards available. *Faculty research:* Science of advanced materials, polymer physics, laser spectroscopy, observational astronomy, nuclear physics. *Unit head:* Dr. Christopher Tycner, Chairperson, 989-774-3321, Fax: 989-774-2697, E-mail: tycne1c@cmich.edu. *Application contact:* Jessica Lapp, Graduate Coordinator, 989-774-2221, Fax: 989-774-2657, E-mail: lapp1jw@cmich.edu. Website: http://www.phy.cmich.edu/.

Christopher Newport University, Graduate Studies, Department of Physics, Computer Science, and Engineering, Newport News, VA 23606-2998. Offers applied physics and computer science (MS). Part-time and evening/weekend programs available. *Degree requirements:* For master's, comprehensive exam (for some programs), thesis optional. *Entrance requirements:* For master's, GRE General Test, minimum GPA of 3.0. Additional exam requirements/recommendations for international students: Required—TOEFL (minimum score 580 paper-based; 92 iBT). Electronic applications accepted. *Faculty research:* Advanced programming methodologies, experimental nuclear physics, computer architecture, semiconductor nanophysics, laser and optical fiber sensors.

City College of the City University of New York, Graduate School, College of Liberal Arts and Science, Division of Science, Department of Physics, New York, NY 10031-9198. Offers MA, PhD. PhD program offered jointly with Graduate School and University Center of the City University of New York. Terminal master's awarded for partial completion of doctoral program. *Degree requirements:* For master's, comprehensive exam; for doctorate, thesis/dissertation. *Entrance requirements:* For doctorate, GRE. Additional exam requirements/recommendations for international students: Required—TOEFL (minimum score 500 paper-based; 61 iBT). Electronic applications accepted.

Clark Atlanta University, School of Arts and Sciences, Department of Physics, Atlanta, GA 30314. Offers MS. Part-time programs available. *Faculty:* 5 full-time (0 women). *Students:* 5 full-time (2 women), 2 part-time (1 woman); includes 4 minority (all Black or African American, non-Hispanic/Latino), 3 international. Average age 28. 6 applicants, 100% accepted, 4 enrolled. In 2012, 1 master's awarded. *Degree requirements:* For master's, one foreign language, comprehensive exam, thesis optional. *Entrance requirements:* For master's, GRE General Test, minimum GPA of 2.5. Additional exam requirements/recommendations for international students: Required—TOEFL (minimum score 500 paper-based; 61 iBT). *Application deadline:* For fall admission, 4/1 for domestic and international students; for spring admission, 11/1 for domestic and international students. Applications are processed on a rolling basis. Application fee: $40 ($55 for international students). *Expenses: Tuition:* Full-time $14,256; part-time $792 per credit hour. *Required fees:* $818; $409 per semester. *Financial support:* Scholarships/grants and unspecified assistantships available. Financial award application deadline: 4/30; financial award applicants required to submit FAFSA. *Faculty research:* Fusion energy, investigations of nonlinear differential equations, difference schemes, collisions in dense plasma. *Unit head:* Dr. Swaraj Tayal, Chairperson, 404-880-6877, E-mail: stayal@cau.edu. *Application contact:* Michelle Clark-Davis, Graduate Program Admissions, 404-880-6605, E-mail: cauadmissions@cau.edu.

Clarkson University, Graduate School, School of Arts and Sciences, Department of Physics, Potsdam, NY 13699. Offers MS, PhD. Part-time programs available. *Faculty:* 14 full-time (1 woman), 1 part-time/adjunct (0 women). *Students:* 13 full-time (3 women), 6 international. Average age 25. 22 applicants, 50% accepted, 5 enrolled. In 2012, 4 master's, 1 doctorate awarded. Terminal master's awarded for partial completion of doctoral program. *Degree requirements:* For doctorate, thesis/dissertation, departmental qualifying exam. *Entrance requirements:* For master's and doctorate, GRE, transcripts of all college coursework, three letters of recommendation; resume and personal statement (recommended). Additional exam requirements/recommendations for international students: Required—TOEFL. *Application deadline:* For fall admission, 1/30 priority date for domestic students, 1/30 for international students; for spring admission, 9/1 priority date for domestic students, 9/1 for international students. Applications are processed on a rolling basis. Application fee: $25 ($35 for international students). Electronic applications accepted. *Expenses: Tuition:* Full-time $15,108; part-time $1259 per credit hour. *Required fees:* $295 per semester. *Financial support:* In 2012–13, 13 students received support, including fellowships with full tuition reimbursements available (averaging $22,650 per year), 3 research assistantships with full tuition reimbursements available (averaging $22,650 per year), 10 teaching assistantships with full tuition reimbursements available (averaging $22,650 per year); scholarships/grants, tuition waivers (partial), and unspecified assistantships also available. *Faculty research:* Cost reduction of silicon-based photovoltaic devices, self-assembled, microthermometers, error correction and digitalization concepts, novel particle tracers. *Total annual research expenditures:* $376,981. *Unit head:* Dr. Dipankar Roy, Chair, 315-268-2396, Fax: 315-268-7754, E-mail: samoy@clarkson.edu. *Application contact:* Jennifer Reed, Graduate Coordinator, School of Arts and Sciences, 315-268-3802, Fax: 315-268-3989, E-mail: sciencegrad@clarkson.edu. Website: http://www.clarkson.edu/physics/.

Clark University, Graduate School, Department of Physics, Worcester, MA 01610-1477. Offers MA, PhD. Part-time programs available. *Faculty:* 6 full-time (0 women). *Students:* 6 full-time (3 women), 2 part-time (0 women); includes 1 minority (Black or African American, non-Hispanic/Latino), 5 international. Average age 35. 16 applicants, 44% accepted, 1 enrolled. In 2012, 1 master's, 2 doctorates awarded. Terminal master's awarded for partial completion of doctoral program. *Degree requirements:* For master's, thesis or alternative; for doctorate, one foreign language, thesis/dissertation. *Entrance requirements:* Additional exam requirements/recommendations for international students: Required—TOEFL. *Application deadline:* For fall admission, 2/1 for domestic students. Application fee: $50. *Expenses: Tuition:* Full-time $38,100; part-time $4762.50 per course. *Required fees:* $30. Tuition and fees vary according to course load and program. *Financial support:* In 2012–13, 2 research assistantships with full tuition reimbursements (averaging $18,280 per year), 5 teaching assistantships with full tuition reimbursements (averaging $18,280 per year) were awarded; fellowships with full and partial tuition reimbursements, Federal Work-Study, and tuition waivers (full and partial) also available. Financial award application deadline: 4/1. *Faculty research:* Statistical and thermal physics, magnetic properties of materials, computer simulation, particle diffusion. *Total annual research expenditures:* $280,000. *Unit head:* Dr. Charles Agosta, Chair, 508-793-7169, Fax: 508-793-8861, E-mail: cagosta@clarku.edu. *Application contact:* Sujata Davis, Department Secretary, 508-793-7169, Fax: 508-793-8861, E-mail: sdavis1@clarku.edu. Website: http://www.clarku.edu/departments/physics/graduate/index.cfm.

Clemson University, Graduate School, College of Engineering and Science, Department of Physics and Astronomy, Clemson, SC 29634. Offers physics (MS, PhD), including astronomy and astrophysics, atmospheric physics, biophysics. Part-time programs available. *Faculty:* 24 full-time (3 women). *Students:* 62 full-time (15 women), 1 part-time (0 women); includes 2 minority (1 Black or African American, non-Hispanic/Latino; 1 Hispanic/Latino), 28 international. Average age 26. 66 applicants, 41% accepted, 12 enrolled. In 2012, 8 master's, 5 doctorates awarded. Terminal master's awarded for partial completion of doctoral program. *Degree requirements:* For master's, thesis or alternative; for doctorate, thesis/dissertation. *Entrance requirements:* For master's and doctorate, GRE General Test. Additional exam requirements/recommendations for international students: Required—TOEFL. *Application deadline:* For fall admission, 1/15 priority date for domestic students; for spring admission, 9/15 priority date for domestic students. Applications are processed on a rolling basis. Application fee: $70 ($80 for international students). Electronic applications accepted. *Financial support:* In 2012–13, 60 students received support, including 1 fellowship with full and partial tuition reimbursement available (averaging $7,000 per year), 25 research assistantships with partial tuition reimbursements available (averaging $13,151 per year), 44 teaching assistantships with partial tuition reimbursements available (averaging $15,956 per year); career-related internships or fieldwork, institutionally sponsored loans, scholarships/grants, health care benefits, and unspecified assistantships also available. Support available to part-time students. Financial award application deadline: 6/1; financial award applicants required to submit FAFSA. *Faculty research:* Radiation physics, solid-state physics, nuclear physics, radar and lidar studies of atmosphere. *Total annual research expenditures:* $2.6 million. *Unit head:* Dr. Peter Barnes, Chair, 864-656-3419, Fax: 864-656-0805, E-mail: peterb@clemson.edu. *Application contact:* Graduate Coordinator, 864-656-6702, Fax: 864-656-0805, E-mail: physgradinfo-l@clemson.edu. Website: http://physicsnt.clemson.edu/.

Cleveland State University, College of Graduate Studies, College of Sciences and Health Professions, Department of Physics, Cleveland, OH 44115. Offers applied optics (MS); condensed matter physics (MS); medical physics (MS); optics and materials (MS); optics and medical imaging (MS). Part-time and evening/weekend programs available. *Faculty:* 4 full-time (0 women), 1 part-time/adjunct (0 women). *Students:* 2 full-time (1 woman), 18 part-time (3 women); includes 1 minority (Asian, non-Hispanic/Latino), 3 international. Average age 31. 30 applicants, 87% accepted, 7 enrolled. In 2012, 3 master's awarded. *Entrance requirements:* For master's, undergraduate degree in engineering, physics, chemistry or mathematics. Additional exam requirements/recommendations for international students: Required—TOEFL (minimum score 525 paper-based). *Application deadline:* For fall admission, 7/15 priority date for domestic students, 7/15 for international students. Applications are processed on a rolling basis. Application fee: $30. Electronic applications accepted. *Expenses:* Tuition, state resident: full-time $8172; part-time $510.75 per credit hour. Tuition, nonresident: full-time $15,372; part-time $960.75 per credit hour. *Required fees:* $25 per semester. Tuition and fees vary according to course load and program. *Financial support:* In 2012–13, 1 research assistantship with full and partial tuition reimbursement (averaging $5,666 per year) was awarded; fellowships with tuition reimbursements, teaching assistantships, and tuition waivers (full) also available. *Faculty research:* Statistical physics, experimental solid-state physics, theoretical optics, experimental biological physics (macromolecular crystallography), experimental optics. *Total annual research expenditures:* $350,000. *Unit head:* Dr. Miron Kaufman, Chairperson, 216-687-2436, Fax: 216-523-7268, E-mail: m.kaufman@csuohio.edu. *Application contact:* Dr. James A. Lock, Director, 216-687-2420, Fax: 216-523-7268, E-mail: j.lock@csuohio.edu. Website: http://www.csuohio.edu/sciences/dept/physics/index.html.

The College of William and Mary, Faculty of Arts and Sciences, Department of Physics, Williamsburg, VA 23187-8795. Offers MS, PhD. *Faculty:* 37 full-time (5 women). *Students:* 71 full-time (18 women); includes 3 minority (2 Asian, non-Hispanic/Latino; 1 Hispanic/Latino), 26 international. Average age 26. 108

applicants, 38% accepted, 15 enrolled. In 2012, 9 master's, 6 doctorates awarded. Terminal master's awarded for partial completion of doctoral program. *Degree requirements:* For master's, minimum GPA of 3.0, 32 credit hours; for doctorate, comprehensive exam, thesis/dissertation, 1-year residency, 2 semesters of physics teaching. *Entrance requirements:* For doctorate, GRE General Test, GRE Subject Test, minimum GPA of 2.5. Additional exam requirements/recommendations for international students: Required—TOEFL. *Application deadline:* For fall admission, 1/15 priority date for domestic students, 1/15 for international students. Applications are processed on a rolling basis. Application fee: $45. Electronic applications accepted. *Expenses:* Tuition, state resident: full-time $6779; part-time $385 per credit hour. Tuition, nonresident: full-time $20,608; part-time $1000 per credit hour. *Required fees:* $4625. *Financial support:* In 2012–13, 65 students received support, including 30 research assistantships with full tuition reimbursements available, 36 teaching assistantships with full tuition reimbursements available; career-related internships or fieldwork, health care benefits, tuition waivers (full), and unspecified assistantships also available. *Faculty research:* Nuclear/particle, condensed-matter, atomic, and plasma physics; accelerator physics; molecular/optical physics; computational/nonlinear physics. *Total annual research expenditures:* $3.9 million. *Unit head:* Dr. David Armstrong, Chair, 757-221-3500, Fax: 757-221-3540, E-mail: chair@physics.wm.edu. *Application contact:* Dr. Keith Griffioen, Chair of Admissions, 757-221-3538, Fax: 757-221-3540, E-mail: grad@physics.wm.edu. Website: http://www.wm.edu/physics/.

Colorado School of Mines, Graduate School, Department of Physics, Golden, CO 80401-1887. Offers applied physics (MS, PhD); materials science (MS, PhD); nuclear engineering (MS, PhD). Part-time programs available. *Faculty:* 37 full-time (4 women), 9 part-time/adjunct (5 women). *Students:* 65 full-time (21 women), 10 part-time (1 woman); includes 5 minority (1 Asian, non-Hispanic/Latino; 4 Hispanic/Latino), 16 international. Average age 27. 102 applicants, 34% accepted, 16 enrolled. In 2012, 10 master's, 3 doctorates awarded. *Degree requirements:* For master's, thesis (for some programs); for doctorate, comprehensive exam, thesis/dissertation. *Entrance requirements:* For master's and doctorate, GRE General Test, GRE Subject Test. Additional exam requirements/recommendations for international students: Required—TOEFL (minimum score 550 paper-based; 80 iBT). *Application deadline:* For fall admission, 1/15 priority date for domestic students, 1/15 for international students; for spring admission, 10/15 priority date for domestic students, 10/15 for international students. Application fee: $50 ($70 for international students). Electronic applications accepted. *Financial support:* In 2012–13, 52 students received support, including fellowships with full tuition reimbursements available (averaging $21,120 per year), 40 research assistantships with full tuition reimbursements available (averaging $21,120 per year), 12 teaching assistantships with full tuition reimbursements available (averaging $21,120 per year); scholarships/grants, health care benefits, and unspecified assistantships also available. Financial award application deadline: 1/15; financial award applicants required to submit FAFSA. *Faculty research:* Light scattering, low-energy nuclear physics, high fusion plasma diagnostics, laser operations, mathematical physics. *Total annual research expenditures:* $7.1 million. *Unit head:* Dr. Thomas Furtak, Head, 303-273-3843, Fax: 303-273-3919, E-mail: tfurtak@mines.edu. *Application contact:* Dr. David Wood, Professor, 303-273-3853, Fax: 303-273-3919, E-mail: dwood@mines.edu. Website: http://physics.mines.edu.

Colorado State University, Graduate School, College of Natural Sciences, Department of Physics, Fort Collins, CO 80523-1875. Offers MS, PhD. *Faculty:* 20 full-time (2 women), 1 part-time/adjunct (0 women). *Students:* 31 full-time (4 women), 40 part-time (8 women); includes 7 minority (2 Asian, non-Hispanic/Latino; 2 Hispanic/Latino; 3 Two or more races, non-Hispanic/Latino), 17 international. Average age 27. 22 applicants, 41% accepted, 9 enrolled. In 2012, 5 master's, 4 doctorates awarded. *Degree requirements:* For doctorate, thesis/dissertation. *Entrance requirements:* For master's, GRE General Test or GRE Subject Test (physics), minimum GPA of 3.0; 3 letters of recommendation; for doctorate, GRE General Test or GRE Subject Test (physics), minimum GPA of 3.0; transcripts; 3 letters of recommendation; BA (for domestic students); statement of purpose. Additional exam requirements/recommendations for international students: Required—TOEFL (minimum score 600 paper-based; 100 iBT). *Application deadline:* For fall admission, 2/1 priority date for domestic students, 2/1 for international students. Application fee: $50. Electronic applications accepted. *Expenses:* Tuition, state resident: full-time $8811; part-time $490 per credit. Tuition, nonresident: full-time $21,600; part-time $1200 per credit. *Required fees:* $1819; $61 per credit. *Financial support:* In 2012–13, 68 students received support, including 4 fellowships (averaging $45,011 per year), 32 research assistantships with full tuition reimbursements available (averaging $14,477 per year), 32 teaching assistantships with full tuition reimbursements available (averaging $13,850 per year); scholarships/grants, health care benefits, and unspecified assistantships also available. Financial award application deadline: 1/1; financial award applicants required to submit FAFSA. *Faculty research:* Condensed-matter physics, theoretical physics, particle and astroparticle physics. *Total annual research expenditures:* $2.8 million. *Unit head:* Dr. John Harton, Chair, 970-491-6246, Fax: 970-491-7947, E-mail: john.harton@colostate.edu. *Application contact:* Veronica Nicholsen, Graduate Contact, 970-491-6207, Fax: 970-491-7947, E-mail: veronica.nicholson@colostate.edu. Website: http://www.physics.colostate.edu/.

Columbia University, Graduate School of Arts and Sciences, Division of Natural Sciences, Department of Physics, New York, NY 10027. Offers philosophical foundations of physics (MA); physics (M Phil, PhD). *Degree requirements:* For doctorate, thesis/dissertation. *Entrance requirements:* For master's and doctorate, GRE General Test, GRE Subject Test, 3 years of course work in physics. Additional exam requirements/recommendations for international students: Required—TOEFL. *Faculty research:* Theoretical physics; astrophysics; low-, medium-, and high-energy physics.

Concordia University, School of Graduate Studies, Faculty of Arts and Science, Department of Physics, Montréal, QC H3G 1M8, Canada. Offers M Sc, PhD.

Cornell University, Graduate School, Graduate Fields of Arts and Sciences, Field of Physics, Ithaca, NY 14853-0001. Offers experimental physics (MS, PhD); physics (MS, PhD); theoretical physics (MS, PhD). *Faculty:* 56 full-time (6 women). *Students:* 166 full-time (29 women); includes 13 minority (1 Black or African American, non-Hispanic/Latino; 6 Asian, non-Hispanic/Latino; 4 Hispanic/Latino; 2 Two or more races, non-Hispanic/Latino), 75 international. Average age 26. 467 applicants, 20% accepted, 32 enrolled. In 2012, 23 master's, 21 doctorates awarded. *Degree requirements:* For doctorate, comprehensive exam, thesis/dissertation. *Entrance requirements:* For doctorate, GRE General Test, GRE Subject Test (physics), 3 letters of recommendation. Additional exam requirements/recommendations for international students: Required—TOEFL (minimum score 620 paper-based; 105 iBT). *Application deadline:* For fall admission, 1/3 for domestic students. Application fee: $95. Electronic applications accepted. *Financial support:* In 2012–13, 157 students received support, including 43 fellowships with full tuition reimbursements available, 56 research assistantships with full tuition reimbursements available, 58 teaching assistantships with full tuition reimbursements available; institutionally sponsored loans, scholarships/grants, health care benefits, tuition waivers (full and partial), and unspecified assistantships also available. Financial award applicants required to submit FAFSA. *Faculty research:* Experimental condensed matter physics, theoretical condensed matter physics, experimental high energy particle physics, theoretical particle physics and field theory, theoretical astrophysics. *Unit head:* Director of Graduate Studies, 607-255-7561. *Application contact:* Graduate Field Assistant, 607-255-7561, E-mail: physics-grad-adm@cornell.edu. Website: http://www.gradschool.cornell.edu/fields.php?id-36&a-2.

Creighton University, Graduate School, College of Arts and Sciences, Program in Physics, Omaha, NE 68178-0001. Offers MS. Part-time programs available. *Faculty:* 11 full-time (2 women). *Students:* 7 full-time (0 women), 2 part-time (0 women); includes 1 minority (Asian, non-Hispanic/Latino). Average age 25. 14 applicants, 64% accepted, 5 enrolled. In 2012, 7 master's awarded. *Degree requirements:* For master's, comprehensive exam, thesis (for some programs). *Entrance requirements:* For master's, GRE General Test, 3 letters of recommendation. Additional exam requirements/recommendations for international students: Required—TOEFL (minimum score 550 paper-based; 80 iBT). *Application deadline:* For fall admission, 3/1 for domestic and international students. Applications are processed on a rolling basis. Application fee: $50. Electronic applications accepted. *Expenses: Tuition:* Full-time $13,250; part-time $730 per credit hour. *Required fees:* $144 per semester. Tuition and fees vary according to course load, campus/location, program, reciprocity agreements and student's religious affiliation. *Financial support:* In 2012–13, 8 students received support, including 8 teaching assistantships with full tuition reimbursements available (averaging $11,633 per year). Financial award applicants required to submit FAFSA. *Unit head:* Dr. Michael Nichols, Chair, 402-280-2159, E-mail: mnichols@creighton.edu. *Application contact:* Taunya Plater, Senior Program Coordinator, 402-280-2870, Fax: 402-280-2423, E-mail: taunyaplater@creighton.edu.

Dalhousie University, Faculty of Science, Department of Physics and Atmospheric Science, Halifax, NS B3H 4R2, Canada. Offers M Sc, PhD. *Degree requirements:* For master's, thesis; for doctorate, thesis/dissertation. *Entrance requirements:* Additional exam requirements/recommendations for international students: Required—TOEFL, IELTS, CANTEST, CAEL, or Michigan English Language Assessment Battery. Electronic applications accepted. *Faculty research:* Applied, experimental, and solid-state physics.

Dartmouth College, Arts and Sciences Graduate Programs, Department of Physics and Astronomy, Hanover, NH 03755. Offers MS, PhD. Terminal master's awarded for partial completion of doctoral program. *Degree requirements:* For master's, thesis; for doctorate, thesis/dissertation. *Entrance requirements:* For master's and doctorate, GRE General Test, GRE Subject Test. Additional exam requirements/recommendations for international students: Required—TOEFL. *Faculty research:* Matter physics, plasma and beam physics, space physics, astronomy, cosmology.

Delaware State University, Graduate Programs, Department of Physics, Dover, DE 19901-2277. Offers applied optics (MS); optics (PhD); physics (MS); physics teaching (MS). Part-time and evening/weekend programs available. *Entrance requirements:* For master's, minimum GPA of 3.0 in major, 2.75 overall. Additional exam requirements/recommendations for international students: Required—TOEFL. Electronic applications accepted. *Faculty research:* Thermal properties of solids, nuclear physics, radiation damage in solids.

DePaul University, College of Science and Health, Department of Physics, Chicago, IL 60614. Offers MS. Part-time and evening/weekend programs available. *Students:* 5 full-time (1 woman), 7 part-time (4 women); includes 1 minority (Black or African American, non-Hispanic/Latino), 3 international. Average age 30. In 2012, 2 master's awarded. *Degree requirements:* For master's, thesis, oral exams. *Entrance requirements:* For master's, 2 letters of

Peterson's Graduate Programs in the Physical Sciences, Mathematics, Agricultural Sciences, the Environment & Natural Resources 2014

www.petersonsbooks.com **231**

recommendation, BA in physics or closely-related field. Additional exam requirements/recommendations for international students: Required—TOEFL. *Application deadline:* For fall admission, 5/1 priority date for domestic students, 4/1 for international students. Application fee: $40. Electronic applications accepted. *Financial support:* In 2012–13, teaching assistantships with full tuition reimbursements (averaging $9,000 per year) were awarded; tuition waivers (full) also available. Financial award applicants required to submit FAFSA. *Faculty research:* Optics, solid-state physics, cosmology, atomic physics, nuclear physics. *Total annual research expenditures:* $54,000. *Unit head:* Dr. Jesus Pando, Chairperson, 773-325-7330, Fax: 773-325-7334, E-mail: graddepaul@depaul.edu. *Application contact:* Ann Spittle, Director of Graduate Admission, 773-325-7315, Fax: 312-476-3244, E-mail: graddepaul@depaul.edu. Website: http://csh.depaul.edu/academics/graduate/physics/Pages/default.aspx.

Drew University, Caspersen School of Graduate Studies, Program in Education, Madison, NJ 07940-1493. Offers biology (MAT); chemistry (MAT); English (MAT); French (MAT); Italian (MAT); math (MAT); physics (MAT); social studies (MAT); Spanish (MAT); theatre arts (MAT). Part-time programs available. *Entrance requirements:* For master's, transcripts, personal statement, recommendations. Additional exam requirements/recommendations for international students: Required—TOEFL, TWE. *Expenses:* Contact institution.

Drexel University, College of Arts and Sciences, Department of Physics, Philadelphia, PA 19104-2875. Offers MS, PhD. Terminal master's awarded for partial completion of doctoral program. *Degree requirements:* For doctorate, thesis/dissertation. *Entrance requirements:* For master's and doctorate, GRE. Additional exam requirements/recommendations for international students: Required—TOEFL. Electronic applications accepted. *Faculty research:* Nuclear structure, mesoscale meteorology, numerical astrophysics, numerical weather prediction, earth energy radiation budget.

Duke University, Graduate School, Department of Physics, Durham, NC 27708. Offers PhD. *Faculty:* 36 full-time. *Students:* 73 full-time (21 women); includes 3 minority (all Asian, non-Hispanic/Latino), 47 international. 271 applicants, 16% accepted, 10 enrolled. In 2012, 11 doctorates awarded. *Degree requirements:* For doctorate, thesis/dissertation. *Entrance requirements:* For doctorate, GRE General Test, GRE Subject Test. Additional exam requirements/recommendations for international students: Required—TOEFL (minimum score 550 paper-based; 83 iBT), IELTS (minimum score 7). *Application deadline:* For fall admission, 12/8 priority date for domestic students, 12/8 for international students. Application fee: $80. *Financial support:* Fellowships, research assistantships, teaching assistantships, and Federal Work-Study available. Financial award application deadline: 12/8. *Unit head:* Dr. Shailesh Chandrasekharan, Director of Graduate Studies, 919-660-2502, Fax: 919-606-2525, E-mail: donna@phy.duke.edu. *Application contact:* Elizabeth Hutton, Director of Admissions, 919-684-3913, Fax: 919-684-2277, E-mail: grad-admissions@duke.edu. Website: http://www.phy.duke.edu/graduate/.

East Carolina University, Graduate School, Thomas Harriot College of Arts and Sciences, Department of Physics, Greenville, NC 27858-4353. Offers applied physics (MS); biomedical physics (PhD); health physics (MS); medical physics (MS). Part-time programs available. *Degree requirements:* For master's, one foreign language, comprehensive exam. *Entrance requirements:* For master's, GRE General Test. Additional exam requirements/recommendations for international students: Required—TOEFL. *Expenses:* Tuition, state resident: full-time $4009. Tuition, nonresident: full-time $15,840. *Required fees:* $2111.

Eastern Michigan University, Graduate School, College of Arts and Sciences, Department of Physics and Astronomy, Ypsilanti, MI 48197. Offers general science (MS); physics (MS); physics education (MS). Part-time and evening/weekend programs available. Postbaccalaureate distance learning degree programs offered (minimal on-campus study). *Faculty:* 10 full-time (3 women). *Students:* 2 full-time (1 woman), 11 part-time (3 women); includes 3 minority (1 Black or African American, non-Hispanic/Latino; 1 Asian, non-Hispanic/Latino; 1 Two or more races, non-Hispanic/Latino). Average age 31. 14 applicants, 64% accepted, 4 enrolled. In 2012, 1 master's awarded. *Entrance requirements:* Additional exam requirements/recommendations for international students: Required—TOEFL. *Application deadline:* Applications are processed on a rolling basis. Application fee: $35. *Expenses:* Tuition, state resident: full-time $10,776; part-time $449 per credit hour. Tuition, nonresident: full-time $21,242; part-time $885 per credit hour. *Required fees:* $41 per credit hour. $48 per term. One-time fee: $100. Tuition and fees vary according to course level, degree level and reciprocity agreements. *Financial support:* Fellowships, research assistantships with full tuition reimbursements, teaching assistantships with full tuition reimbursements, career-related internships or fieldwork, Federal Work-Study, institutionally sponsored loans, scholarships/grants, tuition waivers, and unspecified assistantships available. Support available to part-time students. Financial award applicants required to submit FAFSA. *Unit head:* Dr. Alexandria Oakes, Department Head, 734-487-4144, Fax: 734-487-0989, E-mail: aoakes@emich.edu. Website: http://www.emich.edu/physics/.

Emory University, Laney Graduate School, Department of Physics, Atlanta, GA 30322-1100. Offers biophysics (PhD); experimental condensed matter physics (PhD); theoretical and computational statistical physics (PhD); MS/PhD. *Faculty:* 11 full-time (2 women), 1 part-time/adjunct (0 women). *Students:* 30 full-time (12 women); includes 2 minority (1 Black or African American, non-Hispanic/Latino; 1 Asian, non-Hispanic/Latino), 20 international. Average age 26. 51 applicants, 35% accepted, 4 enrolled. In 2012, 3 doctorates awarded. *Degree requirements:* For doctorate, thesis/dissertation, qualifier proposal. *Entrance requirements:* For doctorate, GRE General Test, minimum GPA of 3.0. Additional exam requirements/recommendations for international students: Required—TOEFL (minimum score 600 paper-based). *Application deadline:* For fall admission, 1/3 priority date for domestic students, 1/3 for international students. Application fee: $75. Electronic applications accepted. *Financial support:* Fellowships, teaching assistantships, institutionally sponsored loans, scholarships/grants, health care benefits, and tuition waivers (full) available. Financial award application deadline: 1/3; financial award applicants required to submit FAFSA. *Faculty research:* Experimental studies of the structure and function of metalloproteins, soft condensed matter, granular materials, biophotonics and fluorescence correlation spectroscopy, single molecule studies of DNA-protein systems. *Unit head:* Prof. Eric Weeks, Chair, 404-727-4479, Fax: 404-727-0873, E-mail: erweeks@emory.edu. *Application contact:* Prof. Stefan Boettcher, Director of Graduate Studies, 404-727-4298, Fax: 404-727-0873, E-mail: sboettc@emory.edu. Website: http://www.physics.emory.edu.

Fisk University, Division of Graduate Studies, Department of Physics, Nashville, TN 37208-3051. Offers MA. *Degree requirements:* For master's, thesis. *Entrance requirements:* For master's, GRE General Test, GRE Subject Test, minimum GPA of 3.0. Electronic applications accepted. *Faculty research:* Molecular physics, astrophysics, surface physics, nanobase materials, optical processing.

Florida Agricultural and Mechanical University, Division of Graduate Studies, Research, and Continuing Education, College of Arts and Sciences, Department of Physics, Tallahassee, FL 32307-3200. Offers MS, PhD. *Degree requirements:* For master's, comprehensive exam, thesis optional; for doctorate, comprehensive exam, thesis/dissertation. *Entrance requirements:* For master's, GRE General Test, minimum GPA of 3.0; for doctorate, GRE General Test, minimum GPA of 3.0, letters of recommendation (2). Additional exam requirements/recommendations for international students: Required—TOEFL (minimum score 550 paper-based). *Faculty research:* Plasma physics, quantum mechanics, condensed matter physics, astrophysics, laser ablation.

Florida Atlantic University, Charles E. Schmidt College of Science, Department of Physics, Boca Raton, FL 33431-0991. Offers MS, PhD. Part-time programs available. *Faculty:* 13 full-time (3 women), 4 part-time/adjunct (1 woman). *Students:* 24 full-time (6 women), 9 part-time (2 women); includes 4 minority (2 Black or African American, non-Hispanic/Latino; 1 Hispanic/Latino; 1 Two or more races, non-Hispanic/Latino), 16 international. Average age 30. 20 applicants, 30% accepted, 3 enrolled. In 2012, 9 master's, 6 doctorates awarded. *Degree requirements:* For master's, thesis; for doctorate, thesis/dissertation. *Entrance requirements:* For master's, GRE General Test, minimum GPA of 3.0; for doctorate, GRE General Test. Additional exam requirements/recommendations for international students: Required—TOEFL (minimum score 500 paper-based). *Application deadline:* For fall admission, 7/1 for domestic students, 2/15 for international students; for spring admission, 11/1 for domestic students, 7/15 for international students. Applications are processed on a rolling basis. Application fee: $30. *Expenses:* Tuition, state resident: full-time $8876; part-time $369.82 per credit hour. Tuition, nonresident: full-time $24,595; part-time $1024.81 per credit hour. *Financial support:* Fellowships, research assistantships with tuition reimbursements, teaching assistantships with tuition reimbursements, Federal Work-Study, and unspecified assistantships available. *Faculty research:* Astrophysics, spectroscopy, mathematical physics, theory of metals, superconductivity. *Unit head:* Dr. Warner A. Miller, Chair, 561-297-3382, Fax: 561-297-2662, E-mail: wam@physics.fau.edu. *Application contact:* Dr. Wolfgang Tichy, Graduate Programs, 561-297-3353, Fax: 561-297-2662. Website: http://physics.fau.edu/.

Florida Institute of Technology, Graduate Programs, College of Science, Department of Physics and Space Sciences, Melbourne, FL 32901-6975. Offers physics (MS, PhD); space sciences (MS, PhD). Part-time programs available. *Faculty:* 12 full-time (1 woman). *Students:* 33 full-time (11 women), 7 part-time (4 women); includes 5 minority (3 Asian, non-Hispanic/Latino; 2 Hispanic/Latino), 9 international. Average age 31. 90 applicants, 24% accepted, 10 enrolled. In 2012, 7 master's, 1 doctorate awarded. Terminal master's awarded for partial completion of doctoral program. *Degree requirements:* For master's, comprehensive exam, thesis optional, oral exam, 6 credits of math methodology; for doctorate, one foreign language, comprehensive exam, thesis/dissertation, publication in referred journal, seminar on dissertation research, dissertation published in a major journal. *Entrance requirements:* For master's, minimum GPA of 3.0, resume, 3 letters of recommendation, vector analysis, statement of objectives; for doctorate, GRE General and Subject Tests (recommended), minimum GPA of 3.2, resume, 3 letters of recommendation, statement of objectives. Additional exam requirements/recommendations for international students: Required—TOEFL (minimum score 550 paper-based; 79 iBT). *Application deadline:* For fall admission, 4/1 for international students; for spring admission, 9/30 for international students. Applications are processed on a rolling basis. Electronic applications accepted. *Expenses: Tuition:* Full-time $20,214; part-time $1123 per credit hour. Tuition and fees vary according to campus/location. *Financial support:* In 2012–13, 14 research assistantships with full and partial tuition reimbursements (averaging $12,502 per year), 12 teaching assistantships with full and partial tuition reimbursements (averaging $12,510 per year) were awarded; career-related internships or fieldwork, institutionally sponsored loans, tuition waivers (partial), unspecified assistantships, and tuition remissions also available. Support available to part-time students. Financial award application deadline: 3/1; financial award applicants required to submit

FAFSA. *Faculty research:* Lasers, semiconductors, magnetism, quantum devices, high energy physics. *Total annual research expenditures:* $1.9 million. *Unit head:* Dr. Terry D. Oswalt, Department Head, 321-674-7325, Fax: 321-674-7482, E-mail: toswalt@fit.edu. *Application contact:* Cheryl A. Brown, Associate Director of Graduate Admissions, 321-674-7581, Fax: 321-723-9468, E-mail: cbrown@fit.edu. Website: http://cos.fit.edu/pss/.

Florida International University, College of Arts and Sciences, Department of Physics, Miami, FL 33199. Offers MS, PhD. Part-time and evening/weekend programs available. *Degree requirements:* For master's, one foreign language, thesis; for doctorate, one foreign language, comprehensive exam, thesis/dissertation. *Entrance requirements:* For master's and doctorate, GRE General Test, 2 letters of recommendation. Additional exam requirements/recommendations for international students: Required—TOEFL (minimum score 550 paper-based; 80 iBT). Electronic applications accepted. *Faculty research:* Molecular collision processes (molecular beams), biophysical optics.

Florida State University, The Graduate School, College of Arts and Sciences, Department of Physics, Tallahassee, FL 32306. Offers MS, PhD. *Faculty:* 44 full-time (2 women), 3 part-time/adjunct (1 woman). *Students:* 144 full-time (26 women); includes 8 minority (1 Black or African American, non-Hispanic/Latino; 1 American Indian or Alaska Native, non-Hispanic/Latino; 3 Asian, non-Hispanic/Latino; 3 Hispanic/Latino), 89 international. Average age 28. 299 applicants, 20% accepted, 30 enrolled. In 2012, 29 master's, 15 doctorates awarded. *Degree requirements:* For doctorate, comprehensive exam, thesis/dissertation. *Entrance requirements:* For master's and doctorate, GRE General Test, minimum GPA of 3.0. Additional exam requirements/recommendations for international students: Required—TOEFL (minimum score 550 paper-based; 80 iBT). *Application deadline:* For fall admission, 4/15 for domestic and international students. Application fee: $30. Electronic applications accepted. *Expenses:* Tuition, state resident: full-time $7263; part-time $403.51 per credit hour. Tuition, nonresident: full-time $18,087; part-time $1004.85 per credit hour. *Required fees:* $1335.42; $74.19 per credit hour. $445.14 per semester. One-time fee: $40 full-time; $20 part-time. Tuition and fees vary according to program. *Financial support:* In 2012–13, 144 students received support, including 86 research assistantships with full tuition reimbursements available (averaging $21,000 per year), 44 teaching assistantships with full tuition reimbursements available (averaging $18,000 per year); fellowships, career-related internships or fieldwork, Federal Work-Study, and scholarships/grants also available. Financial award application deadline: 2/15; financial award applicants required to submit FAFSA. *Faculty research:* High energy physics, computational physics, biophysics, condensed matter physics, nuclear physics, astrophysics. *Total annual research expenditures:* $3.4 million. *Unit head:* Dr. Mark A. Riley, Chairman, 850-644-2867, Fax: 850-644-8630, E-mail: chair@physics.fsu.edu. *Application contact:* Eleanor C. Speirs, Academic Support Assistant, 850-644-4473, Fax: 850-644-8630, E-mail: graduate@phy.fsu.edu. Website: http://www.physics.fsu.edu/.

Florida State University, The Graduate School, College of Arts and Sciences, Department of Scientific Computing, Tallahassee, FL 32306-4120. Offers computational science (MS, PSM, PhD), including atmospheric science (PhD), biochemistry (PhD), biological science (PhD), computational molecular biology/bioinformatics (PSM), computational science (PhD), geological science (PhD), materials science (PhD), physics (PhD). Part-time programs available. *Faculty:* 14 full-time (2 women). *Students:* 28 full-time (5 women), 4 part-time (0 women); includes 12 minority (10 Asian, non-Hispanic/Latino; 2 Hispanic/Latino). Average age 28. 28 applicants, 43% accepted, 7 enrolled. In 2012, 11 master's, 5 doctorates awarded. Terminal master's awarded for partial completion of doctoral program. *Degree requirements:* For master's, thesis (for some programs); for doctorate, comprehensive exam, thesis/dissertation. *Entrance requirements:* For master's and doctorate, GRE General Test, knowledge of at least one object-oriented computing language, 3 letters of recommendations. Additional exam requirements/recommendations for international students: Required—TOEFL (minimum score 550 paper-based; 80 iBT). *Application deadline:* For fall admission, 1/15 for domestic and international students. Application fee: $30. Electronic applications accepted. *Expenses:* Tuition, state resident: full-time $7263; part-time $403.51 per credit hour. Tuition, nonresident: full-time $18,087; part-time $1004.85 per credit hour. *Required fees:* $1335.42; $74.19 per credit hour. $445.14 per semester. One-time fee: $40 full-time; $20 part-time. Tuition and fees vary according to program. *Financial support:* In 2012–13, 32 students received support, including 12 research assistantships with full tuition reimbursements available (averaging $20,000 per year), 17 teaching assistantships with full tuition reimbursements available (averaging $20,000 per year); scholarships/grants and unspecified assistantships also available. Financial award application deadline: 4/15. *Faculty research:* Morphometrics, mathematical and systems biology, mining proteomic and metabolic data, computational materials research, advanced 4-D Var data-assimilation methods in dynamic meteorology and oceanography, computational fluid dynamics, astrophysics. *Unit head:* Dr. Max Gunzburger, Chair, 850-644-1010, E-mail: mgunzburger@fsu.edu. *Application contact:* Maribel Amwake, Academic Coordinator, 850-644-0143, Fax: 850-644-0098, E-mail: mamwake@fsu.edu. Website: http://www.sc.fsu.edu.

George Mason University, College of Science, School of Physics, Astronomy and Computational Sciences, Fairfax, VA 22030. Offers applied and engineering physics (MS); computational science (MS); computational science and informatics (PhD); computational techniques and applications (Certificate); physics (PhD). *Faculty:* 48 full-time (11 women), 10 part-time/adjunct (1 woman). *Students:* 58 full-time (16 women), 97 part-time (19 women); includes 25 minority (6 Black or African American, non-Hispanic/Latino; 11 Asian, non-Hispanic/Latino; 6 Hispanic/Latino; 2 Two or more races, non-Hispanic/Latino), 26 international. Average age 35. 105 applicants, 49% accepted, 22 enrolled. In 2012, 20 master's, 15 doctorates, 1 other advanced degree awarded. *Degree requirements:* For master's, thesis optional; for doctorate, comprehensive exam, thesis/dissertation. *Entrance requirements:* For master's and doctorate, GRE, baccalaureate degree in related field with minimum GPA of 3.0 in last 60 credit hours; 3 letters of recommendation; expanded goals statement; resume; 2 copies of official transcripts. Additional exam requirements/recommendations for international students: Required—TOEFL (minimum score 570 paper-based; 88 iBT), IELTS (minimum score 6.5), Pearson Test of English. *Application deadline:* For fall admission, 4/15 priority date for domestic students; for spring admission, 11/15 priority date for domestic students. Application fee: $65 ($80 for international students). Electronic applications accepted. *Expenses:* Tuition, state resident: full-time $9080; part-time $378.33 per credit hour. Tuition, nonresident: full-time $25,010; part-time $1042.08 per credit hour. *Required fees:* $2610; $108.75 per credit hour. Tuition and fees vary according to program. *Financial support:* In 2012–13, 51 students received support, including 1 fellowship (averaging $8,000 per year), 37 research assistantships with full and partial tuition reimbursements available (averaging $18,917 per year), 16 teaching assistantships with full and partial tuition reimbursements available (averaging $13,676 per year); career-related internships or fieldwork, Federal Work-Study, scholarships/grants, unspecified assistantships, and health care benefits (for full-time research or teaching assistantship recipients) also available. Support available to part-time students. Financial award application deadline: 3/1; financial award applicants required to submit FAFSA. *Faculty research:* Particle and nuclear physics; computational statistics; astronomy, astrophysics, and space and planetary science; astronomy and physics education; atomic physics; biophysics and neuroscience; optical physics; fundamental theoretical studies; multidimensional data analysis. *Total annual research expenditures:* $5.8 million. *Unit head:* Dr. Michael Summers, Director, 703-993-3971, Fax: 703-993-1269, E-mail: msummers@gmu.edu. *Application contact:* Dr. Paul So, Graduate Advisor, 703-993-4377, Fax: 703-993-1269, E-mail: paso@gmu.edu. Website: http://spacs.gmu.edu/.

The George Washington University, Columbian College of Arts and Sciences, Department of Physics, Washington, DC 20052. Offers MA, PhD. Part-time and evening/weekend programs available. *Faculty:* 23 full-time (5 women), 1 part-time/adjunct (0 women). *Students:* 21 full-time (4 women), 8 part-time (3 women); includes 2 minority (1 Black or African American, non-Hispanic/Latino; 1 Native Hawaiian or other Pacific Islander, non-Hispanic/Latino), 18 international. Average age 26. 74 applicants, 38% accepted, 11 enrolled. In 2012, 3 master's, 5 doctorates awarded. *Degree requirements:* For doctorate, thesis/dissertation, general exam. *Entrance requirements:* For master's and doctorate, GRE General Test, minimum GPA of 3.0. Additional exam requirements/recommendations for international students: Required—TOEFL (minimum score 550 paper-based; 80 iBT). *Application deadline:* For fall admission, 1/15 priority date for domestic students, 1/15 for international students; for spring admission, 10/1 priority date for domestic students, 9/1 for international students. Applications are processed on a rolling basis. Application fee: $75. Electronic applications accepted. *Financial support:* In 2012–13, 24 students received support. Fellowships with full tuition reimbursements available, research assistantships, teaching assistantships with tuition reimbursements available, Federal Work-Study, and tuition waivers available. Financial award application deadline: 1/15. *Unit head:* Dr. Cornelius Bennhold, Chair, 202-994-6274. *Application contact:* Dr. Mark Reeves, Director, 202-994-6279, Fax: 202-994-3001, E-mail: reevesme@gwu.edu. Website: http://www.gwu.edu/~physics/.

Georgia Institute of Technology, Graduate Studies and Research, College of Sciences, School of Physics, Atlanta, GA 30332-0001. Offers MS, PhD. Part-time programs available. Terminal master's awarded for partial completion of doctoral program. *Degree requirements:* For doctorate, comprehensive exam, thesis/dissertation. *Entrance requirements:* For master's, GRE General Test, GRE Subject Test, minimum GPA of 3.0; for doctorate, GRE General Test, GRE Subject Test, minimum GPA of 3.4. Additional exam requirements/recommendations for international students: Required—TOEFL. Electronic applications accepted. *Faculty research:* Atomic and molecular physics, chemical physics, condensed matter, optics, nonlinear physics and chaos.

Georgia State University, College of Arts and Sciences, Department of Physics and Astronomy, Program in Physics, Atlanta, GA 30302-3083. Offers MS, PhD. Part-time and evening/weekend programs available. *Faculty:* 13 full-time (0 women), 2 part-time/adjunct (0 women). *Students:* 39 full-time (9 women), 2 part-time (0 women); includes 6 minority (1 Black or African American, non-Hispanic/Latino; 3 Asian, non-Hispanic/Latino; 2 Hispanic/Latino), 26 international. Average age 33. 44 applicants, 25% accepted, 3 enrolled. In 2012, 13 master's, 1 doctorate awarded. Terminal master's awarded for partial completion of doctoral program. *Degree requirements:* For master's, one foreign language, thesis optional; for doctorate, 2 foreign languages, comprehensive exam, thesis/dissertation. *Entrance requirements:* For master's and doctorate, GRE General Test, GRE Subject Test. Additional exam requirements/recommendations for international students: Required—TOEFL (minimum score 550 paper-based; 80 iBT). *Application deadline:* For fall admission, 7/1 for domestic and international students; for spring admission, 11/15 for domestic and international students. Applications are processed on a rolling basis. Application fee: $50. Electronic applications accepted. *Expenses:* Tuition, state resident: full-time $8064; part-time $336 per credit hour. Tuition, nonresident: full-time $28,800; part-time $1200

Peterson's Graduate Programs in the Physical Sciences, Mathematics, Agricultural Sciences, the Environment & Natural Resources 2014

www.petersonsbooks.com **233**

per credit hour. *Required fees:* $2128; $1064 per semester. Tuition and fees vary according to course load and program. *Financial support:* In 2012–13, 1 fellowship with full tuition reimbursement (averaging $21,000 per year), 2 research assistantships with full tuition reimbursements (averaging $20,000 per year), 2 teaching assistantships with full tuition reimbursements (averaging $20,000 per year) were awarded; scholarships/grants and unspecified assistantships also available. Financial award application deadline: 2/15. *Faculty research:* Experimental and theoretical condensed matter physics, nuclear physics (relativistic heavy ion collisions, proton and neutron spin, cosmic ray radiation), biophysics and brain sciences, theoretical atomic and molecular structure and collisions, physics education research. *Total annual research expenditures:* $1.5 million. *Unit head:* Dr. Xiaochun He, Physics Graduate Director, 404-413-6051, Fax: 404-413-6025, E-mail: xhe@gsu.edu. Website: http://www.phy-astr.gsu.edu/.

Georgia State University, College of Education, Department of Middle-Secondary Education and Instructional Technology, Atlanta, GA 30302-3083. Offers English education (M Ed, MAT); English speakers of other languages (MAT); instructional design and technology (online) (MS); instructional technology (PhD), including alternative instructional delivery systems, consulting, instructional design, management, research; mathematics education (M Ed, MAT); middle level education (MAT); reading, language and literacy education (M Ed), including reading instruction; science education (MAT), including biology, broad field science, chemistry, earth science, physics; social studies education (M Ed, MAT), including economics (MAT), geography (MAT), history (MAT), political science (MAT); teaching and learning (PhD), including language and literacy, mathematics education, music education, science education, social studies, teaching and teacher education. *Accreditation:* NCATE. Part-time and evening/weekend programs available. Postbaccalaureate distance learning degree programs offered (minimal on-campus study). *Faculty:* 38 full-time (30 women), 7 part-time/adjunct (all women). *Students:* 268 full-time (191 women), 243 part-time (172 women); includes 212 minority (148 Black or African American, non-Hispanic/Latino; 1 American Indian or Alaska Native, non-Hispanic/Latino; 26 Asian, non-Hispanic/Latino; 20 Hispanic/Latino; 1 Native Hawaiian or other Pacific Islander, non-Hispanic/Latino; 16 Two or more races, non-Hispanic/Latino), 15 international. Average age 34. 149 applicants, 67% accepted, 67 enrolled. In 2012, 253 master's, 18 doctorates awarded. *Degree requirements:* For master's, comprehensive exam (for some programs), thesis or alternative, exit portfolio; for doctorate, comprehensive exam, thesis/dissertation. *Entrance requirements:* For master's, GRE; GACE I (for initial teacher preparation degree programs), baccalaureate degree or equivalent, resume, goals statement, two letters of recommendation, minimum undergraduate GPA of 2.5; proof of initial teacher certification in the content area (for M Ed); for doctorate, GRE, resume, goals statement, writing sample, two letters of recommendation, minimum graduate GPA of 3.3, interview. Additional exam requirements/recommendations for international students: Required—TOEFL (minimum score 550 paper-based, 79 iBT) or IELTS (minimum score 6.5). *Application deadline:* For fall admission, 1/15 priority date for domestic students, 1/15 for international students; for spring admission, 10/1 for domestic and international students. Application fee: $50. Electronic applications accepted. *Expenses:* Tuition, state resident: full-time $8064; part-time $336 per credit hour. Tuition, nonresident: full-time $28,800; part-time $1200 per credit hour. *Required fees:* $2128; $1064 per semester. Tuition and fees vary according to course load and program. *Financial support:* In 2012–13, 110 students received support, including 3 fellowships with full tuition reimbursements available (averaging $19,667 per year), 68 research assistantships with full tuition reimbursements available (averaging $5,436 per year), 29 teaching assistantships with full tuition reimbursements available (averaging $2,779 per year); career-related internships or fieldwork, Federal Work-Study, scholarships/grants, health care benefits, tuition waivers (full and partial), and unspecified assistantships also available. Financial award application deadline: 3/15. *Faculty research:* Teacher education in language and literacy, mathematics, science, and social studies in urban middle and secondary school settings; learning technologies in school, community, and corporate settings; multicultural education and education for social justice; urban education; international education. *Total annual research expenditures:* $761,493. *Unit head:* Dr. Dana L. Fox, Chair, 404-413-8060, Fax: 404-413-8063, E-mail: dfox@gsu.edu. *Application contact:* Bobbie Turner, Administrative Coordinator I, 404-413-8405, Fax: 404-413-8063, E-mail: bnturner@gsu.edu. Website: http://msit.gsu.edu/msit_programs.htm.

Graduate School and University Center of the City University of New York, Graduate Studies, Program in Physics, New York, NY 10016-4039. Offers PhD. *Degree requirements:* For doctorate, thesis/dissertation. *Entrance requirements:* For doctorate, GRE General Test. Additional exam requirements/recommendations for international students: Required—TOEFL. Electronic applications accepted. *Faculty research:* Condensed-matter, particle, nuclear, and atomic physics.

Hampton University, Graduate College, Department of Physics, Hampton, VA 23668. Offers atmospheric physics (MS, PhD); medical physics (MS, PhD); nuclear physics (MS, PhD); optical physics (MS, PhD). Part-time and evening/weekend programs available. Terminal master's awarded for partial completion of doctoral program. *Degree requirements:* For master's, thesis optional; for doctorate, thesis/dissertation, oral defense, qualifying exam. *Entrance requirements:* For master's, GRE General Test; for doctorate, GRE General Test, minimum GPA of 3.0 or master's degree in physics or related field. *Faculty research:* Laser optics, remote sensing.

Harvard University, Graduate School of Arts and Sciences, Department of Physics, Cambridge, MA 02138. Offers experimental physics (PhD); medical engineering/medical physics (PhD), including applied physics, engineering sciences, physics; theoretical physics (PhD). *Degree requirements:* For doctorate, thesis/dissertation, final exams, laboratory experience. *Entrance requirements:* For doctorate, GRE General Test, GRE Subject Test. Additional exam requirements/recommendations for international students: Required—TOEFL. *Expenses: Tuition:* Full-time $37,576. *Required fees:* $930. Tuition and fees vary according to program and student level. *Faculty research:* Particle physics, condensed matter physics, atomic physics.

Hofstra University, School of Education, Programs in Teaching - Secondary Education, Hempstead, NY 11549. Offers business education (MS Ed); education technology (Advanced Certificate); English education (MA, MS Ed); foreign language and TESOL (MS Ed); foreign language education (MA, MS Ed), including French, German, Russian, Spanish; mathematics education (MA, MS Ed); science education (MA, MS Ed), including biology, chemistry, earth science, geology, physics; secondary education (Advanced Certificate); social studies education (MA, MS Ed); technology for learning (MA). Part-time and evening/weekend programs available. Postbaccalaureate distance learning degree programs offered (minimal on-campus study). *Students:* 64 full-time (36 women), 41 part-time (22 women); includes 17 minority (9 Black or African American, non-Hispanic/Latino; 3 Asian, non-Hispanic/Latino; 4 Hispanic/Latino; 1 Native Hawaiian or other Pacific Islander, non-Hispanic/Latino). Average age 28. 87 applicants, 87% accepted, 46 enrolled. In 2012, 57 master's, 7 other advanced degrees awarded. *Degree requirements:* For master's, one foreign language, comprehensive exam (for some programs), thesis (for some programs), exit project, electronic portfolio, student teaching, fieldwork, curriculum project, minimum GPA of 3.0; for Advanced Certificate, 3 foreign languages, comprehensive exam (for some programs), thesis project. *Entrance requirements:* For master's, 2 letters of recommendation, teacher certification (MA), essay; for Advanced Certificate, 2 letters of recommendation, essay, interview and/or portfolio. Additional exam requirements/recommendations for international students: Required—TOEFL (minimum score 550 paper-based; 80 iBT); Recommended—IELTS (minimum score 6.5). *Application deadline:* Applications are processed on a rolling basis. Application fee: $70 ($75 for international students). Electronic applications accepted. *Expenses: Tuition:* Full-time $19,800; part-time $1100 per credit hour. *Required fees:* $970; $165 per term. Tuition and fees vary according to program. *Financial support:* In 2012–13, 82 students received support, including 17 fellowships with full and partial tuition reimbursements available (averaging $3,142 per year), 1 research assistantship with full and partial tuition reimbursement available (averaging $16,527 per year); career-related internships or fieldwork, Federal Work-Study, institutionally sponsored loans, scholarships/grants, tuition waivers (full and partial), and unspecified assistantships also available. Support available to part-time students. Financial award applicants required to submit FAFSA. *Faculty research:* Appropriate content in secondary school disciplines, appropriate pedagogy in secondary school disciplines, adolescent development, secondary school organization, preparation for EDTPA addition to the curriculum. *Unit head:* Dr. Esther Fusco, Chairperson, 516-463-7704, Fax: 516-463-6196, E-mail: catezf@hofstra.edu. *Application contact:* Carol Drummer, Dean of Graduate Admissions, 516-463-4876, Fax: 516-463-4664, E-mail: gradstudent@hofstra.edu. Website: http://www.hofstra.edu/education/.

Howard University, Graduate School, Department of Physics and Astronomy, Washington, DC 20059-0002. Offers physics (MS, PhD). *Degree requirements:* For master's, comprehensive exam (for some programs), thesis (for some programs); for doctorate, comprehensive exam, thesis/dissertation, departmental qualifying exam. *Entrance requirements:* For master's, GRE General Test, bachelor's degree in physics or related field, minimum GPA of 3.0; for doctorate, GRE General Test, bachelor's or master's degree in physics or related field, minimum GPA of 3.0. Additional exam requirements/recommendations for international students: Required—TOEFL (minimum score 550 paper-based). Electronic applications accepted. *Faculty research:* Atmospheric physics, spectroscopy and optical physics, high energy physics, condensed matter.

Hunter College of the City University of New York, Graduate School, School of Arts and Sciences, Department of Physics, New York, NY 10021-5085. Offers MA, PhD. PhD offered jointly with Graduate School and University Center of the City University of New York. Part-time programs available. *Faculty:* 11 full-time (3 women). *Students:* 3 full-time (2 women), 1 part-time (0 women); includes 1 minority (Black or African American, non-Hispanic/Latino), 1 international. Average age 31. 8 applicants, 63% accepted, 1 enrolled. In 2012, 5 master's awarded. Terminal master's awarded for partial completion of doctoral program. *Degree requirements:* For master's, comprehensive exam or thesis. *Entrance requirements:* For master's, minimum 36 credits of course work in mathematics and physics. Additional exam requirements/recommendations for international students: Required—TOEFL. *Application deadline:* For fall admission, 4/1 for domestic students, 2/1 for international students; for spring admission, 11/1 for domestic students, 9/1 for international students. Application fee: $125. *Expenses:* Tuition, state resident: full-time $8690; part-time $365 per credit. Tuition, nonresident: full-time $16,200; part-time $675 per credit. *Required fees:* $320 per semester. One-time fee: $125. Tuition and fees vary according to class time, campus/location and program. *Financial support:* In 2012–13, research assistantships (averaging $20,000 per year), teaching assistantships (averaging $9,000 per year) were awarded; Federal Work-Study, scholarships/grants, and tuition waivers (partial) also available. Support available to part-time students.

Faculty research: Experimental and theoretical quantum optics, experimental and theoretical condensed matter, mathematical physics. *Unit head:* Ying-Chin Chen, Chairperson, 212-772-5248, Fax: 212-772-5390, E-mail: y.c.chen@hunter.cuny.edu. *Application contact:* William Zlata, Director for Graduate Admissions, 212-772-4482, Fax: 212-650-3336, E-mail: admissions@hunter.cuny.edu. Website: http://www.hunter.cuny.edu/physics/.

Idaho State University, Office of Graduate Studies, College of Science and Engineering, Department of Physics, Pocatello, ID 83209-8106. Offers applied physics (PhD); health physics (MS); physics (MNS). Part-time programs available. *Degree requirements:* For master's, comprehensive exam, thesis (for some programs), oral exam (for some programs); for doctorate, comprehensive exam, thesis/dissertation (for some programs), oral exam, written qualifying exam in physics or health physics after 1st year. *Entrance requirements:* For master's, GRE General Test, 3 letters of recommendation, BS or BA in physics, teaching certificate (MNS); for doctorate, GRE General Test (minimum 50th percentile), 3 letters of recommendation, statement of career goals. Additional exam requirements/recommendations for international students: Required—TOEFL (minimum score 550 paper-based; 80 iBT). Electronic applications accepted. *Faculty research:* Ion beam applications, low-energy nuclear physics, relativity and cosmology, observational astronomy.

Illinois Institute of Technology, Graduate College, College of Science and Letters, Department of Physics, Chicago, IL 60616. Offers applied physics (MS); health physics (MHP); physics (MS, PhD). Part-time and evening/weekend programs available. Postbaccalaureate distance learning degree programs offered (minimal on-campus study). *Faculty:* 17 full-time (1 woman), 4 part-time/adjunct (1 woman). *Students:* 47 full-time (12 women), 36 part-time (5 women); includes 10 minority (2 Black or African American, non-Hispanic/Latino; 4 Asian, non-Hispanic/Latino; 1 Hispanic/Latino; 3 Two or more races, non-Hispanic/Latino), 27 international. Average age 31. 104 applicants, 83% accepted, 27 enrolled. In 2012, 13 master's, 2 doctorates awarded. Terminal master's awarded for partial completion of doctoral program. *Degree requirements:* For master's, comprehensive exam (for some programs), thesis (for some programs); for doctorate, comprehensive exam, thesis/dissertation. *Entrance requirements:* For master's, GRE General Test (minimum score 1000 Quantitative and Verbal, 2.5 Analytical Writing), minimum undergraduate GPA of 3.0; for doctorate, GRE General Test (minimum score 1100 Quantitative and Verbal, 3.0 Analytical Writing), minimum undergraduate GPA of 3.0. Additional exam requirements/recommendations for international students: Required—TOEFL (minimum score 523 paper-based; 70 iBT); Recommended—IELTS (minimum score 5.5). *Application deadline:* For fall admission, 5/1 for domestic and international students; for spring admission, 10/15 for domestic and international students. Applications are processed on a rolling basis. Application fee: $40. Electronic applications accepted. *Expenses: Tuition:* Full-time $20,142; part-time $1119 per credit hour. *Required fees:* $605 per semester. One-time fee: $255. Tuition and fees vary according to program and student level. *Financial support:* In 2012–13, 6 fellowships with full and partial tuition reimbursements (averaging $9,547 per year), 3 research assistantships with full and partial tuition reimbursements (averaging $9,848 per year), 3 teaching assistantships with full and partial tuition reimbursements (averaging $7,586 per year) were awarded; Federal Work-Study, institutionally sponsored loans, scholarships/grants, health care benefits, and unspecified assistantships also available. Support available to part-time students. Financial award applicants required to submit FAFSA. *Faculty research:* Elementary particle physics, accelerator and plasma physics, condensed-matter physics, biological physics, x-ray optics, x-ray imaging, quantum theory. *Total annual research expenditures:* $4.6 million. *Unit head:* Dr. Christopher White, Professor, 312-567-3734, Fax: 312-567-3289, E-mail: whitec@iit.edu. *Application contact:* Deborah Gibson, Director, Graduate Admission, 866-472-3448, Fax: 312-567-3138, E-mail: inquiry.grad@iit.edu. Website: http://www.iit.edu/csl/physics.

Indiana University Bloomington, University Graduate School, College of Arts and Sciences, Department of Physics, Bloomington, IN 47405. Offers medical physics (MS); physics (MAT, MS, PhD). Part-time programs available. Postbaccalaureate distance learning degree programs offered (no on-campus study). *Faculty:* 35 full-time (4 women), 11 part-time/adjunct (1 woman). *Students:* 95 full-time (19 women); includes 8 minority (4 Asian, non-Hispanic/Latino; 4 Hispanic/Latino), 45 international. Average age 27. 222 applicants, 27% accepted, 23 enrolled. In 2012, 13 master's, 12 doctorates awarded. Terminal master's awarded for partial completion of doctoral program. *Degree requirements:* For master's, comprehensive exam (for some programs), thesis (for some programs), qualifying exam; for doctorate, comprehensive exam, thesis/dissertation, qualifying exam. *Entrance requirements:* For master's and doctorate, GRE General Test, GRE Subject Test (physics), minimum GPA of 3.0. Additional exam requirements/recommendations for international students: Required—TOEFL (minimum score 550 paper-based, 80 iBT) or IELTS (minimum score 6.5). *Application deadline:* For fall admission, 1/15 priority date for domestic students, 12/1 for international students; for spring admission, 10/1 priority date for domestic students, 9/1 for international students. Applications are processed on a rolling basis. Application fee: $55 ($65 for international students). Electronic applications accepted. *Financial support:* In 2012–13, 14 students received support, including 1 fellowship with full and partial tuition reimbursement available (averaging $18,000 per year), 54 research assistantships with partial tuition reimbursements available (averaging $19,240 per year), 28 teaching assistantships with partial tuition reimbursements available (averaging $16,659 per year); health care benefits also available. Financial award application deadline: 4/15. *Faculty research:* Accelerator physics, astrophysics and cosmology, biophysics (biocomplexity, neural networks, visual systems, chemical signaling), condensed matter physics (neutron scattering, complex fluids, quantum computing), particle physics (collider physics, hybrid mesons, lattice gauge, symmetries, collider phenomenology), neutrino physics, nuclear physics (proton and neutron physics, neutrinos, symmetries, nuclear astrophysics, hadron structure). *Total annual research expenditures:* $13.2 million. *Unit head:* Prof. Rob de Ruyter, Department Chair, 812-855-1247, Fax: 812-855-5533, E-mail: iubphys@indiana.edu. *Application contact:* June Dizer, Director of Academic Support, 812-856-7059, Fax: 812-855-5533, E-mail: gradphys@indiana.edu. Website: http://physics.indiana.edu/.

Indiana University of Pennsylvania, School of Graduate Studies and Research, College of Natural Sciences and Mathematics, Department of Physics, MS Program in Physics, Indiana, PA 15705-1087. Offers MS. Part-time programs available. *Faculty:* 3 full-time (0 women). *Students:* 6 full-time (2 women), 4 international. Average age 25. 16 applicants, 44% accepted, 4 enrolled. In 2012, 3 degrees awarded. *Degree requirements:* For master's, comprehensive exam (for some programs), thesis (for some programs). *Entrance requirements:* Additional exam requirements/recommendations for international students: Required—TOEFL (minimum score 540 paper-based). *Application deadline:* Applications are processed on a rolling basis. Application fee: $50. Electronic applications accepted. *Expenses:* Tuition, state resident: part-time $429 per credit hour. Tuition, nonresident: part-time $644 per credit hour. *Required fees:* $110.60 per credit hour. One-time fee: $180 part-time. *Financial support:* Research assistantships with full and partial tuition reimbursements and Federal Work-Study available. Support available to part-time students. Financial award application deadline: 4/15; financial award applicants required to submit FAFSA. *Unit head:* Dr. Greg Kenning, Graduate Coordinator, 724-357-2318, E-mail: greg.kenning@iup.edu. *Application contact:* Dr. Muhammad Numan, Graduate Coordinator, 724-357-2318, E-mail: mznuman@iup.edu. Website: http://www.iup.edu/upper.aspx?id=93742.

Indiana University–Purdue University Indianapolis, School of Science, Department of Physics, Indianapolis, IN 46202. Offers MS, PhD. PhD offered jointly with Purdue University. Part-time programs available. *Faculty:* 13 full-time (1 woman), 3 part-time/adjunct (0 women). *Students:* 18 full-time (1 woman), 2 part-time (1 woman); includes 3 minority (1 Black or African American, non-Hispanic/Latino; 2 Hispanic/Latino), 8 international. Average age 29. 17 applicants, 35% accepted, 3 enrolled. In 2012, 5 master's awarded. Terminal master's awarded for partial completion of doctoral program. *Degree requirements:* For master's, thesis optional; for doctorate, thesis/dissertation. *Entrance requirements:* For master's and doctorate, GRE. Additional exam requirements/recommendations for international students: Required—TOEFL (minimum score 79 iBT). *Application deadline:* For fall admission, 2/1 priority date for domestic students, 3/1 for international students. Applications are processed on a rolling basis. Application fee: $55 ($65 for international students). *Financial support:* In 2012–13, 6 fellowships with full tuition reimbursements (averaging $14,204 per year), 6 teaching assistantships with full tuition reimbursements (averaging $6,245 per year) were awarded; research assistantships with full tuition reimbursements, Federal Work-Study, institutionally sponsored loans, and tuition waivers (full and partial) also available. Support available to part-time students. Financial award application deadline: 2/1. *Faculty research:* Magnetic resonance, photosynthesis, optical physics, biophysics, physics of materials. *Unit head:* Dr. Andrew Gavrin, Chair, 317-274-6900, E-mail: agavrin@iupui.edu. *Application contact:* Dr. Sherry Queener, Director, Graduate Studies and Associate Dean, 317-274-1577, Fax: 317-278-2380. Website: http://physics.iupui.edu/.

Iowa State University of Science and Technology, Department of Physics and Astronomy, Ames, IA 50011. Offers applied physics (MS, PhD); astrophysics (MS, PhD); condensed matter physics (MS, PhD); high energy physics (MS, PhD); nuclear physics (MS, PhD); physics (MS, PhD). *Degree requirements:* For master's, thesis (for some programs); for doctorate, thesis/dissertation. *Entrance requirements:* For master's and doctorate, GRE General Test, GRE Subject Test (physics). Additional exam requirements/recommendations for international students: Required—TOEFL (minimum score 550 paper-based; 79 iBT), IELTS (minimum score 6.5). *Application deadline:* For fall admission, 2/15 priority date for domestic students, 2/15 for international students; for spring admission, 10/15 for domestic and international students. Applications are processed on a rolling basis. Application fee: $60 ($90 for international students). Electronic applications accepted. *Financial support:* Application deadline: 2/15. *Faculty research:* Condensed-matter physics, including superconductivity and new materials; high-energy and nuclear physics; astronomy and astrophysics; atmospheric and environmental physics. *Total annual research expenditures:* $8.8 million. *Application contact:* Lori Hockett, Application Contact, 515-294-5870, Fax: 515-294-6027, E-mail: physastro@iastate.edu. Website: http://www.physastro.iastate.edu.

Iowa State University of Science and Technology, Program in High Energy Physics, Ames, IA 50011. Offers MS, PhD. *Entrance requirements:* For master's and doctorate, GRE. Additional exam requirements/recommendations for international students: Required—TOEFL (minimum score 550 paper-based; 79 iBT), IELTS (minimum score 6.5). *Application deadline:* For fall admission, 2/15 for domestic students; for spring admission, 10/15 for domestic students. Application fee: $60 ($90 for international students). Electronic applications accepted. *Application contact:* Lori Hockett, Application Contact, 515-294-5870,

Fax: 515-294-6027, E-mail: physastro@iastate.edu. Website: http://www.physastro.iastate.edu.

Iowa State University of Science and Technology, Program in Nuclear Physics, Ames, IA 50011. Offers MS, PhD. *Entrance requirements:* For master's and doctorate, GRE. Additional exam requirements/recommendations for international students: Required—TOEFL (minimum score 550 paper-based; 79 iBT), IELTS (minimum score 6.5). *Application deadline:* For fall admission, 2/15 for domestic students; for spring admission, 10/15 for domestic students. Application fee: $60 ($90 for international students). Electronic applications accepted. *Application contact:* Lori Hockett, Application Contact, 515-294-5870, Fax: 515-294-6027, E-mail: physastro@iastate.edu. Website: http://www.physastro.iastate.edu.

The Johns Hopkins University, Zanvyl Krieger School of Arts and Sciences, Henry A. Rowland Department of Physics and Astronomy, Baltimore, MD 21218-2699. Offers astronomy (PhD); physics (PhD). *Degree requirements:* For doctorate, comprehensive exam, thesis/dissertation, minimum B- average on required coursework. *Entrance requirements:* For doctorate, GRE General Test, GRE Subject Test. Additional exam requirements/recommendations for international students: Required—TOEFL (minimum score 600 paper-based; 100 iBT), IELTS. Electronic applications accepted. *Faculty research:* High-energy physics, condensed-matter, astrophysics, particle and experimental physics, plasma physics.

Kansas State University, Graduate School, College of Arts and Sciences, Department of Physics, Manhattan, KS 66506. Offers MS, PhD. *Faculty:* 25 full-time (2 women), 5 part-time/adjunct (1 woman). *Students:* 59 full-time (21 women), 4 part-time (0 women); includes 1 minority (Asian, non-Hispanic/Latino), 42 international. Average age 28. 119 applicants, 23% accepted, 9 enrolled. In 2012, 2 master's, 7 doctorates awarded. Terminal master's awarded for partial completion of doctoral program. *Degree requirements:* For master's, thesis; for doctorate, thesis/dissertation, preliminary exams. *Entrance requirements:* For master's, GRE Subject Test, BS in physics, minimum GPA of 3.0 in math, chemistry or engineering; for doctorate, GRE Subject Test. Additional exam requirements/recommendations for international students: Required—TOEFL (minimum score 550 paper-based). *Application deadline:* For fall admission, 2/1 for domestic and international students; for spring admission, 10/1 for domestic students, 8/1 for international students. Applications are processed on a rolling basis. Application fee: $50 ($75 for international students). Electronic applications accepted. *Financial support:* In 2012–13, 40 research assistantships with partial tuition reimbursements (averaging $18,819 per year), 18 teaching assistantships with full tuition reimbursements (averaging $13,723 per year) were awarded; fellowships, career-related internships or fieldwork, Federal Work-Study, institutionally sponsored loans, scholarships/grants, and unspecified assistantships also available. Support available to part-time students. Financial award application deadline: 3/1; financial award applicants required to submit FAFSA. *Faculty research:* Atomic, molecular, optical physics; soft matter and biological physics; high energy physics; physics education; cosmology. *Total annual research expenditures:* $4.9 million. *Unit head:* Amit Chakrabarti, Head, 785-532-6786, Fax: 785-532-6806, E-mail: amitc@ksu.edu. *Application contact:* Jane Peterson, Graduate Secretary, 785-532-6786, Fax: 785-532-6806, E-mail: janie@ksu.edu. Website: http://www.phys.ksu.edu/.

Kent State University, College of Arts and Sciences, Department of Physics, Kent, OH 44242-0001. Offers MA, MS, PhD. Terminal master's awarded for partial completion of doctoral program. *Degree requirements:* For master's, thesis; for doctorate, comprehensive exam, thesis/dissertation. *Entrance requirements:* For master's and doctorate, GRE, minimum GPA of 3.0. Additional exam requirements/recommendations for international students: Required—TOEFL. Electronic applications accepted. *Expenses:* Tuition, state resident: full-time $8424; part-time $468 per credit hour. Tuition, nonresident: full-time $14,580; part-time $810 per credit hour. Tuition and fees vary according to course load. *Faculty research:* Correlated electron materials physics, liquid crystals, complex fluids, computational biophysics, QCD-Hadranphysics.

Lakehead University, Graduate Studies, Department of Physics, Thunder Bay, ON P7B 5E1, Canada. Offers M Sc. *Degree requirements:* For master's, thesis or alternative. *Entrance requirements:* For master's, minimum B average. Additional exam requirements/recommendations for international students: Required—TOEFL. *Faculty research:* Absorbed water, radiation reaction, superlattices and quantum well structures, polaron interactions.

Lehigh University, College of Arts and Sciences, Department of Physics, Bethlehem, PA 18015. Offers photonics (MS); physics (MS, PhD); polymer science (MS, PhD). Part-time programs available. *Faculty:* 14 full-time (1 woman). *Students:* 41 full-time (14 women), 1 part-time (0 women); includes 1 minority (Black or African American, non-Hispanic/Latino), 15 international. Average age 26. 101 applicants, 20% accepted, 9 enrolled. In 2012, 6 master's, 5 doctorates awarded. *Degree requirements:* For doctorate, comprehensive exam, thesis/dissertation. *Entrance requirements:* For master's and doctorate, GRE General Test. Additional exam requirements/recommendations for international students: Required—TOEFL (minimum score 79 iBT). *Application deadline:* For fall admission, 2/15 priority date for domestic students, 2/15 for international students. Applications are processed on a rolling basis. Application fee: $75. Electronic applications accepted. *Financial support:* In 2012–13, 40 students received support, including 4 fellowships with full tuition reimbursements available (averaging $26,000 per year), 15 research assistantships with full tuition reimbursements available (averaging $25,640 per year), 21 teaching assistantships with full tuition reimbursements available (averaging $25,640 per year); career-related internships or fieldwork, Federal Work-Study, institutionally sponsored loans, scholarships/grants, tuition waivers (full and partial), and unspecified assistantships also available. Support available to part-time students. Financial award application deadline: 1/15. *Faculty research:* Condensed matter physics; atomic, molecular and optical physics; plasma physics; nonlinear optics and photonics; astronomy and astrophysics. *Total annual research expenditures:* $1.8 million. *Unit head:* Dr. Volkmar Dierolf, Chair, 610-758-3915, Fax: 610-758-5730, E-mail: vod2@lehigh.edu. *Application contact:* Dr. Dimitrios Vavylonis, Graduate Admissions Officer, 610-758-3724, Fax: 610-758-5730, E-mail: div206@lehigh.edu. Website: http://www.physics.lehigh.edu/.

Louisiana State University and Agricultural and Mechanical College, Graduate School, College of Science, Department of Physics and Astronomy, Baton Rouge, LA 70803. Offers astronomy (PhD); astrophysics (PhD); medical physics (MS); physics (MS, PhD). *Faculty:* 45 full-time (5 women), 1 part-time/adjunct (0 women). *Students:* 106 full-time (21 women), 3 part-time (1 woman); includes 5 minority (1 Black or African American, non-Hispanic/Latino; 4 Hispanic/Latino), 52 international. Average age 27. 135 applicants, 16% accepted, 20 enrolled. In 2012, 8 master's, 8 doctorates awarded. Terminal master's awarded for partial completion of doctoral program. *Degree requirements:* For master's, thesis or alternative; for doctorate, thesis/dissertation. *Entrance requirements:* For master's and doctorate, GRE General Test, minimum GPA of 3.0. Additional exam requirements/recommendations for international students: Required—TOEFL (minimum score 550 paper-based; 79 iBT) or IELTS (minimum score 6.5). *Application deadline:* For fall admission, 1/25 priority date for domestic students, 5/15 for international students; for spring admission, 10/15 for international students. Applications are processed on a rolling basis. Application fee: $50 ($70 for international students). Electronic applications accepted. *Financial support:* In 2012–13, 108 students received support, including 12 fellowships with full tuition reimbursements available (averaging $26,748 per year), 60 research assistantships with full and partial tuition reimbursements available (averaging $22,794 per year), 35 teaching assistantships with full and partial tuition reimbursements available (averaging $19,046 per year); Federal Work-Study, institutionally sponsored loans, health care benefits, tuition waivers (full and partial), and unspecified assistantships also available. Financial award application deadline: 3/15; financial award applicants required to submit FAFSA. *Faculty research:* Experimentation and numerical relativity, condensed matter astrophysics, quantum computing, medical physics. *Total annual research expenditures:* $9.6 million. *Unit head:* Dr. Michael Cherry, Chair, 225-578-2262, Fax: 225-578-5855, E-mail: cherry@phys.lsu.edu. *Application contact:* Arnell Dangerfield, Administrative Coordinator, 225-578-1193, Fax: 225-578-5855, E-mail: adanger@lsu.edu. Website: http://www.phys.lsu.edu/.

Louisiana Tech University, Graduate School, College of Engineering and Science, Department of Physics, Ruston, LA 71272. Offers applied computational analysis and modeling (PhD); physics (MS). Part-time programs available. *Degree requirements:* For master's, thesis or alternative; for doctorate, thesis/dissertation. *Entrance requirements:* For master's, GRE General Test, minimum GPA of 3.0 in last 60 hours. Additional exam requirements/recommendations for international students: Required—TOEFL. *Faculty research:* Experimental high energy physics, laser/optics, computational physics, quantum gravity.

Marshall University, Academic Affairs Division, College of Science, Department of Physical Science and Physics, Huntington, WV 25755. Offers physical science (MS). *Faculty:* 9 full-time (2 women). *Students:* 10 full-time (4 women), 5 part-time (1 woman), 2 international. Average age 37. In 2012, 11 master's awarded. *Degree requirements:* For master's, thesis optional. Application fee: $40. *Unit head:* Dr. Nicola Orsini, Chairperson, 304-696-2756, E-mail: orsini@marshall.edu. *Application contact:* Dr. Ralph Oberly, Information Contact, 304-696-2757, Fax: 304-746-1902, E-mail: oberly@marshall.edu.

Massachusetts Institute of Technology, School of Science, Department of Physics, Cambridge, MA 02139. Offers SM, PhD. *Faculty:* 68 full-time (5 women). *Students:* 227 full-time (41 women); includes 22 minority (1 Black or African American, non-Hispanic/Latino; 11 Asian, non-Hispanic/Latino; 8 Hispanic/Latino; 2 Two or more races, non-Hispanic/Latino), 114 international. Average age 26. 744 applicants, 12% accepted, 34 enrolled. In 2012, 2 master's, 37 doctorates awarded. Terminal master's awarded for partial completion of doctoral program. *Degree requirements:* For master's, thesis; for doctorate, comprehensive exam, thesis/dissertation. *Entrance requirements:* For master's and doctorate, GRE General Test, GRE Subject Test (physics). Additional exam requirements/recommendations for international students: Required—TOEFL (minimum score 600 paper-based; 100 iBT), IELTS (minimum score 7). *Application deadline:* For fall admission, 12/15 for domestic and international students; for spring admission, 11/1 for domestic and international students. Application fee: $75. Electronic applications accepted. *Expenses: Tuition:* Full-time $41,770; part-time $650 per credit hour. *Required fees:* $280. *Financial support:* In 2012–13, 213 students received support, including 57 fellowships (averaging $36,300 per year), 129 research assistantships (averaging $33,200 per year), 34 teaching assistantships (averaging $34,000 per year); Federal Work-Study, institutionally sponsored loans, scholarships/grants, traineeships, health care benefits, and unspecified assistantships also available. *Faculty research:* High-energy and nuclear physics; condensed matter physics; astrophysics; atomic physics; biophysics; plasma physics. *Total annual research expenditures:* $101 million. *Unit head:* Prof. Edmund Bertschinger, Head, 617-253-4800, Fax: 617-253-8554,

E-mail: physics@mit.edu. *Application contact:* Graduate Admissions, 617-253-4851, Fax: 617-258-8319, E-mail: physics-grad@mit.edu. Website: http://web.mit.edu/physics/.

McGill University, Faculty of Graduate and Postdoctoral Studies, Faculty of Science, Department of Physics, Montréal, QC H3A 2T5, Canada. Offers M Sc, PhD.

McMaster University, School of Graduate Studies, Faculty of Science, Department of Physics and Astronomy, Hamilton, ON L8S 4M2, Canada. Offers astrophysics (PhD); physics (PhD). Part-time programs available. *Degree requirements:* For doctorate, comprehensive exam, thesis/dissertation. *Entrance requirements:* For doctorate, minimum B+ average. Additional exam requirements/recommendations for international students: Required—TOEFL (minimum score 550 paper-based). *Faculty research:* Condensed matter, astrophysics, nuclear, medical, nonlinear dynamics.

Memorial University of Newfoundland, School of Graduate Studies, Department of Physics and Physical Oceanography, St. John's, NL A1C 5S7, Canada. Offers atomic and molecular physics (M Sc, PhD); condensed matter physics (M Sc, PhD); physical oceanography (M Sc, PhD); physics (M Sc). Part-time programs available. *Degree requirements:* For master's, thesis, seminar presentation on thesis topic; for doctorate, comprehensive exam, thesis/dissertation, oral defense of thesis. *Entrance requirements:* For master's, honors B Sc or equivalent; for doctorate, M Sc or equivalent. Electronic applications accepted. *Faculty research:* Experiment and theory in atomic and molecular physics, condensed matter physics, physical oceanography, theoretical geophysics and applied nuclear physics.

Miami University, College of Arts and Science, Department of Physics, Oxford, OH 45056. Offers MAT. Part-time programs available. *Students:* 20 full-time (2 women), 3 international. Average age 26. In 2012, 9 master's awarded. *Entrance requirements:* For master's, GRE (recommended), minimum undergraduate cumulative GPA of 2.75, bachelor's degree in physics or a cognate discipline. Additional exam requirements/recommendations for international students: Required—TOEFL (minimum score 550 paper-based). *Application deadline:* For fall admission, 3/15 for domestic and international students. Application fee: $50. Electronic applications accepted. *Expenses:* Tuition, state resident: full-time $12,444; part-time $519 per credit hour. Tuition, nonresident: full-time $27,484; part-time $1145 per credit hour. *Required fees:* $468. Part-time tuition and fees vary according to course load, campus/location and program. *Financial support:* Fellowships with full tuition reimbursements, research assistantships, teaching assistantships, Federal Work-Study, institutionally sponsored loans, health care benefits, tuition waivers (full), and unspecified assistantships available. Financial award application deadline: 2/15; financial award applicants required to submit FAFSA. *Unit head:* Dr. Herbert Jaeger, Chair, 513-529-5515, E-mail: jaegerh@miamioh.edu. *Application contact:* Dr. Samir Bali, Graduate Director, 513-529-5635, E-mail: balis@miamioh.edu. Website: http://www.MiamiOH.edu/physics.

Michigan State University, The Graduate School, College of Natural Science, Department of Physics and Astronomy, East Lansing, MI 48824. Offers astrophysics and astronomy (MS, PhD); physics (MS, PhD). *Entrance requirements:* Additional exam requirements/recommendations for international students: Required—TOEFL (minimum score 550 paper-based), Michigan State University ELT (minimum score 85), Michigan English Language Assessment Battery (minimum score 83). Electronic applications accepted. *Faculty research:* Nuclear and accelerator physics, high energy physics, condensed matter physics, biophysics, astrophysics and astronomy.

Michigan State University, National Superconducting Cyclotron Laboratory, East Lansing, MI 48824. Offers chemistry (PhD); physics (PhD).

Michigan Technological University, Graduate School, College of Sciences and Arts, Department of Physics, Houghton, MI 49931. Offers engineering physics (PhD); physics (MS, PhD). Part-time programs available. Terminal master's awarded for partial completion of doctoral program. *Degree requirements:* For master's, comprehensive exam (for some programs), thesis (for some programs); for doctorate, comprehensive exam, thesis/dissertation, preliminary exam, research proposal. *Entrance requirements:* For master's and doctorate, GRE (recommended minimum quantitative score of 156 [720 old version] and analytical score of 3.0), statement of purpose, official transcripts, 3 letters of recommendation. Additional exam requirements/recommendations for international students: Required—TOEFL (minimum score 88 iBT) or IELTS. Electronic applications accepted. *Faculty research:* Atmospheric physics, astrophysics, biophysics, materials physics, atomic/molecular physics.

Minnesota State University Mankato, College of Graduate Studies, College of Science, Engineering and Technology, Department of Physics and Astronomy, Mankato, MN 56001. Offers MS. *Students:* 2 full-time (0 women), 8 part-time (0 women). *Degree requirements:* For master's, one foreign language, comprehensive exam, thesis or alternative. *Entrance requirements:* For master's, minimum GPA of 3.0 during previous 2 years, recommendation letters. Additional exam requirements/recommendations for international students: Required—TOEFL. *Application deadline:* For fall admission, 7/1 priority date for domestic students; for spring admission, 11/1 for domestic students. Applications are processed on a rolling basis. Application fee: $40. Electronic applications accepted. *Financial support:* Research assistantships, teaching assistantships with full tuition reimbursements, Federal Work-Study, and unspecified assistantships available. Support available to part-time students. Financial award

application deadline: 3/15; financial award applicants required to submit FAFSA. *Unit head:* Dr. Mark Pickar, Chairperson, 507-389-2721. *Application contact:* 507-389-2321, E-mail: grad@mnsu.edu. Website: http://cset.mnsu.edu/pa/.

Mississippi State University, College of Arts and Sciences, Department of Physics and Astronomy, Mississippi State, MS 39762. Offers engineering (PhD), including applied physics; physics (MS, PhD). Part-time programs available. *Faculty:* 12 full-time (0 women), 2 part-time/adjunct (0 women). *Students:* 42 full-time (6 women), 3 part-time (1 woman); includes 2 minority (both Hispanic/Latino), 35 international. Average age 30. 75 applicants, 17% accepted, 11 enrolled. In 2012, 7 master's, 3 doctorates awarded. *Degree requirements:* For master's, thesis optional, comprehensive oral or written exam; for doctorate, thesis/dissertation, comprehensive oral or written exam. *Entrance requirements:* For master's, GRE, minimum GPA of 2.75 on last two years of undergraduate courses; for doctorate, GRE. Additional exam requirements/recommendations for international students: Required—TOEFL (minimum score 477 paper-based; 53 iBT); Recommended—IELTS (minimum score 4.5). *Application deadline:* For fall admission, 7/1 priority date for domestic students, 5/1 for international students; for spring admission, 11/1 priority date for domestic students, 9/1 for international students. Applications are processed on a rolling basis. Application fee: $60. Electronic applications accepted. *Financial support:* In 2012–13, 14 research assistantships with full tuition reimbursements (averaging $14,594 per year), 20 teaching assistantships with full tuition reimbursements (averaging $13,950 per year) were awarded; Federal Work-Study, institutionally sponsored loans, and unspecified assistantships also available. Financial award application deadline: 3/15; financial award applicants required to submit FAFSA. *Faculty research:* Atomic/molecular spectroscopy, theoretical optics, gamma-ray astronomy, experimental nuclear physics, computational physics. *Total annual research expenditures:* $2.6 million. *Unit head:* Dr. Mark A. Novotny, Department Head and Professor, 662-325-2806, Fax: 662-325-8898, E-mail: man40@ra.msstate.edu. *Application contact:* Dr. David Monts, Professor and Graduate Coordinator, 662-325-2931, Fax: 662-325-8898, E-mail: physics@msstate.edu. Website: http://www.msstate.edu/dept/physics/.

Missouri University of Science and Technology, Graduate School, Department of Physics, Rolla, MO 65409. Offers MS, MST, PhD. *Entrance requirements:* For master's, GRE (minimum score 600 quantitative, 3 writing); for doctorate, GRE (minimum score: 600 quantitative, 3.5 writing). Additional exam requirements/recommendations for international students: Required—TOEFL (minimum score 550 paper-based).

Montana State University, College of Graduate Studies, College of Letters and Science, Department of Physics, Bozeman, MT 59717. Offers MS, PhD. Part-time programs available. *Degree requirements:* For master's, comprehensive exam, thesis (for some programs); for doctorate, comprehensive exam, thesis/dissertation. *Entrance requirements:* For master's and doctorate, GRE General Test, GRE Subject Test (physics). Additional exam requirements/recommendations for international students: Required—TOEFL (minimum score 550 paper-based). Electronic applications accepted. *Faculty research:* Nanotechnology, gravitational wave, astronomy, photodynamic theory, diode laser development, solar radiation transfer.

Naval Postgraduate School, Departments and Academic Groups, Department of Physics, Monterey, CA 93943. Offers applied physics (MS, PhD); combat systems technology (MS); engineering acoustics (MS, PhD); physics (MS, PhD). Program only open to commissioned officers of the United States and friendly nations and selected United States federal civilian employees. Part-time programs available. *Degree requirements:* For master's, thesis; for doctorate, thesis/dissertation. *Faculty research:* Acoustics, free electron laser, sensors, weapons and effects.

New Mexico Institute of Mining and Technology, Graduate Studies, Department of Physics, Socorro, NM 87801. Offers astrophysics (PhD); atmospheric physics (PhD); instrumentation (MS); mathematical physics (PhD); physics (MS). *Faculty:* 12 full-time (3 women), 1 part-time/adjunct (0 women). *Students:* 30 full-time (12 women), 2 part-time (1 woman); includes 1 minority (Asian, non-Hispanic/Latino), 6 international. Average age 29. 15 applicants, 47% accepted, 4 enrolled. In 2012, 1 master's, 2 doctorates awarded. *Degree requirements:* For master's, thesis optional; for doctorate, thesis/dissertation. *Entrance requirements:* For master's, GRE General Test; for doctorate, GRE General Test, GRE Subject Test. Additional exam requirements/recommendations for international students: Required—TOEFL (minimum score 540 paper-based). *Application deadline:* For fall admission, 3/1 priority date for domestic students; for spring admission, 6/1 for domestic students. Applications are processed on a rolling basis. Application fee: $16 ($30 for international students). *Expenses:* Tuition, state resident: full-time $5043; part-time $280 per credit hour. Tuition, nonresident: full-time $16,682; part-time $927 per credit hour. *Required fees:* $648; $18 per credit hour. $108 per semester. Part-time tuition and fees vary according to course load. *Financial support:* In 2012–13, 19 research assistantships (averaging $18,770 per year), 13 teaching assistantships with full and partial tuition reimbursements (averaging $14,078 per year) were awarded; fellowships, Federal Work-Study, institutionally sponsored loans, and unspecified assistantships also available. Financial award application deadline: 3/1; financial award applicants required to submit CSS PROFILE or FAFSA. *Faculty research:* Cloud physics, stellar and extragalactic processes. *Total annual research expenditures:* $3 million. *Unit head:* Dr. Kenneth Eack, Chairman, 575-835-5328, Fax: 575-835-5707, E-mail: dwestpfa@nmt.edu. *Application contact:* Dr. Lorie

Peterson's Graduate Programs in the Physical Sciences, Mathematics, Agricultural Sciences, the Environment & Natural Resources 2014

www.petersonsbooks.com **237**

Physics

Liebrock, Dean of Graduate Studies, 575-835-5513, Fax: 575-835-5476, E-mail: graduate@nmt.edu. Website: http://www.physics.nmt.edu/.

New Mexico State University, Graduate School, College of Arts and Sciences, Department of Physics, Las Cruces, NM 88003-8001. Offers physics (MS, PhD); space physics (MS). Part-time programs available. *Faculty:* 13 full-time (1 woman), 3 part-time/adjunct (0 women). *Students:* 39 full-time (13 women), 1 part-time (0 women); includes 5 minority (1 Black or African American, non-Hispanic/Latino; 4 Hispanic/Latino), 26 international. Average age 29. 73 applicants, 25% accepted, 9 enrolled. In 2012, 4 master's, 6 doctorates awarded. Terminal master's awarded for partial completion of doctoral program. *Degree requirements:* For master's, comprehensive exam, thesis optional, written qualifying exam; for doctorate, comprehensive exam, thesis/dissertation. *Entrance requirements:* For master's and doctorate, GRE General Test, GRE Subject Test. Additional exam requirements/recommendations for international students: Required—TOEFL (minimum score 550 paper-based; 79 iBT), IELTS (minimum score 6.5). *Application deadline:* For fall admission, 2/15 priority date for domestic students, 2/15 for international students; for spring admission, 9/1 priority date for domestic students, 9/1 for international students. Applications are processed on a rolling basis. Application fee: $40 ($50 for international students). Electronic applications accepted. *Expenses:* Tuition, state resident: full-time $5239; part-time $218 per credit. Tuition, nonresident: full-time $18,266; part-time $761 per credit. *Required fees:* $1274; $53 per credit. *Financial support:* In 2012–13, 39 students received support, including 1 fellowship (averaging $3,930 per year), 20 research assistantships (averaging $18,980 per year), 16 teaching assistantships (averaging $17,206 per year); scholarships/grants, health care benefits, tuition waivers (partial), and unspecified assistantships also available. Financial award application deadline: 2/15; financial award applicants required to submit FAFSA. *Faculty research:* Nuclear and particle physics, optics, materials science, geophysics, physics education, atmospheric physics. *Total annual research expenditures:* $1.8 million. *Unit head:* Dr. Stefan Zollner, Head, 575-646-7627, Fax: 575-646-1934, E-mail: zollner@nmsu.edu. *Application contact:* Dr. Vassilios Papavassiliou, Associate Professor/Recruiting Contact, 575-646-3831, Fax: 575-646-1934, E-mail: graduate_advisor@physics.nmsu.edu. Website: http://physics.nmsu.edu.

New York University, Graduate School of Arts and Science, Department of Physics, New York, NY 10012-1019. Offers MS, PhD. Part-time programs available. *Faculty:* 25 full-time (1 woman), 5 part-time/adjunct (0 women). *Students:* 78 full-time (9 women), 3 part-time (0 women); includes 2 minority (1 Asian, non-Hispanic/Latino; 1 Two or more races, non-Hispanic/Latino), 59 international. Average age 27. 266 applicants, 19% accepted, 14 enrolled. In 2012, 7 master's, 8 doctorates awarded. Terminal master's awarded for partial completion of doctoral program. *Degree requirements:* For master's, thesis (for some programs); for doctorate, one foreign language, thesis/dissertation, research seminar, teaching experience. *Entrance requirements:* For master's, GRE General Test, GRE Subject Test, bachelor's degree in physics; for doctorate, GRE General Test, GRE Subject Test. Additional exam requirements/recommendations for international students: Required—TOEFL. *Application deadline:* For fall admission, 12/12 for domestic and international students. Application fee: $90. *Expenses: Tuition:* Full-time $34,488; part-time $1437 per credit. *Required fees:* $2332; $1437 per credit. Tuition and fees vary according to program. *Financial support:* Fellowships with tuition reimbursements, research assistantships with tuition reimbursements, teaching assistantships with tuition reimbursements, Federal Work-Study, institutionally sponsored loans, scholarships/grants, health care benefits, and unspecified assistantships available. Financial award application deadline: 12/12; financial award applicants required to submit FAFSA. *Faculty research:* Atomic physics, elementary particles and fields, astrophysics, condensed-matter physics, neuromagnetism. *Unit head:* David Grier, Chairman, 212-998-7700, Fax: 212-995-4016, E-mail: dgphys@nyu.edu. *Application contact:* Evette Ma, Graduate Program Administrator, 212-998-7700, Fax: 212-995-4016, E-mail: dgsphys@nyu.edu. Website: http://www.physics.nyu.edu/.

North Carolina Agricultural and Technical State University, School of Graduate Studies, College of Arts and Sciences, Department of Physics, Greensboro, NC 27411. Offers computational sciences (MS); physics (MS).

North Carolina Central University, Division of Academic Affairs, College of Science and Technology, Department of Physics, Durham, NC 27707-3129. Offers MS.

North Carolina State University, Graduate School, College of Physical and Mathematical Sciences, Department of Physics, Raleigh, NC 27695. Offers MS, PhD. Part-time programs available. Terminal master's awarded for partial completion of doctoral program. *Degree requirements:* For master's, thesis (for some programs); for doctorate, thesis/dissertation. *Entrance requirements:* For master's and doctorate, GRE General Test, GRE Subject Test. Electronic applications accepted. *Faculty research:* Astrophysics, optics, physics education, biophysics, geophysics.

North Dakota State University, College of Graduate and Interdisciplinary Studies, College of Science and Mathematics, Department of Physics, Fargo, ND 58108. Offers MS, PhD. Part-time programs available. *Faculty:* 6 full-time (1 woman), 2 part-time/adjunct (0 women). *Students:* 8 full-time (1 woman), 2 part-time (0 women); includes 1 minority (Black or African American, non-Hispanic/Latino), 5 international. Average age 30. 10 applicants, 50% accepted, 4 enrolled. In 2012, 1 master's, 1 doctorate awarded. Terminal master's awarded for partial completion of doctoral program. *Degree requirements:* For master's, thesis; for

doctorate, comprehensive exam, thesis/dissertation. *Entrance requirements:* Additional exam requirements/recommendations for international students: Required—TOEFL (minimum score 550 paper-based; 79 iBT). *Application deadline:* For fall admission, 5/1 for international students; for spring admission, 8/1 for international students. Applications are processed on a rolling basis. Application fee: $35. Electronic applications accepted. *Financial support:* In 2012–13, 2 students received support, including 2 research assistantships with tuition reimbursements available (averaging $16,000 per year), teaching assistantships with tuition reimbursements available (averaging $12,000 per year); career-related internships or fieldwork, scholarships/grants, and unspecified assistantships also available. Support available to part-time students. Financial award application deadline: 4/15; financial award applicants required to submit FAFSA. *Faculty research:* Biophysics; condensed matter; surface physics; general relativity, gravitation, and space physics; nonlinear physics. *Unit head:* Dr. Daniel Kroll, Director, 701-231-8968, Fax: 701-231-7088, E-mail: daniel.kroll@ndsu.edu. *Application contact:* Dr. Alexander Wagner, Graduate Advisory Committee Chair, 701-231-9582, Fax: 701-231-7088, E-mail: alexander.wagner@ndsu.edu. Website: http://www.physics.ndsu.nodak.edu/.

Northeastern University, College of Science, Department of Physics, Boston, MA 02115-5096. Offers MS, PhD. Part-time programs available. *Faculty:* 30 full-time (3 women), 10 part-time/adjunct (2 women). *Students:* 75 full-time (11 women). Average age 30. 171 applicants, 32% accepted, 23 enrolled. In 2012, 12 master's, 5 doctorates awarded. Terminal master's awarded for partial completion of doctoral program. *Degree requirements:* For master's, thesis optional; for doctorate, thesis/dissertation, qualifying exam. *Entrance requirements:* For master's and doctorate, GRE General Test, GRE Subject Test. Additional exam requirements/recommendations for international students: Required—TOEFL (minimum score 100 iBT). *Application deadline:* For fall admission, 2/1 priority date for domestic students, 2/1 for international students. Application fee: $75. Electronic applications accepted. *Financial support:* In 2012–13, 72 students received support, including 33 research assistantships with tuition reimbursements available (averaging $19,000 per year), 39 teaching assistantships with tuition reimbursements available (averaging $19,000 per year); Federal Work-Study, health care benefits, tuition waivers (full and partial), and unspecified assistantships also available. Financial award application deadline: 3/1; financial award applicants required to submit FAFSA. *Faculty research:* Elementary particles and astroparticle physics, nanophysics and condensed matter physics, biological and biomedical physics. *Unit head:* Dr. Mark Williams, Graduate Coordinator, 617-373-7323, Fax: 617-373-2943, E-mail: gradphysics@neu.edu. *Application contact:* Nancy Wong, Administrative Assistant for Graduate Affairs, 617-363-4240, Fax: 617-373-2943, E-mail: gradphysics@neu.edu. Website: http://www.physics.neu.edu/.

Northern Arizona University, Graduate College, College of Engineering, Forestry and Natural Sciences, Department of Physics and Astronomy, Flagstaff, AZ 86011. Offers applied physics (MS). Part-time programs available. *Degree requirements:* For master's, thesis optional. *Entrance requirements:* Additional exam requirements/recommendations for international students: Required—TOEFL (minimum score 550 paper-based; 80 iBT), IELTS (minimum score 7). Electronic applications accepted.

Northern Illinois University, Graduate School, College of Liberal Arts and Sciences, Department of Physics, De Kalb, IL 60115-2854. Offers MS, PhD. Part-time programs available. *Faculty:* 18 full-time (3 women), 3 part-time/adjunct (0 women). *Students:* 33 full-time (6 women), 14 part-time (3 women); includes 5 minority (1 Black or African American, non-Hispanic/Latino; 2 Asian, non-Hispanic/Latino; 2 Hispanic/Latino), 16 international. Average age 31. 69 applicants, 52% accepted, 13 enrolled. In 2012, 10 master's, 5 doctorates awarded. Terminal master's awarded for partial completion of doctoral program. *Degree requirements:* For master's, comprehensive exam, thesis or alternative, research seminar; for doctorate, thesis/dissertation, candidacy exam, dissertation defense, research seminar. *Entrance requirements:* For master's, GRE General Test, minimum GPA of 2.75; for doctorate, GRE General Test, GRE Subject Test (physics), bachelor's degree in physics or related field; minimum undergraduate GPA of 2.75, graduate 3.2. Additional exam requirements/recommendations for international students: Required—TOEFL (minimum score 550 paper-based). *Application deadline:* For fall admission, 6/1 for domestic students, 5/1 for international students; for spring admission, 11/1 for domestic students, 10/1 for international students. Applications are processed on a rolling basis. Application fee: $40. Electronic applications accepted. *Financial support:* In 2012–13, 21 research assistantships with full tuition reimbursements, 20 teaching assistantships with full tuition reimbursements were awarded; fellowships with full tuition reimbursements, career-related internships or fieldwork, Federal Work-Study, scholarships/grants, and unspecified assistantships also available. Support available to part-time students. Financial award applicants required to submit FAFSA. *Faculty research:* Band-structure interpolation schemes, nonlinear procession beams, Mossbauer spectroscopy, beam physics. *Unit head:* Dr. Laurence Lurio, Chair, 815-753-6470, Fax: 815-753-8565, E-mail: lluio@niu.edu. *Application contact:* Graduate School Office, 815-753-0395, E-mail: gradsch@niu.edu. Website: http://www.physics.niu.edu/.

Northwestern University, The Graduate School, Judd A. and Marjorie Weinberg College of Arts and Sciences, Department of Physics and Astronomy, Evanston, IL 60208. Offers astrophysics (PhD); physics (MS, PhD). Admissions and degrees offered through The Graduate School. *Degree requirements:* For doctorate, thesis/dissertation, qualifying exam. *Entrance requirements:* For doctorate, GRE

238 www.petersonsbooks.com

Peterson's Graduate Programs in the Physical Sciences, Mathematics, Agricultural Sciences, the Environment & Natural Resources 2014

General Test, GRE Subject Test. Additional exam requirements/ recommendations for international students: Required—TOEFL. *Faculty research:* Nuclear and particle physics, condensed-matter physics, nonlinear physics, astrophysics.

Oakland University, Graduate Study and Lifelong Learning, College of Arts and Sciences, Department of Physics, Rochester, MI 48309-4401. Offers medical physics (PhD); physics (MS). *Degree requirements:* For doctorate, thesis/ dissertation. *Entrance requirements:* For master's, minimum GPA of 3.0 for unconditional admission; for doctorate, GRE Subject Test, GRE General Test, minimum GPA of 3.0 for unconditional admission. Additional exam requirements/ recommendations for international students: Required—TOEFL (minimum score 550 paper-based). Electronic applications accepted. *Expenses:* Contact institution. *Faculty research:* Quantitative molecular imagings of articular cartilage, multifunctional ferrite-ferroelectric layered structures for microwave and millimeter wave devices, magnoelectric materials for antenna structures.

The Ohio State University, Graduate School, College of Arts and Sciences, Division of Natural and Mathematical Sciences, Department of Physics, Columbus, OH 43210. Offers MS, PhD. *Faculty:* 55. *Students:* 100 full-time (15 women), 92 part-time (19 women); includes 16 minority (1 American Indian or Alaska Native, non-Hispanic/Latino; 11 Asian, non-Hispanic/Latino; 4 Hispanic/ Latino), 81 international. Average age 28. In 2012, 35 master's, 24 doctorates awarded. *Degree requirements:* For master's, thesis optional; for doctorate, thesis/dissertation. *Entrance requirements:* For doctorate, GRE General Test, GRE Subject Test (physics). Additional exam requirements/recommendations for international students: Required—TOEFL (minimum score 550 paper-based; 79 iBT), Michigan English Language Assessment Battery (minimum score 82); Recommended—IELTS (minimum score 7). *Application deadline:* For fall admission, 1/1 priority date for domestic students, 11/30 for international students; for winter admission, 12/1 for domestic students, 11/1 for international students; for spring admission, 3/1 for domestic students, 2/1 for international students. Applications are processed on a rolling basis. Application fee: $40 ($50 for international students). Electronic applications accepted. *Financial support:* Fellowships, research assistantships, teaching assistantships, Federal Work-Study, and institutionally sponsored loans available. Support available to part-time students. *Unit head:* James J. Beatty, Chair, 614-292-2653, E-mail: beatty@ mps.ohio-state.edu. *Application contact:* Graduate Admissions, 614-292-9444, Fax: 614-292-3895, E-mail: gradadmissions@osu.edu. Website: http:// www.physics.ohio-state.edu/.

Ohio University, Graduate College, College of Arts and Sciences, Department of Physics and Astronomy, Athens, OH 45701. Offers astronomy (MS, PhD); physics (MS, PhD). Terminal master's awarded for partial completion of doctoral program. *Degree requirements:* For master's, thesis or alternative; for doctorate, comprehensive exam, thesis/dissertation. *Entrance requirements:* For master's and doctorate, minimum GPA of 3.0. Additional exam requirements/ recommendations for international students: Required—TOEFL (minimum score 600 paper-based; 100 iBT), IELTS (minimum score 7), TWE (minimum score 4). Electronic applications accepted. Application fee is waived when completed online. *Faculty research:* Nuclear physics, condensed-matter physics, nonlinear systems, astrophysics, biophysics.

See Display on next page and Close-Up on page 259.

Oklahoma State University, College of Arts and Sciences, Department of Physics, Stillwater, OK 74078. Offers photonics (MS, PhD); physics (MS, PhD). *Faculty:* 27 full-time (4 women), 2 part-time/adjunct (0 women). *Students:* 3 full-time (0 women), 38 part-time (3 women); includes 2 minority (both Two or more races, non-Hispanic/Latino), 26 international. Average age 29. 65 applicants, 23% accepted, 9 enrolled. In 2012, 2 master's, 8 doctorates awarded. *Degree requirements:* For master's, thesis; for doctorate, comprehensive exam, thesis/ dissertation, oral defense of dissertation, preliminary exam, qualifying exam. *Entrance requirements:* For master's and doctorate, GRE. Additional exam requirements/recommendations for international students: Required—TOEFL (minimum score 550 paper-based; 79 iBT). *Application deadline:* For fall admission, 3/1 for international students; for spring admission, 8/1 for international students. Applications are processed on a rolling basis. Application fee: $40 ($75 for international students). Electronic applications accepted. *Expenses:* Tuition, state resident: full-time $4272; part-time $178 per credit hour. Tuition, nonresident: full-time $17,016; part-time $709 per credit hour. *Required fees:* $2188; $91.17 per credit hour. One-time fee: $50 full-time. Part-time tuition and fees vary according to course load and campus/location. *Financial support:* In 2012–13, 16 research assistantships (averaging $19,560 per year), 35 teaching assistantships (averaging $16,530 per year) were awarded; career-related internships or fieldwork, Federal Work-Study, scholarships/grants, health care benefits, tuition waivers (partial), and unspecified assistantships also available. Support available to part-time students. Financial award application deadline: 3/1; financial award applicants required to submit FAFSA. *Faculty research:* Lasers and photonics, non-linear optical materials, turbulence, structure and function of biological membranes, particle theory. *Unit head:* Dr. John Mintmire, Head, 405-744-5796, Fax: 405-744-6811. *Application contact:* Dr. Sheryl Tucker, Dean, 405-744-7099, Fax: 405-744-0355, E-mail: grad-i@okstate.edu. Website: http:// physics.okstate.edu/.

Old Dominion University, College of Sciences, Program in Physics, Norfolk, VA 23529. Offers MS, PhD. *Faculty:* 21 full-time (2 women), 9 part-time/adjunct (2 women). *Students:* 47 full-time (12 women), 2 part-time (1 woman); includes 16 minority (2 Black or African American, non-Hispanic/Latino; 11 Asian, non-Hispanic/Latino; 3 Hispanic/Latino), 28 international. Average age 32. 73 applicants, 26% accepted, 5 enrolled. In 2012, 7 master's, 6 doctorates awarded. Terminal master's awarded for partial completion of doctoral program. *Degree requirements:* For master's, comprehensive exam, thesis optional; for doctorate, comprehensive exam, thesis/dissertation. *Entrance requirements:* For master's, BS in physics or related field, minimum GPA of 3.0 in major, 2 reference letters; for doctorate, GRE General Test; GRE Subject Test (strongly recommended), minimum GPA of 3.0; three reference letters. Additional exam requirements/ recommendations for international students: Required—TOEFL (minimum score 550 paper-based; 79 iBT). *Application deadline:* For fall admission, 2/15 for domestic and international students. Applications are processed on a rolling basis. Application fee: $50. Electronic applications accepted. *Expenses:* Tuition, state resident: full-time $9432; part-time $393 per credit hour. Tuition, nonresident: full-time $23,928; part-time $997 per credit hour. *Required fees:* $59 per semester. One-time fee: $50. *Financial support:* In 2012–13, 42 students received support, including 2 fellowships with full tuition reimbursements available (averaging $7,500 per year), 33 research assistantships with full and partial tuition reimbursements available (averaging $25,000 per year), 16 teaching assistantships with full tuition reimbursements available (averaging $23,000 per year); career-related internships or fieldwork, scholarships/grants, tuition waivers (full), and unspecified assistantships also available. Support available to part-time students. Financial award application deadline: 2/15; financial award applicants required to submit FAFSA. *Faculty research:* Nuclear and particle physics, atomic physics, condensed-matter physics, plasma physics, accelerator physics. *Unit head:* Dr. Lepsha Vuskovic, Graduate Program Director, 757-683-4611, Fax: 757-683-3038, E-mail: vuskovic@odu.edu. *Application contact:* Dr. Mark Havey, Graduate Recruitment and Admissions Director, 757-683-4612, Fax: 757-683-3038, E-mail: mhavey@odu.edu. Website: http://sci.odu.edu/physics/graduate/ graduate_overview.shtml.

Oregon State University, College of Science, Department of Physics, Program in Physics, Corvallis, OR 97331. Offers MS, PhD. *Faculty:* 17 full-time (4 women), 1 (woman) part-time/adjunct. *Students:* 38 full-time (9 women), 1 part-time (0 women); includes 3 minority (1 Asian, non-Hispanic/Latino; 2 Hispanic/Latino), 9 international. Average age 29. 81 applicants, 22% accepted, 10 enrolled. In 2012, 4 master's, 6 doctorates awarded. *Expenses:* Tuition, state resident: full-time $11,367; part-time $421 per credit hour. Tuition, nonresident: full-time $18,279; part-time $677 per credit hour. *Required fees:* $1478. One-time fee: $300 full-time. Tuition and fees vary according to course load and program. *Unit head:* Dr. Henri J. F. Jansen, Chair, 541-737-1668, Fax: 541-737-1683, E-mail: physics.chair@science.oregonstate.edu. *Application contact:* Dr. Yun-Shik Lee, Head Graduate Advisor/Professor, 541-737-5057, E-mail: leeys@ physics.oregonstate.edu.

Penn State University Park, Graduate School, Eberly College of Science, Department of Physics, State College, University Park, PA 16802-1503. Offers M Ed, MS, PhD. *Unit head:* Dr. Nitin Samarth, Head, 814-865-7533, Fax: 814-865-0978. *Application contact:* Rick Robinett, Director of Graduate Studies, 814-863-0965, E-mail: rq9@psu.edu. Website: http://www.phys.psu.edu.

Pittsburg State University, Graduate School, College of Arts and Sciences, Department of Physics, Pittsburg, KS 66762. Offers applied physics (MS); physics (MS); professional physics (MS). *Degree requirements:* For master's, thesis or alternative.

Portland State University, Graduate Studies, College of Liberal Arts and Sciences, Department of Physics, Portland, OR 97207-0751. Offers MA, MS, PhD. Part-time programs available. *Degree requirements:* For master's, variable foreign language requirement, thesis, oral exam, written report; for doctorate, thesis/dissertation. *Entrance requirements:* For master's, GRE General Test, minimum GPA of 3.0 in upper-division course work or 2.75 overall, 2 letters of recommendation. Additional exam requirements/recommendations for international students: Required—TOEFL (minimum score 550 paper-based). *Faculty research:* Statistical physics, membrane biophysics, low-temperature physics, electron microscopy, atmospheric physics.

Princeton University, Graduate School, Department of Physics, Princeton, NJ 08544-1019. Offers PhD. *Degree requirements:* For doctorate, thesis/dissertation, qualifying exam. *Entrance requirements:* For doctorate, GRE General Test, GRE Subject Test. Additional exam requirements/recommendations for international students: Required—TOEFL (minimum score 600 paper-based). Electronic applications accepted.

Purdue University, Graduate School, College of Science, Department of Physics, West Lafayette, IN 47907. Offers MS, PhD. Part-time programs available. *Faculty:* 51 full-time (5 women), 3 part-time/adjunct (0 women). *Students:* 132 full-time (21 women), 19 part-time (2 women); includes 5 minority (1 Black or African American, non-Hispanic/Latino; 2 Asian, non-Hispanic/Latino; 1 Hispanic/Latino; 1 Two or more races, non-Hispanic/Latino), 74 international. Average age 27. 313 applicants, 21% accepted, 21 enrolled. In 2012, 8 master's, 11 doctorates awarded. Terminal master's awarded for partial completion of doctoral program. *Degree requirements:* For master's, thesis optional, qualifying exam; for doctorate, thesis/dissertation, qualifying exam. *Entrance requirements:* For master's and doctorate, GRE General Test, GRE Subject Test (physics), minimum undergraduate GPA of 3.0 or equivalent. Additional exam requirements/ recommendations for international students: Required—TOEFL (minimum score 550 paper-based; 77 iBT). *Application deadline:* For fall admission, 1/15 for

Peterson's Graduate Programs in the Physical Sciences, Mathematics, Agricultural Sciences, the Environment & Natural Resources 2014

www.petersonsbooks.com **239**

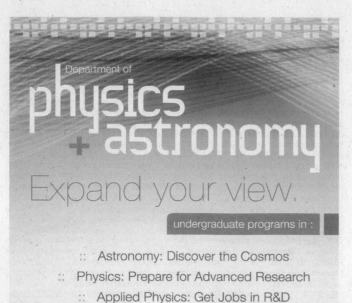

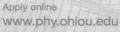

domestic and international students; for spring admission, 8/1 for domestic and international students. Applications are processed on a rolling basis. Application fee: $60 ($75 for international students). Electronic applications accepted. *Financial support:* Fellowships with partial tuition reimbursements, research assistantships with partial tuition reimbursements, and teaching assistantships with partial tuition reimbursements available. Support available to part-time students. Financial award application deadline: 2/1; financial award applicants required to submit FAFSA. *Faculty research:* Solid-state, elementary particle, and nuclear physics; biological physics; acoustics; astrophysics. *Unit head:* Dr. Nicholas J. Giordano, Head, 765-494-3000, Fax: 765-494-0706, E-mail: giordano@purdue.edu. *Application contact:* Sandy J. Formica, Graduate Coordinator, 765-494-3099, E-mail: physcontacts@purdue.edu. Website: http://www.physics.purdue.edu/.

Queens College of the City University of New York, Division of Graduate Studies, Mathematics and Natural Sciences Division, Department of Physics, Flushing, NY 11367-1597. Offers MA, PhD. Part-time and evening/weekend programs available. *Faculty:* 10 full-time (1 woman), 9 part-time/adjunct (0 women). *Students:* 5 part-time (2 women); includes 3 minority (2 Asian, non-Hispanic/Latino; 1 Hispanic/Latino). 8 applicants, 88% accepted, 5 enrolled. In 2012, 2 master's awarded. *Degree requirements:* For master's, comprehensive exam. *Entrance requirements:* For master's, previous course work in calculus, minimum GPA of 3.0. Additional exam requirements/recommendations for international students: Required—TOEFL. *Application deadline:* For fall admission, 4/1 for domestic students; for spring admission, 11/1 for domestic students. Applications are processed on a rolling basis. Application fee: $125. *Expenses:* Tuition, state resident: full-time $8690; part-time $365 per credit. Tuition, nonresident: full-time $16,200; part-time $675 per credit. Full-time tuition and fees vary according to course load. *Financial support:* Career-related internships or fieldwork, Federal Work-Study, institutionally sponsored loans, and tuition waivers (partial) available. Support available to part-time students. Financial award application deadline: 4/1; financial award applicants required to submit FAFSA. *Unit head:* Dr. Alexander Lisyansky, Chairperson, 718-997-3350, E-mail: alexander_lisyansky@qc.edu. *Application contact:* Dr. J. Marion Dickey, Graduate Adviser, 718-997-3350.

Queen's University at Kingston, School of Graduate Studies and Research, Faculty of Arts and Sciences, Department of Physics, Kingston, ON K7L 3N6, Canada. Offers M Sc, M Sc Eng, PhD. Part-time programs available. *Degree requirements:* For master's, thesis; for doctorate, comprehensive exam, thesis/dissertation. *Entrance requirements:* For master's, first or upper second class honours in Physics; for doctorate, M Sc or M Sc Eng. Additional exam requirements/recommendations for international students: Required—TOEFL (minimum score 550 paper-based). *Faculty research:* Theoretical physics, astronomy and astrophysics, subatomic, condensed matter, applied and engineering.

Rensselaer Polytechnic Institute, Graduate School, School of Science, Department of Physics, Applied Physics and Astronomy, Troy, NY 12180-3590. Offers MS, PhD. *Faculty:* 23 full-time (4 women), 3 part-time/adjunct (0 women). *Students:* 53 full-time (8 women); includes 29 minority (1 Black or African American, non-Hispanic/Latino; 25 Asian, non-Hispanic/Latino; 3 Two or more races, non-Hispanic/Latino). Average age 26. 167 applicants, 27% accepted, 8 enrolled. In 2012, 10 master's, 13 doctorates awarded. *Degree requirements:* For doctorate, thesis/dissertation. *Entrance requirements:* For master's and doctorate, GRE General Test, GRE Subject Test (physics). Additional exam requirements/recommendations for international students: Required—TOEFL (minimum score 600 paper-based, 100 iBT), IELTS (minimum score 7), or Pearson Test of English (minimum score 68). *Application deadline:* For fall admission, 1/1 priority date for domestic students, 1/1 for international students; for spring admission, 8/15 priority date for domestic students, 8/15 for international students. Applications are processed on a rolling basis. Application fee: $75. Electronic applications accepted. *Financial support:* In 2012–13, research assistantships (averaging $18,500 per year), teaching assistantships (averaging $18,500 per year) were awarded; fellowships also available. Financial award application deadline: 1/1. *Faculty research:* Astronomy and astrophysics, biological physics, condensed matter physics, optical physics, particle physics, stochastic dynamic on complex networks. *Application contact:* Office of Graduate Admissions, 518-276-6216, E-mail: gradadmissions@rpi.edu. Website: http://www.rpi.edu/dept/phys/graduate/index.html.

Rice University, Graduate Programs, Wiess School of Natural Sciences, Department of Physics and Astronomy, Houston, TX 77251-1892. Offers nanoscale physics (MS); physics and astronomy (PhD); science teaching (MST). Part-time programs available. *Degree requirements:* For master's, thesis (for some programs); for doctorate, thesis/dissertation, minimum B average. *Entrance requirements:* For master's, GRE General Test; for doctorate, GRE General Test, GRE Subject Test. Additional exam requirements/recommendations for international students: Required—TOEFL (minimum score 600 paper-based; 90 iBT). Electronic applications accepted. *Faculty research:* Optical physics; ultra cold atoms; membrane electr-statics, peptides, proteins and lipids; solar astrophysics; stellar activity; magnetic fields; young stars.

Rice University, Graduate Programs, Wiess School–Professional Science Master's Programs, Professional Master's Program in Nanoscale Physics, Houston, TX 77251-1892. Offers MS. *Degree requirements:* For master's, internship. *Entrance requirements:* For master's, GRE General Test, bachelor's degree in physics and related field, 4 letters of recommendation. Additional exam

240 www.petersonsbooks.com

Peterson's Graduate Programs in the Physical Sciences, Mathematics, Agricultural Sciences, the Environment & Natural Resources 2014

requirements/recommendations for international students: Required—TOEFL (minimum score 600 paper-based; 90 iBT). Electronic applications accepted. *Faculty research:* Atomic, molecular, and applied physics, surface and condensed matter physics.

Royal Military College of Canada, Division of Graduate Studies and Research, Science Division, Department of Physics, Kingston, ON K7K 7B4, Canada. Offers M Sc. *Degree requirements:* For master's, thesis. *Entrance requirements:* For master's, honour's degree with second-class standing. Electronic applications accepted.

Rutgers, The State University of New Jersey, New Brunswick, Graduate School-New Brunswick, Department of Physics and Astronomy, Piscataway, NJ 08854-8097. Offers astronomy (MS, PhD); biophysics (PhD); condensed matter physics (MS, PhD); elementary particle physics (MS, PhD); intermediate energy nuclear physics (MS); nuclear physics (MS, PhD); physics (MST); surface science (PhD); theoretical physics (MS, PhD). Part-time programs available. Terminal master's awarded for partial completion of doctoral program. *Degree requirements:* For master's, comprehensive exam, thesis or alternative; for doctorate, comprehensive exam, thesis/dissertation. *Entrance requirements:* For master's and doctorate, GRE General Test, GRE Subject Test. Additional exam requirements/recommendations for international students: Required—TOEFL (minimum score 500 paper-based). Electronic applications accepted. *Faculty research:* Astronomy, high energy, condensed matter, surface, nuclear physics.

St. Francis Xavier University, Graduate Studies, Department of Physics, Antigonish, NS B2G 2W5, Canada. Offers M Sc. *Degree requirements:* For master's, thesis. *Entrance requirements:* For master's, minimum B average in undergraduate course work, honors degree in physics or related area. Additional exam requirements/recommendations for international students: Required—TOEFL (minimum score 580 paper-based). *Faculty research:* Atomic and molecular spectroscopy, quantum theory, many body theory, mathematical physics, phase transitions.

San Diego State University, Graduate and Research Affairs, College of Sciences, Department of Physics, Program in Physics, San Diego, CA 92182. Offers MA, MS. Part-time programs available. *Degree requirements:* For master's, thesis, oral exam. *Entrance requirements:* For master's, GRE General Test, GRE Subject Test (physics), 2 letters of recommendation. Additional exam requirements/recommendations for international students: Required—TOEFL. Electronic applications accepted.

San Francisco State University, Division of Graduate Studies, College of Science and Engineering, Department of Physics and Astronomy, San Francisco, CA 94132-1722. Offers physics (MS). Part-time programs available. *Application deadline:* Applications are processed on a rolling basis. Electronic applications accepted. *Unit head:* Dr. Susan Lea, Chair, 415-338-1659, E-mail: slea@sfsu.edu. *Application contact:* Maarten Golterman, Graduate Coordinator, 415-338-1659, E-mail: maarten@stars.sfsu.edu. Website: http://www.physics.sfsu.edu/.

San Jose State University, Graduate Studies and Research, College of Science, Department of Physics and Astronomy, San Jose, CA 95192-0001. Offers computational physics (MS); physics (MS). Part-time and evening/weekend programs available. *Degree requirements:* For master's, thesis optional. *Entrance requirements:* For master's, GRE. Electronic applications accepted. *Faculty research:* Astrophysics, atmospheric physics, elementary particles, dislocation theory, general relativity.

Simon Fraser University, Office of Graduate Studies, Faculty of Science, Department of Physics, Burnaby, BC V5A 1S6, Canada. Offers M Sc, PhD. *Faculty:* 29 full-time (6 women). *Students:* 63 full-time (26 women), 1 part-time (0 women). 70 applicants, 30% accepted, 12 enrolled. In 2012, 7 master's, 7 doctorates awarded. *Degree requirements:* For master's, thesis; for doctorate, thesis/dissertation. *Entrance requirements:* For master's, minimum GPA of 3.0 (on scale of 4.33), or 3.33 based on last 60 credits of undergraduate courses; for doctorate, minimum GPA of 3.5 (on scale of 4.33). Additional exam requirements/recommendations for international students: Recommended—TOEFL (minimum score 580 paper-based; 93 iBT), IELTS (minimum score 7), TWE (minimum score 5). *Application deadline:* Applications are processed on a rolling basis. Application fee: $90 ($125 for international students). Electronic applications accepted. Tuition and fees charges are reported in Canadian dollars. *Expenses: Tuition, area resident:* Full-time $5000 Canadian dollars; part-time $275 Canadian dollars per credit hour. *Required fees:* $780 Canadian dollars. *Financial support:* In 2012–13, 45 students received support, including 39 fellowships (averaging $6,250 per year), teaching assistantships (averaging $5,008 per year); research assistantships and scholarships/grants also available. Financial award application deadline: 3/15. *Faculty research:* Biophysics and soft condensed matter, particle physics, quantum matter, superconductivity, theoretical physics. *Unit head:* Dr. J. Steven Dodge, Graduate Chair, 778-782-4736, Fax: 778-782-3592, E-mail: physgrad-chair@sfu.ca. *Application contact:* Rose Evans, Graduate Secretary, 778-782-4310, Fax: 778-782-3592, E-mail: physgrad@sfu.ca. Website: http://www.physics.sfu.ca/.

South Dakota School of Mines and Technology, Graduate Division, Program in Physics, Rapid City, SD 57701-3995. Offers MS, PhD. Part-time programs available. *Faculty:* 6 full-time (0 women). *Students:* 10 full-time (1 woman), 1 international. Average age 30. 4 applicants, 100% accepted, 4 enrolled. In 2012, 2 master's awarded. *Degree requirements:* For master's, thesis (for some programs). *Entrance requirements:* Additional exam requirements/recommendations for international students: Required—TOEFL (minimum score 520 paper-based; 68 iBT). *Application deadline:* For fall admission, 7/1 for domestic students, 4/1 for international students; for spring admission, 11/1 for domestic students, 9/1 for international students. Applications are processed on a rolling basis. Application fee: $35. Electronic applications accepted. *Expenses:* Tuition, state resident: full-time $4720; part-time $196.80 per credit hour. Tuition, nonresident: full-time $10,000; part-time $416.55 per credit hour. *Required fees:* $4360. *Financial support:* Application deadline: 5/15. *Unit head:* Dr. Andre G. Petukhov, Director, 605-394-2364, E-mail: andre.petukhov@sdsmt.edu. *Application contact:* Linda Carlson, Office of Graduate Education, 605-355-3468, Fax: 605-394-1767, E-mail: linda.carlson@sdsmt.edu. Website: http://www.sdsmt.edu/Academics/Departments/Physics/Graduate-Education/.

South Dakota State University, Graduate School, College of Engineering, Department of Physics, Brookings, SD 57007. Offers engineering (MS). Part-time programs available. *Degree requirements:* For master's, comprehensive exam (for some programs), thesis (for some programs), oral exam. *Entrance requirements:* Additional exam requirements/recommendations for international students: Required—TOEFL (minimum score 580 paper-based). *Faculty research:* Materials science, astrophysics, remote sensing and atmospheric corrections, theoretical and computational physics, applied physics.

Southern Illinois University Carbondale, Graduate School, College of Science, Department of Physics, Carbondale, IL 62901-4701. Offers MS, PhD. *Faculty:* 9 full-time (0 women). *Students:* 6 full-time (1 woman), 24 part-time (5 women); includes 2 minority (1 Asian, non-Hispanic/Latino; 1 Hispanic/Latino), 14 international. 37 applicants, 19% accepted, 5 enrolled. In 2012, 7 master's, 5 doctorates awarded. *Degree requirements:* For master's, one foreign language, thesis. *Entrance requirements:* For master's, minimum GPA of 2.7. Additional exam requirements/recommendations for international students: Required—TOEFL. *Application deadline:* Applications are processed on a rolling basis. Application fee: $50. *Financial support:* In 2012–13, 1 fellowship with full tuition reimbursement, 9 teaching assistantships with full tuition reimbursements were awarded; research assistantships with full tuition reimbursements, career-related internships or fieldwork, Federal Work-Study, institutionally sponsored loans, and tuition waivers (full) also available. Support available to part-time students. Financial award application deadline: 2/15. *Faculty research:* Atomic, molecular, nuclear, and mathematical physics; statistical mechanics; solid-state and low-temperature physics; rheology; material science. *Total annual research expenditures:* $773,352. *Unit head:* Dr. Naushad Ali, Chairperson, 618-453-1053, E-mail: nali@physics.siu.edu. Website: http://siuphysics.physics.siu.edu/.

Southern Methodist University, Dedman College, Department of Physics, Dallas, TX 75275. Offers MS, PhD. Part-time programs available. Terminal master's awarded for partial completion of doctoral program. *Degree requirements:* For master's, thesis optional, oral exam; for doctorate, thesis/dissertation, written exam. *Entrance requirements:* For master's and doctorate, GRE General Test, GRE Subject Test (physics), minimum GPA of 3.0. Additional exam requirements/recommendations for international students: Required—TOEFL. Electronic applications accepted. *Faculty research:* Particle physics, cosmology, astrophysics, mathematics physics, computational physics.

Southern University and Agricultural and Mechanical College, Graduate School, College of Sciences, Department of Physics, Baton Rouge, LA 70813. Offers MS. *Degree requirements:* For master's, thesis. *Entrance requirements:* For master's, GMAT or GRE General Test. Additional exam requirements/recommendations for international students: Required—TOEFL (minimum score 525 paper-based). *Faculty research:* Piezoelectric materials and devices, predictive ab-instio calculations, high energy physics, surface growth studies, semiconductor and intermetallics.

Stanford University, School of Humanities and Sciences, Department of Physics, Stanford, CA 94305-9991. Offers PhD. *Degree requirements:* For doctorate, thesis/dissertation, oral exam, qualifying exam. *Entrance requirements:* For doctorate, GRE General Test, GRE Subject Test. Additional exam requirements/recommendations for international students: Required—TOEFL. Electronic applications accepted. *Expenses: Tuition:* Full-time $41,250; part-time $917 per credit hour.

Stephen F. Austin State University, Graduate School, College of Sciences and Mathematics, Department of Physics and Astronomy, Nacogdoches, TX 75962. Offers physics (MS). Part-time programs available. *Degree requirements:* For master's, comprehensive exam. *Entrance requirements:* For master's, GRE General Test, minimum GPA of 2.8 in last 60 hours, 2.5 overall. Additional exam requirements/recommendations for international students: Required—TOEFL. *Faculty research:* Low-temperature physics, x-ray spectroscopy and metallic glasses, infrared spectroscopy.

Stevens Institute of Technology, Graduate School, Charles V. Schaefer Jr. School of Engineering, Department of Physics and Engineering Physics, Hoboken, NJ 07030. Offers applied optics (Certificate); engineering physics (M Eng); microdevices and microsystems (Certificate); physics (MS, PhD); plasma and surface physics (Certificate). Part-time and evening/weekend programs available. Terminal master's awarded for partial completion of doctoral program. *Degree requirements:* For master's, thesis optional; for doctorate, thesis/dissertation. *Entrance requirements:* For master's and doctorate, GRE. Additional exam requirements/recommendations for international students: Required—TOEFL. Electronic applications accepted. *Faculty research:* Laser spectroscopy, physical kinetics, semiconductor-device physics, condensed-matter theory.

Stony Brook University, State University of New York, Graduate School, College of Arts and Sciences, Department of Physics and Astronomy, Program in Physics, Stony Brook, NY 11794. Offers modern research instrumentation (MS); physics (MA, PhD); physics education (MAT). *Students:* 171 full-time (29 women), 2 part-time (0 women); includes 10 minority (1 Black or African American, non-Hispanic/Latino; 4 Asian, non-Hispanic/Latino; 4 Hispanic/Latino; 1 Two or more races, non-Hispanic/Latino), 115 international. *Degree requirements:* For doctorate, one foreign language, thesis/dissertation. *Entrance requirements:* For master's and doctorate, GRE General Test. Additional exam requirements/ recommendations for international students: Required—TOEFL. *Application deadline:* For fall admission, 1/15 for domestic students. Application fee: $100. *Expenses:* Tuition, state resident: full-time $9370. Tuition, nonresident: full-time $16,680. *Required fees:* $1214. *Financial support:* Fellowships, research assistantships, and teaching assistantships available. Financial award application deadline: 2/1. *Unit head:* Dr. Laszlo Mihaly, Chair, 631-632-8100, Fax: 631-632-8176, E-mail: lazlo.mihaly@stonybrook.edu. *Application contact:* Dr. Jacobus Verbaarschot, Director, 631-632-8279, Fax: 631-632-8176, E-mail: verbaarschot@stonybrook.edu.

Syracuse University, College of Arts and Sciences, Program in Physics, Syracuse, NY 13244. Offers MS, PhD. Part-time programs available. Terminal master's awarded for partial completion of doctoral program. *Degree requirements:* For master's, thesis or alternative; for doctorate, comprehensive exam, thesis/dissertation. *Entrance requirements:* For master's and doctorate, GRE General Test, GRE Subject Test. Additional exam requirements/ recommendations for international students: Required—TOEFL (minimum score 100 iBT). Electronic applications accepted.

Temple University, College of Science and Technology, Department of Physics, Philadelphia, PA 19122-6096. Offers MA, PhD. *Faculty:* 33 full-time (8 women). *Students:* 48 full-time (13 women), 1 part-time (0 women); includes 8 minority (1 Black or African American, non-Hispanic/Latino; 5 Asian, non-Hispanic/Latino; 1 Hispanic/Latino; 1 Two or more races, non-Hispanic/Latino), 20 international. 31 applicants, 65% accepted, 11 enrolled. In 2012, 1 master's, 4 doctorates awarded. Terminal master's awarded for partial completion of doctoral program. *Degree requirements:* For master's, comprehensive exam, thesis or alternative; for doctorate, thesis/dissertation, 2 comprehensive exams. *Entrance requirements:* For master's and doctorate, GRE General Test, minimum GPA of 3.0. Additional exam requirements/recommendations for international students: Required—TOEFL (minimum score 550 paper-based; 79 iBT). *Application deadline:* For fall admission, 7/15 for domestic students, 12/15 for international students; for spring admission, 11/15 for domestic students, 8/1 for international students. Applications are processed on a rolling basis. Application fee: $60. Electronic applications accepted. *Financial support:* Fellowships, research assistantships, teaching assistantships, and tuition waivers (full and partial) available. Financial award application deadline: 1/15; financial award applicants required to submit FAFSA. *Faculty research:* Laser-based molecular spectroscopy, elementary particle physics, statistical mechanics, solid-state physics. *Unit head:* Dr. Rongjia Tao, Chair, 215-204-7634, Fax: 215-204-5652, E-mail: physics@temple.edu. *Application contact:* Karen E. Woods-Wilson, Department Administrative Specialist, 215-204-4770, E-mail: karen.woods-wilson@temple.edu. Website: http://www.temple.edu/physics/.

Texas A&M University, College of Science, Department of Physics and Astronomy, College Station, TX 77843. Offers applied physics (PhD); physics (MS, PhD). *Faculty:* 54. *Students:* 177 full-time (21 women), 7 part-time (0 women); includes 28 minority (3 Black or African American, non-Hispanic/Latino; 1 American Indian or Alaska Native, non-Hispanic/Latino; 5 Asian, non-Hispanic/ Latino; 13 Hispanic/Latino; 6 Two or more races, non-Hispanic/Latino), 90 international. Average age 27. In 2012, 13 master's, 10 doctorates awarded. Terminal master's awarded for partial completion of doctoral program. *Degree requirements:* For master's, thesis (for some programs); for doctorate, thesis/ dissertation. *Entrance requirements:* For master's and doctorate, GRE General Test, GRE Subject Test. Additional exam requirements/recommendations for international students: Required—TOEFL. *Application deadline:* For fall admission, 3/1 priority date for domestic students; for spring admission, 8/1 for domestic students. Application fee: $50 ($75 for international students). Electronic applications accepted. *Financial support:* In 2012–13, research assistantships (averaging $16,200 per year), teaching assistantships (averaging $16,200 per year) were awarded; fellowships also available. Financial award application deadline: 3/1; financial award applicants required to submit FAFSA. *Faculty research:* Condensed-matter, atomic/molecular, high-energy, and nuclear physics; quantum optics. *Unit head:* Dr. Edward S. Fry, Head, 979-845-7717, E-mail: fry@physics.tamu.edu. *Application contact:* Dr. George W. Kattawar, Professor, 979-845-1180, Fax: 979-845-2590, E-mail: kattawar@tamu.edu. Website: http://physics.tamu.edu/.

Texas A&M University–Commerce, Graduate School, College of Science, Engineering and Agriculture, Department of Physics and Astronomy, Commerce, TX 75429-3011. Offers M Ed, MS. Part-time programs available. *Degree requirements:* For master's, comprehensive exam, thesis (for some programs). *Entrance requirements:* For master's, GRE General Test. Electronic applications accepted. *Expenses:* Tuition, state resident: full-time $3630; part-time $2420 per year. Tuition, nonresident: full-time $9948; part-time $6632.16 per year. *Required fees:* $1006 per year.

Texas Christian University, College of Science and Engineering, Department of Physics and Astronomy, Fort Worth, TX 76129. Offers physics (MA, MS, PhD), including astrophysics (PhD), biophysics (PhD), business (PhD), physics (PhD); PhD/MBA. *Faculty:* 7 full-time (0 women). *Students:* 14 part-time (4 women); includes 2 minority (1 Asian, non-Hispanic/Latino; 1 Hispanic/Latino), 7 international. Average age 30. 31 applicants, 90% accepted, 2 enrolled. In 2012, 1 degree awarded. Terminal master's awarded for partial completion of doctoral program. *Median time to degree:* Of those who began their doctoral program in fall 2004, 100% received their degree in 8 years or less. *Degree requirements:* For master's, comprehensive exam, thesis; for doctorate, comprehensive exam, thesis/dissertation, paper submitted to scientific journal. *Entrance requirements:* For master's and doctorate, GRE General Test, minimum GPA of 3.0. Additional exam requirements/recommendations for international students: Required—TOEFL (minimum score 600 paper-based). *Application deadline:* For fall admission, 2/1 for domestic and international students; for spring admission, 10/1 for domestic and international students. Applications are processed on a rolling basis. Application fee: $60. Electronic applications accepted. *Expenses: Tuition:* Full-time $21,600; part-time $1200 per credit. *Required fees:* $48. Tuition and fees vary according to program. *Financial support:* In 2012–13, 14 students received support, including 1 research assistantship with full tuition reimbursement available (averaging $20,500 per year), 11 teaching assistantships with full tuition reimbursements available (averaging $19,500 per year); tuition waivers also available. Financial award application deadline: 2/1. *Faculty research:* Biophysics, astrophysics, molecular physics, solid state physics, spectroscopy. *Total annual research expenditures:* $190,000. *Unit head:* Dr. William R. Graham, Professor and Chair, 817-257-7375 Ext. 6383, Fax: 817-257-7742, E-mail: w.graham@tcu.edu. *Application contact:* Dr. Yuri Strzhemechny, Associate Professor and Director, Graduate Program, 817-257-7375 Ext. 5793, Fax: 817-257-7742, E-mail: y.strzhemechny@tcu.edu. Website: http://www.phys.tcu.edu/grad_program.asp.

Texas State University–San Marcos, Graduate School, College of Science and Engineering, Department of Physics, San Marcos, TX 78666. Offers material physics (MS); physics (MS). Part-time programs available. *Faculty:* 9 full-time (1 woman), 2 part-time/adjunct (1 woman). *Students:* 12 full-time (0 women), 6 part-time (0 women); includes 1 minority (Hispanic/Latino), 2 international. Average age 28. 9 applicants, 78% accepted, 6 enrolled. *Degree requirements:* For master's, comprehensive exam, thesis (for some programs). *Entrance requirements:* For master's, minimum GPA of 2.75 in junior- and senior-level physics courses or 2.5 with GRE (minimum combined score of 900 Verbal and Quantitative). Additional exam requirements/recommendations for international students: Required—TOEFL (minimum score 550 paper-based; 78 iBT). *Application deadline:* For fall admission, 6/15 priority date for domestic students, 6/1 for international students; for spring admission, 10/15 priority date for domestic students, 10/1 for international students. Applications are processed on a rolling basis. Application fee: $40 ($90 for international students). Electronic applications accepted. *Expenses:* Tuition, state resident: full-time $6408; part-time $3204 per semester. Tuition, nonresident: full-time $14,832; part-time $7416 per semester. *Required fees:* $1824; $618. Tuition and fees vary according to course load. *Financial support:* In 2012–13, 8 students received support, including 6 research assistantships (averaging $11,280 per year), 8 teaching assistantships (averaging $11,280 per year); career-related internships or fieldwork, Federal Work-Study, and institutionally sponsored loans also available. Support available to part-time students. Financial award application deadline: 4/1; financial award applicants required to submit FAFSA. *Faculty research:* New math tools, redesign and development, novel HEMT-based GaN. *Total annual research expenditures:* $52,025. *Unit head:* Dr. David Donnelly, Chair, 512-245-2131, Fax: 512-245-2131, E-mail: dd14@txstate.edu. *Application contact:* Dr. J. Michael Willoughby, Dean of Graduate School, 512-245-2581, Fax: 512-245-8365, E-mail: gradcollege@txstate.edu. Website: http://www.txstate.edu/physics/.

Texas Tech University, Graduate School, College of Arts and Sciences, Department of Physics, Lubbock, TX 79409. Offers applied physics (MS); physics (MS, PhD). Part-time programs available. *Degree requirements:* For master's, variable foreign language requirement, thesis or alternative; for doctorate, variable foreign language requirement, thesis/dissertation. *Entrance requirements:* For master's and doctorate, GRE General Test. Additional exam requirements/recommendations for international students: Required—TOEFL (minimum score 550 paper-based; 79 iBT). Electronic applications accepted. *Faculty research:* Biophysics, high energy and nuclear physics, condensed matter physics, atomic and molecular physics, physics education.

Trent University, Graduate Studies, Program in Applications of Modeling in the Natural and Social Sciences, Department of Physics, Peterborough, ON K9J 7B8, Canada. Offers M Sc. Part-time programs available. *Degree requirements:* For master's, thesis. *Entrance requirements:* For master's, honours degree. *Faculty research:* Radiation physics, chemical physics.

Tufts University, Graduate School of Arts and Sciences, Department of Physics and Astronomy, Medford, MA 02155. Offers physics (MS, PhD). Terminal master's awarded for partial completion of doctoral program. *Degree requirements:* For master's, thesis optional; for doctorate, thesis/dissertation. *Entrance requirements:* For master's and doctorate, GRE General Test. Additional exam requirements/recommendations for international students: Required—TOEFL (minimum score 550 paper-based; 80 iBT). Electronic applications accepted. *Expenses: Tuition:* Full-time $42,856; part-time $1072 per credit hour. *Required fees:* $730. Full-time tuition and fees vary according to degree level, program and student level. Part-time tuition and fees vary according to course load.

Tulane University, School of Science and Engineering, Department of Physics and Engineering Physics, New Orleans, LA 70118-5669. Offers physics (PhD). *Degree requirements:* For doctorate, thesis/dissertation. *Entrance requirements:* For doctorate, GRE General Test. Additional exam requirements/recommendations for international students: Required—TOEFL. Electronic applications accepted. *Faculty research:* Surface physics, condensed-matter experiment, condensed-matter theory, nuclear theory, polymers.

Université de Moncton, Faculty of Sciences, Department of Physics and Astronomy, Moncton, NB E1A 3E9, Canada. Offers M Sc. Part-time programs available. *Degree requirements:* For master's, thesis. *Entrance requirements:* For master's, proficiency in French. Electronic applications accepted. *Faculty research:* Thin films, optical properties, solar selective surfaces, microgravity and photonic materials.

Université de Montréal, Faculty of Arts and Sciences, Department of Physics, Montréal, QC H3C 3J7, Canada. Offers M Sc, PhD. *Degree requirements:* For doctorate, thesis/dissertation, general exam. Electronic applications accepted. *Faculty research:* Astronomy; biophysics; solid-state, plasma, and nuclear physics.

Université de Sherbrooke, Faculty of Sciences, Department of Physics, Sherbrooke, QC J1K 2R1, Canada. Offers M Sc, PhD. *Degree requirements:* For master's, thesis; for doctorate, comprehensive exam, thesis/dissertation. *Entrance requirements:* For doctorate, master's degree. Electronic applications accepted. *Faculty research:* Solid-state physics, quantum computing.

Université du Québec à Trois-Rivières, Graduate Programs, Program in Physics, Trois-Rivières, QC G9A 5H7, Canada. Offers matter and energy (MS, PhD).

Université Laval, Faculty of Sciences and Engineering, Department of Physics, Physical Engineering, and Optics, Programs in Physics, Québec, QC G1K 7P4, Canada. Offers M Sc, PhD. Terminal master's awarded for partial completion of doctoral program. *Degree requirements:* For master's, thesis; for doctorate, comprehensive exam, thesis/dissertation. *Entrance requirements:* For master's and doctorate, knowledge of French, comprehension of written English. Electronic applications accepted.

University at Albany, State University of New York, College of Arts and Sciences, Department of Physics, Albany, NY 12222-0001. Offers MS, PhD. *Degree requirements:* For master's, one foreign language; for doctorate, one foreign language, thesis/dissertation. *Entrance requirements:* Additional exam requirements/recommendations for international students: Required—TOEFL (minimum score 550 paper-based). Electronic applications accepted. *Faculty research:* Condensed-matter physics, high-energy physics, applied physics, electronic materials, theoretical particle physics.

University at Buffalo, the State University of New York, Graduate School, College of Arts and Sciences, Department of Physics, Buffalo, NY 14260-1500. Offers MS, PhD. Part-time programs available. *Faculty:* 26 full-time (3 women), 2 part-time/adjunct (0 women). *Students:* 77 full-time (11 women); includes 47 minority (1 Black or African American, non-Hispanic/Latino; 1 American Indian or Alaska Native, non-Hispanic/Latino; 44 Asian, non-Hispanic/Latino; 1 Hispanic/Latino), 5 international. Average age 29. 135 applicants, 26% accepted, 13 enrolled. In 2012, 1 master's, 9 doctorates awarded. Terminal master's awarded for partial completion of doctoral program. *Median time to degree:* Of those who began their doctoral program in fall 2004, 57% received their degree in 8 years or less. *Degree requirements:* For master's, thesis optional; for doctorate, comprehensive exam, thesis/dissertation. *Entrance requirements:* For master's and doctorate, GRE General Test, GRE Subject Test, undergraduate degree, letters of recommendaion, statement of purpose. Additional exam requirements/recommendations for international students: Required—TOEFL (minimum score 550 paper-based; 79 iBT). *Application deadline:* For fall admission, 2/1 priority date for domestic students, 2/1 for international students. Application fee: $75. Electronic applications accepted. *Financial support:* In 2012–13, 3 fellowships with full tuition reimbursements (averaging $6,000 per year), 29 research assistantships with full tuition reimbursements (averaging $17,000 per year), 45 teaching assistantships with full tuition reimbursements (averaging $16,500 per year) were awarded; institutionally sponsored loans, scholarships/grants, health care benefits, and unspecified assistantships also available. Financial award application deadline: 2/1; financial award applicants required to submit FAFSA. *Faculty research:* Condensed-matter physics (experimental and theoretical), cosmology (theoretical), high energy and particle physics (experimental and theoretical), computational physics, biophysics (experimental and theoretical), materials physics. *Total annual research expenditures:* $2.6 million. *Unit head:* Dr. Hong Luo, Chairman, 716-645-3421, Fax: 716-645-2507, E-mail: luo@buffalo.edu. *Application contact:* Dr. Xuedong Hu, Director of Graduate Studies, 716-645-5444, Fax: 716-645-2507, E-mail: xhu@buffalo.edu. Website: http://www.physics.buffalo.edu/.

The University of Akron, Graduate School, Buchtel College of Arts and Sciences, Department of Physics, Akron, OH 44325. Offers MS. Part-time and evening/weekend programs available. *Faculty:* 9 full-time (1 woman). *Students:* 15 full-time (7 women), 1 (woman) part-time, 8 international. Average age 25. 35 applicants, 49% accepted, 8 enrolled. In 2012, 5 master's awarded. *Degree requirements:* For master's, thesis, written exam or formal report. *Entrance requirements:* For master's, baccalaureate degree in physics or related field, letters of recommendation, resume, statement of purpose. Additional exam requirements/recommendations for international students: Required—TOEFL (minimum score 550 paper-based; 79 iBT). *Application deadline:* For fall admission, 3/15 for domestic and international students. Applications are processed on a rolling basis. Application fee: $40 ($60 for international students). Electronic applications accepted. *Expenses:* Tuition, state resident: full-time $7285; part-time $404.70 per credit hour. Tuition, nonresident: full-time $12,473; part-time $692.95 per credit hour. *Required fees:* $34.05 per credit hour. Tuition and fees vary according to course load. *Financial support:* In 2012–13, 14 teaching assistantships with full tuition reimbursements were awarded. *Faculty research:* Materials physics, surface physics, nanotechnology, polymer physics, condensed matter physics. *Total annual research expenditures:* $12,949. *Unit head:* Dr. Purushottam D. Gujrati, Interim Chair, 330-972-7136, E-mail: pdg@uakron.edu. *Application contact:* Dr. Ben Hu, Graduate Director, 330-972-8093, E-mail: byhu@uakron.edu. Website: http://www.uakron.edu/physics/.

The University of Alabama, Graduate School, College of Arts and Sciences, Department of Physics and Astronomy, Tuscaloosa, AL 35487-0324. Offers physics (MS, PhD). *Faculty:* 24 full-time (2 women). *Students:* 41 full-time (8 women), 2 part-time (0 women); includes 2 minority (1 American Indian or Alaska Native, non-Hispanic/Latino; 1 Hispanic/Latino), 25 international. Average age 28. 43 applicants, 26% accepted, 5 enrolled. In 2012, 6 master's, 5 doctorates awarded. Terminal master's awarded for partial completion of doctoral program. *Degree requirements:* For master's, thesis optional, oral exam; for doctorate, thesis/dissertation, oral and written exams. *Entrance requirements:* For master's and doctorate, GRE General Test, minimum GPA of 3.0. Additional exam requirements/recommendations for international students: Required—TOEFL (minimum score 550 paper-based; 79 iBT). *Application deadline:* For fall admission, 2/15 priority date for domestic students, 2/15 for international students; for spring admission, 11/1 for domestic students, 6/1 for international students. Applications are processed on a rolling basis. Application fee: $50 ($60 for international students). Electronic applications accepted. *Expenses:* Tuition, state resident: full-time $9200. Tuition, nonresident: full-time $22,950. *Financial support:* In 2012–13, 39 students received support, including 3 fellowships with full tuition reimbursements available (averaging $18,000 per year), 9 research assistantships with full tuition reimbursements available (averaging $23,040 per year), 29 teaching assistantships with full tuition reimbursements available (averaging $23,040 per year); career-related internships or fieldwork, institutionally sponsored loans, and health care benefits also available. Financial award application deadline: 2/1. *Faculty research:* Condensed matter, high-energy physics, astrophysics, particle astrophysics, collider physics. *Total annual research expenditures:* $2.3 million. *Unit head:* Dr. Raymond E. White, III, Chairman and Professor, 205-348-5050, Fax: 205-348-5051, E-mail: rwhite@ua.edu. Website: http://physics.ua.edu/.

The University of Alabama at Birmingham, College of Arts and Sciences, Program in Physics, Birmingham, AL 35294-1170. Offers MS, PhD. *Students:* 35 full-time (3 women); includes 1 minority (Hispanic/Latino), 8 international. Average age 28. In 2012, 6 master's, 2 doctorates awarded. Terminal master's awarded for partial completion of doctoral program. *Degree requirements:* For master's, thesis optional; for doctorate, thesis/dissertation. *Entrance requirements:* For master's and doctorate, GRE General Test; GRE Subject Test (recommended), minimum GPA of 3.0. Additional exam requirements/recommendations for international students: Required—TOEFL, TWE. *Application deadline:* For fall admission, 5/1 for domestic students; for spring admission, 10/1 for domestic students. Applications are processed on a rolling basis. Application fee: $45 ($60 for international students). Electronic applications accepted. *Expenses:* Tuition, state resident: full-time $6420; part-time $335 per credit hour. Tuition, nonresident: full-time $14,574; part-time $788 per credit hour. Tuition and fees vary according to course load and program. *Financial support:* Fellowships with full tuition reimbursements, research assistantships with full tuition reimbursements, teaching assistantships with full tuition reimbursements, career-related internships or fieldwork, Federal Work-Study, institutionally sponsored loans, scholarships/grants, traineeships, health care benefits, and unspecified assistantships available. Support available to part-time students. Financial award application deadline: 4/15; financial award applicants required to submit FAFSA. *Faculty research:* Biophysics, computational and theoretical physics, condensed matter and material physics, optics and laser physics. *Unit head:* Dr. Mary Ellen Zvanut, Graduate Program Director, 205-934-6661, E-mail: mezvanut@uab.edu. Website: http://www.uab.edu/cas/physics/.

The University of Alabama in Huntsville, School of Graduate Studies, College of Science, Department of Physics, Huntsville, AL 35899. Offers education (MS); optics and photonics technology (MS); physics (MS, PhD). Part-time and evening/weekend programs available. *Faculty:* 18 full-time (0 women), 1 part-time/adjunct (0 women). *Students:* 41 full-time (11 women), 17 part-time (4 women); includes 3 minority (2 Asian, non-Hispanic/Latino; 1 Hispanic/Latino), 16 international. Average age 28. 41 applicants, 76% accepted, 17 enrolled. In 2012, 10 master's, 2 doctorates awarded. *Degree requirements:* For master's, comprehensive exam, thesis or alternative, oral and written exams; for doctorate, comprehensive exam, thesis/dissertation, oral and written exams. *Entrance requirements:* For master's and doctorate, GRE General Test, minimum GPA of 3.0. Additional exam requirements/recommendations for international students: Required—TOEFL (minimum score 550 paper-based; 80 iBT), IELTS (minimum score 6.5). *Application deadline:* For fall admission, 7/15 priority date for domestic students, 4/1 for international students; for spring admission, 11/30 priority date for

Peterson's Graduate Programs in the Physical Sciences, Mathematics, Agricultural Sciences, the Environment & Natural Resources 2014

www.petersonsbooks.com **243**

domestic students, 9/1 for international students. Applications are processed on a rolling basis. Application fee: $40 ($50 for international students). Electronic applications accepted. *Expenses:* Tuition, state resident: full-time $8516; part-time $515 per credit hour. Tuition, nonresident: full-time $20,384; part-time $1229 per credit hour. *Required fees:* $148 per semester. One-time fee: $150. *Financial support:* In 2012–13, 34 students received support, including 1 fellowship with full tuition reimbursement available (averaging $17,455 per year), 22 research assistantships with full and partial tuition reimbursements available (averaging $16,424 per year), 12 teaching assistantships with full and partial tuition reimbursements available (averaging $17,547 per year); career-related internships or fieldwork, Federal Work-Study, institutionally sponsored loans, scholarships/grants, health care benefits, and unspecified assistantships also available. Support available to part-time students. Financial award application deadline: 4/1; financial award applicants required to submit FAFSA. *Faculty research:* Space and solar physics, computational physics, optics, high energy astrophysics. *Total annual research expenditures:* $6.5 million. *Unit head:* Dr. Gary Zank, Chair, 256-824-2481, Fax: 256-824-6873, E-mail: gary.zank@uah.edu. *Application contact:* Kim Gray, Graduate Studies Admissions Coordinator, 256-824-6002, Fax: 256-824-6405, E-mail: deangrad@uah.edu. Website: http://physics.uah.edu/.

University of Alaska Fairbanks, College of Natural Sciences and Mathematics, Department of Physics, Fairbanks, AK 99775-5920. Offers computational physics (MS); physics (MAT, MS, PhD); space physics (MS, PhD). Part-time programs available. *Faculty:* 10 full-time (2 women). *Students:* 22 full-time (5 women), 3 part-time (0 women); includes 2 minority (1 American Indian or Alaska Native, non-Hispanic/Latino; 1 Asian, non-Hispanic/Latino), 7 international. Average age 30. 17 applicants, 24% accepted, 4 enrolled. In 2012, 3 master's, 2 doctorates awarded. Terminal master's awarded for partial completion of doctoral program. *Degree requirements:* For master's, comprehensive exam, thesis or alternative; for doctorate, comprehensive exam, thesis/dissertation, oral defense. *Entrance requirements:* Additional exam requirements/recommendations for international students: Required—TOEFL (minimum score 550 paper-based; 80 iBT). *Application deadline:* For fall admission, 6/1 for domestic students, 3/1 for international students; for spring admission, 10/15 for domestic students, 9/1 for international students. Applications are processed on a rolling basis. Application fee: $60. Electronic applications accepted. *Expenses:* Tuition, state resident: full-time $7038. Tuition, nonresident: full-time $14,382. Tuition and fees vary according to course level, course load and reciprocity agreements. *Financial support:* In 2012–13, 12 research assistantships with tuition reimbursements (averaging $16,543 per year), 10 teaching assistantships with tuition reimbursements (averaging $10,640 per year) were awarded; fellowships with tuition reimbursements, Federal Work-Study, scholarships/grants, health care benefits, and unspecified assistantships also available. Support available to part-time students. Financial award application deadline: 2/15; financial award applicants required to submit FAFSA. *Faculty research:* Atmospheric and ionospheric radar studies, space plasma theory, magnetospheric dynamics, space weather and auroral studies, turbulence and complex systems. *Unit head:* Ataur Chowdhury, Chair, 907-474-7339, Fax: 907-474-6130, E-mail: physics@uaf.edu. *Application contact:* Libby Eddy, Registrar and Director of Admissions, 907-474-7500, Fax: 907-474-7097, E-mail: admissions@uaf.edu. Website: http://www.uaf.edu/physics/.

University of Alberta, Faculty of Graduate Studies and Research, Department of Physics, Edmonton, AB T6G 2E1, Canada. Offers astrophysics (M Sc, PhD); condensed matter (M Sc, PhD); geophysics (M Sc, PhD); medical physics (M Sc, PhD); subatomic physics (M Sc, PhD). *Degree requirements:* For master's, thesis; for doctorate, thesis/dissertation. *Entrance requirements:* For master's and doctorate, minimum GPA of 7.0 on a 9.0 scale. Additional exam requirements/recommendations for international students: Required—TOEFL. *Faculty research:* Cosmology, astroparticle physics, high-intermediate energy, magnetism, superconductivity.

The University of Arizona, College of Science, Department of Physics, Tucson, AZ 85721. Offers applied and industrial physics (PSM); physics (MS, PhD). Part-time programs available. *Faculty:* 24 full-time (2 women), 1 part-time/adjunct (0 women). *Students:* 68 full-time (12 women), 3 part-time (0 women); includes 1 minority (Hispanic/Latino), 32 international. Average age 28. 179 applicants, 8% accepted, 11 enrolled. In 2012, 5 master's, 9 doctorates awarded. Terminal master's awarded for partial completion of doctoral program. *Degree requirements:* For master's, comprehensive exam (for some programs), thesis optional; for doctorate, comprehensive exam, thesis/dissertation. *Entrance requirements:* For master's and doctorate, GRE General Test, GRE Subject Test, minimum GPA of 3.2, 3 letters of recommendation. Additional exam requirements/recommendations for international students: Required—TOEFL (minimum score 550 paper-based; 79 iBT). *Application deadline:* For fall admission, 2/1 for domestic students, 12/1 for international students. Applications are processed on a rolling basis. Application fee: $75. Electronic applications accepted. *Financial support:* In 2012–13, 23 research assistantships with full tuition reimbursements (averaging $21,722 per year), 36 teaching assistantships with full tuition reimbursements (averaging $22,599 per year) were awarded; career-related internships or fieldwork, scholarships/grants, health care benefits, tuition waivers (full and partial), and unspecified assistantships also available. Financial award application deadline: 5/1. *Faculty research:* Astrophysics; high-energy, condensed-matter, atomic and molecular physics; optics. *Total annual research expenditures:* $4.8 million. *Unit head:* Dr. Sumit Mazumdar, Head, 520-621-6803, E-mail: sumit@physics.arizona.edu. *Application contact:* Lisa Shapouri, Graduate Coordinator, 520-621-2290, Fax: 520-621-4721, E-mail: lisas@physics.arizona.edu. Website: http://www.physics.arizona.edu.

University of Arkansas, Graduate School, J. William Fulbright College of Arts and Sciences, Department of Physics, Fayetteville, AR 72701-1201. Offers applied physics (MS); physics (MS, PhD); physics education (MA). *Students:* 7 full-time (3 women), 45 part-time (7 women); includes 4 minority (1 American Indian or Alaska Native, non-Hispanic/Latino; 1 Asian, non-Hispanic/Latino; 1 Hispanic/Latino; 1 Two or more races, non-Hispanic/Latino), 31 international. In 2012, 3 master's, 1 doctorate awarded. *Degree requirements:* For master's, thesis; for doctorate, thesis/dissertation. *Application deadline:* For fall admission, 4/1 for international students; for spring admission, 10/1 for international students. Applications are processed on a rolling basis. Application fee: $40 ($50 for international students). Electronic applications accepted. *Financial support:* In 2012–13, 21 research assistantships, 22 teaching assistantships were awarded; fellowships with tuition reimbursements, career-related internships or fieldwork, and Federal Work-Study also available. Support available to part-time students. Financial award application deadline: 4/1; financial award applicants required to submit FAFSA. *Unit head:* Dr. Julio Gea-Banacloche, Departmental Chairperson, 479-575-2506, Fax: 479-575-4580, E-mail: jgeabana@uark.edu. *Application contact:* Dr. Reeta Vyas, Graduate Coordinator, 479-575-6058, E-mail: rvyas@uark.edu. Website: http://www.uark.edu/depts/physics/.

The University of British Columbia, Faculty of Science, Program in Physics, Vancouver, BC V6T 1Z1, Canada. Offers M Sc, PhD. *Degree requirements:* For master's, thesis; for doctorate, comprehensive exam, thesis/dissertation. *Entrance requirements:* For master's, GRE General Test, honors degree; for doctorate, GRE General Test, master's degree. Additional exam requirements/recommendations for international students: Required—TOEFL. *Faculty research:* Applied physics, astrophysics, condensed matter, plasma physics, subatomic physics, astronomy.

University of Calgary, Faculty of Graduate Studies, Faculty of Science, Department of Physics and Astronomy, Calgary, AB T2N 1N4, Canada. Offers M Sc, PhD. Part-time programs available. *Degree requirements:* For master's, thesis; for doctorate, thesis/dissertation, oral candidacy exam, written qualifying exam. *Entrance requirements:* For master's and doctorate, GRE General Test, GRE Subject Test. Additional exam requirements/recommendations for international students: Required—TOEFL (minimum score 550 paper-based). Electronic applications accepted. *Faculty research:* Astronomy and astrophysics, mass spectrometry, atmospheric physics, space physics, medical physics.

University of California, Berkeley, Graduate Division, College of Letters and Science, Department of Physics, Berkeley, CA 94720-1500. Offers PhD. *Degree requirements:* For doctorate, thesis/dissertation, qualifying exam. *Entrance requirements:* For doctorate, GRE General Test, GRE Subject Test, minimum GPA of 3.0, 3 letters of recommendation. Additional exam requirements/recommendations for international students: Required—TOEFL (minimum score 570 paper-based). *Faculty research:* Astrophysics (experimental and theoretical), condensed matter physics (experimental and theoretical), particle physics (experimental and theoretical), atomic/molecular physics, biophysics and complex systems.

University of California, Davis, Graduate Studies, Program in Physics, Davis, CA 95616. Offers MS, PhD. Terminal master's awarded for partial completion of doctoral program. *Degree requirements:* For master's, comprehensive exam (for some programs), thesis (for some programs); for doctorate, thesis/dissertation. *Entrance requirements:* For master's and doctorate, GRE General Test, GRE Subject Test, minimum GPA of 3.0. Additional exam requirements/recommendations for international students: Required—TOEFL (minimum score 550 paper-based). Electronic applications accepted. *Faculty research:* Astrophysics, condensed-matter physics, nuclear physics, particle physics, quantum optics.

University of California, Irvine, School of Physical Sciences, Department of Physics and Astronomy, Irvine, CA 92697. Offers physics (MS, PhD); MD/PhD. *Students:* 98 full-time (13 women); includes 25 minority (1 Black or African American, non-Hispanic/Latino; 17 Asian, non-Hispanic/Latino; 4 Hispanic/Latino; 3 Two or more races, non-Hispanic/Latino), 16 international. Average age 27. 265 applicants, 22% accepted, 18 enrolled. In 2012, 7 master's, 15 doctorates awarded. Terminal master's awarded for partial completion of doctoral program. *Degree requirements:* For doctorate, thesis/dissertation. *Entrance requirements:* For master's and doctorate, GRE General Test, GRE Subject Test, minimum GPA of 3.0. Additional exam requirements/recommendations for international students: Required—TOEFL (minimum score 550 paper-based). *Application deadline:* For fall admission, 1/15 priority date for domestic students, 1/15 for international students. Application fee: $80 ($100 for international students). Electronic applications accepted. *Financial support:* Fellowships with full tuition reimbursements, research assistantships with full tuition reimbursements, teaching assistantships with partial tuition reimbursements, institutionally sponsored loans, traineeships, health care benefits, and unspecified assistantships available. Financial award application deadline: 3/1; financial award applicants required to submit FAFSA. *Faculty research:* Condensed-matter physics, plasma physics, astrophysics, particle physics, chemical and materials physics, biophysics. *Unit head:* Peter Taborek, Chair, 949-824-2254, Fax: 949-824-2174, E-mail: ptaborek@uci.edu. *Application contact:* My Banh, Graduate Student Affairs Officer, 949-824-3496, Fax: 949-824-7988, E-mail: mbanh@uci.edu. Website: http://www.ps.uci.edu/physics/.

University of California, Los Angeles, Graduate Division, College of Letters and Science, Department of Physics and Astronomy, Program in Physics, Los Angeles, CA 90095. Offers MS, PhD. *Faculty:* 58 full-time (7 women). *Students:* 134 full-time (15 women); includes 29 minority (2 Black or African American, non-Hispanic/Latino; 16 Asian, non-Hispanic/Latino; 5 Hispanic/Latino; 1 Native Hawaiian or other Pacific Islander, non-Hispanic/Latino; 5 Two or more races, non-Hispanic/Latino), 36 international. Average age 26. 382 applicants, 21% accepted, 21 enrolled. In 2012, 19 master's, 17 doctorates awarded. Terminal master's awarded for partial completion of doctoral program. *Degree requirements:* For master's, comprehensive exam, thesis; for doctorate, thesis/dissertation, oral and written qualifying exams. *Entrance requirements:* For master's and doctorate, GRE General Test; GRE Subject Test (physics), bachelor's degree; minimum undergraduate GPA of 3.0 (or its equivalent if letter grade system not used). Additional exam requirements/recommendations for international students: Required—TOEFL. *Application deadline:* For fall admission, 12/15 for domestic and international students. Application fee: $80 ($100 for international students). Electronic applications accepted. *Expenses:* Tuition, nonresident: full-time $15,102. *Required fees:* $14,809.19. Full-time tuition and fees vary according to program. *Financial support:* In 2012–13, 136 students received support, including 118 fellowships with full and partial tuition reimbursements available, 96 research assistantships with full and partial tuition reimbursements available, 78 teaching assistantships with full and partial tuition reimbursements available; Federal Work-Study, scholarships/grants, health care benefits, tuition waivers (full and partial), and unspecified assistantships also available. Financial award application deadline: 3/2; financial award applicants required to submit FAFSA. *Unit head:* Dr. James Rosenzweig, Chair, 310-825-3440, E-mail: rosenzweig@physics.ucla.edu. *Application contact:* Student Affairs Officer, 310-825-2307, E-mail: apply@physics.ucla.edu.

University of California, Merced, Graduate Division, School of Natural Sciences, Merced, CA 95343. Offers applied mathematics (MS, PhD); physics and chemistry (MS, PhD); quantitative and systems biology (MS, PhD). *Students:* 121 full-time (50 women); includes 38 minority (3 Black or African American, non-Hispanic/Latino; 12 Asian, non-Hispanic/Latino; 18 Hispanic/Latino; 5 Two or more races, non-Hispanic/Latino), 34 international. Average age 28. 161 applicants, 47% accepted, 42 enrolled. In 2012, 9 master's, 5 doctorates awarded. *Financial support:* In 2012–13, 120 students received support, including 108 fellowships with full and partial tuition reimbursements available (averaging $11,590 per year), 34 research assistantships with full and partial tuition reimbursements available (averaging $8,960 per year), 103 teaching assistantships with partial tuition reimbursements available (averaging $12,560 per year); health care benefits also available. Financial award applicants required to submit FAFSA. *Unit head:* Dr. Juan Meza, Dean, 209-228-4487, Fax: 209-228-4060, E-mail: jcmeza@ucmerced.edu. *Application contact:* Tsu Ya, Graduate Admissions and Academic Services Manager, 209-228-4723, Fax: 209-228-6906, E-mail: tya@ucmerced.edu.

University of California, Riverside, Graduate Division, Department of Physics and Astronomy, Riverside, CA 92521-0102. Offers physics (MS, PhD). Part-time programs available. Terminal master's awarded for partial completion of doctoral program. *Degree requirements:* For master's, comprehensive exams or thesis; for doctorate, thesis/dissertation, qualifying exams. *Entrance requirements:* For master's and doctorate, GRE General Test, GRE Subject Test, minimum GPA of 3.2. Additional exam requirements/recommendations for international students: Required—TOEFL (minimum score 550 paper-based; 80 iBT). Electronic applications accepted. *Expenses:* Tuition, state resident: full-time $14,646. Tuition, nonresident: full-time $29,748. *Faculty research:* Laser physics and surface science, elementary particle and heavy ion physics, plasma physics, optical physics, astrophysics.

University of California, San Diego, Office of Graduate Studies, Department of Physics, La Jolla, CA 92093. Offers biophysics (MS, PhD); physics (MS, PhD); physics/materials physics (MS). *Degree requirements:* For doctorate, thesis/dissertation. *Entrance requirements:* For master's and doctorate, GRE General Test, GRE Subject Test. Additional exam requirements/recommendations for international students: Required—TOEFL. Electronic applications accepted.

University of California, Santa Barbara, Graduate Division, College of Letters and Sciences, Division of Mathematics, Life, and Physical Sciences, Department of Physics, Santa Barbara, CA 93106-9530. Offers astrophysics (PhD); physics (PhD). *Faculty:* 49 full-time (6 women), 3 part-time/adjunct (0 women). *Students:* 127 full-time (19 women); includes 18 minority (15 Asian, non-Hispanic/Latino; 3 Hispanic/Latino), 13 international. Average age 26. 651 applicants, 17% accepted, 26 enrolled. In 2012, 13 doctorates awarded. Terminal master's awarded for partial completion of doctoral program. *Degree requirements:* For doctorate, comprehensive exam, thesis/dissertation. *Entrance requirements:* For doctorate, GRE General Test, GRE Subject Test (physics). Additional exam requirements/recommendations for international students: Required—TOEFL (minimum score 550 paper-based; 80 iBT), IELTS (minimum score 7). *Application deadline:* For fall admission, 12/15 priority date for domestic students, 12/15 for international students. Application fee: $80 ($100 for international students). Electronic applications accepted. *Financial support:* In 2012–13, 57 students received support, including 11 fellowships with full tuition reimbursements available (averaging $30,000 per year), 65 research assistantships with full tuition reimbursements available (averaging $21,888 per year), 41 teaching assistantships with partial tuition reimbursements available (averaging $17,655 per year); Federal Work-Study, scholarships/grants, health care benefits, and unspecified assistantships also available. Financial award application deadline: 12/15; financial award applicants required to submit FAFSA. *Faculty research:* High energy theoretical/experimental physics, condensed matter theoretical/experimental physics, astrophysics and cosmology, biophysics, gravity and relativity. *Total annual research expenditures:* $29.7 million. *Unit head:* Prof. Omer Blaes, Chair/Professor, 805-893-7239, Fax: 805-893-7239, E-mail: blaes@physics.ucsb.edu. *Application contact:* Prof. Mark Srednicki, Admissions Chair, 805-893-2165, Fax: 805-893-2165, E-mail: mark@physics.ucsb.edu. Website: http://www.physics.ucsb.edu.

University of California, Santa Cruz, Division of Graduate Studies, Division of Physical and Biological Sciences, Department of Physics, Santa Cruz, CA 95064. Offers MS, PhD. Terminal master's awarded for partial completion of doctoral program. *Degree requirements:* For master's, thesis; for doctorate, one foreign language, thesis/dissertation, qualifying exam. *Entrance requirements:* For master's and doctorate, GRE General Test, GRE Subject Test. Additional exam requirements/recommendations for international students: Required—TOEFL (minimum score 550 paper-based; 83 iBT); Recommended—IELTS (minimum score 8). Electronic applications accepted. *Faculty research:* Theoretical and experimental particle physics, astrophysics and cosmology, condensed matter physics.

University of Central Florida, College of Sciences, Department of Physics, Orlando, FL 32816. Offers MS, PhD. Part-time and evening/weekend programs available. *Faculty:* 41 full-time (8 women), 1 (woman) part-time/adjunct. *Students:* 90 full-time (27 women), 2 part-time (0 women); includes 6 minority (2 Asian, non-Hispanic/Latino; 4 Hispanic/Latino), 60 international. Average age 29. 97 applicants, 30% accepted, 11 enrolled. In 2012, 10 master's, 9 doctorates awarded. *Degree requirements:* For master's, thesis or alternative; for doctorate, thesis/dissertation, candidacy and qualifying exams. *Entrance requirements:* For master's, GRE General Test, minimum GPA of 3.0 in last 60 hours of course work; for doctorate, GRE General Test, GRE Subject Test, minimum GPA of 3.0 in last 60 hours or master's qualifying exam. Additional exam requirements/recommendations for international students: Required—TOEFL. *Application deadline:* For fall admission, 2/15 priority date for domestic students. Application fee: $30. Electronic applications accepted. *Financial support:* In 2012–13, 70 students received support, including 21 fellowships with partial tuition reimbursements available (averaging $5,000 per year), 49 research assistantships with partial tuition reimbursements available (averaging $10,900 per year), 32 teaching assistantships with partial tuition reimbursements available (averaging $12,200 per year); career-related internships or fieldwork, Federal Work-Study, institutionally sponsored loans, tuition waivers (partial), and unspecified assistantships also available. Financial award application deadline: 3/1; financial award applicants required to submit FAFSA. *Faculty research:* Atomic-molecular physics, condensed-matter physics, biophysics of proteins, laser physics. *Unit head:* Dr. Talat Rahman, Chair, 407-823-2325, E-mail: talat.rahman@ucf.edu. *Application contact:* Barbara Rodriguez, Director, Admissions and Registration, 407-823-2766, Fax: 407-823-6442, E-mail: gradadmissions@ucf.edu. Website: http://www.physics.ucf.edu/.

University of Chicago, Division of the Physical Sciences, Department of Physics, Chicago, IL 60637-1513. Offers PhD. *Degree requirements:* For doctorate, comprehensive exam, thesis/dissertation. *Entrance requirements:* For doctorate, bachelor's degree in physics or related area. Additional exam requirements/recommendations for international students: Required—TOEFL (minimum score 102 iBT).

University of Chicago, Division of the Physical Sciences, Program in the Physical Sciences, Chicago, IL 60637-1513. Offers MS. Part-time programs available. *Degree requirements:* For master's, thesis. *Entrance requirements:* For master's, GRE. Additional exam requirements/recommendations for international students: Required—TOEFL.

University of Cincinnati, Graduate School, McMicken College of Arts and Sciences, Department of Physics, Cincinnati, OH 45221. Offers MS, PhD. Terminal master's awarded for partial completion of doctoral program. *Degree requirements:* For master's, thesis optional; for doctorate, thesis/dissertation. *Entrance requirements:* For master's and doctorate, GRE General Test, GRE Subject Test. Additional exam requirements/recommendations for international students: Required—TOEFL (minimum score 540 paper-based). Electronic applications accepted. *Faculty research:* Condensed matter physics, experimental particle physics, theoretical high energy physics, astronomy and astrophysics, computational physics.

University of Colorado Boulder, Graduate School, College of Arts and Sciences, Department of Physics, Boulder, CO 80309. Offers chemical physics (PhD); geophysics (PhD); liquid crystal science and technology (PhD); mathematical physics (PhD); medical physics (PhD); optical sciences and engineering (PhD); physics (MS, PhD). *Faculty:* 50 full-time (7 women). *Students:* 158 full-time (32 women), 64 part-time (9 women); includes 11 minority (6 Asian, non-Hispanic/Latino; 5 Hispanic/Latino), 74 international. Average age 27. 600 applicants, 21% accepted, 32 enrolled. Terminal master's awarded for partial completion of doctoral program. *Degree requirements:* For master's, comprehensive exam, thesis or alternative; for doctorate, comprehensive exam, thesis/dissertation. *Entrance requirements:* For master's and doctorate, GRE General Test, GRE Subject Test, minimum undergraduate GPA of 3.0. Additional exam requirements/recommendations for international students: Required—TOEFL. *Application deadline:* For fall admission, 12/15 priority date for domestic

Peterson's Graduate Programs in the Physical Sciences, Mathematics, Agricultural Sciences, the Environment & Natural Resources 2014

www.petersonsbooks.com **245**

students, 12/15 for international students. Applications are processed on a rolling basis. Application fee: $50 ($60 for international students). Electronic applications accepted. *Financial support:* In 2012–13, 38 fellowships (averaging $14,995 per year), 156 research assistantships with full and partial tuition reimbursements (averaging $25,043 per year), 48 teaching assistantships with full and partial tuition reimbursements (averaging $18,902 per year) were awarded; institutionally sponsored loans, scholarships/grants, health care benefits, and unspecified assistantships also available. Financial award application deadline: 1/15; financial award applicants required to submit FAFSA. *Faculty research:* Atomic and molecular physics, nuclear physics, condensed matter, elementary particle physics, laser or optical physics, plasma physics, geophysics, astrophysics and chemical physics. *Total annual research expenditures:* $23.7 million. *Application contact:* E-mail: physics@colorado.edu. Website: http://physics.colorado.edu/.

University of Colorado Colorado Springs, College of Letters, Arts and Sciences, Master of Sciences Program, Colorado Springs, CO 80933-7150. Offers biology (M Sc); chemistry (M Sc); education (M Sc); forensic science (M Sc); health promotion (M Sc); mathematics (M Sc); physics (M Sc); sports medicine (M Sc); sports nutrition (M Sc). Part-time programs available. *Students:* 67 full-time (48 women), 27 part-time (17 women); includes 12 minority (2 American Indian or Alaska Native, non-Hispanic/Latino; 2 Asian, non-Hispanic/Latino; 6 Hispanic/Latino; 2 Two or more races, non-Hispanic/Latino), 5 international. Average age 28. In 2012, 41 master's awarded. *Degree requirements:* For master's, thesis or alternative. *Entrance requirements:* For master's, minimum GPA of 2.75. Additional exam requirements/recommendations for international students: Required—TOEFL (minimum score 525 paper-based). *Application deadline:* For fall admission, 6/1 priority date for domestic students; for spring admission, 12/1 for domestic students. Applications are processed on a rolling basis. Application fee: $60 ($75 for international students). Electronic applications accepted. *Expenses:* Contact institution. *Financial support:* In 2012–13, 17 students received support, including 2 fellowships; research assistantships, teaching assistantships, career-related internships or fieldwork, Federal Work-Study, and scholarships/grants also available. Support available to part-time students. Financial award application deadline: 3/1; financial award applicants required to submit FAFSA. *Faculty research:* Biomechanics and physiology of elite athletic training, genetic engineering in yeast and bacteria including phage display and DNA repair, immunology and cell biology, synthetic organic chemistry. *Unit head:* Dr. Peter A. Braza, Dean, 719-255-4550, Fax: 719-255-4200, E-mail: pbraza@uccs.edu. *Application contact:* Taryn Bailey, Graduate Recruitment Specialist, 719-255-3702, Fax: 719-255-3037, E-mail: gradinfo@uccs.edu.

University of Connecticut, Graduate School, College of Liberal Arts and Sciences, Department of Physics, Storrs, CT 06269. Offers MS, PhD. *Degree requirements:* For master's, comprehensive exam; for doctorate, thesis/dissertation. *Entrance requirements:* For master's and doctorate, GRE General Test, GRE Subject Test. Additional exam requirements/recommendations for international students: Required—TOEFL (minimum score 550 paper-based). Electronic applications accepted.

University of Delaware, College of Arts and Sciences, Department of Physics and Astronomy, Newark, DE 19716. Offers MS, PhD. Part-time programs available. Terminal master's awarded for partial completion of doctoral program. *Degree requirements:* For master's, thesis; for doctorate, thesis/dissertation. *Entrance requirements:* For master's and doctorate, GRE General Test, GRE Subject Test. Additional exam requirements/recommendations for international students: Required—TOEFL (minimum score 600 paper-based). Electronic applications accepted. *Faculty research:* Magnetoresistance and magnetic materials, ultrafast optical phenomena, superfluidity, elementary particle physics, stellar atmospheres and interiors.

University of Denver, Faculty of Natural Sciences and Mathematics, Department of Physics and Astronomy, Denver, CO 80208. Offers applied physics (MS); physics (MS, PhD). Part-time programs available. *Faculty:* 11 full-time (3 women), 5 part-time/adjunct (0 women). *Students:* 7 full-time (4 women), 7 part-time (3 women), 2 international. Average age 30. 41 applicants, 37% accepted, 4 enrolled. In 2012, 1 master's, 2 doctorates awarded. Terminal master's awarded for partial completion of doctoral program. *Degree requirements:* For master's, thesis optional; for doctorate, thesis/dissertation. *Entrance requirements:* For master's and doctorate, GRE General Test, GRE Subject Test in physics (strongly preferred), three letters of recommendation, personal statement. Additional exam requirements/recommendations for international students: Required—TOEFL (minimum score 550 paper-based; 80 iBT). *Application deadline:* For fall admission, 3/1 priority date for domestic students. Applications are processed on a rolling basis. Application fee: $60. Electronic applications accepted. *Expenses: Tuition:* Full-time $38,232; part-time $1062 per credit hour. *Required fees:* $744. Tuition and fees vary according to program. *Financial support:* In 2012–13, 15 students received support, including 7 research assistantships with full and partial tuition reimbursements available (averaging $15,683 per year), 10 teaching assistantships with full and partial tuition reimbursements available (averaging $23,085 per year); career-related internships or fieldwork, Federal Work-Study, institutionally sponsored loans, scholarships/grants, and unspecified assistantships also available. Support available to part-time students. Financial award application deadline: 2/15; financial award applicants required to submit FAFSA. *Faculty research:* Atomic and molecular beams and collisions, infrared astronomy, acoustic emission from stressed solids, nano materials. *Unit head:* Dr. Davor Balzar, Chair, 303-871-2238, E-mail: davor.balzar@du.edu. *Application contact:* Barbara Stephen, Assistant to the Chair, 303-871-2238, E-mail: barbara.stephen@du.edu. Website: http://www.physics.du.edu.

University of Florida, Graduate School, College of Liberal Arts and Sciences, Department of Physics, Gainesville, FL 32611. Offers MS, MST, PhD. Terminal master's awarded for partial completion of doctoral program. *Degree requirements:* For doctorate, comprehensive exam, thesis/dissertation. *Entrance requirements:* For master's and doctorate, GRE General Test, minimum GPA of 3.0. Additional exam requirements/recommendations for international students: Required—TOEFL (minimum score 550 paper-based; 80 iBT), IELTS (minimum score 6). Electronic applications accepted. *Faculty research:* Astrophysics, biological physics (molecular, magnetic resonance imaging, spectroscopy, biomagnetism), chemical physics (molecular, nano-scale physics, solid state, surface physics, quantum chemistry, quantum electron dynamics, molecular biology), experimental and theory condensed matter physics, low temperature physics (theory and experimental, mathematical physics.

University of Georgia, Franklin College of Arts and Sciences, Department of Physics and Astronomy, Athens, GA 30602. Offers physics (MS, PhD). *Degree requirements:* For master's, thesis; for doctorate, one foreign language, thesis/dissertation. *Entrance requirements:* For master's and doctorate, GRE General Test. Electronic applications accepted.

University of Guelph, Graduate Studies, College of Physical and Engineering Science, Guelph-Waterloo Physics Institute, Guelph, ON N1G 2W1, Canada. Offers M Sc, PhD. M Sc, PhD offered jointly with University of Waterloo. Part-time programs available. *Degree requirements:* For master's, project or thesis; for doctorate, comprehensive exam, thesis/dissertation. *Entrance requirements:* For master's, GRE Subject Test, minimum B average for honors degree; for doctorate, GRE Subject Test, minimum B average. Additional exam requirements/recommendations for international students: Required—TOEFL (minimum score 550 paper-based), TWE (minimum score 4). *Faculty research:* Condensed matter and material physics, quantum computing, astrophysics and gravitation, industrial and applied physics, subatomic physics.

University of Hawaii at Manoa, Graduate Division, College of Natural Sciences, Department of Physics and Astronomy, Program in Physics, Honolulu, HI 96822. Offers MS, PhD. Part-time programs available. *Degree requirements:* For master's, thesis optional; for doctorate, comprehensive exam, thesis/dissertation. *Entrance requirements:* For master's and doctorate, GRE General Test. Additional exam requirements/recommendations for international students: Required—TOEFL (minimum score 560 paper-based; 83 iBT), IELTS (minimum score 5).

University of Houston, College of Natural Sciences and Mathematics, Department of Physics, Houston, TX 77204. Offers MA, PhD. Part-time programs available. Terminal master's awarded for partial completion of doctoral program. *Entrance requirements:* For master's and doctorate, GRE General Test. Electronic applications accepted. *Faculty research:* Condensed-matter, particle physics; high-temperature superconductivity; material/space physics; chaos.

University of Houston–Clear Lake, School of Science and Computer Engineering, Program in Physics, Houston, TX 77058-1098. Offers MS. Part-time and evening/weekend programs available. *Entrance requirements:* For master's, GRE General Test. Additional exam requirements/recommendations for international students: Required—TOEFL (minimum score 550 paper-based).

University of Idaho, College of Graduate Studies, College of Science, Department of Physics, Moscow, ID 83844-0903. Offers MS, PhD. *Faculty:* 5 full-time. *Students:* 22 full-time, 7 part-time. Average age 35. In 2012, 3 master's, 3 doctorates awarded. *Degree requirements:* For master's, thesis; for doctorate, thesis/dissertation. *Entrance requirements:* For master's, GRE, minimum GPA of 2.8; for doctorate, GRE, minimum undergraduate GPA of 2.8, 3.0 graduate. *Application deadline:* For fall admission, 8/1 for domestic students; for spring admission, 12/15 for domestic students. Applications are processed on a rolling basis. Application fee: $60. Electronic applications accepted. *Expenses:* Tuition, state resident: full-time $4230; part-time $252 per credit hour. Tuition, nonresident: full-time $17,018; part-time $891 per credit hour. *Required fees:* $2932; $107 per credit hour. *Financial support:* Research assistantships and teaching assistantships available. Financial award applicants required to submit FAFSA. *Faculty research:* Condensed matter physics, nuclear physics, biological physics, astronomy/planetary science. *Unit head:* Dr. David McIlroy, Chair, 208-885-6380, E-mail: physics@uidaho.edu. *Application contact:* Erick Larson, Director of Graduate Admissions, 208-885-4723, E-mail: gadms@uidaho.edu. Website: http://www.uidaho.edu/sci/physics.

University of Illinois at Chicago, Graduate College, College of Liberal Arts and Sciences, Department of Physics, Chicago, IL 60607-7128. Offers MS, PhD. *Students:* 72 full-time (17 women), 11 part-time (4 women); includes 6 minority (4 Asian, non-Hispanic/Latino; 1 Hispanic/Latino; 1 Two or more races, non-Hispanic/Latino), 48 international. Average age 28. 176 applicants, 23% accepted, 20 enrolled. In 2012, 8 master's, 10 doctorates awarded. Terminal master's awarded for partial completion of doctoral program. *Degree requirements:* For doctorate, thesis/dissertation. *Entrance requirements:* For master's and doctorate, GRE General Test, minimum GPA of 3.0. Additional exam requirements/recommendations for international students: Required—TOEFL. *Application deadline:* For fall admission, 5/15 for domestic students, 2/15 for international students; for spring admission, 11/1 for domestic students, 7/15 for international students. Applications are processed on a rolling basis.

Application fee: $40 ($50 for international students). Electronic applications accepted. *Expenses:* Tuition, state resident: full-time $10,882; part-time $3627 per term. Tuition, nonresident: full-time $22,880; part-time $7627 per term. *Required fees:* $1170 per semester. Tuition and fees vary according to course load, degree level and program. *Financial support:* Fellowships with full tuition reimbursements, research assistantships with full tuition reimbursements, teaching assistantships with full tuition reimbursements, Federal Work-Study, scholarships/grants, traineeships, tuition waivers (full), and unspecified assistantships available. Financial award application deadline: 3/1; financial award applicants required to submit FAFSA. *Faculty research:* High-energy, laser, and solid-state physics. *Unit head:* Prof. David Jonathan Hofman, Acting Head, 312-413-2798, E-mail: hofman@uic.edu. Website: http://physicsweb.phy.uic.edu/.

University of Illinois at Urbana–Champaign, Graduate College, College of Engineering, Department of Physics, Champaign, IL 61820. Offers physics (MS, PhD); teaching of physics (MS). *Students:* 253 (42 women). Application fee: $75 ($90 for international students). *Unit head:* Dale J. VanHarlingen, Head, 217-333-3760, Fax: 217-244-4293, E-mail: dvh@illinois.edu. *Application contact:* Melodee Jo Schweighart, Office Manager, 217-333-3645, Fax: 217-244-5073, E-mail: mschweig@illinois.edu. Website: http://www.physics.illinois.edu/.

The University of Iowa, Graduate College, College of Liberal Arts and Sciences, Department of Physics and Astronomy, Program in Physics, Iowa City, IA 52242-1316. Offers MS, PhD. *Degree requirements:* For master's, thesis optional, exam; for doctorate, comprehensive exam, thesis/dissertation. *Entrance requirements:* For master's and doctorate, GRE General Test, minimum GPA of 3.0. Additional exam requirements/recommendations for international students: Required—TOEFL (minimum score 550 paper-based; 81 iBT). Electronic applications accepted.

The University of Kansas, Graduate Studies, College of Liberal Arts and Sciences, Department of Physics and Astronomy, Lawrence, KS 66045. Offers computational physics and astronomy (MS); physics (MS, PhD). *Faculty:* 27. *Students:* 47 full-time (5 women), 3 part-time (0 women); includes 3 minority (1 Black or African American, non-Hispanic/Latino; 2 Two or more races, non-Hispanic/Latino), 13 international. Average age 29. 69 applicants, 39% accepted, 14 enrolled. In 2012, 1 master's, 5 doctorates awarded. Terminal master's awarded for partial completion of doctoral program. *Degree requirements:* For master's, thesis (for some programs); for doctorate, comprehensive exam, thesis/dissertation, computer skills, communication skills. *Entrance requirements:* For master's and doctorate, GRE Subject Test (physics), undergraduate degree. Additional exam requirements/recommendations for international students: Required—TOEFL (minimum score 53 paper-based; 20 iBT). *Application deadline:* For fall admission, 12/1 priority date for domestic students, 12/1 for international students; for spring admission, 10/1 priority date for domestic students, 10/1 for international students. Applications are processed on a rolling basis. Application fee: $55 ($65 for international students). Electronic applications accepted. *Financial support:* Fellowships with full and partial tuition reimbursements, research assistantships with full and partial tuition reimbursements, teaching assistantships with full and partial tuition reimbursements, health care benefits, and unspecified assistantships available. Financial award application deadline: 4/1; financial award applicants required to submit FAFSA. *Faculty research:* Astrophysics, biophysics, high energy physics, nanophysics, nuclear physics. *Unit head:* Dr. Stephen J. Sanders, Chair, 785-864-4626, Fax: 785-864-5262, E-mail: ssanders@ku.edu. *Application contact:* Hume Feldman, Graduate Director, 785-864-4626, Fax: 785-864-5262, E-mail: humef@ku.edu. Website: http://www.physics.ku.edu.

University of Kentucky, Graduate School, College of Arts and Sciences, Program in Physics and Astronomy, Lexington, KY 40506-0032. Offers physics (MS, PhD). *Degree requirements:* For master's, comprehensive exam, thesis optional; for doctorate, comprehensive exam, thesis/dissertation. *Entrance requirements:* For master's, GRE General Test, minimum undergraduate GPA of 2.75; for doctorate, GRE General Test, minimum graduate GPA of 3.0. Additional exam requirements/recommendations for international students: Required—TOEFL (minimum score 550 paper-based). Electronic applications accepted. *Faculty research:* Astrophysics, active galactic nuclei, and radio astronomy; Rydbert atoms, and electron scattering; TOF spectroscopy, hyperon interactions and muons; particle theory, lattice gauge theory, quark, and skyrmion models.

University of Lethbridge, School of Graduate Studies, Lethbridge, AB T1K 3M4, Canada. Offers accounting (MScM); addictions counseling (M Sc); agricultural biotechnology (M Sc); agricultural studies (M Sc, MA); anthropology (MA); archaeology (MA); art (MA, MFA); biochemistry (M Sc); biological sciences (M Sc); biomolecular science (PhD); biosystems and biodiversity (PhD); Canadian studies (MA); chemistry (M Sc); computer science (M Sc); computer science and geographical information science (M Sc); counseling psychology (M Ed); dramatic arts (MA); earth, space, and physical science (PhD); economics (MA); educational leadership (M Ed); English (MA); environmental science (M Sc); evolution and behavior (PhD); exercise science (M Sc); finance (MScM); French (MA); French/German (MA); French/Spanish (MA); general education (M Ed); general management (MScM); geography (M Sc, MA); German (MA); health science (M Sc); history (MA); human resource management and labour relations (MScM); individualized multidisciplinary (M Sc, MA); information systems (MScM); international management (MScM); kinesiology (M Sc, MA); management (M Sc, MA); marketing (MScM); mathematics (M Sc); music (M Mus, MA); Native American studies (MA); neuroscience (M Sc, PhD); new media (MA); nursing (M Sc); philosophy (MA); physics (M Sc); policy and strategy (MScM); political science (MA); psychology (M Sc, MA); religious studies (MA); social sciences (MA); sociology (MA); theatre and dramatic arts (MFA); theoretical and computational science (PhD); urban and regional studies (MA); women's studies (MA). Part-time and evening/weekend programs available. *Degree requirements:* For doctorate, comprehensive exam, thesis/dissertation. *Entrance requirements:* For master's, GMAT (M Sc in management), bachelor's degree in related field, minimum GPA of 3.0 during previous 20 graded semester courses, 2 years teaching or related experience (M Ed); for doctorate, master's degree, minimum graduate GPA of 3.5. Additional exam requirements/recommendations for international students: Required—TOEFL. *Faculty research:* Movement and brain plasticity, gibberellin physiology, photosynthesis, carbon cycling, molecular properties of main-group ring components.

University of Louisiana at Lafayette, College of Sciences, Department of Physics, Lafayette, LA 70504. Offers MS. Part-time programs available. *Degree requirements:* For master's, thesis. *Entrance requirements:* For master's, GRE General Test, minimum GPA of 2.75. Additional exam requirements/recommendations for international students: Required—TOEFL (minimum score 550 paper-based). Electronic applications accepted. *Faculty research:* Environmental physics, geophysics, astrophysics, acoustics, atomic physics.

University of Louisville, Graduate School, College of Arts and Sciences, Department of Physics and Astronomy, Louisville, KY 40292. Offers physics (MS, PhD). Part-time programs available. *Students:* 29 full-time (6 women), 1 part-time (0 women); includes 2 minority (1 Black or African American, non-Hispanic/Latino; 1 Hispanic/Latino), 12 international. Average age 31. 39 applicants, 33% accepted, 8 enrolled. In 2012, 7 master's awarded. Terminal master's awarded for partial completion of doctoral program. *Degree requirements:* For master's, thesis optional; for doctorate, comprehensive exam, thesis/dissertation. *Entrance requirements:* For master's, GRE General Test. Additional exam requirements/recommendations for international students: Required—TOEFL (minimum score 550 paper-based; 80 iBT). *Application deadline:* For fall admission, 3/1 priority date for domestic students, 3/1 for international students. Applications are processed on a rolling basis. Application fee: $60. Electronic applications accepted. *Financial support:* In 2012–13, 17 students received support. Fellowships, research assistantships, and teaching assistantships available. *Faculty research:* Condensed matter physics; atmospheric science; high energy physics; astrophysics, atomic, molecular, and optical physics. *Unit head:* Dr. Chakram S. Jayanthi, Professor/Chair, 502-852-6790, Fax: 502-852-0742, E-mail: csjaya01@louisville.edu. *Application contact:* Dr. Chris L. Davis, Professor of Physics, 502-852-0852, Fax: 502-852-0742, E-mail: c.l.davis@louisville.edu. Website: http://www.physics.louisville.edu/.

University of Maine, Graduate School, College of Education and Human Development, Master of Science in Teaching Program, Orono, ME 04469. Offers earth sciences (MST); general (MST); mathematics (MST); physics (MST). Part-time programs available. *Students:* 20 full-time (8 women), 5 part-time (2 women); includes 1 minority (Asian, non-Hispanic/Latino). Average age 40. 17 applicants, 71% accepted, 9 enrolled. In 2012, 3 master's awarded. *Degree requirements:* For master's, thesis. *Entrance requirements:* For master's, GRE General Test, MAT. Additional exam requirements/recommendations for international students: Required—TOEFL. Application fee: $65. *Financial support:* Application deadline: 3/1. *Unit head:* Dr. Susan McKay, Director, 207-581-1016. *Application contact:* Scott G. Delcourt, Associate Dean of the Graduate School, 207-581-3291, Fax: 207-581-3232, E-mail: graduate@maine.edu. Website: http://umaine.edu/center/mst-program/.

University of Maine, Graduate School, College of Liberal Arts and Sciences, Department of Physics and Astronomy, Orono, ME 04469. Offers engineering physics (ME); physics (MS, PhD). *Faculty:* 20 full-time (1 woman), 3 part-time/adjunct (0 women). *Students:* 33 full-time (9 women), 1 part-time (0 women); includes 2 minority (1 Asian, non-Hispanic/Latino; 1 Two or more races, non-Hispanic/Latino), 4 international. Average age 28. 31 applicants, 19% accepted, 6 enrolled. In 2012, 5 master's, 3 doctorates awarded. Terminal master's awarded for partial completion of doctoral program. *Degree requirements:* For master's, thesis; for doctorate, comprehensive exam, thesis/dissertation. *Entrance requirements:* For master's, GRE General Test, GRE Subject Test; for doctorate, GRE General Test. Additional exam requirements/recommendations for international students: Required—TOEFL. *Application deadline:* For fall admission, 2/1 priority date for domestic students. Applications are processed on a rolling basis. Application fee: $65. Electronic applications accepted. *Financial support:* In 2012–13, 4 research assistantships with full tuition reimbursements (averaging $18,220 per year), 15 teaching assistantships with full tuition reimbursements (averaging $15,300 per year) were awarded; tuition waivers (full and partial) also available. Financial award application deadline: 3/1. *Faculty research:* Solid-state physics, fluids, biophysics, plasma physics, surface physics. *Total annual research expenditures:* $592,151. *Unit head:* Dr. David Batuski, Chair, 207-581-1015, Fax: 207-581-3410. *Application contact:* Scott G. Delcourt, Associate Dean of the Graduate School, 207-581-3291, Fax: 207-581-3232, E-mail: graduate@maine.edu. Website: http://www.physics.umaine.edu/.

The University of Manchester, School of Earth, Atmospheric and Environmental Sciences, Manchester, United Kingdom. Offers atmospheric sciences (M Phil, M Sc, PhD); basin studies and petroleum geosciences (M Phil, M Sc, PhD); earth, atmospheric and environmental sciences (M Phil, M Sc, PhD); environmental geochemistry and cosmochemistry (M Phil, M Sc, PhD); isotope geochemistry and cosmochemistry (M Phil, M Sc, PhD); paleontology (M Phil, M Sc, PhD);

physics and chemistry of minerals and fluids (M Phil, M Sc, PhD); structural and petrological geosciences (M Phil, M Sc, PhD).

The University of Manchester, School of Physics and Astronomy, Manchester, United Kingdom. Offers astronomy and astrophysics (M Sc, PhD); biological physics (M Sc, PhD); condensed matter physics (M Sc, PhD); nonlinear and liquid crystals physics (M Sc, PhD); nuclear physics (M Sc, PhD); particle physics (M Sc, PhD); photon physics (M Sc, PhD); physics (M Sc, PhD); theoretical physics (M Sc, PhD).

University of Manitoba, Faculty of Graduate Studies, Faculty of Science, Department of Physics and Astronomy, Winnipeg, MB R3T 2N2, Canada. Offers M Sc, PhD. *Degree requirements:* For master's, thesis; for doctorate, one foreign language, thesis/dissertation.

University of Maryland, Baltimore County, Graduate School, College of Arts, Humanities and Social Sciences, Department of Education, Program in Teaching, Baltimore, MD 21250. Offers early childhood education (MAT); elementary education (MAT); secondary education (MAT), including art, biology, chemistry, dance, earth/space science, English, foreign language, mathematics, music, physics, social studies, theatre. Part-time and evening/weekend programs available. *Faculty:* 24 full-time (18 women), 25 part-time/adjunct (19 women). *Students:* 53 full-time (40 women), 43 part-time (28 women); includes 22 minority (14 Black or African American, non-Hispanic/Latino; 3 Asian, non-Hispanic/Latino; 4 Hispanic/Latino; 1 Two or more races, non-Hispanic/Latino), 1 international. Average age 30. 40 applicants, 95% accepted, 35 enrolled. In 2012, 106 master's awarded. *Degree requirements:* For master's, comprehensive exam (for some programs), thesis (for some programs). *Entrance requirements:* For master's, PRAXIS I or SAT (minimum score of 1000), minimum GPA of 3.0. Additional exam requirements/recommendations for international students: Required—TOEFL. *Application deadline:* For fall admission, 6/1 for domestic students; for spring admission, 11/1 for domestic students. Applications are processed on a rolling basis. Application fee: $50. Electronic applications accepted. *Financial support:* In 2012–13, 6 students received support, including teaching assistantships with full and partial tuition reimbursements available (averaging $12,000 per year); career-related internships or fieldwork, Federal Work-Study, scholarships/grants, tuition waivers, and unspecified assistantships also available. Financial award application deadline: 3/1. *Faculty research:* STEM teacher education, culturally sensitive pedagogy, ESOL/bilingual education, early childhood education, language, literacy and culture. *Unit head:* Dr. Susan M. Blunck, Graduate Program Director, 410-455-2869, Fax: 410-455-3986, E-mail: blunck@umbc.edu. Website: http://www.umbc.edu/education/.

University of Maryland, Baltimore County, Graduate School, College of Natural and Mathematical Sciences, Department of Physics, Baltimore, MD 21250. Offers applied physics (MS, PhD); atmospheric physics (MS, PhD). Part-time programs available. *Faculty:* 22 full-time (3 women), 18 part-time/adjunct (3 women). *Students:* 46 full-time (13 women), 2 part-time (0 women); includes 2 minority (both Black or African American, non-Hispanic/Latino), 17 international. Average age 24. 47 applicants, 32% accepted, 6 enrolled. In 2012, 7 master's, 7 doctorates awarded. Terminal master's awarded for partial completion of doctoral program. *Degree requirements:* For master's, thesis optional; for doctorate, comprehensive exam, thesis/dissertation. *Entrance requirements:* For master's and doctorate, GRE General Test, GRE Subject Test (recommended), minimum GPA of 3.0. Additional exam requirements/recommendations for international students: Required—TOEFL. *Application deadline:* For fall admission, 1/1 for domestic and international students; for spring admission, 11/30 for domestic students. Applications are processed on a rolling basis. Application fee: $50. Electronic applications accepted. *Financial support:* In 2012–13, 40 students received support, including 5 fellowships with full tuition reimbursements available (averaging $30,000 per year), 21 research assistantships with full tuition reimbursements available (averaging $26,000 per year), 16 teaching assistantships with full tuition reimbursements available (averaging $22,000 per year); career-related internships or fieldwork, scholarships/grants, health care benefits, and unspecified assistantships also available. Support available to part-time students. Financial award application deadline: 10/1. *Faculty research:* Quantum optics and quantum information science, astrophysics, atmospheric physics, nanoscale physics. *Total annual research expenditures:* $7.5 million. *Unit head:* Dr. L. Michael Hayden, Chairman, 410-455-2513, Fax: 410-455-1072, E-mail: hayden@umbc.edu. *Application contact:* Dr. Lazlo Takacs, Graduate Admissions Director, 410-455-2524, Fax: 410-455-1072, E-mail: takacs@umbc.edu. Website: http://www.physics.umbc.edu/.

University of Maryland, College Park, Academic Affairs, College of Computer, Mathematical and Natural Sciences, Department of Physics, College Park, MD 20742. Offers MS, PhD. Part-time and evening/weekend programs available. *Faculty:* 187 full-time (26 women), 38 part-time/adjunct (5 women). *Students:* 222 full-time (34 women), 5 part-time (0 women); includes 16 minority (4 Black or African American, non-Hispanic/Latino; 10 Asian, non-Hispanic/Latino; 1 Hispanic/Latino; 1 Two or more races, non-Hispanic/Latino), 83 international. 728 applicants, 14% accepted, 33 enrolled. In 2012, 14 master's, 27 doctorates awarded. Terminal master's awarded for partial completion of doctoral program. *Degree requirements:* For master's, thesis optional; for doctorate, thesis/dissertation. *Entrance requirements:* For master's, GRE General Test, GRE Subject Test (physics), minimum GPA of 3.0, 3 letters of recommendation; for doctorate, GRE General Test, GRE Subject Test (physics), 3 letters of recommendation. *Application deadline:* For fall admission, 1/15 for domestic and international students. Applications are processed on a rolling basis. Application fee: $75. Electronic applications accepted. *Expenses:* Tuition, state resident: part-time $551 per credit. Tuition, nonresident: part-time $1188 per credit. Part-time tuition and fees vary according to program. *Financial support:* In 2012–13, 13 fellowships with full and partial tuition reimbursements (averaging $13,122 per year), 169 research assistantships (averaging $20,767 per year), 53 teaching assistantships (averaging $18,155 per year) were awarded; Federal Work-Study and scholarships/grants also available. Support available to part-time students. Financial award applicants required to submit FAFSA. *Faculty research:* Astrometeorology, superconductivity, particle astrophysics, plasma physics, elementary particle theory. *Total annual research expenditures:* $35.9 million. *Unit head:* Dr. Drew Baden, Chair, 301-405-5946, Fax: 301-405-0327, E-mail: drew@umd.edu. *Application contact:* Dr. Charles A. Caramello, Dean of the Graduate School, 301-401-0358, Fax: 301-314-9305.

University of Massachusetts Amherst, Graduate School, College of Natural Sciences, Department of Physics, Amherst, MA 01003. Offers MS, PhD. Part-time programs available. *Faculty:* 42 full-time (5 women). *Students:* 79 full-time (17 women), 3 part-time (1 woman); includes 3 minority (2 Hispanic/Latino; 1 Two or more races, non-Hispanic/Latino), 45 international. Average age 28. 222 applicants, 20% accepted, 10 enrolled. In 2012, 5 master's, 8 doctorates awarded. Terminal master's awarded for partial completion of doctoral program. *Degree requirements:* For master's, thesis or alternative; for doctorate, comprehensive exam, thesis/dissertation. *Entrance requirements:* For master's and doctorate, GRE General Test, GRE Subject Test (physics). Additional exam requirements/recommendations for international students: Required—TOEFL (minimum score 550 paper-based; 80 iBT), IELTS (minimum score 6.5). *Application deadline:* For fall admission, 1/15 for domestic and international students. Applications are processed on a rolling basis. Application fee: $75. Electronic applications accepted. *Expenses:* Tuition, state resident: full-time $1980; part-time $110 per credit. Tuition, nonresident: full-time $13,314; part-time $414 per credit. *Required fees:* $10,338; $3594 per semester. One-time fee: $357. *Financial support:* Fellowships with full and partial tuition reimbursements, research assistantships with full and partial tuition reimbursements, teaching assistantships with full and partial tuition reimbursements, career-related internships or fieldwork, Federal Work-Study, scholarships/grants, traineeships, health care benefits, tuition waivers (full and partial), and unspecified assistantships available. Support available to part-time students. Financial award application deadline: 1/15. *Unit head:* Dr. Carlo Dallapiccola, Graduate Program Director, 413-545-2548, Fax: 413-545-0648. *Application contact:* Lindsay DeSantis, Supervisor of Admissions, 413-545-0722, Fax: 413-577-0010, E-mail: gradadm@grad.umass.edu. Website: http://www.physics.umass.edu/.

University of Massachusetts Dartmouth, Graduate School, College of Engineering, Department of Physics, North Dartmouth, MA 02747-2300. Offers MS. Part-time programs available. *Faculty:* 10 full-time (1 woman), 1 (woman) part-time/adjunct. *Students:* 12 full-time (2 women), 7 part-time (0 women); includes 2 minority (1 Asian, non-Hispanic/Latino; 1 Two or more races, non-Hispanic/Latino), 4 international. Average age 29. 18 applicants, 89% accepted, 9 enrolled. In 2012, 7 master's awarded. *Degree requirements:* For master's, thesis or alternative. *Entrance requirements:* For master's, GRE (recommended), statement of purpose (minimum of 300 words), resume, 3 letters of recommendation, official transcripts. Additional exam requirements/recommendations for international students: Required—TOEFL (minimum score 533 paper-based; 72 iBT). *Application deadline:* For fall admission, 3/31 priority date for domestic students, 2/28 for international students; for spring admission, 11/15 priority date for domestic students, 10/15 for international students. Applications are processed on a rolling basis. Application fee: $60. Electronic applications accepted. *Expenses:* Tuition, state resident: part-time $86.29 per credit. Tuition, nonresident: part-time $337.46 per credit. *Required fees:* $631.03 per credit. Tuition and fees vary according to course load and reciprocity agreements. *Financial support:* In 2012–13, 8 teaching assistantships with full and partial tuition reimbursements (averaging $7,000 per year) were awarded; Federal Work-Study also available. Support available to part-time students. Financial award application deadline: 3/1; financial award applicants required to submit FAFSA. *Faculty research:* Atomic, molecular, and optical physics; ocean physics; experimental nuclear physics; theoretical particle physics; astrophysics. *Total annual research expenditures:* $824,000. *Unit head:* Gaurav Khanna, Graduate Program Director, 508-910-6605, Fax: 508-999-9115, E-mail: gkhanna@umassd.edu. *Application contact:* Steven Briggs, Director of Marketing and Recruitment, 508-999-8604, Fax: 508-999-8183, E-mail: graduate@umassd.edu. Website: http://www.umassd.edu/engineering/phy/.

University of Massachusetts Lowell, College of Sciences, Department of Physics and Applied Physics, Program in Physics, Lowell, MA 01854-2881. Offers MS, PhD. *Degree requirements:* For master's, thesis; for doctorate, 2 foreign languages, thesis/dissertation. *Entrance requirements:* For master's, GRE General Test, 3 letters of reference; for doctorate, GRE General Test, transcripts, 3 letters of reference. Additional exam requirements/recommendations for international students: Required—TOEFL.

University of Memphis, Graduate School, College of Arts and Sciences, Department of Physics, Memphis, TN 38152. Offers MS. Part-time programs available. *Degree requirements:* For master's, comprehensive exam, thesis or alternative. *Entrance requirements:* For master's, GRE General Test or MAT, 20 undergraduate hours of course work in physics. Electronic applications accepted. *Faculty research:* Solid-state physics, materials science, biophysics, astrophysics, physics education.

University of Miami, Graduate School, College of Arts and Sciences, Department of Physics, Coral Gables, FL 33124. Offers MS, PhD. Terminal master's awarded for partial completion of doctoral program. *Degree requirements:* For master's, comprehensive exam; for doctorate, comprehensive exam, thesis/dissertation. *Entrance requirements:* For master's and doctorate, GRE General Test, GRE Subject Test. Additional exam requirements/recommendations for international students: Required—TOEFL (minimum score 550 paper-based; 80 iBT). Electronic applications accepted. *Faculty research:* High-energy theory, marine and atmospheric optics, plasma physics, solid-state physics.

University of Michigan, Horace H. Rackham School of Graduate Studies, College of Literature, Science, and the Arts, Department of Physics, Ann Arbor, MI 48109. Offers PhD. *Faculty:* 68 full-time (14 women). *Students:* 149 full-time (37 women); includes 16 minority (2 Black or African American, non-Hispanic/Latino; 7 Asian, non-Hispanic/Latino; 7 Hispanic/Latino), 68 international. Average age 27. 450 applicants, 22% accepted, 35 enrolled. In 2012, 16 doctorates awarded. Terminal master's awarded for partial completion of doctoral program. *Degree requirements:* For doctorate, thesis/dissertation, oral defense of dissertation, preliminary exam. *Entrance requirements:* For doctorate, GRE General Test, GRE Subject Test in physics (recommended). Additional exam requirements/recommendations for international students: Required—TOEFL (minimum score 600 paper-based; 90 iBT). *Application deadline:* For fall admission, 12/14 for domestic and international students. Application fee: $65 ($75 for international students). Electronic applications accepted. *Financial support:* In 2012–13, fellowships with full tuition reimbursements (averaging $54,702 per year), research assistantships with full tuition reimbursements (averaging $54,702 per year), teaching assistantships with full tuition reimbursements (averaging $54,702 per year) were awarded. *Faculty research:* Elementary particle, solid-state, atomic, and molecular physics (theoretical and experimental). *Total annual research expenditures:* $14 million. *Unit head:* Dr. Bradford Orr, Chair, 734-764-4437. *Application contact:* Christina A. Zigulis, Graduate Coordinator, 734-936-0658, Fax: 734-763-9694, E-mail: physics.inquiries@umich.edu. Website: http://www.lsa.umich.edu/physics/.

University of Minnesota, Duluth, Graduate School, Swenson College of Science and Engineering, Department of Physics, Duluth, MN 55812-2496. Offers MS. Part-time programs available. *Degree requirements:* For master's, thesis optional, final oral exam. *Entrance requirements:* For master's, minimum GPA of 3.0 (preferred). Additional exam requirements/recommendations for international students: Required—TOEFL (minimum score 550 paper-based; 79 iBT), IELTS (minimum score 6.5), or Michigan English Language Assessment Battery (minimum score 80). Electronic applications accepted. *Faculty research:* Computational physics, neutrino physics, oceanography, computational particle physics, optics, condensed matter.

University of Minnesota, Twin Cities Campus, College of Science and Engineering, School of Physics and Astronomy, Program in Physics, Minneapolis, MN 55455-0213. Offers MS, PhD. Part-time programs available. *Degree requirements:* For master's, thesis; for doctorate, thesis/dissertation. *Entrance requirements:* For master's and doctorate, GRE General Test, GRE Subject Test. Additional exam requirements/recommendations for international students: Required—TOEFL. Electronic applications accepted. *Faculty research:* Elementary particles, condensed matter, cosmology, nuclear physics, space physics, biological physics, physics education.

University of Mississippi, Graduate School, College of Liberal Arts, Department of Physics and Astronomy, Oxford, University, MS 38677. Offers physics (MA, MS, PhD). *Faculty:* 17 full-time (1 woman), 2 part-time/adjunct (1 woman). *Students:* 29 full-time (6 women), 2 part-time (0 women); includes 2 minority (1 Asian, non-Hispanic/Latino; 1 Two or more races, non-Hispanic/Latino), 20 international. In 2012, 7 master's, 2 doctorates awarded. *Degree requirements:* For master's, thesis (for some programs); for doctorate, thesis/dissertation. *Entrance requirements:* For master's, GRE General Test, minimum GPA of 3.0; for doctorate, GRE General Test. Additional exam requirements/recommendations for international students: Required—TOEFL. *Application deadline:* For fall admission, 4/1 for domestic students; for spring admission, 10/1 for domestic students. Applications are processed on a rolling basis. Application fee: $25. Electronic applications accepted. *Expenses:* Tuition, state resident: full-time $6282; part-time $349 per credit hour. Tuition, nonresident: full-time $16,266; part-time $903.50 per credit hour. *Financial support:* Scholarships/grants available. Financial award application deadline: 3/1; financial award applicants required to submit FAFSA. *Unit head:* Dr. Lucien M. Cremaldi, Chairman, 662-915-7046, Fax: 662-915-5045, E-mail: physics@phy.olemiss.edu. *Application contact:* Dr. Christy M. Wyandt, Associate Dean, 662-915-7474, Fax: 662-915-7577, E-mail: cwyandt@olemiss.edu.

University of Missouri, Graduate School, College of Arts and Sciences, Department of Physics and Astronomy, Columbia, MO 65211. Offers MS, PhD. *Faculty:* 27 full-time (8 women), 1 (woman) part-time/adjunct. *Students:* 35 full-time (7 women), 19 part-time (2 women); includes 5 minority (1 Black or African American, non-Hispanic/Latino; 1 Asian, non-Hispanic/Latino; 1 Hispanic/Latino; 2 Two or more races, non-Hispanic/Latino), 26 international. Average age 28. 63 applicants, 16% accepted, 9 enrolled. In 2012, 6 master's, 8 doctorates awarded. Terminal master's awarded for partial completion of doctoral program. *Degree requirements:* For doctorate, one foreign language, comprehensive exam, thesis/dissertation. *Entrance requirements:* For master's and doctorate, GRE General Test, minimum GPA of 3.0. Additional exam requirements/recommendations for international students: Required—TOEFL (minimum score 550 paper-based; 80 iBT). *Application deadline:* For fall admission, 3/15 priority date for domestic students, 3/15 for international students. Applications are processed on a rolling basis. Application fee: $55 ($75 for international students). Electronic applications accepted. *Expenses:* Tuition, state resident: full-time $6057. Tuition, nonresident: full-time $15,683. *Required fees:* $1000. *Financial support:* In 2012–13, 35 research assistantships with full tuition reimbursements, 10 teaching assistantships with full tuition reimbursements were awarded; institutionally sponsored loans, health care benefits, and unspecified assistantships also available. *Faculty research:* Experimental and theoretical condensed-matter physics, biological physics, astronomy/astrophysics. *Unit head:* Dr. Peter Pfeifer, Department Chair, 573-882-2335, E-mail: pfeiferp@missouri.edu. *Application contact:* Dr. Carsten Ullrich, Director of Graduate Studies, 573-882-3335, E-mail: ullrichc@missouri.edu. Website: http://physics.missouri.edu/graduate/.

University of Missouri–Kansas City, College of Arts and Sciences, Department of Physics and Astronomy, Kansas City, MO 64110-2499. Offers physics (MS, PhD). PhD (interdisciplinary) offered through the School of Graduate Studies. Part-time and evening/weekend programs available. *Faculty:* 11 full-time (1 woman), 1 part-time/adjunct (0 women). *Students:* 8 full-time (2 women), 19 part-time (1 woman); includes 1 minority (Asian, non-Hispanic/Latino), 9 international. Average age 29. 20 applicants, 65% accepted, 8 enrolled. In 2012, 1 master's awarded. Terminal master's awarded for partial completion of doctoral program. *Degree requirements:* For master's, comprehensive exam, thesis optional; for doctorate, comprehensive exam, thesis/dissertation. *Entrance requirements:* For master's and doctorate, GRE General Test. Additional exam requirements/recommendations for international students: Required—TOEFL (minimum score 550 paper-based; 80 iBT). *Application deadline:* For fall admission, 4/1 priority date for domestic students, 4/1 for international students; for spring admission, 11/1 priority date for domestic students, 11/1 for international students. Applications are processed on a rolling basis. Application fee: $45 ($50 for international students). Electronic applications accepted. *Expenses:* Tuition, state resident: full-time $5972.40; part-time $331.80 per credit hour. Tuition, nonresident: full-time $15,417; part-time $856.50 per credit hour. *Required fees:* $95.89 per credit hour. Full-time tuition and fees vary according to program. *Financial support:* In 2012–13, 5 research assistantships with full and partial tuition reimbursements (averaging $15,995 per year), 19 teaching assistantships with full and partial tuition reimbursements (averaging $15,906 per year) were awarded; Federal Work-Study, institutionally sponsored loans, and tuition waivers (full and partial) also available. Support available to part-time students. Financial award application deadline: 3/1; financial award applicants required to submit FAFSA. *Faculty research:* Surface physics, material science, statistical mechanics, computational physics, relativity and quantum theory. *Unit head:* Dr. Michael Kruger, Chair, 816-235-5441, E-mail: krugerm@umkc.edu. *Application contact:* Dr. Da Ming Zhu, Principal Graduate Advisor, 816-235-5326, Fax: 816-235-5221, E-mail: zhud@umkc.edu. Website: http://cas.umkc.edu/physics/.

University of Missouri–St. Louis, College of Arts and Sciences, Department of Physics and Astronomy, St. Louis, MO 63121. Offers applied physics (MS); astrophysics (MS); physics (PhD). Part-time and evening/weekend programs available. *Faculty:* 9 full-time (2 women), 5 part-time/adjunct (0 women). *Students:* 14 full-time (3 women), 9 part-time (5 women); includes 2 minority (1 American Indian or Alaska Native, non-Hispanic/Latino; 1 Asian, non-Hispanic/Latino), 4 international. Average age 31. 21 applicants, 48% accepted, 6 enrolled. In 2012, 7 master's, 1 doctorate awarded. Terminal master's awarded for partial completion of doctoral program. *Degree requirements:* For master's, thesis optional; for doctorate, thesis/dissertation. *Entrance requirements:* For master's, GRE General Test; for doctorate, GRE General Test, 2 letters of recommendation. Additional exam requirements/recommendations for international students: Required—TOEFL (minimum score 550 paper-based; 79 iBT), IELTS (minimum score 6.5). *Application deadline:* For fall admission, 7/1 for domestic and international students; for spring admission, 12/1 for domestic students, 11/1 for international students. Application fee: $35 ($40 for international students). Electronic applications accepted. *Expenses:* Tuition, state resident: full-time $7364; part-time $409.10 per credit hour. Tuition, nonresident: full-time $18,153; part-time $1008.50 per credit hour. *Financial support:* In 2012–13, 5 research assistantships with full and partial tuition reimbursements (averaging $17,125 per year), 11 teaching assistantships with full and partial tuition reimbursements (averaging $14,500 per year) were awarded; fellowships with full tuition reimbursements and career-related internships or fieldwork also available. Financial award applicants required to submit FAFSA. *Faculty research:* Biophysics, atomic physics, nonlinear dynamics, materials science. *Unit head:* Dr. Bruce Wilking, Director of Graduate Studies, 314-516-5931, Fax: 314-516-6152, E-mail: bwilking@umsl.edu. *Application contact:* 314-516-5458, Fax: 314-516-6996, E-mail: gradadm@umsl.edu. Website: http://www.umsl.edu/~physics/.

University of Nebraska–Lincoln, Graduate College, College of Arts and Sciences, Department of Physics and Astronomy, Lincoln, NE 68588. Offers astronomy (MS, PhD); physics (MS, PhD). *Degree requirements:* For master's, thesis optional; for doctorate, comprehensive exam, thesis/dissertation. *Entrance requirements:* For master's and doctorate, GRE General Test. Additional exam requirements/recommendations for international students: Required—TOEFL (minimum score 550 paper-based). Electronic applications accepted. *Faculty research:* Electromagnetics of solids and thin films, photoionization, ion collisions with atoms, molecules and surfaces, nanostructures.

Peterson's Graduate Programs in the Physical Sciences, Mathematics, Agricultural Sciences, the Environment & Natural Resources 2014

www.petersonsbooks.com **249**

Physics

University of Nevada, Las Vegas, Graduate College, College of Science, Department of Physics, Las Vegas, NV 89154-4002. Offers astronomy (MS, PhD); physics (MS, PhD). Part-time programs available. *Faculty:* 23 full-time (3 women), 10 part-time/adjunct (5 women). *Students:* 12 full-time (1 woman), 4 part-time (0 women); includes 7 minority (all Two or more races, non-Hispanic/Latino), 6 international. Average age 31. 15 applicants, 47% accepted, 4 enrolled. In 2012, 4 master's, 2 doctorates awarded. *Degree requirements:* For master's, thesis, oral exam; for doctorate, comprehensive exam, thesis/dissertation. *Entrance requirements:* For master's and doctorate, GRE General Test. Additional exam requirements/recommendations for international students: Required—TOEFL (minimum score 550 paper-based; 80 iBT), IELTS (minimum score 7). *Application deadline:* For fall admission, 8/1 priority date for domestic students, 5/1 for international students; for spring admission, 10/1 priority date for domestic students, 10/1 for international students. Applications are processed on a rolling basis. Application fee: $60 ($95 for international students). Electronic applications accepted. *Expenses:* Tuition, state resident: full-time $4752; part-time $264 per credit. Tuition, nonresident: full-time $18,662; part-time $527.50 per credit. *Required fees:* $12 per credit. $266 per semester. One-time fee: $35. Tuition and fees vary according to course load, program and reciprocity agreements. *Financial support:* In 2012–13, 14 students received support, including 14 teaching assistantships with partial tuition reimbursements available (averaging $16,120 per year); institutionally sponsored loans, scholarships/grants, health care benefits, and unspecified assistantships also available. Financial award application deadline: 3/1. *Faculty research:* Gamma-ray bursters astrophysics, cosmology and dark matter astrophysics, experimental high pressure physics, theoretical condensed matter physics, laser-plasma atomic physics. *Total annual research expenditures:* $4.2 million. *Unit head:* Stephen Lepp, Chair/Professor, 702-895-4455, E-mail: lepp@physics.unlv.edu. *Application contact:* Graduate College Admissions Evaluator, 702-895-3320, Fax: 702-895-4180, E-mail: gradcollege@unlv.edu. Website: http://www.physics.unlv.edu/graduate.html.

University of Nevada, Reno, Graduate School, College of Science, Department of Physics, Reno, NV 89557. Offers MS, PhD. Terminal master's awarded for partial completion of doctoral program. *Degree requirements:* For master's, thesis optional; for doctorate, thesis/dissertation. *Entrance requirements:* For master's, GRE General Test, GRE Subject Test, minimum GPA of 2.75; for doctorate, GRE General Test, GRE Subject Test, minimum GPA of 3.0. Additional exam requirements/recommendations for international students: Required—TOEFL (minimum score 500 paper-based; 61 iBT), IELTS (minimum score 6). Electronic applications accepted. *Faculty research:* Atomic and molecular physics.

University of New Brunswick Fredericton, School of Graduate Studies, Faculty of Science, Department of Physics, Fredericton, NB E3B 5A3, Canada. Offers M Sc, PhD. Part-time programs available. *Faculty:* 9 full-time (2 women). *Students:* 18 full-time (4 women). In 2012, 3 master's awarded. *Degree requirements:* For master's, thesis; for doctorate, comprehensive exam, thesis/dissertation. *Entrance requirements:* For master's, B Sc with minimum B average; for doctorate, M Sc, minimum GPA of 3.0. Additional exam requirements/recommendations for international students: Required—TOEFL, TWE. *Application deadline:* For fall admission, 3/1 for domestic students. Applications are processed on a rolling basis. Application fee: $50 Canadian dollars. Electronic applications accepted. Tuition and fees charges are reported in Canadian dollars. *Expenses: Tuition, area resident:* Full-time $3956 Canadian dollars. *Required fees:* $579.50 Canadian dollars; $55 Canadian dollars per semester. *Financial support:* In 2012–13, 17 fellowships with tuition reimbursements, 31 research assistantships, 49 teaching assistantships were awarded. *Faculty research:* Optical and laser spectroscopy, infrared and microwave spectroscopy, magnetic resonance and magnetic resonance imaging, space and atmospheric physics, theoretical atomic and molecular physics, space plasma theory, theoretical molecular spectroscopy. *Unit head:* Dr. Igor Mastikhin, Director of Graduate Studies, 506-458-7927, Fax: 506-453-4581, E-mail: mast@unb.ca. *Application contact:* Elinor MacFarlane, Graduate Secretary, 506-453-4723, Fax: 506-453-4581, E-mail: elinor@unb.ca. Website: http://go.unb.ca/gradprograms.

University of New Hampshire, Graduate School, College of Engineering and Physical Sciences, Department of Physics, Durham, NH 03824. Offers MS, PhD. *Faculty:* 32 full-time (4 women). *Students:* 38 full-time (6 women), 31 part-time (7 women); includes 3 minority (2 American Indian or Alaska Native, non-Hispanic/Latino; 1 Asian, non-Hispanic/Latino), 25 international. Average age 26. 96 applicants, 35% accepted, 13 enrolled. In 2012, 4 master's, 6 doctorates awarded. Terminal master's awarded for partial completion of doctoral program. *Degree requirements:* For master's, thesis or alternative; for doctorate, thesis/dissertation. *Entrance requirements:* For master's and doctorate, GRE General Test. Additional exam requirements/recommendations for international students: Required—TOEFL (minimum score 550 paper-based; 80 iBT). *Application deadline:* For fall admission, 4/1 priority date for domestic students, 4/1 for international students; for spring admission, 12/1 for domestic students. Applications are processed on a rolling basis. Application fee: $65. Electronic applications accepted. *Expenses:* Tuition, state resident: full-time $13,500; part-time $750 per credit. Tuition, nonresident: full-time $25,940; part-time $1089 per credit. *Required fees:* $1699; $424.75 per semester. *Financial support:* In 2012–13, 60 students received support, including 3 fellowships, 42 research assistantships, 21 teaching assistantships; Federal Work-Study, scholarships/grants, and tuition waivers (full and partial) also available. Support available to part-time students. Financial award application deadline: 2/15. *Faculty research:* Astrophysics and space physics, nuclear physics, atomic and molecular physics, nonlinear dynamical systems. *Unit head:* Mark McConnell, Chairperson, 603-862-

2047. *Application contact:* Katie Makem-Boucher, Administrative Assistant, 603-862-2669, E-mail: physics.grad.info@unh.edu. Website: http://www.physics.unh.edu/.

University of New Mexico, Graduate School, College of Arts and Sciences, Department of Physics and Astronomy, Albuquerque, NM 87131. Offers physics (MS, PhD). Part-time programs available. *Faculty:* 31 full-time (5 women), 6 part-time/adjunct (0 women). *Students:* 53 full-time (9 women), 31 part-time (2 women); includes 9 minority (3 Asian, non-Hispanic/Latino; 5 Hispanic/Latino; 1 Native Hawaiian or other Pacific Islander, non-Hispanic/Latino), 23 international. Average age 28. 90 applicants, 17% accepted, 14 enrolled. In 2012, 11 master's, 13 doctorates awarded. Terminal master's awarded for partial completion of doctoral program. *Degree requirements:* For master's, comprehensive exam (for some programs), thesis optional, preliminary exams (for non-thesis option); for doctorate, comprehensive exam, thesis/dissertation. *Entrance requirements:* For master's and doctorate, GRE General Test; GRE Subject Test (physics). Additional exam requirements/recommendations for international students: Required—TOEFL (minimum score 550 paper-based; 80 iBT), IELTS (minimum score 7). *Application deadline:* For fall admission, 1/15 for domestic and international students; for spring admission, 8/1 for domestic and international students. Application fee: $50. Electronic applications accepted. *Expenses:* Tuition, state resident: full-time $3296; part-time $276.73 per credit hour. Tuition, nonresident: full-time $10,604; part-time $885.74 per credit hour. *Required fees:* $628. *Financial support:* In 2012–13, 90 students received support, including 4 fellowships (averaging $30,000 per year), 58 research assistantships with full tuition reimbursements available (averaging $23,630 per year), 29 teaching assistantships with full tuition reimbursements available (averaging $15,196 per year); career-related internships or fieldwork, scholarships/grants, traineeships, health care benefits, and unspecified assistantships also available. Support available to part-time students. Financial award application deadline: 2/1; financial award applicants required to submit FAFSA. *Faculty research:* Astronomy and astrophysics, biological physics, condensed-matter physics, nonlinear science and complexity, optics and photonics, quantum information, subatomic physics. *Total annual research expenditures:* $6 million. *Unit head:* Dr. Wolfgang Rudolph, Chair, 505-277-1517, Fax: 505-277-1520, E-mail: wrudolph@unm.edu. *Application contact:* Alisa Gibson, Coordinator, Academic Programs, 505-277-1514, Fax: 505-277-1520, E-mail: agibson@unm.edu. Website: http://panda.unm.edu.

University of New Orleans, Graduate School, College of Sciences, Department of Physics, New Orleans, LA 70148. Offers MS, PhD. Part-time and evening/weekend programs available. *Students:* 8 (1 woman). Average age 32. 7 applicants, 43% accepted, 1 enrolled. In 2012, 4 master's awarded. *Degree requirements:* For master's, thesis (for some programs). *Entrance requirements:* For master's, GRE General Test. Additional exam requirements/recommendations for international students: Required—TOEFL (minimum score 550 paper-based; 79 iBT), IELTS. *Application deadline:* For fall admission, 7/1 priority date for domestic students, 6/1 for international students; for spring admission, 11/1 priority date for domestic students, 10/1 for international students. Applications are processed on a rolling basis. Application fee: $20. Electronic applications accepted. *Expenses: Required fees:* $2165 per semester. *Financial support:* Research assistantships, teaching assistantships, and career-related internships or fieldwork available. Financial award application deadline: 3/15; financial award applicants required to submit FAFSA. *Faculty research:* Underwater acoustics, applied electromagnetics, experimental atomic beams, digital signal processing, astrophysics. *Unit head:* Dr. Kevin Stokes, Chairperson, 504-280-6713, Fax: 504-280-6048, E-mail: kstokes@uno.edu. *Application contact:* Dr. Kevin Stokes, Graduate Coordinator, 504-280-6713, Fax: 504-280-6048, E-mail: kstokes@uno.edu. Website: http://physics.uno.edu.

The University of North Carolina at Chapel Hill, Graduate School, College of Arts and Sciences, Department of Physics and Astronomy, Chapel Hill, NC 27599. Offers physics (MS, PhD). Terminal master's awarded for partial completion of doctoral program. *Degree requirements:* For master's, comprehensive exam; for doctorate, comprehensive exam, thesis/dissertation. *Entrance requirements:* For master's and doctorate, GRE General Test, minimum GPA of 3.0. Electronic applications accepted. *Faculty research:* Observational astronomy, fullerenes, polarized beams, nanotubes, nucleosynthesis in stars and supernovae, superstring theory, ballistic transport in semiconductors, gravitation.

University of North Dakota, Graduate School, College of Arts and Sciences, Department of Physics, Grand Forks, ND 58202. Offers MS, PhD. *Degree requirements:* For master's, thesis, final exam; for doctorate, comprehensive exam, thesis/dissertation, final exam. *Entrance requirements:* For master's, minimum GPA of 3.0; for doctorate, minimum GPA of 3.5. Additional exam requirements/recommendations for international students: Required—TOEFL (minimum score 550 paper-based; 79 iBT), IELTS (minimum score 6.5). Electronic applications accepted. *Faculty research:* Solid state physics, atomic and molecular physics, astrophysics, health physics.

University of Northern Iowa, Graduate College, College of Humanities, Arts and Sciences, Department of Physics, Cedar Falls, IA 50614. Offers applied physics (PSM). *Students:* 2 full-time (1 woman), 1 part-time (0 women), 1 international. 5 applicants, 40% accepted, 1 enrolled. In 2012, 5 degrees awarded. *Degree requirements:* For master's, comprehensive exam (for some programs), thesis or alternative. *Entrance requirements:* For master's, minimum GPA of 3.0. Additional exam requirements/recommendations for international students: Required—TOEFL (minimum score 500 paper-based; 61 iBT). *Application deadline:* For fall

250 www.petersonsbooks.com

Peterson's Graduate Programs in the Physical Sciences, Mathematics, Agricultural Sciences, the Environment & Natural Resources 2014

admission, 8/1 priority date for domestic students. Applications are processed on a rolling basis. Application fee: $50 ($70 for international students). Electronic applications accepted. *Financial support:* Career-related internships or fieldwork, Federal Work-Study, scholarships/grants, and tuition waivers (full and partial) available. Support available to part-time students. Financial award application deadline: 2/1. *Unit head:* Dr. C. Clifton Chancey, Head, 319-273-2420, E-mail: c.chancey@uni.edu. *Application contact:* Laurie S. Russell, Record Analyst, 319-273-2623, Fax: 319-273-2885, E-mail: laurie.russell@uni.edu. Website: http://www.physics.uni.edu/.

University of Northern Iowa, Graduate College, College of Humanities, Arts and Sciences, Program in Science Education, Cedar Falls, IA 50614. Offers earth science education (MA); physics education (MA); science education (MA). *Students:* 4 full-time (2 women), 8 part-time (2 women); includes 1 minority (Two or more races, non-Hispanic/Latino). 1 applicant, 100% accepted, 1 enrolled. In 2012, 8 master's awarded. *Degree requirements:* For master's, comprehensive exam (for some programs), thesis or alternative. *Entrance requirements:* For master's, minimum GPA of 3.0. Additional exam requirements/recommendations for international students: Required—TOEFL (minimum score 500 paper-based; 61 iBT). *Application deadline:* For fall admission, 8/1 priority date for domestic students. Applications are processed on a rolling basis. Application fee: $50 ($70 for international students). Electronic applications accepted. *Financial support:* Application deadline: 2/1. *Unit head:* Dr. Cherin A. Lee, Director, 319-273-7357, Fax: 319-273-3051, E-mail: cherin.lee@uni.edu. *Application contact:* Laurie S. Russell, Record Analyst, 319-273-2623, Fax: 319-273-2885, E-mail: laurie.russell@uni.edu. Website: http://www.uni.edu/science-ed/.

University of North Texas, Robert B. Toulouse School of Graduate Studies, Denton, TN 750603. Offers accounting (MS, PhD); applied anthropology (MA, MS); applied behavior analysis (Certificate); applied technology and performance improvement (M Ed, MS, PhD); art education (MA, PhD); art history (MA); art museum education (Certificate); arts leadership (Certificate); audiology (Au D); behavior analysis (MS); biochemistry and molecular biology (MS, PhD); biology (MA, MS, PhD); business (PhD); business computer information systems (PhD); chemistry (MS, PhD); clinical psychology (PhD); communication studies (MA, MS); computer engineering (MS); computer science (MS); computer science and engineering (PhD); counseling (M Ed, MS, PhD), including clinical mental health counseling (MS), college and university counseling (M Ed, MS), elementary school counseling (M Ed, MS), secondary school counseling (M Ed, MS); counseling psychology (PhD); creative writing (MA); criminal justice (MS); curriculum and instruction (M Ed, PhD), including curriculum studies (PhD), early childhood studies (PhD), language and literacy studies (PhD); decision sciences (MBA); design (MA, MFA), including fashion design (MFA), innovation studies, interior design (MFA); early childhood studies (MS); economics (MS); educational leadership (M Ed, Ed D, PhD); educational psychology (MS), including family studies, gifted and talented (MS, PhD), human development, learning and cognition, research, measurement and evaluation; educational research (PhD), including gifted and talented (MS, PhD), human development and family studies, psychological aspects of sports and exercise, research, measurement and statistics; electrical engineering (MS); emergency management (MPA); engineering systems (MS); English (MA, PhD); environmental science (MS, PhD); experimental psychology (PhD); finance (MBA, MS, PhD); financial management (MPA); French (MA); health psychology and behavioral medicine (PhD); health services management (MBA); higher education (M Ed, Ed D, PhD); history (MA, MS, PhD), including European history (PhD), military history (PhD), United States history (PhD); hospitality management (MS); human resources management (MPA); information science (MS, PhD); information technologies (MBA); information technology and decision sciences (MS); interdisciplinary studies (MA, MS); international sustainable tourism (MS); jazz studies (MM); journalism (MA, MJ, Graduate Certificate), including interactive and virtual digital communication (Graduate Certificate), narrative journalism (Graduate Certificate), public relations (Graduate Certificate); kinesiology (MS); learning technologies (MS, PhD); library science (MS); local government management (MPA); logistics and supply chain management (MBA, PhD); long-term care, senior housing, and aging services (MA, MS); management science (PhD); marketing (MBA, PhD); materials science and engineering (MS, PhD); mathematics (MA, PhD); merchandising (MS); music (MA, MM Ed, PhD), including ethnomusicology (MA), music education (MM Ed, PhD), music theory (MA, PhD), musicology (MA, PhD), performance (MA); nonprofit management (MPA); operations and supply chain management (MBA); performance (MM, DMA); philosophy (MA, PhD); physics (MS, PhD); political science (MA, MS, PhD); public administration and management (PhD), including emergency management, nonprofit management, public financial management, urban management; radio, television and film (MA, MFA); recreation, event and sport management (MS); rehabilitation counseling (MS, Certificate); sociology (MA, MS, PhD); Spanish (MA); special education (M Ed, PhD), including autism intervention (PhD), emotional/behavioral disorders (PhD), mild/moderate disabilities (PhD); speech-language pathology (MA, MS); strategic management (MBA); studio art (MFA); taxation (MS); teaching (M Ed); MBA/MS; MS/MPH; MSES/MBA. Part-time and evening/weekend programs available. Postbaccalaureate distance learning degree programs offered. *Faculty:* 665 full-time (219 women), 237 part-time/adjunct (135 women). *Students:* 3,206 full-time (1,712 women), 3,623 part-time (2,305 women); includes 1,742 minority (575 Black or African American, non-Hispanic/Latino; 16 American Indian or Alaska Native, non-Hispanic/Latino; 294 Asian, non-Hispanic/Latino; 690 Hispanic/Latino; 2 Native Hawaiian or other Pacific Islander, non-Hispanic/Latino; 165 Two or more races, non-Hispanic/Latino), 1,125 international. Average age 32. 6,094 applicants, 43% accepted, 1692 enrolled. In 2012, 1,910 master's, 237 doctorates awarded. Terminal master's awarded for partial completion of doctoral program. *Degree requirements:* For master's, variable foreign language requirement, comprehensive exam (for some programs), thesis (for some programs); for doctorate, variable foreign language requirement, comprehensive exam (for some programs), thesis/dissertation; for other advanced degree, variable foreign language requirement, comprehensive exam (for some programs). *Entrance requirements:* For master's and doctorate, GRE, GMAT. Additional exam requirements/recommendations for international students: Required—TOEFL (minimum score 550 paper-based; 79 iBT). *Application deadline:* For fall admission, 7/15 for domestic students, 3/15 for international students; for spring admission, 11/15 for domestic students, 9/15 for international students. Applications are processed on a rolling basis. Application fee: $60. Electronic applications accepted. *Expenses:* Tuition, state resident: full-time $5242; part-time $216 per credit hour. Tuition, nonresident: full-time $11,560; part-time $567 per credit hour. *Required fees:* $730 per semester. *Financial support:* Fellowships with partial tuition reimbursements, research assistantships with partial tuition reimbursements, teaching assistantships, career-related internships or fieldwork, Federal Work-Study, institutionally sponsored loans, scholarships/grants, and library assistantships available. Support available to part-time students. Financial award applicants required to submit FAFSA. *Unit head:* Mark Wardell, Dean, 940-565-2383, E-mail: mark.wardell@unt.edu. *Application contact:* Toulouse School of Graduate Studies, 940-565-2383, Fax: 940-565-2141, E-mail: gradsch@unt.edu. Website: http://www.tsgs.unt.edu/.

University of Notre Dame, Graduate School, College of Science, Department of Physics, Notre Dame, IN 46556. Offers MS, PhD. *Degree requirements:* For doctorate, thesis/dissertation, candidacy exam. *Entrance requirements:* For doctorate, GRE General Test, GRE Subject Test. Additional exam requirements/recommendations for international students: Required—TOEFL (minimum score 600 paper-based; 80 iBT). Electronic applications accepted. *Faculty research:* High energy, nuclear, atomic, condensed-matter physics; astrophysics; biophysics.

University of Oklahoma, College of Arts and Sciences, Department of Physics and Astronomy, Norman, OK 73019. Offers physics (MS, PhD). Part-time programs available. *Faculty:* 31 full-time (5 women). *Students:* 52 full-time (12 women), 30 part-time (15 women); includes 1 minority (Asian, non-Hispanic/Latino), 31 international. Average age 27. 25 applicants, 56% accepted, 14 enrolled. In 2012, 8 master's, 11 doctorates awarded. Terminal master's awarded for partial completion of doctoral program. *Degree requirements:* For master's, thesis or alternative, departmental qualifying exam; for doctorate, thesis/dissertation, comprehensive, departmental qualifying, oral, and written exams. *Entrance requirements:* For master's and doctorate, GRE General Test, GRE Subject Test, 3 letters of recommendation. Additional exam requirements/recommendations for international students: Required—TOEFL (minimum score 550 paper-based; 79 iBT). *Application deadline:* For fall admission, 3/1 for domestic and international students; for spring admission, 11/1 for domestic students, 9/1 for international students. Applications are processed on a rolling basis. Application fee: $40 ($90 for international students). Electronic applications accepted. *Expenses:* Tuition, state resident: full-time $4205; part-time $175.20 per credit hour. Tuition, nonresident: full-time $15,667; part-time $653 per credit hour. *Required fees:* $2745; $103.85 per credit hour. Tuition and fees vary according to course load and degree level. *Financial support:* In 2012–13, 29 research assistantships with partial tuition reimbursements (averaging $16,298 per year), 34 teaching assistantships with partial tuition reimbursements (averaging $14,595 per year) were awarded; health care benefits and unspecified assistantships also available. Financial award application deadline: 6/1; financial award applicants required to submit FAFSA. *Faculty research:* Astronomy and astrophysics, condensed matter physics, atomic molecular and optical physics, high energy physics. *Total annual research expenditures:* $4.6 million. *Unit head:* Greg Parker, Chair, 405-325-3961, Fax: 405-325-7557, E-mail: parker@nhn.ou.edu. *Application contact:* Debbie Barnhill, University Student Services Assistant, 405-325-3961 Ext. 36101, Fax: 405-325-7557, E-mail: dbarnhill@ou.edu. Website: http://www.nhn.ou.edu.

University of Oregon, Graduate School, College of Arts and Sciences, Department of Physics, Eugene, OR 97403. Offers MA, MS, PhD. Terminal master's awarded for partial completion of doctoral program. *Degree requirements:* For doctorate, thesis/dissertation. *Entrance requirements:* For master's and doctorate, GRE General Test, GRE Subject Test, minimum GPA of 3.0. Additional exam requirements/recommendations for international students: Required—TOEFL. *Faculty research:* Solid-state and chemical physics, optical physics, elementary particle physics, astrophysics, atomic and molecular physics.

University of Ottawa, Faculty of Graduate and Postdoctoral Studies, Faculty of Science, Ottawa-Carleton Institute for Physics, Ottawa, ON K1N 6N5, Canada. Offers M Sc, PhD. M Sc, PhD offered jointly with Carleton University. *Degree requirements:* For master's, thesis or alternative; for doctorate, comprehensive exam, thesis/dissertation, seminar. *Entrance requirements:* For master's, honors B Sc degree or equivalent, minimum B average; for doctorate, M Sc, minimum B+ average. Electronic applications accepted. Tuition and fees charges are reported in Canadian dollars. *Expenses: Tuition, area resident:* Full-time $7074 Canadian dollars; part-time $256 Canadian dollars per credit. *International tuition:* $16,334 Canadian dollars full-time. *Required fees:* $738 Canadian dollars; $110 Canadian dollars per term. Part-time tuition and fees vary according to course load, program and student level. *Faculty research:* Condensed matter physics and statistical physics (CMS), subatomic physics (SAP), medical physics (Med).

University of Pennsylvania, School of Arts and Sciences, Graduate Group in Physics and Astronomy, Philadelphia, PA 19104. Offers medical physics (MS); physics (PhD). Part-time programs available. *Faculty:* 42 full-time (7 women), 13 part-time/adjunct (0 women). *Students:* 101 full-time (20 women), 1 part-time (0 women); includes 14 minority (10 Asian, non-Hispanic/Latino; 3 Hispanic/Latino; 1 Two or more races, non-Hispanic/Latino), 16 international. 488 applicants, 12% accepted, 13 enrolled. In 2012, 14 master's, 17 doctorates awarded. *Degree requirements:* For doctorate, thesis/dissertation, oral, preliminary, and final exams. *Entrance requirements:* For doctorate, GRE General Test, GRE Subject Test (recommended). Additional exam requirements/recommendations for international students: Required—TOEFL. *Application deadline:* For fall admission, 12/1 priority date for domestic students. Application fee: $70. Electronic applications accepted. *Financial support:* Fellowships, research assistantships, teaching assistantships, institutionally sponsored loans, scholarships/grants, traineeships, health care benefits, and unspecified assistantships available. Financial award application deadline: 12/15. *Faculty research:* Astrophysics, condensed matter experiment, condensed matter theory, particle experiment, particle theory. *Total annual research expenditures:* $7.3 million. *Application contact:* Arts and Sciences Graduate Admissions, 215-573-5816, Fax: 215-573-8068, E-mail: gdasadmis@sas.upenn.edu. Website: http://www.sas.upenn.edu/graduate-division.

University of Pittsburgh, Dietrich School of Arts and Sciences, Department of Physics and Astronomy, Pittsburgh, PA 15260. Offers physics (MS, PhD). *Faculty:* 41 full-time (5 women), 1 (woman) part-time/adjunct. *Students:* 93 full-time (18 women), 3 part-time (2 women); includes 3 minority (1 Asian, non-Hispanic/Latino; 2 Hispanic/Latino), 57 international. Average age 25. 313 applicants, 27% accepted, 26 enrolled. In 2012, 19 master's, 11 doctorates awarded. Terminal master's awarded for partial completion of doctoral program. *Degree requirements:* For master's, comprehensive exam, thesis optional; for doctorate, preliminary and comprehensive exams, 2 terms of student teaching, seminar and/or professional talk presentations, annual committee review meeting, oral/written dissertation. *Entrance requirements:* For master's and doctorate, GRE General Test, GRE Subject Test, minimum GPA of 3.0. Additional exam requirements/recommendations for international students: Required—TOEFL, IELTS. *Application deadline:* For fall admission, 1/31 priority date for domestic students, 1/31 for international students. Applications are processed on a rolling basis. Application fee: $0 ($50 for international students). Electronic applications accepted. *Expenses:* Tuition, state resident: full-time $19,336; part-time $782 per credit. Tuition, nonresident: full-time $31,658; part-time $1295 per credit. *Required fees:* $740; $200 per term. Tuition and fees vary according to program. *Financial support:* In 2012–13, 10 fellowships with full tuition reimbursements (averaging $29,071 per year), 47 research assistantships with full tuition reimbursements (averaging $24,450 per year), 32 teaching assistantships with full tuition reimbursements (averaging $24,450 per year) were awarded; scholarships/grants, health care benefits, tuition waivers, and unspecified assistantships also available. Financial award application deadline: 1/31. *Faculty research:* Astrophysics and cosmology, particle and astroparticle physics, condensed matter and solid-state physics, quantum information, biological physics, nanoscience. *Total annual research expenditures:* $6.1 million. *Unit head:* Dr. David Turnshek, Department Chair, 412-624-6381, Fax: 412-624-9163, E-mail: davidt@pitt.edu. *Application contact:* Dr. Robert P. Devaty, Graduate Admissions Committee Chair, 412-624-9009, Fax: 412-624-9163, E-mail: devaty@pitt.edu. Website: http://www.physicsandastronomy.pitt.edu/.

See Display below and Close-Up on page 263.

University of Puerto Rico, Mayagüez Campus, Graduate Studies, College of Arts and Sciences, Department of Physics, Mayagüez, PR 00681-9000. Offers MS. Part-time programs available. *Faculty:* 25 full-time (0 women). *Students:* 32 full-time (11 women); includes 29 minority (all Hispanic/Latino), 21 international. 7 applicants, 100% accepted, 4 enrolled. In 2012, 1 master's awarded. *Degree requirements:* For master's, comprehensive exam. *Entrance requirements:* For master's, bachelor's degree in physics or its equivalent. *Application deadline:* For fall admission, 2/15 for domestic and international students; for spring admission, 9/15 for domestic and international students. Applications are processed on a rolling basis. Application fee: $25. Tuition and fees vary according to course level and course load. *Financial support:* In 2012–13, 13 students received support, including 6 research assistantships (averaging $15,000 per year), 13 teaching assistantships (averaging $8,500 per year); Federal Work-Study and institutionally sponsored loans also available. *Faculty research:* Atomic and molecular physics, nuclear physics, nonlinear thermostatics, fluid dynamics, molecular spectroscopy. *Total annual research expenditures:* $1.8 million. *Unit head:* Dr. Dorial Castellanos, Interim Director, 787-265-3844, Fax: 787-832-1135, E-mail: dorial.castellanos@upr.edu. *Application contact:* Vanessa Gonzalez, Secretary, 787-832-4040 Ext. 3073, Fax: 787-832-1135, E-mail: vanessa@uprm.edu. Website: http://www.uprm.edu/fisica/.

University of Puerto Rico, Río Piedras, College of Natural Sciences, Department of Physics, San Juan, PR 00931-3300. Offers chemical physics (PhD); physics (MS). Part-time programs available. *Degree requirements:* For master's, comprehensive exam, thesis; for doctorate, comprehensive exam, thesis/dissertation. *Entrance requirements:* For master's, GRE General Test, GRE Subject Test, interview, minimum GPA of 3.0, letter of recommendation (3); for doctorate, GRE, master's degree, minimum GPA of 3.0, letter of recommendation (3). Additional exam requirements/recommendations for international students: Required—TOEFL. *Faculty research:* Energy transfer

252 www.petersonsbooks.com

Peterson's Graduate Programs in the Physical Sciences, Mathematics, Agricultural Sciences, the Environment & Natural Resources 2014

process through Van der Vacqs interactions, study of the photodissociation of ketene.

University of Regina, Faculty of Graduate Studies and Research, Faculty of Science, Department of Physics, Regina, SK S4S 0A2, Canada. Offers M Sc, PhD. *Faculty:* 9 full-time (0 women), 3 part-time/adjunct (0 women). *Students:* 5 full-time (1 woman), 2 part-time (0 women). 9 applicants, 33% accepted. In 2012, 1 master's awarded. *Degree requirements:* For master's, thesis; for doctorate, thesis/dissertation. *Entrance requirements:* For master's, honors degree in physics or engineering physics; for doctorate, M Sc or equivalent. Additional exam requirements/recommendations for international students: Required—TOEFL (minimum score 580 paper-based; 80 iBT), IELTS (minimum score 6.5). *Application deadline:* For fall admission, 5/15 for domestic and international students; for winter admission, 8/15 for domestic and international students. Application fee: $100. Electronic applications accepted. Tuition and fees charges are reported in Canadian dollars. *Expenses: Tuition, area resident:* Full-time $3942 Canadian dollars; part-time $219 Canadian dollars per credit hour. *International tuition:* $4742 Canadian dollars full-time. *Required fees:* $421.55 Canadian dollars; $93.60 Canadian dollars per credit hour. Tuition and fees vary according to course load, degree level and program. *Financial support:* In 2012–13, 1 fellowship (averaging $7,000 per year), 3 teaching assistantships (averaging $2,393 per year) were awarded; research assistantships, career-related internships or fieldwork, and scholarships/grants also available. Financial award application deadline: 6/15. *Faculty research:* Quantum mechanics, theoretical nuclear physics, quantum field theory, relativistic astrophysics and cosmology, classical electrodynamics. *Unit head:* Dr. Neil Ashton, Head, 306-585-4252, Fax: 306-585-5659, E-mail: neil.ashton@uregina.ca. *Application contact:* Dr. Zisis Papandreaou, Graduate Program Coordinator, 306-585-5379, Fax: 306-585-5659, E-mail: grad@phys.uregina.ca. Website: http://www.phys.uregina.ca.

University of Rhode Island, Graduate School, College of Arts and Sciences, Department of Physics, Kingston, RI 02881. Offers MS, PhD. Part-time and evening/weekend programs available. *Faculty:* 17 full-time (3 women). *Students:* 19 full-time (6 women), 3 part-time (0 women), includes 1 minority (Black or African American, non-Hispanic/Latino), 8 international. In 2012, 1 master's, 4 doctorates awarded. *Degree requirements:* For master's, comprehensive exam (for some programs), thesis optional; for doctorate, comprehensive exam, thesis/dissertation. *Entrance requirements:* For master's and doctorate, 2 letters of recommendation. Additional exam requirements/recommendations for international students: Required—TOEFL (minimum score 550 paper-based). *Application deadline:* For fall admission, 4/15 for domestic students, 2/1 for international students. Application fee: $65. Electronic applications accepted. *Expenses: Tuition,* state resident: full-time $11,532; part-time $641 per credit. Tuition, nonresident: full-time $23,606; part-time $1311 per credit. *Required fees:* $1388; $36 per credit. $35 per semester. One-time fee: $130. *Financial support:* In 2012–13, 1 research assistantship with full tuition reimbursement (averaging $15,344 per year), 16 teaching assistantships with full tuition reimbursements (averaging $15,515 per year) were awarded. Financial award application deadline: 3/1; financial award applicants required to submit FAFSA. *Total annual research expenditures:* $910,861. *Unit head:* Dr. Oleg Andreev, Chair, 401-874-2060, Fax: 401-874-2380, E-mail: andreev@mail.uri.edu. *Application contact:* Dr. Leonard M Kahn, Director of Graduate Studies, 401-874-2503, Fax: 401-874-2380, E-mail: lkahn@uri.edu. Website: http://www.phys.uri.edu/index.html.

University of Rochester, School of Arts and Sciences, Department of Physics and Astronomy, Rochester, NY 14627. Offers physics (MA, MS, PhD); physics and astronomy (PhD). Part-time programs available. Terminal master's awarded for partial completion of doctoral program. *Degree requirements:* For master's, comprehensive exam, thesis (for some programs); for doctorate, comprehensive exam, thesis/dissertation, qualifying exam. *Entrance requirements:* For master's and doctorate, GRE General Test. Additional exam requirements/recommendations for international students: Required—TOEFL. *Faculty research:* Astronomy and astrophysics, biological physics, condensed matter physics, high energy/nuclear physics, quantum optics.

University of Saskatchewan, College of Graduate Studies and Research, College of Arts and Science, Department of Physics and Engineering Physics, Saskatoon, SK S7N 5A2, Canada. Offers M Sc, PhD. *Degree requirements:* For master's, thesis; for doctorate, comprehensive exam (for some programs), thesis/dissertation. *Entrance requirements:* Additional exam requirements/recommendations for international students: Required—TOEFL (minimum score 80 iBT); Recommended—IELTS (minimum score 6.5). Electronic applications accepted.

University of South Carolina, The Graduate School, College of Arts and Sciences, Department of Physics and Astronomy, Columbia, SC 29208. Offers IMA, MAT, MS, PSM, PhD. IMA and MAT offered in cooperation with the College of Education. Part-time programs available. Terminal master's awarded for partial completion of doctoral program. *Degree requirements:* For master's, comprehensive exam, thesis; for doctorate, one foreign language, comprehensive exam, thesis/dissertation. *Entrance requirements:* For master's and doctorate, GRE General Test, GRE Subject Test. Additional exam requirements/recommendations for international students: Required—TOEFL (minimum score 570 paper-based; 75 iBT). Electronic applications accepted. *Faculty research:* Condensed matter, intermediate-energy nuclear physics, foundations of quantum mechanics, astronomy/astrophysics.

The University of South Dakota, Graduate School, College of Arts and Sciences, Department of Physics, Vermillion, SD 57069-2390. Offers MS, PhD. PhD program offered jointly with South Dakota School of Mines and Technology and South Dakota State University. *Entrance requirements:* For master's and doctorate, GRE.

University of Southern California, Graduate School, Dana and David Dornsife College of Letters, Arts and Sciences, Department of Physics and Astronomy, Los Angeles, CA 90089. Offers physics (MA, MS, PhD). Part-time programs available. Terminal master's awarded for partial completion of doctoral program. *Degree requirements:* For master's, comprehensive exam, thesis (for some programs); for doctorate, comprehensive exam, thesis/dissertation. *Entrance requirements:* For doctorate, GRE General Test, GRE Subject Test (physics), 3 letters of recommendation, statement of purpose. Additional exam requirements/recommendations for international students: Required—TOEFL (minimum score 550 paper-based; 80 iBT). Electronic applications accepted. *Faculty research:* High-energy particle theory, condensed matter physics, astrophysics, solar and cosmology, biophysics, computational physics.

University of Southern Mississippi, Graduate School, College of Science and Technology, Department of Physics and Astronomy, Hattiesburg, MS 39406-0001. Offers computational science (PhD); physics (MS). *Faculty:* 10 full-time (1 woman). *Students:* 10 full-time (2 women), 2 part-time (1 woman), 5 international. Average age 30. 47 applicants, 38% accepted, 3 enrolled. In 2012, 3 master's awarded. *Degree requirements:* For master's, comprehensive exam, thesis; for doctorate, comprehensive exam, thesis/dissertation. *Entrance requirements:* For master's, GRE General Test, minimum GPA of 2.75 in last 60 hours; for doctorate, GRE General Test, minimum GPA of 3.5. Additional exam requirements/recommendations for international students: Required—TOEFL, IELTS. *Application deadline:* For fall admission, 3/1 priority date for domestic students, 3/1 for international students; for spring admission, 1/10 priority date for domestic students, 1/10 for international students. Applications are processed on a rolling basis. Application fee: $50. *Financial support:* In 2012–13, research assistantships with full tuition reimbursements (averaging $11,800 per year), 15 teaching assistantships with full tuition reimbursements (averaging $11,800 per year) were awarded; Federal Work-Study, scholarships/grants, health care benefits, and unspecified assistantships also available. Financial award application deadline: 3/15; financial award applicants required to submit FAFSA. *Faculty research:* Polymers, atomic physics, fluid mechanics, liquid crystals, refractory materials. *Unit head:* Dr. Khin Maung, Chair, 601-266-4934, Fax: 601-266-5149. Website: http://www.usm.edu/graduateschool/table.php.

University of South Florida, Graduate School, College of Arts and Sciences, Department of Physics, Tampa, FL 33620-9951. Offers applied physics (PhD); physics (MS). Part-time programs available. *Degree requirements:* For master's, comprehensive exam, thesis optional; for doctorate, comprehensive exam, thesis/dissertation. *Entrance requirements:* For master's and doctorate, GRE, minimum GPA of 3.0, three letters of recommendation, statement of purpose. Additional exam requirements/recommendations for international students: Required—TOEFL (minimum score 550 paper-based; 79 iBT) or IELTS (minimum score 6.5). Electronic applications accepted. *Faculty research:* Biophysics and biomedical physics, atomic molecular and optical physics, solid state and materials physics, physics education.

The University of Tennessee, Graduate School, College of Arts and Sciences, Department of Physics and Astronomy, Knoxville, TN 37996. Offers physics (MS, PhD). Part-time programs available. *Degree requirements:* For master's, thesis or alternative; for doctorate, thesis/dissertation. *Entrance requirements:* For master's and doctorate, minimum GPA of 2.7. Additional exam requirements/recommendations for international students: Required—TOEFL. Electronic applications accepted. *Expenses:* Tuition, state resident: full-time $9000; part-time $501 per credit hour. Tuition, nonresident: full-time $27,188; part-time $1512 per credit hour. *Required fees:* $1280; $62 per credit hour. Tuition and fees vary according to program.

The University of Tennessee Space Institute, Graduate Programs, Program in Physics, Tullahoma, TN 37388-9700. Offers MS, PhD. *Degree requirements:* For master's, thesis (for some programs); for doctorate, one foreign language, thesis/dissertation. *Entrance requirements:* For master's and doctorate, GRE General Test, GRE Subject Test. Additional exam requirements/recommendations for international students: Required—TOEFL (minimum score 550 paper-based; 80 iBT), IELTS (minimum score 6.5). Electronic applications accepted.

The University of Texas at Arlington, Graduate School, College of Science, Department of Physics, Arlington, TX 76019-0059. Offers physics (MS); physics and applied physics (PhD). Part-time programs available. Terminal master's awarded for partial completion of doctoral program. *Degree requirements:* For master's, thesis optional; for doctorate, comprehensive exam, thesis/dissertation, internship or substitute. *Entrance requirements:* For master's, GRE General Test, minimum GPA of 3.0 in last 60 hours of course work; for doctorate, GRE General Test, minimum GPA of 3.0 in last 60 hours of course work, 30 hours graduate course work in physics. Additional exam requirements/recommendations for international students: Required—TOEFL (minimum score 550 paper-based; 79 iBT). *Faculty research:* Particle physics, astrophysics, condensed matter theory and experiment.

The University of Texas at Austin, Graduate School, College of Natural Sciences, Department of Physics, Austin, TX 78712-1111. Offers MA, MS, PhD. *Degree requirements:* For master's, thesis; for doctorate, thesis/dissertation.

Peterson's Graduate Programs in the Physical Sciences, Mathematics, Agricultural Sciences, the Environment & Natural Resources 2014

www.petersonsbooks.com **253**

Entrance requirements: For master's and doctorate, GRE General Test, GRE Subject Test (physics). Electronic applications accepted.

The University of Texas at Brownsville, Graduate Studies, College of Science, Mathematics and Technology, Brownsville, TX 78520-4991. Offers biological sciences (MS, MSIS); mathematics (MS); physics (MS). Part-time and evening/weekend programs available. Postbaccalaureate distance learning degree programs offered (no on-campus study). *Faculty:* 51 full-time (10 women). *Students:* 58 full-time (18 women), 48 part-time (24 women); includes 80 minority (1 Black or African American, non-Hispanic/Latino; 4 Asian, non-Hispanic/Latino; 69 Hispanic/Latino; 6 Native Hawaiian or other Pacific Islander, non-Hispanic/Latino), 1 international. 61 applicants, 52% accepted, 32 enrolled. In 2012, 20 master's awarded. *Degree requirements:* For master's, comprehensive exam (for some programs), thesis optional, project (for some programs). *Entrance requirements:* For master's, GRE General Test, letters of recommendation. Additional exam requirements/recommendations for international students: Required—TOEFL (minimum score 550 paper-based; 77 iBT). *Application deadline:* For fall admission, 7/1 priority date for domestic students, 7/1 for international students; for spring admission, 12/1 priority date for domestic students, 12/1 for international students. Applications are processed on a rolling basis. Application fee: $30. Electronic applications accepted. *Financial support:* In 2012–13, 2 research assistantships with partial tuition reimbursements (averaging $10,000 per year) were awarded; Federal Work-Study, scholarships/grants, tuition waivers (partial), and unspecified assistantships also available. Support available to part-time students. Financial award application deadline: 3/1; financial award applicants required to submit FAFSA. *Faculty research:* Fish, insects, barrier islands, algae. *Unit head:* Dr. Mikhail M. Bouniaev, Dean, 956-882-6701, Fax: 956-882-6657, E-mail: mikhail.bouniaev@utb.edu. *Application contact:* Mari Montelongo, Graduate Studies Specialist, 956-882-7787, Fax: 956-882-7279, E-mail: mari.montelongo@utb.edu. Website: http://www.utb.edu/vpaa/csmt/Pages/UTB-College-of-Science-Mathematics-and-Technology.aspx.

The University of Texas at Dallas, School of Natural Sciences and Mathematics, Department of Physics, Richardson, TX 75080. Offers MS, PhD. Part-time and evening/weekend programs available. *Faculty:* 18 full-time (1 woman), 2 part-time/adjunct (1 woman). *Students:* 57 full-time (10 women), 8 part-time (4 women); includes 2 minority (1 Black or African American, non-Hispanic/Latino; 1 Two or more races, non-Hispanic/Latino), 25 international. Average age 29. 78 applicants, 27% accepted, 14 enrolled. In 2012, 12 master's, 6 doctorates awarded. *Degree requirements:* For master's, thesis optional, industrial internship; for doctorate, thesis/dissertation, publishable paper. *Entrance requirements:* For master's and doctorate, GRE General Test, minimum GPA of 3.0 in upper-level coursework in field. Additional exam requirements/recommendations for international students: Required—TOEFL (minimum score 550 paper-based). *Application deadline:* For fall admission, 7/15 for domestic students, 5/1 for international students; for spring admission, 11/15 for domestic students, 9/1 for international students. Applications are processed on a rolling basis. Application fee: $50 ($100 for international students). Electronic applications accepted. *Expenses:* Tuition, state resident: full-time $11,940; part-time $663.33 per credit hour. Tuition, nonresident: full-time $21,606; part-time $1200.33 per credit hour. Tuition and fees vary according to course load. *Financial support:* In 2012–13, 48 students received support, including 30 research assistantships with partial tuition reimbursements available (averaging $21,333 per year), 23 teaching assistantships with partial tuition reimbursements available (averaging $15,522 per year); career-related internships or fieldwork, Federal Work-Study, institutionally sponsored loans, scholarships/grants, and unspecified assistantships also available. Support available to part-time students. Financial award application deadline: 4/30; financial award applicants required to submit FAFSA. *Faculty research:* Ionospheric and magnetospheric electrodynamics; high-energy proton collisions and muon detector design and construction; condensed matter physics with emphasis on nanoscience; optical properties of solids including semiconductors, thermoelectric materials and nanomaterials; gravitational lensing and applications to cosmology. *Unit head:* Dr. Robert Glosser, Department Head, 972-883-2876, Fax: 972-883-2848, E-mail: physweb@utdallas.edu. *Application contact:* Dr. Phil Anderson, Graduate Advisor, 972-883-2875, Fax: 972-883-2848, E-mail: phillip.anderson1@utdallas.edu. Website: http://www.utdallas.edu/physics/.

The University of Texas at El Paso, Graduate School, College of Science, Department of Physics, El Paso, TX 79968-0001. Offers MS. Part-time and evening/weekend programs available. *Degree requirements:* For master's, thesis optional. *Entrance requirements:* For master's, GRE, minimum GPA of 3.0. Additional exam requirements/recommendations for international students: Required—TOEFL; Recommended—IELTS. Electronic applications accepted.

The University of Texas at San Antonio, College of Sciences, Department of Physics and Astronomy, San Antonio, TX 78249-0617. Offers physics (MS, PhD). Part-time programs available. *Faculty:* 14 full-time (3 women), 14 part-time/adjunct (4 women). *Students:* 64 full-time (13 women), 16 part-time (4 women); includes 16 minority (1 Black or African American, non-Hispanic/Latino; 3 Asian, non-Hispanic/Latino; 11 Hispanic/Latino; 1 Two or more races, non-Hispanic/Latino), 33 international. Average age 30. 55 applicants, 73% accepted, 20 enrolled. In 2012, 3 master's, 3 doctorates awarded. Terminal master's awarded for partial completion of doctoral program. *Degree requirements:* For master's, comprehensive exam, thesis or alternative; for doctorate, comprehensive exam, thesis/dissertation or alternative. *Entrance requirements:* For master's, GRE, resume, two letters of recommendation, statement of purpose; for doctorate, GRE, minimum GPA of 3.0 on last 60 hours of undergraduate or graduate coursework, resume, two letters of recommendation, statement of purpose. Additional exam requirements/recommendations for international students: Required—TOEFL (minimum score 500 paper-based; 61 iBT), IELTS (minimum score 6.5). *Application deadline:* For fall admission, 7/1 for domestic students, 4/1 for international students; for spring admission, 11/1 for domestic students, 9/1 for international students. Application fee: $45 ($85 for international students). *Financial support:* In 2012–13, 32 students received support, including 20 fellowships with full and partial tuition reimbursements available (averaging $25,000 per year), 5 research assistantships with full and partial tuition reimbursements available (averaging $27,000 per year), 7 teaching assistantships with full tuition reimbursements available (averaging $27,000 per year); institutionally sponsored loans, scholarships/grants, and unspecified assistantships also available. *Faculty research:* Ultramicroscopy, computational physics, terahertz spectroscopy, space physics, biophysics, nanotechnology materials physics, astrophysics and cosmology, theoretical condensed matter and experimental condensed matter. *Total annual research expenditures:* $1.9 million. *Unit head:* Dr. Miguel Yacaman, Chair, 210-458-5451, Fax: 210-458-4919, E-mail: miguel.yacaman@utsa.edu. *Application contact:* Dr. Lorenzo Brancaleon, Graduate Advisor of Record, 210-458-5694, Fax: 210-458-5694, E-mail: lorenzo.brancaleon@utsa.edu.

The University of Toledo, College of Graduate Studies, College of Natural Sciences and Mathematics, Department of Physics and Astronomy, Toledo, OH 43606-3390. Offers photovoltaics (PSM); physics (MS, PhD), including astrophysics (PhD), materials science, medical physics (PhD); MS/PhD. *Faculty:* 35. *Students:* 60 full-time (12 women), 8 part-time (1 woman); includes 2 minority (1 Black or African American, non-Hispanic/Latino; 1 Asian, non-Hispanic/Latino), 30 international. Average age 28. 75 applicants, 49% accepted, 19 enrolled. In 2012, 2 master's, 6 doctorates awarded. *Degree requirements:* For master's, thesis; for doctorate, thesis/dissertation, departmental qualifying exam. *Entrance requirements:* For master's and doctorate, GRE General Test, GRE Subject Test, minimum cumulative point-hour ratio of 2.7 for all previous academic work, three letters of recommendation, statement of purpose, transcripts from all prior institutions attended. Additional exam requirements/recommendations for international students: Required—TOEFL (minimum score 550 paper-based; 80 iBT), IELTS (minimum score 6.5). *Application deadline:* For fall admission, 1/15 priority date for domestic students, 1/15 for international students. Applications are processed on a rolling basis. Application fee: $45 ($75 for international students). Electronic applications accepted. *Financial support:* In 2012–13, 39 research assistantships with full and partial tuition reimbursements (averaging $17,207 per year), 25 teaching assistantships with full and partial tuition reimbursements (averaging $15,130 per year) were awarded; Federal Work-Study, institutionally sponsored loans, scholarships/grants, tuition waivers (full), and unspecified assistantships also available. Support available to part-time students. *Faculty research:* Atomic physics, solid-state physics, materials science, astrophysics. *Unit head:* Dr. Lawrence Anderson-Huang, Chair, 419-530-7257, E-mail: lawrence.anderson@utoledo.edu. *Application contact:* Graduate School Office, 419-530-4723, Fax: 419-537-4724, E-mail: grdsch@utnet.utoledo.edu. Website: http://www.utoledo.edu/nsm/.

University of Toronto, School of Graduate Studies, Faculty of Arts and Science, Department of Physics, Toronto, ON M5S 1A1, Canada. Offers M Sc, PhD. *Degree requirements:* For master's, thesis optional; for doctorate, thesis/dissertation. *Entrance requirements:* For master's, minimum B+ average in an honors physics program or equivalent, 2 letters of reference; for doctorate, M Sc in physics or related field, 2 letters of reference. Additional exam requirements/recommendations for international students: Required—TOEFL (minimum score 580 paper-based; 93 iBT), TWE (minimum score 4). Electronic applications accepted.

University of Tulsa, Graduate School, College of Engineering and Natural Sciences, Department of Physics and Engineering Physics, Program in Physics, Tulsa, OK 74104-3189. Offers MS, PhD. Part-time programs available. *Faculty:* 7 full-time (0 women). *Students:* 8 full-time (2 women); includes 1 minority (American Indian or Alaska Native, non-Hispanic/Latino), 5 international. Average age 26. 13 applicants, 46% accepted, 3 enrolled. *Degree requirements:* For master's, thesis. *Entrance requirements:* For master's, GRE General Test. Additional exam requirements/recommendations for international students: Required—TOEFL (minimum score 550 paper-based; 80 iBT), IELTS (minimum score 6). *Application deadline:* Applications are processed on a rolling basis. Application fee: $40. Electronic applications accepted. *Expenses: Tuition:* Full-time $18,630. *Required fees:* $1340; $5 per credit hour. $75 per semester. Tuition and fees vary according to course load. *Financial support:* In 2012–13, 10 students received support, including 3 fellowships (averaging $1,125 per year), 6 research assistantships (averaging $9,996 per year), 3 teaching assistantships (averaging $8,389 per year); career-related internships or fieldwork, Federal Work-Study, scholarships/grants, health care benefits, tuition waivers, and unspecified assistantships also available. Support available to part-time students. Financial award application deadline: 2/1. *Faculty research:* Nanotechnology, theoretical plasma physics, theoretical and experimental condensed matter, optics, applications of laser spectroscopy to environmental applications. *Total annual research expenditures:* $656,124. *Unit head:* Dr. George Miller, Program Chair, 918-631-3021, Fax: 918-631-2995, E-mail: george-miller@utulsa.edu. *Application contact:* Dr. Scott Holmstrom, Advisor, 918-631-3031, Fax: 918-631-2995, E-mail: scott-holmstrom@utulsa.edu.

University of Utah, Graduate School, College of Science, Department of Physics and Astronomy, Salt Lake City, UT 84112. Offers chemical physics (PhD); medical physics (MS, PhD); physics (MA, MS, PhD); physics teaching (PhD). Part-time programs available. *Faculty:* 33 full-time (3 women), 3 part-time/adjunct (0 women). *Students:* 74 full-time (20 women), 17 part-time (4 women); includes 5 minority (4 Asian, non-Hispanic/Latino; 1 Hispanic/Latino), 45 international. Average age 29. 188 applicants, 14% accepted, 14 enrolled. In 2012, 9 master's, 11 doctorates awarded. Terminal master's awarded for partial completion of doctoral program. *Degree requirements:* For master's, comprehensive exam (for some programs), thesis or alternative, teaching experience, departmental exam; for doctorate, comprehensive exam, thesis/dissertation, departmental qualifying exam. *Entrance requirements:* For master's and doctorate, GRE General Test, GRE Subject Test, minimum GPA of 3.0. Additional exam requirements/recommendations for international students: Required—TOEFL (minimum score 500 paper-based; 69 iBT). *Application deadline:* For fall admission, 4/1 priority date for domestic students, 4/1 for international students. Applications are processed on a rolling basis. Application fee: $55 ($65 for international students). Electronic applications accepted. *Financial support:* In 2012–13, 41 research assistantships with full tuition reimbursements (averaging $23,500 per year); 31 teaching assistantships with full tuition reimbursements (averaging $20,641 per year) were awarded; Federal Work-Study, institutionally sponsored loans, and scholarships/grants also available. Financial award application deadline: 2/15; financial award applicants required to submit FAFSA. *Faculty research:* High-energy, cosmic-ray, astrophysics, medical physics, condensed matter, relativity applied physics, biophysics, astronomy. *Total annual research expenditures:* $6.8 million. *Unit head:* Dr. David Kieda, Chair, 801-581-6901, Fax: 801-581-4801, E-mail: kieda@physics.utah.edu. *Application contact:* Jackie Hadley, Graduate Secretary, 801-581-6861, Fax: 801-581-4801, E-mail: jackie@physics.utah.edu. Website: http://www.physics.utah.edu/.

University of Vermont, Graduate College, College of Arts and Sciences, Department of Physics, Burlington, VT 05405. Offers MS. *Students:* 3 (1 woman); includes 1 minority (Two or more races, non-Hispanic/Latino). 10 applicants, 40% accepted, 2 enrolled. In 2012, 2 master's awarded. *Entrance requirements:* For master's, GRE General Test. Additional exam requirements/recommendations for international students: Required—TOEFL (minimum score 550 paper-based; 80 iBT). *Application deadline:* For fall admission, 4/1 priority date for domestic students, 4/1 for international students. Applications are processed on a rolling basis. Application fee: $40. Electronic applications accepted. *Expenses: Tuition, area resident:* Part-time $572 per credit. Tuition, nonresident: part-time $1444 per credit. *Financial support:* Fellowships, research assistantships, and teaching assistantships available. Financial award application deadline: 3/1. *Unit head:* Dr. Dennis Clougherty, Chairperson, 802-656-2644. *Application contact:* Prof. Kevork Spartalian, Coordinator, 802-656-2644.

University of Victoria, Faculty of Graduate Studies, Faculty of Science, Department of Physics and Astronomy, Victoria, BC V8W 2Y2, Canada. Offers astronomy and astrophysics (M Sc, PhD); condensed matter physics (M Sc, PhD); experimental particle physics (M Sc, PhD); medical physics (M Sc, PhD); ocean physics (M Sc, PhD); theoretical physics (M Sc, PhD). *Degree requirements:* For master's, thesis; for doctorate, comprehensive exam, thesis/dissertation, candidacy exam. *Entrance requirements:* For master's and doctorate, GRE. Additional exam requirements/recommendations for international students: Required—TOEFL (minimum score 575 paper-based), IELTS (minimum score 7). Electronic applications accepted. *Faculty research:* Old stellar populations; observational cosmology and large scale structure; cp violation; atlas.

University of Virginia, College and Graduate School of Arts and Sciences, Department of Physics, Charlottesville, VA 22903. Offers physics (MA, MS, PhD); physics education (MA). *Faculty:* 33 full-time (4 women). *Students:* 89 full-time (19 women); includes 5 minority (4 Asian, non-Hispanic/Latino; 1 Two or more races, non-Hispanic/Latino), 65 international. Average age 26. 211 applicants, 41% accepted, 23 enrolled. In 2012, 27 master's, 10 doctorates awarded. *Degree requirements:* For master's, thesis (for some programs); for doctorate, comprehensive exam, thesis/dissertation. *Entrance requirements:* For master's and doctorate, GRE General Test, GRE Subject Test, 2 or more letters of recommendation. Additional exam requirements/recommendations for international students: Required—TOEFL (minimum score 600 paper-based; 90 iBT), IELTS. *Application deadline:* For fall admission, 1/7 for domestic and international students. Applications are processed on a rolling basis. Application fee: $60. Electronic applications accepted. *Expenses:* Tuition, state resident: full-time $13,278; part-time $717 per credit hour. Tuition, nonresident: full-time $22,602; part-time $1235 per credit hour. *Required fees:* $2384. *Financial support:* Fellowships, research assistantships, and teaching assistantships available. Financial award applicants required to submit FAFSA. *Unit head:* Joe Poon, Chair, 434-924-3781, Fax: 434-924-4576, E-mail: phys-chair@physics.virginia.edu. *Application contact:* Despina Louca, Associate Chair for Graduate Studies, 434-924-3781, Fax: 434-924-4576, E-mail: grad-info-request@physics.virginia.edu. Website: http://www.phys.virginia.edu/.

University of Washington, Graduate School, College of Arts and Sciences, Department of Physics, Seattle, WA 98195. Offers MS, PhD. Part-time and evening/weekend programs available. Terminal master's awarded for partial completion of doctoral program. *Degree requirements:* For doctorate, thesis/dissertation. *Entrance requirements:* For master's, GRE; for doctorate, GRE General Test, GRE Subject Test. Additional exam requirements/

recommendations for international students: Required—TOEFL. Electronic applications accepted. *Faculty research:* Astro-, atomic, condensed-matter, nuclear, and particle physics; physics education.

University of Waterloo, Graduate Studies, Faculty of Science, Guelph-Waterloo Physics Institute, Waterloo, ON N2L 3G1, Canada. Offers M Sc, PhD. M Sc, PhD offered jointly with University of Guelph. Part-time programs available. *Degree requirements:* For master's, project or thesis; for doctorate, thesis/dissertation. *Entrance requirements:* For master's, GRE Subject Test, honors degree, minimum B average; for doctorate, GRE Subject Test, master's degree, minimum B average. Additional exam requirements/recommendations for international students: Required—TOEFL, TWE. Electronic applications accepted. *Faculty research:* Condensed-matter and materials physics; industrial and applied physics; subatomic physics; astrophysics and gravitation; atomic, molecular, and optical physics.

The University of Western Ontario, Faculty of Graduate Studies, Physical Sciences Division, Department of Applied Mathematics, London, ON N6A 5B8, Canada. Offers applied mathematics (M Sc, PhD); theoretical physics (PhD). *Degree requirements:* For master's, thesis or alternative; for doctorate, comprehensive exam, thesis/dissertation. *Entrance requirements:* For master's and doctorate, minimum B average. Additional exam requirements/recommendations for international students: Required—TOEFL. *Faculty research:* Fluid dynamics, mathematical and computational methods, theoretical physics.

The University of Western Ontario, Faculty of Graduate Studies, Physical Sciences Division, Department of Physics and Astronomy, Program in Physics, London, ON N6A 5B8, Canada. Offers M Sc, PhD. Terminal master's awarded for partial completion of doctoral program. *Degree requirements:* For master's, thesis; for doctorate, comprehensive exam, thesis/dissertation. *Entrance requirements:* For master's, GRE Subject Test (physics), honors B Sc degree, minimum B average (Canadian), A- (international); for doctorate, minimum B average (Canadian), A- (international). Additional exam requirements/recommendations for international students. Required—TOEFL (minimum score 580 paper-based). *Faculty research:* Condensed-matter and surface science, space and atmospheric physics, atomic and molecular physics, medical physics, theoretical physics.

University of Windsor, Faculty of Graduate Studies, Faculty of Science, Department of Physics, Windsor, ON N9B 3P4, Canada. Offers M Sc, PhD. Part-time programs available. *Degree requirements:* For master's, thesis or alternative; for doctorate, thesis/dissertation. *Entrance requirements:* For master's, GRE General Test, minimum B average; for doctorate, GRE General Test, master's degree. Additional exam requirements/recommendations for international students: Required—TOEFL (minimum score 560 paper-based). Electronic applications accepted. *Faculty research:* Electrodynamics, plasma physics, atomic structure/particles, spectroscopy, quantum mechanics.

University of Wisconsin–Madison, Graduate School, College of Letters and Science, Department of Physics, Madison, WI 53706-1380. Offers MA, MS, PhD. Terminal master's awarded for partial completion of doctoral program. *Degree requirements:* For master's, qualifying exam, thesis (MS); for doctorate, thesis/dissertation, preliminary and qualifying exams. *Entrance requirements:* For master's and doctorate, GRE, minimum GPA of 3.0. Additional exam requirements/recommendations for international students: Required—TOEFL. Electronic applications accepted. *Expenses:* Tuition, state resident: full-time $10,728; part-time $743 per credit. Tuition, nonresident: full-time $24,054; part-time $1575 per credit. *Required fees:* $1111; $72 per credit. *Faculty research:* Atomic, physics, condensed matter, astrophysics, particles and fields.

University of Wisconsin–Milwaukee, Graduate School, College of Letters and Sciences, Department of Physics, Milwaukee, WI 53201-0413. Offers MS, PhD. *Faculty:* 19 full-time (2 women), 1 (woman) part-time/adjunct. *Students:* 36 full-time (10 women), 9 part-time (1 woman); includes 2 minority (1 Asian, non-Hispanic/Latino; 1 Two or more races, non-Hispanic/Latino), 23 international. Average age 29. 69 applicants, 20% accepted, 8 enrolled. In 2012, 2 master's, 3 doctorates awarded. *Degree requirements:* For master's, thesis or alternative; for doctorate, one foreign language, thesis/dissertation. *Entrance requirements:* For master's, GRE General Test, curriculum vitae; for doctorate, GRE General Test. Additional exam requirements/recommendations for international students: Required—TOEFL (minimum score 550 paper-based; 79 iBT), IELTS (minimum score 6.5). *Application deadline:* For fall admission, 1/1 priority date for domestic students; for spring admission, 9/1 for domestic students. Applications are processed on a rolling basis. Application fee: $56 ($96 for international students). Electronic applications accepted. *Financial support:* In 2012–13, 1 fellowship, 14 research assistantships, 20 teaching assistantships were awarded; career-related internships or fieldwork and unspecified assistantships also available. Support available to part-time students. Financial award application deadline: 4/15; financial award applicants required to submit FAFSA. *Faculty research:* Gravitation, biophysics, condensed matter, optics, medical. *Unit head:* Valerica Raicu, Department Chair, 414-229-4969, E-mail: vraicu@uwm.edu. *Application contact:* General Information Contact, 414-229-4982, Fax: 414-229-6967, E-mail: gradschool@uwm.edu. Website: http://www.uwm.edu/dept/physics/.

Utah State University, School of Graduate Studies, College of Science, Department of Physics, Logan, UT 84322. Offers MS, PhD. Part-time programs available. Terminal master's awarded for partial completion of doctoral program. *Degree requirements:* For master's, thesis; for doctorate, comprehensive exam,

Peterson's Graduate Programs in the Physical Sciences, Mathematics, Agricultural Sciences, the Environment & Natural Resources 2014

www.petersonsbooks.com **255**

thesis/dissertation. *Entrance requirements:* For master's and doctorate, GRE General Test, minimum GPA of 3.0. Additional exam requirements/ recommendations for international students: Required—TOEFL (minimum score 550 paper-based). Electronic applications accepted. *Faculty research:* Upper-atmosphere physics, relativity, gravitational magnetism, particle physics, nanotechnology.

Vanderbilt University, Graduate School, Department of Physics and Astronomy, Nashville, TN 37240-1001. Offers astronomy (MS); health physics (MA); physics (MAT, MS, PhD). *Faculty:* 33 full-time (4 women). *Students:* 78 full-time (21 women), 1 part-time (0 women); includes 12 minority (5 Black or African American, non-Hispanic/Latino; 1 Asian, non-Hispanic/Latino; 4 Hispanic/Latino; 2 Two or more races, non-Hispanic/Latino), 24 international. Average age 28. 199 applicants, 17% accepted, 12 enrolled. In 2012, 7 master's, 7 doctorates awarded. *Degree requirements:* For master's, thesis; for doctorate, comprehensive exam, thesis/dissertation, final and qualifying exams. *Entrance requirements:* For master's, GRE General Test; for doctorate, GRE General Test, GRE Subject Test. Additional exam requirements/recommendations for international students: Required—TOEFL (minimum score 570 paper-based; 88 iBT). *Application deadline:* For fall admission, 1/15 for domestic and international students. Electronic applications accepted. *Financial support:* Fellowships with full and partial tuition reimbursements, research assistantships with full tuition reimbursements, teaching assistantships with full tuition reimbursements, career-related internships or fieldwork, Federal Work-Study, and institutionally sponsored loans available. Financial award application deadline: 1/15; financial award applicants required to submit CSS PROFILE or FAFSA. *Faculty research:* Experimental and theoretical physics, free electron laser, living-state physics, heavy-ion physics, nuclear structure. *Unit head:* Dr. Julia Velkovska, Director of Graduate Studies, 615-322-0656, Fax: 615-343-7263, E-mail: julia.velkovska@vanderbilt.edu. *Application contact:* Donald Pickert, Administrative Assistant, 615-343-1026, Fax: 615-343-7263, E-mail: donald.pickert@vanderbilt.edu. Website: http://www.vanderbilt.edu/physics/.

Virginia Commonwealth University, Graduate School, College of Humanities and Sciences, Department of Physics, Program in Physics and Applied Physics, Richmond, VA 23284-9005. Offers MS. *Entrance requirements:* For master's, GRE. Additional exam requirements/recommendations for international students: Required—TOEFL (minimum score 600 paper-based; 100 iBT); Recommended—IELTS (minimum score 6.5). Electronic applications accepted. *Faculty research:* Theoretical and experimental condensed matter physics, general relativity and cosmology, physics education.

Virginia Polytechnic Institute and State University, Graduate School, College of Science, Blacksburg, VA 24061. Offers biological sciences (MS, PhD); biomedical technology development and management (MS); chemistry (MS, PhD); economics (MA, PhD); geosciences (MS, PhD); mathematics (MS, PhD); physics (MS, PhD); psychology (MS, PhD); statistics (MS, PhD). *Faculty:* 259 full-time (68 women), 3 part-time/adjunct (all women). *Students:* 555 full-time (230 women), 31 part-time (12 women); includes 44 minority (10 Black or African American, non-Hispanic/Latino; 1 American Indian or Alaska Native, non-Hispanic/Latino; 11 Asian, non-Hispanic/Latino; 14 Hispanic/Latino; 8 Two or more races, non-Hispanic/Latino), 250 international. Average age 28. 1,091 applicants, 24% accepted, 137 enrolled. In 2012, 65 master's, 89 doctorates awarded. *Median time to degree:* Of those who began their doctoral program in fall 2004, 68% received their degree in 8 years or less. *Degree requirements:* For master's, comprehensive exam (for some programs), thesis (for some programs); for doctorate, comprehensive exam (for some programs), thesis/dissertation (for some programs). *Entrance requirements:* For master's and doctorate, GRE/ GMAT (may vary by department). Additional exam requirements/ recommendations for international students: Required—TOEFL (minimum score 550 paper-based). *Application deadline:* For fall admission, 8/1 for domestic students, 4/1 for international students; for spring admission, 1/1 for domestic students, 9/1 for international students. Applications are processed on a rolling basis. Application fee: $65. Electronic applications accepted. *Expenses:* Tuition, state resident: full-time $10,677; part-time $593.25 per credit hour. Tuition, nonresident: full-time $20,926; part-time $1162.50 per credit hour. *Required fees:* $427.75 per semester. Tuition and fees vary according to course load, campus/ location and program. *Financial support:* In 2012–13, 1 fellowship with full tuition reimbursement (averaging $21,606 per year), 159 research assistantships with full tuition reimbursements (averaging $19,950 per year), 331 teaching assistantships with full tuition reimbursements (averaging $17,426 per year) were awarded. Financial award application deadline: 3/1; financial award applicants required to submit FAFSA. *Total annual research expenditures:* $23.4 million. *Unit head:* Dr. Lay Nam Chang, Dean, 540-231-5422, Fax: 540-231-3380, E-mail: laynam@vt.edu. *Application contact:* Diane Stearns, Assistant to the Dean, 540-231-7515, Fax: 540-231-3380, E-mail: dstearns@vt.edu. Website: http://www.science.vt.edu/.

Virginia State University, School of Graduate Studies, Research, and Outreach, School of Engineering, Science and Technology, Department of Chemistry and Physics, Petersburg, VA 23806-0001. Offers physics (MS). *Degree requirements:* For master's, one foreign language, thesis. *Entrance requirements:* For master's, GRE General Test.

Wake Forest University, Graduate School of Arts and Sciences, Department of Physics, Winston-Salem, NC 27109. Offers MS, PhD. Part-time programs available. *Degree requirements:* For master's, thesis; for doctorate, comprehensive exam, thesis/dissertation. *Entrance requirements:* For master's and doctorate, GRE General Test. Additional exam requirements/ recommendations for international students: Required—TOEFL (minimum score 79 iBT). Electronic applications accepted.

Washington State University, Graduate School, College of Arts and Sciences, Department of Physics and Astronomy, Pullman, WA 99164-2814. Offers physics (MS, PhD), including astrophysics (PhD), extreme matter (PhD), materials and optics (PhD). *Faculty:* 18 full-time (2 women), 2 part-time/adjunct (1 woman). *Students:* 68 full-time (16 women), 5 part-time (2 women); includes 1 minority (Hispanic/Latino), 30 international. Average age 29. 89 applicants, 45% accepted, 17 enrolled. In 2012, 9 master's, 6 doctorates awarded. Terminal master's awarded for partial completion of doctoral program. *Degree requirements:* For master's, comprehensive exam (for some programs), thesis optional, oral exam; for doctorate, comprehensive exam, thesis/dissertation, oral exam, written exam. *Entrance requirements:* For master's and doctorate, GRE General Test, GRE Subject Test (recommended), minimum GPA of 3.0 in last half of undergraduate work completed. Additional exam requirements/recommendations for international students: Required—TOEFL (minimum score 550 paper-based; 80 iBT), IELTS. *Application deadline:* For fall admission, 3/1 priority date for domestic students, 3/ 1 for international students; for spring admission, 11/1 for domestic and international students. Applications are processed on a rolling basis. Application fee: $75. Electronic applications accepted. *Financial support:* In 2012–13, 67 students received support, including 1 fellowship with full and partial tuition reimbursement available (averaging $18,000 per year), 15 research assistantships with full and partial tuition reimbursements available (averaging $16,169 per year), 25 teaching assistantships with full and partial tuition reimbursements available (averaging $15,075 per year); Federal Work-Study, institutionally sponsored loans, scholarships/grants, health care benefits, and unspecified assistantships also available. Financial award application deadline: 2/ 1; financial award applicants required to submit FAFSA. *Faculty research:* Linear and nonlinear acoustics and optics, shock wave dynamics, solid-state physics, surface physics, high-pressure and semiconductor physics. *Total annual research expenditures:* $3.1 million. *Unit head:* Matthew D. McCluskey, Chair, 509-335-5356, Fax: 509-335-7816, E-mail: mattmcc@wsu.edu. *Application contact:* Graduate School Admissions, 800-GRADWSU, Fax: 509-335-1949, E-mail: gradsch@wsu.edu. Website: http://www.physics.wsu.edu/.

Washington University in St. Louis, Graduate School of Arts and Sciences, Department of Physics, St. Louis, MO 63130-4899. Offers PhD. Terminal master's awarded for partial completion of doctoral program. *Degree requirements:* For doctorate, thesis/dissertation. *Entrance requirements:* For doctorate, GRE General Test. Electronic applications accepted.

Wayne State University, College of Liberal Arts and Sciences, Department of Physics and Astronomy, Detroit, MI 48202. Offers physics (MA, MS, PhD). *Students:* 56 full-time (14 women), 6 part-time (2 women); includes 7 minority (3 Black or African American, non-Hispanic/Latino; 1 American Indian or Alaska Native, non-Hispanic/Latino; 2 Asian, non-Hispanic/Latino; 1 Hispanic/Latino), 33 international. Average age 29. 88 applicants, 17% accepted, 10 enrolled. In 2012, 7 master's, 10 doctorates awarded. *Degree requirements:* For master's, comprehensive exam (for some programs), thesis (for some programs); for doctorate, thesis/dissertation. *Entrance requirements:* For master's and doctorate, GRE General Test; GRE Subject Test in physics (recommended), bachelor's degree from recognized college or university, completion of general college physics with laboratory, fifteen credits in intermediate physics courses. Additional exam requirements/recommendations for international students: Required—TOEFL (minimum score 550 paper-based; 79 iBT); Recommended—TWE (minimum score 5.5). *Application deadline:* For fall admission, 1/15 for domestic and international students; for winter admission, 10/1 for domestic students, 9/1 for international students; for spring admission, 2/1 for domestic students, 1/1 for international students. Applications are processed on a rolling basis. Application fee: $50. Electronic applications accepted. *Expenses:* Tuition, state resident: full-time $12,788; part-time $532.85 per credit hour. Tuition, nonresident: full-time $28,243; part-time $1176.80 per credit hour. *Required fees:* $1367.30; $39.75 per credit hour. $206.65 per semester. Tuition and fees vary according to course load and program. *Financial support:* In 2012–13, 56 students received support, including 5 fellowships with tuition reimbursements available (averaging $13,632 per year), 26 research assistantships with tuition reimbursements available (averaging $18,193 per year), 25 teaching assistantships with tuition reimbursements available (averaging $17,391 per year); Federal Work-Study, scholarships/grants, health care benefits, and unspecified assistantships also available. Financial award application deadline: 1/15; financial award applicants required to submit FAFSA. *Faculty research:* High energy particle physics, relativistic heavy ion physics, theoretical physics, positron and atomic physics, condensed matter and nano-scale physics. *Total annual research expenditures:* $3.1 million. *Unit head:* Dr. Ratna Naik, Chair, 313-577-2721, Fax: 313-577-3932, E-mail: ad5847@wayne.edu. *Application contact:* Dr. Ashis Mukhopadhay, Chair of the Physics Graduate Admissions Committee, 313-577-2775, Fax: 313-577-3932, E-mail: ar8678@wayne.edu. Website: http://physics.clas.wayne.edu/.

Wesleyan University, Graduate Studies, Department of Physics, Middletown, CT 06459. Offers PhD. Terminal master's awarded for partial completion of doctoral program. *Degree requirements:* For doctorate, thesis/dissertation. *Entrance requirements:* For doctorate, GRE General and Subject Tests (recommended). Additional exam requirements/recommendations for international students: Required—TOEFL (minimum score 550 paper-based; 80 iBT). *Application deadline:* Applications are processed on a rolling basis. Application fee: $0.

Electronic applications accepted. *Financial support:* Fellowships, institutionally sponsored loans, and tuition waivers (full) available. Financial award application deadline: 4/15; financial award applicants required to submit FAFSA. *Faculty research:* Biophysics, computational soft matter physics, mesoscopic transport, semiclassical methods and quantum chaos, disordered systems, theoretical atomic physics, low-temperature physics, magnetic resonance, atomic collisions, laser spectroscopy, surface physics, turbulence, granular media. *Unit head:* Brian Stewart, Chair, 860-685-2054, E-mail: bstewart@wesleyan.edu. Website: http://www.wesleyan.edu/physics/.

Western Illinois University, School of Graduate Studies, College of Arts and Sciences, Department of Physics, Macomb, IL 61455-1390. Offers MS. Part-time programs available. *Students:* 31 full-time (7 women); includes 1 minority (Two or more races, non-Hispanic/Latino), 29 international. Average age 30. In 2012, 6 master's awarded. *Degree requirements:* For master's, thesis or alternative. *Entrance requirements:* Additional exam requirements/recommendations for international students: Required—TOEFL (minimum score 550 paper-based; 80, iBT). *Application deadline:* Applications are processed on a rolling basis. Application fee: $30. Electronic applications accepted. *Financial support:* In 2012–13, 12 students received support, including 12 research assistantships with full tuition reimbursements available (averaging $7,544 per year); health care benefits also available. Financial award applicants required to submit FAFSA. *Unit head:* Dr. Mark Boley, Interim Chairperson, 309-298-1538. *Application contact:* Dr. Nancy Parsons, Interim Associate Provost and Director of Graduate Studies, 309-298-1806, Fax: 309-298-2345, E-mail: grad-office@wiu.edu. Website: http://wiu.edu/physics.

Western Kentucky University, Graduate Studies, Ogden College of Science and Engineering, Department of Physics and Astronomy, Bowling Green, KY 42101. Offers homeland security sciences (MS); physics (MA Ed).

Western Michigan University, Graduate College, College of Arts and Sciences, Department of Physics, Kalamazoo, MI 49008. Offers MA, PhD. *Degree requirements:* For master's, thesis; for doctorate, thesis/dissertation, oral exam. *Entrance requirements:* For doctorate, GRE General Test.

Western Michigan University, Graduate College, College of Arts and Sciences, Mallinson Institute for Science Education, Kalamazoo, MI 49008. Offers science education (MA, PhD); science education: biological sciences (PhD); science education: chemistry (PhD); science education: geosciences (PhD); science education: physical geography (PhD); science education: physics (PhD). *Degree requirements:* For doctorate, thesis/dissertation, oral and written exams. *Entrance requirements:* For master's, undergraduate degree in a science or science education, teacher certification (or appropriate education courses); for doctorate, GRE General Test, master's degree in a science or science education. Additional exam requirements/recommendations for international students: Recommended—TOEFL. Electronic applications accepted. *Faculty research:* History and philosophy of science, curriculum and instruction, science content learning, college science teaching and learning, social and cultural factors in science education.

West Virginia University, Eberly College of Arts and Sciences, Department of Physics, Morgantown, WV 26506. Offers applied physics (MS, PhD); astrophysics (MS, PhD); chemical physics (MS, PhD); condensed matter physics (MS, PhD); elementary particle physics (MS, PhD); materials physics (MS, PhD); plasma physics (MS, PhD); solid state physics (MS, PhD); statistical physics (MS, PhD);

theoretical physics (MS, PhD). Terminal master's awarded for partial completion of doctoral program. *Degree requirements:* For master's, thesis or alternative, qualifying exam; for doctorate, thesis/dissertation, qualifying exam. *Entrance requirements:* For master's and doctorate, GRE General Test, minimum GPA of 3.0. Additional exam requirements/recommendations for international students: Required—TOEFL. *Faculty research:* Experimental and theoretical condensed-matter, plasma, high-energy theory, nonlinear dynamics, space physics.

Worcester Polytechnic Institute, Graduate Studies and Research, Department of Physics, Worcester, MA 01609-2280. Offers physics (MS, PhD); physics for educators (MS). *Faculty:* 10 full-time (2 women), 1 part-time/adjunct (0 women). *Students:* 19 full-time (7 women), 4 part-time (3 women); includes 2 minority (1 Black or African American, non-Hispanic/Latino; 1 Hispanic/Latino), 6 international. 34 applicants, 35% accepted, 7 enrolled. In 2012, 7 master's, 3 doctorates awarded. *Degree requirements:* For master's, thesis; for doctorate, comprehensive exam, thesis/dissertation. *Entrance requirements:* For master's, GRE (recommended), 3 letters of recommendation; for doctorate, GRE (recommended), 3 letters of recommendation, statement of purpose (recommended). Additional exam requirements/recommendations for international students: Required—TOEFL (minimum score 563 paper-based; 84 iBT), IELTS (minimum score 7). *Application deadline:* For fall admission, 1/1 priority date for domestic students, 1/1 for international students; for spring admission, 10/1 priority date for domestic students, 10/1 for international students. Applications are processed on a rolling basis. Application fee: $70. Electronic applications accepted. *Financial support:* Research assistantships, teaching assistantships, career-related internships or fieldwork, institutionally sponsored loans, scholarships/grants, and unspecified assistantships available. Financial award application deadline: 1/1; financial award applicants required to submit FAFSA. *Faculty research:* Soft-condensed matter, complex fluids, bio- and medical physics, quantum and atom optics, wave function engineering, mechanical properties of nanostructures, or nanomechanics. *Unit head:* Dr. Germano S. Iannacchione, Head, 508-831-5258, Fax: 508-831-5886, E-mail: gsiannac@wpi.edu. *Application contact:* Dr. I. R. Ram-Mohan, Graduate Coordinator, 508-831-5258, Fax: 508-831-5886, E-mail: lrram@wpi.edu. Website: http://www.wpi.edu/Academics/Depts/Physics/.

Wright State University, School of Graduate Studies, College of Science and Mathematics, Department of Physics, Program in Physics, Dayton, OH 45435. Offers geophysics (MS); medical physics (MS). Part-time and evening/weekend programs available. *Degree requirements:* For master's, thesis. *Entrance requirements:* Additional exam requirements/recommendations for international students: Required—TOEFL. *Faculty research:* Solid-state physics, optics, geophysics.

Yale University, Graduate School of Arts and Sciences, Department of Physics, New Haven, CT 06520. Offers PhD. *Degree requirements:* For doctorate, thesis/dissertation. *Entrance requirements:* For doctorate, GRE General Test, GRE Subject Test.

York University, Faculty of Graduate Studies, Faculty of Science and Engineering, Program in Physics and Astronomy, Toronto, ON M3J 1P3, Canada. Offers M Sc, PhD. Part-time and evening/weekend programs available. *Degree requirements:* For master's, thesis or alternative; for doctorate, comprehensive exam, thesis/dissertation. Electronic applications accepted.

Plasma Physics

Princeton University, Graduate School, Department of Astrophysical Sciences, Program in Plasma Physics, Princeton, NJ 08544-1019. Offers PhD. *Degree requirements:* For doctorate, thesis/dissertation. *Entrance requirements:* For doctorate, GRE General Test, GRE Subject Test. Additional exam requirements/recommendations for international students: Required—TOEFL (minimum score 600 paper-based). *Faculty research:* Magnetic fusion energy research, plasma physics, x-ray laser studies.

University of Colorado Boulder, Graduate School, College of Arts and Sciences, Department of Astrophysical and Planetary Sciences, Boulder, CO 80309. Offers astrophysics (MS, PhD); planetary science (MS, PhD). *Faculty:* 22 full-time (3 women). *Students:* 53 full-time (13 women); includes 3 minority (1 Black or African American, non-Hispanic/Latino; 1 American Indian or Alaska Native, non-Hispanic/Latino; 1 Asian, non-Hispanic/Latino), 5 international. Average age 26. 175 applicants, 21% accepted, 11 enrolled. Terminal master's awarded for partial completion of doctoral program. *Degree requirements:* For master's, comprehensive exam, thesis or alternative; for doctorate, one foreign language, thesis/dissertation. *Entrance requirements:* For master's, GRE General Test, GRE Subject Test, minimum undergraduate GPA of 3.0; for doctorate, GRE General Test, GRE Subject Test. *Application deadline:* For fall admission, 1/15 priority date for domestic students, 12/1 for international students. Applications are processed on a rolling basis. Application fee: $50 ($60 for international students). Electronic applications accepted. *Financial support:* In 2012–13, 23

fellowships (averaging $13,475 per year), 31 research assistantships with full and partial tuition reimbursements (averaging $25,396 per year), 15 teaching assistantships with full and partial tuition reimbursements (averaging $23,435 per year) were awarded; institutionally sponsored loans, scholarships/grants, health care benefits, and unspecified assistantships also available. Financial award application deadline: 1/15; financial award applicants required to submit FAFSA. *Faculty research:* Astrophysics, astronomy, galaxies: stellar systems, infrared/optical astronomy, spectroscopy. *Total annual research expenditures:* $40 million. *Application contact:* E-mail: apsgradsec@colorado.edu. Website: http://aps.colorado.edu/.

West Virginia University, Eberly College of Arts and Sciences, Department of Physics, Morgantown, WV 26506. Offers applied physics (MS, PhD); astrophysics (MS, PhD); chemical physics (MS, PhD); condensed matter physics (MS, PhD); elementary particle physics (MS, PhD); materials physics (MS, PhD); plasma physics (MS, PhD); solid state physics (MS, PhD); statistical physics (MS, PhD); theoretical physics (MS, PhD). Terminal master's awarded for partial completion of doctoral program. *Degree requirements:* For master's, thesis or alternative, qualifying exam; for doctorate, thesis/dissertation, qualifying exam. *Entrance requirements:* For master's and doctorate, GRE General Test, minimum GPA of 3.0. Additional exam requirements/recommendations for international students: Required—TOEFL. *Faculty research:* Experimental and theoretical condensed-matter, plasma, high-energy theory, nonlinear dynamics, space physics.

Peterson's Graduate Programs in the Physical Sciences, Mathematics, Agricultural Sciences, the Environment & Natural Resources 2014

www.petersonsbooks.com **257**

Theoretical Physics

American University of Beirut, Graduate Programs, Faculty of Arts and Sciences, Beirut, Lebanon. Offers anthropology (MA); Arab and Middle Eastern history (PhD); Arabic language and literature (MA, PhD); archaeology (MA); biology (MS); cell and molecular biology (PhD); chemistry (MS); clinical psychology (MA); computational science (MS); computer science (MS); economics (MA); education (MA); English language (MA); English literature (MA); environmental policy planning (MSES); financial economics (MAFE); general psychology (MA); geology (MS); history (MA); mathematics (MA, MS); media studies (MA); Middle Eastern studies (MA); philosophy (MA); physics (MS); political studies (MA); public administration (MA); sociology (MA); statistics (MA, MS); theoretical physics (PhD); transnational American studies (MA). Part-time programs available. *Faculty:* 238 full-time (80 women), 7 part-time/adjunct (3 women). *Students:* 253 full-time (169 women), 139 part-time (105 women). Average age 26. 306 applicants, 47% accepted, 90 enrolled. In 2012, 126 degrees awarded. *Degree requirements:* For master's, one foreign language, comprehensive exam, thesis (for some programs); for doctorate, one foreign language, comprehensive exam, thesis/dissertation. *Entrance requirements:* For master's, GRE, letter of recommendation; for doctorate, GRE, letters of recommendation. Additional exam requirements/recommendations for international students: Required—TOEFL (minimum score 600 paper-based; 97 iBT), IELTS (minimum score 7). *Application deadline:* For fall admission, 4/30 for domestic students, 4/18 for international students; for spring admission, 11/1 for domestic and international students. Application fee: $50. *Expenses: Tuition:* Full-time $13,896; part-time $772 per credit. *Financial support:* In 2012–13, 20 students received support. Career-related internships or fieldwork, institutionally sponsored loans, scholarships/grants, health care benefits, and unspecified assistantships available. Financial award application deadline: 2/4; financial award applicants required to submit FAFSA. *Faculty research:* Modern Middle East history; Near Eastern archaeology; Islamic history; European history; software engineering; scientific computing; data mining; the applications of cooperative learning in language teaching and teacher education; world/comparative literature; rhetoric and composition; creative writing; public management; public policy and international affairs; hydrogeology; mineralogy, petrology, and geochemistry; tectonics and structural geology; cell and molecular biology; ecology. *Unit head:* Dr. Patrick McGreevy, Dean, 961-1374374 Ext. 3800, Fax: 961-1744461, E-mail: pm07@aub.edu.lb. *Application contact:* Dr. Salim Kanaan, Director, Admissions Office, 961-1-350000 Ext. 2594, Fax: 961-1750775, E-mail: sk00@aub.edu.lb. Website: http://staff.aub.edu.lb/~webfas.

Cornell University, Graduate School, Graduate Fields of Arts and Sciences, Field of Physics, Ithaca, NY 14853-0001. Offers experimental physics (MS, PhD); physics (MS, PhD); theoretical physics (MS, PhD). *Faculty:* 56 full-time (6 women). *Students:* 166 full-time (29 women); includes 13 minority (1 Black or African American, non-Hispanic/Latino; 6 Asian, non-Hispanic/Latino; 4 Hispanic/Latino; 2 Two or more races, non-Hispanic/Latino), 75 international. Average age 26. 467 applicants, 20% accepted, 32 enrolled. In 2012, 23 master's, 21 doctorates awarded. *Degree requirements:* For doctorate, comprehensive exam, thesis/dissertation. *Entrance requirements:* For doctorate, GRE General Test, GRE Subject Test (physics), 3 letters of recommendation. Additional exam requirements/recommendations for international students: Required—TOEFL (minimum score 620 paper-based; 105 iBT). *Application deadline:* For fall admission, 1/3 for domestic students. Application fee: $95. Electronic applications accepted. *Financial support:* In 2012–13, 157 students received support, including 43 fellowships with full tuition reimbursements available, 56 research assistantships with full tuition reimbursements available, 58 teaching assistantships with full tuition reimbursements available; institutionally sponsored loans, scholarships/grants, health care benefits, tuition waivers (full and partial), and unspecified assistantships also available. Financial award applicants required to submit FAFSA. *Faculty research:* Experimental condensed matter physics, theoretical condensed matter physics, experimental high energy particle physics, theoretical particle physics and field theory, theoretical astrophysics. *Unit head:* Director of Graduate Studies, 607-255-7561. *Application contact:* Graduate Field Assistant, 607-255-7561, E-mail: physics-grad-adm@cornell.edu. Website: http://www.gradschool.cornell.edu/fields.php?id-36&a-2.

Delaware State University, Graduate Programs, Department of Mathematics, Interdisciplinary Program in Applied Mathematics and Theoretical Physics, Dover, DE 19901-2277. Offers PhD. *Degree requirements:* For doctorate, one foreign language, thesis defense. *Entrance requirements:* For doctorate, GRE General Test, MS degree in physics or mathematics. Additional exam requirements/recommendations for international students: Required—TOEFL (minimum score 550 paper-based).

Emory University, Laney Graduate School, Department of Physics, Atlanta, GA 30322-1100. Offers biophysics (PhD); experimental condensed matter physics (PhD); theoretical and computational statistical physics (PhD); MS/PhD. *Faculty:* 11 full-time (2 women), 1 part-time/adjunct (0 women). *Students:* 30 full-time (12 women); includes 2 minority (1 Black or African American, non-Hispanic/Latino; 1 Asian, non-Hispanic/Latino), 20 international. Average age 26. 51 applicants, 35% accepted, 4 enrolled. In 2012, 3 doctorates awarded. *Degree requirements:* For doctorate, thesis/dissertation, qualifier proposal. *Entrance requirements:* For doctorate, GRE General Test, minimum GPA of 3.0. Additional exam requirements/recommendations for international students: Required—TOEFL (minimum score 600 paper-based). *Application deadline:* For fall admission, 1/3 priority date for domestic students, 1/3 for international students. Application fee: $75. Electronic applications accepted. *Financial support:* Fellowships, teaching assistantships, institutionally sponsored loans, scholarships/grants, health care benefits, and tuition waivers (full) available. Financial award application deadline: 1/3; financial award applicants required to submit FAFSA. *Faculty research:* Experimental studies of the structure and function of metalloproteins, soft condensed matter, granular materials, biophotonics and fluorescence correlation spectroscopy, single molecule studies of DNA-protein systems. *Unit head:* Prof. Eric Weeks, Chair, 404-727-4479, Fax: 404-727-0873, E-mail: erweeks@emory.edu. *Application contact:* Prof. Stefan Boettcher, Director of Graduate Studies, 404-727-4298, Fax: 404-727-0873, E-mail: sboettc@emory.edu. Website: http://www.physics.emory.edu.

Harvard University, Graduate School of Arts and Sciences, Department of Physics, Cambridge, MA 02138. Offers experimental physics (PhD); medical engineering/medical physics (PhD), including applied physics, engineering sciences, physics; theoretical physics (PhD). *Degree requirements:* For doctorate, thesis/dissertation, final exams, laboratory experience. *Entrance requirements:* For doctorate, GRE General Test, GRE Subject Test. Additional exam requirements/recommendations for international students: Required—TOEFL. *Expenses: Tuition:* Full-time $37,576. *Required fees:* $930. Tuition and fees vary according to program and student level. *Faculty research:* Particle physics, condensed matter physics, atomic physics.

Rutgers, The State University of New Jersey, New Brunswick, Graduate School-New Brunswick, Department of Physics and Astronomy, Piscataway, NJ 08854-8097. Offers astronomy (MS, PhD); biophysics (PhD); condensed matter physics (MS, PhD); elementary particle physics (MS, PhD); intermediate energy nuclear physics (MS); nuclear physics (MS, PhD); physics (MST); surface science (PhD); theoretical physics (MS, PhD). Part-time programs available. Terminal master's awarded for partial completion of doctoral program. *Degree requirements:* For master's, comprehensive exam, thesis or alternative; for doctorate, comprehensive exam, thesis/dissertation. *Entrance requirements:* For master's and doctorate, GRE General Test, GRE Subject Test. Additional exam requirements/recommendations for international students: Required—TOEFL (minimum score 560 paper-based). Electronic applications accepted. *Faculty research:* Astronomy, high energy, condensed matter, surface, nuclear physics.

The University of Manchester, School of Physics and Astronomy, Manchester, United Kingdom. Offers astronomy and astrophysics (M Sc, PhD); biological physics (M Sc, PhD); condensed matter physics (M Sc, PhD); nonlinear and liquid crystals physics (M Sc, PhD); nuclear physics (M Sc, PhD); particle physics (M Sc, PhD); photon physics (M Sc, PhD); physics (M Sc, PhD); theoretical physics (M Sc, PhD).

University of Victoria, Faculty of Graduate Studies, Faculty of Science, Department of Physics and Astronomy, Victoria, BC V8W 2Y2, Canada. Offers astronomy and astrophysics (M Sc, PhD); condensed matter physics (M Sc, PhD); experimental particle physics (M Sc, PhD); medical physics (M Sc, PhD); ocean physics (M Sc, PhD); theoretical physics (M Sc, PhD). *Degree requirements:* For master's, thesis; for doctorate, comprehensive exam, thesis/dissertation, candidacy exam. *Entrance requirements:* For master's and doctorate, GRE. Additional exam requirements/recommendations for international students: Required—TOEFL (minimum score 575 paper-based), IELTS (minimum score 7). Electronic applications accepted. *Faculty research:* Old stellar populations; observational cosmology and large scale structure; cp violation; atlas.

West Virginia University, Eberly College of Arts and Sciences, Department of Physics, Morgantown, WV 26506. Offers applied physics (MS, PhD); astrophysics (MS, PhD); chemical physics (MS, PhD); condensed matter physics (MS, PhD); elementary particle physics (MS, PhD); materials physics (MS, PhD); plasma physics (MS, PhD); solid state physics (MS, PhD); statistical physics (MS, PhD); theoretical physics (MS, PhD). Terminal master's awarded for partial completion of doctoral program. *Degree requirements:* For master's, thesis or alternative, qualifying exam; for doctorate, thesis/dissertation, qualifying exam. *Entrance requirements:* For master's and doctorate, GRE General Test, minimum GPA of 3.0. Additional exam requirements/recommendations for international students: Required—TOEFL. *Faculty research:* Experimental and theoretical condensed-matter, plasma, high-energy theory, nonlinear dynamics, space physics.

258 www.petersonsbooks.com

Peterson's Graduate Programs in the Physical Sciences, Mathematics, Agricultural Sciences, the Environment & Natural Resources 2014

OHIO UNIVERSITY
Department of Physics and Astronomy

Programs of Study

The Department of Physics and Astronomy offers graduate study and research programs leading to the Master of Arts, Master of Science, and Doctor of Philosophy degrees. The program of study emphasizes individual needs and interests in addition to essential general requirements of the discipline. Major areas of current research are experimental and theoretical condensed-matter and surface physics, nanoscience, mathematical and computational physics, biological physics, astronomy and astrophysics.

At the end of a student's first year of graduate study, his or her suitability to continue toward the Ph.D. is evaluated by the full faculty. This evaluation is based primarily on the student's GPA in the core courses. The courses in the second year cover more advanced topics. Master's degrees require completion of 30 graduate credits in physics and have both thesis and nonthesis options.

Prospective students can listen to what current students have to say about the program on the Department of Physics and Astronomy's YouTube page at http://www.youtube.com/OhioUPhysics.

Research Facilities

The physics department occupies two wings of Clippinger Laboratories, a modern, well-equipped research building; the Edwards Accelerator Building, which contains Ohio University's 4.5-MV high-intensity tandem Van de Graaff accelerator; and the Surface Science Research Laboratory, which is isolated from mechanical and electrical disturbances. Specialized facilities for measuring structural, thermal, transport, optical, and magnetic properties of condensed matter are available. In addition to research computers in laboratories, students have access to a Beowulf cluster and the Ohio Supercomputer Center, where massively parallel systems are located. Ohio University is a partner in the MDM Observatory at Kitt Peak, Arizona, which provides guaranteed access to major research telescopes.

Financial Aid

Financial aid is available in the form of teaching assistantships (TAs) and research assistantships (RAs). All cover the full cost of tuition plus a stipend from which a semester fee of $696 must be paid by the student. The current stipend level for TAs and RAs is $22,639 per year. TAs require approximately 15 to 20 hours per week of laboratory and/or teaching duties.

Cost of Study

Tuition and fees are $4,722 per semester for Ohio residents and $8,718 per semester for out-of-state students. Students on TA or RA support receive full tuition waivers. Students not otherwise covered by health insurance must pay a $1,370 annual premium for student health insurance.

Living and Housing Costs

On-campus rooms for single students start at $2,807 per semester. A number of off-campus apartments and rooms are available at various costs.

Student Group

About 21,724 students study on the main campus of the University, and 4,204 of these are graduate students. The graduate student enrollment in the physics department ranges from 70 to 80 students.

Location

Athens is a city of about 25,000, situated in the rolling Appalachian foothills of southeastern Ohio. The surrounding landscape consists of wooded hills rising about the Hocking River valley, and the area offers many outdoor recreational opportunities. Eight state parks lie within easy driving distance of the campus and are popular spots for relaxation. The outstanding intellectual and cultural activities sponsored by this diverse university community are pleasantly blended in Athens with a vibrant tradition in the visual and performing arts.

The University and The Department

Ohio University, founded in 1804 and the oldest institution of higher education in the Northwest Territory, is a comprehensive university with a wide range of graduate and undergraduate programs. The Ph.D. program in physics began in 1959, and more than 250 doctoral degrees have been awarded. Currently, the Department has 25 regular faculty members and additional part-time faculty and postdoctoral fellows. Sponsored research in the Department amounts to approximately $4.13 million per year and comes from NSF, DOE, NASA, and the state of Ohio. Further information can be found at the Department's home page (http://www.phy.ohiou.edu).

Applying

Online application procedures and downloadable forms can be found at http://www.ohio.edu/graduate/apply.cfm. Information can also be obtained by e-mailing the Department of Physics and Astronomy at gradapp@helios.phy.ohiou.edu.

Correspondence and Information

Graduate Admissions Chair
Department of Physics and Astronomy
Ohio University
Athens, Ohio 45701
Phone: 740-593-1718
E-mail: gradapp@helios.phy.ohio.edu
Website: http://www.phy.ohiou.edu

THE FACULTY AND THEIR RESEARCH

Professors

Carl R. Brune, Ph.D., Caltech, 1994. Experimental nuclear astrophysics.

David A. Drabold, Distinguished Professor; Ph.D., Washington (St. Louis), 1989. Theoretical condensed matter, computational methodology for electronic structure, theory of topologically disordered materials.

Charlotte Elster, Dr.rer.nat., Bonn, 1986. Nuclear and intermediate-energy theory.

Peterson's Graduate Programs in the Physical Sciences, Mathematics, Agricultural Sciences, the Environment & Natural Resources 2014

www.petersonsbooks.com **259**

Ohio University

Alexander O. Govorov, Ph.D., Novosibirsk (Russia), 1991. Theoretical condensed-matter physics, nanoscience.

Steven M. Grimes, Distinguished Professor, Emeritus; Ph.D., Wisconsin–Madison, 1968. Nuclear physics.

Kenneth H. Hicks, Ph.D., Colorado, 1984. Nuclear and intermediate-energy physics.

Saw-Wai Hla, Ph.D., Ljubljana (Slovenia), 1997. Experimental condensed-matter and surface physics, nanoscience.

David C. Ingram, Ph.D., Chair of the Department; Salford (England), 1980. Atomic collisions in solids, thin films, deposition and analysis, surface physics.

Peter Jung, Distinguished Professor; Ph.D., Ulm (Germany), 1985. Nonequilibrium statistical physics, nonlinear stochastic processes, pattern formation, biophysics.

Martin E. Kordesch, Ph.D., Case Western Reserve, 1984. Surface physics, wide-gap materials.

Daniel Phillips, Ph.D., Flinders (Australia), 1995. Theoretical nuclear and particle physics.

M. Prakash, Ph.D., Bombay, 1979. Theoretical nuclear and particle astrophysics.

Joseph C. Shields, Ph.D., Berkeley, 1991. Astrophysics, interstellar medium, active galactic nuclei.

Arthur Smith, Ph.D., Texas at Austin, 1995. Experimental semiconductors, thin film.

Thomas S. Statler, Ph.D., Princeton, 1986. Astrophysics, galactic structure and dynamics.

Sergio E. Ulloa, Ph.D., SUNY at Buffalo, 1984. Theoretical condensed-matter physics.

Associate Professors

Horacio E. Castillo, Ph.D., Illinois, 1998. Theoretical condensed-matter physics.

Gang Chen, Ph.D., Lehigh, 2004. Experimental condensed-matter physics.

Douglas Clowe, Ph.D., Hawaii, 1998. Observational astrophysics.

Mark Lucas, Ph.D., Illinois, 1994. Experimental nuclear physics, physics education.

Alexander Neiman, Ph.D., Saratov State (Russia), 1991. Biophysics, nonlinear dynamics, stochastic processes.

Julie Roche, Ph.D., Un. B. Pascal (France), 1998. Nuclear and intermediate-energy physics.

Nancy Sandler, Ph.D., Illinois, 1998. Theoretical condensed-matter physics.

Eric Stinaff, Ph.D., Iowa State, 2002. Experimental nanoscience.

David F. J. Tees, Ph.D., McGill, 1996. Experimental biophysics, nanoscience.

Assistant Professors

Justin Frantz, Ph.D., Columbia, 2005. Experimental nuclear physics.

THEORETICAL RESEARCH ACTIVITIES

Astrophysics. Studies of galaxies and galaxy clusters, with emphasis on galaxy structure, dynamics, and interactions; dark matter and dark energy; quasars and supermassive black holes in galaxy nuclei; high-energy astrophysics related to accretion onto compact objects, relativistic jets, and gamma-ray bursts; asteroids and solar system dynamics. Investigations into these topics employ multiwavelength observations with major facilities (Hubble Space Telescope, Chandra X-ray Observatory, MDM Observatory at Kitt Peak, Arizona) as well as theoretical efforts, including analytic calculations and large-scale numerical simulations.

Biophysics. Computational modeling of complex cellular signaling networks, especially intracellular and intercellular calcium signaling, modeling of neural and glial functions in healthy and epileptic tissue, stochastic modeling of electroreceptors in paddle fish, modeling of the neuronal circuitry of the cat's retina, stochastic and coherence resonance in excitable biologic systems, nanoscale ion channel and receptor clusters, and modeling slow axonal transport.

Condensed-Matter Theory. Statistical mechanics and nonequilibrium dynamics of disordered systems and glassy materials. Some areas of interest include nanoscale-sized dynamical heterogeneities in glassy materials, slow activation-controlled motion of topological defects (e.g., vortices, dislocations), and disordered electronic systems; methodology

of first principles simulation: development of local basis density functional methods, time-dependent density functional theory and efficient computation of Wannier functions, and the single-particle-density matrix; theory of disordered insulators: Anderson transition, photo-structural response, novel schemes for structural modeling of glasses, and studies of pressure-induced polyamorphism; and optical and transport phenomena in nanoscale systems, including quantum dots, rings, and channels. Recent activity covers excitons in quantum rings, spin transport in nanocrystals, and quantum acoustoelectric interactions on nanoscale. Other nanoscience problems of interest include electronic transport in complex molecule systems, the role of controlled disorder on the metallic or insulating nature of one- and two-dimensional systems, and the role of collective effects on the optical and transport properties of quantum dot arrays and studies of low-dimensional strongly correlated electron systems, disordered electronic systems, and quantum-Hall-effect physics.

Mathematical and Computational Physics. Quantum simulation, ab initio calculations, and visualization of many-body and few-body systems in condensed-matter and nuclear physics; numerical methods and algorithmic development for high-performance vector and parallel computers; analytical and algorithmic studies in differential and integral equations, probability theory, and series expansions.

Nuclear/Particle Physics and Astrophysics. Research in theoretical nuclear/particle physics at Ohio University focuses on the dynamics of the matter that makes up the atomic nucleus, and examines manifestations of these dynamics in systems ranging in size from a single proton to a neutron star. Researchers combine data from laboratory experiments, astronomical observations, and theoretical studies in order to examine the role of the fundamental forces of nature within these systems. Current topics of interest include models of the nucleon-nucleon force; structure of light nuclei, especially as probed in proton, electron, and photon scattering; proton and neutron structure; reactions on exotic nuclei; relativistic heavy-ion collisions; physics and astrophysics of neutron stars and supernovae; and gravitational waves.

EXPERIMENTAL RESEARCH ACTIVITIES

Astrophysics. Spectroscopic observations of stellar motions and stellar populations in elliptical galaxies and evidence for dark matter, ionized gas in galaxies, gravitational lensing studies of galaxy clusters, nuclear physics applied to astrophysics.

Biological Physics. Stochastic resonance in psychophysics and animal behavior, studies of stochastic nonlinear dynamics in paddlefish electroreceptors, experimental determination of the response of single-cell-adhesion molecules to applied forces using a microcantilever device, lipid bilayer tether pulling on leukocytes and platelets using micropipette aspiration, studies of cell adhesion in pressure gradients in micropipettes, determination of cell membrane mechanical properties, optical studies of biomolecules at the single-molecule level using total internal reflection fluorescence microscopy and fluorescence resonance energy transfer, biomineralization, studies of ice-modifying antifreeze proteins, studies of DNA-protein interactions using optical methods.

Condensed-Matter and Surface Science. Current projects encompass various areas in nanoscale science; scanning-probe techniques; and synthesis and characterization of photonic, composite, and electronic materials. Relevant projects are illustrated by the following list: thin-film growth (by molecular-beam epitaxy) and characterization (using scanning-probe microscopy techniques, including spin-polarized) of the structural, electronic, and magnetic properties of transition-metal nitride layers and magnetic-doped nitride semiconductors; single-atom/molecule manipulation using ultrahigh-vacuum, low-temperature scanning-tunneling microscopy; development of single-molecule electronics; molecular and metal thin films; surface science; electron microscopy of nanoscale structures; amorphous semiconductors and their photonics and electronic properties; MeV ion-beam analysis of materials and measurement of relevant cross-sections; ion-beam and plasma deposition of materials and their characterization; effect of hydrogen and nitrogen to the properties of amorphous carbon; optical spectroscopy and ultrafast laser studies of semiconductor nanostructures and nanostructure-based devices; optical spin manipulation and nanophotonics of individual and coupled nanostructures; growth of semiconducting chalcogenide nanowires for nonvolatile electric memory; synthesis of periodic mesoporous materials through a self-assembly approach; atomic and nanoscale structure characterization by X-ray absorption, fine structure, and small/wide angle X-ray scattering; and study of transparent conductive oxides, low work function surfaces, and thermionic cathodes.

Nuclear and Intermediate-Energy Physics. Contemporary research in experimental nuclear physics involves collaboration with scientists from many different institutions and heavy use of specialized accelerator facilities around the world. Ohio University nuclear physicists are recognized leaders in a variety of experimental programs spanning a broad energy domain. At higher energies, Ohio University's faculty members are leading research programs at Jefferson Laboratory in Virginia. These include the study of electromagnetic production of strange baryons and the search for new

260 www.petersonsbooks.com

Peterson's Graduate Programs in the Physical Sciences, Mathematics, Agricultural Sciences, the Environment & Natural Resources 2014

exotic baryons in Hall B, precision measurements of the weak charge of the proton in Hall C, and the study of the nature of the gluonic flux tube in Hall D; an active program studying the photoexcitation of the nucleon is also ongoing at the SPring-8 experiment in Japan. At lower energies, faculty members are directing research programs in several distinct areas, including fundamental symmetries in nuclear reactions via precision tests of charge symmetry breaking at TRIUMF in Canada, exotic nuclei far from the line of stability at GANIL and the Hahn-Meitner Institute in Europe, measurements of neutron cross sections at Los Alamos in New Mexico, studies of nuclear level densities at the Holifield Radioactive Ion Beam Facility in Tennessee, and studies of pion photoproduction and QCD sum rules with the LEGS facility at Brookhaven National Laboratory in New York. The Department also operates the high-intensity Ohio University Tandem Van de Graaff accelerator with its unique beam swinger magnet and long flight path for high-precision measurements of various nuclear cross sections and projects in medical physics. The research program is supported by the Ohio University Institute for Nuclear and Particle Physics. Grants are provided by the U.S. National Science Foundation and the U.S. Department of Energy.

SELECTED PUBLICATIONS

Azuma, R. F., et al (**C. R. Brune**). AZURE: An R matrix code for nuclear astrophysics. *Phys. Rev. C* 81(4):045805, 2010.

Tang, X. D., et al. (**C. R. Brune**). Determination of the $E1$ component of the low-energy $^{12}C(\alpha,\gamma)^{16}O$ cross section. *Phys. Rev. C* 81(4):045809, 2010.

Boyd, Richard, Lee Bernstein, and **C. R. Brune.** Studying nuclear astrophysics at NIF. *Phys. Today* 62(6):60–61, 2009.

Parsaeian, A., and **H. E. Castillo.** Equilibrium and nonequilibrium fluctuations in a glass-forming liquid. *Phys. Rev. Lett.* 102(5):055704, 2009.

Castillo, H. E. Time reparametrization symmetry in spin-glass models. *Phys. Rev. B.* 78(21):214430, 2008.

Castillo, H. E., and A. Parsaeian. Local fluctuations in the ageing of a simple structural glass. *Nat. Phys.* 3(1):26–28, 2007.

Yan, Y., **G. Chen,** and P. G. Van Patten. Ultrafast exciton dynamics in CdTe nanocrystals and CdTe/CdS core/shell nanocrystals, *J. Phys. Chem. C.* 115(46):22717–28, 2011.

Chen, G. in *X-ray Scattering.* New York: Nova Science Publishers, 2011.

Hall, N., et al. (**D. Clowe**). Using the bullet cluster as a gravitational telescope to study z >~ 7 Lyman break galaxies. *Astrophys. J.* 745(2):id155, 2012.

Ragozzine, B., et al. (**D. Clowe**). Weak-lensing results for the merging cluster A1758. *Astrophys. J.* 744(2):id94, 2012.

Gennou, L., et al. (**D. Clowe**). Intracluster light in clusters of galaxies at redshifts 0.4 < z < 0.8. *Astron. Astrophys.* 537:idA64, 2012.

Zhang, M., and **D. A. Drabold.** Approximate theory of temperature coefficient of resistivity and conductivity for amorphous semiconductors. *Phys. Rev. B* 85:125135, 2012.

Prasai, B., and **D. A. Drabold.** Ab initio simulation of solid electrolyte materials in liquid and glassy phases. *Phys. Rev. B* 83(9):094202, 2011.

Cliffe, M., M. T. Dove, **D. A. Drabold,** and **A. L. Goodwin.** Structure determination of disordered materials from diffraction data. *Phys. Rev. Lett.* 104:125501, 2010.

Weppner, S. P. and **Ch. Elster.** Elastic Scattering of 6He based on a cluster description. *Phys. Rev. C* 85:044617, 2012.

Skibinski, R., et al. (**Ch. Elster**). Recent developments of a three-dimensional description of the NN system. *Few Body Syst.* 50:279–81, 2011.

Polyzou, W. et al. (**Ch. Elster**). Mini review of Poincaré invariant quantum theory. *Few Body Syst.* 49:129–47, 2011.

Kuzyk, A., et al. (**A. O. Govorov**). DNA-based self-assembly of chiral plasmonic nanostructures with tailored optical response. *Nature* 483:311–14, 2012.

Türeci H., et al. (**A. Govorov**). Many-body dynamics of exciton creation in a quantum dot by optical absorption: A quantum quench towards Kondo correlations. *Phys. Rev. Lett.* 106:107402, 2011.

Hicks, K. H. On the conundrum of the pentaquark. *Eur. Phys. J. H* February, 2012.

Hwang, S. H., and **K. Hicks** et al. Spin-density matrix elements for $\gamma p \rightarrow K^*0\Sigma+$ at $E\gamma$=1.85–3.0 GeV with evidence for the $\kappa(800)$ meson exchange. *Phys. Rev. Lett.* 108:092001, 2012.

Daniel, A., and **K. Hicks** et al. Measurement of the nuclear multiplicity ratio for K0 hadronization at CLAS. *Phys. Lett. B* 706:26–31, 2011.

Serrate, D., et al. (**S.-W. Hla**). Imaging and manipulating the spin direction of individual atoms. *Nature Nanotechnology* 5(5):350–3, 2010.

Clark, K., et al. (**S.-W. Hla**). Superconductivity in just four pairs of (BETS)$_2$-GaCl$_4$ molecules. *Nature Nanotechnology* 5(4):261–5, 2010.

Newkome, G., et al. (**S.-W. Hla**). Nanoassembly of a fractal polymer: A molecular "Sierpinski hexagonal gasket". *Science* 312:1782–85, 2006.

Pak, J., et al. (**D. C. Ingram**). Growth of expitaxial iron nitride ultrathin film on zinc-blende gallium nitride. *J. Vac. Sci. Tech.* 28(4):536, 2010.

Jadwisienczak, W., et al. (**D. C. Ingram**). Optical properties, luminescence quenching mechanism and radiation hardness of Eu-doped GaN red powder phosphor. *Radiat. Meas.* 45(3-6):500–02, 2010.

Kayani, A., et al. (**D. C. Ingram**). Effect of bias and hydrogenation on the elemental concentration and the thermal stability of amorphous thin carbon films, deposited on Si substrate. *Diam. Relat. Mater.* 18(11):1333–37, 2009.

Lunderberg, E., et.al. (**S. M. Grimes**). Evidence for the ground-state resonance of 26O. *Phys. Rev. Lett.* 108(14):2503, 2012.

Grimes, S. M., and T. N. Massey. Novel investigation of iron cross sections via spherical shell transmission measurements and particle transport calculations for material embrittlement studies. *Nucl. Sci. Eng.* 170:207–33, 2012.

Voinov, A., et al. (**S. M. Grimes**). g-strength functions in 60Ni from two-step cascades following proton capture. *Phys. Rev. C* 81:024319, 2010.

Li, Y., **P. Jung** and A. Brown. Axonal transport of neurofilaments: A single population of intermittently moving polymers. *J. Neurosci.* 32(2):746–58, 2012.

Sun, L., et al. (**P. Jung**). Endoplasmic reticulum remodeling tunes IP3-dependent Ca^{2+} release sensitivity. *PLoS One* 6(11):e27928, 2011.

Swaminathan, D., and **P. Jung.** The role of agonist-independent conformational transformation (AICT) in IP3 cluster behavior. *Cell Calcium* 49(3):145–52, 2011.

Masson, E., et al. (**M. Kordesch**). "Supramolecular circuitry": Three chemiluminescent, cucurbit[7]uril-controlled on/off switches. *Org. Lett.* 13(15):3872–5, 2011.

Vaughn, J. M., et al. (**M. Kordesch**). Thermionic electron emission microscopy of metal-oxide multilayers on tungsten. *IBM Journal of Research and Development* 55(4):421–6, 2011.

Kordesch, M. E., et al. Model scandate cathodes investigated by thermionic-emission microscopy. *J. Vac. Sci. Tech. B,* 29(4):04E102–7, 2011.

Blanpied, G., et al. (**M. Lucas**). The N $\rightarrow \Delta$ transition from simultaneous measurements of p(γ,π^+) and p(γ,γ). *Phys. Rev. Lett.* 79:4337, 1997.

Feldman, G., et al. (**M. Lucas**). Compton scattering, meson-exchange, and the polarizabilities of bound nucleons. *Phys. Rev. C: Nucl. Phys.* 54:2124, 1996.

Neiman, A. B., and D. F. Russell. Sensory coding in oscillatory electroreceptors of paddlefish. *Chaos* 21:047505, 2011.

Neiman, A. B., et al. Spontaneous voltage oscillations and response dynamics of a Hodgkin-Huxley type model of sensory hair cells. *J. Math. Neurosci.* 1:11, 2011.

Neiman, A. B., D. F. Russell, and M. H. Rowe. Identifying temporal codes in spontaneously active sensory neurons. *PLoS One* 6(11):e27380, 2011.

Griesshammer, H. W., J. A. McGovern, **D. R. Phillips,** and G. Feldman. Using effective field theory to analyse low-energy Compton scattering data from protons and light nuclei. *Prog. Part. Nucl. Phys.* doi.org/10.1016/j.ppnp.2012.04.003, 2012.

Ji, C., **D. R. Phillips,** and L. Platter. The three-boson system at next-to-leading order in an effective field theory for systems with a large scattering length. *Ann. Phys.* 327(7):1803–24, 2012.

Baru, V., et al. (**D. R. Phillips**). Precision calculation of threshold pi^-d scattering, pi N scattering lengths, and the GMO sum rule. *Nucl. Phys. A*872:69–116, 2011.

Androic, D., et al. (**J. Roche**) (G0 Collaboration). The G0 experiment: Apparatus for parity-violating electron scattering measurements at forward and backward angles. *Nuclear Instruments and Methods in Physics Research Section A: Accelerators, Spectrometers, Detectors and Associated Equipment* 646(1):59–86, 2011.

Fuchey, E., et al. (**J. Roche**) Exclusive neutral pion electroproduction in the deeply virtual regime. *Phys. Rev. C* 83(2):025201, 2011.

Androic, D., et al. (**J. Roche**) (G0 Collaboration). Strange quark contributions to parity-violating asymmetries in the backward angle G0 electron scattering experiment. *Phys. Rev. Lett.* 104(1):012001, 2010.

Wong, A., et. Al. (**N. Sandler**). Signatures of quantum phase transitions in parallel quantum dots: Crossover from local moment to underscreened spin-1 Kondo physics. *Phys. Rev. B* 85:115316–22, 2012.

Peterson's Graduate Programs in the Physical Sciences, Mathematics, Agricultural Sciences, the Environment & Natural Resources 2014

www.petersonsbooks.com **261**

Zarea, M., **S. E. Ulloa,** and **N. Sandler.** Enhancement of Kondo effect through Rashba spin-orbit interactions. *Phys. Rev. Lett.* 108:04660–4, 2012.

Zarea, M. and **N. Sandler.** Graphene zigzag ribbons, square lattice models and quantum spin chains. *New J. Phys.* 11:095014, 2009.

Schmidt, K. B., et al. **(J. C. Shields).** The color variability of quasars. *Astrophys. J.* 744:147, 2012.

Capellupo, D. M., et al. **(J. C. Shields).** Variability in quasar broad absorption line outflows - I. Trends in the short-term versus long-term data. *Mon. Not. Roy. Astron. Soc.* 413:908, 2012.

Wang, K.,and **A. R. Smith.** Three-dimensional spin mapping of antiferromagnetic nanopyramids having spatially alternating surface anisotropy at room temperature. *Nano Letters*, 2012. doi.org/10.1021/nl204192n.

Chinchore, A., et al. **(A. R. Smith).** Spontaneous formation of quantum height manganese gallium islands and atomic chains on N-polar gallium nitride(000-1). *Appl. Phys. Lett.* 100:061602, 2012.

Wang, K., et al. **(A. R. Smith).** A modular designed ultra-high-vacuum spin-polarized scanning tunneling microscope with controllable magnetic fields for investigating epitaxial thin films. *Rev. Sci. Instrum.* 82(5):053703, 2011.

Statler, T. S. Extreme sensitivity of the YORP effect to small-scale topography. *Icarus* 202(2):502–13, 2009.

Diehl, S., and **T. S. Statler.** The hot interstellar medium in normal elliptical galaxies. III. The thermal structure of the gas. *Astrophys. J.* 687(2):986–96, 2008.

Diehl, S., and **T. S. Statler.** The hot interstellar medium in normal elliptical galaxies. II. Morphological evidence for AGN feedback. *Astrophys. J.* 680(2):897–910, 2008.

Rolon, J. E., et al. **(S. E. Ulloa** and **E. A. Stinaff).** Oscillatory acoustic phonon relaxation of excitons in quantum dot molecules. *J. Opt. Soc. Am. B* 29(2):A146–53, 2012.

Wijesundara, K. C., et al. **(E. A. Stinaff).** Tunable exciton relaxation in vertically coupled semiconductor InAs quantum dots. *Phys. Rev. B* 84(8):081404(R), 2011.

Garrido, M., et al. **(E. A. Stinaff).** Electric field control of a quantum dot molecule through optical excitation. *Appl. Phys. Lett.* 96(21):211115, 2010.

Pai, A., P. Sundd, and **D. F. J. Tees.** In situ microrheological determination of neutrophil stiffening following adhesion in a model capillary. *Ann. Biomed. Eng.* 36:596–603, 2008.

Sundd, P., X. Zou, D.J. Goetz, and **D. F. J. Tees.** Leukocyte adhesion in capillary-sized, P-selectin-coated micropipettes. *Microcirculation* 15:109–22, 2008.

Tees, D. F. J., R. E. Waugh, and D. A. Hammer. A microcantilever device to assess the effect of force on the lifetime of selectin-carbohydrate bonds. *Biophys. J.* 80:668–82, 2001.

Diniz, G. S., A. Latgé, and **S. E. Ulloa.** Helicoidal fields and spin polarized currents in carbon nanotube–DNA hybrids. *Phys. Rev. Lett.* 108:126601, 2012.

Wong, A., et al. **(N. Sandler** and **S. E. Ulloa).** Signatures of quantum phase transitions in parallel quantum dots: Crossover from local moment to underscreened spin-1 Kondo physics. *Phys. Rev. B* 85:115316, 2012.

Ngo, A. T., J. Rodriguez-Laguna, **S. E. Ulloa,** and E. H. Kim. Quantum manipulation via atomic-scale magnetoelectric effects. *Nano Letters* 12:13–16, 2012.

262 www.petersonsbooks.com

Peterson's Graduate Programs in the Physical Sciences, Mathematics, Agricultural Sciences, the Environment & Natural Resources 2014

UNIVERSITY OF PITTSBURGH
Department of Physics and Astronomy

Programs of Study

The graduate programs in the Department of Physics and Astronomy are designed primarily for students who wish to obtain the Ph.D. degree, although the M.S. degree is also offered. The Ph.D. program provides high-quality training for students without needlessly emphasizing formal requirements. Upon arrival, each graduate student is appointed a faculty adviser to provide personalized guidance through the core curriculum. A set of basic courses is to be taken by all graduate students unless the equivalent material has been demonstrably mastered in other ways. These basic courses include mathematical methods, dynamical systems, quantum mechanics, electromagnetic theory, and statistical physics and thermodynamics. More advanced and special-topics courses are offered in a range of areas, including, but not limited to, condensed-matter, statistical, solid-state, and biological physics; high-energy and particle physics; nanoscience; astrophysics; cosmology; particle astrophysics; relativity; and astronomical techniques.

Students have a wide variety of programs from which to choose a thesis topic. University faculty members have active research programs in astrophysics/cosmology, condensed matter physics, particle physics, and physics education research. Topics in astrophysics/cosmology include: observational, numerical, and theoretical cosmology; dark matter and dark energy; galaxies; active galactic nuclei and quasars; galactic and intergalactic medium; stellar atmospheres and massive stars; supernovae; and physics of the early universe. Topics in condensed matter physics include: biological physics; nanoscience; quantum information; quantum kinetics; quantum optics; quantum states of matter; semiconductor physics; soft condensed matter physics; statistical physics; superconductivity and superfluidity; and ultrafast optics. Topics in particle physics include: the origin of mass and flavor; the search for new symmetries of nature; neutrino physics; CP violation; heavy quarks; leptoquarks; supersymmetry; extra dimensions; baryogenesis; effective field theory; and strongly interacting field theory. Topics in physics education research include: cognitive issues in learning physics; and development and evaluation of research-based curricula for introductory and advanced physics courses. Multidisciplinary thesis research may also be carried out in, for example, particle astrophysics, biophysics, chemical physics, laser physics, materials science, nanoscience, and surface science. This research may be done in cooperation with faculty from other departments of the University.

Interdisciplinary research programs may be arranged on a case-by-case basis. There have been physics doctorates awarded for work done in collaboration with faculty members in the Department of Biological Sciences, the Department of Chemistry, the Department of Mathematics, the Department of Mechanical Engineering and Materials Science, the Departments of Electrical and Chemical Engineering, the Department of Computational Biology, the Department of Radiological Sciences, and the Department of Radiology in the School of Medicine, among others.

Research Facilities

The Department of Physics and Astronomy includes three professionally staffed shops (a machine shop, electronics shop, and glass-blowing shop). Departmental students have access to the local facilities and expertise available at the Peterson Institute of NanoScience and Engineering (PINSE) and its Nanoscale Fabrication and Characterization Facility (NFCF), as well as the Pittsburgh Supercomputing Center (PSC) and Allegheny Observatory. Experiments in particle physics are carried out at national and international facilities such as Fermilab near Chicago, J-PARC in Japan, and CERN in Switzerland. Similarly, astrophysics/cosmology ground-based programs are conducted at such locations as Kitt Peak and Mount Hopkins in Arizona, Cerro Tololo in Chile, Mauna Kea in Hawaii, and Apache Point in New Mexico. Pitt faculty members use space-based telescopes including the Hubble Space Telescope, the Chandra X-ray Observatory, and the GALEX UV Telescope. They also belong to several large-telescope consortia: the Sloan Digital Sky Survey (SDSS), the Atacama Cosmology Telescope (ACT), the Panoramic Survey Telescope and Rapid Response System (Pan-STARRS), and the Large Synoptic Survey Telescope (LSST).

Financial Aid

Financial aid is normally provided through teaching assistantships during the first year and through research assistantships thereafter. These awards carry automatic tuition scholarships and benefits. The University provides individual health insurance under the Graduate Student Plan. The Department's fellowships include the Arts and Sciences Graduate Fellowships, and the A&S Summer Fellowship for entering graduate students. They are awarded on a competitive basis with all qualified applicants automatically considered. Some University fellowships are also available through University-wide competition. Students are generally supported throughout their entire graduate career, provided they maintain good academic standing, make progress toward their degree, and are in residence in the Department or at an appropriate research facility. Teaching and research assistantship appointments carried a stipend of $8,150 per term in 2012, bringing the annual stipend to $24,450 for students supported throughout the year. This includes a full-tuition scholarship and benefits. Similar research assistantship appointments may be held in connection with most of the Department's research programs.

Cost of Study

For full-time students who are not Pennsylvania residents, tuition and fees per term in 2012–13 were $15,829. Part-time students paid $1,295 per credit plus fees. Full-time students who are Pennsylvania residents paid $9,668 per term, including fees, and part-time students who are Pennsylvania residents paid $782 per credit plus fees.

Living and Housing Costs

Most University of Pittsburgh students live in rooms or apartments in the Oakland area. The typical cost of rooms or apartments ranges from $400 to $600 per month for housing. Meals range from $350 to $450 per month. Further information may be found online at http://www.ocl.pitt.edu.

Student Group

The Department's graduate student body in 2011–12 consisted of 83 students, all of whom received financial support. These figures are typical of the Department's graduate enrollment.

Student Outcomes

Many Ph.D. graduates accept postdoctoral positions at major research universities, often leading to teaching and research positions at outstanding universities in the United States and around the world. Other recent graduates have entered research careers in the private sector. One former graduate received the American Physical Society's Nicholas Metropolis Award for Outstanding Doctoral Thesis Work in Computational Physics.

Location

Pittsburgh, nicknamed the City of Bridges, is a hilly urban center located in western Pennsylvania and was ranked the Most Livable City in the U.S. in 2013 by Forbes.com. Surrounded by nine state parks, the woodland city offers a variety of outdoor activites including cycling, hiking, downhill and cross-country skiing, white-water rafting and kayaking, rock climbing, hunting, and fishing. The University is located about 3 miles east of downtown Pittsburgh in the city's cultural center. Adjacent to the campus are Carnegie Mellon University and the Carnegie, comprising the Museum of Art, the Museum of Natural History, the Carnegie Library, and the Carnegie Music Hall. Schenley Park adjoins the campus; it has picnic areas, playing fields, jogging trails, and an excellent botanical conservatory. The Pittsburgh area has several professional sports teams; for detailed information, students should visit http://www.pitt.edu/about.html.

The Department

The Department has long been active in research; guided by faculty mentors, it has trained more than 600 recipients for the Ph.D. degree. Close cooperation exists between this Department and the physics department of Carnegie Mellon University; all seminars, colloquiums, and courses are shared. The graduate students of both institutions benefit from belonging to one of the largest communities of active physicists in the country. Furthermore, basic research, conducted at the University of Pittsburgh Medical Center and the School of Medicine, provides additional opportunities for research with multidisciplinary perspectives.

Applying

Students who wish to apply for admission or financial aid should apply online and take the GRE, including the Subject Test in physics. Applicants should request that the registrars of their undergraduate and graduate schools send transcripts of their records to the Department. Three letters of recommendation are required for admission with aid. Unless English is the applicant's native language, the TOEFL (IBT) or IELTS exam is required, except in cases in which an international applicant has received an advanced degree from a U.S. institution. Acceptable minimum scores are listed in the application instructions. The application deadline is January 31. Late applications are accepted on the basis of space availability.

Peterson's Graduate Programs in the Physical Sciences, Mathematics, Agricultural Sciences, the Environment & Natural Resources 2014

www.petersonsbooks.com **263**

University of Pittsburgh

Correspondence and Information

Professor Robert Devaty
Admissions Committee
Department of Physics and Astronomy
University of Pittsburgh
Pittsburgh, Pennsylvania 15260
United States
Phone: 412-624-9009
Web site: http://www.physicsandastronomy.pitt.edu/

THE FACULTY AND THEIR RESEARCH

Carles Badeness, Assistant Professor; Ph.D., Spain. Type 1a supernovae, supernova remnants, large astronomoical data bases, extragalactic astronomy, observational cosmology.

Joseph Boudreau, Professor; Ph.D., Wisconsin. Experimental particle physics.

Daniel Boyanovsky, Professor; Ph.D., California, Santa Barbara. Theoretical condensed-matter physics, particle astrophysics, astrophysics and cosmology.

Matteo Broccio, Lecturer; Ph.D., Italy. Biophysics, physics, other science education.

Wolfgang J. Choyke, Research Professor; Ph.D., Ohio State. Experimental solid-state physics, defect states in semiconductors, large-bandgap spectroscopy.

Russell Clark, Lecturer/Lab Supervisor; Ph.D., LSU. Physics education research, neutrino physics.

Rob Coalson, Professor; Ph.D., Harvard. Chemical physics.

Andrew Daley, Assistant Professor; Ph.D., Innsbruck (Austria). Theoretical many-body physics, quantum optics, AMO.

Istvan Danko, Research Assistant Professor; Ph.D., Vanderbilt. Experimental neutrino physics.

Robert P. Devaty, Associate Professor and Chair of the Graduate Admissions Committee; Ph.D., Cornell. Experimental solid-state physics, semiconductor physics.

H. E. Anthony Duncan, Professor; Ph.D., MIT. Theoretical particle physics.

Brian D'Urso, Assistant Professor; Ph.D., Harvard. Experimental condensed-matter physics, nanoscience.

Gurudev Dutt, Assistant Professor; Ph.D., Michigan. Quantum optics, quantum information.

Steven A. Dytman, Professor; Ph.D., Carnegie Mellon. Experimental particle physics, neutrino physics.

Min Feng, Research Assistant Professor; Ph.D., Chinese Academy of Sciences (Beijing). Experimental condensed matter.

Ayres Freitas, Assistant Professor; Ph.D., Hamburg. Theoretical particle physics.

Sergey Frolov, Assistant Professor; Ph.D., Illinois. Experimental condensed matter physics, quantum nanwires, Majorana fermions in nanowires, nanowire quantum bits.

Tao Han, Professor and Director of the PITTsburgh Particle Physics, Astrophysics, and Cosmology Center (PACC); Ph.D., Wisconsin. Theoretical particle physics.

D. John Hillier, Professor; Ph.D., Australian National. Theoretical and observational astrophysics, computational physics.

Patrick Irvin, Research Assistant Professor; Ph.D., Pittsburgh. Experimental condensed matter physics.

David M. Jasnow, Professor; Ph.D., Illinois. Theory of phase transitions, statistical physics, biological physics.

Arthur Kosowsky, Professor and Associate Director of the PITTsburgh Particle Physics, Astrophysics, and Cosmology Center (PACC); Ph.D., Chicago. Theoretical and experimental cosmology and astrophysics.

Adam Leibovich, Associate Professor and Associate Department Chair; Ph.D., Caltech. Theoretical particle physics.

Jeremy Levy, Professor; Ph.D., California, Santa Barbara. Experimental condensed matter, nanoscience, quantum information.

W. Vincent Liu, Associate Professor; Ph.D., Texas at Austin. Theoretical condensed matter physics, cold atoms.

James V. Maher, Professor; Ph.D., Yale. Experimental statistical physics, critical phenomena, physics of fluids.

James Mueller, Associate Professor and Undergraduate Program Director; Ph.D., Cornell. Experimental particle physics.

Donna Naples, Associate Professor; Ph.D., Maryland. Experimental neutrino physics.

David Nero, Lecturer; Ph.D., Toledo. Astronomy, physics, other science education.

Jeffrey Newman, Associate Professor; Ph.D., Berkeley. Astrophysics, extragalactic astronomy, observational cosmology.

Vittorio Paolone, Associate Professor; Ph.D., California, Davis. Experimental particle physics, neutrino physics.

David Pekker, Assistant Professor; Ph.D., Illinois. Atomic, molecular, and optical physics; computational physics; condensed matter physics.

Hrvoje Petek, Professor and Co-Director of PINSE (Peterson Institute of Nanoscience and Engineering); Ph.D., Berkeley. Experimental condensed matter/AMO, nanoscience, solid-state physics.

Richard H. Pratt, Research Professor; Ph.D., Chicago. Theoretical atomic physics.

Sandhya Rao, Research Professor; Ph.D., Pittsburgh. Astrophysics, extragalactic astronomy, observational cosmology.

Ralph Z. Roskies, Professor and Co-Director of the Pittsburgh Supercomputing Center; Ph.D., Princeton. Theoretical particle physics, use of computers in theoretical physics.

Hanna Salman, Assistant Professor; Ph.D., Weizmann Institute (Israel). Experimental biological physics.

Vladimir Savinov, Associate Professor; Ph.D., Minnesota. Experimental particle physics.

Regina E. Schulte-Ladbeck, Professor; Ph.D., Heidelberg. Extragalactic astronomy, observational cosmology.

Chandralekha Singh, Professor; Ph.D., California, Santa Barbara. Physics education research, polymer physics.

David Snoke, Professor; Ph.D., Illinois at Urbana-Champaign. Experimental condensed-matter, nanoscience, solid-state physics.

Eric Swanson, Associate Professor; Ph.D., Toronto. Theoretical particle physics.

David A. Turnshek, Professor and Department Chair; Ph.D., Arizona. Astrophysics, extragalactic astronomy, observational cosmology.

Michael Wood-Vasey, Assistant Professor; Ph.D., Berkeley. Astrophysics, extragalactic astronomy, observational cosmology.

Xiao-Lun Wu, Professor; Ph.D., Cornell. Experimental condensed-matter physics, biological physics.

Judith Yang, Professor; Ph.D., Cornell. Materials science and engineering.

Andrew Zentner, Associate Professor and Director of the Graduate Program; Ph.D., Ohio State. Theoretical cosmology.

Jin Zhao, Adjunct Assistant Professor; Ph.D., University of Sciences and Technology of China. Theoretical condensed matter.

EMERITUS FACULTY

Wilfred W. Cleland, Professor; Ph.D., Yale. Experimental particle physics.

Eugene Engels Jr., Professor; Ph.D., Princeton. Experimental particle physics.

Edward Gerjuoy, Professor; Ph.D., Berkeley. Theoretical atomic physics.

Walter I. Goldburg, Professor; Ph.D., Duke. Experimental solid-state physics, phase transitions, light scattering, turbulence.

Allen I. Janis, Professor; Ph.D., Syracuse. General relativity, philosophy of science.

Rainer Johnsen, Professor; Ph.D., Kiel (Germany). Experimental atomic and plasma physics.

Peter F. M. Koehler, Professor and Graduate Program Director; Ph.D., Rochester. Experimental high-energy physics, physics education research.

Ezra T. Newman, Professor; Ph.D., Syracuse. General relativity, gravitational lensing.

Paul Shepard, Professor; Ph.D., Princeton. Experimental particle physics.

C. Martin Vincent, Professor; Ph.D., Witwatersrand (South Africa). Theoretical intermediate-energy physics.

Jeffrey Winicour, Professor; Ph.D., Syracuse. General relativity, numerical relativity.

Allen Hall, the recently renovated home to the Department.

Presentation by a graduate student.

264   www.petersonsbooks.com

Peterson's Graduate Programs in the Physical Sciences, Mathematics, Agricultural Sciences, the Environment & Natural Resources 2014

ACADEMIC AND PROFESSIONAL PROGRAMS IN MATHEMATICS

Section 7
Mathematical Sciences

This section contains a directory of institutions offering graduate work in mathematical sciences, followed by in-depth entries submitted by institutions that chose to prepare detailed program descriptions. Additional information about programs listed in the directory but not augmented by an in-depth entry may be obtained by writing directly to the dean of a graduate school or chair of a department at the address given in the directory.

For programs offering work in related fields, see all other areas in this book. In the other guides in this series:

Graduate Programs in the Humanities, Arts & Social Sciences
See *Economics* and *Psychology and Counseling*

Graduate Programs in the Biological/Biomedical Sciences & Health-Related Medical Professions
See *Biological and Biomedical Sciences; Biophysics; Genetics, Developmental Biology, and Reproductive Biology; Pharmacology and Toxicology* and *Public Health*

Graduate Programs in Engineering & Applied Sciences
See *Biomedical Engineering and Biotechnology; Chemical Engineering (Biochemical Engineering); Computer Science and Information Technology; Electrical and Computer Engineering; Engineering and Applied Sciences;* and *Industrial Engineering*

Graduate Programs In Business, Education, Information Studies, Law & Social Work
See *Business Administration and Management* and *Library and Information Studies*

CONTENTS

Program Directories

Applied Mathematics

Acadia University, Faculty of Pure and Applied Science, Department of Mathematics and Statistics, Wolfville, NS B4P 2R6, Canada. Offers applied mathematics and statistics (M Sc). *Faculty:* 12 full-time (3 women), 2 part-time/adjunct (0 women). *Students:* 3 full-time (2 women), 3 part-time (0 women). 19 applicants, 47% accepted, 3 enrolled. In 2012, 2 master's awarded. *Degree requirements:* For master's, thesis. *Entrance requirements:* For master's, honors degree in mathematics, statistics or equivalent. Additional exam requirements/recommendations for international students: Required—TOEFL (minimum score 580 paper-based; 93 iBT), IELTS (minimum score 6.5). *Application deadline:* For fall admission, 2/1 priority date for domestic students, 2/1 for international students. Applications are processed on a rolling basis. Application fee: $50. *Financial support:* Fellowships, research assistantships, teaching assistantships, career-related internships or fieldwork, and unspecified assistantships available. Financial award application deadline: 2/1. *Faculty research:* Geophysical fluid dynamics, machine scheduling problems, control theory, stochastic optimization, survival analysis. *Unit head:* Dr. Jeff Hooper, Head, 902-585-1382, Fax: 902-585-1074, E-mail: jeff.hooper@acadiau.ca. *Application contact:* Dr. Franklin Mendivil, Graduate Coordinator, 902-585-1368, Fax: 902-585-1074, E-mail: franklin.mendivil@acadiau.ca. Website: http://math.acadiau.ca/.

Air Force Institute of Technology, Graduate School of Engineering and Management, Department of Mathematics and Statistics, Dayton, OH 45433-7765. Offers applied mathematics (MS, PhD). Part-time programs available. *Degree requirements:* For master's, thesis; for doctorate, thesis/dissertation. *Entrance requirements:* For master's, GRE General Test, minimum GPA of 3.0, U.S. citizenship or permanent U.S. residency; for doctorate, GRE General Test, minimum GPA of 3.5, U.S. citizenship or permanent U.S. residency. *Faculty research:* Electromagnetics, groundwater modeling, nonlinear diffusion, goodness of fit, finite element analysis.

Arizona State University, College of Liberal Arts and Sciences, Department of Mathematics and Statistics, Tempe, AZ 85287-1804. Offers applied mathematics (PhD); computational biosciences (PhD); mathematics (MA, MNS, PhD); mathematics education (PhD); statistics (PhD). Part-time programs available. Terminal master's awarded for partial completion of doctoral program. *Degree requirements:* For master's, thesis or alternative, interactive Program of Study (iPOS) submitted before completing 50 percent of required credit hours; for doctorate, comprehensive exam, thesis/dissertation, interactive Program of Study (iPOS) submitted before completing 50 percent of required credit hours. *Entrance requirements:* For master's and doctorate, GRE General Test, minimum GPA of 3.0 or equivalent in last 2 years of work leading to bachelor's degree. Additional exam requirements/recommendations for international students: Required—TOEFL (minimum score 80 iBT), TOEFL, IELTS, or Pearson Test of English. Electronic applications accepted. *Expenses:* Contact institution.

Arizona State University, College of Liberal Arts and Sciences, School of Human Evolution and Social Change, Tempe, AZ 85287-2402. Offers anthropology (PhD); anthropology (archaeology) (PhD); anthropology (bioarchaeology) (PhD); anthropology (museum studies) (MA); anthropology (physical) (PhD); applied mathematics for the life and social sciences (PhD); environmental social science (PhD); environmental social science (urbanism) (PhD); global health (MA); global health (health and culture) (PhD); global health (urbanism) (PhD); immigration studies (Graduate Certificate). Terminal master's awarded for partial completion of doctoral program. *Degree requirements:* For master's, thesis or alternative, interactive Program of Study (iPOS) submitted before completing 50 percent of required credit hours; for doctorate, comprehensive exam, thesis/dissertation, interactive Program of Study (iPOS) submitted before completing 50 percent of required credit hours. *Entrance requirements:* For master's and doctorate, GRE, minimum GPA of 3.0 or equivalent in last 2 years of work leading to bachelor's degree. Additional exam requirements/recommendations for international students: Required—TOEFL (minimum score 80 iBT), TOEFL, IELTS, or Pearson Test of English. Electronic applications accepted.

Auburn University, Graduate School, College of Sciences and Mathematics, Department of Mathematics and Statistics, Auburn University, AL 36849. Offers applied mathematics (MAM, MS); mathematics (MS, PhD); probability and statistics (M Prob S); statistics (MS). *Faculty:* 50 full-time (7 women), 6 part-time/adjunct (4 women). *Students:* 56 full-time (14 women), 52 part-time (14 women); includes 4 minority (3 Black or African American, non-Hispanic/Latino; 1 Hispanic/Latino), 43 international. Average age 28. 160 applicants, 59% accepted, 37 enrolled. In 2012, 17 master's, 9 doctorates awarded. *Degree requirements:* For doctorate, thesis/dissertation. *Entrance requirements:* For master's, GRE General Test, undergraduate mathematics background; for doctorate, GRE General Test, GRE Subject Test. *Application deadline:* For fall admission, 7/7 priority date for domestic students; for spring admission, 11/24 for domestic students. Applications are processed on a rolling basis. Application fee: $50 ($60 for international students). Electronic applications accepted. *Expenses:* Tuition, state resident: full-time $7866; part-time $437 per credit. Tuition, nonresident: full-time $23,598; part-time $1311 per credit. *Required fees:* $787 per semester. Tuition and fees vary according to degree level and program. *Financial support:* Fellowships and teaching assistantships available. Financial award applicants

required to submit FAFSA. *Faculty research:* Pure and applied mathematics. *Unit head:* Dr. Tin Yau Tam, Chair, 334-844-6572, Fax: 334-844-6655. *Application contact:* Dr. George Flowers, Dean of the Graduate School, 334-844-2125. Website: http://www.auburn.edu/~math/.

Bowie State University, Graduate Programs, Program in Applied and Computational Mathematics, Bowie, MD 20715-9465. Offers MS. Part-time and evening/weekend programs available. *Degree requirements:* For master's, comprehensive exam. *Entrance requirements:* For master's, calculus sequence, differential equations, linear algebra, mathematical probability and statistics. Electronic applications accepted.

Brown University, Graduate School, Division of Applied Mathematics, Providence, RI 02912. Offers Sc M, PhD. *Degree requirements:* For master's, thesis or alternative; for doctorate, one foreign language, thesis/dissertation, oral exam. *Entrance requirements:* For master's and doctorate, GRE General Test.

California Institute of Technology, Division of Engineering and Applied Science, Option in Applied and Computational Mathematics, Pasadena, CA 91125-0001. Offers MS, PhD. *Degree requirements:* For doctorate, thesis/dissertation. *Entrance requirements:* For doctorate, GRE Subject Test. Electronic applications accepted. *Faculty research:* Theoretical and computational fluid mechanics, numerical analysis, ordinary and partial differential equations, linear and nonlinear wave propagation, perturbation and asymptotic methods.

California State Polytechnic University, Pomona, Academic Affairs, College of Science, Program in Mathematics, Pomona, CA 91768-2557. Offers applied mathematics (MS); pure mathematics (MS). Part-time programs available. *Students:* 17 full-time (10 women), 32 part-time (10 women); includes 27 minority (1 Black or African American, non-Hispanic/Latino; 7 Asian, non-Hispanic/Latino; 16 Hispanic/Latino; 3 Two or more races, non-Hispanic/Latino), 2 international. Average age 32. 68 applicants, 47% accepted, 16 enrolled. In 2012, 13 master's awarded. *Degree requirements:* For master's, thesis or alternative. *Entrance requirements:* For master's, GRE General Test. *Application deadline:* For fall admission, 5/1 priority date for domestic students; for winter admission, 10/15 priority date for domestic students; for spring admission, 1/20 priority date for domestic students. Applications are processed on a rolling basis. Application fee: $55. Electronic applications accepted. *Financial support:* Career-related internships or fieldwork, Federal Work-Study, and institutionally sponsored loans available. Support available to part-time students. Financial award application deadline: 3/2; financial award applicants required to submit FAFSA. *Unit head:* Dr. John Rock, Graduate Coordinator, 909-869-2404, E-mail: jarock@csupomona.edu. *Application contact:* Deborah L. Brandon, Executive Director, Admissions and Outreach, 909-869-3427, Fax: 909-869-5315, E-mail: dlbrandon@csupomona.edu. Website: http://www.csupomona.edu/~math/.

California State University, East Bay, Office of Academic Programs and Graduate Studies, College of Science, Department of Mathematics and Computer Science, Mathematics Program, Hayward, CA 94542-3000. Offers applied math (MS); mathematics (MS); mathematics teaching (MS). Part-time and evening/weekend programs available. *Degree requirements:* For master's, comprehensive exam or thesis. *Entrance requirements:* For master's, minimum GPA of 3.0 in field. Additional exam requirements/recommendations for international students: Required—TOEFL (minimum score 550 paper-based). Electronic applications accepted.

California State University, Fullerton, Graduate Studies, College of Natural Science and Mathematics, Department of Mathematics, Fullerton, CA 92834-9480. Offers applied mathematics (MA); mathematics (MA); teaching (MA). Part-time programs available. *Students:* 34 full-time (17 women), 41 part-time (17 women); includes 35 minority (2 Black or African American, non-Hispanic/Latino; 21 Asian, non-Hispanic/Latino; 12 Hispanic/Latino), 6 international. Average age 31. 95 applicants, 68% accepted, 39 enrolled. In 2012, 30 master's awarded. *Degree requirements:* For master's, comprehensive exam or project. *Entrance requirements:* For master's, minimum GPA of 2.5 in last 60 units of course work, major in mathematics or related field. Application fee: $55. *Financial support:* Research assistantships, teaching assistantships, career-related internships or fieldwork, Federal Work-Study, institutionally sponsored loans, and scholarships/grants available. Support available to part-time students. Financial award application deadline: 3/1; financial award applicants required to submit FAFSA. *Unit head:* Dr. Stephen W. Goode, Chair, 657-278-3631. *Application contact:* Admissions/Applications, 657-278-2371.

California State University, Long Beach, Graduate Studies, College of Engineering, Department of Mechanical and Aerospace Engineering, Long Beach, CA 90840. Offers aerospace engineering (MSAE); engineering and industrial applied mathematics (PhD); interdisciplinary engineering (MSE); management engineering (MSE); mechanical engineering (MSME). Part-time programs available. *Entrance requirements:* Additional exam requirements/recommendations for international students: Required—TOEFL. Electronic applications accepted. *Faculty research:* Unsteady turbulent flows, solar energy, energy conversion, CAD/CAM, computer-assisted instruction.

268 www.petersonsbooks.com

Peterson's Graduate Programs in the Physical Sciences, Mathematics, Agricultural Sciences, the Environment & Natural Resources 2014

California State University, Long Beach, Graduate Studies, College of Natural Sciences and Mathematics, Department of Mathematics and Statistics, Long Beach, CA 90840. Offers mathematics (MS), including applied mathematics, applied statistics, mathematics education for secondary school teachers. Part-time programs available. *Degree requirements:* For master's, comprehensive exam or thesis. Electronic applications accepted. *Faculty research:* Algebra, functional analysis, partial differential equations, operator theory, numerical analysis.

California State University, Los Angeles, Graduate Studies, College of Natural and Social Sciences, Department of Mathematics, Los Angeles, CA 90032-8530. Offers mathematics (MS), including applied mathematics, mathematics. Part-time and evening/weekend programs available. *Faculty:* 8 full-time (3 women). *Students:* 37 full-time (12 women), 35 part-time (10 women); includes 39 minority (2 Black or African American, non-Hispanic/Latino; 17 Asian, non-Hispanic/Latino; 15 Hispanic/Latino; 2 Native Hawaiian or other Pacific Islander, non-Hispanic/Latino; 3 Two or more races, non-Hispanic/Latino), 8 international. Average age 33. 64 applicants, 73% accepted, 24 enrolled. In 2012, 17 master's awarded. *Degree requirements:* For master's, comprehensive exam or thesis. *Entrance requirements:* For master's, previous course work in mathematics. Additional exam requirements/recommendations for international students: Required—TOEFL (minimum score 500 paper-based). *Application deadline:* For fall admission, 5/1 for domestic and international students. Applications are processed on a rolling basis. Application fee: $55. Electronic applications accepted. *Financial support:* Teaching assistantships and Federal Work-Study available. Support available to part-time students. Financial award application deadline: 3/1. *Faculty research:* Group theory, functional analysis, convexity theory, ordered geometry. *Unit head:* Dr. Grant Fraser, Chair, 323-343-2150, Fax: 323-343-5071, E-mail: gfraser@calstatela.edu. *Application contact:* Dr. Larry Fritz, Dean of Graduate Studies, 323-343-3820, Fax: 323-343-5653, E-mail: lfritz@calstatela.edu. Website: http://www.calstatela.edu/academic/math/.

California State University, Northridge, Graduate Studies, College of Science and Mathematics, Department of Mathematics, Northridge, CA 91330. Offers applied mathematics (MS); mathematics (MS); mathematics for educational careers (MS). Part-time and evening/weekend programs available. *Degree requirements:* For master's, thesis (for some programs). *Entrance requirements:* For master's, GRE (if cumulative undergraduate GPA less than 3.0). Additional exam requirements/recommendations for international students: Required—TOEFL.

Carnegie Mellon University, Mellon College of Science, Department of Mathematical Sciences, Pittsburgh, PA 15213-3891. Offers algorithms, combinatorics, and optimization (PhD); applied mathematics (PhD); computational finance (MS); mathematical finance (PhD); mathematical sciences (MS, DA, PhD); pure and applied logic (PhD). Part-time programs available. Terminal master's awarded for partial completion of doctoral program. *Degree requirements:* For doctorate, thesis/dissertation. *Entrance requirements:* For master's and doctorate, GRE General Test, GRE Subject Test. Additional exam requirements/recommendations for international students: Required—TOEFL. Electronic applications accepted. *Faculty research:* Continuum mechanics, discrete mathematics, applied and computational mathematics.

Case Western Reserve University, School of Graduate Studies, Department of Mathematics, Cleveland, OH 44106. Offers applied mathematics (MS, PhD); mathematics (MS, PhD). Part-time programs available. *Faculty:* 19 full-time (5 women), 1 part-time/adjunct (0 women). *Students:* 22 full-time (9 women), 1 part-time (0 women); includes 1 minority (Two or more races, non-Hispanic/Latino), 10 international. Average age 27. 58 applicants, 19% accepted, 6 enrolled. In 2012, 2 master's, 2 doctorates awarded. Terminal master's awarded for partial completion of doctoral program. *Degree requirements:* For master's, thesis or alternative, thesis (for applied mathematics); for doctorate, comprehensive exam, thesis/dissertation. *Entrance requirements:* For master's and doctorate, GRE General Test, 3 letters of recommendation. Additional exam requirements/recommendations for international students: Required—TOEFL (minimum score 577 paper-based; 90 iBT); Recommended—IELTS (minimum score 7). *Application deadline:* For fall admission, 1/15 priority date for domestic students; for spring admission, 11/1 priority date for domestic students. Applications are processed on a rolling basis. Application fee: $50. Electronic applications accepted. *Financial support:* Research assistantships, teaching assistantships, institutionally sponsored loans, and unspecified assistantships available. Financial award application deadline: 12/15. *Faculty research:* Probability theory, convexity and high-dimensional phenomena, imaging, geometric evaluation of curves, dynamical systems, large scale scientific computing, life sciences. *Unit head:* Daniela Calvetti, Chair, 216-368-2880, Fax: 216-368-5163, E-mail: daniela.calvetti@case.edu. *Application contact:* Gaythresa Lewis, Admissions, 216-368-5014, Fax: 216-368-5163, E-mail: gxl34@case.edu. Website: http://www.case.edu/artsci/math/.

Central European University, Graduate Studies, Department of Mathematics and its Applications, Budapest, Hungary. Offers applied mathematics (MS); mathematics and its applications (PhD). *Faculty:* 2 full-time (0 women), 9 part-time/adjunct (1 woman). *Students:* 38 full-time (7 women). Average age 27. 140 applicants, 15% accepted, 12 enrolled. In 2012, 7 master's, 4 doctorates awarded. *Degree requirements:* For master's, one foreign language, thesis (for some programs); for doctorate, comprehensive exam, thesis/dissertation. *Entrance requirements:* For master's and doctorate, entrance exam or GRE, statement of purpose. Additional exam requirements/recommendations for international students: Required—TOEFL (minimum score 570 paper-based); Recommended—IELTS (minimum score 6.5). *Application deadline:* For fall admission, 1/24 for domestic and international students. Electronic applications accepted. *Financial support:* In 2012–13, 37 students received support, including 37 fellowships (averaging $6,100 per year); career-related internships or fieldwork, scholarships/grants, health care benefits, and tuition waivers (full and partial) also available. *Faculty research:* Applied mathematics, such as: algebra, algebraic geometry, bioinformatics, calculus of variations, computational biology, cryptography, discrete mathematics, evolutions equations, fluid mechanics, geometry, number theory, numerical analysis, optimization, ordinary and partial differential equations, probability theory, quantum mechanics, statistics, stochastic processes. *Unit head:* Karoly Boroczky, Head, 36 1 327-3053, E-mail: mathematics@ceu.hu. *Application contact:* Zsuzsanna Jaszberenyi, Admissions Officer, 361-324-3009, Fax: 367-327-3211, E-mail: admissions@ceu.hu. Website: http://mathematics.ceu.hu/.

Claremont Graduate University, Graduate Programs, School of Mathematical Sciences, Claremont, CA 91711-6160. Offers computational and systems biology (PhD); computational mathematics and numerical analysis (MA, MS); computational science (PhD); engineering and industrial applied mathematics (PhD); mathematics (PhD); operations research and statistics (MA, MS); physical applied mathematics (MA, MS); pure mathematics (MA, MS), scientific computing (MA, MS); systems and control theory (MA, MS). Part-time programs available. *Faculty:* 6 full-time (1 woman), 1 part-time/adjunct (0 women). *Students:* 54 full-time (16 women), 35 part-time (18 women); includes 29 minority (3 Black or African American, non-Hispanic/Latino; 10 Asian, non-Hispanic/Latino; 12 Hispanic/Latino; 4 Two or more races, non-Hispanic/Latino), 21 international. Average age 33. In 2012, 13 master's, 7 doctorates awarded. Terminal master's awarded for partial completion of doctoral program. *Entrance requirements:* For master's and doctorate, GRE General Test. Additional exam requirements/recommendations for international students: Required—TOEFL (minimum score 550 paper-based; 80 iBT). *Application deadline:* For fall admission, 2/1 priority date for domestic students. Applications are processed on a rolling basis. Application fee: $60. Electronic applications accepted. *Expenses: Tuition:* Full-time $37,640; part-time $1636 per unit. *Required fees:* $500; $250 per semester. *Financial support:* Fellowships, research assistantships, Federal Work-Study, institutionally sponsored loans, scholarships/grants, and tuition waivers (full and partial) available. Support available to part-time students. Financial award application deadline: 2/15; financial award applicants required to submit FAFSA. *Unit head:* Henry Schellhorn, Director, 909-607-4168, E-mail: henry.schellhorn@cgu.edu. *Application contact:* Charlotte Ballesteros, Program Coordinator, 909-621-8080, Fax: 909-607-8261, E-mail: charlotte.ballesteros@cgu.edu. Website: http://www.cgu.edu/pages/168.asp.

Clemson University, Graduate School, College of Engineering and Science, Department of Mathematical Sciences, Clemson, SC 29634. Offers applied and pure mathematics (MS, PhD); computational mathematics (MS, PhD); operations research (MS, PhD); statistics (MS, PhD). Part-time programs available. *Faculty:* 44 full-time (13 women), 4 part-time/adjunct (2 women). *Students:* 117 full-time (43 women), 3 part-time (2 women); includes 6 minority (2 Black or African American, non-Hispanic/Latino; 1 American Indian or Alaska Native, non-Hispanic/Latino; 1 Asian, non-Hispanic/Latino; 1 Hispanic/Latino; 1 Two or more races, non-Hispanic/Latino), 50 international. Average age 26. 188 applicants, 76% accepted, 45 enrolled. In 2012, 41 master's, 11 doctorates awarded. *Degree requirements:* For master's, thesis optional, final project; for doctorate, thesis/dissertation, qualifying exams. *Entrance requirements:* For master's and doctorate, GRE General Test. Additional exam requirements/recommendations for international students: Required—TOEFL. *Application deadline:* For fall admission, 1/15 priority date for domestic students, 1/15 for international students; for spring admission, 10/1 priority date for domestic students, 9/15 for international students. Applications are processed on a rolling basis. Application fee: $70 ($80 for international students). Electronic applications accepted. *Financial support:* In 2012–13, 111 students received support, including 2 fellowships with full and partial tuition reimbursements available (averaging $10,000 per year), 8 research assistantships with partial tuition reimbursements available (averaging $17,943 per year), 104 teaching assistantships with partial tuition reimbursements available (averaging $18,793 per year); career-related internships or fieldwork, institutionally sponsored loans, scholarships/grants, health care benefits, and unspecified assistantships also available. Support available to part-time students. Financial award application deadline: 4/15. *Faculty research:* Applied and computational analysis, cryptography, discrete mathematics, optimization, statistics. *Total annual research expenditures:* $780,865. *Unit head:* Dr. Robert L. Taylor, Chair, 864-656-5240, Fax: 864-656-5230, E-mail: rtaylo2@clemson.edu. *Application contact:* Dr. K. B. Kulasekera, Graduate Coordinator, 864-656-5231, Fax: 864-656-5230, E-mail: kk@clemson.edu. Website: http://www.clemson.edu/ces/departments/math/index.html.

The College of William and Mary, Faculty of Arts and Sciences, Department of Applied Science, Williamsburg, VA 23187-8795. Offers accelerator science (PhD); applied mathematics (PhD); applied mechanics (PhD); applied robotics (PhD); applied science (MS); atmospheric and environmental science (PhD); computational neuroscience (PhD); interface, thin film and surface science (PhD); lasers and optics (PhD); magnetic resonance (PhD); materials science and engineering (PhD); mathematical and computational biology (PhD); medical imaging (PhD); nanotechnology (PhD); neuroscience (PhD); non-destructive evaluation (PhD); polymer chemistry (PhD); remote sensing (PhD). *Faculty:* 13

full-time (2 women), 1 part-time/adjunct (0 women). *Students:* 36 full-time (11 women); includes 2 minority (1 Black or African American, non-Hispanic/Latino; 1 Asian, non-Hispanic/Latino), 22 international. Average age 26. 40 applicants, 45% accepted, 8 enrolled. In 2012, 3 master's, 2 doctorates awarded. *Median time to degree:* Of those who began their doctoral program in fall 2004, 95% received their degree in 8 years or less. *Degree requirements:* For master's, comprehensive exam, thesis; for doctorate, comprehensive exam, thesis/dissertation, 4 core courses. *Entrance requirements:* For master's and doctorate, GRE General Test, GRE Subject Test. Additional exam requirements/recommendations for international students: Required—TOEFL, TWE. *Application deadline:* For fall admission, 2/3 priority date for domestic students, 2/3 for international students; for spring admission, 10/15 priority date for domestic students, 10/14 for international students. Applications are processed on a rolling basis. Application fee: $45. Electronic applications accepted. *Expenses:* Tuition, state resident: full-time $6779; part-time $385 per credit hour. Tuition, nonresident: full-time $20,608; part-time $1000 per credit hour. *Required fees:* $4625. *Financial support:* Fellowships, research assistantships, teaching assistantships, Federal Work-Study, health care benefits, tuition waivers (full), and unspecified assistantships available. Financial award application deadline: 4/15; financial award applicants required to submit FAFSA. *Faculty research:* Computational biology, non-destructive evaluation, neurophysiology, lasers and optics. *Unit head:* Dr. Christopher Del Negro, Chair, 757-221-7808, Fax: 757-221-2050, E-mail: cadeln@wm.edu. *Application contact:* Rosario Fox, Graduate Program Coordinator, 757-221-2563, Fax: 757-221-2050, E-mail: rxfoxx@wm.edu. Website: http://www.wm.edu/as/appliedscience.

Colorado School of Mines, Graduate School, Department of Mathematical and Computer Sciences, Golden, CO 80401-1887. Offers nuclear engineering (MS, PhD). Part-time programs available. *Faculty:* 20 full-time (6 women), 7 part-time/adjunct (4 women). *Students:* 44 full-time (15 women), 5 part-time (1 woman); includes 3 minority (1 Asian, non-Hispanic/Latino; 2 Hispanic/Latino), 2 international. Average age 26. 64 applicants, 67% accepted, 22 enrolled. In 2012, 10 master's, 1 doctorate awarded. *Degree requirements:* For master's, thesis (for some programs); for doctorate, comprehensive exam, thesis/dissertation. *Entrance requirements:* For master's and doctorate, GRE General Test. Additional exam requirements/recommendations for international students: Required—TOEFL (minimum score 550 paper-based; 80 iBT). *Application deadline:* For fall admission, 1/15 priority date for domestic students, 1/15 for international students; for spring admission, 10/15 priority date for domestic students, 10/15 for international students. Application fee: $50 ($70 for international students). Electronic applications accepted. *Financial support:* In 2012–13, 21 students received support, including 4 fellowships with full tuition reimbursements available (averaging $21,120 per year), 10 research assistantships with full tuition reimbursements available (averaging $21,120 per year), 7 teaching assistantships with full tuition reimbursements available (averaging $21,120 per year); scholarships/grants, health care benefits, and unspecified assistantships also available. Financial award application deadline: 1/15; financial award applicants required to submit FAFSA. *Faculty research:* Applied statistics, numerical computation, artificial intelligence, linear optimization. *Total annual research expenditures:* $1.5 million. *Unit head:* Dr. Willy Hereman, Head, 303-273-3881, Fax: 303-273-3875, E-mail: whereman@mines.edu. *Application contact:* William Navidi, Professor, 303-273-3489, Fax: 303-273-3875, E-mail: wnavidi@mines.edu. Website: http://ams.mines.edu/.

Columbia University, Fu Foundation School of Engineering and Applied Science, Department of Applied Physics and Applied Mathematics, New York, NY 10027. Offers applied physics (Eng Sc D); applied physics and applied mathematics (MS, PhD, Engr); materials science and engineering (MS, Eng Sc D, PhD); medical physics (MS). Part-time programs available. Postbaccalaureate distance learning degree programs offered (no on-campus study). *Faculty:* 32 full-time (2 women), 23 part-time/adjunct (2 women). *Students:* 111 full-time (22 women), 17 part-time (5 women); includes 19 minority (17 Asian, non-Hispanic/Latino; 1 Hispanic/Latino; 1 Two or more races, non-Hispanic/Latino), 53 international. Average age 28. 460 applicants, 26% accepted, 54 enrolled. In 2012, 41 master's, 17 doctorates awarded. Terminal master's awarded for partial completion of doctoral program. *Degree requirements:* For master's, comprehensive exam; for doctorate, thesis/dissertation, qualifying exam. *Entrance requirements:* For master's, GRE General Test, GRE Subject Test (strongly recommended); for doctorate, GRE General Test, GRE Subject Test (applied physics); for Engr, GRE General Test. Additional exam requirements/recommendations for international students: Required—TOEFL, IELTS. *Application deadline:* For fall admission, 12/15 priority date for domestic students, 12/15 for international students; for spring admission, 10/1 priority date for domestic students, 10/1 for international students. Application fee: $95. Electronic applications accepted. *Financial support:* In 2012–13, 73 students received support, including 2 fellowships with full tuition reimbursements available (averaging $31,140 per year), 55 research assistantships with full tuition reimbursements available (averaging $31,133 per year), 16 teaching assistantships with full tuition reimbursements available (averaging $31,133 per year); health care benefits also available. Financial award application deadline: 12/15; financial award applicants required to submit FAFSA. *Faculty research:* Plasma physics and fusion energy; optical and laser physics; atmospheric, oceanic and earth physics; applied mathematics; solid state science and processing of materials, their properties, and their structure; medical physics. *Unit head:* Dr. I. Cevdet Noyan, Professor/Chair, 212-854-8919, E-mail: icn2@columbia.edu. *Application contact:* Montserrat Fernandez-Pinkley, Student Services Coordinator, 212-854-4457, Fax: 212-854-8257, E-mail: mf2157@columbia.edu. Website: http://www.apam.columbia.edu/.

Cornell University, Graduate School, Graduate Fields of Arts and Sciences, Center for Applied Mathematics, Ithaca, NY 14853-0001. Offers PhD. *Faculty:* 95 full-time (8 women). *Students:* 34 full-time (12 women); includes 7 minority (2 Black or African American, non-Hispanic/Latino; 1 Asian, non-Hispanic/Latino; 3 Hispanic/Latino; 1 Two or more races, non-Hispanic/Latino), 12 international. Average age 26. 189 applicants, 9% accepted, 3 enrolled. In 2012, 8 doctorates awarded. *Degree requirements:* For doctorate, one foreign language, comprehensive exam, thesis/dissertation. *Entrance requirements:* For doctorate, GRE General Test, GRE Subject Test (mathematics recommended), 3 letters of recommendation. Additional exam requirements/recommendations for international students: Required—TOEFL (minimum score 550 paper-based; 77 iBT). *Application deadline:* For fall admission, 1/15 for domestic students. Application fee: $95. Electronic applications accepted. *Financial support:* In 2012–13, 32 students received support, including 15 fellowships with full tuition reimbursements available, 7 research assistantships with full tuition reimbursements available, 10 teaching assistantships with full tuition reimbursements available; institutionally sponsored loans, scholarships/grants, health care benefits, tuition waivers (full and partial), and unspecified assistantships also available. Financial award applicants required to submit FAFSA. *Faculty research:* Nonlinear systems and PDEs, numerical methods, signal and image processing, mathematical biology, discrete mathematics and optimization. *Unit head:* Director of Graduate Studies, 607-255-4756, Fax: 607-255-9860. *Application contact:* Graduate Field Assistant, 607-255-4756, Fax: 607-255-9860, E-mail: appliedmath@cornell.edu. Website: http://www.gradschool.cornell.edu/academics/fields-study/catalog/?fid-22#tabs-1.

Cornell University, Graduate School, Graduate Fields of Engineering, Field of Chemical Engineering, Ithaca, NY 14853-0001. Offers advanced materials processing (M Eng, MS, PhD); applied mathematics and computational methods (M Eng, MS, PhD); biochemical engineering (M Eng, MS, PhD); chemical reaction engineering (M Eng, MS, PhD); classical and statistical thermodynamics (M Eng, MS, PhD); fluid dynamics, rheology and biorheology (M Eng, MS, PhD); heat and mass transfer (M Eng, MS, PhD); kinetics and catalysis (M Eng, MS, PhD); polymers (M Eng, MS, PhD); surface science (M Eng, MS, PhD). *Faculty:* 32 full-time (4 women). *Students:* 123 full-time (41 women); includes 25 minority (3 Black or African American, non-Hispanic/Latino; 17 Asian, non-Hispanic/Latino; 4 Hispanic/Latino; 1 Two or more races, non-Hispanic/Latino), 65 international. Average age 25. 456 applicants, 40% accepted, 66 enrolled. In 2012, 43 master's, 13 doctorates awarded. *Degree requirements:* For master's, thesis (MS); for doctorate, comprehensive exam, thesis/dissertation. *Entrance requirements:* For master's and doctorate, GRE General Test, 2 letters of recommendation. Additional exam requirements/recommendations for international students: Required—TOEFL (minimum score 600 paper-based; 77 iBT). *Application deadline:* For fall admission, 1/15 priority date for domestic students. Application fee: $95. Electronic applications accepted. *Financial support:* In 2012–13, 69 students received support, including 42 fellowships with full tuition reimbursements available, 15 research assistantships with full tuition reimbursements available, 12 teaching assistantships with full tuition reimbursements available; institutionally sponsored loans, scholarships/grants, health care benefits, tuition waivers (full and partial), and unspecified assistantships also available. Financial award applicants required to submit FAFSA. *Faculty research:* Biochemical, biomedical and metabolic engineering; fluid and polymer dynamics; surface science and chemical kinetics; electronics materials; microchemical systems and nanotechnology. *Unit head:* Director of Graduate Studies, 607-255-4550. *Application contact:* Graduate Field Assistant, 607-255-4550, E-mail: dgs@cheme.cornell.edu. Website: http://www.gradschool.cornell.edu/fields.php?id-25&a-2.

Cornell University, Graduate School, Graduate Fields of Engineering, Field of Operations Research and Information Engineering, Ithaca, NY 14853. Offers applied probability and statistics (PhD); manufacturing systems engineering (PhD); mathematical programming (PhD); operations research and industrial engineering (M Eng). *Faculty:* 39 full-time (6 women). *Students:* 155 full-time (43 women); includes 24 minority (2 Black or African American, non-Hispanic/Latino; 17 Asian, non-Hispanic/Latino; 4 Hispanic/Latino; 1 Two or more races, non-Hispanic/Latino), 106 international. Average age 24. 1,077 applicants, 22% accepted, 84 enrolled. In 2012, 96 master's, 6 doctorates awarded. *Degree requirements:* For doctorate, comprehensive exam, thesis/dissertation. *Entrance requirements:* For master's and doctorate, GRE General Test, 3 letters of recommendation. Additional exam requirements/recommendations for international students: Required—TOEFL (minimum score 600 paper-based; 100 iBT). *Application deadline:* For fall admission, 12/15 for domestic students. Application fee: $95. Electronic applications accepted. *Financial support:* In 2012–13, 41 students received support, including 20 fellowships with full tuition reimbursements available, 21 teaching assistantships with full tuition reimbursements available; research assistantships with full tuition reimbursements available, institutionally sponsored loans, scholarships/grants, health care benefits, tuition waivers (full and partial), and unspecified assistantships also available. Financial award applicants required to submit FAFSA. *Faculty research:* Mathematical programming and combinatorial optimization, statistics, stochastic processes, mathematical finance, simulation, manufacturing, e-commerce. *Unit head:* Director of Graduate Studies, 607-255-9128, Fax: 607-255-9129. *Application contact:* Graduate Field Assistant, 607-255-

270 www.petersonsbooks.com

Peterson's Graduate Programs in the Physical Sciences, Mathematics, Agricultural Sciences, the Environment & Natural Resources 2014

9128, Fax: 607-255-9129, E-mail: orie@cornell.edu. Website: http://www.gradschool.cornell.edu/fields.php?id-35&a-2.

Dalhousie University, Faculty of Engineering, Department of Engineering Mathematics, Halifax, NS B3J 2X4, Canada. Offers M Sc, PhD. *Degree requirements:* For master's, thesis; for doctorate, thesis/dissertation. *Entrance requirements:* Additional exam requirements/recommendations for international students: Required—TOEFL, IELTS, CANTEST, CAEL, or Michigan English Language Assessment Battery. Electronic applications accepted. *Faculty research:* Piecewise regression and robust statistics, random field theory, dynamical systems, wave loads on offshore structures, digital signal processing.

Delaware State University, Graduate Programs, Department of Mathematics, Interdisciplinary Program in Applied Mathematics and Theoretical Physics, Dover, DE 19901-2277. Offers PhD. *Degree requirements:* For doctorate, one foreign language, thesis defense. *Entrance requirements:* For doctorate, GRE General Test, MS degree in physics or mathematics. Additional exam requirements/recommendations for international students: Required—TOEFL (minimum score 550 paper-based).

Delaware State University, Graduate Programs, Department of Mathematics, Program in Applied Mathematics, Dover, DE 19901-2277. Offers MS. *Entrance requirements:* Additional exam requirements/recommendations for international students: Required—TOEFL (minimum score 550 paper-based). Electronic applications accepted.

DePaul University, College of Science and Health, Department of Mathematical Sciences, Chicago, IL 60614. Offers applied mathematics (MS), including actuarial science, statistics; applied statistics (MS, Certificate); mathematics education (MA); pure mathematics (MS). Part-time and evening/weekend programs available. *Students:* 120 full-time (51 women), 64 part-time (26 women); includes 54 minority (21 Black or African American, non-Hispanic/Latino; 21 Asian, non-Hispanic/Latino; 10 Hispanic/Latino; 1 Native Hawaiian or other Pacific Islander, non-Hispanic/Latino; 1 Two or more races, non-Hispanic/Latino), 26 international. Average age 31. In 2012, 35 master's awarded. *Degree requirements:* For master's, comprehensive exam. *Entrance requirements:* For master's, bachelor's degree. Additional exam requirements/recommendations for international students: Required—TOEFL (minimum score 550 paper-based; 80 iBT). *Application deadline:* For fall admission, 7/30 for domestic students, 6/30 for international students; for winter admission, 11/30 for domestic students, 10/31 for international students; for spring admission, 2/15 for domestic students. Applications are processed on a rolling basis. Application fee: $40. Electronic applications accepted. *Financial support:* In 2012–13, research assistantships with partial tuition reimbursements (averaging $6,000 per year) were awarded; teaching assistantships and tuition waivers (full) also available. Financial award application deadline: 4/30; financial award applicants required to submit FAFSA. *Faculty research:* Verbally prime algebras, enveloping algebras of Lie, superalgebras and related rings, harmonic analysis, estimation theory. *Total annual research expenditures:* $30,000. *Unit head:* Dr. Ahmed I. Zayed, Chairperson, 773-325-7806, Fax: 773-325-7807, E-mail: azayed@depaul.edu. *Application contact:* Ann Spittle, Director of Graduate Admissions, 773-325-7315, Fax: 312-476-3244, E-mail: graddepaul@depaul.edu. Website: http://csh.depaul.edu/departments/mathematical-sciences/Pages/default.aspx.

École Polytechnique de Montréal, Graduate Programs, Department of Mathematics and Industrial Engineering, Montréal, QC H3C 3A7, Canada. Offers ergonomy (M Eng, M Sc A, DESS); mathematical method in CA engineering (M Eng, M Sc A, PhD); operational research (M Eng, M Sc A, PhD); production (M Eng, M Sc A); technology management (M Eng, M Sc A). DESS program offered jointly with HEC Montreal and Université de Montréal. Part-time programs available. *Degree requirements:* For master's, one foreign language, thesis. *Entrance requirements:* For master's, minimum GPA of 2.75. *Faculty research:* Use of computers in organizations.

Elizabeth City State University, School of Mathematics, Science and Technology, Master of Science in Mathematics Program, Elizabeth City, NC 27909-7806. Offers applied mathematics (MS); community college teaching (MS); mathematics education (MS); remote sensing (MS). Part-time and evening/weekend programs available. *Faculty:* 7 full-time (2 women). *Students:* 3 full-time (1 woman), 27 part-time (16 women); includes 23 minority (22 Black or African American, non-Hispanic/Latino; 1 Two or more races, non-Hispanic/Latino). Average age 25. 7 applicants, 71% accepted, 5 enrolled. In 2012, 9 master's awarded. *Degree requirements:* For master's, thesis. *Entrance requirements:* For master's, MAT and/or GRE, minimum GPA of 3.0, 3 letters of recommendation, two official transcripts from all undergraduate/graduate schools attended, health form for all students taking more than four credit hours of course work on university campus, typewritten one-page request for entry into the program that includes a description of student's educational preparation. Additional exam requirements/recommendations for international students: Required—TOEFL (minimum score 550 paper-based, 80 iBT) or IELTS (minimum score 6.5). *Application deadline:* For fall admission, 7/15 priority date for domestic students, 7/15 for international students; for spring admission, 11/15 priority date for domestic students, 11/15 for international students. Applications are processed on a rolling basis. Application fee: $30. Electronic applications accepted. *Expenses:* Tuition, state resident: full-time $5700. Tuition, nonresident: full-time $16,840. Full-time tuition and fees vary according to campus/location. *Financial support:* In 2012–13, 8 students received support, including 3 research assistantships (averaging $19,000 per year), 2 teaching assistantships (averaging

$18,000 per year); scholarships/grants and tuition waivers also available. Financial award application deadline: 6/30; financial award applicants required to submit FAFSA. *Faculty research:* Oceanic temperature effects, mathematics strategies in elementary schools, multimedia, Antarctic temperature mapping, computer networks, water quality, remote sensing, polar ice, satellite imagery. *Total annual research expenditures:* $25,000. *Unit head:* Dr. Farrah Jackson, Chair, 252-335-8549, Fax: 252-335-3487, E-mail: fmjackson@mail.ecsu.edu. *Application contact:* Dr. Paula S. Viltz, Director of Graduate Education, 252-335-3455, Fax: 252-335-3146, E-mail: psviltz@mail.ecsu.edu. Website: http://www.ecsu.edu/academics/graduate/ma.

Florida Atlantic University, Charles E. Schmidt College of Science, Department of Mathematical Sciences, Boca Raton, FL 33431-0991. Offers applied mathematics and statistics (MS); mathematical sciences (MS, MST, PhD). Part-time programs available. *Faculty:* 42 full-time (6 women), 38 part-time/adjunct (11 women). *Students:* 42 full-time (10 women), 27 part-time (10 women); includes 18 minority (7 Black or African American, non-Hispanic/Latino; 5 Asian, non-Hispanic/Latino; 5 Hispanic/Latino; 1 Two or more races, non-Hispanic/Latino), 21 international. Average age 31. 83 applicants, 48% accepted, 19 enrolled. In 2012, 23 master's, 7 doctorates awarded. Terminal master's awarded for partial completion of doctoral program. *Degree requirements:* For master's, comprehensive exam (for some programs), thesis (for some programs); for doctorate, comprehensive exam, thesis/dissertation. *Entrance requirements:* For master's and doctorate, GRE General Test, minimum GPA of 3.0. Additional exam requirements/recommendations for international students: Required—TOEFL (minimum score 500 paper-based). *Application deadline:* For fall admission, 7/1 priority date for domestic students, 2/15 for international students; for spring admission, 11/1 priority date for domestic students, 7/15 for international students. Applications are processed on a rolling basis. Application fee: $30. Electronic applications accepted. *Expenses:* Tuition, state resident: full-time $8876; part-time $369.82 per credit hour. Tuition, nonresident: full-time $24,595; part-time $1024.81 per credit hour. *Financial support:* In 2012–13, fellowships with partial tuition reimbursements (averaging $20,000 per year), teaching assistantships with partial tuition reimbursements (averaging $20,000 per year) were awarded; Federal Work-Study also available. Financial award application deadline: 4/1. *Faculty research:* Cryptography, statistics, algebra, analysis, combinatorics. *Unit head:* Dr. Lee Klingler, Chair, 561-297-0274, Fax: 561-297-2436, E-mail: klingler@fau.edu. *Application contact:* Dr. Rainer Steinwandt, Graduate Director, 561-297-3353, Fax: 561-297-2436, E-mail: rsteinwa@fau.edu. Website: http://www.math.fau.edu/.

Florida Institute of Technology, Graduate Programs, College of Science, Department of Mathematical Sciences, Melbourne, FL 32901-6975. Offers applied mathematics (MS, PhD); operations research (MS, PhD). Part-time and evening/weekend programs available. *Faculty:* 11 full-time (2 women). *Students:* 29 full-time (7 women), 11 part-time (4 women); includes 4 minority (2 Black or African American, non-Hispanic/Latino; 2 Hispanic/Latino), 18 international. Average age 31. 86 applicants, 53% accepted, 9 enrolled. In 2012, 13 master's, 6 doctorates awarded. *Degree requirements:* For master's, comprehensive exam (for some programs), thesis optional; for doctorate, comprehensive exam, thesis/dissertation, preliminary exam. *Entrance requirements:* For master's, minimum GPA of 3.0, computer programming literacy; for doctorate, minimum GPA of 3.2, resume, 3 letters of recommendation, statement of objectives. Additional exam requirements/recommendations for international students: Required—TOEFL (minimum score 550 paper-based; 79 iBT). *Application deadline:* For fall admission, 4/1 for international students; for spring admission, 9/30 for international students. Applications are processed on a rolling basis. Electronic applications accepted. *Expenses:* Tuition: Full-time $20,214; part-time $1123 per credit hour. Tuition and fees vary according to campus/location. *Financial support:* In 2012–13, 18 teaching assistantships with full and partial tuition reimbursements (averaging $8,217 per year) were awarded; research assistantships, career-related internships or fieldwork, institutionally sponsored loans, tuition waivers (partial), unspecified assistantships, and tuition remissions also available. Support available to part-time students. Financial award application deadline: 3/1; financial award applicants required to submit FAFSA. *Faculty research:* Real analysis, numerical analysis, statistics, data analysis, combinatorics, artificial intelligence, simulation. *Total annual research expenditures:* $2,921. *Unit head:* Dr. Semen Koksal, Department Head, 321-674-8765, Fax: 321-674-7412, E-mail: skoksal@fit.edu. *Application contact:* Cheryl A. Brown, Associate Director of Graduate Admissions, 321-674-7581, Fax: 321-723-9468, E-mail: cbrown@fit.edu. Website: http://cos.fit.edu/math/.

Florida State University, The Graduate School, College of Arts and Sciences, Department of Mathematics, Tallahassee, FL 32306-4510. Offers applied computational mathematics (MS, PhD); biomathematics (MS, PhD); financial mathematics (MS, PhD); pure mathematics (MS, PhD). Part-time programs available. *Faculty:* 52 full-time (12 women). *Students:* 145 full-time (38 women), 6 part-time (2 women); includes 13 minority (6 Black or African American, non-Hispanic/Latino; 3 Asian, non-Hispanic/Latino; 4 Hispanic/Latino), 93 international. 322 applicants, 30% accepted, 41 enrolled. In 2012, 30 master's, 13 doctorates awarded. Terminal master's awarded for partial completion of doctoral program. *Degree requirements:* For master's, comprehensive exam (for some programs), thesis optional; for doctorate, comprehensive exam, thesis/dissertation, candidacy exam including written qualifying examinations which differ by degree concentrations. *Entrance requirements:* For master's and doctorate, GRE General Test, minimum upper-division GPA of 3.0, 4-year bachelor's degree. Additional exam requirements/recommendations for

Peterson's Graduate Programs in the Physical Sciences, Mathematics, Agricultural Sciences, the Environment & Natural Resources 2014

www.petersonsbooks.com **271**

international students: Required—TOEFL (minimum score 550 paper-based; 80 iBT) or IELTS (minimum score 6.5). *Application deadline:* For fall admission, 1/1 priority date for domestic students, 1/1 for international students; for spring admission, 10/1 priority date for domestic students, 11/1 for international students. Applications are processed on a rolling basis. Application fee: $30. Electronic applications accepted. *Expenses:* Tuition, state resident: full-time $7263; part-time $403.51 per credit hour. Tuition, nonresident: full-time $18,087; part-time $1004.85 per credit hour. *Required fees:* $1335.42; $74.19 per credit hour. $445.14 per semester. One-time fee: $40 full-time; $20 part-time. Tuition and fees vary according to program. *Financial support:* In 2012–13, 115 students received support, including 9 fellowships with full tuition reimbursements available (averaging $22,600 per year), 14 research assistantships with full tuition reimbursements available (averaging $22,000 per year), 88 teaching assistantships with full tuition reimbursements available (averaging $19,300 per year); career-related internships or fieldwork, institutionally sponsored loans, scholarships/grants, health care benefits, and unspecified assistantships also available. *Faculty research:* Algebra and algebraic geometry; applied, financial, numerical, and classical analysis; biomathematics, including shape analysis and anatomical imaging; computational mathematics and numerical algorithms; geometric topology. *Unit head:* Dr. Xiaoming Wang, Chairperson, 850-645-3338, Fax: 850-644-4053, E-mail: wxm@math.fsu.edu. *Application contact:* Dr. Giray Okten, Associate Chair for Graduate Studies, 850-644-8713, Fax: 850-644-4053, E-mail: okten@math.fsu.edu. Website: http://www.math.fsu.edu/.

The George Washington University, Columbian College of Arts and Sciences, Department of Mathematics, Washington, DC 20052. Offers applied mathematics (MA, MS, PhD); pure mathematics (MA, MS, PhD). Part-time and evening/weekend programs available. *Faculty:* 18 full-time (4 women), 2 part-time/adjunct (0 women). *Students:* 22 full-time (4 women), 12 part-time (4 women); includes 7 minority (3 Black or African American, non-Hispanic/Latino; 1 American Indian or Alaska Native, non-Hispanic/Latino; 1 Asian, non-Hispanic/Latino; 2 Hispanic/Latino), 17 international. Average age 26. 96 applicants, 79% accepted, 13 enrolled. In 2012, 6 master's, 2 doctorates awarded. Terminal master's awarded for partial completion of doctoral program. *Degree requirements:* For master's, comprehensive exam; for doctorate, one foreign language, thesis/dissertation, general exam. *Entrance requirements:* For master's and doctorate, GRE General Test, minimum GPA of 3.0, interview. Additional exam requirements/recommendations for international students: Required—TOEFL (minimum score 550 paper-based; 80 iBT). *Application deadline:* For fall admission, 1/15 priority date for domestic students, 1/15 for international students; for spring admission, 10/1 priority date for domestic students, 9/1 for international students. Applications are processed on a rolling basis. Application fee: $75. Electronic applications accepted. *Financial support:* In 2012–13, 17 students received support. Fellowships with full tuition reimbursements available, teaching assistantships with tuition reimbursements available, Federal Work-Study, and tuition waivers available. Financial award application deadline: 1/15. *Unit head:* John B. Conway, Chair, 202-994-0553, E-mail: conway@gwu.edu. *Application contact:* 202-994-6210, Fax: 202-994-6213, E-mail: askccas@gwu.edu. Website: http://www.gwu.edu/~math/.

Georgia Institute of Technology, Graduate Studies and Research, College of Sciences, School of Mathematics, Atlanta, GA 30332-0001. Offers algorithms, combinatorics, and optimization (PhD); applied mathematics (MS); bioinformatics (PhD); mathematics (PhD); quantitative and computational finance (MS); statistics (MS Stat). Terminal master's awarded for partial completion of doctoral program. *Degree requirements:* For master's, thesis or alternative; for doctorate, one foreign language, thesis/dissertation. *Entrance requirements:* For master's, GRE General Test, minimum GPA of 3.0; for doctorate, GRE General Test, GRE Subject Test, minimum GPA of 3.0. Additional exam requirements/recommendations for international students: Required—TOEFL. Electronic applications accepted. *Faculty research:* Dynamical systems, discrete mathematics, probability and statistics, mathematical physics.

Hampton University, Graduate College, Program in Applied Mathematics, Hampton, VA 23668. Offers computational mathematics (MS); nonlinear science (MS); statistics and probability (MS). *Degree requirements:* For master's, thesis optional. *Entrance requirements:* For master's, GRE General Test.

Harvard University, Graduate School of Arts and Sciences, School of Engineering and Applied Sciences, Cambridge, MA 02138. Offers applied mathematics (ME, SM, PhD); applied physics (ME, SM, PhD); computer science (ME, SM, PhD); engineering science (ME); engineering sciences (SM, PhD). Part-time programs available. Terminal master's awarded for partial completion of doctoral program. *Degree requirements:* For master's, thesis optional; for doctorate, comprehensive exam, thesis/dissertation. *Entrance requirements:* For master's and doctorate, GRE General Test, GRE Subject Test (recommended), 3 letters of recommendation. Additional exam requirements/recommendations for international students: Required—TOEFL (minimum score 80 iBT). Electronic applications accepted. *Expenses: Tuition:* Full-time $37,576. *Required fees:* $930. Tuition and fees vary according to program and student level. *Faculty research:* Applied mathematics, applied physics, computer science and electrical engineering, environmental engineering, mechanical and biomedical engineering.

Howard University, Graduate School, Department of Mathematics, Washington, DC 20059-0002. Offers applied mathematics (MS, PhD); mathematics (MS, PhD). Part-time programs available. Terminal master's awarded for partial completion of doctoral program. *Degree requirements:* For master's, comprehensive exam, thesis or alternative, qualifying exam; for doctorate, 2 foreign languages, comprehensive exam, thesis/dissertation, qualifying exams. *Entrance requirements:* For master's, GRE General Test, minimum GPA of 3.0; for doctorate, GRE General Test. Additional exam requirements/recommendations for international students: Required—TOEFL. Electronic applications accepted.

Hunter College of the City University of New York, Graduate School, School of Arts and Sciences, Department of Mathematics and Statistics, New York, NY 10021-5085. Offers applied mathematics (MA); mathematics for secondary education (MA); pure mathematics (MA). Part-time and evening/weekend programs available. *Faculty:* 13 full-time (2 women), 2 part-time/adjunct (1 woman). *Students:* 17 full-time (12 women), 62 part-time (34 women); includes 41 minority (6 Black or African American, non-Hispanic/Latino; 29 Asian, non-Hispanic/Latino; 6 Hispanic/Latino), 3 international. Average age 32. 54 applicants, 61% accepted, 16 enrolled. In 2012, 53 master's awarded. *Degree requirements:* For master's, one foreign language, comprehensive exam, thesis (for some programs). *Entrance requirements:* For master's, GRE General Test, 24 credits in mathematics. Additional exam requirements/recommendations for international students: Required—TOEFL. *Application deadline:* For fall admission, 4/1 for domestic students, 2/1 for international students; for spring admission, 11/1 for domestic students, 9/1 for international students. Application fee: $125. *Expenses:* Tuition, state resident: full-time $8690; part-time $365 per credit. Tuition, nonresident: full-time $16,200; part-time $675 per credit. *Required fees:* $320 per semester. One-time fee: $125. Tuition and fees vary according to class time, campus/location and program. *Financial support:* Federal Work-Study, institutionally sponsored loans, scholarships/grants, and tuition waivers (partial) available. Support available to part-time students. *Faculty research:* Data analysis, dynamical systems, computer graphics, topology, statistical decision theory. *Unit head:* Ada Peluso, Chairperson, 212-772-5300, Fax: 212-772-4858, E-mail: peluso@math.hunter.cuny.edu. *Application contact:* William Zlata, Director for Graduate Admissions, 212-772-4482, Fax: 212-650-3336, E-mail: admissions@hunter.cuny.edu. Website: http://math.hunter.cuny.edu/.

Illinois Institute of Technology, Graduate College, College of Science and Letters, Department of Applied Mathematics, Chicago, IL 60616. Offers applied mathematics (MS, PhD); collegiate mathematics (PhD); mathematical finance (MMF). MMF program held jointly with Stuart School of Business, PhD (collegiate mathematics) with Department of Mathematics and Science Education. *Faculty:* 20 full-time (1 woman), 8 part-time/adjunct (0 women). *Students:* 51 full-time (13 women), 3 part-time (0 women); includes 1 minority (Two or more races, non-Hispanic/Latino), 42 international. Average age 27. 101 applicants, 89% accepted, 19 enrolled. In 2012, 3 master's, 7 doctorates awarded. Terminal master's awarded for partial completion of doctoral program. *Degree requirements:* For master's, comprehensive exam, thesis; for doctorate, comprehensive exam, thesis/dissertation. *Entrance requirements:* For master's, GRE General Test (minimum scores: 1100 Quantitative and Verbal, 2.5 Analytical Writing), minimum undergraduate GPA of 3.0; for doctorate, GRE General Test (minimum scores: 1100 Quantitative and Verbal, 3.0 Analytical Writing), minimum undergraduate GPA of 3.5. Additional exam requirements/recommendations for international students: Required—TOEFL (minimum score 523 paper-based; 70 iBT); Recommended—IELTS (minimum score 5.5). *Application deadline:* For fall admission, 5/1 for domestic and international students; for spring admission, 10/15 for domestic and international students. Applications are processed on a rolling basis. Application fee: $50. Electronic applications accepted. *Expenses: Tuition:* Full-time $20,142; part-time $1119 per credit hour. *Required fees:* $605 per semester. One-time fee: $255. Tuition and fees vary according to program and student level. *Financial support:* In 2012–13, 5 teaching assistantships with full and partial tuition reimbursements (averaging $9,193 per year) were awarded; fellowships with full and partial tuition reimbursements, research assistantships with full and partial tuition reimbursements, career-related internships or fieldwork, Federal Work-Study, institutionally sponsored loans, scholarships/grants, health care benefits, tuition waivers (partial), and unspecified assistantships also available. Support available to part-time students. Financial award applicants required to submit FAFSA. *Faculty research:* Applied analysis, computational mathematics, discrete applied mathematics, stochastics, mathematical finance. *Total annual research expenditures:* $564,742. *Unit head:* Fred J. Hickernell, Chairman/Professor, 312-567-8983, Fax: 312-567-3135, E-mail: hickernell@iit.edu. *Application contact:* Deborah Gibson, Director, Graduate Admission, 866-472-3448, Fax: 312-567-3138, E-mail: inquiry.grad@iit.edu. Website: http://www.math.iit.edu.

Indiana University Bloomington, University Graduate School, College of Arts and Sciences, Department of Mathematics, Bloomington, IN 47405-7000. Offers applied mathematics (MA); mathematical physics (PhD); mathematics education (MAT); pure mathematics (MA, PhD). *Faculty:* 49 full-time (3 women). *Students:* 118 full-time (21 women), 1 part-time (0 women); includes 12 minority (2 Black or African American, non-Hispanic/Latino; 9 Asian, non-Hispanic/Latino; 1 Hispanic/Latino), 72 international. Average age 27. 218 applicants, 25% accepted, 28 enrolled. In 2012, 15 master's, 12 doctorates awarded. Terminal master's awarded for partial completion of doctoral program. *Degree requirements:* For doctorate, one foreign language, thesis/dissertation. *Entrance requirements:* For master's and doctorate, GRE General Test, GRE Subject Test. Additional exam requirements/recommendations for international students: Required—TOEFL. *Application deadline:* For fall admission, 1/15 priority date for domestic students, 1/15 for international students. Applications are processed on a rolling basis. Application fee: $55 ($65 for international students). Electronic applications accepted. *Financial support:* In 2012–13, 2 students received support, including 9 fellowships with full tuition reimbursements available (averaging $21,450 per year), 11 research assistantships with full tuition reimbursements available (averaging $16,045 per year), 96 teaching assistantships with full tuition reimbursements available (averaging $15,870 per year); scholarships/grants, health care benefits, and unspecified assistantships also available. Financial award application deadline: 1/15. *Faculty research:* Topology, geometry, algebra, applied, analysis. *Unit head:* Kevin Zumbrun, Chair, 812-855-2200. *Application contact:* Kate Forrest, Graduate Secretary, 812-855-2645, Fax: 812-855-0046, E-mail: gradmath@indiana.edu. Website: http://www.math.indiana.edu/.

Indiana University of Pennsylvania, School of Graduate Studies and Research, College of Natural Sciences and Mathematics, Department of Mathematics, Program in Applied Mathematics, Indiana, PA 15705-1087. Offers MS. Part-time programs available. *Faculty:* 9 full-time (2 women). *Students:* 12 full-time (1 woman), 7 part-time (2 women); includes 1 minority (Asian, non-Hispanic/Latino), 4 international. Average age 30. 43 applicants, 67% accepted, 11 enrolled. In 2012, 11 master's awarded. *Degree requirements:* For master's, thesis optional. *Entrance requirements:* For master's, 2 letters of recommendation. Additional exam requirements/recommendations for international students: Required—TOEFL (minimum score 540 paper-based). *Application deadline:* Applications are processed on a rolling basis. Application fee: $50. Electronic applications accepted. *Expenses:* Tuition, state resident: part-time $429 per credit hour. Tuition, nonresident: part-time $644 per credit hour. *Required fees:* $110.60 per credit hour. One-time fee: $180 part-time. *Financial support:* In 2012–13, 10 research assistantships with full and partial tuition reimbursements (averaging $3,406 per year) were awarded; Federal Work-Study, scholarships/grants, and unspecified assistantships also available. Support available to part-time students. Financial award application deadline: 4/15; financial award applicants required to submit FAFSA. *Unit head:* Dr. Yu-Ju Kuo, Graduate Coordinator, 724-357-4765, E-mail: yu-ju.kuo@iup.edu. Website: http://www.iup.edu/grad/appliedmath/default.aspx.

Indiana University–Purdue University Fort Wayne, College of Arts and Sciences, Department of Mathematical Sciences, Fort Wayne, IN 46805-1499. Offers applied mathematics (MS); applied statistics (Certificate); mathematics (MS); operations research (MS); teaching (MAT). Part-time and evening/weekend programs available. *Faculty:* 19 full-time (5 women). *Students:* 1 (woman) full-time, 10 part-time (2 women), 1 international. Average age 30. 6 applicants, 100% accepted, 4 enrolled. In 2012, 5 master's, 1 other advanced degree awarded. *Entrance requirements:* For master's, minimum GPA of 3.0, major or minor in mathematics, three letters of recommendation. Additional exam requirements/recommendations for international students: Required—TOEFL (minimum score 550 paper-based; 79 iBT); Recommended—TWE. *Application deadline:* For fall admission, 8/1 priority date for domestic students, 7/1 for international students; for spring admission, 12/1 for domestic students, 10/1 for international students. Applications are processed on a rolling basis. Application fee: $55 ($60 for international students). Electronic applications accepted. *Expenses:* Tuition, state resident: full-time $6279; part-time $313.95 per credit hour. Tuition, nonresident: full-time $14,219; part-time $710.95 per credit hour. *Financial support:* In 2012–13, 4 teaching assistantships with partial tuition reimbursements (averaging $13,190 per year) were awarded; scholarships/grants and unspecified assistantships also available. Support available to part-time students. Financial award application deadline: 3/1; financial award applicants required to submit FAFSA. *Faculty research:* Equilibrium measures, group graphs and split-stars, arrangement graphs. *Unit head:* Dr. Peter Dragnev, Interim Chair and Professor, 260-481-6382, Fax: 260-481-0155, E-mail: dragnevp@ipfw.edu. *Application contact:* Dr. W. Douglas Weakley, Director of Graduate Studies, 260-481-6233, Fax: 260-481-0155, E-mail: weakley@ipfw.edu. Website: http://www.ipfw.edu/math/.

Indiana University–Purdue University Indianapolis, School of Science, Department of Mathematical Sciences, Indianapolis, IN 46202-3216. Offers mathematics (MS, PhD), including applied mathematics, applied statistics (MS), mathematical statistics (PhD), mathematics, mathematics education (MS). *Faculty:* 30 full-time (2 women). *Students:* 25 full-time (8 women), 35 part-time (13 women); includes 11 minority (2 Black or African American, non-Hispanic/Latino; 7 Asian, non-Hispanic/Latino; 2 Hispanic/Latino), 23 international. Average age 33. 52 applicants, 67% accepted, 21 enrolled. In 2012, 22 master's awarded. Terminal master's awarded for partial completion of doctoral program. *Degree requirements:* For master's, thesis optional; for doctorate, one foreign language, thesis/dissertation. *Entrance requirements:* For doctorate, GRE General Test. Additional exam requirements/recommendations for international students: Required—TOEFL. *Application deadline:* For fall admission, 2/1 priority date for domestic students. Application fee: $55 ($65 for international students). *Financial support:* In 2012–13, 14 students received support, including 1 fellowships with tuition reimbursements available (averaging $15,375 per year), 4 teaching assistantships with tuition reimbursements available (averaging $13,088 per year); research assistantships with tuition reimbursements available and tuition waivers (full and partial) also available. Financial award application deadline: 2/1. *Faculty research:* Mathematical physics, integrable systems, partial differential equations, noncommutative geometry, biomathematics, computational neurosciences. *Unit head:* Dr. Zhongmin Shen, Chair, 317-278-1065, Fax: 317-274-3460, E-mail: zshen@math.iupui.edu. *Application contact:* Dr. Sherry Queener, Director, Graduate Studies and Associate Dean, 317-274-1577, Fax: 317-278-2380. Website: http://www.math.iupui.edu/.

Indiana University South Bend, College of Liberal Arts and Sciences, South Bend, IN 46634-7111. Offers applied mathematics and computer science (MS); English (MA); liberal studies (MLS); public affairs (MPA). Part-time and evening/weekend programs available. *Faculty:* 79 full-time (33 women). *Students:* 36 full-time (22 women), 91 part-time (66 women); includes 23 minority (13 Black or African American, non-Hispanic/Latino; 4 Asian, non-Hispanic/Latino; 4 Hispanic/Latino; 1 Native Hawaiian or other Pacific Islander, non-Hispanic/Latino; 1 Two or more races, non-Hispanic/Latino), 7 international. Average age 37. 65 applicants, 60% accepted, 27 enrolled. In 2012, 36 master's awarded. *Degree requirements:* For master's, thesis (for some programs). *Entrance requirements:* For master's, minimum GPA of 3.0. Additional exam requirements/recommendations for international students: Required—TOEFL. *Application deadline:* For fall admission, 7/31 priority date for domestic students, 7/1 for international students; for spring admission, 3/31 priority date for domestic students, 11/1 for international students. Applications are processed on a rolling basis. Application fee: $50 ($60 for international students). *Financial support:* In 2012–13, 5 teaching assistantships were awarded; Federal Work-Study also available. Support available to part-time students. *Faculty research:* Artificial intelligence, bioinformatics, English language and literature, creative writing, computer networks. *Total annual research expenditures:* $127,000. *Unit head:* Dr. Elizabeth E. Dunn, Dean, 574-520-4290, E-mail: elizdunn@iusb.edu. *Application contact:* Admissions Counselor, 574-520-4839, Fax: 574-520-4834, E-mail: graduate@iusb.edu. Website: https://www.iusb.edu/clas/index.php.

Inter American University of Puerto Rico, San Germán Campus, Graduate Studies Center, Program in Mathematics Education, San Germán, PR 00683-5008. Offers applied mathematics (MA). Part-time and evening/weekend programs available. *Faculty:* 4 full-time (0 women). *Students:* 25 full-time (8 women), 3 part-time (2 women); all minorities (all Hispanic/Latino). Average age 33. 9 applicants, 67% accepted, 6 enrolled. *Degree requirements:* For master's, comprehensive exam. *Entrance requirements:* For master's, EXADEP or GRE General Test, minimum GPA of 3.0. *Application deadline:* For fall admission, 4/30 priority date for domestic students; for spring admission, 11/15 for domestic students. Application fee: $31. *Expenses: Tuition:* Full-time $202; part-time $202 per credit hour. *Required fees:* $260 per semester. Tuition and fees vary according to degree level. *Financial support:* Teaching assistantships, Federal Work-Study, and unspecified assistantships available. *Unit head:* Dr. Elba T. Irizarry, Director of Graduate Studies Center, 787-264-1912 Ext. 7357, Fax: 787-892-6350, E-mail: elbat@sg.inter.edu. *Application contact:* Dr. Alvaro Locompte, Coordinator, 787-264-1912 Ext. 7547, E-mail: alvarolecompte@cs.com.

Iowa State University of Science and Technology, Department of Mathematics, Ames, IA 50011. Offers applied mathematics (MS, PhD); mathematics (MS, PhD); school mathematics (MSM). *Degree requirements:* For master's, thesis or alternative; for doctorate, thesis/dissertation. *Entrance requirements:* For master's and doctorate, GRE General Test. Additional exam requirements/recommendations for international students: Required—TOEFL (minimum score 550 paper-based; 79 iBT), IELTS (minimum score 6.5). *Application deadline:* For fall admission, 2/1 priority date for domestic students, 2/1 for international students. Application fee: $60 ($90 for international students). Electronic applications accepted. *Financial support:* Scholarships/grants, health care benefits, and unspecified assistantships available. *Application contact:* Melanie Erickson, Application Contact, 515-294-0393, Fax: 515-294-5454, E-mail: gradmath@iastate.edu. Website: http://www.math.iastate.edu/Graduate/Programs.html.

Iowa State University of Science and Technology, Program in Applied Mathematics, Ames, IA 50011. Offers MS, PhD. *Entrance requirements:* For master's and doctorate, GRE. Additional exam requirements/recommendations for international students: Required—TOEFL (minimum score 550 paper-based; 79 iBT), IELTS (minimum score 6.5). *Application deadline:* For fall admission, 2/1 for domestic and international students. Electronic applications accepted. *Application contact:* Melanie Erickson, Application Contact, 515-294-0393, Fax: 515-294-5454, E-mail: gradmath@iastate.edu. Website: http://math.iastate.edu/Graduate/Prospective.html.

The Johns Hopkins University, Engineering Program for Professionals, Part-time Program in Applied and Computational Mathematics, Baltimore, MD 21218-2699. Offers MS, Post-Master's Certificate. Part-time and evening/weekend programs available. Electronic applications accepted.

The Johns Hopkins University, G. W. C. Whiting School of Engineering, Department of Applied Mathematics and Statistics, Baltimore, MD 21218-2699. Offers computational medicine (PhD); discrete mathematics (MA, MSE, PhD); financial mathematics (MSE); operations research/optimization/decision science (MA, MSE, PhD); statistics/probability/stochastic processes (MA, MSE, PhD). Terminal master's awarded for partial completion of doctoral program. *Degree requirements:* For master's, thesis (for some programs); for doctorate, thesis/dissertation, oral exam, introductory exam. *Entrance requirements:* For master's and doctorate, GRE General Test, GRE Subject Test. Additional exam requirements/recommendations for international students: Required—TOEFL (minimum score 600 paper-based; 100 iBT). Electronic applications accepted. *Faculty research:* Discrete mathematics, probability, statistics, optimization and operations research, scientific computation, financial mathematics.

Kent State University, College of Arts and Sciences, Department of Mathematical Sciences, Kent, OH 44242-0001. Offers applied mathematics (MA, MS, PhD); pure mathematics (MA, MS, PhD). Part-time programs available. *Degree requirements:* For master's, thesis optional; for doctorate, one foreign language, thesis/dissertation. Electronic applications accepted. *Expenses:*

Tuition, state resident: full-time $8424; part-time $468 per credit hour. Tuition, nonresident: full-time $14,580; part-time $810 per credit hour. Tuition and fees vary according to course load. *Faculty research:* Approximation theory, measure theory, ring theory, functional analysis, complex analysis.

Lehigh University, College of Arts and Sciences, Department of Mathematics, Bethlehem, PA 18015. Offers applied mathematics (MS, PhD); mathematics (MS, PhD); statistics (MS). Part-time programs available. *Faculty:* 24 full-time (1 woman), 1 part-time/adjunct (0 women). *Students:* 32 full-time (14 women), 4 part-time (3 women); includes 1 minority (Asian, non-Hispanic/Latino), 15 international. Average age 27. 161 applicants, 41% accepted, 12 enrolled. In 2012, 12 master's, 3 doctorates awarded. Terminal master's awarded for partial completion of doctoral program. *Degree requirements:* For master's, comprehensive exam, thesis optional; for doctorate, comprehensive exam, thesis/dissertation, qualifying exams, general exam, advanced topic exam. *Entrance requirements:* For master's and doctorate, GRE General Test (strongly recommended), minimum undergraduate GPA of 2.75, 3.0 for last two semesters; adequate background in math. Additional exam requirements/recommendations for international students: Required—TOEFL (minimum score 85 iBT). *Application deadline:* For fall admission, 1/1 priority date for domestic students, 1/1 for international students; for spring admission, 12/1 priority date for domestic students, 12/1 for international students. Applications are processed on a rolling basis. Application fee: $75. Electronic applications accepted. *Financial support:* In 2012–13, 35 students received support, including 2 fellowships with full tuition reimbursements available (averaging $25,000 per year), 23 teaching assistantships with full tuition reimbursements available (averaging $17,500 per year); research assistantships with full tuition reimbursements available, scholarships/grants, and tuition waivers (partial) also available. Financial award application deadline: 1/1. *Faculty research:* Probability and statistics, geometry and topology, number theory, algebra, discrete mathematics, differential equations. *Total annual research expenditures:* $278,864. *Unit head:* Dr. Wei-Min Huang, Chairman, 610-758-3730, Fax: 610-758-3767, E-mail: wh02@lehigh.edu. *Application contact:* Dr. Terry Napier, Graduate Coordinator, 610-758-3755, E-mail: mathgrad@lehigh.edu. Website: http://www.lehigh.edu/~math/grad.html.

Long Island University–C. W. Post Campus, College of Liberal Arts and Sciences, Department of Mathematics, Brookville, NY 11548-1300. Offers applied mathematics (MS); mathematics education (MS); mathematics for secondary school teachers (MS). Part-time and evening/weekend programs available. *Degree requirements:* For master's, thesis or alternative, oral presentation. *Entrance requirements:* Additional exam requirements/recommendations for international students: Required—TOEFL. Electronic applications accepted. *Faculty research:* Differential geometry, topological groups, general topology, number theory, analysis and statistics, numerical analysis.

McGill University, Faculty of Graduate and Postdoctoral Studies, Faculty of Science, Department of Mathematics and Statistics, Montréal, QC H3A 2T5, Canada. Offers computational science and engineering (M Sc); mathematics and statistics (M Sc, MA, PhD), including applied mathematics (M Sc, MA), pure mathematics (M Sc, MA), statistics (M Sc, MA).

Michigan State University, The Graduate School, College of Natural Science, Department of Mathematics, East Lansing, MI 48824. Offers applied mathematics (MS, PhD); industrial mathematics (MS); mathematics (MAT, MS, PhD). *Entrance requirements:* Additional exam requirements/recommendations for international students: Required—TOEFL. Electronic applications accepted.

Missouri University of Science and Technology, Graduate School, Department of Mathematics and Statistics, Rolla, MO 65409. Offers applied mathematics (MS); mathematics (MST, PhD), including mathematics (PhD), mathematics education (MST), statistics (PhD). Terminal master's awarded for partial completion of doctoral program. *Degree requirements:* For master's, thesis or alternative; for doctorate, one foreign language, thesis/dissertation. *Entrance requirements:* For master's and doctorate, GRE General Test, GRE Subject Test. Electronic applications accepted. *Faculty research:* Analysis, differential equations, topology, statistics.

Montclair State University, The Graduate School, College of Science and Mathematics, Department of Mathematical Sciences, Program in Mathematics, Montclair, NJ 07043-1624. Offers mathematics education (MS); pure and applied mathematics (MS). Part-time and evening/weekend programs available. *Degree requirements:* For master's, comprehensive exam. *Entrance requirements:* For master's, GRE General Test, 2 letters of recommendation, essay. Additional exam requirements/recommendations for international students: Required—TOEFL (minimum score 83 iBT), IELTS (minimum score 6.5). Electronic applications accepted. *Faculty research:* Computation, applied analysis.

Naval Postgraduate School, Departments and Academic Groups, Department of Applied Mathematics, Monterey, CA 93943. Offers MS, PhD. Program only open to commissioned officers of the United States and friendly nations and selected United States federal civilian employees. Part-time programs available. *Degree requirements:* For master's, thesis; for doctorate, one foreign language, thesis/dissertation. *Faculty research:* Compact S-box for Advanced Encryption Standard (AES), rotation symmetric Boolean functions - count and crytogprahic properties, pseudospectral method for the optimal control of constrained feedback linearizable systems, nodal triangle-based spectral element method for the shallow water equations on the sphere, axisymmetric equilibria of three-dimensional Smoluchowski equation.

Naval Postgraduate School, Departments and Academic Groups, Undersea Warfare Academic Group, Monterey, CA 93943. Offers applied mathematics (MS); applied physics (MS); applied science (MS), including acoustics, operations research, physical oceanography, signal processing; electrical engineering (MS); engineering acoustics (MS, PhD); engineering science (MS), including electrical engineering, mechanical engineering; mechanical engineer (ME); mechanical engineering (MS, MSME); meteorology (MS); operations research (MS); physical oceanography (MS). Program only open to commissioned officers of the United States and friendly nations and selected United States federal civilian employees. Part-time programs available. *Degree requirements:* For master's, thesis. *Faculty research:* Unmanned/autonomous vehicles, sea mines and countermeasures, submarine warfare in the twentieth and twenty-first centuries.

New Jersey Institute of Technology, Office of Graduate Studies, College of Science and Liberal Arts, Department of Mathematical Science, Program in Applied Mathematics, Newark, NJ 07102. Offers MS. Part-time and evening/weekend programs available. *Entrance requirements:* For master's, GRE General Test. Additional exam requirements/recommendations for international students: Required—TOEFL (minimum score 550 paper-based; 79 iBT). Electronic applications accepted. *Expenses:* Tuition, state resident: full-time $16,836; part-time $915 per credit. Tuition, nonresident: full-time $24,370; part-time $1286 per credit. *Required fees:* $2318; $242 per credit.

New Mexico Institute of Mining and Technology, Graduate Studies, Department of Mathematics, Socorro, NM 87801. Offers applied and industrial mathematics (PhD); industrial mathematics (MS); mathematics (MS); operations research and statistics (MS). *Faculty:* 13 full-time (1 woman), 2 part-time/adjunct (0 women). *Students:* 14 full-time (3 women), 5 part-time (1 woman); includes 4 minority (2 American Indian or Alaska Native, non-Hispanic/Latino; 1 Hispanic/Latino; 1 Two or more races, non-Hispanic/Latino), 5 international. Average age 31. 14 applicants, 79% accepted, 8 enrolled. In 2012, 1 master's awarded. *Degree requirements:* For master's, thesis optional; for doctorate, thesis/dissertation. *Entrance requirements:* For master's, GRE General Test. Additional exam requirements/recommendations for international students: Required—TOEFL (minimum score 540 paper-based). *Application deadline:* For fall admission, 3/1 priority date for domestic students; for spring admission, 6/1 for domestic students. Applications are processed on a rolling basis. Application fee: $16 ($30 for international students). *Expenses:* Tuition, state resident: full-time $5043; part-time $280 per credit hour. Tuition, nonresident: full-time $16,682; part-time $927 per credit hour. *Required fees:* $648; $18 per credit hour. $108 per semester. Part-time tuition and fees vary according to course load. *Financial support:* In 2012–13, 2 research assistantships (averaging $5,505 per year), 10 teaching assistantships with full and partial tuition reimbursements (averaging $8,944 per year) were awarded; fellowships, Federal Work-Study, and institutionally sponsored loans also available. Financial award application deadline: 3/1; financial award applicants required to submit CSS PROFILE or FAFSA. *Faculty research:* Applied mathematics, differential equations, industrial mathematics, numerical analysis, stochastic processes. *Total annual research expenditures:* $116,935. *Unit head:* Dr. Anwar Hossain, Chairman, 575-835-5135, Fax: 575-835-5366, E-mail: hossain@nmt.edu. *Application contact:* Dr. Lorie Liebrock, Dean of Graduate Studies, 575-835-5513, Fax: 575-835-5476, E-mail: graduate@nmt.edu. Website: http://www.nmt.edu/~math/.

North Carolina Agricultural and Technical State University, School of Graduate Studies, College of Arts and Sciences, Department of Mathematics, Greensboro, NC 27411. Offers applied mathematics (MS), including secondary education. *Accreditation:* NCATE. Part-time and evening/weekend programs available. *Degree requirements:* For master's, comprehensive exam, thesis or alternative, qualifying exam. *Entrance requirements:* For master's, GRE General Test, minimum GPA of 3.0.

North Carolina Central University, Division of Academic Affairs, College of Science and Technology, Department of Mathematics and Computer Science, Durham, NC 27707-3129. Offers applied mathematics (MS); mathematics education (MS); pure mathematics (MS). Part-time and evening/weekend programs available. *Degree requirements:* For master's, one foreign language, comprehensive exam, thesis. *Entrance requirements:* For master's, minimum GPA of 3.0 in major, 2.5 overall. Additional exam requirements/recommendations for international students: Required—TOEFL. *Faculty research:* Structure theorems for Lie algebra, Kleene monoids and semi-groups, theoretical computer science, mathematics education.

North Carolina State University, Graduate School, College of Physical and Mathematical Sciences, Department of Mathematics, Program in Applied Mathematics, Raleigh, NC 27695. Offers MS, PhD. *Degree requirements:* For master's, thesis (for some programs); for doctorate, thesis/dissertation. *Entrance requirements:* For master's and doctorate, GRE, GRE Subject Test. Electronic applications accepted. *Faculty research:* Biological and physical modeling, numerical analysis, control, stochastic processes, industrial mathematics.

North Dakota State University, College of Graduate and Interdisciplinary Studies, College of Science and Mathematics, Department of Mathematics, Fargo, ND 58108. Offers applied mathematics (MS, PhD); mathematics (MS, PhD). *Faculty:* 12 full-time (1 woman), 1 part-time/adjunct (0 women). *Students:* 23 full-time (8 women), 2 part-time (0 women); includes 3 minority (1 Black or African American, non-Hispanic/Latino; 2 Two or more races, non-Hispanic/Latino), 5 international. Average age 29. 26 applicants, 31% accepted, 4 enrolled. In 2012, 1 master's, 2 doctorates awarded. *Degree requirements:* For master's, comprehensive exam, thesis; for doctorate, one foreign language, comprehensive exam, thesis/dissertation, computer proficiency. *Entrance requirements:* For master's and doctorate, GRE General Test. Additional exam requirements/recommendations for international students: Required—TOEFL (minimum score 525 paper-based; 71 iBT), IELTS. *Application deadline:* For fall admission, 3/1 priority date for domestic students. Applications are processed on a rolling basis. Application fee: $35. Electronic applications accepted. *Financial support:* In 2012–13, 5 fellowships with full tuition reimbursements (averaging $18,000 per year), 1 research assistantship with tuition reimbursement (averaging $14,000 per year), 17 teaching assistantships with full tuition reimbursements (averaging $9,300 per year) were awarded; Federal Work-Study, institutionally sponsored loans, and tuition waivers (full) also available. Support available to part-time students. Financial award application deadline: 3/31. *Faculty research:* Discrete mathematics, number theory, analysis theory, algebra, applied math. *Unit head:* Dr. Dogan Comez, Chair, 701-231-8171, Fax: 701-231-7598, E-mail: dogan.comez@ndsu.edu. *Application contact:* Dr. Sean Sather-Wagstaff, Graduate Program Director, 701-231-8105, Fax: 701-231-7598, E-mail: sean.sather-wagstaff@ndsu.edu. Website: http://www.math.ndsu.nodak.edu/.

Northeastern Illinois University, Graduate College, College of Arts and Sciences, Department of Mathematics, Program in Applied Mathematics, Chicago, IL 60625-4699. Offers MS.

Northeastern University, College of Science, Department of Mathematics, Boston, MA 02115-5096. Offers applied mathematics (MS); mathematics (MS, PhD); operations research (MSOR). Part-time programs available. *Students:* 142 applicants, 30% accepted, 20 enrolled. In 2012, 6 master's, 7 doctorates awarded. Terminal master's awarded for partial completion of doctoral program. *Degree requirements:* For master's, thesis (for some programs), 32 credit hours; for doctorate, one foreign language, comprehensive exam, thesis/dissertation, qualifying exams. *Entrance requirements:* For master's and doctorate, GRE Subject Test, GRE General Test. Additional exam requirements/recommendations for international students: Required—TOEFL (minimum score 100 iBT). *Application deadline:* For fall admission, 2/1 priority date for domestic students, 2/1 for international students; for spring admission, 12/1 for domestic students, 10/1 for international students. Applications are processed on a rolling basis. Application fee: $75. Electronic applications accepted. *Financial support:* In 2012–13, 35 students received support, including 3 research assistantships with tuition reimbursements available (averaging $19,000 per year), 35 teaching assistantships with tuition reimbursements available (averaging $19,000 per year); Federal Work-Study, institutionally sponsored loans, health care benefits, tuition waivers (full and partial), and unspecified assistantships also available. Financial award application deadline: 3/1; financial award applicants required to submit FAFSA. *Faculty research:* Algebra and singularities, combinatorics, topology, probability and statistics, geometric analysis and partial differential equations. *Unit head:* Dr. Gordana Todorov, Graduate Coordinator, 617-373-5642, Fax: 617-373-5668, E-mail: mathdept@neu.edu. *Application contact:* E-mail: gradcos@neu.edu. Website: http://www.math.neu.edu/graduate-programs.

Northwestern University, The Graduate School, Interdepartmental Programs, Program In Mathematical Methods in Social Science, Evanston, IL 60208. Offers MS.

Northwestern University, McCormick School of Engineering and Applied Science, Department of Engineering Sciences and Applied Mathematics, Evanston, IL 60208. Offers MS, PhD. Admissions and degrees offered through The Graduate School. Part-time programs available. *Faculty:* 14 full-time (1 woman). *Students:* 46 full-time (11 women), 4 part-time (0 women); includes 10 minority (8 Asian, non-Hispanic/Latino; 2 Hispanic/Latino), 8 international. Average age 26. 126 applicants, 32% accepted, 14 enrolled. In 2012, 13 master's, 6 doctorates awarded. Terminal master's awarded for partial completion of doctoral program. *Degree requirements:* For master's, comprehensive exam; for doctorate, comprehensive exam, thesis/dissertation. *Entrance requirements:* For master's and doctorate, GRE General Test. Additional exam requirements/recommendations for international students: Required—TOEFL (minimum score 577 paper-based; 90 iBT) or IELTS (minimum score 7). *Application deadline:* For fall admission, 1/12 for domestic and international students. Application fee: $75. Electronic applications accepted. *Financial support:* Fellowships with full tuition reimbursements, research assistantships with full tuition reimbursements, teaching assistantships with full tuition reimbursements, career-related internships or fieldwork, institutionally sponsored loans, health care benefits, and unspecified assistantships available. Financial award application deadline: 1/15; financial award applicants required to submit FAFSA. *Faculty research:* Acoustics, asymptotic analysis, bifurcation theory, combustion theory, fluid dynamics, information technology, math biology, microfluidics, moving boundary problems, nonlinear dynamics, pattern formation, waves. *Total annual research expenditures:* $1.9 million. *Unit head:* Dr. Vladimir Volpert, Chair, 847-491-8095, Fax: 847-491-2178, E-mail: v-volpert@northwestern.edu. *Application contact:* Dr. Ed Olmstead, Admission Officer, 847-491-5865, Fax: 847-491-2178, E-mail: weo@northwestern.edu. Website: http://www.esam.northwestern.edu/.

Oakland University, Graduate Study and Lifelong Learning, College of Arts and Sciences, Department of Mathematics and Statistics, Program in Applied Mathematical Sciences, Rochester, MI 48309-4401. Offers PhD.

Oakland University, Graduate Study and Lifelong Learning, College of Arts and Sciences, Department of Mathematics and Statistics, Program in Industrial Applied Mathematics, Rochester, MI 48309-4401. Offers MS. Part-time and evening/weekend programs available. *Entrance requirements:* For master's, minimum GPA of 3.0 for unconditional admission. Additional exam requirements/recommendations for international students: Required—TOEFL (minimum score 550 paper-based). Electronic applications accepted. *Expenses:* Contact institution.

Oklahoma State University, College of Arts and Sciences, Department of Mathematics, Stillwater, OK 74078. Offers applied mathematics (MS, PhD); mathematics education (MS, PhD); pure mathematics (MS, PhD). *Faculty:* 39 full-time (7 women), 7 part-time/adjunct (6 women). *Students:* 5 full-time (2 women), 31 part-time (12 women); includes 2 minority (1 Asian, non-Hispanic/Latino; 1 Hispanic/Latino), 21 international. Average age 30. 60 applicants, 32% accepted, 12 enrolled. In 2012, 5 master's, 5 doctorates awarded. *Degree requirements:* For master's, thesis, creative component, or report; for doctorate, comprehensive exam, thesis/dissertation. *Entrance requirements:* For master's and doctorate, GRE (recommended). Additional exam requirements/recommendations for international students: Required—TOEFL (minimum score 550 paper-based; 79 iBT). *Application deadline:* For fall admission, 3/1 for domestic and international students; for spring admission, 10/15 for domestic and international students. Applications are processed on a rolling basis. Application fee: $40 ($75 for international students). Electronic applications accepted. *Expenses:* Tuition, state resident: full-time $4272; part-time $178 per credit hour. Tuition, nonresident: full-time $17,016; part-time $709 per credit hour. *Required fees:* $2188; $91.17 per credit hour. One-time fee: $50 full-time. Part-time tuition and fees vary according to course load and campus/location. *Financial support:* In 2012–13, 33 teaching assistantships (averaging $18,444 per year) were awarded; health care benefits and tuition waivers (partial) also available. Financial award application deadline: 3/1; financial award applicants required to submit FAFSA. *Unit head:* Dr. Willam Jaco, Head, 405-744-5688, Fax: 405-744-8275. *Application contact:* Dr. Sheryl Tucker, Dean, 405-744-7099, Fax: 405-744-0355, E-mail: grad-i@okstate.edu. Website: http://www.math.okstate.edu/.

Penn State University Park, Graduate School, Eberly College of Science, Department of Mathematics, State College, University Park, PA 16802-1503. Offers applied mathematics (MA); mathematics (M Ed, D Ed, PhD). *Unit head:* Dr. Yuxi Zheng, Head, 814-865-0361, E-mail: yzheng@psu.edu. *Application contact:* Dr. Dimitri Burago, Associate Head of Graduate Studies, 814-865-7741, E-mail: burago@math.psu.edu. Website: http://www.math.psu.edu.

Princeton University, Graduate School, Program in Applied and Computational Mathematics, Princeton, NJ 08544-1019. Offers PhD. *Degree requirements:* For doctorate, thesis/dissertation. *Entrance requirements:* For doctorate, GRE General Test, GRE Subject Test. Additional exam requirements/recommendations for international students: Required—TOEFL (minimum score 600 paper-based). Electronic applications accepted.

Rensselaer Polytechnic Institute, Graduate School, School of Science, Program in Applied Mathematics, Troy, NY 12180-3590. Offers MS. Part-time programs available. *Faculty:* 23 full-time (4 women), 4 part-time/adjunct (1 woman). *Students:* 2 full-time (0 women), 1 international. Average age 29. 40 applicants, 33% accepted, 3 enrolled. In 2012, 9 master's awarded. *Entrance requirements:* For master's, GRE. Additional exam requirements/recommendations for international students: Required—TOEFL (minimum score 600 paper-based, 100 iBT), IELTS (minimum score 7), or PTE (minimum score 68). *Application deadline:* For fall admission, 1/1 priority date for domestic students, 1/1 for international students; for spring admission, 8/15 priority date for domestic students, 8/15 for international students. Applications are processed on a rolling basis. Application fee: $75. Electronic applications accepted. *Financial support:* In 2012–13, teaching assistantships with full tuition reimbursements (averaging $18,500 per year) were awarded. Financial award application deadline: 1/1. *Faculty research:* Mathematical modeling, differential equations, applications of mathematics in science and engineering, operations research, analysis. *Application contact:* Office of Graduate Admissions, 518-276-6216, E-mail: gradadmissions@rpi.edu. Website: http://www.math.rpi.edu/.

Rice University, Graduate Programs, George R. Brown School of Engineering, Department of Computational and Applied Mathematics, Houston, TX 77251-1892. Offers computational and applied mathematics (MA, MCAM, PhD); computational science and engineering (PhD). *Degree requirements:* For master's, comprehensive exam (for some programs), thesis (for some programs); for doctorate, comprehensive exam, thesis/dissertation. *Entrance requirements:* For master's and doctorate, GRE General Test, minimum GPA of 3.0. Additional exam requirements/recommendations for international students: Required—TOEFL (minimum score 600 paper-based; 90 iBT). Electronic applications accepted. *Faculty research:* Inverse problems, partial differential equations, computer algorithms, computational modeling, optimization theory.

Rochester Institute of Technology, Graduate Enrollment Services, College of Science, School of Mathematical Sciences, Rochester, NY 14623-5603. Offers industrial and applied mathematics (MS). Part-time and evening/weekend programs available. *Students:* 10 full-time (3 women), 9 part-time (5 women); includes 2 minority (1 Hispanic/Latino; 1 Native Hawaiian or other Pacific Islander, non-Hispanic/Latino), 6 international. Average age 24. 30 applicants, 67% accepted, 5 enrolled. In 2012, 9 master's awarded. *Degree requirements:* For master's, thesis. *Entrance requirements:* For master's, GRE General Test (recommended), minimum GPA of 3.0. Additional exam requirements/recommendations for international students: Required—TOEFL (minimum score

Peterson's Graduate Programs in the Physical Sciences, Mathematics, Agricultural Sciences, the Environment & Natural Resources 2014

www.petersonsbooks.com 275

550 paper-based; 79 iBT) or IELTS (minimum score 6.5). *Application deadline:* For fall admission, 2/15 priority date for domestic students, 2/15 for international students. Applications are processed on a rolling basis. Application fee: $60. Electronic applications accepted. *Expenses: Tuition:* Full-time $35,976; part-time $999 per credit hour. *Required fees:* $240; $80 per quarter. *Financial support:* Research assistantships with partial tuition reimbursements, teaching assistantships with partial tuition reimbursements, career-related internships or fieldwork, scholarships/grants, and unspecified assistantships available. Support available to part-time students. Financial award applicants required to submit FAFSA. *Faculty research:* Abstract algebra, bioinformatics, combinatorics and graph theory, complex variables, cryptography, dynamical systems and chaos, statistics, topology. *Unit head:* Dr. Douglas Meadows, Head, 585-475-5129, E-mail: dsmsma@rit.edu. *Application contact:* Diane Ellison, Assistant Vice President, Graduate Enrollment Services, 585-475-2229, Fax: 585-475-7164, E-mail: gradinfo@rit.edu.

Rutgers, The State University of New Jersey, Camden, Graduate School of Arts and Sciences, Program in Mathematical Sciences, Camden, NJ 08102. Offers industrial mathematics (MBS); industrial/applied mathematics (MS); mathematical computer science (MS); pure mathematics (MS); teaching in mathematical sciences (MS). Part-time and evening/weekend programs available. *Degree requirements:* For master's, comprehensive exam, thesis optional, survey paper, 30 credits. *Entrance requirements:* For master's, GRE, BS/BA in math or related subject, 2 letters of recommendation. Additional exam requirements/recommendations for international students: Required—TOEFL (minimum score 550 paper-based), IELTS. Electronic applications accepted. *Faculty research:* Differential geometry, dynamical systems, vertex operator algebra, automorphic forms, CR-structures.

Rutgers, The State University of New Jersey, New Brunswick, Graduate School-New Brunswick, Department of Mathematics, Piscataway, NJ 08854-8097. Offers applied mathematics (MS, PhD); mathematics (MS, PhD). Part-time programs available. *Degree requirements:* For doctorate, one foreign language, comprehensive exam, thesis/dissertation. *Entrance requirements:* For master's and doctorate, GRE General Test, GRE Subject Test. Additional exam requirements/recommendations for international students: Required—TOEFL. *Faculty research:* Logic and set theory, number theory, mathematical physics, control theory, partial differential equations.

San Diego State University, Graduate and Research Affairs, College of Sciences, Department of Mathematics and Statistics, Program in Applied Mathematics, San Diego, CA 92182. Offers MS. Part-time programs available. *Degree requirements:* For master's, comprehensive exam. *Entrance requirements:* For master's, GRE General Test. Additional exam requirements/recommendations for international students: Required—TOEFL. Electronic applications accepted. *Faculty research:* Modeling, computational fluid dynamics, biomathematics, thermodynamics.

San Jose State University, Graduate Studies and Research, College of Science, Department of Mathematics, San Jose, CA 95192-0001. Offers applied mathematics (MS); mathematics (MA, MS); mathematics education (MA); statistics (MA). Part-time and evening/weekend programs available. *Degree requirements:* For master's, comprehensive exam, thesis (for some programs). *Entrance requirements:* For master's, GRE Subject Test. Electronic applications accepted. *Faculty research:* Artificial intelligence, algorithms, numerical analysis, software database, number theory.

Santa Clara University, School of Engineering, Santa Clara, CA 95053. Offers analog circuit design (Certificate); applied mathematics (MS); ASIC design and test (Certificate); bioengineering (Engineer); civil engineering (MS); computer science and engineering (PhD); controls (Certificate); digital signal processing (Certificate); dynamics (Certificate); electrical engineering (MS, PhD); engineering (Engineer); engineering management (MS); fundamentals of electrical engineering (Certificate); information assurance (Certificate); materials engineering (Certificate); mechanical design analysis (Certificate); mechanical engineering (MS, PhD); mechatronics systems engineering (Certificate); microwave and antennas (Certificate); networking (Certificate); renewable energy (Certificate); software engineering (Certificate); sustainable energy (MS); technology jump-start (Certificate); thermofluids (Certificate). Part-time and evening/weekend programs available. *Faculty:* 52 full-time (18 women), 69 part-time/adjunct (14 women). *Students:* 309 full-time (99 women), 398 part-time (93 women); includes 241 minority (10 Black or African American, non-Hispanic/Latino; 193 Asian, non-Hispanic/Latino; 30 Hispanic/Latino; 4 Native Hawaiian or other Pacific Islander, non-Hispanic/Latino; 4 Two or more races, non-Hispanic/Latino), 265 international. Average age 29. 666 applicants, 56% accepted, 227 enrolled. In 2012, 317 master's, 6 doctorates, 17 other advanced degrees awarded. *Degree requirements:* For master's, thesis (for some programs); for doctorate, thesis/dissertation; for other advanced degree, thesis. *Entrance requirements:* For master's, GRE, transcript; for doctorate, GRE, master's degree or equivalent; for other advanced degree, master's degree, published paper. Additional exam requirements/recommendations for international students: Required—TOEFL (minimum score 550 paper-based; 79 iBT). *Application deadline:* For fall admission, 8/1 for domestic students, 7/15 for international students; for winter admission, 10/28 for domestic students, 9/23 for international students; for spring admission, 2/25 for domestic students, 1/21 for international students. Applications are processed on a rolling basis. Application fee: $60. Electronic applications accepted. *Expenses:* Contact institution. *Financial support:* In 2012–13, 93 students received support, including 3 fellowships with full and partial tuition reimbursements available (averaging $29,685 per year), 20 research assistantships with full and partial tuition reimbursements available (averaging $29,685 per year), 25 teaching assistantships with full and partial tuition reimbursements available (averaging $29,685 per year). Financial award application deadline: 3/2; financial award applicants required to submit FAFSA. *Total annual research expenditures:* $1.6 million. *Unit head:* Dr. Alex Zecevic, Associate Dean for Graduate Studies, 408-554-2394, E-mail: azecevic@scu.edu. *Application contact:* Stacey Tinker, Director of Enrollment Management, 408-554-4748, Fax: 408-554-4323, E-mail: stinker@scu.edu. Website: http://www.scu.edu/engineering/graduate/.

Simon Fraser University, Office of Graduate Studies, Faculty of Science, Department of Mathematics, Burnaby, BC V5A 1S6, Canada. Offers applied and computational mathematics (M Sc, PhD); mathematics (M Sc, PhD); operations research (M Sc, PhD). *Faculty:* 38 full-time (6 women). *Students:* 65 full-time (17 women). 81 applicants, 48% accepted, 21 enrolled. In 2012, 15 master's, 3 doctorates awarded. *Degree requirements:* For master's, thesis or alternative; for doctorate, comprehensive exam, thesis/dissertation. *Entrance requirements:* For master's, GRE General Test, GRE Subject Test (mathematics), minimum GPA of 3.0 (on scale of 4.33), or 3.33 based on last 60 credits of undergraduate courses; for doctorate, GRE General Test, GRE Subject Test (mathematics), minimum GPA of 3.5 (on scale of 4.33). Additional exam requirements/recommendations for international students: Recommended—TOEFL (minimum score 580 paper-based; 93 iBT), IELTS (minimum score 7), TWE (minimum score 5). *Application deadline:* For fall admission, 2/1 for domestic and international students. Application fee: $90 Canadian dollars ($125 Canadian dollars for international students). Electronic applications accepted. Tuition and fees charges are reported in Canadian dollars. *Expenses: Tuition, area resident:* Full-time $5000 Canadian dollars; part-time $275 Canadian dollars per credit hour. *Required fees:* $780 Canadian dollars. *Financial support:* In 2012–13, 31 students received support, including 30 fellowships (averaging $6,250 per year), teaching assistantships (averaging $5,608 per year); research assistantships and scholarships/grants also available. *Faculty research:* Computer algebra, discrete mathematics, fluid dynamics, nonlinear partial differential equations and variational methods, numerical analysis and scientific computing. *Unit head:* Dr. Tom Archibald, Graduate Chair, 778-782-3379, Fax: 778-782-4947, E-mail: math-gsc@sfu.ca. *Application contact:* Diane Pogue, Graduate Secretary, 778-782-3059, Fax: 778-782-4947, E-mail: mathgsec@sfu.ca. Website: http://www.math.sfu.ca/.

Southern Methodist University, Dedman College, Department of Mathematics, Dallas, TX 75275. Offers computational and applied mathematics (MS, PhD). *Degree requirements:* For master's, oral exams; for doctorate, thesis/dissertation, oral and written exams. *Entrance requirements:* For master's and doctorate, GRE General Test, minimum GPA of 3.0, 18 undergraduate hours in mathematics beyond first and second year calculus. Additional exam requirements/recommendations for international students: Required—TOEFL. Electronic applications accepted. *Faculty research:* Numerical analysis and scientific computation, fluid dynamics, optics, wave propagation, mathematical biology.

Southern Oregon University, Graduate Studies, College of Arts and Sciences, Department of Mathematics, Ashland, OR 97520. Offers applied mathematics (PSM). Part-time programs available. Postbaccalaureate distance learning degree programs offered (minimal on-campus study). *Faculty:* 12 full-time (4 women), 1 part-time/adjunct (0 women). *Students:* 5 full-time (2 women); includes 2 minority (1 Asian, non-Hispanic/Latino; 1 Two or more races, non-Hispanic/Latino). Average age 35. 5 applicants, 100% accepted, 5 enrolled. *Degree requirements:* For master's, thesis (for some programs). *Entrance requirements:* For master's, GRE General Test, minimum cumulative GPA of 3.0 in the last 90 quarter credits (60 semester credits) of undergraduate coursework. Additional exam requirements/recommendations for international students: Required—TOEFL (minimum score 540 paper-based; 76 iBT), IELTS (minimum score 6), ELPT (minimum score 964) or ELS (minimum score 112). *Application deadline:* For fall admission, 7/31 priority date for domestic students, 6/30 for international students; for winter admission, 11/15 priority date for domestic students, 11/15 for international students; for spring admission, 1/7 priority date for domestic students, 1/7 for international students. Applications are processed on a rolling basis. Application fee: $50. Electronic applications accepted. *Expenses:* Tuition, state resident: full-time $12,960; part-time $360 per credit. Tuition, nonresident: full-time $16,200; part-time $450 per credit. *Required fees:* $423 per quarter. *Financial support:* In 2012–13, 3 students received support, including 3 research assistantships with partial tuition reimbursements available; career-related internships or fieldwork, institutionally sponsored loans, scholarships/grants, and unspecified assistantships also available. *Unit head:* Dr. Kemble Yates, Graduate Program Coordinator, 541-552-6578, E-mail: kyates@sou.edu.

Stevens Institute of Technology, Graduate School, Charles V. Schaefer Jr. School of Engineering, Department of Mathematical Sciences, Program in Applied Mathematics, Hoboken, NJ 07030. Offers MS. *Degree requirements:* For master's, thesis optional. *Entrance requirements:* For master's, GRE. Additional exam requirements/recommendations for international students: Required—TOEFL. Electronic applications accepted.

Stony Brook University, State University of New York, Graduate School, College of Engineering and Applied Sciences, Department of Applied Mathematics and Statistics, Stony Brook, NY 11794. Offers MS, PhD. *Faculty:* 20 full-time (4 women), 2 part-time/adjunct (0 women). *Students:* 268 full-time (101 women), 27 part-time (12 women); includes 24 minority (1 Black or African American, non-Hispanic/Latino; 22 Asian, non-Hispanic/Latino; 1 Hispanic/

276 www.petersonsbooks.com

Peterson's Graduate Programs in the Physical Sciences, Mathematics, Agricultural Sciences, the Environment & Natural Resources 2014

Latino), 233 international. Average age 28. 551 applicants, 56% accepted, 74 enrolled. In 2012, 85 master's, 23 doctorates awarded. *Degree requirements:* For master's, thesis or alternative; for doctorate, one foreign language, comprehensive exam, thesis/dissertation. *Entrance requirements:* For master's and doctorate, GRE General Test. Additional exam requirements/recommendations for international students: Required—TOEFL. *Application deadline:* For fall admission, 1/15 for domestic students. Application fee: $100. *Expenses:* Tuition, state resident: full-time $9370. Tuition, nonresident: full-time $16,680. *Required fees:* $1214. *Financial support:* In 2012–13, 42 research assistantships, 52 teaching assistantships were awarded; fellowships also available. *Faculty research:* Biostatistics, combinatorial analysis, differential equations, modeling. *Total annual research expenditures:* $3.2 million. *Unit head:* Dr. Brent Lindquist, Chair, 631-632-8370, Fax: 632-8490, E-mail: lindquis@ams.stonybrook.edu. *Application contact:* Dr. David Green, Graduate Program Director, 631-632-9344, Fax: 631-632-8490, E-mail: dfgreen@ams.sunysb.edu.

Temple University, College of Science and Technology, Department of Mathematics, Philadelphia, PA 19122-6096. Offers applied mathematics (MA); mathematics (PhD); pure mathematics (MA). Part-time and evening/weekend programs available. *Faculty:* 56 full-time (12 women). *Students:* 27 full-time (6 women), 8 international. 71 applicants, 18% accepted, 7 enrolled. In 2012, 1 master's, 3 doctorates awarded. Terminal master's awarded for partial completion of doctoral program. *Degree requirements:* For master's, thesis optional, written exam; for doctorate, 2 foreign languages, thesis/dissertation, oral and written exams. *Entrance requirements:* For master's, GRE General Test, minimum GPA of 3.0; for doctorate, GRE General Test, GRE Subject Test, minimum GPA of 3.0. Additional exam requirements/recommendations for international students: Required—TOEFL (minimum score 550 paper-based; 79 iBT). *Application deadline:* For fall admission, 2/15 priority date for domestic students, 12/15 for international students; for spring admission, 11/15 priority date for domestic students, 8/1 for international students. Applications are processed on a rolling basis. Application fee: $60. Electronic applications accepted. *Financial support:* Fellowships, research assistantships, teaching assistantships, Federal Work-Study, and institutionally sponsored loans available. Financial award application deadline: 1/15; financial award applicants required to submit FAFSA. *Faculty research:* Differential geometry, numerical analysis. *Unit head:* Dr. Gerardo Mendoza, Graduate Chair, 215-204-5053, Fax: 215-204-6433, E-mail: mathematics@temple.edu. *Application contact:* Alexis Cogan, Administrative Assistant, 215-204-7840, E-mail: cogana@temple.edu. Website: http://math.temple.edu/.

Texas A&M University–Corpus Christi, Graduate Studies and Research, College of Science and Technology, Program in Mathematics, Corpus Christi, TX 78412-5503. Offers applied and computational mathematics (MS); curriculum content (MS). Part-time programs available. *Degree requirements:* For master's, thesis (for some programs). *Entrance requirements:* For master's, 2 letters of recommendation.

Texas Christian University, College of Science and Engineering, Department of Mathematics, Fort Worth, TX 76129-0002. Offers applied mathematics (MS); mathematics (MAT); pure mathematics (MS, PhD). Part-time and evening/weekend programs available. *Faculty:* 12 full-time (2 women). *Students:* 6 full-time (2 women), 9 part-time (3 women); includes 2 minority (1 Asian, non-Hispanic/Latino; 1 Hispanic/Latino), 2 international. Average age 26. 28 applicants, 54% accepted, 6 enrolled. In 2012, 4 master's awarded. Terminal master's awarded for partial completion of doctoral program. *Degree requirements:* For master's, thesis optional; for doctorate, comprehensive exam, thesis/dissertation. *Entrance requirements:* For master's and doctorate, GRE, 24 hours of math, including courses in elementary calculus of one and several variables, linear algebra, abstract algebra and real analysis. Additional exam requirements/recommendations for international students: Required—TOEFL. *Application deadline:* For fall admission, 3/1 priority date for domestic students, 3/1 for international students; for spring admission, 10/15 priority date for domestic students, 10/15 for international students. Applications are processed on a rolling basis. Application fee: $60. Electronic applications accepted. *Expenses: Tuition:* Full-time $21,600; part-time $1200 per credit. *Required fees:* $48. Tuition and fees vary according to program. *Financial support:* In 2012–13, 14 students received support, including 7 research assistantships with full tuition reimbursements available (averaging $17,500 per year), 4 teaching assistantships with full tuition reimbursements available (averaging $10,000 per year); tuition waivers (full) also available. Support available to part-time students. Financial award application deadline: 3/1. *Faculty research:* Differential geometry, topology, analysis, number theory, algebraic geometry. *Unit head:* Dr. George Gilbert, Associate Professor and Chair, 817-257-6061, E-mail: g.gilbert@tcu.edu. *Application contact:* Dr. Ken Richardson, Professor/Director, Graduate Program, 817-257-6128, E-mail: k.richardson@tcu.edu. Website: http://www.math.tcu.edu/.

Texas State University–San Marcos, Graduate School, College of Science and Engineering, Department of Mathematics, Program in Applied Mathematics, San Marcos, TX 78666. Offers MS. Part-time programs available. *Faculty:* 15 full-time (6 women), 1 part-time/adjunct (0 women). *Students:* 1 part-time (0 women). Average age 28. 3 applicants, 33% accepted, 0 enrolled. *Degree requirements:* For master's, comprehensive exam, thesis. *Entrance requirements:* For master's, GRE, minimum GPA of 2.75 in last 60 hours of undergraduate work. Additional exam requirements/recommendations for international students: Required—TOEFL (minimum score 550 paper-based; 78 iBT). *Application deadline:* For fall admission, 6/15 priority date for domestic students, 6/1 for international students; for spring admission, 10/15 priority date for domestic students, 10/1 for international students. Applications are processed on a rolling basis. Application fee: $40 ($90 for international students). Electronic applications accepted. *Expenses:* Tuition, state resident: full-time $6408; part-time $3204 per semester. Tuition, nonresident: full-time $14,832; part-time $7416 per semester. *Required fees:* $1824; $618. Tuition and fees vary according to course load. *Financial support:* In 2012–13, 1 student received support. Research assistantships, teaching assistantships, Federal Work-Study, institutionally sponsored loans, scholarships/grants, health care benefits, and unspecified assistantships available. Support available to part-time students. Financial award application deadline: 4/1; financial award applicants required to submit FAFSA. *Unit head:* Dr. Nathaniel Dean, Graduate Advisor, 512-245-2551, Fax: 512-245-3425, E-mail: nd17@txstate.edu. *Application contact:* Dr. J. Michael Willoughby, Dean of Graduate College, 512-245-2581, E-mail: gradcollege@txstate.edu. Website: http://www.math.txstate.edu/degrees-programs/masters/applied-math.html.

Texas State University–San Marcos, Graduate School, College of Science and Engineering, Department of Mathematics, Program in Mathematics, San Marcos, TX 78666. Offers MS. *Faculty:* 15 full-time (6 women), 1 part-time/adjunct (0 women). *Students:* 11 full-time (6 women), 10 part-time (4 women); includes 8 minority (2 Black or African American, non-Hispanic/Latino; 2 Asian, non-Hispanic/Latino; 4 Hispanic/Latino), 2 international. Average age 30. 10 applicants, 60% accepted, 1 enrolled. *Degree requirements:* For master's, comprehensive exam, thesis (for some programs). *Entrance requirements:* For master's, GRE, minimum GPA of 2.75 in last 60 hours of undergraduate course work. Additional exam requirements/recommendations for international students: Required—TOEFL (minimum score 550 paper-based; 78 iBT). *Application deadline:* For fall admission, 6/15 priority date for domestic students, 6/1 for international students; for spring admission, 10/15 priority date for domestic students, 10/1 for international students. Applications are processed on a rolling basis. Application fee: $40 ($90 for international students). Electronic applications accepted. *Expenses:* Tuition, state resident: full-time $6408; part-time $3204 per semester. Tuition, nonresident: full-time $14,832; part-time $7416 per semester. *Required fees:* $1824; $618. Tuition and fees vary according to course load. *Financial support:* In 2012–13, 8 students received support, including 7 teaching assistantships (averaging $16,160 per year); research assistantships, Federal Work-Study, institutionally sponsored loans, scholarships/grants, health care benefits, and unspecified assistantships also available. Support available to part-time students. Financial award application deadline: 4/1; financial award applicants required to submit FAFSA. *Unit head:* Dr. Nathaniel Dean, Graduate Advisor, 512-245-3555, Fax: 512-245-3425, E-mail: nd17@txstate.edu. *Application contact:* Dr. J. Michael Willoughby, Dean of the Graduate College, 512-245-3446, Fax: 512-245-3425, E-mail: gp02@txstate.edu. Website: http://www.math.txstate.edu/degrees-programs/masters/master-math.html.

Towson University, Program in Applied and Industrial Mathematics, Towson, MD 21252-0001. Offers MS. Part-time and evening/weekend programs available. *Entrance requirements:* For master's, bachelor's degree in mathematics or related field; minimum GPA of 3.0, including 3 terms of calculus, one in linear algebra. Additional exam requirements/recommendations for international students: Required—TOEFL (minimum score 550 paper-based). Electronic applications accepted.

Tulane University, School of Science and Engineering, Department of Mathematics, New Orleans, LA 70118-5669. Offers applied mathematics (MS); mathematics (MS, PhD); statistics (MS). *Degree requirements:* For master's, thesis (for some programs); for doctorate, thesis/dissertation. *Entrance requirements:* For master's, GRE General Test, minimum B average in undergraduate course work; for doctorate, GRE General Test. Additional exam requirements/recommendations for international students: Required—TOEFL. Electronic applications accepted.

The University of Akron, Graduate School, Buchtel College of Arts and Sciences, Department of Theoretical and Applied Mathematics, Program in Applied Mathematics, Akron, OH 44325. Offers MS. *Students:* 16 full-time (5 women), 1 part-time (0 women); includes 1 minority (Asian, non-Hispanic/Latino), 2 international. Average age 25. 12 applicants, 67% accepted, 5 enrolled. In 2012, 8 master's awarded. *Degree requirements:* For master's, seminar and comprehensive exam or thesis. *Entrance requirements:* For master's, minimum GPA of 2.75, three letters of recommendation, statement of purpose. Additional exam requirements/recommendations for international students: Required—TOEFL (minimum score 550 paper-based; 79 iBT). *Application deadline:* Applications are processed on a rolling basis. Application fee: $40 ($60 for international students). Electronic applications accepted. *Expenses:* Tuition, state resident: full-time $7285; part-time $404.70 per credit hour. Tuition, nonresident: full-time $12,473; part-time $692.95 per credit hour. *Required fees:* $34.05 per credit hour. Tuition and fees vary according to course load. *Faculty research:* Analysis of nonlinear partial differential equations, finite groups and character theory, mathematics education, modeling and simulation of continuum and nanoscale systems, numerical analysis and scientific computation. *Unit head:* Dr. Gerald Young, Coordinator, 330-972-5731, Fax: 330-972-8630, E-mail: gyoung1@uakron.edu. *Application contact:* Dr. Mark Tausig, Associate Dean, 330-972-6266, Fax: 330-972-6475, E-mail: mtausig@uakron.edu. Website: http://www.uakron.edu/math/academics/graduate/applied-mathematics-program.dot.

The University of Akron, Graduate School, College of Engineering, Program in Engineering Applied Mathematics, Akron, OH 44325. Offers PhD. *Students:* 1 full-time (0 women), 1 (woman) part-time. Average age 35. 2 applicants, 100%

Peterson's Graduate Programs in the Physical Sciences, Mathematics, Agricultural Sciences, the Environment & Natural Resources 2014

www.petersonsbooks.com 277

accepted, 2 enrolled. In 2012, 2 doctorates awarded. *Degree requirements:* For doctorate, one foreign language, thesis/dissertation, candidacy exam, qualifying exam. *Entrance requirements:* For doctorate, GRE, minimum GPA of 3.0 with bachelor's or master's degree; two letters of recommendation, statement of purpose. Additional exam requirements/recommendations for international students: Required—TOEFL (minimum score 550 paper-based; 79 iBT). *Application deadline:* Applications are processed on a rolling basis. Application fee: $40 ($60 for international students). Electronic applications accepted. *Expenses:* Tuition, state resident: full-time $7285; part-time $404.70 per credit hour. Tuition, nonresident: full-time $12,473; part-time $692.95 per credit hour. *Required fees:* $34.05 per credit hour. Tuition and fees vary according to course load. *Unit head:* Dr. Gerald Young, Coordinator, 330-972-5731, E-mail: jerry@math.uakron.edu. *Application contact:* Dr. Craig Menzemer, Director of Graduate Studies, College of Engineering, 330-972-5536, E-mail: ccmenze@uakron.edu. Website: http://www.uakron.edu/math/academics/graduate/engineering-applied-mathematics-ph.-d.-program.dot.

The University of Alabama, Graduate School, College of Arts and Sciences, Department of Mathematics, Tuscaloosa, AL 35487. Offers applied mathematics (PhD); mathematics (MA, PhD); pure mathematics (PhD). *Faculty:* 29 full-time (1 woman). *Students:* 41 full-time (13 women), 4 part-time (2 women); includes 2 minority (1 Black or African American, non-Hispanic/Latino; 1 Two or more races, non-Hispanic/Latino), 25 international. Average age 28. 35 applicants, 60% accepted, 6 enrolled. In 2012, 7 master's, 5 doctorates awarded. Terminal master's awarded for partial completion of doctoral program. *Degree requirements:* For master's, thesis or alternative; for doctorate, thesis/dissertation. *Entrance requirements:* For master's and doctorate, GRE General Test, minimum GPA of 3.0. Additional exam requirements/recommendations for international students: Required—TOEFL (minimum score 550 paper-based; 79 iBT). *Application deadline:* For fall admission, 7/1 for domestic students, 5/31 for international students; for spring admission, 11/30 for domestic students, 10/31 for international students. Applications are processed on a rolling basis. Application fee: $50 ($60 for international students). Electronic applications accepted. *Expenses:* Tuition, state resident: full-time $9200. Tuition, nonresident: full-time $22,950. *Financial support:* In 2012–13, 1 fellowship with full tuition reimbursement (averaging $30,000 per year), 35 teaching assistantships with full tuition reimbursements (averaging $12,258 per year) were awarded; research assistantships with full tuition reimbursements, Federal Work-Study, institutionally sponsored loans, scholarships/grants, and unspecified assistantships also available. Support available to part-time students. Financial award application deadline: 7/1. *Faculty research:* Analysis, topology, algebra, fluid mechanics and system control theory, optimization, stochastic processes, numerical analysis. *Total annual research expenditures:* $302,468. *Unit head:* Dr. Zhijian Wu, Chairperson and Professor, 205-348-5080, Fax: 205-348-7067, E-mail: zwu@as.ua.edu. *Application contact:* Dr. Vo Liem, Director, 205-348-4898, Fax: 205-348-7067, E-mail: vliem@as.ua.edu.

The University of Alabama at Birmingham, College of Arts and Sciences, Program in Applied Mathematics, Birmingham, AL 35294. Offers PhD. Program offered jointly with The University of Alabama (Tuscaloosa), The University of Alabama in Huntsville. *Students:* 19 full-time (5 women), 4 part-time (0 women); includes 1 minority (Black or African American, non-Hispanic/Latino), 12 international. Average age 30. *Entrance requirements:* For doctorate, GRE General Test (minimum score of 150 on Quantitative Reasoning portion), B average in previous coursework, letters of recommendation. *Application deadline:* For fall admission, 3/15 priority date for domestic students. Applications are processed on a rolling basis. Electronic applications accepted. *Expenses:* Tuition, state resident: full-time $6420; part-time $335 per credit hour. Tuition, nonresident: full-time $14,574; part-time $788 per credit hour. Tuition and fees vary according to course load and program. *Financial support:* Fellowships with tuition reimbursements, teaching assistantships with tuition reimbursements, and health care benefits available. *Faculty research:* Inverse problems, mathematical modeling, mathematical biology. *Unit head:* Dr. Yulia Karpeshina, Graduate Program Coordinator, 205-934-2154, Fax: 205-934-9025, E-mail: karpeshi@math.uab.edu.

The University of Alabama in Huntsville, School of Graduate Studies, College of Science, Department of Mathematical Sciences, Huntsville, AL 35899. Offers applied mathematics (PhD); education (MA, MS); mathematics (MA, MS). PhD offered jointly with The University of Alabama (Tuscaloosa) and The University of Alabama at Birmingham. Part-time and evening/weekend programs available. *Faculty:* 14 full-time (1 woman), 1 part-time/adjunct (0 women). *Students:* 20 full-time (10 women), 9 part-time (1 woman); includes 4 minority (3 Black or African American, non-Hispanic/Latino; 1 Hispanic/Latino), 3 international. Average age 27. 26 applicants, 85% accepted, 12 enrolled. In 2012, 6 master's, 3 doctorates awarded. *Degree requirements:* For master's, comprehensive exam, thesis or alternative, oral and written exams; for doctorate, comprehensive exam, thesis/dissertation, oral and written exams. *Entrance requirements:* For master's and doctorate, GRE General Test, minimum GPA of 3.0. Additional exam requirements/recommendations for international students: Required—TOEFL (minimum score 550 paper-based; 80 iBT), IELTS (minimum score 6.5). *Application deadline:* For fall admission, 7/15 priority date for domestic students, 4/1 for international students; for spring admission, 11/30 priority date for domestic students, 9/1 for international students. Applications are processed on a rolling basis. Application fee: $40 ($50 for international students). Electronic applications accepted. *Expenses:* Tuition, state resident: full-time $8516; part-time $515 per credit hour. Tuition, nonresident: full-time $20,384; part-time $1229 per credit hour. *Required fees:* $148 per semester. One-time fee: $150. *Financial support:* In 2012–13, 14 students received support, including 14 teaching assistantships with full and partial tuition reimbursements available (averaging $10,342 per year); career-related internships or fieldwork, Federal Work-Study, institutionally sponsored loans, scholarships/grants, health care benefits, and unspecified assistantships also available. Support available to part-time students. Financial award application deadline: 4/1; financial award applicants required to submit FAFSA. *Faculty research:* Combinatorics and graph theory, computational mathematics, differential equations and applications, mathematical biology, probability and stochastic processes. *Total annual research expenditures:* $241,477. *Unit head:* Dr. Jia Li, Chair, 256-824-6470, Fax: 256-824-6173, E-mail: li@math.uah.edu. *Application contact:* Kim Gray, Graduate Studies Admissions Coordinator, 256-824-6002, Fax: 256-824-6405, E-mail: deangrad@uah.edu. Website: http://www.math.uah.edu/.

University of Alberta, Faculty of Graduate Studies and Research, Department of Mathematical and Statistical Sciences, Edmonton, AB T6G 2E1, Canada. Offers applied mathematics (M Sc, PhD); biostatistics (M Sc); mathematical finance (M Sc, PhD); mathematical physics (M Sc, PhD); mathematics (M Sc, PhD); statistics (M Sc, PhD, Postgraduate Diploma). Part-time programs available. Terminal master's awarded for partial completion of doctoral program. *Degree requirements:* For master's, thesis (for some programs); for doctorate, comprehensive exam, thesis/dissertation. *Entrance requirements:* Additional exam requirements/recommendations for international students: Required—TOEFL (minimum score 580 paper-based). Electronic applications accepted. *Faculty research:* Classical and functional analysis, algebra, differential equations, geometry.

The University of Arizona, Graduate Interdisciplinary Programs, Graduate Interdisciplinary Program in Applied Mathematics, Tucson, AZ 85721. Offers applied mathematics (MS, PhD); mathematical sciences (PMS). *Students:* 53 full-time (14 women), 1 part-time (0 women); includes 6 minority (2 Asian, non-Hispanic/Latino; 3 Hispanic/Latino; 1 Two or more races, non-Hispanic/Latino), 3 international. Average age 27. 156 applicants, 11% accepted, 8 enrolled. In 2012, 7 master's, 2 doctorates awarded. Terminal master's awarded for partial completion of doctoral program. *Degree requirements:* For master's, thesis (for some programs); for doctorate, comprehensive exam, thesis/dissertation. *Entrance requirements:* For master's, GRE, 3 letters of recommendation; for doctorate, GRE, 3 letters of recommendation, statement of purpose. Additional exam requirements/recommendations for international students: Required—TOEFL (minimum score 575 paper-based; 80 iBT). *Application deadline:* For fall admission, 1/15 for domestic students, 1/30 for international students. Applications are processed on a rolling basis. Application fee: $75. Electronic applications accepted. *Financial support:* In 2012–13, 1 research assistantship with full tuition reimbursement (averaging $17,120 per year) was awarded; institutionally sponsored loans, scholarships/grants, health care benefits, tuition waivers (full), and unspecified assistantships also available. Financial award application deadline: 3/1; financial award applicants required to submit FAFSA. *Faculty research:* Dynamical systems and chaos, partial differential equations, pattern formation, fluid dynamics and turbulence, scientific computation, mathematical physics, mathematical biology, medical imaging, applied probability and stochastic processes. *Unit head:* Dr. Michael Tabor, Head, 520-621-4664, Fax: 520-626-5048, E-mail: tabor@math.arizona.edu. *Application contact:* Graduate Coordinator, 520-621-2016, Fax: 520-626-5048, E-mail: applmath@u.arizona.edu. Website: http://appliedmath.arizona.edu/.

University of Arkansas at Little Rock, Graduate School, College of Science and Mathematics, Department of Mathematics and Statistics, Little Rock, AR 72204-1099. Offers applied statistics (Graduate Certificate); mathematical sciences (MS). Part-time and evening/weekend programs available. *Degree requirements:* For master's, comprehensive exam. *Entrance requirements:* For master's, GRE General Test, GRE Subject Test, minimum GPA of 2.7, previous course work in advanced mathematics.

The University of British Columbia, Institute of Applied Mathematics, Vancouver, BC V6T 1Z1, Canada. Offers M Sc, PhD. *Degree requirements:* For master's, thesis (for some programs); for doctorate, comprehensive exam, thesis/dissertation. *Entrance requirements:* For doctorate, master's degree. Additional exam requirements/recommendations for international students: Required—TOEFL. *Faculty research:* Applied analysis, optimization, mathematical biology, numerical analysis, fluid mechanics.

University of California, Berkeley, Graduate Division, College of Letters and Science, Department of Mathematics, Program in Applied Mathematics, Berkeley, CA 94720-1500. Offers PhD. *Degree requirements:* For doctorate, 2 foreign languages, thesis/dissertation, qualifying exam. *Entrance requirements:* For doctorate, GRE General Test, GRE Subject Test, minimum GPA of 3.0, 3 letters of recommendation.

University of California, Davis, Graduate Studies, Graduate Group in Applied Mathematics, Davis, CA 95616. Offers MS, PhD. Terminal master's awarded for partial completion of doctoral program. *Degree requirements:* For master's, thesis; for doctorate, one foreign language, thesis/dissertation. *Entrance requirements:* For master's, GRE General Test, GRE Subject Test, minimum GPA of 3.0; for doctorate, GRE General Test, GRE Subject Test, master's degree, minimum GPA of 3.0. Additional exam requirements/recommendations for international students: Required—TOEFL (minimum score 550 paper-based). Electronic applications

278 www.petersonsbooks.com

Peterson's Graduate Programs in the Physical Sciences, Mathematics, Agricultural Sciences, the Environment & Natural Resources 2014

accepted. *Faculty research:* Mathematical biology, control and optimization, atmospheric sciences, theoretical chemistry, mathematical physics.

University of California, Merced, Graduate Division, School of Natural Sciences, Merced, CA 95343. Offers applied mathematics (MS, PhD); physics and chemistry (MS, PhD); quantitative and systems biology (MS, PhD). *Students:* 121 full-time (50 women); includes 38 minority (3 Black or African American, non-Hispanic/Latino; 12 Asian, non-Hispanic/Latino; 18 Hispanic/Latino; 5 Two or more races, non-Hispanic/Latino), 34 international. Average age 28. 161 applicants, 47% accepted, 42 enrolled. In 2012, 9 master's, 5 doctorates awarded. *Financial support:* In 2012–13, 120 students received support, including 108 fellowships with full and partial tuition reimbursements available (averaging $11,590 per year), 34 research assistantships with full and partial tuition reimbursements available (averaging $8,960 per year), 103 teaching assistantships with partial tuition reimbursements available (averaging $12,560 per year); health care benefits also available. Financial award applicants required to submit FAFSA. *Unit head:* Dr. Juan Meza, Dean, 209-228-4487, Fax: 209-228-4060, E-mail: jcmeza@ucmerced.edu. *Application contact:* Tsu Ya, Graduate Admissions and Academic Services Manager, 209-228-4723, Fax: 209-228-6906, E-mail: tya@ucmerced.edu.

University of California, San Diego, Office of Graduate Studies, Department of Mathematics, La Jolla, CA 92093. Offers applied mathematics (MA); mathematics (MA, PhD); statistics (MS). *Degree requirements:* For doctorate, thesis/dissertation. *Entrance requirements:* For master's and doctorate, GRE General Test, GRE Subject Test. Electronic applications accepted.

University of California, Santa Barbara, Graduate Division, College of Letters and Sciences, Division of Mathematics, Life, and Physical Sciences, Department of Mathematics, Santa Barbara, CA 93106-3080. Offers applied mathematics (MA), including computational science and engineering; mathematics (MA, PhD), including computational science and engineering; MA/PhD. *Faculty:* 28 full-time (2 women). *Students:* 50 full-time (13 women); includes 12 minority (1 Black or African American, non-Hispanic/Latino; 4 Asian, non-Hispanic/Latino; 7 Hispanic/Latino), 5 international. Average age 26. 186 applicants, 17% accepted, 10 enrolled. In 2012, 6 master's, 2 doctorates awarded. Terminal master's awarded for partial completion of doctoral program. *Degree requirements:* For master's, comprehensive exam (for some programs), thesis (for some programs); for doctorate, comprehensive exam, thesis/dissertation. *Entrance requirements:* For master's and doctorate, GRE General Test, GRE Subject Test (math). Additional exam requirements/recommendations for international students: Required—TOEFL (minimum score 575 paper-based; 80 iBT), IELTS (minimum score 7). *Application deadline:* For fall admission, 1/1 for domestic and international students. Application fee: $80 ($100 for international students). Electronic applications accepted. *Financial support:* In 2012–13, 48 students received support, including 4 fellowships with full tuition reimbursements available (averaging $20,000 per year), 6 research assistantships with full tuition reimbursements available (averaging $18,000 per year), 45 teaching assistantships with partial tuition reimbursements available (averaging $17,655 per year); Federal Work-Study, institutionally sponsored loans, health care benefits, and tuition waivers (full and partial) also available. Financial award application deadline: 3/2; financial award applicants required to submit FAFSA. *Faculty research:* Topology, differential geometry, algebra, applied mathematics, partial differential equations. *Total annual research expenditures:* $205,000. *Unit head:* Prof. David R. Morrison, Chair, 805-893-8340, Fax: 805-893-2385, E-mail: chair@math.ucsb.edu. *Application contact:* Medina Price, Graduate Advisor, 805-893-8192, Fax: 805-893-2385, E-mail: price@math.ucsb.edu. Website: http://www.math.ucsb.edu/.

University of California, Santa Cruz, Division of Graduate Studies, Jack Baskin School of Engineering, Program in Statistics and Applied Mathematics, Santa Cruz, CA 95064. Offers MS, PhD. Terminal master's awarded for partial completion of doctoral program. *Degree requirements:* For master's, seminar, qualifying exam, capstone project; for doctorate, thesis/dissertation, seminar, qualifying exam. *Entrance requirements:* For master's and doctorate, GRE General Test; GRE Subject Test in math (recommended). Additional exam requirements/recommendations for international students: Required—TOEFL (minimum score 570 paper-based; 89 iBT); Recommended—IELTS (minimum score 8). Electronic applications accepted. *Faculty research:* Bayesian nonparametric methods; computationally intensive Bayesian inference, prediction, and decision-making; envirometrics; fluid mechanics; mathematical biology.

University of Central Arkansas, Graduate School, College of Natural Sciences and Math, Department of Mathematics, Conway, AR 72035-0001. Offers applied mathematics (MS); math education (MA). Part-time programs available. *Faculty:* 16 full-time (4 women). *Students:* 18 full-time (10 women), 9 part-time (5 women); includes 2 minority (1 Black or African American, non-Hispanic/Latino; 1 Asian, non-Hispanic/Latino), 2 international. Average age 37. 14 applicants, 100% accepted, 11 enrolled. In 2012, 15 master's awarded. *Degree requirements:* For master's, comprehensive exam, thesis optional. *Entrance requirements:* For master's, GRE General Test, minimum GPA of 2.7. Additional exam requirements/recommendations for international students: Required—TOEFL (minimum score 550 paper-based; 80 iBT). *Application deadline:* For fall admission, 3/1 priority date for domestic students; for spring admission, 10/1 priority date for domestic students. Applications are processed on a rolling basis. Application fee: $25 ($50 for international students). Electronic applications accepted. *Expenses:* Tuition, state resident: full-time $3462; part-time $278.02 per credit hour. Tuition, nonresident: full-time $6172; part-time $503.82 per credit hour. *Financial support:* In 2012–13, 11 teaching assistantships with partial tuition reimbursements (averaging $8,500 per year) were awarded; Federal Work-Study, scholarships/grants, and unspecified assistantships also available. Financial award application deadline: 2/15; financial award applicants required to submit FAFSA. *Unit head:* Dr. Ramesh Garimella, Chair, 501-450-3147, Fax: 501-450-5662, E-mail: rameshg@uca.edu. *Application contact:* Susan Wood, Admissions Assistant, 501-450-3124, Fax: 501-450-5678, E-mail: swood@uca.edu. Website: http://uca.edu/math/.

University of Central Missouri, The Graduate School, Warrensburg, MO 64093. Offers accountancy (MA); accounting (MBA); applied mathematics (MS); aviation safety (MA); biology (MS); business administration (MBA); career and technical education leadership (MS); college student personnel administration (MS); communication (MA); computer science (MS); counseling (MS); criminal justice (MS); educational leadership (Ed D); educational technology (MS); elementary and early childhood education (MSE); English (MA); environmental studies (MA); finance (MBA); history (MA); human services/educational technology (Ed S); human services/learning resources (Ed S); human services/professional counseling (Ed S); industrial hygiene (MS); industrial management (MS); information systems (MBA); information technology (MS); kinesiology (MS); library science and information services (MS); literacy education (MSE); marketing (MBA); mathematics (MS); music (MA); occupational safety management (MS); psychology (MS); rural family nursing (MS); school administration (MSE); social gerontology (MS); sociology (MA); special education (MSE); speech language pathology (MS); superintendency (Ed S); teaching (MAT); teaching English as a second language (MA); technology (MS); technology management (PhD); theatre (MA). Part-time programs available. *Faculty:* 233. *Students:* 583 full-time (327 women), 1,425 part-time (930 women); includes 169 minority (93 Black or African American, non-Hispanic/Latino; 11 American Indian or Alaska Native, non-Hispanic/Latino; 27 Asian, non-Hispanic/Latino; 29 Hispanic/Latino; 3 Native Hawaiian or other Pacific Islander, non-Hispanic/Latino; 6 Two or more races, non-Hispanic/Latino), 234 international. Average age 33. 958 applicants, 80% accepted. In 2012, 567 master's, 56 other advanced degrees awarded. *Degree requirements:* For master's and Ed S, comprehensive exam (for some programs), thesis (for some programs). *Entrance requirements:* Additional exam requirements/recommendations for international students: Required—TOEFL (minimum score 550 paper-based; 79 iBT). *Application deadline:* For fall admission, 6/1 for domestic students; for spring admission, 10/1 for domestic and international students. Applications are processed on a rolling basis. Application fee: $30 ($75 for international students). Electronic applications accepted. *Financial support:* In 2012–13, 118 students received support, including 271 research assistantships with full and partial tuition reimbursements available (averaging $7,500 per year), 109 teaching assistantships with full and partial tuition reimbursements available (averaging $7,500 per year); career-related internships or fieldwork, Federal Work-Study, scholarships/grants, and administrative and laboratory assistantships also available. Support available to part-time students. Financial award application deadline: 3/1; financial award applicants required to submit FAFSA. *Unit head:* Dr. Joseph Vaughn, Assistant Provost for Research/Dean, 660-543-4092, Fax: 660-543-4778, E-mail: vaughn@ucmo.edu. *Application contact:* Brittany Gerbec, Graduate Student Services Coordinator, 660-543-4621, Fax: 660-543-4778, E-mail: gradinfo@ucmo.edu. Website: http://www.ucmo.edu/graduate/.

University of Central Oklahoma, The Jackson College of Graduate Studies, College of Mathematics and Science, Department of Mathematics and Statistics, Edmond, OK 73034-5209. Offers applied mathematical sciences (MS), including computer science, mathematics, mathematics/computer science teaching, statistics. Part-time programs available. *Faculty:* 5 full-time (1 woman), 5 part-time/adjunct (1 woman). *Students:* 24 full-time (10 women), 11 part-time (4 women); includes 6 minority (2 Black or African American, non-Hispanic/Latino; 1 American Indian or Alaska Native, non-Hispanic/Latino; 1 Asian, non-Hispanic/Latino; 2 Two or more races, non-Hispanic/Latino), 15 international. Average age 29. 55 applicants, 58% accepted, 14 enrolled. In 2012, 5 master's awarded. *Degree requirements:* For master's, comprehensive exam (for some programs), thesis (for some programs). *Entrance requirements:* For master's, GRE. Additional exam requirements/recommendations for international students: Required—TOEFL (minimum score 550 paper-based; 79 iBT), IELTS (minimum score 6.5). *Application deadline:* For fall admission, 7/1 for international students; for spring admission, 11/1 for international students. Applications are processed on a rolling basis. Application fee: $50. Electronic applications accepted. *Expenses:* Tuition, state resident: full-time $3718; part-time $195.65 per credit hour. Tuition, nonresident: full-time $9309; part-time $489.95 per credit hour. *Required fees:* $399.95; $21.50 per credit hour. One-time fee: $50. Tuition and fees vary according to program. *Financial support:* In 2012–13, 13 students received support, including research assistantships with partial tuition reimbursements available (averaging $5,083 per year), teaching assistantships with partial tuition reimbursements available (averaging $7,447 per year); Federal Work-Study, scholarships/grants, tuition waivers (partial), and unspecified assistantships also available. Financial award application deadline: 3/31; financial award applicants required to submit FAFSA. *Unit head:* Dr. Jesse Byrne, Chair, 405-974-5294, Fax: 405-974-3824, E-mail: jbyrne@uco.edu. *Application contact:* Dr. Richard Bernard, Dean, Jackson College of Graduate Studies, 405-974-3493, Fax: 405-974-3852, E-mail: gradcoll@uco.edu. Website: http://www.math.uco.edu/.

University of Chicago, Division of the Physical Sciences, Department of Mathematics, Program in Applied Mathematics, Chicago, IL 60637-1513. Offers

SM, PhD. *Degree requirements:* For master's, one foreign language, oral exams; for doctorate, one foreign language, thesis/dissertation, 2 qualifying exams. *Entrance requirements:* For master's and doctorate, GRE General Test, GRE Subject Test. Additional exam requirements/recommendations for international students: Required—TOEFL (minimum score 600 paper-based). Electronic applications accepted. *Faculty research:* Applied analysis, dynamical systems, theoretical biology, math-physics.

University of Cincinnati, Graduate School, McMicken College of Arts and Sciences, Department of Mathematical Sciences, Cincinnati, OH 45221. Offers applied mathematics (MS, PhD); mathematics education (MAT); pure mathematics (MS, PhD); statistics (MS, PhD). Part-time programs available. Terminal master's awarded for partial completion of doctoral program. *Degree requirements:* For master's, comprehensive exam, thesis or alternative; for doctorate, one foreign language, comprehensive exam, thesis/dissertation. *Entrance requirements:* For master's, GRE, teacher certification (MAT); for doctorate, GRE. Additional exam requirements/recommendations for international students: Required—TOEFL. Electronic applications accepted. *Faculty research:* Algebra, analysis, differential equations, numerical analysis, statistics.

University of Colorado Boulder, Graduate School, College of Arts and Sciences, Department of Applied Mathematics, Boulder, CO 80309. Offers MS, PhD. *Faculty:* 16 full-time (2 women). *Students:* 69 full-time (15 women), 7 part-time (1 woman); includes 12 minority (2 Black or African American, non-Hispanic/Latino; 4 Asian, non-Hispanic/Latino; 5 Hispanic/Latino; 1 Two or more races, non-Hispanic/Latino), 15 international. Average age 28. 101 applicants, 25% accepted, 21 enrolled. Terminal master's awarded for partial completion of doctoral program. *Degree requirements:* For master's, comprehensive exam, thesis or alternative; for doctorate, one foreign language, comprehensive exam, thesis/dissertation. *Entrance requirements:* For master's, GRE General Test, minimum undergraduate GPA of 2.75; for doctorate, GRE General Test. Additional exam requirements/recommendations for international students: Required—TOEFL. *Application deadline:* For fall admission, 12/15 priority date for domestic students, 12/1 for international students. Applications are processed on a rolling basis. Application fee: $50 ($60 for international students). Electronic applications accepted. *Financial support:* In 2012–13, 74 students received support, including 25 fellowships (averaging $4,866 per year), 20 research assistantships with full and partial tuition reimbursements available (averaging $25,238 per year), 39 teaching assistantships with full and partial tuition reimbursements available (averaging $21,191 per year); institutionally sponsored loans, scholarships/grants, health care benefits, and unspecified assistantships also available. Financial award applicants required to submit FAFSA. *Faculty research:* Applied mathematics, computer simulation/modeling, nonlinear dynamics, numerical analysis, probability. *Total annual research expenditures:* $3.6 million. *Application contact:* E-mail: appm_app@cboulder.colorado.edu. Website: http://amath.colorado.edu/.

University of Colorado Colorado Springs, College of Letters, Arts and Sciences, Department of Mathematics, Colorado Springs, CO 80933-7150. Offers applied mathematics (MS); applied science (PhD); mathematics (M Sc). Part-time and evening/weekend programs available. *Faculty:* 10 full-time (1 woman), 1 (woman) part-time/adjunct. *Students:* 14 full-time (4 women), 3 part-time (1 woman); includes 3 minority (1 Black or African American, non-Hispanic/Latino; 2 Hispanic/Latino), 2 international. Average age 36. In 2012, 6 master's awarded. *Degree requirements:* For master's, thesis, qualifying exam. *Entrance requirements:* For master's, GRE General Test, minimum GPA of 3.0. Additional exam requirements/recommendations for international students: Required—TOEFL (minimum score 550 paper-based). *Application deadline:* For fall admission, 6/1 for domestic and international students; for spring admission, 11/1 for domestic and international students. Applications are processed on a rolling basis. Application fee: $60 ($75 for international students). Electronic applications accepted. *Expenses:* Tuition, state resident: full-time $6412; part-time $686 per credit hour. Tuition, nonresident: full-time $11,782; part-time $1160 per credit hour. Tuition and fees vary according to course load, degree level, campus/location, program and reciprocity agreements. *Financial support:* In 2012–13, 1 student received support. Teaching assistantships, Federal Work-Study, and scholarships/grants available. Support available to part-time students. Financial award application deadline: 3/1; financial award applicants required to submit FAFSA. *Faculty research:* Associative rings and modules, spectral theory for quantum graphs, spectral theory of integrable systems, percolation theory, interacting particle systems, Abelian groups. *Total annual research expenditures:* $100,194. *Unit head:* Dr. Sarbarish Chakravarty, Chair, 719-255-3549, Fax: 719-255-3605, E-mail: schakrav@uccs.edu. *Application contact:* Kristin Sturm, Graduate Liaison, 719-255-3554, Fax: 719-255-3605, E-mail: ksturm@uccs.edu. Website: http://www.uccs.edu/math.

University of Colorado Denver, College of Liberal Arts and Sciences, Department of Mathematical and Statistical Sciences, Denver, CO 80217. Offers applied mathematics (MS, PhD), including applied mathematics, applied probability (MS), applied statistics (MS), computational biology, computational mathematics (PhD), discrete mathematics, finite geometry (PhD), mathematics education (PhD), mathematics of engineering and science (MS), numerical analysis, operations research (MS), optimization and operations research (PhD), probability (PhD), statistics (PhD). Part-time programs available. *Faculty:* 20 full-time (4 women), 3 part-time/adjunct (0 women). *Students:* 43 full-time (12 women), 13 part-time (2 women); includes 9 minority (1 Black or African American, non-Hispanic/Latino; 4 Asian, non-Hispanic/Latino; 4 Hispanic/Latino),

9 international. Average age 32. 63 applicants, 71% accepted, 14 enrolled. In 2012, 10 master's, 6 doctorates awarded. *Degree requirements:* For master's, comprehensive exam, thesis optional, 30 hours of course work with minimum GPA of 3.0; for doctorate, comprehensive exam, thesis/dissertation, 42 hours of course work with minimum GPA of 3.25. *Entrance requirements:* For master's, GRE General Test; GRE Subject Test in math (recommended), 30 hours of course work in mathematics (24 of which must be upper-division mathematics), bachelor's degree with minimum GPA of 3.0; for doctorate, GRE General Test; GRE Subject Test in math (recommended), 30 hours of course work in mathematics (24 of which must be upper-division mathematics), master's degree with minimum GPA of 3.25. Additional exam requirements/recommendations for international students: Required—TOEFL (minimum score 537 paper-based; 75 iBT); Recommended—IELTS (minimum score 6.5). *Application deadline:* For fall admission, 2/1 for domestic and international students; for spring admission, 10/1 for domestic and international students. Application fee: $50 ($75 for international students). Electronic applications accepted. *Expenses:* Tuition, state resident: full-time $7712; part-time $355 per credit hour. Tuition, nonresident: full-time $22,038; part-time $1087 per credit hour. *Required fees:* $1110; $1. Tuition and fees vary according to course load, campus/location and program. *Financial support:* In 2012–13, 33 students received support. Fellowships with partial tuition reimbursements available, research assistantships with full tuition reimbursements available, teaching assistantships with full tuition reimbursements available, Federal Work-Study, institutionally sponsored loans, scholarships/grants, traineeships, and unspecified assistantships available. Financial award application deadline: 4/1; financial award applicants required to submit FAFSA. *Faculty research:* Computational mathematics, computational biology, discrete mathematics and geometry, probability and statistics, optimization. *Unit head:* Dr. Stephen Billups, Graduate Program Director, 303-556-4814, E-mail: stephen.billups@ucdenver.edu. *Application contact:* Margie Bopp, Graduate Program Assistant, 303-556-2341, E-mail: margie.bopp@ucdenver.edu. Website: http://www.ucdenver.edu/academics/colleges/CLAS/Departments/math/Pages/MathStats.aspx.

University of Connecticut, Graduate School, College of Liberal Arts and Sciences, Department of Mathematics, Field of Applied Financial Mathematics, Storrs, CT 06269. Offers MS. *Degree requirements:* For master's, comprehensive exam. *Entrance requirements:* Additional exam requirements/recommendations for international students: Required—TOEFL (minimum score 550 paper-based). Electronic applications accepted.

University of Dayton, Department of Mathematics, Dayton, OH 45469-1300. Offers applied mathematics (MAS); financial mathematics (MFM); mathematics education (MME). Part-time and evening/weekend programs available. *Faculty:* 15 full-time (5 women). *Students:* 45 full-time (25 women), 6 part-time (3 women); includes 3 minority (2 Black or African American, non-Hispanic/Latino; 1 Asian, non-Hispanic/Latino), 37 international. Average age 26. 108 applicants, 35% accepted, 8 enrolled. In 2012, 12 master's awarded. *Entrance requirements:* For master's, minimum undergraduate GPA of 2.8 (MAS), 3.0 (MFM, MME). Additional exam requirements/recommendations for international students: Required—TOEFL (minimum score 550 paper-based; 80 iBT). *Application deadline:* For fall admission, 3/1 priority date for domestic students, 5/1 for international students; for winter admission, 7/1 for international students; for spring admission, 10/1 for international students. Applications are processed on a rolling basis. Application fee: $0 ($50 for international students). Electronic applications accepted. *Expenses:* Tuition: Part-time $708 per credit hour. *Required fees:* $25 per semester. Tuition and fees vary according to course level, course load, degree level and program. *Financial support:* In 2012–13, 6 teaching assistantships with full tuition reimbursements (averaging $14,075 per year) were awarded; institutionally sponsored loans, health care benefits, and unspecified assistantships also available. Financial award applicants required to submit FAFSA. *Faculty research:* Differential equations, integral equations, general topology, measure theory, graph theory, financial math, math education, numerical analysis. *Unit head:* Dr. Joe D. Mashburn, Chair, 937-229-2511, Fax: 937-229-2566, E-mail: jmashburn1@udayton.edu. *Application contact:* Dr. Paul W. Eloe, Graduate Program Director and Professor, 937-229-2016, E-mail: peloe1@udayton.edu.

University of Delaware, College of Arts and Sciences, Department of Mathematical Sciences, Newark, DE 19716. Offers applied mathematics (MS, PhD); mathematics (MS, PhD). Part-time programs available. Terminal master's awarded for partial completion of doctoral program. *Degree requirements:* For master's, thesis (for some programs); for doctorate, one foreign language, thesis/dissertation, qualifying exam. *Entrance requirements:* For master's and doctorate, GRE General Test. Additional exam requirements/recommendations for international students: Required—TOEFL. Electronic applications accepted. *Faculty research:* Scattering theory, inverse problems, fluid dynamics, numerical analysis, combinatorics.

University of Georgia, Franklin College of Arts and Sciences, Department of Mathematics, Athens, GA 30602. Offers applied mathematical science (MAMS); mathematics (MA, PhD). *Degree requirements:* For master's, one foreign language, thesis (for some programs); for doctorate, 2 foreign languages, thesis/dissertation. *Entrance requirements:* For master's and doctorate, GRE General Test. Electronic applications accepted.

University of Guelph, Graduate Studies, College of Physical and Engineering Science, Department of Mathematics and Statistics, Guelph, ON N1G 2W1, Canada. Offers applied mathematics (PhD); applied statistics (PhD); mathematics

280 www.petersonsbooks.com

Peterson's Graduate Programs in the Physical Sciences, Mathematics, Agricultural Sciences, the Environment & Natural Resources 2014

and statistics (M Sc). Part-time programs available. *Degree requirements:* For master's, thesis (for some programs); for doctorate, thesis/dissertation. *Entrance requirements:* For master's, minimum B- average during previous 2 years of course work; for doctorate, minimum B average. Additional exam requirements/recommendations for international students: Required—TOEFL (minimum score 550 paper-based; 89 iBT), IELTS (minimum score 6.5). *Faculty research:* Dynamical systems, mathematical biology, numerical analysis, linear and nonlinear models, reliability and bioassay.

University of Houston, College of Natural Sciences and Mathematics, Department of Mathematics, Houston, TX 77204. Offers applied mathematics (MS); mathematics (MA, PhD). Part-time programs available. *Degree requirements:* For master's, thesis optional. *Entrance requirements:* For master's and doctorate, GRE (Verbal and Quantitative). Additional exam requirements/recommendations for international students: Required—TOEFL (minimum score 550 paper-based; 79 iBT), IELTS (minimum score 6.5). Electronic applications accepted. *Faculty research:* Applied mathematics, modern analysis, computational science, geometry, dynamical systems.

University of Illinois at Chicago, Graduate College, College of Liberal Arts and Sciences, Department of Mathematics, Statistics, and Computer Science, Chicago, IL 60607-7128. Offers applied mathematics (MS, PhD); computational finance (MS, PhD); computer science (MS, PhD); mathematics (DA), mathematics and information sciences for industry (MS); probability and statistics (PhD); pure mathematics (MS, PhD); statistics (MS); teaching of mathematics (MST), including elementary, secondary. Part-time programs available. *Students:* 125 full-time (34 women), 34 part-time (15 women); includes 23 minority (1 Black or African American, non-Hispanic/Latino; 10 Asian, non-Hispanic/Latino; 10 Hispanic/Latino; 2 Two or more races, non-Hispanic/Latino), 45 international. Average age 29. 226 applicants, 37% accepted, 42 enrolled. In 2012, 30 master's, 19 doctorates awarded. *Degree requirements:* For master's, comprehensive exam; for doctorate, one foreign language, thesis/dissertation. *Entrance requirements:* For master's and doctorate, GRE General Test, minimum GPA of 3.0. Additional exam requirements/recommendations for international students: Required—TOEFL (minimum score 100 iBT). *Application deadline:* For fall admission, 1/1 for domestic and international students; for spring admission, 10/1 for domestic students, 7/15 for international students. Applications are processed on a rolling basis. Application fee: $60. Electronic applications accepted. *Expenses:* Tuition, state resident: full-time $10,882; part-time $3627 per term. Tuition, nonresident: full-time $22,880; part-time $7627 per term. *Required fees:* $1170 per semester. Tuition and fees vary according to course load, degree level and program. *Financial support:* In 2012–13, 109 students received support, including 2 fellowships with full tuition reimbursements available (averaging $20,000 per year), 8 research assistantships with full tuition reimbursements available (averaging $17,000 per year), 87 teaching assistantships with full tuition reimbursements available (averaging $17,000 per year); Federal Work-Study, scholarships/grants, and tuition waivers (full) also available. Financial award application deadline: 1/1. *Total annual research expenditures:* $2.2 million. *Unit head:* Lawrence Ein, Head, 312-996-3044, E-mail: ein@math.uic.edu. *Application contact:* Ramin Takloo-Bighash, Director of Graduate Studies, 312-996-5119, E-mail: dgs@math.uic.edu. Website: http://www.math.uic.edu/.

University of Illinois at Urbana–Champaign, Graduate College, College of Liberal Arts and Sciences, Department of Mathematics, Champaign, IL 61820. Offers applied mathematics (MS); applied mathematics: actuarial science (MS); mathematics (MS, PhD); teaching of mathematics (MS). *Students:* 192 (70 women). Application fee: $75 ($90 for international students). *Unit head:* Matthew Ando, Chair, 217-244-2846, Fax: 217-333-9576, E-mail: mando@illinois.edu. *Application contact:* Marci Blocher, Office Support Specialist, 217-333-5749, Fax: 217-333-9576, E-mail: mblocher@illinois.edu. Website: http://math.illinois.edu/.

The University of Iowa, Graduate College, Program in Applied Mathematical and Computational Sciences, Iowa City, IA 52242-1316. Offers PhD. *Degree requirements:* For doctorate, comprehensive exam, thesis/dissertation. *Entrance requirements:* For doctorate, GRE General Test, minimum GPA of 3.0. Additional exam requirements/recommendations for international students: Required—TOEFL (minimum score 620 paper-based; 105 iBT). Electronic applications accepted.

University of Kentucky, Graduate School, College of Arts and Sciences, Program in Mathematics, Lexington, KY 40506-0032. Offers applied mathematics (MS); mathematics (MA, MS, PhD). *Degree requirements:* For master's, comprehensive exam, thesis optional; for doctorate, one foreign language, comprehensive exam, thesis/dissertation. *Entrance requirements:* For master's, GRE General Test, minimum undergraduate GPA of 2.75; for doctorate, GRE General Test, minimum graduate GPA of 3.0. Additional exam requirements/recommendations for international students: Required—TOEFL (minimum score 550 paper-based). Electronic applications accepted. *Faculty research:* Numerical analysis, combinatorics, partial differential equations, algebra and number theory, real and complex analysis.

University of Louisville, Graduate School, College of Arts and Sciences, Department of Mathematics, Louisville, KY 40292. Offers applied and industrial mathematics (PhD); mathematics (MA). Part-time programs available. *Students:* 31 full-time (9 women), 3 part-time (1 woman), 10 international. Average age 30. 34 applicants, 68% accepted, 9 enrolled. In 2012, 6 master's, 5 doctorates awarded. Terminal master's awarded for partial completion of doctoral program. *Degree requirements:* For master's, comprehensive exam (for some programs), thesis optional; for doctorate, comprehensive exam, thesis/dissertation, internship, project. *Entrance requirements:* For master's and doctorate, GRE General Test. Additional exam requirements/recommendations for international students: Required—TOEFL (minimum score 550 paper-based; 79 iBT). *Application deadline:* For fall admission, 3/15 priority date for domestic students, 3/15 for international students; for winter admission, 8/15 priority date for domestic students, 8/15 for international students. Applications are processed on a rolling basis. Application fee: $60. Electronic applications accepted. *Financial support:* In 2012–13, 25 students received support, including 2 fellowships with full tuition reimbursements available (averaging $20,000 per year), 1 research assistantship (averaging $20,000 per year), 25 teaching assistantships with full tuition reimbursements available (averaging $20,000 per year); health care benefits and unspecified assistantships also available. Financial award application deadline: 3/15. *Faculty research:* Algebra, analysis, bio-mathematics, combinatorics and graph theory, coding theory, consensus theory, financial mathematics, functional equations, partial differential equations. *Total annual research expenditures:* $77,000. *Unit head:* Dr. Thomas Riedel, Chair, 502-852-6826, Fax: 502-852-7132, E-mail: thomas.riedel@louisville.edu. *Application contact:* Dr. Bingtuan Li, Graduate Studies Director, 502-852-6826, Fax: 502-852-7132, E-mail: bing.li@louisville.edu. Website: http://www.math.louisville.edu.

The University of Manchester, School of Mathematics, Manchester, United Kingdom. Offers actuarial science (PhD); applied mathematics (M Phil, PhD); applied numerical computing (M Phil, PhD); financial mathematics (M Phil, PhD); mathematical logic (M Phil); probability (M Phil, PhD); pure mathematics (M Phil, PhD); statistics (M Phil, PhD).

University of Maryland, Baltimore County, Graduate School, College of Natural and Mathematical Sciences, Department of Mathematics and Statistics, Program in Applied Mathematics, Baltimore, MD 21250. Offers MS, PhD. Part-time and evening/weekend programs available. *Faculty:* 22 full-time (4 women). *Students:* 23 full-time (9 women), 11 part-time (2 women); includes 4 minority (2 Black or African American, non-Hispanic/Latino; 2 Asian, non-Hispanic/Latino), 9 international. Average age 28. 39 applicants, 40% accepted, 8 enrolled. In 2012, 11 master's, 1 doctorate awarded. Terminal master's awarded for partial completion of doctoral program. *Degree requirements:* For master's, comprehensive exam (for some programs), thesis (for some programs); for doctorate, comprehensive exam, thesis/dissertation. *Entrance requirements:* For master's and doctorate, GRE General Test, minimum GPA of 3.0. Additional exam requirements/recommendations for international students: Required—TOEFL (minimum score 600 paper-based; 100 iBT). *Application deadline:* For fall admission, 2/15 priority date for domestic students, 1/1 for international students; for spring admission, 10/15 priority date for domestic students, 5/1 for international students. Applications are processed on a rolling basis. Application fee: $50. Electronic applications accepted. *Financial support:* In 2012–13, 20 students received support, including 1 fellowship with full tuition reimbursement available (averaging $15,500 per year), 1 research assistantship with full tuition reimbursement available (averaging $15,500 per year), 18 teaching assistantships with full and partial tuition reimbursements available (averaging $15,500 per year); career-related internships or fieldwork, scholarships/grants, health care benefits, tuition waivers (full and partial), and unspecified assistantships also available. Support available to part-time students. Financial award application deadline: 2/15. *Faculty research:* Numerical analysis and scientific computation, optimization theory and algorithms, differential equations and mathematical modeling, mathematical biology and bioinformatics. *Total annual research expenditures:* $503,890. *Unit head:* Dr. Muruhan Rathinam, Director, 410-455-2423, Fax: 410-455-1066, E-mail: muruhan@umbc.edu. Website: http://www.math.umbc.edu.

University of Maryland, College Park, Academic Affairs, College of Computer, Mathematical and Natural Sciences, Department of Mathematics, Applied Mathematics Program, College Park, MD 20742. Offers MS, PhD. Part-time and evening/weekend programs available. *Students:* 82 full-time (23 women), 11 part-time (3 women); includes 18 minority (2 Black or African American, non-Hispanic/Latino; 1 American Indian or Alaska Native, non-Hispanic/Latino; 11 Asian, non-Hispanic/Latino; 1 Hispanic/Latino; 3 Two or more races, non-Hispanic/Latino), 37 international. 305 applicants, 10% accepted, 18 enrolled. In 2012, 19 master's, 16 doctorates awarded. Terminal master's awarded for partial completion of doctoral program. *Degree requirements:* For master's, thesis optional, seminar, scholarly paper; for doctorate, comprehensive exam, thesis/dissertation, exams, seminars. *Entrance requirements:* For master's and doctorate, GRE General Test, GRE Subject Test, minimum GPA of 3.0, 3 letters of recommendation. *Application deadline:* For fall admission, 1/10 priority date for domestic students, 1/10 for international students. Applications are processed on a rolling basis. Application fee: $75. Electronic applications accepted. *Expenses:* Tuition, state resident: part-time $551 per credit. Tuition, nonresident: part-time $1188 per credit. Part-time tuition and fees vary according to program. *Financial support:* In 2012–13, 2 fellowships with full and partial tuition reimbursements (averaging $18,294 per year), 21 research assistantships (averaging $19,829 per year), 49 teaching assistantships (averaging $17,065 per year) were awarded. Financial award applicants required to submit FAFSA. *Unit head:* Konstantina Travisa, Director, 301-405-4489, E-mail: trivisa@umd.edu. *Application contact:* Dr. Charles A. Caramello, Dean of Graduate School, 301-405-0358, Fax: 301-314-9305.

University of Massachusetts Amherst, Graduate School, College of Natural Sciences, Department of Mathematics and Statistics, Amherst, MA 01003. Offers applied mathematics (MS); mathematics (MS, PhD); statistics (MS, PhD). *Faculty:*

Peterson's Graduate Programs in the Physical Sciences, Mathematics, Agricultural Sciences, the Environment & Natural Resources 2014

www.petersonsbooks.com **281**

41 full-time (5 women). *Students:* 74 full-time (21 women), 1 part-time (0 women); includes 8 minority (2 Black or African American, non-Hispanic/Latino; 5 Asian, non-Hispanic/Latino; 1 Two or more races, non-Hispanic/Latino), 35 international. Average age 27. 302 applicants, 21% accepted, 26 enrolled. In 2012, 17 master's, 6 doctorates awarded. Terminal master's awarded for partial completion of doctoral program. *Degree requirements:* For master's, thesis or alternative; for doctorate, comprehensive exam, thesis/dissertation. *Entrance requirements:* For master's and doctorate, GRE General Test, GRE Subject Test (mathematics). Additional exam requirements/recommendations for international students: Required—TOEFL (minimum score 550 paper-based; 80 iBT), IELTS (minimum score 6.5). *Application deadline:* For fall admission, 2/1 for domestic and international students. Applications are processed on a rolling basis. Application fee: $75. Electronic applications accepted. *Expenses:* Tuition, state resident: full-time $1980; part-time $110 per credit. Tuition, nonresident: full-time $13,314; part-time $414 per credit. *Required fees:* $10,338; $3594 per semester. One-time fee: $357. *Financial support:* Fellowships with full and partial tuition reimbursements, research assistantships with full and partial tuition reimbursements, teaching assistantships with full and partial tuition reimbursements, career-related internships or fieldwork, Federal Work-Study, scholarships/grants, traineeships, health care benefits, tuition waivers (full and partial), and unspecified assistantships available. Support available to part-time students. Financial award application deadline: 2/1. *Unit head:* Dr. Michael Lavine, Department Head, 413-545-2282, Fax: 413-545-1801. *Application contact:* Lindsay DeSantis, Supervisor of Admissions, 413-545-0722, Fax: 413-577-0010, E-mail: gradadm@grad.umass.edu. Website: http://www.math.umass.edu/.

University of Massachusetts Lowell, College of Sciences, Department of Mathematical Sciences, Lowell, MA 01854-2881. Offers applied mathematics (MS); computational mathematics (PhD); mathematics (MS). Part-time programs available. *Entrance requirements:* For master's, GRE General Test.

University of Memphis, Graduate School, College of Arts and Sciences, Department of Mathematical Sciences, Memphis, TN 38152. Offers applied mathematics (MS); applied statistics (PhD); bioinformatics (MS); computer science (PhD); computer sciences (MS); mathematics (MS, PhD); statistics (MS, PhD). Part-time programs available. Terminal master's awarded for partial completion of doctoral program. *Degree requirements:* For master's, comprehensive exam; for doctorate, one foreign language, thesis/dissertation, oral exams. *Entrance requirements:* For master's and doctorate, GRE General Test, minimum GPA of 2.5. Additional exam requirements/recommendations for international students: Required—TOEFL (minimum score 550 paper-based). Electronic applications accepted. *Faculty research:* Combinatorics, ergodic theory, graph theory, Ramsey theory, applied statistics.

University of Michigan–Dearborn, College of Arts, Sciences, and Letters, Master of Science in Applied and Computational Mathematics Program, Dearborn, MI 48128. Offers MS. Part-time and evening/weekend programs available. *Faculty:* 8 full-time (2 women). *Students:* 2 full-time (1 woman), 13 part-time (3 women); includes 2 minority (1 Black or African American, non-Hispanic/Latino; 1 Asian, non-Hispanic/Latino). Average age 36. 14 applicants, 79% accepted, 7 enrolled. In 2012, 3 master's awarded. *Degree requirements:* For master's, thesis or alternative, project. *Entrance requirements:* For master's, 3 letters of recommendation, minimum GPA of 3.0, 2 years course work in math. Additional exam requirements/recommendations for international students: Required—TOEFL (minimum score 560 paper-based). *Application deadline:* For fall admission, 8/1 priority date for domestic students, 4/1 for international students; for winter admission, 12/1 priority date for domestic students, 11/1 for international students; for spring admission, 4/1 for domestic students, 3/1 for international students. Applications are processed on a rolling basis. Application fee: $60. Electronic applications accepted. *Expenses:* Tuition, state resident: full-time $4928; part-time $575 per credit hour. Tuition, nonresident: full-time $9454; part-time $1093 per credit hour. *Required fees:* $187 per semester. Tuition and fees vary according to program. *Financial support:* Federal Work-Study and scholarships/grants available. Support available to part-time students. Financial award application deadline: 4/1; financial award applicants required to submit FAFSA. *Faculty research:* Partial differential equations, statistics, mathematical biology, approximation theory, stochastic processes. *Unit head:* Dr. Thomas Snabb, Director, 313-593-5162, E-mail: tsnabb@umich.edu. *Application contact:* Carol Ligienza, Coordinator, CASL Graduate Programs, 313-593-1183, Fax: 313-583-6700, E-mail: caslgrad@umich.edu. Website: http://www.casl.umd.umich.edu/563801/.

University of Minnesota, Duluth, Graduate School, Swenson College of Science and Engineering, Department of Mathematics and Statistics, Duluth, MN 55812-2496. Offers applied and computational mathematics (MS). Part-time programs available. *Degree requirements:* For master's, thesis or alternative. *Entrance requirements:* For master's, GRE General Test, minimum GPA of 3.0. Additional exam requirements/recommendations for international students: Required—TOEFL (minimum score 550 paper-based; 79 iBT); Recommended—TWE. Electronic applications accepted. *Faculty research:* Discrete mathematics, diagnostic markers, combinatorics, biostatistics, mathematical modeling and scientific computation.

University of Missouri, Graduate School, College of Arts and Sciences, Department of Mathematics, Columbia, MO 65211. Offers applied mathematics (MS); mathematics (MA, MST, PhD). *Faculty:* 40 full-time (6 women), 1 (woman) part-time/adjunct. *Students:* 61 full-time (7 women), 10 part-time (1 woman); includes 2 minority (1 Hispanic/Latino; 1 Two or more races, non-Hispanic/Latino), 24 international. Average age 27. 111 applicants, 23% accepted, 15 enrolled. In 2012, 14 master's, 10 doctorates awarded. *Degree requirements:* For doctorate, 2 foreign languages, comprehensive exam, thesis/dissertation. *Entrance requirements:* For master's and doctorate, GRE General Test, minimum GPA of 3.0; bachelor's degree from accredited institution. Additional exam requirements/recommendations for international students: Required—TOEFL (minimum score 500 paper-based; 61 iBT). *Application deadline:* For fall admission, 1/15 priority date for domestic students, 1/15 for international students. Applications are processed on a rolling basis. Application fee: $55 ($75 for international students). Electronic applications accepted. *Expenses:* Tuition, state resident: full-time $6057. Tuition, nonresident: full-time $15,683. *Required fees:* $1000. *Financial support:* In 2012–13, 7 fellowships with full tuition reimbursements, 4 research assistantships with full tuition reimbursements, 64 teaching assistantships with full tuition reimbursements were awarded; institutionally sponsored loans, health care benefits, and unspecified assistantships also available. Financial award applicants required to submit FAFSA. *Faculty research:* Algebraic geometry, analysis (real, complex, functional and harmonic), analytic functions, applied mathematics, financial mathematics and mathematics of insurance, commutative rings, scattering theory, differential equations (ordinary and partial), differential geometry, dynamical systems, general relativity, mathematical physics, number theory, probabilistic analysis and topology. *Unit head:* Dr. Glen Himmelberg, Department Chair, 573-882-6222, E-mail: himmelbergg@missouri.edu. *Application contact:* Amy Crews, Administrative Assistant, 573-882-6222, E-mail: crewsae@missouri.edu. Website: http://www.math.missouri.edu/.

University of Missouri–St. Louis, College of Arts and Sciences, Department of Mathematics and Computer Science, St. Louis, MO 63121. Offers applied mathematics (PhD), including computer science, mathematics; computer science (MS); mathematics (MA). Part-time and evening/weekend programs available. *Faculty:* 15 full-time (2 women). *Students:* 19 full-time (8 women), 50 part-time (17 women); includes 7 minority (2 Black or African American, non-Hispanic/Latino; 2 Asian, non-Hispanic/Latino; 3 Two or more races, non-Hispanic/Latino), 21 international. Average age 32. 76 applicants, 50% accepted, 18 enrolled. In 2012, 19 master's, 3 doctorates awarded. *Degree requirements:* For master's, thesis optional; for doctorate, thesis/dissertation. *Entrance requirements:* For master's, GRE (for teaching assistantships), 2 letters of recommendation; C programming, C++ or Java (for computer science); for doctorate, GRE General Test, 3 letters of recommendation. Additional exam requirements/recommendations for international students: Required—TOEFL (minimum score 550 paper-based; 79 iBT), IELTS (minimum score 6.5). *Application deadline:* For fall admission, 7/1 priority date for domestic students, 7/1 for international students; for spring admission, 12/1 priority date for domestic students, 12/1 for international students. Applications are processed on a rolling basis. Application fee: $35 ($40 for international students). Electronic applications accepted. *Expenses:* Tuition, state resident: full-time $7364; part-time $409.10 per credit hour. Tuition, nonresident: full-time $18,153; part-time $1008.50 per credit hour. *Financial support:* In 2012–13, 1 research assistantship with full and partial tuition reimbursement (averaging $5,626 per year), 9 teaching assistantships with full and partial tuition reimbursements (averaging $12,667 per year) were awarded; fellowships with full tuition reimbursements also available. Financial award applicants required to submit FAFSA. *Faculty research:* Statistics, algebra, analysis. *Unit head:* Dr. Qingtang Jiang, Director of Graduate Studies, 314-516-5741, Fax: 314-516-5400, E-mail: jiangq@umsl.edu. *Application contact:* 314-516-5458, Fax: 314-516-6996, E-mail: gradadm@umsl.edu.

University of New Hampshire, Graduate School, College of Engineering and Physical Sciences, Department of Mathematics and Statistics, Durham, NH 03824. Offers applied mathematics (MS); industrial statistics (Postbaccalaureate Certificate); mathematics (MS, MST, PhD); mathematics education (PhD); statistics (MS). *Faculty:* 21 full-time (5 women). *Students:* 26 full-time (8 women), 36 part-time (18 women); includes 4 minority (1 American Indian or Alaska Native, non-Hispanic/Latino; 2 Asian, non-Hispanic/Latino; 1 Two or more races, non-Hispanic/Latino), 17 international. Average age 30. 84 applicants, 46% accepted, 14 enrolled. In 2012, 12 master's, 1 doctorate, 3 other advanced degrees awarded. Terminal master's awarded for partial completion of doctoral program. *Degree requirements:* For doctorate, 2 foreign languages, thesis/dissertation. *Entrance requirements:* Additional exam requirements/recommendations for international students: Required—TOEFL (minimum score 550 paper-based; 80 iBT). *Application deadline:* For fall admission, 4/1 priority date for domestic students, 4/1 for international students; for spring admission, 12/1 for domestic students. Applications are processed on a rolling basis. Application fee: $65. Electronic applications accepted. *Expenses:* Tuition, state resident: full-time $13,500; part-time $750 per credit. Tuition, nonresident: full-time $25,940; part-time $1089 per credit. *Required fees:* $1699; $424.75 per semester. *Financial support:* In 2012–13, 41 students received support, including 1 fellowship, 7 research assistantships, 36 teaching assistantships; Federal Work-Study, scholarships/grants, and tuition waivers (full and partial) also available. Support available to part-time students. Financial award application deadline: 2/15. *Faculty research:* Operator theory, complex analysis, algebra, nonlinear dynamics, statistics. *Unit head:* Dr. Edward Hinson, Chairperson, 603-862-2688. *Application contact:* Jan Jankowski, Administrative Assistant, 603-862-2320, E-mail: jan.jankowski@unh.edu. Website: http://www.math.unh.edu/.

The University of North Carolina at Charlotte, The Graduate School, College of Liberal Arts and Sciences, Department of Mathematics and Statistics, Charlotte, NC 28223-0001. Offers applied mathematics (MS, PhD); applied statistics (MS); general mathematics (MS); mathematics education (MA). Part-time and evening/

282 www.petersonsbooks.com

Peterson's Graduate Programs in the Physical Sciences, Mathematics, Agricultural Sciences, the Environment & Natural Resources 2014

weekend programs available. *Faculty:* 42 full-time (5 women). *Students:* 42 full-time (21 women), 32 part-time (16 women); includes 12 minority (6 Black or African American, non-Hispanic/Latino; 4 Asian, non-Hispanic/Latino; 2 Hispanic/Latino), 33 international. Average age 30. 43 applicants, 95% accepted, 23 enrolled. In 2012, 15 master's, 4 doctorates awarded. Terminal master's awarded for partial completion of doctoral program. *Degree requirements:* For master's, comprehensive exam, thesis or alternative; for doctorate, thesis/dissertation. *Entrance requirements:* For master's, GRE General Test, minimum GPA of 3.0 in undergraduate major, 2.75 overall; for doctorate, GRE General Test, minimum overall GPA of 3.0. Additional exam requirements/recommendations for international students: Required—TOEFL (minimum score 557 paper-based; 83 iBT), Michigan English Language Assessment Battery (minimum score 78) or IELTS (minimum score 6.5). *Application deadline:* For fall admission, 7/1 for domestic students, 5/1 for international students; for spring admission, 11/1 for domestic students, 10/1 for international students. Applications are processed on a rolling basis. Application fee: $65 ($75 for international students). Electronic applications accepted. *Expenses:* Tuition, state resident: full-time $3453. Tuition, nonresident: full-time $15,982. *Required fees:* $2420. Tuition and fees vary according to course load and program. *Financial support:* In 2012–13, 44 students received support, including 3 fellowships (averaging $21,035 per year), 4 research assistantships (averaging $8,583 per year), 37 teaching assistantships (averaging $12,104 per year); career-related internships or fieldwork, Federal Work-Study, institutionally sponsored loans, scholarships/grants, and unspecified assistantships also available. Support available to part-time students. Financial award application deadline: 4/1; financial award applicants required to submit FAFSA. *Faculty research:* Numerical analysis and scientific computation, probability and stochastic processes, partial differential equations and mathematical physics, algebra and combinatorics, analysis, biostatistics, topology. *Total annual research expenditures:* $1.2 million. *Unit head:* Dr. Yuanan Diao, Chair, 704-687-4560, Fax: 704-687-6415, E-mail: ydiao@uncc.edu. *Application contact:* Kathy B. Giddings, Director of Graduate Admissions, 704-687-5503, Fax: 704-687-1668, E-mail: gradadm@uncc.edu. Website: http://www.math.uncc.edu/.

University of Northern Iowa, Graduate College, College of Humanities, Arts and Sciences, Department of Mathematics, Cedar Falls, IA 50614. Offers industrial mathematics (PSM), including actuarial science, continuous quality improvement, mathematical computing and modeling; mathematics (MA), including mathematics, secondary; mathematics for middle grades 4-8 (MA). Part-time programs available. *Students:* 16 full-time (4 women), 17 part-time (13 women); includes 2 minority (1 Black or African American, non-Hispanic/Latino; 1 Hispanic/Latino), 4 international. 20 applicants, 75% accepted, 6 enrolled. In 2012, 22 master's awarded. *Degree requirements:* For master's, comprehensive exam (for some programs), thesis or alternative. *Entrance requirements:* For master's, minimum GPA of 3.0. Additional exam requirements/recommendations for international students: Required—TOEFL (minimum score 600 paper-based; 100 iBT). *Application deadline:* For fall admission, 8/1 priority date for domestic students. Applications are processed on a rolling basis. Application fee: $50 ($70 for international students). Electronic applications accepted. *Financial support:* Career-related internships or fieldwork, Federal Work-Study, scholarships/grants, and tuition waivers (full and partial) available. Support available to part-time students. Financial award application deadline: 2/1. *Unit head:* Dr. Douglas Mupasiri, Head, 319-273-2012, Fax: 319-273-2546, E-mail: douglas.mupasiri@uni.edu. *Application contact:* Laurie S. Russell, Record Analyst, 319-273-2623, Fax: 319-273-2885, E-mail: laurie.russell@uni.edu. Website: http://www.math.uni.edu/.

University of Notre Dame, Graduate School, College of Science, Department of Mathematics, Notre Dame, IN 46556. Offers algebra (PhD); algebraic geometry (PhD); applied mathematics (MSAM); complex analysis (PhD); differential geometry (PhD); logic (PhD); partial differential equations (PhD); topology (PhD). Terminal master's awarded for partial completion of doctoral program. *Degree requirements:* For doctorate, one foreign language, thesis/dissertation, qualifying exam. *Entrance requirements:* For master's and doctorate, GRE General Test, GRE Subject Test. Additional exam requirements/recommendations for international students: Required—TOEFL (minimum score 600 paper-based; 80 iBT). Electronic applications accepted. *Faculty research:* Algebra, analysis, geometry/topology, logic, applied math.

University of Pennsylvania, School of Arts and Sciences, Graduate Group in Applied Mathematics and Computational Science, Philadelphia, PA 19104. Offers PhD. *Faculty:* 26 full-time (2 women), 1 part-time/adjunct (0 women). *Students:* 27 full-time (7 women), 1 (woman) part-time, 26 international. 132 applicants, 11% accepted, 8 enrolled. *Application deadline:* For fall admission, 1/15 for domestic students. *Financial support:* Institutionally sponsored loans, scholarships/grants, traineeships, health care benefits, and unspecified assistantships available. *Application contact:* Arts and Sciences Graduate Admissions, 215-573-5816, Fax: 215-573-8068, E-mail: gdasadmis@sas.upenn.edu. Website: http://www.amcs.upenn.edu.

University of Pittsburgh, Dietrich School of Arts and Sciences, Department of Mathematics, Pittsburgh, PA 15260. Offers applied mathematics (MA, MS); mathematics (MA, MS, PhD). Part-time programs available. *Faculty:* 36 full-time (2 women), 16 part-time/adjunct (2 women). *Students:* 83 full-time (25 women), 2 part-time (1 woman); includes 4 minority (1 Black or African American, non-Hispanic/Latino; 2 Hispanic/Latino; 1 Native Hawaiian or other Pacific Islander, non-Hispanic/Latino), 44 international. 280 applicants, 16% accepted, 15 enrolled. In 2012, 8 master's, 3 doctorates awarded. Terminal master's awarded for partial completion of doctoral program. *Degree requirements:* For master's, comprehensive exam, thesis (for some programs); for doctorate, comprehensive exam, thesis/dissertation, preliminary exams, defense of dissertation. *Entrance requirements:* For master's, GRE General Test, GRE Subject Test (recommended), minimum GPA of 3.0; for doctorate, GRE General Test, GRE Subject Test (recommended), minimum GPA of 3.0, minimum QPA of 3.25 in math curriculum. Additional exam requirements/recommendations for international students: Required—TOEFL (minimum score 577 paper-based; 90 iBT), IELTS (minimum score 7). *Application deadline:* For fall admission, 1/15 priority date for domestic students, 1/15 for international students; for spring admission, 9/1 priority date for domestic students, 9/1 for international students. Applications are processed on a rolling basis. Application fee: $50. Electronic applications accepted. *Expenses:* Tuition, state resident: full-time $19,336; part-time $782 per credit. Tuition, nonresident: full-time $31,658; part-time $1295 per credit. *Required fees:* $740; $200 per term. Tuition and fees vary according to program. *Financial support:* In 2012–13, 77 students received support, including 14 fellowships with full and partial tuition reimbursements available (averaging $19,610 per year), 11 research assistantships with full and partial tuition reimbursements available (averaging $16,600 per year), 51 teaching assistantships with full and partial tuition reimbursements available (averaging $16,050 per year); institutionally sponsored loans, scholarships/grants, traineeships, health care benefits, tuition waivers (partial), and unspecified assistantships also available. Financial award application deadline: 1/15. *Faculty research:* Algebra, analysis, computational math, geometry/topology, math biology. *Unit head:* Ivan Yotov, Chair, 412-624-8361, Fax: 412-624-8397, E-mail: yotov@math.pitt.edu. *Application contact:* Molly Williams, Administrator, 412-624-1175, Fax: 412-624-8397, E-mail: mollyw@pitt.edu. Website: http://www.mathematics.pitt.edu.

University of Puerto Rico, Mayagüez Campus, Graduate Studies, College of Arts and Sciences, Department of Mathematical Sciences, Mayagüez, PR 00681-9000. Offers applied mathematics (MS); pure mathematics (MS); scientific computation (MS); statistics (MS). Part-time programs available. *Faculty:* 45 full-time (7 women), 1 part-time/adjunct (0 women). *Students:* 34 full-time (10 women), 1 part-time (0 women); includes 30 minority (all Hispanic/Latino), 25 international. 8 applicants, 88% accepted, 7 enrolled. In 2012, 5 master's awarded. *Degree requirements:* For master's, one foreign language, comprehensive exam, thesis optional. *Entrance requirements:* For master's, undergraduate degree in mathematics or its equivalent. *Application deadline:* For fall admission, 2/15 for domestic and international students; for spring admission, 9/15 for domestic and international students. Applications are processed on a rolling basis. Application fee: $25. Tuition and fees vary according to course level and course load. *Financial support:* In 2012–13, 31 students received support, including 5 research assistantships (averaging $15,000 per year), 26 teaching assistantships (averaging $8,500 per year); Federal Work-Study and institutionally sponsored loans also available. *Faculty research:* Automata theory, linear algebra, logic. *Unit head:* Dr. Omar Colon, Director, 787-832-4040 Ext. 3848, Fax: 787-265-5454, E-mail: omar.colon.reyes@gmail.com. Website: http://math.uprm.edu/.

University of Rhode Island, Graduate School, College of Arts and Sciences, Department of Computer Science and Statistics, Kingston, RI 02881. Offers applied mathematics (PhD), including computer science, statistics; computer science (MS, PhD); digital forensics (Graduate Certificate); statistics (MS). Part-time programs available. *Faculty:* 13 full-time (6 women). *Students:* 24 full-time (4 women), 35 part-time (4 women); includes 11 minority (2 Black or African American, non-Hispanic/Latino; 5 Asian, non-Hispanic/Latino; 4 Hispanic/Latino), 7 international. In 2012, 14 master's, 1 doctorate awarded. *Degree requirements:* For master's, comprehensive exam (for some programs), thesis optional; for doctorate, comprehensive exam, thesis/dissertation. *Entrance requirements:* For master's and doctorate, GRE, 2 letters of recommendation. Additional exam requirements/recommendations for international students: Required—TOEFL (minimum score 550 paper-based). *Application deadline:* For fall admission, 7/15 for domestic students, 2/1 for international students; for spring admission, 11/15 for domestic students, 7/15 for international students. Application fee: $65. Electronic applications accepted. *Expenses:* Tuition, state resident: full-time $11,532; part-time $641 per credit. Tuition, nonresident: full-time $23,606; part-time $1311 per credit. *Required fees:* $1388; $36 per credit. $35 per semester. One-time fee: $130. *Financial support:* In 2012–13, 10 teaching assistantships with full tuition reimbursements (averaging $13,258 per year) were awarded. Financial award application deadline: 2/1; financial award applicants required to submit FAFSA. *Faculty research:* Bioinformatics, computer and digital forensics, behavioral model of pedestrian dynamics, real-time distributed object computing, cryptography. *Unit head:* Dr. Joan Peckham, Chair, 401-874-2701, Fax: 401-874-4617, E-mail: joan@cs.uri.edu. *Application contact:* E-mail: grad-inquiries@cs.uri.edu. Website: http://www.cs.uri.edu/.

University of Rhode Island, Graduate School, College of Arts and Sciences, Department of Mathematics, Kingston, RI 02881. Offers applied mathematical sciences (MS, PhD); mathematics (MS, PhD). Part-time programs available. *Faculty:* 19 full-time (6 women). *Students:* 15 full-time (5 women), 11 part-time (5 women); includes 1 minority (Hispanic/Latino), 3 international. In 2012, 10 master's, 2 doctorates awarded. *Degree requirements:* For master's, comprehensive exam (for some programs), thesis optional; for doctorate, one foreign language, comprehensive exam, thesis/dissertation optional. *Entrance requirements:* For master's and doctorate, 2 letters of recommendation. Additional

Peterson's Graduate Programs in the Physical Sciences, Mathematics, Agricultural Sciences, the Environment & Natural Resources 2014

www.petersonsbooks.com **283**

exam requirements/recommendations for international students: Required—TOEFL (minimum score 550 paper-based). *Application deadline:* For fall admission, 7/15 for domestic students, 2/1 for international students; for spring admission, 11/15 for domestic students, 7/15 for international students. Application fee: $65. Electronic applications accepted. *Expenses:* Tuition, state resident: full-time $11,532; part-time $641 per credit. Tuition, nonresident: full-time $23,606; part-time $1311 per credit. *Required fees:* $1388; $36 per credit. $35 per semester. One-time fee: $130. *Financial support:* In 2012–13, 13 teaching assistantships with full tuition reimbursements (averaging $15,754 per year) were awarded. Financial award application deadline: 7/15; financial award applicants required to submit FAFSA. *Unit head:* Dr. James Baglama, Chair, 401-874-2709, Fax: 401-874-4454, E-mail: jbaglama@math.uri.edu. *Application contact:* Dr. Woong Kook, Director of Graduate Studies, 401-874-4421, Fax: 401-874-4454, E-mail: andrewk@math.uri.edu. Website: http://www.math.uri.edu/.

University of Southern California, Graduate School, Dana and David Dornsife College of Letters, Arts and Sciences, Department of Mathematics, Los Angeles, CA 90089. Offers applied mathematics (MA, MS, PhD); mathematical finance (MS); mathematics (MA, PhD); statistics (MS). Part-time programs available. Terminal master's awarded for partial completion of doctoral program. *Degree requirements:* For master's, comprehensive exam (for some programs), thesis (for some programs); for doctorate, one foreign language, comprehensive exam, thesis/dissertation. *Entrance requirements:* For master's, GRE General Test, GMAT; for doctorate, GRE General Test, GRE Subject Test (mathematics). Additional exam requirements/recommendations for international students: Required—TOEFL (minimum score 100 iBT). Electronic applications accepted. *Faculty research:* Algebra, algebraic geometry and number theory, analysis/partial differential equations, applied mathematics, financial mathematics, probability, combinatorics and statistics.

The University of Tennessee, Graduate School, College of Arts and Sciences, Department of Mathematics, Knoxville, TN 37996. Offers applied mathematics (MS); mathematical ecology (PhD); mathematics (M Math, MS, PhD). Part-time programs available. *Degree requirements:* For master's, thesis or alternative; for doctorate, one foreign language, thesis/dissertation. *Entrance requirements:* For master's and doctorate, minimum GPA of 2.7. Additional exam requirements/recommendations for international students: Required—TOEFL. Electronic applications accepted. *Expenses:* Tuition, state resident: full-time $9000; part-time $501 per credit hour. Tuition, nonresident: full-time $27,188; part-time $1512 per credit hour. *Required fees:* $1280; $62 per credit hour. Tuition and fees vary according to program.

The University of Tennessee at Chattanooga, Graduate School, College of Arts and Sciences, Program in Mathematics, Chattanooga, TN 37403-2598. Offers applied mathematics (MS); applied statistics (MS); mathematics (MS); mathematics education (MS). Part-time and evening/weekend programs available. Postbaccalaureate distance learning degree programs offered (no on-campus study). *Faculty:* 6 full-time (0 women). *Students:* 10 full-time (2 women), 7 part-time (1 woman); includes 2 minority (1 Black or African American, non-Hispanic/Latino; 1 Asian, non-Hispanic/Latino). Average age 29. 10 applicants, 100% accepted, 7 enrolled. In 2012, 4 master's awarded. *Entrance requirements:* For master's, two letters of recommendation. *Application deadline:* For fall admission, 6/14 for domestic students, 6/1 for international students; for spring admission, 10/25 for domestic students, 10/1 for international students. Applications are processed on a rolling basis. Application fee: $30 ($35 for international students). Electronic applications accepted. *Expenses:* Tuition, state resident: full-time $6860; part-time $381 per credit hour. Tuition, nonresident: full-time $21,206; part-time $1178 per credit hour. *Required fees:* $1490; $180 per credit hour. *Financial support:* In 2012–13, 16 research assistantships with tuition reimbursements (averaging $4,592 per year) were awarded. Financial award applicants required to submit FAFSA. *Total annual research expenditures:* $71,555. *Unit head:* John Graef, Head, 423-425-4545, E-mail: john-graef@utc.edu. *Application contact:* Dr. Jerald Ainsworth, Dean of Graduate Studies, 423-425-4478, Fax: 423-425-5223, E-mail: jerald-ainsworth@utc.edu. Website: http://www.utc.edu/Academic/Mathematics/.

The University of Texas at Arlington, Graduate School, College of Science, Department of Mathematics, Arlington, TX 76019. Offers applied math (MS); mathematics (PhD); mathematics education (MA). Part-time and evening/weekend programs available. *Degree requirements:* For master's, comprehensive exam, thesis or alternative; for doctorate, comprehensive exam, thesis/dissertation, preliminary examinations. *Entrance requirements:* For master's, GRE General Test (minimum score 350 verbal, 650 quantitative); for doctorate, GRE General Test (minimum score 350 verbal, 700 quantitative), 30 hours of graduate course work in mathematics, minimum GPA of 3.0 in last 60 hours of course work. Additional exam requirements/recommendations for international students: Required—TOEFL (minimum score 550 paper-based; 79 iBT). Electronic applications accepted. *Faculty research:* Algebra, combinatorics and geometry, applied mathematics and mathematical biology, computational mathematics, mathematics education, probability and statistics.

The University of Texas at Austin, Graduate School, Program in Computational Science, Engineering, and Mathematics, Austin, TX 78712-1111. Offers MS, PhD. Terminal master's awarded for partial completion of doctoral program. *Degree requirements:* For master's, thesis optional; for doctorate, thesis/dissertation, 3 area qualifying exams. Electronic applications accepted.

The University of Texas at Dallas, School of Natural Sciences and Mathematics, Department of Mathematical Sciences, Richardson, TX 75080. Offers applied mathematics (MS, PhD); engineering mathematics (MS); mathematics (MS); statistics (MS, PhD). Part-time and evening/weekend programs available. *Faculty:* 20 full-time (4 women), 1 part-time/adjunct (0 women). *Students:* 50 full-time (22 women), 27 part-time (9 women); includes 16 minority (4 Black or African American, non-Hispanic/Latino; 7 Asian, non-Hispanic/Latino; 5 Hispanic/Latino), 37 international. Average age 31. 140 applicants, 36% accepted, 29 enrolled. In 2012, 13 master's, 3 doctorates awarded. *Degree requirements:* For master's, thesis optional; for doctorate, thesis/dissertation. *Entrance requirements:* For master's, GRE General Test, minimum GPA of 3.0 in upper-level course work in field; for doctorate, GRE General Test, minimum GPA of 3.5 in upper-level course work in field. Additional exam requirements/recommendations for international students: Required—TOEFL (minimum score 550 paper-based). *Application deadline:* For fall admission, 7/15 for domestic students, 5/1 for international students; for spring admission, 11/15 for domestic students, 9/1 for international students. Applications are processed on a rolling basis. Application fee: $50 ($100 for international students). Electronic applications accepted. *Expenses:* Tuition, state resident: full-time $11,940; part-time $663.33 per credit hour. Tuition, nonresident: full-time $21,606; part-time $1200.33 per credit hour. Tuition and fees vary according to course load. *Financial support:* In 2012–13, 39 students received support, including 4 research assistantships (averaging $19,800 per year), 35 teaching assistantships with partial tuition reimbursements available (averaging $16,124 per year); career-related internships or fieldwork, Federal Work-Study, institutionally sponsored loans, scholarships/grants, and unspecified assistantships also available. Support available to part-time students. Financial award application deadline: 4/30; financial award applicants required to submit FAFSA. *Faculty research:* Sequential analysis, applications in semiconductor manufacturing, medical image analysis, computational anatomy, information theory, probability theory. *Unit head:* Dr. Matthew Goeckner, Department Head, 972-883-4292, Fax: 972-883-6622, E-mail: goeckner@utdallas.edu. *Application contact:* Jacqueline Thiede, Graduate Support Assistant, 972-883-2163, Fax: 972-883-6622, E-mail: utdmath@utdallas.edu. Website: http://www.utdallas.edu/math.

The University of Texas at San Antonio, College of Sciences, Department of Mathematics, San Antonio, TX 78249-0617. Offers applied mathematics (MS), including industrial mathematics; mathematics (MS); mathematics education (MS). Part-time and evening/weekend programs available. *Faculty:* 10 full-time (1 woman). *Students:* 29 full-time (14 women), 26 part-time (15 women); includes 26 minority (1 Black or African American, non-Hispanic/Latino; 3 Asian, non-Hispanic/Latino; 21 Hispanic/Latino; 1 Two or more races, non-Hispanic/Latino), 12 international. Average age 29. 64 applicants, 67% accepted, 11 enrolled. In 2012, 28 master's awarded. *Degree requirements:* For master's, comprehensive exam (for some programs), thesis or alternative. *Entrance requirements:* For master's, GRE General Test, minimum GPA of 3.0 in last 60 hours. Additional exam requirements/recommendations for international students: Required—TOEFL (minimum score 500 paper-based; 61 iBT), IELTS (minimum score 5). *Application deadline:* For fall admission, 7/1 for domestic students, 4/1 for international students; for spring admission, 11/1 for domestic students, 9/1 for international students. Application fee: $45 ($85 for international students). *Financial support:* In 2012–13, 15 teaching assistantships (averaging $13,000 per year) were awarded. *Faculty research:* Differential equations, functional analysis, numerical analysis, number theory, logic. *Unit head:* Dr. F. Alexander Norman, Department Chair, 210-458-7254, Fax: 210-458-4439, E-mail: sandy.norman@utsa.edu.

The University of Toledo, College of Graduate Studies, College of Natural Sciences and Mathematics, Department of Mathematics, Toledo, OH 43606-3390. Offers applied mathematics (MS, PhD); statistics (MS, PhD). Part-time programs available. *Faculty:* 25. *Students:* 38 full-time (13 women), 3 part-time (0 women); includes 2 minority (both Asian, non-Hispanic/Latino), 30 international. Average age 29. 37 applicants, 57% accepted, 11 enrolled. In 2012, 11 master's, 3 doctorates awarded. *Degree requirements:* For master's, comprehensive exam (for some programs), thesis (for some programs); for doctorate, 2 foreign languages, thesis/dissertation. *Entrance requirements:* For master's and doctorate, GRE General Test, GRE Subject Test, minimum cumulative point-hour ratio of 2.7 for all previous academic work, three letters of recommendation, statement of purpose, transcripts from all prior institutions attended. Additional exam requirements/recommendations for international students: Required—TOEFL (minimum score 550 paper-based; 80 iBT), IELTS (minimum score 6.5). *Application deadline:* For fall admission, 1/15 priority date for domestic students, 1/15 for international students. Applications are processed on a rolling basis. Application fee: $45 ($75 for international students). Electronic applications accepted. *Financial support:* In 2012–13, 38 teaching assistantships with full and partial tuition reimbursements (averaging $14,503 per year) were awarded; research assistantships with full and partial tuition reimbursements, Federal Work-Study, institutionally sponsored loans, scholarships/grants, and unspecified assistantships also available. Support available to part-time students. *Unit head:* Dr. Paul Hewitt, Chair, 419-530-2568, E-mail: paul.hewitt@utoledo.edu. *Application contact:* Graduate School Office, 419-530-4723, Fax: 419-530-4723, E-mail: grdsch@utnet.utoledo.edu. Website: http://www.utoledo.edu/nsm/.

University of Tulsa, Graduate School, Collins College of Business, Finance/Applied Mathematics Program, Tulsa, OK 74104-3189. Offers MS/MS. Part-time and evening/weekend programs available. *Students:* 2 full-time (1 woman), 1 (woman) part-time, 2 international. Average age 24. 6 applicants, 17% accepted, 1 enrolled. *Entrance requirements:* Additional exam requirements/recommendations for international students: Required—TOEFL (minimum score 577 paper-based; 91 iBT), IELTS (minimum score 6.5). *Application deadline:* Applications are processed on a rolling basis. Application fee: $40. Electronic applications accepted. *Expenses: Tuition:* Full-time $18,630. *Required fees:* $1340; $5 per credit hour. $75 per semester. Tuition and fees vary according to course load. *Financial support:* Fellowships, teaching assistantships, career-related internships or fieldwork, Federal Work-Study, institutionally sponsored loans, scholarships/grants, health care benefits, tuition waivers (full and partial), and unspecified assistantships available. Support available to part-time students. Financial award application deadline: 2/1; financial award applicants required to submit FAFSA. *Unit head:* Linda Nichols, Associate Dean, 918-631-2242, Fax: 918-631-2142, E-mail: linda-nichols@utulsa.edu. *Application contact:* Information Contact, 918-631-2242, E-mail: graduate-business@utulsa.edu.

University of Washington, Graduate School, College of Arts and Sciences, Department of Applied Mathematics, Seattle, WA 98195. Offers MS, PhD. Terminal master's awarded for partial completion of doctoral program. *Degree requirements:* For master's, thesis optional; for doctorate, thesis/dissertation. *Entrance requirements:* For master's and doctorate, GRE, minimum GPA of 3.0. Additional exam requirements/recommendations for international students: Required—TOEFL. Electronic applications accepted. *Faculty research:* Mathematical modeling for physical, biological, social, and engineering sciences; development of mathematical methods for analysis, including perturbation, asymptotic, transform, vocational, and numerical methods.

University of Washington, Graduate School, College of Arts and Sciences, Department of Mathematics, Seattle, WA 98195. Offers mathematics (MA, MS, PhD); numerical analysis (MS); optimization (MS). Part-time programs available. Terminal master's awarded for partial completion of doctoral program. *Degree requirements:* For master's, thesis optional; for doctorate, 2 foreign languages, thesis/dissertation. *Entrance requirements:* For master's, GRE, minimum GPA of 3.0; for doctorate, GRE General Test, GRE Subject Test (mathematics), minimum GPA of 3.0. Additional exam requirements/recommendations for international students: Required—TOEFL. Electronic applications accepted. *Faculty research:* Algebra, analysis, probability, combinatorics and geometry.

University of Waterloo, Graduate Studies, Faculty of Mathematics, Department of Applied Mathematics, Waterloo, ON N2L 3G1, Canada. Offers M Math, PhD. Part-time programs available. *Degree requirements:* For master's, research paper or thesis; for doctorate, thesis/dissertation. *Entrance requirements:* For master's, honors degree in field, minimum B+ average; for doctorate, master's degree, minimum B+ average. Additional exam requirements/recommendations for international students: Required—TOEFL (minimum score 600 paper-based; 100 iBT), TWE (minimum score 4). Electronic applications accepted. *Faculty research:* Differential equations, quantum theory, statistical mechanics, fluid mechanics, relativity, control theory.

The University of Western Ontario, Faculty of Graduate Studies, Physical Sciences Division, Department of Applied Mathematics, London, ON N6A 5B8, Canada. Offers applied mathematics (M Sc, PhD); theoretical physics (PhD). *Degree requirements:* For master's, thesis or alternative; for doctorate, comprehensive exam, thesis/dissertation. *Entrance requirements:* For master's and doctorate, minimum B average. Additional exam requirements/recommendations for international students: Required—TOEFL. *Faculty research:* Fluid dynamics, mathematical and computational methods, theoretical physics.

University of West Georgia, College of Science and Mathematics, Department of Mathematics, Carrollton, GA 30118. Offers teaching and applied mathematics (MS). Part-time and evening/weekend programs available. *Faculty:* 13 full-time (3 women). *Students:* 2 full-time (1 woman), 7 part-time (3 women); includes 2 minority (1 Black or African American, non-Hispanic/Latino; 1 Asian, non-Hispanic/Latino). Average age 38. 6 applicants, 17% accepted, 1 enrolled. In 2012, 6 master's awarded. *Degree requirements:* For master's, comprehensive exam, thesis optional, 36 credit hours. *Entrance requirements:* For master's, GRE. Additional exam requirements/recommendations for international students: Recommended—TOEFL (minimum score 523 paper-based; 69 iBT), IELTS (minimum score 6). *Application deadline:* For fall admission, 6/1 for domestic and international students; for spring admission, 11/15 for domestic students, 10/15 for international students. Applications are processed on a rolling basis. Application fee: $40. Electronic applications accepted. *Expenses:* Tuition, state resident: full-time $4466; part-time $187 per semester hour. Tuition, nonresident: full-time $17,888; part-time $745 per semester hour. *Required fees:* $1858; $46.34 per semester hour. One-time fee: $512 full-time; $266 part-time. Tuition and fees vary according to course load, degree level and program. *Financial support:* In 2012–13, 3 students received support, including 3 teaching assistantships (averaging $6,800 per year); unspecified assistantships also available. Financial award application deadline: 6/1; financial award applicants required to submit FAFSA. *Faculty research:* Graph coloring problems, labeling and domination in graphs, high dimension regression, Inverse problem, spectral theory of operators, math teacher education. *Unit head:* Dr. Bruce Landman, Chair, 678-839-6489, Fax: 678-839-6490, E-mail: landman@westga.edu. *Application contact:* Alice Wesley, Departmental Assistant, 678-839-5192, E-mail: awesley@westga.edu. Website: http://www.westga.edu/math/.

Utah State University, School of Graduate Studies, College of Science, Department of Mathematics and Statistics, Logan, UT 84322. Offers industrial mathematics (MS); mathematical sciences (PhD); mathematics (M Math, MS); statistics (MS). Part-time programs available. Terminal master's awarded for partial completion of doctoral program. *Degree requirements:* For master's, thesis optional, qualifying exam; for doctorate, one foreign language, comprehensive exam, thesis/dissertation. *Entrance requirements:* For master's and doctorate, GRE General Test, minimum GPA of 3.0. Additional exam requirements/recommendations for international students: Required—TOEFL. *Faculty research:* Differential equations, computational mathematics, dynamical systems, probability and statistics, pure mathematics.

Virginia Commonwealth University, Graduate School, College of Humanities and Sciences, Department of Mathematics and Applied Mathematics, Richmond, VA 23284-9005. Offers applied mathematics (MS); mathematics (MS). *Degree requirements:* For master's, thesis optional. *Entrance requirements:* For master's, GRE General Test, GRE Subject Test, 30 undergraduate semester credits in the mathematical sciences or closely-related fields. Additional exam requirements/recommendations for international students: Required—TOEFL (minimum score 600 paper-based; 100 iBT); Recommended—IELTS (minimum score 6.5). Electronic applications accepted. *Faculty research:* Mathematics, applied mathematics.

Washington State University, Graduate School, College of Arts and Sciences, Department of Mathematics, Pullman, WA 99164. Offers applied mathematics (MS, PhD); mathematics (MS, PhD); mathematics computational finance (MS); mathematics teaching (MS, PhD). Part-time programs available. *Faculty:* 28 full-time (4 women). *Students:* 49 full-time (16 women), 2 part-time (1 woman); includes 5 minority (1 Black or African American, non-Hispanic/Latino; 2 Asian, non-Hispanic/Latino; 1 Hispanic/Latino; 1 Native Hawaiian or other Pacific Islander, non-Hispanic/Latino), 17 international. Average age 27. 117 applicants, 68% accepted, 18 enrolled. In 2012, 5 master's, 6 doctorates awarded. Terminal master's awarded for partial completion of doctoral program. *Degree requirements:* For master's, comprehensive exam (for some programs), thesis or alternative, oral exam, project; for doctorate, 2 foreign languages, comprehensive exam, thesis/dissertation, oral exam, written exam. *Entrance requirements:* For master's and doctorate, minimum GPA of 3.0, 3 letters of recommendation. Additional exam requirements/recommendations for international students: Required—TOEFL (minimum score 600 paper-based; 100 iBT) or IELTS (minimum score 7). *Application deadline:* For fall admission, 1/10 for domestic and international students; for spring admission, 7/1 for domestic and international students. Applications are processed on a rolling basis. Application fee: $75. Electronic applications accepted. *Financial support:* In 2012–13, 43 students received support, including 9 research assistantships with full and partial tuition reimbursements available (averaging $15,500 per year), 34 teaching assistantships with full and partial tuition reimbursements available (averaging $15,000 per year); fellowships, career-related internships or fieldwork, Federal Work-Study, institutionally sponsored loans, scholarships/grants, traineeships, health care benefits, and tuition waivers (partial) also available. Financial award application deadline: 2/15. *Faculty research:* Computational mathematics, operations research, modeling in the natural sciences, applied statistics. *Unit head:* Dr. K. A. Ariyawansa, Chair, 509-335-4918, Fax: 509-335-1188, E-mail: ari@wsu.edu. *Application contact:* Graduate School Admissions, 800-GRADWSU, Fax: 509-335-1949, E-mail: gradsch@wsu.edu. Website: http://www.sci.wsu.edu/math/.

Wayne State University, College of Liberal Arts and Sciences, Department of Mathematics, Detroit, MI 48202. Offers applied mathematics (MA, PhD); mathematical statistics (MA, PhD); mathematics (MA); pure mathematics (PhD). *Students:* 54 full-time (17 women), 34 part-time (14 women); includes 12 minority (9 Black or African American, non-Hispanic/Latino; 3 Asian, non-Hispanic/Latino), 33 international. Average age 31. 120 applicants, 45% accepted, 16 enrolled. In 2012, 17 master's, 7 doctorates awarded. *Degree requirements:* For master's, thesis (for some programs), essays, oral exams; for doctorate, thesis/dissertation, oral exams; French, German, Russian, or Chinese. *Entrance requirements:* For master's, twelve semester credits in mathematics beyond sophomore calculus; for doctorate, master's degree in mathematics or equivalent level of advancement. Additional exam requirements/recommendations for international students: Required—TOEFL (minimum score 550 paper-based; 79 iBT); Recommended—TWE (minimum score 5.5). *Application deadline:* For fall admission, 6/1 priority date for domestic students, 5/1 for international students; for winter admission, 10/1 priority date for domestic students, 9/1 for international students; for spring admission, 2/1 priority date for domestic students, 1/1 for international students. Applications are processed on a rolling basis. Application fee: $50. Electronic applications accepted. *Expenses:* Tuition, state resident: full-time $12,788; part-time $532.85 per credit hour. Tuition, nonresident: full-time $28,243; part-time $1176.80 per credit hour. *Required fees:* $1367.30; $39.75 per credit hour. $206.65 per semester. Tuition and fees vary according to course load and program. *Financial support:* In 2012–13, 43 students received support, including 2 fellowships with tuition reimbursements available (averaging $17,000 per year), 5 research assistantships with tuition reimbursements available (averaging $18,293 per year), 27 teaching assistantships with tuition reimbursements available (averaging $17,391 per year); institutionally sponsored loans, scholarships/grants, health care benefits, tuition waivers (full), and unspecified assistantships also available. Support available to part-time students. *Faculty research:* Harmonic analysis and partial differential equations, group theory and non-commutative ring theory, homotopy theory and applications to topology and

Applied Mathematics

geometry, numerical analysis, control and optimization, statistical estimation theory. *Total annual research expenditures:* $1 million. *Unit head:* Dr. Daniel Frohardt, Professor and Chair, 313-577-2479, E-mail: ad0798@wayne.edu. *Application contact:* Dr. Alexander Korostelov, E-mail: apk@math.wayne.edu. Website: http://clasweb.clas.wayne.edu/math.

Western Illinois University, School of Graduate Studies, College of Arts and Sciences, Department of Mathematics, Macomb, IL 61455-1390. Offers applied math (Certificate); mathematics (MS). Part-time programs available. *Students:* 12 full-time (6 women), 1 part-time (0 women), 8 international. Average age 27. In 2012, 7 master's, 1 other advanced degree awarded. *Degree requirements:* For master's, thesis or alternative. *Entrance requirements:* Additional exam requirements/recommendations for international students: Required—TOEFL (minimum score 500 paper-based; 61 iBT). *Application deadline:* Applications are processed on a rolling basis. Application fee: $30. Electronic applications accepted. *Financial support:* In 2012–13, 5 students received support, including 1 research assistantship with full tuition reimbursement available (averaging $7,544 per year), 4 teaching assistantships with full tuition reimbursements available (averaging $8,688 per year). Financial award applicants required to submit FAFSA. *Unit head:* Dr. Iraj Kalantari, Chairperson, 309-298-1054. *Application contact:* Dr. Nancy Parsons, Interim Associate Provost and Director of Graduate Studies, 309-298-1806, Fax: 309-298-2345, E-mail: grad-office@wiu.edu. Website: http://wiu.edu/mathematics.

Western Michigan University, Graduate College, College of Arts and Sciences, Department of Mathematics, Program in Applied and Computational Mathematics, Kalamazoo, MI 49008. Offers MS.

West Virginia University, Eberly College of Arts and Sciences, Department of Mathematics, Morgantown, WV 26506. Offers applied mathematics (MS, PhD); discrete mathematics (PhD); interdisciplinary mathematics (MS); mathematics for secondary education (MS); pure mathematics (MS). Part-time programs available. Terminal master's awarded for partial completion of doctoral program. *Degree requirements:* For master's, comprehensive exam (for some programs), thesis optional; for doctorate, one foreign language, comprehensive exam, thesis/dissertation. *Entrance requirements:* For master's, GRE Subject Test (recommended), minimum GPA of 2.5; for doctorate, GRE Subject Test (recommended), master's degree in mathematics. Additional exam requirements/recommendations for international students: Required—TOEFL (paper-based 550) or IELTS (6). *Faculty research:* Combinatorics and graph theory, differential equations, applied and computational mathematics.

Wichita State University, Graduate School, Fairmount College of Liberal Arts and Sciences, Department of Mathematics, Statistics and Physics, Wichita, KS 67260. Offers applied mathematics (PhD); mathematics (MS). Part-time programs available. *Unit head:* Dr. Buma Fridman, Chair, 316-978-3160, Fax: 316-978-3748, E-mail: buma.fridman@wichita.edu. *Application contact:* Jordan Oleson, Admissions Coordinator, 316-978-3095, Fax: 316-978-3253, E-mail: jordan.oleson@wichita.edu. Website: http://www.wichita.edu/.

Worcester Polytechnic Institute, Graduate Studies and Research, Department of Mathematical Sciences, Worcester, MA 01609-2280. Offers applied mathematics (MS); applied statistics (MS); financial mathematics (MS); industrial mathematics (MS); mathematical sciences (PhD, Graduate Certificate); mathematics (MME); mathematics for educators (MS). Part-time and evening/weekend programs available. *Faculty:* 19 full-time (3 women), 7 part-time/adjunct

(2 women). *Students:* 93 full-time (45 women), 19 part-time (15 women); includes 5 minority (2 Black or African American, non-Hispanic/Latino; 2 Hispanic/Latino; 1 Two or more races, non-Hispanic/Latino), 71 international. 398 applicants, 53% accepted, 54 enrolled. In 2012, 25 master's, 1 doctorate awarded. *Degree requirements:* For master's, thesis (for some programs); for doctorate, comprehensive exam, thesis/dissertation. *Entrance requirements:* For master's and doctorate, GRE General Test, GRE Subject Test in math (recommended), 3 letters of recommendation. Additional exam requirements/recommendations for international students: Required—TOEFL (minimum score 563 paper-based; 84 iBT), IELTS (minimum score 7). *Application deadline:* For fall admission, 1/1 priority date for domestic students, 1/1 for international students; for spring admission, 10/1 priority date for domestic students, 10/1 for international students. Applications are processed on a rolling basis. Application fee: $70. Electronic applications accepted. *Financial support:* Research assistantships, teaching assistantships, career-related internships or fieldwork, institutionally sponsored loans, scholarships/grants, and unspecified assistantships available. Financial award application deadline: 1/1; financial award applicants required to submit FAFSA. *Faculty research:* Applied analysis and differential equations, computational mathematics, discrete mathematics, applied and computational statistics, industrial and financial mathematics, mathematical biology. *Unit head:* Dr. Bogdan Vernescu, Head, 508-831-5241, Fax: 508-831-5824, E-mail: vernescu@wpi.edu. *Application contact:* Dr. Joseph Fehribach, Graduate Coordinator, 508-831-5241, Fax: 508-831-5824, E-mail: bach@wpi.edu. Website: http://www.wpi.edu/Academics/Depts/Math/.

Wright State University, School of Graduate Studies, College of Science and Mathematics, Department of Mathematics and Statistics, Program in Applied Mathematics, Dayton, OH 45435. Offers MS. *Degree requirements:* For master's, comprehensive exam. *Entrance requirements:* For master's, bachelor's degree in mathematics or related field. Additional exam requirements/recommendations for international students: Required—TOEFL. *Faculty research:* Control theory, ordinary differential equations, partial differential equations, numerical analysis, mathematical modeling.

Yale University, Graduate School of Arts and Sciences, Program in Applied Mathematics, New Haven, CT 06520. Offers M Phil, MS, PhD. *Entrance requirements:* For doctorate, GRE General Test.

York University, Faculty of Graduate Studies, Faculty of Science and Engineering, Program in Mathematics and Statistics, Toronto, ON M3J 1P3, Canada. Offers industrial and applied mathematics (M Sc); mathematics and statistics (MA, PhD). Part-time programs available. *Degree requirements:* For master's, thesis optional; for doctorate, one foreign language, comprehensive exam, thesis/dissertation. Electronic applications accepted.

Youngstown State University, Graduate School, College of Science, Technology, Engineering and Mathematics, Department of Mathematics and Statistics, Youngstown, OH 44555-0001. Offers applied mathematics (MS); computer science (MS); secondary mathematics (MS); statistics (MS). Part-time programs available. *Degree requirements:* For master's, comprehensive exam, thesis optional. *Entrance requirements:* For master's, minimum GPA of 2.7 in computer science and mathematics. Additional exam requirements/recommendations for international students: Required—TOEFL. *Faculty research:* Regression analysis, numerical analysis, statistics, Markov chain, topology and fuzzy sets.

Applied Statistics

American University, College of Arts and Sciences, Department of Mathematics and Statistics, Washington, DC 22016-8050. Offers applied statistics (Certificate); mathematics (MA); statistics (MS). Part-time and evening/weekend programs available. *Faculty:* 28 full-time (12 women), 12 part-time/adjunct (1 woman). *Students:* 14 full-time (5 women), 17 part-time (5 women); includes 8 minority (3 Black or African American, non-Hispanic/Latino; 2 Asian, non-Hispanic/Latino; 2 Hispanic/Latino), 1 international. Average age 27. 39 applicants, 72% accepted, 13 enrolled. In 2012, 3 master's awarded. *Degree requirements:* For master's, comprehensive exam, thesis or alternative, tools of research in foreign language or computer language. *Entrance requirements:* For master's, GRE; for Certificate, bachelor's degree. Additional exam requirements/recommendations for international students: Required—TOEFL. *Application deadline:* For fall admission, 2/1 for domestic students; for spring admission, 10/1 for domestic students. Application fee: $80. *Expenses: Tuition:* Full-time $25,920; part-time $1440 per credit. *Required fees:* $430. Tuition and fees vary according to course load, campus/location and program. *Financial support:* Fellowships, research assistantships, teaching assistantships, career-related internships or fieldwork, Federal Work-Study, institutionally sponsored loans, and unspecified assistantships available. Support available to part-time students. Financial award application deadline: 2/1. *Faculty research:* Logic, random processes, probability analysis, biostatistics, statistical computing. *Unit head:* Dr. Jeffrey D. Adler, Chair, 202-885-3171, Fax: 202-885-3155, E-mail: jadler@american.edu. *Application contact:* Kathleen Clowery, Director, Graduate Admissions, 202-885-3621, Fax:

202-885-1505, E-mail: clowery@american.edu. Website: http://www.american.edu/cas/mathstat/.

Bowling Green State University, Graduate College, College of Arts and Sciences, Department of Mathematics and Statistics, Bowling Green, OH 43403. Offers applied statistics (MS); mathematics (MA, MAT, PhD); statistics (PhD). Part-time programs available. *Degree requirements:* For master's, thesis or alternative; for doctorate, comprehensive exam, thesis/dissertation. *Entrance requirements:* For master's and doctorate, GRE General Test. Additional exam requirements/recommendations for international students: Required—TOEFL. Electronic applications accepted. *Faculty research:* Statistics and probability, algebra, analysis.

Bowling Green State University, Graduate College, College of Business Administration, Department of Applied Statistics and Operations Research, Bowling Green, OH 43403. Offers applied statistics (MS). Part-time programs available. *Degree requirements:* For master's, thesis or alternative. *Entrance requirements:* For master's, GRE General Test. Additional exam requirements/recommendations for international students: Required—TOEFL. Electronic applications accepted. *Faculty research:* Reliability, linear models, time series, statistical quality control.

Brigham Young University, Graduate Studies, College of Physical and Mathematical Sciences, Department of Statistics, Provo, UT 84602-1001. Offers applied statistics (MS). *Faculty:* 15 full-time (3 women). *Students:* 19 full-time (6

286 www.petersonsbooks.com

Peterson's Graduate Programs in the Physical Sciences, Mathematics,
Agricultural Sciences, the Environment & Natural Resources 2014

women). Average age 25. 18 applicants, 50% accepted, 8 enrolled. In 2012, 12 master's awarded. *Degree requirements:* For master's, comprehensive exam, thesis (for some programs). *Entrance requirements:* For master's, GRE General Test, minimum undergraduate GPA of 3.3; course work in statistical methods, theory, multivariable calculus and linear algebra with minimum B- average. Additional exam requirements/recommendations for international students: Required—TOEFL (minimum score 580 paper-based; 85 iBT). *Application deadline:* For fall admission, 2/1 for domestic and international students. Application fee: $50. Electronic applications accepted. *Expenses:* Tuition: Full-time $5950; part-time $331 per credit hour. Tuition and fees vary according to program and student's religious affiliation. *Financial support:* In 2012–13, 16 students received support, including 5 research assistantships with full and partial tuition reimbursements available (averaging $10,000 per year), 11 teaching assistantships with full and partial tuition reimbursements available (averaging $10,000 per year); scholarships/grants and unspecified assistantships also available. Financial award application deadline: 2/1. *Faculty research:* Statistical genetics, reliability and pollution monitoring, Bayesian methods. *Total annual research expenditures:* $198,150. *Unit head:* Dr. Harold Dennis Tolley, Chair, 801-422-6668, Fax: 801-422-0635, E-mail: tolley@byu.edu. *Application contact:* Dr. Gilbert W. Fellingham, Graduate Coordinator, 801-422-2806, Fax: 801-422-0635, E-mail: gwf@stat.byu.edu. Website: http://statistics.byu.edu/.

California State University, East Bay, Office of Academic Programs and Graduate Studies, College of Science, Department of Statistics and Biostatistics, Statistics Program, Hayward, CA 94542-3000. Offers actuarial science (MS); applied statistics (MS); computational statistics (MS); mathematical statistics (MS). Part-time and evening/weekend programs available. *Degree requirements:* For master's, comprehensive exam. *Entrance requirements:* For master's, letters of recommendation, minimum GPA of 3.0, math through lower-division calculus. Additional exam requirements/recommendations for international students: Required—TOEFL (minimum score 550 paper-based). Electronic applications accepted.

California State University, Long Beach, Graduate Studies, College of Natural Sciences and Mathematics, Department of Mathematics and Statistics, Long Beach, CA 90840. Offers mathematics (MS), including applied mathematics, applied statistics, mathematics education for secondary school teachers. Part-time programs available. *Degree requirements:* For master's, comprehensive exam or thesis. Electronic applications accepted. *Faculty research:* Algebra, functional analysis, partial differential equations, operator theory, numerical analysis.

Cleveland State University, College of Graduate Studies, College of Sciences and Health Professions, Department of Mathematics, Cleveland, OH 44115. Offers applied statistics (MS); mathematics (MA, MS). Part-time and evening/weekend programs available. *Faculty:* 11 full-time (4 women), 1 part-time/adjunct (0 women). *Students:* 8 full-time (4 women), 27 part-time (11 women); includes 3 minority (1 Black or African American, non-Hispanic/Latino; 1 Asian, non-Hispanic/Latino; 1 Hispanic/Latino), 9 international. Average age 32. 59 applicants, 80% accepted, 23 enrolled. In 2012, 16 master's awarded. *Degree requirements:* For master's, exit project. *Entrance requirements:* Additional exam requirements/recommendations for international students: Required—TOEFL (minimum score 515 paper-based). *Application deadline:* For fall admission, 6/15 priority date for domestic students, 6/15 for international students. Applications are processed on a rolling basis. Application fee: $30. Electronic applications accepted. *Expenses:* Tuition, state resident: full-time $8172; part-time $510.75 per credit hour. Tuition, nonresident: full-time $15,372; part-time $960.75 per credit hour. *Required fees:* $25 per semester. Tuition and fees vary according to course load and program. *Financial support:* In 2012–13, 12 students received support, including 12 teaching assistantships with full tuition reimbursements available (averaging $10,000 per year). Financial award application deadline: 3/15. *Faculty research:* Algebraic topology, probability and statistics, differential equations, geometry. *Unit head:* Dr. John Peter Holcomb, Jr., Chairperson, 216-687-4681, Fax: 216-523-7340, E-mail: j.p.holcomb@csuohio.edu. *Application contact:* Dr. John F. Oprea, Graduate Program Director, 216-687-4702, Fax: 216-523-7340, E-mail: j.oprea@csuohio.edu. Website: http://www.csuohio.edu/sciences/dept/mathematics/.

Cornell University, Graduate School, Graduate Fields of Engineering, Field of Statistics, Ithaca, NY 14853-0001. Offers applied statistics (MPS); biometry (MS, PhD); decision theory (MS, PhD); economic and social statistics (MS, PhD); engineering statistics (MS, PhD); experimental design (MS, PhD); mathematical statistics (MS, PhD); probability (MS, PhD); sampling (MS, PhD); statistical computing (MS, PhD); stochastic processes (MS, PhD). *Faculty:* 29 full-time (3 women). *Students:* 70 full-time (35 women); includes 7 minority (5 Asian, non-Hispanic/Latino; 1 Hispanic/Latino; 1 Two or more races, non-Hispanic/Latino), 48 international. Average age 25. 681 applicants, 22% accepted, 50 enrolled. In 2012, 51 master's, 5 doctorates awarded. Terminal master's awarded for partial completion of doctoral program. *Degree requirements:* For master's, project (MPS), thesis (MS); for doctorate, one foreign language, thesis/dissertation. *Entrance requirements:* For master's, GRE General Test (for MS), 2 letters of recommendation (MS, MPS); for doctorate, GRE General Test, 2 letters of recommendation. Additional exam requirements/recommendations for international students: Required—TOEFL (minimum score 550 paper-based; 77 iBT). *Application deadline:* For fall admission, 1/15 for domestic students. Applications are processed on a rolling basis. Application fee: $95. Electronic applications accepted. *Financial support:* In 2012–13, 23 students received support, including 2 fellowships with full tuition reimbursements available, 5 research assistantships with full tuition reimbursements available, 16 teaching assistantships with full tuition reimbursements available; institutionally sponsored loans, scholarships/grants, tuition waivers (full and partial), and unspecified assistantships also available. Financial award applicants required to submit FAFSA. *Faculty research:* Bayesian analysis, survival analysis, nonparametric statistics, stochastic processes, mathematical statistics. *Unit head:* Director of Graduate Studies, 607-255-8066. *Application contact:* Graduate Field Assistant, 607-255-8066, E-mail: csc@cornell.edu. Website: http://www.gradschool.cornell.edu/fields.php?id-94&a-2.

DePaul University, College of Science and Health, Department of Mathematical Sciences, Chicago, IL 60614. Offers applied mathematics (MS), including actuarial science, statistics; applied statistics (MS, Certificate); mathematics education (MA); pure mathematics (MS). Part-time and evening/weekend programs available. *Students:* 120 full-time (51 women), 64 part-time (26 women); includes 54 minority (21 Black or African American, non-Hispanic/Latino; 21 Asian, non-Hispanic/Latino; 10 Hispanic/Latino; 1 Native Hawaiian or other Pacific Islander, non-Hispanic/Latino; 1 Two or more races, non-Hispanic/Latino), 26 international. Average age 31. In 2012, 35 master's awarded. *Degree requirements:* For master's, comprehensive exam. *Entrance requirements:* For master's, bachelor's degree. Additional exam requirements/recommendations for international students: Required—TOEFL (minimum score 550 paper-based; 80 iBT). *Application deadline:* For fall admission, 7/30 for domestic students, 6/30 for international students; for winter admission, 11/30 for domestic students, 10/31 for international students; for spring admission, 2/15 for domestic students. Applications are processed on a rolling basis. Application fee: $40. Electronic applications accepted. *Financial support:* In 2012–13, research assistantships with partial tuition reimbursements (averaging $6,000 per year) were awarded; teaching assistantships and tuition waivers (full) also available. Financial award application deadline: 4/30; financial award applicants required to submit FAFSA. *Faculty research:* Verbally prime algebras, enveloping algebras of Lie, superalgebras and related rings, harmonic analysis, estimation theory. *Total annual research expenditures:* $30,000. *Unit head:* Dr. Ahmed I. Zayed, Chairperson, 773-325-7806, Fax: 773-325-7807, E-mail: azayed@depaul.edu. *Application contact:* Ann Spittle, Director of Graduate Admissions, 773-325-7315, Fax: 312-476-3244, E-mail: graddepaul@depaul.edu. Website: http://csh.depaul.edu/departments/mathematical-sciences/Pages/default.aspx.

Eastern Michigan University, Graduate School, College of Arts and Sciences, Department of Mathematics, Ypsilanti, MI 48197. Offers applied statistics (MA); computer science (MA); mathematics (MA); mathematics education (MA). Part-time and evening/weekend programs available. Postbaccalaureate distance learning degree programs offered (minimal on-campus study). *Faculty:* 23 full-time (10 women). *Students:* 7 full-time (6 women), 39 part-time (16 women); includes 9 minority (4 Black or African American, non-Hispanic/Latino; 3 Asian, non-Hispanic/Latino; 1 Hispanic/Latino; 1 Two or more races, non-Hispanic/Latino), 8 international. Average age 30. 34 applicants, 76% accepted, 13 enrolled. In 2012, 10 master's awarded. *Degree requirements:* For master's, thesis optional. *Entrance requirements:* Additional exam requirements/recommendations for international students: Required—TOEFL. *Application deadline:* Applications are processed on a rolling basis. Application fee: $35. *Expenses:* Tuition, state resident: full-time $10,776; part-time $449 per credit hour. Tuition, nonresident: full-time $21,242; part-time $885 per credit hour. *Required fees:* $41 per credit hour. $48 per term. One-time fee: $100. Tuition and fees vary according to course level, degree level and reciprocity agreements. *Financial support:* Fellowships, research assistantships with full tuition reimbursements, teaching assistantships with full tuition reimbursements, career-related internships or fieldwork, Federal Work-Study, institutionally sponsored loans, scholarships/grants, tuition waivers (partial), and unspecified assistantships available. Support available to part-time students. Financial award applicants required to submit FAFSA. *Unit head:* Dr. Christopher Gardiner, Department Head, 734-487-1444, Fax: 734-487-2489, E-mail: cgardiner@emich.edu. *Application contact:* Dr. Bingwu Wang, Graduate Coordinator, 734-487-5044, Fax: 734-487-2489, E-mail: bwang@emich.edu. Website: http://www.math.emich.edu.

Florida State University, The Graduate School, College of Arts and Sciences, Department of Statistics, Tallahassee, FL 32306-4330. Offers applied statistics (MS); biostatistics (MS, PhD); mathematical statistics (MS, PhD). Part-time programs available. *Faculty:* 15 full-time (2 women). *Students:* 62 full-time (26 women), 5 part-time (2 women); includes 25 minority (9 Black or African American, non-Hispanic/Latino; 9 Asian, non-Hispanic/Latino; 7 Hispanic/Latino), 17 international. Average age 29. 138 applicants, 30% accepted, 18 enrolled. In 2012, 17 master's, 9 doctorates awarded. Terminal master's awarded for partial completion of doctoral program. *Degree requirements:* For doctorate, comprehensive exam, thesis/dissertation, departmental qualifying exam. *Entrance requirements:* For master's, GRE General Test, previous course work in calculus, minimum GPA of 3.0; for doctorate, GRE General Test, minimum GPA of 3.0, 1 course in linear algebra (preferred), calculus I-III, real analysis. Additional exam requirements/recommendations for international students: Required—TOEFL (minimum score 80 iBT). *Application deadline:* For fall admission, 7/1 for domestic and international students; for spring admission, 11/1 for domestic and international students. Applications are processed on a rolling basis. Application fee: $30. Electronic applications accepted. *Expenses:* Tuition, state resident: full-time $7263; part-time $403.51 per credit hour. Tuition, nonresident: full-time $18,087; part-time $1004.85 per credit hour. *Required fees:* $1335.42; $74.19 per credit hour. $445.14 per semester. One-time fee: $40 full-time; $20 part-time.

Peterson's Graduate Programs in the Physical Sciences, Mathematics, Agricultural Sciences, the Environment & Natural Resources 2014

www.petersonsbooks.com **287**

Tuition and fees vary according to program. *Financial support:* In 2012–13, 56 students received support, including 9 research assistantships with full tuition reimbursements available (averaging $22,495 per year), 48 teaching assistantships with full tuition reimbursements available (averaging $20,358 per year); Federal Work-Study, institutionally sponsored loans, scholarships/grants, health care benefits, and unspecified assistantships also available. Financial award application deadline: 2/15; financial award applicants required to submit FAFSA. *Faculty research:* Statistical inference, probability theory, biostatistics, nonparametric estimation, automatic target recognition. *Total annual research expenditures:* $693,402. *Unit head:* Dr. Xufeng Niu, Chairman, 850-644-4008, Fax: 850-644-5271, E-mail: niu@stat.fsu.edu. *Application contact:* Alex Cohn, Academic Support Assistant, 850-644-3514, Fax: 850-644-5271, E-mail: acohn@stat.fsu.edu. Website: http://stat.fsu.edu/.

Indiana University Bloomington, University Graduate School, College of Arts and Sciences, Department of Statistics, Bloomington, IN 47405-7000. Offers applied statistics (MS); statistical science (MS, PhD). *Students:* 15 full-time (3 women), 5 part-time (3 women); includes 3 minority (all Asian, non-Hispanic/Latino), 14 international. 44 applicants, 39% accepted, 10 enrolled. In 2012, 6 master's awarded. Application fee: $55 ($65 for international students). *Unit head:* Dr. Bennett Bertenthal, Dean, 812-855-2392, E-mail: bbertent@indiana.edu. *Application contact:* Katie Bowman, Department Secretary, 812-855-7828, E-mail: katibowm@indiana.edu. Website: http://stat.indiana.edu/.

Indiana University–Purdue University Fort Wayne, College of Arts and Sciences, Department of Mathematical Sciences, Fort Wayne, IN 46805-1499. Offers applied mathematics (MS); applied statistics (Certificate); mathematics (MS); operations research (MS); teaching (MAT). Part-time and evening/weekend programs available. *Faculty:* 19 full-time (5 women). *Students:* 1 (woman) full-time, 10 part-time (2 women), 1 international. Average age 30. 6 applicants, 100% accepted, 4 enrolled. In 2012, 5 master's, 1 other advanced degree awarded. *Entrance requirements:* For master's, minimum GPA of 3.0, major or minor in mathematics, three letters of recommendation. Additional exam requirements/recommendations for international students: Required—TOEFL (minimum score 550 paper-based; 79 iBT); Recommended—TWE. *Application deadline:* For fall admission, 8/1 priority date for domestic students, 7/1 for international students; for spring admission, 12/1 for domestic students, 10/1 for international students. Applications are processed on a rolling basis. Application fee: $55 ($60 for international students). Electronic applications accepted. *Expenses:* Tuition, state resident: full-time $6279; part-time $313.95 per credit hour. Tuition, nonresident: full-time $14,219; part-time $710.95 per credit hour. *Financial support:* In 2012–13, 4 teaching assistantships with partial tuition reimbursements (averaging $13,190 per year) were awarded; scholarships/grants and unspecified assistantships also available. Support available to part-time students. Financial award application deadline: 3/1; financial award applicants required to submit FAFSA. *Faculty research:* Equilibrium measures, group graphs and split-stars, arrangement graphs. *Unit head:* Dr. Peter Dragnev, Interim Chair and Professor, 260-481-6382, Fax: 260-481-0155, E-mail: dragnevp@ipfw.edu. *Application contact:* Dr. W. Douglas Weakley, Director of Graduate Studies, 260-481-6233, Fax: 260-481-0155, E-mail: weakley@ipfw.edu. Website: http://www.ipfw.edu/math/.

Indiana University–Purdue University Indianapolis, School of Science, Department of Mathematical Sciences, Indianapolis, IN 46202-3216. Offers mathematics (MS, PhD), including applied mathematics, applied statistics (MS), mathematical statistics (PhD), mathematics, mathematics education (MS). *Faculty:* 30 full-time (2 women). *Students:* 25 full-time (8 women), 35 part-time (13 women); includes 11 minority (2 Black or African American, non-Hispanic/Latino; 7 Asian, non-Hispanic/Latino; 2 Hispanic/Latino), 23 international. Average age 33. 52 applicants, 67% accepted, 21 enrolled. In 2012, 22 master's awarded. Terminal master's awarded for partial completion of doctoral program. *Degree requirements:* For master's, thesis optional; for doctorate, one foreign language, thesis/dissertation. *Entrance requirements:* For doctorate, GRE General Test. Additional exam requirements/recommendations for international students: Required—TOEFL. *Application deadline:* For fall admission, 2/1 priority date for domestic students. Application fee: $55 ($65 for international students). *Financial support:* In 2012–13, 14 students received support, including 4 fellowships with tuition reimbursements available (averaging $15,375 per year), 4 teaching assistantships with tuition reimbursements available (averaging $13,088 per year); research assistantships with tuition reimbursements available and tuition waivers (full and partial) also available. Financial award application deadline: 2/1. *Faculty research:* Mathematical physics, integrable systems, partial differential equations, noncommutative geometry, biomathematics, computational neurosciences. *Unit head:* Dr. Zhongmin Shen, Chair, 317-278-1065, Fax: 317-274-3460, E-mail: zshen@math.iupui.edu. *Application contact:* Dr. Sherry Queener, Director, Graduate Studies and Associate Dean, 317-274-1577, Fax: 317-278-2380. Website: http://www.math.iupui.edu/.

Instituto Tecnológico y de Estudios Superiores de Monterrey, Campus Monterrey, Graduate and Research Division, Programs in Engineering, Monterrey, Mexico. Offers applied statistics (M Eng); artificial intelligence (PhD); automation engineering (M Eng); chemical engineering (M Eng); civil engineering (M Eng); electrical engineering (M Eng); electronic engineering (M Eng); environmental engineering (M Eng); industrial engineering (M Eng, PhD); manufacturing engineering (M Eng); mechanical engineering (M Eng); systems and quality engineering (M Eng). M Eng program offered jointly with University of Waterloo; PhD in industrial engineering with Texas A&M University. Part-time and evening/weekend programs available. Terminal master's awarded for partial completion of doctoral program. *Degree requirements:* For master's, one foreign language, thesis; for doctorate, one foreign language, thesis/dissertation. *Entrance requirements:* For master's, EXADEP; for doctorate, GRE, master's degree in related field. Additional exam requirements/recommendations for international students: Required—TOEFL. *Faculty research:* Flexible manufacturing cells, materials, statistical methods, environmental prevention, control and evaluation.

Kennesaw State University, College of Science and Mathematics, Program in Applied Statistics, Kennesaw, GA 30144-5591. Offers MSAS. Part-time and evening/weekend programs available. *Students:* 28 full-time (11 women), 59 part-time (27 women); includes 26 minority (17 Black or African American, non-Hispanic/Latino; 1 American Indian or Alaska Native, non-Hispanic/Latino; 6 Asian, non-Hispanic/Latino; 1 Hispanic/Latino; 1 Two or more races, non-Hispanic/Latino), 1 international. Average age 34. 36 applicants, 75% accepted, 20 enrolled. In 2012, 32 master's awarded. *Entrance requirements:* For master's, GRE, minimum GPA of 2.75, resume. Additional exam requirements/recommendations for international students: Required—TOEFL (minimum score 550 paper-based; 80 iBT), IELTS (minimum score 6). *Application deadline:* For fall admission, 6/1 for domestic and international students; for spring admission, 11/1 for domestic and international students. Applications are processed on a rolling basis. Application fee: $60. Electronic applications accepted. *Expenses:* Tuition, state resident: full-time $4662; part-time $259 per semester hour. Tuition, nonresident: full-time $16,794; part-time $933 per semester hour. *Required fees:* $817 per semester. *Financial support:* In 2012–13, 2 research assistantships (averaging $8,000 per year) were awarded; unspecified assistantships also available. Financial award application deadline: 4/1; financial award applicants required to submit FAFSA. *Unit head:* Dr. Lewis Van Brackle, Director, 678-797-2409, E-mail: lvanbrac@kennesaw.edu. *Application contact:* Calla Pavlidis, Admissions Counselor, 770-420-4377, Fax: 770-423-6885, E-mail: cpavlidi@kennesaw.edu. Website: http://www.kennesaw.edu.

Louisiana State University and Agricultural and Mechanical College, Graduate School, College of Agriculture, Department of Experimental Statistics, Baton Rouge, LA 70803. Offers applied statistics (M App St). Part-time programs available. *Faculty:* 8 full-time (0 women). *Students:* 22 full-time (6 women), 3 part-time (2 women); includes 1 minority (Asian, non-Hispanic/Latino), 11 international. Average age 28. 17 applicants, 59% accepted, 7 enrolled. In 2012, 10 master's awarded. *Degree requirements:* For master's, project. *Entrance requirements:* For master's, GRE General Test, minimum GPA of 3.0. Additional exam requirements/recommendations for international students: Required—TOEFL (minimum score 550 paper-based; 79 iBT) or IELTS (minimum score 6.5). *Application deadline:* For fall admission, 1/25 priority date for domestic students, 5/15 for international students; for spring admission, 10/15 priority date for domestic students, 10/15 for international students. Applications are processed on a rolling basis. Application fee: $50 ($70 for international students). Electronic applications accepted. *Financial support:* In 2012–13, 17 students received support, including 1 research assistantship with partial tuition reimbursement available (averaging $20,000 per year), 15 teaching assistantships with partial tuition reimbursements available (averaging $9,853 per year); fellowships, career-related internships or fieldwork, Federal Work-Study, institutionally sponsored loans, tuition waivers (full and partial), and unspecified assistantships also available. Financial award application deadline: 4/1; financial award applicants required to submit FAFSA. *Faculty research:* Linear models, statistical computing, ecological statistics. *Unit head:* Dr. James Geaghan, Head, 225-578-8303, Fax: 225-578-8344, E-mail: jgeaghan@lsu.edu. *Application contact:* Dr. Brian Marx, Graduate Adviser, 225-578-8366, Fax: 225-578-8344, E-mail: bmarx@lsu.edu. Website: http://www.stat.lsu.edu/.

Loyola University Chicago, Graduate School, Department of Mathematical Sciences and Statistics, Chicago, IL 60660. Offers applied statistics (MS); mathematics (MS), including pure and applied mathematics. Part-time programs available. *Faculty:* 19 full-time (4 women). *Students:* 31 full-time (17 women), 7 part-time (4 women); includes 5 minority (2 Black or African American, non-Hispanic/Latino; 2 Asian, non-Hispanic/Latino; 1 Hispanic/Latino), 11 international. Average age 29. 62 applicants, 74% accepted, 17 enrolled. In 2012, 24 master's awarded. *Entrance requirements:* For master's, GRE General Test. Additional exam requirements/recommendations for international students: Required—TOEFL. *Application deadline:* For fall admission, 8/1 for domestic students; for spring admission, 12/1 for domestic students. Applications are processed on a rolling basis. Application fee: $0. Electronic applications accepted. *Expenses: Tuition:* Full-time $16,290. *Required fees:* $128 per semester. Tuition and fees vary according to course load and program. *Financial support:* In 2012–13, 13 students received support, including 6 teaching assistantships with tuition reimbursements available (averaging $10,000 per year); career-related internships or fieldwork, Federal Work-Study, institutionally sponsored loans, and tuition waivers (partial) also available. Financial award application deadline: 3/15. *Faculty research:* Probability and statistics, differential equations, algebra, combinatorics. *Total annual research expenditures:* $70,000. *Unit head:* Dr. Anthony Giaquinto, Chair, 773-508-3578, Fax: 773-508-2123, E-mail: agiaqui@luc.edu. *Application contact:* Dr. W. Cary Huffman, Graduate Program Director, 773-508-3563, Fax: 773-508-2123, E-mail: whuffma@luc.edu. Website: http://math.luc.edu/.

McMaster University, School of Graduate Studies, Faculty of Science, Department of Mathematics and Statistics, Program in Statistics, Hamilton, ON

L8S 4M2, Canada. Offers applied statistics (M Sc); medical statistics (M Sc); statistical theory (M Sc). *Degree requirements:* For master's, thesis or alternative. *Entrance requirements:* For master's, honors degree background in mathematics and statistics. Additional exam requirements/recommendations for international students: Required—TOEFL (minimum score 550 paper-based). *Faculty research:* Development of polymer production technology, quality of life in patients who use pharmaceutical agents, mathematical modeling, order statistics from progressively censored samples, nonlinear stochastic model in genetics.

Michigan State University, The Graduate School, College of Natural Science, Department of Statistics and Probability, East Lansing, MI 48824. Offers applied statistics (MS); statistics (MS, PhD). *Entrance requirements:* Additional exam requirements/recommendations for international students: Required—TOEFL. Electronic applications accepted.

New Jersey Institute of Technology, Office of Graduate Studies, College of Science and Liberal Arts, Department of Mathematical Science, Program in Applied Statistics, Newark, NJ 07102. Offers MS. Part-time and evening/weekend programs available. *Entrance requirements:* For master's, GRE General Test. Additional exam requirements/recommendations for international students: Required—TOEFL (minimum score 550 paper-based; 79 iBT). Electronic applications accepted. *Expenses:* Tuition, state resident: full-time $16,836; part-time $915 per credit. Tuition, nonresident: full-time $24,670; part-time $1286 per credit. *Required fees:* $2318; $242 per credit.

New Mexico State University, Graduate School, College of Business, Department of Economics, Applied Statistics and International Business, Las Cruces, NM 88003. Offers applied statistics (MS); economic development (DED); economics (MA). Part-time programs available. *Faculty:* 20 full-time (7 women). *Students:* 47 full-time (18 women), 24 part-time (5 women); includes 29 minority (3 Black or African American, non-Hispanic/Latino; 2 Asian, non-Hispanic/Latino; 23 Hispanic/Latino; 1 Two or more races, non-Hispanic/Latino), 27 international. Average age 34. 62 applicants, 68% accepted, 26 enrolled. In 2012, 23 master's, 4 doctorates awarded. Terminal master's awarded for partial completion of doctoral program. *Degree requirements:* For master's, comprehensive exam, thesis or alternative; for doctorate, comprehensive exam, thesis/dissertation, internship, written project. *Entrance requirements:* For master's, minimum GPA of 3.0; for doctorate, appropriate master's degree, minimum GPA of 3.0. Additional exam requirements/recommendations for international students: Required—TOEFL (minimum score 550 paper-based; 79 iBT), IELTS (minimum score 6.5). *Application deadline:* For fall admission, 3/1 priority date for domestic students, 3/1 for international students. Applications are processed on a rolling basis. Application fee: $40 ($50 for international students). Electronic applications accepted. *Expenses:* Tuition, state resident: full-time $5239; part-time $218 per credit. Tuition, nonresident: full-time $18,266; part-time $761 per credit. *Required fees:* $1274; $53 per credit. *Financial support:* In 2012–13, 43 students received support, including 1 fellowship (averaging $3,930 per year), 26 teaching assistantships (averaging $10,967 per year); career-related internships or fieldwork, Federal Work-Study, and health care benefits also available. Support available to part-time students. Financial award application deadline: 3/1. *Faculty research:* Public utilities, environment, linear models, biological sampling, public policy, economic development, energy, regional economics. *Unit head:* Dr. Richard V. Adkisson, Head, 575-646-4988, Fax: 575-646-1915, E-mail: radkisso@nmsu.edu. *Application contact:* Coordinator, 575-646-2736, Fax: 575-646-7721, E-mail: gradinfo@nmsu.edu. Website: http://business.nmsu.edu/academics/economics-ib/.

North Dakota State University, College of Graduate and Interdisciplinary Studies, College of Science and Mathematics, Department of Statistics, Fargo, ND 58108. Offers applied statistics (MS, Certificate); statistics (PhD); MS/MS. *Faculty:* 7 full-time (4 women). *Students:* 32 full-time (16 women), 4 part-time (1 woman); includes 5 minority (3 Black or African American, non-Hispanic/Latino; 1 Asian, non-Hispanic/Latino; 1 Two or more races, non-Hispanic/Latino), 18 international. Average age 30. 37 applicants, 78% accepted, 15 enrolled. In 2012, 8 master's, 1 doctorate, 2 other advanced degrees awarded. *Degree requirements:* For master's, comprehensive exam, thesis; for doctorate, comprehensive exam, thesis/dissertation. *Entrance requirements:* For master's and doctorate, minimum GPA of 3.0. Additional exam requirements/recommendations for international students: Required—TOEFL (minimum score 550 paper-based; 79 iBT). *Application deadline:* For fall admission, 3/15 for international students. Applications are processed on a rolling basis. Application fee: $35. Electronic applications accepted. *Financial support:* In 2012–13, 2 fellowships with full tuition reimbursements, 7 research assistantships with full tuition reimbursements, 9 teaching assistantships with full tuition reimbursements were awarded; career-related internships or fieldwork, Federal Work-Study, institutionally sponsored loans, and tuition waivers (full) also available. Financial award application deadline: 4/15. *Faculty research:* Nonparametric statistics, survival analysis, multivariate analysis, distribution theory, inference modeling, biostatistics. *Unit head:* Dr. Rhonda Magel, Chair, 701-231-7532, Fax: 701-231-8734, E-mail: ndsu.stats@ndsu.edu. *Application contact:* Dawn Halle, Academic Assistant, 701-231-7532, Fax: 702-231-8734, E-mail: ndsu.stats@ndsu.edu. Website: http://www.ndsu.edu/statistics/.

Northern Arizona University, Graduate College, College of Engineering, Forestry and Natural Sciences, Department of Mathematics and Statistics, Flagstaff, AZ 86011. Offers applied statistics (Certificate); mathematics (MAT, MS); statistics (MS). Part-time programs available. *Degree requirements:* For master's, comprehensive exam (for some programs), thesis (for some programs). *Entrance requirements:* For master's, minimum GPA of 3.0. Additional exam requirements/recommendations for international students: Required—TOEFL (minimum score 550 paper-based; 80 iBT), IELTS (minimum score 7). Electronic applications accepted. *Faculty research:* Topology, statistics, groups, ring theory, number theory.

Oakland University, Graduate Study and Lifelong Learning, College of Arts and Sciences, Department of Mathematics and Statistics, Program in Applied Statistics, Rochester, MI 48309-4401. Offers MS. Part-time and evening/weekend programs available. *Entrance requirements:* For master's, minimum GPA of 3.0 for unconditional admission. Additional exam requirements/recommendations for international students: Required—TOEFL (minimum score 550 paper-based). Electronic applications accepted. *Expenses:* Contact institution.

Penn State University Park, Graduate School, Eberly College of Science, Department of Statistics, State College, University Park, PA 16802-1503. Offers MA, MAS, MS, PhD. *Unit head:* Dr. David R. Hunter, Head, 814-863-0979, E-mail: drh20@psu.edu. *Application contact:* Information Contact, 814-865-8630, E-mail: b2a@psu.edu. Website: http://stat.psu.edu/.

Rochester Institute of Technology, Graduate Enrollment Services, Kate Gleason College of Engineering, Center of Quality and Applied Statistics, Rochester, NY 14623-5603. Offers applied statistics (MS); statistical quality (AC). Part-time and evening/weekend programs available. Postbaccalaureate distance learning degree programs offered (no on-campus study). *Students:* 4 full-time (3 women), 44 part-time (15 women); includes 5 minority (1 Black or African American, non-Hispanic/Latino; 2 Asian, non-Hispanic/Latino; 2 Hispanic/Latino), 13 international. Average age 30. 70 applicants, 59% accepted, 20 enrolled. In 2012, 24 master's awarded. *Degree requirements:* For master's, oral exam. *Entrance requirements:* For master's, course work in calculus, minimum GPA of 3.0. Additional exam requirements/recommendations for international students: Required—TOEFL (minimum score 570 paper-based; 88 iBT) or IELTS (minimum score 6.5). *Application deadline:* For fall admission, 2/15 priority date for domestic students, 2/15 for international students; for winter admission, 10/15 for domestic students; for spring admission, 2/1 for domestic students. Applications are processed on a rolling basis. Application fee: $60. *Expenses: Tuition:* Full-time $35,976; part-time $999 per credit hour. *Required fees:* $240; $80 per quarter. *Financial support:* Research assistantships with partial tuition reimbursements, career-related internships or fieldwork, institutionally sponsored loans, scholarships/grants, and unspecified assistantships available. Support available to part-time students. Financial award applicants required to submit FAFSA. *Faculty research:* Industrial statistics, quality control; experimental design; reliability; regression techniques; multivariate analysis; nonparametric methods. *Unit head:* Dr. Donald Baker, Director, 585-475-6990, Fax: 585-475-5959, E-mail: cqas@rit.edu. *Application contact:* Diane Ellison, Assistant Vice President, Graduate Enrollment Services, 585-475-2229, Fax: 585-475-7164, E-mail: gradinfo@rit.edu. Website: http://www.rit.edu/kgcoe/cqas/academics/msappliedstatistics.htm.

Rutgers, The State University of New Jersey, New Brunswick, Graduate School-New Brunswick, Program in Statistics, Piscataway, NJ 08854-8097. Offers applied statistics (MS); biostatistics (MS); data mining (MS); quality and productivity management (MS); statistics (MS, PhD). Part-time programs available. Terminal master's awarded for partial completion of doctoral program. *Degree requirements:* For master's, comprehensive exam, essay, exam, non-thesis essay paper; for doctorate, one foreign language, thesis/dissertation, qualifying oral and written exams. *Entrance requirements:* For master's, GRE General Test; for doctorate, GRE General Test, GRE Subject Test (recommended). Additional exam requirements/recommendations for international students: Required—TOEFL (minimum score 550 paper-based). Electronic applications accepted. *Faculty research:* Probability, decision theory, linear models, multivariate statistics, statistical computing.

St. Cloud State University, School of Graduate Studies, College of Science and Engineering, Program in Applied Statistics, St. Cloud, MN 56301-4498. Offers MS.

Stevens Institute of Technology, Graduate School, Charles V. Schaefer Jr. School of Engineering, Department of Mathematical Sciences, Program in Applied Statistics, Hoboken, NJ 07030. Offers Certificate. *Entrance requirements:* Additional exam requirements/recommendations for international students: Required—TOEFL. Electronic applications accepted.

Syracuse University, College of Arts and Sciences, Program in Applied Statistics, Syracuse, NY 13244. Offers MS. Part-time programs available. *Entrance requirements:* For master's, GRE General Test. Additional exam requirements/recommendations for international students: Required—TOEFL (minimum score 100 iBT). Electronic applications accepted.

The University of Alabama, Graduate School, Manderson Graduate School of Business, Department of Information Systems, Statistics, and Management Science, Program in Applied Statistics, Tuscaloosa, AL 35487. Offers MS, PhD. Part-time programs available. *Faculty:* 8 full-time (0 women). *Students:* 19 full-time (7 women), 5 part-time (1 woman), 11 international. Average age 29. 49 applicants, 41% accepted, 8 enrolled. In 2012, 5 master's, 4 doctorates awarded. Terminal master's awarded for partial completion of doctoral program. *Degree requirements:* For master's, comprehensive exam; for doctorate, comprehensive exam, thesis/dissertation. *Entrance requirements:* For master's and doctorate, GMAT or GRE, 3 semesters of calculus and linear algebra. Additional exam requirements/recommendations for international students: Required—TOEFL (minimum score 550 paper-based), IELTS (minimum score 6.5). *Application deadline:* For spring admission, 3/1 priority date for domestic students, 3/1 for international students. Applications are processed on a rolling basis. Application fee: $50 ($60 for international students). Electronic applications accepted. *Expenses:* Tuition, state resident: full-time $9200. Tuition, nonresident: full-time $22,950. *Financial support:* In 2012–13, 9 students received support, including 7 teaching assistantships with tuition reimbursements available (averaging $13,500 per year); scholarships/grants and health care benefits also available. Financial award application deadline: 3/1. *Faculty research:* Data mining, regression analysis, statistical quality control, nonparametric statistics, design of experiments. *Unit head:* Dr. Charles R. Sox, Professor and Department Head, 205-348-8992, E-mail: csox@cba.ua.edu. *Application contact:* Dana Merchant, Administrative Secretary, 205-348-8904, E-mail: dmerchan@cba.ua.edu. Website: http://www.cba.ua.edu/stats.

University of Arkansas at Little Rock, Graduate School, College of Science and Mathematics, Department of Mathematics and Statistics, Little Rock, AR 72204-1099. Offers applied statistics (Graduate Certificate); mathematical sciences (MS). Part-time and evening/weekend programs available. *Degree requirements:* For master's, comprehensive exam. *Entrance requirements:* For master's, GRE General Test, GRE Subject Test, minimum GPA of 2.7, previous course work in advanced mathematics.

University of California, Riverside, Graduate Division, Department of Statistics, Riverside, AB 92521-0219. Offers applied statistics (PhD); statistics (MS). *Faculty:* 45 full-time (28 women), 1 (woman) part-time/adjunct. *Students:* 45 full-time (28 women), 1 (woman) part-time; includes 37 minority (29 Asian, non-Hispanic/Latino; 2 Hispanic/Latino; 2 Native Hawaiian or other Pacific Islander, non-Hispanic/Latino; 4 Two or more races, non-Hispanic/Latino), 2 international. Average age 26. 206 applicants, 25% accepted, 16 enrolled. In 2012, 4 master's, 12 doctorates awarded. Terminal master's awarded for partial completion of doctoral program. *Degree requirements:* For master's, comprehensive exam; for doctorate, comprehensive exam, thesis/dissertation. *Entrance requirements:* For master's, GRE (minimum score 300), strong background in statistics and sufficient training in mathematics or upper-division statistical courses to meet deficiencies; minimum GPA of 3.0; for doctorate, GRE (minimum score 300), BS in statistics, computer science, mathematics, or other quantitatively-based discipline; minimum GPA of 3.25. Additional exam requirements/recommendations for international students: Required—TOEFL (minimum score 550 paper-based; 80 iBT). *Application deadline:* For fall admission, 12/1 priority date for domestic students, 12/1 for international students; for winter admission, 11/15 for domestic students, 7/1 for international students; for spring admission, 3/1 for domestic students, 10/1 for international students. Application fee: $80 ($100 for international students). Electronic applications accepted. *Expenses:* Tuition, state resident: full-time $14,646. Tuition, nonresident: full-time $29,748. *Financial support:* In 2012–13, 7 students received support, including 7 fellowships (averaging $20,951 per year), 7 teaching assistantships (averaging $17,309 per year); research assistantships and tuition waivers also available. Financial award application deadline: 12/1; financial award applicants required to submit FAFSA. *Faculty research:* Design and analysis of gene expression experiments using DNA microarrays, statistical design and analysis of experiments, linear models, probability models and statistical inference, SNP/SFP discovery using DNA microarray, genetic mapping. *Unit head:* Dr. Daniel Jeske, Chair, 951-827-3014, E-mail: daniel.jeske@ucr.edu. *Application contact:* Perla Fabelo, Graduate Student Affairs Assistant, 951-827-4716, Fax: 951-827-5517, E-mail: fabelo@ucr.edu. Website: http://www.statistics.ucr.edu/.

University of California, Santa Barbara, Graduate Division, College of Letters and Sciences, Division of Mathematics, Life, and Physical Sciences, Department of Statistics and Applied Probability, Santa Barbara, CA 93106-3110. Offers financial mathematics and statistics (PhD); quantitative methods in the social sciences (PhD); statistics (MA), including applied statistics, mathematical statistics; statistics and applied probability (PhD); MA/PhD. *Faculty:* 11 full-time (3 women). *Students:* 57 full-time (28 women); includes 47 minority (42 Asian, non-Hispanic/Latino; 3 Hispanic/Latino; 1 Native Hawaiian or other Pacific Islander, non-Hispanic/Latino; 1 Two or more races, non-Hispanic/Latino), 43 international. Average age 27. 298 applicants, 17% accepted, 16 enrolled. In 2012, 12 master's, 2 doctorates awarded. Terminal master's awarded for partial completion of doctoral program. *Degree requirements:* For master's, comprehensive exam, thesis optional; for doctorate, comprehensive exam, thesis/dissertation. *Entrance requirements:* For master's and doctorate, GRE General Test. Additional exam requirements/recommendations for international students: Required—TOEFL (minimum score 550 paper-based; 80 iBT), IELTS (minimum score 7). *Application deadline:* For fall admission, 1/1 priority date for domestic students, 1/1 for international students; for winter admission, 11/1 priority date for domestic students, 11/1 for international students; for spring admission, 2/1 priority date for domestic students, 2/1 for international students. Application fee: $80 ($100 for international students). Electronic applications accepted. *Financial support:* In 2012–13, 23 students received support, including 6 fellowships with full tuition reimbursements available (averaging $11,285 per year), 1 research assistantship with full and partial tuition reimbursement available (averaging $2,790 per year), 28 teaching assistantships with partial tuition reimbursements available (averaging $14,557 per year); Federal Work-Study, scholarships/grants, and health care benefits also available. Financial award application deadline: 1/1; financial award applicants required to submit FAFSA. *Faculty research:* Bayesian inference, financial mathematics, stochastic processes, environmental statistics, biostatistical modeling. *Total annual research expenditures:* $139,480. *Unit head:* Dr. John Hsu, Chair, 805-893-4055, E-mail: hsu@pstat.ucsb.edu. *Application contact:* Dolly J. Cook, Graduate Program Assistant, 805-893-2129, Fax: 805-893-2334, E-mail: gradinfo@pstat.ucsb.edu. Website: http://www.pstat.ucsb.edu/.

University of Chicago, Graham School of Continuing Liberal and Professional Studies, Program in Analytics, Chicago, IL 60637-1513. Offers M Sc. Part-time programs available. *Degree requirements:* For master's, capstone project. *Entrance requirements:* For master's, baccalaureate degree from accredited college or university, three letters of recommendation, official transcripts, resume or curriculum vitae, interview. Additional exam requirements/recommendations for international students: Required—TOEFL. Electronic applications accepted.

University of Colorado Denver, College of Liberal Arts and Sciences, Department of Mathematical and Statistical Sciences, Denver, CO 80217. Offers applied mathematics (MS, PhD), including applied mathematics, applied probability (MS), applied statistics (MS), computational biology, computational mathematics (PhD), discrete mathematics, finite geometry (PhD), mathematics education (PhD), mathematics of engineering and science (MS), numerical analysis, operations research (MS), optimization and operations research (PhD), probability (PhD), statistics (PhD). Part-time programs available. *Faculty:* 20 full-time (4 women), 3 part-time/adjunct (0 women). *Students:* 43 full-time (12 women), 13 part-time (2 women); includes 9 minority (1 Black or African American, non-Hispanic/Latino; 4 Asian, non-Hispanic/Latino; 4 Hispanic/Latino), 9 international. Average age 32. 63 applicants, 71% accepted, 14 enrolled. In 2012, 10 master's, 6 doctorates awarded. *Degree requirements:* For master's, comprehensive exam, thesis optional, 30 hours of course work with minimum GPA of 3.0; for doctorate, comprehensive exam, thesis/dissertation, 42 hours of course work with minimum GPA of 3.25. *Entrance requirements:* For master's, GRE General Test; GRE Subject Test in math (recommended), 30 hours of course work in mathematics (24 of which must be upper-division mathematics), bachelor's degree with minimum GPA of 3.0; for doctorate, GRE General Test; GRE Subject Test in math (recommended), 30 hours of course work in mathematics (24 of which must be upper-division mathematics), master's degree with minimum GPA of 3.25. Additional exam requirements/recommendations for international students: Required—TOEFL (minimum score 537 paper-based; 75 iBT); Recommended—IELTS (minimum score 6.5). *Application deadline:* For fall admission, 2/1 for domestic and international students; for spring admission, 10/1 for domestic and international students. Application fee: $50 ($75 for international students). Electronic applications accepted. *Expenses:* Tuition, state resident: full-time $7712; part-time $355 per credit hour. Tuition, nonresident: full-time $22,038; part-time $1087 per credit hour. *Required fees:* $1110; $1. Tuition and fees vary according to course load, campus/location and program. *Financial support:* In 2012–13, 33 students received support. Fellowships with partial tuition reimbursements available, research assistantships with full tuition reimbursements available, teaching assistantships with full tuition reimbursements available, Federal Work-Study, institutionally sponsored loans, scholarships/grants, traineeships, and unspecified assistantships available. Financial award application deadline: 4/1; financial award applicants required to submit FAFSA. *Faculty research:* Computational mathematics, computational biology, discrete mathematics and geometry, probability and statistics, optimization. *Unit head:* Dr. Stephen Billups, Graduate Program Director, 303-556-4814, E-mail: stephen.billups@ucdenver.edu. *Application contact:* Margie Bopp, Graduate Program Assistant, 303-556-2341, E-mail: margie.bopp@ucdenver.edu. Website: http://www.ucdenver.edu/academics/colleges/CLAS/Departments/math/Pages/MathStats.aspx.

University of Guelph, Graduate Studies, College of Physical and Engineering Science, Department of Mathematics and Statistics, Guelph, ON N1G 2W1, Canada. Offers applied mathematics (PhD); applied statistics (PhD); mathematics and statistics (M Sc). Part-time programs available. *Degree requirements:* For master's, thesis (for some programs); for doctorate, thesis/dissertation. *Entrance requirements:* For master's, minimum B- average during previous 2 years of course work; for doctorate, minimum B average. Additional exam requirements/recommendations for international students: Required—TOEFL (minimum score 550 paper-based; 89 iBT), IELTS (minimum score 6.5). *Faculty research:* Dynamical systems, mathematical biology, numerical analysis, linear and nonlinear models, reliability and bioassay.

University of Illinois at Urbana–Champaign, Graduate College, College of Liberal Arts and Sciences, Department of Statistics, Champaign, IL 61820. Offers analytics (MS); applied statistics (MS); statistics (MS, PhD). *Students:* 106 (47 women). Application fee: $75 ($90 for international students). *Unit head:* Douglas G. Simpson, Chair, 217-244-0885, Fax: 217-244-7190, E-mail: dgs@illinois.edu. *Application contact:* Liza Booker, Office Support Specialist, 217-333-2167, Fax: 217-244-7190, E-mail: booker1@illinois.edu. Website: http://www.stat.illinois.edu/.

University of Memphis, Graduate School, College of Arts and Sciences, Department of Mathematical Sciences, Memphis, TN 38152. Offers applied mathematics (MS); applied statistics (PhD); bioinformatics (MS); computer science (PhD); computer sciences (MS); mathematics (MS, PhD); statistics (MS, PhD). Part-time programs available. Terminal master's awarded for partial completion of doctoral program. *Degree requirements:* For master's, comprehensive exam; for doctorate, one foreign language, thesis/dissertation, oral exams. *Entrance requirements:* For master's and doctorate, GRE General Test, minimum GPA of 2.5. Additional exam requirements/recommendations for international students: Required—TOEFL (minimum score 550 paper-based).

Electronic applications accepted. *Faculty research:* Combinatorics, ergodic theory, graph theory, Ramsey theory, applied statistics.

University of Michigan, Horace H. Rackham School of Graduate Studies, College of Literature, Science, and the Arts, Department of Statistics, Ann Arbor, MI 48109. Offers applied statistics (AM); statistics (AM, PhD). *Faculty:* 19 full-time (4 women). *Students:* 136 full-time (55 women); includes 105 minority (1 Black or African American, non-Hispanic/Latino; 99 Asian, non-Hispanic/Latino; 4 Hispanic/Latino; 1 Two or more races, non-Hispanic/Latino). Average age 27. 633 applicants, 18% accepted, 54 enrolled. In 2012, 27 master's, 7 doctorates awarded. Terminal master's awarded for partial completion of doctoral program. *Degree requirements:* For master's, thesis; for doctorate, thesis/dissertation, oral defense of dissertation, preliminary exam. *Entrance requirements:* For master's and doctorate, GRE General Test. Additional exam requirements/recommendations for international students: Required—TOEFL (minimum score 560 paper-based; 84 iBT), IELTS (minimum score 6.5). *Application deadline:* For fall admission, 1/10 priority date for domestic students, 1/10 for international students. Applications are processed on a rolling basis. Application fee: $65 ($75 for international students). Electronic applications accepted. *Financial support:* In 2012–13, 68 students received support, including 7 fellowships with full and partial tuition reimbursements available (averaging $25,000 per year), 17 research assistantships with full and partial tuition reimbursements available (averaging $17,270 per year), 44 teaching assistantships with full and partial tuition reimbursements available (averaging $17,270 per year); career-related internships or fieldwork, Federal Work-Study, institutionally sponsored loans, scholarships/grants, health care benefits, and unspecified assistantships also available. Financial award application deadline: 1/10. *Faculty research:* Reliability and degradation modeling, biological and legal applications, bioinformatics, statistical computing, covariance estimation. *Unit head:* Prof. Tailen Hsing, Chair, 734-763-3519, Fax: 734-763-4676, E-mail: statchair@umich.edu. *Application contact:* Judy McDonald, Graduate Program Coordinator, 734-763-3520, Fax: 734-763-4676, E-mail: stat-grad-coordinator@umich.edu. Website: http://www.stat.lsa.umich.edu/.

The University of North Carolina at Charlotte, The Graduate School, College of Liberal Arts and Sciences, Department of Mathematics and Statistics, Charlotte, NC 28223-0001. Offers applied mathematics (MS, PhD); applied statistics (MS); general mathematics (MS); mathematics education (MA). Part-time and evening/weekend programs available. *Faculty:* 42 full-time (5 women). *Students:* 42 full-time (21 women), 32 part-time (16 women); includes 12 minority (6 Black or African American, non-Hispanic/Latino; 4 Asian, non-Hispanic/Latino; 2 Hispanic/Latino), 33 international. Average age 30. 43 applicants, 95% accepted, 23 enrolled. In 2012, 15 master's, 4 doctorates awarded. Terminal master's awarded for partial completion of doctoral program. *Degree requirements:* For master's, comprehensive exam, thesis or alternative; for doctorate, thesis/dissertation. *Entrance requirements:* For master's, GRE General Test, minimum GPA of 3.0 in undergraduate major, 2.75 overall; for doctorate, GRE General Test, minimum overall GPA of 3.0. Additional exam requirements/recommendations for international students: Required—TOEFL (minimum score 557 paper-based; 83 iBT), Michigan English Language Assessment Battery (minimum score 78) or IELTS (minimum score 6.5). *Application deadline:* For fall admission, 7/1 for domestic students, 5/1 for international students; for spring admission, 11/1 for domestic students, 10/1 for international students. Applications are processed on a rolling basis. Application fee: $65 ($75 for international students). Electronic applications accepted. *Expenses:* Tuition, state resident: full-time $3453. Tuition, nonresident: full-time $15,982. *Required fees:* $2420. Tuition and fees vary according to course load and program. *Financial support:* In 2012–13, 44 students received support, including 3 fellowships (averaging $21,035 per year), 4 research assistantships (averaging $8,583 per year), 37 teaching assistantships (averaging $12,104 per year); career-related internships or fieldwork, Federal Work-Study, institutionally sponsored loans, scholarships/grants, and unspecified assistantships also available. Support available to part-time students. Financial award application deadline: 4/1; financial award applicants required to submit FAFSA. *Faculty research:* Numerical analysis and scientific computation, probability and stochastic processes, partial differential equations and mathematical physics, algebra and combinatorics, analysis, biostatistics, topology. *Total annual research expenditures:* $1.2 million. *Unit head:* Dr. Yuanan Diao, Chair, 704-687-4560, Fax: 704-687-6415, E-mail: ydiao@uncc.edu. *Application contact:* Kathy B. Giddings, Director of Graduate Admissions, 704-687-5503, Fax: 704-687-1668, E-mail: gradadm@uncc.edu. Website: http://www.math.uncc.edu/.

University of Northern Colorado, Graduate School, College of Education and Behavioral Sciences, Department of Applied Statistics and Research Methods, Greeley, CO 80639. Offers MS, PhD. Part-time programs available. *Degree requirements:* For master's, comprehensive exam; for doctorate, comprehensive exam, thesis/dissertation. *Entrance requirements:* For master's, 3 letters of reference; for doctorate, GRE General Test, 3 letters of reference. Electronic applications accepted.

University of Notre Dame, Graduate School, College of Science, Department of Applied and Computational Mathematics and Statistics, Notre Dame, IN 46556. Offers applied and computational mathematics and statistics (PhD); applied statistics (MS); computational finance (MS).

University of Pittsburgh, Dietrich School of Arts and Sciences, Department of Statistics, Pittsburgh, PA 15260. Offers applied statistics (MA, MS); statistics (MA, MS, PhD). Part-time programs available. *Faculty:* 9 full-time (2 women). *Students:* 44 full-time (21 women), 5 part-time (0 women); includes 2 minority (both Black or African American, non-Hispanic/Latino), 27 international. Average age 26. 428 applicants, 15% accepted, 20 enrolled. In 2012, 18 master's, 8 doctorates awarded. Terminal master's awarded for partial completion of doctoral program. *Degree requirements:* For master's, comprehensive exam, thesis (for some programs); for doctorate, comprehensive exam, thesis/dissertation. *Entrance requirements:* For master's and doctorate, 3 semesters of calculus, 1 semester of linear algebra, 1 year of mathematical statistics. Additional exam requirements/recommendations for international students: Required—TOEFL (minimum score 90 iBT). *Application deadline:* For fall admission, 1/15 priority date for domestic students, 1/15 for international students; for spring admission, 10/1 priority date for domestic students, 10/1 for international students. Application fee: $50. Electronic applications accepted. *Expenses:* Tuition, state resident: full-time $19,336; part-time $782 per credit. Tuition, nonresident: full-time $31,658; part-time $1295 per credit. *Required fees:* $740; $200 per term. Tuition and fees vary according to program. *Financial support:* In 2012–13, 24 students received support, including 1 fellowship with full tuition reimbursement available (averaging $16,950 per year), 9 research assistantships with full tuition reimbursements available (averaging $16,950 per year), 16 teaching assistantships with full tuition reimbursements available (averaging $16,300 per year); career-related internships or fieldwork, Federal Work-Study, institutionally sponsored loans, scholarships/grants, health care benefits, and unspecified assistantships also available. Financial award application deadline: 1/15. *Faculty research:* Multivariate statistics, time series, reliability, meta-analysis, linear and nonlinear regression modeling. *Unit head:* Dr. Satish Iyengar, Chair, 412-624-8341, Fax: 412-648-8814, E-mail: ssi@pitt.edu. *Application contact:* Dr. Leon J. Gleser, Director of Graduate Studies, 412-624-3925, Fax: 412-648-8814, E-mail: gleser@pitt.edu. Website: http://www.stat.pitt.edu/.

University of South Carolina, The Graduate School, College of Arts and Sciences, Department of Statistics, Columbia, SC 29208. Offers applied statistics (CAS); industrial statistics (MIS); statistics (MS, PhD). Part-time and evening/weekend programs available. Postbaccalaureate distance learning degree programs offered (minimal on-campus study). Terminal master's awarded for partial completion of doctoral program. *Degree requirements:* For master's, thesis; for doctorate, comprehensive exam, thesis/dissertation. *Entrance requirements:* For master's, GRE General Test or GMAT, 2 years of work experience (MIS); for doctorate, GRE General Test; for CAS, GRE General Test or GMAT. Additional exam requirements/recommendations for international students: Required—TOEFL (minimum score 600 paper-based; 100 iBT). Electronic applications accepted. *Expenses:* Contact institution. *Faculty research:* Reliability, environmentrics, statistics computing, psychometrics, bioinformatics.

The University of Tennessee at Chattanooga, Graduate School, College of Arts and Sciences, Program in Mathematics, Chattanooga, TN 37403-2598. Offers applied mathematics (MS); applied statistics (MS); mathematics (MS); mathematics education (MS). Part-time and evening/weekend programs available. Postbaccalaureate distance learning degree programs offered (no on-campus study). *Faculty:* 6 full-time (0 women). *Students:* 10 full-time (2 women), 7 part-time (1 woman); includes 2 minority (1 Black or African American, non-Hispanic/Latino; 1 Asian, non-Hispanic/Latino). Average age 29. 10 applicants, 100% accepted, 7 enrolled. In 2012, 4 master's awarded. *Entrance requirements:* For master's, two letters of recommendation. *Application deadline:* For fall admission, 6/14 for domestic students, 6/1 for international students; for spring admission, 10/25 for domestic students, 10/1 for international students. Applications are processed on a rolling basis. Application fee: $30 ($35 for international students). Electronic applications accepted. *Expenses:* Tuition, state resident: full-time $6860; part-time $381 per credit hour. Tuition, nonresident: full-time $21,206; part-time $1178 per credit hour. *Required fees:* $1490; $180 per credit hour. *Financial support:* In 2012–13, 16 research assistantships with tuition reimbursements (averaging $4,592 per year) were awarded. Financial award applicants required to submit FAFSA. *Total annual research expenditures:* $71,555. *Unit head:* John Graef, Head, 423-425-4545, E-mail: john-graef@utc.edu. *Application contact:* Dr. Jerald Ainsworth, Dean of Graduate Studies, 423-425-4478, Fax: 423-425-5223, E-mail: jerald-ainsworth@utc.edu. Website: http://www.utc.edu/Academic/Mathematics/.

The University of Texas at San Antonio, College of Business, Department of Management Science and Statistics, San Antonio, TX 78249-0617. Offers applied statistics (MS, PhD); management science (MBA). *Accreditation:* AACSB. Part-time and evening/weekend programs available. *Faculty:* 13 full-time (3 women), 3 part-time/adjunct (1 woman). *Students:* 34 full-time (11 women), 27 part-time (8 women); includes 22 minority (1 Black or African American, non-Hispanic/Latino; 7 Asian, non-Hispanic/Latino; 14 Hispanic/Latino), 18 international. Average age 30. 54 applicants, 61% accepted, 22 enrolled. In 2012, 10 master's, 3 doctorates awarded. *Degree requirements:* For master's, comprehensive exam (for some programs), thesis or alternative; for doctorate, comprehensive exam, thesis/dissertation. *Entrance requirements:* For master's, GMAT, minimum of 36 semester credit hours of coursework beyond any hours acquired in the MBA-leveling courses; statement of purpose; for doctorate, GRE, minimum cumulative GPA of 3.3 in the last 60 hours of coursework; transcripts from all colleges and universities attended; curriculum vitae; statement of academic work experiences, interests, and goals; three letters of recommendation; BA, BS, or MS in mathematics, statistics, or closely-related field. Additional exam requirements/recommendations for international students: Required—TOEFL (minimum score 500 paper-based; 61 iBT), IELTS (minimum score 5). *Application deadline:* For fall admission, 7/1 for domestic students, 4/1 for international students; for spring

Applied Statistics

admission, 11/1 for domestic students, 9/1 for international students. Applications are processed on a rolling basis. Application fee: $45 ($85 for international students). Electronic applications accepted. *Financial support:* In 2012–13, fellowships (averaging $22,000 per year), research assistantships (averaging $10,000 per year), teaching assistantships (averaging $10,000 per year) were awarded; scholarships/grants, health care benefits, and unspecified assistantships also available. *Faculty research:* Statistical signal processing, reliability and life-testing experiments, modeling decompression sickness using survival analysis. *Unit head:* Dr. Raydel Tullous, Chair, 210-458-6345, Fax: 210-458-6350, E-mail: raydel.tullous@utsa.edu. *Application contact:* Katherine Pope, Graduate Assistant of Record, 210-458-7316, Fax: 210-458-4398, E-mail: katherine.pope@utsa.edu.

University of the District of Columbia, College of Arts and Sciences, Department of Mathematics, Program in Applied Statistics, Washington, DC 20008-1175. Offers MS. *Degree requirements:* For master's, internship or thesis.

University of West Florida, College of Arts and Sciences: Sciences, Department of Mathematics and Statistics, Pensacola, FL 32514-5750. Offers applied statistics (MS); mathematical sciences (MS). Part-time and evening/weekend programs available. *Degree requirements:* For master's, thesis optional. *Entrance requirements:* For master's, GRE (minimum score: verbal 420; quantitative 580), minimum GPA of 3.0; official transcripts. Additional exam requirements/recommendations for international students: Required—TOEFL (minimum score 550 paper-based).

Villanova University, Graduate School of Liberal Arts and Sciences, Department of Mathematical Sciences, Program in Applied Statistics, Villanova, PA 19085-1699. Offers MS. Part-time and evening/weekend programs available. *Students:* 31 full-time (15 women), 11 part-time (3 women); includes 4 minority (2 Black or African American, non-Hispanic/Latino; 1 Asian, non-Hispanic/Latino; 1 Hispanic/Latino), 4 international. Average age 28. 24 applicants, 100% accepted, 17 enrolled. In 2012, 9 master's awarded. *Degree requirements:* For master's, comprehensive exam. *Entrance requirements:* For master's, GRE, minimum GPA of 3.0. Additional exam requirements/recommendations for international students: Required—TOEFL. *Application deadline:* For fall admission, 5/1 for international students; for spring admission, 10/15 for international students. Applications are processed on a rolling basis. Application fee: $50. Electronic applications accepted. *Financial support:* Research assistantships, teaching assistantships, scholarships/grants, and unspecified assistantships available. Financial award applicants required to submit FAFSA. *Unit head:* Dr. Michael Levitan, Director, 610-519-4818. Website: http://www.villanova.edu/artsci/mathematics/graduate/msapplied/.

West Chester University of Pennsylvania, College of Arts and Sciences, Department of Mathematics, West Chester, PA 19383. Offers applied statistics (MS, Certificate); mathematics (MS, Teaching Certificate). Part-time and evening/weekend programs available. *Faculty:* 10 full-time (1 woman). *Students:* 4 full-time (3 women), 83 part-time (34 women); includes 18 minority (7 Black or African American, non-Hispanic/Latino; 9 Asian, non-Hispanic/Latino; 2 Hispanic/Latino), 4 international. Average age 31. 49 applicants, 98% accepted, 31 enrolled. In 2012, 1 master's, 25 other advanced degrees awarded. *Degree requirements:* For master's, thesis optional. *Entrance requirements:* For master's, GMAT, GRE General Test, or MAT (for MA), interview (for mathematics MS); for other advanced degree, GMAT, GRE General Test, or MAT (for Teaching Certificate). Additional exam requirements/recommendations for international students: Required—TOEFL (minimum score 550 paper-based; 80 iBT). *Application deadline:* For fall admission, 4/15 priority date for domestic students, 3/15 for international students; for spring admission, 10/15 priority date for domestic students, 9/1 for international students. Applications are processed on a rolling basis. Application fee: $45. Electronic applications accepted. *Expenses:* Tuition, state resident: full-time $7722; part-time $429 per credit. Tuition, nonresident: full-time $11,592; part-time $644 per credit. *Required fees:* $2108; $105.05 per credit. Tuition and fees vary according to campus/location and program. *Financial support:* Unspecified assistantships available. Support available to part-time students. Financial award application deadline: 2/15; financial award applicants required to submit FAFSA. *Faculty research:* Teachers teaching with technology in service training program, biostatistics, hierarchical linear models, clustered binary outcome date. *Unit head:* Dr. Kathleen Jackson, Chair, 610-436-2537, Fax: 610-738-0578, E-mail: kjackson@wcupa.edu. *Application contact:* Dr. Gail Gallitano, Graduate Coordinator, 610-436-2452, Fax: 610-738-0578, E-mail: ggallitano@wcupa.edu. Website: http://www.wcupa.edu/_academics/sch_cas.mat/.

Worcester Polytechnic Institute, Graduate Studies and Research, Department of Mathematical Sciences, Worcester, MA 01609-2280. Offers applied mathematics (MS); applied statistics (MS); financial mathematics (MS); industrial mathematics (MS); mathematical sciences (PhD, Graduate Certificate); mathematics (MME); mathematics for educators (MS). Part-time and evening/weekend programs available. *Faculty:* 19 full-time (3 women), 7 part-time/adjunct (2 women). *Students:* 93 full-time (45 women), 19 part-time (15 women); includes 5 minority (2 Black or African American, non-Hispanic/Latino; 2 Hispanic/Latino; 1 Two or more races, non-Hispanic/Latino), 71 international. 398 applicants, 53% accepted, 54 enrolled. In 2012, 25 master's, 1 doctorate awarded. *Degree requirements:* For master's, thesis (for some programs); for doctorate, comprehensive exam, thesis/dissertation. *Entrance requirements:* For master's and doctorate, GRE General Test, GRE Subject Test in math (recommended), 3 letters of recommendation. Additional exam requirements/recommendations for international students: Required—TOEFL (minimum score 563 paper-based; 84 iBT), IELTS (minimum score 7). *Application deadline:* For fall admission, 1/1 priority date for domestic students, 1/1 for international students; for spring admission, 10/1 priority date for domestic students, 10/1 for international students. Applications are processed on a rolling basis. Application fee: $70. Electronic applications accepted. *Financial support:* Research assistantships, teaching assistantships, career-related internships or fieldwork, institutionally sponsored loans, scholarships/grants, and unspecified assistantships available. Financial award application deadline: 1/1; financial award applicants required to submit FAFSA. *Faculty research:* Applied analysis and differential equations, computational mathematics, discrete mathematics, applied and computational statistics, industrial and financial mathematics, mathematical biology. *Unit head:* Dr. Bogdan Vernescu, Head, 508-831-5241, Fax: 508-831-5824, E-mail: vernescu@wpi.edu. *Application contact:* Dr. Joseph Fehribach, Graduate Coordinator, 508-831-5241, Fax: 508-831-5824, E-mail: bach@wpi.edu. Website: http://www.wpi.edu/Academics/Depts/Math/.

Wright State University, School of Graduate Studies, College of Science and Mathematics, Department of Mathematics and Statistics, Program in Applied Statistics, Dayton, OH 45435. Offers MS. *Degree requirements:* For master's, comprehensive exam. *Entrance requirements:* For master's, 1 year of course work in calculus and matrix algebra, previous course work in computer programming and statistics. Additional exam requirements/recommendations for international students: Required—TOEFL. *Faculty research:* Reliability theory, stochastic process, nonparametric statistics, design of experiments, multivariate statistics.

Biomathematics

North Carolina State University, Graduate School, College of Physical and Mathematical Sciences, Program in Biomathematics, Raleigh, NC 27695. Offers M Biomath, MS, PhD. Part-time programs available. Terminal master's awarded for partial completion of doctoral program. *Degree requirements:* For master's, thesis (for some programs); for doctorate, thesis/dissertation. *Entrance requirements:* For master's and doctorate, GRE General Test. Additional exam requirements/recommendations for international students: Required—TOEFL. Electronic applications accepted. *Faculty research:* Theory and methods of biological modeling, theoretical biology (genetics, ecology, neurobiology), applied biology (wildlife).

University of California, Los Angeles, David Geffen School of Medicine and Graduate Division, Graduate Programs in Medicine, Department of Biomathematics, Program in Biomathematics, Los Angeles, CA 90095. Offers MS, PhD. *Faculty:* 5 full-time (0 women), 1 part-time/adjunct (0 women). *Students:* 11 full-time (2 women); includes 6 minority (4 Asian, non-Hispanic/Latino; 2 Hispanic/Latino), 2 international. Average age 27. 29 applicants, 31% accepted, 3 enrolled. In 2012, 1 master's, 1 doctorate awarded. *Degree requirements:* For master's, comprehensive exam, thesis; for doctorate, thesis/dissertation, written and oral qualifying exams; 2 quarters of teaching experience. *Entrance requirements:* For master's and doctorate, GRE General and Subject Tests, bachelor's degree; minimum undergraduate GPA of 3.0 (or its equivalent if letter grade system not used). Additional exam requirements/recommendations for international students: Required—TOEFL. *Application deadline:* For fall admission, 1/15 for domestic and international students. Application fee: $80 ($100 for international students). Electronic applications accepted. *Expenses:* Tuition, nonresident: full-time $15,102. *Required fees:* $14,809.19. Full-time tuition and fees vary according to program. *Financial support:* In 2012–13, 10 students received support, including 10 fellowships with full and partial tuition reimbursements available, 3 research assistantships with full and partial tuition reimbursements available; teaching assistantships with full and partial tuition reimbursements available, Federal Work-Study, scholarships/grants, health care benefits, tuition waivers (full and partial), and unspecified assistantships also available. Financial award application deadline: 3/2; financial award applicants required to submit FAFSA. *Unit head:* Dr. Elliot Landaw, Chair, 310-825-6743, E-mail: elandaw@biomath.ucla.edu. *Application contact:* Student Affairs Officer, 310-825-5554, Fax: 310-825-8685, E-mail: gradprog@biomath.ucla.edu. Website: http://www.biomath.ucla.edu.

The University of Texas Health Science Center at Houston, Graduate School of Biomedical Sciences, Program in Biomathematics and Biostatistics, Houston, TX 77225-0036. Offers MS, PhD, MD/PhD. Terminal master's awarded for partial

292 www.petersonsbooks.com

Peterson's Graduate Programs in the Physical Sciences, Mathematics, Agricultural Sciences, the Environment & Natural Resources 2014

completion of doctoral program. *Degree requirements:* For master's, thesis; for doctorate, thesis/dissertation. *Entrance requirements:* For master's and doctorate, GRE General Test. Additional exam requirements/recommendations for international students: Required—TOEFL. Electronic applications accepted. *Faculty research:* Biostatistics, biomarkers, epidemiology, bioinformatics, computational biology.

Biometry

Cornell University, Graduate School, Graduate Fields of Agriculture and Life Sciences, Field of Biometry, Ithaca, NY 14853-0001. Offers MS, PhD. *Faculty:* 10 full-time (0 women). *Students:* 1 full-time (0 women). 10 applicants. Terminal master's awarded for partial completion of doctoral program. *Degree requirements:* For master's, thesis; for doctorate, comprehensive exam, thesis/dissertation. *Entrance requirements:* For master's and doctorate, GRE General Test, 2 letters of recommendation. Additional exam requirements/recommendations for international students: Required—TOEFL (minimum score 550 paper-based; 77 iBT). *Application deadline:* For fall admission, 1/15 for domestic students. Application fee: $95. Electronic applications accepted. *Financial support:* Fellowships with full tuition reimbursements, research assistantships with full tuition reimbursements, teaching assistantships with full tuition reimbursements, institutionally sponsored loans, scholarships/grants, health care benefits, tuition waivers (full and partial), and unspecified assistantships available. Financial award applicants required to submit FAFSA. *Faculty research:* Environmental, agricultural, and biological statistics; biomathematics; modern nonparametric statistics; statistical genetics; computational statistics. *Unit head:* Director of Graduate Studies, 607-255-8066. *Application contact:* Graduate Field Assistant, 607-255-8066, E-mail: bscb@cornell.edu. Website: http://www.gradschool.cornell.edu/fields.php?id-44&a-2.

Cornell University, Graduate School, Graduate Fields of Engineering, Field of Statistics, Ithaca, NY 14853-0001. Offers applied statistics (MPS); biometry (MS, PhD); decision theory (MS, PhD); economic and social statistics (MS, PhD); engineering statistics (MS, PhD); experimental design (MS, PhD); mathematical statistics (MS, PhD); probability (MS, PhD); sampling (MS, PhD); statistical computing (MS, PhD); stochastic processes (MS, PhD). *Faculty:* 29 full-time (3 women). *Students:* 70 full-time (35 women); includes 7 minority (5 Asian, non-Hispanic/Latino; 1 Hispanic/Latino; 1 Two or more races, non-Hispanic/Latino), 48 international. Average age 25. 681 applicants, 22% accepted, 50 enrolled. In 2012, 51 master's, 5 doctorates awarded. Terminal master's awarded for partial completion of doctoral program. *Degree requirements:* For master's, project (MPS), thesis (MS); for doctorate, one foreign language, thesis/dissertation. *Entrance requirements:* For master's, GRE General Test (for MS), 2 letters of recommendation (MS, MPS); for doctorate, GRE General Test, 2 letters of recommendation. Additional exam requirements/recommendations for international students: Required—TOEFL (minimum score 550 paper-based; 77 iBT). *Application deadline:* For fall admission, 1/15 for domestic students. Applications are processed on a rolling basis. Application fee: $95. Electronic applications accepted. *Financial support:* In 2012–13, 23 students received support, including 2 fellowships with full tuition reimbursements available, 5 research assistantships with full tuition reimbursements available, 16 teaching assistantships with full tuition reimbursements available; institutionally sponsored loans, scholarships/grants, tuition waivers (full and partial), and unspecified assistantships also available. Financial award applicants required to submit FAFSA. *Faculty research:* Bayesian analysis, survival analysis, nonparametric statistics, stochastic processes, mathematical statistics. *Unit head:* Director of Graduate Studies, 607-255-8066. *Application contact:* Graduate Field Assistant, 607-255-8066, E-mail: csc@cornell.edu. Website: http://www.gradschool.cornell.edu/fields.php?id-94&a-2.

San Diego State University, Graduate and Research Affairs, College of Health and Human Services, Program in Biostatistics and Biometry, San Diego, CA 92182. Offers biometry (MPH). Electronic applications accepted.

University of Wisconsin–Madison, Graduate School, College of Letters and Science, Department of Statistics, Biometry Program, Madison, WI 53706-1380. Offers MS. *Expenses:* Tuition, state resident: full-time $10,728; part-time $743 per credit. Tuition, nonresident: full-time $24,054; part-time $1575 per credit. *Required fees:* $1111; $72 per credit.

Biostatistics

American University of Beirut, Graduate Programs, Faculty of Health Sciences, Beirut, Lebanon. Offers environmental sciences (MS), including environmental health; epidemiology (MS); epidemiology and biostatistics (MPH); health management and policy (MPH); health promotion and community health (MPH); population health (MS). Part-time programs available. *Faculty:* 31 full-time (22 women), 5 part-time/adjunct (3 women). *Students:* 48 full-time (44 women), 87 part-time (69 women). Average age 27. 166 applicants, 58% accepted, 42 enrolled. In 2012, 70 master's awarded. *Degree requirements:* For master's, one foreign language, comprehensive exam, thesis (for some programs). *Entrance requirements:* For master's, 2 letters of recommendation, personal statement, transcripts. Additional exam requirements/recommendations for international students: Required—TOEFL (minimum score 600 paper-based; 97 iBT), IELTS (minimum score 7). *Application deadline:* For fall admission, 2/7 priority date for domestic students, 2/7 for international students; for spring admission, 11/1 for domestic and international students. Application fee: $50. Electronic applications accepted. *Expenses:* Tuition: Full-time $13,896; part-time $772 per credit. *Financial support:* In 2012–13, 52 students received support. Scholarships/grants, health care benefits, and unspecified assistantships available. Financial award application deadline: 2/7. *Faculty research:* Tobacco control; health of the elderly; youth health; mental health; women's health; reproductive and sexual health, including HIV/AIDS; water quality; health systems; quality in health care delivery; health human resources; health policy; occupational and environmental health; social inequality; social determinants of health; non-communicable diseases. *Total annual research expenditures:* $1.1 million. *Unit head:* Iman Adel Nuwayhid, Dean, 961-1340119, Fax: 961-1744470, E-mail: nuwayhid@aub.edu.lb. *Application contact:* Mitra Tauk, Administrative Coordinator, 961-1-350000 Ext. 4687, Fax: 961-1744470, E-mail: mt12@aub.edu.lb.

Boston University, Graduate School of Arts and Sciences, Intercollegiate Program in Biostatistics, Boston, MA 02215. Offers MA, PhD. *Students:* 56 full-time (31 women), 33 part-time (24 women); includes 15 minority (14 Asian, non-Hispanic/Latino; 1 Two or more races, non-Hispanic/Latino), 24 international. Average age 29. 194 applicants, 25% accepted, 12 enrolled. In 2012, 19 master's, 8 doctorates awarded. Terminal master's awarded for partial completion of doctoral program. *Degree requirements:* For master's, one foreign language, comprehensive exam; for doctorate, one foreign language, comprehensive exam, thesis/dissertation. *Entrance requirements:* For master's and doctorate, GRE General Test, 3 letters of recommendation. Additional exam requirements/recommendations for international students: Required—TOEFL (minimum score 550 paper-based; 84 iBT). *Application deadline:* For fall admission, 12/15 for domestic and international students. Application fee: $80. Electronic applications accepted. *Expenses:* Tuition: Full-time $42,400; part-time $1325 per credit. *Required fees:* $40 per semester. *Financial support:* In 2012–13, 35 students received support, including 28 research assistantships with full tuition reimbursements available (averaging $19,800 per year); fellowships, teaching assistantships, traineeships, and health care benefits also available. Support available to part-time students. Financial award application deadline: 12/15. *Unit head:* Lisa Sullivan, Chairman, 617-638-5047, Fax: 617-638-4458, E-mail: lsull@bu.edu. *Application contact:* Amanda Velez, Curriculum Coordinator, 617-638-5207, Fax: 617-638-6484, E-mail: aavelez@bu.edu. Website: http://sph.bu.edu/Biostatistics/department-of-biostatistics/menu-id-617603.html.

Boston University, School of Public Health, Biostatistics Department, Boston, MA 02215. Offers MA, MPH, PhD. Part-time and evening/weekend programs available. *Faculty:* 26 full-time, 18 part-time/adjunct. *Students:* 56 full-time (31 women), 33 part-time (24 women); includes 18 minority (2 Black or African American, non-Hispanic/Latino; 14 Asian, non-Hispanic/Latino; 1 Hispanic/Latino; 1 Two or more races, non-Hispanic/Latino), 24 international. Average age 29. 79 applicants, 46% accepted, 14 enrolled. In 2012, 19 master's, 8 doctorates awarded. *Entrance requirements:* For master's, GRE, GMAT, LSAT, DAT, or MCAT; for doctorate, GRE. Additional exam requirements/recommendations for international students: Required—TOEFL (minimum score 600 paper-based; 100 iBT), IELTS (minimum score 6). *Application deadline:* For fall admission, 2/1 priority date for domestic students, 2/1 for international students; for spring admission, 10/15 priority date for domestic students, 10/15 for international students. Applications are processed on a rolling basis. Application fee: $115. Electronic applications accepted. *Expenses:* Tuition: Full-time $42,400; part-time $1325 per credit. *Required fees:* $40 per semester. *Financial support:* Career-related internships or fieldwork, Federal Work-Study, institutionally sponsored loans, scholarships/grants, traineeships, health care benefits, and unspecified assistantships available. Support available to part-time students. Financial award application deadline: 3/1; financial award applicants required to submit FAFSA.

Peterson's Graduate Programs in the Physical Sciences, Mathematics, Agricultural Sciences, the Environment & Natural Resources 2014

www.petersonsbooks.com **293**

Biostatistics

Unit head: Dr. Lisa Sullivan, Chair, 617-638-5176, Fax: 617-638-4458, E-mail: biostat@bu.edu. *Application contact:* LePhan Quan, Associate Director of Admissions, 617-638-4640, Fax: 617-638-5299, E-mail: asksph@bu.edu. Website: http://sph.bu.edu/bio.

Brown University, Graduate School, Division of Biology and Medicine, Department of Community Health, Providence, RI 02912. Offers health services research (MS, PhD); public health (MPH); statistical science (MS, PhD), including biostatistics, epidemiology; MD/PhD. *Accreditation:* CEPH. *Degree requirements:* For doctorate, thesis/dissertation, preliminary exam. *Entrance requirements:* For master's and doctorate, GRE General Test. Additional exam requirements/recommendations for international students: Required—TOEFL.

Brown University, Graduate School, Division of Biology and Medicine, Department of Community Health, Center for Statistical Sciences, Program in Biostatistics, Providence, RI 02912. Offers MS, PhD, MD/PhD. *Degree requirements:* For doctorate, thesis/dissertation, preliminary exam. *Entrance requirements:* For master's and doctorate, GRE General Test.

California State University, East Bay, Office of Academic Programs and Graduate Studies, College of Science, Department of Statistics and Biostatistics, Biostatistics Program, Hayward, CA 94542-3000. Offers MS. Part-time and evening/weekend programs available. *Degree requirements:* For master's, comprehensive exam. *Entrance requirements:* For master's, minimum GPA of 3.0; math through lower-division calculus; statement of purpose; 2-3 letters of recommendation or GRE. Additional exam requirements/recommendations for international students: Required—TOEFL (minimum score 550 paper-based). Electronic applications accepted.

Case Western Reserve University, School of Medicine and School of Graduate Studies, Graduate Programs in Medicine, Department of Epidemiology and Biostatistics, Program in Biostatistics, Cleveland, OH 44106. Offers MS, PhD. Part-time programs available. Terminal master's awarded for partial completion of doctoral program. *Degree requirements:* For master's, comprehensive exam, thesis, exam/practicum; for doctorate, comprehensive exam, thesis/dissertation. *Entrance requirements:* For master's, GRE General Test or MCAT, 3 recommendations; for doctorate, GRE General Test, 3 recommendations. Additional exam requirements/recommendations for international students: Required—TOEFL (minimum score 550 paper-based). Electronic applications accepted. *Faculty research:* Survey sampling and statistical computing, generalized linear models, statistical modeling, models in breast cancer survival.

Columbia University, Columbia University Mailman School of Public Health, Department of Biostatistics, New York, NY 10032. Offers MPH, MS, Dr PH, PhD. PhD offered in cooperation with the Graduate School of Arts and Sciences. Part-time programs available. *Students:* 28 full-time (20 women), 80 part-time (44 women); includes 27 minority (7 Black or African American, non-Hispanic/Latino; 15 Asian, non-Hispanic/Latino; 3 Hispanic/Latino; 2 Two or more races, non-Hispanic/Latino), 40 international. Average age 29. 166 applicants, 60% accepted, 38 enrolled. In 2012, 32 master's, 8 doctorates awarded. *Degree requirements:* For doctorate, thesis/dissertation. *Entrance requirements:* For master's, GRE General Test; for doctorate, GRE General Test, MPH or equivalent (Dr PH). Additional exam requirements/recommendations for international students: Required—TOEFL (minimum score 600 paper-based; 100 iBT). *Application deadline:* For fall admission, 12/1 priority date for domestic students, 12/1 for international students. Applications are processed on a rolling basis. Application fee: $120. Electronic applications accepted. *Financial support:* Research assistantships, teaching assistantships, career-related internships or fieldwork, and Federal Work-Study available. Financial award application deadline: 2/1; financial award applicants required to submit FAFSA. *Faculty research:* Statistical methods and public health implications of biomedical experiments, clinical trials, functional data analysis, statistical genetics, and observational studies. *Unit head:* Dr. Roger Vaughan, Chairperson, 212-342-2271, Fax: 212-305-9408. *Application contact:* Dr. Joseph Korevec, Director of Admissions and Financial Aid, 212-305-8698, Fax: 212-342-1861, E-mail: ph-admit@columbia.edu. Website: http://mailman.columbia.edu/biostat/index.html.

Drexel University, School of Biomedical Engineering, Science and Health Systems, Philadelphia, PA 19104-2875. Offers biomedical engineering (MS, PhD); biomedical science (MS, PhD); biostatistics (MS); clinical/rehabilitation engineering (MS); MD/PhD. *Degree requirements:* For doctorate, thesis/dissertation, 1 year of residency, qualifying exam. *Entrance requirements:* For master's, minimum GPA of 3.0; for doctorate, minimum GPA of 3.0, MS. Additional exam requirements/recommendations for international students: Required—TOEFL. Electronic applications accepted. *Faculty research:* Cardiovascular dynamics, diagnostic and therapeutic ultrasound.

Drexel University, School of Public Health, Department of Epidemiology and Biostatistics, Philadelphia, PA 19104-2875. Offers biostatistics (MS); epidemiology (PhD); epidemiology and biostatistics (Certificate).

Duke University, School of Medicine, Program in Biostatistics, Durham, NC 27710. Offers MS. Part-time programs available. *Faculty:* 15 full-time (5 women). *Students:* 36 full-time (23 women), 3 part-time (1 woman); includes 4 minority (1 Black or African American, non-Hispanic/Latino; 3 Asian, non-Hispanic/Latino), 24 international. 59 applicants, 76% accepted, 24 enrolled. *Degree requirements:* For master's, project. *Entrance requirements:* For master's, GRE. Additional exam requirements/recommendations for international students: Required—TOEFL. *Application deadline:* For fall admission, 1/31 priority date for domestic students. Application fee: $75. *Financial support:* Scholarships/grants available. Financial award application deadline: 5/1; financial award applicants required to submit FAFSA. *Unit head:* Dr. Gregory P. Samsa, Associate Professor, 919-613-5212, Fax: 919-660-7040, E-mail: samsa001@mc.duke.edu. *Application contact:* Jonathan Hecht, Program Coordinator, 919-668-5876, E-mail: jonathan.hecht@duke.edu. Website: http://biostat.duke.edu/master-biostatistics-program/program-overview.

East Tennessee State University, School of Graduate Studies, College of Public Health, Master of Public Health Programs, Johnson City, TN 37614. Offers biostatistics (MPH); community health (MPH); environmental health (MPH); epidemiology (MPH). Part-time programs available. Postbaccalaureate distance learning degree programs offered (no on-campus study). *Faculty:* 9 full-time (2 women), 1 part-time/adjunct (0 women). *Students:* 75 full-time (47 women), 41 part-time (28 women); includes 17 minority (13 Black or African American, non-Hispanic/Latino; 2 Asian, non-Hispanic/Latino; 2 Two or more races, non-Hispanic/Latino), 15 international. 82 applicants, 67% accepted, 45 enrolled. In 2012, 32 master's awarded. *Degree requirements:* For master's, comprehensive exam, field experience. *Entrance requirements:* For master's, GRE General Test, SOPHAS application, minimum GPA of 2.75, letters of recommendation. Additional exam requirements/recommendations for international students: Required—TOEFL (minimum score 550 paper-based; 79 iBT). *Application deadline:* For fall admission, 3/1 for domestic and international students. Application fee: $35 ($45 for international students). Electronic applications accepted. *Financial support:* In 2012–13, 31 students received support, including 14 research assistantships with full tuition reimbursements available (averaging $6,000 per year), 2 teaching assistantships with full tuition reimbursements available (averaging $6,000 per year); career-related internships or fieldwork, institutionally sponsored loans, scholarships/grants, and unspecified assistantships also available. Financial award application deadline: 7/1; financial award applicants required to submit FAFSA. *Faculty research:* Skin cancer prevention, chronic disease epidemiology, prescription drug abuse, obesity prevention, school-based intervention. *Unit head:* Dr. Brian Martin, Graduate Program Coordinator, 423-439-4429, Fax: 423-439-6491, E-mail: martinb@etsu.edu. *Application contact:* Mary Duncan, Graduate Specialist, 423-439-4302, Fax: 423-439-5624, E-mail: duncanm@etsu.edu. Website: http://www.etsu.edu/cph/academics/graduate/MPHHome.aspx.

East Tennessee State University, School of Graduate Studies, College of Public Health, Public Health Certificate Programs, Johnson City, TN 37614. Offers biostatistics (Postbaccalaureate Certificate); epidemiology (Postbaccalaureate Certificate); gerontology (Postbaccalaureate Certificate); health care management (Postbaccalaureate Certificate); rural health (Postbaccalaureate Certificate). Part-time programs available. *Students:* 1 full-time (0 women), 6 part-time (4 women); includes 1 minority (Black or African American, non-Hispanic/Latino). 19 applicants, 47% accepted, 3 enrolled. In 2012, 3 Postbaccalaureate Certificates awarded. *Degree requirements:* For Postbaccalaureate Certificate, culminating experience or community-based project. *Entrance requirements:* For degree, minimum GPA of 2.5, 3 letters of recommendation, resume (for gerontology). Additional exam requirements/recommendations for international students: Required—TOEFL (minimum score 550 paper-based; 79 iBT). *Application deadline:* For fall admission, 6/1 for domestic students, 4/29 for international students; for spring admission, 11/1 for domestic students, 9/30 for international students. Application fee: $35 ($45 for international students). Electronic applications accepted. *Financial support:* Institutionally sponsored loans and scholarships/grants available. Financial award application deadline: 7/1; financial award applicants required to submit FAFSA. *Faculty research:* Skin cancer prevention, chronic disease epidemiology, prescription drug abuse, obesity prevention, school-based intervention. *Unit head:* Dr. Randy Wykoff, Dean, 423-439-4243, Fax: 423-439-5238, E-mail: wykoff@etsu.edu. *Application contact:* Mary Duncan, Graduate Specialist, 423-439-4302, Fax: 423-439-5624, E-mail: duncanm@etsu.edu. Website: http://www.etsu.edu/cph/admissions/certificate.aspx.

Emory University, Rollins School of Public Health, Department of Biostatistics and Bioinformatics, Atlanta, GA 30322-1100. Offers bioinformatics (PhD); biostatistics (MPH, MSPH); public health informatics (MSPH). PhD offered through the Graduate School of Arts and Sciences. Part-time programs available. *Faculty:* 22 full-time (7 women), 1 part-time/adjunct (0 women). *Students:* 30 full-time (22 women); includes 6 minority (3 Black or African American, non-Hispanic/Latino; 3 Asian, non-Hispanic/Latino), 15 international. Average age 27. 140 applicants, 10% accepted, 7 enrolled. In 2012, 3 master's, 2 doctorates awarded. *Degree requirements:* For master's, thesis, practicum. *Entrance requirements:* For master's, GRE General Test. Additional exam requirements/recommendations for international students: Required—TOEFL (minimum score 550 paper-based; 80 iBT). *Application deadline:* For fall admission, 1/3 priority date for domestic students, 1/3 for international students. Application fee: $75. Electronic applications accepted. *Financial support:* Fellowships with full and partial tuition reimbursements, career-related internships or fieldwork, Federal Work-Study, institutionally sponsored loans, scholarships/grants, traineeships, health care benefits, and unspecified assistantships available. Support available to part-time students. Financial award application deadline: 1/3; financial award applicants required to submit FAFSA. *Unit head:* Lance A. Waller, Chair, 404-727-1057, Fax: 404-727-1370, E-mail: lwaller@emory.edu.

Florida International University, Robert Stempel College of Public Health and Social Work, Programs in Public Health, Miami, FL 33199. Offers biostatistics

(MPH); environmental and occupational health (MPH, PhD); epidemiology (MPH, PhD); health policy and management (MPH); health promotion and disease prevention (PhD); health promotion and diseases prevention (MPH). Ph D is fall admission only; MPH offered jointly with University of Miami. *Accreditation:* CEPH. Part-time and evening/weekend programs available. Postbaccalaureate distance learning degree programs offered (no on-campus study). *Degree requirements:* For master's, thesis optional; for doctorate, comprehensive exam, thesis/dissertation. *Entrance requirements:* For master's, minimum GPA of 3.0, letters of recommendation; for doctorate, GRE, resume, minimum GPA of 3.0, letters of recommendation, letter of intent. Additional exam requirements/recommendations for international students: Required—TOEFL (minimum score 550 paper-based; 80 iBT). Electronic applications accepted. *Expenses:* Contact institution. *Faculty research:* Drugs/AIDS intervention among migrant workers, provision of services for active/recovering drug users with HIV.

Florida State University, The Graduate School, College of Arts and Sciences, Department of Statistics, Tallahassee, FL 32306-4330. Offers applied statistics (MS); biostatistics (MS, PhD); mathematical statistics (MS, PhD). Part-time programs available. *Faculty:* 15 full-time (2 women). *Students:* 62 full-time (26 women), 5 part-time (2 women); includes 25 minority (9 Black or African American, non-Hispanic/Latino; 9 Asian, non-Hispanic/Latino; 7 Hispanic/Latino), 17 international. Average age 29. 138 applicants, 30% accepted, 18 enrolled. In 2012, 17 master's, 9 doctorates awarded. Terminal master's awarded for partial completion of doctoral program. *Degree requirements:* For doctorate, comprehensive exam, thesis/dissertation, departmental qualifying exam. *Entrance requirements:* For master's, GRE General Test, previous course work in calculus, minimum GPA of 3.0; for doctorate, GRE General Test, minimum GPA of 3.0, 1 course in linear algebra (preferred), calculus I-III, real analysis. Additional exam requirements/recommendations for international students: Required—TOEFL (minimum score 80 iBT). *Application deadline:* For fall admission, 7/1 for domestic and international students; for spring admission, 11/1 for domestic and international students. Applications are processed on a rolling basis. Application fee: $30. Electronic applications accepted. *Expenses:* Tuition, state resident: full-time $7263; part-time $403.51 per credit hour. Tuition, nonresident: full-time $18,087; part-time $1004.85 per credit hour. *Required fees:* $1335.42; $74.19 per credit hour. $445.14 per semester. One-time fee: $40 full-time; $20 part-time. Tuition and fees vary according to program. *Financial support:* In 2012–13, 56 students received support, including 9 research assistantships with full tuition reimbursements available (averaging $22,495 per year), 48 teaching assistantships with full tuition reimbursements available (averaging $20,358 per year); Federal Work-Study, institutionally sponsored loans, scholarships/grants, health care benefits, and unspecified assistantships also available. Financial award application deadline: 2/15; financial award applicants required to submit FAFSA. *Faculty research:* Statistical inference, probability theory, biostatistics, nonparametric estimation, automatic target recognition. *Total annual research expenditures:* $693,402. *Unit head:* Dr. Xufeng Niu, Chairman, 850-644-4008, Fax: 850-644-5271, E-mail: niu@stat.fsu.edu. *Application contact:* Alex Cohn, Academic Support Assistant, 850-644-3514, Fax: 850-644-5271, E-mail: acohn@stat.fsu.edu. Website: http://stat.fsu.edu/.

George Mason University, College of Health and Human Services, Department of Global and Community Health, Fairfax, VA 22030. Offers biostatistics (Certificate); epidemiology (Certificate); gerontology (Certificate); global health (MS, Certificate); nutrition (Certificate); public health (MPH, Certificate). *Faculty:* 10 full-time (6 women), 13 part-time/adjunct (10 women). *Students:* 73 full-time (63 women), 99 part-time (79 women); includes 73 minority (34 Black or African American, non-Hispanic/Latino; 23 Asian, non-Hispanic/Latino; 13 Hispanic/Latino; 1 Native Hawaiian or other Pacific Islander, non-Hispanic/Latino; 2 Two or more races, non-Hispanic/Latino), 6 international. Average age 31. 144 applicants, 76% accepted, 58 enrolled. In 2012, 97 master's, 26 other advanced degrees awarded. *Degree requirements:* For master's, comprehensive exam (for some programs), thesis or practicum. *Entrance requirements:* For master's, GRE, 2 official transcripts; expanded goals statement; 3 letters of recommendation; resume; 1 completed course in health science, statistics, natural sciences and social science (for MPH); 6 credits of foreign language if not fluent (for MS in global health); for Certificate, 2 official transcripts; expanded goals statement; 3 letters of recommendation; resume; bachelor's degree from regionally-accredited institution with minimum GPA of 3.0; statistics and college-level algebra with minimum B grade (for Certificate in biostatistics). Additional exam requirements/recommendations for international students: Required—TOEFL (minimum score 570 paper-based; 88 iBT), IELTS (minimum score 6.5), Pearson Test of English. *Application deadline:* For fall admission, 4/1 priority date for domestic students; for spring admission, 11/1 priority date for domestic students. Applications are processed on a rolling basis. Application fee: $65 ($80 for international students). Electronic applications accepted. *Expenses:* Contact institution. *Financial support:* In 2012–13, 10 students received support, including 1 fellowship (averaging $1,500 per year), 6 research assistantships with full and partial tuition reimbursements available (averaging $16,085 per year), 3 teaching assistantships with full and partial tuition reimbursements available (averaging $21,333 per year); career-related internships or fieldwork, Federal Work-Study, scholarships/grants, unspecified assistantships, and health care benefits (for full-time research or teaching assistantship recipients) also available. Financial award application deadline: 3/1; financial award applicants required to submit FAFSA. *Faculty research:* Health issues and the needs of affected populations at the regional and global level. *Total annual research expenditures:* $54,697. *Unit head:* Dr. Carlos Sluzki, Dean, 703-993-1920, Fax: 703-993-1943, E-mail: csluzki@gmu.edu. *Application contact:* Allan Weiss, Office Manager, 703-993-3126, Fax: 703-993-1908, E-mail: aweiss2@gmu.edu. Website: http://chhs.gmu.edu/gch/index.

Georgetown University, Graduate School of Arts and Sciences, Programs in Biomedical Sciences, Department of Biostatistics, Bioinformatics and Biomathematics, Washington, DC 20057-1484. Offers biostatistics (MS), including bioinformatics, epidemiology. *Entrance requirements:* For master's, GRE General Test. Additional exam requirements/recommendations for international students: Required—TOEFL. *Faculty research:* Occupation epidemiology, cancer.

The George Washington University, Columbian College of Arts and Sciences, Program in Biostatistics, Washington, DC 20052. Offers MS, PhD. *Students:* 9 full-time (6 women), 14 part-time (10 women); includes 5 minority (all Asian, non-Hispanic/Latino), 10 international. Average age 33. 68 applicants, 72% accepted, 9 enrolled. In 2012, 3 master's, 4 doctorates awarded. *Degree requirements:* For master's, comprehensive exam; for doctorate, thesis/dissertation, general exam. *Entrance requirements:* For master's and doctorate, GRE General Test, minimum GPA of 3.0. Additional exam requirements/recommendations for international students: Required—TOEFL (minimum score 550 paper-based; 80 iBT). *Application deadline:* For fall admission, 1/15 priority date for domestic students, 1/15 for international students; for spring admission, 10/1 priority date for domestic students, 9/1 for international students. Applications are processed on a rolling basis. Application fee: $75. Electronic applications accepted. *Financial support:* In 2012–13, 1 student received support. Fellowships with full tuition reimbursements available, teaching assistantships, and tuition waivers available. *Unit head:* Dr. Zhaohai Li, Director, 202-994-7844, Fax: 202-994-6917, E-mail: zli@gwu.edu. *Application contact:* 202-994-6210, Fax: 202-994-6213, E-mail: askccas@gwu.edu.

The George Washington University, School of Public Health and Health Services, Department of Epidemiology and Biostatistics, Washington, DC 20052. Offers biostatistics (MPH); epidemiology (MPH); microbiology and emerging infectious diseases (MSPH). *Faculty:* 25 full-time (16 women). *Students:* 61 full-time (49 women), 58 part-time (45 women); includes 36 minority (21 Black or African American, non-Hispanic/Latino; 12 Asian, non-Hispanic/Latino; 1 Hispanic/Latino; 1 Native Hawaiian or other Pacific Islander, non-Hispanic/Latino; 1 Two or more races, non-Hispanic/Latino), 9 international. Average age 28. 273 applicants, 74% accepted, 34 enrolled. In 2012, 46 master's awarded. *Degree requirements:* For master's, case study or special project. *Entrance requirements:* For master's, GMAT, GRE General Test, or MCAT. Additional exam requirements/recommendations for international students: Required—TOEFL. *Application deadline:* For fall admission, 4/15 priority date for domestic students, 4/15 for international students; for spring admission, 11/1 for domestic and international students. Applications are processed on a rolling basis. Application fee: $75. *Financial support:* In 2012–13, 6 students received support. Tuition waivers available. Financial award application deadline: 2/15. *Unit head:* Dr. Alan E. Greenberg, Chair, 202-994-0612, E-mail: aeg1@gwu.edu. *Application contact:* Jane Smith, Director of Admissions, 202-994-0248, Fax: 202-994-1860, E-mail: sphhsinfo@gwumc.edu.

Georgia Regents University, College of Graduate Studies, Program in Biostatistics, Augusta, GA 30912. Offers MS, PhD. *Degree requirements:* For master's, thesis or alternative. *Entrance requirements:* For master's, GRE General Test, substantial mathematics background, computer literacy. Additional exam requirements/recommendations for international students: Required—TOEFL (minimum score 550 paper-based; 79 iBT). Electronic applications accepted. *Faculty research:* Computational biology, clinical trials, statistical genetics, statistical epidemiology, survival analysis.

Georgia Southern University, Jack N. Averitt College of Graduate Studies, Jiann-Ping Hsu College of Public Health, Program in Public Health, Statesboro, GA 30460. Offers biostatistics (MPH, Dr PH); community health behavior and education (Dr PH); community health education (MPH); environmental health sciences (MPH); epidemiology (MPH); health services policy management (MPH); public health leadership (Dr PH). *Accreditation:* CEPH. Part-time programs available. *Students:* 123 full-time (85 women), 39 part-time (30 women); includes 89 minority (76 Black or African American, non-Hispanic/Latino; 8 Asian, non-Hispanic/Latino; 4 Hispanic/Latino; 1 Two or more races, non-Hispanic/Latino), 23 international. Average age 29. 208 applicants, 80% accepted, 55 enrolled. In 2012, 28 master's, 4 doctorates awarded. *Degree requirements:* For master's, thesis optional, practicum; for doctorate, comprehensive exam, thesis/dissertation, practicum. *Entrance requirements:* For master's, GRE General Test, minimum GPA of 2.75, resume, 3 letters of reference; for doctorate, GRE, GMAT, MCAT, LSAT, 3 letters of reference, statement of purpose, resume or curriculum vitae. Additional exam requirements/recommendations for international students: Required—TOEFL (minimum score 550 paper-based; 80 iBT), IELTS (minimum score 6). *Application deadline:* For fall admission, 3/1 priority date for domestic students, 3/1 for international students; for spring admission, 10/1 priority date for domestic students, 10/1 for international students. Applications are processed on a rolling basis. Application fee: $50. Electronic applications accepted. *Expenses:* Contact institution. *Financial support:* In 2012–13, 57 students received support, including research assistantships with partial tuition reimbursements available (averaging $7,200 per year), teaching assistantships with partial tuition reimbursements available (averaging $7,200 per year); career-related internships or fieldwork, Federal Work-Study, scholarships/grants, tuition waivers (partial), and unspecified assistantships also available. Support available to part-time students. Financial award application deadline: 4/15; financial award applicants required to submit FAFSA. *Faculty research:* Rural public health best practices, health disparity elimination, community initiatives to enhance public health, cost effectiveness analysis, epidemiology of rural public health, environmental health issues, health care system assessment, rural health care, health policy and healthcare financing, survival analysis, nonparametric statistics and resampling methods, micro-arrays and genomics, data imputation techniques and clinical trial methodology. *Unit head:* Sarah Peterson, Dean, 912-478-2413, Fax: 912-478-5811, E-mail: speterson@georgiasouthern.edu. *Application contact:* Amanda Gilliland, Coordinator for Graduate Student Recruitment, 912-478-5384, Fax: 912-478-0740, E-mail: gradadmissions@georgiasouthern.edu. Website: http://chhs.georgiasouthern.edu/health/.

Georgia State University, College of Arts and Sciences, Department of Mathematics and Statistics, Atlanta, GA 30302-3083. Offers bioinformatics (MS, PhD); biostatistics (MS, PhD); discrete mathematics (MS); mathematics (MS, PhD); scientific computing (MS); statistics (MS). Part-time programs available. *Faculty:* 23 full-time (6 women), 1 (woman) part-time/adjunct. *Students:* 79 full-time (42 women), 34 part-time (11 women); includes 38 minority (23 Black or African American, non-Hispanic/Latino; 13 Asian, non-Hispanic/Latino; 2 Hispanic/Latino), 48 international. Average age 32. 97 applicants, 56% accepted, 21 enrolled. In 2012, 19 master's, 2 doctorates awarded. Terminal master's awarded for partial completion of doctoral program. *Degree requirements:* For master's, comprehensive exam (for some programs), thesis optional; for doctorate, comprehensive exam, thesis/dissertation. *Entrance requirements:* For master's and doctorate, GRE. Additional exam requirements/recommendations for international students: Required—TOEFL (minimum score 550 paper-based; 80 iBT). *Application deadline:* For fall admission, 7/1 priority date for domestic students, 7/1 for international students; for spring admission, 11/15 priority date for domestic students, 11/15 for international students. Application fee: $50. Electronic applications accepted. *Expenses:* Tuition, state resident: full-time $8064; part-time $336 per credit hour. Tuition, nonresident: full-time $28,800; part-time $1200 per credit hour. *Required fees:* $2128; $1064 per semester. Tuition and fees vary according to course load and program. *Financial support:* In 2012–13, 15 students received support, including 3 fellowships with full tuition reimbursements available (averaging $22,000 per year), 20 research assistantships with full tuition reimbursements available (averaging $9,000 per year), 50 teaching assistantships with full tuition reimbursements available (averaging $9,000 per year); institutionally sponsored loans, scholarships/grants, health care benefits, and unspecified assistantships also available. Financial award application deadline: 2/1. *Faculty research:* Algebra, matrix theory, graph theory and combinatorics; applied mathematics and analysis; collegiate mathematics education; statistics, biostatistics and applications; bioinformatics, dynamical systems. *Total annual research expenditures:* $491,077. *Unit head:* Dr. Guantao Chen, Chair, 404-413-6436, Fax: 404-413-6403, E-mail: gchen@gsu.edu. *Application contact:* Dr. Zhongshan Li, Graduate Director, 404-413-6437, Fax: 404-413-6403, E-mail: zli@gsu.edu. Website: http://www2.gsu.edu/~wwwmat/.

Grand Valley State University, College of Liberal Arts and Sciences, Program in Biostatistics, Allendale, MI 49401-9403. Offers MS. *Faculty:* 5 full-time (1 woman). *Students:* 28 full-time (14 women), 13 part-time (8 women); includes 3 minority (1 Black or African American, non-Hispanic/Latino; 1 Asian, non-Hispanic/Latino; 1 Two or more races, non-Hispanic/Latino), 1 international. Average age 28. 24 applicants, 83% accepted, 16 enrolled. In 2012, 12 master's awarded. *Entrance requirements:* For master's, minimum GPA of 3.0. Application fee: $30. *Financial support:* In 2012–13, 21 students received support, including 2 fellowships (averaging $325 per year), 20 research assistantships with tuition reimbursements available (averaging $8,000 per year); unspecified assistantships also available. *Faculty research:* Biometrical models, spatial methods, medical statistics, design of experiments. *Unit head:* Dr. Robert Downer, Director, 616-331-2247. *Application contact:* Dr. David Elrod, PSM Coordinator, 616-331-8643, E-mail: elrodd@gvsu.edu.

Harvard University, Cyprus International Institute for the Environment and Public Health in Association with Harvard School of Public Health, Cambridge, MA 02138. Offers environmental health (MS); environmental/public health (PhD); epidemiology and biostatistics (MS). *Entrance requirements:* For master's and doctorate, GRE, resume/curriculum vitae, 3 letters of recommendation, BA or BS (including diploma and official transcripts). Additional exam requirements/recommendations for international students: Required—TOEFL, IELTS (minimum score 7). Electronic applications accepted. *Expenses: Tuition:* Full-time $37,576. *Required fees:* $930. Tuition and fees vary according to program and student level. *Faculty research:* Air pollution, climate change, biostatistics, sustainable development, environmental management.

Harvard University, Graduate School of Arts and Sciences, Department of Biostatistics, Cambridge, MA 02138. Offers PhD. *Expenses: Tuition:* Full-time $37,576. *Required fees:* $930. Tuition and fees vary according to program and student level.

Harvard University, Harvard School of Public Health, Department of Biostatistics, Boston, MA 02115-6096. Offers SM, PhD. Part-time programs available. *Faculty:* 45 full-time (14 women), 19 part-time/adjunct (9 women). *Students:* 88 full-time, 6 part-time; includes 24 minority (2 Black or African American, non-Hispanic/Latino; 16 Asian, non-Hispanic/Latino; 3 Hispanic/Latino; 3 Two or more races, non-Hispanic/Latino), 34 international. Average age 26. 199 applicants, 22% accepted, 28 enrolled. In 2012, 5 master's, 17 doctorates awarded. *Degree requirements:* For doctorate, thesis/dissertation, oral and written qualifying exams. *Entrance requirements:* For master's, GRE, MCAT, prior training in mathematics and/or statistics; for doctorate, GRE, prior training in mathematics and/or statistics. Additional exam requirements/recommendations for international students: Required—TOEFL (minimum score 600 paper-based; 100 iBT); Recommended—IELTS (minimum score 7). *Application deadline:* For fall admission, 12/15 for domestic and international students. Application fee: $120. Electronic applications accepted. *Expenses: Tuition:* Full-time $37,576. *Required fees:* $930. Tuition and fees vary according to program and student level. *Financial support:* Fellowships, research assistantships, teaching assistantships, Federal Work-Study, scholarships/grants, traineeships, and unspecified assistantships available. Support available to part-time students. Financial award application deadline: 2/15; financial award applicants required to submit FAFSA. *Faculty research:* Statistical genetics, clinical trials, cancer and AIDS research, environmental and mental health, dose response modeling. *Unit head:* Dr. Victor DeGruttola, Chair, 617-432-1056, Fax: 617-432-5619, E-mail: degrut@hsph.harvard.edu. *Application contact:* Vincent W. James, Director of Admissions, 617-432-1031, Fax: 617-432-7080, E-mail: admissions@hsph.harvard.edu. Website: http://www.hsph.harvard.edu/biostatistics/.

Hunter College of the City University of New York, Graduate School, Schools of the Health Professions, School of Health Sciences, Programs in Urban Public Health, Program in Epidemiology and Biostatistics, New York, NY 10021-5085. Offers MPH. *Accreditation:* CEPH. Part-time and evening/weekend programs available. *Faculty:* 4 full-time (1 woman). *Students:* 6 full-time (2 women), 43 part-time (25 women); includes 18 minority (5 Black or African American, non-Hispanic/Latino; 9 Asian, non-Hispanic/Latino; 4 Hispanic/Latino), 3 international. Average age 32. 71 applicants, 23% accepted, 8 enrolled. In 2012, 15 master's awarded. *Degree requirements:* For master's, comprehensive exam, thesis optional, internship. *Entrance requirements:* For master's, GRE General Test, previous course work in calculus and statistics. Additional exam requirements/recommendations for international students: Required—TOEFL. *Application deadline:* For fall admission, 4/1 for domestic students; for spring admission, 11/1 for domestic students. Application fee: $125. *Expenses:* Tuition, state resident: full-time $8690; part-time $365 per credit. Tuition, nonresident: full-time $16,200; part-time $675 per credit. *Required fees:* $320 per semester. One-time fee: $125. Tuition and fees vary according to class time, campus/location and program. *Financial support:* In 2012–13, 6 fellowships were awarded; career-related internships or fieldwork, Federal Work-Study, institutionally sponsored loans, and tuition waivers (partial) also available. Support available to part-time students. Financial award application deadline: 3/1. *Unit head:* Prof. Lorna Thorpe, Program Director, 212-396-7746, Fax: 212-481-5260, E-mail: lthor@hunter.cuny.edu. *Application contact:* Milena Solo, Director for Graduate Admissions, 212-772-4288, Fax: 212-650-3336, E-mail: milena.solo@hunter.cuny.edu. Website: http://www.hunter.cuny.edu/uph/grad-test/epidemiology-biostatistics.

Indiana University Bloomington, School of Public Health, Department of Epidemiology and Biostatistics, Bloomington, IN 47405. Offers biostatistics (MPH); epidemiology (MPH, PhD). *Faculty:* 7 full-time (3 women), 3 part-time/adjunct (all women). *Students:* 21 full-time (14 women), 1 part-time (0 women); includes 7 minority (4 Black or African American, non-Hispanic/Latino; 1 Asian, non-Hispanic/Latino; 2 Hispanic/Latino), 7 international. 35 applicants, 54% accepted, 16 enrolled. In 2012, 2 master's, 1 doctorate awarded. *Degree requirements:* For master's, thesis or alternative; for doctorate, comprehensive exam, thesis/dissertation. *Entrance requirements:* For master's, GRE (for applicants with cumulative undergraduate GPA less than 2.8); for doctorate, GRE. Additional exam requirements/recommendations for international students: Required—TOEFL (minimum score 550 paper-based; 80 iBT). *Application deadline:* For fall admission, 2/1 priority date for domestic students, 12/1 for international students. Application fee: $55 ($65 for international students). Electronic applications accepted. *Financial support:* In 2012–13, 15 students received support, including 3 fellowships (averaging $12,000 per year), 12 research assistantships with partial tuition reimbursements available (averaging $8,600 per year); Federal Work-Study, institutionally sponsored loans, and health care benefits also available. Financial award application deadline: 3/15; financial award applicants required to submit FAFSA. *Faculty research:* Nutritional epidemiology, cancer epidemiology, global health, biostatistics. *Unit head:* Dr. Ka He, Chair, 812-856-2448, E-mail: kahe@indiana.edu. *Application contact:* Julie Wilson, Assistant Director of Student Services, 812-856-2448, E-mail: jaw@indiana.edu. Website: http://www.publichealth.indiana.edu/departments/epidemiology/index.shtml.

Indiana University–Purdue University Indianapolis, Indiana University School of Medicine, Department of Biostatistics, Indianapolis, IN 46202-2896. Offers PhD. Program offered jointly with Purdue University Department of Mathematical Sciences. *Students:* 20 full-time (12 women), 3 part-time (0 women); includes 4 minority (all Asian, non-Hispanic/Latino), 17 international. 22 applicants, 27% accepted, 4 enrolled. *Degree requirements:* For doctorate, thesis/dissertation. *Entrance requirements:* For doctorate, GRE General Test. Additional exam requirements/recommendations for international students: Required—TOEFL. *Application deadline:* For fall admission, 1/15 for domestic and international students. Application fee: $55 ($65 for international students). Electronic applications accepted. *Unit head:* Barry Katz, Chair, 317-274-2674, E-mail: bkatz@iupui.edu. *Application contact:* Benzion Boukai, Co-Director, 317-274-2661, E-mail: bboukai@iupui.edu. Website: http://biostatgradprograms.iupui.edu/.

Iowa State University of Science and Technology, Bioinformatics and Computational Biology Program, Ames, IA 50011. Offers MS, PhD. *Degree* *requirements:* For doctorate, thesis/dissertation. *Entrance requirements:* For master's and doctorate, GRE General Test. Additional exam requirements/ recommendations for international students: Recommended—TOEFL, IELTS. *Application deadline:* For fall admission, 1/15 priority date for domestic students, 1/15 for international students; for spring admission, 10/15 for domestic and international students. Application fee: $40 ($90 for international students). Electronic applications accepted. *Faculty research:* Functional and structural genomics, genome evolution, macromolecular structure and function, mathematical biology and biological statistics, metabolic and developmental networks. *Application contact:* Trish Stauble, Information Contact, 515-294-5836, Fax: 515-294-2592, E-mail: grad_admissions@iastate.edu. Website: http:// www.bcb.iastate.edu/.

The Johns Hopkins University, Bloomberg School of Public Health, Department of Biostatistics, Baltimore, MD 21205-2179. Offers bioinformatics (MHS); biostatistics (MHS, Sc M, PhD). Part-time programs available. *Degree requirements:* For master's, comprehensive exam (for some programs), thesis (for some programs), written exam, final project; for doctorate, comprehensive exam, thesis/dissertation, 1 year full-time residency, oral and written exams. *Entrance requirements:* For master's and doctorate, GRE General Test, course work in calculus and matrix algebra, 3 letters of recommendation, curriculum vitae. Additional exam requirements/recommendations for international students: Required—TOEFL (minimum score 600 paper-based). Electronic applications accepted. *Faculty research:* Statistical genetics, bioinformatics, statistical computing, statistical methods, environmental statistics.

Loma Linda University, School of Public Health, Programs in Epidemiology and Biostatistics, Loma Linda, CA 92350. Offers MPH, MSPH, Dr PH, Postbaccalaureate Certificate. *Entrance requirements:* Additional exam requirements/recommendations for international students: Required—Michigan English Language Assessment Battery or TOEFL.

Louisiana State University Health Sciences Center, School of Public Health, New Orleans, LA 70112. Offers behavioral and community health sciences (MPH); biostatistics (MPH, MS, PhD); community health sciences (PhD); environmental and occupational health sciences (MPH); epidemiology (MPH, PhD); health policy and systems management (MPH). Part-time programs available. *Entrance requirements:* For master's, GRE General Test.

McGill University, Faculty of Graduate and Postdoctoral Studies, Faculty of Medicine, Department of Epidemiology and Biostatistics, Montréal, QC H3A 2T5, Canada. Offers community health (M Sc); environmental health (M Sc); epidemiology and biostatistics (M Sc, PhD, Diploma); health care evaluation (M Sc); medical statistics (M Sc). *Accreditation:* CEPH (one or more programs are accredited).

Medical College of Wisconsin, Graduate School of Biomedical Sciences, Department of Population Health, Division of Biostatistics, Milwaukee, WI 53226-0509. Offers PhD. Part-time programs available. *Degree requirements:* For doctorate, comprehensive exam, thesis/dissertation. *Entrance requirements:* For doctorate, GRE, official transcripts, three letters of recommendation. Additional exam requirements/recommendations for international students: Required—TOEFL. Electronic applications accepted. *Faculty research:* Survival analysis, spatial statistics, time series, genetic statistics, Bayesian statistics.

Medical University of South Carolina, College of Graduate Studies, Division of Biostatistics and Epidemiology, Charleston, SC 29425. Offers biostatistics (MS, PhD); epidemiology (MS, PhD); DMD/PhD; MD/PhD. Terminal master's awarded for partial completion of doctoral program. *Degree requirements:* For master's, comprehensive exam, thesis (for some programs); for doctorate, comprehensive exam, oral and written exams. *Entrance requirements:* For master's, GRE General Test, two semesters of college-level calculus; for doctorate, GRE General Test, interview, minimum GPA of 3.0, two semesters of college-level calculus. Additional exam requirements/recommendations for international students: Required—TOEFL (minimum score 600 paper-based; 100 iBT). Electronic applications accepted. *Faculty research:* Health disparities, central nervous system injuries, radiation exposure, analysis of clinical trial data, biomedical information.

Middle Tennessee State University, College of Graduate Studies, College of Basic and Applied Sciences, Program in Professional Science, Murfreesboro, TN 37132. Offers biostatistics (MS); health care informatics (MS). Part-time and evening/weekend programs available. Postbaccalaureate distance learning degree programs offered. *Degree requirements:* For master's, comprehensive exam. *Entrance requirements:* For master's, GRE. Additional exam requirements/ recommendations for international students: Required—TOEFL (minimum score 525 paper-based; 71 iBT) or IELTS (minimum score 6). *Faculty research:* Biotechnology, biostatistics, informatics.

New Jersey Institute of Technology, Office of Graduate Studies, College of Science and Liberal Arts, Department of Mathematical Science, Program in Biostatistics, Newark, NJ 07102. Offers MS. Part-time and evening/weekend programs available. Postbaccalaureate distance learning degree programs offered. Terminal master's awarded for partial completion of doctoral program. *Degree requirements:* For master's, thesis optional. *Entrance requirements:* For master's, GRE General Test. Additional exam requirements/recommendations for international students: Required—TOEFL (minimum score 550 paper-based; 79 iBT). Electronic applications accepted. *Expenses:* Tuition, state resident: full-time $16,836; part-time $915 per credit. Tuition, nonresident: full-time $24,370; part-time $1286 per credit. *Required fees:* $2318; $242 per credit.

The Ohio State University, Graduate School, College of Arts and Sciences, Division of Natural and Mathematical Sciences, Department of Statistics, Columbus, OH 43210. Offers biostatistics (PhD); statistics (M Appl Stat, MS, PhD). *Faculty:* 22. *Students:* 90 full-time (49 women), 24 part-time (11 women); includes 4 minority (all Asian, non-Hispanic/Latino), 58 international. Average age 26. In 2012, 43 master's, 10 doctorates awarded. *Degree requirements:* For master's, thesis optional; for doctorate, thesis/dissertation. *Entrance requirements:* For master's and doctorate, GRE General Test. Additional exam requirements/recommendations for international students: Required—TOEFL (minimum score 600 paper-based; 100 iBT); Recommended—IELTS (minimum score 8). *Application deadline:* For fall admission, 12/28 priority date for domestic students, 11/30 for international students; for winter admission, 12/1 for domestic students, 11/1 for international students; for spring admission, 12/1 priority date for domestic students, 11/1 for international students. Applications are processed on a rolling basis. Application fee: $40 ($50 for international students). Electronic applications accepted. *Financial support:* Fellowships, research assistantships, teaching assistantships, Federal Work-Study, and institutionally sponsored loans available. Support available to part-time students. *Unit head:* L. Mark Berliner, Chair, 614-247-4075, Fax: 614-292-2096, E-mail: berliner.1@osu.edu. *Application contact:* Graduate Admissions, 614-292-9444, Fax: 614-292-3895, E-mail: gradadmissions@osu.edu. Website: http://www.stat.osu.edu/.

Oregon Health & Science University, School of Medicine, Graduate Programs in Medicine, Department of Public Health and Preventive Medicine, Biostatistics Program, Portland, OR 97239-3098. Offers MS, Graduate Certificate. Part-time programs available. Postbaccalaureate distance learning degree programs offered. *Faculty:* 6 full-time (5 women), 5 part-time/adjunct (1 woman). *Students:* 1 full-time (0 women), 19 part-time (12 women); includes 7 minority (1 Black or African American, non-Hispanic/Latino; 1 American Indian or Alaska Native, non-Hispanic/Latino; 2 Asian, non-Hispanic/Latino; 2 Hispanic/Latino; 1 Two or more races, non-Hispanic/Latino), 1 international. Average age 34. 11 applicants, 64% accepted, 7 enrolled. *Degree requirements:* For master's, thesis. *Entrance requirements:* For master's, GRE (minimum scores: 153 Verbal, 148 Quantitative, 4.5 Analytical Writing), minimum GPA of 3.0. Additional exam requirements/ recommendations for international students: Required—TOEFL (minimum score 550 paper-based; 80 iBT). *Application deadline:* For fall admission, 2/15 for domestic and international students. Application fee: $70. Electronic applications accepted. *Financial support:* Applicants required to submit FAFSA. *Unit head:* Dr. Thomas M. Becker, Professor/Chair, 503-494-8257, Fax: 503-494-4981, E-mail: pmph@ohsu.edu. *Application contact:* Tree Triano, Education Manager, 503-494-2012, Fax: 503-494-4981, E-mail: pmph@ohsu.edu. Website: http:// www.ohsu.edu/msbiostat.

Oregon State University, College of Public Health and Human Sciences, School of Social and Behavioral Health Sciences, Program in Public Health, Corvallis, OR 97331. Offers biostatistics (MPH); environmental and occupational health and safety (MPH, PhD); epidemiology (MPH); international health (MPH). *Accreditation:* CEPH. *Faculty:* 17 full-time (10 women), 2 part-time/adjunct (0 women). *Students:* 133 full-time (97 women), 30 part-time (23 women); includes 30 minority (5 Black or African American, non-Hispanic/Latino; 8 Asian, non-Hispanic/Latino; 8 Hispanic/Latino; 1 Native Hawaiian or other Pacific Islander, non-Hispanic/Latino; 8 Two or more races, non-Hispanic/Latino), 10 international. Average age 33. 225 applicants, 60% accepted, 80 enrolled. In 2012, 51 master's, 8 doctorates awarded. Terminal master's awarded for partial completion of doctoral program. *Degree requirements:* For doctorate, one foreign language, thesis/dissertation. *Entrance requirements:* For master's and doctorate, minimum GPA of 3.0 in last 90 hours. Additional exam requirements/recommendations for international students: Required—TOEFL. *Application deadline:* For fall admission, 3/1 for domestic students. Applications are processed on a rolling basis. Application fee: $50. *Expenses:* Tuition, state resident: full-time $11,367; part-time $421 per credit hour. Tuition, nonresident: full-time $18,279; part-time $677 per credit hour. *Required fees:* $1478. One-time fee: $300 full-time. Tuition and fees vary according to course load and program. *Financial support:* Fellowships, research assistantships, teaching assistantships, career-related internships or fieldwork, Federal Work-Study, and institutionally sponsored loans available. Support available to part-time students. Financial award application deadline: 2/1. *Faculty research:* Traffic safety, health safety, injury control, health promotion. *Unit head:* Dr. S. Marie Harvey, Associate Dean for Research and Graduate Programs, 541-737-3824, Fax: 541-737-4001, E-mail: marie.harvey@ oregonstate.edu.

Rice University, Graduate Programs, George R. Brown School of Engineering, Department of Statistics, Houston, TX 77251-1892. Offers bioinformatics (PhD); biostatistics (PhD); computational finance (PhD); general statistics (PhD); statistics (M Stat, MA); MBA/M Stat. Part-time programs available. *Degree requirements:* For master's, comprehensive exam; for doctorate, comprehensive exam, thesis/dissertation. *Entrance requirements:* For master's and doctorate, GRE General Test, minimum GPA of 3.0. Additional exam requirements/ recommendations for international students: Required—TOEFL (minimum score 630 paper-based; 90 iBT). Electronic applications accepted. *Faculty research:* Statistical genetics, non parametric function estimation, computational statistics and visualization, stochastic processes.

Rutgers, The State University of New Jersey, New Brunswick, Graduate School-New Brunswick, BioMaPS Institute for Quantitative Biology, Piscataway,

NJ 08854-8097. Offers computational biology and molecular biophysics (PhD). *Degree requirements:* For doctorate, comprehensive exam, thesis/dissertation. *Entrance requirements:* For doctorate, GRE. Additional exam requirements/ recommendations for international students: Required—TOEFL. Electronic applications accepted. *Faculty research:* Structural biology, systems biology, bioinformatics, translational medicine, genomics.

Rutgers, The State University of New Jersey, New Brunswick, Graduate School-New Brunswick, Program in Statistics, Piscataway, NJ 08854-8097. Offers applied statistics (MS); biostatistics (MS); data mining (MS); quality and productivity management (MS); statistics (MS, PhD). Part-time programs available. Terminal master's awarded for partial completion of doctoral program. *Degree requirements:* For master's, comprehensive exam, essay, exam, non-thesis essay paper; for doctorate, one foreign language, thesis/dissertation, qualifying oral and written exams. *Entrance requirements:* For master's, GRE General Test; for doctorate, GRE General Test, GRE Subject Test (recommended). Additional exam requirements/recommendations for international students: Required—TOEFL (minimum score 550 paper-based). Electronic applications accepted. *Faculty research:* Probability, decision theory, linear models, multivariate statistics, statistical computing.

San Diego State University, Graduate and Research Affairs, College of Health and Human Services, Graduate School of Public Health, San Diego, CA 92182. Offers environmental health (MPH); epidemiology (MPH, PhD), including biostatistics (MPH); global emergency preparedness and response (MS); global health (PhD); health behavior (PhD); health promotion (MPH); health services administration (MPH); toxicology (MS); MPH/MA; MSW/MPH. *Accreditation:* CAHME (one or more programs are accredited); CEPH (one or more programs are accredited). Part-time programs available. *Degree requirements:* For master's, comprehensive exam (for some programs), thesis (for some programs); for doctorate, thesis/dissertation. *Entrance requirements:* For master's, GMAT (MPH in health services administration), GRE General Test; for doctorate, GRE General Test. Additional exam requirements/recommendations for international students: Required—TOEFL. *Faculty research:* Evaluation of tobacco, AIDS prevalence and prevention, mammography, infant death project, Alzheimer's in elderly Chinese.

Tufts University, Sackler School of Graduate Biomedical Sciences, Clinical and Translational Science Program, Medford, MA 02155. Offers MS, PhD. *Faculty:* 34 full-time (10 women). *Students:* 31 full-time (17 women), 2 part-time (0 women); includes 5 minority (1 Black or African American, non-Hispanic/Latino; 3 Asian, non-Hispanic/Latino; 1 Hispanic/Latino), 9 international. Average age 33. In 2012, 10 master's awarded. Terminal master's awarded for partial completion of doctoral program. *Degree requirements:* For master's, thesis; for doctorate, comprehensive exam, thesis/dissertation. *Entrance requirements:* For master's and doctorate, MD or PhD, strong clinical research background. Additional exam requirements/recommendations for international students: Required—TOEFL (minimum score 600 paper-based; 100 iBT). *Application deadline:* For fall admission, 12/15 for domestic and international students. Application fee: $70. Electronic applications accepted. *Expenses: Tuition:* Full-time $42,856; part-time $1072 per credit hour. *Required fees:* $730. Full-time tuition and fees vary according to degree level, program and student level. Part-time tuition and fees vary according to course load. *Financial support:* Application deadline: 12/15. *Faculty research:* Clinical study design, mathematical modeling, meta analysis, epidemiologic research, coronary heart disease. *Unit head:* Dr. David Kent, Program Director, 617-636-3234, Fax: 617-636-8023, E-mail: dkent@tuftsmedicalcenter.edu. *Application contact:* Kellie Melchin, Associate Director of Admissions, 617-636-6767, Fax: 617-636-0375, E-mail: sackler-school@tufts.edu. Website: http://sackler.tufts.edu/Academics/Degree-Programs/PhD-Programs/Clinical-and-Translational-Science.

Tulane University, School of Public Health and Tropical Medicine, Department of Biostatistics, New Orleans, LA 70118-5669. Offers MS, MSPH, PhD, Sc D. MS and PhD offered through the Graduate School. Part-time programs available. *Degree requirements:* For doctorate, comprehensive exam, thesis/dissertation. *Entrance requirements:* For master's and doctorate, GRE General Test. Additional exam requirements/recommendations for international students: Required—TOEFL. Electronic applications accepted. *Faculty research:* Clinical trials, measurement, longitudinal analyses.

University at Albany, State University of New York, School of Public Health, Department of Epidemiology and Biostatistics, Albany, NY 12222-0001. Offers MS, PhD. *Degree requirements:* For master's, thesis; for doctorate, thesis/ dissertation. *Entrance requirements:* For master's and doctorate, GRE General Test. Additional exam requirements/recommendations for international students: Required—TOEFL (minimum score 550 paper-based). Electronic applications accepted.

University at Buffalo, the State University of New York, Graduate School, School of Public Health and Health Professions, Department of Biostatistics, Buffalo, NY 14260. Offers MA, MPH, PhD. *Faculty:* 17 full-time (4 women), 2 part-time/adjunct (0 women). *Students:* 41 full-time (24 women), 8 part-time (1 woman); includes 9 minority (3 Black or African American, non-Hispanic/Latino; 3 Asian, non-Hispanic/Latino; 1 Hispanic/Latino; 2 Native Hawaiian or other Pacific Islander, non-Hispanic/Latino), 26 international. Average age 31. 109 applicants, 74% accepted, 21 enrolled. In 2012, 4 master's, 4 doctorates awarded. Terminal master's awarded for partial completion of doctoral program. *Degree requirements:* For master's, comprehensive exam, thesis optional, final oral exam, practical data analysis experience; for doctorate, comprehensive exam, thesis/ dissertation, final oral exam. *Entrance requirements:* For master's, GRE, 3 semesters of course work in calculus (for mathematics), course work in real analysis (preferred), course work in linear algebra; for doctorate, GRE, master's degree in statistics, biostatistics or equivalent. Additional exam requirements/ recommendations for international students: Required—TOEFL (minimum score 640 paper-based; 79 iBT). *Application deadline:* For fall admission, 4/1 priority date for domestic students, 4/1 for international students. Application fee: $50. Electronic applications accepted. *Financial support:* In 2012–13, 12 students received support, including 2 fellowships with full tuition reimbursements available (averaging $4,000 per year), 6 research assistantships with full tuition reimbursements available (averaging $24,000 per year), 5 teaching assistantships with full tuition reimbursements available (averaging $20,000 per year); institutionally sponsored loans, scholarships/grants, and tuition waivers (partial) also available. Financial award application deadline: 2/1; financial award applicants required to submit FAFSA. *Faculty research:* Biostatistics, longitudinal data analysis, nonparametrics, statistical genetics, epidemiology. *Unit head:* Dr. Alan D. Hutson, Chair and Associate Professor, 716-829-2594, Fax: 716-829-2200, E-mail: ahutson@buffalo.edu. *Application contact:* Dr. Lili Tian, Director of Graduate Studies and Professor, 716-829-2715, Fax: 716-829-2200, E-mail: ltian@buffalo.edu. Website: http://sphhp.buffalo.edu/biostat/index.php.

The University of Alabama at Birmingham, School of Public Health, Program in Biostatistics, Birmingham, AL 35294. Offers MS, PhD. *Students:* 25 full-time (8 women), 9 part-time (6 women); includes 9 minority (4 Black or African American, non-Hispanic/Latino; 5 Asian, non-Hispanic/Latino), 12 international. Average age 32. In 2012, 9 master's, 5 doctorates awarded. *Degree requirements:* For master's, variable foreign language requirement, thesis, fieldwork, research project; for doctorate, variable foreign language requirement, comprehensive exam, thesis/dissertation. *Entrance requirements:* For master's, GRE (minimum revised GRE scores of 146 verbal and 146 quantitative), minimum undergraduate GPA of 3.0; for doctorate, GRE General Test, MPH or MSPH, minimum GPA of 3.0, interview. Additional exam requirements/recommendations for international students: Recommended—TOEFL (minimum score 550 paper-based; 79 iBT), IELTS (minimum score 6.5). *Application deadline:* For fall admission, 4/1 for domestic students. Application fee: $60 ($75 for international students). *Expenses:* Contact institution. *Financial support:* Fellowships and career-related internships or fieldwork available. *Unit head:* Dr. Inmaculada Aban, Director, 205-934-2732, Fax: 205-975-2540, E-mail: bstgrad@uab.edu. Website: http://www.soph.uab.edu/bst.

The University of Alabama at Birmingham, School of Public Health, Program in Public Health, Birmingham, AL 35294. Offers accelerated industrial hygiene (MPH); applied epidemiology (MSPH); biostatistics (MPH); clinical and translational science (MSPH); environmental health (MPH); environmental health and toxicology (MSPH); epidemiology (MPH); general theory and practice (MPH); health behavior (MPH); health care organization (MPH); health policy quantitative policy analysis (MPH); industrial hygiene (MPH, MSPH); maternal and child health policy (Dr PH); maternal and child health policy and leadership (MPH); occupational health and safety (MPH); outcomes research (MSPH, Dr PH); pharmacoepidemiology and comparative effectiveness research (MSPH); public health (PhD); public health management (Dr PH); public health preparedness management (MPH). *Accreditation:* CEPH. *Students:* 223 full-time (153 women), 66 part-time (41 women); includes 76 minority (48 Black or African American, non-Hispanic/Latino; 19 Asian, non-Hispanic/Latino; 8 Hispanic/Latino; 1 Two or more races, non-Hispanic/Latino), 44 international. Average age 28. In 2012, 99 master's, 4 doctorates awarded. *Entrance requirements:* For master's and doctorate, GRE, evaluations. Additional exam requirements/recommendations for international students: Recommended—TOEFL (minimum score 550 paper-based; 79 iBT), IELTS (minimum score 6.5). *Expenses:* Tuition, state resident: full-time $6420; part-time $335 per credit hour. Tuition, nonresident: full-time $14,574; part-time $788 per credit hour. Tuition and fees vary according to course load and program. Website: http://www.soph.uab.edu.

University of Alberta, Faculty of Graduate Studies and Research, Department of Mathematical and Statistical Sciences, Edmonton, AB T6G 2E1, Canada. Offers applied mathematics (M Sc, PhD); biostatistics (M Sc); mathematical finance (M Sc, PhD); mathematical physics (M Sc, PhD); mathematics (M Sc, PhD); statistics (M Sc, PhD, Postgraduate Diploma). Part-time programs available. Terminal master's awarded for partial completion of doctoral program. *Degree requirements:* For master's, thesis (for some programs); for doctorate, comprehensive exam, thesis/dissertation. *Entrance requirements:* Additional exam requirements/recommendations for international students: Required—TOEFL (minimum score 580 paper-based). Electronic applications accepted. *Faculty research:* Classical and functional analysis, algebra, differential equations, geometry.

The University of Arizona, Mel and Enid Zuckerman College of Public Health, Program in Biostatistics, Tucson, AZ 85721. Offers PhD. *Faculty:* 12 full-time (7 women), 1 (woman) part-time/adjunct. *Students:* 12 full-time (8 women), 3 part-time (all women); includes 5 minority (1 Black or African American, non-Hispanic/ Latino; 1 Asian, non-Hispanic/Latino; 2 Hispanic/Latino; 1 Two or more races, non-Hispanic/Latino), 3 international. Average age 33. 30 applicants, 20% accepted, 3 enrolled. *Entrance requirements:* Additional exam requirements/ recommendations for international students: Required—TOEFL (minimum score 550 paper-based; 79 iBT). *Application deadline:* For fall admission, 1/1 for domestic and international students. Applications are processed on a rolling basis. Application fee: $75. Electronic applications accepted. *Financial support:* In 2012–13, 4 research assistantships (averaging $18,151 per year), 12 teaching assistantships (averaging $18,469 per year) were awarded. *Total annual research expenditures:* $2.8 million. *Unit head:* Dr. Iman Hakim, Interim Dean, 520-626-7083, E-mail: ihakim@email.arizona.edu. *Application contact:* Lorraine Varela, Special Assistant to the Dean, 520-626-3201, E-mail: coph-admit@email.arizona.edu.

University of California, Berkeley, Graduate Division, School of Public Health, Group in Biostatistics, Berkeley, CA 94720-1500. Offers MA, PhD. *Accreditation:* CEPH (one or more programs are accredited). *Degree requirements:* For master's, oral exam; for doctorate, thesis/dissertation, oral exam. *Entrance requirements:* For master's and doctorate, GRE General Test, minimum GPA of 3.0, 3 letters of recommendation. Additional exam requirements/recommendations for international students: Required—TOEFL.

University of California, Davis, Graduate Studies, Graduate Group in Biostatistics, Davis, CA 95616. Offers MS, PhD. *Degree requirements:* For master's, comprehensive exam; for doctorate, thesis/dissertation. *Entrance requirements:* Additional exam requirements/recommendations for international students: Required—TOEFL (minimum score 550 paper-based). Electronic applications accepted.

University of California, Los Angeles, Graduate Division, School of Public Health, Department of Biostatistics, Los Angeles, CA 90095. Offers MPH, MS, Dr PH, PhD. *Degree requirements:* For master's, comprehensive exam; for doctorate, thesis/dissertation, oral and written qualifying exams. *Entrance requirements:* For master's, GRE General Test, minimum GPA of 3.0; for doctorate, GRE General Test, minimum undergraduate GPA of 3.0. Electronic applications accepted. *Expenses:* Tuition, nonresident: full-time $15,102. *Required fees:* $14,809.19. Full-time tuition and fees vary according to program.

University of Cincinnati, Graduate School, College of Medicine, Graduate Programs in Biomedical Sciences, Department of Environmental Health, Cincinnati, OH 45221. Offers environmental and industrial hygiene (MS, PhD); environmental and occupational medicine (MS); environmental genetics and molecular toxicology (MS, PhD); epidemiology and biostatistics (MS, PhD); occupational safety and ergonomics (MS, PhD). *Accreditation:* ABET (one or more programs are accredited). Terminal master's awarded for partial completion of doctoral program. *Degree requirements:* For master's, thesis; for doctorate, thesis/dissertation, qualifying exam. *Entrance requirements:* For master's, GRE General Test, bachelor's degree in science; for doctorate, GRE General Test. Additional exam requirements/recommendations for international students: Required—TOEFL (minimum score 600 paper-based; 100 iBT). Electronic applications accepted. *Faculty research:* Carcinogens and mutagenesis, pulmonary studies, reproduction and development.

University of Colorado Denver, Colorado School of Public Health, Department of Biostatistics and Informatics, Aurora, CO 80045. Offers MS, PhD. Part-time programs available. *Students:* 20 full-time (11 women), 15 part-time (6 women); includes 8 minority (1 American Indian or Alaska Native, non-Hispanic/Latino; 4 Asian, non-Hispanic/Latino; 2 Hispanic/Latino; 1 Two or more races, non-Hispanic/Latino), 5 international. Average age 33. 29 applicants, 31% accepted, 9 enrolled. In 2012, 6 master's awarded. Terminal master's awarded for partial completion of doctoral program. *Degree requirements:* For master's, 34 credit hours, project or thesis; for doctorate, comprehensive exam, thesis/dissertation, 78 credit hours (25 of which can be completed while completing a master's degree). *Entrance requirements:* For master's, GRE General Test, baccalaureate degree in scientific field, minimum GPA of 3.0, math course work through integral calculus, two official copies of all academic transcripts, four letters of recommendation/reference, essays describing the applicant's career goals and reasons for applying to the program, resume; for doctorate, GRE General Test, baccalaureate degree in scientific field; master's degree in biostatistics, statistics or equivalent; minimum GPA of 3.0; math course work through integral calculus; two official copies of all academic transcripts; four letters of recommendation/reference; essays; resume. Additional exam requirements/recommendations for international students: Required—TOEFL (minimum score 550 paper-based; 80 iBT). *Application deadline:* For fall admission, 2/1 for domestic students. Application fee: $65 ($75 for international students). Electronic applications accepted. *Expenses:* Contact institution. *Financial support:* In 2012–13, 22 students received support. Fellowships, research assistantships, teaching assistantships, Federal Work-Study, institutionally sponsored loans, scholarships/grants, traineeships, and unspecified assistantships available. Financial award application deadline: 3/1; financial award applicants required to submit FAFSA. *Faculty research:* Health policy research, nonlinear mixed effects models for longitudinal data, statistical methods in nutrition, clinical trials. *Unit head:* Dr. Dennis Lezotte, Chair, 303-724-4365, Fax: 303-724-4620, E-mail: dennis.lezotte@ucdenver.edu. *Application contact:* John Neal, Department Assistant, 303-724-4370, Fax: 303-724-4620, E-mail: john.neal@ucdenver.edu. Website: http://www.ucdenver.edu/academics/colleges/PublicHealth/departments/Biostatistics/Pages/welcome.aspx.

University of Florida, Graduate School, College of Public Health and Health Professions, Programs in Public Health, Gainesville, FL 32611. Offers biostatistics (MPH); environmental health (MPH); epidemiology (MPH); public health management and policy (MPH); public health practice (MPH); social and behavioral sciences (MPH). *Accreditation:* CEPH. Postbaccalaureate distance learning degree programs offered. *Degree requirements:* For master's, internship.

Entrance requirements: For master's, GRE General Test, minimum GPA of 3.0. Additional exam requirements/recommendations for international students: Required—TOEFL (minimum score 550 paper-based; 80 iBT), IELTS (minimum score 6).

University of Illinois at Chicago, Graduate College, School of Public Health, Biostatistics Section, Chicago, IL 60607-7128. Offers biostatistics (MS, PhD); quantitative methods (MPH). Part-time programs available. *Students:* 23 full-time (13 women), 14 part-time (8 women); includes 10 minority (2 Black or African American, non-Hispanic/Latino; 7 Asian, non-Hispanic/Latino; 1 Two or more races, non-Hispanic/Latino), 12 international. Average age 32. 63 applicants, 56% accepted, 8 enrolled. In 2012, 10 master's, 5 doctorates awarded. Terminal master's awarded for partial completion of doctoral program. *Degree requirements:* For master's, thesis, field practicum; for doctorate, thesis/dissertation, independent research, internship. *Entrance requirements:* For master's and doctorate, GRE General Test, minimum GPA of 2.75. Additional exam requirements/recommendations for international students: Required—TOEFL. *Application deadline:* For fall admission, 2/1 for domestic students, 1/1 for international students. Application fee: $40 ($50 for international students). Electronic applications accepted. *Expenses:* Tuition, state resident: full-time $10,882; part-time $3627 per term. Tuition, nonresident: full-time $22,880; part-time $7627 per term. *Required fees:* $1170 per semester. Tuition and fees vary according to course load, degree level and program. *Financial support:* In 2012–13, 17 students received support. Fellowships with full tuition reimbursements available, research assistantships with full tuition reimbursements available, teaching assistantships with full tuition reimbursements available, career-related internships or fieldwork, Federal Work-Study, institutionally sponsored loans, scholarships/grants, traineeships, tuition waivers (full), and unspecified assistantships available. Support available to part-time students. Financial award application deadline: 3/1; financial award applicants required to submit FAFSA. *Faculty research:* Quantitative methods. *Total annual research expenditures:* $842,000. *Unit head:* Dr. Sally Freels, Section Coordinator, 312-996-4763, E-mail: sallyf@uic.edu. Website: http://publichealth.uic.edu/departments/epidemiologyandbiostatistics/.

The University of Iowa, Graduate College, College of Public Health, Department of Biostatistics, Iowa City, IA 52242-1316. Offers MS, PhD. *Degree requirements:* For master's, thesis optional, exam; for doctorate, comprehensive exam, thesis/dissertation. *Entrance requirements:* For master's and doctorate, GRE General Test, minimum GPA of 3.0. Additional exam requirements/recommendations for international students: Required—TOEFL (minimum score 600 paper-based; 100 iBT). Electronic applications accepted.

The University of Kansas, University of Kansas Medical Center, School of Medicine, Department of Biostatistics, Kansas City, KS 66160. Offers MS, PhD. *Faculty:* 13. *Students:* 10 full-time (6 women), 2 part-time (both women); includes 1 minority (Asian, non-Hispanic/Latino), 6 international. Average age 28. 17 applicants, 88% accepted, 5 enrolled. In 2012, 1 master's awarded. *Degree requirements:* For master's, comprehensive exam; for doctorate, comprehensive exam, thesis/dissertation. *Entrance requirements:* For master's, GRE, coursework in calculus, computer programming, linear algebra, differential equations, and numerical analysis; for doctorate, master's degree. Additional exam requirements/recommendations for international students: Required—TOEFL. *Application deadline:* For fall admission, 3/1 for domestic and international students. Application fee: $60. Electronic applications accepted. *Financial support:* Research assistantships with full tuition reimbursements, scholarships/grants, traineeships, and unspecified assistantships available. Financial award application deadline: 3/1; financial award applicants required to submit FAFSA. *Faculty research:* Biostatistics, clinical trials. *Total annual research expenditures:* $398,000. *Unit head:* Dr. Matthew Mayo, Chair and Professor, 913-588-4735 Ext. 913, Fax: 913-588-0252, E-mail: mmayo@kumc.edu. *Application contact:* Dr. Jo A. Wick, Assistant Director of Graduate Education, 913-588-4790, Fax: 913-588-0252, E-mail: jwick@kumc.edu. Website: http://biostatistics.kumc.edu/.

The University of Kansas, University of Kansas Medical Center, School of Medicine, Department of Preventive Medicine and Public Health, Kansas City, KS 66160. Offers biostatistics (MPH); clinical research (MS); environmental health sciences (MPH); epidemiology (MPH); public health management (MPH); social and behavioral health (MPH); MD/MPH; PhD/MPH. Part-time programs available. *Faculty:* 81. *Students:* 42 full-time (28 women), 66 part-time (47 women); includes 35 minority (10 Black or African American, non-Hispanic/Latino; 3 American Indian or Alaska Native, non-Hispanic/Latino; 7 Asian, non-Hispanic/Latino; 8 Hispanic/Latino; 7 Two or more races, non-Hispanic/Latino), 6 international. Average age 34. 83 applicants, 61% accepted, 36 enrolled. In 2012, 47 master's awarded. *Degree requirements:* For master's, thesis, capstone practicum defense. *Entrance requirements:* For master's, GRE, MCAT, LSAT, GMAT or other equivalent graduate professional exam. Additional exam requirements/recommendations for international students: Required—TOEFL. *Application deadline:* For fall admission, 3/1 for domestic and international students. Applications are processed on a rolling basis. Application fee: $60. Electronic applications accepted. *Financial support:* Research assistantships, career-related internships or fieldwork, Federal Work-Study, scholarships/grants, and unspecified assistantships available. Financial award application deadline: 3/1; financial award applicants required to submit FAFSA. *Faculty research:* Cancer screening and prevention, smoking cessation, obesity and physical activity, health services/outcomes research, health disparities. *Total annual research expenditures:* $8.6 million. *Unit head:* Dr. Edward F. Ellerbeck, Chairman, 913-

Peterson's Graduate Programs in the Physical Sciences, Mathematics, Agricultural Sciences, the Environment & Natural Resources 2014

www.petersonsbooks.com   **299**

588-2774, Fax: 913-588-2780, E-mail: eellerbe@kumc.edu. *Application contact:* Tanya Honderick, MPH Director, 913-588-2720, Fax: 913-588-8505, E-mail: thonderick@kumc.edu. Website: http://ph.kumc.edu/.

University of Louisville, Graduate School, School of Public Health and Information Sciences, Department of Bioinformatics and Biostatistics, Louisville, KY 40292-0001. Offers biostatistics (MS, PhD); decision science (MS). Part-time programs available. *Students:* 21 full-time (7 women), 2 part-time (both women); includes 5 minority (all Asian, non-Hispanic/Latino), 12 international. Average age 31. 26 applicants, 50% accepted, 8 enrolled. In 2012, 5 master's, 1 doctorate awarded. *Degree requirements:* For master's, thesis; for doctorate, comprehensive exam, thesis/dissertation. *Entrance requirements:* For master's and doctorate, GRE, official transcripts, statement of purpose, resume/curriculum vitae, letters of recommendation. Additional exam requirements/ recommendations for international students: Required—TOEFL (minimum score 600 paper-based; 100 iBT). *Application deadline:* For fall admission, 3/1 for domestic and international students. Application fee: $60. Electronic applications accepted. *Financial support:* In 2012–13, 9 students received support, including 3 research assistantships with full tuition reimbursements available (averaging $20,000 per year); health care benefits and unspecified assistantships also available. Financial award applicants required to submit FAFSA. *Faculty research:* Bioinformatics, compound decision problems, infectious disease modeling, inference, statistical genetics, genomics, clinical trials, information theory, utility theory and measurement. *Total annual research expenditures:* $173,590. *Unit head:* Dr. Robert Esterhay, Interim Department Chair, 502-852-6135, Fax: 502-852-3294, E-mail: robert.esterhay@louisville.edu. *Application contact:* Lynne Dosker, Administrative Assistant, 502-852-1827, Fax: 502-852-3294, E-mail: lcdosk01@louisville.edu. Website: http://www.louisville.edu/sphis.

University of Maryland, Baltimore, School of Medicine, Department of Epidemiology and Public Health, Baltimore, MD 21201. Offers biostatistics (MS); clinical research (MS); epidemiology and preventive medicine (MPH, MS, PhD); gerontology (PhD); human genetics and genomic medicine (MS, PhD); molecular epidemiology (MS, PhD); toxicology (MS, PhD); JD/MS; MD/PhD; MS/PhD. *Accreditation:* CEPH. Part-time programs available. *Students:* 80 full-time (54 women), 71 part-time (50 women); includes 50 minority (21 Black or African American, non-Hispanic/Latino; 23 Asian, non-Hispanic/Latino; 6 Hispanic/Latino), 25 international. Average age 32. 145 applicants, 29% accepted, 24 enrolled. In 2012, 25 master's, 12 doctorates awarded. *Degree requirements:* For doctorate, comprehensive exam, thesis/dissertation. *Entrance requirements:* For master's and doctorate, GRE General Test. Additional exam requirements/ recommendations for international students: Required—TOEFL (minimum score 550 paper-based; 80 iBT); Recommended—IELTS (minimum score 7). *Application deadline:* For fall admission, 2/1 for domestic students, 1/15 for international students. Application fee: $50. Electronic applications accepted. *Expenses:* Contact institution. *Financial support:* In 2012–13, research assistantships with partial tuition reimbursements (averaging $25,000 per year) were awarded; fellowships, Federal Work-Study, scholarships/grants, and unspecified assistantships also available. Financial award application deadline: 3/ 1; financial award applicants required to submit FAFSA. *Unit head:* Dr. Laura Hungerford, Program Director, 410-706-8492, Fax: 410-706-4225. *Application contact:* Danielle Fitzpatrick, Program Coordinator, 410-706-8492, Fax: 410-706-4225, E-mail: dfitzpatrick@epi.umaryland.edu. Website: http:// medschool.umaryland.edu/Epidemiology/.

University of Maryland, Baltimore County, Graduate School, College of Natural and Mathematical Sciences, Department of Mathematics and Statistics, Program in Statistics, Baltimore, MD 21250. Offers biostatistics (PhD); environmental statistics (MS); statistics (MS, PhD). Part-time and evening/weekend programs available. *Faculty:* 10 full-time (3 women). *Students:* 29 full-time (16 women), 20 part-time (9 women); includes 10 minority (5 Black or African American, non-Hispanic/Latino; 5 Asian, non-Hispanic/Latino), 19 international. Average age 33. 47 applicants, 49% accepted, 5 enrolled. In 2012, 9 master's, 1 doctorate awarded. Terminal master's awarded for partial completion of doctoral program. *Degree requirements:* For master's, comprehensive exam (for some programs), thesis (for some programs); for doctorate, comprehensive exam, thesis/ dissertation. *Entrance requirements:* For master's and doctorate, GRE General Test, minimum GPA of 3.0. Additional exam requirements/recommendations for international students: Required—TOEFL (minimum score 600 paper-based; 100 iBT). *Application deadline:* For fall admission, 2/15 priority date for domestic students, 1/1 for international students; for spring admission, 10/15 priority date for domestic students, 5/1 for international students. Applications are processed on a rolling basis. Application fee: $50. Electronic applications accepted. *Financial support:* In 2012–13, 22 students received support, including 1 fellowship with full tuition reimbursement available (averaging $15,500 per year), 4 research assistantships with full tuition reimbursements available (averaging $15,500 per year), 17 teaching assistantships with full and partial tuition reimbursements available (averaging $15,500 per year); career-related internships or fieldwork, scholarships/grants, health care benefits, tuition waivers (full and partial), and unspecified assistantships also available. Support available to part-time students. Financial award application deadline: 2/15. *Faculty research:* Design of experiments, statistical decision theory and inference, time series analysis, biostatistics and environmental statistics, bioinformatics. *Total annual research expenditures:* $690,828. *Unit head:* Dr. Anindya Roy, Director, 410-455-2435, Fax: 410-455-1066, E-mail: anindya@umbc.edu. Website: http:// www.math.umbc.edu.

University of Maryland, College Park, Academic Affairs, School of Public Health, Department of Epidemiology and Biostatistics, College Park, MD 20742. Offers biostatistics (MPH); epidemiology (MPH, PhD). *Faculty:* 15 full-time (7 women), 3 part-time/adjunct (1 woman). *Students:* 18 full-time (10 women), 13 part-time (11 women); includes 10 minority (5 Asian, non-Hispanic/Latino; 2 Hispanic/Latino; 3 Two or more races, non-Hispanic/Latino), 5 international. 184 applicants, 6% accepted, 9 enrolled. In 2012, 7 master's awarded. *Application deadline:* For fall admission, 1/15 for domestic and international students. Application fee: $75. *Expenses:* Tuition, state resident: part-time $551 per credit. Tuition, nonresident: part-time $1188 per credit. Part-time tuition and fees vary according to program. *Financial support:* In 2012–13, 3 fellowships with full tuition reimbursements (averaging $26,735 per year), 6 research assistantships (averaging $15,997 per year), 2 teaching assistantships (averaging $16,259 per year) were awarded. *Total annual research expenditures:* $1 million. *Unit head:* Dr. Mei-Ling Lee, Chair, 301-405-4581, E-mail: mltlee@umd.edu. *Application contact:* Dr. Charles A. Caramello, Dean of Graduate School, 301-405-0358, Fax: 301-314-9305. Website: http://www.sph.umd.edu/epib/.

University of Massachusetts Amherst, Graduate School, School of Public Health and Health Sciences, Department of Public Health, Amherst, MA 01003. Offers biostatistics (MPH, MS, PhD); community health education (MPH, MS, PhD); environmental health sciences (MPH, MS, PhD); epidemiology (MPH, MS, PhD); health policy and management (MPH, MS, PhD); nutrition (MPH, PhD); public health practice (MPH); MPH/MPPA. *Accreditation:* CEPH (one or more programs are accredited). Part-time and evening/weekend programs available. Postbaccalaureate distance learning degree programs offered (no on-campus study). *Faculty:* 50 full-time (29 women). *Students:* 113 full-time (82 women), 262 part-time (193 women); includes 80 minority (34 Black or African American, non-Hispanic/Latino; 19 Asian, non-Hispanic/Latino; 18 Hispanic/Latino; 9 Two or more races, non-Hispanic/Latino), 50 international. Average age 36. 367 applicants, 62% accepted, 87 enrolled. In 2012, 83 master's, 6 doctorates awarded. Terminal master's awarded for partial completion of doctoral program. *Degree requirements:* For master's, thesis (for some programs); for doctorate, comprehensive exam, thesis/dissertation. *Entrance requirements:* For master's and doctorate, GRE General Test. Additional exam requirements/ recommendations for international students: Required—TOEFL (minimum score 550 paper-based; 80 iBT), IELTS (minimum score 6.5). *Application deadline:* For fall admission, 2/1 for domestic and international students. Applications are processed on a rolling basis. Application fee: $75. Electronic applications accepted. *Expenses:* Tuition, state resident: full-time $1980; part-time $110 per credit. Tuition, nonresident: full-time $13,314; part-time $414 per credit. *Required fees:* $10,338; $3594 per semester. One-time fee: $357. *Financial support:* Fellowships with full and partial tuition reimbursements, research assistantships with full and partial tuition reimbursements, teaching assistantships with full and partial tuition reimbursements, career-related internships or fieldwork, Federal Work-Study, scholarships/grants, traineeships, health care benefits, tuition waivers (full and partial), and unspecified assistantships available. Support available to part-time students. Financial award application deadline: 2/1; financial award applicants required to submit FAFSA. *Unit head:* Dr. Paula Stamps, Graduate Program Director, 413-545-2861, Fax: 413-545-1645. *Application contact:* Lindsay DeSantis, Supervisor of Admissions, 413-545-0722, Fax: 413-577-0010, E-mail: gradadm@grad.umass.edu. Website: http://www.umass.edu/ sphhs/public_health/.

University of Medicine and Dentistry of New Jersey, UMDNJ–School of Public Health (UMDNJ, Rutgers, NJIT) Piscataway/New Brunswick Campus, Piscataway, NJ 08854. Offers biostatistics (MPH, MS, Dr PH, PhD); clinical epidemiology (Certificate); environmental and occupational health (MPH, Dr PH, PhD, Certificate); epidemiology (MPH, Dr PH, PhD); general public health (Certificate); health education and behavioral science (MPH, Dr PH, PhD); health systems and policy (MPH, PhD); public health preparedness (Certificate); DO/ MPH; JD/MPH; MD/MPH; MPH/MBA; MPH/MSPA; MS/MPH; Psy D/MPH. *Accreditation:* CEPH. Part-time and evening/weekend programs available. *Degree requirements:* For master's, thesis, internship; for doctorate, comprehensive exam, thesis/dissertation. *Entrance requirements:* For master's, GRE General Test; for doctorate, GRE General Test, MPH (Dr PH); MA, MPH, or MS (PhD). Additional exam requirements/recommendations for international students: Required—TOEFL. Electronic applications accepted.

University of Memphis, Graduate School, School of Public Health, Memphis, TN 38152. Offers biostatistics (MPH); environmental health (MPH); epidemiology (MPH); health systems management (MPH); public health (MHA); social and behavioral sciences (MPH). Part-time and evening/weekend programs available. Postbaccalaureate distance learning degree programs offered. *Degree requirements:* For master's, comprehensive exam, thesis. *Entrance requirements:* For master's, GRE, letters of recommendation. Additional exam requirements/ recommendations for international students: Required—TOEFL. Electronic applications accepted. *Faculty research:* Health and medical savings accounts, adoption rates, health informatics, Telehealth technologies, biostatistics, environmental health, epidemiology, health systems management, social and behavioral sciences.

University of Michigan, School of Public Health, Department of Biostatistics, Ann Arbor, MI 48109. Offers MPH, MS, PhD. MS and PhD offered through the Horace H. Rackham School of Graduate Studies. Terminal master's awarded for partial completion of doctoral program. *Degree requirements:* For doctorate, oral defense of dissertation, qualifying exam. *Entrance requirements:* For master's,

GRE General Test; for doctorate, GRE General Test, master's degree. Additional exam requirements/recommendations for international students: Required—TOEFL (minimum score 560 paper-based; 100 iBT). Electronic applications accepted. *Faculty research:* Statistical genetics, categorical data analysis, incomplete data, survival analysis, modeling.

University of Michigan, School of Public Health, Program in Clinical Research Design and Statistical Analysis, Ann Arbor, MI 48109. Offers MS. Offered through the Horace H. Rackham School of Graduate Studies; program admits applicants in odd-numbered calendar years only. Evening/weekend programs available. *Degree requirements:* For master's, comprehensive exam. *Entrance requirements:* For master's, GRE General Test or MCAT. Additional exam requirements/recommendations for international students: Recommended—TOEFL (minimum score 560 paper-based; 100 iBT). Electronic applications accepted. *Expenses:* Contact institution. *Faculty research:* Survival analysis, missing data, Bayesian inference, health economics, quality of life.

University of Minnesota, Twin Cities Campus, School of Public Health, Major in Biostatistics, Minneapolis, MN 55455-0213. Offers MPH, MS, PhD. Part-time programs available. Terminal master's awarded for partial completion of doctoral program. *Degree requirements:* For master's, comprehensive exam; for doctorate, comprehensive exam, thesis/dissertation. *Entrance requirements:* For master's, GRE General Test, course work in applied statistics, computer programming, multivariable calculus, linear algebra; for doctorate, GRE General Test, bachelor's or master's degree in statistics, biostatistics or mathematics. Additional exam requirements/recommendations for international students: Required—TOEFL (minimum score 600 paper-based; 90 iBT). Electronic applications accepted. *Faculty research:* Analysis of spatial and longitudinal data, Bayes/Empirical Bayes methods, survival analysis, longitudinal models, generalized linear models.

The University of North Carolina at Chapel Hill, Graduate School, Gillings School of Global Public Health, Department of Biostatistics, Chapel Hill, NC 27599. Offers MPH, MS, Dr PH, PhD. *Faculty:* 34. *Students:* 154 full-time (75 women); includes 38 minority (9 Black or African American, non-Hispanic/Latino; 18 Asian, non-Hispanic/Latino; 3 Hispanic/Latino; 4 Native Hawaiian or other Pacific Islander, non-Hispanic/Latino; 4 Two or more races, non-Hispanic/Latino), 54 international. Average age 26. 292 applicants, 33% accepted, 41 enrolled. In 2012, 13 master's, 14 doctorates awarded. *Degree requirements:* For master's, comprehensive exam, thesis, major paper; for doctorate, comprehensive exam, thesis/dissertation. *Entrance requirements:* For master's and doctorate, GRE General Test, minimum GPA of 3.0 (recommended). Additional exam requirements/recommendations for international students: Required—TOEFL, IELTS. *Application deadline:* For fall admission, 12/10 priority date for domestic students, 12/10 for international students. Applications are processed on a rolling basis. Application fee: $85. Electronic applications accepted. *Financial support:* Fellowships with tuition reimbursements, research assistantships with tuition reimbursements, teaching assistantships with tuition reimbursements, Federal Work-Study, institutionally sponsored loans, traineeships, health care benefits, and unspecified assistantships available. Financial award application deadline: 1/1; financial award applicants required to submit FAFSA. *Faculty research:* Cancer, cardiovascular, environmental biostatistics; AIDS and other infectious diseases; statistical genetics; demography and population studies. *Unit head:* Dr. Michael R. Kosorok, Chair, 919-966-7254, Fax: 919-966-3804. *Application contact:* Melissa Hobgood, Student Services Manager, 919-966-7256, Fax: 919-966-3804, E-mail: hobgood@unc.edu. Website: http://www2.sph.unc.edu/bios/.

University of North Texas Health Science Center at Fort Worth, School of Public Health, Fort Worth, TX 76107-2699. Offers biostatistics (MPH); community health (MPH); disease control and prevention (Dr PH); environmental and occupational health sciences (MPH); epidemiology (MPH); health administration (MHA); health policy and management (MPH, Dr PH); DO/MPH; MS/MPH; MSN/MPH. MPH offered jointly with University of North Texas; DO/MPH with Texas College of Osteopathic Medicine. *Accreditation:* CEPH. Part-time and evening/weekend programs available. *Degree requirements:* For master's, thesis or alternative, supervised internship; for doctorate, thesis/dissertation, supervised internship. *Entrance requirements:* For master's, GRE General Test. Additional exam requirements/recommendations for international students: Required—TOEFL. Electronic applications accepted.

University of Oklahoma Health Sciences Center, Graduate College, College of Public Health, Program in Biostatistics and Epidemiology, Oklahoma City, OK 73190. Offers biostatistics (MPH, MS, Dr PH, PhD); epidemiology (MPH, MS, Dr PH, PhD). *Accreditation:* CEPH (one or more programs are accredited). Part-time programs available. *Faculty:* 12 full-time (8 women), 1 (woman) part-time/adjunct. *Students:* 17 full-time (12 women), 21 part-time (13 women); includes 11 minority (2 Black or African American, non-Hispanic/Latino; 2 Asian, non-Hispanic/Latino; 2 Hispanic/Latino; 5 Two or more races, non-Hispanic/Latino), 8 international. Average age 32. 44 applicants, 27% accepted, 5 enrolled. In 2012, 11 master's, 1 doctorate awarded. *Degree requirements:* For master's, comprehensive exam, thesis (for some programs); for doctorate, comprehensive exam, thesis/dissertation. *Entrance requirements:* For master's, 3 letters of recommendation, resume; for doctorate, GRE General Test, letters of recommendation. Additional exam requirements/recommendations for international students: Required—TOEFL (minimum score 570 paper-based), TWE. *Application deadline:* For fall admission, 7/1 for domestic students; for winter admission, 4/1 for domestic students; for spring admission, 12/1 for domestic students. Applications are processed on a rolling basis. Application fee: $50. *Financial support:* In 2012–13, 7 research assistantships (averaging $14,000 per year) were awarded; career-related internships or fieldwork, institutionally sponsored loans, and traineeships also available. Support available to part-time students. Financial award application deadline: 5/1. *Faculty research:* Statistical methodology, applied statistics, acute and chronic disease epidemiology. *Unit head:* Dr. Willis Owen, Interim Chair, 405-271-2229, E-mail: willis-owen@ouhsc.edu. *Application contact:* Robin Howell, Information Contact, 405-271-2308, E-mail: robin_howell@ouhsc.edu.

University of Pennsylvania, Perelman School of Medicine, Biomedical Graduate Studies, Graduate Group in Epidemiology and Biostatistics, Philadelphia, PA 19104. Offers biostatistics (MS, PhD). Part-time programs available. *Faculty:* 103 full-time (41 women). *Students:* 28 full-time (18 women), 7 part-time (1 woman); includes 19 minority (all Asian, non-Hispanic/Latino). Average age 25. 94 applicants, 23% accepted, 10 enrolled. In 2012, 6 master's, 8 doctorates awarded. Terminal master's awarded for partial completion of doctoral program. *Degree requirements:* For master's, thesis, evaluations examination; for doctorate, thesis/dissertation, evaluations exam, preliminary exam. *Entrance requirements:* For master's and doctorate, GRE, 1 year of course work in calculus, 1 semester of course work in linear algebra, working knowledge of programming language. Additional exam requirements/recommendations for international students: Required—TOEFL. *Application deadline:* For fall admission, 12/1 for domestic and international students. Application fee: $70. *Financial support:* In 2012–13, 24 students received support, including 7 fellowships with full and partial tuition reimbursements available (averaging $24,500 per year), 12 research assistantships with full and partial tuition reimbursements available (averaging $24,500 per year), teaching assistantships with full and partial tuition reimbursements available (averaging $24,500 per year); career-related internships or fieldwork, institutionally sponsored loans, scholarships/grants, traineeships, health care benefits, and unspecified assistantships also available. Financial award application deadline: 12/1. *Faculty research:* Randomized clinical trials, data coordinating centers, methodological approaches to non-experimental epidemiologic studies, theoretical research in biostatistics. *Total annual research expenditures:* $43 million. *Unit head:* Dr. Mary Putt, Director, 215-573-7020, Fax: 215-573-4865, E-mail: mputt@mail.med.upenn.edu. *Application contact:* Catherine Vallejo, Coordinator, Educational Programs in Biostatistics, 215-573-3881, Fax: 215-573-4865, E-mail: vallejo@mail.med.upenn.edu. Website: http://www.cceb.upenn.edu/.

University of Pittsburgh, Graduate School of Public Health, Department of Biostatistics, Pittsburgh, PA 15260. Offers MPH, MS, PhD. Part-time programs available. *Faculty:* 26 full-time (10 women), 20 part-time/adjunct (8 women). *Students:* 85 full-time (50 women), 12 part-time (9 women); includes 17 minority (4 Black or African American, non-Hispanic/Latino; 11 Asian, non-Hispanic/Latino; 1 Hispanic/Latino; 1 Two or more races, non-Hispanic/Latino), 56 international. Average age 31. 176 applicants, 72% accepted, 22 enrolled. In 2012, 9 master's, 8 doctorates awarded. Terminal master's awarded for partial completion of doctoral program. *Degree requirements:* For master's, comprehensive exam, thesis; for doctorate, one foreign language, comprehensive exam, thesis/dissertation. *Entrance requirements:* For master's, GRE General Test, previous course work in biology, calculus and computer science; prior professional degree (for MPH); for doctorate, GRE General Test, previous course work in biology, calculus, and computer science. Additional exam requirements/recommendations for international students: Required—TOEFL (minimum score 550 paper-based; 80 iBT) or IELTS (minimum score 6.5). *Application deadline:* For fall admission, 3/30 priority date for domestic students, 3/1 for international students; for spring admission, 11/30 for domestic students, 4/5 for international students. Applications are processed on a rolling basis. Application fee: $115. Electronic applications accepted. *Expenses:* Tuition, state resident: full-time $19,336; part-time $782 per credit. Tuition, nonresident: full-time $31,658; part-time $1295 per credit. *Required fees:* $740; $200 per term. Tuition and fees vary according to program. *Financial support:* In 2012–13, 62 students received support, including 53 research assistantships with full and partial tuition reimbursements available (averaging $11,732 per year), 9 teaching assistantships with full and partial tuition reimbursements available (averaging $11,891 per year); scholarships/grants also available. Financial award application deadline: 4/15; financial award applicants required to submit FAFSA. *Faculty research:* Survival analysis, environmental risk assessment, statistical computing, longitudinal data analysis, experimental design. *Total annual research expenditures:* $3.6 million. *Unit head:* Dr. Sally C. Morton, Chair, 412-624-3022, Fax: 412-624-2183, E-mail: scmorton@pitt.edu. *Application contact:* Renee N. Valenti, Academic Affairs Administrator, 412-624-3023, Fax: 412-624-0184, E-mail: rmn4@pitt.edu. Website: http://www.biostat.pitt.edu/.

University of Puerto Rico, Medical Sciences Campus, Graduate School of Public Health, Department of Social Sciences, Program in Biostatistics, San Juan, PR 00936-5067. Offers MPH. Part-time programs available. *Entrance requirements:* For master's, GRE, previous course work in algebra. *Expenses:* Contact institution.

University of Rochester, School of Medicine and Dentistry, Graduate Programs in Medicine and Dentistry, Department of Biostatistics and Computational Biology, Program in Medical Statistics, Rochester, NY 14627. Offers MS. *Degree requirements:* For master's, internship/applied project.

University of South Carolina, The Graduate School, Arnold School of Public Health, Department of Epidemiology and Biostatistics, Program in Biostatistics, Columbia, SC 29208. Offers MPH, MSPH, Dr PH, PhD. Part-time programs available. *Degree requirements:* For master's, comprehensive exam, thesis (for some programs), practicum (MPH); for doctorate, comprehensive exam, thesis/dissertation (for some programs), practicum (Dr PH). *Entrance requirements:* For master's, GRE General Test; for doctorate, GRE General Test, master's degree. Additional exam requirements/recommendations for international students: Required—TOEFL (minimum score 570 paper-based; 88 iBT). Electronic applications accepted. *Faculty research:* Bayesian methods, biometric modeling, nonlinear regression, health survey methodology, measurement of health status.

University of Southern California, Keck School of Medicine and Graduate School, Graduate Programs in Medicine, Department of Preventive Medicine, Division of Biostatistics, Los Angeles, CA 90089. Offers applied biostatistics/epidemiology (MS); biostatistics (MS, PhD); epidemiology (PhD); molecular epidemiology (MS). *Faculty:* 71 full-time (30 women). *Students:* 102 full-time (60 women); includes 31 minority (1 Black or African American, non-Hispanic/Latino; 23 Asian, non-Hispanic/Latino; 3 Hispanic/Latino; 1 Native Hawaiian or other Pacific Islander, non-Hispanic/Latino; 3 Two or more races, non-Hispanic/Latino), 52 international. Average age 29. 87 applicants, 48% accepted, 23 enrolled. In 2012, 9 master's, 10 doctorates awarded. Terminal master's awarded for partial completion of doctoral program. *Degree requirements:* For master's, thesis; for doctorate, thesis/dissertation. *Entrance requirements:* For master's, GRE General Test, GRE Subject Test, minimum GPA of 3.0; for doctorate, GRE General Test, GRE Subject Test, minimum GPA of 3.5. Additional exam requirements/recommendations for international students: Required—TOEFL (minimum score 600 paper-based; 100 iBT), IELTS (minimum score 7). *Application deadline:* For fall admission, 12/1 priority date for domestic students, 12/1 for international students; for winter admission, 5/15 priority date for domestic students, 5/15 for international students; for spring admission, 11/1 priority date for domestic students, 11/1 for international students. Applications are processed on a rolling basis. Application fee: $85. Electronic applications accepted. *Financial support:* In 2012–13, 3 fellowships with full tuition reimbursements (averaging $30,000 per year), 37 research assistantships with full tuition reimbursements (averaging $30,000 per year), 23 teaching assistantships with full and partial tuition reimbursements (averaging $30,000 per year) were awarded; career-related internships or fieldwork, Federal Work-Study, institutionally sponsored loans, scholarships/grants, traineeships, health care benefits, and unspecified assistantships also available. Financial award application deadline: 12/1; financial award applicants required to submit CSS PROFILE or FAFSA. *Faculty research:* Clinical trials in ophthalmology and cancer research, methods of analysis for epidemiological studies, genetic epidemiology. *Total annual research expenditures:* $1.3 million. *Unit head:* Dr. William Gauderman, Director, 323-442-2633, Fax: 323-442-2993, E-mail: mtrujill@usc.edu. *Application contact:* Mary L. Trujillo, Student Adviser, 323-442-2633, Fax: 323-442-2993, E-mail: mtrujill@usc.edu. Website: http://keck.usc.edu/Education/Academic_Department_and_Divisions/Department_of_Preventive_Medicine/Divisions/Biostatistics.aspx.

University of Southern California, Keck School of Medicine and Graduate School, Graduate Programs in Medicine, Department of Preventive Medicine, Master of Public Health Program, Los Angeles, CA 91803. Offers biostatistics/epidemiology (MPH); child and family health (MPH); environmental health (MPH); global health leadership (MPH); health communication (MPH); health education and promotion (MPH); public health policy (MPH). *Accreditation:* CEPH. Part-time and evening/weekend programs available. *Faculty:* 22 full-time (12 women), 3 part-time/adjunct (0 women). *Students:* 179 full-time (137 women), 51 part-time (37 women); includes 127 minority (13 Black or African American, non-Hispanic/Latino; 1 American Indian or Alaska Native, non-Hispanic/Latino; 73 Asian, non-Hispanic/Latino; 40 Hispanic/Latino), 33 international. Average age 24. 233 applicants, 71% accepted, 78 enrolled. In 2012, 93 master's awarded. *Degree requirements:* For master's, practicum, final report, oral presentation. *Entrance requirements:* For master's, GRE General Test, MCAT, GMAT, minimum GPA of 3.0. Additional exam requirements/recommendations for international students: Required—TOEFL (minimum score 600 paper-based; 90 iBT). *Application deadline:* For fall admission, 6/1 priority date for domestic students, 6/1 for international students; for spring admission, 11/1 priority date for domestic students, 10/1 for international students. Applications are processed on a rolling basis. Application fee: $85. Electronic applications accepted. *Financial support:* Career-related internships or fieldwork, Federal Work-Study, institutionally sponsored loans, and scholarships/grants available. Support available to part-time students. Financial award application deadline: 5/4; financial award applicants required to submit CSS PROFILE or FAFSA. *Faculty research:* Substance abuse prevention, cancer and heart disease prevention, mass media and health communication research, health promotion, treatment compliance. *Unit head:* Dr. Louise A. Rohrbach, Director, 323-442-8237, Fax: 323-442-8297, E-mail: rohrbac@usc.edu. *Application contact:* Chrystal Martinez, Admissions Counselor, 323-442-7257, Fax: 323-442-8297, E-mail: ccromero@usc.edu. Website: http://mph.usc.edu/main.php.

University of Southern Mississippi, Graduate School, College of Health, Department of Community Health Sciences, Hattiesburg, MS 39406-0001. Offers epidemiology and biostatistics (MPH); health education (MPH); health policy/administration (MPH); occupational/environmental health (MPH); public health nutrition (MPH). *Accreditation:* CEPH. Part-time and evening/weekend programs available. *Faculty:* 8 full-time (4 women), 1 part-time/adjunct (0 women). *Students:* 86 full-time (68 women), 12 part-time (7 women); includes 41 minority (34 Black or African American, non-Hispanic/Latino; 3 Asian, non-Hispanic/Latino; 4 Two or more races, non-Hispanic/Latino), 7 international. Average age 33. 100 applicants, 55% accepted, 43 enrolled. In 2012, 48 master's awarded. *Degree requirements:* For master's, comprehensive exam, thesis (for some programs). *Entrance requirements:* For master's, GRE General Test, minimum GPA of 2.75 in last 60 hours. Additional exam requirements/recommendations for international students: Required—TOEFL, IELTS. *Application deadline:* For fall admission, 3/1 priority date for domestic students, 3/1 for international students; for spring admission, 1/10 priority date for domestic students, 1/10 for international students. Applications are processed on a rolling basis. Application fee: $50. Electronic applications accepted. *Financial support:* In 2012–13, 5 research assistantships with full tuition reimbursements (averaging $7,000 per year), 1 teaching assistantship with full tuition reimbursement (averaging $8,263 per year) were awarded; career-related internships or fieldwork, Federal Work-Study, institutionally sponsored loans, scholarships/grants, health care benefits, and unspecified assistantships also available. Financial award application deadline: 3/15; financial award applicants required to submit FAFSA. *Faculty research:* Rural health care delivery, school health, nutrition of pregnant teens, risk factor reduction, sexually transmitted diseases. *Unit head:* Dr. Emanual Ahua, Interim Chair, 601-266-5437, Fax: 601-266-5043. *Application contact:* Shonna Breland, Manager of Graduate Admissions, 601-266-6563, Fax: 601-266-5138. Website: http://www.usm.edu/chs.

University of South Florida, Graduate School, College of Public Health, Department of Epidemiology and Biostatistics, Tampa, FL 33620-9951. Offers MPH, MSPH, PhD. *Accreditation:* CEPH (one or more programs are accredited). Part-time and evening/weekend programs available. *Degree requirements:* For master's, comprehensive exam, thesis (for some programs); for doctorate, comprehensive exam, thesis/dissertation. *Entrance requirements:* For master's, GRE General Test, minimum GPA of 3.0 in upper-level course work, goal statement letter, two professional letters of recommendation, resume/curriculum vitae; for doctorate, GRE General Test, minimum GPA of 3.0 in upper-level course work, 3 professional letters of recommendation, resume/curriculum vitae, writing sample. Additional exam requirements/recommendations for international students: Required—TOEFL (minimum score 550 paper-based; 79 iBT). Electronic applications accepted. *Faculty research:* Dementia, mental illness, mental health preventative trails, rural health outreach, clinical and administrative studies.

The University of Texas Health Science Center at Houston, Graduate School of Biomedical Sciences, Program in Biomathematics and Biostatistics, Houston, TX 77225-0036. Offers MS, PhD, MD/PhD. Terminal master's awarded for partial completion of doctoral program. *Degree requirements:* For master's, thesis; for doctorate, thesis/dissertation. *Entrance requirements:* For master's and doctorate, GRE General Test. Additional exam requirements/recommendations for international students: Required—TOEFL. Electronic applications accepted. *Faculty research:* Biostatistics, biomarkers, epidemiology, bioinformatics, computational biology.

The University of Toledo, College of Graduate Studies, College of Medicine and Life Sciences, Department of Public Health and Preventative Medicine, Toledo, OH 43606-3390. Offers biostatistics and epidemiology (Certificate); contemporary gerontological practice (Certificate); environmental and occupational health and safety (MPH); epidemiology (Certificate); global public health (Certificate); health promotion and education (MPH); industrial hygiene (MSOH); medical and health science teaching and learning (Certificate); occupational health (Certificate); public health administration (MPH); public health and emergency response (Certificate); public health epidemiology (MPH); public health nutrition (MPH); MD/MPH. Part-time and evening/weekend programs available. *Faculty:* 8. *Students:* 90 full-time (66 women), 50 part-time (33 women); includes 42 minority (28 Black or African American, non-Hispanic/Latino; 11 Asian, non-Hispanic/Latino; 2 Hispanic/Latino; 1 Two or more races, non-Hispanic/Latino), 8 international. Average age 30. 101 applicants, 66% accepted, 50 enrolled. In 2012, 57 master's, 19 other advanced degrees awarded. *Degree requirements:* For master's, thesis or alternative. *Entrance requirements:* For master's, GRE, minimum undergraduate GPA of 3.0, three letters of recommendation, statement of purpose, transcripts from all prior institutions attended, resume; for Certificate, minimum undergraduate GPA of 3.0, three letters of recommendation, statement of purpose, transcripts from all prior institutions attended, resume. Additional exam requirements/recommendations for international students: Required—TOEFL (minimum score 550 paper-based; 80 iBT), IELTS (minimum score 6.5). *Application deadline:* For fall admission, 3/15 for domestic and international students. Applications are processed on a rolling basis. Application fee: $45 ($75 for international students). Electronic applications accepted. *Financial support:* In 2012–13, 5 research assistantships with full tuition reimbursements (averaging $10,000 per year) were awarded; Federal Work-Study, institutionally sponsored loans, scholarships/grants, tuition waivers (full and partial), and unspecified assistantships also available. *Unit head:* Dr. Sheryl A. Milz, Chair, 419-383-3976, Fax: 419-383-6140, E-mail: sheryl.milz@utoledo.edu. *Application contact:* Admissions Analyst, 419-383-4112, Fax: 419-383-6140. Website: http://nocphmph.org/.

University of Toronto, School of Graduate Studies, Dalla Lana School of Public Health, Toronto, ON M5S 1A1, Canada. Offers biostatistics (M Sc, PhD); community health (M Sc); epidemiology (MPH, PhD); health and behavioral science (PhD); health promotion (MPH); social science and health (PhD). *Accreditation:* CAHME (one or more programs are accredited); CEPH (one or more programs are accredited). Part-time programs available. *Degree requirements:* For master's, thesis (for some programs), practicum; for doctorate, comprehensive exam, thesis/dissertation, oral thesis defense. *Entrance requirements:* For master's, 2 letters of reference, relevant professional/research experience, minimum B average in final year; for doctorate, 2 letters of reference, relevant professional/research experience, minimum B+ average. Additional exam requirements/recommendations for international students: Required—TOEFL (minimum score 580 paper-based; 93 iBT), TWE (minimum score 5). Electronic applications accepted. *Expenses:* Contact institution.

University of Utah, Graduate School, Interdepartmental Program in Statistics, Salt Lake City, UT 84112-1107. Offers biostatistics (M Stat); econometrics (M Stat); educational psychology (M Stat); mathematics (M Stat); sociology (M Stat). Part-time programs available. *Students:* 30 full-time (11 women), 29 part-time (12 women); includes 13 minority (3 Black or African American, non-Hispanic/Latino; 7 Asian, non-Hispanic/Latino; 2 Hispanic/Latino; 1 Two or more races, non-Hispanic/Latino), 15 international. Average age 33. 59 applicants, 44% accepted, 16 enrolled. In 2012, 14 master's awarded. *Degree requirements:* For master's, comprehensive exam, projects. *Entrance requirements:* For master's, GRE General Test (for all but biostatistics); GRE Subject Test (for mathematics), minimum GPA of 3.0; course work in calculus, matrix theory, statistics. Additional exam requirements/recommendations for international students: Required—TOEFL (minimum score 500 paper-based; 61 iBT). *Application deadline:* For fall admission, 7/1 for domestic students, 4/1 for international students. Applications are processed on a rolling basis. Application fee: $55 ($65 for international students). *Financial support:* Career-related internships or fieldwork available. *Faculty research:* Biostatistics, management, economics, educational psychology, mathematics. *Unit head:* Richard Fowles, Chair, University Statistics Committee, 801-581-4577, E-mail: fowles@economics.utah.edu. *Application contact:* Laura Egbert, Coordinator, 801-585-6853, E-mail: laura.egbert@utah.edu. Website: http://www.mstat.utah.edu.

University of Utah, School of Medicine and Graduate School, Graduate Programs in Medicine, Programs in Public Health, Salt Lake City, UT 84112-1107. Offers biostatistics (M Stat); public health (MPH, MSPH, PhD). *Accreditation:* CEPH (one or more programs are accredited). Part-time programs available. *Degree requirements:* For master's, comprehensive exam, thesis or project (MSPH); for doctorate, comprehensive exam, thesis/dissertation. *Entrance requirements:* For master's and doctorate, GRE General Test, 3 letters of reference, in-person interviews, minimum GPA of 3.0. Additional exam requirements/recommendations for international students: Required—TOEFL (minimum score 550 paper-based). Electronic applications accepted. *Faculty research:* Health services, health policy, epidemiology of chronic disease, infectious disease epidemiology, cancer epidemiology.

University of Vermont, Graduate College, College of Engineering and Mathematics, Department of Mathematics and Statistics, Program in Biostatistics, Burlington, VT 05405. Offers MS. *Students:* 9 (4 women); includes 2 minority (1 Black or African American, non-Hispanic/Latino; 1 Asian, non-Hispanic/Latino). 33 applicants, 61% accepted, 1 enrolled. In 2012, 1 master's awarded. *Degree requirements:* For master's, thesis or alternative. *Entrance requirements:* For master's, GRE General Test. Additional exam requirements/recommendations for international students: Required—TOEFL (minimum score 90 iBT). *Application deadline:* For fall admission, 4/1 priority date for domestic students, 4/1 for international students. Applications are processed on a rolling basis. Application fee: $40. Electronic applications accepted. *Expenses: Tuition, area resident:* Part-time $572 per credit. Tuition, nonresident: part-time $1444 per credit. *Financial support:* Fellowships, research assistantships, and teaching assistantships available. Financial award application deadline: 3/1. *Unit head:* Dr. James Burgmeier, Chair, 802-656-2940. *Application contact:* Prof. Ruth Mickey, Coordinator, 802-656-2940.

University of Washington, Graduate School, Interdisciplinary Graduate Program in Quantitative Ecology and Resource Management, Seattle, WA 98195. Offers MS, PhD. *Degree requirements:* For master's, thesis; for doctorate, thesis/dissertation. *Entrance requirements:* For master's and doctorate, GRE General Test, minimum GPA of 3.0. Additional exam requirements/recommendations for international students: Required—TOEFL. Electronic applications accepted. *Faculty research:* Population dynamics, statistical analysis, ecological modeling and systems analysis of aquatic and terrestrial ecosystems.

University of Washington, Graduate School, School of Public Health, Department of Biostatistics, Seattle, WA 98195. Offers biostatistics (MPH, MS, PhD); clinical research (MS), including biostatistics; statistical genetics (PhD). Part-time programs available. *Faculty:* 39 full-time (18 women), 17 part-time/adjunct (7 women). *Students:* 76 full-time (41 women), 2 part-time (1 woman); includes 12 minority (1 Black or African American, non-Hispanic/Latino; 8 Asian, non-Hispanic/Latino; 3 Hispanic/Latino), 28 international. Average age 28. 128 applicants, 41% accepted, 19 enrolled. In 2012, 9 master's, 7 doctorates awarded. Terminal master's awarded for partial completion of doctoral program. *Degree requirements:* For master's, comprehensive exam, thesis, practicum (MPH); for doctorate, comprehensive exam, thesis/dissertation. *Entrance requirements:* For master's and doctorate, GRE General Test, coursework on

multivariate calculus, linear algebra and probability; minimum GPA of 3.0. Additional exam requirements/recommendations for international students: Required—TOEFL. *Application deadline:* For fall admission, 1/2 for domestic students. Application fee: $75. Electronic applications accepted. *Financial support:* In 2012–13, 70 research assistantships with full tuition reimbursements (averaging $21,000 per year), 17 teaching assistantships with full tuition reimbursements (averaging $21,000 per year) were awarded; scholarships/grants, traineeships, health care benefits, and tuition waivers (partial) also available. *Faculty research:* Statistical methods for survival data analysis, clinical trials, epidemiological case control and cohort studies, statistical genetics. *Unit head:* Dr. Bruce Weir, Department Chair, 206-543-1044. *Application contact:* Alex MacKenzie, Curriculum Coordinator, 206-543-1044, Fax: 206-543-3286, E-mail: alexam@u.washington.edu. Website: http://www.biostat.washington.edu/.

University of Waterloo, Graduate Studies, Faculty of Mathematics, Department of Statistics and Actuarial Science, Waterloo, ON N2L 3G1, Canada. Offers actuarial science (M Math, PhD); biostatistics (PhD); statistics (M Math, PhD); statistics-biostatistics (M Math); statistics-computing (M Math); statistics-finance (M Math). *Degree requirements:* For master's, research paper or thesis; for doctorate, comprehensive exam, thesis/dissertation. *Entrance requirements:* For master's, honors degree in field, minimum B+ average; for doctorate, master's degree, minimum B+ average. Additional exam requirements/recommendations for international students: Required—TOEFL (minimum score 600 paper-based; 90 iBT), TWE (minimum score 4.5). Electronic applications accepted. *Faculty research:* Data analysis, risk theory, inference, stochastic processes, quantitative finance.

The University of Western Ontario, Faculty of Graduate Studies, Biosciences Division, Department of Epidemiology and Biostatistics, London, ON N6A 5B8, Canada. Offers M Sc, PhD. *Accreditation:* CEPH (one or more programs are accredited). Part-time programs available. *Degree requirements:* For master's, thesis; for doctorate, comprehensive exam, thesis proposal defense. *Entrance requirements:* For master's, BA or B Sc honors degree, minimum B+ average in last 10 courses; for doctorate, M Sc or equivalent, minimum B+ average in last 10 courses. *Faculty research:* Chronic disease epidemiology, clinical epidemiology.

Virginia Commonwealth University, Medical College of Virginia-Professional Programs, School of Medicine, School of Medicine Graduate Programs, Department of Biostatistics, Richmond, VA 23284-9005. Offers MS, PhD, MD/PhD. Part-time programs available. Terminal master's awarded for partial completion of doctoral program. *Degree requirements:* For master's, thesis; for doctorate, thesis/dissertation, comprehensive oral and written exams. *Entrance requirements:* For master's and doctorate, GRE, MCAT or DAT. Additional exam requirements/recommendations for international students: Required—TOEFL (minimum score 600 paper-based; 100 iBT). Electronic applications accepted. *Faculty research:* Health services, linear models, response surfaces, design and analysis of drug/chemical combinations, clinical trials.

Washington University in St. Louis, School of Medicine, Division of Biostatistics, St. Louis, MO 63110. Offers biostatistics (MS); genetic epidemiology (Certificate). Part-time programs available. *Entrance requirements:* For master's, GRE, proficiency in computer programming, statistics and biology/genetics. Additional exam requirements/recommendations for international students: Required—TOEFL (minimum score 600 paper-based; 100 iBT), TWE. Electronic applications accepted. *Expenses:* Contact institution. *Faculty research:* Biostatistics, clinical trials, cardiovascular diseases, genetics, genetic epidemiology.

Yale University, School of Medicine, Yale School of Public Health, New Haven, CT 06520. Offers applied biostatistics and epidemiology (APMPH); biostatistics (MPH, MS, PhD), including global health (MPH); chronic disease epidemiology (MPH, PhD), including global health (MPH); environmental health sciences (MPH, PhD), including global health (MPH); epidemiology of microbial diseases (MPH, PhD), including global health (MPH); global health (APMPH); health management (MPH), including global health; health policy (MPH), including global health; health policy and administration (APMPH, PhD); occupational and environmental medicine (APMPH); preventive medicine (APMPH); social and behavioral sciences (APMPH, MPH), including global health (MPH); JD/MPH; M Div/MPH; MBA/MPH; MD/MPH; MEM/MPH; MFS/MPH; MM Sc/MPH; MPH/MA; MSN/MPH. MS and PhD offered through the Graduate School. *Accreditation:* CEPH. Part-time programs available. Terminal master's awarded for partial completion of doctoral program. *Degree requirements:* For master's, thesis, summer internship; for doctorate, comprehensive exam, thesis/dissertation, residency. *Entrance requirements:* For master's, GMAT, GRE, or MCAT, two years of undergraduate coursework in math and science; for doctorate, GRE General Test. Additional exam requirements/recommendations for international students: Required—TOEFL (minimum score 100 iBT). Electronic applications accepted. *Expenses:* Contact institution. *Faculty research:* Genetic and emerging infections epidemiology, virology, cost/quality, vector biology, quantitative methods, aging, asthma, cancer.

Peterson's Graduate Programs in the Physical Sciences, Mathematics, Agricultural Sciences, the Environment & Natural Resources 2014

www.petersonsbooks.com **303**

Computational Sciences

American University of Beirut, Graduate Programs, Faculty of Arts and Sciences, Beirut, Lebanon. Offers anthropology (MA); Arab and Middle Eastern history (PhD); Arabic language and literature (MA, PhD); archaeology (MA); biology (MS); cell and molecular biology (PhD); chemistry (MS); clinical psychology (MA); computational science (MS); computer science (MS); economics (MA); education (MA); English language (MA); English literature (MA); environmental policy planning (MSES); financial economics (MAFE); general psychology (MA); geology (MS); history (MA); mathematics (MA, MS); media studies (MA); Middle Eastern studies (MA); philosophy (MA); physics (MS); political studies (MA); public administration (MA); sociology (MA); statistics (MA, MS); theoretical physics (PhD); transnational American studies (MA). Part-time programs available. *Faculty:* 238 full-time (80 women), 7 part-time/adjunct (3 women). *Students:* 253 full-time (169 women), 139 part-time (105 women). Average age 26. 306 applicants, 47% accepted, 90 enrolled. In 2012, 126 degrees awarded. *Degree requirements:* For master's, one foreign language, comprehensive exam, thesis (for some programs); for doctorate, one foreign language, comprehensive exam, thesis/dissertation. *Entrance requirements:* For master's, GRE, letter of recommendation; for doctorate, GRE, letters of recommendation. Additional exam requirements/recommendations for international students: Required—TOEFL (minimum score 600 paper-based; 97 iBT), IELTS (minimum score 7). *Application deadline:* For fall admission, 4/30 for domestic students, 4/18 for international students; for spring admission, 11/1 for domestic and international students. Application fee: $50. *Expenses: Tuition:* Full-time $13,896; part-time $772 per credit. *Financial support:* In 2012–13, 20 students received support. Career-related internships or fieldwork, institutionally sponsored loans, scholarships/grants, health care benefits, and unspecified assistantships available. Financial award application deadline: 2/4; financial award applicants required to submit FAFSA. *Faculty research:* Modern Middle East history; Near Eastern archaeology; Islamic history; European history; software engineering; scientific computing; data mining; the applications of cooperative learning in language teaching and teacher education; world/comparative literature; rhetoric and composition; creative writing; public management; public policy and international affairs; hydrogeology; mineralogy, petrology, and geochemistry; tectonics and structural geology; cell and molecular biology; ecology. *Unit head:* Dr. Patrick McGreevy, Dean, 961-1374374 Ext. 3800, Fax: 961-1744461, E-mail: pm07@aub.edu.lb. *Application contact:* Dr. Salim Kanaan, Director, Admissions Office, 961-1-350000 Ext. 2594, Fax: 961-1750775, E-mail: sk00@aub.edu.lb. Website: http://staff.aub.edu.lb/~webfas.

California Institute of Technology, Division of Engineering and Applied Science, Option in Computation and Neural Systems, Pasadena, CA 91125-0001. Offers MS, PhD. Terminal master's awarded for partial completion of doctoral program. *Degree requirements:* For doctorate, thesis/dissertation, qualifying exam. *Entrance requirements:* For doctorate, GRE General Test. *Faculty research:* Biological and artificial computational devices, modeling of sensory processes and learning, theory of collective computation.

Carnegie Mellon University, Tepper School of Business, Program in Algorithms, Combinatorics, and Optimization, Pittsburgh, PA 15213-3891. Offers PhD. *Degree requirements:* For doctorate, thesis/dissertation. *Entrance requirements:* For doctorate, GRE General Test.

Chapman University, Schmid College of Science and Technology, Computational Sciences Program, Orange, CA 92866. Offers MS. *Faculty:* 14 full-time (1 woman), 3 part-time/adjunct (1 woman). *Students:* 13 full-time (5 women), 17 part-time (6 women); includes 8 minority (2 Asian, non-Hispanic/Latino; 5 Hispanic/Latino; 1 Native Hawaiian or other Pacific Islander, non-Hispanic/Latino), 5 international. Average age 29. 28 applicants, 71% accepted, 15 enrolled. *Entrance requirements:* Additional exam requirements/recommendations for international students: Required—TOEFL (minimum score 550 paper-based; 80 iBT). Application fee: $60. *Financial support:* Fellowships, Federal Work-Study, and scholarships/grants available. Financial award applicants required to submit FAFSA. *Unit head:* Dr. Michael Fahy, Associate Dean, 714-628-7223, E-mail: jhill@chapman.edu. *Application contact:* Saundra Hoover, Director of Graduate Admissions, 714-997-6786, Fax: 714-997-6713, E-mail: shoover@chapman.edu. Website: http://www.chapman.edu/SCS/CS/MSCS.asp.

Claremont Graduate University, Graduate Programs, School of Mathematical Sciences, Claremont, CA 91711-6160. Offers computational and systems biology (PhD); computational mathematics and numerical analysis (MA, MS); computational science (PhD); engineering and industrial applied mathematics (PhD); mathematics (PhD); operations research and statistics (MA, MS); physical applied mathematics (MA, MS); pure mathematics (MA, MS); scientific computing (MA, MS); systems and control theory (MA, MS). Part-time programs available. *Faculty:* 6 full-time (1 woman), 1 part-time/adjunct (0 women). *Students:* 54 full-time (16 women), 35 part-time (18 women); includes 29 minority (3 Black or African American, non-Hispanic/Latino; 10 Asian, non-Hispanic/Latino; 12 Hispanic/Latino; 4 Two or more races, non-Hispanic/Latino), 21 international. Average age 33. In 2012, 13 master's, 7 doctorates awarded. Terminal master's awarded for partial completion of doctoral program. *Entrance requirements:* For master's and doctorate, GRE General Test. Additional exam requirements/recommendations for international students: Required—TOEFL (minimum score 550 paper-based; 80 iBT). *Application deadline:* For fall admission, 2/1 priority date for domestic students. Applications are processed on a rolling basis. Application fee: $60. Electronic applications accepted. *Expenses: Tuition:* Full-time $37,640; part-time $1636 per unit. *Required fees:* $500; $250 per semester. *Financial support:* Fellowships, research assistantships, Federal Work-Study, institutionally sponsored loans, scholarships/grants, and tuition waivers (full and partial) available. Support available to part-time students. Financial award application deadline: 2/15; financial award applicants required to submit FAFSA. *Unit head:* Henry Schellhorn, Director, 909-607-4168, E-mail: henry.schellhorn@cgu.edu. *Application contact:* Charlotte Ballesteros, Program Coordinator, 909-621-8080, Fax: 909-607-8261, E-mail: charlotte.ballesteros@cgu.edu. Website: http://www.cgu.edu/pages/168.asp.

Clemson University, Graduate School, College of Engineering and Science, Department of Mathematical Sciences, Clemson, SC 29634. Offers applied and pure mathematics (MS, PhD); computational mathematics (MS, PhD); operations research (MS, PhD); statistics (MS, PhD). Part-time programs available. *Faculty:* 44 full-time (13 women), 4 part-time/adjunct (2 women). *Students:* 117 full-time (43 women), 3 part-time (2 women); includes 6 minority (2 Black or African American, non-Hispanic/Latino; 1 American Indian or Alaska Native, non-Hispanic/Latino; 1 Asian, non-Hispanic/Latino; 1 Hispanic/Latino; 1 Two or more races, non-Hispanic/Latino), 50 international. Average age 26. 188 applicants, 76% accepted, 45 enrolled. In 2012, 41 master's, 11 doctorates awarded. *Degree requirements:* For master's, thesis optional, final project; for doctorate, thesis/dissertation, qualifying exams. *Entrance requirements:* For master's and doctorate, GRE General Test. Additional exam requirements/recommendations for international students: Required—TOEFL. *Application deadline:* For fall admission, 1/15 priority date for domestic students, 1/15 for international students; for spring admission, 10/1 priority date for domestic students, 9/15 for international students. Applications are processed on a rolling basis. Application fee: $70 ($80 for international students). Electronic applications accepted. *Financial support:* In 2012–13, 111 students received support, including 2 fellowships with full and partial tuition reimbursements available (averaging $10,000 per year), 8 research assistantships with partial tuition reimbursements available (averaging $17,943 per year), 104 teaching assistantships with partial tuition reimbursements available (averaging $18,793 per year); career-related internships or fieldwork, institutionally sponsored loans, scholarships/grants, health care benefits, and unspecified assistantships also available. Support available to part-time students. Financial award application deadline: 4/15. *Faculty research:* Applied and computational analysis, cryptography, discrete mathematics, optimization, statistics. *Total annual research expenditures:* $780,865. *Unit head:* Dr. Robert L. Taylor, Chair, 864-656-5240, Fax: 864-656-5230, E-mail: rtaylo2@clemson.edu. *Application contact:* Dr. K. B. Kulasekera, Graduate Coordinator, 864-656-5231, Fax: 864-656-5230, E-mail: kk@clemson.edu. Website: http://www.clemson.edu/ces/departments/math/index.html.

The College of William and Mary, Faculty of Arts and Sciences, Department of Computer Science, Program in Computational Operations Research, Williamsburg, VA 23187-8795. Offers computer science (MS), including operations research. Part-time programs available. *Faculty:* 7 full-time (1 woman), 3 part-time/adjunct (1 woman). *Students:* 20 full-time (9 women); includes 4 minority (2 Black or African American, non-Hispanic/Latino; 2 Two or more races, non-Hispanic/Latino), 4 international. Average age 25. 27 applicants, 74% accepted, 14 enrolled. In 2012, 10 master's awarded. *Degree requirements:* For master's, research project. *Entrance requirements:* For master's, GRE General Test, minimum GPA of 2.5. Additional exam requirements/recommendations for international students: Required—TOEFL. *Application deadline:* For fall admission, 3/1 priority date for domestic students, 3/15 for international students; for spring admission, 11/1 for domestic and international students. Applications are processed on a rolling basis. Application fee: $45. Electronic applications accepted. *Expenses:* Tuition, state resident: full-time $6779; part-time $385 per credit hour. Tuition, nonresident: full-time $20,608; part-time $1000 per credit hour. *Required fees:* $4625. *Financial support:* In 2012–13, 13 students received support, including 6 fellowships (averaging $9,000 per year), 7 teaching assistantships with full tuition reimbursements available (averaging $11,500 per year); scholarships/grants, tuition waivers (full), and unspecified assistantships also available. Financial award application deadline: 3/1; financial award applicants required to submit FAFSA. *Faculty research:* Metaheuristics, reliability, optimization, statistics, networks. *Unit head:* Dr. Rex Kincaid, Professor, 757-221-2038, Fax: 757-221-1717, E-mail: rrkinc@math.wm.edu. *Application contact:* Vanessa Godwin, Administrative Director, 757-221-3455, Fax: 757-221-1717, E-mail: cor@cs.wm.edu. Website: http://www.wm.edu/computerscience/grad/.

Cornell University, Graduate School, Graduate Fields of Engineering, Field of Chemical Engineering, Ithaca, NY 14853-0001. Offers advanced materials processing (M Eng, MS, PhD); applied mathematics and computational methods (M Eng, MS, PhD); biochemical engineering (M Eng, MS, PhD); chemical reaction engineering (M Eng, MS, PhD); classical and statistical thermodynamics (M Eng, MS, PhD); fluid dynamics, rheology and biorheology (M Eng, MS, PhD); heat and mass transfer (M Eng, MS, PhD); kinetics and catalysis (M Eng, MS, PhD);

polymers (M Eng, MS, PhD); surface science (M Eng, MS, PhD). *Faculty:* 32 full-time (4 women). *Students:* 123 full-time (41 women); includes 25 minority (3 Black or African American, non-Hispanic/Latino; 17 Asian, non-Hispanic/Latino; 4 Hispanic/Latino; 1 Two or more races, non-Hispanic/Latino), 65 international. Average age 25. 456 applicants, 40% accepted, 66 enrolled. In 2012, 43 master's, 13 doctorates awarded. *Degree requirements:* For master's, thesis (MS); for doctorate, comprehensive exam, thesis/dissertation. *Entrance requirements:* For master's and doctorate, GRE General Test, 2 letters of recommendation. Additional exam requirements/recommendations for international students: Required—TOEFL (minimum score 600 paper-based; 77 iBT). *Application deadline:* For fall admission, 1/15 priority date for domestic students. Application fee: $95. Electronic applications accepted. *Financial support:* In 2012–13, 69 students received support, including 42 fellowships with full tuition reimbursements available, 15 research assistantships with full tuition reimbursements available, 12 teaching assistantships with full tuition reimbursements available; institutionally sponsored loans, scholarships/grants, health care benefits, tuition waivers (full and partial), and unspecified assistantships also available. Financial award applicants required to submit FAFSA. *Faculty research:* Biochemical, biomedical and metabolic engineering; fluid and polymer dynamics; surface science and chemical kinetics; electronics materials; microchemical systems and nanotechnology. *Unit head:* Director of Graduate Studies, 607-255-4550. *Application contact:* Graduate Field Assistant, 607-255-4550, E-mail: dgs@cheme.cornell.edu. Website: http://www.gradschool.cornell.edu/fields.php?id-25&a-2.

Emory University, Laney Graduate School, Department of Physics, Atlanta, GA 30322-1100. Offers biophysics (PhD); experimental condensed matter physics (PhD); theoretical and computational statistical physics (PhD); MS/PhD. *Faculty:* 11 full-time (2 women), 1 part-time/adjunct (0 women). *Students:* 30 full-time (12 women); includes 2 minority (1 Black or African American, non-Hispanic/Latino; 1 Asian, non-Hispanic/Latino), 20 international. Average age 26. 51 applicants, 35% accepted, 4 enrolled. In 2012, 3 doctorates awarded. *Degree requirements:* For doctorate, thesis/dissertation, qualifier proposal. *Entrance requirements:* For doctorate, GRE General Test, minimum GPA of 3.0. Additional exam requirements/recommendations for international students: Required—TOEFL (minimum score 600 paper-based). *Application deadline:* For fall admission, 1/3 priority date for domestic students, 1/3 for international students. Application fee: $75. Electronic applications accepted. *Financial support:* Fellowships, teaching assistantships, institutionally sponsored loans, scholarships/grants, health care benefits, and tuition waivers (full) available. Financial award application deadline: 1/3; financial award applicants required to submit FAFSA. *Faculty research:* Experimental studies of the structure and function of metalloproteins, soft condensed matter, granular materials, biophotonics and fluorescence correlation spectroscopy, single molecule studies of DNA-protein systems. *Unit head:* Prof. Eric Weeks, Chair, 404-727-4479, Fax: 404-727-0873, E-mail: erweeks@emory.edu. *Application contact:* Prof. Stefan Boettcher, Director of Graduate Studies, 404-727-4298, Fax: 404-727-0873, E-mail: sboettc@emory.edu. Website: http://www.physics.emory.edu.

Florida State University, The Graduate School, College of Arts and Sciences, Department of Scientific Computing, Tallahassee, FL 32306-4120. Offers computational science (MS, PSM, PhD), including atmospheric science (PhD), biochemistry (PhD), biological science (PhD), computational molecular biology/bioinformatics (PSM), computational science (PhD), geological science (PhD), materials science (PhD), physics (PhD). Part-time programs available. *Faculty:* 14 full-time (2 women). *Students:* 28 full-time (5 women), 4 part-time (0 women); includes 12 minority (10 Asian, non-Hispanic/Latino; 2 Hispanic/Latino). Average age 28. 28 applicants, 43% accepted, 7 enrolled. In 2012, 11 master's, 5 doctorates awarded. Terminal master's awarded for partial completion of doctoral program. *Degree requirements:* For master's, thesis (for some programs); for doctorate, comprehensive exam, thesis/dissertation. *Entrance requirements:* For master's and doctorate, GRE General Test, knowledge of at least one object-oriented computing language, 3 letters of recommendations. Additional exam requirements/recommendations for international students: Required—TOEFL (minimum score 550 paper-based; 80 iBT). *Application deadline:* For fall admission, 1/15 for domestic and international students. Application fee: $30. Electronic applications accepted. *Expenses:* Tuition, state resident: full-time $7263; part-time $403.51 per credit hour. Tuition, nonresident: full-time $18,087; part-time $1004.85 per credit hour. *Required fees:* $1335.42; $74.19 per credit hour. $445.14 per semester. One-time fee: $40 full-time; $20 part-time. Tuition and fees vary according to program. *Financial support:* In 2012–13, 32 students received support, including 12 research assistantships with full tuition reimbursements available (averaging $20,000 per year), 17 teaching assistantships with full tuition reimbursements available (averaging $20,000 per year); scholarships/grants and unspecified assistantships also available. Financial award application deadline: 4/15. *Faculty research:* Morphometrics, mathematical and systems biology, mining proteomic and metabolic data, computational materials research, advanced 4-D Var data-assimilation methods in dynamic meteorology and oceanography, computational fluid dynamics, astrophysics. *Unit head:* Dr. Max Gunzburger, Chair, 850-644-1010, E-mail: mgunzburger@fsu.edu. *Application contact:* Maribel Amwake, Academic Coordinator, 850-644-0143, Fax: 850-644-0098, E-mail: mamwake@fsu.edu. Website: http://www.sc.fsu.edu.

George Mason University, College of Science, School of Physics, Astronomy and Computational Sciences, Fairfax, VA 22030. Offers applied and engineering physics (MS); computational science (MS); computational science and informatics (PhD); computational techniques and applications (Certificate); physics (PhD).

Faculty: 48 full-time (11 women), 10 part-time/adjunct (1 woman). *Students:* 58 full-time (16 women), 97 part-time (19 women); includes 25 minority (6 Black or African American, non-Hispanic/Latino; 11 Asian, non-Hispanic/Latino; 6 Hispanic/Latino; 2 Two or more races, non-Hispanic/Latino), 26 international. Average age 35. 105 applicants, 49% accepted, 22 enrolled. In 2012, 20 master's, 15 doctorates, 1 other advanced degree awarded. *Degree requirements:* For master's, thesis optional; for doctorate, comprehensive exam, thesis/dissertation. *Entrance requirements:* For master's and doctorate, GRE, baccalaureate degree in related field with minimum GPA of 3.0 in last 60 credit hours; 3 letters of recommendation; expanded goals statement; resume; 2 copies of official transcripts. Additional exam requirements/recommendations for international students: Required—TOEFL (minimum score 570 paper-based; 88 iBT), IELTS (minimum score 6.5), Pearson Test of English. *Application deadline:* For fall admission, 4/15 priority date for domestic students; for spring admission, 11/15 priority date for domestic students. Application fee: $65 ($80 for international students). Electronic applications accepted. *Expenses:* Tuition, state resident: full-time $9080; part-time $378.33 per credit hour. Tuition, nonresident: full-time $25,010; part-time $1042.08 per credit hour. *Required fees:* $2610; $108.75 per credit hour. Tuition and fees vary according to program. *Financial support:* In 2012–13, 51 students received support, including 1 fellowship (averaging $8,000 per year), 37 research assistantships with full and partial tuition reimbursements available (averaging $18,917 per year), 16 teaching assistantships with full and partial tuition reimbursements available (averaging $13,676 per year); career-related internships or fieldwork, Federal Work-Study, scholarships/grants, unspecified assistantships, and health care benefits (for full-time research or teaching assistantship recipients) also available. Support available to part-time students. Financial award application deadline: 3/1; financial award applicants required to submit FAFSA. *Faculty research:* Particle and nuclear physics; computational statistics; astronomy, astrophysics, and space and planetary science; astronomy and physics education; atomic physics; biophysics and neuroscience; optical physics; fundamental theoretical studies; multidimensional data analysis. *Total annual research expenditures:* $5.8 million. *Unit head:* Dr. Michael Summers, Director, 703-993-3971, Fax: 703-993-1269, E-mail: msummers@gmu.edu. *Application contact:* Dr. Paul So, Graduate Advisor, 703-993-4377, Fax: 703-993-1269, E-mail: paso@gmu.edu. Website: http://spacs.gmu.edu/.

Hampton University, Graduate College, Program in Applied Mathematics, Hampton, VA 23668. Offers computational mathematics (MS); nonlinear science (MS); statistics and probability (MS). *Degree requirements:* For master's, thesis optional. *Entrance requirements:* For master's, GRE General Test.

Lehigh University, P.C. Rossin College of Engineering and Applied Science, Department of Mechanical Engineering and Mechanics, Bethlehem, PA 18015. Offers computational engineering and mechanics (MS, PhD); mechanical engineering (M Eng, MS, PhD, MBA/E); polymer science/engineering (M Eng, MS, PhD, MBA/E); MBA/E. Part-time and evening/weekend programs available. Postbaccalaureate distance learning degree programs offered. *Faculty:* 22 full-time (0 women), 1 part-time/adjunct (0 women). *Students:* 115 full-time (18 women), 37 part-time (3 women); includes 6 minority (2 Black or African American, non-Hispanic/Latino; 3 Asian, non-Hispanic/Latino; 1 Hispanic/Latino), 86 international. Average age 27. 789 applicants, 10% accepted, 30 enrolled. In 2012, 43 master's, 4 doctorates awarded. Terminal master's awarded for partial completion of doctoral program. *Degree requirements:* For master's, thesis; for doctorate, thesis/dissertation, general exam. *Entrance requirements:* Additional exam requirements/recommendations for international students: Required—TOEFL (minimum score 550 paper-based; 79 iBT). *Application deadline:* For fall admission, 7/15 for domestic and international students; for spring admission, 12/1 for domestic and international students. Application fee: $75. Electronic applications accepted. *Financial support:* In 2012–13, 38 students received support, including 5 fellowships with full and partial tuition reimbursements available (averaging $18,819 per year), 24 research assistantships with full and partial tuition reimbursements available (averaging $20,700 per year), 12 teaching assistantships with full and partial tuition reimbursements available (averaging $19,341 per year); unspecified assistantships and dean's doctoral assistantships also available. Financial award application deadline: 1/15. *Faculty research:* Thermofluids, dynamic systems, CAD/CAM, computational mechanics, solid mechanics. *Total annual research expenditures:* $3.3 million. *Unit head:* Dr. D. Gary Harlow, Chairman, 610-758-4102, Fax: 610-758-6224, E-mail: dgh0@lehigh.edu. *Application contact:* Jo Ann M. Casciano, Graduate Coordinator, 610-758-4107, Fax: 610-758-6224, E-mail: jmc4@lehigh.edu. Website: http://www.lehigh.edu/~inmem/.

Marquette University, Graduate School, College of Arts and Sciences, Department of Mathematics, Statistics, and Computer Science, Milwaukee, WI 53201-1881. Offers bioinformatics (MS); computational sciences (MS, PhD); computing (MS); mathematics education (MS). Part-time and evening/weekend programs available. Postbaccalaureate distance learning degree programs offered (minimal on-campus study). Terminal master's awarded for partial completion of doctoral program. *Degree requirements:* For master's, thesis (for some programs), essay with oral presentation; for doctorate, comprehensive exam, thesis/dissertation, qualifying examination. *Entrance requirements:* For master's, official transcripts from all current and previous colleges/universities except Marquette, three letters of recommendation; for doctorate, GRE General Test, official transcripts from all current and previous colleges/universities except Marquette, three letters of recommendation. Additional exam requirements/recommendations for international students: Required—TOEFL (minimum score

Peterson's Graduate Programs in the Physical Sciences, Mathematics, Agricultural Sciences, the Environment & Natural Resources 2014

www.petersonsbooks.com **305**

530 paper-based). Electronic applications accepted. *Faculty research:* Models of physiological systems, mathematical immunology, computational group theory, mathematical logic, computational science.

Massachusetts Institute of Technology, School of Engineering and School of Science and MIT Sloan School of Management, Program in Computation for Design and Optimization, Cambridge, MA 02139. Offers SM. *Faculty:* 55 full-time (6 women). *Students:* 19 full-time (4 women); includes 4 minority (3 Asian, non-Hispanic/Latino; 1 Hispanic/Latino), 14 international. Average age 25. 74 applicants, 27% accepted, 12 enrolled. In 2012, 5 master's awarded. *Degree requirements:* For master's, thesis. *Entrance requirements:* For master's, GRE General Test. Additional exam requirements/recommendations for international students: Required—IELTS. *Application deadline:* For fall admission, 1/10 for domestic and international students. Application fee: $75. Electronic applications accepted. *Expenses: Tuition:* Full-time $41,770; part-time $650 per credit hour. *Required fees:* $280. *Financial support:* In 2012–13, 14 students received support, including 7 fellowships, 12 research assistantships (averaging $30,400 per year); teaching assistantships, Federal Work-Study, institutionally sponsored loans, scholarships/grants, health care benefits, and unspecified assistantships also available. *Faculty research:* Finite element methods; partial differential equations; applied optimization; computational mechanics; optimization theory. *Unit head:* Prof. Nicolas Hadjiconstantinou, Co-Director, 617-258-5808, E-mail: cdo_info@mit.edu. *Application contact:* 617-253-3725, E-mail: cdo_info@mit.edu. Website: http://computationalengineering.mit.edu/education/.

McGill University, Faculty of Graduate and Postdoctoral Studies, Faculty of Science, Department of Mathematics and Statistics, Montréal, QC H3A 2T5, Canada. Offers computational science and engineering (M Sc); mathematics and statistics (M Sc, MA, PhD), including applied mathematics (M Sc, MA), pure mathematics (M Sc, MA), statistics (M Sc, MA).

Memorial University of Newfoundland, School of Graduate Studies, Interdisciplinary Program in Computational Science, St. John's, NL A1C 5S7, Canada. Offers computational science (M Sc); computational science (cooperative) (M Sc). *Degree requirements:* For master's, thesis optional. *Entrance requirements:* For master's, honors B Sc or significant background in the field. Electronic applications accepted. *Faculty research:* Scientific computing, modeling and simulation, computational fluid dynamics, polymer physics, computational chemistry.

Miami University, School of Engineering and Applied Science, Computational Science and Engineering Program, Oxford, OH 45056. Offers MS. *Students:* 22 full-time (6 women), 1 part-time (0 women); includes 1 minority (Asian, non-Hispanic/Latino), 11 international. Average age 24. In 2012, 8 master's awarded. *Entrance requirements:* For master's, GRE. Additional exam requirements/recommendations for international students: Required—TOEFL (minimum score 550 paper-based). *Application deadline:* For fall admission, 2/1 for domestic and international students. Application fee: $50. Electronic applications accepted. *Expenses:* Tuition, state resident: full-time $12,444; part-time $519 per credit hour. Tuition, nonresident: full-time $27,484; part-time $1145 per credit hour. *Required fees:* $468. Part-time tuition and fees vary according to course load, campus/location and program. *Financial support:* Research assistantships with full tuition reimbursements, teaching assistantships with full tuition reimbursements, health care benefits, and unspecified assistantships available. Financial award application deadline: 2/1; financial award applicants required to submit FAFSA. *Unit head:* Dr. Marek Dollar, Dean, 513-529-0700, E-mail: seas@miamioh.edu. *Application contact:* School of Engineering and Applied Science, 513-529-0700, E-mail: seas@miamioh.edu. Website: http://www.eas.miamioh.edu/tabs/future/graduatestudents/computationalscienceandengine/.

Michigan Technological University, Graduate School, Interdisciplinary Programs, Houghton, MI 49931. Offers atmospheric sciences (PhD); biochemistry and molecular biology (PhD); computational science and engineering (PhD); environmental engineering (PhD). *Degree requirements:* For doctorate, comprehensive exam, thesis/dissertation. *Entrance requirements:* For doctorate, GRE, statement of purpose, official transcripts, 3 letters of recommendation. Additional exam requirements/recommendations for international students: Required—TOEFL or IELTS.

North Carolina Agricultural and Technical State University, School of Graduate Studies, College of Arts and Sciences, Department of Physics, Greensboro, NC 27411. Offers computational sciences (MS); physics (MS).

Princeton University, Graduate School, Program in Applied and Computational Mathematics, Princeton, NJ 08544-1019. Offers PhD. *Degree requirements:* For doctorate, thesis/dissertation. *Entrance requirements:* For doctorate, GRE General Test, GRE Subject Test. Additional exam requirements/recommendations for international students: Required—TOEFL (minimum score 600 paper-based). Electronic applications accepted.

Purdue University, Graduate School, College of Health and Human Sciences, Department of Psychological Sciences, West Lafayette, IN 47907. Offers behavioral neuroscience (PhD); clinical psychology (PhD); cognitive psychology (PhD); industrial/organizational psychology (PhD); mathematical and computational cognitive science (PhD). *Accreditation:* APA. *Faculty:* 41 full-time (15 women), 17 part-time/adjunct (8 women). *Students:* 62 full-time (45 women), 8 part-time (7 women); includes 7 minority (2 Black or African American, non-Hispanic/Latino; 1 American Indian or Alaska Native, non-Hispanic/Latino; 1 Asian, non-Hispanic/Latino; 2 Hispanic/Latino; 1 Two or more races, non-Hispanic/Latino), 19 international. Average age 27. 410 applicants, 7% accepted, 12 enrolled. In 2012, 11 doctorates awarded. Terminal master's awarded for partial completion of doctoral program. *Degree requirements:* For doctorate, thesis/dissertation. *Entrance requirements:* For doctorate, GRE General Test, minimum undergraduate GPA of 3.0 or equivalent. Additional exam requirements/recommendations for international students: Required—TOEFL (minimum score 550 paper-based; 77 iBT); Recommended—TWE. *Application deadline:* For fall admission, 12/3 for domestic and international students. Applications are processed on a rolling basis. Application fee: $60 ($75 for international students). Electronic applications accepted. *Financial support:* Fellowships with partial tuition reimbursements, research assistantships with partial tuition reimbursements, teaching assistantships with partial tuition reimbursements, and career-related internships or fieldwork available. Support available to part-time students. Financial award applicants required to submit FAFSA. *Faculty research:* Career development of women in science, development of friendships during childhood and adolescence, social competence, human information processing. *Unit head:* Dr. Christopher R. Agnew, Head, 765-494-6061, Fax: 765-496-1264, E-mail: agnew@psych.purdue.edu. *Application contact:* Nancy A. O'Brien, Graduate Contact, 765-494-6067, Fax: 765-496-1264, E-mail: nobrien@psych.pardue.edu. Website: http://www.psych.purdue.edu/.

Rice University, Graduate Programs, George R. Brown School of Engineering, Department of Computational and Applied Mathematics, Houston, TX 77251-1892. Offers computational and applied mathematics (MA, MCAM, PhD); computational science and engineering (PhD). *Degree requirements:* For master's, comprehensive exam (for some programs), thesis (for some programs); for doctorate, comprehensive exam, thesis/dissertation. *Entrance requirements:* For master's and doctorate, GRE General Test, minimum GPA of 3.0. Additional exam requirements/recommendations for international students: Required—TOEFL (minimum score 600 paper-based; 90 iBT). Electronic applications accepted. *Faculty research:* Inverse problems, partial differential equations, computer algorithms, computational modeling, optimization theory.

Rice University, Graduate Programs, George R. Brown School of Engineering, Program in Computational Science and Engineering, Houston, TX 77251-1892. Offers MCSE.

The Richard Stockton College of New Jersey, School of Graduate and Continuing Studies, Program in Computational Science, Galloway, NJ 08205-9441. Offers MS. Part-time and evening/weekend programs available. *Faculty:* 4 full-time (0 women), 1 part-time/adjunct (0 women). *Students:* 2 full-time (both women), 24 part-time (6 women); includes 3 minority (1 Asian, non-Hispanic/Latino; 1 Hispanic/Latino; 1 Two or more races, non-Hispanic/Latino), 1 international. Average age 29. 7 applicants, 86% accepted, 6 enrolled. In 2012, 2 master's awarded. *Degree requirements:* For master's, thesis optional. *Entrance requirements:* For master's, GRE. Additional exam requirements/recommendations for international students: Required—TOEFL. *Application deadline:* For fall admission, 7/1 for domestic and international students; for spring admission, 12/1 for domestic and international students. Applications are processed on a rolling basis. Application fee: $50. Electronic applications accepted. *Financial support:* In 2012–13, 3 students received support, including 7 research assistantships with partial tuition reimbursements available; fellowships, career-related internships or fieldwork, Federal Work-Study, scholarships/grants, and unspecified assistantships also available. Financial award application deadline: 3/1; financial award applicants required to submit FAFSA. *Unit head:* Dr. J. Russell Manson, Program Director, 609-626-3640, E-mail: gradschool@stockton.edu. *Application contact:* Tara Williams, Assistant Director of Enrollment Management, 609-626-3640, Fax: 609-626-6050, E-mail: gradschool@stockton.edu. Website: http://www.stockton.edu/grad.

Sam Houston State University, College of Sciences, Department of Computer Science, Huntsville, TX 77341. Offers computing and information science (MS); digital forensics (MS); information assurance and security (MS). Part-time programs available. *Faculty:* 12 full-time (3 women). *Students:* 24 full-time (6 women), 46 part-time (14 women); includes 19 minority (9 Black or African American, non-Hispanic/Latino; 2 Asian, non-Hispanic/Latino; 8 Hispanic/Latino), 22 international. Average age 30. 65 applicants, 63% accepted, 20 enrolled. In 2012, 21 master's awarded. *Degree requirements:* For master's, comprehensive exam, thesis optional. *Entrance requirements:* For master's, GRE General Test. Additional exam requirements/recommendations for international students: Required—TOEFL (minimum score 550 paper-based; 79 iBT), IELTS (minimum score 6.5). *Application deadline:* For fall admission, 8/1 for domestic students, 6/25 for international students; for spring admission, 12/1 for domestic students, 11/12 for international students. Applications are processed on a rolling basis. Application fee: $45 ($75 for international students). Electronic applications accepted. *Expenses:* Tuition, state resident: full-time $2205; part-time $245 per credit hour. Tuition, nonresident: full-time $5391; part-time $599 per credit hour. *Required fees:* $67 per credit hour. $367 per semester. Tuition and fees vary according to course load and campus/location. *Financial support:* In 2012–13, 7 research assistantships (averaging $8,950 per year), 9 teaching assistantships (averaging $7,415 per year) were awarded; career-related internships or fieldwork, Federal Work-Study, institutionally sponsored loans, scholarships/grants, tuition waivers (partial), and unspecified assistantships also available. Support available to part-time students. Financial award application deadline: 5/31; financial award applicants required to submit FAFSA. *Total annual research expenditures:* $177,855. *Unit head:* Dr. Peter Cooper, Chair, 936-294-1569, Fax:

936-294-4312, E-mail: css_pac@shsu.edu. *Application contact:* Dr. Jiuhung Ji, Advisor, 936-294-1579, E-mail: csc_jxj@shsu.edu. Website: http://cs.shsu.edu/.

San Diego State University, Graduate and Research Affairs, College of Sciences, Program in Computational Science, San Diego, CA 92182. Offers MS, PhD. *Degree requirements:* For master's, thesis; for doctorate, thesis/dissertation. *Entrance requirements:* For master's, GRE General Test, 3 letters of recommendation; for doctorate, GRE, 3 letters of recommendation. Additional exam requirements/recommendations for international students: Required—TOEFL. Electronic applications accepted.

Simon Fraser University, Office of Graduate Studies, Faculty of Science, Department of Mathematics, Burnaby, BC V5A 1S6, Canada. Offers applied and computational mathematics (M Sc, PhD); mathematics (M Sc, PhD); operations research (M Sc, PhD). *Faculty:* 38 full-time (6 women). *Students:* 65 full-time (17 women). 81 applicants, 48% accepted, 21 enrolled. In 2012, 15 master's, 3 doctorates awarded. *Degree requirements:* For master's, thesis or alternative; for doctorate, comprehensive exam, thesis/dissertation. *Entrance requirements:* For master's, GRE General Test, GRE Subject Test (mathematics), minimum GPA of 3.0 (on scale of 4.33), or 3.33 based on last 60 credits of undergraduate courses; for doctorate, GRE General Test, GRE Subject Test (mathematics), minimum GPA of 3.5 (on scale of 4.33). Additional exam requirements/recommendations for international students: Recommended—TOEFL (minimum score 580 paper-based; 93 iBT), IELTS (minimum score 7), TWE (minimum score 5). *Application deadline:* For fall admission, 2/1 for domestic and international students. Application fee: $90 Canadian dollars ($125 Canadian dollars for international students). Electronic applications accepted. Tuition and fees charges are reported in Canadian dollars. *Expenses: Tuition, area resident:* Full-time $5000 Canadian dollars; part-time $275 Canadian dollars per credit hour. *Required fees:* $780 Canadian dollars. *Financial support:* In 2012–13, 31 students received support, including 30 fellowships (averaging $6,250 per year), teaching assistantships (averaging $5,608 per year); research assistantships and scholarships/grants also available. *Faculty research:* Computer algebra, discrete mathematics, fluid dynamics, nonlinear partial differential equations and variational methods, numerical analysis and scientific computing. *Unit head:* Dr. Tom Archibald, Graduate Chair, 778-782-3379, Fax: 778-782-4947, E-mail: math-gsc@sfu.ca. *Application contact:* Diane Pogue, Graduate Secretary, 778-782-3059, Fax: 778-782-4947, E-mail: mathgsec@sfu.ca. Website: http://www.math.sfu.ca/.

South Dakota State University, Graduate School, College of Engineering, Department of Mathematics and Statistics, Brookings, SD 57007. Offers computational science and statistics (PhD); mathematics (MS); statistics (MS). Part-time programs available. Terminal master's awarded for partial completion of doctoral program. *Degree requirements:* For master's, thesis (for some programs), oral exam; for doctorate, comprehensive exam, thesis/dissertation, oral and written exams. *Entrance requirements:* Additional exam requirements/recommendations for international students: Required—TOEFL (minimum score 550 paper-based; 80 iBT); Recommended—IELTS. *Faculty research:* Financial mathematics, predictive analytics, operations research, bioinformatics, biostatistics, computational science, statistics, number theory, abstract algebra.

Southern Illinois University Edwardsville, Graduate School, College of Arts and Sciences, Department of Mathematics and Statistics, Edwardsville, IL 62026. Offers mathematics (MS), including computational mathematics, postsecondary mathematics education, pure math, statistics and operations research. Part-time programs available. *Faculty:* 17 full-time (6 women). *Students:* 4 full-time (1 woman), 27 part-time (14 women); includes 4 minority (3 Black or African American, non-Hispanic/Latino; 1 Two or more races, non-Hispanic/Latino), 7 international. 22 applicants, 55% accepted. In 2012, 11 master's awarded. *Degree requirements:* For master's, thesis (for some programs), research paper/project. *Entrance requirements:* Additional exam requirements/recommendations for international students: Required—TOEFL (minimum score 550 paper-based; 79 iBT), IELTS (minimum score 6.5). *Application deadline:* For fall admission, 7/26 for domestic students, 6/1 for international students; for spring admission, 12/6 for domestic students, 10/1 for international students. Applications are processed on a rolling basis. Application fee: $30. Electronic applications accepted. *Expenses:* Tuition, state resident: full-time $6504; part-time $3252 per semester. Tuition, nonresident: full-time $8130; part-time $4065 per semester. *Required fees:* $705.50 per semester. Tuition and fees vary according to course level, course load, degree level, program and student level. *Financial support:* In 2012–13, research assistantships with full tuition reimbursements (averaging $9,585 per year), 13 teaching assistantships with full tuition reimbursements (averaging $9,585 per year) were awarded; fellowships with full tuition reimbursements, institutionally sponsored loans, scholarships/grants, and unspecified assistantships also available. Financial award application deadline: 3/1; financial award applicants required to submit FAFSA. *Unit head:* Dr. Krzysztof Jarosz, Chair, 618-650-2354, E-mail: kjarosz@siue.edu. *Application contact:* Dr. Myung Sin Song, Director, 618-650-2580, E-mail: msong@siue.edu. Website: http://www.siue.edu/artsandsciences/math/.

Southern Methodist University, Dedman College, Department of Mathematics, Dallas, TX 75275. Offers computational and applied mathematics (MS, PhD). *Degree requirements:* For master's, oral exams; for doctorate, thesis/dissertation, oral and written exams. *Entrance requirements:* For master's and doctorate, GRE General Test, minimum GPA of 3.0, 18 undergraduate hours in mathematics beyond first and second year calculus. Additional exam requirements/recommendations for international students: Required—TOEFL. Electronic applications accepted. *Faculty research:* Numerical analysis and scientific computation, fluid dynamics, optics, wave propagation, mathematical biology.

Stanford University, School of Engineering, Program in Scientific Computing and Computational Mathematics, Stanford, CA 94305-9991. Offers MS, PhD. Terminal master's awarded for partial completion of doctoral program. *Degree requirements:* For doctorate, thesis/dissertation, qualifying exam. *Entrance requirements:* For master's, GRE General Test; for doctorate, GRE General Test, GRE Subject Test. Additional exam requirements/recommendations for international students: Required—TOEFL. Electronic applications accepted. *Expenses: Tuition:* Full-time $41,250; part-time $917 per credit hour.

Temple University, College of Science and Technology, Department of Mathematics, Philadelphia, PA 19122-6096. Offers applied mathematics (MA); mathematics (PhD); pure mathematics (MA). Part-time and evening/weekend programs available. *Faculty:* 56 full-time (12 women). *Students:* 27 full-time (6 women), 8 international. 71 applicants, 18% accepted, 7 enrolled. In 2012, 1 master's, 3 doctorates awarded. Terminal master's awarded for partial completion of doctoral program. *Degree requirements:* For master's, thesis optional, written exam; for doctorate, 2 foreign languages, thesis/dissertation, oral and written exams. *Entrance requirements:* For master's, GRE General Test, minimum GPA of 3.0; for doctorate, GRE General Test, GRE Subject Test, minimum GPA of 3.0. Additional exam requirements/recommendations for international students: Required—TOEFL (minimum score 550 paper-based; 79 iBT). *Application deadline:* For fall admission, 2/15 priority date for domestic students, 12/15 for international students; for spring admission, 11/15 priority date for domestic students, 8/1 for international students. Applications are processed on a rolling basis. Application fee: $60. Electronic applications accepted. *Financial support:* Fellowships, research assistantships, teaching assistantships, Federal Work-Study, and institutionally sponsored loans available. Financial award application deadline: 1/15; financial award applicants required to submit FAFSA. *Faculty research:* Differential geometry, numerical analysis. *Unit head:* Dr. Gerardo Mendoza, Graduate Chair, 215-204-5053, Fax: 215-204-6433, E-mail: mathematics@temple.edu. *Application contact:* Alexis Cogan, Administrative Assistant, 215-204-7840, E-mail: cogana@temple.edu. Website: http://math.temple.edu/.

University at Buffalo, the State University of New York, Graduate School, College of Arts and Sciences, Center for Computational Research, Buffalo, NY 14260. Offers computational science (Advanced Certificate). *Unit head:* Bruce Pitman, Program Coordinator, 716-881-8966, Fax: 716-881-6656, E-mail: pitman@buffalo.edu. *Application contact:* Joseph C. Syracuse, Graduate Enrollment Manager, 716-645-2711, Fax: 716-645-3888, E-mail: jcs32@buffalo.edu. Website: http://www.ccr.buffalo.edu/display/WEB/Contact.

The University of Alabama at Birmingham, School of Engineering, Program in Interdisciplinary Engineering, Birmingham, AL 35294. Offers computational engineering (PhD); environmental health and safety engineering (PhD). *Students:* 14 full-time (4 women), 16 part-time (2 women); includes 7 minority (5 Black or African American, non-Hispanic/Latino; 1 Asian, non-Hispanic/Latino; 1 Hispanic/Latino), 5 international. Average age 35. In 2012, 1 doctorate awarded. *Degree requirements:* For doctorate, comprehensive exam, thesis/dissertation. *Entrance requirements:* For doctorate, GRE, undergraduate degree in a supporting field, official transcripts, evaluation forms. Additional exam requirements/recommendations for international students: Required—TOEFL (minimum score 550 paper-based; 100 iBT). *Application deadline:* For fall admission, 7/1 for domestic students; for spring admission, 4/1 for domestic students. *Expenses:* Tuition, state resident: full-time $6420; part-time $335 per credit hour. Tuition, nonresident: full-time $14,574; part-time $788 per credit hour. Tuition and fees vary according to course load and program. *Unit head:* Dr. Bharat Soni, Graduate Program Director, 205-934-8460, E-mail: bsoni@uab.edu. Website: http://www.uab.edu/engineering/degrees-cert/189-phd-in-interdisciplinary-engineering.

University of Alaska Fairbanks, College of Natural Sciences and Mathematics, Department of Physics, Fairbanks, AK 99775-5920. Offers computational physics (MS); physics (MAT, MS, PhD); space physics (MS, PhD). Part-time programs available. *Faculty:* 10 full-time (2 women). *Students:* 22 full-time (5 women), 3 part-time (0 women); includes 2 minority (1 American Indian or Alaska Native, non-Hispanic/Latino; 1 Asian, non-Hispanic/Latino), 7 international. Average age 30. 17 applicants, 24% accepted, 4 enrolled. In 2012, 3 master's, 2 doctorates awarded. Terminal master's awarded for partial completion of doctoral program. *Degree requirements:* For master's, comprehensive exam, thesis or alternative; for doctorate, comprehensive exam, thesis/dissertation, oral defense. *Entrance requirements:* Additional exam requirements/recommendations for international students: Required—TOEFL (minimum score 550 paper-based; 80 iBT). *Application deadline:* For fall admission, 6/1 for domestic students, 3/1 for international students; for spring admission, 10/15 for domestic students, 9/1 for international students. Applications are processed on a rolling basis. Application fee: $60. Electronic applications accepted. *Expenses:* Tuition, state resident: full-time $7038. Tuition, nonresident: full-time $14,382. Tuition and fees vary according to course level, course load and reciprocity agreements. *Financial support:* In 2012–13, 12 research assistantships with tuition reimbursements (averaging $16,543 per year), 10 teaching assistantships with tuition reimbursements (averaging $10,640 per year) were awarded; fellowships with tuition reimbursements, Federal Work-Study, scholarships/grants, health care benefits, and unspecified assistantships also available. Support available to part-time students. Financial award application deadline: 2/15; financial award applicants required to submit FAFSA. *Faculty research:* Atmospheric and ionospheric radar studies, space plasma theory, magnetospheric dynamics, space weather and auroral studies, turbulence and complex systems. *Unit head:* Ataur Chowdhury, Chair, 907-474-7339, Fax: 907-474-6130, E-mail: physics@uaf.edu. *Application contact:* Libby Eddy, Registrar and Director of Admissions, 907-474-7500, Fax: 907-474-7097, E-mail: admissions@uaf.edu. Website: http://www.uaf.edu/physics/.

University of California, Santa Barbara, Graduate Division, College of Engineering, Department of Computer Science, Santa Barbara, CA 93106-5110. Offers cognitive science (PhD); computational science and engineering (PhD); computer science (MS, PhD); technology and society (PhD). *Faculty:* 32 full-time (5 women), 5 part-time/adjunct (0 women). *Students:* 144 full-time (31 women); includes 8 minority (2 American Indian or Alaska Native, non-Hispanic/Latino; 5 Asian, non-Hispanic/Latino; 1 Hispanic/Latino), 95 international. Average age 27. 927 applicants, 10% accepted, 36 enrolled. In 2012, 36 master's, 12 doctorates awarded. Terminal master's awarded for partial completion of doctoral program. *Degree requirements:* For master's, comprehensive exam (for some programs), thesis (for some programs), project (for some programs); for doctorate, thesis/dissertation. *Entrance requirements:* For master's and doctorate, GRE. Additional exam requirements/recommendations for international students: Required—TOEFL (minimum score 600 paper-based; 100 iBT), IELTS (minimum score 7). *Application deadline:* For fall admission, 12/15 for domestic and international students. Application fee: $80 ($100 for international students). Electronic applications accepted. *Financial support:* In 2012–13, 116 students received support, including 36 fellowships with full and partial tuition reimbursements available (averaging $12,330 per year), 63 research assistantships with full and partial tuition reimbursements available (averaging $14,876 per year), 44 teaching assistantships with partial tuition reimbursements available (averaging $17,309 per year); career-related internships or fieldwork, Federal Work-Study, institutionally sponsored loans, scholarships/grants, health care benefits, tuition waivers (full and partial), and unspecified assistantships also available. Financial award application deadline: 12/15; financial award applicants required to submit FAFSA. *Faculty research:* Networking and security, database systems, computational science and engineering, programming languages and software engineering, human-computer interaction. *Unit head:* Subhash Suri, Chair, 805-893-5334, Fax: 805-893-8553, E-mail: suri@cs.ucsb.edu. *Application contact:* Katie Ellis, Graduate Advisor, 805-893-4322, Fax: 805-893-8553, E-mail: kellis@cs.ucsb.edu. Website: http://www.cs.ucsb.edu/.

University of California, Santa Barbara, Graduate Division, College of Engineering, Department of Mechanical Engineering, Santa Barbara, CA 93106-5070. Offers computational science and engineering (MS, PhD); mechanical engineering (MS, PhD); MS/PhD. *Faculty:* 27 full-time (4 women), 6 part-time/adjunct (2 women). *Students:* 77 full-time (7 women); includes 9 minority (7 Asian, non-Hispanic/Latino; 2 Hispanic/Latino), 27 international. Average age 26. 310 applicants, 11% accepted, 15 enrolled. In 2012, 5 master's, 6 doctorates awarded. *Degree requirements:* For master's, thesis; for doctorate, comprehensive exam, thesis/dissertation. *Entrance requirements:* For master's and doctorate, GRE. Additional exam requirements/recommendations for international students: Required—TOEFL (minimum score 550 paper-based; 80 iBT), IELTS (minimum score 7). *Application deadline:* For fall admission, 12/15 for domestic and international students. Application fee: $80 ($100 for international students). Electronic applications accepted. *Financial support:* In 2012–13, 71 students received support, including 9 fellowships with full and partial tuition reimbursements available (averaging $22,000 per year), 44 research assistantships with full and partial tuition reimbursements available (averaging $19,099 per year), 18 teaching assistantships with full and partial tuition reimbursements available (averaging $17,654 per year); scholarships/grants, health care benefits, tuition waivers (full and partial), and unspecified assistantships also available. Financial award application deadline: 12/15; financial award applicants required to submit FAFSA. *Faculty research:* Micro/nanoscale technology; computational science and engineering; dynamics systems, controls and robotics; thermofluid sciences; solid mechanics, materials, and structures. *Total annual research expenditures:* $4 million. *Unit head:* Dr. Kimberly Turner, Chair, 805-893-8080, Fax: 805-893-8651, E-mail: turner@engineering.ucsb.edu. *Application contact:* Laura L. Reynolds, Staff Graduate Program Advisor, 805-893-2239, Fax: 805-893-8651, E-mail: megrad@engineering.ucsb.edu. Website: http://www.me.ucsb.edu/.

University of California, Santa Barbara, Graduate Division, College of Letters and Sciences, Division of Mathematics, Life, and Physical Sciences, Department of Ecology, Evolution, and Marine Biology, Santa Barbara, CA 93106-9620. Offers computational science and engineering (MA); computational sciences and engineering (PhD); ecology, evolution, and marine biology (MA, PhD); MA/PhD. *Faculty:* 33 full-time (8 women). *Students:* 56 full-time (39 women); includes 11 minority (1 Black or African American, non-Hispanic/Latino; 5 Asian, non-Hispanic/Latino; 5 Hispanic/Latino), 3 international. Average age 30. 126 applicants, 15% accepted, 10 enrolled. In 2012, 5 master's, 4 doctorates awarded. *Degree requirements:* For master's, comprehensive exam (for some programs), thesis (for some programs); for doctorate, comprehensive exam, thesis/dissertation. *Entrance requirements:* For master's and doctorate, GRE General Test. Additional exam requirements/recommendations for international students: Required—TOEFL (minimum score 550 paper-based; 80 iBT), IELTS. *Application deadline:* For fall admission, 12/15 for domestic and international students. Application fee: $80 ($100 for international students). Electronic applications accepted. *Financial support:* In 2012–13, 50 students received support, including 50 fellowships with full and partial tuition reimbursements

available (averaging $10,812 per year), 13 research assistantships with full and partial tuition reimbursements available (averaging $8,441 per year), 95 teaching assistantships with partial tuition reimbursements available (averaging $9,346 per year); Federal Work-Study, scholarships/grants, traineeships, health care benefits, and tuition waivers (full and partial) also available. Financial award application deadline: 12/15; financial award applicants required to submit FAFSA. *Faculty research:* Community ecology, evolution, marine biology, population genetics, stream ecology. *Unit head:* Dr. Cheryl Briggs, Chair, 805-893-2415, Fax: 805-893-5885, E-mail: eembchair@lifesci.ucsb.edu. *Application contact:* Melanie Fujii, Student Affairs Officer, 805-893-2979, Fax: 805-893-5885, E-mail: eemb-info@lifesci.ucsb.edu. Website: http://www.lifesci.ucsb.edu/EEMB/index.html.

University of California, Santa Barbara, Graduate Division, College of Letters and Sciences, Division of Mathematics, Life, and Physical Sciences, Department of Mathematics, Santa Barbara, CA 93106-3080. Offers applied mathematics (MA), including computational science and engineering; mathematics (MA, PhD), including computational science and engineering; MA/PhD. *Faculty:* 28 full-time (2 women). *Students:* 50 full-time (13 women); includes 12 minority (1 Black or African American, non-Hispanic/Latino; 4 Asian, non-Hispanic/Latino; 7 Hispanic/Latino), 5 international. Average age 26. 186 applicants, 17% accepted, 10 enrolled. In 2012, 6 master's, 2 doctorates awarded. Terminal master's awarded for partial completion of doctoral program. *Degree requirements:* For master's, comprehensive exam (for some programs), thesis (for some programs); for doctorate, comprehensive exam, thesis/dissertation. *Entrance requirements:* For master's and doctorate, GRE General Test, GRE Subject Test (math). Additional exam requirements/recommendations for international students: Required—TOEFL (minimum score 575 paper-based; 80 iBT), IELTS (minimum score 7). *Application deadline:* For fall admission, 1/1 for domestic and international students. Application fee: $80 ($100 for international students). Electronic applications accepted. *Financial support:* In 2012–13, 48 students received support, including 4 fellowships with full tuition reimbursements available (averaging $20,000 per year), 6 research assistantships with full tuition reimbursements available (averaging $18,000 per year), 45 teaching assistantships with partial tuition reimbursements available (averaging $17,655 per year); Federal Work-Study, institutionally sponsored loans, health care benefits, and tuition waivers (full and partial) also available. Financial award application deadline: 3/2; financial award applicants required to submit FAFSA. *Faculty research:* Topology, differential geometry, algebra, applied mathematics, partial differential equations. *Total annual research expenditures:* $205,000. *Unit head:* Prof. David R. Morrison, Chair, 805-893-8340, Fax: 805-893-2385, E-mail: chair@math.ucsb.edu. *Application contact:* Medina Price, Graduate Advisor, 805-893-8192, Fax: 805-893-2385, E-mail: price@math.ucsb.edu. Website: http://www.math.ucsb.edu/.

University of Colorado Denver, College of Liberal Arts and Sciences, Department of Mathematical and Statistical Sciences, Denver, CO 80217. Offers applied mathematics (MS, PhD), including applied mathematics, applied probability (MS), applied statistics (MS), computational biology, computational mathematics (PhD), discrete mathematics, finite geometry (PhD), mathematics education (PhD), mathematics of engineering and science (MS), numerical analysis, operations research (MS), optimization and operations research (PhD), probability (PhD), statistics (PhD). Part-time programs available. *Faculty:* 20 full-time (4 women), 3 part-time/adjunct (0 women). *Students:* 43 full-time (12 women), 13 part-time (2 women); includes 9 minority (1 Black or African American, non-Hispanic/Latino; 4 Asian, non-Hispanic/Latino; 4 Hispanic/Latino), 9 international. Average age 32. 63 applicants, 71% accepted, 14 enrolled. In 2012, 10 master's, 6 doctorates awarded. *Degree requirements:* For master's, comprehensive exam, thesis optional; 30 hours of course work with minimum GPA of 3.0; for doctorate, comprehensive exam, thesis/dissertation, 42 hours of course work with minimum GPA of 3.25. *Entrance requirements:* For master's, GRE General Test; GRE Subject Test in math (recommended), 30 hours of course work in mathematics (24 of which must be upper-division mathematics), bachelor's degree with minimum GPA of 3.0; for doctorate, GRE General Test; GRE Subject Test in math (recommended), 30 hours of course work in mathematics (24 of which must be upper-division mathematics), master's degree with minimum GPA of 3.25. Additional exam requirements/recommendations for international students: Required—TOEFL (minimum score 537 paper-based; 75 iBT); Recommended—IELTS (minimum score 6.5). *Application deadline:* For fall admission, 2/1 for domestic and international students; for spring admission, 10/1 for domestic and international students. Application fee: $50 ($75 for international students). Electronic applications accepted. *Expenses:* Tuition, state resident: full-time $7712; part-time $355 per credit hour. Tuition, nonresident: full-time $22,038; part-time $1087 per credit hour. *Required fees:* $1110; $1. Tuition and fees vary according to course load, campus/location and program. *Financial support:* In 2012–13, 33 students received support. Fellowships with partial tuition reimbursements available, research assistantships with full tuition reimbursements available, teaching assistantships with full tuition reimbursements available, Federal Work-Study, institutionally sponsored loans, scholarships/grants, traineeships, and unspecified assistantships available. Financial award application deadline: 4/1; financial award applicants required to submit FAFSA. *Faculty research:* Computational mathematics, computational biology, discrete mathematics and geometry, probability and statistics, optimization. *Unit head:* Dr. Stephen Billups, Graduate Program Director, 303-556-4814, E-mail: stephen.billups@ucdenver.edu. *Application contact:* Margie Bopp, Graduate Program Assistant, 303-556-2341, E-mail: margie.bopp@

308 www.petersonsbooks.com

Peterson's Graduate Programs in the Physical Sciences, Mathematics, Agricultural Sciences, the Environment & Natural Resources 2014

ucdenver.edu. Website: http://www.ucdenver.edu/academics/colleges/CLAS/Departments/math/Pages/MathStats.aspx.

The University of Iowa, Graduate College, Program in Applied Mathematical and Computational Sciences, Iowa City, IA 52242-1316. Offers PhD. *Degree requirements:* For doctorate, comprehensive exam, thesis/dissertation. *Entrance requirements:* For doctorate, GRE General Test, minimum GPA of 3.0. Additional exam requirements/recommendations for international students: Required—TOEFL (minimum score 620 paper-based; 105 iBT). Electronic applications accepted.

The University of Kansas, Graduate Studies, College of Liberal Arts and Sciences, Department of Physics and Astronomy, Lawrence, KS 66045. Offers computational physics and astronomy (MS); physics (MS, PhD). *Faculty:* 27. *Students:* 47 full-time (5 women), 3 part-time (0 women); includes 3 minority (1 Black or African American, non-Hispanic/Latino; 2 Two or more races, non-Hispanic/Latino), 13 international. Average age 29. 69 applicants, 39% accepted, 14 enrolled. In 2012, 1 master's, 5 doctorates awarded. Terminal master's awarded for partial completion of doctoral program. *Degree requirements:* For master's, thesis (for some programs); for doctorate, comprehensive exam, thesis/dissertation, computer skills, communication skills. *Entrance requirements:* For master's and doctorate, GRE Subject Test (physics), undergraduate degree. Additional exam requirements/recommendations for international students: Required—TOEFL (minimum score 53 paper-based; 20 iBT). *Application deadline:* For fall admission, 12/1 priority date for domestic students, 12/1 for international students; for spring admission, 10/1 priority date for domestic students, 10/1 for international students. Applications are processed on a rolling basis. Application fee: $55 ($65 for international students). Electronic applications accepted. *Financial support:* Fellowships with full and partial tuition reimbursements, research assistantships with full and partial tuition reimbursements, teaching assistantships with full and partial tuition reimbursements, health care benefits, and unspecified assistantships available. Financial award application deadline: 4/1; financial award applicants required to submit FAFSA. *Faculty research:* Astrophysics, biophysics, high energy physics, nanophysics, nuclear physics. *Unit head:* Dr. Stephen J. Sanders, Chair, 785-864-4626, Fax: 785-864-5262, E-mail: ssanders@ku.edu. *Application contact:* Hume Feldman, Graduate Director, 785-864-4626, Fax: 785-864-5262, E-mail: humef@ku.edu. Website: http://www.physics.ku.edu.

University of Lethbridge, School of Graduate Studies, Lethbridge, AB T1K 3M4, Canada. Offers accounting (MScM); addictions counseling (M Sc); agricultural biotechnology (M Sc); agricultural studies (M Sc, MA); anthropology (MA); archaeology (MA); art (MA, MFA); biochemistry (M Sc); biological sciences (M Sc); biomolecular science (PhD); biosystems and biodiversity (PhD); Canadian studies (MA); chemistry (M Sc); computer science (M Sc); computer science and geographical information science (M Sc); counseling psychology (M Ed); dramatic arts (MA); earth, space, and physical science (PhD); economics (MA); educational leadership (M Ed); English (MA); environmental science (M Sc); evolution and behavior (PhD); exercise science (M Sc); finance (MScM); French (MA); French/German (MA); French/Spanish (MA); general education (M Ed); general management (MScM); geography (M Sc, MA); German (MA); health science (M Sc); history (MA); human resource management and labour relations (MScM); individualized multidisciplinary (M Sc, MA); information systems (MScM); international management (MScM); kinesiology (M Sc, MA); management (M Sc, MA); marketing (MScM); mathematics (M Sc); music (M Mus, MA); Native American studies (MA); neuroscience (M Sc, PhD); new media (MA); nursing (M Sc); philosophy (MA); physics (M Sc); policy and strategy (MScM); political science (MA); psychology (M Sc, MA); religious studies (MA); social sciences (MA); sociology (MA); theatre and dramatic arts (MFA); theoretical and computational science (PhD); urban and regional studies (MA); women's studies (MA). Part-time and evening/weekend programs available. *Degree requirements:* For doctorate, comprehensive exam, thesis/dissertation. *Entrance requirements:* For master's, GMAT (M Sc in management), bachelor's degree in related field, minimum GPA of 3.0 during previous 20 graded semester courses, 2 years teaching or related experience (M Ed); for doctorate, master's degree, minimum graduate GPA of 3.5. Additional exam requirements/recommendations for international students: Required—TOEFL. *Faculty research:* Movement and brain plasticity, gibberellin physiology, photosynthesis, carbon cycling, molecular properties of main-group ring components.

University of Manitoba, Faculty of Graduate Studies, Faculty of Science, Program in Mathematical, Computational and Statistical Sciences, Winnipeg, MB R3T 2N2, Canada. Offers MMCSS.

University of Massachusetts Lowell, College of Sciences, Department of Mathematical Sciences, Lowell, MA 01854-2881. Offers applied mathematics (MS); computational mathematics (PhD); mathematics (MS). Part-time programs available. *Entrance requirements:* For master's, GRE General Test.

University of Michigan–Dearborn, College of Arts, Sciences, and Letters, Master of Science in Applied and Computational Mathematics Program, Dearborn, MI 48128. Offers MS. Part-time and evening/weekend programs available. *Faculty:* 8 full-time (2 women). *Students:* 2 full-time (1 woman), 13 part-time (3 women); includes 2 minority (1 Black or African American, non-Hispanic/Latino; 1 Asian, non-Hispanic/Latino). Average age 36. 14 applicants, 79% accepted, 7 enrolled. In 2012, 3 master's awarded. *Degree requirements:* For master's, thesis or alternative, project. *Entrance requirements:* For master's, 3 letters of recommendation, minimum GPA of 3.0, 2 years course work in math. Additional exam requirements/recommendations for international students: Required—TOEFL (minimum score 560 paper-based). *Application deadline:* For fall admission, 8/1 priority date for domestic students, 4/1 for international students; for winter admission, 12/1 priority date for domestic students, 11/1 for international students; for spring admission, 4/1 for domestic students, 3/1 for international students. Applications are processed on a rolling basis. Application fee: $60. Electronic applications accepted. *Expenses:* Tuition, state resident: full-time $4928; part-time $575 per credit hour. Tuition, nonresident: full-time $9454; part-time $1093 per credit hour. *Required fees:* $187 per semester. Tuition and fees vary according to program. *Financial support:* Federal Work-Study and scholarships/grants available. Support available to part-time students. Financial award application deadline: 4/1; financial award applicants required to submit FAFSA. *Faculty research:* Partial differential equations, statistics, mathematical biology, approximation theory, stochastic processes. *Unit head:* Dr. Thomas Snabb, Director, 313-593-5162, E-mail: tsnabb@umich.edu. *Application contact:* Carol Ligienza, Coordinator, CASL Graduate Programs, 313-593-1183, Fax: 313-583-6700, E-mail: caslgrad@umich.edu. Website: http://www.casl.umd.umich.edu/563801/.

University of Minnesota, Duluth, Graduate School, Swenson College of Science and Engineering, Department of Mathematics and Statistics, Duluth, MN 55812-2496. Offers applied and computational mathematics (MS). Part-time programs available. *Degree requirements:* For master's, thesis or alternative. *Entrance requirements:* For master's, GRE General Test, minimum GPA of 3.0. Additional exam requirements/recommendations for international students: Required—TOEFL (minimum score 550 paper-based; 79 iBT); Recommended—TWE. Electronic applications accepted. *Faculty research:* Discrete mathematics, diagnostic markers, combinatorics, biostatistics, mathematical modeling and scientific computation.

University of Minnesota, Twin Cities Campus, Graduate School, Scientific Computation Program, Minneapolis, MN 55455-0213. Offers MS, PhD. Part-time programs available. *Degree requirements:* For master's, thesis; for doctorate, thesis/dissertation. *Entrance requirements:* For doctorate, GRE General Test. Additional exam requirements/recommendations for international students: Required—TOEFL (minimum score 550 paper-based; 79 iBT), IELTS (minimum score 6.5). Electronic applications accepted. *Faculty research:* Parallel computations, quantum mechanical dynamics, computational materials science, computational fluid dynamics, computational neuroscience.

University of New Mexico, Graduate School, School of Engineering, Program in Computational Science and Engineering, Albuquerque, NM 87106. Offers Post-Doctoral Certificate. In 2012, 1 Post-Doctoral Certificate awarded. *Degree requirements:* For Post-Doctoral Certificate, thesis. *Entrance requirements:* For degree, admission to master's or doctoral program at the University of New Mexico or completion of bachelor's degree. *Application deadline:* For fall admission, 6/30 for domestic students; for spring admission, 11/15 for domestic students. Application fee: $50. Electronic applications accepted. *Expenses:* Tuition, state resident: full-time $3296; part-time $276.73 per credit hour. Tuition, nonresident: full-time $10,604; part-time $885.74 per credit hour. *Required fees:* $628. *Financial support:* Application deadline: 3/1. *Faculty research:* Arts technology, biophysics and nanoscale systems, chemistry and chemical biology, civil engineering, climate and weather modeling, computational biology and bioinformatics, cyberinfrastructure, digital arts and humanities, electromagnetics, energy grid modeling, high performance computing and scalable systems, image processing, materials physics, visualization and virtual environments, observational astronomy, open science grid, particle physics, quantum materials and devices, systems biology. *Unit head:* Prof. Susan R. Atlas, Director, Center for Advanced Research Computing (CARC), 505-277-8249, Fax: 505-277-8235, E-mail: director@carc.unm.edu. *Application contact:* Abra Altman, Program Coordinator, 505-277-8245, Fax: 505-277-8235, E-mail: aaltman@carc.unm.edu. Website: http://www.carc.unm.edu/education/cse-program.

University of Notre Dame, Graduate School, College of Science, Department of Applied and Computational Mathematics and Statistics, Notre Dame, IN 46556. Offers applied and computational mathematics and statistics (PhD); applied statistics (MS); computational finance (MS).

University of Pennsylvania, School of Arts and Sciences, Graduate Group in Applied Mathematics and Computational Science, Philadelphia, PA 19104. Offers PhD. *Faculty:* 26 full-time (2 women), 1 part-time/adjunct (0 women). *Students:* 27 full-time (7 women), 1 (woman) part-time, 26 international. 132 applicants, 11% accepted, 8 enrolled. *Application deadline:* For fall admission, 1/15 for domestic students. *Financial support:* Institutionally sponsored loans, scholarships/grants, traineeships, health care benefits, and unspecified assistantships available. *Application contact:* Arts and Sciences Graduate Admissions, 215-573-5816, Fax: 215-573-8068, E-mail: gdasadmis@sas.upenn.edu. Website: http://www.amcs.upenn.edu.

University of Puerto Rico, Mayagüez Campus, Graduate Studies, College of Arts and Sciences, Department of Mathematical Sciences, Mayagüez, PR 00681-9000. Offers applied mathematics (MS); pure mathematics (MS); scientific computation (MS); statistics (MS). Part-time programs available. *Faculty:* 45 full-time (7 women), 1 part-time/adjunct (0 women). *Students:* 34 full-time (10 women), 1 part-time (0 women); includes 30 minority (all Hispanic/Latino), 25 international. 8 applicants, 88% accepted, 7 enrolled. In 2012, 5 master's awarded. *Degree requirements:* For master's, one foreign language, comprehensive exam, thesis optional. *Entrance requirements:* For master's, undergraduate degree in mathematics or its equivalent. *Application deadline:* For fall admission, 2/15 for domestic and international students; for spring admission, 9/15 for domestic and international students. Applications are processed on a rolling basis. Application fee: $25. Tuition and fees vary according to course level and course load. *Financial support:* In 2012–13, 31 students received support, including 5 research assistantships (averaging $15,000 per year), 26 teaching assistantships (averaging $8,500 per year); Federal Work-Study and institutionally sponsored loans also available. *Faculty research:* Automata theory, linear algebra, logic. *Unit head:* Dr. Omar Colon, Director, 787-832-4040 Ext. 3848, Fax: 787-265-5454, E-mail: omar.colon.reyes@gmail.com. Website: http://math.uprm.edu/.

University of Southern Mississippi, Graduate School, College of Science and Technology, Department of Mathematics, Hattiesburg, MS 39406-0001. Offers computational science (PhD); mathematics (MS). Part-time programs available. *Faculty:* 11 full-time (3 women), 1 part-time/adjunct (0 women). *Students:* 20 full-time (9 women), 6 part-time (3 women); includes 6 minority (5 Black or African American, non-Hispanic/Latino; 1 Two or more races, non-Hispanic/Latino), 9 international. Average age 33. 29 applicants, 59% accepted, 13 enrolled. In 2012, 5 master's, 1 doctorate awarded. *Degree requirements:* For master's, comprehensive exam, thesis or alternative; for doctorate, comprehensive exam, thesis/dissertation. *Entrance requirements:* For master's, GRE General Test, minimum GPA of 2.75 in last 60 hours; for doctorate, GRE General Test, minimum GPA of 3.5. Additional exam requirements/recommendations for international students: Required—TOEFL, IELTS. *Application deadline:* For fall admission, 3/15 priority date for domestic students, 3/15 for international students; for spring admission, 1/10 priority date for domestic students, 1/10 for international students. Applications are processed on a rolling basis. Application fee: $50. Electronic applications accepted. *Financial support:* In 2012–13, fellowships (averaging $18,000 per year), research assistantships with full tuition reimbursements (averaging $11,500 per year), teaching assistantships with full tuition reimbursements (averaging $11,408 per year) were awarded; Federal Work-Study, scholarships/grants, health care benefits, and unspecified assistantships also available. Financial award application deadline: 3/15; financial award applicants required to submit FAFSA. *Faculty research:* Dynamical systems, numerical analysis and multigrid methods, random number generation, matrix theory, group theory. *Unit head:* Dr. Joseph Kolibal, Interim Chair, 601-266-4289, Fax: 601-266-5818. *Application contact:* Dr. James Lambers, Director, Graduate Admissions, 601-266-4289, Fax: 601-266-5818. Website: http://www.usm.edu/graduateschool/table.php.

University of Southern Mississippi, Graduate School, College of Science and Technology, Department of Physics and Astronomy, Hattiesburg, MS 39406-0001. Offers computational science (PhD); physics (MS). *Faculty:* 10 full-time (1 woman). *Students:* 10 full-time (2 women), 2 part-time (1 woman), 5 international. Average age 30. 47 applicants, 38% accepted, 3 enrolled. In 2012, 3 master's awarded. *Degree requirements:* For master's, comprehensive exam, thesis; for doctorate, comprehensive exam, thesis/dissertation. *Entrance requirements:* For master's, GRE General Test, minimum GPA of 2.75 in last 60 hours; for doctorate, GRE General Test, minimum GPA of 3.5. Additional exam requirements/recommendations for international students: Required—TOEFL, IELTS. *Application deadline:* For fall admission, 3/1 priority date for domestic students, 3/1 for international students; for spring admission, 1/10 priority date for domestic students, 1/10 for international students. Applications are processed on a rolling basis. Application fee: $50. *Financial support:* In 2012–13, research assistantships with full tuition reimbursements (averaging $11,800 per year), 15 teaching assistantships with full tuition reimbursements (averaging $11,800 per year) were awarded; Federal Work-Study, scholarships/grants, health care benefits, and unspecified assistantships also available. Financial award application deadline: 3/15; financial award applicants required to submit FAFSA. *Faculty research:* Polymers, atomic physics, fluid mechanics, liquid crystals, refractory materials. *Unit head:* Dr. Khin Maung, Chair, 601-266-4934, Fax: 601-266-5149. Website: http://www.usm.edu/graduateschool/table.php.

University of Southern Mississippi, Graduate School, College of Science and Technology, School of Computing, Hattiesburg, MS 39406-0001. Offers computational science (MS, PhD); computer science (MS). *Faculty:* 18 full-time (3 women), 1 (woman) part-time/adjunct. *Students:* 50 full-time (15 women), 9 part-time (2 women); includes 4 minority (1 Black or African American, non-Hispanic/Latino; 2 Asian, non-Hispanic/Latino; 1 Hispanic/Latino), 42 international. Average age 27. 134 applicants, 60% accepted, 22 enrolled. In 2012, 23 master's, 3 doctorates awarded. *Degree requirements:* For master's, comprehensive exam, thesis; for doctorate, comprehensive exam, thesis/dissertation. *Entrance requirements:* For master's, GRE General Test, minimum GPA of 2.75 in last 60 hours; for doctorate, GRE General Test, minimum GPA of 3.5. Additional exam requirements/recommendations for international students: Required—TOEFL, IELTS. *Application deadline:* For fall admission, 3/15 priority date for domestic students, 3/15 for international students; for spring admission, 1/10 priority date for domestic students, 1/10 for international students. Applications are processed on a rolling basis. Application fee: $50. Electronic applications accepted. *Financial support:* In 2012–13, 29 research assistantships with full tuition reimbursements (averaging $8,800 per year), 7 teaching assistantships with full tuition reimbursements (averaging $10,000 per year) were awarded; Federal Work-Study, institutionally sponsored loans, scholarships/grants, health care benefits, and unspecified assistantships also available. Financial award application deadline: 3/15; financial award applicants required to submit FAFSA. *Faculty research:* Satellite telecommunications, advanced life-support systems, artificial intelligence. *Application contact:* Dr. Chaoyang Zhang, Manager of Graduate Admissions, 601-266-4949, Fax: 601-266-6452. Website: http://www.usm.edu/graduateschool/table.php.

The University of Tennessee at Chattanooga, Graduate School, College of Engineering and Computer Science, Program in Computational Engineering, Chattanooga, TN 37403. Offers PhD. *Faculty:* 10 full-time (0 women). *Students:* 14 full-time (2 women), 11 part-time (1 woman); includes 2 minority (1 Asian, non-Hispanic/Latino; 1 Two or more races, non-Hispanic/Latino), 14 international. Average age 30. 11 applicants, 36% accepted, 3 enrolled. In 2012, 1 doctorate awarded. *Degree requirements:* For doctorate, comprehensive exam, thesis/dissertation. *Entrance requirements:* For doctorate, GRE General Test. Additional exam requirements/recommendations for international students: Required—TOEFL (minimum score 550 paper-based; 79 iBT), IELTS (minimum score 6). *Application deadline:* For fall admission, 6/14 priority date for domestic students, 6/1 for international students; for spring admission, 10/25 priority date for domestic students, 10/1 for international students. Applications are processed on a rolling basis. Application fee: $30 ($35 for international students). Electronic applications accepted. *Expenses:* Tuition, state resident: full-time $6860; part-time $381 per credit hour. Tuition, nonresident: full-time $21,206; part-time $1178 per credit hour. *Required fees:* $1490; $180 per credit hour. *Financial support:* In 2012–13, 19 research assistantships with tuition reimbursements (averaging $6,953 per year) were awarded; career-related internships or fieldwork, scholarships/grants, and unspecified assistantships also available. Support available to part-time students. *Faculty research:* Computational fluid dynamics, design optimization, solution algorithms, hydronamics and propulsion. *Unit head:* Dr. Tim Swafford, Department Head, 423-425-5507, Fax: 423-425-5517, E-mail: tim-swafford@utc.edu. *Application contact:* Dr. Jerald Ainsworth, Dean of Graduate Studies, 423-425-4478, Fax: 423-425-5223, E-mail: jerald-ainsworth@utc.edu. Website: http://www.utc.edu/Academic/EngineeringAndComputerScience/grad/.

The University of Tennessee at Chattanooga, Graduate School, College of Engineering and Computer Science, Program in Engineering, Chattanooga, TN 37403. Offers chemical engineering (MS Engr); civil engineering (MS Engr); computational engineering (MS Engr); electrical engineering (MS Engr); industrial engineering (MS Engr); mechanical engineering (MS Engr). Part-time and evening/weekend programs available. *Faculty:* 23 full-time (3 women), 2 part-time/adjunct (0 women). *Students:* 33 full-time (8 women), 63 part-time (13 women); includes 14 minority (5 Black or African American, non-Hispanic/Latino; 5 Asian, non-Hispanic/Latino; 4 Hispanic/Latino), 23 international. Average age 30. 82 applicants, 52% accepted, 27 enrolled. In 2012, 20 master's awarded. *Degree requirements:* For master's, comprehensive exam, thesis or alternative, engineering project. *Entrance requirements:* For master's, GRE General Test, minimum undergraduate GPA of 2.5 or 3.0 in last 30 hours of coursework. Additional exam requirements/recommendations for international students: Required—TOEFL (minimum score 550 paper-based; 79 iBT), IELTS (minimum score 6). *Application deadline:* For fall admission, 6/14 priority date for domestic students, 6/1 for international students; for spring admission, 10/25 priority date for domestic students, 10/1 for international students. Applications are processed on a rolling basis. Application fee: $30 ($35 for international students). Electronic applications accepted. *Expenses:* Tuition, state resident: full-time $6860; part-time $381 per credit hour. Tuition, nonresident: full-time $21,206; part-time $1178 per credit hour. *Required fees:* $1490; $180 per credit hour. *Financial support:* In 2012–13, 25 research assistantships with tuition reimbursements (averaging $7,672 per year), 7 teaching assistantships with tuition reimbursements (averaging $5,740 per year) were awarded; career-related internships or fieldwork, scholarships/grants, and unspecified assistantships also available. Support available to part-time students. *Faculty research:* Quality control and reliability engineering, financial management, thermal science, energy conservation, structural analysis. *Total annual research expenditures:* $1.6 million. *Unit head:* Dr. William Sutton, Dean, 423-425-2256, Fax: 423-425-5229, E-mail: will-sutton@utc.edu. *Application contact:* Dr. Jerald Ainsworth, Dean of Graduate Studies, 423-425-4478, Fax: 423-425-5223, E-mail: jerald-ainsworth@utc.edu. Website: http://www.utc.edu/Departments/engrcs/ms_engr.php.

The University of Texas at Austin, Graduate School, Program in Computational Science, Engineering, and Mathematics, Austin, TX 78712-1111. Offers MS, PhD. Terminal master's awarded for partial completion of doctoral program. *Degree requirements:* For master's, thesis optional; for doctorate, thesis/dissertation, 3 area qualifying exams. Electronic applications accepted.

The University of Texas at El Paso, Graduate School, College of Science, Computational Science Program, El Paso, TX 79968-0001. Offers MS, PhD. *Degree requirements:* For master's, thesis or internship; for doctorate, thesis/dissertation. *Entrance requirements:* For doctorate, GRE, statement of purpose, letters of recommendation. Additional exam requirements/recommendations for international students: Required—TOEFL; Recommended—IELTS. Electronic applications accepted.

University of Utah, Graduate School, College of Engineering, School of Computing, Computational Engineering and Science Program, Salt Lake City, UT 84112. Offers MS. *Students:* 10 full-time (1 woman), 9 part-time (1 woman); includes 3 minority (1 American Indian or Alaska Native, non-Hispanic/Latino; 2 Two or more races, non-Hispanic/Latino), 8 international. Average age 33. 12 applicants, 83% accepted, 5 enrolled. In 2012, 3 master's awarded. *Degree requirements:* For master's, comprehensive exam, thesis (for some programs). *Entrance requirements:* For master's, minimum GPA of 3.0. Additional exam requirements/recommendations for international students: Required—TOEFL (minimum score 500 paper-based; 61 iBT), IELTS (minimum score 6). *Application deadline:* For fall admission, 1/15 priority date for domestic students, 1/15 for international students. Application fee: $55 ($65 for international students). Electronic applications accepted. *Expenses:* Contact institution. *Financial support:* In 2012–13, 1 student received support, including 1 fellowship (averaging $15,000 per year), 2 research assistantships with full tuition reimbursements available (averaging $12,000 per year), 1 teaching assistantship with full tuition reimbursement available (averaging $12,000 per year); health care benefits and unspecified assistantships also available. Financial award application deadline: 12/15; financial award applicants required to submit FAFSA. *Faculty research:* Mathematical modeling, the formulation of the numerical methodology for solving the problem, the selection of the appropriate computer architecture and algorithms, and the effective interpretation of the results through visualization and/or statistical reduction. *Unit head:* Dr. Kris Sikorski, Director, 801-581-8579, Fax: 801-581-5843, E-mail: sikorski@cs.utah.edu. *Application contact:* Ann Carlstrom, Graduate Advisor, 801-581-7631, Fax: 801-581-5843, E-mail: annc@cs.utah.edu. Website: http://www.ces.utah.edu.

University of Utah, Graduate School, Professional Master of Science and Technology Program, Salt Lake City, UT 84112-1107. Offers biotechnology (PSM); computational science (PSM); environmental science (PSM); science instrumentation (PSM). Part-time programs available. *Students:* 20 full-time (11 women), 36 part-time (9 women); includes 4 minority (3 Hispanic/Latino; 1 Native Hawaiian or other Pacific Islander, non-Hispanic/Latino), 3 international. Average age 32. 53 applicants, 55% accepted, 23 enrolled. In 2012, 25 master's awarded. *Degree requirements:* For master's, internship. *Entrance requirements:* For master's, GRE (recommended), minimum undergraduate GPA of 3.0, bachelor's degree from accredited university or college. Additional exam requirements/recommendations for international students: Required—TOEFL (minimum score 500 paper-based; 61 iBT), IELTS (minimum score 6). *Application deadline:* For fall

admission, 2/1 for domestic and international students. Application fee: $55 ($65 for international students). Electronic applications accepted. *Financial support:* Fellowships, research assistantships, teaching assistantships, and unspecified assistantships available. *Unit head:* Jennifer Schmidt, Program Director, 801-585-5630, E-mail: jennifer.schmidt@gradschool.utah.edu. *Application contact:* Jay Derek Payne, Project Coordinator, 801-585-3650, Fax: 801-585-6749, E-mail: derek.payne@gradschool.utah.edu. Website: http://pmst.utah.edu/.

University of Washington, Graduate School, College of Arts and Sciences, Department of Mathematics, Seattle, WA 98195. Offers mathematics (MA, MS, PhD); numerical analysis (MS); optimization (MS). Part-time programs available. Terminal master's awarded for partial completion of doctoral program. *Degree requirements:* For master's, thesis optional; for doctorate, 2 foreign languages, thesis/dissertation. *Entrance requirements:* For master's, GRE, minimum GPA of 3.0; for doctorate, GRE General Test, GRE Subject Test (mathematics), minimum GPA of 3.0. Additional exam requirements/recommendations for international students: Required—TOEFL. Electronic applications accepted. *Faculty research:* Algebra, analysis, probability, combinatorics and geometry.

Western Kentucky University, Graduate Studies, Ogden College of Science and Engineering, Department of Mathematics and Computer Science, Bowling Green, KY 42101. Offers computational mathematics (MS); computer science (MS); mathematics (MA, MS). *Degree requirements:* For master's, comprehensive exam, thesis optional, written exam. *Entrance requirements:* For master's, GRE General Test, minimum GPA of 2.75. Additional exam requirements/recommendations for international students: Required—TOEFL (minimum score 555 paper-based; 79 iBT). *Faculty research:* Differential equations numerical analysis, probability statistics, algebra, typology, knot theory.

Western Michigan University, Graduate College, College of Arts and Sciences, Department of Mathematics, Program in Applied and Computational Mathematics, Kalamazoo, MI 49008. Offers MS.

Mathematical and Computational Finance

Baruch College of the City University of New York, Weissman School of Arts and Sciences, Program in Financial Engineering, New York, NY 10010-5585. Offers MS. *Entrance requirements:* For master's, GRE General Test or GMAT, 3 recommendations. Additional exam requirements/recommendations for international students: Required—TOEFL, TWE.

Boston University, School of Management, Boston, MA 02215. Offers business administration (MBA); executive business administration (EMBA); investment management (MS); management (PhD); mathematical finance (MS, PhD); JD/MBA; MBA/MA; MBA/MPH; MBA/MS; MBA/MSIS; MD/MBA; MS/MBA. *Accreditation:* AACSB. Part-time and evening/weekend programs available. *Faculty:* 185 full-time (49 women), 60 part-time/adjunct (15 women). *Students:* 504 full-time (162 women), 750 part-time (269 women); includes 180 minority (18 Black or African American, non-Hispanic/Latino; 120 Asian, non-Hispanic/Latino; 29 Hispanic/Latino; 13 Two or more races, non-Hispanic/Latino), 256 international. Average age 29. 1,387 applicants, 28% accepted, 160 enrolled. In 2012, 498 master's, 5 doctorates awarded. *Degree requirements:* For doctorate, comprehensive exam, thesis/dissertation. *Entrance requirements:* For master's, GMAT (for MBA and MS in investment management); GMAT or GRE General Test (for MS in mathematical finance), resume, 2 letters of recommendation; for doctorate, GMAT or GRE General Test, resume, personal statement, 3 letters of recommendation, 3 essays, official transcripts. *Application deadline:* For fall admission, 1/5 for domestic and international students; for spring admission, 11/1 for domestic students. Application fee: $125. Electronic applications accepted. *Expenses:* Tuition: Full-time $42,400; part-time $1325 per credit. *Required fees:* $40 per semester. *Financial support:* Career-related internships or fieldwork, Federal Work-Study, institutionally sponsored loans, scholarships/grants, and tuition waivers (partial) available. Financial award applicants required to submit FAFSA. *Faculty research:* Innovation policy and productivity, corporate social responsibility, risk management, information systems, entrepreneurship, clean energy, sustainability. *Unit head:* Kenneth W. Freeman, Professor/Dean, 617-353-9720, Fax: 617-353-5581, E-mail: kfreeman@bu.edu. *Application contact:* Patti Cudney, Assistant Dean, Graduate Admissions, 617-353-2670, Fax: 617-353-7368, E-mail: mba@bu.edu. Website: http://management.bu.edu/.

Carnegie Mellon University, Mellon College of Science, Department of Mathematical Sciences, Pittsburgh, PA 15213-3891. Offers algorithms, combinatorics, and optimization (PhD); applied mathematics (PhD); computational finance (MS); mathematical finance (PhD); mathematical sciences (MS, DA, PhD); pure and applied logic (PhD). Part-time programs available. Terminal master's awarded for partial completion of doctoral program. *Degree requirements:* For doctorate, thesis/dissertation. *Entrance requirements:* For master's and doctorate, GRE General Test, GRE Subject Test. Additional exam requirements/recommendations for international students: Required—TOEFL. Electronic applications accepted. *Faculty research:* Continuum mechanics, discrete mathematics, applied and computational mathematics.

Carnegie Mellon University, Tepper School of Business, Pittsburgh, PA 15213-3891. Offers accounting (PhD); algorithms, combinatorics, and optimization (MS, PhD); business management and software engineering (MBMSE); civil engineering and industrial management (MS); computational finance (MSCF); economics (MS, PhD); electronic commerce (MS); environmental engineering and management (MEEM); finance (PhD); financial economics (PhD); industrial administration (MBA), including administration and public management; information systems (PhD); management of manufacturing and automation (PhD); marketing (PhD); mathematical finance (PhD); operations research (PhD); organizational behavior and theory (PhD); political economy (PhD); production and operations management (PhD); public policy and management (MS, MSED); software engineering and business management (MS); JD/MS; JD/MSIA; M Div/MS; MOM/MSIA; MSCF/MSIA. JD/MSIA offered jointly with University of Pittsburgh. Part-time programs available. Terminal master's awarded for partial completion of doctoral program. *Degree requirements:* For doctorate, thesis/dissertation. *Entrance requirements:* For master's, GMAT. Additional exam requirements/recommendations for international students: Required—TOEFL. *Expenses:* Contact institution.

DePaul University, Charles H. Kellstadt Graduate School of Business, Department of Finance, Chicago, IL 60604-2287. Offers banking (MBA); behavioral finance (MBA); computational finance (MS); finance (MBA, MS); financial analysis (MBA); financial management and control (MBA); investment management (MBA); real estate finance and investment (MBA); wealth management (MS). Part-time and evening/weekend programs available. *Faculty:* 13 full-time (1 woman), 12 part-time/adjunct (2 women). *Students:* 492 full-time (210 women), 173 part-time (43 women); includes 72 minority (15 Black or African American, non-Hispanic/Latino; 27 Asian, non-Hispanic/Latino; 23 Hispanic/Latino; 7 Two or more races, non-Hispanic/Latino), 262 international. Average age 28. *Entrance requirements:* For master's, GMAT, 2 letters of recommendation, resume. Additional exam requirements/recommendations for international students: Required—TOEFL (minimum score 550 paper-based; 80 iBT). *Application deadline:* For fall admission, 7/1 for domestic students, 6/1 for international students; for winter admission, 10/1 for domestic students, 9/1 for international students; for spring admission, 2/1 for domestic students, 1/1 for international students. Applications are processed on a rolling basis. Application fee: $60. Electronic applications accepted. *Financial support:* Application deadline: 6/1; applicants required to submit FAFSA. *Unit head:* Ali M. Fatemi, Professor and Chair, 312-362-8826, Fax: 312-362-6566, E-mail: afatemi@depaul.edu. *Application contact:* Melissa Booth, Director of Admission and Recruitment, 312-362-6353, Fax: 312-362-6677, E-mail: kgsb@depaul.edu. Website: http://finance.depaul.edu/index.asp.

DePaul University, College of Computing and Digital Media, Chicago, IL 60604. Offers animation (MA, MFA); applied technology (MS); business information technology (MS); cinema (MFA); cinema production (MS); computational finance (MS); computer and information sciences (PhD); computer game development

Peterson's Graduate Programs in the Physical Sciences, Mathematics, Agricultural Sciences, the Environment & Natural Resources 2014

www.petersonsbooks.com **311**

(MS); computer information and network security (MS); computer science (MS); e-commerce technology (MS); human-computer interaction (MS); information systems (MS); information technology project management (MS); network engineering and management (MS); predictive analytics (MS); screenwriting (MFA); software engineering (MS); JD/MS. Part-time and evening/weekend programs available. Postbaccalaureate distance learning degree programs offered (no on-campus study). *Faculty:* 59 full-time (15 women), 52 part-time/adjunct (8 women). *Students:* 969 full-time (264 women), 932 part-time (242 women); includes 597 minority (230 Black or African American, non-Hispanic/Latino; 3 American Indian or Alaska Native, non-Hispanic/Latino; 170 Asian, non-Hispanic/Latino; 135 Hispanic/Latino; 10 Native Hawaiian or other Pacific Islander, non-Hispanic/Latino; 49 Two or more races, non-Hispanic/Latino), 286 international. Average age 32. 1,231 applicants, 56% accepted, 372 enrolled. In 2012, 502 master's, 5 doctorates awarded. *Degree requirements:* For master's, thesis (for some programs); for doctorate, comprehensive exam, thesis/dissertation. *Entrance requirements:* For master's, GRE or GMAT (MS in computational finance only), bachelor's degree, resume (MS in predictive analytics only), IT experience (MS in information technology project management only), portfolio review (all MFA programs and MA in animation); for doctorate, GRE, master's degree in computer science. Additional exam requirements/recommendations for international students: Required—TOEFL (minimum score 550 paper-based; 80 iBT), IELTS (minimum score 6.5), Pearson Test of English (minimum score 53). *Application deadline:* For fall admission, 8/1 priority date for domestic students, 6/15 for international students; for winter admission, 12/1 priority date for domestic students, 10/15 for international students; for spring admission, 3/1 priority date for domestic students, 1/15 for international students. Applications are processed on a rolling basis. Application fee: $25. Electronic applications accepted. *Expenses:* Contact institution. *Financial support:* In 2012–13, 89 students received support, including 3 fellowships with full tuition reimbursements available (averaging $25,946 per year), 4 research assistantships with full tuition reimbursements available (averaging $21,750 per year), 82 teaching assistantships with full and partial tuition reimbursements available (averaging $4,998 per year); Federal Work-Study, scholarships/grants, tuition waivers (full and partial), and unspecified assistantships also available. Support available to part-time students. Financial award application deadline: 4/30; financial award applicants required to submit FAFSA. *Faculty research:* Data mining, computer science, human-computer interaction, security, animation and film. *Total annual research expenditures:* $4.1 million. *Unit head:* Elly Kafritsas-Wessels, Senior Administrative Assistant, 312-362-5816, Fax: 312-362-5185, E-mail: ekafrits@cdm.depaul.edu. *Application contact:* James Parker, Director of Graduate Admission, 312-362-8714, Fax: 312-362-5179, E-mail: jparke29@cdm.depaul.edu. Website: http://cdm.depaul.edu.

Florida State University, The Graduate School, College of Arts and Sciences, Department of Mathematics, Tallahassee, FL 32306-4510. Offers applied computational mathematics (MS, PhD); biomathematics (MS, PhD); financial mathematics (MS, PhD); pure mathematics (MS, PhD). Part-time programs available. *Faculty:* 52 full-time (12 women). *Students:* 145 full-time (38 women), 6 part-time (2 women); includes 13 minority (6 Black or African American, non-Hispanic/Latino; 3 Asian, non-Hispanic/Latino; 4 Hispanic/Latino), 93 international. 322 applicants, 30% accepted, 41 enrolled. In 2012, 30 master's, 13 doctorates awarded. Terminal master's awarded for partial completion of doctoral program. *Degree requirements:* For master's, comprehensive exam (for some programs), thesis optional; for doctorate, comprehensive exam, thesis/dissertation, candidacy exam including written qualifying examinations which differ by degree concentrations. *Entrance requirements:* For master's and doctorate, GRE General Test, minimum upper-division GPA of 3.0, 4-year bachelor's degree. Additional exam requirements/recommendations for international students: Required—TOEFL (minimum score 550 paper-based; 80 iBT) or IELTS (minimum score 6.5). *Application deadline:* For fall admission, 1/1 priority date for domestic students, 1/1 for international students; for spring admission, 10/1 priority date for domestic students, 11/1 for international students. Applications are processed on a rolling basis. Application fee: $30. Electronic applications accepted. *Expenses:* Tuition, state resident: full-time $7263; part-time $403.51 per credit hour. Tuition, nonresident: full-time $18,087; part-time $1004.85 per credit hour. *Required fees:* $1335.42; $74.19 per credit hour. $445.14 per semester. One-time fee: $40 full-time; $20 part-time. Tuition and fees vary according to program. *Financial support:* In 2012–13, 115 students received support, including 9 fellowships with full tuition reimbursements available (averaging $22,600 per year), 14 research assistantships with full tuition reimbursements available (averaging $22,000 per year), 88 teaching assistantships with full tuition reimbursements available (averaging $19,300 per year); career-related internships or fieldwork, institutionally sponsored loans, scholarships/grants, health care benefits, and unspecified assistantships also available. *Faculty research:* Algebra and algebraic geometry; applied, financial, numerical, and classical analysis; biomathematics, including shape analysis and anatomical imaging; computational mathematics and numerical algorithms; geometric topology. *Unit head:* Dr. Xiaoming Wang, Chairperson, 850-645-3338, Fax: 850-644-4053, E-mail: wxm@math.fsu.edu. *Application contact:* Dr. Giray Okten, Associate Chair for Graduate Studies, 850-644-8713, Fax: 850-644-4053, E-mail: okten@math.fsu.edu. Website: http://www.math.fsu.edu/.

Georgia Institute of Technology, Graduate Studies and Research, College of Management, Program in Management, Atlanta, GA 30332-0001. Offers accounting (PhD); finance (PhD); information technology management (PhD); marketing (PhD); operations management (PhD); organizational behavior (PhD); quantitative and computational finance (MS); strategic management (PhD). *Accreditation:* AACSB. *Degree requirements:* For doctorate, comprehensive exam, thesis/dissertation, oral exams. *Entrance requirements:* For master's and doctorate, GMAT. Additional exam requirements/recommendations for international students: Required—TOEFL. *Faculty research:* MIS, management of technology, international business, entrepreneurship, operations management.

Georgia Institute of Technology, Graduate Studies and Research, College of Sciences, School of Mathematics, Atlanta, GA 30332-0001. Offers algorithms, combinatorics, and optimization (PhD); applied mathematics (MS); bioinformatics (PhD); mathematics (PhD); quantitative and computational finance (MS); statistics (MS Stat). Terminal master's awarded for partial completion of doctoral program. *Degree requirements:* For master's, thesis or alternative; for doctorate, one foreign language, thesis/dissertation. *Entrance requirements:* For master's, GRE General Test, minimum GPA of 3.0; for doctorate, GRE General Test, GRE Subject Test, minimum GPA of 3.0. Additional exam requirements/recommendations for international students: Required—TOEFL. Electronic applications accepted. *Faculty research:* Dynamical systems, discrete mathematics, probability and statistics, mathematical physics.

Illinois Institute of Technology, Stuart School of Business, Program in Mathematical Finance, Chicago, IL 60661. Offers MMF. Part-time and evening/weekend programs available. *Faculty:* 32 full-time (5 women), 19 part-time/adjunct (2 women). *Students:* 51 full-time (17 women), 2 part-time (1 woman), all international. Average age 23. 127 applicants, 95% accepted, 29 enrolled. In 2012, 13 master's awarded. *Entrance requirements:* For master's, GRE (minimum score 1200). Additional exam requirements/recommendations for international students: Required—TOEFL (minimum score 600 paper-based; 85 iBT); Recommended—IELTS (minimum score 7). *Application deadline:* For fall admission, 8/1 for domestic students, 5/1 for international students; for spring admission, 12/15 for domestic students, 10/15 for international students. Applications are processed on a rolling basis. Application fee: $75. Electronic applications accepted. *Expenses:* Contact institution. *Financial support:* Career-related internships or fieldwork, Federal Work-Study, institutionally sponsored loans, scholarships/grants, traineeships, health care benefits, and tuition waivers (partial) available. Support available to part-time students. Financial award applicants required to submit FAFSA. *Faculty research:* Factor models for investment management, credit rating and credit risk management, hedge fund performance analysis, option trading and risk management, global asset allocation strategies. *Unit head:* Tomasz Bielecki, Professor, 312-567-3165, Fax: 312-567-3135, E-mail: bielecki@iit.edu. *Application contact:* Deborah Gibson, Director, Graduate Admission, 866-472-3448, Fax: 312-567-3138, E-mail: inquiry.grad@iit.edu. Website: http://www.stuart.iit.edu/graduateprograms/prof_masters/index.shtml.

The Johns Hopkins University, G. W. C. Whiting School of Engineering, Department of Applied Mathematics and Statistics, Baltimore, MD 21218-2699. Offers computational medicine (PhD); discrete mathematics (MA, MSE, PhD); financial mathematics (MSE); operations research/optimization/decision science (MA, MSE, PhD); statistics/probability/stochastic processes (MA, MSE, PhD). Terminal master's awarded for partial completion of doctoral program. *Degree requirements:* For master's, thesis (for some programs); for doctorate, thesis/dissertation, oral exam, introductory exam. *Entrance requirements:* For master's and doctorate, GRE General Test, GRE Subject Test. Additional exam requirements/recommendations for international students: Required—TOEFL (minimum score 600 paper-based; 100 iBT). Electronic applications accepted. *Faculty research:* Discrete mathematics, probability, statistics, optimization and operations research, scientific computation, financial mathematics.

Monmouth University, The Graduate School, Department of Mathematics, West Long Branch, NJ 07764-1898. Offers financial mathematics (MS). Part-time and evening/weekend programs available. *Faculty:* 2 full-time (0 women). *Students:* 1 full-time (0 women), 3 part-time (1 woman); includes 1 minority (Asian, non-Hispanic/Latino), 3 international. Average age 30. In 2012, 10 master's awarded. *Degree requirements:* For master's, 6 credits of financial mathematics practicum. *Entrance requirements:* For master's, minimum GPA of 3.0 in major, 2.5 overall; undergraduate degree in mathematics or related field with substantial component of math; coursework in calculus, linear algebra, differential equations (with some exposure to partial differential equations), and a course in calculus-based statistics. Additional exam requirements/recommendations for international students: Required—TOEFL (minimum score 550 paper-based; 79 iBT), IELTS (minimum score 6) or Michigan English Language Assessment Battery (minimum score 77), Cambridge A, B, C. *Application deadline:* For fall admission, 7/15 priority date for domestic students, 6/1 for international students; for spring admission, 10/15 priority date for domestic students, 11/1 for international students. Application fee: $50. *Financial support:* In 2012–13, 2 students received support, including 3 fellowships (averaging $1,167 per year); research assistantships, career-related internships or fieldwork, scholarships/grants, and unspecified assistantships also available. Support available to part-time students. Financial award applicants required to submit FAFSA. *Faculty research:* Mathematics and computational finance, economics, Monte Carlo methods. *Unit head:* Dr. Joseph Coyle, Program Director, 732-263-5306, E-mail: jcoyle@monmouth.edu. *Application contact:* Kevin Roane, Director, Office of Graduate Admission, 732-571-3452, Fax: 732-263-5123, E-mail: gradadm@monmouth.edu. Website: http://www.monmouth.edu/academics/schools/science/graduate_programs/mathematics/msfm.asp.

312 www.petersonsbooks.com

Peterson's Graduate Programs in the Physical Sciences, Mathematics, Agricultural Sciences, the Environment & Natural Resources 2014

New Jersey Institute of Technology, Office of Graduate Studies, College of Science and Liberal Arts, Department of Mathematical Science, Program in Mathematical and Computational Finance, Newark, NJ 07102. Offers MS. *Degree requirements:* For master's, project. *Entrance requirements:* Additional exam requirements/recommendations for international students: Required—TOEFL (minimum score 550 paper-based; 79 iBT). Electronic applications accepted. *Expenses:* Tuition, state resident: full-time $16,836; part-time $915 per credit. Tuition, nonresident: full-time $24,370; part-time $1286 per credit. *Required fees:* $2318; $242 per credit.

New York University, Graduate School of Arts and Science, Courant Institute of Mathematical Sciences, Department of Mathematics, New York, NY 10012-1019. Offers atmosphere ocean science and mathematics (PhD); mathematics (MS, PhD); mathematics and statistics/operations research (MS); mathematics in finance (MS); scientific computing (MS). Part-time and evening/weekend programs available. *Faculty:* 46 full-time (0 women). *Students:* 228 full-time (41 women), 140 part-time (25 women); includes 51 minority (2 Black or African American, non-Hispanic/Latino; 39 Asian, non-Hispanic/Latino; 5 Hispanic/Latino; 5 Two or more races, non-Hispanic/Latino), 216 international. Average age 28. 1,681 applicants, 25% accepted, 121 enrolled. In 2012, 77 master's, 11 doctorates awarded. *Degree requirements:* For master's, thesis optional; for doctorate, one foreign language, thesis/dissertation, oral and written exams. *Entrance requirements:* For master's and doctorate, GRE General Test, GRE Subject Test. Additional exam requirements/recommendations for international students: Required—TOEFL. *Application deadline:* For fall admission, 1/4 for domestic and international students; for spring admission, 11/1 for domestic and international students. Application fee: $90. *Expenses: Tuition:* Full-time $34,488; part-time $1437 per credit. *Required fees:* $2332; $1437 per credit. Tuition and fees vary according to program. *Financial support:* Fellowships with tuition reimbursements, research assistantships with tuition reimbursements, teaching assistantships with tuition reimbursements, Federal Work-Study, institutionally sponsored loans, scholarships/grants, health care benefits, and unspecified assistantships available. Financial award application deadline: 1/4; financial award applicants required to submit FAFSA. *Faculty research:* Partial differential equations, computational science, applied mathematics, geometry and topology, probability and stochastic processes. *Unit head:* Fedor Bogomolov, Director of Graduate Studies, 212-998-3238, Fax: 212-995-4121, E-mail: admissions@math.nyu.edu. *Application contact:* Tamar Arnon, Graduate Program Administrator, 212-998-3238, Fax: 212-995-4121, E-mail: admissions@math.nyu.edu. Website: http://www.math.nyu.edu/.

North Carolina State University, Graduate School, College of Agriculture and Life Sciences and College of Engineering and College of Physical and Mathematical Sciences, Program in Financial Mathematics, Raleigh, NC 27695. Offers MFM. Part-time programs available. *Degree requirements:* For master's, thesis optional, project/internship. *Entrance requirements:* For master's, GRE General Test. Additional exam requirements/recommendations for international students: Required—TOEFL (minimum score 550 paper-based). Electronic applications accepted. *Faculty research:* Financial mathematics modeling and computation, futures, options and commodities markets, real options, credit risk, portfolio optimization.

Polytechnic Institute of New York University, Department of Finance and Risk Engineering, Brooklyn, NY 11201-2990. Offers financial engineering (MS, Advanced Certificate), including capital markets (MS), computational finance (MS), financial technology (MS); financial technology management (Advanced Certificate); organizational behavior (Advanced Certificate); risk management (Advanced Certificate); technology management (Advanced Certificate). Part-time and evening/weekend programs available. *Faculty:* 12 full-time (4 women), 23 part-time/adjunct (6 women). *Students:* 190 full-time (52 women), 51 part-time (13 women); includes 22 minority (4 Black or African American, non-Hispanic/Latino; 16 Asian, non-Hispanic/Latino; 2 Hispanic/Latino), 189 international. Average age 27. 701 applicants, 31% accepted, 109 enrolled. In 2012, 60 master's awarded. *Degree requirements:* For master's, comprehensive exam (for some programs), thesis (for some programs). *Entrance requirements:* For master's, GMAT, minimum B average in undergraduate course work. Additional exam requirements/recommendations for international students: Required—TOEFL (minimum score 550 paper-based; 80 iBT); Recommended—IELTS (minimum score 6.5). *Application deadline:* For fall admission, 7/31 priority date for domestic students, 4/30 for international students; for spring admission, 12/31 priority date for domestic students, 11/30 for international students. Applications are processed on a rolling basis. Application fee: $75. Electronic applications accepted. *Financial support:* Institutionally sponsored loans, scholarships/grants, and unspecified assistantships available. Support available to part-time students. Financial award applicants required to submit FAFSA. *Total annual research expenditures:* $201,720. *Unit head:* Prof. Charles S. Tapiero, Academic Director, 718-260-3653, Fax: 718-260-3874, E-mail: ctapiero@poly.edu. *Application contact:* Raymond Lutzky, Director, Graduate Enrollment Management, 718-637-5984, Fax: 718-260-3624, E-mail: rlutzky@poly.edu.

Rice University, Graduate Programs, George R. Brown School of Engineering, Department of Statistics, Houston, TX 77251-1892. Offers bioinformatics (PhD); biostatistics (PhD); computational finance (PhD); general statistics (PhD); statistics (M Stat, MA); MBA/M Stat. Part-time programs available. *Degree requirements:* For master's, comprehensive exam; for doctorate, comprehensive exam, thesis/dissertation. *Entrance requirements:* For master's and doctorate, GRE General Test, minimum GPA of 3.0. Additional exam requirements/recommendations for international students: Required—TOEFL (minimum score 630 paper-based; 90 iBT). Electronic applications accepted. *Faculty research:* Statistical genetics, non parametric function estimation, computational statistics and visualization, stochastic processes.

Stanford University, School of Humanities and Sciences, Department of Mathematics, Stanford, CA 94305-9991. Offers financial mathematics (MS); mathematics (MS, PhD). Terminal master's awarded for partial completion of doctoral program. *Degree requirements:* For doctorate, 2 foreign languages, thesis/dissertation, oral exam. *Entrance requirements:* For master's, GRE General Test; for doctorate, GRE General Test, GRE Subject Test. Additional exam requirements/recommendations for international students: Required—TOEFL. Electronic applications accepted. *Expenses: Tuition:* Full-time $41,250; part-time $917 per credit hour.

Université de Montréal, Faculty of Arts and Sciences, Department of Economic Sciences, Montréal, QC H3C 3J7, Canada. Offers economics (M Sc, PhD); mathematical and computational finance (M Sc). *Degree requirements:* For master's, one foreign language, thesis; for doctorate, one foreign language, thesis/dissertation, general exam. Electronic applications accepted. *Faculty research:* Applied and economic theory, public choice, international trade, labor economics, industrial organization.

Université de Montréal, Faculty of Arts and Sciences, Department of Mathematics and Statistics, Montréal, QC H3C 3J7, Canada. Offers mathematical and computational finance (M Sc, DESS); mathematics (M Sc, PhD); statistics (M Sc, PhD). *Degree requirements:* For master's, thesis; for doctorate, thesis/dissertation, general exam. *Entrance requirements:* For master's and doctorate, proficiency in French. Electronic applications accepted. *Faculty research:* Pure and applied mathematics, actuarial mathematics.

University of Alberta, Faculty of Graduate Studies and Research, Department of Mathematical and Statistical Sciences, Edmonton, AB T6G 2E1, Canada. Offers applied mathematics (M Sc, PhD); biostatistics (M Sc); mathematical finance (M Sc, PhD); mathematical physics (M Sc, PhD); mathematics (M Sc, PhD); statistics (M Sc, PhD, Postgraduate Diploma). Part-time programs available. Terminal master's awarded for partial completion of doctoral program. *Degree requirements:* For master's, thesis (for some programs); for doctorate, comprehensive exam, thesis/dissertation. *Entrance requirements:* Additional exam requirements/recommendations for international students: Required—TOEFL (minimum score 580 paper-based). Electronic applications accepted. *Faculty research:* Classical and functional analysis, algebra, differential equations, geometry.

University of California, Santa Barbara, Graduate Division, College of Letters and Sciences, Division of Mathematics, Life, and Physical Sciences, Department of Statistics and Applied Probability, Santa Barbara, CA 93106-3110. Offers financial mathematics and statistics (PhD); quantitative methods in the social sciences (PhD); statistics (MA), including applied statistics, mathematical statistics; statistics and applied probability (PhD); MA/PhD. *Faculty:* 11 full-time (3 women). *Students:* 57 full-time (28 women); includes 47 minority (42 Asian, non-Hispanic/Latino; 3 Hispanic/Latino; 1 Native Hawaiian or other Pacific Islander, non-Hispanic/Latino; 1 Two or more races, non-Hispanic/Latino), 43 international. Average age 27. 298 applicants, 17% accepted, 16 enrolled. In 2012, 12 master's, 2 doctorates awarded. Terminal master's awarded for partial completion of doctoral program. *Degree requirements:* For master's, comprehensive exam, thesis optional; for doctorate, comprehensive exam, thesis/dissertation. *Entrance requirements:* For master's and doctorate, GRE General Test. Additional exam requirements/recommendations for international students: Required—TOEFL (minimum score 550 paper-based; 80 iBT), IELTS (minimum score 7). *Application deadline:* For fall admission, 1/1 priority date for domestic students, 1/1 for international students; for winter admission, 11/1 priority date for domestic students, 11/1 for international students; for spring admission, 2/1 priority date for domestic students, 2/1 for international students. Application fee: $80 ($100 for international students). Electronic applications accepted. *Financial support:* In 2012–13, 23 students received support, including 6 fellowships with full tuition reimbursements available (averaging $11,285 per year), 1 research assistantship with full and partial tuition reimbursement available (averaging $2,790 per year), 28 teaching assistantships with partial tuition reimbursements available (averaging $14,557 per year); Federal Work-Study, scholarships/grants, and health care benefits also available. Financial award application deadline: 1/1; financial award applicants required to submit FAFSA. *Faculty research:* Bayesian inference, financial mathematics, stochastic processes, environmental statistics, biostatistical modeling. *Total annual research expenditures:* $139,480. *Unit head:* Dr. John Hsu, Chair, 805-893-4055, E-mail: hsu@pstat.ucsb.edu. *Application contact:* Dolly J. Cook, Graduate Program Assistant, 805-893-2129, Fax: 805-893-2334, E-mail: gradinfo@pstat.ucsb.edu. Website: http://www.pstat.ucsb.edu/.

University of Chicago, Division of the Physical Sciences, Department of Mathematics, Master of Science in Financial Mathematics Program, Chicago, IL 60637. Offers MS. Part-time and evening/weekend programs available. *Entrance requirements:* For master's, GRE General Test, GRE Subject Test (math). Additional exam requirements/recommendations for international students: Required—TOEFL (minimum score 600 paper-based). Electronic applications accepted.

University of Connecticut, Graduate School, College of Liberal Arts and Sciences, Department of Mathematics, Field of Applied Financial Mathematics, Storrs, CT 06269. Offers MS. *Degree requirements:* For master's, comprehensive

Mathematical and Computational Finance

exam. *Entrance requirements:* Additional exam requirements/recommendations for international students: Required—TOEFL (minimum score 550 paper-based). Electronic applications accepted.

University of Dayton, Department of Mathematics, Dayton, OH 45469-1300. Offers applied mathematics (MAS); financial mathematics (MFM); mathematics education (MME). Part-time and evening/weekend programs available. *Faculty:* 15 full-time (5 women). *Students:* 45 full-time (25 women), 6 part-time (3 women); includes 3 minority (2 Black or African American, non-Hispanic/Latino; 1 Asian, non-Hispanic/Latino), 37 international. Average age 26. 108 applicants, 35% accepted, 8 enrolled. In 2012, 12 master's awarded. *Entrance requirements:* For master's, minimum undergraduate GPA of 2.8 (MAS), 3.0 (MFM, MME). Additional exam requirements/recommendations for international students: Required—TOEFL (minimum score 550 paper-based; 80 iBT). *Application deadline:* For fall admission, 3/1 priority date for domestic students, 5/1 for international students; for winter admission, 7/1 for international students; for spring admission, 10/1 for international students. Applications are processed on a rolling basis. Application fee: $0 ($50 for international students). Electronic applications accepted. *Expenses: Tuition:* Part-time $708 per credit hour. *Required fees:* $25 per semester. Tuition and fees vary according to course level, course load, degree level and program. *Financial support:* In 2012–13, 6 teaching assistantships with full tuition reimbursements (averaging $14,075 per year) were awarded; institutionally sponsored loans, health care benefits, and unspecified assistantships also available. Financial award applicants required to submit FAFSA. *Faculty research:* Differential equations, integral equations, general topology, measure theory, graph theory, financial math, math education, numerical analysis. *Unit head:* Dr. Joe D. Mashburn, Chair, 937-229-2511, Fax: 937-229-2566, E-mail: jmashburn1@udayton.edu. *Application contact:* Dr. Paul W. Eloe, Graduate Program Director and Professor, 937-229-2016, E-mail: peloe1@udayton.edu.

University of Illinois at Chicago, Graduate College, College of Liberal Arts and Sciences, Department of Mathematics, Statistics, and Computer Science, Chicago, IL 60607-7128. Offers applied mathematics (MS, PhD); computational finance (MS, PhD); computer science (MS, PhD); mathematics (DA); mathematics and information sciences for industry (MS); probability and statistics (PhD); pure mathematics (MS, PhD); statistics (MS); teaching of mathematics (MST), including elementary, secondary. Part-time programs available. *Students:* 125 full-time (34 women), 34 part-time (15 women); includes 23 minority (1 Black or African American, non-Hispanic/Latino; 10 Asian, non-Hispanic/Latino; 10 Hispanic/Latino; 2 Two or more races, non-Hispanic/Latino), 45 international. Average age 29. 226 applicants, 37% accepted, 42 enrolled. In 2012, 30 master's, 19 doctorates awarded. *Degree requirements:* For master's, comprehensive exam; for doctorate, one foreign language, thesis/dissertation. *Entrance requirements:* For master's and doctorate, GRE General Test, minimum GPA of 3.0. Additional exam requirements/recommendations for international students: Required—TOEFL (minimum score 100 iBT). *Application deadline:* For fall admission, 1/1 for domestic and international students; for spring admission, 10/1 for domestic students, 7/15 for international students. Applications are processed on a rolling basis. Application fee: $60. Electronic applications accepted. *Expenses:* Tuition, state resident: full-time $10,882; part-time $3627 per term. Tuition, nonresident: full-time $22,880; part-time $7627 per term. *Required fees:* $1170 per semester. Tuition and fees vary according to course load, degree level and program. *Financial support:* In 2012–13, 109 students received support, including 2 fellowships with full tuition reimbursements available (averaging $20,000 per year), 8 research assistantships with full tuition reimbursements available (averaging $17,000 per year), 87 teaching assistantships with full tuition reimbursements available (averaging $17,000 per year); Federal Work-Study, scholarships/grants, and tuition waivers (full) also available. Financial award application deadline: 1/1. *Total annual research expenditures:* $2.2 million. *Unit head:* Lawrence Ein, Head, 312-996-3044, E-mail: ein@math.uic.edu. *Application contact:* Ramin Takloo-Bighash, Director of Graduate Studies, 312-996-5119, E-mail: dgs@math.uic.edu. Website: http://www.math.uic.edu/.

The University of Manchester, School of Mathematics, Manchester, United Kingdom. Offers actuarial science (PhD); applied mathematics (M Phil, PhD); applied numerical computing (M Phil, PhD); financial mathematics (M Phil, PhD); mathematical logic (M Phil); probability (M Phil, PhD); pure mathematics (M Phil, PhD); statistics (M Phil, PhD).

The University of North Carolina at Charlotte, The Graduate School, Belk College of Business, Interdisciplinary Business Programs, Charlotte, NC 28223-0001. Offers mathematical finance (MS, PhD); real estate (MS). *Faculty:* 15 full-time (1 woman), 1 part-time/adjunct (0 women). *Students:* 98 full-time (34 women), 57 part-time (19 women); includes 13 minority (7 Black or African American, non-Hispanic/Latino; 5 Asian, non-Hispanic/Latino; 1 Two or more races, non-Hispanic/Latino), 96 international. Average age 27. 200 applicants, 71% accepted, 78 enrolled. In 2012, 34 master's, 2 doctorates awarded. *Degree requirements:* For master's, thesis or alternative, project; for doctorate, thesis/dissertation. *Entrance requirements:* For master's and doctorate, GRE or GMAT, minimum GPA of 2.75, letters of recommendation. Additional exam requirements/

recommendations for international students: Required—TOEFL (minimum score 557 paper-based; 87 iBT). Application fee: $65 ($75 for international students). *Expenses:* Tuition, state resident: full-time $3453. Tuition, nonresident: full-time $15,982. *Required fees:* $2420. Tuition and fees vary according to course load and program. *Unit head:* Dr. Christie Amato, 704-687-7712, Fax: 704-687-4014, E-mail: chamato@uncc.edu. *Application contact:* Kathy B. Giddings, Director of Graduate Admissions, 704-687-5503, Fax: 704-687-1668, E-mail: gradadm@uncc.edu. Website: http://belkcollege.uncc.edu/.

University of Notre Dame, Graduate School, College of Science, Department of Applied and Computational Mathematics and Statistics, Notre Dame, IN 46556. Offers applied and computational mathematics and statistics (PhD); applied statistics (MS); computational finance (MS).

University of Southern California, Graduate School, Dana and David Dornsife College of Letters, Arts and Sciences, Department of Economics, Los Angeles, CA 90089. Offers economic development programming (MA, PhD); mathematical finance (MS); M PI/MA; MA/JD. Terminal master's awarded for partial completion of doctoral program. *Degree requirements:* For master's, comprehensive exam; for doctorate, comprehensive exam, thesis/dissertation. *Entrance requirements:* For master's and doctorate, GRE. Additional exam requirements/recommendations for international students: Required—TOEFL (minimum score 93 iBT). Electronic applications accepted. *Faculty research:* Macro theory, development economics, econometrics.

University of Southern California, Graduate School, Dana and David Dornsife College of Letters, Arts and Sciences, Department of Mathematics, Los Angeles, CA 90089. Offers applied mathematics (MA, MS, PhD); mathematical finance (MS); mathematics (MA, PhD); statistics (MS). Part-time programs available. Terminal master's awarded for partial completion of doctoral program. *Degree requirements:* For master's, comprehensive exam (for some programs), thesis (for some programs); for doctorate, one foreign language, comprehensive exam, thesis/dissertation. *Entrance requirements:* For master's, GRE General Test, GMAT; for doctorate, GRE General Test, GRE Subject Test (mathematics). Additional exam requirements/recommendations for international students: Required—TOEFL (minimum score 100 iBT). Electronic applications accepted. *Faculty research:* Algebra, algebraic geometry and number theory, analysis/partial differential equations, applied mathematics, financial mathematics, probability, combinatorics and statistics.

University of Toronto, School of Graduate Studies, Program in Mathematical Finance, Toronto, ON M5S 1A1, Canada. Offers MMF. *Entrance requirements:* For master's, four-year bachelor's degree in a quantitative, technical discipline from recognized university with minimum of the equivalent of the University of Toronto mid-B (75%) standing in final two years of program or equivalent number of most senior courses. Additional exam requirements/recommendations for international students: Required—TOEFL (minimum score 580 paper-based; 93 iBT), TWE (minimum score 5). Electronic applications accepted.

Washington State University, Graduate School, College of Arts and Sciences, Department of Mathematics, Pullman, WA 99164. Offers applied mathematics (MS, PhD); mathematics (MS, PhD); mathematics computational finance (MS); mathematics teaching (MS, PhD). Part-time programs available. *Faculty:* 28 full-time (4 women). *Students:* 49 full-time (16 women), 2 part-time (1 woman); includes 5 minority (1 Black or African American, non-Hispanic/Latino; 2 Asian, non-Hispanic/Latino; 1 Hispanic/Latino; 1 Native Hawaiian or other Pacific Islander, non-Hispanic/Latino), 17 international. Average age 27. 117 applicants, 68% accepted, 18 enrolled. In 2012, 5 master's, 6 doctorates awarded. Terminal master's awarded for partial completion of doctoral program. *Degree requirements:* For master's, comprehensive exam (for some programs), thesis or alternative, oral exam, project; for doctorate, 2 foreign languages, comprehensive exam, thesis/dissertation, oral exam, written exam. *Entrance requirements:* For master's and doctorate, minimum GPA of 3.0, 3 letters of recommendation. Additional exam requirements/recommendations for international students: Required—TOEFL (minimum score 600 paper-based; 100 iBT) or IELTS (minimum score 7). *Application deadline:* For fall admission, 1/10 for domestic and international students; for spring admission, 7/1 for domestic and international students. Applications are processed on a rolling basis. Application fee: $75. Electronic applications accepted. *Financial support:* In 2012–13, 43 students received support, including 9 research assistantships with full and partial tuition reimbursements available (averaging $15,500 per year), 34 teaching assistantships with full and partial tuition reimbursements available (averaging $15,000 per year); fellowships, career-related internships or fieldwork, Federal Work-Study, institutionally sponsored loans, scholarships/grants, traineeships, health care benefits, and tuition waivers (partial) also available. Financial award application deadline: 2/15. *Faculty research:* Computational mathematics, operations research, modeling in the natural sciences, applied statistics. *Unit head:* Dr. K. A. Ariyawansa, Chair, 509-335-4918, Fax: 509-335-1188, E-mail: ari@wsu.edu. *Application contact:* Graduate School Admissions, 800-GRADWSU, Fax: 509-335-1949, E-mail: gradsch@wsu.edu. Website: http://www.sci.wsu.edu/math/.

314 www.petersonsbooks.com

Peterson's Graduate Programs in the Physical Sciences, Mathematics, Agricultural Sciences, the Environment & Natural Resources 2014

Mathematics

Alabama State University, College of Science, Mathematics and Technology, Department of Mathematics and Computer Science, Montgomery, AL 36101-0271. Offers mathematics (MS, Ed S). Part-time programs available. *Faculty:* 5 full-time (0 women). *Students:* 1 (woman) full-time; minority (Black or African American, non-Hispanic/Latino). Average age 23. 3 applicants, 33% accepted, 1 enrolled. In 2012, 3 master's awarded. *Degree requirements:* For Ed S, thesis. *Entrance requirements:* For master's, GRE General Test, GRE Subject Test, writing competency test; for Ed S, GRE General Test, MAT, writing competency test. Additional exam requirements/recommendations for international students: Required—TOEFL (minimum score 500 paper-based). *Application deadline:* For fall admission, 7/15 for domestic students; for spring admission, 12/15 for domestic students. Applications are processed on a rolling basis. Application fee: $27. *Expenses:* Tuition, state resident: full-time $7236. Tuition, nonresident: full-time $12,852. *Financial support:* In 2012–13, 1 research assistantship (averaging $9,450 per year) was awarded. *Faculty research:* Discrete mathematics, symbolic dynamics, mathematical social sciences. *Total annual research expenditures:* $25,000. *Unit head:* Dr. Carl S. Pettis, Chair, 334-229-4484, Fax: 334-229-4902, E-mail: cpettis@alasu.edu. *Application contact:* Dr. William Person, Dean of Graduate Studies, 334-229-4274, Fax: 334-229-4928, E-mail: wperson@alasu.edu. Website: http://www.alasu.edu/academics/colleges—departments/science-mathematics—technology/mathematics—computer-science/index.aspx.

American University, College of Arts and Sciences, Department of Mathematics and Statistics, Washington, DC 22016-8050. Offers applied statistics (Certificate); mathematics (MA); statistics (MS). Part-time and evening/weekend programs available. *Faculty:* 28 full-time (12 women), 12 part-time/adjunct (1 woman). *Students:* 14 full-time (5 women), 17 part-time (5 women); includes 8 minority (3 Black or African American, non-Hispanic/Latino; 3 Asian, non-Hispanic/Latino; 2 Hispanic/Latino), 1 international. Average age 27. 39 applicants, 72% accepted, 13 enrolled. In 2012, 3 master's awarded. *Degree requirements:* For master's, comprehensive exam, thesis or alternative, tools of research in foreign language or computer language. *Entrance requirements:* For master's, GRE; for Certificate, bachelor's degree. Additional exam requirements/recommendations for international students: Required—TOEFL. *Application deadline:* For fall admission, 2/1 for domestic students; for spring admission, 10/1 for domestic students. Application fee: $80. *Expenses: Tuition:* Full-time $25,920; part-time $1440 per credit. *Required fees:* $430. Tuition and fees vary according to course load, campus/location and program. *Financial support:* Fellowships, research assistantships, teaching assistantships, career-related internships or fieldwork, Federal Work-Study, institutionally sponsored loans, and unspecified assistantships available. Support available to part-time students. Financial award application deadline: 2/1. *Faculty research:* Logic, random processes, probability analysis, biostatistics, statistical computing. *Unit head:* Dr. Jeffrey D. Adler, Chair, 202-885-3171, Fax: 202-885-3155, E-mail: jadler@american.edu. *Application contact:* Kathleen Clowery, Director, Graduate Admissions, 202-885-3621, Fax: 202-885-1505, E-mail: clowery@american.edu. Website: http://www.american.edu/cas/mathstat/.

American University of Beirut, Graduate Programs, Faculty of Arts and Sciences, Beirut, Lebanon. Offers anthropology (MA); Arab and Middle Eastern history (PhD); Arabic language and literature (MA, PhD); archaeology (MA); biology (MS); cell and molecular biology (PhD); chemistry (MS); clinical psychology (MA); computational science (MS); computer science (MS); economics (MA); education (MA); English language (MA); English literature (MA); environmental policy planning (MSES); financial economics (MAFE); general psychology (MA); geology (MS); history (MA); mathematics (MA, MS); media studies (MA); Middle Eastern studies (MA); philosophy (MA); physics (MS); political studies (MA); public administration (MA); sociology (MA); statistics (MA, MS); theoretical physics (PhD); transnational American studies (MA). Part-time programs available. *Faculty:* 238 full-time (80 women), 7 part-time/adjunct (3 women). *Students:* 253 full-time (169 women), 139 part-time (105 women). Average age 26. 306 applicants, 47% accepted, 90 enrolled. In 2012, 126 degrees awarded. *Degree requirements:* For master's, one foreign language, comprehensive exam, thesis (for some programs); for doctorate, one foreign language, comprehensive exam, thesis/dissertation. *Entrance requirements:* For master's, GRE, letter of recommendation; for doctorate, GRE, letters of recommendation. Additional exam requirements/recommendations for international students: Required—TOEFL (minimum score 600 paper-based; 97 iBT), IELTS (minimum score 7). *Application deadline:* For fall admission, 4/30 for domestic students, 4/18 for international students; for spring admission, 11/1 for domestic and international students. Application fee: $50. *Expenses: Tuition:* Full-time $13,896; part-time $772 per credit. *Financial support:* In 2012–13, 20 students received support. Career-related internships or fieldwork, institutionally sponsored loans, scholarships/grants, health care benefits, and unspecified assistantships available. Financial award application deadline: 2/4; financial award applicants required to submit FAFSA. *Faculty research:* Modern Middle East history; Near Eastern archaeology; Islamic history; European history; software engineering; scientific computing; data mining; the applications of cooperative learning in language teaching and teacher education; world/comparative literature; rhetoric and composition; creative writing; public management; public policy and international affairs; hydrogeology; mineralogy, petrology, and geochemistry; tectonics and structural geology; cell and molecular biology; ecology. *Unit head:* Dr. Patrick McGreevy, Dean, 961-1374374 Ext. 3800, Fax: 961-1744461, E-mail: pm07@aub.edu.lb. *Application contact:* Dr. Salim Kanaan, Director, Admissions Office, 961-1-350000 Ext. 2594, Fax: 961-1750775, E-mail: sk00@aub.edu.lb. Website: http://staff.aub.edu.lb/~webfas.

Andrews University, School of Graduate Studies, College of Arts and Sciences, Interdisciplinary Studies in Mathematics and Physical Science Program, Berrien Springs, MI 49104. Offers MS. *Students:* 1 (woman) full-time, 2 part-time (0 women), 1 international. Average age 26. 4 applicants, 25% accepted, 1 enrolled. *Application deadline:* Applications are processed on a rolling basis. Application fee: $40. *Unit head:* Dr. Margarita Mattingly, Chairman, 269-471-3431. *Application contact:* Carolyn Hurst, Supervisor of Graduate Admission, 800-253-3430, Fax: 269-471-3228, E-mail: enroll@andrews.edu.

Appalachian State University, Cratis D. Williams Graduate School, Department of Mathematical Sciences, Boone, NC 28608. Offers mathematics (MA); mathematics education (MA). Part-time programs available. Postbaccalaureate distance learning degree programs offered (no on-campus study). *Degree requirements:* For master's, comprehensive exam, thesis optional. *Entrance requirements:* For master's, GRE General Test, 3 letters of recommendation. Additional exam requirements/recommendations for international students: Required—TOEFL (minimum score 570 paper-based; 79 iBT), IELTS (minimum score 6.5). Electronic applications accepted. *Faculty research:* Graph theory, differential equations, logic, geometry, complex analysis, topology, algebra, mathematics education.

Arizona State University, College of Liberal Arts and Sciences, Department of Mathematics and Statistics, Tempe, AZ 85287-1804. Offers applied mathematics (PhD); computational biosciences (PhD); mathematics (MA, MNS, PhD); mathematics education (PhD); statistics (PhD). Part-time programs available. Terminal master's awarded for partial completion of doctoral program. *Degree requirements:* For master's, thesis or alternative, interactive Program of Study (iPOS) submitted before completing 50 percent of required credit hours; for doctorate, comprehensive exam, thesis/dissertation, interactive Program of Study (iPOS) submitted before completing 50 percent of required credit hours. *Entrance requirements:* For master's and doctorate, GRE General Test, minimum GPA of 3.0 or equivalent in last 2 years of work leading to bachelor's degree. Additional exam requirements/recommendations for international students: Required—TOEFL (minimum score 80 iBT), TOEFL, IELTS, or Pearson Test of English. Electronic applications accepted. *Expenses:* Contact institution.

Arkansas State University, Graduate School, College of Sciences and Mathematics, Department of Mathematics and Statistics, Jonesboro, State University, AR 72467. Offers mathematics (MS); mathematics education (MSE). Part-time programs available. *Faculty:* 11 full-time (5 women). *Students:* 13 full-time (8 women), 5 part-time (3 women); includes 2 minority (1 Black or African American, non-Hispanic/Latino; 1 Hispanic/Latino), 1 international. Average age 31. 15 applicants, 80% accepted, 8 enrolled. In 2012, 6 master's awarded. *Degree requirements:* For master's, comprehensive exam, thesis or alternative. *Entrance requirements:* For master's, GRE General Test or MAT, appropriate bachelor's degree, official transcripts, immunization records, valid teaching certificate (for MSE). Additional exam requirements/recommendations for international students: Required—TOEFL (minimum score 550 paper-based; 79 iBT), IELTS (minimum score 6), Pearson Test of English (minimum score 56). *Application deadline:* For fall admission, 7/1 for domestic and international students; for spring admission, 11/15 for domestic students, 11/14 for international students. Applications are processed on a rolling basis. Application fee: $30 ($40 for international students). Electronic applications accepted. *Expenses:* Tuition, state resident: full-time $4140; part-time $230 per credit hour. Tuition, nonresident: full-time $8280; part-time $460 per credit hour. *Required fees:* $56 per credit hour. $25 per term. Tuition and fees vary according to course load and program. *Financial support:* In 2012–13, 10 students received support. Teaching assistantships, career-related internships or fieldwork, scholarships/grants, and unspecified assistantships available. Financial award application deadline: 7/1; financial award applicants required to submit FAFSA. *Unit head:* Dr. Debra Ingram, Chair, 870-972-3090, Fax: 870-972-3950, E-mail: dingram@astate.edu. *Application contact:* Vickey Ring, Graduate Admissions Coordinator, 870-972-3029, Fax: 870-972-3857, E-mail: vickeyring@astate.edu. Website: http://www.astate.edu/college/sciences-and-mathematics/departments/math-statistics/index.dot.

Auburn University, Graduate School, College of Sciences and Mathematics, Department of Mathematics and Statistics, Auburn University, AL 36849. Offers applied mathematics (MAM, MS); mathematics (MS, PhD); probability and statistics (M Prob S); statistics (MS). *Faculty:* 50 full-time (7 women), 6 part-time/adjunct (4 women). *Students:* 56 full-time (14 women), 52 part-time (14 women); includes 4 minority (3 Black or African American, non-Hispanic/Latino; 1 Hispanic/Latino), 43 international. Average age 28. 160 applicants, 59% accepted, 37 enrolled. In 2012, 17 master's, 9 doctorates awarded. *Degree requirements:* For doctorate, thesis/dissertation. *Entrance requirements:* For master's, GRE General Test, undergraduate mathematics background; for doctorate, GRE General Test,

GRE Subject Test. *Application deadline:* For fall admission, 7/7 priority date for domestic students; for spring admission, 11/24 for domestic students. Applications are processed on a rolling basis. Application fee: $50 ($60 for international students). Electronic applications accepted. *Expenses:* Tuition, state resident: full-time $7866; part-time $437 per credit. Tuition, nonresident: full-time $23,598; part-time $1311 per credit. *Required fees:* $787 per semester. Tuition and fees vary according to degree level and program. *Financial support:* Fellowships and teaching assistantships available. Financial award applicants required to submit FAFSA. *Faculty research:* Pure and applied mathematics. *Unit head:* Dr. Tin Yau Tam, Chair, 334-844-6572, Fax: 334-844-6655. *Application contact:* Dr. George Flowers, Dean of the Graduate School, 334-844-2125. Website: http://www.auburn.edu/~math/.

Aurora University, College of Arts and Sciences, Aurora, IL 60506-4892. Offers elementary math and science (MATL); life science (MATL); mathematics (MATL, MS). Part-time and evening/weekend programs available. *Entrance requirements:* Additional exam requirements/recommendations for international students: Required—TOEFL (minimum score 550 paper-based). Electronic applications accepted. *Expenses:* Contact institution.

Ball State University, Graduate School, College of Sciences and Humanities, Department of Mathematical Sciences, Program in Mathematics, Muncie, IN 47306-1099. Offers mathematics (MA, MS); mathematics education (MA). *Students:* 14 full-time (6 women), 39 part-time (29 women); includes 2 minority (1 American Indian or Alaska Native, non-Hispanic/Latino; 1 Two or more races, non-Hispanic/Latino), 6 international. Average age 39. 16 applicants, 50% accepted, 4 enrolled. In 2012, 7 master's awarded. Application fee: $50. *Expenses:* Tuition, state resident: full-time $7666. Tuition, nonresident: full-time $19,114. *Required fees:* $782. *Financial support:* In 2012–13, 4 students received support, including 5 teaching assistantships with tuition reimbursements available (averaging $4,246 per year). Financial award application deadline: 3/1. *Unit head:* Dr. Sheryl Stump, Director, 765-285-8680, Fax: 765-285-1721, E-mail: sstump@bsu.edu. *Application contact:* Dr. Hanspeter Fischer, Director, 765-285-8640, Fax: 765-285-1721, E-mail: hfischer@bsu.edu. Website: http://cms.bsu.edu/Academics/CollegesandDepartments/Math/AcademicsAdmissions/Programs/Masters/MAorMSinMath.aspx.

Baylor University, Graduate School, College of Arts and Sciences, Department of Mathematics, Waco, TX 76798. Offers MS, PhD. *Faculty:* 23 full-time (1 woman). *Students:* 24 full-time (7 women), 3 part-time (0 women); includes 2 minority (1 Asian, non-Hispanic/Latino; 1 Two or more races, non-Hispanic/Latino), 3 international. 39 applicants, 18% accepted, 5 enrolled. In 2012, 3 master's, 3 doctorates awarded. *Degree requirements:* For master's, final oral exam. *Entrance requirements:* For master's and doctorate, GRE General Test. *Application deadline:* For fall admission, 2/15 for domestic students. Applications are processed on a rolling basis. Application fee: $50. Electronic applications accepted. *Expenses: Tuition:* Full-time $24,426; part-time $1357 per semester hour. *Required fees:* $2556; $142 per semester hour. *Financial support:* Teaching assistantships, career-related internships or fieldwork, Federal Work-Study, and institutionally sponsored loans available. Support available to part-time students. Financial award application deadline: 5/1. *Faculty research:* Algebra, statistics, probability, applied mathematics, numerical analysis. *Unit head:* Dr. Mark Spenski, Graduate Program Director, 254-710-6577, Fax: 254-710-3569, E-mail: ronald_stanke@baylor.edu. *Application contact:* Rita Massey, Graduate Associate, 254-710-3146, Fax: 254-710-3870, E-mail: rita_massey@baylor.edu. Website: http://www.baylor.edu/math/.

Bemidji State University, School of Graduate Studies, Bemidji, MN 56601-2699. Offers biology (MS); education (M Ed, MS); English (MA, MS); environmental studies (MS); mathematics (MS); mathematics (elementary and middle level education) (MS); science (junior high) (MS); special education (M Sp Ed, MS). Part-time programs available. Postbaccalaureate distance learning degree programs offered (no on-campus study). *Faculty:* 114 full-time (47 women), 22 part-time/adjunct (16 women). *Students:* 51 full-time (31 women), 222 part-time (163 women); includes 12 minority (2 Black or African American, non-Hispanic/Latino; 2 American Indian or Alaska Native, non-Hispanic/Latino; 2 Asian, non-Hispanic/Latino; 2 Hispanic/Latino; 4 Two or more races, non-Hispanic/Latino), 5 international. Average age 33. 84 applicants, 93% accepted, 51 enrolled. In 2012, 66 master's awarded. *Degree requirements:* For master's, comprehensive exam, thesis (for some programs). *Entrance requirements:* For master's, GRE, letters of recommendation, letters of interest. Additional exam requirements/recommendations for international students: Required—TOEFL (minimum score 550 paper-based; 80 iBT). *Application deadline:* Applications are processed on a rolling basis. Application fee: $20. Electronic applications accepted. *Expenses:* Tuition, state resident: full-time $6400; part-time $355.50 per credit. Tuition, nonresident: full-time $6400; part-time $355.50 per credit. *Required fees:* $960. *Financial support:* In 2012–13, 131 students received support, including 42 research assistantships with partial tuition reimbursements available (averaging $6,729 per year), 42 teaching assistantships with partial tuition reimbursements available (averaging $6,729 per year); career-related internships or fieldwork, scholarships/grants, health care benefits, and unspecified assistantships also available. Support available to part-time students. Financial award application deadline: 3/31; financial award applicants required to submit FAFSA. *Faculty research:* Human performance, sport, and health: physical education teacher education, continuum models, spiritual health, intellectual health, resiliency, health priorities; psychology: health psychology, college student drinking behavior, micro-aggressions, infant cognition, false memories, leadership assessment; biology: structure and dynamics of forest communities, aquatic and riverine ecology, interaction between animal populations and aquatic environments, cellular motility. *Unit head:* Dr. Patricia Rogers, Dean of Health Sciences and Human Ecology, 218-755-2027, Fax: 218-755-2258, E-mail: progers@bemidjistate.edu. *Application contact:* Joan Miller, Director, School of Graduate Studies, 218-755-2027, Fax: 218-755-2258, E-mail: jmiller@bemidjistate.edu. Website: http://www.bemidjistate.edu/academics/graduate_studies/.

Binghamton University, State University of New York, Graduate School, School of Arts and Sciences, Department of Mathematical Sciences, Binghamton, NY 13902-6000. Offers MA, PhD. Part-time programs available. *Faculty:* 29 full-time (3 women), 21 part-time/adjunct (4 women). *Students:* 51 full-time (13 women), 24 part-time (8 women); includes 4 minority (1 Black or African American, non-Hispanic/Latino; 1 Asian, non-Hispanic/Latino; 2 Hispanic/Latino), 32 international. Average age 27. 101 applicants, 40% accepted, 22 enrolled. In 2012, 10 master's, 8 doctorates awarded. Terminal master's awarded for partial completion of doctoral program. *Degree requirements:* For master's, thesis or alternative; for doctorate, 2 foreign languages, thesis/dissertation. *Entrance requirements:* For master's and doctorate, GRE General Test, GRE Subject Test. Additional exam requirements/recommendations for international students: Required—TOEFL (minimum score 550 paper-based; 80 iBT). *Application deadline:* For fall admission, 4/15 priority date for domestic students, 4/15 for international students; for spring admission, 11/30 priority date for domestic students, 11/30 for international students. Applications are processed on a rolling basis. Application fee: $75. Electronic applications accepted. *Expenses:* Tuition, state resident: full-time $9370. Tuition, nonresident: full-time $16,680. *Financial support:* In 2012–13, 51 students received support, including 50 teaching assistantships with full tuition reimbursements available (averaging $16,500 per year); career-related internships or fieldwork, Federal Work-Study, institutionally sponsored loans, scholarships/grants, health care benefits, tuition waivers (full and partial), and unspecified assistantships also available. Financial award application deadline: 2/15; financial award applicants required to submit FAFSA. *Unit head:* Dr. Anton Schick, Chairperson, 607-777-2983, E-mail: anton@math.binghamton.edu. *Application contact:* Kishan Zuber, Recruiting and Admissions Coordinator, 607-777-2151, Fax: 607-777-2501, E-mail: kzuber@binghamton.edu.

Boise State University, College of Arts and Sciences, Department of Mathematics, Boise, ID 83725-0399. Offers mathematics (MS); mathematics education (MS). *Faculty:* 20 full-time, 5 part-time/adjunct. *Students:* 13 full-time (4 women), 17 part-time (10 women); includes 4 minority (1 Asian, non-Hispanic/Latino; 3 Hispanic/Latino). 17 applicants, 53% accepted, 4 enrolled. In 2012, 5 master's awarded. Application fee: $55. *Expenses:* Tuition, state resident: full-time $3486; part-time $312 per credit. Tuition, nonresident: full-time $5720; part-time $413 per credit. *Financial support:* In 2012–13, 11 students received support, including 11 teaching assistantships. *Unit head:* Leming Qu, Chair, 208-426-1172, E-mail: lqu@boisestate.edu. *Application contact:* Linda Platt, Office Services Supervisor, Graduate Admission and Degree Services, 208-426-1074, Fax: 208-426-2789, E-mail: lplatt@boisestate.edu. Website: http://math.boisestate.edu/.

Boston College, Graduate School of Arts and Sciences, Department of Mathematics, Chestnut Hill, MA 02467-3800. Offers PhD, MBA/MA. *Entrance requirements:* Additional exam requirements/recommendations for international students: Required—TOEFL (minimum score 600 paper-based; 100 iBT). Electronic applications accepted. *Faculty research:* Abstract algebra and number theory, topology, probability and statistics, computer science, analysis.

Boston University, Graduate School of Arts and Sciences, Department of Mathematics and Statistics, Boston, MA 02215. Offers mathematics (MA, PhD). *Students:* 57 full-time (20 women), 2 part-time (1 woman); includes 4 minority (1 Black or African American, non-Hispanic/Latino; 3 Asian, non-Hispanic/Latino), 23 international. Average age 26. 469 applicants, 8% accepted, 10 enrolled. In 2012, 7 master's, 7 doctorates awarded. Terminal master's awarded for partial completion of doctoral program. *Degree requirements:* For master's, one foreign language, comprehensive exam; for doctorate, one foreign language, comprehensive exam, thesis/dissertation. *Entrance requirements:* For master's and doctorate, GRE General Test, GRE Subject Test, 3 letters of recommendation. Additional exam requirements/recommendations for international students: Required—TOEFL (minimum score 600 paper-based). *Application deadline:* For fall admission, 1/15 for domestic and international students; for spring admission, 9/30 for domestic and international students. Application fee: $80. Electronic applications accepted. *Expenses: Tuition:* Full-time $42,400; part-time $1325 per credit. *Required fees:* $40 per semester. *Financial support:* In 2012–13, 2 fellowships with full tuition reimbursements (averaging $20,300 per year), 14 research assistantships with full tuition reimbursements (averaging $19,800 per year), 37 teaching assistantships with full tuition reimbursements (averaging $19,800 per year) were awarded; Federal Work-Study, scholarships/grants, and health care benefits also available. Support available to part-time students. Financial award application deadline: 1/15. *Unit head:* Tasso Kaper, Chairman, 617-353-9552, Fax: 617-353-8100, E-mail: tasso@bu.edu. *Application contact:* Kathleen Heavey, Staff Coordinator, 617-353-2560, Fax: 617-353-8100, E-mail: kheavey@bu.edu. Website: http://math.bu.edu/.

Bowling Green State University, Graduate College, College of Arts and Sciences, Department of Mathematics and Statistics, Bowling Green, OH 43403. Offers applied statistics (MS); mathematics (MA, MAT, PhD); statistics (PhD).

Part-time programs available. *Degree requirements:* For master's, thesis or alternative; for doctorate, comprehensive exam, thesis/dissertation. *Entrance requirements:* For master's and doctorate, GRE General Test. Additional exam requirements/recommendations for international students: Required—TOEFL. Electronic applications accepted. *Faculty research:* Statistics and probability, algebra, analysis.

Brandeis University, Graduate School of Arts and Sciences, Department of Mathematics, Waltham, MA 02454-9110. Offers MA, PhD, Postbaccalaureate Certificate. Part-time programs available. *Faculty:* 12 full-time (2 women), 2 part-time/adjunct (1 woman). *Students:* 39 full-time (13 women), 1 (woman) part-time; includes 3 minority (2 Asian, non-Hispanic/Latino; 1 Hispanic/Latino), 16 international. 141 applicants, 17% accepted, 13 enrolled. In 2012, 2 master's, 7 doctorates, 3 other advanced degrees awarded. Terminal master's awarded for partial completion of doctoral program. *Degree requirements:* For master's, one foreign language; for doctorate, 2 foreign languages, comprehensive exam, thesis/dissertation, qualifying exam. *Entrance requirements:* For master's, resume, 3 letters of recommendation, statement of purpose, transcript(s); for doctorate, GRE General Test and GRE Subject Test (recommended), resume, 3 letters of recommendation, statement of purpose, transcript(s); for Postbaccalaureate Certificate, resume, letter of recommendation, statement of purpose, transcript(s). Additional exam requirements/recommendations for international students: Required—TOEFL (minimum score 600 paper-based; 100 iBT); Recommended—IELTS (minimum score 7). *Application deadline:* For fall admission, 1/15 priority date for domestic students. Application fee: $75. Electronic applications accepted. *Financial support:* In 2012–13, 26 fellowships with full tuition reimbursements (averaging $20,400 per year) were awarded; research assistantships, Federal Work-Study, scholarships/grants, health care benefits, and tuition waivers (partial) also available. Support available to part-time students. Financial award application deadline: 4/15; financial award applicants required to submit FAFSA. *Unit head:* Prof. Kiyoshi Igusa, Director of Graduate Studies, 781-736-3051, Fax: 781-736-3085, E-mail: igusa@brandeis.edu. *Application contact:* Janet Ledda, Department Administrator, 781-736-3051, Fax: 781-736-3085, E-mail: ledda@brandeis.edu. Website: http://www.brandeis.edu/gsas.

Brigham Young University, Graduate Studies, College of Physical and Mathematical Sciences, Department of Mathematics, Provo, UT 84602-1001. Offers MS, PhD. Part-time programs available. *Faculty:* 32 full-time (2 women). *Students:* 14 full-time (3 women), 19 part-time (2 women), 4 international. Average age 24. 19 applicants, 84% accepted, 14 enrolled. In 2012, 19 master's, 6 doctorates awarded. Terminal master's awarded for partial completion of doctoral program. *Degree requirements:* For master's, comprehensive exam, thesis (for some programs), project; written exams; for doctorate, comprehensive exam, thesis/dissertation, qualifying exams. *Entrance requirements:* For master's, GRE General Test, GRE Subject Test (math; minimum score of 600), minimum GPA of 3.0 in last 60 hours, bachelor's degree in mathematics; for doctorate, GRE General Test, GRE Subject Test (math; minimum score of 600), master's degree in mathematics or related field. Additional exam requirements/recommendations for international students: Required—TOEFL (minimum score 600 paper-based; 85 iBT). *Application deadline:* For fall admission, 2/15 priority date for domestic students, 1/15 for international students; for winter admission, 9/15 priority date for domestic students, 9/15 for international students; for spring admission, 2/15 for domestic students, 1/15 for international students. Applications are processed on a rolling basis. Application fee: $50. Electronic applications accepted. *Expenses: Tuition:* Full-time $5950; part-time $331 per credit hour. Tuition and fees vary according to program and student's religious affiliation. *Financial support:* In 2012–13, 30 students received support, including 10 research assistantships (averaging $17,400 per year), 30 teaching assistantships with full tuition reimbursements available (averaging $17,400 per year); institutionally sponsored loans also available. Support available to part-time students. Financial award application deadline: 2/15. *Faculty research:* Algebraic geometry/number theory, applied math/nonlinear PDEs, combinatorics/matrix theory, geometric group theory/topology. Total annual research expenditures: $65,560. *Unit head:* Dr. Robin O. Roundy, Chairperson, 801-422-1747, Fax: 801-422-0504, E-mail: robin@math.byu.edu. *Application contact:* Lonette Stoddard, Graduate Secretary, 801-422-2062, Fax: 801-422-0504, E-mail: gradschool@math.byu.edu. Website: http://www.math.byu.edu/.

Brock University, Faculty of Graduate Studies, Faculty of Mathematics and Science, Program in Mathematics and Statistics, St. Catharines, ON L2S 3A1, Canada. Offers M Sc. Part-time programs available. *Degree requirements:* For master's, thesis or project. *Entrance requirements:* For master's, honors degree. Additional exam requirements/recommendations for international students: Required—TOEFL (minimum score 550 paper-based; 80 iBT), IELTS (minimum score 6.5), TWE (minimum score 4). Electronic applications accepted.

Brooklyn College of the City University of New York, Division of Graduate Studies, Department of Mathematics, Brooklyn, NY 11210-2889. Offers mathematics (MA, PhD). Part-time and evening/weekend programs available. *Degree requirements:* For master's, comprehensive exam (mathematics). *Entrance requirements:* For master's, minimum GPA of 3.0, 2 letters of recommendation. Additional exam requirements/recommendations for international students: Required—TOEFL (minimum score 500 paper-based; 61 iBT). Electronic applications accepted. *Faculty research:* Differential geometry, gauge theory, complex analysis, orthogonal functions.

Brown University, Graduate School, Department of Mathematics, Providence, RI 02912. Offers M Sc, MA, PhD. *Degree requirements:* For doctorate, one foreign language, thesis/dissertation. *Entrance requirements:* For doctorate, GRE. Additional exam requirements/recommendations for international students: Required—TOEFL (minimum score 900 paper-based; 100 iBT) or IELTS (minimum score 7). Electronic applications accepted. *Faculty research:* Algebraic geometry, number theory, functional analysis, geometry, topology, theoretical PDE.

Bryn Mawr College, Graduate School of Arts and Sciences, Department of Mathematics, Bryn Mawr, PA 19010-2899. Offers MA, PhD. Part-time programs available. *Faculty:* 6. *Students:* 2 full-time (both women), 5 part-time (4 women). Average age 26. 17 applicants, 12% accepted, 1 enrolled. *Degree requirements:* For master's, one foreign language, thesis; for doctorate, 2 foreign languages, comprehensive exam, thesis/dissertation. *Entrance requirements:* For master's and doctorate, GRE General Test. Additional exam requirements/recommendations for international students: Required—TOEFL (minimum score 600 paper-based). *Application deadline:* For fall admission, 1/3 for domestic and international students. Application fee: $50. *Expenses: Tuition:* Full-time $35,280. *Financial support:* In 2012–13, 1 research assistantship with full tuition reimbursement (averaging $15,500 per year), 4 teaching assistantships with partial tuition reimbursements (averaging $15,500 per year) were awarded; Federal Work-Study, scholarships/grants, tuition waivers (full and partial), unspecified assistantships, and tuition awards also available. Support available to part-time students. Financial award application deadline: 1/3. *Unit head:* Dr. Paul Melvin, Chair, 610-526-5353, E-mail: pmelvin@brynmawr.edu. *Application contact:* Maria Dantis, Administrative Assistant to the Graduate School of Arts and Sciences Dean, 610-526-5074, Fax: 610-526-5074, E-mail: mdantis@brynmawr.edu.

Bucknell University, Graduate Studies, College of Arts and Sciences, Department of Mathematics, Lewisburg, PA 17837. Offers MA, MS. *Degree requirements:* For master's, comprehensive exam, thesis or alternative. *Entrance requirements:* For master's, GRE General Test, GRE Subject Test, minimum GPA of 3.0. Additional exam requirements/recommendations for international students: Required—TOEFL (minimum score 600 paper-based).

California Institute of Technology, Division of Physics, Mathematics and Astronomy, Department of Mathematics, Pasadena, CA 91125-0001. Offers PhD. *Degree requirements:* For doctorate, one foreign language, thesis/dissertation, candidacy and final exams. *Entrance requirements:* For doctorate, GRE General Test, GRE Subject Test. Additional exam requirements/recommendations for international students: Required—TOEFL. *Faculty research:* Number theory, combinatorics, differential geometry, dynamical systems, finite groups.

California Polytechnic State University, San Luis Obispo, College of Science and Mathematics, Department of Mathematics, San Luis Obispo, CA 93407. Offers MS. Part-time programs available. *Faculty:* 11 full-time (2 women), 1 (woman) part-time/adjunct. *Students:* 9 full-time (4 women), 5 part-time (3 women); includes 5 minority (2 Asian, non-Hispanic/Latino; 2 Hispanic/Latino; 1 Two or more races, non-Hispanic/Latino), 1 international. Average age 23. 28 applicants, 43% accepted, 9 enrolled. In 2012, 7 master's awarded. *Degree requirements:* For master's, comprehensive exam, qualifying exams. *Entrance requirements:* For master's, minimum GPA of 2.5 in last 90 quarter units of course work. Additional exam requirements/recommendations for international students: Required—TOEFL (minimum score 550 paper-based) or IELTS (minimum score 6). *Application deadline:* For fall admission, 7/1 for domestic students, 11/30 for international students; for winter admission, 11/1 for domestic students, 6/30 for international students; for spring admission, 2/1 for domestic students. Applications are processed on a rolling basis. Application fee: $55. *Expenses:* Tuition, state resident: full-time $6738; part-time $3906 per year. Tuition, nonresident: full-time $17,898; part-time $8370 per year. *Required fees:* $3051; $874 per term. One-time fee: $3051 full-time; $2622 part-time. *Financial support:* Fellowships, teaching assistantships, career-related internships or fieldwork, Federal Work-Study, and scholarships/grants available. Support available to part-time students. Financial award application deadline: 3/2; financial award applicants required to submit FAFSA. *Faculty research:* Combinatorics, dynamical systems, ordinary and partial differential equations, operator theory, topology. *Unit head:* Dr. Dylan Retsek, Graduate Coordinator, 805-756-2072, Fax: 805-756-6537, E-mail: dretsek@calpoly.edu. *Application contact:* Dr. James Maraviglia, Associate Vice Provost for Marketing and Enrollment Development, 805-756-2311, Fax: 805-756-5400, E-mail: admissions@calpoly.edu. Website: http://math.calpoly.edu/mathematicsms.html.

California State Polytechnic University, Pomona, Academic Affairs, College of Science, Program in Mathematics, Pomona, CA 91768-2557. Offers applied mathematics (MS); pure mathematics (MS). Part-time programs available. *Students:* 17 full-time (10 women), 32 part-time (10 women); includes 27 minority (1 Black or African American, non-Hispanic/Latino; 7 Asian, non-Hispanic/Latino; 16 Hispanic/Latino; 3 Two or more races, non-Hispanic/Latino), 2 international. Average age 32. 68 applicants, 47% accepted, 16 enrolled. In 2012, 13 master's awarded. *Degree requirements:* For master's, thesis or alternative. *Entrance requirements:* For master's, GRE General Test. *Application deadline:* For fall admission, 5/1 priority date for domestic students; for winter admission, 10/15 priority date for domestic students; for spring admission, 1/20 priority date for domestic students. Applications are processed on a rolling basis. Application fee: $55. Electronic applications accepted. *Financial support:* Career-related internships or fieldwork, Federal Work-Study, and institutionally sponsored loans

Peterson's Graduate Programs in the Physical Sciences, Mathematics, Agricultural Sciences, the Environment & Natural Resources 2014

www.petersonsbooks.com **317**

available. Support available to part-time students. Financial award application deadline: 3/2; financial award applicants required to submit FAFSA. *Unit head:* Dr. John Rock, Graduate Coordinator, 909-869-2404, E-mail: jarock@csupomona.edu. *Application contact:* Deborah L. Brandon, Executive Director, Admissions and Outreach, 909-869-3427, Fax: 909-869-5315, E-mail: dlbrandon@csupomona.edu. Website: http://www.csupomona.edu/~math/.

California State University Channel Islands, Extended University and International Programs, Program in Mathematics, Camarillo, CA 93012. Offers MS. Part-time and evening/weekend programs available. *Students:* 40. *Degree requirements:* For master's, thesis. *Entrance requirements:* For master's, BA in math. Additional exam requirements/recommendations for international students: Required—TOEFL (minimum score 550 paper-based; 80 iBT), IELTS (minimum score 6). *Application deadline:* For fall admission, 6/1 for domestic and international students; for spring admission, 12/1 for international students. Applications are processed on a rolling basis. Application fee: $55. *Financial support:* Applicants required to submit FAFSA. *Unit head:* Dr. Cindy Wyels, Associate Professor of Mathematics, 805-437-2748, E-mail: msmath@csuci.edu. *Application contact:* Christian Cash, 805-437-2748, E-mail: exed@csuci.edu.

California State University, East Bay, Office of Academic Programs and Graduate Studies, College of Science, Department of Mathematics and Computer Science, Mathematics Program, Hayward, CA 94542-3000. Offers applied math (MS); mathematics (MS); mathematics teaching (MS). Part-time and evening/weekend programs available. *Degree requirements:* For master's, comprehensive exam or thesis. *Entrance requirements:* For master's, minimum GPA of 3.0 in field. Additional exam requirements/recommendations for international students: Required—TOEFL (minimum score 550 paper-based). Electronic applications accepted.

California State University, Fresno, Division of Graduate Studies, College of Science and Mathematics, Department of Mathematics, Fresno, CA 93740-8027. Offers mathematics (MA); teaching (MA). Part-time programs available. *Degree requirements:* For master's, thesis or alternative. *Entrance requirements:* For master's, GRE General Test. Additional exam requirements/recommendations for international students: Required—TOEFL. Electronic applications accepted. *Faculty research:* Diagnostic testing project.

California State University, Fullerton, Graduate Studies, College of Natural Science and Mathematics, Department of Mathematics, Fullerton, CA 92834-9480. Offers applied mathematics (MA); mathematics (MA); teaching (MA). Part-time programs available. *Students:* 34 full-time (17 women), 41 part-time (17 women); includes 35 minority (2 Black or African American, non-Hispanic/Latino; 21 Asian, non-Hispanic/Latino; 12 Hispanic/Latino), 6 international. Average age 31. 95 applicants, 68% accepted, 39 enrolled. In 2012, 30 master's awarded. *Degree requirements:* For master's, comprehensive exam or project. *Entrance requirements:* For master's, minimum GPA of 2.5 in last 60 units of course work, major in mathematics or related field. Application fee: $55. *Financial support:* Research assistantships, teaching assistantships, career-related internships or fieldwork, Federal Work-Study, institutionally sponsored loans, and scholarships/grants available. Support available to part-time students. Financial award application deadline: 3/1; financial award applicants required to submit FAFSA. *Unit head:* Dr. Stephen W. Goode, Chair, 657-278-3631. *Application contact:* Admissions/Applications, 657-278-2371.

California State University, Long Beach, Graduate Studies, College of Natural Sciences and Mathematics, Department of Mathematics and Statistics, Long Beach, CA 90840. Offers mathematics (MS), including applied mathematics, applied statistics, mathematics education for secondary school teachers. Part-time programs available. *Degree requirements:* For master's, comprehensive exam or thesis. Electronic applications accepted. *Faculty research:* Algebra, functional analysis, partial differential equations, operator theory, numerical analysis.

California State University, Los Angeles, Graduate Studies, College of Natural and Social Sciences, Department of Mathematics, Los Angeles, CA 90032-8530. Offers mathematics (MS), including applied mathematics, mathematics. Part-time and evening/weekend programs available. *Faculty:* 8 full-time (3 women). *Students:* 37 full-time (12 women), 35 part-time (10 women); includes 39 minority (2 Black or African American, non-Hispanic/Latino; 17 Asian, non-Hispanic/Latino; 15 Hispanic/Latino; 2 Native Hawaiian or other Pacific Islander, non-Hispanic/Latino; 3 Two or more races, non-Hispanic/Latino), 8 international. Average age 33. 64 applicants, 73% accepted, 24 enrolled. In 2012, 17 master's awarded. *Degree requirements:* For master's, comprehensive exam or thesis. *Entrance requirements:* For master's, previous course work in mathematics. Additional exam requirements/recommendations for international students: Required—TOEFL (minimum score 500 paper-based). *Application deadline:* For fall admission, 5/1 for domestic and international students. Applications are processed on a rolling basis. Application fee: $55. Electronic applications accepted. *Financial support:* Teaching assistantships and Federal Work-Study available. Support available to part-time students. Financial award application deadline: 3/1. *Faculty research:* Group theory, functional analysis, convexity theory, ordered geometry. *Unit head:* Dr. Grant Fraser, Chair, 323-343-2150, Fax: 323-343-5071, E-mail: gfraser@calstatela.edu. *Application contact:* Dr. Larry Fritz, Dean of Graduate Studies, 323-343-3820, Fax: 323-343-5653, E-mail: lfritz@calstatela.edu. Website: http://www.calstatela.edu/academic/math/.

California State University, Northridge, Graduate Studies, College of Science and Mathematics, Department of Mathematics, Northridge, CA 91330. Offers applied mathematics (MS); mathematics (MS); mathematics for educational careers (MS). Part-time and evening/weekend programs available. *Degree requirements:* For master's, thesis (for some programs). *Entrance requirements:* For master's, GRE (if cumulative undergraduate GPA less than 3.0). Additional exam requirements/recommendations for international students: Required—TOEFL.

California State University, Sacramento, Office of Graduate Studies, College of Natural Sciences and Mathematics, Department of Mathematics and Statistics, Sacramento, CA 95819-6051. Offers MA. Part-time programs available. *Degree requirements:* For master's, thesis or alternative, directed reading program preparing for written proficiency exam. *Entrance requirements:* For master's, minimum GPA of 3.0 in mathematics, 2.5 overall during previous 2 years; BA in mathematics or equivalent. Additional exam requirements/recommendations for international students: Required—TOEFL. Electronic applications accepted. *Faculty research:* Algebra, applied mathematics, methods in mathematical finance, subelliptic analysis, topology.

California State University, San Bernardino, Graduate Studies, College of Natural Sciences, Department of Mathematics, San Bernardino, CA 92407-2397. Offers mathematics (MA); teaching mathematics (MAT). Part-time programs available. *Students:* 9 full-time (2 women), 58 part-time (31 women); includes 31 minority (2 Black or African American, non-Hispanic/Latino; 4 Asian, non-Hispanic/Latino; 23 Hispanic/Latino; 2 Two or more races, non-Hispanic/Latino), 2 international. Average age 31. 33 applicants, 55% accepted, 14 enrolled. In 2012, 8 master's awarded. *Degree requirements:* For master's, advancement to candidacy. *Entrance requirements:* For master's, writing exam, minimum GPA of 3.0 in math courses. Application fee: $55. *Financial support:* Teaching assistantships available. *Faculty research:* Mathematics education, technology in education, algebra, combinatorics, real analysis. *Unit head:* Dr. Peter D. Williams, Chair, 909-537-5361, Fax: 909-537-7119, E-mail: pwilliam@csusb.edu. *Application contact:* Dr. Jeffrey Thompson, Assistant Dean of Graduate Studies, 909-537-5058, E-mail: jthompso@csusb.edu.

California State University, San Marcos, College of Arts and Sciences, Program in Mathematics, San Marcos, CA 92096-0001. Offers MS. Part-time and evening/weekend programs available. *Degree requirements:* For master's, thesis optional. *Entrance requirements:* Additional exam requirements/recommendations for international students: Required—TOEFL, TWE. Tuition and fees vary according to program. *Faculty research:* Combinatorics, graph theory, partial differential equations, numerical analysis, computational linear algebra.

Carleton University, Faculty of Graduate Studies, Faculty of Science, School of Mathematics and Statistics, Ottawa, ON K1S 5B6, Canada. Offers mathematics (M Sc, PhD). Programs offered jointly with University of Ottawa. *Degree requirements:* For master's, thesis optional; for doctorate, one foreign language, comprehensive exam, thesis/dissertation. *Entrance requirements:* For master's, honors degree; for doctorate, master's degree. Additional exam requirements/recommendations for international students: Required—TOEFL. *Faculty research:* Pure mathematics, applied mathematics, probability and statistics.

Carnegie Mellon University, Mellon College of Science, Department of Mathematical Sciences, Pittsburgh, PA 15213-3891. Offers algorithms, combinatorics, and optimization (PhD); applied mathematics (PhD); computational finance (MS); mathematical finance (PhD); mathematical sciences (MS, DA, PhD); pure and applied logic (PhD). Part-time programs available. Terminal master's awarded for partial completion of doctoral program. *Degree requirements:* For doctorate, thesis/dissertation. *Entrance requirements:* For master's and doctorate, GRE General Test, GRE Subject Test. Additional exam requirements/recommendations for international students: Required—TOEFL. Electronic applications accepted. *Faculty research:* Continuum mechanics, discrete mathematics, applied and computational mathematics.

Case Western Reserve University, School of Graduate Studies, Department of Mathematics, Cleveland, OH 44106. Offers applied mathematics (MS, PhD); mathematics (MS, PhD). Part-time programs available. *Faculty:* 19 full-time (5 women), 1 part-time/adjunct (0 women). *Students:* 22 full-time (9 women), 1 part-time (0 women); includes 1 minority (Two or more races, non-Hispanic/Latino), 10 international. Average age 27. 58 applicants, 19% accepted, 6 enrolled. In 2012, 2 master's, 2 doctorates awarded. Terminal master's awarded for partial completion of doctoral program. *Degree requirements:* For master's, thesis or alternative, thesis (for applied mathematics); for doctorate, comprehensive exam, thesis/dissertation. *Entrance requirements:* For master's and doctorate, GRE General Test, 3 letters of recommendation. Additional exam requirements/recommendations for international students: Required—TOEFL (minimum score 577 paper-based; 90 iBT); Recommended—IELTS (minimum score 7). *Application deadline:* For fall admission, 1/15 priority date for domestic students; for spring admission, 11/1 priority date for domestic students. Applications are processed on a rolling basis. Application fee: $50. Electronic applications accepted. *Financial support:* Research assistantships, teaching assistantships, institutionally sponsored loans, and unspecified assistantships available. Financial award application deadline: 12/15. *Faculty research:* Probability theory, convexity and high-dimensional phenomena, imaging, geometric evaluation of curves, dynamical systems, large scale scientific computing, life sciences. *Unit head:* Daniela Calvetti, Chair, 216-368-2880, Fax: 216-368-5163, E-mail: daniela.calvetti@case.edu. *Application contact:* Gaythresa Lewis, Admissions,

318 www.petersonsbooks.com

Peterson's Graduate Programs in the Physical Sciences, Mathematics, Agricultural Sciences, the Environment & Natural Resources 2014

216-368-5014, Fax: 216-368-5163, E-mail: gxl34@case.edu. Website: http://www.case.edu/artsci/math/.

Central Connecticut State University, School of Graduate Studies, School of Arts and Sciences, Department of Mathematical Sciences, New Britain, CT 06050-4010. Offers data mining (MS, Certificate); mathematics (MA, MS, Certificate, Sixth Year Certificate), including actuarial science (MA), computer science (MA), statistics (MA). Part-time and evening/weekend programs available. *Faculty:* 13 full-time (4 women). *Students:* 18 full-time (8 women), 87 part-time (44 women); includes 18 minority (6 Black or African American, non-Hispanic/Latino; 4 Asian, non-Hispanic/Latino; 7 Hispanic/Latino; 1 Two or more races, non-Hispanic/Latino), 7 international. Average age 35. 59 applicants, 58% accepted, 24 enrolled. In 2012, 34 master's, 5 other advanced degrees awarded. *Degree requirements:* For master's, comprehensive exam, thesis or alternative; for other advanced degree, qualifying exam. *Entrance requirements:* For master's, minimum undergraduate GPA of 2.7; for other advanced degree, minimum undergraduate GPA of 3.0, essay, letters of recommendation. Additional exam requirements/recommendations for international students: Required—TOEFL (minimum score 550 paper-based; 79 iBT). *Application deadline:* For fall admission, 5/1 for domestic and international students; for spring admission, 11/1 for domestic and international students. Applications are processed on a rolling basis. Application fee: $50. Electronic applications accepted. *Expenses: Tuition, area resident:* Full-time $5337, part-time $498 per credit. Tuition, state resident: full-time $8008; part-time $510 per credit. Tuition, nonresident: full-time $14,869; part-time $510 per credit. *Required fees:* $3970. One-time fee: $62 part-time. *Financial support:* In 2012–13, 4 students received support. Career-related internships or fieldwork, Federal Work-Study, scholarships/grants, and unspecified assistantships available. Support available to part-time students. Financial award application deadline: 3/1; financial award applicants required to submit FAFSA. *Faculty research:* Statistics, actuarial mathematics, computer systems and engineering, computer programming techniques, operations research. *Unit head:* Dr. Jeffrey McGowan, Chair, 860-832-2835, E-mail: mcgowan@ccsu.edu. *Application contact:* Patricia Gardner, Associate Director of Graduate Studies, 860-832-2350, Fax: 860-832-2362, E-mail: graduateadmissions@ccsu.edu. Website: http://www.math.ccsu.edu/.

Central European University, Graduate Studies, Department of Mathematics and its Applications, Budapest, Hungary. Offers applied mathematics (MS); mathematics and its applications (PhD). *Faculty:* 2 full-time (0 women), 9 part-time/adjunct (1 woman). *Students:* 38 full-time (7 women). Average age 27. 140 applicants, 15% accepted, 12 enrolled. In 2012, 7 master's, 4 doctorates awarded. *Degree requirements:* For master's, one foreign language, thesis (for some programs); for doctorate, comprehensive exam, thesis/dissertation. *Entrance requirements:* For master's and doctorate, entrance exam or GRE, statement of purpose. Additional exam requirements/recommendations for international students: Required—TOEFL (minimum score 570 paper-based); Recommended—IELTS (minimum score 6.5). *Application deadline:* For fall admission, 1/24 for domestic and international students. Electronic applications accepted. *Financial support:* In 2012–13, 37 students received support, including 37 fellowships (averaging $6,100 per year); career-related internships or fieldwork, scholarships/grants, health care benefits, and tuition waivers (full and partial) also available. *Faculty research:* Applied mathematics, such as: algebra, algebraic geometry, bioinformatics, calculus of variations, computational biology, cryptography, discrete mathematics, evolutions equations, fluid mechanics, geometry, number theory, numerical analysis, optimization, ordinary and partial differential equations, probability theory, quantum mechanics, statistics, stochastic processes. *Unit head:* Karoly Boroczky, Head, 36 1 327-3053, E-mail: mathematics@ceu.hu. *Application contact:* Zsuzsanna Jaszberenyi, Admissions Officer, 361-324-3009, Fax: 367-327-3211, E-mail: admissions@ceu.hu. Website: http://mathematics.ceu.hu/.

Central Michigan University, College of Graduate Studies, College of Science and Technology, Department of Mathematics, Mount Pleasant, MI 48859. Offers mathematics (MA, PhD), including teaching of college mathematics (PhD). Part-time programs available. *Faculty:* 28 full-time (10 women). *Students:* 64 (15 women); includes 6 minority (1 American Indian or Alaska Native, non-Hispanic/Latino; 4 Asian, non-Hispanic/Latino; 1 Hispanic/Latino), 29 international. Average age 29. 82 applicants, 52% accepted, 24 enrolled. In 2012, 9 master's, 5 doctorates awarded. *Degree requirements:* For master's, thesis or alternative; for doctorate, thesis/dissertation. *Entrance requirements:* For master's, minimum GPA of 2.7, 20 hours of course work in mathematics; for doctorate, GRE, minimum GPA of 3.0, 20 hours of course work in mathematics. *Application deadline:* For fall admission, 7/1 for international students; for spring admission, 10/1 for international students. Applications are processed on a rolling basis. Application fee: $35 ($45 for international students). Electronic applications accepted. *Expenses:* Tuition, state resident: full-time $8730; part-time $485 per credit hour. Tuition, nonresident: full-time $13,788; part-time $766 per credit hour. One-time fee: $75. Tuition and fees vary according to degree level, campus/location and reciprocity agreements. *Financial support:* Research assistantships, teaching assistantships, career-related internships or fieldwork, Federal Work-Study, unspecified assistantships, and out-of-state merit awards available. *Faculty research:* Combinatorics, approximation theory, applied mathematics, statistics, functional analysis and operator theory. *Unit head:* Dr. En-Bing Lin, Chairperson, 989-774-3596, Fax: 989-774-2414, E-mail: lin1e@cmich.edu. *Application contact:* Dr. Brad Safnuk, Graduate Program Coordinator, 989-774-6518, Fax: 989-774-2414, E-mail: safnu1b@cmich.edu. Website: http://www.cst.cmich.edu/units/mth/.

Central Washington University, Graduate Studies and Research, College of the Sciences, Department of Mathematics, Ellensburg, WA 98926. Offers MAT. Program offered during summer only. *Faculty:* 13 full-time (3 women). *Students:* 1 (woman) part-time. In 2012, 2 master's awarded. *Degree requirements:* For master's, thesis or alternative. *Entrance requirements:* For master's, minimum GPA of 3.0. Additional exam requirements/recommendations for international students: Required—TOEFL (minimum score 550 paper-based; 79 iBT). *Application deadline:* For fall admission, 2/1 priority date for domestic students; for winter admission, 10/1 for domestic students; for spring admission, 1/1 for domestic students. Applications are processed on a rolling basis. Application fee: $50. Electronic applications accepted. *Expenses:* Tuition, state resident: full-time $8517. Tuition, nonresident: full-time $18,972. *Required fees:* $978. *Financial support:* Federal Work-Study and health care benefits available. Financial award application deadline: 3/1; financial award applicants required to submit FAFSA. *Unit head:* Dr. Michael Lundin, Professor, 509-963-1398, E-mail: lundin@cwu.edu. *Application contact:* Justine Eason, Admissions Program Coordinator, 509-963-3103, Fax: 509-963-1799, E-mail: masters@cwu.edu.

Chicago State University, School of Graduate and Professional Studies, College of Arts and Sciences, Department of Mathematics and Computer Science, Chicago, IL 60628. Offers computer science (MS); mathematics (MS). *Degree requirements:* For master's, thesis optional, oral exam. *Entrance requirements:* For master's, minimum GPA of 2.75.

City College of the City University of New York, Graduate School, College of Liberal Arts and Science, Division of Science, Department of Mathematics, New York, NY 10031-9198. Offers MA. Part-time programs available. *Degree requirements:* For master's, one foreign language. *Entrance requirements:* Additional exam requirements/recommendations for international students: Required—TOEFL (minimum score 500 paper-based; 61 iBT). Electronic applications accepted. *Faculty research:* Group theory, number theory, logic, statistics, computational geometry.

Claremont Graduate University, Graduate Programs, School of Mathematical Sciences, Claremont, CA 91711-6160. Offers computational and systems biology (PhD); computational mathematics and numerical analysis (MA, MS); computational science (PhD); engineering and industrial applied mathematics (PhD); mathematics (PhD); operations research and statistics (MA, MS); physical applied mathematics (MA, MS); pure mathematics (MA, MS); scientific computing (MA, MS); systems and control theory (MA, MS). Part-time programs available. *Faculty:* 6 full-time (1 woman), 1 part-time/adjunct (0 women). *Students:* 54 full-time (16 women), 35 part-time (18 women); includes 29 minority (3 Black or African American, non-Hispanic/Latino; 10 Asian, non-Hispanic/Latino; 12 Hispanic/Latino; 4 Two or more races, non-Hispanic/Latino), 21 international. Average age 33. In 2012, 13 master's, 7 doctorates awarded. Terminal master's awarded for partial completion of doctoral program. *Entrance requirements:* For master's and doctorate, GRE General Test. Additional exam requirements/recommendations for international students: Required—TOEFL (minimum score 550 paper-based; 80 iBT). *Application deadline:* For fall admission, 2/1 priority date for domestic students. Applications are processed on a rolling basis. Application fee: $60. Electronic applications accepted. *Expenses: Tuition:* Full-time $37,640; part-time $1636 per unit. *Required fees:* $500; $250 per semester. *Financial support:* Fellowships, research assistantships, Federal Work-Study, institutionally sponsored loans, scholarships/grants, and tuition waivers (full and partial) available. Support available to part-time students. Financial award application deadline: 2/15; financial award applicants required to submit FAFSA. *Unit head:* Henry Schellhorn, Director, 909-607-4168, E-mail: henry.schellhorn@cgu.edu. *Application contact:* Charlotte Ballesteros, Program Coordinator, 909-621-8080, Fax: 909-607-8261, E-mail: charlotte.ballesteros@cgu.edu. Website: http://www.cgu.edu/pages/168.asp.

Clark Atlanta University, School of Arts and Sciences, Department of Mathematical Sciences, Atlanta, GA 30314. Offers MS. Part-time programs available. *Faculty:* 2 full-time (1 woman), 1 part-time/adjunct (0 women). *Students:* 2 full-time (1 woman), 1 (woman) part-time; all minorities (all Black or African American, non-Hispanic/Latino). Average age 31. 5 applicants, 80% accepted, 2 enrolled. In 2012, 2 master's awarded. *Degree requirements:* For master's, one foreign language, thesis optional. *Entrance requirements:* For master's, GRE General Test, minimum GPA of 2.5. Additional exam requirements/recommendations for international students: Required—TOEFL (minimum score 500 paper-based; 61 iBT). *Application deadline:* For fall admission, 4/1 for domestic and international students; for spring admission, 11/1 for domestic and international students. Applications are processed on a rolling basis. Application fee: $40 ($55 for international students). *Expenses: Tuition:* Full-time $14,256; part-time $792 per credit hour. *Required fees:* $818; $409 per semester. *Financial support:* In 2012–13, 3 fellowships were awarded; scholarships/grants and unspecified assistantships also available. Financial award application deadline: 4/30; financial award applicants required to submit FAFSA. *Faculty research:* Numerical methods for operator equations, Ada language development. *Unit head:* Dr. Charles Pierre, Chairperson, 404-880-8195, E-mail: cpierre@cau.edu. *Application contact:* Michelle Clark-Davis, Graduate Program Admissions, 404-880-6605, E-mail: cauadmissions@cau.edu.

Clarkson University, Graduate School, School of Arts and Sciences, Department of Mathematics, Potsdam, NY 13699. Offers MS, PhD. Part-time programs available. *Faculty:* 13 full-time (4 women), 2 part-time/adjunct (0 women). *Students:* 28 full-time (8 women), 20 international. Average age 29. 24 applicants, 83% accepted, 9 enrolled. In 2012, 4 master's, 3 doctorates awarded.

Peterson's Graduate Programs in the Physical Sciences, Mathematics, Agricultural Sciences, the Environment & Natural Resources 2014

www.petersonsbooks.com 319

Terminal master's awarded for partial completion of doctoral program. *Degree requirements:* For doctorate, thesis/dissertation, departmental qualifying exam. *Entrance requirements:* For master's and doctorate, GRE, transcripts of all college coursework, three letters of recommendation; resume and personal statement (recommended). Additional exam requirements/recommendations for international students: Required—TOEFL. *Application deadline:* For fall admission, 1/30 priority date for domestic students, 1/30 for international students; for spring admission, 9/1 priority date for domestic students, 9/1 for international students. Applications are processed on a rolling basis. Application fee: $25 ($35 for international students). Electronic applications accepted. *Expenses: Tuition:* Full-time $15,108; part-time $1259 per credit hour. *Required fees:* $295 per semester. *Financial support:* In 2012–13, 25 students received support, including fellowships with full tuition reimbursements available (averaging $22,650 per year), 6 research assistantships with full tuition reimbursements available (averaging $22,650 per year), 15 teaching assistantships with full tuition reimbursements available (averaging $22,650 per year); scholarships/grants, tuition waivers (partial), and unspecified assistantships also available. *Faculty research:* Mission security, psychophysical models, data mining, multilinear algebra. *Total annual research expenditures:* $680,813. *Unit head:* Dr. Christopher Lynch, Chair, 315-268-2395, Fax: 315-268-2371, E-mail: clynch@clarkson.edu. *Application contact:* Jennifer Reed, Graduate Coordinator, School of Arts and Sciences, 315-268-3802, Fax: 315-268-3989, E-mail: sciencegrad@clarkson.edu. Website: http://www.clarkson.edu/math/.

Clemson University, Graduate School, College of Engineering and Science, Department of Mathematical Sciences, Clemson, SC 29634. Offers applied and pure mathematics (MS, PhD); computational mathematics (MS, PhD); operations research (MS, PhD); statistics (MS, PhD). Part-time programs available. *Faculty:* 44 full-time (13 women), 4 part-time/adjunct (2 women). *Students:* 117 full-time (43 women), 3 part-time (2 women); includes 6 minority (2 Black or African American, non-Hispanic/Latino; 1 American Indian or Alaska Native, non-Hispanic/Latino; 1 Asian, non-Hispanic/Latino; 1 Hispanic/Latino; 1 Two or more races, non-Hispanic/Latino), 50 international. Average age 26. 188 applicants, 76% accepted, 45 enrolled. In 2012, 41 master's, 11 doctorates awarded. *Degree requirements:* For master's, thesis optional, final project; for doctorate, thesis/dissertation, qualifying exams. *Entrance requirements:* For master's and doctorate, GRE General Test. Additional exam requirements/recommendations for international students: Required—TOEFL. *Application deadline:* For fall admission, 1/15 priority date for domestic students, 1/15 for international students; for spring admission, 10/1 priority date for domestic students, 9/15 for international students. Applications are processed on a rolling basis. Application fee: $70 ($80 for international students). Electronic applications accepted. *Financial support:* In 2012–13, 111 students received support, including 2 fellowships with full and partial tuition reimbursements available (averaging $10,000 per year), 8 research assistantships with partial tuition reimbursements available (averaging $17,943 per year), 104 teaching assistantships with partial tuition reimbursements available (averaging $18,793 per year); career-related internships or fieldwork, institutionally sponsored loans, scholarships/grants, health care benefits, and unspecified assistantships also available. Support available to part-time students. Financial award application deadline: 4/15. *Faculty research:* Applied and computational analysis, cryptography, discrete mathematics, optimization, statistics. *Total annual research expenditures:* $780,865. *Unit head:* Dr. Robert L. Taylor, Chair, 864-656-5240, Fax: 864-656-5230, E-mail: rtaylo2@clemson.edu. *Application contact:* Dr. K. B. Kulasekera, Graduate Coordinator, 864-656-5231, Fax: 864-656-5230, E-mail: kk@clemson.edu. Website: http://www.clemson.edu/ces/departments/math/index.html.

Cleveland State University, College of Graduate Studies, College of Sciences and Health Professions, Department of Mathematics, Cleveland, OH 44115. Offers applied statistics (MS); mathematics (MA, MS). Part-time and evening/weekend programs available. *Faculty:* 11 full-time (4 women), 1 part-time/adjunct (0 women). *Students:* 8 full-time (4 women), 27 part-time (11 women); includes 3 minority (1 Black or African American, non-Hispanic/Latino; 1 Asian, non-Hispanic/Latino; 1 Hispanic/Latino), 9 international. Average age 32. 59 applicants, 80% accepted, 23 enrolled. In 2012, 16 master's awarded. *Degree requirements:* For master's, exit project. *Entrance requirements:* Additional exam requirements/recommendations for international students: Required—TOEFL (minimum score 515 paper-based). *Application deadline:* For fall admission, 6/15 priority date for domestic students, 6/15 for international students. Applications are processed on a rolling basis. Application fee: $30. Electronic applications accepted. *Expenses:* Tuition, state resident: full-time $8172; part-time $510.75 per credit hour. Tuition, nonresident: full-time $15,372; part-time $960.75 per credit hour. *Required fees:* $25 per semester. Tuition and fees vary according to course load and program. *Financial support:* In 2012–13, 12 students received support, including 12 teaching assistantships with full tuition reimbursements available (averaging $10,000 per year). Financial award application deadline: 3/15. *Faculty research:* Algebraic topology, probability and statistics, differential equations, geometry. *Unit head:* Dr. John Peter Holcomb, Jr., Chairperson, 216-687-4681, Fax: 216-523-7340, E-mail: j.p.holcomb@csuohio.edu. *Application contact:* Dr. John F. Oprea, Graduate Program Director, 216-687-4702, Fax: 216-523-7340, E-mail: j.oprea@csuohio.edu. Website: http://www.csuohio.edu/sciences/dept/mathematics/.

The College at Brockport, State University of New York, School of Science and Mathematics, Department of Mathematics, Brockport, NY 14420-2997. Offers MA. Part-time programs available. *Students:* 9 full-time (5 women), 9 part-time (6 women); includes 4 minority (2 Asian, non-Hispanic/Latino; 2 Hispanic/Latino), 1 international. 9 applicants, 89% accepted, 5 enrolled. In 2012, 4 master's awarded. *Degree requirements:* For master's, comprehensive exam. *Entrance requirements:* For master's, minimum GPA of 3.0, letters of recommendation; statement of objectives. Additional exam requirements/recommendations for international students: Required—TOEFL (minimum score 550 paper-based; 79 iBT). *Application deadline:* For fall admission, 4/15 priority date for domestic students, 4/15 for international students; for spring admission, 11/15 priority date for domestic students, 11/15 for international students. Application fee: $50. Electronic applications accepted. *Expenses:* Tuition, state resident: full-time $9370; part-time $390 per credit. Tuition, nonresident: full-time $16,680; part-time $695 per credit. *Required fees:* $2882; $226 per semester. *Financial support:* In 2012–13, 3 teaching assistantships with full tuition reimbursements (averaging $6,000 per year) were awarded; Federal Work-Study, scholarships/grants, and unspecified assistantships also available. Support available to part-time students. Financial award application deadline: 3/15; financial award applicants required to submit FAFSA. *Faculty research:* Mathematical modeling, dynamical systems, complex/functional analysis, graph theory and combinations, algebra and number theory. *Unit head:* Dr. Mihail Barbosu, Chairperson, 585-395-5675, Fax: 585-395-2304, E-mail: mbarbosu@brockport.edu. *Application contact:* Dr. Howard Skogman, Graduate Director, 585-395-2046, Fax: 585-395-2304, E-mail: hskogman@brockport.edu. Website: http://www.brockport.edu/math/grad/.

College of Charleston, Graduate School, School of Sciences and Mathematics, Program in Mathematics, Charleston, SC 29424-0001. Offers mathematics (MS). Part-time and evening/weekend programs available. *Degree requirements:* For master's, thesis optional. *Entrance requirements:* For master's, GRE, BS in mathematics or equivalent, 2 letters of recommendation. Additional exam requirements/recommendations for international students: Required—TOEFL (minimum score 81 iBT). Electronic applications accepted. *Faculty research:* Algebra, dynamical systems, probability, analysis and topology, combinatorics.

Colorado School of Mines, Graduate School, Department of Mathematical and Computer Sciences, Golden, CO 80401-1887. Offers nuclear engineering (MS, PhD). Part-time programs available. *Faculty:* 20 full-time (6 women), 7 part-time/adjunct (4 women). *Students:* 44 full-time (15 women), 5 part-time (1 woman); includes 3 minority (1 Asian, non-Hispanic/Latino; 2 Hispanic/Latino), 2 international. Average age 26. 64 applicants, 67% accepted, 22 enrolled. In 2012, 10 master's, 1 doctorate awarded. *Degree requirements:* For master's, thesis (for some programs); for doctorate, comprehensive exam, thesis/dissertation. *Entrance requirements:* For master's and doctorate, GRE General Test. Additional exam requirements/recommendations for international students: Required—TOEFL (minimum score 550 paper-based; 80 iBT). *Application deadline:* For fall admission, 1/15 priority date for domestic students, 1/15 for international students; for spring admission, 10/15 priority date for domestic students, 10/15 for international students. Application fee: $50 ($70 for international students). Electronic applications accepted. *Financial support:* In 2012–13, 21 students received support, including 4 fellowships with full tuition reimbursements available (averaging $21,120 per year), 10 research assistantships with full tuition reimbursements available (averaging $21,120 per year), 7 teaching assistantships with full tuition reimbursements available (averaging $21,120 per year); scholarships/grants, health care benefits, and unspecified assistantships also available. Financial award application deadline: 1/15; financial award applicants required to submit FAFSA. *Faculty research:* Applied statistics, numerical computation, artificial intelligence, linear optimization. *Total annual research expenditures:* $1.5 million. *Unit head:* Dr. Willy Hereman, Head, 303-273-3881, Fax: 303-273-3875, E-mail: whereman@mines.edu. *Application contact:* William Navidi, Professor, 303-273-3489, Fax: 303-273-3875, E-mail: wnavidi@mines.edu. Website: http://ams.mines.edu/.

Colorado State University, Graduate School, College of Natural Sciences, Department of Mathematics, Fort Collins, CO 80523-1874. Offers MAT, MS, PhD. Part-time programs available. *Faculty:* 24 full-time (6 women). *Students:* 32 full-time (10 women), 19 part-time (8 women); includes 3 minority (1 Black or African American, non-Hispanic/Latino; 1 Asian, non-Hispanic/Latino; 1 Hispanic/Latino), 6 international. Average age 28. 114 applicants, 17% accepted, 8 enrolled. In 2012, 5 master's, 9 doctorates awarded. Terminal master's awarded for partial completion of doctoral program. *Degree requirements:* For master's, comprehensive exam (for some programs), thesis (for some programs); for doctorate, comprehensive exam, thesis/dissertation. *Entrance requirements:* For master's, GRE General Test, minimum GPA of 3.0; for doctorate, GRE General Test, minimum GPA of 3.0. Additional exam requirements/recommendations for international students: Required—TOEFL (minimum score 550 paper-based; 80 iBT), IELTS (minimum score 6.5). *Application deadline:* For fall admission, 2/1 priority date for domestic students, 2/15 for international students; for spring admission, 7/15 priority date for domestic students, 7/15 for international students. Application fee: $50. Electronic applications accepted. *Expenses:* Tuition, state resident: full-time $8811; part-time $490 per credit. Tuition, nonresident: full-time $21,600; part-time $1200 per credit. *Required fees:* $1819; $61 per credit. *Financial support:* In 2012–13, 62 students received support, including 10 fellowships (averaging $34,804 per year), 11 research assistantships with full tuition reimbursements available (averaging $8,480 per year), 41 teaching assistantships with full tuition reimbursements available (averaging $14,414 per year); institutionally sponsored loans, scholarships/grants, health care benefits, and unspecified assistantships also available. Financial award application deadline: 2/1; financial award applicants required to submit FAFSA. *Faculty research:* Algebra, analysis, differential equations, inverse problems, scientific computation. *Total annual research expenditures:* $941,200. *Unit head:* Dr. Gerhard Dangelmayr, Chair, 970-491-6452, Fax: 970-491-2161, E-mail: gerhard@math.colostate.edu. *Application contact:* Bryan Elder, Graduate Coordinator, 970-491-7925, Fax: 970-491-2161, E-mail: elder@math.colostate.edu. Website: http://www.math.colostate.edu/.

Columbia University, Graduate School of Arts and Sciences, Division of Natural Sciences, Department of Mathematics, New York, NY 10027. Offers M Phil, MA, PhD. *Degree requirements:* For master's, written exam; for doctorate, 2 foreign languages, thesis/dissertation. *Entrance requirements:* For master's and doctorate, GRE General Test, major in mathematics. Additional exam requirements/recommendations for international students: Required—TOEFL. *Faculty research:* Algebra, topology, analysis.

Concordia University, School of Graduate Studies, Faculty of Arts and Science, Department of Mathematics and Statistics, Montréal, QC H3G 1M8, Canada. Offers mathematics (M Sc, MA, PhD); teaching of mathematics (MTM). *Degree requirements:* For master's, thesis optional; for doctorate, comprehensive exam, thesis/dissertation. *Entrance requirements:* For master's, honors degree in mathematics or equivalent. *Faculty research:* Number theory, computational algebra, mathematical physics, differential geometry, dynamical systems and statistics.

Cornell University, Graduate School, Graduate Fields of Arts and Sciences, Field of Mathematics, Ithaca, NY 14853-0001. Offers PhD. *Faculty:* 50 full-time (4 women). *Students:* 63 full-time (18 women); includes 5 minority (4 Asian, non-Hispanic/Latino; 1 Hispanic/Latino), 40 international. Average age 25. 293 applicants, 18% accepted, 21 enrolled. In 2012, 11 doctorates awarded. *Degree requirements:* For doctorate, one foreign language, comprehensive exam, thesis/dissertation, teaching experience. *Entrance requirements:* For doctorate, GRE General Test, GRE Subject Test (mathematics), 3 letters of recommendation. Additional exam requirements/recommendations for international students: Required—TOEFL (minimum score 600 paper-based; 95 iBT). *Application deadline:* For fall admission, 1/15 for domestic students. Application fee: $95. Electronic applications accepted. *Financial support:* In 2012–13, 61 students received support, including 20 fellowships with full tuition reimbursements available, 2 research assistantships with full tuition reimbursements available, 39 teaching assistantships with full tuition reimbursements available; institutionally sponsored loans, scholarships/grants, health care benefits, tuition waivers (full and partial), and unspecified assistantships also available. Financial award applicants required to submit FAFSA. *Faculty research:* Analysis, dynamical systems, Lie theory, logic, topology and geometry. *Unit head:* Director of Graduate Studies, 607-255-6757, Fax: 607-255-7149. *Application contact:* Graduate Field Assistant, 607-255-6757, Fax: 607-255-7149, E-mail: gradinfo@math.cornell.edu. Website: http://www.gradschool.cornell.edu/fields.php?id-32&a-2.

Dalhousie University, Faculty of Science, Department of Mathematics and Statistics, Program in Mathematics, Halifax, NS B3H 4R2, Canada. Offers M Sc, PhD. *Degree requirements:* For master's, thesis; for doctorate, thesis/dissertation. *Entrance requirements:* Additional exam requirements/recommendations for international students: Required—TOEFL, IELTS, CANTEST, CAEL, or Michigan English Language Assessment Battery. Electronic applications accepted. *Faculty research:* Applied mathematics, category theory, algebra, analysis, graph theory.

Dartmouth College, Arts and Sciences Graduate Programs, Department of Mathematics, Hanover, NH 03755. Offers PhD. *Degree requirements:* For doctorate, 2 foreign languages, thesis/dissertation. *Entrance requirements:* For doctorate, GRE General Test, GRE Subject Test. Additional exam requirements/recommendations for international students: Required—TOEFL. *Faculty research:* Mathematical logic, set theory, combinations, number theory.

Delaware State University, Graduate Programs, Department of Mathematics, Program in Mathematics, Dover, DE 19901-2277. Offers MS. *Entrance requirements:* Additional exam requirements/recommendations for international students: Required—TOEFL (minimum score 550 paper-based). Electronic applications accepted.

DePaul University, College of Science and Health, Department of Mathematical Sciences, Chicago, IL 60614. Offers applied mathematics (MS), including actuarial science, statistics; applied statistics (MS, Certificate); mathematics education (MA); pure mathematics (MS). Part-time and evening/weekend programs available. *Students:* 120 full-time (51 women), 64 part-time (26 women); includes 54 minority (21 Black or African American, non-Hispanic/Latino; 21 Asian, non-Hispanic/Latino; 10 Hispanic/Latino; 1 Native Hawaiian or other Pacific Islander, non-Hispanic/Latino; 1 Two or more races, non-Hispanic/Latino), 26 international. Average age 31. In 2012, 35 master's awarded. *Degree requirements:* For master's, comprehensive exam. *Entrance requirements:* For master's, bachelor's degree. Additional exam requirements/recommendations for international students: Required—TOEFL (minimum score 550 paper-based; 80 iBT). *Application deadline:* For fall admission, 7/30 for domestic students, 6/30 for international students; for winter admission, 11/30 for domestic students, 10/31 for international students; for spring admission, 2/15 for domestic students. Applications are processed on a rolling basis. Application fee: $40. Electronic applications accepted. *Financial support:* In 2012–13, research assistantships with partial tuition reimbursements (averaging $6,000 per year) were awarded; teaching assistantships and tuition waivers (full) also available. Financial award application deadline: 4/30; financial award applicants required to submit FAFSA. *Faculty research:* Verbally prime algebras, enveloping algebras of Lie, superalgebras and related rings, harmonic analysis, estimation theory. *Total annual research expenditures:* $30,000. *Unit head:* Dr. Ahmed I. Zayed, Chairperson, 773-325-7806, Fax: 773-325-7807, E-mail: azayed@depaul.edu. *Application contact:* Ann Spittle, Director of Graduate Admissions, 773-325-7315, Fax: 312-476-3244, E-mail: graddepaul@depaul.edu. Website: http://csh.depaul.edu/departments/mathematical-sciences/Pages/default.aspx.

Dowling College, Programs in Arts and Sciences, Oakdale, NY 11769-1999. Offers environmental microbiology (MS); integrated math and science (MS); liberal studies (MA). Part-time and evening/weekend programs available. *Faculty:* 3 full-time (1 woman), 1 part-time/adjunct (0 women). *Students:* 6 full-time (3 women), 1 part-time (0 women); includes 3 minority (1 Asian, non-Hispanic/Latino; 1 Hispanic/Latino; 1 Native Hawaiian or other Pacific Islander, non-Hispanic/Latino). Average age 26. 21 applicants, 57% accepted, 6 enrolled. In 2012, 1 master's awarded. *Degree requirements:* For master's, comprehensive exam, thesis. *Entrance requirements:* For master's, minimum undergraduate GPA of 3.0, 2 letters of recommendation. Additional exam requirements/recommendations for international students: Required—TOEFL (minimum score 550 paper-based). *Application deadline:* For fall admission, 9/1 priority date for domestic students; for winter admission, 1/1 priority date for domestic students; for spring admission, 2/1 priority date for domestic students. Applications are processed on a rolling basis. Application fee: $50. Electronic applications accepted. *Expenses: Tuition:* Full-time $21,729; part-time $980 per credit. *Required fees:* $956; $478 per term. Tuition and fees vary according to course load. *Financial support:* Federal Work-Study available. Support available to part-time students. Financial award application deadline: 6/30; financial award applicants required to submit FAFSA. *Unit head:* Patricia Sandilands, Director of Operations, School of Arts and Sciences, 631-244-3237, E-mail: sandilap@dowling.edu. *Application contact:* Richard Lebel, Dean of Admissions, 631-244-3480, Fax: 631-244-1059, E-mail: lebelr@dowling.edu.

Drexel University, College of Arts and Sciences, Department of Mathematics, Program in Mathematics, Philadelphia, PA 19104-2875. Offers MS, PhD. *Degree requirements:* For doctorate, one foreign language, thesis/dissertation. *Entrance requirements:* For master's and doctorate, GRE. Additional exam requirements/recommendations for international students: Required—TOEFL. Electronic applications accepted.

Duke University, Graduate School, Department of Mathematics, Durham, NC 27708. Offers PhD. *Faculty:* 27 full-time. *Students:* 48 full-time (13 women); includes 5 minority (3 Asian, non-Hispanic/Latino; 2 Hispanic/Latino), 25 international. 276 applicants, 14% accepted, 10 enrolled. In 2012, 8 doctorates awarded. *Degree requirements:* For doctorate, 2 foreign languages, thesis/dissertation. *Entrance requirements:* For doctorate, GRE General Test, GRE Subject Test. Additional exam requirements/recommendations for international students: Required—TOEFL (minimum score 550 paper-based; 83 iBT), IELTS (minimum score 7). *Application deadline:* For fall admission, 12/8 priority date for domestic students, 12/8 for international students. Application fee: $80. Electronic applications accepted. *Financial support:* Fellowships, research assistantships, teaching assistantships, and Federal Work-Study available. Financial award application deadline: 12/8. *Unit head:* Thomas Witelski, Director of Graduate Studies, 919-660-2801, Fax: 919-660-2821, E-mail: sholder@math.duke.edu. *Application contact:* Elizabeth Hutton, Director of Admissions, 919-684-3913, Fax: 919-684-2277, E-mail: grad-admissions@duke.edu. Website: http://www.math.duke.edu/graduate.

Duquesne University, Graduate School of Liberal Arts, Program in Computational Mathematics, Pittsburgh, PA 15282-0001. Offers MA, MS. *Faculty:* 21 full-time (5 women), 11 part-time/adjunct (5 women). *Students:* 16 full-time (7 women), 3 part-time (2 women); includes 1 minority (Asian, non-Hispanic/Latino), 7 international. Average age 27. 27 applicants, 52% accepted, 6 enrolled. In 2012, 4 master's awarded. *Degree requirements:* For master's, thesis. *Entrance requirements:* For master's, GRE General Test. Additional exam requirements/recommendations for international students: Required—TOEFL. *Application deadline:* For fall admission, 8/1 for domestic students, 5/1 for international students. Applications are processed on a rolling basis. Electronic applications accepted. *Expenses: Tuition:* Full-time $17,388; part-time $966 per credit. *Required fees:* $1656; $92 per credit. Tuition and fees vary according to program. *Financial support:* In 2012–13, 3 research assistantships with full tuition reimbursements (averaging $10,000 per year), 2 teaching assistantships with full tuition reimbursements (averaging $10,000 per year) were awarded; Federal Work-Study, institutionally sponsored loans, scholarships/grants, and unspecified assistantships also available. Financial award application deadline: 5/1. *Unit head:* Dr. John Kern, Chair, 412-396-6467. *Application contact:* Linda Rendulic, Assistant to the Dean, 412-396-6400, E-mail: rendujic@duq.edu. Website: http://www.duq.edu/academics/schools/liberal-arts/graduate-school/programs/computational-math.

East Carolina University, Graduate School, Thomas Harriot College of Arts and Sciences, Department of Mathematics, Greenville, NC 27858-4353. Offers mathematics (MA); mathematics in the community college (MA); statistics (MA, Certificate). Part-time and evening/weekend programs available. *Degree requirements:* For master's, comprehensive exam. *Entrance requirements:* For master's, GRE General Test, MAT. Additional exam requirements/recommendations for international students: Required—TOEFL. *Expenses:* Tuition, state resident: full-time $4009. Tuition, nonresident: full-time $15,840. *Required fees:* $2111.

Mathematics

Eastern Illinois University, Graduate School, College of Sciences, Department of Mathematics and Computer Science, Charleston, IL 61920-3099. Offers mathematics (MA); mathematics education (MA). *Entrance requirements:* For master's, GRE General Test.

Eastern Kentucky University, The Graduate School, College of Arts and Sciences, Department of Mathematics and Statistics, Richmond, KY 40475-3102. Offers mathematical sciences (MS). Part-time programs available. *Degree requirements:* For master's, comprehensive exam. *Entrance requirements:* For master's, GRE General Test, minimum GPA of 2.5. *Faculty research:* Graph theory, number theory, ring theory, topology, statistics, Abstract Algebra.

Eastern Michigan University, Graduate School, College of Arts and Sciences, Department of Mathematics, Ypsilanti, MI 48197. Offers applied statistics (MA); computer science (MA); mathematics (MA); mathematics education (MA). Part-time and evening/weekend programs available. Postbaccalaureate distance learning degree programs offered (minimal on-campus study). *Faculty:* 23 full-time (10 women). *Students:* 7 full-time (6 women), 39 part-time (16 women); includes 9 minority (4 Black or African American, non-Hispanic/Latino; 3 Asian, non-Hispanic/Latino; 1 Hispanic/Latino; 1 Two or more races, non-Hispanic/Latino), 8 international. Average age 30. 34 applicants, 76% accepted, 13 enrolled. In 2012, 10 master's awarded. *Degree requirements:* For master's, thesis optional. *Entrance requirements:* Additional exam requirements/recommendations for international students: Required—TOEFL. *Application deadline:* Applications are processed on a rolling basis. Application fee: $35. *Expenses:* Tuition, state resident: full-time $10,776; part-time $449 per credit hour. Tuition, nonresident: full-time $21,242; part-time $885 per credit hour. *Required fees:* $41 per credit hour. $48 per term. One-time fee: $100. Tuition and fees vary according to course level, degree level and reciprocity agreements. *Financial support:* Fellowships, research assistantships with full tuition reimbursements, teaching assistantships with full tuition reimbursements, career-related internships or fieldwork, Federal Work-Study, institutionally sponsored loans, scholarships/grants, tuition waivers (partial), and unspecified assistantships available. Support available to part-time students. Financial award applicants required to submit FAFSA. *Unit head:* Dr. Christopher Gardiner, Department Head, 734-487-1444, Fax: 734-487-2489, E-mail: cgardiner@emich.edu. *Application contact:* Dr. Bingwu Wang, Graduate Coordinator, 734-487-5044, Fax: 734-487-2489, E-mail: bwang@emich.edu. Website: http://www.math.emich.edu.

Eastern Washington University, Graduate Studies, College of Science, Health and Engineering, Department of Mathematics, Cheney, WA 99004-2431. Offers mathematics (MS); teaching mathematics (MA). Part-time programs available. *Faculty:* 11 full-time (4 women). *Students:* 7 full-time (4 women), 9 part-time (2 women); includes 1 minority (Asian, non-Hispanic/Latino). Average age 32. In 2012, 7 master's awarded. *Degree requirements:* For master's, comprehensive exam, thesis (for some programs). *Entrance requirements:* For master's, GRE General Test, departmental qualifying exam, minimum GPA of 3.0. *Application deadline:* For fall admission, 4/1 priority date for domestic students; for spring admission, 1/15 for domestic students. Applications are processed on a rolling basis. Application fee: $50. *Financial support:* In 2012–13, 12 teaching assistantships with partial tuition reimbursements (averaging $12,000 per year) were awarded; career-related internships or fieldwork, Federal Work-Study, institutionally sponsored loans, scholarships/grants, health care benefits, tuition waivers (partial), and unspecified assistantships also available. Support available to part-time students. Financial award application deadline: 2/1; financial award applicants required to submit FAFSA. *Unit head:* Dr. Christian Hansen, Chair, 509-359-6225, Fax: 509-359-4700. *Application contact:* Dr. Yves Nievergelt, Adviser, 509-359-2219.

East Tennessee State University, School of Graduate Studies, College of Arts and Sciences, Department of Mathematics and Statistics, Johnson City, TN 37614. Offers mathematical sciences (MS). Part-time and evening/weekend programs available. *Faculty:* 16 full-time (5 women). *Students:* 20 full-time (7 women), 1 part-time (0 women); includes 2 minority (1 Black or African American, non-Hispanic/Latino; 1 Hispanic/Latino), 8 international. 28 applicants, 50% accepted, 12 enrolled. In 2012, 7 master's awarded. *Degree requirements:* For master's, comprehensive exam, thesis. *Entrance requirements:* For master's, GRE General Test, bachelor's degree in math or related area, three letters of recommendation. Additional exam requirements/recommendations for international students: Required—TOEFL (minimum score 550 paper-based; 79 iBT). *Application deadline:* For fall admission, 6/1 for domestic students, 4/30 for international students; for spring admission, 11/1 for domestic students, 11/30 for international students. Application fee: $35 ($45 for international students). Electronic applications accepted. *Financial support:* In 2012–13, 18 students received support, including 1 teaching assistantship with full tuition reimbursement available (averaging $9,500 per year); career-related internships or fieldwork, institutionally sponsored loans, scholarships/grants, unspecified assistantships, and laboratory assistantships also available. Financial award application deadline: 7/1; financial award applicants required to submit FAFSA. *Faculty research:* Applied mathematics, applied statistics, discrete mathematics, graph theory, mathematics education, mathematical epidemiology, probability. *Unit head:* Dr. Robert Price, Chair, 423-439-4349, Fax: 423-439-8361, E-mail: pricejr@etsu.edu. *Application contact:* Kimberly Brockman, Graduate Specialist, 423-439-6165, Fax: 423-439-5624, E-mail: brockmank@etsu.edu. Website: http://www.etsu.edu/cas/math/.

Elizabeth City State University, School of Mathematics, Science and Technology, Master of Science in Mathematics Program, Elizabeth City, NC 27909-7806. Offers applied mathematics (MS); community college teaching (MS); mathematics education (MS); remote sensing (MS). Part-time and evening/weekend programs available. *Faculty:* 7 full-time (2 women). *Students:* 3 full-time (1 woman), 27 part-time (16 women); includes 23 minority (22 Black or African American, non-Hispanic/Latino; 1 Two or more races, non-Hispanic/Latino). Average age 25. 7 applicants, 71% accepted, 5 enrolled. In 2012, 9 master's awarded. *Degree requirements:* For master's, thesis. *Entrance requirements:* For master's, MAT and/or GRE, minimum GPA of 3.0, 3 letters of recommendation, two official transcripts from all undergraduate/graduate schools attended, health form for all students taking more than four credit hours of course work on university campus, typewritten one-page request for entry into the program that includes a description of student's educational preparation. Additional exam requirements/recommendations for international students: Required—TOEFL (minimum score 550 paper-based, 80 iBT) or IELTS (minimum score 6.5). *Application deadline:* For fall admission, 7/15 priority date for domestic students, 7/15 for international students; for spring admission, 11/15 priority date for domestic students, 11/15 for international students. Applications are processed on a rolling basis. Application fee: $30. Electronic applications accepted. *Expenses:* Tuition, state resident: full-time $5700. Tuition, nonresident: full-time $16,840. Full-time tuition and fees vary according to campus/location. *Financial support:* In 2012–13, 8 students received support, including 3 research assistantships (averaging $19,000 per year), 2 teaching assistantships (averaging $18,000 per year); scholarships/grants and tuition waivers also available. Financial award application deadline: 6/30; financial award applicants required to submit FAFSA. *Faculty research:* Oceanic temperature effects, mathematics strategies in elementary schools, multimedia, Antarctic temperature mapping, computer networks, water quality, remote sensing, polar ice, satellite imagery. *Total annual research expenditures:* $25,000. *Unit head:* Dr. Farrah Jackson, Chair, 252-335-8549, Fax: 252-335-3487, E-mail: fmjackson@mail.ecsu.edu. *Application contact:* Dr. Paula S. Viltz, Director of Graduate Education, 252-335-3455, Fax: 252-335-3146, E-mail: psviltz@mail.ecsu.edu. Website: http://www.ecsu.edu/academics/graduate/ma.

Emory University, Laney Graduate School, Department of Mathematics and Computer Science, Atlanta, GA 30322-1100. Offers computer science (MS); computer science and informatics (PhD); mathematics (MS, PhD). *Faculty:* 41 full-time (5 women), 14 part-time/adjunct (1 woman). *Students:* 78 full-time (25 women), 2 part-time (0 women); includes 5 minority (2 Asian, non-Hispanic/Latino; 3 Hispanic/Latino), 52 international. Average age 27. 171 applicants, 20% accepted, 15 enrolled. In 2012, 14 master's, 8 doctorates awarded. Terminal master's awarded for partial completion of doctoral program. *Degree requirements:* For master's, thesis; for doctorate, one foreign language, comprehensive exam, thesis/dissertation. *Entrance requirements:* For master's and doctorate, GRE General Test. Additional exam requirements/recommendations for international students: Recommended—TOEFL. *Application deadline:* For fall admission, 1/3 priority date for domestic students, 1/3 for international students. Application fee: $75. Electronic applications accepted. *Financial support:* Fellowships, teaching assistantships, scholarships/grants, and tuition waivers available. Financial award application deadline: 1/3; financial award applicants required to submit FAFSA. *Unit head:* Dr. Vaidy Sunderam, Chair, 404-727-5926, Fax: 404-727-5611, E-mail: vss@emory.edu. *Application contact:* Prof. James Lu, Director of Graduate Studies, 404-712-8638, Fax: 404-727-5611, E-mail: jlu@mathcs.emory.edu. Website: http://www.mathcs.emory.edu/.

Emporia State University, Department of Mathematics, Computer Science and Economics, Emporia, KS 66801-5087. Offers mathematics (MS). Part-time programs available. *Faculty:* 15 full-time (3 women). *Students:* 9 full-time (3 women), 34 part-time (23 women); includes 4 minority (1 Asian, non-Hispanic/Latino; 2 Hispanic/Latino; 1 Native Hawaiian or other Pacific Islander, non-Hispanic/Latino), 4 international. 20 applicants, 95% accepted, 14 enrolled. In 2012, 8 master's awarded. *Degree requirements:* For master's, comprehensive exam or thesis. *Entrance requirements:* For master's, appropriate undergraduate degree. Additional exam requirements/recommendations for international students: Required—TOEFL (minimum score 520 paper-based; 68 iBT). *Application deadline:* For fall admission, 8/15 priority date for domestic students. Applications are processed on a rolling basis. Application fee: $30 ($75 for international students). Electronic applications accepted. *Expenses:* Tuition, state resident: full-time $4968; part-time $207 per credit hour. Tuition, nonresident: full-time $15,432; part-time $643 per credit hour. *Required fees:* $70 per credit hour. Tuition and fees vary according to course load. *Financial support:* In 2012–13, 3 teaching assistantships with full tuition reimbursements (averaging $7,200 per year) were awarded; research assistantships, career-related internships or fieldwork, Federal Work-Study, institutionally sponsored loans, health care benefits, and unspecified assistantships also available. Financial award application deadline: 3/15; financial award applicants required to submit FAFSA. *Unit head:* Dr. H. Joe Yanik, Chair, 620-341-5281, Fax: 620-341-6055, E-mail: hyanik@emporia.edu. Website: http://www.emporia.edu/math-cs/home.htm.

Fairfield University, College of Arts and Sciences, Fairfield, CT 06824-5195. Offers American studies (MA); communication (MA); creative writing (MFA); liberal studies (MA); mathematics (MS); public administration (MA). Part-time and evening/weekend programs available. Postbaccalaureate distance learning degree programs offered (minimal on-campus study). *Faculty:* 15 full-time (5 women), 4 part-time/adjunct (2 women). *Students:* 71 full-time (38 women), 86 part-time (53 women); includes 24 minority (4 Black or African American, non-Hispanic/Latino; 1 American Indian or Alaska Native, non-Hispanic/Latino; 3

322 www.petersonsbooks.com

Peterson's Graduate Programs in the Physical Sciences, Mathematics, Agricultural Sciences, the Environment & Natural Resources 2014

Asian, non-Hispanic/Latino; 13 Hispanic/Latino; 1 Native Hawaiian or other Pacific Islander, non-Hispanic/Latino; 2 Two or more races, non-Hispanic/Latino), 9 international. Average age 38. 70 applicants, 61% accepted, 29 enrolled. In 2012, 59 master's awarded. *Degree requirements:* For master's, capstone research course. *Entrance requirements:* For master's, minimum GPA of 3.0, 2 letters of recommendation, resume. Additional exam requirements/recommendations for international students: Required—TOEFL (minimum score 550 paper-based; 80 iBT) or IELTS (minimum score 6.5). *Application deadline:* For fall admission, 5/14 for international students; for spring admission, 10/15 for international students. Applications are processed on a rolling basis. Application fee: $60. Electronic applications accepted. *Expenses: Tuition:* Part-time $630 per credit hour. *Required fees:* $30 per semester. One-time fee: $35 part-time. Tuition and fees vary according to program. *Financial support:* In 2012–13, 41 students received support. Scholarships/grants and unspecified assistantships available. Financial award applicants required to submit FAFSA. *Faculty research:* Non-commutative algebra, partial differential equations, creative writing (fiction, non-fiction and poetry), communication for social change, health communication, comparative media systems, negotiation and management, regional economic development, community-based teaching and learning, and non-profit management. *Total annual research expenditures:* $1 million. *Unit head:* Dr. Robbin Crabtree, Dean, 203-254-4000 Ext. 3263, Fax: 203-254-4119, E-mail: rcrabtree@fairfield.edu. *Application contact:* Marianne Gumpper, Director of Graduate and Continuing Studies Admission, 203-254-4184, Fax: 203-254-4073, E-mail: gradadmis@fairfield.edu. Website: http://www.fairfield.edu/cas/cas_grad_1.html.

Fairleigh Dickinson University, Metropolitan Campus, University College: Arts, Sciences, and Professional Studies, School of Computer Sciences and Engineering, Program in Mathematical Foundation, Teaneck, NJ 07666-1914. Offers MS.

Fayetteville State University, Graduate School, Department of Mathematics and Computer Science, Fayetteville, NC 28301-4298. Offers mathematics (MS). Part-time and evening/weekend programs available. *Faculty:* 9 full-time (3 women). *Students:* 1 full-time (0 women), 7 part-time (4 women); includes 5 minority (all Black or African American, non-Hispanic/Latino), 1 international. Average age 35. 2 applicants, 100% accepted, 2 enrolled. In 2012, 2 master's awarded. *Degree requirements:* For master's, comprehensive exam, thesis or alternative, internship. *Entrance requirements:* For master's, GRE General Test. *Application deadline:* For fall admission, 4/15 for domestic students; for spring admission, 10/15 for domestic students. Applications are processed on a rolling basis. Application fee: $35. Electronic applications accepted. *Faculty research:* Mathematical modeling in medicine: derivation of mathematical criteria for cure of cancer, AIDS, diabetes; error correcting codes and cryptography; qualitative properties of dynamical systems: ODE, FDE, PDE; homeomorphisms: ring, group; mathematical modeling of military strategy and outcomes for symmetrical warfare. *Unit head:* Dr. Dwight House, Chairperson, 910-672-1664, E-mail: dhouse@uncfsu.edu. *Application contact:* Katrina Hoffman, Graduate Admissions Officer, 910-672-1374, Fax: 910-672-1470, E-mail: khoffma1@uncfsu.edu.

Florida Atlantic University, Charles E. Schmidt College of Science, Department of Mathematical Sciences, Boca Raton, FL 33431-0991. Offers applied mathematics and statistics (MS); mathematical sciences (MS, MST, PhD). Part-time programs available. *Faculty:* 42 full-time (6 women), 38 part-time/adjunct (11 women). *Students:* 42 full-time (10 women), 27 part-time (10 women); includes 18 minority (7 Black or African American, non-Hispanic/Latino; 5 Asian, non-Hispanic/Latino; 5 Hispanic/Latino; 1 Two or more races, non-Hispanic/Latino), 21 international. Average age 31. 83 applicants, 48% accepted, 19 enrolled. In 2012, 23 master's, 7 doctorates awarded. Terminal master's awarded for partial completion of doctoral program. *Degree requirements:* For master's, comprehensive exam (for some programs), thesis (for some programs); for doctorate, comprehensive exam, thesis/dissertation. *Entrance requirements:* For master's and doctorate, GRE General Test, minimum GPA of 3.0. Additional exam requirements/recommendations for international students: Required—TOEFL (minimum score 500 paper-based). *Application deadline:* For fall admission, 7/1 priority date for domestic students, 2/15 for international students; for spring admission, 11/1 priority date for domestic students, 7/15 for international students. Applications are processed on a rolling basis. Application fee: $30. Electronic applications accepted. *Expenses:* Tuition, state resident: full-time $8876; part-time $369.82 per credit hour. Tuition, nonresident: full-time $24,595; part-time $1024.81 per credit hour. *Financial support:* In 2012–13, fellowships with partial tuition reimbursements (averaging $20,000 per year), teaching assistantships with partial tuition reimbursements (averaging $20,000 per year) were awarded; Federal Work-Study also available. Financial award application deadline: 4/1. *Faculty research:* Cryptography, statistics, algebra, analysis, combinatorics. *Unit head:* Dr. Lee Klingler, Chair, 561-297-0274, Fax: 561-297-2436, E-mail: klingler@fau.edu. *Application contact:* Dr. Rainer Steinwandt, Graduate Director, 561-297-3353, Fax: 561-297-2436, E-mail: rsteinwa@fau.edu. Website: http://www.math.fau.edu/.

Florida International University, College of Arts and Sciences, Department of Mathematics and Statistics, Program in Mathematical Sciences, Miami, FL 33199. Offers MS. Part-time and evening/weekend programs available. *Entrance requirements:* For master's, GRE, letter of intent; three letters of recommendation; minimum GPA of 3.0 in upper-division mathematics courses. Additional exam requirements/recommendations for international students: Required—TOEFL (minimum score 550 paper-based; 80 iBT). Electronic applications accepted.

Florida State University, The Graduate School, College of Arts and Sciences, Department of Mathematics, Tallahassee, FL 32306-4510. Offers applied computational mathematics (MS, PhD); biomathematics (MS, PhD); financial mathematics (MS, PhD); pure mathematics (MS, PhD). Part-time programs available. *Faculty:* 52 full-time (12 women). *Students:* 145 full-time (38 women), 6 part-time (2 women); includes 13 minority (6 Black or African American, non-Hispanic/Latino; 3 Asian, non-Hispanic/Latino; 4 Hispanic/Latino), 93 international. 322 applicants, 30% accepted, 41 enrolled. In 2012, 30 master's, 13 doctorates awarded. Terminal master's awarded for partial completion of doctoral program. *Degree requirements:* For master's, comprehensive exam (for some programs), thesis optional; for doctorate, comprehensive exam, thesis/dissertation, candidacy exam including written qualifying examinations which differ by degree concentrations. *Entrance requirements:* For master's and doctorate, GRE General Test, minimum upper-division GPA of 3.0, 4-year bachelor's degree. Additional exam requirements/recommendations for international students: Required—TOEFL (minimum score 550 paper-based; 80 iBT) or IELTS (minimum score 6.5). *Application deadline:* For fall admission, 1/1 priority date for domestic students, 1/1 for international students; for spring admission, 10/1 priority date for domestic students, 11/1 for international students. Applications are processed on a rolling basis. Application fee: $30. Electronic applications accepted. *Expenses:* Tuition, state resident: full-time $7263; part-time $403.51 per credit hour. Tuition, nonresident: full-time $18,087; part-time $1004.85 per credit hour. *Required fees:* $1335.42; $74.19 per credit hour. $445.14 per semester. One-time fee: $40 full-time; $20 part-time. Tuition and fees vary according to program. *Financial support:* In 2012–13, 115 students received support, including 9 fellowships with full tuition reimbursements available (averaging $22,600 per year), 14 research assistantships with full tuition reimbursements available (averaging $22,000 per year), 88 teaching assistantships with full tuition reimbursements available (averaging $19,300 per year); career-related internships or fieldwork, institutionally sponsored loans, scholarships/grants, health care benefits, and unspecified assistantships also available. *Faculty research:* Algebra and algebraic geometry; applied, financial, numerical, and classical analysis; biomathematics, including shape analysis and anatomical imaging; computational mathematics and numerical algorithms; geometric topology. *Unit head:* Dr. Xiaoming Wang, Chairperson, 850-645-3338; Fax: 850-644-4053, E-mail: wxm@math.fsu.edu. *Application contact:* Dr. Giray Okten, Associate Chair for Graduate Studies, 850-644-8713, Fax: 850-644-4053, E-mail: okten@math.fsu.edu. Website: http://www.math.fsu.edu/.

George Mason University, College of Science, Department of Mathematical Sciences, Fairfax, VA 22030. Offers actuarial sciences (Certificate); mathematics (MS, PhD). *Faculty:* 37 full-time (11 women), 5 part-time/adjunct (1 woman). *Students:* 34 full-time (10 women), 36 part-time (14 women); includes 17 minority (4 Black or African American, non-Hispanic/Latino; 6 Asian, non-Hispanic/Latino; 4 Hispanic/Latino; 3 Two or more races, non-Hispanic/Latino), 8 international. Average age 30. 83 applicants, 64% accepted, 25 enrolled. In 2012, 14 master's, 3 doctorates, 3 other advanced degrees awarded. *Degree requirements:* For master's, comprehensive exam, thesis optional; for doctorate, comprehensive exam, thesis/dissertation. *Entrance requirements:* For master's, GRE, 3 letters of recommendation; official college transcripts; expanded goals statement; resume; for doctorate, GRE (recommended), master's degree in math or undergraduate coursework with math preparation with minimum GPA of 3.0 in last 60 credits; 2 copies of official transcripts; 3 letters of recommendation; expanded goals statement; for Certificate, 3 letters of recommendation; official transcripts. Additional exam requirements/recommendations for international students: Required—TOEFL (minimum score 570 paper-based; 88 iBT), IELTS (minimum score 6.5), Pearson Test of English. *Application deadline:* For fall admission, 4/15 priority date for domestic students; for spring admission, 11/1 priority date for domestic students. Application fee: $65 ($80 for international students). Electronic applications accepted. *Expenses:* Tuition, state resident: full-time $9080; part-time $378.33 per credit hour. Tuition, nonresident: full-time $25,010; part-time $1042.08 per credit hour. *Required fees:* $2610; $108.75 per credit hour. Tuition and fees vary according to program. *Financial support:* In 2012–13, 24 students received support, including 2 fellowships (averaging $8,000 per year), 11 research assistantships with full and partial tuition reimbursements available (averaging $19,352 per year), 13 teaching assistantships with full and partial tuition reimbursements available (averaging $16,240 per year); career-related internships or fieldwork, Federal Work-Study, scholarships/grants, unspecified assistantships, and health care benefits (for full-time research or teaching assistantship recipients) also available. Support available to part-time students. Financial award application deadline: 3/1; financial award applicants required to submit FAFSA. *Faculty research:* Nonlinear dynamics and topology, with an emphasis on global bifurcations and chaos; numerical and theoretical methods of dynamical systems. *Total annual research expenditures:* $1.1 million. *Unit head:* Stephen H. Sapperstone, Acting Chair, 703-993-1462, Fax: 703-993-1491, E-mail: sap@gmu.edu. *Application contact:* Walter D. Morris, Jr., Graduate Coordinator, 703-993-1481, Fax: 703-993-1491, E-mail: wmorris@gmu.edu. Website: http://math.gmu.edu/.

Georgetown University, Graduate School of Arts and Sciences, Department of Mathematics, Washington, DC 20057. Offers mathematics and statistics (MS).

The George Washington University, Columbian College of Arts and Sciences, Department of Mathematics, Washington, DC 20052. Offers applied mathematics (MA, MS, PhD); pure mathematics (MA, MS, PhD). Part-time and evening/weekend programs available. *Faculty:* 18 full-time (4 women), 2 part-time/adjunct (0 women). *Students:* 22 full-time (4 women), 12 part-time (4 women); includes 7

Peterson's Graduate Programs in the Physical Sciences, Mathematics, Agricultural Sciences, the Environment & Natural Resources 2014

www.petersonsbooks.com **323**

minority (3 Black or African American, non-Hispanic/Latino; 1 American Indian or Alaska Native, non-Hispanic/Latino; 1 Asian, non-Hispanic/Latino; 2 Hispanic/Latino), 17 international. Average age 26. 96 applicants, 79% accepted, 13 enrolled. In 2012, 6 master's, 2 doctorates awarded. Terminal master's awarded for partial completion of doctoral program. *Degree requirements:* For master's, comprehensive exam; for doctorate, one foreign language, thesis/dissertation, general exam. *Entrance requirements:* For master's and doctorate, GRE General Test, minimum GPA of 3.0, interview. Additional exam requirements/recommendations for international students: Required—TOEFL (minimum score 550 paper-based; 80 iBT). *Application deadline:* For fall admission, 1/15 priority date for domestic students, 1/15 for international students; for spring admission, 10/1 priority date for domestic students, 9/1 for international students. Applications are processed on a rolling basis. Application fee: $75. Electronic applications accepted. *Financial support:* In 2012–13, 17 students received support. Fellowships with full tuition reimbursements available, teaching assistantships with tuition reimbursements available, Federal Work-Study, and tuition waivers available. Financial award application deadline: 1/15. *Unit head:* John B. Conway, Chair, 202-994-0553, E-mail: conway@gwu.edu. *Application contact:* 202-994-6210, Fax: 202-994-6213, E-mail: askccas@gwu.edu. Website: http://www.gwu.edu/~math/.

Georgia Institute of Technology, Graduate Studies and Research, College of Sciences, School of Mathematics, Atlanta, GA 30332-0001. Offers algorithms, combinatorics, and optimization (PhD); applied mathematics (MS); bioinformatics (PhD); mathematics (PhD); quantitative and computational finance (MS); statistics (MS Stat). Terminal master's awarded for partial completion of doctoral program. *Degree requirements:* For master's, thesis or alternative; for doctorate, one foreign language, thesis/dissertation. *Entrance requirements:* For master's, GRE General Test, minimum GPA of 3.0; for doctorate, GRE General Test, GRE Subject Test, minimum GPA of 3.0. Additional exam requirements/recommendations for international students: Required—TOEFL. Electronic applications accepted. *Faculty research:* Dynamical systems, discrete mathematics, probability and statistics, mathematical physics.

Georgia Institute of Technology, Graduate Studies and Research, Multidisciplinary Program in Algorithms, Combinatorics, and Optimization, Atlanta, GA 30332-0001. Offers PhD. *Degree requirements:* For doctorate, thesis/dissertation. *Entrance requirements:* For doctorate, GRE General Test, GRE Subject Test (computer science or mathematics). Additional exam requirements/recommendations for international students: Required—TOEFL. Electronic applications accepted. *Faculty research:* Complexity, graph minors, combinatorial optimization, mathematical programming, probabilistic methods.

Georgia Southern University, Jack N. Averitt College of Graduate Studies, College of Science and Mathematics, Department of Mathematical Sciences, Statesboro, GA 30460. Offers mathematics (MS). Part-time programs available. *Students:* 39 full-time (10 women), 4 part-time (2 women); includes 6 minority (5 Black or African American, non-Hispanic/Latino; 1 Asian, non-Hispanic/Latino), 19 international. Average age 26. 34 applicants, 85% accepted, 19 enrolled. In 2012, 14 master's awarded. *Degree requirements:* For master's, comprehensive exam, thesis, terminal exam, project. *Entrance requirements:* For master's, GRE, BS in engineering, science, or mathematics; course work in calculus, probability, linear algebra; proficiency in a computer programming language. Additional exam requirements/recommendations for international students: Required—TOEFL (minimum score 550 paper-based; 80 iBT). *Application deadline:* For fall admission, 3/1 priority date for domestic students, 3/1 for international students; for spring admission, 10/1 priority date for domestic students, 10/1 for international students. Applications are processed on a rolling basis. Application fee: $50. Electronic applications accepted. *Expenses:* Tuition, state resident: part-time $270 per hour. Tuition, nonresident: part-time $1077 per hour. *Required fees:* $245 per semester. *Financial support:* In 2012–13, 34 students received support, including research assistantships with partial tuition reimbursements available (averaging $7,200 per year), teaching assistantships with partial tuition reimbursements available (averaging $7,200 per year); career-related internships or fieldwork, Federal Work-Study, scholarships/grants, tuition waivers (partial), and unspecified assistantships also available. Support available to part-time students. Financial award application deadline: 4/15; financial award applicants required to submit FAFSA. *Faculty research:* Algebra, number theory, and combinatorics; analysis and differential equations, approximation, optimization and computational mathematics; geometry and topology; mathematics education; statistics. *Total annual research expenditures:* $32,546. *Unit head:* Dr. Sharon Taylor, Chair, 912-478-0266, Fax: 912-478-0654, E-mail: taylors@georgiasouthern.edu. *Application contact:* Amanda Gilliland, Coordinator for Graduate Student Recruitment, 912-478-5384, Fax: 912-478-0740, E-mail: gradadmissions@georgiasouthern.edu. Website: http://cost.georgiasouthern.edu/math.

Georgia State University, College of Arts and Sciences, Department of Mathematics and Statistics, Atlanta, GA 30302-3083. Offers bioinformatics (MS, PhD); biostatistics (MS, PhD); discrete mathematics (MS); mathematics (MS, PhD); scientific computing (MS); statistics (MS). Part-time programs available. *Faculty:* 23 full-time (6 women), 1 (woman) part-time/adjunct. *Students:* 79 full-time (42 women), 34 part-time (11 women); includes 38 minority (23 Black or African American, non-Hispanic/Latino; 13 Asian, non-Hispanic/Latino; 2 Hispanic/Latino), 48 international. Average age 32. 97 applicants, 56% accepted, 21 enrolled. In 2012, 19 master's, 2 doctorates awarded. Terminal master's awarded for partial completion of doctoral program. *Degree requirements:* For master's, comprehensive exam. (for some programs), thesis optional; for doctorate, comprehensive exam, thesis/dissertation. *Entrance requirements:* For master's and doctorate, GRE. Additional exam requirements/recommendations for international students: Required—TOEFL (minimum score 550 paper-based; 80 iBT). *Application deadline:* For fall admission, 7/1 priority date for domestic students, 7/1 for international students; for spring admission, 11/15 priority date for domestic students, 11/15 for international students. Application fee: $50. Electronic applications accepted. *Expenses:* Tuition, state resident: full-time $8064; part-time $336 per credit hour. Tuition, nonresident: full-time $28,800; part-time $1200 per credit hour. *Required fees:* $2128; $1064 per semester. Tuition and fees vary according to course load and program. *Financial support:* In 2012–13, 15 students received support, including 3 fellowships with full tuition reimbursements available (averaging $22,000 per year), 20 research assistantships with full tuition reimbursements available (averaging $9,000 per year), 50 teaching assistantships with full tuition reimbursements available (averaging $9,000 per year); institutionally sponsored loans, scholarships/grants, health care benefits, and unspecified assistantships also available. Financial award application deadline: 2/1. *Faculty research:* Algebra, matrix theory, graph theory and combinatorics; applied mathematics and analysis; collegiate mathematics education; statistics, biostatistics and applications; bioinformatics, dynamical systems. *Total annual research expenditures:* $491,077. *Unit head:* Dr. Guantao Chen, Chair, 404-413-6436, Fax: 404-413-6403, E-mail: gchen@gsu.edu. *Application contact:* Dr. Zhongshan Li, Graduate Director, 404-413-6437, Fax: 404-413-6403, E-mail: zli@gsu.edu. Website: http://www2.gsu.edu/~wwwmat/.

Graduate School and University Center of the City University of New York, Graduate Studies, Program in Mathematics, New York, NY 10016-4039. Offers PhD. *Degree requirements:* For doctorate, 2 foreign languages, thesis/dissertation. *Entrance requirements:* For doctorate, GRE General Test. Additional exam requirements/recommendations for international students: Required—TOEFL. Electronic applications accepted.

Hardin-Simmons University, Graduate School, Holland School of Sciences and Mathematics, Abilene, TX 79698-0001. Offers MS, DPT. Part-time programs available. *Faculty:* 5 full-time (1 woman). *Students:* 6 full-time (2 women), 1 (woman) part-time. Average age 25. 6 applicants, 100% accepted, 5 enrolled. In 2012, 3 master's awarded. *Degree requirements:* For master's, comprehensive exam, thesis or alternative, internship; for doctorate, comprehensive exam, thesis/dissertation or alternative. *Entrance requirements:* For master's, minimum undergraduate GPA of 3.0 in major, 2.7 overall; 2 semesters of course work each in biology, chemistry and geology; interview; writing sample; occupational experience; for doctorate, letters of recommendation, interview, writing sample. Additional exam requirements/recommendations for international students: Required—TOEFL (minimum score 550 paper-based; 75 iBT). *Application deadline:* For fall admission, 8/15 priority date for domestic students, 4/1 for international students; for spring admission, 1/5 priority date for domestic students, 9/1 for international students. Applications are processed on a rolling basis. Application fee: $50. *Expenses: Tuition:* Full-time $12,870; part-time $715 per credit hour. *Required fees:* $650. Tuition and fees vary according to degree level. *Financial support:* In 2012–13, 8 students received support. Fellowships, career-related internships or fieldwork, and scholarships/grants available. Support available to part-time students. Financial award application deadline: 6/30; financial award applicants required to submit FAFSA. *Unit head:* Dr. Christopher McNair, Dean, 325-670-1401, Fax: 325-670-1385, E-mail: cmcnair@hsutx.edu. *Application contact:* Dr. Nancy Kucinski, Dean of Graduate Studies, 325-670-1298, Fax: 325-670-1564, E-mail: gradoff@hsutx.edu. Website: http://www.hsutx.edu/academics/holland.

Harvard University, Graduate School of Arts and Sciences, Department of Mathematics, Cambridge, MA 02138. Offers PhD. *Degree requirements:* For doctorate, 2 foreign languages, thesis/dissertation, qualifying exam. *Entrance requirements:* For doctorate, GRE General Test, GRE Subject Test. Additional exam requirements/recommendations for international students: Required—TOEFL. *Expenses: Tuition:* Full-time $37,576. *Required fees:* $930. Tuition and fees vary according to program and student level.

Howard University, Graduate School, Department of Mathematics, Washington, DC 20059-0002. Offers applied mathematics (MS, PhD); mathematics (MS, PhD). Part-time programs available. Terminal master's awarded for partial completion of doctoral program. *Degree requirements:* For master's, comprehensive exam, thesis or alternative, qualifying exam; for doctorate, 2 foreign languages, comprehensive exam, thesis/dissertation, qualifying exams. *Entrance requirements:* For master's, GRE General Test, minimum GPA of 3.0; for doctorate, GRE General Test. Additional exam requirements/recommendations for international students: Required—TOEFL. Electronic applications accepted.

Hunter College of the City University of New York, Graduate School, School of Arts and Sciences, Department of Mathematics and Statistics, New York, NY 10021-5085. Offers applied mathematics (MA); mathematics for secondary education (MA); pure mathematics (MA). Part-time and evening/weekend programs available. *Faculty:* 13 full-time (2 women), 2 part-time/adjunct (1 woman). *Students:* 17 full-time (12 women), 62 part-time (34 women); includes 41 minority (6 Black or African American, non-Hispanic/Latino; 29 Asian, non-Hispanic/Latino; 6 Hispanic/Latino), 3 international. Average age 32. 54 applicants, 61% accepted, 16 enrolled. In 2012, 53 master's awarded. *Degree requirements:* For master's, one foreign language, comprehensive exam, thesis (for some programs). *Entrance requirements:* For master's, GRE General Test, 24

324 www.petersonsbooks.com

Peterson's Graduate Programs in the Physical Sciences, Mathematics, Agricultural Sciences, the Environment & Natural Resources 2014

credits in mathematics. Additional exam requirements/recommendations for international students: Required—TOEFL. *Application deadline:* For fall admission, 4/1 for domestic students, 2/1 for international students; for spring admission, 11/1 for domestic students, 9/1 for international students. Application fee: $125. *Expenses:* Tuition, state resident: full-time $8690; part-time $365 per credit. Tuition, nonresident: full-time $16,200; part-time $675 per credit. *Required fees:* $320 per semester. One-time fee: $125. Tuition and fees vary according to class time, campus/location and program. *Financial support:* Federal Work-Study, institutionally sponsored loans, scholarships/grants, and tuition waivers (partial) available. Support available to part-time students. *Faculty research:* Data analysis, dynamical systems, computer graphics, topology, statistical decision theory. *Unit head:* Ada Peluso, Chairperson, 212-772-5300, Fax: 212-772-4858, E-mail: peluso@math.hunter.cuny.edu. *Application contact:* William Zlata, Director for Graduate Admissions, 212-772-4482, Fax: 212-650-3336, E-mail: admissions@hunter.cuny.edu. Website: http://math.hunter.cuny.edu/.

Idaho State University, Office of Graduate Studies, College of Science and Engineering, Department of Mathematics, Pocatello, ID 83209-8085. Offers mathematics (MS, DA); mathematics for secondary teachers (MA). Part-time programs available. *Degree requirements:* For master's, comprehensive exam, thesis (for some programs), oral and written exams; for doctorate, comprehensive exam, thesis/dissertation, teaching internships. *Entrance requirements:* For master's, GRE General Test, GRE Subject Test, course work in modern algebra, differential equations, advanced calculus, introductory analysis; for doctorate, GRE General Test, GRE Subject Test, minimum graduate GPA of 3.5, MS in mathematics, teaching experience, 3 letters of recommendation. Additional exam requirements/recommendations for international students: Required—TOEFL (minimum score 550 paper-based; 80 iBT). Electronic applications accepted. *Faculty research:* Algebra, analysis geometry, statistics, applied mathematics.

Illinois State University, Graduate School, College of Arts and Sciences, Department of Mathematics, Program in Mathematics, Normal, IL 61790-2200. Offers MA, MS. *Degree requirements:* For master's, thesis or alternative. *Entrance requirements:* For master's, GRE General Test, minimum GPA of 2.8 in last 60 hours of course work.

Indiana State University, College of Graduate and Professional Studies, College of Arts and Sciences, Department of Mathematics and Computer Science, Terre Haute, IN 47809. Offers math teaching (MA, MS); mathematics and computer science (MA); mathematics and computer sciences (MS). Part-time programs available. *Degree requirements:* For master's, thesis or alternative. *Entrance requirements:* For master's, 24 semester hours of course work in undergraduate mathematics. Electronic applications accepted. *Expenses:* Tuition, state resident: full-time $7898; part-time $366 per credit hour. Tuition, nonresident: full-time $9872; part-time $458 per credit hour. *International tuition:* $17,440 full-time. Full-time tuition and fees vary according to course load.

Indiana University Bloomington, University Graduate School, College of Arts and Sciences, Department of Mathematics, Bloomington, IN 47405-7000. Offers applied mathematics (MA); mathematical physics (PhD); mathematics education (MAT); pure mathematics (MA, PhD). *Faculty:* 49 full-time (3 women). *Students:* 118 full-time (21 women), 1 part-time (0 women); includes 12 minority (2 Black or African American, non-Hispanic/Latino; 9 Asian, non-Hispanic/Latino; 1 Hispanic/Latino), 72 international. Average age 27. 218 applicants, 25% accepted, 28 enrolled. In 2012, 15 master's, 12 doctorates awarded. Terminal master's awarded for partial completion of doctoral program. *Degree requirements:* For doctorate, one foreign language, thesis/dissertation. *Entrance requirements:* For master's and doctorate, GRE General Test, GRE Subject Test. Additional exam requirements/recommendations for international students: Required—TOEFL. *Application deadline:* For fall admission, 1/15 priority date for domestic students, 1/15 for international students. Applications are processed on a rolling basis. Application fee: $55 ($65 for international students). Electronic applications accepted. *Financial support:* In 2012–13, 2 students received support, including 9 fellowships with full tuition reimbursements available (averaging $21,450 per year), 11 research assistantships with full tuition reimbursements available (averaging $16,045 per year), 96 teaching assistantships with full tuition reimbursements available (averaging $15,870 per year); scholarships/grants, health care benefits, and unspecified assistantships also available. Financial award application deadline: 1/15. *Faculty research:* Topology, geometry, algebra, applied, analysis. *Unit head:* Kevin Zumbrun, Chair, 812-855-2200. *Application contact:* Kate Forrest, Graduate Secretary, 812-855-2645, Fax: 812-855-0046, E-mail: gradmath@indiana.edu. Website: http://www.math.indiana.edu/.

Indiana University of Pennsylvania, School of Graduate Studies and Research, College of Natural Sciences and Mathematics, Department of Mathematics, Indiana, PA 15705-1087. Offers applied mathematics (MS); elementary and middle school mathematics education (M Ed). Part-time programs available. *Faculty:* 9 full-time (2 women). *Students:* 15 full-time (4 women), 12 part-time (7 women); includes 2 minority (both Asian, non-Hispanic/Latino), 5 international. Average age 29. 59 applicants, 59% accepted, 15 enrolled. In 2012, 18 master's awarded. *Degree requirements:* For master's, thesis optional. *Entrance requirements:* For master's, 2 letters of recommendation. Additional exam requirements/recommendations for international students: Required—TOEFL (minimum score 540 paper-based). *Application deadline:* Applications are processed on a rolling basis. Application fee: $50. Electronic applications accepted. *Expenses:* Tuition, state resident: part-time $429 per credit hour. Tuition, nonresident: part-time $644 per credit hour. *Required fees:* $110.60 per credit hour. One-time fee: $180 part-time. *Financial support:* In 2012–13, 12 research assistantships with full and partial tuition reimbursements (averaging $3,518 per year) were awarded; career-related internships or fieldwork, Federal Work-Study, scholarships/grants, and unspecified assistantships also available. Support available to part-time students. Financial award application deadline: 4/15; financial award applicants required to submit FAFSA. *Unit head:* Dr. Francisco E. Alarcon, Chairperson, 724-357-2608, E-mail: falarcon@iup.edu. *Application contact:* Dr. Yu-Ju Kuo, Program Coordinator, 724-357-3797, E-mail: yjkuo@iup.edu. Website: http://www.iup.edu/math.

Indiana University–Purdue University Fort Wayne, College of Arts and Sciences, Department of Mathematical Sciences, Fort Wayne, IN 46805-1499. Offers applied mathematics (MS); applied statistics (Certificate); mathematics (MS); operations research (MS); teaching (MAT). Part-time and evening/weekend programs available. *Faculty:* 19 full-time (5 women). *Students:* 1 (woman) full-time, 10 part-time (2 women), 1 international. Average age 30. 6 applicants, 100% accepted, 4 enrolled. In 2012, 5 master's, 1 other advanced degree awarded. *Entrance requirements:* For master's, minimum GPA of 3.0, major or minor in mathematics, three letters of recommendation. Additional exam requirements/recommendations for international students: Required—TOEFL (minimum score 550 paper-based; 79 iBT); Recommended—TWE. *Application deadline:* For fall admission, 8/1 priority date for domestic students, 7/1 for international students; for spring admission, 12/1 for domestic students, 10/1 for international students. Applications are processed on a rolling basis. Application fee: $55 ($60 for international students). Electronic applications accepted. *Expenses:* Tuition, state resident: full-time $6279; part-time $313.95 per credit hour. Tuition, nonresident: full-time $14,219; part-time $710.95 per credit hour. *Financial support:* In 2012–13, 4 teaching assistantships with partial tuition reimbursements (averaging $13,190 per year) were awarded; scholarships/grants and unspecified assistantships also available. Support available to part-time students. Financial award application deadline: 3/1; financial award applicants required to submit FAFSA. *Faculty research:* Equilibrium measures, group graphs and split-stars, arrangement graphs. *Unit head:* Dr. Peter Dragnev, Interim Chair and Professor, 260-481-6382, Fax: 260-481-0155, E-mail: dragnevp@ipfw.edu. *Application contact:* Dr. W. Douglas Weakley, Director of Graduate Studies, 260-481-6233, Fax: 260-481-0155, E-mail: weakley@ipfw.edu. Website: http://www.ipfw.edu/math/.

Indiana University–Purdue University Indianapolis, School of Science, Department of Mathematical Sciences, Indianapolis, IN 46202-3216. Offers mathematics (MS, PhD), including applied mathematics, applied statistics (MS), mathematical statistics (PhD), mathematics, mathematics education (MS). *Faculty:* 30 full-time (2 women). *Students:* 25 full-time (8 women), 35 part-time (13 women); includes 11 minority (2 Black or African American, non-Hispanic/Latino; 7 Asian, non-Hispanic/Latino; 2 Hispanic/Latino), 23 international. Average age 33. 52 applicants, 67% accepted, 21 enrolled. In 2012, 22 master's awarded. Terminal master's awarded for partial completion of doctoral program. *Degree requirements:* For master's, thesis optional; for doctorate, one foreign language, thesis/dissertation. *Entrance requirements:* For doctorate, GRE General Test. Additional exam requirements/recommendations for international students: Required—TOEFL. *Application deadline:* For fall admission, 2/1 priority date for domestic students. Application fee: $55 ($65 for international students). *Financial support:* In 2012–13, 14 students received support, including 4 fellowships with tuition reimbursements available (averaging $15,375 per year), 4 teaching assistantships with tuition reimbursements available (averaging $13,088 per year); research assistantships with tuition reimbursements available and tuition waivers (full and partial) also available. Financial award application deadline: 2/1. *Faculty research:* Mathematical physics, integrable systems, partial differential equations, noncommutative geometry, biomathematics, computational neurosciences. *Unit head:* Dr. Zhongmin Shen, Chair, 317-278-1065, Fax: 317-274-3460, E-mail: zshen@math.iupui.edu. *Application contact:* Dr. Sherry Queener, Director, Graduate Studies and Associate Dean, 317-274-1577, Fax: 317-278-2380. Website: http://www.math.iupui.edu/.

Instituto Tecnologico de Santo Domingo, Graduate School, Area of Basic And Environmental Sciences, Santo Domingo, Dominican Republic. Offers environmental science (M En S), including environmental education, environmental management, marine resources, natural resources management; mathematics (MS, PhD); renewable energy technology (MS, Certificate).

Iowa State University of Science and Technology, Department of Mathematics, Ames, IA 50011. Offers applied mathematics (MS, PhD); mathematics (MS, PhD); school mathematics (MSM). *Degree requirements:* For master's, thesis or alternative; for doctorate, thesis/dissertation. *Entrance requirements:* For master's and doctorate, GRE General Test. Additional exam requirements/recommendations for international students: Required—TOEFL (minimum score 550 paper-based; 79 iBT), IELTS (minimum score 6.5). *Application deadline:* For fall admission, 2/1 priority date for domestic students, 2/1 for international students. Application fee: $60 ($90 for international students). Electronic applications accepted. *Financial support:* Scholarships/grants, health care benefits, and unspecified assistantships available. *Application contact:* Melanie Erickson, Application Contact, 515-294-0393, Fax: 515-294-5454, E-mail: gradmath@iastate.edu. Website: http://www.math.iastate.edu/Graduate/Programs.html.

Jackson State University, Graduate School, College of Science, Engineering and Technology, Department of Mathematics, Jackson, MS 39217. Offers mathematics (MS). Part-time and evening/weekend programs available. *Degree requirements:* For master's, comprehensive exam, thesis (for some programs).

Entrance requirements: For master's, GRE General Test. Additional exam requirements/recommendations for international students: Required—TOEFL (minimum score 520 paper-based; 67 iBT).

Jacksonville State University, College of Graduate Studies and Continuing Education, College of Arts and Sciences, Department of Mathematics, Jacksonville, AL 36265-1602. Offers MS. Part-time and evening/weekend programs available. *Faculty:* 13 full-time (3 women). *Students:* 2 full-time (both women), 7 part-time (3 women); includes 1 minority (Black or African American, non-Hispanic/Latino), 1 international. Average age 29. 1 applicant, 100% accepted, 1 enrolled. In 2012, 2 master's awarded. *Degree requirements:* For master's, comprehensive exam, thesis (for some programs). *Entrance requirements:* For master's, GRE General Test or MAT. Additional exam requirements/recommendations for international students: Required—TOEFL (minimum score 61 iBT). *Application deadline:* Applications are processed on a rolling basis. Application fee: $30. Electronic applications accepted. *Expenses:* Tuition, state resident: full-time $8376; part-time $349 per credit hour. Tuition, nonresident: full-time $16,752; part-time $698 per credit hour. *Financial support:* In 2012–13, 6 students received support. Available to part-time students. Application deadline: 4/1; applicants required to submit FAFSA. *Unit head:* Dr. Donnie Ford, Head, 256-782-5242, E-mail: dford@jsu.edu. *Application contact:* Dr. Jean Pugliese, Associate Dean, 256-782-8278, Fax: 256-782-5321, E-mail: pugliese@jsu.edu.

James Madison University, The Graduate School, College of Science and Mathematics, Department of Mathematics and Statistics, Harrisonburg, VA 22807. Offers M Ed. Part-time programs available. *Faculty:* 2 full-time (1 woman). *Students:* 5 part-time (2 women). Average age 27. In 2012, 1 master's awarded. *Degree requirements:* For master's, comprehensive exam. *Entrance requirements:* For master's, undergraduate major in mathematics. *Application deadline:* For fall admission, 5/1 priority date for domestic students; for spring admission, 9/1 priority date for domestic students. Application fee: $55. *Financial support:* Application deadline: 3/1; applicants required to submit FAFSA. *Unit head:* Dr. David C. Carothers, Academic Unit Head, 540-568-6184, E-mail: carothdc@jmu.edu. *Application contact:* Lynette M. Bible, Director of Graduate Admissions, 540-568-6395, Fax: 540-568-7860, E-mail: biblelm@jmu.edu.

John Carroll University, Graduate School, Department of Mathematics, University Heights, OH 44118-4581. Offers MA, MS. Part-time and evening/weekend programs available. *Degree requirements:* For master's, comprehensive exam, thesis (for some programs), research essay. *Entrance requirements:* For master's, minimum GPA of 2.5, teaching certificate (MA). Electronic applications accepted. *Faculty research:* Algebraic topology, algebra, differential geometry, combinatorics, Lie groups.

The Johns Hopkins University, Zanvyl Krieger School of Arts and Sciences, Department of Mathematics, Baltimore, MD 21218-2699. Offers PhD. *Degree requirements:* For doctorate, one foreign language, thesis/dissertation, 3 qualifying exams. *Entrance requirements:* For doctorate, GRE General Test, GRE Subject Test. Additional exam requirements/recommendations for international students: Required—TOEFL (minimum score 600 paper-based; 100 iBT), IELTS. Electronic applications accepted. *Faculty research:* Algebraic geometry, number theory, algebraic topology, differential geometry, partial differential equations.

Kansas State University, Graduate School, College of Arts and Sciences, Department of Mathematics, Manhattan, KS 66506. Offers MS, PhD. Part-time programs available. *Faculty:* 30 full-time (4 women), 3 part-time/adjunct (0 women). *Students:* 46 full-time (13 women), 1 part-time (0 women); includes 5 minority (1 Black or African American, non-Hispanic/Latino; 1 Asian, non-Hispanic/Latino; 3 Hispanic/Latino), 20 international. Average age 28. 68 applicants, 46% accepted, 11 enrolled. In 2012, 3 master's, 5 doctorates awarded. Terminal master's awarded for partial completion of doctoral program. *Degree requirements:* For master's, thesis or alternative; for doctorate, one foreign language, thesis/dissertation. *Entrance requirements:* For master's, GRE, bachelor's degree in mathematics; for doctorate, master's degree in mathematics. Additional exam requirements/recommendations for international students: Required—TOEFL (minimum score 600 paper-based). *Application deadline:* For fall admission, 2/1 priority date for domestic students, 2/1 for international students; for spring admission, 8/1 priority date for domestic students, 8/1 for international students. Applications are processed on a rolling basis. Application fee: $50 ($75 for international students). Electronic applications accepted. *Financial support:* In 2012–13, 38 teaching assistantships with full tuition reimbursements (averaging $15,928 per year) were awarded; research assistantships, Federal Work-Study, institutionally sponsored loans, and scholarships/grants also available. Support available to part-time students. Financial award application deadline: 3/1; financial award applicants required to submit FAFSA. *Faculty research:* Low-dimensional topology, geometry, complex and harmonic analysis, group and representation theory, noncommunicative spaces. *Total annual research expenditures:* $602,775. *Unit head:* Louis Pigno, Department Head, 785-532-6750, Fax: 785-532-0546, E-mail: lpigno@ksu.edu. *Application contact:* Kathy Roeser, Graduate Studies Administrative Assistant, 785-532-0556, Fax: 785-532-0546, E-mail: math@math.ksu.edu. Website: http://www.math.ksu.edu/.

Kent State University, College of Arts and Sciences, Department of Mathematical Sciences, Kent, OH 44242-0001. Offers applied mathematics (MA, MS, PhD); pure mathematics (MA, MS, PhD). Part-time programs available. *Degree requirements:* For master's, thesis optional; for doctorate, one foreign language, thesis/dissertation. Electronic applications accepted. *Expenses:* Tuition, state resident: full-time $8424; part-time $468 per credit hour. Tuition, nonresident: full-time $14,580; part-time $810 per credit hour. Tuition and fees vary according to course load. *Faculty research:* Approximation theory, measure theory, ring theory, functional analysis, complex analysis.

Kent State University, Graduate School of Education, Health, and Human Services, School of Teaching, Learning and Curriculum Studies, Program in Math Specialization, Kent, OH 44242-0001. Offers M Ed, MA. Part-time programs available. *Faculty:* 3 full-time (2 women). *Students:* 1 full-time (0 women), 2 part-time (both women). 3 applicants, 100% accepted. In 2012, 4 master's awarded. *Entrance requirements:* For master's, 2 letters of reference, goals statement. Additional exam requirements/recommendations for international students: Required—TOEFL (minimum score 550 paper-based; 80 iBT). *Application deadline:* Applications are processed on a rolling basis. Application fee: $30 ($60 for international students). Electronic applications accepted. *Expenses:* Tuition, state resident: full-time $8424; part-time $468 per credit hour. Tuition, nonresident: full-time $14,580; part-time $810 per credit hour. Tuition and fees vary according to course load. *Financial support:* In 2012–13, 1 research assistantship (averaging $9,000 per year) was awarded. *Unit head:* Dr. Mike Mikusa, Coordinator, 330-672-0647, E-mail: mmikusa@kent.edu. *Application contact:* Nancy Miller, Academic Program Coordinator, Office of Graduate Student Services, 330-672-2576, Fax: 330-672-9162, E-mail: ogs@kent.edu.

Lakehead University, Graduate Studies, School of Mathematical Sciences, Thunder Bay, ON P7B 5E1, Canada. Offers computer science (M Sc); mathematical science (MA). Part-time and evening/weekend programs available. *Degree requirements:* For master's, thesis optional. *Entrance requirements:* For master's, minimum B average, honours degree in mathematics or computer science. Additional exam requirements/recommendations for international students: Required—TOEFL. *Faculty research:* Numerical analysis, classical analysis, theoretical computer science, abstract harmonic analysis, functional analysis.

Lamar University, College of Graduate Studies, College of Arts and Sciences, Department of Mathematics, Beaumont, TX 77710. Offers MS. *Faculty:* 6 full-time (3 women). *Students:* 13 full-time (2 women), 2 part-time (1 woman); includes 2 minority (1 Black or African American, non-Hispanic/Latino; 1 Asian, non-Hispanic/Latino), 7 international. Average age 30. 18 applicants, 72% accepted, 6 enrolled. In 2012, 4 master's awarded. *Degree requirements:* For master's, comprehensive exam (for some programs), thesis optional. *Entrance requirements:* For master's, GRE General Test, minimum GPA of 2.5 in last 60 hours of undergraduate course work. Additional exam requirements/recommendations for international students: Required—TOEFL. *Application deadline:* For fall admission, 5/15 priority date for domestic students; for spring admission, 10/1 priority date for domestic students. Applications are processed on a rolling basis. Application fee: $25 ($50 for international students). *Expenses:* Tuition, state resident: full-time $5364; part-time $298 per credit hour. Tuition, nonresident: full-time $12,582; part-time $699 per credit hour. *Required fees:* $1844. *Financial support:* In 2012–13, 4 teaching assistantships (averaging $12,000 per year) were awarded; fellowships and research assistantships also available. Financial award application deadline: 4/1. *Faculty research:* Complex analysis, differential equations, algebra, topology statistics. *Total annual research expenditures:* $43,585. *Unit head:* Charles F. Coppin, Chair, 409-880-8792, Fax: 409-880-8794, E-mail: chair@math.lamar.edu. *Application contact:* Dr. Paul Chiou, Professor, 409-880-8800, Fax: 409-880-8794, E-mail: chiou@math.lamar.edu.

Lehigh University, College of Arts and Sciences, Department of Mathematics, Bethlehem, PA 18015. Offers applied mathematics (MS, PhD); mathematics (MS, PhD); statistics (MS). Part-time programs available. *Faculty:* 24 full-time (1 woman), 1 part-time/adjunct (0 women). *Students:* 32 full-time (14 women), 4 part-time (3 women); includes 1 minority (Asian, non-Hispanic/Latino), 15 international. Average age 27. 161 applicants, 41% accepted, 12 enrolled. In 2012, 12 master's, 3 doctorates awarded. Terminal master's awarded for partial completion of doctoral program. *Degree requirements:* For master's, comprehensive exam, thesis optional; for doctorate, comprehensive exam, thesis/dissertation, qualifying exams, general exam, advanced topic exam. *Entrance requirements:* For master's and doctorate, GRE General Test (strongly recommended), minimum undergraduate GPA of 2.75, 3.0 for last two semesters; adequate background in math. Additional exam requirements/recommendations for international students: Required—TOEFL (minimum score 85 iBT). *Application deadline:* For fall admission, 1/1 priority date for domestic students, 1/1 for international students; for spring admission, 12/1 priority date for domestic students, 12/1 for international students. Applications are processed on a rolling basis. Application fee: $75. Electronic applications accepted. *Financial support:* In 2012–13, 35 students received support, including 2 fellowships with full tuition reimbursements available (averaging $25,000 per year), 23 teaching assistantships with full tuition reimbursements available (averaging $17,500 per year); research assistantships with full tuition reimbursements available, scholarships/grants, and tuition waivers (partial) also available. Financial award application deadline: 1/1. *Faculty research:* Probability and statistics, geometry and topology, number theory, algebra, discrete mathematics, differential equations. *Total annual research expenditures:* $278,864. *Unit head:* Dr. Wei-Min Huang, Chairman, 610-758-3730, Fax: 610-758-3767, E-mail: wh02@lehigh.edu. *Application contact:* Dr. Terry Napier, Graduate Coordinator, 610-758-3755, E-mail: mathgrad@lehigh.edu. Website: http://www.lehigh.edu/~math/grad.html.

326 www.petersonsbooks.com

Peterson's Graduate Programs in the Physical Sciences, Mathematics, Agricultural Sciences, the Environment & Natural Resources 2014

Lehman College of the City University of New York, School of Natural and Social Sciences, Department of Mathematics and Computer Science, Program in Mathematics, Bronx, NY 10468-1589. Offers MA. Part-time and evening/weekend programs available. *Degree requirements:* For master's, one foreign language, thesis or alternative.

Long Island University–C. W. Post Campus, College of Liberal Arts and Sciences, Department of Mathematics, Brookville, NY 11548-1300. Offers applied mathematics (MS); mathematics education (MS); mathematics for secondary school teachers (MS). Part-time and evening/weekend programs available. *Degree requirements:* For master's, thesis or alternative, oral presentation. *Entrance requirements:* Additional exam requirements/recommendations for international students: Required—TOEFL. Electronic applications accepted. *Faculty research:* Differential geometry, topological groups, general topology, number theory, analysis and statistics, numerical analysis.

Louisiana State University and Agricultural and Mechanical College, Graduate School, College of Science, Department of Mathematics, Baton Rouge, LA 70803. Offers MS, PhD. *Faculty:* 55 full-time (4 women), 1 part-time/adjunct (0 women). *Students:* 88 full-time (24 women), 4 part-time (1 woman); includes 9 minority (1 Black or African American, non-Hispanic/Latino; 1 American Indian or Alaska Native, non-Hispanic/Latino; 4 Asian, non-Hispanic/Latino; 3 Hispanic/Latino), 36 international. Average age 27. 131 applicants, 60% accepted, 19 enrolled. In 2012, 15 master's, 12 doctorates awarded. Terminal master's awarded for partial completion of doctoral program. *Degree requirements:* For doctorate, 2 foreign languages, thesis/dissertation. *Entrance requirements:* For master's and doctorate, GRE General Test, minimum GPA of 3.0. Additional exam requirements/recommendations for international students: Required—TOEFL (minimum score 550 paper-based; 79 iBT) or IELTS (minimum score 6.5). *Application deadline:* For fall admission, 1/25 priority date for domestic students, 5/15 for international students; for spring admission, 10/15 for international students. Applications are processed on a rolling basis. Application fee: $50 ($70 for international students). Electronic applications accepted. *Financial support:* In 2012–13, 85 students received support, including 22 fellowships with full and partial tuition reimbursements available (averaging $25,984 per year), 4 research assistantships with full and partial tuition reimbursements available (averaging $21,625 per year), 51 teaching assistantships with full and partial tuition reimbursements available (averaging $17,959 per year); Federal Work-Study, institutionally sponsored loans, scholarships/grants, health care benefits, tuition waivers (full), and unspecified assistantships also available. Financial award application deadline: 3/1; financial award applicants required to submit FAFSA. *Faculty research:* Algebra, graph theory and combinatorics, algebraic topology, analysis and probability, topological algebra. *Total annual research expenditures:* $1.5 million. *Unit head:* Dr. Robert Perlis, Chair, 225-578-1618, Fax: 225-578-4276, E-mail: perlis@math.lsu.edu. *Application contact:* Dr. William Adkins, Graduate Adviser, 225-578-1601, Fax: 225-578-4276, E-mail: adkins@math.lsu.edu. Website: http://www.math.lsu.edu/.

Louisiana Tech University, Graduate School, College of Engineering and Science, Department of Mathematics and Statistics, Ruston, LA 71272. Offers MS. Part-time programs available. *Degree requirements:* For master's, thesis or alternative. *Entrance requirements:* For master's, GRE General Test, minimum GPA of 3.0 in last 60 hours. Additional exam requirements/recommendations for international students: Required—TOEFL.

Loyola University Chicago, Graduate School, Department of Mathematical Sciences and Statistics, Chicago, IL 60660. Offers applied statistics (MS); mathematics (MS), including pure and applied mathematics. Part-time programs available. *Faculty:* 19 full-time (4 women). *Students:* 31 full-time (17 women), 7 part-time (4 women); includes 5 minority (2 Black or African American, non-Hispanic/Latino; 2 Asian, non-Hispanic/Latino; 1 Hispanic/Latino), 11 international. Average age 29. 62 applicants, 74% accepted, 17 enrolled. In 2012, 24 master's awarded. *Entrance requirements:* For master's, GRE General Test. Additional exam requirements/recommendations for international students: Required—TOEFL. *Application deadline:* For fall admission, 8/1 for domestic students; for spring admission, 12/1 for domestic students. Applications are processed on a rolling basis. Application fee: $0. Electronic applications accepted. *Expenses: Tuition:* Full-time $16,290. *Required fees:* $128 per semester. Tuition and fees vary according to course load and program. *Financial support:* In 2012–13, 13 students received support, including 6 teaching assistantships with tuition reimbursements available (averaging $10,000 per year); career-related internships or fieldwork, Federal Work-Study, institutionally sponsored loans, and tuition waivers (partial) also available. Financial award application deadline: 3/15. *Faculty research:* Probability and statistics, differential equations, algebra, combinatorics. *Total annual research expenditures:* $70,000. *Unit head:* Dr. Anthony Giaquinto, Chair, 773-508-3578, Fax: 773-508-2123, E-mail: agiaqui@luc.edu. *Application contact:* Dr. W. Cary Huffman, Graduate Program Director, 773-508-3563, Fax: 773-508-2123, E-mail: whuffma@luc.edu. Website: http://math.luc.edu/.

Marquette University, Graduate School, College of Arts and Sciences, Department of Mathematics, Statistics, and Computer Science, Milwaukee, WI 53201-1881. Offers bioinformatics (MS); computational sciences (MS, PhD); computing (MS); mathematics education (MS). Part-time and evening/weekend programs available. Postbaccalaureate distance learning degree programs offered (minimal on-campus study). Terminal master's awarded for partial completion of doctoral program. *Degree requirements:* For master's, thesis (for some programs), essay with oral presentation; for doctorate, comprehensive exam, thesis/dissertation, qualifying examination. *Entrance requirements:* For master's, official transcripts from all current and previous colleges/universities except Marquette, three letters of recommendation; for doctorate, GRE General Test, official transcripts from all current and previous colleges/universities except Marquette, three letters of recommendation. Additional exam requirements/recommendations for international students: Required—TOEFL (minimum score 530 paper-based). Electronic applications accepted. *Faculty research:* Models of physiological systems, mathematical immunology, computational group theory, mathematical logic, computational science.

Marshall University, Academic Affairs Division, College of Science, Department of Mathematics, Huntington, WV 25755. Offers MA. *Faculty:* 24 full-time (7 women), 1 (woman) part-time/adjunct. *Students:* 12 full-time (2 women), 1 part-time (0 women); includes 4 minority (2 Black or African American, non-Hispanic/Latino; 2 Two or more races, non-Hispanic/Latino), 4 international. Average age 26. In 2012, 8 master's awarded. *Degree requirements:* For master's, thesis (for some programs). *Entrance requirements:* For master's, GRE General Test. Application fee: $40. *Unit head:* Dr. Alfred Akinsete, Chairperson, 304-696-3285, E-mail: akinsete@marshall.edu. *Application contact:* Dr. Peter Savaliev, Information Contact, 304-696-4639, Fax: 304-746-1902, E-mail: lawrence@marshall.edu.

Massachusetts Institute of Technology, School of Science, Department of Mathematics, Cambridge, MA 02139. Offers PhD. *Faculty:* 50 full-time (5 women), 1 part-time/adjunct (0 women). *Students:* 108 full-time (19 women); includes 13 minority (9 Asian, non-Hispanic/Latino; 2 Hispanic/Latino; 2 Two or more races, non-Hispanic/Latino), 56 international. Average age 25. 465 applicants, 13% accepted, 20 enrolled. In 2012, 22 doctorates awarded. *Degree requirements:* For doctorate, one foreign language, comprehensive exam, thesis/dissertation, language exam in one of the following languages: Chinese, French, German, or Russian. *Entrance requirements:* For doctorate, GRE General Test, GRE Subject Test (mathematics). Additional exam requirements/recommendations for international students: Required—IELTS (minimum score 6). *Application deadline:* For fall admission, 12/15 for domestic and international students. Application fee: $75. Electronic applications accepted. *Expenses: Tuition:* Full-time $41,770; part-time $650 per credit hour. *Required fees:* $280. *Financial support:* In 2012–13, 105 students received support, including 54 fellowships (averaging $31,500 per year), 10 research assistantships (averaging $33,400 per year), 38 teaching assistantships (averaging $35,200 per year); Federal Work-Study, institutionally sponsored loans, scholarships/grants, health care benefits, and unspecified assistantships also available. *Faculty research:* Analysis, geometry and topology; algebra and number theory; representation theory; combinatorics, theoretical computer science and computational biology; physical applied mathematics and computational science. *Total annual research expenditures:* $6.4 million. *Unit head:* Prof. Michael Sipser, Head, 617-253-4381, Fax: 617-253-4358, E-mail: math@mit.edu. *Application contact:* Graduate Education, 617-253-2689, Fax: 617-253-4358, E-mail: gradofc@math.mit.edu. Website: http://math.mit.edu.

McGill University, Faculty of Graduate and Postdoctoral Studies, Faculty of Science, Department of Mathematics and Statistics, Montréal, QC H3A 2T5, Canada. Offers computational science and engineering (M Sc); mathematics and statistics (M Sc, MA, PhD), including applied mathematics (M Sc, MA), pure mathematics (M Sc, MA), statistics (M Sc, MA).

McMaster University, School of Graduate Studies, Faculty of Science, Department of Mathematics and Statistics, Hamilton, ON L8S 4M2, Canada. Offers mathematics (M Sc, PhD); statistics (M Sc), including applied statistics, medical statistics, statistical theory. Part-time programs available. *Degree requirements:* For master's, thesis or alternative, oral exam; for doctorate, comprehensive exam, thesis/dissertation. *Entrance requirements:* For master's, minimum B+ average in last year of honors degree; for doctorate, minimum B+ average, M Sc in mathematics or statistics. Additional exam requirements/recommendations for international students: Required—TOEFL (minimum score 550 paper-based). *Faculty research:* Algebra, analysis, applied mathematics, geometry and topology, probability and statistics.

McNeese State University, Doré School of Graduate Studies, College of Science, Department of Mathematics, Computer Science, and Statistics, Lake Charles, LA 70609. Offers computer science (MS); mathematics (MS); statistics (MS). Evening/weekend programs available. *Faculty:* 11 full-time (4 women). *Students:* 17 full-time (8 women), 3 part-time (1 woman); includes 1 minority (Black or African American, non-Hispanic/Latino), 3 international. In 2012, 9 master's awarded. *Degree requirements:* For master's, comprehensive exam, thesis or alternative, written exam. *Entrance requirements:* For master's, GRE. *Application deadline:* For fall admission, 5/15 priority date for domestic students, 5/15 for international students; for spring admission, 10/15 priority date for domestic students, 10/15 for international students. Applications are processed on a rolling basis. Application fee: $20 ($30 for international students). *Expenses:* Tuition, state resident: full-time $4287; part-time $587 per credit hour. *Required fees:* $1177. Tuition and fees vary according to course load. *Financial support:* Teaching assistantships available. Financial award application deadline: 5/1. *Unit head:* Dr. Karen Aucoin, Head, 337-475-5803, Fax: 337-475-5799, E-mail: aucoin@mcneese.edu. *Application contact:* Dr. Dustin M. Hebert, Director of Dore' School of Graduate Studies, 337-475-5396, Fax: 337-475-5397, E-mail: admissions@mcneese.edu.

Memorial University of Newfoundland, School of Graduate Studies, Department of Mathematics and Statistics, St. John's, NL A1C 5S7, Canada.

Mathematics

Offers mathematics (M Sc, PhD); statistics (M Sc, MAS, PhD). Part-time programs available. *Degree requirements:* For master's, thesis, practicum and report (MAS); for doctorate, comprehensive exam, thesis/dissertation, oral defense of thesis. *Entrance requirements:* For master's, 2nd class honors degree (MAS); for doctorate, MAS or M Sc in mathematics and statistics. Electronic applications accepted. *Faculty research:* Algebra, topology, applied mathematics, mathematical statistics, applied statistics and probability.

Miami University, College of Arts and Science, Department of Mathematics, Oxford, OH 45056. Offers MA, MAT, MS. *Students:* 22 full-time (6 women), 8 part-time (2 women); includes 1 minority (Two or more races, non-Hispanic/Latino), 5 international. Average age 24. In 2012, 10 master's awarded. *Entrance requirements:* For master's, minimum undergraduate GPA of 2.75 overall. Additional exam requirements/recommendations for international students: Required—TOEFL (minimum score 550 paper-based). *Application deadline:* For fall admission, 2/1 for domestic and international students. Application fee: $50. Electronic applications accepted. *Expenses:* Tuition, state resident: full-time $12,444; part-time $519 per credit hour. Tuition, nonresident: full-time $27,484; part-time $1145 per credit hour. *Required fees:* $468. Part-time tuition and fees vary according to course load, campus/location and program. *Financial support:* Research assistantships, teaching assistantships, health care benefits, and unspecified assistantships available. Financial award application deadline: 2/1; financial award applicants required to submit FAFSA. *Unit head:* Dr. Patrick Dowling, Department Chair, 513-529-5818, E-mail: dowlinpn@miamioh.edu. *Application contact:* Dr. Doug Ward, Director of Graduate Studies, 513-529-3534, E-mail: wardde@miamioh.edu. Website: http://www.MiamiOH.edu/mathematics.

Michigan State University, The Graduate School, College of Natural Science, Department of Mathematics, East Lansing, MI 48824. Offers applied mathematics (MS, PhD); industrial mathematics (MS); mathematics (MAT, MS, PhD). *Entrance requirements:* Additional exam requirements/recommendations for international students: Required—TOEFL. Electronic applications accepted.

Michigan Technological University, Graduate School, College of Sciences and Arts, Department of Mathematical Sciences, Houghton, MI 49931. Offers MS, PhD. Part-time programs available. Terminal master's awarded for partial completion of doctoral program. *Degree requirements:* For master's, comprehensive exam (for some programs), thesis (for some programs); for doctorate, comprehensive exam, thesis/dissertation, proficiency exam. *Entrance requirements:* For master's and doctorate, GRE, statement of purpose, official transcripts, 3 letters of recommendation. Additional exam requirements/recommendations for international students: Required—TOEFL (minimum score 79 iBT). Electronic applications accepted. *Faculty research:* Fluid dynamics, mathematical modeling, design theory, coding theory, statistical genetics.

Middle Tennessee State University, College of Graduate Studies, College of Basic and Applied Sciences, Department of Mathematical Sciences, Murfreesboro, TN 37132. Offers mathematics (MS, MST, PhD). Part-time and evening/weekend programs available. Postbaccalaureate distance learning degree programs offered. *Degree requirements:* For master's, comprehensive exam, thesis optional; for doctorate, comprehensive exam, thesis/dissertation. *Entrance requirements:* For master's, GRE General Test or MAT. Additional exam requirements/recommendations for international students: Required—TOEFL (minimum score 525 paper-based; 71 iBT) or IELTS (minimum score 6). Electronic applications accepted. *Faculty research:* Graph theory, computational science.

Minnesota State University Mankato, College of Graduate Studies, College of Science, Engineering and Technology, Department of Mathematics and Statistics, Program in Mathematics, Mankato, MN 56001. Offers MA, MS. *Students:* 6 full-time (5 women), 14 part-time (3 women). *Degree requirements:* For master's, one foreign language, comprehensive exam, thesis or alternative. *Entrance requirements:* For master's, GRE General Test, minimum GPA of 3.0 during previous 2 years. Additional exam requirements/recommendations for international students: Required—TOEFL. *Application deadline:* For fall admission, 7/1 priority date for domestic students; for spring admission, 11/1 for domestic students. Applications are processed on a rolling basis. Application fee: $40. Electronic applications accepted. *Financial support:* Research assistantships with partial tuition reimbursements, teaching assistantships with partial tuition reimbursements, and unspecified assistantships available. Financial award application deadline: 3/15; financial award applicants required to submit FAFSA. *Unit head:* Dr. Han Wu, Graduate Coordinator, 507-389-1453. *Application contact:* 507-389-2321, E-mail: grad@mnsu.edu. Website: http://cset.mnsu.edu/mathstat/program/grad.html.

Mississippi College, Graduate School, College of Arts and Sciences, School of Science and Mathematics, Department of Mathematics, Clinton, MS 39058. Offers M Ed, MCS, MS. Part-time programs available. *Degree requirements:* For master's, comprehensive exam, thesis optional. *Entrance requirements:* For master's, GRE or NTE, minimum GPA of 2.5. Additional exam requirements/recommendations for international students: Recommended—TOEFL, IELTS. Electronic applications accepted.

Mississippi State University, College of Arts and Sciences, Department of Mathematics and Statistics, Mississippi State, MS 39762. Offers mathematical sciences (PhD); mathematics (MS); statistics (MS). Part-time programs available. *Faculty:* 18 full-time (3 women). *Students:* 34 full-time (17 women), 5 part-time (3 women); includes 7 minority (4 Black or African American, non-Hispanic/Latino; 3 Asian, non-Hispanic/Latino), 18 international. Average age 29. 59 applicants, 42%

accepted, 15 enrolled. In 2012, 13 master's, 3 doctorates awarded. Terminal master's awarded for partial completion of doctoral program. *Degree requirements:* For master's, thesis optional, comprehensive oral or written exam; for doctorate, one foreign language, thesis/dissertation, comprehensive oral and written exam. *Entrance requirements:* For master's, minimum GPA of 2.75 on last two years of undergraduate courses; for doctorate, GRE. Additional exam requirements/recommendations for international students: Required—TOEFL (minimum score 477 paper-based; 53 iBT); Recommended—IELTS (minimum score 4.5). *Application deadline:* For fall admission, 3/15 priority date for domestic students, 5/1 for international students; for spring admission, 11/1 for domestic students, 9/1 for international students. Applications are processed on a rolling basis. Application fee: $60. Electronic applications accepted. *Financial support:* In 2012–13, 26 teaching assistantships with full tuition reimbursements (averaging $13,309 per year) were awarded; Federal Work-Study, institutionally sponsored loans, tuition waivers (partial), and unspecified assistantships also available. Financial award application deadline: 4/1; financial award applicants required to submit FAFSA. *Faculty research:* Differential equations, algebra, numerical analysis, functional analysis, applied statistics. *Total annual research expenditures:* $1 million. *Unit head:* Dr. Mohsen Razzaghi, Interim Head, 662-325-3414, Fax: 662-325-0005, E-mail: razzaghi@math.msstate.edu. *Application contact:* Dr. Corlis Johnson, Associate Department Head/Graduate Coordinator, 662-325-3414, Fax: 662-325-0005, E-mail: office@math.msstate.edu. Website: http://www.math.msstate.edu.

Missouri State University, Graduate College, College of Natural and Applied Sciences, Department of Mathematics, Springfield, MO 65897. Offers mathematics (MS); natural and applied science (MNAS), including mathematics (MNAS, MS Ed); secondary education (MS Ed), including mathematics (MNAS, MS Ed). Part-time programs available. *Degree requirements:* For master's, comprehensive exam, thesis or alternative. *Entrance requirements:* For master's, GRE (MS, MNAS), minimum undergraduate GPA of 3.0 (MS, MNAS), 9-12 teacher certification (MS Ed). Additional exam requirements/recommendations for international students: Required—TOEFL (minimum score 550 paper-based; 79 iBT). Electronic applications accepted. *Faculty research:* Harmonic analysis, commutative algebra, number theory, K-theory, probability.

Missouri University of Science and Technology, Graduate School, Department of Mathematics and Statistics, Rolla, MO 65409. Offers applied mathematics (MS); mathematics (MST, PhD), including mathematics (PhD), mathematics education (MST), statistics (PhD). Terminal master's awarded for partial completion of doctoral program. *Degree requirements:* For master's, thesis or alternative; for doctorate, one foreign language, thesis/dissertation. *Entrance requirements:* For master's and doctorate, GRE General Test, GRE Subject Test. Electronic applications accepted. *Faculty research:* Analysis, differential equations, topology, statistics.

Montana State University, College of Graduate Studies, College of Letters and Science, Department of Mathematical Sciences, Bozeman, MT 59717. Offers mathematics (MS, PhD), including mathematics education option (MS); statistics (MS, PhD). Part-time programs available. Postbaccalaureate distance learning degree programs offered (minimal on-campus study). *Degree requirements:* For master's, comprehensive exam, thesis (for some programs); for doctorate, comprehensive exam, thesis/dissertation. *Entrance requirements:* For master's and doctorate, GRE General Test. Additional exam requirements/recommendations for international students: Required—TOEFL (minimum score 550 paper-based). Electronic applications accepted. *Faculty research:* Applied mathematics, dynamical systems, statistics, mathematics education, mathematical and computational biology.

Montclair State University, The Graduate School, College of Science and Mathematics, Department of Mathematical Sciences, Program in Mathematics, Montclair, NJ 07043-1624. Offers mathematics education (MS); pure and applied mathematics (MS). Part-time and evening/weekend programs available. *Degree requirements:* For master's, comprehensive exam. *Entrance requirements:* For master's, GRE General Test, 2 letters of recommendation, essay. Additional exam requirements/recommendations for international students: Required—TOEFL (minimum score 83 iBT), IELTS (minimum score 6.5). Electronic applications accepted. *Faculty research:* Computation, applied analysis.

Morgan State University, School of Graduate Studies, School of Computer, Mathematical, and Natural Sciences, Department of Mathematics, Baltimore, MD 21251. Offers MA. Part-time and evening/weekend programs available. *Degree requirements:* For master's, comprehensive exam, thesis. *Entrance requirements:* For master's, GRE. Additional exam requirements/recommendations for international students: Required—TOEFL (minimum score 550 paper-based). *Faculty research:* Number theory, semigroups, analysis, operations research.

Murray State University, College of Science, Engineering and Technology, Program in Mathematics and Statistics, Murray, KY 42071. Offers MA, MAT, MS. Part-time programs available. *Degree requirements:* For master's, comprehensive exam, thesis optional. *Entrance requirements:* For master's, GRE General Test. Additional exam requirements/recommendations for international students: Required—TOEFL. *Faculty research:* Algebraic structures, mathematical biology, topolgy.

New Jersey Institute of Technology, Office of Graduate Studies, College of Science and Liberal Arts, Department of Mathematical Science, Program in Mathematics Science, Newark, NJ 07102. Offers PhD. Part-time and evening/weekend programs available. *Entrance requirements:* For doctorate, GRE

328 www.petersonsbooks.com

Peterson's Graduate Programs in the Physical Sciences, Mathematics, Agricultural Sciences, the Environment & Natural Resources 2014

General Test, minimum graduate GPA of 3.5. Additional exam requirements/recommendations for international students: Required—TOEFL (minimum score 550 paper-based; 79 iBT). Electronic applications accepted. *Expenses:* Tuition, state resident: full-time $16,836; part-time $915 per credit. Tuition, nonresident: full-time $24,370; part-time $1286 per credit. *Required fees:* $2318; $242 per credit.

New Mexico Institute of Mining and Technology, Graduate Studies, Department of Mathematics, Socorro, NM 87801. Offers applied and industrial mathematics (PhD); industrial mathematics (MS); mathematics (MS); operations research and statistics (MS). *Faculty:* 13 full-time (1 woman), 2 part-time/adjunct (0 women). *Students:* 14 full-time (3 women), 5 part-time (1 woman); includes 4 minority (2 American Indian or Alaska Native, non-Hispanic/Latino; 1 Hispanic/Latino; 1 Two or more races, non-Hispanic/Latino), 5 international. Average age 31. 14 applicants, 79% accepted, 8 enrolled. In 2012, 1 master's awarded. *Degree requirements:* For master's, thesis optional; for doctorate, thesis/dissertation. *Entrance requirements:* For master's, GRE General Test. Additional exam requirements/recommendations for international students: Required—TOEFL (minimum score 540 paper-based). *Application deadline:* For fall admission, 3/1 priority date for domestic students; for spring admission, 6/1 for domestic students. Applications are processed on a rolling basis. Application fee: $16 ($30 for international students). *Expenses:* Tuition, state resident: full-time $5040; part-time $280 per credit hour. Tuition, nonresident: full-time $16,682; part-time $927 per credit hour. *Required fees:* $648; $18 per credit hour. $108 per semester. Part-time tuition and fees vary according to course load. *Financial support:* In 2012–13, 2 research assistantships (averaging $5,505 per year), 10 teaching assistantships with full and partial tuition reimbursements (averaging $8,944 per year) were awarded; fellowships, Federal Work-Study, and institutionally sponsored loans also available. Financial award application deadline: 3/1; financial award applicants required to submit CSS PROFILE or FAFSA. *Faculty research:* Applied mathematics, differential equations, industrial mathematics, numerical analysis, stochastic processes. *Total annual research expenditures:* $116,935. *Unit head:* Dr. Anwar Hossain, Chairman, 575-835-5135, Fax: 575-835-5366, E-mail: hossain@nmt.edu. *Application contact:* Dr. Lorie Liebrock, Dean of Graduate Studies, 575-835-5513, Fax: 575-835-5476, E-mail: graduate@nmt.edu. Website: http://www.nmt.edu/~math/.

New Mexico State University, Graduate School, College of Arts and Sciences, Department of Mathematical Sciences, Las Cruces, NM 88003-8001. Offers MS, PhD. Part-time programs available. *Faculty:* 21 full-time (6 women). *Students:* 34 full-time (11 women), 3 part-time (0 women); includes 5 minority (1 American Indian or Alaska Native, non-Hispanic/Latino; 1 Asian, non-Hispanic/Latino; 3 Hispanic/Latino), 23 international. Average age 32. 55 applicants, 60% accepted, 6 enrolled. In 2012, 5 master's, 6 doctorates awarded. *Degree requirements:* For master's, thesis optional, final oral exam; for doctorate, one foreign language, comprehensive exam, thesis/dissertation, final oral exam. *Entrance requirements:* For master's, GRE Subject Test (preferred), 24 credits of upper-division math/statistics, including real analysis and modern algebra. Additional exam requirements/recommendations for international students: Required—TOEFL (minimum score 550 paper-based; 79 iBT), IELTS (minimum score 6.5). *Application deadline:* For fall admission, 2/1 priority date for domestic students, 2/1 for international students; for spring admission, 10/1 for domestic and international students. Applications are processed on a rolling basis. Application fee: $40 ($50 for international students). Electronic applications accepted. *Expenses:* Tuition, state resident: full-time $5239; part-time $218 per credit. Tuition, nonresident: full-time $18,266; part-time $761 per credit. *Required fees:* $1274; $53 per credit. *Financial support:* In 2012–13, 33 students received support, including 5 fellowships (averaging $3,920 per year), 3 research assistantships (averaging $11,403 per year), 29 teaching assistantships (averaging $15,441 per year); scholarships/grants, health care benefits, and unspecified assistantships also available. Financial award application deadline: 2/1. *Faculty research:* Commutative algebra, dynamical systems, harmonic analysis and applications, partial differential equations, algebraic topology, probability and statistics. *Total annual research expenditures:* $125,916. *Unit head:* Dr. Joseph Lakey, Head, 575-646-3901, Fax: 575-646-1064, E-mail: jlakey@nmsu.edu. *Application contact:* Dr. John Harding, Professor, 575-646-4315, Fax: 575-646-1064, E-mail: jharding@nmsu.edu. Website: http://www.math.nmsu.edu/.

New York University, Graduate School of Arts and Science, Courant Institute of Mathematical Sciences, Department of Mathematics, New York, NY 10012-1019. Offers atmosphere ocean science and mathematics (PhD); mathematics (MS, PhD); mathematics and statistics/operations research (MS); mathematics in finance (MS); scientific computing (MS). Part-time and evening/weekend programs available. *Faculty:* 46 full-time (0 women). *Students:* 228 full-time (41 women), 140 part-time (25 women); includes 51 minority (2 Black or African American, non-Hispanic/Latino; 39 Asian, non-Hispanic/Latino; 5 Hispanic/Latino; 5 Two or more races, non-Hispanic/Latino), 216 international. Average age 28. 1,681 applicants, 25% accepted, 121 enrolled. In 2012, 77 master's, 11 doctorates awarded. *Degree requirements:* For master's, thesis optional; for doctorate, one foreign language, thesis/dissertation, oral and written exams. *Entrance requirements:* For master's and doctorate, GRE General Test, GRE Subject Test. Additional exam requirements/recommendations for international students: Required—TOEFL. *Application deadline:* For fall admission, 1/4 for domestic and international students; for spring admission, 11/1 for domestic and international students. Application fee: $90. *Expenses: Tuition:* Full-time $34,488; part-time $1437 per credit. *Required fees:* $2332; $1437 per credit. Tuition and fees vary according to program. *Financial support:* Fellowships with tuition reimbursements, research assistantships with tuition reimbursements, teaching assistantships with tuition reimbursements, Federal Work-Study, institutionally sponsored loans, scholarships/grants, health care benefits, and unspecified assistantships available. Financial award application deadline: 1/4; financial award applicants required to submit FAFSA. *Faculty research:* Partial differential equations, computational science, applied mathematics, geometry and topology, probability and stochastic processes. *Unit head:* Fedor Bogomolov, Director of Graduate Studies, 212-998-3238, Fax: 212-995-4121, E-mail: admissions@math.nyu.edu. *Application contact:* Tamar Arnon, Graduate Program Administrator, 212-998-3238, Fax: 212-995-4121, E-mail: admissions@math.nyu.edu. Website: http://www.math.nyu.edu/.

Nicholls State University, Graduate Studies, College of Arts and Sciences, Department of Mathematics and Computer Science, Thibodaux, LA 70310. Offers community/technical college mathematics (MS). Part-time and evening/weekend programs available. *Degree requirements:* For master's, comprehensive exam. *Entrance requirements:* For master's, GRE General Test. Electronic applications accepted. *Faculty research:* Operations research, statistics, numerical analysis, algebra, topology.

North Carolina Agricultural and Technical State University, School of Graduate Studies, College of Arts and Sciences, Department of Mathematics, Greensboro, NC 27411. Offers applied mathematics (MS), including secondary education. *Accreditation:* NCATE. Part-time and evening/weekend programs available. *Degree requirements:* For master's, comprehensive exam, thesis or alternative, qualifying exam. *Entrance requirements:* For master's, GRE General Test, minimum GPA of 3.0.

North Carolina Central University, Division of Academic Affairs, College of Science and Technology, Department of Mathematics and Computer Science, Durham, NC 27707-3129. Offers applied mathematics (MS); mathematics education (MS); pure mathematics (MS). Part-time and evening/weekend programs available. *Degree requirements:* For master's, one foreign language, comprehensive exam, thesis. *Entrance requirements:* For master's, minimum GPA of 3.0 in major, 2.5 overall. Additional exam requirements/recommendations for international students: Required—TOEFL. *Faculty research:* Structure theorems for Lie algebra, Kleene monoids and semi-groups, theoretical computer science, mathematics education.

North Carolina State University, Graduate School, College of Agriculture and Life Sciences and College of Engineering and College of Physical and Mathematical Sciences, Program in Financial Mathematics, Raleigh, NC 27695. Offers MFM. Part-time programs available. *Degree requirements:* For master's, thesis optional, project/internship. *Entrance requirements:* For master's, GRE General Test. Additional exam requirements/recommendations for international students: Required—TOEFL (minimum score 550 paper-based). Electronic applications accepted. *Faculty research:* Financial mathematics modeling and computation, futures, options and commodities markets, real options, credit risk, portfolio optimization.

North Carolina State University, Graduate School, College of Physical and Mathematical Sciences, Department of Mathematics, Program in Mathematics, Raleigh, NC 27695. Offers MS, PhD. *Degree requirements:* For master's, thesis (for some programs); for doctorate, thesis/dissertation. *Entrance requirements:* For master's and doctorate, GRE, GRE Subject Test (recommended). Electronic applications accepted.

North Dakota State University, College of Graduate and Interdisciplinary Studies, College of Science and Mathematics, Department of Mathematics, Fargo, ND 58108. Offers applied mathematics (MS, PhD); mathematics (MS, PhD). *Faculty:* 12 full-time (1 woman), 1 part-time/adjunct (0 women). *Students:* 23 full-time (8 women), 2 part-time (0 women); includes 3 minority (1 Black or African American, non-Hispanic/Latino; 2 Two or more races, non-Hispanic/Latino), 5 international. Average age 29. 26 applicants, 31% accepted, 4 enrolled. In 2012, 1 master's, 2 doctorates awarded. *Degree requirements:* For master's, comprehensive exam, thesis; for doctorate, one foreign language, comprehensive exam, thesis/dissertation, computer proficiency. *Entrance requirements:* For master's and doctorate, GRE General Test. Additional exam requirements/recommendations for international students: Required—TOEFL (minimum score 525 paper-based; 71 iBT), IELTS. *Application deadline:* For fall admission, 3/1 priority date for domestic students. Applications are processed on a rolling basis. Application fee: $35. Electronic applications accepted. *Financial support:* In 2012–13, 5 fellowships with full tuition reimbursements (averaging $18,000 per year), 1 research assistantship with tuition reimbursement (averaging $14,000 per year), 17 teaching assistantships with full tuition reimbursements (averaging $9,300 per year) were awarded; Federal Work-Study, institutionally sponsored loans, and tuition waivers (full) also available. Support available to part-time students. Financial award application deadline: 3/31. *Faculty research:* Discrete mathematics, number theory, analysis theory, algebra, applied math. *Unit head:* Dr. Dogan Comez, Chair, 701-231-8171, Fax: 701-231-7598, E-mail: dogan.comez@ndsu.edu. *Application contact:* Dr. Sean Sather-Wagstaff, Graduate Program Director, 701-231-8105, Fax: 701-231-7598, E-mail: sean.sather-wagstaff@ndsu.edu. Website: http://www.math.ndsu.nodak.edu/.

Northeastern Illinois University, Graduate College, College of Arts and Sciences, Department of Mathematics, Programs in Mathematics, Chicago, IL 60625-4699. Offers mathematics (MS); mathematics for elementary school teachers (MA). Part-time and evening/weekend programs available. *Degree requirements:* For master's, comprehensive exam, thesis optional, project.

Mathematics

Entrance requirements: For master's, minimum GPA of 2.75, 6 undergraduate courses in mathematics. Additional exam requirements/recommendations for international students: Required—TOEFL (minimum score 550 paper-based; 79 iBT). Electronic applications accepted. Faculty research: Numerical analysis, mathematical biology, operations research, statistics, geometry and mathematics of finance.

Northeastern University, College of Science, Department of Mathematics, Boston, MA 02115-5096. Offers applied mathematics (MS); mathematics (MS, PhD); operations research (MSOR). Part-time programs available. Students: 142 applicants, 30% accepted, 20 enrolled. In 2012, 6 master's, 7 doctorates awarded. Terminal master's awarded for partial completion of doctoral program. Degree requirements: For master's, thesis (for some programs), 32 credit hours; for doctorate, one foreign language, comprehensive exam, thesis/dissertation, qualifying exams. Entrance requirements: For master's and doctorate, GRE Subject Test, GRE General Test. Additional exam requirements/recommendations for international students: Required—TOEFL (minimum score 100 iBT). Application deadline: For fall admission, 2/1 priority date for domestic students, 2/1 for international students; for spring admission, 12/1 for domestic students, 10/1 for international students. Applications are processed on a rolling basis. Application fee: $75. Electronic applications accepted. Financial support: In 2012–13, 35 students received support, including 3 research assistantships with tuition reimbursements available (averaging $19,000 per year), 35 teaching assistantships with tuition reimbursements available (averaging $19,000 per year); Federal Work-Study, institutionally sponsored loans, health care benefits, tuition waivers (full and partial), and unspecified assistantships also available. Financial award application deadline: 3/1; financial award applicants required to submit FAFSA. Faculty research: Algebra and singularities, combinatorics, topology, probability and statistics, geometric analysis and partial differential equations. Unit head: Dr. Gordana Todorov, Graduate Coordinator, 617-373-5642, Fax: 617-373-5668, E-mail: mathdept@neu.edu. Application contact: E-mail: gradcos@neu.edu. Website: http://www.math.neu.edu/graduate-programs.

Northern Arizona University, Graduate College, College of Engineering, Forestry and Natural Sciences, Department of Mathematics and Statistics, Flagstaff, AZ 86011. Offers applied statistics (Certificate); mathematics (MAT, MS); statistics (MS). Part-time programs available. Degree requirements: For master's, comprehensive exam (for some programs), thesis (for some programs). Entrance requirements: For master's, minimum GPA of 3.0. Additional exam requirements/recommendations for international students: Required—TOEFL (minimum score 550 paper-based; 80 iBT), IELTS (minimum score 7). Electronic applications accepted. Faculty research: Topology, statistics, groups, ring theory, number theory.

Northern Illinois University, Graduate School, College of Liberal Arts and Sciences, Department of Mathematical Sciences, De Kalb, IL 60115-2854. Offers mathematical sciences (PhD); mathematics (MS); statistics (MS). Part-time programs available. Faculty: 43 full-time (10 women), 4 part-time/adjunct (0 women). Students: 64 full-time (26 women), 33 part-time (15 women); includes 6 minority (1 Black or African American, non-Hispanic/Latino; 3 Asian, non-Hispanic/Latino; 1 Native Hawaiian or other Pacific Islander, non-Hispanic/Latino; 1 Two or more races, non-Hispanic/Latino), 26 international. Average age 30. 66 applicants, 64% accepted, 19 enrolled. In 2012, 29 master's, 6 doctorates awarded. Terminal master's awarded for partial completion of doctoral program. Degree requirements: For master's, comprehensive exam, thesis optional; for doctorate, one foreign language, thesis/dissertation, candidacy exam, dissertation defense, internship. Entrance requirements: For master's, GRE General Test, minimum GPA of 2.75; for doctorate, GRE General Test, minimum GPA of 2.75 (undergraduate), 3.2 (graduate). Additional exam requirements/recommendations for international students: Required—TOEFL (minimum score 550 paper-based). Application deadline: For fall admission, 6/1 for domestic students, 5/1 for international students; for spring admission, 11/1 for domestic students, 10/1 for international students. Applications are processed on a rolling basis. Application fee: $40. Electronic applications accepted. Financial support: In 2012–13, 42 teaching assistantships with full tuition reimbursements were awarded; fellowships with full tuition reimbursements, research assistantships with full tuition reimbursements, career-related internships or fieldwork, Federal Work-Study, scholarships/grants, tuition waivers (full), and unspecified assistantships also available. Support available to part-time students. Financial award applicants required to submit FAFSA. Faculty research: Numerical linear algebra, noncommutative rings, nonlinear partial differential equations, finite group theory, abstract harmonic analysis. Unit head: Dr. Bernie Harris, Chair, 815-753-0566, Fax: 815-753-1112, E-mail: harris@math.niu.edu. Application contact: Dr. John Ye, Director, Graduate Studies, 815-753-0568, E-mail: ye@math.niu.edu. Website: http://www.math.niu.edu/.

Northwestern University, The Graduate School, Judd A. and Marjorie Weinberg College of Arts and Sciences, Department of Mathematics, Evanston, IL 60208. Offers PhD. Admissions and degrees offered through The Graduate School. Part-time programs available. Degree requirements: For doctorate, thesis/dissertation, preliminary exam. Entrance requirements: For doctorate, GRE General Test, GRE Subject Test. Additional exam requirements/recommendations for international students: Required—TOEFL. Faculty research: Algebra, algebraic topology, analysis dynamical systems, partial differential equations.

Oakland University, Graduate Study and Lifelong Learning, College of Arts and Sciences, Department of Mathematics and Statistics, Program in Mathematics,

Rochester, MI 48309-4401. Offers MA. Entrance requirements: Additional exam requirements/recommendations for international students: Required—TOEFL (minimum score 550 paper-based). Electronic applications accepted. Expenses: Contact institution.

The Ohio State University, Graduate School, College of Arts and Sciences, Division of Natural and Mathematical Sciences, Department of Mathematics, Columbus, OH 43210. Offers MS, PhD. Faculty: 62. Students: 53 full-time (9 women), 80 part-time (22 women); includes 5 minority (2 Black or African American, non-Hispanic/Latino; 3 Hispanic/Latino), 54 international. Average age 27. In 2012, 11 master's, 16 doctorates awarded. Degree requirements: For master's, thesis optional; for doctorate, 2 foreign languages, thesis/dissertation. Entrance requirements: For master's, GRE General Test; for doctorate, GRE General Test, GRE Subject Test (mathematics). Additional exam requirements/recommendations for international students: Required—TOEFL (minimum score 550 paper-based; 79 iBT), Michigan English Language Assessment Battery (minimum score 82); Recommended—IELTS (minimum score 7). Application deadline: For fall admission, 1/2 priority date for domestic students, 11/30 for international students; for winter admission, 12/1 for domestic students, 11/1 for international students; for spring admission, 3/1 for domestic students, 2/1 for international students. Applications are processed on a rolling basis. Application fee: $40 ($50 for international students). Electronic applications accepted. Financial support: Fellowships, research assistantships, teaching assistantships, Federal Work-Study, institutionally sponsored loans, and unspecified assistantships available. Support available to part-time students. Unit head: Luis Casian, Chair, 614-292-7173, E-mail: casian@math.ohio-state.edu. Application contact: Roman Nitze, Graduate Studies Coordinator, 614-292-6274, Fax: 614-292-1479, E-mail: nitze.1@math.ohio-state.edu. Website: http://www.math.osu.edu/.

Ohio University, Graduate College, College of Arts and Sciences, Department of Mathematics, Athens, OH 45701-2979. Offers MS, PhD. Part-time and evening/weekend programs available. Terminal master's awarded for partial completion of doctoral program. Degree requirements: For master's, thesis optional; for doctorate, comprehensive exam, thesis/dissertation. Entrance requirements: For master's and doctorate, minimum GPA of 3.0. Additional exam requirements/recommendations for international students: Required—TOEFL (minimum score 550 paper-based; 80 iBT) or IELTS (minimum score 6.5). Electronic applications accepted. Faculty research: Algebra (group and ring theory), functional analysis, topology, differential equations, computational math.

Oklahoma State University, College of Arts and Sciences, Department of Mathematics, Stillwater, OK 74078. Offers applied mathematics (MS, PhD); mathematics education (MS, PhD); pure mathematics (MS, PhD). Faculty: 39 full-time (7 women), 7 part-time/adjunct (6 women). Students: 5 full-time (2 women), 31 part-time (12 women); includes 2 minority (1 Asian, non-Hispanic/Latino; 1 Hispanic/Latino), 21 international. Average age 30. 60 applicants, 32% accepted, 12 enrolled. In 2012, 5 master's, 5 doctorates awarded. Degree requirements: For master's, thesis, creative component, or report; for doctorate, comprehensive exam, thesis/dissertation. Entrance requirements: For master's and doctorate, GRE (recommended). Additional exam requirements/recommendations for international students: Required—TOEFL (minimum score 550 paper-based; 79 iBT). Application deadline: For fall admission, 3/1 for domestic and international students; for spring admission, 10/15 for domestic and international students. Applications are processed on a rolling basis. Application fee: $40 ($75 for international students). Electronic applications accepted. Expenses: Tuition, state resident: full-time $4272; part-time $178 per credit hour. Tuition, nonresident: full-time $17,016; part-time $709 per credit hour. Required fees: $2188; $91.17 per credit hour. One-time fee: $50 full-time. Part-time tuition and fees vary according to course load and campus/location. Financial support: In 2012–13, 33 teaching assistantships (averaging $18,444 per year) were awarded; health care benefits and tuition waivers (partial) also available. Financial award application deadline: 3/1; financial award applicants required to submit FAFSA. Unit head: Dr. Willam Jaco, Head, 405-744-5688, Fax: 405-744-8275. Application contact: Dr. Sheryl Tucker, Dean, 405-744-7099, Fax: 405-744-0355, E-mail: grad-i@okstate.edu. Website: http://www.math.okstate.edu/.

Old Dominion University, College of Sciences, Programs in Computational and Applied Mathematics, Norfolk, VA 23529. Offers MS, PhD. Part-time programs available. Faculty: 23 full-time (3 women), 2 part-time/adjunct (0 women). Students: 22 full-time (8 women), 15 part-time (4 women); includes 5 minority (2 Black or African American, non-Hispanic/Latino; 2 Asian, non-Hispanic/Latino; 1 Hispanic/Latino), 15 international. Average age 29. 31 applicants, 55% accepted, 8 enrolled. In 2012, 4 master's, 3 doctorates awarded. Terminal master's awarded for partial completion of doctoral program. Degree requirements: For master's, project; for doctorate, comprehensive exam, thesis/dissertation, candidacy exam. Entrance requirements: For master's, minimum GPA of 3.0 in major, 2.5 overall; for doctorate, GRE General Test, 3 recommendation letters, transcripts, essay. Additional exam requirements/recommendations for international students: Required—TOEFL. Application deadline: For fall admission, 6/1 for domestic students, 5/15 for international students; for winter admission, 11/1 for domestic students, 10/1 for international students; for spring admission, 3/1 for domestic students, 2/1 for international students. Applications are processed on a rolling basis. Application fee: $40. Electronic applications accepted. Expenses: Tuition, state resident: full-time $9432; part-time $393 per credit hour. Tuition, nonresident: full-time $23,928; part-time $997 per credit hour. Required fees: $59 per semester. One-time fee: $50. Financial support: In 2012–13, 4 fellowships

330 www.petersonsbooks.com

Peterson's Graduate Programs in the Physical Sciences, Mathematics, Agricultural Sciences, the Environment & Natural Resources 2014

with full tuition reimbursements (averaging $17,000 per year), 4 research assistantships with full tuition reimbursements (averaging $16,000 per year), 12 teaching assistantships with full tuition reimbursements (averaging $15,000 per year) were awarded; scholarships/grants also available. Financial award application deadline: 2/15; financial award applicants required to submit FAFSA. *Faculty research:* Numerical analysis, integral equations, continuum mechanics. *Total annual research expenditures:* $506,890. *Unit head:* Dr. Raymond Cheng, Graduate Program Director, 757-683-3882, Fax: 757-683-3885, E-mail: rcheng@odu.edu. *Application contact:* William Heffelfinger, Director of Graduate Admissions, 757-683-5554, Fax: 757-683-3255, E-mail: gradadmit@odu.edu. Website: http://sci.odu.edu/math/academics/grad.shtml.

Oregon State University, College of Science, Department of Mathematics, Corvallis, OR 97331. Offers MA, MAIS, MS, PhD. *Faculty:* 45 full-time (15 women), 5 part-time/adjunct (3 women). *Students:* 61 full-time (18 women), 2 part-time (1 woman); includes 7 minority (2 Black or African American, non-Hispanic/Latino; 1 Asian, non-Hispanic/Latino; 2 Hispanic/Latino; 1 Native Hawaiian or other Pacific Islander, non-Hispanic/Latino; 1 Two or more races, non-Hispanic/Latino), 14 international. Average age 28. 127 applicants, 33% accepted, 19 enrolled. In 2012, 13 master's, 5 doctorates awarded. Terminal master's awarded for partial completion of doctoral program. *Degree requirements:* For master's, variable foreign language requirement, thesis or alternative; for doctorate, one foreign language, thesis/dissertation, qualifying exams. *Entrance requirements:* For master's and doctorate, minimum GPA of 3.0 in last 90 hours. Additional exam requirements/recommendations for international students: Required—TOEFL. *Application deadline:* For fall admission, 3/1 for domestic students. Applications are processed on a rolling basis. Application fee: $50. *Expenses:* Tuition, state resident: full-time $11,367; part-time $421 per credit hour. Tuition, nonresident: full-time $18,279; part-time $677 per credit hour. *Required fees:* $1478. One-time fee: $300 full-time. Tuition and fees vary according to course load and program. *Financial support:* Research assistantships, teaching assistantships, Federal Work-Study, and institutionally sponsored loans available. Support available to part-time students. Financial award application deadline: 2/1. *Unit head:* Dr. Thomas P. Dick, Chair, 541-737-1570, E-mail: tpdick@math.oregonstate.edu. *Application contact:* Dr. David V. Finch, Graduate Chair, 541-737-5157, E-mail: finch@math.oregonstate.edu.

Penn State University Park, Graduate School, Eberly College of Science, Department of Mathematics, State College, University Park, PA 16802-1503. Offers applied mathematics (MA); mathematics (M Ed, D Ed, PhD). *Unit head:* Dr. Yuxi Zheng, Head, 814-865-0361, E-mail: yzheng@psu.edu. *Application contact:* Dr. Dimitri Burago, Associate Head of Graduate Studies, 814-865-7741, E-mail: burago@math.psu.edu. Website: http://www.math.psu.edu.

Pittsburg State University, Graduate School, College of Arts and Sciences, Department of Mathematics, Pittsburg, KS 66762. Offers MS. *Degree requirements:* For master's, thesis or alternative. *Faculty research:* Operations research, numerical analysis, applied analysis, applied algebra.

Polytechnic Institute of New York University, Department of Mathematics, Brooklyn, NY 11201-2990. Offers MS, PhD. Part-time and evening/weekend programs available. *Faculty:* 3 full-time (1 woman), 2 part-time/adjunct (0 women). *Students:* 15 full-time (2 women), 17 part-time (4 women); includes 11 minority (4 Black or African American, non-Hispanic/Latino; 5 Asian, non-Hispanic/Latino; 2 Hispanic/Latino), 12 international. Average age 32. 68 applicants, 41% accepted, 16 enrolled. In 2012, 4 master's, 1 doctorate awarded. *Degree requirements:* For master's, comprehensive exam (for some programs), thesis (for some programs); for doctorate, comprehensive exam, thesis/dissertation. *Entrance requirements:* Additional exam requirements/recommendations for international students: Required—TOEFL (minimum score 550 paper-based; 80 iBT); Recommended—IELTS (minimum score 6.5). *Application deadline:* For fall admission, 7/31 priority date for domestic students, 4/30 for international students; for spring admission, 12/31 priority date for domestic students, 11/30 for international students. Applications are processed on a rolling basis. Application fee: $75. Electronic applications accepted. *Financial support:* Institutionally sponsored loans, scholarships/grants, and unspecified assistantships available. Support available to part-time students. Financial award applicants required to submit FAFSA. *Total annual research expenditures:* $135,157. *Unit head:* Dr. Erwin Lutwak, Head, 718-260-3366, Fax: 718-260-3139, E-mail: lutwak@magnus.poly.edu. *Application contact:* Raymond Lutzky, Director of Graduate Enrollment Management, 718-637-5984, Fax: 718-260-3624, E-mail: rlutzky@poly.edu.

Portland State University, Graduate Studies, College of Liberal Arts and Sciences, Department of Mathematics and Statistics, Portland, OR 97207-0751. Offers mathematical sciences (PhD); mathematics education (PhD); statistics (MS); MA/MS. *Degree requirements:* For master's, thesis or alternative, exams; for doctorate, 2 foreign languages, thesis/dissertation, exams. *Entrance requirements:* For master's, GRE General Test, GRE Subject Test, minimum GPA of 3.0 in upper-division course work or 2.75 overall; for doctorate, GRE General Test. Additional exam requirements/recommendations for international students: Required—TOEFL (minimum score 550 paper-based). *Faculty research:* Algebra, topology, statistical distribution theory, control theory, statistical robustness.

Portland State University, Graduate Studies, Systems Science Program, Portland, OR 97207-0751. Offers computational intelligence (Certificate); computer modeling and simulation (Certificate); systems science (MS); systems science/anthropology (PhD); systems science/business administration (PhD); systems science/civil engineering (PhD); systems science/economics (PhD); systems science/engineering management (PhD); systems science/general (PhD); systems science/mathematical sciences (PhD); systems science/mechanical engineering (PhD); systems science/psychology (PhD); systems science/sociology (PhD). *Degree requirements:* For doctorate, variable foreign language requirement, thesis/dissertation. *Entrance requirements:* For master's, 2 letters of recommendation; for doctorate, GMAT, GRE General Test, minimum undergraduate GPA of 3.0. Additional exam requirements/recommendations for international students: Required—TOEFL. *Faculty research:* Systems theory and methodology, artificial intelligence neural networks, information theory, nonlinear dynamics/chaos, modeling and simulation.

Prairie View A&M University, College of Arts and Sciences, Department of Mathematics, Prairie View, TX 77446-0519. Offers MS. Part-time and evening/weekend programs available. *Degree requirements:* For master's, comprehensive exam, thesis. *Entrance requirements:* For master's, GRE General Test, bachelor's degree in mathematics. *Faculty research:* Stochastic processor, queuing theory, waveler numeric analyses, delay systems mathematic modeling.

Princeton University, Graduate School, Department of Mathematics, Princeton, NJ 08544-1019. Offers PhD. *Degree requirements:* For doctorate, 2 foreign languages, thesis/dissertation. *Entrance requirements:* For doctorate, GRE General Test, GRE Subject Test, 3 letters of recommendation. Additional exam requirements/recommendations for international students: Required—TOEFL (minimum score 600 paper-based). Electronic applications accepted.

Purdue University, Graduate School, College of Science, Department of Mathematics, West Lafayette, IN 47907. Offers MS, PhD. *Faculty:* 66 full-time (10 women), 13 part-time/adjunct (4 women). *Students:* 148 full-time (32 women), 11 part-time (1 woman); includes 14 minority (2 Black or African American, non-Hispanic/Latino; 4 Asian, non-Hispanic/Latino; 6 Hispanic/Latino; 2 Two or more races, non-Hispanic/Latino), 83 international. Average age 27. 533 applicants, 11% accepted, 21 enrolled. In 2012, 6 master's, 15 doctorates awarded. Terminal master's awarded for partial completion of doctoral program. *Degree requirements:* For doctorate, one foreign language, thesis/dissertation, oral and written exams. *Entrance requirements:* For master's and doctorate, GRE General Test, GRE Subject Test in advanced mathematics (strongly recommended), minimum undergraduate GPA of 3.0 or equivalent. Additional exam requirements/recommendations for international students: Required—TOEFL (minimum score 570 paper-based; 77 iBT). *Application deadline:* For fall admission, 1/15 for domestic and international students; for spring admission, 12/1 for domestic students, 10/15 for international students. Application fee: $60 ($75 for international students). Electronic applications accepted. *Financial support:* In 2012–13, fellowships with full and partial tuition reimbursements (averaging $16,000 per year), teaching assistantships with partial tuition reimbursements (averaging $16,020 per year) were awarded. Support available to part-time students. Financial award application deadline: 3/1; financial award applicants required to submit FAFSA. *Faculty research:* Algebra, analysis, topology, differential equations, applied mathematics. *Unit head:* Dr. Laszlo Lempert, Head, 765-494-1908, Fax: 765-494-0548, E-mail: lempert@purdue.edu. *Application contact:* Rebecca A. Lank, Graduate Contact, 765-494-1961, Fax: 765-494-0548, E-mail: lankr@purdue.edu. Website: http://www.math.purdue.edu/.

Purdue University Calumet, Graduate Studies Office, School of Engineering, Mathematics, and Science, Department of Mathematics, Computer Science, and Statistics, Hammond, IN 46323-2094. Offers computer science (MS); mathematics (MAT, MS). Part-time programs available. *Entrance requirements:* Additional exam requirements/recommendations for international students: Required—TOEFL. *Faculty research:* Topology, analysis, algebra, mathematics education.

Queens College of the City University of New York, Division of Graduate Studies, Mathematics and Natural Sciences Division, Department of Mathematics, Flushing, NY 11367-1597. Offers MA. Part-time and evening/weekend programs available. *Faculty:* 32 full-time (8 women), 51 part-time/adjunct (19 women). *Students:* 2 full-time (1 woman), 53 part-time (25 women); includes 31 minority (5 Black or African American, non-Hispanic/Latino; 21 Asian, non-Hispanic/Latino; 5 Hispanic/Latino), 5 international. 42 applicants, 74% accepted, 17 enrolled. In 2012, 13 master's awarded. *Degree requirements:* For master's, comprehensive exam. *Entrance requirements:* For master's, minimum GPA of 3.0. Additional exam requirements/recommendations for international students: Required—TOEFL. *Application deadline:* For fall admission, 4/1 for domestic students; for spring admission, 11/1 for domestic students. Applications are processed on a rolling basis. Application fee: $125. *Expenses:* Tuition, state resident: full-time $8090; part-time $365 per credit. Tuition, nonresident: full-time $16,200; part-time $675 per credit. Full-time tuition and fees vary according to course load. *Financial support:* Career-related internships or fieldwork available. Financial award application deadline: 4/1; financial award applicants required to submit FAFSA. *Unit head:* Dr. Wallace Goldberg, Chairperson, 718-997-5800, E-mail: wallace_goldberg@qc.edu. *Application contact:* Dr. Nick Metas, Graduate Adviser, 718-997-5800, E-mail: nick_metas@qc.edu.

Queen's University at Kingston, School of Graduate Studies and Research, Faculty of Arts and Sciences, Department of Mathematics and Statistics, Kingston, ON K7L 3N6, Canada. Offers mathematics (M Sc, M Sc Eng, PhD); statistics (M Sc, M Sc Eng, PhD). Part-time programs available. *Degree requirements:* For master's, thesis; for doctorate, comprehensive exam, thesis/dissertation. *Entrance requirements:* Additional exam requirements/

Peterson's Graduate Programs in the Physical Sciences, Mathematics, Agricultural Sciences, the Environment & Natural Resources 2014

www.petersonsbooks.com **331**

recommendations for international students: Required—TOEFL. *Faculty research:* Algebra, analysis, applied mathematics, statistics.

Rensselaer Polytechnic Institute, Graduate School, School of Science, Program in Mathematics, Troy, NY 12180-3590. Offers MS, PhD. *Faculty:* 23 full-time (4 women), 4 part-time/adjunct (1 woman). *Students:* 54 full-time (16 women), 4 part-time; includes 6 minority (2 Black or African American, non-Hispanic/Latino; 2 Asian, non-Hispanic/Latino; 1 Hispanic/Latino; 1 Two or more races, non-Hispanic/Latino), 7 international. Average age 27. 121 applicants, 42% accepted, 18 enrolled. In 2012, 11 master's, 8 doctorates awarded. Terminal master's awarded for partial completion of doctoral program. *Degree requirements:* For doctorate, comprehensive exam, thesis/dissertation. *Entrance requirements:* For master's and doctorate, GRE. Additional exam requirements/recommendations for international students: Required—TOEFL (minimum score 600 paper-based, 100 iBT), IELTS (minimum score 7), or Pearson Test of English (minimum score 68). *Application deadline:* For fall admission, 1/1 priority date for domestic students, 1/1 for international students; for spring admission, 8/15 priority date for domestic students, 8/15 for international students. Applications are processed on a rolling basis. Application fee: $75. Electronic applications accepted. *Financial support:* In 2012–13, research assistantships (averaging $18,500 per year), teaching assistantships (averaging $18,500 per year) were awarded; fellowships also available. Financial award application deadline: 1/1. *Faculty research:* Acoustics, applied geometry, approximation theory, bioinformatics, biomathematics, chemically-reacting flows, data-driven modeling, dynamical systems, environmental problems, fluid dynamics, inverse problems, machine learning, math education, mathematical physics, multiphase flows, nonlinear analysis, nonlinear materials, nonlinear waves, operations research and mathematical programming, optimization, perturbation methods, scientific computing. *Application contact:* Office of Graduate Admissions, 518-276-6216, E-mail: gradadmissions@rpi.edu. Website: http://www.math.rpi.edu/.

Rhode Island College, School of Graduate Studies, Faculty of Arts and Sciences, Department of Mathematics and Computer Science, Providence, RI 02908-1991. Offers mathematics (MA); mathematics content specialist (CGS). Part-time and evening/weekend programs available. *Faculty:* 3 full-time (1 woman). *Students:* 2 full-time (0 women), 8 part-time (3 women). Average age 30. In 2012, 5 master's awarded. *Degree requirements:* For master's, comprehensive exam. *Entrance requirements:* For master's, GRE General Test or MAT, minimum of 30 hours beyond pre-calculus math, 3 letters of recommendation, interview. Additional exam requirements/recommendations for international students: Recommended—TOEFL (minimum score 550 paper-based; 79 iBT). *Application deadline:* For fall admission, 3/1 for domestic students; for spring admission, 11/1 for domestic students. Applications are processed on a rolling basis. Application fee: $50. *Expenses:* Tuition, state resident: full-time $8928; part-time $372 per credit hour. Tuition, nonresident: full-time $17,376; part-time $724 per credit hour. *Required fees:* $602; $22 per credit. $72 per term. *Financial support:* In 2012–13, 3 teaching assistantships with full tuition reimbursements (averaging $4,550 per year) were awarded; Federal Work-Study, scholarships/grants, health care benefits, and unspecified assistantships also available. Support available to part-time students. Financial award application deadline: 5/15; financial award applicants required to submit FAFSA. *Unit head:* Dr. Raimundo Kovac, Chair, 401-456-8038. *Application contact:* Graduate Studies, 401-456-8700. Website: http://www.ric.edu/mathComputerScience/index.php.

Rice University, Graduate Programs, Wiess School of Natural Sciences, Department of Mathematics, Houston, TX 77251-1892. Offers PhD. Terminal master's awarded for partial completion of doctoral program. *Degree requirements:* For doctorate, one foreign language, comprehensive exam, thesis/dissertation. *Entrance requirements:* For doctorate, GRE Subject Test, GRE General Test. Additional exam requirements/recommendations for international students: Required—TOEFL (minimum score 600 paper-based; 90 iBT). Electronic applications accepted. *Faculty research:* Algebraic geometry/algebra, complex analysis and Teichmuller theory, dynamical systems and Ergodic theory, topology, differential geometry and geometric analysis.

Rivier University, School of Graduate Studies, Department of Computer Science and Mathematics, Nashua, NH 03060. Offers computer science (MS); mathematics (MAT). Part-time and evening/weekend programs available. *Entrance requirements:* For master's, GRE Subject Test. Electronic applications accepted.

Roosevelt University, Graduate Division, College of Arts and Sciences, Department of Mathematics and Actuarial Science, Program in Mathematics, Chicago, IL 60605. Offers mathematical sciences (MS), including actuarial science. Part-time and evening/weekend programs available. *Faculty research:* Statistics, mathematics education, finite groups, computers in mathematics.

Rowan University, Graduate School, College of Science and Mathematics, MA Program in Mathematics, Glassboro, NJ 08028-1701. Offers MA. Part-time and evening/weekend programs available. *Degree requirements:* For master's, thesis. *Entrance requirements:* For master's, GRE General Test. Additional exam requirements/recommendations for international students: Required—TOEFL. Electronic applications accepted.

Royal Military College of Canada, Division of Graduate Studies and Research, Science Division, Department of Mathematics and Computer Science, Kingston, ON K7K 7B4, Canada. Offers computer science (M Sc); mathematics (M Sc). *Degree requirements:* For master's, thesis. *Entrance requirements:* For master's, honours degree with second-class standing. Electronic applications accepted.

Rutgers, The State University of New Jersey, Camden, Graduate School of Arts and Sciences, Program in Mathematical Sciences, Camden, NJ 08102. Offers industrial mathematics (MBS); industrial/applied mathematics (MS); mathematical computer science (MS); pure mathematics (MS); teaching in mathematical sciences (MS). Part-time and evening/weekend programs available. *Degree requirements:* For master's, comprehensive exam, thesis optional, survey paper, 30 credits. *Entrance requirements:* For master's, GRE, BS/BA in math or related subject, 2 letters of recommendation. Additional exam requirements/recommendations for international students: Required—TOEFL (minimum score 550 paper-based), IELTS. Electronic applications accepted. *Faculty research:* Differential geometry, dynamical systems, vertex operator algebra, automorphic forms, CR-structures.

Rutgers, The State University of New Jersey, Newark, Graduate School, Program in Mathematical Sciences, Newark, NJ 07102. Offers PhD. *Degree requirements:* For doctorate, thesis/dissertation, written qualifying exam. *Entrance requirements:* For doctorate, GRE General Test, minimum B average. Additional exam requirements/recommendations for international students: Required—TOEFL. Electronic applications accepted. *Faculty research:* Number theory, automorphic form, low-dimensional topology, Kleinian groups, representation theory.

Rutgers, The State University of New Jersey, New Brunswick, Graduate School-New Brunswick, Department of Mathematics, Piscataway, NJ 08854-8097. Offers applied mathematics (MS, PhD); mathematics (MS, PhD). Part-time programs available. *Degree requirements:* For doctorate, one foreign language, comprehensive exam, thesis/dissertation. *Entrance requirements:* For master's and doctorate, GRE General Test, GRE Subject Test. Additional exam requirements/recommendations for international students: Required—TOEFL. *Faculty research:* Logic and set theory, number theory, mathematical physics, control theory, partial differential equations.

St. Cloud State University, School of Graduate Studies, College of Science and Engineering, Program in Mathematics, St. Cloud, MN 56301-4498. Offers MS. *Degree requirements:* For master's, comprehensive exam (for some programs), thesis or alternative. *Entrance requirements:* For master's, GRE General Test, minimum GPA of 2.75. Additional exam requirements/recommendations for international students: Required—Michigan English Language Assessment Battery; Recommended—TOEFL (minimum score 550 paper-based), IELTS (minimum score 6.5). Electronic applications accepted.

Saint Joseph's University, College of Arts and Sciences, Department of Mathematics and Computer Science, Philadelphia, PA 19131-1395. Offers computer science (MS); mathematics and computer science (Post-Master's Certificate). Part-time and evening/weekend programs available. *Faculty:* 5 full-time (2 women). *Students:* 48 full-time (17 women), 23 part-time (8 women); includes 7 minority (3 Black or African American, non-Hispanic/Latino; 4 Asian, non-Hispanic/Latino), 48 international. Average age 27. 109 applicants, 32% accepted, 24 enrolled. In 2012, 26 master's awarded. *Entrance requirements:* For master's, 2 letters of recommendation, resume, personal statement, official transcripts. Additional exam requirements/recommendations for international students: Required—TOEFL (minimum score 550 paper-based; 80 iBT), IELTS (minimum score 6.2). *Application deadline:* For fall admission, 7/15 priority date for domestic students, 4/15 for international students; for winter admission, 4/15 for domestic students, 1/15 for international students; for spring admission, 11/15 priority date for domestic students, 10/15 for international students. Applications are processed on a rolling basis. Application fee: $35. Electronic applications accepted. *Expenses: Tuition:* Part-time $786 per credit hour. Tuition and fees vary according to degree level and program. *Financial support:* Teaching assistantships with partial tuition reimbursements and unspecified assistantships available. Financial award applicants required to submit FAFSA. *Faculty research:* Computer vision, pathways to careers. *Unit head:* Dr. George Grevera, Director, Graduate Computer Science, 610-660-1535, Fax: 610-660-3082, E-mail: ggrevera@sju.edu. *Application contact:* Elisabeth Woodward, Director of Marketing and Admissions, Graduate Arts and Sciences, 610-660-3131, Fax: 610-660-3230, E-mail: gradstudies@sju.edu. Website: http://sju.edu/majors-programs/graduate-arts-sciences/masters/computer-science-ms.

Saint Louis University, Graduate Education, College of Arts and Sciences and Graduate Education, Department of Mathematics and Computer Science, St. Louis, MO 63103-2097. Offers mathematics (MA, MA-R, PhD). Part-time programs available. *Degree requirements:* For master's, comprehensive exam, thesis (for some programs); for doctorate, one foreign language, thesis/dissertation, preliminary exams. *Entrance requirements:* For master's, GRE General Test, letters of recommendation, resume, interview; for doctorate, GRE General Test, letters of recommendation, resumé, interview, transcripts, goal statement. Additional exam requirements/recommendations for international students: Required—TOEFL (minimum score 525 paper-based). Electronic applications accepted. *Faculty research:* Algebra, groups and rings, analysis, differential geometry, topology.

Salem State University, School of Graduate Studies, Program in Mathematics, Salem, MA 01970-5353. Offers MAT, MS. Part-time and evening/weekend programs available. *Students:* 12 part-time (5 women); includes 3 minority (all Black or African American, non-Hispanic/Latino), 2 international. 6 applicants, 100% accepted, 5 enrolled. In 2012, 10 master's awarded. *Entrance requirements:* For master's, GRE or MAT. Additional exam requirements/recommendations for international students: Required—TOEFL (minimum score

550 paper-based; 80 iBT) or IELTS (minimum score 5.5). *Application deadline:* For fall admission, 5/1 for domestic students; for spring admission, 10/1 for domestic students. Applications are processed on a rolling basis. Application fee: $50. *Expenses:* Tuition, state resident: part-time $140 per credit. Tuition, nonresident: part-time $230 per credit. *Required fees:* $190 per credit. *Financial support:* Career-related internships or fieldwork, Federal Work-Study, scholarships/grants, health care benefits, and unspecified assistantships available. Financial award application deadline: 5/1; financial award applicants required to submit FAFSA. *Unit head:* Julie Belock, Program Coordinator, 978-542-6321, Fax: 978-542-7175, E-mail: jbelock@salemstate.edu. *Application contact:* Dr. Lee A. Brossoit, Assistant Dean of Graduate Admissions, 978-542-6675, Fax: 978-542-7215, E-mail: lbrossoit@salemstate.edu. Website: http://www.salemstate.edu/academics/schools/890.php.

Sam Houston State University, College of Sciences, Department of Mathematics and Statistics, Huntsville, TX 77341. Offers mathematics (MA, MS); statistics (MS). Part-time programs available. *Faculty:* 26 full-time (7 women). *Students:* 25 full-time (9 women), 17 part-time (10 women); includes 5 minority (1 Black or African American, non-Hispanic/Latino; 3 Asian, non-Hispanic/Latino; 1 Hispanic/Latino), 16 international. Average age 31. 40 applicants, 65% accepted, 16 enrolled. In 2012, 14 master's awarded. *Degree requirements:* For master's, comprehensive exam, thesis optional. *Entrance requirements:* For master's, GRE General Test. Additional exam requirements/recommendations for international students: Required—TOEFL (minimum score 550 paper-based; 79 iBT). *Application deadline:* For fall admission, 8/1 for domestic students, 6/25 for international students; for spring admission, 12/1 for domestic students, 11/12 for international students. Applications are processed on a rolling basis. Application fee: $45 ($75 for international students). Electronic applications accepted. *Expenses:* Tuition, state resident: full-time $2205; part-time $245 per credit hour. Tuition, nonresident: full-time $5391; part-time $599 per credit hour. *Required fees:* $67 per credit hour. $367 per semester. Tuition and fees vary according to course load and campus/location. *Financial support:* In 2012–13, 20 teaching assistantships (averaging $10,081 per year) were awarded; career-related internships or fieldwork, institutionally sponsored loans, scholarships/grants, and unspecified assistantships also available. Support available to part-time students. Financial award application deadline: 5/31; financial award applicants required to submit FAFSA. *Total annual research expenditures:* $402,573. *Unit head:* Dr. Brian Loft, Chair, 936-294-1465, Fax: 936-294-1882, E-mail: loft@shsu.edu. *Application contact:* Dr. Ken Smith, Advisor, 936-294-4869, Fax: 936-294-1882, E-mail: kws006@shsu.edu. Website: http://www.shsu.edu/~mcss_www/.

San Diego State University, Graduate and Research Affairs, College of Sciences, Department of Mathematics and Statistics, San Diego, CA 92182. Offers applied mathematics (MS); mathematics (MA); mathematics and science education (PhD); statistics (MS). PhD offered jointly wtih University of California, San Diego. Part-time programs available. *Degree requirements:* For doctorate, thesis/dissertation. *Entrance requirements:* For master's, GRE General Test; for doctorate, GRE, minimum GPA of 3.25 in last 30 undergraduate semester units, minimum graduate GPA of 3.5, MSE recommendation form, 3 letters of recommendation. Additional exam requirements/recommendations for international students: Required—TOEFL. Electronic applications accepted. *Faculty research:* Teacher education in mathematics.

San Francisco State University, Division of Graduate Studies, College of Science and Engineering, Department of Mathematics, San Francisco, CA 94132-1722. Offers MA. *Application deadline:* Applications are processed on a rolling basis. *Unit head:* Dr. David Bao, Chair, 415-338-2251, E-mail: statmath@math.sfsu.edu. *Application contact:* Dr. Eric Hayashi, Graduate Coordinator, 415-338-2251, E-mail: hayashi@math.sfsu.edu. Website: http://math.sfsu.edu.

San Jose State University, Graduate Studies and Research, College of Science, Department of Mathematics, San Jose, CA 95192-0001. Offers applied mathematics (MS); mathematics (MA, MS); mathematics education (MA); statistics (MA). Part-time and evening/weekend programs available. *Degree requirements:* For master's, comprehensive exam, thesis (for some programs). *Entrance requirements:* For master's, GRE Subject Test. Electronic applications accepted. *Faculty research:* Artificial intelligence, algorithms, numerical analysis, software database, number theory.

Simon Fraser University, Office of Graduate Studies, Faculty of Science, Department of Mathematics, Burnaby, BC V5A 1S6, Canada. Offers applied and computational mathematics (M Sc, PhD); mathematics (M Sc, PhD); operations research (M Sc, PhD). *Faculty:* 38 full-time (6 women). *Students:* 65 full-time (17 women). 81 applicants, 48% accepted, 21 enrolled. In 2012, 15 master's, 3 doctorates awarded. *Degree requirements:* For master's, thesis or alternative; for doctorate, comprehensive exam, thesis/dissertation. *Entrance requirements:* For master's, GRE General Test, GRE Subject Test (mathematics), minimum GPA of 3.0 (on scale of 4.33), or 3.33 based on last 60 credits of undergraduate courses; for doctorate, GRE General Test, GRE Subject Test (mathematics), minimum GPA of 3.5 (on scale of 4.33). Additional exam requirements/recommendations for international students: Recommended—TOEFL (minimum score 580 paper-based; 93 iBT), IELTS (minimum score 7), TWE (minimum score 5). *Application deadline:* For fall admission, 2/1 for domestic and international students. Application fee: $90 Canadian dollars ($125 Canadian dollars for international students). Electronic applications accepted. Tuition and fees charges are reported in Canadian dollars. *Expenses: Tuition, area resident:* Full-time $5000 Canadian dollars; part-time $275 Canadian dollars per credit hour. *Required fees:* $780 Canadian dollars. *Financial support:* In 2012–13, 31 students received support, including 30 fellowships (averaging $6,250 per year), teaching assistantships (averaging $5,608 per year); research assistantships and scholarships/grants also available. *Faculty research:* Computer algebra, discrete mathematics, fluid dynamics, nonlinear partial differential equations and variational methods, numerical analysis and scientific computing. *Unit head:* Dr. Tom Archibald, Graduate Chair, 778-782-3379, Fax: 778-782-4947, E-mail: math-gsc@sfu.ca. *Application contact:* Diane Pogue, Graduate Secretary, 778-782-3059, Fax: 778-782-4947, E-mail: mathgsec@sfu.ca. Website: http://www.math.sfu.ca/.

Smith College, Graduate and Special Programs, Center for Women in Mathematics Post-Baccalaureate Program, Northampton, MA 01063. Offers Postbaccalaureate Certificate. Part-time programs available. *Faculty:* 12 full-time (5 women). *Students:* 10 full-time (all women); includes 3 minority (2 Hispanic/Latino; 1 Two or more races, non-Hispanic/Latino). Average age 25. 27 applicants, 26% accepted, 6 enrolled. In 2012, 14 Postbaccalaureate Certificates awarded. *Application deadline:* For fall admission, 7/1 for domestic students; for spring admission, 12/15 for domestic students. Applications are processed on a rolling basis. Application fee: $60. *Expenses: Tuition:* Full-time $15,480; part-time $1290 per credit. *Financial support:* In 2012–13, 10 students received support. Scholarships/grants and tuition waivers (full) available. Support available to part-time students. *Unit head:* Ruth Haas, Director, 413-585-3872, E-mail: rhaas@smith.edu. *Application contact:* Jim Henle, Director, 413-585-3867, E-mail: jhenle@smith.edu.

South Dakota State University, Graduate School, College of Engineering, Department of Mathematics and Statistics, Brookings, SD 57007. Offers computational science and statistics (PhD); mathematics (MS); statistics (MS). Part-time programs available. Terminal master's awarded for partial completion of doctoral program. *Degree requirements:* For master's, thesis (for some programs), oral exam; for doctorate, comprehensive exam, thesis/dissertation, oral and written exams. *Entrance requirements:* Additional exam requirements/recommendations for international students: Required—TOEFL (minimum score 550 paper-based; 80 iBT); Recommended—IELTS. *Faculty research:* Financial mathematics, predictive analytics, operations research, bioinformatics, biostatistics, computational science, statistics, number theory, abstract algebra.

Southeast Missouri State University, School of Graduate Studies, Department of Mathematics, Cape Girardeau, MO 63701-4799. Offers MNS. Part-time and evening/weekend programs available. Postbaccalaureate distance learning degree programs offered (minimal on-campus study). *Faculty:* 12 full-time (4 women). *Students:* 2 full-time (both women), 4 part-time (3 women); includes 1 minority (Asian, non-Hispanic/Latino). Average age 33. 8 applicants, 50% accepted, 2 enrolled. In 2012, 6 master's awarded. *Degree requirements:* For master's, comprehensive exam or thesis. *Entrance requirements:* For master's, minimum undergraduate GPA of 2.5, 2.75 in last 30 hours of undergraduate course work in mathematics and science; major in mathematics or minimum C grade in prerequisite courses; 2 letters of recommendation. Additional exam requirements/recommendations for international students: Required—TOEFL (minimum score 550 paper-based; 79 iBT), IELTS (minimum score 6). *Application deadline:* For fall admission, 8/1 for domestic students, 6/1 for international students; for spring admission, 11/21 for domestic students, 10/1 for international students. Applications are processed on a rolling basis. Application fee: $30 ($40 for international students). Electronic applications accepted. *Financial support:* In 2012–13, 4 students received support, including 8 teaching assistantships with full tuition reimbursements available (averaging $7,900 per year); career-related internships or fieldwork, Federal Work-Study, scholarships/grants, traineeships, tuition waivers (full), and unspecified assistantships also available. Financial award application deadline: 6/30; financial award applicants required to submit FAFSA. *Faculty research:* Algebraic geometry, combinatorics, mathematics education, statistics, topology. *Unit head:* Dr. Tamela Randolph, Chairperson, 573-651-2164, E-mail: trandolph@semo.edu. *Application contact:* Alisa Aleen McFerron, Assistant Director of Admissions for Operations, 573-651-5937, E-mail: amcferron@semo.edu. Website: http://www5.semo.edu/math/.

Southern Connecticut State University, School of Graduate Studies, School of Arts and Sciences, Department of Mathematics, New Haven, CT 06515-1355. Offers MS. Part-time and evening/weekend programs available. *Degree requirements:* For master's, thesis or alternative. *Entrance requirements:* For master's, interview. Electronic applications accepted. *Expenses:* Tuition, state resident: full-time $5617; part-time $314 per credit. Tuition, nonresident: full-time $15,650. *Required fees:* $4355; $253 per credit. $55 per semester.

Southern Illinois University Carbondale, Graduate School, College of Science, Department of Mathematics, Carbondale, IL 62901-4701. Offers mathematics (MA, MS, PhD); statistics (MS). PhD offered jointly with Southeast Missouri State University. Part-time programs available. *Faculty:* 32 full-time (2 women), 1 part-time/adjunct (0 women). *Students:* 35 full-time (13 women), 9 part-time (3 women); includes 3 minority (1 American Indian or Alaska Native, non-Hispanic/Latino; 1 Asian, non-Hispanic/Latino; 1 Hispanic/Latino), 28 international. Average age 26. 44 applicants, 25% accepted, 9 enrolled. In 2012, 3 master's, 5 doctorates awarded. *Degree requirements:* For master's, thesis; for doctorate, 2 foreign languages, thesis/dissertation. *Entrance requirements:* For master's, minimum GPA of 2.7; for doctorate, minimum GPA of 3.25. Additional exam requirements/recommendations for international students: Required—TOEFL. *Application deadline:* Applications are processed on a rolling basis. Application fee: $50. *Financial support:* In 2012–13, 28 students received support, including 24 teaching assistantships with full tuition reimbursements available; fellowships with full tuition reimbursements available, research assistantships with full tuition

Peterson's Graduate Programs in the Physical Sciences, Mathematics, Agricultural Sciences, the Environment & Natural Resources 2014

www.petersonsbooks.com **333**

reimbursements available, Federal Work-Study, institutionally sponsored loans, and tuition waivers (full) also available. Support available to part-time students. *Faculty research:* Differential equations, combinatorics, probability, algebra, numerical analysis. *Unit head:* Dr. Michael Sullivan, Chairperson, 618-453-6517, E-mail: siu950@siu.edu. *Application contact:* Rachel Kubiak, Graduate Studies Office Specialist, 618-453-6597, Fax: 618-453-5300, E-mail: gradinfo@math.siu.edu. Website: http://www.math.siu.edu/.

Southern Illinois University Edwardsville, Graduate School, College of Arts and Sciences, Department of Mathematics and Statistics, Edwardsville, IL 62026. Offers mathematics (MS), including computational mathematics, postsecondary mathematics education, pure math, statistics and operations research. Part-time programs available. *Faculty:* 17 full-time (6 women). *Students:* 4 full-time (1 woman), 27 part-time (14 women); includes 4 minority (3 Black or African American, non-Hispanic/Latino; 1 Two or more races, non-Hispanic/Latino), 7 international. 22 applicants, 55% accepted. In 2012, 11 master's awarded. *Degree requirements:* For master's, thesis (for some programs), research paper/project. *Entrance requirements:* Additional exam requirements/recommendations for international students: Required—TOEFL (minimum score 550 paper-based; 79 iBT), IELTS (minimum score 6.5). *Application deadline:* For fall admission, 7/26 for domestic students, 6/1 for international students; for spring admission, 12/6 for domestic students, 10/1 for international students. Applications are processed on a rolling basis. Application fee: $30. Electronic applications accepted. *Expenses:* Tuition, state resident: full-time $6504; part-time $3252 per semester. Tuition, nonresident: full-time $8130; part-time $4065 per semester. *Required fees:* $705.50 per semester. Tuition and fees vary according to course level, course load, degree level, program and student level. *Financial support:* In 2012–13, research assistantships with full tuition reimbursements (averaging $9,585 per year), 13 teaching assistantships with full tuition reimbursements (averaging $9,585 per year) were awarded; fellowships with full tuition reimbursements, institutionally sponsored loans, scholarships/grants, and unspecified assistantships also available. Financial award application deadline: 3/1; financial award applicants required to submit FAFSA. *Unit head:* Dr. Krzysztof Jarosz, Chair, 618-650-2354, E-mail: kjarosz@siue.edu. *Application contact:* Dr. Myung Sin Song, Director, 618-650-2580, E-mail: msong@siue.edu. Website: http://www.siue.edu/artsandsciences/math/.

Southern Methodist University, Dedman College, Department of Mathematics, Dallas, TX 75275. Offers computational and applied mathematics (MS, PhD). *Degree requirements:* For master's, oral exams; for doctorate, thesis/dissertation, oral and written exams. *Entrance requirements:* For master's and doctorate, GRE General Test, minimum GPA of 3.0, 18 undergraduate hours in mathematics beyond first and second year calculus. Additional exam requirements/recommendations for international students: Required—TOEFL. Electronic applications accepted. *Faculty research:* Numerical analysis and scientific computation, fluid dynamics, optics, wave propagation, mathematical biology.

Southern University and Agricultural and Mechanical College, Graduate School, College of Sciences, Department of Mathematics, Baton Rouge, LA 70813. Offers MS. *Degree requirements:* For master's, comprehensive exam, thesis optional. *Entrance requirements:* For master's, GMAT, GRE General Test. Additional exam requirements/recommendations for international students: Required—TOEFL. *Faculty research:* Algebraic number theory, abstract algebra, computer analysis, probability, mathematics education.

Stanford University, School of Engineering, Program in Scientific Computing and Computational Mathematics, Stanford, CA 94305-9991. Offers MS, PhD. Terminal master's awarded for partial completion of doctoral program. *Degree requirements:* For doctorate, thesis/dissertation, qualifying exam. *Entrance requirements:* For master's, GRE General Test; for doctorate, GRE General Test, GRE Subject Test. Additional exam requirements/recommendations for international students: Required—TOEFL. Electronic applications accepted. *Expenses: Tuition:* Full-time $41,250; part-time $917 per credit hour.

Stanford University, School of Humanities and Sciences, Department of Mathematics, Stanford, CA 94305-9991. Offers financial mathematics (MS); mathematics (MS, PhD). Terminal master's awarded for partial completion of doctoral program. *Degree requirements:* For doctorate, 2 foreign languages, thesis/dissertation, oral exam. *Entrance requirements:* For master's, GRE General Test; for doctorate, GRE General Test, GRE Subject Test. Additional exam requirements/recommendations for international students: Required—TOEFL. Electronic applications accepted. *Expenses: Tuition:* Full-time $41,250; part-time $917 per credit hour.

State University of New York at Fredonia, Graduate Studies, Department of Mathematical Sciences, Fredonia, NY 14063-1136. Offers MS Ed. Part-time and evening/weekend programs available. *Degree requirements:* For master's, thesis optional. *Expenses:* Tuition, state resident: full-time $7020; part-time $390 per credit hour. Tuition, nonresident: full-time $12,510; part-time $695 per credit hour. *Required fees:* $1113.30; $61.85 per credit hour. Tuition and fees vary according to course load.

State University of New York College at Cortland, Graduate Studies, School of Arts and Sciences, Department of Mathematics, Cortland, NY 13045. Offers MAT, MS Ed.

State University of New York College at Potsdam, School of Arts and Sciences, Department of Mathematics, Potsdam, NY 13676. Offers MA. Part-time and evening/weekend programs available. *Faculty:* 6 full-time (2 women). *Students:* 1 full-time (0 women), 2 part-time (1 woman); includes 1 minority (Two or more races, non-Hispanic/Latino). 1 applicant, 100% accepted, 1 enrolled. In 2012, 3 master's awarded. *Entrance requirements:* For master's, minimum GPA of 3.0 in all undergraduate math courses, 2.75 in last 60 hours of undergraduate coursework. Additional exam requirements/recommendations for international students: Required—TOEFL (minimum score 550 paper-based; 80 iBT), IELTS (minimum score 6). *Application deadline:* For fall admission, 4/1 priority date for domestic students, 4/1 for international students; for winter admission, 10/15 for domestic and international students; for spring admission, 3/1 priority date for domestic students, 3/1 for international students. Applications are processed on a rolling basis. Application fee: $50. Electronic applications accepted. *Expenses:* Tuition, state resident: full-time $9870; part-time $411 per credit hour. Tuition, nonresident: full-time $18,350; part-time $764 per credit hour. *Required fees:* $1146; $47.70 per credit hour. One-time fee: $3. *Financial support:* In 2012–13, 1 student received support. Teaching assistantships with full tuition reimbursements available, Federal Work-Study, and unspecified assistantships available. Support available to part-time students. Financial award application deadline: 3/1; financial award applicants required to submit FAFSA. *Unit head:* Dr. Joel Foisy, Chairperson, 315-267-2084, Fax: 315-267-3176, E-mail: foisyjs@potsdam.edu. *Application contact:* Heather teRiele, Graduate Admissions Counselor, 315-267-2165, Fax: 315-267-4802, E-mail: graduate@potsdam.edu.

Stephen F. Austin State University, Graduate School, College of Sciences and Mathematics, Department of Mathematics and Statistics, Nacogdoches, TX 75962. Offers mathematics (MS); mathematics education (MS); statistics (MS). *Degree requirements:* For master's, comprehensive exam, thesis optional. *Entrance requirements:* For master's, GRE General Test, minimum GPA of 2.8 in last 60 hours, 2.5 overall. Additional exam requirements/recommendations for international students: Required—TOEFL. *Faculty research:* Kernel type estimators, fractal mappings, spline curve fitting, robust regression continua theory.

Stevens Institute of Technology, Graduate School, Charles V. Schaefer Jr. School of Engineering, Department of Mathematical Sciences, Program in Mathematics, Hoboken, NJ 07030. Offers MS, PhD. *Degree requirements:* For master's, thesis optional; for doctorate, one foreign language, thesis/dissertation. *Entrance requirements:* For master's and doctorate, GRE. Additional exam requirements/recommendations for international students: Required—TOEFL. Electronic applications accepted.

Stony Brook University, State University of New York, Graduate School, College of Arts and Sciences, Department of Mathematics, Stony Brook, NY 11794. Offers MA, MAT, PhD. *Faculty:* 35 full-time (5 women), 6 part-time/adjunct (1 woman). *Students:* 67 full-time (12 women), 22 part-time (16 women); includes 8 minority (1 Black or African American, non-Hispanic/Latino; 3 Asian, non-Hispanic/Latino; 3 Hispanic/Latino; 1 Two or more races, non-Hispanic/Latino), 41 international. Average age 27. 329 applicants, 12% accepted, 24 enrolled. In 2012, 12 master's, 12 doctorates awarded. *Degree requirements:* For doctorate, 2 foreign languages, thesis/dissertation. *Entrance requirements:* For master's and doctorate, GRE General Test. Additional exam requirements/recommendations for international students: Required—TOEFL. *Application deadline:* For fall admission, 1/15 for domestic students. Application fee: $100. *Expenses:* Tuition, state resident: full-time $9370. Tuition, nonresident: full-time $16,680. *Required fees:* $1214. *Financial support:* In 2012–13, 14 research assistantships, 44 teaching assistantships were awarded; fellowships also available. *Faculty research:* Real analysis, relativity and mathematical physics, complex analysis, topology, combinatorics. *Total annual research expenditures:* $1.5 million. *Unit head:* Dr. Leon Takhtajan, Chair, 631-632-8290, E-mail: leon.takhtajan@stonybrook.edu. *Application contact:* Dr. Claude LeBrun, Director, 631-632-8254, Fax: 631-632-7631, E-mail: claude.lebrun@stonybrook.edu. Website: http://www.math.sunysb.edu/html/index.shtml.

Syracuse University, College of Arts and Sciences, Program in Mathematics, Syracuse, NY 13244. Offers MS, PhD. Part-time programs available. Terminal master's awarded for partial completion of doctoral program. *Degree requirements:* For doctorate, 2 foreign languages, thesis/dissertation, qualifying exam. *Entrance requirements:* For master's and doctorate, GRE General Test, GRE Subject Test (recommended). Additional exam requirements/recommendations for international students: Required—TOEFL (minimum score 100 iBT). Electronic applications accepted. *Faculty research:* Pure mathematics, numerical mathematics, computing statistics.

Tarleton State University, College of Graduate Studies, College of Science and Technology, Department of Mathematics, Stephenville, TX 76402. Offers mathematics (MS). Part-time and evening/weekend programs available. *Faculty:* 7 full-time (1 woman). *Students:* 16 full-time (6 women), 5 part-time (4 women); includes 4 minority (3 Hispanic/Latino; 1 Two or more races, non-Hispanic/Latino), 1 international. Average age 26. 7 applicants, 86% accepted, 5 enrolled. In 2012, 1 master's awarded. *Degree requirements:* For master's, comprehensive exam, thesis (for some programs). *Entrance requirements:* For master's, GRE General Test, minimum GPA of 3.0. Additional exam requirements/recommendations for international students: Required—TOEFL (minimum score 550 paper-based; 80 iBT). *Application deadline:* For fall admission, 8/15 priority date for domestic students; for spring admission, 1/7 for domestic students. Applications are processed on a rolling basis. Application fee: $30 ($130 for international students). Electronic applications accepted. *Expenses:* Tuition, state resident: full-time $3311; part-time $184 per credit hour. Tuition, nonresident: full-time $9090; part-time $505 per credit hour. *Required fees:* $1446. Tuition and fees vary according to course load and campus/location. *Financial support:* Research assistantships, teaching assistantships, career-related internships or fieldwork, and Federal Work-Study available. Support available to part-time students. Financial award application deadline: 5/1; financial award applicants required to submit FAFSA. *Unit head:* Dr. Bryant Wyatt, Department Head, 254-968-9168, Fax: 254-968-9534, E-mail: wyatt@tarleton.edu. *Application contact:* Information Contact, 254-968-9104, Fax: 254-968-9670, E-mail: gradoffice@tarleton.edu. Website: http://www.tarleton.edu/COSTWEB/math.

Temple University, College of Science and Technology, Department of Mathematics, Philadelphia, PA 19122-6096. Offers applied mathematics (MA); mathematics (PhD); pure mathematics (MA). Part-time and evening/weekend programs available. *Faculty:* 56 full-time (12 women). *Students:* 27 full-time (6 women), 8 international. 71 applicants, 18% accepted, 7 enrolled. In 2012, 1 master's, 3 doctorates awarded. Terminal master's awarded for partial completion of doctoral program. *Degree requirements:* For master's, thesis optional, written exam; for doctorate, 2 foreign languages, thesis/dissertation, oral and written exams. *Entrance requirements:* For master's, GRE General Test, minimum GPA of 3.0; for doctorate, GRE General Test, GRE Subject Test, minimum GPA of 3.0. Additional exam requirements/recommendations for international students: Required—TOEFL (minimum score 550 paper-based; 79 iBT). *Application deadline:* For fall admission, 2/15 priority date for domestic students, 12/15 for international students; for spring admission, 11/15 priority date for domestic students, 8/1 for international students. Applications are processed on a rolling basis. Application fee: $60. Electronic applications accepted. *Financial support:* Fellowships, research assistantships, teaching assistantships, Federal Work-Study, and institutionally sponsored loans available. Financial award application deadline: 1/15; financial award applicants required to submit FAFSA. *Faculty research:* Differential geometry, numerical analysis. *Unit head:* Dr. Gerardo Mendoza, Graduate Chair, 215-204-5053, Fax: 215-204-6433, E-mail: mathematics@temple.edu. *Application contact:* Alexis Cogan, Administrative Assistant, 215-204-7840, E-mail: cogana@temple.edu. Website: http://math.temple.edu/.

Tennessee State University, The School of Graduate Studies and Research, College of Arts and Sciences, Department of Physics and Mathematics, Nashville, TN 37209-1561. Offers mathematical sciences (MS). *Entrance requirements:* For master's, GRE General Test. Electronic applications accepted.

Tennessee Technological University, Graduate School, College of Arts and Sciences, Department of Mathematics, Cookeville, TN 38505. Offers MS. Part-time programs available. *Faculty:* 17 full-time (4 women). *Students:* 10 full-time (1 woman), 1 part-time (0 women); includes 2 minority (1 Hispanic/Latino; 1 Two or more races, non-Hispanic/Latino), 2 international. Average age 27. 25 applicants, 52% accepted, 6 enrolled. In 2012, 2 master's awarded. *Degree requirements:* For master's, thesis or alternative. *Entrance requirements:* For master's, GRE General Test. Additional exam requirements/recommendations for international students: Required—TOEFL (minimum score 527 paper-based; 71 iBT), IELTS (minimum score 5.5), Pearson Test of English. *Application deadline:* For fall admission, 8/1 for domestic students, 5/1 for international students; for spring admission, 12/1 for domestic students, 10/1 for international students. Application fee: $35 ($40 for international students). Electronic applications accepted. *Expenses:* Tuition, state resident: full-time $8444; part-time $441 per credit hour. Tuition, nonresident: full-time $21,404; part-time $1089 per credit hour. *Financial support:* In 2012–13, 3 research assistantships (averaging $7,500 per year), 7 teaching assistantships (averaging $7,500 per year) were awarded. Financial award application deadline: 4/1. *Unit head:* Dr. Allan Mills, Interim Chairperson, 931-372-3441, Fax: 931-372-6353, E-mail: amills@tntech.edu. *Application contact:* Shelia K. Kendrick, Coordinator of Graduate Admissions, 931-372-3808, Fax: 931-372-3497, E-mail: skendrick@tntech.edu.

Texas A&M International University, Office of Graduate Studies and Research, College of Arts and Sciences, Department of Engineering, Mathematics, and Physics, Laredo, TX 78041-1900. Offers mathematics (MS). *Degree requirements:* For master's, comprehensive exam, thesis (for some programs). *Entrance requirements:* For master's, GRE General Test. Additional exam requirements/recommendations for international students: Required—TOEFL (minimum score 550 paper-based; 79 iBT).

Texas A&M University, College of Science, Department of Mathematics, College Station, TX 77843. Offers MS, PhD. Part-time programs available. Postbaccalaureate distance learning degree programs offered (minimal on-campus study). *Faculty:* 54. *Students:* 126 full-time (39 women), 29 part-time (12 women); includes 9 minority (1 Black or African American, non-Hispanic/Latino; 3 Asian, non-Hispanic/Latino; 3 Hispanic/Latino; 2 Two or more races, non-Hispanic/Latino), 85 international. Average age 28. In 2012, 19 master's, 17 doctorates awarded. Terminal master's awarded for partial completion of doctoral program. *Degree requirements:* For master's, comprehensive exam, thesis optional; for doctorate, one foreign language, comprehensive exam, thesis/dissertation. *Entrance requirements:* For master's and doctorate, GRE General Test. Additional exam requirements/recommendations for international students: Required—TOEFL (minimum score 550 paper-based). *Application deadline:* For fall admission, 3/1 for domestic and international students; for spring admission, 8/1 for domestic and international students. Applications are processed on a rolling basis. Application fee: $50 ($75 for international students). Electronic applications accepted. *Financial support:* In 2012–13, fellowships with partial tuition reimbursements (averaging $17,850 per year), research assistantships

with partial tuition reimbursements (averaging $17,850 per year), teaching assistantships with partial tuition reimbursements (averaging $17,850 per year) were awarded; career-related internships or fieldwork, institutionally sponsored loans, scholarships/grants, and unspecified assistantships also available. Financial award application deadline: 3/1; financial award applicants required to submit FAFSA. *Faculty research:* Functional analysis, numerical analysis, algebra, geometry/topology, applied mathematics. *Unit head:* Dr. Emil Straube, Head, 979-845-9424, Fax: 979-845-6028, E-mail: e-straube@tamu.edu. *Application contact:* Monique Stewart, Academic Advisor I, 979-862-4137, Fax: 979-862-4190, E-mail: stewart@math.tamu.edu. Website: http://www.math.tamu.edu/.

Texas A&M University–Commerce, Graduate School, College of Science, Engineering and Agriculture, Department of Mathematics, Commerce, TX 75429-3011. Offers MA, MS. Part-time programs available. *Degree requirements:* For master's, comprehensive exam, thesis (for some programs). *Entrance requirements:* For master's, GRE General Test. Electronic applications accepted. *Expenses:* Tuition, state resident: full-time $3630; part-time $2420 per year. Tuition, nonresident: full-time $9948; part-time $6632.16 per year. *Required fees:* $1006 per year.

Texas A&M University–Corpus Christi, Graduate Studies and Research, College of Science and Technology, Program in Mathematics, Corpus Christi, TX 78412-5503. Offers applied and computational mathematics (MS); curriculum content (MS). Part-time programs available. *Degree requirements:* For master's, thesis (for some programs). *Entrance requirements:* For master's, 2 letters of recommendation.

Texas A&M University–Kingsville, College of Graduate Studies, College of Arts and Sciences, Department of Mathematics, Kingsville, TX 78363. Offers MS. Part-time programs available. *Degree requirements:* For master's, comprehensive exam, thesis or alternative. *Entrance requirements:* For master's, GRE General Test. Additional exam requirements/recommendations for international students: Required—TOEFL. *Faculty research:* Complex analysis, multivariate analysis, algebra, numerical analysis, applied statistics.

Texas Christian University, College of Science and Engineering, Department of Mathematics, Fort Worth, TX 76129-0002. Offers applied mathematics (MS); mathematics (MAT); pure mathematics (MS, PhD). Part-time and evening/weekend programs available. *Faculty:* 12 full-time (2 women). *Students:* 6 full-time (2 women), 9 part-time (3 women); includes 2 minority (1 Asian, non-Hispanic/Latino; 1 Hispanic/Latino), 2 international. Average age 26. 28 applicants, 54% accepted, 6 enrolled. In 2012, 4 master's awarded. Terminal master's awarded for partial completion of doctoral program. *Degree requirements:* For master's, thesis optional; for doctorate, comprehensive exam, thesis/dissertation. *Entrance requirements:* For master's and doctorate, GRE, 24 hours of math, including courses in elementary calculus of one and several variables, linear algebra, abstract algebra and real analysis. Additional exam requirements/recommendations for international students: Required—TOEFL. *Application deadline:* For fall admission, 3/1 priority date for domestic students, 3/1 for international students; for spring admission, 10/15 priority date for domestic students, 10/15 for international students. Applications are processed on a rolling basis. Application fee: $60. Electronic applications accepted. *Expenses: Tuition:* Full-time $21,600; part-time $1200 per credit. *Required fees:* $48. Tuition and fees vary according to program. *Financial support:* In 2012–13, 14 students received support, including 7 research assistantships with full tuition reimbursements available (averaging $17,500 per year), 4 teaching assistantships with full tuition reimbursements available (averaging $10,000 per year); tuition waivers (full) also available. Support available to part-time students. Financial award application deadline: 3/1. *Faculty research:* Differential geometry, topology, analysis, number theory, algebraic geometry. *Unit head:* Dr. George Gilbert, Associate Professor and Chair, 817-257-6061, E-mail: g.gilbert@tcu.edu. *Application contact:* Dr. Ken Richardson, Professor/Director, Graduate Program, 817-257-6128, E-mail: k.richardson@tcu.edu. Website: http://www.math.tcu.edu/.

Texas Southern University, School of Science and Technology, Department of Mathematics, Houston, TX 77004-4584. Offers MS. Part-time and evening/weekend programs available. *Faculty:* 7 full-time (2 women). *Students:* 1 full-time (0 women), 2 part-time (1 woman); all minorities (2 Black or African American, non-Hispanic/Latino; 1 Asian, non-Hispanic/Latino). Average age 30. 2 applicants. In 2012, 2 master's awarded. *Degree requirements:* For master's, comprehensive exam, thesis. *Entrance requirements:* For master's, GRE General Test, minimum GPA of 2.5. Additional exam requirements/recommendations for international students: Required—TOEFL. *Application deadline:* For fall admission, 7/1 for domestic and international students; for spring admission, 11/1 for domestic and international students. Applications are processed on a rolling basis. Application fee: $50 ($75 for international students). Electronic applications accepted. *Expenses:* Tuition, state resident: full-time $1836; part-time $100 per credit hour. Tuition, nonresident: full-time $7128; part-time $360 per credit hour. *Required fees:* $6268. *Financial support:* In 2012–13, 1 research assistantship (averaging $6,000 per year) was awarded; fellowships, teaching assistantships, scholarships/grants, and unspecified assistantships also available. Financial award application deadline: 5/1. *Faculty research:* Statistics, number theory, topology, differential equations, numerical analysis. *Unit head:* Dr. Azime Saydam, Chair, 713-313-1396, E-mail: saydamas@tsu.edu. *Application contact:* Nia Eakins, Administrative Assistant, 713-313-7002, E-mail: eakinsnm@tsu.edu. Website: http://www.cost.tsu.edu/WebPages/Mathematics.html.

Peterson's Graduate Programs in the Physical Sciences, Mathematics, Agricultural Sciences, the Environment & Natural Resources 2014

www.petersonsbooks.com **335**

Mathematics

Texas State University–San Marcos, Graduate School, College of Science and Engineering, Department of Mathematics, San Marcos, TX 78666. Offers applied mathematics (MS); mathematics (MS); mathematics education (PhD); middle school mathematics teaching (M Ed). Part-time programs available. *Faculty:* 18 full-time (5 women). *Students:* 39 full-time (25 women), 18 part-time (10 women); includes 13 minority (1 Black or African American, non-Hispanic/Latino; 2 Asian, non-Hispanic/Latino; 8 Hispanic/Latino; 2 Two or more races, non-Hispanic/Latino), 5 international. Average age 33. 34 applicants, 56% accepted, 10 enrolled. In 2012, 12 master's, 3 doctorates awarded. *Degree requirements:* For master's, comprehensive exam, thesis (for some programs). *Entrance requirements:* For master's, GRE General Test, minimum GPA of 2.75 in last 60 hours of course work. Additional exam requirements/recommendations for international students: Required—TOEFL (minimum score 550 paper-based; 78 iBT). *Application deadline:* For fall admission, 6/15 priority date for domestic students, 6/1 for international students; for spring admission, 10/15 priority date for domestic students, 10/1 for international students. Applications are processed on a rolling basis. Application fee: $40 ($90 for international students). Electronic applications accepted. *Expenses:* Tuition, state resident: full-time $6408; part-time $3204 per semester. Tuition, nonresident: full-time $14,832; part-time $7416 per semester. *Required fees:* $1824; $618. Tuition and fees vary according to course load. *Financial support:* In 2012–13, 15 students received support, including 2 research assistantships (averaging $29,750 per year), 33 teaching assistantships (averaging $25,430 per year); Federal Work-Study and institutionally sponsored loans also available. Support available to part-time students. Financial award application deadline: 4/1; financial award applicants required to submit FAFSA. *Faculty research:* Dynamic geometry, mathematics education, Mathworks/3M podcasts, math initiative, science teacher preparation. *Total annual research expenditures:* $1.4 million. *Unit head:* Dr. Nathaniel Dean, Chair, 512-245-2551, Fax: 512-245-3425, E-mail: nd17@txstate.edu. *Application contact:* Dr. J. Michael Willoughby, Dean of the Graduate College, 512-245-2581, Fax: 512-245-3425, E-mail: gradcollege@txstate.edu. Website: http://www.math.txstate.edu/.

Texas Tech University, Graduate School, College of Arts and Sciences, Department of Mathematics and Statistics, Lubbock, TX 79409. Offers mathematics (MA, MS, PhD); statistics (MS). Part-time programs available. Postbaccalaureate distance learning degree programs offered (minimal on-campus study). *Degree requirements:* For master's, thesis or alternative; for doctorate, comprehensive exam, thesis/dissertation. *Entrance requirements:* For master's and doctorate, GRE General Test. Additional exam requirements/recommendations for international students: Required—TOEFL (minimum score 550 paper-based; 79 iBT). Electronic applications accepted. *Faculty research:* Numerical analysis, mathematical biology, complex analysis, algebra and geometry, ordinary and partial differential equations.

Texas Woman's University, Graduate School, College of Arts and Sciences, Department of Mathematics and Computer Science, Denton, TX 76201. Offers mathematics (MA, MS); mathematics teaching (MS). Part-time and evening/weekend programs available. *Degree requirements:* For master's, comprehensive exam, thesis. *Entrance requirements:* For master's, 2 letters of reference. Additional exam requirements/recommendations for international students: Required—TOEFL (minimum score 550 paper-based; 79 iBT). Electronic applications accepted. *Faculty research:* Biopharmaceutical statistics, dynamic systems and control theory, Bayesian inference, math and computer science curriculum innovation, computer modeling of physical phenomenon.

Tufts University, Graduate School of Arts and Sciences, Department of Mathematics, Medford, MA 02155. Offers MA, MS, PhD. Terminal master's awarded for partial completion of doctoral program. *Degree requirements:* For master's, one foreign language, thesis; for doctorate, 2 foreign languages, thesis/dissertation. *Entrance requirements:* For master's, GRE General Test; for doctorate, GRE General Test, GRE Subject Tests. Additional exam requirements/recommendations for international students: Required—TOEFL (minimum score 550 paper-based; 80 iBT). Electronic applications accepted. *Expenses: Tuition:* Full-time $42,856; part-time $1072 per credit hour. *Required fees:* $730. Full-time tuition and fees vary according to degree level, program and student level. Part-time tuition and fees vary according to course load.

Tulane University, School of Science and Engineering, Department of Mathematics, New Orleans, LA 70118-5669. Offers applied mathematics (MS); mathematics (MS, PhD); statistics (MS). *Degree requirements:* For master's, thesis (for some programs); for doctorate, thesis/dissertation. *Entrance requirements:* For master's, GRE General Test, minimum B average in undergraduate course work; for doctorate, GRE General Test. Additional exam requirements/recommendations for international students: Required—TOEFL. Electronic applications accepted.

Université de Moncton, Faculty of Sciences, Department of Mathematics and Statistics, Moncton, NB E1A 3E9, Canada. Offers mathematics (M Sc). *Degree requirements:* For master's, one foreign language, thesis. *Entrance requirements:* For master's, minimum GPA of 3.0. Electronic applications accepted. *Faculty research:* Statistics, numerical analysis, fixed point theory, mathematical physics.

Université de Montréal, Faculty of Arts and Sciences, Department of Mathematics and Statistics, Montréal, QC H3C 3J7, Canada. Offers mathematical and computational finance (M Sc, DESS); mathematics (M Sc, PhD); statistics (M Sc, PhD). *Degree requirements:* For master's, thesis; for doctorate, thesis/dissertation, general exam. *Entrance requirements:* For master's and doctorate, proficiency in French. Electronic applications accepted. *Faculty research:* Pure and applied mathematics, actuarial mathematics.

Université de Sherbrooke, Faculty of Sciences, Department of Mathematics, Sherbrooke, QC J1K 2R1, Canada. Offers M Sc, PhD. *Degree requirements:* For master's, thesis; for doctorate, comprehensive exam, thesis/dissertation. *Entrance requirements:* For doctorate, master's degree. Electronic applications accepted. *Faculty research:* Measure theory, differential equations, probability, statistics, error control codes.

Université du Québec à Montréal, Graduate Programs, Program in Mathematics, Montréal, QC H3C 3P8, Canada. Offers M Sc, PhD. Part-time programs available. *Degree requirements:* For master's, thesis; for doctorate, thesis/dissertation. *Entrance requirements:* For master's, appropriate bachelor's degree or equivalent, proficiency in French; for doctorate, appropriate master's degree or equivalent, proficiency in French.

Université du Québec à Trois-Rivières, Graduate Programs, Program in Mathematics and Computer Science, Trois-Rivières, QC G9A 5H7, Canada. Offers M Sc. *Faculty research:* Probability, statistics.

Université Laval, Faculty of Sciences and Engineering, Department of Mathematics and Statistics, Programs in Mathematics, Québec, QC G1K 7P4, Canada. Offers M Sc, PhD. Terminal master's awarded for partial completion of doctoral program. *Degree requirements:* For master's, thesis (for some programs); for doctorate, comprehensive exam, thesis/dissertation. *Entrance requirements:* For master's and doctorate, knowledge of French and English. Electronic applications accepted.

University at Albany, State University of New York, College of Arts and Sciences, Department of Mathematics and Statistics, Albany, NY 12222-0001. Offers mathematics (PhD); secondary teaching (MA); statistics (MA). *Degree requirements:* For doctorate, one foreign language, thesis/dissertation. *Entrance requirements:* For doctorate, GRE General Test. Additional exam requirements/recommendations for international students: Required—TOEFL (minimum score 550 paper-based). Electronic applications accepted.

University at Buffalo, the State University of New York, Graduate School, College of Arts and Sciences, Department of Mathematics, Buffalo, NY 14260. Offers MA, PhD. *Faculty:* 34 full-time (3 women), 18 part-time/adjunct (7 women). *Students:* 69 full-time (21 women), 2 part-time (0 women); includes 24 minority (23 Asian, non-Hispanic/Latino; 1 Hispanic/Latino). Average age 29. 166 applicants, 36% accepted, 29 enrolled. In 2012, 10 master's, 13 doctorates awarded. Terminal master's awarded for partial completion of doctoral program. *Degree requirements:* For master's, comprehensive exam (for some programs), thesis (for some programs), project (for some programs); for doctorate, comprehensive exam, thesis/dissertation. *Entrance requirements:* Additional exam requirements/recommendations for international students: Required—TOEFL (minimum score 550 paper-based; 79 iBT). *Application deadline:* For fall admission, 1/15 priority date for domestic students, 1/15 for international students; for spring admission, 9/15 priority date for domestic students, 9/15 for international students. Applications are processed on a rolling basis. Application fee: $75. Electronic applications accepted. *Financial support:* In 2012–13, 33 students received support, including fellowships with full tuition reimbursements available (averaging $4,000 per year), 50 teaching assistantships with full tuition reimbursements available (averaging $16,188 per year); research assistantships, Federal Work-Study, institutionally sponsored loans, and unspecified assistantships also available. Financial award application deadline: 1/15; financial award applicants required to submit FAFSA. *Faculty research:* Algebra, analysis, applied mathematics, logic, number theory, topology. *Unit head:* Dr. David Hemmer, Chairman, 716-645-8780, Fax: 716-645-5039, E-mail: chair@math.buffalo.edu. *Application contact:* Dr. Gino Biondini, Director of Graduate Studies, 716-645-8783, Fax: 716-645-5039, E-mail: graduatedirector@math.buffalo.edu. Website: http://www.math.buffalo.edu/.

The University of Akron, Graduate School, Buchtel College of Arts and Sciences, Department of Theoretical and Applied Mathematics, Program in Mathematics, Akron, OH 44325. Offers MS. Part-time and evening/weekend programs available. *Students:* 12 full-time (4 women), 1 (woman) part-time; includes 2 minority (1 Black or African American, non-Hispanic/Latino; 1 Two or more races, non-Hispanic/Latino). Average age 28. 15 applicants, 67% accepted, 6 enrolled. In 2012, 7 master's awarded. *Degree requirements:* For master's, seminar and comprehensive exam or thesis. *Entrance requirements:* For master's, minimum GPA of 2.75, three letters of recommendation, statement of purpose. Additional exam requirements/recommendations for international students: Required—TOEFL (minimum score 550 paper-based; 79 iBT). *Application deadline:* Applications are processed on a rolling basis. Application fee: $40 ($60 for international students). Electronic applications accepted. *Expenses:* Tuition, state resident: full-time $7285; part-time $404.70 per credit hour. Tuition, nonresident: full-time $12,473; part-time $692.95 per credit hour. *Required fees:* $34.05 per credit hour. Tuition and fees vary according to course load. *Unit head:* Dr. Curtis Clemons, Coordinator, 330-972-8353, E-mail: curtis2@uakron.edu. Website: http://www.uakron.edu/math/academics/graduate/index.dot.

The University of Alabama, Graduate School, College of Arts and Sciences, Department of Mathematics, Tuscaloosa, AL 35487. Offers applied mathematics (PhD); mathematics (MA, PhD); pure mathematics (PhD). *Faculty:* 29 full-time (1 woman). *Students:* 41 full-time (13 women), 4 part-time (2 women); includes 2 minority (1 Black or African American, non-Hispanic/Latino; 1 Two or more races, non-Hispanic/Latino), 25 international. Average age 28. 35 applicants, 60% accepted, 6 enrolled. In 2012, 7 master's, 5 doctorates awarded. Terminal master's awarded for partial completion of doctoral program. *Degree requirements:* For master's, thesis or alternative; for doctorate, thesis/dissertation. *Entrance requirements:* For master's and doctorate, GRE General Test, minimum GPA of 3.0. Additional exam requirements/recommendations for international students: Required—TOEFL (minimum score 550 paper-based; 79 iBT). *Application deadline:* For fall admission, 7/1 for domestic students, 5/31 for international students; for spring admission, 11/30 for domestic students, 10/31 for international students. Applications are processed on a rolling basis. Application fee: $50 ($60 for international students). Electronic applications accepted. *Expenses:* Tuition, state resident: full-time $9200. Tuition, nonresident: full-time $22,950. *Financial support:* In 2012–13, 1 fellowship with full tuition reimbursement (averaging $30,000 per year), 35 teaching assistantships with full tuition reimbursements (averaging $12,258 per year) were awarded; research assistantships with full tuition reimbursements, Federal Work-Study, institutionally sponsored loans, scholarships/grants, and unspecified assistantships also available. Support available to part-time students. Financial award application deadline: 7/1. *Faculty research:* Analysis, topology, algebra, fluid mechanics and system control theory, optimization, stochastic processes, numerical analysis. *Total annual research expenditures:* $302,468. *Unit head:* Dr. Zhijian Wu, Chairperson and Professor, 205-348-5080, Fax: 205-348-7067, E-mail: zwu@as.ua.edu. *Application contact:* Dr. Vo Liem, Director, 205-348-4898, Fax: 205-348-7067, E-mail: vliem@as.ua.edu.

The University of Alabama at Birmingham, College of Arts and Sciences, Program in Mathematics, Birmingham, AL 35294. Offers MS. *Students:* 15 full-time (5 women), 1 part-time (0 women); includes 2 minority (both Black or African American, non-Hispanic/Latino), 3 international. Average age 27. In 2012, 6 master's awarded. Terminal master's awarded for partial completion of doctoral program. *Degree requirements:* For master's, thesis optional. *Entrance requirements:* For master's, GRE General Test, minimum GPA of 3.0, letters of recommendation. Additional exam requirements/recommendations for international students: Required—TOEFL, TWE. *Application deadline:* For fall admission, 3/15 priority date for domestic students. Applications are processed on a rolling basis. Application fee: $45 ($60 for international students). Electronic applications accepted. *Expenses:* Tuition, state resident: full-time $6420; part-time $335 per credit hour. Tuition, nonresident: full-time $14,574; part-time $788 per credit hour. Tuition and fees vary according to course load and program. *Financial support:* Fellowships with full tuition reimbursements, research assistantships, teaching assistantships with full tuition reimbursements, career-related internships or fieldwork, Federal Work-Study, institutionally sponsored loans, scholarships/grants, traineeships, health care benefits, tuition waivers (full and partial), and unspecified assistantships available. Support available to part-time students. Financial award application deadline: 8/1; financial award applicants required to submit FAFSA. *Faculty research:* Differential equations, topology, mathematical physics, dynamic systems. *Unit head:* Dr. Yulia Karpechina, Graduate Program Director, 205-934-2154, Fax: 205-934-9025, E-mail: karpeshi@math.uab.edu. *Application contact:* Dr. Gunter Stolz, Graduate Recruitment Coordinator/Professor, 205-934-2154, Fax: 205-934-9025, E-mail: stolz@math.uab.edu. Website: http://www.uab.edu/mathematics/masters-program.

The University of Alabama in Huntsville, School of Graduate Studies, College of Science, Department of Mathematical Sciences, Huntsville, AL 35899. Offers applied mathematics (PhD); education (MA, MS); mathematics (MA, MS). PhD offered jointly with The University of Alabama (Tuscaloosa) and The University of Alabama at Birmingham. Part-time and evening/weekend programs available. *Faculty:* 14 full-time (1 woman), 1 part-time/adjunct (0 women). *Students:* 20 full-time (10 women), 9 part-time (1 woman); includes 4 minority (3 Black or African American, non-Hispanic/Latino; 1 Hispanic/Latino), 3 international. Average age 27. 26 applicants, 85% accepted, 12 enrolled. In 2012, 6 master's, 3 doctorates awarded. *Degree requirements:* For master's, comprehensive exam, thesis or alternative, oral and written exams; for doctorate, comprehensive exam, thesis/dissertation, oral and written exams. *Entrance requirements:* For master's and doctorate, GRE General Test, minimum GPA of 3.0. Additional exam requirements/recommendations for international students: Required—TOEFL (minimum score 550 paper-based; 80 iBT), IELTS (minimum score 6.5). *Application deadline:* For fall admission, 7/15 priority date for domestic students, 4/1 for international students; for spring admission, 11/30 priority date for domestic students, 9/1 for international students. Applications are processed on a rolling basis. Application fee: $40 ($50 for international students). Electronic applications accepted. *Expenses:* Tuition, state resident: full-time $8516; part-time $515 per credit hour. Tuition, nonresident: full-time $20,384; part-time $1229 per credit hour. *Required fees:* $148 per semester. One-time fee: $150. *Financial support:* In 2012–13, 14 students received support, including 14 teaching assistantships with full and partial tuition reimbursements available (averaging $10,342 per year); career-related internships or fieldwork, Federal Work-Study, institutionally sponsored loans, scholarships/grants, health care benefits, and unspecified assistantships also available. Support available to part-time students. Financial award application deadline: 4/1; financial award applicants required to submit FAFSA. *Faculty research:* Combinatorics and graph theory, computational mathematics, differential equations and applications, mathematical biology, probability and stochastic processes. *Total annual research expenditures:* $241,477. *Unit head:* Dr. Jia Li, Chair, 256-824-6470, Fax: 256-824-6173, E-mail: li@math.uah.edu. *Application contact:* Kim Gray, Graduate Studies Admissions Coordinator, 256-824-6002, Fax: 256-824-6405, E-mail: deangrad@uah.edu. Website: http://www.math.uah.edu/.

University of Alaska Fairbanks, College of Natural Sciences and Mathematics, Department of Mathematics and Statistics, Fairbanks, AK 99775-6660. Offers mathematics (MAT, PhD); statistics (MS, Graduate Certificate). Part-time programs available. *Faculty:* 13 full-time (6 women), 1 (woman) part-time/adjunct. *Students:* 12 full-time (4 women), 5 part-time (3 women); includes 1 minority (Asian, non-Hispanic/Latino), 6 international. Average age 26. 24 applicants, 42% accepted, 7 enrolled. In 2012, 1 master's, 1 doctorate awarded. Terminal master's awarded for partial completion of doctoral program. *Degree requirements:* For master's, comprehensive exam, thesis or alternative; for doctorate, comprehensive exam, thesis/dissertation, oral defense. *Entrance requirements:* Additional exam requirements/recommendations for international students: Required—TOEFL (minimum score 550 paper-based; 80 iBT). *Application deadline:* For fall admission, 6/1 for domestic students, 3/1 for international students; for spring admission, 10/15 for domestic students, 9/1 for international students. Applications are processed on a rolling basis. Application fee: $60. Electronic applications accepted. *Expenses:* Tuition, state resident: full-time $7038. Tuition, nonresident: full-time $14,382. Tuition and fees vary according to course level, course load and reciprocity agreements. *Financial support:* In 2012–13, 1 research assistantship with tuition reimbursement (averaging $6,031 per year), 10 teaching assistantships with tuition reimbursements (averaging $17,987 per year) were awarded; fellowships with tuition reimbursements, career-related internships or fieldwork, Federal Work-Study, scholarships/grants, health care benefits, and unspecified assistantships also available. Support available to part-time students. Financial award application deadline: 2/15; financial award applicants required to submit FAFSA. *Faculty research:* Kriging, arrangements of hyperplanes, bifurcation analysis of time-periodic differential-delay equations, inverse problems, phylogenic tree construction. *Total annual research expenditures:* $2,000. *Unit head:* Dr. Anthony Rickard, Department Chair, 907-474-7332, Fax: 907-474-5394, E-mail: uaf-mathandstat-dept@alaska.edu. *Application contact:* Libby Eddy, Registrar and Director of Admissions, 907-474-7500, Fax: 907-474-7097, E-mail: admissions@uaf.edu. Website: http://www.uaf.edu/dms/.

University of Alberta, Faculty of Graduate Studies and Research, Department of Mathematical and Statistical Sciences, Edmonton, AB T6G 2E1, Canada. Offers applied mathematics (M Sc, PhD); biostatistics (M Sc); mathematical finance (M Sc, PhD); mathematical physics (M Sc, PhD); mathematics (M Sc, PhD); statistics (M Sc, PhD, Postgraduate Diploma). Part-time programs available. Terminal master's awarded for partial completion of doctoral program. *Degree requirements:* For master's, thesis (for some programs); for doctorate, comprehensive exam, thesis/dissertation. *Entrance requirements:* Additional exam requirements/recommendations for international students: Required—TOEFL (minimum score 580 paper-based). Electronic applications accepted. *Faculty research:* Classical and functional analysis, algebra, differential equations, geometry.

The University of Arizona, College of Science, Department of Mathematics, Tucson, AZ 85721. Offers mathematics (MA, MS, PhD); middle school mathematics teaching leadership (MA). Part-time programs available. *Faculty:* 50 full-time (6 women), 6 part-time/adjunct (1 woman). *Students:* 52 full-time (10 women), 2 part-time (0 women); includes 7 minority (3 Hispanic/Latino; 4 Two or more races, non-Hispanic/Latino), 17 international. Average age 30. 109 applicants, 21% accepted, 11 enrolled. In 2012, 7 master's, 3 doctorates awarded. *Degree requirements:* For master's, thesis; for doctorate, 2 foreign languages, thesis/dissertation. *Entrance requirements:* For master's, GRE; for doctorate, GRE, statement of purpose. Additional exam requirements/recommendations for international students: Required—TOEFL (minimum score 550 paper-based; 79 iBT). *Application deadline:* For fall admission, 2/1 for domestic students, 12/1 for international students; for spring admission, 10/1 for domestic students, 6/1 for international students. Applications are processed on a rolling basis. Application fee: $75. Electronic applications accepted. *Financial support:* In 2012–13, 14 research assistantships (averaging $22,256 per year), 59 teaching assistantships (averaging $21,751 per year) were awarded; scholarships/grants, health care benefits, tuition waivers (full and partial), and unspecified assistantships also available. Financial award application deadline: 3/5. *Faculty research:* Algebra/number theory, computational science, dynamical systems, geometry, analysis. *Total annual research expenditures:* $8.4 million. *Unit head:* Department Head's Office, 520-621-2713. *Application contact:* Sandy Sutton, Graduate Coordinator, 520-621-2068, Fax: 520-621-8322, E-mail: gradoffice@math.arizona.edu. Website: http://math.arizona.edu/.

The University of Arizona, Graduate Interdisciplinary Programs, Graduate Interdisciplinary Program in Applied Mathematics, Tucson, AZ 85721. Offers applied mathematics (MS, PhD); mathematical sciences (PMS). *Students:* 53 full-time (14 women), 1 part-time (0 women); includes 6 minority (2 Asian, non-Hispanic/Latino; 3 Hispanic/Latino; 1 Two or more races, non-Hispanic/Latino), 3 international. Average age 27. 156 applicants, 11% accepted, 8 enrolled. In 2012, 7 master's, 2 doctorates awarded. Terminal master's awarded for partial completion of doctoral program. *Degree requirements:* For master's, thesis (for some programs); for doctorate, comprehensive exam, thesis/dissertation. *Entrance requirements:* For master's, GRE, 3 letters of recommendation; for doctorate, GRE, 3 letters of recommendation, statement of purpose. Additional exam requirements/recommendations for international students: Required—TOEFL (minimum score 575 paper-based; 80 iBT). *Application deadline:* For fall admission, 1/15 for domestic students, 1/30 for international students. Applications are processed on a rolling basis. Application fee: $75. Electronic applications accepted. *Financial support:* In 2012–13, 1 research assistantship with full tuition reimbursement (averaging $17,120 per year) was awarded; institutionally sponsored loans, scholarships/grants, health care benefits, tuition waivers (full), and unspecified assistantships also available. Financial award application deadline: 3/1; financial award applicants required to submit FAFSA. *Faculty research:* Dynamical systems and chaos, partial differential equations, pattern formation, fluid dynamics and turbulence, scientific computation, mathematical physics, mathematical biology, medical imaging, applied probability and stochastic processes. *Unit head:* Dr. Michael Tabor, Head, 520-621-4664, Fax: 520-626-5048, E-mail: tabor@math.arizona.edu. *Application contact:* Graduate Coordinator, 520-621-2016, Fax: 520-626-5048, E-mail: applmath@u.arizona.edu. Website: http://appliedmath.arizona.edu/.

University of Arkansas, Graduate School, J. William Fulbright College of Arts and Sciences, Department of Mathematical Sciences, Program in Mathematics, Fayetteville, AR 72701-1201. Offers MS, PhD. *Students:* 16 full-time (7 women), 37 part-time (15 women); includes 5 minority (1 Black or African American, non-Hispanic/Latino; 3 Hispanic/Latino; 1 Two or more races, non-Hispanic/Latino), 17 international. In 2012, 7 master's, 5 doctorates awarded. *Degree requirements:* For master's, thesis or alternative; for doctorate, 2 foreign languages, thesis/dissertation. *Application deadline:* For fall admission, 4/1 for international students; for spring admission, 10/1 for international students. Applications are processed on a rolling basis. Application fee: $40 ($50 for international students). Electronic applications accepted. *Financial support:* In 2012–13, 2 research assistantships, 44 teaching assistantships were awarded; fellowships with tuition reimbursements, career-related internships or fieldwork, and Federal Work-Study also available. Support available to part-time students. Financial award application deadline: 4/1; financial award applicants required to submit FAFSA. *Unit head:* Dr. Chaim Goodman-Strauss, Chair, 479-575-3351, Fax: 479-575-8630, E-mail: strauss@uark.edu. *Application contact:* Dr. Phil Harrington, Graduate Coordinator, 479-575-3488, Fax: 479-575-8630, E-mail: psharrin@uark.edu. Website: http://math.uark.edu/.

University of Arkansas at Little Rock, Graduate School, College of Science and Mathematics, Department of Mathematics and Statistics, Little Rock, AR 72204-1099. Offers applied statistics (Graduate Certificate); mathematical sciences (MS). Part-time and evening/weekend programs available. *Degree requirements:* For master's, comprehensive exam. *Entrance requirements:* For master's, GRE General Test, GRE Subject Test, minimum GPA of 2.7, previous course work in advanced mathematics.

University of Arkansas at Little Rock, Graduate School, College of Science and Mathematics, Program in Integrated Science and Mathematics, Little Rock, AR 72204-1099. Offers MS.

The University of British Columbia, Faculty of Science, Program in Mathematics, Vancouver, BC V6T 1Z2, Canada. Offers M Sc, MA, PhD. Part-time programs available. *Degree requirements:* For master's, thesis or alternative, essay, qualifying exam; for doctorate, comprehensive exam, thesis/dissertation, qualifying exam, thesis proposal. *Entrance requirements:* Additional exam requirements/recommendations for international students: Required—TOEFL (minimum score 600 paper-based; 100 iBT). Electronic applications accepted. *Faculty research:* Applied mathematics, financial mathematics, pure mathematics.

University of Calgary, Faculty of Graduate Studies, Faculty of Science, Department of Mathematics and Statistics, Calgary, AB T2N 1N4, Canada. Offers M Sc, PhD. *Degree requirements:* For master's, comprehensive exam, thesis; for doctorate, thesis/dissertation, candidacy exam, preliminary exams. *Entrance requirements:* For master's, honors degree in applied math, pure math, or statistics; for doctorate, MA or M Sc. Additional exam requirements/recommendations for international students: Required—TOEFL (minimum score 600 paper-based) or IELTS (minimum score 7). *Faculty research:* Combinatorics, applied mathematics, statistics, probability, analysis.

University of California, Berkeley, Graduate Division, College of Letters and Science, Department of Mathematics, Berkeley, CA 94720-1500. Offers applied mathematics (PhD); mathematics (MA, PhD). Terminal master's awarded for partial completion of doctoral program. *Degree requirements:* For master's, exam or thesis; for doctorate, 2 foreign languages, thesis/dissertation, qualifying exam. *Entrance requirements:* For master's and doctorate, GRE General Test, GRE Subject Test, minimum GPA of 3.0, 3 letters of recommendation. *Faculty research:* Algebra, analysis, logic, geometry/topology.

University of California, Davis, Graduate Studies, Program in Mathematics, Davis, CA 95616. Offers MA, MAT, PhD. Terminal master's awarded for partial completion of doctoral program. *Degree requirements:* For master's, comprehensive exam; for doctorate, one foreign language, thesis/dissertation. *Entrance requirements:* For master's and doctorate, GRE General Test, GRE Subject Test, minimum GPA of 3.0. Additional exam requirements/recommendations for international students: Required—TOEFL (minimum score 550 paper-based). Electronic applications accepted. *Faculty research:* Mathematical physics, geometric topology, probability, partial differential equations, applied mathematics.

University of California, Irvine, School of Physical Sciences, Department of Mathematics, Irvine, CA 92697. Offers MS, PhD. *Students:* 105 full-time (25 women), 2 part-time (1 woman); includes 22 minority (2 Black or African American, non-Hispanic/Latino; 15 Asian, non-Hispanic/Latino; 4 Hispanic/Latino; 1 Two or more races, non-Hispanic/Latino), 43 international. Average age 28. 247 applicants, 18% accepted, 22 enrolled. In 2012, 12 master's, 14 doctorates awarded. *Degree requirements:* For doctorate, thesis/dissertation. *Entrance requirements:* For master's and doctorate, GRE General Test, GRE Subject Test, minimum GPA of 3.0. Additional exam requirements/recommendations for international students: Required—TOEFL (minimum score 550 paper-based). *Application deadline:* For fall admission, 1/15 priority date for domestic students, 1/15 for international students. Applications are processed on a rolling basis. Application fee: $80 ($100 for international students). Electronic applications accepted. *Financial support:* Fellowships, research assistantships with full tuition reimbursements, teaching assistantships, institutionally sponsored loans, traineeships, health care benefits, and unspecified assistantships available. Financial award application deadline: 3/1; financial award applicants required to submit FAFSA. *Faculty research:* Algebra and logic, geometry and topology, probability, mathematical physics. *Unit head:* Prof. Hongkai Zhao, Chair, 949-824-5510, Fax: 949-824-7993, E-mail: zhao@uci.edu. *Application contact:* Donna M. McConnell, Graduate Affairs Officer, 949-824-5544, Fax: 949-824-7993, E-mail: dmcconne@uci.edu. Website: http://www.math.uci.edu/.

University of California, Los Angeles, Graduate Division, College of Letters and Science, Department of Mathematics, Los Angeles, CA 90095. Offers MA, MAT, PhD. *Faculty:* 49 full-time (4 women). *Students:* 142 full-time (16 women); includes 18 minority (15 Asian, non-Hispanic/Latino; 1 Hispanic/Latino; 2 Two or more races, non-Hispanic/Latino), 43 international. Average age 25. 503 applicants, 21% accepted, 39 enrolled. In 2012, 18 master's, 33 doctorates awarded. Terminal master's awarded for partial completion of doctoral program. *Degree requirements:* For master's, comprehensive exam or thesis; for doctorate, one foreign language, thesis/dissertation, oral and written qualifying exams. *Entrance requirements:* For master's, GRE General Test; GRE Subject Test (mathematics), bachelor's degree; minimum undergraduate GPA of 3.0, 3.2 in upper-division mathematics courses (or its equivalent if letter grade system not used); for doctorate, GRE General Test; GRE Subject Test (mathematics), bachelor's degree; minimum undergraduate GPA of 3.0, 3.5 in upper-division mathematics courses (or its equivalent if letter grade system not used). Additional exam requirements/recommendations for international students: Required—TOEFL. *Application deadline:* For fall admission, 12/15 for domestic and international students. Application fee: $80 ($100 for international students). Electronic applications accepted. *Expenses:* Tuition, nonresident: full-time $15,102. *Required fees:* $14,809.19. Full-time tuition and fees vary according to program. *Financial support:* In 2012–13, 141 students received support, including 127 fellowships with full and partial tuition reimbursements available, 67 research assistantships with full and partial tuition reimbursements available, 108 teaching assistantships with full and partial tuition reimbursements available; Federal Work-Study, scholarships/grants, health care benefits, tuition waivers (full and partial), and unspecified assistantships also available. Financial award application deadline: 3/2; financial award applicants required to submit FAFSA. *Unit head:* Dr. Shlyakhtenko Dimitri, Chair, 310-825-4298 Ext. 310, Fax: 310-206-6673, E-mail: shlyakht@math.ucla.edu. *Application contact:* Student Affairs Officer, 310-825-4971, Fax: 310-206-6673, E-mail: gradapps@math.ucla.edu. Website: http://www.math.ucla.edu.

University of California, Riverside, Graduate Division, Department of Mathematics, Riverside, CA 92521-0102. Offers MA, MS, PhD. Part-time programs available. *Faculty:* 22 full-time (4 women), 21 part-time/adjunct (4 women). *Students:* 65 full-time (15 women); includes 18 minority (1 Black or African American, non-Hispanic/Latino; 7 Asian, non-Hispanic/Latino; 10 Hispanic/Latino), 3 international. Average age 28. 107 applicants, 50% accepted, 23 enrolled. In 2012, 13 master's, 13 doctorates awarded. Terminal master's awarded for partial completion of doctoral program. *Degree requirements:* For master's, comprehensive exam; for doctorate, thesis/dissertation, qualifying exams. *Entrance requirements:* For master's and doctorate, GRE General Test, minimum GPA of 3.2. Additional exam requirements/recommendations for international students: Required—TOEFL (minimum score 550 paper-based; 80 iBT). *Application deadline:* For fall admission, 5/1 for domestic students, 2/1 for international students; for winter admission, 9/1 for domestic students, 7/1 for international students; for spring admission, 12/1 for domestic students, 10/1 for international students. Applications are processed on a rolling basis. Application fee: $80 ($100 for international students). Electronic applications accepted. *Expenses:* Tuition, state resident: full-time $14,646. Tuition, nonresident: full-time $29,748. *Financial support:* In 2012–13, fellowships with tuition reimbursements (averaging $12,000 per year), teaching assistantships with full and partial tuition reimbursements (averaging $16,500 per year) were awarded; research assistantships, career-related internships or fieldwork, Federal Work-Study, institutionally sponsored loans, health care benefits, and tuition waivers (full and partial) also available. Financial award application deadline: 1/5; financial award applicants required to submit FAFSA. *Faculty research:* Algebraic geometry, commutative algebra, Lie algebra, differential equations, differential geometry. *Unit head:* Dr. Gerhard Gierz, Chair, 951-827-6463, Fax: 951-827-7314, E-mail: gerhard.gierz@ucr.edu. *Application contact:* Graduate Assistant, Graduate Program Assistant, 951-827-7378, Fax: 951-827-7314, E-mail: gradmath@ucr.edu. Website: http://www.math.ucr.edu/.

University of California, San Diego, Office of Graduate Studies, Department of Mathematics, La Jolla, CA 92093. Offers applied mathematics (MA); mathematics (MA, PhD); statistics (MS). *Degree requirements:* For doctorate, thesis/

338 www.petersonsbooks.com

Peterson's Graduate Programs in the Physical Sciences, Mathematics, Agricultural Sciences, the Environment & Natural Resources 2014

dissertation. *Entrance requirements:* For master's and doctorate, GRE General Test, GRE Subject Test. Electronic applications accepted.

University of California, Santa Barbara, Graduate Division, College of Letters and Sciences, Division of Mathematics, Life, and Physical Sciences, Department of Mathematics, Santa Barbara, CA 93106-3080. Offers applied mathematics (MA), including computational science and engineering; mathematics (MA, PhD), including computational science and engineering; MA/PhD. *Faculty:* 28 full-time (2 women). *Students:* 50 full-time (13 women); includes 12 minority (1 Black or African American, non-Hispanic/Latino; 4 Asian, non-Hispanic/Latino; 7 Hispanic/Latino), 5 international. Average age 26. 186 applicants, 17% accepted, 10 enrolled. In 2012, 6 master's, 2 doctorates awarded. Terminal master's awarded for partial completion of doctoral program. *Degree requirements:* For master's, comprehensive exam (for some programs), thesis (for some programs); for doctorate, comprehensive exam, thesis/dissertation. *Entrance requirements:* For master's and doctorate, GRE General Test, GRE Subject Test (math). Additional exam requirements/recommendations for international students: Required—TOEFL (minimum score 575 paper-based; 80 iBT), IELTS (minimum score 7). *Application deadline:* For fall admission, 1/1 for domestic and international students. Application fee: $80 ($100 for international students). Electronic applications accepted. *Financial support:* In 2012–13, 48 students received support, including 4 fellowships with full tuition reimbursements available (averaging $20,000 per year), 6 research assistantships with full tuition reimbursements available (averaging $18,000 per year), 45 teaching assistantships with partial tuition reimbursements available (averaging $17,655 per year); Federal Work-Study, institutionally sponsored loans, health care benefits, and tuition waivers (full and partial) also available. Financial award application deadline: 3/2; financial award applicants required to submit FAFSA. *Faculty research:* Topology, differential geometry, algebra, applied mathematics, partial differential equations. *Total annual research expenditures:* $205,000. *Unit head:* Prof. David R. Morrison, Chair, 805-893-8340, Fax: 805-893-2385, E-mail: chair@math.ucsb.edu. *Application contact:* Medina Price, Graduate Advisor, 805-893-8192, Fax: 805-893-2385, E-mail: price@math.ucsb.edu. Website: http://www.math.ucsb.edu/.

University of California, Santa Cruz, Division of Graduate Studies, Division of Physical and Biological Sciences, Department of Mathematics, Santa Cruz, CA 95064. Offers MA, PhD. Terminal master's awarded for partial completion of doctoral program. *Degree requirements:* For master's, thesis; for doctorate, one foreign language, thesis/dissertation, qualifying exam. *Entrance requirements:* For doctorate, GRE General Test, GRE Subject Test. Additional exam requirements/recommendations for international students: Required—TOEFL (minimum score 550 paper-based; 83 iBT); Recommended—IELTS (minimum score 8). Electronic applications accepted. *Faculty research:* Vertex operator algebras, algebraic topology, elliptic cohomology, quantum field theory, automorphic forms, dynamical systems, celestial mechanics, geometric mechanics, bifurcation theory, control theory, representations of Lie and p-adic groups, applications to number theory, Bessel functions, Rankin-Selberg integrals, Gelfand-Graev models, differential geometry, nonlinear analysis, harmonic maps, Ginzburg-Landau problem.

University of Central Arkansas, Graduate School, College of Natural Sciences and Math, Department of Mathematics, Conway, AR 72035-0001. Offers applied mathematics (MS); math education (MA). Part-time programs available. *Faculty:* 16 full-time (4 women). *Students:* 18 full-time (10 women), 9 part-time (5 women); includes 2 minority (1 Black or African American, non-Hispanic/Latino; 1 Asian, non-Hispanic/Latino), 2 international. Average age 37. 14 applicants, 100% accepted, 11 enrolled. In 2012, 15 master's awarded. *Degree requirements:* For master's, comprehensive exam, thesis optional. *Entrance requirements:* For master's, GRE General Test, minimum GPA of 2.7. Additional exam requirements/recommendations for international students: Required—TOEFL (minimum score 550 paper-based; 80 iBT). *Application deadline:* For fall admission, 3/1 priority date for domestic students; for spring admission, 10/1 priority date for domestic students. Applications are processed on a rolling basis. Application fee: $25 ($50 for international students). Electronic applications accepted. *Expenses:* Tuition, state resident: full-time $3462; part-time $278.02 per credit hour. Tuition, nonresident: full-time $6172; part-time $503.82 per credit hour. *Financial support:* In 2012–13, 11 teaching assistantships with partial tuition reimbursements (averaging $8,500 per year) were awarded; Federal Work-Study, scholarships/grants, and unspecified assistantships also available. Financial award application deadline: 2/15; financial award applicants required to submit FAFSA. *Unit head:* Dr. Ramesh Garimella, Chair, 501-450-3147, Fax: 501-450-5662, E-mail: rameshg@uca.edu. *Application contact:* Susan Wood, Admissions Assistant, 501-450-3124, Fax: 501-450-5678, E-mail: swood@uca.edu. Website: http://uca.edu/math/.

University of Central Florida, College of Sciences, Department of Mathematics, Orlando, FL 32816. Offers mathematical science (MS); mathematics (PhD, Certificate). Part-time and evening/weekend programs available. *Faculty:* 42 full-time (5 women), 4 part-time/adjunct (1 woman). *Students:* 55 full-time (23 women), 28 part-time (15 women); includes 13 minority (1 Black or African American, non-Hispanic/Latino; 3 Asian, non-Hispanic/Latino; 8 Hispanic/Latino; 1 Two or more races, non-Hispanic/Latino), 17 international. Average age 31. 89 applicants, 65% accepted, 34 enrolled. In 2012, 17 master's, 5 doctorates, 1 other advanced degree awarded. *Degree requirements:* For master's, thesis or alternative; for doctorate, thesis/dissertation, candidacy exam. *Entrance requirements:* For master's, GRE General Test, minimum GPA of 3.0 in last 60 hours; for doctorate, GRE Subject Test, minimum GPA of 3.0 in last 60 hours or master's qualifying exam. Additional exam requirements/recommendations for international students: Required—TOEFL. *Application deadline:* For fall admission, 7/15 for domestic students; for spring admission, 12/1 for domestic students. Application fee: $30. Electronic applications accepted. *Financial support:* In 2012–13, 41 students received support, including 3 fellowships with partial tuition reimbursements available (averaging $12,700 per year), 4 research assistantships with partial tuition reimbursements available (averaging $9,200 per year), 36 teaching assistantships with partial tuition reimbursements available (averaging $14,200 per year); career-related internships or fieldwork, Federal Work-Study, institutionally sponsored loans, tuition waivers (partial), and unspecified assistantships also available. Financial award application deadline: 3/1; financial award applicants required to submit FAFSA. *Faculty research:* Applied mathematics, analysis, approximation theory, graph theory, mathematical statistics. *Unit head:* Dr. Piotr Mikusinski, Chair, 407-823-6284, Fax: 407-823-6253, E-mail: piotr.mikusinski@mail.ucf.edu. *Application contact:* Barbara Rodriguez, Director, Admissions and Registration, 407-823-2766, Fax: 407-823-6442, E-mail: gradadmissions@ucf.edu. Website: http://www.math.ucf.edu/.

University of Central Missouri, The Graduate School, Warrensburg, MO 64093. Offers accountancy (MA); accounting (MBA); applied mathematics (MS); aviation safety (MA); biology (MS), business administration (MBA); career and technical education leadership (MS); college student personnel administration (MS); communication (MA); computer science (MS); counseling (MS); criminal justice (MS); educational leadership (Ed D); educational technology (MS); elementary and early childhood education (MSE); English (MA); environmental studies (MA); finance (MBA); history (MA); human services/educational technology (Ed S); human services/learning resources (Ed S); human services/professional counseling (Ed S); industrial hygiene (MS); industrial management (MS); information systems (MBA); information technology (MS); kinesiology (MS); library science and information services (MS); literacy education (MSE); marketing (MBA); mathematics (MS); music (MA); occupational safety management (MS); psychology (MS); rural family nursing (MS); school administration (MSE); social gerontology (MS); sociology (MA); special education (MSE); speech language pathology (MS); superintendency (Ed S); teaching (MAT); teaching English as a second language (MA); technology (MS); technology management (PhD); theatro (MA). Part-time programs available. *Faculty:* 233. *Students:* 583 full-time (327 women), 1,425 part-time (930 women); includes 169 minority (93 Black or African American, non-Hispanic/Latino; 11 American Indian or Alaska Native, non-Hispanic/Latino; 27 Asian, non-Hispanic/Latino; 29 Hispanic/Latino; 3 Native Hawaiian or other Pacific Islander, non-Hispanic/Latino; 6 Two or more races, non-Hispanic/Latino), 234 international. Average age 33. 958 applicants, 80% accepted. In 2012, 567 master's, 56 other advanced degrees awarded. *Degree requirements:* For master's and Ed S, comprehensive exam (for some programs), thesis (for some programs). *Entrance requirements:* Additional exam requirements/recommendations for international students: Required—TOEFL (minimum score 550 paper-based; 79 iBT). *Application deadline:* For fall admission, 6/1 for domestic students; for spring admission, 10/1 for domestic and international students. Applications are processed on a rolling basis. Application fee: $30 ($75 for international students). Electronic applications accepted. *Financial support:* In 2012–13, 118 students received support, including 271 research assistantships with full and partial tuition reimbursements available (averaging $7,500 per year), 109 teaching assistantships with full and partial tuition reimbursements available (averaging $7,500 per year); career-related internships or fieldwork, Federal Work-Study, scholarships/grants, and administrative and laboratory assistantships also available. Support available to part-time students. Financial award application deadline: 3/1; financial award applicants required to submit FAFSA. *Unit head:* Dr. Joseph Vaughn, Assistant Provost for Research/Dean, 660-543-4092, Fax: 660-543-4778, E-mail: vaughn@ucmo.edu. *Application contact:* Brittany Gerbec, Graduate Student Services Coordinator, 660-543-4621, Fax: 660-543-4778, E-mail: gradinfo@ucmo.edu. Website: http://www.ucmo.edu/graduate/.

University of Central Oklahoma, The Jackson College of Graduate Studies, College of Mathematics and Science, Department of Mathematics and Statistics, Edmond, OK 73034-5209. Offers applied mathematical sciences (MS), including computer science, mathematics, mathematics/computer science teaching, statistics. Part-time programs available. *Faculty:* 5 full-time (1 woman), 5 part-time/adjunct (1 woman). *Students:* 24 full-time (10 women), 11 part-time (4 women); includes 6 minority (2 Black or African American, non-Hispanic/Latino; 1 American Indian or Alaska Native, non-Hispanic/Latino; 1 Asian, non-Hispanic/Latino; 2 Two or more races, non-Hispanic/Latino), 15 international. Average age 29. 55 applicants, 58% accepted, 14 enrolled. In 2012, 5 master's awarded. *Degree requirements:* For master's, comprehensive exam (for some programs), thesis (for some programs). *Entrance requirements:* For master's, GRE. Additional exam requirements/recommendations for international students: Required—TOEFL (minimum score 550 paper-based; 79 iBT), IELTS (minimum score 6.5). *Application deadline:* For fall admission, 7/1 for international students; for spring admission, 11/1 for international students. Applications are processed on a rolling basis. Application fee: $50. Electronic applications accepted. *Expenses:* Tuition, state resident: full-time $3718; part-time $195.65 per credit hour. Tuition, nonresident: full-time $9309; part-time $489.95 per credit hour. *Required fees:* $399.95; $21.50 per credit hour. One-time fee: $50. Tuition and fees vary according to program. *Financial support:* In 2012–13, 13 students received support, including research assistantships with partial tuition reimbursements available (averaging $5,083 per year), teaching assistantships with partial tuition reimbursements available (averaging $7,447 per year); Federal Work-Study, scholarships/grants, tuition waivers (partial), and unspecified assistantships also available. Financial award application deadline: 3/31; financial award applicants required to submit FAFSA. *Unit head:* Dr. Jesse Byrne, Chair, 405-974-5294, Fax: 405-974-3824, E-mail: jbyrne@uco.edu. *Application contact:* Dr. Richard Bernard, Dean, Jackson College of Graduate Studies, 405-974-3493, Fax: 405-974-3852, E-mail: gradcoll@uco.edu. Website: http://www.math.uco.edu/.

University of Chicago, Division of the Physical Sciences, Department of Mathematics, Chicago, IL 60637-1513. Offers applied mathematics (SM, PhD); financial mathematics (MS); mathematics (SM, PhD). *Degree requirements:* For master's, one foreign language; for doctorate, one foreign language, thesis/dissertation, 2 qualifying exams, oral topic presentation. *Entrance requirements:* For master's and doctorate, GRE General Test, GRE Subject Test. Additional exam requirements/recommendations for international students: Required—TOEFL (minimum score 600 paper-based). Electronic applications accepted. *Faculty research:* Analysis, differential geometry, algebra number theory, topology, algebraic geometry.

University of Cincinnati, Graduate School, McMicken College of Arts and Sciences, Department of Mathematical Sciences, Cincinnati, OH 45221. Offers applied mathematics (MS, PhD); mathematics education (MAT); pure mathematics (MS, PhD); statistics (MS, PhD). Part-time programs available. Terminal master's awarded for partial completion of doctoral program. *Degree requirements:* For master's, comprehensive exam, thesis or alternative; for doctorate, one foreign language, comprehensive exam, thesis/dissertation. *Entrance requirements:* For master's, GRE, teacher certification (MAT); for doctorate, GRE. Additional exam requirements/recommendations for international students: Required—TOEFL. Electronic applications accepted. *Faculty research:* Algebra, analysis, differential equations, numerical analysis, statistics.

University of Colorado Boulder, Graduate School, College of Arts and Sciences, Department of Mathematics, Boulder, CO 80309. Offers MA, MS, PhD. *Faculty:* 25 full-time (5 women). *Students:* 53 full-time (9 women), 11 part-time (1 woman); includes 8 minority (1 Black or African American, non-Hispanic/Latino; 1 American Indian or Alaska Native, non-Hispanic/Latino; 3 Asian, non-Hispanic/Latino; 2 Hispanic/Latino; 1 Two or more races, non-Hispanic/Latino), 4 international. Average age 27. 134 applicants, 18% accepted, 22 enrolled. Terminal master's awarded for partial completion of doctoral program. *Degree requirements:* For master's, comprehensive exam, thesis or alternative; for doctorate, one foreign language, comprehensive exam, thesis/dissertation, 2 preliminary exams. *Entrance requirements:* For master's, minimum undergraduate GPA of 3.0. *Application deadline:* For fall admission, 1/15 priority date for domestic students, 12/15 for international students; for spring admission, 11/1 for domestic and international students. Applications are processed on a rolling basis. Application fee: $50 ($60 for international students). Electronic applications accepted. *Financial support:* In 2012–13, 25 fellowships (averaging $1,120 per year), 1 research assistantship with full and partial tuition reimbursement (averaging $30,965 per year), 57 teaching assistantships with full and partial tuition reimbursements (averaging $23,691 per year) were awarded; institutionally sponsored loans, scholarships/grants, health care benefits, and unspecified assistantships also available. Financial award application deadline: 2/1; financial award applicants required to submit FAFSA. *Faculty research:* Pure mathematics, applied mathematics and mathematical physics (including algebra, algebraic geometry, differential equations, differential geometry, logic and foundations). *Total annual research expenditures:* $351,617. *Application contact:* E-mail: gradmath@colorado.edu. Website: http://math.colorado.edu/.

University of Colorado Colorado Springs, College of Letters, Arts and Sciences, Department of Mathematics, Colorado Springs, CO 80933-7150. Offers applied mathematics (MS); applied science (PhD); mathematics (M Sc). Part-time and evening/weekend programs available. *Faculty:* 10 full-time (1 woman), 1 (woman) part-time/adjunct. *Students:* 14 full-time (4 women), 3 part-time (1 woman); includes 3 minority (1 Black or African American, non-Hispanic/Latino; 2 Hispanic/Latino), 2 international. Average age 36. In 2012, 6 master's awarded. *Degree requirements:* For master's, thesis, qualifying exam. *Entrance requirements:* For master's, GRE General Test, minimum GPA of 3.0. Additional exam requirements/recommendations for international students: Required—TOEFL (minimum score 550 paper-based). *Application deadline:* For fall admission, 6/1 for domestic and international students; for spring admission, 11/1 for domestic and international students. Applications are processed on a rolling basis. Application fee: $60 ($75 for international students). Electronic applications accepted. *Expenses:* Tuition, state resident: full-time $6412; part-time $686 per credit hour. Tuition, nonresident: full-time $11,782; part-time $1160 per credit hour. Tuition and fees vary according to course load, degree level, campus/location, program and reciprocity agreements. *Financial support:* In 2012–13, 1 student received support. Teaching assistantships, Federal Work-Study, and scholarships/grants available. Support available to part-time students. Financial award application deadline: 3/1; financial award applicants required to submit FAFSA. *Faculty research:* Associative rings and modules, spectral theory for quantum graphs, spectral theory of integrable systems, percolation theory, interacting particle systems, Abelian groups. *Total annual research expenditures:* $100,194. *Unit head:* Dr. Sarbarish Chakravarty, Chair, 719-255-3549, Fax: 719-255-3605, E-mail: schakrav@uccs.edu. *Application contact:* Kristin Sturm, Graduate Liaison, 719-255-3554, Fax: 719-255-3605, E-mail: ksturm@uccs.edu. Website: http://www.uccs.edu/math.

University of Colorado Colorado Springs, College of Letters, Arts and Sciences, Master of Sciences Program, Colorado Springs, CO 80933-7150. Offers biology (M Sc); chemistry (M Sc); education (M Sc); forensic science (M Sc); health promotion (M Sc); mathematics (M Sc); physics (M Sc); sports medicine (M Sc); sports nutrition (M Sc). Part-time programs available. *Students:* 67 full-time (48 women), 27 part-time (17 women); includes 12 minority (2 American Indian or Alaska Native, non-Hispanic/Latino; 2 Asian, non-Hispanic/Latino; 6 Hispanic/Latino; 2 Two or more races, non-Hispanic/Latino), 5 international. Average age 28. In 2012, 41 master's awarded. *Degree requirements:* For master's, thesis or alternative. *Entrance requirements:* For master's, minimum GPA of 2.75. Additional exam requirements/recommendations for international students: Required—TOEFL (minimum score 525 paper-based). *Application deadline:* For fall admission, 6/1 priority date for domestic students; for spring admission, 12/1 for domestic students. Applications are processed on a rolling basis. Application fee: $60 ($75 for international students). Electronic applications accepted. *Expenses:* Contact institution. *Financial support:* In 2012–13, 17 students received support, including 2 fellowships; research assistantships, teaching assistantships, career-related internships or fieldwork, Federal Work-Study, and scholarships/grants also available. Support available to part-time students. Financial award application deadline: 3/1; financial award applicants required to submit FAFSA. *Faculty research:* Biomechanics and physiology of elite athletic training, genetic engineering in yeast and bacteria including phage display and DNA repair, immunology and cell biology, synthetic organic chemistry. *Unit head:* Dr. Peter A. Braza, Dean, 719-255-4550, Fax: 719-255-4200, E-mail: pbraza@uccs.edu. *Application contact:* Taryn Bailey, Graduate Recruitment Specialist, 719-255-3702, Fax: 719-255-3037, E-mail: gradinfo@uccs.edu.

University of Colorado Denver, College of Liberal Arts and Sciences, Department of Mathematical and Statistical Sciences, Denver, CO 80217. Offers applied mathematics (MS, PhD), including applied mathematics, applied probability (MS), applied statistics (MS), computational biology, computational mathematics (PhD), discrete mathematics, finite geometry (PhD), mathematics education (PhD), mathematics of engineering and science (MS), numerical analysis, operations research (MS), optimization and operations research (PhD), probability (PhD), statistics (PhD). Part-time programs available. *Faculty:* 20 full-time (4 women), 3 part-time/adjunct (0 women). *Students:* 43 full-time (12 women), 13 part-time (2 women); includes 9 minority (1 Black or African American, non-Hispanic/Latino; 4 Asian, non-Hispanic/Latino; 4 Hispanic/Latino), 9 international. Average age 32. 63 applicants, 71% accepted, 14 enrolled. In 2012, 10 master's, 6 doctorates awarded. *Degree requirements:* For master's, comprehensive exam, thesis optional, 30 hours of course work with minimum GPA of 3.0; for doctorate, comprehensive exam, thesis/dissertation, 42 hours of course work with minimum GPA of 3.25. *Entrance requirements:* For master's, GRE General Test; GRE Subject Test in math (recommended), 30 hours of course work in mathematics (24 of which must be upper-division mathematics), bachelor's degree with minimum GPA of 3.0; for doctorate, GRE General Test; GRE Subject Test in math (recommended), 30 hours of course work in mathematics (24 of which must be upper-division mathematics), master's degree with minimum GPA of 3.25. Additional exam requirements/recommendations for international students: Required—TOEFL (minimum score 537 paper-based; 75 iBT); Recommended—IELTS (minimum score 6.5). *Application deadline:* For fall admission, 2/1 for domestic and international students; for spring admission, 10/1 for domestic and international students. Application fee: $50 ($75 for international students). Electronic applications accepted. *Expenses:* Tuition, state resident: full-time $7712; part-time $355 per credit hour. Tuition, nonresident: full-time $22,038; part-time $1087 per credit hour. *Required fees:* $1110; $1. Tuition and fees vary according to course load, campus/location and program. *Financial support:* In 2012–13, 33 students received support. Fellowships with partial tuition reimbursements available, research assistantships with full tuition reimbursements available, teaching assistantships with full tuition reimbursements available, Federal Work-Study, institutionally sponsored loans, scholarships/grants, traineeships, and unspecified assistantships available. Financial award application deadline: 4/1; financial award applicants required to submit FAFSA. *Faculty research:* Computational mathematics, computational biology, discrete mathematics and geometry, probability and statistics, optimization. *Unit head:* Dr. Stephen Billups, Graduate Program Director, 303-556-4814, E-mail: stephen.billups@ucdenver.edu. *Application contact:* Margie Bopp, Graduate Program Assistant, 303-556-2341, E-mail: margie.bopp@ucdenver.edu. Website: http://www.ucdenver.edu/academics/colleges/CLAS/Departments/math/Pages/MathStats.aspx.

University of Colorado Denver, College of Liberal Arts and Sciences, Program in Integrated Sciences, Denver, CO 80217. Offers applied science (MIS); computer science (MIS); mathematics (MIS). Part-time and evening/weekend programs available. *Students:* 2 full-time (1 woman), 8 part-time (2 women); includes 4 minority (1 Black or African American, non-Hispanic/Latino; 1 Asian, non-Hispanic/Latino; 1 Hispanic/Latino; 1 Two or more races, non-Hispanic/Latino). Average age 40. 3 applicants, 100% accepted, 2 enrolled. In 2012, 1 master's awarded. *Degree requirements:* For master's, 30 credit hours; thesis or project. *Entrance requirements:* For master's, GRE if undergraduate GPA is 3.0 or less, minimum of 40 semester hours in mathematics, computer science, physics, biology, chemistry and/or geology; essay; three letters of recommendation. Additional exam requirements/recommendations for international students: Required—TOEFL (minimum score 537 paper-based; 75 iBT); Recommended—IELTS (minimum score 6.5). *Application deadline:* For fall admission, 4/15 for domestic and international students; for spring admission, 10/15 for domestic and international students. Application fee: $50 ($75 for international students). Electronic applications accepted. *Expenses:* Tuition, state resident: full-time $7712; part-time $355 per credit hour. Tuition, nonresident: full-time $22,038; part-time $1087 per credit hour. *Required fees:* $1110; $1. Tuition and fees vary according to course load, campus/location and program. *Financial support:* In 2012–13, 2 students received support. Fellowships, research assistantships, teaching assistantships, Federal Work-Study, institutionally sponsored loans, scholarships/grants, traineeships, and unspecified assistantships available. Financial award application deadline: 4/1; financial award applicants required to submit FAFSA. *Faculty research:* Computer science, applied science, mathematics. *Unit head:* Dr. Martin Huber, Director of Integrated Sciences, 303-556-3561, E-mail: martin.huber@ucdenver.edu. *Application contact:* 303-556-2557, Fax: 303-556-4861, E-mail: clas@ucdenver.edu. Website: http://www.ucdenver.edu/academics/colleges/CLAS/Programs/MastersofIntegratedSciences/Pages/ProgramOverview.aspx.

University of Connecticut, Graduate School, College of Liberal Arts and Sciences, Department of Mathematics, Field of Mathematics, Storrs, CT 06269. Offers actuarial science (MS, PhD); mathematics (MS, PhD). Terminal master's awarded for partial completion of doctoral program. *Degree requirements:* For master's, comprehensive exam; for doctorate, thesis/dissertation. *Entrance requirements:* For master's and doctorate, GRE General Test. Additional exam requirements/recommendations for international students: Required—TOEFL (minimum score 550 paper-based). Electronic applications accepted.

University of Delaware, College of Arts and Sciences, Department of Mathematical Sciences, Newark, DE 19716. Offers applied mathematics (MS, PhD); mathematics (MS, PhD). Part-time programs available. Terminal master's awarded for partial completion of doctoral program. *Degree requirements:* For master's, thesis (for some programs); for doctorate, one foreign language, thesis/dissertation, qualifying exam. *Entrance requirements:* For master's and doctorate, GRE General Test. Additional exam requirements/recommendations for international students: Required—TOEFL. Electronic applications accepted. *Faculty research:* Scattering theory, inverse problems, fluid dynamics, numerical analysis, combinatorics.

University of Denver, Faculty of Natural Sciences and Mathematics, Department of Mathematics, Denver, CO 80208. Offers MA, MS, PhD. Part-time programs available. *Faculty:* 16 full-time (5 women), 3 part-time/adjunct (2 women). *Students:* 3 full-time (2 women), 19 part-time (6 women); includes 1 minority (Hispanic/Latino), 9 international. Average age 28. 38 applicants, 79% accepted, 9 enrolled. In 2012, 7 master's awarded. Terminal master's awarded for partial completion of doctoral program. *Degree requirements:* For master's, computer language, foreign language, or laboratory experience; for doctorate, one foreign language, comprehensive exam, thesis/dissertation, oral and written exams. *Entrance requirements:* For master's, GRE General Test, BA or BS in mathematics or related field; for doctorate, GRE General Test. Additional exam requirements/recommendations for international students: Required—TOEFL (minimum score 550 paper-based; 80 iBT). *Application deadline:* Applications are processed on a rolling basis. Application fee: $60. Electronic applications accepted. *Expenses:* Tuition: Full-time $38,232; part-time $1062 per credit hour. *Required fees:* $744. Tuition and fees vary according to program. *Financial support:* In 2012–13, 15 students received support, including 16 teaching assistantships with full and partial tuition reimbursements available (averaging $21,482 per year); career-related internships or fieldwork, Federal Work-Study, institutionally sponsored loans, scholarships/grants, and unspecified assistantships also available. Support available to part-time students. Financial award application deadline: 2/15; financial award applicants required to submit FAFSA. *Faculty research:* Real-time software, convex bodies, multidimensional data, parallel computer clusters. *Unit head:* Dr. Petr Vojtechovsky, Interim Chair, 303-871-2911, Fax: 303-871-3173, E-mail: petr@math.du.edu. *Application contact:* Liane Beights, Information Contact, 303-871-2911, Fax: 303-871-3173, E-mail: math-info@math.du.edu. Website: http://www.du.edu/nsm/departments/mathematics/.

University of Florida, Graduate School, College of Liberal Arts and Sciences, Department of Mathematics, Gainesville, FL 32611. Offers MA, MAT, MS, MST, PhD. Part-time programs available. Terminal master's awarded for partial completion of doctoral program. *Degree requirements:* For master's, comprehensive exam, thesis optional, first-year exam; for doctorate, one foreign language, comprehensive exam, thesis/dissertation. *Entrance requirements:* For master's and doctorate, GRE General Test, minimum GPA of 3.0. Additional exam requirements/recommendations for international students: Required—TOEFL (minimum score 550 paper-based; 80 iBT), IELTS (minimum score 6). Electronic applications accepted. *Faculty research:* Combinatorics and number theory, group theory, probability theory, logic, differential geometry and mathematical physics.

University of Georgia, Franklin College of Arts and Sciences, Department of Mathematics, Athens, GA 30602. Offers applied mathematical science (MAMS); mathematics (MA, PhD). *Degree requirements:* For master's, one foreign language, thesis (for some programs); for doctorate, 2 foreign languages, thesis/dissertation. *Entrance requirements:* For master's and doctorate, GRE General Test. Electronic applications accepted.

University of Guelph, Graduate Studies, College of Physical and Engineering Science, Department of Mathematics and Statistics, Guelph, ON N1G 2W1, Canada. Offers applied mathematics (PhD); applied statistics (PhD); mathematics and statistics (M Sc). Part-time programs available. *Degree requirements:* For master's, thesis (for some programs); for doctorate, thesis/dissertation. *Entrance requirements:* For master's, minimum B- average during previous 2 years of course work; for doctorate, minimum B average. Additional exam requirements/recommendations for international students: Required—TOEFL (minimum score 550 paper-based; 89 iBT), IELTS (minimum score 6.5). *Faculty research:* Dynamical systems, mathematical biology, numerical analysis, linear and nonlinear models, reliability and bioassay.

University of Hawaii at Manoa, Graduate Division, College of Natural Sciences, Department of Mathematics, Honolulu, HI 96822. Offers MA, PhD. Part-time programs available. *Degree requirements:* For doctorate, one foreign language, comprehensive exam, thesis/dissertation. *Entrance requirements:* For master's and doctorate, GRE General Test, minimum GPA of 3.0. Additional exam requirements/recommendations for international students: Required—TOEFL (minimum score 500 paper-based; 61 iBT), IELTS (minimum score 5). *Faculty research:* Analysis, algebra, lattice theory, logic topology, differential geometry.

University of Houston, College of Natural Sciences and Mathematics, Department of Mathematics, Houston, TX 77204. Offers applied mathematics (MS); mathematics (MA, PhD). Part-time programs available. *Degree requirements:* For master's, thesis optional. *Entrance requirements:* For master's and doctorate, GRE (Verbal and Quantitative). Additional exam requirements/recommendations for international students: Required—TOEFL (minimum score 550 paper-based; 79 iBT), IELTS (minimum score 6.5). Electronic applications accepted. *Faculty research:* Applied mathematics, modern analysis, computational science, geometry, dynamical systems.

University of Houston–Clear Lake, School of Science and Computer Engineering, Program in Mathematical Sciences, Houston, TX 77058-1098. Offers MS. Part-time and evening/weekend programs available. *Entrance requirements:* For master's, GRE General Test. Additional exam requirements/recommendations for international students: Required—TOEFL (minimum score 550 paper-based).

University of Idaho, College of Graduate Studies, College of Science, Department of Mathematics, Moscow, ID 83844-1103. Offers MAT, MS, PhD. *Faculty:* 9 full-time. *Students:* 17 full-time, 10 part-time. Average age 36. In 2012, 8 master's, 1 doctorate awarded. *Degree requirements:* For doctorate, 2 foreign languages, thesis/dissertation. *Entrance requirements:* For master's, minimum GPA of 2.8; for doctorate, minimum undergraduate GPA of 2.8, 3.0 graduate. *Application deadline:* For fall admission, 8/1 for domestic students; for spring admission, 12/15 for domestic students. Applications are processed on a rolling basis. Application fee: $60. Electronic applications accepted. *Expenses:* Tuition, state resident: full-time $4230; part-time $252 per credit hour. Tuition, nonresident: full-time $17,018; part-time $891 per credit hour. *Required fees:* $2932; $107 per credit hour. *Financial support:* Research assistantships and teaching assistantships available. Financial award applicants required to submit FAFSA. *Faculty research:* Bioinformatics and mathematical biology, analysis and differential equations, combinatorics, probability and stochastic processes, discrete geometry. *Unit head:* Dr. Monte Boisen, Chair, 208-885-6742, E-mail: math@uidaho.edu. *Application contact:* Erick Larson, Director of Graduate Admissions, 208-885-4723, E-mail: gadms@uidaho.edu. Website: http://www.uidaho.edu/sci/math.

University of Illinois at Chicago, Graduate College, College of Liberal Arts and Sciences, Department of Mathematics, Statistics, and Computer Science, Chicago, IL 60607-7128. Offers applied mathematics (MS, PhD); computational finance (MS, PhD); computer science (MS, PhD); mathematics (DA); mathematics and information sciences for industry (MS); probability and statistics (PhD); pure mathematics (MS, PhD); statistics (MS); teaching of mathematics (MST), including elementary, secondary. Part-time programs available. *Students:* 125 full-time (34 women), 34 part-time (15 women); includes 23 minority (1 Black or African American, non-Hispanic/Latino; 10 Asian, non-Hispanic/Latino; 10 Hispanic/Latino; 2 Two or more races, non-Hispanic/Latino), 45 international. Average age 29. 226 applicants, 37% accepted, 42 enrolled. In 2012, 30 master's, 19 doctorates awarded. *Degree requirements:* For master's, comprehensive exam; for doctorate, one foreign language, thesis/dissertation. *Entrance requirements:* For master's and doctorate, GRE General Test, minimum GPA of 3.0. Additional exam requirements/recommendations for international students: Required—TOEFL (minimum score 100 iBT). *Application deadline:* For fall admission, 1/1 for domestic and international students; for spring admission, 10/1 for domestic students, 7/15 for international students. Applications are processed on a rolling basis. Application fee: $60. Electronic applications accepted. *Expenses:* Tuition, state resident: full-time $10,882; part-time $3627 per term. Tuition, nonresident: full-time $22,880; part-time $7627 per term. *Required fees:* $1170 per semester. Tuition and fees vary according to course load, degree level and program. *Financial support:* In 2012–13, 109 students received support, including 2 fellowships with full tuition reimbursements available (averaging $20,000 per year), 8 research assistantships with full tuition reimbursements available (averaging $17,000 per year), 87 teaching assistantships with full tuition reimbursements available (averaging $17,000 per year); Federal Work-Study, scholarships/grants, and tuition waivers (full) also available. Financial award application deadline: 1/1. *Total annual research expenditures:* $2.2 million. *Unit head:* Lawrence Ein, Head, 312-996-3044, E-mail: ein@math.uic.edu. *Application contact:* Ramin Takloo-Bighash, Director of Graduate Studies, 312-996-5119, E-mail: dgs@math.uic.edu. Website: http://www.math.uic.edu/.

Mathematics

University of Illinois at Urbana–Champaign, Graduate College, College of Liberal Arts and Sciences, Department of Mathematics, Champaign, IL 61820. Offers applied mathematics (MS); applied mathematics: actuarial science (MS); mathematics (MS, PhD); teaching of mathematics (MS). *Students:* 192 (70 women). Application fee: $75 ($90 for international students). *Unit head:* Matthew Ando, Chair, 217-244-2846, Fax: .217-333-9576, E-mail: mando@illinois.edu. *Application contact:* Marci Blocher, Office Support Specialist, 217-333-5749, Fax: 217-333-9576, E-mail: mblocher@illinois.edu. Website: http://math.illinois.edu/.

The University of Iowa, Graduate College, College of Liberal Arts and Sciences, Department of Mathematics, Iowa City, IA 52242-1316. Offers MS, PhD. *Degree requirements:* For master's, thesis optional, exam; for doctorate, comprehensive exam, thesis/dissertation. *Entrance requirements:* For master's and doctorate, GRE General Test, minimum GPA of 3.0. Additional exam requirements/recommendations for international students: Required—TOEFL (minimum score 620 paper-based; 105 iBT). Electronic applications accepted.

The University of Kansas, Graduate Studies, College of Liberal Arts and Sciences, Department of Mathematics, Lawrence, KS 66045. Offers mathematics (MA, PhD). *Faculty:* 32. *Students:* 75 full-time (12 women), 7 part-time (0 women); includes 3 minority (1 Black or African American, non-Hispanic/Latino; 2 Asian, non-Hispanic/Latino), 41 international. Average age 28. 106 applicants, 44% accepted, 18 enrolled. In 2012, 13 master's, 3 doctorates awarded. Terminal master's awarded for partial completion of doctoral program. *Degree requirements:* For master's, comprehensive exam, thesis or alternative; for doctorate, one foreign language, comprehensive exam, thesis/dissertation, 1 computer language. *Entrance requirements:* For master's and doctorate, GRE. Additional exam requirements/recommendations for international students: Required—TOEFL. *Application deadline:* For fall admission, 8/4 priority date for domestic students, 5/2 for international students; for spring admission, 1/4 priority date for domestic students, 10/15 for international students. Applications are processed on a rolling basis. Application fee: $55 ($65 for international students). Electronic applications accepted. *Financial support:* Fellowships with full tuition reimbursements, research assistantships with full and partial tuition reimbursements, teaching assistantships with full tuition reimbursements, institutionally sponsored loans, scholarships/grants, health care benefits, and unspecified assistantships available. Support available to part-time students. Financial award application deadline: 1/31. *Faculty research:* Algebra and algebraic geometry; analysis, partial differential equations and dynamical systems; probability, stochastic analysis and stochastic control; numerical analysis; geometry. *Unit head:* Daniel Katz, Chair, 785-864-3651, Fax: 785-864-5255, E-mail: dlk@math.ku.edu. *Application contact:* Prof. Milena Stanislavova, Graduate Director, 785-864-3651, Fax: 785-864-5255, E-mail: stanis@math.ku.edu. Website: http://www.math.ku.edu/.

University of Kentucky, Graduate School, College of Arts and Sciences, Program in Mathematics, Lexington, KY 40506-0032. Offers applied mathematics (MS); mathematics (MA, MS, PhD). *Degree requirements:* For master's, comprehensive exam, thesis optional; for doctorate, one foreign language, comprehensive exam, thesis/dissertation. *Entrance requirements:* For master's, GRE General Test, minimum undergraduate GPA of 2.75; for doctorate, GRE General Test, minimum graduate GPA of 3.0. Additional exam requirements/recommendations for international students: Required—TOEFL (minimum score 550 paper-based). Electronic applications accepted. *Faculty research:* Numerical analysis, combinatorics, partial differential equations, algebra and number theory, real and complex analysis.

University of Lethbridge, School of Graduate Studies, Lethbridge, AB T1K 3M4, Canada. Offers accounting (MScM); addictions counseling (M Sc); agricultural biotechnology (M Sc); agricultural studies (M Sc, MA); anthropology (MA); archaeology (MA); art (MA, MFA); biochemistry (M Sc); biological sciences (M Sc); biomolecular science (PhD); biosystems and biodiversity (PhD); Canadian studies (MA); chemistry (M Sc); computer science (M Sc); computer science and geographical information science (M Sc); counseling psychology (M Ed); dramatic arts (MA); earth, space, and physical science (PhD); economics (MA); educational leadership (M Ed); English (MA); environmental science (M Sc); evolution and behavior (PhD); exercise science (M Sc); finance (MScM); French (MA); French/German (MA); French/Spanish (MA); general education (M Ed); general management (MScM); geography (M Sc, MA); German (MA); health science (M Sc); history (MA); human resource management and labour relations (MScM); individualized multidisciplinary (M Sc, MA); information systems (MScM); international management (MScM); kinesiology (M Sc, MA); management (M Sc, MA); marketing (MScM); mathematics (M Sc); music (M Mus, MA); Native American studies (MA); neuroscience (M Sc, PhD); new media (MA); nursing (M Sc); philosophy (MA); physics (M Sc); policy and strategy (MScM); political science (MA); psychology (M Sc, MA); religious studies (MA); social sciences (MA); sociology (MA); theatre and dramatic arts (MFA); theoretical and computational science (PhD); urban and regional studies (MA); women's studies (MA). Part-time and evening/weekend programs available. *Degree requirements:* For doctorate, comprehensive exam, thesis/dissertation. *Entrance requirements:* For master's, GMAT (M Sc in management), bachelor's degree in related field, minimum GPA of 3.0 during previous 20 graded semester courses, 2 years teaching or related experience (M Ed); for doctorate, master's degree, minimum graduate GPA of 3.5. Additional exam requirements/recommendations for international students: Required—TOEFL. *Faculty research:* Movement and brain plasticity, gibberellin physiology, photosynthesis, carbon cycling, molecular properties of main-group ring components.

University of Louisiana at Lafayette, College of Sciences, Department of Mathematics, Lafayette, LA 70504. Offers MS, PhD. Terminal master's awarded for partial completion of doctoral program. *Degree requirements:* For master's, thesis or alternative; for doctorate, 2 foreign languages, comprehensive exam, thesis/dissertation. *Entrance requirements:* For master's, GRE General Test, minimum GPA of 2.75; for doctorate, GRE General Test, minimum GPA of 3.0. Additional exam requirements/recommendations for international students: Required—TOEFL (minimum score 550 paper-based). Electronic applications accepted. *Faculty research:* Topology, algebra, applied mathematics, analysis.

University of Louisville, Graduate School, College of Arts and Sciences, Department of Mathematics, Louisville, KY 40292. Offers applied and industrial mathematics (PhD); mathematics (MA). Part-time programs available. *Students:* 31 full-time (9 women), 3 part-time (1 woman), 10 international. Average age 30. 34 applicants, 68% accepted, 9 enrolled. In 2012, 6 master's, 5 doctorates awarded. Terminal master's awarded for partial completion of doctoral program. *Degree requirements:* For master's, comprehensive exam (for some programs), thesis optional; for doctorate, comprehensive exam, thesis/dissertation, internship, project. *Entrance requirements:* For master's and doctorate, GRE General Test. Additional exam requirements/recommendations for international students: Required—TOEFL (minimum score 550 paper-based; 79 iBT). *Application deadline:* For fall admission, 3/15 priority date for domestic students, 3/15 for international students; for winter admission, 8/15 priority date for domestic students, 8/15 for international students. Applications are processed on a rolling basis. Application fee: $60. Electronic applications accepted. *Financial support:* In 2012–13, 25 students received support, including 2 fellowships with full tuition reimbursements available (averaging $20,000 per year), 1 research assistantship (averaging $20,000 per year), 25 teaching assistantships with full tuition reimbursements available (averaging $20,000 per year); health care benefits and unspecified assistantships also available. Financial award application deadline: 3/15. *Faculty research:* Algebra, analysis, bio-mathematics, combinatorics and graph theory, coding theory, consensus theory, financial mathematics, functional equations, partial differential equations. *Total annual research expenditures:* $77,000. *Unit head:* Dr. Thomas Riedel, Chair, 502-852-6826, Fax: 502-852-7132, E-mail: thomas.riedel@louisville.edu. *Application contact:* Dr. Bingtuan Li, Graduate Studies Director, 502-852-6826, Fax: 502-852-7132, E-mail: bing.li@louisville.edu. Website: http://www.math.louisville.edu.

University of Maine, Graduate School, College of Liberal Arts and Sciences, Department of Mathematics and Statistics, Orono, ME 04469. Offers mathematics (MA). *Faculty:* 12 full-time (1 woman), 1 part-time/adjunct (0 women). *Students:* 12 full-time (5 women), 2 part-time (0 women), 1 international. Average age 28. 11 applicants, 64% accepted, 3 enrolled. In 2012, 4 master's awarded. *Degree requirements:* For master's, thesis optional. *Entrance requirements:* For master's, GRE General Test. Additional exam requirements/recommendations for international students: Required—TOEFL. *Application deadline:* For fall admission, 2/1 priority date for domestic students. Applications are processed on a rolling basis. Application fee: $65. Electronic applications accepted. *Financial support:* In 2012–13, 7 teaching assistantships with full tuition reimbursements (averaging $13,600 per year) were awarded; tuition waivers (full and partial) also available. Financial award application deadline: 3/1. *Total annual research expenditures:* $144,295. *Unit head:* Dr. Robert Franzosa, Co-Chair, 207-581-3916, Fax: 207-581-4977, E-mail: franzosa@math.umaine.edu. *Application contact:* Scott G. Delcourt, Associate Dean of the Graduate School, 207-581-3291, Fax: 207-581-3232, E-mail: graduate@maine.edu. Website: http://umaine.edu/mathematics/.

The University of Manchester, School of Mathematics, Manchester, United Kingdom. Offers actuarial science (PhD); applied mathematics (M Phil, PhD); applied numerical computing (M Phil, PhD); financial mathematics (M Phil, PhD); mathematical logic (M Phil); probability (M Phil, PhD); pure mathematics (M Phil, PhD); statistics (M Phil, PhD).

University of Manitoba, Faculty of Graduate Studies, Faculty of Science, Department of Mathematics, Winnipeg, MB R3T 2N2, Canada. Offers M Sc, PhD. *Degree requirements:* For master's, one foreign language, thesis or alternative; for doctorate, one foreign language, thesis/dissertation.

University of Manitoba, Faculty of Graduate Studies, Faculty of Science, Program in Mathematical, Computational and Statistical Sciences, Winnipeg, MB R3T 2N2, Canada. Offers MMCSS.

University of Maryland, College Park, Academic Affairs, College of Computer, Mathematical and Natural Sciences, Department of Mathematics, Program in Mathematics, College Park, MD 20742. Offers MA, PhD. Part-time and evening/weekend programs available. *Students:* 72 full-time (12 women), 8 part-time (3 women); includes 9 minority (6 Asian, non-Hispanic/Latino; 3 Hispanic/Latino), 24 international. 239 applicants, 14% accepted, 14 enrolled. In 2012, 9 master's, 9 doctorates awarded. Terminal master's awarded for partial completion of doctoral program. *Degree requirements:* For master's, thesis or alternative; for doctorate, one foreign language, thesis/dissertation, written exam, oral exam. *Entrance requirements:* For master's, GRE General Test, GRE Subject Test, minimum GPA of 3.0, 3 letters of recommendation; for doctorate, GRE General Test, GRE Subject Test, 3 letters of recommendation. *Application deadline:* For fall admission, 1/15 priority date for domestic students, 1/15 for international students; for spring admission, 10/1 for domestic students, 6/1 for international students. Applications are processed on a rolling basis. Application fee: $75. Electronic applications accepted. *Expenses:* Tuition, state resident: part-time $551 per credit. Tuition, nonresident: part-time $1188 per credit. Part-time tuition and fees vary according to program. *Financial support:* In 2012–13, 2 fellowships with partial tuition reimbursements (averaging $11,650 per year), 10 research assistantships (averaging $18,541 per year), 49 teaching assistantships (averaging $17,202 per year) were awarded. Financial award applicants required to submit FAFSA. *Unit head:* James Yorke, Director, 301-405-5048, E-mail: yorke@umd.edu. *Application contact:* Dr. Charles A. Caramello, Dean of Graduate School, 301-405-0358, Fax: 301-314-9305.

University of Massachusetts Amherst, Graduate School, College of Natural Sciences, Department of Mathematics and Statistics, Amherst, MA 01003. Offers applied mathematics (MS); mathematics (MS, PhD); statistics (MS, PhD). *Faculty:* 41 full-time (5 women). *Students:* 74 full-time (21 women), 1 part-time (0 women); includes 8 minority (2 Black or African American, non-Hispanic/Latino; 5 Asian, non-Hispanic/Latino; 1 Two or more races, non-Hispanic/Latino), 35 international. Average age 27. 302 applicants, 21% accepted, 26 enrolled. In 2012, 17 master's, 6 doctorates awarded. Terminal master's awarded for partial completion of doctoral program. *Degree requirements:* For master's, thesis or alternative; for doctorate, comprehensive exam, thesis/dissertation. *Entrance requirements:* For master's and doctorate, GRE General Test, GRE Subject Test (mathematics). Additional exam requirements/recommendations for international students: Required—TOEFL (minimum score 550 paper-based; 80 iBT), IELTS (minimum score 6.5). *Application deadline:* For fall admission, 2/1 for domestic and international students. Applications are processed on a rolling basis. Application fee: $75. Electronic applications accepted. *Expenses:* Tuition, state resident: full-time $1980; part-time $110 per credit. Tuition, nonresident: full-time $13,314; part-time $414 per credit. *Required fees:* $10,338; $3594 per semester. One-time fee: $357. *Financial support:* Fellowships with full and partial tuition reimbursements, research assistantships with full and partial tuition reimbursements, teaching assistantships with full and partial tuition reimbursements, career-related internships or fieldwork, Federal Work-Study, scholarships/grants, traineeships, health care benefits, tuition waivers (full and partial), and unspecified assistantships available. Support available to part-time students. Financial award application deadline: 2/1. *Unit head:* Dr. Michael Lavine, Department Head, 413-545-2282, Fax: 413-545-1801. *Application contact:* Lindsay DeSantis, Supervisor of Admissions, 413-545-0722, Fax: 413-577-0010, E-mail: gradadm@grad.umass.edu. Website: http://www.math.umass.edu/.

University of Massachusetts Lowell, College of Sciences, Department of Mathematical Sciences, Lowell, MA 01854-2881. Offers applied mathematics (MS); computational mathematics (PhD); mathematics (MS). Part-time programs available. *Entrance requirements:* For master's, GRE General Test.

University of Memphis, Graduate School, College of Arts and Sciences, Department of Mathematical Sciences, Memphis, TN 38152. Offers applied mathematics (MS); applied statistics (PhD); bioinformatics (MS); computer science (PhD); computer sciences (MS); mathematics (MS, PhD); statistics (MS, PhD). Part-time programs available. Terminal master's awarded for partial completion of doctoral program. *Degree requirements:* For master's, comprehensive exam; for doctorate, one foreign language, thesis/dissertation, oral exams. *Entrance requirements:* For master's and doctorate, GRE General Test, minimum GPA of 2.5. Additional exam requirements/recommendations for international students: Required—TOEFL (minimum score 550 paper-based). Electronic applications accepted. *Faculty research:* Combinatorics, ergodic theory, graph theory, Ramsey theory, applied statistics.

University of Miami, Graduate School, College of Arts and Sciences, Department of Mathematics, Coral Gables, FL 33124. Offers MA, MS, PhD. Part-time and evening/weekend programs available. Terminal master's awarded for partial completion of doctoral program. *Degree requirements:* For master's, comprehensive exam, qualifying exams; for doctorate, one foreign language, thesis/dissertation, qualifying exams. *Entrance requirements:* For master's and doctorate, GRE General Test, minimum GPA of 3.0. Additional exam requirements/recommendations for international students: Required—TOEFL (minimum score 550 paper-based; 59 iBT). Electronic applications accepted. *Faculty research:* Applied mathematics, probability, geometric analysis, differential equations, algebraic combinatorics.

University of Michigan, Horace H. Rackham School of Graduate Studies, College of Literature, Science, and the Arts, Department of Mathematics, Ann Arbor, MI 48109. Offers applied and interdisciplinary mathematics (AM, MS, PhD); mathematics (AM, MS, PhD). Part-time programs available. *Faculty:* 65 full-time (9 women). *Students:* 144 full-time (33 women); includes 18 minority (3 Black or African American, non-Hispanic/Latino; 8 Asian, non-Hispanic/Latino; 4 Hispanic/Latino; 1 Native Hawaiian or other Pacific Islander, non-Hispanic/Latino; 2 Two or more races, non-Hispanic/Latino), 56 international. Average age 26. 675 applicants, 18% accepted, 31 enrolled. In 2012, 18 master's, 20 doctorates awarded. *Degree requirements:* For doctorate, one foreign language, comprehensive exam, thesis/dissertation, oral defense of dissertation, preliminary exam. *Entrance requirements:* For master's and doctorate, GRE General Test, GRE Subject Test. Additional exam requirements/recommendations for international students: Required—TOEFL (minimum score 560 paper-based; 84 iBT). *Application deadline:* For fall admission, 1/15 for domestic and international students. Applications are processed on a rolling basis. Application fee: $65 ($75 for international students). Electronic applications accepted. *Financial support:* In 2012–13, 126 students received support, including 12 fellowships with full tuition reimbursements available (averaging $25,000 per year), 22 research assistantships with full tuition reimbursements available (averaging $18,234 per year), 92 teaching assistantships with full tuition reimbursements available (averaging $18,234 per year). Financial award application deadline: 3/15. *Faculty research:* Algebra, analysis, topology, applied mathematics, geometry. *Unit head:* Prof. Mel Hochster, Chair, 734-936-1310, Fax: 734-763-0937, E-mail: math-chair@umich.edu. *Application contact:* Prof. Sergey Fomin, Admissions Director, 734-764-7436, Fax: 734-763-0937, E-mail: math-admissionsdir@umich.edu. Website: http://www.lsa.umich.edu/math/.

University of Minnesota, Twin Cities Campus, College of Science and Engineering, School of Mathematics, Minneapolis, MN 55455-0213. Offers mathematics (MS, PhD); quantitative finance (Certificate). Part-time programs available. Terminal master's awarded for partial completion of doctoral program. *Degree requirements:* For master's, thesis (for some programs); for doctorate, 2 foreign languages, thesis/dissertation. *Entrance requirements:* For master's, GRE Subject Test (recommended); for doctorate, GRE Subject Test. Additional exam requirements/recommendations for international students: Required—TOEFL. Electronic applications accepted. *Faculty research:* Partial and ordinary differential equations, algebra and number theory, geometry, combinatorics, numerical analysis, probability.

University of Mississippi, Graduate School, College of Liberal Arts, Department of Mathematics, Oxford, University, MS 38677. Offers MA, MS, PhD. *Faculty:* 36 full-time (17 women). *Students:* 28 full-time (12 women), 5 part-time (2 women); includes 3 minority (all Black or African American, non-Hispanic/Latino), 7 international. In 2012, 5 master's, 1 doctorate awarded. *Degree requirements:* For master's, thesis (for some programs); for doctorate, thesis/dissertation. *Entrance requirements:* For master's, GRE General Test, minimum GPA of 3.0; for doctorate, GRE General Test. Additional exam requirements/recommendations for international students: Required—TOEFL. *Application deadline:* For fall admission, 4/1 for domestic students; for spring admission, 10/1 for domestic students. Applications are processed on a rolling basis. Application fee: $25. Electronic applications accepted. *Expenses:* Tuition, state resident: full-time $6282; part-time $349 per credit hour. Tuition, nonresident: full-time $16,266; part-time $903.50 per credit hour. *Financial support:* Scholarships/grants available. Financial award application deadline: 3/1; financial award applicants required to submit FAFSA. *Unit head:* Dr. Iwo M. Labuda, Interim Chairman, 662-915-7071, Fax: 662-915-5491, E-mail: mdept@olemiss.edu. *Application contact:* Dr. Christy M. Wyandt, Associate Dean, 662-915-7474, Fax: 662-915-7577, E-mail: cwyandt@olemiss.edu.

University of Missouri, Graduate School, College of Arts and Sciences, Department of Mathematics, Columbia, MO 65211. Offers applied mathematics (MS); mathematics (MA, MST, PhD). *Faculty:* 40 full-time (6 women), 1 (woman) part-time/adjunct. *Students:* 61 full-time (7 women), 10 part-time (1 woman); includes 2 minority (1 Hispanic/Latino; 1 Two or more races, non-Hispanic/Latino), 24 international. Average age 27. 111 applicants, 23% accepted, 15 enrolled. In 2012, 14 master's, 10 doctorates awarded. *Degree requirements:* For doctorate, 2 foreign languages, comprehensive exam, thesis/dissertation. *Entrance requirements:* For master's and doctorate, GRE General Test, minimum GPA of 3.0; bachelor's degree from accredited institution. Additional exam requirements/recommendations for international students: Required—TOEFL (minimum score 500 paper-based; 61 iBT). *Application deadline:* For fall admission, 1/15 priority date for domestic students, 1/15 for international students. Applications are processed on a rolling basis. Application fee: $55 ($75 for international students). Electronic applications accepted. *Expenses:* Tuition, state resident: full-time $6057. Tuition, nonresident: full-time $15,683. *Required fees:* $1000. *Financial support:* In 2012–13, 7 fellowships with full tuition reimbursements, 4 research assistantships with full tuition reimbursements, 64 teaching assistantships with full tuition reimbursements were awarded; institutionally sponsored loans, health care benefits, and unspecified assistantships also available. Financial award applicants required to submit FAFSA. *Faculty research:* Algebraic geometry, analysis (real, complex, functional and harmonic), analytic functions, applied mathematics, financial mathematics and mathematics of insurance, commutative rings, scattering theory, differential equations (ordinary and partial), differential geometry, dynamical systems, general relativity, mathematical physics, number theory, probabilistic analysis and topology. *Unit head:* Dr. Glen Himmelberg, Department Chair, 573-882-6222, E-mail: himmelbergg@missouri.edu. *Application contact:* Amy Crews, Administrative Assistant, 573-882-6222, E-mail: crewsae@missouri.edu. Website: http://www.math.missouri.edu/.

University of Missouri–Kansas City, College of Arts and Sciences, Department of Mathematics and Statistics, Kansas City, MO 64110-2499. Offers MA, MS, PhD. PhD (interdisciplinary) offered through the School of Graduate Studies. Part-time programs available. *Faculty:* 14 full-time (4 women), 2 part-time/adjunct (0 women). *Students:* 6 full-time (3 women), 25 part-time (12 women); includes 3 minority (all Asian, non-Hispanic/Latino), 5 international. Average age 31. 31 applicants, 58% accepted, 9 enrolled. In 2012, 11 master's awarded. Terminal master's awarded for partial completion of doctoral program. *Degree requirements:* For master's, written exam; for doctorate, 2 foreign languages, thesis/dissertation, oral and written exams. *Entrance requirements:* For master's, bachelor's degree in mathematics, minimum GPA of 3.0; for doctorate, GMAT or GRE General Test. Additional exam requirements/recommendations for international students: Required—TOEFL (minimum score 550 paper-based; 80 iBT). *Application deadline:* For fall admission, 3/15 for domestic and international students; for spring admission, 10/15 for domestic and international students. Applications are processed on a rolling basis. Application fee: $45 ($50 for international students). Electronic applications accepted. *Expenses:* Tuition, state

Peterson's Graduate Programs in the Physical Sciences, Mathematics, Agricultural Sciences, the Environment & Natural Resources 2014

www.petersonsbooks.com **343**

resident: full-time $5972.40; part-time $331.80 per credit hour. Tuition, nonresident: full-time $15,417; part-time $856.50 per credit hour. *Required fees:* $95.89 per credit hour. Full-time tuition and fees vary according to program. *Financial support:* In 2012–13, 9 teaching assistantships with full tuition reimbursements (averaging $18,061 per year) were awarded; research assistantships, Federal Work-Study, institutionally sponsored loans, and tuition waivers (full and partial) also available. Support available to part-time students. Financial award application deadline: 3/1; financial award applicants required to submit FAFSA. *Faculty research:* Numerical analysis, statistics, biostatistics, commutative algebra, differential equations. *Unit head:* Dr. Eric Hall, Interim Chair, 816-235-5852, Fax: 816-235-5517, E-mail: umkcmathdept@umkc.edu. *Application contact:* Dr. Hristo Voulov, Associate Professor, 816-235-1641, Fax: 816-235-5517, E-mail: umkcmathdept@umkc.edu. Website: http://cas.umkc.edu/math/.

University of Missouri–St. Louis, College of Arts and Sciences, Department of Mathematics and Computer Science, St. Louis, MO 63121. Offers applied mathematics (PhD), including computer science, mathematics; computer science (MS); mathematics (MA). Part-time and evening/weekend programs available. *Faculty:* 15 full-time (2 women). *Students:* 19 full-time (8 women), 50 part-time (17 women); includes 7 minority (2 Black or African American, non-Hispanic/Latino; 2 Asian, non-Hispanic/Latino; 3 Two or more races, non-Hispanic/Latino), 21 international. Average age 32. 76 applicants, 50% accepted, 18 enrolled. In 2012, 19 master's, 3 doctorates awarded. *Degree requirements:* For master's, thesis optional; for doctorate, thesis/dissertation. *Entrance requirements:* For master's, GRE (for teaching assistantships), 2 letters of recommendation; C programming, C++ or Java (for computer science); for doctorate, GRE General Test, 3 letters of recommendation. Additional exam requirements/recommendations for international students: Required—TOEFL (minimum score 550 paper-based; 79 iBT), IELTS (minimum score 6.5). *Application deadline:* For fall admission, 7/1 priority date for domestic students, 7/1 for international students; for spring admission, 12/1 priority date for domestic students, 12/1 for international students. Applications are processed on a rolling basis. Application fee: $35 ($40 for international students). Electronic applications accepted. *Expenses:* Tuition, state resident: full-time $7364; part-time $409.10 per credit hour. Tuition, nonresident: full-time $18,153; part-time $1008.50 per credit hour. *Financial support:* In 2012–13, 1 research assistantship with full and partial tuition reimbursement (averaging $5,626 per year), 9 teaching assistantships with full and partial tuition reimbursements (averaging $12,667 per year) were awarded; fellowships with full tuition reimbursements also available. Financial award applicants required to submit FAFSA. *Faculty research:* Statistics, algebra, analysis. *Unit head:* Dr. Qingtang Jiang, Director of Graduate Studies, 314-516-5741, Fax: 314-516-5400, E-mail: jiangq@umsl.edu. *Application contact:* 314-516-5458, Fax: 314-516-6996, E-mail: gradadm@umsl.edu.

The University of Montana, Graduate School, College of Arts and Sciences, Department of Mathematical Sciences, Missoula, MT 59812-0002. Offers mathematics (MA, PhD), including college teaching (PhD), traditional mathematics research (PhD); mathematics education (MA). Part-time programs available. Terminal master's awarded for partial completion of doctoral program. *Degree requirements:* For doctorate, thesis/dissertation. *Entrance requirements:* For master's and doctorate, GRE General Test. Additional exam requirements/recommendations for international students: Required—TOEFL (minimum score 525 paper-based).

University of Nebraska at Omaha, Graduate Studies, College of Arts and Sciences, Department of Mathematics, Omaha, NE 68182. Offers MA, MAT, MS. Part-time programs available. *Faculty:* 17 full-time (3 women). *Students:* 11 full-time (4 women), 28 part-time (7 women); includes 7 minority (3 Black or African American, non-Hispanic/Latino; 1 Asian, non-Hispanic/Latino; 3 Hispanic/Latino), 3 international. Average age 30. 20 applicants, 70% accepted, 9 enrolled. In 2012, 11 master's awarded. *Degree requirements:* For master's, comprehensive exam, thesis (for some programs). *Entrance requirements:* For master's, minimum GPA of 3.0, 15 undergraduate math hours. Additional exam requirements/recommendations for international students: Required—TOEFL (minimum score 500 paper-based; 61 iBT). *Application deadline:* For fall admission, 7/31 priority date for domestic students; for spring admission, 11/30 priority date for domestic students. Applications are processed on a rolling basis. Application fee: $45. Electronic applications accepted. *Expenses:* Tuition, state resident: full-time $4469; part-time $248.25 per credit. Tuition, nonresident: full-time $11,763; part-time $653.50 per credit. *Required fees:* $1270. *Financial support:* In 2012–13, 11 students received support, including 1 research assistantship with tuition reimbursement available, 8 teaching assistantships with tuition reimbursements available; Federal Work-Study, institutionally sponsored loans, traineeships, tuition waivers (partial), and unspecified assistantships also available. Support available to part-time students. Financial award application deadline: 3/1; financial award applicants required to submit FAFSA. *Unit head:* Dr. John Konvalina, Chairperson, 402-554-3430. *Application contact:* Dr. Steve From, Professor, 402-554-2341, Fax: 402-554-3143, E-mail: graduate@unomaha.edu.

University of Nebraska–Lincoln, Graduate College, College of Arts and Sciences, Department of Mathematics, Lincoln, NE 68588. Offers mathematics (MA, MAT, MS, PhD); mathematics and computer science (PhD). *Degree requirements:* For master's, thesis optional; for doctorate, variable foreign language requirement, comprehensive exam, thesis/dissertation. *Entrance requirements:* Additional exam requirements/recommendations for international students: Required—TOEFL (minimum score 550 paper-based). Electronic

applications accepted. *Faculty research:* Applied mathematics, commutative algebra, algebraic geometry, Bayesian statistics, biostatistics.

University of Nevada, Las Vegas, Graduate College, College of Science, Department of Mathematical Sciences, Las Vegas, NV 89154-4020. Offers MS, PhD. Part-time programs available. *Faculty:* 29 full-time (5 women), 6 part-time/adjunct (3 women). *Students:* 43 full-time (11 women), 7 part-time (3 women); includes 27 minority (4 Hispanic/Latino; 23 Two or more races, non-Hispanic/Latino), 13 international. Average age 31. 57 applicants, 65% accepted, 15 enrolled. In 2012, 15 master's, 1 doctorate awarded. *Degree requirements:* For master's, comprehensive exam (for some programs), thesis (for some programs), oral exam. *Entrance requirements:* For master's and doctorate, GRE General Test. Additional exam requirements/recommendations for international students: Required—TOEFL (minimum score 550 paper-based; 80 iBT), IELTS (minimum score 7). *Application deadline:* For fall admission, 2/1 priority date for domestic students, 5/1 for international students; for spring admission, 10/1 for domestic and international students. Applications are processed on a rolling basis. Application fee: $60 ($75 for international students). Electronic applications accepted. *Expenses:* Tuition, state resident: full-time $4752; part-time $264 per credit. Tuition, nonresident: full-time $18,662; part-time $527.50 per credit. *Required fees:* $12 per credit. $266 per semester. One-time fee: $35. Tuition and fees vary according to course load, program and reciprocity agreements. *Financial support:* In 2012–13, 44 students received support, including 44 teaching assistantships with partial tuition reimbursements available (averaging $11,432 per year); institutionally sponsored loans, scholarships/grants, health care benefits, and unspecified assistantships also available. Financial award application deadline: 3/1. *Faculty research:* Statistics and biostatistics, numerical analysis and scientific computing, partial differential equations, number theory, mathematical logic. *Total annual research expenditures:* $112,646. *Unit head:* Dr. Derrick Dubose, Chair/Professor, 702-895-0382, Fax: 702-895-4343, E-mail: dubose@unlv.nevada.edu. *Application contact:* Graduate College Admissions Evaluator, 702-895-3320, Fax: 702-895-4180, E-mail: gradcollege@unlv.edu. Website: http://math.unlv.edu/.

University of Nevada, Reno, Graduate School, College of Science, Department of Mathematics and Statistics, Reno, NV 89557. Offers mathematics (MS); teaching mathematics (MATM). *Degree requirements:* For master's, thesis optional. *Entrance requirements:* For master's, GRE General Test, minimum GPA of 2.75. Additional exam requirements/recommendations for international students: Required—TOEFL (minimum score 500 paper-based; 61 iBT), IELTS (minimum score 6). Electronic applications accepted. *Faculty research:* Operator algebra, nonlinear systems, differential equations.

University of New Brunswick Fredericton, School of Graduate Studies, Faculty of Science, Department of Mathematics and Statistics, Fredericton, NB E3B 5A3, Canada. Offers M Sc, PhD. *Faculty:* 17 full-time (0 women), 1 part-time/adjunct (0 women). *Students:* 16 full-time (5 women), 2 part-time (1 woman). In 2012, 5 master's, 1 doctorate awarded. *Degree requirements:* For master's, thesis; for doctorate, comprehensive exam, thesis/dissertation. *Entrance requirements:* For master's and doctorate, minimum GPA of 3.0. Additional exam requirements/recommendations for international students: Required—TOEFL (minimum score 550 paper-based), TWE (minimum score 4); Recommended—IELTS (minimum score 7). *Application deadline:* For fall admission, 3/1 for domestic students. Applications are processed on a rolling basis. Application fee: $50 Canadian dollars. Electronic applications accepted. Tuition and fees charges are reported in Canadian dollars. *Expenses:* Tuition, area resident: Full-time $3956 Canadian dollars. *Required fees:* $579.50 Canadian dollars; $55 Canadian dollars per semester. *Financial support:* In 2012–13, 35 research assistantships, 21 teaching assistantships were awarded; fellowships also available. *Faculty research:* Commutative and non-commutative algebra, combinatorics, mathematical modeling and computation, mathematical biology, classical and quantum gravity, multivariate statistics and spatial statistics. *Unit head:* Dr. James Watmough, Director of Graduate Studies, 506-458-7363, Fax: 506-453-4705, E-mail: watmough@unb.ca. *Application contact:* Marilyn Hetherington, Graduate Secretary, 506-458-7373, Fax: 506-453-4705, E-mail: mhetheri@unb.ca. Website: http://go.unb.ca/gradprograms.

University of New Hampshire, Graduate School, College of Engineering and Physical Sciences, Department of Mathematics and Statistics, Durham, NH 03824. Offers applied mathematics (MS); industrial statistics (Postbaccalaureate Certificate); mathematics (MS, MST, PhD); mathematics education (PhD); statistics (MS). *Faculty:* 21 full-time (5 women). *Students:* 26 full-time (8 women), 36 part-time (18 women); includes 4 minority (1 American Indian or Alaska Native, non-Hispanic/Latino; 2 Asian, non-Hispanic/Latino; 1 Two or more races, non-Hispanic/Latino), 17 international. Average age 30. 84 applicants, 46% accepted, 14 enrolled. In 2012, 12 master's, 1 doctorate, 3 other advanced degrees awarded. Terminal master's awarded for partial completion of doctoral program. *Degree requirements:* For doctorate, 2 foreign languages, thesis/dissertation. *Entrance requirements:* Additional exam requirements/recommendations for international students: Required—TOEFL (minimum score 550 paper-based; 80 iBT). *Application deadline:* For fall admission, 4/1 priority date for domestic students, 4/1 for international students; for spring admission, 12/1 for domestic students. Applications are processed on a rolling basis. Application fee: $65. Electronic applications accepted. *Expenses:* Tuition, state resident: full-time $13,500; part-time $750 per credit. Tuition, nonresident: full-time $25,940; part-time $1089 per credit. *Required fees:* $1699; $424.75 per semester. *Financial support:* In 2012–13, 41 students received support, including 1 fellowship, 7

344 www.petersonsbooks.com

Peterson's Graduate Programs in the Physical Sciences, Mathematics, Agricultural Sciences, the Environment & Natural Resources 2014

research assistantships, 36 teaching assistantships; Federal Work-Study, scholarships/grants, and tuition waivers (full and partial) also available. Support available to part-time students. Financial award application deadline: 2/15. *Faculty research:* Operator theory, complex analysis, algebra, nonlinear dynamics, statistics. *Unit head:* Dr. Edward Hinson, Chairperson, 603-862-2688. *Application contact:* Jan Jankowski, Administrative Assistant, 603-862-2320, E-mail: jan.jankowski@unh.edu. Website: http://www.math.unh.edu/.

University of New Mexico, Graduate School, College of Arts and Sciences, Department of Mathematics and Statistics, Albuquerque, NM 87131-2039. Offers mathematics (MS, PhD); statistics (MS, PhD). Part-time programs available. *Faculty:* 25 full-time (8 women), 4 part-time/adjunct (0 women). *Students:* 52 full-time (15 women), 28 part-time (8 women); includes 17 minority (2 Black or African American, non-Hispanic/Latino; 1 Asian, non-Hispanic/Latino; 14 Hispanic/Latino), 23 international. Average age 32. 84 applicants, 52% accepted, 15 enrolled. In 2012, 11 master's, 6 doctorates awarded. Terminal master's awarded for partial completion of doctoral program. *Degree requirements:* For master's, comprehensive exam (for some programs), thesis or alternative; for doctorate, one foreign language, comprehensive exam, thesis/dissertation, 4 department seminars. *Entrance requirements:* For master's and doctorate, minimum GPA of 3.0, 3 letters of recommendation, letter of intent. Additional exam requirements/recommendations for international students: Required—TOEFL (minimum score 550 paper-based). *Application deadline:* For fall admission, 2/15 priority date for domestic students, 2/15 for international students; for spring admission, 11/1 priority date for domestic students, 11/1 for international students. Application fee: $50. Electronic applications accepted. *Expenses:* Tuition, state resident: full-time $3296; part-time $276.73 per credit hour. Tuition, nonresident: full-time $10,604; part-time $885.74 per credit hour. *Required fees:* $628. *Financial support:* In 2012–13, 59 students received support, including 15 research assistantships with tuition reimbursements available (averaging $8,419 per year), 46 teaching assistantships with tuition reimbursements available (averaging $14,812 per year); health care benefits and unspecified assistantships also available. Financial award application deadline: 2/15; financial award applicants required to submit FAFSA. *Faculty research:* Pure and applied mathematics, applied statistics, numerical analysis, biostatistics, differential geometry, fluid dynamics, nonparametric curve estimation. *Total annual research expenditures:* $1.5 million. *Unit head:* Dr. Terry Loring, Chair, 505-277-4613, Fax: 505-277-5505, E-mail: loring@math.unm.edu. *Application contact:* Ana Parra Lombard, Coordinator, Program Advisement, 505-277-5250, Fax: 505-277-5505, E-mail: aparra@math.unm.edu. Website: http://math.unm.edu/.

University of New Orleans, Graduate School, College of Sciences, Department of Mathematics, New Orleans, LA 70148. Offers MS. Part-time programs available. *Students:* 18 (9 women). Average age 31. In 2012, 10 master's awarded. *Entrance requirements:* For master's, BA or BS in mathematics. Additional exam requirements/recommendations for international students: Required—TOEFL (minimum score 550 paper-based; 79 iBT), IELTS (minimum score 6.5). *Application deadline:* For fall admission, 7/1 priority date for domestic students, 6/1 for international students; for spring admission, 11/1 priority date for domestic students, 10/1 for international students. Applications are processed on a rolling basis. Application fee: $20. Electronic applications accepted. *Expenses: Required fees:* $2165 per semester. *Financial support:* Teaching assistantships available. Financial award application deadline: 5/15; financial award applicants required to submit FAFSA. *Faculty research:* Differential equations, combinatorics, statistics, complex analysis, algebra. *Unit head:* Dr. Tumulesh Solanky, Chairperson, 504-280-6331, Fax: 504-280-5516, E-mail: tsolanky@uno.edu. *Application contact:* Dr. Linxiong Li, Graduate Coordinator, 504-280-6331, Fax: 504-280-5516, E-mail: lli@math.uno.edu. Website: http://www.math.uno.edu.

The University of North Carolina at Chapel Hill, Graduate School, College of Arts and Sciences, Department of Mathematics, Chapel Hill, NC 27599. Offers MA, MS, PhD. *Faculty:* 33 full-time (4 women). *Students:* 74 full-time (23 women), 1 part-time (0 women). Average age 25. In 2012, 3 master's, 7 doctorates awarded. *Degree requirements:* For master's, comprehensive exam, thesis or alternative, computer language proficiency; for doctorate, one foreign language, thesis/dissertation, 3 comprehensive exams, computer language proficiency, instructional service. *Entrance requirements:* For master's and doctorate, GRE General Test, minimum GPA of 3.0. Additional exam requirements/recommendations for international students: Required—TOEFL. *Application deadline:* For fall admission, 1/1 priority date for domestic students, 1/1 for international students; for spring admission, 10/15 for domestic students. Application fee: $85. Electronic applications accepted. *Financial support:* In 2012–13, 11 fellowships with full tuition reimbursements (averaging $18,000 per year), 17 research assistantships with full tuition reimbursements (averaging $17,500 per year), 41 teaching assistantships with full tuition reimbursements (averaging $17,500 per year) were awarded; scholarships/grants and health care benefits also available. Financial award application deadline: 1/1; financial award applicants required to submit FAFSA. *Faculty research:* Algebraic geometry, topology, analysis, lie theory, applied math. *Unit head:* Dr. Richard McLaughlin, Chairman, 919-962-9816, Fax: 919-962-2568, E-mail: rmm@amath.unc.edu. *Application contact:* Laurie Straube, Student Services Manager, 919-962-4178, Fax: 919-962-2568, E-mail: straube@live.unc.edu. Website: http://www.math.unc.edu/.

The University of North Carolina at Charlotte, The Graduate School, College of Liberal Arts and Sciences, Department of Mathematics and Statistics, Charlotte, NC 28223-0001. Offers applied mathematics (MS, PhD); applied statistics (MS); general mathematics (MS); mathematics education (MA). Part-time and evening/weekend programs available. *Faculty:* 42 full-time (5 women). *Students:* 42 full-time (21 women), 32 part-time (16 women); includes 12 minority (6 Black or African American, non-Hispanic/Latino; 4 Asian, non-Hispanic/Latino; 2 Hispanic/Latino), 33 international. Average age 30. 43 applicants, 95% accepted, 23 enrolled. In 2012, 15 master's, 4 doctorates awarded. Terminal master's awarded for partial completion of doctoral program. *Degree requirements:* For master's, comprehensive exam, thesis or alternative; for doctorate, thesis/dissertation. *Entrance requirements:* For master's, GRE General Test, minimum GPA of 3.0 in undergraduate major, 2.75 overall; for doctorate, GRE General Test, minimum overall GPA of 3.0. Additional exam requirements/recommendations for international students: Required—TOEFL (minimum score 557 paper-based; 83 iBT), Michigan English Language Assessment Battery (minimum score 78) or IELTS (minimum score 6.5). *Application deadline:* For fall admission, 7/1 for domestic students, 5/1 for international students; for spring admission, 11/1 for domestic students, 10/1 for international students. Applications are processed on a rolling basis. Application fee: $65 ($75 for international students). Electronic applications accepted. *Expenses:* Tuition, state resident: full-time $3453. Tuition, nonresident: full-time $15,982. *Required fees:* $2420. Tuition and fees vary according to course load and program. *Financial support:* In 2012–13, 44 students received support, including 3 fellowships (averaging $21,035 per year), 4 research assistantships (averaging $8,583 per year), 37 teaching assistantships (averaging $12,104 per year); career-related internships or fieldwork, Federal Work-Study, institutionally sponsored loans, scholarships/grants, and unspecified assistantships also available. Support available to part-time students. Financial award application deadline: 4/1; financial award applicants required to submit FAFSA. *Faculty research:* Numerical analysis and scientific computation, probability and stochastic processes, partial differential equations and mathematical physics, algebra and combinatorics, analysis, biostatistics, topology. *Total annual research expenditures:* $1.2 million. *Unit head:* Dr. Yuanan Diao, Chair, 704-687-4560, Fax: 704-687-6415, E-mail: ydiao@uncc.edu. *Application contact:* Kathy B. Giddings, Director of Graduate Admissions, 704-687-5503, Fax: 704-687-1668, E-mail: gradadm@uncc.edu. Website: http://www.math.uncc.edu/.

The University of North Carolina at Charlotte, The Graduate School, College of Liberal Arts and Sciences, Department of Sociology, Charlotte, NC 28223-0001. Offers health research (MA); mathematical sociology and quantitative methods (MA); organizations, occupations, and work (MA); political sociology (MA); race and gender (MA); social psychology (MA); social theory (MA); sociology of education (MA); stratification (MA). Part-time and evening/weekend programs available. *Faculty:* 15 full-time (9 women). *Students:* 11 full-time (6 women), 13 part-time (6 women); includes 2 minority (1 Black or African American, non-Hispanic/Latino; 1 Asian, non-Hispanic/Latino). Average age 32. 27 applicants, 48% accepted, 6 enrolled. In 2012, 3 master's awarded. *Degree requirements:* For master's, thesis or comprehensive exam. *Entrance requirements:* For master's, GRE or MAT, minimum GPA of 3.0 in last 2 years, 2.75 overall. Additional exam requirements/recommendations for international students: Required—TOEFL (minimum score 557 paper-based; 83 iBT). *Application deadline:* For fall admission, 7/1 for domestic students, 5/1 for international students; for spring admission, 11/1 for domestic students, 10/1 for international students. Applications are processed on a rolling basis. Application fee: $65 ($75 for international students). Electronic applications accepted. *Expenses:* Tuition, state resident: full-time $3453. Tuition, nonresident: full-time $15,982. *Required fees:* $2420. Tuition and fees vary according to course load and program. *Financial support:* In 2012–13, 8 students received support, including 3 research assistantships (averaging $9,333 per year), 5 teaching assistantships (averaging $9,200 per year); career-related internships or fieldwork, institutionally sponsored loans, scholarships/grants, and unspecified assistantships also available. Support available to part-time students. Financial award application deadline: 4/1; financial award applicants required to submit FAFSA. *Faculty research:* Impact of race on high school course selection; income inequality within the United States and cross-nationally; small group interaction, nonverbal behaviors, identity, emotions, gender, and expectations; mathematical models of social processes. *Total annual research expenditures:* $494,898. *Unit head:* Dr. Lisa Walker, Chair, 704-687-2288, Fax: 704-687-3091, E-mail: lisa.walker@uncc.edu. *Application contact:* Kathy B. Giddings, Director of Graduate Admissions, 704-687-5503, Fax: 704-687-1668, E-mail: gradadm@uncc.edu. Website: http://sociology.uncc.edu/.

The University of North Carolina at Greensboro, Graduate School, College of Arts and Sciences, Department of Mathematics and Statistics, Greensboro, NC 27412-5001. Offers mathematics (MA, PhD). Part-time programs available. *Degree requirements:* For master's, comprehensive exam, thesis (for some programs). *Entrance requirements:* For master's, GRE General Test. Additional exam requirements/recommendations for international students: Required—TOEFL. Electronic applications accepted. *Faculty research:* General and geometric topology, statistics, computer networks, symbolic logic, mathematics education.

The University of North Carolina Wilmington, College of Arts and Sciences, Department of Mathematics and Statistics, Wilmington, NC 28403-3297. Offers MS. *Degree requirements:* For master's, comprehensive exam, thesis. *Entrance requirements:* For master's, GRE General Test, GRE Subject Test, minimum B average in undergraduate major. Additional exam requirements/recommendations for international students: Required—TOEFL (minimum score 550 paper-based; 79 iBT), IELTS (minimum score 6.5).

Peterson's Graduate Programs in the Physical Sciences, Mathematics, Agricultural Sciences, the Environment & Natural Resources 2014

www.petersonsbooks.com **345**

Mathematics

University of North Dakota, Graduate School, College of Arts and Sciences, Department of Mathematics, Grand Forks, ND 58202. Offers M Ed, MS. Part-time programs available. *Degree requirements:* For master's, thesis or alternative, final exam. *Entrance requirements:* For master's, minimum GPA of 3.0. Additional exam requirements/recommendations for international students: Required—TOEFL (minimum score 550 paper-based; 79 iBT), IELTS (minimum score 6.5). Electronic applications accepted. *Faculty research:* Statistics, measure theory, topological vector spaces, algebra, applied math.

University of Northern British Columbia, Office of Graduate Studies, Prince George, BC V2N 4Z9, Canada. Offers business administration (Diploma); community health science (M Sc); disability management (MA); education (M Ed); first nations studies (MA); gender studies (MA); history (MA); interdisciplinary studies (MA); international studies (MA); mathematical, computer and physical sciences (M Sc); natural resources and environmental studies (M Sc, MA, MNRES, PhD); political science (MA); psychology (M Sc, PhD); social work (MSW). Part-time and evening/weekend programs available. Postbaccalaureate distance learning degree programs offered (no on-campus study). *Degree requirements:* For master's, thesis; for doctorate, thesis/dissertation. *Entrance requirements:* For master's, GRE, minimum B average in undergraduate course work; for doctorate, candidacy exam, minimum A average in graduate course work.

University of Northern Colorado, Graduate School, College of Natural and Health Sciences, School of Mathematical Sciences, Greeley, CO 80639. Offers mathematical teaching (MA); mathematics (MA, PhD); mathematics education (PhD); mathematics: liberal arts (MA). Part-time programs available. *Degree requirements:* For master's, comprehensive exam, thesis or alternative; for doctorate, comprehensive exam, thesis/dissertation. *Entrance requirements:* For master's, GRE General Test (liberal arts), 3 letters of recommendation; for doctorate, GRE General Test, 3 letters of recommendation. Electronic applications accepted.

University of Northern Iowa, Graduate College, College of Humanities, Arts and Sciences, Department of Mathematics, Cedar Falls, IA 50614. Offers industrial mathematics (PSM), including actuarial science, continuous quality improvement, mathematical computing and modeling; mathematics (MA), including mathematics, secondary; mathematics for middle grades 4-8 (MA). Part-time programs available. *Students:* 16 full-time (4 women), 17 part-time (13 women); includes 2 minority (1 Black or African American, non-Hispanic/Latino; 1 Hispanic/Latino), 4 international. 20 applicants, 75% accepted, 6 enrolled. In 2012, 22 master's awarded. *Degree requirements:* For master's, comprehensive exam (for some programs), thesis or alternative. *Entrance requirements:* For master's, minimum GPA of 3.0. Additional exam requirements/recommendations for international students: Required—TOEFL (minimum score 600 paper-based; 100 iBT). *Application deadline:* For fall admission, 8/1 priority date for domestic students. Applications are processed on a rolling basis. Application fee: $50 ($70 for international students). Electronic applications accepted. *Financial support:* Career-related internships or fieldwork, Federal Work-Study, scholarships/grants, and tuition waivers (full and partial) available. Support available to part-time students. Financial award application deadline: 2/1. *Unit head:* Dr. Douglas Mupasiri, Head, 319-273-2012, Fax: 319-273-2546, E-mail: douglas.mupasiri@uni.edu. *Application contact:* Laurie S. Russell, Record Analyst, 319-273-2623, Fax: 319-273-2885, E-mail: laurie.russell@uni.edu. Website: http://www.math.uni.edu/.

University of North Florida, College of Arts and Sciences, Department of Mathematics and Statistics, Jacksonville, FL 32224. Offers mathematical sciences (MS); statistics (MS). Part-time and evening/weekend programs available. *Faculty:* 10 full-time (5 women). *Students:* 18 full-time (5 women), 7 part-time (1 woman); includes 3 minority (all Black or African American, non-Hispanic/Latino), 11 international. Average age 30. 38 applicants, 66% accepted, 12 enrolled. In 2012, 5 master's awarded. *Degree requirements:* For master's, comprehensive exam, thesis optional. *Entrance requirements:* For master's, GRE General Test, minimum GPA of 3.0 in last 60 hours of course work. Additional exam requirements/recommendations for international students: Required—TOEFL (minimum score 500 paper-based; 61 iBT). *Application deadline:* For fall admission, 7/1 priority date for domestic students, 6/1 for international students; for spring admission, 11/1 priority date for domestic students, 10/1 for international students. Applications are processed on a rolling basis. Application fee: $30. Electronic applications accepted. *Expenses:* Tuition, state resident: full-time $9630.72; part-time $401.28 per credit hour. Tuition, nonresident: full-time $23,020; part-time $959.17 per credit hour. *Required fees:* $1962.72; $81.78 per credit hour. Tuition and fees vary according to course load and program. *Financial support:* In 2012–13, 12 students received support, including 6 teaching assistantships (averaging $5,738 per year); Federal Work-Study, scholarships/grants, tuition waivers (partial), and unspecified assistantships also available. Support available to part-time students. Financial award application deadline: 4/1; financial award applicants required to submit FAFSA. *Faculty research:* Real analysis, number theory, Euclidean geometry. *Total annual research expenditures:* $357. *Unit head:* Dr. Scott H. Hochwald, Chair, 904-620-2653, Fax: 904-620-2818, E-mail: shochwal@unf.edu. *Application contact:* Lillith Richardson, Interim Director, The Graduate School, 904-620-1360, Fax: 904-620-1362, E-mail: graduateschool@unf.edu. Website: http://www.unf.edu/coas/math-stat/.

University of North Texas, Robert B. Toulouse School of Graduate Studies, Denton, TN 750603. Offers accounting (MS, PhD); applied anthropology (MA, MS); applied behavior analysis (Certificate); applied technology and performance improvement (M Ed, MS, PhD); art education (MA, PhD); art history (MA); art museum education (Certificate); arts leadership (Certificate); audiology (Au D); behavior analysis (MS); biochemistry and molecular biology (MS, PhD); biology (MA, MS, PhD); business (PhD); business computer information systems (PhD); chemistry (MS, PhD); clinical psychology (PhD); communication studies (MA, MS); computer engineering (MS); computer science (MS); computer science and engineering (PhD); counseling (M Ed, MS, PhD), including clinical mental health counseling (MS), college and university counseling (M Ed, MS), elementary school counseling (M Ed, MS), secondary school counseling (M Ed, MS); counseling psychology (PhD); creative writing (MA); criminal justice (MS); curriculum and instruction (M Ed, PhD), including curriculum studies (PhD), early childhood studies (PhD), language and literacy studies (PhD); decision sciences (MBA); design (MA, MFA), including fashion design (MFA), innovation studies, interior design (MFA); early childhood studies (MS); economics (MS); educational leadership (M Ed, Ed D, PhD); educational psychology (MS), including family studies, gifted and talented (MS, PhD), human development, learning and cognition, research, measurement and evaluation; educational research (PhD), including gifted and talented (MS, PhD), human development and family studies, psychological aspects of sports and exercise, research, measurement and statistics; electrical engineering (MS); emergency management (MPA); engineering systems (MS); English (MA, PhD); environmental science (MS, PhD); experimental psychology (PhD); finance (MBA, MS, PhD); financial management (MPA); French (MA); health psychology and behavioral medicine (PhD); health services management (MBA); higher education (M Ed, Ed D, PhD); history (MA, MS, PhD), including European history (PhD), military history (PhD), United States history (PhD); hospitality management (MS); human resources management (MPA); information science (MS, PhD); information technologies (MBA); information technology and decision sciences (MS); interdisciplinary studies (MA, MS); international sustainable tourism (MS); jazz studies (MM); journalism (MA, MJ, Graduate Certificate), including interactive and virtual digital communication (Graduate Certificate), narrative journalism (Graduate Certificate), public relations (Graduate Certificate); kinesiology (MS); learning technologies (MS, PhD); library science (MS); local government management (MPA); logistics and supply chain management (MBA, PhD); long-term care, senior housing, and aging services (MA, MS); management science (PhD); marketing (MBA, PhD); materials science and engineering (MS, PhD); mathematics (MA, PhD); merchandising (MS); music (MA, MM Ed, PhD), including ethnomusicology (MA), music education (MM Ed, PhD), music theory (MA, PhD), musicology (MA, PhD), performance (MA); nonprofit management (MPA); operations and supply chain management (MBA); performance (MM, DMA); philosophy (MA, PhD); physics (MS, PhD); political science (MA, MS, PhD); public administration and management (PhD), including emergency management, nonprofit management, public financial management, urban management; radio, television and film (MA, MFA); recreation, event and sport management (MS); rehabilitation counseling (MS, Certificate); sociology (MA, MS, PhD); Spanish (MA); special education (M Ed, PhD), including autism intervention (PhD), emotional/behavioral disorders (PhD), mild/moderate disabilities (PhD); speech-language pathology (MA, MS); strategic management (MBA); studio art (MFA); taxation (MS); teaching (M Ed); MBA/MS; MS/MPH; MSES/MBA. Part-time and evening/weekend programs available. Postbaccalaureate distance learning degree programs offered. *Faculty:* 665 full-time (219 women), 237 part-time/adjunct (135 women). *Students:* 3,206 full-time (1,712 women), 3,623 part-time (2,305 women); includes 1,742 minority (575 Black or African American, non-Hispanic/Latino; 16 American Indian or Alaska Native, non-Hispanic/Latino; 294 Asian, non-Hispanic/Latino; 690 Hispanic/Latino; 2 Native Hawaiian or other Pacific Islander, non-Hispanic/Latino; 165 Two or more races, non-Hispanic/Latino), 1,125 international. Average age 32. 6,094 applicants, 43% accepted, 1692 enrolled. In 2012, 1,910 master's, 237 doctorates awarded. Terminal master's awarded for partial completion of doctoral program. *Degree requirements:* For master's, variable foreign language requirement, comprehensive exam (for some programs), thesis (for some programs); for doctorate, variable foreign language requirement, comprehensive exam (for some programs), thesis/dissertation; for other advanced degree, variable foreign language requirement, comprehensive exam (for some programs). *Entrance requirements:* For master's and doctorate, GRE, GMAT. Additional exam requirements/recommendations for international students: Required—TOEFL (minimum score 550 paper-based; 79 iBT). *Application deadline:* For fall admission, 7/15 for domestic students, 3/15 for international students; for spring admission, 11/15 for domestic students, 9/15 for international students. Applications are processed on a rolling basis. Application fee: $60. Electronic applications accepted. *Expenses:* Tuition, state resident: full-time $5242; part-time $216 per credit hour. Tuition, nonresident: full-time $11,560; part-time $567 per credit hour. *Required fees:* $730 per semester. *Financial support:* Fellowships with partial tuition reimbursements, research assistantships with partial tuition reimbursements, teaching assistantships, career-related internships or fieldwork, Federal Work-Study, institutionally sponsored loans, scholarships/grants, and library assistantships available. Support available to part-time students. Financial award applicants required to submit FAFSA. *Unit head:* Mark Wardell, Dean, 940-565-2383, E-mail: mark.wardell@unt.edu. *Application contact:* Toulouse School of Graduate Studies, 940-565-2383, Fax: 940-565-2141, E-mail: gradsch@unt.edu. Website: http://www.tsgs.unt.edu/.

University of Notre Dame, Graduate School, College of Science, Department of Mathematics, Notre Dame, IN 46556. Offers algebra (PhD); algebraic geometry (PhD); applied mathematics (MSAM); complex analysis (PhD); differential geometry (PhD); logic (PhD); partial differential equations (PhD); topology (PhD). Terminal master's awarded for partial completion of doctoral program. *Degree* *requirements:* For doctorate, one foreign language, thesis/dissertation, qualifying exam. *Entrance requirements:* For master's and doctorate, GRE General Test, GRE Subject Test. Additional exam requirements/recommendations for international students: Required—TOEFL (minimum score 600 paper-based; 80 iBT). Electronic applications accepted. *Faculty research:* Algebra, analysis, geometry/topology, logic, applied math.

University of Oklahoma, College of Arts and Sciences, Department of Mathematics, Norman, OK 73019. Offers MA, MS, PhD, MBA/MS. *Faculty:* 32 full-time (3 women), 1 (woman) part-time/adjunct. *Students:* 53 full-time (26 women), 10 part-time (3 women); includes 5 minority (1 American Indian or Alaska Native, non-Hispanic/Latino; 3 Asian, non-Hispanic/Latino; 1 Hispanic/Latino), 30 international. Average age 29. 45 applicants, 47% accepted, 14 enrolled. In 2012, 10 master's, 8 doctorates awarded. Terminal master's awarded for partial completion of doctoral program. *Degree requirements:* For master's, comprehensive exam, thesis optional; for doctorate, 2 foreign languages, comprehensive exam, thesis/dissertation. *Entrance requirements:* Additional exam requirements/recommendations for international students: Required—TOEFL (minimum score 550 paper-based; 79 iBT). *Application deadline:* For fall admission, 1/31 for domestic and international students; for spring admission, 11/1 for domestic students, 9/1 for international students. Applications are processed on a rolling basis. Application fee: $40 ($90 for international students). Electronic applications accepted. *Expenses:* Tuition, state resident: full-time $4205; part-time $175.20 per credit hour. Tuition, nonresident: full-time $15,667; part-time $653 per credit hour. *Required fees:* $2745; $103.85 per credit hour. Tuition and fees vary according to course load and degree level. *Financial support:* In 2012–13, 5 fellowships with full tuition reimbursements (averaging $3,200 per year), 50 teaching assistantships with partial tuition reimbursements (averaging $14,658 per year) were awarded; scholarships/grants and unspecified assistantships also available. Financial award application deadline: 6/1; financial award applicants required to submit FAFSA. *Faculty research:* Representation theory, number theory, topology, geometry, analysis. *Total annual research expenditures:* $332,171. *Unit head:* Andy Miller, Chair, 405-325-6711, Fax: 405-325-7484, E-mail: amiller@math.ou.edu. *Application contact:* Cristin Yates, Assistant to the Graduate Director, 405-325-2719, Fax: 405-325-7484, E-mail: csloan@ou.edu. Website: http://www.math.ou.edu.

See Display below and Close-Up on page 377.

University of Oregon, Graduate School, College of Arts and Sciences, Department of Mathematics, Eugene, OR 97403. Offers MA, MS, PhD. Part-time programs available. Terminal master's awarded for partial completion of doctoral program. *Degree requirements:* For doctorate, 2 foreign languages, thesis/dissertation. *Entrance requirements:* For master's and doctorate, GRE General Test, GRE Subject Test. Additional exam requirements/recommendations for

international students: Required—TOEFL. *Faculty research:* Algebra, topology, analytic geometry, numerical analysis, statistics.

University of Ottawa, Faculty of Graduate and Postdoctoral Studies, Faculty of Science, Ottawa-Carleton Institute of Mathematics and Statistics, Ottawa, ON K1N 6N5, Canada. Offers M Sc, PhD. M Sc, PhD offered jointly with Carleton University. Part-time programs available. *Degree requirements:* For master's, thesis optional; for doctorate, one foreign language, comprehensive exam, thesis/dissertation. *Entrance requirements:* For master's, honors B Sc degree or equivalent, minimum B average; for doctorate, M Sc, minimum B+ average. Electronic applications accepted. Tuition and fees charges are reported in Canadian dollars. *Expenses: Tuition, area resident:* Full-time $7074 Canadian dollars; part-time $256 Canadian dollars per credit. *International tuition:* $16,334 Canadian dollars full-time. *Required fees:* $738 Canadian dollars; $110 Canadian dollars per term. Part-time tuition and fees vary according to course load, program and student level. *Faculty research:* Pure mathematics, applied mathematics, probability and statistics.

University of Pennsylvania, School of Arts and Sciences, Graduate Group in Mathematics, Philadelphia, PA 19104. Offers AM, PhD. *Faculty:* 28 full-time (2 women), 5 part-time/adjunct (0 women). *Students:* 53 full-time (7 women); includes 5 minority (all Asian, non-Hispanic/Latino), 28 international. 287 applicants, 11% accepted, 7 enrolled. In 2012, 8 master's, 8 doctorates awarded. Terminal master's awarded for partial completion of doctoral program. *Degree requirements:* For master's, one foreign language, thesis or alternative; for doctorate, 2 foreign languages, thesis/dissertation. *Entrance requirements:* For master's and doctorate, GRE General Test, GRE Subject Test. Additional exam requirements/recommendations for international students: Required—TOEFL. *Application deadline:* For fall admission, 12/1 priority date for domestic students. Application fee: $70. Electronic applications accepted. *Financial support:* In 2012–13, 13 fellowships, 27 teaching assistantships were awarded; institutionally sponsored loans, scholarships/grants, traineeships, health care benefits, and unspecified assistantships also available. Financial award application deadline: 12/15. *Faculty research:* Geometry-topology, analysis, algebra, logic, combinatorics. *Application contact:* Arts and Sciences Graduate Admissions, 215-573-5816, Fax: 215-573-8068, E-mail: gdasadmis@sas.upenn.edu. Website: http://www.sas.upenn.edu/graduate-division.

University of Pittsburgh, Dietrich School of Arts and Sciences, Department of Mathematics, Pittsburgh, PA 15260. Offers applied mathematics (MA, MS); mathematics (MA, MS, PhD). Part-time programs available. *Faculty:* 36 full-time (2 women), 16 part-time/adjunct (2 women). *Students:* 83 full-time (25 women), 2 part-time (1 woman); includes 4 minority (1 Black or African American, non-Hispanic/Latino; 2 Hispanic/Latino; 1 Native Hawaiian or other Pacific Islander, non-Hispanic/Latino), 44 international. 280 applicants, 16% accepted, 15 enrolled. In 2012, 8 master's, 3 doctorates awarded. Terminal master's awarded for partial

Peterson's Graduate Programs in the Physical Sciences, Mathematics, Agricultural Sciences, the Environment & Natural Resources 2014

www.petersonsbooks.com **347**

completion of doctoral program. *Degree requirements:* For master's, comprehensive exam, thesis (for some programs); for doctorate, comprehensive exam, thesis/dissertation, preliminary exams, defense of dissertation. *Entrance requirements:* For master's, GRE General Test, GRE Subject Test (recommended), minimum GPA of 3.0; for doctorate, GRE General Test, GRE Subject Test (recommended), minimum GPA of 3.0, minimum QPA of 3.25 in math curriculum. Additional exam requirements/recommendations for international students: Required—TOEFL (minimum score 577 paper-based; 90 iBT), IELTS (minimum score 7). *Application deadline:* For fall admission, 1/15 priority date for domestic students, 1/15 for international students; for spring admission, 9/1 priority date for domestic students, 9/1 for international students. Applications are processed on a rolling basis. Application fee: $50. Electronic applications accepted. *Expenses:* Tuition, state resident: full-time $19,336; part-time $782 per credit. Tuition, nonresident: full-time $31,658; part-time $1295 per credit. *Required fees:* $740; $200 per term. Tuition and fees vary according to program. *Financial support:* In 2012–13, 77 students received support, including 14 fellowships with full and partial tuition reimbursements available (averaging $19,610 per year), 11 research assistantships with full and partial tuition reimbursements available (averaging $16,600 per year), 51 teaching assistantships with full and partial tuition reimbursements available (averaging $16,950 per year); institutionally sponsored loans, scholarships/grants, traineeships, health care benefits, tuition waivers (partial), and unspecified assistantships also available. Financial award application deadline: 1/15. *Faculty research:* Algebra, analysis, computational math, geometry/topology, math biology. *Unit head:* Ivan Yotov, Chair, 412-624-8361, Fax: 412-624-8397, E-mail: yotov@math.pitt.edu. *Application contact:* Molly Williams, Administrator, 412-624-1175, Fax: 412-624-8397, E-mail: mollyw@pitt.edu. Website: http://www.mathematics.pitt.edu.

University of Puerto Rico, Mayagüez Campus, Graduate Studies, College of Arts and Sciences, Department of Mathematical Sciences, Mayagüez, PR 00681-9000. Offers applied mathematics (MS); pure mathematics (MS); scientific computation (MS); statistics (MS). Part-time programs available. *Faculty:* 45 full-time (7 women), 1 part-time/adjunct (0 women). *Students:* 34 full-time (10 women), 1 part-time (0 women); includes 30 minority (all Hispanic/Latino), 25 international. 8 applicants, 88% accepted, 7 enrolled. In 2012, 5 master's awarded. *Degree requirements:* For master's, one foreign language, comprehensive exam, thesis optional. *Entrance requirements:* For master's, undergraduate degree in mathematics or its equivalent. *Application deadline:* For fall admission, 2/15 for domestic and international students; for spring admission, 9/15 for domestic and international students. Applications are processed on a rolling basis. Application fee: $25. Tuition and fees vary according to course level and course load. *Financial support:* In 2012–13, 31 students received support, including 5 research assistantships (averaging $15,000 per year), 26 teaching assistantships (averaging $8,500 per year); Federal Work-Study and institutionally sponsored loans also available. *Faculty research:* Automata theory, linear algebra, logic. *Unit head:* Dr. Omar Colon, Director, 787-832-4040 Ext. 3848, Fax: 787-265-5454, E-mail: omar.colon.reyes@gmail.com. Website: http://math.uprm.edu/.

University of Puerto Rico, Río Piedras, College of Natural Sciences, Department of Mathematics, San Juan, PR 00931-3300. Offers MS, PhD. Part-time programs available. *Degree requirements:* For master's, comprehensive exam, thesis; for doctorate, comprehensive exam, thesis/dissertation. *Entrance requirements:* For master's and doctorate, GRE General Test and GRE Subject Test, interview, minimum GPA of 3.0, 3 letters of recommendation. *Faculty research:* Investigation of database logistics, cryptograph systems, distribution and spectral theory, Boolean function, differential equations.

University of Regina, Faculty of Graduate Studies and Research, Faculty of Science, Department of Mathematics and Statistics, Regina, SK S4S 0A2, Canada. Offers mathematics (M Sc, MA, PhD); statistics (M Sc, MA, PhD). *Faculty:* 21 full-time (2 women), 4 part-time/adjunct (2 women). *Students:* 28 full-time (7 women), 2 part-time (0 women). 40 applicants, 63% accepted. In 2012, 5 master's awarded. *Degree requirements:* For master's, thesis; for doctorate, comprehensive exam, thesis/dissertation. *Entrance requirements:* Additional exam requirements/recommendations for international students: Required—TOEFL (minimum score 580 paper-based; 80 iBT), IELTS (minimum score 6.5). *Application deadline:* For fall admission, 1/31 for domestic and international students; for winter admission, 8/31 for domestic and international students. Applications are processed on a rolling basis. Application fee: $100. Electronic applications accepted. Tuition and fees charges are reported in Canadian dollars. *Expenses: Tuition, area resident:* Full-time $3942 Canadian dollars; part-time $219 Canadian dollars per credit hour. *International tuition:* $4742 Canadian dollars full-time. *Required fees:* $421.55 Canadian dollars; $93.60 Canadian dollars per credit hour. Tuition and fees vary according to course load, degree level and program. *Financial support:* In 2012–13, 7 fellowships (averaging $7,000 per year), 7 teaching assistantships (averaging $2,436 per year) were awarded; research assistantships and scholarships/grants also available. Financial award application deadline: 6/15. *Faculty research:* Discrete mathematics, actuarial science and statistics, matrix theory, mathematical science, numerical analysis. *Unit head:* Dr. Douglas Farenick, Head, 306-585-4425, Fax: 306-585-4020, E-mail: douglas.farenick@uregina.ca. *Application contact:* Dr. Martin Argerami, Graduate Program Coordinator, 306-585-4340, Fax: 306-585-4020, E-mail: martin.argerami@math.uregina.ca. Website: http://www.math.uregina.ca.

University of Rhode Island, Graduate School, College of Arts and Sciences, Department of Mathematics, Kingston, RI 02881. Offers applied mathematical sciences (MS, PhD); mathematics (MS, PhD). Part-time programs available. *Faculty:* 19 full-time (6 women). *Students:* 15 full-time (5 women), 11 part-time (5 women); includes 1 minority (Hispanic/Latino), 3 international. In 2012, 10 master's, 2 doctorates awarded. *Degree requirements:* For master's, comprehensive exam (for some programs), thesis optional; for doctorate, one foreign language, comprehensive exam, thesis/dissertation optional. *Entrance requirements:* For master's and doctorate, 2 letters of recommendation. Additional exam requirements/recommendations for international students: Required—TOEFL (minimum score 550 paper-based). *Application deadline:* For fall admission, 7/15 for domestic students, 2/1 for international students; for spring admission, 11/15 for domestic students, 7/15 for international students. Application fee: $65. Electronic applications accepted. *Expenses:* Tuition, state resident: full-time $11,532; part-time $641 per credit. Tuition, nonresident: full-time $23,606; part-time $1311 per credit. *Required fees:* $1388; $36 per credit. $35 per semester. One-time fee: $130. *Financial support:* In 2012–13, 13 teaching assistantships with full tuition reimbursements (averaging $15,754 per year) were awarded. Financial award application deadline: 7/15; financial award applicants required to submit FAFSA. *Unit head:* Dr. James Baglama, Chair, 401-874-2709, Fax: 401-874-4454, E-mail: jbaglama@math.uri.edu. *Application contact:* Dr. Woong Kook, Director of Graduate Studies, 401-874-4421, Fax: 401-874-4454, E-mail: andrewk@math.uri.edu. Website: http://www.math.uri.edu/.

University of Rochester, School of Arts and Sciences, Department of Mathematics, Rochester, NY 14627. Offers PhD. Terminal master's awarded for partial completion of doctoral program. *Degree requirements:* For doctorate, thesis/dissertation, qualifying exam. *Entrance requirements:* For doctorate, GRE General Test. Additional exam requirements/recommendations for international students: Required—TOEFL. Electronic applications accepted. *Faculty research:* Algebra and number theory, analysis, geometry, mathematical physics and probability, topology.

University of Saskatchewan, College of Graduate Studies and Research, College of Arts and Science, Department of Mathematics and Statistics, Saskatoon, SK S7N 5A2, Canada. Offers M Math, MA, PhD. *Degree requirements:* For master's, thesis (for some programs); for doctorate, comprehensive exam (for some programs), thesis/dissertation. *Entrance requirements:* Additional exam requirements/recommendations for international students: Required—TOEFL (minimum score 80 iBT); Recommended—IELTS (minimum score 6.5). Electronic applications accepted.

University of South Alabama, Graduate School, College of Arts and Sciences, Department of Mathematics and Statistics, Mobile, AL 36688. Offers mathematics (MS). Part-time and evening/weekend programs available. *Faculty:* 14 full-time (3 women). *Students:* 8 full-time (2 women); includes 3 minority (1 Asian, non-Hispanic/Latino; 1 Hispanic/Latino; 1 Two or more races, non-Hispanic/Latino), 2 international. 6 applicants, 67% accepted, 3 enrolled. In 2012, 5 master's awarded. *Degree requirements:* For master's, comprehensive exam, thesis optional. *Entrance requirements:* For master's, GRE, BS in mathematics or a mathematics-related field. Additional exam requirements/recommendations for international students: Required—TOEFL. *Application deadline:* For fall admission, 7/15 priority date for domestic students, 6/15 for international students; for spring admission, 12/1 priority date for domestic students, 11/1 for international students. Applications are processed on a rolling basis. Application fee: $35. *Expenses:* Tuition, state resident: full-time $8592; part-time $358 per credit hour. Tuition, nonresident: full-time $17,184; part-time $716 per credit hour. *Financial support:* Fellowships and research assistantships available. Support available to part-time students. Financial award application deadline: 4/1. *Faculty research:* Knot theory, chaos theory. *Unit head:* Dr. Madhuri Mulekar, Chair, 251-460-6264, Fax: 251-460-7969. *Application contact:* Dr. Dan Silver, Graduate Coordinator, 251-460-6264. Website: http://www.southalabama.edu/mathstat.

University of South Carolina, The Graduate School, College of Arts and Sciences, Department of Mathematics, Columbia, SC 29208. Offers mathematics (MA, MS, PhD); mathematics education (M Math, MAT). MAT offered in cooperation with the College of Education. Part-time programs available. Terminal master's awarded for partial completion of doctoral program. *Degree requirements:* For master's, comprehensive exam, thesis (for some programs); for doctorate, one foreign language, comprehensive exam, thesis/dissertation, admission to candidacy exam, residency. *Entrance requirements:* For master's and doctorate, GRE General Test. Additional exam requirements/recommendations for international students: Required—TOEFL (minimum score 600 paper-based; 100 iBT). Electronic applications accepted. *Faculty research:* Computational mathematics, analysis (classical/modern), discrete mathematics, algebra, number theory.

The University of South Dakota, Graduate School, College of Arts and Sciences, Department of Mathematics, Vermillion, SD 57069-2390. Offers MA, MS. Part-time programs available. *Degree requirements:* For master's, thesis (for some programs). *Entrance requirements:* For master's, GRE, minimum GPA of 2.7. Additional exam requirements/recommendations for international students: Required—TOEFL (minimum score 550 paper-based; 79 iBT). Electronic applications accepted.

University of Southern California, Graduate School, Dana and David Dornsife College of Letters, Arts and Sciences, Department of Mathematics, Los Angeles, CA 90089. Offers applied mathematics (MA, MS, PhD); mathematical finance

(MS); mathematics (MA, PhD); statistics (MS). Part-time programs available. Terminal master's awarded for partial completion of doctoral program. *Degree requirements:* For master's, comprehensive exam (for some programs), thesis (for some programs); for doctorate, one foreign language, comprehensive exam, thesis/dissertation. *Entrance requirements:* For master's, GRE General Test, GMAT; for doctorate, GRE General Test, GRE Subject Test (mathematics). Additional exam requirements/recommendations for international students: Required—TOEFL (minimum score 100 iBT). Electronic applications accepted. *Faculty research:* Algebra, algebraic geometry and number theory, analysis/partial differential equations, applied mathematics, financial mathematics, probability, combinatorics and statistics.

University of Southern Mississippi, Graduate School, College of Science and Technology, Department of Mathematics, Hattiesburg, MS 39406-0001. Offers computational science (PhD); mathematics (MS). Part-time programs available. *Faculty:* 11 full-time (3 women), 1 part-time/adjunct (0 women). *Students:* 20 full-time (9 women), 6 part-time (3 women); includes 6 minority (5 Black or African American, non-Hispanic/Latino; 1 Two or more races, non-Hispanic/Latino), 9 international. Average age 33. 29 applicants, 59% accepted, 13 enrolled. In 2012, 5 master's, 1 doctorate awarded. *Degree requirements:* For master's, comprehensive exam, thesis or alternative; for doctorate, comprehensive exam, thesis/dissertation. *Entrance requirements:* For master's, GRE General Test, minimum GPA of 2.75 in last 60 hours; for doctorate, GRE General Test, minimum GPA of 3.5. Additional exam requirements/recommendations for international students: Required—TOEFL, IELTS. *Application deadline:* For fall admission, 3/15 priority date for domestic students, 3/15 for international students; for spring admission, 1/10 priority date for domestic students, 1/10 for international students. Applications are processed on a rolling basis. Application fee: $50. Electronic applications accepted. *Financial support:* In 2012–13, fellowships (averaging $18,000 per year), research assistantships with full tuition reimbursements (averaging $11,500 per year), teaching assistantships with full tuition reimbursements (averaging $11,408 per year) were awarded; Federal Work-Study, scholarships/grants, health care benefits, and unspecified assistantships also available. Financial award application deadline: 3/15; financial award applicants required to submit FAFSA. *Faculty research:* Dynamical systems, numerical analysis and multigrid methods, random number generation, matrix theory, group theory. *Unit head:* Dr. Joseph Kolibal, Interim Chair, 601-266-4289, Fax: 601-266-5818. *Application contact:* Dr. James Lambers, Director, Graduate Admissions, 601-266-4289, Fax: 601-266-5818. Website: http://www.usm.edu/graduateschool/table.php.

University of South Florida, Graduate School, College of Arts and Sciences, Department of Mathematics and Statistics, Tampa, FL 33620-9951. Offers mathematics (MA, PhD); statistics (MA). Part-time and evening/weekend programs available. Terminal master's awarded for partial completion of doctoral program. *Degree requirements:* For master's, comprehensive exam, thesis optional; for doctorate, comprehensive exam, thesis/dissertation. *Entrance requirements:* For master's, GRE, minimum GPA of 3.0; for doctorate, GRE, minimum GPA of 3.5, three letters of recommendation, personal statement of goals. Additional exam requirements/recommendations for international students: Required—TOEFL (minimum score 550 paper-based; 79 iBT) or IELTS (minimum score 6.5). Electronic applications accepted. *Faculty research:* Approximation theory, differential equations, discrete mathematics, functional analysis topology.

The University of Tennessee, Graduate School, College of Arts and Sciences, Department of Mathematics, Knoxville, TN 37996. Offers applied mathematics (MS); mathematical ecology (PhD); mathematics (M Math, MS, PhD). Part-time programs available. *Degree requirements:* For master's, thesis or alternative; for doctorate, one foreign language, thesis/dissertation. *Entrance requirements:* For master's and doctorate, minimum GPA of 2.7. Additional exam requirements/recommendations for international students: Required—TOEFL. Electronic applications accepted. *Expenses:* Tuition, state resident: full-time $9000; part-time $501 per credit hour. Tuition, nonresident: full-time $27,188; part-time $1512 per credit hour. *Required fees:* $1280; $62 per credit hour. Tuition and fees vary according to program.

The University of Tennessee at Chattanooga, Graduate School, College of Arts and Sciences, Program in Mathematics, Chattanooga, TN 37403-2598. Offers applied mathematics (MS); applied statistics (MS); mathematics (MS); mathematics education (MS). Part-time and evening/weekend programs available. Postbaccalaureate distance learning degree programs offered (no on-campus study). *Faculty:* 6 full-time (0 women). *Students:* 10 full-time (2 women), 7 part-time (1 woman); includes 2 minority (1 Black or African American, non-Hispanic/Latino; 1 Asian, non-Hispanic/Latino). Average age 29. 10 applicants, 100% accepted, 7 enrolled. In 2012, 4 master's awarded. *Entrance requirements:* For master's, two letters of recommendation. *Application deadline:* For fall admission, 6/14 for domestic students, 6/1 for international students; for spring admission, 10/25 for domestic students, 10/1 for international students. Applications are processed on a rolling basis. Application fee: $30 ($35 for international students). Electronic applications accepted. *Expenses:* Tuition, state resident: full-time $6860; part-time $381 per credit hour. Tuition, nonresident: full-time $21,206; part-time $1178 per credit hour. *Required fees:* $1490; $180 per credit hour. *Financial support:* In 2012–13, 16 research assistantships with tuition reimbursements (averaging $4,592 per year) were awarded. Financial award applicants required to submit FAFSA. *Total annual research expenditures:* $71,555. *Unit head:* John Graef, Head, 423-425-4545, E-mail: john-graef@utc.edu. *Application contact:* Dr. Jerald Ainsworth, Dean of Graduate Studies, 423-425-4478, Fax: 423-425-5223, E-mail: jerald-ainsworth@utc.edu. Website: http://www.utc.edu/Academic/Mathematics/.

The University of Texas at Arlington, Graduate School, College of Engineering, Department of Computer Science and Engineering, Arlington, TX 76019. Offers computer engineering (MS, PhD); computer science (MS, PhD); mathematical sciences, computer science (PhD); software engineering (MS). Part-time programs available. Postbaccalaureate distance learning degree programs offered (minimal on-campus study). Terminal master's awarded for partial completion of doctoral program. *Degree requirements:* For master's, comprehensive exam (for some programs), thesis; for doctorate, comprehensive exam, thesis/dissertation. *Entrance requirements:* For master's, GRE General Test, minimum GPA of 3.0 (3.2 in computer science-related classes); for doctorate, GRE General Test, minimum GPA of 3.5. Additional exam requirements/recommendations for international students: Required—TOEFL (minimum score 550 paper-based; 92 iBT), IELTS (minimum score 6.5). *Faculty research:* Algorithms, homeland security, mobile pervasive computing, high performance computing bioinformation.

The University of Texas at Arlington, Graduate School, College of Science, Department of Mathematics, Arlington, TX 76019. Offers applied math (MS); mathematics (PhD); mathematics education (MA). Part-time and evening/weekend programs available. *Degree requirements:* For master's, comprehensive exam, thesis or alternative; for doctorate, comprehensive exam, thesis/dissertation, preliminary examinations. *Entrance requirements:* For master's, GRE General Test (minimum score 350 verbal, 650 quantitative); for doctorate, GRE General Test (minimum score 350 verbal, 700 quantitative), 30 hours of graduate course work in mathematics, minimum GPA of 3.0 in last 60 hours of course work. Additional exam requirements/recommendations for international students: Required—TOEFL (minimum score 550 paper-based; 79 iBT). Electronic applications accepted. *Faculty research:* Algebra, combinatorics and geometry, applied mathematics and mathematical biology, computational mathematics, mathematics education, probability and statistics.

The University of Texas at Austin, Graduate School, College of Natural Sciences, Department of Mathematics, Austin, TX 78712-1111. Offers MA, PhD. *Entrance requirements:* For master's and doctorate, GRE General Test. Electronic applications accepted.

The University of Texas at Brownsville, Graduate Studies, College of Science, Mathematics and Technology, Brownsville, TX 78520-4991. Offers biological sciences (MS, MSIS); mathematics (MS); physics (MS). Part-time and evening/weekend programs available. Postbaccalaureate distance learning degree programs offered (no on-campus study). *Faculty:* 51 full-time (10 women). *Students:* 58 full-time (18 women), 48 part-time (24 women); includes 80 minority (1 Black or African American, non-Hispanic/Latino; 4 Asian, non-Hispanic/Latino; 69 Hispanic/Latino; 6 Native Hawaiian or other Pacific Islander, non-Hispanic/Latino), 1 international. 61 applicants, 52% accepted, 32 enrolled. In 2012, 20 master's awarded. *Degree requirements:* For master's, comprehensive exam (for some programs), thesis optional, project (for some programs). *Entrance requirements:* For master's, GRE General Test, letters of recommendation. Additional exam requirements/recommendations for international students: Required—TOEFL (minimum score 550 paper-based; 77 iBT). *Application deadline:* For fall admission, 7/1 priority date for domestic students, 7/1 for international students; for spring admission, 12/1 priority date for domestic students, 12/1 for international students. Applications are processed on a rolling basis. Application fee: $30. Electronic applications accepted. *Financial support:* In 2012–13, 2 research assistantships with partial tuition reimbursements (averaging $10,000 per year) were awarded; Federal Work-Study, scholarships/grants, tuition waivers (partial), and unspecified assistantships also available. Support available to part-time students. Financial award application deadline: 3/1; financial award applicants required to submit FAFSA. *Faculty research:* Fish, insects, barrier islands, algae. *Unit head:* Dr. Mikhail M. Bouniaev, Dean, 956-882-6701, Fax: 956-882-6657, E-mail: mikhail.bouniaev@utb.edu. *Application contact:* Mari Montelongo, Graduate Studies Specialist, 956-882-7787, Fax: 956-882-7279, E-mail: mari.montelongo@utb.edu. Website: http://www.utb.edu/vpaa/csmt/Pages/UTB-College-of-Science-Mathematics-and-Technology.aspx.

The University of Texas at Dallas, School of Natural Sciences and Mathematics, Department of Mathematical Sciences, Richardson, TX 75080. Offers applied mathematics (MS, PhD); engineering mathematics (MS); mathematics (MS); statistics (MS, PhD). Part-time and evening/weekend programs available. *Faculty:* 20 full-time (4 women), 1 part-time/adjunct (0 women). *Students:* 50 full-time (22 women), 27 part-time (9 women); includes 16 minority (4 Black or African American, non-Hispanic/Latino; 7 Asian, non-Hispanic/Latino; 5 Hispanic/Latino), 37 international. Average age 31. 140 applicants, 36% accepted, 29 enrolled. In 2012, 13 master's, 3 doctorates awarded. *Degree requirements:* For master's, thesis optional; for doctorate, thesis/dissertation. *Entrance requirements:* For master's, GRE General Test, minimum GPA of 3.0 in upper-level course work in field; for doctorate, GRE General Test, minimum GPA of 3.5 in upper-level course work in field. Additional exam requirements/recommendations for international students: Required—TOEFL (minimum score 550 paper-based). *Application deadline:* For fall admission, 7/15 for domestic students, 5/1 for international students; for spring admission, 11/15 for domestic students, 9/1 for international students. Applications are processed on a rolling basis. Application fee: $50 ($100 for international students). Electronic applications accepted. *Expenses:* Tuition, state resident: full-time $11,940; part-time $663.33 per credit hour. Tuition, nonresident:

Peterson's Graduate Programs in the Physical Sciences, Mathematics, Agricultural Sciences, the Environment & Natural Resources 2014

www.petersonsbooks.com **349**

full-time $21,606; part-time $1200.33 per credit hour. Tuition and fees vary according to course load. *Financial support:* In 2012–13, 39 students received support, including 4 research assistantships (averaging $19,800 per year), 35 teaching assistantships with partial tuition reimbursements available (averaging $16,124 per year); career-related internships or fieldwork, Federal Work-Study, institutionally sponsored loans, scholarships/grants, and unspecified assistantships also available. Support available to part-time students. Financial award application deadline: 4/30; financial award applicants required to submit FAFSA. *Faculty research:* Sequential analysis, applications in semiconductor manufacturing, medical image analysis, computational anatomy, information theory, probability theory. *Unit head:* Dr. Matthew Goeckner, Department Head, 972-883-4292, Fax: 972-883-6622, E-mail: goeckner@utdallas.edu. *Application contact:* Jacqueline Thiede, Graduate Support Assistant, 972-883-2163, Fax: 972-883-6622, E-mail: utdmath@utdallas.edu. Website: http://www.utdallas.edu/math.

The University of Texas at El Paso, Graduate School, College of Science, Department of Mathematical Sciences, El Paso, TX 79968-0001. Offers mathematical sciences (MS); mathematics (teaching) (MAT); statistics (MS). Part-time and evening/weekend programs available. *Degree requirements:* For master's, thesis optional. *Entrance requirements:* For master's, minimum GPA of 3.0, letters of recommendation. Additional exam requirements/recommendations for international students: Required—TOEFL; Recommended—IELTS. Electronic applications accepted.

The University of Texas at San Antonio, College of Sciences, Department of Mathematics, San Antonio, TX 78249-0617. Offers applied mathematics (MS), including industrial mathematics; mathematics (MS); mathematics education (MS). Part-time and evening/weekend programs available. *Faculty:* 10 full-time (1 woman). *Students:* 29 full-time (14 women), 26 part-time (15 women); includes 26 minority (1 Black or African American, non-Hispanic/Latino; 3 Asian, non-Hispanic/Latino; 21 Hispanic/Latino; 1 Two or more races, non-Hispanic/Latino), 12 international. Average age 29. 64 applicants, 67% accepted, 11 enrolled. In 2012, 28 master's awarded. *Degree requirements:* For master's, comprehensive exam (for some programs), thesis or alternative. *Entrance requirements:* For master's, GRE General Test, minimum GPA of 3.0 in last 60 hours. Additional exam requirements/recommendations for international students: Required—TOEFL (minimum score 500 paper-based; 61 iBT), IELTS (minimum score 5). *Application deadline:* For fall admission, 7/1 for domestic students, 4/1 for international students; for spring admission, 11/1 for domestic students, 9/1 for international students. Application fee: $45 ($85 for international students). *Financial support:* In 2012–13, 15 teaching assistantships (averaging $13,000 per year) were awarded. *Faculty research:* Differential equations, functional analysis, numerical analysis, number theory, logic. *Unit head:* Dr. F. Alexander Norman, Department Chair, 210-458-7254, Fax: 210-458-4439, E-mail: sandy.norman@utsa.edu.

The University of Texas at Tyler, College of Arts and Sciences, Department of Mathematics, Tyler, TX 75799-0001. Offers MS, MSIS. *Degree requirements:* For master's, comprehensive exam, thesis optional. *Entrance requirements:* For master's, GRE General Test. Additional exam requirements/recommendations for international students: Required—TOEFL. *Faculty research:* Discrete geometry, knot theory, commutative algebra, noncommutative rings, group theory, mathematical biology, mathematical physics.

The University of Texas–Pan American, College of Science and Mathematics, Department of Mathematics, Edinburg, TX 78539. Offers mathematical sciences (MS); mathematics teaching (MS). Part-time and evening/weekend programs available. *Degree requirements:* For master's, comprehensive exam. *Entrance requirements:* For master's, GRE General Test, minimum GPA of 3.0. *Expenses:* Tuition, state resident: full-time $1800; part-time $100 per credit hour. Tuition, nonresident: full-time $8118; part-time $451 per credit hour. *Required fees:* $403.45 per credit hour. Tuition and fees vary according to course load. *Faculty research:* Boundary value problems in differential equations, training of public school teachers in methods of presenting mathematics, harmonic analysis, inverse problems, commulative algebra.

University of the Incarnate Word, School of Graduate Studies and Research, School of Mathematics, Science, and Engineering, Program in Mathematics, San Antonio, TX 78209-6397. Offers research statistics (MS); teaching (MA). Part-time and evening/weekend programs available. *Faculty:* 4 full-time (2 women), 1 (woman) part-time/adjunct. *Students:* 5 part-time (3 women); includes 3 minority (all Hispanic/Latino). Average age 35. 6 applicants, 17% accepted, 0 enrolled. In 2012, 7 master's awarded. *Degree requirements:* For master's, capstone or prerequisite knowledge (for research statistics). *Entrance requirements:* For master's, GRE (minimum score 800 verbal and quantitative), 18 hours of undergraduate mathematics with minimum GPA of 3.0; letter of recommendation by a professional in the field, writing sample, teaching experience at the precollege level. Additional exam requirements/recommendations for international students: Required—TOEFL (minimum score 560 paper-based; 83 iBT). *Application deadline:* Applications are processed on a rolling basis. Application fee: $20. Electronic applications accepted. *Expenses: Tuition:* Full-time $9060; part-time $755 per credit hour. *Required fees:* $960; $40 per credit hour. Tuition and fees vary according to degree level, program and student level. *Financial support:* Federal Work-Study and scholarships/grants available. Financial award applicants required to submit FAFSA. *Faculty research:* Scholarship and career development for undergraduate mathematics majors. *Total annual research expenditures:* $140,844. *Unit head:* Dr. Zhanbo Yang, Mathematics Graduate Program Coordinator, 210-283-5008, Fax: 210-829-3153, E-mail: yang@uiwtx.edu. *Application contact:* Andrea Cyterski-Acosta, Dean of Enrollment, 210-829-6005, Fax: 210-829-3921, E-mail: admis@uiwtx.edu. Website: http://www.uiw.edu/math/mathprogramsgrad.html.

The University of Toledo, College of Graduate Studies, College of Natural Sciences and Mathematics, Department of Mathematics, Toledo, OH 43606-3390. Offers applied mathematics (MS, PhD); statistics (MS, PhD). Part-time programs available. *Faculty:* 25. *Students:* 38 full-time (13 women), 3 part-time (0 women); includes 2 minority (both Asian, non-Hispanic/Latino), 30 international. Average age 29. 37 applicants, 57% accepted, 11 enrolled. In 2012, 11 master's, 3 doctorates awarded. *Degree requirements:* For master's, comprehensive exam (for some programs), thesis (for some programs); for doctorate, 2 foreign languages, thesis/dissertation. *Entrance requirements:* For master's and doctorate, GRE General Test, GRE Subject Test, minimum cumulative point-hour ratio of 2.7 for all previous academic work, three letters of recommendation, statement of purpose, transcripts from all prior institutions attended. Additional exam requirements/recommendations for international students: Required—TOEFL (minimum score 550 paper-based; 80 iBT), IELTS (minimum score 6.5). *Application deadline:* For fall admission, 1/15 priority date for domestic students, 1/15 for international students. Applications are processed on a rolling basis. Application fee: $45 ($75 for international students). Electronic applications accepted. *Financial support:* In 2012–13, 38 teaching assistantships with full and partial tuition reimbursements (averaging $14,503 per year) were awarded; research assistantships with full and partial tuition reimbursements, Federal Work-Study, institutionally sponsored loans, scholarships/grants, and unspecified assistantships also available. Support available to part-time students. *Unit head:* Dr. Paul Hewitt, Chair, 419-530-2568, E-mail: paul.hewitt@utoledo.edu. *Application contact:* Graduate School Office, 419-530-4723, Fax: 419-530-4723, E-mail: grdsch@utnet.utoledo.edu. Website: http://www.utoledo.edu/nsm/.

University of Toronto, School of Graduate Studies, Faculty of Arts and Science, Department of Mathematics, Toronto, ON M5S 1A1, Canada. Offers M Sc, MMF, PhD. Part-time programs available. *Degree requirements:* For master's, thesis optional, research project; for doctorate, thesis/dissertation. *Entrance requirements:* For master's, minimum B average in final year, bachelor's degree in mathematics or a related area, 3 letters of reference; for doctorate, master's degree in mathematics or a related area, minimum A- average, 3 letters of reference. Additional exam requirements/recommendations for international students: Required—TOEFL (minimum score 580 paper-based; 93 iBT), TWE (minimum score 4). Electronic applications accepted.

University of Tulsa, Graduate School, College of Arts and Sciences, School of Education, Program in Teaching Arts, Tulsa, OK 74104-3189. Offers art (MTA); biology (MTA); English (MTA); history (MTA); mathematics (MTA); theatre (MTA). Part-time programs available. *Entrance requirements:* For master's, GRE General Test. Additional exam requirements/recommendations for international students: Required—TOEFL (minimum score 577 paper-based), IELTS (minimum score 6.5). *Application deadline:* Applications are processed on a rolling basis. Application fee: $40. Electronic applications accepted. *Expenses: Tuition:* Full-time $18,630. *Required fees:* $1340; $5 per credit hour. $75 per semester. Tuition and fees vary according to course load. *Financial support:* Fellowships with full and partial tuition reimbursements, research assistantships with full and partial tuition reimbursements, teaching assistantships with full and partial tuition reimbursements, career-related internships or fieldwork, Federal Work-Study, scholarships/grants, health care benefits, tuition waivers (full and partial), and unspecified assistantships available. Support available to part-time students. Financial award application deadline: 2/1; financial award applicants required to submit FAFSA. *Application contact:* Dr. David Brown, Advisor, 918-631-2719, Fax: 918-631-2133, E-mail: david-brown@utulsa.edu.

University of Tulsa, Graduate School, College of Engineering and Natural Sciences, Department of Mathematics, Tulsa, OK 74104-3189. Offers MS, MTA, PhD, MSF/MSAM. Part-time programs available. *Faculty:* 12 full-time (3 women). *Students:* 4 full-time (1 woman), 3 part-time (1 woman); includes 2 minority (both Hispanic/Latino), 3 international. Average age 24. 10 applicants, 80% accepted, 4 enrolled. In 2012, 2 master's awarded. *Degree requirements:* For master's, thesis (for some programs). *Entrance requirements:* For master's, GRE General Test. Additional exam requirements/recommendations for international students: Required—TOEFL (minimum score 550 paper-based; 80 iBT), IELTS (minimum score 6). *Application deadline:* Applications are processed on a rolling basis. Application fee: $40. Electronic applications accepted. *Expenses: Tuition:* Full-time $18,630. *Required fees:* $1340; $5 per credit hour. $75 per semester. Tuition and fees vary according to course load. *Financial support:* In 2012–13, 5 students received support, including 5 teaching assistantships with full and partial tuition reimbursements available (averaging $9,915 per year); fellowships with full and partial tuition reimbursements available, research assistantships with full and partial tuition reimbursements available, career-related internships or fieldwork, Federal Work-Study, scholarships/grants, health care benefits, tuition waivers (full and partial), and unspecified assistantships also available. Support available to part-time students. Financial award application deadline: 2/1; financial award applicants required to submit FAFSA. *Faculty research:* Optimization theory, numerical analysis, mathematical physics, modeling, Bayesian statistical inference. *Unit head:* Dr. Bill Coberly, Department Chair, 918-631-3119, Fax: 918-631-3077, E-mail: coberly@utulsa.edu. *Application contact:* Dr. Shirley Pomeranz, Advisor, 918-631-2990, Fax: 918-631-3077, E-mail: shirley-pomeranz@utulsa.edu. Website: http://www.utulsa.edu/academics/colleges/

college-of-engineering-and-natural-sciences/departments-and-schools/department-of-mathematics.aspx.

University of Utah, Graduate School, College of Science, Department of Mathematics, Salt Lake City, UT 84112-0090. Offers M Stat, MA, MS, PhD. Part-time programs available. *Faculty:* 37 full-time (5 women), 3 part-time/adjunct (0 women). *Students:* 78 full-time (22 women), 59 part-time (31 women); includes 8 minority (4 Asian, non-Hispanic/Latino; 3 Hispanic/Latino; 1 Two or more races, non-Hispanic/Latino), 32 international. Average age 30. 211 applicants, 16% accepted, 25 enrolled. In 2012, 11 master's, 10 doctorates awarded. *Degree requirements:* For master's, thesis or alternative, written or oral exam; for doctorate, comprehensive exam, thesis/dissertation, written and oral exams. *Entrance requirements:* For master's and doctorate, GRE Subject Test (math), minimum undergraduate GPA of 3.0. Additional exam requirements/recommendations for international students: Required—TOEFL (minimum score 500 paper-based; 61 iBT). *Application deadline:* For fall admission, 1/1 priority date for domestic students, 1/1 for international students; for spring admission, 11/1 for domestic and international students. Application fee: $55 ($65 for international students). *Financial support:* In 2012–13, 71 students received support, including 19 research assistantships with full tuition reimbursements available (averaging $17,000 per year), 52 teaching assistantships with full tuition reimbursements available (averaging $17,000 per year); fellowships, health care benefits, and unspecified assistantships also available. Financial award application deadline: 1/1. *Faculty research:* Algebraic geometry, geometry and topology materials and microstructure, mathematical biology, probability and statistics. *Total annual research expenditures:* $3.4 million. *Unit head:* Dr. Peter Trapa, Chairman, 801-581-6851, Fax: 801-581-4148, E-mail: ptrapa@math.utah.edu. *Application contact:* Dr. Andrejs Treibergs, Graduate Advisor, 801-581-8350, Fax: 801-581-4148, E-mail: treiberg@math.utah.edu. Website: http://www.math.utah.edu/.

University of Utah, Graduate School, Interdepartmental Program in Statistics, Salt Lake City, UT 84112-1107. Offers biostatistics (M Stat); econometrics (M Stat); educational psychology (M Stat); mathematics (M Stat); sociology (M Stat). Part-time programs available. *Students:* 30 full-time (11 women), 29 part-time (12 women); includes 13 minority (3 Black or African American, non-Hispanic/Latino; 7 Asian, non-Hispanic/Latino; 2 Hispanic/Latino; 1 Two or more races, non-Hispanic/Latino), 15 international. Average age 33. 59 applicants, 44% accepted, 16 enrolled. In 2012, 14 master's awarded. *Degree requirements:* For master's, comprehensive exam, projects. *Entrance requirements:* For master's, GRE General Test (for all but biostatistics); GRE Subject Test (for mathematics), minimum GPA of 3.0; course work in calculus, matrix theory, statistics. Additional exam requirements/recommendations for international students: Required—TOEFL (minimum score 500 paper-based; 61 iBT). *Application deadline:* For fall admission, 7/1 for domestic students, 4/1 for international students. Applications are processed on a rolling basis. Application fee: $55 ($65 for international students). *Financial support:* Career-related internships or fieldwork available. *Faculty research:* Biostatistics, management, economics, educational psychology, mathematics. *Unit head:* Richard Fowles, Chair, University Statistics Committee, 801-581-4577, E-mail: fowles@economics.utah.edu. *Application contact:* Laura Egbert, Coordinator, 801-585-6853, E-mail: laura.egbert@utah.edu. Website: http://www.mstat.utah.edu.

University of Vermont, Graduate College, College of Engineering and Mathematics, Department of Mathematics and Statistics, Program in Mathematics, Burlington, VT 05405. Offers mathematics (MS, PhD); mathematics education (MST). *Students:* 27 (8 women), 3 international. 61 applicants, 52% accepted, 13 enrolled. In 2012, 7 master's, 1 doctorate awarded. *Degree requirements:* For doctorate, thesis/dissertation. *Entrance requirements:* For master's and doctorate, GRE General Test. Additional exam requirements/recommendations for international students: Required—TOEFL (minimum score 550 paper-based; 80 iBT). *Application deadline:* For fall admission, 1/15 priority date for domestic students, 1/15 for international students. Applications are processed on a rolling basis. Application fee: $40. Electronic applications accepted. *Expenses: Tuition, area resident:* Part-time $572 per credit. Tuition, nonresident: part-time $1444 per credit. *Financial support:* Fellowships, research assistantships, and teaching assistantships available. Financial award application deadline: 3/1. *Unit head:* Dr. James Burgmeier, Chair, 802-656-2940. *Application contact:* Prof. Jonathan Sands, Coordinator, 802-656-2940.

University of Victoria, Faculty of Graduate Studies, Faculty of Science, Department of Mathematics and Statistics, Victoria, BC V8W 2Y2, Canada. Offers M Sc, MA, PhD. Part-time programs available. *Degree requirements:* For master's, thesis; for doctorate, one foreign language, thesis/dissertation, 3 qualifying exams, candidacy exam. *Entrance requirements:* Additional exam requirements/recommendations for international students: Required—TOEFL (minimum score 575 paper-based), IELTS (minimum score 7). Electronic applications accepted. *Faculty research:* Functional analysis and operator theory, applied ordinary and partial differential equations, discrete mathematics and graph theory.

University of Virginia, College and Graduate School of Arts and Sciences, Department of Mathematics, Charlottesville, VA 22903. Offers math education (MA); mathematics (MA, MS, PhD). *Faculty:* 22 full-time (2 women). *Students:* 53 full-time (13 women); includes 5 minority (2 Asian, non-Hispanic/Latino; 1 Hispanic/Latino; 2 Two or more races, non-Hispanic/Latino), 9 international. Average age 25. 125 applicants, 19% accepted, 12 enrolled. In 2012, 8 master's, 5 doctorates awarded. *Degree requirements:* For master's, one foreign language, comprehensive exam, thesis optional; for doctorate, one foreign language, comprehensive exam, thesis/dissertation. *Entrance requirements:* For master's and doctorate, GRE General Test, GRE Subject Test, 2-3 letters of recommendation. Additional exam requirements/recommendations for international students: Required—TOEFL (minimum score 600 paper-based; 90 iBT), IELTS. *Application deadline:* For fall admission, 1/15 for domestic and international students. Applications are processed on a rolling basis. Application fee: $60. Electronic applications accepted. *Expenses:* Tuition, state resident: full-time $13,278; part-time $717 per credit hour. Tuition, nonresident: full-time $22,602; part-time $1235 per credit hour. *Required fees:* $2384. *Financial support:* Fellowships, teaching assistantships, and unspecified assistantships available. Financial award application deadline: 1/15; financial award applicants required to submit FAFSA. *Unit head:* John Imbrie, Chair, 434-924-4919, Fax: 434-982-3084, E-mail: imbrie@virginia.edu. *Application contact:* Julie Riddleberger, Administrative and Office Specialist, 434-924-4918, Fax: 434-982-3084, E-mail: julier@virginia.edu. Website: http://www.math.virginia.edu/.

University of Washington, Graduate School, College of Arts and Sciences, Department of Mathematics, Seattle, WA 98195. Offers mathematics (MA, MS, PhD); numerical analysis (MS); optimization (MS). Part-time programs available. Terminal master's awarded for partial completion of doctoral program. *Degree requirements:* For master's, thesis optional; for doctorate, 2 foreign languages, thesis/dissertation. *Entrance requirements:* For master's, GRE, minimum GPA of 3.0; for doctorate, GRE General Test, GRE Subject Test (mathematics), minimum GPA of 3.0. Additional exam requirements/recommendations for international students: Required—TOEFL. Electronic applications accepted. *Faculty research:* Algebra, analysis, probability, combinatorics and geometry.

University of Washington, Graduate School, Interdisciplinary Graduate Program in Quantitative Ecology and Resource Management, Seattle, WA 98195. Offers MS, PhD. *Degree requirements:* For master's, thesis; for doctorate, thesis/dissertation. *Entrance requirements:* For master's and doctorate, GRE General Test, minimum GPA of 3.0. Additional exam requirements/recommendations for international students: Required—TOEFL. Electronic applications accepted. *Faculty research:* Population dynamics, statistical analysis, ecological modeling and systems analysis of aquatic and terrestrial ecosystems.

University of Waterloo, Graduate Studies, Faculty of Mathematics, Department of Combinatorics and Optimization, Waterloo, ON N2L 3G1, Canada. Offers M Math, PhD. *Degree requirements:* For master's, research paper or thesis; for doctorate, comprehensive exam, thesis/dissertation. *Entrance requirements:* For master's, GRE General Test, honors degree in field, minimum B+ average; for doctorate, GRE General Test, master's degree, minimum A average. Additional exam requirements/recommendations for international students: Required—TOEFL, TWE. Electronic applications accepted. *Faculty research:* Algebraic and enumerative combinatorics, continuous optimization, cryptography, discrete optimization and graph theory.

University of Waterloo, Graduate Studies, Faculty of Mathematics, Department of Pure Mathematics, Waterloo, ON N2L 3G1, Canada. Offers M Math, PhD. Part-time programs available. Terminal master's awarded for partial completion of doctoral program. *Degree requirements:* For master's, thesis optional; for doctorate, comprehensive exam, thesis/dissertation. *Entrance requirements:* For master's, honors degree in field, minimum B+ average; for doctorate, master's degree, minimum B+ average. Additional exam requirements/recommendations for international students: Required—TOEFL (minimum score 580 paper-based; 92 iBT), TWE (minimum score 4). Electronic applications accepted. *Faculty research:* Algebra, algebraic and differential geometry, functional and harmonic analysis, logic and universal algebra, number theory.

The University of Western Ontario, Faculty of Graduate Studies, Physical Sciences Division, Department of Mathematics, London, ON N6A 5B8, Canada. Offers M Sc, PhD. Terminal master's awarded for partial completion of doctoral program. *Degree requirements:* For master's, thesis or alternative; for doctorate, one foreign language, comprehensive exam, thesis/dissertation, qualifying exam. *Entrance requirements:* For master's, minimum B average, honors degree; for doctorate, master's degree. Additional exam requirements/recommendations for international students: Required—TOEFL (minimum score 550 paper-based). *Faculty research:* Algebra and number theory, analysis, geometry and topology.

University of West Florida, College of Arts and Sciences: Sciences, Department of Mathematics and Statistics, Pensacola, FL 32514-5750. Offers applied statistics (MS); mathematical sciences (MS). Part-time and evening/weekend programs available. *Degree requirements:* For master's, thesis optional. *Entrance requirements:* For master's, GRE (minimum score: verbal 420; quantitative 580), minimum GPA of 3.0; official transcripts. Additional exam requirements/recommendations for international students: Required—TOEFL (minimum score 550 paper-based).

University of West Georgia, College of Science and Mathematics, Department of Mathematics, Carrollton, GA 30118. Offers teaching and applied mathematics (MS). Part-time and evening/weekend programs available. *Faculty:* 13 full-time (3 women). *Students:* 2 full-time (1 woman), 7 part-time (3 women); includes 2 minority (1 Black or African American, non-Hispanic/Latino; 1 Asian, non-Hispanic/Latino). Average age 38. 6 applicants, 17% accepted, 1 enrolled. In 2012, 6 master's awarded. *Degree requirements:* For master's, comprehensive exam, thesis optional, 36 credit hours. *Entrance requirements:* For master's, GRE. Additional exam requirements/recommendations for international students: Recommended—TOEFL (minimum score 523 paper-based; 69 iBT), IELTS (minimum score 6). *Application deadline:* For fall admission, 6/1 for domestic and international students; for spring admission, 11/15 for domestic students, 10/15 for international students. Applications are processed on a rolling basis. Application fee: $40. Electronic applications accepted. *Expenses:* Tuition, state resident: full-time $4466; part-time $187 per semester hour. Tuition, nonresident: full-time $17,888; part-time $745 per semester hour. *Required fees:* $1858; $46.34 per semester hour. One-time fee: $512 full-time; $266 part-time. Tuition and fees vary according to course load, degree level and program. *Financial support:* In 2012–13, 3 students received support, including 3 teaching assistantships (averaging $6,800 per year); unspecified assistantships also available. Financial award application deadline: 6/1; financial award applicants required to submit FAFSA. *Faculty research:* Graph coloring problems, labeling and domination in graphs, high dimension regression, Inverse problem, spectral theory of operators, math teacher education. *Unit head:* Dr. Bruce Landman, Chair, 678-839-6489, Fax: 678-839-6490, E-mail: landman@westga.edu. *Application contact:* Alice Wesley, Departmental Assistant, 678-839-5192, E-mail: awesley@westga.edu. Website: http://www.westga.edu/math/.

University of Windsor, Faculty of Graduate Studies, Faculty of Science, Department of Mathematics and Statistics, Windsor, ON N9B 3P4, Canada. Offers mathematics (M Sc); statistics (M Sc, PhD). *Degree requirements:* For master's, thesis or alternative; for doctorate, comprehensive exam, thesis/dissertation. *Entrance requirements:* For master's, minimum B average; for doctorate, minimum A average. Additional exam requirements/recommendations for international students: Required—TOEFL (minimum score 560 paper-based). Electronic applications accepted. *Faculty research:* Applied mathematics, operational research, fluid dynamics.

University of Wisconsin–Madison, Graduate School, College of Letters and Science, Department of Mathematics, Madison, WI 53706. Offers PhD. *Degree requirements:* For doctorate, comprehensive exam, thesis/dissertation, classes in a minor field; minimum GPA of 3.3. *Entrance requirements:* For doctorate, GRE General Test, GRE Subject Test (math). Additional exam requirements/recommendations for international students: Required—TOEFL (minimum score 580 paper-based; 92 iBT), IELTS. Electronic applications accepted. *Expenses:* Tuition, state resident: full-time $10,728; part-time $743 per credit. Tuition, nonresident: full-time $24,054; part-time $1575 per credit. *Required fees:* $1111; $72 per credit. *Faculty research:* Analysis, applied/computational mathematics, geometry/topology, logic, algebra/number theory, probability.

University of Wisconsin–Milwaukee, Graduate School, College of Letters and Sciences, Department of Mathematical Sciences, Milwaukee, WI 53201-0413. Offers mathematics (MS, PhD). *Faculty:* 32 full-time (3 women), 2 part-time/adjunct (1 woman). *Students:* 74 full-time (21 women), 15 part-time (5 women); includes 8 minority (3 Black or African American, non-Hispanic/Latino; 4 Asian, non-Hispanic/Latino; 1 Two or more races, non-Hispanic/Latino), 26 international. Average age 30. 138 applicants, 33% accepted, 21 enrolled. In 2012, 23 master's, 4 doctorates awarded. *Degree requirements:* For master's, comprehensive exam, thesis optional; for doctorate, 2 foreign languages, thesis/dissertation. *Entrance requirements:* Additional exam requirements/recommendations for international students: Required—TOEFL (minimum score 550 paper-based; 79 iBT), IELTS (minimum score 6.5). *Application deadline:* For fall admission, 1/1 priority date for domestic students; for spring admission, 9/1 for domestic students. Applications are processed on a rolling basis. Application fee: $56 ($96 for international students). Electronic applications accepted. *Financial support:* In 2012–13, 23 fellowships, 9 research assistantships, 56 teaching assistantships were awarded; career-related internships or fieldwork, health care benefits, and unspecified assistantships also available. Support available to part-time students. Financial award application deadline: 4/15; financial award applicants required to submit FAFSA. *Faculty research:* Algebra, applied mathematics, atmospheric science, probability and statistics, topology. *Unit head:* Richard Stockbridge, Department Chair, 414-229-4568, E-mail: stockbri@uwm.edu. *Application contact:* General Information Contact, 414-229-4982, Fax: 414-229-6967, E-mail: gradschool@uwm.edu. Website: http://www.uwm.edu/dept/math/.

University of Wyoming, College of Arts and Sciences, Department of Mathematics, Laramie, WY 82071. Offers mathematics (MA, MAT, MS, MST, PhD); mathematics/computer science (PhD). Part-time programs available. Terminal master's awarded for partial completion of doctoral program. *Degree requirements:* For master's, comprehensive exam, thesis, qualifying exam; for doctorate, comprehensive exam, thesis/dissertation, preliminary exam. *Entrance requirements:* For master's and doctorate, GRE General Test, minimum GPA of 3.0. Additional exam requirements/recommendations for international students: Required—TOEFL (minimum score 540 paper-based; 76 iBT). *Faculty research:* Numerical analysis, classical analysis, mathematical modeling, algebraic combinations.

Utah State University, School of Graduate Studies, College of Science, Department of Mathematics and Statistics, Logan, UT 84322. Offers industrial mathematics (MS); mathematical sciences (PhD); mathematics (M Math, MS); statistics (MS). Part-time programs available. Terminal master's awarded for partial completion of doctoral program. *Degree requirements:* For master's, thesis optional, qualifying exam; for doctorate, one foreign language, comprehensive exam, thesis/dissertation. *Entrance requirements:* For master's and doctorate, GRE General Test, minimum GPA of 3.0. Additional exam requirements/recommendations for international students: Required—TOEFL. *Faculty research:* Differential equations, computational mathematics, dynamical systems, probability and statistics, pure mathematics.

Vanderbilt University, Graduate School, Department of Mathematics, Nashville, TN 37240-1001. Offers MA, MAT, MS, PhD. *Faculty:* 31 full-time (2 women). *Students:* 39 full-time (7 women); includes 3 minority (1 Asian, non-Hispanic/Latino; 1 Hispanic/Latino; 1 Two or more races, non-Hispanic/Latino), 22 international. Average age 26. 167 applicants, 11% accepted, 7 enrolled. In 2012, 5 master's, 4 doctorates awarded. *Degree requirements:* For master's, one foreign language, thesis or alternative; for doctorate, one foreign language, comprehensive exam, thesis/dissertation. *Entrance requirements:* For master's and doctorate, GRE General Test, GRE Subject Test. Additional exam requirements/recommendations for international students: Required—TOEFL (minimum score 570 paper-based; 88 iBT). *Application deadline:* For fall admission, 1/15 for domestic and international students. Application fee: $0. Electronic applications accepted. *Financial support:* Fellowships with full and partial tuition reimbursements, research assistantships with full tuition reimbursements, teaching assistantships with full tuition reimbursements, Federal Work-Study, institutionally sponsored loans, scholarships/grants, and health care benefits available. Financial award application deadline: 1/15; financial award applicants required to submit CSS PROFILE or FAFSA. *Faculty research:* Algebra, topology, applied mathematics, graph theory, analytical mathematics. *Unit head:* Dr. Mike Neamtu, Director of Graduate Studies, 615-322-6655, Fax: 615-343-0215, E-mail: mike.neamtu@vanderbilt.edu. *Application contact:* Carrie Litsey, Administrative Assistant, 615-322-6672, Fax: 315-343-0215, E-mail: carrie.litsey@vanderbilt.edu. Website: http://www.vanderbilt.edu/math/.

Villanova University, Graduate School of Liberal Arts and Sciences, Department of Mathematical Sciences, Program in Mathematical Sciences, Villanova, PA 19085-1699. Offers MA. Part-time and evening/weekend programs available. *Students:* 18 full-time (6 women), 10 part-time (4 women). Average age 29. 21 applicants, 100% accepted, 12 enrolled. In 2012, 11 master's awarded. *Degree requirements:* For master's, comprehensive exam. *Entrance requirements:* For master's, GRE, minimum GPA of 3.0. Additional exam requirements/recommendations for international students: Required—TOEFL. *Application deadline:* For fall admission, 5/1 for international students; for spring admission, 10/15 for international students. Applications are processed on a rolling basis. Application fee: $50. Electronic applications accepted. *Financial support:* Research assistantships and Federal Work-Study available. Financial award applicants required to submit FAFSA. *Unit head:* Dr. Douglas Norton, Chair, 610-519-4850. Website: http://www.villanova.edu/artsci/mathematics/graduate/mamath.htm.

Virginia Commonwealth University, Graduate School, College of Humanities and Sciences, Department of Mathematics and Applied Mathematics, Richmond, VA 23284-9005. Offers applied mathematics (MS); mathematics (MS). *Degree requirements:* For master's, thesis optional. *Entrance requirements:* For master's, GRE General Test, GRE Subject Test, 30 undergraduate semester credits in the mathematical sciences or closely-related fields. Additional exam requirements/recommendations for international students: Required—TOEFL (minimum score 600 paper-based; 100 iBT); Recommended—IELTS (minimum score 6.5). Electronic applications accepted. *Faculty research:* Mathematics, applied mathematics.

Virginia Polytechnic Institute and State University, Graduate School, College of Science, Blacksburg, VA 24061. Offers biological sciences (MS, PhD); biomedical technology development and management (MS); chemistry (MS, PhD); economics (MA, PhD); geosciences (MS, PhD); mathematics (MS, PhD); physics (MS, PhD); psychology (MS, PhD); statistics (MS, PhD). *Faculty:* 259 full-time (68 women), 3 part-time/adjunct (all women). *Students:* 555 full-time (230 women), 31 part-time (12 women); includes 44 minority (10 Black or African American, non-Hispanic/Latino; 1 American Indian or Alaska Native, non-Hispanic/Latino; 11 Asian, non-Hispanic/Latino; 14 Hispanic/Latino; 8 Two or more races, non-Hispanic/Latino), 250 international. Average age 28. 1,091 applicants, 24% accepted, 137 enrolled. In 2012, 65 master's, 89 doctorates awarded. *Median time to degree:* Of those who began their doctoral program in fall 2004, 68% received their degree in 8 years or less. *Degree requirements:* For master's, comprehensive exam (for some programs), thesis (for some programs); for doctorate, comprehensive exam (for some programs), thesis/dissertation (for some programs). *Entrance requirements:* For master's and doctorate, GRE/GMAT (may vary by department). Additional exam requirements/recommendations for international students: Required—TOEFL (minimum score 550 paper-based). *Application deadline:* For fall admission, 8/1 for domestic students, 4/1 for international students; for spring admission, 1/1 for domestic students, 9/1 for international students. Applications are processed on a rolling basis. Application fee: $65. Electronic applications accepted. *Expenses:* Tuition, state resident: full-time $10,677; part-time $593.25 per credit hour. Tuition, nonresident: full-time $20,926; part-time $1162.50 per credit hour. *Required fees:* $427.75 per semester. Tuition and fees vary according to course load, campus/location and program. *Financial support:* In 2012–13, 1 fellowship with full tuition reimbursement (averaging $21,606 per year), 159 research assistantships with full tuition reimbursements (averaging $19,950 per year), 331 teaching assistantships with full tuition reimbursements (averaging $17,426 per year) were awarded. Financial award application deadline: 3/1; financial award applicants required to submit FAFSA. *Total annual research expenditures:* $23.4 million. *Unit head:* Dr. Lay Nam Chang, Dean, 540-231-5422, Fax: 540-231-3380, E-mail: laynam@vt.edu. *Application contact:* Diane Stearns, Assistant to the Dean, 540-231-7515, Fax: 540-231-3380, E-mail: dstearns@vt.edu. Website: http://www.science.vt.edu/.

Virginia State University, School of Graduate Studies, Research, and Outreach, School of Engineering, Science and Technology, Department of Mathematics and Computer Science, Petersburg, VA 23806-0001. Offers computer science (MS); mathematics (MS); mathematics education (M Ed). *Degree requirements:* For master's, thesis (for some programs).

Wake Forest University, Graduate School of Arts and Sciences, Department of Mathematics, Winston-Salem, NC 27109. Offers MA. Part-time programs available. *Degree requirements:* For master's, one foreign language, thesis optional. *Entrance requirements:* For master's, GRE General Test. Additional exam requirements/recommendations for international students: Required—TOEFL (minimum score 79 iBT). Electronic applications accepted. *Faculty research:* Algebra, ring theory, topology, differential equations.

Washington State University, Graduate School, College of Arts and Sciences, Department of Mathematics, Pullman, WA 99164. Offers applied mathematics (MS, PhD); mathematics (MS, PhD); mathematics computational finance (MS); mathematics teaching (MS, PhD). Part-time programs available. *Faculty:* 28 full-time (4 women). *Students:* 49 full-time (16 women), 2 part-time (1 woman); includes 5 minority (1 Black or African American, non-Hispanic/Latino; 2 Asian, non-Hispanic/Latino; 1 Hispanic/Latino; 1 Native Hawaiian or other Pacific Islander, non-Hispanic/Latino), 17 international. Average age 27. 117 applicants, 68% accepted, 18 enrolled. In 2012, 5 master's, 6 doctorates awarded. Terminal master's awarded for partial completion of doctoral program. *Degree requirements:* For master's, comprehensive exam (for some programs), thesis or alternative, oral exam, project; for doctorate, 2 foreign languages, comprehensive exam, thesis/dissertation, oral exam, written exam. *Entrance requirements:* For master's and doctorate, minimum GPA of 3.0, 3 letters of recommendation. Additional exam requirements/recommendations for international students: Required—TOEFL (minimum score 600 paper-based; 100 iBT) or IELTS (minimum score 7). *Application deadline:* For fall admission, 1/10 for domestic and international students; for spring admission, 7/1 for domestic and international students. Applications are processed on a rolling basis. Application fee: $75. Electronic applications accepted. *Financial support:* In 2012–13, 43 students received support, including 9 research assistantships with full and partial tuition reimbursements available (averaging $15,500 per year), 34 teaching assistantships with full and partial tuition reimbursements available (averaging $15,000 per year); fellowships, career-related internships or fieldwork, Federal Work-Study, institutionally sponsored loans, scholarships/grants, traineeships, health care benefits, and tuition waivers (partial) also available. Financial award application deadline: 2/15. *Faculty research:* Computational mathematics, operations research, modeling in the natural sciences, applied statistics. *Unit head:* Dr. K. A. Ariyawansa, Chair, 509-335-4918, Fax: 509-335-1188, E-mail: ari@wsu.edu. *Application contact:* Graduate School Admissions, 800-GRADWSU, Fax: 509-335-1949, E-mail: gradsch@wsu.edu. Website: http://www.sci.wsu.edu/math/.

Washington University in St. Louis, Graduate School of Arts and Sciences, Department of Mathematics, St. Louis, MO 63130-4899. Offers mathematics (MA, PhD); statistics (MA). Terminal master's awarded for partial completion of doctoral program. *Degree requirements:* For master's, thesis or alternative; for doctorate, thesis/dissertation. *Entrance requirements:* For master's and doctorate, GRE General Test. Electronic applications accepted.

Wayne State University, College of Liberal Arts and Sciences, Department of Mathematics, Detroit, MI 48202. Offers applied mathematics (MA, PhD); mathematical statistics (MA, PhD); mathematics (MA); pure mathematics (PhD). *Students:* 54 full-time (17 women), 34 part-time (14 women); includes 12 minority (9 Black or African American, non-Hispanic/Latino; 3 Asian, non-Hispanic/Latino), 33 international. Average age 31. 120 applicants, 45% accepted, 16 enrolled. In 2012, 17 master's, 7 doctorates awarded. *Degree requirements:* For master's, thesis (for some programs), essays, oral exams; for doctorate, thesis/dissertation, oral exams; French, German, Russian, or Chinese. *Entrance requirements:* For master's, twelve semester credits in mathematics beyond sophomore calculus; for doctorate, master's degree in mathematics or equivalent level of advancement. Additional exam requirements/recommendations for international students: Required—TOEFL (minimum score 550 paper-based; 79 iBT); Recommended—TWE (minimum score 5.5). *Application deadline:* For fall admission, 6/1 priority date for domestic students, 5/1 for international students; for winter admission, 10/1 priority date for domestic students, 9/1 for international students; for spring admission, 2/1 priority date for domestic students, 1/1 for international students. Applications are processed on a rolling basis. Application fee: $50. Electronic applications accepted. *Expenses:* Tuition, state resident: full-time $12,788; part-time $532.85 per credit hour. Tuition, nonresident: full-time $28,243; part-time $1176.80 per credit hour. *Required fees:* $1367.30; $39.75 per credit hour. $206.65 per semester. Tuition and fees vary according to course load and program. *Financial support:* In 2012–13, 43 students received support, including 2 fellowships with tuition reimbursements available (averaging $17,000 per year), 5 research assistantships with tuition reimbursements available (averaging $18,293 per year), 27 teaching assistantships with tuition reimbursements available (averaging $17,391 per year); institutionally sponsored loans, scholarships/grants, health care benefits, tuition waivers (full), and unspecified assistantships also available. Support available to part-time students. *Faculty research:* Harmonic analysis and partial differential equations, group theory and non-commutative ring theory, homotopy theory and applications to topology and geometry, numerical analysis, control and optimization, statistical estimation theory. *Total annual research expenditures:* $1 million. *Unit head:* Dr. Daniel Frohardt, Professor and Chair, 313-577-2479, E-mail: ad0798@wayne.edu. *Application contact:* Dr. Alexander Korostelev, E-mail: apk@math.wayne.edu. Website: http://clasweb.clas.wayne.edu/math.

Wesleyan University, Graduate Studies, Department of Mathematics and Computer Science, Middletown, CT 06459. Offers computer science (MA); mathematics (MA, PhD). Terminal master's awarded for partial completion of doctoral program. *Degree requirements:* For master's, one foreign language, thesis; for doctorate, 2 foreign languages, thesis/dissertation. *Entrance requirements:* For master's, GRE General Test, GRE Subject Test; for doctorate, GRE Subject Test. Additional exam requirements/recommendations for international students: Required—TOEFL. *Application deadline:* For fall admission, 2/15 for domestic and international students. Applications are processed on a rolling basis. Application fee: $0. Electronic applications accepted. *Financial support:* Teaching assistantships with full tuition reimbursements and tuition waivers (full and partial) available. Financial award application deadline: 4/15; financial award applicants required to submit FAFSA. *Faculty research:* Topology, analysis. *Unit head:* Dr. Mark Hovey, Chair, 860-685-2198, E-mail: mhovey@wesleyan.edu. *Application contact:* Caryn Canalia, Administrative Assistant, 860-685-2182, Fax: 860-685-2571, E-mail: ccanalia@wesleyan.edu. Website: http://www.wesleyan.edu/mathcs/index.html.

See Display on next page and Close-Up on page 379.

West Chester University of Pennsylvania, College of Arts and Sciences, Department of Mathematics, West Chester, PA 19383. Offers applied statistics (MS, Certificate); mathematics (MS, Teaching Certificate). Part-time and evening/weekend programs available. *Faculty:* 10 full-time (1 woman). *Students:* 4 full-time (3 women), 83 part-time (34 women); includes 18 minority (7 Black or African American, non-Hispanic/Latino; 9 Asian, non-Hispanic/Latino; 2 Hispanic/Latino), 4 international. Average age 31. 49 applicants, 98% accepted, 31 enrolled. In 2012, 1 master's, 25 other advanced degrees awarded. *Degree requirements:* For master's, thesis optional. *Entrance requirements:* For master's, GMAT, GRE General Test, or MAT (for MA), interview (for mathematics MS); for other advanced degree, GMAT, GRE General Test, or MAT (for Teaching Certificate). Additional exam requirements/recommendations for international students: Required—TOEFL (minimum score 550 paper-based; 80 iBT). *Application deadline:* For fall admission, 4/15 priority date for domestic students, 3/15 for international students; for spring admission, 10/15 priority date for domestic students, 9/1 for international students. Applications are processed on a rolling basis. Application fee: $45. Electronic applications accepted. *Expenses:* Tuition, state resident: full-time $7722; part-time $429 per credit. Tuition, nonresident: full-time $11,592; part-time $644 per credit. *Required fees:* $2108; $105.05 per credit. Tuition and fees vary according to campus/location and program. *Financial support:* Unspecified assistantships available. Support available to part-time students. Financial award application deadline: 2/15; financial award applicants required to submit FAFSA. *Faculty research:* Teachers teaching with technology in service training program, biostatistics, hierarchical linear models, clustered binary outcome date. *Unit head:* Dr. Kathleen Jackson, Chair, 610-436-2537, Fax: 610-738-0578, E-mail: kjackson@wcupa.edu. *Application contact:* Dr. Gail Gallitano, Graduate Coordinator, 610-436-2452, Fax: 610-738-0578, E-mail: ggallitano@wcupa.edu. Website: http://www.wcupa.edu/_academics/sch_cas.mat/.

Western Carolina University, Graduate School, College of Arts and Sciences, Department of Mathematics and Computer Science, Cullowhee, NC 28723. Offers applied mathematics (MS). Part-time and evening/weekend programs available. *Degree requirements:* For master's, thesis or alternative. *Entrance requirements:* For master's, GRE General Test, appropriate undergraduate degree, 3 letters of recommendation. Additional exam requirements/recommendations for international students: Required—TOEFL (minimum score 550 paper-based; 79 iBT).

Western Connecticut State University, Division of Graduate Studies, School of Arts and Sciences, Department of Mathematics, Danbury, CT 06810-6885. Offers mathematics (MA); theoretical mathematics (MA). Part-time programs available. *Faculty:* 2 full-time (1 woman). *Students:* 2 full-time (0 women), 9 part-time (3 women); includes 2 minority (both Hispanic/Latino). Average age 31. 10 applicants, 70% accepted, 7 enrolled. In 2012, 4 master's awarded. *Degree requirements:* For master's, thesis or research project, completion of program in 6 years. *Entrance requirements:* For master's, minimum GPA of 2.5. Additional exam requirements/recommendations for international students: Recommended—TOEFL (minimum score 550 paper-based; 79 iBT), IELTS (minimum score 6). *Application deadline:* For fall admission, 8/5 priority date for domestic students; for spring admission, 1/5 priority date for domestic students. Applications are processed on a rolling basis. Application fee: $50. *Expenses:* Tuition, state resident: full-time $5337; part-time $296 per credit hour. Tuition, nonresident: full-time $14,869; part-time $302 per credit hour. *Required fees:* $4155; $301 per credit hour. Tuition and fees vary according to course level, degree level and program. *Financial support:* Application deadline: 5/1; applicants required to submit FAFSA. *Faculty research:* Eulerian mathematical principles. *Unit head:* Dr. Josephine Hamer, Graduate Coordinator, 203-837-9347, Fax: 203-837-8525, E-mail: hamerj@wcsu.edu. *Application contact:* Chris Shankle, Associate Director of Graduate Studies, 203-837-9005, Fax: 203-837-8326, E-mail: shanklec@wcsu.edu. Website: http://www.wcsu.edu/math/.

Western Illinois University, School of Graduate Studies, College of Arts and Sciences, Department of Mathematics, Macomb, IL 61455-1390. Offers applied

Mathematics

math (Certificate); mathematics (MS). Part-time programs available. *Students:* 12 full-time (6 women), 1 part-time (0 women), 8 international. Average age 27. In 2012, 7 master's, 1 other advanced degree awarded. *Degree requirements:* For master's, thesis or alternative. *Entrance requirements:* Additional exam requirements/recommendations for international students: Required—TOEFL (minimum score 500 paper-based; 61 iBT). *Application deadline:* Applications are processed on a rolling basis. Application fee: $30. Electronic applications accepted. *Financial support:* In 2012–13, 5 students received support, including 1 research assistantship with full tuition reimbursement available (averaging $7,544 per year), 4 teaching assistantships with full tuition reimbursements available (averaging $8,688 per year). Financial award applicants required to submit FAFSA. *Unit head:* Dr. Iraj Kalantari, Chairperson, 309-298-1054. *Application contact:* Dr. Nancy Parsons, Interim Associate Provost and Director of Graduate Studies, 309-298-1806, Fax: 309-298-2345, E-mail: grad-office@wiu.edu. Website: http://wiu.edu/mathematics.

Western Kentucky University, Graduate Studies, Ogden College of Science and Engineering, Department of Mathematics and Computer Science, Bowling Green, KY 42101. Offers computational mathematics (MS); computer science (MS); mathematics (MA, MS). *Degree requirements:* For master's, comprehensive exam, thesis optional, written exam. *Entrance requirements:* For master's, GRE General Test, minimum GPA of 2.75. Additional exam requirements/recommendations for international students: Required—TOEFL (minimum score 555 paper-based; 79 iBT). *Faculty research:* Differential equations numerical analysis, probability statistics, algebra, typology, knot theory.

Western Michigan University, Graduate College, College of Arts and Sciences, Department of Mathematics, Programs in Mathematics, Kalamazoo, MI 49008. Offers mathematics (MA, PhD); mathematics education (MA, PhD). *Degree requirements:* For master's, oral exams; for doctorate, one foreign language, thesis/dissertation, oral exams, 3 comprehensive exams, internship. *Entrance requirements:* For doctorate, GRE General Test.

Western Washington University, Graduate School, College of Sciences and Technology, Department of Mathematics, Bellingham, WA 98225-5996. Offers MS. Part-time programs available. *Degree requirements:* For master's, thesis (for some programs), project, qualifying examination. *Entrance requirements:* For master's, GRE General Test, minimum GPA of 3.0 in last 60 semester hours or last 90 quarter hours. Additional exam requirements/recommendations for international students: Required—TOEFL (minimum score 567 paper-based). Electronic applications accepted. *Faculty research:* Numerical analysis, combinatorics, harmonic analysis, inverse problems, reliability testing.

West Texas A&M University, College of Agriculture, Science and Engineering, Department of Mathematics, Physical Sciences and Engineering Technology, Program in Mathematics, Canyon, TX 79016-0001. Offers MS. Part-time

programs available. *Degree requirements:* For master's, comprehensive exam, thesis optional. *Entrance requirements:* For master's, GRE General Test. Additional exam requirements/recommendations for international students: Required—TOEFL (minimum score 550 paper-based). Electronic applications accepted.

West Virginia University, Eberly College of Arts and Sciences, Department of Mathematics, Morgantown, WV 26506. Offers applied mathematics (MS, PhD); discrete mathematics (PhD); interdisciplinary mathematics (MS); mathematics for secondary education (MS); pure mathematics (MS). Part-time programs available. Terminal master's awarded for partial completion of doctoral program. *Degree requirements:* For master's, comprehensive exam (for some programs), thesis optional; for doctorate, one foreign language, comprehensive exam, thesis/dissertation. *Entrance requirements:* For master's, GRE Subject Test (recommended), minimum GPA of 2.5; for doctorate, GRE Subject Test (recommended), master's degree in mathematics. Additional exam requirements/recommendations for international students: Required—TOEFL (paper-based 550) or IELTS (6). *Faculty research:* Combinatorics and graph theory, differential equations, applied and computational mathematics.

Wichita State University, Graduate School, Fairmount College of Liberal Arts and Sciences, Department of Mathematics, Statistics and Physics, Wichita, KS 67260. Offers applied mathematics (PhD); mathematics (MS). Part-time programs available. *Unit head:* Dr. Buma Fridman, Chair, 316-978-3160, Fax: 316-978-3748, E-mail: buma.fridman@wichita.edu. *Application contact:* Jordan Oleson, Admissions Coordinator, 316-978-3095, Fax: 316-978-3253, E-mail: jordan.oleson@wichita.edu. Website: http://www.wichita.edu/.

Wilfrid Laurier University, Faculty of Graduate and Postdoctoral Studies, Faculty of Science, Department of Mathematics, Waterloo, ON N2L 3C5, Canada. Offers mathematics for science and finance (M Sc). Part-time programs available. *Degree requirements:* For master's, thesis optional. *Entrance requirements:* For master's, 4-year honors degree in mathematics, minimum B+ average. Additional exam requirements/recommendations for international students: Required—TOEFL (minimum score 89 iBT). Electronic applications accepted. *Faculty research:* Modeling, analysis, resolution, and generalization of financial and scientific problems.

Wilkes University, College of Graduate and Professional Studies, College of Science and Engineering, Department of Mathematics and Computer Science, Wilkes-Barre, PA 18766-0002. Offers mathematics (MS, MS Ed). Part-time programs available. *Students:* 1 full-time (0 women). Average age 25. In 2012, 1 master's awarded. *Degree requirements:* For master's, thesis or alternative. *Entrance requirements:* For master's, GRE General Test. Additional exam requirements/recommendations for international students: Required—TOEFL (minimum score 550 paper-based; 79 iBT). *Application deadline:* Applications are

354 www.petersonsbooks.com

Peterson's Graduate Programs in the Physical Sciences, Mathematics, Agricultural Sciences, the Environment & Natural Resources 2014

processed on a rolling basis. Application fee: $45 ($65 for international students). Electronic applications accepted. *Financial support:* Federal Work-Study and unspecified assistantships available. Financial award application deadline: 3/1; financial award applicants required to submit FAFSA. *Unit head:* Dr. Barbara Bracken, Chair, 570-408-4836, Fax: 570-408-7883, E-mail: barbara.bracken@wilkes.edu. *Application contact:* Erin Sutzko, Director of Extended Learning, 570-408-4253, Fax: 570-408-7846, E-mail: erin.sutzko@wilkes.edu. Website: http://www.wilkes.edu/pages/389.asp.

Worcester Polytechnic Institute, Graduate Studies and Research, Department of Mathematical Sciences, Worcester, MA 01609-2280. Offers applied mathematics (MS); applied statistics (MS); financial mathematics (MS); industrial mathematics (MS); mathematical sciences (PhD, Graduate Certificate); mathematics (MME); mathematics for educators (MS). Part-time and evening/weekend programs available. *Faculty:* 19 full-time (3 women), 7 part-time/adjunct (2 women). *Students:* 93 full-time (45 women), 19 part-time (15 women); includes 5 minority (2 Black or African American, non-Hispanic/Latino; 2 Hispanic/Latino; 1 Two or more races, non-Hispanic/Latino), 71 international. 398 applicants, 53% accepted, 54 enrolled. In 2012, 25 master's, 1 doctorate awarded. *Degree requirements:* For master's, thesis (for some programs); for doctorate, comprehensive exam, thesis/dissertation. *Entrance requirements:* For master's and doctorate, GRE General Test, GRE Subject Test in math (recommended), 3 letters of recommendation. Additional exam requirements/recommendations for international students: Required—TOEFL (minimum score 563 paper-based; 84 iBT), IELTS (minimum score 7). *Application deadline:* For fall admission, 1/1 priority date for domestic students, 1/1 for international students; for spring admission, 10/1 priority date for domestic students, 10/1 for international students. Applications are processed on a rolling basis. Application fee: $70. Electronic applications accepted. *Financial support:* Research assistantships, teaching assistantships, career-related internships or fieldwork, institutionally sponsored loans, scholarships/grants, and unspecified assistantships available. Financial award application deadline: 1/1; financial award applicants required to submit FAFSA. *Faculty research:* Applied analysis and differential equations, computational mathematics, discrete mathematics, applied and computational statistics, industrial and financial mathematics, mathematical biology. *Unit head:*

Dr. Bogdan Vernescu, Head, 508-831-5241, Fax: 508-831-5824, E-mail: vernescu@wpi.edu. *Application contact:* Dr. Joseph Fehribach, Graduate Coordinator, 508-831-5241, Fax: 508-831-5824, E-mail: bach@wpi.edu. Website: http://www.wpi.edu/Academics/Depts/Math/.

Wright State University, School of Graduate Studies, College of Science and Mathematics, Department of Mathematics and Statistics, Program in Mathematics, Dayton, OH 45435. Offers MS. *Degree requirements:* For master's, comprehensive exam. *Entrance requirements:* For master's, previous course work in mathematics beyond calculus. Additional exam requirements/recommendations for international students: Required—TOEFL. *Faculty research:* Analysis, algebraic combinatorics, graph theory, operator theory.

Yale University, Graduate School of Arts and Sciences, Department of Mathematics, New Haven, CT 06520. Offers M Phil, MS, PhD. *Degree requirements:* For doctorate, 2 foreign languages, thesis/dissertation. *Entrance requirements:* For doctorate, GRE General Test, GRE Subject Test.

York University, Faculty of Graduate Studies, Faculty of Science and Engineering, Program in Mathematics and Statistics, Toronto, ON M3J 1P3, Canada. Offers industrial and applied mathematics (M Sc); mathematics and statistics (MA, PhD). Part-time programs available. *Degree requirements:* For master's, thesis optional; for doctorate, one foreign language, comprehensive exam, thesis/dissertation. Electronic applications accepted.

Youngstown State University, Graduate School, College of Science, Technology, Engineering and Mathematics, Department of Mathematics and Statistics, Youngstown, OH 44555-0001. Offers applied mathematics (MS); computer science (MS); secondary mathematics (MS); statistics (MS). Part-time programs available. *Degree requirements:* For master's, comprehensive exam, thesis optional. *Entrance requirements:* For master's, minimum GPA of 2.7 in computer science and mathematics. Additional exam requirements/recommendations for international students: Required—TOEFL. *Faculty research:* Regression analysis, numerical analysis, statistics, Markov chain, topology and fuzzy sets.

Statistics

Acadia University, Faculty of Pure and Applied Science, Department of Mathematics and Statistics, Wolfville, NS B4P 2R6, Canada. Offers applied mathematics and statistics (M Sc). *Faculty:* 12 full-time (3 women), 2 part-time/adjunct (0 women). *Students:* 3 full-time (2 women), 3 part-time (0 women). 19 applicants, 47% accepted, 3 enrolled. In 2012, 2 master's awarded. *Degree requirements:* For master's, thesis. *Entrance requirements:* For master's, honors degree in mathematics, statistics or equivalent. Additional exam requirements/recommendations for international students: Required—TOEFL (minimum score 580 paper-based; 93 iBT), IELTS (minimum score 6.5). *Application deadline:* For fall admission, 2/1 priority date for domestic students, 2/1 for international students. Applications are processed on a rolling basis. Application fee: $50. *Financial support:* Fellowships, research assistantships, teaching assistantships, career-related internships or fieldwork, and unspecified assistantships available. Financial award application deadline: 2/1. *Faculty research:* Geophysical fluid dynamics, machine scheduling problems, control theory, stochastic optimization, survival analysis. *Unit head:* Dr. Jeff Hooper, Head, 902-585-1382, Fax: 902-585-1074, E-mail: jeff.hooper@acadiau.ca. *Application contact:* Dr. Franklin Mendivil, Graduate Coordinator, 902-585-1368, Fax: 902-585-1074, E-mail: franklin.mendivil@acadiau.ca. Website: http://math.acadiau.ca/.

American University, College of Arts and Sciences, Department of Mathematics and Statistics, Washington, DC 22016-8050. Offers applied statistics (Certificate); mathematics (MA); statistics (MS). Part-time and evening/weekend programs available. *Faculty:* 28 full-time (12 women), 12 part-time/adjunct (1 woman). *Students:* 14 full-time (5 women), 17 part-time (5 women); includes 8 minority (3 Black or African American, non-Hispanic/Latino; 3 Asian, non-Hispanic/Latino; 2 Hispanic/Latino), 1 international. Average age 27. 39 applicants, 72% accepted, 13 enrolled. In 2012, 3 master's awarded. *Degree requirements:* For master's, comprehensive exam, thesis or alternative, tools of research in foreign language or computer language. *Entrance requirements:* For master's, GRE; for Certificate, bachelor's degree. Additional exam requirements/recommendations for international students: Required—TOEFL. *Application deadline:* For fall admission, 2/1 for domestic students; for spring admission, 10/1 for domestic students. Application fee: $80. *Expenses: Tuition:* Full-time $25,920; part-time $1440 per credit. *Required fees:* $430. Tuition and fees vary according to course load, campus/location and program. *Financial support:* Fellowships, research assistantships, teaching assistantships, career-related internships or fieldwork, Federal Work-Study, institutionally sponsored loans, and unspecified assistantships available. Support available to part-time students. Financial award application deadline: 2/1. *Faculty research:* Logic, random processes, probability analysis, biostatistics, statistical computing. *Unit head:* Dr. Jeffrey D. Adler, Chair, 202-885-3171, Fax: 202-885-3155, E-mail: jadler@american.edu. *Application*

contact: Kathleen Clowery, Director, Graduate Admissions, 202-885-3621, Fax: 202-885-1505, E-mail: clowery@american.edu. Website: http://www.american.edu/cas/mathstat/.

American University of Beirut, Graduate Programs, Faculty of Arts and Sciences, Beirut, Lebanon. Offers anthropology (MA); Arab and Middle Eastern history (PhD); Arabic language and literature (MA, PhD); archaeology (MA); biology (MS); cell and molecular biology (PhD); chemistry (MS); clinical psychology (MA); computational science (MS); computer science (MS); economics (MA); education (MA); English language (MA); English literature (MA); environmental policy planning (MSES); financial economics (MAFE); general psychology (MA); geology (MS); history (MA); mathematics (MA, MS); media studies (MA); Middle Eastern studies (MA); philosophy (MA); physics (MS); political studies (MA); public administration (MA); sociology (MA); statistics (MA, MS); theoretical physics (PhD); transnational American studies (MA). Part-time programs available. *Faculty:* 238 full-time (80 women), 7 part-time/adjunct (3 women). *Students:* 253 full-time (169 women), 139 part-time (105 women). Average age 26. 306 applicants, 47% accepted, 90 enrolled. In 2012, 126 degrees awarded. *Degree requirements:* For master's, one foreign language, comprehensive exam, thesis (for some programs); for doctorate, one foreign language, comprehensive exam, thesis/dissertation. *Entrance requirements:* For master's, GRE, letter of recommendation; for doctorate, GRE, letters of recommendation. Additional exam requirements/recommendations for international students: Required—TOEFL (minimum score 600 paper-based; 97 iBT), IELTS (minimum score 7). *Application deadline:* For fall admission, 4/30 for domestic students, 4/18 for international students; for spring admission, 11/1 for domestic and international students. Application fee: $50. *Expenses: Tuition:* Full-time $13,896; part-time $772 per credit. *Financial support:* In 2012–13, 20 students received support. Career-related internships or fieldwork, institutionally sponsored loans, scholarships/grants, health care benefits, and unspecified assistantships available. Financial award application deadline: 2/4; financial award applicants required to submit FAFSA. *Faculty research:* Modern Middle East history; Near Eastern archaeology; Islamic history; European history; software engineering; scientific computing; data mining; the applications of cooperative learning in language teaching and teacher education; world/comparative literature; rhetoric and composition; creative writing; public management; public policy and international affairs; hydrogeology; mineralogy, petrology, and geochemistry; tectonics and structural geology; cell and molecular biology; ecology. *Unit head:* Dr. Patrick McGreevy, Dean, 961-1374374 Ext. 3800, Fax: 961-1744461, E-mail: pm07@aub.edu.lb. *Application contact:* Dr. Salim Kanaan, Director, Admissions Office, 961-1-350000 Ext. 2594, Fax: 961-1750775, E-mail: sk00@aub.edu.lb. Website: http://staff.aub.edu.lb/~webfas.

Peterson's Graduate Programs in the Physical Sciences, Mathematics, Agricultural Sciences, the Environment & Natural Resources 2014

www.petersonsbooks.com **355**

Statistics

Arizona State University, College of Liberal Arts and Sciences, Department of Mathematics and Statistics, Tempe, AZ 85287-1804. Offers applied mathematics (PhD); computational biosciences (PhD); mathematics (MA, MNS, PhD); mathematics education (PhD); statistics (PhD). Part-time programs available. Terminal master's awarded for partial completion of doctoral program. *Degree requirements:* For master's, thesis or alternative, interactive Program of Study (iPOS) submitted before completing 50 percent of required credit hours; for doctorate, comprehensive exam, thesis/dissertation, interactive Program of Study (iPOS) submitted before completing 50 percent of required credit hours. *Entrance requirements:* For master's and doctorate, GRE General Test, minimum GPA of 3.0 or equivalent in last 2 years of work leading to bachelor's degree. Additional exam requirements/recommendations for international students: Required—TOEFL (minimum score 80 iBT), TOEFL, IELTS, or Pearson Test of English. Electronic applications accepted. *Expenses:* Contact institution.

Arizona State University, Graduate College, Interdisciplinary Program in Statistics, Tempe, AZ 85287-1003. Offers MS, Graduate Certificate. Part-time and evening/weekend programs available. Postbaccalaureate distance learning degree programs offered (minimal on-campus study). *Degree requirements:* For master's, thesis and oral defense/examination or applied project with oral defense/examination; interactive Program of Study (iPOS) submitted before completing 50 percent of required credit hours. *Entrance requirements:* For master's, minimum GPA of 3.0 in the last 2 years of work leading to the bachelor's degree, 3 letters of recommendation, statement of goals; for Graduate Certificate, bachelor's degree, completion of intro to applied statistics, 1 semester of calculus. Additional exam requirements/recommendations for international students: Required—TOEFL (minimum score 550 paper-based; 80 iBT), IELTS (minimum score 6.5). Electronic applications accepted.

Auburn University, Graduate School, College of Sciences and Mathematics, Department of Mathematics and Statistics, Auburn University, AL 36849. Offers applied mathematics (MAM, MS); mathematics (MS, PhD); probability and statistics (M Prob S); statistics (MS). *Faculty:* 50 full-time (7 women), 6 part-time/adjunct (4 women). *Students:* 56 full-time (14 women), 52 part-time (14 women); includes 4 minority (3 Black or African American, non-Hispanic/Latino; 1 Hispanic/Latino), 43 international. Average age 28. 160 applicants, 59% accepted, 37 enrolled. In 2012, 17 master's, 9 doctorates awarded. *Degree requirements:* For doctorate, thesis/dissertation. *Entrance requirements:* For master's, GRE General Test, undergraduate mathematics background; for doctorate, GRE General Test, GRE Subject Test. *Application deadline:* For fall admission, 7/7 priority date for domestic students; for spring admission, 11/24 for domestic students. Applications are processed on a rolling basis. Application fee: $50 ($60 for international students). Electronic applications accepted. *Expenses:* Tuition, state resident: full-time $7866; part-time $437 per credit. Tuition, nonresident: full-time $23,598; part-time $1311 per credit. *Required fees:* $787 per semester. Tuition and fees vary according to degree level and program. *Financial support:* Fellowships and teaching assistantships available. Financial award applicants required to submit FAFSA. *Faculty research:* Pure and applied mathematics. *Unit head:* Dr. Tin Yau Tam, Chair, 334-844-6572, Fax: 334-844-6655. *Application contact:* Dr. George Flowers, Dean of the Graduate School, 334-844-2125. Website: http://www.auburn.edu/~math/.

Ball State University, Graduate School, College of Sciences and Humanities, Department of Mathematical Sciences, Program in Statistics, Muncie, IN 47306-1099. Offers MA. *Students:* 17 full-time (5 women), 5 part-time (2 women), 14 international. Average age 27. 16 applicants, 100% accepted, 4 enrolled. In 2012, 8 master's awarded. Application fee: $50. *Expenses:* Tuition, state resident: full-time $7666. Tuition, nonresident: full-time $19,114. *Required fees:* $782. *Financial support:* In 2012–13, 11 students received support, including 11 teaching assistantships with tuition reimbursements available (averaging $9,915 per year). Financial award application deadline: 3/1. *Faculty research:* Robust methods. *Unit head:* Dr. Sheryl Stump, Director, 765-285-8680, Fax: 765-285-1721, E-mail: sstump@bsu.edu. *Application contact:* Dr. Hanspeter Fischer, Director, 765-285-8640, Fax: 765-285-1721, E-mail: hfischer@bsu.edu. Website: http://cms.bsu.edu/Academics/CollegesandDepartments/Math/AcademicsAdmissions/Programs/Masters/MAorMSinStatistics.aspx.

Baruch College of the City University of New York, Zicklin School of Business, Department of Statistics and Computer Information Systems, Program in Statistics, New York, NY 10010-5585. Offers MBA, MS. Part-time and evening/weekend programs available. *Entrance requirements:* For master's, GMAT, 2 letters of recommendation, resume, 2 years of work experience. Additional exam requirements/recommendations for international students: Required—TOEFL (minimum score 590 paper-based), TWE.

Baylor University, Graduate School, College of Arts and Sciences, Department of Statistics, Waco, TX 76798. Offers MA, PhD. *Faculty:* 7 full-time (1 woman), 4 part-time/adjunct (1 woman). *Students:* 23 full-time (12 women), 2 part-time (0 women); includes 3 minority (1 Asian, non-Hispanic/Latino; 1 Hispanic/Latino; 1 Two or more races, non-Hispanic/Latino), 3 international. Average age 24. 38 applicants, 16% accepted. In 2012, 4 master's, 2 doctorates awarded. *Degree requirements:* For doctorate, thesis/dissertation. *Entrance requirements:* For master's, GRE General Test, 3 semesters of course work in calculus; for doctorate, GRE General Test. *Application deadline:* Applications are processed on a rolling basis. Application fee: $25. *Expenses: Tuition:* Full-time $24,426; part-time $1357 per semester hour. *Required fees:* $2556; $142 per semester hour. *Financial support:* In 2012–13, 1 fellowship, 5 research assistantships, 7 teaching assistantships were awarded; institutionally sponsored loans also available. *Faculty research:* Mathematical statistics, probability theory, biostatistics, linear models, time series. *Application contact:* Dr. James Stamey, Graduate Program Director, 254-710-7405, E-mail: james_stamey@baylor.edu. Website: http://www.baylor.edu/statistics/.

Bowling Green State University, Graduate College, College of Arts and Sciences, Department of Mathematics and Statistics, Bowling Green, OH 43403. Offers applied statistics (MS); mathematics (MA, MAT, PhD); statistics (PhD). Part-time programs available. *Degree requirements:* For master's, thesis or alternative; for doctorate, comprehensive exam, thesis/dissertation. *Entrance requirements:* For master's and doctorate, GRE General Test. Additional exam requirements/recommendations for international students: Required—TOEFL. Electronic applications accepted. *Faculty research:* Statistics and probability, algebra, analysis.

Brigham Young University, Graduate Studies, College of Physical and Mathematical Sciences, Department of Statistics, Provo, UT 84602-1001. Offers applied statistics (MS). *Faculty:* 15 full-time (3 women). *Students:* 19 full-time (6 women). Average age 25. 18 applicants, 50% accepted, 8 enrolled. In 2012, 12 master's awarded. *Degree requirements:* For master's, comprehensive exam, thesis (for some programs). *Entrance requirements:* For master's, GRE General Test, minimum undergraduate GPA of 3.3; course work in statistical methods, theory, multivariable calculus and linear algebra with minimum B- average. Additional exam requirements/recommendations for international students: Required—TOEFL (minimum score 580 paper-based; 85 iBT). *Application deadline:* For fall admission, 2/1 for domestic and international students. Application fee: $50. Electronic applications accepted. *Expenses: Tuition:* Full-time $5950; part-time $331 per credit hour. Tuition and fees vary according to program and student's religious affiliation. *Financial support:* In 2012–13, 16 students received support, including 5 research assistantships with full and partial tuition reimbursements available (averaging $10,000 per year), 11 teaching assistantships with full and partial tuition reimbursements available (averaging $10,000 per year); scholarships/grants and unspecified assistantships also available. Financial award application deadline: 2/1. *Faculty research:* Statistical genetics, reliability and pollution monitoring, Bayesian methods. *Total annual research expenditures:* $198,150. *Unit head:* Dr. Harold Dennis Tolley, Chair, 801-422-6668, Fax: 801-422-0635, E-mail: tolley@byu.edu. *Application contact:* Dr. Gilbert W. Fellingham, Graduate Coordinator, 801-422-2806, Fax: 801-422-0635, E-mail: gwf@stat.byu.edu. Website: http://statistics.byu.edu/.

Brock University, Faculty of Graduate Studies, Faculty of Mathematics and Science, Program in Mathematics and Statistics, St. Catharines, ON L2S 3A1, Canada. Offers M Sc. Part-time programs available. *Degree requirements:* For master's, thesis or project. *Entrance requirements:* For master's, honors degree. Additional exam requirements/recommendations for international students: Required—TOEFL (minimum score 550 paper-based; 80 iBT), IELTS (minimum score 6.5), TWE (minimum score 4). Electronic applications accepted.

California State University, East Bay, Office of Academic Programs and Graduate Studies, College of Science, Department of Statistics and Biostatistics, Statistics Program, Hayward, CA 94542-3000. Offers actuarial science (MS); applied statistics (MS); computational statistics (MS); mathematical statistics (MS). Part-time and evening/weekend programs available. *Degree requirements:* For master's, comprehensive exam. *Entrance requirements:* For master's, letters of recommendation, minimum GPA of 3.0, math through lower-division calculus. Additional exam requirements/recommendations for international students: Required—TOEFL (minimum score 550 paper-based). Electronic applications accepted.

California State University, Sacramento, Office of Graduate Studies, College of Natural Sciences and Mathematics, Department of Mathematics and Statistics, Sacramento, CA 95819-6051. Offers MA. Part-time programs available. *Degree requirements:* For master's, thesis or alternative, directed reading program preparing for written proficiency exam. *Entrance requirements:* For master's, minimum GPA of 3.0 in mathematics, 2.5 overall during previous 2 years; BA in mathematics or equivalent. Additional exam requirements/recommendations for international students: Required—TOEFL. Electronic applications accepted. *Faculty research:* Algebra, applied mathematics, methods in mathematical finance, subelliptic analysis, topology.

Carnegie Mellon University, College of Humanities and Social Sciences, Department of Statistics, Pittsburgh, PA 15213-3891. Offers machine learning and statistics (PhD); mathematical finance (PhD); statistics (MS, PhD), including applied statistics (PhD), computational statistics (PhD), theoretical statistics (PhD); statistics and public policy (PhD). Terminal master's awarded for partial completion of doctoral program. *Degree requirements:* For doctorate, comprehensive exam, thesis/dissertation. *Entrance requirements:* For master's and doctorate, GRE General Test. Additional exam requirements/recommendations for international students: Required—TOEFL. *Faculty research:* Stochastic processes, Bayesian statistics, statistical computing, decision theory, psychiatric statistics.

Case Western Reserve University, School of Graduate Studies, Department of Statistics, Cleveland, OH 44106. Offers MS, PhD. *Faculty:* 3 full-time (2 women), 6 part-time/adjunct (1 woman). *Students:* 2 full-time (0 women), 6 part-time (2 women); includes 1 minority (Asian, non-Hispanic/Latino), 1 international. In 2012, 3 master's, 1 doctorate awarded. *Degree requirements:* For master's, thesis (for some programs); for doctorate, thesis/dissertation. *Entrance requirements:* Additional exam requirements/recommendations for international students:

Required—TOEFL (minimum score 577 paper-based; 90 iBT); Recommended—IELTS (minimum score 7). *Application deadline:* For fall admission, 3/1 priority date for domestic students. Application fee: $50. Electronic applications accepted. *Financial support:* Teaching assistantships and career-related internships or fieldwork available. Support available to part-time students. Financial award application deadline: 3/1. *Faculty research:* Generalized linear models, asymptotics for restricted maximum-likelihood estimation (MLE) Bayesian inference, sample survey theory, statistical computing, nonparametric inference, projection pursuit, stochastic processes, dynamical systems and chaotic behavior. *Unit head:* Jill Korbin, Interim Chair, 216-368-6942, Fax: 216-368-0252, E-mail: jill.korbin@case.edu. *Application contact:* Sharon Dingess, Admissions, 216-368-6941, Fax: 216-368-0252, E-mail: skd@case.edu. Website: http://stat.case.edu/.

Central Connecticut State University, School of Graduate Studies, School of Arts and Sciences, Department of Mathematical Sciences, New Britain, CT 06050-4010. Offers data mining (MS, Certificate); mathematics (MA, MS, Certificate, Sixth Year Certificate), including actuarial science (MA), computer science (MA), statistics (MA). Part-time and evening/weekend programs available. *Faculty:* 13 full-time (4 women). *Students:* 18 full-time (8 women), 87 part-time (44 women); includes 18 minority (6 Black or African American, non-Hispanic/Latino; 4 Asian, non-Hispanic/Latino; 7 Hispanic/Latino; 1 Two or more races, non-Hispanic/Latino), 7 international. Average age 35. 59 applicants, 58% accepted, 24 enrolled. In 2012, 34 master's, 5 other advanced degrees awarded. *Degree requirements:* For master's, comprehensive exam, thesis or alternative; for other advanced degree, qualifying exam. *Entrance requirements:* For master's, minimum undergraduate GPA of 2.7; for other advanced degree, minimum undergraduate GPA of 3.0, essay, letters of recommendation. Additional exam requirements/recommendations for international students: Required—TOEFL (minimum score 550 paper-based; 79 iBT). *Application deadline:* For fall admission, 5/1 for domestic and international students; for spring admission, 11/1 for domestic and international students. Applications are processed on a rolling basis. Application fee: $50. Electronic applications accepted. *Expenses: Tuition,* area resident: Full-time $5337; part-time $498 per credit. Tuition, state resident: full-time $8008; part-time $510 per credit. Tuition, nonresident: full time $14,069; part-time $510 per credit. *Required fees:* $3970. One-time fee: $62 part-time. *Financial support:* In 2012–13, 4 students received support. Career-related internships or fieldwork, Federal Work-Study, scholarships/grants, and unspecified assistantships available. Support available to part-time students. Financial award application deadline: 3/1; financial award applicants required to submit FAFSA. *Faculty research:* Statistics, actuarial mathematics, computer systems and engineering, computer programming techniques, operations research. *Unit head:* Dr. Jeffrey McGowan, Chair, 860-832-2835, E-mail: mcgowan@ccsu.edu. *Application contact:* Patricia Gardner, Associate Director of Graduate Studies, 860-832-2350, Fax: 860-832-2362, E-mail: graduateadmissions@ccsu.edu. Website: http://www.math.ccsu.edu/.

Claremont Graduate University, Graduate Programs, School of Mathematical Sciences, Claremont, CA 91711-6160. Offers computational and systems biology (PhD); computational mathematics and numerical analysis (MA, MS); computational science (PhD); engineering and industrial applied mathematics (PhD); mathematics (PhD); operations research and statistics (MA, MS); physical applied mathematics (MA, MS); pure mathematics (MA, MS); scientific computing (MA, MS); systems and control theory (MA, MS). Part-time programs available. *Faculty:* 6 full-time (1 woman), 1 part-time/adjunct (0 women). *Students:* 54 full-time (16 women), 35 part-time (18 women); includes 29 minority (3 Black or African American, non-Hispanic/Latino; 10 Asian, non-Hispanic/Latino; 12 Hispanic/Latino; 4 Two or more races, non-Hispanic/Latino), 21 international. Average age 33. In 2012, 13 master's, 7 doctorates awarded. Terminal master's awarded for partial completion of doctoral program. *Entrance requirements:* For master's and doctorate, GRE General Test. Additional exam requirements/recommendations for international students: Required—TOEFL (minimum score 550 paper-based; 80 iBT). *Application deadline:* For fall admission, 2/1 priority date for domestic students. Applications are processed on a rolling basis. Application fee: $60. Electronic applications accepted. *Expenses: Tuition:* Full-time $37,640; part-time $1636 per unit. *Required fees:* $500; $250 per semester. *Financial support:* Fellowships, research assistantships, Federal Work-Study, institutionally sponsored loans, scholarships/grants, and tuition waivers (full and partial) available. Support available to part-time students. Financial award application deadline: 2/15; financial award applicants required to submit FAFSA. *Unit head:* Henry Schellhorn, Director, 909-607-4168, E-mail: henry.schellhorn@cgu.edu. *Application contact:* Charlotte Ballesteros, Program Coordinator, 909-621-8080, Fax: 909-607-8261, E-mail: charlotte.ballesteros@cgu.edu. Website: http://www.cgu.edu/pages/168.asp.

Clemson University, Graduate School, College of Business and Behavioral Science, Department of Economics, Clemson, SC 29634. Offers applied economics (PhD), including applied economics, applied economics and statistics; applied economics and statistics (MS, PhD); economics (MA, PhD). Part-time programs available. *Faculty:* 17 full-time (0 women), 5 part-time/adjunct (0 women). *Students:* 124 full-time (48 women), 15 part-time (7 women); includes 6 minority (1 Black or African American, non-Hispanic/Latino; 1 Asian, non-Hispanic/Latino; 2 Hispanic/Latino; 2 Two or more races, non-Hispanic/Latino), 73 international. Average age 26. 259 applicants, 77% accepted, 51 enrolled. In 2012, 41 master's, 13 doctorates awarded. Terminal master's awarded for partial completion of doctoral program. *Degree requirements:* For master's, thesis (for some programs); for doctorate, comprehensive exam, thesis/dissertation. *Entrance requirements:* For master's, GRE General Test or GMAT; for doctorate,

GRE General Test. Additional exam requirements/recommendations for international students: Required—TOEFL. *Application deadline:* For fall admission, 4/15 for international students; for spring admission, 9/15 for international students. Application fee: $70 ($80 for international students). Electronic applications accepted. *Expenses:* Contact institution. *Financial support:* In 2012–13, 72 students received support, including 10 fellowships with partial tuition reimbursements available (averaging $8,500 per year), 4 research assistantships with partial tuition reimbursements available (averaging $18,133 per year), 61 teaching assistantships with partial tuition reimbursements available (averaging $24,693 per year); career-related internships or fieldwork, institutionally sponsored loans, scholarships/grants, health care benefits, and unspecified assistantships also available. Support available to part-time students. Financial award applicants required to submit FAFSA. *Faculty research:* Applied price theory, industrial organization, international economics, labor economics, public economics. *Total annual research expenditures:* $153,240. *Unit head:* Dr. Raymond Sauer, Interim Chair, 864-656-3969, Fax: 864-656-4192, E-mail: sauerr@clemson.edu. *Application contact:* Dr. Curtis J. Simon, Director of Graduate Programs, 864-656-3966, Fax: 864-656-4192, E-mail: cjsmn@clemson.edu. Website: http://www.clemson.edu/econ.

Clemson University, Graduate School, College of Engineering and Science, Department of Mathematical Sciences, Clemson, SC 29634. Offers applied and pure mathematics (MS, PhD); computational mathematics (MS, PhD); operations research (MS, PhD); statistics (MS, PhD). Part-time programs available. *Faculty:* 44 full-time (13 women), 4 part-time/adjunct (2 women). *Students:* 117 full-time (43 women), 3 part-time (2 women); includes 6 minority (2 Black or African American, non-Hispanic/Latino; 1 American Indian or Alaska Native, non-Hispanic/Latino; 1 Asian, non-Hispanic/Latino; 1 Hispanic/Latino; 1 Two or more races, non-Hispanic/Latino), 50 international. Average age 26. 188 applicants, 76% accepted, 45 enrolled. In 2012, 41 master's, 11 doctorates awarded. *Degree requirements:* For master's, thesis optional, final project; for doctorate, thesis/dissertation, qualifying exams. *Entrance requirements:* For master's and doctorate, GRE General Test. Additional exam requirements/recommendations for international students: Required—TOEFL. *Application deadline:* For fall admission, 1/15 priority date for domestic students, 1/15 for international students; for spring admission, 10/1 priority date for domestic students, 9/15 for international students. Applications are processed on a rolling basis. Application fee: $70 ($80 for international students). Electronic applications accepted. *Financial support:* In 2012–13, 111 students received support, including 2 fellowships with full and partial tuition reimbursements available (averaging $10,000 per year), 8 research assistantships with partial tuition reimbursements available (averaging $17,943 per year), 104 teaching assistantships with partial tuition reimbursements available (averaging $18,793 per year); career-related internships or fieldwork, institutionally sponsored loans, scholarships/grants, health care benefits, and unspecified assistantships also available. Support available to part-time students. Financial award application deadline: 4/15. *Faculty research:* Applied and computational analysis, cryptography, discrete mathematics, optimization, statistics. *Total annual research expenditures:* $780,865. *Unit head:* Dr. Robert L. Taylor, Chair, 864-656-5240, Fax: 864-656-5230, E-mail: rtaylo2@clemson.edu. *Application contact:* Dr. K. B. Kulasekera, Graduate Coordinator, 864-656-5231, Fax: 864-656-5230, E-mail: kk@clemson.edu. Website: http://www.clemson.edu/ces/departments/math/index.html.

Colorado State University, Graduate School, College of Natural Sciences, Department of Statistics, Fort Collins, CO 80523-1877. Offers MS, PhD. Postbaccalaureate distance learning degree programs offered (no on-campus study). *Faculty:* 12 full-time (3 women), 1 part-time/adjunct (0 women). *Students:* 36 full-time (13 women), 91 part-time (30 women); includes 23 minority (3 Black or African American, non-Hispanic/Latino; 11 Asian, non-Hispanic/Latino; 8 Hispanic/Latino; 1 Two or more races, non-Hispanic/Latino), 20 international. Average age 34. 243 applicants, 33% accepted, 52 enrolled. In 2012, 13 master's, 2 doctorates awarded. Terminal master's awarded for partial completion of doctoral program. *Degree requirements:* For master's, comprehensive exam (for some programs), thesis (for some programs), project, seminar; for doctorate, comprehensive exam, thesis/dissertation, candidacy exam, preliminary exam, seminar. *Entrance requirements:* For master's and doctorate, GRE General Test, minimum GPA of 3.0, background in math and statistics. Additional exam requirements/recommendations for international students: Required—TOEFL (minimum score 550 paper-based; 80 iBT). *Application deadline:* For fall admission, 2/1 priority date for domestic students, 2/1 for international students. Application fee: $50. Electronic applications accepted. *Expenses:* Tuition, state resident: full-time $8811; part-time $490 per credit. Tuition, nonresident: full-time $21,600; part-time $1200 per credit. *Required fees:* $1819; $61 per credit. *Financial support:* In 2012–13, 34 students received support, including 2 fellowships (averaging $16,388 per year), 9 research assistantships with full tuition reimbursements available (averaging $12,647 per year), 23 teaching assistantships with full tuition reimbursements available (averaging $14,854 per year); health care benefits also available. Financial award application deadline: 1/15; financial award applicants required to submit FAFSA. *Faculty research:* Applied probability, linear models and experimental design, time-series analysis, non-parametric statistical inference, statistical consulting. *Total annual research expenditures:* $1.2 million. *Unit head:* Dr. Jean Opsomer, Professor and Chair, 970-491-3841, Fax: 970-491-7895, E-mail: jopsomer@stat.colostate.edu. *Application contact:* Kristin Stephens, Graduate Admissions Coordinator, 970-

Peterson's Graduate Programs in the Physical Sciences, Mathematics, Agricultural Sciences, the Environment & Natural Resources 2014

www.petersonsbooks.com **357**

491-6546, Fax: 970-491-7895, E-mail: stephens@stat.colostate.edu. Website: http://www.stat.colostate.edu/.

Columbia University, Graduate School of Arts and Sciences, Division of Natural Sciences, Department of Statistics, New York, NY 10027. Offers M Phil, MA, PhD, MD/PhD. Part-time programs available. *Degree requirements:* For doctorate, thesis/dissertation. *Entrance requirements:* For master's and doctorate, GRE General Test, GRE Subject Test. Additional exam requirements/recommendations for international students: Required—TOEFL.

Columbia University, Graduate School of Arts and Sciences, Program in Quantitative Methods in the Social Sciences, New York, NY 10027. Offers MA. Part-time programs available.

Cornell University, Graduate School, Graduate Fields of Engineering, Field of Operations Research and Information Engineering, Ithaca, NY 14853. Offers applied probability and statistics (PhD); manufacturing systems engineering (PhD); mathematical programming (PhD); operations research and industrial engineering (M Eng). *Faculty:* 39 full-time (6 women). *Students:* 155 full-time (43 women); includes 24 minority (2 Black or African American, non-Hispanic/Latino; 17 Asian, non-Hispanic/Latino; 4 Hispanic/Latino; 1 Two or more races, non-Hispanic/Latino), 106 international. Average age 24. 1,077 applicants, 22% accepted, 84 enrolled. In 2012, 96 master's, 6 doctorates awarded. *Degree requirements:* For doctorate, comprehensive exam, thesis/dissertation. *Entrance requirements:* For master's and doctorate, GRE General Test, 3 letters of recommendation. Additional exam requirements/recommendations for international students: Required—TOEFL (minimum score 600 paper-based; 100 iBT). *Application deadline:* For fall admission, 12/15 for domestic students. Application fee: $95. Electronic applications accepted. *Financial support:* In 2012–13, 41 students received support, including 20 fellowships with full tuition reimbursements available, 21 teaching assistantships with full tuition reimbursements available; research assistantships with full tuition reimbursements available, institutionally sponsored loans, scholarships/grants, health care benefits, tuition waivers (full and partial), and unspecified assistantships also available. Financial award applicants required to submit FAFSA. *Faculty research:* Mathematical programming and combinatorial optimization, statistics, stochastic processes, mathematical finance, simulation, manufacturing, e-commerce. *Unit head:* Director of Graduate Studies, 607-255-9128, Fax: 607-255-9129. *Application contact:* Graduate Field Assistant, 607-255-9128, Fax: 607-255-9129, E-mail: orie@cornell.edu. Website: http://www.gradschool.cornell.edu/fields.php?id-35&a-2.

Cornell University, Graduate School, Graduate Fields of Engineering, Field of Statistics, Ithaca, NY 14853-0001. Offers applied statistics (MPS); biometry (MS, PhD); decision theory (MS, PhD); economic and social statistics (MS, PhD); engineering statistics (MS, PhD); experimental design (MS, PhD); mathematical statistics (MS, PhD); probability (MS, PhD); sampling (MS, PhD); statistical computing (MS, PhD); stochastic processes (MS, PhD). *Faculty:* 29 full-time (3 women). *Students:* 70 full-time (35 women); includes 7 minority (5 Asian, non-Hispanic/Latino; 1 Hispanic/Latino; 1 Two or more races, non-Hispanic/Latino), 48 international. Average age 25. 681 applicants, 22% accepted, 50 enrolled. In 2012, 51 master's, 5 doctorates awarded. Terminal master's awarded for partial completion of doctoral program. *Degree requirements:* For master's, project (MPS), thesis (MS); for doctorate, one foreign language, thesis/dissertation. *Entrance requirements:* For master's, GRE General Test (for MS), 2 letters of recommendation (MS, MPS); for doctorate, GRE General Test, 2 letters of recommendation. Additional exam requirements/recommendations for international students: Required—TOEFL (minimum score 550 paper-based; 77 iBT). *Application deadline:* For fall admission, 1/15 for domestic students. Applications are processed on a rolling basis. Application fee: $95. Electronic applications accepted. *Financial support:* In 2012–13, 23 students received support, including 2 fellowships with full tuition reimbursements available, 5 research assistantships with full tuition reimbursements available, 16 teaching assistantships with full tuition reimbursements available; institutionally sponsored loans, scholarships/grants, tuition waivers (full and partial), and unspecified assistantships also available. Financial award applicants required to submit FAFSA. *Faculty research:* Bayesian analysis, survival analysis, nonparametric statistics, stochastic processes, mathematical statistics. *Unit head:* Director of Graduate Studies, 607-255-8066. *Application contact:* Graduate Field Assistant, 607-255-8066, E-mail: csc@cornell.edu. Website: http://www.gradschool.cornell.edu/fields.php?id-94&a-2.

Dalhousie University, Faculty of Science, Department of Mathematics and Statistics, Program in Statistics, Halifax, NS B3H 4R2, Canada. Offers M Sc, PhD. *Degree requirements:* For master's, thesis, 50 hours of consulting; for doctorate, thesis/dissertation, 50 hours of consulting. *Entrance requirements:* Additional exam requirements/recommendations for international students: Required—TOEFL, IELTS, CANTEST, CAEL, or Michigan English Language Assessment Battery. Electronic applications accepted. *Faculty research:* Data analysis, multivariate analysis, robustness, time series, statistical genetics.

Duke University, Graduate School, Department of Statistical Science, Durham, NC 27708. Offers PhD. Part-time programs available. *Faculty:* 20 full-time. *Students:* 41 full-time (14 women); includes 4 minority (1 Black or African American, non-Hispanic/Latino; 1 American Indian or Alaska Native, non-Hispanic/Latino; 2 Asian, non-Hispanic/Latino), 22 international. 196 applicants, 8% accepted, 11 enrolled. In 2012, 4 doctorates awarded. *Degree requirements:* For doctorate, thesis/dissertation. *Entrance requirements:* For doctorate, GRE General Test. Additional exam requirements/recommendations for international students: Required—TOEFL (minimum score 550 paper-based; 83 iBT), IELTS (minimum score 7). *Application deadline:* For fall admission, 12/8 priority date for domestic students, 12/8 for international students. Application fee: $80. Electronic applications accepted. *Financial support:* Fellowships, research assistantships, and teaching assistantships available. Financial award application deadline: 12/8. *Unit head:* Dr. Mike West, Director of Graduate Studies, 919-684-8029, Fax: 919-684-8594, E-mail: karen@stat.duke.edu. *Application contact:* Elizabeth Hutton, Director of Graduate Admissions, 919-681-1557, E-mail: elizabeth.hutton@duke.edu. Website: http://www.stat.duke.edu/.

East Carolina University, Graduate School, Thomas Harriot College of Arts and Sciences, Department of Mathematics, Greenville, NC 27858-4353. Offers mathematics (MA); mathematics in the community college (MA); statistics (MA, Certificate). Part-time and evening/weekend programs available. *Degree requirements:* For master's, comprehensive exam. *Entrance requirements:* For master's, GRE General Test, MAT. Additional exam requirements/recommendations for international students: Required—TOEFL. *Expenses:* Tuition, state resident: full-time $4009. Tuition, nonresident: full-time $15,840. *Required fees:* $2111.

Florida Atlantic University, Charles E. Schmidt College of Science, Department of Mathematical Sciences, Boca Raton, FL 33431-0991. Offers applied mathematics and statistics (MS); mathematical sciences (MS, MST, PhD). Part-time programs available. *Faculty:* 42 full-time (6 women), 38 part-time/adjunct (11 women). *Students:* 42 full-time (10 women), 27 part-time (10 women); includes 18 minority (7 Black or African American, non-Hispanic/Latino; 5 Asian, non-Hispanic/Latino; 5 Hispanic/Latino; 1 Two or more races, non-Hispanic/Latino), 21 international. Average age 31. 83 applicants, 48% accepted, 19 enrolled. In 2012, 23 master's, 7 doctorates awarded. Terminal master's awarded for partial completion of doctoral program. *Degree requirements:* For master's, comprehensive exam (for some programs), thesis (for some programs); for doctorate, comprehensive exam, thesis/dissertation. *Entrance requirements:* For master's and doctorate, GRE General Test, minimum GPA of 3.0. Additional exam requirements/recommendations for international students: Required—TOEFL (minimum score 500 paper-based). *Application deadline:* For fall admission, 7/1 priority date for domestic students, 2/15 for international students; for spring admission, 11/1 priority date for domestic students, 7/15 for international students. Applications are processed on a rolling basis. Application fee: $30. Electronic applications accepted. *Expenses:* Tuition, state resident: full-time $8876; part-time $369.82 per credit hour. Tuition, nonresident: full-time $24,595; part-time $1024.81 per credit hour. *Financial support:* In 2012–13, fellowships with partial tuition reimbursements (averaging $20,000 per year), teaching assistantships with partial tuition reimbursements (averaging $20,000 per year) were awarded; Federal Work-Study also available. Financial award application deadline: 4/1. *Faculty research:* Cryptography, statistics, algebra, analysis, combinatorics. *Unit head:* Dr. Lee Klingler, Chair, 561-297-0274, Fax: 561-297-2436, E-mail: klingler@fau.edu. *Application contact:* Dr. Rainer Steinwandt, Graduate Director, 561-297-3353, Fax: 561-297-2436, E-mail: rsteinwa@fau.edu. Website: http://www.math.fau.edu/.

Florida International University, College of Arts and Sciences, Department of Mathematics and Statistics, Program in Statistics, Miami, FL 33199. Offers MS. Part-time and evening/weekend programs available. *Degree requirements:* For master's, thesis optional. *Entrance requirements:* For master's, GRE General Test, minimum GPA of 3.0, 3 letters of recommendation, resume. Additional exam requirements/recommendations for international students: Required—TOEFL (minimum score 550 paper-based; 80 iBT). Electronic applications accepted.

Florida State University, The Graduate School, College of Arts and Sciences, Department of Statistics, Tallahassee, FL 32306-4330. Offers applied statistics (MS); biostatistics (MS, PhD); mathematical statistics (MS, PhD). Part-time programs available. *Faculty:* 15 full-time (2 women). *Students:* 62 full-time (26 women), 5 part-time (2 women); includes 25 minority (9 Black or African American, non-Hispanic/Latino; 9 Asian, non-Hispanic/Latino; 7 Hispanic/Latino), 17 international. Average age 29. 138 applicants, 30% accepted, 18 enrolled. In 2012, 17 master's, 9 doctorates awarded. Terminal master's awarded for partial completion of doctoral program. *Degree requirements:* For doctorate, comprehensive exam, thesis/dissertation, departmental qualifying exam. *Entrance requirements:* For master's, GRE General Test, previous course work in calculus, minimum GPA of 3.0; for doctorate, GRE General Test, minimum GPA of 3.0, 1 course in linear algebra (preferred), calculus I-III, real analysis. Additional exam requirements/recommendations for international students: Required—TOEFL (minimum score 80 iBT). *Application deadline:* For fall admission, 7/1 for domestic and international students; for spring admission, 11/1 for domestic and international students. Applications are processed on a rolling basis. Application fee: $30. Electronic applications accepted. *Expenses:* Tuition, state resident: full-time $7263; part-time $403.51 per credit hour. Tuition, nonresident: full-time $18,087; part-time $1004.85 per credit hour. *Required fees:* $1335.42; $74.19 per credit hour. $445.14 per semester. One-time fee: $40 full-time; $20 part-time. Tuition and fees vary according to program. *Financial support:* In 2012–13, 56 students received support, including 9 research assistantships with full tuition reimbursements available (averaging $22,495 per year), 48 teaching assistantships with full tuition reimbursements available (averaging $20,358 per year); Federal Work-Study, institutionally sponsored loans, scholarships/grants, health care benefits, and unspecified assistantships also available. Financial award application deadline: 2/15; financial award applicants required to submit

FAFSA. *Faculty research:* Statistical inference, probability theory, biostatistics, nonparametric estimation, automatic target recognition. *Total annual research expenditures:* $693,402. *Unit head:* Dr. Xufeng Niu, Chairman, 850-644-4008, Fax: 850-644-5271, E-mail: niu@stat.fsu.edu. *Application contact:* Alex Cohn, Academic Support Assistant, 850-644-3514, Fax: 850-644-5271, E-mail: acohn@stat.fsu.edu. Website: http://stat.fsu.edu/.

Florida State University, The Graduate School, College of Education, Department of Educational Psychology and Learning Systems, Program in Measurement and Statistics, Tallahassee, FL 32306. Offers MS, PhD, Ed S. *Faculty:* 5 full-time (3 women). *Students:* 19 full-time (11 women), 16 part-time (8 women); includes 3 minority (2 Black or African American, non-Hispanic/Latino; 1 Asian, non-Hispanic/Latino), 24 international. Average age 32. 28 applicants, 54% accepted, 3 enrolled. In 2012, 4 master's, 2 doctorates awarded. *Degree requirements:* For master's, comprehensive exam; for doctorate, comprehensive exam, thesis/dissertation, preliminary exam, prospectus. *Entrance requirements:* Additional exam requirements/recommendations for international students: Required—TOEFL (minimum score 550 paper-based; 80 iBT). *Application deadline:* For fall admission, 7/1 for domestic and international students; for winter admission, 11/1 for domestic and international students; for spring admission, 3/1 for domestic and international students. Application fee: $30. Electronic applications accepted. *Expenses:* Tuition, state resident: full-time $7263; part-time $403.51 per credit hour. Tuition, nonresident: full-time $18,087; part-time $1004.85 per credit hour. *Required fees:* $1335.42; $74.19 per credit hour. $445.14 per semester. One-time fee: $40 full-time; $20 part-time. Tuition and fees vary according to program. *Financial support:* Fellowships with full and partial tuition reimbursements, research assistantships with full and partial tuition reimbursements, teaching assistantships with full and partial tuition reimbursements, Federal Work-Study, scholarships/grants, health care benefits, and unspecified assistantships available. *Faculty research:* Methods for meta analysis; item response theory (IRT)/mixture IRT; cognitive behavioral therapy (CBT); modeling, especially of large data sets. *Unit head:* Dr. Betsy Becker, Program Leader, 850-645-2371, Fax: 850-644-8776, E-mail: bbecker@fsu.edu. *Application contact:* Peggy Lollie, Program Assistant, 850-644-8786, Fax: 850-644-8776, E-mail: plollie@fsu.edu. Website: http://www.coe.fsu.edu/Academic-Programs/Departments/Educational-Psychology-and-Learning-Systems-EPLS/Degree-Programs/Educational-Psychology.

George Mason University, Volgenau School of Engineering, Department of Statistics, Fairfax, VA 22030. Offers federal statistics (Certificate); statistical science (MS, PhD). *Faculty:* 16 full-time (3 women), 4 part-time/adjunct (0 women). *Students:* 32 full-time (14 women), 42 part-time (15 women); includes 20 minority (5 Black or African American, non-Hispanic/Latino; 12 Asian, non-Hispanic/Latino; 2 Hispanic/Latino; 1 Two or more races, non-Hispanic/Latino), 17 international. Average age 32. 68 applicants, 65% accepted, 27 enrolled. In 2012, 11 master's, 3 doctorates, 8 other advanced degrees awarded. *Degree requirements:* For master's, comprehensive exam, thesis optional, qualifying exams; for doctorate, comprehensive exam, thesis/dissertation, qualifying exams. *Entrance requirements:* For master's, GRE/GMAT, bachelor's degree from accredited institution with minimum of GPA of 3.0 in a major that includes calculus, matrix algebra, calculus-based probability and statistics; personal goal statement; 2 official copies of transcripts; 3 letters of recommendation; resume; official bank statement; proof of financial support; photocopy of passport; for doctorate, GRE, MS in math intensive discipline with minimum GPA of 3.5, personal goals statement, 2 official copies of transcripts, 3 letters of recommendation, resume, official bank statement, proof of financial support, photocopy of passport; for Certificate, bachelor's degree with 2 courses in calculus and probability or statistics, personal goals statement, 2 official copies of transcripts, 1-3 letters of recommendation (depending on program) resume, official bank statement, proof of financial support, photocopy of passport. Additional exam requirements/recommendations for international students: Required—TOEFL (minimum score 575 paper-based; 88 iBT), IELTS (minimum score 6.5), Pearson Test of English. *Application deadline:* For fall admission, 1/15 priority date for domestic students; for spring admission, 8/1 for domestic students. Applications are processed on a rolling basis. Application fee: $65 ($80 for international students). Electronic applications accepted. *Expenses:* Contact institution. *Financial support:* In 2012–13, 25 students received support, including 6 fellowships (averaging $12,521 per year), 8 research assistantships with full and partial tuition reimbursements available (averaging $17,479 per year), 16 teaching assistantships with full and partial tuition reimbursements available (averaging $12,200 per year); career-related internships or fieldwork, Federal Work-Study, scholarships/grants, unspecified assistantships, and health care benefits (for full-time research or teaching assistantship recipients) also available. Support available to part-time students. Financial award application deadline: 3/1; financial award applicants required to submit FAFSA. *Faculty research:* Computational statistics, nonparametric function estimation, scientific and statistical visualization, statistical applications to engineering, survey research. *Total annual research expenditures:* $345,602. *Unit head:* Dr. William Rosenberger, Chair, 703-993-3645, Fax: 703-993-1700, E-mail: wrosenbe@gmu.edu. *Application contact:* Elizabeth Quigley, Administrative Assistant, 703-993-9107, Fax: 703-993-1700, E-mail: equigley@gmu.edu. Website: http://statistics.gmu.edu/.

Georgetown University, Graduate School of Arts and Sciences, Department of Mathematics, Washington, DC 20057. Offers mathematics and statistics (MS).

The George Washington University, Columbian College of Arts and Sciences, Department of Statistics, Washington, DC 20052. Offers statistics (MS, PhD); survey design and data analysis (Graduate Certificate). Part-time and evening/weekend programs available. *Faculty:* 21 full-time (6 women), 15 part-time/adjunct (4 women). *Students:* 224 full-time (107 women), 49 part-time (21 women); includes 16 minority (4 Black or African American, non-Hispanic/Latino; 10 Asian, non-Hispanic/Latino; 2 Hispanic/Latino), 220 international. Average age 25. 541 applicants, 85% accepted, 146 enrolled. In 2012, 29 master's, 1 doctorate, 22 other advanced degrees awarded. Terminal master's awarded for partial completion of doctoral program. *Degree requirements:* For master's, comprehensive exam; for doctorate, thesis/dissertation, general exam. *Entrance requirements:* For master's and doctorate, GRE General Test, interview, minimum GPA of 3.0. Additional exam requirements/recommendations for international students: Required—TOEFL (minimum score 550 paper-based; 80 iBT). *Application deadline:* For fall admission, 1/15 priority date for domestic students, 1/15 for international students; for spring admission, 10/1 priority date for domestic students, 9/1 for international students. Applications are processed on a rolling basis. Application fee: $75. Electronic applications accepted. *Financial support:* In 2012–13, 13 students received support. Fellowships with tuition reimbursements available, teaching assistantships with tuition reimbursements available, Federal Work-Study, and tuition waivers available. Financial award application deadline: 1/15. *Unit head:* Dr. Reza Modarres, Chair, 202-994-6888, E-mail: reza@gwu.edu. *Application contact:* Information Contact, 202-994-6356, Fax: 202-994-6917. Website: http://www.gwu.edu/~stat/.

Georgia Institute of Technology, Graduate Studies and Research, College of Sciences, School of Mathematics, Atlanta, GA 30332-0001. Offers algorithms, combinatorics, and optimization (PhD); applied mathematics (MS); bioinformatics (PhD); mathematics (PhD); quantitative and computational finance (MS); statistics (MS Stat). Terminal master's awarded for partial completion of doctoral program. *Degree requirements:* For master's, thesis or alternative; for doctorate, one foreign language, thesis/dissertation. *Entrance requirements:* For master's, GRE General Test, minimum GPA of 3.0; for doctorate, GRE General Test, GRE Subject Test, minimum GPA of 3.0. Additional exam requirements/recommendations for international students: Required—TOEFL. Electronic applications accepted. *Faculty research:* Dynamical systems, discrete mathematics, probability and statistics, mathematical physics.

Georgia Institute of Technology, Graduate Studies and Research, Multidisciplinary Program in Statistics, Atlanta, GA 30332-0001. Offers MS Stat. Part-time programs available. *Degree requirements:* For master's, thesis optional. *Entrance requirements:* For master's, GRE General Test, minimum GPA of 3.0. Additional exam requirements/recommendations for international students: Required—TOEFL. *Faculty research:* Statistical control procedures, statistical modeling of transportation systems.

Georgia State University, College of Arts and Sciences, Department of Mathematics and Statistics, Atlanta, GA 30302-3083. Offers bioinformatics (MS, PhD); biostatistics (MS, PhD); discrete mathematics (MS); mathematics (MS, PhD); scientific computing (MS); statistics (MS). Part-time programs available. *Faculty:* 23 full-time (6 women), 1 (woman) part-time/adjunct. *Students:* 79 full-time (42 women), 34 part-time (11 women); includes 38 minority (23 Black or African American, non-Hispanic/Latino; 13 Asian, non-Hispanic/Latino; 2 Hispanic/Latino), 48 international. Average age 32. 97 applicants, 56% accepted, 21 enrolled. In 2012, 19 master's, 2 doctorates awarded. Terminal master's awarded for partial completion of doctoral program. *Degree requirements:* For master's, comprehensive exam (for some programs), thesis optional; for doctorate, comprehensive exam, thesis/dissertation. *Entrance requirements:* For master's and doctorate, GRE. Additional exam requirements/recommendations for international students: Required—TOEFL (minimum score 550 paper-based; 80 iBT). *Application deadline:* For fall admission, 7/1 priority date for domestic students, 7/1 for international students; for spring admission, 11/15 priority date for domestic students, 11/15 for international students. Application fee: $50. Electronic applications accepted. *Expenses:* Tuition, state resident: full-time $8064; part-time $336 per credit hour. Tuition, nonresident: full-time $28,800; part-time $1200 per credit hour. *Required fees:* $2128; $1064 per semester. Tuition and fees vary according to course load and program. *Financial support:* In 2012–13, 15 students received support, including 3 fellowships with full tuition reimbursements available (averaging $22,000 per year), 20 research assistantships with full tuition reimbursements available (averaging $9,000 per year), 50 teaching assistantships with full tuition reimbursements available (averaging $9,000 per year); institutionally sponsored loans, scholarships/grants, health care benefits, and unspecified assistantships also available. Financial award application deadline: 2/1. *Faculty research:* Algebra, matrix theory, graph theory and combinatorics; applied mathematics and analysis; collegiate mathematics education; statistics, biostatistics and applications; bioinformatics, dynamical systems. *Total annual research expenditures:* $491,077. *Unit head:* Dr. Guantao Chen, Chair, 404-413-6436, Fax: 404-413-6403, E-mail: gchen@gsu.edu. *Application contact:* Dr. Zhongshan Li, Graduate Director, 404-413-6437, Fax: 404-413-6403, E-mail: zli@gsu.edu. Website: http://www2.gsu.edu/~wwwmat/.

Hampton University, Graduate College, Program in Applied Mathematics, Hampton, VA 23668. Offers computational mathematics (MS); nonlinear science (MS); statistics and probability (MS). *Degree requirements:* For master's, thesis optional. *Entrance requirements:* For master's, GRE General Test.

Harvard University, Graduate School of Arts and Sciences, Department of Statistics, Cambridge, MA 02138. Offers AM, PhD. Terminal master's awarded for partial completion of doctoral program. *Degree requirements:* For master's, one

Peterson's Graduate Programs in the Physical Sciences, Mathematics, Agricultural Sciences, the Environment & Natural Resources 2014

www.petersonsbooks.com **359**

foreign language; for doctorate, one foreign language, thesis/dissertation, exam, qualifying paper. *Entrance requirements:* For master's and doctorate, GRE General Test, GRE Subject Test (recommended). Additional exam requirements/ recommendations for international students: Required—TOEFL. *Expenses: Tuition:* Full-time $37,576. *Required fees:* $930. Tuition and fees vary according to program and student level. *Faculty research:* Interactive graphic analysis of multidimensional data, data analysis, modeling and inference, statistical modeling of U.S. economic time series.

Indiana University Bloomington, University Graduate School, College of Arts and Sciences, Department of Statistics, Bloomington, IN 47405-7000. Offers applied statistics (MS); statistical science (MS, PhD). *Students:* 15 full-time (3 women), 5 part-time (3 women); includes 3 minority (all Asian, non-Hispanic/ Latino), 14 international. 44 applicants, 39% accepted, 10 enrolled. In 2012, 6 master's awarded. Application fee: $55 ($65 for international students). *Unit head:* Dr. Bennett Bertenthal, Dean, 812-855-2392, E-mail: bbertent@indiana.edu. *Application contact:* Katie Bowman, Department Secretary, 812-855-7828, E-mail: katibowm@indiana.edu. Website: http://stat.indiana.edu/.

Indiana University–Purdue University Indianapolis, School of Science, Department of Mathematical Sciences, Indianapolis, IN 46202-3216. Offers mathematics (MS, PhD), including applied mathematics, applied statistics (MS), mathematical statistics (PhD), mathematics, mathematics education (MS). *Faculty:* 30 full-time (2 women). *Students:* 25 full-time (8 women), 35 part-time (13 women); includes 11 minority (2 Black or African American, non-Hispanic/Latino; 7 Asian, non-Hispanic/Latino; 2 Hispanic/Latino), 23 international. Average age 33. 52 applicants, 67% accepted, 21 enrolled. In 2012, 22 master's awarded. Terminal master's awarded for partial completion of doctoral program. *Degree requirements:* For master's, thesis optional; for doctorate, one foreign language, thesis/dissertation. *Entrance requirements:* For doctorate, GRE General Test. Additional exam requirements/recommendations for international students: Required—TOEFL. *Application deadline:* For fall admission, 2/1 priority date for domestic students. Application fee: $55 ($65 for international students). *Financial support:* In 2012–13, 14 students received support, including 4 fellowships with tuition reimbursements available (averaging $15,375 per year), 4 teaching assistantships with tuition reimbursements available (averaging $13,088 per year); research assistantships with tuition reimbursements available and tuition waivers (full and partial) also available. Financial award application deadline: 2/1. *Faculty research:* Mathematical physics, integrable systems, partial differential equations, noncommutative geometry, biomathematics, computational neurosciences. *Unit head:* Dr. Zhongmin Shen, Chair, 317-278-1065, Fax: 317-274-3460, E-mail: zshen@math.iupui.edu. *Application contact:* Dr. Sherry Queener, Director, Graduate Studies and Associate Dean, 317-274-1577, Fax: 317-278-2380. Website: http://www.math.iupui.edu/.

Iowa State University of Science and Technology, Department of Statistics, Ames, IA 50011. Offers MS, PhD, MBA/MS. *Entrance requirements:* For master's and doctorate, GRE General Test. Additional exam requirements/ recommendations for international students: Required—TOEFL (minimum score 570 paper-based; 79 iBT), IELTS (minimum score 6.5). *Application deadline:* For fall admission, 1/15 priority date for domestic students, 1/15 for international students; for spring admission, 9/15 priority date for domestic students, 9/15 for international students. Application fee: $60 ($90 for international students). Electronic applications accepted. *Application contact:* Jessica Higgins, Secretary II, 515-294-5044, Fax: 515-294-4040, E-mail: statistics@iastate.edu. Website: http://www.stat.iastate.edu/.

James Madison University, The Graduate School, College of Science and Mathematics, Department of Mathematics and Statistics, Harrisonburg, VA 22807. Offers M Ed. Part-time programs available. *Faculty:* 2 full-time (1 woman). *Students:* 5 part-time (2 women). Average age 27. In 2012, 1 master's awarded. *Degree requirements:* For master's, comprehensive exam. *Entrance requirements:* For master's, undergraduate major in mathematics. *Application deadline:* For fall admission, 5/1 priority date for domestic students; for spring admission, 9/1 priority date for domestic students. Application fee: $55. *Financial support:* Application deadline: 3/1; applicants required to submit FAFSA. *Unit head:* Dr. David C. Carothers, Academic Unit Head, 540-568-6184, E-mail: carothdc@jmu.edu. *Application contact:* Lynette M. Bible, Director of Graduate Admissions, 540-568-6395, Fax: 540-568-7860, E-mail: biblelm@jmu.edu.

The Johns Hopkins University, G. W. C. Whiting School of Engineering, Department of Applied Mathematics and Statistics, Baltimore, MD 21218-2699. Offers computational medicine (PhD); discrete mathematics (MA, MSE, PhD); financial mathematics (MSE); operations research/optimization/decision science (MA, MSE, PhD); statistics/probability/stochastic processes (MA, MSE, PhD). Terminal master's awarded for partial completion of doctoral program. *Degree requirements:* For master's, thesis (for some programs); for doctorate, thesis/ dissertation, oral exam, introductory exam. *Entrance requirements:* For master's and doctorate, GRE General Test, GRE Subject Test. Additional exam requirements/recommendations for international students: Required—TOEFL (minimum score 600 paper-based; 100 iBT). Electronic applications accepted. *Faculty research:* Discrete mathematics, probability, statistics, optimization and operations research, scientific computation, financial mathematics.

The Johns Hopkins University, G. W. C. Whiting School of Engineering, Program in Engineering Management, Baltimore, MD 21218-2699. Offers biomaterials (MSEM); communications science (MSEM); computer science (MSEM); fluid mechanics (MSEM); materials science and engineering (MSEM); mechanical engineering (MSEM); mechanics and materials (MSEM); nanobiotechnology (MSEM); nanomaterials and nanotechnology (MSEM); probability and statistics (MSEM); smart product and device design (MSEM); systems analysis, management and environmental policy (MSEM). *Entrance requirements:* For master's, GRE, 3 letters of recommendation, resume. Additional exam requirements/recommendations for international students: Required—TOEFL (minimum score 600 paper-based; 100 iBT) or IELTS (minimum score 7). Electronic applications accepted.

Kansas State University, Graduate School, College of Arts and Sciences, Department of Statistics, Manhattan, KS 66506. Offers MS, PhD. *Faculty:* 13 full-time (7 women), 4 part-time/adjunct (0 women). *Students:* 46 full-time (27 women), 16 part-time (6 women); includes 6 minority (1 Black or African American, non-Hispanic/Latino; 5 Asian, non-Hispanic/Latino), 40 international. Average age 32. 105 applicants, 54% accepted, 19 enrolled. In 2012, 12 master's, 5 doctorates awarded. Terminal master's awarded for partial completion of doctoral program. *Degree requirements:* For master's, thesis optional; for doctorate, thesis/dissertation, qualifying and preliminary exams. *Entrance requirements:* For master's, GRE; for doctorate, GRE, previous course work in statistics and mathematics. Additional exam requirements/recommendations for international students: Required—TOEFL (minimum score 550 paper-based). *Application deadline:* For fall admission, 2/1 priority date for domestic students, 2/ 1 for international students; for spring admission, 7/1 priority date for domestic students, 8/1 for international students. Applications are processed on a rolling basis. Application fee: $50 ($75 for international students). Electronic applications accepted. *Financial support:* In 2012–13, 3 research assistantships (averaging $16,439 per year), 34 teaching assistantships with full tuition reimbursements (averaging $14,030 per year) were awarded; Federal Work-Study, institutionally sponsored loans, and scholarships/grants also available. Support available to part-time students. Financial award application deadline: 3/1; financial award applicants required to submit FAFSA. *Faculty research:* Linear and nonlinear statistical models, design analysis of experiments, nonparametric methods for reliability and survival data, resampling methods and their application, categorical data analysis. *Total annual research expenditures:* $14,514. *Unit head:* James Neill, Head, 785-532-6883, Fax: 785-532-7336, E-mail: jwneill@ksu.edu. *Application contact:* Teresa Zerbe, Coordinator, 785-532-0511, Fax: 785-532-7336, E-mail: tzerbe@ksu.edu. Website: http://www.k-state.edu/stats/.

Lehigh University, College of Arts and Sciences, Department of Mathematics, Bethlehem, PA 18015. Offers applied mathematics (MS, PhD); mathematics (MS, PhD); statistics (MS). Part-time programs available. *Faculty:* 24 full-time (1 woman), 1 part-time/adjunct (0 women). *Students:* 32 full-time (14 women), 4 part-time (3 women); includes 1 minority (Asian, non-Hispanic/Latino), 15 international. Average age 27. 161 applicants, 41% accepted, 12 enrolled. In 2012, 12 master's, 3 doctorates awarded. Terminal master's awarded for partial completion of doctoral program. *Degree requirements:* For master's, comprehensive exam, thesis optional; for doctorate, comprehensive exam, thesis/dissertation, qualifying exams, general exam, advanced topic exam. *Entrance requirements:* For master's and doctorate, GRE General Test (strongly recommended), minimum undergraduate GPA of 2.75, 3.0 for last two semesters; adequate background in math. Additional exam requirements/recommendations for international students: Required—TOEFL (minimum score 85 iBT). *Application deadline:* For fall admission, 1/1 priority date for domestic students, 1/1 for international students; for spring admission, 12/1 priority date for domestic students, 12/1 for international students. Applications are processed on a rolling basis. Application fee: $75. Electronic applications accepted. *Financial support:* In 2012–13, 35 students received support, including 2 fellowships with full tuition reimbursements available (averaging $25,000 per year), 23 teaching assistantships with full tuition reimbursements available (averaging $17,500 per year); research assistantships with full tuition reimbursements available, scholarships/grants, and tuition waivers (partial) also available. Financial award application deadline: 1/1. *Faculty research:* Probability and statistics, geometry and topology, number theory, algebra, discrete mathematics, differential equations. *Total annual research expenditures:* $278,864. *Unit head:* Dr. Wei-Min Huang, Chairman, 610-758-3730, Fax: 610-758-3767, E-mail: wh02@lehigh.edu. *Application contact:* Dr. Terry Napier, Graduate Coordinator, 610-758-3755, E-mail: mathgrad@lehigh.edu. Website: http://www.lehigh.edu/~math/grad.html.

Louisiana State University and Agricultural and Mechanical College, Graduate School, College of Agriculture, Department of Experimental Statistics, Baton Rouge, LA 70803. Offers applied statistics (M App St). Part-time programs available. *Faculty:* 8 full-time (0 women). *Students:* 22 full-time (6 women), 3 part-time (2 women); includes 1 minority (Asian, non-Hispanic/Latino), 11 international. Average age 28. 17 applicants, 59% accepted, 7 enrolled. In 2012, 10 master's awarded. *Degree requirements:* For master's, project. *Entrance requirements:* For master's, GRE General Test, minimum GPA of 3.0. Additional exam requirements/recommendations for international students: Required—TOEFL (minimum score 550 paper-based; 79 iBT) or IELTS (minimum score 6.5). *Application deadline:* For fall admission, 1/25 priority date for domestic students, 5/15 for international students; for spring admission, 10/15 priority date for domestic students, 10/15 for international students. Applications are processed on a rolling basis. Application fee: $50 ($70 for international students). Electronic applications accepted. *Financial support:* In 2012–13, 17 students received support, including 1 research assistantship with partial tuition reimbursement available (averaging $20,000 per year), 15 teaching assistantships with partial tuition reimbursements available (averaging $9,853 per year); fellowships, career-related internships or fieldwork, Federal Work-Study, institutionally sponsored loans, tuition waivers (full and partial), and unspecified assistantships also available. Financial award application deadline: 4/1; financial award applicants required to submit FAFSA. *Faculty research:* Linear models, statistical computing, ecological statistics. *Unit head:* Dr. James Geaghan, Head, 225-578-8303, Fax: 225-578-8344, E-mail: jgeaghan@lsu.edu. *Application contact:* Dr. Brian Marx, Graduate Adviser, 225-578-8366, Fax: 225-578-8344, E-mail: bmarx@lsu.edu. Website: http://www.stat.lsu.edu/.

Louisiana Tech University, Graduate School, College of Engineering and Science, Department of Mathematics and Statistics, Ruston, LA 71272. Offers MS. Part-time programs available. *Degree requirements:* For master's, thesis or alternative. *Entrance requirements:* For master's, GRE General Test, minimum GPA of 3.0 in last 60 hours. Additional exam requirements/recommendations for international students: Required—TOEFL.

Loyola University Chicago, Graduate School, Department of Mathematical Sciences and Statistics, Chicago, IL 60660. Offers applied statistics (MS); mathematics (MS), including pure and applied mathematics. Part-time programs available. *Faculty:* 19 full-time (4 women). *Students:* 31 full-time (17 women), 7 part-time (4 women); includes 5 minority (2 Black or African American, non-Hispanic/Latino; 2 Asian, non-Hispanic/Latino; 1 Hispanic/Latino), 11 international. Average age 29. 62 applicants, 74% accepted, 17 enrolled. In 2012, 24 master's awarded. *Entrance requirements:* For master's, GRE General Test. Additional exam requirements/recommendations for international students: Required—TOEFL. *Application deadline:* For fall admission, 8/1 for domestic students; for spring admission, 12/1 for domestic students. Applications are processed on a rolling basis. Application fee: $0. Electronic applications accepted. *Expenses: Tuition:* Full-time $16,290. *Required fees:* $128 per semester. Tuition and fees vary according to course load and program. *Financial support:* In 2012–13, 13 students received support, including 6 teaching assistantships with tuition reimbursements available (averaging $10,000 per year); career-related internships or fieldwork, Federal Work-Study, institutionally sponsored loans, and tuition waivers (partial) also available. Financial award application deadline: 3/15. *Faculty research:* Probability and statistics, differential equations, algebra, combinatorics. *Total annual research expenditures:* $70,000. *Unit head:* Dr. Anthony Giaquinto, Chair, 773-508-3578, Fax: 773-508-2123, E-mail: agiaqui@luc.edu. *Application contact:* Dr. W. Cary Huffman, Graduate Program Director, 773-508-3563, Fax: 773-508-2123, E-mail: whuffma@luc.edu. Website: http://math.luc.edu/.

McGill University, Faculty of Graduate and Postdoctoral Studies, Faculty of Arts, Department of Economics, Montréal, QC H3A 2T5, Canada. Offers economics (MA, PhD); social statistics (MA).

McGill University, Faculty of Graduate and Postdoctoral Studies, Faculty of Arts, Department of Sociology, Montréal, QC H3A 2T5, Canada. Offers medical sociology (MA); neo-tropical environment (MA); social statistics (MA); sociology (MA, PhD, Diploma).

McGill University, Faculty of Graduate and Postdoctoral Studies, Faculty of Science, Department of Mathematics and Statistics, Montréal, QC H3A 2T5, Canada. Offers computational science and engineering (M Sc); mathematics and statistics (M Sc, MA, PhD), including applied mathematics (M Sc, MA), pure mathematics (M Sc, MA), statistics (M Sc, MA).

McMaster University, School of Graduate Studies, Faculty of Science, Department of Mathematics and Statistics, Program in Statistics, Hamilton, ON L8S 4M2, Canada. Offers applied statistics (M Sc); medical statistics (M Sc); statistical theory (M Sc). *Degree requirements:* For master's, thesis or alternative. *Entrance requirements:* For master's, honors degree background in mathematics and statistics. Additional exam requirements/recommendations for international students: Required—TOEFL (minimum score 550 paper-based). *Faculty research:* Development of polymer production technology, quality of life in patients who use pharmaceutical agents, mathematical modeling, order statistics from progressively censored samples, nonlinear stochastic model in genetics.

McNeese State University, Doré School of Graduate Studies, College of Science, Department of Mathematics, Computer Science, and Statistics, Lake Charles, LA 70609. Offers computer science (MS); mathematics (MS); statistics (MS). Evening/weekend programs available. *Faculty:* 11 full-time (4 women). *Students:* 17 full-time (8 women), 3 part-time (1 woman); includes 1 minority (Black or African American, non-Hispanic/Latino), 3 international. In 2012, 9 master's awarded. *Degree requirements:* For master's, comprehensive exam, thesis or alternative, written exam. *Entrance requirements:* For master's, GRE. *Application deadline:* For fall admission, 5/15 priority date for domestic students, 5/15 for international students; for spring admission, 10/15 priority date for domestic students, 10/15 for international students. Applications are processed on a rolling basis. Application fee: $20 ($30 for international students). *Expenses:* Tuition, state resident: full-time $4287; part-time $587 per credit hour. *Required fees:* $1177. Tuition and fees vary according to course load. *Financial support:* Teaching assistantships available. Financial award application deadline: 5/1. *Unit head:* Dr. Karen Aucoin, Head, 337-475-5803, Fax: 337-475-5799, E-mail: aucoin@mcneese.edu. *Application contact:* Dr. Dustin M. Hebert, Director of Dore' School of Graduate Studies, 337-475-5396, Fax: 337-475-5397, E-mail: admissions@mcneese.edu.

Memorial University of Newfoundland, School of Graduate Studies, Department of Mathematics and Statistics, St. John's, NL A1C 5S7, Canada. Offers mathematics (M Sc, PhD); statistics (M Sc, MAS, PhD). Part-time programs available. *Degree requirements:* For master's, thesis, practicum and report (MAS); for doctorate, comprehensive exam, thesis/dissertation, oral defense of thesis. *Entrance requirements:* For master's, 2nd class honors degree (MAS); for doctorate, MAS or M Sc in mathematics and statistics. Electronic applications accepted. *Faculty research:* Algebra, topology, applied mathematics, mathematical statistics, applied statistics and probability.

Miami University, College of Arts and Science, Department of Statistics, Oxford, OH 45056. Offers MS. *Students:* 20 full-time (10 women), 2 part-time (1 woman); includes 3 minority (1 Black or African American, non-Hispanic/Latino; 2 Asian, non-Hispanic/Latino), 9 international. Average age 27. In 2012, 9 master's awarded. *Entrance requirements:* For master's, minimum undergraduate GPA of 2.75 overall. Additional exam requirements/recommendations for international students: Required—TOEFL (minimum score 550 paper-based). *Application deadline:* For fall admission, 2/1 for domestic and international students. Application fee: $50. Electronic applications accepted. *Expenses:* Tuition, state resident: full-time $12,444; part-time $519 per credit hour. Tuition, nonresident: full-time $27,484; part-time $1145 per credit hour. *Required fees:* $468. Part-time tuition and fees vary according to course load, campus/location and program. *Financial support:* Research assistantships, teaching assistantships, health care benefits, and unspecified assistantships available. Financial award application deadline: 2/1; financial award applicants required to submit FAFSA. *Unit head:* Dr. A. John Bailer, Professor/Chair, 513-529-3538, E-mail: baileraj@miamioh.edu. *Application contact:* Dr. David J. Groggel, Associate Professor and Director of Graduate Studies, 513-529-6087, E-mail: groggedj@miamioh.edu. Website: http://www.MiamiOH.edu/sta/.

Michigan State University, The Graduate School, College of Natural Science, Department of Statistics and Probability, East Lansing, MI 48824. Offers applied statistics (MS); statistics (MS, PhD). *Entrance requirements:* Additional exam requirements/recommendations for international students: Required—TOEFL. Electronic applications accepted.

Minnesota State University Mankato, College of Graduate Studies, College of Science, Engineering and Technology, Department of Mathematics and Statistics, Program In Statistics, Mankato, MN 56001. Offers MS. *Students:* 4 full-time (3 women), 8 part-time (3 women). *Degree requirements:* For master's, one foreign language, comprehensive exam, thesis or alternative. *Entrance requirements:* For master's, GRE General Test, minimum GPA of 3.0 during previous 2 years. Additional exam requirements/recommendations for international students: Required—TOEFL. *Application deadline:* For fall admission, 7/1 priority date for domestic students; for spring admission, 11/1 for domestic students. Applications are processed on a rolling basis. Application fee: $40. Electronic applications accepted. *Financial support:* Research assistantships with partial tuition reimbursements, teaching assistantships with partial tuition reimbursements, and unspecified assistantships available. Financial award application deadline: 3/15; financial award applicants required to submit FAFSA. *Unit head:* Dr. Han Wu, Chairperson, 507-389-1453. *Application contact:* 507-389-2321, E-mail: grad@mnsu.edu. Website: http://cset.mnsu.edu/mathstat/program/grad.html.

Mississippi State University, College of Arts and Sciences, Department of Mathematics and Statistics, Mississippi State, MS 39762. Offers mathematical sciences (PhD); mathematics (MS); statistics (MS). Part-time programs available. *Faculty:* 18 full-time (3 women). *Students:* 34 full-time (17 women), 5 part-time (3 women); includes 7 minority (4 Black or African American, non-Hispanic/Latino; 3 Asian, non-Hispanic/Latino), 18 international. Average age 29. 59 applicants, 42% accepted, 15 enrolled. In 2012, 13 master's, 3 doctorates awarded. Terminal master's awarded for partial completion of doctoral program. *Degree requirements:* For master's, thesis optional, comprehensive oral or written exam; for doctorate, one foreign language, thesis/dissertation, comprehensive oral and written exam. *Entrance requirements:* For master's, minimum GPA of 2.75 on last two years of undergraduate courses; for doctorate, GRE. Additional exam requirements/recommendations for international students: Required—TOEFL (minimum score 477 paper-based; 53 iBT); Recommended—IELTS (minimum score 4.5). *Application deadline:* For fall admission, 3/15 priority date for domestic students, 5/1 for international students; for spring admission, 11/1 for domestic students, 9/1 for international students. Applications are processed on a rolling basis. Application fee: $60. Electronic applications accepted. *Financial support:* In 2012–13, 26 teaching assistantships with full tuition reimbursements (averaging $13,309 per year) were awarded; Federal Work-Study, institutionally sponsored loans, tuition waivers (partial), and unspecified assistantships also available. Financial award application deadline: 4/1; financial award applicants required to submit FAFSA. *Faculty research:* Differential equations, algebra, numerical analysis, functional analysis, applied statistics. *Total annual research expenditures:* $1 million. *Unit head:* Dr. Mohsen Razzaghi, Interim Head, 662-325-3414, Fax: 662-325-0005, E-mail: razzaghi@math.msstate.edu. *Application contact:* Dr. Corlis Johnson, Associate Department Head/Graduate Coordinator, 662-325-3414, Fax: 662-325-0005, E-mail: office@math.msstate.edu. Website: http://www.math.msstate.edu.

Missouri University of Science and Technology, Graduate School, Department of Mathematics and Statistics, Rolla, MO 65409. Offers applied mathematics (MS); mathematics (MST, PhD), including mathematics (PhD), mathematics education (MST), statistics (PhD). Terminal master's awarded for partial completion of doctoral program. *Degree requirements:* For master's, thesis or alternative; for doctorate, one foreign language, thesis/dissertation. *Entrance requirements:* For master's and doctorate, GRE General Test, GRE Subject Test. Electronic applications accepted. *Faculty research:* Analysis, differential equations, topology, statistics.

Montana State University, College of Graduate Studies, College of Letters and Science, Department of Ecology, Bozeman, MT 59717. Offers ecological and environmental statistics (MS); ecology and environmental sciences (PhD); fish and wildlife biology (PhD); fish and wildlife management (MS). Part-time programs available. *Degree requirements:* For master's, comprehensive exam, thesis (for some programs); for doctorate, comprehensive exam, thesis/dissertation. *Entrance requirements:* For master's and doctorate, GRE, minimum GPA of 3.0, letters of recommendation, essay. Additional exam requirements/ recommendations for international students: Required—TOEFL (minimum score 550 paper-based). Electronic applications accepted. *Faculty research:* Community ecology, population ecology, land-use effects, management and conservation, environmental modeling.

Montana State University, College of Graduate Studies, College of Letters and Science, Department of Mathematical Sciences, Bozeman, MT 59717. Offers mathematics (MS, PhD), including mathematics education option (MS); statistics (MS, PhD). Part-time programs available. Postbaccalaureate distance learning degree programs offered (minimal on-campus study). *Degree requirements:* For master's, comprehensive exam, thesis (for some programs); for doctorate, comprehensive exam, thesis/dissertation. *Entrance requirements:* For master's and doctorate, GRE General Test. Additional exam requirements/ recommendations for international students: Required—TOEFL (minimum score 550 paper-based). Electronic applications accepted. *Faculty research:* Applied mathematics, dynamical systems, statistics, mathematics education, mathematical and computational biology.

Montclair State University, The Graduate School, College of Science and Mathematics, Department of Mathematical Sciences, Program in Statistics, Montclair, NJ 07043-1624. Offers MS. Part-time and evening/weekend programs available. *Degree requirements:* For master's, comprehensive exam, thesis or alternative. *Entrance requirements:* For master's, GRE General Test, 2 letters of recommendation, essay. Additional exam requirements/recommendations for international students: Required—TOEFL (minimum score 83 iBT), IELTS (minimum score 6.5). Electronic applications accepted. *Faculty research:* Biostatisics, time series.

Murray State University, College of Science, Engineering and Technology, Program in Mathematics and Statistics, Murray, KY 42071. Offers MA, MAT, MS. Part-time programs available. *Degree requirements:* For master's, comprehensive exam, thesis optional. *Entrance requirements:* For master's, GRE General Test. Additional exam requirements/recommendations for international students: Required—TOEFL. *Faculty research:* Algebraic structures, mathematical biology, topolgy.

New Mexico Institute of Mining and Technology, Graduate Studies, Department of Mathematics, Socorro, NM 87801. Offers applied and industrial mathematics (PhD); industrial mathematics (MS); mathematics (MS); operations research and statistics (MS). *Faculty:* 13 full-time (1 woman), 2 part-time/adjunct (0 women). *Students:* 14 full-time (3 women), 5 part-time (1 woman); includes 4 minority (2 American Indian or Alaska Native, non-Hispanic/Latino; 1 Hispanic/ Latino; 1 Two or more races, non-Hispanic/Latino), 5 international. Average age 31. 14 applicants, 79% accepted, 8 enrolled. In 2012, 1 master's awarded. *Degree requirements:* For master's, thesis optional; for doctorate, thesis/ dissertation. *Entrance requirements:* For master's, GRE General Test. Additional exam requirements/recommendations for international students: Required—TOEFL (minimum score 540 paper-based). *Application deadline:* For fall admission, 3/1 priority date for domestic students; for spring admission, 6/1 for domestic students. Applications are processed on a rolling basis. Application fee: $16 ($30 for international students). *Expenses:* Tuition, state resident: full-time $5043; part-time $280 per credit hour. Tuition, nonresident: full-time $16,682; part-time $927 per credit hour. *Required fees:* $648; $18 per credit hour. $108 per semester. Part-time tuition and fees vary according to course load. *Financial support:* In 2012–13, 2 research assistantships (averaging $5,505 per year), 10 teaching assistantships with full and partial tuition reimbursements (averaging $8,944 per year) were awarded; fellowships, Federal Work-Study, and institutionally sponsored loans also available. Financial award application deadline: 3/1; financial award applicants required to submit CSS PROFILE or FAFSA. *Faculty research:* Applied mathematics, differential equations, industrial mathematics, numerical analysis, stochastic processes. *Total annual research expenditures:* $116,935. *Unit head:* Dr. Anwar Hossain, Chairman, 575-835-5135, Fax: 575-835-5366, E-mail: hossain@nmt.edu. *Application contact:* Dr. Lorie Liebrock, Dean of Graduate Studies, 575-835-5513, Fax: 575-835-5476, E-mail: graduate@nmt.edu. Website: http://www.nmt.edu/~math/.

New York University, Leonard N. Stern School of Business, Department of Information, Operations and Management Sciences, New York, NY 10012-1019. Offers information systems (MBA, PhD); operations management (MBA, PhD); statistics (MBA, PhD). *Expenses: Tuition:* Full-time $34,488; part-time $1437 per credit. *Required fees:* $2332; $1437 per credit. Tuition and fees vary according to program. *Faculty research:* Knowledge management, economics of information, computer-supported groups and communities financial information systems, data mining and business intelligence.

North Carolina State University, Graduate School, College of Physical and Mathematical Sciences, Department of Statistics, Raleigh, NC 27695. Offers M Stat, MS, PhD. Part-time programs available. *Degree requirements:* For master's, comprehensive exam, thesis (for some programs), final oral exam; for doctorate, thesis/dissertation, final oral and written exams, written and oral preliminary exams. *Entrance requirements:* For master's and doctorate, GRE General Test. Additional exam requirements/recommendations for international students: Required—TOEFL. Electronic applications accepted. *Faculty research:* Biostatistics; time series; spatial, inference, environmental, industrial, genetics applications; nonlinear models; DOE.

North Dakota State University, College of Graduate and Interdisciplinary Studies, College of Science and Mathematics, Department of Statistics, Fargo, ND 58108. Offers applied statistics (MS, Certificate); statistics (PhD); MS/MS. *Faculty:* 7 full-time (4 women). *Students:* 32 full-time (16 women), 4 part-time (1 woman); includes 5 minority (3 Black or African American, non-Hispanic/Latino; 1 Asian, non-Hispanic/Latino; 1 Two or more races, non-Hispanic/Latino), 18 international. Average age 30. 37 applicants, 78% accepted, 15 enrolled. In 2012, 8 master's, 1 doctorate, 2 other advanced degrees awarded. *Degree requirements:* For master's, comprehensive exam, thesis; for doctorate, comprehensive exam, thesis/dissertation. *Entrance requirements:* For master's and doctorate, minimum GPA of 3.0. Additional exam requirements/ recommendations for international students: Required—TOEFL (minimum score 550 paper-based; 79 iBT). *Application deadline:* For fall admission, 3/15 for international students. Applications are processed on a rolling basis. Application fee: $35. Electronic applications accepted. *Financial support:* In 2012–13, 2 fellowships with full tuition reimbursements, 7 research assistantships with full tuition reimbursements, 9 teaching assistantships with full tuition reimbursements were awarded; career-related internships or fieldwork, Federal Work-Study, institutionally sponsored loans, and tuition waivers (full) also available. Financial award application deadline: 4/15. *Faculty research:* Nonparametric statistics, survival analysis, multivariate analysis, distribution theory, inference modeling, biostatistics. *Unit head:* Dr. Rhonda Magel, Chair, 701-231-7532, Fax: 701-231-8734, E-mail: ndsu.stats@ndsu.edu. *Application contact:* Dawn Halle, Academic Assistant, 701-231-7532, Fax: 702-231-8734, E-mail: ndsu.stats@ndsu.edu. Website: http://www.ndsu.edu/statistics/.

Northern Arizona University, Graduate College, College of Engineering, Forestry and Natural Sciences, Department of Mathematics and Statistics, Flagstaff, AZ 86011. Offers applied statistics (Certificate); mathematics (MAT, MS); statistics (MS). Part-time programs available. *Degree requirements:* For master's, comprehensive exam (for some programs), thesis (for some programs). *Entrance requirements:* For master's, minimum GPA of 3.0. Additional exam requirements/recommendations for international students: Required—TOEFL (minimum score 550 paper-based; 80 iBT), IELTS (minimum score 7). Electronic applications accepted. *Faculty research:* Topology, statistics, groups, ring theory, number theory.

Northern Illinois University, Graduate School, College of Liberal Arts and Sciences, Department of Mathematical Sciences, Division of Statistics, De Kalb, IL 60115-2854. Offers MS. Part-time programs available. *Faculty:* 8 full-time (1 woman), 1 part-time/adjunct (0 women). *Students:* 20 full-time (11 women), 7 part-time (5 women); includes 1 minority (Hispanic/Latino), 717 international. Average age 29. In 2012, 12 master's awarded. *Degree requirements:* For master's, comprehensive exam, thesis optional. *Entrance requirements:* For master's, GRE General Test, minimum GPA of 2.75, course work in statistics, calculus, linear algebra. Additional exam requirements/recommendations for international students: Required—TOEFL (minimum score 550 paper-based). *Application deadline:* For fall admission, 6/1 for domestic students, 5/1 for international students; for spring admission, 11/1 for domestic students, 10/1 for international students. Applications are processed on a rolling basis. Application fee: $40. Electronic applications accepted. *Financial support:* In 2012–13, 3 research assistantships with full tuition reimbursements, 18 teaching assistantships with full tuition reimbursements were awarded; fellowships with full tuition reimbursements, career-related internships or fieldwork, Federal Work-Study, scholarships/grants, tuition waivers (full), and unspecified assistantships also available. Support available to part-time students. Financial award applicants required to submit FAFSA. *Faculty research:* Reality and life testing, quality control, statistical inference from stochastic process, nonparametric statistics. *Unit head:* Dr. Rama T. Lingham, Director, 815-753-6773, Fax: 815-753-6776. *Application contact:* Dr. Sanjib Basu, Director, Graduate Studies, 815-753-6799, E-mail: basu@math.niu.edu. Website: http://www.niu.edu/stat/.

Northwestern University, The Graduate School, Judd A. and Marjorie Weinberg College of Arts and Sciences, Department of Statistics, Evanston, IL 60208. Offers MS, PhD. Admissions and degrees offered through The Graduate School. Part-time programs available. Terminal master's awarded for partial completion of doctoral program. *Degree requirements:* For master's, final exam; for doctorate, thesis/dissertation, preliminary exam, final exam. *Entrance requirements:* For master's and doctorate, GRE General Test. Additional exam requirements/ recommendations for international students: Required—TOEFL. *Faculty research:* Theoretical statistics, applied statistics, computational methods, statistical designs, complex models.

Northwestern University, McCormick School of Engineering and Applied Science, Department of Industrial Engineering and Management Sciences, MS in Analytics Program, Evanston, IL 60208. Offers MS. *Students:* 31 full-time (9 women); includes 7 minority (1 Black or African American, non-Hispanic/Latino; 4 Asian, non-Hispanic/Latino; 1 Hispanic/Latino; 1 Two or more races, non-Hispanic/Latino), 11 international. Average age 24. 208 applicants, 25% accepted, 31 enrolled. *Entrance requirements:* Additional exam requirements/ recommendations for international students: Required—TOEFL (minimum score 80 iBT), IELTS (minimum score 7). *Application deadline:* For fall admission, 2/28 for domestic and international students. Application fee: $50. *Financial support:* Institutionally sponsored loans and scholarships/grants available. Financial award application deadline: 1/15; financial award applicants required to submit FAFSA. *Unit head:* Dr. Diego Klabjan, Director, 847-491-7205, E-mail: d-klabjan@northwestern.edu. *Application contact:* Dr. Diego Klabjan, Director, 847-491-7205, E-mail: d-klabjan@northwestern.edu. Website: http://www.analytics.northwestern.edu/.

Oakland University, Graduate Study and Lifelong Learning, College of Arts and Sciences, Department of Mathematics and Statistics, Program in Statistical Methods, Rochester, MI 48309-4401. Offers Certificate. *Entrance requirements:* Additional exam requirements/recommendations for international students: Required—TOEFL (minimum score 550 paper-based). *Expenses:* Contact institution.

The Ohio State University, Graduate School, College of Arts and Sciences, Division of Natural and Mathematical Sciences, Department of Statistics, Columbus, OH 43210. Offers biostatistics (PhD); statistics (M Appl Stat, MS, PhD). *Faculty:* 22. *Students:* 90 full-time (49 women), 24 part-time (11 women); includes 4 minority (all Asian, non-Hispanic/Latino), 58 international. Average age 26. In 2012, 43 master's, 10 doctorates awarded. *Degree requirements:* For master's, thesis optional; for doctorate, thesis/dissertation. *Entrance requirements:* For master's and doctorate, GRE General Test. Additional exam requirements/recommendations for international students: Required—TOEFL (minimum score 600 paper-based; 100 iBT); Recommended—IELTS (minimum score 8). *Application deadline:* For fall admission, 12/28 priority date for domestic students, 11/30 for international students; for winter admission, 12/1 for domestic students, 11/1 for international students; for spring admission, 12/1 priority date for domestic students, 11/1 for international students. Applications are processed on a rolling basis. Application fee: $40 ($50 for international students). Electronic applications accepted. *Financial support:* Fellowships, research assistantships, teaching assistantships, Federal Work-Study, and institutionally sponsored loans available. Support available to part-time students. *Unit head:* L. Mark Berliner, Chair, 614-247-4075, Fax: 614-292-2096, E-mail: berliner.1@osu.edu. *Application contact:* Graduate Admissions, 614-292-9444, Fax: 614-292-3895, E-mail: gradadmissions@osu.edu. Website: http://www.stat.osu.edu/.

Oklahoma State University, College of Arts and Sciences, Department of Statistics, Stillwater, OK 74078. Offers MS, PhD. *Faculty:* 9 full-time (3 women), 1 (woman) part-time/adjunct. *Students:* 18 full-time (3 women), 8 part-time (4 women); includes 3 minority (2 Asian, non-Hispanic/Latino; 1 Hispanic/Latino), 13 international. Average age 30. 76 applicants, 28% accepted, 5 enrolled. In 2012, 2 master's, 2 doctorates awarded. *Degree requirements:* For master's, comprehensive exam, thesis optional; for doctorate, comprehensive exam, thesis/dissertation. *Entrance requirements:* For master's and doctorate, GRE. Additional exam requirements/recommendations for international students: Required—TOEFL (minimum score 550 paper-based), IELTS (minimum score 7). *Application deadline:* For fall admission, 3/1 for international students; for spring admission, 8/1 for international students. Applications are processed on a rolling basis. Application fee: $40 ($75 for international students). Electronic applications accepted. *Expenses:* Tuition, state resident: full time $4272; part-time $178 per credit hour. Tuition, nonresident: full-time $17,016; part-time $709 per credit hour. *Required fees:* $2188; $91.17 per credit hour. One-time fee: $50 full-time. Part-time tuition and fees vary according to course load and campus/location. *Financial support:* In 2012–13, 1 research assistantship (averaging $15,354 per year), 18 teaching assistantships (averaging $15,154 per year) were awarded; career-related internships or fieldwork, Federal Work-Study, scholarships/grants, health care benefits, tuition waivers (partial), and unspecified assistantships also available. Support available to part-time students. Financial award application deadline: 3/1; financial award applicants required to submit FAFSA. *Faculty research:* Linear models, sampling methods, ranking and selections procedures, categorical data, multiple comparisons. *Unit head:* Dr. Ibrahim Ahmad, Head, 405-744-5684, Fax: 405-744-3533. *Application contact:* Dr. Sheryl Tucker, Dean, 405-744-7099, Fax: 405-744-0355, E-mail: grad-i@okstate.edu. Website: http://statistics.okstate.edu.

Oregon State University, College of Science, Department of Statistics, Corvallis, OR 97331. Offers statistics (MA, MAIS, MS, PhD). Part-time programs available. *Faculty:* 11 full-time (6 women), 3 part-time/adjunct (2 women). *Students:* 36 full-time (13 women); includes 2 minority (1 Asian, non-Hispanic/Latino; 1 Two or more races, non-Hispanic/Latino), 12 international. Average age 28. 176 applicants, 25% accepted, 19 enrolled. In 2012, 14 master's, 3 doctorates awarded. *Degree requirements:* For master's, consulting experience; for doctorate, thesis/dissertation, consulting experience. *Entrance requirements:* For master's and doctorate, minimum GPA of 3.0 in last 90 hours. Additional exam requirements/recommendations for international students: Required—TOEFL. *Application deadline:* For fall admission, 2/15 for domestic students. Applications are processed on a rolling basis. Application fee: $50. *Expenses:* Tuition, state resident: full-time $11,367; part-time $421 per credit hour. Tuition, nonresident: full-time $18,279; part-time $677 per credit hour. *Required fees:* $1478. One-time fee: $300 full-time. Tuition and fees vary according to course load and program. *Financial support:* In 2012–13, 8 research assistantships, 19 teaching assistantships were awarded; Federal Work-Study and institutionally sponsored loans also available. Financial award application deadline: 2/15. *Faculty research:* Analysis of enumerative data, nonparametric statistics, asymptotics, experimental design, generalized regression models, linear model theory, reliability theory, survival analysis, wildlife and general survey methodology. *Unit head:* Dr. Virginia

Lesser, Professor and Chair, 541-737-3584, Fax: 541-737-3489, E-mail: lesser@science.oregonstate.edu. Website: http://oregonstate.edu/dept/statistics/.

Penn State University Park, Graduate School, Eberly College of Science, Department of Statistics, State College, University Park, PA 16802-1503. Offers MA, MAS, MS, PhD. *Unit head:* Dr. David R. Hunter, Head, 814-863-0979, E-mail: drh20@psu.edu. *Application contact:* Information Contact, 814-865-8630, E-mail: b2a@psu.edu. Website: http://stat.psu.edu/.

Portland State University, Graduate Studies, College of Liberal Arts and Sciences, Department of Mathematics and Statistics, Portland, OR 97207-0751. Offers mathematical sciences (PhD); mathematics education (PhD); statistics (MS); MA/MS. *Degree requirements:* For master's, thesis or alternative, exams; for doctorate, 2 foreign languages, thesis/dissertation, exams. *Entrance requirements:* For master's, GRE General Test, GRE Subject Test, minimum GPA of 3.0 in upper-division course work or 2.75 overall; for doctorate, GRE General Test. Additional exam requirements/recommendations for international students: Required—TOEFL (minimum score 550 paper-based). *Faculty research:* Algebra, topology, statistical distribution theory, control theory, statistical robustness.

Purdue University, Graduate School, College of Science, Department of Statistics, West Lafayette, IN 47909. Offers MS, PhD. Part-time programs available. *Faculty:* 32 full-time (7 women). *Students:* 102 full-time (37 women); includes 86 minority (3 Black or African American, non-Hispanic/Latino; 2 American Indian or Alaska Native, non-Hispanic/Latino; 76 Asian, non-Hispanic/Latino; 2 Hispanic/Latino; 1 Native Hawaiian or other Pacific Islander, non-Hispanic/Latino; 2 Two or more races, non-Hispanic/Latino). Average age 27. 535 applicants, 7% accepted, 32 enrolled. In 2012, 24 master's, 7 doctorates awarded. Terminal master's awarded for partial completion of doctoral program. *Degree requirements:* For master's, comprehensive exam; for doctorate, thesis/dissertation, qualifying exams. *Entrance requirements:* For master's and doctorate, GRE General Test. Additional exam requirements/recommendations for international students: Required—TOEFL (minimum score 7 iBT); Recommended—IELTS. *Application deadline:* For fall admission, 1/15 for domestic and international students; for spring admission, 10/15 for domestic students, 9/15 for international students. Application fee: $65. Electronic applications accepted. *Financial support:* In 2012–13, 5 students received support, including 5 fellowships with full tuition reimbursements available (averaging $20,000 per year), research assistantships with full tuition reimbursements available (averaging $20,000 per year), 3 teaching assistantships with full tuition reimbursements available (averaging $20,000 per year); career-related internships or fieldwork and unspecified assistantships also available. Support available to part-time students. Financial award application deadline: 1/15; financial award applicants required to submit FAFSA. *Faculty research:* Nonparametric models, computational finance, design of experiments, probability theory, bioinformatics. *Unit head:* Dr. Rebecca W. Doerge, Head, 765-494-3141, Fax: 765-494-0558, E-mail: doerge@purdue.edu. *Application contact:* Becca Pillion, Graduate Secretary, 765-494-5794, Fax: 765-494-0558, E-mail: rpillion@purdue.edu. Website: http://www.stat.purdue.edu/.

Queen's University at Kingston, School of Graduate Studies and Research, Faculty of Arts and Sciences, Department of Mathematics and Statistics, Kingston, ON K7L 3N6, Canada. Offers mathematics (M Sc, M Sc Eng, PhD); statistics (M Sc, M Sc Eng, PhD). Part-time programs available. *Degree requirements:* For master's, thesis; for doctorate, comprehensive exam, thesis/dissertation. *Entrance requirements:* Additional exam requirements/recommendations for international students: Required—TOEFL. *Faculty research:* Algebra, analysis, applied mathematics, statistics.

Rice University, Graduate Programs, George R. Brown School of Engineering, Department of Statistics, Houston, TX 77251-1892. Offers bioinformatics (PhD); biostatistics (PhD); computational finance (PhD); general statistics (PhD); statistics (M Stat, MA); MBA/M Stat. Part-time programs available. *Degree requirements:* For master's, comprehensive exam; for doctorate, comprehensive exam, thesis/dissertation. *Entrance requirements:* For master's and doctorate, GRE General Test, minimum GPA of 3.0. Additional exam requirements/recommendations for international students: Required—TOEFL (minimum score 630 paper-based; 90 iBT). Electronic applications accepted. *Faculty research:* Statistical genetics, non parametric function estimation, computational statistics and visualization, stochastic processes.

Rochester Institute of Technology, Graduate Enrollment Services, Kate Gleason College of Engineering, Center of Quality and Applied Statistics, Rochester, NY 14623-5603. Offers applied statistics (MS); statistical quality (AC). Part-time and evening/weekend programs available. Postbaccalaureate distance learning degree programs offered (no on-campus study). *Students:* 4 full-time (3 women), 44 part-time (15 women); includes 5 minority (1 Black or African American, non-Hispanic/Latino; 2 Asian, non-Hispanic/Latino; 2 Hispanic/Latino), 13 international. Average age 30. 70 applicants, 59% accepted, 20 enrolled. In 2012, 24 master's awarded. *Degree requirements:* For master's, oral exam. *Entrance requirements:* For master's, course work in calculus, minimum GPA of 3.0. Additional exam requirements/recommendations for international students: Required—TOEFL (minimum score 570 paper-based; 88 iBT) or IELTS (minimum score 6.5). *Application deadline:* For fall admission, 2/15 priority date for domestic students, 2/15 for international students; for winter admission, 10/15 for domestic students; for spring admission, 2/1 for domestic students. Applications are processed on a rolling basis. Application fee: $60. *Expenses:* Tuition: Full-time $35,976; part-time $999 per credit hour. *Required fees:* $240; $80 per quarter.

Peterson's Graduate Programs in the Physical Sciences, Mathematics, Agricultural Sciences, the Environment & Natural Resources 2014

www.petersonsbooks.com **363**

Financial support: Research assistantships with partial tuition reimbursements, career-related internships or fieldwork, institutionally sponsored loans, scholarships/grants, and unspecified assistantships available. Support available to part-time students. Financial award applicants required to submit FAFSA. *Faculty research:* Industrial statistics, quality control; experimental design; reliability; regression techniques; multivariate analysis; nonparametric methods. *Unit head:* Dr. Donald Baker, Director, 585-475-6990, Fax: 585-475-5959, E-mail: cqas@rit.edu. *Application contact:* Diane Ellison, Assistant Vice President, Graduate Enrollment Services, 585-475-2229, Fax: 585-475-7164, E-mail: gradinfo@rit.edu. Website: http://www.rit.edu/kgcoe/cqas/academics/msappliedstatistics.htm.

Rutgers, The State University of New Jersey, New Brunswick, Graduate School-New Brunswick, Program in Statistics, Piscataway, NJ 08854-8097. Offers applied statistics (MS); biostatistics (MS); data mining (MS); quality and productivity management (MS); statistics (MS, PhD). Part-time programs available. Terminal master's awarded for partial completion of doctoral program. *Degree requirements:* For master's, comprehensive exam, essay, exam, non-thesis essay paper; for doctorate, one foreign language, thesis/dissertation, qualifying oral and written exams. *Entrance requirements:* For master's, GRE General Test; for doctorate, GRE General Test, GRE Subject Test (recommended). Additional exam requirements/recommendations for international students: Required—TOEFL (minimum score 550 paper-based). Electronic applications accepted. *Faculty research:* Probability, decision theory, linear models, multivariate statistics, statistical computing.

Sam Houston State University, College of Sciences, Department of Mathematics and Statistics, Huntsville, TX 77341. Offers mathematics (MA, MS); statistics (MS). Part-time programs available. *Faculty:* 26 full-time (7 women). *Students:* 25 full-time (9 women), 17 part-time (10 women); includes 5 minority (1 Black or African American, non-Hispanic/Latino; 3 Asian, non-Hispanic/Latino; 1 Hispanic/Latino), 16 international. Average age 31. 40 applicants, 65% accepted, 16 enrolled. In 2012, 14 master's awarded. *Degree requirements:* For master's, comprehensive exam, thesis optional. *Entrance requirements:* For master's, GRE General Test. Additional exam requirements/recommendations for international students: Required—TOEFL (minimum score 550 paper-based; 79 iBT). *Application deadline:* For fall admission, 8/1 for domestic students, 6/25 for international students; for spring admission, 12/1 for domestic students, 11/12 for international students. Applications are processed on a rolling basis. Application fee: $45 ($75 for international students). Electronic applications accepted. *Expenses:* Tuition, state resident: full-time $2205; part-time $245 per credit hour. Tuition, nonresident: full-time $5391; part-time $599 per credit hour. *Required fees:* $67 per credit hour. $367 per semester. Tuition and fees vary according to course load and campus/location. *Financial support:* In 2012–13, 20 teaching assistantships (averaging $10,081 per year) were awarded; career-related internships or fieldwork, institutionally sponsored loans, scholarships/grants, and unspecified assistantships also available. Support available to part-time students. Financial award application deadline: 5/31; financial award applicants required to submit FAFSA. *Total annual research expenditures:* $402,573. *Unit head:* Dr. Brian Loft, Chair, 936-294-4465, Fax: 936-294-1882, E-mail: loft@shsu.edu. *Application contact:* Dr. Ken Smith, Advisor, 936-294-4869, Fax: 936-294-1882, E-mail: kws006@shsu.edu. Website: http://www.shsu.edu/~mcss_www/.

San Diego State University, Graduate and Research Affairs, College of Sciences, Department of Mathematics and Statistics, Program in Statistics, San Diego, CA 92182. Offers MS. Part-time programs available. *Degree requirements:* For master's, comprehensive exam. *Entrance requirements:* For master's, GRE General Test. Additional exam requirements/recommendations for international students: Required—TOEFL. Electronic applications accepted.

San Jose State University, Graduate Studies and Research, College of Science, Department of Mathematics, San Jose, CA 95192-0001. Offers applied mathematics (MS); mathematics (MA, MS); mathematics education (MA); statistics (MA). Part-time and evening/weekend programs available. *Degree requirements:* For master's, comprehensive exam, thesis (for some programs). *Entrance requirements:* For master's, GRE Subject Test. Electronic applications accepted. *Faculty research:* Artificial intelligence, algorithms, numerical analysis, software database, number theory.

Simon Fraser University, Office of Graduate Studies, Faculty of Science, Department of Statistics and Actuarial Science, Burnaby, BC V5A 1S6, Canada. Offers actuarial science (M Sc); statistics (M Sc, PhD). *Faculty:* 21 full-time (5 women). *Students:* 39 full-time (24 women). 159 applicants, 14% accepted, 14 enrolled. In 2012, 10 master's, 2 doctorates awarded. *Degree requirements:* For master's, participation in consulting, project; for doctorate, comprehensive exam, thesis/dissertation. *Entrance requirements:* For master's, minimum GPA of 3.0 (on scale of 4.33), or 3.33 based on last 60 credits of undergraduate courses; for doctorate, minimum GPA of 3.5 (on scale of 4.33). Additional exam requirements/recommendations for international students: Recommended—TOEFL (minimum score 580 paper-based; 93 iBT), IELTS (minimum score 7), TWE (minimum score 5). *Application deadline:* For fall admission, 2/1 for domestic and international students. Application fee: $90 ($125 for international students). Electronic applications accepted. Tuition and fees charges are reported in Canadian dollars. *Expenses: Tuition, area resident:* Full-time $5000 Canadian dollars; part-time $275 Canadian dollars per credit hour. *Required fees:* $780 Canadian dollars. *Financial support:* In 2012–13, 27 students received support, including 31 fellowships (averaging $6,250 per year), teaching assistantships (averaging $5,608 per year); research assistantships, career-related internships or fieldwork, and scholarships/grants also available. *Faculty research:* Biostatistics, experimental design, envirometrics, statistical computing, statistical theory. *Unit head:* Dr. Tim Swartz, Graduate Chair, 778-782-4579, Fax: 778-782-4368, E-mail: stat-grad-chair@sfu.ca. *Application contact:* Kelly Jay, Graduate Secretary, 778-782-3801, Fax: 778-782-4368, E-mail: stat_grad_sec@sfu.ca. Website: http://www.stat.sfu.ca/.

South Dakota State University, Graduate School, College of Engineering, Department of Mathematics and Statistics, Brookings, SD 57007. Offers computational science and statistics (PhD); mathematics (MS); statistics (MS). Part-time programs available. Terminal master's awarded for partial completion of doctoral program. *Degree requirements:* For master's, thesis (for some programs), oral exam; for doctorate, comprehensive exam, thesis/dissertation, oral and written exams. *Entrance requirements:* Additional exam requirements/recommendations for international students: Required—TOEFL (minimum score 550 paper-based; 80 iBT); Recommended—IELTS. *Faculty research:* Financial mathematics, predictive analytics, operations research, bioinformatics, biostatistics, computational science, statistics, number theory, abstract algebra.

Southern Illinois University Carbondale, Graduate School, College of Science, Department of Mathematics, Carbondale, IL 62901-4701. Offers mathematics (MA, MS, PhD); statistics (MS). PhD offered jointly with Southeast Missouri State University. Part-time programs available. *Faculty:* 32 full-time (2 women), 1 part-time/adjunct (0 women). *Students:* 35 full-time (13 women), 9 part-time (3 women); includes 3 minority (1 American Indian or Alaska Native, non-Hispanic/Latino; 1 Asian, non-Hispanic/Latino; 1 Hispanic/Latino), 28 international. Average age 26. 44 applicants, 25% accepted, 9 enrolled. In 2012, 3 master's, 5 doctorates awarded. *Degree requirements:* For master's, thesis; for doctorate, 2 foreign languages, thesis/dissertation. *Entrance requirements:* For master's, minimum GPA of 2.7; for doctorate, minimum GPA of 3.25. Additional exam requirements/recommendations for international students: Required—TOEFL. *Application deadline:* Applications are processed on a rolling basis. Application fee: $50. *Financial support:* In 2012–13, 28 students received support, including 24 teaching assistantships with full tuition reimbursements available; fellowships with full tuition reimbursements available, research assistantships with full tuition reimbursements available, Federal Work-Study, institutionally sponsored loans, and tuition waivers (full) also available. Support available to part-time students. *Faculty research:* Differential equations, combinatorics, probability, algebra, numerical analysis. *Unit head:* Dr. Michael Sullivan, Chairperson, 618-453-6517, E-mail: siu950@siu.edu. *Application contact:* Rachel Kubiak, Graduate Studies Office Specialist, 618-453-6597, Fax: 618-453-5300, E-mail: gradinfo@math.siu.edu. Website: http://www.math.siu.edu/.

Southern Illinois University Edwardsville, Graduate School, College of Arts and Sciences, Department of Mathematics and Statistics, Edwardsville, IL 62026. Offers mathematics (MS), including computational mathematics, postsecondary mathematics education, pure math, statistics and operations research. Part-time programs available. *Faculty:* 17 full-time (6 women). *Students:* 4 full-time (1 woman), 27 part-time (14 women); includes 4 minority (3 Black or African American, non-Hispanic/Latino; 1 Two or more races, non-Hispanic/Latino), 7 international. 22 applicants, 55% accepted. In 2012, 11 master's awarded. *Degree requirements:* For master's, thesis (for some programs), research paper/project. *Entrance requirements:* Additional exam requirements/recommendations for international students: Required—TOEFL (minimum score 550 paper-based; 79 iBT), IELTS (minimum score 6.5). *Application deadline:* For fall admission, 7/26 for domestic students, 6/1 for international students; for spring admission, 12/6 for domestic students, 10/1 for international students. Applications are processed on a rolling basis. Application fee: $30. Electronic applications accepted. *Expenses:* Tuition, state resident: full-time $6504; part-time $3252 per semester. Tuition, nonresident: full-time $8130; part-time $4065 per semester. *Required fees:* $705.50 per semester. Tuition and fees vary according to course level, course load, degree level, program and student level. *Financial support:* In 2012–13, research assistantships with full tuition reimbursements (averaging $9,585 per year), 13 teaching assistantships with full tuition reimbursements (averaging $9,585 per year) were awarded; fellowships with full tuition reimbursements, institutionally sponsored loans, scholarships/grants, and unspecified assistantships also available. Financial award application deadline: 3/1; financial award applicants required to submit FAFSA. *Unit head:* Dr. Krzysztof Jarosz, Chair, 618-650-2354, E-mail: kjarosz@siue.edu. *Application contact:* Dr. Myung Sin Song, Director, 618-650-2580, E-mail: msong@siue.edu. Website: http://www.siue.edu/artsandsciences/math/.

Southern Methodist University, Dedman College, Department of Statistical Science, Dallas, TX 75275-0332. Offers MS, PhD. Part-time programs available. *Degree requirements:* For master's, thesis, oral and written exams; for doctorate, thesis/dissertation, oral and written exams. *Entrance requirements:* For master's, GRE General Test, 12 hours of advanced math courses; for doctorate, GRE General Test, minimum GPA of 3.0. Additional exam requirements/recommendations for international students: Required—TOEFL. Electronic applications accepted. *Faculty research:* Regression, time series, linear models sampling, nonparametrics, biostatistics.

Stanford University, School of Humanities and Sciences, Department of Statistics, Stanford, CA 94305-9991. Offers MS, PhD. Terminal master's awarded for partial completion of doctoral program. *Degree requirements:* For doctorate, thesis/dissertation, oral exam, qualifying exams. *Entrance requirements:* For master's, GRE General Test; for doctorate, GRE General Test, GRE Subject Test. Additional exam requirements/recommendations for international students:

364 www.petersonsbooks.com

Peterson's Graduate Programs in the Physical Sciences, Mathematics, Agricultural Sciences, the Environment & Natural Resources 2014

Required—TOEFL. Electronic applications accepted. *Expenses: Tuition:* Full-time $41,250; part-time $917 per credit hour.

Stephen F. Austin State University, Graduate School, College of Sciences and Mathematics, Department of Mathematics and Statistics, Nacogdoches, TX 75962. Offers mathematics (MS); mathematics education (MS); statistics (MS). *Degree requirements:* For master's, comprehensive exam, thesis optional. *Entrance requirements:* For master's, GRE General Test, minimum GPA of 2.8 in last 60 hours, 2.5 overall. Additional exam requirements/recommendations for international students: Required—TOEFL. *Faculty research:* Kernel type estimators, fractal mappings, spline curve fitting, robust regression continua theory.

Stevens Institute of Technology, Graduate School, Charles V. Schaefer Jr. School of Engineering, Department of Mathematical Sciences, Program in Stochastic Systems, Hoboken, NJ 07030. Offers MS, Certificate.

Stony Brook University, State University of New York, Graduate School, College of Engineering and Applied Sciences, Department of Applied Mathematics and Statistics, Stony Brook, NY 11794. Offers MS, PhD. *Faculty:* 20 full-time (4 women), 2 part-time/adjunct (0 women). *Students:* 268 full-time (101 women), 27 part-time (12 women); includes 24 minority (1 Black or African American, non-Hispanic/Latino; 22 Asian, non-Hispanic/Latino; 1 Hispanic/Latino), 233 international. Average age 28. 551 applicants, 56% accepted, 74 enrolled. In 2012, 85 master's, 23 doctorates awarded. *Degree requirements:* For master's, thesis or alternative; for doctorate, one foreign language, comprehensive exam, thesis/dissertation. *Entrance requirements:* For master's and doctorate, GRE General Test. Additional exam requirements/recommendations for international students: Required—TOEFL. *Application deadline:* For fall admission, 1/15 for domestic students. Application fee: $100. *Expenses:* Tuition, state resident: full-time $9370. Tuition, nonresident: full-time $16,680. *Required fees:* $1214. *Financial support:* In 2012–13, 42 research assistantships, 52 teaching assistantships were awarded; fellowships also available. *Faculty research:* Biostatistics, combinatorial analysis, differential equations, modeling. *Total annual research expenditures:* $3.2 million. *Unit head:* Dr. Brent Lindquist, Chair, 631-632-8370, Fax: 632-8490, E-mail: lindquis@ams.stonybrook.edu. *Application contact:* Dr. David Green, Graduate Program Director, 631-632-9344, Fax: 631-632-8490, E-mail: dfgreen@ams.sunysb.edu.

Temple University, Fox School of Business, Doctoral Programs in Business, Philadelphia, PA 19122-6096. Offers accounting (PhD); entrepreneurship (PhD); finance (PhD); international business (PhD); management information systems (PhD); marketing (PhD); risk management and insurance (PhD); statistics (PhD); strategic management (PhD); tourism and sport (PhD). *Accreditation:* AACSB. *Degree requirements:* For doctorate, thesis/dissertation. *Entrance requirements:* For doctorate, GRE General Test, GMAT, minimum GPA of 3.0, master's degree. Additional exam requirements/recommendations for international students: Required—TOEFL (minimum score 600 paper-based; 100 iBT), IELTS (minimum score 7.5). Electronic applications accepted.

Temple University, Fox School of Business, Specialized Master's Programs, Philadelphia, PA 19122-6096. Offers accountancy (MS); actuarial science (MS); finance (MS); financial engineering (MS); human resource management (MS); marketing (MS); statistics (MS). *Accreditation:* AACSB. Part-time programs available. *Entrance requirements:* For master's, GRE General Test or GMAT, minimum undergraduate GPA of 3.0. Additional exam requirements/recommendations for international students: Required—TOEFL (minimum score 600 paper-based; 100 iBT), IELTS (minimum score 7.5).

Texas A&M University, College of Science, Department of Statistics, College Station, TX 77843. Offers MS, PhD. Part-time programs available. *Faculty:* 28. *Students:* 61 full-time (29 women), 101 part-time (35 women); includes 27 minority (4 Black or African American, non-Hispanic/Latino; 16 Asian, non-Hispanic/Latino; 5 Hispanic/Latino; 2 Two or more races, non-Hispanic/Latino), 46 international. Average age 33. In 2012, 36 master's, 12 doctorates awarded. Terminal master's awarded for partial completion of doctoral program. *Degree requirements:* For doctorate, thesis/dissertation. *Entrance requirements:* For master's and doctorate, GRE General Test. Additional exam requirements/recommendations for international students: Required—TOEFL. *Application deadline:* For fall admission, 3/1 priority date for domestic students; for spring admission, 8/1 for domestic students. Applications are processed on a rolling basis. Application fee: $50 ($75 for international students). *Financial support:* Fellowships, research assistantships, teaching assistantships, and career-related internships or fieldwork available. Financial award application deadline: 3/1. *Faculty research:* Time series, chemometrics, biometrics, smoothing, linear models. *Unit head:* Dr. Simon Sheather, Head, 979-845-3141, Fax: 979-845-3144, E-mail: sheather@stat.tamu.edu. *Application contact:* P. Fred Dahm, Graduate Director, 979-845-7251, Fax: 979-845-3144, E-mail: fdahm@stat.tamu.edu. Website: http://www.stat.tamu.edu/.

Texas Tech University, Graduate School, College of Arts and Sciences, Department of Mathematics and Statistics, Lubbock, TX 79409. Offers mathematics (MA, MS, PhD); statistics (MS). Part-time programs available. Postbaccalaureate distance learning degree programs offered (minimal on-campus study). *Degree requirements:* For master's, thesis or alternative; for doctorate, comprehensive exam, thesis/dissertation. *Entrance requirements:* For master's and doctorate, GRE General Test. Additional exam requirements/recommendations for international students: Required—TOEFL (minimum score 550 paper-based; 79 iBT). Electronic applications accepted. *Faculty research:*

Numerical analysis, mathematical biology, complex analysis, algebra and geometry, ordinary and partial differential equations.

Texas Tech University, Graduate School, Rawls College of Business Administration, Programs in Business Administration, Lubbock, TX 79409. Offers agricultural business (MBA); business administration (IMBA); business statistics (MBA); entrepreneurship and innovation (MBA); general business (MBA); health organization management (MBA); international business (MBA); management and leadership skills (MBA); management information systems (MBA); marketing (MBA); real estate (MBA); JD/MBA; MBA/M Arch; MBA/MA; MBA/MD; MBA/MS; MBA/Pharm D. Part-time and evening/weekend programs available. *Degree requirements:* For master's, capstone course. *Entrance requirements:* For master's, GMAT, holistic review of academic credentials. Additional exam requirements/recommendations for international students: Required—TOEFL (minimum score 550 paper-based; 79 iBT). Electronic applications accepted.

Tulane University, School of Science and Engineering, Department of Mathematics, New Orleans, LA 70118-5669. Offers applied mathematics (MS); mathematics (MS, PhD); statistics (MS). *Degree requirements:* For master's, thesis (for some programs); for doctorate, thesis/dissertation. *Entrance requirements:* For master's, GRE General Test, minimum B average in undergraduate course work; for doctorate, GRE General Test. Additional exam requirements/recommendations for international students: Required—TOEFL. Electronic applications accepted.

Université de Montréal, Faculty of Arts and Sciences, Department of Mathematics and Statistics, Montréal, QC H3C 3J7, Canada. Offers mathematical and computational finance (M Sc, DESS); mathematics (M Sc, PhD); statistics (M Sc, PhD). *Degree requirements:* For master's, thesis; for doctorate, thesis/dissertation, general exam. *Entrance requirements:* For master's and doctorate, proficiency in French. Electronic applications accepted. *Faculty research:* Pure and applied mathematics, actuarial mathematics.

Université Laval, Faculty of Sciences and Engineering, Department of Mathematics and Statistics, Program in Statistics, Québec, QC G1K 7P4, Canada. Offers M Sc. *Degree requirements:* For master's, thesis (for some programs). *Entrance requirements:* For master's, knowledge of French and English. Electronic applications accepted.

University at Albany, State University of New York, College of Arts and Sciences, Department of Mathematics and Statistics, Albany, NY 12222-0001. Offers mathematics (PhD); secondary teaching (MA); statistics (MA). *Degree requirements:* For doctorate, one foreign language, thesis/dissertation. *Entrance requirements:* For doctorate, GRE General Test. Additional exam requirements/recommendations for international students: Required—TOEFL (minimum score 550 paper-based). Electronic applications accepted.

University at Albany, State University of New York, School of Education, Department of Educational and Counseling Psychology, Albany, NY 12222-0001. Offers counseling psychology (MS, PhD, CAS); educational psychology (Ed D); educational psychology and statistics (MS); measurements and evaluation (Ed D); rehabilitation counseling (MS), including counseling psychology; school counselor (CAS); school psychology (Psy D, CAS); special education (MS); statistics and research design (Ed D). *Accreditation:* APA (one or more programs are accredited). Evening/weekend programs available. *Degree requirements:* For doctorate, thesis/dissertation. *Entrance requirements:* For doctorate, GRE General Test. Additional exam requirements/recommendations for international students: Required—TOEFL (minimum score 550 paper-based). Electronic applications accepted.

University of Alaska Fairbanks, College of Natural Sciences and Mathematics, Department of Mathematics and Statistics, Fairbanks, AK 99775-6660. Offers mathematics (MAT, PhD); statistics (MS, Graduate Certificate). Part-time programs available. *Faculty:* 13 full-time (6 women), 1 (woman) part-time/adjunct. *Students:* 12 full-time (4 women), 5 part-time (3 women); includes 1 minority (Asian, non-Hispanic/Latino), 6 international. Average age 26. 24 applicants, 42% accepted, 7 enrolled. In 2012, 1 master's, 1 doctorate awarded. Terminal master's awarded for partial completion of doctoral program. *Degree requirements:* For master's, comprehensive exam, thesis or alternative; for doctorate, comprehensive exam, thesis/dissertation, oral defense. *Entrance requirements:* Additional exam requirements/recommendations for international students: Required—TOEFL (minimum score 550 paper-based; 80 iBT). *Application deadline:* For fall admission, 6/1 for domestic students, 3/1 for international students; for spring admission, 10/15 for domestic students, 9/1 for international students. Applications are processed on a rolling basis. Application fee: $60. Electronic applications accepted. *Expenses:* Tuition, state resident: full-time $7038. Tuition, nonresident: full-time $14,382. Tuition and fees vary according to course level, course load and reciprocity agreements. *Financial support:* In 2012–13, 1 research assistantship with tuition reimbursement (averaging $5,034 per year), 10 teaching assistantships with tuition reimbursements (averaging $17,987 per year) were awarded; fellowships with tuition reimbursements, career-related internships or fieldwork, Federal Work-Study, scholarships/grants, health care benefits, and unspecified assistantships also available. Support available to part-time students. Financial award application deadline: 2/15; financial award applicants required to submit FAFSA. *Faculty research:* Kriging, arrangements of hyperplanes, bifurcation analysis of time-periodic differential-delay equations, inverse problems, phylogenic tree construction. *Total annual research expenditures:* $2,000. *Unit head:* Dr. Anthony Rickard, Department Chair, 907-474-7332, Fax: 907-474-5394, E-mail: uaf-mathandstat-dept@alaska.edu.

Peterson's Graduate Programs in the Physical Sciences, Mathematics, Agricultural Sciences, the Environment & Natural Resources 2014

www.petersonsbooks.com **365**

Application contact: Libby Eddy, Registrar and Director of Admissions, 907-474-7500, Fax: 907-474-7097, E-mail: admissions@uaf.edu. Website: http://www.uaf.edu/dms/.

University of Alberta, Faculty of Graduate Studies and Research, Department of Mathematical and Statistical Sciences, Edmonton, AB T6G 2E1, Canada. Offers applied mathematics (M Sc, PhD); biostatistics (M Sc); mathematical finance (M Sc, PhD); mathematical physics (M Sc, PhD); mathematics (M Sc, PhD); statistics (M Sc, PhD, Postgraduate Diploma). Part-time programs available. Terminal master's awarded for partial completion of doctoral program. *Degree requirements:* For master's, thesis (for some programs); for doctorate, comprehensive exam, thesis/dissertation. *Entrance requirements:* Additional exam requirements/recommendations for international students: Required—TOEFL (minimum score 580 paper-based). Electronic applications accepted. *Faculty research:* Classical and functional analysis, algebra, differential equations, geometry.

The University of Arizona, Graduate Interdisciplinary Programs, Graduate Interdisciplinary Program in Statistics, Tucson, AZ 85721. Offers MS, PhD. *Students:* 21 full-time (6 women), 3 part-time (0 women); includes 4 minority (all Asian, non-Hispanic/Latino), 8 international. Average age 33. 28 applicants, 61% accepted, 5 enrolled. *Application deadline:* For fall admission, 2/1 for domestic and international students; for spring admission, 8/1 for domestic and international students. Application fee: $75. *Unit head:* Dr. Joseph Watkins, Chair, 520-621-5245, Fax: 520-621-4101, E-mail: gidp-stat@email.arizona.edu. *Application contact:* Dr. Andrew Carnie, Faculty Director, 520-621-8368, E-mail: gidp@email.arizona.edu. Website: http://stat.bio5.org/.

University of Arkansas, Graduate School, J. William Fulbright College of Arts and Sciences, Department of Mathematical Sciences, Program in Statistics, Fayetteville, AR 72701-1201. Offers MS. *Students:* 13 full-time (3 women), 4 part-time (1 woman); includes 1 minority (Black or African American, non-Hispanic/Latino), 11 international. In 2012, 8 master's awarded. *Degree requirements:* For master's, thesis. *Application deadline:* For fall admission, 4/1 for international students; for spring admission, 10/1 for international students. Applications are processed on a rolling basis. Application fee: $40 ($50 for international students). Electronic applications accepted. *Financial support:* In 2012–13, 4 research assistantships, 65 teaching assistantships were awarded; fellowships, career-related internships or fieldwork, and Federal Work-Study also available. Support available to part-time students. Financial award application deadline: 4/1; financial award applicants required to submit FAFSA. *Unit head:* Dr. Laurie Meaux, Chair of Studies, 479-575-3352, Fax: 479-575-8630, E-mail: lmeaux@uark.edu. *Application contact:* Dr. Phil Harrington, Graduate Coordinator, 479-575-3351, Fax: 479-575-8630, E-mail: psharrin@uark.edu. Website: http://stat.uark.edu/.

The University of British Columbia, Faculty of Science, Department of Statistics, Vancouver, BC V6T 1Z2, Canada. Offers M Sc, PhD. *Degree requirements:* For master's, thesis or alternative, seminar; for doctorate, comprehensive exam, thesis/dissertation. *Entrance requirements:* Additional exam requirements/recommendations for international students: Required—TOEFL (minimum score 600 paper-based; 100 iBT), IELTS (minimum score 7.5). Electronic applications accepted. *Faculty research:* Theoretical, applied, biostatistical, and computational statistics.

University of Calgary, Faculty of Graduate Studies, Faculty of Science, Department of Mathematics and Statistics, Calgary, AB T2N 1N4, Canada. Offers M Sc, PhD. *Degree requirements:* For master's, comprehensive exam, thesis; for doctorate, thesis/dissertation, candidacy exam, preliminary exams. *Entrance requirements:* For master's, honors degree in applied math, pure math, or statistics; for doctorate, MA or M Sc. Additional exam requirements/recommendations for international students: Required—TOEFL (minimum score 600 paper-based) or IELTS (minimum score 7). *Faculty research:* Combinatorics, applied mathematics, statistics, probability, analysis.

University of California, Berkeley, Graduate Division, College of Letters and Science, Department of Statistics, Berkeley, CA 94720-1500. Offers MA, PhD. *Degree requirements:* For doctorate, thesis/dissertation, qualifying exam, written preliminary exam. *Entrance requirements:* For master's and doctorate, GRE General Test, minimum GPA of 3.0, 3 letters of recommendation.

University of California, Davis, Graduate Studies, Program in Statistics, Davis, CA 95616. Offers MS, PhD. Terminal master's awarded for partial completion of doctoral program. *Degree requirements:* For master's, comprehensive exam; for doctorate, thesis/dissertation. *Entrance requirements:* For master's and doctorate, GRE General Test, minimum GPA of 3.0. Additional exam requirements/recommendations for international students: Required—TOEFL (minimum score 550 paper-based). Electronic applications accepted. *Faculty research:* Nonparametric analysis, time series analysis, biostatistics, curve estimation, reliability.

University of California, Irvine, Donald Bren School of Information and Computer Sciences, Department of Statistics, Irvine, CA 92697. Offers MS, PhD. *Students:* 35 full-time (13 women), 3 part-time (all women); includes 5 minority (4 Asian, non-Hispanic/Latino; 1 Hispanic/Latino), 19 international. Average age 27. 199 applicants, 20% accepted, 13 enrolled. In 2012, 12 master's, 1 doctorate awarded. Application fee: $80 ($100 for international students). *Unit head:* Jessica M. Utts, Chair, 949-824-0649, Fax: 949-824-9863, E-mail: jutts@uci.edu. *Application contact:* Kris Bolcer, Assistant Director, Graduate Affairs, 949-824-5156, Fax: 949-824-4163, E-mail: kbolcer@uci.edu. Website: http://www.stat.uci.edu/.

University of California, Los Angeles, Graduate Division, College of Letters and Science, Department of Statistics, Los Angeles, CA 90095. Offers MS, PhD. *Faculty:* 11 full-time (0 women). *Students:* 79 full-time (32 women); includes 20 minority (15 Asian, non-Hispanic/Latino; 3 Hispanic/Latino; 2 Two or more races, non-Hispanic/Latino), 28 international. Average age 28. 444 applicants, 10% accepted, 18 enrolled. In 2012, 23 master's, 11 doctorates awarded. Terminal master's awarded for partial completion of doctoral program. *Degree requirements:* For master's, comprehensive exam, thesis; for doctorate, thesis/dissertation, oral and written qualifying exams; 1 quarter of teaching experience. *Entrance requirements:* For master's, GRE General Test, bachelor's degree; minimum undergraduate GPA of 3.0, 3.2 in upper-division courses (or its equivalent if letter grade system not used); for doctorate, GRE General Test, bachelor's degree; minimum GPA of 3.5 (or its equivalent if letter grade system not used). Additional exam requirements/recommendations for international students: Required—TOEFL. Application fee: $80 ($100 for international students). Electronic applications accepted. *Expenses:* Tuition, nonresident: full-time $15,102. *Required fees:* $14,809.19. Full-time tuition and fees vary according to program. *Financial support:* In 2012–13, 75 students received support, including 28 fellowships with full and partial tuition reimbursements available, 29 research assistantships with full and partial tuition reimbursements available, 50 teaching assistantships with full and partial tuition reimbursements available; Federal Work-Study, scholarships/grants, health care benefits, tuition waivers (full and partial), and unspecified assistantships also available. Financial award application deadline: 3/2; financial award applicants required to submit FAFSA. *Unit head:* Dr. Rick Schoenberg, Chair, 310-794-5193, E-mail: frederic@stat.ucla.edu. *Application contact:* Student Affairs Officer, 310-206-3742, Fax: 310-206-5658, E-mail: sao@stat.ucla.edu. Website: http://www.stat.ucla.edu.

University of California, Riverside, Graduate Division, Department of Statistics, Riverside, AB 92521-0219. Offers applied statistics (PhD); statistics (MS). *Faculty:* 45 full-time (28 women), 1 (woman) part-time/adjunct. *Students:* 45 full-time (28 women), 1 (woman) part-time; includes 37 minority (29 Asian, non-Hispanic/Latino; 2 Hispanic/Latino; 2 Native Hawaiian or other Pacific Islander, non-Hispanic/Latino; 4 Two or more races, non-Hispanic/Latino), 2 international. Average age 26. 206 applicants, 25% accepted, 16 enrolled. In 2012, 4 master's, 12 doctorates awarded. Terminal master's awarded for partial completion of doctoral program. *Degree requirements:* For master's, comprehensive exam; for doctorate, comprehensive exam, thesis/dissertation. *Entrance requirements:* For master's, GRE (minimum score 300), strong background in statistics and sufficient training in mathematics or upper-division statistical courses to meet deficiencies; minimum GPA of 3.0; for doctorate, GRE (minimum score 300), BS in statistics, computer science, mathematics, or other quantitatively-based discipline; minimum GPA of 3.25. Additional exam requirements/recommendations for international students: Required—TOEFL (minimum score 550 paper-based; 80 iBT). *Application deadline:* For fall admission, 12/1 priority date for domestic students, 12/1 for international students; for winter admission, 11/15 for domestic students, 7/1 for international students; for spring admission, 3/1 for domestic students, 10/1 for international students. Application fee: $80 ($100 for international students). Electronic applications accepted. *Expenses:* Tuition, state resident: full-time $14,646. Tuition, nonresident: full-time $29,748. *Financial support:* In 2012–13, 7 students received support, including 7 fellowships (averaging $20,951 per year), 7 teaching assistantships (averaging $17,309 per year); research assistantships and tuition waivers also available. Financial award application deadline: 12/1; financial award applicants required to submit FAFSA. *Faculty research:* Design and analysis of gene expression experiments using DNA microarrays, statistical design and analysis of experiments, linear models, probability models and statistical inference, SNP/SFP discovery using DNA microarray, genetic mapping. *Unit head:* Dr. Daniel Jeske, Chair, 951-827-3014, E-mail: daniel.jeske@ucr.edu. *Application contact:* Perla Fabelo, Graduate Student Affairs Assistant, 951-827-4716, Fax: 951-827-5517, E-mail: fabelo@ucr.edu. Website: http://www.statistics.ucr.edu/.

University of California, San Diego, Office of Graduate Studies, Department of Mathematics, La Jolla, CA 92093. Offers applied mathematics (MA); mathematics (MA, PhD); statistics (MS). *Degree requirements:* For doctorate, thesis/dissertation. *Entrance requirements:* For master's and doctorate, GRE General Test, GRE Subject Test. Electronic applications accepted.

University of California, Santa Barbara, Graduate Division, College of Letters and Sciences, Division of Mathematics, Life, and Physical Sciences, Department of Statistics and Applied Probability, Santa Barbara, CA 93106-3110. Offers financial mathematics and statistics (PhD); quantitative methods in the social sciences (PhD); statistics (MA), including applied statistics, mathematical statistics; statistics and applied probability (PhD); MA/PhD. *Faculty:* 11 full-time (3 women). *Students:* 57 full-time (28 women); includes 47 minority (42 Asian, non-Hispanic/Latino; 3 Hispanic/Latino; 1 Native Hawaiian or other Pacific Islander, non-Hispanic/Latino; 1 Two or more races, non-Hispanic/Latino), 43 international. Average age 27. 298 applicants, 17% accepted, 16 enrolled. In 2012, 12 master's, 2 doctorates awarded. Terminal master's awarded for partial completion of doctoral program. *Degree requirements:* For master's, comprehensive exam, thesis optional; for doctorate, comprehensive exam, thesis/dissertation. *Entrance requirements:* For master's and doctorate, GRE General Test. Additional exam requirements/recommendations for international students: Required—TOEFL (minimum score 550 paper-based; 80 iBT), IELTS (minimum score 7). *Application*

366 www.petersonsbooks.com

Peterson's Graduate Programs in the Physical Sciences, Mathematics, Agricultural Sciences, the Environment & Natural Resources 2014

deadline: For fall admission, 1/1 priority date for domestic students, 1/1 for international students; for winter admission, 11/1 priority date for domestic students, 11/1 for international students; for spring admission, 2/1 priority date for domestic students, 2/1 for international students. Application fee: $80 ($100 for international students). Electronic applications accepted. *Financial support:* In 2012–13, 23 students received support, including 6 fellowships with full tuition reimbursements available (averaging $11,285 per year), 1 research assistantship with full and partial tuition reimbursement available (averaging $2,790 per year), 28 teaching assistantships with partial tuition reimbursements available (averaging $14,557 per year); Federal Work-Study, scholarships/grants, and health care benefits also available. Financial award application deadline: 1/1; financial award applicants required to submit FAFSA. *Faculty research:* Bayesian inference, financial mathematics, stochastic processes, environmental statistics, biostatistical modeling. *Total annual research expenditures:* $139,480. *Unit head:* Dr. John Hsu, Chair, 805-893-4055, E-mail: hsu@pstat.ucsb.edu. *Application contact:* Dolly J. Cook, Graduate Program Assistant, 805-893-2129, Fax: 805-893-2334, E-mail: gradinfo@pstat.ucsb.edu. Website: http://www.pstat.ucsb.edu/.

University of California, Santa Cruz, Division of Graduate Studies, Jack Baskin School of Engineering, Program in Statistics and Applied Mathematics, Santa Cruz, CA 95064. Offers MS, PhD. Terminal master's awarded for partial completion of doctoral program. *Degree requirements:* For master's, seminar, qualifying exam, capstone project; for doctorate, thesis/dissertation, seminar, qualifying exam. *Entrance requirements:* For master's and doctorate, GRE General Test; GRE Subject Test in math (recommended). Additional exam requirements/recommendations for international students: Required—TOEFL (minimum score 570 paper-based; 89 iBT); Recommended—IELTS (minimum score 8). Electronic applications accepted. *Faculty research:* Bayesian nonparametric methods; computationally intensive Bayesian inference, prediction, and decision-making; envirometrics; fluid mechanics; mathematical biology.

University of Central Florida, College of Sciences, Department of Statistics and Actuarial Science, Orlando, FL 32816. Offers SAS data mining (Certificate); statistical computing (MS). Part-time and evening/weekend programs available. *Faculty:* 10 full-time (2 women), 2 part-time/adjunct (0 women). *Students:* 44 full-time (18 women), 23 part-time (11 women); includes 14 minority (5 Black or African American, non-Hispanic/Latino; 7 Asian, non-Hispanic/Latino; 2 Hispanic/Latino), 18 international. Average age 30. 70 applicants, 74% accepted, 33 enrolled. In 2012, 16 master's, 3 other advanced degrees awarded. *Degree requirements:* For master's, comprehensive exam. *Entrance requirements:* For master's, GRE General Test, minimum GPA of 3.0 in last 60 hours. Additional exam requirements/recommendations for international students: Required—TOEFL. *Application deadline:* For fall admission, 7/15 for domestic students; for spring admission, 12/1 for domestic students. Application fee: $30. Electronic applications accepted. *Financial support:* In 2012–13, 23 students received support, including 5 fellowships with partial tuition reimbursements available (averaging $3,800 per year), 2 research assistantships with partial tuition reimbursements available (averaging $6,300 per year), 18 teaching assistantships with partial tuition reimbursements available (averaging $12,300 per year); career-related internships or fieldwork, Federal Work-Study, institutionally sponsored loans, tuition waivers (partial), and unspecified assistantships also available. Financial award application deadline: 3/1; financial award applicants required to submit FAFSA. *Faculty research:* Multivariate analysis, quality control, shrinkage estimation. *Unit head:* Dr. David Nickerson, Chair, 407-823-2289, Fax: 407-823-5419, E-mail: david.nickerson@ucf.edu. *Application contact:* Barbara Rodriguez, Director, Admissions and Registration, 407-823-2766, Fax: 407-823-6442, E-mail: gradadmissions@ucf.edu. Website: http://statistics.cos.ucf.edu/.

University of Central Oklahoma, The Jackson College of Graduate Studies, College of Mathematics and Science, Department of Mathematics and Statistics, Edmond, OK 73034-5209. Offers applied mathematical sciences (MS), including computer science, mathematics, mathematics/computer science teaching, statistics. Part-time programs available. *Faculty:* 5 full-time (1 woman), 5 part-time/adjunct (1 woman). *Students:* 24 full-time (10 women), 11 part-time (4 women); includes 6 minority (2 Black or African American, non-Hispanic/Latino; 1 American Indian or Alaska Native, non-Hispanic/Latino; 1 Asian, non-Hispanic/Latino; 2 Two or more races, non-Hispanic/Latino), 15 international. Average age 29. 55 applicants, 58% accepted, 14 enrolled. In 2012, 5 master's awarded. *Degree requirements:* For master's, comprehensive exam (for some programs), thesis (for some programs). *Entrance requirements:* For master's, GRE. Additional exam requirements/recommendations for international students: Required—TOEFL (minimum score 550 paper-based; 79 iBT), IELTS (minimum score 6.5). *Application deadline:* For fall admission, 7/1 for international students; for spring admission, 11/1 for international students. Applications are processed on a rolling basis. Application fee: $50. Electronic applications accepted. *Expenses:* Tuition, state resident: full-time $3718; part-time $195.65 per credit hour. Tuition, nonresident: full-time $9309; part-time $489.95 per credit hour. *Required fees:* $399.95; $21.50 per credit hour. One-time fee: $50. Tuition and fees vary according to program. *Financial support:* In 2012–13, 13 students received support, including research assistantships with partial tuition reimbursements available (averaging $5,083 per year), teaching assistantships with partial tuition reimbursements available (averaging $7,447 per year); Federal Work-Study, scholarships/grants, tuition waivers (partial), and unspecified assistantships also available. Financial award application deadline: 3/31; financial award applicants required to submit FAFSA. *Unit head:* Dr. Jesse Byrne, Chair, 405-974-5294, Fax: 405-974-3824, E-mail: jbyrne@uco.edu. *Application contact:* Dr. Richard Bernard, Dean, Jackson College of Graduate Studies, 405-974-3493, Fax: 405-974-3852, E-mail: gradcoll@uco.edu. Website: http://www.math.uco.edu/.

University of Chicago, Booth School of Business, Full-Time MBA Program, Chicago, IL 60637. Offers accounting (MBA); analytic finance (MBA); analytic management (MBA); econometrics and statistics (MBA); economics (MBA); entrepreneurship (MBA); finance (MBA); general management (MBA); health administration and policy (Certificate); human resource management (MBA); international business (MBA); managerial and organizational behavior (MBA); marketing management (MBA); operations management (MBA); strategic management (MBA); MBA/AM; MBA/JD; MBA/MA; MBA/MD; MBA/MPP. *Accreditation:* AACSB. Part-time and evening/weekend programs available. Terminal master's awarded for partial completion of doctoral program. *Entrance requirements:* For master's, GMAT, 2 letters of recommendation, 3 essays, resume, interview. Additional exam requirements/recommendations for international students: Required—TOEFL (minimum score 600 paper-based; 104 iBT), IELTS. Electronic applications accepted. *Expenses:* Contact institution. *Faculty research:* Finance, marketing, economics, entrepreneurship, strategy, management.

University of Chicago, Division of the Physical Sciences, Department of Statistics, Chicago, IL 60637. Offers SM, PhD. Part-time programs available. Terminal master's awarded for partial completion of doctoral program. *Degree requirements:* For master's, thesis; for doctorate, thesis/dissertation. *Entrance requirements:* For master's and doctorate, GRE General Test. Additional exam requirements/recommendations for international students: Required—TOEFL. Electronic applications accepted. *Faculty research:* Genetics, econometrics, generalized linear models, history of statistics, probability theory.

University of Cincinnati, Graduate School, McMicken College of Arts and Sciences, Department of Mathematical Sciences, Cincinnati, OH 45221. Offers applied mathematics (MS, PhD); mathematics education (MAT); pure mathematics (MS, PhD); statistics (MS, PhD). Part-time programs available. Terminal master's awarded for partial completion of doctoral program. *Degree requirements:* For master's, comprehensive exam, thesis or alternative; for doctorate, one foreign language, comprehensive exam, thesis/dissertation. *Entrance requirements:* For master's, GRE, teacher certification (MAT); for doctorate, GRE. Additional exam requirements/recommendations for international students: Required—TOEFL. Electronic applications accepted. *Faculty research:* Algebra, analysis, differential equations, numerical analysis, statistics.

University of Colorado Denver, College of Liberal Arts and Sciences, Department of Mathematical and Statistical Sciences, Denver, CO 80217. Offers applied mathematics (MS, PhD), including applied mathematics, applied probability (MS), applied statistics (MS), computational biology, computational mathematics (PhD), discrete mathematics, finite geometry (PhD), mathematics education (PhD), mathematics of engineering and science (MS), numerical analysis, operations research (MS), optimization and operations research (PhD), probability (PhD), statistics (PhD). Part-time programs available. *Faculty:* 20 full-time (4 women), 3 part-time/adjunct (0 women). *Students:* 43 full-time (12 women), 13 part-time (2 women); includes 9 minority (1 Black or African American, non-Hispanic/Latino; 4 Asian, non-Hispanic/Latino; 4 Hispanic/Latino), 9 international. Average age 32. 63 applicants, 71% accepted, 14 enrolled. In 2012, 10 master's, 6 doctorates awarded. *Degree requirements:* For master's, comprehensive exam, thesis optional, 30 hours of course work with minimum GPA of 3.0; for doctorate, comprehensive exam, thesis/dissertation, 42 hours of course work with minimum GPA of 3.25. *Entrance requirements:* For master's, GRE General Test; GRE Subject Test in math (recommended), 30 hours of course work in mathematics (24 of which must be upper-division mathematics), bachelor's degree with minimum GPA of 3.0; for doctorate, GRE General Test; GRE Subject Test in math (recommended), 30 hours of course work in mathematics (24 of which must be upper-division mathematics), master's degree with minimum GPA of 3.25. Additional exam requirements/recommendations for international students: Required—TOEFL (minimum score 537 paper-based; 75 iBT); Recommended—IELTS (minimum score 6.5). *Application deadline:* For fall admission, 2/1 for domestic and international students; for spring admission, 10/1 for domestic and international students. Application fee: $50 ($75 for international students). Electronic applications accepted. *Expenses:* Tuition, state resident: full-time $7712; part-time $355 per credit hour. Tuition, nonresident: full-time $22,038; part-time $1087 per credit hour. *Required fees:* $1110; $1. Tuition and fees vary according to course load, campus/location and program. *Financial support:* In 2012–13, 33 students received support. Fellowships with partial tuition reimbursements available, research assistantships with full tuition reimbursements available, teaching assistantships with full tuition reimbursements available, Federal Work-Study, institutionally sponsored loans, scholarships/grants, traineeships, and unspecified assistantships available. Financial award application deadline: 4/1; financial award applicants required to submit FAFSA. *Faculty research:* Computational mathematics, computational biology, discrete mathematics and geometry, probability and statistics, optimization. *Unit head:* Dr. Stephen Billups, Graduate Program Director, 303-556-4814, E-mail: stephen.billups@ucdenver.edu. *Application contact:* Margie Bopp, Graduate Program Assistant, 303-556-2341, E-mail: margie.bopp@ucdenver.edu. Website: http://www.ucdenver.edu/academics/colleges/CLAS/Departments/math/Pages/MathStats.aspx.

University of Connecticut, Graduate School, College of Liberal Arts and Sciences, Department of Statistics, Storrs, CT 06269. Offers MS, PhD. Terminal master's awarded for partial completion of doctoral program. *Degree requirements:* For master's, comprehensive exam; for doctorate, thesis/dissertation. *Entrance requirements:* For master's and doctorate, GRE General Test. Additional exam requirements/recommendations for international students: Required—TOEFL (minimum score 550 paper-based). Electronic applications accepted.

University of Delaware, College of Agriculture and Natural Resources, Department of Food and Resource Economics, Program in Statistics, Newark, DE 19716. Offers MS. Part-time programs available. *Entrance requirements:* For master's, GRE General Test, 3 letters of recommendation. Additional exam requirements/recommendations for international students: Required—TOEFL (minimum score 550 paper-based). Electronic applications accepted.

University of Denver, Daniels College of Business, Department of Business Information and Analytics, Denver, CO 80208. Offers business intelligence (MS); data mining (MS). *Faculty:* 11 full-time (2 women), 2 part-time/adjunct (0 women). *Students:* 11 full-time (6 women), 3 part-time (all women), 9 international. Average age 26. 47 applicants, 66% accepted, 13 enrolled. In 2012, 7 master's awarded. *Entrance requirements:* Additional exam requirements/recommendations for international students: Required—TOEFL (minimum score 570 paper-based; 88 iBT). *Application deadline:* For fall admission, 1/15 priority date for domestic students. Applications are processed on a rolling basis. Application fee: $60. Electronic applications accepted. *Expenses: Tuition:* Full-time $38,232; part-time $1062 per credit hour. *Required fees:* $744. Tuition and fees vary according to program. *Financial support:* In 2012–13, 2 teaching assistantships (averaging $9,234 per year) were awarded; career-related internships or fieldwork, Federal Work-Study, institutionally sponsored loans, and scholarships/grants also available. Support available to part-time students. Financial award application deadline: 2/15; financial award applicants required to submit FAFSA. *Unit head:* Dr. Daniel Connolly, Interim Chair, 303-871-4341, E-mail: anthony.hayter@du.edu. *Application contact:* Victoria Chen, Assistant Director of Graduate Recruitment, 303-871-3416, E-mail: victoria.chen@du.edu. Website: http://daniels.du.edu/schoolsdepartments/dbia/index.html.

University of Denver, Morgridge College of Education, Denver, CO 80208. Offers advanced study in law librarianship (Certificate); child and family studies (MA, PhD); counseling psychology (MA, PhD); curriculum and instruction (MA, PhD, Certificate); educational leadership (Ed D, PhD); educational leadership and policy studies (MA, Certificate); higher education (MA, PhD); library and information science (MLIS); research methods and statistics (MA, PhD); school administration (PhD); school psychology (Ed S). *Accreditation:* ALA; APA (one or more programs are accredited). Part-time and evening/weekend programs available. Postbaccalaureate distance learning degree programs offered (no on-campus study). *Faculty:* 35 full-time (25 women), 57 part-time/adjunct (43 women). *Students:* 409 full-time (324 women), 396 part-time (303 women); includes 167 minority (44 Black or African American, non-Hispanic/Latino; 7 American Indian or Alaska Native, non-Hispanic/Latino; 19 Asian, non-Hispanic/Latino; 75 Hispanic/Latino; 1 Native Hawaiian or other Pacific Islander, non-Hispanic/Latino; 21 Two or more races, non-Hispanic/Latino), 20 international. Average age 32. 1,038 applicants, 73% accepted, 388 enrolled. In 2012, 252 master's, 43 doctorates, 63 other advanced degrees awarded. Terminal master's awarded for partial completion of doctoral program. *Degree requirements:* For master's, comprehensive exam; for doctorate, 2 foreign languages, comprehensive exam, thesis/dissertation. *Entrance requirements:* For master's and doctorate, GRE General Test or GMAT. Additional exam requirements/recommendations for international students: Required—TOEFL (minimum score 550 paper-based; 80 iBT). *Application deadline:* Applications are processed on a rolling basis. Application fee: $60. Electronic applications accepted. *Expenses: Tuition:* Full-time $38,232; part-time $1062 per credit hour. *Required fees:* $744. Tuition and fees vary according to program. *Financial support:* In 2012–13, 468 students received support, including 19 research assistantships with full and partial tuition reimbursements available (averaging $11,135 per year), 79 teaching assistantships with full and partial tuition reimbursements available (averaging $7,262 per year); career-related internships or fieldwork, Federal Work-Study, institutionally sponsored loans, scholarships/grants, and unspecified assistantships also available. Support available to part-time students. Financial award application deadline: 2/15; financial award applicants required to submit FAFSA. *Faculty research:* Parkinson's disease, personnel training, development and assessments, gifted education, service-learning, transportation, public schools. *Unit head:* Dr. Gregory M. Anderson, Dean, 303-871-3665, E-mail: gregory.m.anderson@du.edu. *Application contact:* Jodi Dye, Assistant Director, MCE Admission Office, 303-871-2510, E-mail: jodi.dye@du.edu. Website: http://www.du.edu/education/.

University of Florida, Graduate School, College of Liberal Arts and Sciences, Department of Statistics, Gainesville, FL 32611. Offers M Stat, MS Stat, PhD. Part-time programs available. Terminal master's awarded for partial completion of doctoral program. *Degree requirements:* For master's, variable foreign language requirement, comprehensive exam, final oral exam; thesis (for MS Stat); for doctorate, comprehensive exam, thesis/dissertation. *Entrance requirements:* For master's and doctorate, GRE General Test, minimum GPA of 3.0. Additional exam requirements/recommendations for international students: Required—TOEFL (minimum score 550 paper-based; 80 iBT), IELTS (minimum score 6). Electronic applications accepted. *Faculty research:* Bayesian statistics, biostatistics, Markov Chain Monte Carlo (MCMC), nonparametric statistics, statistical genetics/genomics.

University of Georgia, Franklin College of Arts and Sciences, Department of Statistics, Athens, GA 30602. Offers MS, PhD. *Degree requirements:* For master's, thesis (for some programs); for doctorate, one foreign language, thesis/dissertation. *Entrance requirements:* For master's and doctorate, GRE General Test. Electronic applications accepted.

University of Guelph, Graduate Studies, College of Physical and Engineering Science, Department of Mathematics and Statistics, Guelph, ON N1G 2W1, Canada. Offers applied mathematics (PhD); applied statistics (PhD); mathematics and statistics (M Sc). Part-time programs available. *Degree requirements:* For master's, thesis (for some programs); for doctorate, thesis/dissertation. *Entrance requirements:* For master's, minimum B- average during previous 2 years of course work; for doctorate, minimum B average. Additional exam requirements/recommendations for international students: Required—TOEFL (minimum score 550 paper-based; 89 iBT), IELTS (minimum score 6.5). *Faculty research:* Dynamical systems, mathematical biology, numerical analysis, linear and nonlinear models, reliability and bioassay.

University of Houston–Clear Lake, School of Science and Computer Engineering, Program in Statistics, Houston, TX 77058-1098. Offers MS. *Entrance requirements:* For master's, GRE General Test. Additional exam requirements/recommendations for international students: Required—TOEFL (minimum score 550 paper-based).

University of Idaho, College of Graduate Studies, College of Science, Department of Statistics, Moscow, ID 83844-1104. Offers MS. *Faculty:* 4 full-time, 2 part-time/adjunct. *Students:* 17 full-time, 8 part-time. Average age 38. In 2012, 9 master's awarded. *Degree requirements:* For master's, thesis or alternative. *Entrance requirements:* For master's, minimum GPA of 2.8. *Application deadline:* For fall admission, 8/1 for domestic students; for spring admission, 12/15 for domestic students. Applications are processed on a rolling basis. Application fee: $60. Electronic applications accepted. *Expenses:* Tuition, state resident: full-time $4230; part-time $252 per credit hour. Tuition, nonresident: full-time $17,018; part-time $891 per credit hour. *Required fees:* $2932; $107 per credit hour. *Financial support:* Research assistantships and teaching assistantships available. Financial award applicants required to submit FAFSA. *Faculty research:* Statistical genetics, biostatistics, nonlinear population dynamics, multivariate and computational statistics, Six Sigma innovation and design. *Unit head:* Dr. Christopher J. Williams, Chair, 208-885-2929, E-mail: stat@uidaho.edu. *Application contact:* Erick Larson, Director of Graduate Admissions, 208-885-4723, E-mail: gadms@uidaho.edu. Website: http://www.uidaho.edu/sci/stat/.

University of Illinois at Chicago, Graduate College, College of Liberal Arts and Sciences, Department of Mathematics, Statistics, and Computer Science, Chicago, IL 60607-7128. Offers applied mathematics (MS, PhD); computational finance (MS, PhD); computer science (MS, PhD); mathematics (DA); mathematics and information sciences for industry (MS); probability and statistics (PhD); pure mathematics (MS, PhD); statistics (MS); teaching of mathematics (MST), including elementary, secondary. Part-time programs available. *Students:* 125 full-time (34 women), 34 part-time (15 women); includes 23 minority (1 Black or African American, non-Hispanic/Latino; 10 Asian, non-Hispanic/Latino; 10 Hispanic/Latino; 2 Two or more races, non-Hispanic/Latino), 45 international. Average age 29. 226 applicants, 37% accepted, 42 enrolled. In 2012, 30 master's, 19 doctorates awarded. *Degree requirements:* For master's, comprehensive exam; for doctorate, one foreign language, thesis/dissertation. *Entrance requirements:* For master's and doctorate, GRE General Test, minimum GPA of 3.0. Additional exam requirements/recommendations for international students: Required—TOEFL (minimum score 100 iBT). *Application deadline:* For fall admission, 1/1 for domestic and international students; for spring admission, 10/1 for domestic students, 7/15 for international students. Applications are processed on a rolling basis. Application fee: $60. Electronic applications accepted. *Expenses:* Tuition, state resident: full-time $10,882; part-time $3627 per term. Tuition, nonresident: full-time $22,880; part-time $7627 per term. *Required fees:* $1170 per semester. Tuition and fees vary according to course load, degree level and program. *Financial support:* In 2012–13, 109 students received support, including 2 fellowships with full tuition reimbursements available (averaging $20,000 per year), 8 research assistantships with full tuition reimbursements available (averaging $17,000 per year), 87 teaching assistantships with full tuition reimbursements available (averaging $17,000 per year); Federal Work-Study, scholarships/grants, and tuition waivers (full) also available. Financial award application deadline: 1/1. *Total annual research expenditures:* $2.2 million. *Unit head:* Lawrence Ein, Head, 312-996-3044, E-mail: ein@math.uic.edu. *Application contact:* Ramin Takloo-Bighash, Director of Graduate Studies, 312-996-5119, E-mail: dgs@math.uic.edu. Website: http://www.math.uic.edu/.

University of Illinois at Urbana–Champaign, Graduate College, College of Liberal Arts and Sciences, Department of Statistics, Champaign, IL 61820. Offers analytics (MS); applied statistics (MS); statistics (MS, PhD). *Students:* 106 (47 women). Application fee: $75 ($90 for international students). *Unit head:* Douglas G. Simpson, Chair, 217-244-0885, Fax: 217-244-7190, E-mail: dgs@illinois.edu. *Application contact:* Liza Booker, Office Support Specialist, 217-333-2167, Fax: 217-244-7190, E-mail: booker1@illinois.edu. Website: http://www.stat.illinois.edu/.

The University of Iowa, Graduate College, College of Education, Department of Psychological and Quantitative Foundations, Iowa City, IA 52242-1316. Offers counseling psychology (PhD); educational measurement and statistics (MA, PhD); educational psychology (MA, PhD); school psychology (PhD, Ed S); JD/PhD. *Accreditation:* APA. *Degree requirements:* For master's, thesis optional, exam; for doctorate, comprehensive exam, thesis/dissertation; for Ed S, exam. *Entrance requirements:* For master's, doctorate, and Ed S, GRE General Test, minimum GPA of 3.0. Additional exam requirements/recommendations for international students: Required—TOEFL (minimum score 550 paper-based; 81 iBT). Electronic applications accepted.

The University of Iowa, Graduate College, College of Liberal Arts and Sciences, Department of Statistics and Actuarial Science, Iowa City, IA 52242-1316. Offers MS, PhD. *Degree requirements:* For master's, thesis optional, exam; for doctorate, comprehensive exam, thesis/dissertation. *Entrance requirements:* For master's and doctorate, GRE General Test, minimum GPA of 3.0. Additional exam requirements/recommendations for international students: Required—TOEFL (minimum score 550 paper-based; 81 iBT). Electronic applications accepted.

University of Kentucky, Graduate School, College of Arts and Sciences, Program in Statistics, Lexington, KY 40506-0032. Offers MS, PhD. *Degree requirements:* For master's, comprehensive exam, thesis optional; for doctorate, comprehensive exam, thesis/dissertation. *Entrance requirements:* For master's, GRE General Test, minimum undergraduate GPA of 2.75; for doctorate, GRE General Test, minimum graduate GPA of 3.0. Additional exam requirements/recommendations for international students: Required—TOEFL (minimum score 550 paper-based). Electronic applications accepted. *Faculty research:* Computer intensive statistical inference, biostatistics, mathematical and applied statistics, applied probability.

The University of Manchester, School of Mathematics, Manchester, United Kingdom. Offers actuarial science (PhD); applied mathematics (M Phil, PhD); applied numerical computing (M Phil, PhD); financial mathematics (M Phil, PhD); mathematical logic (M Phil); probability (M Phil, PhD); pure mathematics (M Phil, PhD); statistics (M Phil, PhD).

The University of Manchester, School of Social Sciences, Manchester, United Kingdom. Offers ethnographic documentary (M Phil); interdisciplinary study of culture (PhD); philosophy (PhD); politics (PhD); social anthropology (PhD); social anthropology with visual media (PhD); social change (PhD); social statistics (PhD); sociology (PhD); visual anthropology (M Phil).

University of Manitoba, Faculty of Graduate Studies, Faculty of Science, Department of Statistics, Winnipeg, MB R3T 2N2, Canada. Offers M Sc, PhD. *Degree requirements:* For master's, thesis or alternative; for doctorate, one foreign language, thesis/dissertation.

University of Manitoba, Faculty of Graduate Studies, Faculty of Science, Program in Mathematical, Computational and Statistical Sciences, Winnipeg, MB R3T 2N2, Canada. Offers MMCSS.

University of Maryland, Baltimore County, Graduate School, College of Natural and Mathematical Sciences, Department of Mathematics and Statistics, Program in Statistics, Baltimore, MD 21250. Offers biostatistics (PhD); environmental statistics (MS); statistics (MS, PhD). Part-time and evening/weekend programs available. *Faculty:* 10 full-time (3 women). *Students:* 29 full-time (16 women), 20 part-time (9 women); includes 10 minority (5 Black or African American, non-Hispanic/Latino; 5 Asian, non-Hispanic/Latino), 19 international. Average age 33. 47 applicants, 49% accepted, 5 enrolled. In 2012, 9 master's, 1 doctorate awarded. Terminal master's awarded for partial completion of doctoral program. *Degree requirements:* For master's, comprehensive exam (for some programs), thesis (for some programs); for doctorate, comprehensive exam, thesis/dissertation. *Entrance requirements:* For master's and doctorate, GRE General Test, minimum GPA of 3.0. Additional exam requirements/recommendations for international students: Required—TOEFL (minimum score 600 paper-based; 100 iBT). *Application deadline:* For fall admission, 2/15 priority date for domestic students, 1/1 for international students; for spring admission, 10/15 priority date for domestic students, 5/1 for international students. Applications are processed on a rolling basis. Application fee: $50. Electronic applications accepted. *Financial support:* In 2012–13, 22 students received support, including 1 fellowship with full tuition reimbursement available (averaging $15,500 per year), 4 research assistantships with full tuition reimbursements available (averaging $15,500 per year), 17 teaching assistantships with full and partial tuition reimbursements available (averaging $15,500 per year); career-related internships or fieldwork, scholarships/grants, health care benefits, tuition waivers (full and partial), and unspecified assistantships also available. Support available to part-time students. Financial award application deadline: 2/15. *Faculty research:* Design of experiments, statistical decision theory and inference, time series analysis, biostatistics and environmental statistics, bioinformatics. *Total annual research expenditures:* $690,828. *Unit head:* Dr. Anindya Roy, Director, 410-455-2435, Fax: 410-455-1066, E-mail: anindya@umbc.edu. Website: http://www.math.umbc.edu.

University of Maryland, College Park, Academic Affairs, College of Computer, Mathematical and Natural Sciences, Department of Mathematics, Program in Mathematical Statistics, College Park, MD 20742. Offers MA, PhD. Part-time and evening/weekend programs available. *Students:* 23 full-time (9 women), 3 part-time (2 women); includes 6 minority (1 Black or African American, non-Hispanic/Latino; 5 Asian, non-Hispanic/Latino), 15 international. 99 applicants, 6% accepted, 5 enrolled. In 2012, 4 master's, 2 doctorates awarded. Terminal master's awarded for partial completion of doctoral program. *Degree requirements:* For master's, thesis or comprehensive exams, scholarly paper; for doctorate, one foreign language, thesis/dissertation, written and oral exams. *Entrance requirements:* For master's and doctorate, GRE General Test, GRE Subject Test (mathematics), minimum GPA of 3.0, 3 letters of recommendation. *Application deadline:* For fall admission, 5/1 for domestic students, 2/1 for international students; for spring admission, 10/1 for domestic students, 6/1 for international students. Applications are processed on a rolling basis. Application fee: $75. Electronic applications accepted. *Expenses:* Tuition, state resident: part-time $551 per credit. Tuition, nonresident: part-time $1188 per credit. Part-time tuition and fees vary according to program. *Financial support:* In 2012–13, 2 research assistantships (averaging $17,472 per year), 11 teaching assistantships (averaging $17,512 per year) were awarded. Financial award applicants required to submit FAFSA. *Faculty research:* Statistics and probability, stochastic processes, nonparametric statistics, space-time statistics. *Unit head:* James Yorke, Director, 301-405-5048, Fax: 301-314-0827, E-mail: yorke@math.umd.edu. *Application contact:* Dr. Charles A. Caramello, Dean of Graduate School, 301-405-0358, Fax: 301-314-9305.

University of Massachusetts Amherst, Graduate School, College of Natural Sciences, Department of Mathematics and Statistics, Amherst, MA 01003. Offers applied mathematics (MS); mathematics (MS, PhD); statistics (MS, PhD). *Faculty:* 41 full-time (5 women). *Students:* 74 full-time (21 women), 1 part-time (0 women); includes 8 minority (2 Black or African American, non-Hispanic/Latino; 5 Asian, non-Hispanic/Latino, 1 Two or more races, non-Hispanic/Latino), 35 international. Average age 27. 302 applicants, 21% accepted, 26 enrolled. In 2012, 17 master's, 6 doctorates awarded. Terminal master's awarded for partial completion of doctoral program. *Degree requirements:* For master's, thesis or alternative; for doctorate, comprehensive exam, thesis/dissertation. *Entrance requirements:* For master's and doctorate, GRE General Test, GRE Subject Test (mathematics). Additional exam requirements/recommendations for international students: Required—TOEFL (minimum score 550 paper-based; 80 iBT), IELTS (minimum score 6.5). *Application deadline:* For fall admission, 2/1 for domestic and international students. Applications are processed on a rolling basis. Application fee: $75. Electronic applications accepted. *Expenses:* Tuition, state resident: full-time $1980; part-time $110 per credit. Tuition, nonresident: full-time $13,314; part-time $414 per credit. *Required fees:* $10,338; $3594 per semester. One-time fee: $357. *Financial support:* Fellowships with full and partial tuition reimbursements, research assistantships with full and partial tuition reimbursements, teaching assistantships with full and partial tuition reimbursements, career-related internships or fieldwork, Federal Work-Study, scholarships/grants, traineeships, health care benefits, tuition waivers (full and partial), and unspecified assistantships available. Support available to part-time students. Financial award application deadline: 2/1. *Unit head:* Dr. Michael Lavine, Department Head, 413-545-2282, Fax: 413-545-1801. *Application contact:* Lindsay DeSantis, Supervisor of Admissions, 413-545-0722, Fax: 413-577-0010, E-mail: gradadm@grad.umass.edu. Website: http://www.math.umass.edu/.

University of Memphis, Graduate School, College of Arts and Sciences, Department of Mathematical Sciences, Memphis, TN 38152. Offers applied mathematics (MS); applied statistics (PhD); bioinformatics (MS); computer science (PhD); computer sciences (MS); mathematics (MS, PhD); statistics (MS, PhD). Part-time programs available. Terminal master's awarded for partial completion of doctoral program. *Degree requirements:* For master's, comprehensive exam; for doctorate, one foreign language, thesis/dissertation, oral exams. *Entrance requirements:* For master's and doctorate, GRE General Test, minimum GPA of 2.5. Additional exam requirements/recommendations for international students: Required—TOEFL (minimum score 550 paper-based). Electronic applications accepted. *Faculty research:* Combinatorics, ergodic theory, graph theory, Ramsey theory, applied statistics.

University of Michigan, Horace H. Rackham School of Graduate Studies, College of Literature, Science, and the Arts, Department of Statistics, Ann Arbor, MI 48109. Offers applied statistics (AM); statistics (AM, PhD). *Faculty:* 19 full-time (4 women). *Students:* 136 full-time (55 women); includes 105 minority (1 Black or African American, non-Hispanic/Latino; 99 Asian, non-Hispanic/Latino; 4 Hispanic/Latino; 1 Two or more races, non-Hispanic/Latino). Average age 27. 633 applicants, 18% accepted, 54 enrolled. In 2012, 27 master's, 7 doctorates awarded. Terminal master's awarded for partial completion of doctoral program. *Degree requirements:* For master's, thesis; for doctorate, thesis/dissertation, oral defense of dissertation, preliminary exam. *Entrance requirements:* For master's and doctorate, GRE General Test. Additional exam requirements/recommendations for international students: Required—TOEFL (minimum score 560 paper-based; 84 iBT), IELTS (minimum score 6.5). *Application deadline:* For fall admission, 1/10 priority date for domestic students, 1/10 for international students. Applications are processed on a rolling basis. Application fee: $65 ($75 for international students). Electronic applications accepted. *Financial support:* In 2012–13, 68 students received support, including 7 fellowships with full and partial tuition reimbursements available (averaging $25,000 per year), 17 research assistantships with full and partial tuition reimbursements available (averaging $17,270 per year), 44 teaching assistantships with full and partial tuition reimbursements available (averaging $17,270 per year); career-related internships or fieldwork, Federal Work-Study, institutionally sponsored loans, scholarships/grants, health care benefits, and unspecified assistantships also available. Financial award application deadline: 1/10. *Faculty research:* Reliability and degradation modeling, biological and legal applications, bioinformatics, statistical computing, covariance estimation. *Unit head:* Prof. Tailen Hsing, Chair, 734-763-3519, Fax: 734-763-4676, E-mail: statchair@umich.edu. *Application contact:* Judy McDonald, Graduate Program Coordinator, 734-763-3520, Fax:

734-763-4676, E-mail: stat-grad-coordinator@umich.edu. Website: http://www.stat.lsa.umich.edu/.

University of Minnesota, Twin Cities Campus, Graduate School, College of Liberal Arts, School of Statistics, Minneapolis, MN 55455-0213. Offers MS, PhD. Part-time programs available. Terminal master's awarded for partial completion of doctoral program. *Degree requirements:* For doctorate, comprehensive exam, thesis/dissertation. *Entrance requirements:* For master's and doctorate, GRE General Test. Additional exam requirements/recommendations for international students: Required—TOEFL (minimum score 100 iBT). Electronic applications accepted. *Faculty research:* Data analysis, statistical computing, experimental design, probability theory, Bayesian inference, risk analysis.

University of Missouri, Graduate School, College of Arts and Sciences, Department of Statistics, Columbia, MO 65211. Offers MA, PhD. *Faculty:* 15 full-time (4 women), 1 part-time/adjunct (0 women). *Students:* 84 full-time (30 women), 10 part-time (4 women); includes 4 minority (2 Black or African American, non-Hispanic/Latino; 2 Asian, non-Hispanic/Latino), 70 international. Average age 26. 176 applicants, 43% accepted, 46 enrolled. In 2012, 12 master's, 3 doctorates awarded. *Degree requirements:* For doctorate, comprehensive exam, thesis/dissertation. *Entrance requirements:* For master's, GRE General Test, minimum GPA of 3.0 in math and statistics courses; bachelor's degree from accredited college/university in related area; for doctorate, GRE General Test, minimum GPA of 3.0, 3.5 in math/statistics. Additional exam requirements/recommendations for international students: Required—TOEFL (minimum score 535 paper-based; 73 iBT). *Application deadline:* For fall admission, 1/15 priority date for domestic students, 1/15 for international students; for winter admission, 10/15 priority date for domestic students, 10/15 for international students. Applications are processed on a rolling basis. Application fee: $55 ($75 for international students). Electronic applications accepted. *Expenses:* Tuition, state resident: full-time $6057. Tuition, nonresident: full-time $15,683. *Required fees:* $1000. *Financial support:* In 2012–13, 7 fellowships with full tuition reimbursements, 8 research assistantships with full tuition reimbursements, 26 teaching assistantships with full tuition reimbursements were awarded; institutionally sponsored loans, health care benefits, and tuition waivers (full and partial) also available. *Faculty research:* Statistical problems in the fields of ecology, genetics, economics, meteorology, wildlife management, epidemiology, AIDS research, geophysics, climatology. *Unit head:* Dr. Nancy Flournoy, Department Chair, 573-882-7385, E-mail: flournoyn@missouri.edu. *Application contact:* Tracy Pickens, Office Support Staff IV, 573-882-6377, E-mail: pickenst@missouri.edu. Website: http://www.stat.missouri.edu/.

University of Missouri–Kansas City, College of Arts and Sciences, Department of Mathematics and Statistics, Kansas City, MO 64110-2499. Offers MA, MS, PhD. PhD (interdisciplinary) offered through the School of Graduate Studies. Part-time programs available. *Faculty:* 14 full-time (4 women), 2 part-time/adjunct (0 women). *Students:* 6 full-time (3 women), 25 part-time (12 women); includes 3 minority (all Asian, non-Hispanic/Latino), 5 international. Average age 31. 31 applicants, 58% accepted, 9 enrolled. In 2012, 11 master's awarded. Terminal master's awarded for partial completion of doctoral program. *Degree requirements:* For master's, written exam; for doctorate, 2 foreign languages, thesis/dissertation, oral and written exams. *Entrance requirements:* For master's, bachelor's degree in mathematics, minimum GPA of 3.0; for doctorate, GMAT or GRE General Test. Additional exam requirements/recommendations for international students: Required—TOEFL (minimum score 550 paper-based; 80 iBT). *Application deadline:* For fall admission, 3/15 for domestic and international students; for spring admission, 10/15 for domestic and international students. Applications are processed on a rolling basis. Application fee: $45 ($50 for international students). Electronic applications accepted. *Expenses:* Tuition, state resident: full-time $5972.40; part-time $331.80 per credit hour. Tuition, nonresident: full-time $15,417; part-time $856.50 per credit hour. *Required fees:* $95.89 per credit hour. Full-time tuition and fees vary according to program. *Financial support:* In 2012–13, 9 teaching assistantships with full tuition reimbursements (averaging $18,061 per year) were awarded; research assistantships, Federal Work-Study, institutionally sponsored loans, and tuition waivers (full and partial) also available. Support available to part-time students. Financial award application deadline: 3/1; financial award applicants required to submit FAFSA. *Faculty research:* Numerical analysis, statistics, biostatistics, commutative algebra, differential equations. *Unit head:* Dr. Eric Hall, Interim Chair, 816-235-5852, Fax: 816-235-5517, E-mail: umkcmathdept@umkc.edu. *Application contact:* Dr. Hristo Voulov, Associate Professor, 816-235-1641, Fax: 816-235-5517, E-mail: umkcmathdept@umkc.edu. Website: http://cas.umkc.edu/math/.

University of Nebraska–Lincoln, Graduate College, College of Agricultural Sciences and Natural Resources, Department of Statistics, Lincoln, NE 68588. Offers MS, PhD. *Degree requirements:* For master's, thesis optional. *Entrance requirements:* For master's, GRE General Test. Additional exam requirements/recommendations for international students: Required—TOEFL (minimum score 550 paper-based). Electronic applications accepted. *Faculty research:* Design of experiments, linear models, spatial variability, statistical modeling and inference, sampling.

University of New Brunswick Fredericton, School of Graduate Studies, Faculty of Science, Department of Mathematics and Statistics, Fredericton, NB E3B 5A3, Canada. Offers M Sc, PhD. *Faculty:* 17 full-time (0 women), 1 part-time/adjunct (0 women). *Students:* 16 full-time (5 women), 2 part-time (1 woman). In 2012, 5 master's, 1 doctorate awarded. *Degree requirements:* For master's, thesis; for doctorate, comprehensive exam, thesis/dissertation. *Entrance requirements:* For master's and doctorate, minimum GPA of 3.0. Additional exam requirements/recommendations for international students: Required—TOEFL (minimum score 550 paper-based), TWE (minimum score 4); Recommended—IELTS (minimum score 7). *Application deadline:* For fall admission, 3/1 for domestic students. Applications are processed on a rolling basis. Application fee: $50 Canadian dollars. Electronic applications accepted. Tuition and fees charges are reported in Canadian dollars. *Expenses: Tuition, area resident:* Full-time $3956 Canadian dollars. *Required fees:* $579.50 Canadian dollars; $55 Canadian dollars per semester. *Financial support:* In 2012–13, 35 research assistantships, 21 teaching assistantships were awarded; fellowships also available. *Faculty research:* Commutative and non-commutative algebra, combinatorics, mathematical modeling and computation, mathematical biology, classical and quantum gravity, multivariate statistics and spatial statistics. *Unit head:* Dr. James Watmough, Director of Graduate Studies, 506-458-7363, Fax: 506-453-4705, E-mail: watmough@unb.ca. *Application contact:* Marilyn Hetherington, Graduate Secretary, 506-458-7373, Fax: 506-453-4705, E-mail: mhetheri@unb.ca. Website: http://go.unb.ca/gradprograms.

University of New Hampshire, Graduate School, College of Engineering and Physical Sciences, Department of Mathematics and Statistics, Durham, NH 03824. Offers applied mathematics (MS); industrial statistics (Postbaccalaureate Certificate); mathematics (MS, MST, PhD); mathematics education (PhD); statistics (MS). *Faculty:* 21 full-time (5 women). *Students:* 26 full-time (8 women), 36 part-time (18 women); includes 4 minority (1 American Indian or Alaska Native, non-Hispanic/Latino; 2 Asian, non-Hispanic/Latino; 1 Two or more races, non-Hispanic/Latino), 17 international. Average age 30. 84 applicants, 46% accepted, 14 enrolled. In 2012, 12 master's, 1 doctorate, 3 other advanced degrees awarded. Terminal master's awarded for partial completion of doctoral program. *Degree requirements:* For doctorate, 2 foreign languages, thesis/dissertation. *Entrance requirements:* Additional exam requirements/recommendations for international students: Required—TOEFL (minimum score 550 paper-based; 80 iBT). *Application deadline:* For fall admission, 4/1 priority date for domestic students, 4/1 for international students; for spring admission, 12/1 for domestic students. Applications are processed on a rolling basis. Application fee: $65. Electronic applications accepted. *Expenses:* Tuition, state resident: full-time $13,500; part-time $750 per credit. Tuition, nonresident: full-time $25,940; part-time $1089 per credit. *Required fees:* $1699; $424.75 per semester. *Financial support:* In 2012–13, 41 students received support, including 1 fellowship, 7 research assistantships, 36 teaching assistantships; Federal Work-Study, scholarships/grants, and tuition waivers (full and partial) also available. Support available to part-time students. Financial award application deadline: 2/15. *Faculty research:* Operator theory, complex analysis, algebra, nonlinear dynamics, statistics. *Unit head:* Dr. Edward Hinson, Chairperson, 603-862-2688. *Application contact:* Jan Jankowski, Administrative Assistant, 603-862-2320, E-mail: jan.jankowski@unh.edu. Website: http://www.math.unh.edu/.

University of New Mexico, Graduate School, College of Arts and Sciences, Department of Mathematics and Statistics, Albuquerque, NM 87131-2039. Offers mathematics (MS, PhD); statistics (MS, PhD). Part-time programs available. *Faculty:* 25 full-time (8 women), 4 part-time/adjunct (0 women). *Students:* 52 full-time (15 women), 28 part-time (8 women); includes 17 minority (2 Black or African American, non-Hispanic/Latino; 1 Asian, non-Hispanic/Latino; 14 Hispanic/Latino), 23 international. Average age 32. 84 applicants, 52% accepted, 15 enrolled. In 2012, 11 master's, 6 doctorates awarded. Terminal master's awarded for partial completion of doctoral program. *Degree requirements:* For master's, comprehensive exam (for some programs), thesis or alternative; for doctorate, one foreign language, comprehensive exam, thesis/dissertation, 4 department seminars. *Entrance requirements:* For master's and doctorate, minimum GPA of 3.0, 3 letters of recommendation, letter of intent. Additional exam requirements/recommendations for international students: Required—TOEFL (minimum score 550 paper-based). *Application deadline:* For fall admission, 2/15 priority date for domestic students, 2/15 for international students; for spring admission, 11/1 priority date for domestic students, 11/1 for international students. Application fee: $50. Electronic applications accepted. *Expenses:* Tuition, state resident: full-time $3296; part-time $276.73 per credit hour. Tuition, nonresident: full-time $10,604; part-time $885.74 per credit hour. *Required fees:* $628. *Financial support:* In 2012–13, 59 students received support, including 15 research assistantships with tuition reimbursements available (averaging $8,419 per year), 46 teaching assistantships with tuition reimbursements available (averaging $14,812 per year); health care benefits and unspecified assistantships also available. Financial award application deadline: 2/15; financial award applicants required to submit FAFSA. *Faculty research:* Pure and applied mathematics, applied statistics, numerical analysis, biostatistics, differential geometry, fluid dynamics, nonparametric curve estimation. *Total annual research expenditures:* $1.5 million. *Unit head:* Dr. Terry Loring, Chair, 505-277-4613, Fax: 505-277-5505, E-mail: loring@math.unm.edu. *Application contact:* Ana Parra Lombard, Coordinator, Program Advisement, 505-277-5250, Fax: 505-277-5505, E-mail: aparra@math.unm.edu. Website: http://math.unm.edu/.

The University of North Carolina at Chapel Hill, Graduate School, College of Arts and Sciences, Department of Statistics, Chapel Hill, NC 27599. Offers MS, PhD. *Degree requirements:* For master's, comprehensive exam, essay or thesis; for doctorate, comprehensive exam, thesis/dissertation. *Entrance requirements:* For master's and doctorate, GRE General Test, GRE Subject Test, minimum GPA of 3.0. Additional exam requirements/recommendations for international students: Required—TOEFL.

The University of North Carolina Wilmington, College of Arts and Sciences, Department of Mathematics and Statistics, Wilmington, NC 28403-3297. Offers MS. *Degree requirements:* For master's, comprehensive exam, thesis. *Entrance requirements:* For master's, GRE General Test, GRE Subject Test, minimum B average in undergraduate major. Additional exam requirements/recommendations for international students: Required—TOEFL (minimum score 550 paper-based; 79 iBT), IELTS (minimum score 6.5).

University of North Florida, College of Arts and Sciences, Department of Mathematics and Statistics, Jacksonville, FL 32224. Offers mathematical sciences (MS); statistics (MS). Part-time and evening/weekend programs available. *Faculty:* 10 full-time (5 women). *Students:* 18 full-time (5 women), 7 part-time (1 woman); includes 3 minority (all Black or African American, non-Hispanic/Latino), 11 international. Average age 30. 38 applicants, 66% accepted, 12 enrolled. In 2012, 5 master's awarded. *Degree requirements:* For master's, comprehensive exam, thesis optional. *Entrance requirements:* For master's, GRE General Test, minimum GPA of 3.0 in last 60 hours of course work. Additional exam requirements/recommendations for international students: Required—TOEFL (minimum score 500 paper-based; 61 iBT). *Application deadline:* For fall admission, 7/1 priority date for domestic students, 6/1 for international students; for spring admission, 11/1 priority date for domestic students, 10/1 for international students. Applications are processed on a rolling basis. Application fee: $30. Electronic applications accepted. *Expenses:* Tuition, state resident: full-time $9630.72; part-time $401.28 per credit hour. Tuition, nonresident: full-time $23,020; part-time $959.17 per credit hour. *Required fees:* $1962.72; $81.78 per credit hour. Tuition and fees vary according to course load and program. *Financial support:* In 2012–13, 12 students received support, including 6 teaching assistantships (averaging $5,738 per year); Federal Work-Study, scholarships/grants, tuition waivers (partial), and unspecified assistantships also available. Support available to part-time students. Financial award application deadline: 4/1; financial award applicants required to submit FAFSA. *Faculty research:* Real analysis, number theory, Euclidean geometry. *Total annual research expenditures:* $357. *Unit head:* Dr. Scott H. Hochwald, Chair, 904-620-2653, Fax: 904-620-2818, E-mail: shochwal@unf.edu. *Application contact:* Lillith Richardson, Interim Director, The Graduate School, 904-620-1360, Fax: 904-620-1362, E-mail: graduateschool@unf.edu. Website: http://www.unf.edu/coas/math-stat/.

University of North Texas, Robert B. Toulouse School of Graduate Studies, Denton, TN 750603. Offers accounting (MS, PhD); applied anthropology (MA, MS); applied behavior analysis (Certificate); applied technology and performance improvement (M Ed, MS, PhD); art education (MA, PhD); art history (MA); art museum education (Certificate); arts leadership (Certificate); audiology (Au D); behavior analysis (MS); biochemistry and molecular biology (MS, PhD); biology (MA, MS, PhD); business (PhD); business computer information systems (PhD); chemistry (MS, PhD); clinical psychology (PhD); communication studies (MA, MS); computer engineering (MS); computer science (MS); computer science and engineering (PhD); counseling (M Ed, MS, PhD), including clinical mental health counseling (MS), college and university counseling (M Ed, MS), elementary school counseling (M Ed, MS), secondary school counseling (M Ed, MS); counseling psychology (PhD); creative writing (MA); criminal justice (MS); curriculum and instruction (M Ed, PhD), including curriculum studies (PhD), early childhood studies (PhD), language and literacy studies (PhD); decision sciences (MBA); design (MA, MFA), including fashion design (MFA), innovation studies, interior design (MFA); early childhood studies (MS); economics (MS); educational leadership (M Ed, Ed D, PhD); educational psychology (MS), including family studies, gifted and talented (MS, PhD), human development, learning and cognition, research, measurement and evaluation; educational research (PhD), including gifted and talented (MS, PhD), human development and family studies, psychological aspects of sports and exercise, research, measurement and statistics; electrical engineering (MS); emergency management (MPA); engineering systems (MS); English (MA, PhD); environmental science (MS, PhD); experimental psychology (PhD); finance (MBA, MS, PhD); financial management (MPA); French (MA); health psychology and behavioral medicine (PhD); health services management (MBA); higher education (M Ed, Ed D, PhD); history (MA, MS, PhD), including European history (PhD), military history (PhD), United States history (PhD); hospitality management (MS); human resources management (MPA); information science (MS, PhD); information technologies (MBA); information technology and decision sciences (MS); interdisciplinary studies (MA, MS); international sustainable tourism (MS); jazz studies (MM); journalism (MA, MJ, Graduate Certificate), including interactive and virtual digital communication (Graduate Certificate), narrative journalism (Graduate Certificate), public relations (Graduate Certificate); kinesiology (MS); learning technologies (MS, PhD); library science (MS); local government management (MPA); logistics and supply chain management (MBA, PhD); long-term care, senior housing, and aging services (MA, MS); management science (PhD); marketing (MBA, PhD); materials science and engineering (MS, PhD); mathematics (MA, PhD); merchandising (MS); music (MA, MM Ed, PhD), including ethnomusicology (MA), music education (MM Ed, PhD), music theory (MA, PhD), musicology (MA, PhD), performance (MA); nonprofit management (MPA); operations and supply chain management (MBA); performance (MM, DMA); philosophy (MA, PhD); physics (MS, PhD); political science (MA, MS, PhD); public administration and management (PhD), including emergency management, nonprofit management, public financial management, urban management; radio, television and film (MA, MFA); recreation, event and sport management (MS); rehabilitation counseling (MS, Certificate); sociology (MA, MS, PhD); Spanish (MA); special education (M Ed, PhD), including autism intervention (PhD), emotional/behavioral disorders (PhD), mild/moderate disabilities (PhD); speech-language pathology (MA, MS); strategic management (MBA); studio art (MFA); taxation (MS); teaching (M Ed); MBA/MS; MS/MPH; MSES/MBA. Part-time and evening/weekend programs available. Postbaccalaureate distance learning degree programs offered. *Faculty:* 665 full-time (219 women), 237 part-time/adjunct (135 women). *Students:* 3,206 full-time (1,712 women), 3,623 part-time (2,305 women); includes 1,742 minority (575 Black or African American, non-Hispanic/Latino; 16 American Indian or Alaska Native, non-Hispanic/Latino; 294 Asian, non-Hispanic/Latino; 690 Hispanic/Latino; 2 Native Hawaiian or other Pacific Islander, non-Hispanic/Latino; 165 Two or more races, non-Hispanic/Latino), 1,125 international. Average age 32. 6,094 applicants, 43% accepted, 1692 enrolled. In 2012, 1,910 master's, 237 doctorates awarded. Terminal master's awarded for partial completion of doctoral program. *Degree requirements:* For master's, variable foreign language requirement, comprehensive exam (for some programs), thesis (for some programs); for doctorate, variable foreign language requirement, comprehensive exam (for some programs), thesis/dissertation; for other advanced degree, variable foreign language requirement, comprehensive exam (for some programs). *Entrance requirements:* For master's and doctorate, GRE, GMAT. Additional exam requirements/recommendations for international students: Required—TOEFL (minimum score 550 paper-based; 79 iBT). *Application deadline:* For fall admission, 7/15 for domestic students, 3/15 for international students; for spring admission, 11/15 for domestic students, 9/15 for international students. Applications are processed on a rolling basis. Application fee: $60. Electronic applications accepted. *Expenses:* Tuition, state resident: full-time $5242; part-time $216 per credit hour. Tuition, nonresident: full-time $11,560; part-time $567 per credit hour. *Required fees:* $730 per semester. *Financial support:* Fellowships with partial tuition reimbursements, research assistantships with partial tuition reimbursements, teaching assistantships, career-related internships or fieldwork, Federal Work-Study, institutionally sponsored loans, scholarships/grants, and library assistantships available. Support available to part-time students. Financial award applicants required to submit FAFSA. *Unit head:* Mark Wardell, Dean, 940-565-2383, E-mail: mark.wardell@unt.edu. *Application contact:* Toulouse School of Graduate Studies, 940-565-2383, Fax: 940-565-2141, E-mail: gradsch@unt.edu. Website: http://www.tsgs.unt.edu/.

University of Notre Dame, Graduate School, College of Science, Department of Applied and Computational Mathematics and Statistics, Notre Dame, IN 46556. Offers applied and computational mathematics and statistics (PhD); applied statistics (MS); computational finance (MS).

University of Ottawa, Faculty of Graduate and Postdoctoral Studies, Faculty of Science, Ottawa-Carleton Institute of Mathematics and Statistics, Ottawa, ON K1N 6N5, Canada. Offers M Sc, PhD. M Sc, PhD offered jointly with Carleton University. Part-time programs available. *Degree requirements:* For master's, thesis optional; for doctorate, one foreign language, comprehensive exam, thesis/dissertation. *Entrance requirements:* For master's, honors B Sc degree or equivalent, minimum B average; for doctorate, M Sc, minimum B+ average. Electronic applications accepted. Tuition and fees charges are reported in Canadian dollars. *Expenses: Tuition, area resident:* Full-time $7074 Canadian dollars; part-time $256 Canadian dollars per credit. *International tuition:* $16,334 Canadian dollars full-time. *Required fees:* $738 Canadian dollars; $110 Canadian dollars per term. Part-time tuition and fees vary according to course load, program and student level. *Faculty research:* Pure mathematics, applied mathematics, probability and statistics.

University of Pennsylvania, Wharton School, Department of Statistics, Philadelphia, PA 19104. Offers MBA, PhD. *Degree requirements:* For doctorate, comprehensive exam, thesis/dissertation. *Entrance requirements:* For master's and doctorate, GRE. Additional exam requirements/recommendations for international students: Required—TOEFL, TWE. *Faculty research:* Nonparametric function estimation, analysis of algorithms, time series analysis, observational studies, inference.

University of Pittsburgh, Dietrich School of Arts and Sciences, Department of Statistics, Pittsburgh, PA 15260. Offers applied statistics (MA, MS); statistics (MA, MS, PhD). Part-time programs available. *Faculty:* 9 full-time (2 women). *Students:* 44 full-time (21 women), 5 part-time (0 women); includes 2 minority (both Black or African American, non-Hispanic/Latino), 27 international. Average age 26. 428 applicants, 15% accepted, 20 enrolled. In 2012, 18 master's, 8 doctorates awarded. Terminal master's awarded for partial completion of doctoral program. *Degree requirements:* For master's, comprehensive exam, thesis (for some programs); for doctorate, comprehensive exam, thesis/dissertation. *Entrance requirements:* For master's and doctorate, 3 semesters of calculus, 1 semester of linear algebra, 1 year of mathematical statistics. Additional exam requirements/recommendations for international students: Required—TOEFL (minimum score 90 iBT). *Application deadline:* For fall admission, 1/15 priority date for domestic students, 1/15 for international students; for spring admission, 10/1 priority date for domestic students, 10/1 for international students. Application fee: $50. Electronic applications accepted. *Expenses:* Tuition, state resident: full-time $19,336; part-time $782 per credit. Tuition, nonresident: full-time $31,658; part-time $1295 per credit. *Required fees:* $740; $200 per term. Tuition and fees vary according to program. *Financial support:* In 2012–13, 24 students received support, including 1 fellowship with full tuition reimbursement available (averaging $16,950 per year), 9 research assistantships with full tuition reimbursements available (averaging $16,950 per year), 16 teaching assistantships with full tuition reimbursements available (averaging $16,300 per year); career-related internships or fieldwork, Federal Work-Study, institutionally sponsored loans, scholarships/grants, health care benefits, and unspecified assistantships also available. Financial award application deadline: 1/15. *Faculty research:* Multivariate statistics, time series, reliability, meta-analysis, linear and nonlinear regression modeling. *Unit head:* Dr. Satish Iyengar, Chair, 412-624-8341, Fax: 412-648-8814, E-mail: ssi@pitt.edu. *Application contact:* Dr. Leon J. Gleser, Director of Graduate Studies, 412-624-3925, Fax: 412-648-8814, E-mail: gleser@pitt.edu. Website: http://www.stat.pitt.edu/.

University of Puerto Rico, Mayagüez Campus, Graduate Studies, College of Arts and Sciences, Department of Mathematical Sciences, Mayagüez, PR 00681-9000. Offers applied mathematics (MS); pure mathematics (MS); scientific computation (MS); statistics (MS). Part-time programs available. *Faculty:* 45 full-time (7 women), 1 part-time/adjunct (0 women). *Students:* 34 full-time (10 women), 1 part-time (0 women); includes 30 minority (all Hispanic/Latino), 25 international. 8 applicants, 88% accepted, 7 enrolled. In 2012, 5 master's awarded. *Degree requirements:* For master's, one foreign language, comprehensive exam, thesis optional. *Entrance requirements:* For master's, undergraduate degree in mathematics or its equivalent. *Application deadline:* For fall admission, 2/15 for domestic and international students; for spring admission, 9/15 for domestic and international students. Applications are processed on a rolling basis. Application fee: $25. Tuition and fees vary according to course level and course load. *Financial support:* In 2012–13, 31 students received support, including 5 research assistantships (averaging $15,000 per year), 26 teaching assistantships (averaging $8,500 per year); Federal Work-Study and institutionally sponsored loans also available. *Faculty research:* Automata theory, linear algebra, logic. *Unit head:* Dr. Omar Colon, Director, 787-832-4040 Ext. 3848, Fax: 787-265-5454, E-mail: omar.colon.reyes@gmail.com. Website: http://math.uprm.edu/.

University of Regina, Faculty of Graduate Studies and Research, Faculty of Science, Department of Mathematics and Statistics, Regina, SK S4S 0A2, Canada. Offers mathematics (M Sc, MA, PhD); statistics (M Sc, MA, PhD). *Faculty:* 21 full-time (2 women), 4 part-time/adjunct (2 women). *Students:* 28 full-time (7 women), 2 part-time (0 women). 40 applicants, 63% accepted. In 2012, 5 master's awarded. *Degree requirements:* For master's, thesis; for doctorate, comprehensive exam, thesis/dissertation. *Entrance requirements:* Additional exam requirements/recommendations for international students: Required—TOEFL (minimum score 580 paper-based; 80 iBT), IELTS (minimum score 6.5). *Application deadline:* For fall admission, 1/31 for domestic and international students; for winter admission, 8/31 for domestic and international students. Applications are processed on a rolling basis. Application fee: $100. Electronic applications accepted. Tuition and fees charges are reported in Canadian dollars. *Expenses: Tuition, area resident:* Full-time $3942 Canadian dollars; part-time $219 Canadian dollars per credit hour. *International tuition:* $4742 Canadian dollars full-time. *Required fees:* $421.55 Canadian dollars; $93.60 Canadian dollars per credit hour. Tuition and fees vary according to course load, degree level and program. *Financial support:* In 2012–13, 7 fellowships (averaging $7,000 per year), 7 teaching assistantships (averaging $2,436 per year) were awarded; research assistantships and scholarships/grants also available. Financial award application deadline: 6/15. *Faculty research:* Discrete mathematics, actuarial science and statistics, matrix theory, mathematical science, numerical analysis. *Unit head:* Dr. Douglas Farenick, Head, 306-585-4425, Fax: 306-585-4020, E-mail: douglas.farenick@uregina.ca. *Application contact:* Dr. Martin Argerami, Graduate Program Coordinator, 306-585-4340, Fax: 306-585-4020, E-mail: martin.argerami@math.uregina.ca. Website: http://www.math.uregina.ca.

University of Rhode Island, Graduate School, College of Arts and Sciences, Department of Computer Science and Statistics, Kingston, RI 02881. Offers applied mathematics (PhD), including computer science, statistics; computer science (MS, PhD); digital forensics (Graduate Certificate); statistics (MS). Part-time programs available. *Faculty:* 13 full-time (6 women). *Students:* 24 full-time (4 women), 35 part-time (4 women); includes 11 minority (2 Black or African American, non-Hispanic/Latino; 5 Asian, non-Hispanic/Latino; 4 Hispanic/Latino), 7 international. In 2012, 14 master's, 1 doctorate awarded. *Degree requirements:* For master's, comprehensive exam (for some programs), thesis optional; for doctorate, comprehensive exam, thesis/dissertation. *Entrance requirements:* For master's and doctorate, GRE, 2 letters of recommendation. Additional exam requirements/recommendations for international students: Required—TOEFL (minimum score 550 paper-based). *Application deadline:* For fall admission, 7/15 for domestic students, 2/1 for international students; for spring admission, 11/15 for domestic students, 7/15 for international students. Application fee: $65. Electronic applications accepted. *Expenses:* Tuition, state resident: full-time $11,532; part-time $641 per credit. Tuition, nonresident: full-time $23,606; part-time $1311 per credit. *Required fees:* $1388; $36 per credit. $35 per semester. One-time fee: $130. *Financial support:* In 2012–13, 10 teaching assistantships with full tuition reimbursements (averaging $13,258 per year) were awarded. Financial award application deadline: 2/1; financial award applicants required to submit FAFSA. *Faculty research:* Bioinformatics, computer and digital forensics, behavioral model of pedestrian dynamics, real-time distributed object computing, cryptography. *Unit head:* Dr. Joan Peckham, Chair, 401-874-2701, Fax: 401-874-4617, E-mail: joan@cs.uri.edu. *Application contact:* E-mail: grad-inquiries@cs.uri.edu. Website: http://www.cs.uri.edu/.

University of Rochester, School of Medicine and Dentistry, Graduate Programs in Medicine and Dentistry, Department of Biostatistics and Computational Biology, Programs in Statistics, Rochester, NY 14627. Offers MA, PhD.

University of Saskatchewan, College of Graduate Studies and Research, College of Arts and Science, Department of Mathematics and Statistics, Saskatoon, SK S7N 5A2, Canada. Offers M Math, MA, PhD. *Degree requirements:* For master's, thesis (for some programs); for doctorate, comprehensive exam (for some programs), thesis/dissertation. *Entrance requirements:* Additional exam requirements/recommendations for international students: Required—TOEFL (minimum score 80 iBT); Recommended—IELTS (minimum score 6.5). Electronic applications accepted.

University of South Africa, College of Economic and Management Sciences, Pretoria, South Africa. Offers accounting (D Admin, D Com); accounting science (DA); auditing (D Admin, D Com); business administration (M Tech); business economics (D Admin); business leadership (DBL); business management (D Admin, D Com); economic management analysis (M Tech); economics (D Admin, D Com, PhD); human resource development (M Tech); industrial psychology (D Admin, D Com, PhD); logistics (D Com); marketing (M Tech); public administration (D Admin, D Com, DPA, PhD); public management (M Tech); quantitative management (D Admin, D Com); real estate (M Tech); statistics (D Admin, PhD); tourism management (D Admin, D Com); transport economics (D Admin, D Com).

University of South Carolina, The Graduate School, College of Arts and Sciences, Department of Statistics, Columbia, SC 29208. Offers applied statistics (CAS); industrial statistics (MIS); statistics (MS, PhD). Part-time and evening/weekend programs available. Postbaccalaureate distance learning degree programs offered (minimal on-campus study). Terminal master's awarded for partial completion of doctoral program. *Degree requirements:* For master's, thesis; for doctorate, comprehensive exam, thesis/dissertation. *Entrance requirements:* For master's, GRE General Test or GMAT, 2 years of work experience (MIS); for doctorate, GRE General Test; for CAS, GRE General Test or GMAT. Additional exam requirements/recommendations for international students: Required—TOEFL (minimum score 600 paper-based; 100 iBT). Electronic applications accepted. *Expenses:* Contact institution. *Faculty research:* Reliability, environmentrics, statistics computing, psychometrics, bioinformatics.

University of Southern California, Graduate School, Dana and David Dornsife College of Letters, Arts and Sciences, Department of Mathematics, Los Angeles, CA 90089. Offers applied mathematics (MA, MS, PhD); mathematical finance (MS); mathematics (MA, PhD); statistics (MS). Part-time programs available. Terminal master's awarded for partial completion of doctoral program. *Degree requirements:* For master's, comprehensive exam (for some programs), thesis (for some programs); for doctorate, one foreign language, comprehensive exam, thesis/dissertation. *Entrance requirements:* For master's, GRE General Test, GMAT; for doctorate, GRE General Test, GRE Subject Test (mathematics). Additional exam requirements/recommendations for international students: Required—TOEFL (minimum score 100 iBT). Electronic applications accepted. *Faculty research:* Algebra, algebraic geometry and number theory, analysis/partial differential equations, applied mathematics, financial mathematics, probability, combinatorics and statistics.

University of Southern Maine, College of Science, Technology, and Health, Department of Mathematics and Statistics, Portland, ME 04104-9300. Offers statistics (MS).

University of South Florida, Graduate School, College of Arts and Sciences, Department of Mathematics and Statistics, Tampa, FL 33620-9951. Offers mathematics (MA, PhD); statistics (MA). Part-time and evening/weekend programs available. Terminal master's awarded for partial completion of doctoral program. *Degree requirements:* For master's, comprehensive exam, thesis optional; for doctorate, comprehensive exam, thesis/dissertation. *Entrance requirements:* For master's, GRE, minimum GPA of 3.0; for doctorate, GRE, minimum GPA of 3.5, three letters of recommendation, personal statement of goals. Additional exam requirements/recommendations for international students: Required—TOEFL (minimum score 550 paper-based; 79 iBT) or IELTS (minimum score 6.5). Electronic applications accepted. *Faculty research:* Approximation theory, differential equations, discrete mathematics, functional analysis topology.

The University of Tennessee, Graduate School, College of Business Administration, Department of Statistics, Knoxville, TN 37996. Offers industrial statistics (MS); statistics (MS). Part-time programs available. *Degree requirements:* For master's, thesis or alternative. *Entrance requirements:* For master's, GMAT or GRE General Test, minimum GPA of 2.7. Additional exam requirements/recommendations for international students: Required—TOEFL. Electronic applications accepted. *Expenses:* Tuition, state resident: full-time $9000; part-time $501 per credit hour. Tuition, nonresident: full-time $27,188; part-time $1512 per credit hour. *Required fees:* $1280; $62 per credit hour. Tuition and fees vary according to program.

The University of Tennessee, Graduate School, College of Business Administration, Program in Business Administration, Knoxville, TN 37996. Offers accounting (PhD); finance (MBA, PhD); logistics and transportation (MBA, PhD); management (PhD); marketing (MBA, PhD); operations management (MBA); professional business administration (MBA); statistics (PhD); JD/MBA; MS/MBA; Pharm D/MBA. Pharm D/MBA offered jointly with The University of Tennessee Health Science Center. *Accreditation:* AACSB. Postbaccalaureate distance learning degree programs offered. *Degree requirements:* For master's, thesis or alternative; for doctorate, thesis/dissertation. *Entrance requirements:* For master's and doctorate, GMAT, minimum GPA of 2.7. Additional exam requirements/recommendations for international students: Required—TOEFL. Electronic applications accepted. *Expenses:* Tuition, state resident: full-time $9000; part-time $501 per credit hour. Tuition, nonresident: full-time $27,188; part-time $1512 per credit hour. *Required fees:* $1280; $62 per credit hour. Tuition and fees vary according to program.

The University of Texas at Austin, Graduate School, College of Natural Sciences, Division of Statistics and Scientific Computation, Austin, TX 78712-1111. Offers statistics (MS, PhD). *Entrance requirements:* For master's, GRE General Test; for doctorate, GRE General Test, letters of recommendation, bachelor's degree from accredited college or university, minimum GPA of 3.0, statement of purpose, curriculum vitae or resume. Additional exam requirements/recommendations for international students: Required—TOEFL or IELTS.

The University of Texas at Dallas, School of Natural Sciences and Mathematics, Department of Mathematical Sciences, Richardson, TX 75080. Offers applied mathematics (MS, PhD); engineering mathematics (MS); mathematics (MS); statistics (MS, PhD). Part-time and evening/weekend programs available. *Faculty:* 20 full-time (4 women), 1 part-time/adjunct (0 women). *Students:* 50 full-time (22 women), 27 part-time (9 women); includes 16 minority (4 Black or African American, non-Hispanic/Latino; 7 Asian, non-Hispanic/Latino; 5 Hispanic/Latino), 37 international. Average age 31. 140 applicants, 36% accepted, 29 enrolled. In 2012, 13 master's, 3 doctorates awarded. *Degree requirements:* For master's, thesis optional; for doctorate, thesis/dissertation. *Entrance requirements:* For master's, GRE General Test, minimum GPA of 3.0 in upper-level course work in field; for doctorate, GRE General Test, minimum GPA of 3.5 in upper-level course work in field. Additional exam requirements/recommendations for international students: Required—TOEFL (minimum score 550 paper-based). *Application deadline:* For fall admission, 7/15 for domestic students, 5/1 for international students; for spring admission, 11/15 for domestic students, 9/1 for international students. Applications are processed on a rolling basis. Application fee: $50 ($100 for international students). Electronic applications accepted. *Expenses:* Tuition, state resident: full-time $11,940; part-time $663.33 per credit hour. Tuition, nonresident: full-time $21,606; part-time $1200.33 per credit hour. Tuition and fees vary according to course load. *Financial support:* In 2012–13, 39 students received support, including 4 research assistantships (averaging $19,800 per year), 35 teaching assistantships with partial tuition reimbursements available (averaging $16,124 per year); career-related internships or fieldwork, Federal Work-Study, institutionally sponsored loans, scholarships/grants, and unspecified assistantships also available. Support available to part-time students. Financial award application deadline: 4/30; financial award applicants required to submit FAFSA. *Faculty research:* Sequential analysis, applications in semiconductor manufacturing, medical image analysis, computational anatomy, information theory, probability theory. *Unit head:* Dr. Matthew Goeckner, Department Head, 972-883-4292, Fax: 972-883-6622, E-mail: goeckner@utdallas.edu. *Application contact:* Jacqueline Thiede, Graduate Support Assistant, 972-883-2163, Fax: 972-883-6622, E-mail: utdmath@utdallas.edu. Website: http://www.utdallas.edu/math.

The University of Texas at El Paso, Graduate School, College of Science, Department of Mathematical Sciences, El Paso, TX 79968-0001. Offers mathematical sciences (MS); mathematics (teaching) (MAT); statistics (MS). Part-time and evening/weekend programs available. *Degree requirements:* For master's, thesis optional. *Entrance requirements:* For master's, minimum GPA of 3.0, letters of recommendation. Additional exam requirements/recommendations for international students: Required—TOEFL; Recommended—IELTS. Electronic applications accepted.

The University of Texas at San Antonio, College of Business, Department of Management Science and Statistics, San Antonio, TX 78249-0617. Offers applied statistics (MS, PhD); management science (MBA). *Accreditation:* AACSB. Part-time and evening/weekend programs available. *Faculty:* 13 full-time (3 women), 3 part-time/adjunct (1 woman). *Students:* 34 full-time (11 women), 27 part-time (8 women); includes 22 minority (1 Black or African American, non-Hispanic/Latino; 7 Asian, non-Hispanic/Latino; 14 Hispanic/Latino), 18 international. Average age 30. 54 applicants, 61% accepted, 22 enrolled. In 2012, 10 master's, 3 doctorates awarded. *Degree requirements:* For master's, comprehensive exam (for some programs), thesis or alternative; for doctorate, comprehensive exam, thesis/dissertation. *Entrance requirements:* For master's, GMAT, minimum of 36 semester credit hours of coursework beyond any hours acquired in the MBA-leveling courses; statement of purpose; for doctorate, GRE, minimum cumulative GPA of 3.3 in the last 60 hours of coursework; transcripts from all colleges and universities attended; curriculum vitae; statement of academic work experiences, interests, and goals; three letters of recommendation; BA, BS, or MS in mathematics, statistics, or closely-related field. Additional exam requirements/recommendations for international students: Required—TOEFL (minimum score 500 paper-based; 61 iBT), IELTS (minimum score 5). *Application deadline:* For fall admission, 7/1 for domestic students, 4/1 for international students; for spring admission, 11/1 for domestic students, 9/1 for international students. Applications are processed on a rolling basis. Application fee: $45 ($85 for international students). Electronic applications accepted. *Financial support:* In 2012–13, fellowships (averaging $22,000 per year), research assistantships (averaging $10,000 per year), teaching assistantships (averaging $10,000 per year) were awarded; scholarships/grants, health care benefits, and unspecified assistantships also available. *Faculty research:* Statistical signal processing, reliability and life-testing experiments, modeling decompression sickness using survival analysis. *Unit head:* Dr. Raydel Tullous, Chair, 210-458-6345, Fax: 210-458-6350, E-mail: raydel.tullous@utsa.edu. *Application contact:* Katherine Pope, Graduate Assistant of Record, 210-458-7316, Fax: 210-458-4398, E-mail: katherine.pope@utsa.edu.

University of the Incarnate Word, School of Graduate Studies and Research, School of Mathematics, Science, and Engineering, Program in Mathematics, San Antonio, TX 78209-6397. Offers research statistics (MS); teaching (MA). Part-time and evening/weekend programs available. *Faculty:* 4 full-time (2 women), 1 (woman) part-time/adjunct. *Students:* 5 part-time (3 women); includes 3 minority (all Hispanic/Latino). Average age 35. 6 applicants, 17% accepted, 0 enrolled. In 2012, 7 master's awarded. *Degree requirements:* For master's, capstone or prerequisite knowledge (for research statistics). *Entrance requirements:* For master's, GRE (minimum score 800 verbal and quantitative), 18 hours of undergraduate mathematics with minimum GPA of 3.0; letter of recommendation by a professional in the field, writing sample, teaching experience at the precollege level. Additional exam requirements/recommendations for international students: Required—TOEFL (minimum score 560 paper-based; 83 iBT). *Application deadline:* Applications are processed on a rolling basis. Application fee: $20. Electronic applications accepted. *Expenses: Tuition:* Full-time $9060; part-time $755 per credit hour. *Required fees:* $960; $40 per credit hour. Tuition and fees vary according to degree level, program and student level. *Financial support:* Federal Work-Study and scholarships/grants available. Financial award applicants required to submit FAFSA. *Faculty research:* Scholarship and career development for undergraduate mathematics majors. *Total annual research expenditures:* $140,844. *Unit head:* Dr. Zhanbo Yang, Mathematics Graduate Program Coordinator, 210-283-5008, Fax: 210-829-3153, E-mail: yang@uiwtx.edu. *Application contact:* Andrea Cyterski-Acosta, Dean of Enrollment, 210-829-6005, Fax: 210-829-3921, E-mail: admis@uiwtx.edu. Website: http://www.uiw.edu/math/mathprogramsgrad.html.

The University of Toledo, College of Graduate Studies, College of Natural Sciences and Mathematics, Department of Mathematics, Toledo, OH 43606-3390. Offers applied mathematics (MS, PhD); statistics (MS, PhD). Part-time programs available. *Faculty:* 25. *Students:* 38 full-time (13 women), 3 part-time (0 women); includes 2 minority (both Asian, non-Hispanic/Latino), 30 international. Average age 29. 37 applicants, 57% accepted, 11 enrolled. In 2012, 11 master's, 3 doctorates awarded. *Degree requirements:* For master's, comprehensive exam (for some programs), thesis (for some programs); for doctorate, 2 foreign languages, thesis/dissertation. *Entrance requirements:* For master's and doctorate, GRE General Test, GRE Subject Test, minimum cumulative point-hour ratio of 2.7 for all previous academic work, three letters of recommendation, statement of purpose, transcripts from all prior institutions attended. Additional exam requirements/recommendations for international students: Required—TOEFL (minimum score 550 paper-based; 80 iBT), IELTS (minimum score 6.5). *Application deadline:* For fall admission, 1/15 priority date for domestic students, 1/15 for international students. Applications are processed on a rolling basis. Application fee: $45 ($75 for international students). Electronic applications accepted. *Financial support:* In 2012–13, 38 teaching assistantships with full and partial tuition reimbursements (averaging $14,503 per year) were awarded; research assistantships with full and partial tuition reimbursements, Federal Work-Study, institutionally sponsored loans, scholarships/grants, and unspecified assistantships also available. Support available to part-time students. *Unit head:* Dr. Paul Hewitt, Chair, 419-530-2568, E-mail: paul.hewitt@utoledo.edu. *Application contact:* Graduate School Office, 419-530-4723, Fax: 419-530-4723, E-mail: grdsch@utnet.utoledo.edu. Website: http://www.utoledo.edu/nsm/.

University of Toronto, School of Graduate Studies, Faculty of Arts and Science, Department of Statistics, Toronto, ON M5S 1A1, Canada. Offers M Sc, PhD. Part-time programs available. *Degree requirements:* For doctorate, comprehensive exam, thesis/dissertation. *Entrance requirements:* For master's, GRE (recommended for students educated outside of Canada), 3 letters of reference; for doctorate, GRE (recommended for students educated outside of Canada), 3 letters of reference, M Stat or equivalent, minimum B+ average. Additional exam requirements/recommendations for international students: Required—TOEFL (minimum score 580 paper-based; 93 iBT), TWE (minimum score 4). Electronic applications accepted.

University of Utah, Graduate School, College of Education, Department of Educational Psychology, Salt Lake City, UT 84112. Offers clinical mental health counseling (M Ed); counseling psychology (PhD); educational psychology (M Ed, MA, MS, PhD); elementary education (M Ed); instructional design and educational technology (M Ed); instructional design and technology (MS); learning and cognition (PhD); reading and literacy (M Ed, MS, PhD); school counseling (M Ed); school psychology (M Ed, MS, PhD); statistics (M Stat). *Accreditation:* APA (one or more programs are accredited). *Faculty:* 19 full-time (8 women). *Students:* 110 full-time (86 women), 97 part-time (75 women); includes 25 minority (2 Black or African American, non-Hispanic/Latino; 1 American Indian or Alaska Native, non-Hispanic/Latino; 6 Asian, non-Hispanic/Latino; 15 Hispanic/Latino; 1 Two or more races, non-Hispanic/Latino), 7 international. Average age 32. 254 applicants, 33% accepted, 45 enrolled. In 2012, 78 master's, 18 doctorates awarded. *Degree requirements:* For master's, variable foreign language requirement, comprehensive exam (for some programs), thesis (for some programs), projects; for doctorate, variable foreign language requirement, thesis/dissertation, oral exam. *Entrance requirements:* For master's and doctorate, GRE General Test, minimum GPA of 3.0. Additional exam requirements/recommendations for international students: Required—TOEFL (minimum score 61 iBT). *Application deadline:* For fall admission, 4/1 for domestic and international students; for winter admission, 11/1 for domestic and international students; for spring admission, 3/15 for domestic and international students. Application fee: $55 ($65 for international students). Electronic applications accepted. *Expenses:* Contact institution. *Financial support:* In 2012–13, 61 students received support, including 17 fellowships with full tuition reimbursements available (averaging $14,200 per year), 9 research assistantships with full and partial tuition reimbursements available (averaging $12,500 per year), 24 teaching assistantships with full and partial tuition reimbursements available (averaging $12,500 per year); career-related internships or fieldwork, Federal Work-Study, institutionally sponsored loans, scholarships/grants, health care benefits, and unspecified assistantships also available. Financial award application deadline: 4/1; financial award applicants required to submit FAFSA. *Faculty research:* Autism, computer technology and instruction, cognitive behavior, aging, group counseling. *Total annual research expenditures:* $415,396. *Unit head:* Dr. Elaine Clark, Chair, 801-581-7148, Fax: 801-581-5566, E-mail: elclark@utah.edu. *Application contact:* JoLynn N. Yates, Academic Program Specialist, 801-581-7148, Fax: 801-581-5566, E-mail: jo.yates@utah.edu. Website: http://www.ed.utah.edu/edps/.

University of Utah, Graduate School, David Eccles School of Business, Business Administration Program, Salt Lake City, UT 84112. Offers accounting (PhD); business administration (EMBA, MBA, PMBA); business administration engineering (MBA/MS); finance (PhD); information systems (PhD); marketing (PhD); operations management (PhD); organizational behavior (PhD); statistics (M Stat); strategic management (PhD); MBA/JD; MBA/MHA; MBA/MS. Part-time and evening/weekend programs available. *Faculty:* 60 full-time (21 women), 3 part-time/adjunct (0 women). *Students:* 522 full-time (96 women), 97 part-time (15 women); includes 42 minority (2 Black or African American, non-Hispanic/Latino; 14 Asian, non-Hispanic/Latino; 15 Hispanic/Latino; 2 Native Hawaiian or other Pacific Islander, non-Hispanic/Latino; 9 Two or more races, non-Hispanic/Latino), 39 international. Average age 32. 532 applicants, 60% accepted, 228 enrolled. In 2012, 312 master's, 7 doctorates awarded. *Degree requirements:* For doctorate, comprehensive exam, thesis/dissertation. *Entrance requirements:* For master's, GMAT, statistics course with minimum B grade, minimum undergraduate GPA of 3.0; for doctorate, GMAT. Additional exam requirements/recommendations for international students: Required—TOEFL (minimum score 600 paper-based; 100 iBT), IELTS (minimum score 7). *Application deadline:* For fall admission, 12/1 priority date for domestic students, 12/1 for international students; for spring admission, 11/1 for domestic and international students. Applications are processed on a rolling basis. Application fee: $55 ($65 for international students). Electronic applications accepted. *Expenses:* Contact institution. *Financial support:* In 2012–13, 124 students received support, including 32 fellowships with partial tuition reimbursements available (averaging $6,378 per year), 35 research assistantships with partial tuition reimbursements available (averaging $6,378 per year), 57 teaching assistantships with full tuition reimbursements available (averaging $17,000 per year); scholarships/grants and unspecified assistantships also available. Financial award application deadline: 2/1; financial award applicants required to submit FAFSA. *Faculty research:* Corporate finance, strategy services, consumer behavior, financial disclosures, operations. *Unit head:* Dr. William Hesterly, Associate Dean, PhD Program, 801-581-7676, Fax: 801-581-3380, E-mail: mastersinfo@business.utah.edu. *Application contact:* Andrea Miller, Coordinator, 801-581-7785, Fax: 801-581-3666, E-mail: mastersinfo@business.utah.edu. Website: http://business.utah.edu/full-time-mba.

University of Utah, Graduate School, Interdepartmental Program in Statistics, Salt Lake City, UT 84112-1107. Offers biostatistics (M Stat); econometrics (M Stat); educational psychology (M Stat); mathematics (M Stat); sociology (M Stat). Part-time programs available. *Students:* 30 full-time (11 women), 29 part-time (12 women); includes 13 minority (3 Black or African American, non-Hispanic/Latino; 7 Asian, non-Hispanic/Latino; 2 Hispanic/Latino; 1 Two or more races, non-Hispanic/Latino), 15 international. Average age 33. 59 applicants, 44% accepted, 16 enrolled. In 2012, 14 master's awarded. *Degree requirements:* For master's, comprehensive exam, projects. *Entrance requirements:* For master's, GRE General Test (for all but biostatistics); GRE Subject Test (for mathematics), minimum GPA of 3.0; course work in calculus, matrix theory, statistics. Additional exam requirements/recommendations for international students: Required—TOEFL (minimum score 500 paper-based; 61 iBT). *Application deadline:* For fall admission, 7/1 for domestic students, 4/1 for international students. Applications are processed on a rolling basis. Application fee: $55 ($65 for international students). *Financial support:* Career-related internships or fieldwork available. *Faculty research:* Biostatistics, management, economics, educational psychology, mathematics. *Unit head:* Richard Fowles, Chair, University Statistics Committee, 801-581-4577, E-mail: fowles@economics.utah.edu. *Application contact:* Laura Egbert, Coordinator, 801-585-6853, E-mail: laura.egbert@utah.edu. Website: http://www.mstat.utah.edu.

University of Utah, Graduate School, Professional Master of Science and Technology Program, Salt Lake City, UT 84112-1107. Offers biotechnology (PSM); computational science (PSM); environmental science (PSM); science instrumentation (PSM). Part-time programs available. *Students:* 20 full-time (11 women), 36 part-time (9 women); includes 4 minority (3 Hispanic/Latino; 1 Native Hawaiian or other Pacific Islander, non-Hispanic/Latino), 3 international. Average age 32. 53 applicants, 55% accepted, 23 enrolled. In 2012, 25 master's awarded. *Degree requirements:* For master's, internship. *Entrance requirements:* For master's, GRE (recommended), minimum undergraduate GPA of 3.0, bachelor's degree from accredited university or college. Additional exam requirements/recommendations for international students: Required—TOEFL (minimum score 500 paper-based; 61 iBT), IELTS (minimum score 6). *Application deadline:* For fall admission, 2/1 for domestic and international students. Application fee: $55 ($65 for international students). Electronic applications accepted. *Financial support:* Fellowships, research assistantships, teaching assistantships, and unspecified assistantships available. *Unit head:* Jennifer Schmidt, Program Director, 801-585-5630, E-mail: jennifer.schmidt@gradschool.utah.edu. *Application contact:* Jay Derek Payne, Project Coordinator, 801-585-3650, Fax: 801-585-6749, E-mail: derek.payne@gradschool.utah.edu. Website: http://pmst.utah.edu/.

University of Vermont, Graduate College, College of Engineering and Mathematics, Department of Mathematics and Statistics, Program in Statistics, Burlington, VT 05405. Offers MS. *Students:* 12 (5 women); includes 1 minority (Black or African American, non-Hispanic/Latino), 4 international. 48 applicants, 31% accepted, 4 enrolled. In 2012, 3 master's awarded. *Entrance requirements:* For master's, GRE General Test. Additional exam requirements/recommendations for international students: Required—TOEFL (minimum score 550 paper-based; 90 iBT). *Application deadline:* For fall admission, 4/1 priority date for domestic students, 4/1 for international students. Applications are processed on a rolling basis. Application fee: $40. Electronic applications accepted. *Expenses: Tuition, area resident:* Part-time $572 per credit. Tuition, nonresident: part-time $1444 per credit. *Financial support:* Fellowships, research assistantships, and teaching assistantships available. Financial award application deadline: 3/1. *Faculty research:* Applied statistics. *Unit head:* Dr. James Burgmeier, Chair, 802-656-2940. *Application contact:* Prof. Ruth Mlckey, Coordinator, 802-656-2940.

University of Victoria, Faculty of Graduate Studies, Faculty of Science, Department of Mathematics and Statistics, Victoria, BC V8W 2Y2, Canada. Offers M Sc, MA, PhD. Part-time programs available. *Degree requirements:* For master's, thesis; for doctorate, one foreign language, thesis/dissertation, 3 qualifying exams, candidacy exam. *Entrance requirements:* Additional exam requirements/recommendations for international students: Required—TOEFL (minimum score 575 paper-based), IELTS (minimum score 7). Electronic applications accepted. *Faculty research:* Functional analysis and operator theory, applied ordinary and partial differential equations, discrete mathematics and graph theory.

University of Virginia, College and Graduate School of Arts and Sciences, Department of Statistics, Charlottesville, VA 22903. Offers MS, PhD. *Faculty:* 7 full-time (1 woman). *Students:* 36 full-time (14 women), 1 part-time (0 women); includes 7 minority (all Asian, non-Hispanic/Latino), 21 international. Average age 26. 218 applicants, 17% accepted, 12 enrolled. In 2012, 23 master's, 2 doctorates awarded. *Degree requirements:* For master's, exam; for doctorate, comprehensive exam, thesis/dissertation. *Entrance requirements:* For master's and doctorate, GRE General Test, 3 letters of recommendation. Additional exam requirements/recommendations for international students: Required—TOEFL (minimum score 600 paper-based; 90 iBT), IELTS (minimum score 7). *Application deadline:* For fall admission, 2/1 for domestic and international students. Applications are processed on a rolling basis. Application fee: $60. Electronic applications accepted. *Expenses:* Tuition, state resident: full-time $13,278; part-time $717 per credit hour. Tuition, nonresident: full-time $22,602; part-time $1235 per credit hour. *Required fees:* $2384. *Financial support:* Fellowships and teaching assistantships available. Financial award applicants required to submit FAFSA. *Unit head:* Jeffrey Holt, Chairman, 434-924-3222, Fax: 434-924-3076, E-mail: jjholt@virginia.edu. *Application contact:* Dan Spitzner, Director of Graduate Studies, 434-924-3222, Fax: 434-924-3076, E-mail: spitzner@virginia.edu. Website: http://www.stat.virginia.edu/.

University of Washington, Graduate School, College of Arts and Sciences, Department of Statistics, Seattle, WA 98195. Offers MS, PhD. Terminal master's awarded for partial completion of doctoral program. *Degree requirements:* For master's, thesis optional; for doctorate, one foreign language, thesis/dissertation. *Entrance requirements:* For master's and doctorate, GRE General Test, minimum GPA of 3.0. Additional exam requirements/recommendations for international students: Required—TOEFL. *Faculty research:* Mathematical statistics, stochastic modeling, spatial statistics, statistical computing.

University of Washington, Graduate School, School of Public Health, Department of Biostatistics, Seattle, WA 98195. Offers biostatistics (MPH, MS, PhD); clinical research (MS), including biostatistics; statistical genetics (PhD). Part-time programs available. *Faculty:* 39 full-time (18 women), 17 part-time/adjunct (7 women). *Students:* 76 full-time (41 women), 2 part-time (1 woman); includes 12 minority (1 Black or African American, non-Hispanic/Latino; 8 Asian, non-Hispanic/Latino; 3 Hispanic/Latino), 28 international. Average age 28. 128 applicants, 41% accepted, 19 enrolled. In 2012, 9 master's, 7 doctorates awarded. Terminal master's awarded for partial completion of doctoral program. *Degree requirements:* For master's, comprehensive exam, thesis, practicum (MPH); for doctorate, comprehensive exam, thesis/dissertation. *Entrance requirements:* For master's and doctorate, GRE General Test, coursework on multivariate calculus, linear algebra and probability; minimum GPA of 3.0. Additional exam requirements/recommendations for international students: Required—TOEFL. *Application deadline:* For fall admission, 1/2 for domestic students. Application fee: $75. Electronic applications accepted. *Financial support:* In 2012–13, 70 research assistantships with full tuition reimbursements (averaging $21,000 per year), 17 teaching assistantships with full tuition reimbursements (averaging $21,000 per year) were awarded; scholarships/grants, traineeships, health care benefits, and tuition waivers (partial) also available. *Faculty research:* Statistical methods for survival data analysis, clinical trials, epidemiological case control and cohort studies, statistical genetics. *Unit* *head:* Dr. Bruce Weir, Department Chair, 206-543-1044. *Application contact:* Alex MacKenzie, Curriculum Coordinator, 206-543-1044, Fax: 206-543-3286, E-mail: alexam@u.washington.edu. Website: http://www.biostat.washington.edu/.

University of Waterloo, Graduate Studies, Faculty of Mathematics, Department of Statistics and Actuarial Science, Waterloo, ON N2L 3G1, Canada. Offers actuarial science (M Math, PhD); biostatistics (PhD); statistics (M Math, PhD); statistics-biostatistics (M Math); statistics-computing (M Math); statistics-finance (M Math). *Degree requirements:* For master's, research paper or thesis; for doctorate, comprehensive exam, thesis/dissertation. *Entrance requirements:* For master's, honors degree in field, minimum B+ average; for doctorate, master's degree, minimum B+ average. Additional exam requirements/recommendations for international students: Required—TOEFL (minimum score 600 paper-based; 90 iBT), TWE (minimum score 4.5). Electronic applications accepted. *Faculty research:* Data analysis, risk theory, inference, stochastic processes, quantitative finance.

The University of Western Ontario, Faculty of Graduate Studies, Physical Sciences Division, Department of Statistical and Actuarial Sciences, London, ON N6A 5B8, Canada. Offers M Sc, PhD. *Degree requirements:* For master's, thesis (for some programs); for doctorate, comprehensive exam, thesis/dissertation. *Entrance requirements:* For master's, honours BA with B+ average. Additional exam requirements/recommendations for international students: Required—TOEFL. *Faculty research:* Statistical theory, statistical applications, probability, actuarial science.

University of Windsor, Faculty of Graduate Studies, Faculty of Science, Department of Mathematics and Statistics, Windsor, ON N9B 3P4, Canada. Offers mathematics (M Sc); statistics (M Sc, PhD). *Degree requirements:* For master's, thesis or alternative; for doctorate, comprehensive exam, thesis/dissertation. *Entrance requirements:* For master's, minimum B average; for doctorate, minimum A average. Additional exam requirements/recommendations for international students: Required—TOEFL (minimum score 560 paper-based). Electronic applications accepted. *Faculty research:* Applied mathematics, operational research, fluid dynamics.

University of Wisconsin–Madison, Graduate School, College of Letters and Science, Department of Statistics, Madison, WI 53706-1380. Offers biometry (MS); statistics (MS, PhD). Part-time programs available. *Degree requirements:* For master's, exam; for doctorate, thesis/dissertation. *Entrance requirements:* For master's and doctorate, GRE. Additional exam requirements/recommendations for international students: Required—TOEFL. Electronic applications accepted. *Expenses:* Tuition, state resident: full-time $10,728; part-time $743 per credit. Tuition, nonresident: full-time $24,054; part-time $1575 per credit. *Required fees:* $1111; $72 per credit. *Faculty research:* Biostatistics, bootstrap and other resampling theory and methods, linear and nonlinear models, nonparametrics, time series and stochastic processes.

University of Wyoming, College of Arts and Sciences, Department of Statistics, Laramie, WY 82070. Offers MS, PhD. Terminal master's awarded for partial completion of doctoral program. *Degree requirements:* For master's, comprehensive exam (for some programs), thesis (for some programs); for doctorate, comprehensive exam, thesis/dissertation. *Entrance requirements:* For master's, GMAT, GRE General Test, minimum GPA of 3.0; for doctorate, GRE General Test, minimum GPA of 3.0. Additional exam requirements/recommendations for international students: Required—TOEFL; Recommended—TWE. Electronic applications accepted. *Faculty research:* Linear models categorical, Baysain, spatial biological sciences and engineering, multivariate.

Utah State University, School of Graduate Studies, College of Science, Department of Mathematics and Statistics, Logan, UT 84322. Offers industrial mathematics (MS); mathematical sciences (PhD); mathematics (M Math, MS); statistics (MS). Part-time programs available. Terminal master's awarded for partial completion of doctoral program. *Degree requirements:* For master's, thesis optional, qualifying exam; for doctorate, one foreign language, comprehensive exam, thesis/dissertation. *Entrance requirements:* For master's and doctorate, GRE General Test, minimum GPA of 3.0. Additional exam requirements/recommendations for international students: Required—TOEFL. *Faculty research:* Differential equations, computational mathematics, dynamical systems, probability and statistics, pure mathematics.

Virginia Commonwealth University, Graduate School, College of Humanities and Sciences, Department of Statistical Sciences and Operations Research, Richmond, VA 23284-9005. Offers operations research (MS); statistics (MS); systems modeling and analysis (PhD). *Entrance requirements:* For master's, GRE General Test, 30 undergraduate credits in mathematics, statistics, or operations research, including calculus I and II, multivariate calculus, linear algebra, probability and statistics. Additional exam requirements/recommendations for international students: Required—TOEFL (minimum score 600 paper-based; 100 iBT); Recommended—IELTS (minimum score 6.5). Electronic applications accepted.

Virginia Polytechnic Institute and State University, Graduate School, College of Science, Blacksburg, VA 24061. Offers biological sciences (MS, PhD); biomedical technology development and management (MS); chemistry (MS, PhD); economics (MA, PhD); geosciences (MS, PhD); mathematics (MS, PhD); physics (MS, PhD); psychology (MS, PhD); statistics (MS, PhD). *Faculty:* 259 full-time (68 women), 3 part-time/adjunct (all women). *Students:* 555 full-time (230 women), 31 part-time (12 women); includes 44 minority (10 Black or African American, non-Hispanic/Latino; 1 American Indian or Alaska Native, non-Hispanic/Latino; 11 Asian, non-Hispanic/Latino; 14 Hispanic/Latino; 8 Two or more races, non-Hispanic/Latino), 250 international. Average age 28. 1,091 applicants, 24% accepted, 137 enrolled. In 2012, 65 master's, 89 doctorates awarded. *Median time to degree:* Of those who began their doctoral program in fall 2004, 68% received their degree in 8 years or less. *Degree requirements:* For master's, comprehensive exam (for some programs), thesis (for some programs); for doctorate, comprehensive exam (for some programs), thesis/dissertation (for some programs). *Entrance requirements:* For master's and doctorate, GRE/GMAT (may vary by department). Additional exam requirements/recommendations for international students: Required—TOEFL (minimum score 550 paper-based). *Application deadline:* For fall admission, 8/1 for domestic students, 4/1 for international students; for spring admission, 1/1 for domestic students, 9/1 for international students. Applications are processed on a rolling basis. Application fee: $65. Electronic applications accepted. *Expenses:* Tuition, state resident: full-time $10,677; part-time $593.25 per credit hour. Tuition, nonresident: full-time $20,926; part-time $1162.50 per credit hour. *Required fees:* $427.75 per semester. Tuition and fees vary according to course load, campus/location and program. *Financial support:* In 2012–13, 1 fellowship with full tuition reimbursement (averaging $21,606 per year), 159 research assistantships with full tuition reimbursements (averaging $19,950 per year), 331 teaching assistantships with full tuition reimbursements (averaging $17,426 per year) were awarded. Financial award application deadline: 3/1; financial award applicants required to submit FAFSA. *Total annual research expenditures:* $23.4 million. *Unit head:* Dr. Lay Nam Chang, Dean, 540-231-5422, Fax: 540-231-3380, E-mail: laynam@vt.edu. *Application contact:* Diane Stearns, Assistant to the Dean, 540-231-7515, Fax: 540-231-3380, E-mail: dstearns@vt.edu. Website: http://www.science.vt.edu/.

Washington University in St. Louis, Graduate School of Arts and Sciences, Department of Mathematics, St. Louis, MO 63130-4899. Offers mathematics (MA, PhD); statistics (MA). Terminal master's awarded for partial completion of doctoral program. *Degree requirements:* For master's, thesis or alternative; for doctorate, thesis/dissertation. *Entrance requirements:* For master's and doctorate, GRE General Test. Electronic applications accepted.

Wayne State University, College of Liberal Arts and Sciences, Department of Mathematics, Detroit, MI 48202. Offers applied mathematics (MA, PhD); mathematical statistics (MA, PhD); mathematics (MA); pure mathematics (PhD). *Students:* 54 full-time (17 women), 34 part-time (14 women); includes 12 minority (9 Black or African American, non-Hispanic/Latino; 3 Asian, non-Hispanic/Latino), 33 international. Average age 31. 120 applicants, 45% accepted, 16 enrolled. In 2012, 17 master's, 7 doctorates awarded. *Degree requirements:* For master's, thesis (for some programs), essays, oral exams; for doctorate, thesis/dissertation, oral exams; French, German, Russian, or Chinese. *Entrance requirements:* For master's, twelve semester credits in mathematics beyond sophomore calculus; for doctorate, master's degree in mathematics or equivalent level of advancement. Additional exam requirements/recommendations for international students: Required—TOEFL (minimum score 550 paper-based; 79 iBT); Recommended—TWE (minimum score 5.5). *Application deadline:* For fall admission, 6/1 priority date for domestic students, 5/1 for international students; for winter admission, 10/1 priority date for domestic students, 9/1 for international students; for spring admission, 2/1 priority date for domestic students, 1/1 for international students. Applications are processed on a rolling basis. Application fee: $50. Electronic applications accepted. *Expenses:* Tuition, state resident: full-time $12,788; part-time $532.85 per credit hour. Tuition, nonresident: full-time $28,243; part-time $1176.80 per credit hour. *Required fees:* $1367.30; $39.75 per credit hour. $206.65 per semester. Tuition and fees vary according to course load and program. *Financial support:* In 2012–13, 43 students received support, including 2 fellowships with tuition reimbursements available (averaging $17,000 per year), 5 research assistantships with tuition reimbursements available (averaging $18,293 per year), 27 teaching assistantships with tuition reimbursements available (averaging $17,391 per year); institutionally sponsored loans, scholarships/grants, health care benefits, tuition waivers (full), and unspecified assistantships also available. Support available to part-time students. *Faculty research:* Harmonic analysis and partial differential equations, group theory and non-commutative ring theory, homotopy theory and applications to topology and geometry, numerical analysis, control and optimization, statistical estimation theory. *Total annual research expenditures:* $1 million. *Unit head:* Dr. Daniel Frohardt, Professor and Chair, 313-577-2479, E-mail: ad0798@wayne.edu. *Application contact:* Dr. Alexander Korostelev, E-mail: apk@math.wayne.edu. Website: http://clasweb.clas.wayne.edu/math.

Western Michigan University, Graduate College, College of Arts and Sciences, Department of Statistics, Kalamazoo, MI 49008. Offers MS, PhD.

West Virginia University, College of Business and Economics, Division of Economics and Finance, Morgantown, WV 26506. Offers business analysis (MA); developmental financial economics (PhD); environmental and resource economics (PhD); international economics (PhD); mathematical economics (MA); monetary economics (PhD); public finance (PhD); public policy (MA); regional and urban economics (PhD); statistics and economics (MA). Terminal master's awarded for partial completion of doctoral program. *Degree requirements:* For master's, thesis optional; for doctorate, comprehensive exam, thesis/dissertation. *Entrance requirements:* For master's and doctorate, GRE General Test, minimum GPA of 3.0; course work in intermediate microeconomics, intermediate

Statistics

macroeconomics, calculus, and statistics. Additional exam requirements/ recommendations for international students: Required—TOEFL. Electronic applications accepted. *Faculty research:* Financial economics, regional/urban development, public economics, international trade/international finance/ development economics, monetary economics.

West Virginia University, Eberly College of Arts and Sciences, Department of Statistics, Morgantown, WV 26506. Offers MS. *Degree requirements:* For master's, comprehensive exam, thesis. *Entrance requirements:* For master's, minimum GPA of 3.0, course work in linear algebra and multivariable calculus. Additional exam requirements/recommendations for international students: Required—TOEFL. *Faculty research:* Linear models, categorical data analysis, statistical computing, experimental design, non parametric analysis.

Yale University, Graduate School of Arts and Sciences, Department of Statistics, New Haven, CT 06520. Offers MA, PhD. Terminal master's awarded for partial completion of doctoral program. *Degree requirements:* For doctorate, thesis/ dissertation. *Entrance requirements:* For doctorate, GRE General Test, GRE Subject Test.

York University, Faculty of Graduate Studies, Faculty of Science and Engineering, Program in Mathematics and Statistics, Toronto, ON M3J 1P3, Canada. Offers industrial and applied mathematics (M Sc); mathematics and statistics (MA, PhD). Part-time programs available. *Degree requirements:* For master's, thesis optional; for doctorate, one foreign language, comprehensive exam, thesis/dissertation. Electronic applications accepted.

Youngstown State University, Graduate School, College of Science, Technology, Engineering and Mathematics, Department of Mathematics and Statistics, Youngstown, OH 44555-0001. Offers applied mathematics (MS); computer science (MS); secondary mathematics (MS); statistics (MS). Part-time programs available. *Degree requirements:* For master's, comprehensive exam, thesis optional. *Entrance requirements:* For master's, minimum GPA of 2.7 in computer science and mathematics. Additional exam requirements/ recommendations for international students: Required—TOEFL. *Faculty research:* Regression analysis, numerical analysis, statistics, Markov chain, topology and fuzzy sets.

376 www.petersonsbooks.com

Peterson's Graduate Programs in the Physical Sciences, Mathematics, Agricultural Sciences, the Environment & Natural Resources 2014

UNIVERSITY OF OKLAHOMA
Department of Mathematics

Programs of Study

While the Mathematics Department at the University of Oklahoma (OU) offers three different graduate degrees—M.S., M.A., and Ph.D.—students are considered to be on either two tracks, the M.S. track or the M.A./Ph.D. track.

The M.A./Ph.D track is the standard program for most students seeking a Ph.D. in mathematics. All students in the program (regardless of their future specialization) need to pass the three Ph.D. qualifying examinations in algebra, analysis, and topology. Each of these exams is associated with a two-semester graduate course sequence that forms the core of the M.A. degree and also count toward the Ph.D. degree. Students who pass all three qualifying examinations can go into the Ph.D. program in one of the following two options.

Ph.D. program (traditional option): This is essentially the same as the M.A./Ph.D. program above. The main difference is that students who already have a master's degree in mathematics may apply directly to this program. Students with a baccalaureate degree apply to the M.A./Ph.D. program and move into to the Ph.D. program on successful completion of the Ph.D. qualifying examinations. The student's ultimate goal in this program is to write and defend a dissertation representing an original contribution to research in mathematics.

Ph.D. program (RUME—research in undergraduate mathematics—option): As is the case with the traditional option, students who already have a master's degree in mathematics may apply to this program, while students with a baccalaureate degree apply to the M.A./Ph.D. program. The student's ultimate goal in this program is to write and defend a dissertation representing an original contribution to research in undergraduate mathematics education.

Students with strong mathematical backgrounds are encouraged to take "free shot" attempts at the Ph.D. qualifying examinations, usually held in August, the week before classes start. These attempts are only offered to students when they first enter the program, and results do not go on the student's record unless they pass.

The M.S. track (Master of Science program) is offered by the Mathematics Department for students who want to pursue studies in mathematics beyond the undergraduate level, but who do not plan to obtain a doctorate in mathematics. Recent graduates of the M.S. program have gone on to careers as actuaries, statistical analysts, and software engineers. Some become mathematics teachers in settings ranging from middle school to two- and four-year colleges. Still others have gone on to obtain doctorates and academic positions in fields other than mathematics, such as economics, mathematics education, and computer science.

Students will be able to select from a broad range of options in pure and applied mathematics and in research in undergraduate mathematics education as they pursue their graduate degree, including: (1) Algebra and Number Theory: algebraic geometry, algebraic groups, combinatorics, modular forms, representation theory (real, p-adic, Lie, automorphic); (2) Analysis: global analysis, harmonic analysis, integrable systems, PDEs, signal processing, spectral theory, wavelets and frames; (3) Applied Mathematics and Mathematical Physics: control theory, dynamical systems, modeling; (4) Geometry: convexity, harmonic maps, Riemannian geometry, group actions, non-negative curvature; (5) RUME: research in undergraduate mathematics education, diversity and equity, international comparative education; (6) Topology: algebraic and geometric topology, dimension theory, geometric group theory, hyperbolic geometry, low-dimensional topology, Teichmuller theory.

Additional information about the University's graduate programs in mathematics can be found at http://math.ou.edu/grad/programs.html.

Research Facilities

Students in the Department have a wide range of facilities and resources to support their study and research efforts. The department maintains two servers, Aftermath and Zeus, both of which run the Linux operating system. The Aftermath server hosts login shells and some software, while Zeus is the primary file server and provides NFS service to workstations throughout the department. The file system is protected by a RAID backup system. The systems manager should be able to recover a user's lost data for up to three or four weeks. There are two workstation clusters for graduate students in the department.

The library's LORA system gives students access to MathSciNet, the definitive database of mathematics literature reviews and bibliographical information (available in BibTeX format); JSTOR, and numerous other online databases and resources from off-campus locations.

Financial Aid

Most students are employed as graduate teaching assistants while earning their degrees. The students' transition into their new roles as educators is facilitated by a lighter course load in the first year and participation in the Department's graduate teaching seminar. Other graduate teaching assistant duties include grading, working in the Mathematics Help Center, and assisting in multisection courses.

In recent years, stipends for graduate teaching assistants who were fully English-language qualified to teach ranged from $15,038 to $16,187. Stipends for graduate teaching assistants who were not fully English-language qualified started at $14,030.

Other opportunities include graduate assistantships. A variable number of teaching assistantships are available for the summer semester in June and July each year, with a stipend of approximately $2500. Several faculty members also provide support for research assistants using funds from research grants. Research assistants usually participate in research-related projects under the supervision of the faculty member.

Further details regarding financial support for graduate students can be found at http://math.ou.edu/grad/finance.html.

Cost of Study

In the 2011–12 academic year, tuition and fees for graduate students totaled $310.55 per credit hour for Oklahoma students and $760.05 per credit hour for nonresident students.

Peterson's Graduate Programs in the Physical Sciences, Mathematics, Agricultural Sciences, the Environment & Natural Resources 2014

www.petersonsbooks.com **377**

Living and Housing Costs

The University offers several on-campus apartment choices. In addition, there are a large number of privately owned apartments, duplexes, and houses available in Norman. Many off-campus housing locations are served by CART, the Cleveland Area Rapid Transit system, which is free for OU students.

Student Group

The OU mathematics graduate program is comprised of about 70 students, representing over a dozen different countries from around the globe. There is an active Mathematics Graduate Student Association which provides guidance and mentoring and organizes various events for graduate students. Additional details about the association can be found online at http://math.ou.edu/~mgsa/.

Location

As part of the dynamic Southwest, Oklahoma benefits from both its rich historic heritage and the vital and modern growth of its metropolitan areas. Although by location a suburb of Oklahoma City, Norman is an independent community with a permanent population of more than 95,000. Norman residents enjoy extensive parks and recreation programs and a 10,000-acre lake and park area. *Money* magazine named Norman as the nation's sixth best place to live in the 2008 edition of its annual rankings.

The University and The Department

The Mathematics Department at the University of Oklahoma has a long and rich academic tradition dating back to the mid-1890s. Students who pursue a graduate degree in mathematics at OU become part of a team that is responsible for the instruction of 10,000–12,000 OU undergraduate students annually. The Department's faculty members strive to maintain a vibrant and collegial research atmosphere and also serve as sources of inspiration, mentoring, and advice. The strong sense of community is enhanced by having faculty, postdoctoral, and student offices, as well as a common room and instructional classrooms, all housed in the same building. Prospective graduate students can experience the Mathematics Department in person during OU MathFest, an annual two-day open house for prospective graduate students. Dates, schedules, and a registration form for MathFest are available at http://www.math.ou.edu/grad/mathfest/2010/ou_mathfest_2010.html.

Applying

Prospective students should submit the Mathematics Department graduate application form online, or may also download, print, and mail the form with the required materials listed below to the Mathematics Department. To ensure full consideration, the complete application and all supporting material needs to be received by the Department by January 31. The Department will forward everything to the Office of Admissions. Applications after this date will be considered, but those received after May 31 are rarely considered. International applicants are subject to the University's April 1 deadline.

In addition to the application form, students must submit official transcripts from all colleges and universities attended, GRE scores, TOEFL scores (if English is not the student's native language), and letters of reference from 3 people familiar with the student's work in mathematics (using the form found at http://math.ou.edu/grad/gradapp/Reference_Request.pdf). While the University's forms indicate an application fee is necessary, the Mathematics Department prescreens all applications and makes qualified applicants an offer; the application fee can be submitted then.

Correspondence and Information

Director of Graduate Studies
University of Oklahoma
Department of Mathematics
601 Elm Street, PHSC 423
Norman, Oklahoma 73019
Phone: 800-522-0772 (toll-free)
E-mail: mathgraddir@ou.edu
Web site: http://www.math.ou.edu

THE FACULTY

The Mathematics Department at the University of Oklahoma has 34 permanent faculty members, 8 visiting faculty members, and a support staff of 6 (including a full-time undergraduate adviser). Virtually all of the department's faculty have active research programs (many externally funded) and regularly publish articles in mathematical journals and participate in conferences around the world.

Additional details regarding the Mathematics Department faculty can be found at http://www.math.ou.edu/people/faculty_research.html.

Students walk to class on the Norman campus.

378 www.petersonsbooks.com

Peterson's Graduate Programs in the Physical Sciences, Mathematics, Agricultural Sciences, the Environment & Natural Resources 2014

WESLEYAN UNIVERSITY
Department of Mathematics and Computer Science

Programs of Study

The Department of Mathematics and Computer Science offers a program of courses and research leading to the degrees of Master of Arts and Doctor of Philosophy.

The Ph.D. degree demands breadth of knowledge, intensive specialization in one field, original contribution to that field, and expository skill. First-year courses are designed to provide a strong foundation in algebra, analysis, and topology. Students have the option to substitute computer science for one of these three. Written preliminary examinations are taken after the first year. During the second year, the student continues with a variety of courses, sampling areas of possible concentration. The student must choose a thesis adviser by the end of the second year and pass the special preliminary examination, which is an oral exam managed by the student's adviser and examination committee, by the end of the third year. Also required is the ability to read mathematics in at least one of the following languages: French, German, and Russian. The usual time required for completion of all requirements for a Ph.D., including the dissertation, is five years.

During their time in the program, most Ph.D. candidates teach one course per year, typically small sections (fewer than 20 students) of calculus.

The M.A. degree is designed to ensure basic knowledge and the capacity for sustained scholarly study; requirements are six semester courses at the graduate level and the writing and oral presentation of a thesis. The thesis requires (at least) independent search and study of the literature.

Students are also involved in a variety of Departmental activities, including seminars and colloquiums. The small size of the program contributes to an atmosphere of informality and accessibility.

The emphasis at Wesleyan is in pure mathematics and theoretical computer science, and most Wesleyan Ph.D.'s have chosen academic careers.

Research Facilities

The Department is housed in the Science Center, where all graduate students and faculty members have offices. Computer facilities are available for both learning and research purposes. The Science Library collection has about 120,000 volumes, with extensive mathematics holdings; there are more than 200 subscriptions to mathematics journals, and approximately sixty new mathematics books arrive each month. The proximity of students and faculty and the daily gatherings at teatime are also key elements of the research environment.

Financial Aid

Each applicant for admission is automatically considered for appointment to an assistantship. For the 2013–14 academic year, a nine-month stipend is $19,494, plus a dependency allowance when appropriate, and an additional three-month stipend of $6,498 is usually available for the student who wishes to remain on campus to study during the summer. Costs of tuition and health fees are borne by the University. All students in good standing are given financial support for the duration of their studies.

Cost of Study

The only academic costs to the student are books and other educational materials.

Living and Housing Costs

The University provides some subsidized housing and assists in finding private housing. The monthly rent of a single student's housing (a private room in a 2- or 4-person house, with common kitchen and living area) is about $640.

Student Group

The number of graduate students in mathematics ranges from 18 to 22, with an entering class of 3 to 5 each year. There have always been both male and female students, graduates of small colleges and large universities, and U.S. and international students, including, in recent years, students from Bulgaria, Chile, China, Germany, India, Iran, Sri Lanka, and Israel.

Location

Middletown, Connecticut, is a small city of 40,000 by the Connecticut River, about 19 miles southeast of Hartford and 25 miles northeast of New Haven, midway between New York and Boston. The University provides many cultural and recreational opportunities, supplemented by those in the countryside and in larger cities nearby.

The University

Founded in 1831, Wesleyan is an independent coeducational institution of liberal arts and sciences, with Ph.D. programs in biology, chemistry, ethnomusicology, mathematics, and physics and master's programs in a number of departments. Current enrollments show about 2,800 undergraduates and 145 graduate students.

Peterson's Graduate Programs in the Physical Sciences, Mathematics, Agricultural Sciences, the Environment & Natural Resources 2014

www.petersonsbooks.com **379**

Wesleyan University

Applying

No specific courses are required for admission, but it is expected that the equivalent of an undergraduate major in mathematics will have been completed. The complete application consists of the application form, transcripts of all previous academic work at or beyond the college level, letters of recommendation from 3 college instructors familiar with the applicant's mathematical ability and performance, and GRE scores (if available). Applications should be submitted by February 15 in order to receive adequate consideration, but requests for admission from outstanding candidates are welcome at any time. Preference is given to Ph.D. candidates.

Correspondence and Information

Department of Mathematics and Computer Science
Graduate Education Committee
Wesleyan University
Middletown, Connecticut 06459-0128
United States
Phone: 860-685-2620
E-mail: ccanalia@wesleyan.edu
Website: http://www.math.wesleyan.edu

THE FACULTY AND THEIR RESEARCH

Professors

Petra Bonfert-Taylor, Ph.D., Berlin Technical. Complex analysis, complex dynamics, geometric function theory, discrete groups.

Wai Kiu Chan, Ph.D., Ohio State. Number theory, quadratic forms.

Karen L. Collins, Ph.D., MIT. Combinatorics.

Adam Fieldsteel, Ph.D., Berkeley. Ergodic theory.

Mark Hovey, Ph.D., MIT. Algebraic topology and homological algebra.

Philip H. Scowcroft, Ph.D., Cornell. Foundations of mathematics, model-theoretic algebra.

Edward C. Taylor, Ph.D., SUNY at Stony Brook. Analysis, low-dimensional geometry and topology.

Associate Professors

David Pollack, Ph.D., Harvard. Number theory, automorphic forms, representation of p-adic groups.

Constance Leidy, Ph.D., Rice. Knot theory, low-dimensional topography.

Assistant Professors

Ilesanmi Adeboye, Ph.D., Michigan. Topology and geometry, Hyperbolic geometry.

David Constantine, Ph.D., Michigan. Riemannian geometry, dynamics, rigidity, homogeneous dynamics, Lie groups, symmetric spaces.

Cameron Hill, Ph.D., Berkeley. Model theory.

Christopher Rasmussen, Ph.D., Arizona. Algebraic geometry.

Professors of Computer Science

Danny Krizanc, Ph.D., Harvard. Theoretical computer science.

Associate Professors of Computer Science

James Lipton, Ph.D., Cornell. Logic and computation, logic programming, type theory, linear logic.

Norman Danner, Ph.D., Indiana Bloomington. Logic, theoretical computer science.

Janet Burge, Ph.D., Worcester Polytechnic. Design rationale, software engineering, artificial intelligence in design, knowledge elicitation.

Assistant Professor of Computer Science

Daniel Licata, Ph.D. Carnegie Mellon. Homotopy type theory, combining type theory, homotopy theory, and category theory.

Professors Emeriti

W. Wistar Comfort, Ph.D., Washington (Seattle). Point-set topology, ultrafilters, set theory, topological groups.

Ethan M. Coven, Ph.D., Yale. Dynamical systems.

Anthony W. Hager, Ph.D., Penn State. Lattice-ordered algebraic structures, general and categorical topology.

Michael S. Keane, Dr.rer.nat, Erlangen-Nuremberg. Ergodic theory, random walks, statistical physics.

F. E. J. Linton, Ph.D., Columbia. Categorical algebra, functorial semantics, topoi.

James D. Reid, Ph.D., Washington (Seattle). Abelian groups, module theory.

Michael Rice, Ph.D., Wesleyan. Parallel computing, formal specification methods.

Lewis C. Robertson, Ph.D., UCLA. Lie groups, topological groups, representation theory.

Robert A. Rosenbaum, Ph.D., Yale. Geometry, mathematics and science education.

Carol Wood, Ph.D., Yale. Mathematical logic, applications of model theory to algebra.

380   www.petersonsbooks.com

Peterson's Graduate Programs in the Physical Sciences, Mathematics, Agricultural Sciences, the Environment & Natural Resources 2014

ACADEMIC AND PROFESSIONAL PROGRAMS IN THE AGRICULTURAL SCIENCES

Section 8
Agricultural and Food Sciences

This section contains a directory of institutions offering graduate work in agricultural and food sciences. Additional information about programs listed in the directory may be obtained by writing directly to the dean of a graduate school or chair of a department at the address given in the directory.

For programs offering related work, see also in this book *Natural Resources.* In the other guides in this series:

Graduate Programs in the Humanities, Arts & Social Sciences

See *Architecture (Landscape Architecture)* and *Economics (Agricultural Economics and Agribusiness)*

Graduate Programs in the Biological/Biomedical Sciences & Health-Related Medical Professions

See *Biological and Biomedical Sciences; Botany and Plant Biology; Ecology, Environmental Biology, and Evolutionary Biology; Entomology; Genetics, Developmental Biology, and Reproductive Biology; Nutrition; Pathology and Pathobiology; Physiology; Veterinary Medicine and Sciences;* and *Zoology*

Graduate Programs in Engineering & Applied Sciences

See *Agricultural Engineering and Bioengineering* and *Biomedical Engineering and Biotechnology*

Graduate Programs in Business, Education, Information Studies, Law & Social Work

See *Education (Agricultural Education)*

CONTENTS

Program Directories

Agricultural Sciences—General

Alabama Agricultural and Mechanical University, School of Graduate Studies, College of Agricultural, Life and Natural Sciences, Huntsville, AL 35811. Offers MS, MURP, PhD. Part-time and evening/weekend programs available. Terminal master's awarded for partial completion of doctoral program. *Degree requirements:* For doctorate, one foreign language, thesis/dissertation. *Entrance requirements:* For master's, GRE General Test; for doctorate, GRE General Test, MS. Additional exam requirements/recommendations for international students: Required—TOEFL (minimum score 500 paper-based; 61 iBT). Electronic applications accepted. *Faculty research:* Remote sensing, environmental pollutants, food biotechnology, plant growth.

Alcorn State University, School of Graduate Studies, School of Agriculture and Applied Science, Alcorn State, MS 39096-7500. Offers agricultural economics (MS Ag); agronomy (MS Ag); animal science (MS Ag). *Degree requirements:* For master's, thesis optional. *Faculty research:* Aquatic systems, dairy herd improvement, fruit production, alternative farming practices.

Angelo State University, College of Graduate Studies, College of Arts and Sciences, Department of Agriculture, San Angelo, TX 76909. Offers animal science (MS). Part-time and evening/weekend programs available. *Students:* 11 full-time (4 women), 11 part-time (6 women); includes 1 minority (Hispanic/Latino). Average age 23. 9 applicants, 78% accepted, 7 enrolled. In 2012, 11 master's awarded. *Degree requirements:* For master's, comprehensive exam, thesis optional. *Entrance requirements:* For master's, GRE General Test, essay. Additional exam requirements/recommendations for international students: Required—TOEFL or IELTS. *Application deadline:* For fall admission, 7/15 priority date for domestic students, 6/10 for international students; for spring admission, 12/1 priority date for domestic students, 11/1 for international students. Applications are processed on a rolling basis. Application fee: $40 ($50 for international students). Electronic applications accepted. *Financial support:* In 2012–13, 10 students received support, including 11 research assistantships (averaging $7,490 per year); Federal Work-Study, scholarships/grants, and unspecified assistantships also available. Support available to part-time students. Financial award application deadline: 3/1. *Faculty research:* Effect of protein and energy on feedlot performance, bitterweed toxicosis in sheep, meat laboratory, North Concho Watershed Project, baseline vegetation. *Unit head:* Dr. Micheal Salisbury, Department Head, 325-942-2027 Ext. 227, E-mail: mike.salisbury@angelo.edu. *Application contact:* Dr. Cody B. Scott, Graduate Advisor, 325-942-2027 Ext. 284, E-mail: cody.scott@angelo.edu. Website: http://www.angelo.edu/dept/agriculture/.

Arkansas State University, Graduate School, College of Agriculture and Technology, Jonesboro, State University, AR 72467. Offers agricultural education (SCCT); agriculture (MSA); vocational-technical administration (SCCT). Part-time programs available. *Faculty:* 15 full-time (3 women). *Students:* 10 full-time (7 women), 16 part-time (7 women); includes 6 minority (5 Black or African American, non-Hispanic/Latino; 1 Hispanic/Latino), 5 international. Average age 35. 16 applicants, 63% accepted, 7 enrolled. In 2012, 19 master's awarded. *Degree requirements:* For master's, comprehensive exam, thesis or alternative; for SCCT, comprehensive exam. *Entrance requirements:* For master's, GRE General Test or MAT, appropriate bachelor's degree, official transcripts, immunization records; for SCCT, GRE General Test or MAT, interview, master's degree, official transcript, immunization records. Additional exam requirements/recommendations for international students: Required—TOEFL (minimum score 550 paper-based; 79 iBT), IELTS (minimum score 6), Pearson Test of English (minimum score 56). *Application deadline:* For fall admission, 7/1 for domestic and international students; for spring admission, 11/15 for domestic students, 11/14 for international students. Applications are processed on a rolling basis. Application fee: $30 ($40 for international students). Electronic applications accepted. *Expenses:* Tuition, state resident: full-time $4140; part-time $230 per credit hour. Tuition, nonresident: full-time $8280; part-time $460 per credit hour. *Required fees:* $56 per credit hour. $25 per term. Tuition and fees vary according to course load and program. *Financial support:* In 2012–13, 2 students received support. Teaching assistantships, career-related internships or fieldwork, scholarships/grants, and unspecified assistantships available. Financial award application deadline: 7/1; financial award applicants required to submit FAFSA. *Unit head:* Dr. Donald Kennedy, Interim Dean, 870-972-2085, Fax: 870-972-3885, E-mail: dkennedy@astate.edu. *Application contact:* Vickey Ring, Graduate Admissions Coordinator, 870-972-3029, Fax: 870-972-3857, E-mail: vickeyring@astate.edu. Website: http://www.astate.edu/college/agriculture-and-technology.

Auburn University, Graduate School, College of Agriculture, Auburn University, AL 36849. Offers M Ag, M Aq, MS, PhD. Part-time programs available. *Faculty:* 109 full-time (24 women), 10 part-time/adjunct (1 woman). *Students:* 134 full-time (57 women), 147 part-time (62 women); includes 22 minority (11 Black or African American, non-Hispanic/Latino; 7 Asian, non-Hispanic/Latino; 4 Hispanic/Latino), 122 international. Average age 29. 232 applicants, 51% accepted, 72 enrolled. In 2012, 38 master's, 20 doctorates awarded. *Degree requirements:* For doctorate, thesis/dissertation. *Entrance requirements:* For master's and doctorate, GRE General Test. *Application deadline:* For fall admission, 7/7 for domestic students; for spring admission, 11/24 for domestic students. Applications are processed on a rolling basis. Application fee: $50 ($60 for international students). Electronic applications accepted. *Expenses:* Tuition, state resident: full-time $7866; part-time $437 per credit. Tuition, nonresident: full-time $23,598; part-time $1311 per credit. *Required fees:* $787 per semester. Tuition and fees vary according to degree level and program. *Financial support:* Fellowships, research assistantships, teaching assistantships, and Federal Work-Study available. Support available to part-time students. Financial award application deadline: 3/15; financial award applicants required to submit FAFSA. *Unit head:* William Batchelor, Dean, 334-844-2345. *Application contact:* Dr. George Flowers, Dean of the Graduate School, 334-844-2125. Website: http://www.ag.auburn.edu/.

Brigham Young University, Graduate Studies, College of Life Sciences, Provo, UT 84602-1001. Offers MPH, MS, PhD. *Faculty:* 128 full-time (17 women), 3 part-time/adjunct (1 woman). *Students:* 248 full-time (112 women), 9 part-time (5 women); includes 48 minority (2 American Indian or Alaska Native, non-Hispanic/Latino; 22 Asian, non-Hispanic/Latino; 19 Hispanic/Latino; 3 Native Hawaiian or other Pacific Islander, non-Hispanic/Latino; 2 Two or more races, non-Hispanic/Latino), 7 international. Average age 27. 186 applicants, 49% accepted, 78 enrolled. In 2012, 57 master's, 7 doctorates awarded. *Degree requirements:* For master's, comprehensive exam, thesis, prospectus. defense of research, defense of thesis; for doctorate, comprehensive exam, thesis/dissertation, prospectus, defense of research, defense of dissertation. *Entrance requirements:* For master's, GRE General Test, minimum GPA of 3.0 for last 60 hours of course work; for doctorate, GRE General Test, GRE Subject Test (biology), minimum GPA of 3.0 for last 60 hours of course work. Additional exam requirements/recommendations for international students: Required—TOEFL (minimum score 580 paper-based; 85 iBT), IELTS. *Application deadline:* For fall admission, 2/1 for domestic and international students. Application fee: $50. Electronic applications accepted. *Expenses: Tuition:* Full-time $5950; part-time $331 per credit hour. Tuition and fees vary according to program and student's religious affiliation. *Financial support:* In 2012–13, 220 students received support, including 35 fellowships with full and partial tuition reimbursements available (averaging $8,200 per year), 27 research assistantships with full and partial tuition reimbursements available (averaging $11,846 per year), 21 teaching assistantships with full and partial tuition reimbursements available (averaging $13,468 per year); career-related internships or fieldwork, institutionally sponsored loans, scholarships/grants, tuition waivers (full and partial), and unspecified assistantships also available. Financial award application deadline: 2/1. *Total annual research expenditures:* $4.5 million. *Unit head:* Dr. Rodney J. Brown, Dean, 801-422-3963, Fax: 801-422-0050. *Application contact:* Sue Pratley, Application Contact, 801-422-3963, Fax: 801-422-0050, E-mail: sue_pratley@byu.edu. Website: http://lifesciences.byu.edu/home/.

California Polytechnic State University, San Luis Obispo, College of Agriculture, Food and Environmental Sciences, Program in Agriculture, San Luis Obispo, CA 93407. Offers MS. Part-time programs available. *Faculty:* 18 full-time (7 women). *Students:* 21 full-time (16 women), 26 part-time (17 women); includes 12 minority (1 Black or African American, non-Hispanic/Latino; 1 American Indian or Alaska Native, non-Hispanic/Latino; 4 Asian, non-Hispanic/Latino; 5 Hispanic/Latino; 1 Native Hawaiian or other Pacific Islander, non-Hispanic/Latino), 2 international. Average age 27. 61 applicants, 25% accepted, 9 enrolled. In 2012, 23 master's awarded. *Degree requirements:* For master's, comprehensive exam, thesis. *Entrance requirements:* For master's, GRE, minimum GPA of 2.75 in last 90 quarter units of course work. Additional exam requirements/recommendations for international students: Required—TOEFL (minimum score 550 paper-based) or IELTS (minimum score 6). *Application deadline:* For fall admission, 4/1 for domestic students, 11/30 for international students; for winter admission, 10/1 for domestic students, 6/30 for international students; for spring admission, 10/1 for domestic students. Applications are processed on a rolling basis. Application fee: $55. Electronic applications accepted. *Expenses:* Tuition, state resident: full-time $6738; part-time $3906 per year. Tuition, nonresident: full-time $17,898; part-time $8370 per year. *Required fees:* $3051; $874 per term. One-time fee: $3051 full-time; $2622 part-time. *Financial support:* Fellowships, research assistantships, teaching assistantships, career-related internships or fieldwork, Federal Work-Study, institutionally sponsored loans, scholarships/grants, and unspecified assistantships available. Support available to part-time students. Financial award application deadline: 3/2; financial award applicants required to submit FAFSA. *Faculty research:* Sustainability; specialty crops; dairy products technology; irrigation training; recreation, parks, and tourism management. *Unit head:* Dr. Mark Shelton, Associate Dean/Graduate Coordinator, 805-756-2161, Fax: 805-756-6577, E-mail: mshelton@calpoly.edu.

California State Polytechnic University, Pomona, Academic Affairs, College of Agriculture, Pomona, CA 91768-2557. Offers MS. Part-time programs available. *Faculty:* 35 full-time (15 women), 25 part-time/adjunct (21 women). *Students:* 15 full-time (12 women), 34 part-time (28 women); includes 19 minority (3 Black or African American, non-Hispanic/Latino; 7 Asian, non-Hispanic/Latino; 8 Hispanic/Latino; 1 Native Hawaiian or other Pacific Islander, non-Hispanic/Latino), 4 international. Average age 29. 92 applicants, 37% accepted, 27 enrolled. In 2012, 18 master's awarded. *Degree requirements:* For master's, thesis or alternative. *Application deadline:* For fall admission, 5/1 priority date for domestic students; for winter admission, 10/15 priority date for domestic students; for spring admission,

384 www.petersonsbooks.com

Peterson's Graduate Programs in the Physical Sciences, Mathematics, Agricultural Sciences, the Environment & Natural Resources 2014

1/2 priority date for domestic students. Applications are processed on a rolling basis. Application fee: $55. Electronic applications accepted. *Financial support:* Career-related internships or fieldwork, Federal Work-Study, and institutionally sponsored loans available. Support available to part-time students. Financial award application deadline: 3/2; financial award applicants required to submit FAFSA. *Faculty research:* Equine nutrition, physiology, and reproduction; leadership development; bioartificial pancreas; plant science; ruminant and human nutrition. *Unit head:* Dr. Lester C. Young, Dean, 909-869-2203, E-mail: lcyoung@csupomona.edu. *Application contact:* Dan Hostetler, Chair/Professor, 909-869-2189, Fax: 909-869-5036, E-mail: dghostetler@csupomona.edu. Website: http://www.csupomona.edu/~agri/.

Clemson University, Graduate School, College of Agriculture, Forestry and Life Sciences, Clemson, SC 29634. Offers M Ag Ed, MBS, MFR, MS, PhD. Part-time programs available. Postbaccalaureate distance learning degree programs offered. *Faculty:* 153 full-time (46 women), 21 part-time/adjunct (8 women). *Students:* 276 full-time (149 women), 122 part-time (68 women); includes 90 minority (13 Black or African American, non-Hispanic/Latino; 9 Asian, non-Hispanic/Latino; 9 Hispanic/Latino; 59 Two or more races, non-Hispanic/Latino), 97 international. Average age 30. 481 applicants, 34% accepted, 121 enrolled. In 2012, 84 master's, 34 doctorates awarded. Terminal master's awarded for partial completion of doctoral program. *Degree requirements:* For master's, thesis (for some programs); for doctorate, thesis/dissertation. *Entrance requirements:* For master's and doctorate, GRE General Test. Additional exam requirements/recommendations for international students: Required—TOEFL. *Application deadline:* For fall admission, 4/15 for domestic and international students; for spring admission, 10/1 for domestic students, 9/15 for international students. Applications are processed on a rolling basis. Application fee: $70 ($80 for international students). Electronic applications accepted. *Expenses:* Contact institution. *Financial support:* In 2012–13, 236 students received support, including 32 fellowships with full and partial tuition reimbursements available (averaging $8,042 per year), 131 research assistantships with partial tuition reimbursements available (averaging $15,062 per year), 115 teaching assistantships with partial tuition reimbursements available (averaging $14,714 per year); career-related internships or fieldwork, Federal Work-Study, institutionally sponsored loans, scholarships/grants, and unspecified assistantships also available. Financial award applicants required to submit FAFSA. *Total annual research expenditures:* $10.9 million. *Unit head:* Dr. Thomas Scott, Dean, 864-656-7592, Fax: 864-656-1286. *Application contact:* Dr. Joseph Culin, Associate Dean for Research and Graduate Studies, 864-656-2810, E-mail: jculin@clemson.edu. Website: http://www.clemson.edu/cafls/.

Colorado State University, Graduate School, College of Agricultural Sciences, Fort Collins, CO 80523-1101. Offers M Agr, MLA, MS, PhD. Part-time and evening/weekend programs available. Postbaccalaureate distance learning degree programs offered (no on-campus study). *Faculty:* 106 full-time (22 women), 1 part-time/adjunct (0 women). *Students:* 144 full-time (82 women), 225 part-time (120 women); includes 29 minority (9 Black or African American, non-Hispanic/Latino; 1 American Indian or Alaska Native, non-Hispanic/Latino; 1 Asian, non-Hispanic/Latino; 13 Hispanic/Latino; 5 Two or more races, non-Hispanic/Latino), 53 international. Average age 32. 279 applicants, 67% accepted, 103 enrolled. In 2012, 71 master's, 17 doctorates awarded. *Degree requirements:* For master's, thesis (for some programs); for doctorate, comprehensive exam (for some programs), thesis/dissertation. *Entrance requirements:* For master's and doctorate, GRE General Test, minimum GPA of 3.0, 3 letters of recommendation, bachelor's degree. Additional exam requirements/recommendations for international students: Recommended—TOEFL (minimum score 550 paper-based). *Application deadline:* For fall admission, 7/1 for domestic and international students; for spring admission, 1/1 for domestic and international students. Applications are processed on a rolling basis. Application fee: $50. Electronic applications accepted. *Expenses:* Tuition, state resident: full-time $8811; part-time $490 per credit. Tuition, nonresident: full-time $21,600; part-time $1200 per credit. *Required fees:* $1819; $61 per credit. *Financial support:* In 2012–13, 134 students received support, including 17 fellowships (averaging $35,696 per year), 90 research assistantships (averaging $14,398 per year), 27 teaching assistantships (averaging $10,050 per year); scholarships/grants and unspecified assistantships also available. Financial award applicants required to submit FAFSA. *Faculty research:* Systems methodology, biotechnology, plant and animal breeding, water management, plant protection. *Total annual research expenditures:* $9.9 million. *Unit head:* Dr. Craig Beyrouty, Dean, 970-491-6274, Fax: 970-491-4895, E-mail: craig.beyrouty@colostate.edu. *Application contact:* Pam Schell, Administrative Assistant, 970-491-2410, Fax: 970-491-4895, E-mail: pam.schell@colostate.edu. Website: http://home.agsci.colostate.edu/.

Dalhousie University, Faculty of Agriculture, Halifax, NS B3H 4R2, Canada. Offers agriculture (M Sc), including air quality, animal behavior, animal molecular genetics, animal nutrition, animal technology, aquaculture, botany, crop management, crop physiology, ecology, environmental microbiology, food science, horticulture, nutrient management, pest management, physiology, plant biotechnology, plant pathology, soil chemistry, soil fertility, waste management and composting, water quality. Part-time programs available. *Degree requirements:* For master's, thesis, ATC Exam Teaching Assistantship. *Entrance requirements:* For master's, honors B Sc, minimum GPA of 3.0. Additional exam requirements/recommendations for international students: Required—TOEFL (minimum score 580 paper-based; 92 iBT), IELTS, Michigan English Language Assessment Battery, CanTEST, CAEL. *Faculty research:* Bio-product development, organic agriculture, nutrient management, air and water quality, agricultural biotechnology.

Illinois State University, Graduate School, College of Applied Science and Technology, Department of Agriculture, Normal, IL 61790-2200. Offers agribusiness (MS). *Degree requirements:* For master's, thesis optional. *Entrance requirements:* For master's, GRE General Test, minimum GPA of 3.0 in last 60 hours. *Faculty research:* Engineering-economic system models for rural ethanol production facilities, development and evaluation of a propane-fueled, production scale, on-site thermal destruction system C-FAR 2007; field scale evaluation and technology transfer of economically, ecologically systems; sound liquid swine manure treatment and application.

Instituto Tecnológico y de Estudios Superiores de Monterrey, Campus Monterrey, Graduate and Research Division, Program in Agriculture, Monterrey, Mexico. Offers agricultural parasitology (PhD); agricultural sciences (MS); farming productivity (MS); food processing engineering (MS); phytopathology (MS). Part-time programs available. *Degree requirements:* For master's, one foreign language, thesis; for doctorate, one foreign language, thesis/dissertation. *Entrance requirements:* For master's, EXADEP; for doctorate, GMAT or GRE, master's degree in related field. Additional exam requirements/recommendations for international students: Required—TOEFL. *Faculty research:* Animal embryos and reproduction, crop entomology, tropical agriculture, agricultural productivity, induced mutation in oleaginous plants.

Iowa State University of Science and Technology, Program in Sustainable Agriculture, Ames, IA 50011. Offers MS, PhD. *Entrance requirements:* For master's and doctorate, GRE General Test. Additional exam requirements/recommendations for international students: Required—TOEFL (minimum score 570 paper-based; 80 iBT), IELTS (minimum score 6.5). *Application deadline:* For fall admission, 2/1 for domestic and international students; for spring admission, 6/1 priority date for domestic students, 6/1 for international students. Application fee: $60 ($90 for international students). Electronic applications accepted. *Application contact:* Charles Sauer, Application Contact, 515-294-6518, Fax: 515-294-6390, E-mail: gpsa@iastate.edu. Website: http://www.sust.ag.iastate.edu/gpsa/application.html.

Kansas State University, Graduate School, College of Agriculture, Manhattan, KS 66506. Offers MAB, MS, PhD. Part-time programs available. Postbaccalaureate distance learning degree programs offered (minimal on-campus study). *Faculty:* 172 full-time (37 women), 45 part-time/adjunct (4 women). *Students:* 303 full-time (136 women), 213 part-time (104 women); includes 45 minority (10 Black or African American, non-Hispanic/Latino; 2 American Indian or Alaska Native, non-Hispanic/Latino; 11 Asian, non-Hispanic/Latino; 17 Hispanic/Latino; 5 Two or more races, non-Hispanic/Latino), 151 international. Average age 30. 383 applicants, 38% accepted, 88 enrolled. In 2012, 101 master's, 29 doctorates awarded. Terminal master's awarded for partial completion of doctoral program. *Degree requirements:* For doctorate, thesis/dissertation. *Entrance requirements:* For master's, GRE, minimum undergraduate GPA of 3.0; for doctorate, GRE, minimum undergraduate GPA of 3.5. Additional exam requirements/recommendations for international students: Required—TOEFL (minimum score 550 paper-based). *Application deadline:* For fall admission, 2/1 priority date for domestic students, 2/1 for international students; for spring admission, 8/1 priority date for domestic students, 8/1 for international students. Applications are processed on a rolling basis. Application fee: $50 ($75 for international students). Electronic applications accepted. *Financial support:* In 2012–13, 258 research assistantships (averaging $20,435 per year), 29 teaching assistantships (averaging $18,437 per year) were awarded; career-related internships or fieldwork, Federal Work-Study, institutionally sponsored loans, scholarships/grants, and tuition waivers (partial) also available. Support available to part-time students. Financial award application deadline: 3/1; financial award applicants required to submit FAFSA. *Total annual research expenditures:* $26.1 million. *Unit head:* Dr. John Floros, Dean, 785-532-7137, Fax: 785-532-6897, E-mail: floros@ksu.edu. *Application contact:* Shannon Fox, Administrative Assistant, 785-532-6191, Fax: 785-532-2983, E-mail: grad@ksu.edu. Website: http://www.kstateag@k-state.edu.

Louisiana State University and Agricultural and Mechanical College, Graduate School, College of Agriculture, Baton Rouge, LA 70803. Offers M App St, MS, MSBAE, PhD. Part-time programs available. *Students:* 293 full-time (134 women), 55 part-time (30 women); includes 31 minority (16 Black or African American, non-Hispanic/Latino; 5 Asian, non-Hispanic/Latino; 7 Hispanic/Latino; 3 Two or more races, non-Hispanic/Latino), 161 international. Average age 30. 222 applicants, 36% accepted, 74 enrolled. In 2012, 115 master's, 36 doctorates awarded. Terminal master's awarded for partial completion of doctoral program. *Degree requirements:* For doctorate, thesis/dissertation. *Entrance requirements:* For master's and doctorate, GRE General Test, minimum GPA of 3.0. Additional exam requirements/recommendations for international students: Required—TOEFL (minimum score 550 paper-based; 79 iBT) or IELTS (minimum score 6.5). *Application deadline:* For fall admission, 5/15 for domestic and international students; for spring admission, 10/15 for domestic and international students. Applications are processed on a rolling basis. Application fee: $50 ($70 for international students). Electronic applications accepted. *Financial support:* In 2012–13, 313 students received support, including 4 fellowships with full tuition reimbursements available (averaging $15,996 per year), 225 research assistantships with partial tuition reimbursements available (averaging $18,046 per year), 37 teaching assistantships with partial tuition reimbursements available (averaging $12,231 per year); career-related internships or fieldwork, Federal

Work-Study, institutionally sponsored loans, health care benefits, tuition waivers (full), and unspecified assistantships also available. Support available to part-time students. Financial award applicants required to submit FAFSA. *Faculty research:* Biotechnology, resource economics and marketing, aquaculture, food science and technology. *Total annual research expenditures:* $420,504. *Unit head:* Dr. Kenneth Koonce, Dean, 225-578-2362, Fax: 225-578-2526, E-mail: kkoonce@lsu.edu. *Application contact:* Paula Beecher, Recruiting Coordinator, 225-578-2468, E-mail: pbeeche@lsu.edu. Website: http://www.coa.lsu.edu/.

McGill University, Faculty of Graduate and Postdoctoral Studies, Faculty of Agricultural and Environmental Sciences, Montréal, QC H3A 2T5, Canada. Offers M Sc, M Sc A, PhD, Certificate, Graduate Diploma.

McNeese State University, Doré School of Graduate Studies, College of Science, Dripps Department of Agricultural Sciences, Program in Environmental and Chemical Sciences, Lake Charles, LA 70609. Offers agricultural sciences (MS); environmental science (MS). Evening/weekend programs available. *Students:* 17 full-time (11 women), 9 part-time (4 women); includes 4 minority (3 Black or African American, non-Hispanic/Latino; 1 American Indian or Alaska Native, non-Hispanic/Latino), 1 international. In 2012, 18 master's awarded. *Degree requirements:* For master's, comprehensive exam, thesis or alternative. *Entrance requirements:* For master's, GRE. *Application deadline:* For fall admission, 5/15 priority date for domestic students, 5/15 for international students; for spring admission, 10/15 priority date for domestic students, 10/15 for international students. Applications are processed on a rolling basis. Application fee: $20 ($30 for international students). *Expenses:* Tuition, state resident: full-time $4287; part-time $587 per credit hour. *Required fees:* $1177. Tuition and fees vary according to course load. *Financial support:* Application deadline: 5/1. *Unit head:* Dr. Frederick LeMieux, Department Head, 337-475-5690, Fax: 337-475-5699, E-mail: flemieux@mcneese.edu.

Michigan State University, The Graduate School, College of Agriculture and Natural Resources, East Lansing, MI 48824. Offers MA, MIPS, MS, MURP, PhD. *Faculty research:* Plant science, animal sciences, forestry, fisheries and wildlife, recreation and tourism.

Mississippi State University, College of Agriculture and Life Sciences, Department of Animal Dairy Sciences, Mississippi State, MS 39762. Offers agricultural life sciences (MS), including animal physiology (MS, PhD), genetics (MS, PhD); agricultural science (PhD), including animal dairy sciences, animal nutrition (MS, PhD); agriculture (MS), including animal nutrition (MS, PhD), animal science; life sciences (PhD), including animal physiology (MS, PhD), genetics (MS, PhD). *Faculty:* 11 full-time (5 women). *Students:* 22 full-time (15 women), 15 part-time (8 women); includes 3 minority (2 Black or African American, non-Hispanic/Latino; 1 Hispanic/Latino), 8 international. Average age 30. 22 applicants, 45% accepted, 8 enrolled. In 2012, 9 master's, 2 doctorates awarded. *Degree requirements:* For master's, comprehensive exam (for some programs), thesis, written proposal of intended research area; for doctorate, comprehensive exam, thesis/dissertation, written proposal of intended research area. *Entrance requirements:* For master's, GRE General Test, minimum GPA of 3.0; for doctorate, GRE General Test. Additional exam requirements/recommendations for international students: Required—TOEFL (minimum score 575 paper-based; 84 iBT), IELTS (minimum score 7). *Application deadline:* For fall admission, 7/1 for domestic students, 5/1 for international students; for spring admission, 11/1 for domestic students, 9/1 for international students. Applications are processed on a rolling basis. Application fee: $60. Electronic applications accepted. *Financial support:* In 2012–13, 12 research assistantships (averaging $11,261 per year), 1 teaching assistantship (averaging $10,014 per year) were awarded; Federal Work-Study, institutionally sponsored loans, and unspecified assistantships also available. Financial award application deadline: 4/1; financial award applicants required to submit FAFSA. *Faculty research:* Ecology and population dynamics, physiology, biochemistry and behavior, systematics. *Unit head:* Dr. John Blanton, Interim Department Head, 662-325-2802, Fax: 662-325-8873, E-mail: jblanton@ads.msstate.edu. *Application contact:* Dr. Brian Rude, Professor and Graduate Coordinator, 662-325-2802, Fax: 662-325-8873, E-mail: brude@ads.msstate.edu. Website: http://www.ads.msstate.edu/.

Mississippi State University, College of Agriculture and Life Sciences, Department of Biochemistry, Molecular Biology, Entomology and Plant Pathology, Mississippi State, MS 39762. Offers agriculture life sciences (MS), including biochemistry (MS, PhD), entomology (MS, PhD), plant pathology (MS, PhD); life science (PhD), including biochemistry (MS, PhD), entomology (MS, PhD), plant pathology (MS, PhD); molecular biology (PhD). *Faculty:* 25 full-time (1 woman). *Students:* 44 full-time (18 women), 13 part-time (8 women); includes 5 minority (4 Black or African American, non-Hispanic/Latino; 1 Hispanic/Latino), 18 international. Average age 29. 42 applicants, 26% accepted, 9 enrolled. In 2012, 9 master's, 4 doctorates awarded. Terminal master's awarded for partial completion of doctoral program. *Degree requirements:* For master's, thesis (for some programs), final oral exam; for doctorate, thesis/dissertation, preliminary oral and written exam. *Entrance requirements:* For master's, GRE General Test, minimum GPA of 2.75; for doctorate, GRE. Additional exam requirements/recommendations for international students: Required—TOEFL (minimum score 500 paper-based; 61 iBT); Recommended—IELTS (minimum score 5.5). *Application deadline:* For fall admission, 7/1 for domestic students, 5/1 for international students; for spring admission, 11/1 for domestic students, 9/1 for international students. Applications are processed on a rolling basis. Application fee: $60. Electronic applications accepted. *Financial support:* In 2012–13, 39 research assistantships with full tuition reimbursements (averaging $16,268 per year) were awarded; Federal Work-Study, institutionally sponsored loans, and unspecified assistantships also available. Financial award application deadline: 4/1; financial award applicants required to submit FAFSA. *Faculty research:* Fish nutrition, plant and animal molecular biology, plant biochemistry, enzymology, lipid metabolism, chromatin, cell wall synthesis in rice, a model grass bioenergy species and the source of rice stover residues, using reverse genetic and functional genomic and proteomic approaches. *Unit head:* Dr. Scott T. Willard, Professor and Department Head, 662-325-2640, Fax: 662-325-8664, E-mail: swilliard@ads.msstate.edu. *Application contact:* Dr. Din-Pow Ma, Professor/Graduate Coordinator, 662-325-7739, Fax: 662-325-8664, E-mail: dm1@ra.msstate.edu. Website: http://www.biochemistry.msstate.edu.

Mississippi State University, College of Agriculture and Life Sciences, Department of Plant and Soil Sciences, Mississippi State, MS 39762. Offers agriculture (MS, PhD); including agronomy, horticulture, weed science. *Faculty:* 26 full-time (1 woman), 1 part-time/adjunct (0 women). *Students:* 49 full-time (18 women), 22 part-time (7 women); includes 5 minority (2 Black or African American, non-Hispanic/Latino; 2 American Indian or Alaska Native, non-Hispanic/Latino; 1 Asian, non-Hispanic/Latino), 16 international. Average age 31. 49 applicants, 35% accepted, 16 enrolled. In 2012, 6 master's, 4 doctorates awarded. *Degree requirements:* For master's, comprehensive exam, thesis, oral and/or written exams; for doctorate, comprehensive exam, thesis/dissertation, minimum 20 semester hours of research for dissertation. *Entrance requirements:* For master's, GRE (weed science), minimum GPA of 2.75 (agronomy/horticulture), 3.0 (weed science); for doctorate, GRE (weed science), minimum GPA of 3.0 (agronomy/horticulture), 3.25 (weed science). Additional exam requirements/recommendations for international students: Required—TOEFL (minimum score 500 paper-based; 61 iBT), TOEFL (minimum score 550 paper-based, 79 iBT) or IELTS (minimum score 6.5) for weed science; Recommended—IELTS (minimum score 5.5). *Application deadline:* For fall admission, 7/1 for domestic students, 5/1 for international students; for spring admission, 10/1 for domestic students, 9/1 for international students. Applications are processed on a rolling basis. Application fee: $60. Electronic applications accepted. *Financial support:* In 2012–13, 35 research assistantships (averaging $14,968 per year), 3 teaching assistantships (averaging $14,315 per year) were awarded; Federal Work-Study, institutionally sponsored loans, scholarships/grants, and unspecified assistantships also available. Financial award application deadline: 4/1; financial award applicants required to submit FAFSA. *Unit head:* Dr. J. Mike Phillips, Professor and Head, 662-325-2311, Fax: 662-325-8742, E-mail: jmp657@msstate.edu. *Application contact:* Dr. William Kingery, Graduate Coordinator, 662-325-2748, Fax: 662-325-8742, E-mail: wkingery@pss.msstate.edu. Website: http://www.pss.msstate.edu/.

Mississippi State University, College of Agriculture and Life Sciences, Department of Poultry Science, Mississippi State, MS 39762. Offers agricultural sciences (PhD), including poultry science (MS, PhD); agriculture (MS), including poultry science (MS, PhD); animal physiology (MS, PhD); genetics (MS, PhD). *Faculty:* 1 full-time (0 women). *Students:* 7 full-time (3 women), 1 (woman) part-time; includes 1 minority (Asian, non-Hispanic/Latino), 5 international. Average age 28. 17 applicants, 12% accepted, 2 enrolled. In 2012, 2 master's, 1 doctorate awarded. *Degree requirements:* For master's, comprehensive exam, thesis optional; for doctorate, comprehensive exam, thesis/dissertation. *Entrance requirements:* Additional exam requirements/recommendations for international students: Required—TOEFL (minimum score 477 paper-based; 53 iBT); Recommended—IELTS (minimum score 4.5). *Application deadline:* For fall admission, 7/1 for domestic students, 5/1 for international students; for spring admission, 10/1 for domestic students, 11/1 for international students. Applications are processed on a rolling basis. Application fee: $60. Electronic applications accepted. *Financial support:* In 2012–13, 5 research assistantships with partial tuition reimbursements (averaging $11,943 per year), 1 teaching assistantship with partial tuition reimbursement (averaging $16,360 per year) were awarded; Federal Work-Study, institutionally sponsored loans, scholarships/grants, and unspecified assistantships also available. Financial award application deadline: 4/1; financial award applicants required to submit FAFSA. *Unit head:* Dr. Mary Beck, Professor and Head, 662-325-5430, Fax: 662-325-8292, E-mail: mbeck@poultry.msstate.edu. *Application contact:* Dr. Chris McDaniel, Professor and Graduate Coordinator, 662-325-1839, Fax: 662-325-8292, E-mail: cmcdaniel@poultry.msstate.edu. Website: http://www.poultry.msstate.edu/.

Mississippi State University, College of Agriculture and Life Sciences, School of Human Sciences, Mississippi State, MS 39762. Offers agricultural sciences (PhD), including agriculture and extension education; agriculture and extension education (MS, PhD); human development and family studies (MS, PhD). *Accreditation:* NCATE (one or more programs are accredited). Part-time programs available. *Faculty:* 12 full-time (5 women). *Students:* 15 full-time (7 women), 53 part-time (34 women); includes 11 minority (all Black or African American, non-Hispanic/Latino), 2 international. Average age 37. 36 applicants, 69% accepted, 22 enrolled. In 2012, 15 master's awarded. *Degree requirements:* For master's, thesis optional, comprehensive oral or written exam. *Entrance requirements:* For master's, GRE, minimum GPA of 2.75 in last 4 semesters of course work; for doctorate, minimum GPA of 3.0 on prior graduate work. Additional exam requirements/recommendations for international students: Required—TOEFL (minimum score 477 paper-based; 53 iBT); Recommended—IELTS (minimum score 4.5). *Application deadline:* For fall admission, 7/1 for domestic students, 5/1 for international students; for spring admission, 11/1 for domestic students, 9/1 for international students. Applications are processed on a rolling basis. Application fee: $60. Electronic applications accepted. *Financial support:* In 2012–13, 6 research assistantships (averaging $13,117 per year), 3 teaching assistantships with full tuition reimbursements (averaging $12,095 per year) were awarded; Federal Work-Study, institutionally sponsored loans, and unspecified assistantships also available. Financial award application deadline: 4/1; financial award applicants required to submit FAFSA. *Faculty research:* Animal welfare, agroscience, information technology, learning styles, problem solving. *Unit head:* Dr. Michael Newman, Director and Professor, 662-325-2950, E-mail: mnewman@humansci.msstate.edu. *Application contact:* Emily Shaw, Student Services Coordinator, 662-325-7703, E-mail: eshaw@humansci.msstate.edu. Website: http://www.humansci.msstate.edu.

Missouri State University, Graduate College, William H. Darr School of Agriculture, Springfield, MO 65897. Offers plant science (MS); secondary education (MS Ed), including agriculture. Part-time programs available. *Degree requirements:* For master's, comprehensive exam, thesis or alternative. *Entrance requirements:* For master's, GRE (MS in plant science, MNAS), 9-12 teacher certification (MS Ed), minimum GPA of 3.0 (MS plant science, MNAS). Additional exam requirements/recommendations for international students: Required—TOEFL (minimum score 550 paper-based; 79 iBT). Electronic applications accepted. *Faculty research:* Grapevine biotechnology, agricultural marketing, Asian elephant reproduction, poultry science, integrated pest management.

Montana State University, College of Graduate Studies, College of Agriculture, Bozeman, MT 59717. Offers MS, PhD. Part-time programs available. Postbaccalaureate distance learning degree programs offered (minimal on-campus study). *Degree requirements:* For master's, comprehensive exam; for doctorate, comprehensive exam, thesis/dissertation. *Entrance requirements:* For master's and doctorate, GRE General Test. Additional exam requirements/recommendations for international students: Required—TOEFL (minimum score 550 paper-based). Electronic applications accepted.

Morehead State University, Graduate Programs, College of Science and Technology, Department of Agricultural Sciences, Morehead, KY 40351. Offers career and technical agricultural education (MS). Part-time and evening/weekend programs available. *Degree requirements:* For master's, comprehensive exam, thesis or alternative, exit exam. *Entrance requirements:* For master's, GRE, minimum GPA of 3.0 for undergraduate major. Additional exam requirements/recommendations for international students: Required—TOEFL (minimum score 500 paper-based). Electronic applications accepted.

Murray State University, School of Agriculture, Murray, KY 42071. Offers agriculture (MS); agriculture education (MS). Evening/weekend programs available. Postbaccalaureate distance learning degree programs offered (minimal on-campus study). *Degree requirements:* For master's, comprehensive exam, thesis (for some programs). *Entrance requirements:* Additional exam requirements/recommendations for international students: Required—TOEFL. *Faculty research:* Ultrasound in beef, corn and soybean research, tobacco research.

New Mexico State University, Graduate School, College of Agricultural, Consumer and Environmental Sciences, Department of Entomology, Plant Pathology and Weed Science, Las Cruces, NM 88003-8001. Offers agricultural biology (MS). Part-time programs available. *Faculty:* 10 full-time (2 women), 1 (woman) part-time/adjunct. *Students:* 9 full-time (3 women), 4 part-time (2 women); includes 5 minority (4 Hispanic/Latino; 1 Two or more races, non-Hispanic/Latino), 2 international. Average age 26. 2 applicants, 100% accepted, 1 enrolled. In 2012, 5 master's awarded. *Degree requirements:* For master's, comprehensive exam, thesis. *Entrance requirements:* For master's, GRE General Test. Additional exam requirements/recommendations for international students: Required—TOEFL (minimum score 550 paper-based; 79 iBT), IELTS (minimum score 6.5). *Application deadline:* For fall admission, 7/1 priority date for domestic students; for spring admission, 11/1 priority date for domestic students. Applications are processed on a rolling basis. Application fee: $40 ($50 for international students). Electronic applications accepted. *Expenses:* Tuition, state resident: full-time $5239; part-time $218 per credit. Tuition, nonresident: full-time $18,266; part-time $761 per credit. *Required fees:* $1274; $53 per credit. *Financial support:* In 2012–13, 8 students received support, including 10 research assistantships (averaging $20,660 per year); teaching assistantships, career-related internships or fieldwork, and health care benefits also available. Financial award application deadline: 3/1. *Faculty research:* Integrated pest management, pesticide application and safety, livestock ectoparasite research, biotechnology, nematology. *Total annual research expenditures:* $2.6 million. *Unit head:* Dr. Gerald K. Sims, Interim Head, 575-646-3225, Fax: 575-646-8087, E-mail: gksims@nmsu.edu. *Application contact:* Cindy Bullard, Intermediate Administrative Assistant/Recruiting Contact, 575-646-1145, Fax: 575 646 8087, E-mail: cbullard@nmsu.edu. Website: http://eppws.nmsu.edu/.

North Carolina Agricultural and Technical State University, School of Graduate Studies, School of Agriculture and Environmental Sciences, Greensboro, NC 27411. Offers MAT, MS. Part-time and evening/weekend programs available. *Degree requirements:* For master's, comprehensive exam, qualifying exam. *Entrance requirements:* For master's, GRE General Test. *Faculty research:* Aid for small farmers, agricultural technology, housing, food science, nutrition.

North Carolina State University, Graduate School, College of Agriculture and Life Sciences, Raleigh, NC 27695. Offers M Tox, MAE, MB, MBAE, MFG, MFM, MFS, MG, MMB, MN, MP, MS, MZS, Ed D, PhD, Certificate. Part-time programs available. Electronic applications accepted.

North Dakota State University, College of Graduate and Interdisciplinary Studies, College of Agriculture, Food Systems, and Natural Resources, Fargo, ND 58108. Offers MS, PhD. Part-time programs available. *Faculty:* 89 full-time (21 women), 1 (woman) part-time/adjunct. *Students:* 175 full-time (79 women), 67 part-time (35 women); includes 11 minority (1 Black or African American, non-Hispanic/Latino; 1 American Indian or Alaska Native, non-Hispanic/Latino; 1 Asian, non-Hispanic/Latino; 1 Hispanic/Latino; 7 Two or more races, non-Hispanic/Latino), 106 international. Average age 29. 140 applicants, 44% accepted, 47 enrolled. In 2012, 39 master's, 14 doctorates awarded. *Degree requirements:* For doctorate, thesis/dissertation. *Entrance requirements:* Additional exam requirements/recommendations for international students: Required—TOEFL. *Application deadline:* Applications are processed on a rolling basis. Application fee: $35. Electronic applications accepted. *Financial support:* Fellowships with full tuition reimbursements, research assistantships with full tuition reimbursements, teaching assistantships with full tuition reimbursements, career-related internships or fieldwork, Federal Work-Study, and institutionally sponsored loans available. Support available to part-time students. *Faculty research:* Horticulture and forestry, plant and wheat breeding, diseases of insects, animal and range sciences, soil science, veterinary medicine. *Unit head:* Dr. Kenneth F. Grafton, Dean, 701-231-8790, Fax: 701-231-8520, E-mail: k.grafton@ndsu.edu. *Application contact:* Sonya Goergen, Marketing, Recruitment, and Public Relations Coordinator, 701-231-7033, Fax: 701-231-6524. Website: http://www.ag.ndsu.nodak.edu/.

Northwest Missouri State University, Graduate School, Melvin and Valorie Booth College of Business and Professional Studies, Department of Agriculture, Maryville, MO 64468-6001. Offers agricultural economics (MBA); agriculture (MS); teaching agriculture (MS Ed). Part-time programs available. *Faculty:* 7 full-time (2 women). *Students:* 5 full-time (2 women), 4 part-time (0 women). 6 applicants, 67% accepted, 3 enrolled. In 2012, 3 master's awarded. *Degree requirements:* For master's, comprehensive exam, thesis (for some programs). *Entrance requirements:* For master's, GRE General Test, minimum undergraduate GPA of 2.5, writing sample. Additional exam requirements/recommendations for international students: Required—TOEFL (minimum score 550 paper-based). *Application deadline:* For fall admission, 7/1 for domestic and international students; for spring admission, 11/15 for domestic and international students. Applications are processed on a rolling basis. Application fee: $0 ($50 for international students). *Expenses:* Tuition, state resident: part-time $324.72 per credit. Tuition, nonresident: part-time $561.94 per credit. *Required fees:* $87.50 per credit. Tuition and fees vary according to course load. *Financial support:* In 2012–13, 4 research assistantships with full tuition reimbursements (averaging $6,000 per year), 2 teaching assistantships with full tuition reimbursements (averaging $6,000 per year) were awarded; unspecified assistantships also available. Financial award application deadline: 4/1; financial award applicants required to submit FAFSA. *Unit head:* Dr. Arley Larson, Chairperson, 660-562-1161. *Application contact:* Dr. Gregory Haddock, Dean of Graduate School, 660-562-1145, Fax: 660-562-1096, E-mail: gradsch@nwmissouri.edu.

The Ohio State University, Graduate School, College of Food, Agricultural, and Environmental Sciences, Columbus, OH 43210. Offers M Ed, MENR, MPHM, MS, PhD. Part-time programs available. *Faculty:* 201. *Students:* 378 full-time (205 women), 135 part-time (71 women); includes 46 minority (15 Black or African American, non-Hispanic/Latino; 1 American Indian or Alaska Native, non-Hispanic/Latino; 14 Asian, non-Hispanic/Latino; 10 Hispanic/Latino; 6 Two or more races, non-Hispanic/Latino), 180 international. Average age 29. In 2012, 119 master's, 53 doctorates awarded. *Degree requirements:* For doctorate, thesis/dissertation. *Application deadline:* For fall admission, 8/15 for domestic students, 7/1 for international students; for winter admission, 12/1 for domestic students, 11/1 for international students; for spring admission, 3/1 for domestic students, 2/1 for international students. Applications are processed on a rolling basis. Application fee: $40 ($50 for international students). Electronic applications accepted. *Financial support:* Fellowships, research assistantships, teaching assistantships, career-related internships or fieldwork, Federal Work-Study, institutionally sponsored loans, and unspecified assistantships available. Support available to part-time students. *Unit head:* Bruce A. McPheron, Vice President of Agricultural Administration and Dean, 614-292-6891, Fax: 614-292-0452, E-mail: mcpheron.24@osu.edu. *Application contact:* Graduate Admissions, 614-292-6031, Fax: 614-292-3656, E-mail: gradadmissions@osu.edu. Website: http://cfaes.osu.edu/.

Oklahoma State University, College of Agricultural Science and Natural Resources, Stillwater, OK 74078. Offers M Ag, MS, PhD. Postbaccalaureate distance learning degree programs offered. *Faculty:* 242 full-time (57 women), 12 part-time/adjunct (1 woman). *Students:* 161 full-time (78 women), 349 part-time (168 women); includes 62 minority (9 Black or African American, non-Hispanic/Latino; 15 American Indian or Alaska Native, non-Hispanic/Latino; 10 Asian, non-Hispanic/Latino; 7 Hispanic/Latino; 21 Two or more races, non-Hispanic/Latino), 162 international. Average age 29. 497 applicants, 35% accepted, 122 enrolled. In 2012, 137 master's, 48 doctorates awarded. *Degree requirements:* For master's, thesis (for some programs); for doctorate, comprehensive exam, thesis/dissertation. *Entrance requirements:* For master's and doctorate, GRE or GMAT. Additional exam requirements/recommendations for international students: Required—TOEFL (minimum score 550 paper-based; 79 iBT). *Application deadline:* For fall admission, 3/1 for international students; for spring admission, 8/1 for international students. Applications are processed on a rolling basis. Application fee: $40 ($75 for international students). Electronic applications accepted. *Expenses:* Tuition, state resident: full-time $4272; part-time $178 per credit hour. Tuition, nonresident: full-time $17,016; part-time $709 per credit hour. *Required fees:* $2188; $91.17 per credit hour. One-time fee: $50 full-time. Part-time tuition and fees vary according to course load and campus/location. *Financial support:* In 2012–13, 258 research assistantships (averaging $16,184 per year), 47 teaching assistantships (averaging $12,835 per year) were awarded; fellowships, career-related internships or fieldwork, Federal Work-Study, scholarships/grants, health care benefits, tuition waivers (partial), and unspecified assistantships also available. Support available to part-time students. Financial award application deadline: 3/1; financial award applicants required to submit FAFSA. *Unit head:* Dr. Cynda E. Clary, Associate Dean, 405-744-5395, E-mail: cynda.clary@okstate.edu. *Application contact:* Dr. Sheryl Tucker, Dean, 405-744-7099, Fax: 405-744-0355, E-mail: grad-i@okstate.edu. Website: http://www.dasnr.okstate.edu.

Oregon State University, College of Agricultural Sciences, Corvallis, OR 97331. Offers M Ag, M Agr, MA, MAIS, MS, PSM, PhD. Part-time programs available. *Faculty:* 100 full-time (28 women), 32 part-time/adjunct (12 women). *Students:* 294 full-time (166 women), 43 part-time (20 women); includes 44 minority (4 Black or African American, non-Hispanic/Latino; 4 American Indian or Alaska Native, non-Hispanic/Latino; 8 Asian, non-Hispanic/Latino; 24 Hispanic/Latino; 1 Native Hawaiian or other Pacific Islander, non-Hispanic/Latino; 3 Two or more races, non-Hispanic/Latino), 61 international. Average age 30. 465 applicants, 24% accepted, 89 enrolled. In 2012, 64 master's, 21 doctorates awarded. Terminal master's awarded for partial completion of doctoral program. *Degree requirements:* For doctorate, thesis/dissertation. *Entrance requirements:* For master's and doctorate, GRE, minimum GPA of 3.0 in last 90 hours of course work. Additional exam requirements/recommendations for international students: Required—TOEFL. Application fee: $50. *Expenses:* Tuition, state resident: full-time $11,367; part-time $421 per credit hour. Tuition, nonresident: full-time $18,279; part-time $677 per credit hour. *Required fees:* $1478. One-time fee: $300 full-time. Tuition and fees vary according to course load and program. *Financial support:* Fellowships, research assistantships, teaching assistantships, career-related internships or fieldwork, Federal Work-Study, and institutionally sponsored loans available. Support available to part-time students. Financial award application deadline: 2/1. *Faculty research:* Fish and wildlife biology, food science, soil/water/plant relationships, natural resources, animal biochemistry. *Unit head:* Dr. Dan Arp, Dean, 541-737-2331, E-mail: dan.arp@oregonstate.edu. *Application contact:* Dr. Stella Coakley, Associate Dean, 541-737-5264, Fax: 541-737-3178, E-mail: stella.coakley@oregonstate.edu. Website: http://agsci.oregonstate.edu.

Oregon State University, College of Agricultural Sciences, Department of Agricultural Education and Agricultural Sciences, Program in Agricultural Sciences, Corvallis, OR 97331. Offers M Agr. *Expenses:* Tuition, state resident: full-time $11,367; part-time $421 per credit hour. Tuition, nonresident: full-time $18,279; part-time $677 per credit hour. *Required fees:* $1478. One-time fee: $300 full-time. Tuition and fees vary according to course load and program. *Unit head:* Dr. Greg Thompson, Head, 541-737-1337, Fax: 541-737-3178, E-mail: greg.thompson@oregonstate.edu.

Penn State University Park, Graduate School, College of Agricultural Sciences, State College, University Park, PA 16802-1503. Offers M Ed, MPS, MS, PhD, Certificate. Part-time and evening/weekend programs available. Postbaccalaureate distance learning degree programs offered. *Students:* 332 full-time (202 women), 33 part-time (12 women). Average age 29. 622 applicants, 22% accepted, 88 enrolled. In 2012, 63 master's, 41 doctorates awarded. *Entrance requirements:* Additional exam requirements/recommendations for international students: Required—TOEFL (minimum score 550 paper-based; 80 iBT). *Application deadline:* Applications are processed on a rolling basis. Application fee: $65. Electronic applications accepted. *Financial support:* Fellowships, research assistantships, teaching assistantships, career-related internships or fieldwork, Federal Work-Study, and unspecified assistantships available. Support available to part-time students. Financial award application deadline: 2/15; financial award applicants required to submit FAFSA. *Unit head:* Dr. Barbara J. Christ, Interim Dean, 814-865-2541, Fax: 814-865-3103, E-mail: ebf@psu.edu. *Application contact:* Cynthia E. Nicosia, Director of Graduate Enrollment Services, 814-865-1834, E-mail: cey1@psu.edu. Website: http://agsci.psu.edu/.

Prairie View A&M University, College of Agriculture and Human Sciences, Prairie View, TX 77446-0519. Offers agricultural economics (MS); animal sciences (MS); interdisciplinary human sciences (MS); soil science (MS). Part-time and evening/weekend programs available. *Degree requirements:* For master's, comprehensive exam, thesis (for some programs), field placement. *Entrance requirements:* For master's, GRE General Test, minimum GPA of 2.45. Additional exam requirements/recommendations for international students: Required—TOEFL (minimum score 550 paper-based). *Faculty research:* Domestic violence prevention, water quality, food growth regulators, wetland dynamics, biochemistry, obesity and nutrition, family therapy.

Purdue University, Graduate School, College of Agriculture, West Lafayette, IN 47907. Offers EMBA, M Agr, MA, MS, MSF, PhD. Part-time programs available. *Faculty:* 277 full-time (58 women), 81 part-time/adjunct (19 women). *Students:* 490 full-time (220 women), 141 part-time (59 women); includes 45 minority (12 Black or African American, non-Hispanic/Latino; 1 American Indian or Alaska Native, non-Hispanic/Latino; 10 Asian, non-Hispanic/Latino; 17 Hispanic/Latino; 5 Two or more races, non-Hispanic/Latino), 260 international. Average age 28. 780 applicants, 30% accepted, 183 enrolled. In 2012, 138 master's, 68 doctorates awarded. *Degree requirements:* For doctorate, thesis/dissertation. *Entrance requirements:* Additional exam requirements/recommendations for international students: Required—TOEFL. *Application deadline:* Applications are processed on a rolling basis. Application fee: $60 ($75 for international students). Electronic applications accepted. *Financial support:* Fellowships with tuition reimbursements, research assistantships with tuition reimbursements, teaching assistantships with tuition reimbursements, career-related internships or fieldwork, and tuition waivers (partial) available. Support available to part-time students. Financial award applicants required to submit FAFSA. *Unit head:* Dr. Jay W. Akridge, Dean, 765-494-8391, E-mail: akridge@purdue.edu. Website: http://www.ag.purdue.edu/Pages/default.aspx.

Sam Houston State University, College of Sciences, Department of Agricultural Sciences, Huntsville, TX 77341. Offers agriculture (MS). Part-time and evening/weekend programs available. *Faculty:* 16 full-time (3 women). *Students:* 14 full-time (10 women), 10 part-time (6 women); includes 2 minority (1 Asian, non-Hispanic/Latino; 1 Hispanic/Latino). Average age 24. 24 applicants, 75% accepted, 11 enrolled. In 2012, 14 master's awarded. *Degree requirements:* For master's, comprehensive exam, thesis optional. *Entrance requirements:* For master's, GRE General Test, minimum GPA of 2.5. Additional exam requirements/recommendations for international students: Required—TOEFL (minimum score 550 paper-based; 79 iBT), IELTS (minimum score 6.5). *Application deadline:* For fall admission, 8/1 for domestic students, 6/25 for international students; for spring admission, 12/1 for domestic students, 11/12 for international students. Applications are processed on a rolling basis. Application fee: $45 ($75 for international students). Electronic applications accepted. *Expenses:* Tuition, state resident: full-time $2205; part-time $245 per credit hour. Tuition, nonresident: full-time $5391; part-time $599 per credit hour. *Required fees:* $67 per credit hour. $367 per semester. Tuition and fees vary according to course load and campus/location. *Financial support:* In 2012–13, 1 research assistantship (averaging $2,314 per year), 9 teaching assistantships (averaging $8,242 per year) were awarded; career-related internships or fieldwork, Federal Work-Study, institutionally sponsored loans, scholarships/grants, and unspecified assistantships also available. Support available to part-time students. Financial award application deadline: 5/31; financial award applicants required to submit FAFSA. *Total annual research expenditures:* $215,361. *Unit head:* Dr. Stanley F. Kelley, Chair, 936-294-1189, Fax: 936-294-1232, E-mail: sfkelley@shsu.edu. Website: http://www.shsu.edu/~agr_www/.

South Dakota State University, Graduate School, College of Agriculture and Biological Sciences, Brookings, SD 57007. Offers MS, PhD. Part-time programs available. *Degree requirements:* For master's, thesis, oral exam; for doctorate, thesis/dissertation, preliminary oral and written exams. *Entrance requirements:* Additional exam requirements/recommendations for international students: Required—TOEFL.

Southern Arkansas University–Magnolia, Graduate Programs, Magnolia, AR 71754. Offers agriculture (MS); business administration (MBA); computer and information sciences (MS); education (M Ed), including counseling and development, curriculum and instruction, educational administration and supervision, elementary education, reading, secondary education, TESOL; kinesiology (M Ed); library media and information specialist (M Ed); mental health and clinical counseling (MS); public administration (MPA); school counseling (M Ed); teaching (MAT). *Accreditation:* NCATE. Part-time and evening/weekend programs available. Postbaccalaureate distance learning degree programs offered. *Faculty:* 34 full-time (15 women), 8 part-time/adjunct (5 women). *Students:* 69 full-time (42 women), 363 part-time (256 women); includes 128 minority (120 Black or African American, non-Hispanic/Latino; 2 American Indian or Alaska Native, non-Hispanic/Latino; 3 Asian, non-Hispanic/Latino; 1 Hispanic/Latino; 1 Native Hawaiian or other Pacific Islander, non-Hispanic/Latino; 1 Two or more races, non-Hispanic/Latino), 13 international. Average age 33. 137 applicants, 72% accepted, 98 enrolled. In 2012, 149 master's awarded. *Degree requirements:* For master's, comprehensive exam (for some programs), thesis optional. *Entrance requirements:* For master's, GRE, MAT or GMAT, minimum GPA of 2.5. Additional exam requirements/recommendations for international students: Required—TOEFL. *Application deadline:* For fall admission, 7/10 for domestic and international students; for winter admission, 12/1 for domestic and international students; for spring admission, 12/1 for domestic and international students. Applications are processed on a rolling basis. Application fee: $25 ($50 for international students). Electronic applications accepted. *Expenses:* Tuition, state resident: full-time $5856; part-time $244 per credit hour. Tuition, nonresident: full-time $8544; part-time $356 per credit hour. *Required fees:* $1023; $136 per credit hour. *Financial support:* Career-related internships or fieldwork, Federal Work-Study, scholarships/grants, tuition waivers (full), and unspecified assistantships available. Financial award applicants required to submit FAFSA. *Faculty research:* Alternative certification for teachers, supervision of instruction, instructional leadership, counseling. *Unit head:* Dr. Kim Bloss, Dean, School of Graduate Studies, 870-235-4150, Fax: 870-235-5227, E-mail: kkbloss@saumag.edu. *Application contact:* Shrijana Malakar, Admissions Specialist, 870-235-4150, Fax: 870-235-5227, E-mail: gradstudies@saumag.edu. Website: http://www.saumag.edu/graduate.

Southern Illinois University Carbondale, Graduate School, College of Agriculture, Carbondale, IL 62901-4701. Offers MS, MBA/MS. Part-time programs available. *Faculty:* 41 full-time (8 women). *Students:* 41 full-time (31 women), 48 part-time (26 women); includes 3 minority (2 Black or African American, non-

388 www.petersonsbooks.com

Peterson's Graduate Programs in the Physical Sciences, Mathematics, Agricultural Sciences, the Environment & Natural Resources 2014

Hispanic/Latino; 1 Hispanic/Latino), 9 international. 53 applicants, 47% accepted, 16 enrolled. In 2012, 24 master's awarded. *Entrance requirements:* For master's, minimum GPA of 2.7. Additional exam requirements/recommendations for international students: Required—TOEFL. *Application deadline:* Applications are processed on a rolling basis. Application fee: $50. *Financial support:* In 2012–13, 35 students received support, including 31 research assistantships; fellowships, teaching assistantships, career-related internships or fieldwork, Federal Work-Study, institutionally sponsored loans, and tuition waivers (full) also available. Support available to part-time students. *Faculty research:* Production and studies in crops, animal nutrition, agribusiness economics and management, forest biology and ecology, microcomputers in agriculture. *Unit head:* Gary L. Minish, Dean, 618-453-2469.

Southern University and Agricultural and Mechanical College, Graduate School, College of Agricultural, Family and Consumer Sciences, Baton Rouge, LA 70813. Offers urban forestry (MS). *Degree requirements:* For master's, thesis. *Entrance requirements:* For master's, GRE, minimum GPA of 3.0. Additional exam requirements/recommendations for international students: Required—TOEFL (minimum score 525 paper-based). *Faculty research:* Urban forest interactions with environment, social and economic impacts of urban forests, tree biology/pathology, development of urban forest management tools.

Tarleton State University, College of Graduate Studies, College of Agricultural and Environmental Sciences, Department of Agricultural and Consumer Sciences, Stephenville, TX 76402. Offers agriculture education (MS). Part-time and evening/weekend programs available. Postbaccalaureate distance learning degree programs offered (minimal on-campus study). *Faculty:* 7 full-time (2 women), 5 part-time/adjunct (2 women). *Students:* 16 full-time (11 women), 25 part-time (15 women); includes 1 minority (Black or African American, non-Hispanic/Latino). Average age 26. 21 applicants, 90% accepted, 16 enrolled. In 2012, 18 master's awarded. *Degree requirements:* For master's, comprehensive exam. *Entrance requirements:* For master's, GRE General Test, minimum GPA of 3.0. Additional exam requirements/recommendations for international students: Required—TOEFL (minimum score 550 paper-based; 80 iBT). *Application deadline:* For fall admission, 8/5 priority date for domestic students; for spring admission, 12/1 for domestic students. Applications are processed on a rolling basis. Application fee: $30 ($130 for international students). Electronic applications accepted. *Expenses:* Tuition, state resident: full-time $3311; part-time $184 per credit hour. Tuition, nonresident: full-time $9090; part-time $505 per credit hour. *Required fees:* $1446. Tuition and fees vary according to course load and campus/location. *Financial support:* Research assistantships, Federal Work-Study, institutionally sponsored loans, scholarships/grants, and unspecified assistantships available. Financial award application deadline: 5/1; financial award applicants required to submit FAFSA. *Unit head:* Dr. Rudy Tarpley, Head, 254-968-9201, Fax: 254-968-9199, E-mail: tarpley@tarleton.edu. *Application contact:* Information Contact, 254-968-9104, Fax: 254-968-9670, E-mail: gradoffice@tarleton.edu. Website: http://www.tarleton.edu/COAHSWEB/agservices/.

Tarleton State University, College of Graduate Studies, College of Agricultural and Environmental Sciences, Department of Environmental and Agricultural Management, Stephenville, TX 76402. Offers agriculture (MS). Part-time and evening/weekend programs available. *Faculty:* 4 full-time (0 women). *Students:* 8 full-time (4 women), 9 part-time (5 women); includes 1 minority (Hispanic/Latino). Average age 30. 6 applicants, 100% accepted, 5 enrolled. In 2012, 11 master's awarded. *Degree requirements:* For master's, comprehensive exam. *Entrance requirements:* For master's, GRE, minimum GPA of 3.0. Additional exam requirements/recommendations for international students: Required—TOEFL (minimum score 550 paper-based; 80 iBT). *Application deadline:* For fall admission, 8/15 priority date for domestic students; for spring admission, 1/7 for domestic students. Applications are processed on a rolling basis. Application fee: $30 ($130 for international students). Electronic applications accepted. *Expenses:* Tuition, state resident: full-time $3311; part-time $184 per credit hour. Tuition, nonresident: full-time $9090; part-time $505 per credit hour. *Required fees:* $1446. Tuition and fees vary according to course load and campus/location. *Financial support:* Research assistantships available. Financial award application deadline: 5/1; financial award applicants required to submit FAFSA. *Unit head:* Dr. Ashley Lovell, Interim Department Head, 254-968-9931, Fax: 254-968-9228, E-mail: lovell@tarleton.edu. *Application contact:* Information Contact, 254-968-9104, Fax: 254-968-9670, E-mail: gradoffice@tarleton.edu. Website: http://www.tarleton.edu/COAHSWEB/env-ag-mgmt/.

Tennessee State University, The School of Graduate Studies and Research, School of Agriculture and Consumer Sciences, Nashville, TN 37209-1561. Offers agricultural sciences (MS), including agribusiness, agricultural education, animal science, plant science. Part-time and evening/weekend programs available. *Degree requirements:* For master's, thesis. *Entrance requirements:* For master's, GRE General Test, GRE Subject Test, MAT. *Faculty research:* Small farm economics, ornamental horticulture, beef cattle production, rural elderly.

Texas A&M University, College of Agriculture and Life Sciences, College Station, TX 77843. Offers M Agr, M Ed, M Eng, MAB, MS, DE, Ed D, PhD. Part-time programs available. Postbaccalaureate distance learning degree programs offered (minimal on-campus study). *Faculty:* 303. *Students:* 950 full-time (486 women), 341 part-time (160 women); includes 200 minority (41 Black or African American, non-Hispanic/Latino; 2 American Indian or Alaska Native, non-Hispanic/Latino; 29 Asian, non-Hispanic/Latino; 120 Hispanic/Latino; 8 Two or more races, non-Hispanic/Latino), 4,393 international. Average age 29. In 2012, 1,182 master's, 100 doctorates awarded. *Entrance requirements:* Additional exam requirements/recommendations for international students: Required—TOEFL (minimum score 550 paper-based). *Application deadline:* For fall admission, 7/21 priority date for domestic students, 6/1 for international students; for spring admission, 12/1 priority date for domestic students, 10/1 for international students. Applications are processed on a rolling basis. Application fee: $50 ($75 for international students). Electronic applications accepted. *Financial support:* Fellowships, research assistantships, teaching assistantships, career-related internships or fieldwork, Federal Work-Study, institutionally sponsored loans, scholarships/grants, tuition waivers (partial), and unspecified assistantships available. Support available to part-time students. Financial award applicants required to submit FAFSA. *Faculty research:* Plant sciences, animal sciences, environmental natural resources, biological and agricultural engineering, agricultural economics. *Unit head:* Dr. Mark Hussey, Vice Chancellor/Dean, 979-845-4747, Fax: 979-845-9938, E-mail: mhussey@tamu.edu. *Application contact:* Graduate Admissions, 979-845-1044, E-mail: admissions@tamu.edu. Website: http://aglifesciences.tamu.edu/.

Texas A&M University–Commerce, Graduate School, College of Science, Engineering and Agriculture, Department of Agricultural Sciences, Commerce, TX 75429-3011. Offers agricultural education (M Ed, MS); agricultural sciences (M Ed, MS). Part-time programs available. *Degree requirements:* For master's, comprehensive exam, thesis (for some programs). *Entrance requirements:* For master's, GRE General Test. Electronic applications accepted. *Expenses:* Tuition, state resident: full-time $3630; part-time $2420 per year. Tuition, nonresident: full-time $9948; part-time $6632.16 per year. *Required fees:* $1006 per year. *Faculty research:* Soil conservation, retention.

Texas A&M University–Kingsville, College of Graduate Studies, College of Agriculture and Home Economics, Kingsville, TX 78363. Offers MS, PhD. Part-time and evening/weekend programs available. *Degree requirements:* For master's, comprehensive exam, thesis or alternative; for doctorate, one foreign language, comprehensive exam, thesis/dissertation. *Entrance requirements:* For master's, GRE General Test, minimum GPA of 3.0; for doctorate, GRE General Test, minimum GPA of 3.5. Additional exam requirements/recommendations for international students: Required—TOEFL. *Faculty research:* Mesquite cloning; genesis of soil salinity; dove management; bone development; egg, meat, and milk consumption versus price.

Texas Tech University, Graduate School, College of Agricultural Sciences and Natural Resources, Lubbock, TX 79409. Offers M Agr, MAB, MLA, MS, Ed D, PhD, JD/MS. Part-time programs available. Postbaccalaureate distance learning degree programs offered (minimal on-campus study). *Degree requirements:* For master's, thesis or alternative; for doctorate, thesis/dissertation. *Entrance requirements:* For master's and doctorate, GRE General Test, formal approval from departmental committee. Additional exam requirements/recommendations for international students: Required—TOEFL (minimum score 550 paper-based; 79 iBT). Electronic applications accepted. *Expenses:* Contact institution. *Faculty research:* Biotechnology and genomics, water management, food safety, policy, ecology.

Tropical Agriculture Research and Higher Education Center, Graduate School, Turrialba, Costa Rica. Offers agribusiness management (MS); agroforestry systems (PhD); development practices (MS); ecological agriculture (MS); environmental socioeconomics (MS); forestry in tropical and subtropical zones (PhD); integrated watershed management (MS); international sustainable tourism (MS); management and conservation of tropical rainforests and biodiversity (MS); tropical agriculture (PhD); tropical agroforestry (MS). *Entrance requirements:* For master's, GRE, 2 years of related professional experience, letters of recommendation; for doctorate, GRE, 4 letters of recommendation, letter of support from employing organization, master's degree in agronomy, biological sciences, forestry, natural resources or related field. Additional exam requirements/recommendations for international students: Required—TOEFL (minimum score 550 paper-based). Electronic applications accepted. *Faculty research:* Biodiversity in fragmented landscapes, ecosystem management, integrated pest management, environmental livestock production, biotechnology carbon balances in diverse land uses.

Universidad Nacional Pedro Henriquez Urena, Graduate School, Santo Domingo, Dominican Republic. Offers agricultural diversity (MS), including horticultural/fruit production, tropical animal production; conservation of monuments and cultural assets (M Arch); ecology and environment (MS); environmental engineering (MEE); international relations (MA); natural resource management (MS); political science (MA); project optimization (MPM); project feasibility (MPM); project management (MPM); sanitation engineering (ME); science for teachers (MS); tropical Caribbean architecture (M Arch).

Université Laval, Faculty of Agricultural and Food Sciences, Québec, QC G1K 7P4, Canada. Offers M Sc, PhD, Diploma. Part-time programs available. *Degree requirements:* For doctorate, comprehensive exam, thesis/dissertation. Electronic applications accepted.

University of Alberta, Faculty of Graduate Studies and Research, Department of Agricultural, Food and Nutritional Science, Edmonton, AB T6G 2E1, Canada. Offers M Ag, M Eng, M Sc, PhD, MBA/M Ag. *Degree requirements:* For master's, thesis; for doctorate, comprehensive exam, thesis/dissertation. *Entrance requirements:* For master's, minimum GPA of 3.3; for doctorate, minimum GPA of 3.5. Additional exam requirements/recommendations for international students: Required—IELTS (minimum score 6.5), TOEFL (minimum score of 550 paper-based or a total iBT score of 88 with a score of at least 20 on each of the individual skill areas), Michigan English Language Assessment Battery (minimum score 85); CAEL (overall minimum score 60). *Faculty research:* Animal science, food science, nutrition and metabolism, bioresource engineering, plant science and range management.

The University of Arizona, College of Agriculture and Life Sciences, Tucson, AZ 85721. Offers M Ag Ed, MHE Ed, MS, PhD. Part-time programs available. *Faculty:* 113 full-time (37 women), 6 part-time/adjunct (2 women). *Students:* 240 full-time (129 women), 52 part-time (22 women); includes 64 minority (7 Black or African American, non-Hispanic/Latino; 1 American Indian or Alaska Native, non-Hispanic/Latino; 8 Asian, non-Hispanic/Latino; 27 Hispanic/Latino; 21 Two or more races, non-Hispanic/Latino), 62 international. Average age 30. 341 applicants, 34% accepted, 60 enrolled. In 2012, 55 master's, 27 doctorates awarded. *Degree requirements:* For doctorate, thesis/dissertation. *Entrance requirements:* For master's, GRE, GMAT, or MAT, bachelor's degree or equivalent, minimum GPA of 3.0. Additional exam requirements/recommendations for international students: Required—TOEFL (minimum score 550 paper-based; 79 iBT). *Application deadline:* For fall admission, 1/1 for domestic students, 12/1 for international students. Applications are processed on a rolling basis. Application fee: $75. Electronic applications accepted. *Financial support:* In 2012–13, 135 research assistantships with full and partial tuition reimbursements (averaging $19,963 per year), 59 teaching assistantships with full and partial tuition reimbursements (averaging $19,737 per year) were awarded; fellowships with full and partial tuition reimbursements, career-related internships or fieldwork, Federal Work-Study, institutionally sponsored loans, scholarships/grants, traineeships, health care benefits, tuition waivers (full and partial), and unspecified assistantships also available. *Faculty research:* Regulation of skeletal muscle mass during growth, bone health and osteoporosis prevention, regulation of gene expression, development of new crops for arid and semi-arid lands, molecular genetics and pathogenesis of the opportunistic pathogen. *Total annual research expenditures:* $48.1 million. *Unit head:* Dr. Shane Burgess, Dean, 520-621-7621, Fax: 520-621-7196, E-mail: dean@cals.arizona.edu. *Application contact:* 520-621-3612, Fax: 520-621-8662. Website: http://www.ag.arizona.edu/.

University of Arkansas, Graduate School, Dale Bumpers College of Agricultural, Food and Life Sciences, Fayetteville, AR 72701-1201. Offers MS, PhD. *Students:* 103 full-time (55 women), 207 part-time (98 women); includes 28 minority (9 Black or African American, non-Hispanic/Latino; 5 Asian, non-Hispanic/Latino; 9 Hispanic/Latino; 5 Two or more races, non-Hispanic/Latino), 88 international. 164 applicants, 59% accepted. In 2012, 82 master's, 13 doctorates awarded. *Degree requirements:* For doctorate, thesis/dissertation. *Application deadline:* For fall admission, 4/1 for international students; for spring admission, 10/1 for international students. Applications are processed on a rolling basis. Application fee: $40 ($50 for international students). Electronic applications accepted. *Financial support:* In 2012–13, 167 research assistantships, 7 teaching assistantships were awarded; fellowships with tuition reimbursements, career-related internships or fieldwork, Federal Work-Study, scholarships/grants, and unspecified assistantships also available. Support available to part-time students. Financial award application deadline: 4/1; financial award applicants required to submit FAFSA. *Unit head:* Dr. Michael E. Vayda, Dean, 479-575-2034, Fax: 479-575-7273, E-mail: mvayda@uark.edu. *Application contact:* Graduate Admissions, 479-575-6246, Fax: 479-575-5908, E-mail: gradinfo@uark.edu. Website: http://bumperscollege.uark.edu/.

The University of British Columbia, Faculty of Land and Food Systems, Vancouver, BC V6T 1Z1, Canada. Offers M Sc, MFS, PhD. *Degree requirements:* For master's, thesis; for doctorate, comprehensive exam, thesis/dissertation. *Entrance requirements:* Additional exam requirements/recommendations for international students: Required—TOEFL (minimum score 577 paper-based; 90 iBT), IELTS (minimum score 6.5). Electronic applications accepted.

University of California, Davis, Graduate Studies, Graduate Group in International Agricultural Development, Davis, CA 95616. Offers MS. *Degree requirements:* For master's, comprehensive exam (for some programs), thesis (for some programs). *Entrance requirements:* For master's, GRE General Test, minimum GPA of 3.0. Additional exam requirements/recommendations for international students: Required—TOEFL (minimum score 550 paper-based). Electronic applications accepted. *Faculty research:* Aspects of agricultural, environmental and social sciences on agriculture and related issues in developing countries.

University of Connecticut, Graduate School, College of Agriculture and Natural Resources, Storrs, CT 06269. Offers MS, PhD. Terminal master's awarded for partial completion of doctoral program. *Degree requirements:* For master's, comprehensive exam; for doctorate, comprehensive exam, thesis/dissertation. *Entrance requirements:* For master's and doctorate, GRE General Test. Additional exam requirements/recommendations for international students: Required—TOEFL (minimum score 550 paper-based). Electronic applications accepted.

University of Delaware, College of Agriculture and Natural Resources, Newark, DE 19716. Offers MA, MS, PhD. Part-time programs available. *Degree requirements:* For master's, thesis; for doctorate, thesis/dissertation. *Entrance requirements:* For master's and doctorate, GRE General Test. Electronic applications accepted.

University of Florida, Graduate School, College of Agricultural and Life Sciences, Gainesville, FL 32611. Offers M Ag, MAB, MFAS, MFRC, MFYCS, MS, DPM, PhD, JD/MFRC, JD/MS, JD/PhD. Part-time programs available. *Degree requirements:* For master's, comprehensive exam (for some programs), thesis (for some programs); for doctorate, comprehensive exam, thesis/dissertation. *Entrance requirements:* For master's and doctorate, GRE General Test, minimum GPA of 3.0. Additional exam requirements/recommendations for international students: Required—TOEFL (minimum score 550 paper-based; 80 iBT), IELTS (minimum score 6). Electronic applications accepted. *Faculty research:* Agriculture, human and natural resources, and the life sciences.

University of Georgia, College of Agricultural and Environmental Sciences, Athens, GA 30602. Offers MA Ext, MADS, MAE, MAL, MFT, MPPPM, MS, PhD. *Degree requirements:* For doctorate, thesis/dissertation. *Entrance requirements:* For master's and doctorate, GRE General Test. Electronic applications accepted.

University of Guelph, Graduate Studies, Ontario Agricultural College, Guelph, ON N1G 2W1, Canada. Offers M Sc, MLA, PhD, Diploma, MA/M Sc. Part-time programs available. Postbaccalaureate distance learning degree programs offered (minimal on-campus study). *Degree requirements:* For doctorate, thesis/dissertation.

University of Hawaii at Manoa, Graduate Division, College of Tropical Agriculture and Human Resources, Honolulu, HI 96822. Offers MS, PhD. Part-time programs available. *Entrance requirements:* Additional exam requirements/recommendations for international students: Required—TOEFL or IELTS.

University of Illinois at Urbana–Champaign, Graduate College, College of Agricultural, Consumer and Environmental Sciences, Program in Agricultural Production, Champaign, IL 61820. Offers MS. Applications accepted for Fall semester only. Part-time programs available. *Students:* 5 full-time (3 women). Application fee: $75 ($90 for international students). *Unit head:* Robert Knox, Associate Professor, 217-244-5177. *Application contact:* Lori Kelso, Resource and Policy Analyst, 217-244-0418, E-mail: lkelso@illinois.edu.

University of Kentucky, Graduate School, College of Agriculture, Lexington, KY 40506-0032. Offers MS, MSFOR, PhD. Part-time programs available. Terminal master's awarded for partial completion of doctoral program. *Degree requirements:* For master's, comprehensive exam, thesis (for some programs); for doctorate, comprehensive exam, thesis/dissertation. *Entrance requirements:* For master's, GRE General Test, minimum undergraduate GPA of 2.75; for doctorate, GRE General Test, minimum undergraduate GPA of 2.75, graduate 3.0. Additional exam requirements/recommendations for international students: Required—TOEFL (minimum score 550 paper-based). Electronic applications accepted.

University of Lethbridge, School of Graduate Studies, Lethbridge, AB T1K 3M4, Canada. Offers accounting (MScM); addictions counseling (M Sc); agricultural biotechnology (M Sc); agricultural studies (M Sc, MA); anthropology (MA); archaeology (MA); art (MA, MFA); biochemistry (M Sc); biological sciences (M Sc); biomolecular science (PhD); biosystems and biodiversity (PhD); Canadian studies (MA); chemistry (M Sc); computer science (M Sc); computer science and geographical information science (M Sc); counseling psychology (M Ed); dramatic arts (MA); earth, space, and physical science (PhD); economics (MA); educational leadership (M Ed); English (MA); environmental science (M Sc); evolution and behavior (PhD); exercise science (M Sc); finance (MScM); French (MA); French/German (MA); French/Spanish (MA); general education (M Ed); general management (MScM); geography (M Sc, MA); German (MA); health science (M Sc); history (MA); human resource management and labour relations (MScM); individualized multidisciplinary (M Sc, MA); information systems (MScM); international management (MScM); kinesiology (M Sc, MA); management (M Sc, MA); marketing (MScM); mathematics (M Sc); music (M Mus, MA); Native American studies (MA); neuroscience (M Sc, PhD); new media (MA); nursing (M Sc); philosophy (MA); physics (M Sc); policy and strategy (MScM); political science (MA); psychology (M Sc, MA); religious studies (MA); social sciences (MA); sociology (MA); theatre and dramatic arts (MFA); theoretical and computational science (PhD); urban and regional studies (MA); women's studies (MA). Part-time and evening/weekend programs available. *Degree requirements:* For doctorate, comprehensive exam, thesis/dissertation. *Entrance requirements:* For master's, GMAT (M Sc in management), bachelor's degree in related field, minimum GPA of 3.0 during previous 20 graded semester courses, 2 years teaching or related experience (M Ed); for doctorate, master's degree, minimum graduate GPA of 3.5. Additional exam requirements/recommendations for international students: Required—TOEFL. *Faculty research:* Movement and brain plasticity, gibberellin physiology, photosynthesis, carbon cycling, molecular properties of main-group ring components.

University of Maine, Graduate School, College of Natural Sciences, Forestry, and Agriculture, Orono, ME 04469. Offers MA, MF, MPS, MS, MSW, MWC, PhD, CAS, CGS. *Accreditation:* SAF (one or more programs are accredited). Part-time and evening/weekend programs available. *Faculty:* 285 full-time (104 women), 182 part-time/adjunct (50 women). *Students:* 448 full-time (287 women), 80 part-time (56 women); includes 19 minority (1 Black or African American, non-Hispanic/Latino; 9 American Indian or Alaska Native, non-Hispanic/Latino; 4 Asian, non-Hispanic/Latino; 3 Hispanic/Latino; 1 Native Hawaiian or other Pacific Islander, non-Hispanic/Latino; 1 Two or more races, non-Hispanic/Latino), 58 international. Average age 31. 529 applicants, 39% accepted, 147 enrolled. In 2012, 147 master's, 19 doctorates, 2 other advanced degrees awarded. *Degree requirements:* For doctorate, thesis/dissertation. *Entrance requirements:* For master's and doctorate, GRE General Test. Additional exam requirements/recommendations for international students: Required—TOEFL. *Application* *deadline:* For fall admission, 2/1 priority date for domestic students. Applications are processed on a rolling basis. Application fee: $65. Electronic applications accepted. *Financial support:* Career-related internships or fieldwork, Federal Work-Study, institutionally sponsored loans, scholarships/grants, tuition waivers (full and partial), and unspecified assistantships available. Support available to part-time students. Financial award application deadline: 3/1. *Unit head:* Dr. Edward Ashworth, Dean, 207-581-3206, Fax: 207-581-3207. *Application contact:* Scott G. Delcourt, Associate Dean of the Graduate School, 207-581-3291, Fax: 207-581-3232, E-mail: graduate@maine.edu. Website: http://www2.umaine.edu/graduate/.

University of Manitoba, Faculty of Graduate Studies, Faculty of Agricultural and Food Sciences, Winnipeg, MB R3T 2N2, Canada. Offers M Sc, PhD. *Degree requirements:* For master's, thesis or alternative; for doctorate, variable foreign language requirement, thesis/dissertation.

University of Maryland, College Park, Academic Affairs, College of Agriculture and Natural Resources, College Park, MD 20742. Offers MS, DVM, PhD. Part-time and evening/weekend programs available. *Faculty:* 370 full-time (177 women), 40 part-time/adjunct (22 women). *Students:* 367 full-time (240 women), 28 part-time (17 women); includes 55 minority (6 Black or African American, non-Hispanic/Latino; 24 Asian, non-Hispanic/Latino; 17 Hispanic/Latino; 1 Native Hawaiian or other Pacific Islander, non-Hispanic/Latino; 7 Two or more races, non-Hispanic/Latino), 114 international. 525 applicants, 27% accepted, 101 enrolled. In 2012, 34 master's, 42 doctorates awarded. *Degree requirements:* For doctorate, thesis/dissertation. *Entrance requirements:* For master's, minimum GPA of 3.0. Additional exam requirements/recommendations for international students: Required—TOEFL. *Application deadline:* For fall admission, 2/1 priority date for domestic students, 2/1 for international students; for spring admission, 6/1 for domestic and international students. Applications are processed on a rolling basis. Application fee: $75. Electronic applications accepted. *Expenses:* Tuition, state resident: part-time $551 per credit. Tuition, nonresident: part-time $1188 per credit. Part-time tuition and fees vary according to program. *Financial support:* In 2012–13, 4 fellowships with full and partial tuition reimbursements (averaging $13,100 per year), 80 research assistantships with tuition reimbursements (averaging $17,198 per year), 112 teaching assistantships with tuition reimbursements (averaging $16,581 per year) were awarded; career-related internships or fieldwork, Federal Work-Study, and scholarships/grants also available. Support available to part-time students. Financial award applicants required to submit FAFSA. *Total annual research expenditures:* $37.4 million. *Unit head:* Dr. Cheng-i Wei, Dean, 301-405-2072, Fax: 301-314-9146, E-mail: wei@umd.edu. *Application contact:* Dr. Charles A. Caramello, Dean of Graduate School, 301-405-0358, Fax: 301-314-9305.

University of Maryland Eastern Shore, Graduate Programs, Department of Agriculture, Princess Anne, MD 21853-1299. Offers food and agricultural sciences (MS); food science and technology (PhD). *Degree requirements:* For master's, comprehensive exam, thesis (for some programs), oral exam; for doctorate, comprehensive exam, thesis/dissertation. *Entrance requirements:* For master's, GRE, minimum GPA of 3.0. Additional exam requirements/recommendations for international students: Required—TOEFL (minimum score 80 iBT). Electronic applications accepted. *Faculty research:* Poultry and swine nutrition and management, soybean specialty products, farm management practices, aquaculture technology.

University of Minnesota, Twin Cities Campus, Graduate School, College of Food, Agricultural and Natural Resource Sciences, Saint Paul, MN 55108. Offers MS, PhD. Part-time programs available. *Faculty:* 741 full-time (180 women). *Students:* 817 full-time (406 women); includes 40 minority (6 Black or African American, non-Hispanic/Latino; 5 American Indian or Alaska Native, non-Hispanic/Latino; 20 Asian, non-Hispanic/Latino; 9 Hispanic/Latino), 267 international. Average age 30. 1,176 applicants, 20% accepted, 160 enrolled. In 2012, 340 master's, 393 doctorates awarded. Terminal master's awarded for partial completion of doctoral program. *Degree requirements:* For master's, comprehensive exam, thesis; for doctorate, comprehensive exam, thesis/dissertation. *Entrance requirements:* For master's and doctorate, GRE General Test. Additional exam requirements/recommendations for international students: Required—TOEFL (minimum score 550 paper-based; 79 iBT), IELTS (minimum score 6.5). *Application deadline:* For fall admission, 12/15 priority date for domestic students, 12/15 for international students; for spring admission, 10/15 for domestic and international students. Applications are processed on a rolling basis. Application fee: $75 ($95 for international students). Electronic applications accepted. *Financial support:* In 2012–13, fellowships with full tuition reimbursements (averaging $40,000 per year), research assistantships with full and partial tuition reimbursements (averaging $40,000 per year), teaching assistantships with full and partial tuition reimbursements (averaging $40,000 per year) were awarded; career-related internships or fieldwork, institutionally sponsored loans, scholarships/grants, health care benefits, tuition waivers (full), and unspecified assistantships also available. Support available to part-time students. Financial award application deadline: 12/15. *Total annual research expenditures:* $38.9 million. *Unit head:* Dr. F. Abel Ponce de Leon, Senior Associate Dean, 612-625-4772, Fax: 612-625-1260, E-mail: apl@umn.edu. *Application contact:* Lisa Wiley, Graduate Programs Coordinator, 612-624-2748, Fax: 612-625-1260, E-mail: lwiley@umn.edu. Website: http://www.cfans.umn.edu/GraduateStudents/index.htm.

University of Missouri, Graduate School, College of Agriculture, Food and Natural Resources, Columbia, MO 65211. Offers MS, PhD, Graduate Certificate,

MD/PhD. Part-time programs available. *Faculty:* 431 full-time (121 women), 40 part-time/adjunct (11 women). *Students:* 339 full-time (164 women), 105 part-time (42 women); includes 24 minority (5 Black or African American, non-Hispanic/Latino; 1 American Indian or Alaska Native, non-Hispanic/Latino; 5 Asian, non-Hispanic/Latino; 7 Hispanic/Latino; 6 Two or more races, non-Hispanic/Latino), 138 international. Average age 29. 268 applicants, 37% accepted, 70 enrolled. In 2012, 51 master's, 24 doctorates, 1 other advanced degree awarded. Terminal master's awarded for partial completion of doctoral program. *Degree requirements:* For master's, thesis (for some programs); for doctorate, variable foreign language requirement, comprehensive exam (for some programs), thesis/dissertation. *Entrance requirements:* For master's and doctorate, GRE General Test, minimum GPA of 3.0. Additional exam requirements/recommendations for international students: Required—TOEFL (minimum score 500 paper-based; 61 iBT), IELTS (minimum score 5.5). *Application deadline:* Applications are processed on a rolling basis. Application fee: $55 ($75 for international students). Electronic applications accepted. *Expenses:* Tuition, state resident: full-time $6057. Tuition, nonresident: full-time $15,683. *Required fees:* $1000. *Financial support:* Fellowships with tuition reimbursements, research assistantships with tuition reimbursements, teaching assistantships with tuition reimbursements, institutionally sponsored loans, scholarships/grants, traineeships, health care benefits, and unspecified assistantships available. Support available to part-time students. *Unit head:* Dr. Thomas L. Payne, Dean, 573-882-3846, E-mail: paynet@missouri.edu. *Application contact:* Dr. Bryan L. Garton, Associate Dean, 573-882-0089, E-mail: gartonb@missouri.edu. Website: http://cafnr.missouri.edu/.

University of Nebraska–Lincoln, Graduate College, College of Agricultural Sciences and Natural Resources, Lincoln, NE 68588. Offers M Ag, MA, MBA, MS, PhD. *Degree requirements:* For doctorate, comprehensive exam, thesis/dissertation. *Entrance requirements:* Additional exam requirements/recommendations for international students: Required—TOEFL. Electronic applications accepted. *Faculty research:* Environmental sciences, animal sciences, human resources and family sciences, plant breeding and genetics, food and nutrition.

University of Nevada, Reno, Graduate School, College of Agriculture, Biotechnology and Natural Resources, Reno, NV 89557. Offers MS, PhD. Terminal master's awarded for partial completion of doctoral program. *Degree requirements:* For master's, thesis optional; for doctorate, thesis/dissertation. *Entrance requirements:* For master's, GRE General Test, minimum GPA of 2.75; for doctorate, GRE General Test, minimum GPA of 3.0. Additional exam requirements/recommendations for international students: Required—TOEFL (minimum score 500 paper-based; 61 iBT), IELTS (minimum score 6). Electronic applications accepted.

University of Puerto Rico, Mayagüez Campus, Graduate Studies, College of Agricultural Sciences, Mayagüez, PR 00681-9000. Offers MS. Part-time programs available. *Students:* 158 full-time (89 women), 7 part-time (4 women); includes 137 minority (all Hispanic/Latino), 31 international. 58 applicants, 91% accepted, 39 enrolled. In 2012, 14 master's awarded. *Degree requirements:* For master's, comprehensive exam, thesis. *Application deadline:* For fall admission, 2/15 for domestic and international students; for spring admission, 9/15 for domestic and international students. Applications are processed on a rolling basis. Application fee: $25. Tuition and fees vary according to course level and course load. *Financial support:* In 2012–13, 36 research assistantships with tuition reimbursements (averaging $15,000 per year), 69 teaching assistantships with tuition reimbursements (averaging $8,500 per year) were awarded; career-related internships or fieldwork, Federal Work-Study, and institutionally sponsored loans also available. *Total annual research expenditures:* $459,210. *Unit head:* Prof. Aristides Armstrong, Associate Dean, 787-832-4040 Ext. 2181, E-mail: aristides.armstrong@upr.edu. *Application contact:* Carmen Figueroa, Student Affairs Official, 787-265-3809, Fax: 787-265-5489, E-mail: carmen.figueroa11@upr.edu. Website: http://www.uprm.edu/agricultura.

University of Saskatchewan, College of Graduate Studies and Research, College of Agriculture, Saskatoon, SK S7N 5A2, Canada. Offers M Ag, M Sc, MA, PhD, Diploma, PGD. Part-time programs available. *Degree requirements:* For master's, thesis (for some programs); for doctorate, comprehensive exam (for some programs), thesis/dissertation. *Entrance requirements:* Additional exam requirements/recommendations for international students: Required—TOEFL (minimum score 80 iBT); Recommended—IELTS (minimum score 6.5).

University of South Africa, College of Agriculture and Environmental Sciences, Pretoria, South Africa. Offers agriculture (MS); consumer science (MCS); environmental management (MA, MS, PhD); environmental science (MA, MS, PhD); geography (MA, MS, PhD); horticulture (M Tech); human ecology (MHE); life sciences (MS); nature conservation (M Tech).

The University of Tennessee, Graduate School, College of Agricultural Sciences and Natural Resources, Knoxville, TN 37996. Offers MS, PhD. Part-time programs available. Postbaccalaureate distance learning degree programs offered (minimal on-campus study). *Degree requirements:* For master's, thesis (for some programs); for doctorate, thesis/dissertation. *Entrance requirements:* For master's and doctorate, minimum GPA of 2.7. Additional exam requirements/recommendations for international students: Required—TOEFL. Electronic applications accepted. *Expenses:* Tuition, state resident: full-time $9000; part-time $501 per credit hour. Tuition, nonresident: full-time $27,188; part-time $1512 per credit hour. *Required fees:* $1280; $62 per credit hour. Tuition and fees vary according to program.

Peterson's Graduate Programs in the Physical Sciences, Mathematics, Agricultural Sciences, the Environment & Natural Resources 2014

www.petersonsbooks.com **391**

Agricultural Sciences—General

The University of Tennessee at Martin, Graduate Programs, College of Agriculture and Applied Sciences, Program in Agricultural and Natural Resources Management, Martin, TN 38238-1000. Offers MSANR. Part-time programs available. Postbaccalaureate distance learning degree programs offered (no on-campus study). *Faculty:* 20. *Students:* 44 (18 women); includes 3 minority (2 Black or African American, non-Hispanic/Latino; 1 Hispanic/Latino). 16 applicants, 88% accepted, 14 enrolled. In 2012, 7 master's awarded. *Degree requirements:* For master's, comprehensive exam, thesis optional. *Entrance requirements:* For master's, GRE General Test, minimum GPA of 2.5. Additional exam requirements/recommendations for international students: Required—TOEFL (minimum score 525 paper-based; 71 iBT). *Application deadline:* For fall admission, 8/10 priority date for domestic students, 8/10 for international students; for spring admission, 12/15 priority date for domestic students, 12/15 for international students. Applications are processed on a rolling basis. Application fee: $30 ($130 for international students). Electronic applications accepted. *Expenses:* Tuition, state resident: full-time $8194; part-time $457 per credit hour. Tuition, nonresident: full-time $21,348; part-time $1188 per credit hour. *Financial support:* In 2012–13, 3 students received support, including 2 research assistantships with full tuition reimbursements available (averaging $7,540 per year), 1 teaching assistantship with tuition reimbursement available (averaging $9,801 per year); scholarships/grants and unspecified assistantships also available. Support available to part-time students. Financial award application deadline: 2/15; financial award applicants required to submit FAFSA. *Unit head:* Dr. Joey Melhorn, Interim Coordinator, 731-881-7275, Fax: 731-881-7968, E-mail: melhorn@utm.edu. *Application contact:* Jolene L. Cunningham, Student Services Specialist, 731-881-7012, Fax: 731-881-7499, E-mail: jcunningham@utm.edu. Website: http://www.utm.edu/departments/caas/msanr.

University of Vermont, Graduate College, College of Agriculture and Life Sciences, Burlington, VT 05405. Offers MPA, MS, MSD, PhD, MD/MS, MD/PhD. Part-time programs available. *Students:* 151 (98 women); includes 10 minority (6 Asian, non-Hispanic/Latino; 2 Hispanic/Latino; 2 Two or more races, non-Hispanic/Latino), 23 international. 225 applicants, 44% accepted, 47 enrolled. In 2012, 56 master's, 3 doctorates awarded. *Degree requirements:* For doctorate, one foreign language, thesis/dissertation. *Entrance requirements:* For master's and doctorate, GRE General Test. Additional exam requirements/recommendations for international students: Required—TOEFL (minimum score 550 paper-based; 80 iBT). Application fee: $40. Electronic applications accepted. *Expenses: Tuition, area resident:* Part-time $572 per credit. Tuition, nonresident: part-time $1444 per credit. *Financial support:* Fellowships, research assistantships, teaching assistantships, career-related internships or fieldwork, Federal Work-Study, and tuition waivers (full and partial) available. Financial award application deadline: 3/1. *Unit head:* Dr. Thomas C. Vogelmann, Dean, 802-656-2980. *Application contact:* Ralph Swenson, Director of Graduate Admissions, 802-656-2699, Fax: 802-656-0519, E-mail: graduate.admissions@uvm.edu.

University of Wisconsin–Madison, Graduate School, College of Agricultural and Life Sciences, Madison, WI 53706-1380. Offers MA, MPS, MS, PhD. Part-time programs available. *Entrance requirements:* For master's and doctorate, GRE. Additional exam requirements/recommendations for international students: Required—TOEFL. Electronic applications accepted. *Expenses:* Tuition, state resident: full-time $10,728; part-time $743 per credit. Tuition, nonresident: full-time $24,054; part-time $1575 per credit. *Required fees:* $1111; $72 per credit.

University of Wisconsin–River Falls, Outreach and Graduate Studies, College of Agriculture, Food, and Environmental Sciences, River Falls, WI 54022. Offers MS. Part-time programs available. *Degree requirements:* For master's, comprehensive exam, thesis (for some programs). *Entrance requirements:* For master's, minimum GPA of 2.75. Additional exam requirements/recommendations for international students: Required—TOEFL (minimum score 500 paper-based; 65 iBT), IELTS (minimum score 5.4). Electronic applications accepted.

University of Wyoming, College of Agriculture and Natural Resources, Laramie, WY 82070. Offers MA, MS, PhD. Part-time programs available. Terminal master's awarded for partial completion of doctoral program. *Degree requirements:* For doctorate, thesis/dissertation. *Entrance requirements:* For master's and doctorate, GRE General Test, minimum GPA of 3.0. Electronic applications accepted. *Faculty research:* Nutrition, molecular biology, animal science, plant science, entomology.

Utah State University, School of Graduate Studies, College of Agriculture, Logan, UT 84322. Offers MDA, MS, PhD. Part-time programs available. Postbaccalaureate distance learning degree programs offered (minimal on-campus study). Terminal master's awarded for partial completion of doctoral program. *Degree requirements:* For doctorate, thesis/dissertation. *Entrance requirements:* For master's and doctorate, GRE General Test, minimum GPA of 3.0. Additional exam requirements/recommendations for international students: Required—TOEFL. *Faculty research:* Low-input agriculture, anti-viral chemotherapy, lactic culture, environmental biophysics and climate.

Virginia Polytechnic Institute and State University, Graduate School, College of Agriculture and Life Sciences, Blacksburg, VA 24124. Offers agricultural and applied economics (MS); agricultural and life sciences (MS); animal and poultry science (MS, PhD); crop and soil environmental sciences (MS, PhD); dairy science (MS); entomology (PhD); horticulture (MS, PhD); human nutrition, foods and exercise (MS, PhD); life sciences (MS, PhD); plant pathology, physiology and weed science (PhD). *Faculty:* 233 full-time (65 women), 1 (woman) part-time/adjunct. *Students:* 343 full-time (199 women), 74 part-time (47 women); includes 48 minority (20 Black or African American, non-Hispanic/Latino; 1 American Indian or Alaska Native, non-Hispanic/Latino; 15 Asian, non-Hispanic/Latino; 7 Hispanic/Latino; 5 Two or more races, non-Hispanic/Latino), 105 international. Average age 29. 387 applicants, 33% accepted, 98 enrolled. In 2012, 81 master's, 52 doctorates awarded. *Degree requirements:* For master's, comprehensive exam (for some programs), thesis (for some programs); for doctorate, comprehensive exam (for some programs), thesis/dissertation (for some programs). *Entrance requirements:* For master's and doctorate, GRE/GMAT (may vary by department). Additional exam requirements/recommendations for international students: Required—TOEFL (minimum score 550 paper-based). *Application deadline:* For fall admission, 8/1 for domestic students, 4/1 for international students; for spring admission, 1/1 for domestic students, 9/1 for international students. Applications are processed on a rolling basis. Application fee: $65. Electronic applications accepted. *Expenses:* Tuition, state resident: full-time $10,677; part-time $593.25 per credit hour. Tuition, nonresident: full-time $20,926; part-time $1162.50 per credit hour. *Required fees:* $427.75 per semester. Tuition and fees vary according to course load, campus/location and program. *Financial support:* In 2012–13, 1 fellowship with full tuition reimbursement (averaging $21,000 per year), 229 research assistantships with full tuition reimbursements (averaging $18,998 per year), 77 teaching assistantships with full tuition reimbursements (averaging $18,174 per year) were awarded. Financial award application deadline: 3/1; financial award applicants required to submit FAFSA. *Total annual research expenditures:* $41.8 million. *Unit head:* Dr. Alan L. Grant, Dean, 540-231-4152, Fax: 540-231-4163, E-mail: algrant@vt.edu. *Application contact:* Sheila Norman, Administrative Assistant, 540-231-4152, Fax: 540-231-4163, E-mail: snorman@vt.edu. Website: http://www.cals.vt.edu/.

Virginia Polytechnic Institute and State University, VT Online, Blacksburg, VA 24061. Offers advanced transportation systems (Certificate); aerospace engineering (MS); agricultural and life sciences (MSLFS); business information systems (Graduate Certificate); career and technical education (MS); civil engineering (MS); computer engineering (M Eng, MS); decision support systems (Graduate Certificate); eLearning leadership (MA); electrical engineering (M Eng, MS); engineering administration (MEA); environmental engineering (Certificate); environmental politics and policy (Graduate Certificate); environmental sciences and engineering (MS); foundations of political analysis (Graduate Certificate); health product risk management (Graduate Certificate); industrial and systems engineering (MS); information policy and society (Graduate Certificate); information security (Graduate Certificate); information technology (MIT); instructional technology (MA); integrative STEM education (MA Ed); liberal arts (Graduate Certificate); life sciences: health product risk management (MS); natural resources (MNR, Graduate Certificate); networking (Graduate Certificate); nonprofit and nongovernmental organization management (Graduate Certificate); ocean engineering (MS); political science (MA); security studies (Graduate Certificate); software development (Graduate Certificate). *Expenses:* Tuition, state resident: full-time $10,677; part-time $593.25 per credit hour. Tuition, nonresident: full-time $20,926; part-time $1162.50 per credit hour. *Required fees:* $427.75 per semester. Tuition and fees vary according to course load, campus/location and program. Website: http://www.vto.vt.edu/.

Virginia State University, School of Graduate Studies, Research, and Outreach, School of Agriculture, Petersburg, VA 23806-0001. Offers MS.

Washington State University, Graduate School, College of Agricultural, Human, and Natural Resource Sciences, Department of Crop and Soil Sciences, Program in Agriculture, Pullman, WA 99164. Offers MS. *Degree requirements:* For master's, comprehensive exam (for some programs), thesis (for some programs), oral defense. *Entrance requirements:* For master's, transcripts of all college course work, three letters of reference, personal statement describing intent and interest area(s). Additional exam requirements/recommendations for international students: Required—TOEFL, IELTS.

Western Kentucky University, Graduate Studies, Ogden College of Science and Engineering, Department of Agriculture, Bowling Green, KY 42101. Offers MA Ed, MS. Part-time and evening/weekend programs available. *Degree requirements:* For master's, comprehensive exam, thesis optional. *Entrance requirements:* For master's, GRE General Test, minimum GPA of 2.75. Additional exam requirements/recommendations for international students: Required—TOEFL (minimum score 555 paper-based; 79 iBT). *Faculty research:* Establishment of warm season grasses, heat composting, enrichment activities in agricultural education.

West Texas A&M University, College of Agriculture, Science and Engineering, Department of Agricultural Sciences, Canyon, TX 79016-0001. Offers agricultural business and economics (MS); agriculture (MS, PhD); animal science (MS); plant, soil and environmental science (MS). Part-time programs available. *Degree requirements:* For master's, comprehensive exam, thesis optional. *Entrance requirements:* For master's, GRE General Test. Additional exam requirements/recommendations for international students: Required—TOEFL (minimum score 550 paper-based). Electronic applications accepted.

West Virginia University, Davis College of Agriculture, Forestry and Consumer Sciences, Morgantown, WV 26506. Offers M Agr, MS, MSF, PhD. Part-time programs available. *Degree requirements:* For master's, thesis; for doctorate, thesis/dissertation. *Entrance requirements:* Additional exam requirements/recommendations for international students: Required—TOEFL. Electronic applications accepted. *Faculty research:* Reproductive physiology, soil and water quality, human nutrition, aquaculture, wildlife management.

Agronomy and Soil Sciences

Alabama Agricultural and Mechanical University, School of Graduate Studies, College of Agricultural, Life and Natural Sciences, Department of Biological and Environmental Sciences, Huntsville, AL 35811. Offers plant and soil science (MS, PhD). Evening/weekend programs available. Terminal master's awarded for partial completion of doctoral program. *Degree requirements:* For master's, thesis; for doctorate, one foreign language, thesis/dissertation. *Entrance requirements:* For master's, GRE General Test, BS in agriculture; for doctorate, GRE General Test, master's degree. Additional exam requirements/recommendations for international students: Required—TOEFL (minimum score 500 paper-based; 61 iBT). Electronic applications accepted. *Faculty research:* Plant breeding, cytogenetics, crop production, soil chemistry and fertility, remote sensing.

Alcorn State University, School of Graduate Studies, School of Agriculture and Applied Science, Alcorn State, MS 39096-7500. Offers agricultural economics (MS Ag); agronomy (MS Ag); animal science (MS Ag). *Degree requirements:* For master's, thesis optional. *Faculty research:* Aquatic systems, dairy herd improvement, fruit production, alternative farming practices.

Auburn University, Graduate School, College of Agriculture, Department of Agronomy and Soils, Auburn University, AL 36849. Offers M Ag, MS, PhD. Part-time programs available. *Faculty:* 26 full-time (6 women). *Students:* 16 full-time (7 women), 27 part-time (8 women); includes 3 minority (2 Asian, non-Hispanic/Latino; 1 Hispanic/Latino), 17 international. Average age 28. 28 applicants, 54% accepted, 12 enrolled. In 2012, 6 master's, 2 doctorates awarded. *Degree requirements:* For master's, thesis (for some programs); for doctorate, thesis/dissertation. *Entrance requirements:* For master's and doctorate, GRE General Test. *Application deadline:* For fall admission, 7/7 for domestic students; for spring admission, 11/24 for domestic students. Applications are processed on a rolling basis. Application fee: $50 ($60 for international students). Electronic applications accepted. *Expenses:* Tuition, state resident: full-time $7866; part-time $437 per credit. Tuition, nonresident: full-time $23,598; part-time $1311 per credit. *Required fees:* $787 per semester. Tuition and fees vary according to degree level and program. *Financial support:* Research assistantships, teaching assistantships, and Federal Work-Study available. Support available to part-time students. Financial award application deadline: 3/15; financial award applicants required to submit FAFSA. *Faculty research:* Plant breeding and genetics; weed science; crop production; soil fertility and plant nutrition; soil genesis, morphology, and classification. *Unit head:* Dr. Joseph T. Touchton, Head, 334-844-4100, E-mail: jtouchto@ag.auburn.edu. *Application contact:* Dr. George Flowers, Dean of the Graduate School, 334-844-2125.

Colorado State University, Graduate School, College of Agricultural Sciences, Department of Soil and Crop Sciences, Fort Collins, CO 80523-1170. Offers MS, PhD. Part-time programs available. *Faculty:* 19 full-time (4 women), 1 part-time/adjunct (0 women). *Students:* 23 full-time (9 women), 18 part-time (7 women); includes 4 minority (2 Black or African American, non-Hispanic/Latino; 1 Asian, non-Hispanic/Latino; 1 Hispanic/Latino), 12 international. Average age 35. 24 applicants, 29% accepted, 7 enrolled. In 2012, 6 master's, 5 doctorates awarded. Terminal master's awarded for partial completion of doctoral program. *Degree requirements:* For master's, thesis; for doctorate, comprehensive exam, thesis/dissertation, student teaching. *Entrance requirements:* For master's, GRE, minimum GPA of 3.0, appropriate bachelor's degree, letters of recommendation, statement of purpose; for doctorate, GRE, minimum GPA of 3.0, appropriate master's degree, letters of recommendation. Additional exam requirements/recommendations for international students: Required—TOEFL (minimum score 550 paper-based; 80 iBT). *Application deadline:* For fall admission, 4/1 priority date for domestic students, 5/1 for international students; for spring admission, 9/1 priority date for domestic students, 10/1 for international students. Application fee: $50. Electronic applications accepted. *Expenses:* Tuition, state resident: full-time $8811; part-time $490 per credit. Tuition, nonresident: full-time $21,600; part-time $1200 per credit. *Required fees:* $1819; $61 per credit. *Financial support:* In 2012–13, 19 students received support, including 5 fellowships with full tuition reimbursements available (averaging $26,683 per year), 15 research assistantships with full tuition reimbursements available (averaging $18,547 per year), 1 teaching assistantship with full tuition reimbursement available (averaging $8,924 per year); scholarships/grants and unspecified assistantships also available. Financial award application deadline: 2/15; financial award applicants required to submit FAFSA. *Faculty research:* Water quality, soil fertility, soil/plant ecosystems, plant breeding and genetics, cropping systems. *Total annual research expenditures:* $3.4 million. *Unit head:* Dr. Eugene Kelly, Head, 970-491-6517, Fax: 970-491-0564, E-mail: eugene.kelly@colostate.edu. *Application contact:* Karen Allison, Graduate Contact, 970-491-6295, Fax: 970-491-0564, E-mail: karen.allison@colostate.edu. Website: http://www.soilcrop.colostate.edu/.

Cornell University, Graduate School, Graduate Fields of Agriculture and Life Sciences, Field of Soil and Crop Sciences, Ithaca, NY 14853-0001. Offers agronomy (MS, PhD); environmental information science (MS, PhD);

environmental management (MPS); field crop science (MS, PhD); soil science (MS, PhD). *Faculty:* 41 full-time (10 women). *Students:* 16 full-time (10 women); includes 4 minority (all Hispanic/Latino), 5 international. Average age 30. 54 applicants, 17% accepted, 5 enrolled. In 2012, 10 master's, 5 doctorates awarded. *Degree requirements:* For master's, thesis (MS); for doctorate, comprehensive exam, thesis/dissertation. *Entrance requirements:* For master's and doctorate, GRE General Test, 2 letters of recommendation. Additional exam requirements/recommendations for international students: Required—TOEFL (minimum score 550 paper-based; 77 iBT). *Application deadline:* For fall admission, 2/1 priority date for domestic students. Applications are processed on a rolling basis. Application fee: $95. Electronic applications accepted. *Financial support:* In 2012–13, 12 students received support, including 7 fellowships with full tuition reimbursements available, 5 teaching assistantships with full tuition reimbursements available; research assistantships with full tuition reimbursements available, institutionally sponsored loans, traineeships, health care benefits, tuition waivers (full and partial), and unspecified assistantships also available. *Faculty research:* Soil chemistry, physics and biology; crop physiology and management; environmental information science and modeling; international agriculture; weed science. *Unit head:* Director of Graduate Studies, 607-255-3267, Fax: 607-255-8615. *Application contact:* Graduate Field Assistant, 607-255-3267, Fax: 607-255-8615, E-mail: ljh4@cornell.edu. Website: http://www.gradschool.cornell.edu/fields.php?id=5A&a-2

Dalhousie University, Faculty of Agriculture, Halifax, NS B3H 4R2, Canada. Offers agriculture (M Sc), including air quality, animal behavior, animal molecular genetics, animal nutrition, animal technology, aquaculture, botany, crop management, crop physiology, ecology, environmental microbiology, food science, horticulture, nutrient management, pest management, physiology, plant biotechnology, plant pathology, soil chemistry, soil fertility, waste management and composting, water quality. Part-time programs available. *Degree requirements:* For master's, thesis, ATC Exam Teaching Assistantship. *Entrance requirements:* For master's, honors B Sc, minimum GPA of 3.0. Additional exam requirements/recommendations for international students: Required—TOEFL (minimum score 580 paper-based; 92 iBT), IELTS, Michigan English Language Assessment Battery, CanTEST, CAEL. *Faculty research:* Bio-product development, organic agriculture, nutrient management, air and water quality, agricultural biotechnology.

Iowa State University of Science and Technology, Department of Agronomy, Ames, IA 50011. Offers agricultural meteorology (MS, PhD); agronomy (MS); crop production and physiology (MS, PhD); plant breeding (MS, PhD); soil science (MS, PhD). *Degree requirements:* For master's, thesis or alternative. *Entrance requirements:* Additional exam requirements/recommendations for international students: Recommended—TOEFL (minimum score 550 paper-based; 79 iBT), IELTS (minimum score 6.5). *Application deadline:* For fall admission, 4/15 priority date for domestic students, 4/15 for international students; for spring admission, 10/1 priority date for domestic students, 10/1 for international students. Application fee: $60 ($90 for international students). Electronic applications accepted. *Application contact:* Jaci Severson, Application Contact, 515-294-1361, Fax: 515-294-5506, E-mail: msagron@iastate.edu. Website: http://www.masters.agron.iastate.edu/.

Iowa State University of Science and Technology, Program in Crop Production and Physiology, Ames, IA 50011. Offers MS, PhD. *Entrance requirements:* Additional exam requirements/recommendations for international students: Required—TOEFL (minimum score 550 paper-based; 79 iBT), IELTS (minimum score 6.5). *Application deadline:* Applications are processed on a rolling basis. Application fee: $60 ($90 for international students). Electronic applications accepted. *Application contact:* Jaci Severson, Application Contact, 515-294-1361, Fax: 515-294-8146, E-mail: gradprograms@agron.iastate.edu. Website: http://www.agron.iastate.edu.

Iowa State University of Science and Technology, Program in Soil Science, Ames, IA 50011. Offers MS, PhD. *Entrance requirements:* Additional exam requirements/recommendations for international students: Required—TOEFL (minimum score 550 paper-based; 79 iBT), IELTS (minimum score 6.5). *Application deadline:* Applications are processed on a rolling basis. Application fee: $60 ($90 for international students). Electronic applications accepted. *Application contact:* Jaci Severson, Application Contact, 515-294-1361, Fax: 515-294-8146, E-mail: gradprograms@agron.iastate.edu. Website: http://www.agron.iastate.edu.

Kansas State University, Graduate School, College of Agriculture, Department of Agronomy, Manhattan, KS 66506. Offers crop science (MS, PhD); plant breeding and genetics (MS, PhD); range management (MS, PhD); soil science (MS, PhD); weed science (MS, PhD). Part-time programs available. *Faculty:* 29 full-time (6 women), 13 part-time/adjunct (0 women). *Students:* 62 full-time (21

Peterson's Graduate Programs in the Physical Sciences, Mathematics, Agricultural Sciences, the Environment & Natural Resources 2014

www.petersonsbooks.com **393**

women), 15 part-time (4 women); includes 5 minority (2 Black or African American, non-Hispanic/Latino; 2 Asian, non-Hispanic/Latino; 1 Hispanic/Latino), 34 international. Average age 31. 38 applicants, 29% accepted, 10 enrolled. In 2012, 15 master's, 1 doctorate awarded. *Degree requirements:* For master's, thesis or alternative, oral exam; for doctorate, thesis/dissertation, preliminary exams. *Entrance requirements:* For master's, minimum GPA of 3.0 in BS; for doctorate, minimum GPA of 3.0 in master's program. Additional exam requirements/recommendations for international students: Required—TOEFL (minimum score 550 paper-based; 79 iBT). *Application deadline:* For fall admission, 2/1 priority date for domestic students, 2/1 for international students; for spring admission, 8/1 priority date for domestic students, 8/1 for international students. Applications are processed on a rolling basis. Application fee: $50 ($75 for international students). Electronic applications accepted. *Financial support:* In 2012–13, 62 research assistantships (averaging $23,500 per year) were awarded; institutionally sponsored loans and scholarships/grants also available. Support available to part-time students. Financial award application deadline: 3/1; financial award applicants required to submit FAFSA. *Faculty research:* Range and forage science, soil and environmental science, crop physiology, weed science, plant breeding and genetics. *Total annual research expenditures:* $6.5 million. *Unit head:* Dr. Gary Pierzynski, Head, 785-532-6101, Fax: 785-532-6094, E-mail: gmp@k-state.edu. *Application contact:* Dr. Gerard Kluitenberg, Graduate Coordinator, 785-532-7215, Fax: 785-532-6094, E-mail: gjk@ksu.edu. Website: http://www.agronomy.k-state.edu/DesktopDefault.aspx.

Louisiana State University and Agricultural and Mechanical College, Graduate School, College of Agriculture, School of Plant, Environmental and Soil Sciences, Department of Agronomy and Environmental Management, Baton Rouge, LA 70803. Offers agronomy (MS, PhD). Part-time programs available. *Faculty:* 32 full-time (4 women). *Students:* 39 full-time (11 women), 5 part-time (1 woman); includes 4 minority (1 Asian, non-Hispanic/Latino; 2 Hispanic/Latino; 1 Two or more races, non-Hispanic/Latino), 19 international. Average age 29. 27 applicants, 37% accepted, 4 enrolled. In 2012, 3 master's, 5 doctorates awarded. *Degree requirements:* For master's, thesis or alternative; for doctorate, thesis/dissertation. *Entrance requirements:* For master's and doctorate, GRE General Test, minimum GPA of 3.0. Additional exam requirements/recommendations for international students: Required—TOEFL (minimum score 550 paper-based; 79 iBT) or IELTS (minimum score 6.5). *Application deadline:* For fall admission, 1/25 priority date for domestic students, 5/15 for international students; for spring admission, 10/15 for international students. Applications are processed on a rolling basis. Application fee: $50 ($70 for international students). Electronic applications accepted. *Financial support:* In 2012–13, 41 students received support, including 34 research assistantships with partial tuition reimbursements available (averaging $19,212 per year), 1 teaching assistantship with partial tuition reimbursement available (averaging $16,000 per year); fellowships, Federal Work-Study, scholarships/grants, tuition waivers (full), and unspecified assistantships also available. Support available to part-time students. Financial award applicants required to submit FAFSA. *Faculty research:* Crop production, resource management, environmental studies, soil science, plant genetics. *Total annual research expenditures:* $54,474. *Unit head:* Dr. Don LaBonte, Director, 225-578-2110, Fax: 225-578-1403, E-mail: dlabonte@lsu.edu. *Application contact:* Dr. David Weindorf, Graduate Coordinator, 225-578-0396, Fax: 225-578-1403, E-mail: dweindorf@agcenter.lsu.edu. Website: http://www.agronomy.lsu.edu/.

McGill University, Faculty of Graduate and Postdoctoral Studies, Faculty of Agricultural and Environmental Sciences, Department of Bioresource Engineering, Montréal, QC H3A 2T5, Canada. Offers computer applications (M Sc, M Sc A, PhD); food engineering (M Sc, M Sc A, PhD); grain drying (M Sc, M Sc A, PhD); irrigation and drainage (M Sc, M Sc A, PhD); machinery (M Sc, M Sc A, PhD); pollution control (M Sc, M Sc A, PhD); post-harvest technology (M Sc, M Sc A, PhD); soil dynamics (M Sc, M Sc A, PhD); structure and environment (M Sc, M Sc A, PhD); vegetable and fruit storage (M Sc, M Sc A, PhD).

McGill University, Faculty of Graduate and Postdoctoral Studies, Faculty of Agricultural and Environmental Sciences, Department of Natural Resource Sciences, Montréal, QC H3A 2T5, Canada. Offers entomology (M Sc, PhD); environmental assessment (M Sc); forest science (M Sc, PhD); microbiology (M Sc, PhD); micrometeorology (M Sc, PhD); neotropical environment (M Sc, PhD); soil science (M Sc, PhD); wildlife biology (M Sc, PhD).

Michigan State University, The Graduate School, College of Agriculture and Natural Resources, Department of Crop and Soil Sciences, East Lansing, MI 48824. Offers crop and soil sciences (MS, PhD); crop and soil sciences-environmental toxicology (PhD); plant breeding and genetics-crop and soil sciences (MS); plant breeding, genetics and biotechnology-crop and soil sciences (PhD). *Entrance requirements:* Additional exam requirements/recommendations for international students: Required—TOEFL (minimum score 550 paper-based), Michigan State University ELT (minimum score 85), Michigan Michigan English Language Assessment Battery (minimum score 83). Electronic applications accepted.

Michigan State University, The Graduate School, College of Agriculture and Natural Resources, MSU-DOE Plant Research Laboratory, East Lansing, MI 48824. Offers biochemistry and molecular biology (PhD); cellular and molecular biology (PhD); crop and soil sciences (PhD); genetics (PhD); microbiology and molecular genetics (PhD); plant biology (PhD); plant physiology (PhD). Offered jointly with the Department of Energy. *Degree requirements:* For doctorate, comprehensive exam, thesis/dissertation, laboratory rotation, defense of dissertation. *Entrance requirements:* For doctorate, GRE General Test, acceptance into one of the affiliated department programs; 3 letters of recommendation; bachelor's degree or equivalent in life sciences, chemistry, biochemistry, or biophysics; research experience. Electronic applications accepted. *Faculty research:* Role of hormones in the regulation of plant development and physiology, molecular mechanisms associated with signal recognition, development and application of genetic methods and materials, protein routing and function.

Mississippi State University, College of Agriculture and Life Sciences, Department of Plant and Soil Sciences, Mississippi State, MS 39762. Offers agriculture (MS, PhD), including agronomy, horticulture, weed science. *Faculty:* 26 full-time (1 woman), 1 part-time/adjunct (0 women). *Students:* 49 full-time (18 women), 22 part-time (7 women); includes 5 minority (2 Black or African American, non-Hispanic/Latino; 2 American Indian or Alaska Native, non-Hispanic/Latino; 1 Asian, non-Hispanic/Latino), 16 international. Average age 31. 49 applicants, 35% accepted, 16 enrolled. In 2012, 6 master's, 4 doctorates awarded. *Degree requirements:* For master's, comprehensive exam, thesis, oral and/or written exams; for doctorate, comprehensive exam, thesis/dissertation, minimum 20 semester hours of research for dissertation. *Entrance requirements:* For master's, GRE (weed science), minimum GPA of 2.75 (agronomy/horticulture), 3.0 (weed science); for doctorate, GRE (weed science), minimum GPA of 3.0 (agronomy/horticulture), 3.25 (weed science). Additional exam requirements/recommendations for international students: Required—TOEFL (minimum score 500 paper-based; 61 iBT), TOEFL (minimum score 550 paper-based, 79 iBT) or IELTS (minimum score 6.5) for weed science; Recommended—IELTS (minimum score 5.5). *Application deadline:* For fall admission, 7/1 for domestic students, 5/1 for international students; for spring admission, 10/1 for domestic students, 9/1 for international students. Applications are processed on a rolling basis. Application fee: $60. Electronic applications accepted. *Financial support:* In 2012–13, 35 research assistantships (averaging $14,968 per year), 3 teaching assistantships (averaging $14,315 per year) were awarded; Federal Work-Study, institutionally sponsored loans, scholarships/grants, and unspecified assistantships also available. Financial award application deadline: 4/1; financial award applicants required to submit FAFSA. *Unit head:* Dr. J. Mike Phillips, Professor and Head, 662-325-2311, Fax: 662-325-8742, E-mail: jmp657@msstate.edu. *Application contact:* Dr. William Kingery, Graduate Coordinator, 662-325-2748, Fax: 662-325-8742, E-mail: wkingery@pss.msstate.edu. Website: http://www.pss.msstate.edu/.

North Carolina Agricultural and Technical State University, School of Graduate Studies, School of Agriculture and Environmental Sciences, Department of Natural Resources and Environmental Design, Greensboro, NC 27411. Offers plant, soil and environmental science (MS). Part-time and evening/weekend programs available. *Degree requirements:* For master's, comprehensive exam, thesis optional, qualifying exam. *Entrance requirements:* For master's, GRE General Test, minimum GPA of 3.0. *Faculty research:* Soil parameters and compaction of forest site, controlled traffic effects on soil, improving soybean and vegetable crops.

North Carolina State University, Graduate School, College of Agriculture and Life Sciences, Department of Crop Science, Raleigh, NC 27695. Offers MS, PhD. Part-time programs available. Terminal master's awarded for partial completion of doctoral program. *Degree requirements:* For master's, thesis; for doctorate, thesis/dissertation. *Entrance requirements:* For master's and doctorate, GRE. Electronic applications accepted. *Faculty research:* Crop breeding and genetics, application of biotechnology to crop improvement, plant physiology, crop physiology and management, agroecology.

North Carolina State University, Graduate School, College of Agriculture and Life Sciences, Department of Soil Science, Raleigh, NC 27695. Offers MS, PhD. Part-time programs available. Postbaccalaureate distance learning degree programs offered. *Degree requirements:* For master's, thesis (for some programs); for doctorate, thesis/dissertation. *Entrance requirements:* For master's and doctorate, GRE, minimum GPA of 3.0. Additional exam requirements/recommendations for international students: Required—TOEFL (minimum score 75 iBT). Electronic applications accepted. *Faculty research:* Soil management, soil-environmental relations, chemical and physical properties of soils, nutrient and water management, land use.

North Dakota State University, College of Graduate and Interdisciplinary Studies, College of Agriculture, Food Systems, and Natural Resources, Department of Soil Science, Fargo, ND 58108. Offers soil sciences (MS, PhD). Part-time programs available. *Students:* 9 full-time (5 women), 3 part-time (2 women), 5 international. Average age 32. 1 applicant. In 2012, 2 master's awarded. *Degree requirements:* For master's, comprehensive exam, thesis, classroom teaching; for doctorate, comprehensive exam, thesis/dissertation, classroom teaching. *Entrance requirements:* Additional exam requirements/recommendations for international students: Required—TOEFL (minimum score 525 paper-based; 71 iBT). *Application deadline:* For fall admission, 5/1 for international students; for winter admission, 8/1 for international students. Applications are processed on a rolling basis. Application fee: $35. Electronic applications accepted. *Financial support:* In 2012–13, 7 research assistantships with full tuition reimbursements (averaging $14,300 per year) were awarded; fellowships, Federal Work-Study, institutionally sponsored loans, and scholarships/grants also available. Financial award application deadline: 3/15. *Faculty research:* Microclimate, nitrogen management, landscape studies, water quality, soil management. *Unit head:* Dr. Donald Kirby, Interim Chair, 701-231-8901, Fax: 701-231-7861. *Application contact:* Sonya Goergen, Marketing, Recruitment, and Public Relations Coordinator, 701-231-7033, Fax: 701-231-6524. Website: http://www.ndsu.edu/ndsu/academic/factsheets/ag/soilsci.shtml.

The Ohio State University, Graduate School, College of Food, Agricultural, and Environmental Sciences, School of Environment and Natural Resources, Program in Soil Science, Columbus, OH 43210. Offers MS, PhD. *Faculty:* 9. *Students:* 1 (woman) full-time, 1 (woman) part-time, 1 international. Average age 29. In 2012, 3 master's, 4 doctorates awarded. *Degree requirements:* For doctorate, thesis/dissertation. *Entrance requirements:* For master's and doctorate, GRE General Test. Additional exam requirements/recommendations for international students: Required—TOEFL (minimum score 550 paper-based), IELTS (minimum score 6.5), or Michigan English Language Assessment Battery (minimum score 82). *Application deadline:* For fall admission, 8/15 priority date for domestic students, 7/1 for international students; for winter admission, 12/1 priority date for domestic students, 11/1 for international students; for spring admission, 3/1 priority date for domestic students, 2/1 for international students. Applications are processed on a rolling basis. Application fee: $40 ($50 for international students). Electronic applications accepted. *Unit head:* Ronald Hendrick, Director, 614-292-8522, E-mail: hendrick.15@osu.edu. *Application contact:* Amy Schmidt, Graduate Program Coordinator, 614-292-0000, Fax: 614-292-7432, E-mail: schmidt.442@osu.edu. Website: http://senr.osu.edu/Future_Graduate_Students/Graduate_Areas_of_Specialization/Soil_Science_.htm.

Oklahoma State University, College of Agricultural Science and Natural Resources, Department of Horticulture and Landscape Architecture, Stillwater, OK 74078. Offers agriculture (M Ag); crop science (PhD); environmental science (PhD); horticulture (MS); plant science (PhD). *Faculty:* 19 full-time (3 women), 2 part-time/adjunct (1 woman). *Students:* 1 (woman) full-time, 7 part-time (5 women), 4 international. Average age 27. 11 applicants, 27% accepted, 2 enrolled. In 2012, 6 master's awarded. *Degree requirements:* For master's, thesis (for some programs); for doctorate, comprehensive exam, thesis/dissertation. *Entrance requirements:* For master's and doctorate, GRE or GMAT. Additional exam requirements/recommendations for international students: Required—TOEFL (minimum score 550 paper-based; 79 iBT). *Application deadline:* For fall admission, 3/1 for international students; for spring admission, 8/1 for international students. Applications are processed on a rolling basis. Application fee: $40 ($75 for international students). Electronic applications accepted. *Expenses:* Tuition, state resident: full-time $4272; part-time $178 per credit hour. Tuition, nonresident: full-time $17,016; part-time $709 per credit hour. *Required fees:* $2188; $91.17 per credit hour. One-time fee: $50 full-time. Part-time tuition and fees vary according to course load and campus/location. *Financial support:* In 2012–13, 3 research assistantships (averaging $14,964 per year), 3 teaching assistantships (averaging $14,964 per year) were awarded; career-related internships or fieldwork, Federal Work-Study, scholarships/grants, health care benefits, tuition waivers (partial), and unspecified assistantships also available. Support available to part-time students. Financial award application deadline: 3/1; financial award applicants required to submit FAFSA. *Faculty research:* Stress and postharvest physiology; water utilization and runoff; integrated pest management (IPM) systems and nursery, turf, floriculture, vegetable, net and fruit produces and natural resources, food extraction, and processing; public garden management. *Unit head:* Dr. Dale Maronek, Head, 405-744-5414, Fax: 405-744-9709. *Application contact:* Dr. Sheryl Tucker, Dean, 405-744-7099, Fax: 405-744-0355, E-mail: grad-i@okstate.edu. Website: http://www.hortla.okstate.edu/.

Oklahoma State University, College of Agricultural Science and Natural Resources, Department of Plant and Soil Sciences, Stillwater, OK 74078. Offers crop science (PhD); environmental science (PhD); plant and soil sciences (MS); plant science (PhD); soil science (M Ag, PhD). *Faculty:* 33 full-time (5 women), 1 part-time/adjunct (0 women). *Students:* 20 full-time (6 women), 37 part-time (14 women); includes 6 minority (1 Black or African American, non-Hispanic/Latino; 2 Asian, non-Hispanic/Latino; 3 Two or more races, non-Hispanic/Latino), 31 international. Average age 29. 37 applicants, 27% accepted, 6 enrolled. In 2012, 20 master's, 3 doctorates awarded. *Degree requirements:* For master's, thesis; for doctorate, comprehensive exam, thesis/dissertation. *Entrance requirements:* For master's and doctorate, GRE or GMAT. Additional exam requirements/recommendations for international students: Required—TOEFL (minimum score 550 paper-based; 79 iBT). *Application deadline:* For fall admission, 3/1 for international students; for spring admission, 8/1 for international students. Applications are processed on a rolling basis. Application fee: $40 ($75 for international students). Electronic applications accepted. *Expenses:* Tuition, state resident: full-time $4272; part-time $178 per credit hour. Tuition, nonresident: full-time $17,016; part-time $709 per credit hour. *Required fees:* $2188; $91.17 per credit hour. One-time fee: $50 full-time. Part-time tuition and fees vary according to course load and campus/location. *Financial support:* In 2012–13, 44 research assistantships (averaging $15,985 per year), 2 teaching assistantships (averaging $17,760 per year) were awarded; career-related internships or fieldwork, Federal Work-Study, scholarships/grants, health care benefits, tuition waivers (partial), and unspecified assistantships also available. Support available to part-time students. Financial award application deadline: 3/1; financial award applicants required to submit FAFSA. *Faculty research:* Crop science, weed science, rangeland ecology and management, biotechnology, breeding and genetics. *Unit head:* Dr. David Porter, Interim Head, 405-744-6130, Fax: 405-744-5269. *Application contact:* Dr. Sheryl Tucker, Dean, 405-744-7099, Fax: 405-744-0355, E-mail: grad-i@okstate.edu. Website: http://www.pss.okstate.edu.

Oregon State University, College of Agricultural Sciences, Department of Crop and Soil Science, Program in Crop Science, Corvallis, OR 97331. Offers M Agr, MAIS, MS, PhD. Part-time programs available. *Students:* 17 full-time (9 women); includes 2 minority (both Hispanic/Latino), 6 international. Average age 35. 15 applicants, 27% accepted, 2 enrolled. In 2012, 3 master's, 2 doctorates awarded. *Degree requirements:* For master's, thesis (for some programs); for doctorate, variable foreign language requirement, thesis/dissertation. *Entrance requirements:* For master's and doctorate, GRE, minimum GPA of 3.0 in last 90 hours of course work. Additional exam requirements/recommendations for international students: Required—TOEFL. *Application deadline:* For fall admission, 3/1 for domestic students. Applications are processed on a rolling basis. Application fee: $50. *Expenses:* Tuition, state resident: full-time $11,367; part-time $421 per credit hour. Tuition, nonresident: full-time $18,279; part-time $677 per credit hour. *Required fees:* $1478. One-time fee: $300 full-time. Tuition and fees vary according to course load and program. *Financial support:* Fellowships, research assistantships, teaching assistantships, career-related internships or fieldwork, Federal Work-Study, and institutionally sponsored loans available. Support available to part-time students. Financial award application deadline: 2/1. *Faculty research:* Cereal and new crops breeding and genetics; weed science; seed technology and production; potato, new crops, and general crop production; plant physiology. *Unit head:* Dr. Russ Karow, Head, 541-737-2821, E-mail: russell.s.karow@oregonstate.edu.

Oregon State University, College of Agricultural Sciences, Department of Crop and Soil Science, Program in Soil Science, Corvallis, OR 97331. Offers M Agr, MAIS, MS, PhD. Part-time programs available. *Faculty:* 9 full-time (2 women). *Students:* 21 full-time (11 women), 2 part-time (0 women); includes 2 minority (both Hispanic/Latino), 4 international. Average age 29. 24 applicants, 38% accepted, 6 enrolled. In 2012, 3 master's awarded. *Degree requirements:* For master's, thesis (for some programs); for doctorate, variable foreign language requirement, thesis/dissertation. *Entrance requirements:* For master's and doctorate, GRE, minimum GPA of 3.0 in last 90 hours of course work. Additional exam requirements/recommendations for international students: Required—TOEFL. *Application deadline:* For fall admission, 3/1 for domestic students. Applications are processed on a rolling basis. Application fee: $50. *Expenses:* Tuition, state resident: full-time $11,367; part-time $421 per credit hour. Tuition, nonresident: full-time $18,279; part-time $677 per credit hour. *Required fees:* $1478. One-time fee: $300 full-time. Tuition and fees vary according to course load and program. *Financial support:* Fellowships, research assistantships, teaching assistantships, career-related internships or fieldwork, Federal Work-Study, and institutionally sponsored loans available. Support available to part-time students. Financial award application deadline: 2/1. *Faculty research:* Soil physics, chemistry, biology, fertility, and genesis. *Unit head:* Dr. Jay Stratton Noller, Associate Department Head, 541-737-6187, E-mail: jay.noller@oregonstate.edu.

Penn State University Park, Graduate School, College of Agricultural Sciences, Department of Ecosystem Science and Management, State College, University Park, PA 16802-1503. Offers forest resources (MS, PhD); soil science (MS, PhD); wildlife and fisheries science (MS, PhD). *Unit head:* Dr. Barbara J. Christ, Interim Dean, 814-865-2541, Fax: 814-865-3103, E-mail: ebf@psu.edu. *Application contact:* Cynthia E. Nicosia, Director of Graduate Enrollment Services, 814-865-1834, E-mail: cey1@psu.edu. Website: http://ecosystems.psu.edu.

Prairie View A&M University, College of Agriculture and Human Sciences, Prairie View, TX 77446-0519. Offers agricultural economics (MS); animal sciences (MS); interdisciplinary human sciences (MS); soil science (MS). Part-time and evening/weekend programs available. *Degree requirements:* For master's, comprehensive exam, thesis (for some programs), field placement. *Entrance requirements:* For master's, GRE General Test, minimum GPA of 2.45. Additional exam requirements/recommendations for international students: Required—TOEFL (minimum score 550 paper-based). *Faculty research:* Domestic violence prevention, water quality, food growth regulators, wetland dynamics, biochemistry, obesity and nutrition, family therapy.

Purdue University, Graduate School, College of Agriculture, Department of Agronomy, West Lafayette, IN 47907. Offers MS, PhD. Part-time programs available. *Faculty:* 34 full-time (7 women), 21 part-time/adjunct (6 women). *Students:* 57 full-time (23 women), 10 part-time (4 women); includes 3 minority (1 Black or African American, non-Hispanic/Latino; 2 Hispanic/Latino), 24 international. Average age 29. 49 applicants, 16% accepted, 7 enrolled. In 2012, 10 master's, 2 doctorates awarded. *Degree requirements:* For doctorate, thesis/dissertation. *Entrance requirements:* For master's and doctorate, GRE General Test, minimum undergraduate GPA of 3.0 or equivalent. Additional exam requirements/recommendations for international students: Recommended—TOEFL (minimum score 550 paper-based; 77 iBT), TWE. *Application deadline:* For fall admission, 4/15 for domestic and international students; for spring admission, 10/15 for domestic students, 9/15 for international students. Applications are processed on a rolling basis. Application fee: $60 ($75 for international students). Electronic applications accepted. *Financial support:* Fellowships with tuition reimbursements, research assistantships with tuition reimbursements, and teaching assistantships with tuition reimbursements available. Support available to part-time students. Financial award applicants required to submit FAFSA. *Faculty research:* Plant genetics and breeding, crop physiology and ecology, agricultural meteorology, soil microbiology. *Unit head:* Dr. Joseph M. Anderson, Head, 765-494-4774, E-mail: janderson@purdue.edu.

Peterson's Graduate Programs in the Physical Sciences, Mathematics, Agricultural Sciences, the Environment & Natural Resources 2014

www.petersonsbooks.com   **395**

Application contact: Karen N. Clymer, Graduate Coordinator, 765-494-4775, E-mail: kclymer@purdue.edu.

South Dakota State University, Graduate School, College of Agriculture and Biological Sciences, Department of Plant Science, Brookings, SD 57007. Offers agronomy (PhD); biological sciences (PhD); plant science (MS). *Degree requirements:* For master's, thesis (for some programs), oral exam; for doctorate, comprehensive exam, thesis/dissertation, preliminary oral and written exams. *Entrance requirements:* Additional exam requirements/recommendations for international students: Required—TOEFL (minimum score 560 paper-based; 83 iBT).

Southern Illinois University Carbondale, Graduate School, College of Agriculture, Department of Plant, Soil, and General Agriculture, Carbondale, IL 62901-4701. Offers horticultural science (MS); plant and soil science (MS). *Faculty:* 12 full-time (1 woman), 8 part-time/adjunct (0 women). *Students:* 2 full-time (1 woman), 32 part-time (11 women); includes 3 minority (2 Black or African American, non-Hispanic/Latino; 1 Hispanic/Latino), 6 international. 12 applicants, 42% accepted, 1 enrolled. In 2012, 7 master's awarded. *Degree requirements:* For master's, thesis. *Entrance requirements:* For master's, minimum GPA of 2.7. Additional exam requirements/recommendations for international students: Required—TOEFL. *Application deadline:* Applications are processed on a rolling basis. Application fee: $50. *Financial support:* In 2012–13, 22 students received support, including 15 research assistantships with full tuition reimbursements available, 6 teaching assistantships with full tuition reimbursements available; fellowships with full tuition reimbursements available, Federal Work-Study, institutionally sponsored loans, and tuition waivers (full) also available. Support available to part-time students. *Faculty research:* Herbicides, fertilizers, agriculture education, landscape design, plant breeding. *Total annual research expenditures:* $2 million. *Unit head:* Dr. Brian Klubek, Chair, 618-453-2496, E-mail: bklubek@siu.edu. *Application contact:* Lisa Hartline, Administrative Clerk, 618-453-1770, E-mail: lisah@siu.edu.

Texas A&M University, College of Agriculture and Life Sciences, Department of Soil and Crop Sciences, College Station, TX 77843. Offers agronomy (M Agr, MS, PhD); food science and technology (MS, PhD); genetics (PhD); molecular and environmental plant sciences (MS, PhD); plant breeding (MS, PhD); soil science (MS, PhD). *Faculty:* 31. *Students:* 97 full-time (39 women), 21 part-time (6 women); includes 7 minority (1 Black or African American, non-Hispanic/Latino; 2 Asian, non-Hispanic/Latino; 4 Hispanic/Latino), 42 international. Average age 29. In 2012, 8 master's, 7 doctorates awarded. *Degree requirements:* For master's, thesis; for doctorate, thesis/dissertation. *Entrance requirements:* For master's and doctorate, GRE General Test. Additional exam requirements/recommendations for international students: Required—TOEFL. *Application deadline:* For fall admission, 3/1 priority date for domestic students; for spring admission, 8/1 for domestic students. Applications are processed on a rolling basis. Application fee: $50 ($75 for international students). *Financial support:* In 2012–13, fellowships (averaging $16,000 per year), research assistantships with partial tuition reimbursements (averaging $15,000 per year) were awarded; career-related internships or fieldwork, Federal Work-Study, and institutionally sponsored loans also available. *Faculty research:* Soil and crop management, turfgrass science, weed science, cereal chemistry, food protein chemistry. *Unit head:* Dr. David D. Baltensperger, Department Head, 979-845-3001, E-mail: dbaltensperger@ag.tamu.edu. *Application contact:* Graduate Admissions, 979-845-1044, E-mail: admissions@tamu.edu. Website: http://soilcrop.tamu.edu.

Texas A&M University–Kingsville, College of Graduate Studies, College of Agriculture and Home Economics, Program in Plant and Soil Sciences, Kingsville, TX 78363. Offers MS, PhD. *Degree requirements:* For master's, comprehensive exam, thesis or alternative. *Entrance requirements:* For master's, GRE General Test, minimum GPA of 3.0. Additional exam requirements/recommendations for international students: Required—TOEFL.

Texas Tech University, Graduate School, College of Agricultural Sciences and Natural Resources, Department of Plant and Soil Science, Lubbock, TX 79409. Offers crop science (MS); horticulture (MS); plant and soil science (PhD); plant protection (MS); soil science (MS); JD/MS. Part-time programs available. Postbaccalaureate distance learning degree programs offered (no on-campus study). *Degree requirements:* For master's, thesis or alternative; for doctorate, thesis/dissertation. *Entrance requirements:* For master's and doctorate, GRE General Test, formal approval from departmental committee. Additional exam requirements/recommendations for international students: Required—TOEFL (minimum score 550 paper-based; 79 iBT). Electronic applications accepted. *Faculty research:* Molecular and cellular biology of plant stress, physiology/genetics of crop production in semi-arid conditions, improvement of native plants, soil science and management, fibers and biopolymers.

Tuskegee University, Graduate Programs, College of Agricultural, Environmental and Natural Sciences, Department of Agricultural Sciences, Program in Plant and Soil Sciences, Tuskegee, AL 36088. Offers MS. *Degree requirements:* For master's, thesis. *Entrance requirements:* For master's, GRE General Test. Additional exam requirements/recommendations for international students: Required—TOEFL (minimum score 500 paper-based). *Expenses: Tuition:* Full-time $18,100; part-time $575 per credit hour. *Required fees:* $800.

Université Laval, Faculty of Agricultural and Food Sciences, Department of Soils and Agricultural Engineering, Programs in Soils and Environment Science, Québec, QC G1K 7P4, Canada. Offers environmental technology (M Sc); soils and environment science (M Sc, PhD). Terminal master's awarded for partial completion of doctoral program. *Degree requirements:* For master's, thesis (for some programs); for doctorate, comprehensive exam, thesis/dissertation. *Entrance requirements:* For master's and doctorate, knowledge of French and English. Electronic applications accepted.

Université Laval, Faculty of Forestry, Geography and Geomatics, Program in Agroforestry, Québec, QC G1K 7P4, Canada. Offers M Sc. *Degree requirements:* For master's, thesis (for some programs). *Entrance requirements:* For master's, English exam (comprehension of English), knowledge of French, knowledge of a third language. Electronic applications accepted.

University of Alberta, Faculty of Graduate Studies and Research, Department of Renewable Resources, Edmonton, AB T6G 2E1, Canada. Offers agroforestry (M Ag, M Sc, MF); conservation biology (M Sc, PhD); forest biology and management (M Sc, PhD); land reclamation and remediation (M Sc, PhD); protected areas and wildlands management (M Sc, PhD); soil science (M Ag, M Sc, PhD); water and land resources (M Ag, M Sc, PhD); wildlife ecology and management (M Sc, PhD); MBA/M Ag; MBA/MF. Part-time programs available. *Degree requirements:* For master's, thesis (for some programs); for doctorate, comprehensive exam, thesis/dissertation. *Entrance requirements:* For master's, minimum 2 years of relevant professional experiences, minimum GPA of 3.0; for doctorate, minimum GPA of 3.0. Additional exam requirements/recommendations for international students: Required—TOEFL (minimum score 550 paper-based). Electronic applications accepted. *Faculty research:* Natural and managed landscapes.

The University of Arizona, College of Agriculture and Life Sciences, Department of Soil, Water and Environmental Science, Tucson, AZ 85721. Offers MS, PhD. *Faculty:* 5 full-time (2 women), 1 (woman) part-time/adjunct. *Students:* 51 full-time (28 women), 10 part-time (4 women); includes 17 minority (4 Black or African American, non-Hispanic/Latino; 1 American Indian or Alaska Native, non-Hispanic/Latino; 1 Asian, non-Hispanic/Latino; 7 Hispanic/Latino; 4 Two or more races, non-Hispanic/Latino), 15 international. Average age 29. 29 applicants, 55% accepted, 13 enrolled. In 2012, 10 master's, 9 doctorates awarded. *Degree requirements:* For master's, thesis; for doctorate, comprehensive exam, thesis/dissertation. *Entrance requirements:* For master's, GRE (recommended), minimum GPA of 3.0, letter of interest, 3 letters of recommendation; for doctorate, GRE (recommended), MS, minimum GPA of 3.0, letter of interest, 3 letters of recommendation. Additional exam requirements/recommendations for international students: Required—TOEFL (minimum score 550 paper-based; 80 iBT). *Application deadline:* For fall admission, 6/1 for domestic students, 12/1 for international students; for spring admission, 10/1 for domestic students, 6/1 for international students. Applications are processed on a rolling basis. Application fee: $75. *Financial support:* In 2012–13, 14 students received support, including 25 research assistantships with full and partial tuition reimbursements available (averaging $17,098 per year), 8 teaching assistantships with full and partial tuition reimbursements available (averaging $17,044 per year); fellowships, Federal Work-Study, institutionally sponsored loans, scholarships/grants, health care benefits, tuition waivers (full and partial), and unspecified assistantships also available. Financial award application deadline: 5/1. *Faculty research:* Plant production, environmental microbiology, contaminant flow and transport, aquaculture. *Total annual research expenditures:* $2.8 million. *Unit head:* Dr. Jonathan D. Chorover, Interim Department Head, 520-626-5635, E-mail: chorover@cals.arizona.edu. *Application contact:* Alicia Velasquez, Program Coordinator, 520-621-1606, Fax: 520-621-1647, E-mail: avelasqu@ag.arizona.edu. Website: http://ag.arizona.edu/SWES/.

University of Arkansas, Graduate School, Dale Bumpers College of Agricultural, Food and Life Sciences, Department of Crop, Soil and Environmental Sciences, Fayetteville, AR 72701-1201. Offers agronomy (MS, PhD). *Students:* 7 full-time (2 women), 48 part-time (19 women); includes 1 minority (Two or more races, non-Hispanic/Latino), 23 international. In 2012, 10 master's, 4 doctorates awarded. *Degree requirements:* For master's, thesis optional; for doctorate, variable foreign language requirement, thesis/dissertation. *Application deadline:* For fall admission, 4/1 for international students; for spring admission, 10/1 for international students. Applications are processed on a rolling basis. Application fee: $40 ($50 for international students). Electronic applications accepted. *Financial support:* In 2012–13, 36 research assistantships were awarded; fellowships with tuition reimbursements, teaching assistantships, career-related internships or fieldwork, and Federal Work-Study also available. Support available to part-time students. Financial award application deadline: 4/1; financial award applicants required to submit FAFSA. *Unit head:* Dr. Robert Bacon, Interim Departmental Chairperson, 479-575-2347, Fax: 479-575-7465, E-mail: rbacon@uark.edu. *Application contact:* Dr. Kristofor Brye, Graduate Coordinator, 479-575-5742, E-mail: kbrye@uark.edu. Website: http://cses.uark.edu.

The University of British Columbia, Faculty of Land and Food Systems, Program in Soil Science, Vancouver, BC V6T 1Z1, Canada. Offers M Sc, PhD. *Degree requirements:* For master's, thesis; for doctorate, comprehensive exam, thesis/dissertation. *Entrance requirements:* Additional exam requirements/recommendations for international students: Required—TOEFL (minimum score 577 paper-based; 90 iBT), IELTS (minimum score 6.5). Electronic applications accepted. *Faculty research:* Soil and water conservation, land use, land use and land classification, soil physics, soil chemistry and mineralogy.

University of California, Davis, Graduate Studies, Graduate Group in Horticulture and Agronomy, Davis, CA 95616. Offers MS. *Degree requirements:* For master's, comprehensive exam (for some programs), thesis (for some programs). *Entrance requirements:* For master's, GRE General Test. Additional exam requirements/recommendations for international students: Required—TOEFL (minimum score 550 paper-based). Electronic applications accepted. *Faculty research:* Postharvest physiology, mineral nutrition, crop improvement, plant growth and development.

University of California, Davis, Graduate Studies, Graduate Group in Soils and Biogeochemistry, Davis, CA 95616. Offers MS, PhD. Terminal master's awarded for partial completion of doctoral program. *Degree requirements:* For master's, comprehensive exam (for some programs), thesis (for some programs); for doctorate, thesis/dissertation. *Entrance requirements:* For master's, minimum GPA of 3.3; for doctorate, GRE, minimum GPA of 3.3. Additional exam requirements/recommendations for international students: Required—TOEFL (minimum score 550 paper-based). Electronic applications accepted. *Faculty research:* Rhizosphere ecology, soil transport processes, biogeochemical cycling, sustainable agriculture.

University of California, Riverside, Graduate Division, Environmental Sciences Department, Riverside, CA 92521-0102. Offers MS, PhD. *Faculty:* 19 full-time (2 women). *Students:* 22 full-time (12 women); includes 4 minority (1 Asian, non-Hispanic/Latino; 3 Hispanic/Latino), 11 international. Average age 29. In 2012, 5 master's, 1 doctorate awarded. *Degree requirements:* For doctorate, thesis/dissertation. *Entrance requirements:* For master's and doctorate, minimum GPA of 3.2. Additional exam requirements/recommendations for international students: Required—TOEFL (minimum score 550 paper-based; 80 iBT). *Application deadline:* For fall admission, 12/1 priority date for domestic students, 12/1 for international students; for winter admission, 9/1 for domestic students, 7/1 for international students; for spring admission, 12/1 for domestic students, 10/1 for international students. Application fee: $80 ($100 for international students). Electronic applications accepted. *Expenses:* Tuition, state resident: full-time $14,646. Tuition, nonresident: full-time $29,748. *Financial support:* Fellowships with tuition reimbursements and research assistantships with tuition reimbursements available. *Faculty research:* Environmental chemistry and ecotoxicology, environmental microbiology, environmental and natural resource economics and policy, soil and water science, environmental sciences and management. *Unit head:* Dr. Michael Anderson, Chair, 951-827-3757. *Application contact:* John Herring, Program Assistant, 951-827-2441, E-mail: soilwater@ucr.edu. Website: http://envisci.ucr.edu/.

University of Connecticut, Graduate School, College of Agriculture and Natural Resources, Department of Plant Science, Storrs, CT 06269. Offers plant and soil sciences (MS, PhD). Terminal master's awarded for partial completion of doctoral program. *Degree requirements:* For master's, comprehensive exam; for doctorate, thesis/dissertation. *Entrance requirements:* For master's and doctorate, GRE General Test, GRE Subject Test. Additional exam requirements/recommendations for international students: Required—TOEFL (minimum score 550 paper-based). Electronic applications accepted.

University of Delaware, College of Agriculture and Natural Resources, Department of Plant and Soil Sciences, Newark, DE 19716. Offers MS, PhD. Part-time programs available. Terminal master's awarded for partial completion of doctoral program. *Degree requirements:* For master's, thesis; for doctorate, thesis/dissertation. *Entrance requirements:* For master's and doctorate, GRE General Test. Additional exam requirements/recommendations for international students: Required—TOEFL (minimum score 550 paper-based). Electronic applications accepted. *Faculty research:* Soil chemistry, plant and cell tissue culture, plant breeding and genetics, soil physics, soil biochemistry, plant molecular biology, soil microbiology.

University of Florida, Graduate School, College of Agricultural and Life Sciences, Department of Agronomy, Gainesville, FL 32611. Offers M Ag, MS, PhD. Part-time programs available. Terminal master's awarded for partial completion of doctoral program. *Degree requirements:* For master's, thesis (for some programs); for doctorate, comprehensive exam, thesis/dissertation (for some programs). *Entrance requirements:* For master's and doctorate, GRE General Test, minimum GPA of 3.0. Additional exam requirements/recommendations for international students: Required—TOEFL (minimum score 550 paper-based; 80 iBT), IELTS (minimum score 6). Electronic applications accepted. *Faculty research:* Plant breeding and genetics weed science, crop physiology and ecology, crop management and nutrition.

University of Florida, Graduate School, College of Agricultural and Life Sciences, Department of Soil and Water Science, Gainesville, FL 32611. Offers MS, PhD. Part-time and evening/weekend programs available. Postbaccalaureate distance learning degree programs offered (no on-campus study). Terminal master's awarded for partial completion of doctoral program. *Degree requirements:* For master's, thesis optional; for doctorate, comprehensive exam, thesis/dissertation. *Entrance requirements:* For master's and doctorate, GRE General Test (minimum score 1000 taken within last 5 years), minimum GPA of 3.0. Additional exam requirements/recommendations for international students: Required—TOEFL (minimum score 550 paper-based; 80 iBT), IELTS (minimum score 6). Electronic applications accepted. *Faculty research:* Nutrient, pesticide, and waste management; soil, water, and aquifer remediation; carbon dynamics and ecosystem services; landscape analysis and modeling; wetlands and aquatic ecosystems.

University of Georgia, College of Agricultural and Environmental Sciences, Department of Crop and Soil Sciences, Athens, GA 30602. Offers crop and soil sciences (MS, PhD); plant protection and pest management (MPPPM). Part-time programs available. *Degree requirements:* For master's, thesis (MS); for doctorate, comprehensive exam, thesis/dissertation. *Entrance requirements:* For master's and doctorate, GRE General Test. Additional exam requirements/recommendations for international students: Required—TOEFL (minimum score 550 paper-based). Electronic applications accepted. *Faculty research:* Plant breeding, genomics, nutrient management, water quality, soil chemistry.

University of Guelph, Graduate Studies, Ontario Agricultural College, Department of Land Resource Science, Guelph, ON N1G 2W1, Canada. Offers atmospheric science (M Sc, PhD); environmental and agricultural earth sciences (M Sc, PhD); land resources management (M Sc, PhD); soil science (M Sc, PhD). Part-time programs available. *Degree requirements:* For master's, thesis (for some programs), research project (non-thesis track); for doctorate, comprehensive exam, thesis/dissertation. *Entrance requirements:* For master's, minimum B- average during previous 2 years of course work; for doctorate, minimum B average during previous 2 years of course work. Additional exam requirements/recommendations for international students: Required—TOEFL (minimum score 550 paper-based). Electronic applications accepted. *Faculty research:* Soil science, environmental earth science, land resource management.

University of Idaho, College of Graduate Studies, College of Agricultural and Life Sciences, Department of Plant, Soil, and Entomological Sciences, Moscow, ID 83844-2339. Offers entomology (MS, PhD); plant science (MS, PhD); soil and land resources (MS, PhD). *Faculty:* 28 full-time, 1 part-time/adjunct. *Students:* 33 full-time, 13 part-time. Average age 30. In 2012, 9 master's, 2 doctorates awarded. *Degree requirements:* For doctorate, thesis/dissertation. *Entrance requirements:* For master's and doctorate, GRE General Test, minimum GPA of 3.0. *Application deadline:* For fall admission, 7/1 for domestic students; for spring admission, 11/1 for domestic students. Applications are processed on a rolling basis. Application fee: $60. Electronic applications accepted. *Expenses:* Tuition, state resident: full-time $4230; part-time $252 per credit hour. Tuition, nonresident: full-time $17,018; part-time $891 per credit hour. *Required fees:* $2932; $107 per credit hour. *Financial support:* Research assistantships and teaching assistantships available. Financial award applicants required to submit FAFSA. *Faculty research:* Entomological sciences, crop and weed science, horticultural science, soil and land resources. *Unit head:* Dr. James B. Johnson, Department Head, 208-885-6274, Fax: 208-885-7760, E-mail: nthompson@uidaho.edu. *Application contact:* Erick Larson, Director of Graduate Admissions, 208-885-4723, E-mail: gadms@uidaho.edu. Website: http://www.uidaho.edu/pses.

University of Illinois at Urbana–Champaign, Graduate College, College of Agricultural, Consumer and Environmental Sciences, Department of Crop Sciences, Champaign, IL 61820. Offers bioinformatics: crop sciences (MS); crop sciences (MS, PhD). Postbaccalaureate distance learning degree programs offered (no on-campus study). *Students:* 142 (50 women). Application fee: $75 ($90 for international students). *Unit head:* German A. Bollero, Head, 217-333-9475, Fax: 217-333-9817, E-mail: gbollero@illinois.edu. *Application contact:* S. Dianne Carson, Office Support Specialist, 217-244-0396, Fax: 217-333-9817, E-mail: sdcarson@illinois.edu. Website: http://www.cropsci.illinois.edu.

University of Kentucky, Graduate School, College of Agriculture, Program in Crop Science, Lexington, KY 40506-0032. Offers MS, PhD. *Degree requirements:* For master's, comprehensive exam, thesis optional; for doctorate, comprehensive exam, thesis/dissertation. *Entrance requirements:* For master's, GRE General Test, minimum GPA of 2.75; for doctorate, GRE General Test, minimum GPA of 3.0. Additional exam requirements/recommendations for international students: Required—TOEFL (minimum score 550 paper-based). Electronic applications accepted. *Faculty research:* Crop physiology, crop ecology, crop management, crop breeding and genetics, weed science.

University of Kentucky, Graduate School, College of Agriculture, Program in Plant and Soil Science, Lexington, KY 40506-0032. Offers MS. *Degree requirements:* For master's, comprehensive exam, thesis optional. *Entrance requirements:* For master's, GRE General Test, minimum undergraduate GPA of 2.75, graduate 3.0. Additional exam requirements/recommendations for international students: Required—TOEFL (minimum score 550 paper-based). Electronic applications accepted.

University of Kentucky, Graduate School, College of Agriculture, Program in Soil Science, Lexington, KY 40506-0032. Offers PhD. *Degree requirements:* For doctorate, comprehensive exam, thesis/dissertation. *Entrance requirements:* For doctorate, GRE General Test, minimum graduate GPA of 3.0, undergraduate 2.75. Additional exam requirements/recommendations for international students: Required—TOEFL (minimum score 550 paper-based). Electronic applications accepted. *Faculty research:* Soil fertility and plant nutrition, soil chemistry and physics, soil genesis and morphology, soil management and conservation, water and environmental quality.

University of Maine, Graduate School, College of Natural Sciences, Forestry, and Agriculture, Department of Plant, Soil, and Environmental Sciences, Orono, ME 04469. Offers ecology and environmental sciences (MS); horticulture (MS); plant, soil, and environmental sciences (MS). *Faculty:* 18 full-time (6 women), 3 part-time/adjunct. *Students:* 9 full-time (7 women), 2 part-time (0 women), 1 international. Average age 30. 11 applicants, 9% accepted, 1 enrolled. In 2012, 3 master's awarded. *Degree requirements:* For master's, thesis (for some programs). *Entrance requirements:* For master's, GRE General Test. Additional exam requirements/recommendations for international students: Required—TOEFL. *Application deadline:* Applications are processed on a rolling basis.

Application fee: $65. Electronic applications accepted. *Financial support:* In 2012–13, 16 research assistantships with full tuition reimbursements (averaging $17,336 per year), 1 teaching assistantship with full tuition reimbursement (averaging $13,600 per year) were awarded; scholarships/grants, tuition waivers (full and partial), and unspecified assistantships also available. *Total annual research expenditures:* $179,065. *Unit head:* Dr. Eric Gallandt, Chair, 207-581-2933, Fax: 207-581-3207. *Application contact:* Scott G. Delcourt, Associate Dean of the Graduate School, 207-581-3291, Fax: 207-581-3232, E-mail: graduate@maine.edu. Website: http://umaine.edu/pse/.

University of Manitoba, Faculty of Graduate Studies, Faculty of Agricultural and Food Sciences, Department of Plant Science, Winnipeg, MB R3T 2N2, Canada. Offers agronomy and plant protection (M Sc, PhD); horticulture (M Sc, PhD); plant breeding and genetics (M Sc, PhD); plant physiology-biochemistry (M Sc, PhD). *Degree requirements:* For master's, thesis; for doctorate, one foreign language, thesis/dissertation.

University of Manitoba, Faculty of Graduate Studies, Faculty of Agricultural and Food Sciences, Department of Soil Science, Winnipeg, MB R3T 2N2, Canada. Offers M Sc, PhD. *Degree requirements:* For master's, thesis; for doctorate, one foreign language, thesis/dissertation.

University of Minnesota, Twin Cities Campus, Graduate School, College of Food, Agricultural and Natural Resource Sciences, Land and Atmospheric Science Graduate Program, Saint Paul, MN 55108. Offers MS, PhD. *Faculty:* 46 full-time. *Students:* 36 full-time (14 women); includes 4 minority (2 Asian, non-Hispanic/Latino; 2 Hispanic/Latino), 9 international. Average age 30. 29 applicants, 28% accepted, 7 enrolled. In 2012, 19 master's, 15 doctorates awarded. Terminal master's awarded for partial completion of doctoral program. *Degree requirements:* For master's, comprehensive exam, thesis; for doctorate, comprehensive exam, thesis/dissertation. *Entrance requirements:* For master's and doctorate, GRE General Test, minimum GPA of 3.0. Additional exam requirements/recommendations for international students: Required—TOEFL (minimum score 550 paper-based; 79 iBT), IELTS (minimum score 6.5). *Application deadline:* For fall admission, 12/15 priority date for domestic students, 12/15 for international students; for spring admission, 10/15 priority date for domestic students, 10/15 for international students. Applications are processed on a rolling basis. Application fee: $75 ($95 for international students). Electronic applications accepted. *Financial support:* In 2012–13, fellowships with full tuition reimbursements (averaging $40,000 per year), research assistantships with full and partial tuition reimbursements (averaging $40,000 per year), teaching assistantships with full and partial tuition reimbursements (averaging $40,000 per year) were awarded; scholarships/grants, traineeships, health care benefits, tuition waivers (full), and unspecified assistantships also available. Support available to part-time students. Financial award application deadline: 12/15. *Faculty research:* Soil water and atmospheric resources, soil physical management, agricultural chemicals and their management, plant nutrient management, biological nitrogen fixation. *Total annual research expenditures:* $3,271. *Unit head:* Dr. David Mulla, Co-Director of Graduate Studies, 612-625-6721, Fax: 612-625-2208, E-mail: mulla003@umn.edu. *Application contact:* Kari Jarco, Program Coordinator, 612-625-5251, Fax: 612-625-2208, E-mail: kjarcho@umn.edu. Website: http://www.laas.umn.edu/.

University of Missouri, Graduate School, College of Agriculture, Food and Natural Resources, Division of Plant Sciences, Columbia, MO 65211. Offers crop, soil and pest management (MS, PhD); entomology (MS, PhD); horticulture (MS, PhD); plant biology and genetics (MS, PhD); plant stress biology (MS, PhD). *Faculty:* 40 full-time (11 women). *Students:* 75 full-time (36 women), 10 part-time (2 women); includes 4 minority (2 Black or African American, non-Hispanic/Latino; 1 American Indian or Alaska Native, non-Hispanic/Latino; 1 Hispanic/Latino), 28 international. Average age 28. 67 applicants, 22% accepted, 15 enrolled. In 2012, 8 master's, 9 doctorates awarded. Terminal master's awarded for partial completion of doctoral program. *Degree requirements:* For master's, thesis; for doctorate, comprehensive exam, thesis/dissertation. *Entrance requirements:* For master's and doctorate, GRE General Test, minimum GPA of 3.0; bachelor's degree from accredited college. Additional exam requirements/recommendations for international students: Required—TOEFL (minimum score 500 paper-based; 61 iBT), IELTS (minimum score 5.5). *Application deadline:* For fall admission, 1/15 priority date for domestic students, 1/15 for international students. Applications are processed on a rolling basis. Application fee: $55 ($75 for international students). Electronic applications accepted. *Expenses:* Tuition, state resident: full-time $6057. Tuition, nonresident: full-time $15,683. *Required fees:* $1000. *Financial support:* In 2012–13, 2 fellowships with tuition reimbursements, 59 research assistantships with tuition reimbursements, 1 teaching assistantship with tuition reimbursement were awarded; institutionally sponsored loans, scholarships/grants, health care benefits, and unspecified assistantships also available. Support available to part-time students. *Faculty research:* Crop, soil and pest management; entomology; horticulture; plant biology and genetics; plant microbiology and pathology. *Unit head:* Dr. Michael Collins, Director, 573-882-1957, E-mail: collinsm@missouri.edu. *Application contact:* Dr. James Schoelz, Director of Graduate Studies, 573-882-1185, E-mail: schoelzj@missouri.edu. Website: http://plantsci.missouri.edu/graduate/.

University of Missouri, Graduate School, School of Natural Resources, Department of Soil, Environmental, and Atmospheric Sciences, Columbia, MO 65211. Offers atmospheric science (MS, PhD); soil science (MS, PhD). *Faculty:* 9 full-time (0 women). *Students:* 24 full-time (10 women), 8 part-time (5 women); includes 4 minority (1 Black or African American, non-Hispanic/Latino; 1 Asian, non-Hispanic/Latino; 1 Hispanic/Latino; 1 Two or more races, non-Hispanic/Latino), 6 international. Average age 30. 22 applicants, 45% accepted, 9 enrolled. In 2012, 6 master's, 2 doctorates awarded. *Degree requirements:* For doctorate, thesis/dissertation. *Entrance requirements:* For master's and doctorate, GRE General Test, minimum GPA of 3.0. Additional exam requirements/recommendations for international students: Required—TOEFL (minimum score 530 paper-based; 71 iBT). *Application deadline:* Applications are processed on a rolling basis. Application fee: $55 ($75 for international students). *Expenses:* Tuition, state resident: full-time $6057. Tuition, nonresident: full-time $15,683. *Required fees:* $1000. *Financial support:* Fellowships, research assistantships, teaching assistantships, institutionally sponsored loans, and scholarships/grants available. *Faculty research:* Soil physics; x-ray tomography of soil systems; use of radar in forecasting; soil and water conservation and management and applied soil physics; soil chemical and biogeochemical investigations; fresh water supply regimes (quantity, timing); water quality disturbance mechanisms; best management practices (BMP's); environmental biophysics and ecohydrology; hydrologic scaling, modeling, and change; synoptic and mesoscale dynamics. *Unit head:* Dr. Stephen Anderson, Department Chair, 573-882-6303, E-mail: andersons@missouri.edu. Website: http://www.snr.missouri.edu/seas/academics/graduate-program.php.

University of Nebraska–Lincoln, Graduate College, College of Agricultural Sciences and Natural Resources, Department of Agronomy and Horticulture, Program in Agronomy, Lincoln, NE 68588. Offers MS, PhD. *Degree requirements:* For master's, thesis; for doctorate, comprehensive exam, thesis/dissertation. *Entrance requirements:* Additional exam requirements/recommendations for international students: Required—TOEFL (minimum score 500 paper-based). Electronic applications accepted. *Faculty research:* Crop physiology and production, plant breeding and genetics, range and forage management, soil and water science, weed science.

University of Puerto Rico, Mayagüez Campus, Graduate Studies, College of Agricultural Sciences, Department of Agronomy and Soils, Mayagüez, PR 00681-9000. Offers agronomy (MS); soils (MS). Part-time programs available. *Faculty:* 9 full-time (2 women). *Students:* 12 full-time (6 women); all minorities (all Hispanic/Latino), 1 international. 4 applicants, 100% accepted, 3 enrolled. In 2012, 2 master's awarded. *Degree requirements:* For master's, comprehensive exam, thesis. *Application deadline:* For fall admission, 2/15 for domestic and international students; for spring admission, 9/15 for domestic and international students. Applications are processed on a rolling basis. Application fee: $25. Tuition and fees vary according to course level and course load. *Financial support:* In 2012–13, 4 research assistantships with tuition reimbursements (averaging $15,000 per year), 4 teaching assistantships with tuition reimbursements (averaging $8,500 per year) were awarded; Federal Work-Study and institutionally sponsored loans also available. *Faculty research:* Soil physics and chemistry, soil management, plant physiology, ecology, plant breeding. *Total annual research expenditures:* $330,000. *Unit head:* Dr. Skip Van Bloem, Director, 787-265-3851, E-mail: skip.vanbloem@upr.edu. *Application contact:* Dr. Carmen Figueroa, Student Affairs Official, 787-265-3809, Fax: 787-265-5489, E-mail: carmen.figueroa11@upr.edu. Website: http://www.uprm.edu/agricultura/agrosuelos/.

University of Puerto Rico, Mayagüez Campus, Graduate Studies, College of Agricultural Sciences, Department of Crop Protection, Mayagüez, PR 00681-9000. Offers MS. Part-time programs available. *Faculty:* 3 full-time (1 woman). *Students:* 24 full-time (15 women); includes 23 minority (all Hispanic/Latino), 6 international. 6 applicants, 100% accepted, 6 enrolled. In 2012, 4 master's awarded. *Degree requirements:* For master's, comprehensive exam, thesis. *Entrance requirements:* For master's, minimum GPA of 2.75, BS in agricultural science or its equivalent. *Application deadline:* For fall admission, 2/15 for domestic and international students; for spring admission, 9/15 for domestic and international students. Applications are processed on a rolling basis. Application fee: $25. Tuition and fees vary according to course level and course load. *Financial support:* Career-related internships or fieldwork, Federal Work-Study, and institutionally sponsored loans available. Financial award application deadline: 5/30. *Faculty research:* Nematology, virology, plant pathology, weed control, peas and soybean seed diseases. *Unit head:* Dr. Skip Van Bloem, Director, 787-265-3859, Fax: 787-265-5490, E-mail: skip.vanbloem@upr.edu. *Application contact:* Prof. Nydia Vicente, Coordinator, 787-832-4040 Ext. 3104, Fax: 787-265-5490, E-mail: nvicente@uprm.edu. Website: http://www.uprm.edu/agricultura/proteccion.

University of Saskatchewan, College of Graduate Studies and Research, College of Agriculture, Department of Soil Science, Saskatoon, SK S7N 5A2, Canada. Offers M Ag, M Sc, PhD, Diploma. *Degree requirements:* For master's, thesis (for some programs); for doctorate, comprehensive exam (for some programs), thesis/dissertation. *Entrance requirements:* Additional exam requirements/recommendations for international students: Required—TOEFL (minimum score 80 iBT); Recommended—IELTS (minimum score 6.5).

University of Vermont, Graduate College, College of Agriculture and Life Sciences, Department of Plant and Soil Science, Burlington, VT 05405. Offers MS, PhD. *Students:* 25 (17 women); includes 1 minority (Asian, non-Hispanic/Latino), 3 international. 28 applicants, 36% accepted, 4 enrolled. In 2012, 4 master's, 1 doctorate awarded. *Degree requirements:* For master's, thesis; for doctorate, one foreign language, thesis/dissertation. *Entrance requirements:* For master's and doctorate, GRE General Test. Additional exam requirements/recommendations for international students: Required—TOEFL (minimum score

550 paper-based; 80 iBT). *Application deadline:* For fall admission, 2/15 priority date for domestic students, 2/15 for international students. Applications are processed on a rolling basis. Application fee: $40. Electronic applications accepted. *Expenses: Tuition, area resident:* Part-time $572 per credit. Tuition, nonresident: part-time $1444 per credit. *Financial support:* Fellowships, research assistantships, and teaching assistantships available. Financial award application deadline: 3/1. *Faculty research:* Soil chemistry, plant nutrition. *Unit head:* Dr. Ernesto Mendez, Acting Chairperson, 802-656-2630. *Application contact:* Dr. Josef Gorres, Coordinator, 802-656-2630. Website: http://www.uvm.edu/~pss.

University of Wisconsin–Madison, Graduate School, College of Agricultural and Life Sciences, Department of Agronomy, Madison, WI 53706-1380. Offers agronomy (MS, PhD); plant breeding and plant genetics (MS, PhD). *Degree requirements:* For master's, thesis or alternative; for doctorate, thesis/dissertation. *Entrance requirements:* For master's and doctorate, GRE, minimum GPA of 3.0. Additional exam requirements/recommendations for international students: Required—TOEFL (minimum score 580 paper-based). Electronic applications accepted. *Expenses:* Tuition, state resident: full-time $10,728; part-time $743 per credit. Tuition, nonresident: full-time $24,054; part-time $1575 per credit. *Required fees:* $1111; $72 per credit. *Faculty research:* Plant breeding and genetics, plant molecular biology and physiology, cropping systems and management, weed science.

University of Wisconsin–Madison, Graduate School, College of Agricultural and Life Sciences, Department of Soil Science, Madison, WI 53706. Offers MS, PhD. *Degree requirements:* For master's, comprehensive exam, thesis; for doctorate, comprehensive exam, thesis/dissertation. *Entrance requirements:* For master's and doctorate, GRE General Test. Additional exam requirements/ recommendations for international students: Required—TOEFL. Electronic applications accepted. *Expenses:* Tuition, state resident: full-time $10,728; part-time $743 per credit. Tuition, nonresident: full-time $24,054; part-time $1575 per credit. *Required fees:* $1111; $72 per credit. *Faculty research:* Soil characterization and mapping, fate of toxicants in the environment, soil microbiology, permafrost, water quality and quantity.

University of Wyoming, College of Agriculture and Natural Resources, Department of Plant Sciences, Laramie, WY 82070. Offers agronomy (MS, PhD). *Degree requirements:* For master's, thesis; for doctorate, thesis/dissertation. *Entrance requirements:* For master's and doctorate, GRE General Test, minimum GPA of 3.0. Additional exam requirements/recommendations for international students: Required—TOEFL (minimum score 525 paper-based). Electronic applications accepted. *Faculty research:* Crops, weeds, plant diseases.

University of Wyoming, College of Agriculture and Natural Resources, Department of Renewable Resources, Laramie, WY 82070. Offers agroecology (MS); entomology (MS, PhD); entomology/water resources (MS, PhD); rangeland ecology and watershed management (MS, PhD), including soil sciences (PhD); soil sciences and water resources (MS); rangeland ecology and watershed management/water resources (MS, PhD); soil science (MS); soil science/water resources (PhD). Part-time programs available. *Degree requirements:* For master's, comprehensive exam, thesis, oral examination; for doctorate, comprehensive exam, thesis/dissertation, preliminary oral and written exam, oral final exam. *Entrance requirements:* For master's and doctorate, GRE General Test, minimum GPA of 3.0. Additional exam requirements/recommendations for international students: Required—TOEFL. Electronic applications accepted. *Faculty research:* Plant control, grazing management, riparian restoration, riparian management, reclamation.

Utah State University, School of Graduate Studies, College of Agriculture, Department of Plants, Soils, and Biometeorology, Logan, UT 84322. Offers biometeorology (MS, PhD); ecology (MS, PhD); plant science (MS, PhD); soil science (MS, PhD). Part-time programs available. Terminal master's awarded for partial completion of doctoral program. *Degree requirements:* For master's, thesis; for doctorate, thesis/dissertation. *Entrance requirements:* For master's, GRE General Test, BS in plant, soil, atmospheric science, or related field; minimum GPA of 3.0; for doctorate, GRE General Test, minimum GPA of 3.0. Additional exam requirements/recommendations for international students: Required— TOEFL. Electronic applications accepted. *Faculty research:* Biotechnology and genomics, plant physiology and biology, nutrient and water efficient landscapes, physical-chemical-biological processes in soil, environmental biophysics and climate.

Virginia Polytechnic Institute and State University, Graduate School, College of Agriculture and Life Sciences, Blacksburg, VA 24124. Offers agricultural and applied economics (MS); agricultural and life sciences (MS); animal and poultry science (MS, PhD); crop and soil environmental sciences (MS, PhD); dairy science (MS); entomology (PhD); horticulture (MS, PhD); human nutrition, foods and exercise (MS, PhD); life sciences (MS, PhD); plant pathology, physiology and weed science (PhD). *Faculty:* 233 full-time (65 women), 1 (woman) part-time/ adjunct. *Students:* 343 full-time (199 women), 74 part-time (47 women); includes 48 minority (20 Black or African American, non-Hispanic/Latino; 1 American

Indian or Alaska Native, non-Hispanic/Latino; 15 Asian, non-Hispanic/Latino; 7 Hispanic/Latino; 5 Two or more races, non-Hispanic/Latino), 105 international. Average age 29. 387 applicants, 33% accepted, 98 enrolled. In 2012, 81 master's, 52 doctorates awarded. *Degree requirements:* For master's, comprehensive exam (for some programs), thesis (for some programs); for doctorate, comprehensive exam (for some programs), thesis/dissertation (for some programs). *Entrance requirements:* For master's and doctorate, GRE/GMAT (may vary by department). Additional exam requirements/recommendations for international students: Required—TOEFL (minimum score 550 paper-based). *Application deadline:* For fall admission, 8/1 for domestic students, 4/1 for international students; for spring admission, 1/1 for domestic students, 9/1 for international students. Applications are processed on a rolling basis. Application fee: $65. Electronic applications accepted. *Expenses:* Tuition, state resident: full-time $10,677; part-time $593.25 per credit hour. Tuition, nonresident: full-time $20,926; part-time $1162.50 per credit hour. *Required fees:* $427.75 per semester. Tuition and fees vary according to course load, campus/location and program. *Financial support:* In 2012–13, 1 fellowship with full tuition reimbursement (averaging $21,000 per year), 229 research assistantships with full tuition reimbursements (averaging $18,998 per year), 77 teaching assistantships with full tuition reimbursements (averaging $18,174 per year) were awarded. Financial award application deadline: 3/1; financial award applicants required to submit FAFSA. *Total annual research expenditures:* $41.8 million. *Unit head:* Dr. Alan L. Grant, Dean, 540-231-4152, Fax: 540-231-4163, E-mail: algrant@vt.edu. *Application contact:* Sheila Norman, Administrative Assistant, 540-231-4152, Fax: 540-231-4163, E-mail: snorman@vt.edu. Website: http://www.cals.vt.edu/.

Washington State University, Graduate School, College of Agricultural, Human, and Natural Resource Sciences, Department of Crop and Soil Sciences, Program in Crop Sciences, Pullman, WA 99164. Offers MS, PhD. Terminal master's awarded for partial completion of doctoral program. *Degree requirements:* For master's, comprehensive exam (for some programs), thesis (for some programs), oral exam; for doctorate, comprehensive exam, thesis/dissertation, oral exam, written exam. *Entrance requirements:* For master's and doctorate, GRE General Test, personal statement of educational goals and professional expectations. Additional exam requirements/recommendations for international students: Required—TOEFL (minimum score 550 paper-based), IELTS. Electronic applications accepted. *Faculty research:* Barley genetics, soil biology, soil fertility, winter wheat breeding, weed science.

Washington State University, Graduate School, College of Agricultural, Human, and Natural Resource Sciences, Department of Crop and Soil Sciences, Program in Soil Sciences, Pullman, WA 99164. Offers MS, PhD. *Faculty:* 25. *Students:* 36 full-time (14 women), 2 part-time (0 women), 11 international. Average age 30. 25 applicants, 32% accepted, 8 enrolled. In 2012, 2 master's, 2 doctorates awarded. Terminal master's awarded for partial completion of doctoral program. *Degree requirements:* For master's, comprehensive exam (for some programs), thesis (for some programs), oral exam; for doctorate, comprehensive exam, thesis/ dissertation, oral exam, written exam. *Entrance requirements:* For master's and doctorate, GRE General Test, minimum cumulative GPA of 3.0, 3 letters of reference, statement of intent. Additional exam requirements/recommendations for international students: Required—TOEFL (minimum score 550 paper-based). *Application deadline:* For fall admission, 1/10 priority date for domestic students, 1/10 for international students; for spring admission, 7/1 priority date for domestic students, 7/1 for international students. Applications are processed on a rolling basis. Application fee: $75. Electronic applications accepted. *Financial support:* In 2012–13, 30 students received support, including 5 fellowships (averaging $30,000 per year), 22 research assistantships with full and partial tuition reimbursements available (averaging $18,204 per year), 3 teaching assistantships with full and partial tuition reimbursements available (averaging $18,204 per year); career-related internships or fieldwork, Federal Work-Study, institutionally sponsored loans, scholarships/grants, health care benefits, and unspecified assistantships also available. Financial award application deadline: 4/ 1; financial award applicants required to submit FAFSA. *Faculty research:* Environmental soils, soil/water quality, soil microbiology, soil physics. *Total annual research expenditures:* $8 million. *Unit head:* Dr. James Harsh, Chair, 509-335-3475, Fax: 509-335-8674, E-mail: harsh@wsu.edu. *Application contact:* Graduate School Admissions, 800-GRADWSU, Fax: 509-335-1949, E-mail: gradsch@wsu.edu. Website: http://css.wsu.edu/.

West Virginia University, Davis College of Agriculture, Forestry and Consumer Sciences, Division of Plant and Soil Sciences, Program in Agricultural Sciences, Morgantown, WV 26506. Offers animal and food sciences (PhD); plant and soil sciences (PhD). *Degree requirements:* For doctorate, thesis/dissertation, oral and written exams. *Entrance requirements:* Additional exam requirements/ recommendations for international students: Required—TOEFL. *Faculty research:* Ruminant nutrition, metabolism, forage utilization, physiology, reproduction.

Peterson's Graduate Programs in the Physical Sciences, Mathematics, Agricultural Sciences, the Environment & Natural Resources 2014

www.petersonsbooks.com **399**

Animal Sciences

Alcorn State University, School of Graduate Studies, School of Agriculture and Applied Science, Alcorn State, MS 39096-7500. Offers agricultural economics (MS Ag); agronomy (MS Ag); animal science (MS Ag). *Degree requirements:* For master's, thesis optional. *Faculty research:* Aquatic systems, dairy herd improvement, fruit production, alternative farming practices.

American University of Beirut, Graduate Programs, Faculty of Agricultural and Food Sciences, Beirut, Lebanon. Offers agricultural economics (MS); animal sciences (MS); ecosystem management (MSES); food technology (MS); irrigation (MS); nutrition (MS); plant protection (MS); plant science (MS); poultry science (MS). Part-time programs available. *Faculty:* 22 full-time (6 women), 1 part-time/adjunct (0 women). *Students:* 11 full-time (10 women), 89 part-time (74 women). Average age 25. 97 applicants, 64% accepted, 18 enrolled. In 2012, 35 master's awarded. *Degree requirements:* For master's, one foreign language, comprehensive exam, thesis (for some programs). *Entrance requirements:* Additional exam requirements/recommendations for international students: Required—TOEFL (minimum score 600 paper-based; 100 iBT), IELTS (minimum score 7.5). *Application deadline:* For fall admission, 2/7 for domestic and international students; for spring admission, 11/15 for domestic and international students. Applications are processed on a rolling basis. Application fee: $50. Electronic applications accepted. *Expenses: Tuition:* Full-time $13,896; part-time $772 per credit. *Financial support:* In 2012–13, 18 research assistantships with partial tuition reimbursements (averaging $1,500 per year), 49 teaching assistantships with full and partial tuition reimbursements (averaging $1,000 per year) were awarded; scholarships/grants, health care benefits, and unspecified assistantships also available. Financial award application deadline: 2/2. *Faculty research:* Evidence-based nutrition intervention; studies related to immunopotentiation, protection and production in broilers; nutritional food-based dietary guidelines; production of biodiesel from algae; regional knowledge management and knowledge sharing network. *Total annual research expenditures:* $560,850. *Unit head:* Prof. Nahla Hwalla, Dean, 961-1343002 Ext. 4400, Fax: 961-1744460, E-mail: nahla@aub.edu.lb. *Application contact:* Dr. Salim Kanaan, Director, Admissions Office, 961-1-350000 Ext. 2594, Fax: 961-1750775, E-mail: sk00@aub.edu.lb. Website: http://www.aub.edu.lb/fafs/fafs_home/Pages/index.aspx.

Angelo State University, College of Graduate Studies, College of Arts and Sciences, Department of Agriculture, San Angelo, TX 76909. Offers animal science (MS). Part-time and evening/weekend programs available. *Students:* 11 full-time (4 women), 11 part-time (6 women); includes 1 minority (Hispanic/Latino). Average age 23. 9 applicants, 78% accepted, 7 enrolled. In 2012, 11 master's awarded. *Degree requirements:* For master's, comprehensive exam, thesis optional. *Entrance requirements:* For master's, GRE General Test, essay. Additional exam requirements/recommendations for international students: Required—TOEFL or IELTS. *Application deadline:* For fall admission, 7/15 priority date for domestic students, 6/10 for international students; for spring admission, 12/1 priority date for domestic students, 11/1 for international students. Applications are processed on a rolling basis. Application fee: $40 ($50 for international students). Electronic applications accepted. *Financial support:* In 2012–13, 10 students received support, including 11 research assistantships (averaging $7,490 per year); Federal Work-Study, scholarships/grants, and unspecified assistantships also available. Support available to part-time students. Financial award application deadline: 3/1. *Faculty research:* Effect of protein and energy on feedlot performance, bitterweed toxicosis in sheep, meat laboratory, North Concho Watershed Project, baseline vegetation. *Unit head:* Dr. Micheal Salisbury, Department Head, 325-942-2027 Ext. 227, E-mail: mike.salisbury@angelo.edu. *Application contact:* Dr. Cody B. Scott, Graduate Advisor, 325-942-2027 Ext. 284, E-mail: cody.scott@angelo.edu. Website: http://www.angelo.edu/dept/agriculture/.

Auburn University, Graduate School, College of Agriculture, Department of Animal Sciences, Auburn University, AL 36849. Offers M Ag, MS, PhD. Part-time programs available. *Faculty:* 23 full-time (5 women), 1 part-time/adjunct (0 women). *Students:* 5 full-time (1 woman), 9 part-time (8 women). Average age 25. 30 applicants, 30% accepted, 6 enrolled. In 2012, 2 master's awarded. *Degree requirements:* For master's, thesis (for some programs); for doctorate, thesis/dissertation. *Entrance requirements:* For master's and doctorate, GRE General Test. *Application deadline:* For fall admission, 7/7 for domestic students; for spring admission, 11/24 for domestic students. Applications are processed on a rolling basis. Application fee: $50 ($60 for international students). Electronic applications accepted. *Expenses:* Tuition, state resident: full-time $7866; part-time $437 per credit. Tuition, nonresident: full-time $23,598; part-time $1311 per credit. *Required fees:* $787 per semester. Tuition and fees vary according to degree level and program. *Financial support:* Research assistantships, teaching assistantships, and Federal Work-Study available. Support available to part-time students. Financial award application deadline: 3/15; financial award applicants required to submit FAFSA. *Faculty research:* Animal breeding and genetics, animal biochemistry and nutrition, physiology of reproduction, animal production. *Unit head:* Dr. L. Wayne Greene, Head, 334-844-1528. *Application contact:* Dr. George Flowers, Dean of the Graduate School, 334-844-2125.

Auburn University, Graduate School, College of Agriculture, Department of Poultry Science, Auburn University, AL 36849. Offers M Ag, MS, PhD. Part-time programs available. *Faculty:* 16 full-time (3 women). *Students:* 11 full-time (6 women), 10 part-time (6 women); includes 2 minority (both Asian, non-Hispanic/Latino), 8 international. Average age 29. 26 applicants, 15% accepted, 2 enrolled. In 2012, 1 doctorate awarded. *Degree requirements:* For master's, thesis (for some programs); for doctorate, thesis/dissertation. *Entrance requirements:* For master's, GRE General Test; for doctorate, GRE General Test, MS. *Application deadline:* For fall admission, 7/7 for domestic students; for spring admission, 11/24 for domestic students. Applications are processed on a rolling basis. Application fee: $50 ($60 for international students). Electronic applications accepted. *Expenses:* Tuition, state resident: full-time $7866; part-time $437 per credit. Tuition, nonresident: full-time $23,598; part-time $1311 per credit. *Required fees:* $787 per semester. Tuition and fees vary according to degree level and program. *Financial support:* Research assistantships and Federal Work-Study available. Support available to part-time students. Financial award application deadline: 3/15; financial award applicants required to submit FAFSA. *Faculty research:* Poultry nutrition, poultry breeding, poultry physiology, poultry diseases and parasites, processing/food science. *Unit head:* Dr. Donald E. Conner, Head, 334-844-4133, E-mail: connede@auburn.edu. *Application contact:* Dr. George Flowers, Dean of the Graduate School, 334-844-2125. Website: http://www.ag.auburn.edu/poul/.

Bergin University of Canine Studies, Program in Canine Life Sciences, Rohnert Park, CA 94928. Offers MS. Postbaccalaureate distance learning degree programs offered (minimal on-campus study). *Degree requirements:* For master's, thesis or culminating project.

Boise State University, College of Arts and Sciences, Department of Biology, Boise, ID 83725-0399. Offers biology (MA, MS); raptor biology (MS). Part-time programs available. *Faculty:* 23 full-time, 64 part-time/adjunct. *Students:* 38 full-time (20 women), 17 part-time (13 women); includes 5 minority (1 Black or African American, non-Hispanic/Latino; 1 American Indian or Alaska Native, non-Hispanic/Latino; 1 Asian, non-Hispanic/Latino; 2 Hispanic/Latino), 4 international. Average age 32. 57 applicants, 79% accepted, 22 enrolled. In 2012, 12 master's awarded. *Degree requirements:* For master's, thesis. *Entrance requirements:* For master's, GRE General Test, minimum GPA of 3.0. *Application deadline:* For fall admission, 7/17 priority date for domestic students; for spring admission, 12/5 priority date for domestic students. Applications are processed on a rolling basis. Application fee: $55. Electronic applications accepted. *Expenses:* Tuition, state resident: full-time $3486; part-time $312 per credit. Tuition, nonresident: full-time $5720; part-time $413 per credit. *Financial support:* In 2012–13, 2 fellowships, 6 research assistantships with full tuition reimbursements (averaging $11,348 per year), 10 teaching assistantships with full and partial tuition reimbursements (averaging $11,348 per year) were awarded; career-related internships or fieldwork, Federal Work-Study, institutionally sponsored loans, and unspecified assistantships also available. Support available to part-time students. Financial award application deadline: 3/1. *Faculty research:* Soil and stream microbial ecology, avian ecology. *Unit head:* Dr. James Belthoff, Coordinator, 208-426-4033, Fax: 208-426-3117. *Application contact:* Linda Platt, Office Services Supervisor, Graduate Admission and Degree Services, 208-426-1074, Fax: 208-426-2789, E-mail: lplatt@boisestate.edu.

Brigham Young University, Graduate Studies, College of Life Sciences, Department of Plant and Wildlife Sciences, Provo, UT 84602. Offers environmental science (MS); genetics and biotechnology (MS); wildlife and wildlands conservation (MS, PhD). *Faculty:* 24 full-time (1 woman), 2 part-time/adjunct (1 woman). *Students:* 47 full-time (18 women); includes 6 minority (3 Asian, non-Hispanic/Latino; 2 Hispanic/Latino; 1 Native Hawaiian or other Pacific Islander, non-Hispanic/Latino), 2 international. Average age 28. 29 applicants, 41% accepted, 9 enrolled. In 2012, 15 master's, 2 doctorates awarded. *Degree requirements:* For master's, thesis; for doctorate, comprehensive exam, thesis/dissertation, minimum GPA of 3.2, 54 hours (18 dissertation, 36 coursework). *Entrance requirements:* For master's, GRE General Test, minimum GPA of 3.2 during last 60 hours of course work; for doctorate, GRE, minimum GPA of 3.2. Additional exam requirements/recommendations for international students: Required—TOEFL (minimum score 580 paper-based; 85 iBT). *Application deadline:* 2/1 for domestic and international students. Applications are processed on a rolling basis. Application fee: $50. Electronic applications accepted. *Expenses: Tuition:* Full-time $5950; part-time $331 per credit hour. Tuition and fees vary according to program and student's religious affiliation. *Financial support:* In 2012–13, 47 students received support, including 64 research assistantships with partial tuition reimbursements available (averaging $17,840 per year), 52 teaching assistantships with partial tuition reimbursements available (averaging $17,840 per year); scholarships/grants and tuition waivers (partial) also available. Financial award application deadline: 2/1. *Faculty research:* Environmental science, plant genetics, plant ecology, plant nutrition and pathology, wildlife and wildlands conservation. *Total annual research expenditures:* $1.9 million. *Unit head:* Dr. Eric N. Jellen, Chair, 801-422-3527, Fax: 801-422-0008, E-mail: rick_jellen@byu.edu. *Application contact:* Dr. Brock R. McMillan, Graduate Coordinator, 801-422-1228, Fax: 801-422-0008, E-mail: brock_mcmillan@byu.edu. Website: http://pws.byu.edu/home/.

California State University, Fresno, Division of Graduate Studies, College of Agricultural Sciences and Technology, Department of Animal Science and Agricultural Education, Fresno, CA 93740-8027. Offers animal science (MS). Part-time and evening/weekend programs available. *Degree requirements:* For master's, thesis. *Entrance requirements:* For master's, GRE General Test, minimum GPA of 3.0 in last 60 hours. Additional exam requirements/recommendations for international students: Required—TOEFL. Electronic applications accepted. *Faculty research:* Horse nutrition, animal health and welfare, electronic monitoring.

Clemson University, Graduate School, College of Agriculture, Forestry and Life Sciences, Department of Animal and Veterinary Sciences, Clemson, SC 29634. Offers animal and veterinary sciences (MS, PhD). *Faculty:* 9 full-time (5 women), 2 part-time/adjunct (0 women). *Students:* 12 full-time (9 women), 1 part-time (0 women); includes 1 minority (Black or African American, non-Hispanic/Latino), 31 international. Average age 28. 12 applicants, 50% accepted, 6 enrolled. In 2012, 1 master's, 3 doctorates awarded. *Degree requirements:* For doctorate, thesis/dissertation. *Entrance requirements:* For master's and doctorate, GRE General Test. Additional exam requirements/recommendations for international students: Required—TOEFL. *Application deadline:* For fall admission, 4/15 for international students; for spring admission, 9/15 for international students. Applications are processed on a rolling basis. Application fee: $70 ($80 for international students). Electronic applications accepted. *Expenses:* Contact institution. *Financial support:* In 2012–13, 9 students received support, including 2 fellowships with full and partial tuition reimbursements available (averaging $10,000 per year), 6 research assistantships with partial tuition reimbursements available (averaging $17,250 per year), 2 teaching assistantships with partial tuition reimbursements available (averaging $14,500 per year); career-related internships or fieldwork, Federal Work-Study, institutionally sponsored loans, scholarships/grants, and unspecified assistantships also available. Financial award applicants required to submit FAFSA. *Total annual research expenditures:* $1.1 million. *Unit head:* Dr. Susan K. Duckett, Chair, 864-656-2570, Fax: 864-656-3131, E-mail: sducket@clemson.edu. Website: http://www.clemson.edu/avs.

Colorado State University, Graduate School, College of Agricultural Sciences, Department of Animal Sciences, Fort Collins, CO 80523-1171. Offers MS, PhD. *Faculty:* 23 full-time (3 women). *Students:* 31 full-time (23 women), 11 part-time (6 women); includes 3 minority (1 Black or African American, non-Hispanic/Latino; 2 Hispanic/Latino), 10 international. Average age 28. 37 applicants, 27% accepted, 10 enrolled. In 2012, 13 master's, 5 doctorates awarded. *Degree requirements:* For master's, variable foreign language requirement, comprehensive exam, thesis, one article prepared for publication in a refereed scientific journal with degree candidate as senior author and approval of on-campus graduate committee consisting of three faculty members; for doctorate, variable foreign language requirement, comprehensive exam, thesis/dissertation, two articles prepared for publication in refereed scientific publication with degree candidate as senior author and approval of on-campus graduate committee consisting of three faculty members. *Entrance requirements:* For master's, GRE General Test (minimum score 1000 verbal and quantitative), minimum GPA of 3.0; reference letters; for doctorate, GRE General Test (combined minimum score of 1000 on the Verbal and Quantitative sections), minimum GPA of 3.0; reference letters. Additional exam requirements/recommendations for international students: Required—TOEFL (minimum score 525 paper-based), IELTS (minimum score 6.5). *Application deadline:* For fall admission, 4/1 for domestic and international students; for spring admission, 10/1 for domestic and international students. Applications are processed on a rolling basis. Application fee: $50. Electronic applications accepted. *Expenses:* Tuition, state resident: full-time $8811; part-time $490 per credit. Tuition, nonresident: full-time $21,600; part-time $1200 per credit. *Required fees:* $1819; $61 per credit. *Financial support:* In 2012–13, 39 students received support, including 3 fellowships with full tuition reimbursements available (averaging $26,798 per year), 28 research assistantships with full tuition reimbursements available (averaging $13,143 per year), 8 teaching assistantships with full tuition reimbursements available (averaging $8,495 per year); scholarships/grants and unspecified assistantships also available. Financial award applicants required to submit FAFSA. *Faculty research:* Meat science, food safety, livestock management systems, equine science, breeding and genetics. *Total annual research expenditures:* $1.6 million. *Unit head:* Dr. Kevin Pond, Department Head, 970-491-7295, Fax: 970-491-5326, E-mail: kevin.pond@colostate.edu. *Application contact:* Melissa Weiss, Administrative Assistant, 970-491-1442, Fax: 970-491-5326, E-mail: m.weiss@colostate.edu. Website: http://ansci.agsci.colostate.edu/.

Cornell University, Graduate School, Graduate Fields of Agriculture and Life Sciences, Field of Animal Science, Ithaca, NY 14853-0001. Offers agriculture and life sciences (MPS); animal breeding (MS, PhD); animal genetics (MS, PhD); animal genomics (PhD); animal nutrition (PhD); physiology of reproduction (PhD). *Faculty:* 36 full-time (9 women). *Students:* 31 full-time (14 women); includes 5 minority (2 Asian, non-Hispanic/Latino; 2 Hispanic/Latino; 1 Two or more races, non-Hispanic/Latino), 11 international. Average age 29. 42 applicants, 29% accepted, 10 enrolled. In 2012, 2 master's, 7 doctorates awarded. *Degree requirements:* For master's, thesis, teaching experience; for doctorate, comprehensive exam, thesis/dissertation, teaching experience. *Entrance requirements:* For master's and doctorate, 2 letters of recommendation. Additional exam requirements/recommendations for international students: Required—TOEFL (minimum score 550 paper-based; 77 iBT). *Application deadline:* For fall admission, 4/1 for domestic students; for spring admission, 9/1 for domestic students. Application fee: $95. Electronic applications accepted. *Financial support:* In 2012–13, 25 students received support, including 2 fellowships with full tuition reimbursements available, 12 research assistantships with full tuition reimbursements available, 11 teaching assistantships with full tuition reimbursements available; institutionally sponsored loans, scholarships/grants, health care benefits, tuition waivers (full and partial), and unspecified assistantships also available. Financial award applicants required to submit FAFSA. *Faculty research:* Quantitative genetics, genetic improvement of animal populations, statistical genetics. *Unit head:* Director of Graduate Studies, 607-255-4416, Fax: 607-254-5413, E-mail: shh4@cornell.edu. *Application contact:* Graduate Field Assistant, 607-255-4416, Fax: 607-254-5413, E-mail: shh4@cornell.edu. Website: http://www.gradschool.cornell.edu/fields.php?id-41&a-2.

Dalhousie University, Faculty of Agriculture, Halifax, NS B3H 4R2, Canada. Offers agriculture (M Sc), including air quality, animal behavior, animal molecular genetics, animal nutrition, animal technology, aquaculture, botany, crop management, crop physiology, ecology, environmental microbiology, food science, horticulture, nutrient management, pest management, physiology, plant biotechnology, plant pathology, soil chemistry, soil fertility, waste management and composting, water quality. Part-time programs available. *Degree requirements:* For master's, thesis, ATC Exam Teaching Assistantship. *Entrance requirements:* For master's, honors B Sc, minimum GPA of 3.0. Additional exam requirements/recommendations for international students: Required—TOEFL (minimum score 580 paper-based; 92 iBT), IELTS, Michigan English Language Assessment Battery, CanTEST, CAEL. *Faculty research:* Bio-product development, organic agriculture, nutrient management, air and water quality, agricultural biotechnology.

Fort Valley State University, College of Graduate Studies and Extended Education, Program in Animal Science, Fort Valley, GA 31030. Offers MS. *Degree requirements:* For master's, thesis. *Entrance requirements:* For master's, GRE General Test. Additional exam requirements/recommendations for international students: Recommended—TOEFL.

Iowa State University of Science and Technology, Department of Animal Science, Ames, IA 50011. Offers animal breeding and genetics (MS, PhD); animal physiology (MS); animal psychology (PhD); animal science (MS, PhD); meat science (MS, PhD). *Degree requirements:* For master's, thesis or alternative; for doctorate, thesis/dissertation. *Entrance requirements:* For master's and doctorate, GRE General Test. Additional exam requirements/recommendations for international students: Required—TOEFL (minimum score 550 paper-based; 80 iBT), IELTS (minimum score 6.5). *Application deadline:* For fall admission, 2/1 priority date for domestic students, 2/1 for international students; for spring admission, 9/1 priority date for domestic students, 9/1 for international students. Application fee: $60 ($90 for international students). Electronic applications accepted. *Faculty research:* Animal breeding, animal nutrition, meat science, muscle biology, nutritional physiology. *Application contact:* Donna Nelson, Application Contact, 515-294-2160, Fax: 515-294-6994, E-mail: dlnelson@iastate.edu. Website: http://www.ans.iastate.edu/stud/prosp_grad/.

Iowa State University of Science and Technology, Program in Animal Breeding and Genetics, Ames, IA 50011. Offers animal breeding and genetics (MS); immunogenetics (PhD); molecular genetics (PhD); quantitative genetics (PhD). *Entrance requirements:* For master's and doctorate, GRE. Additional exam requirements/recommendations for international students: Required—TOEFL (minimum score 550 paper-based; 80 iBT), IELTS (minimum score 6.5). *Application deadline:* For fall admission, 2/1 for domestic and international students; for spring admission, 9/1 for domestic and international students. Electronic applications accepted. *Application contact:* Donna Nelson, Application Contact, 515-294-2160, Fax: 515-294-6994, E-mail: dlnelson@iastate.edu. Website: http://www.ans.iastate.edu/stud/prosp_grad/.

Iowa State University of Science and Technology, Program in Animal Physiology, Ames, IA 50011. Offers MS, PhD. *Entrance requirements:* For master's and doctorate, GRE. Additional exam requirements/recommendations for international students: Required—TOEFL (minimum score 550 paper-based; 80 iBT), IELTS (minimum score 6.5). *Application deadline:* For fall admission, 2/1 for domestic and international students; for spring admission, 9/1 for domestic and international students. Application fee: $60 ($90 for international students). Electronic applications accepted. *Application contact:* Donna Nelson, Application Contact, 515-294-2160, Fax: 515-294-6994, E-mail: dlnelson@iastate.edu. Website: http://www.fshn.hs.iastate.edu/graduate-program/food-safety-defense/.

Iowa State University of Science and Technology, Program in Meat Science, Ames, IA 50011. Offers MS, PhD. *Entrance requirements:* For master's and doctorate, GRE. Additional exam requirements/recommendations for international students: Required—TOEFL (minimum score 550 paper-based; 80 iBT), IELTS (minimum score 6.5). *Application deadline:* For fall admission, 2/1 for domestic students; for spring admission, 9/1 for domestic students. Electronic applications accepted. *Application contact:* Donna Nelson, Application Contact, 515-294-2160, Fax: 515-294-6994, E-mail: dlnelson@iastate.edu. Website: http://www.ans.iastate.edu/stud/prosp_grad/.

Kansas State University, Graduate School, College of Agriculture, Department of Animal Sciences and Industry, Manhattan, KS 66506. Offers animal breeding and genetics (MS, PhD); meat science (MS, PhD); monogastric nutrition (MS, PhD); physiology (MS, PhD); ruminant nutrition (MS, PhD). *Faculty:* 40 full-time (10 women), 6 part-time/adjunct (0 women). *Students:* 54 full-time (25 women), 5 part-time (2 women); includes 3 minority (2 Hispanic/Latino; 1 Two or more races, non-Hispanic/Latino), 9 international. Average age 27. 60 applicants, 30%

accepted, 12 enrolled. In 2012, 22 master's, 5 doctorates awarded. *Degree requirements:* For master's, thesis, oral exam; for doctorate, thesis/dissertation, preliminary exams. *Entrance requirements:* Additional exam requirements/recommendations for international students: Required—TOEFL (minimum score 550 paper-based). *Application deadline:* For fall admission, 2/1 priority date for domestic students, 2/1 for international students; for spring admission, 8/1 priority date for domestic students, 8/1 for international students. Applications are processed on a rolling basis. Application fee: $50 ($75 for international students). Electronic applications accepted. *Financial support:* In 2012–13, 1 fellowship, 45 research assistantships (averaging $17,652 per year), 5 teaching assistantships with full tuition reimbursements (averaging $13,397 per year) were awarded; health care benefits and unspecified assistantships also available. Financial award application deadline: 3/1; financial award applicants required to submit FAFSA. *Faculty research:* Animal nutrition, animal physiology, meat science, animal genetics. *Total annual research expenditures:* $1.3 million. *Unit head:* Dr. Ken Odde, Head, 785-532-1227, Fax: 785-532-7059, E-mail: kenodde@ksu.edu. *Application contact:* Dr. Evan Titgemeyer, Director, 785-532-1220, Fax: 785-532-7059, E-mail: etitgeme@ksu.edu. Website: http://www.asi.k-state.edu/DesktopDefault.aspx.

Louisiana State University and Agricultural and Mechanical College, Graduate School, College of Agriculture, School of Animal Sciences, Baton Rouge, LA 70803. Offers MS, PhD. Part-time programs available. *Faculty:* 17 full-time (2 women). *Students:* 29 full-time (16 women), 6 part-time (5 women); includes 4 minority (1 Black or African American, non-Hispanic/Latino; 3 Hispanic/Latino), 9 international. Average age 28. 18 applicants, 44% accepted, 4 enrolled. In 2012, 11 master's, 3 doctorates awarded. Terminal master's awarded for partial completion of doctoral program. *Degree requirements:* For master's, thesis; for doctorate, thesis/dissertation. *Entrance requirements:* For master's and doctorate, GRE General Test, minimum GPA of 3.0. Additional exam requirements/recommendations for international students: Required—TOEFL (minimum score 550 paper-based; 79 iBT) or IELTS (minimum score 6.5). *Application deadline:* For fall admission, 1/25 priority date for domestic students, 5/15 for international students; for spring admission, 10/15 for international students. Applications are processed on a rolling basis. Application fee: $50 ($70 for international students). Electronic applications accepted. *Financial support:* In 2012–13, 30 students received support, including 13 research assistantships with partial tuition reimbursements available (averaging $14,769 per year), 9 teaching assistantships with partial tuition reimbursements available (averaging $14,390 per year); fellowships, Federal Work-Study, institutionally sponsored loans, scholarships/grants, health care benefits, tuition waivers (full and partial), and unspecified assistantships also available. Support available to part-time students. Financial award applicants required to submit FAFSA. *Faculty research:* Reproductive physiology, biotechnology, meats, non-ruminant and ruminant nutrition, daily science. *Total annual research expenditures:* $23,055. *Unit head:* Dr. Gary Hay, Director, 225-578-3241, Fax: 225-578-3279, E-mail: ghay@agcenter.lsu.edu. *Application contact:* Dr. Donald L. Thompson, Jr., Graduate Coordinator, 225-578-3445, Fax: 225-578-2794, E-mail: dthompson@agcenter.lsu.edu. Website: http://www.lsuagcenter.com/en/our_offices/departments/Animal_Sciences/.

McGill University, Faculty of Graduate and Postdoctoral Studies, Faculty of Agricultural and Environmental Sciences, Department of Animal Science, Montréal, QC H3A 2T5, Canada. Offers M Sc, M Sc A, PhD.

Michigan State University, College of Veterinary Medicine and The Graduate School, Graduate Programs in Veterinary Medicine, Department of Large Animal Clinical Sciences, East Lansing, MI 48824. Offers MS, PhD. *Entrance requirements:* Additional exam requirements/recommendations for international students: Required—TOEFL (minimum score 550 paper-based), Michigan State University ELT (minimum score 85), Michigan English Language Assessment Battery (minimum score 83). Electronic applications accepted.

Michigan State University, College of Veterinary Medicine and The Graduate School, Graduate Programs in Veterinary Medicine, Department of Small Animal Clinical Sciences, East Lansing, MI 48824. Offers MS. *Degree requirements:* For master's, thesis. *Entrance requirements:* Additional exam requirements/recommendations for international students: Required—TOEFL, Michigan State University ELT (minimum score 85), Michigan English Language Assessment Battery (minimum score 83).

Michigan State University, The Graduate School, College of Agriculture and Natural Resources, Department of Animal Science, East Lansing, MI 48824. Offers animal science (MS, PhD); animal science-environmental toxicology (PhD). *Entrance requirements:* Additional exam requirements/recommendations for international students: Required—TOEFL (minimum score 550 paper-based), Michigan State University ELT (minimum score 85), Michigan English Language Assessment Battery (minimum score 83). Electronic applications accepted.

Mississippi State University, College of Agriculture and Life Sciences, Department of Animal Dairy Sciences, Mississippi State, MS 39762. Offers agricultural life sciences (MS), including animal physiology (MS, PhD), genetics (MS, PhD); agricultural science (PhD), including animal dairy sciences, animal nutrition (MS, PhD); agriculture (MS), including animal nutrition (MS, PhD), animal science; life sciences (PhD), including animal physiology (MS, PhD), genetics (MS, PhD). *Faculty:* 11 full-time (5 women). *Students:* 22 full-time (15 women), 15 part-time (8 women); includes 3 minority (2 Black or African American, non-Hispanic/Latino; 1 Hispanic/Latino), 8 international. Average age 30. 22 applicants, 45% accepted, 8 enrolled. In 2012, 9 master's, 2 doctorates awarded. *Degree requirements:* For master's, comprehensive exam (for some programs), thesis, written proposal of intended research area; for doctorate, comprehensive exam, thesis/dissertation, written proposal of intended research area. *Entrance requirements:* For master's, GRE General Test, minimum GPA of 3.0; for doctorate, GRE General Test. Additional exam requirements/recommendations for international students: Required—TOEFL (minimum score 575 paper-based; 84 iBT), IELTS (minimum score 7). *Application deadline:* For fall admission, 7/1 for domestic students, 5/1 for international students; for spring admission, 11/1 for domestic students, 9/1 for international students. Applications are processed on a rolling basis. Application fee: $60. Electronic applications accepted. *Financial support:* In 2012–13, 12 research assistantships (averaging $11,261 per year), 1 teaching assistantship (averaging $10,014 per year) were awarded; Federal Work-Study, institutionally sponsored loans, and unspecified assistantships also available. Financial award application deadline: 4/1; financial award applicants required to submit FAFSA. *Faculty research:* Ecology and population dynamics, physiology, biochemistry and behavior, systematics. *Unit head:* Dr. John Blanton, Interim Department Head, 662-325-2802, Fax: 662-325-8873, E-mail: jblanton@ads.msstate.edu. *Application contact:* Dr. Brian Rude, Professor and Graduate Coordinator, 662-325-2802, Fax: 662-325-8873, E-mail: brude@ads.msstate.edu. Website: http://www.ads.msstate.edu/.

Mississippi State University, College of Agriculture and Life Sciences, Department of Poultry Science, Mississippi State, MS 39762. Offers agricultural sciences (PhD), including poultry science (MS, PhD); agriculture (MS), including poultry science (MS, PhD); animal physiology (MS, PhD); genetics (MS, PhD). *Faculty:* 1 full-time (0 women). *Students:* 7 full-time (3 women), 1 (woman) part-time; includes 1 minority (Asian, non-Hispanic/Latino), 5 international. Average age 28. 17 applicants, 12% accepted, 2 enrolled. In 2012, 2 master's, 1 doctorate awarded. *Degree requirements:* For master's, comprehensive exam, thesis optional; for doctorate, comprehensive exam, thesis/dissertation. *Entrance requirements:* Additional exam requirements/recommendations for international students; Required—TOEFL (minimum score 477 paper-based; 53 iBT); Recommended—IELTS (minimum score 4.5). *Application deadline:* For fall admission, 7/1 for domestic students, 5/1 for international students; for spring admission, 10/1 for domestic students, 11/1 for international students. Applications are processed on a rolling basis. Application fee: $60. Electronic applications accepted. *Financial support:* In 2012–13, 5 research assistantships with partial tuition reimbursements (averaging $11,943 per year), 1 teaching assistantship with partial tuition reimbursement (averaging $16,360 per year) were awarded; Federal Work-Study, institutionally sponsored loans, scholarships/grants, and unspecified assistantships also available. Financial award application deadline: 4/1; financial award applicants required to submit FAFSA. *Unit head:* Dr. Mary Beck, Professor and Head, 662-325-5430, Fax: 662-325-8292, E-mail: mbeck@poultry.msstate.edu. *Application contact:* Dr. Chris McDaniel, Professor and Graduate Coordinator, 662-325-1839, Fax: 662-325-8292, E-mail: cmcdaniel@poultry.msstate.edu. Website: http://www.poultry.msstate.edu/.

Montana State University, College of Graduate Studies, College of Agriculture, Department of Animal and Range Sciences, Bozeman, MT 59717. Offers MS, PhD. Part-time programs available. *Degree requirements:* For master's, comprehensive exam; for doctorate, comprehensive exam, thesis/dissertation. *Entrance requirements:* For master's, GRE, minimum GPA of 3.0; undergraduate coursework in animal science, range science or closely-related field; faculty adviser; for doctorate, GRE. Additional exam requirements/recommendations for international students: Required—TOEFL (minimum score 550 paper-based; 80 iBT). Electronic applications accepted. *Faculty research:* Rangeland ecology, wildlife habitat management, residual feed intake, post-partum effect of bulls, increasing efficiency of sheep production systems.

New Mexico State University, Graduate School, College of Agricultural, Consumer and Environmental Sciences, Department of Animal and Range Sciences, Las Cruces, NM 88003-8001. Offers animal science (MS, PhD); domestic animal biology (M Ag); range science (M Ag, MS, PhD). Part-time programs available. *Faculty:* 17 full-time (5 women). *Students:* 28 full-time (18 women), 8 part-time (4 women); includes 5 minority (1 Black or African American, non-Hispanic/Latino; 4 Hispanic/Latino), 8 international. Average age 27. 24 applicants, 50% accepted, 8 enrolled. In 2012, 6 master's, 4 doctorates awarded. *Degree requirements:* For master's, thesis, seminar, experimental statistics; for doctorate, thesis/dissertation, research tool. *Entrance requirements:* For master's, minimum GPA of 3.0 in last 60 hours of undergraduate course work (MS); for doctorate, minimum graduate GPA of 3.2, MS with thesis. Additional exam requirements/recommendations for international students: Required—TOEFL (minimum score 530 paper-based; 71 iBT), IELTS (minimum score 6). *Application deadline:* For fall admission, 2/15 priority date for domestic students, 2/15 for international students; for winter admission, 10/1 priority date for domestic students, 10/1 for international students; for spring admission, 11/1 for domestic and international students. Applications are processed on a rolling basis. Application fee: $40 ($50 for international students). Electronic applications accepted. *Expenses:* Tuition, state resident: full-time $5239; part-time $218 per credit. Tuition, nonresident: full-time $18,266; part-time $761 per credit. *Required fees:* $1274; $53 per credit. *Financial support:* In 2012–13, 25 students received support, including 1 fellowship (averaging $3,930 per year), 14 research assistantships (averaging $21,914 per year), 6 teaching assistantships (averaging $14,892 per year); career-related internships or fieldwork, Federal Work-Study, scholarships/grants, traineeships, health care benefits, and unspecified assistantships also available. Support available to part-time students. Financial award application deadline: 3/15. *Faculty research:* Reproductive physiology, ruminant nutrition, nutrition toxicology, range ecology, wildland hydrology. *Total annual research expenditures:* $3.8 million. *Unit head:* Dr. Tim Ross, Head, 575-646-2515, Fax: 575-646-5441, E-mail: tross@nmsu.edu. Website: http://aces.nmsu.edu/academics/anrs.

North Carolina Agricultural and Technical State University, School of Graduate Studies, School of Agriculture and Environmental Sciences, Department of Animal Sciences, Greensboro, NC 27411. Offers animal health science (MS).

North Carolina State University, Graduate School, College of Agriculture and Life Sciences, Department of Animal Science, Raleigh, NC 27695. Offers animal and poultry science (PhD); animal science (MS). *Degree requirements:* For master's, thesis optional. *Entrance requirements:* For master's, GRE, minimum GPA of 3.0. Electronic applications accepted. *Faculty research:* Nutrient utilization, mineral nutrition, genomics, endocrinology, reproductive physiology.

North Carolina State University, Graduate School, College of Agriculture and Life Sciences, Department of Poultry Science, Raleigh, NC 27695. Offers MS. Part-time programs available. *Degree requirements:* For master's, thesis. Electronic applications accepted. *Faculty research:* Reproductive physiology, nutrition, toxicology, immunology, molecular biology.

North Dakota State University, College of Graduate and Interdisciplinary Studies, College of Agriculture, Food Systems, and Natural Resources, Department of Animal and Range Sciences, Fargo, ND 58108. Offers animal science (MS, PhD); range sciences (MS, PhD). *Faculty:* 17 full-time (6 women). *Students:* 28 full-time (19 women), 8 part-time (4 women); includes 1 minority (Two or more races, non-Hispanic/Latino), 3 international. Average age 27. 27 applicants, 41% accepted, 10 enrolled. In 2012, 7 master's, 3 doctorates awarded. *Degree requirements:* For master's, thesis; for doctorate, comprehensive exam, thesis/dissertation. *Entrance requirements:* For master's and doctorate, GRE General Test. Additional exam requirements/recommendations for international students: Required—TOEFL (minimum score 71 iBT). *Application deadline:* Applications are processed on a rolling basis. Application fee: $35. *Financial support:* In 2012–13, 1 fellowship with tuition reimbursement (averaging $18,000 per year), 29 research assistantships with tuition reimbursements (averaging $13,000 per year) were awarded; teaching assistantships, Federal Work-Study, institutionally sponsored loans, and tuition waivers (partial) also available. Financial award application deadline: 3/15. *Faculty research:* Reproduction, nutrition, meat and muscle biology, breeding/genetics. *Unit head:* Dr. Gregory Lardy, Chair, 701-231-7641, Fax: 701-231-7590, E-mail: gregory.lardy@ndsu.edu. *Application contact:* Sonya Goergen, Marketing, Recruitment, and Public Relations Coordinator, 701-231-7033, Fax: 701-231-6524.

The Ohio State University, Graduate School, College of Food, Agricultural, and Environmental Sciences, Department of Animal Sciences, Columbus, OH 43210. Offers MS, PhD. *Faculty:* 31. *Students:* 31 full-time (19 women), 13 part-time (7 women); includes 6 minority (1 Black or African American, non-Hispanic/Latino; 4 Hispanic/Latino; 1 Two or more races, non-Hispanic/Latino), 15 international. Average age 27. In 2012, 14 master's, 9 doctorates awarded. *Degree requirements:* For master's, thesis; for doctorate, thesis/dissertation. *Entrance requirements:* For master's and doctorate, GRE General Test. Additional exam requirements/recommendations for international students: Required—TOEFL (minimum score 550 paper-based; 79 iBT), Michigan English Language Assessment Battery (minimum score 82); Recommended—IELTS (minimum score 7). *Application deadline:* For fall admission, 1/1 priority date for domestic students, 11/30 for international students; for winter admission, 12/1 priority date for domestic students, 11/1 for international students; for spring admission, 5/15 priority date for domestic students, 4/1 for international students. Applications are processed on a rolling basis. Application fee: $40 ($50 for international students). Electronic applications accepted. *Financial support:* Fellowships, research assistantships, teaching assistantships, Federal Work-Study, and institutionally sponsored loans available. Support available to part-time students. *Unit head:* Ronald Kensinger, Chair, 614-292-6401, E-mail: kensinger.4@osu.edu. *Application contact:* Animal Science Graduate Programs, 614-292-6401, Fax: 614-292-2929, E-mail: gradadmissions@osu.edu. Website: http://ansci.osu.edu/.

Oklahoma State University, College of Agricultural Science and Natural Resources, Department of Animal Science, Stillwater, OK 74078. Offers animal sciences (M Ag, MS); food science (MS, PhD). *Faculty:* 33 full-time (10 women), 2 part-time/adjunct (0 women). *Students:* 20 full-time (14 women), 45 part-time (20 women); includes 6 minority (2 Asian, non-Hispanic/Latino; 2 Hispanic/Latino; 2 Two or more races, non-Hispanic/Latino), 22 international. Average age 27. 94 applicants, 28% accepted, 20 enrolled. In 2012, 15 master's, 7 doctorates awarded. *Degree requirements:* For master's, thesis; for doctorate, comprehensive exam, thesis/dissertation. *Entrance requirements:* For master's and doctorate, GRE or GMAT. Additional exam requirements/recommendations for international students: Required—TOEFL (minimum score 550 paper-based; 79 iBT). *Application deadline:* For fall admission, 3/1 for international students; for spring admission, 8/1 for international students. Applications are processed on a rolling basis. Application fee: $40 ($75 for international students). Electronic applications accepted. *Expenses:* Tuition, state resident: full-time $4272; part-time $178 per credit hour. Tuition, nonresident: full-time $17,016; part-time $709 per credit hour. *Required fees:* $2188; $91.17 per credit hour. One-time fee: $50 full-time. Part-time tuition and fees vary according to course load and campus/location. *Financial support:* In 2012–13, 23 research assistantships (averaging $14,693 per year), 8 teaching assistantships (averaging $15,496 per year) were awarded; career-related internships or fieldwork, Federal Work-Study, scholarships/grants, health care benefits, tuition waivers (partial), and unspecified assistantships also available. Support available to part-time students. Financial award application deadline: 3/1; financial award applicants required to submit FAFSA. *Faculty research:* Quantitative trait loci identification for economical traits in swing/beef; waste management strategies in livestock; endocrine control of reproductive processes in farm animals; cholesterol synthesis, inhibition, and reduction; food safety research. *Unit head:* Dr. Clint Rusk, Head, 405-744-6062, Fax: 405-744-7390. *Application contact:* Dr. Sheryl Tucker, Dean, 405-744-7099, Fax: 405-744-0355, E-mail: grad-i@okstate.edu. Website: http://www.ansi.okstate.edu.

Oregon State University, College of Agricultural Sciences, Department of Animal and Rangeland Sciences, Program in Animal Sciences, Corvallis, OR 97331. Offers M Agr, MS, PhD. *Faculty:* 6 full-time (3 women), 3 part-time/adjunct (1 woman). *Students:* 13 full-time (7 women), 2 part-time (1 woman); includes 2 minority (1 Asian, non-Hispanic/Latino; 1 Hispanic/Latino), 3 international. Average age 27. 25 applicants, 12% accepted, 1 enrolled. In 2012, 7 master's awarded. *Expenses:* Tuition, state resident: full-time $11,367; part-time $421 per credit hour. Tuition, nonresident: full-time $18,279; part-time $677 per credit hour. *Required fees:* $1478. One-time fee: $300 full-time. Tuition and fees vary according to course load and program. *Unit head:* Dr. John Killefer, Professor and Department Head, 541-737-1891, E-mail: john.killefer@oregonstate.edu.

Penn State University Park, Graduate School, College of Agricultural Sciences, Department of Animal Science, State College, University Park, PA 16802-1503. Offers MPS, MS, PhD. *Unit head:* Dr. Barbara J. Christ, Interim Dean, 814-865-2541, Fax: 814-865-3103, E-mail: ebf@psu.edu. *Application contact:* Cynthia E. Nicosia, Director of Graduate Enrollment Services, 814-865-1834, E-mail: cey1@psu.edu. Website: http://www.animalscience.psu.edu/.

Prairie View A&M University, College of Agriculture and Human Sciences, Prairie View, TX 77446-0519. Offers agricultural economics (MS); animal sciences (MS); interdisciplinary human sciences (MS); soil science (MS). Part-time and evening/weekend programs available. *Degree requirements:* For master's, comprehensive exam, thesis (for some programs), field placement. *Entrance requirements:* For master's, GRE General Test, minimum GPA of 2.45. Additional exam requirements/recommendations for international students: Required—TOEFL (minimum score 550 paper-based). *Faculty research:* Domestic violence prevention, water quality, food growth regulators, wetland dynamics, biochemistry, obesity and nutrition, family therapy.

Purdue University, Graduate School, College of Agriculture, Department of Animal Sciences, West Lafayette, IN 47907. Offers MS, PhD. Part-time programs available. *Faculty:* 30 full-time (5 women), 7 part-time/adjunct (2 women). *Students:* 47 full-time (26 women), 8 part-time (6 women); includes 5 minority (3 Black or African American, non-Hispanic/Latino; 1 Asian, non-Hispanic/Latino; 1 Two or more races, non-Hispanic/Latino), 27 international. Average age 28. 59 applicants, 25% accepted, 11 enrolled. In 2012, 14 master's, 6 doctorates awarded. Terminal master's awarded for partial completion of doctoral program. *Degree requirements:* For master's, thesis optional; for doctorate, thesis/dissertation. *Entrance requirements:* For master's, GRE General Test, minimum undergraduate GPA of 3.0 or equivalent; for doctorate, GRE General Test, minimum undergraduate GPA of 3.0 or equivalent; master's degree with minimum GPA of 3.0 or equivalent. Additional exam requirements/recommendations for international students: Required—TOEFL (minimum score 550 paper-based; 77 iBT), TWE. *Application deadline:* For fall admission, 6/1 priority date for domestic students, 3/1 for international students; for spring admission, 10/1 priority date for domestic students, 8/1 for international students. Applications are processed on a rolling basis. Application fee: $60 ($75 for international students). Electronic applications accepted. *Financial support:* In 2012–13, 35 students received support, including fellowships with full tuition reimbursements available (averaging $17,475 per year), 29 research assistantships with full tuition reimbursements available (averaging $18,577 per year). Support available to part-time students. Financial award applicants required to submit FAFSA. *Faculty research:* Genetics, meat science, nutrition, management, ethology. *Unit head:* Dr. Nancy F. Gabin, Head, 765-494-4806. *Application contact:* Delayne K. Graham, Graduate Contact, 765-494-4863, E-mail: dkgraham@purdue.edu. Website: http://www.ansc.purdue.edu/.

Purdue University, Graduate School, College of Health and Human Sciences, Department of Nutrition Science, West Lafayette, IN 47907. Offers animal health (MS, PhD); biochemical and molecular nutrition (MS, PhD); growth and development (MS, PhD); human and clinical nutrition (MS, PhD); public health and education (MS, PhD). *Faculty:* 17 full-time (11 women), 16 part-time/adjunct (14 women). *Students:* 39 full-time (35 women), 3 part-time (2 women); includes 4 minority (2 Black or African American, non-Hispanic/Latino; 1 Asian, non-Hispanic/Latino; 1 Hispanic/Latino), 21 international. Average age 27. 94 applicants, 23% accepted, 18 enrolled. In 2012, 1 master's, 7 doctorates awarded. *Degree requirements:* For master's, thesis; for doctorate, thesis/dissertation. *Entrance requirements:* For master's and doctorate, GRE General Test (minimum scores in verbal and quantitative areas of 1000 or 300 on new scoring), minimum undergraduate GPA of 3.0 or equivalent. Additional exam requirements/recommendations for international students: Required—TOEFL (minimum score 600 paper-based; 77 iBT). *Application deadline:* For fall admission, 1/15 for domestic and international students. Applications are processed on a rolling basis. Application fee: $60 ($75 for international students). Electronic applications accepted. *Financial support:* Fellowships, research assistantships, and teaching assistantships available. Support available to part-time students. Financial award applicants required to submit FAFSA. *Faculty research:* Nutrient requirements, nutrient metabolism, nutrition and disease prevention. *Unit head:* Dr. Connie M. Weaver, Head, 765-494-8237, Fax: 765-494-0674, E-mail: weavercm@purdue.edu. *Application contact:* Marilyn McCammack, Graduate Secretary, 765-476-7492, E-mail: mccammac@purdue.edu. Website: http://www.cfs.purdue.edu/fn/.

Rutgers, The State University of New Jersey, New Brunswick, Graduate School-New Brunswick, Program in Endocrinology and Animal Biosciences, Piscataway, NJ 08854-8097. Offers MS, PhD. Terminal master's awarded for partial completion of doctoral program. *Degree requirements:* For master's, thesis; for doctorate, comprehensive exam, thesis/dissertation. *Entrance requirements:* For master's and doctorate, GRE General Test. Additional exam requirements/recommendations for international students: Required—TOEFL. Electronic applications accepted. *Faculty research:* Comparative and behavioral endocrinology, epigenetic regulation of the endocrine system, exercise physiology and immunology, fetal and neonatal developmental programming, mammary gland biology and breast cancer, neuroendocrinology and alcohol studies, reproductive and developmental toxicology.

South Dakota State University, Graduate School, College of Agriculture and Biological Sciences, Department of Animal and Range Sciences, Brookings, SD 57007. Offers animal science (MS, PhD); biological sciences (PhD). Part-time programs available. *Degree requirements:* For master's, thesis, oral exam; for doctorate, comprehensive exam, thesis/dissertation, preliminary oral and written exams. *Entrance requirements:* Additional exam requirements/recommendations for international students: Required—TOEFL (minimum score 550 paper-based; 79 iBT). *Faculty research:* Ruminant and nonruminant nutrition, meat science, reproductive physiology, range utilization, ecology genetics, muscle biology, animal production.

South Dakota State University, Graduate School, College of Agriculture and Biological Sciences, Department of Dairy Science, Brookings, SD 57007. Offers animal sciences (MS, PhD); biological sciences (MS, PhD). Part-time programs available. *Degree requirements:* For master's, thesis, oral exam; for doctorate, comprehensive exam, thesis/dissertation, preliminary oral and written exams. *Entrance requirements:* Additional exam requirements/recommendations for international students: Required—TOEFL (minimum score 550 paper-based). *Faculty research:* Dairy cattle nutrition, energy metabolism, food safety, dairy processing technology.

Southern Illinois University Carbondale, Graduate School, College of Agriculture, Department of Animal Science, Food and Nutrition, Program in Animal Science, Carbondale, IL 62901-4701. Offers MS. *Faculty:* 12 full-time (4 women). *Students:* 4 full-time (2 women), 7 part-time (6 women). Average age 29. 5 applicants. In 2012, 1 master's awarded. *Degree requirements:* For master's, thesis. *Entrance requirements:* For master's, GRE, minimum GPA of 2.7. Additional exam requirements/recommendations for international students: Required—TOEFL. *Application deadline:* For fall admission, 3/1 for domestic students; for spring admission, 9/2 for domestic students. Applications are processed on a rolling basis. Application fee: $50. *Financial support:* In 2012–13, 13 research assistantships with full tuition reimbursements, 2 teaching assistantships with full tuition reimbursements were awarded; fellowships with full tuition reimbursements, career-related internships or fieldwork, Federal Work-Study, institutionally sponsored loans, and tuition waivers (full) also available. Support available to part-time students. *Faculty research:* Nutrition, reproductive physiology, animal biotechnology, phytoestrogens and animal reproduction. *Unit head:* Dr. Todd A. Winters, Interim Chair, 618-453-1760, Fax: 618-453-5231, E-mail: tw3a@siu.edu. *Application contact:* Ruth Cook, Administrative Clerk, 618-453-1762, E-mail: racook@siu.edu. Website: http://www.coas.siu.edu/default2.asp?active_page_id-112.

Sul Ross State University, Division of Agricultural and Natural Resource Science, Program in Animal Science, Alpine, TX 79832. Offers equine (M Ag, MS); meat science (M Ag, MS); production (M Ag, MS); reproductive physiology (M Ag, MS). Part-time programs available. *Degree requirements:* For master's, thesis (for some programs). *Entrance requirements:* For master's, GRE General Test, minimum GPA of 2.5 in last 60 hours of undergraduate work. *Faculty research:* Reproductive physiology, meat processing, animal nutrition, equine foot and motion studies, Spanish goat and Barbado sheep studies.

Texas A&M University, College of Agriculture and Life Sciences, Department of Animal Science, College Station, TX 77843. Offers M Agr, MS, PhD. *Faculty:* 29. *Students:* 81 full-time (55 women), 28 part-time (16 women); includes 14 minority (3 Black or African American, non-Hispanic/Latino; 10 Hispanic/Latino; 1 Two or more races, non-Hispanic/Latino), 16 international. Average age 27. In 2012, 24 master's, 6 doctorates awarded. *Degree requirements:* For master's, thesis; for doctorate, thesis/dissertation. *Entrance requirements:* For master's and doctorate, GRE General Test. Additional exam requirements/recommendations for international students: Required—TOEFL. *Application deadline:* For fall admission, 2/1 priority date for domestic students; for spring admission, 10/1 priority date for domestic students. Applications are processed on a rolling basis. Application fee: $50 ($75 for international students). *Financial support:* In 2012–13, fellowships (averaging $15,000 per year), research assistantships (averaging $12,950 per year), teaching assistantships (averaging $11,500 per year) were awarded; career-related internships or fieldwork, Federal Work-Study, institutionally sponsored loans, and scholarships/grants also available. Financial award application deadline: 2/1; financial award applicants required to submit FAFSA. *Faculty research:* Genetic engineering/gene markers, dietary effects on colon cancer, biotechnology. *Unit head:* Dr. H. Russell Cross, Interim Head, 979-845-1543, Fax: 979-845-6433, E-mail: hrcross@tamu.edu. *Application contact:* Graduate Admissions, 979-845-1044, E-mail: admissions@tamu.edu. Website: http://animalscience.tamu.edu/.

Texas A&M University, College of Agriculture and Life Sciences, Department of Poultry Science, College Station, TX 77843. Offers M Agr, MS, PhD. Part-time and evening/weekend programs available. Postbaccalaureate distance learning degree programs offered (no on-campus study). *Faculty:* 12. *Students:* 26 full-time (15 women), 11 part-time (6 women); includes 8 minority (2 Black or African American, non-Hispanic/Latino; 1 Asian, non-Hispanic/Latino; 5 Hispanic/Latino), 9 international. Average age 28. In 2012, 3 master's, 4 doctorates awarded. Terminal master's awarded for partial completion of doctoral program. *Degree requirements:* For master's, thesis (for some programs); for doctorate, thesis/dissertation. *Entrance requirements:* For master's and doctorate, GRE General Test. Additional exam requirements/recommendations for international students: Required—TOEFL. Application fee: $50 ($75 for international students). Electronic applications accepted. *Financial support:* In 2012–13, fellowships with partial tuition reimbursements (averaging $18,000 per year) were awarded; research assistantships with partial tuition reimbursements, teaching assistantships, scholarships/grants, and unspecified assistantships also available. Financial award application deadline: 4/1; financial award applicants required to submit FAFSA. *Faculty research:* Poultry diseases and immunology, avian genetics and physiology, nutrition and metabolism, poultry processing and food safety, waste management. *Unit head:* Dr. John B. Carey, Head, 979-845-1931, E-mail: jcarey@poultry.tamu.edu. *Application contact:* Jennifer Allen, Academic Advisor II, 979-845-1654, E-mail: jallen@poultry.tamu.edu. Website: http://gallus.tamu.edu/.

Texas A&M University–Kingsville, College of Graduate Studies, College of Agriculture and Home Economics, Program in Animal Sciences, Kingsville, TX 78363. Offers MS. *Degree requirements:* For master's, comprehensive exam, thesis or alternative. *Entrance requirements:* For master's, GRE General Test, minimum GPA of 3.0. Additional exam requirements/recommendations for international students: Required—TOEFL.

Texas Tech University, Graduate School, College of Agricultural Sciences and Natural Resources, Department of Animal and Food Sciences, Lubbock, TX 79409-2141. Offers animal science (MS, PhD); food science (MS). *Degree requirements:* For master's, thesis or alternative, internship (M Agr); for doctorate, thesis/dissertation. *Entrance requirements:* For master's and doctorate, GRE General Test, formal approval from departmental committee. Additional exam requirements/recommendations for international students: Required—TOEFL (minimum score 550 paper-based; 79 iBT). Electronic applications accepted. *Faculty research:* Animal nutrition, health and welfare (species of emphasis: beef cattle, dairy cattle, swine, horse, sheep and goat); animal physiology and reproduction; meat science and muscle biology; food safety, security and public health, food science.

Tufts University, Cummings School of Veterinary Medicine, Program in Conservation Medicine, Medford, MA 02155. Offers MS. *Degree requirements:* For master's, case study, preceptorship. *Entrance requirements:* For master's, GRE, official transcripts, curriculum vitae. Additional exam requirements/recommendations for international students: Required—TOEFL or IELTS. Electronic applications accepted. *Expenses: Tuition:* Full-time $42,856; part-time $1072 per credit hour. *Required fees:* $730. Full-time tuition and fees vary according to degree level, program and student level. Part-time tuition and fees vary according to course load. *Faculty research:* Non-invasive saliva collection techniques for free-ranging mountain gorillas and captive eastern gorillas, animal sentinels for infectious diseases.

Tuskegee University, Graduate Programs, College of Agricultural, Environmental and Natural Sciences, Department of Agricultural Sciences, Program in Animal and Poultry Sciences, Tuskegee, AL 36088. Offers MS. *Degree requirements:* For master's, thesis. *Entrance requirements:* For master's, GRE General Test. Additional exam requirements/recommendations for international students: Required—TOEFL (minimum score 500 paper-based). *Expenses: Tuition:* Full-time $18,100; part-time $575 per credit hour. *Required fees:* $800.

Universidad Nacional Pedro Henriquez Urena, Graduate School, Santo Domingo, Dominican Republic. Offers agricultural diversity (MS), including horticultural/fruit production, tropical animal production; conservation of monuments and cultural assets (M Arch); ecology and environment (MS); environmental engineering (MEE); international relations (MA); natural resource management (MS); political science (MA); project optimization (MPM); project feasibility (MPM); project management (MPM); sanitation engineering (ME); science for teachers (MS); tropical Caribbean architecture (M Arch).

Université Laval, Faculty of Agricultural and Food Sciences, Department of Animal Sciences, Programs in Animal Sciences, Québec, QC G1K 7P4, Canada. Offers M Sc, PhD. Part-time programs available. Terminal master's awarded for partial completion of doctoral program. *Degree requirements:* For master's, thesis; for doctorate, comprehensive exam, thesis/dissertation. *Entrance requirements:*

For master's and doctorate, knowledge of French and English. Electronic applications accepted.

The University of Arizona, College of Agriculture and Life Sciences, Department of Animal Sciences, Tucson, AZ 85721. Offers MS, PhD. Part-time programs available. *Faculty:* 6 full-time (0 women), 1 part-time/adjunct (0 women). *Students:* 15 full-time (9 women), 3 part-time (1 woman); includes 2 minority (both Hispanic/Latino), 2 international. Average age 27. 23 applicants, 43% accepted, 5 enrolled. In 2012, 3 master's, 2 doctorates awarded. *Degree requirements:* For master's, thesis; for doctorate, thesis/dissertation. *Entrance requirements:* For master's, GRE Subject Test, 3 letters of recommendation, minimum GPA of 3.0; for doctorate, GRE Subject Test (biology or chemistry recommended), 3 letters of recommendation, statement of purpose, minimum GPA of 3.0. Additional exam requirements/recommendations for international students: Required—TOEFL (minimum score 550 paper-based; 79 iBT). *Application deadline:* Applications are processed on a rolling basis. Application fee: $75. Electronic applications accepted. *Financial support:* In 2012–13, 10 students received support, including 6 research assistantships with partial tuition reimbursements available (averaging $16,413 per year), 3 teaching assistantships with partial tuition reimbursements available (averaging $21,174 per year); fellowships, scholarships/grants, health care benefits, and unspecified assistantships also available. Financial award application deadline: 4/1. *Faculty research:* Nutrition of beef and dairy cattle, reproduction and breeding, muscle growth and function, animal stress, meat science. *Total annual research expenditures:* $872,066. *Unit head:* Dr. Ronald E. Allen, Professor and Head, 520-621-7626, Fax: 520-621-9435, E-mail: rallen@ag.arizona.edu. *Application contact:* Dr. Sean Limesand, Graduate Committee Chair, 520-626-8903, Fax: 520-621-9435, E-mail: limesand@ag.arizona.edu. Website: http://animal.cals.arizona.edu/.

University of Arkansas, Graduate School, Dale Bumpers College of Agricultural, Food and Life Sciences, Department of Animal Science, Fayetteville, AR 72701-1201. Offers MS, PhD. *Students:* 8 full-time (7 women), 17 part-time (7 women); includes 1 minority (Two or more races, non-Hispanic/Latino), 4 international. In 2012, 11 master's, 1 doctorate awarded. *Degree requirements:* For master's, thesis; for doctorate, variable foreign language requirement, thesis/dissertation. *Entrance requirements:* For master's, GRE General Test or minimum GPA of 2.7. *Application deadline:* For fall admission, 4/1 for international students; for spring admission, 10/1 for international students. Applications are processed on a rolling basis. Application fee: $40 ($50 for international students). Electronic applications accepted. *Financial support:* In 2012–13, 11 research assistantships, 2 teaching assistantships were awarded; fellowships with tuition reimbursements, career-related internships or fieldwork, and Federal Work-Study also available. Support available to part-time students. Financial award application deadline: 4/1; financial award applicants required to submit FAFSA. *Unit head:* Dr. Michael Looper, Chair, 479-575-4351, E-mail: looper@uark.edu. *Application contact:* Dr. David Kreider, Graduate Coordinator, 479-575-6323, E-mail: dkreider@uark.edu. Website: http://animalscience.uark.edu.

University of Arkansas, Graduate School, Dale Bumpers College of Agricultural, Food and Life Sciences, Department of Poultry Science, Fayetteville, AR 72701-1201. Offers MS, PhD. *Students:* 10 full-time (6 women), 28 part-time (13 women); includes 1 minority (Hispanic/Latino), 18 international. In 2012, 5 master's, 4 doctorates awarded. *Degree requirements:* For master's, thesis; for doctorate, variable foreign language requirement, thesis/dissertation. *Application deadline:* For fall admission, 4/1 for international students; for spring admission, 10/1 for international students. Applications are processed on a rolling basis. Application fee: $40 ($50 for international students). Electronic applications accepted. *Financial support:* In 2012–13, 25 research assistantships were awarded; fellowships with tuition reimbursements, teaching assistantships, career-related internships or fieldwork, and Federal Work-Study also available. Support available to part-time students. Financial award application deadline: 4/1; financial award applicants required to submit FAFSA. *Unit head:* Dr. Mike Kidd, Department Head, 479-575-4952, E-mail: mkidd@uark.edu. *Application contact:* Dr. Mike Slavik, Graduate Coordinator, 479-575-4952, E-mail: mslavik@uark.edu. Website: http://www.poultryscience.uark.edu/.

The University of British Columbia, Faculty of Land and Food Systems, Animal Science Graduate Program, Vancouver, BC V6T 1Z1, Canada. Offers M Sc, PhD. *Degree requirements:* For master's, thesis; for doctorate, comprehensive exam, thesis/dissertation. *Entrance requirements:* Additional exam requirements/recommendations for international students: Required—TOEFL (minimum score 577 paper-based; 90 iBT), IELTS (minimum score 6.5). Electronic applications accepted. *Faculty research:* Animal production, animal behavior and welfare, reproductive physiology, animal genetics, aquaculture and fish physiology.

University of California, Davis, Graduate Studies, Graduate Group in Animal Biology, Davis, CA 95616. Offers MAM, MS, PhD. Terminal master's awarded for partial completion of doctoral program. *Degree requirements:* For master's, comprehensive exam (for some programs), thesis (for some programs); for doctorate, thesis/dissertation. *Entrance requirements:* For master's, GRE General Test, minimum GPA of 3.0. Additional exam requirements/recommendations for international students: Required—TOEFL (minimum score 550 paper-based). Electronic applications accepted. *Faculty research:* Genetics, nutrition, physiology and behavior in domestic and aquatic animals.

University of Connecticut, Graduate School, College of Agriculture and Natural Resources, Department of Animal Science, Storrs, CT 06269. Offers MS, PhD. Terminal master's awarded for partial completion of doctoral program. *Degree requirements:* For master's, comprehensive exam, thesis; for doctorate, comprehensive exam, thesis/dissertation. *Entrance requirements:* For master's and doctorate, GRE General Test, GRE Subject Test. Additional exam requirements/recommendations for international students: Required—TOEFL (minimum score 550 paper-based). Electronic applications accepted.

University of Delaware, College of Agriculture and Natural Resources, Department of Animal and Food Sciences, Newark, DE 19716. Offers animal sciences (MS, PhD); food sciences (MS). Part-time programs available. Terminal master's awarded for partial completion of doctoral program. *Degree requirements:* For master's, thesis; for doctorate, comprehensive exam, thesis/dissertation. *Entrance requirements:* For master's and doctorate, GRE General Test. Additional exam requirements/recommendations for international students: Required—TOEFL. Electronic applications accepted. *Faculty research:* Food chemistry, food microbiology, process engineering technology, packaging, food analysis, microbial genetics, molecular endocrinology, growth physiology, avian immunology and virology, monogastric nutrition, avian genomics.

University of Florida, Graduate School, College of Agricultural and Life Sciences, Department of Animal Sciences, Gainesville, FL 32611. Offers MS, PhD. Part-time programs available. *Degree requirements:* For master's, variable foreign language requirement, comprehensive exam (for some programs), thesis optional, one departmental and one exit seminar; for doctorate, comprehensive exam, thesis/dissertation, two departmental seminars, one exit seminar. *Entrance requirements:* For master's and doctorate, GRE General Test, minimum GPA of 3.0. Additional exam requirements/recommendations for international students: Required—TOEFL (minimum score 550 paper-based; 80 iBT), IELTS (minimum score 6). Electronic applications accepted. *Faculty research:* Ruminal metabolism and fermentation, enteric greenhouse gas emissions, beef cattle nutrition; embryonic development, fertility, uterine biology, dairy cattle, heat stress; genetic and genomic evaluation of animals in multibreed populations; prostaglandin and immune response to lipopolysaccharides in dairy cattle, dietary fatty acids and their effects on reproduction, immunity and energy metabolism; metabolic influences of nutrients on reproduction.

University of Florida, Interdisciplinary Concentration in Animal Molecular and Cellular Biology, Gainesville, FL 32611. Offers MS, PhD. Program offered jointly by College of Agricultural and Life Sciences, College of Liberal Arts and Sciences, College of Medicine, and College of Veterinary Medicine. *Entrance requirements:* For master's and doctorate, GRE General Test (minimum score 1000), minimum GPA of 3.0. Additional exam requirements/recommendations for international students: Required—TOEFL (minimum score 550 paper-based; 80 iBT), IELTS (minimum score 6). Electronic applications accepted.

University of Georgia, College of Agricultural and Environmental Sciences, Department of Animal and Dairy Sciences, Athens, GA 30602. Offers animal and dairy science (PhD); animal and dairy sciences (MADS); animal science (MS); dairy science (MS). *Degree requirements:* For master's, thesis; for doctorate, one foreign language, thesis/dissertation. *Entrance requirements:* For master's and doctorate, GRE General Test. Electronic applications accepted.

University of Georgia, College of Agricultural and Environmental Sciences, Department of Poultry Science, Athens, GA 30602. Offers animal nutrition (PhD); poultry science (MS, PhD). *Degree requirements:* For master's, thesis; for doctorate, one foreign language, thesis/dissertation. *Entrance requirements:* For master's and doctorate, GRE General Test. Electronic applications accepted.

University of Guelph, Graduate Studies, Ontario Agricultural College, Department of Animal and Poultry Science, Guelph, ON N1G 2W1, Canada. Offers M Sc, PhD. Part-time programs available. *Degree requirements:* For master's, thesis (for some programs); for doctorate, comprehensive exam, thesis/dissertation. *Entrance requirements:* For master's, minimum B- average during previous 2 years of course work; for doctorate, minimum B- average. Additional exam requirements/recommendations for international students: Required—TOEFL (minimum score 550 paper-based; 89 iBT), IELTS (minimum score 6.5). *Faculty research:* Animal breeding and genetics (quantitative or molecular), animal nutrition (monogastric or ruminant), animal physiology (environmental, reproductive or behavioral), behavior and welfare.

University of Hawaii at Manoa, Graduate Division, College of Tropical Agriculture and Human Resources, Department of Human Nutrition, Food and Animal Sciences, Program in Animal Sciences, Honolulu, HI 96822. Offers MS. Part-time programs available. *Entrance requirements:* For master's, GRE General Test. Additional exam requirements/recommendations for international students: Required—TOEFL (minimum score 580 paper-based; 100 iBT), IELTS (minimum score 5). *Faculty research:* Nutritional biochemistry, food composition, nutrition education, nutritional epidemiology, international nutrition, food toxicology.

University of Idaho, College of Graduate Studies, College of Agricultural and Life Sciences, Department of Animal and Veterinary Science, Moscow, ID 83844-2330. Offers animal physiology (PhD); animal science (MS), including production. *Faculty:* 4 full-time. *Students:* 13 full-time, 12 part-time. Average age 31. In 2012, 5 master's, 2 doctorates awarded. *Degree requirements:* For doctorate, thesis/dissertation. *Entrance requirements:* For master's, GRE General Test, minimum GPA of 2.8; for doctorate, minimum undergraduate GPA of 2.8, graduate 3.0. *Application deadline:* For fall admission, 8/1 for domestic students; for spring admission, 12/15 for domestic students. Applications are processed on a rolling basis. Application fee: $60. Electronic applications accepted. *Expenses:* Tuition, state resident: full-time $4230; part-time $252 per credit hour. Tuition, nonresident: full-time $17,018; part-time $891 per credit hour. *Required fees:* $2932; $107 per credit hour. *Financial support:* Research assistantships and teaching assistantships available. Financial award applicants required to submit FAFSA. *Faculty research:* Reproductive biology, muscle and growth physiology, meat science, aquaculture, ruminant nutrition. *Unit head:* Dr. Mark A. McGuire, Interim Department Head, 208-885-6345, E-mail: avs-students@uidaho.edu. *Application contact:* Erick Larson, Director of Graduate Admissions, 208-885-4723, E-mail: gadms@uidaho.edu. Website: http://www.uidaho.edu/cals/avs.

University of Illinois at Urbana–Champaign, Graduate College, College of Agricultural, Consumer and Environmental Sciences, Department of Animal Sciences, Champaign, IL 61820. Offers animal sciences (MS, PhD); bioinformatics: animal sciences (MS). *Students:* 82 (30 women). Application fee: $75 ($90 for international students). *Unit head:* Douglas F. Parrett, Interim Head, 217-333-2647, Fax: 217-244-2871, E-mail: dparrett@illinois.edu. *Application contact:* Lori Kelso, Resource and Policy Analyst, 217-244-0418, Fax: 217-333-5044, E-mail: lkelso@illinois.edu. Website: http://www.ansci.illinois.edu/.

University of Kentucky, Graduate School, College of Agriculture, Program in Animal Sciences, Lexington, KY 40506-0032. Offers MS, PhD. Terminal master's awarded for partial completion of doctoral program. *Degree requirements:* For master's, comprehensive exam, thesis optional; for doctorate, comprehensive exam, thesis/dissertation. *Entrance requirements:* For master's, GRE General Test, minimum undergraduate GPA of 2.75; for doctorate, GRE General Test, minimum graduate GPA of 3.0. Additional exam requirements/recommendations for international students: Required—TOEFL (minimum score 550 paper-based). Electronic applications accepted. *Faculty research:* Nutrition of horses, cattle, swine, poultry, and sheep; physiology of reproduction and lactation; food science; microbiology.

University of Maine, Graduate School, College of Natural Sciences, Forestry, and Agriculture, Department of Animal and Veterinary Sciences, Orono, ME 04469. Offers animal sciences (MPS, MS). Part-time programs available. *Faculty:* 12 full-time (2 women), 3 part-time/adjunct (1 woman). *Students:* 3 full-time (1 woman), 1 (woman) part-time, 1 international. Average age 35. 5 applicants. In 2012, 1 master's awarded. *Entrance requirements:* For master's, GRE General Test. Additional exam requirements/recommendations for international students: Required—TOEFL. *Application deadline:* For fall admission, 2/1 priority date for domestic students. Applications are processed on a rolling basis. Application fee: $65. Electronic applications accepted. *Financial support:* In 2012–13, 4 research assistantships with full tuition reimbursements (averaging $16,794 per year), 1 teaching assistantship with full tuition reimbursement (averaging $13,600 per year) were awarded; Federal Work-Study, institutionally sponsored loans, and tuition waivers (full and partial) also available. Financial award application deadline: 3/1. *Faculty research:* Animal nutrition, parasitology, veterinary pathology, reproductive physiology, marine life nutrition and management. *Unit head:* Dr. James Weber, Chair, 207-581-2774, Fax: 207-581-2770. *Application contact:* Scott G. Delcourt, Associate Dean of the Graduate School, 207-581-3291, Fax: 207-581-3232, E-mail: graduate@maine.edu. Website: http://umaine.edu/animalveterinarysciences/.

University of Manitoba, Faculty of Graduate Studies, Faculty of Agricultural and Food Sciences, Department of Animal Science, Winnipeg, MB R3T 2N2, Canada. Offers M Sc, PhD. *Degree requirements:* For master's, thesis; for doctorate, one foreign language, thesis/dissertation.

University of Maryland, College Park, Academic Affairs, College of Agriculture and Natural Resources, Department of Animal and Avian Sciences, Program in Animal Sciences, College Park, MD 20742. Offers MS, PhD. *Students:* 37 full-time (22 women), 3 part-time (all women); includes 3 minority (2 Asian, non-Hispanic/Latino; 1 Hispanic/Latino), 17 international. 49 applicants, 29% accepted, 13 enrolled. In 2012, 2 master's, 3 doctorates awarded. *Degree requirements:* For master's, thesis, oral exam or written comprehensive exam; for doctorate, thesis/dissertation, journal publication, scientific paper. *Entrance requirements:* For master's, GRE General Test, minimum GPA of 3.0; for doctorate, GRE General Test. Additional exam requirements/recommendations for international students: Required—TOEFL. *Application deadline:* For fall admission, 2/1 for domestic and international students; for spring admission, 10/1 for domestic students, 6/1 for international students. Applications are processed on a rolling basis. Application fee: $75. Electronic applications accepted. *Expenses:* Tuition, state resident: part-time $551 per credit. Tuition, nonresident: part-time $1188 per credit. Part-time tuition and fees vary according to program. *Financial support:* In 2012–13, 33 teaching assistantships (averaging $16,491 per year) were awarded; fellowships and research assistantships also available. Financial award applicants required to submit FAFSA. *Faculty research:* Animal physiology, cell biology and biochemistry, reproduction, biometrics, animal behavior. *Unit head:* Dr. Tom Porter, Chairman, 301-405-1366, Fax: 301-314-9059, E-mail: teporter@umd.edu. *Application contact:* Dr. Charles A. Caramello, Dean of Graduate School, 301-405-0358, Fax: 301-314-9305, E-mail: ccaramel@umd.edu.

University of Massachusetts Amherst, Graduate School, College of Natural Sciences, Department of Animal Biotechnology and Biomedical Sciences, Amherst, MA 01003. Offers MS, PhD. Part-time programs available. *Faculty:* 23 full-time (10 women). *Students:* 17 full-time (11 women), 6 international. Average age 32. 31 applicants, 10% accepted, 3 enrolled. In 2012, 2 master's, 1 doctorate awarded. Terminal master's awarded for partial completion of doctoral program. *Degree requirements:* For master's, thesis or alternative; for doctorate, comprehensive exam, thesis/dissertation. *Entrance requirements:* For master's and doctorate, GRE General Test. Additional exam requirements/recommendations for international students: Required—TOEFL (minimum score 550 paper-based; 80 iBT), IELTS (minimum score 6.5). *Application deadline:* For fall admission, 2/1 for domestic and international students; for spring admission, 10/1 for domestic and international students. Applications are processed on a rolling basis. Application fee: $75. Electronic applications accepted. *Expenses:* Tuition, state resident: full-time $1980; part-time $110 per credit. Tuition, nonresident: full-time $13,314; part-time $414 per credit. *Required fees:* $10,338; $3594 per semester. One-time fee: $357. *Financial support:* Fellowships with full and partial tuition reimbursements, research assistantships with full and partial tuition reimbursements, teaching assistantships with full and partial tuition reimbursements, career-related internships or fieldwork, Federal Work-Study, scholarships/grants, traineeships, health care benefits, tuition waivers (full and partial), and unspecified assistantships available. Support available to part-time students. Financial award application deadline: 2/1. *Unit head:* Dr. Lisa Minter, Graduate Program Director, 413-577-1193, Fax: 413-577-1150. *Application contact:* Lindsay DeSantis, Supervisor of Admissions, 413-545-0722, Fax: 413-577-0010, E-mail: gradadm@grad.umass.edu. Website: http://www.vasci.umass.edu/graduate-program-overview.

University of Minnesota, Twin Cities Campus, Graduate School, College of Food, Agricultural and Natural Resource Sciences, Program in Animal Science, Minneapolis, MN 55455-0213. Offers MS, PhD. Part-time programs available. *Faculty:* 40 full-time. *Students:* 50 full-time (24 women); includes 1 minority (Asian, non-Hispanic/Latino), 22 international. Average age 30. 36 applicants, 42% accepted, 14 enrolled. In 2012, 21 master's, 22 doctorates awarded. Terminal master's awarded for partial completion of doctoral program. *Degree requirements:* For master's, comprehensive exam, thesis; for doctorate, comprehensive exam, thesis/dissertation. *Entrance requirements:* For master's and doctorate, GRE. Additional exam requirements/recommendations for international students: Required—TOEFL (minimum score 550 paper-based; 79 iBT), IELTS (minimum score 6.5). *Application deadline:* For fall admission, 12/15 priority date for domestic students, 12/15 for international students; for spring admission, 10/15 priority date for domestic students, 10/15 for international students. Applications are processed on a rolling basis. Application fee: $75 ($95 for international students). Electronic applications accepted. *Financial support:* In 2012–13, fellowships with full tuition reimbursements (averaging $40,000 per year), research assistantships with full tuition reimbursements (averaging $40,000 per year), teaching assistantships with full tuition reimbursements (averaging $40,000 per year) were awarded; scholarships/grants, traineeships, tuition waivers, and unspecified assistantships also available. Support available to part-time students. *Faculty research:* Physiology, growth biology, nutrition, genetics, production systems. *Total annual research expenditures:* $1,957. *Unit head:* Dr. William Dayton, Director of Graduate Studies, 612-624-2234, Fax: 612-625-5789, E-mail: wdayton@umn.edu. *Application contact:* Kim Reno, Assistant to the Director of Graduate Studies, 612-624-3491, E-mail: renox001@umn.edu. Website: http://www.ansci.umn.edu/gradprogram/.

University of Missouri, Graduate School, College of Agriculture, Food and Natural Resources, Department of Animal Sciences, Columbia, MO 65211. Offers MS, PhD. *Faculty:* 28 full-time (3 women), 2 part-time/adjunct (0 women). *Students:* 52 full-time (27 women), 5 part-time (3 women); includes 4 minority (1 Asian, non-Hispanic/Latino; 2 Hispanic/Latino; 1 Two or more races, non-Hispanic/Latino), 13 international. Average age 26. 35 applicants, 29% accepted, 9 enrolled. In 2012, 10 master's, 6 doctorates awarded. Terminal master's awarded for partial completion of doctoral program. *Degree requirements:* For doctorate, 2 foreign languages, comprehensive exam, thesis/dissertation. *Entrance requirements:* For master's, GRE General Test, minimum GPA of 3.0; for doctorate, GRE General Test (minimum score: Verbal 400, Quantitative 550), minimum GPA of 3.0. Additional exam requirements/recommendations for international students: Required—TOEFL (minimum score 500 paper-based; 61 iBT), IELTS (minimum score 5.5). *Application deadline:* Applications are processed on a rolling basis. Application fee: $55 ($75 for international students). Electronic applications accepted. *Expenses:* Tuition, state resident: full-time $6057. Tuition, nonresident: full-time $15,683. *Required fees:* $1000. *Financial support:* Fellowships, research assistantships with full tuition reimbursements, teaching assistantships with full tuition reimbursements, institutionally sponsored loans, scholarships/grants, health care benefits, and unspecified assistantships available. Support available to part-time students. Financial award application deadline: 3/1; financial award applicants required to submit FAFSA. *Faculty research:* Reproductive and environmental physiology; ruminant and monogastric nutrition; genetics/genomics; meat science and livestock production across swine, dairy cattle, beef cattle, poultry, companion animals and horses. *Unit head:* Dr. Rod Geisert, Department Chair, 573-884-0934, E-mail: geisertr@missouri.edu. *Application contact:* Cinda Hudlow, Administrative Assistant, 573-882-7446, E-mail: hudlowc@missouri.edu. Website: http://animalsciences.missouri.edu/academics/graduates.php.

University of Nebraska–Lincoln, Graduate College, College of Agricultural Sciences and Natural Resources, Department of Animal Science, Lincoln, NE 68588. Offers MS, PhD. *Degree requirements:* For master's, thesis; for doctorate, comprehensive exam, thesis/dissertation. *Entrance requirements:* For master's and doctorate, GRE General Test. Additional exam requirements/recommendations for international students: Required—TOEFL (minimum score 525 paper-based). Electronic applications accepted. *Faculty research:* Animal breeding and genetics, meat and poultry products, nonruminant and ruminant nutrition, physiology.

University of Nevada, Reno, Graduate School, College of Agriculture, Biotechnology and Natural Resources, Department of Animal Science, Reno, NV 89557. Offers MS. *Degree requirements:* For master's, thesis optional. *Entrance requirements:* For master's, GRE, minimum GPA of 2.75. Additional exam requirements/recommendations for international students: Required—TOEFL (minimum score 500 paper-based; 61 iBT), IELTS (minimum score 6). Electronic applications accepted. *Faculty research:* Sperm fertility, embryo development, ruminant utilization of forages.

University of New Hampshire, Graduate School, College of Life Sciences and Agriculture, Department of Biological Sciences, Program in Animal Science, Durham, NH 03824. Offers MS. Part-time programs available. *Faculty:* 23 full-time. *Students:* 2 full-time (both women), 4 part-time (3 women). Average age 28. 16 applicants, 6% accepted, 1 enrolled. In 2012, 2 master's awarded. *Entrance requirements:* For master's, GRE General Test. Additional exam requirements/recommendations for international students: Required—TOEFL (minimum score 550 paper-based; 80 iBT). *Application deadline:* For fall admission, 6/1 priority date for domestic students, 4/1 for international students; for spring admission, 12/1 for domestic students. Applications are processed on a rolling basis. Application fee: $65. Electronic applications accepted. *Expenses:* Tuition, state resident: full-time $13,500; part-time $750 per credit. Tuition, nonresident: full-time $25,940; part-time $1089 per credit. *Required fees:* $1699; $424.75 per semester. *Financial support:* In 2012–13, 5 students received support, including 1 research assistantship, 4 teaching assistantships; fellowships, career-related internships or fieldwork, Federal Work-Study, scholarships/grants, and tuition waivers (full and partial) also available. Support available to part-time students. Financial award application deadline: 2/15. *Unit head:* Dr. Larry Harris, Chair, 603-862-3897. *Application contact:* Diane Lavalliere, Administrative Assistant, 603-862-2100. Website: http://www.mcbs.unh.edu/.

University of New Hampshire, Graduate School, College of Life Sciences and Agriculture, Department of Molecular, Cellular and Biomedical Sciences, Program in Animal and Nutritional Sciences, Durham, NH 03824. Offers PhD. Part-time programs available. *Faculty:* 23 full-time. *Students:* 4 full-time (2 women), 3 part-time (all women); includes 2 minority (both Hispanic/Latino). Average age 38. 7 applicants, 57% accepted, 2 enrolled. *Entrance requirements:* For doctorate, GRE. Additional exam requirements/recommendations for international students: Required—TOEFL (minimum score 550 paper-based; 80 iBT). *Application deadline:* For fall admission, 6/1 priority date for domestic students, 4/1 for international students; for spring admission, 12/1 for domestic students. Application fee: $65. Electronic applications accepted. *Expenses:* Tuition, state resident: full-time $13,500; part-time $750 per credit. Tuition, nonresident: full-time $25,940; part-time $1089 per credit. *Required fees:* $1699; $424.75 per semester. *Financial support:* In 2012–13, 4 students received support, including 1 fellowship, 2 teaching assistantships; research assistantships, scholarships/grants, traineeships, and unspecified assistantships also available. Support available to part-time students. *Unit head:* Dr. Rick Cote, Chairperson, 603-862-2458. *Application contact:* Flora Joyal, Administrative Assistant, 603-862-4095, E-mail: ansc.grad.program.info@unh.edu. Website: http://www.biolsci.unh.edu/.

University of Puerto Rico, Mayagüez Campus, Graduate Studies, College of Agricultural Sciences, Department of Animal Industries, Mayagüez, PR 00681-9000. Offers MS. Part-time programs available. *Faculty:* 8 full-time (3 women). *Students:* 30 full-time (18 women), 2 part-time (1 woman); includes 31 minority (all Hispanic/Latino), 1 international. 11 applicants, 100% accepted, 9 enrolled. In 2012, 1 master's awarded. *Degree requirements:* For master's, comprehensive exam, thesis. *Entrance requirements:* For master's, minimum GPA of 2.75, BS in agricultural science or closely-related field. *Application deadline:* For fall admission, 2/15 for domestic and international students; for spring admission, 9/15 for domestic and international students. Applications are processed on a rolling basis. Application fee: $25. Tuition and fees vary according to course level and course load. *Financial support:* In 2012–13, 12 students received support, including 6 research assistantships with tuition reimbursements available (averaging $15,000 per year), 6 teaching assistantships with tuition reimbursements available (averaging $8,500 per year); Federal Work-Study and institutionally sponsored loans also available. *Faculty research:* Swine production and nutrition, poultry production, dairy science and technology, microbiology. *Unit head:* Dr. Jose LaTorre, Director, 787-265-3854, Fax: 787-834-4548, E-mail: jose.latorre1@upr.edu. *Application contact:* Dr. Teodoro Ruiz, Coordinator, 787-832-4040 Ext. 2574, Fax: 787-834-4548, E-mail: truiz@uprm.edu. Website: http://www.uprm.edu/agricultura/inpe/.

University of Rhode Island, Graduate School, College of the Environment and Life Sciences, Department of Fisheries, Animal and Veterinary Science, Kingston, RI 02881. Offers animal health and disease (MS); animal science (MS); aquaculture (MS); aquatic pathology (MS); environmental sciences (PhD), including animal science, aquacultural science, aquatic pathology, fisheries science; fisheries (MS). *Faculty:* 9 full-time (4 women). *Students:* 6 full-time (2 women), 1 part-time (0 women), 2 international. In 2012, 6 master's, 1 doctorate awarded. *Degree requirements:* For master's, comprehensive exam (for some programs), thesis optional; for doctorate, comprehensive exam, thesis/dissertation. *Entrance requirements:* For master's and doctorate, GRE, 2 letters of recommendation. Additional exam requirements/recommendations for international students: Required—TOEFL (minimum score 550 paper-based). *Application deadline:* For fall admission, 7/15 for domestic students, 2/1 for international students; for spring admission, 11/15 for domestic students, 7/15 for international students. Application fee: $65. Electronic applications accepted. *Expenses:* Tuition, state resident: full-time $11,532; part-time $641 per credit. Tuition, nonresident: full-time $23,606; part-time $1311 per credit. *Required fees:* $1388; $36 per credit. $35 per semester. One-time fee: $130. *Financial support:* In 2012–13, 3 research assistantships with full and partial tuition reimbursements (averaging $11,679 per year), 1 teaching assistantship with full and partial tuition reimbursement (averaging $9,818 per year) were awarded. Financial award application deadline: 7/15; financial award applicants required to submit FAFSA. *Unit head:* Dr. David Bengtson, Chair, 401-874-2668, Fax: 401-874-7575, E-mail: bengtson@uri.edu. Website: http://www.uri.edu/cels/favs/.

University of Saskatchewan, College of Graduate Studies and Research, College of Agriculture, Department of Animal and Poultry Science, Saskatoon, SK S7N 5A2, Canada. Offers M Ag, M Sc, PhD. *Degree requirements:* For master's, thesis; for doctorate, thesis/dissertation. *Entrance requirements:* Additional exam requirements/recommendations for international students: Required—TOEFL.

University of Saskatchewan, Western College of Veterinary Medicine and College of Graduate Studies and Research, Graduate Programs in Veterinary Medicine, Department of Large Animal Clinical Sciences, Saskatoon, SK S7N 5A2, Canada. Offers M Sc, M Vet Sc, PhD. *Degree requirements:* For master's, thesis (for some programs); for doctorate, comprehensive exam (for some programs), thesis/dissertation. *Entrance requirements:* Additional exam requirements/recommendations for international students: Required—TOEFL (minimum score 80 iBT); Recommended—IELTS (minimum score 6.5). Electronic applications accepted. *Faculty research:* Reproduction, infectious diseases, epidemiology, food safety.

University of Saskatchewan, Western College of Veterinary Medicine and College of Graduate Studies and Research, Graduate Programs in Veterinary Medicine, Department of Small Animal Clinical Sciences, Saskatoon, SK S7N 5A2, Canada. Offers small animal clinical sciences (M Sc, PhD); veterinary anesthesiology, radiology and surgery (M Vet Sc); veterinary internal medicine (M Vet Sc). *Degree requirements:* For master's, thesis (for some programs); for doctorate, comprehensive exam (for some programs), thesis/dissertation. *Entrance requirements:* Additional exam requirements/recommendations for international students: Required—TOEFL (minimum score 80 iBT); Recommended—IELTS (minimum score 6.5). Electronic applications accepted. *Faculty research:* Orthopedics, wildlife, cardiovascular exercise/myelopathy, ophthalmology.

The University of Tennessee, Graduate School, College of Agricultural Sciences and Natural Resources, Department of Animal Science, Knoxville, TN 37996. Offers animal anatomy (PhD); breeding (MS, PhD); management (MS, PhD); nutrition (MS, PhD); physiology (MS, PhD). Part-time programs available. *Degree requirements:* For master's, thesis; for doctorate, thesis/dissertation. *Entrance requirements:* For master's and doctorate, GRE General Test, minimum GPA of 2.7. Additional exam requirements/recommendations for international students: Required—TOEFL. Electronic applications accepted. *Expenses:* Tuition, state resident: full-time $9000; part-time $501 per credit hour. Tuition, nonresident: full-time $27,188; part-time $1512 per credit hour. *Required fees:* $1280; $62 per credit hour. Tuition and fees vary according to program.

University of Vermont, Graduate College, College of Agriculture and Life Sciences, Department of Animal Sciences, Burlington, VT 05405. Offers MS, PhD. *Students:* 4 applicants. In 2012, 1 master's awarded. *Degree requirements:* For master's, thesis; for doctorate, one foreign language, thesis/dissertation. *Entrance requirements:* For master's and doctorate, GRE General Test. Additional exam requirements/recommendations for international students: Required—TOEFL (minimum score 550 paper-based; 80 iBT). *Application deadline:* For fall admission, 4/1 priority date for domestic students. Applications are processed on a rolling basis. Application fee: $40. Electronic applications accepted. *Expenses: Tuition, area resident:* Part-time $572 per credit. Tuition, nonresident: part-time $1444 per credit. *Financial support:* Fellowships, research assistantships, and teaching assistantships available. Financial award application deadline: 3/1. *Faculty research:* Animal nutrition, dairy production. *Unit head:* Dr. Andre-Denis Wright, Chairperson, 802-656-2070. *Application contact:* Dr. David Kerr, Coordinator, 802-656-2070.

University of Vermont, Graduate College, College of Agriculture and Life Sciences, Program in Animal, Nutrition and Food Sciences, Burlington, VT 05405. Offers PhD. *Students:* 21 (9 women); includes 2 minority (both Asian, non-Hispanic/Latino), 11 international. 13 applicants, 23% accepted, 3 enrolled. In 2012, 2 doctorates awarded. *Degree requirements:* For doctorate, one foreign language, thesis/dissertation. *Entrance requirements:* For doctorate, GRE General Test. Additional exam requirements/recommendations for international students: Required—TOEFL (minimum score 550 paper-based; 80 iBT). *Application deadline:* For fall admission, 4/1 priority date for domestic students, 4/1 for international students. Applications are processed on a rolling basis. Application fee: $40. Electronic applications accepted. *Expenses: Tuition, area resident:* Part-time $572 per credit. Tuition, nonresident: part-time $1444 per credit. *Financial support:* Application deadline: 3/1. *Unit head:* Dr. Andre-Denis Wright, Chairperson, 802-656-2070. *Application contact:* Dr. David Kerr, Coordinator, 802-656-2070.

University of Wisconsin–Madison, Graduate School, College of Agricultural and Life Sciences, Department of Animal Sciences, Madison, WI 53706-1380. Offers MS, PhD. Part-time programs available. Terminal master's awarded for partial completion of doctoral program. *Degree requirements:* For master's, thesis; for doctorate, thesis/dissertation. *Entrance requirements:* For master's and doctorate, GRE General Test. Additional exam requirements/recommendations for international students: Required—TOEFL (minimum score 550 paper-based; 80 iBT). Electronic applications accepted. *Expenses:* Tuition, state resident: full-time $10,728; part-time $743 per credit. Tuition, nonresident: full-time $24,054; part-time $1575 per credit. *Required fees:* $1111; $72 per credit. *Faculty research:* Animal biology, immunity and toxicology, endocrinology and reproductive physiology, genetics-animal breeding, meat science, muscle biology.

University of Wisconsin–Madison, Graduate School, College of Agricultural and Life Sciences, Department of Dairy Science, Madison, WI 53706-1380. Offers MS, PhD. Part-time programs available. Terminal master's awarded for partial completion of doctoral program. *Degree requirements:* For master's, thesis; for doctorate, thesis/dissertation. *Entrance requirements:* For master's and doctorate, GRE General Test. Additional exam requirements/recommendations for international students: Required—TOEFL (minimum score 550 paper-based; 80 iBT). Electronic applications accepted. *Expenses:* Tuition, state resident: full-time $10,728; part-time $743 per credit. Tuition, nonresident: full-time $24,054; part-time $1575 per credit. *Required fees:* $1111; $72 per credit. *Faculty research:* Genetics, nutrition, lactation, reproduction, management of dairy cattle.

University of Wyoming, College of Agriculture and Natural Resources, Department of Animal Sciences, Program in Animal Sciences, Laramie, WY 82070. Offers MS, PhD. *Degree requirements:* For master's, comprehensive exam, thesis; for doctorate, comprehensive exam, thesis/dissertation. *Entrance requirements:* For master's, GRE General Test, minimum GPA of 3.0; for doctorate, GRE General Test or MS degree, minimum GPA of 3.0. Additional exam requirements/recommendations for international students: Required—TOEFL (minimum score 525 paper-based). *Faculty research:* Reproductive biology, ruminant nutrition meat science, muscle biology, food microbiology, lipid metabolism.

Utah State University, School of Graduate Studies, College of Agriculture, Department of Animal, Dairy and Veterinary Sciences, Logan, UT 84322. Offers animal science (MS, PhD); bioveterinary science (MS, PhD); dairy science (MS). Part-time programs available. *Degree requirements:* For master's, thesis (for some programs); for doctorate, comprehensive exam, thesis/dissertation. *Entrance requirements:* For master's and doctorate, GRE General Test, minimum GPA of 3.0. Additional exam requirements/recommendations for international students: Required—TOEFL. Electronic applications accepted. *Faculty research:* Monoclonal antibodies, antiviral chemotherapy, management systems, biotechnology, rumen fermentation manipulation.

Virginia Polytechnic Institute and State University, Graduate School, College of Agriculture and Life Sciences, Blacksburg, VA 24124. Offers agricultural and applied economics (MS); agricultural and life sciences (MS); animal and poultry science (MS, PhD); crop and soil environmental sciences (MS, PhD); dairy science (MS); entomology (PhD); horticulture (MS, PhD); human nutrition, foods and exercise (MS, PhD); life sciences (MS, PhD); plant pathology, physiology and weed science (PhD). *Faculty:* 233 full-time (65 women), 1 (woman) part-time/adjunct. *Students:* 343 full-time (199 women), 74 part-time (47 women); includes 48 minority (20 Black or African American, non-Hispanic/Latino; 1 American Indian or Alaska Native, non-Hispanic/Latino; 15 Asian, non-Hispanic/Latino; 7 Hispanic/Latino; 5 Two or more races, non-Hispanic/Latino), 105 international. Average age 29. 387 applicants, 33% accepted, 98 enrolled. In 2012, 81 master's, 52 doctorates awarded. *Degree requirements:* For master's, comprehensive exam (for some programs), thesis (for some programs); for doctorate, comprehensive exam (for some programs), thesis/dissertation (for some programs). *Entrance requirements:* For master's and doctorate, GRE/GMAT (may vary by department). Additional exam requirements/recommendations for international students: Required—TOEFL (minimum score 550 paper-based). *Application deadline:* For fall admission, 8/1 for domestic students, 4/1 for international students; for spring admission, 1/1 for domestic students, 9/1 for international students. Applications are processed on a rolling basis. Application fee: $65. Electronic applications accepted. *Expenses:* Tuition, state resident: full-time $10,677; part-time $593.25 per credit hour. Tuition, nonresident: full-time $20,926; part-time $1162.50 per credit hour. *Required fees:* $427.75 per semester. Tuition and fees vary according to course load, campus/location and program. *Financial support:* In 2012–13, 1 fellowship with full tuition reimbursement (averaging $21,000 per year), 229 research assistantships with full tuition reimbursements (averaging $18,998 per year), 77 teaching assistantships with full tuition reimbursements (averaging $18,174 per year) were awarded. Financial award application deadline: 3/1; financial award applicants required to submit FAFSA. *Total annual research expenditures:* $41.8 million. *Unit head:* Dr. Alan L. Grant, Dean, 540-231-4152, Fax: 540-231-4163, E-mail: algrant@vt.edu. *Application contact:* Sheila Norman, Administrative Assistant, 540-231-4152, Fax: 540-231-4163, E-mail: snorman@vt.edu. Website: http://www.cals.vt.edu/.

Washington State University, College of Veterinary Medicine, Paul G. Allen School for Global Animal Health, Pullman, WA 99164-7090. Offers global animal health (PhD); immunology and infectious diseases (MS). Part-time programs available. *Faculty:* 8 full-time (3 women), 26 part-time/adjunct (10 women). *Students:* 20 full-time (10 women); includes 3 minority (1 Black or African American, non-Hispanic/Latino; 1 Hispanic/Latino; 1 Native Hawaiian or other Pacific Islander, non-Hispanic/Latino). Average age 31. Terminal master's awarded for partial completion of doctoral program. *Degree requirements:* For master's, thesis; for doctorate, thesis/dissertation. *Entrance requirements:* For master's and doctorate, GRE or GMAT. Additional exam requirements/recommendations for international students: Required—TOEFL. *Application deadline:* For fall admission, 1/10 priority date for domestic students, 1/10 for international students; for spring admission, 7/1 priority date for domestic students, 7/1 for international students. Application fee: $75. Electronic applications accepted. *Financial support:* In 2012–13, 6 fellowships (averaging $42,732 per year), 10 research assistantships (averaging $22,842 per year), 1 teaching assistantship were awarded. *Faculty research:* Immunology, infectious disease, virology, disease surveillance, vaccine development. *Total annual research expenditures:* $668,662. *Unit head:* Dr. Guy H. Palmer, Director, Paul G. Allen School for Global Animal Health, 509-335-5861, Fax: 509-335-6328, E-mail: gpalmer@vetmed.wsu.edu. *Application contact:* Jill Griffin, Administrative Manager, 509-335-5861, Fax: 509-335-6328, E-mail: griffinj@vetmed.wsu.edu. Website: http://globalhealth.wsu.edu/.

Washington State University, Graduate School, College of Agricultural, Human, and Natural Resource Sciences, Department of Animal Sciences, Pullman, WA 99164. Offers MS, PhD. Part-time programs available. *Faculty:* 13 full-time (3 women). *Students:* 34 full-time (18 women); includes 11 minority (all Asian, non-Hispanic/Latino), 15 international. Average age 23. 26 applicants, 38% accepted, 7 enrolled. In 2012, 3 master's, 4 doctorates awarded. *Degree requirements:* For master's, comprehensive exam (for some programs), thesis (for some programs), oral exam; for doctorate, comprehensive exam, thesis/dissertation, oral and written exam. *Entrance requirements:* For master's, GRE, minimum GPA of 3.0, 3 letters of recommendation, department questionnaire; for doctorate, GRE General Test, minimum GPA of 3.0. Additional exam requirements/recommendations for international students: Required—TOEFL, IELTS. *Application deadline:* For fall admission, 1/10 priority date for domestic students, 1/10 for international students; for spring admission, 7/1 priority date for domestic students, 7/1 for international students. Applications are processed on a rolling basis. Application fee: $75. Electronic applications accepted. *Financial support:* In 2012–13, 28 students received support, including research assistantships with full and partial tuition reimbursements available (averaging $18,204 per year), teaching assistantships with full and partial tuition reimbursements available (averaging $18,204 per year); career-related internships or fieldwork, Federal Work-Study, institutionally sponsored loans, scholarships/grants, health care benefits, tuition waivers (partial), unspecified assistantships, and teaching assistantships also available. Financial award application deadline: 4/1; financial award applicants required to submit FAFSA. *Faculty research:* Reproduction, genetics, equine cytokines, fish diseases and vaccines. *Total annual research expenditures:* $682,000. *Unit head:* Dr. Margaret Benson, Professor and Chair, 509-335-5523, Fax: 509-335-1082, E-mail: m_benson@wsu.edu. *Application contact:* Graduate School Admissions, 800-GRADWSU, Fax: 509-335-1949, E-mail: gradsch@wsu.edu. Website: http://www.asci.wsu.edu/.

West Texas A&M University, College of Agriculture, Science and Engineering, Department of Agricultural Sciences, Emphasis in Animal Science, Canyon, TX 79016-0001. Offers MS. Part-time programs available. *Degree requirements:* For master's, comprehensive exam, thesis optional. *Entrance requirements:* For master's, GRE General Test. Additional exam requirements/recommendations for international students: Required—TOEFL (minimum score 550 paper-based). Electronic applications accepted. *Faculty research:* Nutrition, animal breeding, meat science, reproduction physiology, feedlots.

West Virginia University, Davis College of Agriculture, Forestry and Consumer Sciences, Division of Animal and Nutritional Sciences, Program in Animal and Nutritional Sciences, Morgantown, WV 26506. Offers breeding (MS); food sciences (MS); nutrition (MS); physiology (MS); production management (MS); reproduction (MS). Part-time programs available. *Degree requirements:* For master's, thesis, oral and written exams. *Entrance requirements:* For master's, GRE, minimum GPA of 2.5. Additional exam requirements/recommendations for international students: Required—TOEFL. *Faculty research:* Animal nutrition, reproductive physiology, food science.

West Virginia University, Davis College of Agriculture, Forestry and Consumer Sciences, Division of Plant and Soil Sciences, Program in Agricultural Sciences, Morgantown, WV 26506. Offers animal and food sciences (PhD); plant and soil sciences (PhD). *Degree requirements:* For doctorate, thesis/dissertation, oral and written exams. *Entrance requirements:* Additional exam requirements/recommendations for international students: Required—TOEFL. *Faculty research:* Ruminant nutrition, metabolism, forage utilization, physiology, reproduction.

408 www.petersonsbooks.com

Peterson's Graduate Programs in the Physical Sciences, Mathematics, Agricultural Sciences, the Environment & Natural Resources 2014

Aquaculture

American University of Beirut, Graduate Programs, Faculty of Agricultural and Food Sciences, Beirut, Lebanon. Offers agricultural economics (MS); animal sciences (MS); ecosystem management (MSES); food technology (MS); irrigation (MS); nutrition (MS); plant protection (MS); plant science (MS); poultry science (MS). Part-time programs available. *Faculty:* 22 full-time (6 women), 1 part-time/adjunct (0 women). *Students:* 11 full-time (10 women), 89 part-time (74 women). Average age 25. 97 applicants, 64% accepted, 18 enrolled. In 2012, 35 master's awarded. *Degree requirements:* For master's, one foreign language, comprehensive exam, thesis (for some programs). *Entrance requirements:* Additional exam requirements/recommendations for international students: Required—TOEFL (minimum score 600 paper-based; 100 iBT), IELTS (minimum score 7.5). *Application deadline:* For fall admission, 2/7 for domestic and international students; for spring admission, 11/15 for domestic and international students. Applications are processed on a rolling basis. Application fee: $50. Electronic applications accepted. *Expenses: Tuition:* Full-time $13,896; part-time $772 per credit. *Financial support:* In 2012–13, 18 research assistantships with partial tuition reimbursements (averaging $1,500 per year), 49 teaching assistantships with full and partial tuition reimbursements (averaging $1,000 per year) were awarded; scholarships/grants, health care benefits, and unspecified assistantships also available. Financial award application deadline: 2/2. *Faculty research:* Evidence-based nutrition intervention; studies related to immunopotentiation, protection and production in broilers; nutritional food-based dietary guidelines; production of biodiesel from algae; regional knowledge management and knowledge sharing network. *Total annual research expenditures:* $560,850. *Unit head:* Prof. Nahla Hwalla, Dean, 961-1343002 Ext. 4400, Fax: 961-1744460, E-mail: nahla@aub.edu.lb. *Application contact:* Dr. Salim Kanaan, Director, Admissions Office, 961-1-350000 Ext. 2594, Fax: 961-1750775, E-mail: sk00@aub.edu.lb. Website: http://www.aub.edu.lb/fafs/fafs_home/Pages/index.aspx.

Auburn University, Graduate School, College of Agriculture, Department of Fisheries and Allied Aquacultures, Auburn University, AL 36849. Offers M Aq, MS, PhD. Part-time programs available. *Faculty:* 20 full-time (3 women). *Students:* 33 full-time (15 women), 53 part-time (24 women); includes 4 minority (1 Black or African American, non-Hispanic/Latino; 1 Asian, non-Hispanic/Latino; 2 Hispanic/Latino), 49 international. Average age 28. 48 applicants, 48% accepted, 19 enrolled. In 2012, 15 master's, 5 doctorates awarded. *Degree requirements:* For master's, thesis (for some programs); for doctorate, 2 foreign languages, thesis/dissertation. *Entrance requirements:* For master's and doctorate, GRE General Test. *Application deadline:* For fall admission, 7/7 for domestic students; for spring admission, 11/24 for domestic students. Applications are processed on a rolling basis. Application fee: $50 ($60 for international students). Electronic applications accepted. *Expenses:* Tuition, state resident: full-time $7866; part-time $437 per credit. Tuition, nonresident: full-time $23,598; part-time $1311 per credit. *Required fees:* $787 per semester. Tuition and fees vary according to degree level and program. *Financial support:* Fellowships, research assistantships, teaching assistantships, and Federal Work-Study available. Support available to part-time students. Financial award application deadline: 3/15; financial award applicants required to submit FAFSA. *Faculty research:* Channel catfish production; aquatic animal health; community and population ecology; pond management; production hatching, breeding and genetics. *Total annual research expenditures:* $8 million. *Unit head:* Dr. David B. Rouse, Head, 334-844-4786. *Application contact:* Dr. George Flowers, Dean of the Graduate School, 334-844-2125. Website: http://www.ag.auburn.edu/fish/.

Clemson University, Graduate School, College of Agriculture, Forestry and Life Sciences, Department of Forestry and Natural Resources, Program in Wildlife and Fisheries Biology, Clemson, SC 29634. Offers MS, PhD. *Students:* 11 full-time (10 women), 5 part-time (3 women); includes 1 minority (Black or African American, non-Hispanic/Latino), 2 international. Average age 32. 6 applicants, 33% accepted, 2 enrolled. In 2012, 4 doctorates awarded. *Degree requirements:* For master's, thesis; for doctorate, thesis/dissertation. *Entrance requirements:* For master's, GRE General Test, minimum undergraduate GPA of 3.0; for doctorate, GRE General Test. Additional exam requirements/recommendations for international students: Required—TOEFL, IELTS. *Application deadline:* For fall admission, 6/1 for domestic students, 4/15 for international students; for spring admission, 9/15 for international students. Applications are processed on a rolling basis. Application fee: $70 ($80 for international students). Electronic applications accepted. *Expenses:* Contact institution. *Financial support:* In 2012–13, 10 students received support, including 6 research assistantships with partial tuition reimbursements available (averaging $15,833 per year), 5 teaching assistantships with partial tuition reimbursements available (averaging $16,500 per year); fellowships with full and partial tuition reimbursements available, career-related internships or fieldwork, institutionally sponsored loans, scholarships/grants, health care benefits, and unspecified assistantships also available. Support available to part-time students. Financial award applicants required to submit FAFSA. *Faculty research:* Intensive freshwater culture systems, conservation biology, stream management, applied wildlife management. *Unit head:* Dr. Patricia Layton, Chair, 864-656-3303, Fax: 864-656-3304, E-mail: playton@clemson.edu. *Application contact:* Dr. David Guynn, Graduate Program Coordinator, 864-656-4830, Fax: 864-656-5344, E-mail: dguynn@clemson.edu. Website: http://www.clemson.edu/cafls/departments/forestry/.

Dalhousie University, Faculty of Agriculture, Halifax, NS B3H 4R2, Canada. Offers agriculture (M Sc), including air quality, animal behavior, animal molecular genetics, animal nutrition, animal technology, aquaculture, botany, crop management, crop physiology, ecology, environmental microbiology, food science, horticulture, nutrient management, pest management, physiology, plant biotechnology, plant pathology, soil chemistry, soil fertility, waste management and composting, water quality. Part-time programs available. *Degree requirements:* For master's, thesis, ATC Exam Teaching Assistantship. *Entrance requirements:* For master's, honors B Sc, minimum GPA of 3.0. Additional exam requirements/recommendations for international students: Required—TOEFL (minimum score 580 paper-based; 92 iBT), IELTS, Michigan English Language Assessment Battery, CanTEST, CAEL. *Faculty research:* Bio-product development, organic agriculture, nutrient management, air and water quality, agricultural biotechnology.

Kentucky State University, College of Agriculture, Food Science and Sustainable Systems, Frankfort, KY 40601. Offers aquaculture (MS); environmental studies (MS). Part-time and evening/weekend programs available. *Faculty:* 5 full-time (1 woman). *Students:* 15 full-time (7 women), 11 part-time (4 women); includes 4 minority (3 Black or African American, non-Hispanic/Latino; 1 Two or more races, non-Hispanic/Latino), 4 international. Average age 31. 27 applicants, 48% accepted, 12 enrolled. In 2012, 11 master's awarded. *Degree requirements:* For master's, comprehensive exam, thesis optional. *Entrance requirements:* For master's, GRE, GMAT. Additional exam requirements/recommendations for international students: Required—TOEFL (minimum score 525 paper-based). *Application deadline:* Applications are processed on a rolling basis. Application fee: $30 ($100 for international students). Electronic applications accepted. *Expenses:* Tuition, state resident: full-time $6516; part-time $362 per credit hour. Tuition, nonresident: full-time $10,026; part-time $557 per credit hour. *Required fees:* $450; $25 per credit hour. Tuition and fees vary according to course load. *Financial support:* In 2012–13, 16 students received support, including 19 research assistantships (averaging $11,335 per year); scholarships/grants, tuition waivers (partial), and unspecified assistantships also available. Financial award application deadline: 4/15; financial award applicants required to submit FAFSA. *Unit head:* Dr. Teferi Tsegaye, Dean, 502-597-6310, E-mail: teferi.tsegaye@kysu.edu. *Application contact:* Dr. Beverly Downing, Acting Director of Graduate Studies, 502-597-6443, E-mail: beverly.downing@kysu.edu. Website: http://www.kysu.edu/academics/collegesAndSchools/CAFSSS/.

Memorial University of Newfoundland, School of Graduate Studies, Interdisciplinary Program in Aquaculture, St. John's, NL A1C 5S7, Canada. Offers M Sc. Part-time programs available. *Degree requirements:* For master's, thesis, seminar or thesis topic. *Entrance requirements:* For master's, honors B Sc or diploma in aquaculture from the Marine Institute of Memorial University of Newfoundland. Electronic applications accepted. *Faculty research:* Marine fish larval biology, fin fish nutrition, shellfish culture, fin fish virology, fin fish reproductive biology.

Purdue University, Graduate School, College of Agriculture, Department of Forestry and Natural Resources, West Lafayette, IN 47907. Offers fisheries and aquatic sciences (MS, MSF, PhD); forest biology (MS, MSF, PhD); natural resource social science (MS, PhD); natural resources social science (MSF); quantitative ecology (MS, MSF, PhD); wildlife science (MS, MSF, PhD); wood products and wood products manufacturing (MS, MSF, PhD). *Faculty:* 25 full-time (3 women), 10 part-time/adjunct (1 woman). *Students:* 61 full-time (24 women), 11 part-time (6 women); includes 3 minority (1 American Indian or Alaska Native, non-Hispanic/Latino; 2 Hispanic/Latino), 18 international. Average age 29. 57 applicants, 28% accepted, 15 enrolled. In 2012, 18 master's, 7 doctorates awarded. *Degree requirements:* For master's, thesis; for doctorate, thesis/dissertation. *Entrance requirements:* For master's and doctorate, GRE General Test (minimum score: verbal 50th percentile; quantitative 50th percentile; analytical writing 4.0), minimum undergraduate GPA of 3.2 or equivalent. Additional exam requirements/recommendations for international students: Required—TOEFL (minimum score 550 paper-based; 77 iBT). *Application deadline:* For fall admission, 1/5 for domestic students, 1/15 for international students; for spring admission, 9/15 for domestic and international students. Applications are processed on a rolling basis. Application fee: $60 ($75 for international students). Electronic applications accepted. *Financial support:* In 2012–13, 10 research assistantships (averaging $15,259 per year) were awarded; fellowships, teaching assistantships, career-related internships or fieldwork, and scholarships/grants also available. Support available to part-time students. Financial award application deadline: 1/5; financial award applicants required to submit FAFSA. *Faculty research:* Wildlife management, forest management, forest ecology, forest soils, limnology. *Unit head:* Dr. Robert K. Swihart, Interim Head, 765-494-3590, Fax: 765-494-9461, E-mail: rswihart@purdue.edu. *Application contact:* Kelly J. Wrede, Graduate Secretary, 765-494-3572, Fax: 765-494-9461, E-mail: kgarrett@purdue.edu. Website: http://www.fnr.purdue.edu/.

Peterson's Graduate Programs in the Physical Sciences, Mathematics, Agricultural Sciences, the Environment & Natural Resources 2014

www.petersonsbooks.com **409**

Aquaculture

Texas A&M University–Corpus Christi, Graduate Studies and Research, College of Science and Technology, Program in Mariculture, Corpus Christi, TX 78412-5503. Offers MS.

University of Arkansas at Pine Bluff, School of Agriculture, Fisheries and Human Sciences, Pine Bluff, AR 71601-2799. Offers aquaculture and fisheries (MS).

University of Florida, Graduate School, College of Agricultural and Life Sciences, Department of Fisheries and Aquatic Sciences, Gainesville, FL 32611. Offers MFAS, MS, PhD. Part-time programs available. *Degree requirements:* For master's, thesis (for MS); technical paper (for MFAS); for doctorate, comprehensive exam, thesis/dissertation. *Entrance requirements:* For master's and doctorate, GRE General Test, minimum GPA of 3.0. Additional exam requirements/recommendations for international students: Required—TOEFL (minimum score 550 paper-based; 80 iBT), IELTS (minimum score 6). Electronic applications accepted. *Faculty research:* Conservation and management of aquatic ecosystems; aquatic animal health; water quality, nutrients, and eutrophication; sustainable and quantitative fisheries; aquaculture or ornamental fish, marine baitfish, and shellfish.

University of Guelph, Graduate Studies, Ontario Agricultural College, Program in Aquaculture, Guelph, ON N1G 2W1, Canada. Offers M Sc. *Degree requirements:* For master's, practicum, research project. *Entrance requirements:* For master's, minimum B- average during previous 2 years of course work. *Faculty research:* Protein and amino acid metabolism, genetics, gamete cryogenics, pathology, epidemiology.

University of Rhode Island, Graduate School, College of the Environment and Life Sciences, Department of Fisheries, Animal and Veterinary Science, Kingston, RI 02881. Offers animal health and disease (MS); animal science (MS); aquaculture (MS); aquatic pathology (MS); environmental sciences (PhD), including animal science, aquacultural science, aquatic pathology, fisheries science; fisheries (MS). *Faculty:* 9 full-time (4 women). *Students:* 6 full-time (2 women), 1 part-time (0 women), 2 international. In 2012, 6 master's, 1 doctorate awarded. *Degree requirements:* For master's, comprehensive exam (for some programs), thesis optional; for doctorate, comprehensive exam, thesis/dissertation. *Entrance requirements:* For master's and doctorate, GRE, 2 letters of recommendation. Additional exam requirements/recommendations for international students: Required—TOEFL (minimum score 550 paper-based). *Application deadline:* For fall admission, 7/15 for domestic students, 2/1 for international students; for spring admission, 11/15 for domestic students, 7/15 for international students. Application fee: $65. Electronic applications accepted. *Expenses:* Tuition, state resident: full-time $11,532; part-time $641 per credit. Tuition, nonresident: full-time $23,606; part-time $1311 per credit. *Required fees:* $1388; $36 per credit. $35 per semester. One-time fee: $130. *Financial support:* In 2012–13, 3 research assistantships with full and partial tuition reimbursements (averaging $11,679 per year), 1 teaching assistantship with full and partial tuition reimbursement (averaging $9,818 per year) were awarded. Financial award application deadline: 7/15; financial award applicants required to submit FAFSA. *Unit head:* Dr. David Bengtson, Chair, 401-874-2668, Fax: 401-874-7575, E-mail: bengtson@uri.edu. Website: http://www.uri.edu/cels/favs/.

Food Science and Technology

Alabama Agricultural and Mechanical University, School of Graduate Studies, College of Agricultural, Life and Natural Sciences, Department of Family and Consumer Sciences, Huntsville, AL 35811. Offers family and consumer sciences (MS); food science (MS, PhD). Part-time and evening/weekend programs available. *Degree requirements:* For master's, comprehensive exam, thesis optional; for doctorate, one foreign language, thesis/dissertation. *Entrance requirements:* For master's, GRE General Test; for doctorate, GRE General Test, MS. Additional exam requirements/recommendations for international students: Required—TOEFL (minimum score 500 paper-based; 61 iBT). Electronic applications accepted. *Faculty research:* Food biotechnology, nutrition, food microbiology, food engineering, food chemistry.

Alabama Agricultural and Mechanical University, School of Graduate Studies, College of Agricultural, Life and Natural Sciences, Department of Food and Animal Sciences, Huntsville, AL 35811. Offers food science (MS, PhD). *Entrance requirements:* Additional exam requirements/recommendations for international students: Required—TOEFL (minimum score 500 paper-based; 61 iBT).

American University of Beirut, Graduate Programs, Faculty of Agricultural and Food Sciences, Beirut, Lebanon. Offers agricultural economics (MS); animal sciences (MS); ecosystem management (MSES); food technology (MS); irrigation (MS); nutrition (MS); plant protection (MS); plant science (MS); poultry science (MS). Part-time programs available. *Faculty:* 22 full-time (6 women), 1 part-time/adjunct (0 women). *Students:* 11 full-time (10 women), 89 part-time (74 women). Average age 25. 97 applicants, 64% accepted, 18 enrolled. In 2012, 35 master's awarded. *Degree requirements:* For master's, one foreign language, comprehensive exam, thesis (for some programs). *Entrance requirements:* Additional exam requirements/recommendations for international students: Required—TOEFL (minimum score 600 paper-based; 100 iBT), IELTS (minimum score 7.5). *Application deadline:* For fall admission, 2/7 for domestic and international students; for spring admission, 11/15 for domestic and international students. Applications are processed on a rolling basis. Application fee: $50. Electronic applications accepted. *Expenses: Tuition:* Full-time $13,896; part-time $772 per credit. *Financial support:* In 2012–13, 18 research assistantships with partial tuition reimbursements (averaging $1,500 per year), 49 teaching assistantships with full and partial tuition reimbursements (averaging $1,000 per year) were awarded; scholarships/grants, health care benefits, and unspecified assistantships also available. Financial award application deadline: 2/2. *Faculty research:* Evidence-based nutrition intervention; studies related to immunopotentiation, protection and production in broilers; nutritional food-based dietary guidelines; production of biodiesel from algae; regional knowledge management and knowledge sharing network. *Total annual research expenditures:* $560,850. *Unit head:* Prof. Nahla Hwalla, Dean, 961-1343002 Ext. 4400, Fax: 961-1744460, E-mail: nahla@aub.edu.lb. *Application contact:* Dr. Salim Kanaan, Director, Admissions Office, 961-1-350000 Ext. 2594, Fax: 961-1750775, E-mail: sk00@aub.edu.lb. Website: http://www.aub.edu.lb/fafs/fafs_home/Pages/index.aspx.

Auburn University, Graduate School, College of Human Sciences, Department of Nutrition and Food Science, Auburn University, AL 36849. Offers global hospitality and retailing (Graduate Certificate); nutrition (MS, PhD). Part-time programs available. *Faculty:* 13 full-time (5 women). *Students:* 23 full-time (15 women), 25 part-time (16 women); includes 5 minority (4 Black or African

American, non-Hispanic/Latino; 1 Asian, non-Hispanic/Latino), 19 international. Average age 29. 56 applicants, 38% accepted, 11 enrolled. In 2012, 4 master's, 2 doctorates awarded. *Degree requirements:* For master's, thesis (for some programs); for doctorate, thesis/dissertation. *Entrance requirements:* For master's and doctorate, GRE General Test. *Application deadline:* For fall admission, 7/7 for domestic students; for spring admission, 11/24 for domestic students. Applications are processed on a rolling basis. Application fee: $50 ($60 for international students). Electronic applications accepted. *Expenses:* Tuition, state resident: full-time $7866; part-time $437 per credit. Tuition, nonresident: full-time $23,598; part-time $1311 per credit. *Required fees:* $787 per semester. Tuition and fees vary according to degree level and program. *Financial support:* Research assistantships, teaching assistantships, career-related internships or fieldwork, and Federal Work-Study available. Support available to part-time students. Financial award application deadline: 3/15; financial award applicants required to submit FAFSA. *Faculty research:* Food quality and safety, diet, food supply, physical activity in maintenance of health, prevention of selected chronic disease states. *Unit head:* Dr. Martin O'Neill, Head, 334-844-3266. *Application contact:* Dr. George Flowers, Dean of the Graduate School, 334-844-2125. Website: http://www.humsci.auburn.edu/nufs/.

Boston University, Metropolitan College, Program in Gastronomy, Boston, MA 02215. Offers business (MLA); communications (MLA); food policy (MLA); history and culture (MLA). Part-time and evening/weekend programs available. *Faculty:* 4 full-time (3 women), 11 part-time/adjunct (6 women). *Students:* 4 full-time (3 women), 79 part-time (66 women); includes 14 minority (1 Black or African American, non-Hispanic/Latino; 3 Asian, non-Hispanic/Latino; 6 Hispanic/Latino; 4 Two or more races, non-Hispanic/Latino), 4 international. Average age 40. 58 applicants, 76% accepted, 27 enrolled. In 2012, 49 master's awarded. *Degree requirements:* For master's, thesis optional. *Entrance requirements:* Additional exam requirements/recommendations for international students: Required—TOEFL. *Application deadline:* Applications are processed on a rolling basis. Application fee: $80. Electronic applications accepted. *Expenses: Tuition:* Full-time $42,400; part-time $1325 per credit. *Required fees:* $40 per semester. *Financial support:* In 2012–13, 3 research assistantships (averaging $5,000 per year) were awarded; career-related internships or fieldwork, scholarships/grants, and unspecified assistantships also available. Support available to part-time students. Financial award applicants required to submit FAFSA. *Faculty research:* Food studies. *Unit head:* Dr. Rachel Black, Assistant Professor, 617-353-6291, Fax: 617-353-4130, E-mail: rblack@bu.edu. Website: http://www.bu.edu/met/gastronomy.

Brigham Young University, Graduate Studies, College of Life Sciences, Department of Nutrition, Dietetics and Food Science, Provo, UT 84602. Offers food science (MS); nutrition (MS). *Faculty:* 12 full-time (5 women). *Students:* 10 full-time (7 women). Average age 24. 3 applicants, 67% accepted, 2 enrolled. In 2012, 3 master's awarded. *Degree requirements:* For master's, comprehensive exam, thesis. *Entrance requirements:* For master's, GRE General Test. Additional exam requirements/recommendations for international students: Required—TOEFL (minimum score 550 paper-based). *Application deadline:* For fall admission, 2/1 for domestic and international students; for winter admission, 6/30 for domestic and international students. Application fee: $50. Electronic applications accepted. *Expenses: Tuition:* Full-time $5950; part-time $331 per

410 www.petersonsbooks.com

Peterson's Graduate Programs in the Physical Sciences, Mathematics, Agricultural Sciences, the Environment & Natural Resources 2014

credit hour. Tuition and fees vary according to program and student's religious affiliation. *Financial support:* In 2012–13, 9 students received support, including 4 research assistantships (averaging $20,325 per year), 3 teaching assistantships (averaging $20,325 per year); career-related internships or fieldwork, institutionally sponsored loans, and scholarships/grants also available. Financial award application deadline: 4/1. *Faculty research:* Dairy foods, lipid oxidation, food processes, magnesium and selenium nutrition, nutrient effect on gene expression. *Total annual research expenditures:* $382,427. *Unit head:* Dr. Michael L. Dunn, Chair, 801-422-6670, Fax: 801-422-0258, E-mail: michael_dunn@byu.edu. *Application contact:* Dr. Susan Fullmer, Graduate Coordinator, 801-422-3349, Fax: 801-422-0258, E-mail: susan_fullmer@byu.edu.

California State University, Fresno, Division of Graduate Studies, College of Agricultural Sciences and Technology, Department of Food Science and Nutritional Sciences, Fresno, CA 93740-8027. Offers MS. Part-time programs available. *Degree requirements:* For master's, thesis. *Entrance requirements:* For master's, GRE General Test, minimum GPA of 3.0 in last 60 units. Additional exam requirements/recommendations for international students: Required—TOEFL. Electronic applications accepted. *Faculty research:* Liquid foods, analysis, mushrooms, gaseous ozone, natamycin.

California State University, Long Beach, Graduate Studies, College of Health and Human Services, Department of Family and Consumer Sciences, Master of Science in Nutritional Science Program, Long Beach, CA 90840. Offers food science (MS); hospitality foodservice and hotel management (MS); nutritional science (MS). Part-time programs available. *Degree requirements:* For master's, thesis, oral presentation of thesis or directed project. *Entrance requirements:* For master's, GRE, minimum GPA of 2.5 in last 60 units. Electronic applications accepted. *Faculty research:* Protein and water-soluble vitamins, sensory evaluation of foods, mineral deficiencies in humans, child nutrition, minerals and blood pressure.

Chapman University, Schmid College of Science and Technology, Food Science Program, Orange, CA 92866. Offers MS, MBA/MS. Part-time and evening/weekend programs available. *Faculty:* 4 full-time (3 women), 5 part-time/adjunct (all women). *Students:* 20 full-time (17 women), 31 part-time (22 women); includes 22 minority (1 Black or African American, non-Hispanic/Latino; 18 Asian, non-Hispanic/Latino; 3 Hispanic/Latino), 12 international. Average age 27. 35 applicants, 66% accepted, 15 enrolled. In 2012, 14 master's awarded. *Degree requirements:* For master's, comprehensive exam, thesis optional. *Entrance requirements:* For master's, GRE or GMAT, minimum undergraduate GPA of 3.0. Additional exam requirements/recommendations for international students: Required—TOEFL (minimum score 550 paper-based; 80 iBT). *Application deadline:* For fall admission, 5/2 priority date for domestic students; for spring admission, 11/1 priority date for domestic students. Application fee: $60. Electronic applications accepted. *Financial support:* Fellowships, Federal Work-Study, and scholarships/grants available. Financial award applicants required to submit FAFSA. *Unit head:* Dr. Anuradha Prakash, Program Director, 714-744-7895, E-mail: prakash@chapman.edu. *Application contact:* Gianne Diosomito, Graduate Admission Counselor, 714-997-6711, E-mail: diosomit@chapman.edu.

Clemson University, Graduate School, College of Agriculture, Forestry and Life Sciences, Department of Food, Nutrition and Packaging Sciences, Program in Food, Nutrition, and Culinary Science, Clemson, SC 29634. Offers MS. *Students:* 31 full-time (21 women), 8 part-time (5 women); includes 2 minority (1 Asian, non-Hispanic/Latino; 1 Hispanic/Latino), 18 international. Average age 26. 90 applicants, 24% accepted, 16 enrolled. In 2012, 18 master's awarded. *Degree requirements:* For master's, thesis. *Entrance requirements:* For master's, GRE General Test. Additional exam requirements/recommendations for international students: Required—TOEFL, IELTS. *Application deadline:* For fall admission, 6/1 for domestic students, 4/15 for international students; for spring admission, 9/15 for international students. Applications are processed on a rolling basis. Application fee: $70 ($80 for international students). Electronic applications accepted. *Expenses:* Contact institution. *Financial support:* In 2012–13, 15 students received support, including 5 research assistantships with partial tuition reimbursements available (averaging $13,817 per year), 8 teaching assistantships with partial tuition reimbursements available (averaging $10,546 per year); fellowships with full and partial tuition reimbursements available, career-related internships or fieldwork, institutionally sponsored loans, scholarships/grants, health care benefits, and unspecified assistantships also available. Support available to part-time students. Financial award applicants required to submit FAFSA. *Unit head:* Dr. Anthony Pometto, III, Chair, 864-656-4382, Fax: 864-656-3131, E-mail: pometto@clemson.edu. *Application contact:* Dr. Paul Dawson, Coordinator, 864-656-1138, Fax: 864-656-3131, E-mail: pdawson@clemson.edu. Website: http://www.clemson.edu/foodscience.

Clemson University, Graduate School, College of Agriculture, Forestry and Life Sciences, Department of Food, Nutrition and Packaging Sciences and Department of Animal and Veterinary Sciences, Program in Food Technology, Clemson, SC 29634. Offers PhD. *Students:* 12 full-time (9 women), 9 part-time (4 women); includes 6 minority (2 Black or African American, non-Hispanic/Latino; 1 Asian, non-Hispanic/Latino; 3 Hispanic/Latino), 6 international. Average age 37. 24 applicants, 33% accepted, 6 enrolled. In 2012, 2 doctorates awarded. *Degree requirements:* For doctorate, thesis/dissertation. *Entrance requirements:* For doctorate, GRE General Test. Additional exam requirements/recommendations for international students: Required—TOEFL, IELTS. *Application deadline:* For fall admission, 6/1 for domestic students, 4/15 for international students; for spring admission, 9/15 for international students. Applications are processed on a rolling basis. Application fee: $70 ($80 for international students). Electronic applications accepted. *Expenses:* Contact institution. *Financial support:* In 2012–13, 9 students received support, including 1 fellowship with full and partial tuition reimbursement available (averaging $10,000 per year), 4 research assistantships with partial tuition reimbursements available (averaging $16,750 per year), 5 teaching assistantships with partial tuition reimbursements available (averaging $12,000 per year); career-related internships or fieldwork, institutionally sponsored loans, scholarships/grants, health care benefits, and unspecified assistantships also available. Support available to part-time students. Financial award applicants required to submit FAFSA. *Unit head:* Dr. Anthony Pometto, III, Coordinator, 864-656-4382, Fax: 864-656-3131, E-mail: pometto@clemson.edu. *Application contact:* Dr. Paul Dawson, Coordinator, 864-656-1138, Fax: 864-656-3131, E-mail: pdawson@clemson.edu. Website: http://www.clemson.edu/foodscience/.

Colorado State University, Graduate School, College of Health and Human Sciences, Department of Food Science and Human Nutrition, Fort Collins, CO 80523-1571. Offers MS, PhD. *Accreditation:* AND. Part-time programs available. Postbaccalaureate distance learning degree programs offered (no on-campus study). *Faculty:* 17 full-time (9 women), 1 part-time/adjunct (0 women). *Students:* 54 full-time (45 women), 39 part-time (29 women); includes 6 minority (1 Black or African American, non-Hispanic/Latino; 1 Asian, non-Hispanic/Latino; 3 Hispanic/Latino; 1 Two or more races, non-Hispanic/Latino), 3 international. Average age 30. 116 applicants, 41% accepted, 25 enrolled. In 2012, 28 master's, 1 doctorate awarded. *Degree requirements:* For master's, thesis; for doctorate, thesis/dissertation. *Entrance requirements:* For master's and doctorate, GRE (minimum 50th percentile), minimum GPA of 3.0, overall and in science. Additional exam requirements/recommendations for international students: Required—TOEFL (minimum score 550 paper-based; 80 iBT), IELTS (minimum score 6.5). *Application deadline:* For fall admission, 2/1 priority date for domestic students, 2/1 for international students; for spring admission, 8/1 priority date for domestic students, 8/1 for international students. Application fee: $50. Electronic applications accepted. *Expenses:* Tuition, state resident: full-time $8811; part-time $490 per credit. Tuition, nonresident: full-time $21,600; part-time $1200 per credit. *Required fees:* $1819; $61 per credit. *Financial support:* In 2012–13, 23 students received support, including 15 research assistantships with tuition reimbursements available (averaging $12,690 per year), 8 teaching assistantships with tuition reimbursements available (averaging $8,229 per year); fellowships, Federal Work-Study, scholarships/grants, and unspecified assistantships also available. Financial award application deadline: 3/1; financial award applicants required to submit FAFSA. *Faculty research:* Nutrition education in schools and communities, food safety, limited resource audiences, cellular/molecular nutrition and chronic disease (CVD, obesity, diabetes), gastrointestinal microbiota and chronic disease. *Total annual research expenditures:* $2.3 million. *Unit head:* Dr. Garry Auld, Head, 970-491-7429, Fax: 970-491-7252, E-mail: garry.auld@colostate.edu. *Application contact:* Paula Coleman, Graduate Coordinator, 970-491-3819, Fax: 970-491-3875, E-mail: pcoleman@cahs.colostate.edu. Website: http://www.fshn.chhs.colostate.edu/.

Cornell University, Graduate School, Graduate Fields of Agriculture and Life Sciences, Field of Food Science and Technology, Ithaca, NY 14853-0001. Offers dairy science (MPS, MS, PhD); enology (MS, PhD); food chemistry (MPS, MS, PhD); food engineering (MPS, MS, PhD); food microbiology (MPS, MS, PhD); food processing waste technology (MPS, MS, PhD); food science (MFS, MPS, MS, PhD); international food science (MPS, MS, PhD); sensory evaluation (MPS, MS, PhD). *Faculty:* 43 full-time (10 women). *Students:* 81 full-time (51 women); includes 11 minority (3 Black or African American, non-Hispanic/Latino; 2 Asian, non-Hispanic/Latino; 3 Hispanic/Latino; 3 Two or more races, non-Hispanic/Latino), 41 international. Average age 27. 211 applicants, 15% accepted, 27 enrolled. In 2012, 22 master's, 7 doctorates awarded. Terminal master's awarded for partial completion of doctoral program. *Degree requirements:* For master's, thesis (MS), teaching experience; for doctorate, comprehensive exam, thesis/dissertation, teaching experience. *Entrance requirements:* For master's and doctorate, GRE General Test, 3 letters of recommendation. Additional exam requirements/recommendations for international students: Required—TOEFL (minimum score 550 paper-based; 77 iBT). *Application deadline:* For fall admission, 1/30 priority date for domestic students. Application fee: $95. Electronic applications accepted. *Financial support:* In 2012–13, 53 students received support, including 4 fellowships with full tuition reimbursements available, 37 research assistantships with full tuition reimbursements available, 12 teaching assistantships with full tuition reimbursements available; institutionally sponsored loans, scholarships/grants, health care benefits, tuition waivers (full and partial), and unspecified assistantships also available. Financial award applicants required to submit FAFSA. *Faculty research:* Food microbiology/biotechnology, food engineering/processing, food safety/toxicology, sensory science/flavor chemistry, food packaging. *Unit head:* Director of Graduate Studies, 607-255-7637, Fax: 607-254-4868. *Application contact:* Graduate Field Assistant, 607-255-7637, Fax: 607-254-4868, E-mail: fdscigrad@cornell.edu. Website: http://www.gradschool.cornell.edu/fields.php?id-50&a-2.

Dalhousie University, Faculty of Agriculture, Halifax, NS B3H 4R2, Canada. Offers agriculture (M Sc), including air quality, animal behavior, animal molecular genetics, animal nutrition, animal technology, aquaculture, botany, crop management, crop physiology, ecology, environmental microbiology, food science, horticulture, nutrient management, pest management, physiology, plant biotechnology, plant pathology, soil chemistry, soil fertility, waste management and composting, water quality. Part-time programs available. *Degree* *requirements:* For master's, thesis, ATC Exam Teaching Assistantship. *Entrance requirements:* For master's, honors B Sc, minimum GPA of 3.0. Additional exam requirements/recommendations for international students: Required—TOEFL (minimum score 580 paper-based; 92 iBT), IELTS, Michigan English Language Assessment Battery, CanTEST, CAEL. *Faculty research:* Bio-product development, organic agriculture, nutrient management, air and water quality, agricultural biotechnology.

Dalhousie University, Faculty of Engineering, Department of Food Science and Technology, Halifax, NS B3J 1Z1, Canada. Offers M Sc, PhD. *Degree requirements:* For master's, thesis; for doctorate, thesis/dissertation. *Entrance requirements:* Additional exam requirements/recommendations for international students: Required—TOEFL, IELTS, CANTEST, CAEL, or Michigan English Language Assessment Battery. Electronic applications accepted. *Faculty research:* Food microbiology, food safety/HALLP, rheology and rheometry, food processing, seafood processing.

Drexel University, Goodwin College of Professional Studies, School of Technology and Professional Studies, Philadelphia, PA 19104-2875. Offers construction management (MS); creativity and innovation (MS); engineering technology (MS); food science (MS); hospitality management (MS); professional studies: creativity studies (MS); professional studies: e-learning leadership (MS); professional studies: homeland security management (MS); project management (MS); property management (MS); sport management (MS). Part-time and evening/weekend programs available. *Faculty:* 37 full-time (14 women). *Students:* 13 full-time, 462 part-time; includes 133 minority (86 Black or African American, non-Hispanic/Latino; 24 Asian, non-Hispanic/Latino; 23 Hispanic/Latino). 456 applicants, 46% accepted, 138 enrolled. In 2012, 88 master's awarded. *Entrance requirements:* Additional exam requirements/recommendations for international students: Required—TOEFL, IELTS. *Application deadline:* For fall admission, 9/1 for domestic students; for winter admission, 12/1 for domestic students; for spring admission, 3/1 for domestic students. Applications are processed on a rolling basis. Application fee: $75. Electronic applications accepted. Application fee is waived when completed online. *Financial support:* Applicants required to submit FAFSA. *Unit head:* Dr. William F. Lynch, Dean, 215-895-2159, E-mail: goodwin@drexel.edu. *Application contact:* Matthew Gray, Manager, Recruitment and Enrollment, 215-895-6255, Fax: 215-895-2153, E-mail: mdg67@drexel.edu. Website: http://www.drexel.edu/taps.aspx.

Florida State University, The Graduate School, College of Human Sciences, Department of Nutrition, Food and Exercise Sciences, Tallahassee, FL 32306-1493. Offers exercise physiology (MS, PhD); nutrition and food science (MS, PhD), including clinical nutrition (MS), food science, human nutrition (PhD), nutrition education and health promotion (MS), nutrition science (MS), sports nutrition (MS); sports sciences (MS). Part-time programs available. *Faculty:* 16 full-time (9 women). *Students:* 97 full-time (60 women), 10 part-time (6 women); includes 24 minority (9 Black or African American, non-Hispanic/Latino; 2 Asian, non-Hispanic/Latino; 11 Hispanic/Latino; 1 Native Hawaiian or other Pacific Islander, non-Hispanic/Latino; 1 Two or more races, non-Hispanic/Latino), 24 international. Average age 26. 162 applicants, 69% accepted, 49 enrolled. In 2012, 41 master's, 8 doctorates awarded. *Degree requirements:* For master's, comprehensive exam (for some programs), thesis optional; for doctorate, thesis/dissertation. *Entrance requirements:* For master's, GRE General Test, minimum upper-division GPA of 3.0; for doctorate, GRE General Test, minimum upper-division GPA of 3.0, MS. Additional exam requirements/recommendations for international students: Required—TOEFL (minimum score 550 paper-based; 80 iBT). *Application deadline:* For fall admission, 7/1 for domestic students, 3/1 for international students; for spring admission, 11/1 for domestic students, 5/1 for international students. Applications are processed on a rolling basis. Application fee: $30. Electronic applications accepted. *Expenses:* Tuition, state resident: full-time $7263; part-time $403.51 per credit hour. Tuition, nonresident: full-time $18,087; part-time $1004.85 per credit hour. *Required fees:* $1335.42; $74.19 per credit hour. $445.14 per semester. One-time fee: $40 full-time; $20 part-time. Tuition and fees vary according to program. *Financial support:* In 2012–13, 64 students received support, including 1 fellowship with full tuition reimbursement available (averaging $17,000 per year), 10 research assistantships with partial tuition reimbursements available (averaging $8,000 per year), 39 teaching assistantships with partial tuition reimbursements available (averaging $8,000 per year); career-related internships or fieldwork, Federal Work-Study, institutionally sponsored loans, scholarships/grants, and unspecified assistantships also available. Financial award application deadline: 2/1; financial award applicants required to submit FAFSA. *Faculty research:* Body composition, functional food, chronic disease and aging response; food safety, food allergy, and safety/quality detection methods; sports nutrition, energy and human performance; strength training, functional performance, cardiovascular physiology, sarcopenia. *Unit head:* Dr. Bahram H. Arjmandi, Professor/Chair, 850-645-1517, Fax: 850-645-5000, E-mail: barjmandi@fsu.edu. *Application contact:* Ann R. Smith, Office Administrator, 850-644-1828, Fax: 850-645-5000, E-mail: asmith@fsu.edu. Website: http://www.chs.fsu.edu/.

Framingham State University, Division of Graduate and Continuing Education, Programs in Food and Nutrition, Food Science and Nutrition Science Program, Framingham, MA 01701-9101. Offers MS. Part-time and evening/weekend programs available. *Entrance requirements:* For master's, GRE General Test. *Expenses: Required fees:* $1045 per course. Part-time tuition and fees vary according to course load and program.

Illinois Institute of Technology, Graduate College, College of Science and Letters, Program in Food Safety and Technology, Bedford Park, IL 60501. Offers MFPE, MFST, MS. Part-time programs available. *Faculty:* 8 full-time (1 woman). *Students:* 75 full-time (45 women), 29 part-time (22 women); includes 1 minority (Black or African American, non-Hispanic/Latino), 95 international. Average age 25. 103 applicants, 91% accepted, 34 enrolled. In 2012, 25 master's awarded. *Degree requirements:* For master's, comprehensive exam (for some programs), thesis (for some programs). *Entrance requirements:* For master's, GRE General Test, minimum undergraduate GPA of 3.0. Additional exam requirements/recommendations for international students: Required—TOEFL (minimum score 523 paper-based; 70 iBT). *Application deadline:* For fall admission, 5/1 for domestic and international students; for spring admission, 10/15 for domestic and international students. Applications are processed on a rolling basis. Application fee: $50. Electronic applications accepted. *Expenses: Tuition:* Full-time $20,142; part-time $1119 per credit hour. *Required fees:* $605 per semester. One-time fee: $255. Tuition and fees vary according to program and student level. *Financial support:* Fellowships with partial tuition reimbursements, research assistantships with full and partial tuition reimbursements, Federal Work-Study, institutionally sponsored loans, scholarships/grants, health care benefits, and unspecified assistantships available. Support available to part-time students. Financial award applicants required to submit FAFSA. *Faculty research:* Microbial food safety and security, food virology, interfacial colloidial phenomena, development of DNA-based methods for detection, differentiation and tracking of food borne pathogens in food systems and environment, appetite and obesity management and vascular disease. *Total annual research expenditures:* $5.7 million. *Unit head:* Dr. Robert E. Brackett, Vice President and Director, 708-563-1533, E-mail: rbrackett@iit.edu. *Application contact:* Deborah Gibson, Director, Graduate Admission, 866-472-3448, Fax: 312-567-3138, E-mail: inquiry.grad@iit.edu. Website: http://www.ncfstgradprogram.iit.edu/.

Iowa State University of Science and Technology, Department of Food Science and Human Nutrition, Ames, IA 50011. Offers food science and technology (MS, PhD); nutrition (MS, PhD). *Degree requirements:* For master's, thesis; for doctorate, thesis/dissertation. *Entrance requirements:* For master's and doctorate, GRE General Test. Additional exam requirements/recommendations for international students: Required—TOEFL (minimum score 550 paper-based; 79 iBT), IELTS (minimum score 6.5). *Application deadline:* For fall admission, 1/15 priority date for domestic students, 1/15 for international students. Applications are processed on a rolling basis. Application fee: $60 ($90 for international students). Electronic applications accepted. *Application contact:* Brenda Emery, Director of Graduate Education, 515-294-6442, Fax: 515-294-6193, E-mail: gradsecretary@iastate.edu. Website: http://www.fshn.hs.iastate.edu.

Kansas State University, Graduate School, College of Agriculture, Food Science Institute, Manhattan, KS 66506. Offers MS, PhD. Part-time programs available. Postbaccalaureate distance learning degree programs offered (minimal on-campus study). *Faculty:* 27 full-time (7 women). *Students:* 30 full-time (17 women), 94 part-time (62 women); includes 15 minority (3 Black or African American, non-Hispanic/Latino; 6 Asian, non-Hispanic/Latino; 4 Hispanic/Latino; 2 Two or more races, non-Hispanic/Latino), 18 international. Average age 31. 108 applicants, 38% accepted, 26 enrolled. In 2012, 26 master's, 4 doctorates awarded. *Degree requirements:* For master's, thesis, residency; for doctorate, thesis/dissertation, preliminary exams, residency. *Entrance requirements:* For master's, GRE General Test, minimum GPA of 3.0 in undergraduate course work, course work in mathematics; for doctorate, GRE General Test, minimum GPA of 3.5 in master's course work. Additional exam requirements/recommendations for international students: Required—TOEFL (minimum score 550 paper-based; 90 iBT). *Application deadline:* For fall admission, 2/1 priority date for domestic students, 12/15 for international students; for spring admission, 7/1 priority date for domestic students, 6/5 for international students. Applications are processed on a rolling basis. Application fee: $50 ($75 for international students). Electronic applications accepted. *Financial support:* Research assistantships with partial tuition reimbursements, teaching assistantships with partial tuition reimbursements, Federal Work-Study, institutionally sponsored loans, and scholarships/grants available. Support available to part-time students. Financial award application deadline: 3/1; financial award applicants required to submit FAFSA. *Faculty research:* Food safety and defense, food chemistry, ingredient technology, food nutrients and bioactive compounds, new product development, meat and dairy technology, sensory evaluation, food microbiology. *Total annual research expenditures:* $438,204. *Unit head:* Curtis Kastner, Director, 785-532-4057, Fax: 785-532-5861, E-mail: ckastner@ksu.edu. *Application contact:* J. Scott Smith, Program Chair, 785-532-1219, Fax: 785-532-5861, E-mail: jsschem@ksu.edu. Website: http://foodsci.k-state.edu.

Louisiana State University and Agricultural and Mechanical College, Graduate School, College of Agriculture, Department of Food Science, Baton Rouge, LA 70803. Offers MS, PhD. Part-time programs available. *Faculty:* 12 full-time (4 women). *Students:* 36 full-time (19 women), 7 part-time (4 women); includes 3 minority (2 Black or African American, non-Hispanic/Latino; 1 Two or more races, non-Hispanic/Latino), 29 international. Average age 29. 53 applicants, 13% accepted, 6 enrolled. In 2012, 7 master's awarded. *Degree requirements:* For master's, thesis; for doctorate, thesis/dissertation. *Entrance requirements:* For master's and doctorate, GRE General Test, minimum GPA of 3.0. Additional exam requirements/recommendations for international students: Required—TOEFL (minimum score 550 paper-based; 79 iBT), IELTS (minimum score 6.5). *Application deadline:* For fall admission, 1/25 priority date for domestic students, 5/15 for international students; for spring admission, 10/15 for international students. Applications are processed on a rolling basis. Application fee: $50 ($70 for international students). Electronic applications accepted. *Financial support:* In 2012–13, 36 students received support, including 1 fellowship (averaging $19,027 per year), 28 research assistantships with partial tuition reimbursements available (averaging $17,607 per year), 2 teaching assistantships with partial tuition reimbursements available (averaging $12,250 per year); Federal Work-Study, institutionally sponsored loans, scholarships/grants, health care benefits, tuition waivers (full and partial), and unspecified assistantships also available. Support available to part-time students. Financial award application deadline: 4/1; financial award applicants required to submit FAFSA. *Faculty research:* Food chemistry/analysis, food microbiology, food processing/engineering, sensory science, product development. *Total annual research expenditures:* $12,062. *Unit head:* Dr. John W. Finley, Head, 225-578-5206, Fax: 225-578-5300, E-mail: jfinley@agcenter.lsu.edu. *Application contact:* Dr. Kenneth McMillan, Graduate Coordinator, 225-578-3438, Fax: 225-578-5300, E-mail: kmcmill@lsu.edu. Website: http://www.lsu.edu/foodscience/.

McGill University, Faculty of Graduate and Postdoctoral Studies, Faculty of Agricultural and Environmental Sciences, Department of Food Science and Agricultural Chemistry, Montréal, QC H3A 2T5, Canada. Offers M Sc, PhD.

Memorial University of Newfoundland, School of Graduate Studies, Department of Biochemistry, St. John's, NL A1C 5S7, Canada. Offers biochemistry (M Sc, PhD); food science (M Sc, PhD). Part-time programs available. *Degree requirements:* For master's, thesis; for doctorate, comprehensive exam, thesis/dissertation, oral defense of thesis. *Entrance requirements:* For master's, 2nd class degree in related field; for doctorate, M Sc. Electronic applications accepted. *Faculty research:* Toxicology, cell and molecular biology, food engineering, marine biotechnology, lipid biology.

Michigan State University, College of Veterinary Medicine and The Graduate School, Graduate Programs in Veterinary Medicine, National Food Safety and Toxicology Center, East Lansing, MI 48824. Offers food safety (MS). *Entrance requirements:* Additional exam requirements/recommendations for international students: Required—TOEFL, Michigan State University ELT (minimum score 85), Michigan English Language Assessment Battery (minimum score 83). Electronic applications accepted.

Michigan State University, The Graduate School, College of Agriculture and Natural Resources and College of Natural Science, Department of Food Science and Human Nutrition, East Lansing, MI 48824. Offers food science (MS, PhD); food science - environmental toxicology (PhD); human nutrition (MS, PhD); human nutrition-environmental toxicology (PhD). *Entrance requirements:* Additional exam requirements/recommendations for international students: Required—TOEFL (minimum score 550 paper-based), Michigan State University ELT (minimum score 85), Michigan English Language Assessment Battery (minimum score 83). Electronic applications accepted.

Mississippi State University, College of Agriculture and Life Sciences, Department of Food Science, Nutrition and Health Promotion, Mississippi State, MS 39762. Offers food science and technology (MS, PhD); health promotion (MS); nutrition (MS, PhD). Postbaccalaureate distance learning degree programs offered (no on-campus study). *Faculty:* 9 full-time (3 women), 3 part-time/adjunct (1 woman). *Students:* 53 full-time (37 women), 39 part-time (35 women); includes 17 minority (10 Black or African American, non-Hispanic/Latino; 2 American Indian or Alaska Native, non-Hispanic/Latino; 1 Asian, non-Hispanic/Latino; 3 Hispanic/Latino; 1 Two or more races, non-Hispanic/Latino), 17 international. Average age 29. 120 applicants, 30% accepted, 30 enrolled. In 2012, 23 master's, 4 doctorates awarded. *Degree requirements:* For master's, comprehensive exam, thesis; for doctorate, comprehensive exam, thesis/dissertation. *Entrance requirements:* For master's, GRE General Test, minimum GPA of 2.75; for doctorate, GRE General Test, minimum GPA of 2.75 undergraduate, 3.0 graduate. Additional exam requirements/recommendations for international students: Required—TOEFL (minimum score 550 paper-based; 79 iBT); Recommended—IELTS (minimum score 6.5). *Application deadline:* For fall admission, 7/1 for domestic students, 5/1 for international students; for spring admission, 11/1 for domestic students, 9/1 for international students. Applications are processed on a rolling basis. Application fee: $60. Electronic applications accepted. *Financial support:* In 2012–13, 12 research assistantships with full tuition reimbursements (averaging $13,388 per year), 3 teaching assistantships with full tuition reimbursements (averaging $13,669 per year) were awarded; Federal Work-Study, institutionally sponsored loans, scholarships/grants, and unspecified assistantships also available. Financial award application deadline: 4/1; financial award applicants required to submit FAFSA. *Faculty research:* Food preservation, food chemistry, food safety, food processing, product development. *Unit head:* Dr. Sam Chang, Professor and Head, 662-325-3200, Fax: 662-325-8728, E-mail: sc1690@msstate.edu. *Application contact:* Dr. Juan Silva, Graduate Coordinator, 662-325-3200, E-mail: jls@msstate.edu. Website: http://www.fsnhp.msstate.edu.

New Mexico State University, Graduate School, College of Agricultural, Consumer and Environmental Sciences, Department of Family and Consumer Sciences, Las Cruces, NM 88003-8001. Offers family and child science (MS); family and consumer science education (MS); food science and technology (MS); marriage and family therapy (MS); nutrition and dietetic science (MS). Part-time programs available. *Faculty:* 12 full-time (10 women), 2 part-time/adjunct (1 woman). *Students:* 25 full-time (24 women), 20 part-time (19 women); includes 24 minority (all Hispanic/Latino), 3 international. Average age 31. 26 applicants, 58% accepted, 14 enrolled. In 2012, 15 master's awarded. *Degree requirements:* For master's, comprehensive exam (for some programs), thesis (for some programs), oral exam. *Entrance requirements:* For master's, GRE, 3 letters of reference, resume. Additional exam requirements/recommendations for international students: Required—TOEFL (minimum score 550 paper-based; 79 iBT), IELTS (minimum score 6.5). *Application deadline:* For fall admission, 3/1 priority date for domestic students, 3/1 for international students; for spring admission, 11/30 for domestic and international students. Applications are processed on a rolling basis. Application fee: $40 ($50 for international students). Electronic applications accepted. *Expenses:* Tuition, state resident: full-time $5239; part-time $218 per credit. Tuition, nonresident: full-time $18,266; part-time $761 per credit. *Required fees:* $1274; $53 per credit. *Financial support:* In 2012–13, 20 students received support, including 7 teaching assistantships (averaging $8,579 per year); career-related internships or fieldwork, Federal Work-Study, scholarships/grants, health care benefits, and unspecified assistantships also available. Support available to part-time students. Financial award application deadline: 3/1; financial award applicants required to submit FAFSA. *Faculty research:* Food product analysis, childhood obesity, couple relationship education, military families, Latino college students. *Total annual research expenditures:* $362,394. *Unit head:* Dr. Esther Lynn Devall, Head, 575-646-3936, Fax: 575-646-1889, E-mail: edevall@nmsu.edu. *Application contact:* Dr. Roselyn Smitley, Coordinator, 575-646-1183, Fax: 575-646-1889, E-mail: rosmile@nmsu.edu. Website: http://fcs.nmsu.edu.

New York University, Steinhardt School of Culture, Education, and Human Development, Department of Nutrition, Food Studies, and Public Health, Program in Food Studies and Food Management, New York, NY 10012-1019. Offers food studies (MA), including food culture, food systems; food studies and food management (PhD). Part-time programs available. *Faculty:* 4 full-time (2 women). *Students:* 26 full-time (23 women), 120 part-time (106 women); includes 37 minority (4 Black or African American, non-Hispanic/Latino; 1 American Indian or Alaska Native, non-Hispanic/Latino; 7 Asian, non-Hispanic/Latino; 19 Hispanic/Latino; 2 Native Hawaiian or other Pacific Islander, non-Hispanic/Latino; 4 Two or more races, non-Hispanic/Latino), 6 international. Average age 32. 155 applicants, 43% accepted, 32 enrolled. In 2012, 40 master's awarded. *Degree requirements:* For master's, thesis (for some programs); for doctorate, thesis/dissertation. *Entrance requirements:* For doctorate, GRE General Test, interview. Additional exam requirements/recommendations for international students: Required—TOEFL. *Application deadline:* For fall admission, 12/1 priority date for domestic students, 12/1 for international students; for spring admission, 10/1 for domestic and international students. Applications are processed on a rolling basis. Application fee: $75. Electronic applications accepted. *Expenses: Tuition:* Full-time $34,488; part-time $1437 per credit. *Required fees:* $2332; $1437 per credit. Tuition and fees vary according to program. *Financial support:* Fellowships with full and partial tuition reimbursements, career-related internships or fieldwork, Federal Work-Study, institutionally sponsored loans, scholarships/grants, tuition waivers (partial), and unspecified assistantships available. Financial award application deadline: 2/1; financial award applicants required to submit FAFSA. *Faculty research:* Cultural and social history of food, food systems and agriculture, food and aesthetics, political economy of food. *Unit head:* Dr. Jennifer Berg, Director, 212-998-5580, Fax: 212-995-4194. *Application contact:* 212-998-5030, Fax: 212-995-4328, E-mail: steinhardt.gradadmissions@nyu.edu. Website: http://steinhardt.nyu.edu/nutrition/food.

North Carolina State University, Graduate School, College of Agriculture and Life Sciences, Department of Food Science, Raleigh, NC 27695. Offers MFS, MS, PhD. *Degree requirements:* For master's, thesis (for some programs); for doctorate, thesis/dissertation. *Entrance requirements:* For master's and doctorate, GRE. Electronic applications accepted. *Faculty research:* Food safety, value-added food products, environmental quality, nutrition and health, biotechnology.

North Dakota State University, College of Graduate and Interdisciplinary Studies, College of Agriculture, Food Systems, and Natural Resources, Department of Cereal and Food Sciences, Fargo, ND 58108. Offers cereal science (MS, PhD). Part-time programs available. *Faculty:* 4 full-time (1 woman). *Students:* 16 full-time (10 women), 8 part-time (6 women); includes 2 minority (1 Black or African American, non-Hispanic/Latino; 1 Two or more races, non-Hispanic/Latino), 14 international. Average age 28. 16 applicants, 44% accepted, 6 enrolled. In 2012, 3 master's, 1 doctorate awarded. Terminal master's awarded for partial completion of doctoral program. *Degree requirements:* For master's, comprehensive exam, thesis; for doctorate, comprehensive exam, thesis/dissertation. *Entrance requirements:* Additional exam requirements/recommendations for international students: Required—TOEFL (minimum score 550 paper-based; 79 iBT), IELTS (minimum score 6). *Application deadline:* For fall admission, 3/15 priority date for domestic students; for spring admission, 9/30 for domestic students. Application fee: $35. *Financial support:* In 2012–13, 15 research assistantships with full tuition reimbursements (averaging $12,000 per year) were awarded; career-related internships or fieldwork and unspecified assistantships also available. Support available to part-time students. *Faculty research:* Legume food products, cereal proteins and product quality, oilseeds functional components. *Unit head:* Dr. Deland Myers, Chair, 701-231-7711, Fax: 701-231-5171, E-mail: deland.myers@ndsu.edu. *Application contact:* Sonya Goergen, Marketing, Recruitment, and Public Relations Coordinator, 701-231-7033, Fax: 701-231-6524.

North Dakota State University, College of Graduate and Interdisciplinary Studies, Interdisciplinary Program in Food Safety, Fargo, ND 58108. Offers food protection (Certificate); food safety (MS, PhD). Part-time programs available.

Food Science and Technology

Postbaccalaureate distance learning degree programs offered (minimal on-campus study). *Faculty:* 10 full-time (5 women), 3 part-time/adjunct (2 women). *Students:* 6 full-time (4 women), 3 part-time (2 women); includes 1 minority (Asian, non-Hispanic/Latino), 4 international. Average age 31. 19 applicants, 11% accepted, 1 enrolled. In 2012, 2 master's, 1 doctorate, 3 other advanced degrees awarded. Terminal master's awarded for partial completion of doctoral program. *Degree requirements:* For master's, thesis; for doctorate, comprehensive exam, thesis/dissertation. *Entrance requirements:* Additional exam requirements/recommendations for international students: Required—TOEFL (minimum score 525 paper-based; 71 iBT), TWE (minimum score 5). *Application deadline:* Applications are processed on a rolling basis. Application fee: $35. Electronic applications accepted. *Financial support:* In 2012–13, 9 research assistantships with full tuition reimbursements (averaging $16,000 per year) were awarded; scholarships/grants also available. *Faculty research:* Mycotoxins in grain, pathogens in meat systems, sensor development for food pathogens. *Unit head:* Dr. Clifford Hall, Associate Director, 701-231-6359, Fax: 701-231-5171, E-mail: clifford.hall@ndsu.edu. *Application contact:* Sonya Goergen, Marketing, Recruitment, and Public Relations Coordinator, 701-231-7033, Fax: 701-231-6524.

The Ohio State University, Graduate School, College of Food, Agricultural, and Environmental Sciences, Department of Food Science and Technology, Columbus, OH 43210. Offers food science (MS, PhD). *Accreditation:* AND. *Faculty:* 15. *Students:* 61 full-time (36 women), 11 part-time (5 women); includes 11 minority (7 Black or African American, non-Hispanic/Latino; 3 Asian, non-Hispanic/Latino; 1 Two or more races, non-Hispanic/Latino), 36 international. Average age 26. In 2012, 22 master's, 9 doctorates awarded. *Degree requirements:* For master's, thesis optional; for doctorate, thesis/dissertation. *Entrance requirements:* For master's and doctorate, GRE General Test. Additional exam requirements/recommendations for international students: Required—TOEFL (minimum score 550 paper-based; 79 iBT), Michigan English Language Assessment Battery (minimum score 82); Recommended—IELTS (minimum score 7). *Application deadline:* For fall admission, 1/7 priority date for domestic students, 11/30 for international students; for winter admission, 12/1 for domestic students, 11/1 for international students; for spring admission, 6/1 priority date for domestic students, 4/1 for international students. Applications are processed on a rolling basis. Application fee: $40 ($50 for international students). Electronic applications accepted. *Financial support:* Fellowships, research assistantships, Federal Work-Study, and institutionally sponsored loans available. Support available to part-time students. *Unit head:* Monica Giusti, Chair, 614-247-8016, E-mail: guisti.6@osu.edu. *Application contact:* Graduate Admissions, 614-292-6031, Fax: 614-292-3656, E-mail: gradadmissions@osu.edu. Website: http://fst.osu.edu/.

Oklahoma State University, College of Agricultural Science and Natural Resources, Department of Animal Science, Stillwater, OK 74078. Offers animal sciences (M Ag, MS); food science (MS, PhD). *Faculty:* 33 full-time (10 women), 2 part-time/adjunct (0 women). *Students:* 20 full-time (14 women), 45 part-time (20 women); includes 6 minority (2 Asian, non-Hispanic/Latino; 2 Hispanic/Latino; 2 Two or more races, non-Hispanic/Latino), 22 international. Average age 27. 94 applicants, 28% accepted, 20 enrolled. In 2012, 15 master's, 7 doctorates awarded. *Degree requirements:* For master's, thesis; for doctorate, comprehensive exam, thesis/dissertation. *Entrance requirements:* For master's and doctorate, GRE or GMAT. Additional exam requirements/recommendations for international students: Required—TOEFL (minimum score 550 paper-based; 79 iBT). *Application deadline:* For fall admission, 3/1 for international students; for spring admission, 8/1 for international students. Applications are processed on a rolling basis. Application fee: $40 ($75 for international students). Electronic applications accepted. *Expenses:* Tuition, state resident: full-time $4272; part-time $178 per credit hour. Tuition, nonresident: full-time $17,016; part-time $709 per credit hour. *Required fees:* $2188; $91.17 per credit hour. One-time fee: $50 full-time. Part-time tuition and fees vary according to course load and campus/location. *Financial support:* In 2012–13, 23 research assistantships (averaging $14,693 per year), 8 teaching assistantships (averaging $15,496 per year) were awarded; career-related internships or fieldwork, Federal Work-Study, scholarships/grants, health care benefits, tuition waivers (partial), and unspecified assistantships also available. Support available to part-time students. Financial award application deadline: 3/1; financial award applicants required to submit FAFSA. *Faculty research:* Quantitative trait loci identification for economical traits in swing/beef; waste management strategies in livestock; endocrine control of reproductive processes in farm animals; cholesterol synthesis, inhibition, and reduction; food safety research. *Unit head:* Dr. Clint Rusk, Head, 405-744-6062, Fax: 405-744-7390. *Application contact:* Dr. Sheryl Tucker, Dean, 405-744-7099, Fax: 405-744-0355, E-mail: grad-i@okstate.edu. Website: http://www.ansi.okstate.edu.

Oregon State University, College of Agricultural Sciences, Department of Food Science and Technology, Corvallis, OR 97331. Offers M Agr, MAIS, MS, PhD. *Faculty:* 10 full-time (2 women). *Students:* 37 full-time (25 women), 3 part-time (2 women); includes 4 minority (2 Asian, non-Hispanic/Latino; 2 Hispanic/Latino), 22 international. Average age 26. 146 applicants, 8% accepted, 12 enrolled. In 2012, 11 master's, 2 doctorates awarded. *Degree requirements:* For master's, thesis (for some programs); for doctorate, thesis/dissertation. *Entrance requirements:* For master's and doctorate, GRE General Test, minimum GPA of 3.0 in last 90 hours. Additional exam requirements/recommendations for international students: Required—TOEFL. *Application deadline:* For fall admission, 3/1 for domestic students. Applications are processed on a rolling basis. Application fee: $50.

Expenses: Tuition, state resident: full-time $11,367; part-time $421 per credit hour. Tuition, nonresident: full-time $18,279; part-time $677 per credit hour. *Required fees:* $1478. One-time fee: $300 full-time. Tuition and fees vary according to course load and program. *Financial support:* Fellowships, research assistantships, teaching assistantships, career-related internships or fieldwork, Federal Work-Study, and institutionally sponsored loans available. Support available to part-time students. Financial award application deadline: 2/1. *Faculty research:* Diet, cancer, and anticarcinogenesis; sensory analysis; chemistry and biochemistry. *Unit head:* Dr. Robert McGorrin, Department Head, 541-737-3131, Fax: 541-737-1877, E-mail: robert.mcgorrin@orst.edu. *Application contact:* Dr. Stella Coakley, Associate Dean, 541-737-5264, Fax: 541-737-3178, E-mail: stella.coakley@oregonstate.edu. Website: http://www.orst.edu/dept/foodsci/.

Penn State University Park, Graduate School, College of Agricultural Sciences, Department of Food Science, State College, University Park, PA 16802-1503. Offers MS, PhD. *Unit head:* Dr. Barbara J. Christ, Interim Dean, 814-865-2541, Fax: 814-865-3103, E-mail: ebf@psu.edu. *Application contact:* Cynthia E. Nicosia, Director of Graduate Enrollment Services, 814-865-1834, E-mail: cey1@psu.edu. Website: http://foodscience.psu.edu.

Purdue University, Graduate School, College of Agriculture, Department of Food Science, West Lafayette, IN 47907. Offers MS, PhD. *Faculty:* 19 full-time (7 women), 14 part-time/adjunct (0 women). *Students:* 57 full-time (40 women), 5 part-time (4 women); includes 6 minority (3 Black or African American, non-Hispanic/Latino; 3 Asian, non-Hispanic/Latino), 40 international. Average age 26. 147 applicants, 16% accepted, 21 enrolled. In 2012, 6 master's, 10 doctorates awarded. *Degree requirements:* For master's, thesis (for some programs); for doctorate, thesis/dissertation, teaching assistantship. *Entrance requirements:* For master's, GRE General Test (minimum score Verbal 400, Quantitative 500, Analytical 4.0 old scoring; 146/144, 4.0 new scoring), minimum undergraduate GPA of 3.0 or equivalent; for doctorate, GRE General Test (minimum score Verbal 400, Quantitative 500, Analytical 4.0 old scoring; 146/144, 4.0 new scoring), minimum undergraduate GPA of 3.0 or equivalent; master's degree with minimum GPA of 3.0 or equivalent. Additional exam requirements/recommendations for international students: Required—TOEFL (minimum score 575 paper-based; 77 iBT). *Application deadline:* For fall admission, 7/15 priority date for domestic students, 7/15 for international students; for spring admission, 11/15 for domestic and international students. Applications are processed on a rolling basis. Application fee: $60 ($75 for international students). Electronic applications accepted. *Financial support:* In 2012–13, 4 fellowships (averaging $24,500 per year), 38 research assistantships (averaging $13,500 per year), 1 teaching assistantship (averaging $13,500 per year) were awarded; career-related internships or fieldwork also available. Support available to part-time students. Financial award application deadline: 4/1; financial award applicants required to submit FAFSA. *Faculty research:* Processing, technology, microbiology, chemistry of foods, carbohydrate chemistry. *Unit head:* Dr. R. Chandrasekaran, Head/Graduate Committee Chair, 765-494-8328, Fax: 765-494-7953, E-mail: nielsens@foodsci.purdue.edu. *Application contact:* Dr. Mitzi L. Barnett, Graduate Contact for Admissions, 765-494-8256, E-mail: mbarnett@purdue.edu.

Purdue University, Graduate School, Food Science Interdepartmental Program, West Lafayette, IN 47907. Offers MS, PhD. *Students:* 57 full-time (40 women), 5 part-time (4 women); includes 6 minority (3 Black or African American, non-Hispanic/Latino; 3 Asian, non-Hispanic/Latino), 40 international. Average age 26. 147 applicants, 16% accepted, 21 enrolled. *Degree requirements:* For master's, thesis (for some programs); for doctorate, thesis/dissertation, teaching assistantship. *Entrance requirements:* For master's, GRE General Test (minimum scores: Verbal 400, Quantitative 500, Analytical 4.0 old scoring; 146/144/4.0 new scoring), minimum undergraduate GPA of 3.0 or equivalent; for doctorate, GRE General Test (minimum scores: Verbal 400, Quantitative 500, Analytical 4.0 old scoring; 146/144/4.0 new scoring), minimum undergraduate GPA of 3.0 or equivalent; master's degree with minimum GPA of 3.0 or equivalent. Additional exam requirements/recommendations for international students: Required—TOEFL (minimum score 575 paper-based; 77 iBT). *Application deadline:* For fall admission, 7/15 for domestic and international students; for spring admission, 11/15 for domestic and international students. Applications are processed on a rolling basis. Application fee: $60 ($75 for international students). Electronic applications accepted. *Financial support:* Application deadline: 4/1; applicants required to submit FAFSA. *Unit head:* Dr. R. J.T. Chandrasekaran, Head/Graduate Committee Chair, 765-494-8328, Fax: 765-494-7953, E-mail: nielsens@foodsci.purdue.edu. *Application contact:* Dr. Mitzi L. Barnett, Graduate Contact for Admissions, 765-494-8256, E-mail: mbarnett@purdue.edu.

Rutgers, The State University of New Jersey, New Brunswick, Graduate School-New Brunswick, Program in Food Science, Piscataway, NJ 08854-8097. Offers M Phil, MS, PhD. Part-time and evening/weekend programs available. Postbaccalaureate distance learning degree programs offered (minimal on-campus study). *Degree requirements:* For master's, thesis or alternative; for doctorate, thesis/dissertation. *Entrance requirements:* For master's and doctorate, GRE General Test. *Faculty research:* Nutraceuticals and functional foods, food and flavor analysis, food chemistry and biochemistry, food nanotechnology, food engineering and processing.

South Dakota State University, Graduate School, College of Education and Human Sciences, Department of Nutrition, Food Science and Hospitality, Brookings, SD 57007. Offers dietetics (MS); nutrition, food science and hospitality (MFCS); nutritional sciences (MS, PhD). Part-time programs available. *Degree*

414 www.petersonsbooks.com

Peterson's Graduate Programs in the Physical Sciences, Mathematics, Agricultural Sciences, the Environment & Natural Resources 2014

requirements: For master's, comprehensive exam (for some programs), thesis (for some programs), oral exam. *Entrance requirements:* Additional exam requirements/recommendations for international students: Required—TOEFL (minimum score 525 paper-based). *Faculty research:* Food chemistry, bone density, functional food, nutrition education, nutrition biochemistry.

Texas A&M University, College of Agriculture and Life Sciences, Department of Nutrition and Food Science, College Station, TX 77843. Offers food science and technology (M Agr), nutrition (MS, PhD). *Faculty:* 13. *Students:* 41 full-time (32 women), 20 part-time (16 women); includes 12 minority (4 Black or African American, non-Hispanic/Latino; 4 Asian, non-Hispanic/Latino; 3 Hispanic/Latino; 1 Two or more races, non-Hispanic/Latino), 21 international. Average age 26. *Degree requirements:* For master's, thesis; for doctorate, thesis/dissertation. *Entrance requirements:* For master's and doctorate, GRE General Test. Additional exam requirements/recommendations for international students: Required—TOEFL. *Application deadline:* For fall admission, 2/1 priority date for domestic students; for spring admission, 10/1 priority date for domestic students. Applications are processed on a rolling basis. Application fee: $50 ($75 for international students). *Financial support:* Fellowships, research assistantships, teaching assistantships, career-related internships or fieldwork, and scholarships/grants available. *Faculty research:* Food safety, microbiology, product development. *Unit head:* Dr. Jimmy T. Keeton, Department Head, 979-458-3128, E-mail: jkeeton@tamu.edu. *Application contact:* Graduate Admissions, 979-845-1044, E-mail: admissions@tamu.edu. Website: http://nfs.tamu.edu.

Texas A&M University, College of Agriculture and Life Sciences, Department of Soil and Crop Sciences, College Station, TX 77843. Offers agronomy (M Agr, MS, PhD); food science and technology (MS, PhD); genetics (PhD); molecular and environmental plant sciences (MS, PhD); plant breeding (MS, PhD); soil science (MS, PhD). *Faculty:* 31. *Students:* 97 full-time (39 women), 21 part-time (6 women); includes 7 minority (1 Black or African American, non-Hispanic/Latino; 2 Asian, non-Hispanic/Latino; 4 Hispanic/Latino), 42 international. Average age 29. In 2012, 8 master's, 7 doctorates awarded. *Degree requirements:* For master's, thesis; for doctorate, thesis/dissertation. *Entrance requirements:* For master's and doctorate, GRE General Test. Additional exam requirements/recommendations for international students: Required—TOEFL. *Application deadline:* For fall admission, 3/1 priority date for domestic students; for spring admission, 8/1 for domestic students. Applications are processed on a rolling basis. Application fee: $50 ($75 for international students). *Financial support:* In 2012–13, fellowships (averaging $16,000 per year), research assistantships with partial tuition reimbursements (averaging $15,000 per year) were awarded; career-related internships or fieldwork, Federal Work-Study, and institutionally sponsored loans also available. *Faculty research:* Soil and crop management, turfgrass science, weed science, cereal chemistry, food protein chemistry. *Unit head:* Dr. David D. Baltensperger, Department Head, 979-845-3001, E-mail: dbaltensperger@ag.tamu.edu. *Application contact:* Graduate Admissions, 979-845-1044, E-mail: admissions@tamu.edu. Website: http://soilcrop.tamu.edu.

Texas Tech University, Graduate School, College of Agricultural Sciences and Natural Resources, Department of Animal and Food Sciences, Lubbock, TX 79409-2141. Offers animal science (MS, PhD); food science (MS). *Degree requirements:* For master's, thesis or alternative, internship (M Agr); for doctorate, thesis/dissertation. *Entrance requirements:* For master's and doctorate, GRE General Test, formal approval from departmental committee. Additional exam requirements/recommendations for international students: Required—TOEFL (minimum score 550 paper-based; 79 iBT). Electronic applications accepted. *Faculty research:* Animal nutrition, health and welfare (species of emphasis: beef cattle, dairy cattle, swine, horse, sheep and goat); animal physiology and reproduction; meat science and muscle biology; food safety, security and public health, food science.

Texas Woman's University, Graduate School, College of Health Sciences, Department of Nutrition and Food Sciences, Denton, TX 76201. Offers exercise and sports nutrition (MS); food science (MS); food systems administration (MS); nutrition (MS, PhD). Part-time and evening/weekend programs available. *Degree requirements:* For master's, comprehensive exam, thesis or alternative; for doctorate, comprehensive exam, thesis/dissertation, qualifying exam. *Entrance requirements:* For master's, GRE General Test (preferred minimum score 143 [350 old version] Verbal, 141 [450 old version] Quantitative), minimum GPA of 3.25, resume; for doctorate, GRE General Test (preferred minimum score 150 [450 old version] Verbal, 141 [550 old version] Quantitative), minimum GPA of 3.5 on last 60 undergraduate hours and graduate course work, 2 letters of reference, resume. Additional exam requirements/recommendations for international students: Required—TOEFL (minimum score 550 paper-based; 79 iBT). Electronic applications accepted. *Faculty research:* Bioactive food components and cancer, nutraceuticals and functional foods in diabetes, obesity and bone health, food safety, dietary modulation of dyslipidemia, childhood obesity prevention.

Tuskegee University, Graduate Programs, College of Agricultural, Environmental and Natural Sciences, Department of Food and Nutritional Sciences, Tuskegee, AL 36088. Offers MS. *Degree requirements:* For master's, thesis. *Entrance requirements:* For master's, GRE General Test. Additional exam requirements/recommendations for international students: Required—TOEFL (minimum score 500 paper-based). *Expenses: Tuition:* Full-time $18,100; part-time $575 per credit hour. *Required fees:* $800.

Universidad de las Américas Puebla, Division of Graduate Studies, School of Engineering, Program in Chemical Engineering, Puebla, Mexico. Offers chemical engineering (MS); food technology (MS). Part-time and evening/weekend programs available. *Degree requirements:* For master's, one foreign language, thesis. *Faculty research:* Food science, reactors, oil industry, biotechnology.

Universidad de las Américas Puebla, Division of Graduate Studies, School of Engineering, Program in Food Sciences, Puebla, Mexico. Offers MS.

Université de Moncton, School of Food Science, Nutrition and Family Studies, Moncton, NB E1A 3E9, Canada. Offers foods/nutrition (M Sc). Part-time programs available. *Degree requirements:* For master's, one foreign language, thesis. *Entrance requirements:* For master's, previous course work in statistics. Electronic applications accepted. *Faculty research:* Clinic nutrition (anemia, elderly, osteoporosis), applied nutrition, metabolic activities of lactic bacteria, solubility of low density lipoproteins, bile acids.

Université Laval, Faculty of Agricultural and Food Sciences, Department of Food Sciences and Nutrition, Programs in Food Sciences and Technology, Québec, QC G1K 7P4, Canada. Offers M Sc, PhD. Terminal master's awarded for partial completion of doctoral program. *Degree requirements:* For master's, thesis (for some programs); for doctorate, comprehensive exam, thesis/dissertation. *Entrance requirements:* For master's and doctorate, knowledge of French and English. Electronic applications accepted.

University of Arkansas, Graduate School, Dale Bumpers College of Agricultural, Food and Life Sciences, Department of Food Science, Fayetteville, AR 72701-1201. Offers MS, PhD. *Students:* 11 full-time (8 women), 22 part-time (13 women); includes 5 minority (2 Black or African American, non-Hispanic/Latino; 1 Asian, non-Hispanic/Latino; 2 Hispanic/Latino), 16 international. In 2012, 10 master's, 3 doctorates awarded. *Degree requirements:* For master's, thesis; for doctorate, thesis/dissertation. *Application deadline:* For fall admission, 4/1 for international students; for spring admission, 10/1 for international students. Applications are processed on a rolling basis. Application fee: $40 ($50 for international students). Electronic applications accepted. *Financial support:* In 2012–13, 25 research assistantships were awarded; fellowships with tuition reimbursements, teaching assistantships, career-related internships or fieldwork, Federal Work-Study, scholarships/grants, and unspecified assistantships also available. Support available to part-time students. Financial award application deadline: 4/1; financial award applicants required to submit FAFSA. *Unit head:* Dr. Jean-Francois Meullenet, Department Head, 479-575-4605, E-mail: jfmeull@uark.edu. *Application contact:* Graduate Admissions, 479-575-6246, Fax: 479-575-5908, E-mail: gradinfo@uark.edu. Website: http://www.foodscience.uark.edu/.

University of Arkansas, Graduate School, Dale Bumpers College of Agricultural, Food and Life Sciences, Program in Agricultural, Food and Life Sciences, Fayetteville, AR 72701-1201. Offers MS. Part-time and evening/weekend programs available. Postbaccalaureate distance learning degree programs offered (minimal on-campus study). *Students:* 2 full-time (1 woman), 19 part-time (10 women); includes 2 minority (both Hispanic/Latino), 2 international. In 2012, 3 master's awarded. *Degree requirements:* For master's, thesis optional. *Application deadline:* For fall admission, 4/1 for international students; for spring admission, 10/1 for international students. Applications are processed on a rolling basis. Application fee: $40 ($50 for international students). Electronic applications accepted. *Financial support:* Fellowships, research assistantships, teaching assistantships, career-related internships or fieldwork, and Federal Work-Study available. Support available to part-time students. Financial award application deadline: 4/1; financial award applicants required to submit FAFSA. *Unit head:* Dr. Michael E. Vayda, Dean, 479-575-2034, E-mail: mvayda@uark.edu. *Application contact:* Diana Bisbee, Program Coordinator, 479-575-2025, E-mail: dbisbee@uark.edu. Website: http://bumperscollege.uark.edu/.

The University of British Columbia, Faculty of Land and Food Systems, Program in Food Science, Vancouver, BC V6T 1Z1, Canada. Offers M Sc, MFS, PhD. *Degree requirements:* For master's, thesis; for doctorate, comprehensive exam, thesis/dissertation. *Entrance requirements:* Additional exam requirements/recommendations for international students: Required—TOEFL (minimum score 577 paper-based; 90 iBT), IELTS (minimum score 6.5). Electronic applications accepted. *Faculty research:* Food chemistry and biochemistry, food process science, food toxicology and safety, food microbiology, food biotechnology.

University of California, Davis, Graduate Studies, Graduate Group in Food Science, Davis, CA 95616. Offers MS, PhD. Terminal master's awarded for partial completion of doctoral program. *Degree requirements:* For master's, comprehensive exam (for some programs), thesis (for some programs); for doctorate, thesis/dissertation. *Entrance requirements:* For master's and doctorate, GRE General Test, minimum GPA of 3.0. Additional exam requirements/recommendations for international students: Required—TOEFL (minimum score 550 paper-based). Electronic applications accepted.

University of Delaware, College of Agriculture and Natural Resources, Department of Animal and Food Sciences, Newark, DE 19716. Offers animal sciences (MS, PhD); food sciences (MS). Part-time programs available. Terminal master's awarded for partial completion of doctoral program. *Degree requirements:* For master's, thesis; for doctorate, comprehensive exam, thesis/dissertation. *Entrance requirements:* For master's and doctorate, GRE General Test. Additional exam requirements/recommendations for international students: Required—TOEFL. Electronic applications accepted. *Faculty research:* Food chemistry, food microbiology, process engineering technology, packaging, food analysis, microbial genetics, molecular endocrinology, growth physiology, avian immunology and virology, monogastric nutrition, avian genomics.

University of Florida, Graduate School, College of Agricultural and Life Sciences, Department of Food Science and Human Nutrition, Gainesville, FL 32611. Offers nutritional sciences (MS, PhD). *Degree requirements:* For master's, thesis optional; for doctorate, thesis/dissertation. *Entrance requirements:* For master's and doctorate, GRE General Test, minimum GPA of 3.0. Additional exam requirements/recommendations for international students: Required—TOEFL. Electronic applications accepted. *Faculty research:* Pesticide research, nutritional biochemistry and microbiology, food safety and toxicology assessment and dietetics, food chemistry.

University of Georgia, College of Agricultural and Environmental Sciences, Department of Food Science and Technology, Athens, GA 30602. Offers food science (MS, PhD); food technology (MFT). Part-time programs available. *Degree requirements:* For master's, thesis; for doctorate, thesis/dissertation. *Entrance requirements:* For master's and doctorate, GRE General Test. Additional exam requirements/recommendations for international students: Required—TOEFL (minimum score 550 paper-based). Electronic applications accepted.

University of Guelph, Graduate Studies, Ontario Agricultural College, Department of Food Science, Guelph, ON N1G 2W1, Canada. Offers food safety and quality assurance (M Sc); food science (M Sc, PhD). *Degree requirements:* For master's, thesis; for doctorate, comprehensive exam, thesis/dissertation. *Entrance requirements:* For master's, minimum B- average during previous 2 years of honors B Sc degree; for doctorate, minimum B average. Additional exam requirements/recommendations for international students: Required—TOEFL (minimum score 550 paper-based), IELTS (minimum score 6.5). Electronic applications accepted. *Faculty research:* Food chemistry, food microbiology, food processing, preservation and utilization.

University of Hawaii at Manoa, Graduate Division, College of Tropical Agriculture and Human Resources, Department of Human Nutrition, Food and Animal Sciences, Program in Food Science, Honolulu, HI 96822. Offers MS. Part-time programs available. *Degree requirements:* For master's, thesis optional. *Entrance requirements:* For master's, GRE General Test. Additional exam requirements/recommendations for international students: Required—TOEFL (minimum score 580 paper-based; 92 iBT), IELTS (minimum score 5). *Faculty research:* Biochemistry of natural products, sensory evaluation, food processing, food chemistry, food safety.

University of Idaho, College of Graduate Studies, College of Agricultural and Life Sciences, Bistate School of Food Science, Moscow, ID 83844-2312. Offers MS, PhD. *Faculty:* 3 full-time. *Students:* 4 full-time, 2 part-time. Average age 29. In 2012, 1 master's, 1 doctorate awarded. *Entrance requirements:* For master's, minimum GPA of 2.8. Additional exam requirements/recommendations for international students: Required—TOEFL (minimum score 550 paper-based). *Application deadline:* For fall admission, 8/1 for domestic students; for spring admission, 12/15 for domestic students. Applications are processed on a rolling basis. Application fee: $60. Electronic applications accepted. *Expenses:* Tuition, state resident: full-time $4230; part-time $252 per credit hour. Tuition, nonresident: full-time $17,018; part-time $891 per credit hour. *Required fees:* $2932; $107 per credit hour. *Financial support:* Research assistantships and teaching assistantships available. Financial award applicants required to submit FAFSA. *Faculty research:* Food biotechnology, food and environmental toxicology, bio-preservation of food products, conversion of biomass. *Unit head:* Dr. Denise Smith, Director, 208-885-0707, E-mail: foodscience@uidaho.edu. *Application contact:* Erick Larson, Director of Graduate Admissions, 208-885-4723, E-mail: gadms@uidaho.edu. Website: http://sfs.wsu.edu/.

University of Illinois at Urbana–Champaign, Graduate College, College of Agricultural, Consumer and Environmental Sciences, Department of Food Science and Human Nutrition, Champaign, IL 61820. Offers food science (MS); food science and human nutrition (MS, PhD), including professional science (MS); human nutrition (MS). Part-time programs available. Postbaccalaureate distance learning degree programs offered (no on-campus study). *Students:* 111 (74 women). Application fee: $75 ($90 for international students). *Unit head:* Nicki Engeseth, Head, 217-244-6788, Fax: 217-265-0925, E-mail: engeseth@illinois.edu. *Application contact:* Terri Cummings, Director of Student Services, 217-244-4405, Fax: 217-265-0925, E-mail: tcumming@illinois.edu. Website: http://fshn.illinois.edu/.

University of Maine, Graduate School, College of Natural Sciences, Forestry, and Agriculture, Department of Food Science and Human Nutrition, Orono, ME 04469. Offers food and nutrition sciences (PhD); food science and human nutrition (MS); foods and nutrition (CGS). Part-time programs available. *Faculty:* 22 full-time (13 women), 18 part-time/adjunct (9 women). *Students:* 37 full-time (29 women), 7 part-time (all women); includes 3 minority (2 American Indian or Alaska Native, non-Hispanic/Latino; 1 Asian, non-Hispanic/Latino), 4 international. Average age 27. 43 applicants, 58% accepted, 15 enrolled. In 2012, 12 master's, 3 doctorates awarded. *Degree requirements:* For master's, thesis; for doctorate, comprehensive exam, thesis/dissertation. *Entrance requirements:* For master's, GRE General Test, minimum GPA of 3.0; for doctorate, GRE General Test. Additional exam requirements/recommendations for international students: Required—TOEFL. *Application deadline:* For fall admission, 2/1 priority date for domestic students. Applications are processed on a rolling basis. Application fee: $65. Electronic applications accepted. *Financial support:* In 2012–13, 4 research assistantships with full tuition reimbursements (averaging $18,596 per year), 3 teaching assistantships with full tuition reimbursements (averaging $13,600 per year) were awarded; scholarships/grants and tuition waivers (full and partial) also available. Financial award application deadline: 3/1. *Faculty research:* Product development of fruit and vegetables, lipid oxidation in fish and meat, analytical methods development, metabolism of potato glycoalkaloids, seafood quality. *Unit head:* Rodney Bushway, Chair, 207-581-1626, Fax: 207-581-1636, E-mail: rbushway@maine.edu. *Application contact:* Scott G. Delcourt, Associate Dean of the Graduate School, 207-581-3291, Fax: 207-581-3232, E-mail: graduate@maine.edu. Website: http://foodsciencehumannutrition.umaine.edu/.

University of Manitoba, Faculty of Graduate Studies, Faculty of Agricultural and Food Sciences, Department of Food Science, Winnipeg, MB R3T 2N2, Canada. Offers food and nutritional sciences (PhD); food science (M Sc); foods and nutrition (M Sc). *Degree requirements:* For master's, thesis.

University of Maryland, College Park, Academic Affairs, College of Agriculture and Natural Resources, Department of Nutrition and Food Science, Program in Food Science, College Park, MD 20742. Offers MS, PhD. *Students:* 30 full-time (17 women), 1 (woman) part-time; includes 3 minority (1 Black or African American, non-Hispanic/Latino; 1 Asian, non-Hispanic/Latino; 1 Hispanic/Latino), 23 international. 58 applicants, 12% accepted, 6 enrolled. In 2012, 2 master's, 3 doctorates awarded. *Degree requirements:* For master's, comprehensive exam, research-based thesis or equivalent paper; for doctorate, comprehensive exam, thesis/dissertation. *Entrance requirements:* For master's, GRE General Test, minimum GPA of 3.0, professional experience, 3 letters of recommendation; for doctorate, GRE General Test, minimum GPA of 3.0. Additional exam requirements/recommendations for international students: Required—TOEFL. *Application deadline:* For fall admission, 12/15 for domestic and international students; for spring admission, 6/1 for domestic and international students. Applications are processed on a rolling basis. Application fee: $75. Electronic applications accepted. *Expenses:* Tuition, state resident: part-time $551 per credit. Tuition, nonresident: part-time $1188 per credit. Part-time tuition and fees vary according to program. *Financial support:* In 2012–13, 2 fellowships (averaging $10,800 per year), 11 research assistantships (averaging $15,907 per year), 14 teaching assistantships (averaging $15,864 per year) were awarded. Financial award applicants required to submit FAFSA. *Faculty research:* Food chemistry, engineering, microbiology, and processing technology; quality assurance; membrane separations, rheology and texture measurement. *Unit head:* Robert Jackson, Acting Chair, 301-405-0773, E-mail: bojack@umd.edu. *Application contact:* Dr. Charles A. Caramello, Dean of Graduate School, 301-405-0358, Fax: 301-314-9305, E-mail: ccaramel@umd.edu.

University of Maryland Eastern Shore, Graduate Programs, Department of Agriculture, Program in Food and Agricultural Sciences, Princess Anne, MD 21853-1299. Offers MS. *Degree requirements:* For master's, comprehensive exam, thesis or alternative, oral exams. *Entrance requirements:* For master's, GRE General Test, minimum GPA of 3.0. Additional exam requirements/recommendations for international students: Required—TOEFL (minimum score 80 iBT). Electronic applications accepted. *Faculty research:* Poultry and swine nutrition and management, soybean specialty products, farm management practices, agriculture technology.

University of Maryland Eastern Shore, Graduate Programs, Department of Agriculture, Program in Food Science and Technology, Princess Anne, MD 21853-1299. Offers PhD. *Degree requirements:* For doctorate, comprehensive exam, thesis/dissertation. *Entrance requirements:* For doctorate, minimum GPA of 3.0, strong background in food science and related fields, intended dissertation research. Additional exam requirements/recommendations for international students: Required—TOEFL (minimum score 80 iBT). Electronic applications accepted. *Faculty research:* Prevalence, growth, survival and control of listeria; microbial models of the effect of storage temperature.

University of Massachusetts Amherst, Graduate School, College of Natural Sciences, Department of Food Science, Amherst, MA 01003. Offers MS, PhD. Part-time programs available. *Faculty:* 17 full-time (5 women). *Students:* 46 full-time (31 women), 13 part-time (6 women); includes 8 minority (1 Black or African American, non-Hispanic/Latino; 5 Asian, non-Hispanic/Latino; 2 Hispanic/Latino), 38 international. Average age 26. 165 applicants, 24% accepted, 23 enrolled. In 2012, 7 master's, 1 doctorate awarded. Terminal master's awarded for partial completion of doctoral program. *Degree requirements:* For master's, thesis or alternative; for doctorate, comprehensive exam, thesis/dissertation. *Entrance requirements:* For master's and doctorate, GRE General Test. Additional exam requirements/recommendations for international students: Required—TOEFL (minimum score 550 paper-based; 80 iBT), IELTS (minimum score 6.5). *Application deadline:* For fall admission, 2/1 for domestic and international students; for spring admission, 10/1 for domestic and international students. Applications are processed on a rolling basis. Application fee: $50 ($65 for international students). Electronic applications accepted. *Expenses:* Tuition, state resident: full-time $1980; part-time $110 per credit. Tuition, nonresident: full-time $13,314; part-time $414 per credit. *Required fees:* $10,338; $3594 per semester. One-time fee: $357. *Financial support:* Fellowships with full and partial tuition reimbursements, research assistantships with full and partial tuition reimbursements, teaching assistantships with full and partial tuition reimbursements, career-related internships or fieldwork, Federal Work-Study, scholarships/grants, traineeships, health care benefits, tuition waivers (full and partial), and unspecified assistantships available. Support available to part-time students. Financial award application deadline: 2/1. *Unit head:* Dr. Ronald G.

Labbe, Graduate Program Director, 413-545-2276, Fax: 413-545-1262. *Application contact:* Lindsay DeSantis, Interim Supervisor of Admissions, 413-545-0721, Fax: 413-577-0010, E-mail: gradadm@grad.umass.edu. Website: http://www.umass.edu/foodsci/.

University of Minnesota, Twin Cities Campus, Graduate School, College of Food, Agricultural and Natural Resource Sciences, Program in Food Science, Minneapolis, MN 55455-0213. Offers MS, PhD. Part-time programs available. *Faculty:* 24 full-time. *Students:* 72 full-time (49 women); includes 4 minority (3 Asian, non-Hispanic/Latino; 1 Hispanic/Latino), 34 international. Average age 30. 459 applicants, 4% accepted, 20 enrolled. In 2012, 50 master's, 16 doctorates awarded. Terminal master's awarded for partial completion of doctoral program. *Degree requirements:* For master's, comprehensive exam, thesis; for doctorate, comprehensive exam, thesis/dissertation. *Entrance requirements:* For master's and doctorate, GRE General Test, previous course work in general chemistry, organic chemistry, calculus, physics, and biology. Additional exam requirements/recommendations for international students: Required—TOEFL (minimum score 550 paper-based; 79 iBT), IELTS (minimum score 6.5). *Application deadline:* For fall admission, 12/15 for domestic and international students; for spring admission, 10/15 for domestic and international students. Applications are processed on a rolling basis. Application fee: $75 ($95 for international students). Electronic applications accepted. *Financial support:* In 2012–13, fellowships with full tuition reimbursements (averaging $40,000 per year), research assistantships with full and partial tuition reimbursements (averaging $40,000 per year), teaching assistantships with full and partial tuition reimbursements (averaging $40,000 per year) were awarded; career-related internships or fieldwork, scholarships/grants, traineeships, health care benefits, and unspecified assistantships also available. Support available to part-time students. *Faculty research:* Food chemistry, food microbiology, food technology, grain science, dairy science, food safety. *Total annual research expenditures:* $5,849. *Unit head:* Dr. David E. Smith, Director of Graduate Studies, 612-624-3260, Fax: 612-625-5272, E-mail: desmith@umn.edu. *Application contact:* Nancy L. Toedt, Program Coordinator, 612-624-6753, Fax: 612-625-5272, E-mail: ntoedt@umn.edu. Website: http://fscn.cfans.umn.edu/education/foodsciencegraduate/index.htm.

University of Missouri, Graduate School, College of Agriculture, Food and Natural Resources, Department of Food Science, Columbia, MO 65211. Offers food science (MS, PhD); foods and food systems management (MS); human nutrition (MS). *Faculty:* 12 full-time (4 women), 2 part-time/adjunct (0 women). *Students:* 35 full-time (26 women), 12 part-time (7 women), 36 international. Average age 27. 87 applicants, 16% accepted, 11 enrolled. In 2012, 7 master's awarded. Terminal master's awarded for partial completion of doctoral program. *Degree requirements:* For doctorate, comprehensive exam, thesis/dissertation. *Entrance requirements:* For master's, GRE General Test (minimum score: Verbal and Quantitative 1000 with neither section below 400, Analytical 3.5), minimum GPA of 3.0; BS in food science from accredited university; for doctorate, GRE General Test (minimum score: Verbal and Quantitative 1000 with neither section below 400, Analytical 3.5), minimum GPA of 3.0; BS and MS in food science from accredited university. Additional exam requirements/recommendations for international students: Required—TOEFL (minimum score 550 paper-based; 79 iBT). *Application deadline:* For fall admission, 4/1 priority date for domestic students; for winter admission, 10/1 priority date for domestic students. Applications are processed on a rolling basis. Application fee: $55 ($75 for international students). Electronic applications accepted. *Expenses:* Tuition, state resident: full-time $6057. Tuition, nonresident: full-time $15,683. *Required fees:* $1000. *Financial support:* Fellowships, research assistantships with tuition reimbursements, teaching assistantships with tuition reimbursements, institutionally sponsored loans, scholarships/grants, health care benefits, and unspecified assistantships available. Support available to part-time students. *Faculty research:* Food chemistry, food analysis, food microbiology, food engineering and process control, functional foods, meat science and processing technology. *Unit head:* Dr. Jinglu Tan, Department Chair, 573-882-2369, E-mail: tanj@missouri.edu. Website: http://foodscience.missouri.edu/graduate/.

University of Nebraska–Lincoln, Graduate College, College of Agricultural Sciences and Natural Resources, Department of Food Science and Technology, Lincoln, NE 68588. Offers MS, PhD. *Degree requirements:* For master's, thesis optional; for doctorate, comprehensive exam, thesis/dissertation. *Entrance requirements:* For master's and doctorate, GRE General Test. Additional exam requirements/recommendations for international students: Required—TOEFL (minimum score 505 paper-based). Electronic applications accepted. *Faculty research:* Food chemistry, microbiology, processing, engineering, and biotechnology.

University of Puerto Rico, Mayagüez Campus, Graduate Studies, College of Agricultural Sciences, Department of Food Science and Technology, Mayagüez, PR 00681-9000. Offers MS. Part-time programs available. *Faculty:* 1 (woman) full-time. *Students:* 42 full-time (27 women), 2 part-time (both women); includes 28 minority (all Hispanic/Latino), 13 international. 29 applicants, 83% accepted, 15 enrolled. In 2012, 3 master's awarded. *Degree requirements:* For master's, comprehensive exam, thesis. *Entrance requirements:* For master's, minimum GPA of 2.5. *Application deadline:* For fall admission, 2/15 for domestic and international students; for spring admission, 9/15 for domestic and international students. Applications are processed on a rolling basis. Application fee: $25. Tuition and fees vary according to course level and course load. *Financial support:* Federal Work-Study and institutionally sponsored loans available. *Faculty research:* Food microbiology, food science, seafood technology, food engineering and packaging, fermentation. *Total annual research expenditures:* $128,100. *Unit head:* Dr. Edna Negron, Director, 787-265-5410, Fax: 787-265-5410, E-mail: edna.negron1@upr.edu. *Application contact:* Gloria Aguilar, Administrative Assistant, 787-832-4040 Ext. 3078, Fax: 787-265-5410, E-mail: gloriag.aguilar@upr.edu. Website: http://www.uprm.edu/agricultura/cita/.

University of Rhode Island, Graduate School, College of the Environment and Life Sciences, Department of Nutrition and Food Sciences, Kingston, RI 02881. Offers food science (MS, PhD); nutrition (MS, PhD). Part-time programs available. *Faculty:* 7 full-time (5 women), 1 (woman) part-time/adjunct. *Students:* 11 full-time (9 women), 12 part-time (8 women); includes 2 minority (1 Asian, non-Hispanic/Latino; 1 Hispanic/Latino). In 2012, 13 master's awarded. *Degree requirements:* For master's, comprehensive exam (for some programs), thesis optional; for doctorate, thesis/dissertation. *Entrance requirements:* For master's and doctorate, GRE, 2 letters of recommendation. Additional exam requirements/recommendations for international students: Required—TOEFL (minimum score 550 paper-based). *Application deadline:* For fall admission, 7/15 for domestic students, 2/1 for international students; for spring admission, 11/15 for domestic students, 7/15 for international students. Application fee: $65. Electronic applications accepted. *Expenses:* Tuition, state resident: full-time $11,532; part-time $641 per credit. Tuition, nonresident: full-time $23,606; part-time $1311 per credit. *Required fees:* $1388; $36 per credit. $35 per semester. One-time fee: $130. *Financial support:* In 2012–13, 5 teaching assistantships with full and partial tuition reimbursements (averaging $13,901 per year) were awarded; research assistantships also available. Financial award application deadline: 7/15; financial award applicants required to submit FAFSA. *Faculty research:* Food safety and quality, marine resource utilization, nutrition in underserved populations, eating behavior, lipid metabolism. *Unit head:* Dr. Geoffrey Greene, Chair, 401-874-4028, Fax: 401-874-5974, E-mail: gwg@uri.edu. Website: http://cels.uri.edu/nfs/.

University of Saskatchewan, College of Graduate Studies and Research, College of Agriculture, Department of Applied Microbiology and Food Science, Saskatoon, SK S7N 5A2, Canada. Offers M Ag, M Sc, PhD. *Degree requirements:* For master's, thesis; for doctorate, comprehensive exam (for some programs), thesis/dissertation. *Entrance requirements:* Additional exam requirements/recommendations for international students: Required—TOEFL (minimum score 80 iBT); Recommended—IELTS (minimum score 6.5).

University of Southern California, Graduate School, School of Pharmacy, Regulatory Science Programs, Los Angeles, CA 90089. Offers clinical research design and management (Graduate Certificate); food safety (Graduate Certificate); patient and product safety (Graduate Certificate); preclinical drug development (Graduate Certificate); regulatory and clinical affairs (Graduate Certificate); regulatory science (MS, DRSc). Part-time and evening/weekend programs available. Postbaccalaureate distance learning degree programs offered (minimal on-campus study). Terminal master's awarded for partial completion of doctoral program. *Degree requirements:* For master's, thesis optional; for doctorate, comprehensive exam, thesis/dissertation. *Entrance requirements:* For master's, GRE. Additional exam requirements/recommendations for international students: Required—TOEFL (minimum score 603 paper-based; 100 iBT). Electronic applications accepted.

The University of Tennessee, Graduate School, College of Agricultural Sciences and Natural Resources, Department of Food Science and Technology, Knoxville, TN 37996. Offers food science and technology (MS, PhD), including food chemistry (PhD), food microbiology (PhD), food processing (PhD), sensory evaluation of foods (PhD). Part-time programs available. *Degree requirements:* For master's, thesis or alternative; for doctorate, thesis/dissertation. *Entrance requirements:* For master's and doctorate, GRE General Test, minimum GPA of 2.7. Additional exam requirements/recommendations for international students: Required—TOEFL. Electronic applications accepted. *Expenses:* Tuition, state resident: full-time $9000; part-time $501 per credit hour. Tuition, nonresident: full-time $27,188; part-time $1512 per credit hour. *Required fees:* $1280; $62 per credit hour. Tuition and fees vary according to program.

The University of Tennessee at Martin, Graduate Programs, College of Agriculture and Applied Sciences, Department of Family and Consumer Sciences, Martin, TN 38238-1000. Offers dietetics (MSFCS); general family and consumer sciences (MSFCS). Part-time programs available. Postbaccalaureate distance learning degree programs offered (minimal on-campus study). *Faculty:* 9. *Students:* 34 (32 women); includes 10 minority (8 Black or African American, non-Hispanic/Latino; 1 Hispanic/Latino; 1 Two or more races, non-Hispanic/Latino), 1 international. 30 applicants, 73% accepted, 15 enrolled. In 2012, 10 master's awarded. *Degree requirements:* For master's, comprehensive exam, thesis optional. *Entrance requirements:* For master's, GRE General Test, minimum GPA of 2.5. Additional exam requirements/recommendations for international students: Required—TOEFL (minimum score 525 paper-based; 71 iBT). *Application deadline:* For fall admission, 8/10 priority date for domestic students, 8/10 for international students; for spring admission, 12/15 priority date for domestic students, 12/15 for international students. Applications are processed on a rolling basis. Application fee: $30 ($130 for international students). Electronic applications accepted. *Expenses:* Tuition, state resident: full-time $8194; part-time $457 per credit hour. Tuition, nonresident: full-time $21,348; part-time $1188 per credit hour. *Financial support:* In 2012–13, 1 student received support, including 1 teaching assistantship with full tuition reimbursement available (averaging $7,540 per year); scholarships/grants and unspecified assistantships also available. Support available to part-time students. Financial award application deadline: 2/15; financial award applicants required to submit FAFSA.

Food Science and Technology

Faculty research: Children with developmental disabilities, regional food product development and marketing, parent education. *Unit head:* Dr. Lisa LeBleu, Coordinator, 731-881-7116, Fax: 731-881-7106, E-mail: llebleu@utm.edu. *Application contact:* Jolene L. Cunningham, Student Services Specialist, 731-881-7012, Fax: 731-881-7499, E-mail: jcunningham@utm.edu. Website: http://www.utm.edu/departments/caas/fcs/index.php.

University of Vermont, Graduate College, College of Agriculture and Life Sciences, Program in Animal, Nutrition and Food Sciences, Burlington, VT 05405. Offers PhD. *Students:* 21 (9 women); includes 2 minority (both Asian, non-Hispanic/Latino), 11 international. 13 applicants, 23% accepted, 3 enrolled. In 2012, 2 doctorates awarded. *Degree requirements:* For doctorate, one foreign language, thesis/dissertation. *Entrance requirements:* For doctorate, GRE General Test. Additional exam requirements/recommendations for international students: Required—TOEFL (minimum score 550 paper-based; 80 iBT). *Application deadline:* For fall admission, 4/1 priority date for domestic students, 4/1 for international students. Applications are processed on a rolling basis. Application fee: $40. Electronic applications accepted. *Expenses: Tuition,* area resident: Part-time $572 per credit. Tuition, nonresident: part-time $1444 per credit. *Financial support:* Application deadline: 3/1. *Unit head:* Dr. Andre-Denis Wright, Chairperson, 802-656-2070. *Application contact:* Dr. David Kerr, Coordinator, 802-656-2070.

University of Wisconsin–Madison, Graduate School, College of Agricultural and Life Sciences, Department of Food Science, Madison, WI 53706-1380. Offers MS, PhD. Part-time programs available. *Degree requirements:* For master's, thesis; for doctorate, thesis/dissertation. *Entrance requirements:* For master's and doctorate, GRE General Test. Additional exam requirements/recommendations for international students: Required—TOEFL. Electronic applications accepted. *Expenses:* Tuition, state resident: full-time $10,728; part-time $743 per credit. Tuition, nonresident: full-time $24,054; part-time $1575 per credit. *Required fees:* $1111; $72 per credit. *Faculty research:* Food chemistry, food engineering, food microbiology, food processing.

University of Wisconsin–Stout, Graduate School, College of Human Development, Program in Food and Nutritional Sciences, Menomonie, WI 54751. Offers MS. Part-time programs available. *Degree requirements:* For master's, thesis. *Entrance requirements:* For master's, minimum GPA of 3.0. Additional exam requirements/recommendations for international students: Required—TOEFL (minimum score 500 paper-based; 61 iBT). Electronic applications accepted. *Faculty research:* Disease states and nutrition, childhood obesity, nutraceuticals, food safety, nanotechnology.

University of Wyoming, College of Agriculture and Natural Resources, Department of Animal Sciences, Program in Food Science and Human Nutrition, Laramie, WY 82070. Offers MS. *Degree requirements:* For master's, thesis. *Entrance requirements:* For master's, GRE General Test, minimum GPA of 3.0. Additional exam requirements/recommendations for international students: Required—TOEFL (minimum score 525 paper-based). Electronic applications accepted. *Faculty research:* Protein and lipid metabolism, food microbiology, food safety, meat science.

Utah State University, School of Graduate Studies, College of Agriculture, Department of Nutrition, Dietetics, and Food Sciences, Logan, UT 84322. Offers dietetic administration (MDA); nutrition and food sciences (MS, PhD). Postbaccalaureate distance learning degree programs offered. *Degree requirements:* For master's, thesis; for doctorate, comprehensive exam, thesis/dissertation, teaching experience. *Entrance requirements:* For master's, GRE General Test, minimum GPA of 3.0, course work in chemistry, biochemistry, physics, math, bacteriology, physiology; for doctorate, GRE General Test, minimum GPA of 3.2, course work in chemistry, MS or manuscript in referred journal. Additional exam requirements/recommendations for international students: Required—TOEFL (minimum score 550 paper-based). Electronic applications accepted. *Faculty research:* Mineral balance, meat microbiology and nitrate interactions, milk ultrafiltration, lactic culture, milk coagulation.

Washington State University, Graduate School, College of Agricultural, Human, and Natural Resource Sciences, School of Food Science, Pullman, WA 99164-6376. Offers MS, PhD, *Faculty:* 19 full-time (7 women), 2 part-time/adjunct (both women). *Students:* 29 full-time (12 women), 7 part-time (4 women); includes 1 minority (Asian, non-Hispanic/Latino), 21 international. Average age 28. 93 applicants, 25% accepted, 13 enrolled. In 2012, 12 master's, 3 doctorates awarded. *Degree requirements:* For master's, comprehensive exam, thesis, oral exam, written exam; for doctorate, comprehensive exam, thesis/dissertation, oral exam, written exam. *Entrance requirements:* For master's, GRE General Test, official transcripts; letter of interest; minimum GPA of 3.0; resume; 3 letters of recommendation, 1 from major advisor; for doctorate, GRE General Test, MS demonstrating ability to conduct and report research; minimum GPA of 3.0; resume; 3 letters of recommendation, 1 from major advisor. Additional exam

requirements/recommendations for international students: Required—TOEFL (minimum score 550 paper-based; 80 iBT). *Application deadline:* For fall admission, 1/10 priority date for domestic students, 1/10 for international students; for spring admission, 7/1 priority date for domestic students, 7/1 for international students. Applications are processed on a rolling basis. Application fee: $75. Electronic applications accepted. *Financial support:* In 2012–13, 24 students received support, including fellowships with tuition reimbursements available (averaging $4,250 per year), 5 research assistantships with full tuition reimbursements available (averaging $19,000 per year), 5 teaching assistantships with full tuition reimbursements available (averaging $19,000 per year); career-related internships or fieldwork, Federal Work-Study, institutionally sponsored loans, scholarships/grants, tuition waivers, and unspecified assistantships also available. Support available to part-time students. Financial award application deadline: 1/10; financial award applicants required to submit CSS PROFILE or FAFSA. *Faculty research:* Improving food safety, developing healthy and sustainable foods, fundamental approaches to enhance food quality. *Total annual research expenditures:* $1.8 million. *Unit head:* Dr. Denise Smith, Director, 509-335-2101, Fax: 509-335-4815, E-mail: denise.smith@wsu.edu. *Application contact:* Graduate School Admissions, 800-GRADWSU, Fax: 509-335-1949, E-mail: gradsch@wsu.edu. Website: http://sfs.wsu.edu/.

Wayne State University, College of Liberal Arts and Sciences, Department of Nutrition and Food Science, Detroit, MI 48202. Offers MA, MS, PhD. *Students:* 53 full-time (42 women), 12 part-time (all women); includes 11 minority (3 Black or African American, non-Hispanic/Latino; 7 Asian, non-Hispanic/Latino; 1 Two or more races, non-Hispanic/Latino), 22 international. Average age 29. 93 applicants, 41% accepted, 20 enrolled. In 2012, 12 master's, 2 doctorates awarded. *Degree requirements:* For master's, thesis (for some programs), essay (for MA); for doctorate, thesis/dissertation. *Entrance requirements:* For master's, GRE General Test, minimum GPA of 3.0, undergraduate degree with major in science, courses in human nutrition and metabolism, food chemistry, introductory microbiology, anatomy and physiology, organic chemistry; for doctorate, GRE General Test, MS (in exceptional cases, an outstanding undergraduate record), two letters of recommendation; personal statement. Additional exam requirements/recommendations for international students: Required—TOEFL (minimum score 550 paper-based; 79 iBT); Recommended—TWE (minimum score 5.5). *Application deadline:* For fall admission, 6/1 priority date for domestic students, 5/1 for international students; for winter admission, 10/1 for domestic students, 9/1 for international students; for spring admission, 2/1 for domestic students, 1/1 for international students. Applications are processed on a rolling basis. Application fee: $50. Electronic applications accepted. *Expenses:* Tuition, state resident: full-time $12,788; part-time $532.85 per credit hour. Tuition, nonresident: full-time $28,243; part-time $1176.80 per credit hour. *Required fees:* $1367.30; $39.75 per credit hour. $206.65 per semester. Tuition and fees vary according to course load and program. *Financial support:* In 2012–13, 23 students received support, including 1 fellowship with tuition reimbursement available (averaging $17,000 per year), 2 research assistantships with tuition reimbursements available (averaging $16,352 per year), 8 teaching assistantships with tuition reimbursements available (averaging $17,391 per year); career-related internships or fieldwork, Federal Work-Study, scholarships/grants, health care benefits, and unspecified assistantships also available. Financial award application deadline: 3/1. *Faculty research:* Nutrition, cancer and gene expression, food microbiology and food safety, lipids, lipoprotein and cholesterol metabolism, obesity and diabetes, metabolomics. *Total annual research expenditures:* $329,056. *Unit head:* Dr. Kai-Lin Catherine Jen, Chair, 313-577-2500, E-mail: ac1578@wayne.edu. *Application contact:* Dr. Pramod Khosla, Graduate Director, E-mail: nfsgradprogram@wayne.edu. Website: http://clasweb.clas.wayne.edu/nfs.

West Virginia University, Davis College of Agriculture, Forestry and Consumer Sciences, Division of Animal and Nutritional Sciences, Program in Animal and Nutritional Sciences, Morgantown, WV 26506. Offers breeding (MS); food sciences (MS); nutrition (MS); physiology (MS); production management (MS); reproduction (MS). Part-time programs available. *Degree requirements:* For master's, thesis, oral and written exams. *Entrance requirements:* For master's, GRE, minimum GPA of 2.5. Additional exam requirements/recommendations for international students: Required—TOEFL. *Faculty research:* Animal nutrition, reproductive physiology, food science.

West Virginia University, Davis College of Agriculture, Forestry and Consumer Sciences, Division of Plant and Soil Sciences, Program in Agricultural Sciences, Morgantown, WV 26506. Offers animal and food sciences (PhD); plant and soil sciences (PhD). *Degree requirements:* For doctorate, thesis/dissertation, oral and written exams. *Entrance requirements:* Additional exam requirements/recommendations for international students: Required—TOEFL. *Faculty research:* Ruminant nutrition, metabolism, forage utilization, physiology, reproduction.

418 www.petersonsbooks.com

Peterson's Graduate Programs in the Physical Sciences, Mathematics, Agricultural Sciences, the Environment & Natural Resources 2014

Horticulture

Auburn University, Graduate School, College of Agriculture, Department of Horticulture, Auburn University, AL 36849. Offers M Ag, MS, PhD. Part-time programs available. *Faculty:* 19 full-time (4 women). *Students:* 9 full-time (3 women), 20 part-time (6 women); includes 3 minority (1 Black or African American, non-Hispanic/Latino; 1 Asian, non-Hispanic/Latino; 1 Hispanic/Latino), 5 international. Average age 29. 17 applicants, 47% accepted, 4 enrolled. In 2012, 6 master's, 3 doctorates awarded. *Degree requirements:* For master's, thesis (for some programs); for doctorate, thesis/dissertation. *Entrance requirements:* For master's and doctorate, GRE General Test. *Application deadline:* For fall admission, 7/7 for domestic students; for spring admission, 11/24 for domestic students. Applications are processed on a rolling basis. Application fee: $50 ($60 for international students). Electronic applications accepted. *Expenses:* Tuition, state resident: full-time $7866; part-time $437 per credit. Tuition, nonresident: full-time $23,598; part-time $1311 per credit. *Required fees:* $787 per semester. Tuition and fees vary according to degree level and program. *Financial support:* Research assistantships, teaching assistantships, and Federal Work-Study available. Support available to part-time students. Financial award application deadline: 3/15; financial award applicants required to submit FAFSA. *Faculty research:* Environmental regulators, water quality, weed control, growth regulators, plasticulture. *Unit head:* Dr. Jeffrey L. Sibley, Head, 334-844-3132. *Application contact:* Dr. George Flowers, Dean of the Graduate School, 334-844-2125. Website: http://www.ag.auburn.edu/dept/hf/index.html.

Colorado State University, Graduate School, College of Agricultural Sciences, Department of Horticulture and Landscape Architecture, Fort Collins, CO 80523-1173. Offers horticulture (MS, PhD); landscape architecture (MLA). Part-time programs available. *Faculty:* 26 full-time (6 women). *Students:* 31 full-time (19 women), 17 part-time (9 women); includes 5 minority (1 American Indian or Alaska Native, non-Hispanic/Latino; 2 Hispanic/Latino; 2 Two or more races, non-Hispanic/Latino), 10 international. Average age 32. 40 applicants, 75% accepted, 12 enrolled. In 2012, 3 master's awarded. *Degree requirements:* For master's, thesis (for some programs); for doctorate, comprehensive exam, thesis/dissertation. *Entrance requirements:* For master's, GRE General Test (minimum score in upper 50th percentile, 1100 verbal and quantitative), minimum GPA of 3.0, letters of reference, related bachelor's degree or experience; for doctorate, GRE General Test (upper 50th percentile and combined minimum score of 1100 for the Verbal and Quantitative sections), minimum GPA of 3.0, letters of reference, statement of purpose, related bachelor's degree or experience. Additional exam requirements/recommendations for international students: Required—TOEFL (minimum score 550 paper-based; 80 iBT). *Application deadline:* For fall admission, 1/15 for domestic and international students; for spring admission, 9/1 for domestic and international students. Applications are processed on a rolling basis. Application fee: $50. Electronic applications accepted. *Expenses:* Tuition, state resident: full-time $8811; part-time $490 per credit. Tuition, nonresident: full-time $21,600; part-time $1200 per credit. *Required fees:* $1819; $61 per credit. *Financial support:* In 2012–13, 19 students received support, including 4 fellowships with full tuition reimbursements available (averaging $31,685 per year), 9 research assistantships with partial tuition reimbursements available (averaging $14,556 per year), 6 teaching assistantships with partial tuition reimbursements available (averaging $9,540 per year); scholarships/grants and unspecified assistantships also available. Financial award applicants required to submit FAFSA. *Faculty research:* Antioxidants in food crops, environmental physiology, water conservation, tissue culture, rhizosphere biology, cancer prevention through dietary intervention. *Total annual research expenditures:* $1.6 million. *Unit head:* Dr. Stephen J. Wallner, Head, 970-491-7018, Fax: 970-491-7745, E-mail: stephen.wallner@colostate.edu. *Application contact:* Kathi Nietfeld, Coordinator, 970-491-7018, Fax: 970-491-7745, E-mail: kathi.nietfeld@colostate.edu. Website: http://hla.agsci.colostate.edu/.

Cornell University, Graduate School, Graduate Fields of Agriculture and Life Sciences, Field of Horticulture, Ithaca, NY 14853-0001. Offers controlled environment agriculture (MPS, PhD); controlled environment horticulture (MS); greenhouse crops (MPS); horticultural business management (MPS, MS, PhD); horticultural physiology (MPS, MS, PhD); landscape horticulture (MPS, MS, PhD); nursery crops (MPS); nutrition of horticultural crops (MPS, MS, PhD); plant propagation (MPS, MS, PhD); public garden management (MPS); restoration ecology (MPS); taxonomy of ornamental plants (MPS); turfgrass science (MPS); urban horticulture (MPS, MS, PhD); weed science (MPS). *Faculty:* 50 full-time (13 women). *Students:* 36 full-time (18 women); includes 3 minority (2 Hispanic/Latino; 1 Two or more races, non-Hispanic/Latino), 11 international. Average age 28. 63 applicants, 17% accepted, 10 enrolled. In 2012, 5 master's, 8 doctorates awarded. *Degree requirements:* For master's, thesis (MS); for doctorate, comprehensive exam, thesis/dissertation. *Entrance requirements:* For master's and doctorate, GRE General Test, 3 letters of recommendation. Additional exam requirements/recommendations for international students: Required—TOEFL (minimum score 550 paper-based; 77 iBT). *Application deadline:* For fall admission, 1/15 for domestic students; for spring admission, 8/15 for domestic students. Application fee: $95. Electronic applications accepted. *Financial support:* In 2012–13, 28 students received support, including 6 fellowships with full tuition reimbursements available, 13 research assistantships with full tuition reimbursements available, 9 teaching assistantships with full tuition reimbursements available; institutionally sponsored loans, scholarships/grants, health care benefits, tuition waivers (full and partial), and unspecified assistantships also available. Financial award applicants required to submit FAFSA. *Faculty research:* Plant selection/plant materials, greenhouse management, greenhouse crop production, urban landscape management, turfgrass management. *Unit head:* Director of Graduate Studies, 607-255-4568, Fax: 607-255-0599. *Application contact:* Graduate Field Assistant, 607-255-4568, Fax: 607-255-0599, E-mail: hortgrad@cornell.edu. Website: http://www.gradschool.cornell.edu/fields.php?id-XX&a-2.

Dalhousie University, Faculty of Agriculture, Halifax, NS B3H 4R2, Canada. Offers agriculture (M Sc), including air quality, animal behavior, animal molecular genetics, animal nutrition, animal technology, aquaculture, botany, crop management, crop physiology, ecology, environmental microbiology, food science, horticulture, nutrient management, pest management, physiology, plant biotechnology, plant pathology, soil chemistry, soil fertility, waste management and composting, water quality. Part-time programs available. *Degree requirements:* For master's, thesis, ATC Exam Teaching Assistantship. *Entrance requirements:* For master's, honors B Sc, minimum GPA of 3.0. Additional exam requirements/recommendations for international students: Required—TOEFL (minimum score 580 paper-based; 92 iBT), IELTS, Michigan English Language Assessment Battery, CanTEST, CAEL. *Faculty research:* Bio-product development, organic agriculture, nutrient management, air and water quality, agricultural biotechnology.

Iowa State University of Science and Technology, Department of Horticulture, Ames, IA 50011. Offers MS, PhD. *Degree requirements:* For master's, thesis; for doctorate, thesis/dissertation. *Entrance requirements:* For master's and doctorate, GRE General Test. Additional exam requirements/recommendations for international students: Required—TOEFL (minimum score 550 paper-based; 79 iBT), IELTS (minimum score 6.5). *Application deadline:* Applications are processed on a rolling basis. Application fee: $60 ($90 for international students). Electronic applications accepted. *Application contact:* Kim Gaul, Director of Graduate Education, 515-294-3718, Fax: 515-294-0730, E-mail: kimgaul@iastate.edu. Website: http://www.hort.iastate.edu/programs/graduate.html.

Kansas State University, Graduate School, College of Agriculture, Department of Horticulture, Forestry and Recreation Resources, Manhattan, KS 66506. Offers horticulture (MS, PhD). *Faculty:* 20 full-time (6 women). *Students:* 25 full-time (11 women), 6 part-time (4 women), 6 international. Average age 40. 23 applicants, 43% accepted, 8 enrolled. In 2012, 5 master's, 2 doctorates awarded. *Degree requirements:* For master's, thesis, oral exam; for doctorate, thesis/dissertation, preliminary exams. *Entrance requirements:* For master's and doctorate, GRE General Test. Additional exam requirements/recommendations for international students: Required—TOEFL (minimum score 550 paper-based; 79 iBT); Recommended—IELTS (minimum score 6.5). *Application deadline:* For fall admission, 2/1 priority date for domestic students, 2/1 for international students; for spring admission, 8/1 priority date for domestic students, 8/1 for international students. Applications are processed on a rolling basis. Application fee: $50 ($75 for international students). Electronic applications accepted. *Financial support:* In 2012–13, 22 research assistantships (averaging $18,444 per year), 7 teaching assistantships (averaging $20,000 per year) were awarded; career-related internships or fieldwork, institutionally sponsored loans, and scholarships/grants also available. Support available to part-time students. Financial award application deadline: 3/1; financial award applicants required to submit FAFSA. *Faculty research:* Environmental stress, phytochemicals and health, crop nutrition, sustainable horticulture, turfgrass science. *Total annual research expenditures:* $810,475. *Unit head:* Stuart Warren, Head, 785-532-6170, Fax: 785-532-6949, E-mail: slwarren@ksu.edu. Website: http://www.hfrr.k-state.edu/DesktopDefault.aspx.

Louisiana State University and Agricultural and Mechanical College, Graduate School, College of Agriculture, School of Plant, Environmental and Soil Sciences, Department of Horticulture, Baton Rouge, LA 70803. Offers MS, PhD. Part-time programs available. *Faculty:* 10 full-time (1 woman). *Students:* 4 full-time (1 woman), 3 part-time (2 women); includes 1 minority (Black or African American, non-Hispanic/Latino), 2 international. Average age 32. 4 applicants, 25% accepted, 0 enrolled. In 2012, 1 master's, 1 doctorate awarded. Terminal master's awarded for partial completion of doctoral program. *Degree requirements:* For master's, thesis (for some programs); for doctorate, thesis/dissertation. *Entrance requirements:* For master's and doctorate, GRE General Test, minimum GPA of 3.0. Additional exam requirements/recommendations for international students: Required—TOEFL (minimum score 550 paper-based; 79 iBT) or IELTS (minimum score 6.5). *Application deadline:* For fall admission, 7/1 priority date for domestic students, 5/15 for international students; for spring admission, 10/15 for international students. Applications are processed on a rolling basis. Application fee: $50 ($70 for international students). Electronic applications accepted. *Financial support:* In 2012–13, 5 students received support, including 3 research assistantships with partial tuition reimbursements available (averaging $19,333 per year); fellowships, Federal Work-Study, health care benefits, tuition waivers (full and partial), and unspecified assistantships also available. Financial award application deadline: 4/15; financial award applicants required to submit FAFSA. *Faculty research:* Plant breeding, stress physiology, postharvest physiology, biotechnology. *Unit head:* Dr. Don LaBonte, Director, 225-578-1043, Fax: 225-578-1403, E-mail: dlabont@lsu.edu. *Application contact:* Dr. David Weindorf, Graduate Coordinator, 225-578-0396, Fax: 225-578-1403, E-mail: dweindorf@agcenter.lsu.edu. Website: http://www.lsuagcenter.com/en/our_offices/departments/SPESS/Horticulture/.

Michigan State University, The Graduate School, College of Agriculture and Natural Resources, Department of Horticulture, East Lansing, MI 48824. Offers horticulture (MS, PhD); plant breeding, genetics and biotechnology-horticulture (MS, PhD). *Entrance requirements:* Additional exam requirements/recommendations for international students: Required—TOEFL. Electronic applications accepted.

Mississippi State University, College of Agriculture and Life Sciences, Department of Plant and Soil Sciences, Mississippi State, MS 39762. Offers agriculture (MS, PhD), including agronomy, horticulture, weed science. *Faculty:* 26 full-time (1 woman), 1 part-time/adjunct (0 women). *Students:* 49 full-time (18 women), 22 part-time (7 women); includes 5 minority (2 Black or African American, non-Hispanic/Latino; 2 American Indian or Alaska Native, non-Hispanic/Latino; 1 Asian, non-Hispanic/Latino), 16 international. Average age 31. 49 applicants, 35% accepted, 16 enrolled. In 2012, 6 master's, 4 doctorates awarded. *Degree requirements:* For master's, comprehensive exam, thesis, oral and/or written exams; for doctorate, comprehensive exam, thesis/dissertation, minimum 20 semester hours of research for dissertation. *Entrance requirements:* For master's, GRE (weed science), minimum GPA of 2.75 (agronomy/horticulture), 3.0 (weed science); for doctorate, GRE (weed science), minimum GPA of 3.0 (agronomy/horticulture), 3.25 (weed science). Additional exam requirements/recommendations for international students: Required—TOEFL (minimum score 500 paper-based; 61 iBT), TOEFL (minimum score 550 paper-based, 79 iBT) or IELTS (minimum score 6.5) for weed science; Recommended—IELTS (minimum score 5.5). *Application deadline:* For fall admission, 7/1 for domestic students, 5/1 for international students; for spring admission, 10/1 for domestic students, 9/1 for international students. Applications are processed on a rolling basis. Application fee: $60. Electronic applications accepted. *Financial support:* In 2012–13, 35 research assistantships (averaging $14,968 per year), 3 teaching assistantships (averaging $14,315 per year) were awarded; Federal Work-Study, institutionally sponsored loans, scholarships/grants, and unspecified assistantships also available. Financial award application deadline: 4/1; financial award applicants required to submit FAFSA. *Unit head:* Dr. J. Mike Phillips, Professor and Head, 662-325-2311, Fax: 662-325-8742, E-mail: jmp657@msstate.edu. *Application contact:* Dr. William Kingery, Graduate Coordinator, 662-325-2748, Fax: 662-325-8742, E-mail: wkingery@pss.msstate.edu. Website: http://www.pss.msstate.edu/.

New Mexico State University, Graduate School, College of Agricultural, Consumer and Environmental Sciences, Department of Plant and Environmental Sciences, Las Cruces, NM 88003-8001. Offers horticulture (MS); plant and environmental sciences (MS, PhD). Part-time programs available. *Faculty:* 19 full-time (3 women). *Students:* 41 full-time (18 women), 15 part-time (5 women); includes 6 minority (3 American Indian or Alaska Native, non-Hispanic/Latino; 3 Hispanic/Latino), 19 international. Average age 32. 19 applicants, 32% accepted, 5 enrolled. In 2012, 6 master's, 5 doctorates awarded. Terminal master's awarded for partial completion of doctoral program. *Degree requirements:* For master's, thesis; for doctorate, one foreign language, comprehensive exam, thesis/dissertation, qualifying exam, 2 seminars. *Entrance requirements:* For master's, GRE, minimum GPA of 3.0, 3 letters of reference, letter of purpose or intent; for doctorate, GRE, minimum GPA of 3.3; 3 letters of reference, letter of purpose or intent. Additional exam requirements/recommendations for international students: Required—TOEFL (minimum score 550 paper-based; 79 iBT), IELTS (minimum score 6.5). *Application deadline:* Applications are processed on a rolling basis. Application fee: $40 ($50 for international students). Electronic applications accepted. *Expenses:* Tuition, state resident: full-time $5239; part-time $218 per credit. Tuition, nonresident: full-time $18,266; part-time $761 per credit. *Required fees:* $1274; $53 per credit. *Financial support:* In 2012–13, 39 students received support, including 1 fellowship (averaging $3,930 per year), 26 research assistantships (averaging $21,062 per year), 9 teaching assistantships (averaging $13,700 per year); career-related internships or fieldwork, Federal Work-Study, scholarships/grants, health care benefits, and unspecified assistantships also available. Support available to part-time students. Financial award application deadline: 3/1. *Faculty research:* Plant breeding and genetics, molecular biology, plant physiology, soil science and environmental remediation, urban horticulture and turfgrass management. *Total annual research expenditures:* $6.2 million. *Unit head:* Dr. Richard Pratt, Head, 575-646-3406, Fax: 575-646-6041, E-mail: ricpratt@nmsu.edu. *Application contact:* Esther Ramirez, Information Contact, 575-646-3406, Fax: 575-646-6041, E-mail: esramire@nmsu.edu. Website: http://aces.nmsu.edu/pes.

North Carolina State University, Graduate School, College of Agriculture and Life Sciences, Department of Horticultural Science, Raleigh, NC 27695. Offers MS, PhD, Certificate. Postbaccalaureate distance learning degree programs offered. Terminal master's awarded for partial completion of doctoral program. *Degree requirements:* For master's, thesis (for some programs); for doctorate, thesis/dissertation. *Entrance requirements:* For master's and doctorate, GRE General Test, bachelor's degree in agriculture or biology, minimum GPA of 3.0. Electronic applications accepted. *Faculty research:* Plant physiology, breeding and genetics, tissue culture, herbicide physiology, propagation.

The Ohio State University, Graduate School, College of Food, Agricultural, and Environmental Sciences, Department of Horticulture and Crop Science, Columbus, OH 43210. Offers MS, PhD. *Faculty:* 38. *Students:* 46 full-time (25 women), 16 part-time (7 women); includes 1 minority (American Indian or Alaska Native, non-Hispanic/Latino), 26 international. Average age 29. In 2012, 7 master's, 9 doctorates awarded. *Degree requirements:* For master's, thesis optional; for doctorate, thesis/dissertation. *Entrance requirements:* For master's and doctorate, GRE General Test. Additional exam requirements/recommendations for international students: Required—TOEFL (minimum score 550 paper-based; 79 iBT), Michigan English Language Assessment Battery (minimum score 82); Recommended—IELTS (minimum score 7). *Application deadline:* For fall admission, 12/14 priority date for domestic students, 11/30 for international students; for winter admission, 12/1 for domestic students, 11/1 for international students; for spring admission, 6/1 priority date for domestic students, 4/1 for international students. Applications are processed on a rolling basis. Application fee: $40 ($50 for international students). Electronic applications accepted. *Financial support:* Fellowships, research assistantships, teaching assistantships, Federal Work-Study, and institutionally sponsored loans available. Support available to part-time students. *Unit head:* Jim Metzger, Interim Chair, 614-292-3854, E-mail: metzger.72@osu.edu. *Application contact:* Graduate Admissions, 614-292-6031, Fax: 614-292-3656, E-mail: gradadmissions@osu.edu. Website: http://hcs.osu.edu/.

Oklahoma State University, College of Agricultural Science and Natural Resources, Department of Horticulture and Landscape Architecture, Stillwater, OK 74078. Offers agriculture (M Ag); crop science (PhD); environmental science (PhD); horticulture (MS); plant science (PhD). *Faculty:* 19 full-time (3 women), 2 part-time/adjunct (1 woman). *Students:* 1 (woman) full-time, 7 part-time (5 women), 4 international. Average age 27. 11 applicants, 27% accepted, 2 enrolled. In 2012, 6 master's awarded. *Degree requirements:* For master's, thesis (for some programs); for doctorate, comprehensive exam, thesis/dissertation. *Entrance requirements:* For master's and doctorate, GRE or GMAT. Additional exam requirements/recommendations for international students: Required—TOEFL (minimum score 550 paper-based; 79 iBT). *Application deadline:* For fall admission, 3/1 for international students; for spring admission, 8/1 for international students. Applications are processed on a rolling basis. Application fee: $40 ($75 for international students). Electronic applications accepted. *Expenses:* Tuition, state resident: full-time $4272; part-time $178 per credit hour. Tuition, nonresident: full-time $17,016; part-time $709 per credit hour. *Required fees:* $2188; $91.17 per credit hour. One-time fee: $50 full-time. Part-time tuition and fees vary according to course load and campus/location. *Financial support:* In 2012–13, 3 research assistantships (averaging $14,964 per year), 3 teaching assistantships (averaging $14,964 per year) were awarded; career-related internships or fieldwork, Federal Work-Study, scholarships/grants, health care benefits, tuition waivers (partial), and unspecified assistantships also available. Support available to part-time students. Financial award application deadline: 3/1; financial award applicants required to submit FAFSA. *Faculty research:* Stress and postharvest physiology; water utilization and runoff; integrated pest management (IPM) systems and nursery, turf, floriculture, vegetable, net and fruit produces and natural resources, food extraction, and processing; public garden management. *Unit head:* Dr. Dale Maronek, Head, 405-744-5414, Fax: 405-744-9709. *Application contact:* Dr. Sheryl Tucker, Dean, 405-744-7099, Fax: 405-744-0355, E-mail: grad-i@okstate.edu. Website: http://www.hortla.okstate.edu/.

Oregon State University, College of Agricultural Sciences, Department of Horticulture, Corvallis, OR 97331. Offers M Ag, MAIS, MS, PhD. *Faculty:* 11 full-time (0 women), 2 part-time/adjunct (1 woman). *Students:* 34 full-time (20 women), 2 part-time (0 women); includes 4 minority (2 Asian, non-Hispanic/Latino; 2 Hispanic/Latino), 10 international. Average age 31. 36 applicants, 28% accepted, 9 enrolled. In 2012, 3 master's awarded. *Degree requirements:* For master's, thesis (for some programs); for doctorate, thesis/dissertation. *Entrance requirements:* For master's and doctorate, GRE General Test, minimum GPA of 3.0 in last 90 hours. Additional exam requirements/recommendations for international students: Required—TOEFL. *Application deadline:* For fall admission, 3/1 for domestic students. Applications are processed on a rolling basis. Application fee: $50. *Expenses:* Tuition, state resident: full-time $11,367; part-time $421 per credit hour. Tuition, nonresident: full-time $18,279; part-time $677 per credit hour. *Required fees:* $1478. One-time fee: $300 full-time. Tuition and fees vary according to course load and program. *Financial support:* Research assistantships, teaching assistantships, career-related internships or fieldwork, Federal Work-Study, and institutionally sponsored loans available. Support available to part-time students. Financial award application deadline: 2/1. *Unit head:* Dr. Bill Braunworth, Interim Department Head, 541-737-1317, E-mail: bill.braunworth@oregonstate.edu. Website: http://hort.oregonstate.edu.

Penn State University Park, Graduate School, College of Agricultural Sciences, Department of Horticulture, State College, University Park, PA 16802-1503. Offers MS, PhD. *Unit head:* Dr. Bruce A. McPheron, Dean, 814-865-2541, Fax: 814-865-3103, E-mail: bam10@psu.edu. *Application contact:* Cynthia E. Nicosia, Director of Graduate Enrollment Services, 814-865-1834, E-mail: cey1@psu.edu. Website: http://horticulture.psu.edu.

Penn State University Park, Graduate School, College of Agricultural Sciences, Department of Plant Science, State College, University Park, PA 16802-1503. Offers agronomy (MS, PhD); horticulture (MS, PhD); turfgrass management

(MPS). *Unit head:* Dr. Barbara J. Christ, Interim Dean, 814-865-2541, Fax: 814-865-3103, E-mail: ebf@psu.edu. *Application contact:* Cynthia E. Nicosia, Director of Graduate Enrollment Services, 814-865-1834, E-mail: cey1@psu.edu. Website: http://plantscience.psu.edu/.

Purdue University, Graduate School, College of Agriculture, Department of Horticulture, West Lafayette, IN 47907. Offers M Agr, MS, PhD. Part-time programs available. *Faculty:* 25 full-time (4 women), 7 part-time/adjunct (2 women). *Students:* 25 full-time (13 women), 1 part-time (0 women), 14 international. Average age 28. 39 applicants, 18% accepted, 6 enrolled. In 2012, 3 master's, 4 doctorates awarded. Terminal master's awarded for partial completion of doctoral program. *Degree requirements:* For master's, thesis optional; for doctorate, thesis/dissertation. *Entrance requirements:* For master's and doctorate, GRE General Test, minimum undergraduate GPA of 3.0 or equivalent. Additional exam requirements/recommendations for international students: Required—TOEFL (minimum score 550 paper-based; 77 iBT); Recommended—TWE. *Application deadline:* For fall admission, 5/1 for domestic and international students; for spring admission, 10/1 for domestic and international students. Applications are processed on a rolling basis. Application fee: $60 ($75 for international students). Electronic applications accepted. *Financial support:* Fellowships, research assistantships with tuition reimbursements, and teaching assistantships with tuition reimbursements available. Support available to part-time students. Financial award applicants required to submit FAFSA. *Faculty research:* Floral scent and plant volatile biosynthesis, mineral nutrient utilization from cellular to global scales, hormone signaling and transport, regulation of plant architecture and reproduction, plant cell cycle regulation, water utilization and stress responses, sustainable biofuel production, enhancement of salt tolerance in crop plants, natural genetic variation, plant epigenetics, mechanisms of heterosis; hybridization and species breeding barriers. *Unit head:* Dr. Robert J. Joly, Interim Head, 765-494-1306, Fax: 765-494-0391, E-mail: joly@purdue.edu. *Application contact:* Colleen K. Flynn, Graduate Contact, 765-494-1306, Fax: 765-494-0391, E-mail: martinck@purdue.edu. Website: http://www.hort.purdue.edu/hort/hort.html.

Rutgers, The State University of New Jersey, New Brunswick, Graduate School-New Brunswick, Program in Plant Biology, Piscataway, NJ 08854-8097. Offers horticulture and plant technology (MS, PhD); molecular and cellular biology (MS, PhD); organismal and population biology (MS, PhD); plant pathology (MS, PhD). Part-time programs available. Terminal master's awarded for partial completion of doctoral program. *Degree requirements:* For master's, comprehensive exam, thesis or alternative; for doctorate, comprehensive exam, thesis/dissertation. *Entrance requirements:* For master's and doctorate, GRE General Test, GRE Subject Test (recommended). Additional exam requirements/recommendations for international students: Required—TOEFL (minimum score 600 paper-based). Electronic applications accepted. *Faculty research:* Molecular biology and biochemistry of plants, plant development and genomics, plant protection, plant improvement, plant management of horticultural and field crops.

Southern Illinois University Carbondale, Graduate School, College of Agriculture, Department of Plant, Soil, and General Agriculture, Carbondale, IL 62901-4701. Offers horticultural science (MS); plant and soil science (MS). *Faculty:* 12 full-time (1 woman), 8 part-time/adjunct (0 women). *Students:* 2 full-time (1 woman), 32 part-time (11 women); includes 3 minority (2 Black or African American, non-Hispanic/Latino; 1 Hispanic/Latino), 6 international. 12 applicants, 42% accepted, 1 enrolled. In 2012, 7 master's awarded. *Degree requirements:* For master's, thesis. *Entrance requirements:* For master's, minimum GPA of 2.7. Additional exam requirements/recommendations for international students: Required—TOEFL. *Application deadline:* Applications are processed on a rolling basis. Application fee: $50. *Financial support:* In 2012–13, 22 students received support, including 15 research assistantships with full tuition reimbursements available, 6 teaching assistantships with full tuition reimbursements available; fellowships with full tuition reimbursements available, Federal Work-Study, institutionally sponsored loans, and tuition waivers (full) also available. Support available to part-time students. *Faculty research:* Herbicides, fertilizers, agriculture education, landscape design, plant breeding. *Total annual research expenditures:* $2 million. *Unit head:* Dr. Brian Klubek, Chair, 618-453-2496, E-mail: bklubek@siu.edu. *Application contact:* Lisa Hartline, Administrative Clerk, 618-453-1770, E-mail: lisah@siu.edu.

Texas A&M University, College of Agriculture and Life Sciences, Department of Horticultural Sciences, College Station, TX 77843. Offers M Agr, MS, PhD. *Faculty:* 14. *Students:* 31 full-time (16 women), 8 part-time (4 women); includes 3 minority (1 Asian, non-Hispanic/Latino; 2 Hispanic/Latino), 17 international. Average age 29. In 2012, 3 master's, 4 doctorates awarded. Terminal master's awarded for partial completion of doctoral program. *Degree requirements:* For master's, thesis (for some programs), professional internship; for doctorate, thesis/dissertation. *Entrance requirements:* For master's and doctorate, GRE General Test. Additional exam requirements/recommendations for international students: Required—TOEFL. Application fee: $50 ($75 for international students). Electronic applications accepted. *Financial support:* In 2012–13, 30 students received support, including fellowships with full tuition reimbursements available (averaging $15,000 per year), research assistantships with partial tuition reimbursements available (averaging $14,000 per year), teaching assistantships with partial tuition reimbursements available (averaging $14,000 per year); career-related internships or fieldwork and tuition waivers (partial) also available. Financial award application deadline: 4/1. *Faculty research:* Plant breeding, molecular biology, plant nutrition, post-harvest physiology, plant physiology. *Unit head:* Dr. Leland S. Pierson, III, Head, 979-458-2048, Fax: 979-845-0627, E-mail: plpm-head@ag.tamu.edu. *Application contact:* Dr. Michael Arnold, Professor, 979-845-1499, Fax: 979-845-0627, E-mail: ma-arnold@tamu.edu. Website: http://hortsciences.tamu.edu/.

Texas Tech University, Graduate School, College of Agricultural Sciences and Natural Resources, Department of Plant and Soil Science, Lubbock, TX 79409. Offers crop science (MS); horticulture (MS); plant and soil science (PhD); plant protection (MS); soil science (MS); JD/MS. Part-time programs available. Postbaccalaureate distance learning degree programs offered (no on-campus study). *Degree requirements:* For master's, thesis or alternative; for doctorate, thesis/dissertation. *Entrance requirements:* For master's and doctorate, GRE General Test, formal approval from departmental committee. Additional exam requirements/recommendations for international students: Required—TOEFL (minimum score 550 paper-based; 79 iBT). Electronic applications accepted. *Faculty research:* Molecular and cellular biology of plant stress, physiology/genetics of crop production in semi-arid conditions, improvement of native plants, soil science and management, fibers and biopolymers.

Universidad Nacional Pedro Henriquez Urena, Graduate School, Santo Domingo, Dominican Republic. Offers agricultural diversity (MS), including horticultural/fruit production, tropical animal production; conservation of monuments and cultural assets (M Arch); ecology and environment (MS); environmental engineering (MEE); international relations (MA); natural resource management (MS); political science (MA); project optimization (MPM); project feasibility (MPM); project management (MPM); sanitation engineering (ME); science for teachers (MS); tropical Caribbean architecture (M Arch).

University of Arkansas, Graduate School, Dale Bumpers College of Agricultural, Food and Life Sciences, Department of Horticulture, Fayetteville, AR 72701-1201. Offers MS. *Students:* 2 full-time (1 woman), 6 part-time (2 women), 4 international. In 2012, 5 master's awarded. *Degree requirements:* For master's, thesis. *Application deadline:* For fall admission, 4/1 for international students; for spring admission, 10/1 for international students. Applications are processed on a rolling basis. Application fee: $40 ($50 for international students). Electronic applications accepted. *Financial support:* In 2012–13, 7 research assistantships were awarded; fellowships, teaching assistantships, career-related internships or fieldwork, and Federal Work-Study also available. Support available to part-time students. Financial award application deadline: 4/1; financial award applicants required to submit FAFSA. *Unit head:* Dr. David Hensley, Department Head, 479-575-2603, E-mail: dhensley@uark.edu. *Application contact:* Dr. J. Brad Murphy, Graduate Coordinator, 479-575-2603, E-mail: jbmurph@comp.uark.edu. Website: http://hort.uark.edu.

University of California, Davis, Graduate Studies, Graduate Group in Horticulture and Agronomy, Davis, CA 95616. Offers MS. *Degree requirements:* For master's, comprehensive exam (for some programs), thesis (for some programs). *Entrance requirements:* For master's, GRE General Test. Additional exam requirements/recommendations for international students: Required—TOEFL (minimum score 550 paper-based). Electronic applications accepted. *Faculty research:* Postharvest physiology, mineral nutrition, crop improvement, plant growth and development.

University of Delaware, College of Agriculture and Natural Resources, Longwood Graduate Program in Public Horticulture, Newark, DE 19716. Offers MS. *Degree requirements:* For master's, thesis, internship. *Entrance requirements:* For master's, GRE General Test, introductory taxonomy course. Additional exam requirements/recommendations for international students: Required—TOEFL. Electronic applications accepted. *Faculty research:* Management and development of publicly oriented horticultural institutions.

University of Florida, Graduate School, College of Agricultural and Life Sciences, Department of Environmental Horticulture, Gainesville, FL 32611. Offers MS, PhD. Postbaccalaureate distance learning degree programs offered (no on-campus study). *Degree requirements:* For master's, comprehensive exam, thesis optional, teaching experience; for doctorate, comprehensive exam, thesis/dissertation, teaching experience. *Entrance requirements:* For master's and doctorate, GRE General Test, minimum GPA of 3.0. Additional exam requirements/recommendations for international students: Required—TOEFL (minimum score 550 paper-based; 80 iBT), IELTS (minimum score 6). Electronic applications accepted. *Faculty research:* Breeding and genetics, conservation horticulture landscape design and ecology, floriculture, nursery and foliage crop production, turfgrasses, urban horticulture.

University of Florida, Graduate School, College of Agricultural and Life Sciences, Department of Horticultural Sciences, Gainesville, FL 32611. Offers MS, PhD. *Degree requirements:* For master's, thesis optional; for doctorate, comprehensive exam, thesis/dissertation. *Entrance requirements:* For master's and doctorate, GRE General Test, minimum GPA of 3.0. Additional exam requirements/recommendations for international students: Required—TOEFL (minimum score 550 paper-based; 80 iBT), IELTS (minimum score 6). Electronic applications accepted. *Faculty research:* Breeding and genetics, crop production, organic/sustainable agriculture and nutrition, physiology and biochemistry, plant molecular and cellular biology, postharvest biology.

University of Georgia, College of Agricultural and Environmental Sciences, Department of Horticulture, Athens, GA 30602. Offers horticulture (MS, PhD); plant protection and pest management (MPPPM). Part-time programs available. *Degree requirements:* For master's, thesis (MS); for doctorate, one foreign language, thesis/dissertation. *Entrance requirements:* For master's and doctorate, GRE General Test. Electronic applications accepted.

University of Guelph, Graduate Studies, Ontario Agricultural College, Department of Plant Agriculture, Guelph, ON N1G 2W1, Canada. Offers M Sc, PhD. Part-time programs available. *Degree requirements:* For master's, thesis; for doctorate, comprehensive exam, thesis/dissertation. *Entrance requirements:* For master's, minimum B average during previous 2 years of course work; for doctorate, minimum B average. Additional exam requirements/recommendations for international students: Required—TOEFL (minimum score 550 paper-based; 89 iBT), IELTS (minimum score 6.5), Michigan English Language Assessment Battery (minimum score: 85). Electronic applications accepted. *Faculty research:* Plant physiology, biochemistry, taxonomy, morphology, genetics, production, ecology, breeding and biotechnology.

University of Hawaii at Manoa, Graduate Division, College of Tropical Agriculture and Human Resources, Department of Tropical Plant and Soil Sciences, Honolulu, HI 96822. Offers MS, PhD. Part-time programs available. *Degree requirements:* For master's, thesis optional; for doctorate, comprehensive exam, thesis/dissertation. *Entrance requirements:* For master's and doctorate, GRE General Test. Additional exam requirements/recommendations for international students: Required—TOEFL (minimum score 520 paper-based; 79 iBT), IELTS (minimum score 5). *Faculty research:* Genetics and breeding; physiology, culture, and management; weed science; turfgrass and landscape; sensory evaluation.

University of Maine, Graduate School, College of Natural Sciences, Forestry, and Agriculture, Department of Plant, Soil, and Environmental Sciences, Orono, ME 04469. Offers ecology and environmental sciences (MS); horticulture (MS); plant, soil, and environmental sciences (MS). *Faculty:* 18 full-time (6 women), 3 part-time/adjunct. *Students:* 9 full-time (7 women), 2 part-time (0 women), 1 international. Average age 30. 11 applicants, 9% accepted, 1 enrolled. In 2012, 3 master's awarded. *Degree requirements:* For master's, thesis (for some programs). *Entrance requirements:* For master's, GRE General Test. Additional exam requirements/recommendations for international students: Required—TOEFL. *Application deadline:* Applications are processed on a rolling basis. Application fee: $65. Electronic applications accepted. *Financial support:* In 2012–13, 16 research assistantships with full tuition reimbursements (averaging $17,336 per year), 1 teaching assistantship with full tuition reimbursement (averaging $13,600 per year) were awarded; scholarships/grants, tuition waivers (full and partial), and unspecified assistantships also available. *Total annual research expenditures:* $179,065. *Unit head:* Dr. Eric Gallandt, Chair, 207-581-2933, Fax: 207-581-3207. *Application contact:* Scott G. Delcourt, Associate Dean of the Graduate School, 207-581-3291, Fax: 207-581-3232, E-mail: graduate@maine.edu. Website: http://umaine.edu/pse/.

University of Manitoba, Faculty of Graduate Studies, Faculty of Agricultural and Food Sciences, Department of Plant Science, Winnipeg, MB R3T 2N2, Canada. Offers agronomy and plant protection (M Sc, PhD); horticulture (M Sc, PhD); plant breeding and genetics (M Sc, PhD); plant physiology-biochemistry (M Sc, PhD). *Degree requirements:* For master's, thesis; for doctorate, one foreign language, thesis/dissertation.

University of Maryland, College Park, Academic Affairs, College of Agriculture and Natural Resources, Department of Plant Science and Landscape Architecture, Plant Science Program, College Park, MD 20742. Offers MS, PhD. *Students:* 26 full-time (19 women), 5 part-time (1 woman); includes 7 minority (1 Black or African American, non-Hispanic/Latino; 1 Asian, non-Hispanic/Latino; 3 Hispanic/Latino; 2 Two or more races, non-Hispanic/Latino), 8 international. 43 applicants, 42% accepted, 12 enrolled. In 2012, 3 master's, 1 doctorate awarded. *Entrance requirements:* For doctorate, GRE General Test. Additional exam requirements/recommendations for international students: Required—TOEFL. *Application deadline:* For fall admission, 2/1 priority date for domestic students, 2/1 for international students; for spring admission, 6/1 for domestic and international students. Applications are processed on a rolling basis. Application fee: $75. Electronic applications accepted. *Expenses:* Tuition, state resident: part-time $551 per credit. Tuition, nonresident: part-time $1188 per credit. Part-time tuition and fees vary according to program. *Financial support:* In 2012–13, 22 research assistantships (averaging $16,909 per year), 4 teaching assistantships (averaging $16,807 per year) were awarded; fellowships and career-related internships or fieldwork also available. Financial award applicants required to submit FAFSA. *Faculty research:* Mineral nutrition, genetics and breeding, chemical growth, histochemistry, postharvest physiology. *Unit head:* Susan Burk, Coordinator, 301-405-6244, Fax: 301-314-9308, E-mail: sburk@umd.edu. *Application contact:* Dr. Charles A. Caramello, Dean of Graduate School, 301-405-0358, Fax: 301-314-9305.

University of Missouri, Graduate School, College of Agriculture, Food and Natural Resources, Division of Plant Sciences, Columbia, MO 65211. Offers crop, soil and pest management (MS, PhD); entomology (MS, PhD); horticulture (MS, PhD); plant biology and genetics (MS, PhD); plant stress biology (MS, PhD). *Faculty:* 40 full-time (11 women). *Students:* 75 full-time (36 women), 10 part-time (2 women); includes 4 minority (2 Black or African American, non-Hispanic/Latino; 1 American Indian or Alaska Native, non-Hispanic/Latino; 1 Hispanic/Latino), 28 international. Average age 28. 67 applicants, 22% accepted, 15 enrolled. In 2012, 8 master's, 9 doctorates awarded. Terminal master's awarded for partial completion of doctoral program. *Degree requirements:* For master's, thesis; for doctorate, comprehensive exam, thesis/dissertation. *Entrance requirements:* For master's and doctorate, GRE General Test, minimum GPA of 3.0; bachelor's degree from accredited college. Additional exam requirements/recommendations for international students: Required—TOEFL (minimum score 500 paper-based; 61 iBT), IELTS (minimum score 5.5). *Application deadline:* For fall admission, 1/15 priority date for domestic students, 1/15 for international students. Applications are processed on a rolling basis. Application fee: $55 ($75 for international students). Electronic applications accepted. *Expenses:* Tuition, state resident: full-time $6057. Tuition, nonresident: full-time $15,683. *Required fees:* $1000. *Financial support:* In 2012–13, 2 fellowships with tuition reimbursements, 59 research assistantships with tuition reimbursements, 1 teaching assistantship with tuition reimbursement were awarded; institutionally sponsored loans, scholarships/grants, health care benefits, and unspecified assistantships also available. Support available to part-time students. *Faculty research:* Crop, soil and pest management; entomology; horticulture; plant biology and genetics; plant microbiology and pathology. *Unit head:* Dr. Michael Collins, Director, 573-882-1957, E-mail: collinsm@missouri.edu. *Application contact:* Dr. James Schoelz, Director of Graduate Studies, 573-882-1185, E-mail: schoelzj@missouri.edu. Website: http://plantsci.missouri.edu/graduate/.

University of Nebraska–Lincoln, Graduate College, College of Agricultural Sciences and Natural Resources, Department of Agronomy and Horticulture, Program in Horticulture, Lincoln, NE 68588. Offers MS, PhD. *Degree requirements:* For master's, thesis optional. *Entrance requirements:* For master's, GRE General Test. Additional exam requirements/recommendations for international students: Required—TOEFL (minimum score 600 paper-based). Electronic applications accepted. *Faculty research:* Horticultural crops: production, management, cultural, and ecological aspects; tissue and cell culture; plant nutrition and anatomy; postharvest physiology and ecology.

University of Puerto Rico, Mayagüez Campus, Graduate Studies, College of Agricultural Sciences, Department of Horticulture, Mayagüez, PR 00681-9000. Offers MS. Part-time programs available. *Faculty:* 6 full-time (4 women). *Students:* 15 full-time (9 women); includes 13 minority (all Hispanic/Latino), 2 international. 1 applicant. *Degree requirements:* For master's, comprehensive exam, thesis. *Entrance requirements:* For master's, BS in agricultural science or its equivalent. *Application deadline:* For fall admission, 2/15 for domestic and international students; for spring admission, 9/15 for domestic and international students. Applications are processed on a rolling basis. Application fee: $25. Tuition and fees vary according to course level and course load. *Financial support:* In 2012–13, 3 research assistantships (averaging $15,000 per year), 5 teaching assistantships (averaging $8,500 per year) were awarded; Federal Work-Study and institutionally sponsored loans also available. *Faculty research:* Growth regulators, floriculture, starchy crops, coffee and fruit technology. *Unit head:* Dr. Skip Van Bloem, Director, 787-265-3852, Fax: 787-265-0860, E-mail: skip.vanbloem@upr.edu. *Application contact:* Janice Perez, Secretary, 787-832-4040 Ext. 3511, E-mail: japerez@uprm.edu. Website: http://www.uprm.edu/agricultura/horticultura/.

University of South Africa, College of Agriculture and Environmental Sciences, Pretoria, South Africa. Offers agriculture (MS); consumer science (MCS); environmental management (MA, MS, PhD); environmental science (MA, MS, PhD); geography (MA, MS, PhD); horticulture (M Tech); human ecology (MHE); life sciences (MS); nature conservation (M Tech).

University of Vermont, Graduate College, College of Agriculture and Life Sciences, Department of Plant and Soil Science, Burlington, VT 05405. Offers MS, PhD. *Students:* 25 (17 women); includes 1 minority (Asian, non-Hispanic/Latino), 3 international. 28 applicants, 36% accepted, 4 enrolled. In 2012, 4 master's, 1 doctorate awarded. *Degree requirements:* For master's, thesis; for doctorate, one foreign language, thesis/dissertation. *Entrance requirements:* For master's and doctorate, GRE General Test. Additional exam requirements/recommendations for international students: Required—TOEFL (minimum score 550 paper-based; 80 iBT). *Application deadline:* For fall admission, 2/15 priority date for domestic students, 2/15 for international students. Applications are processed on a rolling basis. Application fee: $40. Electronic applications accepted. *Expenses: Tuition, area resident:* Part-time $572 per credit. Tuition, nonresident: part-time $1444 per credit. *Financial support:* Fellowships, research assistantships, and teaching assistantships available. Financial award application deadline: 3/1. *Faculty research:* Soil chemistry, plant nutrition. *Unit head:* Dr. Ernesto Mendez, Acting Chairperson, 802-656-2630. *Application contact:* Dr. Josef Gorres, Coordinator, 802-656-2630. Website: http://www.uvm.edu/~pss.

University of Washington, Graduate School, College of the Environment, School of Environmental and Forest Sciences, Seattle, WA 98195. Offers bioresource science and engineering (MS, PhD); environmental horticulture (MEH); forest ecology (MS, PhD); forest management (MFR); forest soils (MS, PhD); restoration ecology (MS, PhD); restoration ecology and environmental horticulture (MS, PhD); social sciences (MS, PhD); sustainable resource management (MS, PhD); wildlife science (MS, PhD); MFR/MAIS; MPA/MS. *Accreditation:* SAF. Part-time programs available. *Degree requirements:* For master's, thesis; for doctorate, comprehensive exam (for some programs), thesis/dissertation. *Entrance requirements:* For master's and doctorate, GRE, minimum GPA of 3.0. Additional exam requirements/recommendations for international students: Required—TOEFL, GRE. Electronic applications accepted. *Faculty research:* Ecosystem analysis, silviculture and forest protection, paper science and engineering, environmental horticulture and urban forestry, natural resource policy and economics, restoration ecology and environment horticulture, conservation, human dimensions, wildlife, bioresource science and engineering.

University of Wisconsin–Madison, Graduate School, College of Agricultural and Life Sciences, Department of Horticulture, Madison, WI 53706-1380. Offers MS, PhD. Part-time programs available. Terminal master's awarded for partial completion of doctoral program. *Degree requirements:* For master's, comprehensive exam, thesis (for some programs); for doctorate, comprehensive exam, thesis/dissertation. *Entrance requirements:* For master's and doctorate, minimum GPA of 3.0. Additional exam requirements/recommendations for international students: Required—TOEFL (minimum score 580 paper-based). Electronic applications accepted. *Expenses:* Tuition, state resident: full-time $10,728; part-time $743 per credit. Tuition, nonresident: full-time $24,054; part-time $1575 per credit. *Required fees:* $1111; $72 per credit. *Faculty research:* Biotechnology, crop breeding/genetics, environmental physiology, crop management, cytogenetics.

Virginia Polytechnic Institute and State University, Graduate School, College of Agriculture and Life Sciences, Blacksburg, VA 24124. Offers agricultural and applied economics (MS); agricultural and life sciences (MS); animal and poultry science (MS, PhD); crop and soil environmental sciences (MS, PhD); dairy science (MS); entomology (PhD); horticulture (MS, PhD); human nutrition, foods and exercise (MS, PhD); life sciences (MS, PhD); plant pathology, physiology and weed science (PhD). *Faculty:* 233 full-time (65 women), 1 (woman) part-time/adjunct. *Students:* 343 full-time (199 women), 74 part-time (47 women); includes 48 minority (20 Black or African American, non-Hispanic/Latino; 1 American Indian or Alaska Native, non-Hispanic/Latino; 15 Asian, non-Hispanic/Latino; 7 Hispanic/Latino; 5 Two or more races, non-Hispanic/Latino), 105 international. Average age 29. 387 applicants, 33% accepted, 98 enrolled. In 2012, 81 master's, 52 doctorates awarded. *Degree requirements:* For master's, comprehensive exam (for some programs), thesis (for some programs); for doctorate, comprehensive exam (for some programs), thesis/dissertation (for some programs). *Entrance requirements:* For master's and doctorate, GRE/GMAT (may vary by department). Additional exam requirements/recommendations for international students: Required—TOEFL (minimum score 550 paper-based). *Application deadline:* For fall admission, 8/1 for domestic students, 4/1 for international students; for spring admission, 1/1 for domestic students, 9/1 for international students. Applications are processed on a rolling basis. Application fee: $65. Electronic applications accepted. *Expenses:* Tuition, state resident: full-time $10,677; part-time $593.25 per credit hour. Tuition, nonresident: full-time $20,926; part-time $1162.50 per credit hour. *Required fees:* $427.75 per semester. Tuition and fees vary according to course load, campus/location and program. *Financial support:* In 2012–13, 1 fellowship with full tuition reimbursement (averaging $21,000 per year), 229 research assistantships with full tuition reimbursements (averaging $18,998 per year), 77 teaching assistantships with full tuition reimbursements (averaging $18,174 per year) were awarded. Financial award application deadline: 3/1; financial award applicants

required to submit FAFSA. *Total annual research expenditures:* $41.8 million. *Unit head:* Dr. Alan L. Grant, Dean, 540-231-4152, Fax: 540-231-4163, E-mail: algrant@vt.edu. *Application contact:* Sheila Norman, Administrative Assistant, 540-231-4152, Fax: 540-231-4163, E-mail: snorman@vt.edu. Website: http://www.cals.vt.edu/.

Washington State University, Graduate School, College of Agricultural, Human, and Natural Resource Sciences, Department of Horticulture, Pullman, WA 99164. Offers MS, PhD. Part-time programs available. *Faculty:* 18. *Students:* 27 full-time (14 women), 2 part-time (both women), 12 international. Average age 27. 38 applicants, 18% accepted, 7 enrolled. In 2012, 6 master's, 1 doctorate awarded. *Degree requirements:* For master's, comprehensive exam (for some programs), thesis (for some programs), oral exam; for doctorate, comprehensive exam, thesis/dissertation, oral exam, written exam. *Entrance requirements:* For master's and doctorate, GRE General Test, GRE Subject Test, minimum GPA of 3.0, 3 letters of recommendation, statement of purpose/intent. Additional exam requirements/recommendations for international students: Required—TOEFL (minimum score 550 paper-based). *Application deadline:* For fall admission, 1/10 priority date for domestic students, 1/10 for international students; for spring admission, 7/1 priority date for domestic students, 7/1 for international students. Applications are processed on a rolling basis. Application fee: $75. Electronic applications accepted. *Financial support:* In 2012–13, 18 research assistantships with full and partial tuition reimbursements (averaging $18,204 per year), 4 teaching assistantships with full and partial tuition reimbursements (averaging $18,204 per year) were awarded; fellowships, career-related internships or fieldwork, Federal Work-Study, institutionally sponsored loans, scholarships/grants, health care benefits, and unspecified assistantships also available. Financial award application deadline: 4/1; financial award applicants required to submit FAFSA. *Faculty research:* Post-harvest physiology, genetics/plant breeding, molecular biology. *Unit head:* Dr. N. Richard Knowles, Chair, 509-335-9502, Fax: 509-335-8690, E-mail: rknowles@wsu.edu. *Application contact:* Graduate School Admissions, 800-GRADWSU, Fax: 509-335-1949, E-mail: gradsch@wsu.edu. Website: http://horticulture.wsu.edu.

West Virginia University, Davis College of Agriculture, Forestry and Consumer Sciences, Division of Plant and Soil Sciences, Morgantown, WV 26506. Offers agricultural sciences (PhD), including animal and food sciences, plant and soil sciences; agronomy (MS); entomology (MS); environmental microbiology (MS); horticulture (MS); plant pathology (MS). *Degree requirements:* For master's, thesis. *Entrance requirements:* For master's, GRE, minimum GPA of 2.5. Additional exam requirements/recommendations for international students: Required—TOEFL. *Faculty research:* Water quality, reclamation of disturbed land, crop production, pest control, environmental protection.

Plant Sciences

Alabama Agricultural and Mechanical University, School of Graduate Studies, College of Agricultural, Life and Natural Sciences, Department of Biological and Environmental Sciences, Huntsville, AL 35811. Offers plant and soil science (MS, PhD). Evening/weekend programs available. Terminal master's awarded for partial completion of doctoral program. *Degree requirements:* For master's, thesis; for doctorate, one foreign language, thesis/dissertation. *Entrance requirements:* For master's, GRE General Test, BS in agriculture; for doctorate, GRE General Test, master's degree. Additional exam requirements/recommendations for international students: Required—TOEFL (minimum score 500 paper-based; 61 iBT). Electronic applications accepted. *Faculty research:* Plant breeding, cytogenetics, crop production, soil chemistry and fertility, remote sensing.

American University of Beirut, Graduate Programs, Faculty of Agricultural and Food Sciences, Beirut, Lebanon. Offers agricultural economics (MS); animal sciences (MS); ecosystem management (MSES); food technology (MS); irrigation (MS); nutrition (MS); plant protection (MS); plant science (MS); poultry science (MS). Part-time programs available. *Faculty:* 22 full-time (6 women), 1 part-time/adjunct (0 women). *Students:* 11 full-time (10 women), 89 part-time (74 women). Average age 25. 97 applicants, 64% accepted, 18 enrolled. In 2012, 35 master's awarded. *Degree requirements:* For master's, one foreign language, comprehensive exam, thesis (for some programs). *Entrance requirements:* Additional exam requirements/recommendations for international students: Required—TOEFL (minimum score 600 paper-based; 100 iBT), IELTS (minimum score 7.5). *Application deadline:* For fall admission, 2/7 for domestic and international students; for spring admission, 11/15 for domestic and international students. Applications are processed on a rolling basis. Application fee: $50. Electronic applications accepted. *Expenses: Tuition:* Full-time $13,896; part-time $772 per credit. *Financial support:* In 2012–13, 18 research assistantships with partial tuition reimbursements (averaging $1,500 per year), 49 teaching assistantships with full and partial tuition reimbursements (averaging $1,000 per year) were awarded; scholarships/grants, health care benefits, and unspecified assistantships also available. Financial award application deadline: 2/2. *Faculty research:* Evidence-based nutrition intervention; studies related to immunopotentiation, protection and production in broilers; nutritional food-based

dietary guidelines; production of biodiesel from algae; regional knowledge management and knowledge sharing network. *Total annual research expenditures:* $560,850. *Unit head:* Prof. Nahla Hwalla, Dean, 961-1343002 Ext. 4400, Fax: 961-1744460, E-mail: nahla@aub.edu.lb. *Application contact:* Dr. Salim Kanaan, Director, Admissions Office, 961-1-350000 Ext. 2594, Fax: 961-1750775, E-mail: sk00@aub.edu.lb. Website: http://www.aub.edu.lb/fafs/fafs_home/Pages/index.aspx.

Brigham Young University, Graduate Studies, College of Life Sciences, Department of Plant and Wildlife Sciences, Provo, UT 84602. Offers environmental science (MS); genetics and biotechnology (MS); wildlife and wildlands conservation (MS, PhD). *Faculty:* 24 full-time (1 woman), 2 part-time/adjunct (1 woman). *Students:* 47 full-time (18 women); includes 6 minority (3 Asian, non-Hispanic/Latino; 2 Hispanic/Latino; 1 Native Hawaiian or other Pacific Islander, non-Hispanic/Latino), 2 international. Average age 28. 29 applicants, 41% accepted, 9 enrolled. In 2012, 15 master's, 2 doctorates awarded. *Degree requirements:* For master's, thesis; for doctorate, comprehensive exam, thesis/dissertation, minimum GPA of 3.2, 54 hours (18 dissertation, 36 coursework). *Entrance requirements:* For master's, GRE General Test, minimum GPA of 3.2 during last 60 hours of course work; for doctorate, GRE, minimum GPA of 3.2. Additional exam requirements/recommendations for international students: Required—TOEFL (minimum score 580 paper-based; 85 iBT). *Application deadline:* 2/1 for domestic and international students. Applications are processed on a rolling basis. Application fee: $50. Electronic applications accepted. *Expenses: Tuition:* Full-time $5950; part-time $331 per credit hour. Tuition and fees vary according to program and student's religious affiliation. *Financial support:* In 2012–13, 47 students received support, including 64 research assistantships with partial tuition reimbursements available (averaging $17,840 per year), 52 teaching assistantships with partial tuition reimbursements available (averaging $17,840 per year); scholarships/grants and tuition waivers (partial) also available. Financial award application deadline: 2/1. *Faculty research:* Environmental science, plant genetics, plant ecology, plant nutrition and pathology, wildlife and wildlands conservation. *Total annual research expenditures:* $1.9 million. *Unit head:* Dr. Eric N. Jellen, Chair, 801-422-3527,

Peterson's Graduate Programs in the Physical Sciences, Mathematics, Agricultural Sciences, the Environment & Natural Resources 2014

www.petersonsbooks.com   **423**

Fax: 801-422-0008, E-mail: rick_jellen@byu.edu. *Application contact:* Dr. Brock R. McMillan, Graduate Coordinator, 801-422-1228, Fax: 801-422-0008, E-mail: brock_mcmillan@byu.edu. Website: http://pws.byu.edu/home/.

California State University, Fresno, Division of Graduate Studies, College of Agricultural Sciences and Technology, Department of Plant Science, Fresno, CA 93740-8027. Offers MS. Part-time programs available. *Degree requirements:* For master's, thesis. *Entrance requirements:* For master's, GRE General Test, minimum GPA of 2.5. Additional exam requirements/recommendations for international students: Required—TOEFL. Electronic applications accepted. *Faculty research:* Crop patterns, small watershed management, electronic monitoring of feedlot cattle, disease control, dairy operations.

Clemson University, Graduate School, College of Agriculture, Forestry and Life Sciences, Department of Forestry and Natural Resources, Program in Plant and Environmental Sciences, Clemson, SC 29634. Offers MS, PhD. *Students:* 50 full-time (20 women), 8 part-time (0 women); includes 2 minority (1 Hispanic/Latino; 1 Two or more races, non-Hispanic/Latino), 22 international. Average age 29. 39 applicants, 44% accepted, 13 enrolled. In 2012, 6 master's, 5 doctorates awarded. *Degree requirements:* For master's, thesis; for doctorate, comprehensive exam, thesis/dissertation. *Entrance requirements:* For master's, GRE General Test, bachelor's degree in biological science or related disciplines; for doctorate, GRE General Test. Additional exam requirements/recommendations for international students: Required—TOEFL, IELTS. *Application deadline:* Applications are processed on a rolling basis. Electronic applications accepted. *Expenses:* Contact institution. *Financial support:* In 2012–13, 42 students received support, including 4 fellowships with full and partial tuition reimbursements available (averaging $10,709 per year), 35 research assistantships with partial tuition reimbursements available (averaging $16,948 per year), 8 teaching assistantships with partial tuition reimbursements available (averaging $10,780 per year); career-related internships or fieldwork, institutionally sponsored loans, scholarships/grants, health care benefits, and unspecified assistantships also available. Support available to part-time students. Financial award application deadline: 3/15; financial award applicants required to submit FAFSA. *Faculty research:* Sustainable agroecology, horticulture and turfgrass, physiology and pathology of plants. *Unit head:* Dr. Patricia Layton, School Director, 864-656-3302, Fax: 864-656-3304, E-mail: playton@clemson.edu. *Application contact:* Dr. Halina Knap, Coordinator, 864-656-3523, Fax: 864-656-3443, E-mail: hskrpsk@clemson.edu. Website: http://www.clemson.edu/cafls/departments/pes/.

Colorado State University, Graduate School, College of Agricultural Sciences, Department of Bioagricultural Sciences and Pest Management, Fort Collins, CO 80523-1177. Offers entomology (MS, PhD); plant pathology and weed science (MS, PhD). Part-time programs available. *Faculty:* 20 full-time (5 women). *Students:* 10 full-time (4 women), 21 part-time (11 women); includes 3 minority (1 Black or African American, non-Hispanic/Latino; 2 Hispanic/Latino), 5 international. Average age 32. 8 applicants, 75% accepted, 6 enrolled. In 2012, 6 master's, 6 doctorates awarded. *Degree requirements:* For master's, comprehensive exam, thesis; for doctorate, comprehensive exam, thesis/dissertation. *Entrance requirements:* For master's, GRE General Test, minimum GPA of 3.0, letters of recommendation; for doctorate, GRE General Test, minimum GPA of 3.0, letters of recommendation, essay. Additional exam requirements/recommendations for international students: Required—TOEFL (minimum score 550 paper-based; 79 iBT). *Application deadline:* For fall admission, 1/15 priority date for domestic students, 1/1 for international students; for spring admission, 9/1 priority date for domestic students, 9/1 for international students. Applications are processed on a rolling basis. Application fee: $50. Electronic applications accepted. *Expenses:* Tuition, state resident: full-time $8811; part-time $490 per credit. Tuition, nonresident: full-time $21,600; part-time $1200 per credit. *Required fees:* $1819; $61 per credit. *Financial support:* In 2012–13, 37 students received support, including 6 fellowships with full tuition reimbursements available (averaging $41,908 per year), 23 research assistantships with full tuition reimbursements available (averaging $14,438 per year), 8 teaching assistantships with full tuition reimbursements available (averaging $11,046 per year); unspecified assistantships also available. Financial award application deadline: 3/1; financial award applicants required to submit FAFSA. *Faculty research:* Genomics and molecular biology, ecology and biodiversity, biology and management of invasive species, integrated pest management. *Total annual research expenditures:* $2.4 million. *Unit head:* Dr. Thomas O. Holtzer, Department Head and Professor, 970-491-5261, Fax: 970-491-3862, E-mail: tholtzer@lamar.colostate.edu. *Application contact:* Janet Dill, Education Coordinator, 970-491-0402, Fax: 970-491-3862, E-mail: janet.dill@colostate.edu. Website: http://bspm.agsci.colostate.edu/.

Colorado State University, Graduate School, College of Agricultural Sciences, Department of Soil and Crop Sciences, Fort Collins, CO 80523-1170. Offers MS, PhD. Part-time programs available. *Faculty:* 19 full-time (4 women), 1 part-time/adjunct (0 women). *Students:* 23 full-time (9 women), 18 part-time (7 women); includes 4 minority (2 Black or African American, non-Hispanic/Latino; 1 Asian, non-Hispanic/Latino; 1 Hispanic/Latino), 12 international. Average age 35. 24 applicants, 29% accepted, 7 enrolled. In 2012, 6 master's, 5 doctorates awarded. Terminal master's awarded for partial completion of doctoral program. *Degree requirements:* For master's, thesis; for doctorate, comprehensive exam, thesis/dissertation, student teaching. *Entrance requirements:* For master's, GRE, minimum GPA of 3.0, appropriate bachelor's degree, letters of recommendation, statement of purpose; for doctorate, GRE, minimum GPA of 3.0, appropriate master's degree, letters of recommendation. Additional exam requirements/recommendations for international students: Required—TOEFL (minimum score 550 paper-based; 80 iBT). *Application deadline:* For fall admission, 4/1 priority date for domestic students, 5/1 for international students; for spring admission, 9/1 priority date for domestic students, 10/1 for international students. Application fee: $50. Electronic applications accepted. *Expenses:* Tuition, state resident: full-time $8811; part-time $490 per credit. Tuition, nonresident: full-time $21,600; part-time $1200 per credit. *Required fees:* $1819; $61 per credit. *Financial support:* In 2012–13, 19 students received support, including 5 fellowships with full tuition reimbursements available (averaging $26,683 per year), 15 research assistantships with full tuition reimbursements available (averaging $18,547 per year), 1 teaching assistantship with full tuition reimbursement available (averaging $8,924 per year); scholarships/grants and unspecified assistantships also available. Financial award application deadline: 2/15; financial award applicants required to submit FAFSA. *Faculty research:* Water quality, soil fertility, soil/plant ecosystems, plant breeding and genetics, cropping systems. *Total annual research expenditures:* $3.4 million. *Unit head:* Dr. Eugene Kelly, Head, 970-491-6517, Fax: 970-491-0564, E-mail: eugene.kelly@colostate.edu. *Application contact:* Karen Allison, Graduate Contact, 970-491-6295, Fax: 970-491-0564, E-mail: karen.allison@colostate.edu. Website: http://www.soilcrop.colostate.edu/.

Cornell University, Graduate School, Graduate Fields of Agriculture and Life Sciences, Field of Plant Breeding, Ithaca, NY 14853-0001. Offers plant breeding (MPS, MS, PhD); plant genetics (MPS, MS, PhD). *Faculty:* 30 full-time (7 women). *Students:* 39 full-time (19 women); includes 7 minority (3 Asian, non-Hispanic/Latino; 4 Hispanic/Latino), 17 international. Average age 27. 67 applicants, 22% accepted, 11 enrolled. In 2012, 9 master's, 2 doctorates awarded. Terminal master's awarded for partial completion of doctoral program. *Degree requirements:* For master's, thesis (MS), project paper (MPS); for doctorate, comprehensive exam, thesis/dissertation. *Entrance requirements:* For master's and doctorate, GRE General Test, GRE Subject Test (recommended), 3 letters of recommendation. Additional exam requirements/recommendations for international students: Required—TOEFL (minimum score 550 paper-based; 77 iBT). *Application deadline:* For fall admission, 1/15 priority date for domestic students. Application fee: $95. Electronic applications accepted. *Financial support:* In 2012–13, 28 students received support, including 10 fellowships with full tuition reimbursements available, 14 research assistantships with full tuition reimbursements available, 4 teaching assistantships with full tuition reimbursements available; institutionally sponsored loans, scholarships/grants, health care benefits, tuition waivers (full and partial), and unspecified assistantships also available. Financial award applicants required to submit FAFSA. *Faculty research:* Crop breeding for improved yield, stress resistance and quality; genetics and genomics of crop plants; applications of molecular biology and bioinformatics to crop improvement; genetic diversity and utilization of wild germplasm; international agriculture. *Unit head:* Director of Graduate Studies, 607-255-2180. *Application contact:* Graduate Field Assistant, 607-255-2180, E-mail: plbrgrad@cornell.edu. Website: http://www.gradschool.cornell.edu/fields.php?id-58&a-2.

Cornell University, Graduate School, Graduate Fields of Agriculture and Life Sciences, Field of Plant Protection, Ithaca, NY 14853-0001. Offers MPS. *Faculty:* 22 full-time (4 women). *Students:* 1 applicant. *Degree requirements:* For master's, internship, final exam. *Entrance requirements:* For master's, GRE General Test, 3 letters of recommendation. Additional exam requirements/recommendations for international students: Required—TOEFL (minimum score 550 paper-based; 77 iBT). *Application deadline:* For fall admission, 4/1 for domestic students. Application fee: $95. Electronic applications accepted. *Financial support:* Fellowships with full tuition reimbursements, research assistantships with full tuition reimbursements, teaching assistantships with full tuition reimbursements, institutionally sponsored loans, scholarships/grants, health care benefits, tuition waivers (full and partial), and unspecified assistantships available. Financial award applicants required to submit FAFSA. *Faculty research:* Fruit and vegetable crop insects and diseases, systems modeling, biological control, plant protection economics, integrated pest management. *Unit head:* Director of Graduate Studies, 315-787-2323, Fax: 315-787-2326. *Application contact:* Graduate Field Assistant, 315-787-2323, Fax: 315-787-2326, E-mail: plprotection@cornell.edu. Website: http://www.gradschool.cornell.edu/fields.php?id-60&a-2.

Delaware State University, Graduate Programs, Department of Agriculture and Natural Resources, Program in Plant Science, Dover, DE 19901-2277. Offers MS. *Entrance requirements:* For master's, GRE. Additional exam requirements/recommendations for international students: Required—TOEFL (minimum score 550 paper-based).

Illinois State University, Graduate School, College of Arts and Sciences, Department of Biological Sciences, Normal, IL 61790-2200. Offers animal behavior (MS); bacteriology (MS); biochemistry (MS); biological sciences (MS); biology (PhD); biophysics (MS); biotechnology (MS); botany (MS, PhD); cell biology (MS); conservation biology (MS); developmental biology (MS); ecology (MS, PhD); entomology (MS); evolutionary biology (MS); genetics (MS, PhD); immunology (MS); microbiology (MS, PhD); molecular biology (MS); molecular genetics (MS); neurobiology (MS); neuroscience (MS); parasitology (MS); physiology (MS, PhD); plant biology (MS); plant molecular biology (MS); plant sciences (MS); structural biology (MS); zoology (MS, PhD). Part-time programs available. *Degree requirements:* For master's, thesis or alternative; for doctorate, variable foreign language requirement, thesis/dissertation, 2 terms of residency.

Entrance requirements: For master's, GRE General Test, minimum GPA of 2.6 in last 60 hours of course work; for doctorate, GRE General Test. *Faculty research:* Redoc balance and drug development in schistosoma mansoni, control of the growth of listeria monocytogenes at low temperature, regulation of cell expansion and microtubule function by SPRI, CRUI: physiology and fitness consequences of different life history phenotypes.

Iowa State University of Science and Technology, Program in Plant Breeding, Ames, IA 50011. Offers MS, PhD. *Degree requirements:* For master's, thesis optional. *Entrance requirements:* For master's and doctorate, GRE. Additional exam requirements/recommendations for international students: Required—TOEFL (minimum score 550 paper-based; 79 iBT), IELTS (minimum score 6.5). *Application deadline:* Applications are processed on a rolling basis. Application fee: $60 ($90 for international students). Electronic applications accepted. *Application contact:* Jaci Severson, Application Contact, 515-294-1361, Fax: 515-294-8146, E-mail: gradprograms@agron.iastate.edu. Website: http://www.agron.iastate.edu.

Kansas State University, Graduate School, College of Agriculture, Department of Agronomy, Manhattan, KS 66506. Offers crop science (MS, PhD); plant breeding and genetics (MS, PhD); range management (MS, PhD); soil science (MS, PhD); weed science (MS, PhD). Part-time programs available. *Faculty:* 29 full-time (0 women), 13 part-time/adjunct (0 women). *Students:* 62 full-time (21 women), 15 part-time (4 women); includes 5 minority (2 Black or African American, non-Hispanic/Latino; 2 Asian, non-Hispanic/Latino; 1 Hispanic/Latino), 34 international. Average age 31. 38 applicants, 29% accepted, 10 enrolled. In 2012, 15 master's, 1 doctorate awarded. *Degree requirements:* For master's, thesis or alternative, oral exam; for doctorate, thesis/dissertation, preliminary exams. *Entrance requirements:* For master's, minimum GPA of 3.0 in BS; for doctorate, minimum GPA of 3.0 in master's program. Additional exam requirements/recommendations for international students: Required—TOEFL (minimum score 550 paper-based; 79 iBT). *Application deadline:* For fall admission, 2/1 priority date for domestic students, 2/1 for international students; for spring admission, 8/1 priority date for domestic students, 8/1 for international students. Applications are processed on a rolling basis. Application fee: $50 ($75 for international students). Electronic applications accepted. *Financial support:* In 2012–13, 62 research assistantships (averaging $23,500 per year) were awarded; institutionally sponsored loans and scholarships/grants also available. Support available to part-time students. Financial award application deadline: 3/1; financial award applicants required to submit FAFSA. *Faculty research:* Range and forage science, soil and environmental science, crop physiology, weed science, plant breeding and genetics. *Total annual research expenditures:* $6.5 million. *Unit head:* Dr. Gary Pierzynski, Head, 785-532-6101, Fax: 785-532-6094, E-mail: gmp@k-state.edu. *Application contact:* Dr. Gerard Kluitenberg, Graduate Coordinator, 785-532-7215, Fax: 785-532-6094, E-mail: gjk@ksu.edu. Website: http://www.agronomy.k-state.edu/DesktopDefault.aspx.

Lehman College of the City University of New York, School of Natural and Social Sciences, Department of Biological Sciences, Program in Plant Sciences, Bronx, NY 10468-1589. Offers PhD. *Degree requirements:* For doctorate, 2 foreign languages, thesis/dissertation. *Entrance requirements:* For doctorate, GRE General Test.

McGill University, Faculty of Graduate and Postdoctoral Studies, Faculty of Agricultural and Environmental Sciences, Department of Plant Science, Montréal, QC H3A 2T5, Canada. Offers M Sc, M Sc A, PhD, Certificate.

Miami University, College of Arts and Science, Department of Botany, Oxford, OH 45056. Offers MA, MAT, MS, PhD. *Students:* 64 full-time (34 women), 2 part-time (1 woman); includes 4 minority (2 Black or African American, non-Hispanic/Latino; 1 Asian, non-Hispanic/Latino; 1 Two or more races, non-Hispanic/Latino), 26 international. Average age 28. In 2012, 4 master's, 5 doctorates awarded. *Entrance requirements:* For master's and doctorate, GRE General Test, minimum undergraduate GPA of 2.75. Additional exam requirements/recommendations for international students: Required—TOEFL (minimum score 550 paper-based). *Application deadline:* For fall admission, 1/1 for domestic and international students. Applications are processed on a rolling basis. Application fee: $50. Electronic applications accepted. *Expenses:* Tuition, state resident: full-time $12,444; part-time $519 per credit hour. Tuition, nonresident: full-time $27,484; part-time $1145 per credit hour. *Required fees:* $468. Part-time tuition and fees vary according to course load, campus/location and program. *Financial support:* Research assistantships, teaching assistantships with full tuition reimbursements, Federal Work-Study, institutionally sponsored loans, health care benefits, and unspecified assistantships available. Financial award application deadline: 2/15; financial award applicants required to submit FAFSA. *Faculty research:* Evolution of plants, fungi and algae; bioinformatics; molecular biology of plants and cyanobacteria; food web dynamics; plant science education. *Unit head:* Dr. John Kiss, Chair, 513-529-4200, E-mail: kissjz@miamioh.edu. *Application contact:* Dr. Richard C. Moore, Graduate Advisor, 513-529-4278, E-mail: moorerc@miamioh.edu. Website: http://www.MiamiOH.edu/botany/.

Michigan State University, The Graduate School, College of Agriculture and Natural Resources, MSU-DOE Plant Research Laboratory, East Lansing, MI 48824. Offers biochemistry and molecular biology (PhD); cellular and molecular biology (PhD); crop and soil sciences (PhD); genetics (PhD); microbiology and molecular genetics (PhD); plant biology (PhD); plant physiology (PhD). Offered jointly with the Department of Energy. *Degree requirements:* For doctorate, comprehensive exam, thesis/dissertation, laboratory rotation, defense of dissertation. *Entrance requirements:* For doctorate, GRE General Test, acceptance into one of the affiliated department programs; 3 letters of recommendation; bachelor's degree or equivalent in life sciences, chemistry, biochemistry, or biophysics; research experience. Electronic applications accepted. *Faculty research:* Role of hormones in the regulation of plant development and physiology, molecular mechanisms associated with signal recognition, development and application of genetic methods and materials, protein routing and function.

Michigan State University, The Graduate School, College of Agriculture and Natural Resources, Program in Plant Breeding and Genetics, East Lansing, MI 48824. Offers MS, PhD. *Entrance requirements:* Additional exam requirements/recommendations for international students: Required—TOEFL. Electronic applications accepted. *Faculty research:* Applied plant breeding and genetics; disease, insect and herbicide resistances; gene isolation and genomics; abiotic stress factors; molecular mapping.

Mississippi State University, College of Agriculture and Life Sciences, Department of Plant and Soil Sciences, Mississippi State, MS 39762. Offers agriculture (MS, PhD), including agronomy, horticulture, weed science. *Faculty:* 26 full-time (1 woman), 1 part-time/adjunct (0 women). *Students:* 49 full-time (18 women), 22 part-time (7 women); includes 5 minority (2 Black or African American, non-Hispanic/Latino; 2 American Indian or Alaska Native, non-Hispanic/Latino; 1 Asian, non-Hispanic/Latino), 16 international. Average age 31. 49 applicants, 35% accepted, 16 enrolled. In 2012, 6 master's, 4 doctorates awarded. *Degree requirements:* For master's, comprehensive exam, thesis, oral and/or written exams; for doctorate, comprehensive exam, thesis/dissertation, minimum 20 semester hours of research for dissertation. *Entrance requirements:* For master's, GRE (weed science), minimum GPA of 2.75 (agronomy/horticulture), 3.0 (weed science); for doctorate, GRE (weed science), minimum GPA of 3.0 (agronomy/horticulture), 3.25 (weed science). Additional exam requirements/recommendations for international students: Required—TOEFL (minimum score 500 paper-based; 61 iBT), TOEFL (minimum score 550 paper-based, 79 iBT) or IELTS (minimum score 6.5) for weed science; Recommended—IELTS (minimum score 5.5). *Application deadline:* For fall admission, 7/1 for domestic students, 5/1 for international students; for spring admission, 10/1 for domestic students, 9/1 for international students. Applications are processed on a rolling basis. Application fee: $60. Electronic applications accepted. *Financial support:* In 2012–13, 35 research assistantships (averaging $14,968 per year), 3 teaching assistantships (averaging $14,315 per year) were awarded; Federal Work-Study, institutionally sponsored loans, scholarships/grants, and unspecified assistantships also available. Financial award application deadline: 4/1; financial award applicants required to submit FAFSA. *Unit head:* Dr. J. Mike Phillips, Professor and Head, 662-325-2311, Fax: 662-325-8742, E-mail: jmp657@msstate.edu. *Application contact:* Dr. William Kingery, Graduate Coordinator, 662-325-2748, Fax: 662-325-8742, E-mail: wkingery@pss.msstate.edu. Website: http://www.pss.msstate.edu/.

Missouri State University, Graduate College, William H. Darr School of Agriculture, Springfield, MO 65897. Offers plant science (MS); secondary education (MS Ed), including agriculture. Part-time programs available. *Degree requirements:* For master's, comprehensive exam, thesis or alternative. *Entrance requirements:* For master's, GRE (MS in plant science, MNAS), 9-12 teacher certification (MS Ed), minimum GPA of 3.0 (MS plant science, MNAS). Additional exam requirements/recommendations for international students: Required—TOEFL (minimum score 550 paper-based; 79 iBT). Electronic applications accepted. *Faculty research:* Grapevine biotechnology, agricultural marketing, Asian elephant reproduction, poultry science, integrated pest management.

Montana State University, College of Graduate Studies, College of Agriculture, Department of Plant Sciences and Plant Pathology, Bozeman, MT 59717. Offers plant pathology (MS); plant sciences (MS, PhD), including plant genetics (PhD), plant pathology (PhD). Part-time programs available. *Degree requirements:* For master's, comprehensive exam; for doctorate, comprehensive exam, thesis/dissertation. *Entrance requirements:* For master's, GRE General Test, minimum GPA of 3.0; for doctorate, GRE General Test. Additional exam requirements/recommendations for international students: Required—TOEFL (minimum score 550 paper-based). Electronic applications accepted. *Faculty research:* Plant genetics, plant metabolism, plant microbe interactions, plant pathology, entomology research.

New Mexico State University, Graduate School, College of Agricultural, Consumer and Environmental Sciences, Department of Entomology, Plant Pathology and Weed Science, Las Cruces, NM 88003-8001. Offers agricultural biology (MS). Part-time programs available. *Faculty:* 10 full-time (2 women), 1 (woman) part-time/adjunct. *Students:* 9 full-time (3 women), 4 part-time (2 women); includes 5 minority (4 Hispanic/Latino; 1 Two or more races, non-Hispanic/Latino), 2 international. Average age 26. 2 applicants, 100% accepted, 1 enrolled. In 2012, 5 master's awarded. *Degree requirements:* For master's, comprehensive exam, thesis. *Entrance requirements:* For master's, GRE General Test. Additional exam requirements/recommendations for international students: Required—TOEFL (minimum score 550 paper-based; 79 iBT), IELTS (minimum score 6.5). *Application deadline:* For fall admission, 7/1 priority date for domestic students; for spring admission, 11/1 priority date for domestic students. Applications are processed on a rolling basis. Application fee: $40 ($50 for international students). Electronic applications accepted. *Expenses:* Tuition, state resident: full-time $5239; part-time $218 per credit. Tuition, nonresident: full-time $18,266; part-time $761 per credit. *Required fees:* $1274; $53 per credit.

Financial support: In 2012–13, 8 students received support, including 10 research assistantships (averaging $20,660 per year); teaching assistantships, career-related internships or fieldwork, and health care benefits also available. Financial award application deadline: 3/1. *Faculty research:* Integrated pest management, pesticide application and safety, livestock ectoparasite research, biotechnology, nematology. *Total annual research expenditures:* $2.6 million. *Unit head:* Dr. Gerald K. Sims, Interim Head, 575-646-3225, Fax: 575-646-8087, E-mail: gksims@nmsu.edu. *Application contact:* Cindy Bullard, Intermediate Administrative Assistant/Recruiting Contact, 575-646-1145, Fax: 575-646-8087, E-mail: cbullard@nmsu.edu. Website: http://eppws.nmsu.edu/.

New Mexico State University, Graduate School, College of Agricultural, Consumer and Environmental Sciences, Department of Plant and Environmental Sciences, Las Cruces, NM 88003-8001. Offers horticulture (MS); plant and environmental sciences (MS, PhD). Part-time programs available. *Faculty:* 19 full-time (3 women). *Students:* 41 full-time (18 women), 15 part-time (5 women); includes 6 minority (3 American Indian or Alaska Native, non-Hispanic/Latino; 3 Hispanic/Latino), 19 international. Average age 32. 19 applicants, 32% accepted, 5 enrolled. In 2012, 6 master's, 5 doctorates awarded. Terminal master's awarded for partial completion of doctoral program. *Degree requirements:* For master's, thesis; for doctorate, one foreign language, comprehensive exam, thesis/dissertation, qualifying exam, 2 seminars. *Entrance requirements:* For master's, GRE, minimum GPA of 3.0, 3 letters of reference, letter of purpose or intent; for doctorate, GRE, minimum GPA of 3.3; 3 letters of reference, letter of purpose or intent. Additional exam requirements/recommendations for international students: Required—TOEFL (minimum score 550 paper-based; 79 iBT), IELTS (minimum score 6.5). *Application deadline:* Applications are processed on a rolling basis. Application fee: $40 ($50 for international students). Electronic applications accepted. *Expenses:* Tuition, state resident: full-time $5239; part-time $218 per credit. Tuition, nonresident: full-time $18,266; part-time $761 per credit. *Required fees:* $1274; $53 per credit. *Financial support:* In 2012–13, 39 students received support, including 1 fellowship (averaging $3,930 per year), 26 research assistantships (averaging $21,062 per year), 9 teaching assistantships (averaging $13,700 per year); career-related internships or fieldwork, Federal Work-Study, scholarships/grants, health care benefits, and unspecified assistantships also available. Support available to part-time students. Financial award application deadline: 3/1. *Faculty research:* Plant breeding and genetics, molecular biology, plant physiology, soil science and environmental remediation, urban horticulture and turfgrass management. *Total annual research expenditures:* $6.2 million. *Unit head:* Dr. Richard Pratt, Head, 575-646-3406, Fax: 575-646-6041, E-mail: ricpratt@nmsu.edu. *Application contact:* Esther Ramirez, Information Contact, 575-646-3406, Fax: 575-646-6041, E-mail: esramire@nmsu.edu. Website: http://aces.nmsu.edu/pes.

North Carolina Agricultural and Technical State University, School of Graduate Studies, School of Agriculture and Environmental Sciences, Department of Natural Resources and Environmental Design, Greensboro, NC 27411. Offers plant, soil and environmental science (MS). Part-time and evening/weekend programs available. *Degree requirements:* For master's, comprehensive exam, thesis optional, qualifying exam. *Entrance requirements:* For master's, GRE General Test, minimum GPA of 3.0. *Faculty research:* Soil parameters and compaction of forest site, controlled traffic effects on soil, improving soybean and vegetable crops.

North Dakota State University, College of Graduate and Interdisciplinary Studies, College of Agriculture, Food Systems, and Natural Resources, Department of Plant Sciences, Fargo, ND 58108. Offers horticulture (MS); plant science (MS); plant sciences (PhD). Part-time programs available. *Faculty:* 31 full-time (5 women). *Students:* 51 full-time (12 women), 18 part-time (8 women); includes 5 minority (1 Hispanic/Latino; 4 Two or more races, non-Hispanic/Latino), 39 international. Average age 30. 29 applicants, 38% accepted, 8 enrolled. In 2012, 16 master's, 3 doctorates awarded. *Degree requirements:* For master's, thesis; for doctorate, thesis/dissertation. *Entrance requirements:* Additional exam requirements/recommendations for international students: Required—TOEFL (minimum score 525 paper-based; 71 iBT). *Application deadline:* For fall admission, 5/1 for international students; for winter admission, 8/1 for international students. Applications are processed on a rolling basis. Application fee: $35. Electronic applications accepted. *Financial support:* In 2012–13, 2 fellowships (averaging $19,950 per year), 64 research assistantships were awarded; teaching assistantships, Federal Work-Study, and institutionally sponsored loans also available. Financial award application deadline: 4/15. *Faculty research:* Biotechnology, weed control science, plant breeding, plant genetics, crop physiology. *Unit head:* Dr. Richard Horsley, Head, 701-231-7971, Fax: 701-231-8474, E-mail: richard.horsley@ndsu.edu. *Application contact:* Sonya Goergen, Marketing, Recruitment, and Public Relations Coordinator, 701-231-7033, Fax: 701-231-6524. Website: http://www.ndsu.nodak.edu/.

Oklahoma State University, College of Agricultural Science and Natural Resources, Department of Horticulture and Landscape Architecture, Stillwater, OK 74078. Offers agriculture (M Ag); crop science (PhD); environmental science (PhD); horticulture (MS); plant science (PhD). *Faculty:* 19 full-time (3 women), 2 part-time/adjunct (1 woman). *Students:* 1 (woman) full-time, 7 part-time (5 women), 4 international. Average age 27. 11 applicants, 27% accepted, 2 enrolled. In 2012, 6 master's awarded. *Degree requirements:* For master's, thesis (for some programs); for doctorate, comprehensive exam, thesis/dissertation. *Entrance requirements:* For master's and doctorate, GRE or GMAT. Additional exam requirements/recommendations for international students: Required—TOEFL (minimum score 550 paper-based; 79 iBT). *Application deadline:* For fall admission, 3/1 for international students; for spring admission, 8/1 for international students. Applications are processed on a rolling basis. Application fee: $40 ($75 for international students). Electronic applications accepted. *Expenses:* Tuition, state resident: full-time $4272; part-time $178 per credit hour. Tuition, nonresident: full-time $17,016; part-time $709 per credit hour. *Required fees:* $2188; $91.17 per credit hour. One-time fee: $50 full-time. Part-time tuition and fees vary according to course load and campus/location. *Financial support:* In 2012–13, 3 research assistantships (averaging $14,964 per year), 3 teaching assistantships (averaging $14,964 per year) were awarded; career-related internships or fieldwork, Federal Work-Study, scholarships/grants, health care benefits, tuition waivers (partial), and unspecified assistantships also available. Support available to part-time students. Financial award application deadline: 3/1; financial award applicants required to submit FAFSA. *Faculty research:* Stress and postharvest physiology; water utilization and runoff; integrated pest management (IPM) systems and nursery, turf, floriculture, vegetable, net and fruit produces and natural resources, food extraction, and processing; public garden management. *Unit head:* Dr. Dale Maronek, Head, 405-744-5414, Fax: 405-744-9709. *Application contact:* Dr. Sheryl Tucker, Dean, 405-744-7099, Fax: 405-744-0355, E-mail: grad-i@okstate.edu. Website: http://www.hortla.okstate.edu/.

Oklahoma State University, College of Agricultural Science and Natural Resources, Department of Plant and Soil Sciences, Stillwater, OK 74078. Offers crop science (PhD); environmental science (PhD); plant and soil sciences (MS); plant science (PhD); soil science (M Ag, PhD). *Faculty:* 33 full-time (5 women), 1 part-time/adjunct (0 women). *Students:* 20 full-time (6 women), 37 part-time (14 women); includes 6 minority (1 Black or African American, non-Hispanic/Latino; 2 Asian, non-Hispanic/Latino; 3 Two or more races, non-Hispanic/Latino), 31 international. Average age 29. 37 applicants, 27% accepted, 6 enrolled. In 2012, 20 master's, 3 doctorates awarded. *Degree requirements:* For master's, thesis; for doctorate, comprehensive exam, thesis/dissertation. *Entrance requirements:* For master's and doctorate, GRE or GMAT. Additional exam requirements/recommendations for international students: Required—TOEFL (minimum score 550 paper-based; 79 iBT). *Application deadline:* For fall admission, 3/1 for international students; for spring admission, 8/1 for international students. Applications are processed on a rolling basis. Application fee: $40 ($75 for international students). Electronic applications accepted. *Expenses:* Tuition, state resident: full-time $4272; part-time $178 per credit hour. Tuition, nonresident: full-time $17,016; part-time $709 per credit hour. *Required fees:* $2188; $91.17 per credit hour. One-time fee: $50 full-time. Part-time tuition and fees vary according to course load and campus/location. *Financial support:* In 2012–13, 44 research assistantships (averaging $15,985 per year), 2 teaching assistantships (averaging $17,760 per year) were awarded; career-related internships or fieldwork, Federal Work-Study, scholarships/grants, health care benefits, tuition waivers (partial), and unspecified assistantships also available. Support available to part-time students. Financial award application deadline: 3/1; financial award applicants required to submit FAFSA. *Faculty research:* Crop science, weed science, rangeland ecology and management, biotechnology, breeding and genetics. *Unit head:* Dr. David Porter, Interim Head, 405-744-6130, Fax: 405-744-5269. *Application contact:* Dr. Sheryl Tucker, Dean, 405-744-7099, Fax: 405-744-0355, E-mail: grad-i@okstate.edu. Website: http://www.pss.okstate.edu.

Oklahoma State University, College of Arts and Sciences, Department of Botany, Stillwater, OK 74078. Offers botany (MS); environmental science (MS, PhD); plant science (PhD). *Faculty:* 15 full-time (6 women), 2 part-time/adjunct (1 woman). *Students:* 5 full-time (2 women), 6 part-time (3 women); includes 4 minority (1 American Indian or Alaska Native, non-Hispanic/Latino; 1 Hispanic/Latino; 2 Two or more races, non-Hispanic/Latino). Average age 28. 13 applicants, 46% accepted, 4 enrolled. In 2012, 3 master's awarded. *Degree requirements:* For master's, thesis; for doctorate, comprehensive exam, thesis/dissertation. *Entrance requirements:* For master's and doctorate, GRE or GMAT. Additional exam requirements/recommendations for international students: Required—TOEFL (minimum score 550 paper-based; 79 iBT). *Application deadline:* For fall admission, 3/1 for international students; for spring admission, 8/1 for international students. Applications are processed on a rolling basis. Application fee: $40 ($75 for international students). Electronic applications accepted. *Expenses:* Tuition, state resident: full-time $4272; part-time $178 per credit hour. Tuition, nonresident: full-time $17,016; part-time $709 per credit hour. *Required fees:* $2188; $91.17 per credit hour. One-time fee: $50 full-time. Part-time tuition and fees vary according to course load and campus/location. *Financial support:* In 2012–13, 3 research assistantships (averaging $15,770 per year), 11 teaching assistantships (averaging $14,941 per year) were awarded; career-related internships or fieldwork, Federal Work-Study, scholarships/grants, health care benefits, tuition waivers (partial), and unspecified assistantships also available. Support available to part-time students. Financial award application deadline: 3/1; financial award applicants required to submit FAFSA. *Faculty research:* Ethnobotany, developmental genetics of Arabidopsis, biological roles of Plasmodesmata, community ecology and biodiversity, nutrient cycling in grassland ecosystems. *Unit head:* Dr. Linda Watson, Head, 405-744-5559, Fax: 405-744-7074. *Application contact:* Dr. Sheryl Tucker, Dean, 405-744-7099, Fax: 405-744-0355, E-mail: grad-i@okstate.edu. Website: http://botany.okstate.edu.

Oklahoma State University, Graduate College, Stillwater, OK 74078. Offers aerospace security (Graduate Certificate); biobased products and bioenergy (Graduate Certificate); bioinformatics (Graduate Certificate); business data mining (Graduate Certificate); engineering and technology management (Graduate Certificate); environmental science (MS); global issues (Graduate Certificate);

information assurance (Graduate Certificate); international studies (MS); natural and applied science (MS); photonics (PhD); plant science (PhD); teaching English to speakers of other languages (Graduate Certificate). Programs are interdisciplinary. *Faculty:* 3 full-time (2 women), 2 part-time/adjunct (0 women). *Students:* 83 full-time (50 women), 169 part-time (90 women); includes 64 minority (16 Black or African American, non-Hispanic/Latino; 13 American Indian or Alaska Native, non-Hispanic/Latino; 13 Asian, non-Hispanic/Latino; 6 Hispanic/Latino; 1 Native Hawaiian or other Pacific Islander, non-Hispanic/Latino; 15 Two or more races, non-Hispanic/Latino), 51 international. Average age 32. 605 applicants, 71% accepted, 82 enrolled. In 2012, 76 master's, 7 doctorates awarded. *Degree requirements:* For master's, thesis (for some programs); for doctorate, comprehensive exam, thesis/dissertation. *Entrance requirements:* For master's and doctorate, GRE or GMAT. Additional exam requirements/recommendations for international students: Required—TOEFL (minimum score 550 paper-based; 79 iBT). *Application deadline:* For fall admission, 3/1 for international students; for spring admission, 8/1 for international students. Applications are processed on a rolling basis. Application fee: $40 ($75 for international students). Electronic applications accepted. *Expenses:* Tuition, state resident: full-time $4272; part-time $178 per credit hour. Tuition, nonresident: full-time $17,016; part-time $709 per credit hour. *Required fees:* $2188; $91.17 per credit hour. One-time fee: $50 full-time. Part-time tuition and fees vary according to course load and campus/location. *Financial support:* In 2012–13, 6 research assistantships (averaging $6,600 per year) were awarded; career-related internships or fieldwork, Federal Work-Study, scholarships/grants, health care benefits, tuition waivers (partial), and unspecified assistantships also available. Support available to part-time students. Financial award application deadline: 3/1; financial award applicants required to submit FAFSA. *Unit head:* Dr. Sheryl Tucker, Dean, 405-744-7099, Fax: 405-744-0355, E-mail: grad-i@okstate.edu. *Application contact:* Dr. Susan Mathew, Coordinator of Admissions, 405-744-6368, Fax: 405-744-0355, E-mail: grad-i@okstate.edu. Website: http://gradcollege.okstate.edu/.

Penn State University Park, Graduate School, College of Agricultural Sciences, Department of Plant Science, State College, University Park, PA 16802-1503. Offers agronomy (MS, PhD); horticulture (MS, PhD); turfgrass management (MPS). *Unit head:* Dr. Barbara J. Christ, Interim Dean, 814-865-2541, Fax: 814-865-3103, E-mail: ebf@psu.edu. *Application contact:* Cynthia E. Nicosia, Director of Graduate Enrollment Services, 814-865-1834, E-mail: cey1@psu.edu. Website: http://plantscience.psu.edu/.

Purdue University, Graduate School, PULSe - Purdue University Life Sciences Program, West Lafayette, IN 47907. Offers biomolecular structure and biophysics (PhD); biotechnology (PhD); chemical biology (PhD); chromatin and regulation of gene expression (PhD); integrative neuroscience (PhD); integrative plant sciences (PhD); membrane biology (PhD); microbiology (PhD); molecular evolutionary and cancer biology (PhD); molecular evolutionary genetics (PhD); molecular virology (PhD). *Students:* 152 full-time (72 women), 2 part-time (1 woman); includes 17 minority (4 Black or African American, non-Hispanic/Latino; 3 Asian, non-Hispanic/Latino; 8 Hispanic/Latino; 2 Two or more races, non-Hispanic/Latino), 70 international. Average age 27. 372 applicants, 25% accepted, 34 enrolled. *Entrance requirements:* For doctorate, GRE, minimum undergraduate GPA of 3.0. Additional exam requirements/recommendations for international students: Required—TOEFL (minimum score 550 paper-based; 77 iBT). *Application deadline:* For fall admission, 1/15 priority date for domestic students, 1/15 for international students. Applications are processed on a rolling basis. Application fee: $60 ($75 for international students). Electronic applications accepted. *Financial support:* In 2012–13, research assistantships with tuition reimbursements (averaging $22,500 per year), teaching assistantships with tuition reimbursements (averaging $22,500 per year) were awarded. *Unit head:* Dr. Christine A. Hrycyna, Head, 765-494-7322, E-mail: hrycyna@purdue.edu. *Application contact:* Colleen Gabauer, Graduate Contact, 765-494-9256, E-mail: cgabauer@purdue.edu. Website: http://www.gradschool.purdue.edu/pulse.

South Dakota State University, Graduate School, College of Agriculture and Biological Sciences, Department of Plant Science, Brookings, SD 57007. Offers agronomy (PhD); biological sciences (PhD); plant science (MS). *Degree requirements:* For master's, thesis (for some programs), oral exam; for doctorate, comprehensive exam, thesis/dissertation, preliminary oral and written exams. *Entrance requirements:* Additional exam requirements/recommendations for international students: Required—TOEFL (minimum score 560 paper-based; 83 iBT).

Southern Illinois University Carbondale, Graduate School, College of Agriculture, Department of Plant, Soil, and General Agriculture, Carbondale, IL 62901-4701. Offers horticultural science (MS); plant and soil science (MS). *Faculty:* 12 full-time (1 woman), 8 part-time/adjunct (0 women). *Students:* 2 full-time (1 woman), 32 part-time (11 women); includes 3 minority (2 Black or African American, non-Hispanic/Latino; 1 Hispanic/Latino), 6 international. 12 applicants, 42% accepted, 1 enrolled. In 2012, 7 master's awarded. *Degree requirements:* For master's, thesis. *Entrance requirements:* For master's, minimum GPA of 2.7. Additional exam requirements/recommendations for international students: Required—TOEFL. *Application deadline:* Applications are processed on a rolling basis. Application fee: $50. *Financial support:* In 2012–13, 22 students received support, including 15 research assistantships with full tuition reimbursements available, 6 teaching assistantships with full tuition reimbursements available; fellowships with full tuition reimbursements available, Federal Work-Study, institutionally sponsored loans, and tuition waivers (full) also available. Support available to part-time students. *Faculty research:* Herbicides, fertilizers, agriculture education, landscape design, plant breeding. *Total annual research expenditures:* $2 million. *Unit head:* Dr. Brian Klubek, Chair, 618-453-2496, E-mail: bklubek@siu.edu. *Application contact:* Lisa Hartline, Administrative Clerk, 618-453-1770, E-mail: lisah@siu.edu.

State University of New York College of Environmental Science and Forestry, Department of Environmental and Forest Biology, Syracuse, NY 13210-2779. Offers applied ecology (MPS); chemical ecology (MPS, MS, PhD); conservation biology (MPS, MS, PhD); ecology (MPS, MS, PhD); entomology (MPS, MS, PhD); environmental interpretation (MPS, MS, PhD); environmental physiology (MPS, MS, PhD); fish and wildlife biology and management (MPS, MS, PhD); forest pathology and mycology (MPS, MS, PhD); plant biotechnology (MPS); plant science and biotechnology (MPS, MS, PhD). *Degree requirements:* For master's, thesis (for some programs); for doctorate, comprehensive exam, thesis/dissertation. *Entrance requirements:* For master's and doctorate, GRE General Test, GRE Subject Test, minimum GPA of 3.0. Additional exam requirements/recommendations for international students: Required—TOEFL (minimum score 550 paper-based; 80 iBT), IELTS (minimum score 6). *Expenses:* Tuition, state resident: full-time $9370; part-time $390 per credit hour. Tuition, nonresident: full-time $16,680; part-time $695 per credit hour. *Required fees:* $981. Tuition and fees vary according to course load and program. *Faculty research:* Ecology, fish and wildlife biology and management, plant science, entomology.

Texas A&M University, College of Agriculture and Life Sciences, Department of Soil and Crop Sciences, College Station, TX 77843. Offers agronomy (M Agr, MS, PhD); food science and technology (MS, PhD); genetics (PhD); molecular and environmental plant sciences (MS, PhD); plant breeding (MS, PhD); soil science (MS, PhD). *Faculty:* 31. *Students:* 97 full-time (39 women), 21 part-time (6 women); includes 7 minority (1 Black or African American, non-Hispanic/Latino; 2 Asian, non-Hispanic/Latino; 4 Hispanic/Latino), 42 international. Average age 29. In 2012, 8 master's, 7 doctorates awarded. *Degree requirements:* For master's, thesis; for doctorate, thesis/dissertation. *Entrance requirements:* For master's and doctorate, GRE General Test. Additional exam requirements/recommendations for international students: Required—TOEFL. *Application deadline:* For fall admission, 3/1 priority date for domestic students; for spring admission, 8/1 for domestic students. Applications are processed on a rolling basis. Application fee: $50 ($75 for international students). *Financial support:* In 2012–13, fellowships (averaging $16,000 per year), research assistantships with partial tuition reimbursements (averaging $15,000 per year) were awarded; career-related internships or fieldwork, Federal Work-Study, and institutionally sponsored loans also available. *Faculty research:* Soil and crop management, turfgrass science, weed science, cereal chemistry, food protein chemistry. *Unit head:* Dr. David D. Baltensperger, Department Head, 979-845-3001, E-mail: dbaltensperger@ag.tamu.edu. *Application contact:* Graduate Admissions, 979-845-1044, E-mail: admissions@tamu.edu. Website: http://soilcrop.tamu.edu.

Texas A&M University–Kingsville, College of Graduate Studies, College of Agriculture and Home Economics, Program in Plant and Soil Sciences, Kingsville, TX 78363. Offers MS, PhD. *Degree requirements:* For master's, comprehensive exam, thesis or alternative. *Entrance requirements:* For master's, GRE General Test, minimum GPA of 3.0. Additional exam requirements/recommendations for international students: Required—TOEFL.

Texas Tech University, Graduate School, College of Agricultural Sciences and Natural Resources, Department of Plant and Soil Science, Lubbock, TX 79409. Offers crop science (MS); horticulture (MS); plant and soil science (PhD); plant protection (MS); soil science (MS); JD/MS. Part-time programs available. Postbaccalaureate distance learning degree programs offered (no on-campus study). *Degree requirements:* For master's, thesis or alternative; for doctorate, thesis/dissertation. *Entrance requirements:* For master's and doctorate, GRE General Test, formal approval from departmental committee. Additional exam requirements/recommendations for international students: Required—TOEFL (minimum score 550 paper-based; 79 iBT). Electronic applications accepted. *Faculty research:* Molecular and cellular biology of plant stress, physiology/genetics of crop production in semi-arid conditions, improvement of native plants, soil science and management, fibers and biopolymers.

Tuskegee University, Graduate Programs, College of Agricultural, Environmental and Natural Sciences, Department of Agricultural Sciences, Program in Plant and Soil Sciences, Tuskegee, AL 36088. Offers MS. *Degree requirements:* For master's, thesis. *Entrance requirements:* For master's, GRE General Test. Additional exam requirements/recommendations for international students: Required—TOEFL (minimum score 500 paper-based). *Expenses: Tuition:* Full-time $18,100; part-time $575 per credit hour. *Required fees:* $800.

The University of Arizona, College of Agriculture and Life Sciences, School of Plant Sciences, Program in Plant Sciences, Tucson, AZ 85721. Offers MS, PhD. *Faculty:* 19 full-time (5 women), 3 part-time/adjunct (1 woman). *Students:* 12 full-time (4 women), 1 part-time (0 women); includes 2 minority (1 Hispanic/Latino; 1 Two or more races, non-Hispanic/Latino), 4 international. Average age 29. 24 applicants, 13% accepted, 3 enrolled. *Entrance requirements:* Additional exam requirements/recommendations for international students: Required—TOEFL (minimum score 550 paper-based; 79 iBT). *Application deadline:* For fall admission, 12/15 for domestic and international students; for spring admission, 6/15 for domestic and international students. Application fee: $75. Electronic applications accepted. *Financial support:* In 2012–13, 13 research assistantships with full and partial tuition reimbursements (averaging $21,988 per year), 9 teaching assistantships with full and partial tuition reimbursements (averaging $21,988 per year) were awarded. *Faculty research:* Biochemistry and physiology, biodiversity and evolutionarily biology, cell and developmental biology, controlled environmental agriculture, crop and horticultural management and production, environmental and stress biology. *Total annual research expenditures:* $600,208. *Unit head:* Dr. Brian Larkins, Department Head, 520-621-9958, E-mail: larkins@email.arizona.edu. *Application contact:* Georgina Lambert, Graduate Coordinator, 520-621-1219, E-mail: georgina@cals.arizona.edu.

University of Arkansas, Graduate School, Dale Bumpers College of Agricultural, Food and Life Sciences, Interdepartmental Program in Plant Science, Fayetteville, AR 72701-1201. Offers PhD. *Students:* 2 full-time (1 woman), 10 part-time (4 women), 4 international. In 2012, 1 doctorate awarded. *Degree requirements:* For doctorate, thesis/dissertation. *Application deadline:* For fall admission, 4/1 for international students; for spring admission, 10/1 for international students. Applications are processed on a rolling basis. Application fee: $40 ($50 for international students). Electronic applications accepted. *Financial support:* In 2012–13, 9 research assistantships were awarded; fellowships with tuition reimbursements, teaching assistantships, career-related internships or fieldwork, and Federal Work-Study also available. Support available to part-time students. Financial award application deadline: 4/1; financial award applicants required to submit FAFSA. *Unit head:* Dr. A. Rick Bennett, Department Head, 479-575-2445, E-mail: rbennett@uark.edu. *Application contact:* Dr. Ioannis Tzanetakis, Graduate Coordinator, 479-575-3180, E-mail: itzaneta@uark.edu. Website: http://plantpathology.uark.edu/.

The University of British Columbia, Faculty of Land and Food Systems, Plant Science Program, Vancouver, BC V6T 1Z1, Canada. Offers M Sc, PhD. Part-time programs available. *Degree requirements:* For master's, thesis; for doctorate, comprehensive exam, thesis/dissertation. *Entrance requirements:* Additional exam requirements/recommendations for international students: Required—TOEFL (minimum score 577 paper-based; 90 iBT), IELTS (minimum score 6.5). Electronic applications accepted. *Faculty research:* Plant physiology and biochemistry, biotechnology, plant protection (insect, weeds, and diseases), plant breeding, plant-environment interaction.

University of California, Riverside, Graduate Division, Department of Botany and Plant Sciences, Riverside, CA 92521-0102. Offers plant biology (MS, PhD), including plant cell, molecular, and developmental biology (PhD), plant ecology (PhD), plant genetics (PhD). Part-time programs available. Terminal master's awarded for partial completion of doctoral program. *Degree requirements:* For master's, comprehensive exams or thesis; for doctorate, thesis/dissertation, qualifying exams. *Entrance requirements:* For master's and doctorate, GRE General Test, minimum GPA of 3.2. Additional exam requirements/recommendations for international students: Required—TOEFL (minimum score 550 paper-based; 80 iBT). Electronic applications accepted. *Expenses:* Tuition, state resident: full-time $14,646. Tuition, nonresident: full-time $29,748. *Faculty research:* Agricultural plant biology; biochemistry and physiology; cellular, molecular and developmental biology; ecology, evolution, systematics and ethnobotany; genetics, genomics and bioinformatics.

University of Connecticut, Graduate School, College of Agriculture and Natural Resources, Department of Plant Science, Storrs, CT 06269. Offers plant and soil sciences (MS, PhD). Terminal master's awarded for partial completion of doctoral program. *Degree requirements:* For master's, comprehensive exam; for doctorate, thesis/dissertation. *Entrance requirements:* For master's and doctorate, GRE General Test, GRE Subject Test. Additional exam requirements/recommendations for international students: Required—TOEFL (minimum score 550 paper-based). Electronic applications accepted.

University of Delaware, College of Agriculture and Natural Resources, Department of Plant and Soil Sciences, Newark, DE 19716. Offers MS, PhD. Part-time programs available. Terminal master's awarded for partial completion of doctoral program. *Degree requirements:* For master's, thesis; for doctorate, thesis/dissertation. *Entrance requirements:* For master's and doctorate, GRE General Test. Additional exam requirements/recommendations for international students: Required—TOEFL (minimum score 550 paper-based). Electronic applications accepted. *Faculty research:* Soil chemistry, plant and cell tissue culture, plant breeding and genetics, soil physics, soil biochemistry, plant molecular biology, soil microbiology.

University of Florida, Graduate School, College of Agricultural and Life Sciences, Program in Plant Medicine, Gainesville, FL 32611. Offers plant medicine (DPM); tropical conservation and development (DPM). Part-time programs available. *Degree requirements:* For doctorate, comprehensive exam, thesis/dissertation. *Entrance requirements:* For doctorate, GRE General Test, minimum GPA of 3.0. Additional exam requirements/recommendations for international students: Required—TOEFL (minimum score 550 paper-based; 80 iBT), IELTS (minimum score 6).

University of Georgia, College of Agricultural and Environmental Sciences, Institute of Plant Breeding, Genetics and Genomics, Athens, GA 30602. Offers MS, PhD.

University of Hawaii at Manoa, Graduate Division, College of Tropical Agriculture and Human Resources, Department of Plant and Environmental Protection Sciences, Honolulu, HI 96822. Offers entomology (MS, PhD); tropical plant pathology (MS, PhD). Part-time programs available. Terminal master's awarded for partial completion of doctoral program. *Degree requirements:* For master's, thesis optional; for doctorate, comprehensive exam, thesis/dissertation. *Entrance requirements:* For master's and doctorate, GRE General Test. Additional exam requirements/recommendations for international students: Required—TOEFL (minimum score 500 paper-based; 61 iBT), IELTS (minimum score 5). *Faculty research:* Nematology, virology, mycology, bacteriology, epidemiology.

University of Idaho, College of Graduate Studies, College of Agricultural and Life Sciences, Department of Plant, Soil, and Entomological Sciences, Moscow, ID 83844-2339. Offers entomology (MS, PhD); plant science (MS, PhD); soil and land resources (MS, PhD). *Faculty:* 28 full-time, 1 part-time/adjunct. *Students:* 33 full-time, 13 part-time. Average age 30. In 2012, 9 master's, 2 doctorates awarded. *Degree requirements:* For doctorate, thesis/dissertation. *Entrance requirements:* For master's and doctorate, GRE General Test, minimum GPA of 3.0. *Application deadline:* For fall admission, 7/1 for domestic students; for spring admission, 11/1 for domestic students. Applications are processed on a rolling basis. Application fee: $60. Electronic applications accepted. *Expenses:* Tuition, state resident: full-time $4230; part-time $252 per credit hour. Tuition, nonresident: full-time $17,018; part-time $891 per credit hour. *Required fees:* $2932; $107 per credit hour. *Financial support:* Research assistantships and teaching assistantships available. Financial award applicants required to submit FAFSA. *Faculty research:* Entomological sciences, crop and weed science, horticultural science, soil and land resources. *Unit head:* Dr. James B. Johnson, Department Head, 208-885-6274, Fax: 208-885-7760, E-mail: nthompson@uidaho.edu. *Application contact:* Erick Larson, Director of Graduate Admissions, 208-885-4723, E-mail: gadms@uidaho.edu. Website: http://www.uidaho.edu/pses.

University of Kentucky, Graduate School, College of Agriculture, Program in Plant and Soil Science, Lexington, KY 40506-0032. Offers MS. *Degree requirements:* For master's, comprehensive exam, thesis optional. *Entrance requirements:* For master's, GRE General Test, minimum undergraduate GPA of 2.75, graduate 3.0. Additional exam requirements/recommendations for international students: Required—TOEFL (minimum score 550 paper-based). Electronic applications accepted.

University of Maine, Graduate School, College of Natural Sciences, Forestry, and Agriculture, Department of Plant, Soil, and Environmental Sciences, Orono, ME 04469. Offers ecology and environmental sciences (MS); horticulture (MS); plant, soil, and environmental sciences (MS). *Faculty:* 18 full-time (6 women), 3 part-time/adjunct. *Students:* 9 full-time (7 women), 2 part-time (0 women), 1 international. Average age 30. 11 applicants, 9% accepted, 1 enrolled. In 2012, 3 master's awarded. *Degree requirements:* For master's, thesis (for some programs). *Entrance requirements:* For master's, GRE General Test. Additional exam requirements/recommendations for international students: Required—TOEFL. *Application deadline:* Applications are processed on a rolling basis. Application fee: $65. Electronic applications accepted. *Financial support:* In 2012–13, 16 research assistantships with full tuition reimbursements (averaging $17,336 per year), 1 teaching assistantship with full tuition reimbursement (averaging $13,600 per year) were awarded; scholarships/grants, tuition waivers (full and partial), and unspecified assistantships also available. *Total annual research expenditures:* $179,065. *Unit head:* Dr. Eric Gallandt, Chair, 207-581-2933, Fax: 207-581-3207. *Application contact:* Scott G. Delcourt, Associate Dean of the Graduate School, 207-581-3291, Fax: 207-581-3232, E-mail: graduate@maine.edu. Website: http://umaine.edu/pse/.

University of Maine, Graduate School, College of Natural Sciences, Forestry, and Agriculture, School of Biology and Ecology, Orono, ME 04469. Offers biological sciences (PhD); botany and plant pathology (MS); ecology and environmental science (MS, PhD); entomology (MS); plant science (PhD); zoology (MS, PhD). Part-time programs available. *Faculty:* 33 full-time (13 women), 26 part-time/adjunct (5 women). *Students:* 60 full-time (38 women), 9 part-time (5 women); includes 3 minority (1 American Indian or Alaska Native, non-Hispanic/Latino; 1 Asian, non-Hispanic/Latino; 1 Hispanic/Latino), 6 international. Average age 29. 71 applicants, 20% accepted, 12 enrolled. In 2012, 16 master's, 6 doctorates awarded. *Degree requirements:* For doctorate, comprehensive exam, thesis/dissertation. *Entrance requirements:* For master's and doctorate, GRE General Test. Additional exam requirements/recommendations for international students: Required—TOEFL. *Application deadline:* For fall admission, 2/1 priority date for domestic students. Applications are processed on a rolling basis. Application fee: $65. Electronic applications accepted. *Financial support:* In 2012–13, 1 fellowship with full tuition reimbursement (averaging $18,000 per year), 5 research assistantships with full tuition reimbursements (averaging $18,000 per year), 19 teaching assistantships with full tuition reimbursements (averaging $13,600 per year) were awarded; career-related internships or fieldwork, Federal Work-Study, institutionally sponsored loans, and tuition waivers (full and partial) also available. Financial award application deadline: 3/1. *Total annual research expenditures:* $569,533. *Unit head:* Dr. Ellie Groden, Director, 207-581-2551, Fax: 207-581-2537. *Application contact:* Scott G. Delcourt, Associate Dean of the Graduate School, 207-581-3291, Fax: 207-581-3232, E-mail: graduate@maine.edu. Website: http://sbe.umaine.edu/.

The University of Manchester, Faculty of Life Sciences, Manchester, United Kingdom. Offers adaptive organismal biology (M Phil, PhD); animal biology (M Phil, PhD); biochemistry (M Phil, PhD); bioinformatics (M Phil, PhD); biomolecular sciences (M Phil, PhD); biotechnology (M Phil, PhD); cell biology (M Phil, PhD); cell matrix research (M Phil, PhD); channels and transporters

(M Phil, PhD); developmental biology (M Phil, PhD); Egyptology (M Phil, PhD); environmental biology (M Phil, PhD); evolutionary biology (M Phil, PhD); gene expression (M Phil, PhD); genetics (M Phil, PhD); history of science, technology and medicine (M Phil, PhD); immunology (M Phil, PhD); integrative neurobiology and behavior (M Phil, PhD); membrane trafficking (M Phil, PhD); microbiology (M Phil, PhD); molecular and cellular neuroscience (M Phil, PhD); molecular biology (M Phil, PhD); molecular cancer studies (M Phil, PhD); neuroscience (M Phil, PhD); ophthalmology (M Phil, PhD); optometry (M Phil, PhD); organelle function (M Phil, PhD); pharmacology (M Phil, PhD); physiology (M Phil, PhD); plant sciences (M Phil, PhD); stem cell research (M Phil, PhD); structural biology (M Phil, PhD); systems neuroscience (M Phil, PhD); toxicology (M Phil, PhD).

University of Manitoba, Faculty of Graduate Studies, Faculty of Agricultural and Food Sciences, Department of Plant Science, Winnipeg, MB R3T 2N2, Canada. Offers agronomy and plant protection (M Sc, PhD); horticulture (M Sc, PhD); plant breeding and genetics (M Sc, PhD); plant physiology-biochemistry (M Sc, PhD). *Degree requirements:* For master's, thesis; for doctorate, one foreign language, thesis/dissertation.

University of Massachusetts Amherst, Graduate School, Interdisciplinary Programs, Program in Plant Biology, Amherst, MA 01003. Offers biochemistry and metabolism (MS, PhD); cell biology and physiology (MS, PhD); environmental, ecological and integrative biology (MS, PhD); genetics and evolution (MS, PhD). *Students:* 20 full-time (12 women), 1 (woman) part-time; includes 1 minority (Two or more races, non-Hispanic/Latino), 8 international. Average age 27. 35 applicants, 29% accepted, 8 enrolled. In 2012, 1 master's, 3 doctorates awarded. *Degree requirements:* For master's, thesis; for doctorate, 2 foreign languages, comprehensive exam, thesis/dissertation. *Entrance requirements:* For master's and doctorate, GRE General Test. Additional exam requirements/recommendations for international students: Required—TOEFL (minimum score 550 paper-based; 80 iBT), IELTS (minimum score 6.5). *Application deadline:* For fall admission, 12/15 for domestic and international students; for spring admission, 10/1 for domestic and international students. Applications are processed on a rolling basis. Application fee: $75. Electronic applications accepted. *Expenses:* Tuition, state resident: full-time $1980; part-time $110 per credit. Tuition, nonresident: full-time $13,314; part-time $414 per credit. *Required fees:* $10,338; $3594 per semester. One-time fee: $357. *Financial support:* Fellowships with full and partial tuition reimbursements, research assistantships with full and partial tuition reimbursements, teaching assistantships with full and partial tuition reimbursements, career-related internships or fieldwork, Federal Work-Study, scholarships/grants, traineeships, health care benefits, tuition waivers (full and partial), and unspecified assistantships available. Support available to part-time students. Financial award application deadline: 12/15; financial award applicants required to submit FAFSA. *Unit head:* Dr. Elsbeth L. Walker, Graduate Program Director, 413-577-3217, Fax: 413-545-3243. *Application contact:* Lindsay DeSantis, Supervisor of Admissions, 413-545-0722, Fax: 413-577-0010, E-mail: gradadm@grad.umass.edu. Website: http://www.bio.umass.edu/plantbio/.

University of Minnesota, Twin Cities Campus, Graduate School, College of Food, Agricultural and Natural Resource Sciences, Program in Applied Plant Sciences, Minneapolis, MN 55455-0213. Offers MS, PhD. Part-time programs available. *Faculty:* 59 full-time. *Students:* 72 full-time (31 women); includes 5 minority (1 Black or African American, non-Hispanic/Latino; 1 American Indian or Alaska Native, non-Hispanic/Latino; 3 Asian, non-Hispanic/Latino), 13 international. Average age 30. 64 applicants, 19% accepted, 11 enrolled. In 2012, 3 master's, 1 doctorate awarded. Terminal master's awarded for partial completion of doctoral program. *Degree requirements:* For master's, comprehensive exam, thesis; for doctorate, comprehensive exam, thesis/dissertation. *Entrance requirements:* For master's and doctorate, GRE General Test. Additional exam requirements/recommendations for international students: Required—TOEFL (minimum score 550 paper-based; 79 iBT), IELTS (minimum score 6.5). *Application deadline:* For fall admission, 12/1 priority date for domestic students, 12/1 for international students; for spring admission, 10/15 priority date for domestic students, 10/15 for international students. Applications are processed on a rolling basis. Application fee: $75 ($95 for international students). Electronic applications accepted. *Financial support:* In 2012–13, fellowships with full tuition reimbursements (averaging $40,000 per year), research assistantships with full and partial tuition reimbursements (averaging $40,000 per year), teaching assistantships (averaging $40,000 per year) were awarded; scholarships/grants, traineeships, health care benefits, tuition waivers, and unspecified assistantships also available. *Faculty research:* Weed science, horticulture, crop management, sustainable agriculture, biotechnology, plant breeding. *Total annual research expenditures:* $8,529. *Unit head:* Dr. Alan Smith, Director of Graduate Studies, 612-624-9290, Fax: 612-625-1268, E-mail: smith022@umn.edu. *Application contact:* Lynne Medgaarden, Assistant to the Director of Graduate Studies, 612-625-4742, Fax: 612-625-1268, E-mail: medga001@umn.edu. Website: http://www.appliedplantsciences.umn.edu/.

University of Missouri, Graduate School, College of Agriculture, Food and Natural Resources, Division of Plant Sciences, Columbia, MO 65211. Offers crop, soil and pest management (MS, PhD); entomology (MS, PhD); horticulture (MS, PhD); plant biology and genetics (MS, PhD); plant stress biology (MS, PhD). *Faculty:* 40 full-time (11 women). *Students:* 75 full-time (36 women), 10 part-time (2 women); includes 4 minority (2 Black or African American, non-Hispanic/Latino; 1 American Indian or Alaska Native, non-Hispanic/Latino; 1 Hispanic/Latino), 28 international. Average age 28. 67 applicants, 22% accepted, 15 enrolled. In 2012, 8 master's, 9 doctorates awarded. Terminal master's awarded for partial completion of doctoral program. *Degree requirements:* For master's, thesis; for doctorate, comprehensive exam, thesis/dissertation. *Entrance requirements:* For master's and doctorate, GRE General Test, minimum GPA of 3.0; bachelor's degree from accredited college. Additional exam requirements/recommendations for international students: Required—TOEFL (minimum score 500 paper-based; 61 iBT), IELTS (minimum score 5.5). *Application deadline:* For fall admission, 1/15 priority date for domestic students, 1/15 for international students. Applications are processed on a rolling basis. Application fee: $55 ($75 for international students). Electronic applications accepted. *Expenses:* Tuition, state resident: full-time $6057. Tuition, nonresident: full-time $15,683. *Required fees:* $1000. *Financial support:* In 2012–13, 2 fellowships with tuition reimbursements, 59 research assistantships with tuition reimbursements, 1 teaching assistantship with tuition reimbursement were awarded; institutionally sponsored loans, scholarships/grants, health care benefits, and unspecified assistantships also available. Support available to part-time students. *Faculty research:* Crop, soil and pest management; entomology; horticulture; plant biology and genetics; plant microbiology and pathology. *Unit head:* Dr. Michael Collins, Director, 573-882-1957, E-mail: collinsm@missouri.edu. *Application contact:* Dr. James Schoelz, Director of Graduate Studies, 573-882-1185, E-mail: schoelzj@missouri.edu. Website: http://plantsci.missouri.edu/graduate/.

University of Saskatchewan, College of Graduate Studies and Research, College of Agriculture, Department of Plant Sciences, Saskatoon, SK S7N 5A2, Canada. Offers M Sc, PhD. *Degree requirements:* For master's, thesis; for doctorate, comprehensive exam (for some programs), thesis/dissertation. *Entrance requirements:* Additional exam requirements/recommendations for international students: Required—TOEFL (minimum score 80 iBT); Recommended—IELTS (minimum score 6.5).

The University of Tennessee, Graduate School, College of Agricultural Sciences and Natural Resources, Department of Plant Sciences, Knoxville, TN 37996. Offers floriculture (MS); landscape design (MS); public horticulture (MS); turfgrass (MS); woody ornamentals (MS). Part-time programs available. *Degree requirements:* For master's, thesis or alternative. *Entrance requirements:* For master's, minimum GPA of 2.7. Additional exam requirements/recommendations for international students: Required—TOEFL. Electronic applications accepted. *Expenses:* Tuition, state resident: full-time $9000; part-time $501 per credit hour. Tuition, nonresident: full-time $27,188; part-time $1512 per credit hour. *Required fees:* $1280; $62 per credit hour. Tuition and fees vary according to program.

University of Vermont, Graduate College, College of Agriculture and Life Sciences, Department of Plant and Soil Science, Burlington, VT 05405. Offers MS, PhD. *Students:* 25 (17 women); includes 1 minority (Asian, non-Hispanic/Latino), 3 international. 28 applicants, 36% accepted, 4 enrolled. In 2012, 4 master's, 1 doctorate awarded. *Degree requirements:* For master's, thesis; for doctorate, one foreign language, thesis/dissertation. *Entrance requirements:* For master's and doctorate, GRE General Test. Additional exam requirements/recommendations for international students: Required—TOEFL (minimum score 550 paper-based; 80 iBT). *Application deadline:* For fall admission, 2/15 priority date for domestic students, 2/15 for international students. Applications are processed on a rolling basis. Application fee: $40. Electronic applications accepted. *Expenses: Tuition, area resident:* Part-time $572 per credit. Tuition, nonresident: part-time $1444 per credit. *Financial support:* Fellowships, research assistantships, and teaching assistantships available. Financial award application deadline: 3/1. *Faculty research:* Soil chemistry, plant nutrition. *Unit head:* Dr. Ernesto Mendez, Acting Chairperson, 802-656-2630. *Application contact:* Dr. Josef Gorres, Coordinator, 802-656-2630. Website: http://www.uvm.edu/~pss.

The University of Western Ontario, Faculty of Graduate Studies, Biosciences Division, Department of Plant Sciences, London, ON N6A 5B8, Canada. Offers plant and environmental sciences (M Sc); plant sciences (M Sc, PhD); plant sciences and environmental sciences (PhD); plant sciences and molecular biology (M Sc, PhD). *Degree requirements:* For master's, thesis; for doctorate, thesis/dissertation. *Entrance requirements:* For doctorate, M Sc or equivalent. Additional exam requirements/recommendations for international students: Required—TOEFL. *Faculty research:* Ecology systematics, plant biochemistry and physiology, yeast genetics, molecular biology.

University of Wisconsin–Madison, Graduate School, College of Agricultural and Life Sciences, Department of Agronomy, Madison, WI 53706-1380. Offers agronomy (MS, PhD); plant breeding and plant genetics (MS, PhD). *Degree requirements:* For master's, thesis or alternative; for doctorate, thesis/dissertation. *Entrance requirements:* For master's and doctorate, GRE, minimum GPA of 3.0. Additional exam requirements/recommendations for international students: Required—TOEFL (minimum score 580 paper-based). Electronic applications accepted. *Expenses:* Tuition, state resident: full-time $10,728; part-time $743 per credit. Tuition, nonresident: full-time $24,054; part-time $1575 per credit. *Required fees:* $1111; $72 per credit. *Faculty research:* Plant breeding and genetics, plant molecular biology and physiology, cropping systems and management, weed science.

University of Wisconsin–Madison, Graduate School, College of Agricultural and Life Sciences, Plant Breeding and Plant Genetics Program, Madison, WI 53706-1380. Offers MS, PhD. Part-time programs available. Terminal master's awarded for partial completion of doctoral program. *Degree requirements:* For master's, comprehensive exam, thesis; for doctorate, comprehensive exam, thesis/dissertation, formal exit seminar. *Entrance requirements:* For master's and

Plant Sciences

doctorate, GRE, minimum GPA of 3.0. Additional exam requirements/ recommendations for international students: Required—TOEFL (minimum: 550 paper, 80 iBT), IELTS (minimum: 6) or Michigan English Language Assessment Battery (minimum: 77). Electronic applications accepted. *Expenses:* Tuition, state resident: full-time $10,728; part-time $743 per credit. Tuition, nonresident: full-time $24,054; part-time $1575 per credit. *Required fees:* $1111; $72 per credit. *Faculty research:* Plant improvement, classical and molecular genetics, quantitative and statistical genetics, cytogenetics, stress and pest resistances.

Utah State University, School of Graduate Studies, College of Agriculture, Department of Plants, Soils, and Biometeorology, Logan, UT 84322. Offers biometeorology (MS, PhD); ecology (MS, PhD); plant science (MS, PhD); soil science (MS, PhD). Part-time programs available. Terminal master's awarded for partial completion of doctoral program. *Degree requirements:* For master's, thesis; for doctorate, thesis/dissertation. *Entrance requirements:* For master's, GRE General Test, BS in plant, soil, atmospheric science, or related field; minimum GPA of 3.0; for doctorate, GRE General Test, minimum GPA of 3.0. Additional exam requirements/recommendations for international students: Required— TOEFL. Electronic applications accepted. *Faculty research:* Biotechnology and genomics, plant physiology and biology, nutrient and water efficient landscapes, physical-chemical-biological processes in soil, environmental biophysics and climate.

Virginia State University, School of Graduate Studies, Research, and Outreach, School of Agriculture, Department of Agriculture and Human Ecology, Petersburg, VA 23806-0001. Offers plant science (MS).

West Texas A&M University, College of Agriculture, Science and Engineering, Department of Agricultural Sciences, Emphasis in Plant, Soil and Environmental Science, Canyon, TX 79016-0001. Offers MS. Part-time programs available. *Degree requirements:* For master's, comprehensive exam, thesis optional. *Entrance requirements:* For master's, GRE General Test. Additional exam requirements/recommendations for international students: Required—TOEFL (minimum score 550 paper-based). Electronic applications accepted. *Faculty research:* Crop and soil disciplines.

West Virginia University, Davis College of Agriculture, Forestry and Consumer Sciences, Division of Plant and Soil Sciences, Program in Agricultural Sciences, Morgantown, WV 26506. Offers animal and food sciences (PhD); plant and soil sciences (PhD). *Degree requirements:* For doctorate, thesis/dissertation, oral and written exams. *Entrance requirements:* Additional exam requirements/recommendations for international students: Required—TOEFL. *Faculty research:* Ruminant nutrition, metabolism, forage utilization, physiology, reproduction.

Viticulture and Enology

California State University, Fresno, Division of Graduate Studies, College of Agricultural Sciences and Technology, Department of Viticulture and Enology, Fresno, CA 93740-8027. Offers MS. Part-time and evening/weekend programs available. *Degree requirements:* For master's, comprehensive exam (for some programs), thesis (for some programs). *Entrance requirements:* For master's, GRE General Test, minimum GPA of 2.5. Additional exam requirements/recommendations for international students: Required—TOEFL. Electronic applications accepted. *Faculty research:* Ethel carbonate formation, clinical an physiological characterization, grape and wine quality.

University of California, Davis, Graduate Studies, Graduate Group in Viticulture and Enology, Davis, CA 95616. Offers MS, PhD. *Degree requirements:* For master's, comprehensive exam (for some programs), thesis (for some programs). *Entrance requirements:* Additional exam requirements/recommendations for international students: Required—TOEFL (minimum score 550 paper-based).

430 www.petersonsbooks.com

Peterson's Graduate Programs in the Physical Sciences, Mathematics, Agricultural Sciences, the Environment & Natural Resources 2014

ACADEMIC AND PROFESSIONAL PROGRAMS IN THE ENVIRONMENT AND NATURAL RESOURCES

Section 9
Environmental Sciences and Management

This section contains a directory of institutions offering graduate work in environmental sciences and management, followed by an in-depth entry submitted by an institution that chose to prepare a detailed program description. Additional information about programs listed in the directory but not augmented by an in-depth entry may be obtained by writing directly to the dean of a graduate school or chair of a department at the address given in the directory.

For programs offering related work, see also in this book *Natural Resources.* In the other guides in this series:

Graduate Programs in the Humanities, Arts & Social Sciences
See *Political Science and International Affairs* and *Public, Regional, and Industrial Affairs*

Graduate Programs in the Biological/Biomedical Sciences & Health-Related Medical Professions
See *Ecology, Environmental Biology, and Evolutionary Biology*

Graduate Programs in Engineering & Applied Sciences
See *Management of Engineering and Technology*

CONTENTS

Program Directories

Display and Close-Up

Environmental Management and Policy

Adelphi University, College of Arts and Sciences, Program in Environmental Studies, Garden City, NY 11530-0701. Offers MS. *Students:* 10 full-time (5 women), 6 part-time (2 women); includes 3 minority (1 Black or African American, non-Hispanic/Latino; 1 Asian, non-Hispanic/Latino; 1 Hispanic/Latino), 1 international. Average age 27. In 2012, 6 master's awarded. *Degree requirements:* For master's, thesis optional. *Entrance requirements:* For master's, GRE General Test, 2 letters of recommendation; course work in microeconomics, political science, statistics/calculus, and either chemistry or physics; computer literacy. Additional exam requirements/recommendations for international students: Required—TOEFL (minimum score 550 paper-based; 80 iBT). *Application deadline:* For fall admission, 5/1 for international students; for spring admission, 11/1 for international students. Applications are processed on a rolling basis. Application fee: $50. Electronic applications accepted. *Financial support:* Research assistantships with full and partial tuition reimbursements, teaching assistantships, career-related internships or fieldwork, Federal Work-Study, institutionally sponsored loans, and unspecified assistantships available. Financial award application deadline: 2/15; financial award applicants required to submit FAFSA. *Faculty research:* Contaminates sites, workplace exposure level of contaminants, climate change and human health. *Unit head:* Dr. Anagnostis Agelarakis, Director, 516-877-4112, E-mail: agelarak@adelphi.edu. *Application contact:* Christine Murphy, Director of Admissions, 516-877-3050, Fax: 516-877-3039, E-mail: graduateadmissions@adelphi.edu. Website: http://academics.adelphi.edu/arts-sciences-programs/ms-environmental-study.php.

See Display on page 461 and Close-Up on page 491.

Air Force Institute of Technology, Graduate School of Engineering and Management, Department of Systems and Engineering Management, Dayton, OH 45433-7765. Offers cost analysis (MS); environmental and engineering management (MS); environmental engineering science (MS); information resource/systems management (MS). *Accreditation:* ABET. Part-time programs available. *Degree requirements:* For master's, thesis. *Entrance requirements:* For master's, GRE, GMAT, minimum GPA of 3.0.

American Public University System, AMU/APU Graduate Programs, Charles Town, WV 25414. Offers accounting (MBA, MS); criminal justice (MA), including business administration, emergency and disaster management, general (MA, MS); educational leadership (M Ed); emergency and disaster management (MA); entrepreneurship (MBA); environmental policy and management (MS), including environmental planning, environmental sustainability, fish and wildlife management, general (MA, MS), global environmental management; finance (MBA); general (MBA); global business management (MBA); history (MA), including American history, ancient and classical history, European history, global history, public history; homeland security (MA), including business administration, counter-terrorism studies, criminal justice, cyber, emergency management and public health, intelligence studies, transportation security; homeland security resource allocation (MBA); humanities (MA); information technology (MS), including digital forensics, enterprise software development, information assurance and security, IT project management; information technology management (MBA); intelligence studies (MA), including criminal intelligence, cyber, general (MA, MS), homeland security, intelligence analysis, intelligence collection, intelligence management, intelligence operations, terrorism studies; international relations and conflict resolution (MA), including comparative and security issues, conflict resolution, international and transnational security issues, peacekeeping; legal studies (MA); management (MA), including defense management, general (MA, MS), human resource management, organizational leadership, public administration; marketing (MBA); military history (MA), including American military history, American Revolution, civil war, war since 1945, World War II; military studies (MA), including joint warfare, strategic leadership; national security studies (MA), including general (MA, MS), homeland security, regional security studies, security and intelligence analysis, terrorism studies; nonprofit management (MBA); political science (MA), including American politics and government, comparative government and development, general (MA, MS), international relations, public policy; psychology (MA), including general (MA, MS), maritime engineering management, reverse logistics management; public administration (MPA), including disaster management, environmental policy, health policy, human resources, national security, organizational management, security management; public health (MPH); reverse logistics management (MA); school counseling (M Ed); security management (MA); space studies (MS), including aerospace science, general (MA, MS), planetary science; sports and health sciences (MS); sports management (MS), including coaching theory and strategy, general (MA, MS), sports administration; teaching (M Ed), including curriculum and instruction for elementary teachers, elementary reading, English language learners, instructional leadership, online learning, special education; transportation and logistics management (MA), including general (MA, MS), maritime engineering management, reverse logistics management. Programs offered via distance learning only. Part-time and evening/weekend programs available. Postbaccalaureate distance learning degree programs offered (no on-campus study). *Faculty:* 439 full-time (246 women), 1,493 part-time/adjunct (708 women). *Students:* 611 full-time (284 women), 11,732 part-time (4,476 women); includes 3,985 minority (2,112 Black or African American, non-Hispanic/Latino; 103 American Indian or Alaska Native, non-Hispanic/Latino; 336 Asian, non-Hispanic/Latino; 915 Hispanic/Latino; 113 Native Hawaiian or other Pacific Islander, non-Hispanic/Latino; 406 Two or more races, non-Hispanic/Latino), 167 international. Average age 36. In 2012, 2,761 master's awarded. *Degree requirements:* For master's, comprehensive exam or practicum. *Entrance requirements:* For master's, official transcript showing earned bachelor's degree from institution accredited by recognized accrediting body. Additional exam requirements/recommendations for international students: Required—TOEFL (minimum score 550 paper-based), IELTS (minimum score 6.5). *Application deadline:* Applications are processed on a rolling basis. Application fee: $0. Electronic applications accepted. *Financial support:* Applicants required to submit FAFSA. *Faculty research:* Military history, criminal justice, management performance, national security. *Unit head:* Dr. Karan Powell, Executive Vice President and Provost, 877-468-6268, Fax: 304-724-3780. *Application contact:* Terry Grant, Vice President of Enrollment Management, 877-468-6268, Fax: 304-724-3780, E-mail: info@apus.edu. Website: http://www.apus.edu.

American University, College of Arts and Sciences, Department of Environmental Science, Washington, DC 20016-8070. Offers environmental assessment (Graduate Certificate); environmental science (MS). *Faculty:* 6 full-time (1 woman), 4 part-time/adjunct (1 woman). *Students:* 7 full-time (4 women), 6 part-time (5 women); includes 3 minority (1 Black or African American, non-Hispanic/Latino; 1 Asian, non-Hispanic/Latino; 1 Two or more races, non-Hispanic/Latino), 2 international. Average age 30. 16 applicants, 75% accepted, 3 enrolled. In 2012, 7 master's awarded. *Degree requirements:* For master's, comprehensive exam, thesis (for some programs). *Entrance requirements:* For master's, GRE General Test, GRE Subject Test, one year of calculus, lab science. Additional exam requirements/recommendations for international students: Required—TOEFL. *Application deadline:* For fall admission, 2/1 for domestic students; for spring admission, 10/1 for domestic students. Application fee: $80. *Expenses: Tuition:* Full-time $25,920; part-time $1440 per credit. *Required fees:* $430. Tuition and fees vary according to course load, campus/location and program. *Financial support:* Research assistantships and teaching assistantships available. Financial award application deadline: 2/1. *Unit head:* Dr. Albert Mei-Chu Cheh, Chair, 202-885-8014, Fax: 202-885-1752, E-mail: acheh@american.edu. *Application contact:* Kathleen Clowery, Director, Graduate Admissions, 202-885-3621, Fax: 202-885-1505, E-mail: clowery@american.edu. Website: http://www.american.edu/cas/environmental/.

American University, School of International Service, Washington, DC 20016-8071. Offers comparative and international disability policy (MA); comparative and regional studies (Certificate); cross-cultural communication (Certificate); development management (MS); ethics, peace, and global affairs (MA); European studies (Certificate); global environmental policy (MA, Certificate); global information technology (Certificate); international affairs (MA), including comparative and international disability policy, comparative and regional studies, international economic relations, international politics, natural resources and sustainable development, U.S. foreign policy; international communication (MA, Certificate); international development (MA, Certificate); international economic policy (Certificate); international economic relations (Certificate); international media (MA); international peace and conflict resolution (MA, Certificate); international politics (Certificate); international relations (PhD); international service (MIS); peacebuilding (Certificate); social enterprise (MA); the Americas (Certificate); United States foreign policy (Certificate); JD/MA. Part-time and evening/weekend programs available. Postbaccalaureate distance learning degree programs offered (no on-campus study). *Faculty:* 111 full-time (47 women), 58 part-time/adjunct (31 women). *Students:* 673 full-time (429 women), 376 part-time (227 women); includes 258 minority (82 Black or African American, non-Hispanic/Latino; 8 American Indian or Alaska Native, non-Hispanic/Latino; 71 Asian, non-Hispanic/Latino; 77 Hispanic/Latino; 1 Native Hawaiian or other Pacific Islander, non-Hispanic/Latino; 19 Two or more races, non-Hispanic/Latino), 142 international. Average age 27. 2,074 applicants, 64% accepted, 391 enrolled. In 2012, 367 master's, 7 doctorates, 12 other advanced degrees awarded. Terminal master's awarded for partial completion of doctoral program. *Degree requirements:* For master's, one foreign language, comprehensive exam, thesis or alternative; for doctorate, one foreign language, comprehensive exam, thesis/dissertation, research practicum; for Certificate, minimum 15 credit hours of related course work. *Entrance requirements:* For master's, GRE, 24 credits of course work in related social sciences, minimum GPA of 3.5, 2 letters of recommendation, bachelor's degree, resume, statement of purpose; for doctorate, GRE, 3 letters of recommendation, 24 credits in related social sciences; for Certificate, bachelor's degree. Additional exam requirements/recommendations for international students: Required—TOEFL (minimum score 600 paper-based; 100 iBT). *Application deadline:* For fall admission, 1/15 priority date for domestic students; for spring admission, 10/1 priority date for domestic students. Applications are processed on a rolling basis. Application fee: $50. *Expenses: Tuition:* Full-time $25,920; part-time $1440 per credit. *Required fees:* $430. Tuition and fees vary according to course load, campus/location and program. *Financial support:* Fellowships with partial tuition reimbursements, research assistantships with partial tuition reimbursements, teaching assistantships with partial tuition reimbursements, career-related internships or fieldwork, Federal

Work-Study, institutionally sponsored loans, and scholarships/grants available. Financial award application deadline: 1/15. *Faculty research:* International intellectual property, international environmental issues, international law and legal order, international telecommunications/technology, international sustainable development. *Unit head:* Dr. James Goldgeier, Dean, 202-885-1603, Fax: 202-885-2494, E-mail: goldgeier@american.edu. *Application contact:* Amanda Taylor, Director of Graduate Admissions and Financial Aid, 202-885-2496, Fax: 202-885-1109, E-mail: ataylor@american.edu. Website: http://www.american.edu/sis/.

American University of Beirut, Graduate Programs, Faculty of Arts and Sciences, Beirut, Lebanon. Offers anthropology (MA); Arab and Middle Eastern history (PhD); Arabic language and literature (MA, PhD); archaeology (MA); biology (MS); cell and molecular biology (PhD); chemistry (MS); clinical psychology (MA); computational science (MS); computer science (MS); economics (MA); education (MA); English language (MA); English literature (MA); environmental policy planning (MSES); financial economics (MAFE); general psychology (MA); geology (MS); history (MA); mathematics (MA, MS); media studies (MA); Middle Eastern studies (MA); philosophy (MA); physics (MS); political studies (MA); public administration (MA); sociology (MA); statistics (MA, MS); theoretical physics (PhD); transnational American studies (MA). Part-time programs available. *Faculty:* 238 full-time (80 women), 7 part-time/adjunct (3 women). *Students:* 253 full-time (169 women), 139 part-time (105 women). Average age 26. 306 applicants, 47% accepted, 90 enrolled. In 2012, 126 degrees awarded. *Degree requirements:* For master's, one foreign language, comprehensive exam, thesis (for some programs); for doctorate, one foreign language, comprehensive exam, thesis/dissertation. *Entrance requirements:* For master's, GRE, letter of recommendation; for doctorate, GRE, letters of recommendation. Additional exam requirements/recommendations for international students: Required—TOEFL (minimum score 600 paper-based; 97 iBT), IELTS (minimum score 7). *Application deadline:* For fall admission, 4/30 for domestic students, 4/18 for international students; for spring admission, 11/1 for domestic and international students. Application fee: $50. *Expenses: Tuition:* Full-time $13,896; part-time $772 per credit. *Financial support:* In 2012–13, 20 students received support. Career-related internships or fieldwork, institutionally sponsored loans, scholarships/grants, health care benefits, and unspecified assistantships available. Financial award application deadline: 2/4; financial award applicants required to submit FAFSA. *Faculty research:* Modern Middle East history; Near Eastern archaeology; Islamic history; European history; software engineering; scientific computing; data mining; the applications of cooperative learning in language teaching and teacher education; world/comparative literature; rhetoric and composition; creative writing; public management; public policy and international affairs; hydrogeology; mineralogy, petrology, and geochemistry; tectonics and structural geology; cell and molecular biology; ecology. *Unit head:* Dr. Patrick McGreevy, Dean, 961-1374374 Ext. 3800, Fax: 961-1744461, E-mail: pm07@aub.edu.lb. *Application contact:* Dr. Salim Kanaan, Director, Admissions Office, 961-1-350000 Ext. 2594, Fax: 961-1750775, E-mail: sk00@aub.edu.lb. Website: http://staff.aub.edu.lb/~webfas.

Antioch University New England, Graduate School, Department of Environmental Studies, Doctoral Program in Environmental Studies, Keene, NH 03431-3552. Offers PhD. *Degree requirements:* For doctorate, thesis/dissertation, practicum. *Entrance requirements:* For doctorate, master's degree and previous experience in the environmental field. Additional exam requirements/recommendations for international students: Required—TOEFL (minimum score 600 paper-based). Electronic applications accepted. *Expenses:* Contact institution. *Faculty research:* Environmental history, green politics, ecopsychology.

Antioch University New England, Graduate School, Department of Environmental Studies, Individualized Program, Keene, NH 03431-3552. Offers MS. *Degree requirements:* For master's, practicum, seminar, thesis or project. *Entrance requirements:* For master's, detailed proposal.

Antioch University New England, Graduate School, Department of Environmental Studies, Program in Environmental Advocacy and Organizing, Keene, NH 03431-3552. Offers MS. *Degree requirements:* For master's, practicum, seminar. *Entrance requirements:* For master's, samples of written work, portfolio, letters of recommendation, interview.

Antioch University New England, Graduate School, Department of Environmental Studies, Program in Resource Management and Conservation, Keene, NH 03431-3552. Offers MS. *Degree requirements:* For master's, thesis optional, practicum. *Entrance requirements:* For master's, previous undergraduate course work in science and math. Additional exam requirements/recommendations for international students: Required—TOEFL (minimum score 600 paper-based). Electronic applications accepted. *Expenses:* Contact institution. *Faculty research:* Waste management, land use.

Antioch University New England, Graduate School, Department of Organization and Management, Program in Organizational and Environmental Sustainability (Green MBA), Keene, NH 03431-3552. Offers MBA. Part-time programs available. *Entrance requirements:* For master's, GRE, resume, 3 letters of recommendation. Additional exam requirements/recommendations for international students: Required—TOEFL (minimum score 600 paper-based).

Antioch University Seattle, Graduate Programs, Center for Creative Change, Seattle, WA 98121-1814. Offers environment and community (MA); organizational development (MA); whole system design (MA). Evening/weekend programs available. *Faculty:* 7 full-time (3 women), 10 part-time/adjunct (6 women). *Students:* 46 full-time (37 women), 32 part-time (24 women); includes 18 minority (4 Black or African American, non-Hispanic/Latino; 7 American Indian or Alaska Native, non-Hispanic/Latino; 2 Asian, non-Hispanic/Latino; 2 Hispanic/Latino; 2 Native Hawaiian or other Pacific Islander, non-Hispanic/Latino; 1 Two or more races, non-Hispanic/Latino). Average age 39. 71 applicants, 66% accepted. In 2012, 87 master's awarded. *Application deadline:* For fall admission, 8/15 priority date for domestic students; for spring admission, 2/3 priority date for domestic students. Applications are processed on a rolling basis. Application fee: $50. Electronic applications accepted. *Expenses:* Contact institution. *Financial support:* Research assistantships, Federal Work-Study, institutionally sponsored loans, and unspecified assistantships available. Financial award application deadline: 6/15. *Unit head:* Betsy Geist, Director, 206-268-4904, E-mail: bgeist@antioch.edu. *Application contact:* Eileen Knight, Recruitment and Admissions Director, 206-268-4200, E-mail: eknight@antioch.edu. Website: http://www.antiochseattle.edu/academics/center-for-creative-change/.

Appalachian State University, Cratis D. Williams Graduate School, Department of Government and Justice Studies, Boone, NC 28608. Offers criminal justice (MS); political science (MA), including American government, environmental politics and policy analysis, international relations; public administration (MPA), including public management, town, city and county management. Part-time programs available. Postbaccalaureate distance learning degree programs offered (no on-campus study). *Degree requirements:* For master's, variable foreign language requirement, comprehensive exam, thesis optional. *Entrance requirements:* For master's, GRE General Test, 3 letters of recommendation. Additional exam requirements/recommendations for international students: Required—TOEFL (minimum score 570 paper-based; 79 iBT), IELTS (minimum score 6.5). Electronic applications accepted. *Faculty research:* Campaign finance, emerging democracies, bureaucratic politics, judicial behavior, administration of justice.

Aquinas College, School of Management, Grand Rapids, MI 49506-1799. Offers health care administration (MM); marketing management (MM); organizational leadership (MM); sustainable business (MM, MSB). Part-time and evening/weekend programs available. *Students:* 4 full-time (0 women), 77 part-time (49 women); includes 14 minority (8 Black or African American, non-Hispanic/Latino; 1 American Indian or Alaska Native, non-Hispanic/Latino; 4 Hispanic/Latino; 1 Two or more races, non-Hispanic/Latino). Average age 35. In 2012, 28 master's awarded. *Entrance requirements:* For master's, GMAT, minimum undergraduate GPA of 2.75, 2 years of work experience. Additional exam requirements/recommendations for international students: Required—TOEFL (minimum score 550 paper-based). *Application deadline:* Applications are processed on a rolling basis. Application fee: $0. *Expenses:* Contact institution. *Financial support:* Scholarships/grants available. Support available to part-time students. Financial award application deadline: 3/15; financial award applicants required to submit FAFSA. *Unit head:* Brian DiVita, Director, 616-632-2922, Fax: 616-732-4489. *Application contact:* Lynn Atkins-Rykert, Administrative Assistant, 616-632-2924, Fax: 616-732-4489, E-mail: atkinlyn@aquinas.edu.

Arizona State University, College of Technology and Innovation, Department of Technology Management, Mesa, AZ 85212. Offers technology (aviation management and human factors) (MS); technology (environmental technology management) (MS); technology (global technology and development) (MS); technology (graphic information technology) (MS); technology (management of technology) (MS). Part-time and evening/weekend programs available. Postbaccalaureate distance learning degree programs offered (minimal on-campus study). *Degree requirements:* For master's, thesis or applied project and oral defense; interactive Program of Study (iPOS) submitted before completing 50 percent of required credit hours. *Entrance requirements:* For master's, GRE, minimum GPA of 3.0 or equivalent in last 2 years of work leading to bachelor's degree. Additional exam requirements/recommendations for international students: Required—TOEFL (minimum score 83 iBT), TOEFL, IELTS, or Pearson Test of English. Electronic applications accepted. *Faculty research:* Digital imaging, digital publishing, Internet development/e-commerce, information aviation human factors, pilot selection, databases, multimedia, commercial digital photography, digital workflow, computer graphics modeling and animation, information design, sociotechnology, visual and technical literacy, environmental management, quality management, project management, industrial ethics, hazardous materials, environmental chemistry.

Arizona State University, W. P. Carey School of Business, Morrison School of Agribusiness and Resource Management, Mesa, AZ 85212. Offers agribusiness (MS). Part-time and evening/weekend programs available. *Degree requirements:* For master's, thesis, oral defense, interactive Program of Study (iPOS) submitted before completing 50 percent of required credit hours. *Entrance requirements:* For master's, GMAT or GRE General Test, minimum GPA of 3.0 in last 2 years of work leading to bachelor's degree, 3 letters of recommendation, resume, official transcripts, statement of intent. Additional exam requirements/recommendations for international students: Required—TOEFL (minimum score 550 paper-based; 80 iBT), IELTS (minimum score 6.5); Recommended—TWE. Electronic applications accepted. *Faculty research:* Consumer behavior and marketing strategies in food markets, supply-chain management, derivatives and risk management, and international agricultural trade and policy.

Bard College, Bard Center for Environmental Policy, Annandale-on-Hudson, NY 12504. Offers climate science and policy (MS, Professional Certificate), including agriculture (MS), ecosystems (MS); environmental policy (MS, Professional Certificate); sustainability (MBA); MS/JD; MS/MAT. Part-time programs available.

Degree requirements: For master's, thesis, 4-month, full-time internship. *Entrance requirements:* For master's, GRE, coursework in statistics, chemistry and one other semester of college science; personal statement; curriculum vitae; 3 letters of recommendation; sample of written work. Additional exam requirements/ recommendations for international students: Required—TOEFL (minimum score 600 paper-based; 100 iBT). Electronic applications accepted. *Expenses:* Contact institution. *Faculty research:* Climate and agriculture, alternative energy, environmental economics, environmental toxicology, EPA law, sustainable development, international relations, literature and composition, human rights, agronomy, advocacy, leadership.

Baylor University, Graduate School, College of Arts and Sciences, Department of Environmental Science, Waco, TX 76798. Offers MES, MS. *Students:* 13 full-time (6 women), 2 part-time (0 women); includes 2 minority (both Hispanic/Latino), 3 international. In 2012, 3 master's awarded. *Degree requirements:* For master's, thesis. *Entrance requirements:* For master's, GRE General Test. *Application deadline:* For fall admission, 2/14 priority date for domestic students; for spring admission, 8/15 for domestic students. Applications are processed on a rolling basis. Application fee: $25. *Expenses: Tuition:* Full-time $24,426; part-time $1357 per semester hour. *Required fees:* $2556; $142 per semester hour. *Financial support:* Research assistantships, teaching assistantships, career-related internships or fieldwork, Federal Work-Study, and institutionally sponsored loans available. *Faculty research:* Renewable energy/waste management policies, Third World environmental problem solving, ecotourism. *Unit head:* Dr. Joe Yelderman, Graduate Program Director, 254-710-1385, Fax: 254-710-3409, E-mail: joe_yelderman@baylor.edu. *Application contact:* Glenda Plemons, Administrative Assistant, 254-710-3405, Fax: 254-710-3870, E-mail: glenda_plemons@baylor.edu. Website: http://www.baylor.edu/environmental%5Fstudies/.

Baylor University, Graduate School, College of Arts and Sciences, Program in Air Science and Environment, Waco, TX 76798. Offers IMES. *Expenses: Tuition:* Full-time $24,426; part-time $1357 per semester hour. *Required fees:* $2556; $142 per semester hour. *Unit head:* Dr. Larry Lyon, Dean, 254-710-3588, Fax: 254-710-3870, E-mail: larry_lyon@baylor.edu. *Application contact:* Suzanne Keener, Administrative Assistant, 254-710-3588, Fax: 254-710-3870.

Bemidji State University, School of Graduate Studies, Bemidji, MN 56601-2699. Offers biology (MS); education (M Ed, MS); English (MA, MS); environmental studies (MS); mathematics (MS); mathematics (elementary and middle level education) (MS); science (junior high) (MS); special education (M Sp Ed, MS). Part-time programs available. Postbaccalaureate distance learning degree programs offered (no on-campus study). *Faculty:* 114 full-time (47 women), 22 part-time/adjunct (16 women). *Students:* 51 full-time (31 women), 222 part-time (163 women); includes 12 minority (2 Black or African American, non-Hispanic/ Latino; 2 American Indian or Alaska Native, non-Hispanic/Latino; 2 Asian, non-Hispanic/Latino; 2 Hispanic/Latino; 4 Two or more races, non-Hispanic/Latino), 5 international. Average age 33. 84 applicants, 93% accepted, 51 enrolled. In 2012, 66 master's awarded. *Degree requirements:* For master's, comprehensive exam, thesis (for some programs). *Entrance requirements:* For master's, GRE, letters of recommendation, letters of interest. Additional exam requirements/ recommendations for international students: Required—TOEFL (minimum score 550 paper-based; 80 iBT). *Application deadline:* Applications are processed on a rolling basis. Application fee: $20. Electronic applications accepted. *Expenses:* Tuition, state resident: full-time $6400; part-time $355.50 per credit. Tuition, nonresident: full-time $6400; part-time $355.50 per credit. *Required fees:* $960. *Financial support:* In 2012–13, 131 students received support, including 42 research assistantships with partial tuition reimbursements available (averaging $6,729 per year), 42 teaching assistantships with partial tuition reimbursements available (averaging $6,729 per year); career-related internships or fieldwork, scholarships/grants, health care benefits, and unspecified assistantships also available. Support available to part-time students. Financial award application deadline: 3/31; financial award applicants required to submit FAFSA. *Faculty research:* Human performance, sport, and health: physical education teacher education, continuum models, spiritual health, intellectual health, resiliency, health priorities; psychology: health psychology, college student drinking behavior, micro-aggressions, infant cognition, false memories, leadership assessment; biology: structure and dynamics of forest communities, aquatic and riverine ecology, interaction between animal populations and aquatic environments, cellular motility. *Unit head:* Dr. Patricia Rogers, Dean of Health Sciences and Human Ecology, 218-755-2027, Fax: 218-755-2258, E-mail: progers@bemidjistate.edu. *Application contact:* Joan Miller, Director, School of Graduate Studies, 218-755-2027, Fax: 218-755-2258, E-mail: jmiller@bemidjistate.edu. Website: http://www.bemidjistate.edu/academics/graduate_studies/.

Boise State University, College of Social Sciences and Public Affairs, Department of Public Policy and Administration, Boise, ID 83725-0399. Offers environmental and natural resources policy and administration (MPA); general public administration (MPA); public policy and administration (Graduate Certificate); state and local government policy and administration (MPA). *Accreditation:* NASPAA. Part-time programs available. *Faculty:* 12 full-time, 16 part-time/adjunct. *Students:* 22 full-time (11 women), 72 part-time (45 women); includes 5 minority (1 Asian, non-Hispanic/Latino; 4 Hispanic/Latino). 52 applicants, 90% accepted, 22 enrolled. In 2012, 27 master's, 6 other advanced degrees awarded. *Degree requirements:* For master's, comprehensive exam, directed research project, internship. *Entrance requirements:* For master's, GRE General Test, minimum GPA of 3.0. Additional exam requirements/ recommendations for international students: Required—TOEFL. *Application deadline:* For fall admission, 3/1 priority date for domestic students; for spring admission, 10/1 priority date for domestic students. Applications are processed on a rolling basis. Application fee: $55. Electronic applications accepted. *Expenses:* Tuition, state resident: full-time $3486; part-time $312 per credit. Tuition, nonresident: full-time $5720; part-time $413 per credit. *Financial support:* In 2012–13, 2 students received support. Federal Work-Study, institutionally sponsored loans, and unspecified assistantships available. Support available to part-time students. Financial award application deadline: 3/1. *Unit head:* Dr. Leslie Alm, Director of Graduate Studies, 208-426-1476, Fax: 208-426-4370. *Application contact:* Linda Platt, Office Services Supervisor, Graduate Admission and Degree Services, 208-426-1074, Fax: 208-426-2789, E-mail: lplatt@boisestate.edu.

Boston University, Graduate School of Arts and Sciences, Department of Earth and Environment, Boston, MA 02215. Offers earth sciences (MA, PhD); energy and environmental analysis (MA); environmental remote sensing and GIS (MA); geography and environment (MA, PhD); global development policy (MA); international relations and environmental policy (MA). *Students:* 77 full-time (39 women), 11 part-time (5 women); includes 2 minority (1 American Indian or Alaska Native, non-Hispanic/Latino; 1 Asian, non-Hispanic/Latino), 25 international. Average age 27. 288 applicants, 33% accepted, 23 enrolled. In 2012, 4 master's, 6 doctorates awarded. *Degree requirements:* For master's, comprehensive exam (for some programs), thesis (for some programs); for doctorate, comprehensive exam, thesis/dissertation. *Entrance requirements:* For master's and doctorate, GRE, 3 letters of recommendation, official transcripts, personal statement. Additional exam requirements/recommendations for international students: Required—TOEFL (minimum score 550 paper-based; 84 iBT). *Application deadline:* For fall admission, 1/15 for domestic students, 11/15 for international students. Application fee: $80. Electronic applications accepted. *Expenses: Tuition:* Full-time $42,400; part-time $1325 per credit. *Required fees:* $40 per semester. *Financial support:* In 2012–13, 2 fellowships with full tuition reimbursements (averaging $20,300 per year), 32 research assistantships with full tuition reimbursements (averaging $19,800 per year), 19 teaching assistantships with full tuition reimbursements (averaging $19,800 per year) were awarded; Federal Work-Study, scholarships/grants, traineeships, and health care benefits also available. Financial award application deadline: 1/15. *Faculty research:* Biogeosciences, climate and surface processes; energy, environment and society; geographical sciences; geology, geochemistry and geophysics. *Unit head:* Curtis Woodcock, Chair, 617-353-5746, E-mail: curtis@bu.edu. *Application contact:* Christian Cole, Graduate Program Coordinator, 617-353-2529, Fax: 617-353-8399, E-mail: ccole@bu.edu. Website: http://www.bu.edu/earth/.

Boston University, Graduate School of Arts and Sciences, Department of International Relations, Boston, MA 02215. Offers African studies (Certificate); Asian studies (Certificate); global development policy (MA); international affairs (MA); international relations and communication (MA); international relations and environmental policy (MA); international relations and religion (MA); Latin American studies (MA); mid-career international relations (MA); JD/MA; MBA/MA. *Students:* 40 full-time (33 women), 10 part-time (6 women); includes 10 minority (1 Black or African American, non-Hispanic/Latino; 3 Asian, non-Hispanic/Latino; 1 Hispanic/Latino; 1 Native Hawaiian or other Pacific Islander, non-Hispanic/ Latino; 4 Two or more races, non-Hispanic/Latino), 14 international. Average age 25. 446 applicants, 65% accepted, 41 enrolled. In 2012, 27 master's awarded. *Degree requirements:* For master's, one foreign language, capstone. *Entrance requirements:* For master's, GRE General Test, 3 letters of recommendation, transcript of all prior college coursework, statement of purpose. Additional exam requirements/recommendations for international students: Required—TOEFL (minimum score 600 paper-based; 94 iBT). *Application deadline:* For fall admission, 4/15 for domestic and international students; for spring admission, 10/ 15 for domestic and international students. Application fee: $80. Electronic applications accepted. *Expenses: Tuition:* Full-time $42,400; part-time $1325 per credit. *Required fees:* $40 per semester. *Financial support:* In 2012–13, 20 students received support. Federal Work-Study, scholarships/grants, and unspecified assistantships available. Financial award application deadline: 12/15; financial award applicants required to submit FAFSA. *Unit head:* Andrew J. Bacevich, Chair, 617-353-9279, Fax: 617-353-9290, E-mail: bacevich@bu.edu. *Application contact:* Michael Williams, Graduate Program Administrator, 617-353-9349, Fax: 617-353-9290, E-mail: mawillia@bu.edu. Website: http://www.bu.edu/ IR/.

California State University, Chico, Office of Graduate Studies, College of Behavioral and Social Sciences, Department of Geography and Planning, Program in Geography, Chico, CA 95929-0722. Offers environmental policy and planning (MA); geography (MA). Part-time programs available. *Faculty:* 5 full-time (2 women). *Students:* 1 (woman) full-time, 4 part-time (3 women); includes 1 minority (American Indian or Alaska Native, non-Hispanic/Latino). Average age 38. 5 applicants, 40% accepted, 2 enrolled. In 2012, 4 master's awarded. *Degree requirements:* For master's, thesis or project. *Entrance requirements:* For master's, GRE General Test, two letters of recommendation, statement of purpose, writing sample. Additional exam requirements/recommendations for international students: Required—TOEFL (minimum score 550 paper-based; 80 iBT), IELTS (minimum score 6.5), Pearson Test of English (minimum score 59). *Application deadline:* For fall admission, 3/1 priority date for domestic students, 3/ 1 for international students; for spring admission, 9/15 priority date for domestic students, 9/15 for international students. Application fee: $55. Electronic applications accepted. *Expenses:* Tuition, state resident: part-time $372 per unit. Tuition, nonresident: part-time $372 per unit. *Required fees:* $2687 per semester.

Tuition and fees vary according to course level and program. *Financial support:* Career-related internships or fieldwork, institutionally sponsored loans, scholarships/grants, and unspecified assistantships available. Financial award application deadline: 3/1; financial award applicants required to submit FAFSA. *Unit head:* Dr. Jacquelyn Chase, Chair, 530-898-5285, Fax: 530-898-6781, E-mail: geop@csuchico.edu. *Application contact:* Judy L. Rice, Graduate Admissions Coordinator, 530-898-6871, E-mail: jlrice@csuchico.edu. Website: http://catalog.csuchico.edu/viewer/11/GEOG/GEOGNONEPN.html.

California State University, Fullerton, Graduate Studies, College of Humanities and Social Sciences, Program in Environmental Studies, Fullerton, CA 92834-9480. Offers MS. Part-time programs available. *Students:* 29 full-time (15 women), 33 part-time (17 women); includes 18 minority (1 Black or African American, non-Hispanic/Latino; 7 Asian, non-Hispanic/Latino; 7 Hispanic/Latino; 3 Two or more races, non-Hispanic/Latino), 2 international. Average age 30. 52 applicants, 56% accepted, 23 enrolled. In 2012, 25 master's awarded. *Degree requirements:* For master's, thesis. *Entrance requirements:* For master's, minimum GPA of 2.5 in last 60 units of course work. Application fee: $55. *Financial support:* Career-related internships or fieldwork, Federal Work-Study, institutionally sponsored loans, and scholarships/grants available. Support available to part-time students. Financial award application deadline: 3/1; financial award applicants required to submit FAFSA. *Unit head:* Dr. John Bock, Coordinator, 657-278-4373. *Application contact:* Admissions/Applications, 657-278-2371.

Central European University, Graduate Studies, Department of Environmental Sciences and Policy, Budapest, Hungary. Offers MS, PhD. Part-time programs available. *Faculty:* 13 full-time (4 women), 5 part-time/adjunct (3 women). *Students:* 101 full-time (73 women), 11 part-time (7 women). Average age 29. 1,101 applicants, 7% accepted, 53 enrolled. In 2012, 37 master's, 10 doctorates awarded. Terminal master's awarded for partial completion of doctoral program. *Degree requirements:* For master's, one foreign language, thesis; for doctorate, one foreign language, comprehensive exam, thesis/dissertation. *Entrance requirements:* For master's and doctorate, interview. Additional exam requirements/recommendations for international students: Required—TOEFL (minimum score 570 paper-based); Recommended—IELTS (minimum score 6.5). *Application deadline:* For fall admission, 1/24 priority date for domestic students, 1/24 for international students. Application fee: $0. Electronic applications accepted. *Financial support:* In 2012–13, 42 students received support, including 42 fellowships with full and partial tuition reimbursements available (averaging $6,100 per year); career-related internships or fieldwork, institutionally sponsored loans, scholarships/grants, health care benefits, and tuition waivers (full and partial) also available. Financial award application deadline: 1/5. *Faculty research:* Management of ecological systems, environmental impact assessment, energy conservation, climate change policy, forest policy in countries in transition. *Unit head:* Dr. Alan Watt, Head, 36-1-327-3021, Fax: 36-1-327-3031, E-mail: envsci@ceu.hu. *Application contact:* Krisztina Szabados, Department Coordinator, 361-327-3021, Fax: 361-327-3031, E-mail: envsci@ceu.hu. Website: http://www.ceu.hu/envsci/.

Clarkson University, Graduate School, Institute for a Sustainable Environment, Program in Environmental Politics and Governance, Potsdam, NY 13699. Offers MS. Part-time programs available. *Students:* 2 full-time (0 women). Average age 26. 4 applicants, 75% accepted, 2 enrolled. Terminal master's awarded for partial completion of doctoral program. *Degree requirements:* For master's, thesis. *Entrance requirements:* For master's, GRE, transcripts of all college coursework, resume, personal statement, three letters of recommendation. Additional exam requirements/recommendations for international students: Required—TOEFL (minimum score 550 paper-based; 80 iBT), IELTS (minimum score 6.5). *Application deadline:* For fall admission, 1/30 priority date for domestic students, 1/30 for international students; for spring admission, 9/1 priority date for domestic students, 9/1 for international students. Applications are processed on a rolling basis. Application fee: $25 ($35 for international students). Electronic applications accepted. *Expenses: Tuition:* Full-time $15,108; part-time $1259 per credit hour. *Required fees:* $295 per semester. *Financial support:* In 2012–13, 2 students received support, including fellowships with full tuition reimbursements available (averaging $22,650 per year), research assistantships with full tuition reimbursements available (averaging $22,650 per year), teaching assistantships with full tuition reimbursements available (averaging $22,650 per year); scholarships/grants, tuition waivers (partial), and unspecified assistantships also available. *Unit head:* Dr. Philip Hopke, Director, 315-268-3856, Fax: 315-268-4291, E-mail: hopkepk@clarkson.edu. *Application contact:* Mary Jane Smalling, Senior Department Secretary, 315-268-2318, Fax: 315-268-4291, E-mail: msmallin@clarkson.edu. Website: http://www.clarkson.edu/epg/.

Clark University, Graduate School, Department of International Development, Community, and Environment, Program in Environmental Science and Policy, Worcester, MA 01610-1477. Offers MA, MA/MBA. Part-time programs available. *Students:* 50 full-time (27 women), 11 part-time (5 women); includes 4 minority (2 Black or African American, non-Hispanic/Latino; 1 Asian, non-Hispanic/Latino; 1 Hispanic/Latino), 27 international. Average age 30. 81 applicants, 78% accepted, 28 enrolled. In 2012, 7 master's awarded. *Degree requirements:* For master's, thesis. *Entrance requirements:* For master's, 3 references, resume or curriculum vitae. Additional exam requirements/recommendations for international students: Required—TOEFL (minimum score 575 paper-based; 90 iBT) or IELTS (minimum score 6.5). *Application deadline:* For fall admission, 1/15 for domestic students. Application fee: $50. *Expenses: Tuition:* Full-time $38,100; part-time $4762.50 per course. *Required fees:* $30. Tuition and fees vary according to course load and program. *Financial support:* In 2012–13, research assistantships with partial tuition reimbursements (averaging $5,000 per year), teaching assistantships with partial tuition reimbursements (averaging $5,000 per year) were awarded; fellowships with partial tuition reimbursements, institutionally sponsored loans, and scholarships/grants also available. *Faculty research:* Environmental justice, children's health and risk assessment, smart grids and energy technology transitions, uncertainty-risk analysis, climate variability modeling. *Unit head:* Dr. David Bell, Director, 508-793-8820, Fax: 508-793-8820, E-mail: dbell@clarku.edu. *Application contact:* Paula Hall, IDCE Graduate Admissions, 508-793-7201, Fax: 508-793-8820, E-mail: idce@clarku.edu. Website: http://clarku.edu/departments/idce/academicsGradESP.cfm.

Clark University, Graduate School, Department of International Development, Community, and Environment, Program in Geographic Information Science for Development and Environment, Worcester, MA 01610-1477. Offers MA. *Students:* 32 full-time (16 women), 5 part-time (2 women); includes 3 minority (1 Black or African American, non-Hispanic/Latino; 2 Asian, non-Hispanic/Latino), 19 international. Average age 26. 96 applicants, 53% accepted, 21 enrolled. In 2012, 7 master's awarded. *Degree requirements:* For master's, thesis. *Entrance requirements:* For master's, 3 references, resume or curriculum vitae. Additional exam requirements/recommendations for international students: Required—TOEFL (minimum score 575 paper-based; 90 iBT) or IELTS (minimum score 6.5). *Application deadline:* For fall admission, 1/15 for domestic students. Application fee: $50. *Expenses: Tuition:* Full-time $38,100; part-time $4762.50 per course. *Required fees:* $30. Tuition and fees vary according to course load and program. *Financial support:* In 2012–13, research assistantships with partial tuition reimbursements (averaging $5,000 per year), teaching assistantships with partial tuition reimbursements (averaging $5,000 per year) were awarded; fellowships with partial tuition reimbursements, institutionally sponsored loans, and scholarships/grants also available. *Faculty research:* Land-use change, the effects of environmental influences on child health and development, quantitative methods, watershed management, brownfields redevelopment, human/environment interactions, biodiversity conservation, climate change. *Unit head:* Dr. David Bell, IDCE Director, 508-793-8820, Fax: 508-793-8820, E-mail: dbell@clarku.edu. *Application contact:* Paula Hall, IDCE Graduate Admissions Office, 508-793-7205, E-mail: idce@clarku.edu. Website: http://clarku.edu/departments/idce/academicsGradGISDE.cfm.

Clemson University, Graduate School, College of Agriculture, Forestry and Life Sciences, Department of Forestry and Natural Resources, Program in Plant and Environmental Sciences, Clemson, SC 29634. Offers MS, PhD. *Students:* 50 full-time (20 women), 8 part-time (0 women); includes 2 minority (1 Hispanic/Latino; 1 Two or more races, non-Hispanic/Latino), 22 international. Average age 29. 39 applicants, 44% accepted, 13 enrolled. In 2012, 6 master's, 5 doctorates awarded. *Degree requirements:* For master's, thesis; for doctorate, comprehensive exam, thesis/dissertation. *Entrance requirements:* For master's, GRE General Test, bachelor's degree in biological science or related disciplines; for doctorate, GRE General Test. Additional exam requirements/recommendations for international students: Required—TOEFL, IELTS. *Application deadline:* Applications are processed on a rolling basis. Electronic applications accepted. *Expenses:* Contact institution. *Financial support:* In 2012–13, 42 students received support, including 4 fellowships with full and partial tuition reimbursements available (averaging $10,709 per year), 35 research assistantships with partial tuition reimbursements available (averaging $16,948 per year), 8 teaching assistantships with partial tuition reimbursements available (averaging $10,780 per year); career-related internships or fieldwork, institutionally sponsored loans, scholarships/grants, health care benefits, and unspecified assistantships also available. Support available to part-time students. Financial award application deadline: 3/15; financial award applicants required to submit FAFSA. *Faculty research:* Sustainable agroecology, horticulture and turfgrass, physiology and pathology of plants. *Unit head:* Dr. Patricia Layton, School Director, 864-656-3302, Fax: 864-656-3304, E-mail: playton@clemson.edu. *Application contact:* Dr. Halina Knap, Coordinator, 864-656-3523, Fax: 864-656-3443, E-mail: hskrpsk@clemson.edu. Website: http://www.clemson.edu/cafls/departments/pes/.

Cleveland State University, College of Graduate Studies, Maxine Goodman Levin College of Urban Affairs, Program in Environmental Studies, Cleveland, OH 44115. Offers environmental nonprofit management (MAES); environmental planning (MAES); geographic information systems (Certificate); policy and administration (MAES); sustainable economic development (MAES); urban economic development (Certificate); urban real estate development and finance (Certificate); JD/MAES. Part-time and evening/weekend programs available. *Faculty:* 24 full-time (10 women), 14 part-time/adjunct (5 women). *Students:* 5 full-time (1 woman), 10 part-time (8 women). Average age 34. 6 applicants, 100% accepted. In 2012, 16 master's awarded. *Degree requirements:* For master's, thesis or alternative, exit project. *Entrance requirements:* For master's, GRE General Test (minimum score: verbal and quantitative combined 40th percentile, analytical writing 4.0), minimum GPA of 3.0. Additional exam requirements/recommendations for international students: Required—TOEFL (minimum score 525 paper-based; 65 iBT). *Application deadline:* For fall admission, 7/15 priority date for domestic students, 5/15 for international students; for spring admission, 11/1 for international students. Applications are processed on a rolling basis. Application fee: $30. Electronic applications accepted. *Expenses:* Tuition, state resident: full-time $8172; part-time $510.75 per credit hour. Tuition, nonresident: full-time $15,372; part-time $960.75 per credit hour. *Required fees:* $25 per semester. Tuition and fees vary according to course load and program. *Financial support:* In 2012–13, 5 students received support, including 3 research assistantships with full and partial tuition reimbursements available (averaging $7,200 per year), 2 teaching assistantships with full and partial tuition reimbursements available (averaging $2,400 per year); career-related internships or fieldwork, scholarships/grants, traineeships, and unspecified assistantships also available. Support available to part-time students. Financial award application deadline: 3/1; financial award applicants required to submit FAFSA. *Faculty research:* Environmental policy and administration, environmental planning, geographic information systems (GIS), urban sustainability planning and management, energy policy, land re-use. *Unit head:* Dr. Sanda Kaufman, Director, 216-687-2367, Fax: 216-687-9342, E-mail: s.kaufman@csuohio.edu. *Application contact:* David Arrighi, Graduate Academic Advisor, 216-523-7522, Fax: 216-687-5398, E-mail: urbanprograms@csuohio.edu. Website: http://urban.csuohio.edu/academics/graduate/maes/.

Cleveland State University, College of Graduate Studies, Maxine Goodman Levin College of Urban Affairs, Program in Urban Planning, Design, and Development, Cleveland, OH 44115. Offers economic development (MUPDD); environmental sustainability (MUPDD); geographic information systems (Certificate); historic preservation (MUPDD); housing and neighborhood development (MUPDD); urban economic development (Certificate); urban real estate development and finance (MUPDD, Certificate); JD/MUPDD. *Accreditation:* ACSP. Part-time and evening/weekend programs available. *Faculty:* 24 full-time (10 women), 14 part-time/adjunct (5 women). *Students:* 30 full-time (10 women), 28 part-time (17 women); includes 9 minority (6 Black or African American, non-Hispanic/Latino; 3 Hispanic/Latino), 5 international. Average age 38. 91 applicants, 45% accepted, 21 enrolled. In 2012, 24 master's awarded. *Degree requirements:* For master's, thesis or alternative, planning studio. *Entrance requirements:* For master's, GRE General Test (minimum score: 50th percentile combined verbal and quantitative, 4.0 analytical writing), minimum GPA of 3.0. Additional exam requirements/recommendations for international students: Required—TOEFL (minimum score 525 paper-based; 65 iBT). *Application deadline:* For fall admission, 7/15 priority date for domestic students, 5/15 for international students; for spring admission, 11/1 for international students. Applications are processed on a rolling basis. Application fee: $30. Electronic applications accepted. *Expenses:* Tuition, state resident: full-time $8172; part-time $510.75 per credit hour. Tuition, nonresident: full-time $15,372; part-time $960.75 per credit hour. *Required fees:* $25 per semester. Tuition and fees vary according to course load and program. *Financial support:* In 2012–13, 11 students received support, including 9 research assistantships with full and partial tuition reimbursements available (averaging $7,200 per year), 2 teaching assistantships with full and partial tuition reimbursements available (averaging $4,800 per year); career-related internships or fieldwork, Federal Work-Study, scholarships/grants, tuition waivers, and unspecified assistantships also available. Support available to part-time students. Financial award application deadline: 3/1; financial award applicants required to submit FAFSA. *Faculty research:* Housing and neighborhood development, urban housing policy, environmental sustainability, economic development, GIS and planning decision support. *Unit head:* Dr. Dennis Keating, Director, 216-687-2298, Fax: 216-687-2013, E-mail: w.keating@csuohio.edu. *Application contact:* David Arrighi, Graduate Academic Advisor, 216-523-7522, Fax: 216-687-5398, E-mail: urbanprograms@csuohio.edu. Website: http://urban.csuohio.edu/academics/graduate/mupdd/.

College of the Atlantic, Program in Human Ecology, Bar Harbor, ME 04609-1198. Offers M Phil. *Degree requirements:* For master's, thesis. *Faculty research:* Conservation of endangered species, public policy/community planning, environmental education, history, philosophy.

Columbia University, Graduate School of Arts and Sciences, Program in Climate and Society, New York, NY 10027. Offers MA.

Columbia University, School of International and Public Affairs, Program in Environmental Science and Policy, New York, NY 10027. Offers MPA. Program admits applicants for late May/early June start only. *Degree requirements:* For master's, workshops. *Entrance requirements:* For master's, GRE, previous course work in biology and chemistry, earth sciences (recommended), economics (strongly recommended). Additional exam requirements/recommendations for international students: Required—TOEFL. Electronic applications accepted. *Faculty research:* Ecological management of enclosed ecosystems vegetation dynamics, environmental policy and management, energy policy, nuclear waste policy, environmental and natural resource economics and policy, carbon sequestration, urban planning, environmental risk assessment/toxicology, environmental justice.

Concordia University, School of Graduate Studies, Faculty of Arts and Science, Department of Geography, Planning and Environment, Montréal, QC H3G 1M8, Canada. Offers environmental impact assessment (Diploma); geography, urban and environmental studies (M Sc).

Cornell University, Graduate School, Graduate Fields of Agriculture and Life Sciences, Field of Natural Resources, Ithaca, NY 14853-0001. Offers community-based natural resources management (MS, PhD); ecosystem biology and biogeochemistry (MPS, MS, PhD); environmental management (MPS); fishery and aquatic science (MPS, MS, PhD); forest science (MPS, MS, PhD); human dimensions of natural resources management (MPS, MS, PhD); program development and evaluation (MPS, MS, PhD); wildlife science (MPS, MS, PhD). *Faculty:* 40 full-time (8 women). *Students:* 56 full-time (23 women); includes 2 minority (1 Asian, non-Hispanic/Latino; 1 Two or more races, non-Hispanic/Latino), 12 international. Average age 32. 61 applicants, 33% accepted, 15 enrolled. In 2012, 7 master's, 6 doctorates awarded. *Degree requirements:* For master's, thesis (MS), project paper (MPS); for doctorate, comprehensive exam, thesis/dissertation. *Entrance requirements:* For master's and doctorate, GRE General Test, 2 letters of recommendation. Additional exam requirements/recommendations for international students: Required—TOEFL (minimum score 550 paper-based; 77 iBT). *Application deadline:* For spring admission, 10/30 for domestic students. Applications are processed on a rolling basis. Application fee: $95. Electronic applications accepted. *Financial support:* In 2012–13, 46 students received support, including 14 fellowships with full tuition reimbursements available, 15 research assistantships with full tuition reimbursements available, 17 teaching assistantships with full tuition reimbursements available; institutionally sponsored loans, scholarships/grants, health care benefits, tuition waivers (full and partial), and unspecified assistantships also available. Financial award applicants required to submit FAFSA. *Faculty research:* Ecosystem-level dynamics, systems modeling, conservation biology/management, resource management's human dimensions, biogeochemistry. *Unit head:* Director of Graduate Studies, 607-255-2807, Fax: 607-255-0349. *Application contact:* Graduate Field Assistant, 607-255-2807, Fax: 607-255-0349, E-mail: nrgrad@cornell.edu. Website: http://www.gradschool.cornell.edu/fields.php?id-54&a-2.

Cornell University, Graduate School, Graduate Fields of Agriculture and Life Sciences, Field of Soil and Crop Sciences, Ithaca, NY 14853-0001. Offers agronomy (MS, PhD); environmental information science (MS, PhD); environmental management (MPS); field crop science (MS, PhD); soil science (MS, PhD). *Faculty:* 41 full-time (10 women). *Students:* 16 full-time (10 women); includes 4 minority (all Hispanic/Latino), 5 international. Average age 30. 54 applicants, 17% accepted, 5 enrolled. In 2012, 10 master's, 5 doctorates awarded. *Degree requirements:* For master's, thesis (MS); for doctorate, comprehensive exam, thesis/dissertation. *Entrance requirements:* For master's and doctorate, GRE General Test, 2 letters of recommendation. Additional exam requirements/recommendations for international students: Required—TOEFL (minimum score 550 paper-based; 77 iBT). *Application deadline:* For fall admission, 2/1 priority date for domestic students. Applications are processed on a rolling basis. Application fee: $95. Electronic applications accepted. *Financial support:* In 2012–13, 12 students received support, including 7 fellowships with full tuition reimbursements available, 5 teaching assistantships with full tuition reimbursements available; research assistantships with full tuition reimbursements available, institutionally sponsored loans, traineeships, health care benefits, tuition waivers (full and partial), and unspecified assistantships also available. *Faculty research:* Soil chemistry, physics and biology; crop physiology and management; environmental information science and modeling; international agriculture; weed science. *Unit head:* Director of Graduate Studies, 607-255-3267, Fax: 607-255-8615. *Application contact:* Graduate Field Assistant, 607-255-3267, Fax: 607-255-8615, E-mail: ljh4@cornell.edu. Website: http://www.gradschool.cornell.edu/fields.php?id-5A&a-2.

Cornell University, Graduate School, Graduate Fields of Architecture, Art and Planning, Field of Regional Science, Ithaca, NY 14853-0001. Offers environmental studies (MA, MS, PhD); international spatial problems (MA, MS, PhD); location theory (MA, MS, PhD); multiregional economic analysis (MA, MS, PhD); peace science (MA, MS, PhD); planning methods (MA, MS, PhD); urban and regional economics (MA, MS, PhD). *Faculty:* 25 full-time (5 women). *Students:* 17 full-time (3 women); includes 1 minority (Two or more races, non-Hispanic/Latino), 15 international. Average age 31. 15 applicants, 53% accepted, 5 enrolled. In 2012, 2 master's, 2 doctorates awarded. Terminal master's awarded for partial completion of doctoral program. *Degree requirements:* For master's, thesis; for doctorate, comprehensive exam, thesis/dissertation. *Entrance requirements:* For master's and doctorate, GRE General Test, 2 letters of recommendation. Additional exam requirements/recommendations for international students: Required—TOEFL (minimum score 600 paper-based; 77 iBT). *Application deadline:* For fall admission, 1/15 priority date for domestic students. Application fee: $95. Electronic applications accepted. *Financial support:* In 2012–13, 5 students received support, including 1 fellowship with full tuition reimbursement available, 1 research assistantship with full tuition reimbursement available, 3 teaching assistantships with full tuition reimbursements available; institutionally sponsored loans, scholarships/grants, health care benefits, tuition waivers (full and partial), and unspecified assistantships also available. Financial award applicants required to submit FAFSA. *Faculty research:* Urban and regional growth, spatial economics, formation of spatial patterns by socioeconomic systems, non-linear dynamics and complex systems, environmental-economic systems. *Unit head:* Director of Graduate Studies, 607-255-6848, Fax: 607-255-1971. *Application contact:* Graduate Field Assistant, 607-255-6848, Fax: 607-255-1971, E-mail: regsci@cornell.edu. Website: http://www.gradschool.cornell.edu/fields.php?id-92&a-2.

Cornell University, Graduate School, Graduate Fields of Arts and Sciences, Field of Archaeology, Ithaca, NY 14853-0001. Offers environmental archaeology (MA); historical archaeology (MA); Latin American archaeology (MA); medieval archaeology (MA); Mediterranean and Near Eastern archaeology (MA); Stone Age archaeology (MA). *Faculty:* 24 full-time (9 women). *Students:* 5 full-time (4 women). Average age 25. 28 applicants, 32% accepted, 4 enrolled. In 2012, 2 master's awarded. *Degree requirements:* For master's, one foreign language, thesis. *Entrance requirements:* For master's, GRE General Test, 3 letters of recommendation, sample of written work. Additional exam requirements/recommendations for international students: Required—TOEFL (minimum score

550 paper-based; 77 iBT). *Application deadline:* For fall admission, 1/15 for domestic students. Application fee: $95. Electronic applications accepted. *Financial support:* In 2012–13, 2 students received support, including 2 teaching assistantships with full tuition reimbursements available; fellowships with full tuition reimbursements available, research assistantships with full tuition reimbursements available, institutionally sponsored loans, scholarships/grants, health care benefits, tuition waivers (full and partial), and unspecified assistantships also available. Financial award applicants required to submit FAFSA. *Faculty research:* Anatolia, Lydia, Sardis, classical and Hellenistic Greece; science in archaeology; North American Indians; Stone Age Africa; Mayan trade. *Unit head:* Director of Graduate Studies, 607-255-6768, E-mail: blj7@cornell.edu. *Application contact:* Graduate Field Assistant, 607-255-6768, E-mail: dsd6@cornell.edu. Website: http://www.gradschool.cornell.edu/fields.php?id-97&a-2.

Dalhousie University, Faculty of Agriculture, Halifax, NS B3H 4R2, Canada. Offers agriculture (M Sc), including air quality, animal behavior, animal molecular genetics, animal nutrition, animal technology, aquaculture, botany, crop management, crop physiology, ecology, environmental microbiology, food science, horticulture, nutrient management, pest management, physiology, plant biotechnology, plant pathology, soil chemistry, soil fertility, waste management and composting, water quality. Part-time programs available. *Degree requirements:* For master's, thesis, ATC Exam Teaching Assistantship. *Entrance requirements:* For master's, honors B Sc, minimum GPA of 3.0. Additional exam requirements/recommendations for international students: Required—TOEFL (minimum score 580 paper-based; 92 iBT), IELTS, Michigan English Language Assessment Battery, CanTEST, CAEL. *Faculty research:* Bio-product development, organic agriculture, nutrient management, air and water quality, agricultural biotechnology.

Dalhousie University, Faculty of Management, School for Resource and Environmental Studies, Halifax, NS B3H 3J5, Canada. Offers MES, MREM, MLIS/MREM. Part-time programs available. *Degree requirements:* For master's, thesis. *Entrance requirements:* For master's, honors degree. Additional exam requirements/recommendations for international students: Required—TOEFL, IELTS, CANTEST, CAEL, or Michigan English Language Assessment Battery. Electronic applications accepted. *Faculty research:* Resource management and ecology, aboriginal resource rights, management of toxic substances, environmental impact assessment, forest management, policy, coastal zone management.

Drexel University, College of Arts and Sciences, Program in Environmental Policy, Philadelphia, PA 19104-2875. Offers MS. Part-time and evening/weekend programs available. *Degree requirements:* For master's, thesis optional. Electronic applications accepted.

Duke University, Graduate School, Nicholas School of the Environment, Durham, NC 27708. Offers environmental management (MEM); forestry (MF); natural resource economics/policy (PhD); natural resource science/ecology (PhD); natural resource systems science (PhD); JD/AM. Part-time programs available. *Faculty:* 28 full-time. *Students:* 59 full-time (33 women); includes 2 minority (both Asian, non-Hispanic/Latino), 18 international. 99 applicants, 19% accepted, 12 enrolled. In 2012, 11 doctorates awarded. *Degree requirements:* For doctorate, variable foreign language requirement, thesis/dissertation. *Entrance requirements:* For master's and doctorate, GRE General Test. Additional exam requirements/recommendations for international students: Required—TOEFL (minimum score 550 paper-based; 83 iBT), IELTS (minimum score 7). *Application deadline:* For fall admission, 12/8 priority date for domestic students, 12/8 for international students. Application fee: $80. Electronic applications accepted. *Financial support:* Fellowships, research assistantships, teaching assistantships, and Federal Work-Study available. Financial award application deadline: 12/8. *Unit head:* Gaby Katul, Director of Graduate Studies, 919-613-8002, Fax: 919-613-8061, E-mail: meg.stephens@duke.edu. *Application contact:* Elizabeth Hutton, Director, Graduate Admissions, 919-684-3913, Fax: 919-684-2277, E-mail: grad-admissions@duke.edu. Website: http://www.nicholas.duke.edu/.

Duke University, Graduate School, Program in Environmental Policy, Durham, NC 27708. Offers PhD. *Faculty:* 29 full-time. *Students:* 11 full-time (6 women); includes 1 minority (Black or African American, non-Hispanic/Latino), 5 international. 65 applicants, 15% accepted, 5 enrolled. *Degree requirements:* For doctorate, comprehensive exam, thesis/dissertation. *Entrance requirements:* For doctorate, GRE General Test. Additional exam requirements/recommendations for international students: Required—TOEFL (minimum score 550 paper-based; 83 iBT), IELTS (minimum score 7). *Application deadline:* For fall admission, 12/8 priority date for domestic students, 12/8 for international students. Application fee: $80. Electronic applications accepted. *Financial support:* Fellowships, research assistantships, and teaching assistantships available. Financial award application deadline: 12/8. *Unit head:* Jeff Vincent, Dean, 919-613-8002, Fax: 919-613-8061, E-mail: meg.stephens@duke.edu. *Application contact:* Elizabeth Hutton, Director of Admissions, 919-684-3913, E-mail: grad-admissions@duke.edu. Website: http://www.nicholas.duke.edu/programs/doctoral/upep/.

Duquesne University, Bayer School of Natural and Environmental Sciences, Environmental Science and Management Program, Pittsburgh, PA 15282-0001. Offers environmental management (Certificate); environmental science (Certificate); environmental science and management (MS); JD/MS; MBA/MS; MS/MS. Part-time and evening/weekend programs available. Postbaccalaureate distance learning degree programs offered (minimal on-campus study). *Faculty:* 2 full-time (0 women), 8 part-time/adjunct (1 woman). *Students:* 19 full-time (12 women), 20 part-time (11 women); includes 4 minority (2 Asian, non-Hispanic/Latino; 2 Hispanic/Latino), 5 international. Average age 26. 41 applicants, 54% accepted, 12 enrolled. In 2012, 18 master's, 3 other advanced degrees awarded. *Degree requirements:* For master's, thesis (for some programs), minimum of 36 credit hours; for Certificate, minimum of 18 credit hours. *Entrance requirements:* For master's, GRE General Test, course work in biology, chemistry, and calculus or statistics; 3 letters of reference, official transcripts, statement of purpose; for Certificate, undergraduate degree, 3 letters of reference, official transcripts, statement of purpose. Additional exam requirements/recommendations for international students: Required—TOEFL (minimum score 80 iBT). *Application deadline:* For fall admission, 4/1 priority date for domestic students, 4/1 for international students; for spring admission, 10/1 priority date for domestic students, 10/1 for international students. Applications are processed on a rolling basis. Application fee: $40. *Expenses:* Contact institution. *Financial support:* In 2012–13, 9 students received support, including 1 fellowship with full tuition reimbursement available (averaging $16,500 per year), 7 research assistantships (averaging $13,350 per year), 1 teaching assistantship with partial tuition reimbursement available; career-related internships or fieldwork, scholarships/grants, tuition waivers (partial), and unspecified assistantships also available. Financial award application deadline: 5/31. *Faculty research:* Watershed management systems, environmental analytical chemistry, environmental endocrinology, environmental microbiology, aquatic biology. *Total annual research expenditures:* $113,953. *Unit head:* Dr. John Stolz, Director, 412-396-4367, Fax: 412-396-4092, E-mail: stolz@duq.edu. *Application contact:* Heather Costello, Graduate Academic Advisor, 412-396-6339, Fax: 412-396-4881, E-mail: costelloh@duq.edu. Website: http://www.duq.edu/academics/schools/natural-and-environmental-sciences/academic-programs/environmental-science-and-management.

Duquesne University, John F. Donahue Graduate School of Business, Pittsburgh, PA 15282-0001. Offers accounting (M Acc); business ethics (MBA); environmental management (MBA); finance (MBA); health care management (MBA); human resources (MBA); information systems management (MBA); international business (MBA); management (MBA); marketing (MBA); supply chain management (MBA); sustainability (MBA); JD/MBA; MBA/M Acc; MBA/MA; MBA/MES; MBA/MHMS; MBA/MSN; MSISM/MBA; Pharm D/MBA. *Accreditation:* AACSB. Part-time and evening/weekend programs available. *Faculty:* 58 full-time (17 women), 40 part-time/adjunct (8 women). *Students:* 91 full-time (40 women), 181 part-time (60 women); includes 15 minority (7 Black or African American, non-Hispanic/Latino; 1 Asian, non-Hispanic/Latino; 5 Hispanic/Latino; 2 Two or more races, non-Hispanic/Latino), 34 international. Average age 28. 410 applicants, 42% accepted, 103 enrolled. In 2012, 135 master's awarded. *Entrance requirements:* For master's, GMAT, undergraduate transcripts, 2 letters of recommendation, current resume, personal statement. Additional exam requirements/recommendations for international students: Required—TOEFL (minimum score 577 paper-based; 90 iBT), TWE, or IELTS (minimum score 7). *Application deadline:* For fall admission, 7/1 priority date for domestic students, 5/1 for international students; for spring admission, 11/1 for domestic and international students. Applications are processed on a rolling basis. Application fee: $0. Electronic applications accepted. *Expenses: Tuition:* Full-time $17,388; part-time $966 per credit. *Required fees:* $1656; $92 per credit. Tuition and fees vary according to program. *Financial support:* In 2012–13, 38 students received support, including 6 fellowships with partial tuition reimbursements available, 32 research assistantships with partial tuition reimbursements available; career-related internships or fieldwork, scholarships/grants, and unspecified assistantships also available. Financial award application deadline: 7/1; financial award applicants required to submit FAFSA. *Faculty research:* International business, investment management, business ethics, technology management, supply chain management, business strategy, finance. *Unit head:* Thomas J. Nist, Director of Graduate Programs, 412-396-6276, Fax: 412-396-1726, E-mail: nist@duq.edu. *Application contact:* Maria W. DeCrosta, Enrollment Manager, 412-396-5529, Fax: 412-396-1726, E-mail: decrostam@duq.edu. Website: http://www.duq.edu/business/graduate.

The Evergreen State College, Graduate Programs, Program in Environmental Studies, Olympia, WA 98505. Offers MES. Part-time and evening/weekend programs available. *Faculty:* 6 full-time (4 women), 4 part-time/adjunct (0 women). *Students:* 77 full-time (44 women), 16 part-time (7 women); includes 9 minority (1 Black or African American, non-Hispanic/Latino; 1 American Indian or Alaska Native, non-Hispanic/Latino; 1 Asian, non-Hispanic/Latino; 3 Hispanic/Latino; 3 Two or more races, non-Hispanic/Latino). Average age 31. 81 applicants, 83% accepted, 36 enrolled. In 2012, 26 master's awarded. *Degree requirements:* For master's, thesis. *Entrance requirements:* For master's, GRE, BA or BS; minimum GPA of 3.0 in last 90 quarter hours toward BA/BS; 15 quarter hours in social sciences and biological or physical science, 4 in statistics, biology, and microeconomics; 3 letters of recommendation; evidence of writing, analytical and general communication skills of high quality and at level appropriate for graduate study. Additional exam requirements/recommendations for international students: Required—TOEFL (minimum score 600 paper-based; 100 iBT). *Application deadline:* For fall admission, 2/15 priority date for domestic students, 2/15 for international students. Applications are processed on a rolling basis. Application fee: $50. Electronic applications accepted. *Expenses:* Contact institution. *Financial support:* In 2012–13, 58 students received support, including 8 fellowships with partial tuition reimbursements available (averaging $2,040 per year); career-related internships or fieldwork, Federal Work-Study, institutionally sponsored loans, scholarships/grants, tuition waivers (partial), and unspecified assistantships also available. Support available to part-time students. Financial award application deadline: 3/1; financial award applicants required to submit FAFSA. *Faculty research:* Science of natural resources management, conservation, restoration riparian forests, ecology and management of headwater streams and wetlands, water quality, hydrology, water supply, watershed functions, climate change, landscape interpretation, political ecology, wildland fire, public lands in western U.S., food security, environmental decision-making bioethics, technology, carbon cycling on land, in rivers, and in the ocean, using carbon to assess organic matter source and age, biomarkers. *Unit head:* Dr. Martha Henderson, Director, 360-867-6225, Fax: 360-867-5430, E-mail: mhenders@evergreen.edu. *Application contact:* Gail Wootan, Assistant Director, 360-867-6225, Fax: 360-867-5430, E-mail: wootang@evergreen.edu. Website: http://www.evergreen.edu/mes/.

Florida Atlantic University, Dorothy F. Schmidt College of Arts and Letters, Department of History, Boca Raton, FL 33431-0991. Offers environmental studies (Certificate); history (MA). Part-time programs available. *Faculty:* 17 full-time (7 women), 6 part-time/adjunct (1 woman). *Students:* 13 full-time (2 women), 15 part-time (5 women); includes 3 minority (1 Asian, non-Hispanic/Latino; 2 Hispanic/Latino), 2 international. Average age 34. 28 applicants, 39% accepted, 7 enrolled. In 2012, 4 master's awarded. *Degree requirements:* For master's, one foreign language, thesis optional. *Entrance requirements:* For master's, GRE General Test, minimum GPA of 3.0. *Application deadline:* For fall admission, 6/1 priority date for domestic students, 2/15 for international students; for spring admission, 10/15 for domestic students, 8/15 for international students. Applications are processed on a rolling basis. Application fee: $30. Electronic applications accepted. *Expenses:* Tuition, state resident: full-time $8876; part-time $369.82 per credit hour. Tuition, nonresident: full-time $24,595; part-time $1024.81 per credit hour. *Financial support:* Fellowships, research assistantships, teaching assistantships with tuition reimbursements, career-related internships or fieldwork, Federal Work-Study, and tuition waivers (partial) available. Support available to part-time students. Financial award application deadline: 3/1. *Faculty research:* Twentieth-century America, U.S. urban history, Florida history, history of socialism, Latin America. *Unit head:* Dr. Patricia Kollander, Chair, 561-297-3841, Fax: 561-297-2704, E-mail: kollande@fau.edu. *Application contact:* Ben Lowe, Director of Graduate Programs, 561-297-3846, Fax: 561-297-2704, E-mail: bplowe@fau.edu. Website: http://www.fau.edu/history/.

Florida Gulf Coast University, College of Professional Studies, Program in Public Administration, Fort Myers, FL 33965-6565. Offers criminal justice (MPA); environmental policy (MPA); general public administration (MPA); management (MPA). *Accreditation:* NASPAA. Part-time programs available. *Faculty:* 39 full-time (16 women), 38 part-time/adjunct (12 women). *Students:* 41 full-time (25 women), 18 part-time (11 women); includes 19 minority (10 Black or African American, non-Hispanic/Latino; 8 Hispanic/Latino; 1 Two or more races, non-Hispanic/Latino), 1 international. Average age 35. 30 applicants, 73% accepted, 20 enrolled. In 2012, 30 master's awarded. *Entrance requirements:* For master's, GRE General Test, MAT, minimum GPA of 3.0. Additional exam requirements/recommendations for international students: Required—TOEFL (minimum score 550 paper-based). *Application deadline:* For fall admission, 7/1 priority date for domestic students; for spring admission, 11/15 for domestic students. Applications are processed on a rolling basis. Application fee: $30. Electronic applications accepted. *Expenses:* Tuition, state resident: full-time $6458. Tuition, nonresident: full-time $28,170. *Required fees:* $1952. Tuition and fees vary according to course load. *Financial support:* In 2012–13, 5 research assistantships were awarded; career-related internships or fieldwork and tuition waivers (full and partial) also available. Support available to part-time students. *Faculty research:* Personnel, public policy, public finance, housing policy. *Unit head:* Roger Green, Chair, 239-590-7838, E-mail: tbusson@fgcu.edu. *Application contact:* Howard Smith, Assistant Professor/Director of MPA Program, 239-590-7837, Fax: 239-590-7846, E-mail: hsmith@fgcu.edu.

Florida Institute of Technology, Graduate Programs, College of Engineering, Department of Marine and Environmental Systems, Melbourne, FL 32901-6975. Offers earth remote sensing (MS); environmental resource management (MS); environmental science (MS, PhD); meteorology (MS); ocean engineering (MS, PhD); oceanography (MS, PhD), including biological oceanography (MS), chemical oceanography (MS), coastal management (MS), geological oceanography (MS), oceanography (PhD), physical oceanography (MS). Part-time programs available. *Faculty:* 15 full-time (0 women), 2 part-time/adjunct (0 women). *Students:* 53 full-time (19 women), 15 part-time (4 women); includes 3 minority (1 Asian, non-Hispanic/Latino; 1 Hispanic/Latino; 1 Two or more races, non-Hispanic/Latino), 23 international. Average age 27. 141 applicants, 45% accepted, 21 enrolled. In 2012, 16 master's, 4 doctorates awarded. *Degree requirements:* For master's, comprehensive exam (for some programs), thesis (for some programs), seminar, field project, written final exam, technical paper, oral presentation, or internship; for doctorate, comprehensive exam, thesis/dissertation, seminar, internships (oceanography and environmental science), publications. *Entrance requirements:* For master's, GRE General Test (environmental science, oceanography, environmental resource management, meteorology, earth remote sensing), 3 letters of recommendation, minimum GPA of 3.0, resume, transcripts, statement of objectives; for doctorate, GRE General Test (oceanography, environmental science), resume, 3 letters of recommendation, minimum GPA of 3.3, statement of objectives, on-campus interview (highly recommended). Additional exam requirements/recommendations for international students: Required—TOEFL (minimum score 550 paper-based; 79 iBT). *Application deadline:* For fall admission, 4/1 for international students; for spring admission, 9/30 for international students. Applications are processed on a rolling basis. Electronic applications accepted. *Expenses: Tuition:* Full-time $20,214; part-time $1123 per credit hour. Tuition and fees vary according to campus/location. *Financial support:* In 2012–13, 5 fellowships with full and partial tuition reimbursements (averaging $5,400 per year), 8 research assistantships with full and partial tuition reimbursements (averaging $7,851 per year), 13 teaching assistantships with full and partial tuition reimbursements (averaging $5,565 per year) were awarded; career-related internships or fieldwork, institutionally sponsored loans, tuition waivers (partial), unspecified assistantships, and tuition remissions also available. Support available to part-time students. Financial award application deadline: 3/1; financial award applicants required to submit FAFSA. *Total annual research expenditures:* $2.2 million. *Unit head:* Dr. George Maul, Department Head, 321-674-7453, Fax: 321-674-7212, E-mail: gmaul@fit.edu. *Application contact:* Cheryl A. Brown, Associate Director of Graduate Admissions, 321-674-7581, Fax: 321-723-9468, E-mail: cbrown@fit.edu. Website: http://coe.fit.edu/dmes/.

Florida International University, College of Arts and Sciences, Department of Earth and Environment, Program in Environmental Studies, Miami, FL 33199. Offers MS. Part-time programs available. *Degree requirements:* For master's, thesis or alternative. *Entrance requirements:* For master's, GRE General Test, minimum GPA of 3.0, 3 letters of recommendation, letter of intent. Additional exam requirements/recommendations for international students: Required—TOEFL (minimum score 550 paper-based; 80 iBT). Electronic applications accepted.

George Mason University, College of Science, Department of Environmental Science and Policy, Fairfax, VA 22030. Offers environmental management (Certificate); environmental science and policy (MS); environmental science and public policy (PhD). *Faculty:* 21 full-time (7 women), 4 part-time/adjunct (1 woman). *Students:* 75 full-time (45 women), 93 part-time (62 women); includes 27 minority (7 Black or African American, non-Hispanic/Latino; 9 Asian, non-Hispanic/Latino; 8 Hispanic/Latino; 1 Native Hawaiian or other Pacific Islander, non-Hispanic/Latino; 2 Two or more races, non-Hispanic/Latino), 12 international. Average age 34. 91 applicants, 51% accepted, 29 enrolled. In 2012, 19 master's, 17 doctorates, 2 other advanced degrees awarded. *Degree requirements:* For doctorate, comprehensive exam, thesis/dissertation, internship; seminar. *Entrance requirements:* For master's, GRE, bachelor's degree with minimum GPA of 3.0 in related field; 3 letters of recommendation; expanded goals statement; 2 official copies of transcripts; for doctorate, GRE, bachelor's degree with minimum GPA of 3.0; 3 letters of recommendation; current resume; expanded goals statement; 2 official copies of transcripts; for Certificate, GRE, 3 letters of recommendation; undergraduate degree in related field; expanded goals statement; resume; 2 official copies of transcripts. Additional exam requirements/recommendations for international students: Required—TOEFL (minimum score 570 paper-based; 88 iBT), IELTS (minimum score 6.5), Pearson Test of English. *Application deadline:* For fall admission, 2/15 priority date for domestic students; for spring admission, 10/1 priority date for domestic students. Application fee: $65 ($80 for international students). Electronic applications accepted. *Expenses:* Tuition, state resident: full-time $9080; part-time $378.33 per credit hour. Tuition, nonresident: full-time $25,010; part-time $1042.08 per credit hour. *Required fees:* $2610; $108.75 per credit hour. Tuition and fees vary according to program. *Financial support:* In 2012–13, 52 students received support, including 10 fellowships (averaging $10,522 per year), 10 research assistantships with full and partial tuition reimbursements available (averaging $18,966 per year), 38 teaching assistantships with full and partial tuition reimbursements available (averaging $14,832 per year); career-related internships or fieldwork, Federal Work-Study, scholarships/grants, unspecified assistantships, and health care benefits (for full-time research or teaching assistantship recipients) also available. Support available to part-time students. Financial award application deadline: 3/1; financial award applicants required to submit FAFSA. *Faculty research:* Wetland ecosystems, comparative physiology, systematics, molecular phylogenetics, conservation genetics, estuarine and oceanic systems, biodiversity of fungi, environmental and resource management, human ecology. *Total annual research expenditures:* $1 million. *Unit head:* Dr. Robert B. Jonas, Chair, 703-993-7590, Fax: 703-993-1066, E-mail: rjonas@gmu.edu. *Application contact:* Sharon Bloomquist, Graduate Program Coordinator, 703-993-3187, Fax: 703-993-1066, E-mail: sbloomqu@gmu.edu. Website: http://esp.gmu.edu/.

The George Washington University, Columbian College of Arts and Sciences, Program in Environmental and Resource Policy, Washington, DC 20052. Offers MA. *Faculty:* 2 full-time (both women). *Students:* 14 full-time (9 women), 7 part-time (4 women); includes 2 minority (1 Black or African American, non-Hispanic/Latino; 1 Asian, non-Hispanic/Latino), 3 international. Average age 25. 57 applicants, 75% accepted, 7 enrolled. In 2012, 13 master's awarded. *Degree requirements:* For master's, capstone course. *Entrance requirements:* For master's, GRE General Test, minimum GPA of 3.0, two letters of recommendation. Additional exam requirements/recommendations for international students: Required—TOEFL (minimum score 600 paper-based; 100 iBT). *Application deadline:* For fall admission, 4/1 priority date for domestic students, 4/1 for international students; for spring admission, 10/1 priority date for domestic students, 9/1 for international students. Applications are processed on a rolling basis. Application fee: $60. Electronic applications accepted. *Financial support:* In 2012–13, 2 students received support. Fellowships with tuition reimbursements available, institutionally sponsored loans, and tuition waivers available. Financial award application deadline: 1/15. *Unit head:* Prof. Henry

Teng, Chair, 202-994-1008. *Application contact:* 202-994-6210, Fax: 202-994-6213, E-mail: askccas@gwu.edu. Website: http://www.gwu.edu/~tspppa/academics/affiliated_environment_policy.cfm.

Georgia Institute of Technology, Graduate Studies and Research, College of Architecture, City and Regional Planning Program, Atlanta, GA 30332-0001. Offers city and regional planning (PhD); economic development (MCRP); environmental planning and management (MCRP); geographic information systems (MCRP); land and community development (MCRP); land use planning (MCRP); transportation (MCRP); urban design (MCRP); MCP/MSCE. *Accreditation:* ACSP. *Degree requirements:* For master's, thesis, internship. *Entrance requirements:* For master's, GRE General Test, minimum GPA of 2.7. Additional exam requirements/recommendations for international students: Required—TOEFL. Electronic applications accepted.

Georgia State University, Andrew Young School of Policy Studies, Department of Economics, Atlanta, GA 30302. Offers economics (MA); environmental economics (PhD); experimental economics (PhD); labor economics (PhD); policy (MA); public finance (PhD); urban and regional economics (PhD). MA offered through the College of Arts and Sciences. Part-time programs available. *Faculty:* 30 full-time (7 women), 6 part-time/adjunct (2 women). *Students:* 138 full-time (52 women), 7 part-time (1 woman); includes 10 minority (6 Black or African American, non-Hispanic/Latino; 2 Asian, non-Hispanic/Latino; 2 Hispanic/Latino), 86 international. Average age 28. 206 applicants, 52% accepted, 52 enrolled. In 2012, 18 master's, 9 doctorates awarded. Terminal master's awarded for partial completion of doctoral program. *Degree requirements:* For master's, thesis optional; for doctorate, comprehensive exam, thesis/dissertation. *Entrance requirements:* For master's, GRE; for doctorate, GRE. Additional exam requirements/recommendations for international students: Required—TOEFL (minimum score 603 paper-based, 100 iBT) or IELTS (minimum score 7). *Application deadline:* For fall admission, 2/15 for domestic and international students; for spring admission, 10/1 for domestic and international students. Application fee: $50. Electronic applications accepted. *Expenses:* Tuition, state resident: full-time $8064; part-time $336 per credit hour. Tuition, nonresident: full-time $28,800; part-time $1200 per credit hour. *Required fees:* $2128; $1064 per semester. Tuition and fees vary according to course load and program. *Financial support:* In 2012–13, 120 students received support, including 5 fellowships with full tuition reimbursements available (averaging $11,333 per year), 112 research assistantships with full tuition reimbursements available (averaging $9,788 per year), 3 teaching assistantships with full tuition reimbursements available (averaging $3,000 per year); career-related internships or fieldwork also available. Financial award application deadline: 2/15. *Faculty research:* Public, experimental, urban/environmental, labor, and health economics. *Total annual research expenditures:* $214,100. *Unit head:* Dr. Sally Wallace, Department Chair, 404-413-0046, Fax: 404-413-0145, E-mail: swallace@gsu.edu. *Application contact:* Charisma Parker, Admissions Coordinator, 404-413-0030, Fax: 404-413-0023, E-mail: cparker28@gsu.edu. Website: http://aysps.gsu.edu/econ.

Georgia State University, Andrew Young School of Policy Studies, Department of Public Management and Policy, Atlanta, GA 30303. Offers criminal justice (MPA); disaster management (Certificate); disaster policy (MPA); environmental policy (PhD); health policy (PhD); management and finance (MPA); nonprofit management (MPA, Certificate); nonprofit policy (MPA); planning and economic development (MPP, Certificate); policy analysis and evaluation (MPA), including planning and economic development; public and nonprofit management (PhD); public finance and budgeting (PhD), including science and technology policy, urban and regional economic development; public finance policy (MPA), including social policy; public health (MPA). *Accreditation:* NASPAA (one or more programs are accredited). Part-time programs available. *Faculty:* 16 full-time (6 women), 9 part-time/adjunct (3 women). *Students:* 141 full-time (77 women), 95 part-time (63 women); includes 99 minority (73 Black or African American, non-Hispanic/Latino; 6 Asian, non-Hispanic/Latino; 10 Hispanic/Latino; 10 Two or more races, non-Hispanic/Latino), 18 international. Average age 30. 296 applicants, 58% accepted, 87 enrolled. In 2012, 75 master's, 10 other advanced degrees awarded. Terminal master's awarded for partial completion of doctoral program. *Degree requirements:* For master's, thesis optional; for doctorate, comprehensive exam, thesis/dissertation. *Entrance requirements:* For master's and doctorate, GRE. Additional exam requirements/recommendations for international students: Required—TOEFL (minimum score 603 paper-based, 100 iBT) or IELTS (minimum score 7). *Application deadline:* For fall admission, 2/15 for domestic and international students; for spring admission, 10/1 for domestic and international students. Application fee: $50. Electronic applications accepted. *Expenses:* Tuition, state resident: full-time $8064; part-time $336 per credit hour. Tuition, nonresident: full-time $28,800; part-time $1200 per credit hour. *Required fees:* $2128; $1064 per semester. Tuition and fees vary according to course load and program. *Financial support:* In 2012–13, 65 students received support, including 8 fellowships (averaging $8,194 per year), 57 research assistantships (averaging $8,068 per year), 7 teaching assistantships (averaging $3,600 per year); institutionally sponsored loans, scholarships/grants, health care benefits, and unspecified assistantships also available. Financial award application deadline: 2/1. *Faculty research:* Public budgeting and finance, public management, nonprofit management, performance measurement and management, urban development. *Total annual research expenditures:* $390,159. *Unit head:* Dr. Gregory Burr Lewis, Chair and Professor, 404-413-0114, Fax: 404-413-0104, E-mail: glewis@gsu.edu. *Application contact:* Charisma Parker, Admissions Coordinator, 404-413-0030, Fax: 404-413-0023, E-mail: cparker28@gsu.edu. Website: http://aysps.gsu.edu/pmap/.

Goddard College, Graduate Division, Master of Arts in Individualized Studies Program, Plainfield, VT 05667-9432. Offers consciousness studies (MA); environmental studies (MA); transformative language arts (MA). Postbaccalaureate distance learning degree programs offered (minimal on-campus study). *Degree requirements:* For master's, thesis. *Entrance requirements:* For master's, 3 letters of recommendation, study plan, bibliography/resource list, interview. Electronic applications accepted. *Expenses:* Contact institution.

Green Mountain College, Program in Environmental Studies, Poultney, VT 05764-1199. Offers MS. Distance learning only. Part-time and evening/weekend programs available. Postbaccalaureate distance learning degree programs offered (no on-campus study). *Entrance requirements:* For master's, portfolio, curriculum vitae, 3 recommendations. Electronic applications accepted. *Faculty research:* Herbarium specimen, solar electricity's value, environmental politics.

Hardin-Simmons University, Graduate School, Holland School of Sciences and Mathematics, Program in Environmental Management, Abilene, TX 79698-0001. Offers MS. Part-time programs available. *Faculty:* 5 full-time (1 woman). *Students:* 6 full-time (2 women), 1 (woman) part-time. Average age 25. 6 applicants, 100% accepted, 5 enrolled. In 2012, 3 master's awarded. *Degree requirements:* For master's, comprehensive exam, thesis or alternative, internship. *Entrance requirements:* For master's, minimum undergraduate GPA of 3.0 in major, 2.7 overall; 2 semesters of course work each in biology, chemistry, and geology; interview; writing sample; occupational experience. Additional exam requirements/recommendations for international students: Required—TOEFL (minimum score 550 paper-based; 75 iBT). *Application deadline:* For fall admission, 8/15 priority date for domestic students, 4/1 for international students; for spring admission, 1/5 priority date for domestic students, 9/1 for international students. Applications are processed on a rolling basis. Application fee: $50. *Expenses: Tuition:* Full-time $12,870; part-time $715 per credit hour. *Required fees:* $650. Tuition and fees vary according to degree level. *Financial support:* In 2012–13, 8 students received support. Fellowships, career-related internships or fieldwork, and scholarships/grants available. Support available to part-time students. Financial award application deadline: 6/30; financial award applicants required to submit FAFSA. *Faculty research:* South American history, herpetology, geology, environmental education, petroleum biodegradation, environmental ecology and microbiology. *Unit head:* Dr. Mark Ouimette, Director, 325-670-1383, Fax: 325-670-1391, E-mail: ouimette@hsutx.edu. *Application contact:* Dr. Nancy Kucinski, Dean of Graduate Studies, 325-670-1298, Fax: 325-670-1564, E-mail: gradoff@hsutx.edu. Website: http://www.hsutx.edu/academics/holland/graduate/environmental.

Harvard University, Extension School, Cambridge, MA 02138-3722. Offers applied sciences (CAS); biotechnology (ALM); educational technologies (ALM); educational technology (CET); English for graduate and professional studies (DGP); environmental management (ALM, CEM); information technology (ALM); journalism (ALM); liberal arts (ALM); management (ALM, CM); mathematics for teaching (ALM); museum studies (ALM); premedical studies (Diploma); publication and communication (CPC). Part-time and evening/weekend programs available. *Degree requirements:* For master's, thesis. *Entrance requirements:* For master's, 3 completed graduate courses with grade of B or higher. Additional exam requirements/recommendations for international students: Required—TOEFL (minimum score 600 paper-based), TWE (minimum score 5). *Expenses:* Contact institution.

Humboldt State University, Academic Programs, College of Natural Resources and Sciences, Programs in Environmental Systems, Arcata, CA 95521-8299. Offers environmental systems (MS), including energy, environment and society, environmental resources engineering, geology, math modeling. *Students:* 35 full-time (11 women), 5 part-time (2 women); includes 4 minority (1 Asian, non-Hispanic/Latino; 3 Two or more races, non-Hispanic/Latino), 1 international. Average age 27. 71 applicants, 42% accepted, 20 enrolled. In 2012, 18 master's awarded. *Degree requirements:* For master's, thesis. *Entrance requirements:* For master's, GRE, appropriate bachelor's degree, minimum GPA of 2.5, 3 letters of recommendation. Additional exam requirements/recommendations for international students: Required—TOEFL. *Application deadline:* For fall admission, 2/15 for domestic students; for spring admission, 10/15 for domestic students. Applications are processed on a rolling basis. Application fee: $55. *Expenses:* Tuition, state resident: full-time $8396. Tuition, nonresident: full-time $17,324. Tuition and fees vary according to program. *Financial support:* Application deadline: 3/1; applicants required to submit FAFSA. *Faculty research:* Mathematical modeling, international development technology, geology, environmental resources engineering. *Unit head:* Dr. Chris Dugaw, Chair, 707-826-4251, Fax: 707-826-4145, E-mail: dugaw@humboldt.edu. *Application contact:* Dr. Dale Oliver, Coordinator, 707-826-4921, Fax: 707-826-3140, E-mail: dale.oliver@humboldt.edu.

Idaho State University, Office of Graduate Studies, College of Science and Engineering, Civil and Environmental Engineering Department, Pocatello, ID 83209-8060. Offers civil engineering (MS); environmental engineering (MS); environmental science and management (MS). Part-time programs available. *Degree requirements:* For master's, comprehensive exam (for some programs), thesis optional, thesis project, 2 semesters of seminar. *Entrance requirements:* For master's, GRE. Additional exam requirements/recommendations for international students: Required—TOEFL (minimum score 550 paper-based; 80 iBT). Electronic applications accepted. *Faculty research:* Floor vibration investigations, earthquake engineering, base isolation systems and seismic risk assessment, infrastructure revitalization (building foundations and damage, bridge structures, highways, and dams), slope stability and soil erosion, pavement rehabilitation, computational fluid dynamics and flood control structures, microbial fuel cells, water treatment and water quality modeling, environmental risk assessment, biotechnology, nanotechnology.

Illinois Institute of Technology, Stuart School of Business, Program in Environmental Management and Sustainability, Chicago, IL 60661. Offers MS, JD/MS, MBA/MS. Part-time and evening/weekend programs available. *Faculty:* 33 full-time (5 women), 19 part-time/adjunct (2 women). *Students:* 16 full-time (9 women), 17 part-time (11 women); includes 6 minority (2 Asian, non-Hispanic/ Latino; 2 Hispanic/Latino; 2 Two or more races, non-Hispanic/Latino), 11 international. Average age 32. 24 applicants, 88% accepted, 5 enrolled. In 2012, 21 master's awarded. *Entrance requirements:* For master's, GRE (minimum score 298) or GMAT (500), one semester of general chemistry and mathematics through calculus. Additional exam requirements/recommendations for international students: Required—TOEFL (minimum score 600 paper-based; 85 iBT); Recommended—IELTS (minimum score 7). *Application deadline:* For fall admission, 8/1 for domestic students, 5/1 for international students; for spring admission, 12/15 for domestic students, 10/15 for international students. Applications are processed on a rolling basis. Application fee: $75. Electronic applications accepted. *Expenses:* Contact institution. *Financial support:* Career-related internships or fieldwork, Federal Work-Study, institutionally sponsored loans, scholarships/grants, traineeships, health care benefits, and tuition waivers (partial) available. Support available to part-time students. Financial award applicants required to submit FAFSA. *Faculty research:* Wind energy, carbon footprint reduction, critical asset management, solar energy, water quality management. *Unit head:* M. Krishna Erramilli, Professor/Director, MBA Program, 312-906-6573, Fax: 312-906-6549, E-mail: krish@stuart.iit.edu. *Application contact:* Deborah Gibson, Director, Graduate Admission, 866-472-3448, Fax: 312-567-3138, E-mail: inquiry.grad@iit.edu. Website: http://www.stuart.iit.edu/ graduateprograms/ms/environmentalmanagement/index.shtml.

Indiana University Bloomington, School of Public and Environmental Affairs, Public Affairs Programs, Bloomington, IN 47405. Offers comparative and international affairs (MPA); economic development (MPA); energy (MPA); environmental policy (PhD); environmental policy and natural resource management (MPA); hazardous materials management (Certificate); information systems (MPA); international development (MPA); local government management (MPA); nonprofit management (MPA, Certificate); policy analysis (MPA); public budgeting and financial management (Certificate); public finance (PhD); public financial administration (MPA); public management (MPA, PhD, Certificate); public policy analysis (PhD); social entrepreneurship (Certificate); specialized public affairs (MPA); sustainability and sustainable development (MPA); JD/MPA; MPA/MA; MPA/MIS; MPA/MLS; MSES/MPA. *Accreditation:* NASPAA (one or more programs are accredited). Part-time programs available. *Faculty:* 80 full-time (30 women), 102 part-time/adjunct (43 women). *Students:* 383 full-time, 34 part-time; includes 51 minority (14 Black or African American, non-Hispanic/Latino; 1 American Indian or Alaska Native, non-Hispanic/Latino; 16 Asian, non-Hispanic/ Latino; 14 Hispanic/Latino; 6 Two or more races, non-Hispanic/Latino), 49 international. Average age 26. 652 applicants, 172 enrolled. In 2012, 172 master's, 12 doctorates awarded. *Degree requirements:* For master's, core classes, capstone, internship; for doctorate, comprehensive exam, thesis/ dissertation. *Entrance requirements:* For master's, GRE General Test or GMAT, official transcripts, 3 letters of recommendation, resume, personal statement; for doctorate, GRE General Test or LSAT, official transcripts, 3 letters of recommendation, resume or curriculum vitae, statement of purpose. Additional exam requirements/recommendations for international students: Required—TOEFL (minimum score 600 paper-based; 96 iBT); Recommended—IELTS (minimum score 7). *Application deadline:* For fall admission, 2/1 priority date for domestic students, 12/1 for international students; for spring admission, 11/15 for domestic students, 9/1 for international students. Applications are processed on a rolling basis. Application fee: $55 ($65 for international students). Electronic applications accepted. *Financial support:* Fellowships with partial tuition reimbursements, research assistantships with partial tuition reimbursements, teaching assistantships with partial tuition reimbursements, career-related internships or fieldwork, Federal Work-Study, scholarships/grants, health care benefits, unspecified assistantships, and Service Corps programs available. Financial award application deadline: 2/1; financial award applicants required to submit FAFSA. *Faculty research:* Comparative and international affairs, environmental policy and resource management, policy analysis, public finance, public management, urban management, nonprofit management, energy policy, social policy, public finance. *Unit head:* Jennifer Forney, Director, Graduate Student Services, 812-855-9485, Fax: 812-856-3665, E-mail: speampo@ indiana.edu. *Application contact:* Lane Bowman, Admissions Services Coordinator, 812-855-2840, Fax: 812-856-3665, E-mail: speaapps@indiana.edu. Website: http://www.indiana.edu/~spea/prospective_students/masters/.

Indiana University Northwest, School of Public and Environmental Affairs, Gary, IN 46408-1197. Offers criminal justice (MPA); environmental affairs (Graduate Certificate); health services (MPA); human services (MPA); nonprofit management (Certificate); public management (MPA). *Accreditation:* NASPAA (one or more programs are accredited). Part-time programs available. *Faculty:* 5 full-time (3 women). *Students:* 17 full-time (10 women), 50 part-time (37 women); includes 42 minority (34 Black or African American, non-Hispanic/Latino; 2 Asian, non-Hispanic/Latino; 6 Hispanic/Latino), 1 international. Average age 38. 32 applicants, 97% accepted, 25 enrolled. In 2012, 36 master's, 29 other advanced degrees awarded. *Entrance requirements:* For master's, GRE General Test or GMAT, letters of recommendation. *Application deadline:* For fall admission, 8/15 priority date for domestic students. Applications are processed on a rolling basis. *Financial support:* Career-related internships or fieldwork, Federal Work-Study, and tuition waivers (partial) available. Support available to part-time students. Financial award application deadline: 3/1. *Faculty research:* Employment in income security policies, evidence in criminal justice, equal employment law, social welfare policy and welfare reform, public finance in developing countries. *Unit head:* Dr. Barbara Peat, Department Chair, 219-981-5645. *Application contact:* Dawn Samson, Assistant to the Director of Graduate Programs and Outreach, 219-981-5668, E-mail: dawnsams@iun.edu. Website: http:// www.iun.edu/spea/index.htm.

Indiana University of Pennsylvania, School of Graduate Studies and Research, College of Humanities and Social Sciences, Department of Geography and Regional Planning, Environmental Planning Track, Indiana, PA 15705-1087. Offers MS. *Faculty:* 8 full-time (1 woman). *Students:* 5 full-time (0 women). Average age 27. 8 applicants, 63% accepted, 2 enrolled. In 2012, 2 master's awarded. *Entrance requirements:* Additional exam requirements/ recommendations for international students: Required—TOEFL (minimum score 540 paper-based). *Application deadline:* Applications are processed on a rolling basis. Application fee: $50. Electronic applications accepted. *Expenses:* Tuition, state resident: part-time $429 per credit hour. Tuition, nonresident: part-time $644 per credit hour. *Required fees:* $110.60 per credit hour. One-time fee: $180 part-time. *Financial support:* In 2012–13, 5 research assistantships (averaging $3,935 per year) were awarded. Financial award application deadline: 4/15; financial award applicants required to submit FAFSA. *Application contact:* Dr. John E. Benhart, Jr., Chairperson, 724-357-2250, E-mail: jbenhart@iup.edu. Website: http://www.iup.edu/upper.aspx?id=90827.

Instituto Tecnologico de Santo Domingo, Graduate School, Area of Basic And Environmental Sciences, Santo Domingo, Dominican Republic. Offers environmental science (M En S), including environmental education, environmental management, marine resources, natural resources management; mathematics (MS, PhD); renewable energy technology (MS, Certificate).

Instituto Tecnológico y de Estudios Superiores de Monterrey, Campus Estado de México, Professional and Graduate Division, Estado de Mexico, Mexico. Offers administration of information technologies (MITA); architecture (M Arch); business administration (GMBA, MBA); computer sciences (MCS, PhD); education (M Ed); educational institution administration (MAD); educational technology and innovation (PhD); electronic commerce (MEC); environmental systems (MS); finance (MAF); humanistic studies (MHS); information sciences and knowledge management (MISKM); information systems (MS); manufacturing systems (MS); marketing (MEM); quality systems and productivity (MS); science and materials engineering (PhD); telecommunications management (MTM). Part-time programs available. Postbaccalaureate distance learning degree programs offered (minimal on-campus study). *Degree requirements:* For master's, one foreign language, thesis (for some programs); for doctorate, one foreign language, thesis/dissertation. *Entrance requirements:* For master's, E-PAEP 500, interview; for doctorate, E-PAEP 500, research proposal. Additional exam requirements/recommendations for international students: Required—TOEFL (minimum score 550 paper-based). *Faculty research:* Surface treatments by plasmas, mechanical properties, robotics, graphical computing, mechatronics security protocols.

Instituto Tecnológico y de Estudios Superiores de Monterrey, Campus Irapuato, Graduate Programs, Irapuato, Mexico. Offers administration (MBA); administration of information technology (MAIT); administration of telecommunications (MAT); architecture (M Arch); computer science (MCS); education (M Ed); educational administration (MEA); educational innovation and technology (DEIT); educational technology (MET); electronic commerce (MBA); environmental administration and planning (MEAP); environmental systems (MES); finances (MBA); humanistic studies (MHS); international management for Latin American executives (MIMLAE); library and information science (MLIS); manufacturing quality management (MMQM); marketing research (MBA).

Inter American University of Puerto Rico, Metropolitan Campus, Graduate Programs, Program in Environmental Evaluation and Protection, San Juan, PR 00919-1293. Offers MS.

The Johns Hopkins University, Engineering Program for Professionals, Part-Time Program in Environmental Planning and Management, Baltimore, MD 21218-2699. Offers MS, Post-Master's Certificate. Part-time and evening/ weekend programs available. Postbaccalaureate distance learning degree programs offered (no on-campus study).

The Johns Hopkins University, G. W. C. Whiting School of Engineering, Program in Engineering Management, Baltimore, MD 21218-2699. Offers biomaterials (MSEM); communications science (MSEM); computer science (MSEM); fluid mechanics (MSEM); materials science and engineering (MSEM); mechanical engineering (MSEM); mechanics and materials (MSEM); nano-biotechnology (MSEM); nanomaterials and nanotechnology (MSEM); probability and statistics (MSEM); smart product and device design (MSEM); systems analysis, management and environmental policy (MSEM). *Entrance requirements:* For master's, GRE, 3 letters of recommendation, resume. Additional exam requirements/recommendations for international students: Required—TOEFL (minimum score 600 paper-based; 100 iBT) or IELTS (minimum score 7). Electronic applications accepted.

The Johns Hopkins University, Zanvyl Krieger School of Arts and Sciences, Advanced Academic Programs, Program in Environmental Sciences and Policy, Baltimore, MD 21218-2699. Offers MS. Part-time and evening/weekend programs available. Postbaccalaureate distance learning degree programs offered (minimal on-campus study). *Degree requirements:* For master's, thesis (for some programs). *Entrance requirements:* For master's, minimum GPA of 3.0, coursework in chemistry and calculus. Additional exam requirements/recommendations for international students: Required—TOEFL.

Kean University, College of Business and Public Management, Program in Public Administration, Union, NJ 07083. Offers environmental management (MPA); health services administration (MPA); non-profit management (MPA); public administration (MPA). *Accreditation:* NASPAA. Part-time programs available. *Faculty:* 14 full-time (6 women). *Students:* 76 full-time (40 women), 78 part-time (48 women); includes 101 minority (69 Black or African American, non-Hispanic/Latino; 6 Asian, non-Hispanic/Latino; 25 Hispanic/Latino; 1 Two or more races, non-Hispanic/Latino), 4 international. Average age 32. 84 applicants, 90% accepted, 44 enrolled. In 2012, 44 master's awarded. *Degree requirements:* For master's, thesis, internship, research seminar. *Entrance requirements:* For master's, minimum cumulative GPA of 3.0, official transcripts from all institutions attended, two letters of recommendation, personal statement, writing sample, professional resume/curriculum vitae. Additional exam requirements/recommendations for international students: Required—TOEFL (minimum score 79 iBT). *Application deadline:* For fall admission, 6/1 for domestic and international students; for spring admission, 12/1 for domestic and international students. Applications are processed on a rolling basis. Application fee: $75 ($150 for international students). Electronic applications accepted. *Expenses:* Tuition, state resident: full-time $11,748; part-time $572 per credit. Tuition, nonresident: full-time $15,923; part-time $701 per credit. *Required fees:* $2961; $135 per credit. Part-time tuition and fees vary according to course load, degree level and program. *Financial support:* In 2012–13, 23 research assistantships with full tuition reimbursements (averaging $3,263 per year) were awarded; unspecified assistantships also available. Financial award applicants required to submit FAFSA. *Unit head:* Dr. Patricia Moore, Program Coordinator, 908-737-4314, E-mail: pmoore@kean.edu. *Application contact:* Reenat Hasan, Admissions Counselor, 908-737-5923, Fax: 908-737-5925, E-mail: hasanr@kean.edu. Website: http://grad.kean.edu/masters-programs/public-administration-0.

Kentucky State University, College of Agriculture, Food Science and Sustainable Systems, Frankfort, KY 40601. Offers aquaculture (MS); environmental studies (MS). Part-time and evening/weekend programs available. *Faculty:* 5 full-time (1 woman). *Students:* 15 full-time (7 women), 11 part-time (4 women); includes 4 minority (3 Black or African American, non-Hispanic/Latino; 1 Two or more races, non-Hispanic/Latino), 4 international. Average age 31. 27 applicants, 48% accepted, 12 enrolled. In 2012, 11 master's awarded. *Degree requirements:* For master's, comprehensive exam, thesis optional. *Entrance requirements:* For master's, GRE, GMAT. Additional exam requirements/recommendations for international students: Required—TOEFL (minimum score 525 paper-based). *Application deadline:* Applications are processed on a rolling basis. Application fee: $30 ($100 for international students). Electronic applications accepted. *Expenses:* Tuition, state resident: full-time $6516; part-time $362 per credit hour. Tuition, nonresident: full-time $10,026; part-time $557 per credit hour. *Required fees:* $450; $25 per credit hour. Tuition and fees vary according to course load. *Financial support:* In 2012–13, 16 students received support, including 19 research assistantships (averaging $11,335 per year); scholarships/grants, tuition waivers (partial), and unspecified assistantships also available. Financial award application deadline: 4/15; financial award applicants required to submit FAFSA. *Unit head:* Dr. Teferi Tsegaye, Dean, 502-597-6310, E-mail: teferi.tsegaye@kysu.edu. *Application contact:* Dr. Beverly Downing, Acting Director of Graduate Studies, 502-597-6443, E-mail: beverly.downing@kysu.edu. Website: http://www.kysu.edu/academics/collegesAndSchools/CAFSSS/.

Lamar University, College of Graduate Studies, College of Engineering, Department of Civil Engineering, Beaumont, TX 77710. Offers civil engineering (ME, MES, DE); environmental engineering (MS); environmental studies (MS). Part-time programs available. *Faculty:* 6 full-time (1 woman), 2 part-time/adjunct (0 women). *Students:* 29 full-time (8 women), 8 part-time (4 women); includes 7 minority (2 Black or African American, non-Hispanic/Latino; 4 Asian, non-Hispanic/Latino; 1 Hispanic/Latino), 27 international. Average age 27. 43 applicants, 77% accepted, 5 enrolled. In 2012, 22 master's awarded. *Degree requirements:* For master's, thesis optional; for doctorate, thesis/dissertation. *Entrance requirements:* For master's and doctorate, GRE General Test. Additional exam requirements/recommendations for international students: Required—TOEFL. *Application deadline:* For fall admission, 5/15 priority date for domestic students; for spring admission, 10/1 priority date for domestic students. Applications are processed on a rolling basis. Application fee: $25 ($50 for international students). *Expenses:* Tuition, state resident: full-time $5364; part-time $298 per credit hour. Tuition, nonresident: full-time $12,582; part-time $699 per credit hour. *Required fees:* $1844. *Financial support:* In 2012–13, 45 fellowships with partial tuition reimbursements (averaging $1,000 per year), 10 research assistantships with partial tuition reimbursements (averaging $7,200 per year), 3 teaching assistantships with partial tuition reimbursements (averaging $7,200 per year) were awarded; scholarships/grants and tuition waivers (partial) also available. Financial award application deadline: 4/1. *Faculty research:* Environmental remediations, construction productivity, geotechnical soil stabilization, lake/reservoir hydrodynamics, air pollution. *Unit head:* Dr. Enno Koehn, Chair, 409-880-8759, Fax: 409-880-8121, E-mail: koehneu@hal.lamar.edu. *Application contact:* Sandy Drane, Coordinator of Graduate Admissions, 409-880-8356, Fax: 409-880-8414, E-mail: gradmissions@hal.lamar.edu.

Lehigh University, College of Arts and Sciences, Environmental Initiative Program, Bethlehem, PA 18015. Offers environmental law and policy (Graduate Certificate); environmental policy design (MA). Part-time programs available. *Students:* 6 full-time (4 women), 1 (woman) part-time; includes 1 minority (Hispanic/Latino), 1 international. Average age 28. 11 applicants, 82% accepted, 5 enrolled. In 2012, 5 master's awarded. *Degree requirements:* For master's, thesis or additional course work. *Entrance requirements:* For master's, GRE, minimum GPA of 2.75, 3.0 for last two undergraduate semesters. Additional exam requirements/recommendations for international students: Required—TOEFL. *Application deadline:* For fall admission, 1/15 for domestic and international students; for spring admission, 12/1 for domestic and international students. Applications are processed on a rolling basis. Application fee: $75. Electronic applications accepted. *Financial support:* In 2012–13, 6 students received support, including 1 teaching assistantship with full tuition reimbursement available (averaging $18,850 per year); scholarships/grants, tuition waivers (partial), and community fellowship and tuition remission (from College of Arts and Sciences) also available. Financial award application deadline: 1/15; financial award applicants required to submit FAFSA. *Faculty research:* Dissolved organic carbon in freshwater ecosystems, environmental law, politics, sustainability, policy (national and local), environmental justice, land use law and planning, paleoclimatology, global hydrology, sea levels and impact on risk management. *Unit head:* Dr. Donald P. Morris, Director, 610-758-5175, E-mail: dpm2@lehigh.edu. *Application contact:* Beth Anne Pelton, Academic Coordinator, 610-758-5119, Fax: 610-758-6232, E-mail: bap212@lehigh.edu. Website: http://ei.cas2.lehigh.edu/.

Long Island University–C. W. Post Campus, College of Liberal Arts and Sciences, Department of Earth and Environmental Science, Brookville, NY 11548-1300. Offers earth science (MS); earth science education (MS); environmental studies (MS).

Louisiana State University and Agricultural and Mechanical College, Graduate School, School of the Coast and Environment, Department of Environmental Sciences, Baton Rouge, LA 70803. Offers environmental planning and management (MS); environmental toxicology (MS). *Faculty:* 9 full-time (3 women), 1 part-time/adjunct (0 women). *Students:* 32 full-time (20 women), 9 part-time (3 women); includes 4 minority (1 Black or African American, non-Hispanic/Latino; 3 Hispanic/Latino), 5 international. Average age 28. 26 applicants, 62% accepted, 11 enrolled. In 2012, 12 master's awarded. *Degree requirements:* For master's, thesis (for some programs). *Entrance requirements:* For master's, GRE General Test, minimum GPA of 3.0. Additional exam requirements/recommendations for international students: Required—TOEFL (minimum score 550 paper-based; 79 iBT) or IELTS (minimum score 6.5). *Application deadline:* For fall admission, 1/25 priority date for domestic students, 5/15 for international students; for spring admission, 10/15 for international students. Applications are processed on a rolling basis. Application fee: $50 ($70 for international students). Electronic applications accepted. *Financial support:* In 2012–13, 33 students received support, including 13 research assistantships with full and partial tuition reimbursements available (averaging $16,700 per year), 8 teaching assistantships with full and partial tuition reimbursements available (averaging $13,562 per year); fellowships with full and partial tuition reimbursements available, career-related internships or fieldwork, Federal Work-Study, institutionally sponsored loans, scholarships/grants, health care benefits, and unspecified assistantships also available. Support available to part-time students. Financial award applicants required to submit FAFSA. *Faculty research:* Environmental toxicology, environmental policy and law, microbial ecology, bioremediation, genetic toxicology. *Total annual research expenditures:* $2.3 million. *Unit head:* Dr. Ed Laws, Chair, 225-578-8800, Fax: 225-578-4286, E-mail: edlaws@lsu.edu. *Application contact:* Charlotte G. St. Romain, Academic Coordinator, 225-578-8522, Fax: 225-578-4286, E-mail: cstrom4@lsu.edu. Website: http://info.envs.lsu.edu/.

Marylhurst University, Department of Business Administration, Marylhurst, OR 97036-0261. Offers finance (MBA); general management (MBA); government policy and administration (MBA); green development (MBA); health care management (MBA); marketing (MBA); natural and organic resources (MBA); nonprofit management (MBA); organizational behavior (MBA); real estate (MBA); renewable energy (MBA); sustainable business (MBA). Part-time and evening/weekend programs available. Postbaccalaureate distance learning degree programs offered (no on-campus study). *Degree requirements:* For master's, comprehensive exam, capstone course. *Entrance requirements:* For master's, GMAT (if GPA less than 3.0 and fewer than 5 years of work experience), interview, resume, 2 letters of recommendation. Additional exam requirements/recommendations for international students: Recommended—TOEFL (minimum score 550 paper-based; 80 iBT). Electronic applications accepted.

McGill University, Faculty of Graduate and Postdoctoral Studies, Faculty of Agricultural and Environmental Sciences, Department of Natural Resource Sciences, Montréal, QC H3A 2T5, Canada. Offers entomology (M Sc, PhD); environmental assessment (M Sc); forest science (M Sc, PhD); microbiology (M Sc, PhD); micrometeorology (M Sc, PhD); neotropical environment (M Sc, PhD); soil science (M Sc, PhD); wildlife biology (M Sc, PhD).

Environmental Management and Policy

Michigan Technological University, Graduate School, College of Sciences and Arts, Department of Social Sciences, Houghton, MI 49931. Offers environmental policy (MS, PhD); industrial archaeology (MS); industrial heritage and archeology (PhD). Part-time programs available. Terminal master's awarded for partial completion of doctoral program. *Degree requirements:* For master's, comprehensive exam (for some programs), thesis (for some programs); for doctorate, comprehensive exam, thesis/dissertation. *Entrance requirements:* For master's and doctorate, GRE, statement of purpose, official transcripts, 3 letters of recommendation, writing sample, resume/curriculum vitae. Additional exam requirements/recommendations for international students: Required—TOEFL (minimum score 79 iBT). Electronic applications accepted. *Faculty research:* Industrial archeology of early American industry, mining history, environmental policy, land-use policy, citizen participation in environmental decision-making.

Millersville University of Pennsylvania, College of Graduate and Professional Studies, School of Science and Mathematics, Department of Earth Sciences, Millersville, PA 17551-0302. Offers integrated scientific applications (MS), including climate science applications, environmental systems management, geoinformatics, weather intelligence and risk management. Part-time and evening/weekend programs available. *Faculty:* 10 full-time (2 women), 2 part-time/adjunct (1 woman). *Students:* 4 part-time (1 woman); includes 1 minority (Asian, non-Hispanic/Latino). Average age 23. 5 applicants, 100% accepted, 3 enrolled. *Degree requirements:* For master's, thesis optional, internship or applied research. *Entrance requirements:* For master's, GRE, MAT, or GMAT (if GPA is lower than 3.0), 3 letters of recommendation, resume, official transcripts, goal statement, telephone interview. Additional exam requirements/recommendations for international students: Required—TOEFL (minimum score 500 paper-based) or IELTS (minimum score 6). *Application deadline:* For fall admission, 1/15 priority date for domestic students, 1/15 for international students; for winter admission, 10/1 priority date for domestic students, 10/1 for international students; for spring admission, 10/1 priority date for domestic students, 10/1 for international students. Applications are processed on a rolling basis. Application fee: $40 ($50 for international students). Electronic applications accepted. *Expenses:* Tuition, state resident: full-time $7722; part-time $429 per credit. Tuition, nonresident: full-time $11,592; part-time $644 per credit. Tuition and fees vary according to course load. *Financial support:* In 2012–13, 2 students received support, including 2 research assistantships (averaging $5,000 per year). Financial award application deadline: 3/15; financial award applicants required to submit FAFSA. *Faculty research:* Climatology and meteorology. *Total annual research expenditures:* $229,000. *Unit head:* Dr. Richard D. Clark, Graduate Program Coordinator, 717-872-3930, E-mail: richard.clark@millersville.edu. *Application contact:* Dr. Victor S. DeSantis, Dean of Graduate and Professional Studies, 717-872-3099, Fax: 717-872-3453, E-mail: victor.desantis@millersville.edu. Website: http://www.millersville.edu/graduate/admissions/MSISA.php.

Millersville University of Pennsylvania, College of Graduate and Professional Studies, School of Science and Mathematics, Program in Integrated Scientific Applications, Millersville, PA 17551-0302. Offers climate science applications (MS); environmental systems management (MS); geoinformatics (MS); weather intelligence and risk management (MS). *Expenses:* Tuition, state resident: full-time $7722; part-time $429 per credit. Tuition, nonresident: full-time $11,592; part-time $644 per credit. Tuition and fees vary according to course load.

Missouri State University, Graduate College, Interdisciplinary Program in Administrative Studies, Springfield, MO 65897. Offers applied communication (MS); criminal justice (MS); environmental management (MS); homeland security (MS); project management (MS); sports management (MS). Part-time and evening/weekend programs available. Postbaccalaureate distance learning degree programs offered (no on-campus study). *Degree requirements:* For master's, comprehensive exam, thesis or alternative. *Entrance requirements:* For master's, GRE, GMAT, 3 years of work experience. Additional exam requirements/recommendations for international students: Required—TOEFL (minimum score 550 paper-based; 79 iBT). Electronic applications accepted.

Montclair State University, The Graduate School, College of Science and Mathematics, Department of Earth and Environmental Studies, PhD Program in Environmental Management, Montclair, NJ 07043-1624. Offers PhD. *Degree requirements:* For doctorate, thesis/dissertation. *Entrance requirements:* For doctorate, GRE General Test, 3 letters of recommendation, essay. Additional exam requirements/recommendations for international students: Required—TOEFL (minimum score 83 iBT) or IELTS (minimum score 6.5). Electronic applications accepted. *Faculty research:* Environmental geochemisty/remediation/forensics, environmental law and policy, regional climate modeling, remote sensing, Cenozoic marine sediment records from polar regions, sustainability science.

Montclair State University, The Graduate School, College of Science and Mathematics, Department of Earth and Environmental Studies, Program in Environmental Studies, Montclair, NJ 07043-1624. Offers environmental education (MA); environmental management (MA); environmental science (MA). Part-time and evening/weekend programs available. *Degree requirements:* For master's, thesis. *Entrance requirements:* For master's, GRE General Test, 2 letters of recommendation, essay. Additional exam requirements/recommendations for international students: Required—TOEFL (minimum score 83 iBT), IELTS (minimum score 6.5). Electronic applications accepted. *Faculty research:* Environmental geochemisty/remediation/forensics, environmental law and policy, regional climate modeling, remote sensing, Cenozoic marine sediment records from polar regions, sustainability science.

Monterey Institute of International Studies, Graduate School of International Policy and Management, Program in International Environmental Policy, Monterey, CA 93940-2691. Offers MA. *Students:* 47 full-time (32 women); includes 12 minority (1 Black or African American, non-Hispanic/Latino; 2 Asian, non-Hispanic/Latino; 4 Hispanic/Latino; 5 Two or more races, non-Hispanic/Latino), 4 international. Average age 27. In 2012, 35 master's awarded. *Degree requirements:* For master's, one foreign language. *Entrance requirements:* For master's, minimum GPA of 3.0, proficiency in a foreign language. Additional exam requirements/recommendations for international students: Required—TOEFL (minimum score 550 paper-based; 80 iBT). *Application deadline:* For fall admission, 3/15 priority date for domestic students, 3/5 for international students; for spring admission, 10/1 priority date for domestic students, 10/1 for international students. Applications are processed on a rolling basis. Application fee: $50. Electronic applications accepted. *Expenses: Tuition:* Full-time $33,950; part-time $1615 per credit. *Required fees:* $28 per semester. *Financial support:* Application deadline: 3/15; applicants required to submit FAFSA. *Unit head:* Dr. Yuwei Shi, Dean, 831-647-4155, Fax: 831-647-4199, E-mail: gsipm@miis.edu. *Application contact:* 831-647-4123, Fax: 831-647-6405, E-mail: admit@miis.edu.

Morehead State University, Graduate Programs, College of Science and Technology, Department of Biology and Chemistry, Morehead, KY 40351. Offers biology (MS); biology regional analysis (MS). Part-time programs available. *Degree requirements:* For master's, comprehensive exam, thesis optional, oral and written final exams. *Entrance requirements:* For master's, GRE General Test, minimum GPA of 3.0 in biology, 2.5 overall; undergraduate major/minor in biology, environmental science, or equivalent. Additional exam requirements/recommendations for international students: Required—TOEFL (minimum score 525 paper-based). Electronic applications accepted. *Faculty research:* Atherosclerosis, RNA evolution, cancer biology, water quality/ecology, immunoparasitology.

Naropa University, Graduate Programs, Program in Environmental Leadership, Boulder, CO 80302-6697. Offers MA. *Faculty:* 2 full-time (both women), 4 part-time/adjunct (1 woman). *Students:* 17 full-time (12 women), 1 (woman) part-time; includes 4 minority (2 Hispanic/Latino; 2 Two or more races, non-Hispanic/Latino). Average age 30. 21 applicants, 76% accepted, 10 enrolled. In 2012, 12 master's awarded. *Degree requirements:* For master's, comprehensive exam, applied leadership project. *Entrance requirements:* For master's, in-person interview, letter of interest, resume, 2 letters of recommendation. Additional exam requirements/recommendations for international students: Required—TOEFL (minimum score 600 paper-based; 80 iBT). *Application deadline:* For fall admission, 1/15 priority date for domestic students, 1/15 for international students. Applications are processed on a rolling basis. Application fee: $60. Electronic applications accepted. *Expenses: Tuition:* Full-time $16,200; part-time $900 per credit. *Required fees:* $310 per semester. *Financial support:* In 2012–13, 9 students received support, including 5 research assistantships with partial tuition reimbursements available (averaging $5,688 per year); Federal Work-Study, scholarships/grants, tuition waivers (partial), and unspecified assistantships also available. Support available to part-time students. Financial award application deadline: 3/1; financial award applicants required to submit FAFSA. *Unit head:* Dr. Jeanine Canty, Director, School of Natural and Social Sciences, 303-245-4735, E-mail: jcanty@naropa.edu. *Application contact:* Office of Admissions, 303-546-3572, Fax: 303-546-3583, E-mail: rregnery@naropa.edu. Website: http://www.naropa.edu/academics/snss/grad/environmental-leadership-ma/index.php.

New Jersey Institute of Technology, Office of Graduate Studies, College of Science and Liberal Arts, Department of Chemistry and Environmental Science, Program in Environmental Policy Studies, Newark, NJ 07102. Offers MS. Part-time and evening/weekend programs available. Terminal master's awarded for partial completion of doctoral program. *Degree requirements:* For master's, thesis or alternative. *Entrance requirements:* For master's, GRE General Test. Additional exam requirements/recommendations for international students: Required—TOEFL (minimum score 550 paper-based; 79 iBT). Electronic applications accepted. *Expenses:* Tuition, state resident: full-time $16,836; part-time $915 per credit. Tuition, nonresident: full-time $24,370; part-time $1286 per credit. *Required fees:* $2318; $242 per credit.

New Mexico Highlands University, Graduate Studies, College of Arts and Sciences, Program in Natural Science, Las Vegas, NM 87701. Offers biology (MS); environmental science and management (MS); geology (MS). *Expenses:* Tuition, state resident: full-time $4277; part-time $178.22 per hour. Tuition, nonresident: full-time $6715; part-time $279.81 per hour. *International tuition:* $8510 full-time. Part-time tuition and fees vary according to campus/location. *Application contact:* Diane Trujillo, Administrative Assistant, Graduate Studies, 505-454-3266, Fax: 505-454-3558, E-mail: dtrujillo@nmhu.edu. Website: http://www.nmhu.edu/academics/graduate/arts_science_grad/natural_science/index.aspx.

The New School, Milano The New School for Management and Urban Policy, Program in Environmental Policy and Sustainability Management, New York, NY 10011. Offers MS. *Expenses: Tuition:* Full-time $30,960; part-time $1755 per credit.

New York Institute of Technology, School of Engineering and Computing Sciences, Department of Energy Management, Old Westbury, NY 11568-8000. Offers energy management (MS); energy technology (Advanced Certificate); environmental management (Advanced Certificate); facilities management (Advanced Certificate); infrastructure security management (MS). Part-time and evening/weekend programs available. Postbaccalaureate distance learning degree programs offered (minimal on-campus study). *Faculty:* 1 full-time (0 women), 6 part-time/adjunct (0 women). *Students:* 43 full-time (9 women), 87 part-time (13 women); includes 34 minority (9 Black or African American, non-Hispanic/Latino; 9 Asian, non-Hispanic/Latino; 16 Hispanic/Latino), 33 international. Average age 32. 129 applicants, 67% accepted, 31 enrolled. In 2012, 58 master's, 20 other advanced degrees awarded. *Degree requirements:* For master's, comprehensive exam, thesis or alternative. *Entrance requirements:* For master's, minimum QPA of 2.85. Additional exam requirements/recommendations for international students: Required—TOEFL (minimum score 550 paper-based; 79 iBT), IELTS (minimum score 6). *Application deadline:* For fall admission, 7/1 priority date for domestic students, 6/1 for international students; for spring admission, 12/1 priority date for domestic students, 12/1 for international students. Applications are processed on a rolling basis. Application fee: $50. Electronic applications accepted. *Expenses: Tuition:* Full-time $17,820; part-time $990 per credit. *Required fees:* $400; $990 per credit. *Financial support:* Research assistantships with partial tuition reimbursements, career-related internships or fieldwork, scholarships/grants, health care benefits, tuition waivers (full and partial), and unspecified assistantships available. Support available to part-time students. Financial award applicants required to submit FAFSA. *Unit head:* Dr. Robert Amundsen, Department Chair, 516-686-7578, E-mail: ramundse@nyit.edu. *Application contact:* Alice Dolitsky, Director, Graduate Admissions, 516-686-7520, Fax: 516-686-1116, E-mail: nyitgrad@nyit.edu. Website: http://www.nyit.edu/engineering/energy_management.

New York University, School of Continuing and Professional Studies, Center for Global Affairs, New York, NY 10012-1019. Offers global affairs (MS), including environment/energy policy, human rights and international law, international development and humanitarian assistance, international relations, peace building, private sector, transnational security. Part-time and evening/weekend programs available. *Faculty:* 8 full-time (3 women), 43 part-time/adjunct (19 women). *Students:* 154 full-time (99 women), 165 part-time (109 women); includes 56 minority (16 Black or African American, non-Hispanic/Latino; 2 American Indian or Alaska Native, non-Hispanic/Latino; 14 Asian, non-Hispanic/Latino; 15 Hispanic/Latino; 8 Native Hawaiian or other Pacific Islander, non-Hispanic/Latino; 1 Two or more races, non-Hispanic/Latino), 51 international. Average age 29. 410 applicants, 79% accepted, 124 enrolled. In 2012, 27 master's awarded. *Degree requirements:* For master's, thesis. *Entrance requirements:* For master's, relevant professional work, internship or volunteer experience. Additional exam requirements/recommendations for international students: Required—TOEFL (minimum score 600 paper-based; 100 iBT), IELTS (minimum score 7). *Application deadline:* For fall admission, 2/1 priority date for domestic students, 2/1 for international students; for spring admission, 10/15 priority date for domestic students, 8/15 for international students. Applications are processed on a rolling basis. Application fee: $150. Electronic applications accepted. *Expenses: Tuition:* Full-time $34,488; part-time $1437 per credit. *Required fees:* $2332; $1437 per credit. Tuition and fees vary according to program. *Financial support:* In 2012–13, 205 students received support, including 199 fellowships (averaging $2,732 per year); scholarships/grants also available. Financial award application deadline: 3/1; financial award applicants required to submit FAFSA. *Application contact:* Office of Admissions, 212-998-7100, E-mail: scps.gradamissions@nyu.edu. Website: http://www.scps.nyu.edu/academics/departments.html.

Northeastern Illinois University, Graduate College, College of Arts and Sciences, Department of Geography, Environmental Studies and Economics, Program in Geography and Environmental Studies, Chicago, IL 60625-4699. Offers MA. Part-time and evening/weekend programs available. *Degree requirements:* For master's, comprehensive exam, thesis optional. *Entrance requirements:* For master's, undergraduate minor in geography or environmental studies, minimum GPA of 2.75. Additional exam requirements/recommendations for international students: Required—TOEFL (minimum score 550 paper-based; 79 iBT). Electronic applications accepted. *Faculty research:* Segregation and urbanization of minority groups in the Chicago area, scale dependence and parameterization in nonpoint source pollution modeling, ecological land classification and mapping, ecosystem restoration, soil-vegetation relationships.

Northeastern State University, College of Business and Technology, Program in Environmental, Health, and Safety Management, Tahlequah, OK 74464-2399. Offers MEHS. Part-time and evening/weekend programs available. *Faculty:* 5 full-time (1 woman), 1 part-time/adjunct (0 women). *Students:* 2 full-time (0 women), 11 part-time (3 women); includes 6 minority (5 American Indian or Alaska Native, non-Hispanic/Latino; 1 Two or more races, non-Hispanic/Latino), 1 international. Average age 33. In 2012, 8 master's awarded. *Degree requirements:* For master's, synergistic experience. *Entrance requirements:* For master's, GRE, MAT, minimum GPA of 2.5. Additional exam requirements/recommendations for international students: Required—TOEFL. *Application deadline:* For fall admission, 6/1 priority date for domestic students. Applications are processed on a rolling basis. Application fee: $25. Electronic applications accepted. *Expenses:* Tuition, state resident: full-time $1451.25; part-time $161.25 per credit hour. Tuition, nonresident: full-time $3701; part-time $411.25 per credit hour. *Required fees:* $36.90 per contact hour. *Financial support:* Teaching assistantships and Federal Work-Study available. Financial award application deadline: 3/1. *Unit head:* Dr. Michael Turner, Chair, 918-456-5511 Ext. 2970, Fax: 918-458-2337, E-mail: turne003@nsuok.edu. *Application contact:* Margie Railey, Administrative Assistant, 918-456-5511 Ext. 2093, Fax: 918-458-2061, E-mail: railey@nsouk.edu. Website: http://academics.nsuok.edu/businesstechnology/Graduate/MEHS.aspx.

Northern Arizona University, Graduate College, College of Engineering, Forestry and Natural Sciences, School of Earth Sciences and Environmental Sustainability, Flagstaff, AZ 86011. Offers climate science and solutions (MS); earth science (MS); earth sciences and environmental sustainability (PhD); environmental sciences and policy (MS); geology (MS). *Degree requirements:* For master's, comprehensive exam (for some programs), thesis (for some programs). *Entrance requirements:* Additional exam requirements/recommendations for international students: Required—TOEFL (minimum score 550 paper-based; 80 iBT), IELTS (minimum score 7). Electronic applications accepted.

Ohio University, Graduate College, College of Arts and Sciences, Department of Geological Sciences, Athens, OH 45701-2979. Offers environmental geochemistry (MS); environmental geology (MS); environmental/hydrology (MS); geology (MS); geology education (MS); geomorphology/surficial processes (MS); geophysics (MS); hydrogeology (MS); sedimentology (MS); structure/tectonics (MS). Part-time programs available. *Degree requirements:* For master's, thesis. *Entrance requirements:* Additional exam requirements/recommendations for international students: Required—TOEFL (minimum score 550 paper-based; 80 iBT) or IELTS (minimum score 6.5). Electronic applications accepted. *Faculty research:* Geoscience education, tectonics, fluvial geomorphology, invertebrate paleontology, mine/hydrology.

Ohio University, Graduate College, Voinovich School of Leadership and Public Affairs, Program in Environmental Studies, Athens, OH 45701-2979. Offers MS. Part-time programs available. *Degree requirements:* For master's, comprehensive exam (for some programs), written exams or thesis, research project. *Entrance requirements:* For master's, minimum GPA of 3.0. Additional exam requirements/recommendations for international students: Required—TOEFL (minimum score 600 paper-based; 100 iBT) or IELTS (minimum score 7). Electronic applications accepted. *Faculty research:* Air quality modeling, conservation biology, environmental policy, geographical information systems, land management and watershed restoration.

Pace University, Dyson College of Arts and Sciences, Department of Public Administration, New York, NY 10038. Offers environmental management (MPA); government management (MPA); health care administration (MPA); management for public safety and homeland security (MA); nonprofit management (MPA); JD/MPA. Offered at White Plains, NY location only. Part-time and evening/weekend programs available. *Faculty:* 5 full-time (2 women), 5 part-time/adjunct (1 woman). *Students:* 54 full-time (39 women), 72 part-time (43 women); includes 75 minority (45 Black or African American, non-Hispanic/Latino; 5 Asian, non-Hispanic/Latino; 21 Hispanic/Latino; 4 Two or more races, non-Hispanic/Latino), 15 international. Average age 31. 89 applicants, 76% accepted, 35 enrolled. In 2012, 62 master's awarded. *Degree requirements:* For master's, capstone project. *Entrance requirements:* For master's, GRE General Test. Additional exam requirements/recommendations for international students: Required—TOEFL. *Application deadline:* For fall admission, 8/1 priority date for domestic students, 6/1 for international students; for spring admission, 12/1 priority date for domestic students, 10/1 for international students. Applications are processed on a rolling basis. Application fee: $70. Electronic applications accepted. *Expenses: Tuition:* Part-time $1035 per credit. *Required fees:* $230 per semester. Tuition and fees vary according to course load, degree level and program. *Financial support:* Research assistantships, career-related internships or fieldwork, Federal Work-Study, and tuition waivers (partial) available. Support available to part-time students. Financial award applicants required to submit FAFSA. *Unit head:* Dr. Farrokh Hormozi, Chairperson, 914-422-4285, E-mail: fhormozi@pace.edu. *Application contact:* Susan Ford-Goldschein, Director of Admissions, 914-422-4283, Fax: 914-422-4287, E-mail: gradwp@pace.edu. Website: http://www.pace.edu/dyson/academic-departments-and-programs/public-admin.

Penn State University Park, Graduate School, Intercollege Graduate Programs, Intercollege Program in Environmental Pollution Control, State College, University Park, PA 16802-1503. Offers MEPC, MS. *Unit head:* Dr. Herschel A. Elliott, Chair, 814-865-1417, Fax: 814-863-1031, E-mail: helliott3@psu.edu. *Application contact:* Cynthia E. Nicosia, Director, Graduate Enrollment Services, 814-865-1795, Fax: 814-865-4627, E-mail: cey1@psu.edu.

Plymouth State University, College of Graduate Studies, Graduate Studies in Education, Program in Science, Plymouth, NH 03264-1595. Offers applied meteorology (MS); environmental science and policy (MS); science education (MS).

Point Park University, School of Arts and Sciences, Department of Natural Science and Engineering Technology, Pittsburgh, PA 15222-1984. Offers engineering management (MS); environmental studies (MS). Part-time and evening/weekend programs available. *Faculty:* 2 full-time, 3 part-time/adjunct. *Students:* 15 full-time (7 women), 13 part-time (3 women); includes 4 minority (2 Black or African American, non-Hispanic/Latino; 1 Hispanic/Latino; 1 Two or more races, non-Hispanic/Latino), 5 international. Average age 33. 84 applicants, 57% accepted, 17 enrolled. In 2012, 16 master's awarded. *Degree requirements:* For master's, comprehensive exam (for some programs), thesis or alternative. *Entrance requirements:* For master's, minimum QPA of 2.75, 2 letters of recommendation, minimum B average in engineering technology or a related field, official undergraduate transcript, statement of intent, resume. Additional exam requirements/recommendations for international students: Required—TOEFL. *Application deadline:* Applications are processed on a rolling basis. Application fee: $30. Electronic applications accepted. *Expenses: Tuition:* Full-time $13,698; part-time $761 per credit. *Required fees:* $900; $50 per credit. *Financial support:*

Environmental Management and Policy

In 2012–13, 2 students received support, including teaching assistantships with full tuition reimbursements available (averaging $6,400 per year); scholarships/grants also available. Financial award application deadline: 3/30; financial award applicants required to submit FAFSA. *Unit head:* Dr. Mark Farrell, Chair, 412-392-3879, Fax: 421-392-3962, E-mail: mfarrell@pointpark.edu. *Application contact:* Jennifer Sellman, Admissions Counselor, Graduate and Adult Enrollment Office, 412-392-4794, Fax: 412-392-6164, E-mail: jseelman@pointpark.edu.

Polytechnic University of Puerto Rico, Graduate School, Hato Rey, PR 00919. Offers business administration (MBA), including computer information systems, general management, management of information systems, management of international enterprises; civil engineering (ME, MS); computer engineering (ME, MS); computer science (MCS, MS); electrical engineering (ME, MS); engineering management (MEM); environmental management (MEM); landscape architecture (M Land Arch); manufacturing competitiveness (MMC, MS); manufacturing engineering (ME, MS); mechanical engineering (M Mech E). Part-time and evening/weekend programs available. *Entrance requirements:* For master's, 3 letters of recommendation.

Polytechnic University of Puerto Rico, Miami Campus, Graduate School, Miami, FL 33166. Offers accounting (MBA); business administration (MBA); construction management (MEM); environmental management (MEM); finance (MBA); human resources management (MBA); logistics and supply chain management (MBA); management of international enterprises (MBA); manufacturing management (MEM); marketing management (MBA); project management (MBA). Part-time and evening/weekend programs available. Postbaccalaureate distance learning degree programs offered (no on-campus study). *Entrance requirements:* For master's, minimum GPA of 3.0. Electronic applications accepted.

Polytechnic University of Puerto Rico, Orlando Campus, Graduate School, Winter Park, FL 32792. Offers accounting (MBA); business administration (MBA); construction management (MEM); engineering management (MEM); environmental management (MEM); finance (MBA); human resources management (MBA); management of international enterprises (MBA); management of technology (MBA); manufacturing management (MEM). Part-time and evening/weekend programs available. Postbaccalaureate distance learning degree programs offered (no on-campus study). *Entrance requirements:* For master's, minimum GPA of 3.0. Additional exam requirements/recommendations for international students: Recommended—TOEFL. Electronic applications accepted.

Portland State University, Graduate Studies, College of Liberal Arts and Sciences, Program in Environmental Sciences and Management, Portland, OR 97207-0751. Offers environmental management (MEM); environmental sciences/biology (PhD); environmental sciences/chemistry (PhD); environmental sciences/civil engineering (PhD); environmental sciences/geography (PhD); environmental sciences/geology (PhD); environmental sciences/physics (PhD); environmental studies (MS); science/environmental science (MST). Part-time programs available. *Degree requirements:* For master's, thesis or alternative; for doctorate, variable foreign language requirement, comprehensive exam, thesis/dissertation, oral and qualifying exams. *Entrance requirements:* For master's, GRE General Test, 3 letters of recommendation; for doctorate, minimum GPA of 3.0 in upper-division course work or 2.75 overall. Additional exam requirements/recommendations for international students: Required—TOEFL (minimum score 550 paper-based). *Faculty research:* Environmental aspects of biology, chemistry, civil engineering, geology, physics.

Prescott College, Graduate Programs, Program in Environmental Studies, Prescott, AZ 86301. Offers environmental studies (MA); student-directed independent study (MA). Part-time programs available. Postbaccalaureate distance learning degree programs offered (minimal on-campus study). *Faculty:* 1 full-time (0 women). *Students:* 4 full-time (2 women), 24 part-time (18 women); includes 3 minority (1 Black or African American, non-Hispanic/Latino; 1 Hispanic/Latino; 1 Two or more races, non-Hispanic/Latino). Average age 34. 15 applicants, 73% accepted, 6 enrolled. In 2012, 8 master's awarded. *Degree requirements:* For master's, thesis, fieldwork or internship, practicum. *Entrance requirements:* For master's, 2 letters of recommendation, resume. Additional exam requirements/recommendations for international students: Required—TOEFL (minimum score 500 paper-based). *Application deadline:* For fall admission, 4/15 priority date for domestic students, 4/15 for international students; for spring admission, 9/15 priority date for domestic students, 9/15 for international students. Applications are processed on a rolling basis. Application fee: $40. Electronic applications accepted. *Expenses: Tuition:* Full-time $17,160; part-time $715 per credit. *Required fees:* $200 per semester. One-time fee: $250. Tuition and fees vary according to course load, degree level and program. *Financial support:* Career-related internships or fieldwork, Federal Work-Study, and scholarships/grants available. Financial award applicants required to submit FAFSA. *Unit head:* Peter Sherman, Interim Chair, 928-350-1014, Fax: 928-776-5151, E-mail: psherman@prescott.edu. *Application contact:* Kerstin Alicki, Admissions Counselor, 928-350-2100, Fax: 928-776-5242, E-mail: admissions@prescott.edu.

Purdue University, Graduate School, College of Agriculture, Department of Forestry and Natural Resources, West Lafayette, IN 47907. Offers fisheries and aquatic sciences (MS, MSF, PhD); forest biology (MS, MSF, PhD); natural resource social science (MS, PhD); natural resources social science (MSF); quantitative ecology (MS, MSF, PhD); wildlife science (MS, MSF, PhD); wood products and wood products manufacturing (MS, MSF, PhD). *Faculty:* 25 full-time (3 women), 10 part-time/adjunct (1 woman). *Students:* 61 full-time (24 women), 11 part-time (6 women); includes 3 minority (1 American Indian or Alaska Native, non-Hispanic/Latino; 2 Hispanic/Latino), 18 international. Average age 29. 57 applicants, 28% accepted, 15 enrolled. In 2012, 18 master's, 7 doctorates awarded. *Degree requirements:* For master's, thesis; for doctorate, thesis/dissertation. *Entrance requirements:* For master's and doctorate, GRE General Test (minimum score: verbal 50th percentile; quantitative 50th percentile; analytical writing 4.0), minimum undergraduate GPA of 3.2 or equivalent. Additional exam requirements/recommendations for international students: Required—TOEFL (minimum score 550 paper-based; 77 iBT). *Application deadline:* For fall admission, 1/5 for domestic students, 1/15 for international students; for spring admission, 9/15 for domestic and international students. Applications are processed on a rolling basis. Application fee: $60 ($75 for international students). Electronic applications accepted. *Financial support:* In 2012–13, 10 research assistantships (averaging $15,259 per year) were awarded; fellowships, teaching assistantships, career-related internships or fieldwork, and scholarships/grants also available. Support available to part-time students. Financial award application deadline: 1/5; financial award applicants required to submit FAFSA. *Faculty research:* Wildlife management, forest management, forest ecology, forest soils, limnology. *Unit head:* Dr. Robert K. Swihart, Interim Head, 765-494-3590, Fax: 765-494-9461, E-mail: rswihart@purdue.edu. *Application contact:* Kelly J. Wrede, Graduate Secretary, 765-494-3572, Fax: 765-494-9461, E-mail: kgarrett@purdue.edu. Website: http://www.fnr.purdue.edu/.

Rice University, Graduate Programs, Wiess School–Professional Science Master's Programs, Professional Master's Program in Environmental Analysis and Decision Making, Houston, TX 77251-1892. Offers MS. Part-time programs available. *Degree requirements:* For master's, internship. *Entrance requirements:* For master's, GRE General Test, letters of recommendation (4). Additional exam requirements/recommendations for international students: Required—TOEFL (minimum score 600 paper-based; 90 iBT). Electronic applications accepted. *Faculty research:* Environmental biotechnology, environmental nanochemistry, environmental statistics, remote sensing.

Rochester Institute of Technology, Graduate Enrollment Services, College of Applied Science and Technology, School of Engineering Technology, Department of Civil Engineering Technology, Environmental Management and Safety, Rochester, NY 14623-5603. Offers environmental health and safety management (MS); facility management (MS). Part-time and evening/weekend programs available. Postbaccalaureate distance learning degree programs offered (minimal on-campus study). *Students:* 25 full-time (12 women), 54 part-time (12 women); includes 14 minority (5 Black or African American, non-Hispanic/Latino; 5 Asian, non-Hispanic/Latino; 4 Hispanic/Latino), 10 international. Average age 36. 70 applicants, 40% accepted, 20 enrolled. In 2012, 29 master's awarded. *Degree requirements:* For master's, thesis or project. *Entrance requirements:* For master's, minimum GPA of 3.0. Additional exam requirements/recommendations for international students: Required—TOEFL (minimum score 550 paper-based; 79 iBT) or IELTS (minimum score 6.5). *Application deadline:* For fall admission, 2/15 priority date for domestic students, 2/15 for international students; for winter admission, 11/1 for domestic students; for spring admission, 2/1 priority date for domestic students, 1/1 for international students. Applications are processed on a rolling basis. Application fee: $60. Electronic applications accepted. *Expenses: Tuition:* Full-time $35,976; part-time $999 per credit hour. *Required fees:* $240; $80 per quarter. *Financial support:* Research assistantships with partial tuition reimbursements, teaching assistantships with partial tuition reimbursements, career-related internships or fieldwork, scholarships/grants, and unspecified assistantships available. Support available to part-time students. Financial award applicants required to submit FAFSA. *Faculty research:* Environmental, health and safety (EHS) issues; regulatory, voluntary and business drivers for EHS programs; design and implementation of effective EHS management systems and programs; design and implementation of performance measurement processes. *Unit head:* Dr. Christy Tyler, Graduate Program Director, 585-475-5042, E-mail: actsbi@rit.edu. *Application contact:* Diane Ellison, Assistant Vice President, Graduate Enrollment Services, 585-475-2229, Fax: 585-475-7164, E-mail: gradinfo@rit.edu. Website: http://www.rit.edu/cast/cetems/.

Royal Roads University, Graduate Studies, Environment and Sustainability Program, Victoria, BC V9B 5Y2, Canada. Offers environment and management (M Sc, MA); environmental education and communication (MA, G Dip, Graduate Certificate); MA/MS. Postbaccalaureate distance learning degree programs offered (minimal on-campus study). *Degree requirements:* For master's, thesis. *Entrance requirements:* For master's, 5-7 years of related work experience. Electronic applications accepted. *Faculty research:* Sustainable development, atmospheric processes, sustainable communities, chemical fate and transport of persistent organic pollutants, educational technology.

Sacred Heart University, Graduate Programs, College of Arts and Sciences, Department of Biology, Fairfield, CT 06825-1000. Offers environmental systems analysis and management (MS). Part-time and evening/weekend programs available. *Faculty:* 4 full-time (2 women), 1 part-time/adjunct (0 women). *Students:* 16 full-time (11 women); includes 1 minority (Asian, non-Hispanic/Latino). 22 applicants, 64% accepted, 9 enrolled. *Entrance requirements:* Additional exam requirements/recommendations for international students: Recommended—TOEFL (minimum score 90 iBT), IELTS (minimum score 6.5). Application fee: $60. Tuition and fees vary according to program. *Financial support:* Career-related internships or fieldwork, institutionally sponsored loans, and unspecified assistantships available. Support available to part-time students. Financial award applicants required to submit FAFSA. *Unit head:* Dr. Jennifer Mattei, Chair, 203-365-7577, E-mail: biology@sacredheart.edu. *Application contact:* Kathy Dilks, Executive Director of Graduate Admissions, 203-365-7619, Fax: 203-365-4732, E-mail: dilksk@sacredheart.edu. Website: http://www.sacredheart.edu/academics/collegeofartssciences/academicdepartments/biology/graduatedegree/.

St. Cloud State University, School of Graduate Studies, College of Science and Engineering, Department of Environmental and Technological Studies, St. Cloud, MN 56301-4498. Offers MS. *Degree requirements:* For master's, thesis or alternative. *Entrance requirements:* For master's, minimum GPA of 2.75. Additional exam requirements/recommendations for international students: Required—TOEFL (minimum score 550 paper-based), Michigan English Language Assessment Battery; Recommended—IELTS (minimum score 6.5). Electronic applications accepted.

St. Edward's University, School of Management and Business, Program in Environmental Management and Sustainability, Austin, TX 78704. Offers PSM. *Students:* 18 full-time (10 women); includes 11 minority (1 Black or African American, non-Hispanic/Latino; 1 Asian, non-Hispanic/Latino; 8 Hispanic/Latino; 1 Two or more races, non-Hispanic/Latino). Average age 26. 38 applicants, 50% accepted, 18 enrolled. *Degree requirements:* For master's, internship. *Entrance requirements:* For master's, GRE or GMAT, 2 letters of recommendation, resume or curriculum vitae, minimum GPA of 3.0 in last 60 hours of course work. Additional exam requirements/recommendations for international students: Required—TOEFL (minimum score 79 iBT) or IELTS (minimum score 6). *Application deadline:* For fall admission, 2/15 priority date for domestic students, 2/15 for international students. Applications are processed on a rolling basis. Application fee: $50. Electronic applications accepted. *Expenses: Tuition:* Full-time $19,044; part-time $1058 per credit hour. *Required fees:* $50 per trimester. Full-time tuition and fees vary according to course load and program. *Unit head:* Dr. William J. Quinn, Director, 512-448-8457, Fax: 512-448-8492, E-mail: billq@stedwards.edu. *Application contact:* Office of Admission, 512-428-1050, Fax: 877-738-4723, E-mail: seu.grad@stedwards.edu. Website: http://www.stedwards.edu.

Samford University, Howard College of Arts and Sciences, Birmingham, AL 35229. Offers energy management and policy (MSEM); JD/MSEM. Part-time and evening/weekend programs available. *Faculty:* 9 full-time (1 woman), 5 part-time/adjunct (0 women). *Students:* 38 full-time (17 women), 14 part-time (10 women); includes 6 minority (4 Black or African American, non-Hispanic/Latino; 1 Asian, non-Hispanic/Latino; 1 Two or more races, non-Hispanic/Latino), 34 international. Average age 28. 37 applicants, 95% accepted, 33 enrolled. In 2012, 19 master's awarded. *Entrance requirements:* For master's, GRE General Test (minimum score 295 combined) or MAT (minimum score 396), minimum GPA of 2.5 with 3 years of work experience or 3.0 for a recent college graduate. Additional exam requirements/recommendations for international students: Required—TOEFL (minimum score 90 iBT); Recommended—IELTS (minimum score 6.5). *Application deadline:* For fall admission, 1/1 for domestic students, 8/1 for international students; for winter admission, 2/1 for domestic students; for spring admission, 1/2 for domestic students, 12/14 for international students. Applications are processed on a rolling basis. Application fee: $35. *Expenses:* Contact institution. *Financial support:* In 2012–13, 18 students received support. Application deadline: 3/1; applicants required to submit FAFSA. *Faculty research:* Mosquito fish as an environmental model for pollutants, PCB contamination, environmental epidemiology and toxicology, GIS, geology and natural resource management, energy management. *Unit head:* Dr. Ronald N. Hunsinger, Professor and Chair, Biological and Environmental Sciences, 205-726-2944, Fax: 205-726-2479, E-mail: rnhunsin@samford.edu. *Application contact:* Dr. Ronald N. Hunsinger, Professor/Chair, Biological and Environmental Sciences, 205-726-2944, Fax: 205-726-2479, E-mail: rnhunsin@samford.edu. Website: http://howard.samford.edu/.

San Francisco State University, Division of Graduate Studies, College of Science and Engineering, Department of Geography and Human Environmental Studies, San Francisco, CA 94132-1722. Offers geographic information science (MS); geography (MA), including resource management and environmental planning. *Unit head:* Dr. Jerry Davis, Chair, 415-338-2049, E-mail: jerry@sfsu.edu. *Application contact:* Dr. Nancy Wilkinson, Graduate Coordinator, 415-338-2049, E-mail: nancyw@sfsu.edu. Website: http://geog.sfsu.edu/.

San Jose State University, Graduate Studies and Research, College of Social Sciences, Department of Environmental Studies, San Jose, CA 95192-0001. Offers MS. Part-time programs available. *Degree requirements:* For master's, comprehensive exam, thesis or alternative. *Entrance requirements:* Additional exam requirements/recommendations for international students: Required—TOEFL (minimum score 580 paper-based). Electronic applications accepted. *Faculty research:* Remote sensing, land use/land cover mapping.

Shippensburg University of Pennsylvania, School of Graduate Studies, College of Arts and Sciences, Department of Geography and Earth Science, Shippensburg, PA 17257-2299. Offers geoenvironmental studies (MS). Part-time and evening/weekend programs available. *Faculty:* 9 full-time (1 woman), 2 part-time/adjunct (1 woman). *Students:* 20 full-time (9 women), 6 part-time (1 woman); includes 2 minority (both Hispanic/Latino), 1 international. Average age 27. 33 applicants, 30% accepted, 1 enrolled. In 2012, 11 master's awarded. *Degree requirements:* For master's, comprehensive exam, thesis (6 credits) or 1 semester research project (3 credits) and internship (6 credits); practicum exam. *Entrance requirements:* For master's, GRE (if GPA less than 2.75), 12 credit hours in geography or earth sciences or 15 credit hours each in social sciences (including 6 hours in geography) and natural sciences (including 6 in the earth sciences) or a combined total of 18 credits in geography and earth science. Additional exam requirements/recommendations for international students: Required—TOEFL (minimum score 580 paper-based); Recommended—IELTS (minimum score 6). *Application deadline:* For fall admission, 3/30 for international students; for spring admission, 9/30 for international students. Applications are processed on a rolling basis. Application fee: $40. Electronic applications accepted. *Expenses: Tuition, area resident:* Part-time $429 per credit. Tuition, state resident: part-time $429 per credit. Tuition, nonresident: part-time $644 per credit. *Required fees:* $123 per credit. *Financial support:* In 2012–13, 10 research assistantships with full tuition reimbursements (averaging $5,000 per year) were awarded; career-related internships or fieldwork, scholarships/grants, unspecified assistantships, and resident hall director and student payroll positions also available. Support available to part-time students. Financial award application deadline: 3/1; financial award applicants required to submit FAFSA. *Unit head:* Dr. Tim Hawkins, Professor, 717-477-1685, Fax: 717-477-4029, E-mail: twhawk@ship.edu. *Application contact:* Jeremy R. Goshorn, Assistant Dean of Graduate Admissions, 717-477-1231, Fax: 717-477-4016, E-mail: jrgoshorn@ship.edu. Website: http://www.ship.edu/geo-ess/.

Shippensburg University of Pennsylvania, School of Graduate Studies, College of Arts and Sciences, Department of Sociology and Anthropology, Shippensburg, PA 17257-2299. Offers organizational development and leadership (MS), including business, communications, environmental management, higher education structure and policy, historical administration, individual and organizational development, management information systems, public organizations, social structures and organizations. Part-time and evening/weekend programs available. *Faculty:* 4 full-time (all women). *Students:* 17 full-time (6 women), 34 part-time (28 women); includes 7 minority (3 Black or African American, non-Hispanic/Latino; 3 Asian, non-Hispanic/Latino; 1 Hispanic/Latino), 2 international. Average age 31. 70 applicants, 43% accepted, 23 enrolled. In 2012, 27 master's awarded. *Degree requirements:* For master's, capstone experience including internship. *Entrance requirements:* For master's, interview (if GPA less than 2.75), resume, personal goals statement. Additional exam requirements/recommendations for international students: Required—TOEFL (minimum score 580 paper-based); Recommended—IELTS (minimum score 6). *Application deadline:* For fall admission, 4/30 for international students; for spring admission, 9/30 for international students. Applications are processed on a rolling basis. Application fee: $40. Electronic applications accepted. *Expenses: Tuition, area resident:* Part-time $429 per credit. Tuition, state resident: part-time $429 per credit. Tuition, nonresident: part-time $644 per credit. *Required fees:* $123 per credit. *Financial support:* In 2012–13, 9 research assistantships with full tuition reimbursements (averaging $5,000 per year) were awarded; career-related internships or fieldwork, scholarships/grants, unspecified assistantships, and resident hall director and student payroll positions also available. Support available to part-time students. Financial award applicants required to submit FAFSA. *Unit head:* Dr. Barbara Denison, Program Coordinator, 717-477-1735, Fax: 717-477-4011, E-mail: bjdeni@ship.edu. *Application contact:* Jeremy R. Goshorn, Assistant Dean of Graduate Admissions, 717-477-1231, Fax: 717-477-4016, E-mail: jrgoshorn@ship.edu. Website: http://www.ship.edu/odl/.

Simon Fraser University, Office of Graduate Studies, Faculty of Environment, School of Resource and Environmental Management, Burnaby, BC V5A 1S6, Canada. Offers quantitative methods in fisheries management (Graduate Diploma); resource and environmental management (MRM, PhD); resource and environmental planning (MRM). *Faculty:* 19 full-time (4 women). *Students:* 121 full-time (66 women), 5 part-time (2 women). 179 applicants, 26% accepted, 34 enrolled. In 2012, 26 master's, 3 doctorates, 1 other advanced degree awarded. *Degree requirements:* For master's, thesis (for some programs); for doctorate, comprehensive exam, thesis/dissertation. *Entrance requirements:* For master's and Graduate Diploma, minimum GPA of 3.0 (on scale of 4.33), or 3.33 based on last 60 credits of undergraduate courses; for doctorate, minimum GPA of 3.5 (on scale of 4.33). Additional exam requirements/recommendations for international students: Recommended—TOEFL (minimum score 580 paper-based; 93 iBT), IELTS (minimum score 7), TWE (minimum score 5). *Application deadline:* For fall admission, 2/15 for domestic and international students. Application fee: $90 ($125 for international students). Electronic applications accepted. Tuition and fees charges are reported in Canadian dollars. *Expenses: Tuition, area resident:* Full-time $5000 Canadian dollars; part-time $275 Canadian dollars per credit hour. *Required fees:* $780 Canadian dollars. *Financial support:* In 2012–13, 35 students received support, including 19 fellowships (averaging $6,250 per year), teaching assistantships (averaging $5,608 per year); research assistantships, career-related internships or fieldwork, and scholarships/grants also available. *Faculty research:* Climate, coastal marine ecology and conservation, environmental toxicology, fisheries science and management, forest ecology. *Unit head:* Dr. Frank Gobas, Director, 778-782-3069, Fax: 778-782-4968, E-mail: rem-grad-chair@sfu.ca. *Application contact:* Devan Huber, Graduate Secretary, 778-782-4780, Fax: 778-782-4968, E-mail: rem_gradasst@sfu.ca. Website: http://www.rem.sfu.ca/.

Slippery Rock University of Pennsylvania, Graduate Studies (Recruitment), College of Health, Environment, and Science, Department of Parks, Recreation, and Environmental Education, Slippery Rock, PA 16057-1383. Offers environmental education (M Ed); park and resource management (MS). Part-time and evening/weekend programs available. Postbaccalaureate distance learning degree programs offered (no on-campus study). *Faculty:* 3 full-time (1 woman), 2 part-time/adjunct (1 woman). *Students:* 24 full-time (14 women), 67 part-time (39 women); includes 4 minority (all Hispanic/Latino), 3 international. Average age 30. 64 applicants, 81% accepted, 36 enrolled. In 2012, 36 master's awarded. *Degree requirements:* For master's, comprehensive exam (for some programs), thesis (for some programs). *Entrance requirements:* For master's, GRE General Test, MAT, minimum GPA of 2.75. Additional exam requirements/recommendations for international students: Required—TOEFL (minimum score 550 paper-based; 80 iBT). *Application deadline:* For fall admission, 3/1 priority date for domestic students, 5/1 for international students; for spring admission, 10/1 priority date for domestic students, 9/1 for international students. Applications are processed on a rolling basis. Application fee: $25 ($30 for international students). Electronic applications accepted. *Expenses:* Tuition, state resident: full-time $7722; part-time $429 per credit. Tuition, nonresident: full-time $11,592; part-time $644 per credit. *Required fees:* $2803; $144 per credit. Tuition and fees vary according to degree level and program. *Financial support:* Career-related internships or fieldwork, Federal Work-Study, institutionally sponsored loans, scholarships/grants, and tuition waivers (partial) available. Support available to part-time students. Financial award application deadline: 5/1; financial award applicants required to submit FAFSA. *Unit head:* Dr. Daniel Dziubek, Graduate Coordinator, 724-738-2958, Fax: 724-738-2938, E-mail: daniel.dziubek@sru.edu. *Application contact:* Brandi Weber-Mortimer, Director of Graduate Admissions, 724-738-2051, Fax: 724-738-2146, E-mail: graduate.admissions@sru.edu.

Southeast Missouri State University, School of Graduate Studies, Department of Human Environmental Studies, Cape Girardeau, MO 63701-4799. Offers human environmental studies (MA). Part-time programs available. *Faculty:* 10 full-time (7 women). *Students:* 3 full-time (all women), 17 part-time (16 women); includes 1 minority (Black or African American, non-Hispanic/Latino), 2 international. Average age 28. 13 applicants, 77% accepted, 9 enrolled. In 2012, 4 master's awarded. *Degree requirements:* For master's, comprehensive exam (for some programs), thesis or alternative, professional practicum (for some programs). *Entrance requirements:* For master's, minimum undergraduate GPA of 2.75; 18 credit hours in human environment studies or related field. Additional exam requirements/recommendations for international students: Required—TOEFL (minimum score 550 paper-based; 79 iBT), IELTS (minimum score 6). *Application deadline:* For fall admission, 8/1 for domestic students, 6/1 for international students; for spring admission, 11/21 for domestic students, 10/1 for international students. Applications are processed on a rolling basis. Application fee: $30 ($40 for international students). Electronic applications accepted. *Financial support:* In 2012–13, 5 students received support, including 8 teaching assistantships with full tuition reimbursements available (averaging $7,900 per year); career-related internships or fieldwork, Federal Work-Study, scholarships/grants, traineeships, tuition waivers (full), and unspecified assistantships also available. Financial award application deadline: 6/30; financial award applicants required to submit FAFSA. *Faculty research:* Gerontology educational models, military families, nutrition education and obesity, domestic violence and abuse, kitchen and bath design, infant stimulation and sensory systems. *Unit head:* Dr. Shelba Y. Branscum, Professor, 573-651-2729, E-mail: sybranscum@semo.edu. *Application contact:* Alisa Aleen McFerron, Assistant Director of Admission for Operations, 573-651-5937, E-mail: amcferron@semo.edu. Website: http://www.semo.edu/hes/.

Southern Illinois University Carbondale, Graduate School, College of Liberal Arts, Department of Geography, Carbondale, IL 62901-4701. Offers environmental resources and policy (PhD); geography and environmental resources (MS). *Faculty:* 7 full-time (1 woman), 1 part-time/adjunct (0 women). *Students:* 18 full-time (5 women), 14 part-time (6 women), 9 international. Average age 27. 20 applicants, 50% accepted, 7 enrolled. In 2012, 10 master's awarded. *Degree requirements:* For master's, thesis; for doctorate, thesis/dissertation. *Entrance requirements:* For master's, minimum GPA of 2.7; for doctorate, minimum GPA of 3.25. Additional exam requirements/recommendations for international students: Required—TOEFL. *Application deadline:* Applications are processed on a rolling basis. Application fee: $50. *Financial support:* In 2012–13, 21 students received support, including 6 research assistantships with full tuition reimbursements available, 11 teaching assistantships with full tuition reimbursements available; fellowships with full tuition reimbursements available, career-related internships or fieldwork, Federal Work-Study, institutionally sponsored loans, and tuition waivers (full) also available. Support available to part-time students. Financial award application deadline: 4/1. *Faculty research:* Natural resources management emphasizing water resources and environmental quality of air, water, and land systems. *Unit head:* Dr. Justin Schoof, Chair, 618-453-6019, E-mail: jschoof@siu.edu. *Application contact:* Jennie Absher, Administrative Clerk, 618-536-3375, E-mail: jabsher@siu.edu. Website: http://info.geography.siu.edu/.

Southern Illinois University Edwardsville, Graduate School, College of Arts and Sciences, Program in Environmental Science Management, Edwardsville, IL 62026-0001. Offers MS. Part-time and evening/weekend programs available. *Students:* 2 full-time (both women), 21 part-time (8 women); includes 2 minority (1 Native Hawaiian or other Pacific Islander, non-Hispanic/Latino; 1 Two or more races, non-Hispanic/Latino). 6 applicants. In 2012, 3 master's awarded. *Degree requirements:* For master's, thesis, internship. *Entrance requirements:* For master's, GRE. Additional exam requirements/recommendations for international students: Required—TOEFL (minimum score 550 paper-based; 79 iBT), IELTS (minimum score 6.5). *Application deadline:* For fall admission, 7/26 for domestic students, 6/1 for international students; for spring admission, 12/6 for domestic students, 10/1 for international students. Applications are processed on a rolling basis. Application fee: $30. Electronic applications accepted. *Expenses:* Tuition, state resident: full-time $6504; part-time $3252 per semester. Tuition, nonresident: full-time $8130; part-time $4065 per semester. *Required fees:* $705.50 per semester. Tuition and fees vary according to course level, course load, degree level, program and student level. *Financial support:* In 2012–13, 6 teaching assistantships with full tuition reimbursements (averaging $9,585 per year) were awarded; fellowships with full tuition reimbursements, research assistantships with full tuition reimbursements, institutionally sponsored loans, scholarships/grants, and unspecified assistantships also available. Financial award application deadline: 3/1; financial award applicants required to submit FAFSA. *Unit head:* Dr. Kevin Johnson, Program Director, 618-650-5934, E-mail: kevjohn@siue.edu. *Application contact:* Michelle Robinson, Coordinator of Graduate Recruitment, 618-650-2811, Fax: 618-650-3523, E-mail: michero@siue.edu. Website: http://www.siue.edu/artsandsciences/environment/psm.shtml.

Stanford University, School of Earth Sciences, Earth Systems Program, Stanford, CA 94305-9991. Offers MS. Students admitted at the undergraduate level. Electronic applications accepted. *Expenses: Tuition:* Full-time $41,250; part-time $917 per credit hour.

State University of New York College of Environmental Science and Forestry, Department of Environmental Resources Engineering, Syracuse, NY 13210-2779. Offers ecological engineering (MPS, MS, PhD); environmental management (MPS); environmental resources engineering (MPS, MS, PhD); geospatial information science and engineering (MPS, MS, PhD); water resources engineering (MS, PhD). Part-time programs available. *Faculty:* 8 full-time (1 woman), 4 part-time/adjunct (0 women). *Students:* 37 full-time (11 women), 6 part-time (3 women); includes 17 minority (1 Black or African American, non-Hispanic/Latino; 16 Asian, non-Hispanic/Latino), 21 international. Average age 25. 120 applicants, 38% accepted, 14 enrolled. In 2012, 15 master's, 5 doctorates awarded. *Degree requirements:* For master's, thesis (for some programs); for doctorate, comprehensive exam, thesis/dissertation. *Entrance requirements:* For master's and doctorate, GRE General Test, minimum GPA of 3.0. Additional exam requirements/recommendations for international students: Required—TOEFL (minimum score 550 paper-based; 80 iBT), IELTS (minimum score 6). *Application deadline:* For fall admission, 1/15 priority date for domestic students, 1/15 for international students; for spring admission, 11/1 priority date for domestic students, 11/1 for international students. Applications are processed on a rolling basis. Application fee: $60. *Expenses:* Tuition, state resident: full-time $9370; part-time $390 per credit hour. Tuition, nonresident: full-time $16,680; part-time $695 per credit hour. *Required fees:* $981. Tuition and fees vary according to course load and program. *Financial support:* Fellowships with full and partial tuition reimbursements, research assistantships with full and partial tuition reimbursements, teaching assistantships with full and partial tuition reimbursements, Federal Work-Study, institutionally sponsored loans, scholarships/grants, health care benefits, and unspecified assistantships available. Financial award application deadline: 6/30; financial award applicants required to submit FAFSA. *Faculty research:* Ecological engineering, environmental resources engineering, geospatial information science and engineering, water resources engineering. *Total annual research expenditures:* $1 million. *Unit head:* Dr. Theodore Endreny, Chair, 315-470-6565, Fax: 315-470-6958, E-mail: te@esf.edu. *Application contact:* Scott Shannon, Dean of the Graduate School, 315-470-6599, Fax: 315-470-6978, E-mail: esfgrad@esf.edu. Website: http://www.esf.edu/ere.

State University of New York College of Environmental Science and Forestry, Department of Environmental Studies, Syracuse, NY 13210-2779. Offers MPS, MS. *Degree requirements:* For master's, thesis (for some programs). *Entrance requirements:* For master's, GRE General Test. *Expenses:* Tuition, state resident: full-time $9370; part-time $390 per credit hour. Tuition, nonresident: full-time $16,680; part-time $695 per credit hour. *Required fees:* $981. Tuition and fees vary according to course load and program.

State University of New York College of Environmental Science and Forestry, Department of Forest and Natural Resources Management, Syracuse, NY 13210-2779. Offers ecology and ecosystems (MPS, MS, PhD); economics, governance and human dimensions (MPS, MS, PhD); environmental and natural resources policy (MPS, MS); forest and natural resources management (MPS, MS, PhD); monitoring, analysis and modeling (MPS, MS, PhD). *Accreditation:* SAF. *Degree requirements:* For master's, thesis (for some programs); for doctorate, comprehensive exam, thesis/dissertation. *Entrance requirements:* For master's and doctorate, GRE General Test, minimum GPA of 3.0. Additional exam requirements/recommendations for international students: Required—TOEFL (minimum score 550 paper-based; 80 iBT), IELTS (minimum score 6). *Expenses:* Tuition, state resident: full-time $9370; part-time $390 per credit hour. Tuition, nonresident: full-time $16,680; part-time $695 per credit hour. *Required fees:* $981. Tuition and fees vary according to course load and program. *Faculty research:* Silviculture recreation management, tree improvement, operations management, economics.

State University of New York College of Environmental Science and Forestry, Program in Environmental Science, Syracuse, NY 13210-2779. Offers biophysical and ecological economics (MPS); coupled natural and human systems (MPS); ecosystem restoration (MPS); environmental and community land planning (MPS, MS); environmental and natural resources policy (PhD); environmental communication and participatory processes (MPS, MS); environmental monitoring and modeling (MPS); environmental policy and democratic processes (MPS, MS); environmental systems and risk management (MS); water and wetland resource studies (MPS, MS). Part-time programs available. *Degree requirements:* For master's, thesis (for some programs); for doctorate, comprehensive exam, thesis/dissertation. *Entrance requirements:* For master's and doctorate, GRE General Test, minimum GPA of 3.0. Additional exam requirements/recommendations for international students: Required—TOEFL (minimum score 550 paper-based; 80 iBT), IELTS (minimum score 6). *Expenses:* Tuition, state resident: full-time $9370; part-time $390 per credit hour. Tuition, nonresident: full-time $16,680; part-time $695 per credit hour. *Required fees:* $981. Tuition and fees vary according to course load and program. *Faculty research:* Environmental education/communications, water resources, land resources, waste management.

Stony Brook University, State University of New York, Graduate School, College of Engineering and Applied Sciences, Department of Technology and Society, Program in Energy and Environmental Systems, Stony Brook, NY 11794. Offers MS, Advanced Certificate. Part-time programs available. *Degree requirements:* For master's, thesis, project. *Application deadline:* For fall admission, 2/1 for domestic students; for spring admission, 10/1 for domestic students. Electronic applications accepted. *Expenses:* Tuition, state resident: full-time $9370. Tuition, nonresident: full-time $16,680. *Required fees:* $1214. *Financial support:* Research assistantships, teaching assistantships, and career-related internships or fieldwork available. *Unit head:* Dr. David Ferguson, Chairman, 631-632-8770, E-mail: david.ferguson@stonybrook.edu. *Application contact:* Dr. Sheldon Reaven, 631-632-8770, E-mail: sheldon.raven@sunysb.edu. Website: http://www.stonybrook.edu/est/graduate/msenergyenv.shtml.

Stony Brook University, State University of New York, School of Professional Development, Stony Brook, NY 11794. Offers biology-grade 7-12 (MAT); chemistry-grade 7-12 (MAT); coaching (Graduate Certificate); computer integrated engineering (Graduate Certificate); earth science-grade 7-12 (MAT); educational computing (Graduate Certificate); educational leadership (Advanced Certificate); English-grade 7-12 (MAT); environmental management (Graduate Certificate); environmental/occupational health and safety (Graduate Certificate); French-grade 7-12 (MAT); German-grade 7-12 (MAT); higher education administration (MA, Certificate); human resource management (MS, Graduate Certificate); information systems management (Graduate Certificate); Italian-grade 7-12 (MAT); liberal studies (MA); mathematics-grade 7-12 (MAT); operation research (Graduate Certificate); physics-grade 7-12 (MAT); school administration and supervision (Graduate Certificate); school building leadership (Graduate Certificate); school district administration (Graduate Certificate); school district business leadership (Advanced Certificate); school district leadership (Graduate Certificate); social science and the professions (MPS), including environmental management, human resource management; social studies-grade 7-12 (MAT); Spanish-grade 7-12 (MAT); waste management (Graduate Certificate). Part-time and evening/weekend programs available. Postbaccalaureate distance learning degree programs offered. *Faculty:* 102 part-time/adjunct (39 women). *Students:* 267 full-time (168 women), 986 part-time (649 women); includes 165 minority (50 Black or African American, non-Hispanic/Latino; 27 Asian, non-Hispanic/Latino; 86 Hispanic/Latino; 2 Two or more races, non-Hispanic/Latino), 4 international. Average age 28. 411 applicants, 96% accepted, 251 enrolled. In 2012, 436 master's, 308 other advanced degrees awarded. *Degree requirements:* For master's, one foreign language, thesis or alternative. *Application deadline:* Applications are processed on a rolling basis. Application fee: $100. *Expenses:* Tuition, state resident: full-time $9370. Tuition, nonresident: full-time $16,680. *Required fees:* $1214. *Financial support:* In 2012–13, 3 teaching assistantships were awarded; fellowships, research assistantships, and career-related internships or fieldwork also available. Support available to part-time students. *Unit head:* Dr. Paul J. Edelson, Dean, 631-632-7052, Fax: 631-632-9046, E-mail: paul.edelson@stonybrook.edu. *Application contact:* 631-632-7050, E-mail: spd@stonybrook.edu. Website: http://www.stonybrook.edu/spd/.

Texas Christian University, College of Science and Engineering, School of Geology, Energy and the Environment, Fort Worth, TX 76129. Offers environmental management (MEM); environmental science (MA, MS); geology (MS). Part-time programs available. *Faculty:* 7 full-time (1 woman). *Students:* 17 full-time (9 women), 24 part-time (11 women); includes 4 minority (1 Black or African American, non-Hispanic/Latino; 1 Asian, non-Hispanic/Latino; 2 Hispanic/Latino), 2 international. Average age 26. 30 applicants, 80% accepted, 16 enrolled. In 2012, 10 master's awarded. *Degree requirements:* For master's, comprehensive exam (for some programs), thesis (for some programs). *Entrance requirements:* For master's, GRE. Additional exam requirements/recommendations for international students: Required—TOEFL (minimum score 550 paper-based; 80 iBT). *Application deadline:* For fall admission, 2/28 priority date for domestic students, 2/28 for international students. Application fee: $60. *Expenses: Tuition:* Full-time $21,600; part-time $1200 per credit. *Required fees:* $48. Tuition and fees vary according to program. *Financial support:* In 2012–13, 15 teaching assistantships with full tuition reimbursements (averaging $15,000 per year) were awarded. Financial award application deadline: 2/28. *Unit head:* Dr. Phil Hartman, Dean, 817-257-7727, E-mail: p.hartman@tcu.edu. *Application contact:* Dr. Magnus Rittby, Associate Dean for Administration and Graduate Programs, 817-257-7729, Fax: 817-257-7736, E-mail: m.rittby@tcu.edu. Website: http://geo1.tcu.edu/graduate/graduate.html.

Texas Southern University, School of Public Affairs, Program in Urban Planning and Environmental Policy, Houston, TX 77004-4584. Offers MS, PhD. *Accreditation:* ACSP. Part-time and evening/weekend programs available. *Faculty:* 7 full-time (4 women). *Students:* 41 full-time (19 women), 32 part-time (15 women); includes 67 minority (55 Black or African American, non-Hispanic/Latino; 8 Asian, non-Hispanic/Latino; 4 Hispanic/Latino), 1 international. Average age 37. 34 applicants, 44% accepted, 11 enrolled. In 2012, 7 master's, 5 doctorates awarded. *Degree requirements:* For master's, comprehensive exam, thesis optional. *Entrance requirements:* For master's, GRE General Test, minimum GPA of 2.5. Additional exam requirements/recommendations for international students: Required—TOEFL. *Application deadline:* For fall admission, 7/1 priority date for domestic students, 7/1 for international students; for spring admission, 11/1 for domestic and international students. Applications are processed on a rolling basis. Application fee: $50 ($75 for international students). Electronic applications accepted. *Expenses:* Tuition, state resident: full-time $1836; part-time $100 per credit hour. Tuition, nonresident: full-time $7128; part-time $360 per credit hour. *Required fees:* $6268. *Financial support:* In 2012–13, 18 research assistantships (averaging $4,412 per year), 2 teaching assistantships (averaging $3,400 per year) were awarded; fellowships, career-related internships or fieldwork, Federal Work-Study, and institutionally sponsored loans also available. Financial award application deadline: 5/1; financial award applicants required to submit FAFSA. *Unit head:* Dr. Qisheng Pan, Chair, 713-313-7221, E-mail: taylor_sa@tsu.edu. *Application contact:* Sheila Taylor, Secretary, 713-313-6842, E-mail: randell_bj@tsu.edu. Website: http://www.tsu.edu/academics/colleges__schools/publicaffairs/upep/.

Texas State University–San Marcos, Graduate School, College of Liberal Arts, Department of Geography, Program in Resource and Environmental Studies, San Marcos, TX 78666. Offers MAG. Part-time and evening/weekend programs available. *Faculty:* 7 full-time (2 women), 1 part-time/adjunct (0 women). *Students:* 9 full-time (2 women), 10 part-time (7 women); includes 3 minority (2 Hispanic/Latino; 1 Two or more races, non-Hispanic/Latino). Average age 29. 8 applicants, 88% accepted, 4 enrolled. In 2012, 5 master's awarded. *Degree requirements:* For master's, comprehensive exam. *Entrance requirements:* For master's, GRE General Test, minimum GPA of 3.0 in last 60 hours of course work, letter of interest, 2 letters of recommendation, curriculum vitae/resume. Additional exam requirements/recommendations for international students: Required—TOEFL (minimum score 550 paper-based; 78 iBT). *Application deadline:* For fall admission, 5/1 priority date for domestic students, 4/15 for international students; for spring admission, 10/15 priority date for domestic students, 10/1 for international students. Applications are processed on a rolling basis. Application fee: $40 ($90 for international students). *Expenses:* Tuition, state resident: full-time $6408; part-time $3204 per semester. Tuition, nonresident: full-time $14,832; part-time $7416 per semester. *Required fees:* $1824; $618. Tuition and fees vary according to course load. *Financial support:* In 2012–13, 14 students received support, including 1 research assistantship (averaging $10,950 per year), 4 teaching assistantships (averaging $12,330 per year); career-related internships or fieldwork, Federal Work-Study, institutionally sponsored loans, and scholarships/grants also available. Support available to part-time students. Financial award application deadline: 4/1; financial award applicants required to submit FAFSA. *Unit head:* Dr. David Butler, Graduate Adviser, 512-245-2170, Fax: 512-245-8353, E-mail: db25@txstate.edu. *Application contact:* Dr. J. Michael Willoughby, Dean of Graduate School, 512-245-2581, Fax: 512-245-8365, E-mail: gradcollege@txstate.edu. Website: http://www.geo.txstate.edu/.

Texas Tech University, Graduate School, College of Architecture, PhD Program in Land-Use Planning, Management, and Design, Lubbock, TX 79409. Offers PhD. *Degree requirements:* For doctorate, comprehensive exam, thesis/dissertation. *Entrance requirements:* For doctorate, GRE General Test. Additional exam requirements/recommendations for international students: Required—TOEFL (minimum score 550 paper-based; 79 iBT). Electronic applications accepted. *Faculty research:* Architecture, landscape architecture, geography, urban planning, environmental policy.

Towson University, Program in Geography and Environmental Planning, Towson, MD 21252-0001. Offers MA. Part-time and evening/weekend programs available. *Degree requirements:* For master's, thesis optional. *Entrance requirements:* For master's, 9 credits of course work in geography, minimum GPA of 3.0 in geography, 2 narrative letters of recommendation. Additional exam requirements/recommendations for international students: Required—TOEFL. Electronic applications accepted.

Trent University, Graduate Studies, Program in Environmental and Life Sciences, Environmental and Resource Studies Program, Peterborough, ON K9J 7B8, Canada. Offers M Sc, PhD. *Degree requirements:* For master's, thesis; for doctorate, thesis/dissertation. *Entrance requirements:* For master's, honours degree; for doctorate, master's degree. *Faculty research:* Environmental biogeochemistry, aquatic organic contaminants, fisheries, wetland ecology, renewable resource management.

Tropical Agriculture Research and Higher Education Center, Graduate School, Turrialba, Costa Rica. Offers agribusiness management (MS); agroforestry systems (PhD); development practices (MS); ecological agriculture (MS); environmental socioeconomics (MS); forestry in tropical and subtropical zones (PhD); integrated watershed management (MS); international sustainable tourism (MS); management and conservation of tropical rainforests and biodiversity (MS); tropical agriculture (PhD); tropical agroforestry (MS). *Entrance requirements:* For master's, GRE, 2 years of related professional experience, letters of recommendation; for doctorate, GRE, 4 letters of recommendation, letter of support from employing organization, master's degree in agronomy, biological sciences, forestry, natural resources or related field. Additional exam requirements/recommendations for international students: Required—TOEFL (minimum score 550 paper-based). Electronic applications accepted. *Faculty research:* Biodiversity in fragmented landscapes, ecosystem management, integrated pest management, environmental livestock production, biotechnology carbon balances in diverse land uses.

Troy University, Graduate School, College of Arts and Sciences, Program in Environmental and Biological Sciences, Troy, AL 36082. Offers biological science (MS); environmental analysis and management (MS); environmental policy (MS); environmental science (MS). Part-time and evening/weekend programs available. *Faculty:* 8 full-time (1 woman). *Students:* 3 full-time (all women), 20 part-time (14 women); includes 1 minority (Hispanic/Latino). Average age 26. 38 applicants, 53% accepted, 5 enrolled. In 2012, 13 master's awarded. *Degree requirements:* For master's, comprehensive exam (for some programs), thesis (for some programs), comprehensive exam or thesis, minimum GPA of 3.0, admission to candidacy. *Entrance requirements:* For master's, GRE (minimum score of 850 on old exam or 286 on new exam), MAT (minimum score of 385) or GMAT (minimum score of 380), bachelor's degree; minimum undergraduate GPA of 2.5 or 3.0 on last 30 semester hours. Additional exam requirements/recommendations for international students: Required—TOEFL (minimum score 523 paper-based; 70 iBT), IELTS (minimum score 5.5). *Application deadline:* Applications are processed on a rolling basis. Application fee: $50. Electronic applications accepted. *Expenses:* Tuition, state resident: full-time $6102; part-time $307 per credit hour. Tuition, nonresident: full-time $12,204; part-time $614 per credit hour. *Required fees:* $32 per credit hour. $50 per term. Tuition and fees vary according to campus/location. *Unit head:* Dr. Glenn Cohen, Chairman, 334-670-3660, Fax: 334-670-3401, E-mail: gcohen@troy.edu. *Application contact:* Brenda K. Campbell, Director of Graduate Admissions, 334-670-3178, Fax: 334-670-3733, E-mail: bcamp@troy.edu.

Troy University, Graduate School, College of Arts and Sciences, Program in Public Administration, Troy, AL 36082. Offers education (MPA); environmental management (MPA); government contracting (MPA); health care administration (MPA); justice administration (MPA); national security affairs (MPA); nonprofit management (MPA); public human resources management (MPA); public management (MPA). *Accreditation:* NASPAA. Part-time and evening/weekend programs available. Postbaccalaureate distance learning degree programs offered (no on-campus study). *Faculty:* 18 full-time (11 women), 7 part-time/adjunct (3 women). *Students:* 118 full-time (80 women), 324 part-time (209 women); includes 260 minority (226 Black or African American, non-Hispanic/Latino; 4 American Indian or Alaska Native, non-Hispanic/Latino; 6 Asian, non-Hispanic/Latino; 14 Hispanic/Latino; 10 Two or more races, non-Hispanic/Latino). Average age 32. 167 applicants, 87% accepted, 92 enrolled. In 2012, 184 master's awarded. *Degree requirements:* For master's, capstone course with a grade of B or better, minimum GPA of 3.0, admission to candidacy. *Entrance requirements:* For master's, GRE (minimum score of 850 on old exam or 286 on new exam), MAT (minimum score of 385) or GMAT (minimum score of 380), bachelor's degree; minimum undergraduate GPA of 2.5 or 3.0 on last 30 semester hours, letter of recommendation; essay. Additional exam requirements/recommendations for international students: Required—TOEFL (minimum score 523 paper-based; 70 iBT), IELTS (minimum score 6). *Application deadline:* Applications are processed on a rolling basis. Application fee: $50. Electronic applications accepted. *Expenses:* Tuition, state resident: full-time $6102; part-time $307 per credit hour. Tuition, nonresident: full-time $12,204; part-time $614 per credit hour. *Required fees:* $32 per credit hour. $50 per term. Tuition and fees vary according to campus/location. *Financial support:* Available to part-time students. Applicants required to submit FAFSA. *Unit head:* Dr. Sam Shelton, Chairman, 334-670-3754, Fax: 334-670-5647, E-mail: ssheltonl@troy.edu. *Application contact:* Brenda K. Campbell, Director of Graduate Admissions, 334-670-3178, Fax: 334-670-3733, E-mail: bcamp@troy.edu.

Tufts University, Graduate School of Arts and Sciences, Department of Urban and Environmental Policy and Planning, Medford, MA 02155. Offers community development (MA); environmental policy (MA); health and human welfare (MA); housing policy (MA); international environment/development policy (MA); public policy (MPP); MA/MS; MALD/MA. *Accreditation:* ACSP (one or more programs are accredited). Part-time programs available. *Degree requirements:* For master's, thesis, internship. *Entrance requirements:* For master's, GRE General Test. Additional exam requirements/recommendations for international students: Required—TOEFL (minimum score 550 paper-based; 80 iBT). Electronic applications accepted. *Expenses:* Contact institution.

Tufts University, Graduate School of Arts and Sciences, Graduate Certificate Programs, Community Environmental Studies Program, Medford, MA 02155. Offers Certificate. Part-time and evening/weekend programs available. Electronic applications accepted. *Expenses:* Contact institution.

Tufts University, Graduate School of Arts and Sciences, Graduate Certificate Programs, Environmental Management Program, Medford, MA 02155. Offers Certificate. Part-time and evening/weekend programs available. Electronic applications accepted. *Expenses: Tuition:* Full-time $42,856; part-time $1072 per credit hour. *Required fees:* $730. Full-time tuition and fees vary according to degree level, program and student level. Part-time tuition and fees vary according to course load.

Tufts University, School of Engineering, Department of Civil and Environmental Engineering, Medford, MA 02155. Offers bioengineering (ME, MS), including environmental technology; civil engineering (ME, MS, PhD), including geotechnical engineering, structural engineering, water diplomacy (PhD); environmental engineering (ME, MS, PhD), including environmental engineering and environmental sciences, environmental geotechnology, environmental health, environmental science and management, hazardous materials management, water diplomacy (PhD), water resources engineering. Part-time programs available. Terminal master's awarded for partial completion of doctoral program. *Degree requirements:* For master's, thesis or alternative; for doctorate, thesis/dissertation. *Entrance requirements:* For master's and doctorate, GRE General Test. Additional exam requirements/recommendations for international students: Required—TOEFL (minimum score 550 paper-based; 80 iBT). Electronic applications accepted. *Expenses: Tuition:* Full-time $42,856; part-time $1072 per credit hour. *Required fees:* $730. Full-time tuition and fees vary according to degree level, program and student level. Part-time tuition and fees vary according to course load. *Faculty research:* Environmental and water resources engineering, environmental health, geotechnical and geoenvironmental engineering, structural engineering and mechanics, water diplomacy.

Universidad Autonoma de Guadalajara, Graduate Programs, Guadalajara, Mexico. Offers administrative law and justice (LL M); advertising and corporate communications (MA); architecture (M Arch); business (MBA); computational science (MCC); education (Ed M, Ed D); English-Spanish translation (MA); entrepreneurship and management (MBA); integrated management of digital animation (MA); international business (MIB); international corporate law (LL M); internet technologies (MS); manufacturing systems (MMS); occupational health (MS); philosophy (MA, PhD); power electronics (MS); quality systems (MQS); renewable energy (MS); social evaluation of projects (MBA); strategic market research (MBA); tax law (MA); teaching mathematics (MA).

Universidad del Turabo, Graduate Programs, Programs in Science and Technology, Gurabo, PR 00778-3030. Offers environmental analysis (MSE), including environmental chemistry; environmental management (MSE), including pollution management; environmental science (D Sc), including environmental biology. *Students:* 12 full-time (10 women), 97 part-time (63 women); all minorities (all Hispanic/Latino). Average age 38. 60 applicants, 90% accepted, 40 enrolled. In 2012, 17 master's, 1 doctorate awarded. *Entrance requirements:* For master's, GRE, EXADEP, interview. *Application deadline:* For fall admission, 8/5 for domestic students. Application fee: $25. *Unit head:* Teresa Lipsett, Dean, 787-743-7979. *Application contact:* Virginia Gonzalez, Admissions Officer, 787-746-3009.

Universidad Metropolitana, School of Environmental Affairs, Program in Environmental Planning, San Juan, PR 00928-1150. Offers MP. Part-time programs available. *Degree requirements:* For master's, thesis. *Entrance requirements:* For master's, EXADEP, interview. Electronic applications accepted.

Universidad Metropolitana, School of Environmental Affairs, Program in Environmental Studies, San Juan, PR 00928-1150. Offers MAES. Part-time programs available. *Degree requirements:* For master's, thesis or alternative. *Entrance requirements:* For master's, EXADEP, interview. Electronic applications accepted.

Université de Montréal, Faculty of Medicine, Programs in Environment and Prevention, Montréal, QC H3C 3J7, Canada. Offers environment, health and disaster management (DESS). Electronic applications accepted. *Faculty research:* Health, environment, pollutants, protection, waste.

Université du Québec à Chicoutimi, Graduate Programs, Program in Renewable Resources, Chicoutimi, QC G7H 2B1, Canada. Offers M Sc. Part-time programs available. *Degree requirements:* For master's, thesis. *Entrance requirements:* For master's, appropriate bachelor's degree, proficiency in French.

Université du Québec, Institut National de la Recherche Scientifique, Graduate Programs, Research Center–Water, Earth and Environment, Québec, QC G1K 9A9, Canada. Offers earth sciences (M Sc, PhD); earth sciences-environmental technologies (M Sc); water sciences (M Sc, PhD). Part-time programs available. *Faculty:* 39. *Students:* 204 full-time (96 women), 20 part-time (9 women), 106 international. Average age 30. In 2012, 24 master's, 6 doctorates awarded. *Degree requirements:* For master's, thesis optional; for doctorate, thesis/dissertation. *Entrance requirements:* For master's, appropriate bachelor's degree, proficiency in French; for doctorate, appropriate master's degree, proficiency in French. *Application deadline:* For fall admission, 3/30 for domestic and international students; for winter admission, 11/1 for domestic and international students; for spring admission, 3/1 for domestic and international students. Application fee: $45. Electronic applications accepted. *Financial support:* In 2012–13, fellowships (averaging $16,500 per year) were awarded; research assistantships also available. *Faculty research:* Land use, impacts of climate change, adaptation to climate change, integrated management of resources (mineral and water). *Unit head:* Yves Begin, Director, 418-654-2524, Fax: 418-654-2600, E-mail: yves.begin@ete.inrs.ca. *Application contact:* Sylvie Richard, Registrar, 418-654-2518, Fax: 418-654-3858, E-mail: sylvie.richard@adm.inrs.ca. Website: http://www.ete.inrs.ca/.

Université Laval, Faculty of Administrative Sciences, Programs in Business Administration, Québec, QC G1K 7P4, Canada. Offers accounting (MBA); agri-food management (MBA); electronic business (MBA, Diploma); factory management and logistics (MBA); finance (MBA); firm management (MBA); geomatic management (MBA); information technology management (MBA); international management (MBA); management (MBA); management accounting (MBA, Diploma); marketing (MBA); modeling and organizational decision (MBA);

occupational health and safety management (MBA); pharmacy management (MBA); social and environmental responsibility (MBA); technological entrepreneurship (Diploma). *Accreditation:* AACSB. Part-time and evening/weekend programs available. Postbaccalaureate distance learning degree programs offered (no on-campus study). *Entrance requirements:* For master's and Diploma, knowledge of French and English. Electronic applications accepted.

Université Laval, Faculty of Agricultural and Food Sciences, Department of Soils and Agricultural Engineering, Programs in Agri-Food Engineering, Québec, QC G1K 7P4, Canada. Offers agri-food engineering (M Sc); environmental technology (M Sc). *Degree requirements:* For master's, thesis (for some programs). *Entrance requirements:* For master's, knowledge of French. Electronic applications accepted.

Université Laval, Faculty of Agricultural and Food Sciences, Department of Soils and Agricultural Engineering, Programs in Soils and Environment Science, Québec, QC G1K 7P4, Canada. Offers environmental technology (M Sc); soils and environment science (M Sc, PhD). Terminal master's awarded for partial completion of doctoral program. *Degree requirements:* For master's, thesis (for some programs); for doctorate, comprehensive exam, thesis/dissertation. *Entrance requirements:* For master's and doctorate, knowledge of French and English. Electronic applications accepted.

University at Albany, State University of New York, College of Arts and Sciences, Department of Biological Sciences, Program in Biodiversity, Conservation, and Policy, Albany, NY 12222-0001. Offers MS. *Degree requirements:* For master's, one foreign language. *Entrance requirements:* For master's, GRE General Test. *Faculty research:* Aquatic ecology, plant community ecology, biodiversity and public policy, restoration ecology, coastal and estuarine science.

University of Alaska Fairbanks, College of Engineering and Mines, Department of Civil and Environmental Engineering, Program in Environmental Engineering, Fairbanks, AK 99775-5900. Offers engineering (PhD), including environmental engineering; environmental engineering (MS), including environmental contaminants, environmental science and management, water supply and waste treatment. Part-time programs available. *Students:* 3 full-time (2 women), 1 part-time (0 women), 1 international. Average age 26. 2 applicants, 50% accepted, 1 enrolled. *Degree requirements:* For master's, comprehensive exam, thesis or alternative; for doctorate, comprehensive exam, thesis/dissertation, oral exam, oral defense. *Entrance requirements:* For master's, basic computer techniques; for doctorate, GRE General Test. Additional exam requirements/recommendations for international students: Required—TOEFL (minimum score 575 paper-based). *Application deadline:* For fall admission, 6/1 for domestic students, 3/1 for international students; for spring admission, 10/15 for domestic students, 9/1 for international students. Applications are processed on a rolling basis. Application fee: $60. Electronic applications accepted. *Expenses:* Tuition, state resident: full-time $7038. Tuition, nonresident: full-time $14,382. Tuition and fees vary according to course level, course load and reciprocity agreements. *Financial support:* In 2012–13, 2 research assistantships (averaging $5,316 per year), 1 teaching assistantship (averaging $3,651 per year) were awarded; fellowships, career-related internships or fieldwork, Federal Work-Study, scholarships/grants, health care benefits, and unspecified assistantships also available. Support available to part-time students. Financial award application deadline: 7/1; financial award applicants required to submit FAFSA. *Unit head:* Dr. David Barnes, Department Chair, 907-474-7241, Fax: 907-474-6087, E-mail: fycee@uaf.edu. *Application contact:* Libby Eddy, Registrar and Director of Admissions, 907-474-7500, Fax: 907-474-7097, E-mail: admissions@uaf.edu. Website: http://cem.uaf.edu/cee/environmental-engineering.aspx.

University of Alaska Fairbanks, College of Liberal Arts, Department of Northern Studies, Fairbanks, AK 99775-6460. Offers environmental politics and policy (MA); Northern history (MA). Part-time programs available. *Faculty:* 1 (woman) full-time. *Students:* 14 full-time (9 women), 16 part-time (7 women); includes 3 minority (2 American Indian or Alaska Native, non-Hispanic/Latino; 1 Two or more races, non-Hispanic/Latino), 2 international. Average age 38. 20 applicants, 65% accepted, 10 enrolled. In 2012, 5 master's awarded. *Degree requirements:* For master's, comprehensive exam, thesis or alternative. *Entrance requirements:* Additional exam requirements/recommendations for international students: Required—TOEFL (minimum score 550 paper-based; 80 iBT). *Application deadline:* For fall admission, 6/1 for domestic students, 3/1 for international students; for spring admission, 10/15 for domestic students, 9/1 for international students. Applications are processed on a rolling basis. Application fee: $60. Electronic applications accepted. *Expenses:* Tuition, state resident: full-time $7038. Tuition, nonresident: full-time $14,382. Tuition and fees vary according to course level, course load and reciprocity agreements. *Financial support:* In 2012–13, 6 research assistantships with tuition reimbursements (averaging $4,782 per year), 8 teaching assistantships with tuition reimbursements (averaging $7,400 per year) were awarded; fellowships with tuition reimbursements, career-related internships or fieldwork, Federal Work-Study, scholarships/grants, health care benefits, and unspecified assistantships also available. Support available to part-time students. Financial award application deadline: 1/1; financial award applicants required to submit FAFSA. *Unit head:* Mary Ehrlander, Director, 907-474-7126, Fax: 907-474-5817, E-mail: fynors@uaf.edu. *Application contact:* Libby Eddy, Registrar and Director of Admissions, 907-474-7500, Fax: 907-474-7097, E-mail: admissions@uaf.edu. Website: http://www.uaf.edu/northern/.

University of Alberta, Faculty of Graduate Studies and Research, Department of Economics, Edmonton, AB T6G 2E1, Canada. Offers economics (MA, PhD); economics and finance (MA); environmental and natural resource economics (PhD). Part-time programs available. *Degree requirements:* For doctorate, thesis/dissertation. *Entrance requirements:* For master's and doctorate, GRE. Additional exam requirements/recommendations for international students: Required—TOEFL. *Faculty research:* Public finance, international trade, industrial organization, Pacific Rim economics, monetary economics.

The University of Arizona, College of Agriculture and Life Sciences, School of Natural Resources, Watershed Resources Program, Tucson, AZ 85721. Offers water, society, and policy (MS); watershed management (MS, PhD). *Faculty:* 19 full-time (3 women), 2 part-time/adjunct (0 women). *Students:* 6 full-time (2 women), 4 part-time (2 women); includes 2 minority (both Hispanic/Latino). Average age 34. 4 applicants, 50% accepted, 0 enrolled. *Degree requirements:* For master's, thesis; for doctorate, comprehensive exam, thesis/dissertation. *Entrance requirements:* For master's, GRE General Test, minimum GPA of 3.0, 3 letters of recommendation; for doctorate, GRE General Test, minimum GPA of 3.0, 3 letters of recommendation, MA or MS. Additional exam requirements/recommendations for international students: Required—TOEFL (minimum score 550 paper-based; 79 iBT). *Application deadline:* For fall admission, 8/1 priority date for domestic students, 12/1 for international students; for spring admission, 7/1 for international students. Applications are processed on a rolling basis. Application fee: $75. *Financial support:* In 2012–13, 6 research assistantships with partial tuition reimbursements (averaging $13,872 per year) were awarded; teaching assistantships with partial tuition reimbursements, career-related internships or fieldwork, scholarships/grants, health care benefits, tuition waivers (partial), and unspecified assistantships also available. *Faculty research:* Forest fuel characteristics, prescribed fire, tree ring-fire scar analysis, erosion, sedimentation. *Total annual research expenditures:* $6.5 million. *Unit head:* Dr. CHarles Hutchinson, Director, 520-621-8568, E-mail: chuck@ag.arizona.edu. *Application contact:* Katie Hughes, Academic Coordinator, 520-621-7260, E-mail: khughes@email.arizona.edu. Website: http://www.ag.arizona.edu/srnr/.

University of Calgary, Faculty of Graduate Studies, Interdisciplinary Graduate Programs, Calgary, AB T2N 1N4, Canada. Offers interdisciplinary research (M Sc, MA, PhD); resources and the environment (M Sc, MA, PhD). Part-time programs available. *Degree requirements:* For master's, thesis; for doctorate, thesis/dissertation, written and oral candidacy exam. *Entrance requirements:* Additional exam requirements/recommendations for international students: Required—TOEFL (minimum score 600 paper-based).

University of Calgary, Faculty of Law, Programs in Natural Resources, Energy and Environmental Law, Calgary, AB T2N 1N4, Canada. Offers LL M, Postbaccalaureate Certificate. Part-time and evening/weekend programs available. *Degree requirements:* For master's, thesis optional. *Entrance requirements:* For master's, JD or LL B. Additional exam requirements/recommendations for international students: Required—TOEFL (minimum score 100 iBT), IELTS (minimum score 7). Electronic applications accepted. *Faculty research:* Natural resources law and regulations; environmental law, ethics and policies; oil and gas and energy law; water and municipal law; Aboriginal law.

University of California, Berkeley, Graduate Division, College of Natural Resources, Department of Environmental Science, Policy, and Management, Berkeley, CA 94720-1500. Offers environmental science, policy, and management (MS, PhD); forestry (MF). Terminal master's awarded for partial completion of doctoral program. *Degree requirements:* For master's, thesis optional; for doctorate, thesis/dissertation, qualifying exam. *Entrance requirements:* For master's and doctorate, GRE General Test, minimum GPA of 3.0, 3 letters of recommendation. Additional exam requirements/recommendations for international students: Required—TOEFL. Electronic applications accepted. *Faculty research:* Biology and ecology of insects; ecosystem function and environmental issues of soils; plant health/interactions from molecular to ecosystem levels; range management and ecology; forest and resource policy, sustainability, and management.

University of California, Berkeley, UC Berkeley Extension, Certificate Programs in Sustainability Studies, Berkeley, CA 94720-1500. Offers leadership in sustainability and environmental management (Professional Certificate); solar energy and green building (Professional Certificate); sustainable design (Professional Certificate).

University of California, Santa Barbara, Graduate Division, College of Letters and Sciences, Division of Social Sciences, Department of Global and International Studies, Santa Barbara, CA 93106-7065. Offers global culture, ideology, and religion (MA); global government and human rights (MA); political economy, sustainable development, and the environment (MA). *Faculty:* 12 full-time (5 women), 5 part-time/adjunct (2 women). *Students:* 23 full-time (14 women); includes 4 minority (1 Asian, non-Hispanic/Latino; 2 Hispanic/Latino; 1 Native Hawaiian or other Pacific Islander, non-Hispanic/Latino), 2 international. Average age 27. 55 applicants, 42% accepted, 9 enrolled. In 2012, 22 master's awarded. *Degree requirements:* For master's, one foreign language, thesis, 2 years of a second language. *Entrance requirements:* For master's, GRE, 2 years of a second language with minimum B grade in the final term, 3 letters of recommendation, resume/curriculum vitae, personal statement. Additional exam requirements/recommendations for international students: Required—TOEFL (minimum score 600 paper-based; 94 iBT), IELTS (minimum score 7). *Application deadline:* For fall admission, 12/15 for domestic and international students.

Application fee: $80 ($100 for international students). Electronic applications accepted. *Financial support:* In 2012–13, 23 students received support, including 29 fellowships with full and partial tuition reimbursements available (averaging $10,000 per year), 47 teaching assistantships with partial tuition reimbursements available (averaging $10,796 per year); career-related internships or fieldwork, Federal Work-Study, and scholarships/grants also available. Financial award application deadline: 12/15; financial award applicants required to submit FAFSA. *Faculty research:* Global culture, ideology, and religion; global governance and human rights; political economy, sustainable development and the environment. *Total annual research expenditures:* $240,000. *Unit head:* Prof. Giles Gunn, Chair, 805-893-4299, Fax: 805-893-8003, E-mail: ggunn@global.ucsb.edu. *Application contact:* Jessea Gay Marie, Graduate Program Advisor/Internship Assistance Officer, 805-893-4668, Fax: 805-893-8003, E-mail: gd-global@global.ucsb.edu. Website: http://www.global.ucsb.edu/home.

University of California, Santa Barbara, Graduate Division, Donald Bren School of Environmental Science and Management, Santa Barbara, CA 93106-5131. Offers economics and environmental science (PhD); environmental science and management (MESM, PhD); technology and society (PhD). *Faculty:* 18 full-time (3 women), 3 part-time/adjunct (0 women). *Students:* 226 full-time (113 women); includes 31 minority (2 Black or African American, non-Hispanic/Latino; 1 American Indian or Alaska Native, non-Hispanic/Latino; 19 Asian, non-Hispanic/Latino; 8 Hispanic/Latino; 1 Native Hawaiian or other Pacific Islander, non-Hispanic/Latino), 26 international. Average age 27. 476 applicants, 46% accepted, 84 enrolled. In 2012, 75 master's, 8 doctorates awarded. *Degree requirements:* For master's, thesis; for doctorate, thesis/dissertation. *Entrance requirements:* For master's and doctorate, GRE. Additional exam requirements/recommendations for international students: Required—TOEFL (minimum score 550 paper-based; 80 iBT), IELTS (minimum score 7). *Application deadline:* For fall admission, 12/15 priority date for domestic students, 12/15 for international students. Application fee: $80 ($100 for international students). Electronic applications accepted. *Financial support:* In 2012–13, 34 students received support, including 53 fellowships with full and partial tuition reimbursements available, 10 research assistantships with full and partial tuition reimbursements available, 18 teaching assistantships with full and partial tuition reimbursements available; career-related internships or fieldwork and tuition waivers (full and partial) also available. Financial award application deadline: 12/15; financial award applicants required to submit FAFSA. *Faculty research:* Coastal marine resources management, conservation planning, corporate environmental management, economics and politics of the environment, energy and climate, pollution prevention and remediation, water resources management. *Unit head:* Bryant Wieneke, Assistant Dean, Planning and Administration, 805-893-2212, Fax: 805-893-7612, E-mail: bryant@bren.ucsb.edu. *Application contact:* Dori Molnar, Graduate Advisor, 805-893-7611, Fax: 805-893-7612, E-mail: admissions@bren.ucsb.edu. Website: http://www.bren.ucsb.edu/.

University of California, Santa Cruz, Division of Graduate Studies, Division of Social Sciences, Program in Environmental Studies, Santa Cruz, CA 95064. Offers PhD. *Degree requirements:* For doctorate, thesis/dissertation, qualifying exam. *Entrance requirements:* For doctorate, GRE General Test. Additional exam requirements/recommendations for international students: Required—TOEFL (minimum score 550 paper-based; 83 iBT); Recommended—IELTS (minimum score 8). Electronic applications accepted. *Faculty research:* Political economy and sustainability, conservation biology, agroecology, environmental policy analysis.

University of Central Missouri, The Graduate School, Warrensburg, MO 64093. Offers accountancy (MA); accounting (MBA); applied mathematics (MS); aviation safety (MA); biology (MS); business administration (MBA); career and technical education leadership (MS); college student personnel administration (MS); communication (MA); computer science (MS); counseling (MS); criminal justice (MS); educational leadership (Ed D); educational technology (MS); elementary and early childhood education (MSE); English (MA); environmental studies (MA); finance (MBA); history (MA); human services/educational technology (Ed S); human services/learning resources (Ed S); human services/professional counseling (Ed S); industrial hygiene (MS); industrial management (MS); information systems (MBA); information technology (MS); kinesiology (MS); library science and information services (MS); literacy education (MSE); marketing (MBA); mathematics (MS); music (MA); occupational safety management (MS); psychology (MS); rural family nursing (MS); school administration (MSE); social gerontology (MS); sociology (MA); special education (MSE); speech language pathology (MS); superintendency (Ed S); teaching (MAT); teaching English as a second language (MA); technology (MS); technology management (PhD); theatre (MA). Part-time programs available. *Faculty:* 233. *Students:* 583 full-time (327 women), 1,425 part-time (930 women); includes 169 minority (93 Black or African American, non-Hispanic/Latino; 11 American Indian or Alaska Native, non-Hispanic/Latino; 27 Asian, non-Hispanic/Latino; 29 Hispanic/Latino; 3 Native Hawaiian or other Pacific Islander, non-Hispanic/Latino; 6 Two or more races, non-Hispanic/Latino), 234 international. Average age 33. 958 applicants, 80% accepted. In 2012, 567 master's, 56 other advanced degrees awarded. *Degree requirements:* For master's and Ed S, comprehensive exam (for some programs), thesis (for some programs). *Entrance requirements:* Additional exam requirements/recommendations for international students: Required—TOEFL (minimum score 550 paper-based; 79 iBT). *Application deadline:* For fall admission, 6/1 for domestic students; for spring admission, 10/1 for domestic and international students. Applications are processed on a rolling basis. Application fee: $30 ($75 for international students). Electronic applications accepted. *Financial support:* In 2012–13, 118 students received support, including 271 research assistantships with full and partial tuition reimbursements available (averaging $7,500 per year), 109 teaching assistantships with full and partial tuition reimbursements available (averaging $7,500 per year); career-related internships or fieldwork, Federal Work-Study, scholarships/grants, and administrative and laboratory assistantships also available. Support available to part-time students. Financial award application deadline: 3/1; financial award applicants required to submit FAFSA. *Unit head:* Dr. Joseph Vaughn, Assistant Provost for Research/Dean, 660-543-4092, Fax: 660-543-4778, E-mail: vaughn@ucmo.edu. *Application contact:* Brittany Gerbec, Graduate Student Services Coordinator, 660-543-4621, Fax: 660-543-4778, E-mail: gradinfo@ucmo.edu. Website: http://www.ucmo.edu/graduate/.

University of Chicago, Irving B. Harris Graduate School of Public Policy Studies, Chicago, IL 60637-1513. Offers environmental science and policy (MS); public policy studies (AM, MPP, PhD); JD/MPP; MBA/MPP; MPP/M Div; MPP/MA. Part-time programs available. *Degree requirements:* For doctorate, thesis/dissertation. *Entrance requirements:* Additional exam requirements/recommendations for international students: Required—TOEFL. Electronic applications accepted. *Expenses:* Contact institution. *Faculty research:* Family and child policy, international security, health policy, social policy.

University of Colorado Boulder, Graduate School, College of Arts and Sciences, Program in Environmental Studies, Boulder, CO 80309. Offers MS, PhD. *Faculty:* 8 full-time (4 women). *Students:* 46 full-time (31 women), 6 part-time (all women); includes 10 minority (3 American Indian or Alaska Native, non-Hispanic/Latino; 4 Asian, non-Hispanic/Latino; 1 Hispanic/Latino; 2 Two or more races, non-Hispanic/Latino), 2 international. Average age 31. 196 applicants, 16% accepted, 18 enrolled. *Entrance requirements:* For master's, minimum undergraduate GPA of 3.0. *Application deadline:* For fall admission, 12/15 for domestic students, 12/1 for international students. Electronic applications accepted. *Financial support:* In 2012–13, 21 fellowships (averaging $6,792 per year), 11 research assistantships with full and partial tuition reimbursements (averaging $21,476 per year), 19 teaching assistantships with full and partial tuition reimbursements (averaging $20,888 per year) were awarded; institutionally sponsored loans, scholarships/grants, health care benefits, and unspecified assistantships also available. Financial award applicants required to submit FAFSA. *Faculty research:* Climate and atmospheric chemistry, water sciences, environmental policy and sustainability, waste management and environmental remediation, biogeochemical cycles. *Total annual research expenditures:* $529,191. *Application contact:* E-mail: envsgrad@colorado.edu. Website: http://envs.colorado.edu/.

University of Colorado Denver, College of Architecture and Planning, Program in Urban and Regional Planning, Denver, CO 80217-3364. Offers economic and community development planning (MURP); land use and environmental planning (MURP); urban place making (MURP). *Accreditation:* ACSP. Part-time programs available. *Students:* 98 full-time (37 women), 6 part-time (3 women); includes 16 minority (4 Black or African American, non-Hispanic/Latino; 1 American Indian or Alaska Native, non-Hispanic/Latino; 1 Asian, non-Hispanic/Latino; 6 Hispanic/Latino; 4 Two or more races, non-Hispanic/Latino), 10 international. Average age 30. 126 applicants, 74% accepted, 41 enrolled. In 2012, 58 master's awarded. *Degree requirements:* For master's, minimum of 51 semester hours; self-directed studio/project/thesis. *Entrance requirements:* For master's, GRE (for students with an undergraduate GPA below 3.0), sample of writing or work project. Additional exam requirements/recommendations for international students: Required—TOEFL (minimum score 550 paper-based; 79 iBT); Recommended—IELTS (minimum score 6.5). *Application deadline:* For fall admission, 2/15 priority date for domestic students, 1/15 for international students; for spring admission, 10/1 for domestic students. Applications are processed on a rolling basis. Application fee: $50 ($75 for international students). Electronic applications accepted. *Expenses:* Contact institution. *Financial support:* In 2012–13, 16 students received support. Fellowships, research assistantships, teaching assistantships, Federal Work-Study, institutionally sponsored loans, scholarships/grants, traineeships, and unspecified assistantships available. Financial award application deadline: 4/1; financial award applicants required to submit FAFSA. *Faculty research:* Physical planning, environmental planning, economic development planning. *Unit head:* Jeremy Nemeth, Assistant Professor/Chair/Director, 303-315-0069, E-mail: jeremy.nemeth@ucdenver.edu. *Application contact:* Michael Harper, Administrative Coordinator, Graduate Admissions and PhD Program, 303-556-6042, E-mail: michael.t.harper@ucdenver.edu. Website: http://www.ucdenver.edu/academics/colleges/ArchitecturePlanning/ExplorePrograms/masters/UrbanRegionalPlanning/Pages/UrbanRegionalPlanning.aspx.

University of Colorado Denver, College of Liberal Arts and Sciences, Program in Humanities, Denver, CO 80217. Offers community health science (MSS); humanities (MH); international studies (MSS); philosophy and theory (MH); social justice (MSS); society and the environment (MSS); visual studies (MH); women's and gender studies (MSS). Part-time and evening/weekend programs available. *Faculty:* 1 (woman) full-time, 2 part-time/adjunct (both women). *Students:* 39 full-time (27 women), 35 part-time (24 women); includes 7 minority (1 Black or African American, non-Hispanic/Latino; 1 American Indian or Alaska Native, non-Hispanic/Latino; 1 Asian, non-Hispanic/Latino; 4 Hispanic/Latino). Average age 34. 20 applicants, 65% accepted, 9 enrolled. In 2012, 14 master's awarded. *Degree requirements:* For master's, 36 credit hours, project or thesis. *Entrance requirements:* For master's, writing sample, statement of purpose/letter of intent, three letters of recommendation. Additional exam requirements/recommendations for international students: Required—TOEFL (minimum score 537 paper-based; 75 iBT); Recommended—IELTS (minimum score 6.5). *Application deadline:* For fall admission, 5/15 for domestic and international students; for spring admission, 10/15 for domestic and international students. Application fee: $50 ($75 for international students). Electronic applications accepted. *Expenses:* Tuition, state resident: full-time $7712; part-time $355 per credit hour. Tuition, nonresident: full-time $22,038; part-time $1087 per credit hour. *Required fees:* $1110; $1. Tuition and fees vary according to course load, campus/location and program. *Financial support:* In 2012–13, 2 students received support. Fellowships, research assistantships, teaching assistantships, Federal Work-Study, institutionally sponsored loans, scholarships/grants, traineeships, and unspecified assistantships available. Financial award application deadline: 4/1; financial award applicants required to submit FAFSA. *Faculty research:* Women and gender in the classical Mediterranean, communication theory and democracy, relationship between psychology and philosophy. *Unit head:* Myra Bookman, Associate Director of Humanities and Social Science, 303-556-2496, Fax: 303-556-8100, E-mail: myra.bookman@ucdenver.edu. *Application contact:* Catherine Osmundson, Program Assistant, 303-556-2305, E-mail: catherine.osmundson@ucdenver.edu. Website: http://www.ucdenver.edu/academics/colleges/CLAS/Programs/HumanitiesSocialSciences/Programs/Pages/MasterofHumanities.aspx.

University of Colorado Denver, School of Public Affairs, Program in Public Affairs and Administration, Denver, CO 80127. Offers public administration (MPA), including domestic violence, emergency management and homeland security, environmental policy, management and law, homeland security and defense, local government, nonprofit management, public administration; public affairs (PhD). *Accreditation:* NASPAA. Part-time and evening/weekend programs available. Postbaccalaureate distance learning degree programs offered (no on-campus study). *Students:* 240 full-time (142 women), 176 part-time (110 women); includes 58 minority (10 Black or African American, non-Hispanic/Latino; 2 American Indian or Alaska Native, non-Hispanic/Latino; 11 Asian, non-Hispanic/Latino; 31 Hispanic/Latino; 1 Native Hawaiian or other Pacific Islander, non-Hispanic/Latino; 3 Two or more races, non-Hispanic/Latino), 27 international. Average age 33. 223 applicants, 65% accepted, 83 enrolled. In 2012, 142 master's, 9 doctorates awarded. *Degree requirements:* For master's, thesis or alternative, 36-39 credit hours; for doctorate, comprehensive exam, thesis/dissertation, minimum of 66 semester hours, including at least 30 hours of dissertation. *Entrance requirements:* For master's, GRE, GMAT or LSAT, resume, essay, transcripts, recommendations; for doctorate, GRE, resume, essay, transcripts, recommendations. Additional exam requirements/recommendations for international students: Required—TOEFL (minimum score 550 paper-based; 80 iBT); Recommended—IELTS (minimum score 6.5). *Application deadline:* For fall admission, 2/1 priority date for domestic students, 1/15 for international students; for spring admission, 10/15 priority date for domestic students, 10/1 for international students. Application fee: $50 ($75 for international students). Electronic applications accepted. *Expenses:* Contact institution. *Financial support:* In 2012–13, 101 students received support. Fellowships with partial tuition reimbursements available, research assistantships with partial tuition reimbursements available, teaching assistantships with partial tuition reimbursements available, Federal Work-Study, institutionally sponsored loans, scholarships/grants, traineeships, and unspecified assistantships available. Financial award application deadline: 4/1; financial award applicants required to submit FAFSA. *Faculty research:* Housing, education and the social and economic issues of vulnerable populations; nonprofit governance and management; education finance, effectiveness and reform; P-20 education initiatives; municipal government accountability. *Unit head:* Dr. Kathleen Beatty, Director of Executive MPA Program, 303-315-2485, Fax: 303-315-2229, E-mail: kathleen.beatty@ucdenver.edu. *Application contact:* Annie Davies, Director of Marketing, Community Outreach and Alumni Affairs, 303-315-2896, Fax: 303-315-2229, E-mail: annie.davies@ucdenver.edu. Website: http://www.ucdenver.edu/academics/colleges/SPA/Academics/programs/PublicAffairsAdmin/Pages/index.aspx.

University of Dayton, Department of Mechanical and Aerospace Engineering, Dayton, OH 45469-1300. Offers aerospace engineering (MSAE, DE, PhD); mechanical engineering (MSME, DE, PhD); renewable and clean energy (MS). Part-time programs available. *Faculty:* 14 full-time (2 women), 9 part-time/adjunct (0 women). *Students:* 146 full-time (23 women), 30 part-time (5 women); includes 8 minority (3 Black or African American, non-Hispanic/Latino; 1 Asian, non-Hispanic/Latino; 4 Hispanic/Latino), 104 international. Average age 27. 299 applicants, 51% accepted, 63 enrolled. In 2012, 67 master's, 6 doctorates awarded. Terminal master's awarded for partial completion of doctoral program. *Degree requirements:* For master's, thesis optional; for doctorate, variable foreign language requirement, thesis/dissertation, departmental qualifying exam. *Entrance requirements:* Additional exam requirements/recommendations for international students: Required—TOEFL (minimum score 550 paper-based; 80 iBT), IELTS (minimum score 6.5). *Application deadline:* For fall admission, 8/1 priority date for domestic students, 5/1 for international students; for winter admission, 9/1 for international students; for spring admission, 11/1 for international students. Applications are processed on a rolling basis. Application fee: $0 ($50 for international students). Electronic applications accepted. *Expenses: Tuition:* Part-time $708 per credit hour. *Required fees:* $25 per semester. Tuition and fees vary according to course level, course load, degree level and program. *Financial support:* In 2012–13, 31 research assistantships with full tuition reimbursements (averaging $12,000 per year), 2 teaching assistantships with full tuition reimbursements (averaging $8,800 per year) were awarded; institutionally sponsored loans, health care benefits, and unspecified assistantships also available. Financial award applicants required to submit FAFSA. *Faculty research:* Jet engine combustion, surface coating friction and wear, aircraft thermal management, aerospace fuels, energy efficient buildings, energy efficient manufacturing, renewable energy. *Total annual research expenditures:* $1.2 million. *Unit head:* Dr. Kelly Kissock, Chair, 937-229-2999, Fax: 937-229-4766, E-mail: jkissock1@udayton.edu. *Application contact:* Dr. Vinod Jain, Graduate Program Director, 937-229-2992, Fax: 937-229-4766, E-mail: vjain1@udayton.edu. Website: http://www.udayton.edu/engineering/mechanical_and_aerospace/.

University of Delaware, Center for Energy and Environmental Policy, Newark, DE 19716. Offers energy and environmental policy (MA, MEEP, PhD); urban affairs and public policy (PhD), including technology, environment, and society. *Degree requirements:* For master's, analytical paper or thesis; for doctorate, comprehensive exam, thesis/dissertation. *Entrance requirements:* For master's, GRE General Test, minimum GPA of 3.0; for doctorate, GRE General Test, minimum GPA of 3.5. Additional exam requirements/recommendations for international students: Required—TOEFL. Electronic applications accepted. *Faculty research:* Sustainable development, renewable energy, climate change, environmental policy, environmental justice, disaster policy.

University of Denver, University College, Denver, CO 80208. Offers arts and culture (MLS, Certificate), including art, literature, and culture, arts development and program management (Certificate), creative writing; environmental policy and management (MAS, Certificate), including energy and sustainability (Certificate), environmental assessment of nuclear power (Certificate), environmental health and safety (Certificate), environmental management, natural resource management (Certificate); geographic information systems (MAS, Certificate); global affairs (MLS, Certificate), including translation studies, world history and culture; healthcare leadership (MPH, Certificate), including healthcare policy, law, and ethics, medical and healthcare information technologies, strategic management of healthcare; information and communications technology (MCIS, Certificate), including database design and administration (Certificate), geographic information systems (MCIS), information security systems security (Certificate), information systems security (MCIS), project management (MCIS, MPS, Certificate), software design and administration (Certificate), software design and programming (MCIS), technology management, telecommunications technology (MCIS), Web design and development; leadership and organizations (MPS, Certificate), including human capital in organizations, philanthropic leadership, project management (MCIS, MPS, Certificate), strategic innovation and change; organizational and professional communication (MPS, Certificate), including alternative dispute resolution, organizational communication, organizational development and training, public relations and marketing; security management (MAS, Certificate), including emergency planning and response, information security (MAS), organizational security; strategic human resource management (MPS, Certificate), including global human resources (MPS), human resource management and development (MPS). Part-time and evening/weekend programs available. Postbaccalaureate distance learning degree programs offered (no on-campus study). *Faculty:* 187 part-time/adjunct (75 women). *Students:* 43 full-time (18 women), 1,125 part-time (670 women); includes 226 minority (78 Black or African American, non-Hispanic/Latino; 3 American Indian or Alaska Native, non-Hispanic/Latino; 31 Asian, non-Hispanic/Latino; 88 Hispanic/Latino; 3 Native Hawaiian or other Pacific Islander, non-Hispanic/Latino; 23 Two or more races, non-Hispanic/Latino), 61 international. Average age 36. 905 applicants, 93% accepted, 358 enrolled. In 2012, 491 master's, 132 other advanced degrees awarded. *Degree requirements:* For master's, capstone project. *Entrance requirements:* For master's, two letters of recommendation, personal statement, resume. Additional exam requirements/recommendations for international students: Required—TOEFL (minimum score 550 paper-based; 80 iBT). *Application deadline:* For fall admission, 7/20 priority date for domestic students, 6/8 for international students; for winter admission, 10/26 priority date for domestic students, 9/14 for international students; for spring admission, 2/1 priority date for domestic students, 12/14 for international students. Applications are processed on a rolling basis. Application fee: $75. Electronic applications accepted. *Expenses:* Contact institution. *Financial support:* In 2012–13, 14 students received support. Applicants required to submit FAFSA. *Unit head:* Dr. Michael McGuire, Interim Dean, 303-871-2291, Fax: 303-871-4047, E-mail: mmcguire@du.edu. *Application contact:* Information Contact, 303-871-2291, Fax: 303-871-4047, E-mail: ucolinfo@du.edu. Website: http://www.universitycollege.du.edu/.

The University of Findlay, Office of Graduate Admissions, College of Sciences, Master of Science Program in Environmental, Safety and Health Management, Findlay, OH 45840-3653. Offers MSEM. Part-time and evening/weekend programs available. Postbaccalaureate distance learning degree programs offered (no on-campus study). *Faculty:* 11 full-time (2 women), 3 part-time/adjunct (1 woman). *Students:* 4 full-time (2 women), 68 part-time (23 women); includes 6 minority (2 Black or African American, non-Hispanic/Latino; 3 Asian, non-Hispanic/Latino; 1 Hispanic/Latino), 23 international. Average age 35. 22 applicants, 82% accepted, 15 enrolled. In 2012, 33 master's awarded. *Degree requirements:* For master's, thesis, cumulative project. *Entrance requirements:* For master's, GRE, bachelor's degree from accredited institution, minimum undergraduate GPA of 3.0 in last 64 hours of course work. Additional exam requirements/recommendations for international students: Required—TOEFL (minimum score 550 paper-based; 80 iBT). *Application deadline:* Applications are processed on a rolling basis. Application fee: $25. Electronic applications accepted. *Expenses: Tuition:* Full-time $15,000; part-time $750 per semester hour. *Required fees:* $201.50 per semester. Tuition and fees vary according to degree level and program. *Financial support:* In 2012–13, 1 research assistantship with full and partial tuition reimbursement (averaging $4,200 per year), 1 teaching assistantship with full and partial tuition reimbursement (averaging $3,600 per year) were awarded; career-related internships or fieldwork, Federal Work-Study, health care benefits, and unspecified assistantships also available. Financial award application deadline: 4/1; financial award applicants required to submit FAFSA. *Unit head:* Dr. William Doyle, Director, 419-434-5747, Fax: 419-434-4822. *Application contact:* Heather Riffle, Assistant Director, Graduate and Professional Studies, 419-434-4640, Fax: 419-434-5517, E-mail: riffle@findlay.edu. Website: http://www.findlay.edu.

University of Guelph, Graduate Studies, Ontario Agricultural College, Department of Land Resource Science, Guelph, ON N1G 2W1, Canada. Offers atmospheric science (M Sc, PhD); environmental and agricultural earth sciences (M Sc, PhD); land resources management (M Sc, PhD); soil science (M Sc, PhD). Part-time programs available. *Degree requirements:* For master's, thesis (for some programs), research project (non-thesis track); for doctorate, comprehensive exam, thesis/dissertation. *Entrance requirements:* For master's, minimum B- average during previous 2 years of course work; for doctorate, minimum B average during previous 2 years of course work. Additional exam requirements/recommendations for international students: Required—TOEFL (minimum score 550 paper-based). Electronic applications accepted. *Faculty research:* Soil science, environmental earth science, land resource management.

University of Hawaii at Manoa, Graduate Division, College of Social Sciences, Department of Urban and Regional Planning, Honolulu, HI 96822. Offers community planning and social policy (MURP); disaster preparedness and emergency management (Graduate Certificate); environmental planning and management (MURP); land use and infrastructure planning (MURP); urban and regional planning (PhD, Graduate Certificate); urban and regional planning in Asia and Pacific (MURP). *Accreditation:* ACSP. Part-time programs available. *Entrance requirements:* For master's, GRE General Test, minimum GPA of 3.0; for doctorate, GRE General Test. Additional exam requirements/recommendations for international students: Required—TOEFL (minimum score 500 paper-based; 61 iBT), IELTS (minimum score 5).

University of Hawaii at Manoa, Graduate Division, College of Tropical Agriculture and Human Resources, Department of Natural Resources and Environmental Management, Honolulu, HI 96822. Offers MS, PhD. Part-time programs available. Terminal master's awarded for partial completion of doctoral program. *Degree requirements:* For master's, thesis optional; for doctorate, comprehensive exam, thesis/dissertation. *Entrance requirements:* For master's and doctorate, GRE General Test, minimum GPA of 3.0 in last 4 semesters of course work. Additional exam requirements/recommendations for international students: Required—TOEFL (minimum score 600 paper-based; 100 iBT), IELTS (minimum score 7). *Faculty research:* Bioeconomics, natural resource management.

University of Houston–Clear Lake, School of Business, Program in Administrative Science, Houston, TX 77058-1098. Offers environmental management (MS); human resource management (MA). Part-time and evening/weekend programs available. *Degree requirements:* For master's, thesis optional. *Entrance requirements:* For master's, GMAT. Additional exam requirements/recommendations for international students: Required—TOEFL (minimum score 550 paper-based). Electronic applications accepted.

University of Idaho, College of Graduate Studies, College of Agricultural and Life Sciences, Department of Agricultural Economics and Rural Sociology, Moscow, ID 83844-2334. Offers agricultural economics (MS); applied economics (MS), including agribusiness, agricultural economics, applied economics, natural resources. *Faculty:* 9 full-time. *Students:* 12 full-time, 2 part-time. Average age 25. In 2012, 7 master's awarded. *Entrance requirements:* For master's, minimum GPA of 2.8. *Application deadline:* For fall admission, 8/1 for domestic students; for spring admission, 12/15 for domestic students. Applications are processed on a rolling basis. Application fee: $60. Electronic applications accepted. *Expenses:* Tuition, state resident: full-time $4230; part-time $252 per credit hour. Tuition, nonresident: full-time $17,018; part-time $891 per credit hour. *Required fees:* $2932; $107 per credit hour. *Financial support:* Research assistantships and teaching assistantships available. Financial award applicants required to submit FAFSA. *Faculty research:* Crops: potatoes, blue grass; livestock: beef, dairy; rural and community development; natural resources and the environment; farm and ranch management. *Unit head:* Dr. Cathy Roheim, Department Head, 208-885-6262, Fax: 208-885-5759, E-mail: cdarby@uidaho.edu. *Application contact:* Erick Larson, Director of Graduate Admissions, 208-885-4723, E-mail: gadms@uidaho.edu. Website: http://www.cals.uidaho.edu/aers/.

University of Illinois at Springfield, Graduate Programs, College of Public Affairs and Administration, Program in Environmental Studies, Springfield, IL 62703-5407. Offers environmental science (MS); environmental studies (MA). Part-time and evening/weekend programs available. Postbaccalaureate distance learning degree programs offered (no on-campus study). *Faculty:* 6 full-time (1 woman). *Students:* 24 full-time (15 women), 70 part-time (46 women); includes 11 minority (3 Black or African American, non-Hispanic/Latino; 3 Asian, non-Hispanic/Latino; 5 Hispanic/Latino), 3 international. Average age 34. 63 applicants, 62% accepted, 32 enrolled. In 2012, 30 master's awarded. *Degree requirements:* For master's, thesis or project. *Entrance requirements:* For master's, minimum undergraduate GPA of 3.0, 2 letters of recommendation, goals essay. Additional exam requirements/recommendations for international students: Required—TOEFL (minimum score 500 paper-based; 61 iBT). *Application deadline:* Applications are processed on a rolling basis. Application fee: $60 ($75 for international students). Electronic applications accepted. *Expenses:* Tuition, state resident: full-time $7314. Tuition, nonresident: full-time $15,618. *Required fees:* $2695. *Financial support:* In 2012–13, fellowships with full tuition reimbursements (averaging $9,900 per year), research assistantships with full tuition reimbursements (averaging $9,000 per year), teaching assistantships with full tuition reimbursements (averaging $9,000 per year) were awarded; career-related internships or fieldwork, Federal Work-Study, scholarships/grants, health care benefits, and unspecified assistantships also available. Support available to part-time students. Financial award application deadline: 11/15; financial award applicants required to submit FAFSA. *Unit head:* Dr. Dennis Ruez, Program Administrator, 217-206-8424, E-mail: druez2@uis.edu. *Application contact:* Dr. Lynn Pardie, Office of Graduate Studies, 800-252-8533, Fax: 217-206-7623, E-mail: lpard1@uis.edu. Website: http://www.uis.edu/environmentalstudies/.

University of Maine, Graduate School, College of Liberal Arts and Sciences, Department of History, Orono, ME 04469. Offers American studies (MA, PhD); Asian studies (MA); Canadian studies (MA, PhD); environmental studies (MA); European (MA); technology (MA). *Faculty:* 17 full-time (2 women), 7 part-time/adjunct (1 woman). *Students:* 43 full-time (17 women), 12 part-time (4 women); includes 1 minority (Hispanic/Latino), 1 international. Average age 38. 24 applicants, 71% accepted, 12 enrolled. In 2012, 3 master's awarded. Terminal master's awarded for partial completion of doctoral program. *Degree requirements:* For master's, variable foreign language requirement, thesis optional; for doctorate, one foreign language, comprehensive exam, thesis/dissertation. *Entrance requirements:* For master's and doctorate, GRE General Test. Additional exam requirements/recommendations for international students: Required—TOEFL. *Application deadline:* For fall admission, 2/1 priority date for domestic students. Applications are processed on a rolling basis. Application fee: $65. Electronic applications accepted. *Financial support:* In 2012–13, 9 teaching assistantships with tuition reimbursements (averaging $12,790 per year) were awarded; career-related internships or fieldwork, Federal Work-Study, and tuition waivers (full and partial) also available. Support available to part-time students. Financial award application deadline: 3/1. *Faculty research:* Canadian labor and working classes; American social, cultural, and urban history. *Unit head:* Dr. Nathan Godfried, Chair, 207-581-1923, Fax: 207-581-1817. *Application contact:* Scott G. Delcourt, Associate Dean of the Graduate School, 207-581-3291, Fax: 207-581-3232, E-mail: graduate@maine.edu. Website: http://www.umaine.edu/history/.

The University of Manchester, School of Environment and Development, Manchester, United Kingdom. Offers architecture (M Phil, PhD); development policy and management (M Phil, PhD); human geography (M Phil, PhD); physical geography (M Phil, PhD); planning and landscape (M Phil, PhD).

University of Maryland, Baltimore County, Graduate School, College of Arts, Humanities and Social Sciences, Department of Geography and Environmental Systems, Program in Geography and Environmental Systems, Baltimore, MD 21250. Offers MS, PhD. *Faculty:* 10 full-time (3 women), 6 part-time/adjunct (1 woman). *Students:* 21 full-time (12 women), 5 part-time (1 woman); includes 1 minority (Black or African American, non-Hispanic/Latino), 1 international. Average age 29. 27 applicants, 37% accepted, 7 enrolled. In 2012, 3 master's, 1 doctorate awarded. Terminal master's awarded for partial completion of doctoral program. *Degree requirements:* For master's, thesis optional, annual faculty evaluation, research paper; for doctorate, comprehensive exam, thesis/dissertation, annual faculty evaluation, qualifying exams, proposal and dissertation defense. *Entrance requirements:* For master's and doctorate, GRE, minimum GPA of 3.0 overall, 3.3 in major. Additional exam requirements/recommendations for international students: Required—TOEFL (minimum score 550 paper-based; 80 iBT). *Application deadline:* For fall admission, 2/1 for domestic students, 1/1 for international students. Application fee: $50. Electronic applications accepted. *Financial support:* In 2012–13, 18 students received support, including 5 research assistantships with full tuition reimbursements available (averaging $18,392 per year), 13 teaching assistantships with full tuition reimbursements available (averaging $18,392 per year); fellowships, scholarships/grants, traineeships, health care benefits, and unspecified assistantships also available. Financial award application deadline: 2/1. *Faculty research:* Watershed processes, climate and weather systems; ecology and biogeography; landscape ecology and land-use change; human geography, urban sustainability and environmental health; environmental policy; geographic information science and remote sensing. *Unit head:* Dr. Christopher M. Swan, Graduate Program Director, 410-455-2002, E-mail: gpd.ges@umbc.edu. *Application contact:* Kathryn Nee, Coordinator of Domestic Admissions, 410-455-2944, E-mail: nee@umbc.edu. Website: http://ges.umbc.edu/graduate/.

University of Maryland University College, Graduate School of Management and Technology, Program in Environmental Management, Adelphi, MD 20783. Offers MS, Certificate. Offered evenings and weekends only. Part-time programs available. Postbaccalaureate distance learning degree programs offered (no on-campus study). *Students:* 10 full-time (6 women), 326 part-time (168 women); includes 103 minority (70 Black or African American, non-Hispanic/Latino; 2 American Indian or Alaska Native, non-Hispanic/Latino; 11 Asian, non-Hispanic/Latino; 18 Hispanic/Latino; 1 Native Hawaiian or other Pacific Islander, non-

Hispanic/Latino; 1 Two or more races, non-Hispanic/Latino), 6 international. Average age 35. 70 applicants, 100% accepted, 48 enrolled. In 2012, 115 master's, 11 other advanced degrees awarded. *Degree requirements:* For master's, thesis or alternative, capstone course. *Application deadline:* Applications are processed on a rolling basis. Application fee: $50. Electronic applications accepted. *Financial support:* Federal Work-Study and scholarships/ grants available. Support available to part-time students. Financial award application deadline: 6/1; financial award applicants required to submit FAFSA. *Unit head:* Rana Khan, Chair, 240-684-2400, Fax: 240-684-2401, E-mail: rana.khan@umuc.edu. *Application contact:* Coordinator, Graduate Admissions, 800-888-8682, Fax: 240-684-2151, E-mail: newgrad@umuc.edu. Website: http://www.umuc.edu/grad/envm.shtml.

University of Massachusetts Amherst, Graduate School, College of Natural Sciences, Department of Environmental Conservation, Amherst, MA 01003. Offers building systems (MS, PhD); environmental policy and human dimensions (MS, PhD); forest resources (MS, PhD); sustainability science (MS); water, wetlands and watersheds (MS, PhD); wildlife and fisheries conservation (MS, PhD). Part-time programs available. *Faculty:* 62 full-time (11 women). *Students:* 52 full-time (18 women), 40 part-time (19 women); includes 2 minority (1 Black or African American, non-Hispanic/Latino; 1 Two or more races, non-Hispanic/ Latino), 17 international. Average age 33. 73 applicants, 40% accepted, 10 enrolled. In 2012, 16 master's, 3 doctorates awarded. Terminal master's awarded for partial completion of doctoral program. *Degree requirements:* For master's, thesis or alternative; for doctorate, comprehensive exam, thesis/dissertation. *Entrance requirements:* For master's and doctorate, GRE General Test. Additional exam requirements/recommendations for international students: Required—TOEFL (minimum score 550 paper-based; 80 iBT), IELTS (minimum score 6.5). *Application deadline:* For fall admission, 2/1 for domestic and international students; for spring admission, 10/1 for domestic and international students. Applications are processed on a rolling basis. Application fee: $75. Electronic applications accepted. *Expenses:* Tuition, state resident: full-time $1980; part-time $110 per credit. Tuition, nonresident: full-time $13,314; part-time $414 per credit. *Required fees:* $10,338; $3594 per semester. One-time fee: $357. *Financial support:* Fellowships with full and partial tuition reimbursements, research assistantships with full and partial tuition reimbursements, teaching assistantships with full and partial tuition reimbursements, career-related internships or fieldwork, Federal Work-Study, scholarships/grants, traineeships, health care benefits, tuition waivers (full and partial), and unspecified assistantships available. Support available to part-time students. Financial award application deadline: 2/1. *Unit head:* Dr. Kevin McGarigal, Graduate Program Director, 413-545-2257, Fax: 413-545-4358. *Application contact:* Lindsay DeSantis, Supervisor of Admissions, 413-546-0721, Fax: 413-577-0100, E-mail: gradadm@grad.umass.edu. Website: http://eco.umass.edu/.

University of Massachusetts Dartmouth, Graduate School, School of Education, Public Policy, and Civic Engagement, Department of Public Policy, North Dartmouth, MA 02747-2300. Offers educational policy (Postbaccalaureate Certificate); environmental policy (Postbaccalaureate Certificate); public policy (MPP). Part-time programs available. Postbaccalaureate distance learning degree programs offered (minimal on-campus study). *Faculty:* 4 full-time (1 woman). *Students:* 15 full-time (7 women), 46 part-time (29 women); includes 9 minority (1 Black or African American, non-Hispanic/Latino; 1 American Indian or Alaska Native, non-Hispanic/Latino; 2 Asian, non-Hispanic/Latino; 3 Hispanic/Latino; 2 Two or more races, non-Hispanic/Latino), 1 international. Average age 34. 65 applicants, 82% accepted, 33 enrolled. In 2012, 10 master's, 8 other advanced degrees awarded. *Entrance requirements:* For master's, GRE or GMAT, statement of purpose (minimum of 300 words), resume, 2 letters of recommendation, official transcripts; for Postbaccalaureate Certificate, GRE or GMAT, statement of purpose (minimum of 300 words), resume, official transcripts. Additional exam requirements/recommendations for international students: Required—TOEFL (minimum score 600 paper-based). *Application deadline:* For fall admission, 3/1 priority date for domestic students, 2/1 for international students; for spring admission, 11/15 priority date for domestic students, 10/15 for international students. Applications are processed on a rolling basis. Application fee: $60. Electronic applications accepted. *Expenses:* Tuition, state resident: part-time $86.29 per credit. Tuition, nonresident: part-time $337.46 per credit. *Required fees:* $631.03 per credit. Tuition and fees vary according to course load and reciprocity agreements. *Financial support:* In 2012–13, 1 teaching assistantship with full tuition reimbursement (averaging $6,000 per year) was awarded; Federal Work-Study and unspecified assistantships also available. Support available to part-time students. Financial award application deadline: 3/1. *Faculty research:* Demographic analysis, legal and regulatory framework. *Total annual research expenditures:* $333,000. *Unit head:* Michael Goodman, Graduate Program Director, 508-990-9660, Fax: 508-999-8374, E-mail: mgoodman@umassd.edu. *Application contact:* Steven Briggs, Director of Marketing and Recruitment, 508-999-8604, Fax: 508-999-8183, E-mail: graduate@umassd.edu. Website: http://www.umassd.edu/seppce/departments/publicpolicy/.

University of Massachusetts Lowell, School of Health and Environment, Department of Work Environment, Lowell, MA 01854-2881. Offers cleaner production and pollution prevention (MS, Sc D); environmental risk assessment (Certificate); epidemiology (MS, Sc D); ergonomics and safety (MS, Sc D); identification and control of ergonomic hazards (Certificate); job stress and healthy job redesign (Certificate); occupational and environmental hygiene (MS, Sc D); radiological health physics and general work environment protection (Certificate); work environment policy (MS, Sc D). *Accreditation:* ABET (one or more programs are accredited). Part-time programs available. Terminal master's awarded for partial completion of doctoral program. *Degree requirements:* For master's, thesis optional; for doctorate, thesis/dissertation. *Entrance requirements:* For master's and doctorate, GRE General Test. Additional exam requirements/recommendations for international students: Required—TOEFL.

University of Miami, Graduate School, School of Business Administration, Department of Economics, Coral Gables, FL 33124. Offers economic development (MA, PhD); environmental economics (PhD); human resource economics (MA, PhD); international economics (MA, PhD); macroeconomics (PhD). Students admitted every two years in the fall semester. Terminal master's awarded for partial completion of doctoral program. *Degree requirements:* For master's, comprehensive exam; for doctorate, comprehensive exam, thesis/ dissertation. *Entrance requirements:* For master's and doctorate, GRE General Test, minimum GPA of 3.0. Additional exam requirements/recommendations for international students: Required—TOEFL (minimum score 550 paper-based). *Faculty research:* International economics/trade, applied microeconomics, development.

University of Michigan, School of Natural Resources and Environment, Program in Natural Resources and Environment, Ann Arbor, MI 48109-1041. Offers aquatic sciences: research and management (MS), behavior, education and communication (MS); conservation biology (MS); conservation ecology (MS); environmental informatics (MS); environmental justice (MS); environmental policy and planning (MS); natural resources and environment (PhD); sustainable systems (MS); terrestrial ecosystems (MS); MS/JD; MS/MBA; MUP/MS. *Faculty:* 45 full-time, 23 part-time/adjunct. *Students:* 399 full-time (221 women); includes 65 minority (4 Black or African American, non-Hispanic/Latino; 29 Asian, non-Hispanic/Latino; 23 Hispanic/Latino; 9 Two or more races, non-Hispanic/Latino), 68 international. Average age 27. 635 applicants. In 2012, 138 master's, 9 doctorates awarded. Terminal master's awarded for partial completion of doctoral program. *Degree requirements:* For master's, practicum or group project; for doctorate, comprehensive exam, thesis/dissertation, oral defense of dissertation, preliminary exam. *Entrance requirements:* For master's, GRE General Test; for doctorate, GRE General Test, master's degree. Additional exam requirements/ recommendations for international students: Required—TOEFL (minimum score 560 paper-based; 84 iBT). *Application deadline:* For fall admission, 1/5 priority date for domestic students, 1/5 for international students. Applications are processed on a rolling basis. Application fee: $65 ($75 for international students). Electronic applications accepted. *Financial support:* Fellowships with tuition reimbursements, research assistantships with tuition reimbursements, teaching assistantships with tuition reimbursements, career-related internships or fieldwork, Federal Work-Study, institutionally sponsored loans, scholarships/ grants, health care benefits, and unspecified assistantships available. Support available to part-time students. Financial award application deadline: 1/5; financial award applicants required to submit FAFSA. *Faculty research:* Stream ecology and fish biology, plant-insect interactions, environmental education, resource control and reproductive success, remote sensing, conservation ecology, sustainable systems. *Unit head:* Dr. Marie Lynn Miranda, Dean, 734-764-2550, Fax: 734-763-8965, E-mail: mlmirand@umich.edu. *Application contact:* Sondra R. Auerbach, Director of Academic Services, 734-764-6453, Fax: 734-936-2195, E-mail: snre.admissions@umich.edu. Website: http://www.snre.umich.edu/.

University of Minnesota, Twin Cities Campus, Graduate School, Hubert H. Humphrey School of Public Affairs, Program in Science, Technology, and Environmental Policy, Minneapolis, MN 55455. Offers MS, JD/MS. Part-time programs available. *Students:* 5 full-time (4 women). Average age 27. 20 applicants, 65% accepted, 5 enrolled. In 2012, 11 master's awarded. *Degree requirements:* For master's, thesis. *Entrance requirements:* For master's, GRE General Test, undergraduate training in the biological or physical sciences or engineering, minimum undergraduate GPA of 3.0. Additional exam requirements/ recommendations for international students: Required—TOEFL (minimum score 600 paper-based; 100 iBT), IELTS (minimum score 7). *Application deadline:* For fall admission, 4/1 for domestic and international students. Applications are processed on a rolling basis. Application fee: $75 ($95 for international students). Electronic applications accepted. *Financial support:* In 2012–13, 6 students received support, including fellowships with full and partial tuition reimbursements available (averaging $8,500 per year), research assistantships with full and partial tuition reimbursements available (averaging $5,270 per year), teaching assistantships with full and partial tuition reimbursements available (averaging $5,270 per year); career-related internships or fieldwork, Federal Work-Study, scholarships/grants, health care benefits, tuition waivers (full and partial), and unspecified assistantships also available. Financial award application deadline: 1/ 15. *Faculty research:* Economics, history, philosophy, and politics of science and technology; organization and management of science and technology. *Unit head:* Laura Bloomberg, Associate Dean, 612-625-0608, Fax: 612-626-0002, E-mail: bloom004@umn.edu. *Application contact:* Amy Luitjens, Director of Recruiting and Admissions, 612-626-7229, Fax: 612-626-0002, E-mail: luitjens@umn.edu.

The University of Montana, Graduate School, College of Arts and Sciences, Program in Environmental Studies (EVST), Missoula, MT 59812-0002. Offers MS, JD/MS. Part-time programs available. *Faculty:* 6 full-time (3 women), 2 part-time/ adjunct (0 women). *Students:* 30 full-time (16 women), 23 part-time (20 women); includes 3 minority (2 American Indian or Alaska Native, non-Hispanic/Latino; 1 Hispanic/Latino). Average age 30. 64 applicants, 67% accepted, 21 enrolled. In 2012, 22 master's awarded. *Degree requirements:* For master's, thesis, portfolio or professional paper. *Entrance requirements:* For master's, GRE General Test (minimum score: 500 verbal on old scoring; 153 verbal new scoring). Additional exam requirements/recommendations for international students: Required—TOEFL (minimum score 580 paper-based; 92 iBT). *Application deadline:* For fall admission, 2/1 priority date for domestic students, 2/1 for international students. Application fee: $51. *Financial support:* In 2012–13, 25 students received support, including 4 fellowships with partial tuition reimbursements available (averaging $4,500 per year), 1 research assistantship with full tuition reimbursement available (averaging $4,800 per year), 6 teaching assistantships with full tuition reimbursements available (averaging $9,000 per year). Financial award application deadline: 4/15. *Faculty research:* Pollution ecology, sustainable agriculture, environmental writing, environmental policy, environmental justice, environmental history, habitat-land management. *Total annual research expenditures:* $145,137. *Unit head:* Prof. Phil Condon, Director, 406-243-2904, Fax: 406-243-6090, E-mail: phil.condon@mso.umt.edu. *Application contact:* Karen Hurd, Administrative Assistant, 406-243-6273, Fax: 406-243-6090, E-mail: karen.hurd@mso.umt.edu. Website: http://www.cas.umt.edu/evst.

University of Nevada, Reno, Graduate School, College of Science, Mackay School of Earth Sciences and Engineering, Department of Geography, Program in Land Use Planning, Reno, NV 89557. Offers MS. *Degree requirements:* For master's, thesis. *Entrance requirements:* For master's, GRE General Test, minimum GPA of 3.0. Additional exam requirements/recommendations for international students: Required—TOEFL (minimum score 500 paper-based; 61 iBT), IELTS (minimum score 6). Electronic applications accepted. *Faculty research:* Contemporary planning, environmental planning.

University of New Brunswick Fredericton, School of Graduate Studies, Faculty of Engineering, Department of Chemical Engineering, Fredericton, NB E3B 5A3, Canada. Offers chemical engineering (M Eng, M Sc E, PhD); environmental studies (M Eng). Part-time programs available. *Faculty:* 10 full-time (1 woman). *Students:* 63 full-time (29 women), 6 part-time (1 woman). In 2012, 11 master's, 3 doctorates awarded. *Degree requirements:* For master's, thesis; for doctorate, comprehensive exam, thesis/dissertation, qualifying exam. *Entrance requirements:* For master's and doctorate, minimum GPA of 3.0. Additional exam requirements/recommendations for international students: Required—TOEFL (minimum score 580 paper-based), TWE (minimum score 5), Michigan English Language Assessment Battery (minimum score 85) or CanTest (minimum score 4.5). *Application deadline:* For fall admission, 3/1 for domestic students. Applications are processed on a rolling basis. Application fee: $50 Canadian dollars. Electronic applications accepted. Tuition and fees charges are reported in Canadian dollars. *Expenses: Tuition, area resident:* Full-time $3956 Canadian dollars. *Required fees:* $579.50 Canadian dollars; $55 Canadian dollars per semester. *Financial support:* In 2012–13, 65 fellowships, 65 research assistantships with tuition reimbursements, 47 teaching assistantships were awarded. *Faculty research:* Processing and characterizing nanoengineered composite materials based on carbon nanotubes, enhanced oil recovery processes and oil sweep strategies for conventional and heavy oils, pulp and paper, waste-water treatment, chemistry and corrosion of high and lower temperature water systems; adsorption; aquaculture systems; bioprocessing and biomass refining; nanotechnologies; nuclear; oil and gas; polymer and recirculation. *Unit head:* Dr. Kecheng Li, Director of Graduate Studies, 506-451-6861, Fax: 506-453-3591, E-mail: kecheng@unb.ca. *Application contact:* Sylvia Demerson, Graduate Secretary, 506-453-4520, Fax: 506-453-3591, E-mail: sdemerso@unb.ca. Website: http://go.unb.ca/gradprograms.

University of New Brunswick Fredericton, School of Graduate Studies, Faculty of Engineering, Department of Civil Engineering, Fredericton, NB E3B 5A3, Canada. Offers construction engineering and management (M Eng, M Sc E, PhD); environmental engineering (M Eng, M Sc E, PhD); environmental studies (M Eng); geotechnical engineering (M Eng, M Sc E, PhD); groundwater/hydrology (M Eng, M Sc E, PhD); materials (M Eng, M Sc E, PhD); pavements (M Eng, M Sc E, PhD); structures (M Eng, M Sc E, PhD); transportation (M Eng, M Sc E, PhD). Part-time programs available. *Faculty:* 18 full-time (1 woman). *Students:* 22 full-time (6 women), 17 part-time (4 women). In 2012, 13 master's, 2 doctorates awarded. *Degree requirements:* For master's, thesis, proposal; for doctorate, comprehensive exam, thesis/dissertation, qualifying exam; proposal; 27 credit hours of courses. *Entrance requirements:* For master's, minimum GPA of 3.0; B Sc E in civil engineering or related engineering degree; for doctorate, minimum GPA of 3.0; graduate degree in engineering or applied science. Additional exam requirements/recommendations for international students: Required—IELTS (minimum score 7.5), TWE (minimum score 4), Michigan English Language Assessment Battery (minimum score 85), Can Test (minimum score 4.75). *Application deadline:* For fall admission, 5/1 for domestic students; for winter admission, 11/1 for domestic students. Applications are processed on a rolling basis. Application fee: $50 Canadian dollars. Electronic applications accepted. Tuition and fees charges are reported in Canadian dollars. *Expenses: Tuition, area resident:* Full-time $3956 Canadian dollars. *Required fees:* $579.50 Canadian dollars; $55 Canadian dollars per semester. *Financial support:* In 2012–13, 35 fellowships, 48 research assistantships, 35 teaching assistantships were awarded; career-related internships or fieldwork and scholarships/grants also available. *Faculty research:* Construction engineering and management; engineering materials and infrastructure renewal; highway and pavement research; structures and solid mechanics; geotechnical and geoenvironmental engineering; structure interaction; transportation and planning; environment, solid waste management; structural engineering; water and environmental engineering. *Unit head:* Dr. Peter Bischoff, Director of Graduate Studies, 506-453-5103, Fax: 506-453-3568, E-mail: bischoff@unb.ca. *Application contact:* Joyce Moore, Graduate Secretary, 506-452-6127, Fax: 506-453-3568, E-mail: joycem@unb.ca. Website: http://go.unb.ca/gradprograms.

University of New Brunswick Fredericton, School of Graduate Studies, Faculty of Forestry and Environmental Management, Fredericton, NB E3B 5A3, Canada. Offers ecological foundations of forest management (PhD); environmental management (MEM); forest engineering (M Sc FE, MFE); forest products marketing (MBA); forest resources (M Sc F, MF, PhD). Part-time programs available. *Faculty:* 27 full-time (2 women). *Students:* 70 full-time (23 women), 15 part-time (10 women). In 2012, 22 master's, 6 doctorates awarded. *Degree requirements:* For master's, thesis; for doctorate, thesis/dissertation. *Entrance requirements:* For master's and doctorate, minimum GPA of 3.0. Additional exam requirements/recommendations for international students: Required—TOEFL (minimum score 550 paper-based; 80 iBT), IELTS (minimum score 7), TWE (minimum score 4). *Application deadline:* For fall admission, 3/1 for domestic students. Applications are processed on a rolling basis. Application fee: $50 Canadian dollars. Electronic applications accepted. Tuition and fees charges are reported in Canadian dollars. *Expenses: Tuition, area resident:* Full-time $3956 Canadian dollars. *Required fees:* $579.50 Canadian dollars; $55 Canadian dollars per semester. *Financial support:* In 2012–13, 98 research assistantships, 36 teaching assistantships were awarded; fellowships also available. *Faculty research:* Forest machines, soils, and ecosystems; integrated forest management; forest meteorology; wood engineering; stream ecosystems dynamics; forest and natural resources policy; forest operations planning; wood technology and mechanics; forest road construction and engineering; forest, wildlife, insect, bird, and fire ecology; remote sensing; insect impacts; Silviculture; LiDAR analytics; integrated pest management; forest tree genetics; genetic resource conservation and sustainable management. *Unit head:* Dr. Dan Quiring, Director of Graduate Studies, 506-453-4922, Fax: 506-453-3538, E-mail: quiring@unb.ca. *Application contact:* Faith Sharpe, Graduate Secretary, 506-458-7520, Fax: 506-453-3538, E-mail: fsharpe@unb.ca. Website: http://go.unb.ca/gradprograms.

University of New Hampshire, Graduate School, College of Life Sciences and Agriculture, Department of Natural Resources, Durham, NH 03824. Offers environmental conservation (MS); forestry (MS); integrated coastal ecosystem science, policy, management (MS); natural resources (MS); water resources (MS); wildlife (MS). Part-time programs available. *Faculty:* 40 full-time. *Students:* 32 full-time (18 women), 29 part-time (16 women); includes 3 minority (all Hispanic/Latino), 3 international. Average age 28. 63 applicants, 43% accepted, 22 enrolled. In 2012, 14 master's awarded. *Degree requirements:* For master's, thesis or alternative. *Entrance requirements:* For master's, GRE General Test. Additional exam requirements/recommendations for international students: Required—TOEFL (minimum score 550 paper-based; 80 iBT). *Application deadline:* For fall admission, 6/1 for domestic students, 4/1 for international students; for spring admission, 12/1 for domestic students. Applications are processed on a rolling basis. Application fee: $65. Electronic applications accepted. *Expenses:* Tuition, state resident: full-time $13,500; part-time $750 per credit. Tuition, nonresident: full-time $25,940; part-time $1089 per credit. *Required fees:* $1699; $424.75 per semester. *Financial support:* In 2012–13, 35 students received support, including 1 fellowship, 15 research assistantships, 23 teaching assistantships; career-related internships or fieldwork, Federal Work-Study, scholarships/grants, and tuition waivers (full and partial) also available. Support available to part-time students. Financial award application deadline: 2/15. *Unit head:* Dr. Ted Howard, Chairperson, 603-862-2700, E-mail: natural.resources@unh.edu. *Application contact:* Nancy Brown, Administrative Assistant, 603-862-1022, E-mail: natural.resources@unh.edu. Website: http://www.nre.unh.edu/academics/.

University of New Haven, Graduate School, College of Arts and Sciences, Program in Environmental Sciences, West Haven, CT 06516-1916. Offers environmental ecology (MS); environmental geoscience (MS); environmental health and management (MS); environmental science (MS); environmental science education (MS); geographical information systems (MS, Certificate). Part-time and evening/weekend programs available. *Students:* 23 full-time (14 women), 13 part-time (6 women); includes 5 minority (3 Black or African American, non-Hispanic/Latino; 2 Asian, non-Hispanic/Latino), 9 international. 43 applicants, 81% accepted, 21 enrolled. In 2012, 9 master's, 4 other advanced degrees awarded. *Degree requirements:* For master's, thesis optional, research project. *Entrance requirements:* Additional exam requirements/recommendations for international students: Required—TOEFL (minimum score 80 iBT), IELTS, Pearson Test of English (minimum score 53). *Application deadline:* For fall admission, 5/31 for international students; for winter admission, 10/15 for international students; for spring admission, 1/15 for international students. Applications are processed on a rolling basis. Application fee: $75. Electronic applications accepted. Application fee is waived when completed online. *Expenses: Tuition:* Part-time $775 per credit. *Required fees:* $45 per trimester. *Financial support:* Research assistantships with partial tuition reimbursements, teaching assistantships with partial tuition reimbursements, career-related internships or fieldwork, Federal Work-Study, scholarships/grants, and unspecified assistantships available. Support available to part-time students. Financial award applicants required to submit FAFSA. *Faculty research:* Mapping and assessing geological and living resources in Long Island Sound, geology, San Salvador Island, Bahamas. *Unit head:* Dr. Roman Zajac, Coordinator, 203-932-7114, E-mail: rzajac@newhaven.edu. *Application contact:* Eloise Gormley, Director of Graduate Admissions, 203-932-7440, E-mail: gradinfo@newhaven.edu. Website: http://www.newhaven.edu/4728/.

University of New Mexico, Graduate School, Water Resources Program, Albuquerque, NM 87131-2039. Offers hydroscience (MWR); policy management (MWR). Part-time programs available. *Faculty:* 1 full-time (0 women). *Students:* 15 full-time (11 women), 27 part-time (14 women); includes 10 minority (1 Black or African American, non-Hispanic/Latino; 3 American Indian or Alaska Native, non-Hispanic/Latino; 1 Asian, non-Hispanic/Latino; 3 Hispanic/Latino; 2 Two or more races, non-Hispanic/Latino). Average age 35. 20 applicants, 70% accepted, 8 enrolled. In 2012, 12 master's awarded. *Degree requirements:* For master's, professional project. *Entrance requirements:* For master's, minimum GPA of 3.0 during last 2 years of undergraduate work, 3 letters of reference. Additional exam requirements/recommendations for international students: Required—TOEFL (minimum score 550 paper-based). *Application deadline:* For fall admission, 7/15 for domestic students; for spring admission, 11/15 for domestic students. Applications are processed on a rolling basis. Application fee: $50. Electronic applications accepted. *Expenses:* Tuition, state resident: full-time $3296; part-time $276.73 per credit hour. Tuition, nonresident: full-time $10,604; part-time $885.74 per credit hour. *Required fees:* $628. *Financial support:* In 2012–13, 24 students received support, including 3 research assistantships with full and partial tuition reimbursements available (averaging $5,791 per year); career-related internships or fieldwork, institutionally sponsored loans, scholarships/grants, and unspecified assistantships also available. Financial award application deadline: 3/1; financial award applicants required to submit FAFSA. *Faculty research:* Sustainable water resources, transboundary water resources, economics, water law, hydrology, developing countries, hydrogeology. *Total annual research expenditures:* $150,557. *Unit head:* Dr. Bruce M. Thomson, Director, 505-277-5249, Fax: 505-277-5226, E-mail: bthomson@unm.edu. *Application contact:* Annamarie Cordova, Administrative Assistant II, 505-277-7759, Fax: 505-277-5226, E-mail: acordova@unm.edu. Website: http://www.unm.edu/~wrp/.

The University of North Carolina at Chapel Hill, Graduate School, Gillings School of Global Public Health, Department of Environmental Sciences and Engineering, Chapel Hill, NC 27599. Offers air, radiation and industrial hygiene (MPH, MS, MSEE, MSPH, PhD); aquatic and atmospheric sciences (MPH, MS, MSPH, PhD); environmental engineering (MPH, MS, MSEE, MSPH, PhD); environmental health sciences (MPH, MS, MSPH, PhD); environmental management and policy (MPH, MS, MSPH, PhD). *Faculty:* 31 full-time. *Students:* 131 full-time (74 women); includes 31 minority (3 Black or African American, non-Hispanic/Latino; 13 Asian, non-Hispanic/Latino; 9 Hispanic/Latino; 1 Native Hawaiian or other Pacific Islander, non-Hispanic/Latino; 5 Two or more races, non-Hispanic/Latino), 24 international. Average age 27. 262 applicants, 26% accepted, 30 enrolled. In 2012, 22 master's, 8 doctorates awarded. Terminal master's awarded for partial completion of doctoral program. *Degree requirements:* For master's, comprehensive exam, thesis (for some programs), research paper; for doctorate, comprehensive exam, thesis/dissertation. *Entrance requirements:* For master's and doctorate, GRE General Test, minimum GPA of 3.0 (recommended). Additional exam requirements/recommendations for international students: Required—TOEFL. *Application deadline:* For fall admission, 12/10 priority date for domestic students, 12/10 for international students; for spring admission, 9/10 for domestic students. Applications are processed on a rolling basis. Application fee: $85. Electronic applications accepted. *Financial support:* Fellowships with tuition reimbursements, research assistantships with tuition reimbursements, teaching assistantships with tuition reimbursements, career-related internships or fieldwork, Federal Work-Study, traineeships, health care benefits, and unspecified assistantships available. Support available to part-time students. Financial award application deadline: 12/10; financial award applicants required to submit FAFSA. *Faculty research:* Air, radiation and industrial hygiene, aquatic and atmospheric sciences, environmental health sciences, environmental management and policy, water resources engineering. *Unit head:* Dr. Michael Aitken, Chair, 919-966-1024, Fax: 919-966-7911, E-mail: mike_aitken@unc.edu. *Application contact:* Jack Whaley, Registrar, 919-966-3844, Fax: 919-966-7911, E-mail: jack_whaley@unc.edu. Website: http://www2.sph.unc.edu/envr/.

The University of North Carolina Wilmington, College of Arts and Sciences, Department of Environmental Studies, Wilmington, NC 28403-3297. Offers coastal management (MA); environmental education and interpretation (MA); environmental management (MA); individualized study (MA). Part-time programs available. *Degree requirements:* For master's, comprehensive exam, thesis or alternative, final project, practicum. *Entrance requirements:* For master's, GRE, 3 letters of recommendation. Additional exam requirements/recommendations for international students: Required—TOEFL (minimum score 550 paper-based; 79 iBT), IELTS (minimum score 6.5). Electronic applications accepted. *Faculty research:* Coastal management, environmental management, environmental education, environmental law, natural resource management.

University of Northern British Columbia, Office of Graduate Studies, Prince George, BC V2N 4Z9, Canada. Offers business administration (Diploma); community health science (M Sc); disability management (MA); education (M Ed); first nations studies (MA); gender studies (MA); history (MA); interdisciplinary studies (MA); international studies (MA); mathematical, computer and physical sciences (M Sc); natural resources and environmental studies (M Sc, MA, MNRES, PhD); political science (MA); psychology (M Sc, PhD); social work (MSW). Part-time and evening/weekend programs available. Postbaccalaureate distance learning degree programs offered (no on-campus study). *Degree requirements:* For master's, thesis; for doctorate, thesis/dissertation. *Entrance requirements:* For master's, GRE, minimum B average in undergraduate course work; for doctorate, candidacy exam, minimum A average in graduate course work.

University of Oregon, Graduate School, College of Arts and Sciences, Environmental Studies Program, Eugene, OR 97403. Offers environmental science, studies, and policy (PhD); environmental studies (MA, MS). *Degree requirements:* For master's, one foreign language, thesis; for doctorate, comprehensive exam, thesis/dissertation. *Entrance requirements:* For master's, GRE General Test, minimum GPA of 3.0; for doctorate, GRE General Test. Additional exam requirements/recommendations for international students: Required—TOEFL (minimum score 550 paper-based). Electronic applications accepted.

University of Pennsylvania, School of Arts and Sciences, College of Liberal and Professional Studies, Philadelphia, PA 19104. Offers environmental studies (MES); individualized study (MLA). *Students:* 136 full-time (80 women), 327 part-time (192 women); includes 77 minority (28 Black or African American, non-Hispanic/Latino; 21 Asian, non-Hispanic/Latino; 12 Hispanic/Latino; 16 Two or more races, non-Hispanic/Latino), 53 international. 749 applicants, 44% accepted, 265 enrolled. In 2012, 222 master's awarded. *Application deadline:* For fall admission, 12/1 priority date for domestic students. Application fee: $70. Electronic applications accepted. *Unit head:* Nora Lewis, Vice Dean, Professional and Liberal Education, 215-898-7326, E-mail: nlewis@sas.upenn.edu. *Application contact:* 215-898-7326, E-mail: lps@sas.upenn.edu. Website: http://www.sas.upenn.edu/lps/graduate.

University of Pittsburgh, Graduate School of Public and International Affairs, Master of International Development Program, Pittsburgh, PA 15260. Offers development planning and environmental sustainability (MID); human security (MID); nongovernmental organizations and civil society (MID); MID/JD; MID/MBA; MID/MPH; MID/MPIA; MID/MSIS; MID/MSW; MPA/MID. Part-time and evening/weekend programs available. *Faculty:* 35 full-time (15 women), 22 part-time/adjunct (7 women). *Students:* 55 full-time (42 women), 6 part-time (4 women); includes 14 minority (4 Black or African American, non-Hispanic/Latino; 3 Asian, non-Hispanic/Latino; 7 Hispanic/Latino), 12 international. Average age 25. 101 applicants, 85% accepted, 30 enrolled. In 2012, 37 master's awarded. *Degree requirements:* For master's, thesis optional, internship, capstone seminar. *Entrance requirements:* For master's, GRE General Test, 2 letters of recommendation; undergraduate transcripts; resume; personal statement. Additional exam requirements/recommendations for international students: Required—TOEFL (minimum score 550 paper-based; 80 iBT), TWE (minimum score 4); Recommended—IELTS (minimum score 7). *Application deadline:* For fall admission, 2/1 for domestic students, 1/15 for international students; for spring admission, 11/1 for domestic students, 8/1 for international students. Application fee: $50. Electronic applications accepted. *Expenses:* Tuition, state resident: full-time $19,336; part-time $782 per credit. Tuition, nonresident: full-time $31,658; part-time $1295 per credit. *Required fees:* $740; $200 per term. Tuition and fees vary according to program. *Financial support:* In 2012–13, 38 students received support, including 5 fellowships; scholarships/grants, unspecified assistantships, and student employment also available. Financial award application deadline: 2/1. *Faculty research:* Nongovernmental organizations, religion and civil society, international development, development economics and policy, human rights and development, humanitarian intervention, ethnic conflict and civil war, post-conflict peace-building, corruption and transnational governance, civil society and public affairs, political constraints on rural development. *Total annual research expenditures:* $760,592. *Unit head:* Dr. Paul J. Nelson, Director, 412-648-7645, Fax: 412-648-2605, E-mail: pjnelson@pitt.edu. *Application contact:* Elizabeth Hruby, Graduate Enrollment Counselor, 412-648-7640, Fax: 412-648-7641, E-mail: eah44@pitt.edu. Website: http://www.gspia.pitt.edu/.

University of Puerto Rico, Río Piedras, Graduate School of Planning, San Juan, PR 00931-3300. Offers economic planning systems (MP); environmental planning (MP); social policy and planning (MP); urban and territorial planning (MP). *Accreditation:* ACSP. Part-time programs available. *Degree requirements:* For master's, comprehensive exam, thesis, planning project defense. *Entrance requirements:* For master's, PAEG, GRE, minimum GPA of 3.0, 2 letters of recommendation. *Faculty research:* Municipalities, historic Atlas, Puerto Rico, economic future.

University of Rhode Island, Graduate School, College of the Environment and Life Sciences, Department of Environmental and Natural Resource Economics, Kingston, RI 02881. Offers MESM, MS, PhD. Part-time programs available. *Faculty:* 6 full-time (2 women). *Students:* 31 full-time (21 women), 1 (woman) part-time; includes 3 minority (2 Asian, non-Hispanic/Latino; 1 Hispanic/Latino), 12 international. In 2012, 10 master's, 3 doctorates awarded. *Degree requirements:* For master's, comprehensive exam (for some programs), thesis optional; for doctorate, comprehensive exam, thesis/dissertation. *Entrance requirements:* For master's, GRE, 2 letters of recommendation; for doctorate, GRE, 3 letters of recommendation. Additional exam requirements/recommendations for international students: Required—TOEFL (minimum score 550 paper-based). *Application deadline:* For fall admission, 7/15 for domestic students, 2/1 for international students; for spring admission, 11/15 for domestic students, 7/15 for international students. Application fee: $65. Electronic applications accepted. *Expenses:* Tuition, state resident: full-time $11,532; part-time $641 per credit. Tuition, nonresident: full-time $23,606; part-time $1311 per credit. *Required fees:* $1388; $36 per credit. $35 per semester. One-time fee: $130. *Financial support:* In 2012–13, 1 research assistantship with full and partial tuition reimbursement (averaging $16,256 per year), 7 teaching assistantships with full and partial tuition reimbursements (averaging $11,939 per year) were awarded. Financial award application deadline: 7/15; financial award applicants required to submit FAFSA. *Faculty research:* Policy simulation, policy actions, experimental economics. *Unit head:* Dr. James Opaluch, Chair, 401-874-4590, Fax: 401-874-4766, E-mail: jimo@uri.edu. Website: http://www.uri.edu/cels/enre/.

University of Rochester, Hajim School of Engineering and Applied Sciences, Master of Science in Technical Entrepreneurship and Management Program, Rochester, NY 14627-0360. Offers biomedical engineering (MS); chemical engineering (MS); computer science (MS); electrical and computer engineering (MS); energy and the environment (MS); materials science (MS); mechanical engineering (MS); optics (MS). Program offered in collaboration with Simons School of Business. Part-time programs available. *Faculty:* 621 full-time, 21 part-time/adjunct. *Students:* 24 full-time (7 women); includes 2 minority (both Asian, non-Hispanic/Latino), 17 international. Average age 24. 170 applicants, 63% accepted, 24 enrolled. In 2012, 1 degree awarded. *Degree requirements:* For master's, comprehensive exam. *Entrance requirements:* For master's, GRE or GMAT, technical concentration of interest, 3 letters of recommendation, personal statement, official transcript, bachelor's degree (or equivalent for international students) in engineering, science, or mathematics. Additional exam requirements/recommendations for international students: Required—TOEFL or IELTS. *Application deadline:* For fall admission, 2/1 for domestic and international students. Applications are processed on a rolling basis. Application fee: $60. Electronic applications accepted. *Financial support:* In 2012–13, 23 students received support. Career-related internships or fieldwork and scholarships/grants available. Financial award application deadline: 2/1. *Faculty research:* High efficiency solar cells, macromolecular self-assembly, digital signal processing, memory hierarchy management, molecular and physical mechanisms in cell migration, optical imaging systems. *Unit head:* Duncan T. Moore, Vice Provost for Entrepreneurship, 585-275-5248, Fax: 585-473-6745, E-mail: moore@optics.rochester.edu. *Application contact:* Andrea M. Galati, Executive Director, 585-276-3407, Fax: 585-276-2357, E-mail: andrea.galati@rochester.edu. Website: http://www.rochester.edu/team.

University of South Africa, College of Agriculture and Environmental Sciences, Pretoria, South Africa. Offers agriculture (MS); consumer science (MCS); environmental management (MA, MS, PhD); environmental science (MA, MS, PhD); geography (MA, MS, PhD); horticulture (M Tech); human ecology (MHE); life sciences (MS); nature conservation (M Tech).

University of South Carolina, The Graduate School, School of the Environment, Program in Earth and Environmental Resources Management, Columbia, SC 29208. Offers MEERM, JD/MEERM. Part-time programs available. Postbaccalaureate distance learning degree programs offered (no on-campus study). *Degree requirements:* For master's, thesis optional. *Entrance requirements:* For master's, GRE General Test. Additional exam requirements/recommendations for international students: Required—TOEFL. Electronic applications accepted. *Faculty research:* Hydrology, sustainable development, environmental geology and engineering, energy/environmental resources management.

University of South Florida, Graduate School, College of Arts and Sciences, Department of Geography, Environment and Planning, Tampa, FL 33620-9951. Offers environmental science and policy (MS); geography (MA); geography and environmental science and policy (PhD); urban and regional planning (MURP). Part-time and evening/weekend programs available. *Degree requirements:* For master's, comprehensive exam, thesis; for doctorate, comprehensive exam, thesis/dissertation. *Entrance requirements:* For master's, GRE General Test, minimum GPA of 3.0, letter of intent, two letters of recommendation (three for MS); for doctorate, GRE General Test, minimum GPA of 3.2 in last 60 hours, letter of intent, two letters of recommendation. Additional exam requirements/recommendations for international students: Required—TOEFL (minimum score 600 paper-based), TOEFL (minimum score 550 paper-based; 79 iBT) or IELTS (minimum score 6.5); TOEFL (minimum score 600 paper-based) for ESP MS and Ph D. *Faculty research:* Natural hazards, geographic information systems models, soil contamination, urban geography and social theory.

University of South Florida–St. Petersburg Campus, College of Arts and Sciences, St. Petersburg, FL 33701. Offers digital journalism and design (MA); environmental science and policy (MA, MS); Florida studies (MLA); journalism and media studies (MA); liberal studies (MLA); psychology (MA). Part-time programs available. Postbaccalaureate distance learning degree programs offered (no on-campus study). *Degree requirements:* For master's, comprehensive exam, thesis or project. *Entrance requirements:* For master's, GRE, LSAT, MCAT (varies by program), letter of intent, 3 letters of recommendation, writing samples, bachelor's degree from regionally-accredited institution with minimum GPA of 3.0 overall or in upper two years. Additional exam requirements/recommendations for international students: Required—TOEFL (minimum score 550 paper-based; 79 iBT); Recommended—IELTS. Electronic applications accepted.

The University of Tennessee, Graduate School, College of Arts and Sciences, Department of Sociology, Knoxville, TN 37996. Offers criminology (MA, PhD); energy, environment, and resource policy (MA, PhD); political economy (MA, PhD). Part-time programs available. *Degree requirements:* For master's, thesis or alternative; for doctorate, thesis/dissertation. *Entrance requirements:* For master's, GRE General Test, minimum GPA of 3.0; for doctorate, GRE General Test, minimum GPA of 3.5. Additional exam requirements/recommendations for international students: Required—TOEFL. Electronic applications accepted. *Expenses:* Tuition, state resident: full-time $9000; part-time $501 per credit hour. Tuition, nonresident: full-time $27,188; part-time $1512 per credit hour. *Required fees:* $1280; $62 per credit hour. Tuition and fees vary according to program.

The University of Texas at Austin, Graduate School, College of Liberal Arts, Teresa Lozano Long Institute of Latin American Studies, Austin, TX 78712-1111. Offers cultural politics of Afro-Latin and indigenous peoples (MA); development studies (MA); environmental studies (MA); human rights (MA); Latin American and international law (LL M); JD/MA; MA/MA; MBA/MA; MP Aff/MA; MSCRP/MA. LL M offered jointly with The University of Texas School of Law. *Entrance requirements:* For master's, GRE General Test.

University of Washington, Graduate School, Interdisciplinary Graduate Program in Quantitative Ecology and Resource Management, Seattle, WA 98195. Offers MS, PhD. *Degree requirements:* For master's, thesis; for doctorate, thesis/dissertation. *Entrance requirements:* For master's and doctorate, GRE General Test, minimum GPA of 3.0. Additional exam requirements/recommendations for international students: Required—TOEFL. Electronic applications accepted. *Faculty research:* Population dynamics, statistical analysis, ecological modeling and systems analysis of aquatic and terrestrial ecosystems.

University of Waterloo, Graduate Studies, Faculty of Environment, Department of Environment and Resource Studies, Waterloo, ON N2L 3G1, Canada. Offers MES. Part-time programs available. *Degree requirements:* For master's, thesis. *Entrance requirements:* For master's, honors degree, minimum B average, resume. Additional exam requirements/recommendations for international students: Required—TOEFL, TWE. Electronic applications accepted. *Faculty research:* Applied sustainability; sustainable water policy; food, agriculture, and the environment; biology studies; environment and business; ecological monitoring; soil ecosystem dynamics; urban water demand management; demand response.

University of Waterloo, Graduate Studies, Faculty of Environment, Program in Tourism Policy and Planning, Waterloo, ON N2L 3G1, Canada. Offers MAES. Part-time programs available. *Degree requirements:* For master's, research paper. *Entrance requirements:* For master's, honors degree in related field, minimum B average. Additional exam requirements/recommendations for international students: Required—TOEFL, TWE. Electronic applications accepted. *Faculty research:* Urban and regional economics, regional economic development, strategic planning, environmental economics, economic geography.

University of Wisconsin–Green Bay, Graduate Studies, Program in Environmental Science and Policy, Green Bay, WI 54311-7001. Offers MS. Part-time programs available. *Faculty:* 16 full-time (3 women), 3 part-time/adjunct (0 women). *Students:* 22 full-time (9 women), 21 part-time (13 women); includes 5 minority (1 Black or African American, non-Hispanic/Latino; 1 American Indian or Alaska Native, non-Hispanic/Latino; 1 Hispanic/Latino; 2 Two or more races, non-Hispanic/Latino). Average age 29. 20 applicants, 90% accepted, 12 enrolled. In 2012, 11 master's awarded. *Degree requirements:* For master's, thesis. *Entrance requirements:* For master's, GRE General Test, minimum GPA of 3.0. *Application deadline:* For fall admission, 8/1 for domestic students; for spring admission, 11/1 for domestic students. Applications are processed on a rolling basis. Application fee: $56. Electronic applications accepted. *Expenses:* Tuition, state resident: full-time $7640; part-time $424 per credit. Tuition, nonresident: full-time $16,771; part-time $932 per credit. *Required fees:* $1350; $75 per credit. Tuition and fees vary according to reciprocity agreements. *Financial support:* In 2012–13, 3 students received support, including 3 teaching assistantships with full tuition reimbursements available; research assistantships with full tuition reimbursements available, career-related internships or fieldwork, Federal Work-Study, and institutionally sponsored loans also available. Financial award application deadline: 7/15; financial award applicants required to submit FAFSA. *Faculty research:* Bald eagle, parasitic population of domestic and wild animals, resource recovery, anaerobic digestion of organic waste. *Unit head:* Dr. Matthew Dornbush, Chair, 920-465-2264, E-mail: dornbusm@uwgb.edu. *Application contact:* Mary Valitchka, Graduate Studies Coordinator, 920-465-2123, E-mail: valitchm@uwgb.edu. Website: http://www.uwgb.edu/graduate/.

Utah State University, School of Graduate Studies, College of Natural Resources, Department of Environment and Society, Logan, UT 84322. Offers bioregional planning (MS); geography (MA, MS); human dimensions of ecosystem science and management (MS, PhD); recreation resource management (MS, PhD). *Degree requirements:* For master's, comprehensive exam, thesis (for some programs). *Entrance requirements:* For master's and doctorate, GRE General Test, minimum GPA of 3.0. Additional exam requirements/recommendations for international students: Required—TOEFL. Electronic applications accepted. *Faculty research:* Geographic information systems/geographic and environmental education, bioregional planning, natural resource and environmental policy, outdoor recreation and tourism, natural resource and environmental management.

Vanderbilt University, School of Engineering, Department of Civil and Environmental Engineering, Program in Environmental Engineering, Nashville, TN 37240-1001. Offers environmental engineering (M Eng); environmental management (MS, PhD). MS and PhD offered through the Graduate School. Part-time programs available. Terminal master's awarded for partial completion of doctoral program. *Degree requirements:* For master's, thesis or alternative; for doctorate, thesis/dissertation. *Entrance requirements:* For master's and doctorate, GRE General Test. Additional exam requirements/recommendations for international students: Required—TOEFL. Electronic applications accepted. *Faculty research:* Waste treatment, hazardous waste management, chemical waste treatment, water quality.

Vermont Law School, Law School, Environmental Law Center, South Royalton, VT 05068-0096. Offers energy law (LL M); energy regulation and law (MERL); environmental law (LL M); environmental law and policy (MELP); JD/MELP. Part-time programs available. *Entrance requirements:* Additional exam requirements/recommendations for international students: Required—TOEFL. *Application deadline:* For fall admission, 3/1 priority date for domestic students. Applications are processed on a rolling basis. Application fee: $60. *Financial support:* Fellowships with full tuition reimbursements, career-related internships or fieldwork, Federal Work-Study, institutionally sponsored loans, scholarships/grants, and tuition waivers (partial) available. Support available to part-time students. Financial award application deadline: 3/1; financial award applicants required to submit FAFSA. *Faculty research:* Environment and technology; takings; international environmental law; interaction among science, law, and environmental policy; air pollution. *Unit head:* Marc B. Mihaly, Dean, 802-831-1237, Fax: 802-763-2490. *Application contact:* Anne Mansfield, Associate Director, 802-831-1338, Fax: 802-763-2940, E-mail: admiss@vermontlaw.edu. Website: http://www.vermontlaw.edu/Academics/Environmental_Law_Center.htm.

Virginia Commonwealth University, Graduate School, School of Life Sciences, Center for Environmental Studies, Richmond, VA 23284-9005. Offers M Env Sc, MS. *Degree requirements:* For master's, thesis. *Entrance requirements:* For master's, GRE General Test. Additional exam requirements/recommendations for international students: Required—TOEFL (minimum score 600 paper-based; 100 iBT). Electronic applications accepted.

Virginia Polytechnic Institute and State University, Graduate School, College of Architecture and Urban Studies, Blacksburg, VA 24061. Offers architecture (MS Arch); architecture and design research (PhD); building/construction science and management (MS); creative technologies (MFA); environmental design and planning (PhD); landscape architecture (MLA); planning, governance, and globalization (PhD); public administration (MPA); public administration/public affairs (PhD, Certificate); public and international affairs (MPIA); urban and regional planning (MURP); MS/MA. *Accreditation:* ASLA (one or more programs are accredited). *Faculty:* 132 full-time (52 women), 3 part-time/adjunct (1 woman). *Students:* 374 full-time (166 women), 268 part-time (128 women); includes 104 minority (57 Black or African American, non-Hispanic/Latino; 2 American Indian or Alaska Native, non-Hispanic/Latino; 19 Asian, non-Hispanic/Latino; 14 Hispanic/Latino; 12 Two or more races, non-Hispanic/Latino), 100 international. Average age 32. 814 applicants, 39% accepted, 141 enrolled. In 2012, 173 master's, 25 doctorates, 2 other advanced degrees awarded. *Degree requirements:* For master's, comprehensive exam (for some programs), thesis (for some programs); for doctorate, comprehensive exam (for some programs), thesis/dissertation (for some programs). *Entrance requirements:* For master's and doctorate, GRE/GMAT (may vary by department). Additional exam requirements/recommendations for international students: Required—TOEFL (minimum score 550 paper-based). *Application deadline:* For fall admission, 8/1 for domestic students, 4/1 for international students; for spring admission, 1/1 for domestic students, 9/1 for international students. Applications are processed on a rolling basis. Application fee: $65. Electronic applications accepted. *Expenses:* Tuition, state resident: full-time $10,677; part-time $593.25 per credit hour. Tuition, nonresident: full-time $20,926; part-time $1162.50 per credit hour. *Required fees:* $427.75 per semester. Tuition and fees vary according to course load, campus/location and program. *Financial support:* In 2012–13, 6 research assistantships with full tuition reimbursements (averaging $15,349 per year), 36 teaching assistantships with full tuition reimbursements (averaging $15,345 per year) were awarded. Financial award application deadline: 3/1; financial award applicants required to submit FAFSA. *Total annual research expenditures:* $1.9 million. *Unit head:* Dr. A. J. Davis, Dean, 540-231-6416, Fax: 540-231-6332, E-mail: davisa@vt.edu. *Application contact:* Christine Mattsson-Coon, Executive Assistant, 540-231-6416, Fax: 540-231-6332, E-mail: cmattsso@vt.edu. Website: http://www.caus.vt.edu/.

Virginia Polytechnic Institute and State University, VT Online, Blacksburg, VA 24061. Offers advanced transportation systems (Certificate); aerospace engineering (MS); agricultural and life sciences (MSLFS); business information systems (Graduate Certificate); career and technical education (MS); civil engineering (MS); computer engineering (M Eng, MS); decision support systems (Graduate Certificate); eLearning leadership (MA); electrical engineering (M Eng, MS); engineering administration (MEA); environmental engineering (Certificate); environmental politics and policy (Graduate Certificate); environmental sciences and engineering (MS); foundations of political analysis (Graduate Certificate); health product risk management (Graduate Certificate); industrial and systems engineering (MS); information policy and society (Graduate Certificate); information security (Graduate Certificate); information technology (MIT); instructional technology (MA); integrative STEM education (MA Ed); liberal arts (Graduate Certificate); life sciences: health product risk management (MS); natural resources (MNR, Graduate Certificate); networking (Graduate Certificate); nonprofit and nongovernmental organization management (Graduate Certificate); ocean engineering (MS); political science (MA); security studies (Graduate Certificate); software development (Graduate Certificate). *Expenses:* Tuition, state resident: full-time $10,677; part-time $593.25 per credit hour. Tuition, nonresident: full-time $20,926; part-time $1162.50 per credit hour. *Required fees:* $427.75 per semester. Tuition and fees vary according to course load, campus/location and program. Website: http://www.vto.vt.edu/.

Webster University, College of Arts and Sciences, Department of Biological Sciences, St. Louis, MO 63119-3194. Offers environmental management (MS); nurse anesthesia (MS); professional science management and leadership (MA). Part-time programs available. Postbaccalaureate distance learning degree programs offered (no on-campus study). *Degree requirements:* For master's, comprehensive exam (for some programs), thesis (for some programs). *Entrance requirements:* Additional exam requirements/recommendations for international students: Required—TOEFL. *Expenses: Tuition:* Full-time $11,250; part-time $625 per credit hour. Tuition and fees vary according to campus/location and program.

Webster University, George Herbert Walker School of Business and Technology, Department of Business, St. Louis, MO 63119-3194. Offers business (MA); business and organizational security management (MBA); computer resources and information management (MBA); environmental management (MBA); finance (MA, MBA); health services management (MBA); human resources development (MBA); human resources management (MBA); international business (MA, MBA); management and leadership (MBA); marketing (MBA); procurement and acquisitions management (MBA); telecommunications management (MBA). *Accreditation:* ACBSP. Part-time and evening/weekend programs available. Postbaccalaureate distance learning degree programs offered (no on-campus study). *Degree requirements:* For master's, comprehensive exam (for some programs), thesis (for some programs). *Entrance requirements:* Additional exam requirements/recommendations for international students: Required—TOEFL. *Expenses: Tuition:* Full-time $11,250; part-time $625 per credit hour. Tuition and fees vary according to campus/location and program.

Webster University, George Herbert Walker School of Business and Technology, Department of Management, St. Louis, MO 63119-3194. Offers business and organizational security management (MA); computer resources and information management (MA); environmental management (MS); government contracting (Certificate); health care management (MA); health services management (MA); human resources development (MA); human resources management (MA); management (DM); management and leadership (MA); marketing (MA); nonprofit leadership (MA); nonprofit management (Certificate); procurement and acquisitions management (MA); public administration (MA); quality management (MA); space systems operations management (MS); telecommunications management (MA). Part-time and evening/weekend programs available. Postbaccalaureate distance learning degree programs offered (no on-campus study). *Degree requirements:* For master's, thesis (for some programs); for doctorate, thesis/dissertation, written exam. *Entrance requirements:* For doctorate, GMAT, 3 years of work experience, MBA. Additional exam requirements/recommendations for international students: Required—TOEFL. *Expenses: Tuition:* Full-time $11,250; part-time $625 per credit hour. Tuition and fees vary according to campus/location and program.

Wesley College, Business Program, Dover, DE 19901-3875. Offers environmental management (MBA); executive leadership (MBA); management (MBA). Executive leadership concentration also offered at New Castle, DE location. Part-time and evening/weekend programs available. *Entrance requirements:* For master's, GMAT or GRE, minimum undergraduate GPA of 2.75.

Wesley College, Environmental Studies Program, Dover, DE 19901-3875. Offers MS. Part-time and evening/weekend programs available. *Entrance requirements:* For master's, BA/BSM in science or engineering field, portfolio.

West Virginia University, Davis College of Agriculture, Forestry and Consumer Sciences, Division of Resource Management and Sustainable Development, Morgantown, WV 26506. Offers agricultural and extension education (MS, PhD), including agricultural and extension education, teaching vocational-agriculture (MS); agricultural and resource economics (MS); human and community development (PhD); natural resource economics (PhD); resource management (PhD); resource management and sustainable development (PhD). Part-time programs available. *Degree requirements:* For master's, thesis; for doctorate, comprehensive exam, thesis/dissertation. *Entrance requirements:* For master's, GRE General Test. Additional exam requirements/recommendations for international students: Required—TOEFL. *Faculty research:* Environmental economics, energy economics, agriculture.

West Virginia University, Eberly College of Arts and Sciences, Department of Geology and Geography, Program in Geography, Morgantown, WV 26506. Offers energy and environmental resources (MA); geographic information systems (PhD); geography-regional development (PhD); GIS/cartographic analysis (MA); regional development (MA). Part-time programs available. *Degree requirements:* For master's, thesis, oral and written exams; for doctorate, comprehensive exam, thesis/dissertation, oral and written exams. *Entrance requirements:* For master's and doctorate, GRE General Test, minimum GPA of 3.0. Additional exam requirements/recommendations for international students: Required—TOEFL. Electronic applications accepted. *Faculty research:* Space, place and development, geographic information science, environmental geography.

Wilfrid Laurier University, Faculty of Graduate and Postdoctoral Studies, Faculty of Arts, Department of Geography and Environmental Studies, Waterloo, ON N2L 3C5, Canada. Offers environmental and resource management (MA,

MES, PhD); environmental science (M Sc, MES, PhD); geomatics (M Sc, MES, PhD); human geography (MES, PhD). Part-time programs available. *Degree requirements:* For master's, thesis optional; for doctorate, thesis/dissertation. *Entrance requirements:* For master's, honors BA in geography, minimum B average in undergraduate course work; honors BSc with minimum B+ or honors BES or BA in physical geography, environmental or earth sciences or the equivalent; for doctorate, MA in geography, minimum A- average. Additional exam requirements/recommendations for international students: Required—TOEFL (minimum score 89 iBT). Electronic applications accepted. *Faculty research:* Resources management, urban, economic, physical, cultural, earth surfaces, geomatics, historical, regional, spatial data handling.

Wilfrid Laurier University, Faculty of Graduate and Postdoctoral Studies, School of International Policy and Governance, International Public Policy Program, Waterloo, ON N2L 3C5, Canada. Offers global governance (MIPP); human security (MIPP); international economic relations (MIPP); international environmental policy (MIPP). Offered jointly with University of Waterloo. *Entrance requirements:* For master's, honours BA with minimum B average. Additional exam requirements/recommendations for international students: Required— TOEFL (minimum score 89 iBT). Electronic applications accepted. *Faculty research:* International environmental policy, international economic relations, human security, global governance.

Willamette University, Graduate School of Education, Salem, OR 97301-3931. Offers environmental literacy (M Ed); reading (M Ed); special education (M Ed); teaching (MAT). *Accreditation:* NCATE. Evening/weekend programs available. *Degree requirements:* For master's, leadership project (action research). *Entrance requirements:* For master's, California Basic Educational Skills Test, Multiple Subject Assessment for Teachers, PRAXIS, minimum GPA of 3.0, classroom experience, 2 letters of reference. Additional exam requirements/ recommendations for international students: Recommended—TOEFL. Electronic applications accepted. *Expenses:* Contact institution. *Faculty research:* Educational leadership, multicultural education, middle school education, clinical supervision, educational technology.

Wilmington University, College of Business, New Castle, DE 19720-6491. Offers accounting (MBA, MS); business administration (MBA, DBA); environmental stewardship (MBA); finance (MBA); health care administration (MBA, MSM); homeland security (MBA, MSM); human resource management (MSM); management information systems (MBA, MSN); marketing (MSM); marketing management (MBA); military leadership (MSM); organizational leadership (MBA, MSM); public administration (MSM). Part-time and evening/ weekend programs available. *Faculty:* 10 full-time (2 women), 111 part-time/ adjunct (45 women). *Students:* 455 full-time (240 women), 1,206 part-time (715 women); includes 626 minority (495 Black or African American, non-Hispanic/ Latino; 5 American Indian or Alaska Native, non-Hispanic/Latino; 88 Asian, non-Hispanic/Latino; 36 Hispanic/Latino; 2 Native Hawaiian or other Pacific Islander, non-Hispanic/Latino), 21 international. Average age 34. 659 applicants, 99% accepted, 446 enrolled. In 2012, 567 master's, 7 doctorates awarded. *Entrance requirements:* Additional exam requirements/recommendations for international students: Required—TOEFL (minimum score 500 paper-based). *Application deadline:* Applications are processed on a rolling basis. Application fee: $35. Electronic applications accepted. *Expenses: Tuition:* Full-time $7452; part-time $411 per credit. *Required fees:* $50; $25 per semester. Tuition and fees vary according to degree level and campus/location. *Financial support:* Applicants required to submit FAFSA. *Unit head:* Dr. Donald W. Durandetta, Dean, 302-356-6780, E-mail: donald.w.durandetta@wilmu.edu. *Application contact:* Chris Ferguson, Director of Admissions, 302-356-4636 Ext. 256, Fax: 302-328-5164, E-mail: inquire@wilmcoll.edu. Website: http://www.wilmu.edu/business/.

Yale University, Graduate School of Arts and Sciences, Department of Forestry and Environmental Studies, New Haven, CT 06520. Offers environmental sciences (PhD); forestry (PhD). *Degree requirements:* For doctorate, thesis/ dissertation. *Entrance requirements:* For doctorate, GRE General Test.

Yale University, School of Forestry and Environmental Studies, New Haven, CT 06511. Offers MEM, MES, MF, MFS, PhD, JD/MEM, MBA/MEM, MBA/MF, MEM/ M Arch, MEM/MA, MEM/MPH, MF/MA. *Accreditation:* SAF (one or more programs are accredited). Part-time programs available. *Faculty:* 49 full-time, 40 part-time/adjunct. *Students:* 301 full-time, 22 part-time; includes 60 minority (5 Black or African American, non-Hispanic/Latino; 7 American Indian or Alaska Native, non-Hispanic/Latino; 29 Asian, non-Hispanic/Latino; 19 Hispanic/Latino). Average age 28. 590 applicants, 163 enrolled. In 2012, 139 master's awarded. Terminal master's awarded for partial completion of doctoral program. *Degree requirements:* For master's, thesis (for some programs); for doctorate, thesis/ dissertation. *Entrance requirements:* For master's, GRE General Test, GMAT or LSAT; for doctorate, GRE General Test. Additional exam requirements/ recommendations for international students: Required—TOEFL (minimum score 600 paper-based, 100 iBT) or IELTS (minimum score of 7.0). *Application deadline:* For fall admission, 12/15 priority date for domestic students, 12/15 for international students. Application fee: $80. Electronic applications accepted. *Expenses:* Contact institution. *Financial support:* In 2012–13, 252 students received support. Fellowships, research assistantships, teaching assistantships, career-related internships or fieldwork, Federal Work-Study, institutionally sponsored loans, scholarships/grants, and health care benefits available. Support available to part-time students. Financial award application deadline: 2/15; financial award applicants required to submit FAFSA. *Faculty research:* Environmental policy, social ecology, industrial environmental management, forestry, environmental health, urban ecology, water science policy. *Unit head:* Peter Crane, Dean, School of Forestry and Environmental Studies, 203-432-5109, Fax: 203-432-3051. *Application contact:* Danielle Curtis, Director of Enrollment Management (Admissions and Financial Aid), 203-432-5106, Fax: 203-432-5528, E-mail: fesinfo@yale.edu. Website: http://environment.yale.edu.

York University, Faculty of Graduate Studies, Program in Environmental Studies, Toronto, ON M3J 1P3, Canada. Offers MES, PhD, MES/LL B, MES/MA. Part-time programs available. *Degree requirements:* For master's, thesis optional; for doctorate, comprehensive exam, thesis/dissertation, research seminar. Electronic applications accepted.

Youngstown State University, Graduate School, College of Liberal Arts and Social Sciences, Program in Environmental Studies, Youngstown, OH 44555-0001. Offers environmental studies (MS); industrial/institutional management (Certificate); risk management (Certificate). *Degree requirements:* For master's, comprehensive exam, thesis, oral defense of dissertation. *Entrance requirements:* For master's, GRE General Test or minimum GPA of 2.7. Additional exam requirements/recommendations for international students: Required—TOEFL.

Environmental Sciences

Adelphi University, College of Arts and Sciences, Program in Environmental Studies, Garden City, NY 11530-0701. Offers MS. *Students:* 10 full-time (5 women), 6 part-time (2 women); includes 3 minority (1 Black or African American, non-Hispanic/Latino; 1 Asian, non-Hispanic/Latino; 1 Hispanic/Latino), 1 international. Average age 27. In 2012, 6 master's awarded. *Degree requirements:* For master's, thesis optional. *Entrance requirements:* For master's, GRE General Test, 2 letters of recommendation; course work in microeconomics, political science, statistics/calculus, and either chemistry or physics; computer literacy. Additional exam requirements/recommendations for international students: Required—TOEFL (minimum score 550 paper-based; 80 iBT). *Application deadline:* For fall admission, 5/1 for international students; for spring admission, 11/1 for international students. Applications are processed on a rolling basis. Application fee: $50. Electronic applications accepted. *Financial support:* Research assistantships with full and partial tuition reimbursements, teaching assistantships, career-related internships or fieldwork, Federal Work-Study, institutionally sponsored loans, and unspecified assistantships available. Financial award application deadline: 2/15; financial award applicants required to submit FAFSA. *Faculty research:* Contaminates sites, workplace exposure level of contaminants, climate change and human health. *Unit head:* Dr. Anagnostis Agelarakis, Director, 516-877-4112, E-mail: agelarak@adelphi.edu. *Application contact:* Christine Murphy, Director of Admissions, 516-877-3050, Fax: 516-877-3039, E-mail: graduateadmissions@adelphi.edu. Website: http:// academics.adelphi.edu/arts-sciences-programs/ms-environmental-study.php.

See Display on next page and Close-Up on page 491.

Alaska Pacific University, Graduate Programs, Environmental Science Department, Program in Environmental Science, Anchorage, AK 99508-4672. Offers MSES. Part-time programs available. *Degree requirements:* For master's, thesis. *Entrance requirements:* For master's, GRE General Test, minimum GPA of 3.0. Additional exam requirements/recommendations for international students: Required—TOEFL (minimum score 550 paper-based).

American University, College of Arts and Sciences, Department of Biology, Washington, DC 20016-8007. Offers applied science (MS), including biotechnology, environmental science assessment; biology (MA, MS). Part-time programs available. *Faculty:* 12 full-time (6 women), 2 part-time/adjunct (both women). *Students:* 9 full-time (4 women), 2 part-time (0 women); includes 5 minority (1 Black or African American, non-Hispanic/Latino; 3 Asian, non-Hispanic/Latino; 1 Two or more races, non-Hispanic/Latino), 1 international. Average age 27. 25 applicants, 52% accepted, 6 enrolled. In 2012, 8 master's awarded. *Degree requirements:* For master's, comprehensive exam, thesis (for some programs). *Entrance requirements:* For master's, GRE General Test, GRE Subject Test. Additional exam requirements/recommendations for international students: Required—TOEFL. *Application deadline:* For fall admission, 2/1 for domestic students; for spring admission, 10/1 for domestic students. Application fee: $80. *Expenses: Tuition:* Full-time $25,920; part-time $1440 per credit. *Required fees:* $430. Tuition and fees vary according to course load, campus/ location and program. *Financial support:* Fellowships, research assistantships with tuition reimbursements, teaching assistantships with tuition reimbursements, career-related internships or fieldwork, Federal Work-Study, and institutionally

460 www.petersonsbooks.com

Peterson's Graduate Programs in the Physical Sciences, Mathematics, Agricultural Sciences, the Environment & Natural Resources 2014

sponsored loans available. Financial award application deadline: 2/1. *Faculty research:* Neurobiology, cave biology, population genetics, vertebrate physiology. *Unit head:* Dr. David Carlini, Chair, 202-885-2194, Fax: 202-885-2182, E-mail: carlini@american.edu. *Application contact:* Kathleen Clowery, Director, Graduate Admissions, 202-885-3621, Fax: 202-885-1505, E-mail: clowery@american.edu. Website: http://www.american.edu/cas/biology/.

American University, College of Arts and Sciences, Department of Environmental Science, Washington, DC 20016-8070. Offers environmental assessment (Graduate Certificate); environmental science (MS). *Faculty:* 6 full-time (1 woman), 4 part-time/adjunct (1 woman). *Students:* 7 full-time (4 women), 6 part-time (5 women); includes 3 minority (1 Black or African American, non-Hispanic/Latino; 1 Asian, non-Hispanic/Latino; 1 Two or more races, non-Hispanic/Latino), 2 international. Average age 30. 16 applicants, 75% accepted, 3 enrolled. In 2012, 7 master's awarded. *Degree requirements:* For master's, comprehensive exam, thesis (for some programs). *Entrance requirements:* For master's, GRE General Test, GRE Subject Test, one year of calculus, lab science. Additional exam requirements/recommendations for international students: Required—TOEFL. *Application deadline:* For fall admission, 2/1 for domestic students; for spring admission, 10/1 for domestic students. Application fee: $80. *Expenses: Tuition:* Full-time $25,920; part-time $1440 per credit. *Required fees:* $430. Tuition and fees vary according to course load, campus/location and program. *Financial support:* Research assistantships and teaching assistantships available. Financial award application deadline: 2/1. *Unit head:* Dr. Albert Mei-Chu Cheh, Chair, 202-885-8014, Fax: 202-885-1752, E-mail: acheh@american.edu. *Application contact:* Kathleen Clowery, Director, Graduate Admissions, 202-885-3621, Fax: 202-885-1505, E-mail: clowery@american.edu. Website: http://www.american.edu/cas/environmental/.

American University of Beirut, Graduate Programs, Faculty of Agricultural and Food Sciences, Beirut, Lebanon. Offers agricultural economics (MS); animal sciences (MS); ecosystem management (MSES); food technology (MS); irrigation (MS); nutrition (MS); plant protection (MS); plant science (MS); poultry science (MS). Part-time programs available. *Faculty:* 22 full-time (6 women), 1 part-time/adjunct (0 women). *Students:* 11 full-time (10 women), 89 part-time (74 women). Average age 25. 97 applicants, 64% accepted, 18 enrolled. In 2012, 35 master's awarded. *Degree requirements:* For master's, one foreign language, comprehensive exam, thesis (for some programs). *Entrance requirements:* Additional exam requirements/recommendations for international students: Required—TOEFL (minimum score 600 paper-based; 100 iBT), IELTS (minimum score 7.5). *Application deadline:* For fall admission, 2/7 for domestic and international students; for spring admission, 11/15 for domestic and international students. Applications are processed on a rolling basis. Application fee: $50. Electronic applications accepted. *Expenses: Tuition:* Full-time $13,896; part-time $772 per credit. *Financial support:* In 2012–13, 18 research assistantships with

partial tuition reimbursements (averaging $1,500 per year), 49 teaching assistantships with full and partial tuition reimbursements (averaging $1,000 per year) were awarded; scholarships/grants, health care benefits, and unspecified assistantships also available. Financial award application deadline: 2/2. *Faculty research:* Evidence-based nutrition intervention; studies related to immunopotentiation, protection and production in broilers; nutritional food-based dietary guidelines; production of biodiesel from algae; regional knowledge management and knowledge sharing network. *Total annual research expenditures:* $560,850. *Unit head:* Prof. Nahla Hwalla, Dean, 961-1343002 Ext. 4400, Fax: 961-1744460, E-mail: nahla@aub.edu.lb. *Application contact:* Dr. Salim Kanaan, Director, Admissions Office, 961-1-350000 Ext. 2594, Fax: 961-1750775, E-mail: sk00@aub.edu.lb. Website: http://www.aub.edu.lb/fafs/fafs_home/Pages/index.aspx.

American University of Beirut, Graduate Programs, Faculty of Engineering and Architecture, Beirut, Lebanon. Offers applied energy (MME); civil engineering (ME, PhD); electrical and computer engineering (ME, PhD); engineering management (MEM); environmental and water resources (ME); environmental and water resources engineering (PhD); environmental technology (MSES); mechanical engineering (ME, PhD); urban design (MUD); urban planning and policy (MUPP). Part-time programs available. *Faculty:* 79 full-time (11 women), 3 part-time/adjunct (1 woman). *Students:* 307 full-time (119 women), 50 part-time (19 women). Average age 26. 370 applicants, 68% accepted, 110 enrolled. In 2012, 114 master's, 6 doctorates awarded. *Degree requirements:* For master's, one foreign language, comprehensive exam, thesis (for some programs); for doctorate, one foreign language, comprehensive exam, thesis/dissertation, publications. *Entrance requirements:* For master's, GRE (for electrical and computer engineering), letters of recommendation; for doctorate, GRE, letters of recommendation, master's degree, transcripts, curriculum vitae, interview. Additional exam requirements/recommendations for international students: Required—TOEFL (minimum score 600 paper-based; 100 iBT), IELTS (minimum score 7.5). *Application deadline:* For fall admission, 2/5 priority date for domestic students, 2/5 for international students; for spring admission, 11/1 priority date for domestic students, 11/1 for international students. Application fee: $50. Electronic applications accepted. *Expenses: Tuition:* Full-time $13,896; part-time $772 per credit. *Financial support:* In 2012–13, 9 fellowships with full tuition reimbursements (averaging $24,800 per year), 33 research assistantships with full tuition reimbursements (averaging $24,800 per year), 74 teaching assistantships with full tuition reimbursements (averaging $9,800 per year) were awarded; career-related internships or fieldwork, institutionally sponsored loans, scholarships/grants, health care benefits, and unspecified assistantships also available. *Total annual research expenditures:* $1.1 million. *Unit head:* Prof. Makram T. Suidan, Dean, 961-1350000 Ext. 3400, Fax: 961-1744462, E-mail: msuidan@aub.edu.lb. *Application contact:* Dr. Salim Kanaan, Director,

Peterson's Graduate Programs in the Physical Sciences, Mathematics, Agricultural Sciences, the Environment & Natural Resources 2014

www.petersonsbooks.com **461**

Admissions Office, 961-1-350000 Ext. 2594, Fax: 961-1750775, E-mail: sk00@aub.edu.lb. Website: http://staff.aub.edu.lb/~webfea.

American University of Beirut, Graduate Programs, Faculty of Health Sciences, Beirut, Lebanon. Offers environmental sciences (MS), including environmental health; epidemiology (MS); epidemiology and biostatistics (MPH); health management and policy (MPH); health promotion and community health (MPH); population health (MS). Part-time programs available. *Faculty:* 31 full-time (22 women), 5 part-time/adjunct (3 women). *Students:* 48 full-time (44 women), 87 part-time (69 women). Average age 27. 166 applicants, 58% accepted, 42 enrolled. In 2012, 70 master's awarded. *Degree requirements:* For master's, one foreign language, comprehensive exam, thesis (for some programs). *Entrance requirements:* For master's, 2 letters of recommendation, personal statement, transcripts. Additional exam requirements/recommendations for international students: Required—TOEFL (minimum score 600 paper-based; 97 iBT), IELTS (minimum score 7). *Application deadline:* For fall admission, 2/7 priority date for domestic students, 2/7 for international students; for spring admission, 11/1 for domestic and international students. Application fee: $50. Electronic applications accepted. *Expenses: Tuition:* Full-time $13,896; part-time $772 per credit. *Financial support:* In 2012–13, 52 students received support. Scholarships/grants, health care benefits, and unspecified assistantships available. Financial award application deadline: 2/7. *Faculty research:* Tobacco control; health of the elderly; youth health; mental health; women's health; reproductive and sexual health, including HIV/AIDS; water quality; health systems; quality in health care delivery; health human resources; health policy; occupational and environmental health; social inequality; social determinants of health; non-communicable diseases. *Total annual research expenditures:* $1.1 million. *Unit head:* Iman Adel Nuwayhid, Dean, 961-1340119, Fax: 961-1744470, E-mail: nuwayhid@aub.edu.lb. *Application contact:* Mitra Tauk, Administrative Coordinator, 961-1-350000 Ext. 4687, Fax: 961-1744470, E-mail: mt12@aub.edu.lb.

Antioch University New England, Graduate School, Department of Environmental Studies, Doctoral Program in Environmental Studies, Keene, NH 03431-3552. Offers PhD. *Degree requirements:* For doctorate, thesis/dissertation, practicum. *Entrance requirements:* For doctorate, master's degree and previous experience in the environmental field. Additional exam requirements/recommendations for international students: Required—TOEFL (minimum score 600 paper-based). Electronic applications accepted. *Expenses:* Contact institution. *Faculty research:* Environmental history, green politics, ecopsychology.

Antioch University New England, Graduate School, Department of Environmental Studies, Program in Environmental Education, Keene, NH 03431-3552. Offers MS. *Degree requirements:* For master's, practicum. *Entrance requirements:* For master's, previous undergraduate course work in biology, chemistry, mathematics (environmental biology); resume; 3 letters of recommendation. Additional exam requirements/recommendations for international students: Required—TOEFL (minimum score 550 paper-based). Electronic applications accepted. *Expenses:* Contact institution. *Faculty research:* Sustainability, natural resources inventory.

Arizona State University, College of Liberal Arts and Sciences, School of Human Evolution and Social Change, Tempe, AZ 85287-2402. Offers anthropology (PhD); anthropology (archaeology) (PhD); anthropology (bioarchaeology) (PhD); anthropology (museum studies) (MA); anthropology (physical) (PhD); applied mathematics for the life and social sciences (PhD); environmental social science (PhD); environmental social science (urbanism) (PhD); global health (MA); global health (health and culture) (PhD); global health (urbanism) (PhD); immigration studies (Graduate Certificate). Terminal master's awarded for partial completion of doctoral program. *Degree requirements:* For master's, thesis or alternative, interactive Program of Study (iPOS) submitted before completing 50 percent of required credit hours; for doctorate, comprehensive exam, thesis/dissertation, interactive Program of Study (iPOS) submitted before completing 50 percent of required credit hours. *Entrance requirements:* For master's and doctorate, GRE, minimum GPA of 3.0 or equivalent in last 2 years of work leading to bachelor's degree. Additional exam requirements/recommendations for international students: Required—TOEFL (minimum score 80 iBT), TOEFL, IELTS, or Pearson Test of English. Electronic applications accepted.

Arkansas State University, Graduate School, College of Sciences and Mathematics, Program in Environmental Sciences, Jonesboro, State University, AR 72467. Offers MS, PhD. Part-time programs available. *Faculty:* 1 (woman) full-time. *Students:* 20 full-time (7 women), 15 part-time (12 women); includes 5 minority (1 Black or African American, non-Hispanic/Latino; 1 Asian, non-Hispanic/Latino; 2 Hispanic/Latino; 1 Two or more races, non-Hispanic/Latino), 7 international. Average age 32. 11 applicants, 73% accepted, 7 enrolled. In 2012, 3 master's, 3 doctorates awarded. *Degree requirements:* For master's, comprehensive exam, thesis (for some programs); for doctorate, comprehensive exam, thesis/dissertation. *Entrance requirements:* For master's, GRE General Test, appropriate bachelor's degree, letters of reference, interview, official transcript, immunization records, letter of intent, resume, statement of purpose; for doctorate, GRE, appropriate bachelor's or master's degree, interview, letters of reference, personal statement, official transcript, immunization records, resume, statement of purpose. Additional exam requirements/recommendations for international students: Required—TOEFL (minimum score 550 paper-based; 79 iBT), IELTS (minimum score 6), Pearson Test of English (minimum score 56). *Application deadline:* For fall admission, 1/15 for domestic and international students; for spring admission, 8/15 for domestic and international students. Applications are processed on a rolling basis. Electronic applications accepted. *Expenses:* Tuition, state resident: full-time $4140; part-time $230 per credit hour. Tuition, nonresident: full-time $8280; part-time $460 per credit hour. *Required fees:* $56 per credit hour. $25 per term. Tuition and fees vary according to course load and program. *Financial support:* In 2012–13, 13 students received support. Fellowships, research assistantships, teaching assistantships, career-related internships or fieldwork, scholarships/grants, and unspecified assistantships available. Financial award application deadline: 7/1; financial award applicants required to submit FAFSA. *Unit head:* Dr. Thomas Risch, Director, 870-972-2007, Fax: 870-972-2008, E-mail: trisch@astate.edu. *Application contact:* Vickey Ring, Graduate Admissions Coordinator, 870-972-3029, Fax: 870-972-3857, E-mail: vickeyring@astate.edu. Website: http://www.astate.edu/college/sciences-and-mathematics/doctoral-programs/environmental-science/.

Ball State University, Graduate School, College of Sciences and Humanities, Program in Environmental Science, Muncie, IN 47306-1099. Offers PhD. *Students:* 3 full-time (0 women), 5 part-time (1 woman), 2 international. 6 applicants, 67% accepted, 1 enrolled. In 2012, 4 doctorates awarded. *Expenses:* Tuition, state resident: full-time $7666. Tuition, nonresident: full-time $19,114. *Required fees:* $782. *Financial support:* In 2012–13, 7 students received support, including 4 teaching assistantships with full and partial tuition reimbursements available (averaging $9,331 per year). Financial award application deadline: 3/1; financial award applicants required to submit FAFSA. *Unit head:* E. Michael Perdue, Director, 765-285-8096, E-mail: emperdue@bsu.edu. *Application contact:* Dr. Robert Morris, Associate Provost for Research and Dean of the Graduate School, 765-285-1300, E-mail: rmorris@bsu.edu. Website: http://cms.bsu.edu/Academics/CollegesandDepartments/EnvironmentalScience.aspx.

Baylor University, Graduate School, College of Arts and Sciences, The Institute of Ecological, Earth and Environmental Sciences, Waco, TX 76798. Offers PhD. *Students:* 10 full-time (3 women); includes 2 minority (1 Hispanic/Latino; 1 Two or more races, non-Hispanic/Latino), 5 international. In 2012, 1 doctorate awarded. *Degree requirements:* For doctorate, variable foreign language requirement, comprehensive exam, thesis/dissertation or alternative. *Entrance requirements:* For doctorate, GRE. Additional exam requirements/recommendations for international students: Required—TOEFL (minimum score 550 paper-based; 80 iBT); Recommended—IELTS (minimum score 6.5). *Application deadline:* For fall admission, 2/15 priority date for domestic students, 2/15 for international students; for spring admission, 11/15 for domestic and international students. Application fee: $40. Electronic applications accepted. *Expenses: Tuition:* Full-time $24,426; part-time $1357 per semester hour. *Required fees:* $2556; $142 per semester hour. *Financial support:* In 2012–13, 5 students received support, including 5 research assistantships with full and partial tuition reimbursements available (averaging $20,000 per year), 5 teaching assistantships with full and partial tuition reimbursements available (averaging $20,000 per year); career-related internships or fieldwork, scholarships/grants, traineeships, health care benefits, tuition waivers (partial), unspecified assistantships, and Presidential Scholarship (Baylor University) also available. Financial award application deadline: 2/15. *Faculty research:* Ecosystem processes, environmental toxicology and risk assessment, biogeochemical cycling, chemical fate and transport, conservation management. *Unit head:* Dr. Joseph D. White, Director, 254-710-2911, E-mail: joseph_d_white@baylor.edu. *Application contact:* Shannon Koehler, Administrative Associate, 254-710-2224, Fax: 254-710-2580, E-mail: shannon_koehler@baylor.edu. Website: http://www.baylor.edu/TIEEES/.

Binghamton University, State University of New York, Graduate School, School of Arts and Sciences, Department of Chemistry, Binghamton, NY 13902-6000. Offers analytical chemistry (PhD); chemistry (MA, MS); environmental (PhD); inorganic chemistry (PhD); organic chemistry (PhD); physical chemistry (PhD). Part-time programs available. *Faculty:* 16 full-time (4 women), 4 part-time/adjunct (1 woman). *Students:* 25 full-time (10 women), 26 part-time (10 women); includes 4 minority (3 Black or African American, non-Hispanic/Latino; 1 Hispanic/Latino), 33 international. Average age 28. 53 applicants, 49% accepted, 11 enrolled. In 2012, 3 master's, 6 doctorates awarded. Terminal master's awarded for partial completion of doctoral program. *Degree requirements:* For master's, thesis or alternative, oral exam, seminar presentation; for doctorate, thesis/dissertation, cumulative exams. *Entrance requirements:* For master's and doctorate, GRE General Test, GRE Subject Test. Additional exam requirements/recommendations for international students: Required—TOEFL (minimum score 550 paper-based; 80 iBT). *Application deadline:* For fall admission, 1/15 priority date for domestic students, 1/15 for international students; for spring admission, 10/15 priority date for domestic students, 10/15 for international students. Applications are processed on a rolling basis. Application fee: $75. Electronic applications accepted. *Expenses:* Tuition, state resident: full-time $9370. Tuition, nonresident: full-time $16,680. *Financial support:* In 2012–13, 47 students received support, including 5 research assistantships with full tuition reimbursements available (averaging $18,000 per year), 34 teaching assistantships with full tuition reimbursements available (averaging $18,000 per year); career-related internships or fieldwork, Federal Work-Study, institutionally sponsored loans, scholarships/grants, health care benefits, tuition waivers (full), and unspecified assistantships also available. Financial award application deadline: 2/15; financial award applicants required to submit FAFSA. *Unit head:* Dr. Wayne E. Jones, Chairperson, 607-777-2421, E-mail: wjones@binghamton.edu. *Application contact:* Kishan Zuber, Recruiting and Admissions Coordinator, 607-777-2151, Fax: 607-777-2501, E-mail: kzuber@binghamton.edu.

Boston University, Graduate School of Arts and Sciences, Department of Earth and Environment, Boston, MA 02215. Offers earth sciences (MA, PhD); energy and environmental analysis (MA); environmental remote sensing and GIS (MA); geography and environment (MA, PhD); global development policy (MA); international relations and environmental policy (MA). *Students:* 77 full-time (39 women), 11 part-time (5 women); includes 2 minority (1 American Indian or Alaska Native, non-Hispanic/Latino; 1 Asian, non-Hispanic/Latino), 25 international. Average age 27. 288 applicants, 33% accepted, 23 enrolled. In 2012, 4 master's, 6 doctorates awarded. *Degree requirements:* For master's, comprehensive exam (for some programs), thesis (for some programs); for doctorate, comprehensive exam, thesis/dissertation. *Entrance requirements:* For master's and doctorate, GRE, 3 letters of recommendation, official transcripts, personal statement. Additional exam requirements/recommendations for international students: Required—TOEFL (minimum score 550 paper-based; 84 iBT). *Application deadline:* For fall admission, 1/15 for domestic students, 11/15 for international students. Application fee: $80. Electronic applications accepted. *Expenses: Tuition:* Full-time $42,400; part-time $1325 per credit. *Required fees:* $40 per semester. *Financial support:* In 2012–13, 2 fellowships with full tuition reimbursements (averaging $20,300 per year), 32 research assistantships with full tuition reimbursements (averaging $19,800 per year), 19 teaching assistantships with full tuition reimbursements (averaging $19,800 per year) were awarded; Federal Work-Study, scholarships/grants, traineeships, and health care benefits also available. Financial award application deadline: 1/15. *Faculty research:* Biogeosciences, climate and surface processes; energy, environment and society; geographical sciences; geology, geochemistry and geophysics. *Unit head:* Curtis Woodcock, Chair, 617-353-5746, E-mail: curtis@bu.edu. *Application contact:* Christian Cole, Graduate Program Coordinator, 617-353-2529, Fax: 617-353-8399, E-mail: ccole@bu.edu. Website: http://www.bu.edu/earth/.

Brigham Young University, Graduate Studies, College of Life Sciences, Department of Plant and Wildlife Sciences, Provo, UT 84602. Offers environmental science (MS); genetics and biotechnology (MS); wildlife and wildlands conservation (MS, PhD). *Faculty:* 24 full-time (1 woman), 2 part-time/adjunct (1 woman). *Students:* 47 full-time (18 women); includes 6 minority (3 Asian, non-Hispanic/Latino; 2 Hispanic/Latino; 1 Native Hawaiian or other Pacific Islander, non-Hispanic/Latino), 2 international. Average age 28. 29 applicants, 41% accepted, 9 enrolled. In 2012, 15 master's, 2 doctorates awarded. *Degree requirements:* For master's, thesis; for doctorate, comprehensive exam, thesis/dissertation, minimum GPA of 3.2, 54 hours (18 dissertation, 36 coursework). *Entrance requirements:* For master's, GRE General Test, minimum GPA of 3.2 during last 60 hours of course work; for doctorate, GRE, minimum GPA of 3.2. Additional exam requirements/recommendations for international students: Required—TOEFL (minimum score 580 paper-based; 85 iBT). *Application deadline:* 2/1 for domestic and international students. Applications are processed on a rolling basis. Application fee: $50. Electronic applications accepted. *Expenses: Tuition:* Full-time $5950; part-time $331 per credit hour. Tuition and fees vary according to program and student's religious affiliation. *Financial support:* In 2012–13, 47 students received support, including 64 research assistantships with partial tuition reimbursements available (averaging $17,840 per year), 52 teaching assistantships with partial tuition reimbursements available (averaging $17,840 per year); scholarships/grants and tuition waivers (partial) also available. Financial award application deadline: 2/1. *Faculty research:* Environmental science, plant genetics, plant ecology, plant nutrition and pathology, wildlife and wildlands conservation. *Total annual research expenditures:* $1.9 million. *Unit head:* Dr. Eric N. Jellen, Chair, 801-422-3527, Fax: 801-422-0008, E-mail: rick_jellen@byu.edu. *Application contact:* Dr. Brock R. McMillan, Graduate Coordinator, 801-422-1228, Fax: 801-422-0008, E-mail: brock_mcmillan@byu.edu. Website: http://pws.byu.edu/home/.

California Institute of Technology, Division of Geological and Planetary Sciences, Pasadena, CA 91125-0001. Offers environmental science and engineering (MS, PhD); geobiology (MS, PhD); geochemistry (MS, PhD); geology (MS, PhD); geophysics (MS, PhD); planetary science (MS, PhD). *Faculty:* 43 full-time (8 women). *Students:* 110 full-time (52 women); includes 9 minority (1 Black or African American, non-Hispanic/Latino; 7 Asian, non-Hispanic/Latino; 1 Hispanic/Latino), 30 international. Average age 26. 225 applicants, 19% accepted, 24 enrolled. In 2012, 7 master's, 13 doctorates awarded. *Degree requirements:* For doctorate, thesis/dissertation. *Entrance requirements:* For doctorate, GRE General Test. Additional exam requirements/recommendations for international students: Required—TOEFL; Recommended—IELTS, TWE. *Application deadline:* For fall admission, 1/1 for domestic and international students. Application fee: $80. Electronic applications accepted. *Financial support:* In 2012–13, 19 fellowships with full tuition reimbursements (averaging $29,000 per year), 72 research assistantships with full tuition reimbursements (averaging $29,000 per year) were awarded; teaching assistantships with full tuition reimbursements, institutionally sponsored loans, scholarships/grants, health care benefits, and unspecified assistantships also available. Financial award applicants required to submit FAFSA. *Faculty research:* Planetary surfaces, evolution of anaerobic respiratory processes, structural geology and tectonics, theoretical and numerical seismology, global biogeochemical cycles. *Unit head:* Dr. Kenneth A. Farley, Chairman, 626-395-6111, Fax: 626-795-6028, E-mail: dianb@gps.caltech.edu. *Application contact:* Dr. Robert W. Clayton, Academic Officer, 626-395-6909, Fax: 626-795-6028, E-mail: dianb@gps.caltech.edu. Website: http://www.gps.caltech.edu/.

California State Polytechnic University, Pomona, Academic Affairs, College of Environmental Design, John T. Lyle Center for Regenerative Studies, Pomona, CA 91768-2557. Offers MS. Part-time programs available. *Students:* 10 full-time (3 women), 22 part-time (13 women); includes 11 minority (1 Black or African American, non-Hispanic/Latino; 3 Asian, non-Hispanic/Latino; 4 Hispanic/Latino; 3 Two or more races, non-Hispanic/Latino), 1 international. Average age 31. 30 applicants, 70% accepted, 9 enrolled. In 2012, 11 master's awarded. *Application deadline:* For fall admission, 5/1 priority date for domestic students; for winter admission, 10/15 priority date for domestic students; for spring admission, 1/20 priority date for domestic students. Applications are processed on a rolling basis. Application fee: $55. Electronic applications accepted. *Financial support:* Application deadline: 3/2; applicants required to submit FAFSA. *Unit head:* Dr. Kyle D. Brown, Director, 909-869-5178, E-mail: kdbrown@csupomona.edu. *Application contact:* Deborah L. Brandon, Executive Director, Admissions and Outreach, 909-869-3427, Fax: 909-869-5315, E-mail: dlbrandon@csupomona.edu. Website: http://www.csupomona.edu/~crs/.

California State University, Chico, Office of Graduate Studies, College of Natural Sciences, Department of Geological and Environmental Sciences, Program in Environmental Science, Chico, CA 95929-0722. Offers MS. Part-time programs available. *Faculty:* 5 full-time (2 women), 3 part-time/adjunct (1 woman). *Students:* 9 full-time (3 women), 4 part-time (1 woman); includes 3 minority (all Asian, non-Hispanic/Latino), 2 international. Average age 31. 9 applicants, 67% accepted, 4 enrolled. In 2012, 0 master's awarded. *Degree requirements:* For master's, comprehensive exam, thesis. *Entrance requirements:* For master's, GRE, two letters of recommendation, faculty mentor, statement of purpose. Additional exam requirements/recommendations for international students: Required—TOEFL (minimum score 550 paper-based; 80 iBT), IELTS (minimum score 6.5), Pearson Test of English (minimum score 59). *Application deadline:* For fall admission, 3/1 priority date for domestic students, 3/1 for international students; for spring admission, 9/15 priority date for domestic students, 9/15 for international students. Application fee: $55. Electronic applications accepted. *Expenses:* Tuition, state resident: part-time $372 per unit. Tuition, nonresident: part-time $372 per unit. *Required fees:* $2687 per semester. Tuition and fees vary according to course level and program. *Financial support:* Research assistantships, teaching assistantships, and career-related internships or fieldwork available. Financial award application deadline: 3/1; financial award applicants required to submit FAFSA. *Unit head:* Dr. David L. Brown, Chair, 530-898-5262, Fax: 530-898-5234, E-mail: geos@csuchico.edu. *Application contact:* Judy L. Rice, Graduate Admissions Coordinator, 530-898-5416, Fax: 530-898-3342, E-mail: jlrice@csuchico.edu. Website: http://catalog.csuchico.edu/viewer/12/GEOS.html.

California State University, Dominguez Hills, College of Natural and Behavioral Sciences, Program in Environmental Science, Carson, CA 90747-0001. Offers MS. *Faculty:* 1 (woman) full-time. *Students:* 3 full-time (1 woman), 11 part-time (4 women); includes 4 minority (1 Black or African American, non-Hispanic/Latino; 3 Hispanic/Latino), 3 international. Average age 34. 4 applicants. In 2012, 1 master's awarded. Application fee: $55. *Expenses:* Tuition, state resident: full-time $6738; part-time $1953 per semester. Tuition, nonresident: full-time $13,434; part-time $372 per unit. *Required fees:* $314 per semester. *Unit head:* Dr. John Keyantash, Chair, 310-243-2363, E-mail: jkeyantash@csudh.edu. *Application contact:* Brandy McLelland, Director of Student Information Services and Registrar, 310-243-3645, E-mail: bmclelland@csudh.edu. Website: http://www.nbs.csudh.edu/.

California State University, East Bay, Office of Academic Programs and Graduate Studies, College of Science, Department of Earth and Environmental Sciences, Hayward, CA 94542-3000. Offers geology (MS), including environmental geology, geology. Part-time and evening/weekend programs available. *Degree requirements:* For master's, thesis or project. *Entrance requirements:* For master's, GRE, minimum GPA of 2.75 in field, 2.5 overall; 2 letters of recommendation. Additional exam requirements/recommendations for international students: Required—TOEFL (minimum score 550 paper-based). Electronic applications accepted. *Faculty research:* Hydrology, seismic activity; origins of life.

California State University, Northridge, Graduate Studies, College of Science and Mathematics, Department of Chemistry and Biochemistry, Northridge, CA 91330. Offers biochemistry (MS); chemistry (MS), including chemistry, environmental chemistry. *Degree requirements:* For master's, thesis. *Entrance requirements:* For master's, GRE General Test or minimum GPA of 3.0. Additional exam requirements/recommendations for international students: Required—TOEFL. Electronic applications accepted.

California State University, San Bernardino, Graduate Studies, College of Social and Behavioral Sciences, Program in Environmental Sciences, San Bernardino, CA 92407-2397. Offers MS. *Students:* 4 full-time (2 women), 12 part-time (6 women); includes 9 minority (3 Asian, non-Hispanic/Latino; 5 Hispanic/Latino; 1 Two or more races, non-Hispanic/Latino), 1 international. Average age 33. 2 applicants, 50% accepted, 0 enrolled. In 2012, 2 master's awarded. *Unit head:* Dr. Joan E. Fryxell, Graduate Coordinator, 909-537-5311, E-mail: jfryxell@csusb.edu. *Application contact:* Dr. Jeffrey Thompson, Dean of Graduate Studies, 909-537-5058, E-mail: jthompso@csusb.edu.

Christopher Newport University, Graduate Studies, Department of Biology, Chemistry and Environmental Science, Newport News, VA 23606-2998. Offers environmental science (MS). Part-time and evening/weekend programs available. *Degree requirements:* For master's, comprehensive exam, thesis optional. *Entrance requirements:* For master's, GRE General Test, minimum GPA of 3.0.

Additional exam requirements/recommendations for international students: Required—TOEFL (minimum score 580 paper-based; 92 iBT). Electronic applications accepted. *Faculty research:* Wetlands ecology and restoration, aquatic ecology, wetlands mitigation, greenhouse gases.

City College of the City University of New York, Graduate School, College of Liberal Arts and Science, Division of Science, Department of Earth and Atmospheric Sciences, New York, NY 10031-9198. Offers earth and environmental science (PhD); earth systems science (MA). PhD program offered jointly with Graduate School and University Center of the City University of New York. *Degree requirements:* For master's, comprehensive exam, thesis. *Entrance requirements:* Additional exam requirements/recommendations for international students: Required—TOEFL (minimum score 500 paper-based; 61 iBT). Electronic applications accepted. *Faculty research:* Water resources, high-temperature geochemistry, sedimentary basin analysis, tectonics.

Clarkson University, Graduate School, Institute for a Sustainable Environment, Program in Environmental Science and Engineering, Potsdam, NY 13699. Offers MS, PhD. Part-time programs available. *Faculty:* 7 full-time (4 women). *Students:* 26 full-time (12 women), 2 part-time (1 woman); includes 2 minority (both Two or more races, non-Hispanic/Latino), 10 international. Average age 27. 58 applicants, 62% accepted, 7 enrolled. In 2012, 12 master's, 1 doctorate awarded. Terminal master's awarded for partial completion of doctoral program. *Degree requirements:* For master's, thesis; for doctorate, comprehensive exam, thesis/dissertation, departmental qualifying exam. *Entrance requirements:* For master's and doctorate, GRE, transcripts of all college coursework, resume, personal statement, three letters of recommendation. Additional exam requirements/recommendations for international students: Required—TOEFL (minimum score 550 paper-based; 80 iBT), IELTS (minimum score 6.5). *Application deadline:* For fall admission, 1/30 priority date for domestic students, 1/30 for international students; for spring admission, 9/1 priority date for domestic students, 9/1 for international students. Applications are processed on a rolling basis. Application fee: $25 ($35 for international students). Electronic applications accepted. *Expenses: Tuition:* Full-time $15,108; part-time $1259 per credit hour. *Required fees:* $295 per semester. *Financial support:* In 2012–13, 23 students received support, including fellowships with full tuition reimbursements available (averaging $22,650 per year), 9 research assistantships with full tuition reimbursements available (averaging $22,650 per year), 6 teaching assistantships with full tuition reimbursements available (averaging $22,650 per year); scholarships/grants, tuition waivers (partial), and unspecified assistantships also available. *Faculty research:* Biological, chemical, physical and social systems, renewable energy, environmental health. *Unit head:* Dr. Philip Hopke, Director, 315-268-3856, Fax: 315-268-4291, E-mail: hopkepk@clarkson.edu. *Application contact:* Mary Jane Smalling, Senior Departmental Secretary, 315-268-2318, Fax: 315-268-4291, E-mail: msmallin@clarkson.edu. Website: http://www.clarkson.edu/ese/.

Clemson University, Graduate School, College of Agriculture, Forestry and Life Sciences, Program in Environmental Toxicology, Clemson, SC 29634. Offers MS, PhD. *Students:* 22 full-time (11 women), 3 part-time (1 woman); includes 2 minority (1 Asian, non-Hispanic/Latino; 1 Two or more races, non-Hispanic/Latino), 5 international. Average age 28. 34 applicants, 21% accepted, 6 enrolled. In 2012, 4 master's, 5 doctorates awarded. *Degree requirements:* For master's, thesis; for doctorate, one foreign language, thesis/dissertation. *Entrance requirements:* For master's and doctorate, GRE General Test. Additional exam requirements/recommendations for international students: Required—TOEFL. *Application deadline:* For fall admission, 2/1 for domestic and international students; for spring admission, 9/15 for domestic and international students. Applications are processed on a rolling basis. Application fee: $70 ($80 for international students). Electronic applications accepted. *Expenses:* Contact institution. *Financial support:* In 2012–13, 19 students received support, including 1 fellowship with full and partial tuition reimbursement available (averaging $7,000 per year), 9 research assistantships with partial tuition reimbursements available (averaging $12,534 per year), 14 teaching assistantships with partial tuition reimbursements available (averaging $15,357 per year); career-related internships or fieldwork, Federal Work-Study, institutionally sponsored loans, scholarships/grants, health care benefits, and unspecified assistantships also available. Financial award applicants required to submit FAFSA. *Faculty research:* Biochemical toxicology, analytical toxicology, ecological risk assessment, aqutic toxicology, environmental engineering. *Total annual research expenditures:* $3 million. *Unit head:* Dr. Lisa J. Bain, Graduate Program Director, 864-656-5050, E-mail: lbain@clemson.edu. Website: http://www.clemson.edu/entox.

Cleveland State University, College of Graduate Studies, College of Sciences and Health Professions, Department of Biological, Geological, and Environmental Sciences, Cleveland, OH 44115. Offers biology (MS); environmental science (MS); museum studies for natural historians (MS); regulatory biology (PhD); JD/MS. Part-time programs available. *Faculty:* 11 full-time (3 women), 1 part-time/adjunct (0 women). *Students:* 3 full-time (1 woman), 98 part-time (55 women); includes 8 minority (2 Black or African American, non-Hispanic/Latino; 5 Asian, non-Hispanic/Latino; 1 Hispanic/Latino), 46 international. Average age 30. 74 applicants, 69% accepted, 16 enrolled. In 2012, 13 master's, 6 doctorates awarded. Terminal master's awarded for partial completion of doctoral program. *Degree requirements:* For master's, comprehensive exam (for some programs), thesis (for some programs); for doctorate, comprehensive exam, thesis/dissertation. *Entrance requirements:* For master's, GRE General Test, 2 letters of recommendation; for doctorate, GRE General Test, 2 letters of recommendation; 1-2 page essay; statement of career goals and research interests. Additional exam requirements/recommendations for international students: Required—TOEFL (minimum score 525 paper-based). *Application deadline:* For fall admission, 4/1 priority date for domestic students, 4/1 for international students; for spring admission, 12/1 priority date for domestic students. Applications are processed on a rolling basis. Application fee: $30. Electronic applications accepted. *Expenses:* Tuition, state resident: full-time $8172; part-time $510.75 per credit hour. Tuition, nonresident: full-time $15,372; part-time $960.75 per credit hour. *Required fees:* $25 per semester. Tuition and fees vary according to course load and program. *Financial support:* In 2012–13, 29 students received support, including research assistantships with full and partial tuition reimbursements available (averaging $16,500 per year), teaching assistantships with full and partial tuition reimbursements available (averaging $16,500 per year); institutionally sponsored loans and unspecified assistantships also available. *Faculty research:* Molecular and cell biology, immunology, urban ecology. *Unit head:* Dr. Jeffrey Dean, Chair, 216-687-2120, Fax: 216-687-6972, E-mail: j.dean@csuohio.edu. *Application contact:* Deborah L. Brown, Interim Assistant Director, Graduate Admissions, 216-523-7572, Fax: 216-687-5400, E-mail: d.l.brown@csuohio.edu. Website: http://www.csuohio.edu/sciences/dept/biology/index.html.

The College at Brockport, State University of New York, School of Science and Mathematics, Department of Environmental Science and Biology, Brockport, NY 14420-2997. Offers MS. Part-time programs available. *Students:* 7 full-time (5 women), 14 part-time (4 women); includes 1 minority (Asian, non-Hispanic/Latino). 10 applicants, 60% accepted, 3 enrolled. In 2012, 4 master's awarded. *Degree requirements:* For master's, comprehensive exam, thesis. *Entrance requirements:* For master's, minimum GPA of 3.0, letters of recommendation, sample of scientific writing; statement of objectives. Additional exam requirements/recommendations for international students: Required—TOEFL (minimum score 550 paper-based; 79 iBT). *Application deadline:* For fall admission, 4/15 priority date for domestic students, 4/15 for international students; for spring admission, 11/15 priority date for domestic students, 11/15 for international students. Application fee: $50. Electronic applications accepted. *Expenses:* Tuition, state resident: full-time $9370; part-time $390 per credit. Tuition, nonresident: full-time $16,680; part-time $695 per credit. *Required fees:* $2882; $226 per semester. *Financial support:* In 2012–13, 2 research assistantships with full tuition reimbursements (averaging $6,000 per year) were awarded; Federal Work-Study, scholarships/grants, and unspecified assistantships also available. Support available to part-time students. Financial award application deadline: 3/15; financial award applicants required to submit FAFSA. *Faculty research:* Aquatic and terrestrial ecology/organismal biology, watersheds and wetlands, persistent toxic chemicals, soil-plant interactions, aquaculture. *Unit head:* Dr. James Haynes, Chairperson, 585-395-5975, Fax: 585-395-5969, E-mail: jhaynes@brockport.edu. *Application contact:* Dr. Joseph Makarewic, Graduate Director, 585-395-5747, Fax: 585-395-5969, E-mail: jmakarew@brockport.edu. Website: http://www.brockport.edu/envsci/grad/.

College of Charleston, Graduate School, School of Sciences and Mathematics, Program in Environmental Studies, Charleston, SC 29424-0001. Offers MS. Part-time and evening/weekend programs available. *Degree requirements:* For master's, thesis optional, thesis or research internship. *Entrance requirements:* For master's, GRE, minimum GPA of 3.0, 3 letters of recommendation. Additional exam requirements/recommendations for international students: Required—TOEFL (minimum score 81 iBT). Electronic applications accepted. *Expenses:* Contact institution.

College of Staten Island of the City University of New York, Graduate Programs, Program in Environmental Science, Staten Island, NY 10314-6600. Offers MS. Part-time and evening/weekend programs available. *Faculty:* 5 full-time (0 women), 1 (woman) part-time/adjunct. *Students:* Average age 29. 20 applicants, 50% accepted, 6 enrolled. In 2012, 10 master's awarded. Terminal master's awarded for partial completion of doctoral program. *Degree requirements:* For master's, thesis. *Entrance requirements:* For master's, GRE General Test, 1 year of course work in chemistry, physics, calculus, and ecology; overall average grade of B-, or the equivalent, in undergraduate work and B average, or the equivalent, in undergraduate science and engineering courses; bachelor's degree in a natural science or engineering; interview. Additional exam requirements/recommendations for international students: Required—TOEFL (minimum score 550 paper-based; 79 iBT), IELTS (minimum score 6.5). *Application deadline:* For fall admission, 4/25 priority date for domestic students, 4/22 for international students; for spring admission, 11/19 priority date for domestic students, 11/19 for international students. Applications are processed on a rolling basis. Application fee: $125. Electronic applications accepted. *Expenses:* Tuition, state resident: full-time $8690; part-time $365 per credit. Tuition, nonresident: part-time $675 per credit. *Required fees:* $428; $128 per semester. *Financial support:* Fellowships, career-related internships or fieldwork, Federal Work-Study, and scholarships/grants available. Support available to part-time students. Financial award applicants required to submit FAFSA. *Faculty research:* Staten Island Cancer Research Initiative. *Total annual research expenditures:* $130,000. *Unit head:* Dr. Alfred Levine, Director, 718-982-2822, Fax: 718-982-3923, E-mail: alfred.levine@csi.cuny.edu. *Application contact:* Sasha Spence, Assistant Director for Graduate Admissions, 718-982-2019, Fax: 718-982-2500, E-mail: sasha.spence@csi.cuny.edu. Website: http://www.csi.cuny.edu/catalog/graduate/master-of-science-in-environmental-science-ms.htm.

Colorado School of Mines, Graduate School, Division of Environmental Science and Engineering, Golden, CO 80401-1887. Offers civil and environmental engineering (MS, PhD); environmental engineering science (MS, PhD). Part-time programs available. *Faculty:* 31 full-time (11 women), 9 part-time/adjunct (6 women). *Students:* 141 full-time (52 women), 33 part-time (9 women); includes 24 minority (3 Black or African American, non-Hispanic/Latino; 7 Asian, non-Hispanic/Latino; 13 Hispanic/Latino; 1 Two or more races, non-Hispanic/Latino), 20 international. Average age 28. 215 applicants, 60% accepted, 65 enrolled. In 2012, 51 master's, 9 doctorates awarded. *Degree requirements:* For master's, thesis (for some programs); for doctorate, comprehensive exam, thesis/dissertation. *Entrance requirements:* For master's and doctorate, GRE General Test. Additional exam requirements/recommendations for international students: Required—TOEFL (minimum score 550 paper-based; 80 iBT). *Application deadline:* For fall admission, 1/15 priority date for domestic students, 1/15 for international students; for spring admission, 10/15 priority date for domestic students, 10/15 for international students. Application fee: $50 ($70 for international students). Electronic applications accepted. *Financial support:* In 2012–13, 77 students received support, including 14 fellowships with full tuition reimbursements available (averaging $21,120 per year), 55 research assistantships with full tuition reimbursements available (averaging $21,120 per year), 8 teaching assistantships with full tuition reimbursements available (averaging $21,120 per year); scholarships/grants, health care benefits, and unspecified assistantships also available. Financial award application deadline: 1/15; financial award applicants required to submit FAFSA. *Faculty research:* Treatment of water and wastes, environmental law: policy and practice, natural environment systems, hazardous waste management, environmental data analysis. *Total annual research expenditures:* $4.9 million. *Unit head:* Dr. John McCray, Director, 303-384-3490, Fax: 303-273-3413, E-mail: jmccray@mines.edu. *Application contact:* Tim VanHaverbeke, Research Faculty, 303-273-3467, Fax: 303-273-3413, E-mail: tvanhave@mines.edu. Website: http://ese.mines.edu.

Columbia University, Graduate School of Arts and Sciences, Program in Climate and Society, New York, NY 10027. Offers MA.

Columbia University, School of International and Public Affairs, Program in Environmental Science and Policy, New York, NY 10027. Offers MPA. Program admits applicants for late May/early June start only. *Degree requirements:* For master's, workshops. *Entrance requirements:* For master's, GRE, previous course work in biology and chemistry, earth sciences (recommended), economics (strongly recommended). Additional exam requirements/recommendations for international students: Required—TOEFL. Electronic applications accepted. *Faculty research:* Ecological management of enclosed ecosystems vegetation dynamics, environmental policy and management, energy policy, nuclear waste policy, environmental and natural resource economics and policy, carbon sequestration, urban planning, environmental risk assessment/toxicology, environmental justice.

Columbus State University, Graduate Studies, College of Letters and Sciences, Environmental Science Program, Columbus, GA 31907-5645. Offers MS. Part-time and evening/weekend programs available. *Degree requirements:* For master's, thesis. *Entrance requirements:* For master's, GRE General Test, minimum GPA of 3.0. Additional exam requirements/recommendations for international students: Required—TOEFL (minimum score 550 paper-based; 79 iBT). Electronic applications accepted.

Cornell University, Graduate School, Graduate Fields of Agriculture and Life Sciences, Field of Soil and Crop Sciences, Ithaca, NY 14853-0001. Offers agronomy (MS, PhD); environmental information science (MS, PhD); environmental management (MPS); field crop science (MS, PhD); soil science (MS, PhD). *Faculty:* 41 full-time (10 women). *Students:* 16 full-time (10 women); includes 4 minority (all Hispanic/Latino), 5 international. Average age 30. 54 applicants, 17% accepted, 5 enrolled. In 2012, 10 master's, 5 doctorates awarded. *Degree requirements:* For master's, thesis (MS); for doctorate, comprehensive exam, thesis/dissertation. *Entrance requirements:* For master's and doctorate, GRE General Test, 2 letters of recommendation. Additional exam requirements/recommendations for international students: Required—TOEFL (minimum score 550 paper-based; 77 iBT). *Application deadline:* For fall admission, 2/1 priority date for domestic students. Applications are processed on a rolling basis. Application fee: $95. Electronic applications accepted. *Financial support:* In 2012–13, 12 students received support, including 7 fellowships with full tuition reimbursements available, 5 teaching assistantships with full tuition reimbursements available; research assistantships with full tuition reimbursements available, institutionally sponsored loans, traineeships, health care benefits, tuition waivers (full and partial), and unspecified assistantships also available. *Faculty research:* Soil chemistry, physics and biology; crop physiology and management; environmental information science and modeling; international agriculture; weed science. *Unit head:* Director of Graduate Studies, 607-255-3267, Fax: 607-255-8615. *Application contact:* Graduate Field Assistant, 607-255-3267, Fax: 607-255-8615, E-mail: ljh4@cornell.edu. Website: http://www.gradschool.cornell.edu/fields.php?id-5A&a-2.

Dalhousie University, Faculty of Agriculture, Halifax, NS B3H 4R2, Canada. Offers agriculture (M Sc), including air quality, animal behavior, animal molecular genetics, animal nutrition, animal technology, aquaculture, botany, crop management, crop physiology, ecology, environmental microbiology, food science, horticulture, nutrient management, pest management, physiology, plant biotechnology, plant pathology, soil chemistry, soil fertility, waste management and composting, water quality. Part-time programs available. *Degree requirements:* For master's, thesis, ATC Exam Teaching Assistantship. *Entrance requirements:* For master's, honors B Sc, minimum GPA of 3.0. Additional exam requirements/recommendations for international students: Required—TOEFL (minimum score 580 paper-based; 92 iBT), IELTS, Michigan English Language Assessment Battery, CanTEST, CAEL. *Faculty research:* Bio-product development, organic agriculture, nutrient management, air and water quality, agricultural biotechnology.

Drexel University, College of Arts and Sciences, Program in Environmental Science, Philadelphia, PA 19104-2875. Offers MS, PhD. Part-time and evening/weekend programs available. Terminal master's awarded for partial completion of doctoral program. *Degree requirements:* For master's, thesis optional; for doctorate, thesis/dissertation. Electronic applications accepted.

Duke University, Graduate School, Nicholas School of the Environment, Durham, NC 27708. Offers environmental management (MEM); forestry (MF); natural resource economics/policy (PhD); natural resource science/ecology (PhD); natural resource systems science (PhD); JD/AM. Part-time programs available. *Faculty:* 28 full-time. *Students:* 59 full-time (33 women); includes 2 minority (both Asian, non-Hispanic/Latino), 18 international. 99 applicants, 19% accepted, 12 enrolled. In 2012, 11 doctorates awarded. *Degree requirements:* For doctorate, variable foreign language requirement, thesis/dissertation. *Entrance requirements:* For master's and doctorate, GRE General Test. Additional exam requirements/recommendations for international students: Required—TOEFL (minimum score 550 paper-based; 83 iBT), IELTS (minimum score 7). *Application deadline:* For fall admission, 12/8 priority date for domestic students, 12/8 for international students. Application fee: $80. Electronic applications accepted. *Financial support:* Fellowships, research assistantships, teaching assistantships, and Federal Work-Study available. Financial award application deadline: 12/8. *Unit head:* Gaby Katul, Director of Graduate Studies, 919-613-8002, Fax: 919-613-8061, E-mail: meg.stephens@duke.edu. *Application contact:* Elizabeth Hutton, Director, Graduate Admissions, 919-684-3913, Fax: 919-684-2277, E-mail: grad-admissions@duke.edu. Website: http://www.nicholas.duke.edu/.

Duquesne University, Bayer School of Natural and Environmental Sciences, Environmental Science and Management Program, Pittsburgh, PA 15282-0001. Offers environmental management (Certificate); environmental science (Certificate); environmental science and management (MS); JD/MS; MBA/MS; MS/MS. Part-time and evening/weekend programs available. Postbaccalaureate distance learning degree programs offered (minimal on-campus study). *Faculty:* 2 full-time (0 women), 8 part-time/adjunct (1 woman). *Students:* 19 full-time (12 women), 20 part-time (11 women); includes 4 minority (2 Asian, non-Hispanic/Latino; 2 Hispanic/Latino), 5 international. Average age 26. 41 applicants, 54% accepted, 12 enrolled. In 2012, 18 master's, 3 other advanced degrees awarded. *Degree requirements:* For master's, thesis (for some programs), minimum of 36 credit hours; for Certificate, minimum of 18 credit hours. *Entrance requirements:* For master's, GRE General Test, course work in biology, chemistry, and calculus or statistics; 3 letters of reference, official transcripts, statement of purpose; for Certificate, undergraduate degree, 3 letters of reference, official transcripts, statement of purpose. Additional exam requirements/recommendations for international students: Required—TOEFL (minimum score 80 iBT). *Application deadline:* For fall admission, 4/1 priority date for domestic students, 4/1 for international students; for spring admission, 10/1 priority date for domestic students, 10/1 for international students. Applications are processed on a rolling basis. Application fee: $40. *Expenses:* Contact institution. *Financial support:* In 2012–13, 9 students received support, including 1 fellowship with full tuition reimbursement available (averaging $16,500 per year), 7 research assistantships (averaging $13,350 per year), 1 teaching assistantship with partial tuition reimbursement available; career-related internships or fieldwork, scholarships/grants, tuition waivers (partial), and unspecified assistantships also available. Financial award application deadline: 5/31. *Faculty research:* Watershed management systems, environmental analytical chemistry, environmental endocrinology, environmental microbiology, aquatic biology. *Total annual research expenditures:* $113,953. *Unit head:* Dr. John Stolz, Director, 412-396-4367, Fax: 412-396-4092, E-mail: stolz@duq.edu. *Application contact:* Heather Costello, Graduate Academic Advisor, 412-396-6339, Fax: 412-396-4881, E-mail: costelloh@duq.edu. Website: http://www.duq.edu/academics/schools/natural-and-environmental-sciences/academic-programs/environmental-science-and-management.

Florida Agricultural and Mechanical University, School of the Environment, Tallahassee, FL 32307. Offers MS, PhD. *Faculty:* 9 full-time (2 women). *Students:* 24 full-time (18 women), 7 part-time (3 women); includes 23 minority (20 Black or African American, non-Hispanic/Latino; 1 Asian, non-Hispanic/Latino; 2 Hispanic/Latino), 5 international. Average age 25. 14 applicants, 64% accepted, 6 enrolled. In 2012, 4 master's, 4 doctorates awarded. *Degree requirements:* For master's, thesis; for doctorate, comprehensive exam, thesis/dissertation, oral exam. *Entrance requirements:* For master's and doctorate, GRE General Test, minimum GPA of 3.0. Additional exam requirements/recommendations for international students: Required—TOEFL. *Application deadline:* For fall admission, 6/30 priority date for domestic students, 3/30 for international students; for spring admission, 11/1 priority date for domestic students, 10/1 for international students. Application fee: $30. *Financial support:* In 2012–13, 29 students received support, including 29 research assistantships with full and partial tuition reimbursements available; career-related internships or fieldwork, institutionally sponsored loans, scholarships/grants, tuition waivers (partial), and unspecified assistantships also available. Financial award application deadline: 6/10; financial award applicants required to submit FAFSA. *Faculty research:* Environmental chemistry, environmental policy and risk management, aquatic and terrestrial ecology, biomolecular sciences. *Unit head:* Dr. Michael Abazinge, Interim Dean, 850-599-3550, Fax: 850-599-8183, E-mail: michael.abazinge@famu.edu. *Application contact:* Hazel Taylor, Coordinator, Research Programs and Services, 850-599-8193, Fax: 850-412-7785, E-mail: hazel.taylor@famu.edu. Website: http://www.famu.edu/index.cfm?environmentalscience.

Florida Gulf Coast University, College of Arts and Sciences, Program in Environmental Science, Fort Myers, FL 33965-6565. Offers MS. Part-time programs available. *Faculty:* 219 full-time (88 women), 155 part-time/adjunct (61 women). *Students:* 36 full-time (21 women), 11 part-time (3 women); includes 2 minority (1 Hispanic/Latino; 1 Two or more races, non-Hispanic/Latino), 1 international. Average age 32. 40 applicants, 55% accepted, 15 enrolled. In 2012, 6 master's awarded. *Entrance requirements:* For master's, GRE General Test, minimum GPA of 3.0. Additional exam requirements/recommendations for international students: Required—TOEFL (minimum score 550 paper-based). *Application deadline:* For fall admission, 2/15 priority date for domestic students. Applications are processed on a rolling basis. Application fee: $30. Electronic applications accepted. *Expenses:* Tuition, state resident: full-time $6458. Tuition, nonresident: full-time $28,170. *Required fees:* $1952. Tuition and fees vary according to course load. *Faculty research:* Political issues in environmental science, recycling, environmentally-friendly buildings, pathophysiology, immunotoxicology of marine organisms. *Unit head:* Dr. Brian Bovard, Chair, 239-590-7564, Fax: 239-590-7200, E-mail: bbovard@fgcu.edu. *Application contact:* Patricia Price, Executive Secretary, 239-590-7196, Fax: 239-590-7200, E-mail: price@fgcu.edu.

Florida Institute of Technology, Graduate Programs, College of Engineering, Department of Marine and Environmental Systems, Melbourne, FL 32901-6975. Offers earth remote sensing (MS); environmental resource management (MS); environmental science (MS, PhD); meteorology (MS); ocean engineering (MS, PhD); oceanography (MS, PhD), including biological oceanography (MS), chemical oceanography (MS), coastal management (MS), geological oceanography (MS), oceanography (PhD), physical oceanography (MS). Part-time programs available. *Faculty:* 15 full-time (0 women), 2 part-time/adjunct (0 women). *Students:* 53 full-time (19 women), 15 part-time (4 women); includes 3 minority (1 Asian, non-Hispanic/Latino; 1 Hispanic/Latino; 1 Two or more races, non-Hispanic/Latino), 23 international. Average age 27. 141 applicants, 45% accepted, 21 enrolled. In 2012, 16 master's, 4 doctorates awarded. *Degree requirements:* For master's, comprehensive exam (for some programs), thesis (for some programs), seminar, field project, written final exam, technical paper, oral presentation, or internship; for doctorate, comprehensive exam, thesis/dissertation, seminar, internships (oceanography and environmental science), publications. *Entrance requirements:* For master's, GRE General Test (environmental science, oceanography, environmental resource management, meteorology, earth remote sensing), 3 letters of recommendation, minimum GPA of 3.0, resume, transcripts, statement of objectives; for doctorate, GRE General Test (oceanography, environmental science), resume, 3 letters of recommendation, minimum GPA of 3.3, statement of objectives, on-campus interview (highly recommended). Additional exam requirements/recommendations for international students: Required—TOEFL (minimum score 550 paper-based; 79 iBT). *Application deadline:* For fall admission, 4/1 for international students; for spring admission, 9/30 for international students. Applications are processed on a rolling basis. Electronic applications accepted. *Expenses: Tuition:* Full-time $20,214; part-time $1123 per credit hour. Tuition and fees vary according to campus/location. *Financial support:* In 2012–13, 5 fellowships with full and partial tuition reimbursements (averaging $5,400 per year), 8 research assistantships with full and partial tuition reimbursements (averaging $7,851 per year), 13 teaching assistantships with full and partial tuition reimbursements (averaging $5,565 per year) were awarded; career-related internships or fieldwork, institutionally sponsored loans, tuition waivers (partial), unspecified assistantships, and tuition remissions also available. Support available to part-time students. Financial award application deadline: 3/1; financial award applicants required to submit FAFSA. *Total annual research expenditures:* $2.2 million. *Unit head:* Dr. George Maul, Department Head, 321-674-7453, Fax: 321-674-7212, E-mail: gmaul@fit.edu. *Application contact:* Cheryl A. Brown, Associate Director of Graduate Admissions, 321-674-7581, Fax: 321-723-9468, E-mail: cbrown@fit.edu. Website: http://coe.fit.edu/dmes/.

Florida International University, College of Arts and Sciences, Department of Earth and Environment, Program in Environmental Studies, Miami, FL 33199. Offers MS. Part-time programs available. *Degree requirements:* For master's, thesis or alternative. *Entrance requirements:* For master's, GRE General Test, minimum GPA of 3.0, 3 letters of recommendation, letter of intent. Additional exam requirements/recommendations for international students: Required—TOEFL (minimum score 550 paper-based; 80 iBT). Electronic applications accepted.

Florida State University, The Graduate School, College of Arts and Sciences, Department of Earth, Ocean and Atmospheric Science, Program in Oceanography, Tallahassee, FL 32306-4320. Offers aquatic environmental science (MS, PSM); oceanography (MS, PhD). *Faculty:* 10 full-time (1 woman), 1 (woman) part-time/adjunct. *Students:* 53 full-time (25 women); includes 5 minority (1 Black or African American, non-Hispanic/Latino; 4 Asian, non-Hispanic/Latino), 15 international. Average age 27. 60 applicants, 23% accepted, 12 enrolled. In 2012, 7 master's, 5 doctorates awarded. *Degree requirements:* For master's, thesis; for doctorate, comprehensive exam, thesis/dissertation. *Entrance requirements:* For master's and doctorate, GRE General Test, minimum upper-division GPA of 3.0. Additional exam requirements/recommendations for international students: Required—TOEFL (minimum score 550 paper-based; 80 iBT). *Application deadline:* For fall admission, 2/15 priority date for domestic students, 2/15 for international students; for spring admission, 7/15 priority date for domestic students, 7/15 for international students. Applications are processed on a rolling basis. Application fee: $35. Electronic applications accepted. *Expenses:* Tuition, state resident: full-time $7263; part-time $403.51 per credit hour. Tuition, nonresident: full-time $18,087; part-time $1004.85 per credit hour. *Required fees:* $1335.42; $74.19 per credit hour. $445.14 per semester. One-time fee: $40 full-time; $20 part-time. Tuition and fees vary according to program. *Financial support:* In 2012–13, 36 students received support, including 1 fellowship with full tuition reimbursement available, 27 research assistantships with full tuition reimbursements available, 10 teaching assistantships with full tuition reimbursements available. Financial award application deadline: 2/15; financial award applicants required to submit FAFSA. *Faculty research:* Trace metals in seawater, currents and waves, modeling, benthic ecology, marine biogeochemistry. *Unit head:* Dr. Jeffrey Chanton, Area Coordinator, 850-644-6700, Fax: 850-644-2581, E-mail: chanton@ocean.fsu.edu. *Application contact:* Michaela Lupiani, Academic Coordinator, 850-644-6700, Fax: 850-644-2581, E-mail: admissions@ocean.fsu.edu. Website: http://www.eoas.fsu.edu.

Friends University, Graduate School, Wichita, KS 67213. Offers accounting (MBA); business administration (MBA); business law (MBL); Christian ministry (MACM); environment science (MSES); family therapy (MSFT); global leadership and management (MA); health care leadership (MHCL); management information systems (MMIS); operations management (MSOM); organization development (MSOD); teaching (MAT). Part-time and evening/weekend programs available. Postbaccalaureate distance learning degree programs offered (no on-campus study). *Faculty:* 18 full-time (6 women), 2 part-time/adjunct (1 woman). *Students:* 142 full-time (104 women), 561 part-time (345 women); includes 158 minority (80 Black or African American, non-Hispanic/Latino; 9 American Indian or Alaska Native, non-Hispanic/Latino; 23 Asian, non-Hispanic/Latino; 21 Hispanic/Latino; 2 Native Hawaiian or other Pacific Islander, non-Hispanic/Latino; 23 Two or more races, non-Hispanic/Latino). Average age 36. 362 applicants, 58% accepted, 174 enrolled. In 2012, 281 master's awarded. *Degree requirements:* For master's, research project. *Entrance requirements:* For master's, bachelor's degree from accredited institution, official transcripts, interview with program director, letter(s) of recommendation. Additional exam requirements/recommendations for international students: Required—TOEFL (minimum score 560 paper-based). *Application deadline:* Applications are processed on a rolling basis. Application fee: $45 ($50 for international students). Electronic applications accepted. *Expenses: Tuition:* Full-time $11,358; part-time $631 per credit hour. One-time fee: $35. Tuition and fees vary according to campus/location and program. *Financial support:* Applicants required to submit FAFSA. *Unit head:* Dr. Dona Gibson, Interim Dean, Graduate School, 800-794-6945 Ext. 5859, Fax: 316-295-5040, E-mail: evelyn_hume@friends.edu. *Application contact:* Lisa Haggard, Manager, Graduate Recruiting Services, 800-794-6945, Fax: 316-295-5967, E-mail: lisa_haggard@friends.edu. Website: http://www.friends.edu/.

Gannon University, School of Graduate Studies, College of Engineering and Business, School of Engineering and Computer Science, Program in Environmental and Occupational Science and Health, Erie, PA 16541-0001. Offers Certificate. Part-time and evening/weekend programs available. *Entrance requirements:* Additional exam requirements/recommendations for international students: Required—TOEFL (minimum score 79 iBT). Electronic applications accepted.

Gannon University, School of Graduate Studies, College of Engineering and Business, School of Engineering and Computer Science, Program in Environmental Science and Engineering, Erie, PA 16541-0001. Offers MS. Part-time and evening/weekend programs available. *Degree requirements:* For master's, thesis, internship, research paper or project. *Entrance requirements:* For master's, GRE. Additional exam requirements/recommendations for international students: Required—TOEFL (minimum score 79 iBT). Electronic applications accepted. *Faculty research:* Water quality, renewable energy, human health risk assessment, solid waste management, soil and groundwater contamination.

George Mason University, College of Science, Department of Environmental Science and Policy, Fairfax, VA 22030. Offers environmental management (Certificate); environmental science and policy (MS); environmental science and public policy (PhD). *Faculty:* 21 full-time (7 women), 4 part-time/adjunct (1 woman). *Students:* 75 full-time (45 women), 93 part-time (62 women); includes 27 minority (7 Black or African American, non-Hispanic/Latino; 9 Asian, non-Hispanic/Latino; 8 Hispanic/Latino; 1 Native Hawaiian or other Pacific Islander, non-Hispanic/Latino; 2 Two or more races, non-Hispanic/Latino), 12 international. Average age 34. 91 applicants, 51% accepted, 29 enrolled. In 2012, 19 master's, 17 doctorates, 2 other advanced degrees awarded. *Degree requirements:* For doctorate, comprehensive exam, thesis/dissertation, internship; seminar. *Entrance requirements:* For master's, GRE, bachelor's degree with minimum GPA of 3.0 in related field; 3 letters of recommendation; expanded goals statement; 2 official copies of transcripts; for doctorate, GRE, bachelor's degree with minimum GPA of 3.0; 3 letters of recommendation; current resume; expanded goals statement; 2 official copies of transcripts; for Certificate, GRE, 3 letters of recommendation; undergraduate degree in related field; expanded goals statement; resume; 2 official copies of transcripts. Additional exam requirements/ recommendations for international students: Required—TOEFL (minimum score 570 paper-based; 88 iBT), IELTS (minimum score 6.5), Pearson Test of English. *Application deadline:* For fall admission, 2/15 priority date for domestic students; for spring admission, 10/1 priority date for domestic students. Application fee: $65 ($80 for international students). Electronic applications accepted. *Expenses:* Tuition, state resident: full-time $9080; part-time $378.33 per credit hour. Tuition, nonresident: full-time $25,010; part-time $1042.08 per credit hour. *Required fees:* $2610; $108.75 per credit hour. Tuition and fees vary according to program. *Financial support:* In 2012–13, 52 students received support, including 10 fellowships (averaging $10,522 per year), 10 research assistantships with full and partial tuition reimbursements available (averaging $18,966 per year), 38 teaching assistantships with full and partial tuition reimbursements available (averaging $14,832 per year); career-related internships or fieldwork, Federal Work-Study, scholarships/grants, unspecified assistantships, and health care benefits (for full-time research or teaching assistantship recipients) also available. Support available to part-time students. Financial award application deadline: 3/1; financial award applicants required to submit FAFSA. *Faculty research:* Wetland ecosystems, comparative physiology, systematics, molecular phylogenetics, conservation genetics, estuarine and oceanic systems, biodiversity of fungi, environmental and resource management, human ecology. *Total annual research expenditures:* $1 million. *Unit head:* Dr. Robert B. Jonas, Chair, 703-993-7500, Fax: 703-993-1066, E-mail: rjonas@gmu.edu. *Application contact:* Sharon Bloomquist, Graduate Program Coordinator, 703-993-3187, Fax: 703-993-1066, E-mail: sbloomqu@gmu.edu. Website: http://esp.gmu.edu/.

Georgia Institute of Technology, Graduate Studies and Research, College of Sciences, School of Earth and Atmospheric Sciences, Atlanta, GA 30332-0340. Offers atmospheric chemistry, aerosols and clouds (MS, PhD); dynamics of weather and climate (MS, PhD); geochemistry (MS, PhD); geophysics (MS, PhD); oceanography (MS, PhD); paleoclimate (MS, PhD); planetary science (MS, PhD); remote sensing (MS, PhD). Part-time programs available. Terminal master's awarded for partial completion of doctoral program. *Degree requirements:* For master's, thesis or alternative; for doctorate, comprehensive exam, thesis/ dissertation. *Entrance requirements:* For master's, GRE, letters of recommendation; for doctorate, GRE, academic transcripts, letters of recommendation, personal statement. Additional exam requirements/ recommendations for international students: Required—TOEFL (minimum score 550 paper-based; 79 iBT). *Faculty research:* Geophysics; atmospheric chemistry, aerosols and clouds; dynamics of weather and climate; geochemistry; oceanography; paleoclimate; planetary science; remote sensing.

Graduate School and University Center of the City University of New York, Graduate Studies, Program in Earth and Environmental Sciences, New York, NY 10016-4039. Offers PhD. *Degree requirements:* For doctorate, one foreign language, comprehensive exam, thesis/dissertation. *Entrance requirements:* For doctorate, GRE General Test. Additional exam requirements/recommendations for international students: Required—TOEFL. Electronic applications accepted.

Harvard University, Cyprus International Institute for the Environment and Public Health in Association with Harvard School of Public Health, Cambridge, MA 02138. Offers environmental health (MS); environmental/public health (PhD); epidemiology and biostatistics (MS). *Entrance requirements:* For master's and doctorate, GRE, resume/curriculum vitae, 3 letters of recommendation, BA or BS (including diploma and official transcripts). Additional exam requirements/ recommendations for international students: Required—TOEFL, IELTS (minimum score 7). Electronic applications accepted. *Expenses: Tuition:* Full-time $37,576. *Required fees:* $930. Tuition and fees vary according to program and student level. *Faculty research:* Air pollution, climate change, biostatistics, sustainable development, environmental management.

Howard University, Graduate School, Department of Chemistry, Washington, DC 20059-0002. Offers analytical chemistry (MS, PhD); atmospheric (MS, PhD); biochemistry (MS, PhD); environmental (MS, PhD); inorganic chemistry (MS, PhD); organic chemistry (MS, PhD); physical chemistry (MS, PhD). Terminal master's awarded for partial completion of doctoral program. *Degree requirements:* For master's, comprehensive exam, thesis, teaching experience; for doctorate, comprehensive exam, thesis/dissertation, teaching experience. *Entrance requirements:* For master's, GRE General Test, minimum GPA of 2.7; for doctorate, GRE General Test, minimum GPA of 3.0. Additional exam requirements/recommendations for international students: Required—TOEFL. Electronic applications accepted. *Faculty research:* Synthetic organics, materials, natural products, mass spectrometry.

Humboldt State University, Academic Programs, College of Natural Resources and Sciences, Programs in Environmental Systems, Arcata, CA 95521-8299. Offers environmental systems (MS), including energy, environment and society, environmental resources engineering, geology, math modeling. *Students:* 35 full-time (11 women), 5 part-time (2 women); includes 4 minority (1 Asian, non-Hispanic/Latino; 3 Two or more races, non-Hispanic/Latino), 1 international. Average age 27. 71 applicants, 42% accepted, 20 enrolled. In 2012, 18 master's awarded. *Degree requirements:* For master's, thesis. *Entrance requirements:* For master's, GRE, appropriate bachelor's degree, minimum GPA of 2.5, 3 letters of recommendation. Additional exam requirements/recommendations for international students: Required—TOEFL. *Application deadline:* For fall admission, 2/15 for domestic students; for spring admission, 10/15 for domestic students. Applications are processed on a rolling basis. Application fee: $55. *Expenses:* Tuition, state resident: full-time $8396. Tuition, nonresident: full-time $17,324. Tuition and fees vary according to program. *Financial support:* Application deadline: 3/1; applicants required to submit FAFSA. *Faculty research:* Mathematical modeling, international development technology, geology, environmental resources engineering. *Unit head:* Dr. Chris Dugaw, Chair, 707-826-4251, Fax: 707-826-4145, E-mail: dugaw@humboldt.edu. *Application contact:* Dr. Dale Oliver, Coordinator, 707-826-4921, Fax: 707-826-3140, E-mail: dale.oliver@humboldt.edu.

Hunter College of the City University of New York, Graduate School, School of Arts and Sciences, Department of Geography, New York, NY 10021-5085. Offers analytical geography (MA); earth system science (MA); environmental and social issues (MA); geographic information science (Certificate); geographic information systems (MA); teaching earth science (MA). Part-time and evening/weekend programs available. *Faculty:* 8 full-time (4 women), 5 part-time/adjunct (0 women). *Students:* 2 full-time (1 woman), 58 part-time (30 women); includes 11 minority (1 Black or African American, non-Hispanic/Latino; 5 Asian, non-Hispanic/Latino; 5 Hispanic/Latino), 3 international. Average age 33. 22 applicants, 68% accepted, 7 enrolled. In 2012, 13 master's, 8 other advanced degrees awarded. *Degree requirements:* For master's, comprehensive exam or thesis. *Entrance requirements:* For master's, GRE General Test, minimum B average in major, B- overall; 18 credits of course work in geography; 2 letters of recommendation; for Certificate, minimum B average in major, B- overall. Additional exam requirements/ recommendations for international students: Required—TOEFL. *Application deadline:* For fall admission, 4/1 for domestic students; for spring admission, 11/1 for domestic students. Applications are processed on a rolling basis. Application fee: $125. *Expenses:* Tuition, state resident: full-time $8690; part-time $365 per credit. Tuition, nonresident: full-time $16,200; part-time $675 per credit. *Required fees:* $320 per semester. One-time fee: $125. Tuition and fees vary according to class time, campus/location and program. *Financial support:* In 2012–13, 1 fellowship (averaging $3,000 per year), 2 research assistantships (averaging $10,000 per year), 10 teaching assistantships (averaging $6,000 per year) were awarded; career-related internships or fieldwork, Federal Work-Study, institutionally sponsored loans, and unspecified assistantships also available. Financial award application deadline: 3/1. *Faculty research:* Urban geography, economic geography, geographic information science, demographic methods, climate change. *Unit head:* Prof. William Solecki, Chair, 212-772-4536, Fax: 212-772-5268, E-mail: wsolecki@hunter.cuny.edu. *Application contact:* Prof. Marianna Pavlovskaya, Graduate Adviser, 212-772-5320, Fax: 212-772-5268, E-mail: mpavlov@geo.hunter.cuny.edu. Website: http://www.geo.hunter.cuny.edu/.

Idaho State University, Office of Graduate Studies, College of Science and Engineering, Civil and Environmental Engineering Department, Pocatello, ID 83209-8060. Offers civil engineering (MS); environmental engineering (MS); environmental science and management (MS). Part-time programs available. *Degree requirements:* For master's, comprehensive exam (for some programs), thesis optional, thesis project, 2 semesters of seminar. *Entrance requirements:* For master's, GRE. Additional exam requirements/recommendations for international students: Required—TOEFL (minimum score 550 paper-based; 80 iBT). Electronic applications accepted. *Faculty research:* Floor vibration investigations, earthquake engineering, base isolation systems and seismic risk assessment, infrastructure revitalization (building foundations and damage, bridge structures, highways, and dams), slope stability and soil erosion, pavement rehabilitation, computational fluid dynamics and flood control structures, microbial fuel cells, water treatment and water quality modeling, environmental risk assessment, biotechnology, nanotechnology.

Idaho State University, Office of Graduate Studies, College of Science and Engineering, Department of Geosciences, Pocatello, ID 83209-8072. Offers geographic information science (MS); geology (MNS, MS); geology with emphasis in environmental geoscience (MS); geophysics/hydrology/geology (MS); geotechnology (Postbaccalaureate Certificate). Part-time programs available. *Degree requirements:* For master's, comprehensive exam, thesis, oral colloquium; for Postbaccalaureate Certificate, thesis optional, minimum 19 credits. *Entrance requirements:* For master's, GRE General Test (minimum 50th percentile in 2 sections), 3 letters of recommendation; for Postbaccalaureate Certificate, GRE General Test, 3 letters of recommendation, bachelor's degree, statement of goals. Additional exam requirements/recommendations for international students: Required—TOEFL (minimum score 550 paper-based; 80 iBT). Electronic applications accepted. *Faculty research:* Quantitative field mapping and sampling: microscopic, geochemical, and isotopic analysis of rocks, minerals and water; remote sensing, geographic information systems, and global positioning systems: environmental and watershed management; surficial and fluvial processes: landscape change; regional tectonics, structural geology; planetary geology.

Idaho State University, Office of Graduate Studies, Department of Interdisciplinary Studies, Pocatello, ID 83209. Offers general interdisciplinary (M Ed, MA, MNS); waste management and environmental science (MS). Part-time programs available. *Degree requirements:* For master's, comprehensive exam, thesis optional. *Entrance requirements:* For master's, GRE General Test or MAT, minimum GPA of 3.0. Additional exam requirements/recommendations for international students: Required—TOEFL (minimum score 550 paper-based; 80 iBT).

Indiana University Bloomington, School of Public and Environmental Affairs, Environmental Science Programs, Bloomington, IN 47405. Offers applied ecology (MSES); energy (MSES); environmental chemistry, toxicology, and risk assessment (MSES); environmental science (PhD); specialized environmental science (MSES); water resources (MSES); JD/MSES; MSES/MA; MSES/MPA; MSES/MS. Part-time programs available. *Faculty:* 80 full-time (30 women), 102 part-time/adjunct (43 women). *Students:* 75 full-time, 9 part-time; includes 13 minority (1 Black or African American, non-Hispanic/Latino; 7 Asian, non-Hispanic/Latino; 5 Hispanic/Latino), 9 international. Average age 26. 193 applicants, 64 enrolled. In 2012, 58 master's, 3 doctorates awarded. Terminal master's awarded for partial completion of doctoral program. *Degree requirements:* For master's, core classes; capstone or thesis; internship; for doctorate, comprehensive exam, thesis/dissertation. *Entrance requirements:* For master's, GRE General Test or GMAT, official transcripts, 3 letters of recommendation, resume, personal statement; for doctorate, GRE General Test or LSAT, official transcripts, 3 letters of recommendation, resume or curriculum vitae, statement of purpose. Additional exam requirements/recommendations for international students: Required—TOEFL (minimum score 600 paper-based; 96 iBT); Recommended—IELTS (minimum score 7). *Application deadline:* For fall admission, 2/1 priority date for domestic students, 12/1 for international students; for spring admission, 11/15 for domestic students, 9/1 for international students. Applications are processed on a rolling basis. Application fee: $55 ($65 for international students). Electronic applications accepted. *Financial support:* Fellowships with partial tuition reimbursements, research assistantships with partial tuition reimbursements, teaching assistantships with partial tuition reimbursements, career-related internships or fieldwork, Federal Work-Study, scholarships/grants, health care benefits, unspecified assistantships, and Service Corps programs available. Financial award application deadline: 2/1; financial award applicants required to submit FAFSA. *Faculty research:* Applied ecology, bio-geo chemistry, toxicology, wetlands ecology, environmental microbiology, forest ecology, environmental chemistry. *Unit head:* Jennifer Forney, Director, Graduate Student Services, 812-855-9485, Fax: 812-856-3665, E-mail: speampo@indiana.edu. *Application contact:* Lane Bowman, Admissions Services Coordinator, 812-855-2840, Fax: 812-856-3665, E-mail: speaapps@indiana.edu. Website: http://www.indiana.edu/~spea/prospective_students/masters/.

Instituto Tecnologico de Santo Domingo, Graduate School, Area of Basic And Environmental Sciences, Santo Domingo, Dominican Republic. Offers environmental science (M En S), including environmental education, environmental management, marine resources, natural resources management; mathematics (MS, PhD); renewable energy technology (MS, Certificate).

Instituto Tecnológico y de Estudios Superiores de Monterrey, Campus Ciudad de México, Virtual University Division, Ciudad de Mexico, Mexico. Offers administration of information technologies (MA); computer sciences (MA); education (MA, PhD); educational technology (MA); environmental engineering (MA); environmental systems (MA); humanistic studies (MA); industrial engineering (MA); international business for Latin America (MA); quality systems (MA); quality systems and productivity (MA). Part-time and evening/weekend programs available. Postbaccalaureate distance learning degree programs offered (minimal on-campus study). *Entrance requirements:* For master's and doctorate, Instituto entrance exam. Additional exam requirements/recommendations for international students: Required—TOEFL.

Inter American University of Puerto Rico, San Germán Campus, Graduate Studies Center, Program in Environmental Sciences, San Germán, PR 00683-5008. Offers MS. Part-time and evening/weekend programs available. *Faculty:* 8 full-time (4 women), 13 part-time/adjunct (7 women). *Students:* 32 full-time (18 women), 23 part-time (14 women); all minorities (all Hispanic/Latino). Average age 30. 2 applicants, 100% accepted, 2 enrolled. *Degree requirements:* For master's, comprehensive exam, thesis. *Entrance requirements:* For master's, GRE General Test or EXADEP, minimum GPA of 3.0. *Application deadline:* For fall admission, 4/30 priority date for domestic students; for spring admission, 11/15 for domestic students. Applications are processed on a rolling basis. Application fee: $31. *Expenses: Tuition:* Full-time $202; part-time $202 per credit hour. *Required fees:* $260 per semester. Tuition and fees vary according to degree level. *Financial support:* Fellowships, research assistantships, teaching assistantships, Federal Work-Study, and unspecified assistantships available. *Faculty research:* Environmental biology, environmental chemistry, water resources and unit operations. *Unit head:* Dr. Elba T. Irizarry, Director of Graduate Studies Center, 787-264-1912 Ext. 7357, Fax: 787-892-6350, E-mail: elbat@sg.inter.edu. *Application contact:* Prof. Marian Espola, Coordinator, 787-264-1912 Ext. 7437, E-mail: marian_espole_sepulveda@intersg.edu.

Iowa State University of Science and Technology, Department of Geological and Atmospheric Sciences, Ames, IA 50011. Offers earth science (MS, PhD); environmental science (MS, PhD); geology (MS, PhD); meteorology (MS, PhD). *Degree requirements:* For master's, thesis (for some programs); for doctorate, thesis/dissertation. *Entrance requirements:* For master's and doctorate, GRE General Test. Additional exam requirements/recommendations for international students: Required—TOEFL (minimum score 550 paper-based; 79 iBT), IELTS (minimum score 6.5). *Application deadline:* For fall admission, 1/1 priority date for domestic students. Application fee: $60 ($90 for international students). Electronic applications accepted. *Application contact:* Deann Frisk, Application Contact, 515-294-4477, Fax: 515-294-6049, E-mail: geology@iastate.edu. Website: http://www.ge-at.iastate.edu/.

Iowa State University of Science and Technology, Program in Environmental Sciences, Ames, IA 50011. Offers MS, PhD. *Degree requirements:* For master's, thesis; for doctorate, thesis/dissertation. *Entrance requirements:* For master's and doctorate, GRE General Test. Additional exam requirements/recommendations for international students: Required—TOEFL (minimum score 550 paper-based; 79 iBT), IELTS (minimum score 6.5). *Application deadline:* For fall admission, 2/1 for domestic and international students; for spring admission, 6/1 for domestic and international students. Application fee: $60 ($90 for international students). Electronic applications accepted. *Application contact:* Charles Sauer, Application Contact, 515-294-6518, Fax: 515-294-6390, E-mail: enscigradoffice@iastate.edu. Website: http://www.ensci.iastate.edu/grad/applying.html.

Jackson State University, Graduate School, College of Science, Engineering and Technology, Department of Biology, Jackson, MS 39217. Offers environmental science (MS, PhD). Part-time and evening/weekend programs available. *Degree requirements:* For master's, comprehensive exam, thesis (alternative accepted for MST); for doctorate, comprehensive exam, thesis/dissertation. *Entrance requirements:* For master's, GRE General Test; for doctorate, MAT. Additional exam requirements/recommendations for international students: Required—TOEFL (minimum score 520 paper-based; 67 iBT). *Faculty research:* Comparative studies on the carbohydrate composition of marine macroalgae, host-parasite relationship between the spruce budworm and entomepathogen fungus.

The Johns Hopkins University, Zanvyl Krieger School of Arts and Sciences, Advanced Academic Programs, Program in Environmental Sciences and Policy, Baltimore, MD 21218-2699. Offers MS. Part-time and evening/weekend programs available. Postbaccalaureate distance learning degree programs offered (minimal on-campus study). *Degree requirements:* For master's, thesis (for some programs). *Entrance requirements:* For master's, minimum GPA of 3.0, coursework in chemistry and calculus. Additional exam requirements/recommendations for international students: Required—TOEFL.

Laurentian University, School of Graduate Studies and Research, Programme in Chemistry and Biochemistry, Sudbury, ON P3E 2C6, Canada. Offers analytical chemistry (M Sc); biochemistry (M Sc); environmental chemistry (M Sc); organic chemistry (M Sc); physical/theoretical chemistry (M Sc). Part-time programs available. *Degree requirements:* For master's, thesis or alternative. *Entrance requirements:* For master's, honors degree with minimum second class. *Faculty research:* Cell cycle checkpoints, kinetic modeling, toxicology to metal stress, quantum chemistry, biogeochemistry metal speciation.

Lehigh University, College of Arts and Sciences, Department of Earth and Environmental Sciences, Bethlehem, PA 18015. Offers MS, PhD. *Faculty:* 15 full-time (2 women). *Students:* 21 full-time (7 women), 4 part-time (2 women), 4 international. Average age 27. 56 applicants, 23% accepted, 5 enrolled. In 2012, 8 master's, 3 doctorates awarded. Terminal master's awarded for partial completion of doctoral program. *Degree requirements:* For master's, thesis; for doctorate, thesis/dissertation. *Entrance requirements:* For master's and doctorate, GRE General Test, transcripts, recommendation letters, research statement, faculty advocates. Additional exam requirements/recommendations for international students: Required—TOEFL (minimum score 85 iBT). *Application deadline:* For fall admission, 1/1 for domestic and international students. Applications are processed on a rolling basis. Application fee: $75. Electronic applications accepted. *Financial support:* In 2012–13, 14 students received support, including 2 fellowships with full tuition reimbursements available (averaging $25,000 per year), 5 research assistantships with full tuition reimbursements available (averaging $25,000 per year), 10 teaching assistantships with full tuition reimbursements available (averaging $25,000 per year); career-related internships or fieldwork, Federal Work-Study, institutionally sponsored loans, scholarships/grants, tuition waivers (full and partial), and unspecified assistantships also available. Support available to part-time students. Financial award application deadline: 1/1. *Faculty research:* Tectonics, surficial processes, ecology, environmental change. *Total annual research expenditures:* $1.6 million. *Unit head:* Dr. Frank J. Pazzaglia, Chairman, 610-758-3667, Fax: 610-758-3677, E-mail: fjp3@lehigh.edu. *Application contact:* Dr. Stephen Peters, Graduate Coordinator, 610-758-3957, Fax: 610-758-3677, E-mail: scp2@lehigh.edu. Website: http://www.ees.lehigh.edu/.

Louisiana State University and Agricultural and Mechanical College, Graduate School, College of Agriculture, School of Renewable Natural Resources, Baton Rouge, LA 70803. Offers fisheries (MS); forestry (MS, PhD); wildlife (MS); wildlife and fisheries science (PhD). *Faculty:* 31 full-time (5 women). *Students:* 51 full-time (15 women), 5 part-time (2 women); includes 3 minority (2 Black or African American, non-Hispanic/Latino; 1 Hispanic/Latino), 12 international. Average age 29. 34 applicants, 41% accepted, 13 enrolled. In 2012, 11 master's, 10 doctorates awarded. *Degree requirements:* For master's, thesis; for doctorate, thesis/dissertation. *Entrance requirements:* For master's, GRE General Test, minimum GPA of 3.0; for doctorate, GRE General Test, MS, minimum GPA of 3.0. Additional exam requirements/recommendations for international students: Required—TOEFL (minimum score 550 paper-based; 79 iBT), IELTS (minimum score 6.5). *Application deadline:* For fall admission, 1/25 priority date for domestic students, 5/15 for international students; for spring admission, 10/15 for international students. Applications are processed on a rolling basis. Application fee: $50 ($70 for international students). Electronic applications accepted. *Financial support:* In 2012–13, 55 students received support, including 49 research assistantships with partial tuition reimbursements available (averaging $19,751 per year), 2 teaching assistantships (averaging $10,250 per year); fellowships, Federal Work-Study, institutionally sponsored loans, scholarships/grants, health care benefits, tuition waivers (full and partial), and unspecified assistantships also available. Financial award application deadline: 4/15; financial award applicants required to submit FAFSA. *Faculty research:* Forest biology and management, aquaculture, fisheries biology and ecology, upland and wetlands wildlife. *Total annual research expenditures:* $163,169. *Unit head:* Dr. Allen Rutherford, Director, 225-578-4131, Fax: 225-578-4227, E-mail: druther@lsu.edu. *Application contact:* Dr. William Kelso, Coordinator of Graduate Studies, 225-578-4176, Fax: 225-578-4227, E-mail: wkelso@lsu.edu. Website: http://www.fwf.lsu.edu/.

Louisiana State University and Agricultural and Mechanical College, Graduate School, School of the Coast and Environment, Department of Environmental Sciences, Baton Rouge, LA 70803. Offers environmental planning and management (MS); environmental toxicology (MS). *Faculty:* 9 full-time (3 women), 1 part-time/adjunct (0 women). *Students:* 32 full-time (20 women), 9 part-time (3 women); includes 4 minority (1 Black or African American, non-Hispanic/Latino; 3 Hispanic/Latino), 5 international. Average age 28. 26 applicants, 62% accepted, 11 enrolled. In 2012, 12 master's awarded. *Degree requirements:* For master's, thesis (for some programs). *Entrance requirements:* For master's, GRE General Test, minimum GPA of 3.0. Additional exam requirements/recommendations for international students: Required—TOEFL (minimum score 550 paper-based; 79 iBT) or IELTS (minimum score 6.5). *Application deadline:* For fall admission, 1/25 priority date for domestic students, 5/15 for international students; for spring admission, 10/15 for international students. Applications are processed on a rolling basis. Application fee: $50 ($70 for international students). Electronic applications accepted. *Financial support:* In 2012–13, 33 students received support, including 13 research assistantships with full and partial tuition reimbursements available (averaging $16,700 per year), 8 teaching assistantships with full and partial tuition reimbursements available (averaging $13,562 per year); fellowships with full and partial tuition reimbursements available, career-related internships or fieldwork, Federal Work-Study, institutionally sponsored loans, scholarships/grants, health care benefits, and unspecified assistantships also available. Support available to part-time students. Financial award applicants required to submit FAFSA. *Faculty research:* Environmental toxicology, environmental policy and law, microbial ecology, bioremediation, genetic toxicology. *Total annual research expenditures:* $2.3 million. *Unit head:* Dr. Ed Laws, Chair, 225-578-8800, Fax: 225-578-4286, E-mail: edlaws@lsu.edu. *Application contact:* Charlotte G. St. Romain, Academic Coordinator, 225-578-8522, Fax: 225-578-4286, E-mail: cstrom4@lsu.edu. Website: http://info.envs.lsu.edu/.

Loyola Marymount University, College of Science and Engineering, Department of Civil Engineering and Environmental Science, Program in Environmental Science, Los Angeles, CA 90045. Offers MS. Part-time programs available. *Faculty:* 7 full-time (1 woman), 5 part-time/adjunct (3 women). *Students:* 17 full-time (12 women), 8 part-time (1 woman); includes 13 minority (3 Black or African American, non-Hispanic/Latino; 5 Asian, non-Hispanic/Latino; 3 Hispanic/Latino; 1 Native Hawaiian or other Pacific Islander, non-Hispanic/Latino; 1 Two or more races, non-Hispanic/Latino), 3 international. Average age 28. 13 applicants, 100% accepted, 10 enrolled. In 2012, 6 master's awarded. *Degree requirements:* For master's, comprehensive exam, thesis or alternative. *Entrance requirements:* For master's, 2 letters of recommendation, personal statement. Additional exam requirements/recommendations for international students: Required—TOEFL (minimum score 550 paper-based; 80 iBT). *Application deadline:* Applications are processed on a rolling basis. Application fee: $50. Electronic applications accepted. *Financial support:* In 2012–13, 6 students received support. Scholarships/grants and unspecified assistantships available. Support available to part-time students. Financial award application deadline: 6/1; financial award applicants required to submit FAFSA. *Total annual research expenditures:* $110,590. *Unit head:* Prof. Joe J. Reichenberger, Graduate Director, 310-338-2830, E-mail: jreichenberger@lmu.edu. *Application contact:* Chake H. Kouyoumjian, Associate Dean of Graduate Studies, 310-338-2721, E-mail: ckouyoum@lmu.edu. Website: http://cse.lmu.edu/department/civilengineering/environmentalscienceprogram/.

Marshall University, Academic Affairs Division, College of Information Technology and Engineering, Division of Applied Science and Technology, Program in Environmental Science, Huntington, WV 25755. Offers MS. Part-time and evening/weekend programs available. *Students:* 21 full-time (10 women), 25 part-time (7 women); includes 2 minority (both Asian, non-Hispanic/Latino), 3 international. Average age 30. In 2012, 13 master's awarded. *Degree requirements:* For master's, final project, oral exam. *Entrance requirements:* For master's, GRE General Test or MAT, minimum GPA of 2.5, course work in calculus. Application fee: $40. *Financial support:* Tuition waivers (full) available. Support available to part-time students. Financial award application deadline: 8/1; financial award applicants required to submit FAFSA. *Unit head:* Dr. D. Scott Simonton, Associate Professor, 304-746-2045, E-mail: simonton@marshall.edu. *Application contact:* Information Contact, 304-746-1900, Fax: 304-746-1902, E-mail: services@marshall.edu. Website: http://www.marshall.edu/cite/.

Massachusetts Institute of Technology, School of Engineering, Department of Civil and Environmental Engineering, Cambridge, MA 02139. Offers biological oceanography (PhD, Sc D); chemical oceanography (PhD, Sc D); civil and environmental engineering (M Eng, SM, PhD, Sc D); civil and environmental systems (PhD, Sc D); civil engineering (PhD, Sc D, CE); coastal engineering (PhD, Sc D); construction engineering and management (PhD, Sc D); environmental biology (PhD, Sc D); environmental chemistry (PhD, Sc D); environmental engineering (PhD, Sc D); environmental fluid mechanics (PhD, Sc D); geotechnical and geoenvironmental engineering (PhD, Sc D); hydrology (PhD, Sc D); information technology (PhD, Sc D); oceanographic engineering (PhD, Sc D); structures and materials (PhD, Sc D); transportation (PhD, Sc D); SM/MBA. *Faculty:* 34 full-time (7 women), 1 part-time/adjunct (0 women). *Students:* 224 full-time (85 women); includes 29 minority (4 Black or African American, non-Hispanic/Latino; 13 Asian, non-Hispanic/Latino; 6 Hispanic/Latino; 6 Two or more races, non-Hispanic/Latino), 129 international. Average age 26. 636 applicants, 25% accepted, 95 enrolled. In 2012, 67 master's, 18 doctorates, 1 other advanced degree awarded. *Degree requirements:* For master's and CE, thesis; for doctorate, comprehensive exam, thesis/dissertation. *Entrance requirements:* For master's and doctorate, GRE General Test. Additional exam requirements/recommendations for international students: Required—TOEFL (minimum score 577 paper-based; 90 iBT), IELTS (minimum score 7). *Application deadline:* For fall admission, 12/15 for domestic and international students. Application fee: $75. Electronic applications accepted. *Expenses: Tuition:* Full-time $41,770; part-time $650 per credit hour. *Required fees:* $280. *Financial support:* In 2012–13, 180 students received support, including 46 fellowships (averaging $32,400 per year), 117 research assistantships (averaging $30,800 per year), 22 teaching assistantships (averaging $31,800 per year); career-related internships or fieldwork, Federal Work-Study, institutionally sponsored loans, scholarships/grants, health care benefits, and unspecified assistantships also available. *Faculty research:* Environmental chemistry; environmental fluid mechanics and coastal engineering; environmental microbiology; geotechnical engineering and geomechanics; hydrology and hydroclimatology; infrastructure systems; mechanics of materials and structures; transportation systems. *Total annual research expenditures:* $20.7 million. *Unit head:* Prof. Markus Buehler, Head, 617-253-7101. *Application contact:* Graduate Admissions Coordinator, 617-253-7119, E-mail: cee-admissions@mit.edu. Website: http://cee.mit.edu/.

McNeese State University, Doré School of Graduate Studies, College of Science, Dripps Department of Agricultural Sciences, Program in Environmental and Chemical Sciences, Lake Charles, LA 70609. Offers agricultural sciences (MS); environmental science (MS). Evening/weekend programs available. *Students:* 17 full-time (11 women), 9 part-time (4 women); includes 4 minority (3 Black or African American, non-Hispanic/Latino; 1 American Indian or Alaska Native, non-Hispanic/Latino), 1 international. In 2012, 18 master's awarded. *Degree requirements:* For master's, comprehensive exam, thesis or alternative. *Entrance requirements:* For master's, GRE. *Application deadline:* For fall admission, 5/15 priority date for domestic students, 5/15 for international students; for spring admission, 10/15 priority date for domestic students, 10/15 for international students. Applications are processed on a rolling basis. Application fee: $20 ($30 for international students). *Expenses:* Tuition, state resident: full-time $4287; part-time $587 per credit hour. *Required fees:* $1177. Tuition and fees vary according to course load. *Financial support:* Application deadline: 5/1. *Unit head:* Dr. Frederick LeMieux, Department Head, 337-475-5690, Fax: 337-475-5699, E-mail: flemieux@mcneese.edu.

Memorial University of Newfoundland, School of Graduate Studies, Interdisciplinary Program in Environmental Science, St. John's, NL A1C 5S7, Canada. Offers M Env Sc, M Sc. Part-time programs available. *Degree requirements:* For master's, thesis (M Sc), project (M Env Sci). *Entrance requirements:* For master's, honors B Sc or 2nd class B Eng. Electronic applications accepted. *Faculty research:* Earth and ocean systems, environmental chemistry and toxicology, environmental engineering.

Mercer University, Graduate Studies, Macon Campus, School of Engineering, Macon, GA 31207-0003. Offers biomedical engineering (MSE); computer engineering (MSE); electrical engineering (MSE); engineering management (MSE); environmental engineering (MSE); environmental systems (MS); mechanical engineering (MSE); software engineering (MSE); software systems (MS); technical communications management (MS); technical management (MS). Part-time and evening/weekend programs available. Postbaccalaureate distance learning degree programs offered (no on-campus study). *Faculty:* 16 full-time (3 women), 1 part-time/adjunct (0 women). *Students:* 18 full-time (2 women), 107 part-time (21 women); includes 9 minority (4 Black or African American, non-Hispanic/Latino; 4 Asian, non-Hispanic/Latino; 1 Hispanic/Latino), 7 international. Average age 32. In 2012, 60 master's awarded. *Degree requirements:* For master's, thesis or alternative. *Entrance requirements:* For master's, minimum undergraduate GPA of 3.0. Additional exam requirements/recommendations for international students: Required—TOEFL. *Application deadline:* For fall admission, 7/1 for domestic students; for spring admission, 11/15 for domestic students. Applications are processed on a rolling basis. Application fee: $35 ($50 for international students). Electronic applications accepted. *Expenses:* Contact institution. *Financial support:* Federal Work-Study available. *Unit head:* Dr. Wade H. Shaw, Dean, 478-301-2459, Fax: 478-301-5593, E-mail: shaw_wh@mercer.edu. *Application contact:* Dr. Richard O. Mines, Director of MSE and Associate MS Programs, 478-301-2347, Fax: 478-301-5433, E-mail: mines_ro@mercer.edu. Website: http://engineering.mercer.edu/.

Miami University, Institute of Environmental Sciences, Oxford, OH 45056. Offers M En. Part-time programs available. *Students:* 60 full-time (40 women), 1 part-time (0 women); includes 6 minority (1 Black or African American, non-Hispanic/Latino; 1 Asian, non-Hispanic/Latino; 1 Hispanic/Latino; 1 Native Hawaiian or other Pacific Islander, non-Hispanic/Latino; 2 Two or more races, non-Hispanic/Latino), 3 international. Average age 28. In 2012, 11 master's awarded. *Entrance requirements:* For master's, minimum undergraduate GPA of 2.75 overall. Additional exam requirements/recommendations for international students: Required—TOEFL (minimum score 550 paper-based). *Application deadline:* For fall admission, 2/1 for domestic and international students. Application fee: $50. Electronic applications accepted. *Expenses:* Tuition, state resident: full-time

$12,444; part-time $519 per credit hour. Tuition, nonresident: full-time $27,484; part-time $1145 per credit hour. *Required fees:* $468. Part-time tuition and fees vary according to course load, campus/location and program. *Financial support:* Fellowships with full and partial tuition reimbursements, research assistantships with full and partial tuition reimbursements, teaching assistantships with full and partial tuition reimbursements, career-related internships or fieldwork, Federal Work-Study, health care benefits, and unspecified assistantships available. Financial award application deadline: 2/15; financial award applicants required to submit FAFSA. *Unit head:* Dr. Thomas Crist, Director of IES and Professor of Zoology, 513-529-5811, Fax: 513-529-5814, E-mail: ies@miamioh.edu. Website: http://www.MiamiOH.edu/ies/.

Michigan State University, The Graduate School, College of Natural Science, Department of Geological Sciences, East Lansing, MI 48824. Offers environmental geosciences (MS, PhD); environmental geosciences-environmental toxicology (PhD); geological sciences (MS, PhD). *Degree requirements:* For master's, thesis (for those without prior thesis work); for doctorate, thesis/dissertation. *Entrance requirements:* For master's, GRE General Test, minimum GPA of 3.0, course work in geoscience, 3 letters of recommendation; for doctorate, GRE General Test, 3 letters of recommendation. Additional exam requirements/recommendations for international students: Required—TOEFL (minimum score 550 paper-based), Michigan State University ELT (minimum score 85), Michigan English Language Assessment Battery (minimum score 83). Electronic applications accepted. *Faculty research:* Water in the environment, global and biological change, crystal dynamics.

Minnesota State University Mankato, College of Graduate Studies, College of Science, Engineering and Technology, Department of Biological Sciences, Program in Environmental Sciences, Mankato, MN 56001. Offers MS. *Students:* 2 full-time (0 women), 7 part-time (2 women). *Degree requirements:* For master's, one foreign language, comprehensive exam, thesis or alternative. *Entrance requirements:* For master's, minimum GPA of 3.0 during previous 2 years. Additional exam requirements/recommendations for international students: Required—TOEFL. *Application deadline:* For fall admission, 7/1 priority date for domestic students; for spring admission, 11/1 for domestic students. Applications are processed on a rolling basis. Application fee: $40. Electronic applications accepted. *Financial support:* Research assistantships with partial tuition reimbursements, teaching assistantships with partial tuition reimbursements, career-related internships or fieldwork, Federal Work-Study, institutionally sponsored loans, and unspecified assistantships available. Financial award application deadline: 3/15; financial award applicants required to submit FAFSA. *Unit head:* Dr. Beth Proctor, Graduate Coordinator, 507-389-5697. *Application contact:* 507-389-2321, E-mail: grad@mnsu.edu.

Montana State University, College of Graduate Studies, College of Agriculture, Department of Land Resources and Environmental Sciences, Bozeman, MT 59717. Offers land rehabilitation (interdisciplinary) (MS); land resources and environmental sciences (MS), including land rehabilitation (interdisciplinary), land resources and environmental sciences. Part-time programs available. *Degree requirements:* For master's, comprehensive exam. *Entrance requirements:* For master's, GRE General Test. Additional exam requirements/recommendations for international students: Required—TOEFL (minimum score 550 paper-based). Electronic applications accepted. *Faculty research:* Soil nutrient management and plant nutrition, isotope biogeochemistry of soils, biodegradation of hydrocarbons in soils and natural waters, remote sensing, GIS systems, managed and natural ecosystems, microbial and metabolic diversity in geothermally heated soils, integrated management of weeds, diversified cropping systems, insect behavior and ecology, river ecology, microbial biogeochemistry, weed ecology.

Montana State University, College of Graduate Studies, College of Letters and Science, Department of Ecology, Bozeman, MT 59717. Offers ecological and environmental statistics (MS); ecology and environmental sciences (PhD); fish and wildlife biology (PhD); fish and wildlife management (MS). Part-time programs available. *Degree requirements:* For master's, comprehensive exam, thesis (for some programs); for doctorate, comprehensive exam, thesis/dissertation. *Entrance requirements:* For master's and doctorate, GRE, minimum GPA of 3.0, letters of recommendation, essay. Additional exam requirements/recommendations for international students: Required—TOEFL (minimum score 550 paper-based). Electronic applications accepted. *Faculty research:* Community ecology, population ecology, land-use effects, management and conservation, environmental modeling.

Montclair State University, The Graduate School, College of Science and Mathematics, Department of Earth and Environmental Studies, Program in Environmental Studies, Montclair, NJ 07043-1624. Offers environmental education (MA); environmental management (MA); environmental science (MA). Part-time and evening/weekend programs available. *Degree requirements:* For master's, thesis. *Entrance requirements:* For master's, GRE General Test, 2 letters of recommendation, essay. Additional exam requirements/recommendations for international students: Required—TOEFL (minimum score 83 iBT), IELTS (minimum score 6.5). Electronic applications accepted. *Faculty research:* Environmental geochemisty/remediation/forensics, environmental law and policy, regional climate modeling, remote sensing, Cenozoic marine sediment records from polar regions, sustainability science.

Murray State University, College of Health Sciences and Human Services, Program in Occupational Safety and Health, Murray, KY 42071. Offers environmental science (MS); industrial hygiene (MS); safety management (MS). *Accreditation:* ABET. Part-time programs available. *Degree requirements:* For master's, comprehensive exam, thesis optional, professional internship. Electronic applications accepted. *Faculty research:* Light effects on plant growth, ergonomics, toxic effects of pets' pesticides, traffic safety.

New Jersey Institute of Technology, Office of Graduate Studies, College of Science and Liberal Arts, Department of Chemistry and Environmental Science, Program in Environmental Science, Newark, NJ 07102. Offers MS, PhD. Part-time and evening/weekend programs available. *Degree requirements:* For doctorate, thesis/dissertation. *Entrance requirements:* For master's, GRE General Test; for doctorate, GRE General Test, minimum graduate GPA of 3.5. Additional exam requirements/recommendations for international students: Required—TOEFL (minimum score 550 paper-based; 79 iBT). Electronic applications accepted. *Expenses:* Tuition, state resident: full-time $16,836; part-time $915 per credit. Tuition, nonresident: full-time $24,370; part-time $1286 per credit. *Required fees:* $2318; $242 per credit.

New Mexico Highlands University, Graduate Studies, College of Arts and Sciences, Program in Natural Science, Las Vegas, NM 87701. Offers biology (MS); environmental science and management (MS); geology (MS). *Expenses:* Tuition, state resident: full-time $4277; part-time $178.22 per hour. Tuition, nonresident: full-time $6715; part-time $279.81 per hour. *International tuition:* $8510 full-time. Part-time tuition and fees vary according to campus/location. *Application contact:* Diane Trujillo, Administrative Assistant, Graduate Studies, 505-454-3266, Fax: 505-454-3558, E-mail: dtrujillo@nmhu.edu. Website: http://www.nmhu.edu/academics/graduate/arts_science_grad/natural_science/index.aspx.

New Mexico State University, Graduate School, College of Agricultural, Consumer and Environmental Sciences, Department of Plant and Environmental Sciences, Las Cruces, NM 88003-8001. Offers horticulture (MS); plant and environmental sciences (MS, PhD). Part-time programs available. *Faculty:* 19 full-time (3 women). *Students:* 41 full-time (18 women), 15 part-time (5 women); includes 6 minority (3 American Indian or Alaska Native, non-Hispanic/Latino; 3 Hispanic/Latino), 19 international. Average age 32. 19 applicants, 32% accepted, 5 enrolled. In 2012, 6 master's, 5 doctorates awarded. Terminal master's awarded for partial completion of doctoral program. *Degree requirements:* For master's, thesis; for doctorate, one foreign language, comprehensive exam, thesis/dissertation, qualifying exam, 2 seminars. *Entrance requirements:* For master's, GRE, minimum GPA of 3.0, 3 letters of reference, letter of purpose or intent; for doctorate, GRE, minimum GPA of 3.3; 3 letters of reference, letter of purpose or intent. Additional exam requirements/recommendations for international students: Required—TOEFL (minimum score 550 paper-based; 79 iBT), IELTS (minimum score 6.5). *Application deadline:* Applications are processed on a rolling basis. Application fee: $40 ($50 for international students). Electronic applications accepted. *Expenses:* Tuition, state resident: full-time $5239; part-time $218 per credit. Tuition, nonresident: full-time $18,266; part-time $761 per credit. *Required fees:* $1274; $53 per credit. *Financial support:* In 2012–13, 39 students received support, including 1 fellowship (averaging $3,930 per year), 26 research assistantships (averaging $21,062 per year), 9 teaching assistantships (averaging $13,700 per year); career-related internships or fieldwork, Federal Work-Study, scholarships/grants, health care benefits, and unspecified assistantships also available. Support available to part-time students. Financial award application deadline: 3/1. *Faculty research:* Plant breeding and genetics, molecular biology, plant physiology, soil science and environmental remediation, urban horticulture and turfgrass management. *Total annual research expenditures:* $6.2 million. *Unit head:* Dr. Richard Pratt, Head, 575-646-3406, Fax: 575-646-6041, E-mail: ricpratt@nmsu.edu. *Application contact:* Esther Ramirez, Information Contact, 575-646-3406, Fax: 575-646-6041, E-mail: esramire@nmsu.edu. Website: http://aces.nmsu.edu/pes.

North Carolina Agricultural and Technical State University, School of Graduate Studies, School of Agriculture and Environmental Sciences, Greensboro, NC 27411. Offers MAT, MS. Part-time and evening/weekend programs available. *Degree requirements:* For master's, comprehensive exam, qualifying exam. *Entrance requirements:* For master's, GRE General Test. *Faculty research:* Aid for small farmers, agricultural technology, housing, food science, nutrition.

North Dakota State University, College of Graduate and Interdisciplinary Studies, Interdisciplinary Program in Environmental and Conservation Sciences, Fargo, ND 58108. Offers MS, PhD. *Faculty:* 4 full-time (0 women), 1 part-time/adjunct (0 women). *Students:* 28 full-time (13 women), 11 part-time (5 women); includes 2 minority (both Two or more races, non-Hispanic/Latino), 16 international. Average age 31. 22 applicants, 23% accepted, 5 enrolled. In 2012, 9 master's, 4 doctorates awarded. *Degree requirements:* For master's, comprehensive exam, thesis. *Entrance requirements:* Additional exam requirements/recommendations for international students: Required—TOEFL (minimum score 550 paper-based; 79 iBT). *Application deadline:* For fall admission, 5/1 for international students; for spring admission, 8/1 for international students. Application fee: $35. *Unit head:* Dr. Craig Stockwell, Director, 701-231-8449, Fax: 701-231-7149, E-mail: craig.stockwell@ndsu.edu. *Application contact:* Madonna Fitzgerald, Administrative Assistant, 701-231-6456, E-mail: madonna.fitzgerald@ndsu.edu. Website: http://www.ndsu.nodak.edu/ecs/.

Northern Arizona University, Graduate College, College of Engineering, Forestry and Natural Sciences, School of Earth Sciences and Environmental Sustainability, Flagstaff, AZ 86011. Offers climate science and solutions (MS);

earth science (MS); earth sciences and environmental sustainability (PhD); environmental sciences and policy (MS); geology (MS). *Degree requirements:* For master's, comprehensive exam (for some programs), thesis (for some programs). *Entrance requirements:* Additional exam requirements/recommendations for international students: Required—TOEFL (minimum score 550 paper-based; 80 iBT), IELTS (minimum score 7). Electronic applications accepted.

Nova Southeastern University, Oceanographic Center, Fort Lauderdale, FL 33314-7796. Offers biological sciences (MS); coastal zone management (MS); marine and coastal studies (MA); marine biology (MS); marine biology and oceanography (PhD), including marine biology, oceanography; marine environmental sciences (MS). Part-time and evening/weekend programs available. *Faculty:* 13 full-time (1 woman), 20 part-time/adjunct (5 women). *Students:* 123 full-time (84 women), 153 part-time (96 women); includes 36 minority (7 Black or African American, non-Hispanic/Latino; 1 American Indian or Alaska Native, non-Hispanic/Latino; 5 Asian, non-Hispanic/Latino; 18 Hispanic/Latino; 5 Two or more races, non-Hispanic/Latino), 6 international. Average age 29. 98 applicants, 81% accepted, 48 enrolled. In 2012, 26 master's, 1 doctorate awarded. *Degree requirements:* For master's, thesis; for doctorate, comprehensive exam, thesis/dissertation, departmental qualifying exam. *Entrance requirements:* For master's, GRE General Test, 3 letters of recommendation, BS/BA in natural science (for marine biology program), BS/BA in biology (for biological sciences program), minor in the natural sciences or equivalent (for coastal zone management and marine environmental sciences); for doctorate, GRE General Test, master's degree. Additional exam requirements/recommendations for international students: Required—TOEFL (minimum score 550 paper-based). *Application deadline:* Applications are processed on a rolling basis. Application fee: $50. *Expenses:* Contact institution. *Financial support:* In 2012–13, 2 fellowships with full and partial tuition reimbursements (averaging $16,300 per year), 50 research assistantships with full and partial tuition reimbursements (averaging $19,000 per year) were awarded; teaching assistantships, career-related internships or fieldwork, Federal Work-Study, scholarships/grants, health care benefits, tuition waivers (full and partial), and unspecified assistantships also available. Support available to part-time students. Financial award applicants required to submit FAFSA. *Faculty research:* Physical, geological, chemical, and biological oceanography. *Unit head:* Dr. Richard Dodge, Dean, 954-262-3600, Fax: 954-262-4020, E-mail: dodge@nsu.nova.edu. *Application contact:* Dr. Richard Spieler, Associate Dean of Academic Programs, 954-262-3600, Fax: 954-262-4020, E-mail: spieler@nova.edu. Website: http://www.nova.edu/ocean/.

Oakland University, Graduate Study and Lifelong Learning, College of Arts and Sciences, Department of Chemistry, Rochester, MI 48309-4401. Offers biological sciences: health and environmental chemistry (PhD); chemistry (MS). *Degree requirements:* For master's, thesis; for doctorate, thesis/dissertation. *Entrance requirements:* For master's, minimum GPA of 3.0 for unconditional admission; for doctorate, GRE Subject Test, minimum GPA of 3.0 for unconditional admission. Additional exam requirements/recommendations for international students: Required—TOEFL (minimum score 550 paper-based). Electronic applications accepted. *Faculty research:* Chemistry of free radical species generated from biological intermediates; fate of toxic organic compounds in the environment; electroanalytical and surface chemistry at solid/liquid interface; computational modeling of intermolecular interactions and surface phenomena; metabolism and biological activity of modified fatty acids and xenobiotic carboxylic acids; physiologic and pathologic mechanisms that modulate immune responses.

The Ohio State University, Graduate School, College of Food, Agricultural, and Environmental Sciences, School of Environment and Natural Resources, Columbus, OH 43210. Offers environment and natural resources (MENR); rural sociology (MS, PhD); soil science (MS, PhD). *Faculty:* 35. *Students:* 73 full-time (40 women), 26 part-time (13 women); includes 11 minority (2 Black or African American, non-Hispanic/Latino; 6 Hispanic/Latino; 3 Two or more races, non-Hispanic/Latino), 14 international. Average age 29. In 2012, 30 master's, 4 doctorates awarded. *Degree requirements:* For master's, thesis; for doctorate, thesis/dissertation. *Entrance requirements:* For master's and doctorate, GRE. Additional exam requirements/recommendations for international students: Required—TOEFL (minimum score 550 paper-based; 79 iBT), Michigan English Language Assessment Battery (minimum score 82); Recommended—IELTS (minimum score 7). *Application deadline:* Applications are processed on a rolling basis. Application fee: $40 ($50 for international students). Electronic applications accepted. *Unit head:* Ronald Hendrick, Director, 614-292-8522, E-mail: hendrick.15@osu.edu. *Application contact:* Amy Schmidt, Graduate Program Coordinator, 614-292-9883, Fax: 614-292-7432, E-mail: schmidt.442@osu.edu. Website: http://senr.osu.edu/default.asp.

Oklahoma State University, College of Agricultural Science and Natural Resources, Department of Horticulture and Landscape Architecture, Stillwater, OK 74078. Offers agriculture (M Ag); crop science (PhD); environmental science (PhD); horticulture (MS); plant science (PhD). *Faculty:* 19 full-time (3 women), 2 part-time/adjunct (1 woman). *Students:* 1 (woman) full-time, 7 part-time (5 women), 4 international. Average age 27. 11 applicants, 27% accepted, 2 enrolled. In 2012, 6 master's awarded. *Degree requirements:* For master's, thesis (for some programs); for doctorate, comprehensive exam, thesis/dissertation. *Entrance requirements:* For master's and doctorate, GRE or GMAT. Additional exam requirements/recommendations for international students: Required—TOEFL (minimum score 550 paper-based; 79 iBT). *Application deadline:* For fall admission, 3/1 for international students; for spring admission, 8/1 for international students. Applications are processed on a rolling basis. Application fee: $40 ($75 for international students). Electronic applications accepted. *Expenses:* Tuition, state resident: full-time $4272; part-time $178 per credit hour. Tuition, nonresident: full-time $17,016; part-time $709 per credit hour. *Required fees:* $2188; $91.17 per credit hour. One-time fee: $50 full-time. Part-time tuition and fees vary according to course load and campus/location. *Financial support:* In 2012–13, 3 research assistantships (averaging $14,964 per year), 3 teaching assistantships (averaging $14,964 per year) were awarded; career-related internships or fieldwork, Federal Work-Study, scholarships/grants, health care benefits, tuition waivers (partial), and unspecified assistantships also available. Support available to part-time students. Financial award application deadline: 3/1; financial award applicants required to submit FAFSA. *Faculty research:* Stress and postharvest physiology; water utilization and runoff; integrated pest management (IPM) systems and nursery, turf, floriculture, vegetable, net and fruit produces and natural resources, food extraction, and processing; public garden management. *Unit head:* Dr. Dale Maronek, Head, 405-744-5414, Fax: 405-744-9709. *Application contact:* Dr. Sheryl Tucker, Dean, 405-744-7099, Fax: 405-744-0355, E-mail: grad-i@okstate.edu. Website: http://www.hortla.okstate.edu/.

Oklahoma State University, College of Agricultural Science and Natural Resources, Department of Plant and Soil Sciences, Stillwater, OK 74078. Offers crop science (PhD); environmental science (PhD); plant and soil sciences (MS); plant science (PhD); soil science (M Ag, PhD). *Faculty:* 33 full-time (5 women), 1 part-time/adjunct (0 women). *Students:* 20 full-time (6 women), 37 part-time (14 women); includes 6 minority (1 Black or African American, non-Hispanic/Latino; 2 Asian, non-Hispanic/Latino; 3 Two or more races, non-Hispanic/Latino), 31 international. Average age 29. 37 applicants, 27% accepted, 6 enrolled. In 2012, 20 master's, 3 doctorates awarded. *Degree requirements:* For master's, thesis; for doctorate, comprehensive exam, thesis/dissertation. *Entrance requirements:* For master's and doctorate, GRE or GMAT. Additional exam requirements/recommendations for international students: Required—TOEFL (minimum score 550 paper-based; 79 iBT). *Application deadline:* For fall admission, 3/1 for international students; for spring admission, 8/1 for international students. Applications are processed on a rolling basis. Application fee: $40 ($75 for international students). Electronic applications accepted. *Expenses:* Tuition, state resident: full-time $4272; part-time $178 per credit hour. Tuition, nonresident: full-time $17,016; part-time $709 per credit hour. *Required fees:* $2188; $91.17 per credit hour. One-time fee: $50 full-time. Part-time tuition and fees vary according to course load and campus/location. *Financial support:* In 2012–13, 44 research assistantships (averaging $15,985 per year), 2 teaching assistantships (averaging $17,760 per year) were awarded; career-related internships or fieldwork, Federal Work-Study, scholarships/grants, health care benefits, tuition waivers (partial), and unspecified assistantships also available. Support available to part-time students. Financial award application deadline: 3/1; financial award applicants required to submit FAFSA. *Faculty research:* Crop science, weed science, rangeland ecology and management, biotechnology, breeding and genetics. *Unit head:* Dr. David Porter, Interim Head, 405-744-6130, Fax: 405-744-5269. *Application contact:* Dr. Sheryl Tucker, Dean, 405-744-7099, Fax: 405-744-0355, E-mail: grad-i@okstate.edu. Website: http://www.pss.okstate.edu.

Oklahoma State University, College of Arts and Sciences, Department of Botany, Stillwater, OK 74078. Offers botany (MS); environmental science (MS, PhD); plant science (PhD). *Faculty:* 15 full-time (6 women), 2 part-time/adjunct (1 woman). *Students:* 5 full-time (2 women), 6 part-time (3 women); includes 4 minority (1 American Indian or Alaska Native, non-Hispanic/Latino; 1 Hispanic/Latino; 2 Two or more races, non-Hispanic/Latino). Average age 28. 13 applicants, 46% accepted, 4 enrolled. In 2012, 3 master's awarded. *Degree requirements:* For master's, thesis; for doctorate, comprehensive exam, thesis/dissertation. *Entrance requirements:* For master's and doctorate, GRE or GMAT. Additional exam requirements/recommendations for international students: Required—TOEFL (minimum score 550 paper-based; 79 iBT). *Application deadline:* For fall admission, 3/1 for international students; for spring admission, 8/1 for international students. Applications are processed on a rolling basis. Application fee: $40 ($75 for international students). Electronic applications accepted. *Expenses:* Tuition, state resident: full-time $4272; part-time $178 per credit hour. Tuition, nonresident: full-time $17,016; part-time $709 per credit hour. *Required fees:* $2188; $91.17 per credit hour. One-time fee: $50 full-time. Part-time tuition and fees vary according to course load and campus/location. *Financial support:* In 2012–13, 3 research assistantships (averaging $15,770 per year), 11 teaching assistantships (averaging $14,941 per year) were awarded; career-related internships or fieldwork, Federal Work-Study, scholarships/grants, health care benefits, tuition waivers (partial), and unspecified assistantships also available. Support available to part-time students. Financial award application deadline: 3/1; financial award applicants required to submit FAFSA. *Faculty research:* Ethnobotany, developmental genetics of Arabidopsis, biological roles of Plasmodesmata, community ecology and biodiversity, nutrient cycling in grassland ecosystems. *Unit head:* Dr. Linda Watson, Head, 405-744-5559, Fax: 405-744-7074. *Application contact:* Dr. Sheryl Tucker, Dean, 405-744-7099, Fax: 405-744-0355, E-mail: grad-i@okstate.edu. Website: http://botany.okstate.edu.

Oklahoma State University, Graduate College, Stillwater, OK 74078. Offers aerospace security (Graduate Certificate); biobased products and bioenergy (Graduate Certificate); bioinformatics (Graduate Certificate); business data mining (Graduate Certificate); engineering and technology management (Graduate Certificate); environmental science (MS); global issues (Graduate Certificate); information assurance (Graduate Certificate); international studies (MS); natural and applied science (MS); photonics (PhD); plant science (PhD); teaching English to speakers of other languages (Graduate Certificate). Programs are interdisciplinary. *Faculty:* 3 full-time (2 women), 2 part-time/adjunct (0 women). *Students:* 83 full-time (50 women), 169 part-time (90 women); includes 64 minority (16 Black or African American, non-Hispanic/Latino; 13 American Indian or Alaska Native, non-Hispanic/Latino; 13 Asian, non-Hispanic/Latino; 6 Hispanic/Latino; 1 Native Hawaiian or other Pacific Islander, non-Hispanic/Latino; 15 Two or more races, non-Hispanic/Latino), 51 international. Average age 32. 605 applicants, 71% accepted, 82 enrolled. In 2012, 76 master's, 7 doctorates awarded. *Degree requirements:* For master's, thesis (for some programs); for doctorate, comprehensive exam, thesis/dissertation. *Entrance requirements:* For master's and doctorate, GRE or GMAT. Additional exam requirements/recommendations for international students: Required—TOEFL (minimum score 550 paper-based; 79 iBT). *Application deadline:* For fall admission, 3/1 for international students; for spring admission, 8/1 for international students. Applications are processed on a rolling basis. Application fee: $40 ($75 for international students). Electronic applications accepted. *Expenses:* Tuition, state resident: full-time $4272; part-time $178 per credit hour. Tuition, nonresident: full-time $17,016; part-time $709 per credit hour. *Required fees:* $2188; $91.17 per credit hour. One-time fee: $50 full-time. Part-time tuition and fees vary according to course load and campus/location. *Financial support:* In 2012–13, 6 research assistantships (averaging $6,600 per year) were awarded; career-related internships or fieldwork, Federal Work-Study, scholarships/grants, health care benefits, tuition waivers (partial), and unspecified assistantships also available. Support available to part-time students. Financial award application deadline: 3/1; financial award applicants required to submit FAFSA. *Unit head:* Dr. Sheryl Tucker, Dean, 405-744-7099, Fax: 405-744-0355, E-mail: grad-i@okstate.edu. *Application contact:* Dr. Susan Mathew, Coordinator of Admissions, 405-744-6368, Fax: 405-744-0355, E-mail: grad-i@okstate.edu. Website: http://gradcollege.okstate.edu/.

Oregon Health & Science University, School of Medicine, Graduate Programs in Medicine, Department of Environmental and Biomolecular Systems, Portland, OR 97239-3098. Offers biochemistry and molecular biology (MS, PhD); environmental science and engineering (MS, PhD). Part-time programs available. *Faculty:* 12 full-time (4 women), 2 part-time/adjunct (1 woman). *Students:* 22 full-time (17 women), 9 part-time (5 women); includes 10 minority (2 Black or African American, non-Hispanic/Latino; 1 American Indian or Alaska Native, non-Hispanic/Latino; 1 Asian, non-Hispanic/Latino; 5 Hispanic/Latino; 1 Two or more races, non-Hispanic/Latino), 4 international. Average age 28. 30 applicants, 33% accepted, 10 enrolled. In 2012, 10 master's, 3 doctorates awarded. Terminal master's awarded for partial completion of doctoral program. *Degree requirements:* For master's, thesis (for some programs); for doctorate, comprehensive exam, thesis/dissertation, qualifying exam. *Entrance requirements:* For master's and doctorate, GRE General Test (minimum scores: 500 Verbal/600 Quantitative/4.5 Analytical) or MCAT (for some programs). Additional exam requirements/recommendations for international students: Required—TOEFL. *Application deadline:* For fall admission, 7/15 for domestic students, 5/15 for international students; for winter admission, 10/15 for domestic students, 9/15 for international students; for spring admission, 1/15 for domestic students, 12/15 for international students. Applications are processed on a rolling basis. Application fee: $70. Electronic applications accepted. *Financial support:* Health care benefits and full tuition and stipends (for PhD students) available. *Unit head:* Dr. Paul Tratnyek, Program Director, 503-748-1070, E-mail: info@ebs.ogi.edu. *Application contact:* Nancy Christie, Program Coordinator, 503-748-1070, E-mail: info@ebs.ogi.edu.

Oregon State University, College of Agricultural Sciences, Department of Environmental and Molecular Toxicology, Corvallis, OR 97331. Offers toxicology (MS, PhD). *Faculty:* 9 full-time (2 women), 4 part-time/adjunct (0 women). *Students:* 28 full-time (12 women), 1 part-time (0 women); includes 4 minority (2 American Indian or Alaska Native, non-Hispanic/Latino; 1 Asian, non-Hispanic/Latino; 1 Hispanic/Latino), 3 international. Average age 29. 37 applicants, 24% accepted, 6 enrolled. In 2012, 1 master's, 2 doctorates awarded. Application fee: $50. *Expenses:* Tuition, state resident: full-time $11,367; part-time $421 per credit hour. Tuition, nonresident: full-time $18,279; part-time $677 per credit hour. *Required fees:* $1478. One-time fee: $300 full-time. Tuition and fees vary according to course load and program. *Unit head:* Dr. Craig Marcus, Department Head, 541-737-1808, E-mail: craig.marcus@oregonstate.edu. Website: http://emt.oregonstate.edu/.

Oregon State University, Graduate School, Program in Environmental Sciences, Corvallis, OR 97331. Offers MA, MS, PhD. *Students:* 47 full-time (29 women), 11 part-time (5 women); includes 5 minority (1 Black or African American, non-Hispanic/Latino; 3 Hispanic/Latino; 1 Two or more races, non-Hispanic/Latino), 6 international. Average age 32. 70 applicants, 33% accepted, 13 enrolled. In 2012, 15 master's, 1 doctorate awarded. Application fee: $50. *Expenses:* Tuition, state resident: full-time $11,367; part-time $421 per credit hour. Tuition, nonresident: full-time $18,279; part-time $677 per credit hour. *Required fees:* $1478. One-time fee: $300 full-time. Tuition and fees vary according to course load and program. *Unit head:* Dr. Andrew R. Blaustein, Director and Professor, 541-737-5356, Fax: 541-737-0501, E-mail: blaustea@science.oregonstate.edu.

Pace University, Dyson College of Arts and Sciences, Program in Environmental Science, New York, NY 10038. Offers MS. Offered at Pleasantville, NY location only. *Students:* 11 full-time (7 women), 19 part-time (10 women); includes 4 minority (2 Asian, non-Hispanic/Latino; 1 Hispanic/Latino; 1 Two or more races, non-Hispanic/Latino), 4 international. Average age 29. 24 applicants, 50% accepted, 8 enrolled. In 2012, 6 master's awarded. *Degree requirements:* For master's, research project. *Entrance requirements:* For master's, GRE. Additional exam requirements/recommendations for international students: Required—TOEFL. *Application deadline:* For fall admission, 8/1 priority date for domestic students, 6/1 for international students; for spring admission, 12/1 priority date for domestic students, 10/1 for international students. Applications are processed on a rolling basis. Application fee: $70. Electronic applications accepted. *Expenses: Tuition:* Part-time $1035 per credit. *Required fees:* $230 per semester. Tuition and fees vary according to course load, degree level and program. *Unit head:* Dr. Melissa Grigione, Program Director, Environmental Science Graduate Program, 914-773-3509, Fax: 914-773-3634, E-mail: mgrigione@pace.edu. *Application contact:* Susan Ford-Goldschein, Director of Graduate Admissions, 914-422-4283, Fax: 914-422-4287, E-mail: gradwp@pace.edu. Website: http://www.pace.edu/dyson/academic-departments-and-programs/environmental-science.

Penn State Harrisburg, Graduate School, School of Science, Engineering and Technology, Middletown, PA 17057-4898. Offers computer science (MS); electrical engineering (MS); engineering management (MPS); environmental engineering (M Eng). Part-time and evening/weekend programs available. *Unit head:* Dr. Jerry F. Shoup, Interim Director, 717-948-6352, E-mail: jfs1@psu.edu. *Application contact:* Robert Coffman, Director of Admissions, 717-948-6250, Fax: 717-948-6325, E-mail: ric1@psu.edu. Website: http://harrisburg.psu.edu/science-engineering-technology.

Penn State University Park, Graduate School, Intercollege Graduate Programs, Intercollege Program in Environmental Pollution Control, State College, University Park, PA 16802-1503. Offers MEPC, MS. *Unit head:* Dr. Herschel A. Elliott, Chair, 814-865-1417, Fax: 814-863-1031, E-mail: helliott3@psu.edu. *Application contact:* Cynthia E. Nicosia, Director, Graduate Enrollment Services, 814-865-1795, Fax: 814-865-4627, E-mail: cey1@psu.edu.

Polytechnic Institute of New York University, Department of Civil and Urban Engineering, Major in Environmental Science, Brooklyn, NY 11201-2990. Offers MS. Part-time and evening/weekend programs available. *Students:* 7 full-time (4 women), 3 part-time (1 woman); includes 2 minority (both Black or African American, non-Hispanic/Latino), 6 international. 25 applicants, 72% accepted, 9 enrolled. In 2012, 1 master's awarded. *Degree requirements:* For master's, comprehensive exam (for some programs), thesis (for some programs). *Entrance requirements:* Additional exam requirements/recommendations for international students: Required—TOEFL (minimum score 550 paper-based; 80 iBT); Recommended—IELTS (minimum score 6.5). *Application deadline:* For fall admission, 7/31 priority date for domestic students, 4/30 for international students; for spring admission, 12/31 priority date for domestic students, 10/30 for international students. Applications are processed on a rolling basis. Application fee: $75. Electronic applications accepted. *Financial support:* Fellowships, research assistantships, teaching assistantships, institutionally sponsored loans, scholarships/grants, and unspecified assistantships available. Support available to part-time students. Financial award applicants required to submit FAFSA. *Unit head:* Dr. Lawrence Chiarelli, Head, 718-260-4040, Fax: 718-260-3433, E-mail: lchiarel@poly.edu. *Application contact:* Raymond Lutzky, Director of Graduate Enrollment Management, 718-637-5984, Fax: 718-260-3624, E-mail: rlutzky@poly.edu.

Pontifical Catholic University of Puerto Rico, College of Sciences, Department of Biology, Ponce, PR 00717-0777. Offers environmental sciences (MS). *Degree requirements:* For master's, thesis. *Entrance requirements:* For master's, GRE, 2 letters of recommendation, interview, minimum GPA of 2.75.

Portland State University, Graduate Studies, College of Liberal Arts and Sciences, Department of Geology, Portland, OR 97207-0751. Offers environmental sciences and resources (PhD); geology (MA, MS); science/geology (MAT, MST). Part-time programs available. *Degree requirements:* For master's, comprehensive exam, thesis, field comprehensive; for doctorate, thesis/dissertation, 2 years of residency. *Entrance requirements:* For master's, GRE General Test, GRE Subject Test, BA/BS in geology, minimum GPA of 3.0 in upper-division course work or 2.75 overall. Additional exam requirements/recommendations for international students: Required—TOEFL (minimum score 550 paper-based). *Faculty research:* Sediment transport, volcanic environmental geology, coastal and fluvial processes.

Portland State University, Graduate Studies, College of Liberal Arts and Sciences, Program in Environmental Sciences and Management, Portland, OR 97207-0751. Offers environmental management (MEM); environmental sciences/biology (PhD); environmental sciences/chemistry (PhD); environmental sciences/civil engineering (PhD); environmental sciences/geography (PhD); environmental sciences/geology (PhD); environmental sciences/physics (PhD); environmental studies (MS); science/environmental science (MST). Part-time programs available. *Degree requirements:* For master's, thesis or alternative; for doctorate, variable foreign language requirement, comprehensive exam, thesis/dissertation, oral and qualifying exams. *Entrance requirements:* For master's, GRE General Test, 3 letters of recommendation; for doctorate, minimum GPA of 3.0 in upper-division course work or 2.75 overall. Additional exam requirements/recommendations for international students: Required—TOEFL (minimum score 550 paper-based). *Faculty research:* Environmental aspects of biology, chemistry, civil engineering, geology, physics.

Queens College of the City University of New York, Division of Graduate Studies, Mathematics and Natural Sciences Division, School of Earth and Environmental Sciences, Flushing, NY 11367-1597. Offers MA. Part-time and evening/weekend programs available. *Faculty:* 16 full-time (4 women), 9 part-time/adjunct (3 women). *Students:* 9 part-time (5 women); includes 4 minority (1 Black or African American, non-Hispanic/Latino; 1 Asian, non-Hispanic/Latino; 2 Hispanic/Latino). 18 applicants, 56% accepted, 4 enrolled. In 2012, 10 master's awarded. *Degree requirements:* For master's, comprehensive exam, thesis. *Entrance requirements:* For master's, GRE, previous course work in calculus, physics, and chemistry; minimum GPA of 3.0. Additional exam requirements/recommendations for international students: Required—TOEFL. *Application deadline:* For fall admission, 4/1 for domestic students; for spring admission, 11/1 for domestic students. Applications are processed on a rolling basis. Application fee: $125. *Expenses:* Tuition, state resident: full-time $8690; part-time $365 per credit. Tuition, nonresident: full-time $16,200; part-time $675 per credit. Full-time tuition and fees vary according to course load. *Financial support:* Career-related internships or fieldwork and unspecified assistantships available. Financial award application deadline: 4/1; financial award applicants required to submit FAFSA. *Unit head:* Dr. Allan Ludman, Chairperson, 718-997-3300. *Application contact:* Dr. Hannes Brueckner, Graduate Adviser, 718-997-3300, E-mail: hannes_brueckner@qc.edu.

Rice University, Graduate Programs, George R. Brown School of Engineering, Department of Civil and Environmental Engineering, Houston, TX 77251-1892. Offers civil engineering (MCE, MS, PhD); environmental engineering (MEE, MES, MS, PhD); environmental science (MEE, MES, MS, PhD). Part-time programs available. *Degree requirements:* For master's, thesis (for some programs); for doctorate, thesis/dissertation. *Entrance requirements:* For master's and doctorate, GRE General Test, GRE Subject Test, minimum GPA of 3.25. Additional exam requirements/recommendations for international students: Required—TOEFL (minimum score 600 paper-based; 90 iBT). Electronic applications accepted. *Faculty research:* Biology and chemistry of groundwater, pollutant fate in groundwater systems, water quality monitoring, urban storm water runoff, urban air quality.

Rice University, Graduate Programs, Wiess School–Professional Science Master's Programs, Houston, TX 77251-1892. Offers MS.

The Richard Stockton College of New Jersey, School of Graduate and Continuing Studies, Program in Environmental Science, Galloway, NJ 08205-9441. Offers PSM. Part-time and evening/weekend programs available. *Faculty:* 3 full-time (1 woman), 2 part-time/adjunct (0 women). *Students:* 7 full-time (3 women), 11 part-time (4 women); includes 1 minority (Hispanic/Latino). Average age 31. 13 applicants, 69% accepted, 8 enrolled. In 2012, 5 master's awarded. *Degree requirements:* For master's, thesis optional, project. *Entrance requirements:* For master's, GRE. Additional exam requirements/recommendations for international students: Required—TOEFL. *Application deadline:* For fall admission, 7/1 for domestic and international students; for spring admission, 12/1 for domestic and international students. Applications are processed on a rolling basis. Application fee: $50. Electronic applications accepted. *Financial support:* In 2012–13, 5 students received support. Fellowships with partial tuition reimbursements available, research assistantships, career-related internships or fieldwork, Federal Work-Study, scholarships/grants, and unspecified assistantships available. Financial award application deadline: 3/1; financial award applicants required to submit FAFSA. *Unit head:* Dr. Kathy Sedia, Program Director, 609-626-3640, E-mail: gradschool@stockton.edu. *Application contact:* Tara Williams, Assistant Director of Graduate Enrollment Management, 609-626-3640, Fax: 609-626-6050, E-mail: gradschool@stockton.edu. Website: http://www.stockton.edu/grad.

Rochester Institute of Technology, Graduate Enrollment Services, College of Science, Thomas H. Gosnell School of Life Sciences, Program in Environmental Science, Rochester, NY 14623-5603. Offers MS. Part-time and evening/weekend programs available. *Students:* 16 full-time (8 women), 6 part-time (2 women); includes 1 minority (Hispanic/Latino), 2 international. Average age 26. 33 applicants, 24% accepted, 4 enrolled. In 2012, 6 master's awarded. *Degree requirements:* For master's, thesis. *Entrance requirements:* For master's, GRE General Test (recommended), minimum GPA of 3.0. Additional exam requirements/recommendations for international students: Required—TOEFL (minimum score 550 paper-based; 79 iBT) or IELTS (minimum score 6.5). *Application deadline:* For fall admission, 2/15 priority date for domestic students, 2/15 for international students; for winter admission, 11/1 for domestic students; for spring admission, 2/1 for domestic students. Applications are processed on a rolling basis. Application fee: $60. Electronic applications accepted. *Expenses: Tuition:* Full-time $35,976; part-time $999 per credit hour. *Required fees:* $240; $80 per quarter. *Financial support:* Fellowships with partial tuition reimbursements, research assistantships with partial tuition reimbursements, teaching assistantships with partial tuition reimbursements, career-related internships or fieldwork, scholarships/grants, and unspecified assistantships available. Support available to part-time students. Financial award applicants required to submit FAFSA. *Faculty research:* Environmental chemistry; digital imaging; environmental biology; remote sensing; mathematics and statistics; environmental public policy; environmental economics; feedbacks among benthic fauna, algae and biogeochemical cycling during eutrophication of a shallow estuary. *Unit head:* Dr. Christy Tyler, Graduate Program Director, 585-475-5042, Fax: 585-475-5000, E-mail: actsbi@rit.edu. *Application contact:* Diane Ellison, Assistant Vice President, Graduate Enrollment Services, 585-475-2229, Fax: 585-475-7164, E-mail: gradinfo@rit.edu. Website: http://www.rit.edu/cos/lifesciences/programs.html#ES.

Royal Military College of Canada, Division of Graduate Studies and Research, Engineering Division, Program in Environmental Science, Kingston, ON K7K 7B4, Canada. Offers M Sc, PhD. *Degree requirements:* For master's, thesis; for doctorate, comprehensive exam, thesis/dissertation. *Entrance requirements:* For master's, honours degree with second-class standing; for doctorate, master's degree. Electronic applications accepted.

Rutgers, The State University of New Jersey, Newark, Graduate School, Program in Environmental Science, Newark, NJ 07102. Offers MS, PhD. MS, PhD offered jointly with New Jersey Institute of Technology. *Entrance requirements:* For master's and doctorate, GRE, minimum B average.

Rutgers, The State University of New Jersey, New Brunswick, Graduate School-New Brunswick, Department of Environmental Sciences, Piscataway, NJ 08854-8097. Offers air pollution and resources (MS, PhD); aquatic biology (MS, PhD); aquatic chemistry (MS, PhD); atmospheric science (MS, PhD); chemistry and physics of aerosol and hydrosol systems (MS, PhD); environmental chemistry (MS, PhD); environmental microbiology (MS, PhD); environmental toxicology (PhD); exposure assessment (PhD); fate and effects of pollutants (MS, PhD); pollution prevention and control (MS, PhD); water and wastewater treatment (MS, PhD); water resources (MS, PhD). Terminal master's awarded for partial completion of doctoral program. *Degree requirements:* For master's, comprehensive exam, thesis or alternative, oral final exam; for doctorate, comprehensive exam, thesis/dissertation, thesis defense, qualifying exam. *Entrance requirements:* For master's and doctorate, GRE General Test. Additional exam requirements/recommendations for international students: Required—TOEFL. Electronic applications accepted. *Faculty research:* Biological waste treatment; contaminant fate and transport; air, soil and water quality.

South Dakota School of Mines and Technology, Graduate Division, PhD Program in Atmospheric and Environmental Sciences, Rapid City, SD 57701-3995. Offers PhD. Program offered jointly with South Dakota State University. Part-time programs available. *Faculty:* 6 full-time (1 woman), 2 part-time/adjunct (1 woman). *Students:* 3 full-time (0 women), 9 part-time (2 women); includes 1 minority (Two or more races, non-Hispanic/Latino), 3 international. Average age 38. 1 applicant. *Degree requirements:* For doctorate, comprehensive exam, thesis/dissertation. *Entrance requirements:* For doctorate, GRE General Test, GRE Subject Test. Additional exam requirements/recommendations for international students: Required—TOEFL (minimum score 520 paper-based; 68 iBT), TWE. *Application deadline:* For fall admission, 7/1 priority date for domestic students, 4/1 for international students; for spring admission, 11/1 for domestic students, 9/1 for international students. Applications are processed on a rolling basis. Application fee: $35. Electronic applications accepted. *Expenses:* Tuition, state resident: full-time $4720; part-time $196.80 per credit hour. Tuition, nonresident: full-time $10,000; part-time $416.55 per credit hour. *Required fees:* $4360. *Financial support:* Fellowships, research assistantships with partial tuition reimbursements, teaching assistantships with partial tuition reimbursements, and unspecified assistantships available. Financial award application deadline: 5/15. *Unit head:* Dr. William Capehart, Program Coordinator, 605-394-1994, E-mail: william.capehart@sdsmt.edu. *Application contact:* Linda Carlson, Office of Graduate Education, 605-355-3468, Fax: 605-394-1767, E-mail: linda.carlson@sdsmt.edu. Website: http://www.sdsmt.edu/Academics/Departments/Atmospheric-Sciences/Graduate-Education/Atmospheric-and-Environmental-Sciences—PhD-/.

Southeast Missouri State University, School of Graduate Studies, Program in Environmental Science, Cape Girardeau, MO 63701-4799. Offers MS. *Faculty:* 15 full-time (3 women). *Students:* 7 full-time (4 women), 5 part-time (4 women), 6 international. Average age 28. 10 applicants, 60% accepted, 5 enrolled. In 2012, 1 master's awarded. *Degree requirements:* For master's, comprehensive exam (for some programs), thesis (for some programs), applied research project. *Entrance requirements:* For master's, GRE, minimum undergraduate GPA of 2.5; letter of intent; 2 letters of recommendation; 20 hours in science with minimum GPA of 3.0. Additional exam requirements/recommendations for international students: Required—TOEFL (minimum score 550 paper-based; 79 iBT), IELTS (minimum score 6). *Application deadline:* For fall admission, 8/1 for domestic students, 6/1 for international students; for spring admission, 11/21 for domestic students, 10/1 for international students. Applications are processed on a rolling basis. Application fee: $30 ($40 for international students). Electronic applications accepted. *Financial support:* In 2012–13, 15 students received support, including 3 teaching assistantships with full tuition reimbursements available (averaging $7,900 per year); career-related internships or fieldwork, Federal Work-Study, scholarships/grants, traineeships, tuition waivers (full), and unspecified assistantships also available. Financial award application deadline: 6/30; financial award applicants required to submit FAFSA. *Faculty research:* Contamination of soils and water with environmental chemicals, influence of environmental factors on respiratory health, determination of energy-related pollutants in environmental samples, economic valuation of water resources, impacts of environmental chemicals on wildlife species. *Total annual research expenditures:* $10,000. *Unit head:* Dr. Stephen R. Overmann, Program Director, 573-651-2386, E-mail: sovermann@semo.edu. *Application contact:* Gail Amick, Administrative Secretary, 573-651-2049, Fax: 573-651-2001, E-mail: gamick@semo.edu. Website: http://www.semo.edu/study/envirosci.

Southern Illinois University Carbondale, Graduate School, College of Science, Department of Geology and Department of Geography, Program in Environmental Resources and Policy, Carbondale, IL 62901-4701. Offers PhD. *Students:* 14 full-time (10 women), 20 part-time (3 women); includes 5 minority (4 Black or African

American, non-Hispanic/Latino; 1 American Indian or Alaska Native, non-Hispanic/Latino), 7 international. 15 applicants, 7% accepted, 0 enrolled. In 2012, 1 doctorate awarded. *Entrance requirements:* For doctorate, GRE. Application fee: $50. *Unit head:* Dr. Steven Esling, Chair, 618-453-3351, Fax: 618-453-7393, E-mail: esling@geo.siu.edu. *Application contact:* Dana Wise, Office Specialist, 618-453-7328, E-mail: dwise@siu.edu.

Southern Illinois University Edwardsville, Graduate School, College of Arts and Sciences, Program in Environmental Sciences, Edwardsville, IL 62026-0001. Offers MS. Part-time and evening/weekend programs available. *Students:* 2 full-time (1 woman), 6 part-time (3 women); includes 1 minority (Black or African American, non-Hispanic/Latino), 5 international. 15 applicants, 60% accepted, 0 enrolled. In 2012, 13 master's awarded. *Degree requirements:* For master's, thesis (for some programs), final exam, oral exam. *Entrance requirements:* For master's, GRE. Additional exam requirements/recommendations for international students: Required—TOEFL (minimum score 550 paper-based; 79 iBT), IELTS (minimum score 6.5). *Application deadline:* For fall admission, 7/26 for domestic students, 6/1 for international students; for spring admission, 12/6 for domestic students, 10/1 for international students. Applications are processed on a rolling basis. Application fee: $30. Electronic applications accepted. *Expenses:* Tuition, state resident: full-time $6504; part-time $3252 per semester. Tuition, nonresident: full-time $8130; part-time $4065 per semester. *Required fees:* $705.50 per semester. Tuition and fees vary according to course level, course load, degree level, program and student level. *Financial support:* In 2012–13, research assistantships with full tuition reimbursements (averaging $9,585 per year), teaching assistantships with full tuition reimbursements (averaging $9,585 per year) were awarded; fellowships with full tuition reimbursements, institutionally sponsored loans, scholarships/grants, and unspecified assistantships also available. Financial award application deadline: 3/1; financial award applicants required to submit FAFSA. *Unit head:* Dr. Kevin Johnson, Program Director, 618-650-5934, E-mail: kevjohn@siue.edu. *Application contact:* Michelle Robinson, Coordinator of Graduate Recruitment, 618-650-2811, Fax: 618-650-3523, E-mail: michero@siue.edu. Website: http://www.siue.edu/artsandsciences/environment/masters.shtml.

Southern Methodist University, Bobby B. Lyle School of Engineering, Department of Environmental and Civil Engineering, Dallas, TX 75275-0340. Offers air pollution control and atmospheric sciences (PhD); civil engineering (MS); environmental engineering (MS); structural engineering (PhD); sustainability and development (MA); water and wastewater engineering (PhD). Part-time and evening/weekend programs available. Postbaccalaureate distance learning degree programs offered (no on-campus study). Terminal master's awarded for partial completion of doctoral program. *Degree requirements:* For master's, thesis optional; for doctorate, thesis/dissertation, oral and written qualifying exams. *Entrance requirements:* For master's, GRE General Test, minimum GPA of 3.0 in last 2 years; bachelor's degree in engineering, mathematics, or sciences; for doctorate, GRE, BS and MS in related field, minimum GPA of 3.3. Additional exam requirements/recommendations for international students: Required—TOEFL. Electronic applications accepted. *Faculty research:* Human and environmental health effects of endocrine disrupters, development of air pollution control systems for diesel engines, structural analysis and design, modeling and design of waste treatment systems.

Southern University and Agricultural and Mechanical College, Graduate School, College of Sciences, Department of Chemistry, Baton Rouge, LA 70813. Offers analytical chemistry (MS); biochemistry (MS); environmental sciences (MS); inorganic chemistry (MS); organic chemistry (MS); physical chemistry (MS). *Degree requirements:* For master's, thesis. *Entrance requirements:* For master's, GMAT or GRE General Test. Additional exam requirements/recommendations for international students: Required—TOEFL (minimum score 525 paper-based). *Faculty research:* Synthesis of macrocyclic ligands, latex accelerators, anticancer drugs, biosensors, absorption isotheums, isolation of specific enzymes from plants.

Stanford University, School of Earth Sciences, Department of Geological and Environmental Sciences, Stanford, CA 94305-9991. Offers MS, PhD, Eng. Terminal master's awarded for partial completion of doctoral program. *Degree requirements:* For master's and Eng, thesis; for doctorate, thesis/dissertation. *Entrance requirements:* For master's, doctorate, and Eng, GRE General Test. Additional exam requirements/recommendations for international students: Required—TOEFL. Electronic applications accepted. *Expenses: Tuition:* Full-time $41,250; part-time $917 per credit hour.

Stanford University, School of Earth Sciences, Earth Systems Program, Stanford, CA 94305-9991. Offers MS. Students admitted at the undergraduate level. Electronic applications accepted. *Expenses: Tuition:* Full-time $41,250; part-time $917 per credit hour.

State University of New York College of Environmental Science and Forestry, Department of Chemistry, Syracuse, NY 13210-2779. Offers biochemistry (MPS, MS, PhD); environmental chemistry (MPS, MS, PhD); organic chemistry of natural products (MPS, MS, PhD); polymer chemistry (MPS, MS, PhD). *Degree requirements:* For master's, thesis; for doctorate, comprehensive exam, thesis/dissertation. *Entrance requirements:* For master's and doctorate, GRE General Test, GRE Subject Test, minimum GPA of 3.0. Additional exam requirements/recommendations for international students: Required—TOEFL (minimum score 550 paper-based; 80 iBT), IELTS (minimum score 6). Electronic applications accepted. *Expenses:* Tuition, state resident: full-time $9370; part-

time $390 per credit hour. Tuition, nonresident: full-time $16,680; part-time $695 per credit hour. *Required fees:* $981. Tuition and fees vary according to course load and program. *Faculty research:* Polymer chemistry, biochemistry.

State University of New York College of Environmental Science and Forestry, Department of Environmental and Forest Biology, Syracuse, NY 13210-2779. Offers applied ecology (MPS); chemical ecology (MPS, MS, PhD); conservation biology (MPS, MS, PhD); ecology (MPS, MS, PhD); entomology (MPS, MS, PhD); environmental interpretation (MPS, MS, PhD); environmental physiology (MPS, MS, PhD); fish and wildlife biology and management (MPS, MS, PhD); forest pathology and mycology (MPS, MS, PhD); plant biotechnology (MPS); plant science and biotechnology (MPS, MS, PhD). *Degree requirements:* For master's, thesis (for some programs); for doctorate, comprehensive exam, thesis/dissertation. *Entrance requirements:* For master's and doctorate, GRE General Test, GRE Subject Test, minimum GPA of 3.0. Additional exam requirements/recommendations for international students: Required—TOEFL (minimum score 550 paper-based; 80 iBT), IELTS (minimum score 6). *Expenses:* Tuition, state resident: full-time $9370; part-time $390 per credit hour. Tuition, nonresident: full-time $16,680; part-time $695 per credit hour. *Required fees:* $981. Tuition and fees vary according to course load and program. *Faculty research:* Ecology, fish and wildlife biology and management, plant science, entomology.

State University of New York College of Environmental Science and Forestry, Program in Environmental Science, Syracuse, NY 13210-2779. Offers biophysical and ecological economics (MPS); coupled natural and human systems (MPS); ecosystem restoration (MPS); environmental and community land planning (MPS, MS); environmental and natural resources policy (PhD); environmental communication and participatory processes (MPS, MS); environmental monitoring and modeling (MPS); environmental policy and democratic processes (MPS, MS); environmental systems and risk management (MS); water and wetland resource studies (MPS, MS). Part-time programs available. *Degree requirements:* For master's, thesis (for some programs); for doctorate, comprehensive exam, thesis/dissertation. *Entrance requirements:* For master's and doctorate, GRE General Test, minimum GPA of 3.0. Additional exam requirements/recommendations for international students: Required—TOEFL (minimum score 550 paper-based; 80 iBT), IELTS (minimum score 6). *Expenses:* Tuition, state resident: full-time $9370; part-time $390 per credit hour. Tuition, nonresident: full-time $16,680; part-time $695 per credit hour. *Required fees:* $981. Tuition and fees vary according to course load and program. *Faculty research:* Environmental education/communications, water resources, land resources, waste management.

Stephen F. Austin State University, Graduate School, College of Sciences and Mathematics, Division of Environmental Science, Nacogdoches, TX 75962. Offers MS. *Degree requirements:* For master's, comprehensive exam. *Entrance requirements:* For master's, GRE General Test, minimum GPA of 2.8 in last 60 hours, 2.5 overall. Additional exam requirements/recommendations for international students: Required—TOEFL.

Tarleton State University, College of Graduate Studies, College of Science and Technology, Department of Chemistry, Geosciences and Environmental Sciences, Stephenville, TX 76402. Offers environmental science (MS); manufacturing quality and leadership (MS). Part-time and evening/weekend programs available. *Faculty:* 1 (woman) full-time. *Students:* 2 full-time (0 women), 13 part-time (3 women); includes 2 minority (1 Black or African American, non-Hispanic/Latino; 1 Hispanic/Latino). Average age 37. 8 applicants, 100% accepted, 7 enrolled. In 2012, 5 master's awarded. *Degree requirements:* For master's, comprehensive exam, thesis optional. *Entrance requirements:* For master's, GRE General Test, minimum GPA of 3.0. Additional exam requirements/recommendations for international students: Required—TOEFL (minimum score 550 paper-based; 80 iBT). *Application deadline:* For fall admission, 8/15 priority date for domestic students; for spring admission, 1/7 for domestic students. Applications are processed on a rolling basis. Application fee: $30 ($130 for international students). Electronic applications accepted. *Expenses:* Tuition, state resident: full-time $3311; part-time $184 per credit hour. Tuition, nonresident: full-time $9090; part-time $505 per credit hour. *Required fees:* $1446. Tuition and fees vary according to course load and campus/location. *Financial support:* Research assistantships, teaching assistantships, career-related internships or fieldwork, and Federal Work-Study available. Support available to part-time students. Financial award application deadline: 5/1; financial award applicants required to submit FAFSA. *Unit head:* Dr. George Mollick, Head, 254-968-9012, Fax: 254-968-9953, E-mail: mollick@tarleton.edu. *Application contact:* Information Contact, 254-968-9104, Fax: 254-968-9670, E-mail: gradoffice@tarleton.edu. Website: http://www.tarleton.edu/COSTWEB/engtech/.

Tennessee Technological University, Graduate School, College of Arts and Sciences, Department of Environmental Sciences, Cookeville, TN 38505. Offers biology (PhD); chemistry (PhD). Part-time programs available. *Students:* 2 full-time (1 woman), 15 part-time (5 women); includes 3 minority (1 Black or African American, non-Hispanic/Latino; 1 American Indian or Alaska Native, non-Hispanic/Latino; 1 Hispanic/Latino), 5 international. 14 applicants, 43% accepted, 3 enrolled. In 2012, 1 doctorate awarded. *Degree requirements:* For doctorate, comprehensive exam, thesis/dissertation. *Entrance requirements:* For doctorate, GRE. Additional exam requirements/recommendations for international students: Required—TOEFL (minimum score 527 paper-based; 71 iBT), IELTS (minimum score 5.5), Pearson Test of English. *Application deadline:* For fall admission, 8/1 for domestic students, 5/1 for international students; for spring admission, 12/1 for domestic students, 10/2 for international students. Application fee: $35 ($40 for international students). Electronic applications accepted. *Expenses:* Tuition, state resident: full-time $8444; part-time $441 per credit hour. Tuition nonresident: full-time $21,404; part-time $1089 per credit hour. *Financial support:* In 2012–13, 5 research assistantships (averaging $10,000 per year), 3 teaching assistantships (averaging $10,000 per year) were awarded; fellowships also available. Financial award application deadline: 4/1. *Application contact:* Shelia K. Kendrick, Coordinator of Graduate Admissions, 931-372-3808, Fax: 931-372-3497, E-mail: skendrick@tntech.edu.

Texas A&M University–Commerce, Graduate School, College of Science, Engineering and Agriculture, Department of Biological and Environmental Sciences, Commerce, TX 75429-3011. Offers biological sciences (M Ed, MS); environmental sciences (Certificate). *Degree requirements:* For master's, comprehensive exam, thesis (for some programs). *Entrance requirements:* For master's, GRE General Test. Electronic applications accepted. *Expenses:* Tuition, state resident: full-time $3630; part-time $2420 per year. Tuition, nonresident: full-time $9948; part-time $6632.16 per year. *Required fees:* $1006 per year. *Faculty research:* Microbiology, botany, environmental science, birds.

Texas A&M University–Corpus Christi, Graduate Studies and Research, College of Science and Technology, Program in Environmental Science, Corpus Christi, TX 70412-5500. Offers MS. Part-time and evening/weekend programs available. *Degree requirements:* For master's, comprehensive exam, thesis (for some programs). *Entrance requirements:* For master's, GRE General Test. Additional exam requirements/recommendations for international students: Required—TOEFL. Electronic applications accepted.

Texas Christian University, College of Science and Engineering, School of Geology, Energy and the Environment, Fort Worth, TX 76129. Offers environmental management (MEM); environmental science (MA, MS); geology (MS). Part-time programs available. *Faculty:* 7 full-time (1 woman). *Students:* 17 full-time (9 women), 24 part-time (11 women); includes 4 minority (1 Black or African American, non-Hispanic/Latino; 1 Asian, non-Hispanic/Latino; 2 Hispanic/Latino), 2 international. Average age 26. 30 applicants, 80% accepted, 16 enrolled. In 2012, 10 master's awarded. *Degree requirements:* For master's, comprehensive exam (for some programs), thesis (for some programs). *Entrance requirements:* For master's, GRE. Additional exam requirements/recommendations for international students: Required—TOEFL (minimum score 550 paper-based; 80 iBT). *Application deadline:* For fall admission, 2/28 priority date for domestic students, 2/28 for international students. Application fee: $60. *Expenses:* Tuition: Full-time $21,600; part-time $1200 per credit. *Required fees:* $48. Tuition and fees vary according to program. *Financial support:* In 2012–13, 15 teaching assistantships with full tuition reimbursements (averaging $15,000 per year) were awarded. Financial award application deadline: 2/28. *Unit head:* Dr. Phil Hartman, Dean, 817-257-7727, E-mail: p.hartman@tcu.edu. *Application contact:* Dr. Magnus Rittby, Associate Dean for Administration and Graduate Programs, 817-257-7729, Fax: 817-257-7736, E-mail: m.rittby@tcu.edu. Website: http://geo1.tcu.edu/graduate/graduate.html.

Texas Tech University, Graduate School, College of Arts and Sciences, Department of Environmental Toxicology, Lubbock, TX 79409. Offers MS, PhD, JD/MS, MBA/MS, MS/MPA. Part-time programs available. *Degree requirements:* For master's, thesis; for doctorate, thesis/dissertation. *Entrance requirements:* For master's and doctorate, GRE General Test. Additional exam requirements/recommendations for international students: Required—TOEFL (minimum score 550 paper-based; 79 iBT). Electronic applications accepted. *Faculty research:* Terrestrial and aquatic toxicology, biochemical and developmental toxicology, advanced materials, countermeasures to biologic and chemical threats, molecular epidemiology and modeling.

Thompson Rivers University, Program in Environmental Science, Kamloops, BC V2C 0C8, Canada. Offers MS. *Entrance requirements:* For master's, personal resume, 2 letters of recommendation. Additional exam requirements/recommendations for international students: Required—TOEFL.

Towson University, Program in Environmental Science, Towson, MD 21252-0001. Offers MS, Postbaccalaureate Certificate. Part-time and evening/weekend programs available. *Entrance requirements:* For master's, GRE (recommended), bachelor's degree in related field, minimum GPA of 3.0. Electronic applications accepted.

Troy University, Graduate School, College of Arts and Sciences, Program in Environmental and Biological Sciences, Troy, AL 36082. Offers biological science (MS); environmental analysis and management (MS); environmental policy (MS); environmental science (MS). Part-time and evening/weekend programs available. *Faculty:* 8 full-time (1 woman). *Students:* 3 full-time (all women), 20 part-time (14 women); includes 1 minority (Hispanic/Latino). Average age 26. 38 applicants, 53% accepted, 5 enrolled. In 2012, 13 master's awarded. *Degree requirements:* For master's, comprehensive exam (for some programs), thesis (for some programs), comprehensive exam or thesis, minimum GPA of 3.0, admission to candidacy. *Entrance requirements:* For master's, GRE (minimum score of 850 on old exam or 286 on new exam), MAT (minimum score of 385) or GMAT (minimum score of 380); bachelor's degree; minimum undergraduate GPA of 2.5 or 3.0 on last 30 semester hours. Additional exam requirements/recommendations for international students: Required—TOEFL (minimum score 523 paper-based; 70 iBT), IELTS (minimum score 5.5). *Application deadline:* Applications are processed on a rolling basis. Application fee: $50. Electronic applications

accepted. *Expenses:* Tuition, state resident: full-time $6102; part-time $307 per credit hour. Tuition, nonresident: full-time $12,204; part-time $614 per credit hour. *Required fees:* $32 per credit hour. $50 per term. Tuition and fees vary according to campus/location. *Unit head:* Dr. Glenn Cohen, Chairman, 334-670-3660, Fax: 334-670-3401, E-mail: gcohen@troy.edu. *Application contact:* Brenda K. Campbell, Director of Graduate Admissions, 334-670-3178, Fax: 334-670-3733, E-mail: bcamp@troy.edu.

Tufts University, School of Engineering, Department of Civil and Environmental Engineering, Medford, MA 02155. Offers bioengineering (ME, MS), including environmental technology; civil engineering (ME, MS, PhD), including geotechnical engineering, structural engineering, water diplomacy (PhD); environmental engineering (ME, MS, PhD), including environmental engineering and environmental sciences, environmental geotechnology, environmental health, environmental science and management, hazardous materials management, water diplomacy (PhD), water resources engineering. Part-time programs available. Terminal master's awarded for partial completion of doctoral program. *Degree requirements:* For master's, thesis or alternative; for doctorate, thesis/dissertation. *Entrance requirements:* For master's and doctorate, GRE General Test. Additional exam requirements/recommendations for international students: Required—TOEFL (minimum score 550 paper-based; 80 iBT). Electronic applications accepted. *Expenses: Tuition:* Full-time $12,856; part-time $1072 per credit hour. *Required fees:* $730. Full-time tuition and fees vary according to degree level, program and student level. Part-time tuition and fees vary according to course load. *Faculty research:* Environmental and water resources engineering, environmental health, geotechnical and geoenvironmental engineering, structural engineering and mechanics, water diplomacy.

Tuskegee University, Graduate Programs, College of Agricultural, Environmental and Natural Sciences, Department of Agricultural Sciences, Program in Environmental Sciences, Tuskegee, AL 36088. Offers MS. *Degree requirements:* For master's, thesis. *Entrance requirements:* For master's, GRE General Test. Additional exam requirements/recommendations for international students: Required—TOEFL (minimum score 500 paper-based). *Expenses: Tuition:* Full-time $18,100; part-time $575 per credit hour. *Required fees:* $800.

Universidad del Turabo, Graduate Programs, Programs in Science and Technology, Gurabo, PR 00778-3030. Offers environmental analysis (MSC), including environmental chemistry; environmental management (MSE), including pollution management; environmental science (D Sc), including environmental biology. *Students:* 12 full-time (10 women), 97 part-time (63 women); all minorities (all Hispanic/Latino). Average age 38. 60 applicants, 90% accepted, 40 enrolled. In 2012, 17 master's, 1 doctorate awarded. *Entrance requirements:* For master's, GRE, EXADEP, interview. *Application deadline:* For fall admission, 8/5 for domestic students. Application fee: $25. *Unit head:* Teresa Lipsett, Dean, 787-743-7979. *Application contact:* Virginia Gonzalez, Admissions Officer, 787-746-3009.

Universidad Nacional Pedro Henriquez Urena, Graduate School, Santo Domingo, Dominican Republic. Offers agricultural diversity (MS), including horticultural/fruit production, tropical animal production; conservation of monuments and cultural assets (M Arch); ecology and environment (MS); environmental engineering (MEE); international relations (MA); natural resource management (MS); political science (MA); project optimization (MPM); project feasibility (MPM); project management (MPM); sanitation engineering (ME); science for teachers (MS); tropical Caribbean architecture (M Arch).

Université de Sherbrooke, Faculty of Sciences, Centre Universitaire de Formation en Environnement, Sherbrooke, QC J1K 2R1, Canada. Offers M Sc, Diploma. Postbaccalaureate distance learning degree programs offered (no on-campus study). Electronic applications accepted. *Faculty research:* Environmental studies.

Université du Québec à Montréal, Graduate Programs, Program in Environmental Sciences, Montréal, QC H3C 3P8, Canada. Offers M Sc, PhD, Certificate. Part-time programs available. *Degree requirements:* For master's, research report; for doctorate, thesis/dissertation. *Entrance requirements:* For master's, appropriate bachelor's degree or equivalent, proficiency in French; for doctorate, appropriate master's degree or equivalent, proficiency in French.

Université du Québec à Trois-Rivières, Graduate Programs, Program in Environmental Sciences, Trois-Rivières, QC G9A 5H7, Canada. Offers M Sc, PhD. Part-time programs available. *Degree requirements:* For master's, thesis. *Entrance requirements:* For master's, appropriate bachelor's degree, proficiency in French.

Université du Québec en Abitibi-Témiscamingue, Graduate Programs, Program in Environmental Sciences, Rouyn-Noranda, QC J9X 5E4, Canada. Offers biology (MS); environmental sciences (PhD); sustainable forest ecosystem management (MS).

Université Laval, Faculty of Sciences and Engineering, Department of Geology and Geological Engineering, Programs in Earth Sciences, Québec, QC G1K 7P4, Canada. Offers earth sciences (M Sc, PhD); environmental technologies (M Sc). Offered jointly with INRS-Géressources. Terminal master's awarded for partial completion of doctoral program. *Degree requirements:* For master's, thesis (for some programs); for doctorate, comprehensive exam, thesis/dissertation. *Entrance requirements:* For master's and doctorate, knowledge of French. Electronic applications accepted.

Peterson's Graduate Programs in the Physical Sciences, Mathematics, Agricultural Sciences, the Environment & Natural Resources 2014

www.petersonsbooks.com **475**

Environmental Sciences

University at Albany, State University of New York, College of Arts and Sciences, Department of Biological Sciences, Program in Biodiversity, Conservation, and Policy, Albany, NY 12222-0001. Offers MS. *Degree requirements:* For master's, one foreign language. *Entrance requirements:* For master's, GRE General Test. *Faculty research:* Aquatic ecology, plant community ecology, biodiversity and public policy, restoration ecology, coastal and estuarine science.

University at Buffalo, the State University of New York, Graduate School, College of Arts and Sciences, Department of Geography, Buffalo, NY 14260. Offers Canadian studies (Certificate); earth systems science (MA, MS); economic geography and business geographics (MS); environmental modeling and analysis (MA); geographic information science (MA, MS); geography (MA, PhD); GIS and environmental analysis (Certificate); health geography (MS); international trade (MA); transportation and business geographics (MA); urban and regional analysis (MA). Part-time programs available. *Faculty:* 16 full-time (7 women), 1 part-time/adjunct (0 women). *Students:* 98 full-time (46 women), 17 part-time (6 women); includes 69 minority (66 Asian, non-Hispanic/Latino; 3 Hispanic/Latino). Average age 29. 157 applicants, 58% accepted, 43 enrolled. In 2012, 30 master's, 10 doctorates awarded. Terminal master's awarded for partial completion of doctoral program. *Degree requirements:* For master's, thesis (for some programs), project or portfolio; for doctorate, thesis/dissertation. *Entrance requirements:* For master's, GRE General Test, minimum GPA of 2.9; for doctorate, GRE General Test, minimum GPA of 3.0. Additional exam requirements/recommendations for international students: Required—TOEFL (minimum score 550 paper-based; 79 iBT). *Application deadline:* For fall admission, 5/1 priority date for domestic students, 3/10 for international students; for spring admission, 11/1 priority date for domestic students, 9/1 for international students. Applications are processed on a rolling basis. Application fee: $75. Electronic applications accepted. *Financial support:* In 2012–13, 13 students received support, including 8 fellowships with full tuition reimbursements available (averaging $5,500 per year), 13 teaching assistantships with full tuition reimbursements available (averaging $13,520 per year); research assistantships with full tuition reimbursements available, career-related internships or fieldwork, Federal Work-Study, institutionally sponsored loans, traineeships, health care benefits, and unspecified assistantships also available. Financial award application deadline: 1/10. *Faculty research:* International business and world trade, geographic information systems and cartography, transportation, urban and regional analysis, physical and environmental geography. *Total annual research expenditures:* $505,189. *Unit head:* Dr. Sharmistha Bagchi-Sen, Chairman, 716-645-0473, Fax: 716-645-2329, E-mail: geosbs@buffalo.edu. *Application contact:* Betsy Crooks, Graduate Secretary, 716-645-0471, Fax: 716-645-2329, E-mail: babraham@buffalo.edu. Website: http://www.geog.buffalo.edu/.

The University of Alabama in Huntsville, School of Graduate Studies, College of Science, Department of Atmospheric Science, Huntsville, AL 35899. Offers atmospheric science (MS, PhD); earth system science (MS). Part-time and evening/weekend programs available. *Faculty:* 10 full-time (0 women), 1 part-time/adjunct (0 women). *Students:* 42 full-time (14 women), 5 part-time (all women); includes 3 minority (1 Black or African American, non-Hispanic/Latino; 1 Asian, non-Hispanic/Latino; 1 Hispanic/Latino), 7 international. Average age 26. 49 applicants, 90% accepted, 17 enrolled. In 2012, 5 master's, 2 doctorates awarded. *Degree requirements:* For master's, comprehensive exam, thesis or alternative, oral and written exams; for doctorate, comprehensive exam, thesis/dissertation, oral and written exams. *Entrance requirements:* For master's, GRE General Test, minimum GPA of 3.0; sequence of courses in calculus (including the calculus of vector-valued functions); courses in linear algebra and ordinary differential equations; two semesters each of chemistry and calculus-based physics; proficiency in at least one high-level computer programming language; for doctorate, GRE General Test, minimum GPA of 3.0. Additional exam requirements/recommendations for international students: Required—TOEFL (minimum score 550 paper-based; 80 iBT), IELTS (minimum score 6.5). *Application deadline:* For fall admission, 7/15 priority date for domestic students, 4/1 for international students; for spring admission, 11/30 priority date for domestic students, 9/1 for international students. Applications are processed on a rolling basis. Application fee: $40 ($50 for international students). Electronic applications accepted. *Expenses:* Tuition, state resident: full-time $8516; part-time $515 per credit hour. Tuition, nonresident: full-time $20,384; part-time $1229 per credit hour. *Required fees:* $148 per semester. One-time fee: $150. *Financial support:* In 2012–13, 36 students received support, including 34 research assistantships with full and partial tuition reimbursements available (averaging $14,797 per year), 2 teaching assistantships with full and partial tuition reimbursements available (averaging $14,400 per year); career-related internships or fieldwork, Federal Work-Study, institutionally sponsored loans, scholarships/grants, health care benefits, and unspecified assistantships also available. Support available to part-time students. Financial award application deadline: 4/1; financial award applicants required to submit FAFSA. *Faculty research:* Severe weather, climate, satellite remote sensing, numerical modeling, air pollution. *Total annual research expenditures:* $9.6 million. *Unit head:* Dr. Sundar Christopher, Chair, 256-922-7872, Fax: 256-922-7755, E-mail: sundar@nsstc.uah.edu. *Application contact:* Kim Gray, Graduate Studies Admissions Coordinator, 256-824-6002, Fax: 256-824-6405, E-mail: deangrad@uah.edu. Website: http://www.nsstc.uah.edu/atmos/index.html.

University of Alaska Anchorage, School of Engineering, Program in Applied Environmental Science and Technology, Anchorage, AK 99508. Offers M AEST, MS. Part-time and evening/weekend programs available. *Degree requirements:* For master's, comprehensive exam, thesis (for some programs). *Entrance requirements:* For master's, GRE General Test. Additional exam requirements/recommendations for international students: Required—TOEFL (minimum score 550 paper-based). *Faculty research:* Wastewater treatment, environmental regulations, water resources management, justification of public facilities, rural sanitation, biological treatment process.

University of Alaska Fairbanks, College of Engineering and Mines, Department of Civil and Environmental Engineering, Program in Environmental Engineering, Fairbanks, AK 99775-5900. Offers engineering (PhD), including environmental engineering; environmental engineering (MS), including environmental contaminants, environmental science and management, water supply and waste treatment. Part-time programs available. *Students:* 3 full-time (2 women), 1 part-time (0 women), 1 international. Average age 26. 2 applicants, 50% accepted, 1 enrolled. *Degree requirements:* For master's, comprehensive exam, thesis or alternative; for doctorate, comprehensive exam, thesis/dissertation, oral exam, oral defense. *Entrance requirements:* For master's, basic computer techniques; for doctorate, GRE General Test. Additional exam requirements/recommendations for international students: Required—TOEFL (minimum score 575 paper-based). *Application deadline:* For fall admission, 6/1 for domestic students, 3/1 for international students; for spring admission, 10/15 for domestic students, 9/1 for international students. Applications are processed on a rolling basis. Application fee: $60. Electronic applications accepted. *Expenses:* Tuition, state resident: full-time $7038. Tuition, nonresident: full-time $14,382. Tuition and fees vary according to course level, course load and reciprocity agreements. *Financial support:* In 2012–13, 2 research assistantships (averaging $5,316 per year), 1 teaching assistantship (averaging $3,651 per year) were awarded; fellowships, career-related internships or fieldwork, Federal Work-Study, scholarships/grants, health care benefits, and unspecified assistantships also available. Support available to part-time students. Financial award application deadline: 7/1; financial award applicants required to submit FAFSA. *Unit head:* Dr. David Barnes, Department Chair, 907-474-7241, Fax: 907-474-6087, E-mail: fycee@uaf.edu. *Application contact:* Libby Eddy, Registrar and Director of Admissions, 907-474-7500, Fax: 907-474-7097, E-mail: admissions@uaf.edu. Website: http://cem.uaf.edu/cee/environmental-engineering.aspx.

University of Alaska Fairbanks, College of Engineering and Mines, Department of Civil and Environmental Engineering, Program in Environmental Quality Science, Fairbanks, AK 99775-5900. Offers MS. Part-time programs available. *Students:* 3 full-time (2 women), 1 (woman) part-time. Average age 30. 3 applicants, 67% accepted, 2 enrolled. In 2012, 1 master's awarded. *Degree requirements:* For master's, comprehensive exam, thesis or alternative. *Entrance requirements:* For master's, calculus, chemistry, basic computer techniques. Additional exam requirements/recommendations for international students: Required—TOEFL (minimum score 575 paper-based). *Application deadline:* For fall admission, 6/1 for domestic students, 3/1 for international students; for spring admission, 10/15 for domestic students, 9/1 for international students. Applications are processed on a rolling basis. Application fee: $60. Electronic applications accepted. *Expenses:* Tuition, state resident: full-time $7038. Tuition, nonresident: full-time $14,382. Tuition and fees vary according to course level, course load and reciprocity agreements. *Financial support:* Fellowships, research assistantships, teaching assistantships, career-related internships or fieldwork, Federal Work-Study, scholarships/grants, health care benefits, and unspecified assistantships available. Support available to part-time students. Financial award application deadline: 7/1; financial award applicants required to submit FAFSA. *Unit head:* Dr. David Barnes, Department Chair, 907-474-7241, Fax: 907-474-6087, E-mail: fycee@uaf.edu. *Application contact:* Libby Eddy, Registrar and Director of Admissions, 907-474-7500, Fax: 907-474-7097, E-mail: admissions@uaf.edu. Website: http://cem.uaf.edu/cee/environmental-engineering.aspx.

University of Alaska Fairbanks, College of Natural Sciences and Mathematics, Department of Chemistry and Biochemistry, Fairbanks, AK 99775-6160. Offers biochemistry and molecular biology (MS, PhD); chemistry (MA, MS); environmental chemistry (MS, PhD). Part-time programs available. *Faculty:* 11 full-time (2 women). *Students:* 29 full-time (14 women), 5 part-time (3 women); includes 6 minority (1 American Indian or Alaska Native, non-Hispanic/Latino; 1 Asian, non-Hispanic/Latino; 4 Hispanic/Latino), 9 international. Average age 29. 34 applicants, 24% accepted, 8 enrolled. In 2012, 8 master's, 2 doctorates awarded. *Degree requirements:* For master's, comprehensive exam, thesis or alternative; for doctorate, comprehensive exam, thesis/dissertation, oral defense. *Entrance requirements:* Additional exam requirements/recommendations for international students: Required—TOEFL (minimum score 550 paper-based). *Application deadline:* For fall admission, 6/1 for domestic students, 3/1 for international students; for spring admission, 10/15 for domestic students, 9/1 for international students. Applications are processed on a rolling basis. Application fee: $60. Electronic applications accepted. *Expenses:* Tuition, state resident: full-time $7038. Tuition, nonresident: full-time $14,382. Tuition and fees vary according to course level, course load and reciprocity agreements. *Financial support:* In 2012–13, 10 research assistantships with tuition reimbursements (averaging $14,528 per year), 17 teaching assistantships with tuition reimbursements (averaging $17,756 per year) were awarded; fellowships with tuition reimbursements, Federal Work-Study, scholarships/grants, health care benefits, and unspecified assistantships also available. Support available to part-time students. Financial award application deadline: 7/1; financial award applicants required to submit FAFSA. *Faculty research:* Atmospheric aerosols, cold adaptation, hibernation and neuroprotection, liganogated ion channels, arctic contaminants. *Unit head:* Bill Simpson, Department Chair, 907-474-5510, Fax:

907-474-5640, E-mail: chemistry.uaf@alaska.edu. *Application contact:* Libby Eddy, Registrar and Director of Admissions, 907-474-7500, Fax: 907-474-7097, E-mail: admissions@uaf.edu. Website: http://www.uaf.edu/chem.

University of Alberta, Faculty of Graduate Studies and Research, Department of Civil and Environmental Engineering, Edmonton, AB T6G 2E1, Canada. Offers construction engineering and management (M Eng, M Sc, PhD); environmental engineering (M Eng, M Sc, PhD); environmental science (M Sc, PhD); geoenvironmental engineering (M Eng, M Sc, PhD); geotechnical engineering (M Eng, M Sc, PhD); mining engineering (M Eng, M Sc, PhD); petroleum engineering (M Eng, M Sc, PhD); structural engineering (M Eng, M Sc, PhD); water resources (M Eng, M Sc, PhD). Part-time programs available. Postbaccalaureate distance learning degree programs offered (minimal on-campus study). *Degree requirements:* For master's, thesis (for some programs); for doctorate, thesis/dissertation. *Entrance requirements:* For master's, minimum GPA of 3.0 in last 2 years of undergraduate studies; for doctorate, minimum GPA of 3.0. Additional exam requirements/recommendations for international students: Required—TOEFL (minimum score 550 paper-based). Electronic applications accepted. *Faculty research:* Mining.

The University of Arizona, College of Agriculture and Life Sciences, Department of Soil, Water and Environmental Science, Tucson, AZ 85721. Offers MS, PhD. *Faculty:* 5 full-time (2 women), 1 (woman) part-time/adjunct. *Students:* 51 full-time (28 women), 10 part-time (4 women); includes 17 minority (4 Black or African American, non-Hispanic/Latino; 1 American Indian or Alaska Native, non-Hispanic/Latino; 1 Asian, non-Hispanic/Latino; 7 Hispanic/Latino; 4 Two or more races, non-Hispanic/Latino), 15 international. Average age 29. 29 applicants, 55% accepted, 13 enrolled. In 2012, 10 master's, 9 doctorates awarded. *Degree requirements:* For master's, thesis; for doctorate, comprehensive exam, thesis/dissertation. *Entrance requirements:* For master's, GRE (recommended), minimum GPA of 3.0, letter of interest, 3 letters of recommendation; for doctorate, GRE (recommended), MS, minimum GPA of 3.0, letter of interest, 3 letters of recommendation. Additional exam requirements/recommendations for international students: Required—TOEFL (minimum score 550 paper-based; 80 iBT). *Application deadline:* For fall admission, 6/1 for domestic students, 12/1 for international students; for spring admission, 10/1 for domestic students, 6/1 for international students. Applications are processed on a rolling basis. Application fee: $75. *Financial support:* In 2012–13, 14 students received support, including 25 research assistantships with full and partial tuition reimbursements available (averaging $17,098 per year), 8 teaching assistantships with full and partial tuition reimbursements available (averaging $17,044 per year); fellowships, Federal Work-Study, institutionally sponsored loans, scholarships/grants, health care benefits, tuition waivers (full and partial), and unspecified assistantships also available. Financial award application deadline: 5/1. *Faculty research:* Plant production, environmental microbiology, contaminant flow and transport, aquaculture. *Total annual research expenditures:* $2.8 million. *Unit head:* Dr. Jonathan D. Chorover, Interim Department Head, 520-626-5635, E-mail: chorover@cals.arizona.edu. *Application contact:* Alicia Velasquez, Program Coordinator, 520-621-1606, Fax: 520-621-1647, E-mail: avelasqu@ag.arizona.edu. Website: http://ag.arizona.edu/SWES/.

The University of Arizona, College of Agriculture and Life Sciences, Graduate Interdisciplinary Program in Arid Lands Resource Sciences, Tucson, AZ 85721. Offers PhD. *Faculty:* 5. *Students:* 21 full-time (12 women), 3 part-time (all women); includes 4 minority (1 Asian, non-Hispanic/Latino; 1 Hispanic/Latino; 2 Two or more races, non-Hispanic/Latino), 10 international. Average age 42. 11 applicants, 64% accepted, 3 enrolled. *Degree requirements:* For doctorate, one foreign language, comprehensive exam, thesis/dissertation. *Entrance requirements:* For doctorate, GRE. Additional exam requirements/recommendations for international students: Required—TOEFL (minimum score 550 paper-based; 79 iBT). *Application deadline:* For fall admission, 2/15 priority date for domestic students, 2/15 for international students; for spring admission, 8/1 priority date for domestic students, 8/15 for international students. Applications are processed on a rolling basis. Application fee: $75. *Financial support:* In 2012–13, 2 research assistantships with full tuition reimbursements (averaging $14,670 per year), 1 teaching assistantship with full tuition reimbursement (averaging $14,164 per year) were awarded; career-related internships or fieldwork, scholarships/grants, health care benefits, and unspecified assistantships also available. Financial award application deadline: 4/1. *Faculty research:* International development; famine, famine early warning systems, and food security; land use, history, change, degradation, desertification, management, and policy; sustainable agriculture and farming systems; remote sensing and spatial analysis; carbon sequestration; political-ecology of natural resources; ethnoecology and other ethno-sciences; economic and agricultural policy and development; economic botany; borderlands issues; globalization; civil conflict; urban development. *Total annual research expenditures:* $147,751. *Unit head:* Dr. Stuart E. Marsh, Chair, 520-621-8574, E-mail: smarsh@ag.arizona.edu. *Application contact:* MaryLou Meyers, Graduate Coordinator, 520-626-4521, E-mail: myersm@email.arizona.edu. Website: http://alrs.arizona.edu/.

University of California, Berkeley, Graduate Division, College of Natural Resources, Department of Environmental Science, Policy, and Management, Berkeley, CA 94720-1500. Offers environmental science, policy, and management (MS, PhD); forestry (MF). Terminal master's awarded for partial completion of doctoral program. *Degree requirements:* For master's, thesis optional; for doctorate, thesis/dissertation, qualifying exam. *Entrance requirements:* For master's and doctorate, GRE General Test, minimum GPA of 3.0, 3 letters of recommendation. Additional exam requirements/recommendations for international students: Required—TOEFL. Electronic applications accepted. *Faculty research:* Biology and ecology of insects; ecosystem function and environmental issues of soils; plant health/interactions from molecular to ecosystem levels; range management and ecology; forest and resource policy, sustainability, and management.

University of California, Davis, Graduate Studies, Graduate Group in Soils and Biogeochemistry, Davis, CA 95616. Offers MS, PhD. Terminal master's awarded for partial completion of doctoral program. *Degree requirements:* For master's, comprehensive exam (for some programs), thesis (for some programs); for doctorate, thesis/dissertation. *Entrance requirements:* For master's, minimum GPA of 3.3; for doctorate, GRE, minimum GPA of 3.3. Additional exam requirements/recommendations for international students: Required—TOEFL (minimum score 550 paper-based). Electronic applications accepted. *Faculty research:* Rhizosphere ecology, soil transport processes, biogeochemical cycling, sustainable agriculture.

University of California, Los Angeles, Graduate Division, School of Public Health, Department of Environmental Health Sciences, Los Angeles, CA 90095. Offers environmental health sciences (MS, PhD); environmental science and engineering (D Env); molecular toxicology (PhD); JD/MPH. *Accreditation:* ABET (one or more programs are accredited). *Degree requirements:* For master's, comprehensive exam or thesis; for doctorate, thesis/dissertation, oral and written qualifying exams. *Entrance requirements:* For master's, GRE General Test, minimum GPA of 3.0; for doctorate, GRE General Test, minimum undergraduate GPA of 3.0. Electronic applications accepted. *Expenses:* Tuition, nonresident: full-time $15,102. *Required fees:* $14,809.19. Full-time tuition and fees vary according to program.

University of California, Los Angeles, Graduate Division, School of Public Health, Program in Environmental Science and Engineering, Los Angeles, CA 90095. Offers D Env. *Degree requirements:* For doctorate, thesis/dissertation, oral and written qualifying exams. *Entrance requirements:* For doctorate, GRE General Test, minimum undergraduate GPA of 3.0, master's degree or equivalent in a natural science, engineering, or public health. *Expenses:* Tuition, nonresident: full-time $15,102. *Required fees:* $14,809.19. Full-time tuition and fees vary according to program. *Faculty research:* Toxic and hazardous substances, air and water pollution, risk assessment/management, water resources, marine science.

University of California, Riverside, Graduate Division, Bourns College of Engineering, Materials Science and Engineering Program, Riverside, CA 92521. Offers MS, PhD. *Entrance requirements:* For master's and doctorate, GRE. Additional exam requirements/recommendations for international students: Required—TOEFL (minimum score 550 paper-based; 80 iBT). Electronic applications accepted. *Expenses:* Tuition, state resident: full-time $14,646. Tuition, nonresident: full-time $29,748.

University of California, Santa Barbara, Graduate Division, College of Letters and Sciences, Division of Social Sciences, Department of Economics, Santa Barbara, CA 93106-9210. Offers economics (MA, PhD); economics and environmental science (PhD); MA/PhD. *Faculty:* 27 full-time (4 women), 21 part-time/adjunct (7 women). *Students:* 109 full-time (49 women); includes 18 minority (7 Asian, non-Hispanic/Latino; 11 Hispanic/Latino), 37 international. Average age 26. 467 applicants, 42% accepted, 51 enrolled. In 2012, 65 master's, 5 doctorates awarded. Terminal master's awarded for partial completion of doctoral program. *Degree requirements:* For master's, comprehensive exam; for doctorate, comprehensive exam, thesis/dissertation. *Entrance requirements:* For master's and doctorate, GRE General Test, 3 letters of recommendation, statement of purpose, personal achievements/contributions statement, resume/curriculum vitae, transcripts for post-secondary institutions attended. Additional exam requirements/recommendations for international students: Required—TOEFL (minimum score 550 paper-based; 80 iBT), IELTS (minimum score 7). *Application deadline:* For fall admission, 12/1 priority date for domestic students, 12/1 for international students. Application fee: $80 ($100 for international students). Electronic applications accepted. *Financial support:* In 2012–13, 65 students received support, including 17 fellowships with full and partial tuition reimbursements available (averaging $19,000 per year), 7 research assistantships with full and partial tuition reimbursements available (averaging $19,000 per year), 106 teaching assistantships with partial tuition reimbursements available (averaging $17,000 per year); Federal Work-Study, institutionally sponsored loans, scholarships/grants, health care benefits, tuition waivers (full and partial), and unspecified assistantships also available. Support available to part-time students. Financial award application deadline: 12/1; financial award applicants required to submit FAFSA. *Faculty research:* Labor economics, econometrics, macroeconomic theory and policy, environmental and natural resources economics, experimental and behavioral economics. *Unit head:* Prof. Olivier Deschenes, Director of Graduate Studies, 805-893-5617, Fax: 805-893-8830, E-mail: olivier@econ.ucsb.edu. *Application contact:* Mark Patterson, Graduate Advisor, 805-893-2205, Fax: 805-893-8830, E-mail: mark@econ.ucsb.edu. Website: http://www.econ.ucsb.edu/.

University of California, Santa Barbara, Graduate Division, Donald Bren School of Environmental Science and Management, Santa Barbara, CA 93106-5131. Offers economics and environmental science (PhD); environmental science and management (MESM, PhD); technology and society (PhD). *Faculty:* 18 full-time (3 women), 3 part-time/adjunct (0 women). *Students:* 226 full-time (113 women); includes 31 minority (2 Black or African American, non-Hispanic/Latino; 1

American Indian or Alaska Native, non-Hispanic/Latino; 19 Asian, non-Hispanic/Latino; 8 Hispanic/Latino; 1 Native Hawaiian or other Pacific Islander, non-Hispanic/Latino), 26 international. Average age 27. 476 applicants, 46% accepted, 84 enrolled. In 2012, 75 master's, 8 doctorates awarded. *Degree requirements:* For master's, thesis; for doctorate, thesis/dissertation. *Entrance requirements:* For master's and doctorate, GRE. Additional exam requirements/recommendations for international students: Required—TOEFL (minimum score 550 paper-based; 80 iBT), IELTS (minimum score 7). *Application deadline:* For fall admission, 12/15 priority date for domestic students, 12/15 for international students. Application fee: $80 ($100 for international students). Electronic applications accepted. *Financial support:* In 2012–13, 34 students received support, including 53 fellowships with full and partial tuition reimbursements available, 10 research assistantships with full and partial tuition reimbursements available, 18 teaching assistantships with full and partial tuition reimbursements available; career-related internships or fieldwork and tuition waivers (full and partial) also available. Financial award application deadline: 12/15; financial award applicants required to submit FAFSA. *Faculty research:* Coastal marine resources management, conservation planning, corporate environmental management, economics and politics of the environment, energy and climate, pollution prevention and remediation, water resources management. *Unit head:* Bryant Wieneke, Assistant Dean, Planning and Administration, 805-893-2212, Fax: 805-893-7612, E-mail: bryant@bren.ucsb.edu. *Application contact:* Dori Molnar, Graduate Advisor, 805-893-7611, Fax: 805-893-7612, E-mail: admissions@bren.ucsb.edu. Website: http://www.bren.ucsb.edu/.

University of Chicago, Irving B. Harris Graduate School of Public Policy Studies, Chicago, IL 60637-1513. Offers environmental science and policy (MS); public policy studies (AM, MPP, PhD); JD/MPP; MBA/MPP; MPP/M Div; MPP/MA. Part-time programs available. *Degree requirements:* For doctorate, thesis/dissertation. *Entrance requirements:* Additional exam requirements/recommendations for international students: Required—TOEFL. Electronic applications accepted. *Expenses:* Contact institution. *Faculty research:* Family and child policy, international security, health policy, social policy.

University of Cincinnati, Graduate School, College of Engineering and Applied Science, Department of Civil and Environmental Engineering, Program in Environmental Sciences, Cincinnati, OH 45221. Offers MS, PhD. Part-time programs available. *Degree requirements:* For master's, thesis or alternative; for doctorate, one foreign language, thesis/dissertation. *Entrance requirements:* For master's and doctorate, GRE General Test. Additional exam requirements/recommendations for international students: Required—TOEFL (minimum score 580 paper-based; 92 iBT). Electronic applications accepted. *Faculty research:* Environmental microbiology, solid-waste management, air pollution control, water pollution control, aerosols.

University of Colorado Colorado Springs, College of Letters, Arts and Sciences, Department of Geography and Environmental Studies, Colorado Springs, CO 80933-7150. Offers MA. Part-time programs available. *Faculty:* 12 full-time (3 women). *Students:* 6 full-time (0 women), 6 part-time (3 women); includes 1 minority (Hispanic/Latino). Average age 35. In 2012, 3 master's awarded. *Degree requirements:* For master's, comprehensive exam (for some programs), thesis (for some programs). *Entrance requirements:* For master's, GRE (recommended minimum combined score for the verbal and quantitative tests of 1000, plus proficiency on the writing requirement), minimum undergraduate GPA of 3.0, statement of intent (essay). Additional exam requirements/recommendations for international students: Recommended—TOEFL. *Application deadline:* For fall admission, 2/1 priority date for domestic students, 2/1 for international students. Applications are processed on a rolling basis. Application fee: $60 ($75 for international students). *Expenses:* Tuition, state resident: full-time $6412; part-time $686 per credit hour. Tuition, nonresident: full-time $11,782; part-time $1160 per credit hour. Tuition and fees vary according to course load, degree level, campus/location, program and reciprocity agreements. *Financial support:* In 2012–13, 5 students received support, including 1 fellowship; Federal Work-Study and scholarships/grants also available. Support available to part-time students. Financial award application deadline: 3/1; financial award applicants required to submit FAFSA. *Faculty research:* Socio-ecological implications of conservation strategies, cultural geography, militarized spaces, geovisualization, geographic information systems, hydrology, biogeography, human-environment interactions, geomorphology, population. *Total annual research expenditures:* $208,755. *Unit head:* Dr. Emily Skop, Associate Professor, 719-255-3789, Fax: 719-255-4066, E-mail: eskop@uccs.edu. *Application contact:* Emily Skop, Program Assistant, 719-255-3789, E-mail: eskop@uccs.edu. Website: http://www.uccs.edu/geography/.

University of Colorado Denver, College of Liberal Arts and Sciences, Department of Geography and Environmental Sciences, Denver, CO 80217. Offers environmental sciences (MS), including air quality, ecosystems, environmental health, environmental science education, geo-spatial analysis, hazardous waste, water quality. Part-time and evening/weekend programs available. *Faculty:* 11 full-time (3 women), 4 part-time/adjunct (0 women). *Students:* 30 full-time (23 women), 6 part-time (3 women); includes 7 minority (1 Black or African American, non-Hispanic/Latino; 2 Asian, non-Hispanic/Latino; 3 Hispanic/Latino; 1 Two or more races, non-Hispanic/Latino), 6 international. Average age 30. 34 applicants, 65% accepted, 12 enrolled. In 2012, 22 master's awarded. *Degree requirements:* For master's, thesis or alternative, 30 credits including 21 of core requirements and 9 of environmental science electives. *Entrance requirements:* For master's, GRE General Test, BA in one of the natural/physical sciences or engineering (or equivalent background); prerequisite coursework in calculus and physics (one semester each), general chemistry with lab and general biology with lab (two semesters each), three letters of recommendation. Additional exam requirements/recommendations for international students: Required—TOEFL (minimum score 537 paper-based; 75 iBT); Recommended—IELTS (minimum score 6.5). *Application deadline:* For fall admission, 4/1 for domestic and international students; for spring admission, 10/1 for domestic and international students. Application fee: $50 ($75 for international students). Electronic applications accepted. *Expenses:* Tuition, state resident: full-time $7712; part-time $355 per credit hour. Tuition, nonresident: full-time $22,038; part-time $1087 per credit hour. *Required fees:* $1110; $1. Tuition and fees vary according to course load, campus/location and program. *Financial support:* In 2012–13, 10 students received support. Fellowships, research assistantships, teaching assistantships, Federal Work-Study, institutionally sponsored loans, scholarships/grants, traineeships, and unspecified assistantships available. Financial award application deadline: 4/1; financial award applicants required to submit FAFSA. *Faculty research:* Air quality, environmental health, ecosystems, hazardous waste, water quality, geo-spatial analysis and environmental science education. *Unit head:* Dr. Frederick Chambers, Director of MS Environmental Sciences Program, 303-556-2619, Fax: 303-556-6197, E-mail: frederick.chambers@ucdenver.edu. *Application contact:* Sue Eddleman, Program Assistant, 303-556-2276, E-mail: sue.eddleman@ucdenver.edu. Website: http://www.ucdenver.edu/academics/colleges/CLAS/Departments/ges/Programs/MasterofScience/Pages/MasterofScience.aspx.

University of Guam, Office of Graduate Studies, College of Natural and Applied Sciences, Program in Environmental Science, Mangilao, GU 96923. Offers MS. Part-time programs available. *Degree requirements:* For master's, thesis. *Entrance requirements:* For master's, GRE General Test. Additional exam requirements/recommendations for international students: Required—TOEFL. *Faculty research:* Water resources, ecology, karst formations, hydrogeology, meteorology.

University of Guelph, Graduate Studies, Ontario Agricultural College, Department of Land Resource Science, Guelph, ON N1G 2W1, Canada. Offers atmospheric science (M Sc, PhD); environmental and agricultural earth sciences (M Sc, PhD); land resources management (M Sc, PhD); soil science (M Sc, PhD). Part-time programs available. *Degree requirements:* For master's, thesis (for some programs), research project (non-thesis track); for doctorate, comprehensive exam, thesis/dissertation. *Entrance requirements:* For master's, minimum B- average during previous 2 years of course work; for doctorate, minimum B average during previous 2 years of course work. Additional exam requirements/recommendations for international students: Required—TOEFL (minimum score 550 paper-based). Electronic applications accepted. *Faculty research:* Soil science, environmental earth science, land resource management.

University of Hawaii at Hilo, Program in Tropical Conservation Biology and Environmental Science, Hilo, HI 96720-4091. Offers MS.

University of Houston–Clear Lake, School of Science and Computer Engineering, Program in Environmental Science, Houston, TX 77058-1098. Offers MS. Part-time and evening/weekend programs available. *Entrance requirements:* For master's, GRE General Test. Additional exam requirements/recommendations for international students: Required—TOEFL (minimum score 550 paper-based).

University of Idaho, College of Graduate Studies, Program in Environmental Science, Moscow, ID 83844-3006. Offers environmental science (MS, PhD); natural resources and environmental science (PSM). *Faculty:* 19 full-time, 1 part-time/adjunct. *Students:* 47 full-time, 51 part-time. Average age 33. In 2012, 16 master's, 2 doctorates awarded. *Application deadline:* For fall admission, 8/1 for domestic students; for spring admission, 12/15 for domestic students. Applications are processed on a rolling basis. Application fee: $60. Electronic applications accepted. *Expenses:* Tuition, state resident: full-time $4230; part-time $252 per credit hour. Tuition, nonresident: full-time $17,018; part-time $891 per credit hour. *Required fees:* $2932; $107 per credit hour. *Financial support:* Research assistantships and teaching assistantships available. Financial award applicants required to submit FAFSA. *Unit head:* Dr. Jan Boll, Director, 208-885-6113, Fax: 208-885-4674, E-mail: envs@uidaho.edu. *Application contact:* Erick Larson, Director of Graduate Admissions, 208-885-4723, E-mail: gadms@uidaho.edu. Website: http://www.uidaho.edu/cogs/envs.

University of Illinois at Springfield, Graduate Programs, College of Public Affairs and Administration, Program in Environmental Studies, Springfield, IL 62703-5407. Offers environmental science (MS); environmental studies (MA). Part-time and evening/weekend programs available. Postbaccalaureate distance learning degree programs offered (no on-campus study). *Faculty:* 6 full-time (1 woman). *Students:* 24 full-time (15 women), 70 part-time (46 women); includes 11 minority (3 Black or African American, non-Hispanic/Latino; 3 Asian, non-Hispanic/Latino; 5 Hispanic/Latino), 3 international. Average age 34. 63 applicants, 62% accepted, 32 enrolled. In 2012, 30 master's awarded. *Degree requirements:* For master's, thesis or project. *Entrance requirements:* For master's, minimum undergraduate GPA of 3.0, 2 letters of recommendation, goals essay. Additional exam requirements/recommendations for international students: Required—TOEFL (minimum score 500 paper-based; 61 iBT). *Application deadline:* Applications are processed on a rolling basis. Application fee: $60 ($75 for international students). Electronic applications accepted. *Expenses:* Tuition, state resident: full-time $7314. Tuition, nonresident: full-time $15,618. *Required* *fees:* $2695. *Financial support:* In 2012–13, fellowships with full tuition reimbursements (averaging $9,900 per year), research assistantships with full tuition reimbursements (averaging $9,000 per year), teaching assistantships with full tuition reimbursements (averaging $9,000 per year) were awarded; career-related internships or fieldwork, Federal Work-Study, scholarships/grants, health care benefits, and unspecified assistantships also available. Support available to part-time students. Financial award application deadline: 11/15; financial award applicants required to submit FAFSA. *Unit head:* Dr. Dennis Ruez, Program Administrator, 217-206-8424, E-mail: druez2@uis.edu. *Application contact:* Dr. Lynn Pardie, Office of Graduate Studies, 800-252-8533, Fax: 217-206-7623, E-mail: lpard1@uis.edu. Website: http://www.uis.edu/environmentalstudies/.

University of Illinois at Urbana–Champaign, Graduate College, College of Agricultural, Consumer and Environmental Sciences, Department of Natural Resources and Environmental Science, Champaign, IL 61820. Offers MS, PhD, MS/JD. Part-time programs available. Postbaccalaureate distance learning degree programs offered (no on-campus study). *Students:* 129 (54 women). Application fee: $75 ($90 for international students). *Unit head:* Jeffrey D. Brawn, Head, 217-244-5937, Fax: 217-244-3219, E-mail: jbrawn@illinois.edu. *Application contact:* Karen M. Claus, Secretary, 217-333-5824, Fax: 217-244-3219, E-mail: kclaus@illinois.edu. Website: http://nres.illinois.edu/.

The University of Kansas, Graduate Studies, School of Engineering, Program in Environmental Science, Lawrence, KS 66045. Offers MS, PhD. Part-time programs available. *Faculty:* 9 full-time (1 woman), 1 part-time/adjunct (0 women). *Students:* 2 full-time (1 woman), 4 part-time (1 woman); includes 2 minority (both Asian, non-Hispanic/Latino), 1 international. Average age 28. 10 applicants, 50% accepted, 1 enrolled. In 2012, 3 master's awarded. *Degree requirements:* For master's, thesis or alternative, exam; for doctorate, comprehensive exam, thesis/dissertation. *Entrance requirements:* For master's, GRE, minimum GPA of 3.0; for doctorate, GRE, minimum GPA of 3.5. Additional exam requirements/recommendations for international students: Required—TOEFL. *Application deadline:* For fall admission, 3/1 priority date for domestic students, 3/1 for international students; for spring admission, 12/1 priority date for domestic students, 8/15 for international students. Applications are processed on a rolling basis. Application fee: $55 ($65 for international students). Electronic applications accepted. *Financial support:* Fellowships with full tuition reimbursements, research assistantships with full tuition reimbursements, teaching assistantships, and career-related internships or fieldwork available. Financial award application deadline: 2/7. *Faculty research:* Water quality, water treatment, wastewater treatment, air quality, air pollution control, solid waste, hazardous waste, water resources engineering, water resources science. *Unit head:* Dave Darwin, Chair, 785-864-3766, Fax: 785-864-5631, E-mail: daved@ku.edu. *Application contact:* Bruce M. McEnroe, Professor and Graduate Advisor, 785-864-3766, Fax: 785-864-5631, E-mail: mcenroe@ku.edu. Website: http://www.ceae.ku.edu/.

University of Lethbridge, School of Graduate Studies, Lethbridge, AB T1K 3M4, Canada. Offers accounting (MScM); addictions counseling (M Sc); agricultural biotechnology (M Sc); agricultural studies (M Sc, MA); anthropology (MA); archaeology (MA); art (MA, MFA); biochemistry (M Sc); biological sciences (M Sc), biomolecular science (PhD), biosystems and biodiversity (PhD); Canadian studies (MA); chemistry (M Sc); computer science (M Sc); computer science and geographical information science (M Sc); counseling psychology (M Ed); dramatic arts (MA); earth, space, and physical science (PhD); economics (MA); educational leadership (M Ed); English (MA); environmental science (M Sc); evolution and behavior (PhD); exercise science (M Sc); finance (MScM); French (MA); French/German (MA); French/Spanish (MA); general education (M Ed); general management (MScM); geography (M Sc, MA); German (MA); health science (M Sc); history (MA); human resource management and labour relations (MScM); individualized multidisciplinary (M Sc, MA); information systems (MScM); international management (MScM); kinesiology (M Sc, MA); management (M Sc, MA); marketing (MScM); mathematics (M Sc); music (M Mus, MA); Native American studies (MA); neuroscience (M Sc, PhD); new media (MA); nursing (M Sc); philosophy (MA); physics (M Sc); policy and strategy (MScM); political science (MA); psychology (M Sc, MA); religious studies (MA); social sciences (MA); sociology (MA); theatre and dramatic arts (MFA); theoretical and computational science (PhD); urban and regional studies (MA); women's studies (MA). Part-time and evening/weekend programs available. *Degree requirements:* For doctorate, comprehensive exam, thesis/dissertation. *Entrance requirements:* For master's, GMAT (M Sc in management), bachelor's degree in related field, minimum GPA of 3.0 during previous 20 graded semester courses, 2 years teaching or related experience (M Ed); for doctorate, master's degree, minimum graduate GPA of 3.5. Additional exam requirements/recommendations for international students: Required—TOEFL. *Faculty research:* Movement and brain plasticity, gibberellin physiology, photosynthesis, carbon cycling, molecular properties of main-group ring components.

University of Maine, Graduate School, College of Natural Sciences, Forestry, and Agriculture, Department of Plant, Soil, and Environmental Sciences, Orono, ME 04469. Offers ecology and environmental sciences (MS); horticulture (MS); plant, soil, and environmental sciences (MS). *Faculty:* 18 full-time (6 women), 3 part-time/adjunct. *Students:* 9 full-time (7 women), 2 part-time (0 women), 1 international. Average age 30. 11 applicants, 9% accepted, 1 enrolled. In 2012, 3 master's awarded. *Degree requirements:* For master's, thesis (for some programs). *Entrance requirements:* For master's, GRE General Test. Additional exam requirements/recommendations for international students: Required—TOEFL. *Application deadline:* Applications are processed on a rolling basis. Application fee: $65. Electronic applications accepted. *Financial support:* In 2012–13, 16 research assistantships with full tuition reimbursements (averaging $17,336 per year), 1 teaching assistantship with full tuition reimbursement (averaging $13,600 per year) were awarded; scholarships/grants, tuition waivers (full and partial), and unspecified assistantships also available. *Total annual research expenditures:* $179,065. *Unit head:* Dr. Eric Gallandt, Chair, 207-581-2933, Fax: 207-581-3207. *Application contact:* Scott G. Delcourt, Associate Dean of the Graduate School, 207-581-3291, Fax: 207-581-3232, E-mail: graduate@maine.edu. Website: http://umaine.edu/pse/.

University of Maine, Graduate School, College of Natural Sciences, Forestry, and Agriculture, School of Biology and Ecology, Orono, ME 04469. Offers biological sciences (PhD); botany and plant pathology (MS); ecology and environmental science (MS, PhD); entomology (MS); plant science (PhD); zoology (MS, PhD). Part-time programs available. *Faculty:* 33 full-time (13 women), 26 part-time/adjunct (5 women). *Students:* 60 full-time (38 women), 9 part-time (5 women); includes 3 minority (1 American Indian or Alaska Native, non-Hispanic/Latino; 1 Asian, non-Hispanic/Latino; 1 Hispanic/Latino), 6 international. Average age 29. 71 applicants, 20% accepted, 12 enrolled. In 2012, 16 master's, 6 doctorates awarded. *Degree requirements:* For doctorate, comprehensive exam, thesis/dissertation. *Entrance requirements:* For master's and doctorate, GRE General Test. Additional exam requirements/recommendations for international students: Required—TOEFL. *Application deadline:* For fall admission, 2/1 priority date for domestic students. Applications are processed on a rolling basis. Application fee: $65. Electronic applications accepted. *Financial support:* In 2012–13, 1 fellowship with full tuition reimbursement (averaging $18,000 per year), 5 research assistantships with full tuition reimbursements (averaging $18,000 per year), 19 teaching assistantships with full tuition reimbursements (averaging $13,600 per year) were awarded; career-related internships or fieldwork, Federal Work-Study, institutionally sponsored loans, and tuition waivers (full and partial) also available. Financial award application deadline: 3/1. *Total annual research expenditures:* $569,533. *Unit head:* Dr. Ellie Groden, Director, 207-581-2551, Fax: 207-581-2537. *Application contact:* Scott G. Delcourt, Associate Dean of the Graduate School, 207-581-3291, Fax: 207-581-3232, E-mail: graduate@maine.edu. Website: http://sbe.umaine.edu/.

The University of Manchester, School of Earth, Atmospheric and Environmental Sciences, Manchester, United Kingdom. Offers atmospheric sciences (M Phil, M Sc, PhD); basin studies and petroleum geosciences (M Phil, M Sc, PhD); earth, atmospheric and environmental sciences (M Phil, M Sc, PhD); environmental geochemistry and cosmochemistry (M Phil, M Sc, PhD); isotope geochemistry and cosmochemistry (M Phil, M Sc, PhD); paleontology (M Phil, M Sc, PhD); physics and chemistry of minerals and fluids (M Phil, M Sc, PhD); structural and petrological geosciences (M Phil, M Sc, PhD).

University of Manitoba, Faculty of Graduate Studies, Clayton H. Riddell Faculty of Environment, Earth, and Resources, Department of Environment and Geography, Winnipeg, MB R3T 2N2, Canada. Offers environment (M Env); environment and geography (M Sc); geography (MA, PhD). *Degree requirements:* For master's, thesis; for doctorate, one foreign language, thesis/dissertation.

University of Maryland, Baltimore, Graduate School, Program in Marine-Estuarine-Environmental Sciences, College Park, MD 20742. Offers MS, PhD. Part-time programs available. *Faculty:* 7. *Students:* 1 applicant. Terminal master's awarded for partial completion of doctoral program. *Degree requirements:* For master's, thesis, oral defense; for doctorate, comprehensive exam, thesis/dissertation, proposal defense, oral defense. *Entrance requirements:* For master's and doctorate, GRE General Test, minimum GPA of 3.0. Additional exam requirements/recommendations for international students: Required—TOEFL. *Application deadline:* For fall admission, 2/1 for domestic students, 1/1 for international students; for spring admission, 9/1 for domestic students. Applications are processed on a rolling basis. Application fee: $50. Electronic applications accepted. *Financial support:* In 2012–13, 1 research assistantship with tuition reimbursement was awarded; fellowships with tuition reimbursements, teaching assistantships with tuition reimbursements, scholarships/grants, and unspecified assistantships also available. *Unit head:* Dr. Kennedy T. Paynter, Jr., Director, 301-405-6938, Fax: 301-314-4139, E-mail: mees@umd.edu. *Application contact:* Keith T. Brooks, Assistant Dean, 410-706-7131, Fax: 410-706-3473, E-mail: kbrooks@umaryland.edu. Website: http://www.mees.umd.edu/.

University of Maryland, Baltimore County, Graduate School, College of Natural and Mathematical Sciences, Department of Biological Sciences, Baltimore, MD 21250. Offers applied molecular biology (MS); biological sciences (MS, PhD); biotechnology (MPS), including biotechnology; biotechnology (Graduate Certificate), including biochemical regulatory engineering, biotechnology management; marine-estuarine-environmental sciences (MS); molecular and cell biology (PhD); neuroscience and cognitive sciences (PhD). Part-time programs available. *Faculty:* 34 full-time (17 women). *Students:* 84 full-time (48 women); includes 33 minority (11 Black or African American, non-Hispanic/Latino; 19 Asian, non-Hispanic/Latino; 3 Hispanic/Latino). Average age 27. 154 applicants, 21% accepted, 19 enrolled. In 2012, 9 master's, 10 doctorates awarded. *Entrance requirements:* For master's and doctorate, GRE General Test, minimum GPA of 3.0. Additional exam requirements/recommendations for international students: Required—TOEFL. *Application deadline:* For fall admission, 1/15 for domestic students, 12/15 for international students. Applications are processed on a rolling basis. Application fee: $50. Electronic applications accepted. *Financial support:* In 2012–13, 77 students received support, including fellowships (averaging $12,000 per year), 33 research assistantships (averaging $22,746 per year), 44 teaching assistantships (averaging $21,726 per year); career-related internships or fieldwork and tuition waivers (partial) also available. *Unit head:* Dr. Philip Farabaugh, Chairman, 410-455-3081, Fax: 410-455-3875, E-mail: farabaug@umbc.edu. *Application contact:* Dr. Stephen Miller, Director, 410-455-3381, Fax: 410-455-3875, E-mail: biograd@umbc.edu.

University of Maryland, Baltimore County, Graduate School, Marine-Estuarine-Environmental Sciences Graduate Program, College Park, MD 20742. Offers MS, PhD. Part-time programs available. *Faculty:* 11. *Students:* 2 full-time (1 woman). 6 applicants, 33% accepted, 2 enrolled. In 2012, 1 doctorate awarded. *Degree requirements:* For master's, thesis, oral defense; for doctorate, comprehensive exam, thesis/dissertation, proposal defense, oral defense. *Entrance requirements:* For master's and doctorate, GRE General Test, minimum GPA of 3.0. Additional exam requirements/recommendations for international students: Required—TOEFL. *Application deadline:* For fall admission, 2/1 for domestic students, 1/1 for international students; for spring admission, 9/1 for domestic students. Applications are processed on a rolling basis. Application fee: $50. Electronic applications accepted. *Financial support:* In 2012–13, 2 fellowships with tuition reimbursements (averaging $22,500 per year), 1 research assistantship with tuition reimbursement (averaging $21,000 per year), 1 teaching assistantship with tuition reimbursement (averaging $20,000 per year) were awarded; career-related internships or fieldwork, scholarships/grants, and unspecified assistantships also available. Financial award application deadline: 12/1. *Unit head:* Dr. Kennedy T. Paynter, Jr., Director, 301-405-6938, Fax: 301-314-4139, E-mail: mees@umd.edu. Website: http://www.mees.umd.edu.

University of Maryland, College Park, Academic Affairs, College of Agriculture and Natural Resources, Department of Environmental Science and Technology, College Park, MD 20742. Offers MS, PhD. *Faculty:* 31 full-time (7 women), 6 part-time/adjunct (3 women). *Students:* 30 full-time (17 women), 9 part-time (6 women); includes 4 minority (1 Black or African American, non-Hispanic/Latino; 1 Asian, non-Hispanic/Latino; 2 Two or more races, non-Hispanic/Latino), 4 international. 66 applicants, 41% accepted, 13 enrolled. In 2012, 8 master's, 1 doctorate awarded. *Application deadline:* For fall admission, 1/15 priority date for domestic students, 1/15 for international students; for spring admission, 8/15 for domestic students, 6/1 for international students. Applications are processed on a rolling basis. Application fee: $75. Electronic applications accepted. *Expenses:* Tuition, state resident: part-time $551 per credit. Tuition, nonresident: part-time $1188 per credit. Part-time tuition and fees vary according to program. *Financial support:* In 2012–13, 6 research assistantships (averaging $17,347 per year), 19 teaching assistantships (averaging $17,241 per year) were awarded; fellowships also available. *Total annual research expenditures:* $4.3 million. *Unit head:* William Bowerman, Chair, 301-405-1306, E-mail: wbowerma@umd.edu. *Application contact:* Dr. Charles A. Caramello, Dean of Graduate School, 301-405-0358, Fax: 301-314-9305, E-mail: ccaramel@umd.edu. Website: http://www.enst.umd.edu/.

University of Maryland, College Park, Academic Affairs, College of Computer, Mathematical and Natural Sciences, Program in Marine-Estuarine-Environmental Sciences, College Park, MD 20742. Offers MS, PhD. Part-time programs available. *Faculty:* 127. *Students:* 113 (73 women); includes 9 minority (3 Black or African American, non-Hispanic/Latino; 4 Asian, non-Hispanic/Latino; 2 Hispanic/Latino), 22 international. 141 applicants, 26% accepted, 23 enrolled. In 2012, 13 master's, 12 doctorates awarded. Terminal master's awarded for partial completion of doctoral program. *Degree requirements:* For master's, thesis, oral defense; for doctorate, comprehensive exam, thesis/dissertation, proposal defense, oral defense. *Entrance requirements:* For master's and doctorate, GRE General Test, minimum GPA of 3.0. Additional exam requirements/recommendations for international students: Required—TOEFL. *Application deadline:* For fall admission, 2/1 for domestic and international students; for spring admission, 9/1 for domestic students, 6/1 for international students. Applications are processed on a rolling basis. Application fee: $75. Electronic applications accepted. *Expenses:* Tuition, state resident: part-time $551 per credit. Tuition, nonresident: part-time $1188 per credit. Part-time tuition and fees vary according to program. *Financial support:* In 2012–13, 9 teaching assistantships with full tuition reimbursements were awarded; fellowships with full tuition reimbursements, research assistantships with full tuition reimbursements, Federal Work-Study, scholarships/grants, traineeships, health care benefits, and unspecified assistantships also available. Financial award application deadline: 1/1; financial award applicants required to submit FAFSA. *Faculty research:* Ecology, environmental chemistry, environmental molecular biology/biotechnology, environmental sciences, fisheries science, oceanography. *Unit head:* Dr. Kennedy T. Paynter, Jr., Director, 301-405-6938, Fax: 301-314-4139, E-mail: mees@umd.edu. Website: http://www.mees.umd.edu/.

University of Maryland Eastern Shore, Graduate Programs, Department of Natural Sciences, Princess Anne, MD 21853-1299. Offers marine-estuarine-environmental sciences (MS, PhD); toxicology (MS, PhD). *Degree requirements:* For master's, thesis; for doctorate, comprehensive exam, thesis/dissertation. *Entrance requirements:* For master's and doctorate, GRE General Test, minimum GPA of 3.0. Additional exam requirements/recommendations for international students: Required—TOEFL (minimum score 80 iBT). Electronic applications accepted. *Faculty research:* Environmental chemistry (air/water pollution), fin fish ecology.

University of Maryland Eastern Shore, Graduate Programs, Program in Marine-Estuarine-Environmental Sciences, College Park, MD 20742. Offers MS, PhD. Part-time programs available. *Faculty:* 26. *Students:* 30 full-time (20 women), 2 part-time (both women); includes 10 minority (8 Black or African American, non-Hispanic/Latino; 1 American Indian or Alaska Native, non-Hispanic/Latino; 1 Hispanic/Latino), 13 international. 12 applicants, 67% accepted, 5 enrolled. In 2012, 3 master's, 3 doctorates awarded. *Degree requirements:* For master's, thesis; for doctorate, comprehensive exam, thesis/dissertation, proposal defense. *Entrance requirements:* For master's and doctorate, GRE General Test, minimum GPA of 3.0. Additional exam requirements/recommendations for international students: Required—TOEFL. *Application deadline:* For fall admission, 2/1 for domestic and international students; for spring admission, 9/1 for domestic students, 8/1 for international students. Applications are processed on a rolling basis. Application fee: $45. Electronic applications accepted. *Financial support:* In 2012–13, 28 students received support. Fellowships with tuition reimbursements available, research assistantships with tuition reimbursements available, teaching assistantships with tuition reimbursements available, career-related internships or fieldwork, scholarships/grants, and unspecified assistantships available. Support available to part-time students. Financial award application deadline: 1/1. *Unit head:* Dr. Kennedy T. Paynter, Jr., Director, 301-405-6938, Fax: 301-314-4139, E-mail: mees@umd.edu. Website: http://www.mees.umd.edu/.

University of Massachusetts Boston, Office of Graduate Studies, College of Science and Mathematics, Department of Environmental, Earth and Ocean Sciences, Track in Environmental, Earth and Ocean Sciences, Boston, MA 02125-3393. Offers PhD. Part-time and evening/weekend programs available. *Degree requirements:* For doctorate, comprehensive exam, thesis/dissertation, oral exams. *Entrance requirements:* For doctorate, GRE General Test, minimum GPA of 2.75. *Faculty research:* Conservation genetics, anthropogenic and natural influences on community structures of coral reef factors, geographical variation in mitochondrial DNA, protein chemistry and enzymology pertaining to insect cuticle.

University of Massachusetts Lowell, College of Engineering, Department of Civil and Environmental Engineering and College of Sciences, Program in Environmental Studies, Lowell, MA 01854-2881. Offers environmental engineering (MSES); environmental studies (PhD, Certificate). Part-time programs available. *Degree requirements:* For master's, thesis optional. *Entrance requirements:* For master's, GRE General Test. *Faculty research:* Remote sensing of air pollutants, atmospheric deposition of toxic metals, contaminant transport in groundwater, soil remediation.

University of Massachusetts Lowell, College of Sciences, Department of Chemistry, Lowell, MA 01854-2881. Offers analytical chemistry (PhD); biochemistry (PhD); chemistry (MS, PhD); environmental studies (PhD); green chemistry (PhD); inorganic chemistry (PhD); organic chemistry (PhD); polymer science (MS). Terminal master's awarded for partial completion of doctoral program. *Degree requirements:* For master's, thesis; for doctorate, 2 foreign languages, thesis/dissertation. *Entrance requirements:* For master's and doctorate, GRE General Test. Electronic applications accepted.

University of Massachusetts Lowell, School of Health and Environment, Department of Work Environment, Lowell, MA 01854-2881. Offers cleaner production and pollution prevention (MS, Sc D); environmental risk assessment (Certificate); epidemiology (MS, Sc D); ergonomics and safety (MS, Sc D); identification and control of ergonomic hazards (Certificate); job stress and healthy job redesign (Certificate); occupational and environmental hygiene (MS, Sc D); radiological health physics and general work environment protection (Certificate); work environment policy (MS, Sc D). *Accreditation:* ABET (one or more programs are accredited). Part-time programs available. Terminal master's awarded for partial completion of doctoral program. *Degree requirements:* For master's, thesis optional; for doctorate, thesis/dissertation. *Entrance requirements:* For master's and doctorate, GRE General Test. Additional exam requirements/recommendations for international students: Required—TOEFL.

University of Medicine and Dentistry of New Jersey, Graduate School of Biomedical Sciences, Graduate Programs in Biomedical Sciences–Piscataway, Program in Exposure Science and Assessment, Piscataway, NJ 08854-5635. Offers PhD, MD/PhD. PhD offered jointly with Rutgers, The State University of New Jersey, New Brunswick. *Entrance requirements:* Additional exam requirements/recommendations for international students: Required—TOEFL. *Application deadline:* For fall admission, 12/1 for domestic students. Applications are processed on a rolling basis. Application fee: $40. Electronic applications accepted. *Financial support:* Application deadline: 5/1; applicants required to submit FAFSA. *Unit head:* Dr. Clifford Weisel, Director, 732-445-0154, Fax: 732-445-0116, E-mail: weisel@eohsi.rutgers.edu.

University of Michigan, Horace H. Rackham School of Graduate Studies, College of Literature, Science, and the Arts, Department of Earth and Environmental Sciences, Ann Arbor, MI 48109-1005. Offers MS, PhD. *Faculty:* 28 full-time (6 women), 10 part-time/adjunct (5 women). *Students:* 67 full-time (31 women); includes 7 minority (1 Black or African American, non-Hispanic/Latino; 1 American Indian or Alaska Native, non-Hispanic/Latino; 1 Asian, non-Hispanic/Latino; 2 Hispanic/Latino; 2 Two or more races, non-Hispanic/Latino), 21 international. 139 applicants, 25% accepted, 24 enrolled. In 2012, 9 master's, 12 doctorates awarded. Terminal master's awarded for partial completion of doctoral program. *Degree requirements:* For master's, thesis; for doctorate, comprehensive exam, thesis/dissertation, oral defense of dissertation. *Entrance requirements:* For master's and doctorate, GRE General Test. Additional exam requirements/recommendations for international students: Required—TOEFL (minimum score 84 iBT). *Application deadline:* For fall admission, 1/5 for domestic and international students; for winter admission, 11/1 for domestic and international students. Application fee: $65 ($75 for international students). Electronic applications accepted. *Financial support:* Fellowships with full tuition reimbursements, research assistantships with full tuition reimbursements, teaching assistantships with full tuition reimbursements, career-related internships or fieldwork, scholarships/grants, health care benefits, and unspecified assistantships available. Financial award application deadline: 1/5; financial award applicants required to submit FAFSA. *Faculty research:* Isotope geochemistry, paleoclimatology, mineral physics, tectonics, paleontology. *Unit head:* Dr. Rebecca Lange, Chair, 734-764-1435, Fax: 734-763-4690, E-mail: michiganearth@umich.edu. *Application contact:* Anne Hudon, Graduate Program Coordinator, 734-615-3034, Fax: 734-763-4690, E-mail: michiganearth@umich.edu. Website: http://www.lsa.umich.edu/earth.

University of Michigan, School of Natural Resources and Environment, Program in Natural Resources and Environment, Ann Arbor, MI 48109-1041. Offers aquatic sciences: research and management (MS); behavior, education and communication (MS); conservation biology (MS); conservation ecology (MS); environmental informatics (MS); environmental justice (MS); environmental policy and planning (MS); natural resources and environment (PhD); sustainable systems (MS); terrestrial ecosystems (MS); MS/JD; MS/MBA; MUP/MS. *Faculty:* 45 full-time, 23 part-time/adjunct. *Students:* 399 full-time (221 women); includes 65 minority (4 Black or African American, non-Hispanic/Latino; 29 Asian, non-Hispanic/Latino; 23 Hispanic/Latino; 9 Two or more races, non-Hispanic/Latino), 68 international. Average age 27. 635 applicants. In 2012, 138 master's, 9 doctorates awarded. Terminal master's awarded for partial completion of doctoral program. *Degree requirements:* For master's, practicum or group project; for doctorate, comprehensive exam, thesis/dissertation, oral defense of dissertation, preliminary exam. *Entrance requirements:* For master's, GRE General Test; for doctorate, GRE General Test, master's degree. Additional exam requirements/recommendations for international students: Required—TOEFL (minimum score 560 paper-based; 84 iBT). *Application deadline:* For fall admission, 1/5 priority date for domestic students, 1/5 for international students. Applications are processed on a rolling basis. Application fee: $65 ($75 for international students). Electronic applications accepted. *Financial support:* Fellowships with tuition reimbursements, research assistantships with tuition reimbursements, teaching assistantships with tuition reimbursements, career-related internships or fieldwork, Federal Work-Study, institutionally sponsored loans, scholarships/grants, health care benefits, and unspecified assistantships available. Support available to part-time students. Financial award application deadline: 1/5; financial award applicants required to submit FAFSA. *Faculty research:* Stream ecology and fish biology, plant-insect interactions, environmental education, resource control and reproductive success, remote sensing, conservation ecology, sustainable systems. *Unit head:* Dr. Marie Lynn Miranda, Dean, 734-764-2550, Fax: 734-763-8965, E-mail: mlmirand@umich.edu. *Application contact:* Sondra R. Auerbach, Director of Academic Services, 734-764-6453, Fax: 734-936-2195, E-mail: snre.admissions@umich.edu. Website: http://www.snre.umich.edu/.

University of Michigan–Dearborn, College of Arts, Sciences, and Letters, Master of Science in Environmental Science Program, Dearborn, MI 48128. Offers MS. Part-time and evening/weekend programs available. *Faculty:* 17 full-time (6 women), 1 part-time/adjunct (0 women). *Students:* 5 full-time (2 women), 24 part-time (16 women); includes 4 minority (1 Black or African American, non-Hispanic/Latino; 3 Asian, non-Hispanic/Latino). Average age 30. 9 applicants, 78% accepted, 5 enrolled. In 2012, 12 master's awarded. *Degree requirements:* For master's, thesis optional. *Entrance requirements:* For master's, 2 letters of reference, minimum GPA of 3.0. Additional exam requirements/recommendations for international students: Required—TOEFL (minimum score 560 paper-based). *Application deadline:* For fall admission, 8/1 priority date for domestic students, 4/1 for international students; for winter admission, 12/1 priority date for domestic students, 11/1 for international students; for spring admission, 4/1 for domestic students, 3/1 for international students. Applications are processed on a rolling basis. Application fee: $60. *Expenses:* Tuition, state resident: full-time $4928; part-time $575 per credit hour. Tuition, nonresident: full-time $9454; part-time $1093 per credit hour. *Required fees:* $187 per semester. Tuition and fees vary according to program. *Financial support:* In 2012–13, 1 fellowship (averaging $2,500 per year), 2 research assistantships (averaging $2,500 per year) were awarded. Financial award application deadline: 4/1; financial award applicants required to submit FAFSA. *Faculty research:* Fate and transport of heavy metals; land use and impact on ground water and surface water quality; ecosystems and management; natural resources; plant, animal and microbial diversity. *Unit head:* Dr. Sonia Tiquia-Arashiro, Director, 313-593-5148, E-mail: smtiquia@umich.edu. *Application contact:* Carol Ligienza, Administrative Coordinator, CASL Graduate Programs, 313-593-1183, Fax: 313-583-6700, E-mail: caslgrad@umich.edu. Website: http://www.umd.umich.edu/envsci_ms/.

The University of Montana, Graduate School, College of Arts and Sciences, Program in Environmental Studies (EVST), Missoula, MT 59812-0002. Offers MS, JD/MS. Part-time programs available. *Faculty:* 6 full-time (3 women), 2 part-time/adjunct (0 women). *Students:* 30 full-time (16 women), 23 part-time (20 women); includes 3 minority (2 American Indian or Alaska Native, non-Hispanic/Latino; 1 Hispanic/Latino). Average age 30. 64 applicants, 67% accepted, 21 enrolled. In 2012, 22 master's awarded. *Degree requirements:* For master's, thesis, portfolio or professional paper. *Entrance requirements:* For master's, GRE General Test (minimum score: 500 verbal on old scoring; 153 verbal new scoring). Additional exam requirements/recommendations for international students: Required—TOEFL (minimum score 580 paper-based; 92 iBT). *Application deadline:* For fall admission, 2/1 priority date for domestic students, 2/1 for international students. Application fee: $51. *Financial support:* In 2012–13, 25 students received support, including 4 fellowships with partial tuition reimbursements available (averaging $4,500 per year), 1 research assistantship with full tuition reimbursement available (averaging $4,800 per year), 6 teaching assistantships with full tuition reimbursements available (averaging $9,000 per year). Financial award application deadline: 4/15. *Faculty research:* Pollution ecology, sustainable agriculture, environmental writing, environmental policy, environmental justice, environmental history, habitat-land management. *Total annual research expenditures:* $145,137. *Unit head:* Prof. Phil Condon, Director, 406-243-2904, Fax: 406-243-6090, E-mail: phil.condon@mso.umt.edu. *Application contact:* Karen Hurd, Administrative Assistant, 406-243-6273, Fax: 406-243-6090, E-mail: karen.hurd@mso.umt.edu. Website: http://www.cas.umt.edu/evst.

University of Nevada, Las Vegas, Graduate College, Greenspun College of Urban Affairs, School of Environmental and Public Affairs, Las Vegas, NV 89154-4030. Offers crisis and emergency management (MS); environmental science (MS, PhD); non-profit management (Certificate); public administration (MPA); public affairs (PhD); public management (Certificate); solar and renewable energy (Certificate); urban leadership (MA); workforce development and organizational leadership (PhD). Part-time programs available. *Faculty:* 15 full-time (9 women), 11 part-time/adjunct (3 women). *Students:* 86 full-time (41 women), 121 part-time (58 women); includes 108 minority (22 Black or African American, non-Hispanic/Latino; 1 American Indian or Alaska Native, non-Hispanic/Latino; 4 Asian, non-Hispanic/Latino; 28 Hispanic/Latino; 53 Two or more races, non-Hispanic/Latino), 11 international. Average age 36. 89 applicants, 83% accepted, 64 enrolled. In 2012, 46 master's, 6 doctorates, 7 other advanced degrees awarded. *Degree requirements:* For master's, comprehensive exam (for some programs), thesis; for doctorate, comprehensive exam (for some programs), thesis/dissertation. *Entrance requirements:* Additional exam requirements/recommendations for international students: Required—TOEFL (minimum score 550 paper-based; 80 iBT), IELTS (minimum score 7). *Application deadline:* For fall admission, 2/15 priority date for domestic students, 5/1 for international students; for spring admission, 11/15 priority date for domestic students, 10/1 for international students. Applications are processed on a rolling basis. Application fee: $60 ($95 for international students). Electronic applications accepted. *Expenses:* Tuition, state resident: full-time $4752; part-time $264 per credit. Tuition, nonresident: full-time $18,662; part-time $527.50 per credit. *Required fees:* $12 per credit. $266 per semester. One-time fee: $35. Tuition and fees vary according to course load, program and reciprocity agreements. *Financial support:* In 2012–13, 33 students received support, including 23 research assistantships with partial tuition reimbursements available (averaging $11,541 per year), 10 teaching assistantships with partial tuition reimbursements available (averaging $12,250 per year); institutionally sponsored loans, scholarships/grants, health care benefits, and unspecified assistantships also available. Financial award application deadline: 3/1. *Faculty research:* Community and organizational resilience; environmental decision-making and management; budgeting and human resource/workforce management; urban design, sustainability and governance; public and non-profit management. *Total annual research expenditures:* $504,127. *Unit head:* Dr. Christopher Stream, Chair/Associate Professor, 702-895-5120, Fax: 702-895-4436, E-mail: chris.stream@unlv.edu. *Application contact:* Graduate College Admissions Evaluator, 702-895-3320, Fax: 702-895-4180, E-mail: gradcollege@unlv.edu. Website: http://sepa.unlv.edu/.

University of Nevada, Reno, Graduate School, College of Agriculture, Biotechnology and Natural Resources, Department of Natural Resources and Environmental Sciences, Reno, NV 89557. Offers MS. *Degree requirements:* For master's, thesis optional. *Entrance requirements:* For master's, GRE, minimum GPA of 2.75. Additional exam requirements/recommendations for international students: Required—TOEFL (minimum score 500 paper-based; 61 iBT), IELTS (minimum score 6). Electronic applications accepted. *Faculty research:* Range management, plant physiology, remote sensing, soils, wildlife.

University of Nevada, Reno, Graduate School, Interdisciplinary Program in Environmental Sciences and Health, Reno, NV 89557. Offers MS, PhD. Terminal master's awarded for partial completion of doctoral program. *Degree requirements:* For master's, thesis; for doctorate, thesis/dissertation. *Entrance requirements:* For master's, GRE General Test, minimum GPA of 2.75; for doctorate, GRE General Test, minimum GPA of 3.0. Additional exam requirements/recommendations for international students: Required—TOEFL (minimum score 500 paper-based; 61 iBT), IELTS (minimum score 6). Electronic applications accepted. *Faculty research:* Environmental chemistry, environmental toxicology, ecological toxicology.

University of New Haven, Graduate School, College of Arts and Sciences, Program in Environmental Sciences, West Haven, CT 06516-1916. Offers environmental ecology (MS); environmental geoscience (MS); environmental health and management (MS); environmental science (MS); environmental science education (MS); geographical information systems (MS, Certificate). Part-time and evening/weekend programs available. *Students:* 23 full-time (14 women), 13 part-time (6 women); includes 5 minority (3 Black or African American, non-Hispanic/Latino; 2 Asian, non-Hispanic/Latino), 9 international. 43 applicants, 81% accepted, 21 enrolled. In 2012, 9 master's, 4 other advanced degrees awarded. *Degree requirements:* For master's, thesis optional, research project. *Entrance requirements:* Additional exam requirements/recommendations for international students: Required—TOEFL (minimum score 80 iBT), IELTS, Pearson Test of English (minimum score 53). *Application deadline:* For fall admission, 5/31 for international students; for winter admission, 10/15 for international students; for spring admission, 1/15 for international students. Applications are processed on a rolling basis. Application fee: $75. Electronic applications accepted. Application fee is waived when completed online. *Expenses: Tuition:* Part-time $775 per credit. *Required fees:* $45 per trimester. *Financial support:* Research assistantships with partial tuition reimbursements, teaching assistantships with partial tuition reimbursements, career-related internships or fieldwork, Federal Work-Study, scholarships/grants, and unspecified assistantships available. Support available to part-time students. Financial award applicants required to submit FAFSA. *Faculty research:* Mapping and assessing geological and living resources in Long Island Sound, geology, San Salvador Island, Bahamas. *Unit head:* Dr. Roman Zajac, Coordinator, 203-932-7114, E-mail: rzajac@newhaven.edu. *Application contact:* Eloise Gormley, Director of Graduate Admissions, 203-932-7440, E-mail: gradinfo@newhaven.edu. Website: http://www.newhaven.edu/4728/.

University of New Orleans, Graduate School, College of Sciences, Department of Earth and Environmental Sciences, New Orleans, LA 70148. Offers MS. Evening/weekend programs available. *Students:* 16 (7 women). Average age 27. 17 applicants, 41% accepted, 3 enrolled. In 2012, 7 master's awarded. *Degree requirements:* For master's, thesis. *Entrance requirements:* For master's, GRE General Test. Additional exam requirements/recommendations for international students: Required—TOEFL (minimum score 550 paper-based; 79 iBT), IELTS. *Application deadline:* For fall admission, 1/1 priority date for domestic students, 1/1 for international students; for spring admission, 10/15 priority date for domestic students, 10/1 for international students. Applications are processed on a rolling basis. Application fee: $20. Electronic applications accepted. *Expenses: Required fees:* $2165 per semester. *Financial support:* Fellowships, research assistantships, teaching assistantships, career-related internships or fieldwork, Federal Work-Study, and institutionally sponsored loans available. Financial award application deadline: 3/15; financial award applicants required to submit FAFSA. *Faculty research:* Continental margin structure and seismology, burial diagenesis of siliclastic sediments, tectonics at convergent plate margins, continental shelf sediment stability, early diagenesis of carbonates. *Unit head:* Dr. William Simmons, Chairperson, 504-280-6791, Fax: 504-280-7396, E-mail: wsimmons@uno.edu. *Application contact:* Dr. Ioannis Georgiou, Graduate Coordinator, 504-280-1373, Fax: 504-280-7396, E-mail: igeorgio@uno.edu. Website: http://ees.uno.edu.

The University of North Carolina at Chapel Hill, Graduate School, Gillings School of Global Public Health, Department of Environmental Sciences and Engineering, Chapel Hill, NC 27599. Offers air, radiation and industrial hygiene (MPH, MS, MSEE, MSPH, PhD); aquatic and atmospheric sciences (MPH, MS, MSPH, PhD); environmental engineering (MPH, MS, MSEE, MSPH, PhD); environmental health sciences (MPH, MS, MSPH, PhD); environmental management and policy (MPH, MS, MSPH, PhD). *Faculty:* 31 full-time. *Students:* 131 full-time (74 women); includes 31 minority (3 Black or African American, non-Hispanic/Latino; 13 Asian, non-Hispanic/Latino; 9 Hispanic/Latino; 1 Native Hawaiian or other Pacific Islander, non-Hispanic/Latino; 5 Two or more races, non-Hispanic/Latino), 24 international. Average age 27. 262 applicants, 26% accepted, 30 enrolled. In 2012, 22 master's, 8 doctorates awarded. Terminal master's awarded for partial completion of doctoral program. *Degree requirements:* For master's, comprehensive exam, thesis (for some programs), research paper; for doctorate, comprehensive exam, thesis/dissertation. *Entrance requirements:* For master's and doctorate, GRE General Test, minimum GPA of 3.0 (recommended). Additional exam requirements/recommendations for international students: Required—TOEFL. *Application deadline:* For fall admission, 12/10 priority date for domestic students, 12/10 for international students; for spring admission, 9/10 for domestic students. Applications are processed on a rolling basis. Application fee: $85. Electronic applications accepted. *Financial support:* Fellowships with tuition reimbursements, research assistantships with tuition reimbursements, teaching assistantships with tuition reimbursements, career-related internships or fieldwork, Federal Work-Study, traineeships, health care benefits, and unspecified assistantships available. Support available to part-time students. Financial award application deadline: 12/10; financial award applicants required to submit FAFSA. *Faculty research:* Air, radiation and industrial hygiene, aquatic and atmospheric sciences, environmental health sciences, environmental management and policy, water resources engineering. *Unit head:* Dr. Michael Aitken, Chair, 919-966-1024, Fax: 919-966-7911, E-mail: mike_aitken@unc.edu. *Application contact:* Jack Whaley, Registrar, 919-966-3844, Fax: 919-966-7911, E-mail: jack_whaley@unc.edu. Website: http://www2.sph.unc.edu/envr/.

University of Northern Iowa, Graduate College, College of Humanities, Arts and Sciences, Environmental Programs, Cedar Falls, IA 50614. Offers environmental health (MS); environmental science (MS). *Students:* 4 full-time (1 woman), 5 part-time (3 women), 3 international. 6 applicants. In 2012, 1 master's awarded. *Degree requirements:* For master's, comprehensive exam, thesis or alternative. *Entrance requirements:* For master's, minimum GPA of 3.0; 3 letters of recommendation. Additional exam requirements/recommendations for international students: Required—TOEFL (minimum score 500 paper-based; 61 iBT). *Application deadline:* For fall admission, 8/1 priority date for domestic students. Applications are processed on a rolling basis. Application fee: $50 ($70 for international students). Electronic applications accepted. *Financial support:* Application deadline: 2/1. *Unit head:* Dr. Maureen Clayton, Head, 319-273-7147, Fax: 319-273-7125, E-mail: maureen.clayton@uni.edu. *Application contact:* Laurie S. Russell, Record Analyst, 319-273-2623, Fax: 319-273-2885, E-mail: laurie.russell@uni.edu.

University of North Texas, Robert B. Toulouse School of Graduate Studies, Denton, TN 750603. Offers accounting (MS, PhD); applied anthropology (MA, MS); applied behavior analysis (Certificate); applied technology and performance improvement (M Ed, MS, PhD); art education (MA, PhD); art history (MA); art museum education (Certificate); arts leadership (Certificate); audiology (Au D); behavior analysis (MS); biochemistry and molecular biology (MS, PhD); biology (MA, MS, PhD); business (PhD); business computer information systems (PhD); chemistry (MS, PhD); clinical psychology (PhD); communication studies (MA, MS); computer engineering (MS); computer science (MS); computer science and engineering (PhD); counseling (M Ed, MS, PhD), including clinical mental health counseling (MS), college and university counseling (M Ed, MS), elementary school counseling (M Ed, MS), secondary school counseling (M Ed, MS); counseling psychology (PhD); creative writing (MA); criminal justice (MS); curriculum and instruction (M Ed, PhD), including curriculum studies (PhD), early childhood studies (PhD), language and literacy studies (PhD); decision sciences (MBA); design (MA, MFA), including fashion design (MFA), innovation studies, interior design (MFA); early childhood studies (MS); economics (MS); educational leadership (M Ed, Ed D, PhD); educational psychology (MS), including family studies, gifted and talented (MS, PhD), human development, learning and cognition, research, measurement and evaluation; educational research (PhD), including gifted and talented (MS, PhD), human development and family studies, psychological aspects of sports and exercise, research, measurement and statistics; electrical engineering (MS); emergency management (MPA); engineering systems (MS); English (MA, PhD); environmental science (MS, PhD); experimental psychology (PhD); finance (MBA, MS, PhD); financial management (MPA); French (MA); health psychology and behavioral medicine (PhD); health services management (MBA); higher education (M Ed, Ed D, PhD); history (MA, MS, PhD), including European history (PhD), military history (PhD), United States history (PhD); hospitality management (MS); human resources management (MPA); information science (MS, PhD); information technologies (MBA); information technology and decision sciences (MS); interdisciplinary studies (MA, MS); international sustainable tourism (MS); jazz studies (MM); journalism (MA, MJ, Graduate Certificate), including interactive and virtual digital communication (Graduate Certificate), narrative journalism (Graduate Certificate), public relations (Graduate Certificate); kinesiology (MS); learning technologies (MS, PhD); library science (MS); local government management (MPA); logistics and supply chain management (MBA, PhD); long-term care, senior housing, and aging services (MA, MS); management science (PhD); marketing (MBA, PhD); materials science and engineering (MS, PhD); mathematics (MA, PhD); merchandising (MS); music (MA, MM Ed, PhD), including ethnomusicology (MA), music education (MM Ed, PhD), music theory (MA, PhD), musicology (MA, PhD), performance (MA); nonprofit management (MPA); operations and supply chain management (MBA); performance (MM, DMA); philosophy (MA, PhD); physics (MS, PhD); political science (MA, MS, PhD); public administration and management (PhD), including emergency management, nonprofit management, public financial management, urban management; radio, television and film (MA, MFA); recreation, event and sport management (MS); rehabilitation counseling (MS, Certificate); sociology (MA, MS, PhD); Spanish (MA); special education (M Ed, PhD), including autism intervention (PhD), emotional/behavioral disorders (PhD), mild/moderate disabilities (PhD); speech-language pathology (MA, MS); strategic management (MBA); studio art (MFA); taxation (MS); teaching (M Ed); MBA/MS; MS/MPH; MSES/MBA. Part-time and evening/weekend programs available. Postbaccalaureate distance learning degree programs offered. *Faculty:* 665 full-time (219 women), 237 part-time/adjunct (135 women). *Students:* 3,206 full-time (1,712 women), 3,623 part-time (2,305 women); includes 1,742 minority (575 Black or African American, non-Hispanic/Latino; 16 American Indian or Alaska Native, non-Hispanic/Latino; 294 Asian, non-Hispanic/Latino; 690 Hispanic/Latino; 2 Native Hawaiian or other Pacific Islander, non-Hispanic/Latino; 165 Two or more races, non-Hispanic/Latino), 1,125 international. Average age 32. 6,094 applicants, 43% accepted, 1692 enrolled. In 2012, 1,910 master's, 237 doctorates awarded. Terminal master's awarded for partial completion of doctoral program. *Degree requirements:* For master's, variable foreign language requirement, comprehensive exam (for some programs), thesis (for some programs); for doctorate, variable foreign language requirement, comprehensive exam (for some programs), thesis/dissertation; for other advanced degree, variable foreign language requirement, comprehensive exam (for some programs). *Entrance requirements:* For master's and doctorate, GRE, GMAT. Additional exam requirements/recommendations for international students: Required—TOEFL (minimum score 550 paper-based; 79 iBT). *Application deadline:* For fall admission, 7/15 for domestic students, 3/15 for international students; for spring admission, 11/15 for domestic students, 9/15 for international students. Applications are processed on a rolling basis. Application fee: $60. Electronic applications accepted. *Expenses:* Tuition, state resident: full-time $5242; part-time $216 per credit hour. Tuition, nonresident: full-time $11,560; part-time $567 per credit hour. *Required fees:* $730 per semester. *Financial support:* Fellowships with partial tuition reimbursements, research assistantships with partial tuition reimbursements, teaching assistantships, career-related internships or fieldwork, Federal Work-Study, institutionally sponsored loans, scholarships/grants, and library assistantships available. Support available to part-time students. Financial award applicants required to submit FAFSA. *Unit head:* Mark Wardell, Dean, 940-565-2383, E-mail: mark.wardell@unt.edu. *Application contact:* Toulouse School of Graduate Studies, 940-565-2383, Fax: 940-565-2141, E-mail: gradsch@unt.edu. Website: http://www.tsgs.unt.edu/.

University of Oklahoma, College of Architecture, Division of Architecture, Norman, OK 73019. Offers architectural urban studies (MS), including architectural urban studies, environmental technology, human resources; architecture (M Arch). *Faculty:* 29 full-time (7 women). *Students:* 16 full-time (8 women), 4 part-time (1 woman); includes 9 minority (1 American Indian or Alaska Native, non-Hispanic/Latino; 2 Hispanic/Latino; 6 Two or more races, non-Hispanic/Latino), 2 international. Average age 32. 28 applicants, 29% accepted, 4 enrolled. In 2012, 14 master's awarded. *Degree requirements:* For master's, thesis or alternative, portfolio, project. *Entrance requirements:* For master's, GRE General Test, portfolio. Additional exam requirements/recommendations for international students: Required—TOEFL (minimum score 550 paper-based; 79 iBT). *Application deadline:* For fall admission, 4/1 for domestic students, 3/1 for international students. Applications are processed on a rolling basis. Application fee: $40 ($90 for international students). Electronic applications accepted. *Expenses:* Tuition, state resident: full-time $4205; part-time $175.20 per credit hour. Tuition, nonresident: full-time $15,667; part-time $653 per credit hour. *Required fees:* $2745; $103.85 per credit hour. Tuition and fees vary according to course load and degree level. *Financial support:* In 2012–13, 1 research assistantship with partial tuition reimbursement (averaging $9,873 per year), 4 teaching assistantships with partial tuition reimbursements (averaging $9,873 per year) were awarded; scholarships/grants and unspecified assistantships also available. Financial award application deadline: 6/1; financial award applicants required to submit FAFSA. *Faculty research:* Rammed earth bricks, energy sustainability, acoustics, Italian architecture, architectural design. *Total annual research expenditures:* $449,593. *Unit head:* Hans Butzer, Director, 405-325-2444, Fax: 405-325-7558, E-mail: butzer@ou.edu. *Application contact:* Connie Matthews, Assistant, 405-325-6493, Fax: 405-325-7558, E-mail: c.matthews@ou.edu. Website: http://arch.ou.edu.

University of Oklahoma, College of Engineering, School of Civil Engineering and Environmental Science, Program in Environmental Science, Norman, OK 73019. Offers air (M Env Sc); environmental science (PhD). Part-time programs available. *Students:* 7 full-time (5 women), 8 part-time (7 women); includes 1 minority (Black or African American, non-Hispanic/Latino), 3 international. Average age 29. 5 applicants, 40% accepted, 1 enrolled. In 2012, 4 master's, 1 doctorate awarded. Terminal master's awarded for partial completion of doctoral program. *Degree requirements:* For master's, comprehensive exam, oral exams; for doctorate, comprehensive exam, thesis/dissertation, oral and qualifying exams. *Entrance requirements:* For master's, minimum GPA of 3.0; for doctorate, minimum graduate GPA of 3.5. Additional exam requirements/recommendations for international students: Required—TOEFL (minimum score 600 paper-based; 100 iBT). *Application deadline:* For fall admission, 4/1 priority date for domestic students, 3/1 for international students; for spring admission, 11/1 for domestic students, 9/1 for international students. Applications are processed on a rolling basis. Application fee: $40 ($90 for international students). Electronic applications accepted. *Expenses:* Tuition, state resident: full-time $4205; part-time $175.20 per credit hour. Tuition, nonresident: full-time $15,667; part-time $653 per credit hour. *Required fees:* $2745; $103.85 per credit hour. Tuition and fees vary according to course load and degree level. *Financial support:* Scholarships/grants available. Financial award application deadline: 6/1; financial award applicants required to submit FAFSA. *Faculty research:* Constructed wetlands, sustainable water treatment technologies, subsurface transport and fate of chemicals. *Unit head:* Robert C. Knox, Director, 405-325-5911, Fax: 405-325-4217, E-mail: rknox@ou.edu. *Application contact:* Susan Williams, Graduate Programs Assistant, 405-325-2344, Fax: 405-325-4147, E-mail: srwilliams@ou.edu. Website: http://cees.ou.edu.

University of Pennsylvania, School of Arts and Sciences, Graduate Group in Earth and Environmental Science, Philadelphia, PA 19104. Offers MS, PhD. Part-time programs available. *Faculty:* 9 full-time (2 women), 4 part-time/adjunct (0 women). *Students:* 15 full-time (11 women), 1 (woman) part-time, 4 international. 31 applicants, 10% accepted, 1 enrolled. In 2012, 3 doctorates awarded. *Degree requirements:* For master's, one foreign language, thesis; for doctorate, one foreign language, thesis/dissertation. *Entrance requirements:* For master's and doctorate, GRE General Test. Additional exam requirements/recommendations for international students: Required—TOEFL. *Application deadline:* For fall admission, 12/1 priority date for domestic students. Application fee: $70. Electronic applications accepted. *Financial support:* Fellowships, research assistantships, teaching assistantships, institutionally sponsored loans, scholarships/grants, traineeships, health care benefits, and unspecified assistantships available. Financial award application deadline: 12/15. *Faculty research:* Isotope geochemistry, regional tectonics, environmental geology, metamorphic and igneous petrology, paleontology. *Application contact:* Arts and Sciences Graduate Admissions, 215-573-5816, Fax: 215-573-8068, E-mail: gdasadmis@sas.upenn.edu. Website: http://www.sas.upenn.edu/graduate-division.

University of Puerto Rico, Río Piedras, College of Natural Sciences, Department of Environmental Sciences, San Juan, PR 00931-3300. Offers MS, PhD.

University of Rhode Island, Graduate School, College of the Environment and Life Sciences, Department of Fisheries, Animal and Veterinary Science, Kingston, RI 02881. Offers animal health and disease (MS); animal science (MS); aquaculture (MS); aquatic pathology (MS); environmental sciences (PhD), including animal science, aquacultural science, aquatic pathology, fisheries science; fisheries (MS). *Faculty:* 9 full-time (4 women). *Students:* 6 full-time (2 women), 1 part-time (0 women), 2 international. In 2012, 6 master's, 1 doctorate awarded. *Degree requirements:* For master's, comprehensive exam (for some programs), thesis optional; for doctorate, comprehensive exam, thesis/dissertation. *Entrance requirements:* For master's and doctorate, GRE, 2 letters of recommendation. Additional exam requirements/recommendations for international students: Required—TOEFL (minimum score 550 paper-based). *Application deadline:* For fall admission, 7/15 for domestic students, 2/1 for international students; for spring admission, 11/15 for domestic students, 7/15 for international students. Application fee: $65. Electronic applications accepted. *Expenses:* Tuition, state resident: full-time $11,532; part-time $641 per credit. Tuition, nonresident: full-time $23,606; part-time $1311 per credit. *Required fees:* $1388; $36 per credit. $35 per semester. One-time fee: $130. *Financial support:* In 2012–13, 3 research assistantships with full and partial tuition reimbursements (averaging $11,679 per year), 1 teaching assistantship with full and partial tuition reimbursement (averaging $9,818 per year) were awarded. Financial award application deadline: 7/15; financial award applicants required to submit FAFSA. *Unit head:* Dr. David Bengtson, Chair, 401-874-2668, Fax: 401-874-7575, E-mail: bengtson@uri.edu. Website: http://www.uri.edu/cels/favs/.

University of Saint Francis, Graduate School, Department of Biology, Fort Wayne, IN 46808-3994. Offers environmental science (MS). Part-time and evening/weekend programs available. Postbaccalaureate distance learning degree programs offered (minimal on-campus study). *Faculty:* 6 full-time (1 woman), 3 part-time/adjunct (0 women). *Students:* 5 part-time (2 women); includes 1 minority (Black or African American, non-Hispanic/Latino). In 2012, 8 master's awarded. *Degree requirements:* For master's, thesis, internship. *Entrance requirements:* For master's, minimum GPA of 3.2, three letters of recommendation, statement of professional goals, resume. *Application deadline:* For fall admission, 7/1 for domestic students. Applications are processed on a rolling basis. Electronic applications accepted. Application fee is waived when completed online. *Expenses:* *Tuition:* Full-time $7065; part-time $785 per semester hour. *Required fees:* $21 per semester hour. $95 per semester. Tuition and fees vary according to course load. *Financial support:* Career-related internships or fieldwork, institutionally sponsored loans, tuition waivers (full and partial), and unspecified assistantships available. Support available to part-time students. *Unit head:* Dr. Joe T. Steensma, Chair, 260-399-7700 Ext. 8305, E-mail: jsteensma@sf.edu. *Application contact:* James Cashdollar, Admissions Counselor, 260-399-7700 Ext. 6302, E-mail: jcashdollar@sf.edu. Website: http://www.sf.edu/sf/arts-sciences/biology.

University of Saskatchewan, College of Graduate Studies and Research, School of Environment and Sustainability, Saskatoon, SK S7N 5A2, Canada. Offers MES.

University of South Africa, College of Agriculture and Environmental Sciences, Pretoria, South Africa. Offers agriculture (MS); consumer science (MCS); environmental management (MA, MS, PhD); environmental science (MA, MS, PhD); geography (MA, MS, PhD); horticulture (M Tech); human ecology (MHE); life sciences (MS); nature conservation (M Tech).

University of South Florida, Graduate School, College of Arts and Sciences, Department of Chemistry, Tampa, FL 33620-9951. Offers analytical chemistry (MS, PhD); biochemistry (MS, PhD); computational chemistry (MS, PhD); environmental chemistry (MS, PhD); inorganic chemistry (MS, PhD); organic chemistry (MS); physical chemistry (MS, PhD); polymer chemistry (PhD). Part-time programs available. Terminal master's awarded for partial completion of doctoral program. *Degree requirements:* For master's, comprehensive exam, thesis (for some programs); for doctorate, comprehensive exam, thesis/dissertation. *Entrance requirements:* For master's and doctorate, GRE General Test, minimum GPA of 3.0. Additional exam requirements/recommendations for international students: Required—TOEFL (minimum score 550 paper-based; 79 iBT) or IELTS (minimum score 6.5). Electronic applications accepted. *Faculty research:* Synthesis, bio-organic chemistry, bioinorganic chemistry, environmental chemistry, nuclear magnetic resonance (NMR).

University of South Florida, Graduate School, College of Arts and Sciences, Department of Geography, Environment and Planning, Tampa, FL 33620-9951. Offers environmental science and policy (MS); geography (MA); geography and environmental science and policy (PhD); urban and regional planning (MURP). Part-time and evening/weekend programs available. *Degree requirements:* For master's, comprehensive exam, thesis; for doctorate, comprehensive exam, thesis/dissertation. *Entrance requirements:* For master's, GRE General Test, minimum GPA of 3.0, letter of intent, two letters of recommendation (three for MS); for doctorate, GRE General Test, minimum GPA of 3.2 in last 60 hours, letter of intent, two letters of recommendation. Additional exam requirements/recommendations for international students: Required—TOEFL (minimum score 600 paper-based), TOEFL (minimum score 550 paper-based; 79 iBT) or IELTS (minimum score 6.5); TOEFL (minimum score 600 paper-based) for ESP MS and Ph D. *Faculty research:* Natural hazards, geographic information systems models, soil contamination, urban geography and social theory.

University of South Florida–St. Petersburg Campus, College of Arts and Sciences, St. Petersburg, FL 33701. Offers digital journalism and design (MA); environmental science and policy (MA, MS); Florida studies (MLA); journalism and media studies (MA); liberal studies (MLA); psychology (MA). Part-time programs available. Postbaccalaureate distance learning degree programs offered (no on-campus study). *Degree requirements:* For master's, comprehensive exam, thesis or project. *Entrance requirements:* For master's,

GRE, LSAT, MCAT (varies by program), letter of intent, 3 letters of recommendation, writing samples, bachelor's degree from regionally-accredited institution with minimum GPA of 3.0 overall or in upper two years. Additional exam requirements/recommendations for international students: Required—TOEFL (minimum score 550 paper-based; 79 iBT); Recommended—IELTS. Electronic applications accepted.

The University of Tennessee at Chattanooga, Graduate School, College of Arts and Sciences, Program in Environmental Science, Chattanooga, TN 37403. Offers environmental science (MS). Part-time and evening/weekend programs available. *Faculty:* 13 full-time (2 women), 1 (woman) part-time/adjunct. *Students:* 17 full-time (12 women), 22 part-time (13 women); includes 2 minority (1 Black or African American, non-Hispanic/Latino; 1 Asian, non-Hispanic/Latino). Average age 29. 14 applicants, 64% accepted, 6 enrolled. In 2012, 8 master's awarded. *Degree requirements:* For master's, thesis optional. *Entrance requirements:* For master's, GRE General Test, minimum undergraduate GPA of 2.75; undergraduate course work in ecology or knowledge equivalent. Additional exam requirements/recommendations for international students: Required—TOEFL (minimum score 550 paper-based; 79 iBT), IELTS (minimum score 6). *Application deadline:* For fall admission, 6/14 priority date for domestic students, 6/1 for international students; for spring admission, 10/25 priority date for domestic students, 10/1 for international students. Applications are processed on a rolling basis. Application fee: $35. Electronic applications accepted. *Expenses:* Tuition, state resident: full-time $6860; part-time $381 per credit hour. Tuition, nonresident: full-time $21,206; part-time $1178 per credit hour. *Required fees:* $1490; $180 per credit hour. *Financial support:* In 2012–13, 7 research assistantships with tuition reimbursements (averaging $6,860 per year), 7 teaching assistantships with tuition reimbursements (averaging $6,860 per year) were awarded; career-related internships or fieldwork, scholarships/grants, and unspecified assistantships also available. Support available to part-time students. Financial award applicants required to submit FAFSA. *Faculty research:* Bioremediation, stream fish ecology and conservation, environmental law and policy, avian conservation and management. *Total annual research expenditures:* $108,685. *Unit head:* Dr. John Tucker, Department Head, 423-425-4341, Fax: 423-425-2285, E-mail: john-tucker@utc.edu. *Application contact:* Dr. Jerald Ainsworth, Dean of Graduate Studies, 423-425-4478, Fax: 423-425-5223, E-mail: jerald-ainsworth@utc.edu. Website: http://www.utc.edu/Academic/BiologicalAndEnvironmentalSciences/.

The University of Texas at Arlington, Graduate School, College of Science, Department of Earth and Environmental Sciences, Program in Environmental and Earth Sciences, Arlington, TX 76019. Offers environmental science (MS, PhD); geology (MS, PhD). Part-time and evening/weekend programs available. Terminal master's awarded for partial completion of doctoral program. *Degree requirements:* For master's, thesis optional; for doctorate, comprehensive exam, thesis/dissertation. *Entrance requirements:* For master's, GRE General Test. Additional exam requirements/recommendations for international students: Required—TOEFL (minimum score 550 paper-based). Electronic applications accepted.

The University of Texas at El Paso, Graduate School, College of Science, Environmental Science Program, El Paso, TX 79968-0001. Offers MS. *Degree requirements:* For master's, thesis. *Entrance requirements:* For master's, GRE, bachelor's degree in a science or engineering discipline, 3 letters of recommendation. Additional exam requirements/recommendations for international students: Required—TOEFL.

The University of Texas at El Paso, Graduate School, Interdisciplinary Program in Environmental Science and Engineering, El Paso, TX 79968-0001. Offers PhD. Part-time and evening/weekend programs available. *Degree requirements:* For doctorate, thesis/dissertation. *Entrance requirements:* For doctorate, GRE, letters of recommendation. Additional exam requirements/recommendations for international students: Required—TOEFL; Recommended—IELTS. Electronic applications accepted.

The University of Texas at San Antonio, College of Engineering, Department of Civil and Environmental Engineering, San Antonio, TX 78249-0617. Offers civil engineering (MCE, MSCE); environmental science and engineering (PhD). Part-time and evening/weekend programs available. *Faculty:* 12 full-time (2 women). *Students:* 35 full-time (11 women), 23 part-time (5 women); includes 18 minority (2 Black or African American, non-Hispanic/Latino; 1 Asian, non-Hispanic/Latino; 14 Hispanic/Latino; 1 Two or more races, non-Hispanic/Latino), 25 international. Average age 31. 37 applicants, 46% accepted, 11 enrolled. In 2012, 17 master's, 8 doctorates awarded. *Degree requirements:* For master's, comprehensive exam (for some programs), thesis (for some programs); for doctorate, comprehensive exam, thesis/dissertation. *Entrance requirements:* For master's, GRE General Test, bachelor's degree with 18 credit hours in field of study or in another appropriate field of study, statement of purpose; for doctorate, GRE, BA or BS and MS from accredited university, minimum GPA of 3.0 in upper-division and graduate courses, resume, three letters of recommendation, statement of purpose. Additional exam requirements/recommendations for international students: Required—TOEFL (minimum score 550 paper-based; 79 iBT), IELTS (minimum score 5). *Application deadline:* For fall admission, 7/1 for domestic students, 4/1 for international students; for spring admission, 11/1 for domestic students, 9/1 for international students. Application fee: $45 ($85 for international students). *Financial support:* In 2012–13, 29 students received support, including 5 fellowships (averaging $4,100 per year), 18 research assistantships with partial tuition reimbursements available (averaging $19,882 per year), 18 teaching assistantships (averaging $4,680 per year); scholarships/grants and unspecified assistantships also available. Financial award application deadline: 3/31. *Faculty research:* Fate, transport and reactivity of chemicals in natural systems/contaminant adsorption/desorption involving nano-particles; transportation infrastructure management and pavement materials; hydrologic analysis; beneficial use of wastes and industrial by-products; pavement-vehicle interaction. *Unit head:* Dr. Athanassio T. Papagiannakis, Chair, 210-458-7517, Fax: 210-458-6475, E-mail: at.papagiannakis@utsa.edu.

The University of Texas at San Antonio, College of Sciences, Department of Biology, San Antonio, TX 78249-0617. Offers biology (MS); biotechnology (MS), including bioprocessing technician; cell and molecular biology (PhD); environmental science (MS); neurobiology (PhD). *Faculty:* 34 full-time (6 women), 5 part-time/adjunct (2 women). *Students:* 123 full-time (62 women), 62 part-time (33 women); includes 77 minority (10 Black or African American, non-Hispanic/Latino; 13 Asian, non-Hispanic/Latino; 48 Hispanic/Latino; 2 Native Hawaiian or other Pacific Islander, non-Hispanic/Latino; 4 Two or more races, non-Hispanic/Latino), 41 international. Average age 28. 285 applicants, 51% accepted, 63 enrolled. In 2012, 61 master's, 6 doctorates awarded. Terminal master's awarded for partial completion of doctoral program. *Degree requirements:* For master's, comprehensive exam, thesis or alternative; for doctorate, thesis/dissertation. *Entrance requirements:* For master's, GRE General Test, bachelor's degree with 18 credit hours in field of study or in another appropriate field of study; for doctorate, GRE General Test, 3 letters of recommendation, statement of purpose, resume. Additional exam requirements/recommendations for international students: Required—TOEFL (minimum score 500 paper-based; 100 iBT), IELTS (minimum score 5). *Application deadline:* For fall admission, 7/1 for domestic students, 4/1 for international students; for spring admission, 11/1 for domestic students, 9/1 for international students. Application fee: $45 ($85 for international students). *Financial support:* In 2012–13, 66 students received support, including 4 fellowships (averaging $22,350 per year), 34 research assistantships (averaging $22,350 per year), 8 teaching assistantships (averaging $22,350 per year). *Faculty research:* Development of human and veterinary vaccines against a fungal disease, mammalian germ cells and stem cells, dopamine neuron physiology and addiction, plant biochemistry, dendritic computation and synaptic plasticity. *Total annual research expenditures:* $2.8 million. *Unit head:* Dr. Edwin J. Barea-Rodriguez, Chair, 210-458-4511, Fax: 210-458-5658, E-mail: edwin.barea@utsa.edu. *Application contact:* Rene Munguia, Program Coordinator, 210-458-4642, Fax: 210-458-5658, E-mail: rene.munguia@utsa.edu.

The University of Texas at San Antonio, College of Sciences, Department of Geological Sciences, San Antonio, TX 78249-0617. Offers MS. Part-time programs available. *Faculty:* 12 full-time (3 women), 2 part-time/adjunct (0 women). *Students:* 21 full-time (10 women), 11 part-time (2 women); includes 5 minority (1 Black or African American, non-Hispanic/Latino; 1 Asian, non-Hispanic/Latino; 2 Hispanic/Latino; 1 Two or more races, non-Hispanic/Latino), 8 international. Average age 29. 33 applicants, 79% accepted, 17 enrolled. In 2012, 6 master's awarded. *Degree requirements:* For master's, comprehensive exam, thesis (for some programs). *Entrance requirements:* For master's, GRE General Test, three letters of recommendation, statement of research interest. Additional exam requirements/recommendations for international students: Required—TOEFL (minimum score 500 paper-based; 61 iBT), IELTS (minimum score 5). *Application deadline:* For fall admission, 7/1 for domestic students, 4/1 for international students; for spring admission, 11/1 for domestic students, 9/1 for international students. Application fee: $45 ($85 for international students). *Financial support:* Tuition waivers available. *Faculty research:* Low temperature geochemistry, aqueous geochemistry, hydrogeology, groundwater modeling, stratigraphy, carbonate petrology, paleontology, micropaleontology, remote sensing, geographic information systems, geoinformatics, tectonics, structural geology, metamorphic petrology, geochronology, sediment transports, methodology. *Unit head:* Dr. Alan R. Dutton, Department Chair, 210-458-4455, Fax: 210-458-4469, E-mail: alan.dutton@utsa.edu. *Application contact:* Graduate Advisor of Record, 210-458-4455, Fax: 210-458-4469, E-mail: geosciences@utsa.edu. Website: http://www.utsa.edu/geosci/.

University of the Virgin Islands, Graduate Programs, Division of Science and Mathematics, Program in Environmental and Marine Science, Saint Thomas, VI 00802-9990. Offers MS. *Entrance requirements:* For master's, GRE. Additional exam requirements/recommendations for international students: Required—TOEFL (minimum score 550 paper-based).

The University of Toledo, College of Graduate Studies, College of Natural Sciences and Mathematics, Department of Environmental Sciences, Toledo, OH 43606-3390. Offers biology - ecology (PhD), including ecology (MS, PhD); geology (MS), including ecology (MS, PhD). Part-time programs available. *Faculty:* 35. *Students:* 6 full-time (0 women), 5 part-time (4 women), 1 international. Average age 30. 4 applicants, 50% accepted, 2 enrolled. In 2012, 3 master's awarded. *Degree requirements:* For master's, thesis or alternative. *Entrance requirements:* For master's, GRE General Test, minimum cumulative point-hour ratio of 2.7 for all previous academic work, three letters of recommendation, statement of purpose, transcripts from all prior institutions attended. Additional exam requirements/recommendations for international students: Required—TOEFL (minimum score 550 paper-based; 80 iBT), IELTS (minimum score 6.5). *Application deadline:* For fall admission, 1/15 priority date for domestic students, 1/15 for international students. Applications are processed on a rolling basis. Application fee: $45 ($75 for international students). Electronic applications accepted. *Financial support:* In 2012–13, 2 research assistantships with full and partial tuition reimbursements (averaging $18,700 per year), 4 teaching assistantships with full and partial tuition reimbursements (averaging $3,038 per year) were awarded; Federal Work-Study, institutionally sponsored loans, scholarships/grants, tuition waivers (full), and unspecified assistantships also available. Support available to part-time students. *Faculty research:* Environmental geochemistry, geophysics, petrology and mineralogy, paleontology, geohydrology. *Unit head:* Dr. Timothy G. Fisher, Chair, 419-530-2883, E-mail: timothy.fisher@utoledo.edu. *Application contact:* Graduate School Office, 419-530-4723, Fax: 419-530-4724, E-mail: grdsch@utnet.utoledo.edu. Website: http://www.utoledo.edu/nsm/.

University of Toronto, School of Graduate Studies, Department of Physical and Environmental Sciences, Toronto, ON M5S 1A1, Canada. Offers environmental science (M Env Sc, PhD). *Entrance requirements:* For master's, bachelor's degree (B Sc or B Eng), minimum B average in last two years of undergraduate program, two half-courses or one full-course each in chemistry, physics, calculus and biology. Additional exam requirements/recommendations for international students: Required—TOEFL (minimum score 580 paper-based; 93 iBT), TWE (minimum score 4). Electronic applications accepted.

University of Utah, Graduate School, Professional Master of Science and Technology Program, Salt Lake City, UT 84112-1107. Offers biotechnology (PSM); computational science (PSM); environmental science (PSM); science instrumentation (PSM). Part-time programs available. *Students:* 20 full-time (11 women), 36 part-time (9 women); includes 4 minority (3 Hispanic/Latino; 1 Native Hawaiian or other Pacific Islander, non-Hispanic/Latino), 3 international. Average age 32. 53 applicants, 55% accepted, 23 enrolled. In 2012, 25 master's awarded. *Degree requirements:* For master's, internship. *Entrance requirements:* For master's, GRE (recommended), minimum undergraduate GPA of 3.0, bachelor's degree from accredited university or college. Additional exam requirements/recommendations for international students: Required—TOEFL (minimum score 500 paper-based; 61 iBT), IELTS (minimum score 6). *Application deadline:* For fall admission, 2/1 for domestic and international students. Application fee: $55 ($65 for international students). Electronic applications accepted. *Financial support:* Fellowships, research assistantships, teaching assistantships, and unspecified assistantships available. *Unit head:* Jennifer Schmidt, Program Director, 801-585-5630, E-mail: jennifer.schmidt@gradschool.utah.edu. *Application contact:* Jay Derek Payne, Project Coordinator, 801-585-3650, Fax: 801-585-6749, E-mail: derek.payne@gradschool.utah.edu. Website: http://pmst.utah.edu/.

University of Virginia, College and Graduate School of Arts and Sciences, Department of Environmental Sciences, Charlottesville, VA 22903. Offers MA, MS, PhD. *Faculty:* 28 full-time (4 women), 2 part-time/adjunct (both women). *Students:* 68 full-time (40 women); includes 4 minority (2 Asian, non-Hispanic/Latino; 1 Hispanic/Latino; 1 Two or more races, non-Hispanic/Latino), 5 international. Average age 28. 91 applicants, 27% accepted, 20 enrolled. In 2012, 8 master's, 10 doctorates awarded. *Degree requirements:* For master's, thesis; for doctorate, comprehensive exam, thesis/dissertation. *Entrance requirements:* For master's and doctorate, GRE General Test, 2 letters of recommendation. Additional exam requirements/recommendations for international students: Required—TOEFL (minimum score 600 paper-based; 90 iBT), IELTS (minimum score 7). *Application deadline:* For fall admission, 12/1 for domestic and international students; for winter admission, 10/15 for domestic and international students. Applications are processed on a rolling basis. Application fee: $60. Electronic applications accepted. *Expenses:* Tuition, state resident: full-time $13,278; part-time $717 per credit hour. Tuition, nonresident: full-time $22,602; part-time $1235 per credit hour. *Required fees:* $2384. *Financial support:* Fellowships, research assistantships, and teaching assistantships available. Financial award application deadline: 12/1; financial award applicants required to submit FAFSA. *Unit head:* Patricia Wiberg, Chairman, 434-924-7761, Fax: 434-982-2137, E-mail: pw3z@virginia.edu. *Application contact:* Graduate Admissions Chair, 434-924-7761, Fax: 434-982-2137. Website: http://www.evsc.virginia.edu/.

The University of Western Ontario, Faculty of Graduate Studies, Biosciences Division, Department of Plant Sciences, London, ON N6A 5B8, Canada. Offers plant and environmental sciences (M Sc); plant sciences (M Sc, PhD); plant sciences and environmental sciences (PhD); plant sciences and molecular biology (M Sc, PhD). *Degree requirements:* For master's, thesis; for doctorate, thesis/dissertation. *Entrance requirements:* For doctorate, M Sc or equivalent. Additional exam requirements/recommendations for international students: Required—TOEFL. *Faculty research:* Ecology systematics, plant biochemistry and physiology, yeast genetics, molecular biology.

The University of Western Ontario, Faculty of Graduate Studies, Physical Sciences Division, Department of Earth Sciences, London, ON N6A 5B8, Canada. Offers environment and sustainability (MES); geology (M Sc, PhD); geology and environmental science (M Sc, PhD); geophysics (M Sc, PhD); geophysics and environmental science (M Sc, PhD). *Degree requirements:* For master's, thesis; for doctorate, thesis/dissertation, qualifying exam. *Entrance requirements:* For master's, honors in B Sc; for doctorate, M Sc. Additional exam requirements/recommendations for international students: Required—TOEFL. *Faculty research:* Geophysics, geochemistry, paleontology, sedimentology/stratigraphy, glaciology/quaternary.

University of West Florida, College of Arts and Sciences: Sciences, Department of Environmental Sciences, Pensacola, FL 32514-5750. Offers MS. Part-time programs available. *Entrance requirements:* For master's, GRE (minimum score: 450 verbal; 550 quantitative), official transcripts; formal letter of interest, background, and professional goals; three letters of recommendation by individuals in professionally-relevant fields (waived for graduates of UWF Department of Environmental Sciences); current curriculum vitae/resume. Additional exam requirements/recommendations for international students: Required—TOEFL (minimum score 550 paper-based).

University of Windsor, Faculty of Graduate Studies, GLIER-Great Lakes Institute for Environmental Research, Windsor, ON N9B 3P4, Canada. Offers environmental science (M Sc, PhD). *Degree requirements:* For master's, thesis; for doctorate, thesis/dissertation. *Entrance requirements:* For master's, minimum B+ average; for doctorate, M Sc degree, minimum B+ average. Additional exam requirements/recommendations for international students: Required—TOEFL (minimum score 560 paper-based). Electronic applications accepted. *Faculty research:* Environmental chemistry and toxicology, conservation and resource management, iron formation geochemistry.

University of Wisconsin–Green Bay, Graduate Studies, Program in Environmental Science and Policy, Green Bay, WI 54311-7001. Offers MS. Part-time programs available. *Faculty:* 16 full-time (3 women), 3 part-time/adjunct (0 women). *Students:* 22 full-time (9 women), 21 part-time (13 women); includes 5 minority (1 Black or African American, non-Hispanic/Latino; 1 American Indian or Alaska Native, non-Hispanic/Latino; 1 Hispanic/Latino; 2 Two or more races, non-Hispanic/Latino). Average age 29. 20 applicants, 90% accepted, 12 enrolled. In 2012, 11 master's awarded. *Degree requirements:* For master's, thesis. *Entrance requirements:* For master's, GRE General Test, minimum GPA of 3.0. *Application deadline:* For fall admission, 8/1 for domestic students; for spring admission, 11/1 for domestic students. Applications are processed on a rolling basis. Application fee: $56. Electronic applications accepted. *Expenses:* Tuition, state resident: full-time $7640; part-time $424 per credit. Tuition, nonresident: full-time $16,771; part-time $932 per credit. *Required fees:* $1350; $75 per credit. Tuition and fees vary according to reciprocity agreements. *Financial support:* In 2012–13, 3 students received support, including 3 teaching assistantships with full tuition reimbursements available; research assistantships with full tuition reimbursements available, career-related internships or fieldwork, Federal Work-Study, and institutionally sponsored loans also available. Financial award application deadline: 7/15; financial award applicants required to submit FAFSA. *Faculty research:* Bald eagle, parasitic population of domestic and wild animals, resource recovery, anaerobic digestion of organic waste. *Unit head:* Dr. Matthew Dornbush, Chair, 920-465-2264, E-mail: dornbusm@uwgb.edu. *Application contact:* Mary Valitchka, Graduate Studies Coordinator, 920-465-2123, E-mail: valitchm@uwgb.edu. Website: http://www.uwgb.edu/graduate/.

University of Wisconsin–Madison, Graduate School, Gaylord Nelson Institute for Environmental Studies, Environmental Monitoring Program, Madison, WI 53706-1380. Offers MS, PhD. Part-time programs available. *Degree requirements:* For master's, thesis or alternative; for doctorate, thesis/dissertation. *Expenses:* Tuition, state resident: full-time $10,728; part-time $743 per credit. Tuition, nonresident: full-time $24,054; part-time $1575 per credit. *Required fees:* $1111; $72 per credit. *Faculty research:* Remote sensing, geographic information systems, climate modeling, natural resource management.

Vanderbilt University, Graduate School, Department of Earth and Environmental Sciences, Nashville, TN 37240-1001. Offers MAT, MS. *Faculty:* 8 full-time (2 women). *Students:* 15 full-time (6 women), 1 (woman) part-time, 1 international. Average age 25. 31 applicants, 32% accepted, 6 enrolled. In 2012, 3 master's awarded. *Degree requirements:* For master's, thesis. *Entrance requirements:* For master's, GRE General Test, GRE Subject Test (recommended). Additional exam requirements/recommendations for international students: Required—TOEFL (minimum score 570 paper-based; 88 iBT). *Application deadline:* For fall admission, 1/15 for domestic and international students. Application fee: $0. Electronic applications accepted. *Financial support:* Fellowships with full and partial tuition reimbursements, research assistantships with full and partial tuition reimbursements, teaching assistantships with full tuition reimbursements, career-related internships or fieldwork, Federal Work-Study, institutionally sponsored loans, and health care benefits available. Financial award application deadline: 1/15; financial award applicants required to submit CSS PROFILE or FAFSA. *Faculty research:* Geochemical processes, magmatic processes and crustal evolution, paleoecology and paleoenvironments, sedimentary systems, transport phenomena, environmental policy. *Unit head:* Dr. Calvin Miller, Director of Graduate Studies, 615-322-2232, E-mail: calvin.miller@vanderbilt.edu. *Application contact:* Teri Sparkman, Office Assistant, 615-322-2976, E-mail: teri.pugh@vanderbilt.edu. Website: http://www.vanderbilt.edu/ees/.

Virginia Polytechnic Institute and State University, Graduate School, College of Engineering, Blacksburg, VA 24061. Offers aerospace engineering (ME, MS, PhD); biological systems engineering (ME, MS, PhD); biomedical engineering (MS, PhD); chemical engineering (ME, MS, PhD); civil engineering (ME, MS, PhD); computer engineering (ME, MS, PhD); computer science and application (MS, PhD); electrical engineering (ME, PhD); engineering education (PhD); engineering mechanics (ME, MS, PhD); environmental engineering (MS); environmental science and engineering (MS); industrial and systems engineering (ME, MS, PhD); materials science and engineering (ME, MS, PhD); mechanical engineering (ME, MS, PhD); mining and minerals engineering (PhD); mining engineering (ME, MS); ocean engineering (MS); systems engineering (ME, MS). *Accreditation:* ABET (one or more programs are accredited). *Faculty:* 351 full-time (56 women), 3 part-time/adjunct (0 women). *Students:* 1,804 full-time (378 women), 336 part-time (67 women); includes 207 minority (35 Black or African

American, non-Hispanic/Latino; 98 Asian, non-Hispanic/Latino; 46 Hispanic/Latino; 28 Two or more races, non-Hispanic/Latino), 1,010 international. Average age 28. 4,841 applicants, 19% accepted, 535 enrolled. In 2012, 469 master's, 172 doctorates awarded. *Degree requirements:* For master's, comprehensive exam (for some programs), thesis (for some programs); for doctorate, comprehensive exam (for some programs), thesis/dissertation (for some programs). *Entrance requirements:* For master's and doctorate, GRE/GMAT (may vary by department). Additional exam requirements/recommendations for international students: Required—TOEFL (minimum score 550 paper-based). *Application deadline:* For fall admission, 8/1 for domestic students, 4/1 for international students; for spring admission, 1/1 for domestic students, 9/1 for international students. Applications are processed on a rolling basis. Application fee: $65. Electronic applications accepted. *Expenses:* Tuition, state resident: full-time $10,677; part-time $593.25 per credit hour. Tuition, nonresident: full-time $20,926; part-time $1162.50 per credit hour. *Required fees:* $427.75 per semester. Tuition and fees vary according to course load, campus/location and program. *Financial support:* In 2012–13, 175 fellowships with full tuition reimbursements (averaging $6,125 per year), 919 research assistantships with full tuition reimbursements (averaging $20,641 per year), 273 teaching assistantships with full tuition reimbursements (averaging $17,546 per year) were awarded. Financial award application deadline: 3/1; financial award applicants required to submit FAFSA. *Total annual research expenditures:* $84.8 million. *Unit head:* Dr. Richard C. Benson, Dean, 540-231-9752, Fax: 540-231-3031, E-mail: deaneng@vt.edu. *Application contact:* Linda Perkins, Executive Assistant, 540-231-9752, Fax: 540-231-3031, E-mail: lperkins@vt.edu. Website: http://www.eng.vt.edu/.

Virginia Polytechnic Institute and State University, Graduate School, College of Natural Resources and Environment, Blacksburg, VA 24061. Offers fisheries and wildlife (MS); forestry and forest products (MF, MS, PhD); geography (MS); geospatial and environmental analysis (PhD); natural resources (MNR). *Faculty:* 68 full-time (14 women). *Students:* 181 full-time (82 women), 78 part-time (47 women); includes 20 minority (5 Black or African American, non-Hispanic/Latino; 1 American Indian or Alaska Native, non-Hispanic/Latino; 4 Asian, non-Hispanic/Latino; 4 Hispanic/Latino; 6 Two or more races, non-Hispanic/Latino), 54 international. Average age 31. 133 applicants, 41% accepted, 48 enrolled. In 2012, 71 master's, 16 doctorates awarded. *Degree requirements:* For master's, comprehensive exam (for some programs), thesis (for some programs); for doctorate, comprehensive exam (for some programs), thesis/dissertation (for some programs). *Entrance requirements:* For master's and doctorate, GRE/GMAT (may vary by department). Additional exam requirements/recommendations for international students: Required—TOEFL (minimum score 550 paper-based). *Application deadline:* For fall admission, 8/1 for domestic students, 4/1 for international students; for spring admission, 1/1 for domestic students, 9/1 for international students. Applications are processed on a rolling basis. Application fee: $65. Electronic applications accepted. *Expenses:* Tuition, state resident: full-time $10,677; part-time $593.25 per credit hour. Tuition, nonresident: full-time $20,926; part-time $1162.50 per credit hour. *Required fees:* $427.75 per semester. Tuition and fees vary according to course load, campus/location and program. *Financial support:* In 2012–13, 92 research assistantships with full tuition reimbursements (averaging $19,523 per year), 43 teaching assistantships with full tuition reimbursements (averaging $16,826 per year) were awarded. Financial award application deadline: 3/1; financial award applicants required to submit FAFSA. *Total annual research expenditures:* $14 million. *Unit head:* Dr. Paul M. Winistorfer, Dean, 540-231-5481, Fax: 540-231-7664, E-mail: pstorfer@vt.edu. *Application contact:* Arlice Banks, Assistant to the Dean, 540-231-5481, Fax: 540-231-7664. Website: http://www.cnre.vt.edu/.

Virginia Polytechnic Institute and State University, VT Online, Blacksburg, VA 24061. Offers advanced transportation systems (Certificate); aerospace engineering (MS); agricultural and life sciences (MSLFS); business information systems (Graduate Certificate); career and technical education (MS); civil engineering (MS); computer engineering (M Eng, MS); decision support systems (Graduate Certificate); eLearning leadership (MA); electrical engineering (M Eng, MS); engineering administration (MEA); environmental engineering (Certificate); environmental politics and policy (Graduate Certificate); environmental sciences and engineering (MS); foundations of political analysis (Graduate Certificate); health product risk management (Graduate Certificate); industrial and systems engineering (MS); information policy and society (Graduate Certificate); information security (Graduate Certificate); information technology (MIT); instructional technology (MA); integrative STEM education (MA Ed); liberal arts (Graduate Certificate); life sciences: health product risk management (MS); natural resources (MNR, Graduate Certificate); networking (Graduate Certificate); nonprofit and nongovernmental organization management (Graduate Certificate); ocean engineering (MS); political science (MA); security studies (Graduate Certificate); software development (Graduate Certificate). *Expenses:* Tuition, state resident: full-time $10,677; part-time $593.25 per credit hour. Tuition, nonresident: full-time $20,926; part-time $1162.50 per credit hour. *Required fees:* $427.75 per semester. Tuition and fees vary according to course load, campus/location and program. Website: http://www.vto.vt.edu/.

Washington State University, Graduate School, College of Agricultural, Human, and Natural Resource Sciences, School of the Environment, Pullman, WA 99164. Offers environmental and natural resource sciences (PhD); environmental sciences (MS); geology (MS, PhD); natural resources (MS). *Faculty:* 27 full-time (5 women), 7 part-time/adjunct (3 women). *Students:* 72 full-time (37 women), 7 part-time (4 women); includes 1 minority (Hispanic/Latino), 6 international. Average age 27. In 2012, 5 master's, 2 doctorates awarded. *Degree requirements:* For master's, comprehensive exam (for some programs), thesis (for some programs), oral exam; for doctorate, comprehensive exam, thesis/dissertation, oral exam. *Entrance requirements:* For master's, GRE General Test, official copies of all college transcripts, three letters of recommendation. Additional exam requirements/recommendations for international students: Required—TOEFL, IELTS. *Application deadline:* For fall admission, 1/10 priority date for domestic students, 1/10 for international students; for spring admission, 7/1 for domestic and international students. Applications are processed on a rolling basis. Application fee: $75. *Financial support:* In 2012–13, fellowships (averaging $2,333 per year), research assistantships with full and partial tuition reimbursements (averaging $13,917 per year), teaching assistantships with full and partial tuition reimbursements (averaging $13,056 per year) were awarded; career-related internships or fieldwork, Federal Work-Study, institutionally sponsored loans, tuition waivers (partial), and unspecified assistantships also available. Financial award application deadline: 2/15; financial award applicants required to submit FAFSA. *Faculty research:* Environmental and natural resources conservation and sustainability; earth sciences: earth systems and geology; wildlife ecology and conservation sciences. *Total annual research expenditures:* $967,000. *Unit head:* Dr. Steve Bollens, Director, 360-546-9116, E-mail: sbollens@vancouver.wsu.edu. *Application contact:* Graduate School Admissions, 800-GRADWSU, Fax: 509-335-1949, E-mail: gradsch@wsu.edu. Website: http://environment.wsu.edu/.

Washington State University, Graduate School, College of Arts and Sciences, School of the Environment, Program in Environmental and Natural Resource Sciences, Pullman, WA 99164. Offers PhD.

Washington State University, Graduate School, College of Arts and Sciences, School of the Environment, Program in Environmental Science, Pullman, WA 99164. Offers environmental and natural resource sciences (PhD); environmental science (MS). *Degree requirements:* For master's, comprehensive exam (for some programs), thesis (for some programs), oral exam; for doctorate, comprehensive exam, thesis/dissertation, oral exam, written exam. *Entrance requirements:* For master's, 3 undergraduate semester hours each in sociology or cultural anthropology, environmental science, biological sciences, and calculus or statistics; 4 in general ecology; and 6 in general chemistry or general physics; for doctorate, minimum GPA of 3.0. Additional exam requirements/recommendations for international students: Required—TOEFL, IELTS.

Washington State University Tri-Cities, Graduate Programs, Program in Agricultural, Human, and Natural Resource Science, Richland, WA 99354. Offers MS. *Degree requirements:* For master's, comprehensive exam (for some programs), thesis (for some programs), special project. *Entrance requirements:* For master's, GRE, minimum GPA of 3.0, 3 letters of recommendation. Additional exam requirements/recommendations for international students: Required—TOEFL.

Washington State University Tri-Cities, Graduate Programs, Program in Environmental Science, Richland, WA 99352-1671. Offers environmental and natural resource sciences (PhD); environmental science (MS). Part-time programs available. *Degree requirements:* For master's, comprehensive exam, thesis (for some programs), oral exam; for doctorate, comprehensive exam, thesis/dissertation. *Entrance requirements:* For master's, GRE General Test, minimum GPA of 3.0, 3 letters of recommendation. Additional exam requirements/recommendations for international students: Required—TOEFL (minimum score 550 paper-based). *Faculty research:* Radiation ecology, cytogenetics.

Washington State University Vancouver, Graduate Programs, Program in Environmental Science, Vancouver, WA 98686. Offers MS. *Degree requirements:* For master's, comprehensive exam, thesis (for some programs). *Entrance requirements:* For master's, GRE General Test, minimum GPA of 3.0, 3 letters of recommendation. Additional exam requirements/recommendations for international students: Required—TOEFL (minimum score 550 paper-based). *Faculty research:* Conservation biology, environmental chemistry.

Wesleyan University, Graduate Studies, Department of Earth and Environmental Sciences, Middletown, CT 06459. Offers MA. *Degree requirements:* For master's, thesis. *Entrance requirements:* For master's, GRE General Test, official transcripts, three recommendation letters, essay. Additional exam requirements/recommendations for international students: Required—TOEFL. *Application deadline:* For fall admission, 2/15 priority date for domestic students, 2/15 for international students. Applications are processed on a rolling basis. Application fee: $0. Electronic applications accepted. *Financial support:* Teaching assistantships with full tuition reimbursements and tuition waivers (full and partial) available. Financial award application deadline: 4/15; financial award applicants required to submit FAFSA. *Faculty research:* Tectonics, volcanology, stratigraphy, coastal processes, geochemistry. *Unit head:* Dr. Martha Gilmore, Chair, 860-685-3129, E-mail: mgilmore@wesleyan.edu. *Application contact:* Ginny Harris, Administrative Assistant, 860-685-2244, E-mail: vharris@wesleyan.edu. Website: http://www.weslean.edu/ees/.

Western Connecticut State University, Division of Graduate Studies, School of Arts and Sciences, Department of Biological and Environmental Sciences, Danbury, CT 06810-6885. Offers MA. Part-time programs available. *Faculty:* 3 full-time (1 woman). *Students:* 6 part-time (5 women). Average age 30. 1 applicant. In 2012, 2 master's awarded. *Degree requirements:* For master's, comprehensive exam or thesis, completion of program in 6 years. *Entrance requirements:* For master's, minimum GPA of 2.5. Additional exam requirements/recommendations for international students: Recommended—TOEFL (minimum score 550 paper-based; 79 iBT), IELTS (minimum score 6). *Application deadline:* For fall admission, 8/5 priority date for domestic students; for spring admission, 1/5 priority date for domestic students. Applications are processed on a rolling basis. Application fee: $50. *Expenses:* Contact institution. *Financial support:* Application deadline: 5/1; applicants required to submit FAFSA. *Faculty research:* Biology, taxonomy and evolution of aquatic flowering plants; aquatic plant reproductive systems, the spread of invasive aquatic plants, aquatic plant structure, and the taxonomy of water starworts (Callitrichaceae) and riverweeds (Podostemaceae). *Unit head:* Dr. Ruth Gyure, Graduate Coordinator, 203-837-8796, Fax: 203-837-8525, E-mail: gyurer@wcsu.edu. *Application contact:* Chris Shankle, Associate Director of Graduate Studies, 203-837-9005, Fax: 203-837-8326, E-mail: shanklec@wcsu.edu. Website: http://www.wcsu.edu/biology/.

Western Washington University, Graduate School, Huxley College of the Environment, Department of Environmental Sciences, Bellingham, WA 98225-5996. Offers environmental science (MS); marine and estuarine science (MS). Part-time programs available. *Degree requirements:* For master's, thesis. *Entrance requirements:* For master's, GRE General Test, minimum GPA of 3.0 in last 60 semester hours or last 90 quarter hours. Additional exam requirements/recommendations for international students: Required—TOEFL (minimum score 567 paper-based). Electronic applications accepted. *Faculty research:* Landscape ecology, climate change, watershed studies, environmental toxicology and risk assessment, aquatic toxicology, toxic algae, invasive species.

Western Washington University, Graduate School, Huxley College of the Environment, Department of Environmental Studies, Bellingham, WA 98225-5996. Offers environmental education (M Ed); geography (MS). Part-time programs available. *Degree requirements:* For master's, thesis. *Entrance requirements:* For master's, GRE General Test, minimum GPA of 3.0 in last 60 semester hours or last 90 quarter hours. Additional exam requirements/recommendations for international students: Required—TOEFL (minimum score 567 paper-based). Electronic applications accepted. *Faculty research:* Geomorphology; pedogenesis; quaternary studies and climate change in the western U.S. landscape ecology, biogeography, pyrogeography, and spatial analysis.

West Texas A&M University, College of Agriculture, Science and Engineering, Department of Agricultural Sciences, Emphasis in Plant, Soil and Environmental Science, Canyon, TX 79016-0001. Offers MS. Part-time programs available. *Degree requirements:* For master's, comprehensive exam, thesis optional. *Entrance requirements:* For master's, GRE General Test. Additional exam requirements/recommendations for international students: Required—TOEFL (minimum score 550 paper-based). Electronic applications accepted. *Faculty research:* Crop and soil disciplines.

West Texas A&M University, College of Agriculture, Science and Engineering, Department of Life, Earth, and Environmental Sciences, Program in Environmental Science, Canyon, TX 79016-0001. Offers MS. Part-time programs available. *Degree requirements:* For master's, comprehensive exam, thesis optional. *Entrance requirements:* For master's, GRE General Test. Additional exam requirements/recommendations for international students: Required—TOEFL (minimum score 550 paper-based). Electronic applications accepted. *Faculty research:* Degradation of presistant pesticides in soils and ground water, air quality.

Wichita State University, Graduate School, Fairmount College of Liberal Arts and Sciences, Department of Geology, Wichita, KS 67260. Offers earth, environmental, and physical sciences (MS). Part-time programs available. *Unit head:* Dr. William Parcell, Chair, 316-978-3140, E-mail: william.parcell@wichita.edu. *Application contact:* Jordan Oleson, Admissions Coordinator, 316-978-3095, Fax: 316-978-3253, E-mail: jordan.oleson@wichita.edu. Website: http://www.wichita.edu/.

Wilfrid Laurier University, Faculty of Graduate and Postdoctoral Studies, Faculty of Arts, Department of Geography and Environmental Studies, Waterloo, ON N2L 3C5, Canada. Offers environmental and resource management (MA, MES, PhD); environmental science (M Sc, MES, PhD); geomatics (M Sc, MES, PhD); human geography (MES, PhD). Part-time programs available. *Degree requirements:* For master's, thesis optional; for doctorate, thesis/dissertation. *Entrance requirements:* For master's, honors BA in geography, minimum B average in undergraduate course work; honors BSc with minimum B+ or honors BES or BA in physical geography, environmental or earth sciences or the equivalent; for doctorate, MA in geography, minimum A- average. Additional exam requirements/recommendations for international students: Required—TOEFL (minimum score 89 iBT). Electronic applications accepted. *Faculty research:* Resources management, urban, economic, physical, cultural, earth surfaces, geomatics, historical, regional, spatial data handling.

Wright State University, School of Graduate Studies, College of Science and Mathematics, Department of Biological Sciences, Dayton, OH 45435. Offers biological sciences (MS); environmental sciences (MS). *Degree requirements:* For master's, thesis optional. *Entrance requirements:* Additional exam requirements/recommendations for international students: Required—TOEFL.

Wright State University, School of Graduate Studies, College of Science and Mathematics, Department of Chemistry, Dayton, OH 45435. Offers chemistry (MS); environmental sciences (MS). Part-time and evening/weekend programs available. *Degree requirements:* For master's, oral defense of thesis, seminar. *Entrance requirements:* Additional exam requirements/recommendations for international students: Required—TOEFL. *Faculty research:* Polymer synthesis and characterization, laser kinetics, organic and inorganic synthesis, analytical and environmental chemistry.

Wright State University, School of Graduate Studies, College of Science and Mathematics, Program in Environmental Sciences, Dayton, OH 45435. Offers PhD.

Yale University, Graduate School of Arts and Sciences, Department of Forestry and Environmental Studies, New Haven, CT 06520. Offers environmental sciences (PhD); forestry (PhD). *Degree requirements:* For doctorate, thesis/dissertation. *Entrance requirements:* For doctorate, GRE General Test.

Yale University, School of Forestry and Environmental Studies, New Haven, CT 06511. Offers MEM, MES, MF, MFS, PhD, JD/MEM, MBA/MEM, MBA/MF, MEM/M Arch, MEM/MA, MEM/MPH, MF/MA. *Accreditation:* SAF (one or more programs are accredited). Part-time programs available. *Faculty:* 49 full-time, 40 part-time/adjunct. *Students:* 301 full-time, 22 part-time; includes 60 minority (5 Black or African American, non-Hispanic/Latino; 7 American Indian or Alaska Native, non-Hispanic/Latino; 29 Asian, non-Hispanic/Latino; 19 Hispanic/Latino). Average age 28. 590 applicants, 163 enrolled. In 2012, 139 master's awarded. Terminal master's awarded for partial completion of doctoral program. *Degree requirements:* For master's, thesis (for some programs); for doctorate, thesis/dissertation. *Entrance requirements:* For master's, GRE General Test, GMAT or LSAT; for doctorate, GRE General Test. Additional exam requirements/recommendations for international students: Required—TOEFL (minimum score 600 paper-based, 100 iBT) or IELTS (minimum score of 7.0). *Application deadline:* For fall admission, 12/15 priority date for domestic students, 12/15 for international students. Application fee: $80. Electronic applications accepted. *Expenses:* Contact institution. *Financial support:* In 2012–13, 252 students received support. Fellowships, research assistantships, teaching assistantships, career-related internships or fieldwork, Federal Work-Study, institutionally sponsored loans, scholarships/grants, and health care benefits available. Support available to part-time students. Financial award application deadline: 2/15; financial award applicants required to submit FAFSA. *Faculty research:* Environmental policy, social ecology, industrial environmental management, forestry, environmental health, urban ecology, water science policy. *Unit head:* Peter Crane, Dean, School of Forestry and Environmental Studies, 203-432-5109, Fax: 203-432-3051. *Application contact:* Danielle Curtis, Director of Enrollment Management (Admissions and Financial Aid), 203-432-5106, Fax: 203-432-5528, E-mail: fesinfo@yale.edu. Website: http://environment.yale.edu.

Marine Affairs

American Public University System, AMU/APU Graduate Programs, Charles Town, WV 25414. Offers accounting (MBA, MS); criminal justice (MA), including business administration, emergency and disaster management, general (MA, MS); educational leadership (M Ed); emergency and disaster management (MA); entrepreneurship (MBA); environmental policy and management (MS), including environmental planning, environmental sustainability, fish and wildlife management, general (MA, MS), global environmental management; finance (MBA); general (MBA); global business management (MBA); history (MA), including American history, ancient and classical history, European history, global history, public history; homeland security (MA), including business administration, counter-terrorism studies, criminal justice, cyber, emergency management and public health, intelligence studies, transportation security; homeland security resource allocation (MBA); humanities (MA); information technology (MS), including digital forensics, enterprise software development, information assurance and security, IT project management; information technology management (MBA); intelligence studies (MA), including criminal intelligence, cyber, general (MA, MS), homeland security, intelligence analysis, intelligence collection, intelligence management, intelligence operations, terrorism studies; international relations and conflict resolution (MA), including comparative and security issues, conflict resolution, international and transnational security issues, peacekeeping; legal studies (MA); management (MA), including defense management, general (MA, MS), human resource management, organizational leadership, public administration; marketing (MBA); military history (MA), including American military history, American Revolution, civil war, war since 1945, World War II; military studies (MA), including joint warfare, strategic leadership; national security studies (MA), including general (MA, MS), homeland security, regional security studies, security and intelligence analysis, terrorism studies; nonprofit management (MBA); political science (MA), including American politics and government, comparative government and development, general (MA, MS), international relations, public policy; psychology (MA), including general (MA,

Peterson's Graduate Programs in the Physical Sciences, Mathematics, Agricultural Sciences, the Environment & Natural Resources 2014

www.petersonsbooks.com **487**

MS), maritime engineering management, reverse logistics management; public administration (MPA), including disaster management, environmental policy, health policy, human resources, national security, organizational management, security management; public health (MPH); reverse logistics management (MA); school counseling (M Ed); security management (MA); space studies (MS), including aerospace science, general (MA, MS), planetary science; sports and health sciences (MS); sports management (MS), including coaching theory and strategy, general (MA, MS), sports administration; teaching (M Ed), including curriculum and instruction for elementary teachers, elementary reading, English language learners, instructional leadership, online learning, special education; transportation and logistics management (MA), including general (MA, MS), maritime engineering management, reverse logistics management. Programs offered via distance learning only. Part-time and evening/weekend programs available. Postbaccalaureate distance learning degree programs offered (no on-campus study). *Faculty:* 439 full-time (246 women), 1,493 part-time/adjunct (708 women). *Students:* 611 full-time (284 women), 11,732 part-time (4,476 women); includes 3,985 minority (2,112 Black or African American, non-Hispanic/Latino; 103 American Indian or Alaska Native, non-Hispanic/Latino; 336 Asian, non-Hispanic/Latino; 915 Hispanic/Latino; 113 Native Hawaiian or other Pacific Islander, non-Hispanic/Latino; 406 Two or more races, non-Hispanic/Latino), 167 international. Average age 36. In 2012, 2,761 master's awarded. *Degree requirements:* For master's, comprehensive exam or practicum. *Entrance requirements:* For master's, official transcript showing earned bachelor's degree from institution accredited by recognized accrediting body. Additional exam requirements/recommendations for international students: Required—TOEFL (minimum score 550 paper-based), IELTS (minimum score 6.5). *Application deadline:* Applications are processed on a rolling basis. Application fee: $0. Electronic applications accepted. *Financial support:* Applicants required to submit FAFSA. *Faculty research:* Military history, criminal justice, management performance, national security. *Unit head:* Dr. Karan Powell, Executive Vice President and Provost, 877-468-6268, Fax: 304-724-3780. *Application contact:* Terry Grant, Vice President of Enrollment Management, 877-468-6268, Fax: 304-724-3780, E-mail: info@apus.edu. Website: http://www.apus.edu.

Dalhousie University, Faculty of Management, Marine Affairs Program, Halifax, NS B3H 3J5, Canada. Offers MMM. *Degree requirements:* For master's, project. *Entrance requirements:* For master's, minimum GPA of 3.0. Additional exam requirements/recommendations for international students: Required—TOEFL, IELTS, CANTEST, CAEL, or Michigan English Language Assessment Battery. Electronic applications accepted. *Faculty research:* Coastal zone management, sea use planning, development of non-living resources, protection and preservation of the coastal and marine environment, marine law and policy, fisheries management, maritime transport, conflict management.

Louisiana State University and Agricultural and Mechanical College, Graduate School, School of the Coast and Environment, Department of Oceanography and Coastal Sciences, Baton Rouge, LA 70803. Offers MS, PhD. *Faculty:* 25 full-time (3 women), 2 part-time/adjunct (0 women). *Students:* 51 full-time (24 women), 11 part-time (6 women); includes 1 minority (Hispanic/Latino), 11 international. Average age 29. 39 applicants, 33% accepted, 12 enrolled. In 2012, 7 master's, 9 doctorates awarded. *Degree requirements:* For master's, thesis (for some programs); for doctorate, one foreign language, thesis/dissertation. *Entrance requirements:* For master's, GRE General Test, minimum GPA of 3.0; for doctorate, GRE General Test, MA or MS, minimum GPA of 3.0. Additional exam requirements/recommendations for international students: Required—TOEFL (minimum score 550 paper-based; 79 iBT) or IELTS (minimum score 6.5). *Application deadline:* For fall admission, 1/25 priority date for domestic students, 5/15 for international students; for spring admission, 10/15 for international students. Applications are processed on a rolling basis. Application fee: $50 ($70 for international students). *Financial support:* In 2012–13, 59 students received support, including 6 fellowships (averaging $37,644 per year), 46 research assistantships with full and partial tuition reimbursements available (averaging $19,426 per year); teaching assistantships with full and partial tuition reimbursements available, Federal Work-Study, institutionally sponsored loans, scholarships/grants, health care benefits, tuition waivers (full and partial), and unspecified assistantships also available. Support available to part-time students. Financial award applicants required to submit FAFSA. *Faculty research:* Physical and geological oceanography, wetland sustainability and restoration fisheries, coastal ecology and biogeochemistry. *Total annual research expenditures:* $9.2 million. *Unit head:* Dr. Donald Baltz, Chair, 225-578-6512, Fax: 225-578-6513, E-mail: dbaltz@lsu.edu. *Application contact:* Dr. Charles Lindau, Graduate Adviser, 225-578-8766, Fax: 225-578-5328, E-mail: clinda1@lsu.edu. Website: http://www.oceanography.lsu.edu/.

Memorial University of Newfoundland, School of Graduate Studies, Department of Sociology, St. John's, NL A1C 5S7, Canada. Offers gender (PhD); maritime sociology (PhD); sociology (M Phil, MA); work and development (PhD). Part-time programs available. *Degree requirements:* For master's, comprehensive exam, thesis optional, program journal (M Phil); for doctorate, one foreign language, comprehensive exam, thesis/dissertation, oral defense of thesis. *Entrance requirements:* For master's, 2nd class degree from university of recognized standing in area of study; for doctorate, MA, M Phil, or equivalent. Electronic applications accepted. *Faculty research:* Work and development, gender, maritime sociology.

Memorial University of Newfoundland, School of Graduate Studies, Interdisciplinary Program in Marine Studies, St. John's, NL A1C 5S7, Canada. Offers fisheries resource management (MMS, Advanced Diploma). Part-time programs available. *Degree requirements:* For master's, report. *Entrance requirements:* For master's and Advanced Diploma, high 2nd class degree from a recognized university. *Faculty research:* Biological, ecological and oceanographic aspects of world fisheries; economics; political science; sociology.

Nova Southeastern University, Oceanographic Center, Fort Lauderdale, FL 33314-7796. Offers biological sciences (MS); coastal zone management (MS); marine and coastal studies (MA); marine biology (MS); marine biology and oceanography (PhD), including marine biology, oceanography; marine environmental sciences (MS). Part-time and evening/weekend programs available. *Faculty:* 13 full-time (1 woman), 20 part-time/adjunct (5 women). *Students:* 123 full-time (84 women), 153 part-time (96 women); includes 36 minority (7 Black or African American, non-Hispanic/Latino; 1 American Indian or Alaska Native, non-Hispanic/Latino; 5 Asian, non-Hispanic/Latino; 18 Hispanic/Latino; 5 Two or more races, non-Hispanic/Latino), 6 international. Average age 29. 98 applicants, 81% accepted, 48 enrolled. In 2012, 26 master's, 1 doctorate awarded. *Degree requirements:* For master's, thesis; for doctorate, comprehensive exam, thesis/dissertation, departmental qualifying exam. *Entrance requirements:* For master's, GRE General Test, 3 letters of recommendation, BS/BA in natural science (for marine biology program), BS/BA in biology (for biological sciences program), minor in the natural sciences or equivalent (for coastal zone management and marine environmental sciences); for doctorate, GRE General Test, master's degree. Additional exam requirements/recommendations for international students: Required—TOEFL (minimum score 550 paper-based). *Application deadline:* Applications are processed on a rolling basis. Application fee: $50. *Expenses:* Contact institution. *Financial support:* In 2012–13, 2 fellowships with full and partial tuition reimbursements (averaging $16,300 per year), 50 research assistantships with full and partial tuition reimbursements (averaging $19,000 per year) were awarded; teaching assistantships, career-related internships or fieldwork, Federal Work-Study, scholarships/grants, health care benefits, tuition waivers (full and partial), and unspecified assistantships also available. Support available to part-time students. Financial award applicants required to submit FAFSA. *Faculty research:* Physical, geological, chemical, and biological oceanography. *Unit head:* Dr. Richard Dodge, Dean, 954-262-3600, Fax: 954-262-4020, E-mail: dodge@nsu.nova.edu. *Application contact:* Dr. Richard Spieler, Associate Dean of Academic Programs, 954-262-3600, Fax: 954-262-4020, E-mail: spieler@nova.edu. Website: http://www.nova.edu/ocean/.

Old Dominion University, College of Business and Public Administration, MBA Program, Norfolk, VA 23529. Offers business and economic forecasting (MBA); financial analysis and valuation (MBA); health sciences administration (MBA); information technology and enterprise integration (MBA); international business (MBA); maritime and port management (MBA); public administration (MBA). *Accreditation:* AACSB. Part-time and evening/weekend programs available. *Faculty:* 83 full-time (19 women), 5 part-time/adjunct (2 women). *Students:* 35 full-time (19 women), 96 part-time (34 women); includes 21 minority (9 Black or African American, non-Hispanic/Latino; 1 American Indian or Alaska Native, non-Hispanic/Latino; 6 Asian, non-Hispanic/Latino; 2 Hispanic/Latino; 1 Native Hawaiian or other Pacific Islander, non-Hispanic/Latino; 2 Two or more races, non-Hispanic/Latino), 14 international. Average age 30. 177 applicants, 43% accepted, 53 enrolled. In 2012, 98 master's awarded. *Entrance requirements:* For master's, GMAT, GRE, letter of reference, resume, coursework in calculus, essay. Additional exam requirements/recommendations for international students: Required—TOEFL (minimum score 550 paper-based; 80 iBT). *Application deadline:* For fall admission, 6/1 priority date for domestic students, 4/15 for international students; for spring admission, 11/1 priority date for domestic students, 10/1 for international students. Applications are processed on a rolling basis. Application fee: $50. Electronic applications accepted. *Expenses:* Tuition, state resident: full-time $9432; part-time $393 per credit hour. Tuition, nonresident: full-time $23,928; part-time $997 per credit hour. *Required fees:* $59 per semester. One-time fee: $50. *Financial support:* In 2012–13, 44 students received support, including 90 research assistantships with partial tuition reimbursements available (averaging $8,900 per year); career-related internships or fieldwork, scholarships/grants, and unspecified assistantships also available. Support available to part-time students. Financial award application deadline: 2/15; financial award applicants required to submit FAFSA. *Faculty research:* International business, buyer behavior, financial markets, strategy, operations research, maritime and transportation economics. *Unit head:* Dr. Larry Filer, Graduate Program Director, 757-683-3585, Fax: 757-683-5750, E-mail: mbainfo@odu.edu. *Application contact:* Shanna Wood, MBA Program Manager, 757-683-3585, Fax: 757-683-5750, E-mail: mbainfo@odu.edu. Website: http://bpa.odu.edu/mba/.

Oregon State University, College of Earth, Ocean, and Atmospheric Sciences, Program in Marine Resource Management, Corvallis, OR 97331. Offers MA, MS, Certificate. *Students:* 23 full-time (15 women), 3 part-time (1 woman); includes 3 minority (2 Asian, non-Hispanic/Latino; 1 Hispanic/Latino), 2 international. Average age 28. 47 applicants, 30% accepted, 10 enrolled. In 2012, 10 master's awarded. *Degree requirements:* For master's, thesis optional. *Entrance requirements:* For master's, GRE General Test, minimum GPA of 3.0 in last 90 hours of course work. Additional exam requirements/recommendations for international students: Required—TOEFL. *Application deadline:* For fall admission, 2/1 priority date for domestic students. Applications are processed on a rolling basis. Application fee: $50. *Expenses:* Tuition, state resident: full-time $11,367; part-time $421 per credit hour. Tuition, nonresident: full-time $18,279;

part-time $677 per credit hour. *Required fees:* $1478. One-time fee: $300 full-time. Tuition and fees vary according to course load and program. *Financial support:* Fellowships, research assistantships, teaching assistantships, career-related internships or fieldwork, Federal Work-Study, and institutionally sponsored loans available. Support available to part-time students. Financial award application deadline: 2/1. *Faculty research:* Ocean and coastal resources, fisheries resources, marine pollution, marine recreation and tourism. *Unit head:* Dr. Flaxen Conway, Director/Professor, 541-737-1339, Fax: 541-737-2540, E-mail: fconway@coas.oregonstate.edu. *Application contact:* Anna Pakenham, Assistant Director, 541-737-8637, Fax: 541-737-2064, E-mail: apakenham@coas.oregonstate.edu.

Stevens Institute of Technology, Graduate School, Charles V. Schaefer Jr. School of Engineering, Department of Civil, Environmental, and Ocean Engineering, Program in Maritime Systems, Hoboken, NJ 07030. Offers MS.

Stony Brook University, State University of New York, Graduate School, School of Marine and Atmospheric Sciences, Program in Marine Conservation and Policy, Stony Brook, NY 11794. Offers MA. *Students:* 11 full-time (9 women), 8 part-time (4 women); includes 1 minority (Hispanic/Latino), 2 international. 25 applicants, 76% accepted, 12 enrolled. In 2012, 6 master's awarded. *Degree requirements:* For master's, capstone project or internship. *Entrance requirements:* For master's, GRE, minimum GPA of 3.0; one semester of college-level biology and three additional semester courses in college-level math or science; personal statement; 3 letters of reference; official transcripts. *Application deadline:* For fall admission, 1/15 for domestic students. Electronic applications accepted. *Expenses:* Tuition, state resident: full-time $9370. Tuition, nonresident: full-time $16,680. *Required fees:* $1214. *Unit head:* Dr. Minghua Zhang, Director, 631-632-8781, Fax: 631-632-8915, E-mail: minghua.zhang@stonybrook.edu. *Application contact:* Dr. Lesley Thorne, Assistant Director, 631-632-5117, Fax: 631-632-8915, E-mail: lesley.thorne@stonybrook.edu. Website: http://somas.stonybrook.edu/MCP/.

Université du Québec à Rimouski, Graduate Programs, Program in Management of Marine Resources, Rimouski, QC G5L 3A1, Canada. Offers M Sc, Diploma. Part-time programs available. *Students:* 29 full-time, 2 part-time, 18 international. In 2012, 18 master's awarded. *Entrance requirements:* For master's, appropriate bachelor's degree, proficiency in French. *Application deadline:* For fall admission, 5/1 priority date for domestic students. Application fee: $50. *Financial support:* Fellowships, research assistantships, and teaching assistantships available. *Unit head:* James Wilson, Director, 418-724-1544, Fax: 418-724-1525, E-mail: james_wilson@uqar.ca. *Application contact:* Jacques d'Astous, Conseiller en Recrutement et en Communication, 800-463-4712, Fax: 418-724-1869, E-mail: jacques_dastous@uqar.ca.

University of Delaware, College of Earth, Ocean, and Environment, School of Marine Science and Policy, Newark, DE 19716. Offers marine policy (MMP); marine studies (MS, PhD), including marine biosciences, oceanography, physical ocean science and engineering; oceanography (PhD).

University of Maine, Graduate School, College of Natural Sciences, Forestry, and Agriculture, School of Marine Sciences, Orono, ME 04469. Offers marine biology (MS, PhD); marine policy (MS); oceanography (MS, PhD). Part-time programs available. *Faculty:* 40 full-time (8 women), 60 part-time/adjunct (16 women). *Students:* 46 full-time (24 women), 16 part-time (5 women); includes 1 minority (Hispanic/Latino), 7 international. Average age 29. 71 applicants, 15% accepted, 10 enrolled. In 2012, 12 master's, 3 doctorates awarded. *Degree requirements:* For master's, thesis; for doctorate, comprehensive exam, thesis/dissertation. *Entrance requirements:* For master's and doctorate, GRE General Test. Additional exam requirements/recommendations for international students: Required—TOEFL. *Application deadline:* For fall admission, 2/1 priority date for domestic students. Applications are processed on a rolling basis. Application fee: $65. Electronic applications accepted. *Financial support:* In 2012–13, 41 research assistantships with tuition reimbursements (averaging $16,713 per year), 6 teaching assistantships with tuition reimbursements (averaging $13,600 per year) were awarded; career-related internships or fieldwork, Federal Work-Study, and tuition waivers (full and partial) also available. Support available to part-time students. Financial award application deadline: 3/1. *Faculty research:* Coastal processes, microbial ecology, crustacean systematics. *Total annual research expenditures:* $2 million. *Unit head:* Dr. Peter Jumars, Director, 207-581-3321, Fax: 207-581-4388. *Application contact:* Scott G. Delcourt, Associate Dean of the Graduate School, 207-581-3291, Fax: 207-581-3232, E-mail: graduate@maine.edu. Website: http://www.umaine.edu/marine/.

University of Massachusetts Dartmouth, Graduate School, School of Marine Science and Technology, North Dartmouth, MA 02747-2300. Offers coastal and ocean administration science and technology (MS); marine science (MS, PhD). Part-time programs available. *Faculty:* 14 full-time (1 woman), 1 part-time/adjunct (0 women). *Students:* 32 full-time (14 women), 26 part-time (7 women); includes 1 minority (Hispanic/Latino), 15 international. Average age 32. 44 applicants, 73% accepted, 8 enrolled. In 2012, 7 master's, 1 doctorate awarded. Terminal master's awarded for partial completion of doctoral program. *Degree requirements:* For master's, thesis or alternative; for doctorate, comprehensive exam, thesis/dissertation. *Entrance requirements:* For master's and doctorate, GRE, resume, 3 letters of recommendation, official transcripts. Additional exam requirements/recommendations for international students: Required—TOEFL (minimum score 577 paper-based; 91 iBT). *Application deadline:* For fall admission, 2/15 priority date for domestic students, 1/15 for international students; for spring admission, 11/15 priority date for domestic students, 10/15 for international students. Applications are processed on a rolling basis. Application fee: $60. Electronic applications accepted. *Expenses:* Tuition, state resident: part-time $86.29 per credit. Tuition, nonresident: part-time $337.46 per credit. *Required fees:* $631.03 per credit. Tuition and fees vary according to course load and reciprocity agreements. *Financial support:* In 2012–13, 1 fellowship with full tuition reimbursement (averaging $30,000 per year), 30 research assistantships with full and partial tuition reimbursements (averaging $6,600 per year) were awarded. Financial award application deadline: 3/1; financial award applicants required to submit FAFSA. *Faculty research:* Storm-forced and internal wave dynamics, estuarine circulation, marine biogeochemical cycles, spatial distributions of marine fishes and invertebrates, plankton communities. *Total annual research expenditures:* $10.5 million. *Unit head:* Louis Goodman, Associate Dean, School of Marine Science and Technology, 508-910-6375, Fax: 508-910-6371, E-mail: lgoodman@umassd.edu. *Application contact:* Steven Briggs, Director of Marketing and Recruitment, 508-999-8604, Fax: 508-999-8183, E-mail: graduate@umassd.edu. Website: http://www.umassd.edu/smast.

University of Miami, Graduate School, Rosenstiel School of Marine and Atmospheric Science, Division of Marine Affairs and Policy, Coral Gables, FL 33124. Offers MA, MS, JD/MA. Part-time programs available. *Degree requirements:* For master's, comprehensive exam, thesis (for some programs), internship, paper. *Entrance requirements:* For master's, GRE General Test. Additional exam requirements/recommendations for international students: Required—TOEFL (minimum score 550 paper-based). Electronic applications accepted.

University of Rhode Island, Graduate School, College of the Environment and Life Sciences, Department of Marine Affairs, Kingston, RI 02881. Offers MA, MESM, MMA, PhD, JD/MMA. Part-time programs available. *Faculty:* 6 full-time (1 woman). *Students:* 23 full-time (15 women), 7 part-time (2 women), 6 international. In 2012, 16 master's, 2 doctorates awarded. *Degree requirements:* For master's, comprehensive exam (for some programs), thesis optional; for doctorate, comprehensive exam, thesis/dissertation. *Entrance requirements:* For master's, GRE (for MA), 2 letters of recommendation (for MMA); for doctorate, GRE, 2 letters of recommendation, writing sample. Additional exam requirements/recommendations for international students: Required—TOEFL (minimum score 550 paper-based). *Application deadline:* For fall admission, 4/7 for domestic students, 2/1 for international students. Application fee: $65. Electronic applications accepted. *Expenses:* Tuition, state resident: full-time $11,532; part-time $641 per credit. Tuition, nonresident: full-time $23,606; part-time $1311 per credit. *Required fees:* $1388; $36 per credit. $35 per semester. One-time fee: $130. *Financial support:* In 2012–13, 1 research assistantship with full tuition reimbursement (averaging $16,265 per year), 1 teaching assistantship with full and partial tuition reimbursement (averaging $7,672 per year) were awarded. Financial award application deadline: 2/1; financial award applicants required to submit FAFSA. *Faculty research:* Assessing change in coastal ecosystems and its impact to society. *Unit head:* Dr. Robert Thompson, Chair, 401-874-4485, Fax: 401-874-2156, E-mail: rob@uri.edu. Website: http://cels.uri.edu/maf/.

University of San Diego, College of Arts and Sciences, Program in Marine Science, San Diego, CA 92110-2492. Offers MS. Part-time programs available. *Faculty:* 4 full-time (1 woman). *Students:* 8 full-time (4 women), 12 part-time (10 women); includes 6 minority (1 Black or African American, non-Hispanic/Latino; 2 Hispanic/Latino; 3 Two or more races, non-Hispanic/Latino). Average age 27. 28 applicants, 21% accepted, 2 enrolled. In 2012, 2 master's awarded. *Degree requirements:* For master's, thesis. *Entrance requirements:* For master's, GRE General Test, minimum GPA of 3.0, 1 semester of biology with lab, 1 year of chemistry with lab, 1 year of physics with lab, 1 semester of calculus. Additional exam requirements/recommendations for international students: Required—TOEFL (minimum score 580 paper-based; 83 iBT), TWE. *Application deadline:* For fall admission, 4/1 for domestic and international students. Applications are processed on a rolling basis. Application fee: $45. Electronic applications accepted. *Expenses: Tuition:* Full-time $23,040; part-time $1280 per unit. *Required fees:* $270. Full-time tuition and fees vary according to course load and degree level. *Financial support:* In 2012–13, 13 students received support. Career-related internships or fieldwork, Federal Work-Study, institutionally sponsored loans, and unspecified assistantships available. Support available to part-time students. Financial award application deadline: 4/1; financial award applicants required to submit FAFSA. *Faculty research:* Marine ecology, environmental geology and geochemistry, climatology, physiological ecology, fisheries and aquaculture. *Unit head:* Dr. Ronald S. Kaufmann, Director, 619-260-4795, Fax: 619-260-6874, E-mail: andrewsk@sandiego.edu. *Application contact:* Monica Mahon, Associate Director of Graduate Admissions, 619-260-4524, Fax: 619-260-4158, E-mail: grads@sandiego.edu. Website: http://www.sandiego.edu/cas/marine_science_ms/.

University of Washington, Graduate School, College of the Environment, School of Marine and Environmental Affairs, Seattle, WA 98195. Offers MMA, Graduate Certificate. *Degree requirements:* For master's, thesis. *Entrance requirements:* For master's, GRE General Test, minimum GPA of 3.0. Additional exam requirements/recommendations for international students: Required—TOEFL. Electronic applications accepted. *Faculty research:* Marine pollution, port authorities, fisheries management, global climate change, marine environmental protection.

University of West Florida, College of Arts and Sciences: Sciences, School of Allied Health and Life Sciences, Department of Biology, Pensacola, FL 32514-

5750. Offers biological chemistry (MS); biology (MS); biology education (MST); biotechnology (MS); coastal zone studies (MS); environmental biology (MS). *Degree requirements:* For master's, thesis. *Entrance requirements:* For master's, GRE (minimum score: verbal 450, quantitative 550), official transcripts; BS in biology or related field; letter of interest; relevant past experience; three letters of recommendation from individuals who can evaluate applicant's academic ability. Additional exam requirements/recommendations for international students: Required—TOEFL (minimum score 550 paper-based).

490 www.petersonsbooks.com

Peterson's Graduate Programs in the Physical Sciences, Mathematics, Agricultural Sciences, the Environment & Natural Resources 2014

ADELPHI UNIVERSITY

College of the Arts and Sciences
Program in Environmental Studies

Program of Study

The M.S. in Environmental Studies is an interdisciplinary program that offers students a firm grounding in issues at the interface of human activity and the environment. The program has an active faculty with expertise in diverse disciplines, including anthropology, biology, chemistry, earth science, physics, and political science. Small class sizes, internship and research opportunities, and the potential to develop marketable expertise in areas such as geographic information systems and Occupational Safety and Health Administration (OSHA) certification are also features of the program.

The M.S. in Environmental Studies provides opportunities to study abroad in Australia with independent research on the Great Barrier Reef and exploration of the coastal and upland rainforests of Queensland. Closer to home, students investigate marine conservation and other environmental issues specific to the tropics in the U.S. Virgin Islands. Additional opportunities can be arranged in concert with undergraduate research investigations by the Department of Anthropology and Sociology in Alaska and Greece.

Research leading to an M.S. in Environmental Studies thesis is field-based and collaborative, with a local focus on the South Shore Estuary Reserve of Long Island. This local research has global applications with respect to environmental pollution, climate change and fisheries management. There is a strong record of student research presentations at national and international conferences, allowing students to develop career networks with other research professionals.

Students with graduate assistantships gain valuable practical experience working on research projects in faculty laboratories and as teaching assistants in undergraduate courses.

The curriculum comprises concentration courses (21–24 credits), courses from outside the concentration designed to add perspective and breadth to the experience (6-credit minimum), and additional advanced offerings (3-credit minimum). Up to 8 credits may be taken in environmentally relevant course work outside the program in consultation with an adviser. Concentration courses focus on directed research, fieldwork, and electives. Advanced offerings include guided or thesis research, a graduate seminar, and an internship option. The environmental studies program works with its graduate students to find internships that match their professional interests and provide a challenging and rewarding experience.

The M.S. in Environmental Studies program offers several options:

- **Global physical environment track:** This concentration involves knowledge of the physical, climatic, and abiotic resources of the world.

- **Global human environment track:** Global human environment studies the complex biological and cultural interactions of human populations through time, within their varied environmental and geographic contexts.

- **Global human environment–environment and health track:** Environmental health is a recently defined area of study that includes diverse fields such as toxicology and ecotoxicology, disease ecology and epidemiology.

- **Global human environment–business and environmental economics track:** Environmental policy makers must have a solid knowledge of financial and management arguments to persuasively influence environmental decision making.

- **Specialization in education/earth science certification:** Students interested in courses for environmental education certification in earth science should contact the department.

Research Facilities

The University's primary research holdings are at Swirbul Library and include 603,000 volumes (including bound periodicals and government publications); 786,000 items in microformats; 35,000 audiovisual items; and online access to more than 80,000 e-book titles, 76,000 electronic journal titles, and 265 research databases.

Financial Aid

The program offers a number of stipends and financial assistance awards to teaching and research assistants on a yearly basis. Further opportunities for financial support over the course of every academic year, including summers, are offered through the research projects and activities of faculty members.

Cost of Study

For the 2013–14 academic year, the tuition rate is $1,005 per credit. University fees range from $330 to $575 per semester.

Living and Housing Costs

The University assists single and married students in finding suitable accommodations whenever possible. The cost of living is dependent on location and number of rooms rented.

Location

Located in historic Garden City, New York, just 23 miles from Manhattan, Adelphi's 75-acre suburban campus is known for the beauty of its landscape and architecture. The campus is a short walk from the Long Island Rail Road and is convenient to New York's major airports and several major highways. Off-campus centers are located in Manhattan, Poughkeepsie, and Suffolk County.

The University and The College

Founded in 1896, Adelphi is a fully accredited, private university with nearly 8,000 undergraduate, graduate, and returning-adult students in the arts and sciences, business, clinical psychology, education, health care, nursing, and social work. Students come from forty states and forty-four countries. The *Fiske Guide to Colleges* has recognized Adelphi as a Best Buy in higher education for the eighth straight year. The University is one of only twenty private institutions in the nation to earn this recognition.

Mindful of the cultural inheritance of the past, the College of Arts and Sciences encompasses those realms of inquiry that have characterized the modern pursuit of knowledge. The faculty members of the College place a high priority on students' intellectual development in and out of the classroom and structure programs to foster that growth. Students analyze original research and other creative work, develop firsthand facility with creative and research methodologies,

Peterson's Graduate Programs in the Physical Sciences, Mathematics, Agricultural Sciences, the Environment & Natural Resources 2014

www.petersonsbooks.com 491

undertake collaborative work with peers and mentors, engage in serious internships, and hone communicative skills.

Applying

Students should have a bachelor's degree in environmental studies or a related field and a demonstrated promise of successful achievement in the field. A student must submit a completed application, a $50 application fee, and official college transcripts. For more information, students should contact the graduate coordinator.

Correspondence and Information

Office of Graduate Admissions
Department of Environmental Sciences
Beth Christensen, Associate Professor and Director
College of Arts and Sciences
Science Building, Room 220
One South Avenue
Adelphi University
Garden City, New York 11530
United States
Phone: 516-877-4174
Fax: 516-877-4485
E-mail: christensen@adelphi.edu
Website: http://academics.adelphi.edu/artsci/env/graduate-environmental-studies.php

THE FACULTY AND THEIR RESEARCH

Anagnostis Agelarakis, Ph.D., Columbia University. Physical anthropology, anthropological archaeology, ethnohistory, environmental studies.

Beth Christensen, Ph.D., University of South Carolina. Climate and sea level change, southern ocean paleoceanography, reef sediments, New Jersey margin geology, influence of African climate on hominid evolution.

Jonna Coombs, associate professor and graduate coordinator; Ph.D., Pennsylvania State University. Environmental studies program, biology, bioremediation.

Jessica Dutton, assistant professor, environmental studies program; Ph.D., Stony Brook University. Guided research metals, toxicology.

John P. Dooher, professor of physics; Ph.D., Stevens Institute of Technology. Physics, electromagnetic theory, biomass gasification, engineering thermodynamics and kinetic theory, energy utilization.

Matthias Foellmer, associate professor, biology; Ph.D., Concordia University, Montreal. Behavioral ecology, mating systems in spiders, salt marsh community ecology, biostatistics.

Gus Kalogrias, adjunct professor; M.S., Polytechnic University. Electric utility: transmission, distribution, electric design, and operations.

Robert Lippman, visiting professor of chemistry; Ph.D., Adelphi University. Safety, managing hazardous materials, environmental impact of hazardous materials.

Matthew Sisk, instructor; Ph.D., Stony Brook University. Geographic information systems, paleolithic archaeology, human evolution.

Andrea Ward, associate professor, biology; Ph.D., University of Massachusetts, Amherst. Functional morphology in fishes, comparative vertebrate anatomy, evolution and development.

Bryan Wygal, assistant professor of anthropology and sociology; Ph.D., University of Nevada, Reno. Human ecology, New World and subarctic archaeology, peopling of the Americas, prehistoric technology, field methods.

Environmental studies students perform field-based research in such areas as the South Shore Estuary Reserve on Long Island.

Research opportunities include study abroad in Australia, research on the Great Barrier Reef, and exploration of the coastal and upland rainforests of Queensland.

492 www.petersonsbooks.com

Peterson's Graduate Programs in the Physical Sciences, Mathematics, Agricultural Sciences, the Environment & Natural Resources 2014

Section 10
Natural Resources

This section contains a directory of institutions offering graduate work in natural resources. Additional information about programs listed in the directory may be obtained by writing directly to the dean of a graduate school or chair of a department at the address given in the directory.

For programs offering related work, see also in this book *Environmental Sciences and Management* and *Meteorology and Atmospheric Sciences*. In the other guides in this series:

Graduate Programs in the Humanities, Arts & Social Sciences

See *Architecture (Landscape Architecture)* and *Public, Regional, and Industrial Affairs*

Graduate Programs in the Biological/Biomedical Sciences & Health-Related Medical Professions

See *Biological and Biomedical Sciences; Botany and Plant Biology; Ecology, Environmental Biology, and Evolutionary Biology; Entomology; Genetics, Developmental Biology, and Reproductive Biology;* *Nutrition; Pathology and Pathobiology; Pharmacology and Toxicology; Physiology; Veterinary Medicine and Sciences;* and *Zoology*

Graduate Programs in Engineering & Applied Sciences

See *Agricultural Engineering and Bioengineering; Civil and Environmental Engineering; Geological, Mineral/Mining, and Petroleum Engineering; Management of Engineering and Technology;* and *Ocean Engineering*

CONTENTS

Program Directories

Fish, Game, and Wildlife Management

American Public University System, AMU/APU Graduate Programs, Charles Town, WV 25414. Offers accounting (MBA, MS); criminal justice (MA), including business administration, emergency and disaster management, general (MA, MS); educational leadership (M Ed); emergency and disaster management (MA); entrepreneurship (MBA); environmental policy and management (MS), including environmental planning, environmental sustainability, fish and wildlife management, general (MA, MS), global environmental management; finance (MBA); general (MBA); global business management (MBA); history (MA), including American history, ancient and classical history, European history, global history, public history; homeland security (MA), including business administration, counter-terrorism studies, criminal justice, cyber, emergency management and public health, intelligence studies, transportation security; homeland security resource allocation (MBA); humanities (MA); information technology (MS), including digital forensics, enterprise software development, information assurance and security, IT project management; information technology management (MBA); intelligence studies (MA), including criminal intelligence, cyber, general (MA, MS), homeland security, intelligence analysis, intelligence collection, intelligence management, intelligence operations, terrorism studies; international relations and conflict resolution (MA), including comparative and security issues, conflict resolution, international and transnational security issues, peacekeeping; legal studies (MA); management (MA), including defense management, general (MA, MS), human resource management, organizational leadership, public administration; marketing (MBA); military history (MA), including American military history, American Revolution, civil war, war since 1945, World War II; military studies (MA), including joint warfare, strategic leadership; national security studies (MA), including general (MA, MS), homeland security, regional security studies, security and intelligence analysis, terrorism studies; nonprofit management (MBA); political science (MA), including American politics and government, comparative government and development, general (MA, MS), international relations, public policy; psychology (MA), including general (MA, MS), maritime engineering management, reverse logistics management; public administration (MPA), including disaster management, environmental policy, health policy, human resources, national security, organizational management, security management; public health (MPH); reverse logistics management (MA); school counseling (M Ed); security management (MA); space studies (MS), including aerospace science, general (MA, MS), planetary science; sports and health sciences (MS); sports management (MS), including coaching theory and strategy, general (MA, MS), sports administration; teaching (M Ed), including curriculum and instruction for elementary teachers, elementary reading, English language learners, instructional leadership, online learning, special education; transportation and logistics management (MA), including general (MA, MS), maritime engineering management, reverse logistics management. Programs offered via distance learning only. Part-time and evening/weekend programs available. Postbaccalaureate distance learning degree programs offered (no on-campus study). *Faculty:* 439 full-time (246 women), 1,493 part-time/adjunct (708 women). *Students:* 611 full-time (284 women), 11,732 part-time (4,476 women); includes 3,985 minority (2,112 Black or African American, non-Hispanic/Latino; 103 American Indian or Alaska Native, non-Hispanic/Latino; 336 Asian, non-Hispanic/Latino; 915 Hispanic/Latino; 113 Native Hawaiian or other Pacific Islander, non-Hispanic/Latino; 406 Two or more races, non-Hispanic/Latino), 167 international. Average age 36. In 2012, 2,761 master's awarded. *Degree requirements:* For master's, comprehensive exam or practicum. *Entrance requirements:* For master's, official transcript showing earned bachelor's degree from institution accredited by recognized accrediting body. Additional exam requirements/recommendations for international students: Required—TOEFL (minimum score 550 paper-based), IELTS (minimum score 6.5). *Application deadline:* Applications are processed on a rolling basis. Application fee: $0. Electronic applications accepted. *Financial support:* Applicants required to submit FAFSA. *Faculty research:* Military history, criminal justice, management performance, national security. *Unit head:* Dr. Karan Powell, Executive Vice President and Provost, 877-468-6268, Fax: 304-724-3780. *Application contact:* Terry Grant, Vice President of Enrollment Management, 877-468-6268, Fax: 304-724-3780, E-mail: info@apus.edu. Website: http://www.apus.edu.

Arkansas Tech University, College of Natural and Health Sciences, Russellville, AR 72801. Offers fisheries and wildlife biology (MS); health informatics (MS); nursing (MSN). Part-time programs available. *Students:* 10 full-time (8 women), 52 part-time (42 women); includes 4 minority (3 Black or African American, non-Hispanic/Latino; 1 American Indian or Alaska Native, non-Hispanic/Latino), 2 international. Average age 40. In 2012, 6 master's awarded. *Degree requirements:* For master's, thesis (for some programs), project. *Entrance requirements:* For master's, GRE General Test. Additional exam requirements/recommendations for international students: Required—TOEFL (minimum score 550 paper-based; 79 iBT), IELTS (minimum score 6). *Application deadline:* For fall admission, 3/1 priority date for domestic students, 5/1 for international students; for spring admission, 10/1 priority date for domestic students, 10/1 for international students. Applications are processed on a rolling basis. Application fee: $25 ($75 for international students). Electronic applications accepted. *Expenses:* Tuition, state resident: full-time $5160; part-time $215 per credit hour. Tuition, nonresident: full-time $10,320; part-time $430 per credit hour. *Required fees:* $399 per semester. Tuition and fees vary according to course load. *Financial support:* In 2012–13, research assistantships with full tuition reimbursements (averaging $4,800 per year), teaching assistantships with full tuition reimbursements (averaging $4,800 per year) were awarded; career-related internships or fieldwork, Federal Work-Study, scholarships/grants, health care benefits, and unspecified assistantships also available. Support available to part-time students. Financial award application deadline: 4/15; financial award applicants required to submit FAFSA. *Unit head:* Dr. Jeff Robertson, Dean, 479-968-0498, E-mail: jrobertson@atu.edu. *Application contact:* Dr. Mary B. Gunter, Dean of Graduate College, 479-968-0398, Fax: 479-964-0542, E-mail: gradcollege@atu.edu. Website: http://www.atu.edu/nhs/.

Auburn University, Graduate School, College of Agriculture, Department of Fisheries and Allied Aquacultures, Auburn University, AL 36849. Offers M Aq, MS, PhD. Part-time programs available. *Faculty:* 20 full-time (3 women). *Students:* 33 full-time (15 women), 53 part-time (24 women); includes 4 minority (1 Black or African American, non-Hispanic/Latino; 1 Asian, non-Hispanic/Latino; 2 Hispanic/Latino), 49 international. Average age 28. 48 applicants, 48% accepted, 19 enrolled. In 2012, 15 master's, 5 doctorates awarded. *Degree requirements:* For master's, thesis (for some programs); for doctorate, 2 foreign languages, thesis/dissertation. *Entrance requirements:* For master's and doctorate, GRE General Test. *Application deadline:* For fall admission, 7/7 for domestic students; for spring admission, 11/24 for domestic students. Applications are processed on a rolling basis. Application fee: $50 ($60 for international students). Electronic applications accepted. *Expenses:* Tuition, state resident: full-time $7866; part-time $437 per credit. Tuition, nonresident: full-time $23,598; part-time $1311 per credit. *Required fees:* $787 per semester. Tuition and fees vary according to degree level and program. *Financial support:* Fellowships, research assistantships, teaching assistantships, and Federal Work-Study available. Support available to part-time students. Financial award application deadline: 3/15; financial award applicants required to submit FAFSA. *Faculty research:* Channel catfish production; aquatic animal health; community and population ecology; pond management; production hatching, breeding and genetics. *Total annual research expenditures:* $8 million. *Unit head:* Dr. David B. Rouse, Head, 334-844-4786. *Application contact:* Dr. George Flowers, Dean of the Graduate School, 334-844-2125. Website: http://www.ag.auburn.edu/fish/.

Auburn University, Graduate School, School of Forestry and Wildlife Sciences, Auburn University, AL 36849. Offers forest economics (PhD); forestry (MS, PhD); natural resource conservation (MNR); wildlife sciences (MS, PhD). *Accreditation:* SAF. Part-time programs available. *Faculty:* 32 full-time (6 women), 2 part-time/adjunct (0 women). *Students:* 28 full-time (12 women), 36 part-time (15 women), 18 international. Average age 28. 28 applicants, 43% accepted, 10 enrolled. In 2012, 22 master's, 5 doctorates awarded. *Degree requirements:* For master's, thesis (MS); for doctorate, thesis/dissertation. *Entrance requirements:* For master's and doctorate, GRE General Test. *Application deadline:* For fall admission, 7/7 for domestic students; for spring admission, 11/24 for domestic students. Applications are processed on a rolling basis. Application fee: $50 ($60 for international students). Electronic applications accepted. *Expenses:* Tuition, state resident: full-time $7866; part-time $437 per credit. Tuition, nonresident: full-time $23,598; part-time $1311 per credit. *Required fees:* $787 per semester. Tuition and fees vary according to degree level and program. *Financial support:* Fellowships, research assistantships, teaching assistantships, and Federal Work-Study available. Support available to part-time students. Financial award application deadline: 3/15; financial award applicants required to submit FAFSA. *Faculty research:* Forest nursery management, silviculture and vegetation management, biological processes and ecological relationships, growth and yield of plantations and natural stands, urban forestry, forest taxation, law and policy. *Unit head:* Dr. James P. Shepard, Dean, 334-844-4000, Fax: 334-844-1084, E-mail: brinker@forestry.auburn.edu. *Application contact:* Dr. George Flowers, Dean of the Graduate School, 334-844-2125. Website: http://www.forestry.auburn.edu/.

Brigham Young University, Graduate Studies, College of Life Sciences, Department of Plant and Wildlife Sciences, Provo, UT 84602. Offers environmental science (MS); genetics and biotechnology (MS); wildlife and wildlands conservation (MS, PhD). *Faculty:* 24 full-time (1 woman), 2 part-time/adjunct (1 woman). *Students:* 47 full-time (18 women); includes 6 minority (3 Asian, non-Hispanic/Latino; 2 Hispanic/Latino; 1 Native Hawaiian or other Pacific Islander, non-Hispanic/Latino), 2 international. Average age 28. 29 applicants, 41% accepted, 9 enrolled. In 2012, 15 master's, 2 doctorates awarded. *Degree requirements:* For master's, thesis; for doctorate, comprehensive exam, thesis/dissertation, minimum GPA of 3.2, 54 hours (18 dissertation, 36 coursework). *Entrance requirements:* For master's, GRE General Test, minimum GPA of 3.2 during last 60 hours of course work; for doctorate, GRE, minimum GPA of 3.2. Additional exam requirements/recommendations for international students: Required—TOEFL (minimum score 580 paper-based; 85 iBT). *Application deadline:* 2/1 for domestic and international students. Applications are processed on a rolling basis. Application fee: $50. Electronic applications accepted. *Expenses: Tuition:* Full-time $5950; part-time $331 per credit hour. Tuition and fees vary according to program and student's religious affiliation. *Financial* *support:* In 2012–13, 47 students received support, including 64 research assistantships with partial tuition reimbursements available (averaging $17,840 per year), 52 teaching assistantships with partial tuition reimbursements available (averaging $17,840 per year); scholarships/grants and tuition waivers (partial) also available. Financial award application deadline: 2/1. *Faculty research:* Environmental science, plant genetics, plant ecology, plant nutrition and pathology, wildlife and wildlands conservation. *Total annual research expenditures:* $1.9 million. *Unit head:* Dr. Eric N. Jellen, Chair, 801-422-3527, Fax: 801-422-0008, E-mail: rick_jellen@byu.edu. *Application contact:* Dr. Brock R. McMillan, Graduate Coordinator, 801-422-1228, Fax: 801-422-0008, E-mail: brock_mcmillan@byu.edu. Website: http://pws.byu.edu/home/.

Clemson University, Graduate School, College of Agriculture, Forestry and Life Sciences, Department of Forestry and Natural Resources, Program in Wildlife and Fisheries Biology, Clemson, SC 29634. Offers MS, PhD. *Students:* 11 full-time (10 women), 5 part-time (3 women); includes 1 minority (Black or African American, non-Hispanic/Latino), 2 international. Average age 32. 6 applicants, 33% accepted, 2 enrolled. In 2012, 4 doctorates awarded. *Degree requirements:* For master's, thesis; for doctorate, thesis/dissertation. *Entrance requirements:* For master's, GRE General Test, minimum undergraduate GPA of 3.0; for doctorate, GRE General Test. Additional exam requirements/recommendations for international students: Required—TOEFL, IELTS. *Application deadline:* For fall admission, 6/1 for domestic students, 4/15 for international students; for spring admission, 9/15 for international students. Applications are processed on a rolling basis. Application fee: $70 ($80 for international students). Electronic applications accepted. *Expenses:* Contact institution. *Financial support:* In 2012–13, 10 students received support, including 6 research assistantships with partial tuition reimbursements available (averaging $15,833 per year), 5 teaching assistantships with partial tuition reimbursements available (averaging $16,500 per year); fellowships with full and partial tuition reimbursements available, career-related internships or fieldwork, institutionally sponsored loans, scholarships/grants, health care benefits, and unspecified assistantships also available. Support available to part-time students. Financial award applicants required to submit FAFSA. *Faculty research:* Intensive freshwater culture systems, conservation biology, stream management, applied wildlife management. *Unit head:* Dr. Patricia Layton, Chair, 864-656-3303, Fax: 864-656-3304, E-mail: playton@clemson.edu. *Application contact:* Dr. David Guynn, Graduate Program Coordinator, 864-656-4830, Fax: 864-656-5344, E-mail: dguynn@clemson.edu. Website: http://www.clemson.edu/cafls/departments/forestry/.

Colorado State University, Graduate School, Warner College of Natural Resources, Department of Fishery and Wildlife Biology, Fort Collins, CO 80523-1474. Offers fish, wildlife and conservation biology (MFWCB); fishery and wildlife biology (MFWB, MS, PhD). *Faculty:* 14 full-time (4 women). *Students:* 8 full-time (1 woman), 22 part-time (8 women); includes 2 minority (both Hispanic/Latino). Average age 30. 10 applicants, 40% accepted, 4 enrolled. In 2012, 5 master's, 1 doctorate awarded. Terminal master's awarded for partial completion of doctoral program. *Degree requirements:* For master's, comprehensive exam, thesis (for some programs); for doctorate, comprehensive exam, thesis/dissertation. *Entrance requirements:* For master's, GRE General Test (combined minimum score of 1200 on the Verbal and Quantitative sections), minimum GPA of 3.0, BA or BS in related field, letters of recommendation, resume, transcripts; for doctorate, GRE General Test (minimum score 1000 verbal and quantitative), minimum GPA of 3.0, MS in related field. Additional exam requirements/recommendations for international students: Required—TOEFL (minimum score 550 paper-based; 80 iBT). *Application deadline:* For fall admission, 2/15 priority date for domestic students, 2/15 for international students. Applications are processed on a rolling basis. Application fee: $50. Electronic applications accepted. *Expenses:* Tuition, state resident: full-time $8811; part-time $490 per credit. Tuition, nonresident: full-time $21,600; part-time $1200 per credit. *Required fees:* $1819; $61 per credit. *Financial support:* In 2012–13, 37 students received support, including 4 fellowships with full and partial tuition reimbursements available (averaging $41,674 per year), 20 research assistantships with full and partial tuition reimbursements available (averaging $15,328 per year), 13 teaching assistantships with full and partial tuition reimbursements available (averaging $6,441 per year); career-related internships or fieldwork, scholarships/grants, tuition waivers (full and partial), and unspecified assistantships also available. Financial award application deadline: 2/15; financial award applicants required to submit FAFSA. *Faculty research:* Conservation biology, aquatic ecology, animal behavior, population modeling, habitat evaluation and management. *Total annual research expenditures:* $2.3 million. *Unit head:* Dr. Kenneth R. Wilson, Professor/Department Head, 970-491-5020, Fax: 970-491-5091, E-mail: kenneth.wilson@colostate.edu. *Application contact:* Joyce Pratt, Graduate Contact, 970-491-5020, Fax: 970-491-5091, E-mail: joyce.pratt@colostate.edu. Website: http://warnercnr.colostate.edu/fwcb-home/.

Cornell University, Graduate School, Graduate Fields of Agriculture and Life Sciences, Field of Natural Resources, Ithaca, NY 14853-0001. Offers community-based natural resources management (MS, PhD); ecosystem biology and biogeochemistry (MPS, MS, PhD); environmental management (MPS); fishery and aquatic science (MPS, MS, PhD); forest science (MPS, MS, PhD); human dimensions of natural resources management (MPS, MS, PhD); program development and evaluation (MPS, MS, PhD); wildlife science (MPS, MS, PhD). *Faculty:* 40 full-time (8 women). *Students:* 56 full-time (23 women); includes 2 minority (1 Asian, non-Hispanic/Latino; 1 Two or more races, non-Hispanic/Latino), 12 international. Average age 32. 61 applicants, 33% accepted, 15 enrolled. In 2012, 7 master's, 6 doctorates awarded. *Degree requirements:* For master's, thesis (MS), project paper (MPS); for doctorate, comprehensive exam, thesis/dissertation. *Entrance requirements:* For master's and doctorate, GRE General Test, 2 letters of recommendation. Additional exam requirements/recommendations for international students: Required—TOEFL (minimum score 550 paper-based; 77 iBT). *Application deadline:* For spring admission, 10/30 for domestic students. Applications are processed on a rolling basis. Application fee: $95. Electronic applications accepted. *Financial support:* In 2012–13, 46 students received support, including 14 fellowships with full tuition reimbursements available, 15 research assistantships with full tuition reimbursements available, 17 teaching assistantships with full tuition reimbursements available; institutionally sponsored loans, scholarships/grants, health care benefits, tuition waivers (full and partial), and unspecified assistantships also available. Financial award applicants required to submit FAFSA. *Faculty research:* Ecosystem-level dynamics, systems modeling, conservation biology/management, resource management's human dimensions, biogeochemistry. *Unit head:* Director of Graduate Studies, 607-255-2807, Fax: 607-255-0349. *Application contact:* Graduate Field Assistant, 607-255-2807, Fax: 607-255-0349, E-mail: nrgrad@cornell.edu. Website: http://www.gradschool.cornell.edu/fields.php?id-54&a-2.

Cornell University, Graduate School, Graduate Fields of Agriculture and Life Sciences, Field of Zoology and Wildlife Conservation, Ithaca, NY 14853-0001. Offers animal cytology (MS, PhD); comparative and functional anatomy (MS, PhD); developmental biology (MS, PhD); ecology (MS, PhD); histology (MS, PhD); wildlife conservation (MS, PhD). *Faculty:* 24 full-time (7 women). *Students:* 3 full-time (all women); includes 1 minority (Two or more races, non-Hispanic/Latino), 1 international. Average age 26. 10 applicants, 10% accepted, 0 enrolled. In 2012, 1 doctorate awarded. *Degree requirements:* For doctorate, comprehensive exam, thesis/dissertation, 2 semesters of teaching experience. *Entrance requirements:* For doctorate, GRE General Test, GRE Subject Test (biology), 2 letters of recommendation. Additional exam requirements/recommendations for international students: Required—TOEFL (minimum score 550 paper-based; 77 iBT). *Application deadline:* For fall admission, 2/1 priority date for domestic students. Application fee: $95. Electronic applications accepted. *Financial support:* In 2012–13, 2 research assistantships with full tuition reimbursements, 1 teaching assistantship with full tuition reimbursement were awarded; fellowships with full tuition reimbursements, institutionally sponsored loans, scholarships/grants, health care benefits, tuition waivers (full and partial), and unspecified assistantships also available. Financial award applicants required to submit FAFSA. *Faculty research:* Organismal biology, functional morphology, biomechanics, comparative vertebrate anatomy, comparative invertebrate anatomy, paleontology. *Unit head:* Director of Graduate Studies, 607-253-3276, Fax: 607-253-3756. *Application contact:* Graduate Field Assistant, 607-253-3276, Fax: 607-253-3756, E-mail: graduate_edcvm@cornell.edu. Website: http://www.gradschool.cornell.edu/fields.php?id-65&a-2.

Frostburg State University, Graduate School, College of Liberal Arts and Sciences, Department of Biology, Program in Fisheries and Wildlife Management, Frostburg, MD 21532-1099. Offers MS. Part-time and evening/weekend programs available. *Degree requirements:* For master's, thesis. *Entrance requirements:* For master's, GRE General Test, resume. Additional exam requirements/recommendations for international students: Required—TOEFL. Electronic applications accepted. *Faculty research:* Evolution and systematics of freshwater fishes, biochemical mechanisms of temperature adaptation in freshwater fishes, wildlife and fish parasitology, biology of freshwater invertebrates, remote sensing.

Humboldt State University, Academic Programs, College of Natural Resources and Sciences, Programs in Natural Resources, Arcata, CA 95521-8299. Offers natural resources (MS), including fisheries, forestry, natural resources planning and interpretation, rangeland resources and wildland soils, wastewater utilization, watershed management, wildlife. *Students:* 36 full-time (18 women), 20 part-time (9 women); includes 2 minority (1 Asian, non-Hispanic/Latino; 1 Two or more races, non-Hispanic/Latino). Average age 30. 51 applicants, 37% accepted, 11 enrolled. In 2012, 29 master's awarded. *Degree requirements:* For master's, thesis or alternative. *Entrance requirements:* For master's, GRE, appropriate bachelor's degree, minimum GPA of 2.5, 3 letters of recommendation, resume. Additional exam requirements/recommendations for international students: Required—TOEFL (minimum score 500 paper-based). *Application deadline:* For fall admission, 2/1 for domestic and international students; for spring admission, 9/30 for domestic and international students. Applications are processed on a rolling basis. Application fee: $55. *Expenses:* Tuition, state resident: full-time $8396. Tuition, nonresident: full-time $17,324. Tuition and fees vary according to program. *Financial support:* Fellowships, career-related internships or fieldwork, and Federal Work-Study available. Support available to part-time students. Financial award application deadline: 3/1; financial award applicants required to submit FAFSA. *Faculty research:* Spotted owl habitat, pre-settlement vegetation, hardwood utilization, tree physiology, fisheries. *Unit head:* Dr. Robert Van Kirk, Coordinator, 707-826-3744, E-mail: rob.vankirk@humboldt.edu. *Application contact:* Julie Tucker, Administrative Support Coordinator, 707-826-3256, E-mail: jlt7002@humboldt.edu. Website: http://www.humboldt.edu/cnrs/graduate_programs.

Iowa State University of Science and Technology, Department of Natural Resource Ecology and Management, Ames, IA 50011. Offers forestry (MS, PhD); wildlife ecology (MS). *Entrance requirements:* For master's and doctorate, GRE General Test. Additional exam requirements/recommendations for international students: Required—TOEFL (minimum score 550 paper-based; 79 iBT), IELTS (minimum score 6.5). *Application deadline:* For fall admission, 4/1 priority date for domestic students, 4/1 for international students; for spring admission, 10/1 priority date for domestic students, 10/1 for international students. Application fee: $60 ($90 for international students). Electronic applications accepted. *Application contact:* Kelly Kyle, Director of Graduate Education, 515-294-7400, Fax: 515-294-7406, E-mail: nremgradinfo@iastate.edu. Website: http://www.nrem.iastate.edu/.

Iowa State University of Science and Technology, Program in Fisheries Biology, Ames, IA 50010. Offers MS, PhD. *Entrance requirements:* For master's and doctorate, GRE. Additional exam requirements/recommendations for international students: Required—TOEFL (minimum score 550 paper-based; 79 iBT), IELTS (minimum score 6.5). *Application deadline:* For fall admission, 4/1 for domestic students; for spring admission, 10/1 for domestic students. Application fee: $60 ($90 for international students). Electronic applications accepted. *Application contact:* Kelly Kyle, Application Contact, 515-294-7400, Fax: 515-294-7406, E-mail: nremgradinfo@iastate.edu. Website: http://www.nrem.iastate.edu.

Louisiana State University and Agricultural and Mechanical College, Graduate School, College of Agriculture, School of Renewable Natural Resources, Baton Rouge, LA 70803. Offers fisheries (MS); forestry (MS, PhD); wildlife (MS); wildlife and fisheries science (PhD). *Faculty:* 31 full-time (5 women). *Students:* 51 full-time (15 women), 5 part-time (2 women); includes 3 minority (2 Black or African American, non-Hispanic/Latino; 1 Hispanic/Latino), 12 international. Average age 29. 34 applicants, 41% accepted, 13 enrolled. In 2012, 11 master's, 10 doctorates awarded. *Degree requirements:* For master's, thesis; for doctorate, thesis/dissertation. *Entrance requirements:* For master's, GRE General Test, minimum GPA of 3.0; for doctorate, GRE General Test, MS, minimum GPA of 3.0. Additional exam requirements/recommendations for international students: Required—TOEFL (minimum score 550 paper-based; 79 iBT), IELTS (minimum score 6.5). *Application deadline:* For fall admission, 1/25 priority date for domestic students, 5/15 for international students; for spring admission, 10/15 for international students. Applications are processed on a rolling basis. Application fee: $50 ($70 for international students). Electronic applications accepted. *Financial support:* In 2012–13, 55 students received support, including 49 research assistantships with partial tuition reimbursements available (averaging $19,751 per year), 2 teaching assistantships (averaging $10,250 per year); fellowships, Federal Work-Study, institutionally sponsored loans, scholarships/grants, health care benefits, tuition waivers (full and partial), and unspecified assistantships also available. Financial award application deadline: 4/15; financial award applicants required to submit FAFSA. *Faculty research:* Forest biology and management, aquaculture, fisheries biology and ecology, upland and wetlands wildlife. *Total annual research expenditures:* $163,169. *Unit head:* Dr. Allen Rutherford, Director, 225-578-4131, Fax: 225-578-4227, E-mail: druther@lsu.edu. *Application contact:* Dr. William Kelso, Coordinator of Graduate Studies, 225-578-4176, Fax: 225-578-4227, E-mail: wkelso@lsu.edu. Website: http://www.fwf.lsu.edu/.

McGill University, Faculty of Graduate and Postdoctoral Studies, Faculty of Agricultural and Environmental Sciences, Department of Natural Resource Sciences, Montréal, QC H3A 2T5, Canada. Offers entomology (M Sc, PhD); environmental assessment (M Sc); forest science (M Sc, PhD); microbiology (M Sc, PhD); micrometeorology (M Sc, PhD); neotropical environment (M Sc, PhD); soil science (M Sc, PhD); wildlife biology (M Sc, PhD).

Memorial University of Newfoundland, School of Graduate Studies, Interdisciplinary Program in Marine Studies, St. John's, NL A1C 5S7, Canada. Offers fisheries resource management (MMS, Advanced Diploma). Part-time programs available. *Degree requirements:* For master's, report. *Entrance requirements:* For master's and Advanced Diploma, high 2nd class degree from a recognized university. *Faculty research:* Biological, ecological and oceanographic aspects of world fisheries; economics; political science; sociology.

Michigan State University, The Graduate School, College of Agriculture and Natural Resources, Department of Fisheries and Wildlife, East Lansing, MI 48824. Offers fisheries and wildlife (MS, PhD); fisheries and wildlife - environmental toxicology (PhD). *Entrance requirements:* Additional exam requirements/recommendations for international students: Required—TOEFL (minimum score 550 paper-based), Michigan State University ELT (minimum score 85), Michigan English Language Assessment Battery (minimum score 83). Electronic applications accepted.

Mississippi State University, College of Forest Resources, Department of Wildlife, Fisheries and Aquaculture, Mississippi State, MS 39762. Offers forest resources (PhD), including wildlife and fisheries; wildlife and fisheries science (MS). Part-time programs available. *Faculty:* 20 full-time (1 woman), 1 part-time/adjunct (0 women). *Students:* 57 full-time (15 women), 20 part-time (8 women); includes 3 minority (1 Black or African American, non-Hispanic/Latino; 1 Hispanic/Latino; 1 Two or more races, non-Hispanic/Latino), 7 international. Average age 29. 25 applicants, 40% accepted, 10 enrolled. In 2012, 12 master's, 4 doctorates awarded. *Degree requirements:* For master's, thesis, comprehensive oral or written exam; for doctorate, comprehensive exam, thesis/dissertation. *Entrance requirements:* For master's, GRE, bachelor's degree, minimum GPA of 3.0 on last 60 hours of undergraduate courses; for doctorate, GRE, master's degree, minimum GPA of 3.2 on prior graduate studies. Additional exam requirements/recommendations for international students: Required—TOEFL (minimum score 550 paper-based; 79 iBT); Recommended—IELTS (minimum score 6.5). *Application deadline:* For fall admission, 7/1 for domestic students, 5/1 for international students; for spring admission, 11/1 for domestic students, 9/1 for international students. Applications are processed on a rolling basis. Application fee: $60. Electronic applications accepted. *Financial support:* In 2012–13, 53 research assistantships with partial tuition reimbursements (averaging $15,410 per year), 1 teaching assistantship with partial tuition reimbursement (averaging $19,223 per year) were awarded; Federal Work-Study, institutionally sponsored loans, and unspecified assistantships also available. Financial award application deadline: 4/1; financial award applicants required to submit FAFSA. *Faculty research:* Spatial technology, habitat restoration, aquaculture, fisheries, wildlife management. *Unit head:* Dr. Bruce D. Leopold, Department Head and Graduate Coordinator, 662-325-2615, Fax: 662-325-8726, E-mail: bleopold@cfr.msstate.edu. *Application contact:* Dr. Eric Dibble, Professor and Coordinator of Graduate Studies, 662-325-7494, Fax: 662-325-8726, E-mail: edibble@cfr.msstate.edu. Website: http://www.cfr.msstate.edu/wildlife/index.asp.

Montana State University, College of Graduate Studies, College of Letters and Science, Department of Ecology, Bozeman, MT 59717. Offers ecological and environmental statistics (MS); ecology and environmental sciences (PhD); fish and wildlife biology (PhD); fish and wildlife management (MS). Part-time programs available. *Degree requirements:* For master's, comprehensive exam, thesis (for some programs); for doctorate, comprehensive exam, thesis/dissertation. *Entrance requirements:* For master's and doctorate, GRE, minimum GPA of 3.0, letters of recommendation, essay. Additional exam requirements/recommendations for international students: Required—TOEFL (minimum score 550 paper-based). Electronic applications accepted. *Faculty research:* Community ecology, population ecology, land-use effects, management and conservation, environmental modeling.

New Mexico State University, Graduate School, College of Agricultural, Consumer and Environmental Sciences, Department of Fish, Wildlife and Conservation Ecology, Las Cruces, NM 88003. Offers wildlife science (MS). *Faculty:* 7 full-time (3 women), 1 (woman) part-time/adjunct. *Students:* 19 full-time (8 women), 7 part-time (2 women); includes 4 minority (1 Black or African American, non-Hispanic/Latino; 3 Hispanic/Latino), 1 international. Average age 27. 26 applicants, 58% accepted, 14 enrolled. In 2012, 5 master's awarded. *Degree requirements:* For master's, thesis (for some programs). *Entrance requirements:* For master's, GRE General Test, minimum GPA of 3.0. Additional exam requirements/recommendations for international students: Required—TOEFL (minimum score 550 paper-based; 79 iBT), IELTS (minimum score 6.5). *Application deadline:* For fall admission, 4/1 priority date for domestic students; for spring admission, 11/1 priority date for domestic students. Applications are processed on a rolling basis. Application fee: $40 ($50 for international students). Electronic applications accepted. *Expenses:* Tuition, state resident: full-time $5239; part-time $218 per credit. Tuition, nonresident: full-time $18,266; part-time $761 per credit. *Required fees:* $1274; $53 per credit. *Financial support:* In 2012–13, 19 students received support, including 18 research assistantships (averaging $19,976 per year), 4 teaching assistantships (averaging $16,100 per year); career-related internships or fieldwork, Federal Work-Study, scholarships/grants, health care benefits, and unspecified assistantships also available. Support available to part-time students. Financial award application deadline: 4/1. *Faculty research:* Ecosystems analyses, landscape and wildlife ecology, wildlife and fish population dynamics, management models, wildlife and fish habitat relationships. *Total annual research expenditures:* $1.6 million. *Unit head:* Dr. Steven Loring, Interim Head/Recruiting Contact, 575-646-1217, Fax: 575-646-1281, E-mail: sloring@nmsu.edu. *Application contact:* Doris J. Morgan, Intermediate Administrative Assistant, 575-646-7051, Fax: 575-646-1281, E-mail: domorgan@nmsu.edu. Website: http://aces.nmsu.edu/academics/FWS.

North Carolina State University, Graduate School, College of Natural Resources, Program in Fisheries and Wildlife Sciences, Raleigh, NC 27695. Offers MFWS, MS, PhD. *Degree requirements:* For master's, thesis optional. *Entrance requirements:* For master's, GRE General Test. Additional exam requirements/recommendations for international students: Required—TOEFL. Electronic applications accepted. *Faculty research:* Fisheries biology; ecology of marine, estuarine, and anadromous fishes; aquaculture pond water quality; larviculture of freshwater and marine finfish; predator/prey interactions.

Oregon State University, College of Agricultural Sciences, Department of Fisheries and Wildlife, Program in Fisheries and Wildlife Administration, Corvallis, OR 97331. Offers PSM. Postbaccalaureate distance learning degree programs offered (no on-campus study). *Students:* 2 applicants, 100% accepted, 1 enrolled. *Expenses:* Tuition, state resident: full-time $11,367; part-time $421 per credit hour. Tuition, nonresident: full-time $18,279; part-time $677 per credit hour. *Required fees:* $1478. One-time fee: $300 full-time. Tuition and fees vary according to course load and program. *Unit head:* Dr. Selina S. Heppell, Program Director, 541-737-9039, E-mail: selina.hoppell@oregonstate.edu.

Oregon State University, College of Agricultural Sciences, Department of Fisheries and Wildlife, Program in Fisheries Science, Corvallis, OR 97331. Offers M Agr, MAIS, MS, PhD. Part-time programs available. *Faculty:* 8 full-time (1 woman), 8 part-time/adjunct (3 women). *Students:* 49 full-time (29 women), 4 part-time (2 women); includes 5 minority (4 Hispanic/Latino; 1 Native Hawaiian or other Pacific Islander, non-Hispanic/Latino), 2 international. Average age 32. 40 applicants, 23% accepted, 9 enrolled. In 2012, 9 master's, 3 doctorates awarded. *Degree requirements:* For master's, thesis (for some programs); for doctorate, thesis/dissertation. *Entrance requirements:* For master's and doctorate, GRE, minimum GPA of 3.0 in last 90 hours. Additional exam requirements/recommendations for international students: Required—TOEFL. *Application deadline:* For fall admission, 3/15 for domestic students; for spring admission, 12/

15 for domestic students. Applications are processed on a rolling basis. Application fee: $50. *Expenses:* Tuition, state resident: full-time $11,367; part-time $421 per credit hour. Tuition, nonresident: full-time $18,279; part-time $677 per credit hour. *Required fees:* $1478. One-time fee: $300 full-time. Tuition and fees vary according to course load and program. *Financial support:* Fellowships, research assistantships, teaching assistantships, career-related internships or fieldwork, Federal Work-Study, and institutionally sponsored loans available. Support available to part-time students. Financial award application deadline: 2/1. *Faculty research:* Fisheries ecology, fish toxicology, stream ecology, quantitative analyses of marine and freshwater fish populations. *Unit head:* Dr. Daniel Edge, Department Head, 541-737-2910, Fax: 541-737-3590, E-mail: daniel.edge@oregonstate.edu. *Application contact:* Dr. Nancy Allen, Head Advisor, 541-737-2910, Fax: 541-737-3590, E-mail: nancy.allen@oregonstate.edu.

Oregon State University, College of Agricultural Sciences, Department of Fisheries and Wildlife, Program in Wildlife Science, Corvallis, OR 97331. Offers MAIS, MS, PhD. *Faculty:* 7 full-time (3 women), 1 (woman) part-time/adjunct. *Students:* 47 full-time (24 women), 1 part-time (0 women); includes 5 minority (1 American Indian or Alaska Native, non-Hispanic/Latino; 3 Hispanic/Latino; 1 Two or more races, non-Hispanic/Latino), 4 international. Average age 32. 35 applicants, 37% accepted, 13 enrolled. In 2012, 7 master's, 4 doctorates awarded. *Degree requirements:* For master's, thesis (for some programs); for doctorate, thesis/dissertation. *Entrance requirements:* For master's and doctorate, GRE, minimum GPA of 3.0 in last 90 hours. Additional exam requirements/recommendations for international students: Required—TOEFL. Application fee: $50. *Expenses:* Tuition, state resident: full-time $11,367; part-time $421 per credit hour. Tuition, nonresident: full-time $18,279; part-time $677 per credit hour. *Required fees:* $1478. One-time fee: $300 full-time. Tuition and fees vary according to course load and program. *Financial support:* Fellowships, research assistantships, teaching assistantships, career-related internships or fieldwork, Federal Work-Study, and institutionally sponsored loans available. Financial award application deadline: 2/1. *Unit head:* Dr. Daniel Edge, Department Head, 541-737-2910, Fax: 541-737-3590, E-mail: daniel.edge@oregonstate.edu. *Application contact:* Dr. Nancy Allen, Head Advisor, 541-737-1941, Fax: 541-737-3590, E-mail: nancy.allen@oregonstate.edu.

Penn State University Park, Graduate School, College of Agricultural Sciences, Department of Ecosystem Science and Management, State College, University Park, PA 16802-1503. Offers forest resources (MS, PhD); soil science (MS, PhD); wildlife and fisheries science (MS, PhD). *Unit head:* Dr. Barbara J. Christ, Interim Dean, 814-865-2541, Fax: 814-865-3103, E-mail: ebf@psu.edu. *Application contact:* Cynthia E. Nicosia, Director of Graduate Enrollment Services, 814-865-1834, E-mail: cey1@psu.edu. Website: http://ecosystems.psu.edu.

Purdue University, Graduate School, College of Agriculture, Department of Forestry and Natural Resources, West Lafayette, IN 47907. Offers fisheries and aquatic sciences (MS, MSF, PhD); forest biology (MS, MSF, PhD); natural resource social science (MS, PhD); natural resources social science (MSF); quantitative ecology (MS, MSF, PhD); wildlife science (MS, MSF, PhD); wood products and wood products manufacturing (MS, MSF, PhD). *Faculty:* 25 full-time (3 women), 10 part-time/adjunct (1 woman). *Students:* 61 full-time (24 women), 11 part-time (6 women); includes 3 minority (1 American Indian or Alaska Native, non-Hispanic/Latino; 2 Hispanic/Latino), 18 international. Average age 29. 57 applicants, 28% accepted, 15 enrolled. In 2012, 18 master's, 7 doctorates awarded. *Degree requirements:* For master's, thesis; for doctorate, thesis/dissertation. *Entrance requirements:* For master's and doctorate, GRE General Test (minimum score: verbal 50th percentile; quantitative 50th percentile; analytical writing 4.0), minimum undergraduate GPA of 3.2 or equivalent. Additional exam requirements/recommendations for international students: Required—TOEFL (minimum score 550 paper-based; 77 iBT). *Application deadline:* For fall admission, 1/5 for domestic students, 1/15 for international students; for spring admission, 9/15 for domestic and international students. Applications are processed on a rolling basis. Application fee: $60 ($75 for international students). Electronic applications accepted. *Financial support:* In 2012–13, 10 research assistantships (averaging $15,259 per year) were awarded; fellowships, teaching assistantships, career-related internships or fieldwork, and scholarships/grants also available. Support available to part-time students. Financial award application deadline: 1/5; financial award applicants required to submit FAFSA. *Faculty research:* Wildlife management, forest management, forest ecology, forest soils, limnology. *Unit head:* Dr. Robert K. Swihart, Interim Head, 765-494-3590, Fax: 765-494-9461, E-mail: rswihart@purdue.edu. *Application contact:* Kelly J. Wrede, Graduate Secretary, 765-494-3572, Fax: 765-494-9461, E-mail: kgarrett@purdue.edu. Website: http://www.fnr.purdue.edu/.

Simon Fraser University, Office of Graduate Studies, Faculty of Environment, School of Resource and Environmental Management, Burnaby, BC V5A 1S6, Canada. Offers quantitative methods in fisheries management (Graduate Diploma); resource and environmental management (MRM, PhD); resource and environmental planning (MRM). *Faculty:* 19 full-time (4 women). *Students:* 121 full-time (66 women), 5 part-time (2 women). 179 applicants, 26% accepted, 34 enrolled. In 2012, 26 master's, 3 doctorates, 1 other advanced degree awarded. *Degree requirements:* For master's, thesis (for some programs); for doctorate, comprehensive exam, thesis/dissertation. *Entrance requirements:* For master's and Graduate Diploma, minimum GPA of 3.0 (on scale of 4.33), or 3.33 based on last 60 credits of undergraduate courses; for doctorate, minimum GPA of 3.5 (on scale of 4.33). Additional exam requirements/recommendations for international students: Recommended—TOEFL (minimum score 580 paper-based; 93 iBT), IELTS (minimum score 7), TWE (minimum score 5). *Application deadline:* For fall admission, 2/15 for domestic and international students. Application fee: $90 ($125 for international students). Electronic applications accepted. Tuition and fees charges are reported in Canadian dollars. *Expenses: Tuition, area resident:* Full-time $5000 Canadian dollars; part-time $275 Canadian dollars per credit hour. *Required fees:* $780 Canadian dollars. *Financial support:* In 2012–13, 35 students received support, including 19 fellowships (averaging $6,250 per year), teaching assistantships (averaging $5,608 per year); research assistantships, career-related internships or fieldwork, and scholarships/grants also available. *Faculty research:* Climate, coastal marine ecology and conservation, environmental toxicology, fisheries science and management, forest ecology. *Unit head:* Dr. Frank Gobas, Director, 778-782-3069, Fax: 778-782-4968, E-mail: rem-grad-chair@sfu.ca. *Application contact:* Devan Huber, Graduate Secretary, 778-782-4780, Fax: 778-782-4968, E-mail: rem_gradasst@sfu.ca. Website: http://www.rem.sfu.ca/.

South Dakota State University, Graduate School, College of Agriculture and Biological Sciences, Department of Wildlife and Fisheries Sciences, Brookings, SD 57007. Offers MS, PhD. Part-time programs available. *Degree requirements:* For master's, thesis, oral exam; for doctorate, comprehensive exam, thesis/dissertation, interim exam, oral and written comprehensive exams. *Entrance requirements:* For master's and doctorate, GRE. Additional exam requirements/recommendations for international students: Required—TOEFL (minimum score 525 paper-based; 71 iBT). *Faculty research:* Agriculture interactions, wetland conservation, biostress, wildlife and fisheries ecology and techniques.

State University of New York College of Environmental Science and Forestry, Department of Environmental and Forest Biology, Syracuse, NY 13210-2779. Offers applied ecology (MPS); chemical ecology (MPS, MS, PhD); conservation biology (MPS, MS, PhD); ecology (MPS, MS, PhD); entomology (MPS, MS, PhD); environmental interpretation (MPS, MS, PhD); environmental physiology (MPS, MS, PhD); fish and wildlife biology and management (MPS, MS, PhD); forest pathology and mycology (MPS, MS, PhD); plant biotechnology (MPS); plant science and biotechnology (MPS, MS, PhD). *Degree requirements:* For master's, thesis (for some programs); for doctorate, comprehensive exam, thesis/dissertation. *Entrance requirements:* For master's and doctorate, GRE General Test, GRE Subject Test, minimum GPA of 3.0. Additional exam requirements/recommendations for international students: Required—TOEFL (minimum score 550 paper-based; 80 iBT), IELTS (minimum score 6). *Expenses:* Tuition, state resident: full-time $9370; part-time $390 per credit hour. Tuition, nonresident: full-time $16,680; part-time $695 per credit hour. *Required fees:* $981. Tuition and fees vary according to course load and program. *Faculty research:* Ecology, fish and wildlife biology and management, plant science, entomology.

Sul Ross State University, Division of Agricultural and Natural Resource Science, Programs in Natural Resource Management, Alpine, TX 79832. Offers range and wildlife management (M Ag, MS). Part-time programs available. *Degree requirements:* For master's, thesis (for some programs). *Entrance requirements:* For master's, GRE General Test, minimum undergraduate GPA of 2.5 in last 60 hours.

Tennessee Technological University, Graduate School, College of Arts and Sciences, Department of Biology, Cookeville, TN 38505. Offers fish, game, and wildlife management (MS). Part-time programs available. *Faculty:* 22 full-time (2 women). *Students:* 3 full-time (1 woman), 12 part-time (8 women), 1 international. Average age 25. 15 applicants, 33% accepted, 4 enrolled. In 2012, 10 master's awarded. *Degree requirements:* For master's, thesis. *Entrance requirements:* For master's, GRE. Additional exam requirements/recommendations for international students: Required—TOEFL (minimum score 527 paper-based; 71 iBT), IELTS (minimum score 5.5), Pearson Test of English. *Application deadline:* For fall admission, 8/1 for domestic students, 5/1 for international students; for spring admission, 12/1 for domestic students, 10/1 for international students. Application fee: $35 ($40 for international students). Electronic applications accepted. *Expenses:* Tuition, state resident: full-time $8444; part-time $441 per credit hour. Tuition, nonresident: full-time $21,404; part-time $1089 per credit hour. *Financial support:* In 2012–13, 17 research assistantships (averaging $9,000 per year), 8 teaching assistantships (averaging $7,500 per year) were awarded. Financial award application deadline: 4/1. *Faculty research:* Aquatics, environmental studies. *Unit head:* Dr. Steven Bradford Cook, Interim Chairperson, 931-372-3134, Fax: 931-372-6257, E-mail: sbcook@tntech.edu. *Application contact:* Shelia K. Kendrick, Coordinator of Graduate Admissions, 931-372-3808, Fax: 931-372-3497, E-mail: skendrick@tntech.edu.

Texas A&M University, College of Agriculture and Life Sciences, Department of Wildlife and Fisheries Sciences, College Station, TX 77843. Offers MS, PhD. Part-time programs available. Postbaccalaureate distance learning degree programs offered (no on-campus study). *Faculty:* 26. *Students:* 84 full-time (49 women), 58 part-time (26 women); includes 35 minority (3 Black or African American, non-Hispanic/Latino; 1 American Indian or Alaska Native, non-Hispanic/Latino; 1 Asian, non-Hispanic/Latino; 30 Hispanic/Latino), 19 international. Average age 31. In 2012, 23 master's, 5 doctorates awarded. Terminal master's awarded for partial completion of doctoral program. *Degree requirements:* For master's, thesis, final oral defense; for doctorate, thesis/dissertation, final oral defense. *Entrance requirements:* For master's and doctorate, GRE General Test, minimum GPA of 3.0. Additional exam requirements/recommendations for international students: Required—TOEFL (minimum score 550 paper-based). *Application deadline:* For fall admission, 3/1 for international students; for spring admission, 8/1 for international students. Applications are processed on a rolling basis. Application fee: $50 ($75 for international students). Electronic applications accepted. *Financial support:* In 2012–13, fellowships with partial tuition reimbursements (averaging $22,000 per year), research assistantships (averaging $14,400 per year), teaching assistantships (averaging $14,400 per year) were awarded; career-related internships or fieldwork, institutionally sponsored loans, and scholarships/grants also available. Financial award application deadline: 3/1; financial award applicants required to submit FAFSA. *Faculty research:* Wildlife ecology and management, fisheries ecology and management, aquaculture, biological inventories and museum collections, biosystematics and genome analysis. *Unit head:* Dr. John Carey, Interim Department Head, 979-845-5777, Fax: 979-845-3786, E-mail: jcarey@poultry.tamu.edu. *Application contact:* Felix Arnold, Academic Advisor II, 979-845-5768, Fax: 979-845-3786, E-mail: fwarnold@tamu.edu. Website: http://wfscnet.tamu.edu/.

Texas A&M University–Kingsville, College of Graduate Studies, College of Agriculture and Home Economics, Program in Range and Wildlife Management, Kingsville, TX 78363. Offers MS. *Degree requirements:* For master's, comprehensive exam, thesis or alternative. *Entrance requirements:* For master's, GRE General Test, minimum GPA of 3.0. Additional exam requirements/recommendations for international students: Required—TOEFL.

Texas A&M University–Kingsville, College of Graduate Studies, College of Agriculture and Home Economics, Program in Wildlife Science, Kingsville, TX 78363. Offers PhD. *Degree requirements:* For doctorate, one foreign language, comprehensive exam, thesis/dissertation. *Entrance requirements:* For doctorate, GRE General Test, minimum GPA of 3.5.

Texas State University–San Marcos, Graduate School, College of Science and Engineering, Department of Biology, Program in Wildlife Ecology, San Marcos, TX 78666. Offers MS. *Faculty:* 5 full-time (0 women). *Students:* 18 full-time (13 women), 8 part-time (2 women); includes 3 minority (1 Black or African American, non-Hispanic/Latino; 2 Hispanic/Latino), 1 international. Average age 29. 14 applicants, 79% accepted, 9 enrolled. In 2012, 8 master's awarded. *Degree requirements:* For master's, thesis. *Entrance requirements:* For master's, GRE General Test (preferred minimum combined score of 1000 Verbal and Quantitative), bachelor's degree in biology or related discipline, minimum GPA of 3.0 in last 60 hours of undergraduate work. Additional exam requirements/recommendations for international students: Required—TOEFL (minimum score 550 paper-based; 78 iBT). *Application deadline:* For fall admission, 6/15 priority date for domestic students, 6/1 for international students; for spring admission, 10/15 priority date for domestic students, 10/1 for international students. Applications are processed on a rolling basis. Application fee: $40 ($90 for international students). Electronic applications accepted. *Expenses:* Tuition, state resident: full-time $6408; part-time $3204 per semester. Tuition, nonresident: full-time $14,832; part-time $7416 per semester. *Required fees:* $1824; $618. Tuition and fees vary according to course load. *Financial support:* In 2012–13, 9 students received support, including 18 teaching assistantships (averaging $14,510 per year); research assistantships, Federal Work-Study, and institutionally sponsored loans also available. Support available to part-time students. Financial award application deadline: 4/1; financial award applicants required to submit FAFSA. *Unit head:* Dr. Thomas Randy Simpson, Graduate Advisor, 512-245-3817, Fax: 512-245-8713, E-mail: r_simpson@txstate.edu. *Application contact:* Dr. J. Michael Willoughby, Dean of the Graduate School, 512-245-2581, Fax: 512-245-8365, E-mail: jw02@swt.edu. Website: http://www.gradcollege.txstate.edu/Prospect_Students/Pgms_Apps/Masters/Science/Wild_Eco.html.

Texas Tech University, Graduate School, College of Agricultural Sciences and Natural Resources, Department of Natural Resources Management, Lubbock, TX 79409. Offers fisheries science (MS, PhD); range science (MS, PhD); wildlife, aquatic, and wildlands science and management (MS, PhD). Part-time programs available. *Degree requirements:* For master's, thesis; for doctorate, thesis/dissertation. *Entrance requirements:* For master's and doctorate, GRE General Test, formal approval from departmental committee. Additional exam requirements/recommendations for international students: Required—TOEFL (minimum score 550 paper-based; 79 iBT). Electronic applications accepted. *Faculty research:* Use of fire on range lands; big game, upland game, and waterfowl; playa lakes in the southern Great Plains; conservation biology; fish ecology and physiology.

Université du Québec à Rimouski, Graduate Programs, Program in Wildlife Resources Management, Rimouski, QC G5L 3A1, Canada. Offers biology (PhD); wildlife resources management (M Sc, Diploma). PhD offered jointly with Université du Québec à Montréal, Université du Québec à Trois-Rivières, and Université du Québec en Abitibi-Témiscamingue. *Students:* 78 full-time, 4 part-time. In 2012, 8 other advanced degrees awarded. *Entrance requirements:* For degree, appropriate bachelor's degree, proficiency in French. *Application deadline:* For fall admission, 5/1 for domestic students. Application fee: $50. *Financial support:* Fellowships, research assistantships, and teaching assistantships available. *Unit head:* Magella Guillemette, Director, 418-724-1592, Fax: 418-724-1525, E-mail: magella_guillemette@uqar.ca. *Application contact:* Jacques d'Astous, Conseiller en Recrutement et en Communication, 800-463-4712, Fax: 418-724-1869, E-mail: jacques_dastous@uqar.ca.

University of Alaska Fairbanks, College of Natural Sciences and Mathematics, Department of Biology and Wildlife, Fairbanks, AK 99775-6100. Offers biological sciences (MS, PhD), including biology, botany, wildlife biology (PhD), zoology; biology (MAT, MS); wildlife biology (MS). Part-time programs available. *Faculty:* 21 full-time (11 women), 1 part-time/adjunct (0 women). *Students:* 77 full-time (46 women), 29 part-time (14 women); includes 8 minority (2 Asian, non-Hispanic/Latino; 3 Hispanic/Latino; 3 Two or more races, non-Hispanic/Latino), 5 international. Average age 30. 55 applicants, 31% accepted, 15 enrolled. In 2012, 10 master's, 10 doctorates awarded. *Degree requirements:* For master's, comprehensive exam, thesis, oral exam, oral defense; for doctorate, comprehensive exam, thesis/dissertation, oral exam, oral defense. *Entrance requirements:* For master's and doctorate, GRE General Test, GRE Subject Test (biology). Additional exam requirements/recommendations for international students: Required—TOEFL (minimum score 550 paper-based; 80 iBT), TWE. *Application deadline:* For fall admission, 6/1 for domestic students, 3/1 for international students; for spring admission, 10/15 for domestic students, 9/1 for international students. Applications are processed on a rolling basis. Application fee: $60. Electronic applications accepted. *Expenses:* Tuition, state resident: full-time $7038. Tuition, nonresident: full-time $14,382. Tuition and fees vary according to course level, course load and reciprocity agreements. *Financial support:* In 2012–13, 33 research assistantships with tuition reimbursements (averaging $13,708 per year), 24 teaching assistantships with tuition reimbursements (averaging $11,139 per year) were awarded; fellowships with tuition reimbursements, career-related internships or fieldwork, Federal Work-Study, scholarships/grants, health care benefits, and unspecified assistantships also available. Support available to part-time students. Financial award application deadline: 7/1; financial award applicants required to submit FAFSA. *Faculty research:* Plant-herbivore interactions, plant metabolic defenses, insect manufacture of glycerol, ice nucleators, structure and functions of arctic and subarctic freshwater ecosystems. *Unit head:* Christa Mulder, Department Chair, 907-474-7671, Fax: 907-474-6716, E-mail: uaf-bw-dept@alaska.edu. *Application contact:* Libby Eddy, Registrar and Director of Admissions, 907-474-7500, Fax: 907-474-7097, E-mail: admissions@uaf.edu. Website: http://www.bw.uaf.edu.

University of Alaska Fairbanks, School of Fisheries and Ocean Sciences, Program in Marine Sciences and Limnology, Fairbanks, AK 99775-7220. Offers marine biology (MS, PhD); oceanography (PhD), including biological oceanography, chemical oceanography, fisheries, geological oceanography, physical oceanography. Part-time programs available. *Faculty:* 5 full-time (2 women), 1 part-time/adjunct (0 women). *Students:* 45 full-time (33 women), 17 part-time (13 women); includes 8 minority (3 Asian, non-Hispanic/Latino; 5 Hispanic/Latino), 8 international. Average age 29. 52 applicants, 25% accepted, 12 enrolled. In 2012, 4 master's, 5 doctorates awarded. *Degree requirements:* For master's, comprehensive exam, thesis, oral defense; for doctorate, comprehensive exam, thesis/dissertation, oral defense. *Entrance requirements:* For master's and doctorate, GRE General Test. Additional exam requirements/recommendations for international students: Required—TOEFL (minimum score 550 paper-based; 80 iBT). *Application deadline:* For fall admission, 6/1 for domestic students, 3/1 for international students; for spring admission, 10/15 for domestic students, 8/1 for international students. Applications are processed on a rolling basis. Application fee: $60. Electronic applications accepted. *Expenses:* Tuition, state resident: full-time $7038. Tuition, nonresident: full-time $14,382. Tuition and fees vary according to course level, course load and reciprocity agreements. *Financial support:* In 2012–13, 31 research assistantships with tuition reimbursements (averaging $11,137 per year), 7 teaching assistantships with tuition reimbursements (averaging $11,750 per year) were awarded; fellowships with tuition reimbursements, career-related internships or fieldwork, Federal Work-Study, scholarships/grants, health care benefits, and unspecified assistantships also available. Support available to part-time students. Financial award application deadline: 7/1; financial award applicants required to submit FAFSA. *Unit head:* Katrin Iken, Co-Chair, 907-474-7289, Fax: 907-474-5863, E-mail: academics@sfos.uaf.edu. *Application contact:* Libby Eddy, Registrar and Director of Admissions, 907-474-7500, Fax: 907-474-7097, E-mail: admissions@alaska.edu. Website: http://www.sfos.uaf.edu/prospective/graduate/marinebio.php.

The University of Arizona, College of Agriculture and Life Sciences, School of Natural Resources, Program in Wildlife, Fisheries Conservation, and Management, Tucson, AZ 85721. Offers wildlife and fisheries science (MS, PhD); wildlife conservation and management (MS, PhD). *Faculty:* 19 full-time (3 women), 2 part-time/adjunct (0 women). *Students:* 1 full-time (0 women), 1 part-time (0 women). Average age 49. In 2012, 1 doctorate awarded. *Degree requirements:* For master's, thesis; for doctorate, comprehensive exam, thesis/dissertation. *Entrance requirements:* For master's, GRE General Test, GRE Subject Test (biology), minimum GPA of 3.0, 3 letters of recommendation; for doctorate, GRE General Test, GRE Subject Test (biology), minimum GPA of 3.0, 3 letters of recommendation, MA or MS. Additional exam requirements/recommendations for international students: Required—TOEFL (minimum score 550 paper-based; 79 iBT). *Application deadline:* For fall admission, 8/1 priority date for domestic students, 12/1 for international students; for spring admission, 7/1 for international students. Applications are processed on a rolling basis. Application fee: $75. *Financial support:* Research assistantships with partial tuition reimbursements, teaching assistantships with partial tuition reimbursements, scholarships/grants, health care benefits, tuition waivers (partial), and unspecified assistantships available. *Faculty research:* Short-term effects of artificial oases on Arizona wildlife, elk response to cattle in northern Arizona, effect of reservoir operation on tailwaters, conservation of wildlife. *Total annual research expenditures:* $6.5 million. *Unit head:* Dr. Charles Hutchinson, Director, 520-621-8568, E-mail: chuck@ag.arizona.edu. *Application contact:*

Katie Hughes, Academic Coordinator, 520-621-7260, Fax: 520-621-8801, E-mail: khughes@email.arizona.edu. Website: http://www.ag.arizona.edu/srnr/.

University of Arkansas at Pine Bluff, School of Agriculture, Fisheries and Human Sciences, Pine Bluff, AR 71601-2799. Offers aquaculture and fisheries (MS).

University of Delaware, College of Agriculture and Natural Resources, Department of Entomology and Wildlife Ecology, Newark, DE 19716. Offers entomology and applied ecology (MS, PhD), including avian ecology, evolution and taxonomy, insect biological control, insect ecology and behavior (MS), insect genetics, pest management, plant-insect interactions, wildlife ecology and management. Part-time programs available. *Degree requirements:* For master's, comprehensive exam, thesis, oral exam, seminar; for doctorate, comprehensive exam, thesis/dissertation, qualifying exam, seminar. *Entrance requirements:* For master's, GRE General Test, minimum GPA of 3.0 in field, 2.8 overall; for doctorate, GRE General Test, GRE Subject Test (biology), minimum GPA of 3.0 in field, 2.8 overall. Additional exam requirements/recommendations for international students: Required—TOEFL. Electronic applications accepted. *Faculty research:* Ecology and evolution of plant-insect interactions, ecology of wildlife conservation management, habitat restoration, biological control, applied ecosystem management.

University of Florida, Graduate School, College of Agricultural and Life Sciences, Department of Wildlife Ecology and Conservation, Gainesville, FL 32611. Offers MS, PhD. *Degree requirements:* For master's, comprehensive exam, thesis optional; for doctorate, comprehensive exam, thesis/dissertation. *Entrance requirements:* For master's and doctorate, GRE General Test, minimum GPA of 3.3. Additional exam requirements/recommendations for international students: Required—TOEFL (minimum score 550 paper-based; 80 iBT), IELTS (minimum score 6). Electronic applications accepted. *Faculty research:* Wildlife biology and management, tropical ecology and conservation, conservation biology, landscape ecology and restoration, conservation education.

University of Maine, Graduate School, College of Natural Sciences, Forestry, and Agriculture, Department of Wildlife Ecology, Orono, ME 04469. Offers wildlife conservation (MWC); wildlife ecology (MS, PhD). Part-time programs available. *Faculty:* 14 full-time (4 women), 11 part-time/adjunct (1 woman). *Students:* 22 full-time (10 women), 1 part-time (0 women); includes 1 minority (Hispanic/Latino), 1 international. Average age 32. 22 applicants, 27% accepted, 6 enrolled. In 2012, 1 master's awarded. *Degree requirements:* For master's, thesis (for some programs); for doctorate, one foreign language, comprehensive exam, thesis/dissertation. *Entrance requirements:* For master's and doctorate, GRE General Test. Additional exam requirements/recommendations for international students: Required—TOEFL. *Application deadline:* For fall admission, 2/1 priority date for domestic students. Applications are processed on a rolling basis. Application fee: $65. Electronic applications accepted. *Financial support:* In 2012–13, 19 research assistantships with full tuition reimbursements (averaging $18,500 per year), 2 teaching assistantships with full tuition reimbursements (averaging $13,600 per year) were awarded; career-related internships or fieldwork, Federal Work-Study, institutionally sponsored loans, and tuition waivers (full and partial) also available. Financial award application deadline: 3/1. *Faculty research:* Integration of wildlife and forest management; population dynamics; behavior, physiology and nutrition; wetland ecology and influence of environmental disturbances. *Total annual research expenditures:* $159,122. *Unit head:* Dr. Judith Rhymer, Chair, 207-581-2863, Fax: 207-581-2858. *Application contact:* Scott G. Delcourt, Associate Dean of the Graduate School, 207-581-3291, Fax: 207-581-3232, E-mail: graduate@maine.edu. Website: http://umaine.edu/wle/.

University of Massachusetts Amherst, Graduate School, College of Natural Sciences, Department of Environmental Conservation, Amherst, MA 01003. Offers building systems (MS, PhD); environmental policy and human dimensions (MS, PhD); forest resources (MS, PhD); sustainability science (MS); water, wetlands and watersheds (MS, PhD); wildlife and fisheries conservation (MS, PhD). Part-time programs available. *Faculty:* 62 full-time (11 women). *Students:* 52 full-time (18 women), 40 part-time (19 women); includes 2 minority (1 Black or African American, non-Hispanic/Latino; 1 Two or more races, non-Hispanic/Latino), 17 international. Average age 33. 73 applicants, 40% accepted, 18 enrolled. In 2012, 16 master's, 3 doctorates awarded. Terminal master's awarded for partial completion of doctoral program. *Degree requirements:* For master's, thesis or alternative; for doctorate, comprehensive exam, thesis/dissertation. *Entrance requirements:* For master's and doctorate, GRE General Test. Additional exam requirements/recommendations for international students: Required—TOEFL (minimum score 550 paper-based; 80 iBT), IELTS (minimum score 6.5). *Application deadline:* For fall admission, 2/1 for domestic and international students; for spring admission, 10/1 for domestic and international students. Applications are processed on a rolling basis. Application fee: $75. Electronic applications accepted. *Expenses:* Tuition, state resident: full-time $1980; part-time $110 per credit. Tuition, nonresident: full-time $13,314; part-time $414 per credit. *Required fees:* $10,338; $3594 per semester. One-time fee: $357. *Financial support:* Fellowships with full and partial tuition reimbursements, research assistantships with full and partial tuition reimbursements, teaching assistantships with full and partial tuition reimbursements, career-related internships or fieldwork, Federal Work-Study, scholarships/grants, traineeships, health care benefits, tuition waivers (full and partial), and unspecified assistantships available. Support available to part-time students. Financial award application deadline: 2/1. *Unit head:* Dr. Kevin McGarigal, Graduate Program Director, 413-545-2257, Fax: 413-545-4358. *Application contact:* Lindsay DeSantis, Supervisor of Admissions, 413-545-0721, Fax: 413-577-0100, E-mail: gradadm@grad.umass.edu. Website: http://eco.umass.edu/.

University of Miami, Graduate School, Rosenstiel School of Marine and Atmospheric Science, Division of Marine Biology and Fisheries, Coral Gables, FL 33124. Offers MA, MS, PhD. Terminal master's awarded for partial completion of doctoral program. *Degree requirements:* For master's, comprehensive exam, thesis; for doctorate, comprehensive exam, thesis/dissertation. *Entrance requirements:* For master's and doctorate, GRE General Test. Additional exam requirements/recommendations for international students: Required—TOEFL (minimum score 550 paper-based). Electronic applications accepted. *Faculty research:* Biochemistry, physiology, plankton, coral, biology.

University of Missouri, Graduate School, School of Natural Resources, Department of Fisheries and Wildlife, Columbia, MO 65211. Offers conservation biology (Certificate); fisheries and wildlife (MS, PhD). *Faculty:* 10 full-time (1 woman). *Students:* 12 full-time (5 women), 18 part-time (9 women); includes 2 minority (1 Black or African American, non-Hispanic/Latino; 1 Two or more races, non-Hispanic/Latino), 3 international. Average age 29. 15 applicants, 40% accepted, 6 enrolled. In 2012, 8 master's, 3 doctorates, 2 other advanced degrees awarded. *Degree requirements:* For doctorate, thesis/dissertation. *Entrance requirements:* For master's and doctorate, GRE General Test, minimum GPA of 3.0. Additional exam requirements/recommendations for international students: Required—TOEFL (minimum score 550 paper-based; 79 iBT). *Application deadline:* Applications are processed on a rolling basis. Application fee: $55 ($75 for international students). Electronic applications accepted. *Expenses:* Tuition, state resident: full-time $6057. Tuition, nonresident: full-time $15,683. *Required fees:* $1000. *Financial support:* Fellowships, research assistantships, teaching assistantships, institutionally sponsored loans, and scholarships/grants available. *Faculty research:* Limnology; conservation biology; landscape ecology; natural resource policy and management; rare species conservation; avian ecology; behavior and conservation; large river ecology; native fish ecology and restoration ecology; wildlife disease ecology; behavioral, population and community ecology; conservation biology; mammalian carnivores; fish bioenergetics; compensatory growth; fish population dynamics and aquaculture; endangered species recovery; wildlife stress physiology. *Unit head:* Dr. Jack Jones, Department Chair, 573-882-3543, E-mail: jonesj@missouri.edu. *Application contact:* Janice Faaborg, Academic Advisor, 573-882-9422, E-mail: faaborgj@missouri.edu. Website: http://www.snr.missouri.edu/fw/academics/graduate-program.php.

The University of Montana, Graduate School, College of Forestry and Conservation, Missoula, MT 59812-0002. Offers ecosystem management (MEM, MS); fish and wildlife biology (PhD); forestry (MS, PhD); recreation management (MS); resource conservation (MS); wildlife biology (MS). *Degree requirements:* For doctorate, thesis/dissertation. *Entrance requirements:* For master's and doctorate, GRE General Test. Additional exam requirements/recommendations for international students: Required—TOEFL (minimum score 575 paper-based).

University of New Hampshire, Graduate School, College of Life Sciences and Agriculture, Department of Natural Resources, Durham, NH 03824. Offers environmental conservation (MS); forestry (MS); integrated coastal ecosystem science, policy, management (MS); natural resources (MS); water resources (MS); wildlife (MS). Part-time programs available. *Faculty:* 40 full-time. *Students:* 32 full-time (18 women), 29 part-time (16 women); includes 3 minority (all Hispanic/Latino), 3 international. Average age 28. 63 applicants, 43% accepted, 22 enrolled. In 2012, 14 master's awarded. *Degree requirements:* For master's, thesis or alternative. *Entrance requirements:* For master's, GRE General Test. Additional exam requirements/recommendations for international students: Required—TOEFL (minimum score 550 paper-based; 80 iBT). *Application deadline:* For fall admission, 6/1 for domestic students, 4/1 for international students; for spring admission, 12/1 for domestic students. Applications are processed on a rolling basis. Application fee: $65. Electronic applications accepted. *Expenses:* Tuition, state resident: full-time $13,500; part-time $750 per credit. Tuition, nonresident: full-time $25,940; part-time $1089 per credit. *Required fees:* $1699; $424.75 per semester. *Financial support:* In 2012–13, 35 students received support, including 1 fellowship, 15 research assistantships, 23 teaching assistantships; career-related internships or fieldwork, Federal Work-Study, scholarships/grants, and tuition waivers (full and partial) also available. Support available to part-time students. Financial award application deadline: 2/15. *Unit head:* Dr. Ted Howard, Chairperson, 603-862-2700, E-mail: natural.resources@unh.edu. *Application contact:* Nancy Brown, Administrative Assistant, 603-862-1022, E-mail: natural.resources@unh.edu. Website: http://www.nre.unh.edu/academics/.

University of North Dakota, Graduate School, College of Arts and Sciences, Department of Biology, Grand Forks, ND 58202. Offers botany (MS, PhD); ecology (MS, PhD); entomology (MS, PhD); environmental biology (MS, PhD); fisheries/wildlife (MS, PhD); genetics (MS, PhD); zoology (MS, PhD). Terminal master's awarded for partial completion of doctoral program. *Degree requirements:* For master's, thesis, final exam; for doctorate, comprehensive exam, thesis/dissertation, final exam. *Entrance requirements:* For master's, GRE General Test, GRE Subject Test, minimum GPA of 3.0; for doctorate, GRE General Test, GRE Subject Test, minimum GPA of 3.5. Additional exam requirements/recommendations for international students: Required—TOEFL (minimum score 550 paper-based; 79 iBT), IELTS (minimum score 6.5). Electronic applications accepted. *Faculty research:* Population biology, wildlife ecology, RNA processing, hormonal control of behavior.

Fish, Game, and Wildlife Management

University of Rhode Island, Graduate School, College of the Environment and Life Sciences, Department of Fisheries, Animal and Veterinary Science, Kingston, RI 02881. Offers animal health and disease (MS); animal science (MS); aquaculture (MS); aquatic pathology (MS); environmental sciences (PhD), including animal science, aquacultural science, aquatic pathology, fisheries science; fisheries (MS). *Faculty:* 9 full-time (4 women). *Students:* 6 full-time (2 women), 1 part-time (0 women), 2 international. In 2012, 6 master's, 1 doctorate awarded. *Degree requirements:* For master's, comprehensive exam (for some programs), thesis optional; for doctorate, comprehensive exam, thesis/dissertation. *Entrance requirements:* For master's and doctorate, GRE, 2 letters of recommendation. Additional exam requirements/recommendations for international students: Required—TOEFL (minimum score 550 paper-based). *Application deadline:* For fall admission, 7/15 for domestic students, 2/1 for international students; for spring admission, 11/15 for domestic students, 7/15 for international students. Application fee: $65. Electronic applications accepted. *Expenses:* Tuition, state resident: full-time $11,532; part-time $641 per credit. Tuition, nonresident: full-time $23,606; part-time $1311 per credit. *Required fees:* $1388; $36 per credit. $35 per semester. One-time fee: $130. *Financial support:* In 2012–13, 3 research assistantships with full and partial tuition reimbursements (averaging $11,679 per year), 1 teaching assistantship with full and partial tuition reimbursement (averaging $9,818 per year) were awarded. Financial award application deadline: 7/15; financial award applicants required to submit FAFSA. *Unit head:* Dr. David Bengtson, Chair, 401-874-2668, Fax: 401-874-7575, E-mail: bengtson@uri.edu. Website: http://www.uri.edu/cels/favs/.

The University of Tennessee, Graduate School, College of Agricultural Sciences and Natural Resources, Department of Forestry, Wildlife, and Fisheries, Program in Wildlife and Fisheries Science, Knoxville, TN 37996. Offers MS. *Degree requirements:* For master's, thesis. *Entrance requirements:* For master's, GRE General Test, minimum GPA of 2.7. Additional exam requirements/recommendations for international students: Required—TOEFL. Electronic applications accepted. *Expenses:* Tuition, state resident: full-time $9000; part-time $501 per credit hour. Tuition, nonresident: full-time $27,188; part-time $1512 per credit hour. *Required fees:* $1280; $62 per credit hour. Tuition and fees vary according to program.

University of Washington, Graduate School, College of the Environment, School of Aquatic and Fishery Sciences, Seattle, WA 98195. Offers MS, PhD. *Degree requirements:* For master's, thesis; for doctorate, thesis/dissertation. *Entrance requirements:* For master's and doctorate, GRE General Test, minimum GPA of 3.0. Additional exam requirements/recommendations for international students: Required—TOEFL. Electronic applications accepted. *Faculty research:* Fish and shellfish ecology, fisheries management, aquatic ecology, conservation biology, genetics.

University of Washington, Graduate School, College of the Environment, School of Environmental and Forest Sciences, Seattle, WA 98195. Offers bioresource science and engineering (MS, PhD); environmental horticulture (MEH); forest ecology (MS, PhD); forest management (MFR); forest soils (MS, PhD); restoration ecology (MS, PhD); restoration ecology and environmental horticulture (MS, PhD); social sciences (MS, PhD); sustainable resource management (MS, PhD); wildlife science (MS, PhD); MFR/MAIS; MPA/MS. *Accreditation:* SAF. Part-time programs available. *Degree requirements:* For master's, thesis; for doctorate, comprehensive exam (for some programs), thesis/dissertation. *Entrance requirements:* For master's and doctorate, GRE, minimum GPA of 3.0. Additional exam requirements/recommendations for international students: Required—TOEFL, GRE. Electronic applications accepted. *Faculty research:* Ecosystem analysis, silviculture and forest protection, paper science and engineering, environmental horticulture and urban forestry, natural resource policy and economics, restoration ecology and environment horticulture, conservation, human dimensions, wildlife, bioresource science and engineering.

University of Wisconsin–Madison, Graduate School, College of Agricultural and Life Sciences, Department of Forest and Wildlife Ecology, Program in Wildlife Ecology, Madison, WI 53706-1380. Offers MS, PhD. *Expenses:* Tuition, state resident: full-time $10,728; part-time $743 per credit. Tuition, nonresident: full-time $24,054; part-time $1575 per credit. *Required fees:* $1111; $72 per credit.

Utah State University, School of Graduate Studies, College of Natural Resources, Department of Watershed Sciences, Logan, UT 84322. Offers ecology (MS, PhD); fisheries biology (MS, PhD); watershed science (MS, PhD). *Degree requirements:* For master's, thesis (for some programs); for doctorate, thesis/dissertation. *Entrance requirements:* For master's and doctorate, GRE General Test, minimum GPA of 3.2. Additional exam requirements/recommendations for international students: Required—TOEFL. Electronic applications accepted. *Faculty research:* Behavior, population ecology, habitat, conservation biology, restoration, aquatic ecology, fisheries management, fluvial geomorphology, remote sensing, conservation biology.

Utah State University, School of Graduate Studies, College of Natural Resources, Department of Wildland Resources, Logan, UT 84322. Offers ecology (MS, PhD); forestry (MS, PhD); range science (MS, PhD); wildlife biology (MS, PhD). Part-time programs available. *Degree requirements:* For master's, thesis; for doctorate, comprehensive exam, thesis/dissertation. *Entrance requirements:* For master's and doctorate, GRE General Test, minimum GPA of 3.0. Additional exam requirements/recommendations for international students: Required—TOEFL. *Faculty research:* Range plant ecophysiology, plant community ecology, ruminant nutrition, population ecology.

Virginia Polytechnic Institute and State University, Graduate School, College of Natural Resources and Environment, Blacksburg, VA 24061. Offers fisheries and wildlife (MS); forestry and forest products (MF, MS, PhD); geography (MS); geospatial and environmental analysis (PhD); natural resources (PhD). *Faculty:* 68 full-time (14 women). *Students:* 181 full-time (82 women), 78 part-time (47 women); includes 20 minority (5 Black or African American, non-Hispanic/Latino; 1 American Indian or Alaska Native, non-Hispanic/Latino; 4 Asian, non-Hispanic/Latino; 4 Hispanic/Latino; 6 Two or more races, non-Hispanic/Latino), 54 international. Average age 31. 133 applicants, 41% accepted, 48 enrolled. In 2012, 71 master's, 16 doctorates awarded. *Degree requirements:* For master's, comprehensive exam (for some programs), thesis (for some programs); for doctorate, comprehensive exam (for some programs), thesis/dissertation (for some programs). *Entrance requirements:* For master's and doctorate, GRE/GMAT (may vary by department). Additional exam requirements/recommendations for international students: Required—TOEFL (minimum score 550 paper-based). *Application deadline:* For fall admission, 8/1 for domestic students, 4/1 for international students; for spring admission, 1/1 for domestic students, 9/1 for international students. Applications are processed on a rolling basis. Application fee: $65. Electronic applications accepted. *Expenses:* Tuition, state resident: full-time $10,677; part-time $593.25 per credit hour. Tuition, nonresident: full-time $20,926; part-time $1162.50 per credit hour. *Required fees:* $427.75 per semester. Tuition and fees vary according to course load, campus/location and program. *Financial support:* In 2012–13, 92 research assistantships with full tuition reimbursements (averaging $19,523 per year), 43 teaching assistantships with full tuition reimbursements (averaging $16,826 per year) were awarded. Financial award application deadline: 3/1; financial award applicants required to submit FAFSA. *Total annual research expenditures:* $14 million. *Unit head:* Dr. Paul M. Winistorfer, Dean, 540-231-5481, Fax: 540-231-7664, E-mail: pstorfer@vt.edu. *Application contact:* Arlice Banks, Assistant to the Dean, 540-231-5481, Fax: 540-231-7664. Website: http://www.cnre.vt.edu/.

West Virginia University, Davis College of Agriculture, Forestry and Consumer Sciences, Division of Forestry, Program in Wildlife and Fisheries Resources, Morgantown, WV 26506. Offers MS. Part-time programs available. *Degree requirements:* For master's, comprehensive exam, thesis. *Entrance requirements:* For master's, GRE, minimum GPA of 3.0. Additional exam requirements/recommendations for international students: Required—TOEFL. Electronic applications accepted. *Faculty research:* Managing habitat for game, nongame, and fish; fish ecology; wildlife ecology.

Forestry

Auburn University, Graduate School, School of Forestry and Wildlife Sciences, Auburn University, AL 36849. Offers forest economics (PhD); forestry (MS, PhD); natural resource conservation (MNR); wildlife sciences (MS, PhD). *Accreditation:* SAF. Part-time programs available. *Faculty:* 32 full-time (6 women), 2 part-time/adjunct (0 women). *Students:* 28 full-time (12 women), 36 part-time (15 women), 18 international. Average age 28. 28 applicants, 43% accepted, 10 enrolled. In 2012, 22 master's, 5 doctorates awarded. *Degree requirements:* For master's, thesis (MS); for doctorate, thesis/dissertation. *Entrance requirements:* For master's and doctorate, GRE General Test. *Application deadline:* For fall admission, 7/7 for domestic students; for spring admission, 11/24 for domestic students. Applications are processed on a rolling basis. Application fee: $50 ($60 for international students). Electronic applications accepted. *Expenses:* Tuition, state resident: full-time $7866; part-time $437 per credit. Tuition, nonresident: full-time $23,598; part-time $1311 per credit. *Required fees:* $787 per semester. Tuition and fees vary according to degree level and program. *Financial support:* Fellowships, research assistantships, teaching assistantships, and Federal Work-Study available. Support available to part-time students. Financial award application deadline: 3/15; financial award applicants required to submit FAFSA. *Faculty research:* Forest nursery management, silviculture and vegetation management, biological processes and ecological relationships, growth and yield of plantations and natural stands, urban forestry, forest taxation, law and policy. *Unit head:* Dr. James P. Shepard, Dean, 334-844-4000, Fax: 334-844-1084, E-mail: brinker@forestry.auburn.edu. *Application contact:* Dr. George Flowers, Dean of the Graduate School, 334-844-2125. Website: http://www.forestry.auburn.edu/.

California Polytechnic State University, San Luis Obispo, College of Agriculture, Food and Environmental Sciences, Department of Natural Resources Management and Environmental Sciences, San Luis Obispo, CA 93407. Offers forestry sciences (MS). Part-time programs available. *Faculty:* 5 full-time (1

500 www.petersonsbooks.com

Peterson's Graduate Programs in the Physical Sciences, Mathematics, Agricultural Sciences, the Environment & Natural Resources 2014

woman), 1 part-time/adjunct (0 women). *Students:* 2 full-time (0 women), 3 part-time (1 woman); includes 1 minority (Two or more races, non-Hispanic/Latino). Average age 32. 5 applicants, 20% accepted, 1 enrolled. In 2012, 4 master's awarded. *Degree requirements:* For master's, comprehensive exam, thesis. *Entrance requirements:* For master's, minimum GPA of 2.75 in last 90 quarter units of course work. Additional exam requirements/recommendations for international students: Required—TOEFL (minimum score 550 paper-based) or IELTS (minimum score 6). *Application deadline:* For fall admission, 4/1 for domestic students, 11/30 for international students; for winter admission, 10/1 for domestic students, 6/30 for international students; for spring admission, 10/1 for domestic students. Applications are processed on a rolling basis. Application fee: $55. Electronic applications accepted. *Expenses:* Tuition, state resident: full-time $6738; part-time $3906 per year. Tuition, nonresident: full-time $17,898; part-time $8370 per year. *Required fees:* $3051; $874 per term. One-time fee: $3051 full-time; $2622 part-time. *Financial support:* Fellowships, research assistantships, career-related internships or fieldwork, Federal Work-Study, institutionally sponsored loans, scholarships/grants, and unspecified assistantships available. Support available to part-time students. Financial award application deadline: 3/2; financial award applicants required to submit FAFSA. *Faculty research:* Hydrology, biometrics, forest health and management, fire science, urban and community forestry. *Unit head:* Dr. Christopher Dicus, Department Head/Graduate Coordinator, 805-756-5104, Fax: 805-756-1402, E-mail: cdicus@calpoly.edu. *Application contact:* Dr. Mark Shelton, Associate Dean/Graduate Coordinator, 805-756-2161, Fax: 805-756-6577, E-mail: mshelton@calpoly.edu. Website: http://nres.calpoly.edu/.

Clemson University, Graduate School, College of Agriculture, Forestry and Life Sciences, Department of Forestry and Natural Resources, Program in Forest Resources, Clemson, SC 29634. Offers MFR, MS, PhD. Part-time programs available. *Students:* 23 full-time (4 women), 12 part-time (4 women); includes 2 minority (both Two or more races, non-Hispanic/Latino), 6 international. Average age 30. 19 applicants, 47% accepted, 6 enrolled. In 2012, 10 master's, 3 doctorates awarded. *Degree requirements:* For master's, thesis; for doctorate, thesis/dissertation. *Entrance requirements:* For master's, GRE General Test, minimum B average in last 2 years of undergraduate course work; for doctorate, GRE General Test, minimum B average in graduate course work. Additional exam requirements/recommendations for international students: Required TOEFL, IELTS. *Application deadline:* For fall admission, 3/1 priority date for domestic students, 4/15 for international students; for spring admission, 10/1 for domestic students, 9/15 for international students. Applications are processed on a rolling basis. Application fee: $70 ($80 for international students). Electronic applications accepted. *Expenses:* Contact institution. *Financial support:* In 2012–13, 20 students received support, including 3 fellowships with full and partial tuition reimbursements available (averaging $6,000 per year), 11 research assistantships with partial tuition reimbursements available (averaging $12,855 per year), 9 teaching assistantships with partial tuition reimbursements available (averaging $8,557 per year); career-related internships or fieldwork, institutionally sponsored loans, scholarships/grants, health care benefits, and unspecified assistantships also available. Support available to part-time students. Financial award application deadline: 5/1; financial award applicants required to submit FAFSA. *Faculty research:* Wetlands management, wood technology, forest management, silviculture, economics. *Unit head:* Dr. Patricia Layton, Chair, 864-656-3303, Fax: 864-656-3304, E-mail: playton@clemson.edu. *Application contact:* Dr. David Guynn, Graduate Program Coordinator, 864-656-4830, E-mail: dguynn@clemson.edu. Website: http://www.clemson.edu/cafls/departments/forestry/.

Colorado State University, Graduate School, Warner College of Natural Resources, Department of Forest and Rangeland Stewardship, Fort Collins, CO 80523-1472. Offers forest sciences (MS, PhD); natural resources stewardship (MNRS); rangeland ecosystem science (MS, PhD); watershed science (MS). Part-time programs available. Postbaccalaureate distance learning degree programs offered (no on-campus study). *Faculty:* 12 full-time (2 women). *Students:* 26 full-time (7 women), 80 part-time (34 women); includes 6 minority (1 American Indian or Alaska Native, non-Hispanic/Latino; 5 Hispanic/Latino), 11 international. Average age 35. 20 applicants, 100% accepted, 17 enrolled. In 2012, 17 master's, 3 doctorates awarded. *Degree requirements:* For master's, thesis (for some programs); for doctorate, comprehensive exam, thesis/dissertation. *Entrance requirements:* For master's, GRE General Test (minimum score 1000 verbal and quantitative), minimum GPA of 3.0, 3 letters of recommendation; for doctorate, GRE General Test (combined minimum score of 1100 on the Verbal and Quantitative sections), minimum GPA of 3.0, 3 letters of recommendation, statement of research interest. Additional exam requirements/recommendations for international students: Required—TOEFL (minimum score 550 paper-based; 80 iBT), IELTS (minimum score 6.5). *Application deadline:* For fall admission, 2/15 priority date for domestic students, 2/15 for international students; for spring admission, 7/15 priority date for domestic students, 7/15 for international students. Applications are processed on a rolling basis. Application fee: $50. Electronic applications accepted. *Expenses:* Tuition, state resident: full-time $8811; part-time $490 per credit. Tuition, nonresident: full-time $21,600; part-time $1200 per credit. *Required fees:* $1819; $61 per credit. *Financial support:* In 2012–13, 53 students received support, including 3 fellowships (averaging $14,767 per year), 36 research assistantships with full and partial tuition reimbursements available (averaging $16,479 per year), 14 teaching assistantships with full and partial tuition reimbursements available (averaging $6,991 per year); Federal Work-Study, scholarships/grants, and unspecified assistantships also available. Financial award application deadline: 2/15; financial award applicants required to submit FAFSA. *Faculty research:* Ecology, natural resource management, hydrology, restoration, human dimensions. *Total annual research expenditures:* $2.4 million. *Unit head:* Dr. Frederick Smith, Department Head and Professor, 970-491-7505, Fax: 970-491-6754, E-mail: fwsmith@colostate.edu. *Application contact:* Sonya LeFebre, Coordinator, 970-491-1907, Fax: 970-491-6754, E-mail: sonya.lefebre@colostate.edu. Website: http://warnercnr.colostate.edu/frws-home/.

Cornell University, Graduate School, Graduate Fields of Agriculture and Life Sciences, Field of Natural Resources, Ithaca, NY 14853-0001. Offers community-based natural resources management (MS, PhD); ecosystem biology and biogeochemistry (MPS, MS, PhD); environmental management (MPS); fishery and aquatic science (MPS, MS, PhD); forest science (MPS, MS, PhD); human dimensions of natural resources management (MPS, MS, PhD); program development and evaluation (MPS, MS, PhD); wildlife science (MPS, MS, PhD). *Faculty:* 40 full-time (8 women). *Students:* 56 full-time (23 women); includes 2 minority (1 Asian, non-Hispanic/Latino; 1 Two or more races, non-Hispanic/Latino), 12 international. Average age 32. 61 applicants, 33% accepted, 15 enrolled. In 2012, 7 master's, 6 doctorates awarded. *Degree requirements:* For master's, thesis (MS), project paper (MPS); for doctorate, comprehensive exam, thesis/dissertation. *Entrance requirements:* For master's and doctorate, GRE General Test, 2 letters of recommendation. Additional exam requirements/recommendations for international students: Required—TOEFL (minimum score 550 paper-based; 77 iBT). *Application deadline:* For spring admission, 10/30 for domestic students. Applications are processed on a rolling basis. Application fee: $95. Electronic applications accepted. *Financial support:* In 2012–13, 46 students received support, including 14 fellowships with full tuition reimbursements available, 15 research assistantships with full tuition reimbursements available, 17 teaching assistantships with full tuition reimbursements available; institutionally sponsored loans, scholarships/grants, health care benefits, tuition waivers (full and partial), and unspecified assistantships also available. Financial award applicants required to submit FAFSA. *Faculty research:* Ecosystem-level dynamics, systems modeling, conservation biology/management, resource management's human dimensions, biogeochemistry. *Unit head:* Director of Graduate Studies, 607-255-2807, Fax: 607-255-0349. *Application contact:* Graduate Field Assistant, 607-255-2807, Fax: 607-255-0349, E-mail: nrgrad@cornell.edu. Website: http://www.gradschool.cornell.edu/fields.php?id-54&a-2.

Duke University, Graduate School, Nicholas School of the Environment, Durham, NC 27708. Offers environmental management (MEM); forestry (MF); natural resource economics/policy (PhD); natural resource science/ecology (PhD); natural resource systems science (PhD); JD/AM. Part-time programs available. *Faculty:* 28 full-time. *Students:* 59 full-time (33 women); includes 2 minority (both Asian, non-Hispanic/Latino), 18 international. 99 applicants, 19% accepted, 12 enrolled. In 2012, 11 doctorates awarded. *Degree requirements:* For doctorate, variable foreign language requirement, thesis/dissertation. *Entrance requirements:* For master's and doctorate, GRE General Test. Additional exam requirements/recommendations for international students: Required—TOEFL (minimum score 550 paper-based; 83 iBT), IELTS (minimum score 7). *Application deadline:* For fall admission, 12/8 priority date for domestic students, 12/8 for international students. Application fee: $80. Electronic applications accepted. *Financial support:* Fellowships, research assistantships, teaching assistantships, and Federal Work-Study available. Financial award application deadline: 12/8. *Unit head:* Gaby Katul, Director of Graduate Studies, 919-613-8002, Fax: 919-613-8061, E-mail: meg.stephens@duke.edu. *Application contact:* Elizabeth Hutton, Director, Graduate Admissions, 919-684-3913, Fax: 919-684-2277, E-mail: grad-admissions@duke.edu. Website: http://www.nicholas.duke.edu/.

Harvard University, Graduate School of Arts and Sciences, Department of Forestry, Cambridge, MA 02138. Offers forest science (MFS). *Degree requirements:* For master's, thesis. *Entrance requirements:* For master's, GRE General Test, bachelor's degree in biology or forestry. Additional exam requirements/recommendations for international students: Required—TOEFL. *Expenses: Tuition:* Full-time $37,576. *Required fees:* $930. Tuition and fees vary according to program and student level. *Faculty research:* Forest ecology, planning, and physiology; forest microbiology.

Humboldt State University, Academic Programs, College of Natural Resources and Sciences, Programs in Natural Resources, Arcata, CA 95521-8299. Offers natural resources (MS), including fisheries, forestry, natural resources planning and interpretation, rangeland resources and wildland soils, wastewater utilization, watershed management, wildlife. *Students:* 36 full-time (18 women), 20 part-time (9 women); includes 2 minority (1 Asian, non-Hispanic/Latino; 1 Two or more races, non-Hispanic/Latino). Average age 30. 51 applicants, 37% accepted, 11 enrolled. In 2012, 29 master's awarded. *Degree requirements:* For master's, thesis or alternative. *Entrance requirements:* For master's, GRE, appropriate bachelor's degree, minimum GPA of 2.5, 3 letters of recommendation, resume. Additional exam requirements/recommendations for international students: Required—TOEFL (minimum score 500 paper-based). *Application deadline:* For fall admission, 2/1 for domestic and international students; for spring admission, 9/30 for domestic and international students. Applications are processed on a rolling basis. Application fee: $55. *Expenses:* Tuition, state resident: full-time $8396. Tuition, nonresident: full-time $17,324. Tuition and fees vary according to program. *Financial support:* Fellowships, career-related internships or fieldwork, and Federal Work-Study available. Support available to part-time students. Financial award application deadline: 3/1; financial award applicants required to submit FAFSA. *Faculty research:* Spotted owl habitat, pre-settlement vegetation, hardwood utilization, tree physiology, fisheries. *Unit head:* Dr. Robert Van Kirk, Coordinator, 707-826-3744, E-mail: rob.vankirk@humboldt.edu. *Application contact:* Julie Tucker, Administrative Support Coordinator, 707-826-3256, E-mail: jlt7002@humboldt.edu. Website: http://www.humboldt.edu/cnrs/graduate_programs.

Iowa State University of Science and Technology, Department of Natural Resource Ecology and Management, Ames, IA 50011. Offers forestry (MS, PhD); wildlife ecology (MS). *Entrance requirements:* For master's and doctorate, GRE General Test. Additional exam requirements/recommendations for international students: Required—TOEFL (minimum score 550 paper-based; 79 iBT), IELTS (minimum score 6.5). *Application deadline:* For fall admission, 4/1 priority date for domestic students, 4/1 for international students; for spring admission, 10/1 priority date for domestic students, 10/1 for international students. Application fee: $60 ($90 for international students). Electronic applications accepted. *Application contact:* Kelly Kyle, Director of Graduate Education, 515-294-7400, Fax: 515-294-7406, E-mail: nremgradinfo@iastate.edu. Website: http://www.nrem.iastate.edu/.

Iowa State University of Science and Technology, Program in Forestry, Ames, IA 50011. Offers MS, PhD. *Entrance requirements:* For master's and doctorate, GRE. Additional exam requirements/recommendations for international students: Required—TOEFL (minimum score 550 paper-based; 79 iBT), IELTS (minimum score 6.5). *Application deadline:* For fall admission, 4/1 for domestic students; for spring admission, 10/1 for domestic students. Application fee: $60 ($90 for international students). Electronic applications accepted. *Application contact:* Kelly Kyle, Application Contact, 515-294-7400, Fax: 515-294-7406, E-mail: nremgradinfo@iastate.edu. Website: http://www.nrem.iastate.edu.

Lakehead University, Graduate Studies, Faculty of Natural Resources Management, Thunder Bay, ON P7B 5E1, Canada. Offers forest sciences (PhD); forestry (M Sc F). Part-time programs available. *Degree requirements:* For master's, thesis. *Entrance requirements:* For master's, minimum B average. Additional exam requirements/recommendations for international students: Required—TOEFL. *Faculty research:* Soils, silviculture, wildlife, ecology, genetics.

Louisiana State University and Agricultural and Mechanical College, Graduate School, College of Agriculture, School of Renewable Natural Resources, Baton Rouge, LA 70803. Offers fisheries (MS); forestry (MS, PhD); wildlife (MS); wildlife and fisheries science (PhD). *Faculty:* 31 full-time (5 women). *Students:* 51 full-time (15 women), 5 part-time (2 women); includes 3 minority (2 Black or African American, non-Hispanic/Latino; 1 Hispanic/Latino), 12 international. Average age 29. 34 applicants, 41% accepted, 13 enrolled. In 2012, 11 master's, 10 doctorates awarded. *Degree requirements:* For master's, thesis; for doctorate, thesis/dissertation. *Entrance requirements:* For master's, GRE General Test, minimum GPA of 3.0; for doctorate, GRE General Test, MS, minimum GPA of 3.0. Additional exam requirements/recommendations for international students: Required—TOEFL (minimum score 550 paper-based; 79 iBT), IELTS (minimum score 6.5). *Application deadline:* For fall admission, 1/25 priority date for domestic students, 5/15 for international students; for spring admission, 10/15 for international students. Applications are processed on a rolling basis. Application fee: $50 ($70 for international students). Electronic applications accepted. *Financial support:* In 2012–13, 55 students received support, including 49 research assistantships with partial tuition reimbursements available (averaging $19,751 per year), 2 teaching assistantships (averaging $10,250 per year); fellowships, Federal Work-Study, institutionally sponsored loans, scholarships/grants, health care benefits, tuition waivers (full and partial), and unspecified assistantships also available. Financial award application deadline: 4/15; financial award applicants required to submit FAFSA. *Faculty research:* Forest biology and management, aquaculture, fisheries biology and ecology, upland and wetlands wildlife. *Total annual research expenditures:* $163,169. *Unit head:* Dr. Allen Rutherford, Director, 225-578-4131, Fax: 225-578-4227, E-mail: druther@lsu.edu. *Application contact:* Dr. William Kelso, Coordinator of Graduate Studies, 225-578-4176, Fax: 225-578-4227, E-mail: wkelso@lsu.edu. Website: http://www.fwf.lsu.edu/.

McGill University, Faculty of Graduate and Postdoctoral Studies, Faculty of Agricultural and Environmental Sciences, Department of Natural Resource Sciences, Montréal, QC H3A 2T5, Canada. Offers entomology (M Sc, PhD); environmental assessment (M Sc); forest science (M Sc, PhD); microbiology (M Sc, PhD); micrometeorology (M Sc, PhD); neotropical environment (M Sc, PhD); soil science (M Sc, PhD); wildlife biology (M Sc, PhD).

Michigan State University, The Graduate School, College of Agriculture and Natural Resources, Department of Forestry, East Lansing, MI 48824. Offers forestry (MS, PhD); forestry-environmental toxicology (PhD); plant breeding, genetics and biotechnology-forestry (MS, PhD). *Entrance requirements:* Additional exam requirements/recommendations for international students: Required—TOEFL (minimum score 550 paper-based), Michigan State University ELT (minimum score 85), Michigan English Language Assessment Battery (minimum score 83). Electronic applications accepted.

Michigan Technological University, Graduate School, School of Forest Resources and Environmental Science, Houghton, MI 49931. Offers applied ecology (MS); forest ecology and management (MS); forest science (PhD); forestry (MF, MS); molecular genetics and biotechnology (MS, PhD). *Accreditation:* SAF. Part-time programs available. Terminal master's awarded for partial completion of doctoral program. *Degree requirements:* For master's, comprehensive exam (for some programs), thesis (for some programs); for doctorate, comprehensive exam, thesis/dissertation. *Entrance requirements:* For master's and doctorate, GRE (minimum scores: 500 in verbal, 500 quantitative, 3.5 in analytical), statement of purpose, official transcripts, 3 letters of recommendation, resume/curriculum vitae. Additional exam requirements/recommendations for international students: Required—TOEFL (minimum score 79 iBT) or IELTS. Electronic applications accepted. *Faculty research:* Forest molecular genetics and biotechnology, forestry, forest ecology and management, applied ecology, wood science.

Mississippi State University, College of Forest Resources, Department of Forest Products, Mississippi State, MS 39762. Offers forest products (MS); forest resources (PhD), including forest products. *Faculty:* 11 full-time (2 women), 2 part-time/adjunct (0 women). *Students:* 19 full-time (8 women), 2 part-time (1 woman), 16 international. Average age 30. 19 applicants, 26% accepted, 4 enrolled. In 2012, 9 master's, 5 doctorates awarded. *Degree requirements:* For master's, thesis optional; for doctorate, comprehensive exam, thesis/dissertation. *Entrance requirements:* For master's, GRE (if undergraduate GPA of last two years less than 3.0); for doctorate, GRE if undergraduate GPA of last two years is below 3.0. Additional exam requirements/recommendations for international students: Required—TOEFL (minimum score 550 paper-based; 79 iBT); Recommended—IELTS (minimum score 6.5). *Application deadline:* For fall admission, 7/1 for domestic students, 5/1 for international students; for spring admission, 11/1 for domestic students, 9/1 for international students. Applications are processed on a rolling basis. Application fee: $60. Electronic applications accepted. *Financial support:* In 2012–13, 17 research assistantships with full tuition reimbursements (averaging $13,579 per year), 1 teaching assistantship with full tuition reimbursement (averaging $15,133 per year) were awarded; Federal Work-Study, institutionally sponsored loans, and unspecified assistantships also available. Financial award application deadline: 4/1; financial award applicants required to submit FAFSA. *Faculty research:* Wood property enhancement and durability, environmental science and chemistry, wood-based composites, primary wood production, furniture manufacturing and management. *Unit head:* Dr. Robin Shmulsky, Department Head, 662-325-2243, Fax: 662-325-8126, E-mail: rshmulsky@cfr.msstate.edu. *Application contact:* Dr. Tor Schultz, Graduate Coordinator, 662-325-2116, Fax: 662-325-8726, E-mail: tschultz@cfr.msstate.edu. Website: http://www.cfr.msstate.edu/forestp/.

Mississippi State University, College of Forest Resources, Department of Forestry, Mississippi State, MS 39762. Offers forest resources (PhD); forestry (MS). Part-time programs available. *Faculty:* 15 full-time (2 women). *Students:* 28 full-time (9 women), 35 part-time (7 women); includes 3 minority (1 Black or African American, non-Hispanic/Latino; 1 American Indian or Alaska Native, non-Hispanic/Latino; 1 Hispanic/Latino), 12 international. Average age 30. 29 applicants, 48% accepted, 12 enrolled. In 2012, 6 master's awarded. *Degree requirements:* For master's, thesis optional, comprehensive oral or written exam; for doctorate, comprehensive exam, thesis/dissertation. *Entrance requirements:* For master's, GRE, BS with minimum GPA of 3.0 on last 60 hours of undergraduate study; for doctorate, minimum GPA of 3.1 on prior graduate courses or 3.25 on last 60 hours of undergraduate study. Additional exam requirements/recommendations for international students: Required—TOEFL (minimum score 550 paper-based; 79 iBT); Recommended—IELTS (minimum score 6.5). *Application deadline:* For fall admission, 7/1 for domestic students, 5/1 for international students; for spring admission, 11/1 for domestic students, 9/1 for international students. Applications are processed on a rolling basis. Application fee: $60. Electronic applications accepted. *Financial support:* In 2012–13, 26 research assistantships with full tuition reimbursements (averaging $13,651 per year) were awarded; Federal Work-Study, institutionally sponsored loans, and unspecified assistantships also available. Financial award application deadline: 4/1; financial award applicants required to submit FAFSA. *Faculty research:* Forest hydrology, forest biometry, forest management/economics, forest biology, industrial forest operations. *Unit head:* Dr. Andrew Ezell, Professor/Head/Graduate Coordinator, 662-325-2949, Fax: 662-325-8126, E-mail: aezell@cfr.msstate.edu. Website: http://www.cfr.msstate.edu/forestry/.

Mississippi State University, College of Forest Resources, Department of Wildlife, Fisheries and Aquaculture, Mississippi State, MS 39762. Offers forest resources (PhD), including wildlife and fisheries; wildlife and fisheries science (MS). Part-time programs available. *Faculty:* 20 full-time (1 woman), 1 part-time/adjunct (0 women). *Students:* 57 full-time (15 women), 20 part-time (8 women); includes 3 minority (1 Black or African American, non-Hispanic/Latino; 1 Hispanic/Latino; 1 Two or more races, non-Hispanic/Latino), 7 international. Average age 29. 25 applicants, 40% accepted, 10 enrolled. In 2012, 12 master's, 4 doctorates awarded. *Degree requirements:* For master's, thesis, comprehensive oral or written exam; for doctorate, comprehensive exam, thesis/dissertation. *Entrance requirements:* For master's, GRE, bachelor's degree, minimum GPA of 3.0 on last 60 hours of undergraduate courses; for doctorate, GRE, master's degree, minimum GPA of 3.2 on prior graduate studies. Additional exam requirements/recommendations for international students: Required—TOEFL (minimum score 550 paper-based; 79 iBT); Recommended—IELTS (minimum score 6.5). *Application deadline:* For fall admission, 7/1 for domestic students, 5/1 for international students; for spring admission, 11/1 for domestic students, 9/1 for international students. Applications are processed on a rolling basis. Application fee: $60. Electronic applications accepted. *Financial support:* In 2012–13, 53 research assistantships with partial tuition reimbursements (averaging $15,410 per year), 1 teaching assistantship with partial tuition reimbursement (averaging $19,223 per year) were awarded; Federal Work-Study, institutionally sponsored loans, and unspecified assistantships also available. Financial award application deadline: 4/1; financial award applicants required to submit FAFSA. *Faculty research:* Spatial technology, habitat restoration, aquaculture, fisheries, wildlife management. *Unit head:* Dr. Bruce D. Leopold, Department Head and Graduate Coordinator, 662-325-2615, Fax: 662-325-8726, E-mail: bleopold@cfr.msstate.edu. *Application contact:* Dr. Eric Dibble, Professor and Coordinator of Graduate Studies, 662-325-7494, Fax: 662-325-8726, E-mail: edibble@cfr.msstate.edu. Website: http://www.cfr.msstate.edu/wildlife/index.asp.

North Carolina State University, Graduate School, College of Natural Resources, Department of Forestry and Environmental Resources, Raleigh, NC 27695. Offers MF, MS, PhD. Part-time programs available. *Degree requirements:* For master's, thesis (for some programs), teaching experience; for doctorate, thesis/dissertation, teaching experience. *Entrance requirements:* For master's and doctorate, GRE General Test. Additional exam requirements/recommendations for international students: Required—TOEFL. Electronic applications accepted. *Faculty research:* Forest genetics, forest ecology and silviculture, forest economics/management/policy, international forestry, remote sensing/geographic information systems.

Northern Arizona University, Graduate College, College of Engineering, Forestry and Natural Sciences, School of Forestry, Flagstaff, AZ 86011. Offers forest science (MF, MSF), forestry (PhD). Part-time programs available. *Degree requirements:* For master's, thesis optional; for doctorate, comprehensive exam, thesis/dissertation. *Entrance requirements:* For master's, GRE General Test; for doctorate, GRE General Test. Additional exam requirements/recommendations for international students: Required—TOEFL (minimum score 550 paper-based; 80 iBT), IELTS (minimum score 7). Electronic applications accepted. *Faculty research:* Multiresource management, ecology, entomology, recreation, hydrology.

Oklahoma State University, College of Agricultural Science and Natural Resources, Department of Natural Resource Ecology and Management, Stillwater, OK 74078. Offers M Ag, MS, PhD. *Faculty:* 32 full-time (2 women), 1 part-time/adjunct (0 women). *Students:* 7 full-time (2 women), 57 part-time (16 women); includes 8 minority (1 Black or African American, non-Hispanic/Latino; 3 American Indian or Alaska Native, non-Hispanic/Latino; 4 Two or more races, non-Hispanic/Latino), 11 international. Average age 30. 31 applicants, 52% accepted, 14 enrolled. In 2012, 8 master's, 2 doctorates awarded. *Degree requirements:* For master's, comprehensive exam (for some programs), thesis; for doctorate, comprehensive exam, thesis/dissertation. *Entrance requirements:* For master's and doctorate, GRE or GMAT. Additional exam requirements/recommendations for international students: Required—TOEFL (minimum score 550 paper-based; 79 iBT). *Application deadline:* For fall admission, 3/1 for international students; for spring admission, 8/1 for international students. Applications are processed on a rolling basis. Application fee: $40 ($75 for international students). Electronic applications accepted. *Expenses:* Tuition, state resident: full-time $4272; part-time $178 per credit hour. Tuition, nonresident: full-time $17,016; part-time $709 per credit hour. *Required fees:* $2188; $91.17 per credit hour. One-time fee: $50 full-time. Part-time tuition and fees vary according to course load and campus/location. *Financial support:* In 2012–13, 53 research assistantships (averaging $16,317 per year), 1 teaching assistantship (averaging $17,496 per year) were awarded; career-related internships or fieldwork, Federal Work-Study, scholarships/grants, health care benefits, tuition waivers (partial), and unspecified assistantships also available. Support available to part-time students. Financial award application deadline: 3/1; financial award applicants required to submit FAFSA. *Faculty research:* Forest ecology, upland bird ecology, forest ecophysiology, urban forestry, molecular forest genetics/biotechnology/tree breeding. *Unit head:* Dr. Keith Owens, Head, 405-744-5438, Fax: 405-744-3530. *Application contact:* Dr. Sheryl Tucker, Dean, 405-744-7099, Fax: 405-744-0355, E-mail: grad-i@okstate.edu. Website: http://nrem.okstate.edu/.

Oregon State University, College of Forestry, Department of Forest Ecosystems and Society, Corvallis, OR 97331. Offers MAIS, MF, MS, PhD. Part-time programs available. *Faculty:* 25 full-time (2 women), 18 part-time/adjunct (6 women). *Students:* 62 full-time (37 women), 36 part-time (20 women); includes 6 minority (1 Black or African American, non-Hispanic/Latino; 3 Asian, non-Hispanic/Latino; 1 Hispanic/Latino; 1 Two or more races, non-Hispanic/Latino), 6 international. Average age 32. 102 applicants, 43% accepted, 30 enrolled. In 2012, 13 master's, 2 doctorates awarded. *Degree requirements:* For master's, thesis (for some programs); for doctorate, thesis/dissertation. *Entrance requirements:* For master's and doctorate, GRE General Test, minimum GPA of 3.0 in last 90 hours. Additional exam requirements/recommendations for international students: Required—TOEFL. *Application deadline:* For fall admission, 8/25 priority date for domestic students; for spring admission, 3/1 for domestic students. Applications are processed on a rolling basis. Application fee: $50. *Expenses:* Tuition, state resident: full-time $11,367; part-time $421 per credit hour. Tuition, nonresident: full-time $18,279; part-time $677 per credit hour. *Required fees:* $1478. One-time fee: $300 full-time. Tuition and fees vary according to course load and program. *Financial support:* Fellowships, research assistantships, career-related internships or fieldwork, Federal Work-Study, and institutionally sponsored loans available. Support available to part-time students. Financial award application deadline: 2/1. *Faculty research:* Ecosystem structure and function, nutrient cycling, biotechnology, vegetation management, integrated forest protection. *Unit head:* Dr. Paul Doescher, Professor/Department Head, 541-737-6583, Fax: 541-737-1393, E-mail: paul.doescher@oregonstate.edu. *Application contact:* Dr. John Bliss, Associate Dean for Graduate and International Programs, 541-737-4427, E-mail: john.bliss@oregonstate.edu. Website: http://fes.forestry.oregonstate.edu/.

Oregon State University, College of Forestry, Department of Forest Engineering, Resources and Management, Program in Sustainable Forest Management, Corvallis, OR 97331. Offers MAIS, MS, PhD. *Students:* 19 full-time (5 women); includes 1 minority (Two or more races, non-Hispanic/Latino), 3 international. Average age 29. 36 applicants, 58% accepted, 17 enrolled. *Expenses:* Tuition, state resident: full-time $11,367; part-time $421 per credit hour. Tuition, nonresident: full-time $18,279; part-time $677 per credit hour. *Required fees:* $1478. One-time fee: $300 full-time. Tuition and fees vary according to course load and program. *Unit head:* Dr. Thomas Maness, Professor and Dean, 541-737-1585, Fax: 541-737-2906, E-mail: thomas.maness@oregonstate.edu. *Application contact:* Dr. John Bliss, Associate Dean for Graduate and International Programs, 541-737-4427, E-mail: john.bliss@oregonstate.edu.

Oregon State University, College of Forestry, Department of Wood Science and Engineering, Corvallis, OR 97331. Offers forest products (MAIS, MF, MS, PhD); wood science and technology (MF, MS, PhD). Part-time programs available. *Faculty:* 16 full-time (2 women). *Students:* 13 full-time (3 women), 4 part-time (0 women), 7 international. Average age 30. 18 applicants, 22% accepted, 4 enrolled. In 2012, 8 master's, 2 doctorates awarded. *Degree requirements:* For master's, thesis (for some programs); for doctorate, thesis/dissertation. *Entrance requirements:* For master's and doctorate, GRE General Test, minimum GPA of 3.0 in last 90 hours. Additional exam requirements/recommendations for international students: Required—TOEFL. *Application deadline:* For fall admission, 3/1 priority date for domestic students. Applications are processed on a rolling basis. Application fee: $50. *Expenses:* Tuition, state resident: full-time $11,367; part-time $421 per credit hour. Tuition, nonresident: full-time $18,279; part-time $677 per credit hour. *Required fees:* $1478. One-time fee: $300 full-time. Tuition and fees vary according to course load and program. *Financial support:* Fellowships, research assistantships, career-related internships or fieldwork, Federal Work-Study, and institutionally sponsored loans available. Support available to part-time students. Financial award application deadline: 2/1. *Faculty research:* Biodeterioration and preservation, timber engineering, process engineering and control, composite materials science, anatomy, chemistry and physical properties. *Unit head:* Dr. Fred Kramke, Professor/Chair of Wood-based Composites Science, 541-737-8422, E-mail: fred.kamke@oregonstate.edu. *Application contact:* Dr. John Bliss, Associate Dean for Graduate and International Programs, 541-737-4427, Fax: 541-737-1393, E-mail: john.bliss@oregonstate.edu. Website: http://www.cof.orst.edu/cof/fp/.

Penn State University Park, Graduate School, College of Agricultural Sciences, Department of Ecosystem Science and Management, State College, University Park, PA 16802-1503. Offers forest resources (MS, PhD); soil science (MS, PhD); wildlife and fisheries science (MS, PhD). *Unit head:* Dr. Barbara J. Christ, Interim Dean, 814-865-2541, Fax: 814-865-3103, E-mail: ebf@psu.edu. *Application contact:* Cynthia E. Nicosia, Director of Graduate Enrollment Services, 814-865-1834, E-mail: cey1@psu.edu. Website: http://ecosystems.psu.edu.

Purdue University, Graduate School, College of Agriculture, Department of Forestry and Natural Resources, West Lafayette, IN 47907. Offers fisheries and aquatic sciences (MS, MSF, PhD); forest biology (MS, MSF, PhD); natural resource social science (MS, PhD); natural resources social science (MSF); quantitative ecology (MS, MSF, PhD); wildlife science (MS, MSF, PhD); wood products and wood products manufacturing (MS, MSF, PhD). *Faculty:* 25 full-time (3 women), 10 part-time/adjunct (1 woman). *Students:* 61 full-time (24 women), 11 part-time (6 women); includes 3 minority (1 American Indian or Alaska Native, non-Hispanic/Latino; 2 Hispanic/Latino), 18 international. Average age 29. 57 applicants, 28% accepted, 15 enrolled. In 2012, 18 master's, 7 doctorates awarded. *Degree requirements:* For master's, thesis; for doctorate, thesis/dissertation. *Entrance requirements:* For master's and doctorate, GRE General Test (minimum score: verbal 50th percentile; quantitative 50th percentile; analytical writing 4.0), minimum undergraduate GPA of 3.2 or equivalent. Additional exam requirements/recommendations for international students: Required—TOEFL (minimum score 550 paper-based; 77 iBT). *Application deadline:* For fall admission, 1/5 for domestic students, 1/15 for international students; for spring admission, 9/15 for domestic and international students. Applications are processed on a rolling basis. Application fee: $60 ($75 for international students). Electronic applications accepted. *Financial support:* In 2012–13, 10 research assistantships (averaging $15,259 per year) were awarded; fellowships, teaching assistantships, career-related internships or fieldwork, and scholarships/grants also available. Support available to part-time students. Financial award application deadline: 1/5; financial award applicants required to submit FAFSA. *Faculty research:* Wildlife management, forest management, forest ecology, forest soils, limnology. *Unit head:* Dr. Robert K. Swihart, Interim Head, 765-494-3590, Fax: 765-494-9461, E-mail: rswihart@purdue.edu. *Application contact:* Kelly J. Wrede, Graduate Secretary, 765-494-3572, Fax: 765-494-9461, E-mail: kgarrett@purdue.edu. Website: http://www.fnr.purdue.edu/.

Southern Illinois University Carbondale, Graduate School, College of Agriculture, Department of Forestry, Carbondale, IL 62901-4701. Offers MS. Part-time programs available. *Faculty:* 9 full-time (0 women). *Students:* 16 full-time (14 women), 4 part-time (all women). Average age 24. 14 applicants, 57% accepted, 7 enrolled. In 2012, 4 master's awarded. *Degree requirements:* For master's, thesis. *Entrance requirements:* For master's, GRE, minimum GPA of 2.7. Additional exam requirements/recommendations for international students:

Required—TOEFL. *Application deadline:* Applications are processed on a rolling basis. Application fee: $50. *Financial support:* In 2012–13, 18 students received support, including 3 fellowships with full tuition reimbursements available, 10 research assistantships with full tuition reimbursements available, 3 teaching assistantships with full tuition reimbursements available; career-related internships or fieldwork, Federal Work-Study, institutionally sponsored loans, and tuition waivers (full) also available. Support available to part-time students. *Faculty research:* Forest recreation, forest ecology, remote sensing, forest management and economics. *Unit head:* Dr. Jim Zaczek, Chair, 618-453-7465, E-mail: zaczek@siu.edu. *Application contact:* Patti Cludray, Administrative Clerk, 618-453-3341, E-mail: plc1@siu.edu.

Southern University and Agricultural and Mechanical College, Graduate School, College of Agricultural, Family and Consumer Sciences, Department of Urban Forestry, Baton Rouge, LA 70813. Offers MS. *Degree requirements:* For master's, thesis. *Entrance requirements:* For master's, GRE, minimum GPA of 3.0. Additional exam requirements/recommendations for international students: Required—TOEFL (minimum score 525 paper-based). *Faculty research:* Biology of plant pathogen, water resources, plant pathology.

State University of New York College of Environmental Science and Forestry, Department of Environmental and Forest Biology, Syracuse, NY 13210-2779. Offers applied ecology (MPS); chemical ecology (MPS, MS, PhD); conservation biology (MPS, MS, PhD); ecology (MPS, MS, PhD); entomology (MPS, MS, PhD); environmental interpretation (MPS, MS, PhD); environmental physiology (MPS, MS, PhD); fish and wildlife biology and management (MPS, MS, PhD); forest pathology and mycology (MPS, MS, PhD); plant biotechnology (MPS); plant science and biotechnology (MPS, MS, PhD). *Degree requirements:* For master's, thesis (for some programs); for doctorate, comprehensive exam, thesis/dissertation. *Entrance requirements:* For master's and doctorate, GRE General Test, GRE Subject Test, minimum GPA of 3.0. Additional exam requirements/recommendations for international students: Required—TOEFL (minimum score 550 paper-based; 80 iBT), IELTS (minimum score 6). *Expenses:* Tuition, state resident: full-time $9370; part-time $390 per credit hour. Tuition, nonresident: full-time $16,680; part-time $695 per credit hour. *Required fees:* $981. Tuition and fees vary according to course load and program. *Faculty research:* Ecology, fish and wildlife biology and management, plant science, entomology.

State University of New York College of Environmental Science and Forestry, Department of Forest and Natural Resources Management, Syracuse, NY 13210-2779. Offers ecology and ecosystems (MPS, MS, PhD); economics, governance and human dimensions (MPS, MS, PhD); environmental and natural resources policy (MPS, MS); forest and natural resources management (MPS, MS, PhD); monitoring, analysis and modeling (MPS, MS, PhD). *Accreditation:* SAF. *Degree requirements:* For master's, thesis (for some programs); for doctorate, comprehensive exam, thesis/dissertation. *Entrance requirements:* For master's and doctorate, GRE General Test, minimum GPA of 3.0. Additional exam requirements/recommendations for international students: Required—TOEFL (minimum score 550 paper-based; 80 iBT), IELTS (minimum score 6). *Expenses:* Tuition, state resident: full-time $9370; part-time $390 per credit hour. Tuition, nonresident: full-time $16,680; part-time $695 per credit hour. *Required fees:* $981. Tuition and fees vary according to course load and program. *Faculty research:* Silviculture recreation management, tree improvement, operations management, economics.

State University of New York College of Environmental Science and Forestry, Department of Sustainable Construction Management and Engineering, Syracuse, NY 13210-2779. Offers construction management (MPS, MS, PhD); engineered wood products and structures (MPS, MS, PhD); sustainable construction (MPS, MS, PhD); tropical timbers (MPS, MS, PhD); wood anatomy and ultrastructure (MPS, MS, PhD); wood science and technology (MPS, MS, PhD); wood treatments (MPS, MS, PhD). *Degree requirements:* For master's, thesis (for some programs); for doctorate, comprehensive exam, thesis/dissertation. *Entrance requirements:* For master's and doctorate, GRE General Test, minimum GPA of 3.0. Additional exam requirements/recommendations for international students: Required—TOEFL (minimum score 550 paper-based; 80 iBT), IELTS (minimum score 6). *Expenses:* Tuition, state resident: full-time $9370; part-time $390 per credit hour. Tuition, nonresident: full-time $16,680; part-time $695 per credit hour. *Required fees:* $981. Tuition and fees vary according to course load and program.

Stephen F. Austin State University, Graduate School, College of Forestry and Agriculture, Department of Forestry, Nacogdoches, TX 75962. Offers MF, MS, PhD. Part-time programs available. *Degree requirements:* For master's, thesis; for doctorate, thesis/dissertation. *Entrance requirements:* For master's and doctorate, GRE General Test. Additional exam requirements/recommendations for international students: Required—TOEFL. *Faculty research:* Wildlife management, basic plant science, forest recreation, multipurpose land management.

Texas A&M University, College of Agriculture and Life Sciences, Department of Ecosystem Science and Management, College Station, TX 77843. Offers forestry (MS, PhD); rangeland ecology and management (M Agr, MS, PhD). Part-time programs available. *Faculty:* 24. *Students:* 52 full-time (31 women), 32 part-time (18 women); includes 24 minority (3 Black or African American, non-Hispanic/Latino; 2 Asian, non-Hispanic/Latino; 18 Hispanic/Latino; 1 Two or more races, non-Hispanic/Latino), 16 international. Average age 32. In 2012, 10 master's, 2 doctorates awarded. Terminal master's awarded for partial completion of doctoral program. *Degree requirements:* For master's, thesis (for some programs); for doctorate, thesis/dissertation. *Entrance requirements:* For master's and doctorate, GRE General Test. Additional exam requirements/recommendations for international students: Required—TOEFL. *Application deadline:* For fall admission, 3/1 priority date for domestic students; for spring admission, 11/1 priority date for domestic students. Applications are processed on a rolling basis. Application fee: $50 ($75 for international students). Electronic applications accepted. *Financial support:* In 2012–13, fellowships with partial tuition reimbursements (averaging $15,000 per year), research assistantships with partial tuition reimbursements (averaging $15,000 per year), teaching assistantships with partial tuition reimbursements (averaging $15,000 per year) were awarded; career-related internships or fieldwork and institutionally sponsored loans also available. Support available to part-time students. Financial award application deadline: 3/1; financial award applicants required to submit FAFSA. *Faculty research:* Expert systems, geographic information systems, economics, biology, genetics. *Unit head:* Dr. Steve Whisenant, Professor and Head, 979-845-5000, Fax: 979-845-6049, E-mail: s-whisenant@tamu.edu. *Application contact:* Dr. Carol Loopstra, Associate Professor, 979-862-2200, Fax: 979-845-6049, E-mail: c-loopstra@tamu.edu. Website: http://essm.tamu.edu.

Tropical Agriculture Research and Higher Education Center, Graduate School, Turrialba, Costa Rica. Offers agribusiness management (MS); agroforestry systems (PhD); development practices (MS); ecological agriculture (MS); environmental socioeconomics (MS); forestry in tropical and subtropical zones (PhD); integrated watershed management (MS); international sustainable tourism (MS); management and conservation of tropical rainforests and biodiversity (MS); tropical agriculture (PhD); tropical agroforestry (MS). *Entrance requirements:* For master's, GRE, 2 years of related professional experience, letters of recommendation; for doctorate, GRE, 4 letters of recommendation, letter of support from employing organization, master's degree in agronomy, biological sciences, forestry, natural resources or related field. Additional exam requirements/recommendations for international students: Required—TOEFL (minimum score 550 paper-based). Electronic applications accepted. *Faculty research:* Biodiversity in fragmented landscapes, ecosystem management, integrated pest management, environmental livestock production, biotechnology carbon balances in diverse land uses.

Université du Québec en Abitibi-Témiscamingue, Graduate Programs, Program in Environmental Sciences, Rouyn-Noranda, QC J9X 5E4, Canada. Offers biology (MS); environmental sciences (PhD); sustainable forest ecosystem management (MS).

Université Laval, Faculty of Forestry, Geography and Geomatics, Department of Wood and Forest Sciences, Programs in Forestry Sciences, Québec, QC G1K 7P4, Canada. Offers M Sc, PhD. Terminal master's awarded for partial completion of doctoral program. *Degree requirements:* For master's, thesis (for some programs); for doctorate, comprehensive exam, thesis/dissertation. *Entrance requirements:* For master's and doctorate, knowledge of French. Additional exam requirements/recommendations for international students: Required—TOEIC or TOEFL. Electronic applications accepted.

Université Laval, Faculty of Forestry, Geography and Geomatics, Department of Wood and Forest Sciences, Programs in Wood Sciences, Québec, QC G1K 7P4, Canada. Offers M Sc, PhD. Terminal master's awarded for partial completion of doctoral program. *Degree requirements:* For master's, thesis; for doctorate, comprehensive exam, thesis/dissertation. *Entrance requirements:* For master's and doctorate, knowledge of French. Electronic applications accepted.

Université Laval, Faculty of Forestry, Geography and Geomatics, Program in Agroforestry, Québec, QC G1K 7P4, Canada. Offers M Sc. *Degree requirements:* For master's, thesis (for some programs). *Entrance requirements:* For master's, English exam (comprehension of English), knowledge of French, knowledge of a third language. Electronic applications accepted.

University of Alberta, Faculty of Graduate Studies and Research, Department of Rural Economy, Edmonton, AB T6G 2E1, Canada. Offers agricultural economics (M Ag, M Sc, PhD); forest economics (M Ag, M Sc, PhD); rural sociology (M Ag, M Sc); MBA/M Ag. Part-time programs available. *Degree requirements:* For doctorate, thesis/dissertation. *Entrance requirements:* Additional exam requirements/recommendations for international students: Required—TOEFL. *Faculty research:* Agroforestry, development, extension education, marketing and trade, natural resources and environment, policy, production economics.

The University of Arizona, College of Agriculture and Life Sciences, School of Natural Resources, Watershed Resources Program, Tucson, AZ 85721. Offers water, society, and policy (MS); watershed management (MS, PhD). *Faculty:* 19 full-time (3 women), 2 part-time/adjunct (0 women). *Students:* 6 full-time (2 women), 4 part-time (2 women); includes 2 minority (both Hispanic/Latino). Average age 34. 4 applicants, 50% accepted, 0 enrolled. *Degree requirements:* For master's, thesis; for doctorate, comprehensive exam, thesis/dissertation. *Entrance requirements:* For master's, GRE General Test, minimum GPA of 3.0, 3 letters of recommendation; for doctorate, GRE General Test, minimum GPA of 3.0, 3 letters of recommendation, MA or MS. Additional exam requirements/recommendations for international students: Required—TOEFL (minimum score 550 paper-based; 79 iBT). *Application deadline:* For fall admission, 8/1 priority date for domestic students, 12/1 for international students; for spring admission, 7/1 for international students. Applications are processed on a rolling basis. Application fee: $75. *Financial support:* In 2012–13, 6 research assistantships with partial tuition reimbursements (averaging $13,872 per year) were awarded; teaching assistantships with partial tuition reimbursements, career-related internships or fieldwork, scholarships/grants, health care benefits, tuition waivers (partial), and unspecified assistantships also available. *Faculty research:* Forest fuel characteristics, prescribed fire, tree ring-fire scar analysis, erosion, sedimentation. *Total annual research expenditures:* $6.5 million. *Unit head:* Dr. CHarles Hutchinson, Director, 520-621-8568, E-mail: chuck@ag.arizona.edu. *Application contact:* Katie Hughes, Academic Coordinator, 520-621-7260, E-mail: khughes@email.arizona.edu. Website: http://www.ag.arizona.edu/srnr/.

University of Arkansas at Monticello, School of Forest Resources, Monticello, AR 71656. Offers MS. Part-time programs available. *Degree requirements:* For master's, comprehensive exam, thesis. *Entrance requirements:* For master's, GRE General Test, minimum GPA of 2.7. Additional exam requirements/recommendations for international students: Required—TOEFL (minimum score 550 paper-based). Electronic applications accepted. *Faculty research:* Geographic information systems/remote sensing, forest ecology, wildlife ecology and management.

The University of British Columbia, Faculty of Forestry, Vancouver, BC V6T 1Z1, Canada. Offers M Sc, MA Sc, MF, PhD. Part-time programs available. *Degree requirements:* For master's, thesis (for some programs); for doctorate, comprehensive exam, thesis/dissertation, thesis exam. *Entrance requirements:* Additional exam requirements/recommendations for international students: Required—TOEFL (minimum score 550 paper-based; 80 iBT). Electronic applications accepted. *Faculty research:* Forest sciences, forest resources management, forest operations, wood sciences, conservation, forests and society.

University of California, Berkeley, Graduate Division, College of Natural Resources, Department of Environmental Science, Policy, and Management, Berkeley, CA 94720-1500. Offers environmental science, policy, and management (MS, PhD); forestry (MF). Terminal master's awarded for partial completion of doctoral program. *Degree requirements:* For master's, thesis optional; for doctorate, thesis/dissertation, qualifying exam. *Entrance requirements:* For master's and doctorate, GRE General Test, minimum GPA of 3.0, 3 letters of recommendation. Additional exam requirements/recommendations for international students: Required—TOEFL. Electronic applications accepted. *Faculty research:* Biology and ecology of insects; ecosystem function and environmental issues of soils; plant health/interactions from molecular to ecosystem levels; range management and ecology; forest and resource policy, sustainability, and management.

University of Florida, Graduate School, College of Agricultural and Life Sciences, School of Forest Resources and Conservation, Gainesville, FL 32611. Offers MFAS, MFRC, MS, PhD, JD/MFRC, JD/MS, JD/PhD. Part-time and evening/weekend programs available. Postbaccalaureate distance learning degree programs offered. Terminal master's awarded for partial completion of doctoral program. *Degree requirements:* For master's, comprehensive exam, thesis optional, project (for MFRC); for doctorate, comprehensive exam, thesis/dissertation. *Entrance requirements:* For master's, GRE General Test (minimum score of 1000), minimum GPA of 3.0; for doctorate, GRE General Test, minimum GPA of 3.25. Additional exam requirements/recommendations for international students: Required—TOEFL (minimum score 550 paper-based; 80 iBT), IELTS (minimum score 6). Electronic applications accepted. *Faculty research:* Forest biology and ecology; natural resource economics and management; human dimensions and resource policy; tropical forestry and agroforestry; geomatics: geospatial, GIS, and remote sensing.

University of Georgia, School of Forestry and Natural Resources, Athens, GA 30602. Offers MFR, MS, PhD. *Degree requirements:* For master's, thesis (MS); for doctorate, one foreign language, thesis/dissertation. *Entrance requirements:* For master's and doctorate, GRE General Test. Electronic applications accepted.

University of Kentucky, Graduate School, College of Agriculture, Program in Forestry, Lexington, KY 40506-0032. Offers MSFOR. *Degree requirements:* For master's, comprehensive exam, thesis optional. *Entrance requirements:* For master's, GRE General Test, minimum undergraduate GPA of 2.75. Additional exam requirements/recommendations for international students: Required—TOEFL (minimum score 550 paper-based). Electronic applications accepted. *Faculty research:* Forest ecology, silviculture, watershed management, forest products utilization, wildlife habitat management.

University of Maine, Graduate School, College of Natural Sciences, Forestry, and Agriculture, School of Forest Resources, Orono, ME 04469. Offers forest resources (MS, PhD); forestry (MF). *Accreditation:* SAF (one or more programs are accredited). Part-time programs available. *Faculty:* 20 full-time (1 woman). *Students:* 40 full-time (9 women), 5 part-time (4 women); includes 1 minority (American Indian or Alaska Native, non-Hispanic/Latino), 10 international. Average age 29. 36 applicants, 53% accepted, 10 enrolled. In 2012, 13 master's, 1 doctorate awarded. *Degree requirements:* For master's, thesis; for doctorate, one foreign language, comprehensive exam, thesis/dissertation. *Entrance requirements:* For master's and doctorate, GRE General Test. Additional exam requirements/recommendations for international students: Required—TOEFL. *Application deadline:* For fall admission, 2/1 priority date for domestic students. Applications are processed on a rolling basis. Application fee: $65. Electronic applications accepted. *Financial support:* In 2012–13, 28 research assistantships with full tuition reimbursements (averaging $20,447 per year), 7 teaching assistantships with full tuition reimbursements (averaging $13,600 per year) were awarded; career-related internships or fieldwork, Federal Work-Study, and institutionally sponsored loans also available. Financial award application deadline: 3/1. *Faculty research:* Forest economics, engineering and operations analysis, biometrics and remote sensing, timber management, wood technology. *Total annual research expenditures:* $336,195. *Unit head:* Dr. Robert Wagner, Director, 207-581-4737. *Application contact:* Scott G. Delcourt, Associate Dean of the Graduate School, 207-581-3291, Fax: 207-581-3232, E-mail: graduate@maine.edu. Website: http://www.forest.umaine.edu/.

University of Massachusetts Amherst, Graduate School, College of Natural Sciences, Department of Environmental Conservation, Amherst, MA 01003. Offers building systems (MS, PhD); environmental policy and human dimensions (MS, PhD); forest resources (MS, PhD); sustainability science (MS); water, wetlands and watersheds (MS, PhD); wildlife and fisheries conservation (MS, PhD). Part-time programs available. *Faculty:* 62 full-time (11 women). *Students:* 52 full-time (18 women), 40 part-time (19 women); includes 2 minority (1 Black or African American, non-Hispanic/Latino; 1 Two or more races, non-Hispanic/Latino), 17 international. Average age 33. 73 applicants, 40% accepted, 18 enrolled. In 2012, 16 master's, 3 doctorates awarded. Terminal master's awarded for partial completion of doctoral program. *Degree requirements:* For master's, thesis or alternative; for doctorate, comprehensive exam, thesis/dissertation. *Entrance requirements:* For master's and doctorate, GRE General Test. Additional exam requirements/recommendations for international students: Required—TOEFL (minimum score 550 paper-based; 80 iBT), IELTS (minimum score 6.5). *Application deadline:* For fall admission, 2/1 for domestic and international students; for spring admission, 10/1 for domestic and international students. Applications are processed on a rolling basis. Application fee: $75. Electronic applications accepted. *Expenses:* Tuition, state resident: full-time $1980; part-time $110 per credit. Tuition, nonresident: full-time $13,314; part-time $414 per credit. *Required fees:* $10,338; $3594 per semester. One-time fee: $357. *Financial support:* Fellowships with full and partial tuition reimbursements, research assistantships with full and partial tuition reimbursements, teaching assistantships with full and partial tuition reimbursements, career-related internships or fieldwork, Federal Work-Study, scholarships/grants, traineeships, health care benefits, tuition waivers (full and partial), and unspecified assistantships available. Support available to part-time students. Financial award application deadline: 2/1. *Unit head:* Dr. Kevin McGarigal, Graduate Program Director, 413-545-2257, Fax: 413-545-4358. *Application contact:* Lindsay DeSantis, Supervisor of Admissions, 413-545-0721, Fax: 413-577-0100, E-mail: gradadm@grad.umass.edu. Website: http://eco.umass.edu/.

University of Missouri, Graduate School, School of Natural Resources, Department of Forestry, Columbia, MO 65211. Offers MS, PhD. *Faculty:* 17 full-time (2 women), 1 part-time/adjunct (0 women). *Students:* 19 full-time (5 women), 18 part-time (2 women); includes 2 minority (both Two or more races, non-Hispanic/Latino), 6 international. Average age 32. 16 applicants, 63% accepted, 8 enrolled. In 2012, 8 master's, 2 doctorates awarded. Terminal master's awarded for partial completion of doctoral program. *Degree requirements:* For master's, thesis; for doctorate, thesis/dissertation. *Entrance requirements:* For master's and doctorate, GRE General Test, minimum GPA of 3.0. Additional exam requirements/recommendations for international students: Required—TOEFL (minimum score 500 paper-based; 61 iBT). *Application deadline:* For fall admission, 5/15 for domestic and international students; for winter admission, 10/15 for domestic and international students; for spring admission, 3/15 for domestic and international students. Applications are processed on a rolling basis. Application fee: $55 ($75 for international students). Electronic applications accepted. *Expenses:* Tuition, state resident: full-time $6057. Tuition, nonresident: full-time $15,683. *Required fees:* $1000. *Financial support:* Fellowships, research assistantships, teaching assistantships, institutionally sponsored loans, and scholarships/grants available. *Faculty research:* Spatial analysis of natural resource-based industries; forest industry corporate responsibility and environmental stewardship programs; consumer preferences for forest products; forest sector economic development; development of improved nut tree cultivars for use in agroforestry-based systems; hardwood tree improvement; tree growth-wood quality interactions; evaluation and development of forest management guidelines to improve forest health, sustainability and value; agroforestry. *Unit head:* Dr. Dave Larsen, Department Chair, 573-882-8835, E-mail: muzikar@missouri.edu. Website: http://www.snr.missouri.edu/forestry/academics/graduate-program.php.

The University of Montana, Graduate School, College of Forestry and Conservation, Missoula, MT 59812-0002. Offers ecosystem management (MEM, MS); fish and wildlife biology (PhD); forestry (MS, PhD); recreation management (MS); resource conservation (MS); wildlife biology (MS). *Degree requirements:* For doctorate, thesis/dissertation. *Entrance requirements:* For master's and doctorate, GRE General Test. Additional exam requirements/recommendations for international students: Required—TOEFL (minimum score 575 paper-based).

University of New Brunswick Fredericton, School of Graduate Studies, Faculty of Forestry and Environmental Management, Fredericton, NB E3B 5A3, Canada. Offers ecological foundations of forest management (PhD); environmental management (MEM); forest engineering (M Sc FE, MFE); forest products marketing (MBA); forest resources (M Sc F, MF, PhD). Part-time programs available. *Faculty:* 27 full-time (2 women). *Students:* 70 full-time (23 women), 15 part-time (10 women). In 2012, 22 master's, 6 doctorates awarded. *Degree requirements:* For master's, thesis; for doctorate, thesis/dissertation. *Entrance requirements:* For master's and doctorate, minimum GPA of 3.0. Additional exam requirements/recommendations for international students: Required—TOEFL (minimum score 550 paper-based; 80 iBT), IELTS (minimum score 7), TWE (minimum score 4). *Application deadline:* For fall admission, 3/1 for domestic students. Applications are processed on a rolling basis. Application fee: $50 Canadian dollars. Electronic applications accepted. Tuition and fees charges are reported in Canadian dollars. *Expenses: Tuition, area resident:* Full-time $3956 Canadian dollars. *Required fees:* $579.50 Canadian dollars; $55 Canadian dollars per semester. *Financial support:* In 2012–13, 98 research assistantships, 36 teaching assistantships were awarded; fellowships also available. *Faculty research:* Forest machines, soils, and ecosystems; integrated forest management; forest meteorology; wood engineering; stream ecosystems dynamics; forest and natural resources policy; forest operations planning; wood technology and mechanics; forest road construction and engineering; forest, wildlife, insect, bird, and fire ecology; remote sensing; insect impacts; Silviculture; LiDAR analytics; integrated pest management; forest tree genetics; genetic resource conservation and sustainable management. *Unit head:* Dr. Dan Quiring, Director of Graduate Studies, 506-453-4922, Fax: 506-453-3538, E-mail: quiring@unb.ca. *Application contact:* Faith Sharpe, Graduate Secretary, 506-458-7520, Fax: 506-453-3538, E-mail: fsharpe@unb.ca. Website: http://go.unb.ca/gradprograms.

University of New Hampshire, Graduate School, College of Life Sciences and Agriculture, Department of Natural Resources, Durham, NH 03824. Offers environmental conservation (MS); forestry (MS); integrated coastal ecosystem science, policy, management (MS); natural resources (MS); water resources (MS); wildlife (MS). Part-time programs available. *Faculty:* 40 full-time. *Students:* 32 full-time (18 women), 29 part-time (16 women); includes 3 minority (all Hispanic/Latino), 3 international. Average age 28. 63 applicants, 43% accepted, 22 enrolled. In 2012, 14 master's awarded. *Degree requirements:* For master's, thesis or alternative. *Entrance requirements:* For master's, GRE General Test. Additional exam requirements/recommendations for international students: Required—TOEFL (minimum score 550 paper-based; 80 iBT). *Application deadline:* For fall admission, 6/1 for domestic students, 4/1 for international students; for spring admission, 12/1 for domestic students. Applications are processed on a rolling basis. Application fee: $65. Electronic applications accepted. *Expenses:* Tuition, state resident: full-time $13,500; part-time $750 per credit. Tuition, nonresident: full-time $25,940; part-time $1089 per credit. *Required fees:* $1699; $424.75 per semester. *Financial support:* In 2012–13, 35 students received support, including 1 fellowship, 15 research assistantships, 23 teaching assistantships; career-related internships or fieldwork, Federal Work-Study, scholarships/grants, and tuition waivers (full and partial) also available. Support available to part-time students. Financial award application deadline: 2/15. *Unit head:* Dr. Ted Howard, Chairperson, 603-862-2700, E-mail: natural.resources@unh.edu. *Application contact:* Nancy Brown, Administrative Assistant, 603-862-1022, E-mail: natural.resources@unh.edu. Website: http://www.nre.unh.edu/academics/.

The University of Tennessee, Graduate School, College of Agricultural Sciences and Natural Resources, Department of Forestry, Wildlife, and Fisheries, Program in Forestry, Knoxville, TN 37996. Offers MS. *Degree requirements:* For master's, thesis or alternative. *Entrance requirements:* For master's, GRE General Test, minimum GPA of 2.7. Additional exam requirements/recommendations for international students: Required—TOEFL. Electronic applications accepted. *Expenses:* Tuition, state resident: full-time $9000; part-time $501 per credit hour. Tuition, nonresident: full-time $27,188; part-time $1512 per credit hour. *Required fees:* $1280; $62 per credit hour. Tuition and fees vary according to program.

University of Toronto, School of Graduate Studies, Faculty of Forestry, Toronto, ON M5S 1A1, Canada. Offers M Sc F, MFC, PhD. *Degree requirements:* For master's, comprehensive exam, thesis, oral thesis/research paper defense; for doctorate, thesis/dissertation, oral defense of thesis. *Entrance requirements:* For master's, bachelor's degree in a related area, minimum B average in final year (M Sc F), final 2 years (MFC); resume, 3 letters of reference; for doctorate, writing sample, minimum A- average, master's in a related area, 3 letters of reference, resume. Additional exam requirements/recommendations for international students: Required—TOEFL (minimum score 580 paper-based; 93 iBT), TWE (minimum score 5). Electronic applications accepted.

University of Vermont, Graduate College, The Rubenstein School of Environment and Natural Resources, Program in Natural Resources, Burlington, VT 05405. Offers natural resources (MS, PhD), including aquatic ecology and watershed science (MS), environment thought and culture (MS), environment, science and public affairs (MS), forestry (MS). *Students:* 90 (48 women); includes 7 minority (1 Black or African American, non-Hispanic/Latino; 1 American Indian or Alaska Native, non-Hispanic/Latino; 4 Asian, non-Hispanic/Latino; 1 Hispanic/Latino), 1 international. 115 applicants, 30% accepted, 17 enrolled. In 2012, 22 master's, 4 doctorates awarded. *Degree requirements:* For master's, thesis or alternative; for doctorate, thesis/dissertation. *Entrance requirements:* For master's and doctorate, GRE General Test. Additional exam requirements/recommendations for international students: Required—TOEFL (minimum score 550 paper-based; 80 iBT). *Application deadline:* For fall admission, 2/1 priority date for domestic students, 2/1 for international students. Applications are processed on a rolling basis. Application fee: $40. Electronic applications accepted. *Expenses: Tuition, area resident:* Part-time $572 per credit. Tuition, nonresident: part-time $1444 per credit. *Financial support:* Fellowships, research assistantships, and teaching assistantships available. Financial award application deadline: 3/1. *Unit head:* Clare Ginger, Chair, 802-656-2620. *Application contact:* Kimberly Wallin, Coordinator, 802-656-2620.

University of Washington, Graduate School, College of the Environment, School of Environmental and Forest Sciences, Seattle, WA 98195. Offers bioresource science and engineering (MS, PhD); environmental horticulture (MEH); forest ecology (MS, PhD); forest management (MFR); forest soils (MS, PhD); restoration ecology (MS, PhD); restoration ecology and environmental horticulture (MS, PhD); social sciences (MS, PhD); sustainable resource management (MS, PhD); wildlife science (MS, PhD); MFR/MAIS; MPA/MS. *Accreditation:* SAF. Part-time programs available. *Degree requirements:* For master's, thesis; for doctorate, comprehensive exam (for some programs), thesis/dissertation. *Entrance requirements:* For master's and doctorate, GRE, minimum GPA of 3.0. Additional exam requirements/recommendations for international students: Required—TOEFL, GRE. Electronic applications accepted. *Faculty research:* Ecosystem analysis, silviculture and forest protection, paper science and engineering, environmental horticulture and urban forestry, natural resource policy and economics, restoration ecology and environment horticulture, conservation, human dimensions, wildlife, bioresource science and engineering.

University of Wisconsin–Madison, Graduate School, College of Agricultural and Life Sciences, Department of Forest and Wildlife Ecology, Program in Forestry, Madison, WI 53706-1380. Offers MS, PhD. *Expenses:* Tuition, state resident: full-time $10,728; part-time $743 per credit. Tuition, nonresident: full-time $24,054; part-time $1575 per credit. *Required fees:* $1111; $72 per credit.

Utah State University, School of Graduate Studies, College of Natural Resources, Department of Wildland Resources, Logan, UT 84322. Offers ecology (MS, PhD); forestry (MS, PhD); range science (MS, PhD); wildlife biology (MS, PhD). Part-time programs available. *Degree requirements:* For master's, thesis; for doctorate, comprehensive exam, thesis/dissertation. *Entrance requirements:* For master's and doctorate, GRE General Test, minimum GPA of 3.0. Additional exam requirements/recommendations for international students: Required—TOEFL. *Faculty research:* Range plant ecophysiology, plant community ecology, ruminant nutrition, population ecology.

Virginia Polytechnic Institute and State University, Graduate School, College of Natural Resources and Environment, Blacksburg, VA 24061. Offers fisheries and wildlife (MS); forestry and forest products (MF, MS, PhD); geography (MS); geospatial and environmental analysis (PhD); natural resources (MNR). *Faculty:* 68 full-time (14 women). *Students:* 181 full-time (82 women), 78 part-time (47 women); includes 20 minority (5 Black or African American, non-Hispanic/Latino; 1 American Indian or Alaska Native, non-Hispanic/Latino; 4 Asian, non-Hispanic/Latino; 4 Hispanic/Latino; 6 Two or more races, non-Hispanic/Latino), 54 international. Average age 31. 133 applicants, 41% accepted, 48 enrolled. In 2012, 71 master's, 16 doctorates awarded. *Degree requirements:* For master's, comprehensive exam (for some programs), thesis (for some programs); for doctorate, comprehensive exam (for some programs), thesis/dissertation (for some programs). *Entrance requirements:* For master's and doctorate, GRE/GMAT (may vary by department). Additional exam requirements/recommendations for international students: Required—TOEFL (minimum score 550 paper-based). *Application deadline:* For fall admission, 8/1 for domestic students, 4/1 for international students; for spring admission, 1/1 for domestic students, 9/1 for international students. Applications are processed on a rolling basis. Application fee: $65. Electronic applications accepted. *Expenses:* Tuition, state resident: full-time $10,677; part-time $593.25 per credit hour. Tuition, nonresident: full-time $20,926; part-time $1162.50 per credit hour. *Required fees:* $427.75 per semester. Tuition and fees vary according to course load, campus/location and program. *Financial support:* In 2012–13, 92 research assistantships with full tuition reimbursements (averaging $19,523 per year), 43 teaching assistantships with full tuition reimbursements (averaging $16,826 per year) were awarded. Financial award application deadline: 3/1; financial award applicants required to submit FAFSA. *Total annual research expenditures:* $14 million. *Unit head:* Dr. Paul M. Winistorfer, Dean, 540-231-5481, Fax: 540-231-7664, E-mail: pstorfer@vt.edu. *Application contact:* Arlice Banks, Assistant to the Dean, 540-231-5481, Fax: 540-231-7664. Website: http://www.cnre.vt.edu/.

West Virginia University, Davis College of Agriculture, Forestry and Consumer Sciences, Division of Forestry, Program in Forest Resource Science, Morgantown, WV 26506. Offers PhD. *Degree requirements:* For doctorate, comprehensive exam, thesis/dissertation. *Entrance requirements:* For doctorate, GRE, minimum GPA of 3.0. Additional exam requirements/recommendations for international students: Required—TOEFL. *Faculty research:* Impact of management on wildlife and fish, forest sampling designs, forest economics and policy, oak regeneration.

West Virginia University, Davis College of Agriculture, Forestry and Consumer Sciences, Division of Forestry, Program in Forestry, Morgantown, WV 26506. Offers MSF. *Degree requirements:* For master's, thesis. *Entrance requirements:* For master's, GRE, minimum GPA of 3.0. Additional exam requirements/recommendations for international students: Required—TOEFL. *Faculty research:* Health and productivity on Appalachian forests, wood industries in Appalachian forests, role of forestry in regional economics.

Yale University, Graduate School of Arts and Sciences, Department of Forestry and Environmental Studies, New Haven, CT 06520. Offers environmental sciences (PhD); forestry (PhD). *Degree requirements:* For doctorate, thesis/dissertation. *Entrance requirements:* For doctorate, GRE General Test.

Yale University, School of Forestry and Environmental Studies, New Haven, CT 06511. Offers MEM, MES, MF, MFS, PhD, JD/MEM, MBA/MEM, MBA/MF, MEM/M Arch, MEM/MA, MEM/MPH, MF/MA. *Accreditation:* SAF (one or more programs are accredited). Part-time programs available. *Faculty:* 49 full-time, 40 part-time/adjunct. *Students:* 301 full-time, 22 part-time; includes 60 minority (5 Black or African American, non-Hispanic/Latino; 7 American Indian or Alaska Native, non-Hispanic/Latino; 29 Asian, non-Hispanic/Latino; 19 Hispanic/Latino). Average age 28. 590 applicants, 163 enrolled. In 2012, 139 master's awarded. Terminal master's awarded for partial completion of doctoral program. *Degree requirements:* For master's, thesis (for some programs); for doctorate, thesis/dissertation. *Entrance requirements:* For master's, GRE General Test, GMAT or LSAT; for doctorate, GRE General Test. Additional exam requirements/recommendations for international students: Required—TOEFL (minimum score 600 paper-based, 100 iBT) or IELTS (minimum score of 7.0). *Application deadline:* For fall admission, 12/15 priority date for domestic students, 12/15 for international students. Application fee: $80. Electronic applications accepted. *Expenses:* Contact institution. *Financial support:* In 2012–13, 252 students received support. Fellowships, research assistantships, teaching assistantships, career-related internships or fieldwork, Federal Work-Study, institutionally sponsored loans, scholarships/grants, and health care benefits available. Support available to part-time students. Financial award application deadline: 2/15; financial award applicants required to submit FAFSA. *Faculty research:* Environmental policy, social ecology, industrial environmental management, forestry, environmental health, urban ecology, water science policy. *Unit head:* Peter Crane, Dean, School of Forestry and Environmental Studies, 203-432-5109, Fax: 203-432-3051. *Application contact:* Danielle Curtis, Director of Enrollment Management (Admissions and Financial Aid), 203-432-5106, Fax: 203-432-5528, E-mail: fesinfo@yale.edu. Website: http://environment.yale.edu.

Natural Resources

American University, School of International Service, Washington, DC 20016-8071. Offers comparative and international disability policy (MA); comparative and regional studies (Certificate); cross-cultural communication (Certificate); development management (MS); ethics, peace, and global affairs (MA); European studies (Certificate); global environmental policy (MA, Certificate); global information technology (Certificate); international affairs (MA), including comparative and international disability policy, comparative and regional studies, international economic relations, international politics, natural resources and sustainable development, U.S. foreign policy; international communication (MA, Certificate); international development (MA, Certificate); international economic policy (Certificate); international economic relations (Certificate); international media (MA); international peace and conflict resolution (MA, Certificate); international politics (Certificate); international relations (PhD); international service (MIS); peacebuilding (Certificate); social enterprise (MA); the Americas (Certificate); United States foreign policy (Certificate); JD/MA. Part-time and evening/weekend programs available. Postbaccalaureate distance learning degree programs offered (no on-campus study). *Faculty:* 111 full-time (47 women), 58 part-time/adjunct (31 women). *Students:* 673 full-time (429 women), 376 part-time (227 women); includes 258 minority (82 Black or African American, non-Hispanic/Latino; 8 American Indian or Alaska Native, non-Hispanic/Latino; 71 Asian, non-Hispanic/Latino; 77 Hispanic/Latino; 1 Native Hawaiian or other Pacific Islander, non-Hispanic/Latino; 19 Two or more races, non-Hispanic/Latino), 142 international. Average age 27. 2,074 applicants, 64% accepted, 391 enrolled. In 2012, 367 master's, 7 doctorates, 12 other advanced degrees awarded. Terminal master's awarded for partial completion of doctoral program. *Degree requirements:* For master's, one foreign language, comprehensive exam, thesis or alternative; for doctorate, one foreign language, comprehensive exam, thesis/dissertation, research practicum; for Certificate, minimum 15 credit hours of related course work. *Entrance requirements:* For master's, GRE, 24 credits of course work in related social sciences, minimum GPA of 3.5, 2 letters of recommendation, bachelor's degree, resume, statement of purpose; for doctorate, GRE, 3 letters of recommendation, 24 credits in related social sciences; for Certificate, bachelor's degree. Additional exam requirements/recommendations for international students: Required—TOEFL (minimum score 600 paper-based; 100 iBT). *Application deadline:* For fall admission, 1/15 priority date for domestic students; for spring admission, 10/1 priority date for domestic students. Applications are processed on a rolling basis. Application fee: $50. *Expenses: Tuition:* Full-time $25,920; part-time $1440 per credit. *Required fees:* $430. Tuition and fees vary according to course load, campus/location and program. *Financial support:* Fellowships with partial tuition reimbursements, research assistantships with partial tuition reimbursements, teaching assistantships with partial tuition reimbursements, career-related internships or fieldwork, Federal Work-Study, institutionally sponsored loans, and scholarships/grants available. Financial award application deadline: 1/15. *Faculty research:* International intellectual property, international environmental issues, international law and legal order, international telecommunications/technology, international sustainable development. *Unit head:* Dr. James Goldgeier, Dean, 202-885-1603, Fax: 202-885-2494, E-mail: goldgeier@american.edu. *Application contact:* Amanda Taylor, Director of Graduate Admissions and Financial Aid, 202-885-2496, Fax: 202-885-1109, E-mail: ataylor@american.edu. Website: http://www.american.edu/sis/.

Auburn University, Graduate School, School of Forestry and Wildlife Sciences, Auburn University, AL 36849. Offers forest economics (PhD); forestry (MS, PhD); natural resource conservation (MNR); wildlife sciences (MS, PhD). *Accreditation:* SAF. Part-time programs available. *Faculty:* 32 full-time (6 women), 2 part-time/adjunct (0 women). *Students:* 28 full-time (12 women), 36 part-time (15 women), 18 international. Average age 28. 28 applicants, 43% accepted, 10 enrolled. In 2012, 22 master's, 5 doctorates awarded. *Degree requirements:* For master's, thesis (MS); for doctorate, thesis/dissertation. *Entrance requirements:* For master's and doctorate, GRE General Test. *Application deadline:* For fall admission, 7/7 for domestic students; for spring admission, 11/24 for domestic students. Applications are processed on a rolling basis. Application fee: $50 ($60 for international students). Electronic applications accepted. *Expenses:* Tuition, state resident: full-time $7866; part-time $437 per credit. Tuition, nonresident: full-time $23,598; part-time $1311 per credit. *Required fees:* $787 per semester. Tuition and fees vary according to degree level and program. *Financial support:* Fellowships, research assistantships, teaching assistantships, and Federal Work-Study available. Support available to part-time students. Financial award application deadline: 3/15; financial award applicants required to submit FAFSA. *Faculty research:* Forest nursery management, silviculture and vegetation management, biological processes and ecological relationships, growth and yield of plantations and natural stands, urban forestry, forest taxation, law and policy. *Unit head:* Dr. James P. Shepard, Dean, 334-844-4000, Fax: 334-844-1084, E-mail: brinker@forestry.auburn.edu. *Application contact:* Dr. George Flowers, Dean of the Graduate School, 334-844-2125. Website: http://www.forestry.auburn.edu/.

Ball State University, Graduate School, College of Sciences and Humanities, Department of Natural Resources, Muncie, IN 47306-1099. Offers MA, MS. *Faculty:* 8 full-time (2 women). *Students:* 14 full-time (11 women), 8 part-time (5 women); includes 2 minority (1 Hispanic/Latino; 1 Two or more races, non-Hispanic/Latino), 2 international. Average age 25. 10 applicants, 50% accepted, 2 enrolled. In 2012, 1 master's awarded. *Entrance requirements:* For master's, GRE General Test. Application fee: $50. *Expenses:* Tuition, state resident: full-time $7666. Tuition, nonresident: full-time $19,114. *Required fees:* $782. *Financial support:* In 2012–13, 8 students received support, including 14 teaching assistantships with full tuition reimbursements available (averaging $9,334 per year); research assistantships with full tuition reimbursements available and career-related internships or fieldwork also available. Financial award application deadline: 3/1. *Faculty research:* Acid rain, indoor air pollution, land reclamation. *Unit head:* Dr. James Eflin, Chairman, 765-285-2327, Fax: 765-285-2606, E-mail: jeflin1@bsu.edu. *Application contact:* Dr. Robert Morris, Associate Provost for Research and Dean of the Graduate School, 765-285-1300, E-mail: rmorris@bsu.edu. Website: http://www.bsu.edu/nrem/.

California Polytechnic State University, San Luis Obispo, College of Agriculture, Food and Environmental Sciences, Department of Natural Resources Management and Environmental Sciences, San Luis Obispo, CA 93407. Offers forestry sciences (MS). Part-time programs available. *Faculty:* 5 full-time (1 woman), 1 part-time/adjunct (1 woman). *Students:* 2 full-time (0 women), 3 part-time (1 woman); includes 1 minority (Two or more races, non-Hispanic/Latino). Average age 32. 5 applicants, 20% accepted, 1 enrolled. In 2012, 4 master's awarded. *Degree requirements:* For master's, comprehensive exam, thesis. *Entrance requirements:* For master's, minimum GPA of 2.75 in last 90 quarter units of course work. Additional exam requirements/recommendations for international students: Required—TOEFL (minimum score 550 paper-based) or IELTS (minimum score 6). *Application deadline:* For fall admission, 4/1 for domestic students, 11/30 for international students; for winter admission, 10/1 for domestic students, 6/30 for international students; for spring admission, 10/1 for domestic students. Applications are processed on a rolling basis. Application fee: $55. Electronic applications accepted. *Expenses:* Tuition, state resident: full-time $6738; part-time $3906 per year. Tuition, nonresident: full-time $17,898; part-time $8370 per year. *Required fees:* $3051; $874 per term. One-time fee: $3051 full-time; $2622 part-time. *Financial support:* Fellowships, research assistantships, career-related internships or fieldwork, Federal Work-Study, institutionally sponsored loans, scholarships/grants, and unspecified assistantships available. Support available to part-time students. Financial award application deadline: 3/2; financial award applicants required to submit FAFSA. *Faculty research:* Hydrology, biometrics, forest health and management, fire science, urban and community forestry. *Unit head:* Dr. Christopher Dicus, Department Head/Graduate Coordinator, 805-756-5104, Fax: 805-756-1402, E-mail: cdicus@calpoly.edu. *Application contact:* Dr. Mark Shelton, Associate Dean/Graduate Coordinator, 805-756-2161, Fax: 805-756-6577, E-mail: mshelton@calpoly.edu. Website: http://nres.calpoly.edu/.

Peterson's Graduate Programs in the Physical Sciences, Mathematics, Agricultural Sciences, the Environment & Natural Resources 2014

www.petersonsbooks.com **507**

Natural Resources

Central Washington University, Graduate Studies and Research, College of the Sciences, Program in Resource Management, Ellensburg, WA 98926. Offers MS. *Faculty:* 25 full-time (7 women). *Students:* 30 full-time (15 women), 15 part-time (10 women); includes 4 minority (3 American Indian or Alaska Native, non-Hispanic/Latino; 1 Asian, non-Hispanic/Latino). 28 applicants, 79% accepted, 22 enrolled. In 2012, 22 master's awarded. *Degree requirements:* For master's, thesis. *Entrance requirements:* For master's, minimum GPA of 3.0. Additional exam requirements/recommendations for international students: Required—TOEFL (minimum score 550 paper-based; 79 iBT). *Application deadline:* For fall admission, 2/1 priority date for domestic students; for spring admission, 1/1 for domestic students. Applications are processed on a rolling basis. Application fee: $50. Electronic applications accepted. *Expenses:* Tuition, state resident: full-time $8517. Tuition, nonresident: full-time $18,972. *Required fees:* $978. *Financial support:* In 2012–13, 4 research assistantships with full and partial tuition reimbursements (averaging $9,677 per year), 14 teaching assistantships with full and partial tuition reimbursements (averaging $9,677 per year) were awarded; career-related internships or fieldwork, Federal Work-Study, health care benefits, and unspecified assistantships also available. Financial award application deadline: 3/1; financial award applicants required to submit FAFSA. *Unit head:* Dr. Karl Lillquist, Co-Director, 509-963-1188, Fax: 509-963-3224, E-mail: lillquis@cwu.edu. *Application contact:* Justine Eason, Admissions Program Coordinator, 509-963-3103, Fax: 509-963-1799, E-mail: masters@cwu.edu.

Colorado State University, Graduate School, Warner College of Natural Resources, Department of Forest and Rangeland Stewardship, Fort Collins, CO 80523-1472. Offers forest sciences (MS, PhD); natural resources stewardship (MNRS); rangeland ecosystem science (MS, PhD); watershed science (MS). Part-time programs available. Postbaccalaureate distance learning degree programs offered (no on-campus study). *Faculty:* 12 full-time (2 women). *Students:* 26 full-time (7 women), 80 part-time (34 women); includes 6 minority (1 American Indian or Alaska Native, non-Hispanic/Latino; 5 Hispanic/Latino), 11 international. Average age 35. 20 applicants, 100% accepted, 17 enrolled. In 2012, 17 master's, 3 doctorates awarded. *Degree requirements:* For master's, thesis (for some programs); for doctorate, comprehensive exam, thesis/dissertation. *Entrance requirements:* For master's, GRE General Test (minimum score 1000 verbal and quantitative), minimum GPA of 3.0, 3 letters of recommendation; for doctorate, GRE General Test (combined minimum score of 1100 on the Verbal and Quantitative sections), minimum GPA of 3.0, 3 letters of recommendation, statement of research interest. Additional exam requirements/recommendations for international students: Required—TOEFL (minimum score 550 paper-based; 80 iBT), IELTS (minimum score 6.5). *Application deadline:* For fall admission, 2/15 priority date for domestic students, 2/15 for international students; for spring admission, 7/15 priority date for domestic students, 7/15 for international students. Applications are processed on a rolling basis. Application fee: $50. Electronic applications accepted. *Expenses:* Tuition, state resident: full-time $8811; part-time $490 per credit. Tuition, nonresident: full-time $21,600; part-time $1200 per credit. *Required fees:* $1819; $61 per credit. *Financial support:* In 2012–13, 53 students received support, including 3 fellowships (averaging $14,767 per year), 36 research assistantships with full and partial tuition reimbursements available (averaging $16,479 per year), 14 teaching assistantships with full and partial tuition reimbursements available (averaging $6,991 per year); Federal Work-Study, scholarships/grants, and unspecified assistantships also available. Financial award application deadline: 2/15; financial award applicants required to submit FAFSA. *Faculty research:* Ecology, natural resource management, hydrology, restoration, human dimensions. *Total annual research expenditures:* $2.4 million. *Unit head:* Dr. Frederick Smith, Department Head and Professor, 970-491-7505, Fax: 970-491-6754, E-mail: fwsmith@colostate.edu. *Application contact:* Sonya LeFebre, Coordinator, 970-491-1907, Fax: 970-491-6754, E-mail: sonya.lefebre@colostate.edu. Website: http://warnercnr.colostate.edu/frws-home/.

Colorado State University, Graduate School, Warner College of Natural Resources, Department of Human Dimensions of Natural Resources, Fort Collins, CO 80523-1480. Offers MS, PhD. Part-time programs available. Postbaccalaureate distance learning degree programs offered. *Faculty:* 11 full-time (3 women). *Students:* 37 full-time (27 women), 23 part-time (13 women); includes 6 minority (1 Black or African American, non-Hispanic/Latino; 1 Asian, non-Hispanic/Latino; 4 Hispanic/Latino), 9 international. Average age 30. 69 applicants, 67% accepted, 31 enrolled. In 2012, 23 master's, 2 doctorates awarded. Terminal master's awarded for partial completion of doctoral program. *Degree requirements:* For master's, comprehensive exam, thesis; for doctorate, comprehensive exam, thesis/dissertation. *Entrance requirements:* For master's, GRE General Test, minimum GPA of 3.0, 3 letters of recommendation, statement of interest; for doctorate, GRE General Test (combined minimum score of 1000 on the Verbal and Quantitative sections), minimum GPA of 3.0, 3 letters of recommendation, copy of master's thesis or professional paper, interview, statement of interest. Additional exam requirements/recommendations for international students: Required—TOEFL (minimum score 550 paper-based; 80 iBT). *Application deadline:* For fall admission, 2/1 priority date for domestic students, 2/1 for international students. Application fee: $50. Electronic applications accepted. *Expenses:* Tuition, state resident: full-time $8811; part-time $490 per credit. Tuition, nonresident: full-time $21,600; part-time $1200 per credit. *Required fees:* $1819; $61 per credit. *Financial support:* In 2012–13, 14 students received support, including 1 fellowship (averaging $38,000 per year), 5 research assistantships with tuition reimbursements available (averaging $9,442 per year), 8 teaching assistantships with tuition reimbursements available (averaging $8,113 per year); career-related internships or fieldwork, Federal Work-Study, scholarships/grants, traineeships, and unspecified assistantships also available. Support available to part-time students. Financial award application deadline: 2/15; financial award applicants required to submit FAFSA. *Faculty research:* International tourism, wilderness preservation, resource interpretation, human dimensions in natural resources, protected areas management. *Total annual research expenditures:* $1.1 million. *Unit head:* Dr. Michael J. Manfredo, Head, 970-491-6591, Fax: 970-491-2255, E-mail: michael.manfredo@colostate.edu. *Application contact:* Jacqie Hasan, Graduate Contact, 970-491-6591, Fax: 970-491-2255, E-mail: jacqie.hasan@colostate.edu. Website: http://warnercnr.colostate.edu/hdnr-home.

Cornell University, Graduate School, Graduate Fields of Agriculture and Life Sciences, Field of Natural Resources, Ithaca, NY 14853-0001. Offers community-based natural resources management (MS, PhD); ecosystem biology and biogeochemistry (MPS, MS, PhD); environmental management (MPS); fishery and aquatic science (MPS, MS, PhD); forest science (MPS, MS, PhD); human dimensions of natural resources management (MPS, MS, PhD); program development and evaluation (MPS, MS, PhD); wildlife science (MPS, MS, PhD). *Faculty:* 40 full-time (8 women). *Students:* 56 full-time (23 women); includes 2 minority (1 Asian, non-Hispanic/Latino; 1 Two or more races, non-Hispanic/Latino), 12 international. Average age 32. 61 applicants, 33% accepted, 15 enrolled. In 2012, 7 master's, 6 doctorates awarded. *Degree requirements:* For master's, thesis (MS), project paper (MPS); for doctorate, comprehensive exam, thesis/dissertation. *Entrance requirements:* For master's and doctorate, GRE General Test, 2 letters of recommendation. Additional exam requirements/recommendations for international students: Required—TOEFL (minimum score 550 paper-based; 77 iBT). *Application deadline:* For spring admission, 10/30 for domestic students. Applications are processed on a rolling basis. Application fee: $95. Electronic applications accepted. *Financial support:* In 2012–13, 46 students received support, including 14 fellowships with full tuition reimbursements available, 15 research assistantships with full tuition reimbursements available, 17 teaching assistantships with full tuition reimbursements available; institutionally sponsored loans, scholarships/grants, health care benefits, tuition waivers (full and partial), and unspecified assistantships also available. Financial award applicants required to submit FAFSA. *Faculty research:* Ecosystem-level dynamics, systems modeling, conservation biology/management, resource management's human dimensions, biogeochemistry. *Unit head:* Director of Graduate Studies, 607-255-2807, Fax: 607-255-0349. *Application contact:* Graduate Field Assistant, 607-255-2807, Fax: 607-255-0349, E-mail: nrgrad@cornell.edu. Website: http://www.gradschool.cornell.edu/fields.php?id-54&a-2.

Dalhousie University, Faculty of Management, Centre for Advanced Management Education, Halifax, NS B3H 3J5, Canada. Offers financial services (MBA); information management (MIM); management (MPA); natural resources (MBA). Part-time programs available. Postbaccalaureate distance learning degree programs offered. *Entrance requirements:* For master's, GMAT, minimum GPA of 3.0, resume. Additional exam requirements/recommendations for international students: Required—TOEFL, IELTS, CANTEST, CAEL, or Michigan English Language Assessment Battery. Electronic applications accepted.

Delaware State University, Graduate Programs, Department of Agriculture and Natural Resources, Program in Natural Resources, Dover, DE 19901-2277. Offers MS. *Entrance requirements:* For master's, GRE. Additional exam requirements/recommendations for international students: Required—TOEFL (minimum score 550 paper-based).

Duke University, Graduate School, Nicholas School of the Environment, Durham, NC 27708. Offers environmental management (MEM); forestry (MF); natural resource economics/policy (PhD); natural resource science/ecology (PhD); natural resource systems science (PhD); JD/AM. Part-time programs available. *Faculty:* 28 full-time. *Students:* 59 full-time (33 women); includes 2 minority (both Asian, non-Hispanic/Latino), 18 international. 99 applicants, 19% accepted, 12 enrolled. In 2012, 11 doctorates awarded. *Degree requirements:* For doctorate, variable foreign language requirement, thesis/dissertation. *Entrance requirements:* For master's and doctorate, GRE General Test. Additional exam requirements/recommendations for international students: Required—TOEFL (minimum score 550 paper-based; 83 iBT), IELTS (minimum score 7). *Application deadline:* For fall admission, 12/8 priority date for domestic students, 12/8 for international students. Application fee: $80. Electronic applications accepted. *Financial support:* Fellowships, research assistantships, teaching assistantships, and Federal Work-Study available. Financial award application deadline: 12/8. *Unit head:* Gaby Katul, Director of Graduate Studies, 919-613-8002, Fax: 919-613-8061, E-mail: meg.stephens@duke.edu. *Application contact:* Elizabeth Hutton, Director, Graduate Admissions, 919-684-3913, Fax: 919-684-2277, E-mail: grad-admissions@duke.edu. Website: http://www.nicholas.duke.edu/.

Georgia Institute of Technology, Graduate Studies and Research, College of Engineering, School of Chemical and Biomolecular Engineering, Atlanta, GA 30332-0001. Offers bioengineering (MS Bio E, PhD); chemical engineering (MS Ch E, PhD); paper science and engineering (MS, PhD); polymers (MS Poly). *Degree requirements:* For master's, thesis; for doctorate, comprehensive exam, thesis/dissertation. *Entrance requirements:* For master's and doctorate, GRE, minimum GPA of 3.0. Additional exam requirements/recommendations for international students: Required—TOEFL (minimum score 550 paper-based). Electronic applications accepted. *Faculty research:* Biochemical engineering; process modeling, synthesis, and control; polymer science and engineering; thermodynamics and separations; surface and particle science.

Humboldt State University, Academic Programs, College of Natural Resources and Sciences, Programs in Natural Resources, Arcata, CA 95521-8299. Offers natural resources (MS), including fisheries, forestry, natural resources planning and interpretation, rangeland resources and wildland soils, wastewater utilization, watershed management, wildlife. *Students:* 36 full-time (18 women), 20 part-time (9 women); includes 2 minority (1 Asian, non-Hispanic/Latino; 1 Two or more races, non-Hispanic/Latino). Average age 30. 51 applicants, 37% accepted, 11 enrolled. In 2012, 29 master's awarded. *Degree requirements:* For master's, thesis or alternative. *Entrance requirements:* For master's, GRE, appropriate bachelor's degree, minimum GPA of 2.5, 3 letters of recommendation, resume. Additional exam requirements/recommendations for international students: Required—TOEFL (minimum score 500 paper-based). *Application deadline:* For fall admission, 2/1 for domestic and international students; for spring admission, 9/30 for domestic and international students. Applications are processed on a rolling basis. Application fee: $55. *Expenses:* Tuition, state resident: full-time $8396. Tuition, nonresident: full-time $17,324. Tuition and fees vary according to program. *Financial support:* Fellowships, career-related internships or fieldwork, and Federal Work-Study available. Support available to part-time students. Financial award application deadline: 3/1; financial award applicants required to submit FAFSA. *Faculty research:* Spotted owl habitat, pre-settlement vegetation, hardwood utilization, tree physiology, fisheries. *Unit head:* Dr. Robert Van Kirk, Coordinator, 707-826-3744, E-mail: rob.vankirk@humboldt.edu. *Application contact:* Julie Tucker, Administrative Support Coordinator, 707-826-3256, E-mail: jlt7002@humboldt.edu. Website: http://www.humboldt.edu/cnrs/graduate_programs.

Instituto Tecnologico de Santo Domingo, Graduate School, Area of Basic And Environmental Sciences, Santo Domingo, Dominican Republic. Offers environmental science (M En S), including environmental education, environmental management, marine resources, natural resources management; mathematics (MS, PhD); renewable energy technology (MS, Certificate).

Iowa State University of Science and Technology, Program in Biorenewable Resources and Technology, Ames, IA 50011. Offers MS, PhD. *Degree requirements:* For master's, thesis or alternative; for doctorate, thesis/dissertation. *Entrance requirements:* For master's and doctorate, GRE General Test. Additional exam requirements/recommendations for international students: Required—TOEFL (minimum score 550 paper-based; 79 iBT), IELTS (minimum score 6.5). *Application deadline:* For fall admission, 1/1 priority date for domestic students, 1/1 for international students; for spring admission, 9/1 for domestic and international students. Applications are processed on a rolling basis. Application fee: $40 ($90 for international students). Electronic applications accepted. *Application contact:* Jan Meyer, Application Contact, 515-294-3859, Fax: 515-294-3091, E-mail: brtgrad@iastate.edu. Website: http://www.biorenew.iastate.edu/.

Laurentian University, School of Graduate Studies and Research, School of Engineering, Sudbury, ON P3E 2C6, Canada. Offers mineral resources engineering (M Eng, MA Sc); natural resources engineering (PhD). Part-time programs available. *Faculty research:* Mining engineering, rock mechanics (tunneling, rockbursts, rock support), metallurgy (mineral processing, hydro and pyrometallurgy), simulations and remote mining, simulations and scheduling.

Louisiana State University and Agricultural and Mechanical College, Graduate School, College of Agriculture, School of Renewable Natural Resources, Baton Rouge, LA 70803. Offers fisheries (MS); forestry (MS, PhD); wildlife (MS); wildlife and fisheries science (PhD). *Faculty:* 31 full-time (5 women). *Students:* 51 full-time (15 women), 5 part-time (2 women); includes 3 minority (2 Black or African American, non-Hispanic/Latino; 1 Hispanic/Latino), 12 international. Average age 29. 34 applicants, 41% accepted, 13 enrolled. In 2012, 11 master's, 10 doctorates awarded. *Degree requirements:* For master's, thesis; for doctorate, thesis/dissertation. *Entrance requirements:* For master's, GRE General Test, minimum GPA of 3.0; for doctorate, GRE General Test, MS, minimum GPA of 3.0. Additional exam requirements/recommendations for international students: Required—TOEFL (minimum score 550 paper-based; 79 iBT), IELTS (minimum score 6.5). *Application deadline:* For fall admission, 1/25 priority date for domestic students, 5/15 for international students; for spring admission, 10/15 for international students. Applications are processed on a rolling basis. Application fee: $50 ($70 for international students). Electronic applications accepted. *Financial support:* In 2012–13, 55 students received support, including 49 research assistantships with partial tuition reimbursements available (averaging $19,751 per year), 2 teaching assistantships (averaging $10,250 per year); fellowships, Federal Work-Study, institutionally sponsored loans, scholarships/grants, health care benefits, tuition waivers (full and partial), and unspecified assistantships also available. Financial award application deadline: 4/15; financial award applicants required to submit FAFSA. *Faculty research:* Forest biology and management, aquaculture, fisheries biology and ecology, upland and wetlands wildlife. *Total annual research expenditures:* $163,169. *Unit head:* Dr. Allen Rutherford, Director, 225-578-4131, Fax: 225-578-4227, E-mail: druther@lsu.edu. *Application contact:* Dr. William Kelso, Coordinator of Graduate Studies, 225-578-4176, Fax: 225-578-4227, E-mail: wkelso@lsu.edu. Website: http://www.fwf.lsu.edu/.

Marylhurst University, Department of Business Administration, Marylhurst, OR 97036-0261. Offers finance (MBA); general management (MBA); government policy and administration (MBA); green development (MBA); health care management (MBA); marketing (MBA); natural and organic resources (MBA); nonprofit management (MBA); organizational behavior (MBA); real estate (MBA); renewable energy (MBA); sustainable business (MBA). Part-time and evening/weekend programs available. Postbaccalaureate distance learning degree programs offered (no on-campus study). *Degree requirements:* For master's, comprehensive exam, capstone course. *Entrance requirements:* For master's, GMAT (if GPA less than 3.0 and fewer than 5 years of work experience), interview, resume, 2 letters of recommendation. Additional exam requirements/recommendations for international students: Recommended—TOEFL (minimum score 550 paper-based; 80 iBT). Electronic applications accepted.

McGill University, Faculty of Graduate and Postdoctoral Studies, Faculty of Agricultural and Environmental Sciences, Department of Natural Resource Sciences, Montréal, QC H3A 2T5, Canada. Offers entomology (M Sc, PhD); environmental assessment (M Sc); forest science (M Sc, PhD); microbiology (M Sc, PhD); micrometeorology (M Sc, PhD); neotropical environment (M Sc, PhD); soil science (M Sc, PhD); wildlife biology (M Sc, PhD).

Michigan State University, The Graduate School, College of Agriculture and Natural Resources, Department of Community, Agriculture, Recreation, and Resource Studies, East Lansing, MI 48824. Offers MS, PhD. *Entrance requirements:* Additional exam requirements/recommendations for international students: Required—TOEFL. Electronic applications accepted.

Missouri State University, Graduate College, College of Natural and Applied Sciences, Department of Geography, Geology, and Planning, Springfield, MO 65897. Offers geospatial sciences (MS, MS Ed), including earth science (MS Ed), geology (MS), human geography and planning (MS), physical geography (MS Ed); natural and applied science (MNAS), including geography, geology and planning; secondary education (MS Ed), including geography. *Accreditation:* ACSP. Part-time and evening/weekend programs available. *Degree requirements:* For master's, comprehensive exam, thesis (for some programs). *Entrance requirements:* For master's, GRE General Test (MS, MNAS), minimum undergraduate GPA of 3.0 (MS, MNAS), 9-12 teacher certification (MS Ed). Additional exam requirements/recommendations for international students: Required—TOEFL (minimum score 550 paper-based; 79 iBT). Electronic applications accepted. *Faculty research:* Stratigraphy and ancient meteorite impacts, environmental geochemistry of karst, hyperspectral image processing, water quality, small town planning.

Montana State University, College of Graduate Studies, College of Agriculture, Department of Land Resources and Environmental Sciences, Bozeman, MT 59717. Offers land rehabilitation (interdisciplinary) (MS); land resources and environmental sciences (MS), including land rehabilitation (interdisciplinary), land resources and environmental sciences. Part-time programs available. *Degree requirements:* For master's, comprehensive exam. *Entrance requirements:* For master's, GRE General Test. Additional exam requirements/recommendations for international students: Required—TOEFL (minimum score 550 paper-based). Electronic applications accepted. *Faculty research:* Soil nutrient management and plant nutrition, isotope biogeochemistry of soils, biodegradation of hydrocarbons in soils and natural waters, remote sensing, GIS systems, managed and natural ecosystems, microbial and metabolic diversity in geothermally heated soils, integrated management of weeds, diversified cropping systems, insect behavior and ecology, river ecology, microbial biogeochemistry, weed ecology.

New Mexico Highlands University, Graduate Studies, College of Arts and Sciences, Program in Natural Science, Las Vegas, NM 87701. Offers biology (MS); environmental science and management (MS); geology (MS). *Expenses:* Tuition, state resident: full-time $4277; part-time $178.22 per hour. Tuition, nonresident: full-time $6715; part-time $279.81 per hour. *International tuition:* $8510 full-time. Part-time tuition and fees vary according to campus/location. *Application contact:* Diane Trujillo, Administrative Assistant, Graduate Studies, 505-454-3266, Fax: 505-454-3558, E-mail: dtrujillo@nmhu.edu. Website: http://www.nmhu.edu/academics/graduate/arts_science_grad/natural_science/index.aspx.

North Carolina State University, Graduate School, College of Natural Resources, Department of Parks, Recreation and Tourism Management, Raleigh, NC 27695. Offers natural resource management (MPRTM, MS); park and recreation management (MPRTM, MS); parks, recreation and tourism management (PhD); recreational sport management (MPRTM, MS); spatial information science (MPRTM, MS); tourism policy and development (MPRTM, MS). *Degree requirements:* For master's, thesis (for some programs); for doctorate, thesis/dissertation. *Entrance requirements:* For master's and doctorate, GRE General Test. Additional exam requirements/recommendations for international students: Required—TOEFL. Electronic applications accepted. *Faculty research:* Tourism policy and development, spatial information systems, natural resource management, recreational sports management, park and recreation management.

North Carolina State University, Graduate School, College of Natural Resources and College of Agriculture and Life Sciences, Program in Natural Resources, Raleigh, NC 27695. Offers MNR, MS. *Degree requirements:* For master's, thesis optional. *Entrance requirements:* For master's, GRE. Electronic applications accepted.

North Dakota State University, College of Graduate and Interdisciplinary Studies, Interdisciplinary Program in Natural Resources Management, Fargo, ND 58108. Offers MS, PhD. Part-time programs available. *Faculty:* 21 full-time (5 women). *Students:* 33 full-time (14 women), 17 part-time (7 women); includes 4 minority (2 Black or African American, non-Hispanic/Latino; 2 Two or more races, non-Hispanic/Latino), 4 international. Average age 31. 17 applicants, 76% accepted, 11 enrolled. In 2012, 18 master's, 1 doctorate awarded. *Degree requirements:* For master's, thesis; for doctorate, comprehensive exam, thesis/dissertation. *Entrance requirements:* Additional exam requirements/recommendations for international students: Required—TOEFL (minimum score 525 paper-based; 71 iBT). *Application deadline:* Applications are processed on a rolling basis. Application fee: $35. Electronic applications accepted. *Financial support:* In 2012–13, 25 students received support. Research assistantships with full tuition reimbursements available and teaching assistantships with full tuition reimbursements available available. Support available to part-time students. Financial award application deadline: 3/15. *Faculty research:* Natural resources economics, wetlands issues, wildlife, prairie ecology, range management. *Unit head:* Dr. Carolyn E. Grygiel, Director, 701-231-8180, Fax: 701-231-7590, E-mail: carolyn.grygiel@ndsu.edu. *Application contact:* Sonya Goergen, Marketing, Recruitment, and Public Relations Coordinator, 701-231-7033, Fax: 701-231-6524. Website: http://www.ag.ndsu.nodak.edu/nrm/grad.htm.

Northeastern State University, College of Science and Health Professions, Department of Natural Sciences, Program in Natural Sciences, Tahlequah, OK 74464-2399. Offers MS. *Faculty:* 10 full-time (3 women). *Students:* 8 full-time (7 women), 1 part-time (0 women); includes 5 minority (3 American Indian or Alaska Native, non-Hispanic/Latino; 2 Two or more races, non-Hispanic/Latino). Average age 27. 12 applicants, 83% accepted, 7 enrolled. *Degree requirements:* For master's, thesis, project. *Application deadline:* For fall admission, 3/1 for domestic students; for spring admission, 10/1 for domestic students. *Expenses:* Tuition, state resident: full-time $1451.25; part-time $161.25 per credit hour. Tuition, nonresident: full-time $3701; part-time $411.25 per credit hour. *Required fees:* $36.90 per contact hour. *Unit head:* Dr. Chris Burba, Department Chair, 918-444-3835, E-mail: burba@nsuok.edu. *Application contact:* Margie Railey, Administrative Assistant, 918-456-5511 Ext. 2093, Fax: 918-458-2061, E-mail: railey@nsouk.edu. Website: http://academics.nsuok.edu/naturalsciences/Degrees/Graduate/MSNaturalScience.aspx.

The Ohio State University, Graduate School, College of Food, Agricultural, and Environmental Sciences, School of Environment and Natural Resources, Columbus, OH 43210. Offers environment and natural resources (MENR); rural sociology (MS, PhD); soil science (MS, PhD). *Faculty:* 35. *Students:* 73 full-time (40 women), 26 part-time (13 women); includes 11 minority (2 Black or African American, non-Hispanic/Latino; 6 Hispanic/Latino; 3 Two or more races, non-Hispanic/Latino), 14 international. Average age 29. In 2012, 30 master's, 4 doctorates awarded. *Degree requirements:* For master's, thesis; for doctorate, thesis/dissertation. *Entrance requirements:* For master's and doctorate, GRE. Additional exam requirements/recommendations for international students: Required—TOEFL (minimum score 550 paper-based; 79 iBT), Michigan English Language Assessment Battery (minimum score 82); Recommended—IELTS (minimum score 7). *Application deadline:* Applications are processed on a rolling basis. Application fee: $40 ($50 for international students). Electronic applications accepted. *Unit head:* Ronald Hendrick, Director, 614-292-8522, E-mail: hendrick.15@osu.edu. *Application contact:* Amy Schmidt, Graduate Program Coordinator, 614-292-9883, Fax: 614-292-7432, E-mail: schmidt.442@osu.edu. Website: http://senr.osu.edu/default.asp.

Oklahoma State University, College of Agricultural Science and Natural Resources, Stillwater, OK 74078. Offers M Ag, MS, PhD. Postbaccalaureate distance learning degree programs offered. *Faculty:* 242 full-time (57 women), 12 part-time/adjunct (1 woman). *Students:* 161 full-time (78 women), 349 part-time (168 women); includes 62 minority (9 Black or African American, non-Hispanic/Latino; 15 American Indian or Alaska Native, non-Hispanic/Latino; 10 Asian, non-Hispanic/Latino; 7 Hispanic/Latino; 21 Two or more races, non-Hispanic/Latino), 162 international. Average age 29. 497 applicants, 35% accepted, 122 enrolled. In 2012, 137 master's, 48 doctorates awarded. *Degree requirements:* For master's, thesis (for some programs); for doctorate, comprehensive exam, thesis/dissertation. *Entrance requirements:* For master's and doctorate, GRE or GMAT. Additional exam requirements/recommendations for international students: Required—TOEFL (minimum score 550 paper-based; 79 iBT). *Application deadline:* For fall admission, 3/1 for international students; for spring admission, 8/1 for international students. Applications are processed on a rolling basis. Application fee: $40 ($75 for international students). Electronic applications accepted. *Expenses:* Tuition, state resident: full-time $4272; part-time $178 per credit hour. Tuition, nonresident: full-time $17,016; part-time $709 per credit hour. *Required fees:* $2188; $91.17 per credit hour. One-time fee: $50 full-time. Part-time tuition and fees vary according to course load and campus/location. *Financial support:* In 2012–13, 258 research assistantships (averaging $16,184 per year), 47 teaching assistantships (averaging $12,835 per year) were awarded; fellowships, career-related internships or fieldwork, Federal Work-Study, scholarships/grants, health care benefits, tuition waivers (partial), and unspecified assistantships also available. Support available to part-time students. Financial award application deadline: 3/1; financial award applicants required to submit FAFSA. *Unit head:* Dr. Cynda E. Clary, Associate Dean, 405-744-5395, E-mail: cynda.clary@okstate.edu. *Application contact:* Dr. Sheryl Tucker, Dean, 405-744-7099, Fax: 405-744-0355, E-mail: grad-i@okstate.edu. Website: http://www.dasnr.okstate.edu.

Oregon State University, College of Forestry, Program in Natural Resources, Corvallis, OR 97331. Offers MNR. Postbaccalaureate distance learning degree programs offered (no on-campus study). *Students:* 8 full-time (6 women), 33 part-time (20 women); includes 2 minority (both Asian, non-Hispanic/Latino). Average age 36. 35 applicants, 51% accepted, 12 enrolled. In 2012, 4 master's awarded. *Expenses:* Tuition, state resident: full-time $11,367; part-time $421 per credit hour. Tuition, nonresident: full-time $18,279; part-time $677 per credit hour. *Required fees:* $1478. One-time fee: $300 full-time. Tuition and fees vary according to course load and program. *Unit head:* Dr. Paul Doescher, Professor/Department Head, 541-737-6583, Fax: 541-737-1393, E-mail: paul.doescher@oregonstate.edu. Website: http://ecampus.oregonstate.edu/online-degrees/graduate/natural-resources/.

Purdue University, Graduate School, College of Agriculture, Department of Forestry and Natural Resources, West Lafayette, IN 47907. Offers fisheries and aquatic sciences (MS, MSF, PhD); forest biology (MS, MSF, PhD); natural resource social science (MS, PhD); natural resources social science (MSF); quantitative ecology (MS, MSF, PhD); wildlife science (MS, MSF, PhD); wood products and wood products manufacturing (MS, MSF, PhD). *Faculty:* 25 full-time (3 women), 10 part-time/adjunct (1 woman). *Students:* 61 full-time (24 women), 11 part-time (6 women); includes 3 minority (1 American Indian or Alaska Native, non-Hispanic/Latino; 2 Hispanic/Latino), 18 international. Average age 29. 57 applicants, 28% accepted, 15 enrolled. In 2012, 18 master's, 7 doctorates awarded. *Degree requirements:* For master's, thesis; for doctorate, thesis/dissertation. *Entrance requirements:* For master's and doctorate, GRE General Test (minimum score: verbal 50th percentile; quantitative 50th percentile; analytical writing 4.0), minimum undergraduate GPA of 3.2 or equivalent. Additional exam requirements/recommendations for international students: Required—TOEFL (minimum score 550 paper-based; 77 iBT). *Application deadline:* For fall admission, 1/5 for domestic students, 1/15 for international students; for spring admission, 9/15 for domestic and international students. Applications are processed on a rolling basis. Application fee: $60 ($75 for international students). Electronic applications accepted. *Financial support:* In 2012–13, 10 research assistantships (averaging $15,259 per year) were awarded; fellowships, teaching assistantships, career-related internships or fieldwork, and scholarships/grants also available. Support available to part-time students. Financial award application deadline: 1/5; financial award applicants required to submit FAFSA. *Faculty research:* Wildlife management, forest management, forest ecology, forest soils, limnology. *Unit head:* Dr. Robert K. Swihart, Interim Head, 765-494-3590, Fax: 765-494-9461, E-mail: rswihart@purdue.edu. *Application contact:* Kelly J. Wrede, Graduate Secretary, 765-494-3572, Fax: 765-494-9461, E-mail: kgarrett@purdue.edu. Website: http://www.fnr.purdue.edu/.

San Francisco State University, Division of Graduate Studies, College of Science and Engineering, Department of Geography and Human Environmental Studies, San Francisco, CA 94132-1722. Offers geographic information science (MS); geography (MA), including resource management and environmental planning. *Unit head:* Dr. Jerry Davis, Chair, 415-338-2049, E-mail: jerry@sfsu.edu. *Application contact:* Dr. Nancy Wilkinson, Graduate Coordinator, 415-338-2049, E-mail: nancyw@sfsu.edu. Website: http://geog.sfsu.edu/.

State University of New York College of Environmental Science and Forestry, Department of Environmental Resources Engineering, Syracuse, NY 13210-2779. Offers ecological engineering (MPS, MS, PhD); environmental management (MPS); environmental resources engineering (MPS, MS, PhD); geospatial information science and engineering (MPS, MS, PhD); water resources engineering (MS, PhD). Part-time programs available. *Faculty:* 8 full-time (1 woman), 4 part-time/adjunct (0 women). *Students:* 37 full-time (11 women), 6 part-time (3 women); includes 17 minority (1 Black or African American, non-Hispanic/Latino; 16 Asian, non-Hispanic/Latino), 21 international. Average age 25. 120 applicants, 38% accepted, 14 enrolled. In 2012, 15 master's, 5 doctorates awarded. *Degree requirements:* For master's, thesis (for some programs); for doctorate, comprehensive exam, thesis/dissertation. *Entrance requirements:* For master's and doctorate, GRE General Test, minimum GPA of 3.0. Additional exam requirements/recommendations for international students: Required—TOEFL (minimum score 550 paper-based; 80 iBT), IELTS (minimum score 6). *Application deadline:* For fall admission, 1/15 priority date for domestic students, 1/15 for international students; for spring admission, 11/1 priority date for domestic students, 11/1 for international students. Applications are processed on a rolling basis. Application fee: $60. *Expenses:* Tuition, state resident: full-time $9370; part-time $390 per credit hour. Tuition, nonresident: full-time $16,680; part-time $695 per credit hour. *Required fees:* $981. Tuition and fees vary according to course load and program. *Financial support:* Fellowships with full and partial tuition reimbursements, research assistantships with full and partial tuition reimbursements, teaching assistantships with full and partial tuition reimbursements, Federal Work-Study, institutionally sponsored loans, scholarships/grants, health care benefits, and unspecified assistantships available. Financial award application deadline: 6/30; financial award applicants required to submit FAFSA. *Faculty research:* Ecological engineering, environmental resources engineering, geospatial information science and engineering, water resources engineering. *Total annual research expenditures:* $1 million. *Unit head:* Dr. Theodore Endreny, Chair, 315-470-6565, Fax: 315-470-6958, E-mail: te@esf.edu. *Application contact:* Scott Shannon, Dean of the Graduate School, 315-470-6599, Fax: 315-470-6978, E-mail: esfgrad@esf.edu. Website: http://www.esf.edu/ere.

State University of New York College of Environmental Science and Forestry, Department of Forest and Natural Resources Management, Syracuse, NY 13210-2779. Offers ecology and ecosystems (MPS, MS, PhD); economics, governance and human dimensions (MPS, MS, PhD); environmental and natural resources policy (MPS, MS); forest and natural resources management (MPS, MS, PhD); monitoring, analysis and modeling (MPS, MS, PhD). *Accreditation:* SAF. *Degree requirements:* For master's, thesis (for some programs); for doctorate, comprehensive exam, thesis/dissertation. *Entrance requirements:* For master's and doctorate, GRE General Test, minimum GPA of 3.0. Additional exam requirements/recommendations for international students: Required—TOEFL (minimum score 550 paper-based; 80 iBT), IELTS (minimum score 6). *Expenses:* Tuition, state resident: full-time $9370; part-time $390 per credit hour. Tuition, nonresident: full-time $16,680; part-time $695 per credit hour. *Required fees:* $981. Tuition and fees vary according to course load and program. *Faculty research:* Silviculture recreation management, tree improvement, operations management, economics.

State University of New York College of Environmental Science and Forestry, Department of Sustainable Construction Management and Engineering, Syracuse, NY 13210-2779. Offers construction management (MPS, MS, PhD); engineered wood products and structures (MPS, MS, PhD); sustainable construction (MPS, MS, PhD); tropical timbers (MPS, MS, PhD); wood anatomy and ultrastructure (MPS, MS, PhD); wood science and technology (MPS, MS, PhD); wood treatments (MPS, MS, PhD). *Degree requirements:* For master's, thesis (for some programs); for doctorate, comprehensive exam, thesis/dissertation. *Entrance requirements:* For master's and doctorate, GRE General Test, minimum GPA of 3.0. Additional exam requirements/recommendations for international students: Required—TOEFL (minimum score 550 paper-based; 80 iBT), IELTS (minimum score 6). *Expenses:* Tuition, state resident: full-time $9370; part-time $390 per credit hour. Tuition, nonresident: full-time $16,680; part-time $695 per credit hour. *Required fees:* $981. Tuition and fees vary according to course load and program.

Sul Ross State University, Division of Agricultural and Natural Resource Science, Programs in Natural Resource Management, Alpine, TX 79832. Offers range and wildlife management (M Ag, MS). Part-time programs available. *Degree requirements:* For master's, thesis (for some programs). *Entrance requirements:* For master's, GRE General Test, minimum undergraduate GPA of 2.5 in last 60 hours.

Texas A&M University, College of Agriculture and Life Sciences, Department of Ecosystem Science and Management, College Station, TX 77843. Offers forestry (MS, PhD); rangeland ecology and management (M Agr, MS, PhD). Part-time programs available. *Faculty:* 24. *Students:* 52 full-time (31 women), 32 part-time (18 women); includes 24 minority (3 Black or African American, non-Hispanic/Latino; 2 Asian, non-Hispanic/Latino; 18 Hispanic/Latino; 1 Two or more races, non-Hispanic/Latino), 16 international. Average age 32. In 2012, 10 master's, 2 doctorates awarded. Terminal master's awarded for partial completion of doctoral program. *Degree requirements:* For master's, thesis (for some programs); for doctorate, thesis/dissertation. *Entrance requirements:* For master's and doctorate, GRE General Test. Additional exam requirements/recommendations for international students: Required—TOEFL. *Application deadline:* For fall admission, 3/1 priority date for domestic students; for spring admission, 11/1 priority date for domestic students. Applications are processed on a rolling basis. Application fee: $50 ($75 for international students). Electronic applications accepted. *Financial support:* In 2012–13, fellowships with partial tuition reimbursements (averaging $15,000 per year), research assistantships with partial tuition reimbursements (averaging $15,000 per year), teaching assistantships with partial tuition reimbursements (averaging $15,000 per year) were awarded; career-related internships or fieldwork and institutionally sponsored loans also available. Support available to part-time students. Financial award application deadline: 3/1; financial award applicants required to submit FAFSA. *Faculty research:* Expert systems, geographic information systems, economics, biology, genetics. *Unit head:* Dr. Steve Whisenant, Professor and Head, 979-845-5000, Fax: 979-845-6049, E-mail: s-whisenant@tamu.edu. *Application contact:* Dr. Carol Loopstra, Associate Professor, 979-862-2200, Fax: 979-845-6049, E-mail: c-loopstra@tamu.edu. Website: http://essm.tamu.edu.

Texas A&M University, College of Agriculture and Life Sciences, Department of Recreation, Park and Tourism Sciences, College Station, TX 77843. Offers natural resources development (M Agr); recreation resources development (M Agr); recreation, park, and tourism sciences (MS, PhD). *Faculty:* 15. *Students:* 61 full-time (33 women), 19 part-time (9 women); includes 10 minority (6 Black or African American, non-Hispanic/Latino; 2 Asian, non-Hispanic/Latino; 2 Hispanic/Latino), 31 international. Average age 31. In 2012, 7 master's, 7 doctorates awarded. *Degree requirements:* For master's, thesis (for some programs), internship and professional paper (M Agr); for doctorate, thesis/dissertation. *Entrance requirements:* For master's and doctorate, GRE General Test. Additional exam requirements/recommendations for international students: Required—TOEFL. *Application deadline:* For fall admission, 4/15 priority date for domestic students; for spring admission, 10/15 priority date for domestic students. Applications are processed on a rolling basis. Application fee: $50 ($75 for international students). Electronic applications accepted. *Financial support:* Fellowships, research assistantships, teaching assistantships, career-related internships or fieldwork, institutionally sponsored loans, and scholarships/grants available. Financial award application deadline: 4/15; financial award applicants required to submit FAFSA. *Faculty research:* Administration and tourism, outdoor recreation, commercial recreation, environmental law, system planning. *Unit head:* Dr. Gary Ellis, Head, 979-845-7324. *Application contact:* Graduate Admissions, 979-845-1044, E-mail: admissions@tamu.edu. Website: http://rpts.tamu.edu/.

Texas Tech University, Graduate School, College of Agricultural Sciences and Natural Resources, Department of Natural Resources Management, Lubbock, TX 79409. Offers fisheries science (MS, PhD); range science (MS, PhD); wildlife, aquatic, and wildlands science and management (MS, PhD). Part-time programs available. *Degree requirements:* For master's, thesis; for doctorate, thesis/dissertation. *Entrance requirements:* For master's and doctorate, GRE General Test, formal approval from departmental committee. Additional exam requirements/recommendations for international students: Required—TOEFL (minimum score 550 paper-based; 79 iBT). Electronic applications accepted. *Faculty research:* Use of fire on range lands; big game, upland game, and waterfowl; playa lakes in the southern Great Plains; conservation biology; fish ecology and physiology.

Universidad Metropolitana, School of Environmental Affairs, Program in Environmental Management, San Juan, PR 00928-1150. Offers MSEM. Part-time programs available. *Degree requirements:* For master's, thesis. Electronic applications accepted.

Universidad Nacional Pedro Henriquez Urena, Graduate School, Santo Domingo, Dominican Republic. Offers agricultural diversity (MS), including horticultural/fruit production, tropical animal production; conservation of monuments and cultural assets (M Arch); ecology and environment (MS); environmental engineering (MEE); international relations (MA); natural resource management (MS); political science (MA); project optimization (MPM); project feasibility (MPM); project management (MPM); sanitation engineering (ME); science for teachers (MS); tropical Caribbean architecture (M Arch).

Université du Québec à Montréal, Graduate Programs, Program in Earth Sciences, Montreal, QC H3C 3P8, Canada. Offers earth sciences (M Sc); mineral resources (PhD); non-renewable resources (DESS). Part-time programs available. Terminal master's awarded for partial completion of doctoral program. *Degree requirements:* For master's, thesis (for some programs); for doctorate, thesis/dissertation. *Entrance requirements:* For master's, appropriate bachelor's degree or equivalent, proficiency in French. *Faculty research:* Economic geology, structural geology, geochemistry, Quaternary geology, isotopic geochemistry.

Université du Québec en Abitibi-Témiscamingue, Graduate Programs, Program in Environmental Sciences, Rouyn-Noranda, QC J9X 5E4, Canada. Offers biology (MS); environmental sciences (PhD); sustainable forest ecosystem management (MS).

University of Alaska Fairbanks, School of Natural Resources and Agricultural Sciences, Fairbanks, AK 99775-7140. Offers natural resource and sustainability (PhD); natural resource management (MS); natural resource management and geography (MNRM, MS). Part-time programs available. *Faculty:* 27 full-time (8 women), 3 part-time/adjunct (2 women). *Students:* 28 full-time (20 women), 26 part-time (13 women); includes 2 minority (1 American Indian or Alaska Native, non-Hispanic/Latino; 1 Hispanic/Latino), 5 international. Average age 35. 34 applicants, 32% accepted, 11 enrolled. In 2012, 7 master's, 3 doctorates awarded. *Degree requirements:* For master's, comprehensive exam, thesis or alternative. *Entrance requirements:* For master's, GRE General Test. Additional exam requirements/recommendations for international students: Required—TOEFL (minimum score 550 paper-based). *Application deadline:* For fall admission, 6/1 for domestic students, 3/1 for international students; for spring admission, 10/15 for domestic students, 9/1 for international students. Applications are processed on a rolling basis. Application fee: $60. Electronic applications accepted. *Expenses:* Tuition, state resident: full-time $7038. Tuition, nonresident: full-time $14,382. Tuition and fees vary according to course level, course load and reciprocity agreements. *Financial support:* In 2012–13, 8 research assistantships (averaging $13,550 per year), 2 teaching assistantships (averaging $5,087 per year) were awarded; fellowships, career-related internships or fieldwork, Federal Work-Study, scholarships/grants, health care benefits, and unspecified assistantships also available. Support available to part-time students. Financial award application deadline: 2/15; financial award applicants required to submit FAFSA. *Faculty research:* Conservation biology, soil/water conservation, land use policy and planning in the arctic and subarctic, forest ecosystem management, subarctic agricultural production. *Total annual research expenditures:* $4.4 million. *Unit head:* Stephen Sparrow, Interim Dean, 907-474-7083, Fax: 907-474-6567, E-mail: fysnras@uaf.edu. *Application contact:* Martha Westphal, Enrollment and Administrative Coordinator, 907-474-7188, Fax: 907-474-6567, E-mail: mmwestphal@alaska.edu. Website: http://www.uaf.edu/snras/.

University of Alberta, Faculty of Graduate Studies and Research, Department of Renewable Resources, Edmonton, AB T6G 2E1, Canada. Offers agroforestry (M Ag, M Sc, MF); conservation biology (M Sc, PhD); forest biology and management (M Sc, PhD); land reclamation and remediation (M Sc, PhD); protected areas and wildlands management (M Sc, PhD); soil science (M Ag, M Sc, PhD); water and land resources (M Ag, M Sc, PhD); wildlife ecology and management (M Sc, PhD); MBA/M Ag; MBA/MF. Part-time programs available. *Degree requirements:* For master's, thesis (for some programs); for doctorate, comprehensive exam, thesis/dissertation. *Entrance requirements:* For master's, minimum 2 years of relevant professional experiences, minimum GPA of 3.0; for doctorate, minimum GPA of 3.0. Additional exam requirements/recommendations for international students: Required—TOEFL (minimum score 550 paper-based). Electronic applications accepted. *Faculty research:* Natural and managed landscapes.

Natural Resources

University of Alberta, Faculty of Graduate Studies and Research, Program in Business Administration, Edmonton, AB T6G 2E1, Canada. Offers international business (MBA); leisure and sport management (MBA); natural resources and energy (MBA); technology commercialization (MBA); MBA/LL B; MBA/M Ag; MBA/M Eng; MBA/MF; MBA/PhD. *Accreditation:* AACSB. Part-time and evening/weekend programs available. *Degree requirements:* For master's, thesis or alternative. *Entrance requirements:* For master's, GMAT. Additional exam requirements/recommendations for international students: Required—TOEFL (minimum score 600 paper-based). Electronic applications accepted. *Faculty research:* Natural resources and energy/management and policy/family enterprise/international business/healthcare research management.

The University of Arizona, College of Agriculture and Life Sciences, School of Natural Resources, Program in Natural Resources, Tucson, AZ 85721. Offers MS, PhD. *Faculty:* 19 full-time (3 women), 2 part-time/adjunct (0 women). *Students:* 72 full-time (39 women), 18 part-time (8 women); includes 17 minority (1 Black or African American, non-Hispanic/Latino; 6 Hispanic/Latino; 10 Two or more races, non-Hispanic/Latino), 10 international. Average age 31. 65 applicants, 29% accepted, 11 enrolled. In 2012, 16 master's, 3 doctorates awarded. *Degree requirements:* For master's, thesis; for doctorate, comprehensive exam, thesis/dissertation. *Entrance requirements:* For master's and doctorate, GRE General Test, minimum GPA of 3.0. Additional exam requirements/recommendations for international students: Required—TOEFL (minimum score 550 paper-based; 79 iBT). *Application deadline:* For fall admission, 2/1 for domestic and international students. Applications are processed on a rolling basis. Application fee: $75. Electronic applications accepted. *Financial support:* In 2012–13, 37 research assistantships with full and partial tuition reimbursements (averaging $16,587 per year), 2 teaching assistantships with full and partial tuition reimbursements (averaging $13,809 per year) were awarded; career-related internships or fieldwork, scholarships/grants, health care benefits, tuition waivers (partial), and unspecified assistantships also available. *Faculty research:* Criteria for defining, mapping, and evaluating range sites; methods of establishing forage plants on southwestern range lands; plants for pollution and erosion control, beautification, and browse. *Total annual research expenditures:* $6.5 million. *Unit head:* Dr. Charles Hutchinson, Director, 520-621-8568, E-mail: chuck@ag.arizona.edu. *Application contact:* Katie Hughes, Academic Coordinator, 520-621-7260, Fax: 520-621-8801, E-mail: khughes@email.arizona.edu. Website: http://grad.arizona.edu/live/programs/description/117.

University of Arkansas at Monticello, School of Forest Resources, Monticello, AR 71656. Offers MS. Part-time programs available. *Degree requirements:* For master's, comprehensive exam, thesis. *Entrance requirements:* For master's, GRE General Test, minimum GPA of 2.7. Additional exam requirements/recommendations for international students: Required—TOEFL (minimum score 550 paper-based). Electronic applications accepted. *Faculty research:* Geographic information systems/remote sensing, forest ecology, wildlife ecology and management.

The University of British Columbia, Program in Resource Management and Environmental Studies, Vancouver, BC, BC V6T 1Z4, Canada. Offers M Sc, MA, PhD. *Degree requirements:* For master's, thesis; for doctorate, comprehensive exam, thesis/dissertation. *Entrance requirements:* Additional exam requirements/recommendations for international students: Required—TOEFL (minimum score 600 paper-based; 100 iBT). Electronic applications accepted. *Faculty research:* Land management, water resources, energy, environmental assessment, risk evaluation.

University of California, Berkeley, Graduate Division, Group in Energy and Resources, Berkeley, CA 94720-1500. Offers MA, MS, PhD. *Degree requirements:* For master's, project or thesis; for doctorate, one foreign language, thesis/dissertation, qualifying exam. *Entrance requirements:* For master's and doctorate, GRE General Test, minimum GPA of 3.0, 3 letters of recommendation. *Faculty research:* Technical, economic, environmental, and institutional aspects of energy conservation in residential and commercial buildings; international patterns of energy use; renewable energy sources; assessment of valuation of energy and environmental resources pricing.

University of Connecticut, Graduate School, College of Agriculture and Natural Resources, Department of Natural Resources Management and Engineering, Storrs, CT 06269. Offers MS, PhD. Terminal master's awarded for partial completion of doctoral program. *Degree requirements:* For master's, comprehensive exam. *Entrance requirements:* For master's, GRE General Test, GRE Subject Test. Additional exam requirements/recommendations for international students: Required—TOEFL (minimum score 550 paper-based). Electronic applications accepted. *Faculty research:* Forest management, forest protection, water resources, biometeorology.

University of Delaware, College of Agriculture and Natural Resources, Department of Bioresources Engineering, Newark, DE 19716. Offers MS.

University of Denver, University College, Denver, CO 80208. Offers arts and culture (MLS, Certificate), including art, literature, and culture, arts development and program management (Certificate), creative writing; environmental policy and management (MAS, Certificate), including energy and sustainability (Certificate), environmental assessment of nuclear power (Certificate), environmental health and safety (Certificate), environmental management, natural resource management (Certificate); geographic information systems (MAS, Certificate); global affairs (MLS, Certificate), including translation studies, world history and culture; healthcare leadership (MPH, Certificate), including healthcare policy, law, and ethics, medical and healthcare information technologies, strategic management of healthcare; information and communications technology (MCIS, Certificate), including database design and administration (Certificate), geographic information systems (MCIS), information security systems security (Certificate), information systems security (MCIS), project management (MCIS, MPS, Certificate), software design and administration (Certificate), software design and programming (MCIS), technology management, telecommunications technology (MCIS), Web design and development; leadership and organizations (MPS, Certificate), including human capital in organizations, philanthropic leadership, project management (MCIS, MPS, Certificate), strategic innovation and change; organizational and professional communication (MPS, Certificate), including alternative dispute resolution, organizational communication, organizational development and training, public relations and marketing; security management (MAS, Certificate), including emergency planning and response, information security (MAS), organizational security; strategic human resource management (MPS, Certificate), including global human resources (MPS), human resource management and development (MPS). Part-time and evening/weekend programs available. Postbaccalaureate distance learning degree programs offered (no on-campus study). *Faculty:* 187 part-time/adjunct (75 women). *Students:* 43 full-time (18 women), 1,125 part-time (670 women); includes 226 minority (78 Black or African American, non-Hispanic/Latino; 3 American Indian or Alaska Native, non-Hispanic/Latino; 31 Asian, non-Hispanic/Latino; 88 Hispanic/Latino; 3 Native Hawaiian or other Pacific Islander, non-Hispanic/Latino; 23 Two or more races, non-Hispanic/Latino), 61 international. Average age 36. 905 applicants, 93% accepted, 358 enrolled. In 2012, 491 master's, 132 other advanced degrees awarded. *Degree requirements:* For master's, capstone project. *Entrance requirements:* For master's, two letters of recommendation, personal statement, resume. Additional exam requirements/recommendations for international students: Required—TOEFL (minimum score 550 paper-based; 80 iBT). *Application deadline:* For fall admission, 7/20 priority date for domestic students, 6/8 for international students; for winter admission, 10/26 priority date for domestic students, 9/14 for international students; for spring admission, 2/1 priority date for domestic students, 12/14 for international students. Applications are processed on a rolling basis. Application fee: $75. Electronic applications accepted. *Expenses:* Contact institution. *Financial support:* In 2012–13, 14 students received support. Applicants required to submit FAFSA. *Unit head:* Dr. Michael McGuire, Interim Dean, 303-871-2291, Fax: 303-871-4047, E-mail: mmcguire@du.edu. *Application contact:* Information Contact, 303-871-2291, Fax: 303-871-4047, E-mail: ucolinfo@du.edu. Website: http://www.universitycollege.du.edu/.

University of Florida, Graduate School, College of Agricultural and Life Sciences, School of Forest Resources and Conservation, Gainesville, FL 32611. Offers MFAS, MFRC, MS, PhD, JD/MFRC, JD/MS, JD/PhD. Part-time and evening/weekend programs available. Postbaccalaureate distance learning degree programs offered. Terminal master's awarded for partial completion of doctoral program. *Degree requirements:* For master's, comprehensive exam, thesis optional, project (for MFRC); for doctorate, comprehensive exam, thesis/dissertation. *Entrance requirements:* For master's, GRE General Test (minimum score of 1000), minimum GPA of 3.0; for doctorate, GRE General Test, minimum GPA of 3.25. Additional exam requirements/recommendations for international students: Required—TOEFL (minimum score 550 paper-based; 80 iBT), IELTS (minimum score 6). Electronic applications accepted. *Faculty research:* Forest biology and ecology; natural resource economics and management; human dimensions and resource policy; tropical forestry and agroforestry; geomatics: geospatial, GIS, and remote sensing.

University of Florida, Graduate School, School of Natural Resources and Environment, Gainesville, FL 32611. Offers interdisciplinary ecology (MS, PhD). *Degree requirements:* For master's, comprehensive exam, thesis; for doctorate, comprehensive exam, thesis/dissertation. *Entrance requirements:* For master's and doctorate, GRE General Test, minimum GPA of 3.0. Additional exam requirements/recommendations for international students: Required—TOEFL (minimum score 550 paper-based; 80 iBT), IELTS (minimum score 6). Electronic applications accepted. *Faculty research:* Natural sciences, social sciences, sustainability studies, research design and methods.

University of Georgia, School of Forestry and Natural Resources, Athens, GA 30602. Offers MFR, MS, PhD. *Degree requirements:* For master's, thesis (MS); for doctorate, one foreign language, thesis/dissertation. *Entrance requirements:* For master's and doctorate, GRE General Test. Electronic applications accepted.

University of Guelph, Graduate Studies, Ontario Agricultural College, Department of Land Resource Science, Guelph, ON N1G 2W1, Canada. Offers atmospheric science (M Sc, PhD); environmental and agricultural earth sciences (M Sc, PhD); land resources management (M Sc, PhD); soil science (M Sc, PhD). Part-time programs available. *Degree requirements:* For master's, thesis (for some programs), research project (non-thesis track); for doctorate, comprehensive exam, thesis/dissertation. *Entrance requirements:* For master's, minimum B- average during previous 2 years of course work; for doctorate, minimum B average during previous 2 years of course work. Additional exam requirements/recommendations for international students: Required—TOEFL (minimum score 550 paper-based). Electronic applications accepted. *Faculty research:* Soil science, environmental earth science, land resource management.

University of Hawaii at Manoa, Graduate Division, College of Tropical Agriculture and Human Resources, Department of Natural Resources and

Environmental Management, Honolulu, HI 96822. Offers MS, PhD. Part-time programs available. Terminal master's awarded for partial completion of doctoral program. *Degree requirements:* For master's, thesis optional; for doctorate, comprehensive exam, thesis/dissertation. *Entrance requirements:* For master's and doctorate, GRE General Test, minimum GPA of 3.0 in last 4 semesters of course work. Additional exam requirements/recommendations for international students: Required—TOEFL (minimum score 600 paper-based; 100 iBT), IELTS (minimum score 7). *Faculty research:* Bioeconomics, natural resource management.

University of Idaho, College of Graduate Studies, College of Natural Resources, Moscow, ID 83844-1138. Offers MNR, MS, PhD. *Faculty:* 33 full-time, 2 part-time/adjunct. *Students:* 101 full-time (52 women), 81 part-time (34 women). Average age 36. In 2012, 55 master's, 9 doctorates awarded. *Degree requirements:* For doctorate, thesis/dissertation. *Entrance requirements:* For master's, minimum GPA of 2.8; for doctorate, minimum undergraduate GPA of 2.8, 3.0 graduate. *Application deadline:* For fall admission, 8/1 for domestic students; for spring admission, 12/15 for domestic students. Applications are processed on a rolling basis. Application fee: $60. Electronic applications accepted. *Expenses:* Tuition, state resident: full-time $4230; part-time $252 per credit hour. Tuition, nonresident: full-time $17,018; part-time $891 per credit hour. *Required fees:* $2932; $107 per credit hour. *Financial support:* Fellowships, research assistantships, teaching assistantships, and Federal Work-Study available. Support available to part-time students. Financial award applicants required to submit FAFSA. *Faculty research:* Aquaculture, forest nursery and seedling research, remote sensing and GIS research, wilderness research, conservation and ecological genetics. *Unit head:* Dr. Kurt Scott Pregitzer, Dean, 208-885-8981, Fax: 208-885-5534, E-mail: cnr@uidaho.edu. *Application contact:* Erick Larson, Director of Graduate Admissions, 208-885-4723, E-mail: gadms@uidaho.edu. Website: http://www.uidaho.edu/cnr.

University of Idaho, College of Graduate Studies, Program in Environmental Science, Moscow, ID 83844-3006. Offers environmental science (MS, PhD); natural resources and environmental science (PSM). *Faculty:* 19 full-time, 1 part-time/adjunct. *Students:* 47 full-time, 51 part-time. Average age 33. In 2012, 16 master's, 2 doctorates awarded. *Application deadline:* For fall admission, 8/1 for domestic students; for spring admission, 12/15 for domestic students. Applications are processed on a rolling basis. Application fee: $60. Electronic applications accepted. *Expenses:* Tuition, state resident: full-time $4230; part-time $252 per credit hour. Tuition, nonresident: full-time $17,018; part-time $891 per credit hour. *Required fees:* $2932; $107 per credit hour. *Financial support:* Research assistantships and teaching assistantships available. Financial award applicants required to submit FAFSA. *Unit head:* Dr. Jan Boll, Director, 208-885-6113, Fax: 208-885-4674, E-mail: envs@uidaho.edu. *Application contact:* Erick Larson, Director of Graduate Admissions, 208-885-4723, E-mail: gadms@uidaho.edu. Website: http://www.uidaho.edu/cogs/envs.

University of Illinois at Urbana–Champaign, Graduate College, College of Agricultural, Consumer and Environmental Sciences, Department of Natural Resources and Environmental Science, Champaign, IL 61820. Offers MS, PhD, MS/JD. Part-time programs available. Postbaccalaureate distance learning degree programs offered (no on-campus study). *Students:* 129 (54 women). Application fee: $75 ($90 for international students). *Unit head:* Jeffrey D. Brawn, Head, 217-244-5937, Fax: 217-244-3219, E-mail: jbrawn@illinois.edu. *Application contact:* Karen M. Claus, Secretary, 217-333-5824, Fax: 217-244-3219, E-mail: kclaus@illinois.edu. Website: http://nres.illinois.edu/.

University of Maine, Graduate School, College of Natural Sciences, Forestry, and Agriculture, School of Forest Resources, Orono, ME 04469. Offers forest resources (MS, PhD); forestry (MF). *Accreditation:* SAF (one or more programs are accredited). Part-time programs available. *Faculty:* 20 full-time (1 woman). *Students:* 40 full-time (9 women), 5 part-time (4 women); includes 1 minority (American Indian or Alaska Native, non-Hispanic/Latino), 10 international. Average age 29. 36 applicants, 53% accepted, 10 enrolled. In 2012, 13 master's, 1 doctorate awarded. *Degree requirements:* For master's, thesis; for doctorate, one foreign language, comprehensive exam, thesis/dissertation. *Entrance requirements:* For master's and doctorate, GRE General Test. Additional exam requirements/recommendations for international students: Required—TOEFL. *Application deadline:* For fall admission, 2/1 priority date for domestic students. Applications are processed on a rolling basis. Application fee: $65. Electronic applications accepted. *Financial support:* In 2012–13, 28 research assistantships with full tuition reimbursements (averaging $20,447 per year), 7 teaching assistantships with full tuition reimbursements (averaging $13,600 per year) were awarded; career-related internships or fieldwork, Federal Work-Study, and institutionally sponsored loans also available. Financial award application deadline: 3/1. *Faculty research:* Forest economics, engineering and operations analysis, biometrics and remote sensing, timber management, wood technology. *Total annual research expenditures:* $336,195. *Unit head:* Dr. Robert Wagner, Director, 207-581-4737. *Application contact:* Scott G. Delcourt, Associate Dean of the Graduate School, 207-581-3291, Fax: 207-581-3232, E-mail: graduate@maine.edu. Website: http://www.forest.umaine.edu/.

The University of Manchester, School of Materials, Manchester, United Kingdom. Offers advanced aerospace materials engineering (M Sc); advanced metallic systems (PhD); biomedical materials (M Phil, M Sc, PhD); ceramics and glass (M Phil, M Sc, PhD); composite materials (M Sc, PhD); corrosion and protection (M Phil, M Sc, PhD); materials (M Phil, PhD); metallic materials (M Phil, M Sc, PhD); nanostructural materials (M Phil, M Sc, PhD); paper science (M Phil, M Sc, PhD); polymer science and engineering (M Phil, M Sc, PhD); technical textiles (M Sc); textile design, fashion and management (M Phil, M Sc, PhD); textile science and technology (M Phil, M Sc, PhD); textiles (M Phil, PhD); textiles and fashion (M Ent).

University of Manitoba, Faculty of Graduate Studies, Clayton H. Riddell Faculty of Environment, Earth, and Resources, Natural Resources Institute, Winnipeg, MB R3T 2N2, Canada. Offers natural resources and environmental management (PhD); natural resources management (MNRM).

University of Maryland, College Park, Academic Affairs, College of Agriculture and Natural Resources, Department of Plant Science and Landscape Architecture, Natural Resource Sciences Program, College Park, MD 20742. Offers MS, PhD. *Expenses:* Tuition, state resident: part-time $551 per credit. Tuition, nonresident: part-time $1188 per credit. Part-time tuition and fees vary according to program. *Financial support:* Fellowships, research assistantships, and teaching assistantships available. *Faculty research:* Wetland soils, acid mine drainage, acid sulfate soil. *Unit head:* Dr. Angus Murphy, Chair, 301-405-6244, Fax: 301-314-9308, E-mail: asmurphy@umd.edu.

University of Michigan, School of Natural Resources and Environment, Program in Natural Resources and Environment, Ann Arbor, MI 48109-1041. Offers aquatic sciences: research and management (MS); behavior, education and communication (MS); conservation biology (MS); conservation ecology (MS); environmental informatics (MS); environmental justice (MS); environmental policy and planning (MS); natural resources and environment (PhD); sustainable systems (MS); terrestrial ecosystems (MS); MS/JD; MS/MBA; MUP/MS. *Faculty:* 45 full-time, 23 part-time/adjunct. *Students:* 399 full-time (221 women); includes 65 minority (4 Black or African American, non-Hispanic/Latino; 29 Asian, non-Hispanic/Latino; 23 Hispanic/Latino; 9 Two or more races, non-Hispanic/Latino), 68 international. Average age 27. 635 applicants. In 2012, 138 master's, 9 doctorates awarded. Terminal master's awarded for partial completion of doctoral program. *Degree requirements:* For master's, practicum or group project; for doctorate, comprehensive exam, thesis/dissertation, oral defense of dissertation, preliminary exam. *Entrance requirements:* For master's, GRE General Test; for doctorate, GRE General Test, master's degree. Additional exam requirements/recommendations for international students: Required—TOEFL (minimum score 500 paper-based; 84 iBT). *Application deadline:* For fall admission, 1/5 priority date for domestic students, 1/5 for international students. Applications are processed on a rolling basis. Application fee: $65 ($75 for international students). Electronic applications accepted. *Financial support:* Fellowships with tuition reimbursements, research assistantships with tuition reimbursements, teaching assistantships with tuition reimbursements, career-related internships or fieldwork, Federal Work-Study, institutionally sponsored loans, scholarships/grants, health care benefits, and unspecified assistantships available. Support available to part-time students. Financial award application deadline: 1/5; financial award applicants required to submit FAFSA. *Faculty research:* Stream ecology and fish biology, plant-insect interactions, environmental education, resource control and reproductive success, remote sensing, conservation ecology, sustainable systems. *Unit head:* Dr. Marie Lynn Miranda, Dean, 734-764-2550, Fax: 734-763-8965, E-mail: mlmirand@umich.edu. *Application contact:* Sondra R. Auerbach, Director of Academic Services, 734-764-6453, Fax: 734-936-2195, E-mail: snre.admissions@umich.edu. Website: http://www.snre.umich.edu/.

University of Minnesota, Twin Cities Campus, Graduate School, College of Food, Agricultural and Natural Resource Sciences, Program in Natural Resources Science and Management, Minneapolis, MN 55455-0213. Offers MS, PhD. Part-time programs available. *Faculty:* 127 full-time. *Students:* 117 full-time (51 women); includes 5 minority (1 Black or African American, non-Hispanic/Latino; 2 American Indian or Alaska Native, non-Hispanic/Latino; 1 Asian, non-Hispanic/Latino; 1 Hispanic/Latino), 22 international. Average age 30. 85 applicants, 38% accepted, 24 enrolled. In 2012, 49 master's, 48 doctorates awarded. Terminal master's awarded for partial completion of doctoral program. *Degree requirements:* For master's, comprehensive exam, thesis; for doctorate, comprehensive exam, thesis/dissertation. *Entrance requirements:* For master's and doctorate, GRE General Test. Additional exam requirements/recommendations for international students: Required—TOEFL (minimum score 500 paper-based; 79 iBT), IELTS (minimum score 6.5). *Application deadline:* For fall admission, 12/15 priority date for domestic students, 12/15 for international students; for spring admission, 10/15 for domestic and international students. Applications are processed on a rolling basis. Application fee: $75 ($95 for international students). Electronic applications accepted. *Financial support:* In 2012–13, fellowships with full tuition reimbursements (averaging $40,000 per year), research assistantships with full tuition reimbursements (averaging $40,000 per year), teaching assistantships with full tuition reimbursements (averaging $40,000 per year) were awarded; scholarships/grants, health care benefits, tuition waivers (full and partial), and unspecified assistantships also available. *Faculty research:* Paper science, forestry, recreation resource management, wildlife ecology, environmental education, hydrology, conservation, tourism, economics, policy, watershed management, GIS, forest products. *Total annual research expenditures:* $4,658. *Unit head:* Dr. Michael Kilgore, Director of Graduate Studies, 612-624-6298, E-mail: mkilgore@umn.edu. *Application contact:* Jennifer Welsh, Program Coordinator, 612-624-7683, Fax: 612-625-5212, E-mail: jwelsh@umn.edu. Website: http://www.nrsm.umn.edu.

University of Missouri, Graduate School, School of Natural Resources, Natural Resources Master's Program, Columbia, MO 65211. Offers MNR. *Students:* 1 part-time (0 women). Average age 35. In 2012, 1 master's awarded. Application fee: $55 ($75 for international students). *Expenses:* Tuition, state resident: full-time $6057. Tuition, nonresident: full-time $15,683. *Required fees:* $1000. *Unit head:* Dr. Bruce Cutter, Associate Director, 573-882-7045, E-mail: cutterb@missouri.edu. *Application contact:* E-mail: snr@missouri.edu.

The University of Montana, Graduate School, College of Forestry and Conservation, Missoula, MT 59812-0002. Offers ecosystem management (MEM, MS); fish and wildlife biology (PhD); forestry (MS, PhD); recreation management (MS); resource conservation (MS); wildlife biology (MS). *Degree requirements:* For doctorate, thesis/dissertation. *Entrance requirements:* For master's and doctorate, GRE General Test. Additional exam requirements/recommendations for international students: Required—TOEFL (minimum score 575 paper-based).

University of Nebraska–Lincoln, Graduate College, College of Agricultural Sciences and Natural Resources, Department of Agricultural Economics, Lincoln, NE 68588. Offers agribusiness (MBA); agricultural economics (MS, PhD); community development (M Ag). *Degree requirements:* For master's, thesis optional; for doctorate, comprehensive exam, thesis/dissertation. *Entrance requirements:* For master's and doctorate, GRE General Test. Additional exam requirements/recommendations for international students: Required—TOEFL (minimum score 550 paper-based). Electronic applications accepted. *Faculty research:* Marketing and agribusiness, production economics, resource law, international trade and development, rural policy and revitalization.

University of Nebraska–Lincoln, Graduate College, College of Agricultural Sciences and Natural Resources, School of Natural Resources, Lincoln, NE 68588. Offers geography (PhD); natural resources (MS, PhD). *Degree requirements:* For master's, thesis optional. *Entrance requirements:* For master's, GRE General Test. Additional exam requirements/recommendations for international students: Required—TOEFL. Electronic applications accepted. *Faculty research:* Wildlife biology, aquatic sciences, landscape ecology, agroforestry.

University of New Brunswick Saint John, Faculty of Business, Saint John, NB E2L 4L5, Canada. Offers administration (MBA); electronic commerce (MBA); international business (MBA); natural resource management (MBA). Part-time programs available. *Faculty:* 7 full-time (3 women), 2 part-time/adjunct (1 woman). *Students:* 55 full-time (26 women), 142 part-time (65 women). In 2012, 106 master's awarded. *Entrance requirements:* For master's, GMAT (minimum score of 550) or GRE (minimum 54th percentile), minimum GPA of 3.0. Additional exam requirements/recommendations for international students: Required—TOEFL (minimum score 580 paper-based; 93 iBT), TWE (minimum score 4.5). *Application deadline:* For fall admission, 5/31 for domestic students, 7/15 for international students. Application fee: $100. Electronic applications accepted. *Expenses:* Contact institution. *Financial support:* In 2012–13, 4 students received support. Career-related internships or fieldwork and scholarships/grants available. *Faculty research:* International business, project management, innovation and technology management; business use of weblogs and podcasts to communicate; corporate governance; high-involvement work systems; international competitiveness; supply chain management and logistics. *Unit head:* Henryk Sterniczuk, Director of Graduate Studies, 506-648-5573, Fax: 506-648-5574, E-mail: sternicz@unbsj.ca. *Application contact:* Tammy Morin, Secretary, 506-648-5746, Fax: 506-648-5574, E-mail: tmorin@unbsj.ca. Website: http://go.unb.ca/gradprograms.

University of New Hampshire, Graduate School, College of Life Sciences and Agriculture, Department of Natural Resources, Durham, NH 03824. Offers environmental conservation (MS); forestry (MS); integrated coastal ecosystem science, policy, management (MS); natural resources (MS); water resources (MS); wildlife (MS). Part-time programs available. *Faculty:* 40 full-time. *Students:* 32 full-time (18 women), 29 part-time (16 women); includes 3 minority (all Hispanic/Latino), 3 international. Average age 28. 63 applicants, 43% accepted, 22 enrolled. In 2012, 14 master's awarded. *Degree requirements:* For master's, thesis or alternative. *Entrance requirements:* For master's, GRE General Test. Additional exam requirements/recommendations for international students: Required—TOEFL (minimum score 550 paper-based; 80 iBT). *Application deadline:* For fall admission, 6/1 for domestic students, 4/1 for international students; for spring admission, 12/1 for domestic students. Applications are processed on a rolling basis. Application fee: $65. Electronic applications accepted. *Expenses:* Tuition, state resident: full-time $13,500; part-time $750 per credit. Tuition, nonresident: full-time $25,940; part-time $1089 per credit. *Required fees:* $1699; $424.75 per semester. *Financial support:* In 2012–13, 35 students received support, including 1 fellowship, 15 research assistantships, 23 teaching assistantships; career-related internships or fieldwork, Federal Work-Study, scholarships/grants, and tuition waivers (full and partial) also available. Support available to part-time students. Financial award application deadline: 2/15. *Unit head:* Dr. Ted Howard, Chairperson, 603-862-2700, E-mail: natural.resources@unh.edu. *Application contact:* Nancy Brown, Administrative Assistant, 603-862-1022, E-mail: natural.resources@unh.edu. Website: http://www.nre.unh.edu/academics/.

University of New Hampshire, Graduate School, College of Life Sciences and Agriculture, Department of Resource Economics and Development, Program in Resource Administration, Durham, NH 03824. Offers MS. Part-time programs available. *Faculty:* 4 full-time (0 women), 1 (woman) part-time/adjunct. *Students:* 2 full-time (both women), 1 part-time (0 women); includes 1 minority (Asian, non-Hispanic/Latino). Average age 31. 2 applicants, 100% accepted, 1 enrolled. In 2012, 2 master's awarded. *Degree requirements:* For master's, thesis or alternative. *Entrance requirements:* For master's, GRE General Test. Additional exam requirements/recommendations for international students: Required—TOEFL (minimum score 550 paper-based; 80 iBT). *Application deadline:* For fall admission, 6/1 priority date for domestic students, 4/1 for international students; for spring admission, 12/1 for domestic students. Applications are processed on a rolling basis. Application fee: $65. Electronic applications accepted. *Expenses:* Tuition, state resident: full-time $13,500; part-time $750 per credit. Tuition, nonresident: full-time $25,940; part-time $1089 per credit. *Required fees:* $1699; $424.75 per semester. *Financial support:* In 2012–13, 2 students received support, including 1 teaching assistantship; fellowships, research assistantships, career-related internships or fieldwork, Federal Work-Study, and scholarships/grants also available. Support available to part-time students. Financial award application deadline: 2/15. *Unit head:* Dr. Serita Frey, Chairperson, 603-862-3880. *Application contact:* Jennifer Bourgeault, Information Contact, 603-862-2227, E-mail: resecon.ms.program@unh.edu. Website: http://www.dred.unh.edu.

University of New Hampshire, Graduate School, College of Life Sciences and Agriculture, Department of Resource Economics and Development, Program in Resource Economics, Durham, NH 03824. Offers MS. Part-time programs available. *Faculty:* 6 full-time. *Students:* 2 full-time (1 woman), 1 (woman) part-time. Average age 22. 4 applicants, 50% accepted, 2 enrolled. *Degree requirements:* For master's, thesis or alternative. *Entrance requirements:* For master's, GRE General Test. Additional exam requirements/recommendations for international students: Required—TOEFL (minimum score 550 paper-based; 80 iBT). *Application deadline:* For fall admission, 6/1 for domestic students, 4/1 for international students; for spring admission, 12/1 for domestic students. Applications are processed on a rolling basis. Application fee: $65. Electronic applications accepted. *Expenses:* Tuition, state resident: full-time $13,500; part-time $750 per credit. Tuition, nonresident: full-time $25,940; part-time $1089 per credit. *Required fees:* $1699; $424.75 per semester. *Financial support:* In 2012–13, 1 student received support, including 2 teaching assistantships; fellowships, research assistantships, career-related internships or fieldwork, and Federal Work-Study also available. Support available to part-time students. Financial award application deadline: 2/15. *Unit head:* Dr. Serita Frey, Chairperson, 603-862-3880. *Application contact:* Jennifer Bourgeault, Information Contact, 603-862-2227, E-mail: resecon.ms.program@unh.edu. Website: http://www.dred.unh.edu.

University of New Hampshire, Graduate School, Interdisciplinary Programs, Doctoral Program in Natural Resources and Earth Systems Science, Durham, NH 03824. Offers earth and environmental science (PhD), including geology, oceanography; natural resources and environmental studies (PhD). *Faculty:* 59 full-time (11 women). *Students:* 51 full-time (26 women), 25 part-time (13 women); includes 4 minority (all Asian, non-Hispanic/Latino), 4 international. Average age 35. 43 applicants, 30% accepted, 9 enrolled. In 2012, 15 doctorates awarded. *Degree requirements:* For doctorate, thesis/dissertation. *Entrance requirements:* For doctorate, GRE (if from a non-U.S. university). Additional exam requirements/recommendations for international students: Required—TOEFL (minimum score 550 paper-based; 80 iBT). *Application deadline:* For fall admission, 6/1 priority date for domestic students, 4/1 for international students; for spring admission, 12/1 for domestic students. Applications are processed on a rolling basis. Application fee: $65. Electronic applications accepted. *Expenses:* Tuition, state resident: full-time $13,500; part-time $750 per credit. Tuition, nonresident: full-time $25,940; part-time $1089 per credit. *Required fees:* $1699; $424.75 per semester. *Financial support:* In 2012–13, 48 students received support, including 1 fellowship, 19 research assistantships, 15 teaching assistantships; Federal Work-Study, scholarships/grants, and tuition waivers (full and partial) also available. Financial award application deadline: 2/15. *Faculty research:* Environmental and natural resource studies and management. *Unit head:* Dr. Serita Frey, Chairperson, 603-862-3880. *Application contact:* Jennifer Bourgeault, Administrative Assistant, 603-862-2227, E-mail: nress.phd.program@unh.edu. Website: http://www.unh.edu/nressphd/.

University of New Mexico, Graduate School, College of Arts and Sciences, Program in Economics, Albuquerque, NM 87131-2039. Offers econometrics (MA); economic theory (MA); environmental/natural resource economics (MA, PhD); international/development and sustainability economics (MA, PhD); public economics (MA, PhD). Part-time programs available. *Faculty:* 19 full-time (10 women), 8 part-time/adjunct (1 woman). *Students:* 35 full-time (9 women), 19 part-time (5 women); includes 8 minority (2 Asian, non-Hispanic/Latino; 5 Hispanic/Latino; 1 Two or more races, non-Hispanic/Latino), 16 international. Average age 32. 36 applicants, 58% accepted, 10 enrolled. In 2012, 10 master's, 4 doctorates awarded. Terminal master's awarded for partial completion of doctoral program. *Degree requirements:* For master's, comprehensive exam, thesis (for some programs); for doctorate, comprehensive exam, thesis/dissertation. *Entrance requirements:* For master's and doctorate, GRE General Test, 3 letters of recommendation, letter of intent, curriculum vitae. Additional exam requirements/recommendations for international students: Required—TOEFL (minimum score 520 paper-based; 68 iBT). *Application deadline:* For fall admission, 3/1 priority date for domestic students, 3/1 for international students. Applications are processed on a rolling basis. Application fee: $50. Electronic applications accepted. *Expenses:* Tuition, state resident: full-time $3296; part-time $276.73 per credit hour. Tuition, nonresident: full-time $10,604; part-time $885.74 per credit hour. *Required fees:* $628. *Financial support:* In 2012–13, 47 students received support, including 3 fellowships with tuition reimbursements available (averaging $6,858 per year), 13 research assistantships with tuition reimbursements available (averaging $6,858 per year), 15 teaching assistantships with tuition reimbursements available (averaging $7,396 per year); career-related internships or fieldwork, Federal Work-Study, scholarships/grants, health care benefits, and unspecified assistantships also available. Support available to part-time students. Financial award application deadline: 3/1; financial award applicants required to submit FAFSA. *Faculty research:* Core theory, econometrics, public finance, international/development economics, labor/human resource economics, environmental/natural resource economics. *Total annual research expenditures:* $388,864. *Unit head:* Dr. Janie Chermak, Chair, 505-277-2037, Fax: 505-277-9445, E-mail: jchermak@unm.edu. *Application contact:* Jeff Newcomer Miller, Academic Advisor, 505-277-3056, Fax: 505-277-9445, E-mail: econgrad@unm.edu. Website: http://econ.unm.edu.

University of Northern British Columbia, Office of Graduate Studies, Prince George, BC V2N 4Z9, Canada. Offers business administration (Diploma); community health science (M Sc); disability management (MA); education (M Ed); first nations studies (MA); gender studies (MA); history (MA); interdisciplinary studies (MA); international studies (MA); mathematical, computer and physical sciences (M Sc); natural resources and environmental studies (M Sc, MA, MNRES, PhD); political science (MA); psychology (M Sc, PhD); social work (MSW). Part-time and evening/weekend programs available. Postbaccalaureate distance learning degree programs offered (no on-campus study). *Degree requirements:* For master's, thesis; for doctorate, thesis/dissertation. *Entrance requirements:* For master's, GRE, minimum B average in undergraduate course work; for doctorate, candidacy exam, minimum A average in graduate course work.

University of Northern Iowa, Graduate College, College of Humanities, Arts and Sciences, Department of Biology, Cedar Falls, IA 50614. Offers biology (MA, MS); biotechnology (PSM); ecosystem management (PSM). Part-time programs available. *Students:* 23 full-time (13 women), 10 part-time (3 women); includes 1 minority (Asian, non-Hispanic/Latino), 7 international. 58 applicants, 31% accepted, 11 enrolled. In 2012, 9 master's awarded. *Degree requirements:* For master's, comprehensive exam (for some programs), thesis or alternative. *Entrance requirements:* For master's, minimum GPA of 3.0; 3 letters of recommendation. Additional exam requirements/recommendations for international students: Required—TOEFL (minimum score 500 paper-based; 61 iBT). *Application deadline:* For fall admission, 8/1 priority date for domestic students. Applications are processed on a rolling basis. Application fee: $50 ($70 for international students). Electronic applications accepted. *Financial support:* Scholarships/grants available. Financial award application deadline: 2/1. *Unit head:* Dr. David Saunders, Head, 319-273-2456, Fax: 319-273-7125, E-mail: david.saunders@uni.edu. *Application contact:* Laurie S. Russell, Record Analyst, 319-273-2623, Fax: 319-273-2885, E-mail: laurie.russell@uni.edu. Website: http://www.biology.uni.edu/.

University of Rhode Island, Graduate School, College of the Environment and Life Sciences, Department of Environmental and Natural Resource Economics, Kingston, RI 02881. Offers MESM, MS, PhD. Part-time programs available. *Faculty:* 6 full-time (2 women). *Students:* 31 full-time (21 women), 1 (woman) part-time; includes 3 minority (2 Asian, non-Hispanic/Latino; 1 Hispanic/Latino), 12 international. In 2012, 10 master's, 3 doctorates awarded. *Degree requirements:* For master's, comprehensive exam (for some programs), thesis optional; for doctorate, comprehensive exam, thesis/dissertation. *Entrance requirements:* For master's, GRE, 2 letters of recommendation; for doctorate, GRE, 3 letters of recommendation. Additional exam requirements/recommendations for international students: Required—TOEFL (minimum score 550 paper-based). *Application deadline:* For fall admission, 7/15 for domestic students, 2/1 for international students; for spring admission, 11/15 for domestic students, 7/15 for international students. Application fee: $65. Electronic applications accepted. *Expenses:* Tuition, state resident: full-time $11,532; part-time $641 per credit. Tuition, nonresident: full-time $23,606; part-time $1311 per credit. *Required fees:* $1388; $36 per credit. $35 per semester. One-time fee: $130. *Financial support:* In 2012–13, 1 research assistantship with full and partial tuition reimbursement (averaging $16,256 per year), 7 teaching assistantships with full and partial tuition reimbursements (averaging $11,939 per year) were awarded. Financial award application deadline: 7/15; financial award applicants required to submit FAFSA. *Faculty research:* Policy simulation, policy actions, experimental economics. *Unit head:* Dr. James Opaluch, Chair, 401-874-4590, Fax: 401-874-4766, E-mail: jimo@uri.edu. Website: http://www.uri.edu/cels/enre/.

University of Rhode Island, Graduate School, College of the Environment and Life Sciences, Department of Natural Resources Science, Kingston, RI 02881. Offers MESM, MS, PhD. Part-time programs available. *Faculty:* 10 full-time (1 woman). *Students:* 40 full-time (25 women), 10 part-time (7 women); includes 3 minority (1 Black or African American, non-Hispanic/Latino; 1 Asian, non-Hispanic/Latino; 1 Hispanic/Latino), 5 international. In 2012, 11 master's, 1 doctorate awarded. *Degree requirements:* For master's, comprehensive exam (for some programs), thesis optional; for doctorate, comprehensive exam, thesis/dissertation. *Entrance requirements:* For master's and doctorate, GRE, 2 letters of recommendation. Additional exam requirements/recommendations for international students: Required—TOEFL (minimum score 550 paper-based). *Application deadline:* For fall admission, 7/15 for domestic students, 2/1 for international students; for spring admission, 11/15 for domestic students, 7/15 for international students. Application fee: $65. Electronic applications accepted. *Expenses:* Tuition, state resident: full-time $11,532; part-time $641 per credit. Tuition, nonresident: full-time $23,606; part-time $1311 per credit. *Required fees:* $1388; $36 per credit. $35 per semester. One-time fee: $130. *Financial support:* In 2012–13, 3 research assistantships with full and partial tuition reimbursements (averaging $9,343 per year), 6 teaching assistantships with full and partial tuition reimbursements (averaging $11,350 per year) were awarded. Financial award application deadline: 7/15; financial award applicants required to submit FAFSA. *Faculty research:* Spatial data modeling, ecological mapping, data integration for environmental applications. *Unit head:* Dr. Arthur Gold, Chair, 401-874-2903, Fax: 401-874-4561, E-mail: agold@uri.edu. *Application contact:* Dr. Peter August, Co-Director of the CELS Master of Environmental Science and Management Graduate Program, 401-874-4794, Fax: 401-874-4561, E-mail: pete@edc.uri.edu. Website: http://nrs.uri.edu/.

University of San Francisco, College of Arts and Sciences, Program in Environmental Management, San Francisco, CA 94117-1080. Offers MS. Evening/weekend programs available. *Faculty:* 8 full-time (7 women), 11 part-time/adjunct (3 women). *Students:* 79 full-time (46 women), 10 part-time (7 women); includes 38 minority (3 Black or African American, non-Hispanic/Latino; 20 Asian, non-Hispanic/Latino; 12 Hispanic/Latino; 2 Native Hawaiian or other Pacific Islander, non-Hispanic/Latino; 1 Two or more races, non-Hispanic/Latino), 5 international. Average age 30. 105 applicants, 47% accepted, 37 enrolled. In 2012, 38 master's awarded. *Degree requirements:* For master's, thesis, project. *Entrance requirements:* For master's, 3 semesters of course work in chemistry, minimum GPA of 2.7, work experience in environmental field. *Application deadline:* For fall admission, 2/15 for domestic students. Applications are processed on a rolling basis. Application fee: $55 ($65 for international students). *Expenses: Tuition:* Full-time $20,340; part-time $1130 per credit hour. Part-time tuition and fees vary according to course load, degree level, campus/location and program. *Financial support:* In 2012–13, 28 students received support. Teaching assistantships and career-related internships or fieldwork available. Financial award application deadline: 3/2; financial award applicants required to submit FAFSA. *Faculty research:* Problems of environmental managers, water quality, hazardous materials, environmental health. *Unit head:* Dr. Stephanie Oshita, Chair, 415-422-5927, Fax: 415-422-6387. *Application contact:* Information Contact, 415-422-5135, Fax: 415-422-2217, E-mail: asgraduate@usfca.edu. Website: http://www.usfca.edu/artsci/msem/.

University of South Africa, College of Agriculture and Environmental Sciences, Pretoria, South Africa. Offers agriculture (MS); consumer science (MCS); environmental management (MA, MS, PhD); environmental science (MA, MS, PhD); geography (MA, MS, PhD); horticulture (M Tech); human ecology (MHE); life sciences (MS); nature conservation (M Tech).

The University of Texas at Austin, Graduate School, Cockrell School of Engineering, Department of Petroleum and Geosystems Engineering, Program in Energy and Earth Resources, Austin, TX 78712-1111. Offers MA. *Degree requirements:* For master's, thesis, seminar. *Entrance requirements:* For master's, GRE General Test. Additional exam requirements/recommendations for international students: Required—TOEFL. Electronic applications accepted.

University of Vermont, Graduate College, The Rubenstein School of Environment and Natural Resources, Program in Natural Resources, Burlington, VT 05405. Offers natural resources (MS, PhD), including aquatic ecology and watershed science (MS), environment thought and culture (MS), environment, science and public affairs (MS), forestry (MS). *Students:* 90 (48 women); includes 7 minority (1 Black or African American, non-Hispanic/Latino; 1 American Indian or Alaska Native, non-Hispanic/Latino; 4 Asian, non-Hispanic/Latino; 1 Hispanic/Latino), 1 international. 115 applicants, 30% accepted, 17 enrolled. In 2012, 22 master's, 4 doctorates awarded. *Degree requirements:* For master's, thesis or alternative; for doctorate, thesis/dissertation. *Entrance requirements:* For master's and doctorate, GRE General Test. Additional exam requirements/recommendations for international students: Required—TOEFL (minimum score 550 paper-based; 80 iBT). *Application deadline:* For fall admission, 2/1 priority date for domestic students, 2/1 for international students. Applications are processed on a rolling basis. Application fee: $40. Electronic applications accepted. *Expenses: Tuition, area resident:* Part-time $572 per credit. Tuition, nonresident: part-time $1444 per credit. *Financial support:* Fellowships, research assistantships, and teaching assistantships available. Financial award application deadline: 3/1. *Unit head:* Clare Ginger, Chair, 802-656-2620. *Application contact:* Kimberly Wallin, Coordinator, 802-656-2620.

University of Washington, Graduate School, College of the Environment, School of Environmental and Forest Sciences, Seattle, WA 98195. Offers bioresource science and engineering (MS, PhD); environmental horticulture (MEH); forest ecology (MS, PhD); forest management (MFR); forest soils (MS, PhD); restoration ecology (MS, PhD); restoration ecology and environmental horticulture (MS, PhD); social sciences (MS, PhD); sustainable resource management (MS, PhD); wildlife science (MS, PhD); MFR/MAIS; MPA/MS. *Accreditation:* SAF. Part-time programs available. *Degree requirements:* For master's, thesis; for doctorate, comprehensive exam (for some programs), thesis/dissertation. *Entrance requirements:* For master's and doctorate, GRE, minimum GPA of 3.0. Additional exam requirements/recommendations for international students: Required—TOEFL, GRE. Electronic applications accepted. *Faculty research:* Ecosystem analysis, silviculture and forest protection, paper science and engineering, environmental horticulture and urban forestry, natural resource policy and economics, restoration ecology and environment horticulture, conservation, human dimensions, wildlife, bioresource science and engineering.

University of Wisconsin–Madison, Graduate School, Gaylord Nelson Institute for Environmental Studies, Environment and Resources Program, Madison, WI

53706-1380. Offers MS, PhD. Part-time programs available. *Degree requirements:* For master's, thesis; for doctorate, thesis/dissertation. *Entrance requirements:* For master's and doctorate, GRE General Test. Additional exam requirements/recommendations for international students: Required—TOEFL (minimum score 550 paper-based; 80 iBT). Electronic applications accepted. *Expenses:* Tuition, state resident: full-time $10,728; part-time $743 per credit. Tuition, nonresident: full-time $24,054; part-time $1575 per credit. *Required fees:* $1111; $72 per credit. *Faculty research:* Land use issues, soil science/watershed management, geographic information systems, environmental law/justice, waste management, restoration ecology, agroecology, energy resources.

University of Wisconsin–Stevens Point, College of Natural Resources, Stevens Point, WI 54481-3897. Offers MS. Part-time programs available. *Students:* 43 full-time (23 women), 38 part-time (27 women); includes 2 minority (1 Hispanic/Latino; 1 Two or more races, non-Hispanic/Latino), 2 international. Average age 31. In 2012, 33 master's awarded. *Degree requirements:* For master's, thesis or alternative. *Entrance requirements:* For master's, GRE. *Application deadline:* For fall admission, 3/15 priority date for domestic students; for spring admission, 11/15 for domestic students. Applications are processed on a rolling basis. Application fee: $45. *Financial support:* Research assistantships, teaching assistantships, career-related internships or fieldwork, Federal Work-Study, and unspecified assistantships available. Support available to part-time students. Financial award application deadline: 5/1; financial award applicants required to submit FAFSA. *Faculty research:* Wildlife management, environmental education, fisheries, forestry, resource policy and planning. *Unit head:* Dr. Christine Thomas, Dean, 715-346-4617, Fax: 715-346-3624. *Application contact:* Catherine Glennon, Director of Admissions, 715-346-2441, E-mail: admiss@uwsp.edu. Website: http://www.uwsp.edu/cnr/.

University of Wyoming, College of Agriculture and Natural Resources, Department of Renewable Resources, Laramie, WY 82070. Offers agroecology (MS); entomology (MS, PhD); entomology/water resources (MS, PhD); rangeland ecology and watershed management (MS, PhD), including soil sciences (PhD), soil sciences and water resources (MS); rangeland ecology and watershed management/water resources (MS, PhD); soil science (MS); soil science/water resources (PhD). Part-time programs available. *Degree requirements:* For master's, comprehensive exam, thesis, oral examination; for doctorate, comprehensive exam, thesis/dissertation, preliminary oral and written exam, oral final exam. *Entrance requirements:* For master's and doctorate, GRE General Test, minimum GPA of 3.0. Additional exam requirements/recommendations for international students: Required—TOEFL. Electronic applications accepted. *Faculty research:* Plant control, grazing management, riparian restoration, riparian management, reclamation.

University of Wyoming, College of Arts and Sciences, Department of Geography, Program in Rural Planning and Natural Resources, Laramie, WY 82070. Offers community and regional planning and natural resources (MP). *Degree requirements:* For master's, thesis or alternative. *Entrance requirements:* For master's, GRE General Test, minimum GPA of 3.0. Additional exam requirements/recommendations for international students: Required—TOEFL. *Faculty research:* Rural and small town planning, public land management.

Utah State University, School of Graduate Studies, College of Natural Resources, Interdisciplinary Program in Natural Resources, Logan, UT 84322. Offers MNR. *Entrance requirements:* For master's, GRE General Test, minimum GPA of 3.0. Additional exam requirements/recommendations for international students: Required—TOEFL. *Faculty research:* Ecosystem management, human dimensions, quantitative methods, informative management.

Virginia Polytechnic Institute and State University, Graduate School, College of Natural Resources and Environment, Blacksburg, VA 24061. Offers fisheries and wildlife (MS); forestry and forest products (MF, MS, PhD); geography (MS); geospatial and environmental analysis (PhD); natural resources (MNR). *Faculty:* 68 full-time (14 women). *Students:* 181 full-time (82 women), 78 part-time (47 women); includes 20 minority (5 Black or African American, non-Hispanic/Latino; 1 American Indian or Alaska Native, non-Hispanic/Latino; 4 Asian, non-Hispanic/Latino; 4 Hispanic/Latino; 6 Two or more races, non-Hispanic/Latino), 54 international. Average age 31. 133 applicants, 41% accepted, 48 enrolled. In 2012, 71 master's, 16 doctorates awarded. *Degree requirements:* For master's, comprehensive exam (for some programs), thesis (for some programs); for doctorate, comprehensive exam (for some programs), thesis/dissertation (for some programs). *Entrance requirements:* For master's and doctorate, GRE/GMAT (may vary by department). Additional exam requirements/recommendations for international students: Required—TOEFL (minimum score 550 paper-based). *Application deadline:* For fall admission, 8/1 for domestic students, 4/1 for international students; for spring admission, 1/1 for domestic students, 9/1 for international students. Applications are processed on a rolling basis. Application fee: $65. Electronic applications accepted. *Expenses:* Tuition, state resident: full-time $10,677; part-time $593.25 per credit hour. Tuition, nonresident: full-time $20,926; part-time $1162.50 per credit hour. *Required fees:* $427.75 per semester. Tuition and fees vary according to course load, campus/location and program. *Financial support:* In 2012–13, 92 research assistantships with full tuition reimbursements (averaging $19,523 per year), 43 teaching assistantships with full tuition reimbursements (averaging $16,826 per year) were awarded. Financial award application deadline: 3/1; financial award applicants required to submit FAFSA. *Total annual research expenditures:* $14 million. *Unit head:* Dr. Paul M. Winistorfer, Dean, 540-231-5481, Fax: 540-231-7664, E-mail: pstorfer@vt.edu. *Application contact:* Arlice Banks, Assistant to the Dean, 540-231-5481, Fax: 540-231-7664. Website: http://www.cnre.vt.edu/.

Virginia Polytechnic Institute and State University, VT Online, Blacksburg, VA 24061. Offers advanced transportation systems (Certificate); aerospace engineering (MS); agricultural and life sciences (MSLFS); business information systems (Graduate Certificate); career and technical education (MS); civil engineering (MS); computer engineering (M Eng, MS); decision support systems (Graduate Certificate); eLearning leadership (MA); electrical engineering (M Eng, MS); engineering administration (MEA); environmental engineering (Certificate); environmental politics and policy (Graduate Certificate); environmental sciences and engineering (MS); foundations of political analysis (Graduate Certificate); health product risk management (Graduate Certificate); industrial and systems engineering (MS); information policy and society (Graduate Certificate); information security (Graduate Certificate); information technology (MIT); instructional technology (MA); integrative STEM education (MA Ed); liberal arts (Graduate Certificate); life sciences: health product risk management (MS); natural resources (MNR, Graduate Certificate); networking (Graduate Certificate); nonprofit and nongovernmental organization management (Graduate Certificate); ocean engineering (MS); political science (MA); security studies (Graduate Certificate); software development (Graduate Certificate). *Expenses:* Tuition, state resident: full-time $10,677; part-time $593.25 per credit hour. Tuition, nonresident: full-time $20,926; part-time $1162.50 per credit hour. *Required fees:* $427.75 per semester. Tuition and fees vary according to course load, campus/location and program. Website: http://www.vto.vt.edu/.

Washington State University, Graduate School, College of Agricultural, Human, and Natural Resource Sciences, School of the Environment, Pullman, WA 99164. Offers environmental and natural resource sciences (PhD); environmental sciences (MS); geology (MS, PhD); natural resources (MS). *Faculty:* 27 full-time (5 women), 7 part-time/adjunct (3 women). *Students:* 72 full-time (37 women), 7 part-time (4 women); includes 1 minority (Hispanic/Latino), 6 international. Average age 27. In 2012, 5 master's, 2 doctorates awarded. *Degree requirements:* For master's, comprehensive exam (for some programs), thesis (for some programs), oral exam; for doctorate, comprehensive exam, thesis/dissertation, oral exam. *Entrance requirements:* For master's, GRE General Test, official copies of all college transcripts, three letters of recommendation. Additional exam requirements/recommendations for international students: Required—TOEFL, IELTS. *Application deadline:* For fall admission, 1/10 priority date for domestic students, 1/10 for international students; for spring admission, 7/1 for domestic and international students. Applications are processed on a rolling basis. Application fee: $75. *Financial support:* In 2012–13, fellowships (averaging $2,333 per year), research assistantships with full and partial tuition reimbursements (averaging $13,917 per year), teaching assistantships with full and partial tuition reimbursements (averaging $13,056 per year) were awarded; career-related internships or fieldwork, Federal Work-Study, institutionally sponsored loans, tuition waivers (partial), and unspecified assistantships also available. Financial award application deadline: 2/15; financial award applicants required to submit FAFSA. *Faculty research:* Environmental and natural resources conservation and sustainability; earth sciences: earth systems and geology; wildlife ecology and conservation sciences. *Total annual research expenditures:* $967,000. *Unit head:* Dr. Steve Bollens, Director, 360-546-9116, E-mail: sbollens@vancouver.wsu.edu. *Application contact:* Graduate School Admissions, 800-GRADWSU, Fax: 509-335-1949, E-mail: gradsch@wsu.edu. Website: http://environment.wsu.edu/.

Washington State University, Graduate School, College of Arts and Sciences, School of the Environment, Program in Environmental and Natural Resource Sciences, Pullman, WA 99164. Offers PhD.

Washington State University, Graduate School, College of Arts and Sciences, School of the Environment, Program in Environmental Science, Pullman, WA 99164. Offers environmental and natural resource sciences (PhD); environmental science (MS). *Degree requirements:* For master's, comprehensive exam (for some programs), thesis (for some programs), oral exam; for doctorate, comprehensive exam, thesis/dissertation, oral exam, written exam. *Entrance requirements:* For master's, 3 undergraduate semester hours each in sociology or cultural anthropology, environmental science, biological sciences, and calculus or statistics; 4 in general ecology; and 6 in general chemistry or general physics; for doctorate, minimum GPA of 3.0. Additional exam requirements/recommendations for international students: Required—TOEFL, IELTS.

Washington State University Tri-Cities, Graduate Programs, Program in Environmental Science, Richland, WA 99352-1671. Offers environmental and natural resource sciences (PhD); environmental science (MS). Part-time programs available. *Degree requirements:* For master's, comprehensive exam, thesis (for some programs), oral exam; for doctorate, comprehensive exam, thesis/dissertation. *Entrance requirements:* For master's, GRE General Test, minimum GPA of 3.0, 3 letters of recommendation. Additional exam requirements/recommendations for international students: Required—TOEFL (minimum score 550 paper-based). *Faculty research:* Radiation ecology, cytogenetics.

West Virginia University, College of Business and Economics, Division of Economics and Finance, Morgantown, WV 26506. Offers business analysis (MA); developmental financial economics (PhD); environmental and resource economics (PhD); international economics (PhD); mathematical economics (MA); monetary economics (PhD); public finance (PhD); public policy (MA); regional and urban economics (PhD); statistics and economics (MA). Terminal master's awarded for partial completion of doctoral program. *Degree requirements:* For master's, thesis optional; for doctorate, comprehensive exam, thesis/dissertation. *Entrance requirements:* For master's and doctorate, GRE General Test, minimum GPA of 3.0; course work in intermediate microeconomics, intermediate macroeconomics, calculus, and statistics. Additional exam requirements/recommendations for international students: Required—TOEFL. Electronic applications accepted. *Faculty research:* Financial economics, regional/urban development, public economics, international trade/international finance/development economics, monetary economics.

West Virginia University, Davis College of Agriculture, Forestry and Consumer Sciences, Division of Resource Management and Sustainable Development, Program in Resource Management and Sustainable Development, Morgantown, WV 26506. Offers PhD. Part-time programs available. *Degree requirements:* For doctorate, thesis/dissertation. *Entrance requirements:* For doctorate, GRE General Test. Additional exam requirements/recommendations for international students: Required—TOEFL.

Range Science

Colorado State University, Graduate School, Warner College of Natural Resources, Department of Forest and Rangeland Stewardship, Fort Collins, CO 80523-1472. Offers forest sciences (MS, PhD); natural resources stewardship (MNRS); rangeland ecosystem science (MS, PhD); watershed science (MS). Part-time programs available. Postbaccalaureate distance learning degree programs offered (no on-campus study). *Faculty:* 12 full-time (2 women). *Students:* 26 full-time (7 women), 80 part-time (34 women); includes 6 minority (1 American Indian or Alaska Native, non-Hispanic/Latino; 5 Hispanic/Latino), 11 international. Average age 35. 20 applicants, 100% accepted, 17 enrolled. In 2012, 17 master's, 3 doctorates awarded. *Degree requirements:* For master's, thesis (for some programs); for doctorate, comprehensive exam, thesis/dissertation. *Entrance requirements:* For master's, GRE General Test (minimum score 1000 verbal and quantitative), minimum GPA of 3.0, 3 letters of recommendation; for doctorate, GRE General Test (combined minimum score of 1100 on the Verbal and Quantitative sections), minimum GPA of 3.0, 3 letters of recommendation, statement of research interest. Additional exam requirements/recommendations for international students: Required—TOEFL (minimum score 550 paper-based; 80 iBT), IELTS (minimum score 6.5). *Application deadline:* For fall admission, 2/15 priority date for domestic students, 2/15 for international students; for spring admission, 7/15 priority date for domestic students, 7/15 for international students. Applications are processed on a rolling basis. Application fee: $50. Electronic applications accepted. *Expenses:* Tuition, state resident: full-time $8811; part-time $490 per credit. Tuition, nonresident: full-time $21,600; part-time $1200 per credit. *Required fees:* $1819; $61 per credit. *Financial support:* In 2012–13, 53 students received support, including 3 fellowships (averaging $14,767 per year), 36 research assistantships with full and partial tuition reimbursements available (averaging $16,479 per year), 14 teaching assistantships with full and partial tuition reimbursements available (averaging $6,991 per year); Federal Work-Study, scholarships/grants, and unspecified assistantships also available. Financial award application deadline: 2/15; financial award applicants required to submit FAFSA. *Faculty research:* Ecology, natural resource management, hydrology, restoration, human dimensions. *Total annual research expenditures:* $2.4 million. *Unit head:* Dr. Frederick Smith, Department Head and Professor, 970-491-7505, Fax: 970-491-6754, E-mail: fwsmith@colostate.edu. *Application contact:* Sonya LeFebre, Coordinator, 970-491-1907, Fax: 970-491-6754, E-mail: sonya.lefebre@colostate.edu. Website: http://warnercnr.colostate.edu/frws-home/.

Kansas State University, Graduate School, College of Agriculture, Department of Agronomy, Manhattan, KS 66506. Offers crop science (MS, PhD); plant breeding and genetics (MS, PhD); range management (MS, PhD); soil science (MS, PhD); weed science (MS, PhD). Part-time programs available. *Faculty:* 29 full-time (6 women), 13 part-time/adjunct (0 women). *Students:* 62 full-time (21 women), 15 part-time (4 women); includes 5 minority (2 Black or African American, non-Hispanic/Latino; 2 Asian, non-Hispanic/Latino; 1 Hispanic/Latino), 34 international. Average age 31. 38 applicants, 29% accepted, 10 enrolled. In 2012, 15 master's, 1 doctorate awarded. *Degree requirements:* For master's, thesis or alternative, oral exam; for doctorate, thesis/dissertation, preliminary exams. *Entrance requirements:* For master's, minimum GPA of 3.0 in BS; for doctorate, minimum GPA of 3.0 in master's program. Additional exam requirements/recommendations for international students: Required—TOEFL (minimum score 550 paper-based; 79 iBT). *Application deadline:* For fall admission, 2/1 priority date for domestic students, 2/1 for international students; for spring admission, 8/1 priority date for domestic students, 8/1 for international students. Applications are processed on a rolling basis. Application fee: $50 ($75 for international students). Electronic applications accepted. *Financial support:* In 2012–13, 62 research assistantships (averaging $23,500 per year) were awarded; institutionally sponsored loans and scholarships/grants also available. Support available to part-time students. Financial award application deadline: 3/1; financial award applicants required to submit FAFSA. *Faculty research:* Range and forage science, soil and environmental science, crop physiology, weed science, plant breeding and genetics. *Total annual research expenditures:* $6.5 million. *Unit head:* Dr. Gary Pierzynski, Head, 785-532-6101, Fax: 785-532-6094, E-mail: gmp@k-state.edu. *Application contact:* Dr. Gerard Kluitenberg, Graduate Coordinator, 785-532-7215, Fax: 785-532-6094, E-mail: gjk@ksu.edu. Website: http://www.agronomy.k-state.edu/DesktopDefault.aspx.

Montana State University, College of Graduate Studies, College of Agriculture, Department of Animal and Range Sciences, Bozeman, MT 59717. Offers MS,

PhD. Part-time programs available. *Degree requirements:* For master's, comprehensive exam; for doctorate, comprehensive exam, thesis/dissertation. *Entrance requirements:* For master's, GRE, minimum GPA of 3.0; undergraduate coursework in animal science, range science or closely-related field; faculty adviser; for doctorate, GRE. Additional exam requirements/recommendations for international students: Required—TOEFL (minimum score 550 paper-based; 80 iBT). Electronic applications accepted. *Faculty research:* Rangeland ecology, wildlife habitat management, residual feed intake, post-partum effect of bulls, increasing efficiency of sheep production systems.

New Mexico State University, Graduate School, College of Agricultural, Consumer and Environmental Sciences, Department of Animal and Range Sciences, Las Cruces, NM 88003-8001. Offers animal science (MS, PhD); domestic animal biology (M Ag); range science (M Ag, MS, PhD). Part-time programs available. *Faculty:* 17 full-time (5 women). *Students:* 28 full-time (18 women), 8 part-time (4 women); includes 5 minority (1 Black or African American, non-Hispanic/Latino; 4 Hispanic/Latino), 8 international. Average age 27. 24 applicants, 50% accepted, 8 enrolled. In 2012, 6 master's, 4 doctorates awarded. *Degree requirements:* For master's, thesis, seminar, experimental statistics; for doctorate, thesis/dissertation, research tool. *Entrance requirements:* For master's, minimum GPA of 3.0 in last 60 hours of undergraduate course work (MS); for doctorate, minimum graduate GPA of 3.2, MS with thesis. Additional exam requirements/recommendations for international students: Required—TOEFL (minimum score 530 paper-based; 71 iBT), IELTS (minimum score 6). *Application deadline:* For fall admission, 2/15 priority date for domestic students, 2/15 for international students; for winter admission, 10/1 priority date for domestic students, 10/1 for international students; for spring admission, 11/1 for domestic and international students. Applications are processed on a rolling basis. Application fee: $40 ($50 for international students). Electronic applications accepted. *Expenses:* Tuition, state resident: full-time $5239; part-time $218 per credit. Tuition, nonresident: full-time $18,266; part-time $761 per credit. *Required fees:* $1274; $53 per credit. *Financial support:* In 2012–13, 25 students received support, including 1 fellowship (averaging $3,930 per year), 14 research assistantships (averaging $21,914 per year), 6 teaching assistantships (averaging $14,892 per year); career-related internships or fieldwork, Federal Work-Study, scholarships/grants, traineeships, health care benefits, and unspecified assistantships also available. Support available to part-time students. Financial award application deadline: 3/15. *Faculty research:* Reproductive physiology, ruminant nutrition, nutrition toxicology, range ecology, wildland hydrology. *Total annual research expenditures:* $3.8 million. *Unit head:* Dr. Tim Ross, Head, 575-646-2515, Fax: 575-646-5441, E-mail: tross@nmsu.edu. Website: http://aces.nmsu.edu/academics/anrs.

North Dakota State University, College of Graduate and Interdisciplinary Studies, College of Agriculture, Food Systems, and Natural Resources, Department of Animal and Range Sciences, Fargo, ND 58108. Offers animal science (MS, PhD); range sciences (MS, PhD). *Faculty:* 17 full-time (6 women). *Students:* 28 full-time (19 women), 8 part-time (4 women); includes 1 minority (Two or more races, non-Hispanic/Latino), 3 international. Average age 27. 27 applicants, 41% accepted, 10 enrolled. In 2012, 7 master's, 3 doctorates awarded. *Degree requirements:* For master's, thesis; for doctorate, comprehensive exam, thesis/dissertation. *Entrance requirements:* For master's and doctorate, GRE General Test. Additional exam requirements/recommendations for international students: Required—TOEFL (minimum score 71 iBT). *Application deadline:* Applications are processed on a rolling basis. Application fee: $35. *Financial support:* In 2012–13, 1 fellowship with tuition reimbursement (averaging $18,000 per year), 29 research assistantships with tuition reimbursements (averaging $13,000 per year) were awarded; teaching assistantships, Federal Work-Study, institutionally sponsored loans, and tuition waivers (partial) also available. Financial award application deadline: 3/15. *Faculty research:* Reproduction, nutrition, meat and muscle biology, breeding/genetics. *Unit head:* Dr. Gregory Lardy, Chair, 701-231-7641, Fax: 701-231-7590, E-mail: gregory.lardy@ndsu.edu. *Application contact:* Sonya Goergen, Marketing, Recruitment, and Public Relations Coordinator, 701-231-7033, Fax: 701-231-6524.

Oregon State University, College of Agricultural Sciences, Department of Animal and Rangeland Sciences, Program in Rangeland Ecology and Management, Corvallis, OR 97331. Offers M Agr, MS, PhD. *Faculty:* 5 full-time (0 women), 1

Peterson's Graduate Programs in the Physical Sciences, Mathematics, Agricultural Sciences, the Environment & Natural Resources 2014

www.petersonsbooks.com **517**

Range Science

part-time/adjunct (0 women). *Students:* 7 full-time (3 women), 2 international. Average age 34. 4 applicants, 50% accepted, 2 enrolled. In 2012, 4 master's, 1 doctorate awarded. Terminal master's awarded for partial completion of doctoral program. *Degree requirements:* For master's, thesis (for some programs); for doctorate, thesis/dissertation. *Entrance requirements:* For master's and doctorate, GRE, minimum GPA of 3.0 in last 90 hours of course work. Additional exam requirements/recommendations for international students: Required—TOEFL. *Application deadline:* For fall admission, 6/1 priority date for domestic students; for spring admission, 12/15 for domestic students. Applications are processed on a rolling basis. Application fee: $50. *Expenses:* Tuition, state resident: full-time $11,367; part-time $421 per credit hour. Tuition, nonresident: full-time $18,279; part-time $677 per credit hour. *Required fees:* $1478. One-time fee: $300 full-time. Tuition and fees vary according to course load and program. *Financial support:* Research assistantships, career-related internships or fieldwork, Federal Work-Study, and institutionally sponsored loans available. Support available to part-time students. Financial award application deadline: 2/1. *Faculty research:* Range ecology, watershed science, animal grazing, agroforestry. *Unit head:* Dr. Michael M. Borman, Head, 541-737-1614, Fax: 541-737-0504, E-mail: michael.borman@oregonstate.edu.

Sul Ross State University, Division of Agricultural and Natural Resource Science, Programs in Natural Resource Management, Alpine, TX 79832. Offers range and wildlife management (M Ag, MS). Part-time programs available. *Degree requirements:* For master's, thesis (for some programs). *Entrance requirements:* For master's, GRE General Test, minimum undergraduate GPA of 2.5 in last 60 hours.

Texas A&M University, College of Agriculture and Life Sciences, Department of Ecosystem Science and Management, College Station, TX 77843. Offers forestry (MS, PhD); rangeland ecology and management (M Agr, MS, PhD). Part-time programs available. *Faculty:* 24. *Students:* 52 full-time (31 women), 32 part-time (18 women); includes 24 minority (3 Black or African American, non-Hispanic/Latino; 2 Asian, non-Hispanic/Latino; 18 Hispanic/Latino; 1 Two or more races, non-Hispanic/Latino), 16 international. Average age 32. In 2012, 10 master's, 2 doctorates awarded. Terminal master's awarded for partial completion of doctoral program. *Degree requirements:* For master's, thesis (for some programs); for doctorate, thesis/dissertation. *Entrance requirements:* For master's and doctorate, GRE General Test. Additional exam requirements/recommendations for international students: Required—TOEFL. *Application deadline:* For fall admission, 3/1 priority date for domestic students; for spring admission, 11/1 priority date for domestic students. Applications are processed on a rolling basis. Application fee: $50 ($75 for international students). Electronic applications accepted. *Financial support:* In 2012–13, fellowships with partial tuition reimbursements (averaging $15,000 per year), research assistantships with partial tuition reimbursements (averaging $15,000 per year), teaching assistantships with partial tuition reimbursements (averaging $15,000 per year) were awarded; career-related internships or fieldwork and institutionally sponsored loans also available. Support available to part-time students. Financial award application deadline: 3/1; financial award applicants required to submit FAFSA. *Faculty research:* Expert systems, geographic information systems, economics, biology, genetics. *Unit head:* Dr. Steve Whisenant, Professor and Head, 979-845-5000, Fax: 979-845-6049, E-mail: s-whisenant@tamu.edu. *Application contact:* Dr. Carol Loopstra, Associate Professor, 979-862-2200, Fax: 979-845-6049, E-mail: c-loopstra@tamu.edu. Website: http://essm.tamu.edu.

Texas A&M University–Kingsville, College of Graduate Studies, College of Agriculture and Home Economics, Program in Range and Wildlife Management, Kingsville, TX 78363. Offers MS. *Degree requirements:* For master's, comprehensive exam, thesis or alternative. *Entrance requirements:* For master's, GRE General Test, minimum GPA of 3.0. Additional exam requirements/recommendations for international students: Required—TOEFL.

Texas Tech University, Graduate School, College of Agricultural Sciences and Natural Resources, Department of Natural Resources Management, Lubbock, TX 79409. Offers fisheries science (MS, PhD); range science (MS, PhD); wildlife, aquatic, and wildlands science and management (MS, PhD). Part-time programs available. *Degree requirements:* For master's, thesis; for doctorate, thesis/dissertation. *Entrance requirements:* For master's and doctorate, GRE General

Test, formal approval from departmental committee. Additional exam requirements/recommendations for international students: Required—TOEFL (minimum score 550 paper-based; 79 iBT). Electronic applications accepted. *Faculty research:* Use of fire on range lands; big game, upland game, and waterfowl; playa lakes in the southern Great Plains; conservation biology; fish ecology and physiology.

The University of Arizona, College of Agriculture and Life Sciences, School of Natural Resources, Program in Natural Resources, Tucson, AZ 85721. Offers MS, PhD. *Faculty:* 19 full-time (3 women), 2 part-time/adjunct (0 women). *Students:* 72 full-time (39 women), 18 part-time (8 women); includes 17 minority (1 Black or African American, non-Hispanic/Latino; 6 Hispanic/Latino; 10 Two or more races, non-Hispanic/Latino), 10 international. Average age 31. 65 applicants, 29% accepted, 11 enrolled. In 2012, 16 master's, 3 doctorates awarded. *Degree requirements:* For master's, thesis; for doctorate, comprehensive exam, thesis/dissertation. *Entrance requirements:* For master's and doctorate, GRE General Test, minimum GPA of 3.0. Additional exam requirements/recommendations for international students: Required—TOEFL (minimum score 550 paper-based; 79 iBT). *Application deadline:* For fall admission, 2/1 for domestic and international students. Applications are processed on a rolling basis. Application fee: $75. Electronic applications accepted. *Financial support:* In 2012–13, 37 research assistantships with full and partial tuition reimbursements (averaging $16,587 per year), 2 teaching assistantships with full and partial tuition reimbursements (averaging $13,809 per year) were awarded; career-related internships or fieldwork, scholarships/grants, health care benefits, tuition waivers (partial), and unspecified assistantships also available. *Faculty research:* Criteria for defining, mapping, and evaluating range sites; methods of establishing forage plants on southwestern range lands; plants for pollution and erosion control, beautification, and browse. *Total annual research expenditures:* $6.5 million. *Unit head:* Dr. Charles Hutchinson, Director, 520-621-8568, E-mail: chuck@ag.arizona.edu. *Application contact:* Katie Hughes, Academic Coordinator, 520-621-7260, Fax: 520-621-8801, E-mail: khughes@email.arizona.edu. Website: http://grad.arizona.edu/live/programs/description/117.

University of California, Berkeley, Graduate Division, College of Natural Resources, Group in Range Management, Berkeley, CA 94720-1500. Offers MS. *Degree requirements:* For master's, thesis. *Entrance requirements:* For master's, GRE General Test, minimum GPA of 3.0, 3 letters of recommendation. Additional exam requirements/recommendations for international students: Required—TOEFL. *Faculty research:* Grassland and savannah ecology, wetland ecology, oak woodland classification, wildlife habitat management.

University of Wyoming, College of Agriculture and Natural Resources, Department of Renewable Resources, Laramie, WY 82070. Offers agroecology (MS); entomology (MS, PhD); entomology/water resources (MS, PhD); rangeland ecology and watershed management (MS, PhD), including soil sciences (PhD), soil sciences and water resources (MS); rangeland ecology and watershed management/water resources (MS, PhD); soil science (MS); soil science/water resources (PhD). Part-time programs available. *Degree requirements:* For master's, comprehensive exam, thesis, oral examination; for doctorate, comprehensive exam, thesis/dissertation, preliminary oral and written exam, oral final exam. *Entrance requirements:* For master's and doctorate, GRE General Test, minimum GPA of 3.0. Additional exam requirements/recommendations for international students: Required—TOEFL. Electronic applications accepted. *Faculty research:* Plant control, grazing management, riparian restoration, riparian management, reclamation.

Utah State University, School of Graduate Studies, College of Natural Resources, Department of Wildland Resources, Logan, UT 84322. Offers ecology (MS, PhD); forestry (MS, PhD); range science (MS, PhD); wildlife biology (MS, PhD). Part-time programs available. *Degree requirements:* For master's, thesis; for doctorate, comprehensive exam, thesis/dissertation. *Entrance requirements:* For master's and doctorate, GRE General Test, minimum GPA of 3.0. Additional exam requirements/recommendations for international students: Required—TOEFL. *Faculty research:* Range plant ecophysiology, plant community ecology, ruminant nutrition, population ecology.

Water Resources

Albany State University, College of Arts and Humanities, Albany, GA 31705-2717. Offers English education (M Ed); public administration (MPA), including community and economic development administration, criminal justice administration, general administration, health administration and policy, human resources management, public policy, water resources management; social work (MSW). Part-time programs available. *Degree requirements:* For master's, comprehensive exam, professional portfolio (for MPA), internship, capstone report. *Entrance requirements:* For master's, GRE, MAT, minimum GPA of 3.0, official transcript, pre-medical record/certificate of immunization, letters of reference. Electronic applications accepted. *Faculty research:* HIV prevention for minority students.

California State University, Monterey Bay, College of Science, Media Arts and Technology, Program in Coastal and Watershed Science and Policy, Seaside, CA 93955-8001. Offers MS, PSM. Part-time programs available. *Degree requirements:* For master's, thesis, thesis defense. *Entrance requirements:* For master's, GRE, recommendations, interview. Additional exam requirements/recommendations for international students: Required—TOEFL (minimum score 525 paper-based; 71 iBT). Electronic applications accepted. *Faculty research:* Remote sensing and geospatial technology, MPA design, efficacy and management, marine science and ecology, watershed process, hydrology, restoration, sedim entology, ecosystem modeling.

518 www.petersonsbooks.com

Peterson's Graduate Programs in the Physical Sciences, Mathematics, Agricultural Sciences, the Environment & Natural Resources 2014

Colorado State University, Graduate School, Warner College of Natural Resources, Department of Forest and Rangeland Stewardship, Fort Collins, CO 80523-1472. Offers forest sciences (MS, PhD); natural resources stewardship (MNRS); rangeland ecosystem science (MS, PhD); watershed science (MS). Part-time programs available. Postbaccalaureate distance learning degree programs offered (no on-campus study). *Faculty:* 12 full-time (2 women). *Students:* 26 full-time (7 women), 80 part-time (34 women); includes 6 minority (1 American Indian or Alaska Native, non-Hispanic/Latino; 5 Hispanic/Latino), 11 international. Average age 35. 20 applicants, 100% accepted, 17 enrolled. In 2012, 17 master's, 3 doctorates awarded. *Degree requirements:* For master's, thesis (for some programs); for doctorate, comprehensive exam, thesis/dissertation. *Entrance requirements:* For master's, GRE General Test (minimum score 1000 verbal and quantitative), minimum GPA of 3.0, 3 letters of recommendation; for doctorate, GRE General Test (combined minimum score of 1100 on the Verbal and Quantitative sections), minimum GPA of 3.0, 3 letters of recommendation, statement of research interest. Additional exam requirements/recommendations for international students: Required—TOEFL (minimum score 550 paper-based; 80 iBT), IELTS (minimum score 6.5). *Application deadline:* For fall admission, 2/15 priority date for domestic students, 2/15 for international students; for spring admission, 7/15 priority date for domestic students, 7/15 for international students. Applications are processed on a rolling basis. Application fee: $50. Electronic applications accepted. *Expenses:* Tuition, state resident: full-time $8811; part-time $490 per credit. Tuition, nonresident: full-time $21,600; part-time $1200 per credit. *Required fees:* $1819; $61 per credit. *Financial support:* In 2012–13, 53 students received support, including 3 fellowships (averaging $14,767 per year), 36 research assistantships with full and partial tuition reimbursements available (averaging $16,479 per year), 14 teaching assistantships with full and partial tuition reimbursements available (averaging $6,991 per year); Federal Work-Study, scholarships/grants, and unspecified assistantships also available. Financial award application deadline: 2/15; financial award applicants required to submit FAFSA. *Faculty research:* Ecology, natural resource management, hydrology, restoration, human dimensions. *Total annual research expenditures:* $2.4 million. *Unit head:* Dr. Frederick Smith, Department Head and Professor, 970-491-7505, Fax: 970-491-6754, E-mail: fwsmith@colostate.edu. *Application contact:* Sonya LeFebre, Coordinator, 970-491-1907, Fax: 970-491-6754, E-mail: sonya.lefebre@colostate.edu. Website: http://warnercnr.colostate.edu/frws-home/.

Dalhousie University, Faculty of Agriculture, Halifax, NS B3H 4R2, Canada. Offers agriculture (M Sc), including air quality, animal behavior, animal molecular genetics, animal nutrition, animal technology, aquaculture, botany, crop management, crop physiology, ecology, environmental microbiology, food science, horticulture, nutrient management, pest management, physiology, plant biotechnology, plant pathology, soil chemistry, soil fertility, waste management and composting, water quality. Part-time programs available. *Degree requirements:* For master's, thesis, ATC Exam Teaching Assistantship. *Entrance requirements:* For master's, honors B Sc, minimum GPA of 3.0. Additional exam requirements/recommendations for international students: Required—TOEFL (minimum score 580 paper-based; 92 iBT), IELTS, Michigan English Language Assessment Battery, CanTEST, CAEL. *Faculty research:* Bio-product development, organic agriculture, nutrient management, air and water quality, agricultural biotechnology.

Eastern Michigan University, Graduate School, College of Arts and Sciences, Department of Biology, Ypsilanti, MI 48197. Offers cell and molecular biology (MS); community college biology teaching (MS); ecology and organismal biology (MS); general biology (MS); water resources (MS). Part-time and evening/weekend programs available. Postbaccalaureate distance learning degree programs offered (minimal on-campus study). *Faculty:* 19 full-time (5 women). *Students:* 11 full-time (4 women), 28 part-time (15 women); includes 3 minority (1 Black or African American, non-Hispanic/Latino; 1 Asian, non-Hispanic/Latino; 1 Hispanic/Latino), 2 international. Average age 26. 56 applicants, 52% accepted, 15 enrolled. In 2012, 16 master's awarded. *Entrance requirements:* For master's, GRE General Test, GRE Subject Test. Additional exam requirements/recommendations for international students: Required—TOEFL. *Application deadline:* Applications are processed on a rolling basis. Application fee: $35. *Expenses:* Tuition, state resident: full-time $10,776; part-time $449 per credit hour. Tuition, nonresident: full-time $21,242; part-time $885 per credit hour. *Required fees:* $41 per credit hour. $48 per term. One-time fee: $100. Tuition and fees vary according to course level, degree level and reciprocity agreements. *Financial support:* Fellowships, research assistantships with full tuition reimbursements, teaching assistantships with full tuition reimbursements, career-related internships or fieldwork, Federal Work-Study, institutionally sponsored loans, scholarships/grants, tuition waivers (partial), and unspecified assistantships available. Support available to part-time students. Financial award applicants required to submit FAFSA. *Unit head:* Dr. Daniel Clemans, Department Head, 734-487-4242, Fax: 734-487-9235, E-mail: dclemans@emich.edu. *Application contact:* Dr. David Kass, Graduate Coordinator, 734-487-4242, Fax: 734-487-9235, E-mail: dkass@emich.edu. Website: http://www.emich.edu/biology.

Eastern Michigan University, Graduate School, College of Arts and Sciences, Department of Geography and Geology, Programs in Geography and Geology, Ypsilanti, MI 48197. Offers geography (MA, MS); water resources (Graduate Certificate). Part-time and evening/weekend programs available. Postbaccalaureate distance learning degree programs offered (minimal on-campus study). In 2012, 1 other advanced degree awarded. *Degree requirements:* For master's, thesis optional. *Entrance requirements:* Additional exam requirements/recommendations for international students: Required—TOEFL. *Application deadline:* Applications are processed on a rolling basis. Application fee: $35. *Expenses:* Tuition, state resident: full-time $10,776; part-time $449 per credit hour. Tuition, nonresident: full-time $21,242; part-time $885 per credit hour. *Required fees:* $41 per credit hour. $48 per term. One-time fee: $100. Tuition and fees vary according to course level, degree level and reciprocity agreements. *Financial support:* Fellowships, research assistantships with full tuition reimbursements, teaching assistantships with full tuition reimbursements, career-related internships or fieldwork, Federal Work-Study, institutionally sponsored loans, traineeships, and unspecified assistantships available. Support available to part-time students. Financial award applicants required to submit FAFSA. *Application contact:* Dr. Andrew Nazzaro, Program Advisor, 734-487-0218, Fax: 734-487-6979, E-mail: andrew.nazzaro@emich.edu.

Humboldt State University, Academic Programs, College of Natural Resources and Sciences, Programs in Natural Resources, Arcata, CA 95521-8299. Offers natural resources (MS), including fisheries, forestry, natural resources planning and interpretation, rangeland resources and wildland soils, wastewater utilization, watershed management, wildlife. *Students:* 36 full-time (18 women), 20 part-time (9 women); includes 2 minority (1 Asian, non-Hispanic/Latino; 1 Two or more races, non-Hispanic/Latino). Average age 30. 51 applicants, 37% accepted, 11 enrolled. In 2012, 29 master's awarded. *Degree requirements:* For master's, thesis or alternative. *Entrance requirements:* For master's, GRE, appropriate bachelor's degree, minimum GPA of 2.5, 3 letters of recommendation, resume. Additional exam requirements/recommendations for international students: Required—TOEFL (minimum score 500 paper-based). *Application deadline:* For fall admission, 2/1 for domestic and international students; for spring admission, 9/30 for domestic and international students. Applications are processed on a rolling basis. Application fee: $55. *Expenses:* Tuition, state resident: full-time $8396. Tuition, nonresident: full-time $17,324. Tuition and fees vary according to program. *Financial support:* Fellowships, career-related internships or fieldwork, and Federal Work-Study available. Support available to part-time students. Financial award application deadline: 3/1; financial award applicants required to submit FAFSA. *Faculty research:* Spotted owl habitat, pre-settlement vegetation, hardwood utilization, tree physiology, fisheries. *Unit head:* Dr. Robert Van Kirk, Coordinator, 707-826-3744, E-mail: rob.vankirk@humboldt.edu. *Application contact:* Julie Tucker, Administrative Support Coordinator, 707-826-3256, E-mail: jlt7002@humboldt.edu. Website: http://www.humboldt.edu/cnrs/graduate_programs.

Marquette University, Graduate School, College of Engineering, Department of Civil and Environmental Engineering, Milwaukee, WI 53201-1881. Offers construction and public works management (MS, PhD); construction engineering and management (Certificate); environmental/water resources engineering (MS, PhD); structural design (Certificate); structural/geotechnical engineering (MS, PhD); transportation planning and engineering (MS, PhD); waste and wastewater treatment processes (Certificate). Part-time and evening/weekend programs available. Terminal master's awarded for partial completion of doctoral program. *Degree requirements:* For master's, comprehensive exam (for some programs), thesis or alternative; for doctorate, thesis/dissertation. *Entrance requirements:* For master's, GRE General Test (recommended), minimum GPA of 3.0, official transcripts from all current and previous colleges/universities except Marquette, three letters of recommendation; for doctorate, GRE General Test, minimum GPA of 3.0, official transcripts from all current and previous colleges/universities except Marquette, three letters of recommendation, brief statement of purpose, submission of any English language publications authored by applicant (strongly recommended). Additional exam requirements/recommendations for international students: Required—TOEFL (minimum score 530 paper-based). Electronic applications accepted. *Faculty research:* Highway safety, highway performance, and intelligent transportation systems; surface mount technology; watershed management.

Missouri University of Science and Technology, Graduate School, Department of Geological Sciences and Engineering, Rolla, MO 65409. Offers geological engineering (MS, DE, PhD); geology and geophysics (MS, PhD), including geochemistry, geology, geophysics, groundwater and environmental geology; petroleum engineering (MS, DE, PhD). Part-time programs available. *Degree requirements:* For master's, thesis optional; for doctorate, comprehensive exam, thesis/dissertation. *Entrance requirements:* For master's, GRE General Test (minimum score 600 quantitative, writing 3.5), minimum GPA of 3.0 in last 4 semesters; for doctorate, GRE General Test (minimum: Q 600, GRE WR 3.5). Additional exam requirements/recommendations for international students: Required—TOEFL. Electronic applications accepted. *Faculty research:* Digital image processing and geographic information systems, mineralogy, igneous and sedimentary petrology-geochemistry, sedimentology groundwater hydrology and contaminant transport.

Oregon State University, Graduate School, Program in Water Resources Policy and Management, Corvallis, OR 97331. Offers MS. *Students:* 19 full-time (10 women), 2 part-time (both women); includes 3 minority (1 Asian, non-Hispanic/Latino; 2 Two or more races, non-Hispanic/Latino), 1 international. Average age 27. 25 applicants, 36% accepted, 6 enrolled. In 2012, 7 master's awarded. *Entrance requirements:* For master's, GRE. *Expenses:* Tuition, state resident: full-time $11,367; part-time $421 per credit hour. Tuition, nonresident: full-time $18,279; part-time $677 per credit hour. *Required fees:* $1478. One-time fee: $300 full-time. Tuition and fees vary according to course load and program. *Unit head:* Dr. Mary Santelmann, Director, 541-737-1215, Fax: 541-737-1200, E-mail:

santlemm@geo.oregonstate.edu. *Application contact:* Dr. Court Smith, Associate Director, 541-737-3858, E-mail: csmith@oregonstate.edu.

Oregon State University, Graduate School, Program in Water Resources Science, Corvallis, OR 97331. Offers MS, PhD. *Students:* 19 full-time (10 women), 2 part-time (both women); includes 3 minority (1 Asian, non-Hispanic/Latino; 2 Two or more races, non-Hispanic/Latino), 1 international. Average age 30. 33 applicants, 27% accepted, 6 enrolled. In 2012, 3 doctorates awarded. *Entrance requirements:* For master's and doctorate, GRE. *Expenses:* Tuition, state resident: full-time $11,367; part-time $421 per credit hour. Tuition, nonresident: full-time $18,279; part-time $677 per credit hour. *Required fees:* $1478. One-time fee: $300 full-time. Tuition and fees vary according to course load and program. *Unit head:* Dr. Mary Santelmann, Director, 541-737-1215, Fax: 541-737-1200, E-mail: santelmm@geo.oregonstate.edu. *Application contact:* Dr. Roy Haggerty, Associate Director, 541-737-1210, Fax: 541-737-1200, E-mail: haggertr@geo.oregonstate.edu.

Rutgers, The State University of New Jersey, New Brunswick, Graduate School-New Brunswick, Department of Environmental Sciences, Piscataway, NJ 08854-8097. Offers air pollution and resources (MS, PhD); aquatic biology (MS, PhD); aquatic chemistry (MS, PhD); atmospheric science (MS, PhD); chemistry and physics of aerosol and hydrosol systems (MS, PhD); environmental chemistry (MS, PhD); environmental microbiology (MS, PhD); environmental toxicology (PhD); exposure assessment (PhD); fate and effects of pollutants (MS, PhD); pollution prevention and control (MS, PhD); water and wastewater treatment (MS, PhD); water resources (MS, PhD). Terminal master's awarded for partial completion of doctoral program. *Degree requirements:* For master's, comprehensive exam, thesis or alternative, oral final exam; for doctorate, comprehensive exam, thesis/dissertation, thesis defense, qualifying exam. *Entrance requirements:* For master's and doctorate, GRE General Test. Additional exam requirements/recommendations for international students: Required—TOEFL. Electronic applications accepted. *Faculty research:* Biological waste treatment; contaminant fate and transport; air, soil and water quality.

State University of New York College of Environmental Science and Forestry, Program in Environmental Science, Syracuse, NY 13210-2779. Offers biophysical and ecological economics (MPS); coupled natural and human systems (MPS); ecosystem restoration (MPS); environmental and community land planning (MPS, MS); environmental and natural resources policy (PhD); environmental communication and participatory processes (MPS, MS); environmental monitoring and modeling (MPS); environmental policy and democratic processes (MPS, MS); environmental systems and risk management (MS); water and wetland resource studies (MPS, MS). Part-time programs available. *Degree requirements:* For master's, thesis (for some programs); for doctorate, comprehensive exam, thesis/dissertation. *Entrance requirements:* For master's and doctorate, GRE General Test, minimum GPA of 3.0. Additional exam requirements/recommendations for international students: Required—TOEFL (minimum score 550 paper-based; 80 iBT), IELTS (minimum score 6). *Expenses:* Tuition, state resident: full-time $9370; part-time $390 per credit hour. Tuition, nonresident: full-time $16,680; part-time $695 per credit hour. *Required fees:* $981. Tuition and fees vary according to course load and program. *Faculty research:* Environmental education/communications, water resources, land resources, waste management.

Tropical Agriculture Research and Higher Education Center, Graduate School, Turrialba, Costa Rica. Offers agribusiness management (MS); agroforestry systems (PhD); development practices (MS); ecological agriculture (MS); environmental socioeconomics (MS); forestry in tropical and subtropical zones (PhD); integrated watershed management (MS); international sustainable tourism (MS); management and conservation of tropical rainforests and biodiversity (MS); tropical agriculture (PhD); tropical agroforestry (MS). *Entrance requirements:* For master's, GRE, 2 years of related professional experience, letters of recommendation; for doctorate, GRE, 4 letters of recommendation, letter of support from employing organization, master's degree in agronomy, biological sciences, forestry, natural resources or related field. Additional exam requirements/recommendations for international students: Required—TOEFL (minimum score 550 paper-based). Electronic applications accepted. *Faculty research:* Biodiversity in fragmented landscapes, ecosystem management, integrated pest management, environmental livestock production, biotechnology carbon balances in diverse land uses.

University of Alaska Fairbanks, College of Engineering and Mines, Department of Civil and Environmental Engineering, Program in Environmental Engineering, Fairbanks, AK 99775-5900. Offers engineering (PhD), including environmental engineering; environmental engineering (MS), including environmental contaminants, environmental science and management, water supply and waste treatment. Part-time programs available. *Students:* 3 full-time (2 women), 1 part-time (0 women), 1 international. Average age 26. 2 applicants, 50% accepted, 1 enrolled. *Degree requirements:* For master's, comprehensive exam, thesis or alternative; for doctorate, comprehensive exam, thesis/dissertation, oral exam, oral defense. *Entrance requirements:* For master's, basic computer techniques; for doctorate, GRE General Test. Additional exam requirements/recommendations for international students: Required—TOEFL (minimum score 575 paper-based). *Application deadline:* For fall admission, 6/1 for domestic students, 3/1 for international students; for spring admission, 10/15 for domestic students, 9/1 for international students. Applications are processed on a rolling basis. Application fee: $60. Electronic applications accepted. *Expenses:* Tuition, state resident: full-time $7038. Tuition, nonresident: full-time $14,382. Tuition and fees vary according to course level, course load and reciprocity agreements. *Financial support:* In 2012–13, 2 research assistantships (averaging $5,316 per year), 1 teaching assistantship (averaging $3,651 per year) were awarded; fellowships, career-related internships or fieldwork, Federal Work-Study, scholarships/grants, health care benefits, and unspecified assistantships also available. Support available to part-time students. Financial award application deadline: 7/1; financial award applicants required to submit FAFSA. *Unit head:* Dr. David Barnes, Department Chair, 907-474-7241, Fax: 907-474-6087, E-mail: fycee@uaf.edu. *Application contact:* Libby Eddy, Registrar and Director of Admissions, 907-474-7500, Fax: 907-474-7097, E-mail: admissions@uaf.edu. Website: http://cem.uaf.edu/cee/environmental-engineering.aspx.

The University of Arizona, College of Agriculture and Life Sciences, Department of Soil, Water and Environmental Science, Tucson, AZ 85721. Offers MS, PhD. *Faculty:* 5 full-time (2 women), 1 (woman) part-time/adjunct. *Students:* 51 full-time (28 women), 10 part-time (4 women); includes 17 minority (4 Black or African American, non-Hispanic/Latino; 1 American Indian or Alaska Native, non-Hispanic/Latino; 1 Asian, non-Hispanic/Latino; 7 Hispanic/Latino; 4 Two or more races, non-Hispanic/Latino), 15 international. Average age 29. 29 applicants, 55% accepted, 13 enrolled. In 2012, 10 master's, 9 doctorates awarded. *Degree requirements:* For master's, thesis; for doctorate, comprehensive exam, thesis/dissertation. *Entrance requirements:* For master's, GRE (recommended), minimum GPA of 3.0, letter of interest, 3 letters of recommendation; for doctorate, GRE (recommended), MS, minimum GPA of 3.0, letter of interest, 3 letters of recommendation. Additional exam requirements/recommendations for international students: Required—TOEFL (minimum score 550 paper-based; 80 iBT). *Application deadline:* For fall admission, 6/1 for domestic students, 12/1 for international students; for spring admission, 10/1 for domestic students, 6/1 for international students. Applications are processed on a rolling basis. Application fee: $75. *Financial support:* In 2012–13, 14 students received support, including 25 research assistantships with full and partial tuition reimbursements available (averaging $17,098 per year), 8 teaching assistantships with full and partial tuition reimbursements available (averaging $17,044 per year); fellowships, Federal Work-Study, institutionally sponsored loans, scholarships/grants, health care benefits, tuition waivers (full and partial), and unspecified assistantships also available. Financial award application deadline: 5/1. *Faculty research:* Plant production, environmental microbiology, contaminant flow and transport, aquaculture. *Total annual research expenditures:* $2.8 million. *Unit head:* Dr. Jonathan D. Chorover, Interim Department Head, 520-626-5635, E-mail: chorover@cals.arizona.edu. *Application contact:* Alicia Velasquez, Program Coordinator, 520-621-1606, Fax: 520-621-1647, E-mail: avelasqu@ag.arizona.edu. Website: http://ag.arizona.edu/SWES/.

The University of Arizona, College of Agriculture and Life Sciences, School of Natural Resources, Watershed Resources Program, Tucson, AZ 85721. Offers water, society, and policy (MS); watershed management (MS, PhD). *Faculty:* 19 full-time (3 women), 2 part-time/adjunct (0 women). *Students:* 6 full-time (2 women), 4 part-time (2 women); includes 2 minority (both Hispanic/Latino). Average age 34. 4 applicants, 50% accepted, 0 enrolled. *Degree requirements:* For master's, thesis; for doctorate, comprehensive exam, thesis/dissertation. *Entrance requirements:* For master's, GRE General Test, minimum GPA of 3.0, 3 letters of recommendation; for doctorate, GRE General Test, minimum GPA of 3.0, 3 letters of recommendation, MA or MS. Additional exam requirements/recommendations for international students: Required—TOEFL (minimum score 550 paper-based; 79 iBT). *Application deadline:* For fall admission, 8/1 priority date for domestic students, 12/1 for international students; for spring admission, 7/1 for international students. Applications are processed on a rolling basis. Application fee: $75. *Financial support:* In 2012–13, 6 research assistantships with partial tuition reimbursements (averaging $13,872 per year) were awarded; teaching assistantships with partial tuition reimbursements, career-related internships or fieldwork, scholarships/grants, health care benefits, tuition waivers (partial), and unspecified assistantships also available. *Faculty research:* Forest fuel characteristics, prescribed fire, tree ring-fire scar analysis, erosion, sedimentation. *Total annual research expenditures:* $6.5 million. *Unit head:* Dr. CHarles Hutchinson, Director, 520-621-8568, E-mail: chuck@ag.arizona.edu. *Application contact:* Katie Hughes, Academic Coordinator, 520-621-7260, E-mail: khughes@email.arizona.edu. Website: http://www.ag.arizona.edu/srnr/.

The University of Arizona, College of Science, Department of Hydrology and Water Resources, Tucson, AZ 85721. Offers MS, PhD. Part-time programs available. *Faculty:* 11 full-time (1 woman), 3 part-time/adjunct (0 women). *Students:* 52 full-time (16 women), 6 part-time (3 women); includes 11 minority (1 American Indian or Alaska Native, non-Hispanic/Latino; 1 Asian, non-Hispanic/Latino; 4 Hispanic/Latino; 5 Two or more races, non-Hispanic/Latino), 13 international. Average age 31. 59 applicants, 29% accepted, 7 enrolled. In 2012, 9 master's, 5 doctorates awarded. *Degree requirements:* For master's, thesis; for doctorate, thesis/dissertation. *Entrance requirements:* For master's, GRE General Test, 3 letters of recommendation, bachelor's degree in related field; for doctorate, GRE General Test, minimum undergraduate GPA of 3.2, graduate 3.4; 3 letters of recommendation; master's degree in related field; master's thesis abstract. Additional exam requirements/recommendations for international students: Required—TOEFL (minimum score 550 paper-based; 79 iBT). *Application deadline:* For fall admission, 5/1 for domestic students, 12/1 for international students; for spring admission, 10/1 for domestic students, 6/1 for international students. Applications are processed on a rolling basis. Application fee: $75. Electronic applications accepted. *Financial support:* In 2012–13, 15 research assistantships with full tuition reimbursements (averaging $23,223 per year), 4 teaching assistantships with full tuition reimbursements (averaging $23,586 per year) were awarded; institutionally sponsored loans, scholarships/ grants, health care benefits, and unspecified assistantships also available. Financial award application deadline: 1/31. *Faculty research:* Subsurface and surface hydrology, hydrometeorology/climatology, applied remote sensing, water resource systems, environmental hydrology and water quality. *Total annual research expenditures:* $1.7 million. *Unit head:* Kevin E. Lansey, Department Head, 520-621-7120, E-mail: lansey@email.arizona.edu. *Application contact:* Terrie Thompson, Academic Advising Coordinator, 520-621-3131, Fax: 520-621-1422, E-mail: programs@hwr.arizona.edu. Website: http://www.hwr.arizona.edu/.

University of California, Riverside, Graduate Division, Environmental Sciences Department, Riverside, CA 92521-0102. Offers MS, PhD. *Faculty:* 19 full-time (2 women). *Students:* 22 full-time (12 women); includes 4 minority (1 Asian, non-Hispanic/Latino; 3 Hispanic/Latino), 11 international. Average age 29. In 2012, 5 master's, 1 doctorate awarded. *Degree requirements:* For doctorate, thesis/ dissertation. *Entrance requirements:* For master's and doctorate, minimum GPA of 3.2. Additional exam requirements/recommendations for international students: Required—TOEFL (minimum score 550 paper-based; 80 iBT). *Application deadline:* For fall admission, 12/1 priority date for domestic students, 12/1 for international students, for winter admission, 9/1 for domestic students, 7/1 for international students; for spring admission, 12/1 for domestic students, 10/1 for international students. Application fee: $80 ($100 for international students). Electronic applications accepted. *Expenses:* Tuition, state resident: full-time $14,646. Tuition, nonresident: full-time $29,748. *Financial support:* Fellowships with tuition reimbursements and research assistantships with tuition reimbursements available. *Faculty research:* Environmental chemistry and ecotoxicology, environmental microbiology, environmental and natural resource economics and policy, soil and water science, environmental sciences and management. *Unit head:* Dr. Michael Anderson, Chair, 951-827-3757. *Application contact:* John Herring, Program Assistant, 951-827-2441, E-mail: soilwater@ ucr.edu. Website: http://envisci.ucr.edu/.

University of Colorado Denver, College of Liberal Arts and Sciences, Department of Geography and Environmental Sciences, Denver, CO 80217. Offers environmental sciences (MS), including air quality, ecosystems, environmental health, environmental science education, geo-spatial analysis, hazardous waste, water quality. Part-time and evening/weekend programs available. *Faculty:* 11 full-time (3 women), 4 part-time/adjunct (0 women). *Students:* 30 full-time (23 women), 6 part-time (3 women); includes 7 minority (1 Black or African American, non-Hispanic/Latino; 2 Asian, non-Hispanic/Latino; 3 Hispanic/Latino; 1 Two or more races, non-Hispanic/Latino), 6 international. Average age 30. 34 applicants, 65% accepted, 12 enrolled. In 2012, 22 master's awarded. *Degree requirements:* For master's, thesis or alternative, 30 credits including 21 of core requirements and 9 of environmental science electives. *Entrance requirements:* For master's, GRE General Test, BA in one of the natural/ physical sciences or engineering (or equivalent background); prerequisite coursework in calculus and physics (one semester each), general chemistry with lab and general biology with lab (two semesters each), three letters of recommendation. Additional exam requirements/recommendations for international students: Required—TOEFL (minimum score 537 paper-based; 75 iBT); Recommended—IELTS (minimum score 6.5). *Application deadline:* For fall admission, 4/1 for domestic and international students; for spring admission, 10/1 for domestic and international students. Application fee: $50 ($75 for international students). Electronic applications accepted. *Expenses:* Tuition, state resident: full-time $7712; part-time $355 per credit hour. Tuition, nonresident: full-time $22,038; part-time $1087 per credit hour. *Required fees:* $1110; $1. Tuition and fees vary according to course load, campus/location and program. *Financial support:* In 2012–13, 10 students received support. Fellowships, research assistantships, teaching assistantships, Federal Work-Study, institutionally sponsored loans, scholarships/grants, traineeships, and unspecified assistantships available. Financial award application deadline: 4/1; financial award applicants required to submit FAFSA. *Faculty research:* Air quality, environmental health, ecosystems, hazardous waste, water quality, geo-spatial analysis and environmental science education. *Unit head:* Dr. Frederick Chambers, Director of MS Environmental Sciences Program, 303-556-2619, Fax: 303-556-6197, E-mail: frederick.chambers@ucdenver.edu. *Application contact:* Sue Eddleman, Program Assistant, 303-556-2276, E-mail: sue.eddleman@ ucdenver.edu. Website: http://www.ucdenver.edu/academics/colleges/CLAS/ Departments/ges/Programs/MasterofScience/Pages/MasterofScience.aspx.

University of Florida, Graduate School, College of Agricultural and Life Sciences, Department of Soil and Water Science, Gainesville, FL 32611. Offers MS, PhD. Part-time and evening/weekend programs available. Postbaccalaureate distance learning degree programs offered (no on-campus study). Terminal master's awarded for partial completion of doctoral program. *Degree requirements:* For master's, thesis optional; for doctorate, comprehensive exam, thesis/dissertation. *Entrance requirements:* For master's and doctorate, GRE General Test (minimum score 1000 taken within last 5 years), minimum GPA of 3.0. Additional exam requirements/recommendations for international students: Required—TOEFL (minimum score 550 paper-based; 80 iBT), IELTS (minimum score 6). Electronic applications accepted. *Faculty research:* Nutrient, pesticide, and waste management; soil, water, and aquifer remediation; carbon dynamics and ecosystem services; landscape analysis and modeling; wetlands and aquatic ecosystems.

University of Maine, Graduate School, College of Natural Sciences, Forestry, and Agriculture, School of Earth and Climate Sciences, Orono, ME 04469. Offers water resources (MS, PhD). Part-time programs available. *Faculty:* 24 full-time (5 women), 25 part-time/adjunct (4 women). *Students:* 34 full-time (20 women), 2 part-time (1 woman); includes 1 minority (Two or more races, non-Hispanic/ Latino), 6 international. Average age 28. 37 applicants, 38% accepted, 7 enrolled. In 2012, 5 master's, 2 doctorates awarded. *Degree requirements:* For master's, thesis; for doctorate, one foreign language, comprehensive exam, thesis/ dissertation. *Entrance requirements:* For master's and doctorate, GRE General Test. Additional exam requirements/recommendations for international students: Required—TOEFL. *Application deadline:* For fall admission, 2/1 priority date for domestic students. Applications are processed on a rolling basis. Application fee: $65. Electronic applications accepted. *Financial support:* In 2012–13, 5 research assistantships with full tuition reimbursements (averaging $16,950 per year), 6 teaching assistantships with full tuition reimbursements (averaging $13,600 per year) were awarded; Federal Work-Study, institutionally sponsored loans, and tuition waivers (full and partial) also available. Financial award application deadline: 3/1. *Faculty research:* Appalachian bedrock geology, Quaternary studies, marine geology. *Unit head:* Dr. Scott Johnson, Chair, 207-581-2142, Fax: 207-581-2202. *Application contact:* Scott G. Delcourt, Associate Dean of the Graduate School, 207-581-3291, Fax: 207-581-3232, E-mail: graduate@ maine.edu. Website: http://umaine.edu/earthclimate/.

University of Massachusetts Amherst, Graduate School, College of Natural Sciences, Department of Environmental Conservation, Amherst, MA 01003. Offers building systems (MS, PhD); environmental policy and human dimensions (MS, PhD); forest resources (MS, PhD); sustainability science (MS); water, wetlands and watersheds (MS, PhD); wildlife and fisheries conservation (MS, PhD). Part-time programs available. *Faculty:* 62 full-time (11 women). *Students:* 52 full-time (18 women), 40 part-time (19 women); includes 2 minority (1 Black or African American, non-Hispanic/Latino; 1 Two or more races, non-Hispanic/ Latino), 17 international. Average age 33. 73 applicants, 40% accepted, 18 enrolled. In 2012, 16 master's, 3 doctorates awarded. Terminal master's awarded for partial completion of doctoral program. *Degree requirements:* For master's, thesis or alternative; for doctorate, comprehensive exam, thesis/dissertation. *Entrance requirements:* For master's and doctorate, GRE General Test. Additional exam requirements/recommendations for international students: Required—TOEFL (minimum score 550 paper-based; 80 iBT), IELTS (minimum score 6.5). *Application deadline:* For fall admission, 2/1 for domestic and international students; for spring admission, 10/1 for domestic and international students. Applications are processed on a rolling basis. Application fee: $75. Electronic applications accepted. *Expenses:* Tuition, state resident: full-time $1980; part-time $110 per credit. Tuition, nonresident: full-time $13,314; part-time $414 per credit. *Required fees:* $10,338; $3594 per semester. One-time fee: $357. *Financial support:* Fellowships with full and partial tuition reimbursements, research assistantships with full and partial tuition reimbursements, teaching assistantships with full and partial tuition reimbursements, career-related internships or fieldwork, Federal Work-Study, scholarships/grants, traineeships, health care benefits, tuition waivers (full and partial), and unspecified assistantships available. Support available to part-time students. Financial award application deadline: 2/1. *Unit head:* Dr. Kevin McGarigal, Graduate Program Director, 413-545-2257, Fax: 413-545-4358. *Application contact:* Lindsay DeSantis, Supervisor of Admissions, 413-545-0721, Fax: 413-577-0100, E-mail: gradadm@grad.umass.edu. Website: http://eco.umass.edu/.

University of Minnesota, Twin Cities Campus, Graduate School, College of Food, Agricultural and Natural Resource Sciences, Program in Water Resources Science, Minneapolis, MN 55455-0213. Offers MS, PhD. Part-time programs available. *Faculty:* 119 full-time. *Students:* 70 full-time (38 women); includes 2 minority (1 American Indian or Alaska Native, non-Hispanic/Latino; 1 Hispanic/ Latino), 8 international. Average age 30. 57 applicants, 21% accepted, 10 enrolled. In 2012, 8 master's, 7 doctorates awarded. *Degree requirements:* For master's, comprehensive exam, thesis; for doctorate, comprehensive exam, thesis/dissertation. *Entrance requirements:* For master's and doctorate, GRE, minimum GPA of 3.0, calculus, chemistry, biology, physics. Additional exam requirements/recommendations for international students: Required—TOEFL (minimum score 550 paper-based; 79 iBT), IELTS (minimum score 6.5). *Application deadline:* For fall admission, 12/15 priority date for domestic students, 12/15 for international students; for spring admission, 12/15 priority date for domestic students, 12/15 for international students. Applications are processed on a rolling basis. Application fee: $75 ($95 for international students). Electronic applications accepted. *Financial support:* In 2012–13, fellowships with full tuition reimbursements (averaging $40,000 per year), research assistantships with full and partial tuition reimbursements (averaging $40,000 per year) were awarded; scholarships/grants, health care benefits, tuition waivers, and unspecified assistantships also available. Financial award application deadline: 12/15. *Faculty research:* Hydrology, limnology, water policy and economics, water quality, water chemistry. *Unit head:* Dr. Deb Swackhamer, Director of Graduate Studies, 612-625-0279, E-mail: dswack@umn.edu. *Application contact:* Carol Stoneburner, Assistant to Director of Graduate Studies, 612-624-7456, Fax: 612-625-1263, E-mail: carols@umn.edu.

University of Nevada, Las Vegas, Graduate College, College of Science, Program in Water Resources Management, Las Vegas, NV 89154-4029. Offers MS. Part-time programs available. *Students:* 4 full-time (2 women), 5 part-time (3 women); includes 3 minority (all Two or more races, non-Hispanic/Latino), 1 international. Average age 32. 8 applicants, 38% accepted, 3 enrolled. In 2012, 1 master's awarded. *Degree requirements:* For master's, comprehensive exam, thesis. *Entrance requirements:* For master's, GRE Subject Test. Additional exam requirements/recommendations for international students: Required—TOEFL (minimum score 550 paper-based; 80 iBT), IELTS (minimum score 7). *Application deadline:* For fall admission, 2/1 priority date for domestic students, 5/1 for international students; for spring admission, 10/1 priority date for domestic students, 10/1 for international students. Applications are processed on a rolling basis. Application fee: $60 ($95 for international students). Electronic applications accepted. *Expenses:* Tuition, state resident: full-time $4752; part-time $264 per credit. Tuition, nonresident: full-time $18,662; part-time $527.50 per credit. *Required fees:* $12 per credit. $266 per semester. One-time fee: $35. Tuition and fees vary according to course load, program and reciprocity agreements. *Financial support:* In 2012–13, 2 students received support, including 2 research assistantships with partial tuition reimbursements available (averaging $6,000 per year); institutionally sponsored loans, scholarships/grants, health care benefits, and unspecified assistantships also available. Financial award application deadline: 3/1. *Faculty research:* Hydrogeology, water conservation, environmental chemistry, water resources planning, hydrology, waste management: hazardous materials management. *Unit head:* Dr. Michael Nicholl, Chair/Associate Professor, 702-895-4616, Fax: 702-895-4064, E-mail: michael.nicholl@unlv.edu. *Application contact:* Graduate College Admissions Evaluator, 702-895-3320, Fax: 702-895-4180, E-mail: gradcollege@unlv.edu. Website: http://www.unlv.edu/sciences/wrm/.

University of New Brunswick Fredericton, School of Graduate Studies, Faculty of Engineering, Department of Civil Engineering, Fredericton, NB E3B 5A3, Canada. Offers construction engineering and management (M Eng, M Sc E, PhD); environmental engineering (M Eng, M Sc E, PhD); environmental studies (M Eng); geotechnical engineering (M Eng, M Sc E, PhD); groundwater/hydrology (M Eng, M Sc E, PhD); materials (M Eng, M Sc E, PhD); pavements (M Eng, M Sc E, PhD); structures (M Eng, M Sc E, PhD); transportation (M Eng, M Sc E, PhD). Part-time programs available. *Faculty:* 18 full-time (1 woman). *Students:* 22 full-time (6 women), 17 part-time (4 women). In 2012, 13 master's, 2 doctorates awarded. *Degree requirements:* For master's, thesis, proposal; for doctorate, comprehensive exam, thesis/dissertation, qualifying exam; proposal; 27 credit hours of courses. *Entrance requirements:* For master's, minimum GPA of 3.0; B Sc E in civil engineering or related engineering degree; for doctorate, minimum GPA of 3.0; graduate degree in engineering or applied science. Additional exam requirements/recommendations for international students: Required—IELTS (minimum score 7.5), TWE (minimum score 4), Michigan English Language Assessment Battery (minimum score 85), Can Test (minimum score 4.75). *Application deadline:* For fall admission, 5/1 for domestic students; for winter admission, 11/1 for domestic students. Applications are processed on a rolling basis. Application fee: $50 Canadian dollars. Electronic applications accepted. Tuition and fees charges are reported in Canadian dollars. *Expenses: Tuition, area resident:* Full-time $3956 Canadian dollars. *Required fees:* $579.50 Canadian dollars; $55 Canadian dollars per semester. *Financial support:* In 2012–13, 35 fellowships, 48 research assistantships, 35 teaching assistantships were awarded; career-related internships or fieldwork and scholarships/grants also available. *Faculty research:* Construction engineering and management; engineering materials and infrastructure renewal; highway and pavement research; structures and solid mechanics; geotechnical and geoenvironmental engineering; structure interaction; transportation and planning; environment, solid waste management; structural engineering; water and environmental engineering. *Unit head:* Dr. Peter Bischoff, Director of Graduate Studies, 506-453-5103, Fax: 506-453-3568, E-mail: bischoff@unb.ca. *Application contact:* Joyce Moore, Graduate Secretary, 506-452-6127, Fax: 506-453-3568, E-mail: joycem@unb.ca. Website: http://go.unb.ca/gradprograms.

University of New Hampshire, Graduate School, College of Life Sciences and Agriculture, Department of Natural Resources, Durham, NH 03824. Offers environmental conservation (MS); forestry (MS); integrated coastal ecosystem science, policy, management (MS); natural resources (MS); water resources (MS); wildlife (MS). Part-time programs available. *Faculty:* 40 full-time. *Students:* 32 full-time (18 women), 29 part-time (16 women); includes 3 minority (all Hispanic/Latino), 3 international. Average age 28. 63 applicants, 43% accepted, 22 enrolled. In 2012, 14 master's awarded. *Degree requirements:* For master's, thesis or alternative. *Entrance requirements:* For master's, GRE General Test. Additional exam requirements/recommendations for international students: Required—TOEFL (minimum score 550 paper-based; 80 iBT). *Application deadline:* For fall admission, 6/1 for domestic students, 4/1 for international students; for spring admission, 12/1 for domestic students. Applications are processed on a rolling basis. Application fee: $65. Electronic applications accepted. *Expenses:* Tuition, state resident: full-time $13,500; part-time $750 per credit. Tuition, nonresident: full-time $25,940; part-time $1089 per credit. *Required fees:* $1699; $424.75 per semester. *Financial support:* In 2012–13, 35 students received support, including 1 fellowship, 15 research assistantships, 23 teaching assistantships; career-related internships or fieldwork, Federal Work-Study, scholarships/grants, and tuition waivers (full and partial) also available. Support available to part-time students. Financial award application deadline: 2/15. *Unit head:* Dr. Ted Howard, Chairperson, 603-862-2700, E-mail: natural.resources@unh.edu. *Application contact:* Nancy Brown, Administrative Assistant, 603-862-1022, E-mail: natural.resources@unh.edu. Website: http://www.nre.unh.edu/academics/.

University of New Mexico, Graduate School, Water Resources Program, Albuquerque, NM 87131-2039. Offers hydroscience (MWR); policy management (MWR). Part-time programs available. *Faculty:* 1 full-time (0 women). *Students:* 15 full-time (11 women), 27 part-time (14 women); includes 10 minority (1 Black or African American, non-Hispanic/Latino; 3 American Indian or Alaska Native, non-Hispanic/Latino; 1 Asian, non-Hispanic/Latino; 3 Hispanic/Latino; 2 Two or more races, non-Hispanic/Latino). Average age 35. 20 applicants, 70% accepted, 8 enrolled. In 2012, 12 master's awarded. *Degree requirements:* For master's, professional project. *Entrance requirements:* For master's, minimum GPA of 3.0 during last 2 years of undergraduate work, 3 letters of reference. Additional exam requirements/recommendations for international students: Required—TOEFL (minimum score 550 paper-based). *Application deadline:* For fall admission, 7/15 for domestic students; for spring admission, 11/15 for domestic students. Applications are processed on a rolling basis. Application fee: $50. Electronic applications accepted. *Expenses:* Tuition, state resident: full-time $3296; part-time $276.73 per credit hour. Tuition, nonresident: full-time $10,604; part-time $885.74 per credit hour. *Required fees:* $628. *Financial support:* In 2012–13, 24 students received support, including 3 research assistantships with full and partial tuition reimbursements available (averaging $5,791 per year); career-related internships or fieldwork, institutionally sponsored loans, scholarships/grants, and unspecified assistantships also available. Financial award application deadline: 3/1; financial award applicants required to submit FAFSA. *Faculty research:* Sustainable water resources, transboundary water resources, economics, water law, hydrology, developing countries, hydrogeology. *Total annual research expenditures:* $150,557. *Unit head:* Dr. Bruce M. Thomson, Director, 505-277-5249, Fax: 505-277-5226, E-mail: bthomson@unm.edu. *Application contact:* Annamarie Cordova, Administrative Assistant II, 505-277-7759, Fax: 505-277-5226, E-mail: acordova@unm.edu. Website: http://www.unm.edu/~wrp/.

University of Southern California, Graduate School, Viterbi School of Engineering, Sonny Astani Department of Civil Engineering, Los Angeles, CA 90089. Offers applied mechanics (MS); civil engineering (MS, PhD); computer-aided engineering (ME, Graduate Certificate); construction management (MCM); engineering technology commercialization (Graduate Certificate); environmental engineering (MS, PhD); environmental quality management (ME); structural design (ME); sustainable cities (Graduate Certificate); transportation systems (MS, Graduate Certificate); water and waste management (MS). Part-time and evening/weekend programs available. Terminal master's awarded for partial completion of doctoral program. *Degree requirements:* For master's, thesis optional; for doctorate, thesis/dissertation. *Entrance requirements:* For master's and doctorate, GRE General Test. Additional exam requirements/recommendations for international students: Recommended—TOEFL. Electronic applications accepted. *Faculty research:* Geotechnical engineering, transportation engineering, structural engineering, construction management, environmental engineering, water resources.

University of the Pacific, McGeorge School of Law, Sacramento, CA 95817. Offers advocacy (JD); criminal justice (JD); experiential law teaching (LL M); intellectual property (JD); international legal studies (JD); international water resources law (LL M, JSD); law (JD); public law and policy (JD); public policy and law (LL M); tax (JD); transnational business practice (LL M); U.S. law and policy (LL M), including public law and policy, U.S. law; water resources law (LL M), including international law, U.S. law; JD/MBA; JD/MPPA. *Accreditation:* ABA. Part-time and evening/weekend programs available. *Faculty:* 46 full-time (21 women), 57 part-time/adjunct (18 women). *Students:* 623 full-time (282 women), 227 part-time (101 women); includes 245 minority (22 Black or African American, non-Hispanic/Latino; 18 American Indian or Alaska Native, non-Hispanic/Latino; 136 Asian, non-Hispanic/Latino; 68 Hispanic/Latino; 1 Two or more races, non-Hispanic/Latino), 28 international. Average age 27. 2,508 applicants, 49% accepted, 255 enrolled. In 2012, 37 master's, 308 doctorates awarded. *Degree requirements:* For master's, thesis (for some programs); for doctorate, thesis/dissertation (for some programs). *Entrance requirements:* For master's, JD; for doctorate, LSAT (for JD), LL M (for JSD). Additional exam requirements/recommendations for international students: Required—TOEFL (minimum score 600 paper-based; 100 iBT). *Application deadline:* For fall admission, 3/15 priority date for domestic students. Applications are processed on a rolling basis. Application fee: $50. Electronic applications accepted. *Expenses:* Contact institution. *Financial support:* Fellowships, research assistantships, teaching assistantships, career-related internships or fieldwork, Federal Work-Study, institutionally sponsored loans, and scholarships/grants available. Support available to part-time students. Financial award applicants required to submit FAFSA. *Faculty research:* International legal studies, public policy and law, advocacy, intellectual property law, taxation, criminal law. *Unit head:* Francis Jay Mootz, III, Dean, 916-739-7151, E-mail: jmootz@pacific.edu. *Application contact:* 916-739-7105, Fax: 916-739-7301, E-mail: mcgeorge@pacific.edu. Website: http://www.mcgeorge.edu/.

University of Wisconsin–Madison, Graduate School, Gaylord Nelson Institute for Environmental Studies, Water Resources Management Program, Madison, WI 53706-1380. Offers MS. Part-time programs available. *Degree requirements:* For master's, summer practicum workshop. *Entrance requirements:* For master's, GRE General Test. Additional exam requirements/recommendations for international students: Required—TOEFL (minimum score 550 paper-based; 80 iBT). Electronic applications accepted. *Expenses:* Tuition, state resident: full-time $10,728; part-time $743 per credit. Tuition, nonresident: full-time $24,054; part-time $1575 per credit. *Required fees:* $1111; $72 per credit. *Faculty research:* Geology, hydrogeology, water chemistry, limnology, oceanography, aquatic ecology, rural sociology, water law and policy.

University of Wisconsin–Milwaukee, Graduate School, School of Freshwater Sciences, Milwaukee, WI 53201-0413. Offers freshwater sciences (PhD); freshwater sciences and technology (MS). *Faculty:* 12 full-time (3 women). *Students:* 30 full-time (14 women), 6 part-time (4 women); includes 1 minority (Black or African American, non-Hispanic/Latino), 1 international. Average age 30. 36 applicants, 61% accepted, 10 enrolled. Application fee: $56 ($96 for international students). *Financial support:* Fellowships, research assistantships, teaching assistantships, and unspecified assistantships available. Financial award applicants required to submit FAFSA. *Total annual research expenditures:* $6.3 million. *Unit head:* David Garman, Founding Dean, 414-382-1700, E-mail: garmand@uwm.edu. *Application contact:* General Information Contact, 414-229-4982, Fax: 414-229-6967, E-mail: gradschool@uwm.edu. Website: http://www4.uwm.edu/freshwater/.

University of Wyoming, College of Agriculture and Natural Resources, Department of Renewable Resources, Laramie, WY 82070. Offers agroecology (MS); entomology (MS, PhD); entomology/water resources (MS, PhD); rangeland ecology and watershed management (MS, PhD), including soil sciences (PhD), soil sciences and water resources (MS); rangeland ecology and watershed management/water resources (MS, PhD); soil science (MS); soil science/water resources (PhD). Part-time programs available. *Degree requirements:* For master's, comprehensive exam, thesis, oral examination; for doctorate, comprehensive exam, thesis/dissertation, preliminary oral and written exam, oral final exam. *Entrance requirements:* For master's and doctorate, GRE General Test, minimum GPA of 3.0. Additional exam requirements/recommendations for international students: Required—TOEFL. Electronic applications accepted. *Faculty research:* Plant control, grazing management, riparian restoration, riparian management, reclamation.

Utah State University, School of Graduate Studies, College of Natural Resources, Department of Watershed Sciences, Logan, UT 84322. Offers ecology (MS, PhD); fisheries biology (MS, PhD); watershed science (MS, PhD). *Degree requirements:* For master's, thesis (for some programs); for doctorate, thesis/dissertation. *Entrance requirements:* For master's and doctorate, GRE General Test, minimum GPA of 3.2. Additional exam requirements/recommendations for international students: Required—TOEFL. Electronic applications accepted. *Faculty research:* Behavior, population ecology, habitat, conservation biology, restoration, aquatic ecology, fisheries management, fluvial geomorphology, remote sensing, conservation biology.

Peterson's Graduate Programs in the Physical Sciences, Mathematics, Agricultural Sciences, the Environment & Natural Resources 2014

www.petersonsbooks.com 523

APPENDIXES

Institutional Changes Since the 2013 Edition

Following is an alphabetical listing of institutions that have recently closed, merged with other institutions, or changed their names or status. In the case of a name change, the former name appears first, followed by the new name.

Academy of Oriental Medicine at Austin (Austin, TX): *name changed to AOMA Graduate School of Integrative Medicine*

The Art Institute of California, a college of Argosy University, San Francisco (San Francisco, CA): *name changed to The Art Institute of California–San Francisco, a campus of Argosy University*

Associated Mennonite Biblical Seminary (Elkhart, IN): *name changed to Anabaptist Mennonnite Biblical Seminary*

Atlantic College (Guaynabo, PR): *name changed to Atlantic University College*

Auburn University Montgomery (Montgomery, AL): *name changed to Auburn University at Montgomery*

Augusta State University (Augusta, GA): *merged into a single entry for Georgia Regents University (Augusta, GA)*

Bernard M. Baruch College of the City University of New York (New York, NY): *name changed to Baruch College of the City University of New York*

Capital Bible Seminary (Lanham, MD): *merged with and became a unit of Lancaster Bible College (Lancaster, PA)*

Carson-Newman College (Jefferson City, TN): *name changed to Carson-Newman University*

Colgate University (Hamilton, NY): *graduate program profile removed by request from the school*

Davenport University (Dearborn, MI): *closed*

Ellis University (Chicago, IL): *name changed to John Hancock University*

Florida Hospital College of Health Sciences (Orlando, FL): *name changed to Adventist University of Health Sciences*

Georgia Health Sciences University (Augusta, GA): *merged into a single entry for Georgia Regents University (Augusta, GA)*

Institute of Transpersonal Psychology (Palo Alto, CA): *name changed to Sofia University*

Laura and Alvin Siegal College of Judaic Studies (Beachwood, OH): *no longer degree granting*

Longy School of Music (Cambridge, MA): *merged with and became a unit of Bard College (Annandale-on-Hudson, NY)*

Manchester College (North Manchester, IN): *name changed to Manchester University*

Mercyhurst College (Erie, PA): *name changed to Mercyhurst University*

Mountain State University (Beckley, WV): *closed*

The Nigerian Baptist Theological Seminary (Ogbomoso, Nigeria): *no longer accredited by agency recognized by USDE or CHEA*

Northeastern Ohio Medical University (Rootstown, OH): *name changed to Northeast Ohio Medical University*

North Georgia College & State University (Dahlonega, GA): *name changed to University of North Georgia*

Nova Scotia Agricultural College (Truro, NS, Canada): *merged with and became a unit of Dalhousie University (Halifax, NS)*

Ohio College of Podiatric Medicine (Independence, OH): *merged with and became a unit of Kent State University (Kent, OH)*

Providence College and Theological Seminary (Otterburne, MB, Canada): *name changed to Providence University College & Theological Seminary*

Saint Peter's College (Jersey City, NJ): *name changed to Saint Peter's University*

Santa Fe University of Art and Design (Santa Fe, NM): *no longer offers graduate degrees*

State University of New York at Binghamton (Binghamton, NY): *name changed to Binghamton University, State University of New York*

Texas College of Traditional Chinese Medicine (Austin, TX): *name changed to Texas Health and Science University*

Traditional Chinese Medical College of Hawaii (Kamuela, HI): *name changed to Hawaii College of Oriental Medicine*

Universidad de las Américas–Puebla (Puebla, Mexico): *name changed to Universidad de las Américas Puebla*

Universidad FLET (Miami, FL): *name changed to Laurel University*

University of Colorado at Colorado Springs (Colorado Springs, CO): *name changed to University of Colorado Colorado Springs*

University of Medicine and Dentistry of New Jersey (Newark, NJ): *units of this school have merged with Rowan University (Glassboro, NJ); Rutgers, The State University of New Jersey, Camden (Camden, NJ); Rutgers, The State University of New Jersey, Newark (Newark, NJ); Rutgers, The State University of New Jersey, New Brunswick (Piscataway, NJ)*

The University of North Carolina at Asheville (Asheville, NC): *name changed to University of North Carolina at Asheville*

University of Phoenix–Vancouver Campus (Burnaby, BC, Canada): *closed*

University of South Florida–Polytechnic (Lakeland, FL): *name changed to University of South Florida in Lakeland and no longer enrolling new students*

University of the Sciences in Philadelphia (Philadelphia, PA): *name changed to University of the Sciences*

Virginia College at Birmingham (Birmingham, AL): *name changed to Virginia College in Birmingham*

Western State College of Colorado (Gunnison, CO): *name changed to Western State Colorado University*

Western State University College of Law (Fullerton, CA): *name changed to Western State University College of Law at Argosy University*

Yorktown University (Denver, CO): *no longer accredited by agency recognized by USDE or CHEA*

Abbreviations Used in the Guides

The following list includes abbreviations of degree names used in the profiles in the 2014 edition of the guides. Because some degrees (e.g., Doctor of Education) can be abbreviated in more than one way (e.g., D.Ed. or Ed.D.), and because the abbreviations used in the guides reflect the preferences of the individual colleges and universities, the list may include two or more abbreviations for a single degree.

DEGREES

A Mus D	Doctor of Musical Arts
AC	Advanced Certificate
AD	Artist's Diploma
	Doctor of Arts
ADP	Artist's Diploma
Adv C	Advanced Certificate
Adv M	Advanced Master
AGC	Advanced Graduate Certificate
AGSC	Advanced Graduate Specialist Certificate
ALM	Master of Liberal Arts
AM	Master of Arts
AMBA	Accelerated Master of Business Administration
	Aviation Master of Business Administration
AMRS	Master of Arts in Religious Studies
APC	Advanced Professional Certificate
APMPH	Advanced Professional Master of Public Health
App Sc	Applied Scientist
App Sc D	Doctor of Applied Science
AstE	Astronautical Engineer
Au D	Doctor of Audiology
B Th	Bachelor of Theology
CAES	Certificate of Advanced Educational Specialization
CAGS	Certificate of Advanced Graduate Studies
CAL	Certificate in Applied Linguistics
CALS	Certificate of Advanced Liberal Studies
CAMS	Certificate of Advanced Management Studies
CAPS	Certificate of Advanced Professional Studies
CAS	Certificate of Advanced Studies
CASPA	Certificate of Advanced Study in Public Administration
CASR	Certificate in Advanced Social Research
CATS	Certificate of Achievement in Theological Studies
CBHS	Certificate in Basic Health Sciences
CBS	Graduate Certificate in Biblical Studies
CCJA	Certificate in Criminal Justice Administration
CCSA	Certificate in Catholic School Administration
CCTS	Certificate in Clinical and Translational Science
CE	Civil Engineer
CEM	Certificate of Environmental Management
CET	Certificate in Educational Technologies
CGS	Certificate of Graduate Studies
Ch E	Chemical Engineer
CM	Certificate in Management
CMH	Certificate in Medical Humanities
CMM	Master of Church Ministries
CMS	Certificate in Ministerial Studies
CNM	Certificate in Nonprofit Management
CPASF	Certificate Program for Advanced Study in Finance
CPC	Certificate in Professional Counseling
	Certificate in Publication and Communication
CPH	Certificate in Public Health
CPM	Certificate in Public Management
CPS	Certificate of Professional Studies
CScD	Doctor of Clinical Science
CSD	Certificate in Spiritual Direction
CSS	Certificate of Special Studies
CTS	Certificate of Theological Studies
CURP	Certificate in Urban and Regional Planning
D Admin	Doctor of Administration
D Arch	Doctor of Architecture
D Be	Doctor in Bioethics
D Com	Doctor of Commerce
D Couns	Doctor of Counseling
D Div	Doctor of Divinity
D Ed	Doctor of Education
D Ed Min	Doctor of Educational Ministry
D Eng	Doctor of Engineering
D Engr	Doctor of Engineering
D Ent	Doctor of Enterprise
D Env	Doctor of Environment
D Law	Doctor of Law
D Litt	Doctor of Letters
D Med Sc	Doctor of Medical Science
D Min	Doctor of Ministry
D Miss	Doctor of Missiology
D Mus	Doctor of Music
D Mus A	Doctor of Musical Arts
D Phil	Doctor of Philosophy
D Prof	Doctor of Professional Studies
D Ps	Doctor of Psychology
D Sc	Doctor of Science
D Sc D	Doctor of Science in Dentistry
D Sc IS	Doctor of Science in Information Systems
D Sc PA	Doctor of Science in Physician Assistant Studies
D Th	Doctor of Theology
D Th P	Doctor of Practical Theology
DA	Doctor of Accounting
	Doctor of Arts
DA Ed	Doctor of Arts in Education
DAH	Doctor of Arts in Humanities
DAOM	Doctorate in Acupuncture and Oriental Medicine
DAT	Doctorate of Athletic Training
DATH	Doctorate of Art Therapy
DBA	Doctor of Business Administration
DBH	Doctor of Behavioral Health
DBL	Doctor of Business Leadership
DBS	Doctor of Buddhist Studies
DC	Doctor of Chiropractic
DCC	Doctor of Computer Science
DCD	Doctor of Communications Design
DCL	Doctor of Civil Law
	Doctor of Comparative Law
DCM	Doctor of Church Music
DCN	Doctor of Clinical Nutrition
DCS	Doctor of Computer Science
DDN	Diplôme du Droit Notarial
DDS	Doctor of Dental Surgery
DE	Doctor of Education
	Doctor of Engineering
DED	Doctor of Economic Development
DEIT	Doctor of Educational Innovation and Technology
DEL	Doctor of Executive Leadership
DEM	Doctor of Educational Ministry
DEPD	Diplôme Études Spécialisées
DES	Doctor of Engineering Science
DESS	Diplôme Études Supérieures Spécialisées

DFA	Doctor of Fine Arts
DGP	Diploma in Graduate and Professional Studies
DH Ed	Doctor of Health Education
DH Sc	Doctor of Health Sciences
DHA	Doctor of Health Administration
DHCE	Doctor of Health Care Ethics
DHL	Doctor of Hebrew Letters
	Doctor of Hebrew Literature
DHS	Doctor of Health Science
DHSc	Doctor of Health Science
Dip CS	Diploma in Christian Studies
DIT	Doctor of Industrial Technology
DJ Ed	Doctor of Jewish Education
DJS	Doctor of Jewish Studies
DLS	Doctor of Liberal Studies
DM	Doctor of Management
	Doctor of Music
DMA	Doctor of Musical Arts
DMD	Doctor of Dental Medicine
DME	Doctor of Music Education
DMEd	Doctor of Music Education
DMFT	Doctor of Marital and Family Therapy
DMH	Doctor of Medical Humanities
DML	Doctor of Modern Languages
DMP	Doctorate in Medical Physics
DMPNA	Doctor of Management Practice in Nurse Anesthesia
DN Sc	Doctor of Nursing Science
DNAP	Doctor of Nurse Anesthesia Practice
DNP	Doctor of Nursing Practice
DNP-A	Doctor of Nursing PracticeAnesthesia
DNS	Doctor of Nursing Science
DO	Doctor of Osteopathy
DOT	Doctor of Occupational Therapy
DPA	Doctor of Public Administration
DPC	Doctor of Pastoral Counseling
DPDS	Doctor of Planning and Development Studies
DPH	Doctor of Public Health
DPM	Doctor of Plant Medicine
	Doctor of Podiatric Medicine
DPPD	Doctor of Policy, Planning, and Development
DPS	Doctor of Professional Studies
DPT	Doctor of Physical Therapy
DPTSc	Doctor of Physical Therapy Science
Dr DES	Doctor of Design
Dr NP	Doctor of Nursing Practice
Dr PH	Doctor of Public Health
Dr Sc PT	Doctor of Science in Physical Therapy
DRSc	Doctor of Regulatory Science
DS	Doctor of Science
DS Sc	Doctor of Social Science
DSJS	Doctor of Science in Jewish Studies
DSL	Doctor of Strategic Leadership
DSW	Doctor of Social Work
DTL	Doctor of Talmudic Law
DV Sc	Doctor of Veterinary Science
DVM	Doctor of Veterinary Medicine
DWS	Doctor of Worship Studies
EAA	Engineer in Aeronautics and Astronautics
EASPh D	Engineering and Applied Science Doctor of Philosophy
ECS	Engineer in Computer Science
Ed D	Doctor of Education
Ed DCT	Doctor of Education in College Teaching
Ed L D	Doctor of Education Leadership
Ed M	Master of Education
Ed S	Specialist in Education
Ed Sp	Specialist in Education
EDB	Executive Doctorate in Business

EDM	Executive Doctorate in Management
EE	Electrical Engineer
EJD	Executive Juris Doctor
EMBA	Executive Master of Business Administration
EMFA	Executive Master of Forensic Accounting
EMHA	Executive Master of Health Administration
EMIB	Executive Master of International Business
EML	Executive Master of Leadership
EMPA	Executive Master of Public Administration
EMS	Executive Master of Science
EMTM	Executive Master of Technology Management
Eng	Engineer
Eng Sc D	Doctor of Engineering Science
Engr	Engineer
Ex Doc	Executive Doctor of Pharmacy
Exec Ed D	Executive Doctor of Education
Exec MBA	Executive Master of Business Administration
Exec MPA	Executive Master of Public Administration
Exec MPH	Executive Master of Public Health
Exec MS	Executive Master of Science
G Dip	Graduate Diploma
GBC	Graduate Business Certificate
GCE	Graduate Certificate in Education
GDM	Graduate Diploma in Management
GDPA	Graduate Diploma in Public Administration
GDRE	Graduate Diploma in Religious Education
GEMBA	Global Executive Master of Business Administration
GEMPA	Gulf Executive Master of Public Administration
GM Acc	Graduate Master of Accountancy
GMBA	Global Master of Business Administration
GP LL M	Global Professional Master of Laws
GPD	Graduate Performance Diploma
GSS	Graduate Special Certificate for Students in Special Situations
IEMBA	International Executive Master of Business Administration
IM Acc	Integrated Master of Accountancy
IMA	Interdisciplinary Master of Arts
IMBA	International Master of Business Administration
IMES	International Master's in Environmental Studies
Ingeniero	Engineer
JCD	Doctor of Canon Law
JCL	Licentiate in Canon Law
JD	Juris Doctor
JSD	Doctor of Juridical Science
	Doctor of Jurisprudence
	Doctor of the Science of Law
JSM	Master of Science of Law
L Th	Licenciate in Theology
LL B	Bachelor of Laws
LL CM	Master of Laws in Comparative Law
LL D	Doctor of Laws
LL M	Master of Laws
LL M in Tax	Master of Laws in Taxation
LL M CL	Master of Laws (Common Law)
M Ac	Master of Accountancy
	Master of Accounting
	Master of Acupuncture
M Ac OM	Master of Acupuncture and Oriental Medicine
M Acc	Master of Accountancy
	Master of Accounting
M Acct	Master of Accountancy
	Master of Accounting
M Accy	Master of Accountancy
M Actg	Master of Accounting
M Acy	Master of Accountancy

530 www.petersonsbooks.com

Peterson's Graduate Programs in the Physical Sciences, Mathematics, Agricultural Sciences, the Environment & Natural Resources 2014

M Ad	Master of Administration	M Med Sc	Master of Medical Science
M Ad Ed	Master of Adult Education	M Mgmt	Master of Management
M Adm	Master of Administration	M Mgt	Master of Management
M Adm Mgt	Master of Administrative Management	M Min	Master of Ministries
M Admin	Master of Administration	M Mtl E	Master of Materials Engineering
M ADU	Master of Architectural Design and Urbanism	M Mu	Master of Music
M Adv	Master of Advertising	M Mus	Master of Music
M Aero E	Master of Aerospace Engineering	M Mus Ed	Master of Music Education
M AEST	Master of Applied Environmental Science and Technology	M Music	Master of Music
		M Nat Sci	Master of Natural Science
M Ag	Master of Agriculture	M Oc E	Master of Oceanographic Engineering
M Ag Ed	Master of Agricultural Education	M Pet E	Master of Petroleum Engineering
M Agr	Master of Agriculture	M Pharm	Master of Pharmacy
M Anesth Ed	Master of Anesthesiology Education	M Phil	Master of Philosophy
M App Comp Sc	Master of Applied Computer Science	M Phil F	Master of Philosophical Foundations
M App St	Master of Applied Statistics	M Pl	Master of Planning
M Appl Stat	Master of Applied Statistics	M Plan	Master of Planning
M Aq	Master of Aquaculture	M Pol	Master of Political Science
M Arc	Master of Architecture	M Pr Met	Master of Professional Meteorology
M Arch	Master of Architecture	M Prob S	Master of Probability and Statistics
M Arch I	Master of Architecture I	M Psych	Master of Psychology
M Arch II	Master of Architecture II	M Pub	Master of Publishing
M Arch E	Master of Architectural Engineering	M Rel	Master of Religion
M Arch H	Master of Architectural History	M Sc	Master of Science
M Bioethics	Master in Bioethics	M Sc A	Master of Science (Applied)
M Biomath	Master of Biomathematics	M Sc AC	Master of Science in Applied Computing
M Ch	Master of Chemistry	M Sc AHN	Master of Science in Applied Human Nutrition
M Ch E	Master of Chemical Engineering	M Sc BMC	Master of Science in Biomedical Communications
M Chem	Master of Chemistry		
M Cl D	Master of Clinical Dentistry	M Sc CS	Master of Science in Computer Science
M Cl Sc	Master of Clinical Science	M Sc E	Master of Science in Engineering
M Comp	Master of Computing	M Sc Eng	Master of Science in Engineering
M Comp Sc	Master of Computer Science	M Sc Engr	Master of Science in Engineering
M Coun	Master of Counseling	M Sc F	Master of Science in Forestry
M Dent	Master of Dentistry	M Sc FE	Master of Science in Forest Engineering
M Dent Sc	Master of Dental Sciences	M Sc Geogr	Master of Science in Geography
M Des	Master of Design	M Sc N	Master of Science in Nursing
M Des S	Master of Design Studies	M Sc OT	Master of Science in Occupational Therapy
M Div	Master of Divinity	M Sc P	Master of Science in Planning
M Ec	Master of Economics	M Sc Pl	Master of Science in Planning
M Econ	Master of Economics	M Sc PT	Master of Science in Physical Therapy
M Ed	Master of Education	M Sc T	Master of Science in Teaching
M Ed T	Master of Education in Teaching	M SEM	Master of Sustainable Environmental Management
M En	Master of Engineering		
	Master of Environmental Science	M Serv Soc	Master of Social Service
M En S	Master of Environmental Sciences	M Soc	Master of Sociology
M Eng	Master of Engineering	M Sp Ed	Master of Special Education
M Eng Mgt	Master of Engineering Management	M Stat	Master of Statistics
M Engr	Master of Engineering	M Sys E	Master of Systems Engineering
M Ent	Master of Enterprise	M Sys Sc	Master of Systems Science
M Env	Master of Environment	M Tax	Master of Taxation
M Env Des	Master of Environmental Design	M Tech	Master of Technology
M Env E	Master of Environmental Engineering	M Th	Master of Theology
M Env Sc	Master of Environmental Science	M Tox	Master of Toxicology
M Fin	Master of Finance	M Trans E	Master of Transportation Engineering
M Geo E	Master of Geological Engineering	M Urb	Master of Urban Planning
M Geoenv E	Master of Geoenvironmental Engineering	M Vet Sc	Master of Veterinary Science
M Geog	Master of Geography	MA	Master of Accounting
M Hum	Master of Humanities		Master of Administration
M Hum Svcs	Master of Human Services		Master of Arts
M IBD	Master of Integrated Building Delivery	MA Comm	Master of Arts in Communication
M IDST	Master's in Interdisciplinary Studies	MA Ed	Master of Arts in Education
M Kin	Master of Kinesiology	MA Ed Ad	Master of Arts in Educational Administration
M Land Arch	Master of Landscape Architecture	MA Ext	Master of Agricultural Extension
M Litt	Master of Letters	MA Islamic	Master of Arts in Islamic Studies
M Mat SE	Master of Material Science and Engineering	MA Min	Master of Arts in Ministry
M Math	Master of Mathematics	MA Miss	Master of Arts in Missiology
M Mech E	Master of Mechanical Engineering	MA Past St	Master of Arts in Pastoral Studies
		MA Ph	Master of Arts in Philosophy

Peterson's Graduate Programs in the Physical Sciences, Mathematics, Agricultural Sciences, the Environment & Natural Resources 2014

www.petersonsbooks.com   **531**

MA Psych	Master of Arts in Psychology
MA Sc	Master of Applied Science
MA Sp	Master of Arts (Spirituality)
MA Th	Master of Arts in Theology
MA-R	Master of Arts (Research)
MAA	Master of Administrative Arts
	Master of Applied Anthropology
	Master of Applied Arts
	Master of Arts in Administration
MAAA	Master of Arts in Arts Administration
MAAAP	Master of Arts Administration and Policy
MAAE	Master of Arts in Art Education
MAAT	Master of Arts in Applied Theology
	Master of Arts in Art Therapy
MAB	Master of Agribusiness
MABC	Master of Arts in Biblical Counseling
	Master of Arts in Business Communication
MABE	Master of Arts in Bible Exposition
MABL	Master of Arts in Biblical Languages
MABM	Master of Agribusiness Management
MABMH	bioethics and medical humanities
MABS	Master of Arts in Biblical Studies
MABT	Master of Arts in Bible Teaching
MAC	Master of Accountancy
	Master of Accounting
	Master of Arts in Communication
	Master of Arts in Counseling
MACC	Master of Arts in Christian Counseling
	Master of Arts in Clinical Counseling
MACCM	Master of Arts in Church and Community Ministry
MACCT	Master of Accounting
MACD	Master of Arts in Christian Doctrine
MACE	Master of Arts in Christian Education
MACFM	Master of Arts in Children's and Family Ministry
MACH	Master of Arts in Church History
MACI	Master of Arts in Curriculum and Instruction
MACIS	Master of Accounting and Information Systems
MACJ	Master of Arts in Criminal Justice
MACL	Master of Arts in Christian Leadership
MACM	Master of Arts in Christian Ministries
	Master of Arts in Christian Ministry
	Master of Arts in Church Music
	Master of Arts in Counseling Ministries
MACN	Master of Arts in Counseling
MACO	Master of Arts in Counseling
MAcOM	Master of Acupuncture and Oriental Medicine
MACP	Master of Arts in Christian Practice
	Master of Arts in Counseling Psychology
MACS	Master of Applied Computer Science
	Master of Arts in Catholic Studies
	Master of Arts in Christian Studies
MACSE	Master of Arts in Christian School Education
MACT	Master of Arts in Christian Thought
	Master of Arts in Communications and Technology
MAD	Master of Art and Design
MAD-Crit	Master of Arts in Design Criticism
MADR	Master of Arts in Dispute Resolution
MADS	Master of Animal and Dairy Science
	Master of Applied Disability Studies
MAE	Master of Aerospace Engineering
	Master of Agricultural Economics
	Master of Agricultural Education
	Master of Architectural Engineering
	Master of Art Education
	Master of Arts in Education
	Master of Arts in English

MAEd	Master of Arts Education
MAEL	Master of Arts in Educational Leadership
MAEM	Master of Arts in Educational Ministries
MAEN	Master of Arts in English
MAEP	Master of Arts in Economic Policy
MAES	Master of Arts in Environmental Sciences
MAET	Master of Arts in English Teaching
MAF	Master of Arts in Finance
MAFE	Master of Arts in Financial Economics
MAFLL	Master of Arts in Foreign Language and Literature
MAFM	Master of Accounting and Financial Management
MAFS	Master of Arts in Family Studies
MAG	Master of Applied Geography
MAGU	Master of Urban Analysis and Management
MAH	Master of Arts in Humanities
MAHA	Master of Arts in Humanitarian Assistance
	Master of Arts in Humanitarian Studies
MAHCM	Master of Arts in Health Care Mission
MAHG	Master of American History and Government
MAHL	Master of Arts in Hebrew Letters
MAHN	Master of Applied Human Nutrition
MAHSR	Master of Applied Health Services Research
MAIA	Master of Arts in International Administration
	Master of Arts in International Affairs
MAIB	Master of Arts in International Business
MAIDM	Master of Arts in Interior Design and Merchandising
MAIH	Master of Arts in Interdisciplinary Humanities
MAIOP	Master of Arts in Industrial/Organizational Psychology
MAIPCR	Master of Arts in International Peace and Conflict Management
MAIS	Master of Arts in Intercultural Studies
	Master of Arts in Interdisciplinary Studies
	Master of Arts in International Studies
MAIT	Master of Administration in Information Technology
	Master of Applied Information Technology
MAJ	Master of Arts in Journalism
MAJ Ed	Master of Arts in Jewish Education
MAJCS	Master of Arts in Jewish Communal Service
MAJE	Master of Arts in Jewish Education
MAJPS	Master of Arts in Jewish Professional Studies
MAJS	Master of Arts in Jewish Studies
MAL	Master in Agricultural Leadership
MALA	Master of Arts in Liberal Arts
MALD	Master of Arts in Law and Diplomacy
MALER	Master of Arts in Labor and Employment Relations
MALM	Master of Arts in Leadership Evangelical Mobilization
MALP	Master of Arts in Language Pedagogy
MALPS	Master of Arts in Liberal and Professional Studies
MALS	Master of Arts in Liberal Studies
MAM	Master of Acquisition Management
	Master of Agriculture and Management
	Master of Applied Mathematics
	Master of Arts in Ministry
	Master of Arts Management
	Master of Avian Medicine
MAMB	Master of Applied Molecular Biology
MAMC	Master of Arts in Mass Communication
	Master of Arts in Ministry and Culture
	Master of Arts in Ministry for a Multicultural Church
	Master of Arts in Missional Christianity
MAME	Master of Arts in Missions/Evangelism

532 www.petersonsbooks.com

Peterson's Graduate Programs in the Physical Sciences, Mathematics, Agricultural Sciences, the Environment & Natural Resources 2014

MAMFC	Master of Arts in Marriage and Family Counseling
MAMFCC	Master of Arts in Marriage, Family, and Child Counseling
MAMFT	Master of Arts in Marriage and Family Therapy
MAMHC	Master of Arts in Mental Health Counseling
MAMI	Master of Arts in Missions
MAMS	Master of Applied Mathematical Sciences
	Master of Arts in Ministerial Studies
	Master of Arts in Ministry and Spirituality
MAMT	Master of Arts in Mathematics Teaching
MAN	Master of Applied Nutrition
MANT	Master of Arts in New Testament
MAOL	Master of Arts in Organizational Leadership
MAOM	Master of Acupuncture and Oriental Medicine
	Master of Arts in Organizational Management
MAOT	Master of Arts in Old Testament
MAP	Master of Applied Psychology
	Master of Arts in Planning
	Master of Psychology
	Master of Public Administration
MAP Min	Master of Arts in Pastoral Ministry
MAPA	Master of Arts in Public Administration
MAPC	Master of Arts in Pastoral Counseling
	Master of Arts in Professional Counseling
MAPE	Master of Arts in Political Economy
MAPM	Master of Arts in Pastoral Ministry
	Master of Arts in Pastoral Music
	Master of Arts in Practical Ministry
MAPP	Master of Arts in Public Policy
MAPPS	Master of Arts in Asia Pacific Policy Studies
MAPS	Master of Arts in Pastoral Counseling/Spiritual Formation
	Master of Arts in Pastoral Studies
	Master of Arts in Public Service
MAPT	Master of Practical Theology
MAPW	Master of Arts in Professional Writing
MAR	Master of Arts in Reading
	Master of Arts in Religion
Mar Eng	Marine Engineer
MARC	Master of Arts in Rehabilitation Counseling
MARE	Master of Arts in Religious Education
MARL	Master of Arts in Religious Leadership
MARS	Master of Arts in Religious Studies
MAS	Master of Accounting Science
	Master of Actuarial Science
	Master of Administrative Science
	Master of Advanced Study
	Master of Aeronautical Science
	Master of American Studies
	Master of Applied Science
	Master of Applied Statistics
	Master of Archival Studies
MASA	Master of Advanced Studies in Architecture
MASD	Master of Arts in Spiritual Direction
MASE	Master of Arts in Special Education
MASF	Master of Arts in Spiritual Formation
MASJ	Master of Arts in Systems of Justice
MASLA	Master of Advanced Studies in Landscape Architecture
MASM	Master of Aging Services Management
	Master of Arts in Specialized Ministries
MASP	Master of Applied Social Psychology
	Master of Arts in School Psychology
MASPAA	Master of Arts in Sports and Athletic Administration
MASS	Master of Applied Social Science
	Master of Arts in Social Science
MAST	Master of Arts in Science Teaching

MASW	Master of Aboriginal Social Work
MAT	Master of Arts in Teaching
	Master of Arts in Theology
	Master of Athletic Training
	Master's in Administration of Telecommunications
Mat E	Materials Engineer
MATCM	Master of Acupuncture and Traditional Chinese Medicine
MATDE	Master of Arts in Theology, Development, and Evangelism
MATDR	Master of Territorial Management and Regional Development
MATE	Master of Arts for the Teaching of English
MATESL	Master of Arts in Teaching English as a Second Language
MATESOL	Master of Arts in Teaching English to Speakers of Other Languages
MATF	Master of Arts in Teaching English as a Foreign Language/Intercultural Studies
MATFL	Master of Arts in Teaching Foreign Language
MATH	Master of Arts in Therapy
MATI	Master of Administration of Information Technology
MATL	Master of Arts in Teacher Leadership
	Master of Arts in Teaching of Languages
	Master of Arts in Transformational Leadership
MATM	Master of Arts in Teaching of Mathematics
MATS	Master of Arts in Theological Studies
	Master of Arts in Transforming Spirituality
MATSL	Master of Arts in Teaching a Second Language
MAUA	Master of Arts in Urban Affairs
MAUD	Master of Arts in Urban Design
MAURP	Master of Arts in Urban and Regional Planning
MAWSHP	Master of Arts in Worship
MAYM	Master of Arts in Youth Ministry
MB	Master of Bioinformatics
	Master of Biology
MBA	Master of Business Administration
MBA-AM	Master of Business Administration in Aviation Management
MBA-EP	Master of Business Administration–Experienced Professionals
MBA/MGPS	Master of Business Administration/Master of Global Policy Studies
MBAA	Master of Business Administration in Aviation
MBAE	Master of Biological and Agricultural Engineering
	Master of Biosystems and Agricultural Engineering
MBAH	Master of Business Administration in Health
MBAi	Master of Business Administration–International
MBAICT	Master of Business Administration in Information and Communication Technology
MBATM	Master of Business Administration in Technology Management
MBC	Master of Building Construction
MBE	Master of Bilingual Education
	Master of Bioengineering
	Master of Bioethics
	Master of Biological Engineering
	Master of Biomedical Engineering
	Master of Business and Engineering
	Master of Business Economics
	Master of Business Education
MBEE	Master in Biotechnology Enterprise and Entrepreneurship
MBET	Master of Business, Entrepreneurship and Technology
MBIOT	Master of Biotechnology
MBiotech	Master of Biotechnology

Peterson's Graduate Programs in the Physical Sciences, Mathematics, Agricultural Sciences, the Environment & Natural Resources 2014

www.petersonsbooks.com **533**

MBL	Master of Business Law
	Master of Business Leadership
MBLE	Master in Business Logistics Engineering
MBMI	Master of Biomedical Imaging and Signals
MBMSE	Master of Business Management and Software Engineering
MBOE	Master of Business Operational Excellence
MBS	Master of Biblical Studies
	Master of Biological Science
	Master of Biomedical Sciences
	Master of Bioscience
	Master of Building Science
	Master of Business and Science
MBST	Master of Biostatistics
MBT	Master of Biblical and Theological Studies
	Master of Biomedical Technology
	Master of Biotechnology
	Master of Business Taxation
MC	Master of Communication
	Master of Counseling
	Master of Cybersecurity
MC Ed	Master of Continuing Education
MC Sc	Master of Computer Science
MCA	Master of Arts in Applied Criminology
	Master of Commercial Aviation
MCAM	Master of Computational and Applied Mathematics
MCC	Master of Computer Science
MCCS	Master of Crop and Soil Sciences
MCD	Master of Communications Disorders
	Master of Community Development
MCE	Master in Electronic Commerce
	Master of Christian Education
	Master of Civil Engineering
	Master of Control Engineering
MCEM	Master of Construction Engineering Management
MCH	Master of Chemical Engineering
MCHE	Master of Chemical Engineering
MCIS	Master of Communication and Information Studies
	Master of Computer and Information Science
	Master of Computer Information Systems
MCIT	Master of Computer and Information Technology
MCJ	Master of Criminal Justice
MCJA	Master of Criminal Justice Administration
MCL	Master in Communication Leadership
	Master of Canon Law
	Master of Comparative Law
MCM	Master of Christian Ministry
	Master of Church Music
	Master of City Management
	Master of Communication Management
	Master of Community Medicine
	Master of Construction Management
	Master of Contract Management
	Master of Corporate Media
MCMP	Master of City and Metropolitan Planning
MCMS	Master of Clinical Medical Science
MCN	Master of Clinical Nutrition
MCOL	Master of Arts in Community and Organizational Leadership
MCP	Master of City Planning
	Master of Community Planning
	Master of Counseling Psychology
	Master of Cytopathology Practice
	Master of Science in Quality Systems and Productivity
MCPC	Master of Arts in Chaplaincy and Pastoral Care

MCPD	Master of Community Planning and Development
MCR	Master in Clinical Research
MCRP	Master of City and Regional Planning
MCRS	Master of City and Regional Studies
MCS	Master of Christian Studies
	Master of Clinical Science
	Master of Combined Sciences
	Master of Communication Studies
	Master of Computer Science
	Master of Consumer Science
MCSE	Master of Computer Science and Engineering
MCSL	Master of Catholic School Leadership
MCSM	Master of Construction Science/Management
MCST	Master of Science in Computer Science and Information Technology
MCTP	Master of Communication Technology and Policy
MCTS	Master of Clinical and Translational Science
MCVS	Master of Cardiovascular Science
MD	Doctor of Medicine
MDA	Master of Development Administration
	Master of Dietetic Administration
MDB	Master of Design-Build
MDE	Master of Developmental Economics
	Master of Distance Education
	Master of the Education of the Deaf
MDH	Master of Dental Hygiene
MDM	Master of Design Methods
	Master of Digital Media
MDP	Master in Sustainable Development Practice
	Master of Development Practice
MDR	Master of Dispute Resolution
MDS	Master of Dental Surgery
	Master of Design Studies
ME	Master of Education
	Master of Engineering
	Master of Entrepreneurship
	Master of Evangelism
ME Sc	Master of Engineering Science
MEA	Master of Educational Administration
	Master of Engineering Administration
MEAP	Master of Environmental Administration and Planning
MEBT	Master in Electronic Business Technologies
MEC	Master of Electronic Commerce
MECE	Master of Electrical and Computer Engineering
Mech E	Mechanical Engineer
MED	Master of Education of the Deaf
MEDS	Master of Environmental Design Studies
MEE	Master in Education
	Master of Electrical Engineering
	Master of Energy Engineering
	Master of Environmental Engineering
MEEM	Master of Environmental Engineering and Management
MEENE	Master of Engineering in Environmental Engineering
MEEP	Master of Environmental and Energy Policy
MEERM	Master of Earth and Environmental Resource Management
MEH	Master in Humanistic Studies
	Master of Environmental Horticulture
MEHP	Master of Education in the Health Professions
MEHS	Master of Environmental Health and Safety
MEIM	Master of Entertainment Industry Management
MEL	Master of Educational Leadership
	Master of English Literature
MELP	Master of Environmental Law and Policy
MEM	Master of Ecosystem Management

	Master of Electricity Markets
	Master of Engineering Management
	Master of Environmental Management
	Master of Marketing
MEME	Master of Engineering in Manufacturing Engineering
	Master of Engineering in Mechanical Engineering
MENG	Master of Arts in English
MENVEGR	Master of Environmental Engineering
MEP	Master of Engineering Physics
MEPC	Master of Environmental Pollution Control
MEPD	Master of EducationNProfessional Development
	Master of Environmental Planning and Design
MER	Master of Employment Relations
MERE	Master of Entrepreneurial Real Estate
MES	Master of Education and Science
	Master of Engineering Science
	Master of Environment and Sustainability
	Master of Environmental Science
	Master of Environmental Studies
	Master of Environmental Systems
	Master of Special Education
MESM	Master of Environmental Science and Management
MET	Master of Educational Technology
	Master of Engineering Technology
	Master of Entertainment Technology
	Master of Environmental Toxicology
METM	Master of Engineering and Technology Management
MEVE	Master of Environmental Engineering
MF	Master of Finance
	Master of Forestry
MFA	Master of Fine Arts
MFAM	Master in Food Animal Medicine
MFAS	Master of Fisheries and Aquatic Science
MFAW	Master of Fine Arts in Writing
MFC	Master of Forest Conservation
MFCS	Master of Family and Consumer Sciences
MFE	Master of Financial Economics
	Master of Financial Engineering
	Master of Forest Engineering
MFG	Master of Functional Genomics
MFHD	Master of Family and Human Development
MFM	Master of Financial Management
	Master of Financial Mathematics
MFMS	Master's in Food Microbiology and Safety
MFPE	Master of Food Process Engineering
MFR	Master of Forest Resources
MFRC	Master of Forest Resources and Conservation
MFS	Master of Food Science
	Master of Forensic Sciences
	Master of Forest Science
	Master of Forest Studies
	Master of French Studies
MFST	Master of Food Safety and Technology
MFT	Master of Family Therapy
	Master of Food Technology
MFWB	Master of Fishery and Wildlife Biology
MFWCB	Master of Fish, Wildlife and Conservation Biology
MFWS	Master of Fisheries and Wildlife Sciences
MFYCS	Master of Family, Youth and Community Sciences
MG	Master of Genetics
MGA	Master of Global Affairs
	Master of Governmental Administration
MGC	Master of Genetic Counseling

MGD	Master of Graphic Design
MGE	Master of Geotechnical Engineering
MGEM	Master of Global Entrepreneurship and Management
MGIS	Master of Geographic Information Science
	Master of Geographic Information Systems
MGM	Master of Global Management
MGP	Master of Gestion de Projet
MGPS	Master of Global Policy Studies
MGPS/MA	Master of Global Policy Studies/Master of Arts
MGPS/MPH	Master of Global Policy Studies/Master of Public Health
MGREM	Master of Global Real Estate Management
MGS	Master of Gerontological Studies
	Master of Global Studies
MH	Master of Humanities
MH Ed	Master of Health Education
MH Sc	Master of Health Sciences
MHA	Master of Health Administration
	Master of Healthcare Administration
	Master of Hospital Administration
	Master of Hospitality Administration
MHAD	Master of Health Administration
MHB	Master of Human Behavior
MHCA	Master of Health Care Administration
MHCI	Master of Health Care Informatics
	Master of Human-Computer Interaction
MHCL	Master of Health Care Leadership
MHE	Master of Health Education
	Master of Human Ecology
MHE Ed	Master of Home Economics Education
MHEA	Master of Higher Education Administration
MHHS	Master of Health and Human Services
MHI	Master of Health Informatics
	Master of Healthcare Innovation
MHIIM	Master of Health Informatics and Information Management
MHIS	Master of Health Information Systems
MHK	Master of Human Kinetics
MIIL	Master of Hebrew Literature
MHM	Master of Healthcare Management
MHMS	Master of Health Management Systems
MHP	Master of Health Physics
	Master of Heritage Preservation
	Master of Historic Preservation
MHPA	Master of Heath Policy and Administration
MHPE	Master of Health Professions Education
MHR	Master of Human Resources
MHRD	Master in Human Resource Development
MHRIR	Master of Human Resources and Industrial Relations
MHRLR	Master of Human Resources and Labor Relations
MHRM	Master of Human Resources Management
MHS	Master of Health Science
	Master of Health Sciences
	Master of Health Studies
	Master of Hispanic Studies
	Master of Human Services
	Master of Humanistic Studies
MHSA	Master of Health Services Administration
MHSM	Master of Health Systems Management
MI	Master of Information
	Master of Instruction
MI Arch	Master of Interior Architecture
MIA	Master of Interior Architecture
	Master of International Affairs
MIAA	Master of International Affairs and Administration

Peterson's Graduate Programs in the Physical Sciences, Mathematics, Agricultural Sciences, the Environment & Natural Resources 2014

www.petersonsbooks.com   **535**

MIAM	Master of International Agribusiness Management
MIAPD	Master of Interior Architecture and Product Design
MIB	Master of International Business
MIBA	Master of International Business Administration
MICM	Master of International Construction Management
MID	Master of Industrial Design
	Master of Industrial Distribution
	Master of Interior Design
	Master of International Development
MIDC	Master of Integrated Design and Construction
MIE	Master of Industrial Engineering
MIH	Master of Integrative Health
MIHTM	Master of International Hospitality and Tourism Management
MIJ	Master of International Journalism
MILR	Master of Industrial and Labor Relations
MiM	Master in Management
MIM	Master of Industrial Management
	Master of Information Management
	Master of International Management
MIMLAE	Master of International Management for Latin American Executives
MIMS	Master of Information Management and Systems
	Master of Integrated Manufacturing Systems
MIP	Master of Infrastructure Planning
	Master of Intellectual Property
	Master of International Policy
MIPA	Master of International Public Affairs
MIPER	Master of International Political Economy of Resources
MIPP	Master of International Policy and Practice
	Master of International Public Policy
MIPS	Master of International Planning Studies
MIR	Master of Industrial Relations
	Master of International Relations
MIRHR	Master of Industrial Relations and Human Resources
MIS	Master of Industrial Statistics
	Master of Information Science
	Master of Information Systems
	Master of Integrated Science
	Master of Interdisciplinary Studies
	Master of International Service
	Master of International Studies
MISE	Master of Industrial and Systems Engineering
MISKM	Master of Information Sciences and Knowledge Management
MISM	Master of Information Systems Management
MIT	Master in Teaching
	Master of Industrial Technology
	Master of Information Technology
	Master of Initial Teaching
	Master of International Trade
	Master of Internet Technology
MITA	Master of Information Technology Administration
MITM	Master of Information Technology and Management
MITO	Master of Industrial Technology and Operations
MJ	Master of Journalism
	Master of Jurisprudence
MJ Ed	Master of Jewish Education
MJA	Master of Justice Administration
MJM	Master of Justice Management

MJS	Master of Judicial Studies
	Master of Juridical Science
MKM	Master of Knowledge Management
ML	Master of Latin
ML Arch	Master of Landscape Architecture
MLA	Master of Landscape Architecture
	Master of Liberal Arts
MLAS	Master of Laboratory Animal Science
	Master of Liberal Arts and Sciences
MLAUD	Master of Landscape Architecture in Urban Development
MLD	Master of Leadership Development
MLE	Master of Applied Linguistics and Exegesis
MLER	Master of Labor and Employment Relations
MLHR	Master of Labor and Human Resources
MLI Sc	Master of Library and Information Science
MLIS	Master of Library and Information Science
	Master of Library and Information Studies
MLM	Master of Library Media
MLRHR	Master of Labor Relations and Human Resources
MLS	Master of Leadership Studies
	Master of Legal Studies
	Master of Liberal Studies
	Master of Library Science
	Master of Life Sciences
MLSP	Master of Law and Social Policy
MLT	Master of Language Technologies
MLTCA	Master of Long Term Care Administration
MM	Master of Management
	Master of Ministry
	Master of Missiology
	Master of Music
MM Ed	Master of Music Education
MM Sc	Master of Medical Science
MM St	Master of Museum Studies
MMA	Master of Marine Affairs
	Master of Media Arts
	Master of Musical Arts
MMAE	Master of Mechanical and Aerospace Engineering
MMAL	Master of Maritime Administration and Logistics
MMAS	Master of Military Art and Science
MMB	Master of Microbial Biotechnology
MMBA	Managerial Master of Business Administration
MMC	Master of Manufacturing Competitiveness
	Master of Mass Communications
	Master of Music Conducting
MMCM	Master of Music in Church Music
MMCSS	Master of Mathematical Computational and Statistical Sciences
MME	Master of Manufacturing Engineering
	Master of Mathematics Education
	Master of Mathematics for Educators
	Master of Mechanical Engineering
	Master of Medical Engineering
	Master of Mining Engineering
	Master of Music Education
MMF	Master of Mathematical Finance
MMFT	Master of Marriage and Family Therapy
MMG	Master of Management
MMH	Master of Management in Hospitality
	Master of Medical Humanities
MMI	Master of Management of Innovation
MMIS	Master of Management Information Systems
MMM	Master of Manufacturing Management
	Master of Marine Management
	Master of Medical Management

536 www.petersonsbooks.com

Peterson's Graduate Programs in the Physical Sciences, Mathematics, Agricultural Sciences, the Environment & Natural Resources 2014

MMME	Master of Metallurgical and Materials Engineering		Master of Professional Accountancy
			Master of Professional Accounting
MMP	Master of Management Practice		Master of Public Administration
	Master of Marine Policy		Master of Public Affairs
	Master of Medical Physics	MPAC	Master of Professional Accounting
	Master of Music Performance	MPAID	Master of Public Administration and International Development
MMPA	Master of Management and Professional Accounting	MPAP	Master of Physician Assistant Practice
MMQM	Master of Manufacturing Quality Management		Master of Public Affairs and Politics
MMR	Master of Marketing Research	MPAS	Master of Physician Assistant Science
MMRM	Master of Marine Resources Management		Master of Physician Assistant Studies
MMS	Master of Management Science	MPC	Master of Pastoral Counseling
	Master of Management Studies		Master of Professional Communication
	Master of Manufacturing Systems		Master of Professional Counseling
	Master of Marine Studies	MPCU	Master of Planning in Civic Urbanism
	Master of Materials Science	MPD	Master of Product Development
	Master of Medical Science		Master of Public Diplomacy
	Master of Medieval Studies	MPDS	Master of Planning and Development Studies
MMSE	Master of Manufacturing Systems Engineering	MPE	Master of Physical Education
	Multidisciplinary Master of Science in Engineering		Master of Power Engineering
		MPEM	Master of Project Engineering and Management
MMSM	Master of Music in Sacred Music		
MMT	Master in Marketing	MPH	Master of Public Health
	Master of Music Teaching	MPHE	Master of Public Health Education
	Master of Music Therapy	MPHTM	Master of Public Health and Tropical Medicine
	Master's in Marketing Technology	MPI	Master of Product Innovation
MMus	Master of Music	MPIA	Master in International Affairs
MN	Master of Nursing		Master of Public and International Affairs
	Master of Nutrition	MPM	Master of Pastoral Ministry
MN NP	Master of Nursing in Nurse Practitioner		Master of Pest Management
MNA	Master of Nonprofit Administration		Master of Policy Management
	Master of Nurse Anesthesia		Master of Practical Ministries
MNAL	Master of Nonprofit Administration and Leadership		Master of Project Management
			Master of Public Management
MNAS	Master of Natural and Applied Science	MPNA	Master of Public and Nonprofit Administration
MNCM	Master of Network and Communications Management	MPO	Master of Prosthetics and Orthotics
		MPOD	Master of Positive Organizational Development
MNE	Master of Network Engineering	MPP	Master of Public Policy
	Master of Nuclear Engineering	MPPA	Master of Public Policy Administration
MNL	Master in International Business for Latin America		Master of Public Policy and Administration
		MPPAL	Master of Public Policy, Administration and Law
MNM	Master of Nonprofit Management	MPPM	Master of Public and Private Management
MNO	Master of Nonprofit Organization		Master of Public Policy and Management
MNPL	Master of Not-for-Profit Leadership	MPPPM	Master of Plant Protection and Pest Management
MNpS	Master of Nonprofit Studies		
MNR	Master of Natural Resources	MPRTM	Master of Parks, Recreation, and Tourism Management
MNRES	Master of Natural Resources and Environmental Studies		
		MPS	Master of Pastoral Studies
MNRM	Master of Natural Resource Management		Master of Perfusion Science
MNRS	Master of Natural Resource Stewardship		Master of Planning Studies
MNS	Master of Natural Science		Master of Political Science
MO	Master of Oceanography		Master of Preservation Studies
MOD	Master of Organizational Development		Master of Professional Studies
MOGS	Master of Oil and Gas Studies		Master of Public Service
MOH	Master of Occupational Health	MPSA	Master of Public Service Administration
MOL	Master of Organizational Leadership	MPSRE	Master of Professional Studies in Real Estate
MOM	Master of Oriental Medicine	MPT	Master of Pastoral Theology
MOR	Master of Operations Research		Master of Physical Therapy
MOT	Master of Occupational Therapy		Master of Practical Theology
MP	Master of Physiology	MPVM	Master of Preventive Veterinary Medicine
	Master of Planning	MPW	Master of Professional Writing
MP Ac	Master of Professional Accountancy		Master of Public Works
MP Acc	Master of Professional Accountancy	MQM	Master of Quality Management
	Master of Professional Accounting	MQS	Master of Quality Systems
	Master of Public Accounting	MR	Master of Recreation
MP Aff	Master of Public Affairs		Master of Retailing
MP Aff/MPH	Master of Public Affairs/Master of Public Health	MRA	Master in Research Administration
		MRC	Master of Rehabilitation Counseling
MP Th	Master of Pastoral Theology	MRCP	Master of Regional and City Planning
MPA	Master of Physician Assistant		

Peterson's Graduate Programs in the Physical Sciences, Mathematics, Agricultural Sciences, the Environment & Natural Resources 2014

www.petersonsbooks.com **537**

	Master of Regional and Community Planning
MRD	Master of Rural Development
MRE	Master of Real Estate
	Master of Religious Education
MRED	Master of Real Estate Development
MREM	Master of Resource and Environmental Management
MRLS	Master of Resources Law Studies
MRM	Master of Resources Management
MRP	Master of Regional Planning
MRS	Master of Religious Studies
MRSc	Master of Rehabilitation Science
MS	Master of Science
MS Cmp E	Master of Science in Computer Engineering
MS Kin	Master of Science in Kinesiology
MS Acct	Master of Science in Accounting
MS Accy	Master of Science in Accountancy
MS Aero E	Master of Science in Aerospace Engineering
MS Ag	Master of Science in Agriculture
MS Arch	Master of Science in Architecture
MS Arch St	Master of Science in Architectural Studies
MS Bio E	Master of Science in Bioengineering
	Master of Science in Biomedical Engineering
MS Bm E	Master of Science in Biomedical Engineering
MS Ch E	Master of Science in Chemical Engineering
MS Chem	Master of Science in Chemistry
MS Cp E	Master of Science in Computer Engineering
MS Eco	Master of Science in Economics
MS Econ	Master of Science in Economics
MS Ed	Master of Science in Education
MS El	Master of Science in Educational Leadership and Administration
MS En E	Master of Science in Environmental Engineering
MS Eng	Master of Science in Engineering
MS Engr	Master of Science in Engineering
MS Env E	Master of Science in Environmental Engineering
MS Exp Surg	Master of Science in Experimental Surgery
MS Int A	Master of Science in International Affairs
MS Mat E	Master of Science in Materials Engineering
MS Mat SE	Master of Science in Material Science and Engineering
MS Met E	Master of Science in Metallurgical Engineering
MS Mgt	Master of Science in Management
MS Min	Master of Science in Mining
MS Min E	Master of Science in Mining Engineering
MS Mt E	Master of Science in Materials Engineering
MS Otal	Master of Science in Otalrynology
MS Pet E	Master of Science in Petroleum Engineering
MS Phys	Master of Science in Physics
MS Poly	Master of Science in Polymers
MS Psy	Master of Science in Psychology
MS Pub P	Master of Science in Public Policy
MS Sc	Master of Science in Social Science
MS Sp Ed	Master of Science in Special Education
MS Stat	Master of Science in Statistics
MS Surg	Master of Science in Surgery
MS Tax	Master of Science in Taxation
MS Tc E	Master of Science in Telecommunications Engineering
MS-R	Master of Science (Research)
MS/CAGS	Master of Science/Certificate of Advanced Graduate Studies
MSA	Master of School Administration
	Master of Science Administration
	Master of Science in Accountancy
	Master of Science in Accounting
	Master of Science in Administration
	Master of Science in Aeronautics

	Master of Science in Agriculture
	Master of Science in Anesthesia
	Master of Science in Architecture
	Master of Science in Aviation
	Master of Sports Administration
MSA Phy	Master of Science in Applied Physics
MSAA	Master of Science in Astronautics and Aeronautics
MSAAE	Master of Science in Aeronautical and Astronautical Engineering
MSABE	Master of Science in Agricultural and Biological Engineering
MSAC	Master of Science in Acupuncture
MSACC	Master of Science in Accounting
MSAE	Master of Science in Aeronautical Engineering
	Master of Science in Aerospace Engineering
	Master of Science in Applied Economics
	Master of Science in Applied Engineering
	Master of Science in Architectural Engineering
MSAH	Master of Science in Allied Health
MSAL	Master of Sport Administration and Leadership
MSAM	Master of Science in Applied Mathematics
MSANR	Master of Science in Agriculture and Natural Resources Systems Management
MSAPM	Master of Security Analysis and Portfolio Management
MSAS	Master of Science in Applied Statistics
	Master of Science in Architectural Studies
MSAT	Master of Science in Accounting and Taxation
	Master of Science in Advanced Technology
	Master of Science in Athletic Training
MSB	Master of Science in Bible
	Master of Science in Biotechnology
	Master of Science in Business
	Master of Sustainable Business
MSBA	Master of Science in Business Administration
	Master of Science in Business Analysis
MSBAE	Master of Science in Biological and Agricultural Engineering
	Master of Science in Biosystems and Agricultural Engineering
MSBC	Master of Science in Building Construction
MSBCB	bioinformatics and computational biology
MSBE	Master of Science in Biological Engineering
	Master of Science in Biomedical Engineering
MSBENG	Master of Science in Bioengineering
MSBIT	Master of Science in Business Information Technology
MSBM	Master of Sport Business Management
MSBME	Master of Science in Biomedical Engineering
MSBMS	Master of Science in Basic Medical Science
MSBS	Master of Science in Biomedical Sciences
MSC	Master of Science in Commerce
	Master of Science in Communication
	Master of Science in Computers
	Master of Science in Counseling
	Master of Science in Criminology
MSCC	Master of Science in Christian Counseling
	Master of Science in Community Counseling
MSCD	Master of Science in Communication Disorders
	Master of Science in Community Development
MSCE	Master of Science in Civil Engineering
	Master of Science in Clinical Epidemiology
	Master of Science in Computer Engineering
	Master of Science in Continuing Education
MSCEE	Master of Science in Civil and Environmental Engineering
MSCF	Master of Science in Computational Finance
MSCH	Master of Science in Chemical Engineering
MSChE	Master of Science in Chemical Engineering

Peterson's Graduate Programs in the Physical Sciences, Mathematics, Agricultural Sciences, the Environment & Natural Resources 2014

MSCI	Master of Science in Clinical Investigation
	Master of Science in Curriculum and Instruction
MSCIS	Master of Science in Computer and Information Systems
	Master of Science in Computer Information Science
	Master of Science in Computer Information Systems
MSCIT	Master of Science in Computer Information Technology
MSCJ	Master of Science in Criminal Justice
MSCJA	Master of Science in Criminal Justice Administration
MSCJS	Master of Science in Crime and Justice Studies
MSCLS	Master of Science in Clinical Laboratory Studies
MSCM	Master of Science in Church Management
	Master of Science in Conflict Management
	Master of Science in Construction Management
MScM	Master of Science in Management
MSCM	Master of Supply Chain Management
MSCNU	Master of Science in Clinical Nutrition
MSCP	Master of Science in Clinical Psychology
	Master of Science in Community Psychology
	Master of Science in Computer Engineering
	Master of Science in Counseling Psychology
MSCPE	Master of Science in Computer Engineering
MSCPharm	Master of Science in Pharmacy
MSCPI	Master in Strategic Planning for Critical Infrastructures
MSCR	Master of Science in Clinical Research
MSCRP	Master of Science in City and Regional Planning
	Master of Science in Community and Regional Planning
MSCRP/MP Aff	Master of Science in Community and Regional Planning/Master of Public Affairs
MSCRP/MSSD	Master of Science in Community and Regional Planning/Master of Science in Sustainable Design
MSCRP/MSUD	Master of Science in Community and Regional Planning/Masters of Science in Urban Design
MSCS	Master of Science in Clinical Science
	Master of Science in Computer Science
MSCSD	Master of Science in Communication Sciences and Disorders
MSCSE	Master of Science in Computer Science and Engineering
MSCTE	Master of Science in Career and Technical Education
MSD	Master of Science in Dentistry
	Master of Science in Design
	Master of Science in Dietetics
MSE	Master of Science Education
	Master of Science in Economics
	Master of Science in Education
	Master of Science in Engineering
	Master of Science in Engineering Management
	Master of Software Engineering
	Master of Special Education
	Master of Structural Engineering
MSECE	Master of Science in Electrical and Computer Engineering
MSED	Master of Sustainable Economic Development
MSEE	Master of Science in Electrical Engineering
	Master of Science in Environmental Engineering
MSEH	Master of Science in Environmental Health
MSEL	Master of Science in Educational Leadership
MSEM	Master of Science in Engineering Management
	Master of Science in Engineering Mechanics

	Master of Science in Environmental Management
MSENE	Master of Science in Environmental Engineering
MSEO	Master of Science in Electro-Optics
MSEP	Master of Science in Economic Policy
MSEPA	Master of Science in Economics and Policy Analysis
MSES	Master of Science in Embedded Software Engineering
	Master of Science in Engineering Science
	Master of Science in Environmental Science
	Master of Science in Environmental Studies
MSESM	Master of Science in Engineering Science and Mechanics
MSET	Master of Science in Educational Technology
	Master of Science in Engineering Technology
MSEV	Master of Science in Environmental Engineering
MSEVH	Master of Science in Environmental Health and Safety
MSF	Master of Science in Finance
	Master of Science in Forestry
	Master of Spiritual Formation
MSFA	Master of Science in Financial Analysis
MSFAM	Master of Science in Family Studies
MSFCS	Master of Science in Family and Consumer Science
MSFE	Master of Science in Financial Engineering
MSFOR	Master of Science in Forestry
MSFP	Master of Science in Financial Planning
MSFS	Master of Science in Financial Sciences
	Master of Science in Forensic Science
MSFSB	Master of Science in Financial Services and Banking
MSFT	Master of Science in Family Therapy
MSGC	Master of Science in Genetic Counseling
MSH	Master of Science in Health
	Master of Science in Hospice
MSHA	Master of Science in Health Administration
MSHCA	Master of Science in Health Care Administration
MSHCI	Master of Science in Human Computer Interaction
MSHCPM	Master of Science in Health Care Policy and Management
MSHE	Master of Science in Health Education
MSHES	Master of Science in Human Environmental Sciences
MSHFID	Master of Science in Human Factors in Information Design
MSHFS	Master of Science in Human Factors and Systems
MSHI	Master of Science in Health Informatics
MSHP	Master of Science in Health Professions
	Master of Science in Health Promotion
MSHR	Master of Science in Human Resources
MSHRL	Master of Science in Human Resource Leadership
MSHRM	Master of Science in Human Resource Management
MSHROD	Master of Science in Human Resources and Organizational Development
MSHS	Master of Science in Health Science
	Master of Science in Health Services
	Master of Science in Health Systems
	Master of Science in Homeland Security
MSHT	Master of Science in History of Technology
MSI	Master of Science in Information
	Master of Science in Instruction
	Master of System Integration
MSIA	Master of Science in Industrial Administration

Peterson's Graduate Programs in the Physical Sciences, Mathematics, Agricultural Sciences, the Environment & Natural Resources 2014

www.petersonsbooks.com **539**

	Master of Science in Information Assurance and Computer Security
MSIB	Master of Science in International Business
MSIDM	Master of Science in Interior Design and Merchandising
MSIDT	Master of Science in Information Design and Technology
MSIE	Master of Science in Industrial Engineering
	Master of Science in International Economics
MSIEM	Master of Science in Information Engineering and Management
MSIID	Master of Science in Information and Instructional Design
MSIM	Master of Science in Information Management
	Master of Science in International Management
MSIMC	Master of Science in Integrated Marketing Communications
MSIR	Master of Science in Industrial Relations
MSIS	Master of Science in Information Science
	Master of Science in Information Studies
	Master of Science in Information Systems
	Master of Science in Interdisciplinary Studies
MSIS/MA	Master of Science in Information Studies/ Master of Arts
MSISE	Master of Science in Infrastructure Systems Engineering
MSISM	Master of Science in Information Systems Management
MSISPM	Master of Science in Information Security Policy and Management
MSIST	Master of Science in Information Systems Technology
MSIT	Master of Science in Industrial Technology
	Master of Science in Information Technology
	Master of Science in Instructional Technology
MSITM	Master of Science in Information Technology Management
MSJ	Master of Science in Journalism
	Master of Science in Jurisprudence
MSJC	Master of Social Justice and Criminology
MSJE	Master of Science in Jewish Education
MSJFP	Master of Science in Juvenile Forensic Psychology
MSJJ	Master of Science in Juvenile Justice
MSJPS	Master of Science in Justice and Public Safety
MSJS	Master of Science in Jewish Studies
MSK	Master of Science in Kinesiology
MSL	Master of School Leadership
	Master of Science in Leadership
	Master of Science in Limnology
	Master of Strategic Leadership
	Master of Studies in Law
MSLA	Master of Science in Landscape Architecture
	Master of Science in Legal Administration
MSLD	Master of Science in Land Development
MSLFS	Master of Science in Life Sciences
MSLP	Master of Speech-Language Pathology
MSLS	Master of Science in Library Science
MSLSCM	Master of Science in Logistics and Supply Chain Management
MSLT	Master of Second Language Teaching
MSM	Master of Sacred Ministry
	Master of Sacred Music
	Master of School Mathematics
	Master of Science in Management
	Master of Science in Organization Management
	Master of Security Management
MSMA	Master of Science in Marketing Analysis
MSMAE	Master of Science in Materials Engineering
MSMC	Master of Science in Mass Communications
MSME	Master of Science in Mathematics Education

	Master of Science in Mechanical Engineering
MSMFE	Master of Science in Manufacturing Engineering
MSMFT	Master of Science in Marriage and Family Therapy
MSMIS	Master of Science in Management Information Systems
MSMIT	Master of Science in Management and Information Technology
MSMLS	Master of Science in Medical Laboratory Science
MSMOT	Master of Science in Management of Technology
MSMS	Master of Science in Management Science
	Master of Science in Medical Sciences
MSMSE	Master of Science in Manufacturing Systems Engineering
	Master of Science in Material Science and Engineering
	Master of Science in Mathematics and Science Education
MSMT	Master of Science in Management and Technology
MSMus	Master of Sacred Music
MSN	Master of Science in Nursing
MSN-R	Master of Science in Nursing (Research)
MSNA	Master of Science in Nurse Anesthesia
MSNE	Master of Science in Nuclear Engineering
MSNED	Master of Science in Nurse Education
MSNM	Master of Science in Nonprofit Management
MSNS	Master of Science in Natural Science
	Master of Science in Nutritional Science
MSOD	Master of Science in Organizational Development
MSOEE	Master of Science in Outdoor and Environmental Education
MSOES	Master of Science in Occupational Ergonomics and Safety
MSOH	Master of Science in Occupational Health
MSOL	Master of Science in Organizational Leadership
MSOM	Master of Science in Operations Management
	Master of Science in Oriental Medicine
MSOR	Master of Science in Operations Research
MSOT	Master of Science in Occupational Technology
	Master of Science in Occupational Therapy
MSP	Master of Science in Pharmacy
	Master of Science in Planning
	Master of Science in Psychology
	Master of Speech Pathology
MSPA	Master of Science in Physician Assistant
	Master of Science in Professional Accountancy
MSPAS	Master of Science in Physician Assistant Studies
MSPC	Master of Science in Professional Communications
	Master of Science in Professional Counseling
MSPE	Master of Science in Petroleum Engineering
MSPG	Master of Science in Psychology
MSPH	Master of Science in Public Health
MSPHR	Master of Science in Pharmacy
MSPM	Master of Science in Professional Management
	Master of Science in Project Management
MSPNGE	Master of Science in Petroleum and Natural Gas Engineering
MSPS	Master of Science in Pharmaceutical Science
	Master of Science in Political Science
	Master of Science in Psychological Services
MSPT	Master of Science in Physical Therapy
MSpVM	Master of Specialized Veterinary Medicine
MSR	Master of Science in Radiology
	Master of Science in Reading
MSRA	Master of Science in Recreation Administration

540 www.petersonsbooks.com

Peterson's Graduate Programs in the Physical Sciences, Mathematics, Agricultural Sciences, the Environment & Natural Resources 2014

MSRC	Master of Science in Resource Conservation		Master of Teaching Arts
MSRE	Master of Science in Real Estate		Master of Tourism Administration
	Master of Science in Religious Education	MTCM	Master of Traditional Chinese Medicine
MSRED	Master of Science in Real Estate Development	MTD	Master of Training and Development
MSRLS	Master of Science in Recreation and Leisure Studies	MTE	Master in Educational Technology
		MTESOL	Master in Teaching English to Speakers of Other Languages
MSRMP	Master of Science in Radiological Medical Physics	MTHM	Master of Tourism and Hospitality Management
MSRS	Master of Science in Rehabilitation Science	MTI	Master of Information Technology
MSS	Master of Science in Software	MTIM	Master of Trust and Investment Management
	Master of Security Studies	MTL	Master of Talmudic Law
	Master of Social Science	MTM	Master of Technology Management
	Master of Social Services		Master of Telecommunications Management
	Master of Software Systems		Master of the Teaching of Mathematics
	Master of Sports Science	MTMH	Master of Tropical Medicine and Hygiene
	Master of Strategic Studies	MTOM	Master of Traditional Oriental Medicine
MSSA	Master of Science in Social Administration	MTP	Master of Transpersonal Psychology
MSSCP	Master of Science in Science Content and Process	MTPC	Master of Technical and Professional Communication
MSSD	Master of Science in Sustainable Design	MTR	Master of Translational Research
MSSE	Master of Science in Software Engineering	MTS	Master of Theatre Studies
	Master of Science in Space Education		Master of Theological Studies
	Master of Science in Special Education	MTSC	Master of Technical and Scientific Communication
MSSEM	Master of Science in Systems and Engineering Management	MTSE	Master of Telecommunications and Software Engineering
MSSI	Master of Science in Security Informatics		
	Master of Science in Strategic Intelligence	MTT	Master in Technology Management
MSSL	Master of Science in School Leadership	MTX	Master of Taxation
	Master of Science in Strategic Leadership	MUA	Master of Urban Affairs
MSSLP	Master of Science in Speech-Language Pathology	MUCD	Master of Urban and Community Design
		MUD	Master of Urban Design
MSSM	Master of Science in Sports Medicine	MUDS	Master of Urban Design Studies
MSSP	Master of Science in Social Policy	MUEP	Master of Urban and Environmental Planning
MSSPA	Master of Science in Student Personnel Administration	MUP	Master of Urban Planning
		MUPDD	Master of Urban Planning, Design, and Development
MSSS	Master of Science in Safety Science		
	Master of Science in Systems Science	MUPP	Master of Urban Planning and Policy
MSST	Master of Science in Security Technologies	MUPRED	Master of Urban Planning and Real Estate Development
MSSW	Master of Science in Social Work		
MSSWE	Master of Science in Software Engineering	MURP	Master of Urban and Regional Planning
MST	Master of Science and Technology		Master of Urban and Rural Planning
	Master of Science in Taxation	MURPL	Master of Urban and Regional Planning
	Master of Science in Teaching	MUS	Master of Urban Studies
	Master of Science in Technology	MUSA	Master of Urban Spatial Analytics
	Master of Science in Telecommunications	MVM	Master of VLSI and Microelectronics
	Master of Science Teaching	MVP	Master of Voice Pedagogy
MSTC	Master of Science in Technical Communication	MVPH	Master of Veterinary Public Health
	Master of Science in Telecommunications	MVS	Master of Visual Studies
MSTCM	Master of Science in Traditional Chinese Medicine	MWC	Master of Wildlife Conservation
		MWE	Master in Welding Engineering
MSTE	Master of Science in Telecommunications Engineering	MWPS	Master of Wood and Paper Science
		MWR	Master of Water Resources
	Master of Science in Transportation Engineering	MWS	Master of Women's Studies
			Master of Worship Studies
MSTM	Master of Science in Technical Management	MZS	Master of Zoological Science
	Master of Science in Technology Management	Nav Arch	Naval Architecture
	Master of Science in Transfusion Medicine	Naval E	Naval Engineer
MSTOM	Master of Science in Traditional Oriental Medicine	ND	Doctor of Naturopathic Medicine
		NE	Nuclear Engineer
MSUD	Master of Science in Urban Design	Nuc E	Nuclear Engineer
MSW	Master of Social Work	OD	Doctor of Optometry
MSWE	Master of Software Engineering	OTD	Doctor of Occupational Therapy
MSWREE	Master of Science in Water Resources and Environmental Engineering	PBME	Professional Master of Biomedical Engineering
		PC	Performer's Certificate
MSX	Master of Science in Exercise Science	PD	Professional Diploma
MT	Master of Taxation	PGC	Post-Graduate Certificate
	Master of Teaching	PGD	Postgraduate Diploma
	Master of Technology	Ph L	Licentiate of Philosophy
	Master of Textiles	Pharm D	Doctor of Pharmacy
MTA	Master of Tax Accounting		

Peterson's Graduate Programs in the Physical Sciences, Mathematics, Agricultural Sciences, the Environment & Natural Resources 2014

www.petersonsbooks.com   **541**

PhD	Doctor of Philosophy
PhD Otal	Doctor of Philosophy in Otalrynology
PhD Surg	Doctor of Philosophy in Surgery
PhDEE	Doctor of Philosophy in Electrical Engineering
PMBA	Professional Master of Business Administration
PMC	Post Master Certificate
PMD	Post-Master's Diploma
PMS	Professional Master of Science
	Professional Master's
Post-Doctoral MS	Post-Doctoral Master of Science
Post-MSN Certificate	Post-Master of Science in Nursing Certificate
PPDPT	Postprofessional Doctor of Physical Therapy
Pro-MS	Professional Science Master's
PSM	Professional Master of Science
	Professional Science Master's
Psy D	Doctor of Psychology
Psy M	Master of Psychology
Psy S	Specialist in Psychology
Psya D	Doctor of Psychoanalysis
Rh D	Doctor of Rehabilitation
S Psy S	Specialist in Psychological Services
Sc D	Doctor of Science
Sc M	Master of Science
SCCT	Specialist in Community College Teaching
ScDPT	Doctor of Physical Therapy Science
SD	Doctor of Science
	Specialist Degree
SJD	Doctor of Juridical Science

SLPD	Doctor of Speech-Language Pathology
SM	Master of Science
SM Arch S	Master of Science in Architectural Studies
SMACT	Master of Science in Art, Culture and Technology
SMBT	Master of Science in Building Technology
SP	Specialist Degree
Sp C	Specialist in Counseling
Sp Ed	Specialist in Education
Sp LIS	Specialist in Library and Information Science
SPA	Specialist in Arts
SPCM	Specialist in Church Music
Spec	Specialist's Certificate
Spec M	Specialist in Music
SPEM	Specialist in Educational Ministries
Spt	Specialist Degree
SPTH	Specialist in Theology
SSP	Specialist in School Psychology
STB	Bachelor of Sacred Theology
STD	Doctor of Sacred Theology
STL	Licentiate of Sacred Theology
STM	Master of Sacred Theology
TDPT	Transitional Doctor of Physical Therapy
Th D	Doctor of Theology
Th M	Master of Theology
VMD	Doctor of Veterinary Medicine
WEMBA	Weekend Executive Master of Business Administration
XMA	Executive Master of Arts

542 www.petersonsbooks.com

Peterson's Graduate Programs in the Physical Sciences, Mathematics, Agricultural Sciences, the Environment & Natural Resources 2014

INDEXES

Displays and Close-Ups

Directories and Subject Areas

Following is an alphabetical listing of directories and subject areas. Also listed are cross-references for subject area names not used in the directory structure of the guides, for example, "City and Regional Planning (see Urban and Regional Planning)."

Graduate Programs in the Humanities, Arts & Social Sciences

Addictions/Substance Abuse Counseling
Administration (see Arts Administration; Public Administration)
African-American Studies
African Languages and Literatures (see African Studies)
African Studies
Agribusiness (see Agricultural Economics and Agribusiness)
Agricultural Economics and Agribusiness
Alcohol Abuse Counseling (see Addictions/Substance Abuse Counseling)
American Indian/Native American Studies
American Studies
Anthropology
Applied Arts and Design—General
Applied Behavior Analysis
Applied Economics
Applied History (see Public History)
Applied Psychology
Applied Social Research
Arabic (see Near and Middle Eastern Languages)
Arab Studies (see Near and Middle Eastern Studies)
Archaeology
Architectural History
Architecture
Archives Administration (see Public History)
Area and Cultural Studies (see African-American Studies; African Studies; American Indian/Native American Studies; American Studies; Asian-American Studies; Asian Studies; Canadian Studies; Cultural Studies; East European and Russian Studies; Ethnic Studies; Folklore; Gender Studies; Hispanic Studies; Holocaust Studies; Jewish Studies; Latin American Studies; Near and Middle Eastern Studies; Northern Studies; Pacific Area/Pacific Rim Studies; Western European Studies; Women's Studies)
Art/Fine Arts
Art History
Arts Administration
Arts Journalism
Art Therapy
Asian-American Studies
Asian Languages
Asian Studies
Behavioral Sciences (see Psychology)
Bible Studies (see Religion; Theology)
Biological Anthropology
Black Studies (see African-American Studies)
Broadcasting (see Communication; Film, Television, and Video Production)
Broadcast Journalism
Building Science
Canadian Studies
Celtic Languages
Ceramics (see Art/Fine Arts)
Child and Family Studies
Child Development
Chinese
Chinese Studies (see Asian Languages; Asian Studies)
Christian Studies (see Missions and Missiology; Religion; Theology)
Cinema (see Film, Television, and Video Production)
City and Regional Planning (see Urban and Regional Planning)
Classical Languages and Literatures (see Classics)
Classics

Clinical Psychology
Clothing and Textiles
Cognitive Psychology (see Psychology—General; Cognitive Sciences)
Cognitive Sciences
Communication—General
Community Affairs (see Urban and Regional Planning; Urban Studies)
Community Planning (see Architecture; Environmental Design; Urban and Regional Planning; Urban Design; Urban Studies)
Community Psychology (see Social Psychology)
Comparative and Interdisciplinary Arts
Comparative Literature
Composition (see Music)
Computer Art and Design
Conflict Resolution and Mediation/Peace Studies
Consumer Economics
Corporate and Organizational Communication
Corrections (see Criminal Justice and Criminology)
Counseling (see Counseling Psychology; Pastoral Ministry and Counseling)
Counseling Psychology
Crafts (see Art/Fine Arts)
Creative Arts Therapies (see Art Therapy; Therapies—Dance, Drama, and Music)
Criminal Justice and Criminology
Cultural Anthropology
Cultural Studies
Dance
Decorative Arts
Demography and Population Studies
Design (see Applied Arts and Design; Architecture; Art/Fine Arts; Environmental Design; Graphic Design; Industrial Design; Interior Design; Textile Design; Urban Design)
Developmental Psychology
Diplomacy (see International Affairs)
Disability Studies
Drama Therapy (see Therapies—Dance, Drama, and Music)
Dramatic Arts (see Theater)
Drawing (see Art/Fine Arts)
Drug Abuse Counseling (see Addictions/Substance Abuse Counseling)
Drug and Alcohol Abuse Counseling (see Addictions/Substance Abuse Counseling)
East Asian Studies (see Asian Studies)
East European and Russian Studies
Economic Development
Economics
Educational Theater (see Theater; Therapies—Dance, Drama, and Music)
Emergency Management
English
Environmental Design
Ethics
Ethnic Studies
Ethnomusicology (see Music)
Experimental Psychology
Family and Consumer Sciences—General
Family Studies (see Child and Family Studies)
Family Therapy (see Child and Family Studies; Clinical Psychology; Counseling Psychology; Marriage and Family Therapy)
Filmmaking (see Film, Television, and Video Production)
Film Studies (see Film, Television, and Video Production)
Film, Television, and Video Production
Film, Television, and Video Theory and Criticism
Fine Arts (see Art/Fine Arts)
Folklore
Foreign Languages (see specific language)
Foreign Service (see International Affairs; International Development)
Forensic Psychology
Forensic Sciences
Forensics (see Speech and Interpersonal Communication)
French

Gender Studies
General Studies (*see* Liberal Studies)
Genetic Counseling
Geographic Information Systems
Geography
German
Gerontology
Graphic Design
Greek (*see* Classics)
Health Communication
Health Psychology
Hebrew (*see* Near and Middle Eastern Languages)
Hebrew Studies (*see* Jewish Studies)
Hispanic and Latin American Languages
Hispanic Studies
Historic Preservation
History
History of Art (*see* Art History)
History of Medicine
History of Science and Technology
Holocaust and Genocide Studies
Home Economics (*see* Family and Consumer Sciences—General)
Homeland Security
Household Economics, Sciences, and Management (*see* Family and Consumer Sciences—General)
Human Development
Humanities
Illustration
Industrial and Labor Relations
Industrial and Organizational Psychology
Industrial Design
Interdisciplinary Studies
Interior Design
International Affairs
International Development
International Economics
International Service (*see* International Affairs; International Development)
International Trade Policy
Internet and Interactive Multimedia
Interpersonal Communication (*see* Speech and Interpersonal Communication)
Interpretation (*see* Translation and Interpretation)
Islamic Studies (*see* Near and Middle Eastern Studies; Religion)
Italian
Japanese
Japanese Studies (*see* Asian Languages; Asian Studies; Japanese)
Jewelry (*see* Art/Fine Arts)
Jewish Studies
Journalism
Judaic Studies (*see* Jewish Studies; Religion)
Labor Relations (*see* Industrial and Labor Relations)
Landscape Architecture
Latin American Studies
Latin (*see* Classics)
Law Enforcement (*see* Criminal Justice and Criminology)
Liberal Studies
Lighting Design
Linguistics
Literature (*see* Classics; Comparative Literature; specific language)
Marriage and Family Therapy
Mass Communication
Media Studies
Medical Illustration
Medieval and Renaissance Studies
Metalsmithing (*see* Art/Fine Arts)
Middle Eastern Studies (*see* Near and Middle Eastern Studies)
Military and Defense Studies
Mineral Economics
Ministry (*see* Pastoral Ministry and Counseling; Theology)
Missions and Missiology
Motion Pictures (*see* Film, Television, and Video Production)
Museum Studies
Music
Musicology (*see* Music)
Music Therapy (*see* Therapies—Dance, Drama, and Music)

National Security
Native American Studies (*see* American Indian/Native American Studies)
Near and Middle Eastern Languages
Near and Middle Eastern Studies
Near Environment (*see* Family and Consumer Sciences)
Northern Studies
Organizational Psychology (*see* Industrial and Organizational Psychology)
Oriental Languages (*see* Asian Languages)
Oriental Studies (*see* Asian Studies)
Pacific Area/Pacific Rim Studies Painting (*see* Art/Fine Arts)
Pastoral Ministry and Counseling
Philanthropic Studies
Philosophy
Photography
Playwriting (*see* Theater; Writing)
Policy Studies (*see* Public Policy)
Political Science
Population Studies (*see* Demography and Population Studies)
Portuguese
Printmaking (*see* Art/Fine Arts)
Product Design (*see* Industrial Design)
Psychoanalysis and Psychotherapy Psychology—General
Public Administration
Public Affairs
Public History
Public Policy
Public Speaking (*see* Mass Communication; Rhetoric; Speech and Interpersonal Communication)
Publishing
Regional Planning (*see* Architecture; Urban and Regional Planning; Urban Design; Urban Studies)
Rehabilitation Counseling
Religion
Renaissance Studies (*see* Medieval and Renaissance Studies)
Rhetoric
Romance Languages
Romance Literatures (*see* Romance Languages)
Rural Planning and Studies
Rural Sociology
Russian
Scandinavian Languages
School Psychology
Sculpture (*see* Art/Fine Arts)
Security Administration (*see* Criminal Justice and Criminology)
Slavic Languages
Slavic Studies (*see* East European and Russian Studies; Slavic Languages)
Social Psychology
Social Sciences
Sociology
Southeast Asian Studies (*see* Asian Studies)
Soviet Studies (*see* East European and Russian Studies; Russian)
Spanish
Speech and Interpersonal Communication
Sport Psychology
Studio Art (*see* Art/Fine Arts)
Substance Abuse Counseling (*see* Addictions/Substance Abuse Counseling)
Survey Methodology
Sustainable Development
Technical Communication
Technical Writing
Telecommunications (*see* Film, Television, and Video Production)
Television (*see* Film, Television, and Video Production)
Textile Design
Textiles (*see* Clothing and Textiles; Textile Design)
Thanatology
Theater
Theater Arts (*see* Theater)
Theology
Therapies—Dance, Drama, and Music
Translation and Interpretation
Transpersonal and Humanistic Psychology
Urban and Regional Planning

548 www.petersonsbooks.com

Peterson's Graduate Programs in the Physical Sciences, Mathematics, Agricultural Sciences, the Environment & Natural Resources 2014

Urban Design
Urban Planning (*see* Architecture; Urban and Regional Planning; Urban Design; Urban Studies)
Urban Studies
Video (*see* Film, Television, and Video Production)
Visual Arts (*see* Applied Arts and Design; Art/Fine Arts; Film, Television, and Video Production; Graphic Design; Illustration; Photography)
Western European Studies
Women's Studies
World Wide Web (*see* Internet and Interactive Multimedia)
Writing

Graduate Programs in the Biological/Biomedical Sciences & Health-Related Medical Professions

Acupuncture and Oriental Medicine
Acute Care/Critical Care Nursing Administration (*see* Health Services Management and Hospital Administration; Nursing and Healthcare Administration; Pharmaceutical Administration)
Adult Nursing
Advanced Practice Nursing (*see* Family Nurse Practitioner Studies)
Allied Health—General
Allied Health Professions (*see* Clinical Laboratory Sciences/Medical Technology; Clinical Research; Communication Disorders; Dental Hygiene; Emergency Medical Services; Occupational Therapy; Physical Therapy; Physician Assistant Studies; Rehabilitation Sciences)
Allopathic Medicine
Anatomy
Anesthesiologist Assistant Studies
Animal Behavior
Bacteriology
Behavioral Sciences (*see* Biopsychology; Neuroscience; Zoology)
Biochemistry
Bioethics
Biological and Biomedical Sciences—General Biological Chemistry (*see* Biochemistry)
Biological Oceanography (*see* Marine Biology)
Biophysics
Biopsychology
Botany
Breeding (*see* Botany; Plant Biology; Genetics)
Cancer Biology/Oncology
Cardiovascular Sciences
Cell Biology
Cellular Physiology (*see* Cell Biology; Physiology)
Child-Care Nursing (*see* Maternal and Child/Neonatal Nursing)
Chiropractic
Clinical Laboratory Sciences/Medical Technology
Clinical Research
Community Health
Community Health Nursing
Computational Biology
Conservation (*see* Conservation Biology; Environmental Biology)
Conservation Biology
Crop Sciences (*see* Botany; Plant Biology)
Cytology (*see* Cell Biology)
Dental and Oral Surgery (*see* Oral and Dental Sciences)
Dental Assistant Studies (*see* Dental Hygiene)
Dental Hygiene
Dental Services (*see* Dental Hygiene)
Dentistry
Developmental Biology Dietetics (*see* Nutrition)
Ecology
Embryology (*see* Developmental Biology)
Emergency Medical Services
Endocrinology (*see* Physiology)
Entomology
Environmental Biology
Environmental and Occupational Health

Epidemiology
Evolutionary Biology
Family Nurse Practitioner Studies
Foods (*see* Nutrition)
Forensic Nursing
Genetics
Genomic Sciences
Gerontological Nursing
Health Physics/Radiological Health
Health Promotion
Health-Related Professions (*see* individual allied health professions)
Health Services Management and Hospital Administration
Health Services Research
Histology (*see* Anatomy; Cell Biology)
HIV/AIDS Nursing
Hospice Nursing
Hospital Administration (*see* Health Services Management and Hospital Administration)
Human Genetics
Immunology
Industrial Hygiene
Infectious Diseases
International Health
Laboratory Medicine (*see* Clinical Laboratory Sciences/Medical Technology; Immunology; Microbiology; Pathology)
Life Sciences (*see* Biological and Biomedical Sciences)
Marine Biology
Maternal and Child Health
Maternal and Child/Neonatal Nursing
Medical Imaging
Medical Microbiology
Medical Nursing (*see* Medical/Surgical Nursing)
Medical Physics
Medical/Surgical Nursing
Medical Technology (*see* Clinical Laboratory Sciences/Medical Technology)
Medical Sciences (*see* Biological and Biomedical Sciences)
Medical Science Training Programs (*see* Biological and Biomedical Sciences)
Medicinal and Pharmaceutical Chemistry
Medicinal Chemistry (*see* Medicinal and Pharmaceutical Chemistry)
Medicine (*see* Allopathic Medicine; Naturopathic Medicine; Osteopathic Medicine; Podiatric Medicine)
Microbiology
Midwifery (*see* Nurse Midwifery)
Molecular Biology
Molecular Biophysics
Molecular Genetics
Molecular Medicine
Molecular Pathogenesis
Molecular Pathology
Molecular Pharmacology
Molecular Physiology
Molecular Toxicology
Naturopathic Medicine
Neural Sciences (*see* Biopsychology; Neurobiology; Neuroscience)
Neurobiology
Neuroendocrinology (*see* Biopsychology; Neurobiology; Neuroscience; Physiology)
Neuropharmacology (*see* Biopsychology; Neurobiology; Neuroscience; Pharmacology)
Neurophysiology (*see* Biopsychology; Neurobiology; Neuroscience; Physiology)
Neuroscience
Nuclear Medical Technology (*see* Clinical Laboratory Sciences/Medical Technology)
Nurse Anesthesia
Nurse Midwifery
Nurse Practitioner Studies (*see* Family Nurse Practitioner Studies)
Nursing Administration (*see* Nursing and Healthcare Administration)
Nursing and Healthcare Administration
Nursing Education
Nursing—General
Nursing Informatics
Nutrition

Peterson's Graduate Programs in the Physical Sciences, Mathematics, Agricultural Sciences, the Environment & Natural Resources 2014

www.petersonsbooks.com **549**

Occupational Health (*see* Environmental and Occupational Health; Occupational Health Nursing)
Occupational Health Nursing
Occupational Therapy
Oncology (*see* Cancer Biology/Oncology)
Oncology Nursing
Optometry
Oral and Dental Sciences
Oral Biology (*see* Oral and Dental Sciences)
Oral Pathology (*see* Oral and Dental Sciences)
Organismal Biology (*see* Biological and Biomedical Sciences; Zoology)
Oriental Medicine and Acupuncture (*see* Acupuncture and Oriental Medicine)
Orthodontics (*see* Oral and Dental Sciences)
Osteopathic Medicine
Parasitology
Pathobiology
Pathology
Pediatric Nursing
Pedontics (*see* Oral and Dental Sciences)
Perfusion
Pharmaceutical Administration
Pharmaceutical Chemistry (*see* Medicinal and Pharmaceutical Chemistry)
Pharmaceutical Sciences
Pharmacology
Pharmacy
Photobiology of Cells and Organelles (*see* Botany; Cell Biology; Plant Biology)
Physical Therapy
Physician Assistant Studies
Physiological Optics (*see* Vision Sciences)
Podiatric Medicine
Preventive Medicine (*see* Community Health and Public Health)
Physiological Optics (*see* Physiology)
Physiology
Plant Biology
Plant Molecular Biology
Plant Pathology
Plant Physiology
Pomology (*see* Botany; Plant Biology)
Psychiatric Nursing
Public Health—General
Public Health Nursing (*see* Community Health Nursing)
Psychiatric Nursing
Psychobiology (*see* Biopsychology)
Psychopharmacology (*see* Biopsychology; Neuroscience; Pharmacology)
Radiation Biology
Radiological Health (*see* Health Physics/Radiological Health)
Rehabilitation Nursing
Rehabilitation Sciences
Rehabilitation Therapy (*see* Physical Therapy)
Reproductive Biology
School Nursing
Sociobiology (*see* Evolutionary Biology)
Structural Biology
Surgical Nursing (*see* Medical/Surgical Nursing)
Systems Biology
Teratology
Therapeutics
Theoretical Biology (*see* Biological and Biomedical Sciences)
Therapeutics (*see* Pharmaceutical Sciences; Pharmacology; Pharmacy)
Toxicology
Transcultural Nursing
Translational Biology
Tropical Medicine (*see* Parasitology)
Veterinary Medicine
Veterinary Sciences
Virology
Vision Sciences
Wildlife Biology (*see* Zoology)
Women's Health Nursing
Zoology

Graduate Programs in the Physical Sciences, Mathematics, Agricultural Sciences, the Environment & Natural Resources

Acoustics
Agricultural Sciences
Agronomy and Soil Sciences
Analytical Chemistry
Animal Sciences
Applied Mathematics
Applied Physics
Applied Statistics
Aquaculture
Astronomy
Astrophysical Sciences (*see* Astrophysics; Atmospheric Sciences; Meteorology; Planetary and Space Sciences)
Astrophysics
Atmospheric Sciences
Biological Oceanography (*see* Marine Affairs; Marine Sciences; Oceanography)
Biomathematics
Biometry
Biostatistics
Chemical Physics
Chemistry
Computational Sciences
Condensed Matter Physics
Dairy Science (*see* Animal Sciences)
Earth Sciences (*see* Geosciences)
Environmental Management and Policy
Environmental Sciences
Environmental Studies (*see* Environmental Management and Policy)
Experimental Statistics (*see* Statistics)
Fish, Game, and Wildlife Management
Food Science and Technology
Forestry
General Science (*see* specific topics)
Geochemistry
Geodetic Sciences
Geological Engineering (*see* Geology)
Geological Sciences (*see* Geology)
Geology
Geophysical Fluid Dynamics (*see* Geophysics)
Geophysics
Geosciences
Horticulture
Hydrogeology
Hydrology
Inorganic Chemistry
Limnology
Marine Affairs
Marine Geology
Marine Sciences
Marine Studies (*see* Marine Affairs; Marine Geology; Marine Sciences; Oceanography)
Mathematical and Computational Finance
Mathematical Physics
Mathematical Statistics (*see* Applied Statistics; Statistics)
Mathematics
Meteorology
Mineralogy
Natural Resource Management (*see* Environmental Management and Policy; Natural Resources)
Natural Resources
Nuclear Physics (*see* Physics)
Ocean Engineering (*see* Marine Affairs; Marine Geology; Marine Sciences; Oceanography)
Oceanography
Optical Sciences
Optical Technologies (*see* Optical Sciences)
Optics (*see* Applied Physics; Optical Sciences; Physics)
Organic Chemistry

550 www.petersonsbooks.com

Peterson's Graduate Programs in the Physical Sciences, Mathematics, Agricultural Sciences, the Environment & Natural Resources 2014

Paleontology
Paper Chemistry (*see* Chemistry)
Photonics
Physical Chemistry
Physics
Planetary and Space Sciences
Plant Sciences
Plasma Physics
Poultry Science (*see* Animal Sciences)
Radiological Physics (*see* Physics)
Range Management (*see* Range Science)
Range Science
Resource Management (*see* Environmental Management and Policy; Natural Resources)
Solid-Earth Sciences (*see* Geosciences)
Space Sciences (*see* Planetary and Space Sciences)
Statistics
Theoretical Chemistry
Theoretical Physics
Viticulture and Enology
Water Resources

Graduate Programs in Engineering & Applied Sciences

Aeronautical Engineering (*see* Aerospace/Aeronautical Engineering)
Aerospace/Aeronautical Engineering
Aerospace Studies (*see* Aerospace/Aeronautical Engineering)
Agricultural Engineering
Applied Mechanics (*see* Mechanics)
Applied Science and Technology
Architectural Engineering
Artificial Intelligence/Robotics
Astronautical Engineering (*see* Aerospace/Aeronautical Engineering)
Automotive Engineering
Aviation
Biochemical Engineering
Bioengineering
Bioinformatics
Biological Engineering (*see* Bioengineering)
Biomedical Engineering
Biosystems Engineering
Biotechnology
Ceramic Engineering (*see* Ceramic Sciences and Engineering)
Ceramic Sciences and Engineering
Ceramics (*see* Ceramic Sciences and Engineering)
Chemical Engineering
Civil Engineering
Computer and Information Systems Security
Computer Engineering
Computer Science
Computing Technology (*see* Computer Science)
Construction Engineering
Construction Management
Database Systems
Electrical Engineering
Electronic Materials
Electronics Engineering (*see* Electrical Engineering)
Energy and Power Engineering
Energy Management and Policy
Engineering and Applied Sciences
Engineering and Public Affairs (*see* Technology and Public Policy)
Engineering and Public Policy (*see* Energy Management and Policy; Technology and Public Policy)
Engineering Design
Engineering Management
Engineering Mechanics (*see* Mechanics)
Engineering Metallurgy (*see* Metallurgical Engineering and Metallurgy)
Engineering Physics
Environmental Design (*see* Environmental Engineering)
Environmental Engineering
Ergonomics and Human Factors

Financial Engineering
Fire Protection Engineering
Food Engineering (*see* Agricultural Engineering)
Game Design and Development
Gas Engineering (*see* Petroleum Engineering)
Geological Engineering
Geophysics Engineering (*see* Geological Engineering)
Geotechnical Engineering
Hazardous Materials Management
Health Informatics
Health Systems (*see* Safety Engineering; Systems Engineering)
Highway Engineering (*see* Transportation and Highway Engineering)
Human-Computer Interaction
Human Factors (*see* Ergonomics and Human Factors)
Hydraulics
Hydrology (*see* Water Resources Engineering)
Industrial Engineering (*see* Industrial/Management Engineering)
Industrial/Management Engineering
Information Science
Internet Engineering
Macromolecular Science (*see* Polymer Science and Engineering)
Management Engineering (*see* Engineering Management; Industrial/ Management Engineering)
Management of Technology
Manufacturing Engineering
Marine Engineering (*see* Civil Engineering)
Materials Engineering
Materials Sciences
Mechanical Engineering
Mechanics
Medical Informatics
Metallurgical Engineering and Metallurgy
Metallurgy (*see* Metallurgical Engineering and Metallurgy)
Mineral/Mining Engineering
Modeling and Simulation
Nanotechnology
Nuclear Engineering
Ocean Engineering
Operations Research
Paper and Pulp Engineering
Petroleum Engineering
Pharmaceutical Engineering
Plastics Engineering (*see* Polymer Science and Engineering)
Polymer Science and Engineering
Public Policy (*see* Energy Management and Policy; Technology and Public Policy)
Reliability Engineering
Robotics (*see* Artificial Intelligence/Robotics)
Safety Engineering
Software Engineering
Solid-State Sciences (*see* Materials Sciences)
Structural Engineering
Surveying Science and Engineering
Systems Analysis (*see* Systems Engineering)
Systems Engineering
Systems Science
Technology and Public Policy
Telecommunications
Telecommunications Management
Textile Sciences and Engineering
Textiles (*see* Textile Sciences and Engineering)
Transportation and Highway Engineering
Urban Systems Engineering (*see* Systems Engineering)
Waste Management (*see* Hazardous Materials Management)
Water Resources Engineering

Graduate Programs in Business, Education, Information Studies, Law & Social Work

Accounting
Actuarial Science

Peterson's Graduate Programs in the Physical Sciences, Mathematics, Agricultural Sciences, the Environment & Natural Resources 2014

www.petersonsbooks.com **551**

Adult Education
Advertising and Public Relations
Agricultural Education
Alcohol Abuse Counseling (*see* Counselor Education)
Archival Management and Studies
Art Education
Athletics Administration (*see* Kinesiology and Movement Studies)
Athletic Training and Sports Medicine
Audiology (*see* Communication Disorders)
Aviation Management
Banking (*see* Finance and Banking)
Business Administration and Management—General
Business Education
Communication Disorders
Community College Education
Computer Education
Continuing Education (*see* Adult Education)
Counseling (*see* Counselor Education)
Counselor Education
Curriculum and Instruction
Developmental Education
Distance Education Development
Drug Abuse Counseling (*see* Counselor Education)
Early Childhood Education
Educational Leadership and Administration
Educational Measurement and Evaluation
Educational Media/Instructional Technology
Educational Policy
Educational Psychology
Education—General
Education of the Blind (*see* Special Education)
Education of the Deaf (*see* Special Education)
Education of the Gifted
Education of the Hearing Impaired (*see* Special Education)
Education of the Learning Disabled (*see* Special Education)
Education of the Mentally Retarded (*see* Special Education)
Education of the Physically Handicapped (*see* Special Education)
Education of Students with Severe/Multiple Disabilities
Education of the Visually Handicapped (*see* Special Education)
Electronic Commerce
Elementary Education
English as a Second Language
English Education
Entertainment Management
Entrepreneurship
Environmental Education
Environmental Law
Exercise and Sports Science
Exercise Physiology (*see* Kinesiology and Movement Studies)
Facilities and Entertainment Management
Finance and Banking
Food Services Management (*see* Hospitality Management)
Foreign Languages Education
Foundations and Philosophy of Education
Guidance and Counseling (*see* Counselor Education)
Health Education
Health Law
Hearing Sciences (*see* Communication Disorders)
Higher Education
Home Economics Education
Hospitality Management
Hotel Management (*see* Travel and Tourism)
Human Resources Development
Human Resources Management
Human Services
Industrial Administration (*see* Industrial and Manufacturing Management)
Industrial and Manufacturing Management
Industrial Education (*see* Vocational and Technical Education)
Information Studies
Instructional Technology (*see* Educational Media/Instructional Technology)
Insurance
Intellectual Property Law
International and Comparative Education
International Business

International Commerce (*see* International Business)
International Economics (*see* International Business)
International Trade (*see* International Business)
Investment and Securities (*see* Business Administration and Management; Finance and Banking; Investment Management)
Investment Management
Junior College Education (*see* Community College Education)
Kinesiology and Movement Studies
Law
Legal and Justice Studies
Leisure Services (*see* Recreation and Park Management)
Leisure Studies
Library Science
Logistics
Management (*see* Business Administration and Management)
Management Information Systems
Management Strategy and Policy
Marketing
Marketing Research
Mathematics Education
Middle School Education
Movement Studies (*see* Kinesiology and Movement Studies)
Multilingual and Multicultural Education
Museum Education
Music Education
Nonprofit Management
Nursery School Education (*see* Early Childhood Education)
Occupational Education (*see* Vocational and Technical Education)
Organizational Behavior
Organizational Management
Parks Administration (*see* Recreation and Park Management)
Personnel (*see* Human Resources Development; Human Resources Management; Organizational Behavior; Organizational Management; Student Affairs)
Philosophy of Education (*see* Foundations and Philosophy of Education)
Physical Education
Project Management
Public Relations (*see* Advertising and Public Relations)
Quality Management
Quantitative Analysis
Reading Education
Real Estate
Recreation and Park Management
Recreation Therapy (*see* Recreation and Park Management)
Religious Education
Remedial Education (*see* Special Education)
Restaurant Administration (*see* Hospitality Management)
Science Education
Secondary Education
Social Sciences Education
Social Studies Education (*see* Social Sciences Education)
Social Work
Special Education
Speech-Language Pathology and Audiology (*see* Communication Disorders)
Sports Management
Sports Medicine (*see* Athletic Training and Sports Medicine)
Sports Psychology and Sociology (*see* Kinesiology and Movement Studies)
Student Affairs
Substance Abuse Counseling (*see* Counselor Education)
Supply Chain Management
Sustainability Management
Systems Management (*see* Management Information Systems)
Taxation
Teacher Education (*see* specific subject areas)
Teaching English as a Second Language (*see* English as a Second Language)
Technical Education (*see* Vocational and Technical Education)
Transportation Management
Travel and Tourism
Urban Education
Vocational and Technical Education
Vocational Counseling (*see* Counselor Education)

552 www.petersonsbooks.com

Peterson's Graduate Programs in the Physical Sciences, Mathematics, Agricultural Sciences, the Environment & Natural Resources 2014

Directories and Subject Areas in This Book

NOTES

NOTES

NOTES

NOTES

NOTES

NOTES

NOTES

NOTES

NOTES

NOTES